Dear Reader

*The present volume is the 17th edition
of the Michelin Guide
Great Britain and Ireland.*

*The unbiased and independent selection
of hotels and restaurants
is the result of local visits and enquiries
by our inspectors.
In addition we receive considerable help
from our readers' invaluable letters
and comments.*

*It is our purpose
to provide up-to-date information
and thus render a service to our readers.
The next edition is already in preparation.*

*Therefore, only the guide of the year
merits your complete confidence,
so please remember to use the latest edition*

Bon voyage

Contents

3   Dear Reader

5 to 12   How to use this guide

43   Starred establishments

44   Further establishments which merit your attention

Hotels, restaurants, town plans, garages, sights... and maps

45   England and Wales

541   Scotland

615   Northern Ireland

627   Channel Islands

637   Isle of Man

639   Republic of Ireland

pages bordered in red   Greater London

674   Motorway hotels

679   Major hotel groups

680   Traffic signs

685   Principal shipping companies

690   Distances

692   Atlas: main roads and principal shipping routes

699   Michelin maps and guides

Choosing
a hotel or restaurant

This guide offers a selection of hotels and restaurants to help the motorist on his travels. In each category establishments are listed in order of preference according to the degree of comfort they offer.

CATEGORIES

🏨	Luxury in the traditional style	XXXXX
🏨	Top class comfort	XXXX
🏨	Very comfortable	XXX
🏨	Comfortable	XX
🏠	Quite comfortable	X
⚲	Simple comfort	
↑	Other recommended accommodation, at moderate prices	

without rest.	The hotel has no restaurant	
	The restaurant also offers accommodation	with rm

PEACEFUL ATMOSPHERE AND SETTING

Certain establishments are distinguished in the guide by the red symbols shown below.
Your stay in such hotels will be particularly pleasant or restful, owing to the character of the building, its decor, the setting, the welcome and services offered, or simply the peace and quiet to be enjoyed there.

🏨 to 🏠	Pleasant hotels
XXXXX to X	Pleasant restaurants
« Park »	Particularly attractive feature
⌣	Very quiet or quiet, secluded hotel
⌣	Quiet hotel
⩽ sea	Exceptional view
⩽	Interesting or extensive view

The maps located at the beginning of each regional section in the guide indicate places with such peaceful, pleasant hotels and restaurants.

By consulting them before setting out and sending us your comments on your return you can help us with our enquiries.

Hotel facilities

In general the hotels we recommend have full bathroom and toilet facilities in each room. However, this may not be the case for certain rooms in categories 🏨, 🏠, ⚘ and ⌂.

30 rm	Number of rooms
	Lift (elevator)
	Air conditioning
TV	Television in room
	Establishment either partly or wholly reserved for non-smokers
	Telephone in room: outside calls connected by the operator
	Telephone in room: direct dialling for outside calls
	Rooms accessible to disabled people
	Outdoor or indoor swimming pool
	Garden
	Hotel tennis court – Golf course and number of holes
	Fishing available to hotel guests. A charge may be made
150	Equipped conference hall: maximum capacity
	Hotel garage (additional charge in most cases)
P	Car park for customers only
	Dogs are not allowed in all or part of the hotel
Fax	Telephone document transmission
May-October	Dates when open, as indicated by the hotelier
season	Probably open for the season – precise dates not available
	Where no date or season is shown, establishments are open all year round
LL35 OSB	Postal code
(T.H.F.)	Hotel Group (See list at end of the Guide)

Animals

It is forbidden to bring domestic animals (dogs, cats...) into Great Britain and Ireland.

Cuisine

STARS

Certain establishments deserve to be brought to your attention for the particularly fine quality of their cooking. **Michelin stars** are awarded for the standard of meals served.

For each of these restaurants we indicate three culinary specialities typical of their style of cooking to assist you in your choice.

❀❀❀ | **Exceptional cuisine, worth a special journey**
Superb food, fine wines, faultless service, elegant surroundings. One will pay accordingly!

❀❀ | **Excellent cooking, worth a detour**
Specialities and wines of first class quality. This will be reflected in the price.

❀ | **A very good restaurant in its category**
The star indicates a good place to stop on your journey.

But beware of comparing the star given to an expensive « de luxe » establishment to that of a simple restaurant where you can appreciate fine cuisine at a reasonable price.

THE RED « M »

Whilst appreciating the quality of the cooking in restaurants with a star, you may, however, wish to find some serving a perhaps less elaborate but nonetheless always carefully prepared meal. Certain restaurants seem to us to answer this requirement.

We bring them to your attention by marking them with a red « **M** » in the text of the Guide.

Please refer to the map of star and **M** *rated restaurants located at the beginning of each regional section in the guide.*

Alcoholic beverages-conditions of sale

The sale of alcoholic drinks is governed in Great Britain and Ireland by licensing laws which vary greatly from country to country.

Allowing for local variations, restaurants may stay open and serve alcohol with a bona fide meal during the afternoon. Hotel bars and public houses are generally open between 11am and 11pm at the discretion of the licensee. Hotel residents, however, may buy drinks outside the permitted hours at the discretion of the hotelier.

Children under the age of 14 are not allowed in bars.

Prices

Prices quoted are valid for autumn 1989. Changes may arise if goods and service costs are revised.

Your recommendation is self-evident if you always walk into a hotel guide in hand.

Hotels and restaurants in bold type have supplied details of all their rates and have assumed responsibility for maintaining them for all travellers in possession of this guide.

Prices are given in £ sterling, except for the Republic of Ireland (Punts)
Where no mentoin s., t., or st. is shown, prices are subject to the addition of service charge, V.A.T., or both (V.A.T. does not apply in the Channel Islands).

MEALS

M 12.00/17.00	**Sets meals** – Lunch 12.00, dinner 17.00 – including cover charge, where applicable
M 14.00/18.00	See page 7
s. t.	Service only included – V.A.T. included
st.	Service and V.A.T. included
5.00	Price of 1/2 bottle or carafe of house wine
M a la carte 17.00/21.00	**A la carte meals** – The prices represent the range of charges from a simple to an elaborate 3 course meal and include a cover charge where applicable
7.50	Charge for full cooked breakfast (i.e. not included in the room rate) Continental breakfast may be available at a lower rate

ROOMS

rm 45.00/65.00	Lowest price 45.00 for a comfortable single and highest price 65.00 for the best double room
rm 50.00/70.00	Full cooked breakfast (whether taken or not) is included in the price of the room
suites 100.00/200.00	Lowest and highest prices for a suite comprising bedroom, bathroom and sitting room

SHORT BREAKS

Many hotels now offer a special rate for a stay of two nights which comprises dinner, room and breakfast usually for a minimum of two people.

SB 60.00/80.00	Prices indicated are lowest and highest per person for two nights.

Some hotels will require a deposit, which confirms the commitment of customer and hotelier alike. Make sure the terms of the agreement are clear.

◪ ⒜Ⓔ ⓓ 𝗩𝗜𝗦𝗔	Credit cards accepted by the establishment: Access – American Express – Diners Club – Visa

Towns

✉ York	Postal address
☎ 0225 Bath	STD dialling code (name of exchange indicated only when different from name of the town). Omit 0 when dialling from abroad
401 M 27, ⑩	Michelin map and co-ordinates or fold
West Country G.	See the Michelin Green Guide England : The West Country
pop. 1057	Population
ECD: Wednesday	Early closing day (shops close at midday)
BX **A**	Letters giving the location of a place on the town map
⛳18	Golf course and number of holes (visitors unrestricted, telephone reservation advisable)
☀, ≼	Panoramic view, viewpoint
✈	Airport
🚗 ✆ 218	Place with a motorail connection; further information from telephone number listed
⛴	Shipping line
🛥	Passenger transport only *see list of companies at the end of the Guide*
🛈	Tourist Information Centre

Standard Time

In winter standard time throughout the British Isles is Greenwich Mean Time (G.M.T.). In summer British clocks are advanced by one hour to give British Summer Time (B.S.T.). The actual dates are announced annually but always occur over weekends in March and October.

Sights

STAR-RATING

★★★	Worth a journey
★★	Worth a detour
★	Interesting
AC	Admission charge

LOCATION

See	Sights in town
Envir.	On the outskirts
Exc.	In the surrounding area
N, S, E, W	The sight lies north, south, east or west of the town
A 22	Take road A 22, indicated by the same symbol on the Guide map
2 m.	Mileage

Town plans

Hotels
Restaurants

Sights

Place of interest and its main entrance

Interesting place of worship :
    Cathedral, church or chapel

Roads

Motorway, dual carriageway
    Interchange : complete, limited

Major through route

One-way street – Unsuitable for traffic

Pedestrian street

Pasteur   P   Shopping street – Car park

Gateway – Street passing under arch – Tunnel

Low headroom (16'6" max.) on major through routes

Station and railway

Funicular – Cable-car

Lever bridge – Car ferry

Various signs

Tourist information Centre

Mosque – Synagogue

Ruins – Windmill

Communications tower or mast

Garden, park, wood – Cemetery – Cross

Stadium – Racecourse – Golf course

Golf course (with restrictions for visitors)

View – Panorama

Monument – Fountain – Hospital

Pleasure boat harbour – Lighthouse

Airport – Underground station

Ferry services :
    passengers and cars

Main post office with poste restante, telephone

Public buildings located by letter :
    Country Council Offices
    Town Hall – Museum – Theatre
    University, College
    Police (in large towns police headquarters)

London

BRENT   SOHO   Borough – Area

Borough boundary – Area boundary

Car, tyres

The wearing of seat belts is obligatory for drivers and front seat passengers in Great Britain and Ireland.

CAR DEALERS, GARAGES AND MICHELIN TYRE SUPPLIERS

In the text of many towns are to be found the names of car dealers, garages and tyre dealers many of which offer a breakdown service.

ATS Tyre dealers

The address of the nearest ATS tyre dealer can be obtained by contacting the address below between 9am and 5pm.

ATS HOUSE 180-188 Northolt Rd.
Harrow,
Middlesex HA2 OED
(01) 423 2000

MOTORING ORGANISATIONS

The major motoring organisations in Great Britain are the Automobile Association and the Royal Automobile Club. Each provides services in varying degrees for non-resident members of affiliated clubs.

AUTOMOBILE ASSOCIATION
Fanum House
BASINGSTOKE, Hants., RG21 2EA
☎ (0256) 20123

ROYAL AUTOMOBILE CLUB
RAC House, Lansdowne Rd.
CROYDON, Surrey CR9 2JA
☎ (01) 686 2525

Ami lecteur

Le présent volume représente la 17e édition
du Guide Michelin
Great Britain and Ireland.

Réalisée en toute indépendance,
sa sélection d'hôtels et de restaurants
est le fruit des recherches de ses inspecteurs,
que complètent
vos précieux courriers et commentaires.

Soucieux d'actualité et de service,
le Guide prépare déjà sa prochaine édition.

Seul le Guide de l'année
mérite ainsi votre confiance.

Pensez à le renouveler...

Bon voyage avec Michelin

Sommaire

13 Ami lecteur

15 à 22 Comment se servir du guide

43 Les établissements à étoiles

44 Autres tables qui méritent votre attention

Hôtels, restaurants, plans de ville, garagistes, curiosités... et cartes

45 England and Wales

541 Scotland

615 Northern Ireland

627 Channel Islands

637 Isle of Man

639 Republic of Ireland

pages bordées de rouge Le Grand Londres

674 Hôtels d'autoroutes

679 Principales chaînes hôtelières

680 Signalisation routière

685 Compagnies de navigation

690 Distances

692 Atlas : principales routes et liaisons maritimes

699 Cartes et Guides Michelin

Le choix
d'un hôtel, d'un restaurant

Ce guide vous propose une sélection d'hôtels et restaurants établie à l'usage de l'automobiliste de passage. Les établissements, classés selon leur confort, sont cités par ordre de préférence dans chaque catégorie.

CATÉGORIES

	Grand luxe et tradition	XXXXX
	Grand confort	XXXX
	Très confortable	XXX
	De bon confort	XX
	Assez confortable	X
	Simple mais convenable	
	Autre ressource hôtelière conseillée, à prix modérés	
Without rest.	L'hôtel n'a pas de restaurant	
	Le restaurant possède des chambres	with rm

AGRÉMENT ET TRANQUILLITÉ

Certains établissements se distinguent dans le guide par les symboles rouges indiqués ci-après. Le séjour dans ces hôtels se révèle particulièrement agréable ou reposant.

Cela peut tenir d'une part au caractère de l'édifice, au décor original, au site, à l'accueil et aux services qui sont proposés, d'autre part à la tranquillité des lieux.

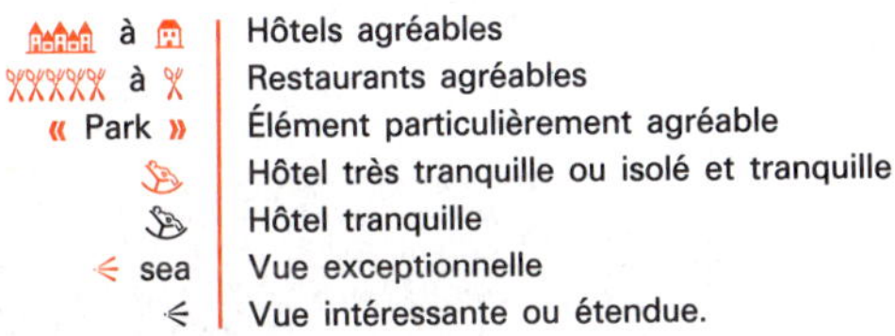

à	Hôtels agréables
à	Restaurants agréables
« Park »	Élément particulièrement agréable
	Hôtel très tranquille ou isolé et tranquille
	Hôtel tranquille
sea	Vue exceptionnelle
	Vue intéressante ou étendue.

Les localités possédant des établissements agréables ou tranquilles sont repérées sur les cartes placées au début de chacune des régions traitées dans ce guide.

Consultez-les pour la préparation de vos voyages et donnez-nous vos appréciations à votre retour, vous faciliterez ainsi nos enquêtes.

L'installation

Les chambres des hôtels que nous recommandons possèdent, en général, des installations sanitaires complètes. Il est toutefois possible que dans les catégories 🏠, 🏡, ⚲ et ⌂, certaines chambres en soient dépourvues.

30 ch	Nombre de chambres
	Ascenseur
	Air conditionné
	Télévision dans la chambre
	Établissement entièrement ou en partie réservé aux non-fumeurs
	Téléphone dans la chambre relié par standard
	Téléphone dans la chambre, direct avec l'extérieur
	Chambres accessibles aux handicapés physiques
	Piscine : de plein air ou couverte
	Jardin de repos
	Tennis à l'hôtel – Golf et nombre de trous
	Pêche ouverte aux clients de l'hôtel (éventuellement payant)
150	Salles de conférences : capacité maximum
	Garage dans l'hôtel (généralement payant)
	Parking réservé à la clientèle
	Accès interdit aux chiens (dans tout ou partie de l'établissement)
Fax	Transmission de documents par télécopie
May-October	Période d'ouverture, communiquée par l'hôtelier
season	Ouverture probable en saison mais dates non précisées. En l'absence de mention, l'établissement est ouvert toute l'année.
LL35 OSB	Code postal de l'établissement
(T.H.F.)	Chaîne hôtelière (voir liste en fin de guide)

Animaux

L'introduction d'animaux domestiques (chiens, chats...) est interdite en Grande-Bretagne et en Irlande.

La table

LES ÉTOILES

Certains établissements méritent d'être signalés à votre attention pour la qualité de leur cuisine. Nous les distinguons par **les étoiles de bonne table**.

Nous indiquons, pour ces établissements, trois spécialités culinaires qui pourront orienter votre choix.

❁❁❁ **Une des meilleures tables, vaut le voyage**

Table merveilleuse, grands vins, service impeccable, cadre élégant... Prix en conséquence.

❁❁ **Table excellente, mérite un détour**

Spécialités et vins de choix... Attendez-vous à une dépense en rapport.

❁ **Une très bonne table dans sa catégorie**

L'étoile marque une bonne étape sur votre itinéraire.

Mais ne comparez pas l'étoile d'un établissement de luxe à prix élevés avec celle d'une petite maison où à prix raisonnables, on sert également une cuisine de qualité.

LE « M » ROUGE

Tout en appréciant les tables à « étoiles », on peut souhaiter trouver sur sa route un repas plus simple mais toujours de préparation soignée. Certaines maisons nous ont paru répondre à cette préoccupation.

Un « **M** » rouge les signale à votre attention dans le texte de ce guide.

Consultez les cartes des localités (étoiles de bonne table et **M**) *placées au début de chacune des régions traitées dans ce guide.*

La vente de boissons alcoolisées

En Grande-Bretagne et en Irlande, la vente de boissons alcoolisées est soumise à des lois pouvant varier d'une région à l'autre.

D'une façon générale, les hôtels, les restaurants et les pubs peuvent demeurer ouverts l'après-midi et servir des boissons alcoolisées dans la mesure où elles accompagnent un repas suffisamment consistant. Les bars ferment après 23 heures.

Néanmoins, l'hôtelier a toujours la possibilité de servir, à sa clientèle, des boissons alcoolisées en dehors des heures légales.

Les enfants au-dessous de 14 ans n'ont pas accès aux bars.

Les prix

Les prix que nous indiquons dans ce guide ont été établis en automne 1989. Ils sont susceptibles de modifications, notamment en cas de variations des prix des biens et services.

Entrez à l'hôtel le Guide à la main, vous montrerez ainsi qu'il vous conduit là en confiance.

Les prix sont indiqués en livres sterling (1 L = 100 pence), sauf en République d'Irlande (Punts).

Lorsque les mentions **s.**, **t.**, ou **st.** ne figurent pas, les prix indiqués peuvent être majorés d'un pourcentage pour le service, la T.V.A., ou les deux. (La T.V.A. n'est pas appliquée dans les Channel Islands.)

Les hôtels et restaurants figurent en gros caractères lorsque les hôteliers nous ont donné tous leurs prix et se sont engagés, sous leur propre responsabilité, à les appliquer aux touristes de passage porteurs de notre guide.

REPAS

M 12.00/17.00	**Repas à prix fixe** – Déjeuner 12.00, diner 17.00. Ces prix s'entendent couvert compris
M 14.00/18.00	Voir page 17
s. t.	Service compris – T.V.A comprise
st.	Service et T.V.A. compris (prix nets)
🍾 5.00	Prix de la 1/2 bouteille ou carafe de vin ordinaire
M à la carte 17.00/21.00	**Repas à la carte** – Le 1er prix correspond à un repas simple mais soigné, comprenant : petite entrée, plat du jour garni, dessert. Le 2e prix concerne un repas plus complet, comprenant : hors-d'œuvre, plat principal, fromage ou dessert. Ces prix s'entendent couvert compris
☕ 7.50	Prix du petit déjeuner à l'anglaise, s'il n'est pas compris dans celui de la chambre Un petit déjeuner continental peut être obtenu à moindre prix

CHAMBRES

rm 45.00/65.00	Prix minimum 45.00 d'une chambre pour une personne et prix maximum 65.00 de la plus belle chambre occupée par deux personnes
rm ☕ 50.00/70.00	Le prix du petit déjeuner à l'anglaise est inclus dans le prix de la chambre, même s'il n'est pas consommé
suites 100.00/200.00	Prix minimum et maximum d'un appartement comprenant chambre, salle de bains et salon

« SHORT BREAKS »

SB 60.00/80.00	Prix minimum et maximum par personne pour un séjour de deux nuits en conditions avantageuses ou « Short Break ». Ce forfait comprend la chambre, le dîner et le petit déjeuner, en général pour un minimum de deux personnes.

Certains hôteliers demandent le versement d'arrhes. Il s'agit d'un dépôt-garantie qui engage l'hôtelier comme le client. Bien faire préciser les dispositions de cette garantie.

⬛ AE ⓓ **VISA**	Cartes de crédit acceptées par l'établissement : Access (Eurocard) – American Express – Diners Club – Visa

Les villes

✉ York	Bureau de poste desservant la localité
✆ 0225 Bath	Indicatif téléphonique interurbain suivi, si nécessaire, de la localité de rattachement (De l'étranger, ne pas composer le 0)
401 M 27, ⑩	Numéro des cartes Michelin et carroyage ou numéro du pli
West Country G.	Voir le guide vert Michelin England : The West Country
pop. 1057	Population
ECD : Wednesday	Jour de fermeture des magasins (après-midi seulement)
BX **A**	Lettres repérant un emplacement sur le plan
🏌18	Golf et nombre de trous (réservation conseillée)
✳, ≤	Panorama, point de vue
✈	Aéroport
🚗 ✆ 218	Localité desservie par train-auto. Renseignements au numéro de téléphone indiqué
🚢	Transports maritimes
⛴	Transports maritimes (pour passagers seulement) *Voir liste des compagnies en fin de guide*
🛈	Information touristique

Heure légale

Les visiteurs devront tenir compte de l'heure officielle en Grande Bretagne : une heure de retard sur l'heure française.

Les curiosités

INTÉRÊT

★★★	Vaut le voyage
★★	Mérite un détour
★	Intéressant
AC	Entrée payante

SITUATION

See	Dans la ville
Envir.	Aux environs de la ville
Exc.	Excursions dans la région
N, S, E, W	La curiosité est située : au Nord, au Sud, à l'Est, à l'Ouest
A 22	On s'y rend par la route A 22, repérée par le même signe sur le plan du Guide
2 m.	Distance en miles

Les plans

Hôtels
Restaurants

Curiosités

Bâtiment intéressant et entrée principale

Édifice religieux intéressant :
  Cathédrale, église ou chapelle

Voirie

Autoroute, route à chaussées séparées
  échangeur : complet, partiel

Grande voie de circulation

Sens unique – Rue impraticable

Rue piétonne

Pasteur   P   Rue commerçante – Parc de stationnement

Porte – Passage sous voûte – Tunnel

Passage bas (inférieur à 16'6") sur les grandes voies de circulation

Gare et voie ferrée

Funiculaire – Téléphérique, télécabine

Pont mobile – Bac pour autos

Signes divers

Information touristique

Mosquée – Synagogue

Ruines – Moulin à vent

Tour ou pylône de télécommunication

Jardin, parc, bois – Cimetière – Calvaire

Stade – Hippodrome – Golf

Golf (réservé)

Vue   Panorama

Monument – Fontaine – Hôpital

Port de plaisance – Phare

Aéroport – Station de métro

Transport par bateau :
  passagers et voitures

Bureau principal de poste restante, téléphone

Bâtiment public repéré par une lettre :
  Bureau de l'Administration du Comté
  Hôtel de ville – Musée – Théâtre
  Université, grande école
  Police (commissariat central)

Londres

BRENT   SOHO   Nom d'arrondissement (borough) – de quartier (area)

Limite de « borough » – d'« area »

La voiture, les pneus

En Grande Bretagne et en Irlande, le port de la ceinture de sécurité est obligatoire pour le conducteur et le passager avant.

GARAGISTES, RÉPARATEURS FOURNISSEURS DE PNEUS MICHELIN

Au texte de la plupart des localités figure une liste des garagistes ou concessionnaires automobiles pouvant, éventuellement, vous aider en cas de panne.

ATS Spécialistes du pneu

Des renseignements sur le plus proche point de vente de pneus ATS pourront être obtenus en s'informant entre 9 h et 17 h à l'adresse indiquée ci-dessous.

ATS HOUSE 180-188 Northolt Rd.
Harrow,
Middlesex HA2 OED
(01) 423 2000

Dans nos agences, nous nous faisons un plaisir de donner à nos clients tous conseils pour la meilleure utilisation de leurs pneus.

AUTOMOBILE CLUBS

Les principales organisations de secours automobile dans le pays sont l'Automobile Association et le Royal Automobile Club, toutes deux offrant certains de leurs services aux membres de clubs affilés.

AUTOMOBILE ASSOCIATION
Fanum House
BASINGSTOKE, Hants., RG21 2EA
☎ (0256) 20123

ROYAL AUTOMOBILE CLUB
RAC House, Lansdowne Rd,
CROYDON, Surrey CR9 2JA
☎ (01) 686 2525

Amico Lettore

Questo volume rappresenta
la 17^{esima} edizione
della Guida Michelin
Great Britain and Ireland.

La sua selezione di alberghi e ristoranti,
realizzata in assoluta indipendenza,
è il risultato
delle indagini dei suoi ispettori,
che completano
le vostre preziose informazioni o giudizi.

Desiderosa di mantenersi sempre aggiornata
per fornire un buon servizio,
la Guida sta già preparando
la sua prossima edizione.

Soltanto la Guida dell'anno merita perciò
la vostra fiducia. Pensate a rinnovarla...

Buon viaggio con Michelin

Sommario

23   Amico Lettore

25 a 32   Come servirsi della guida

43   Gli esercizi con stelle

44   Altre tavole particolarmente interessanti

Alberghi, ristoranti, piante di città, officine di riparazione, curiosità... e Carte

45   England and Wales

541   Scotland

615   Northern Ireland

627   Channel Islands

637   Isle of Man

639   Republic of Ireland

Pagine bordate di rosso   Londra

674   Alberghi sulle autostrade

679   Principali catene alberghiere

680   Segnaletica stradale

685   Compagnie di navigazione

690   Distanze

692   Carta : principali strade e collegamenti marittimi

699   Carte e guide Michelin

La scelta
di un albergo, di un ristorante

Questa guida Vi propone una selezione di alberghi e ristoranti stabilita ad uso dell'automobilista di passaggio. Gli esercizi, classificati in base al confort che offrono, vengono citati in ordine di preferenza per ogni categoria.

CATEGORIE

	Gran lusso e tradizione	XXXXX
	Gran confort	XXXX
	Molto confortevole	XXX
	Di buon confort	XX
	Abbastanza confortevole	X
	Semplice, ma conveniente	
	Altra risorsa, consigliata per prezzi contenuti	
without rest.	L'albergo non ha ristorante	
	Il ristorante dispone di camere	with rm

AMENITÀ E TRANQUILLITÀ

Alcuni esercizi sono evidenziati nella guida dai simboli rossi indicati qui di seguito. Il soggiorno in questi alberghi dovrebbe rivelarsi particolarmente ameno o riposante.
Ciò può dipendere sia dalle caratteristiche dell'edifico, dalle decorazioni non comuni, dalla sua posizione e dal servizio offerto, sia dalla tranquillità dei luoghi.

a	Alberghi ameni
XXXXX a X	Ristoranti ameni
« Park »	Un particolare piacevole
	Albergo molto tranquillo o isolato e tranquillo
	Albergo tranquillo
← sea	Vista eccezionale
←	Vista interessante o estesa

Le località che possiedono degli esercizi ameni o tranquilli sono riportate sulle carte che precedono ciascuna delle regioni trattate nella guida.

Consultatele per la preparazione dei Vostri viaggi e, al ritorno, inviateci i Vostri pareri; in tal modo agevolerete le nostre inchieste.

Installazioni

Le camere degli alberghi che raccomandiamo possiedono, generalmente, delle installazioni sanitarie complete. È possibile tuttavia che nelle categorie 🏠, 🏠, ⚘ e ⌂ alcune camere ne siano sprovviste.

30 rm	Numero di camere
	Ascensore
	Aria condizionata
TV	Televisione in camera
	Esercizio riservato completamente o in parte ai non fumatori
	Telefono in camera collegato con il centralino
	Telefono in camera comunicante direttamente con l'esterno
	Camere di agevole accesso per i minorati fisici
	Piscina : all'aperto, coperta
	Giardino da riposo
9	Tennis appartenente all'albergo – Golf e numero di buche
	Pesca aperta ai clienti dell' albergo (eventualmente a pagamento)
150	Sale per conferenze : capienza massima
	Garage nell'albergo (generalmente a pagamento)
P	Parcheggio riservato alla clientela
	Accesso vietato ai cani (in tutto o in parte dell'esercizio)
Fax	Trasmissione telefonica di documenti
May-October	Periodo di apertura, comunicato dall'albergatore
season	Probabile apertura in stagione, ma periodo non precisato. Gli esercizi senza tali menzioni sono aperti tutto l'anno.
LL35 OSB	Codice postale dell' esercizio
(T.H.F.)	Catena alberghiera (Vedere la lista alla fine della Guida)

Animali

L'introduzione di animali domestici (cani, gatti...),
in Gran Bretagna e in Irlanda, è vietata.

La tavola

LE STELLE

Alcuni esercizi meritano di essere segnalati alla Vostra attenzione per la qualità tutta particolare della loro cucina. Noi li evidenziamo con le « **stelle di ottima tavola** ».

Per questi ristoranti indichiamo tre specialità culinarie e alcuni vini locali che potranno aiutarVi nella scelta.

✿✿✿   **Una delle migliori tavole, vale il viaggio**

Tavola meravigliosa, grandi vini, servizio impeccabile, ambientazione accurata... Prezzi conformi.

✿✿   **Tavola eccellente, merita una deviazione**

Specialità e vini scelti... AspettateVi una spesa in proporzione.

✿   **Un'ottima tavola nella sua categoria**

La stella indica una tappa gastronomica sul Vostro itinerario.

Non mettete però a confronto la stella di un esercizio di lusso, dai prezzi elevati, con quella di un piccolo esercizio dove, a prezzi ragionevoli, viene offerta una cucina di qualità.

LA « M » ROSSA

Pur apprezzando le tavole a « stella », si desidera alle volte consumare un pasto più semplice ma sempre accuratamente preparato.

Alcuni esercizi ci son parsi rispondenti a tale esigenza e sono contraddistinti nella guida da una « **M** » in rosso.

Consultate le carte delle località con stelle e con **M** *che precedono ciascuna delle regioni trattate nella guida.*

La vendita di bevande alcoliche

In Gran Bretagna e Irlanda la vendita di bevande alcoliche è soggetta a leggi che possono variare da una regione all'altra.

In generale gli alberghi, i ristoranti e i pubs possono restare aperti il pomeriggio e servire bevande alcoliche nella misura in cui queste accompagnano un pasto abbastanza consistente. I bars chiudono dopo le ore 23.00.

L'albergatore ha tuttavia la possobilità di servire alla clientela bevande alcoliche anche oltre le ore legali.

Ai ragazzi inferiori ai 14 anni è vietato l'accesso ai bar.

I prezzi

I prezzi che indichiamo in questa guida sono stati stabiliti nel l'autunno 1989. Potranno pertanto subire delle variazioni in relazione ai cambiamenti dei prezzi di beni e servizi.

Entrate nell'albergo o nel ristorante con la Guida alla mano, dimostrando in tal modo la fiducia in chi vi ha indirizzato.

Gli alberghi e i ristoranti vengono menzionati in carattere grassetto quando gli albergatori ci hanno comunicato tutti i loro prezzi e si sono impegnati, sotto la propria responsabilità, ad applicarli ai turisti di passaggio, in possesso della nostra guida.

I prezzi sono indicati in lire sterline (1 £ = 100 pence) ad eccezione per la Repubblica d'Irlanda (Punts).

Quando non figurano le lettere **s.**, **t.**, o **st.** i prezzi indicati possono essere maggiorati per il servizio o per l'I.V.A. o per entrambi. (L'I.V.A. non viene applicata nelle Channel Islands).

PASTI

M 12.00/17.00	**Prezzo fisso** – Pranzo 12.00, cena 17.00. Questi prezzi comprendono il coperto
M 14.00/18.00	Vedere p. 27
s. t.	Servizio compreso. – I.V.A. compresa
st.	Servizio ed I.V.A. compresi (prezzi netti)
5.00	Prezzo della mezza bottiglia o di una caraffa di vino
M a la carte 17.00/21.00	**Alla carta** – Il 1° prezzo corrisponde ad un pasto semplice comprendente : primo piatto, piatto del giorno con contorno, dessert. Il 2° prezzo corrisponde ad un pasto più completo comprendente : antipasto, piatto principale, formaggio e dessert. Questi prezzi comprendono il coperto
7.50	Prezzo della prima colazione inglese se non è compreso nel prezzo della camera. Una prima colazione continentale può essere ottenuta a minor prezzo

CAMERE

rm 45.00/65.00	Prezzo minimo 45.00 per una camera singola e prezzo massimo 65.00 per la camera più bella per due persone
rm 50.00/70.00	Il prezzo della prima colazione inglese è compreso nel prezzo della camera anche se non viene consumata
suites 100.00/200.00	Prezzo minimo e massimo per un appartamento comprendente camera, bagno e salone

« SHORT BREAKS »

SB 60.00/80.00	Prezzo minimo e massimo per persona per un soggiorno di due notti a condizioni vantaggiose o « Short Break ». Questo forfait comprende la camera, la cena e la colazione del mattino generalmente per un minimo di due persone.

LA CAPARRA – CARTE DI CREDITO

Alcuni albergatori chiedono il versamento di una caparra. Si tratta di un deposito-garanzia che impegna tanto l'albergatore che il cliente. Vi raccomandiamo di farVi precisare le norme riguardanti la reciproca garanzia di tale caparra.

🔲 AE ⊙ VISA	Carte di credito accettate dall'esercizio Access (Eurocard) – American Express – Diners Club – Visa

Le città

✉ York	Sede dell'ufficio postale
☎ 0225 Bath	Prefisso telefonico interurbano (nome del centralino indicato solo quando differisce dal nome della località). Dall'estero non formare lo 0
401 M 27, ⑩	Numero della carta Michelin e del riquadro o numero della piega
West Country G.	Vedere la Guida Verde Michelin England : The West Country
pop. 1057	Popolazione
ECD : Wednesday	Giorno di chiusura settimanale dei negozi (solo pomeriggio)
BX **A**	Lettere indicanti l'ubicazione sulla pianta
⛳18	Golf e numero di buche (accesso consentito a tutti, prenotazione consigliata)
☀, ≼	Panorama, punto di vista
✈	Aeroporto
🚗 ☎ 218	Località con servizio auto su treno. Informarsi al numero di telefono indicato
⛴	Trasporti marittimi
⛴	Trasporti marittimi (solo passeggeri) *Vedere la lista delle compagnie alla fine della Guida*
🛈	Ufficio informazioni turistiche

Ora legale

I visitatori dovranno tenere in considerazione l'ora ufficiale in Gran Bretagna : un'ora di ritardo sull'ora italiana.

Le curiosità

GRADO DI INTERESSE

★★★	Vale il viaggio
★★	Merita una deviazione
★	Interessante
AC	Entrata a pagamento

UBICAZIONE

See	Nella città
Envir.	Nei dintorni della città
Exc.	Nella regione
N, S, E, W	La curiosità è situata : a Nord, a Sud, a Est, a Ovest
A 22	Ci si va per la strada A 22 indicata con lo stesso segno sulla pianta
2 m.	Distanza in miglia

Le piante

Alberghi
Ristoranti

Curiosità

Edificio interessante ed entrata principale

Costruzione religiosa interessante :
  Cattedrale, chiesa o cappella

Viabilità

Autostrada, strada a carreggiate separate
  svincolo : completo, parziale,

Grande via di circolazione

Senso unico – Via impraticabile

Via pedonale

Via commerciale – Parcheggio

Porta – Sottopassaggio – Galleria

Sottopassaggio (altezza inferiore a 16'6") sulle grandi
vie di circolazione

Stazione e ferrovia

Funicolare – Funivia, Cabinovia

Ponte mobile – Battello per auto

Simboli vari

Ufficio informazioni turistiche

Moschea – Sinagoga

Ruderi – Mulino a vento

Torre o pilone per telecomunicazione

Giardino, parco, bosco – Cimitero – Calvario

Stadio – Ippodromo – Golf

Golf riservato

Vista – Panorama

Monumento – Fontana – Ospedale

Porto per imbarcazioni da diporto – Faro

Aeroporto – Stazione della Metropolitana

Trasporto con traghetto :
  passeggeri ed autovetture

Ufficio centrale di fermo posta, telefono

Edificio pubblico indicato con lettera :
  Sede dell'Amministrazione di Contea
  Municipio – Museo – Teatro
  Università, grande scuola
  Polizia (Questura, nelle grandi città)

Londra

BRENT SOHO Nome del distretto amministrativo (borough) –
del quartiere (area)

Limite del « borough » – di « area »

L'automobile, I pneumatici

In Gran Bretagna e in Irlanda, l'uso della cintura di sicurezza è obbligatorio per il guidatore e il passeggero che gli siede accanto.

GARAGISTI RIPARATORI
RIVENDITORI DI PNEUMATICI MICHELIN

Nel testo di molte località abbiamo elencato gli indirizzi di garage o concessionari in grado di effettuare, eventualmente, il traino o le riparazioni.

ATS Specialista in pneumatici

Potrete avere delle informazioni sul più vicino punto vendita di pneumatici ATS, rivolgendovi, tra le 9 e le 17, all'indirizzo indicato qui di seguito :

ATS HOUSE   180-188 Northolt Rd.
                Harrow,
                Middlesex HA2 OED
                (01) 423 2000

Le nostre Succursali sono in grado di dare ai nostri clienti tutti i consigli relativi alla migliore utilizzazione dei pneumatici.

AUTOMOBILE CLUBS

Le principali organizzazioni di soccorso automobilistico sono l'Automobile Association ed il Royal Automobile Club : entrambe offrono alcuni loro servizi ai membri dei club affiliati.

AUTOMOBILE ASSOCIATION
Fanum House
BASINGSTOKE, Hants., RG21 2EA
✆ (0256) 20123

ROYAL AUTOMOBILE CLUB
RAC House, Lansdowne Rd,
CROYDON, Surrey CR9 2JA
✆ (01) 686 2525

Lieber Leser

Der Rote Michelin-Führer
Great Britain and Ireland
liegt nun schon in der
17. Ausgabe vor.

Er bringt eine
in voller Unabhängigkeit getroffene,
bewußt begrenzte Auswahl
an Hotels und Restaurants.
Sie basiert auf den regelmäßigen
Überprüfungen durch unsere Inspektoren,
komplettiert durch die zahlreichen
Zuschriften und Erfahrungsberichte
unserer Leser.

Wir sind stets um die Aktualität
unserer Informationen bemüht
und bereiten schon jetzt
den Führer des nächsten Jahres vor.
Nur die neueste Ausgabe
ist wirklich zuverlässig —
denken Sie bitte daran,
wenn der nächste
Rote Michelin-Führer erscheint.

Gute Reise mit Michelin !

Inhaltsverzeichnis

S. 33 — Lieber Leser

S. 35 bis 42 — Zum Gebrauch dieses Führers

S. 43 — Die Stern-Restaurants

S. 44 — Weitere empfehlenswerte Häuser

Hotels, Restaurants, Stadtpläne, Reparatur-
werkstätten, Sehenswürdigkeiten ... Karten

S. 45 — England and Wales

S. 541 — Scotland

S. 615 — Northern Ireland

S. 627 — Channel Islands

S. 637 — Isle of Man

S. 639 — Republic of Ireland

Rot umran-
dete Seiten — Groß-London

S. 674 — Autobahn-Rasthäuser

S. 679 — Die wichtigsten Hotelketten

S. 680 — Verkehrszeichen

S. 685 — Schiffahrtslinien

S. 690 — Entfernungen

S. 692 — Atlas : Hauptverkehrsstraßen und -schiffs-
verbindungen

S. 699 — Michelin-Karten und -Führer

Wahl
eines Hotels, eines Restaurants

Die Auswahl der in diesem Führer aufgeführten Hotels und Restaurants ist für Durchreisende gedacht. In jeder Kategorie drückt die Reihenfolge der Betriebe (sie sind nach ihrem Komfort klassifiziert) eine weitere Rangordnung aus.

KATEGORIEN

🏨	Großer Luxus und Tradition	XXXXX
🏨	Großer Komfort	XXXX
🏨	Sehr komfortabel	XXX
🏨	Mit gutem Komfort	XX
🏨	Mit ausreichendem Komfort	X
	Bürgerlich	
	Preiswerte, empfehlenswerte Gasthäuser und Pensionen	
without rest.	Hotel ohne Restaurant	
	Restaurant vermietet auch Zimmer	with rm

ANNEHMLICHKEITEN

Manche Häuser sind im Führer durch rote Symbole gekennzeichnet (s. unten.). Der Aufenthalt in diesen Hotels ist wegen der schönen, ruhigen Lage, der nicht alltäglichen Einrichtung und Atmosphäre und dem gebotenen Service besonders angenehm und erholsam.

🏨 bis 🏨	Angenehme Hotels
XXXXX bis X	Angenehme Restaurants
« Park »	Besondere Annehmlichkeit
	Sehr ruhiges, oder abgelegenes und ruhiges Hotel
	Ruhiges Hotel
≤ sea	Reizvolle Aussicht
≤	Interessante oder weite Sicht

Die den einzelnen Regionen vorangestellten Übersichtskarten, auf denen die Orte mit besonders angenehmen oder ruhigen Häusern eingezeichnet sind, helfen Ihnen bei der Reisevorbereitung. Teilen Sie uns bitte nach der Reise Ihre Erfahrungen und Meinungen mit. Sie helfen uns damit, den Führer weiter zu verbessern.

Einrichtung

Die meisten der empfohlenen Hotels verfügen über Zimmer, die alle oder doch zum größten Teil mit einer Naßzelle ausgestattet sind. In den Häusern der Kategorien ⌂, ⌂, ⌂ und ⌂ kann diese jedoch in einigen Zimmern fehlen.

30 rm	Anzahl der Zimmer
	Fahrstuhl
	Klimaanlage
TV	Fernsehen im Zimmer
	Hotel ganz oder teilweise reserviert für Nichtraucher
	Zimmertelefon mit Außenverbindung über Telefonzentrale
	Zimmertelefon mit direkter Außenverbindung
	Für Körperbehinderte leicht zugängliche Zimmer
	Freibad, Hallenbad
	Liegewiese, Garten
	Hoteleigener Tennisplatz – Golfplatz und Lochzahl
	Angelmöglichkeit für Hotelgäste, evtl. gegen Gebühr
150	Konferenzräume : Höchstkapazität
	Hotelgarage (wird gewöhnlich berechnet)
P	Parkplatz reserviert für Gäste
	Hunde sind unerwünscht (im ganzen Haus bzw. in den Zimmern oder im Restaurant)
Fax	Telefonische Dokumentenübermittlung
May-October	Öffnungszeit, vom Hotelier mitgeteilt
season	Unbestimmte Öffnungszeit eines Saisonhotels. Die Häuser, für die wir keine Schließungszeiten angeben, sind im allgemeinen ganzjährig geöffnet
LL35 OSB	Angabe des Postbezirks (hinter der Hoteladresse)
(T.H.F.)	Hotelkette (Liste am Ende des Führers)

Tiere

Das Mitführen von Haustieren (Hunde, Katzen u. dgl.) bei der Einreise in Großbritannien und Irland ist untersagt.

Küche

DIE STERNE

Einige Häuser verdienen wegen ihrer überdurchschnittlich guten Küche Ihre besondere Beachtung. Auf diese Häuser weisen die Sterne hin.

Bei den mit « **Stern** » ausgezeichneten Betrieben nennen wir drei kulinarische Spezialitäten, die Sie probieren sollten.

❀❀❀   **Eine der besten Küchen : eine Reise wert**

Ein denkwürdiges Essen, edle Weine, tadelloser Service, gepflegte Atmosphäre ... entsprechende Preise.

❀❀   **Eine hervorragende Küche : verdient einen Umweg**

Ausgesuchte Menus und Weine ... angemessene Preise.

❀   **Eine sehr gute Küche : verdient Ihre besondere Beachtung**

Der Stern bedeutet eine angenehme Unterbrechung Ihrer Reise. Vergleichen Sie aber bitte nicht den Stern eines sehr teuren Luxusrestaurants mit dem Stern eines kleineren oder mittleren Hauses, wo man Ihnen zu einem annehmbaren Preis eine ebenfalls vorzügliche Mahlzeit reicht.

DAS ROTE « M »

Wir glauben, daß Sie neben den Häusen mit « Stern » auch solche Adressen interessieren werden, die einfache, aber sorgfältig zubereitete Mahlzeiten anbieten.

Auf solche Häuser weisen wir im Text durch das rote « **M** » hin.

Siehe Karten der Orte mit « Stern » und « M », die den einzelnen im Führer behandelten Regionen vorangestellt sind.

Ausschank alkoholischer Getränke

In Großbritannien und Irland unterliegt der Ausschank alkoholischer Getränke gesetzlichen Bestimmungen, die in den einzelnen Gegenden verschieden sind.

Generell können Hotels, Restaurants und Pubs nachmittags geöffnet sein und alkoholische Getränke ausschenken, wenn diese zu einer entsprechend gehaltvollen Mahlzeit genossen werden. Die Bars schließen nach 23 Uhr.

Hotelgästen können alkoholische Getränke jedoch auch außerhalb der Ausschankzeiten serviert werden.

Kindern unter 14 Jahren ist der Zutritt zu den Bars untersagt.

Preise

Die in diesem Führer genannten Preise wurden uns im Herbst 1989 angegeben. Sie können sich mit den Preisen von Waren und Dienstleistungen ändern.

Halten Sie beim Betreten des Hotels den Führer in der Hand. Sie zeigen damit, daß Sie aufgrund dieser Empfehlung gekommen sind.

Die Preise sind in Pfund Sterling angegeben (1 £ = 100 pence) mit Ausnahme der Republik Irland (Punts).

Wenn die Buchstaben **s.**, **t.**, oder **st.** nicht hinter den angegebenen Preisen aufgeführt sind, können sich diese um den Zuschlag für Bedienung und/oder MWSt erhöhen (keine MWSt auf den Channel Islands).

Die Namen der Hotels und Restaurants, die ihre Preise genannt haben, sind fett gedruckt. Gleichzeitig haben sich diese Häuser verpflichtet, die von den Hoteliers selbst angegebenen Preise den Benutzern des Michelin-Führers zu berechnen.

MAHLZEITEN

M 12.00/17.00	**Feste Menupreise** – Mittagessen 12.00, Abendessen 17.00 (inkl. Couvert)
M 14.00/18.00	Siehe Seite 37
s. t.	Bedienung inkl. – MWSt inkl.
st.	Bedienung und MWSt inkl.
5.00	Preis für 1/2 Flasche oder eine Karaffe Tafelwein
M a la carte 17.00/21.00	**Mahlzeiten « à la carte »** – Der erste Preis entspricht einer einfachen aber sorgfältig zubereiteten Mahlzeit, bestehend aus kleiner Vorspeise, Tagesgericht mit Beilage und Nachtisch. Der zweite Preis entspricht einer reichlicheren Mahlzeit mit Vorspeise, Hauptgericht, Käse oder Nachtisch (inkl. Couvert)
7.50	Preis des englischen Frühstücks, wenn dieser nicht im Übernachtungspreis enthalten ist Einfaches, billigeres Frühstück (Continental breakfast) erhältlich

ZIMMER

rm 45.00/65.00	Mindestpreis 45.00 für ein Einzelzimmer und Höchstpreis 65.00 für das schönste Doppelzimmer
rm 50.00/70.00	Übernachtung mit englischem Frühstück, selbst wenn dieses nicht eingenommen wird
suites 100.00/200.00	Mindest- und Höchstpreis für ein Appartement bestehend aus Wohnzimmer, Schlafzimmer und Bad

« SHORT BREAKS »

SB 60.00/80.00	Mindest- und Höchstpreis pro Person bei einem Aufenthalt von 2 Nächten (« Short Break »). Diese Pauschalpreise (für mindestens 2 Personen) umfassen Zimmer, Abendessen und Frühstück.

Einige Hoteliers verlangen eine Anzahlung. Diese ist als Garantie sowohl für den Hotelier als auch für den Gast anzusehen.

Vom Haus akzeptierte Kreditkarten :
Access (Eurocard) – American Express – Diners Club – Visa

Städte

⊠ York	Zuständiges Postamt
✆ 0225 Bath	Vorwahlnummer und evtl. zuständiges Fernsprechamt (bei Gesprächen vom Ausland aus wird die erste Null weggelassen)
101 M 27, ⑩	Nummer der Michelin-Karte und Koordinaten des Planfeldes oder Faltseite
West Country G.	Siehe auch den grünen Michelinführer « England : The West Country »
pop. 1057	Einwohnerzahl
ECD : Wednesday	Tag, an dem die Läden nachmittags geschlossen sind
BX A	Markierung auf dem Stadtplan
⚑18	Öffentlicher Golfplatz und Lochzahl (Reservierung ratsam)
✳, ≼	Rundblick, Aussichtspunkt
✈	Flughafen
🚗 ✆ 218	Ladestelle für Autoreisezüge – Nähere Auskünfte unter der angegebenen Telefonnummer
🚢	Autofähre
🚤	Personenfähre *Liste der Schiffahrtsgesellschaften am Ende des Führers*
🛈	Informationsstelle

Uhrzeit

In Großbritannien ist eine Zeitverschiebung zu beachten und die Uhr gegenüber der deutschen Zeit um 1 Stunde zurückzustellen.

Sehenswürdigkeiten

BEWERTUNG

★★★	Eine Reise wert
★★	Verdient einen Umweg
★	Sehenswert
AC	Eintritt (gegen Gebühr)

LAGE

See	In der Stadt
Envir.	In der Umgebung der Stadt
Exc.	Ausflugsziele
N, S, E, W	Im Norden (N), Süden (S), Osten (E), Westen (W) der Stadt
A 22	Zu erreichen über die Straße A 22
2 m.	Entfernung in Meilen

Stadtpläne

Hotels
Restaurants

Sehenswürdigkeiten

Sehenswertes Gebäude mit Haupteingang
Sehenswerter Sakralbau
   Kathedrale, Kirche oder Kapelle

Straßen

Autobahn, Schnellstraße
   Anschlußstelle : Autobahneinfahrt und/oder -ausfahrt,
Hauptverkehrsstraße
Einbahnstraße – nicht befahrbare Straße
Fußgängerzone
Pasteur   P   Einkaufsstraße – Parkplatz
Tor – Passage – Tunnel
Unterführung (Höhe angegeben bis 16'6") auf Hauptverkehrsstraßen
Bahnhof und Bahnlinie
Standseilbahn – Seilschwebebahn
Bewegliche Brücke – Autofähre

Sonstige Zeichen

Informationsstelle
Moschee – Synagoge
Ruine – Windmühle
Funk-, Fernsehturm
Garten, Park, Wäldchen – Friedhof – Bildstock
Stadion – Pferderennbahn – Golfplatz
Golfplatz (Zutritt bedingt erlaubt)
Aussicht – Rundblick
Denkmal – Brunnen – Krankenhaus
Jachthafen – Leuchtturm
Flughafen – U-Bahnstation
Schiffsverbindungen :
   Autofähre
Hauptpostamt (postlagernde Sendungen), Telefon
Öffentliches Gebäude, durch einen Buchstaben gekennzeichnet :
   C   Sitz der Grafschaftsverwaltung
H   M   T   Rathaus – Museum – Theater
U   Universität, Hochschule
POL.   Polizei (in größeren Städten Polizeipräsidium)

London

BRENT SOHO   Name des Verwaltungsbezirks (borough) – des Stadtteils (area)
Grenze des « borough » – des « area »

Das Auto, die Reifen

In Großbritannien und Irland besteht Gurtanlegepflicht für Fahrer und Beifahrer auf den Vordersitzen.

REPARATURWERKSTÄTTEN
LIEFERANTEN VON MICHELIN-REIFEN

Bei den meisten Orten geben wir Adressen von Kfz-Vertragswerkstätten an; viele davon haben einen Abschlepp- bzw. Reparaturdienst.

ATS Reifenhändler

Die Anschrift der nächstgelegenen ATS-Verkaufsstelle erhalten Sie auf Anfrage (9-17 Uhr) bei

ATS HOUSE   180-188 Northolt Rd.
Harrow,
Middlesex HA2 OED
(01) 423 2000

AUTOMOBILCLUBS

Die wichtigsten Automobilclubs des Landes sind die Automobile Association und der Royal Automobile Club, die den Mitgliedern der der FIA angeschlossenen Automobilclubs Pannenhilfe leisten und einige ihrer Dienstleistungen anbieten.

AUTOMOBILE ASSOCIATION
Fanum House
BASINGSTOKE, Hants., RG21 2EA
✆ (0256) 20123

ROYAL AUTOMOBILE CLUB
RAC House, Lansdowne Rd
CROYDON, Surrey CR9 2JA
✆ (01) 686 2525

Starred establishments
Les établissements à étoiles
Gli esercizi con stelle
Die Stern-Restaurants

England and Wales

Bray-on-Thames	Waterside Inn	**London**	Le Gavroche

England and Wales

London	La Tante Claire	**London**	Chez Nico
–	Harvey's	**Oxford**	Le Manoir aux Quat'Saisons

England and Wales

Chester	Arkle
Esher	Les Alouettes
Great Malvern	Croque-en-Bouche
Ilkley	Box-Tree
London	L'Arlequin
–	Capital
–	Cavaliers'
–	Connaught
–	Four Seasons
–	Oak Room
–	Le Soufflé
–	Suntory
–	Sutherlands
New Milton	Chewton Glen
Norwich	Adlard's

Oakham	Hambleton Hall
Plymouth	Chez Nous
Reading	L'Ortolan
Royal Leamington Spa	Mallory Court
South Molton	Whitechapel Manor
Stroud	Oakes
Taunton	Castle
Tetbury	Calcot Manor

Scotland

Fort William	Inverlochy Castle
Peat Inn	Peat Inn
Ullapool	Altnaharrie Inn

Republic of Ireland

Dublin	Patrick Guilbaud
Kenmare	Park

Further establishments which merit your attention

Autres tables qui méritent votre attention
Altre tavole particolarmente interessanti
Weitere empfehlenswerte Häuser

M

England and Wales

Abergavenny	Walnut Tree Inn
Amersham	King's Arms
Bath	Homewood Park
Bath	The Priory
Blackpool	River House
Bradford	Restaurant 19
Bristol	Lettonie
Broadway	Buckland Manor
Brockenhurst	Le Poussin
Cheltenham	Redmond's at Malvern View
Clun	Old Post Office
Dartmouth	Mansion House
Earl Stonham	Mr Underhill's
Eastbourne	Hungry Monk
Emsworth	36 on the Quay
Fowey	Food for Thought
Glemsford	Barretts
Grasmere	Michael's Nook Country House
Grasmere	White Moss House
Hastings	Röser's
Henley-on-Thames	Stonor Arms
King's Lynn	Congham Hall
Knowl Hill	Warrener
London	Candlewick Room
–	Le Caprice
–	Chinon
–	Hilaire
–	Keats
–	Kensington Place
–	Martin's
–	Partners 23
–	Red Fort
–	Turner's
London	Zen Central
Padstow	Seafood
Pool-in-Wharfedale	Pool Court
Pwllheli	Plas Bodegroes
Royal Tunbridge Wells	Cheevers
Storrington	Manley's
Torquay	Table
Truro	Long's
Ullswater	Sharrow Bay Country House
Waterhouses	Old Beams
Williton	White House
Windermere	Miller Howe
Worcester	Brown's
Wrightington Bar	Highmoor

Scotland

Aberfoyle	Braeval Old Mill
Arisaig	Arisaig House
Gullane	La Potinière
Port Appin	Airds
Portpatrick	Knockinaam Lodge

Northern Ireland

Portrush	Ramore

Republic of Ireland

Adare	Mustard Seed
Ahakista	Shiro
Bunratty	McCloskey's
Dingle	Doyle's Seafood Bar
Dublin	Park
Gorey	Marlfield House
Mallow	Longueville House
Moycullen	Drimcong House
Shanagarry	Ballymaloe House

England and Wales

ENGLAND

County	Abbreviation
Avon	Avon
Bedfordshire	Beds.
Berkshire	Berks.
Buckinghamshire	Bucks.
Cambridgeshire	Cambs.
Cheshire	Cheshire
Cleveland	Cleveland
Cornwall	Cornwall
Cumbria	Cumbria
Derbyshire	Derbs.
Devon	Devon
Dorset	Dorset
Durham	Durham
East Sussex	East Sussex
Essex	Essex
Gloucestershire	Glos.
Greater Manchester	Greater Manchester
Hampshire	Hants.
Hereford and Worcester	Heref. and Worc.
Hertfordshire	Herts.
Humberside	Humberside
Isle of Wight	I. O. W.
Kent	Kent
Lancashire	Lancs.
Leicestershire	Leics.
Lincolnshire	Lincs.
Merseyside	Merseyside
Norfolk	Norfolk
Northamptonshire	Northants.
Northumberland	Northumb.
North Yorkshire	North Yorks.
Nottinghamshire	Notts.
Oxfordshire	Oxon.
Shropshire	Shropshire
Somerset	Somerset
South Yorkshire	South Yorks.
Staffordshire	Staffs.
Suffolk	Suffolk
Surrey	Surrey
Tyne and Wear	Tyne and Wear
Warwickshire	Warw.
West Midlands	West Midlands
West Sussex	West Sussex
West Yorkshire	West Yorks.
Wiltshire	Wilts.

WALES

County	Abbreviation
Clwyd	Clwyd
Dyfed	Dyfed
Gwent	Gwent
Gwynedd	Gwynedd
Mid Glamorgan	Mid Glam.
Powys	Powys
South Glamorgan	South Glam.
West Glamorgan	West Glam.

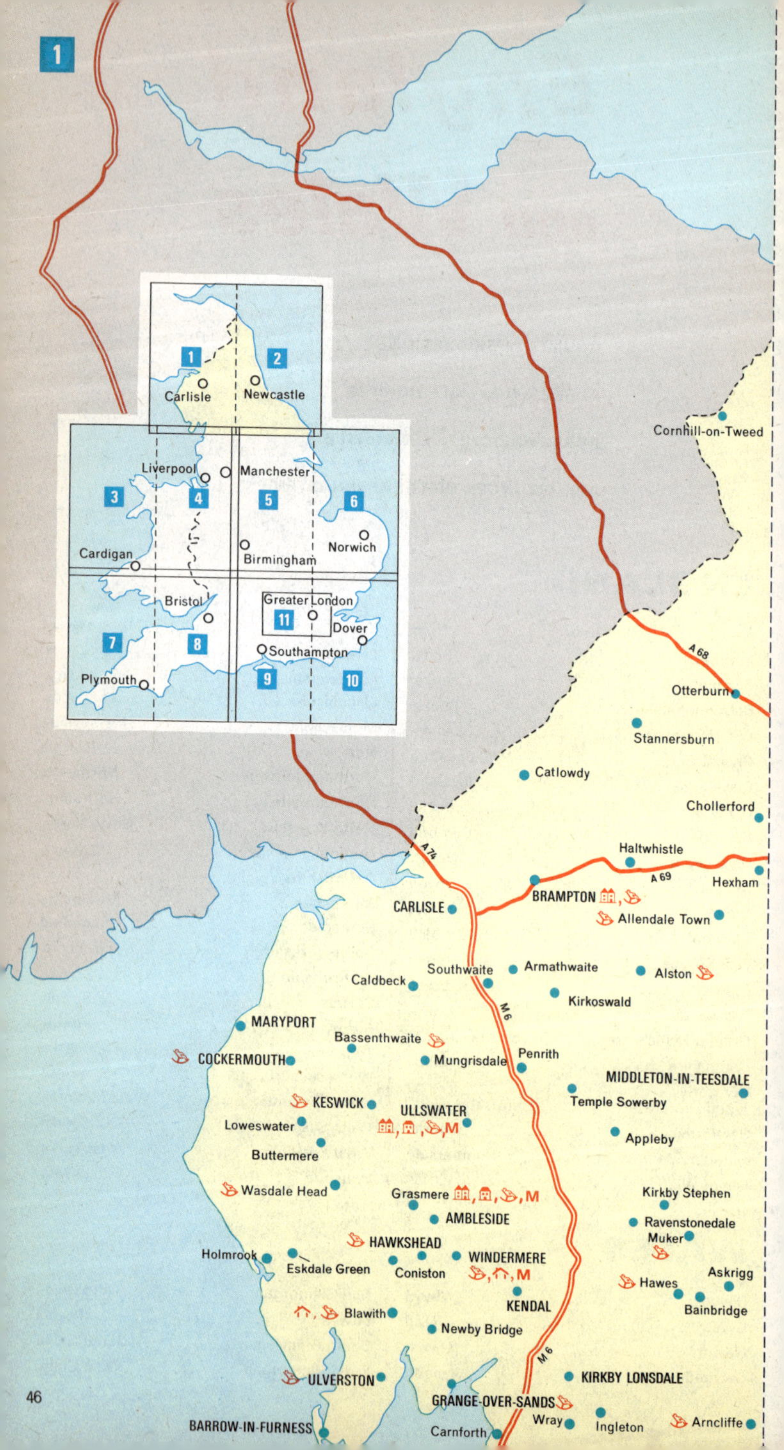

1
1 Carlisle
2 Newcastle
3
4 Liverpool
Manchester
5
6
Cardigan
Birmingham
Norwich
Bristol
7
8
Greater London
11
Dover
Plymouth
Southampton
9
10
Cornhill-on-Tweed
A 68
Otterburn
Stannersburn
Catlowdy
Chollerford
A 74
Haltwhistle
A 69
Hexham
BRAMPTON
Allendale Town
CARLISLE
Southwaite
Armathwaite
Alston
Caldbeck
Kirkoswald
M 6
MARYPORT
Bassenthwaite
Mungrisdale
Penrith
COCKERMOUTH
MIDDLETON-IN-TEESDALE
KESWICK
Temple Sowerby
ULLSWATER
Loweswater
M
Appleby
Buttermere
Wasdale Head
Kirkby Stephen
Grasmere
M
Ravenstonedale
AMBLESIDE
Muker
HAWKSHEAD
Holmrook
WINDERMERE
Askrigg
Eskdale Green
Coniston
M
Hawes
Bainbridge
KENDAL
Blawith
Newby Bridge
M 6
KIRKBY LONSDALE
ULVERSTON
GRANGE-OVER-SANDS
BARROW-IN-FURNESS
Carnforth
Wray
Ingleton
Arncliffe

Place with at least :

one hotel or restaurant .... ● Ripon

one pleasant hotel .... 🏨 , 🏠 . ✗ with rm

one quiet, secluded hotel .... 🦢

one restaurant with .... ✿, ✿✿, ✿✿✿, M

See this town for establishments
located in its vicinity .... LEICESTER

Localité offrant au moins :

une ressource hôtelière .... ● Ripon

un hôtel agréable .... 🏨 , 🏠 . ✗ with rm

un hôtel très tranquille, isolé .... 🦢

une bonne table à .... ✿, ✿✿, ✿✿✿, M

Localité groupant dans le texte
les ressources de ses environs .... LEICESTER

La località possiede come minimo :

una risorsa alberghiera .... ● Ripon

un albergo ameno .... 🏨 , 🏠 . ✗ with rm

un albergo molto tranquillo, isolato .... 🦢

un'ottima tavola con .... ✿, ✿✿, ✿✿✿, M

La località raggruppa nel suo testo
le risorse dei dintorni .... LEICESTER

Ort mit mindestens :

einem Hotel oder Restaurant .... ● Ripon

einem angenehmen Hotel .... 🏨 , 🏠 . ✗ with rm

einem sehr ruhigen und abgelegenen Hotel ...... 🦢

einem Restaurant mit .... ✿, ✿✿, ✿✿✿, M

Ort mit Angaben über Hotels und Restaurants
in seiner Umgebung .... LEICESTER

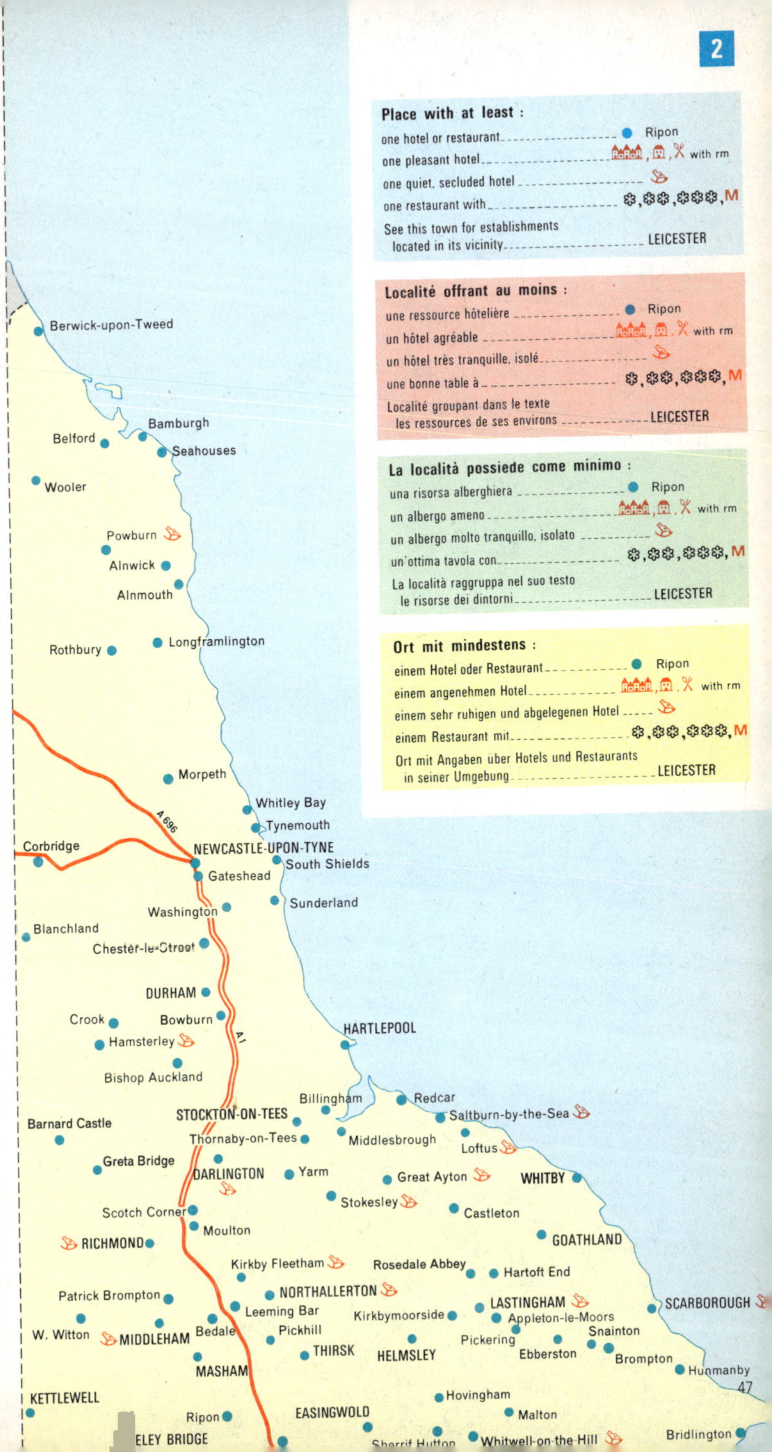

47

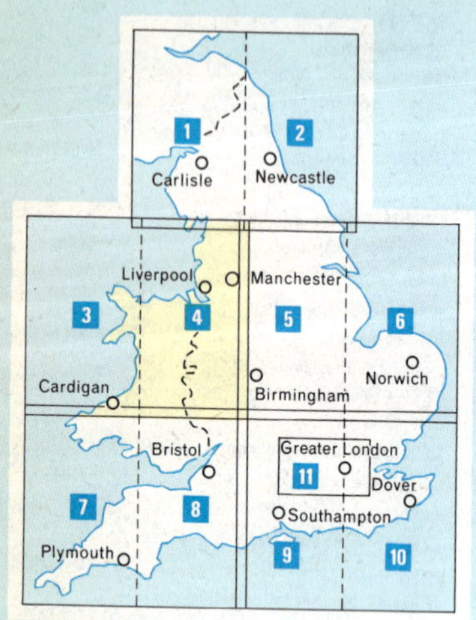

1
2
Carlisle
Newcastle
Liverpool
Manchester
3
4
5
6
Cardigan
Birmingham
Norwich
Bristol
Greater London
11
Dover
7
8
Southampton
9
10
Plymouth

Llanerchymedd
Llangefni
Beaumaris
Rhoscolyn
A 5
Menai Bridge
Port Dinorwic
Bangor
Caernarfon
Llanberis
Beddgelert
Nefyn
Porthmadog
Criccieth
Portmeirion
Tudweiliog
PWLLHELI
Llanbedrog
, M
Harlech
ABERSOCH
Llanbedr
Dyffryn Ardudwy
Barmouth
Tywyn
Aberdovey
ABERYSTWYTH
New Quay
ABERPORTH
CARDIGAN
Pontshaen
FISHGUARD
NEWPORT
Boncath

4
BARROW-IN-FURNESS
Carnforth
Wray
Ingleton
Arncliffe
SETTLE
Malham
Het
Morecambe
Heysham
LANCASTER
Slaidburn
Grindleton
Gisburn
Sawley
Fleetwood
Chipping
St-Michaels-on-Wyre
Hurst Green
Colne
Thornton Cleveleys
Whalley
Burnley
M , BLACKPOOL
Kirkham
PRESTON
BLACKBURN
Clayton-le-Moors
LYTHAM ST. ANNE'S
Leyland
Clayton le Woods
Ramsbottom
Mere Brow
CHORLEY
Southport
Wrightington Bar
Adlington
Bury
Birch
M
Standish
BOLTON
Wigan
Salford
Kirkby
Haydock
Eccles
MANCHESTER
Sale
Birkenhead
LIVERPOOL
M 62
ALTRINCHAM
Greasby
WARRINGTON
Stockport
Llandudno
Rock Ferry
Widnes
Daresbury
Lymm
WILMSLOW
Bromborough
Runcorn
KNUTSFORD
CONWY
Parkgate
Eastham
Frodsham
Alderley Edge
Pres
CULWYN-BAY
Holywell
Puddington
Hartford
MACCLESFIELD
Llansantffraid
Glan Conwy
St.Asaph
CHESTER
HOLMES CHAPEL
Congleto
Llannefydd
Mold
Tattenhall
Tarporley
Sandbach
LLANRWST
Beeston
Alsager
Ruthin
Rossett
Broxton
Crewe
BETWS-Y-COED
A5
Wrexham
Nantwich
STOKE-ON-TRENT
Dolwyddelan
Cerrigydrudion
Malpas
Newcastle-under-Lyme
Llangollen
Hanmer
Whitchurch
Stone
Bala
Llandrillo
Glyn Ceiriog
MARKET DRAYTON
Llanarmon Dyffryn Ceiriog
Weston-under-Redcastle
Hodnet
Staffo
Lake Vyrnwy
Oswestry
NEWPORT
LLANFYLLIN
SHREWSBURY
DOLGELLAU
TELFORD
Tal-y-Llyn
Welshpool
Shifnal
Abergynolwyn
Berriew
WOLVERHAMPTON
MACHYNLLETH
Montgomery
Church Stretton
Darlasto
NEWTOWN
BRIDGNORTH
Dud
Ditton Priors
STOURBRIDGE
Bishops Castle
Pant Mawr
Craven Arms
Diddlebury
Hopton Wafers
KIDDERMINSTER
Llangurig
Clun M
Ludlow
Cleobury Mortimer
Stourport-on-Severn
Knighton
Bewdley
Rhayader
Brimfield
Abberley
Presteigne
Shrawley
Crossgates
Penybont
LEOMINSTER
Bromyard
Droitwich
LLANDRINDOD WELLS
Kington
Ullingswick
M , WORCESTER
Builth Wells
Knightwick
LLANWRTYD WELLS
Weobley
Llangammarch Wells
Bredwardine
GREAT MALVERN
Crug-y-bar
Glasbury
Hay-on-Wye
HEREFORD
Upton upon Severn
49
A40
Three Cocks
Vowchurch
LEDBURY
Llyswen
R. Severn
M 54
M 6
M 6
M 61
M 56
A 483
A 5
A 483
M 5

5
Ripon
EASINGWOLD
Malton
PATELEY BRIDGE
Sherrif Hutton
Whitwell-on-the-Hill
Bridlington
M Boroughbridge
GRASSINGTON
Burnsall
Hetton
Knaresborough
GREAT DRIFFIELD
Skipton
Bolton Abbey
YORK
POCKLINGTON
Ilkley
HARROGATE
Wetherby
Pool in Wharfedale
Otley
With rm., M
Boston Spa
BEVERLEY
Haworth
Bingley
Harewood
Tadcaster
Shipley
LEEDS
Selby
Howden
KINGSTON-UPON-HULL
Hedon
Bradford
Monk Fryston
M 62
A 63
Hebden
Bridge
Brighouse
M 62
HALIFAX
Wakefield
Winteringham
M 62
Wentbridge
Barnsdale Bar
Scunthorpe
HUDDERSFIELD
Meltham
HOLMFIRTH
BARNSLEY
Oldham
DONCASTER
Ashton-under-Lyne
Glossop
Rotherham
Bawtry
Marple
M 18
Clayworth
Castleton
SHEFFIELD
Aston
Blyth
Barnby Moor
Disley
Dinnington
Hathersage
Todwick
Prestbury
Grindleford
Renishaw
Sturton-by-Stow
Dronfield
Clowne
Markham
Moor
Buxton
Eyam
Baslow
Tuxford
LINCOLN
BAKEWELL
Chesterfield
Longnor
Rowsley
Ollerton
Hartington
MATLOCK
Woodhall Spa
Leek
South Normanton
Beckingham
Southwell
NEWARK-ON-TRENT
Thorpe
Waterhouses
with rm., M
Belper
Hucknall
Sleaford
A 17
Ashbourne
NOTTINGHAM
Bottesford
Uttoxeter
DERBY
GRANTHAM
CASTLE DONINGTON
Tutbury
Grimsthorpe
BURTON-UPON-TRENT
LOUGHBOROUGH
Rugeley
Ashby de la Zouch
Melton Mowbray
Bourne
Cannock
Market Deeping
Lichfield
Markfield
Tamworth
STAMFORD
Dordon
LEICESTER
OAKHAM
WALSALL
Aldridge
Earl Shilton
PETERBOROUGH
Countesthorpe
UPPINGHAM
Sutton Coldfield
Hinckley
Coleshill
NUNEATON
MARKET HARBOROUGH
BIRMINGHAM
Bedworth
M 69
Oundle
M 6
Lutterworth
SOLIHULL
Husbands Bosworth
Aldwincle
COVENTRY
Hockley-
Heath
Kenilworth
RUGBY
Kettering
Keyston
Bromsgrove
Dunchurch
Huntingdon
Henley-in-Arden
WELLINGBOROUGH
Buckden
REDDITCH
Royal Leamington Spa
with rm.
ST. NEOTS
Alcester
WARWICK
Weedon-Bec
NORTHAMPTON
Castle Ashby
Priors Hardwick
Horton
A 428
SANDY
STRATFORD-UPON-AVON
Roade
BEDFORD
ERSHORE
Evesham
Towcester
Newport Pagnell
50
SHIPSTON-ON-STOUR
STONY STRATFORD
Milton Keynes
CHIPPING CAMPDEN
BANBURY
Aspley Guise
Flitwick
Blockley
Brackley
Woburn

6
1 Carlisle
2 Newcastle
3
4 Liverpool
5 Manchester
6 Norwich
Cardigan
Birmingham
Bristol
Greater London
11 Dover
7
8 Southampton
9
10
Plymouth
Great Grimsby
Cleethorpes
LOUTH
Skegness
Boston
Sheringham
West Runton
HUNSTANTON
Wells-next-the-Sea
BLAKENEY
Weybourne
Cromer
Little Walsingham
Holt
Docking
Great Snoring
Thorpe Market
Dersingham
Fakenham
Corpusty
NORTH WALSHAM
Guist
Worstead
Sandringham
Cawston
Neatishead
Lenwade
Great Witchingham
Coltishall
Wroxham
Whaplode
Ormesby
St-Margar
Elsing
Horning
KING'S LYNN
East Dereham
A 47
South Walsham
Wisbech
Shipdham
NORWICH
GREAT YARMOUTH
Swaffham
Wymondham
Attleborough
Bunwell
LOWESTOFT
Great Hockham
A 11
Beccles
Thetford
ELY
DISS
Fressingfield
Southwold
Mildenhall
Gislingham
St. Ives
Yoxford
Westleto
Barton Mills
Ixworth
BURY ST. EDMUNDS
Framlingham
NEWMARKET
A 45
Earl Stonham M
Aldebu
CAMBRIDGE
A 45
Needham Market
Otley
Wickham Market
A 11
M Glemsford
LAVENHAM
Chelsworth
Claydon
Woodbridge
Orford
Melbourn
Long Melford
Stoke-by-Nayland
IPSWICH
M 11
Sudbury
Hadleigh
wport
Saffron Walden
Great Yeldham
Higham
East Bergholt
Castle Hedingham
51

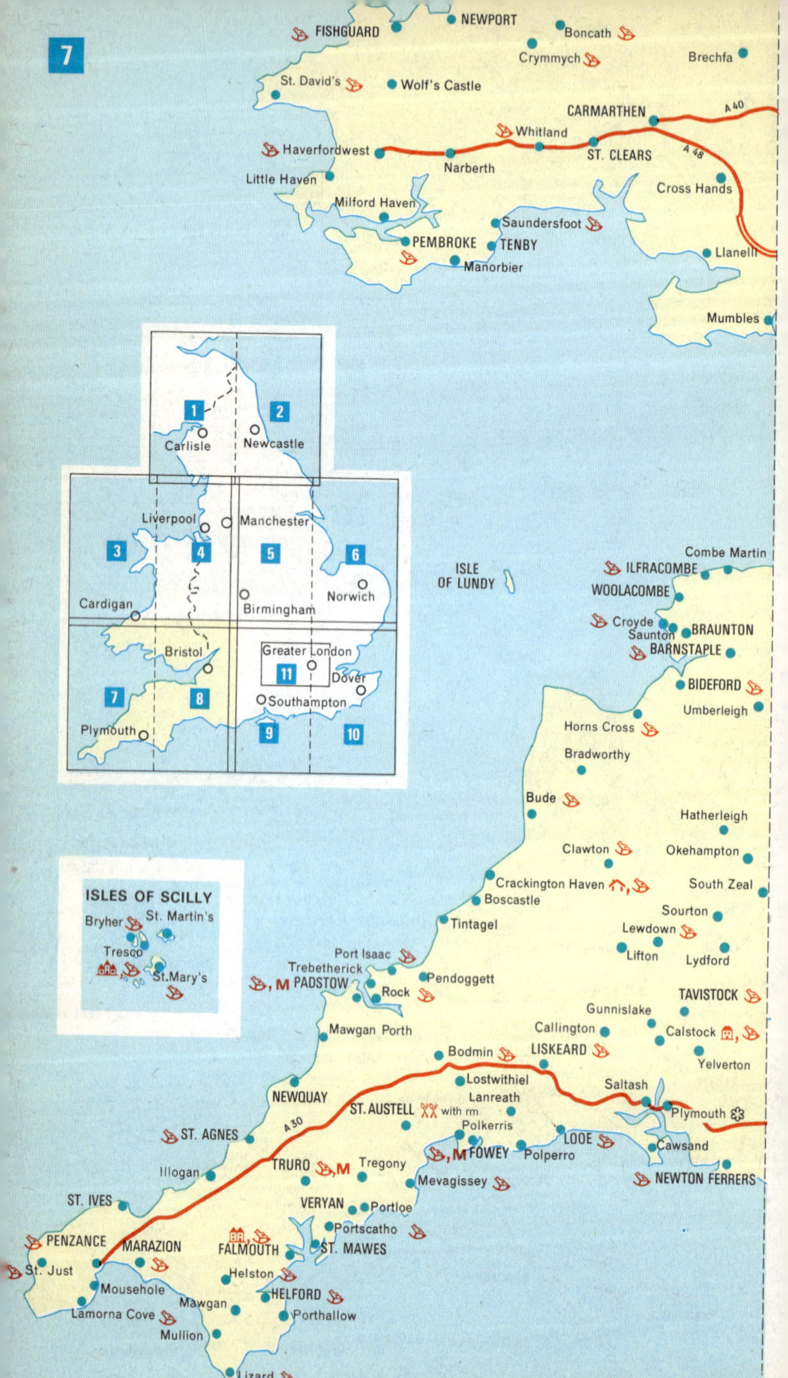

FISHGUARD
NEWPORT
Boncath
Crymmych
Brechfa
St. David's
Wolf's Castle
CARMARTHEN
A 40
Whitland
Haverfordwest
Narberth
ST. CLEARS
A 48
Little Haven
Cross Hands
Milford Haven
Saundersfoot
Llanelli
PEMBROKE
TENBY
Manorbier
Mumbles

1
Carlisle
2
Newcastle

Liverpool
Manchester

3
4
5
6
Norwich
Cardigan
Birmingham

Bristol
Greater London
11
Dover
7
8
Southampton
Plymouth
9
10

ISLE
OF LUNDY

Combe Martin
ILFRACOMBE
WOOLACOMBE
Croyde
Saunton
BRAUNTON
BARNSTAPLE
BIDEFORD
Umberleigh
Horns Cross
Bradworthy
Hatherleigh
Bude
Clawton
Okehampton
Crackington Haven
South Zeal
Boscastle
Sourton
Tintagel
Lewdown
Port Isaac
Lifton
Lydford
Trebetherick
Pendoggett
PADSTOW
Rock
TAVISTOCK
Mawgan Porth
Gunnislake
Callington
Calstock
Bodmin
LISKEARD
Yelverton
Lostwithiel
Saltash
NEWQUAY
Lanreath
A 30
ST. AUSTELL
with rm
Polkerris
Plymouth
ST. AGNES
Polperro
LOOE
Cawsand
Illogan
TRURO
Tregony
FOWEY
Polperro
Mevagissey
NEWTON FERRERS
ST. IVES
VERYAN
Portloe
Portscatho
PENZANCE
MARAZION
FALMOUTH
ST. MAWES
St. Just
Helston
Mousehole
HELFORD
Mawgan
Lamorna Cove
Porthallow
Mullion
Lizard

ISLES OF SCILLY
Bryher
St. Martin's
Tresco
St. Mary's

8
53
Crug-y-bar
A 40
LLANDEILO
Llandybie
Ammanford
Neath
SWANSEA
Port Talbot
Sarn Park
Pencoed
PORTHCAWL
BRIDGEND
Llantwit Major
Trecastle
Talybont-on-Usk
Llangynidr
Merthyr Tydfil
Miskin
Three Cocks
Llyswen
Brecon
Crickhowell
M ABERGAVENNY
Cwmbran
M 4
St. Brides-Super-Ely
CARDIFF
Barry
Hay-on-Wye
Vowchurch
Fownhope
Woolhope
ROSS-ON-WYE
SYMONDS YAT
MONMOUTH
Trelleck
USK
Tintern
Chepstow
NEWPORT
LEDBURY
TEWKESBURY
GLOUCESTER
Birdlip
Withingto
COLEFORD
Painswick
Berkeley
STROUD
Stone
TETBURY
Thornbury
MALMESBURY
Alveston
Badminton
Chipping Sodbury
M 4
Sutt
CASTLE COMBE
Corsham
C
Weston-Super-Mare
M BRISTOL
With rm. Lacock
M BATH
MELKSHAM
Blagdon
Bradford-on-Avon
Trowbrid
LYNTON
PORLOCK
MINEHEAD
Wheddon Cross
DUNSTER
Watchet
Kilve
Simonsbath
Exford
Bilbrook
Holford
Williton
Withypool
Winsford
BRIDGWATER
SOUTH MOLTON
Hawkridge
WIVELISCOMBE
Dulverton
Chittlehamholt
Brushford
TAUNTON
Burrington
Winkleigh
TIVERTON
Bickleigh
Spreyton
Cheriton Bishop
EXETER
CHAGFORD
Fenny Bridges
Gittisham
Ottery St.Mary
Venn Ottery
Colyton
Beer
Branscombe
SIDMOUTH
North Bovey
BOVEY TRACEY
EXMOUTH
Dawlish
A 38
A 30
Brent Knoll
Wedmore
WELLS
GLASTONBURY
Street
Somerton
South Petherton
Donyatt
Yarcombe
HONITON
AXMINSTER
Charmouth
LYME REGIS
Abbotsbury
Chilcompton
FARRINGTON GURNEY
WARMINSTER
SHEPTON MALLET
Bruton
Castle Cary
Mere
Wincanton
GILLINGHAM
West Stour
SHAFTESBU
SHERBORNE
YEOVIL
Seavington St.Mary
CREWKERNE
Chedington
Beaminster
Evershot
BLANDFORD FORUM
with rm,
Sturminster Newton
Maiden Newton
Milton Abbas
BRIDPORT
West Bexington
A 35
DORCHESTER
Affpuddle
WAREHAM
West Lulworth
Weymouth
C
C
Portland
Two Bridges
Ashburton
Kingskerswell
TORQUAY M
TOTNES
SOUTH BRENT
Paignton
Galmpton
Ermington
Brixham
M DARTMOUTH
Kingston
KINGSBRIDGE
Bigbury-on-Sea
SALCOMBE

9
CHIPPING CAMPDEN
BANBURY
Milton Keynes
Aspley Guise
Flitwick
Blockley
Brackley
Woburn
BROADWAY
Moreton-in-Marsh
Buckingham
Toddington
Letchworth
M
Great Tew
Deddington
Leighton Buzzard
HITCHIN
STOW-ON-THE-WOLD
Churchill
Steeple Aston
Whitchurch
STEVENAGE
HELTENHAM
Kingham
Chadlington
Middleton Stoney
Dunstable
Luton
M
BOURTON-ON-THE WATER
Mentmore
Welwyn
Milton-under-Wychwood
Charlbury
Shipton-under-Wychwood
Woodstock
Weston-on-the-Green
Ivinghoe
Flamstead
Harpenden
on
Minster Lovell
Northleach
BURFORD
M 1
Fossebridge
Standlake
Bitbury
Standlake
CIRENCESTER
Stanton-Harcourt
Clanfield
GREATER
Cricklade
Fairford
Highworth
Faringdon
11
SWINDON
Wantage
M 4
Lambourn
Calne
Aldbourne
M 40
ton Benger
HIPPENHAM
Marlborough
Kintbury
M 4
Devizes
Hungerford
M 25
dge
HURSTBOURNE TARRANT
M 3
ANDOVER
Elstead
GODALMING
Middle Wallop
Sutton Scotney
Cranleigh
Gatwick Airport
Hindon
Stockbridge
Alton
Rusper
New Alresford
Four Marks
Grayshott
Chiddingfold
SALISBURY
Winchester
Liss
Haslemere
HORSHAM
Ampfield
Liphook
Billingshurst
Cranborne
ROMSEY
Petersfield
Rogate
Pulborough
Ashington
RY
Bramshaw
M 27
Eastleigh
MIDHURST
West Chiltington
FORDINGBRIDGE
Brook
Cadnam
Steyning
RINGWOOD
A 31
Southampton
M 27
A 27
WIMBORNE
Lyndhurst
WORTHING
MINSTER
Burley
Brockenhurst
M
Ferndown
BEAULIEU
New Milton
Lymington
CHRISTCHURCH
Poole
Milford on Sea
Bournemouth
Freshwater Bay
Studland
Totland Bay
orfe
astle
Swanage
Botley
Shedfield
Amberley
Wickham
Storrington
M,
M 27
Fontwell
ARUNDEL
Sarisbury
Fareham
Havant
Emsworth
M
A 27
CHICHESTER
PORTSMOUTH
Lee-on-the-Solent
Hayling Island
Climping
Bognor Regis
Cowes
East Wittering
NEWPORT
Seaview
Sandown
ISLE OF
Shanklin
WIGHT
54
Chale
VENTNOR
Niton

Saffron Walden
Hadleigh
Newport
Great Yeldham
Higham
East Bergholt
Castle Hedingham
Felixstowe
Baldock
THAXTED
Dedham
10
Manningtree
Clavering
Harwich and
Dovercourt
BISHOP'S STORTFORD
Braintree
Coggeshall
Colchester
Frinton-on-Sea
WARE
Great Dunmow
Clacton-on-Sea
Witham
West Mersea
CHELMSFORD
M 25
Maldon
M 11
South Woodham Ferrers
Burnham-on-Crouch
M 25
Rochford
Basildon
LONDON
Southend-on-Sea
Horndon on the Hill
North Stifford
Gravesend
A 2
Rochester
Broadstairs
Shorne
Herne Bay
Farthing Corner
Whitstable
Hoath
RAMSGATE
Cobham
M 2
FAVERSHAM
M 23
Sittingbourne
Sandwich
Selling
CANTERBURY
Wingham
M 25
MAIDSTONE
Warren Street
DEAL
M 23
Wye
Edenbridge
Tonbridge
A 2
Horley
Penhurst
Pluckley
Ashford
Turners Hill
M ROYAL TUNBRIDGE WELLS
Bethersden
DOVER
EAST GRINSTEAD
Goudhurst
Biddenden
Folkestone
CRAWLEY
Wadhurst
CRANBROOK
Hythe
FOREST ROW
TENTERDEN
Crowborough
Hawkhurst
A 259
Cuckfield
Mayfield
Robertsbridge
Northiam
New Romney
Dallington
SEDLESCOMBE
Uckfield
Heathfield
Rushlake Green
RYE
Halland
Battle
Herstmonceux
Bexhill
A 23
Lewes
A 27
BRIGHTON AND HOVE
HAILSHAM
Hastings and St. Leonards M
Alfriston
Rottingdean
Seaford
EASTBOURNE M
1
2
Carlisle
Newcastle
Liverpool
Manchester
3
4
5
6
Norwich
Cardigan
Birmingham
Bristol
Greater London
11
Dover
7
8
Southampton
9
10
Plymouth

11
56
Horton-cum-Studley
Tring
Welwyn Garden City
Hertingfordbury
HERTFORD
Sawbridgeworth
Stanstead Abbots
OXFORD
With rm
THAME
Berkhamsted
St. Albans
Hatfield
Harlow
HEMEL HEMPSTEAD
Brookmans Park
M 1
Great Missenden
Chesham
South Mimms
Cuffley
Epping
Saunderton
Chipperfield
Radlett
Waltham Abbey
Ingatestone
ABINGDON
Chislehampton
Chinnor
Little Chalfont
M 11
M 40
Chenies
Watford
Brentwood
Dorchester
Watlington
M AMERSHAM
Buckhurst Hill
High Wycombe
East Horndon
WALLINGFORD
BEACONSFIELD
Chalfont St. Peter
GREATER
A 41
A 11
Gerrards Cross
A 40
M 25
Moulsford
Marlow
Cookham
Thames
Streatley
Hurley-on-Thames
MAIDENHEAD
M HENLEY-ON-THAMES
Burnham
M 25
A 4
Purfleet
M KNOWL HILL
Slough
M 4
A 2
Pangbourne
Thames
Bray-on-Thames
WINDSOR
Yattendon
Sonning-on-Thames
A 316
READING
Staines
Ashford
LONDON M
Bracknell
Egham
Thatcham
Wokingham
Shepperton
NEWBURY
Ascot
Walton
Crowthorne
Bagshot
Weybridge
ESHER
Epsom
BRANDS HATCH
Silchester
Yateley
Camberley
COBHAM
Banstead
A 23
Stratfield Turgis
Woking
Leatherhead
WROTHAM HEATH
Frimley
Ripley
Walton-on-the-Hill
Chipstead
Hook
M 3
Fleet
Ockham
SEVENOAKS
Farnborough
East Horsley
M 25
BASINGSTOKE
Aldershot
REDHILL
Westerham
M 23
North Waltham
Odiham
FARNHAM
GUILDFORD
Dorking
Reigate
Godstone

Towns

ABBERLEY Heref. and Worc. **403** **404** M 27 – pop. 604 – ECD : Wednesday – ✉ Worcester – ☎ 0299 Great Witley.
♦ London 137 – ♦Birmingham 27 – Worcester 13.

The Elms (Norfolk Cap.) ⑤, WR6 6AT, W : 2 m. on A 443 ℰ 896666, Telex 337105, Fax 896804, ≤, ☞, park, ✗ – TV ☎ ℗ – 🛏 60. ◪ AE ① VISA ✵
M 12.95/19.00 **st.** and a la carte 17.75/28.20 🍶5.00 – **24 rm** ☎ 75.00/125.00 **st.**, **1 suite** 145.00 **st.** – SB (weekends only) (except Christmas and New Year) 120.00/150.00 **st.**

Manor Arms ⑤, Abberley Village, WR6 6BN, ℰ 896507 – TV ☎ ℗. ◪ VISA
M *(closed Sunday dinner to non-residents and 25-26 December)* 12.50 **t.** and a la carte 🍶 3.50 – **10 rm** ☎ 32.00/42.00 **t.** – SB (except 25 and 26 December) 63.00/85.00 **st.**

ABBOTSBURY Dorset **403** **404** M 32 **The West Country G.** – pop. 401 – ☎ 0305.
See : Site★★.
♦London 146 – Exeter 50 – Bournemouth 44 – Weymouth 10.

Ilchester Arms, 9 Market St., DT3 4JR, ℰ 871243 – ⤢ rest TV & ℗. ◪ VISA
M a la carte 6.70/9.50 **t.** – **10 rm** ☎ 30.00/40.00 **t.** – SB (November-April except December) 40.00 **st.**

FORD, VOLVO Alban Sq. ℰ 570312

ABERDAUGLEDDAU = Milford Haven.

ABERDOVEY (ABERDYFI) Gwynedd **403** H 26 – pop. 778 – ECD : Wednesday – ☎ 065 472.
See : Afon Dovey's mouth (site★★).
Envir. : Llanegryn (church★) N : 8 m. – Dolgoch Falls★ NE : 10 m.
🛈 The Wharf ℰ 72321 (summer only).
♦ London 230 – Dolgellau 25 – Shrewsbury 66.

Plas Penhelig ⑤, LL35 0NA, E : 1 m. by A 493 ℰ 676, Fax 7783, ≤, « Terraced gardens », park, ✗ – ☎ ℗. ◪ AE ① VISA. ✵
March-November – **M** (bar lunch Monday to Saturday)/dinner 14.50 **t.** – **11 rm** ☎ 51.75/98.50 **t.** – SB (except summer) 145.80/163.80 **st.**

Trefeddian, Tywyn Rd, LL35 0SB, W : 1 m. on A 493 ℰ 213, ≤ golf course and sea, ◪, ☞, park, ✗ – 🛗 ⤢ rest TV ☎ ⇌ ℗. ◪ VISA
23 March-December – **M** 7.00/12.00 **t.** – **46 rm** ☎ (dinner included) 35.00/80.00 **t.** – SB 64.00/80.00 **st.**

Penhelig Arms, Terrace Rd, LL35 0LT, ℰ 215, Fax 7761, ≤ – TV ℗. ◪ VISA
closed 4 days at Christmas – **M** (bar lunch Monday to Saturday)/dinner 14.00 **t.** – **11 rm** ☎ 25.00/60.00 **t.** – SB 70.00/80.00 **st.**

Harbour, LL35 0EB, ℰ 250, ≤ – TV. ◪ AE ① VISA
M a la carte 10.10/16.25 **st.** 🍶 3.75 – **12 rm** ☎ 35.00/105.00 **st.**

Maybank, LL35 0PT, E : 1 m. on A 493 ℰ 500, ≤ – TV. ◪ VISA. ✵
closed 9 January-10 February – **M** *(closed Monday May and October and weekdays November-April)* (booking essential)(dinner only and Sunday lunch)/dinner 15.00 **t.** – **5 rm** ☎ 31.95/43.90 **st.** – SB 49.95/66.00 **st.**

Morlan, Tywyn Rd, LL35 0SE, W : 1 ½ m. on A 493 ℰ 7706, ≤, ☞ – ⤢ rm TV ℗. ✵
closed Christmas – **M** 11.00 **st.** – **4 rm** ☎ –/32.00 **st.**

ABERGAVENNY (Y-FENNI) Gwent **403** L 28 – pop. 9 427 – ECD : Thursday – ☎ 0873.
Envir. : Llanthony Priory★ N : 10 m. – Bwlch (≤★ of the Usk Valley), NW : 9 ½ m.
🛈 Monmouthshire, Gypsy Lane, Llanfoist ℰ 3171, S : 2m. off B 4269.
🛈 Swan Meadow, Monmouth Rd ℰ 3254/77588 (summer only).
♦ London 163 – Gloucester 43 – Newport 19 – ♦Swansea 49.

Angel (T.H.F.), Cross St., NP7 5EW, ℰ 7121, Fax 78059 – TV ☎ ℗ – 🛏 60. ◪ AE ① VISA
M 9.50 **st.** (lunch) and a la carte 🍶 3.95 – ☎ 7.00 – **29 rm** 49.00/69.00 **st.** – SB 70.00/90.00 **st.**

Halidon House without rest., 63 Monmouth Rd, NP7 5HR, ℰ 77855, ≤, ◪, ☞ – ℗. ✵
5 rm ☎ 15.00/30.00 **st.**

Bagan Tandoori, 35 Frogmore St., NP7 5AN, ℰ 77389, Indian rest. – ◪ AE VISA
closed 25 and 26 December – **M** 15.00 **t.** and a la carte approx. 10.50 **t.**

    at Llandewi Skirrid NE : 3 ½ m. by A 465 on B 4521 – ✉ ☎ 0873 Abergavenny :

✗ **Walnut Tree Inn,** NP7 8AW, ✆ 2797 – ℗
closed Sunday, Monday, 2 weeks February and 4 days at Christmas – **M** a la carte approx. 22.00/25.00 **t.** 🍷 4.00.

    at Llanwenarth NW : 3 m. on A 40 – ✉ Abergavenny – ☎ 0873 Crickhowell :

🏨 **Llanwenarth Arms,** Brecon Rd, NP8 1EP, ✆ 810550, ≤, ⌕ – 📺 ☎ ℗. 🔲 AE ① VISA. ⋙
M a la carte 9.95/17.95 **st.** 🍷 3.50 – **18 rm** ⚏ 45.00/55.00 **st.**

AUSTIN-ROVER, FORD Brecon Rd ✆ 2126　　　 ⓦ ATS 11 Monmouth Rd ✆ 4348
RENAULT 9 Monmouth Rd ✆ 2323

ABERGWAUN = Fishguard.

ABERGWESYN Powys **403** I 27 – see Llanwrtyd Wells.

ABERGYNOLWYN Gwynedd **402 403** I 26 – ✉ Twywn – ☎ 0654.
◆London 228 – Dolgellau 12 – Shrewsbury 63.

🔼 **Dolgoch Falls,** SW : 2 ½ m. on B 4405 ✆ 782258, ≤, 🐎 – ℗. VISA
March-October – **M** 11.25 **st.** 🍷 3.25 – **6 rm** ⚏ 16.50/45.00 **st.** – SB (weekends only) (except May-September) 42.20 **st.**

ABERHONDDU = Brecon.

ABERLLYNFI = Three Cocks.

ABERMAW = Barmouth.

ABERMULE (ABER-MIWL) Powys **403** K 26 – see Newtown.

ABERPORTH Dyfed **403** G 27 – pop. 1 614 – ECD : Wednesday – ☎ 0239.
See : Site★.
Envir. : Llangranog (cliffs★) NE : 4 m.
◆ London 249 – Carmarthen 29 – Fishguard 26.

🏨 **Penrallt,** SA43 2BS, SW : 1 m. by B 4333 ✆ 810227, Fax 811375, 🏊 heated, 🐎, ✗ – 📺 ☎ ℗. 🔲 AE ① VISA. ⋙
closed 23 to 31 December – **M** (bar lunch)/dinner 11.00 **st.** and a la carte – **16 rm** ⚏ 35.00/52.00 **st.** – SB (September-May) 66.00 **st.**

🏨 **Morlan Motel,** SA43 2EN, ✆ 810611 – 📺 ℗. 🔲 AE ① VISA. ⋙
M (bar lunch)/dinner 8.25 **st.** and a la carte 🍷 2.80 – **15 rm** ⚏ 16.00/32.00 **st.** – SB (October-April) 32.50/35.00 **st.**

    at Tresaith NE : 1 ¾ m. – ✉ ☎ 0239 Aberporth :

🏨 **Glandwr Manor** ⌂, SA43 2JH, ✆ 810197, 🐎 – ℗. ⋙
March-October – **M** *(closed Sunday to non-residents)* (dinner only) a la carte 6.80/11.50 **t.** 🍷 2.95 – **7 rm** ⚏ 15.50/37.00 **t.**

ABERRIW = Berriew.

ABERSOCH Gwynedd **402 403** G 25 – ECD : Wednesday – ✉ Pwllheli – ☎ 075 881.
Envir. : Llanengan (church★ : twin aisles rood screen) W : 2 m. – Hell's Mouth★ W : 3 m. – Aberdaron (site★) W : 10 m. – Braich y Pwll (≤★★ from 2nd car park) W : 12 m.
🏌 Golf Rd, Pwllheli, ✆ 0758 (Pwllheli) 612520, NE : 7 m.
◆ London 265 – Caernarfon 28 – Shrewsbury 101.

🏨 **Riverside,** LL53 7HW, ✆ 2419, 🔲 – 📺 ☎ ℗. 🔲 VISA. ⋙
March-mid November – **M** (bar lunch)/dinner 17.50 **st.** 🍷 4.20 – **12 rm** ⚏ 29.50/105.00 **st.** – SB 84.00/148.00 **st.**

🏨 **Abersoch Harbour,** Long Engan, LL53 7HR, ✆ 2406, ≤ – 📺 ☎ ℗. 🔲 AE VISA. ⋙
M 12.00 **st.** and a la carte 🍷 3.30 – **14 rm** ⚏ 30.00/45.00 **t.**

🔼 **Llwyn Du,** Sarn Bach Rd, LL53 7EL, ✆ 2186, 🐎 – ✗ rm ℗. ⋙
M approx. 5.00 – **3 rm** ⚏ –/28.00 **st.**

    at Bwlchtocyn S : 2 m. – ✉ Pwllheli – ☎ 075 881 Abersoch :

🏨 **Porth Tocyn** ⌂, LL53 7BU, ✆ 3303, ≤ Cardigan Bay and mountains, « Country house atmosphere », 🏊 heated, 🐎, ✗ – 📺 ☎ ℗. 🔲
6 April-mid November – **M** (bar lunch)/dinner 19.00 **t.** – **17 rm** ⚏ 42.00/78.00 **t.**

ABERTAWE = Swansea.

ABERTEIFI = Cardigan.

ABERYSTWYTH Dyfed 403 H 26 – pop. 8 636 – ECD : Wednesday – ☎ 0970.

See : Site★ – ≤★ from the National Library.

Envir. : Vale of Rheidol★, SE : 6 m. – Strata Florida★, SE : 15 m.

18 Bryn-y-mor Rd, ☎ 615104, N : ½ m.

Terrace Rd ☎ 612125 and 611955.

♦ London 238 – Chester 98 – Fishguard 58 – Shrewsbury 74.

Belle Vue Royal, The Promenade, SY23 2BA, ☎ 617558, ≤ – TV ☎. AE VISA. *closed 23 to 27 December* – **M** 7.50/12.50 **t.** and a la carte 3.50 – **42 rm** 24.00/49.00 **t.** – SB (except Bank Holidays) 58.00/67.00 **st.**

The Groves, 44-46 North Par., SY23 2NF, ☎ 617623 – TV ☎ P. AE VISA. *closed Christmas and New Year* – **M** (bar lunch)/dinner a la carte 8.15/13.15 **t.** 3.40 – **11 rm** 28.00/48.00 **t.** – SB (except Bank Holidays) 52.00/60.00 **st.**

Four Seasons, 50-54 Portland St., SY23 2DX, ☎ 612120 – rest TV ☎ P. VISA. *closed first 2 weeks January* – **M** (bar lunch Monday to Saturday)/dinner 10.75 **t.** 3.00 – **14 rm** 23.50/47.00 **t.** – SB (October-April)(weekends only) 57.20/63.80 **st.**

Glyn-Garth, South Rd, SY23 1JS, ☎ 615050 – TV. *closed 1 week Christmas* – **M** *(closed Saturday)* 8.00 **st.** – **10 rm** 13.00/34.00 **st.**

at Chancery (Rhydgaled) S : 4 m. on A 487 – ✉ ☎ 0970 Aberystwyth :

Conrah Country, SY23 4DF, ☎ 617941, Telex 35892, Fax 624546, ≤, « 18C country house », , park – rest TV ☎ P – 100. AE VISA. *closed 23 to 30 December* – **M** 12.50/17.50 **t.** and a la carte 3.00 – **22 rm** 43.00/79.00 **t.** – SB (October-June) 83.00/99.00 **st.**

AUSTIN-ROVER, LAND-ROVER, RANGE-ROVER, JAGUAR-DAIMLER Park Av. ☎ 624841
FIAT Llanfarian ☎ 612311
HONDA North Parade ☎ 624171
ATS Glanyrafon Ind Est., Llandabarn ☎ 611166

Pour voyager rapidement, utilisez les cartes Michelin "Grandes Routes" :
920 *Europe,* 980 *Grèce,* 984 *Allemagne,* 985 *Scandinavie-Finlande,*
986 *Grande-Bretagne-Irlande,* 987 *Allemagne-Autriche-Benelux,* 988 *Italie,*
989 *France,* 990 *Espagne-Portugal,* 991 *Yougoslavie.*

ABINGDON Oxon. 403 404 Q 28 – pop. 29 130 – ECD : Thursday – ☎ 0235.

See : Site★.

The Old Gaol, Bridge St. ☎ 22711.

♦ London 64 – ♦Oxford 6 – Reading 25.

Upper Reaches (T.H.F.), Thames St., OX14 3JA, ☎ 22311, Fax 555182 – TV ☎ P – 40. AE VISA. **M** 10.75/14.95 **st.** and a la carte – 7.00 – **26 rm** 65.00/82.00 **st.** – SB (weekends only) 92.00/100.00 **st.**

Crown and Thistle (B.C.B.), Bridge St., OX14 3HS, ☎ 22556 – TV ☎ P – 30. **21 rm.**

at Clifton Hampden SE : 3 ¾ m. on A 415 – ✉ Abingdon – ☎ 086 730 Clifden Hampden :

Barley Mow (B.C.B.), OX14 3EH, on Long Wittenham Rd ☎ 7847, – TV ☎ P. AE VISA. **M** *(closed Saturday lunch and Sunday)* (dinner only and weekday lunch October-June)/dinner a la carte 9.00/16.35 **t.** 3.65 – **4 rm** 29.00/46.00 **t.**

AUSTIN-ROVER Drayton Rd ☎ 22822
RENAULT Drayton Rd ☎ 28828

ACOCKS GREEN West Midlands 403 404 ⑳ – see Birmingham.

ADLINGTON Lancs. 402 404 M 23 – ECD : Wednesday – ☎ 0257.

♦London 217 – ♦Liverpool 35 – ♦Manchester 21 – Preston 16.

Gladmar, Railway Rd, PR6 9RG, ☎ 480398, Fax 482681, – TV ☎ P. VISA. *closed 25 December-1 January* – **M** (bar lunch)/dinner 8.50 **t.** and a la carte 3.60 – **20 rm** 30.00/45.00 **st.** – SB (weekends only) 26.00/32.00 **st.**

AFFPUDDLE Dorset 403 404 N 31 – pop. 425 – ✉ Dorchester – ☎ 030 584 (3 and 4 fig.) and 0305 (6 fig.) Puddletown.

♦London 121 – Bournemouth 19 – Exeter 60 – ♦Southampton 47 – Weymouth 14.

Old Vicarage without rest., DT2 7HH, ☎ 848315, – TV P. **3 rm** 18.00/35.00 **st.**

AIGBURTH Merseyside – see Liverpool.

ALBRIGHTON Shropshire 402 403 L 25 – see Shrewsbury.

ALCESTER Warw. 403 404 O 27 – pop. 5 207 – ECD : Thursday – ☎ 0789.
Envir. : Ragley Hall✶✶ (17C) *AC*, SW : 2 m.
♦London 104 – ♦Birmingham 20 – ♦Coventry 28 – Gloucester 34.

🏠 **Arrow Mill** ॐ, Arrow, B49 5NL, SW : 1 ¼ m. on A 435 ℘ 762419, Fax 765170, ≼, ॐ, ⇶ –
📺 ☎ 🅿 – 🏄 30. 🔼 AE Ⓞ *VISA*
closed 25 and 26 December – **M** 8.95/14.50 **t.** and a la carte ▯ 3.60 – **15 rm** � 48.00/72.00 **t.**
– SB (except Christmas) 75.00/90.00 **st.**

AUSTIN-ROVER Station Rd ℘ 764146   RENAULT Stratford Rd ℘ 762191
FORD Priory Rd ℘ 762408

ALDBOURNE Wilts. 403 404 P 29 – pop. 1 479 – ☎ 0672 Marlborough.
♦London 77 – ♦Oxford 36 – ♦Southampton 53 – Swindon 9.

❌❌ **Raffles,** 1 The Green, SN8 2BW, ℘ 40700 – 🔼 AE Ⓞ *VISA*
closed lunch Monday and Saturday, Sunday, last 2 weeks August, 25 to 30 December and Bank Holidays – **M** a la carte 12.50/16.70 **t.** ▯ 3.90.

ALDEBURGH Suffolk 404 Y 27 – pop. 2 711 – ECD : Wednesday – ☎ 0728 (6 fig.) and 072 885 (4 fig.).
� at Thorpeness ℘ 2176, N : 2 ½ m.
🅩 The Cinema, High St. ℘ 3637 (summer only).
♦ London 97 – ♦Ipswich 24 – ♦Norwich 41.

🏨 **Wentworth,** Wentworth Rd, IP15 5BD, ℘ 452312, ≼ – 📺 ☎ 🅿. 🔼 AE Ⓞ *VISA*
closed 27 December-12 January – **M** 12.00/13.50 **t.** and a la carte – **31 rm** ⊑ 35.75/85.25 **t.**
– SB 69.00/99.00 **st.**

🏨 **Brudenell** (T.H.F.), The Parade, IP15 5BU, ℘ 452071, ≼ – ▮ 📺 ☎ 🅿 – 🏄 60. 🔼 AE Ⓞ
VISA
M 7.95/11.95 **st.** and a la carte ▯ 3.95 – ⊑ 7.00 – **47 rm** 49.00/74.00 **st.** – SB (except summer) 88.00/96.00 **st.**

🏨 **White Lion** (Best Western), Sea Front, IP15 5BJ, ℘ 452720, Telex 94017152, Fax 452986, ≼
– 📺 ☎ 🅿 – 🏄 80. 🔼 AE Ⓞ *VISA*
M a la carte 13.00/18.70 **t.** – **36 rm** ⊑ 45.00/67.50 **t.** – SB 34.50/50.00 **st.**

🏠 **Uplands,** Victoria Rd, IP15 5DX, ℘ 452420, ⇶ – 📺 ☎ 🅿. 🔼 AE Ⓞ *VISA*. ֍
closed 22 to 31 December – **M** (dinner only) 12.50 **t.** and a la carte – **20 rm** ⊑ 25.00/55.00 **t.**
– SB (October-May) 45.00/62.00 **st.**

VAUXHALL-OPEL ℘ 2721

ALDERLEY EDGE Cheshire 402 403 404 N 24 – pop. 4 272 – ECD : Wednesday – ☎ 0625.
Envir. : Capesthorne Hall✶ (18C) *AC*, S : 4 ½ m.
♦ London 187 – Chester 34 – ♦Manchester 14 – ♦Stoke-on-Trent 25.

🏨 **Alderley Edge,** Macclesfield Rd, SK9 7BJ, ℘ 583033, Fax 586343 – 📺 ☎ 🅿. 🔼 AE Ⓞ
VISA. ֍
M 11.95/14.95 **st.** and a la carte ▯ 4.50 – ⊑ 7.95 – **32 rm** 72.00/120.00 **st.** – SB (weekends only) (except Christmas) 105.00/150.00 **st.**

🏨 De Trafford Arms (De Vere), London Rd, SK9 7AA, ℘ 583881, Group Telex 629462 – ▮ 📺
☎ 🅿
37 rm.

✗ **Octobers,** 47 London Rd, SK9 7JT, ℘ 583942, Bistro – 🔼 *VISA*
closed Sunday – **M** (dinner only) 10.95 **t.** and a la carte 9.00/16.95 **t.** ▯ 3.80.

AUSTIN-ROVER London Rd ℘ 582218   VOLVO 77 London Rd ℘ 583912
VAUXHALL-OPEL 34 Knutsford Rd ℘ 585411

ALDERSHOT Hants. 404 R 30 – pop. 53 665 – ECD : Wednesday – ☎ 0252.
🅩 Military Museum, Queens Av. ℘ 20968.
♦London 43 – Guildford 9 – ♦Southampton 43.

⌂ Glencoe, 4 Eggars Hill, GU11 3NQ, ℘ 20801, ⇶ – 🅿. ֍
15 rm.

AUSTIN-ROVER Victoria Rd ℘ 20581   ⓪ ATS Blackwater Way ℘ 20246
PEUGEOT Arthur Street Rd ℘ 21246
SKODA, SUBARU 20 Waterloo Rd ℘ 311818

ALDRIDGE West Midlands 402 403 404 O 26 – pop. 17 549 – ECD : Thursday – ✉ Walsall –
☎ 0922.
♦London 130 – ♦Birmingham 12 – Derby 32 – ♦Leicester 40 – ♦Stoke-on-Trent 38.

🏨 **Fairlawns,** 178 Little Aston Rd, WS9 0NU, E : 1 m. on A 454 ℘ 55122, Telex 339873, Fax
743210 – ▤ rest 📺 ☎ 🅿 – 🏄 40. 🔼 AE Ⓞ *VISA*
M *(closed Saturday lunch and Sunday dinner to non-residents)* 15.00/16.50 **st.** and a la carte
▯ 4.25 – **36 rm** ⊑ 39.50/75.00 **st.** – SB (weekends only) 65.00 **st.**

FORD Northgate ℘ 743031   ⓪ ATS 106 Leighswood Rd ℘ 51968/53970

ALDWINCLE Northants. 402 404 S 26 – pop. 302 – ⊠ Kettering – ☎ 08015.
♦London 84 – ♦Cambridge 40 – ♦Leicester 40 – Northampton 26 – Peterborough 18.

  ⌂ **The Maltings** ⌘ without rest., NN14 3EP, ☎ 233, 🚗 – ⊱ rm ℗. ⌘
  3 rm ⊡ 18.00/36.00 s.

ALFRISTON East Sussex 404 U 31 – pop. 811 – ECD : Wednesday – ⊠ Polegate – ☎ 0323.
♦ London 66 – Eastbourne 9 – Lewes 10 – Newhaven 8.

  🏨 Deans Place, BN26 5TW, ☎ 870248, ≤, ⌘ heated, 🚗, park, ⌘ – ⊱ TV ☎ ℗ – ⚲ 120.
  ⌘
  40 rm.
  🏨 **Star** (T.H.F.), High St., BN26 5TA, ☎ 870495, Fax 870922 – ⊱ rm TV ☎ ℗. ◩ AE ① VISA
  M 11.00/12.50 **st.** and a la carte ◗ 3.95 – ⊡ 7.00 – **35 rm** 60.00/82.00 **st.** – SB 80.00/100.00 **st.**
  ✗ **Moonrakers,** High St., BN26 5TD, ☎ 870472
  closed Sunday, Monday and 15 January-13 February – **M** (dinner only) 17.40 **t.** ◗ 3.40.

ALLENDALE Northumb. 401 402 N 19 – ⊠ Hexham – ☎ 043 483 (from spring : 0434 683).
🏌 Thornley Gate ☎ 091 (Tyneside) 267 5875, W : ¾ m..
♦London 314 – ♦Carlisle 39 – ♦Newcastle 33.

  🏠 **Bishop Field Country House** ⌘, NE47 9EJ, W : 1 m. on Whitfield rd ☎ 248, Fax 830,
  ⌘, 🚗, park – ⊱ rm TV ☎ ℗. ◩ ①. ⌘
  closed Christmas – **M** 8.00/12.00 **t.** ◗ 3.00 – **11 rm** ⊡ 35.00/60.00 **t.**

ALLESLEY West Midlands 403 404 P 26 – see Coventry.

ALNMOUTH Northumb. 401 402 P 17 – pop. 605 – ECD : Wednesday – ☎ 0665.
🏌 Foxton Hall ☎ 830368 NE : 1 m. – 🏌 Alnmouth Village, Marine Rd ☎ 830370.
♦London 314 – ♦Edinburgh 90 – ♦Newcastle-upon-Tyne 37.

  ⌂ **Marine House,** 1 Marine Rd, NE66 2RW, ☎ 830349, ≤, 🚗 – ℗
  February-October – **8 rm** ⊡ (dinner included) 57.00 **t.** – SB (except summer) 50.00/
  56.00 **st.**

ALNWICK Northumb. 401 402 O 17 – pop. 6 972 – ECD : Wednesday – ☎ 0665.
See : Site ★ – Castle ★★ (Norman) *AC*.
Envir. : Dunstanburgh Castle ★ 14C-15C (ruins, coastal setting ★) *AC*, 1 ¼ m. walk from Craster, no
cars, NE : 7 ½ m. – Warkworth (castle ★ 12C) *AC*, SE : 7 m. – Rothbury (Cragside gardens ★ :
rhododendrons) *AC*, SW : 12 m.
🏌 Swansfield Park ☎ 602632.
🛈 The Shambles ☎ 603129.
♦ London 320 – ♦Edinburgh 86 – ♦Newcastle-upon-Tyne 34.

  🏨 White Swan (Swallow), Bondgate Within, NE66 1TD, ☎ 602109, Group Telex 53168, Fax
  510400 – ⊱ rm TV ☎ ℗ – ⚲ 60. ◩ AE ① VISA
  41 rm ⊡ 50.00/72.00 **st.**
  🏛 **Hotspur,** Bondgate Without, NE66 1PR, ☎ 510101, Fax 605033 – TV ☎ ℗. ◩ VISA
  M a la carte 10.00/13.75 **t.** ◗ 3.00 – **26 rm** ⊡ 25.00/50.00 **t.** – SB 30.00/35.00 **st.**
  ⌂ **Bondgate House,** 20 Bondgate Without, NE66 1PN, ☎ 602025 – TV. ⌘
  M *(closed Sunday)* 8.00 **st.** ◗ 2.50 – **8 rm** ⊡ 18.00/30.00 **st.**

FORD Lagny St. ☎ 602294   VAUXHALL Station Rd ☎ 604737
TOYOTA Pottergate ☎ 604909

ALPORT Derbs. – see Bakewell.

ALSAGER Cheshire 402 403 404 N 24 – pop. 12 944 – ⊠ Stoke-on-Trent – ☎ 093 63 (4 and
5 fig.) or 0270 (Crewe) (6 fig.).
♦ London 180 – Chester 36 – ♦ Liverpool 49 – ♦ Manchester 32 – ♦ Stoke-on-Trent 11.

  🏨 Manor House, Audley Rd, ST7 2QQ, SE : ½ m. ☎ 878013, Fax 882483 – TV ☎ ℗
  27 rm.

AUSTIN-ROVER Lawton Rd ☎ 882146   FORD 52 Sandbach Rd South ☎ 873241

ALSTON Cumbria 401 402 M 19 – pop. 1 968 – ECD : Tuesday – ☎ 0434.
🏌 Alston Moor, The Hermitage ☎ 81675 SE : 1 ¾ m. on B 6277.
🛈 Railway Station ☎ 81696.
♦ London 309 – ♦Carlisle 28 – ♦Newcastle-upon-Tyne 45.

  🏨 **Lovelady Shield Country House** ⌘, Nenthead Rd, CA9 3LF, E : 2 ½ m. on A 689
  ☎ 81203, Fax 81515, ≤, 🚗, ✗ – ⊱ rest TV ☎ ℗. AE ①
  closed 3 January-22 February – **M** (dinner only and Sunday lunch)/dinner 18.00 **t.** – **12 rm**
  ⊡ 28.00/72.00 **t.** – SB (November-April) (except Bank Holidays) 70.00/90.00 **st.**

ALTON Hants. 404 R 30 – pop. 14 163 – ECD : Wednesday – ✆ 0420.

🏌 Old Odiham Rd ✆ 82042, N : 2 m off A 32.

♦London 53 – Reading 24 – ♦Southampton 29 – Winchester 18.

🏨 **Swan** (T.H.F.), High St., GU34 1AT, ✆ 83777, Telex 859916 – ⇔ rm 📺 ☎ Ⓟ – 🛎 60. 🅂 AE ⓪ VISA
M 10.00/14.00 **st.** and a la carte – ⌕ 7.00 – **38 rm** 55.00/70.00 **st.** – SB (weekends only) 76.00 **st.**

🏨 **Alton House**, Normandy St., GU34 1DW, ✆ 80033, ⌇ heated, 🐎, ✻ – 📺 ☎ Ⓟ – 🛎 120. ⅏ – **26 rm**.

🏨 **Grange**, 17 London Rd, Holybourne, GU34 4EG, NE : 1 m. on A 339 ✆ 86565, Fax 541346, 🐎 – ⇔ rest 📺 ☎ Ⓟ. 🅂 AE ⓪ VISA
closed 24 and 31 December – **M** 7.95/9.95 **t.** and a la carte ⒜ 3.75 – **15 rm** ⌕ 39.50/59.50 **t.**

AUSTIN-ROVER, VAUXHALL Butts Rd ✆ 84141   PEUGEOT-TALBOT Four Marks ✆ 62354
FORD Ackender Rd ✆ 83993

ALTRINCHAM Greater Manchester 402 403 404 N 23 – pop. 39 528 – ECD : Wednesday – ✆ 061 Manchester.

🏌 Stockport Rd, Timperley ✆ 928 0761, E : 1 m. – 🏌 Dunham Forest, Oldfield Lane ✆ 928 2605, W : 1 m. – 🏌 Hale Mount, Hale Barns ✆ 980 2630 – 🛈 Stamford New Rd. ✆ 941 7337.

♦London 191 – Chester 30 – ♦Liverpool 30 – ♦Manchester 8.

🏨 **Cresta Court** (Best Western), Church St., WA14 4DP, on A 56 ✆ 927 7272, Telex 667242, Fax 926 9194 – ▤ ⇔ rm 📺 ☎ Ⓟ – 🛎 300. 🅂 AE ⓪ VISA. ⅏
M a la carte 6.80/11.95 **st.** ⒜ 4.25 – **139 rm** ⌕ 50.00/61.00 **st.**

🏨 **George and Dragon** (De Vere), 22 Manchester Rd, WA14 4PH, on A 56 ✆ 928 9933, Telex 665051 – ▤ ⇔ rm 📺 ☎ Ⓟ. 🅂 AE ⓪ VISA. ⅏
M (bar lunch Monday to Saturday)/dinner 10.75 **st.** and a la carte ⒜ 4.25 – **47 rm** ⌕ 52.00/63.50 **st.**

🏨 **Pelican Inn** (De Vere), Manchester Rd, West Timperley, WA14 5NH, N : 2 m. on A 56 ✆ 962 7414, Telex 668014 – 📺 ☎ Ⓟ – **50 rm**.

🏠 **Bollin** without rest., 58 Manchester Rd, WA14 4PJ, on A 56 ✆ 928 2390 – Ⓟ
10 rm ⌕ 18.50/28.75 **st.**

at Timperley NE : 2 m. by A 560 on B 5165 – ✉ Altrincham – ✆ 061 Manchester :

XXX **Le Bon Viveur** (at Hare and Hounds H.), 1 Wood Lane, WA15 2LX, on A 560 ✆ 904 0266 – Ⓟ. 🅂 AE ⓪ VISA
closed Saturday lunch, Sunday and Bank Holidays – **M** 14.25 **st.** and a la carte 13.75/26.00 **st.** ⒜ 3.80.

at Hale SE : 1 m. on B 5163 – ✉ Altrincham – ✆ 061 Manchester :

🏨 **Ashley** (De Vere), Ashley Rd, WA15 9SF, ✆ 928 3794, Group Telex 669406, Fax 926 9046 – ▤ ⇔ rm 📺 ☎ – 🛎 250. 🅂 AE ⓪ VISA. ⅏
M (closed Saturday lunch) 10.00/12.00 **st.** and a la carte ⒜ 4.00 – **49 rm** ⌕ 57.00/68.00 **st.**

at Halebarns SE : 3 m. on A 538 – ✉ Altrincham – ✆ 061 Manchester :

🏨 **Four Seasons**, Manchester Airport, Hale Rd, WA15 8XW, ✆ 904 0301, Telex 665492, Fax 980 1787 – ▤ 📺 ☎ Ⓟ – 🛎 . 🅂 AE ⓪ VISA. ⅏
M (bar lunch Saturday)/dinner 18.95 **t.** and a la carte – **48 rm** ⌕ 84.50/109.50 **st.**

at Bowdon SW : 1 m. – ✉ Altrincham – ✆ 061 Manchester :

🏨 **Bowdon**, Langham Rd, WA14 2HT, ✆ 928 7121, Telex 668208, Fax 927 7560 – 📺 ☎ Ⓟ – 🛎 160. 🅂 AE ⓪ VISA
M 10.75 **t.** and a la carte 10.70/22.00 **t.** ⒜ 3.00 – **82 rm** ⌕ 55.00/65.00 **t.** – SB (except New Year) (weekends only) 60.00 **st.**

🏨 **Bowdon Croft** ⅌, Green Walk, WA14 2SN, ✆ 928 1718, Fax 928 1718, ≼, « Tastefully furnished 19C house », 🐎 – 📺 ☎ Ⓟ. 🅂 AE ⓪ VISA. ⅏
M *(closed Sunday lunch)* (booking essential) 12.50/16.50 and a la carte ⒜ 4.00 – **8 rm** ⌕ 56.50/68.50.

ALFA-ROMEO Money Ash Rd, Hale Bridge ✆ 928 5980
AUSTIN-ROVER Victoria Rd ✆ 928 7124
RENAULT, HYUNDAI Manchester Rd ✆ 973 3021
SAAB Bancroft Rd, Hale ✆ 980 8004
TOYOTA Mobberley Rd, Ashley ✆ 928 3112

VAUXHALL-OPEL 276-280 Stockport Rd, Timperley ✆ 980 3212
VOLVO Manchester Rd ✆ 928 2384

⊛ ATS 74 Oakfield Rd ✆ 928 7024

ALVESTON Avon 403 404 M 29 – pop. 3 154 – ECD : Wednesday – ✉ Bristol – ✆ 0454 Thornbury.

♦London 127 – ♦Bristol 11 – Gloucester 23 – Swindon 42.

🏨 **Alveston House**, BS12 2LJ, on A 38 ✆ 415050, Telex 449212, Fax 415425, 🐎 – 📺 ☎ Ⓟ – 🛎 80. 🅂 AE ⓪ VISA
M 13.95 **st.** and a la carte ⒜ 3.75 – **30 rm** ⌕ 59.50/78.50 **st.** – SB (weekends only) 75.00/88.00 **st.**

🏨 **Post House** (T.H.F.), Thornbury Rd, BS12 2LL, on A 38 ✆ 412521, Telex 444753, Fax 413920, ⌇ heated, 🐎 – ⇔ rm 📺 ☎ Ⓟ – 🛎 80. 🅂 AE ⓪ VISA
M 12.50/14.95 **st.** and a la carte ⒜ 4.00 – ⌕ 7.00 – **75 rm** 62.00/72.00 **st.** – SB (weekends only) 80.00/90.00 **st.**

ALWALTON Cambs. 402 404 T 26 – see Peterborough.

AMBERLEY Glos. – see Stroud.

AMBERLEY West Sussex 404 S 31 – ✉ Arundel – ✆ 0798 Bury.
♦London 56 – ♦Brighton 24 – ♦Portsmouth 31.

Amberley Castle, BN18 9ND, SW : ½ m. on B 2139 ✆ 831992, Fax 831998, « 14C castle of 12C origin », 🍽 – TV ☎ P. 🅿 AE ⓪ VISA. ✖
M (bar lunch Monday to Saturday) 15.00/19.50 t. and a la carte 21.50/38.50 t. – 12 rm ⌂ 85.00/175.00 t. – SB 295.00 st.

AMBLESIDE Cumbria 402 L 20 – pop. 2 689 – ECD : Thursday – ✆ 05394.
Envir. : Tarn Hows★★ (lake) SW : 6 m. by A 593 AY – Langdale Valley★★ W : 7 m. by B 5343 AY – Brantwood★, SW : 6 ½ m. – Helvellyn★, NW : 8 m.
🛈 Old Courthouse, Church St. ✆ 32602 (summer only).
♦London 278 – ♦Carlisle 47 – Kendal 14.

Plan on next page

Kirkstone Foot Country House, Kirkstone Pass Rd, LA22 9EH, NE : ¼ m. ✆ 32232, 🍽 – ✖ rest TV ☎ P. 🅿 AE ⓪ VISA. ✖   AZ c
closed 4 January-8 February – M (dinner only) 14.75 t. ▯ 3.50 – 15 rm ⌂ (dinner included) 56.00/96.00 t. – SB (November-January) 120.00/140.00 st.

Rothay Garth, Rothay Rd, LA22 0EE, ✆ 32217, 🍽 – ✖ TV ☎ P. 🅿 AE ⓪ VISA   AZ e
M (bar lunch)/dinner 14.50 st. ▯ 3.70 – 15 rm ⌂ 28.00/68.00 st., 1 suite 83.00 st. – SB (except 24 August-29 October and Bank Holidays) 48.00/76.00 st.

Elder Grove, Lake Rd, LA22 0DB, ✆ 32504 – ✖ rest TV P. 🅿 VISA   AZ a
Mid February-mid November – M 10.50 t. ▯ 3.50 – 12 rm ⌂ 20.00/40.00 t. – SB 56.00/60.00 st.

Crow How ♨, Rydal Rd, LA22 9PN, NW : ½ m. on A 591 ✆ 32193, ≤, 🍽 – TV P   BY x
Easter-October and weekends in winter – M 10.00 st. ▯ 3.00 – 9 rm ⌂ 17.50/46.25 st. – SB (November-Easter) (weekends only) 45.00/51.50 st.

Chapel House, Kirkstone Rd, LA22 9DZ, ✆ 33143 – ✖ rest. ✖   AZ n
closed January-February and restricted service November-December – M 12.50 st. ▯ 5.00 – 10 rm ⌂ (dinner included) 21.25/53.00 st. – SB (weekdays only) 42.50/45.50 st.

at Rothay Bridge S : ½ m. on A 593 – ✉ ✆ 05394 Ambleside :

Rothay Manor, LA22 0EH, ✆ 33605, ≤, « Elegant Regency interior », 🍽 – ✖ rest TV ☎ ﺝ P. 🅿 AE ⓪ VISA. ✖   BY r
closed 3 January-11 February – M (buffet lunch Monday to Saturday)/dinner 21.00 t. ▯ 4.00 – 15 rm ⌂ 58.00/92.00 t., 3 suites 116.00 t. – SB (November-Easter) 96.00/122.00 st.

Borrans Park, Borrans Rd, LA22 0EN, ✆ 33454, 🍽 – ✖ TV ☎ ﺝ P. ✖   BY a
closed 1 week Christmas – M (dinner only) 11.00 st. ▯ 3.60 – 14 rm ⌂ 44.00/58.00 st. – SB (November-March) 65.00/75.00 st.

Riverside ♨, Under Loughrigg, LA22 9LJ, ✆ 32395, 🍽 – ✖ rest TV ☎ P. 🅿 VISA. ✖   BY s
closed mid November-January – M (bar lunch)/dinner 14.00 t. ▯ 3.50 – 10 rm ⌂ 37.00/72.00 t. – SB 60.00/72.00 st.

at Waterhead S : 1 m. on A 591 – ✉ ✆ 05394 Ambleside :

Wateredge, Borrans Rd, LA22 0EP, ✆ 32332, ≤, « Part 17C Fishermans cottages, lakeside setting », 🍽 – TV ☎ P. 🅿 AE VISA. ✖   BY o
closed mid December-early February – M (bar lunch)/dinner 18.50 t. ▯ 4.30 – 23 rm ⌂ (dinner included) 50.50/114.00 t. – SB (except 11 May-October) 74.00/100.00 st.

Regent, Borrans Rd, LA22 0ES, ✆ 32254, 🅿 – ✖ rest TV ☎ P. 🅿 VISA   BY e
M (dinner only) 15.50 t. – 21 rm ⌂ 38.00/64.00 t. – SB (November-March) 69.00/72.00 st.

at Clappersgate W : 1 m. on A 593 – ✉ ✆ 05394 Ambleside :

Nanny Brow Country House ♨, LA22 9NF, ✆ 32036, ≤, « Landscaped gardens », ♨ – ✖ rest TV ☎ P. 🅿 AE VISA   BY u
M (dinner only) 15.00 t. ▯ 4.25 – 16 rm ⌂ 29.50/72.00 t., 3 suites 80.00/82.00 t. – SB (November-April) 70.00/95.00 st.

Grey Friar Lodge, LA22 9NE, ✆ 33158, ≤, 🍽 – ✖. ✖   BY n
April-October – M (dinner only) 12.50 st. ▯ 4.50 – 8 rm ⌂ (dinner included) 27.00/68.00.

at Skelwith Bridge W : 2 ½ m. on A 593 – ✉ ✆ 05394 Ambleside :

Skelwith Bridge, LA22 9NJ, ✆ 32115, ≤, 🍽 – ✖ rest TV P. 🅿 VISA   AY v
M (bar lunch Monday to Saturday)/dinner 14.75 t. ▯ 3.75 – 24 rm ⌂ 35.00/60.00 t. – SB (except September-October and Bank Holidays) (weekdays only) 58.00/76.00 st.

at Little Langdale W : 4 ½ m. by A 593 – ✉ ✆ 096 67 Langdale :

Three Shires Inn ♨, LA22 9NZ, ✆ 215, ≤, 🍽 – ✖ rest P. ✖   AY z
closed January-mid February except New Year – M (bar lunch)/dinner 15.00 t. ▯ 3.80 – 11 rm ⌂ 24.00/60.00 t. – SB (weekdays only) 62.50 st.

AMBLESIDE
GRASMERE

Lake Rd . . . . AZ

Borrans Rd . . . . **BY** 2
Broadgate . . . . **BZ** 3
Cheapside . . . . **AZ** 4
Church St . . . . **AZ** 6
Compston St . . . . **AZ** 8
Easedale Rd . . . . **BZ** 10
Kelswick Rd . . . . **AZ** 12

King St . . . . **AZ** 13
Market Pl . . . . **AZ** 14
North Rd . . . . **AZ** 17
Old Lake Rd . . . . **AZ** 20
St. Mary's Lane . . . . **AZ** 22
Smithy Brow . . . . **AZ** 23
Swan Hill . . . . **AY** 24

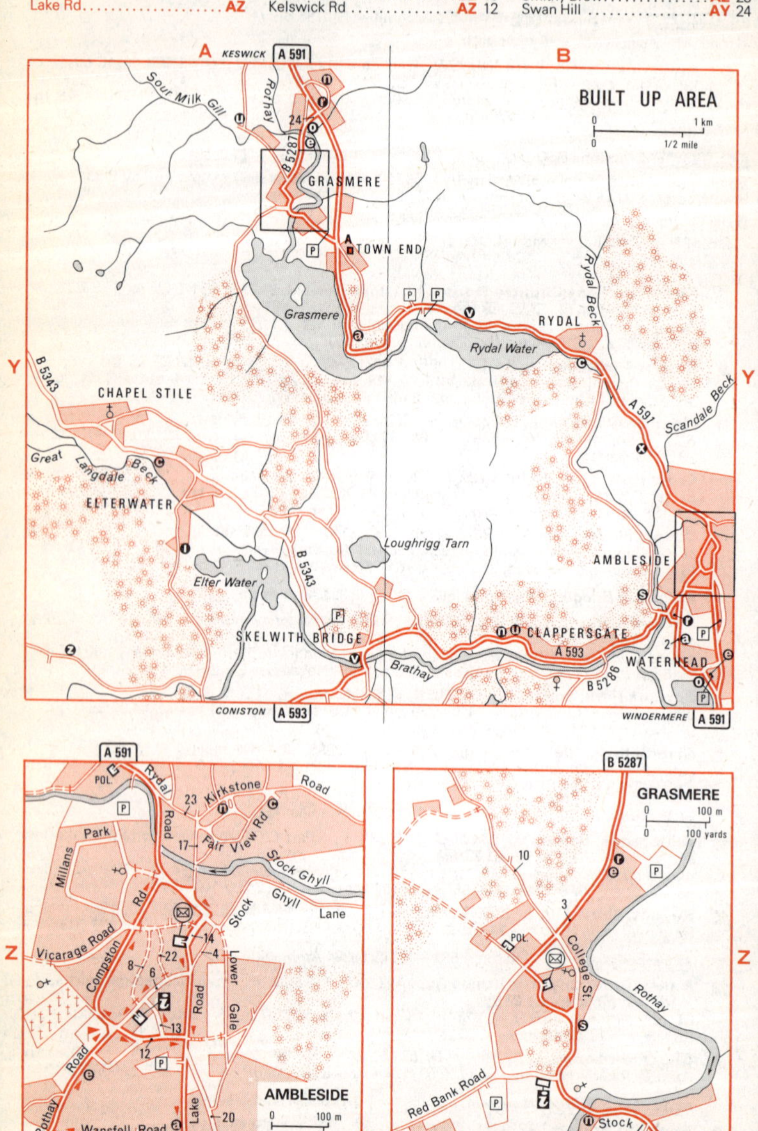

Town plans : roads most used by traffic and those on which guide listed hotels and restaurants stand are fully drawn ; the beginning only of lesser roads is indicated.

at Elterwater W : 4 ½ m. by A 593 off B 5343 – ✉ Ambleside – ☎ 096 67 Langdale :

Langdale H & Country Club ⌘, Great Langdale, LA22 9JD, NW : 1 ¼ m. on B 5343 ✆ 302, Fax 694, 🏊, ✏, park, squash – 🍽 rest 📺 ☎ 🅿 – 👥 100. 🔺 AE ⓪ VISA. ⌘ AY c
M 8.00/17.00 st. and a la carte 11.20/16.50 st. – **41 rm** ☕ 88.00/97.00 st., **12 suites** 88.00/106.00 st. – SB 110.00/138.00 st.

Eltermere Country House ⌘, LA22 9HY, ✆ 207, ≤, ✿ – ✕ rest 📺 🅿. 🔺 VISA ⌘
closed December-January except New Year – **M** (dinner only) 13.95 t. 🍾 4.50 – **15 rm** ☕ 36.00/72.00 t. – SB (winter only) 56.00/60.00 st. AY i

at Rydal NW : 1 ½ m. on A 591 – ✉ ☎ 05394 Ambleside :

Rydal Lodge, LA22 9LR, ✆ 33208, ✿ – ✕ rest 🅿. 🔺 ⓪ VISA BY c
closed January and December except Chistmas-New Year – **M** 10.50 t. 🍾 2.90 – **8 rm** ☕ 19.00/30.00 t.

AMERSHAM (Old Town) Bucks. 404 S 28 – pop. 21 326 – ECD : Thursday – ☎ 0494.
♦London 29 – Aylesbury 16 – ♦Oxford 33.

Crown (T.H.F.), High St., HP7 0DH, ✆ 721541, ✿ – 📺 ☎ 🅿. 🔺 AE ⓪ VISA
M 15.00 st. (dinner) and a la carte 🍾 4.00 – ☕ 7.00 – **23 rm** 65.00/83.00 st., **2 suites** 95.00/120.00 st. – SB (weekends only) 64.00/80.00 st.

King's Arms, High St., HP7 0DJ, ✆ 726333 – 🅿. 🔺 AE ⓪ VISA
closed Sunday dinner and Monday – **M** 10.50 t. (lunch) and a la carte 17.50/22.00 t. 🍾 3.20.

Romna, 20-22 The Broadway, HP7 0HP, ✆ 433732, Indian rest..

at Penn Street SW : 2 m. by A 404 – ✉ ☎ 0494 Amersham :

Hit or Miss Inn, HP7 0PX, ✆ 713109 – 🅿. 🔺 AE ⓪ VISA
closed Saturday lunch, Sunday dinner and Monday – **M** 12.95/17.50 t. and a la carte 11.65/19.05 t. 🍾 3.90.

AUSTIN-ROVER London Rd ✆ 5911
DAIMLER-JAGUAR London Rd ✆ 28013
PEUGEOT-TALBOT 4-8 White Lion Rd ✆ 024 04
(Little Chalfont) 4666

RENAULT The Broadway ✆ 29411

AMMANFORD (RHYDAMAN) Dyfed 403 I 28 – pop. 5 708 – ECD : Thursday – ✉ ☎ 0269 Llandybie.
♦London 208 – Carmarthen 22 – ♦Swansea 15.

Mill at Glynhir ⌘, SA18 2TE, NE : 3 ¼ m. by A 483 and Glynhir Rd ✆ 850672, 🏊, ✿ – 📺 ☎ 🅿. 🔺 VISA
closed Christmas-New Year – **M** (bar lunch)/dinner 12.00 st. 🍾 2.40 – **10 rm** ☕ 27.00/64.00 st. – SB 58.00/69.00 st.

⬡ ATS, Pontamman Rd ✆ 3838

AMPFIELD Hants. 403 404 P 30 – pop. 1 675 – ECD : Wednesday – ✉ Romsey – ☎ 0794 Braishfield.
ℹ8 Winchester Rd ✆ 68480.
♦London 70 – Bournemouth 31 – Salisbury 19 – ♦Southampton 11 – Winchester 7.

Potters Heron (Lansbury), Winchester Rd, SO51 9ZF, on A 31 ✆ 0703 (Southampton) 266611, Telex 47459, Fax 251359 – ✕ rm 🍽 rest 📺 ☎ ♿ 🅿 – 👥 120. 🔺 AE ⓪ VISA ⌘
M *(closed Saturday lunch)* 8.50/12.50 t. and a la carte – **60 rm** ☕ 63.00/73.00 t. – SB (spring and autumn) (weekends only) 76.00/84.00 st.

Keats, Winchester Rd, SO51 9BQ, on A 31 ✆ 68252, Italian rest. – 🅿. 🔺 AE ⓪ VISA
closed Sunday and Monday – **M** 8.50 t. (lunch) and a la carte 12.10/19.25 t. 🍾 3.50.

ANDOVER Hants. 403 404 P 30 – pop. 30 632 – ECD : Wednesday – ☎ 0264.
ℹ9 51 Winchester Rd ✆ 23980, S : 1 m. on A 3057.
ℹ Town Mill car park, Bridge St. ✆ 24320.
♦London 74 – Bath 53 – Salisbury 17 – Winchester 11.

Danebury (Lansbury), High St., SP10 1NX, ✆ 323332, Telex 47587 – 📺 ☎ – 👥 60. 🔺 AE ⓪ VISA ⌘
M 7.95 st. (lunch) and a la carte approx. 11.25 st. 🍾 3.95 – **24 rm** ☕ 55.00/65.00 st. – SB (weekends only) (except Christmas and New Year) 40.00/72.00 st.

Ashley Court, Micheldever Rd, via London Rd, SP11 6LA, ✆ 57344, Fax 56755, ✿ – ✕ rm 📺 ☎ ♿ 🅿 – 👥 120. 🔺 AE VISA
M a la carte 17.00/25.00 🍾 3.00 – ☕ 3.00 – **35 rm** 51.00/70.00 st. – SB (weekends only) 72.00/78.00 st.

White Hart (T.H.F.), Bridge St., SP10 1BH, ✆ 52266 – 📺 ☎ 🅿 – 👥 50. 🔺 AE ⓪ VISA
M (bar lunch)/dinner 13.95 st. and a la carte 🍾 3.95 – ☕ 7.00 – **20 rm** 56.00/66.00 st. – SB (weekends only) (except Easter and Christmas) 64.00/68.00 st.

at Barton Stacey SE : 5 ½ m. by A 303 – ✉ ☎ 0264 Andover :

🏨 **Travelodge** without rest., SO21 3NP, on A 303 ℘ 72260 – TV ৬ P. 🅿 AE VISA
20 rm 21.50/27.00 t.

AUDI-VW Colebrook Way, Weyhill Rd ℘ 55200
AUSTIN-ROVER 278 Weyhill Rd ℘ 23781
FORD West St. ℘ 332144
MERCEDES-BENZ, FIAT Salisbury Rd ℘ 61166

VAUXHALL Newbury Rd ℘ 24233

⊛ ATS 51a New St. ℘ 23606/7

ANDOVERSFORD Glos. 408 404 O 28 – see Cheltenham.

ANSTY Warw. – see Coventry (West Midlands).

APPLEBY Cumbria 402 M 20 – pop. 2 344 – ECD : Thursday – ☎ 07683.
🏌 Blackenber Moor ℘ 51432, S : 2 m. by A 66.
🛈 Moot Hall, Boroughgate ℘ 51177.
♦London 285 – ♦Carlisle 33 – Kendal 24 – ♦Middlesbrough 58.

🏨 **Appleby Manor** (Best Western), Roman Rd, CA16 6JD, E : 1 m. by B 6542 via Station Rd
℘ 51571, ≼, 🚗 – ⊱ rest TV ☎ P. 🅿 AE ① VISA
M 12.25 st. and a la carte ▮ 4.35 – **18 rm** � 48.50/77.00 st. – SB 74.00/94.00 st.

🏠 Royal Oak Inn, Bongate, CA16 6UN, SE : ½ m. on B 6542 ℘ 51463 – TV P.
7 rm.

FORD The Sands ℘ 51133

PEUGEOT-TALBOT ℘ 61435

APPLETON-LE-MOORS North Yorks. 402 R 21 – pop. 166 – ☎ 075 15 Lastingham.
♦London 245 – ♦Middlesbrough 37 – ♦Scarborough 27 – York 33.

🏨 **Dweldapilton Hall** ⑤, YO6 6TF, ℘ 227, Fax 540, 🚗 – ▤ TV ☎ P. 🅿 AE VISA. ⋇
M (bar lunch)/dinner 18.50 st. and a la carte ▮ 3.95 – **12 rm** ⊱ 38.50/77.00 st. –
SB (November-March) 90.00 st.

ARBERTH = Narberth.

ARDSLEY South Yorks. – see Barnsley.

ARMATHWAITE Cumbria 401 402 L 19 – ✉ Carlisle – ☎ 069 92.
♦London 305 – ♦Carlisle 10 – Penrith 12.

🏠 Fox and Pheasant, CA4 9PY, ℘ 400, ≼ – TV P
6 rm.

ARNCLIFFE North Yorks. 402 N 21 – pop. 67 – ✉ Skipton – ☎ 075 677.
♦London 232 – Kendal 41 – ♦Leeds 41 – Preston 50 – York 52.

🏨 **Amerdale House** ⑤, BD23 5QE, ℘ 250, ≼, 🚗 – ⊱ rest TV P. 🅿 VISA. ⋇
Mid March-mid November – **M** (dinner only) 15.00 t. ▮ 3.45 – **11 rm** ⊱ 35.00/70.00 t. –
SB (except summer) 56.00/66.00 st.

ARUNDEL West Sussex 404 S 31 – pop. 2 595 – ECD : Wednesday – ☎ 0903.
See : Castle* (keep 12C, ≼* 119 steps, State apartments*) *AC* – St. Nicholas' Church (chancel
or Fitzalan chapel* 14C).
Envir. : Bignor (Roman Villa : mosaics** *AC*) NW : 7 m.
🛈 61 High St. ℘ 882268.
♦London 58 – ♦Brighton 21 – ♦Southampton 41 – Worthing 9.

🏨 **Norfolk Arms**, 22 High St., BN18 9AD, ℘ 882101, Telex 878436, Fax 884275 – ⊱ rm TV
☎ P. 🅿 AE ① VISA
M 9.00 t. (lunch) and a la carte 12.85/19.85 t. ▮ 4.45 – **34 rm** ⊱ 44.50/65.00 t. –
SB 90.00/110.00 st.

🏨 **Arundel Resort**, Chichester Rd, BN18 0AD, W : 1 m. on A 27 ℘ 882677, Fax 884154 – TV
☎ P. 🅿 AE ① VISA
M 9.95 t. (lunch) and a la carte 15.00/30.00 t. ▮ 5.00 – ⊱ 5.95 – **16 rm** 40.00/50.00 st. –
SB (weekends only) 70.00 st.

🏠 **Swan**, 29 High St., BN18 9AG, ℘ 882314 – ⊱ rest TV ☎. 🅿 AE ① VISA. ⋇
M (bar lunch Monday to Saturday)/dinner 10.00 t. and a la carte ▮ 3.75 – **10 rm**
⊱ 38.00/50.00 t. – SB 63.00/92.00 st.

🏠 **Portreeves Acre** without rest., The Causeway, BN18 9JJ, ℘ 883277, 🚗 – TV P. ⋇
5 rm ⊱ 25.00/36.00 st.

at Burpham NE : 3 m. by A 27 – ✉ ☎ 0903 Arundel :

🏨 **Burpham Country** ⑤, Old Down, BN18 9RJ, ℘ 882160, ≼, 🚗 – ⊱ rest TV P. 🅿 ⋇
M *(closed dinner Sunday and Monday)* (bar lunch)/dinner 11.80 t. ▮ 3.50 – **10 rm**
⊱ 35.00/53.00 t. – SB (October-May) 70.00/80.00 st.

at Walberton W : 3 m. by A 27 on B 2132 – ⊠ Arundel – ✆ 0243 Yapton :

🏨 **Avisford Park,** Yapton Lane, BN18 0LS, ✆ 551215, Telex 86137, Fax 552485, ≼, ⌁ heated,
⬚, 📾9, ⇌, park, ✗, squash – 📺 ☎ 🅿 – 🚣 200. 🄰 AE VISA. ✗
M (buffet lunch Monday to Saturday)/dinner 22.00 **st.** and a la carte ⌑ 4.75 – **97 rm**
⌑ 66.00/118.00 **st.**, **3 suites** 110.00/147.00 **st.** – SB (weekends only) (except Bank Holidays) 107.00/160.50 **st.**

ASCOT Berks. 404 R 29 – pop. 17 930 (inc Sunningdale) – ECD : Wednesday – ✆ 0990 (during 1990 will change to 0344).

📾18 Royal Ascot, Winkfield Rd, on Royal Ascot racecourse ✆ 25175 – 📾9 Lavender Park, Swinley Rd ✆ 0344(Bracknell) 884074, SW : 3 ½ m. on A 332.

♦London 36 – Reading 15.

🏨 **Royal Berkshire** (Hilton) ⌁, London Rd, Sunninghill, SL5 0PP, E : 2 m. on A 329
✆ 23322, Telex 847280, Fax 27100, « Queen Anne mansion in garden », ⬚, park, ✗,
squash – 📺 ☎ 🅿 – 🚣 . 🄰 AE ① VISA
M (see **Stateroom rest.** below) – ⌑ 9.50 – **79 rm** 75.90/139.70 **t.**, **3 suites** 231.00/358.60 **t.**
– SB (weekends only) 128.00 **st.**

🏨 **Berystede** (T.H.F.), Bagshot Rd, Sunninghill, SL5 9JH, S : 1 ¼ m. on A 330 ✆ 23311, Telex
847707, Fax 872301, ⌁ heated, ⇌ – ⧉ ✗ rm 📺 ☎ 🅿 – 🚣 120. 🄰 AE ① VISA
M 14.75/17.50 **st.** and a la carte ⌑ 3.95 – ⌑ 7.60 – **89 rm** 81.00/96.00 **st.**, **2 suites** 165.00 **st.**
– SB (weekends only) 96.00/108.00 **st.**

⚘ **Royal Foresters,** London Rd, SL5 8DR, W : 1 ½ m. on A 329 ✆ 0344 (Winkfield Row)
884747, Fax 884115 – 📺 ☎ 🅿. 🄰 AE ① VISA
accommodation closed 25 and 26 December – **M** a la carte 10.45/15.25 **t.** ⌑ 3.85 – **34 rm**
⌑ 50.00/60.00 **t.** – SB (weekends only) 40.00/60.00 **st.**

XXX **Stateroom** (at Royal Berkshire H.), London Rd, Sunninghill, SL5 0PP, E : 2 m. on A 329
✆ 23322, Telex 847280, Fax 27100 – 🅿. 🄰 AE ① VISA
M 19.50/25.00 **t.** and a la carte 30.50/35.00 **t.** ⌑ 7.00.

XXX **Ascot Guinea,** Mill Ride Estate, Mill Ride, North Ascot, SL5 8LT, ✆ 0344 (Bracknell) 886737
– 🅿. 🄰 AE ① VISA
*closed Saturday lunch, Sunday, Monday, last 2 weeks August, 2 weeks Christmas and Bank
Holidays* – **M** (grill rest.) a la carte 10.50/30.25 **t.** ⌑ 4.00.

XX Hyns Beijing, 4 Brockenhurst Rd, South Ascot, SL5 9DL, S : ½ m. on A 330 ✆ 872583,
Chinese rest. – ▤ 🅿.

XX **Grooms,** 6 Hermitage Par., High St., SL5 7HE, ✆ 22285 – ▤. 🄰 AE ① VISA
closed Saturday lunch, Sunday, 24 December, 2 January and Bank Holidays – **M** a la carte
15.05/20.55 **t.** ⌑ 4.75.

AUSTIN-ROVER Ascot Motor Works ✆ 20324   CITROEN Lyndhurst Rd, South Ascot ✆ 22257

ASHBOURNE Derbs. 402 403 404 O 24 – pop. 5 909 – ✆ 0335.

📾9 Clifton ✆ 42078, SW : 1 ½ m. on A 515.

🛈 13 The Market Pl. ✆ 43666.

♦London 146 – Derby 14 – ♦Manchester 48 – ♦Nottingham 33 – ♦Sheffield 44.

🏨 Ashbourne Lodge (Best Western), Derby Rd, DE6 1XH, SE : 1 m. on A 52 ✆ 46666, Telex
378560, Fax 46549 – ⧉ 📺 ☎ 🅿 – 🚣 200
M (carving lunch) – **49 rm**, **2 suites**.

🏨 **Callow Hall** ⌁, Mapleton Rd, DE6 2AA, W : ¾ m. (via Union St.) ✆ 43103, Fax 43624, ⤸,
⇌, park – 📺 ☎ 🅿. 🄰 AE ① VISA. ✗
closed 2 weeks February and 25-26 December – **M** *(closed Monday lunch and Sunday
dinner to non-residents)* 12.50/19.50 **t.** and a la carte ⌑ 3.50 – **9 rm** ⌑ 50.00/103.00 **t.** –
SB 130.00/170.00 **st.**

🄰 ATS Blenheim Rd ✆ 44644

ASHBURTON Devon 403 I 32 The West Country G. – pop. 3 610 – ECD : Wednesday –
✆ 0364.

♦London 220 – Exeter 20 – ♦Plymouth 23.

🏛 **Holne Chase** ⌁, TQ13 7NS, NW : 3 m. on Two Bridges Rd ✆ 036 43 (Poundsgate) 471,
Fax 453, ≼, « Country house atmosphere », ⤸, ⇌, park – ✗ rest 📺 ☎ 🅿. 🄰 AE ①
VISA. ✗
M 9.50/16.50 **st.** ⌑ 3.35 – **14 rm** ⌑ 50.00/120.00 **t.** – SB 95.00/130.00 **st.**

🏛 **Dartmoor Motel,** Peartree Cross, TQ13 7JW, W : ½ m. ✆ 52232 – ⧉ 📺 ☎ 🅿. 🄰 AE ①
VISA
closed 25 and 26 December – **M** 6.00/6.50 **t.** and a la carte ⌑ 2.70 – **28 rm** ⌑ 32.85/49.85 **t.**

⚘ **Gages Mill Country,** Buckfastleigh Rd, TQ13 7JW, S : ½ m. on old A 38 ✆ 52391, ⇌ –
✗ rest 🅿. ✗
Mid March-October – **M** (dinner only) 8.00 **st.** ⌑ 3.00 – **8 rm** ⌑ 20.00/35.00 **st.**

MITSUBISHI 6 East St. ✆ 52215

ASHBY DE LA ZOUCH Leics. 402 403 404 P 25 – pop. 9 987 – ECD : Wednesday – 0530.
🖪 North St. 510034 (summer only).
♦London 119 – ♦Birmingham 29 – ♦Leicester 18 – ♦Nottingham 22.

Royal Osprey, Station Rd, LE6 5GP, 412833, Telex 341629, ☞ – ❤️ rm ▥ ⬓ Ⓟ – 🛁 60. ☒ AE ⓞ VISA
M (closed Saturday lunch and Bank Holidays) 8.35/11.95 t. and a la carte 2.80 – **31 rm** 44.00/54.00 st. – SB (weekends only) 54.90 st.

ATS Kilwardy St. 412791

ASHFORD Kent 404 W 30 – pop. 45 198 – ECD : Wednesday – 0233.
Envir. : Hothfield (St. Margaret's Church : memorial tomb★ 17C) NW : 3 m. – Lenham (St. Mary's Church : woodwork★) NW : 9 ½ m.
🖪₈ Sandyhurst Lane 620180, NW : 1 ½ m. by A 20 – 🖪 Lower High St. 37311 ext 316/410/209.
♦London 56 – Canterbury 14 – ♦Dover 24 – Hastings 30 – Maidstone 19.

Eastwell Manor (Norfolk Cap.) 🦢, Eastwell Park, TN25 4HR, N : 3 m. by A 28 on A 251 635751, Telex 966281, Fax 635530, ≤, « Reconstructed period mansion in formal gardens », 🦢, park, ✕ – ▤ ▥ ☎ & Ⓟ – 🛁 60. ☒ AE ⓞ VISA
M 15.00/24.00 t. and a la carte – **20 rm** 80.00/120.00 t., **3 suites** 140.00/200.00 t. – SB 157.00/173.00 st.

Post House (T.H.F.), Canterbury Rd, TN24 8QQ, 625790, Telex 966685, Fax 643176, ☞ – ❤️ rm ▥ ☎ Ⓟ – 🛁 120. ☒ AE ⓞ VISA
M 11.95/14.95 st. and a la carte 4.25 – 7.25 – **60 rm** 60.00/90.00 st. – SB (weekends only) 80.00/100.00 st.

Master Spearpoint (Best Western), Canterbury Rd, Kennington, TN24 9QR, NE : 2 m. on A 28 636863, Telex 965978, Fax 610119, ☞ – ▥ ☎ Ⓟ – 🛁 50. ☒ AE ⓞ VISA
M (carving lunch) – **36 rm** 57.00/75.00 st. – SB (weekends only) 73.00/76.00 st.

AUSTIN-ROVER 20-46 New St. 20334
FORD Station Rd 23451
NISSAN Maidstone Rd 34177
SKODA, FIAT Chart Rd 22281

VOLVO Chart Rd 35661

ATS Hythe Rd 622450

ASHFORD Surrey 404 S 29 – ECD : Wednesday – 078 42.
♦London 21 – Reading 27.

Terrazza, 45 Church Rd, TW15 2TY, 2244887, Italian rest. – ▤. ☒ AE ⓞ VISA
closed Saturday lunch, Sunday and Bank Holidays – M 16.50 st. and a la carte 19.55/29.50 st.

CITROEN 594 London Rd 52125
VAUXHALL Staines Rd 41901

VW-AUDI 554 London Rd 50051

ASHINGTON West Sussex 404 S 31 – pop. 1 728 – ECD : Wednesday – ✉ Pulborough – 0903.
♦London 50 – ♦Brighton 20 – Worthing 9.

Mill House 🦢, Mill Lane, RH20 3BZ, 892426, Fax 892855, ☞ – ▥ ☎ Ⓟ. ☒ AE ⓞ VISA ✕
M 8.95/11.55 st. and a la carte 2.95 – **10 rm** 35.00/70.00 st. – SB (weekends only) 85.00 st.

ATS Lintonville Terr. 817013/817038

ASHTON-UNDER-LYNE Greater Manchester 402 403 404 N 23 – pop. 43 605 – ECD : Tuesday – 061 Manchester.
🖪₈ Gorsey Way, Higher Hurst 330 1537 – 🖪₉ Dunkinfield, Lyne Edge 338 2340.
♦London 209 – ♦Leeds 40 – ♦Manchester 7 – ♦Sheffield 34.

York House, York Pl., off Richmond St., OL6 7TT, 330 5899, Fax 343 1613 – ▥ ☎ Ⓟ. ☒ AE ⓞ VISA ✕
closed 26 December and 2 January – M (closed Saturday lunch and Sunday dinner) 8.50 st. (lunch) and a la carte 8.70/19.50 t. 2.50 – **34 rm** 38.00/57.00 st. – SB (weekends only) 58.00 st.

Woodlands, 33 Shepley Rd, Audenshaw, M34 5DJ, S : 2 m. by A 635, Audenshaw Rd and Guide Lane (A 6017) on B 6169 336 4241 – Ⓟ. ☒ VISA
closed Saturday lunch, Sunday, Monday, 1 week after Easter, 2 weeks August and 1 week Christmas – M 10.00/12.50 t. and a la carte 15.05/20.65 t. 3.00.

FORD Manchester Rd 330 0121
LADA Dukinfield Rd 368 3632

PEUGEOT-TALBOT Oldham Rd 343 1333
VAUXHALL 185 Katherine St 330 2222

ASKRIGG North Yorks. 402 N 21 – pop. 404 – ✉ Leyburn – 0969 Wensleydale.
♦London 251 – Kendal 32 – ♦Leeds 70 – York 63.

King's Arms, Market Sq., DL8 3HQ, 50258 – ❤️ rm ▥. ☒ VISA ✕
M 13.75 t. (dinner) and a la carte 3.00 – **10 rm** 30.00/65.00 t. – SB (except Christmas and Bank Holidays) 68.00/72.00 st.

Winville, Main St., DL8 3HG, 50515, ☞ – ▥ Ⓟ. ☒ AE ⓞ VISA
M 6.95/12.95 t. – **6 rm** 31.00/42.00 t. – SB 54.00/62.00 st.

ASPLEY GUISE Beds. **404** S 27 – pop. 2 314 – ⊠ Woburn – ✆ 0908 Milton Keynes.
⚑ Woburn Sands, West Hill ✆ 583596, W : 2 m. off M 1 (junction 13).
♦London 52 – Bedford 13 – Luton 16 – ♦Northampton 22.

   🏨 **Moore Place,** The Square, MK17 8DW, ✆ 282000, Telex 281888, ⇌ – �📺 ☎ 🅿 – 🚶 40.
   ◪ AE ⓞ VISA ⅏
   M *(closed Saturday lunch)* 13.00/17.00 **t.** and a la carte ▮6.75 – **53 rm** ⌑ 75.00/95.00 **t.**,
   1 suite 135.00 **t.** – SB (weekends only) 85.00 **t.**

ASTON South Yorks. **402** **403** **404** Q 23 – ⊠ ✆ 0742 Sheffield.
♦London 161 – Lincoln 39 – ♦Sheffield 8.

   🏨 Aston Hall ⑤, Worksop Rd, S31 0EE, ✆ 872309, Fax 873228, ⇌ – �📺 ☎ 🅿 – 🚶
   21 rm.

ASTON CLINTON Bucks. **404** R 28 – pop. 3 671 – ECD : Wednesday – ⊠ ✆ 0296 Aylesbury.
♦London 42 – Aylesbury 4 – ♦Oxford 26.

   🏨 **Bell Inn,** HP22 5HP, ✆ 630252, Telex 83252, Fax 631250, « Courtyard and gardens » –
   ⇥ rest �📺 ☎ 🅿 – 🚶 200. ◪ VISA
   M *(closed Sunday dinner and Monday to non-residents)* 21.50/22.50 **st.** and a la carte
   30.50/50.00 **st.** – ⌑ 10.00 – **15 rm** 84.00/121.00 **st.**, **6 suites** 121.00/165.00 **st.**

ATTLEBOROUGH Norfolk **404** X 26 – pop. 6 322 – ECD : Wednesday – ✆ 0953.
♦London 94 – ♦Cambridge 47 – ♦Norwich 15.

   🏛 **Sherbourne,** Norwich Rd, NR17 2JX, NE : ½ m. ✆ 454363, ⇌ – ⇥ rest �📺 ☎ 🅿. ◪ AE
   VISA ⅏
   M (bar lunch)/dinner 18.00 **t.** and a la carte ▮3.95 – **8 rm** ⌑ 18.00/65.00 **t.** – SB 50.00/55.00 **st.**

   ⚐ **Griffin,** Church St., NR17 2AH, ✆ 452149 – �📺 🅿
   M *(closed Sunday dinner)* (bar lunch)/dinner a la carte 10.50/17.25 **st.** ▮2.90 – **8 rm**
   ⌑ 20.00/40.00 **st.**

FORD High St. ✆ 452274   🅐 ATS London Rd ✆ 453883
RENAULT Station Rd ✆ 452223

AVENING Glos. **403** **404** N 28 – see Tetbury.

AVON Hants. – see Ringwood.

AXBRIDGE Somerset **403** L 30 The West Country G. – pop. 1 724 – ECD : Wednesday –
✆ 0934 – See : Site★★ – King John's Hunting Lodge★ *AC* – St. John the Baptist Church★.
Envir. : The Cheddar Gorge★★ (The Gorge★★ - Jacob's Ladder ≤★*AC* - The Caves★★*AC*)
– St. Andrews Church★, SE : 1 ½ m.
♦London 142 – ♦Bristol 17 – Taunton 31 – Weston-Super-Mare 10.

   Hotels and restaurants see : Weston-Super-Mare NW : 7 ½ m.

AXMINSTER Devon **403** L 31 – pop. 4 457 – ECD : Wednesday – ✆ 0297.
🛈 Old Court House, Church St. ✆ 34386 (summer only).
♦London 156 – Exeter 27 – Lyme Regis 5.5 – Taunton 22 – Yeovil 24.

   at Hawkchurch NE : 4 ½ m. by A 35 off B 3165 – ⊠ Axminster – ✆ 029 77 Hawkchurch :

   🏨 **Fairwater Head** ⑤, EX13 5TX, S : ¾ m. ✆ 349, ≤ Axe Vale, ⇌ – �📺 ☎ 🅿. ◪ AE ⓞ
   VISA ⅏
   closed January and February – **M** (bar lunch)/dinner 14.00 **st.** ▮4.50 – **18 rm**
   ⌑ 45.00/80.00 **st.** – SB 110.00/120.00 **st.**

AYLESBURY Bucks. **404** R 28 – pop. 51 999 – ECD : Thursday – ✆ 0296.
Envir. : Waddesdon Manor★★ (Rothschild Collection★★★) *AC*, NW : 5 ½ m. – Ascott House★★
(Rothschild Collection★★) and gardens★ *AC*, NE : 8 ½ m. – Stewkley (St. Michael's Church★
12C) NE : 12 m.
⚑ Weston Turville, New Rd ✆ 24084, SE : 2 ½ m – 🛈 County Hall, Walton St. ✆ 395000.
♦London 46 – ♦Birmingham 72 – Northampton 37 – ♦Oxford 22.

   🏰 **Hartwell House** ⑤, Oxford Rd, HP17 8NL, SW : 2 m. on A 418 ✆ 747444, Telex 837108,
   Fax 747450, ≤, « Part Jacobean, part Georgian house, former residence of Louis XVIII »,
   ⑤, ⇌, park – 🕴 �📺 ☎ & 🅿. ◪ AE ⓞ VISA ⅏
   M 15.00/25.00 **st.** and a la carte 24.35/33.40 **st.** ▮5.50 – ⌑ 9.50 – **29 rm** 83.00/145.00 **st.**,
   3 suites 215.00/250.00 **st.** – SB 170.00/220.00 **st.**

   🏨 **Forte** (T.H.F.), Aston Clinton Rd, HP22 5AA, SE : 2 m. on A 41 ✆ 393388, Telex 838820, Fax
   392211, ▨ – ⇥ rm �📺 ☎ & 🅿 – 🚶 140. ◪ AE ⓞ VISA
   M 11.95/19.75 **st.** and a la carte ▮3.95 – ⌑ 7.60 – **98 rm** 69.00/84.00 **st.**, **2 suites** 150.00 **st.**
   – SB (weekends only) 68.00/88.00 **st.**

   🏛 **Horse and Jockey Motel** without rest, Buckingham Rd, HP19 3QL, ✆ 23803 – �📺 🅿. ◪
   AE ⓞ VISA ⅏
   24 rm ⌑ 35.00/45.00 **st.**

   ✗✗ **Pebbles,** 1 Pebble Lane, HP20 2JH, ✆ 86622 – ◪ AE ⓞ VISA
   closed Sunday dinner and Monday – **M** 12.50 **t.** (lunch) and a la carte 27.00/39.50 **t.** ▮7.00.

at Stoke Mandeville S : 3 ¼ m. by A 413 on A 4010 – ⊠ Aylesbury – ☎ 029 661 Stoke Mandeville :

🏠 **Belmore**, Risborough Rd, HP22 5UT, ✆ 2022, ⌇ heated, 🚗 – TV ☎ P. 🔼 AE ⓪ VISA 🛇
closed 6 days at Christmas – **M** (closed Sunday dinner and Monday Lunch) 14.00/17.00 **st.**
🍾 3.50 – ⊆ 3.90 – **15 rm** 31.00/48.00 **st.**

AUSTIN-ROVER, DAIMLER-JAGUAR Buckingham Rd ✆ 84071
CITROEN Park St. ✆ 435331
FORD Griffin Lane ✆ 26162
MERCEDES-BENZ Bicester Rd ✆ 81641

RENAULT Little Kimble ✆ 029 661 (Stoke Mandeville) 2239
VAUXHALL-OPEL 143 Cambridge St. ✆ 82321

🔟 ATS Gatehouse Way ✆ 433177

BABBACOMBE Devon 403 J 32 – see Torquay.

BACKFORD CROSS Cheshire 402 403 L 24 – see Chester.

BADMINTON Avon 403 404 N 29 The West Country G. – pop. 283 – ☎ 045 423 Didmarton.
See : Badminton House ★ AC.
♦London 114 – ♦Bristol 19 – Gloucester 26 – Swindon 33.

🏠 **Petty France**, GL9 1AF, NW : 3 m. on A 46 ✆ 361, Fax 768, 🚗 – TV ☎ P. 🔼 AE ⓪ VISA
M 19.25/18.50 **t.** and a la carte 🍾 4.50 – ⊆ 4.50 – **20 rm** 55.00/110.00 **t.** – SB (weekends only) (except Christmas) 90.00/130.00 **st.**

BAE COLWYN = Colwyn Bay.

BAGINTON Warw. 403 404 P 26 – see Coventry (West Midlands).

BAGSHOT Surrey 404 R 29 – pop. 4 239 – ECD : Wednesday – ☎ 0276.
♦London 37 – Reading 17 – ♦Southampton 49.

🏰 **Pennyhill Park** ⑤, College Ride, GU19 5ET, off A 30 ✆ 71774, Telex 858841, Fax 73217, ⩽, ⌇ heated, 🏌, 🎣, 🚗, park, 🍽 – ⇥ rm TV ☎ P. – 🔺 25. 🔼 AE ⓪ VISA 🛇
M 19.00 **t.** (lunch) and a la carte 25.00/38.00 **t.** 🍾 9.00 – ⊆ 8.95 – **52 rm** 120.00/250.00 **t.** – **2 suites** 250.00/300.00 **t.** – SB (weekends only) (except Christmas) 165.00 **st.**

🏠 **Cricketer's**, London Rd, GU19 5HR, N : ½ m. on A 30 ✆ 73196, Fax 51357, 🚗 – TV ☎ P. 🛇 – **29 rm**.

AUSTIN-ROVER London Rd, Windlesham, Nr Bagshot ✆ 73561
FORD 577 London Rd, Blackwater ✆ 33033

BAINBRIDGE North Yorks. 402 N 21 – pop. 474 – ECD : Wednesday – ⊠ Leyburn – ☎ 0969 Wensleydale.
♦London 249 – Kendal 31 – ♦Leeds 68 – York 61.

🏠 **Rose and Crown**, DL8 3EE, ✆ 50225 – TV P. 🔼 VISA
M (bar lunch Monday to Saturday)/dinner a la carte 11.20/14.85 **t.** 🍾 3.95 – **12 rm** ⊆ 32.00/52.00 **t.** – SB (October-April) 72.00/80.00 **st.**

BAKEWELL Derbs. 402 403 404 O 24 – pop. 3 839 – ECD : Thursday – ☎ 062 981 (4 fig.) or 0629 (6 fig.) – Envir. : Chatsworth ★★★ : site ★★, house ★★★ (Renaissance) garden ★★★ AC, NE : 2 ½ m. – Haddon Hall ★★ (14C-16C) AC, SE : 3 m.
🏌 Station Rd ✆ 2307 – 🅘 Old Market Hall, Bridge St. ✆ 3227.
♦London 160 – Derby 26 – ♦Manchester 37 – ♦Nottingham 33 – ♦Sheffield 17.

🏠 **Rutland Arms** (Best Western), The Square, DE4 1BT, ✆ 2812, Fax 4600 – TV ☎ P. – 🔺 35. 🔼 AE ⓪ VISA 🛇
M 9.95/15.95 **t.** and a la carte 🍾 4.70 – **36 rm** ⊆ 40.00/57.00 **t.** – SB 67.00/69.00 **st.**

🏡 **Milford House**, Mill St., DE4 1DA, ✆ 812130, 🚗 – TV P. 🛇
March-October – **M** (closed Sunday dinner) (dinner only and Sunday lunch)/dinner 11.00 **t.** 🍾 3.50 – **12 rm** ⊆ 25.30/54.00 **t.**

at Hassop N : 3 ½ m. by A 619 on B 6001 – ⊠ Bakewell – ☎ 062 987 Great Longstone :

🏰 **Hassop Hall** ⑤, DE4 1NS, ✆ 488, Telex 378485, ⩽, « Part 16C hall », 🚗, park, 🍽 – ⫞ TV ☎ P. 🔼 AE ⓪ VISA 🛇
closed 3 days at Christmas – **M** (closed Monday lunch and Sunday dinner) 14.00/25.00 **t.** 🍾 4.50 – ⊆ 10.00 – **12 rm** 55.00/90.00 **t.** – SB (November-March) 175.00/210.00 **st.**

at Great Longstone N : 4 m. by A 619 off B 6001 – ⊠ Bakewell – ☎ 062 987 Great Longstone :

🏠 **Croft** ⑤, DE4 1TF, ✆ 278, 🚗 – TV P. 🔼 VISA 🛇
closed January and 21 to 31 December – **M** (closed Monday to Wednesday to non-residents) (dinner only) 14.50 **t.** – **9 rm** ⊆ 44.00/65.00 **t.** – SB 70.00/100.00 **st.**

at Alport S : 4 m. by A 6 off B 5056 – ⊠ Bakewell – ☎ 062 986 Youlgreave :

🏡 **Rock House** without rest., DE4 1LG, ✆ 636736, 🚗 – P. 🛇
3 rm ⊆ 16.00/28.00 **st.**

BALA Gwynedd **402 403** J 25 – pop. 1 852 – ECD : Wednesday – ✆ 0678.

See : Site★.

Envir. : SW : Road ★ from Pandy to Dinas Mawddwy.

☗ Penlan ✆ 520359, SW : ¾ m. off A 494.

🛈 Snowdonia National Park Visitor Centre, High St. ✆ 520367 (summer only).

♦London 216 – Chester 46 – Dolgellau 18 – Shrewsbury 52.

Palé Hall ⌖, Llandderfel, LL23 7PS, E : 4 ¾ m. by A 494 on B 4401 ✆ 067 83 (Llandderfel) 285, ≤, « Ornate decor », ☜, ☞, park – ⧉ ✂ rest ⓣⱱ ☎ ℗. ◪ AE ⓞ VISA ⚡
M 12.50/21.00 **st.** and a la carte ⌕ 3.75 – **15 rm** ⌕ 99.00/150.00 t., **2 suites** 130.00 t. –
SB (except summer) (weekdays only) 135.00/160.00 **st.**

White Lion Royal, 61 High St., LL23 7AE, ✆ 520314 – ⓣⱱ ☎ ℗. ◪ AE ⓞ VISA
closed 25 and 26 December – **M** (buffet lunch)/dinner 9.25 **st.** ⌕ 4.00 – **22 rm**
⌕ 32.00/49.00 **st.** – SB 59.50 **st.**

Plas Coch, High St., LL23 7AB, ✆ 520309 – ✂ rest ⓣⱱ ℗. ◪ AE ⓞ VISA
closed 24 and 25 December – **M** (bar lunch)/dinner 10.50 **st.** and a la carte ⌕ 2.50 – **10 rm**
⌕ 27.00/43.00 **st.** – SB 54.00 **st.**

Fron Feuno Hall, LL23 7YF, SW : 1 m. on A 494 ✆ 521115, ≤, ☜, ☞, park – ℗. ⚡
closed December-February – **M** (communal dining) 15.00 **s.** – **3 rm** ⌕ 21.50/45.00 **s.** –
SB 54.00/70.00 **st.**

Dewis Cyfarfod, Llandderfel, LL23 7DR, E : 3 ¼ m. by A 494 on B 4401 ✆ 067 83 (Llanderfel) 243, ≤, ☞, park – ⓣⱱ ℗
M *(closed Wednesday dinner)* 12.75 **st.** ⌕ 3.00 – **5 rm** ⌕ 19.75/39.00 **st.**

Llidiardau Mawr ⌖, Llidiardau, LL23 7SG, NW : 4 ¼ m. by A 4212 ✆ 520555, « 17C
Stone-built mill house », ☞ – ✂ rest ℗. ⚡
Easter-October – **M** approx. 7.50 – **3 rm** ⌕ –/28.00.

VOLVO High St. ✆ 520210

BALDOCK Herts. **404** T 28 – pop. 6 703 – ECD : Thursday – ✆ 0462.

Envir. : Ashwell (St. Mary's Church★ 14C : Medieval graffiti) NE : 4 ½ m.

♦London 42 – Bedford 20 – ♦Cambridge 21 – Luton 15.

Travelodge without rest., A 1 Great North Road, Hinxworth (southbound carriagway),
SG7 5EX, NW : 3 m. by A 501 on A 1 ✆ 835329 – ⓣⱱ ⅗ ℗. ◪ AE VISA
40 rm 21.50/27.00 t.

COLT High St. ✆ 046 274 (Ashwell) 893305

BALSALL COMMON West Midlands – see Coventry.

BAMBER BRIDGE Lancs. **402** M 22 – see Preston.

BAMBURGH Northumb. **401 402** O 17 – pop. 567 – ECD : Wednesday – ✆ 066 84.

See : Castle★ (12C-18C) *AC*.

☗ Bamburgh Castle ✆ 378/321, N : 1 m.

♦London 337 – ♦Edinburgh 77 – ♦Newcastle-upon-Tyne 51.

Lord Crewe Arms, Front St., NE69 7BL, ✆ 243 – ⓣⱱ ℗. ◪ VISA
March-November – **M** (bar lunch)/dinner 14.50 t. ⌕ 4.00 – **25 rm** ⌕ 28.00/52.00 t. –
SB (April-November) 68.00/72.00 **st.**

BANBURY Oxon. **403 404** P 27 – pop. 37 463 – ECD : Tuesday – ✆ 0295.

Envir. : Upton House★ (pictures★★★, porcelain★★) *AC*, NW : 7 m. – East Adderbury (St. Mary's
Church : corbels★) SE : 3 ½ m. – Broughton Castle (great hall★, white room : 1599 plaster ceiling★★) and St. Mary's Church (memorial tombs★) *AC*, SW : 3 ½ m. – Wroxton (thatched cottages★) NW : 3 m. – Farnborough Hall (interior plasterwork★) *AC*, NW : 6 m.

☗ Cherwell Edge, Chacombe ✆ 711591, NE : 4 m.

🛈 Banbury Museum, 8 Horsefair ✆ 59855.

♦London 76 – ♦Birmingham 40 – ♦Coventry 25 – ♦Oxford 23.

Whately Hall (T.H.F.), Horsefair, by Banbury Cross, OX16 0AN, ✆ 263451, Telex 837149,
Fax 271736, « Part 17C hall », ☞ – ⧉ ✂ ⓣⱱ ☎ ℗ – 🛆 . ◪ AE ⓞ VISA
M 9.95/13.50 **st.** and a la carte ⌕ 3.50 – ⌕ 7.60 – **72 rm** 65.00/84.00 **st.**, **2 suites** 110.00/
150.00 **st.** – SB (weekends only) 68.00/84.00 **st.**

Banbury Moat House (Q.M.H) 27-29 Oxford Rd, OX16 9AH, ✆ 259361, Telex 838967, Fax
270954 – ⓣⱱ ☎ ℗ – 🛆 80. ◪ AE ⓞ VISA
closed 25 December-1 January – **M** *(closed Saturday lunch)* 9.50/10.50 **st.** and a la carte
⌕ 3.25 – **48 rm** ⌕ 59.00/89.00 **st.** – SB (weekends only) 71.00 **st.**

Lismore, 61 Oxford Rd, OX16 9AJ, ✆ 267661 – ⓣⱱ ☎ ℗. ◪ VISA
M 10.50 t. and a la carte ⌕ 3.50 – **21 rm** ⌕ 25.00/50.00 t. – SB 55.00/60.00 **st.**

Cromwell Lodge, North Bar, OX16 0TB, ✆ 259781, ☞ – ⓣⱱ ☎ ℗. ◪ AE ⓞ VISA
closed 8 days at Christmas – **M** *(closed Sunday dinner)* (bar lunch Monday to Saturday)/dinner 13.00 t. and a la carte ⌕ 3.50 – **32 rm** ⌕ 53.00/65.00 t. – SB (weekends
only) 70.00/100.00 **st.**

BANBURY

↟ **Easington House** without rest., 50 Oxford Rd, OX16 9AN, ℰ 259395 – TV ☎. ⬛ VISA
closed 23 December-1 January – **11 rm** � 25.00/55.00 st.

↟ **Tredis**, 15 Broughton Rd, OX16 9QB, ℰ 264632 – TV P
11 rm � 11.00/24.00 s.

at Bloxham SW : 4 ¼ m. on A 361 – ⊠ ✆ 0295 Banbury :

🏠 **Olde School**, Church St., OX15 4ET, ℰ 720369, Fax 721748 – TV ☎ P – 🛎 175. ⬛ AE ⓪
VISA
M 11.50/16.00 **t.** and a la carte 🍷 4.00 – ⊇ 5.50 – **30 rm** 30.00/75.00 t. – SB (weekends
only) 72.00/76.00 st.

at North Newington W : 2 ¼ m. by B 4035 – ⊠ Banbury – ✆ 0295 Banbury :

🏠 **L'Auberge De La Madonette** ⌕ without rest., OX15 6AA, ℰ 730212, 丂 heated, 🐎 –
TV P. ⬛ ⓪ VISA
closed 20 December-4 January – **5 rm** ⊇ 28.00/44.00 st.

at Swalcliffe W : 6 m. on B 4035 – ⊠ Banbury – ✆ 029 578 Swalcliffe :

↟ **Swalcliffe Manor** ⌕, OX15 5EH, on B 4035 ℰ 348, « Part 13C manor house », 丂, 🐎 –
P
March-November – **M** (by arrangement) 16.00 **s.** – **3 rm** ⊇ –/50.00 **s.**

at Wroxton NW : 3 m. by A 41 on A 422 – ⊠ Banbury – ✆ 0295 Banbury :

🏰 **Wroxton House** (Best Western), Silver St., OX15 6QB, ℰ 730482, Fax 730800, 🐎 – TV ☎
P. ⬛ AE ⓪ VISA 🐕
M 14.00/19.00 **st.** and a la carte 🍷 4.50 – **33 rm** ⊇ 70.00/90.00 st. – SB (weekends
only) (except Christmas) 89.00/98.00 **st.**

at Shenington NW : 6 m. by A 41 off A 422 – ⊠ Banbury – ✆ 029 588 Tysoe :

↟ **Sugarswell Farm** ⌕, OX15 6HW, NW : 2 ¼ m. on Edge Hill Rd ℰ 512, ≤, 🐎 – ✑➤ P.
🐕
M 16.00 **st.** – **3 rm** ⊇ 25.00/40.00 **st.**

AUSTIN-ROVER Southam Rd ℰ 51551
DAIHATSU Hook Norton ℰ 0608 (Hook Norton)
737641
FIAT 21-27 Broad St. ℰ 50733
FORD 98 Warwick Rd ℰ 67711
MITSUBISHI, LANCIA Thorpe Rd, Middleton
Cheney ℰ 710325

PEUGEOT-TALBOT Southam Rd ℰ 53511
VAUXHALL-OPEL 8 Middleton Rd ℰ 3551
VW-AUDI 9-16 Southam Rd ℰ 50141

🅐 ATS Beaumont Industrial Est., Beaumont Close
ℰ 53525

BANGOR Gwynedd 402 403 H 24 – pop. 12 126 – ECD : Wednesday – ✆ 0248.

Envir. : Bethesda (slate quarries⋆) SE : 5 m. – Nant Francon Pass⋆⋆, SE : 9 m.

🈁 St. Deiniol ℰ 353098.

🛈 Theatr Gwynedd ℰ 352786 (summer only).

♦London 247 – Birkenhead 68 – Holyhead 23 – Shrewsbury 83.

🏰 **Menai Court**, Craig-Y-Don Rd, LL57 2BG, ℰ 354200 – TV ☎ P – 🛎
12 rm.

🏠 **Telford**, Holyhead Rd, LL57 2HX, ℰ 352543, ≤ Menai Bridge and Isle of Anglesey, 🐎 –
✑➤ rm TV P. ⬛ VISA. 🐕
M (bar lunch)/dinner 12.00 and a la carte 🍷 3.50 – **9 rm** ⊇ 24.95/49.90.

🏠 **Ty-Uchaf**, Tal-y-Bont, LL57 3UR, SE : 2 m. by A 5122 ℰ 352219 – TV ⊛ P. ⬛ VISA 🐕
M *(closed Sunday lunch)* (bar lunch)/dinner 8.50 **t.** and a la carte 🍷 3.50 – **9 rm**
⊇ 20.00/35.00 **t.** – SB (weekends only) 50.00/60.00 **st.**

FORD 49 High St. ℰ 355107

BANSTEAD Surrey 404 T 30 – pop. 35 360 (inc. Tadworth) – ECD : Wednesday – ⊠ Tadworth
– ✆ 0737 Burgh Heath.

♦London 17 – ♦Brighton 39.

🏠 **Heathside** without rest., Brighton Rd, Burgh Heath, KT20 6BW, S : 1 ½ m. on A 217
ℰ 353355, Telex 929908, Fax 370857 – TV ☎ P – 🛎 200. ⬛ AE ⓪ VISA
M a la carte 9.50/12.00 **t.** – ⊇ 4.75 – **44 rm** 52.00/66.00 t.

BANTHAM Devon – see Kingsbridge.

BARFORD Warw. 403 404 P 27 – see Warwick.

BAR HILL Cambs. 404 U 27 – see Cambridge.

BARKSTON Lincs. 402 404 S 25 – see Grantham.

BARMBY MOOR Humberside 402 R 22 – see Pocklington.

BARMOUTH (ABERMAW) Gwynedd 402 403 H 25 – pop. 2 142 – ECD : Wednesday – ✆ 0341.
See : Site★★ – Panorama walk★★.

🛈 The Old Library ✆ 280787 (summer only).

♦London 231 – Chester 74 – Dolgellau 10 – Shrewsbury 67.

🏰 **Ty'r Craig Castle,** Llanaber Rd, LL42 1YN, on A 496 ✆ 280470, ≼ – 📺 ☎ 🅿. 🔼
VISA. 🕸
March-October – **M** (bar lunch Monday to Saturday)/dinner 10.50 **t.** and a la carte ₰ 4.25 –
12 rm ⊑ 30.00/50.00 **t.** – SB 66.00 **st.**

⋔ **Cranbourne,** 9 Marine Par., LL42 1NA, ✆ 280202 – 📺. 🔼 VISA. 🕸
M 7.50 **st.** – **10 rm** ⊑ 16.50/40.00 **st.** – SB (except July and August) 49.50/53.50 **st.**

⋔ **Bryn Melyn** ⌚, Panorama Rd, LL42 1DQ, ✆ 280556, ≼ Mawddach estuary and mountains
– 📺 🅿. 🔼
April-October – **M** 11.00 **st.** ₰ 3.60 – **8 rm** ⊑ 13.50/37.50 **st.** – SB 52.00/56.00 **st.**

AUSTIN-ROVER, DAIMLER-JAGUAR Rover Park COLT Smithy Garage ✆ 034 17 (Dyffryn) 279
Rd ✆ 280449

BARNARD CASTLE Durham 402 O 20 – pop. 6 075 – ECD : Thursday – ✆ 0833 Teesdale.
See : Bowes Museum★ *AC.*

Envir. : High force★★ (waterfalls) *AC*, NW : 14 m. – Raby Castle★ (14C) *AC*, NE : 6 m.

🏌 Marwood, Harmire Rd ✆ 38355, N : ¾ m. on B 6278.

🛈 43 Galgate ✆ 690000 (weekends ✆ 690909).

♦London 258 – ♦Carlisle 63 – ♦Leeds 68 – ♦Middlesbrough 31 – ♦Newcastle-upon-Tyne 39.

🏰 **Jersey Farm** ⌚, Darlington Rd, DL12 8TA, E : 1 ½ m. on A 67 ✆ 38223, Fax 31988, ≼,
« Working farm » – 📺 ☎ 🅿. 🕸
M (dinner only and Sunday lunch)/dinner 12.00 **t.** ₰ 3.75 – **19 rm** ⊑ 35.00/45.00 **t.** –
SB (weekends only) 49.00/56.00 **st.**

at Romaldkirk NW : 6 m. by A 67 on B 6277 – ✉ Barnard Castle – ✆ 0833 Teesdale :

🏰 **Rose and Crown,** DL12 9EB, ✆ 50213 – 📺 ☎ 🅿. 🔼 VISA
M *(closed Sunday dinner)* (bar lunch Monday to Saturday)/dinner 15.50 **st.** ₰ 3.25 – **9 rm**
⊑ 40.00/65.00 **st.**, **2 suites** – SB (weekends only) (except summer) 68.00/75.00 **st.**

VAUXHALL Newgate ✆ 38352

BARNBY MOOR Notts. 402 403 404 Q 23 – pop. 268 – ECD : Wednesday – ✉ ✆ 0777
Retford.

♦London 151 – ♦Leeds 44 – Lincoln 27 – ♦Nottingham 31.

🏰 **Ye Olde Bell** (T.H.F.), DN22 8QS, ✆ 705121, Fax 860424, 🐎 – ⋉ rm 📺 ☎ 🅿 – 🏛 200.
🔼 AE ⓪ VISA
M 7.50/12.95 **st.** and a la carte ₰ 3.95 – ⊑ 7.00 – **55 rm** 49.00/103.00 **st.** – SB (week-
ends only) 60.00/64.00 **st.**

BARNSDALE BAR West Yorks. 402 404 Q 23 – ✉ ✆ 0977 Pontefract.

♦London 181 – ♦Leeds 22 – ♦Nottingham 53 – ♦Sheffield 26.

🏰 **Travelodge** without rest., WF8 3JB, on A 1 ✆ 620711 – 📺 ☎ 🅿. 🔼 AE VISA
56 rm 21.50/27.00 **t.**

BARNSLEY Glos. 403 404 O28 – see Cirencester.

BARNSLEY South Yorks. 402 404 P 23 – pop. 76 783 – ECD : Thursday – ✆ 0226.

🏌 Wakefield Rd, Staincross ✆ 382856, N : 4 m. on A 61.

🛈 56 Eldon St. ✆ 206757.

♦London 177 – ♦Leeds 21 – ♦Manchester 36 – ♦Sheffield 15.

🏰 **Queens,** Regent St., S70 2HY, ✆ 731010, Telex 547348, Fax 248719 – 📺 ☎
48 rm.

at Ardsley E : 2 ½ m. on A 635 – ✉ ✆ 0226 Barnsley :

🏰 **Ardsley Moat House** (Q.M.H.), Doncaster Rd, S71 5EH, ✆ 289401, Telex 547762, Fax
205374, 🐎 – 📺 ☎ 🅿 – 🏛 300. 🔼 AE ⓪ VISA
closed 25 December – **M** (bar lunch Saturday) 10.50/12.50 **t.** and a la carte ₰ 4.00 – ⊑ 7.00
– **73 rm** 49.00/66.00 **t.** – SB (weekends only) 74.00 **st.**

AUSTIN-ROVER Claycliff Rd, Barkgreen ✆ 299891   VAUXHALL New St. ✆ 733833
CITROEN The Cross, Silkstone ✆ 790636   VW-AUDI Huddersfield Rd ✆ 299494
FIAT, PEUGEOT-TALBOT, VOLVO Stairfoot ✆
206675   ⓐ ATS Hoyle Mill, Pontefract Rd ✆ 281888/287406
FORD Dodworth Rd ✆ 732732   ATS Wombwell Lane, Aldham Bridge, Wombwell
HONDA Doncaster Rd ✆ 287417   ✆ 753511
RENAULT Doncaster Rd ✆ 291554

BARNSTAPLE Devon **403** H 30 The West Country G. – pop. 24 490 – ECD : Wednesday – 🕿 0271.

See : Site★ – The Long Bridge★.

Envir. : Arlington Court★★ AC The Carriage Collection★, NE : 8 m. on A 39.

🛈 Library, Tuly St., ℰ 47177.

◆London 222 – Exeter 40 – Taunton 51.

🏨 **Imperial** (T.H.F.), Taw Vale Par., EX32 8NB, ℰ 45861 – 📶 ⇔ rm 📺 ☎ 🅿. 🔼 AE ⓓ VISA
M (bar lunch)/dinner 12.95 **st.** and a la carte 🍷 3.95 – ☕ 7.00 – **56 rm** 56.00/73.00 **st.** – SB (except Easter and Christmas) 86.00/96.00 **st.**

🏛 **North Devon Motel,** Taw Vale, EX32 8NJ, ℰ 72166, Group Telex 42551, Fax 78558 – 📺 ☎ 🅿. 🔼 AE ⓓ VISA
M 9.00 **t.** (dinner) and a la carte – **42 rm** ☕ 35.00/60.00 **t.** – SB (except Christmas) 62.00/70.00 **st.**

XX **Lynwood House** with rm, Bishops Tawton Rd, EX32 9DZ, on A 377 ℰ 43695, Fax 79340, Seafood – ⇔ rest 📺 ☎ 🅿. 🔼 VISA ⚘
M (closed Sunday) a la carte 9.95/23.90 **t.** 🍷 3.80 – **5 rm** ☕ 47.50/67.50 **t.** – SB (except Bank Holidays) (weekends only) 135.00/195.00 **st.**

at Bishop's Tawton S : 2 m. on A 377 – ✉ 🕿 0271 Barnstaple :

🏨 **Downrew House** 🦢, EX32 0DY, SE : 1 ½ m. on Chittlehampton Rd ℰ 42497, ≤, « Country house atmosphere », ⤢ heated, ⚘, park, ⚘ – ⇔ rest 📺 ☎ 🅿. 🔼 VISA
closed January and February – M (bar lunch)/dinner 20.00 **t.** 🍷 3.00 – **12 rm** ☕ 50.00/85.00 **t.** – SB 90.00/105.00 **st.**

🏚 **Halmpstone Manor** 🦢, EX32 0EA, SE : 3 m. by Chittlehampton Rd ℰ 830321, Fax 830826, ≤, « Working farm », ⚘, park – 📺 ☎ 🅿. 🔼 AE VISA ⚘
M (closed Sunday dinner to non-residents) (lunch by arrangement)/dinner 20.00 **st.** and a la carte – **4 rm** ☕ 40.00/80.00 **t.**

AUSTIN-ROVER Hollowtree Rd ℰ 73232
DAIHATSU Newport Rd ℰ 45363
FIAT, TOYOTA, VOLVO Pottington Industrial Estate, Pillandway ℰ 76551

FORD New Rd ℰ 74173
VAUXHALL-OPEL 42 Boutport St. ℰ 74366

🅰 ATS Pottington Ind. Est., Braunton Rd ℰ 42294/5

BARROW-IN-FURNESS Cumbria **402** K 21 – pop. 50 174 – 🕿 0229.

🛈 Rakesmoore Lane, Hawcoat ℰ 25444, N : 2 m. by A 590 – 🛈 Furness, Central Dr., Walney Island ℰ 41232, E : 1 ¾ m. by A 590.

🛈 Civic Hall, 28 Duke St. ℰ 25795.

◆London 295 – Kendal 34 – Lancaster 47.

🏨 **Abbey House,** Abbey Rd, LA13 0PA, NE : 2 m. on A 590 ℰ 38282, Telex 65357, Fax 20403, « Lutyens house », ⚘, park – 📶 📺 ☎ 🅿 – 🔥 100. 🔼 AE ⓓ VISA
M (closed Saturday lunch) 8.50/14.50 **t.** and a la carte 15.25/31.50 **t.** 🍷 3.50 – **32 rm** ☕ 60.50/85.50 **t.** – SB (weekends only) 80.50/95.50 **st.**

at Rampside S : 5 m. by A 5087 – ✉ 🕿 0229 Barrow-in-Furness :

🏩 Clarkes Arms (Whitbread), Rampside St., LA13 0PA, ℰ 20303 – 📺 🅿
10 rm.

🅰 ATS 149-151 Ainslie St. ℰ 28513/28663   ATS Walney Rd ℰ 39034

BARRY (BARRI) South Glam. **403** K 29 – pop. 44 443 – ECD : Wednesday – 🕿 0446.

🛈 The Promenade, Barry Island ℰ 747171 (summer only).

◆London 167 – ◆Cardiff 10 – ◆Swansea 39.

🏨 **Mount Sorrel,** Porthkerry Rd, CF6 8AY, ℰ 740069, Telex 497819, Fax 746600 – 📺 ☎ 🅿. 🔼 AE ⓓ VISA
M 10.95 **t.** (dinner) and a la carte 8.10/12.75 **t.** 🍷 3.50 – **47 rm** ☕ 42.00/65.00 **t.** – SB (weekends only) 55.00/65.00 **st.**

🏨 **Egerton Grey** 🦢, CF6 9BZ, SW : 4 ½ m. by A 4226 and Porthkerry rd via Cardiff Airport ℰ 711666, Fax 711690, ≤, « Country house atmosphere », ⚘, park, ⚘ – ⇔ rest 📺 ☎ 🅿. 🔼 AE VISA ⚘
M (closed Sunday dinner) (booking essential) 15.00/21.00 **st.** and a la carte 🍷 4.50 – **10 rm** ☕ 55.00/120.00 **st.** – SB 95.00/150.00 **st.**

🏚 **Aberthaw House,** 28 Porthkerry Rd, CF6 8AX, ℰ 737314 – 📺 ☎. 🔼 VISA
closed 23 December-2 January – M (closed Sunday and Monday to non-residents) (dinner only) 12.50 **t.** and a la carte 🍷 3.00 – **9 rm** ☕ 37.50/47.50 **t.**

🏩 Cwm Ciddy Toby, Airport Rd, CF6 9BA, NW : 1 ½ m. by B 4266 ℰ 700075 – 📺 ☎ 🅿
14 rm.

BARTON MILLS Suffolk. **404** V 26 – ✆ 0638 Newmarket.

◆London 72 – Cambridge 21 – ◆Ipswich 37 – ◆Norwich 40.

  🏠 **Travelodge** without rest., Fiveways Roundabout, IP28 6AE, on A 11 ✆ 717675 – 📺 ౬ 🅿.
    🔼 AE VISA
    32 rm 21.50/27.00 t.

BARTON STACEY Hants. **403** **404** P 30 – see Andover.

BARTON UNDER NEEDWOOD Staffs. – see Burton-upon-Trent.

BARWICK Somerset **403** **404** M 31 – see Yeovil.

BASCHURCH Shropshire **402** **403** L 25 – see Shrewsbury.

BASFORD Staffs. – see Stoke-on-Trent.

BASILDON Essex **404** V 29 – pop. 94 800 – ECD : Wednesday – ✆ 0268.

See : Basildon Park★.

🏌18 Clay Hill, Kingswood ✆ 3849, S : 1 m. by A 176 – 🏌9 Pipps Hill Country Club, Cranes Farm Rd ✆ 27278, N : off A 127.

◆London 30 – Chelmsford 17 – Southend-on-Sea 13.

  🏨 **Crest** (Crest), Cranes Farm Rd, SS14 3DG, NW : 2 ¼ m. by A 176 off A 1235 ✆ 533955,
    Telex 995141, Fax 530119, 🚗 – 🛗 ✑ 📺 ☎ 🅿 – 🔬 300. 🔼 AE ① VISA
    M (closed Saturday lunch) 11.95/22.15 **st.** and a la carte – ☕ 7.35 – **110 rm** 72.45/86.10 **st.**
    – SB (weekends only) 76.00/80.00 **st.**

  🏨 **Watermill Travel Inn** (Lansbury), Felmores, East Mayne, SS13 1BW, N : 1 ½ m. on A 132
    ✆ 522227, Fax 530092, 🚗 – 📺 🅿. 🔼 AE ① VISA. 🍴
    closed 25 and 26 December – **M** a la carte 10.35/16.25 t. – ☕ 3.95 – **32 rm** 24.50/27.50 t.

  🏠 **Campanile**, A 127 Southend Arterial Rd, Pipp's Hill, SS14 3AE, NW : 1 m. on A 176
    ✆ 530810, Telex 995068 – 📺 ☎ ౬ 🅿 – 🔬 40. 🔼 VISA
    M 8.20/8.90 **st.** and a la carte 🍷 2.90 – ☕ 3.50 – **47 rm** 27.50 **st.**

AUSTIN-ROVER Southern Hay ✆ 22661   ⓐ ATS Archers Field ✆ 525177/8
NISSAN Nethermayne ✆ 22261

BASINGSTOKE Hants. **403** **404** Q 30 – pop. 73 027 – ✆ 0256.

🏌9 Bishopswood, Bishopswood Lane ✆ 073 56 (Tadley) 5213, N : 6 m. by A 340 Z.

◆London 55 – Reading 17 – ◆Southampton 31 – Winchester 18.

Plan on next page

  🏨 **Hilton Lodge** (Hilton), Old Common Rd, Black Dam, RG21 3PR, ✆ 460460, Telex 859038,
    Fax 840441, 🔲 – ✑ 📺 ☎ ౬ 🅿 – 🔬 120. 🔼 AE ① VISA   **Z** **i**
    M (closed Saturday lunch) (carving rest.) 12.50/14.50 **t.** and a la carte 🍷 4.85 – ☕ 7.95 –
    144 rm 76.00/101.00 **st.** – SB (weekends only) 80.00/95.00 **st.**

  🏨 **Hilton National** (Hilton), Aldermaston Roundabout, Ringway North, RG24 9NV, N : 2 m.
    junction A 339 and A 340 ✆ 20212, Telex 858223, Fax 842835 – 🛗 ▤ rest 📺 ☎ 🅿 – 🔬 200.
    🔼 AE ① VISA   **Z** **a**
    M (closed Saturday lunch) (carving rest.) a la carte 14.00/23.50 **t.** 🍷 4.50 – ☕ 7.95 – **138 rm**
    77.00/107.00 **t.**

  🏨 **Crest** (Crest), Grove Rd, RG21 3EE, S : 1 m. junction A 339 and A 30 ✆ 468181, Telex
    858501, Fax 840081 – ✑ rm 📺 ☎ ౬ 🅿 – 🔬 220. 🔼 AE ① VISA   **Z** **e**
    M (closed Saturday lunch) 9.45/15.95 **st.** and a la carte – ☕ 7.35 – **85 rm** 78.00/91.00 **st.** –
    SB (weekends only) 80.00/90.00 **st.**

  🏠 **Travelodge** without rest., Stag & Hounds, Winchester Rd, RG22 6HN, SW : 1 ¾ m. by
    A 30 ✆ 843566 – 📺 ౬ 🅿. 🔼 AE VISA   **Z** **u**
    32 rm 21.50/27.00 t.

  XX Hee's, 23 Westminster House, off Upper Church St., RG21 1CS, ✆ 464410, Chinese (Peking,
    Szechuan) rest. – ▤   **Y** **a**

  at *Nately Scures* E : 5 m. by Black Dam roundabout on A 30 – ✉ Hook – ✆ 0256
  Basingstoke :

  🏨 Basingstoke Country, RG27 9JS, on A 30 ✆ 764161, Telex 859981, Fax 768341, 🔲, 🚗 – 🛗
    ✑ rm ▤ rest 📺 ☎ ౬ 🅿 – 🔬 160. 🔼 AE ① VISA
    M 14.00/16.00 **st.** and a la carte 18.70/24.95 **st.** 🍷 3.50 – **69 rm** ☕ 82.50/150.00 **st.**, **1 suite**
    150.00 **st.** – SB (weekends only) 93.00/153.00 **st.**

  at *Rotherwick* E : 6 ¾ m. by Black Dam roundabout, A 30 – **z** – and Rotherwick Rd – ✉
  – ✆ 0256 Basingstoke :

  🏰 **Tylney Hall** 🦫, RG27 9AJ, W : 1 m. ✆ 764881, Telex 859864, Fax 768141, « 19C mansion in
    extensive gardens », 🏊 heated, 🔲, park, XX – 🛗 📺 ☎ 🅿 – 🔬. 🔼 AE ① VISA 🍴
    M 15.50/22.00 **st.** and a la carte 🍷 6.00 – **81 rm** ☕ 82.00/95.00 **st.**, **9 suites** 115.00/215.00 **st.**
    – SB (weekends only) 120.00/200.00 **st.**

BASINGSTOKE

London Street............... Y 19
Upper Church
   Street.................... Y 24
Winchester Street .... Y 27

Aldermaston Road............ Z 2
Beaconsfield Road .... Y 3
Buckland Avenue............. Z 5
Chequers Road .... Y 6
Church Street .... Y 7
Churchill Way East.......... Z 9
Churchill Way West......... Z 10
Council Road .... Y 12
Cross Street .... Y 13
Fairfields Road............. Y 14
Houndmills Road............. Z 17
New Road .... Y 20
Reading Road .... Z 22
Southern Ringway........... Z 23
Victoria Street............. Y 25
Wote Street................. Y 28

North is at the top on all town plans.

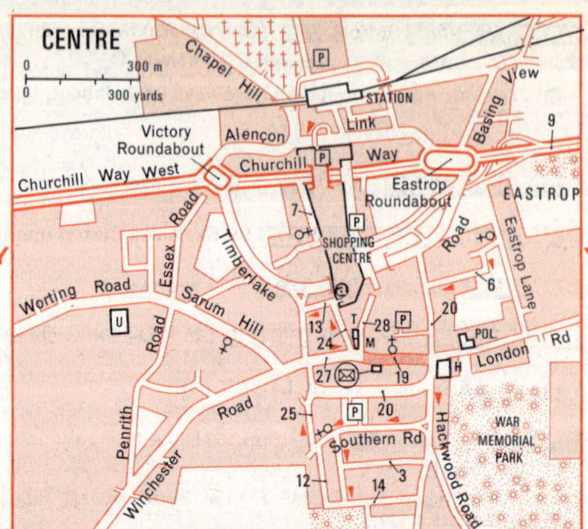

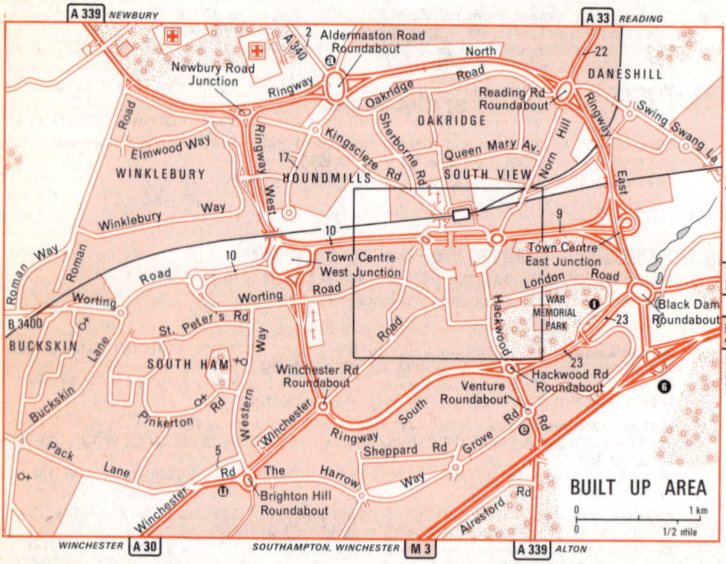

AUDI-VW London Rd ☎ 24444
FIAT, LANCIA, MASERATI London Rd ☎ 55221
FORD Roentgen Rd ☎ 53336
PEUGEOT-TALBOT Houndmills ☎ 465991
RANGE-ROVER, JAGUAR, HONDA New Rd ☎ 24561

VAUXHALL-OPEL West Ham ☎ 840540
VOLVO London Rd ☎ 466111

ATS Moniton Trading Estate ☎ 51431
ATS Armstrong Rd, Daneshill East ☎ 462448

Per visitare una città o una regione : utilizzate le **guide verdi Michelin.**

BASLOW Derbs. 402 403 404 P 24 – pop. 1 205 – ECD : Wednesday – ⊠ Bakewell – ☎ 024 688 – ♦London 161 – Derby 27 – ♦Manchester 35 – ♦Sheffield 13.

  Cavendish, DE4 1SP, on A 619 ☎ 2311, Telex 547150, ≤ Chatsworth Park, 🍴, 🍴 – ☒ rest TV ☎ P. ☒ AE ① VISA ⚹
  M 22.00 t. ↓ 5.00 – � 7.25 – **23 rm** 60.50/83.50 t.. **1 suite.**

  XX **Fischer's at Baslow Hall** with rm, Calver Rd, DE4 1RR, ☎ 3259, 🍴, park – TV ☎ P. ☒ AE ① VISA ⚹
  M *(closed Sunday dinner and Monday to non-residents)* 13.50/25.00 **t.** and a la carte 19.00/25.00 t. ↓ 5.00 – **5 rm** ⊇ 60.00/100.00 t.

BASSENTHWAITE Cumbria **401 402** K 19 – pop. 533 – ✆ 059 681 Bassenthwaite Lake.

♦London 300 – ♦Carlisle 24 – Keswick 7.

🏨 **Armathwaite Hall** ⑤, CA12 4RE, W : 1 ½ m. on B 5291 ✉ Keswick ℘ 551, Telex 64319, Fax 220, ⩽ Bassenthwaite Lake, « Part 18C mansion in extensive grounds », 🏊, 🏌, 🛥, park, 🍴, squash – 🛗 TV ☎ P – 🛎 . 🔁 AE ⓪ VISA
M 10.00/23.00 t. and a la carte 21.90/29.35 t. – **42 rm** ☲ 45.00/160.00 t. – SB (November-April) (except Easter, Christmas and New year) (weekends only) 99.00/105.00 st.

🏨 **Pheasant Inn**, CA13 9YE, SW : 3 ¼ m. by B 5291 off A 66 ✉ Cockermouth ℘ 76234, « 16C inn », 🛥 – ⤬ rest P. ✻
closed 24 and 25 December – **M** 8.20/16.50 **st.** and a la carte 🍾 3.00 – **20 rm** ☲ 39.00/68.00 **st.** – SB (winter only) 84.00/90.00 st.

🏨 **Overwater Hall** ⑤, CA5 1HH, NE : 2 ¼ m. on Uldale Rd ✉ Ireby ℘ 566, ⩽, 🛥, park – TV P. 🔁 VISA
closed 25 December-22 February – **M** (dinner only) 14.50 t. 🍾 2.90 – **13 rm** ☲ 23.00/46.00 t. – SB (except summer) 60.00/64.00 st.

BATH Avon **403 404** M 29 *The West Country G.* – pop. 84 283 – ECD : Monday and Thursday – ✆ 0225.

See : Site★★★ : Royal Crescent★★★ (N° 1 Royal Crescent★★ *AC*) **AV D** – Circus★★★ **AV** – Museum of costume★★★ *AC* **AV M2** – Royal Photographic Society National Centre of Photography★★ *AC* **BV M3** – Roman Baths★★ *AC* **BX B** (Pump Room★ *AC*) **BX A** – Holburne of Menstrie Museum★★ *AC* **Y M1** – Pulteney Bridge★ **BV** – Assembly Rooms★ *AC* **AV** – Bath Abbey★ **BX** – Camden Works Museum★ *AC* **AV M4** – Envir. : Lansdown Crescent★★ (Somerset Place★) **Y** – at Claverton, E : 2 ½ m. by A36 **Y** American Museum★★ *AC* - Claverton Pump★ *AC* – Camden Crescent★ **Y** – Beckford Tower and Museum *AC* (prospect★) **Y M6.**

🏌, 🏌 Tracy Park, Bath Rd, Wick ℘ 027 582 (Abson) 2251, N : 5 m. by Lansdown Rd **Y** – 🏌 Lansdown ℘ 22138, NW : 3 m. by Lansdown Rd **Y.**

🛈 Abbey Church Yard ℘ 462831.

♦London 119 – ♦Bristol 13 – ♦Southampton 63 – Taunton 49.

Plans on following pages

🏨 **Royal Crescent** (Norfolk Cap.), 16 Royal Cres., BA1 2LS, ℘ 319090, Telex 444251, Fax 339401, ⩽, « Tastefully restored Georgian town houses », 🛥 – 🛗 🍽 rest TV ☎ 🚗 – 🛎 30. 🔁 AE ⓪ VISA ✻ **AV a**
M 21.00/33.00 t. and a la carte 31.00/44.50 t. 🍾 8.00 – ☲ 10.00 – **35 rm** 89.00/165.00 st., **9 suites** 225.00/330.00 st. – SB (weekdays only) 209.00/325.00 st.

🏨 **The Priory**, Weston Rd, BA1 2XT, ℘ 331922, Telex 44612, Fax 448276, ⩽, 🏊 heated, 🛥 – ⤬ rest TV ☎ P. 🔁 AE ⓪ VISA ✻ **Y c**
M 18.00/25.00 **st.** and a la carte 27.00/34.75 st. 🍾 4.50 – **21 rm** ☲ 82.00/154.00 st. – SB (November-mid April) 132.00/165.00 st.

🏨 **Queensberry** without rest., Russel St., BA1 2QT, ℘ 447928, Telex 445628, Fax 446065 – 🛗 TV ☎. 🔁 AE ⓪ VISA. ✻ **AV x**
closed 2 weeks Christmas-New Year – **24 rm** 70.00/115.00 st.

🏨 **Fountain House** without rest., 9-11 Fountain Buildings, Lansdown Rd, BA1 5DV, ℘ 338622, Telex 444905 – 🛗 TV ☎ 🚗. 🔁 AE ⓪ VISA **BV e**
14 suites ☲ 83.00/205.00 st.

🏨 **Francis** (T.H.F.), Queen Sq., BA1 2HH, ℘ 24257, Telex 449162, Fax 319715 – 🛗 ⤬ rm TV ☎ P – 🛎 60. 🔁 AE ⓪ VISA **AV i**
M 11.95/16.15 **st.** and a la carte 🍾 4.25 – ☲ 8.25 – **93 rm** 70.00/105.00 st., **1 suite** 175.00 st. – SB (weekends only) 100.00/125.00 st.

🏨 **Hilton National** (Hilton), Walcot St., BA1 5BJ, ℘ 463411, Telex 449519, Fax 464393 – 🛗 ⤬ rm TV ☎ – 🛎 200. 🔁 AE ⓪ VISA **BV i**
M 8.50/13.25 t. and a la carte 🍾 4.20 – ☲ 7.50 – **154 rm** 65.00/84.00 t. – SB 97.00 st.

🏨 **Lansdown Grove** (Best Western), Lansdown Rd, BA1 5EH, ℘ 315891, Telex 444850, Fax 448092, 🛥 – 🛗 TV ☎ P – 🛎 100. 🔁 AE ⓪ VISA **Y o**
M (buffet lunch) 9.00/15.50 t. and a la carte 🍾 3.75 – **45 rm** ☲ 58.00/90.00 t. – SB (weekends only) 88.00/96.00 st.

🏨 **Apsley House**, 141 Newbridge Hill, BA1 3PT, ℘ 336966, ⩽, 🛥 – ⤬ rest TV ☎ P. 🔁 AE ⓪ VISA ✻ **Y e**
closed 1 to 15 January – **M** (dinner only) a la carte approx. 17.50 st. 🍾 3.45 – **7 rm** ☲ 60.00/105.00 st. – SB 85.00/110.00 st.

🏨 **Dukes**, Great Pulteney St., BA2 4DN, ℘ 463512, Telex 449227 – ⤬ rest TV ☎. 🔁 AE VISA
M 12.50/17.95 **st.** and a la carte 🍾 4.50 – **22 rm** 50.00/90.00 st. – SB (November-April) 70.00/80.00 st. **BV s**

🏨 **Bath** (Best Western), Widcombe Basin, BA2 4JP, ℘ 338855, Telex 445876, Fax 28941 – 🛗 TV ☎ P – 🛎 80. 🔁 AE ⓪ VISA **BX a**
M 10.00/13.00 **st.** and a la carte 11.00/20.00 st. 🍾 4.00 – ☲ 6.00 – **94 rm** 60.50/72.50 st. – SB (except Bank Holidays) 80.00/90.00 st.

🏨 Berni Royal (B.C.B.), Manvers St., BA1 1JP, ℘ 63134 – 🛗 TV ☎. ✻ **BX e**
30 rm.

🏨 **Pratt's**, South Par., BA2 4AB, ℘ 460441, Telex 444827, Fax 448807 – 🛗 TV ☎ – 🛎 50. 🔁 AE ⓪ VISA **BX c**
M (bar lunch Monday to Saturday)/dinner 18.00 **st.** and a la carte 🍾 5.25 – **46 rm** ☲ 55.00/70.00 st. – SB (except Christmas) 80.00/95.00 st.

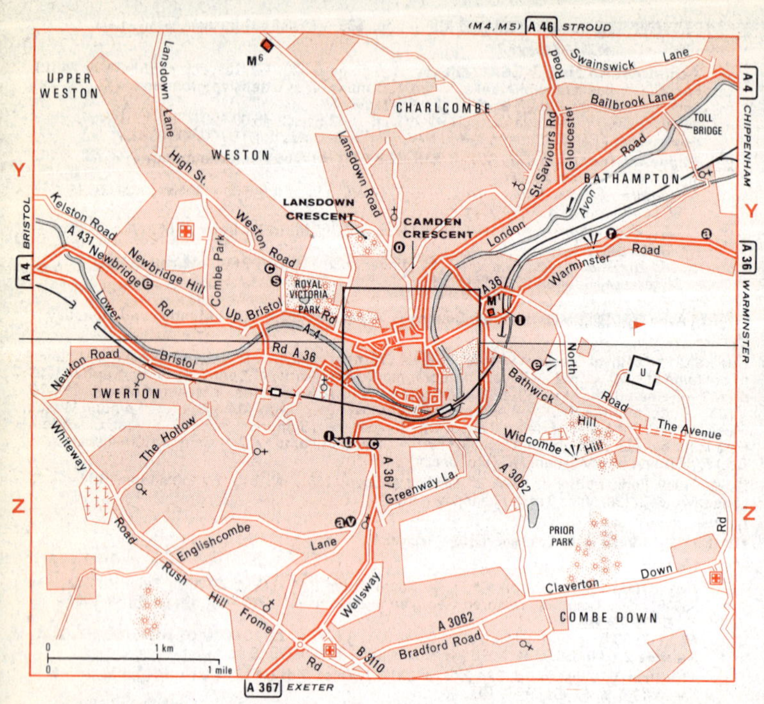

🏠 **Sydney Gardens** without rest., Sydney Rd, BA2 6NT, ℰ 464818, ≤, 🚗 – ✗ 📺 ☎ 🅿. 🔅 VISA
closed Christmas and January – **6 rm** ⬜ 50.00/65.00 **st.**
Y i

🏠 **Holly Lodge** without rest., 8 Upper Oldfield Park, BA2 3JZ, ℰ 24042, ≤, 🚗 – ✗ 📺 ☎ 🅿. 🔅 ⓘ VISA. 🐕
6 rm ⬜ 36.00/60.00 **st.**
Z i

🏠 **Audley House** ⅏, Park Gdns, BA1 2XP, ℰ 333110, 🚗 – ✗ 📺 ☎ 🅿. 🔅 VISA. 🐕
closed January – **M** (unlicensed)(dinner only. residents only) 12.00 **st.** – **3 rm** ⬜ 40.00/52.00 **st.**
Y s

🏠 **Paradise House** ⅏ without rest., 86-88 Holloway, BA2 4PX, ℰ 317723, ≤, 🚗 – 📺 ☎. 🔅 VISA. 🐕
closed Christmas and New Year – **9 rm** ⬜ 40.00/55.00 **t.**
Z c

🏠 **Somerset House,** 35 Bathwick Hill, BA2 6LD, ℰ 466451, ≤, 🚗 – ✗ ☎ 🅿. 🔅 AE VISA
closed 4 January-4 February – **M** (dinner only Monday to Saturday and Sunday lunch)/dinner 14.50 **st.** 🍷 2.55 – **9 rm** ⬜ (dinner included) 38.50/77.00 **st.** – SB (November-mid May) (weekdays only) 67.70/77.00 **st.**
Z e

🏠 **Villa Magdala** without rest., Henrietta Rd, BA2 6LX, ℰ 466329, 🚗 – 📺 ☎ 🅿. 🔅 VISA 🐕
closed Christmas – **17 rm** ⬜ 36.00/58.00 **st.**
BV r

🏠 **Orchard House,** Warminster Rd, Bathampton, BA2 6XG, ℰ 466115 – ✗ rest 📺 ☎ 🅿. 🔅 AE ⓘ VISA
M (*closed 25-26 December and 1 January*) a la carte 8.05/11.50 **t.** 🍷 2.75 – **14 rm** ⬜ 39.00/57.00 **t.** – SB (November-March) 68.00/72.00 **st.**
Y a

🏠 **North Parade,** 10 North Par., BA2 4AL, ℰ 463384 – 📺 ☎. 🔅 AE ⓘ VISA 🐕
M (dinner only) a la carte 10.45/13.70 **t.** 🍷 3.75 – **16 rm** ⬜ 22.00/60.00 **t.**, **2 suites** 72.00/80.00 **t.** – SB (November-June) 60.00/68.00 **st.**
BX i

🏠 **Haydon House** without rest., 9 Bloomfield Park off Bloomfield Rd, BA2 2BY, ℰ 427351, 🚗 – ✗ 📺 ☎. 🔅 VISA 🐕
4 rm ⬜ 30.00/50.00 **s.**
Z a

🏠 **Cheriton House** without rest., 9 Upper Oldfield Park, BA2 3JX, ℰ 429862, 🚗 – 📺 🅿. 🔅 VISA.
8 rm ⬜ 32.00/48.00 **st.**
Z u

🏠 **Oldfields** without rest., 102 Wells Rd, BA2 3AL, ℰ 317984, 🚗 – 📺 🅿. 🔅 VISA 🐕
14 rm ⬜ 38.00/48.00 **st.**
AX n

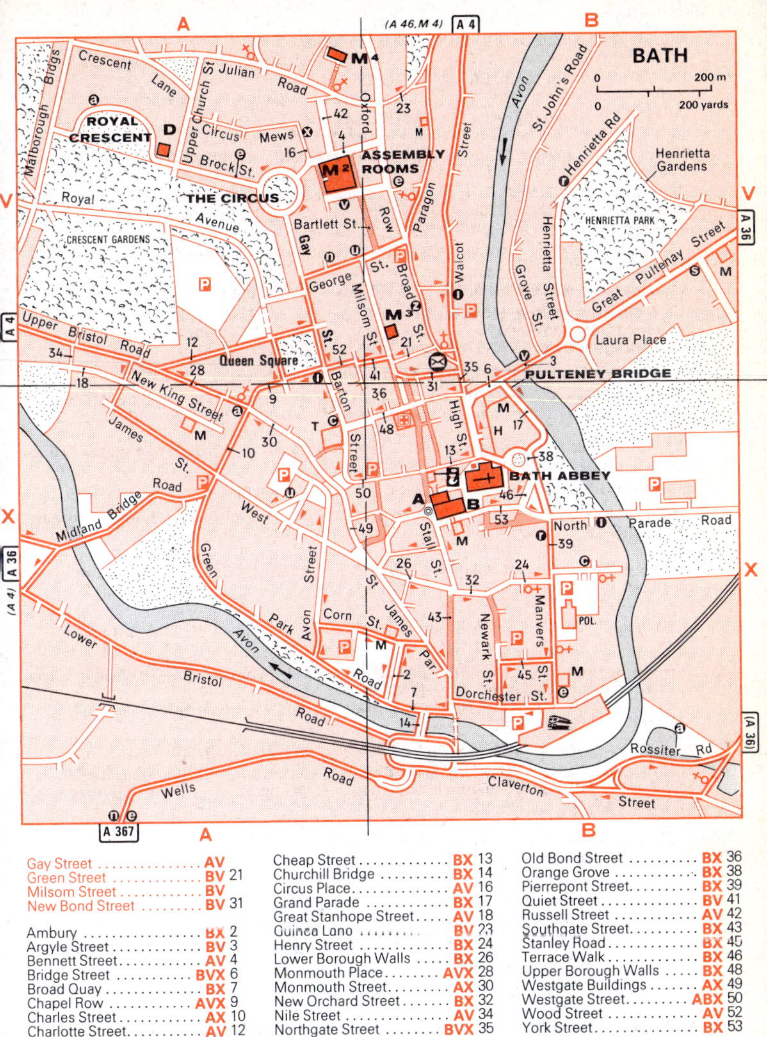

Gay Street	AV	
Green Street	BV	21
Milsom Street	BV	
New Bond Street	BV	31
Ambury	BX	2
Argyle Street	BV	3
Bennett Street	AV	4
Bridge Street	BVX	6
Broad Quay	BX	7
Chapel Row	AVX	9
Charles Street	AX	10
Charlotte Street	AV	12

Cheap Street	BX	13
Churchill Bridge	BX	14
Circus Place	AV	16
Grand Parade	BX	17
Great Stanhope Street	AV	18
Guinea Lane	BV	23
Henry Street	BX	24
Lower Borough Walls	BX	26
Monmouth Place	AVX	28
Monmouth Street	AX	30
New Orchard Street	BX	32
Nile Street	AV	34
Northgate Street	BVX	35

Old Bond Street	BX	36
Orange Grove	BX	38
Pierrepont Street	BX	39
Quiet Street	BV	41
Russell Street	AV	42
Southgate Street	BX	43
Stanley Road	BX	45
Terrace Walk	BX	46
Upper Borough Walls	BX	48
Westgate Buildings	AX	49
Westgate Street	ABX	50
Wood Street	AV	52
York Street	BX	53

Tasburgh without rest., Warminster Rd, Bathampton, BA2 6SH, ℰ 425096, ≤, – TV P. AE ⓪ VISA Y r
13 rm ⚏ 28.00/50.00 st.

Oakleigh without rest., 19 Upper Oldfield Park, BA2 3JX, ℰ 315698 – TV P. VISA Z i
4 rm ⚏ 40.00/45.00 s.

Leighton House without rest., 139 wells Rd, BA2 3AL, ℰ 314769 – TV ☎ P AX e
closed 23 to 29 December – **7 rm** ⚏ 35.00/50.00.

Wentworth House, 106 Bloomfield Rd, BA2 2AP, ℰ 339193, – TV ☎ P. VISA Z v
 – **M** 9.00 st. – **20 rm** ⚏ 26.00/41.00 st. – SB (except Sunday) 53.00/63.00 st.

XXX **Popjoys**, Beau Nash House, Sawclose, BA1 1EU, ℰ 460494, « Former residence of Beau AX c
Nash » – . AE VISA
closed Saturday lunch, Sunday and Monday – **M** 18.50/22.50 t. 5.00.

XX **Pino's Hole in the Wall**, 16 George St., BA1 2EN, ℰ 425242, Italian rest. – AE ⓪ VISA AV u
closed Sunday – **M** a la carte 16.30/24.70 st. 5.00.

XX **Rajpoot**, 4 Argyle St., BA2 4BA, ℰ 466833, Indian rest. – AE ⓪ VISA BV v
closed 25 and 26 December – **M** 16.50 t. and a la carte 15.05/24.50 t. 6.75.

- **Woods**, 9-13 Alfred St., BA1 2QX, ☎ 314812 – ⬛ *VISA* — AV v
  closed Sunday and 5 days at Christmas – **M** 7.95/17.95 **t.** and a la carte 15.95/17.95 **t.** ▮ 3.00.
- **The Circus**, 34 Brock St., BA1 2LN, ☎ 330208 – ⬛ *VISA* — AV e
  closed Sunday dinner – **M** 15.75/17.10 **t.** and a la carte approx. 15.70 **t.** ▮ 3.60.
- **Tarts**, 8 Pierrepont Pl., BA1 1JX, ☎ 330280 – ⬛ *VISA* — BX r
  closed Sunday, 3 days at Christmas and 1 January – **M** a la carte 13.95/17.40 **t.** ▮ 4.30.
- **Moon and Sixpence**, 6a Broad St., BA1 5LJ, ☎ 460962 – ⬛ AE *VISA* — BV z
  closed 25-26 December and 1 January – **M** a la carte 18.25/19.70 **t.** ▮ 3.85.
- **Peking**, 1-2 New St., BA1 2AF, ☎ 466377, Chinese rest. – ▤. ⬛ AE ⓪ *VISA* — AX u
  M 14.95 **t.** and a la carte 11.75/17.20 **t.** ▮ 3.75.
- **Xian**, 28 Charles St., BA1 1HU, ☎ 24917, Chinese rest. – ▤. ⬛ AE ⓪ *VISA* — AX a
  closed Sunday lunch, 25-26 December and 2 weeks in summer – **M** 15.00/20.00 **t.** and a la carte 10.00/20.00 **t.** ▮ 3.00.

at Box (Wilts.) NE : 5 ½ m. on A 4 – Y – ✉ Box – ☎ 0225 Bath :

- **Clos du Roy at Box House**, SN14 9NR, on A 4 ☎ 744447, Fax 743971, « Tastefully converted Georgian rectory », ⌇ heated, ☞ – ✄ ⓟ. ⬛ AE ⓪ *VISA*
  M (booking essential) 14.50/27.50 **st.** and a la carte 23.70/31.95 **st.** ▮ 6.50.

at Colerne (Wilts.) NE : 6 ½ m. by A 4 – Y – and Bannerdown rd – ☎ 0225 Bath :

- **Lucknam Park** ⤳, SN14 8AZ, N : ½ m. on Marshfield rd ☎ 742777, Telex 445648, Fax 743536, ≤, « Early 18C country house in park », ⌇, ☞, ✕ – TV ☎ ⓟ – ⚇ 25. ⬛ AE ⓪ *VISA*. ⌖
  M 16.50/29.50 **t.** and a la carte ▮ 7.50 – ⊡ 4.00 – **35 rm** 80.00/160.00 **t.**, **4 suites** 185.00/250.00 **t.** – SB 160.00/285.00 **st.**

at Bathford E : 3 ½ m. by A 4 – Y – off A 363 – ✉ ☎ 0225 Bath :

- **Eagle House** ⤳ without rest., Church St., BA1 7RS, ☎ 859946, ≤, « Georgian house », ☞ – TV ☎ ⓟ
  closed 23 December-2 January – ⊡ 2.15 – **6 rm** 24.00/70.00 **st.**
- **Orchard** ⤳ without rest., 80 High St., BA1 7TG, ☎ 858765, « Georgian house », ☞ – ✄ TV ⓟ. ⌖
  March-October – **4 rm** ⊡ 49.50 **st.**

at Winsley (Wilts) SE : 6 ½ m. by A 36 – Y – on B 3108 – ✉ Bradford-on-Avon – ☎ 0225 Bath :

- **Burghope Manor** ⤳, on B 3108, BA15 2LA, ☎ 723557, Fax 760593, « 13C manor house, country house atmosphere », ☞ – ⓟ. AE *VISA*. ⌖
  closed Christmas-New Year – **M** (booking essential) (lunch by arrangement)/dinner 30.00 **st.** – **6 rm** ⊡ 35.00/70.00 **st.**

at Hinton Charterhouse S : 5 ¾ m. by A 367 – Z – on B 3110 – ☎ 0225 Bath :

- **Homewood Park** ⤳, BA3 6BB, E : 1 ¼ m. on A 36 (North) ☎ 723731, Telex 444937, Fax 723820, ≤, « Tastefully converted country house », ☞, park, ✕ – ✄ rest TV ☎ ⓟ – ⚇ 25. ⬛ ⓪ *VISA*. ⌖
  closed 23 December-6 January – **M** 17.50/30.00 **st.** ▮ 5.00 – ⊡ 7.50 – **15 rm** 65.00/135.00 **st.** – SB (except summer) (weekdays only) 125.00 **st.**
- **Green Lane House** without rest., Green Lane, BA3 6BL, ☎ 723631 – ⬛ *VISA*. ⌖
  closed December and January – **4 rm** ⊡ 22.00/40.00 **st.**

at Monkton Combe S : 6 m. by A 36 – Y – ✉ Bath – ☎ 0225 Bath :

- **Wheelwrights Arms**, BA2 7HD, ☎ 722287 – TV ☎ ⓟ. ⬛ *VISA*. ⌖
  M (bar lunch)/dinner a la carte approx. 11.10 **t.** ▮ 3.00 – **8 rm** ⊡ 38.00/44.00 **t.** – SB (October-February) 62.00/66.00 **st.**

at Norton St. Philip (Somerset) S : 7 ¼ m. by A 367 – Z – on B 3110 – ✉ Bath (Avon) – ☎ 0225 Limpley Stoke :

- **Bath Lodge**, BA3 6NH, E : 1 ¼ m. by A 366 on A 36 ☎ 723737, « Early 19C gatehouse », ☞ – ✄ TV ☎ ⓟ. ⬛ AE *VISA*. ⌖
  M *(closed Sunday and Monday)* (dinner only) 20.00 **t.** ▮ 4.50 – **4 rm** ⊡ 50.00/95.00 **t.** – SB (November-March) 115.00/180.00 **st.**

at Hunstrete W : 8 ½ m. by A 4 – Y – and A 39 off A 368 – ✉ Pensford – ☎ 076 18 Compton Dando :

- **Hunstrete House** ⤳, BS18 4NS, ☎ 490490, Telex 449540, Fax 490732, ≤, « Country house atmosphere and gardens », ⌇ heated, park, ✕ – ✄ rest TV ☎ ⓖ ⓟ. ⬛ *VISA*. ⌖
  M 17.50/30.00 **t.** – **23 rm** ⊡ 80.00/145.00 **t.**, **1 suite** 175.00 **t.** – SB (November-mid April) 165.00/210.00 **st.**

BATTISBOROUGH CROSS Devon – see Newton Ferrers.

BATTLE East Sussex **404** V 31 – pop. 4 662 – ✆ 042 46.
See : Abbey★ (11C-14C) *AC* (site of the Battle of Hastings 1066).
🛈 88 High St. ℘ 3721 – ♦London 55 – ♦Brighton 34 – Folkestone 43 – Maidstone 30.

🏨 **Netherfield Place** ⑤, TN33 9PP, NW : 1 ¾ m. by A 2100 on Netherfield Rd ℘ 4455, Telex 95284, Fax 4024, ≼, « Gardens », park, ✗ – TV ☎ Ⓟ – ⅍ 60. ☒ AE ① VISA ✾
closed Christmas and New Year – **M** 13.50/16.95 **t.** and a la carte 17.40/23.45 **t.** ⑂ 3.75 –
13 rm � 50.00/100.00 **t.** – SB (October-March) 110.00/130.00 **st.**

🏠 **George,** 23 High St., TN33 0EA, ℘ 4466 – TV ☜ Ⓟ. ☒ AE ① VISA
M 7.75/11.50 **st.** and a la carte 10.45/14.30 **st.** ⑂ 4.00 – ⊃ 3.75 – **21 rm** 29.00/40.00 **st.** –
SB 55.00/65.50 **st.**

↑ **Little Hemingfold Farmhouse** ⑤, Telham, TN33 0TT, SE : 1 ¾ m. on A 2100 ℘ 4338, ≼,
« Lakeside setting », ⑬, ⋈, park, ✗ – ⊱ rest TV ☎ Ⓟ. ☒ VISA
M 15.00 **t.** ⑂ 3.00 – **12 rm** ⊃ 40.00/55.00 **t.** – SB 64.00/78.00 **st.**

XX **La Vieille Auberge** with rm, 27 High St., TN33 0EA, ℘ 5171, Fax 4015 – TV ☎. ☒ AE ①
VISA ✾
M 12.00/21.00 **st.** and a la carte 16.50/31.00 **st.** ⑂ 6.00 – **7 rm** ⊃ 29.50/55.00 **st.** –
SB (October-May) 70.00/80.00 **st.**

AUSTIN-ROVER High St. ℘ 2425
CITROEN Ninfield ℘ 0424 (Ninfield) 892278
CITROEN Whatlington ℘ 042 487 (Sedlescombe)
307

FORD Upper Lake ℘ 3155
SKODA Battle Hill ℘ 2286

BAWTRY South Yorks. **402 403 404** Q 23 – pop. 2 677 – ✉ ✆ 0302 Doncaster.
🛈⒙ Austerfield Park, Cross Lane ℘ 710841, NE : 2 m. by A 614.
♦London 158 – ♦Leeds 39 – Lincoln 32 – ♦Nottingham 36 – ♦Sheffield 22.

🏨 **Crown** (T.H.F.), High St., DN10 6JW, ℘ 710341, Telex 547089, Fax 711798, ⋈ – ⊱ rm TV
☎ ⅋ Ⓟ – ⅍ 150. ☒ AE ① VISA
M 7.95/14.00 **st.** and a la carte – ⊃ 7.00 – **57 rm** 56.00/100.00 **st.** – SB (weekends
only) 70.00/76.00 **st.**

FORD Market Pl. ℘ 710212

RENAULT Bawtry Rd ℘ 710595

BEACONSFIELD Bucks. **404** S 29 – pop. 13 397 – ECD : Wednesday and Saturday – ✆ 049 46
(4 and 5 fig.) or 0494 (6 fig.) – ♦London 26 – Aylesbury 19 – ♦Oxford 32.

🏨 **Bellhouse** (De Vere), Oxford Rd, HP9 2XE, E : 1 ¾ m. on A 40 ℘ 0753 (Gerrard's Cross)
887211, Telex 848719, Fax 888231, ⋈ – ▐⑂ ⊱ rm ☎ Ⓟ – ⅍ 400. ☒ AE ① VISA
M 15.00/17.00 **st.** and a la carte – **133 rm** ⊃ 45.00/82.00 **st.**, **3 suites** 83.00/150.00 **st.** –
SB (July-August and weekends only September-June) 88.50/187.00 **st.**

XX **Wheeler's,** 14 London End, HP9 2JH, ℘ 677077, Seafood – ☒ AE ① VISA
closed Sunday dinner and 25-26 December – **M** a la carte 13.30/23.20 **t.** ⑂ 4.25.

XX **Leigh House,** 53 Wycombe End, ℘ 676348, Chinese (Peking) rest. – ☒ AE ① VISA
M 18.00/20.00 **t.** and a la carte approx. 17.00 **t.**

XX **La Lanterna,** 57 Wycombe End, HP9 1LX, ℘ 675210, Italian rest. – ☒ AE ① VISA
closed Sunday – **M** 8.50 **t.** (lunch) and a la carte 11.50/17.70 **t.** ⑂ 3.85.

XX **China Diner,** 7 The Highway, Station Rd, Beaconsfield New Town, HP9 1LG, ℘ 678346,
Chinese rest. – ☒ AE ① VISA
closed 3 days at Christmas – **M** 12.50 **t.** and a la carte 8.90/15.00 **t.** ⑂ 3.25.

at Wooburn Common SW : 3 ½ m. by A 40 – ✉ Beaconsfield – ✆ 062 85 (5 fig.) or 0628
(6 fig.) Bourne End :

🏠 **Chequers Inn** ⑤, Kiln Lane, HP10 0JQ, ℘ 29575, Telex 849832 – TV ☎ Ⓟ – ⅍ 30. ☒ AE
VISA ✾
M 12.00/15.00 **t.** and a la carte – **16 rm** ⊃ 64.00/70.00 **t.**

FIAT Gregorys Rd ℘ 6171
MERCEDES-BENZ, TOYOTA 55 Station Rd ℘ 2141

VAUXHALL Penn Rd, Knotty Green ℘ 3730

BEAMINSTER Dorset **403** L 31 – ✆ 0308 – ♦London 149 – Dorchester 19 – Exeter 40 – Taunton 31.

↑ **Hams Plot,** DT8 3LU, ℘ 862979, ⌇, ⋈, ✗ – Ⓟ
April-October – **M** (by arrangement)/dinner 16.00 **st.** – **5 rm** ⊃ 30.00/42.00 **st.**

BEARSTED Kent **404** V 30 – see Maidstone.

BEAULIEU Hants. **403 404** P 31 – pop. 1 027 – ECD : Tuesday and Saturday – ✉ Brockenhurst
– ✆ 0590 – See : Site★★ – National Motor Museum★ Buckler's Hard Maritime Museum *AC*.
🛈 John Montagu Building ℘ 612345 – ♦London 102 – Bournemouth 24 – ♦Southampton 13 – Winchester 23.

🏨 **Montagu Arms,** Palace Lane, SO42 7ZL, ℘ 612324, Telex 47276, « Part 18C inn, gardens »
– TV ☎ Ⓟ. ☒ AE ① VISA ✾
M 17.50/35.00 **t.** and a la carte 23.00/33.00 **t.** ⑂ 6.00 – **24 rm** ⊃ 60.00/115.00 **t.**, **1 suite**
150.00 **t.** – SB 120.00/140.00 **st.**

at Bucklers Hard S : 2 ½ m. – ✉ Brockenhurst – ✆ 0590 Bucklers Hard :

🏨 **Master Builder's House,** SO4 7XB, ℘ 616253, ≼, ⋈ – TV ☎ Ⓟ – ⅍ 50. ☒ AE ① VISA
M 10.00 **st.** and a la carte ⑂ 3.45 – **23 rm** ⊃ 40.00/85.00 **st.** – SB 78.00/84.00 **st.**

BEAUMARIS Gwynedd 402 403 H 24 – pop. 1 413 – ECD : Wednesday – ✆ 0248.
See : Castle★★ (13C) *AC* – **Envir.** : Anglesey★★ – Menai Strait★ (Channel), Menai Suspension Bridge ≤★ SW : 4 ½ m. – Bryn Celli Du (burial chamber★) SW : 8 m.
Baron Hill ✆ 810231, SW : 1 m. on A 545.
◆London 253 – Birkenhead 74 – Holyhead 25.

   Bishopsgate House, 54 Castle St., LL58 8AB, ✆ 810302 – TV ☎ ℗. 🅂 VISA
   closed January – **M** (dinner only and Sunday lunch)/dinner 10.95 **t.** and a la carte 🍾 3.75 –
   10 rm ⊇ 20.00/45.00 **t.** – SB (October-May) 55.00/65.00 **st.**

   Liverpool Arms without rest., Castle St., LL58 8BA, ✆ 810362 – TV ☎ ℗. ⌘ – **10 rm**.

BECCLES Suffolk 404 Y 26 – pop. 10 677 – ECD : Wednesday – ✆ 0502.
The Common ✆ 712244 – ⛵ The Quay, Fen Lane ✆ 713196 (summer only).
◆London 113 – Great Yarmouth 15 – ◆Ipswich 40 – ◆Norwich 18.

   King's Head (B.C.B.), New Market Sq., NR34 9HA, ✆ 712147 – ⌿⤬ rest TV ☎ ℗ – 🏖 100.
   ⌘ – **12 rm**.

   Waveney House ⤴, Puddingmoor, NR34 9PL, ✆ 712270 – TV ☎ ℗. 🅂 AE ⓪ VISA
   M 13.00/18.00 **t.** and a la carte 🍾 4.00 – **13 rm** ⊇ 35.00/60.00 **t.** – SB 55.00/65.00 **st.**

   Riverview House without rest., 29 Ballygate, NR34 9ND, ✆ 713519 – TV
   10 rm ⊇ 15.00/35.00 **st.**

LAND ROVER, RANGE ROVER Beccles Rd, Barnby   VAUXHALL-OPEL, FORD Station Rd ✆ 717023
✆ 050 276 (Barnby) 204

BECKINGHAM Lincs. 402 404 R 24 – pop. 255 – ✉ ✆ 063 684 Fenton Claypole.
◆London 124 – Leicester 43 – Lincoln 20 – ◆Nottingham 28 – ◆Sheffield 46.

   Black Swan, Hillside, LN5 0RF, ✆ 474 – ℗. 🅂 VISA
   closed Sunday dinner, Monday, last 2 weeks August and last 2 weeks February – **M** (booking essential)(lunch by arrangement)/dinner 16.90 **t.**

BECKWITHSHAW North Yorks. 402 P 22 – see Harrogate.

BEDALE North Yorks. 402 P 21 – pop. 2 158 – ECD : Thursday – ✉ Darlington – ✆ 0677.
Leyburn Rd ✆ 22451 – ⛵ Bedale Hall ✆ 24604.
◆London 225 – ◆Leeds 45 – ◆Newcastle 30 – York 38.

   Plummer's, North End, DL8 1AF, ✆ 23432 – 🅂 VISA
   closed Sunday and Monday – **M** 12.00/19.00 **t.** and a la carte 13.25/18.60 **t.** 🍾 3.50.

BEDDGELERT Gwynedd 402 403 H 24 – pop. 646 – ECD : Wednesday – ✆ 076 686.
Envir. : NE : Llyn Dinas valley★★ – Llyn Gwynant valley★.
Exc. : Blaenau Ffestiniog (site : slate quarries★) E : 14 m. by Penrhyndeudraeth.
⛵ Llewelyn Cottage ✆ 293.
◆London 249 – Caernarfon 13 – Chester 73.

   Royal Goat, LL55 4YE, ✆ 224, ⤳ – ⌿⤬ rm TV ☎ ℗. 🅂 AE ⓪ VISA
   M 9.00/15.00 **st.** and a la carte 🍾 4.50 – **34 rm** ⊇ 35.00/66.00 **st.** – SB 70.00/94.00 **st.**

   Tanronen, LL55 4YB, ✆ 347 – TV ℗. 🅂 VISA. ⌘
   M 5.25/10.50 **t.** and a la carte 🍾 2.00 – **8 rm** ⊇ 15.75/31.50 **st.** – SB 46.50 **st.**

   Sygun Fawr Country House ⤴, LL55 4NE, NE : ¾ m. by A 498 ✆ 258, ≤ mountains and valley, « Part 16C stone built house », 🌲, park – ℗. ⌘
   M 9.00 **t.** 🍾 3.75 – **7 rm** ⊇ 17.50/35.00 **t.** – SB 47.00/49.00 **st.**

BEDFORD Beds. 404 S 27 – pop. 75 632 – ECD : Thursday – ✆ 0234.
See : Embankment★ – Cecil Higgins Art Gallery (porcelain★ 18C) – **Envir.** : Elstow (Abbey Church★ 11C, Moot Hall : John Bunyan Museum *AC*) S : 1 ¼ m. – Ampthill (Houghton House site★, ≤★) S : 5 m. – Old Warden (St. Leonard's Church : woodwork★ – Aeroplane Museum, near Biggleswade Aerodrome : the Shuttleworth collection★ *AC*) SE : 7 ½ m.
Bedford and County, Green Lane, Clapham ✆ 52617, N : 2 m. by A 6 – Bedfordshire, Bromham Rd, Biddenham ✆ 61669, NE : 1 m. on A 428 – Mowsbury, Cleat Hill, Kimbolton Rd ✆ 771042, N : 2 m. on B 660 – ⛵ 10 St. Paul's Sq. ✆ 215226.
◆London 59 – ◆Cambridge 31 – Colchester 70 – ◆Leicester 51 – Lincoln 95 – Luton 20 – ◆Oxford 52 – Southend-on-Sea 85.

   Barns (Lansbury), Cardington Rd, MK44 3SA, E : 2 m. on A 603 ✆ 270044, Telex 827748, Fax 273102, « Extended 17C manor house with 13C tithe barn », 🌲 – ⌿⤬ TV ☎ & ℗ – 🏖 90. 🅂 AE ⓪ VISA. ⌘
   M (closed Saturday lunch) 10.00/14.50 **st.** and a la carte 🍾 6.00 – **49 rm** ⊇ 60.00/120.00 **st.** – SB (weekends only) (except Christmas) 70.00 **st.**

   Bedford Swan, The Embankment, MK40 1RW, ✆ 46565, Telex 827779, 🔲 – 🛗 TV ☎ ℗ – 🏖 250. 🅂 AE ⓪ VISA
   M 12.55 **st.** and a la carte 🍾 3.95 – **122 rm** ⊇ 59.00/69.00 **st.**, **1 suite** 85.00 **st.**

   De Parys, 41-45 De Parys Av., MK40 2UA, ✆ 52121, Telex 82392, 🌲 – TV ☎ ℗ – 🏖 70. 🅂 AE ⓪ VISA
   closed 1 week at Christmas – **M** 9.00/9.75 **t.** and a la carte 🍾 7.50 – **29 rm** ⊇ 45.00/55.00 **t.**

🏠 **Shakespeare**, 27 Shakespeare Rd, MK40 2DX, ☎ 213147, Telex 82392, Fax 270637, 🚗 –
📺 ☎ 🅿. 🔄 AE VISA. 🚫
M *(closed Sunday and Bank Holidays)* 11.50 **st.** and a la carte 11.35/15.75 **st.** – **19 rm**
⬜ 30.00/54.00 **t.**

🏠 **Wayfarer**, Goldington Rd, Goldington, MK41 0DS, E : 2 m. on A 428 ☎ 272707, Fax
272707, 🚗 – 📺 ☎ ♿ 🅿 – 🔺 35. 🔄 AE ⓪ VISA. 🚫
M *(closed Saturday lunch)* 9.95/12.95 **t.** and a la carte – **29 rm** ⬜ 49.50/59.50 **t.** – SB (weekends only) 68.00 **st.**

🕯 **Edwardian House**, 15 Shakespeare Rd, MK40 2DZ, ☎ 211156 – 📺 ☎ 🅿. 🔄 AE VISA. 🚫
M *(closed Saturday, Sunday and Bank Holidays)* (dinner only) a la carte approx. 10.65 **st.**
🍷 3.55 – **14 rm** ⬜ 35.00/43.00 **st.**

at Houghton Conquest S : 6 ½ m. by A 6 – ✉ ☎ 0234 Bedford :

XX **Knife and Cleaver** with rm., MK45 3LA, ☎ 740387, 🚗 – 📺 ☎ 🅿. 🔄 VISA
closed Sunday dinner – **M** a la carte 9.30/15.15 **t.** 🍷 4.25 – **6 rm** ⬜ 36.00/48.00 **st.**

at Marston Moretaine SW : 6 ¼ m. by A 421 – ✉ ☎ 0234 Bedford :

🏠 **Travelodge** without rest., Beancroft Rd junction, MK43 0PQ, on A 421 ☎ 766755 – 📺 ♿
🅿. 🔄 AE VISA
32 rm 21.50/27.00 **t.**

at Clapham NW : 2 m. on A 6 – ✉ ☎ 0234 Bedford :

🏰 **Woodlands Manor** ⌖, Green Lane, MK41 6EP, ☎ 63281, Telex 825007, Fax 272390, 🚗 –
📺 ☎ 🅿 – 🔺 25. 🔄 AE VISA. 🚫
M *(closed lunch Saturday and Bank Holidays)* 14.95/23.50 **st.** and a la carte 🍷 5.30 – ⬜ 6.50
– **28 rm** 76.00/81.00 **st.**, **1 suite** 100.00/145.00 **st.** – SB (weekends only) 110.00 **st.**

MICHELIN Distribution Centre, Hammond Rd, Elms Farm Industrial Estate, MK41 0LG, ☎
271100, FAX 269453

AUSTIN-ROVER 120 Goldington Rd ☎ 55221
BMW, ROLLS-ROYCE, BENTLEY Shuttleworth Rd,
Goldington ☎ 60411
CITROEN, SUZUKI 89 Brickhill Av ☎ 213381
FIAT, LANCIA 9 Kingsway ☎ 64491
FORD 8-12 The Broadway ☎ 58391
FORD Hudson Rd ☎ 40041
HONDA, VOLVO Windsor Rd ☎ 45454

JAGUAR Bedford Rd, Kempston ☎ 841444
MERCEDES-BENZ Ampthill Rd ☎ 272888
NISSAN 180 Goldington Rd ☎ 60121
RENAULT 87 High St., Clapham ☎ 54257
SAAB Station Rd, Oakley ☎ 023 02 (Oakley) 3118
VAUXHALL-OPEL Barker's Lane ☎ 270000

🛞 ATS 3 London Rd ☎ 58838/9

BEDWORTH Warw 🅾🅾🅾 P 26 – ✉ – ☎ 0203 Nuneaton.
♦London 104 – ♦Birmingham 21 – ♦Coventry 4,5 – ♦Leicester 24.

🏠 **Travelodge** without rest., A 444 Southbound, EX12 0BN, N : 2 m. by B 4113 on A 444
☎ 382541 – 📺 ♿ 🅿. 🔄 AE VISA
40 rm 21.50/27.00 **t.**

🏠 **Travel Inn** without rest., Coventry Rd, CV10 7PJ, N : 1 ½ m. on B 4113 at junction with
A 444 ☎ 343584, Fax 327156, 🚗 – ✂ 📺 ♿ 🅿. 🔄 AE ⓪ VISA. 🚫
⬜ 3.95 – **38 rm** 24.50/27.50 **t.**

BEER Devon 🅾🅾🅾 K 31 – ✉ ☎ 0297 Seaton.
♦London 170 – Exeter 22 – Taunton 28.

🕯 **Anchor Inn**, Fore St., EX12 3ET, ☎ 20386, ⩽ – 📺. 🔄 VISA. 🚫
closed 2 weeks Christmas-New Year – **M** a la carte 8.95/15.15 – **9 rm** ⬜ 24.75/44.00 **t.**

BEESTON Cheshire 🅾🅾🅾🅾 L 24 – pop. 221 – ✉ Tarporley – ☎ 0829 Bunbury.
♦London 186 – Chester 15 – ♦Liverpool 40 – Shrewsbury 32.

🏨 **Wild Boar**, Bunbury, CW6 9NW, on A 49 ☎ 260309, Telex 61222, Fax 261081, 🚗 – 🍽 rest.
📺 ☎ ♿ 🅿 – 🔺. 🔄 AE ⓪ VISA. 🚫
M 22.00 **t.** and a la carte approx. 19.50 🍷 4.95 – **37 rm** ⬜ 62.00/90.00 **t.** – SB 75.00 **st.**

BEESTON Notts. 🅾🅾🅾 Q 25 – see Nottingham.

BELFORD Northumb. 🅾🅾 O 17 – pop. 943 – ECD : Thursday – ☎ 066 83.
🅩 2 Market Pl. ☎ 888 – ♦London 335 – ♦Edinburgh 71 – ♦Newcastle-upon-Tyne 49.

🏨 **Blue Bell**, Market Sq., NE70 7NE, ☎ 543, 🚗 – ✂ 📺 ☎ ♿ 🅿. 🔄 AE ⓪ VISA. 🚫
M 7.50/14.00 **t.** and a la carte 🍷 3.00 – **16 rm** ⬜ 32.00/80.00 **t.**, **1 suite** – SB (November-
mid March) 76.00/86.00 **st.**

BELPER Derbs. 🅾🅾🅾 P 24 – pop. 17 328 – ✉ ☎ 0773.
♦London 141 – Derby 8 – ♦Manchester 55 – ♦Nottingham 17.

XX **Remy**, 84 Bridge St., DE5 1AZ, ☎ 822246 – 🍽. 🔄 AE ⓪ VISA
closed Sunday, 1 week January and 2 weeks July – **M** (dinner only) 16.50 **t.** and a la carte
12.95/16.50 **t.**

BEPTON West Sussex – see Midhurst.

BERKELEY Glos. 403 404 M 28 – pop. 1 498 – ECD : Wednesday – ✆ 0453 Dursley.
♦London 129 – ♦Bristol 20 – ♦Cardiff 50 – Gloucester 18.

  🏠 **Old School House**, Canonbury St., GL13 9BG, ✆ 811711 – 📺 ☎ 🅿. ⑤ VISA. ✕
  closed 26 December-14 January – **M** *(closed Monday lunch)* a la carte lunch 9.40/10.90 **t.**
  /dinner 14.50 **t.** 🍷 4.00 – **7 rm** ☕ 35.00/50.00 **t.** – SB 70.00 **st.**

BERKHAMSTED Herts 404 S 28 – pop. 16 874 – ECD : Wednesday and Saturday – ✆ 0442
(6 fig.) or 044 27 (4 and 5 fig.).
📍 Berkhamstead, The Common ✆ 865832, NE : 1 m – 🅱 Library, Kings Rd ✆ 864545.
♦London 33 – Luton 16 – ♦Oxford 35.

  🏠 **Hamberlin's** ⚶ without rest., Tring Rd, Northchurch, HP4 3TL, NW : 1 ½ m. on A 41
  ✆ 875100, 🚗 – 📺 🅿 – **15 rm**.

  🏠 **Swan**, 135-139 High St., HP4 3HH, ✆ 871451, Telex 82257 – ✕ rest ▤ rest 📺 ☎ 🅿
  19 rm.

AUSTIN-ROVER London Rd ✆ 71234
CITROEN,VAUXHALL Lower Kings Rd ✆ 2232
FORD 33 High St. ✆ 71171

PEUGEOT-TALBOT, SUBARU, ISUZU Ringshall, Nr.
Berkhamsted ✆ 044 284 (Little Gaddesden) 2273/27

BERKSWELL West Midlands 403 404 P 26 – see Coventry.

BERRIEW (ABERRIW) Powys 402 403 K 26 – pop. 1 167 – ✉ Welshpool – ✆ 068 685.
♦London 190 – Chester 49 – Shrewsbury 26.

  ⚘ **Lion**, SY21 8PQ, ✆ 452 – 📺 🅿 VISA ✕
  M (bar lunch Monday to Saturday)/dinner a la carte 10.80/12.05 **t.** 🍷 3.75 – **3 rm**
  ☕ 30.00/55.00 **t.** – SB 75.00/85.00 **st.**

BERWICK-UPON-TWEED Northumb. 401 402 O 16 – pop. 12 772 – ECD : Thursday – ✆ 0289.
See : City Walls★ 16C.
Envir. : Holy Island★ (Lindisfarne Castle★) : 6 m.
📍 Goswick, Beal ✆ 87256, S : 5 m. – 📍 Magdalene Fields ✆ 306384.
🅱 Castlegate Car Park ✆ 330733.
♦London 349 – ♦Edinburgh 57 – ♦Newcastle-upon-Tyne 63.

  🏨 **King's Arms** (Best Western), 43 Hide Hill, TD15 1EJ, ✆ 307454, Fax 308867, 🚗 – 📺 ☎ –
  🔰 120. ⑤ AE ⓪ VISA
  M (carving lunch)/dinner 15.50 **st.** and a la carte 🍷 3.50 – **36 rm** ☕ 42.50/64.50 **st.** –
  SB (weekends only) 75.00 **st.**

  🏠 **Turret House**, Etal Rd, Tweedmouth, TD15 2EG, S : ¾ m. by A 1167 on B 6354 ✆ 330808,
  Fax 330467, 🚗 – 📺 ☎ 🅿. ⑤ AE ⓪ VISA
  M 6.50/14.50 **st.** and a la carte 🍷 3.50 – **13 rm** ☕ 42.50/57.00 **st.** – SB 64.00/73.00 **st.**

AUSTIN-ROVER Tweedside Trading Estate ✆
330707
RENAULT Golden Sq. ✆ 307371
VAUXHALL 12 Silver St. ✆ 307436

VOLVO Tweed St. ✆ 307537

Ⓐ ATS 78-80 Church St. ✆ 305720/308222

BETHERSDEN Kent 404 W 30 – pop. 1 273 – ✉ ✆ 023 382.
♦London 63 – Folkestone 20 – Maidstone 27.

  ⌂ **Little Hodgeham** ⚶, Smarden Rd ✉ Ashford, TN26 3HE, N : 2 m. by A 28 ✆ 0233
  (High Halden) 850323, ≼, « Tastefully decorated 15C cottage, antique furniture », ⊼, 🚗 –
  ✕ rest 🅿
  Mid March-September – **M** 12.50 **s.** 🍷 2.50 – **3 rm** ☕ (dinner included) 50.00/70.00 **s.**

BETWS-Y-COED Gwynedd 402 403 I 24 – pop. 654 – ECD : Thursday – ✆ 069 02.
Envir. : Fairy Glen and Conway Falls★ *AC*, SE : 2 m. – Swallow Falls★ *AC*, NW : 2 m. – Nant-y-
Gwryd Valley★ W : by Capel Curig.
📍 Betws-y-Coed ✆ 556, NE : ½ m. by A 5 – 🅱 Royal Oak Stables ✆ 426 and 665 (summer only).
♦London 226 – Holyhead 44 – Shrewsbury 62.

  🏨 **Royal Oak**, Holyhead Rd, LL24 0AY, ✆ 219 – 📺 ☎ 🅿. ⑤ AE ⓪ VISA. ✕
  closed 25 and 26 December – **M** 7.50/15.00 **t.** and a la carte 🍷 3.75 – **27 rm** ☕ 42.00/128.00 **t.**
  – SB 57.00/74.00 **st.**

  🏠 **Waterloo**, LL24 0AR, on A 5 ✆ 411 – 📺 ☎ 🅿. ✕ – **42 rm**.

  ⚘ **Ty Gwyn**, LL24 0SG, SE : ½ m. on A 5 ✆ 383, « 17C inn » – 🅿. ⑤ VISA
  M (bar lunch) 7.95/10.95 **t.** and a la carte 🍷 3.25 – **13 rm** ☕ 16.00/60.00 **t.** – SB 53.50/81.50 **st.**

  ⌂ **Park Hill**, Llanrwst Rd, LL24 0HD, NE : 1 m. by A 5 on A 470 ✆ 540, ≼ Vale of Conwy, ⊼,
  🚗 – ✕ rest 📺 🅿. ⑤ AE ⓪ VISA. ✕
  M 11.00 **st.** 🍷 3.20 – **11 rm** ☕ 16.00/48.00 **st.** – SB (November-March) 46.00/60.00 **st.**

  at Pont-y-Pant SW : 4 ½ m. on A 470 – ✉ ✆ 069 06 Dolwyddelan :

  🏨 **Plas Hall** ⚶, LL25 0PJ, ✆ 206, Fax 526, ⟍, 🚗 – 📺 ☎ 🕭 🅿. ⑤ VISA ✕
  M (bar lunch)/dinner 11.50 **t.** and a la carte 🍷 3.50 – **18 rm** ☕ 55.50/104.00 **t.** – SB (January-
  March) 66.00 **st.**

BEVERLEY Humberside 402 S 22 – pop. 19 368 – ECD : Thursday – ✉ ☎ 0482 Kingston-upon-Hull.

See : Minster★★ 13C-15C – St. Mary's Church★ 14C-15C.

🛇 The Westwood, Walkington Rd ℰ 867190, SW : 1 m. on B 1230.

🛈 Guildhall, Register Sq. ℰ 867430 – Museum of Army Transport, Flemingate ℰ 867813.

♦London 188 – ♦Kingston-upon-Hull 8 – ♦Leeds 52 – York 29.

🏰 **Beverley Arms** (T.H.F.), North Bar Within, HU17 8DD, ℰ 869241, Telex 597568, Fax 870907 – 🛗 ⇤ rm 🍽 rest 📺 ☎ Ⓟ – 🛏 70. 🔼 AE ⓪ VISA
M 8.50/11.95 **st.** and a la carte 🍷 3.75 – ⌓ 6.50 – **57 rm** 52.00/77.00 **st.** – SB 56.00/80.00 **st.**

🏰 **Lairgate,** 30 Lairgate, HU17 8EP, ℰ 882141, Fax 882141 – 📺 ☎ Ⓟ. 🔼 VISA ⚓
M 7.25/12.95 **st.** and a la carte 🍷 3.00 – **24 rm** ⌓ 25.00/55.00 **t.**

at Tickton NE : 3 ½ m. by A 1035 – ✉ Kingston-upon-Hull – ☎ 0964 Hornsea :

🏰 **Tickton Grange,** HU17 9SH, on A 1035 ℰ 543666, Telex 527254, 🚗 – 📺 ☎ Ⓟ – 🛏 100. 🔼 AE ⓪ VISA
M 19.95 **t.** (dinner) and a la carte 🍷 3.95 – **17 rm** ⌓ 52.00/80.00 **t.** – SB (weekends only) 64.40 **st.**

at South Dalton NW : 6 ¼ m. by A 164 off B 1248 – ✉ ☎ 0430 Howden :

✗ **Pipe and Glass,** West End, HU17 7PN, ℰ 810246 – Ⓟ. 🔼 VISA
closed dinner Sunday and Monday and 25 December – **M** (bar lunch Monday to Friday)/dinner 18.00 **t.** and a la carte 11.50/16.50 **t.** 🍷 3.00.

AUSTIN-ROVER Barmston Rd, Swinemoor Ind Est. ℰ 867922
FORD Wednesday Market ℰ 868311

VAUXHALL-OPEL Swinemoor Lane ℰ 882207
Ⓜ ATS 379 Grovehill Rd ℰ 868655/882644

BEWDLEY Heref. and Worc. 403 404 N 26 – pop. 8 696 – ECD : Wednesday – ☎ 0299.

🛇 Little Lakes Golf and Country Club, Lye Head ℰ 266385, W : 2 ¼ m. by A 456.

🛈 The Library, Load St. ℰ 404740.

♦London 140 – ♦Birmingham 20 – Worcester 16.

🏠 **Black Boy,** Kidderminster Rd, DY12 1AG, ℰ 402119, 🚗 – 📺 Ⓟ. 🔼 AE VISA
closed Christmas Day – **M** (bar lunch Monday to Saturday)/dinner 13.50 **t.** – **25 rm** ⌓ 25.00/54.00 **t.** – SB (weekends only) 65.00/82.00 **t.**

BEXHILL East Sussex 404 V 31 – pop. 34 625 – ECD : Wednesday – ☎ 0424.

🛇 Cooden Beach ℰ 042 43 (Cooden) 2040, W : 2 m. by A 259.

🛈 De La Warr Pavilion, Marina ℰ 212023.

♦London 66 – ♦ Brighton 32 – Folkestone 42.

🏰 **Cooden Resort,** Cooden Sea Rd, Cooden Beach, TN39 4TT, W : 2 m. on B 2182, Fax 6142, 🏊 heated, 🔼, 🚗 – 📺 ☎ Ⓟ – 🛏 80. 🔼 AE ⓪ VISA
M 11.00/15.50 **t.** and a la carte – **34 rm** ⌓ 48.00/70.00 **t.** – SB (except Easter, Christmas and New Year) 80.00 **st.**

✗ **Lychgates,** 5a Church St., Old Town, TN40 2HE, ℰ 212193 – 🔼 VISA
closed Saturday lunch, Sunday and Monday – **M** 7.95/14.95 **t.**

AUDI-VW King Offa Way ℰ 212255
AUSTIN-ROVER 57-69 London Rd ℰ 212000
FORD ℰ 212727
HONDA Sackville Rd ℰ 221330

RENAULT London Rd ℰ 210485
TOYOTA Holliers Hill ℰ 213577
VAUXHALL-OPEL Dorset Rd ℰ 211212

BIBURY Glos. 403 404 O 28 – pop. 603 – ECD : Wednesday – ✉ Cirencester – ☎ 028 574.

See : Arlington Row★ 17C.

♦London 86 – Gloucester 26 – ♦Oxford 30.

🏰 **Swan,** GL7 5NW, ℰ 204, Telex 437360, « Garden and trout stream », 🐟 – 📺 ☎ Ⓟ. 🔼 VISA
M 13.50/16.50 **t.** 🍷 3.50 – **24 rm** ⌓ 38.50/68.50 **t.** – SB (November-Easter) 67.50/75.00 **st.**

🏠 **Bibury Court** 🦢, GL7 5NT, ℰ 337, ≼, « Tudor mansion », 🐟, 🚗, park – 📺 ☎ Ⓟ. 🔼 VISA
closed 2 weeks Christmas – **M** (bar lunch)/dinner a la carte 16.80 **t.** – ⌓ 4.50 – **16 rm** 36.00/60.00 **t.**, **1 suite** 82.00 **t.** – SB (November-March) 74.00/78.00 **st.**

BICKLEIGH Devon 403 J 31 – pop. 205 – ECD : Tuesday – ✉ Tiverton – ☎ 088 45.

See : Site★★ – Bickleigh Mill Craft Centre and Farms★★ AC – Bickleigh Castle★ AC.

♦London 195 – Exeter 9 – Taunton 31.

🏠 **Bickleigh Cottage Country,** Bickleigh Bridge, EX16 8RJ, on A 396 ℰ 230, « Part 17C thatched inn and cottage, riverside setting », 🚗 – Ⓟ. 🔼 VISA ⚓
April-October – **M** (dinner only) (residents only) 7.50 **t.** – **9 rm** ⌓ 15.00/35.00 **t.**

BIDDENDEN Kent **404** V 30 – pop. 2 229 – ⊠ Ashford – ✆ 0580.
♦London 51 – Folkestone 29 – Hastings 23 – Maidstone 14.

XX   **West House**, 28 High St., TN27 8AH, ✆ 291341, Italian rest. – **P**. **△** **VISA**
closed Sunday, Monday, 1 week January, 1 week April and 3 weeks August-September –
M a la carte 10.95/20.50 **st.** ⟨ 3.50.

X   **Ye Maydes**, 13-15 High St., TN27 8AL, ✆ 291306 – **△** **AE** **VISA**
closed Sunday, Monday, 1 week February, 2 weeks August and 1 week November –
M 8.50 **t.** (lunch) and a la carte 14.25/17.75 **t.** ⟨ 3.50.

BIDEFORD Devon **403** H 30 The West Country G. – pop. 13 826 – ECD : Wednesday – ✆ 023 72
(5 fig.) or 0237 (6 fig.).
See : The Bridge★★ – Burton Art Gallery★AC.
Envir. : Clovelly★★, W : 11 m. – Great Torrington : Dartington Glass★AC, SE : 7 m. – at Hartland
(≤★★★) Church★ Quay★ (≤★★), W : 12 m. – at Thornbury, Devon Museum of Mechanical
Music★AC, S : 15 m.
⛴ to the Isle of Lundy (Lundy Co.) 1-2 Weekly (2 h).
🛈 The Quay ✆ 77676/74591 (summer only).
♦London 231 – Exeter 43 – ♦Plymouth 58 – Taunton 60.

🏨   **Durrant House**, Heywood Rd, Northam, EX39 3QB, N : 1 m. on A 386 ✆ 472361, Telex
46740, 🌊 – |🛗| ▤ rest **TV** ☎ **P**. **△** **AE** **①** **VISA**
M 5.50/12.00 **t.** and a la carte – **83 rm** ☲ 51.00/73.50 **t.**, **2 suites** 85.50/100.00 **t.** –
SB (weekends only) 57.00/79.00 **st.**

🏨   **Yeoldon House** (Best Western) 🦊, Durrant Lane, Northam, EX39 2RL, N : 1 ½ m. by A
386 ✆ 474400, Telex 46410, Fax 476618, ≤ Torridge estuary, « Country house atmosphere »,
🚲 – **TV** ☎ **P**. **△** **AE** **①** **VISA**
M 9.95/18.50 **st.** – **10 rm** ☲ 40.50/65.50 **st.** – SB 73.50/81.50 **st.**

🏠   **Riversford** 🦊, Limers Lane, Northam, EX39 2RG, N : 1 m. by A 386 ✆ 474239, ≤ Torridge
estuary, 🚲 – **TV** ☎ **P**. **△** **AE** **①** **VISA** ⠶
M 7.30/16.00 **st.** and a la carte ⟨ 3.65 – **17 rm** ☲ 22.00/68.00 **st.** – SB (20 May-September and Christmas) 66.00/82.00 **st.**

🏠   **Beaconside House** 🦊, Landcross, EX39 5JL, S : 3 m. by A 386 on A 388 ✆ 477205, ≤,
🌊 heated, 🚲, park, ✗ – ✗ **TV** **P**. ⠶
M (lunch by arrangement) 7.95/12.95 ⟨ 3.50 – **8 rm** ☲ (dinner included) 28.00/32.00, **3 suites**
32.00 – SB 25.00/32.00 **st.**

🏠   Orchard Hill, Orchard Hill, EX39 2QY, N : ¾ m. by A 386 ✆ 72872, 🚲 – **TV** **P**. ⠶
9 rm.

at Instow N : 3 m. on A 39 – ⊠ Bideford – ✆ 0271 Instow :

🏨   **Commodore**, Marine Par., EX39 4JN, ✆ 860347, Fax 861233, ≤ Taw and Torridge estuaries,
🚲 – **TV** ☎ **P** – 🔥 50. **△** **AE** **VISA**. ⠶
M 9.50/15.00 **t.** and a la carte – **20 rm** ☲ 45.00/72.00 **t.** – SB (November-
March) 68.00/72.00 **st.**

at Eastleigh NE : 2 ½ m. by A 39 (via Old Barnstaple rd) – ⊠ Bideford – ✆ 0271 Instow :

⩕   **Pines**, EX39 4PA, ✆ 860561, ≤, 🚲 – **P**
M 10.00 **st.** – **8 rm** ☲ 20.00/40.00 **st.** – SB 46.00/58.00 **st.**

at Fairy Cross W : 5 m. on A 39 – ⊠ Bideford – ✆ 023 75 Horns Cross :

🏨   Portledge (Best Western) 🦊, EX39 5BX, ✆ 262, Fax 717, « Part 17C country house in
extensive grounds », 🌊 heated, 🚲, ✗ – **TV** ☎ **P**
24 rm.

AUSTIN-ROVER 6 Queen St. ✆ 73304   🅰 ATS New Rd ✆ 72451
VAUXHALL-OPEL Handy Cross ✆ 72282

BIGBURY-ON-SEA Devon **403** I 33 – pop. 559 – ECD : Thursday – ⊠ Kingsbridge – ✆ 0548.
♦London 196 – Exeter 42 – ♦Plymouth 17.

🏨   **Burgh Island** 🦊, TQ7 4AU, S : ½ m. by sea tractor ✆ 810514, Fax 810243, ≤ Bigbury Bay,
« Idyllic island setting, Art Deco », park, ✗ – |🛗| **TV** ☎. **△** **AE** **VISA**. ⠶
M (booking essential) (bar lunch)/dinner 22.00 **t.** –, **13 suites** ☲ (dinner included)
120.00/160.00 **t.** – SB 116.00/150.00 **st.**

🏠   Seagulls 🦊, Folly Hill, TQ7 4AR, ✆ 810331, ≤ Bigbury Bay and Bolt Head, 🚲 – ✗ rest **P**
9 rm.

⩕   **Henley** 🦊, Folly Hill, TQ7 4AR, ✆ 810240, ≤ Bigbury Bay and Bolt Head, 🚲 – ✗ **P**. **△**
VISA.
M 10.75 **t.** ⟨ 2.40 – **9 rm** ☲ 18.35/42.00 – SB 50.60/56.00 **st.**

BILBROOK Somerset **403** J 30 – ⊠ Minehead – ✆ 0984 Washford.
♦London 181 – Minehead 5 – Taunton 19.

🏨   **Dragon House**, TA24 6HQ, ✆ 40215, « Part 18C house with gardens » – **TV** ☎ **P**. **△** **AE**
① **VISA**
M 12.50 **t.** and a la carte 12.75/18.10 **t.** ⟨ 3.00 – **9 rm** ☲ 36.00/72.00 **t.**, **1 suite** –
SB (except Bank Holidays) 70.00/80.00 **st.**

BILBROUGH North Yorks. **402** Q 22 – see York.

BILLESLEY Warw. – see Stratford-upon-Avon.

BILLINGHAM Cleveland **402** Q 20 – pop. 36 855 – ✉ ✆ 0642 Stockton-on-Tees.
 Sandy Lane ☎ 554494.
♦London 255 – ♦Middlesbrough 3 – Sunderland 26.

    Billingham Arms, The Causeway, TS23 2LH, ☎ 553661, Telex 587746, Fax 552104 – TV ☎
    P – 🛏 250. 🖪 AE ⓞ VISA. ✖
    M (bar lunch) 10.45 **t.** and a la carte 🍷 3.40 – ☲ 2.50 – **63 rm** 18.00/54.00 **st.** – SB (week-
    ends only) 63.90 **st.**

BILLINGSHURST West Sussex **404** S 30 – ECD : Wednesday – ✆ 040 381.
♦London 44 – ♦Brighton 24 – Guildford 25 – ♦Portsmouth 40.

    Travelodge without rest., 51 Oaks, A 29 Staines St., RH14 9AE, N : 1 m. on A 29 ☎ 812711
    – TV ♿ P. 🖪 AE VISA
    26 rm 21.50/27.00 **t.**

    ✗ **Wills,** 92 High St., RH14 9QS, ☎ 2432 – 🖪 AE VISA
    closed Tuesday lunch, Sunday dinner, Monday and 26 to 30 December – **M** a la carte
    18.50/23.00 **t.** 🍷 3.50.

AUSTIN-ROVER Wolviston Rd ☎ 553959   RENAULT Central Garage ☎ 553071
FORD The Green ☎ 550415

BINGLEY West Yorks. **402** O 22 – pop. 18 954 – ECD : Tuesday – ✉ ✆ 0274 Bradford.
 St Ives Mansion, Harden ☎ 562436, W : ¾ m. by B 6429 – Shipley, Beckfoot Lane, Fottingley
Bridge ☎ 568652, NW : 6 m. by A 650.
♦London 204 – Bradford 6 – Skipton 13.

    Bankfield (Embassy), Bradford Rd, BD16 1TV, SE : 1 ½ m. on A 650 ☎ 567123, Fax 551331,
    🚗 – 📶 ✖ rm 🍽 rest TV ☎ ♿ P – 🛏 300. 🖪 AE ⓞ VISA
    M *(closed Saturday lunch)* (carving rest.) 11.00 **st.** and a la carte 🍷 4.40 – ☲ 6.50 – **101 rm**
    58.00/68.00 **st.** – SB (weekends only) 59.00/68.00 **st.**

    ⌂ **Hallbank,** Beck Lane, BD16 4DD, ☎ 565296 – ✖ rest TV ☎ P. ✖
    closed Christmas and New Year – **M** 8.00 **st.** 🍷 3.00 – **10 rm** ☲ 32.50/42.50 **st.** – SB (week-
    ends only) 55.00/75.00 **st.**

BIRCH SERVICE AREA Greater Manchester **402** ㉒ **403** ?3 **404** ⑩ – ✉ Heywood (Lancashire) – ✆ 061 Manchester

    Granada Lodge without rest., OL10 2QH, on M 62, between junctions 18 and 19 ☎ 655 3403
    – ✖ TV ♿ P. 🖪 AE ⓞ VISA. ✖
    37 rm 24.50/27.50 **st.**

BIRDLIP Glos. **403** **404** N 28 – ECD : Saturday – ✉ ✆ 0452 Gloucester.
♦London 107 – ♦Bristol 51 – Gloucester 9 – ♦Oxford 44 – Swindon 24.

    Royal George (Lansbury), GL4 8JH, ☎ 862506, Telex 437238, Fax 862277, 🚗 – ✖ rm TV
    ☎ ♿ P – 🛏 120. 🖪 AE ⓞ VISA. ✖
    M 8.50/12.50 **t.** and a la carte – **36 rm** ☲ 60.00/70.00 **t.**, **1 suite** – SB (week-
    ends only) 74.00/82.00 **st.**

BIRKBY Cumbria – see Maryport.

BIRKENHEAD Merseyside **402** **403** K 23 – pop. 99 075 – ECD : Thursday – ✆ 051 Liverpool.
 Arrowe Park, Woodchurch ☎ 677 1527 – Prenton, Golf Links Rd ☎ 608 1053.
 to Liverpool (Merseyside Transport) frequent services daily (7-8 mn).
🛈 Central Library, Borough Rd ☎ 652 6106 ext 36.
♦London 222 – ♦Liverpool 2.

Plan : see Liverpool p. 3

    Bowler Hat, 2 Talbot Rd, Oxton, L43 2HH, ☎ 652 4931, Telex 628761, 🚗 – TV ☎ P
    🛏 100. 🖪 AE ⓞ VISA
    M 12.50/15.50 **t.** and a la carte 🍷 3.25 – ☲ 5.50 – **28 rm** 35.00/67.50 **t.**, **1 suite** 70.50 **t.** –
    SB (weekends only) (except Christmas) 100.00/150.00 **st.**

    Riverhill, Talbot Rd, Oxton, L43 2HJ, ☎ 653 3773, 🚗 – TV ☎ P. 🖪 AE ⓞ VISA. ✖
    M 7.65/9.90 **st.** and a la carte 🍷 3.75 – **16 rm** ☲ 27.50/46.20 **st.**

    ✗ **Beadles,** 15 Rose Mount, Oxton, L43 5SG, ☎ 653 9010
    closed Sunday, Monday and August – **M** (dinner only) a la carte 15.75/18.75 **t.** 🍷 2.75.

FIAT Claughton Firs ☎ 653 8555   RENAULT Borough Rd ☎ 342 8471
MAZDA Albion St., Wallasey ☎ 638 2234   VAUXHALL-OPEL 6 Woodchurch Rd ☎ 652 2366
MITSUBISHI, COLT New Chester Rd ☎ 645 1025
NISSAN Hoylake Rd ☎ 678 1060   ⓐ ATS 40 Mill Lane, Wallasey ☎ 638 1949/8606

BIRMINGHAM West Midlands 403 404 O 26 – pop. 1 013 995 – ECD : Wednesday – ✆ 021.

See : Museum and Art Gallery★★ JZ M1 – Aston Hall★★ FV – Barber Institute of Fine Arts★★ (at Birmingham University) BX – Museum of Science and Industry★ JY M2 – Cathedral (stained glass windows★ 19C) KYZ E.

🏌 Cocks Moor Woods, Alcester Rd South, King's Heath ✆ 444 3584, S : 6 ½ m. by A 435 FX – 🏌 Edgbaston, Church Rd ✆ 454 1736, S : 1 m. FX – 🏌 Warley, Lightwoods Hill, ✆ 429 2440, W : 5 m. by A 456 BU.

✈ Birmingham Airport : ✆ 767 7145, E : 6 ½ m. by A 45 DU.

🛈 2 City Arcade ✆ 643 2514 – The Piazza, National Exhibition Centre ✆ 780 4321 – Birmingham Airport ✆ 767 7145.

♦London 122 – ♦Bristol 91 – ♦Liverpool 103 – ♦Manchester 86 – ♦Nottingham 50.

Town plans : Birmingham pp. 2-7
Except where otherwise stated see pp. 6 and 7

🏰 **Plough and Harrow** (Crest), 135 Hagley Rd, Edgbaston, B16 8LS, W : 1 ½ m. on A 456 ✆ 454 4111, Telex 338074, Fax 454 1868, 🌴 – 🛗 ⇔ 📺 ☎ Ⓟ – 🛎 60. 🌙 AE ⓞ VISA
p. 4 EX a
M (see **Plough and Harrow** below) – ☲ 9.25 – **41 rm** 88.00/102.00 st., **3 suites** 130.00/160.00 st. – SB (weekends only) 114.00 st.

🏨 **Holiday Inn** (Holiday Inn), Central Sq., Holliday St., B1 1HH, ✆ 631 2000, Telex 337272, Fax 643 9018, ≼, 🌙 – 🛗 ⇔ rm 🗏 📺 ☎ ♿ Ⓟ – 🛎 250. 🌙 AE ⓞ VISA
JZ z
M 12.95/14.95 st. and a la carte 13.75/22.00 st. 🍷 5.00 – ☲ 8.00 – **291 rm** 82.50/92.50 st., **4 suites** 250.00/350.00 st. – SB (weekends only) 80.00/95.00 st.

🏨 **Copthorne** (Best Western), Paradise Circus, B3 3HJ, ✆ 200 2727, Telex 339026, Fax 200 1197, 🌙 – 🛗 ⇔ rm 🗏 rest 📺 ☎ ♿ Ⓟ – 🛎 . 🌙 AE ⓞ VISA 🍴
JZ e
M 10.95/12.95 t. and a la carte 🍷 4.65 – ☲ 7.80 – **213 rm** 79.50/215.00 t.

🏨 **Midland**, 128 New St., B2 4JT, ✆ 643 2601, Telex 338419, Fax 643 5075 – 🛗 📺 ☎ – 🛎 250. 🌙 AE ⓞ VISA
KZ r
M (closed lunch Saturday and Sunday) 16.00 st. and a la carte 🍷 6.00 – ☲ 7.75 – **105 rm** 70.00/82.00 st., **3 suites** 135.00 st.

🏨 **Royal Angus Thistle** (Thistle), St. Chad's, Queensway, B4 6HY, ✆ 236 4211, Telex 336889, Fax 233 2195 – 🛗 ⇔ rm 📺 ☎ – 🛎 180. 🌙 AE ⓞ VISA
KY s
M 13.50 st. and a la carte 18.65/33.90 st. – ☲ 7.25 – **133 rm** 65.00/92.00 st., **2 suites** 95.00 st. – SB 76.00/95.00 st.

🏨 **Strathallan Thistle** (Thistle), 225 Hagley Rd, Edgbaston, B16 9RY, W : 2 m. on A 456 ✆ 455 9777, Telex 336680, Fax 454 9432 – 🛗 ⇔ rm 🗏 rest 📺 ☎ Ⓟ – 🛎 180. 🌙 AE ⓞ VISA
p. 4 EX i
M a la carte 8.95/23.95 st. 🍷 4.00 – ☲ 7.25 – **163 rm** 65.00/82.00 st., **4 suites** 95.00 st. – SB 76.00/95.00 st.

🏨 **Grand** (Q.M.H.), Colmore Row, B3 2DA, ✆ 236 7951, Telex 338174, Fax 233 1465 – 🛗 📺 ☎ – 🛎 450. 🌙 AE ⓞ VISA
JKY c
closed 4 days at Christmas – M 11.55 st. and a la carte 🍷 3.50 – **164 rm** ☲ 70.00/85.00 st., **2 suites** 140.00 st. – SB (January-March) (weekends only) 67.00 st.

🏨 **Apollo** (Mt. Charlotte), Hagley Rd, Edgbaston, B16 9RA, W : 2 ¼ m. on A 456 ✆ 455 0271, Telex 336759 – 🛗 🗏 rest 📺 ☎ Ⓟ – 🛎
p. 4 EX o
128 rm, 2 suites.

🏨 **Penguin**, New St., B2 4RX, ✆ 631 3331, Fax 633 3226 – 🛗 ⇔ rm 📺 ☎ – 🛎 200. 🌙 AE ⓞ VISA
KZ x
M (closed lunch Saturday and Sunday) (carving rest.) 8.50/11.75 t. and a la carte – ☲ 6.95 – **190 rm** 68.00/90.00 st., **2 suites** 105.00/125.00 st. – SB (weekends only) 63.50 st.

🏠 **Asquith House,** 19 Portland Rd, off Hagley Rd, Edgbaston, B16 9HN, W : 2 m. by A 456 ✆ 454 5282, « Attractive decor and furnishings », 🌴 – 📺 ☎. 🌙 AE
p. 4 EX c
M (lunch by arrangement)/dinner 20.00 st. and a la carte 🍷 2.75 – **10 rm** ☲ 37.95/54.40 st.

🏠 **Copperfield House,** 60 Upland Rd, Selly Park, B29 7JS, S : 2 ½ m. by A 441 ✆ 472 8344, 🌴 – ⇔ rest 📺 ☎ Ⓟ. 🌙 VISA
FX a
closed Christmas-New Year – M 8.95 st. – **14 rm** ☲ 32.50/45.00 st.

🏠 Cobden, 166-174 Hagley Rd, Edgbaston, B16 9NZ, W : 2 m. on A 456 ✆ 454 6621, Telex 333851, Fax 454 1910, 🌙, 🌴 – 🛗 📺 ☎ Ⓟ – 🛎
p. 4 EX n
253 rm.

🏠 **Fountain Court,** 339-343 Hagley Rd, Edgbaston, B17 8NH, W : 2 ½ m. on A 456 ✆ 429 1754, 🌴 – 📺 Ⓟ. 🌙 VISA
EX u
M (bar lunch)/dinner 12.00 st. 🍷 5.95 – **25 rm** ☲ 35.00/50.00 st. – SB (weekends only) 84.00 st.

🏠 **Campanile,** 55 Irving St., B1 1DH, ✆ 622 4925, Telex 333701 – 📺 ☎ ♿ Ⓟ. 🌙 VISA
JZ a
M (grill rest.) (restricted menu) approx. 8.90 t. – ☲ 4.50 – **50 rm** 29.00 t.

🏠 **Portland,** 313 Hagley Rd, Edgbaston, B16 9LQ, ✆ 455 0535, Telex 334200, Fax 456 1841 – 🛗 🗏 rest 📺 ☎ Ⓟ – 🛎 70. 🌙 AE ⓞ VISA
p. 4 EX
M (closed Saturday lunch) 11.75 t. and a la carte 🍷 3.25 – **62 rm** ☲ 41.75/55.00 t. – SB (weekends only) 55.50/63.00 st.

🏛 **Hagley Court**, 229 Hagley Rd, Edgbaston, B16 9RP, W : 2 m. on A 456 ℰ 454 6514, Fax 456 2722 – 📺 ☎ ℗. 🆗 AE Ⓞ VISA ⚗️ p. 4 **EX** s
closed 24 December-3 January – **M** (closed Friday to Sunday and Bank Holidays) (bar lunch)/dinner 11.00 **st.** and a la carte ↑ 3.50 – **27 rm** ⊑ 28.00/55.00 **st.**

🏛 **Travelodge** without rest., A 4123, Wolverhampton Rd, Oldbury, B69 2BH, ℰ 552 2967 – 📺 ⅙ ℗. 🆗 AE VISA **BU** n
33 rm 21.50/27.00 **t.**

↑ **Westbourne Lodge**, 27-29 Fountain Rd, Edgbaston, B17 8NJ, ℰ 429 1003, 🚗 – 📺 ℗. 🆗 VISA p. 4 **EV** x
M 13.80 **t.** ↑ 4.00 – **19 rm** ⊑ 34.00/70.00 **t.** – SB (weekends only) 80.40/100.00 **st.**

XXX **Plough and Harrow** (Crest), (at Plough and Harrow H.) 135 Hagley Rd, Edgbaston, B16 8LS, W : 1 ½ m. on A 456 ℰ 454 4111, Telex 338074, Fax 454 1868, 🚗 – ℗ **EX** a

XXX **Jonathans'** with rm, 16-20 Wolverhampton Rd, B68 0LH, W : 4 m. by A 456 ℰ 429 3757, Fax 434 3107, English rest., « Victoriana » – 📺 ☎ ℗. 🆗 AE Ⓞ VISA p. 2 **BU** e
M 18.90 **t.** and a la carte 16.70/24.20 **t.** ↑ 2.50 – ⊑ 8.50 – **4 rm** 69.00/95.00 **t.** – SB (weekends only) 146.20/198.20 **st.**

XXX **Sloans**, Chad Sq., Hawthorne Rd, Edgbaston, B15 3TQ, W : 2 ¾ m. by A 456 ℰ 455 6697 – 🆗 AE Ⓞ VISA p. 4 **EX** v
closed Saturday lunch, Sunday, 23 December-3 January and Bank Holidays – **M** 13.50 **t.** (lunch) and a la carte approx. 20.75 **t.**

XX **Days of the Raj**, 51 Dale End, B4 7LS, ℰ 236 0445, Indian rest. – 🗏. 🆗 AE Ⓞ VISA **KZ** n
closed lunch Saturday and Sunday, and 25-26 December – **M** 5.95/14.00 **t.** and a la carte 12.55/20.25 **t.**

XX **Henry's**, 27 St. Paul's Sq., B3 1RB, ℰ 200 1136, Chinese (Canton) rest. – 🆗 AE Ⓞ VISA **JY** a
closed Sunday, last week August and Bank Holidays – **M** 11.50 **t.** and a la carte 13.20/15.00 **t.** ↑ 3.50.

XX **Maharaja**, 23-25 Hurst St., B5 4AS, ℰ 622 2641, Indian rest. – 🗏. 🆗 AE Ⓞ VISA **KZ** i
closed last 2 weeks July – **M** 7.50/13.50 **t.** and a la carte 8.10/10.50 **t.** ↑ 3.75.

XX **Henry Wong**, 283 High St., Harborne, B17 9QH, W : 3 ¾ m. by A 456 ℰ 427 9799, Chinese (Canton) rest. – 🆗 AE Ⓞ VISA **EX** n
closed Sunday, last week August and Bank Holidays – **M** 11.50 **t.** and a la carte 13.20/15.00 **t.** ↑ 3.50.

XX **Dynasty**, 93-103 Hurst St., B5 4TE, ℰ 622 1410, Chinese rest. – 🆗 AE Ⓞ VISA **KZ** e
closed 25-26 December and Bank Holidays – **M** 9.00/14.00 **st.** and a la carte 11.50/13.70 **t.**

XX **Lorenzo**, 3 Park St., Digbeth, B5 5JD, ℰ 643 0541, Italian rest. – 🆗 AE Ⓞ VISA **KZ** o
closed Saturday lunch, Monday dinner, Sunday, 13 and 16 April, 7 May and 25 December – **M** a la carte 13.30/19.00 **t.** ↑ 3.00.

XX **Rajdoot**, 12-22 Albert St., B4 7UD, ℰ 643 8805, Indian rest. – 🗏. 🆗 AE Ⓞ VISA **KZ** c
closed lunch Sunday and Bank Holidays and 25-26 December – **M** 6.00/14.00 **t.** and a la carte 10.75/18.85 **t.** ↑ 3.00.

MICHELIN Distribution Centre, Valepits Rd, Garretts Green, B33 0YD, ℰ 789 7100, FAX 789 7323 p. 5 **HX**

AUSTIN-ROVER Aston Hall Rd, Aston ℰ 328 0833
AUSTIN-ROVER 71 Aston Rd North, Aston ℰ 359 2011
AUSTIN-ROVER 1306 Bristol Rd South ℰ 441 2777
CITROEN, SUZUKI Barnes Hill, Weoley Castle ℰ 427 5231
FORD 156 182 Bristol St ℰ 666 6000
FORD Long Acre, Nechells ℰ 322 2222
FORD Granby Av., Garretts Green ℰ 789 7000
JAGUAR Bristol St. ℰ 666 6999
MAZDA Rookery Rd, Handsworth ℰ 554 9333
MERCEDES-BENZ Charles Henry St. ℰ 622 3031
NISSAN Walkers Heath Rd, Kings Norton ℰ 451 1411

NISSAN 4 Birmingham Rd ℰ 358 7011
PEUGEOT-TALBOT Charlotte St. ℰ 236 4382
PEUGEOT-TALBOT 30 High St, Deritend ℰ 772 4388
ROLLS-ROYCE, BENTLEY, FERRARI Stratford Rd, Shirley ℰ 745 5566
TOYOTA 138 Soho Hill, Handsworth ℰ 554 6311
VAUXHALL Queslett Rd, Great Barr ℰ 360 5445
VAUXHALL-OPEL 86 Orphanage Rd, Erdington ℰ 373 5241
VW-AUDI Digbeth ℰ 643 7341

🅰 ATS 341 Dudley Rd, Winson Green ℰ 454 2588/2536

Except where otherwise stated see pp. 2 and 3

at Erdington NE : 5 m. by A 5127 – ✉ ☎ 021 Birmingham :

↑ **Willow Tree**, 759 Chester Rd, B24 0BY, ℰ 373 6388, 🚗 – ⌿ rest 📺 ℗. 🆗 VISA. ⚗️ **DT** e
M 10.50 **st.** – **7 rm**.

AUSTIN-ROVER Chester Rd ℰ 353 3231
BMW Jockey Rd, Boldmere ℰ 354 8131
CITROEN Old Kingsbury Rd, Minworth ℰ 351 4367
FIAT 35 Sutton New Rd, Erdington ℰ 377 6533
HONDA Bromford Lane ℰ 328 4211
LADA Wood End Lane, Erdington ℰ 373 5805
MAZDA 29-33 Kings Rd, New Oscott ℰ 354 6781
PEUGEOT-TALBOT Newport Rd, Castle Bromwich ℰ 747 4712

SAAB Eachelhurst Rd, Erdington ℰ 351 1027
VAUXHALL 364 Chester Rd, Castle Bromwich ℰ 749 2222

🅰 ATS 158 Slade Rd, Erdington ℰ 327 2783/4
ATS 1189 Chester Rd ℰ 373 6104

at Castle Bromwich NE : 6 m. by A 47 – ✉ ☎ 021 Birmingham :

🏛 **Bradford Arms Motel**, Chester Rd, B36 0AG, ℰ 747 0227 – 📺 ☎ ℗ – **29 rm**. p. 5 **HV** a

MITSUBISHI, SEAT 127 Chester Rd ℰ 353 3191
RENAULT 62 Chester Rd North ℰ 352 0022

VAUXHALL Lichfield Rd ℰ 308 8282
VW, AUDI 45-51 Kings Rd ℰ 355 1261

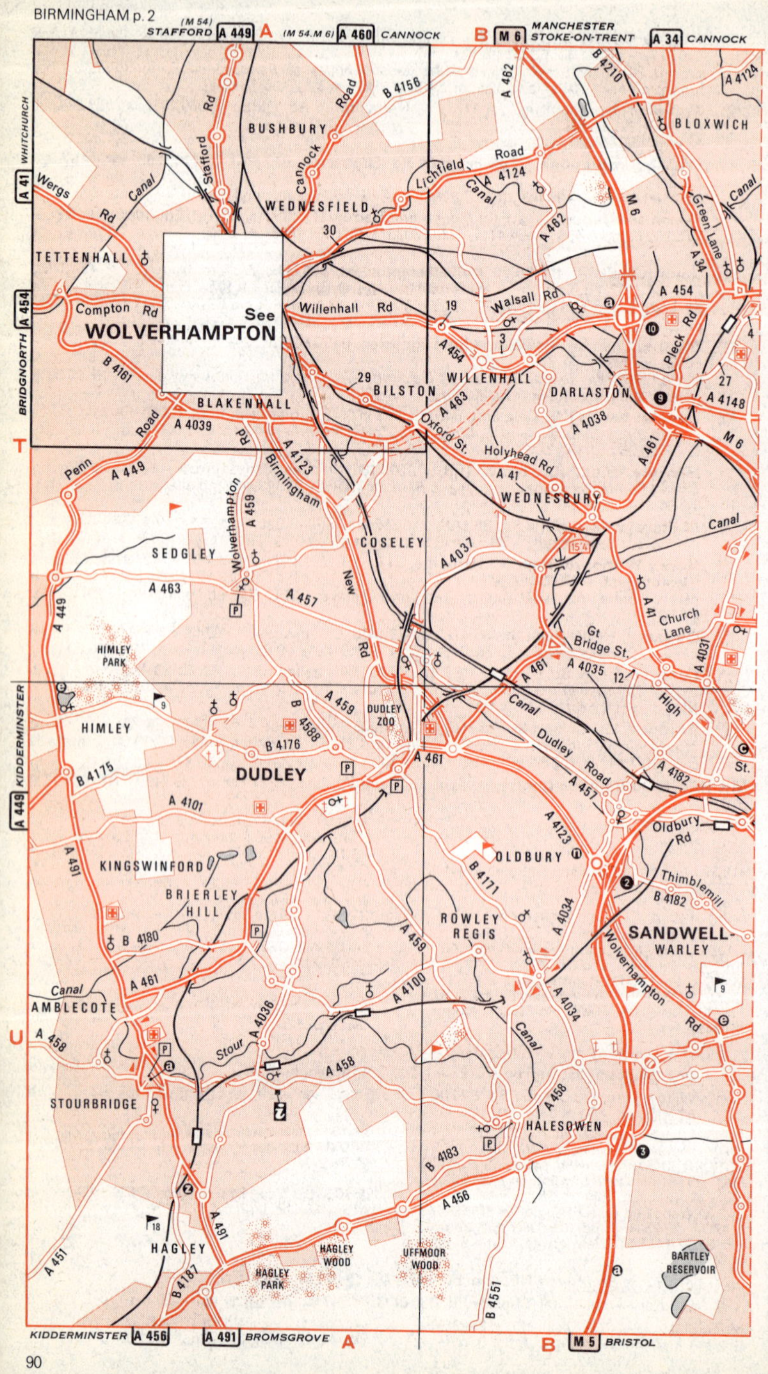
STAFFORD A 449 A (M 54) (M 54.M 6) A 460 CANNOCK B M 6 MANCHESTER STOKE-ON-TRENT A 34 CANNOCK
B 4210
A 4124
BLOXWICH
WHITCHURCH
A 41
Wergs
Rd
Stafford Rd
Cannock Rd
Canal
BUSHBURY
B 4156
A 462
A 4124
Lichfield Road
Canal
M 6
Green Lane
A 34
Canal
WEDNESFIELD
30
A 462
TETTENHALL
See
WOLVERHAMPTON
Compton Rd
Willenhall Rd
19
Walsall Rd
A 454
Pleck Rd
10
A 41
A 454
BRIDGNORTH A 454
B 4161
Willenhall Rd
3
WILLENHALL
DARLASTON
A 4038
27
A 4148
9
M 6
BLAKENHALL
29
BILSTON
A 463
Oxford St.
A 461
A 4039
Penn
A 449
Birmingham Rd
A 4123
Holyhead Rd
A 41
WEDNESBURY
T
Wolverhampton Rd
A 459
COSELEY
New Rd
A 4037
15¾
Canal
SEDGLEY
A 463
A 457
P
Gt Bridge St.
A 41
Church Lane
A 4031
HIMLEY PARK
9
A 459
B 4588
DUDLEY ZOO
A 461
Canal
Dudley Road
A 4035
12
High St.
HIMLEY
B 4176
DUDLEY
P
A 4182
B 4175
A 4101
P
A 461
A 457
A 4123
Oldbury Rd
KIDDERMINSTER A 449
KINGSWINFORD
A 459
OLDBURY
B 4171
A 4034
SANDWELL-WARLEY
Thimblemill
B 4182
2
A 491
BRIERLEY HILL
B 4180
ROWLEY REGIS
A 4034
Wolverhampton Rd
9
A 461
A 4100
Canal
AMBLECOTE
A 4036
A 458
Stour
A 458
A 458
STOURBRIDGE
U
HALESOWEN
P
3
18
A 491
B 4183
HAGLEY
A 456
HAGLEY WOOD
UFFMOOR WOOD
BARTLEY RESERVOIR
A 451
B 4187
HAGLEY PARK
B 4551
KIDDERMINSTER A 456 A 491 BROMSGROVE A B M 5 BRISTOL

BIRMINGHAM AND WOLVERHAMPTON
ENLARGED AREA

Bilston Road . . . . **BT** 3
Bradford Street . . . **BT** 4
Bridge Street . . . . . . **CT** 5
Cape Hill . . . . **CU** 6
Dudley Road . . . . . . **CU** 8
Dudley Street . . . . . . **BT** 12
Harborne Park Rd . . **CU** 14
New Road . . . . **BT** 19
North High Street . . **DT** 21
Wednesbury Road . **BT** 27
Wellington Road . . . **AT** 29
Wolverhampton Rd **AT** 30

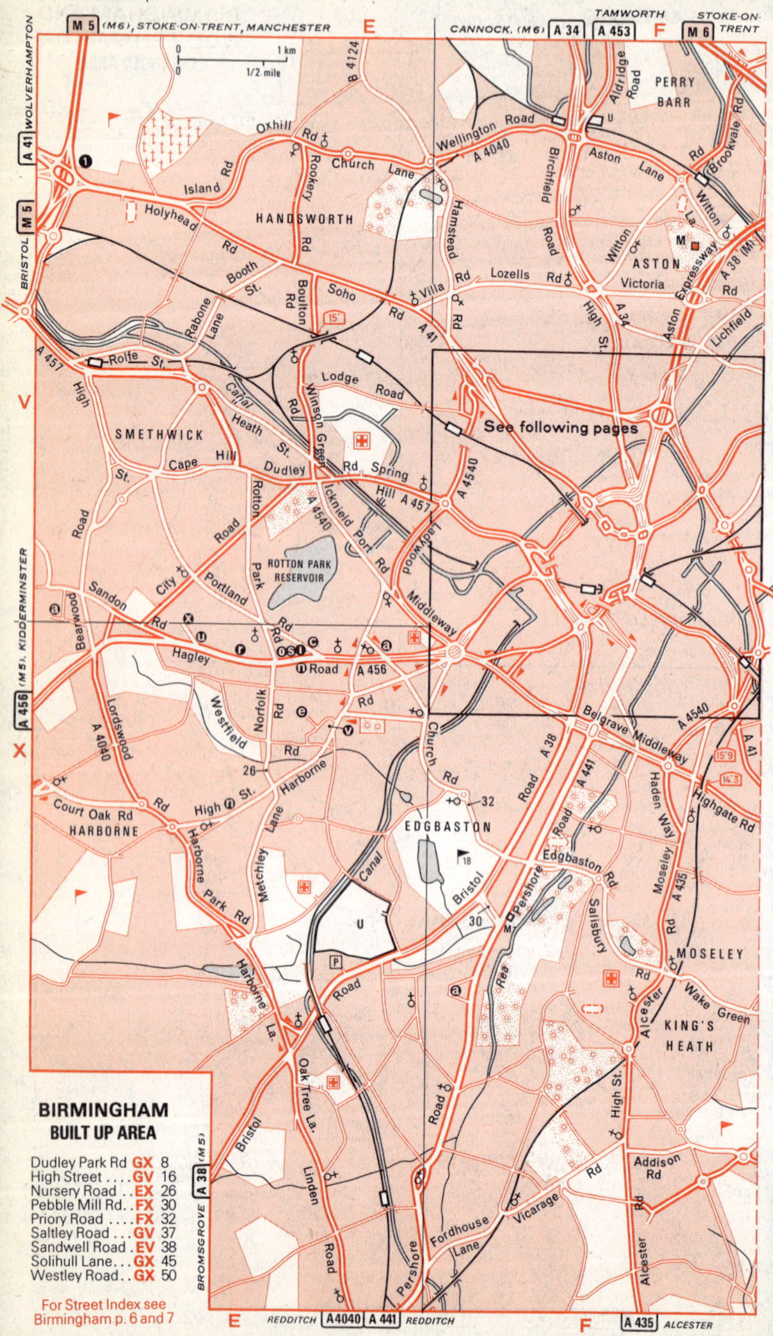

M 5 (M6), STOKE-ON-TRENT, MANCHESTER
E
CANNOCK, (M6) A 34
TAMWORTH A 453
F
M 6 STOKE-ON-TRENT
0 1 km
0 1/2 mile
B 4124
Oxhill Rd
Rookery Rd
Church Lane
Wellington Road
A 4040
Aldridge Road
PERRY BARR
Brookvale Rd
Birchfield Road
Aston Lane
Witton Rd
Island Rd
Holyhead Rd
HANDSWORTH
Hamstead Rd
Witton La.
ASTON
Expressway
A 38 (M)
Booth St.
Boulton Rd
Soho Rd
Villa Rd
Lozells Rd
Victoria Rd
High St.
A 34
Aston
Lichfield
A 41
Rabone Lane
A 457
Rolfe St.
High St.
Lodge Road
Winson Green Rd
Canal
Heath St.
SMETHWICK
See following pages
Cape Hill
Dudley Rd
Spring Hill A 457
A 4540
St. Rd
Rotton Road
A 4540
Icknield Port Rd
Ladywood
ROTTON PARK RESERVOIR
Park
City Rd
Portland Rd
Sandon Rd
Bearwood Rd
Middleway
Hagley Road
A 456
Westfield Rd
Norfolk Rd
Church Rd
Belgrave Middleway
A 4540
A 41
A 38
Lordswood Rd
A 4040
26
Harborne Rd
Court Oak Rd
HARBORNE
High St.
Metchley Lane
32
EDGBASTON
Road
A 441
Haden Way
Highgate Rd
Edgbaston Rd
Moseley Rd
A 435
Canal
Bristol
18
Pershore Road
Harborne Park Rd
U
30
Salisbury
MOSELEY
Rea
Harborne La.
P
Road
Rd
Alcester
Wake Green
KING'S HEATH
Oak Tree La.
Bristol
Road
High St.
Addison Rd
Rd
Linden Road
Vicarage Rd
Fordhouse Lane
Pershore
Alcester Rd
A 41 WOLVERHAMPTON
M 5 BRISTOL
A 456 (M5), KIDDERMINSTER
V
X
BROMSGROVE A 38 (M5)
E
REDDITCH A4040 A 441 REDDITCH
F
A 435 ALCESTER
BIRMINGHAM
BUILT UP AREA
Dudley Park Rd GX 8
High Street . . . . GV 16
Nursery Road . . EX 26
Pebble Mill Rd. . FX 30
Priory Road . . . . FX 32
Saltley Road . . . GV 37
Sandwell Road . EV 38
Solihull Lane. . . GX 45
Westley Road . . GX 50
For Street Index see Birmingham p. 6 and 7

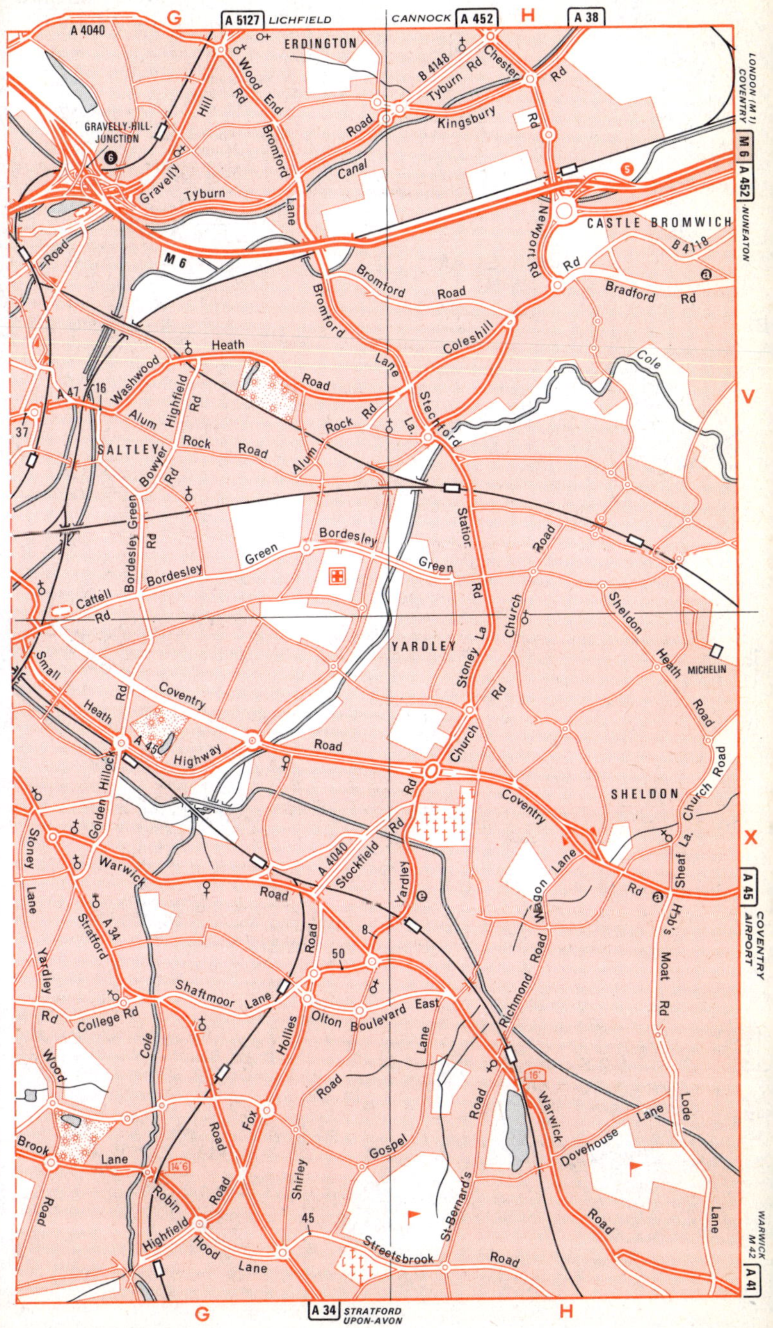
A 4040
G
A 5127 LICHFIELD
CANNOCK A 452
H
A 38
ERDINGTON
B 4148
Tyburn Rd
Chester
Rd
Kingsbury
Rd
LONDON (M 1)
COVENTRY
Wood End
Road
Hill
Bromford
Lane
M 6
A 452
5
Newport Rd
CASTLE BROMWICH
B 4118
GRAVELLY HILL JUNCTION
6
Gravelly
Tyburn
Canal
Bromford
Road
Rd
Bradford
Rd
Road
M 6
Bromford
Lane
Coleshill
Cole
V
Heath
Road
Stechford
A 47
16
Washwood
Highfield
Rd
Rock
Rd
La.
37
Alum
Rock
Road
Alum
Station
Road
SALTLEY
Bowyer
Rd
Bordesley
Green
Rd
Green
Green
Sheldon
Bordesley
Bordesley
Station
Rd
Church
Heath
Cattell
Rd
YARDLEY
Stoney La.
Church Rd
MICHELIN
Road
Small
Heath
Rd
Coventry
Church
SHELDON
A 45
Highway
Road
Coventry
Golden Hillock
Sheaf La.
Church Road
X
A 45
COVENTRY
AIRPORT
Stoney
Lane
Warwick
A 4040
Stockfield
Yardley
Wagon Lane
Rd
Hob's
Rd
Moat
Rd
A 34
Stratford
Road
Road
8
50
Shaftmoor Lane
Olton Boulevard East
Yardley
Lane
Richmond Road
16
Warwick
Lode
Lane
Yardley
Rd
College Rd
Cole
Hollies
Road
Road
Warwick
Dovehouse
Lane
Road
Wood
Fox
Gospel
St. Bernard's Road
WARWICK
M 42
Brook
Lane
14'6
Shirley
Road
A 41
Robin
Highfield
Hood
Lane
45
Streetsbrook
Road
G
A 34 STRATFORD UPON-AVON
H

Bull Ring Centre .... p. 6 **KZ**
Corporation St. .... p. 6 **KY**
Fiveways'
  Shopping Centre ...... p. 6 **JZ**
New St. .... p. 6 **KZ**

Adderley St. ... p. 7 **LZ**
Addison Rd ... p. 4 **FX**
Albert St. ... p. 6 **KZ**
Alcester Rd ... p. 4 **FX**
Alcester St. ... p. 7 **LZ**
Aldridge Rd ... p. 4 **FV**
Alum Rock Rd ... p. 5 **GV**

Aston Expressway ..... p. 4 **FV**
Aston Lane ... p. 4 **FV**
Aston St. ... p. 6 **KY**
Avenue Rd ... p. 7 **LY**
Bagot St. ... p. 6 **KY**
Bath Row ... p. 6 **JZ**
Bearwood Rd. ... p. 4 **EV**
Belgrave Middleway ... p. 4 **FX**
Bell Barn Rd. ... p. 6 **JZ**
Birchfield Rd ... p. 4 **FV**
Bishopsgate St. ... p. 6 **JZ** 2
Booth St. ... p. 4 **EV**
Bordesley Green ...... p. 5 **GV**

Bordesley Green Rd .... p. 5 **GV**
Boulton Rd ... p. 4 **EV**
Bowyer Rd ... p. 5 **GV**
Bradford Rd ... p. 5 **HV**
Bradford St. ... p. 6 **KZ**
Bristol Rd ... p. 4 **EX**
Bristol St. ... p. 6 **JZ**
Broad St. ... p. 6 **JZ**
Bromford Lane ... p. 5 **GV**
Bromford Rd ... p. 5 **HV**
Bromsgrove St. ... p. 6 **KZ**
Brook Lane ... p. 6 **GX**
Brook St. ... p. 6 **JY** 3

BIRMINGHAM
CENTRE

0 400 m
0 400 yards

A 4540

Hockley Circus
Hockley Hill
Heaton St.
Street
Lodge Rd
Icknield
Warstone
Camden
BROOKFIELDS
Summer Hill
Rd
St. Vincent St.
Sand Pits Parade
Summer
Cambridge St.
Hill St.
Sheepcote
Great King Ter.
New John Street
Great Hampton Street
Vyse St.
Caroline St.
George St.
Hall St.
Newhall
Canal
Constitution Hill
Livery Street
Great Charles St.
Colmore Row
Great Charles St.

Hospital St.
Summer Lane
New Town Row
Summer Lane West
Lancaster St.
Bagot St.
Corporation St.
Elkington St.
Aston Rd
Dartmouth
Lister St.
James Watt
Aston St.
Jennen's Rd

St. Chads
Queensway
Steelhouse La.
POL.
POL.

Cambridge St.
Suffolk St.
Granville St.
Broad Street
Holliday St.
Holloway Head
Fair St.
Horse Fair
New St.
Albert St.
Fazeley St.
Corporation St.

NEW STREET STATION
BULL RING CENTRE
MOOR STREET STATION
Digbeth
Bradford St.
Cheapside

Ladywood Middleway
Islington Middleway
Bath Row
Bell
Great Barn St.
Colmore St.
Holloway Head
Wrentham St.
Bromsgrove St.
Macdonald Street
Alcester St.

Calthorpe Rd
James's Road
Canal
Lee Bank Middleway
A 4540
Rickman Drive
Bristol St.
Sherlock St.
Gooch St.
A 441

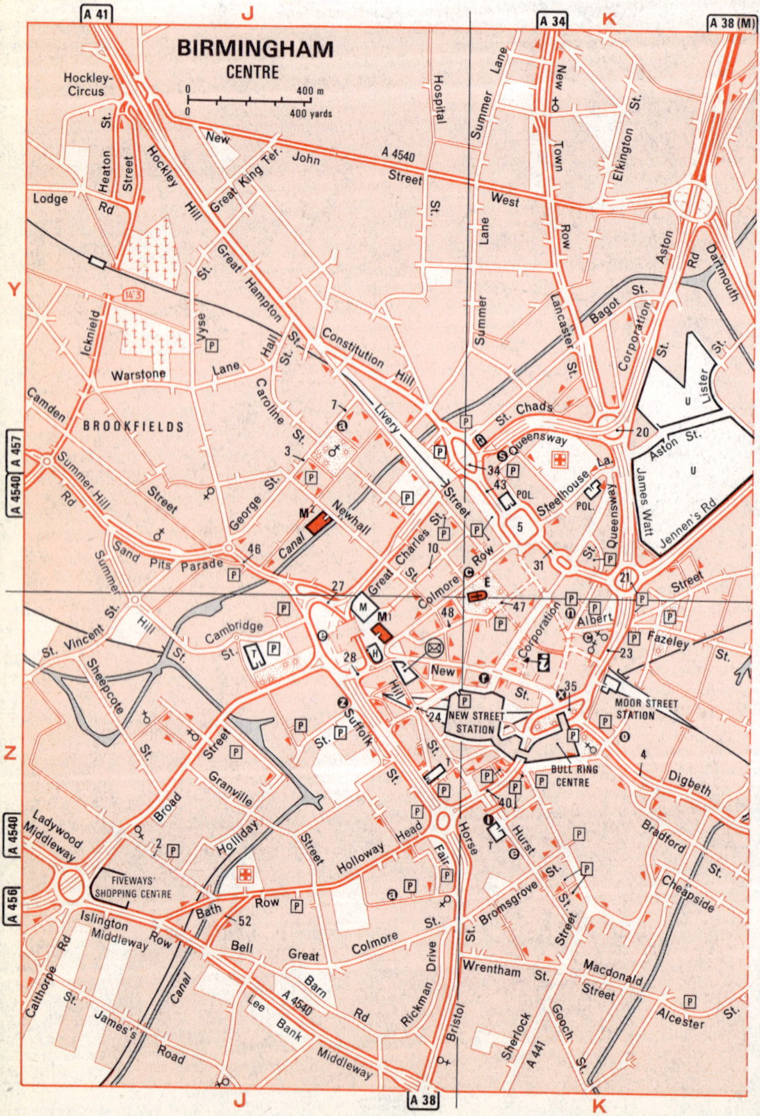

Brookvale Rd . . . . p. 4 **FV**
Bull Ring . . . . p. 6 **KZ** 4
Bull Ring Centre . . . . p. 6 **KZ**
Calthorpe Rd . . . . p. 6 **JZ**
Cambridge St . . . . p. 6 **JZ**
Camden St . . . . p. 6 **JY**
Camp Hill . . . . p. 7 **LZ**
Cape Hill . . . . p. 4 **EV**
Caroline St . . . . p. 6 **JY**
Cattell Rd . . . . p. 5 **GV**
Cheapside . . . . p. 6 **KZ**
Chester St . . . . p. 7 **LY**
Church Lane . . . . p. 4 **EV**

Church Rd
  EDGBASTON . . . . . . p. 4 **FX**
Church Rd SHELDON . p. 5 **HX**
Church Rd YARDLEY . p. 5 **HX**
City Rd . . . . p. 4 **EV**
Coleshill Rd . . . . p. 5 **HV**
College Rd . . . . p. 5 **GX**
Colmore Circus . . . . p. 6 **KY** 5
Colmore Row . . . . p. 6 **JY**
Constitution Hill . . . . p. 6 **JY**
Corporation St . . . . p. 6 **KZ**
Court Oak Rd . . . . p. 4 **EX**
Coventry Rd . . . . p. 7 **LZ** 6
Cox St . . . . p. 6 **JY** 7
Curzon St . . . . p. 7 **LY**
Dartmouth Middleway p. 6 **KY**
Digbeth . . . . p. 6 **KZ**
Dovehouse Lane . . . . p. 5 **HX**
Dudley Park Rd . . . . p. 5 **GX** 8
Dudley Rd . . . . p. 4 **EV**
Edgbaston Rd . . . . p. 4 **FX**
Edmund St . . . . p. 6 **JY** 10
Elkington St . . . . p. 6 **KY**
Fazeley St . . . . p. 6 **KZ**
Fiveways' Shopping
  Centre . . . . p. 6 **JZ**
Fordhouse Lane . . . . p. 4 **FX**
Fox Hollies Rd . . . . p. 5 **GX**
George St . . . . p. 6 **JY**
Golden Hillock Rd . . . . . p. 5 **GX**
Gooch St . . . . p. 6 **KZ**
Gospel Lane . . . . p. 5 **HX**
Granville St . . . . p. 6 **JZ**
Gravelly Hill . . . . p. 5 **GV**
Gravelly Hill Junction . p. 5 **GV**
Great Barr St . . . . p. 7 **LZ**
Great Charles St . . . . . p. 6 **JY**
Great Colmore St . . . . p. 6 **JZ**
Great Hampton St . . . . . p. 6 **JY**
Great King Ter . . . . p. 6 **JY**
Great Lister St . . . . p. 7 **LY**
Hagley Rd . . . . p. 4 **EX**
Hall St . . . . p. 6 **JY**
Hampstead Rd . . . . p. 4 **FV**
Harborne Lane . . . . p. 4 **EX**
Harborne Park Rd . . . p. 4 **EX**
Harborne Rd . . . . p. 4 **EX**
Heath Mill Lane . . . . . . p. 7 **LZ**
Heath St . . . . p. 4 **EV**
Heaton St . . . . p. 6 **JY**
Highfield Rd . . . . p. 5 **GX**
Highfield Rd . . . . p. 5 **GV**
Highgate Rd . . . . p. 4 **FX**
High St. ASTON . . . . . . p. 4 **FV**
High St. BORDESLEY . p. 7 **LZ** 14
High St. DERITEND . . p. 7 **LZ**
High St. HARBORNE . . p. 4 **EX**
High St. KING'S
  HEATH . . . . p. 4 **FX**
High St. SALTLEY . . . . p. 5 **GV** 16
High St. SMETHWICK . p. 4 **EV**
Hill St . . . . p. 6 **JZ**
Hob's Moat Rd . . . . p. 5 **HX**
Hockley Circus . . . . p. 6 **JY**
Hockley Hill . . . . p. 6 **JY**
Holliday St . . . . p. 6 **JZ** 18
Holloway Head . . . . p. 6 **JZ**
Holyhead Rd . . . . p. 4 **EV**
Horse Fair . . . . p. 6 **JZ**
Hospital St . . . . p. 6 **JY**
Hurst St . . . . p. 6 **KZ**
Icknield Port Rd . . . . . . p. 4 **EV**
Icknield St . . . . p. 6 **JY**
Island Rd . . . . p. 4 **EV**
Islington Row
  Middleway . . . . p. 6 **JZ**
James Watt
  Queensway . . . . p. 6 **KY**
Jennen's Rd . . . . p. 6 **KY**
Kingsbury Rd . . . . p. 5 **HV**
Ladywood Middleway p. 4 **EV**
Lancaster Circus . . . . . p. 6 **KY** 20
Lancaster St . . . . p. 6 **KY**
Lawley St . . . . p. 7 **LY**
Lee Bank Middleway . p. 6 **JZ**
Lichfield Rd . . . . p. 4 **FV**
Linden Rd . . . . p. 4 **EX**
Lister St . . . . p. 6 **KY**
Livery St . . . . p. 6 **JY**
Lode Lane . . . . p. 5 **HX**
Lodge Rd . . . . p. 4 **EV**
Lordswood Rd . . . . p. 4 **EX**
Lozells Rd . . . . p. 4 **FV**

Macdonald St . . . . p. 6 **KZ**
Masshouse Circus . . . . p. 6 **KY** 21
Metchley Lane . . . . p. 4 **EX**
Moor St. Queensway . p. 6 **KZ** 23
Moseley Rd . . . . p. 4 **FX**
Navigation St . . . . p. 6 **JZ** 24
Nechell's Parkway . . . . p. 7 **LY**
Newhall St . . . . p. 6 **JY**
New John St. West . . . p. 6 **JY**
Newport Rd . . . . p. 5 **HV**
New St . . . . p. 6 **JZ**
New Town Row . . . . . . p. 6 **KY**
Norfolk Rd . . . . p. 4 **EX**
Nursery Rd . . . . p. 4 **EX** 26
Oak Tree Lane . . . . p. 4 **EX**
Olton Bd East . . . . p. 5 **GX**
Oxhill Rd . . . . p. 4 **EV**
Paradise Circus . . . . . . p. 6 **JY** 27
Paradise St . . . . p. 6 **JZ** 28
Pebble Mill Rd . . . . p. 4 **FX** 30
Pershore Rd . . . . p. 4 **FX**
Portland Rd . . . . p. 4 **EV**
Priory Queensway . . . . p. 6 **KY** 31
Priory Rd . . . . p. 4 **FX** 32
Rabone Lane . . . . p. 4 **EV**
Richmond Rd . . . . p. 5 **HX**
Rickman Drive . . . . p. 6 **JZ**
Robin Hood Lane . . . . . p. 5 **GX**
Rolfe St . . . . p. 4 **EV**
Rookery Rd . . . . p. 4 **EV**
Rotton Park Rd . . . . p. 4 **EV**
St. Bernard's Rd . . . . . p. 5 **HX**
St. Chads Circus . . . . . . p. 6 **KY** 34
St. Chads Ringway . . . p. 6 **KY**
St. James's Rd . . . . p. 6 **JZ**
St. Martin's Circus . . . . p. 6 **KZ** 35
St. Vincent St . . . . p. 6 **JZ**
Salisbury Rd . . . . p. 4 **FX**
Saltley Rd . . . . p. 5 **GV** 37
Sandon Rd . . . . p. 4 **EV**
Sand Pits Parade . . . . . p. 6 **JY**
Sandy Lane . . . . p. 7 **LZ**
Shaftmoor Lane . . . . . . p. 5 **GX**
Sheaf Lane . . . . p. 5 **HX**
Sheepcote St . . . . p. 6 **JZ**
Sheldon Heath Rd . . . . p. 5 **HX**
Sherlock St . . . . p. 6 **KZ**
Shirley Rd . . . . p. 5 **GX**
Smallbrook
  Queensway . . . . p. 6 **KZ** 40
Small Heath Highway . p. 5 **GX**
Snow Hill Queensway . p. 6 **KY** 43
Soho Rd . . . . p. 4 **EV**
Solihull Lane . . . . p. 5 **GX** 45
Spring Hill . . . . p. 4 **EV**
Station Rd . . . . p. 5 **HV**
Stechford Lane . . . . p. 5 **HV**
Steelhouse Lane . . . . . p. 6 **KY**
Stockfield Rd . . . . p. 5 **GX**
Stoney La. MOSELEY . p. 5 **GX**
Stoney La. SHELDON . p. 5 **HX**
Stratford Pl . . . . p. 7 **LZ**
Stratford Rd . . . . p. 5 **GX**
Streetsbrook Rd . . . . . . p. 5 **HX**
Suffolk St . . . . p. 6 **JZ**
Summer Hill Rd, St . . . p. 6 **JY**
Summer Lane . . . . p. 6 **KY**
Summer Row . . . . p. 6 **JY** 46
Temple Row . . . . p. 6 **KZ** 47
Tyburn Rd . . . . p. 5 **GV**
Vauxhall Rd . . . . p. 7 **LY**
Vicarage Rd . . . . p. 4 **FX**
Victoria Rd . . . . p. 4 **FV**
Villa Rd . . . . p. 4 **FV**
Vyse St . . . . p. 6 **JY**
Wagon Lane . . . . p. 5 **HX**
Wake Green Rd . . . . . . p. 4 **FX**
Warstone Lane . . . . p. 6 **JY**
Warwick Rd . . . . p. 5 **GX**
Washwood Heath Rd . p. 5 **GV**
Waterloo St . . . . p. 6 **JZ** 48
Watery Lane . . . . p. 7 **LZ**
Wellington Rd . . . . p. 4 **FV**
Westfield Rd . . . . p. 4 **EX**
Westley Rd . . . . p. 5 **GX** 50
Wheeley's Lane . . . . . . p. 6 **JZ** 52
Winson Green Rd . . . . . p. 4 **EV**
Witton Lane . . . . p. 4 **FV**
Witton Rd . . . . p. 4 **FV**
Wood End Rd . . . . p. 5 **GV**
Wrentham St . . . . p. 6 **KZ**
Yardley Rd . . . . p. 5 **HX**
Yardley Wood Rd . . . . . p. 5 **GX**

at *Acocks Green* SE : 4 ½ m. on B 4146 – DU – ✉ ☎ 021 Birmingham :

⋔ **Atholl Lodge,** 16 Elmdon Rd, off Yardley Rd, B27 6LH, ℰ 707 4417, ☞ – ℗. ✗ HX **e**
M (by arrangement) 8.00 **st.** – **10 rm** ⊄ 15.00/34.00 **st.**

ALFA-ROMEO 683 Stratford Rd, Sparkhill ℰ 778 1295
AUSTIN-ROVER 884 Warwick Rd ℰ 765 4488
DAIHATSU, SKODA 266 Vicarage Rd, Kings Heath ℰ 444 3195
FIAT, LANCIA, LOTUS 979 Stratford Rd, Hall Green ℰ 778 2323
FSO 438 Stratford Rd, Sparkhill ℰ 773 8646

LADA, RELIANT 723-725 Stratford Rd, Sparkhill ℰ 777 6164
MAZDA 32-38 Coventry Rd, Bordesley ℰ 772 5916
RENAULT High St., Bordesley ℰ 773 8251
VAUXHALL 291 Shaftmoor Lane, Hall Green ℰ 777 1074
VAUXHALL-OPEL 870 Stratford Rd, Sparkhill ℰ 702 2345

at *Sheldon* SE : 6 m. on A 45 – HX – ✉ ☎ 021 Birmingham :

🏨 **Wheatsheaf,** 2225 Coventry Rd, B26 3EH, ℰ 742 6201 – 📺 ☎ ℗ – ⛱ p. 5 HX **a**
86 rm.

CITROEN The Radleys ℰ 742 1142

at *Birmingham Airport* SE : 7 m. on A 45 – DU – ✉ ☎ 021 Birmingham :

🏨 **Excelsior** (T.H.F.), Coventry Rd, Elmdon, B26 3QW, ℰ 782 8141, Telex 338005, Fax 782 2476
– ⇤ rm 📺 ☎ ℗ – ⛱ 170. ◪ AE ⓞ VISA
M 10.00/15.00 **st.** and a la carte ⓵ 4.75 – ⊄ 7.00 – **138 rm** 65.00/75.00 **st.**, **3 suites** –
SB (weekends only) 56.00/76.00 **st.**

at *National Exhibition Centre* SE : 9 ½ m. on A 45 – DU – ✉ ☎ 021 Birmingham :

🏨 **Birmingham Metropole,** Bickenhill, B40 1PP, ℰ 780 4242, Telex 336129, Fax 780 3923, ≼,
squash – 🛗 ▤ 📺 ☎ ℗ – ⛱ 1 800. ◪ AE ⓞ VISA
M 15.95 **t.** and a la carte – ⊄ 7.95 – **485 rm** 80.00/120.00 **t.**, **9 suites** 240.00/315.00 **t.** –
SB (weekends only) 86.00 **st.**

🏨 Arden, Coventry Rd, Bickenhill ✉ Solihull, B92 0EH, ℰ 067 55 (Hampton-in-Arden) 3221,
Telex 334913, ◪ – 🛗 📺 ☎ ♿ ℗ – ⛱
76 rm.

at *King's Norton* S : 8 ½ m. by A 435 – FX – ✉ ☎ 021 Birmingham :

XXX **Lombard Room** (at The Patrick Collection), 180 Lifford Lane, B30 3NT, ℰ 451 3991, Fax
433 3048, « Collection of classic motor cars », ☞ – ⇤ ℗. ◪ AE ⓞ VISA
M 13.50/19.50 **st.** and a la carte 19.20/25.85 **st.** ⓵ 4.50.

at *Northfield* SW : 6 m. by A 38 – CU – ✉ ☎ 021 Birmingham :

⋔ **Norwood,** 87-89 Bunbury Rd, B31 2ET, ℰ 411 2202, ☞ – 📺 ☎ ℗. ◪ VISA
M (by arrangement) 15.00 **st.** ⓵ 3.25 – **17 rm** ⊄ 25.75/75.00 **st.** – SB (weekends
only) (except Christmas) 65.00 **st.**

CITROEN Hallam St., Balsall Heath, Kings Heath ℰ 440 4606/523 3421
FORD 82 St. Mary's Row, Moseley, Kings Heath ℰ 442 4000
NISSAN 57 Walkers Heath Rd ℰ 451 1411

SKODA 307 Northfield Rd, Harborne, Kings Heath ℰ 427 4050
VAUXHALL Ryland St., Edgbaston, Kings Heath ℰ 455 7171

at *Frankley Service Station* SW : 8 ¾ m. by A 456 on M 5 (Southbound carriageway) –
✉ ☎ 021 Birmingham :

🏨 Granada Lodge without rest., B32 4AR, ℰ 550 3261, Fax 501 2880 – 📺 ♿ ℗ BU **a**
41 rm.

at *Smethwick* W : 3 ½ m. by A 456 – ✉ ☎ 021 Birmingham :

✕ **Franzl's,** 151 Milcote Rd, Bearwood, B67 5BN, ℰ 429 7920, Austrian rest. – ◪ VISA
closed Sunday, Monday, first 3 weeks August and last week December – **M** (dinner only)
a la carte 12.00/15.00 **t.** ⓵ 3.75. p. 4 EV **a**

at *West Bromwich* NW : 6 m. on A 41 – ✉ West Bromwich – ☎ 021 Birmingham :

🏨 West Bromwich Moat House (Q.M.H.) Birmingham Rd, B70 6RS, W : 1 m. by A 41 ℰ
553 6111, Telex 336232, Fax 525 7403 – 🛗 ▤ rest 📺 ☎ ℗ – ⛱ BU **c**
181 rm.

AUSTIN-ROVER High St. ℰ 553 0778
FERRARI, FIAT Birmingham Rd ℰ 525 9408
FORD 377 High St. ℰ 553 1881

VAUXHALL-OPEL Spon Lane ℰ 553 3777
VOLVO 127 Hill Top ℰ 502 3802

at *Great Barr* NW : 6 m. on A 34 – ✉ Great Barr – ☎ 021 Birmingham :

🏨 **Post House** (T.H.F.), Chapel Lane, B43 7BG, ℰ 357 7444, Telex 338497, Fax 357 7503,
⊒ heated – ⇤ rm 📺 ☎ ℗ – ⛱ 150. ◪ AE ⓞ VISA CT **x**
M 10.00/15.00 **st.** and a la carte ⓵ 4.00 – ⊄ 7.00 – **204 rm** 60.00/140.00 **st.** – SB (weekends only) 60.00/160.00 **st.**

🏨 **Great Barr,** Pear Tree Drive, Newton Rd, B43 6HS, W : 1 m. by A 4041 ℰ 357 1141, Telex
336406, Fax 357 7557, ☞ – 📺 ☎ ℗ – ⛱ 120. ◪ AE ⓞ VISA ✗ CT **z**
M 8.50/12.50 **t.** and a la carte – **114 rm** ⊄ 59.00/69.00 **t.**

🅐 ATS 94 Aldrige Rd, Perry Barr ℰ 356 5925/6632

BISHOP AUCKLAND Durham 401 402 P 20 – pop. 23 560 – ECD : Wednesday – ✪ 0388.
♦London 253 – ♦Carlisle 73 – ♦Middlesbrough 24 – ♦Newcastle-upon-Tyne 28 – Sunderland 25.

🏠 **Park Head,** New Coundon, DL14 8QT, NE : 1 ¾ m. by A 689 on A 688 ℰ 661727 – 📺 ☎
ℙ. 🔄 AE ① VISA
M 10.70/21.40 **t.** and a la carte ⧍ 3.25 – **15 rm** 28.00/42.00 **t.** – SB (weekends only) 50.00 **st.**

ARG Tindale Cres. ℰ 604481
DAIHATSU Station Rd ℰ 832184
FORD St Helens ℰ 605184

RENAULT Holdforth Crest ℰ 602703

⓪ ATS Cockton Hill ℰ 603681

BISHOP'S CASTLE Shropshire 403 L 26 – pop. 1 810 – ✪ 0588.
♦London 182 – ♦Birmingham 71 – Shrewsbury 24.

🏯 Castle, Market Sq., SY9 5BN, ℰ 638403, 🚗 – 📺 ℙ
8 rm.

BISHOP'S HULL Somerset – see Taunton.

BISHOP'S STORTFORD Herts. 404 U 28 – pop. 22 535 – ECD : Wednesday – ✪ 0279.
🏌 Dunmow Rd ℰ 654715, W : 1 m. on A 1250.
✈ Stansted Airport : ℰ 502380, Telex 81102, NE : 3 ½ m.
🛈 2 The Causeway ℰ 655261.
♦London 34 – ♦Cambridge 27 – Chelmsford 19 – Colchester 33.

✗ **Michael Man,** 88 South St., CM23 3PG, ℰ 505799, Chinese rest. – 🔄 AE ① VISA
M 17.00/18.00 **st.** and a la carte 7.20/8.50 **st.** ⧍ 2.50.

at Hatfield Heath SE : 6 m. on A 1060 – ✉ ✪ 0279 Bishop's Stortford :

🏰 **Down Hall Country House** ⚓, CM22 7AS, S : 1 ½ m. ℰ 731441, Telex 681609, Fax
730416, ≤, « 19C Italianate mansion », ⧐ heated, 🚗, park, ✗ – 📺 ☎ ℙ – 🅰 100. 🔄 AE
① VISA
M 14.50/16.00 **st.** and a la carte – **45 rm** ⊇ 75.00/130.00 **st.** – SB 95.00/120.00 **st.**

AUSTIN-ROVER 123-129 South St. ℰ 757777
CITROEN Dunmow Rd ℰ 654335
DAIHATSU, LANCIA London Rd ℰ 654181
FORD London Rd ℰ 652214
PEUGEOT-TALBOT 26 Northgate End ℰ 653494

RENAULT,VAUXHALL Northgate End ℰ 653127
VAUXHALL-OPEL, VOLVO Stansted Rd ℰ 652304
VW, AUDI Dane St. ℰ 654680

⓪ ATS 14 Burnt Mill, Harlow ℰ 21965

BISHOP'S TAWTON Devon 403 H 30 – see Barnstaple.

BLACKBURN Lancs. 402 M 22 – pop. 109 564 – ECD : Thursday – ✪ 0254.
🏌 Beardwood Brow, ℰ 51122, NW : 1 ¼ m. by A 677.
🛈 Tower Block, Town Hall ℰ 55201 and 53277 ext 214.
♦London 228 – ♦Leeds 47 – ♦Liverpool 39 – ♦Manchester 24 – Preston 11.

🏰 **Blackburn Moat House** (Q.M.H.), Yew Tree Drive, Preston New Rd, BB2 7BE, NW : 2 m.
at junction A 677 and A 6119 ℰ 64441, Telex 63271, Fax 682435 – ▐ ↦ rm 📺 ☎ ℙ
– 🅰 350. 🔄 AE ① VISA
M *(closed Saturday lunch)* 8.45/11.45 **st.** and a la carte ⧍ 4.25 – **96 rm** ⊇ 56.00/72.00 **st.**,
2 suites 72.00/82.00 **st.** – SB (weekends only) 63.00 **st.**

at Mellor NW : 4 m. by A 677 – ✉ Blackburn – ✪ 025 481 Mellor :

🏠 **Millstone,** Church Lane, BB2 7JR, ℰ 3333 – ↦ rm 📺 ☎ ℙ – 🅰 . 🔄 AE ① VISA
M *(closed Saturday lunch)* 7.95/17.90 **t.** and a la carte ⧍ 3.95 – **18 rm** ⊇ 44.00/59.00 **st.**,
1 suite 90.00/100.00 **st.** – SB (weekends only) 70.00/76.00 **st.**

AUSTIN-ROVER, DAIMLER-JAGUAR Park Rd ℰ
662721
FIAT 52-56 King St. ℰ 52981
FORD Montague St. ℰ 57021
PEUGEOT, TALBOT Whalley New Rd ℰ 661616
RENAULT Gt. Harwood ℰ 886590
TOYOTA Accrington Rd ℰ 57333

VAUXHALL Quarry St., Eanam ℰ 51191
VAUXHALL-OPEL Montague St. ℰ 53885
VW, AUDI 854 Whalley New Rd ℰ 40621

⓪ ATS Bancroft St., Eanam. ℰ 55963/59272/
665115

BLACKPOOL Lancs. 402 K 22 – pop. 146 297 – ECD : Wednesday – ✪ 0253.
See : Illuminations✶✶ (late September and early October) – Tower✶ (❊✶) *AC* AY **A.**
🏌 Blackpool North Shore, Devonshire Rd ℰ 52054, N : 1 ½ m. from main station BY – 🏌
Blackpool-Stanley Park, North Park Drive, ℰ 33960, E : 1 ½ m. BY – 🏌 Poulton-le-Fylde, Myrtle
Farm, Breck Rd ℰ 0253 (Poulton) 893150, E : 3 m. by A 586 BY.
✈ Blackpool Airport : ℰ 43061, S : 3 m. by A 584.
🛈 1 Clifton St. ℰ 21623 and 25212 (weekdays only) – 87a Coronation St. ℰ 21891 – Blackpool Airport,
Terminal Building, Squires Gate Lane ℰ 43061.
♦London 246 – ♦Leeds 88 – ♦Liverpool 56 – ♦Manchester 51 – ♦Middlesbrough 123.

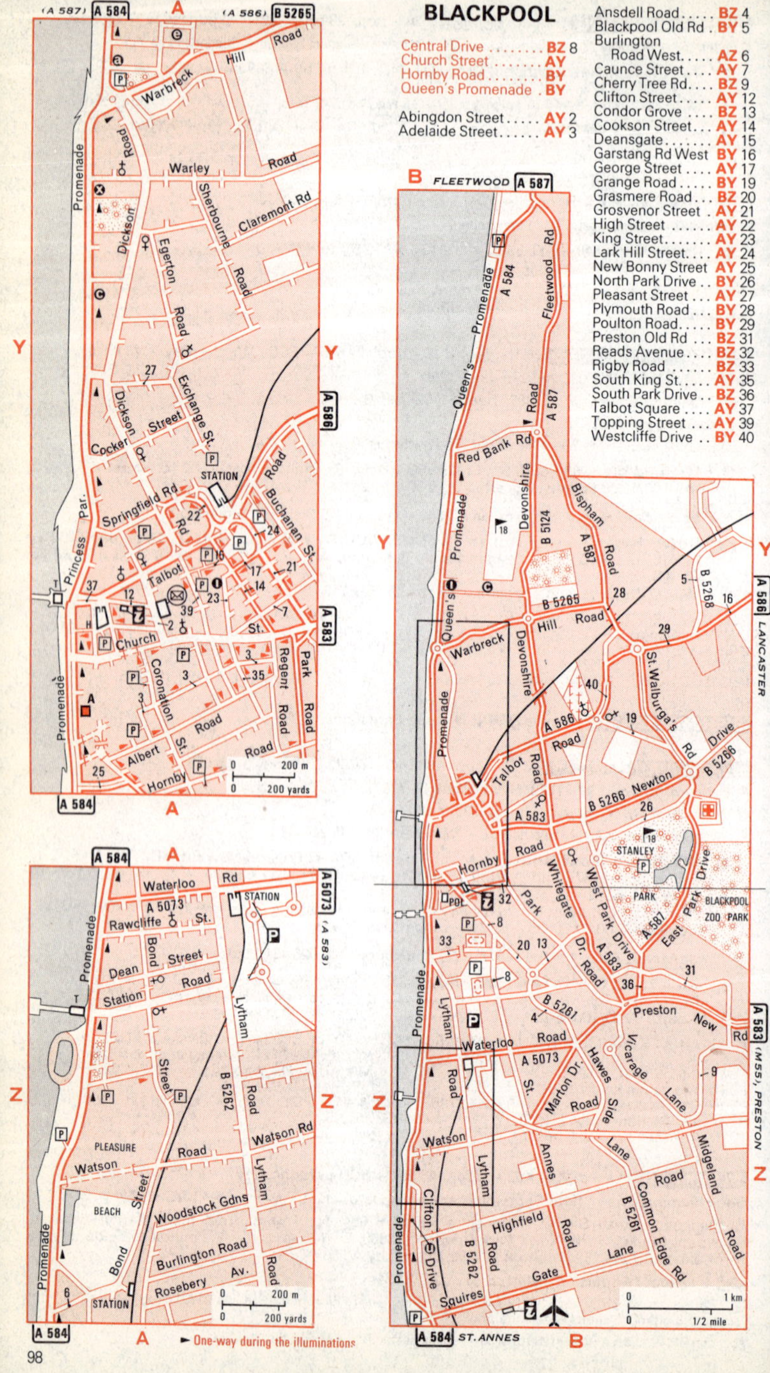

BLACKPOOL

Central Drive . . . . BZ 8
Church Street . . . . AY
Hornby Road . . . . BY
Queen's Promenade . . BY

Abingdon Street . . . . . AY 2
Adelaide Street . . . . . . AY 3

Ansdell Road . . . . . BZ 4
Blackpool Old Rd . BY 5
Burlington
   Road West . . . . . AZ 6
Caunce Street . . . . AY 7
Cherry Tree Rd . . . . BZ 9
Clifton Street . . . . . AY 12
Condor Grove . . . . BZ 13
Cookson Street . . . AY 14
Deansgate . . . . AY 15
Garstang Rd West . BY 16
George Street . . . . AY 17
Grange Road . . . . . BY 19
Grasmere Road . . . BZ 20
Grosvenor Street . . AY 21
High Street . . . . AY 22
King Street . . . . AY 23
Lark Hill Street . . . . AY 24
New Bonny Street . AY 25
North Park Drive . . BY 26
Pleasant Street . . . AY 27
Plymouth Road . . . BY 28
Poulton Road . . . . . BY 29
Preston Old Rd . . . BZ 31
Reads Avenue . . . . BZ 32
Rigby Road . . . . . . BZ 33
South King St. . . . . AY 35
South Park Drive . . BZ 36
Talbot Square . . . . AY 37
Topping Street . . . . AY 39
Westcliffe Drive . . BY 40

FLEETWOOD
ST. ANNES

One-way during the illuminations

Imperial (T.H.F.), North Shore, North Promenade, FY1 2HB, ℰ 23971, Telex 677376, Fax 751784, ≤, ⬚ – 劇 ⤬ rm TV ☎ Ⓟ – 逾 400. ⬚ AE ⓞ VISA **AY c**
M 7.45/10.50 st. and a la carte ⌀ 3.95 – 굧 7.00 – **152 rm** 59.00/89.00 t., **7 suites** 160.00/185.00 t.

Pembroke, North Promenade, FY1 2JQ, ℰ 23434, Telex 677469, Fax 27864, ≤, ⬚ – 劇 ⤬ rm TV ☎ Ⓟ – 逾. ⬚ AE ⓞ VISA **AY x**
M 10.25/11.50 st. and a la carte 17.15/22.45 st. ⌀ 4.65 – **194 rm** 굧 75.00/95.00 st., **6 suites** 190.00/300.00 st. – SB 82.00/122.00 st.

Savoy, Queens Promenade, FY2 9SJ, ℰ 52561, Telex 667570 – 劇 TV ☎ Ⓟ – 逾 150. ⬚ AE ⓞ VISA **AY a**
M 10.00/15.00 st. and a la carte – **145 rm** 굧 45.00/70.00 t., **5 suites** 100.00 t. – SB (except September and October) 70.00 st.

Warwick (Best Western), 603-609 New South Promenade, FY4 1NG, ℰ 42192, Fax 52346, ⬚ – TV ☎ Ⓟ – 逾 50. ⬚ AE ⓞ VISA **BZ u**
M (bar lunch)/dinner 10.95 t. ⌀ 2.30 – **52 rm** 굧 26.50/49.50 t. – SB 58.00 st.

Brabyns, 1-3 Shaftesbury Av., North Shore, FY2 9QQ, ℰ 54263 – TV ☎ Ⓟ. ⬚ ⓞ VISA **BY i**
M 5.00/7.50 t. ⌀ 3.50 – **25 rm** 굧 25.50/45.00 t. – SB (except Bank Holidays) 52.00/62.00 st.

Sunray, 42 Knowle Av., off Queens Promenade, FY2 9TQ, ℰ 51937 – TV ☎ Ⓟ **BY c**
closed 15 December-5 January – **M** 9.00 st. – **9 rm** 굧 19.00/44.00 st. – SB (November-March) 35.00 st.

Denely without rest., 15 King Edward Av., FY2 9TA, ℰ 52757 – Ⓟ. ⤫ **AY e**
9 rm 굧 10.75/35.00.

at Little Thornton NE : 5 m. by A 586 – BY – off A 588 – ✉ ☏ 0253 Blackpool :

XX River House ⚘ with rm, Skippool Creek, Wyre Rd, FY5 5LF, ℰ 883497, ≤, 🚗 – TV ☎ Ⓟ. ⬚ AE
M (closed Sunday) (booking essential) a la carte 22.50/35.00 t. ⌀ 5.50 – **4 rm** 굧 50.00/90.00 t. – SB (weekends only) 80.00/95.00 st.

at Little Singleton NE : 6 m. by A 586 – BY – on A 585 – ✉ ☏ 0253 Blackpool :

Mains Hall ⚘, 86 Mains Lane, FY6 7LE, ℰ 885130, 🚗 – ⤬ rm TV ☎ Ⓟ. ⬚ VISA
M (closed Sunday) (dinner only) 11.00 t. ⌀ 3.00 – **9 rm** 굧 22.00/53.00 t.

AUSTIN-ROVER, DAIMLER-JAGUAR Vicarage Lane ℰ 67811
AUSTIN-ROVER Cherry Tree Rd ℰ 67811
AUSTIN-ROVER 159 Devonshire Rd ℰ 34301
BMW Vicarage Lane ℰ 697101
FIAT 79/83 Breck Rd, Poulton-le-Fylde ℰ 882571
FORD Whitegate Drive ℰ 63333
HONDA Devonshire Rd ℰ 35816

LADA St. Annes Rd ℰ 405119
MERCEDES-BENZ Church St. ℰ 22257
MERCEDES-BENZ Church St. ℰ 28436
PEUGEOT-TALBOT Squires Gate Lane ℰ 45544
VW, AUDI Central Drive ℰ 401226

Ⓜ ATS Clifton Rd, Marton ℰ 695033/4

BLACKWATER Cornwall **403** E 33 – see Truro.

BLAGDON Avon **403** L 30 – pop. 1 192 – ☏ 0761.
♦London 137 – ♦Bristol 16 – Taunton 34.

Butcombe Farm ⚘, Aldwick Lane, BS18 6UW, NE : 1 ½ m. via Station Rd ℰ 62380, ≤, « Farmhouse of 15C origin », ⬚ heated, 🚗, park – TV ☎ Ⓟ. ⤫
M 18.50 ⌀ 3.50 – **8 rm** 굧 27.50/42.00.

BLAKENEY Norfolk **404** X 25 – pop. 1 559 – ECD : Wednesday – ✉ Holt – ☏ 0263 Cley.
♦London 127 – King's Lynn 37 – ♦Norwich 28.

Blakeney, The Quay, NR25 7NE, ℰ 740797, Fax 740795, ≤, ⬚, 🚗 – TV ☎ 🐾 Ⓟ – 逾 150. ⬚ AE ⓞ VISA
M (bar lunch)/dinner 15.00 t. and a la carte ⌀ 3.50 – **50 rm** 굧 42.00/84.00 t., **1 suite** 94.00/114.00 t. – SB (except Christmas and Bank Holidays) 78.00/120.00 st.

Manor, The Quay, NR25 7ND, ℰ 740376, 🚗 – ⤬ rest TV Ⓟ
closed 3 to 28 December – M (bar lunch)/dinner 12.75 st. ⌀ 2.50 – **31 rm** 굧 28.00/66.00 st. – SB (November-May) 45.00/62.00 st.

at Cley next the Sea E : 1 ½ m. on A 149 – ✉ Holt – ☏ 0263 Cley :

George & Dragon, NR25 7RN, ℰ 740652 – Ⓟ
M (bar lunch)/dinner a la carte 7.00/13.70 t. – **8 rm** 굧 20.00/60.00 t.

Cley Mill ⚘, NR25 7NN, ℰ 740209, ≤, « 18C redbrick windmill on saltmarshes » – Ⓟ
closed mid January-February – M 15.00 t. – **4 rm** 굧 22.00/40.00 t.

at Morston W : 1 ½ m. on A 149 – ✉ Holt – ☏ 0263 Cley :

Morston Hall, NR25 7AA, ℰ 741041, Fax 741034, 🚗 – ⤬ rest TV ☎ Ⓟ. ⬚ AE VISA ⤫
M (closed lunch Thursday and dinner Tuesday to Thursday to non-residents) 8.50/15.00 t. ⌀ 2.75 – **3 rm** 굧 40.00/80.00 t. – SB (October-June) (weekends only) 150.00/185.00 st.

BLANCHLAND Northumb. 401 402 N 19 – ECD : Monday and Tuesday – ⊠ Consett (Durham)
– ☎ 043 475.

♦London 298 – ♦Carlisle 47 – ♦Newcastle-upon-Tyne 24.

  🏠 **Lord Crewe Arms** ⑤, DH8 9SP, ✆ 251, Fax 337, « Part 13C Abbey », ⇗ – TV ☎. ⬛ AE
  ⑩ VISA
  M (bar lunch Monday to Saturday)/dinner 19.50 **t.** and a la carte ⌽ 4.50 – **15 rm**
  ⇌ 58.00/76.00 **t.** – SB 46.90/62.90 **st.**

BLANDFORD FORUM Dorset 403 404 N 31 The West Country G. – pop. 7 249 – ECD : Wednesday – ☎ 0258 Blandford.

See : Site★ – Envir. : Royal Blandford Signals Museum★ AC, NE : 2 m. by B 3082.
🏌 Ashley Wood, The Wimborne Rd ✆ 52253, SW : 1 ½ m. on B 3082.
🛈 Marsh and Ham Car Park, West St. ✆ 51989.
♦London 124 – Bournemouth 17 – Dorchester 17 – Salisbury 24.

  🏨 **Crown**, 1 West St., DT11 7AJ, ✆ 456626, Telex 418292, Fax 451084, ⑤, ⇗ – TV ☎ Ⓟ. ⬛
  AE ⑩ VISA
  closed 25 to 27 December – **M** 10.00 **t.** and a la carte ⌽ 3.50 – **28 rm** ⇌ 50.00/60.00 **t.** –
  SB (weekends only) 70.00 **st.**
  XX **La Belle Alliance** with rm, Portman Lodge, Whitecliff Mill St., DT11 7BP, ✆ 452842 –
  ⇤ rest TV ☎ Ⓟ. ⬛ AE VISA ⌘
  closed January – **M** (closed Sunday except Bank Holidays) (dinner only) 20.00 **st.**
  and a la carte 18.50/21.50 **st.** ⌽ 3.95 – **5 rm** ⇌ 38.00/54.00 **st.** – SB 82.00/90.00 **st.**

  at Pimperne NE : 2 ½ m. on A 354 – ⊠ ☎ 0258 Blandford Forum :

  🏠 **Anvil**, Salisbury Rd, DT11 8UQ, ✆ 453431 – TV ☎ Ⓟ. ⬛ AE ⑩ VISA
  M 15.00 **t.** and a la carte 8.95/16.10 **t.** ⌽ 3.30 – **9 rm** ⇌ 35.00/55.00 **t.** – SB (October-
  April) 44.00/51.00 **st.**

  at Tarrant Monkton NE : 5 ½ m. by A 354 – ⊠ Blandford Forum – ☎ 025 889 Tarrant
  Hinton :

  ✗ **Langtons** with rm, DT11 8RX, ✆ 225 – TV ☎ Ⓟ. ⬛ AE ⑩ VISA
  M (bar lunch Monday to Saturday)/dinner a la carte 5.45/12.75 **t.** ⌽ 2.90 – **6 rm**
  ⇌ 27.50/40.00 **t.**

FERRARI Pimperne ✆ 451211   RENAULT St. Leonards Av. ✆ 52311

BLAWITH Cumbria 402 K 21 – pop. 101 – ⊠ Ulverston – ☎ 022 985 Lowick Bridge.
♦London 290 – ♦Carlisle 66 – Kendal 28 – Lancaster 43.

  🏠 Highfield, LA12 8EG, on A 5084 ✆ 238, ≤, ⇗ – TV Ⓟ. ⌘ – **12 rm**.
  ↑ **Appletree Holme** ⑤, LA12 8EL, W : 1 m. ✆ 618, ≤, ⇗ – ⇤ TV ☎ Ⓟ. AE. ⌘
  M 16.50 **st.** ⌽ 3.25 – **4 rm** ⇌ (dinner included) 55.00/96.00 **st.**

BLEDINGTON Glos. 403 404 P 28 – see Stow-on-the-Wold.

BLOCKLEY Glos. 403 404 O 27 – pop. 1 729 – ECD : Thursday – ⊠ Moreton-in-Marsh –
☎ 0386.
♦London 89 – ♦Birmingham 40 – Gloucester 29 – ♦Oxford 33.

  🏨 **Crown Inn**, High St., GL56 9EX, ✆ 700245, Fax 700247, « Converted 17C coach house and
  cottages » – TV ☎ Ⓟ. ⬛ AE ⑩ VISA ⌘
  M 11.95/15.95 **t.** and a la carte ⌽ 3.50 – **15 rm** ⇌ 49.50/78.50 **t.**
  🏠 Lower Brook House ⑤, Lower St., GL56 9DS, ✆ 700286, « Converted 17C cottages », ⇗
  – TV Ⓟ. ⬛ ⑩
  closed January – **M** (bar lunch Monday to Saturday)/dinner 19.00 **t.** and a la carte ⌽ 3.50 –
  8 rm.

BLOXHAM Oxon. 403 404 P 28 – see Banbury.

BLUE ANCHOR Somerset – see Dunster.

BLUNSDON Wilts. 403 404 O 29 – see Swindon.

BLYTH Notts. 402 403 404 Q 23 – pop. 1 179 – ⊠ Worksop – ☎ 090 976.
♦London 166 – Doncaster 13 – Lincoln 30 – ♦Nottingham 32 – ♦Sheffield 20.

  🏠 **Granada Lodge** without rest., Hilltop roundabout, S81 8HG, N : ¾ m. by B 6045 at junction
  A 1 (M) and A 614 ✆ 836, Fax 831 – ⇤ rm TV ⚙ Ⓟ. ⬛ AE ⑩ VISA
  – **37 rm** 24.50/27.50 **st.**
  ♟ Fourways, High St., S81 8EW, ✆ 235 – Ⓟ – **6 rm.**

BODFUAN Gwynedd – see Pwllheli.

BODINNICK-BY-FOWEY Cornwall – see Fowey.

BODMIN Cornwall **403** F 32 The West Country G. – pop. 11 992 – ECD : Wednesday – ✆ 0208.
See : St. Petroc Church★ – Envir. : Lanhydrock★★ *AC*, S : 3 m. – Bodmin Moor★★ – St. Endellion
Church★★, NW : 12 m. – Pencarrow House★ *AC*, NW : 4 m. – Cardinham Church★, NE : 5 m.
– Blisland★ (Church★) NE : 6 m. – St. Mabyn Church★, N : 6 m. – St. Tudy★, N : 8 m.
🛈 Shire House, Mount Folly Sq. ✆ 76616.
♦London 273 – Exeter 63 – Penzance 47 – ♦Plymouth 30.

  🏠 **Westberry**, Rhind St., PL31 2EL, ✆ 72772 – 📺 ☎ Ⓟ. ◪ ⓪ 𝑽𝑰𝑺𝑨
     M (bar lunch Monday to Saturday)/dinner 8.00 **t.** and a la carte ⫶ 2.50 – **20 rm**
     ⊇ 19.50/38.50 **t.** – SB (weekends only) 45.00 **st.**

AUSTIN-ROVER Liskeard Rd ✆ 73145   ⓪ ATS Church Sq. ✆ 74353

BOGNOR REGIS West Sussex **404** R 31 – pop. 50 323 – ECD : Wednesday – ✆ 0243.
🛈 1-2 Place St-Maur des Fossés, Belmont St. ✆ 823140.
♦London 65 – ♦Brighton 29 – ♦Portsmouth 24 – ♦Southampton 37.

  🏨 **Royal Norfolk** (T.H.F), The Esplanade, PO21 2LH, ✆ 826222, Fax 826325, ⤓ heated, 🐎,
     ✗ – ▯ ⤢ rm 📺 ☎ Ⓟ – 🔼 130. ◪ 𝐀𝐄 ⓪ 𝑽𝑰𝑺𝑨
     M 9.95/11.50 **st.** and a la carte ⫶ 3.95 – ⊇ 7.00 – **49 rm** 44.00/65.00 **st.**, **2 suites** 84.00 **st.** –
     SB 84.00/114.00 **st.**

AUSTIN-ROVER 16 Durban Rd, South Bersted   PEUGEOT-TALBOT Shripney Rd, South Bersted
✆ 864041   ✆ 582432
FORD Lennox St. ✆ 864641   VW-AUDI 126 Felpham Way ✆ 583185

BOLHAM Devon **403** J 31 – see Tiverton.

BOLLINGTON Cheshire **402 403 404** N 24 – see Macclesfield.

BOLTON Greater Manchester **402 404** M 23 – pop. 143 960 – ECD : Wednesday – ✆ 0204.
Envir. : Hall I'Th'Wood★ (16C) *AC*, N : 1 ½ m.
🏌 Bolton Municipal, Links Rd, Lostock ✆ 42336, W : 3 m. on A 673 – 🏌 Dunscar, Longworth
Lane, Bromley Cross ✆ 53321, N : 3 m. by A 666 – 🏌 Lostock Park, ✆ 43067, W : 3 ½ m – 🏌 Old
Links, Chorley Old Rd ✆ 42307, NW: on B 6226.
🛈 Town Hall, ✆ 22311 ext 1025/1026/1029 and 384174.
♦London 214 – Burnley 19 – ♦Liverpool 32 – ♦Manchester 11 – Preston 23.

  🏨 **Crest** (Crest), Beaumont Rd, BL3 4TA, SW : 2 ½ m. on A 58 ✆ 651511, Telex 635527, Fax
     61064 – ⤢ rm 📺 ☎ Ⓟ – 🔼 80. ◪ 𝐀𝐄 ⓪ 𝑽𝑰𝑺𝑨
     M (closed Saturday dinner) 10.50/15.50 **st.** and a la carte – ⊇ 8.00 – **100 rm** 68.00/80.00 **st.**
     – SB (weekends only) 60.00/80.00 **st.**

  🏨 **Pack Horse** (De Vere), Nelson Sq., Bradshawgate, BL1 1DP, ✆ 27261, Telex 635168, Fax
     364352 – ▯ ⤢ rm 📺 ☎ – 🔼 200. ◪ 𝐀𝐄 ⓪ 𝑽𝑰𝑺𝑨
     M (bar lunch Saturday) 9.00/12.00 **st.** and a la carte ⫶ 4.50 – **73 rm** ⊇ 63.00/87.00 **st.** –
     SB (weekends only except July and August) 63.00/70.00 **st.**

  🏠 **Broomfield**, 33-35 Wigan Rd, Deane, BL3 5XP, SW : 1 ½ m. on A 6140 ✆ 61570 – 📺 Ⓟ.
     ◪ 𝑽𝑰𝑺𝑨
     M (closed Sunday) (dinner only) 10.50 **t.** and a la carte – ⊇ 3.50 – **15 rm** 25.00/34.00 **t.**

  at Egerton N : 3 ½ m. by A 666 – ✉ ✆ 0204 Bolton :

  🏨 **Egerton House** ⤸, Blackburn Rd, BL7 9PL, ✆ 57171, Fax 593030, ≤, 🐎, park – 📺 ☎ Ⓟ.
     ◪ 𝐀𝐄 ⓪ 𝑽𝑰𝑺𝑨. ✗
     M (closed Saturday lunch) 8.95 **t.** (lunch) and a la carte 14.90/22.75 **t.** ⫶ 4.95 – **29 rm**
     ⊇ 58.00/70.00 **t.** – SB (weekends only) 65.00 **st.**

  at Bromley Cross N : 4 m. by A 666 on B 6472 – ✉ ✆ 0204 Bolton :

  🏨 **Last Drop Village**, Hospital Rd, BL7 9PZ, ✆ 591131, Telex 635322, Fax 54122, « Village
     created from restored farm buildings », ◪, 🐎, squash – 📺 ☎ Ⓟ – 🔼 200. ◪ 𝐀𝐄 ⓪ 𝑽𝑰𝑺𝑨
     M (closed Saturday lunch) 9.25 **st.** (lunch) and a la carte 13.20/19.25 **st.** ⫶ 4.95 – **80 rm**
     ⊇ 64.00/76.00 **st.**, **3 suites** 80.00/100.00 **st.** – SB (weekends only) 69.00 **st.**

AUSTIN-ROVER Manchester Rd ✆ 32241   VW, AUDI Blackburn Rd ✆ 31464
FORD 54-56 Higher Bridge St. ✆ 24474   VW, AUDI St. Helens Rd ✆ 62131
HYUNDAI, SUBARU, YUGO Thynne St. ✆ 32511
LANCIA Halliwell Rd ✆ 26566   ⓪ ATS Foundry St. ✆ 22144/27841/388681
PEUGEOT-TALBOT, RENAULT 157 Bradshawgate   ATS Moss Bank Way, Astley Bridge, Bolton ✆ 50057
✆ 31323   ATS Chorley Rd, Fourgates, Westhoughton ✆
SEAT 154-160 Crook St. ✆ 24686   813024
TOYOTA Radcliffe Rd ✆ 382234

BOLTON ABBEY North Yorks. **402** O 22 – pop. 122 – ✉ Skipton – ✆ 075 671.
See : Bolton Priory★ (ruins) and woods (the Strid★ and nature trails in upper Wharfedale).
♦London 216 – Harrogate 18 – ♦Leeds 23 – Skipton 6.

  🏨 **Devonshire Arms** (Best Western), BD23 6AJ, on A 59 at Bolton Bridge ✆ 441, Telex
     51218, Fax 564, ≤, « Restored former coaching inn », ◪, park – ⤢ 📺 ☎ ♿ Ⓟ – 🔼. ◪
     𝐀𝐄 ⓪ 𝑽𝑰𝑺𝑨
     M 11.95/19.50 **st.** and a la carte ⫶ 5.50 – **40 rm** ⊇ 63.00/85.00 **st.** – SB 47.50/55.00 **st.**

BONCATH Dyfed **403** G 27 – ⊠ ✆ 023 974.
Envir. : Cenarth Falls★, NE : 6 m.
◆London 247 – Carmarthen 27 – Fishguard 17.

⋔ **Pantyderi Farm** ⑤, SA37 0JB, W : 2 ¾ m. by B 4332 ✆ 227, ≼, ⊒, ⬎, ☲, park – TV Ⓟ
⑤⑤
M 7.00 st. 🍷 2.50 – **8 rm** ⊐ 12.00/37.50 st.

BONCHURCH I.O.W. **403 404** Q 32 – see Wight (Isle of) : Ventnor.

BONTDDU Gwynedd **402 403** I 25 – see Dolgellau.

BOOTLE Merseyside **402** ㉜ **403** ② – see Liverpool.

BOROUGHBRIDGE North Yorks. **402** P 21 – pop. 1 835 – ECD : Thursday – ✆ 0423 Harrogate.
🛈 Fishergate ✆ 323373 (summer only).
◆London 216 – ◆Leeds 26 – ◆Middlesbrough 35 – York 17.

🏨 **Crown**, Horsefair, YO5 9LB, ✆ 322328, Telex 57906 – 🛗 TV ☎ ⓰ Ⓟ – 🕍 ⚶ ΑΕ ⓞ VISA
M 9.00/14.50 t. and a la carte 🍷 3.95 – **41 rm** ⊐ 42.00/82.50 t., **1 suite** 90.00/120.00 t. –
SB (weekends only) 75.00/85.00 st.

⋔ **Farndale**, Horsefair, YO5 9AH, ✆ 323463 – TV Ⓟ
M 6.50 t. 🍷 3.25 – **13 rm** ⊐ 15.00/35.00 t.

BORROWDALE Cumbria **402** K 20 – see Keswick.

BOSCASTLE Cornwall **403** F 31 The West Country G. – ✆ 084 05.
See : Site★.
◆London 260 – Bude 14 – Exeter 59 – ◆Plymouth 43.

🏠 **Bottreaux House**, PL35 0BG, on B 3266 ✆ 231 – ⅋ rest TV Ⓟ. ⚶ VISA
March-November – **M** *(closed Monday lunch)* (bar lunch)/dinner a la carte 8.95/12.85 st.
🍷 3.25 – **7 rm** ⊐ 22.50/42.00 st. – SB 56.50 st.

⚓ **Riverside**, The Harbour, PL35 0HE, ✆ 216 – TV Ⓟ. ⚶
M (bar lunch)/dinner 14.00 t. and a la carte 🍷 4.25 – **10 rm** ⊐ 33.00/66.00 t.

⋔ **St. Christopher's Country House**, High St., PL35 0BD, S : ½ m. by B 3266 ✆ 412 – Ⓟ.
⚶ VISA
Easter-October – **M** 7.00 st. 🍷 2.50 – **8 rm** ⊐ 17.00/34.00 st.

BOSHAM West Sussex **404** R 31 – see Chichester.

BOSTON Lincs. **402 404** T 25 – pop. 33 908 – ECD : Thursday – ✆ 0205.
See : St. Botolph's Church★ 14C.
🛈 Cowbridge, Horncastle Rd ✆ 62306, N : 2 m. by B 1183.
◆London 122 – Lincoln 35 – ◆Nottingham 55.

🏨 **White Hart**, Bridge Foot, PE21 8SH, ✆ 64877 – ⅋ rest TV ☎ Ⓟ – 🕍 80. ⚶ ΑΕ ⓞ VISA. ⑤
M (grill rest.) – **23 rm** ⊐ 37.00/49.50 t.

🏨 **New England** (T.H.F.), 49 Wide Bargate, PE21 6SH, ✆ 65255, Fax 310597 – ⅋ rm TV ☎
Ⓟ. ⚶ ΑΕ ⓞ VISA
M 8.90/10.45 st. and a la carte 🍷 3.95 – ⊐ 7.00 – **25 rm** 46.00/56.00 st. – SB (week-
ends only) 68.00/76.00 **st.**

AUSTIN-ROVER, DAIMLER-JAGUAR Tawney St.   PROTON, LADA, RELIANT Frith Bank ✆ 62230
✆ 66677   TOYOTA Tawney St. ✆ 368626
BMW Sleaford Rd ✆ 350000   VAUXHALL Butterwick ✆ 760421
FIAT 200 London Rd ✆ 355500   VW, AUDI-NSU ✆ 63867
FORD 57 High St. ✆ 60404
NISSAN Main Ridge East ✆ 353737   Ⓐ ATS London Rd ✆ 362854

BOSTON SPA West Yorks. **402** P 22 – pop. 6 022 – ⊠ Wetherby – ✆ 0937 Boston Spa.
◆London 205 – Harrogate 11 – ◆Leeds 12 – ◆Middlesbrough 52 – York 14.

🏠 **Royal** (B.C.B.), 182 High St., LS23 6HT, ✆ 842142 – TV ☎ Ⓟ. ⑤
9 rm.

BOTLEY Hants. **403 404** Q 31 – pop. 2 156 – ECD : Thursday – ⊠ Hedge End, Southampton
– ✆ 0489.
◆London 83 – ◆Portsmouth 17 – ◆Southampton 6 – Winchester 11.

XX **Cobbett's**, 13-15 The Square, SO3 2EA, ✆ 782068, French rest. – Ⓟ. ⚶ VISA
*closed lunch Saturday and Monday, Sunday, 2 weeks in summer, 2 weeks in winter and
Bank Holidays* – **M** 13.50/16.00 t. and a la carte 17.80/29.00 t. 🍷 4.65.

AUDI, VW Shamblehurst Lane ✆ 783434   AUSTIN-ROVER Southampton Rd ✆ 785111

BOTTESFORD Leics. 🔲🔲 R 25 – pop. 2 085 – ECD : Wednesday – ✿ 0949.
♦ London 116 – Grantham 75 – Lincoln 26 – ♦ Leicester 32 – ♦ Nottingham 18.
   ✗✗ Thatch, 26 High St., NG13 0AA, ✆ 42330 – ℗.

BOUGHTON Kent – see Faversham.

BOUGHTON MONCHELSEA Kent – see Maidstone.

BOURNE Lincs. 🔲🔲 S 25 – pop. 7 672 – ECD : Wednesday – ✿ 0778.
Envir. : Spalding Parish Church ★, E : 10 m. – Ayscoughfee Hall ★ 15C, E : 10 m.
♦London 101 – ♦Leicester 42 – Lincoln 35 – ♦Nottingham 42.
   🏠 **Bourne Eau House**, 30 South St., PE10 9LY, on A 15 ✆ 423621, « Part Elizabethan and part Georgian house », 🐎 – 📺 ☎ ℗. 🛇
   M *(closed Sunday dinner)* (residents only, communal dining) (lunch by arrangement)/dinner 15.00 s. – **3 rm** ☕ 30.00/60.00 s.
   🏠 **Toft House**, Main Rd, Toft, PE10 0JT, SW : 3 m. on A 6121 ✆ 077 833 (Witham-on-the-Hill) 614, 🐎, squash – 📺 ℗ – 🎪 100. 🖲 VISA. 🛇
   M *(closed Sunday dinner)* 7.00/10.00 t. and a la carte 🍷 2.75 – **22 rm** ☕ 23.00/50.00 t.
AUSTIN-ROVER Thurlby Rd ✆ 422892   ⊚ ATS 18 Abbey Rd ✆ 422811
AUSTIN-ROVER North St. ✆ 422129
FORD Spalding Rd ✆ 424464

BOURNE END Herts. 🔲 S 28 – see Hemel Hempstead.

BOURNEMOUTH Dorset 🔲🔲 O 31 **The West Country G.** – pop. 142 829 – ECD : Wednesday and Saturday – ✿ 0202.
🏌 Meyrick Park ✆ 290871 CY – 🏌 Queen's Park, Queen's Park South Drive ✆ 36198, NE : 2 m. CV.
✈ Hurn Airport : ✆ 579751, Telex 41345, N : 5 m. by Hurn Rd DV.
🛈 Westover Rd ✆ 24571.
♦London 114 – ♦Bristol 76 – ♦Southampton 34.

Plans on following pages

   🏨 **Royal Bath** (De Vere), Bath Rd, BH1 2EW, ✆ 25555, Telex 41375, Fax 24158, ≤, 🖈, 🐎 – 🛗 📺 ☎ 🚗 ℗ – 🎪 300. 🖲 AE ⓞ VISA. 🛇   DZ a
   M (see **Oscars** below) – **123 rm** ☕ 75.00/170.00 st., **8 suites** 170.00/220.00 st. – SB 120.00/225.00 st.
   🏨 **Carlton**, Meyrick Rd, East Overcliff, BH1 3DN, ✆ 22011, Telex 41244, Fax 299573, ≤, 🏊 heated, 🐎 – 🛗 🍽 rest 📺 ☎ 🚗 ℗ – 🎪 140. 🖲 AE ⓞ VISA. 🛇   EZ a
   M 14.50/21.50 t. and a la carte – **61 rm** ☕ 74.00/125.00 t., **4 suites** 195.00 t. – SB (except summer) 135.00 st.
   🏨 **Norfolk Royale**, Richmond Hill, BH2 6EN, ✆ 21521, Telex 418474, Fax 299729, 🖲 – 🛗 ✗ rm 📺 ☎ 🚗 – 🎪 50. 🖲 AE ⓞ VISA. 🛇   CY u
   M 12.75/22.00 t. and a la carte 🍷 5.00 – **90 rm** ☕ 72.50/115.00 st., **5 suites** 165.00/300.00 st. – SB (weekends only) 90.00/120.00 st.
   🏨 **Highcliff** (Best Western), 105 St. Michael's Rd, West Cliff, BH2 5DU, ✆ 27702, Telex 417153, Fax 21233, ≤, 🏊 heated, 🐎, ✗✗ – 🛗 📺 ☎ ℗ – 🎪 180. 🖲 AE ⓞ VISA. 🛇   CZ z
   M 11.50/20.00 st. and a la carte 🍷 3.75 – **107 rm** ☕ 60.00/140.00 st., **3 suites** 90.00/160.00 st. – SB 90.00/120.00 st.
   🏨 **Crest** (Crest), Meyrick Rd, The Lansdowne, BH1 2PR, ✆ 23262, Telex 41232, Fax 27698 – 🛗 ✗ rm 🍽 rest 📺 ☎ ℗ – 🎪 100. 🖲 AE ⓞ VISA   DY a
   M (carving lunch) 6.95/11.95 st. and a la carte – ☕ 7.25 – **102 rm** 61.00/73.00 st. – SB 84.00 st.
   🏨 **Marsham Court**, Russell Cotes Rd, East Cliff, BH1 3AB, ✆ 22111, Telex 41420, Fax 294744, ≤, 🏊 heated – 🛗 📺 ☎ ℗ – 🎪 200. 🖲 AE ⓞ VISA. 🛇   DZ e
   M 8.50/12.50 st. and a la carte – **79 rm** ☕ 43.00/76.00 st., **1 suite** 116.00 st. – SB (except Christmas and New Year) 80.00/94.00 st.
   🏨 Anglo-Swiss, 16 Gervis Rd, East Cliff, BH1 3EQ, ✆ 24794, Fax 299615, 🏊 heated, 🐎 – 🛗 📺 ☎ ℗ – 🎪 250   EY e
   60 rm.
   🏨 **Durley Hall**, 7 Durley Chine Rd, Westcliff, BH2 5JS, ✆ 766886, Fax 762236, 🏊 heated, 🖲, 🐎 – 🛗 📺 ☎ ℗ – 🎪 100. 🖲 AE ⓞ VISA. 🛇   CZ s
   M (bar lunch Monday to Saturday)/dinner 13.50 st. and a la carte 🍷 3.95 – **81 rm** ☕ 42.00/98.00 t. – SB 71.00/112.00 t.
   🏨 Heathlands, 12 Grove Rd, East Cliff, BH1 3AY, ✆ 23336, Fax 25937, 🏊 heated – 🛗 📺 ☎ 🚗 ℗ – 🎪 250   EZ c
   114 rm, 2 suites.
   🏨 **Burley Court**, 29 Bath Rd, BH1 2NP, ✆ 22824, 🏊 heated – 🛗 📺 📠 ℗. 🖲 VISA   DY i
   closed 1 to 8 January – **M** (bar lunch) (lunch weekends only in winter)/dinner 9.00 t. and a la carte 🍷 3.75 – **39 rm** ☕ 31.00/66.00 st. – SB (October-May) (weekends only) 55.00 st.

P.T.O. →

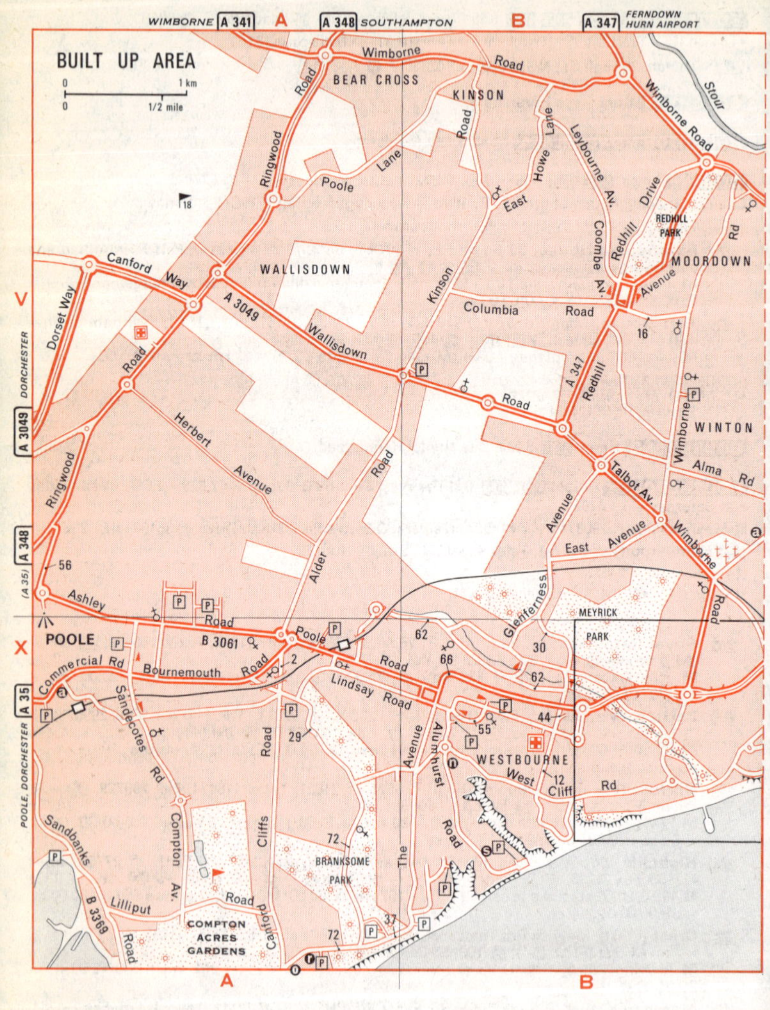

BOURNEMOUTH

Old Christchurch Road .... **DY**
Square (The) .... **CY** 60
Westover Road .... **DZ** 73

Archway Road .... **AX** 2
Boscombe Cliff Road..... **CX** 6
Boscombe Overcliff Road.. **DX** 7
Boscombe Spa Road...... **CX** 8
Branksome Wood Road ... **CY** 10
Clarendon Road .... **BX** 12
Commercial Road .... **CY** 13
Durley Road............. **CZ** 15
Ensbury Park Road ...... **BV** 16
Exeter Road .... **CDZ** 17
Fir Vale Road............ **DY** 18
Gervis Place............. **DY** 20

Gloucester Road.......... **DV** 21
Hinton Road .... **DZ** 25
Lansdowne (The) .... **DY** 26
Lansdowne
  Road .... **DY** 27
Leicester Road .... **AX** 29
Leven Avenue .... **BX** 30
Madeira Road .... **DY** 32
Manor Road............. **EY** 34
Meyrick Road .... **EYZ** 35
Owls Road.............. **CX** 36
Pinecliff Road .... **AX** 37
Post Office Road......... **CY** 41
Priory Road .... **CZ** 43
Queen's Road .... **BX** 44
Richmond Hill .... **CY** 45
Richmond Park Road .... **CV** 46
Russell Cotes Road ...... **DZ** 47
St. Michael's Road .... **CZ** 48

St. Paul's Road .... **EY** 49
St. Peter's Road .... **DY** 50
St. Stephen's Road........ **CY** 51
St. Swithuns Road
  South .... **EY** 52
Saxonbury Road .... **EV** 53
Seabourne Road .... **DV** 54
Seamoor Road .... **BX** 55
Sea View Road .... **AV** 56
Southbourne Grove .... **DX** 57
Southbourne Overcliff
  Drive .... **DX** 59
Suffolk Road .... **CY** 61
Surrey Road............. **BX** 62
Triangle (The) .... **CY** 63
Upper Hinton Road ...... **DZ** 64
Wessex Way .... **BX** 66
West Cliff Promenade ..... **CZ** 67
Western Road .... **AX** 72

Town plans : the names of main shopping streets are indicated in red at the beginning of the list of streets.

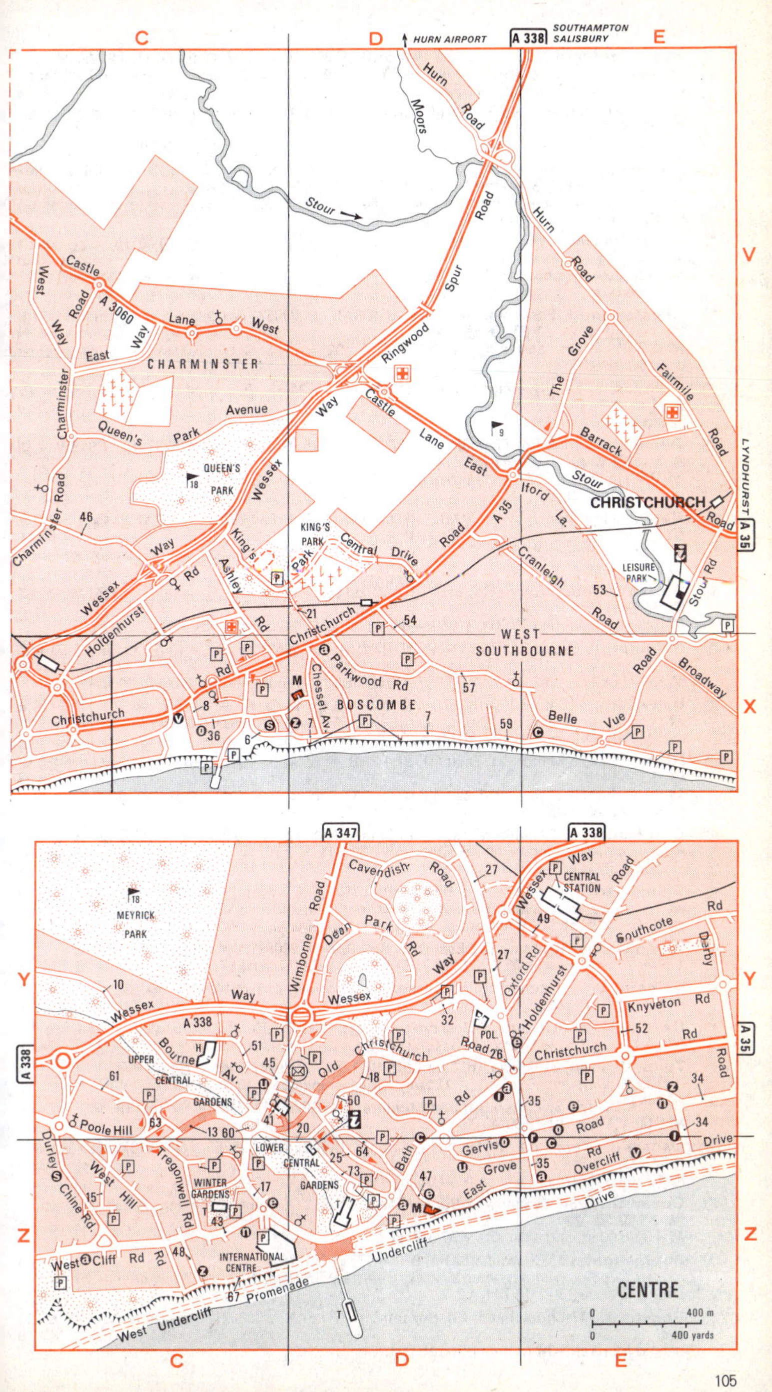

HURN AIRPORT
A 338
SOUTHAMPTON
SALISBURY
Hurn Moors
Hurn Road
Stour
Spur Road
Ringwood
Hurn Road
The Grove
Fairmile Road
West Castle Road
A 3060
Way
Lane
West
Way
East
Charminster Road
CHARMINSTER
Way
Castle
Lane
East
Barrack
Stour
Iford
CHRISTCHURCH
LYNDHURST Road
A 35
9
Queen's Park Avenue
Wessex
Queen's Park Road
18
QUEEN'S PARK
46
King's
King's Park
Central Drive
A 35
Iford La.
Cranleigh Road
LEISURE PARK
53
Wessex Way
Ashley Rd
Holdenhurst
Rd
21
Christchurch Rd
54
WEST SOUTHBOURNE
Road
Broadway
Parkwood Rd
Chessel Av.
57
P
Christchurch
8
M
BOSCOMBE
7
7
59
Belle Vue
36
6
S
V
C
A 347
A 338
Cavendish Road
27
Wessex Way
CENTRAL STATION
Road
Wimborne Road
Dean Park Road
Park Rd
Way
27
49
Oxford Rd
Holdenhurst
Southcote Rd
Darby Rd
MEYRICK PARK
18
Wessex Way
10
A 338
Way
Wessex
32
POL
Knyveton Rd
52
Christchurch
A 35
A 338
61
UPPER CENTRAL GARDENS
Bourne Av.
H
51
45
Old
Christchurch
Road
26
35
34
Poole Hill
63
13 60
41
18
50
Rd
Road
34
Durley Chine Rd
West Hill
Tregonwell Rd
LOWER CENTRAL GARDENS
20
25
64
Bath Rd
Gervis
Grove
Road
Rd
Overcliff Drive
V
WINTER GARDENS
17
73
East
47
West Cliff Rd
15
43
48
M
INTERNATIONAL CENTRE
Undercliff
67 Promenade
West Undercliff
CENTRE
0   400 m
0   400 yards

Royal Exeter (B.C.B.), Exeter Rd, BH2 5AG, ☏ 290566 – ▮ TV ☎ ℗. ◪ AE ① VISA. ⊁
M (grill rest.) a la carte 12.65/15.05 t. – **36 rm** ⊇ 23.00/51.00 t. – SB (weekends only) (except Christmas) 43.00/82.00 t.
CZ e

Cliff End, 99 Manor Rd, East Cliff, BH1 3EX, ☏ 309711, ⊼ heated, ☞, ※ – ▮ TV ☎ ℗. ◪ AE VISA
CX v
M (bar lunch)/dinner 9.00 st. – **40 rm** ⊇ 32.00/64.00 st. – SB 70.00/77.00 st.

Courtlands (Best Western), 16 Boscombe Spa Rd, East Cliff, BH5 1BB, ☏ 302442, Telex 41344, Fax 309880, ⊼ heated – ▮ TV ☎ ℗ – 🔏 50. ◪ AE ① VISA
CX o
M (bar lunch)/dinner 12.60 t. ▮ 3.90 – **60 rm** ⊇ 36.50/68.20 t. – SB (except summer) 59.00/64.00 st.

Winterbourne, Priory Rd, BH2 5DJ, ☏ 296366, ≤, ⊼ heated – ▮ TV ☎ ℗ – 🔏 80. ◪ VISA
CZ n
M (bar lunch)/dinner 8.00 st. ▮ 2.70 – **41 rm** ⊇ 23.00/60.00 st. – SB (October-April) 52.00/56.00 st.

Chesterwood, East Overcliff Drive, BH1 3AR, ☏ 28057, Fax 293457, ≤, ⊼ heated – ▮ ⊁ rest TV ☎ ℗. ◪ AE ① VISA. ⊁
EZ i
M 8.50/11.00 st. and a la carte ▮ 2.95 – **52 rm** ⊇ 39.50/85.00 st. – SB (weekends only) 50.00/86.00 st.

Cliffeside, 32 East Overcliff Drive, BH1 3AQ, ☏ 25724, ≤, ⊼ heated – ▮ ⊁ rest TV ☎ ℗ – 🔏 60
EZ v
62 rm.

Queens, Meyrick Rd, Eastcliff, BH1 3DL, ☏ 24415, Group Telex 418297, Fax 294810 – ▮ ▤ rest TV ☎ ℗ – 🔏. ◪ VISA
EYZ r
M 8.50/15.95 t. ▮ 3.65 – **114 rm** ⊇ 32.50/75.00 t. – SB (weekends only) (except summer) 68.50/73.50 st.

New Durley Dean, Westcliff Rd, BH2 5HE, ☏ 27711, Fax 292815 – TV ☎ ♿ ℗ – 🔏 150. ◪ AE VISA. ⊁
CZ a
M (carving lunch) 8.50/11.00 t. ▮ 3.00 – **112 rm** ⊇ 35.00/95.00 t. – SB (except summer) 65.00/69.00 st.

Durlston Court, Gervis Rd, BH1 3DD, ☏ 291488, Fax 299615, ⊼ heated – ▮ TV ☎ ℗. ◪ AE ① VISA
DZ o
M (bar lunch)/dinner 12.50 t. ▮ 4.50 – **60 rm** ⊇ 40.00/80.00 st. – SB 56.00/75.00 st.

Miramar, 19 Grove Rd, East Overcliff, BH1 3AL, ☏ 26581, ≤, ☞ – ▮ TV ☎ ℗. ◪ AE VISA. ⊁
DZ u
M 6.95/11.50 st. – **42 rm** ⊇ 31.00/67.00 st. – SB (November-April) 68.00/75.00 st.

Belvedere, 14 Bath Rd, BH1 2EU, ☏ 21080 – ▮ TV ☎ ℗. ◪ AE ① VISA. ⊁
DYZ c
M (bar lunch)/dinner 10.50 t. ▮ 3.25 – **35 rm** ⊇ 39.00/76.00 t. – SB (October-mid March) (weekends only) 58.00 st.

Hinton Firs, 9 Manor Rd, Eastcliff, BH1 3HB, ☏ 555409, Fax 299607, ⊼ heated – ▮ TV ☎ ℗. ◪ VISA. ⊁
EY n
M (bar lunch)/dinner 8.75 st. ▮ 3.80 – **52 rm** ⊇ 38.50/87.00 st. – SB (November-May) 56.00/62.00 st.

Cliff House, 113 Alumhurst Rd, Alum Chine, BH4 8HS, ☏ 763003, ≤ – ▮ TV ℗. ⊁
BX s
Mid March-October – **M** (dinner only) 11.50 t. ▮ 2.75 – **11 rm** ⊇ 24.00/50.00 st. – SB 30.00/33.50 st.

Chinehead, 31 Alumhurst Rd, BH4 8EN, ☏ 752777 – ⊁ rm TV ☎ ℗. ◪ VISA. ⊁
BX n
M (lunch by arrangement)/dinner 7.50 st. and a la carte approx. 14.75 st. ▮ 3.00 – **22 rm** ⊇ 26.50/53.00 st. – SB (except summer and Bank Holidays) 48.00/56.00 st.

Wood Lodge, 10 Manor Rd, East Cliff, BH1 3EY, ☏ 290891, ☞ – TV ℗. ◪ VISA. ⊁
EY z
Easter-mid October – **M** 7.50 t. ▮ 3.75 – **15 rm** ⊇ 22.75/45.50 t.

Valberg, 1a Wollstonecraft Rd, Boscombe, BH5 1JQ, ☏ 394644, ☞ – ℗. ⊁
CX t
M 6.00 st. – **10 rm** ⊇ 16.00/28.00 st.

Naseby Nye, 10 Byron Rd, Boscombe, Overcliff, BH5 1JD, ☏ 394079, ☞ – ⊁ rest ℗
DX z
M 10.00 st. ▮ 3.50 – **12 rm** ⊇ 15.00/42.00 st.

Tudor Grange, 31 Gervis Rd, East Cliff, BH1 3EE, ☏ 291472, ☞ – TV ℗. VISA
EY o
closed January and February – **12 rm** ⊇ (dinner included) 18.00/56.00 t.

Clifton Court, 30 Clifton Rd, Southbourne, BH6 3PA, ☏ 427753 – ⊁ rest ℗. ⊁
EX c
M 6.00 – **11 rm** ⊇ 18.00/40.00.

Oscars (De Vere) (at Royal Bath H.), Bath Rd, BH1 2EW, ☏ 25555, Telex 41375, Fax 24158 – ℗. ◪ AE ① VISA
DZ
M 12.50/21.00 st. and a la carte 24.05/29.40 st.

Ocean City, 3-5 Lansdowne Rd, BH1 1RZ, ☏ 291277, Chinese (Peking, Szechuan) rest. – ▤. ◪ AE ① VISA
DY e
M 4.95/8.00 st. and a la carte 9.70/9.80 st.

Sophisticats, 43 Charminster Rd, BH8 8UE, ☏ 291019
BV a
closed Sunday, Monday, first 2 weeks February and first 2 weeks November – **M** (dinner only) a la carte 13.70/16.70 t. ▮ 2.95.

Regent's, 747 Christchurch Rd, Boscombe, BH7 6AN, ☏ 36021, Chinese rest. – ▤. ◪ AE VISA
DX a
closed Monday – **M** (dinner only) 15.50 t.

ALFA-ROMEO, SCIMITAR, MASERATI 33 R. L. Stevenson Av., Westbourne ℰ 752790
AUSTIN-ROVER Castle Lane West, Redhill ℰ 510201
AUSTIN-ROVER 14 Carbery Row ℰ 423243
BENTLEY, ROLLS-ROYCE Ringwood Rd ℰ 570575
CITROEN, PEUGEOT-TALBOT 3 Oxford Rd, Lansdowne ℰ 26566
DAIMLER-JAGUAR 382-6 Charminster Rd ℰ 510252
FIAT 674 Wimborne Rd ℰ 512121

FORD Tower Park, Canford Heath, Poole ℰ 762442
MERCEDES-BENZ Wallisdown Rd ℰ 525111
PORSCHE 282 New Rd ℰ 897688
SEAT 318-320 Holdenhurst Rd ℰ 33304
VAUXHALL Castle Lane West ℰ 526434
VAUXHALL-OPEL Poole Rd ℰ 763361
VOLVO 582-600 Ringwood Rd, Poole ℰ 715733

ⓜ ATS 892 Christchurch Rd, Boscombe ℰ 424457
ATS 1 Fernside Rd, Poole ℰ 733301/733326

BOURTON-ON-THE-WATER Glos. **403** **404** O 28 – pop. 2 538 – ECD : Saturday – ☎ 0451 Cotswold.

♦London 91 – ♦Birmingham 47 – Gloucester 24 – ♦Oxford 36.

⩘ **Camalan House** without rest., Station Rd, GL54 2ER, ℰ 21302 – ⤫ Ⓟ. ⌘
April-October – **5 rm** ⌷ 15.00/24.00 **st.**

⩘ **Triangle** without rest., Station Rd, GL54 2ER, ℰ 21037 – ⤫. ⌘
March-October – **3 rm** ⌷ 15.00/28.00 **s.**

at Great Rissington SE : 3 ¼ m. – ✉ Cheltenham – ☎ 0451 Cotswold :

🏠 **Lamb Inn** ⌘, GL54 2LP, ℰ 20388, ≼, « Attractive part 17C Cotswold-stone inn », ⌷, ⤬
– Ⓟ. ◪ **VISA**
closed 25 and 26 December – **M** (bar lunch)/dinner 12.15 **t.** and a la carte ₰ 3.95 – **8 rm**
⌷ 21.00/44.00 **st.** – SB (winter only) 48.00/65.00 **st.**

FORD Lansdowne Rd ℰ 20366

BOVEY TRACEY Devon **403** I 32 The West Country G. – pop. 3 434 – ECD : Wednesday –
✉ Newton Abbot – ☎ 0626.

See : St. Peter, St. Paul and St. Thomas of Canterbury Church★.

🖪 Lower Car Park, Station Rd ℰ 832047 (summer only).

♦London 214 – Exeter 14 – ♦Plymouth 32.

🏠 **Coombe Cross,** Coombe Cross, TQ13 9EY, SE : on B 3344 ℰ 832476, ⤬ – Ⓣⓥ ☎ Ⓟ. ◪
Ⓐⓔ ⓪ **VISA**
M (bar lunch)/dinner 13.95 **st.** ₰ 4.20 – **26 rm** ⌷ 31.50/49.90 **st.** – SB 62.00/67.80 **st.**

🏠 Edgemoor ⌘, Haytor Rd, TQ13 9LE, ℰ 832466, ⤬ – ⤫ rm Ⓣⓥ Ⓟ. ◪ Ⓐⓔ ⓪ **VISA**
M 10.50 **st.** and a la carte ₰ 3.00 – **18 rm**.

⩘ **Front House Lodge,** East St., TQ13 9EL, ℰ 832202, ⤬ – ⤫ rest Ⓣⓥ Ⓟ. ◪ **VISA**
⌘
M (by arrangement) – **8 rm** ⌷ 17.00/28.00 **st.** – SB (except June-September) 50.00/80.00 **st.**

⩘ **Willmead Farm** ⌘ without rest., TQ13 9NP, NW : 2 ¾ m. by A 382 ℰ 064 77 (Lustleigh) 214,
≼, « Part 14C thatched farmhouse », ⤬, park – ⤫ Ⓟ. ⌘
closed Christmas and New Year – **3 rm** ⌷ 25.00/40.00 **st.**

at Haytor NW : 1 ½ m. on B 3344 – ✉ Bovey Tracey – ☎ 036 46 Haytor :

🏠🏠 **Bel Alp House** ⌘, TQ13 9XX, NW : 1 m. on Widecombe Rd ℰ 217, ≼ countryside,
« Country house atmosphere », ⤬, ✗ – ▯ ⤫ rest Ⓣⓥ ☎ ♿ Ⓟ. ◪ **VISA**
restricted service December-February – **M** (booking essential) 17.50/27.50 **t.** ₰ 4.00 – **9 rm**
⌷ 57.00/106.00 **t.** – SB 68.00/90.00 **st.**

BOWBURN Durham **401** **402** P 19 – pop. 3 748 – ☎ 091 Tyneside.

♦London 265 – Durham 3 – ♦Middlesbrough 20.

🏠 **Bowburn Hall,** DH6 5NH, E : 1 m. ℰ 3770311, ⤬ – ⤫ rest Ⓣⓥ ☎ Ⓟ. ◪ Ⓐⓔ ⓪ **VISA**
M (dinner) a la carte 9.95/13.95 **st.** ₰ 3.50 – **19 rm** ⌷ 30.00/50.00 **st.**

BOWDON Greater Manchester **402** **403** **404** M 23 – see Altrincham.

BOWNESS-ON-WINDERMERE Cumbria **402** L 20 – see Windermere.

BOX Wilts. **403** **404** N 29 – see Bath (Avon).

When travelling for business or pleasure
in England, Wales, Scotland and Ireland :

– *use the series of five maps*
   *(nos **401**, **402**, **403**, **404** and **405**) at a scale of 1:400 000*

– *they are the perfect complement to this Guide*
   as towns underlined in red on the maps will be found in this Guide.

BRACKLEY Northants. **403 404** Q 27 – pop. 6 663 – ECD : Wednesday – ✉ ☎ 0280.
♦London 67 – ♦Birmingham 53 – Northampton 21 – ♦Oxford 21.

🏨 **Crown** (B.C.B.), 20-22 Market Sq., NN13 5DP, ☎ 702210 – 📺 ☎ 🅿. 🔦 AE ⓓ VISA
⇘
M 7.95 **st.** and a la carte ▮ 3.65 – **14 rm** ⊑ 36.00/51.00 **st.** – SB (weekends only) 42.00 **st.**

FORD Burwell Hill ☎ 702268 ▮ ATS Station Building, Northampton Rd ☎ 702000/703188

BRACKNELL Berks. **404** R 29 – pop. 52 257 – ECD : Wednesday – ☎ 0344.
🏌 Downshire Easthampstead Park, Wokingham ☎ 424066, SW : 3 m.
🛈 Central Library, Town Sq., ☎ 423149.
♦London 35 – Reading 11.

🏨 **Hilton National** (Hilton), Bagshot Rd, RG12 3QJ, S : 2 m. on A 322 ☎ 424801, Telex 848058, Fax 487454 – |ᘔ| ⇖ rm ▤ rest 📺 ☎ 🅿 – 🛎 200. 🔦 AE ⓓ VISA
M (closed Saturday lunch) 12.50/20.00 **t.** and a la carte – ⊑ 7.95 – **167 rm** 80.00/96.00 **st.** – SB (weekends only) 100.00 **st.**

NISSAN Downshire Way ☎ 426500 VAUXHALL Lovelace Rd ☎ 481925
RENAULT London Rd ☎ 54444

BRADFIELD COMBUST Suffolk – see Bury St. Edmunds.

BRADFORD West Yorks. **402** O 22 – pop. 293 336 – ECD : Wednesday – ☎ 0274.
Envir. : Corsham Court ★★.
🏌 Phoenix Park, Thornbury ☎ 667573, E : on A 647 BX – 🏌 Bradford Moor, Scarr-Hall, Pollard Lane ☎ 638313 BX – 🏌 West Bowling, Newall Hall, Rooley Lane ☎ 724449, on A 6177 BY.
✈ Leeds and Bradford Airport : ☎ 0532 (Rawdon) 503431, Telex 557868 NE : 6 m. by A 658 BX.
🛈 City Hall, Hall Ings, Channing Way ☎ 753678.
♦ London 212 – ♦Leeds 9 – ♦Manchester 39 – ♦Middlesbrough 75 – ♦Sheffield 45.

Plan of Enlarged Area : see Leeds

Plan opposite

🏨 **Stakis Norfolk Gardens** (Stakis), Hall Ings, BD1 5SH, ☎ 734734, Telex 517573, Fax 306146 – |ᘔ| 📺 ☎ ᘔ – 🛎 750. 🔦 AE ⓓ VISA BZ e
M (closed lunch Saturday and Sunday) – ⊑ 7.25 – **121 rm** 66.00/99.00 **st.**, **5 suites** 125.00 **st.**

🏨 **Guide Post,** Common Rd, Low Moor, BD12 OST, S : 3 m. by A 641 off A 638 ☎ 607866, Telex 517635, Fax 671085 – 📺 ☎ 🅿 – 🛎 80. 🔦 AE ⓓ VISA on plan of Leeds AX c
M (closed Saturday lunch and Sunday dinner) 10.00 **t.** (lunch) and a la carte ▮ 3.45 – **43 rm** ⊑ 39.50/65.00 **t.** – SB (weekends only) 60.00 **st.**

🏨 **Novotel Bradford,** Euroway Trading Estate, Merrydale Rd, BD4 6SA, S : 3 ½ m. by A 641 and A 6117 off M 606 ☎ 683683, Telex 517312, Fax 651342, ⤓ heated – |ᘔ| 📺 ☎ ᘔ 🅿 – 🛎 on plan of Leeds AX a
132 rm.

🏨 **Victoria** (T.H.F.), Bridge St., BD1 1JX, ☎ 728706, Telex 517456, Fax 736358 – |ᘔ| ⇖ rm 📺 ☎ 🅿 – 🛎. 🔦 AE ⓓ VISA BZ c
M (carving rest.) 7.50/9.95 **st.** and a la carte ▮ 3.95 – ⊑ 7.00 – **58 rm** 60.00/85.00 **st.**, **1 suite** 115.00 **st.** – SB (weekends only) 60.00/72.00 **st.**

⚕ **Cartwright,** 308 Manningham Lane, BD8 7AX, ☎ 499908, Fax 481309 – 📺 ☎ 🅿. 🔦 VISA
⇘ BX a
M (closed Sunday dinner) (Indian rest.) (bar lunch Monday to Saturday)/dinner a la carte 6.30/9.55 **st.** ▮ 3.50 – **14 rm** ⊑ 26.00/36.00 **st.**

⚘ **Park Drive,** 12 Park Drive, Heaton, BD9 4DR, ☎ 480194, ⇜ – 📺 🅿. 🔦 AE VISA
⇘ AX e
M 9.50 **st.** ▮ 3.90 – **7 rm** ⊑ 39.00/49.00 **st.** – SB (weekends only) 54.00 **st.**

⚘ **Norland House,** 695 Great Horton Rd, BD7 4DU, ☎ 571698 – 📺 🅿 AY i
M (by arrangement) 5.30 **st.** – **8 rm** ⊑ 15.50/28.75 **st.**

✕✕✕ **Restaurant Nineteen,** North Park Rd, Heaton, BD9 4NT, ☎ 492559 – ⇖. 🔦 AE ⓓ
VISA AX n
closed Sunday, Monday, 1 week June, 2 weeks September and 1 week Christmas – **M** (dinner only) 26.00 **t.** ▮ 5.25.

AUSTIN-ROVER, DAIMLER-JAGUAR Canal Rd ☎ 733488
BMW Oak Lane ☎ 495521
CITROEN Whetley Hill ☎ 495543
COLT St. Enoch's Rd ☎ 678272
FIAT Keighley Rd, Frizinghall ☎ 490031
FORD 44 Bowland St. ☎ 725131
FORD 146-148 Tong St. ☎ 681601
MERCEDES-BENZ Thornton Rd ☎ 494122

NISSAN 77 Otley Rd ☎ 727302
PORSCHE, VAUXHALL-OPEL Neville Rd ☎ 307600
SAAB Apperley Lane, Yeadon ☎ 0532 (Leeds) 502231
VOLVO 221 Sunbridge Rd ☎ 721720
VW, AUDI-NSU Ingleby Rd ☎ 494100

▮ ATS 8 Cranmer Rd ☎ 632233/632106
ATS 177 Thornton Rd ☎ 731141/723015

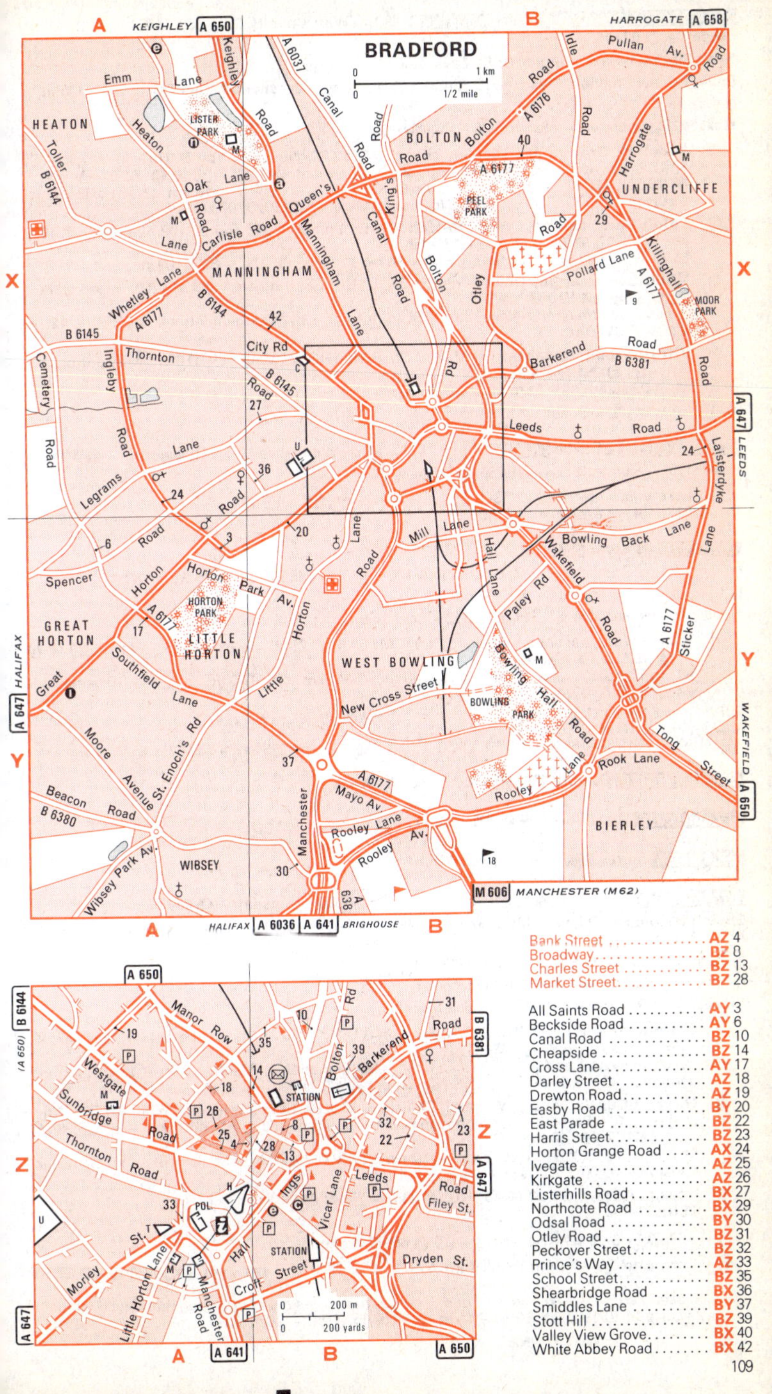

Bank Street . . . . **AZ** 4
Broadway . . . . **BZ** 8
Charles Street . . . . **BZ** 13
Market Street . . . . **BZ** 28

All Saints Road . . . . **AY** 3
Beckside Road . . . . **AY** 6
Canal Road . . . . **BZ** 10
Cheapside . . . . **BZ** 14
Cross Lane . . . . **AY** 17
Darley Street . . . . **AZ** 18
Drewton Road . . . . **AZ** 19
Easby Road . . . . **BY** 20
East Parade . . . . **BZ** 22
Harris Street . . . . **BZ** 23
Horton Grange Road . . . . . . **AX** 24
Ivegate . . . . **AZ** 25
Kirkgate . . . . **AZ** 26
Listerhills Road . . . . **BX** 27
Northcote Road . . . . **BX** 29
Odsal Road . . . . **BY** 30
Otley Road . . . . **BZ** 31
Peckover Street . . . . **BZ** 32
Prince's Way . . . . **AZ** 33
School Street . . . . **BZ** 35
Shearbridge Road . . . . **BX** 36
Smiddles Lane . . . . **BY** 37
Stott Hill . . . . **BZ** 39
Valley View Grove . . . . **BX** 40
White Abbey Road . . . . **BX** 42

BRADFORD-ON-AVON Wilts. 403 404 N 29 The West Country G. – pop. 8 921 – ECD : Wednesday – ✆ 022 16.

See : Site★★ – Saxon Church of St. Lawrence★★ – Bridge★.

Envir. : Great Chalfield Manor★ AC (Church★) NE : 2 m. – Westwood Manor★ AC, SW : 1 ½ m.

🛈 Waterlands, 34 Silver St. ✆ 5797.

◆London 118 – ◆Bristol 24 – Salisbury 35 – Swindon 33.

🏨 **Woolley Grange** ⬠, Woolley Green, BA15 1TX, NE : ¾ m. by B 3107 on Woolley St. ✆ 4705, Fax 4059, ≤, « 17C manor house », ⅃ heated, 🐎, ✗ – TV ☎ Ⓟ. 🖾 AE ① VISA
M 16.00/24.50 st. and dinner a la carte 32.00/37.00 st. � 5.50 – **15 rm** ☑ 78.00/150.00 st.
2 suites 115.00/155.00 st. – SB (November-March) 136.00/200.00 st.

🏨 **Leigh Park**, Leigh Rd West, BA15 2RA, NE : 1 m. by A 363 and B 3109 on B 3105 ✆ 4885, 🐎, ✗ – TV ☎ Ⓟ – 🎿 100. 🖾 AE ① VISA
M 13.50/18.50 t. and a la carte ♸ 3.50 – **20 rm** ☑ 58.00/95.00 t. – SB 92.00 st.

🏠 **Widbrook Grange**, Trowbridge Rd, BA15 1UH, SE : 1 m. on A 363 ✆ 4750, ≤, 🐎, park – TV ☎ & Ⓟ. 🖾 AE VISA ✗✗
closed Christmas and New Year – **M** (dinner only by arrangement) 14.95 ♸ 3.50 – **12 rm** ☑ 21.50/64.00 st.

🏠 **Priory Steps**, Newtown, off Market St., BA15 1NQ, ✆ 2230, ≤, « 17C weavers cottages », 🐎 – TV Ⓟ. 🖾 VISA. ✗✗
M 14.00 st. ♸ 2.75 – **5 rm** ☑ 35.00/48.00 st.

AUSTIN-ROVER St Margarets ✆ 3215

RENAULT Woolley St. ✆ 2352

BRADWORTHY Devon 403 G 31 – pop. 821 – ECD : Wednesday – ✉ Holsworthy – ✆ 040 924.

◆London 251 – Barnstaple 27 – Exeter 50 – ◆Plymouth 47.

✗✗ **Lake Villa** with rm, EX22 7SQ, E : ½ m. ✆ 342, 🐎, ✗ – TV Ⓟ
M (booking essential) – **8 rm**.

BRAINTREE Essex 404 V 28 – pop. 30 975 – ECD : Thursday – ✆ 0376.

🏌 Kings Lane, Stisted ✆ 24117, E: 2 m. by A 120 – 🏌 Towerlands, Panfield Rd ✆ 26802.

🛈 Town Hall Centre, Market Sq. ✆ 550066/43140.

◆London 45 – ◆Cambridge 38 – Chelmsford 12 – Colchester 15.

🏨 **White Hart** (Lansbury), Bocking End, CM7 6AB, ✆ 21401, Telex 988835 – ✗ rm TV ☎ Ⓟ – 🎿. 🖾 AE ① VISA ✗✗
M (grill rest.) a la carte 8.20/15.30 t. – **34 rm** ☑ 47.00/57.00 t. – SB (weekends only) 58.00/62.00 st.

FORD Rayne Rd ✆ 21202
MAZDA Rayne Rd ✆ 42159
VAUXHALL-OPEL 277-281 Rayne Rd ✆ 21456

VOLVO Skitts Hill ✆ 47797

⬡ ATS 271-275 Rayne Rd ✆ 23306

BRAITHWAITE Cumbria 401 402 K 20 – see Keswick.

BRAMHOPE West Yorks. 402 P 22 – see Leeds.

BRAMLEY Surrey 404 S 30 – see Guildford.

BRAMPTON Cumbria 401 402 L 19 – pop. 3 686 – ECD : Thursday – ✆ 069 77.

Envir. : Lanercost : Priory★ (14C ruins) AC, NE : 3 m. – Bewcastle (churchyard Runic Cross★ 8C) N : 12 m.

🏌 Talkin Tarn ✆ 2255, SE : 1 m. on B 6413.

🛈 Moot Hall, Market Place ✆ 3433 (summer only).

◆London 317 – ◆Carlisle 9 – ◆Newcastle-upon-Tyne 49.

🏨 **Farlam Hall** ⬠, CA8 2NG, SE : 2 ¾ m. on A 689 ✆ 069 76 (Hallbankgate) 234, Fax 683, ≤, « Gardens » – TV ☎ Ⓟ. 🖾 AE VISA
closed February and 26 to 31 December – **M** (dinner only) 20.00 t. ♸ 3.75 – **13 rm** ☑ (dinner included) 70.00/160.00 t. – SB (November-April) 110.00/140.00 st.

🏨 **Hayton Castle** ⬠, ✉ Wetheral, Carlisle, CA6 8QD, SW : 2 ½ m. on A 69 ✆ 022 870 (Hayton) 651, ≤, « Part 16C country house in extensive grounds », ⬠, 🐎, park – ✗ TV ☎ Ⓟ – 🎿. 🖾 AE ① VISA ✗✗
M a la carte 13.00/20.00 st. ♸ 3.50 – **10 rm** ☑ 40.00/70.00 st. – SB (except summer) (weekends only) 60.00/110.00 st.

⬡ **Howard Arms**, Front St., CA8 1NG, ✆ 2357 – TV ☎ Ⓟ. ✗✗
11 rm.

at Talkin S : 2 ¾ m. by B 6413 – ✉ ✆ 06977 Brampton :

✗✗ **Tarn End** ⬠ with rm, Talkin Tarn, CA8 1LS, ✆ 2340, ≤ Talkin Tarn, 🐎 – TV Ⓟ. 🖾 AE ① VISA ✗✗
closed February – **M** (closed Sunday dinner to non-residents in winter) (bar lunch)/dinner a la carte 14.20/19.20 st. ♸ 3.50 – **6 rm** ☑ 38.00/55.00 st. – SB 72.00 st.

AUSTIN-ROVER Carlisle Rd ✆ 2508

BRAMSHAW Hants. 408 404 P 31 – pop. 611 – ECD : Tuesday – ⊠ Lyndhurst – ✆ 0703 Southampton.

◆London 93 – Salisbury 13 – ◆Southampton 11 – Winchester 21.

    Bramble Hill ⑤, Bramble Hill, SO43 7JG, W : ½ m. ✆ 813165, ≤, « Former hunting lodge », ☞, park – TV ☎ P. 🅂 VISA
    M *(closed Monday lunch and Sunday dinner)* 12.50 **t.** and a la carte ⱐ 3.95 – **12 rm** ⌕ 30.00/80.00 **t.**

BRANDON Warw. 408 404 P 26 – see Coventry (West Midlands).

BRANDS HATCH Kent – ⊠ Dartford – ✆ 0474 Ash Green.

◆London 22 – Maidstone 18.

    Brands Hatch Thistle (Thistle), on A 20, DA3 8PE, ✆ 854900, Telex 966449, Fax 853220 – ⇆
    ☰ rest TV ☎ & P – ⛛ 300. 🅂 AE ⓞ VISA. ⅜
    M 12.95/14.95 **st.** and a la carte 18.70/23.95 **st.** – ⌕ 7.25 – **130 rm, 2 suites**.

    at Fawkham E : 1 ½ m. by A 20 – ⊠ Dartford – ✆ 0474 Ash Geen :

    Brands Hatch Place, DA3 8NQ, ✆ 872239, Fax 879652, 🔲, ☞, ⁑, squash – ⇆ TV ☎
    P – ⛛ 120. 🅂 AE ⓞ VISA. ⅜
    closed Christmas – **M** *(closed Saturday lunch)* 16.50 **t.** and a la carte – ⌕ 7.00 – **29 rm** 65.00/95.00 **t.**

BRANSCOMBE Devon 408 K 32 The West Country G. – pop. 506 – ECD : Thursday – ⊠ Seaton – ✆ 029 780.

◆London 167 – Exeter 20 – Lyme Regis 11.

    Masons Arms, EX12 3DJ, ✆ 300, « 14C inn », ☞ – TV ☎ P. 🅂 VISA
    M *(bar lunch Monday to Saturday)/dinner* a la carte 16.20/19.50 **t.** ⱐ 3.95 – **21 rm** ⌕ 25.00/84.00 **t.** – SB (except Bank Holidays) (November-April) 65.25/97.00 **st.**

BRANSTON Lincs. 402 404 S 24 – see Lincoln.

BRANSTON Staffs. – see Burton-upon-Trent.

BRAUNSTONE Leics. 402 408 404 Q 26 – see Leicester.

BRAUNTON Devon 408 H 30 – pop. 9 004 – ECD : Wednesday – ✆ 0271.

🛈 The Car Park ✆ 816400 (summer only).

◆London 226 – Exeter 47 – Taunton 58.

    Otter's, 30 Caen St., EX33 1AA, ✆ 813633 – 🅂 VISA
    closed Sunday, Monday, 2 weeks March and 2 weeks October – **M** *(dinner only)* 13.50 **st.** and a la carte 12.50/19.25 **st.** ⱐ 3.25.

    at Wrafton SE : ½ m. on A 361 – ⊠ ✆ 0271 Braunton :

    Poyers, EX33 2DN, ✆ 812149, ☞ – TV ☎ P. 🅂 AE VISA
    M *(closed Sunday to non-residents)* (dinner only) a la carte 13.80/16.50 **t.** ⱐ 3.00 – **10 rm** ⌕ 35.00/50.00 **t.**

    at Knowle N : 1 ¼ m. on A 361 – ⊠ ✆ 0271 Braunton:

    Grays Country, EX33 2NA, ✆ 812809, ☞ – P. 🅂 VISA
    closed lunch Tuesday and Saturday, Sunday and Monday – **M** 15.00 **t.** and a la carte approx. 15.00 **t.**

BRAY-ON-THAMES Berks. 404 R 29 – pop. 9 427 – ⊠ ✆ 0628 Maidenhead.

◆London 34 – Reading 13.

    ❀❀❀ **Waterside Inn** (Roux), Ferry Rd, SL6 2AT, ✆ 20691, Fax 784710, French rest.
    , « ≤ Thames-side setting », ☞ – ☰ P. 🅂 ⓞ VISA
    closed Tuesday lunch, Sunday dinner 16 October-Easter, Monday and 26 December-10 February – **M** 22.50/46.50 **st.** and a la carte 36.50/53.50 **st.** ⱐ 8.00
    Spec. Tronçonnettes de homard poêlées minute au porto blanc, Canoe de poussin aux petits légumes à la senteur d'estragon, Péché gourmand selon ''Michel''.

BRECHFA Dyfed **403** H 28 – ✉ Carmarthen – ☎ 026 789.

♦London 223 – Carmarthen 11 – ♦Swansea 30.

XX **Ty Mawr Country House** ♨ with rm, Abergorlech Rd, SA32 7RA, ✆ 332, ◣, ☞ – **P**.
◣ VISA
M (dinner only) (booking essential) 17.00 **st.** ▮ 3.75 – **5 rm** ⌷ 40.00/55.00 **st.** –
SB 30.00/40.00 **st.**

BRECON (ABERHONDDU) Powys **403** J 28 – pop. 7 166 – ECD : Wednesday – ☎ 0874.
See : Cathedral ★ 13C.
Envir. : Craig-y-Nos (Dan-yr-Ogof Caves★★) SW : 18 m. – Road★ from Brecon to Hirwaun –
Road★ from Brecon to Merthyr Tydfil – Bwlch (≤★ of the Usk Valley) SE : 8 ½ m.
◻9 Newton Park ✆ 2004, W : ¾ m. on A 40 – ◻18 Penoyre Park, Cradoc ✆ 3658, NW : 2 m.
◪ Watton Mount ✆ 4437 (summer only) – Market Car Park ✆ 2485 and 5692 (summer only).
♦London 171 – ♦Cardiff 40 – Carmarthen 31 – Gloucester 65.

⌂ Wellington, The Bulwark, LD3 7AD, ✆ 5225 – TV ☎. ◣ AE VISA. ≫
21 rm ⌷ 30.00/50.00 **st.**

FORD ✆ 2401   VAUXHALL County Garages ✆ 2266

BREDON Heref and Worc. **403 404** N 27 – see Tewkesbury.

BREDWARDINE Heref. and Worc. **403** L 27 – pop. 177 – ✉ Hereford – ☎ 098 17 Moccas.
♦London 150 – Hereford 12 – Newport 51.

⛲ **Red Lion,** HR3 6BU, ✆ 303, ◣, ☞ – TV ☎ **P**. ◣ AE ⓞ VISA
M (bar lunch)/dinner 15.00 **t.** ▮ 3.00 – **9 rm** ⌷ 28.00/45.00 **t.** – SB 39.00 **st.**

BRENDON Devon **403** I 30 – see Lynton.

BRENT ELEIGH Suffolk – see Lavenham.

BRENT KNOLL Somerset **403** L 30 – pop. 1 092 – ECD : Wednesday and Saturday – ✉ Highbridge – ☎ 0278 Bridgwater.
♦London 151 – ♦Bristol 33 – Taunton 21.

⌂ **Battleborough Grange,** Bristol Rd, TA9 4HJ, on A 38 ✆ 760208, Fax 760208, ☞ – TV ☎
P – ⌂ 80. ◣ AE ⓞ VISA ≫
M 9.50 **st.** and a la carte ▮ 3.50 – **18 rm** ⌷ 24.00/48.00 **t.** – SB (except summer) (week-
ends only) 55.00/70.00 **st.**

BRENTWOOD Essex **404** V 29 – pop. 51 212 – ECD : Thursday – ☎ 0277.
◻18 King George's playing fields, Ingrave Rd ✆ 218850.
♦London 22 – Chelmsford 11 – Southend-on-Sea 21.

🏰 **Brentwood Moat House** (Q.M.H.), London Rd, CM14 4NR, SW : 1 ¼ m. on A 1023
✆ 225252, Telex 995182, Fax 262809, ☞ – ✂ rest TV ⅙ **P** – ⌂ 55. ◣ AE ⓞ VISA ≫
M a la carte 19.00/30.00 **t.** ▮ 3.80 – ⌷ 6.75 – **33 rm** 75.00/130.00 **st.**

🏛 **Post House** (T.H.F.), Brook St., CM14 5NF, SW : 1 ¾ m. on A 1023 ✆ 260260, Telex 995379,
Fax 264264, ⊠ heated – ▮ ✂ rm TV ☎ ⅙ **P** – ⌂. ◣ AE ⓞ VISA
M (closed Saturday lunch and Sunday dinner) 11.95/15.50 **st.** and a la carte ▮ 3.95 – ⌷ 7.00
– **117 rm** 80.00/90.00 **st.** – SB (weekends only) 60.00/80.00 **st.**

AUDI-VW. DAIMLER-JAGUAR 2 Brook St. ✆   VAUXHALL-OPEL Brook St. ✆ 263333
216161
AUSTIN-ROVER Ingrave Rd ✆ 221401   ⓦ ATS Fairfield Rd ✆ 211079
FORD 140 London Rd ✆ 261616   ATS Unit 30, Wash Rd ✆ 262877
RENAULT 21 Hutton Rd, Shenfield ✆ 218686

BRERETON Cheshire – see Holmes Chapel.

BRIDGEND (PEN-Y-BONT) Mid Glam. **403** J 29 – pop. 31 008 – ECD : Wednesday – ☎ 0656.
♦London 177 – ♦Cardiff 20 – ♦Swansea 23.

🏛 Heronston, Ewenny, CF35 5AW, S : 2 m. on B 4265 ✆ 668811, Telex 498232, Fax 767391,
⊠ heated, ◪ – TV ☎ **P** – ⌂
78 rm.

at Coychurch (Llangrallo) E : 2 ¼ m. by A 473 – ✉ ☎ 0656 Bridgend :

🏛 **Coed-y-Mwstwr** ♨, CF35 6AF, N : 1 m. ✆ 860621, Fax 863122, ≤, ⊠ heated, ☞, park,
XX – ▮ TV ☎ **P**. ◣ AE ⓞ VISA. ≫
M 16.95/22.90 **st.** and a la carte ▮ 4.95 – ⌷ 7.95 – **28 rm** 65.00/150.00 **st.** – SB (week-
ends only) 100.00/120.00 **st.**

at Laleston W : 2 m. on A 473 – ⊠ ✆ 0656 Bridgend :

XX **Great House,** CF32 OHP, on A 473 ✆ 657644 – **P.** 🚗 ⓘ **VISA**
closed Saturday lunch and Sunday – **M** 8.95/12.95 **t.** and a la carte 13.55/22.95 **t.** 🍷 3.75.

MICHELIN Distribution Centre, Brackla Industrial Estate, CF31 2AG, ✆ **662343,** FAX **645602**

AUSTIN-ROVER Brackla Ind. Est. ✆ 653376
VAUXHALL, OPEL Maesteg Rd, Ind. Est. ✆ 55007
VOLVO Ogmore Rd, Ewenny ✆ 769769

ⓦ ATS Coity Rd ✆ 58775/6

BRIDGNORTH Shropshire 403 404 M 26 – pop. 10 332 – ECD : Thursday – ✆ 074 62 (4 and 5 fig.) or 0746 (6 fig.).

Envir. : Claverley (Parish church : wall paintings★ 13C-15C) E : 5 m. – Much Wenlock : Wenlock priory★ (ruins 11C) *AC*, NW : 8 ½ m.

📷 Stanley Lane ✆ 3315, N : 1 m.

🛈 Bridgnorth Library, Listley St. ✆ 3358.

◆London 146 – ◆Birmingham 26 – Shrewsbury 20 – Worcester 29.

⋔ **Croft,** St. Mary's St., WV16 4DW, ✆ 767155 – TV ☎. 🚗 AE **VISA**
M 12.95 **st.** 🍷 3.25 – **12 rm** ⊑ 20.00/43.00 **st.** – SB 48.00 **st.**

at Worfield NE : 4 m. by A 454 – ⊠ Bridgnorth – ✆ 074 64 Worfield :

🏠 **Old Vicarage** ⑤, WV15 5JZ, ✆ 497, Fax 552, 🚗 – ⭲ TV ☎ **P.** 🚗 AE ⓘ **VISA**
closed Christmas-New Year – **M** (lunch by arrangement) 14.50/23.95 **st.** 🍷 4.75 – **15 rm** ⊑ 54.50/75.00 **st.** – SB 85.00/92.50 **st.**

at Hampton Loade SE : 6 ¼ m. by A 442 – ⊠ Bridgnorth – ✆ 0746 Quatt :

XX **Haywain,** WV15 6HD, ✆ 780404 – **P.** 🚗 AE ⓘ **VISA**
closed Sunday dinner and Monday – **M** (dinner only and Sunday lunch)/dinner 23.00 **t.** 🍷 4.00.

AUSTIN-ROVER Salop St. ✆ 2207
RENAULT Mill St. ✆ 765315/761067

VW, AUDI Hollybush Rd ✆ 4343 (or after 5.30 ✆ 0836 502555)

BRIDGWATER Somerset 403 L 30 The West Country G. – pop. 30 782 – ECD : Thursday – ✆ 0278.

See : Site★ – Castle St.★ – St. Mary's★ – Admiral Blake Museum★*AC*.

Envir. : Stogursey Priory Church★★, NW : 14 m. by A 39 – Westonzoyland Church★★, SE : 3 m. – North Petherton Church Tower★★, S : 3 m.

🛈 Town Hall, High St. ✆ 427652 (summer only).

◆London 160 – ◆Bristol 39 – Taunton 11.

🏠 Friarn Court, 37 St. Mary St., TA6 3LX, ✆ 452859, Fax 452988 – TV ☎ **P**
12 rm.

🏠 Old Vicarage, 45 St. Mary's St., TA6 3LQ, ✆ 458891, 🚗 – TV ☎ **P.** 🚗 **VISA**
M *(closed Sunday lunch)* – **13 rm** ⊑ 35.00/39.50 **st.**

🏠 **Watergate,** 10-11 West Quay, TA6 3DB, ✆ 423847 – TV. 🚗 AE ⓘ **VISA**. 🐾
M *(closed lunch Saturday and Sunday)* 9.50 **t.** and a la carte 🍷 3.00 – **8 rm** ⊑ 29.50/44.00 **t.**

at West Huntspill N : 6 m. on A 38 – ⊠ Highbridge – ✆ 0278 Burnham-on-Sea :

🏠 **Sundowner,** 74 Main Rd, TA9 3QU, on A 38 ✆ 784766 – TV ☎ **P.** 🚗 AE ⓘ **VISA**
M *(closed Sunday dinner October-April)* 7.45/9.45 and a la carte 🍷 2.90 – **8 rm** ⊑ 28.00/56.00 **t.** – SB (except summer) (weekends only) 60.00/66.00 **st.**

at North Petherton S : 3 m. on A 38 – ⊠ ✆ 0278 Bridgwater :

🏠🏠 **Walnut Tree Inn** (Best Western), TA6 6QA, ✆ 662255, Fax 663946 – TV ☎ **P** – 🛁. 🚗
AE ⓘ **VISA**. 🐾
closed 25 and 26 December – **M** a la carte 7.70/16.75 **st.** – **27 rm** ⊑ 37.00/68.00 **st.**, **1 suite** 70.00/90.00 **st.** – SB 74.00/86.00 **st.**

AUDI-VW Taunton Rd ✆ 428110
AUSTIN-ROVER Market St. ✆ 422125
CITROEN Main Rd, Cannington ✆ 0278 (Combwich) 652228
FORD 37 Friar St. ✆ 451332

RENAULT 52 Eastover ✆ 422218
VOLVO Bristol Rd ✆ 455333

ⓦ ATS Polden St ✆ 455795
ATS Friarn St. ✆ 450571

BRIDLINGTON Humberside **402** T 21 – pop. 28 426 – ECD : Thursday – ☎ 0262.

See : Priory Church★ (12C-15C).

Envir. : Burton Agnes Hall★ (Elizabethan) *AC*, SW : 6 m.

ⓘ₈ Belvedere, Belvedere Rd ☎ 672092, S : 1 ½ m. on A 165 – ⓘ₈ Flamborough Head ☎ 850333, NE : 5 m.

ℹ 25 Prince St. ☎ 673474 and 679626.

◆ London 236 – ◆Kingston-upon-Hull 29 – York 41.

　　Expanse, North Marine Drive, YO15 2LS, ☎ 675347, Fax 604928, ≼ – 🛗 📺 ☎ ℗. 🅿 AE
　　　ⓞ **VISA**. ⚙
　　　M 6.25/9.50 **st.** and a la carte 🍷 3.40 – **48 rm** ⊊ 35.00/60.00 **t.** – SB 62.00/76.00 **st.**

　　Monarch, South Marine Drive, YO15 3JJ, ☎ 674447, Fax 604928, ≼ – 🛗 📺 ☎ ℗. 🅿 AE
　　　ⓞ **VISA**. ⚙
　　　closed 24 December-15 January – **M** (bar lunch Monday to Saturday)/dinner 11.00 **t.**
　　　and a la carte 🍷 3.60 – **40 rm** ⊊ 35.00/55.00 **t.** – SB 70.00/80.00 **st.**

FIAT　Quay Rd ☎ 670331　　　　　　　　　　　　　VOLVO　Pinfold Lane ☎ 670351
FORD　Hamilton Rd ☎ 675336
TALBOT　74 Pessingby Rd ☎ 678141　　　　　　　Ⓜ ATS　Springfield Av. ☎ 675571
VAUXHALL-OPEL　52-60 Quay Rd ☎ 672022

BRIDPORT Dorset **403** L 31 The West Country G. – pop. 10 615 – ECD : Thursday – ☎ 0308.

Envir. : Parnham House★★*AC*, N : 6 m. on A 3066.

ⓘ₈ Bridport and West Dorset, West Bay ☎ 22597, S : 1 ½ m.

ℹ 32 South St. ☎ 24901 (summer only).

◆London 150 – Exeter 38 – Taunton 33 – Weymouth 19.

　　Roundham House, Roundham Gdns, West Bay Rd, DT6 4BD, S : 1 m. by B 3157 ☎ 22753,
　　　Fax 421145, ⚘ – ⇔ rest 📺 ☎ ℗. 🅿 AE ⓞ **VISA**. ⚙
　　　February-November – **M** *(closed Sunday lunch)* (bar lunch)/dinner 10.95 **t.** 🍷 4.40 – **8 rm**
　　　⊊ 27.50/43.00 **t.** – SB (except summer) 50.00/59.50 **st.**

　　at Powerstock NE : 4 m. by A 3066 – ✉ Bridport – ☎ 030 885 Powerstock :

※※　**Three Horseshoes Inn** with rm, DT6 3TF, ☎ 328 – ℗. 🅿 AE **VISA**
　　　M *(closed Sunday dinner and Monday)* 9.50/16.50 **t.** 🍷 3.75 – **4 rm** ⊊ 15.00/40.00 **t.**

　　at Nettlecombe NE : 4 m. by A 3066 – ✉ Bridport – ☎ 030 885 Powerstock :

　　Marquis of Lorne ⑤, DT6 3SY, ☎ 236, ⚘ – ℗. ⚙
　　　closed Christmas Day – **M** a la carte 10.95/15.00 **t.** 🍷 3.60 – **6 rm** ⊊ 26.00/41.00 **t.** –
　　　SB (November-March) 37.90/49.00 **st.**

　　at Shipton Gorge SE : 3 m. by A 35 – ✉ ☎ 0308 Bridport :

※※　**Innsacre Farmhouse** ⑤ with rm, Shipton Lane, DT6 4LJ, N : 1 m. ☎ 56137, ⚘ – 📺 ℗.
　　　🅿 AE ⓞ **VISA**
　　　M 18.50 **t.** 🍷 3.50 – **7 rm** ⊊ 36.00/64.00 **t.** – SB (November-February) (except Christ-
　　　mas) (weekdays only) 69.00/73.00 **st.**

　　at West Bay S : 1 ½ m. on B 3157 – ✉ ☎ 0308 Bridport :

　　Haddon House, DT6 4EL, ☎ 23626 – 📺 ☎ ℗. 🅿 AE ⓞ **VISA**
　　　M 9.50/13.95 **t.** and a la carte 🍷 3.25 – **13 rm** ⊊ 32.50/50.00 **t.** – SB (weekends
　　　only) 55.00/70.00 **st.**

　　Britmead House, 154 West Bay Rd, DT6 4EG, N : ½ m. on B 3157 ☎ 22941 – ⇔ rest 📺
　　　℗. 🅿 AE ⓞ **VISA**. ⚙
　　　M 9.25 **st.** 🍷 3.40 – **6 rm** ⊊ 21.50/37.00 **st.**

　　at Chideock W : 3 m. on A 35 – ✉ Bridport – ☎ 0297 Chideock :

　　Betchworth House without rest., Main St., DT6 6JW, ☎ 89478, ⚘ – ℗
　　　6 rm ⊊ 16.00/34.00 **st.**

Ⓜ ATS　Victoria Grove ☎ 23661/2

BRIGHOUSE West Yorks. **402** O 22 – ☎ 0484.

◆London 213 – Bradford 12 – Burnley 28 – ◆Manchester 35 – ◆Sheffield 39.

　　Forte (T.H.F.), HD6 4HW, SE : 1 m. on A 644 ☎ 400400, Telex 518204, Fax 40006, 🔲 –
　　　⇔ rm 📺 ☎ ﮶ ℗ – 🅰 200. 🅿 AE ⓞ **VISA**. ⚙
　　　M 11.15/14.70 **st.** and a la carte 🍷 4.35 – ⊊ 7.60 – **92 rm** 72.00/100.00, **2 suites** 135.00 **st.** –
　　　SB (weekends only) 76.00/90.00 **st.**

See : Sea Front★★ – Royal Pavilion★ (interior★★) *AC* CZ – Booth Museum (bird collection)★ BV M – Preston Manor (Chinese collection★) BV D – The Lanes★ CZ – Aquarium★ *AC* CZ A – St. Bartholomews Church★ CX B – Envir. : Stanmer Park (site★) N : 3 ½ m. by A 27 CV – Clayton (Church of St. John the Baptist : frescoes★ 14C) N : 6 m. by A 23 BV.

🏌 East Brighton, Roedean ✆ 604838 CV – 🏌 Dyke, Dyke Rd ✆ 079 156 (Poynings) 296, N : by Dyke Rd BV – 🏌 Dyke Rd ✆ 556482 BV.

✈ Shoreham Airport : ✆ 452304, W : 8 m. by A 27 A.

🛈 Marlborough House, 54 Old Steine ✆ 23755 – Sea Front, Kings Rd ✆ 23755 (summer only).

🛈 at Hove : Town Hall, Norton Rd ✆ 775400.

King Alfred Leisure Centre, Kingsway ✆ 720371 ext 155.

♦London 53 – ♦Portsmouth 48 – ♦Southampton 61.

Plans on following pages

Grand (De Vere), King's Rd, BN1 2FW, ✆ 21188, Telex 877410, Fax 202694, ⩤, 🏊 – 🛗 📧 rest 📺 ☎ – 🔼 350. 🔼 AE ⓪ VISA BZ v
M 15.00/27.00 **st.** and a la carte ▯5.00 – **157 rm** ⊡ 95.00/135.00 **st.**, **6 suites** 350.00/850.00 **st.** – SB (weekends only) 130.00/220.00 **st.**

Hospitality Inn (Mt. Charlotte), King's Rd, BN1 1JA, ✆ 206700, Telex 878555, Fax 820692, ⩤, CZ n 🏊 – 🛗 ⤢ rm 📧 📺 ☎ ⅙ ⇔ – 🔼 350. 🛇
200 rm, 4 suites.

Brighton Metropole, King's Rd, BN1 2FU, ✆ 775432, Telex 877245, Fax 207764, ⩤, 🏊 – BZ s 🛗 📧 📺 ☎ – 🔼 1200. 🔼 AE ⓪ VISA
M 18.95 **t.** and a la carte 19.30/26.40 **t.** ▯5.25 – **312 rm** ⊡ 99.00/130.00 **st.**, **16 suites** 251.00/341.00 **st.** – SB (weekends only) 105.00 **st.**

Royal Crescent, Marine Parade, BN2 1AX, ✆ 606311, Telex 87253, Fax 601042, ⩤ – 🛗 📺 ☎ CV e – 🔼
64 rm, 2 suites.

Granville, 123-125 King's Rd, BN1 2FA, ✆ 26302, Fax 202541, ⩤ – 🛗 📺 ☎ – 🔼 35 BZ a
25 rm.

Kings, 139-141 King's Rd, BN1 2NA, ✆ 820854, Telex 878802, Fax 28120 – 🛗 📺 ☎ Ⓟ – BZ r 🔼 100. 🔼 AE ⓪ VISA. 🛇
M *(closed Saturday lunch)* (buffet lunch Monday to Friday)/dinner 12.50 **t.** ▯3.50 – **78 rm** ⊡ 55.00/75.00 **st.** – SB (weekends only) (except Easter, Christmas and New Year) 79.00/85.00 **st.**

Twenty One, 21 Charlotte St., BN2 1AG, ✆ 686450 – 📺 ☎. 🔼 AE VISA 🛇 CV i
M *(closed Sunday and Monday)* (dinner only) 21.50 **t.** ▯3.50 – **6 rm** ⊡ 35.00/65.00 **st.**

Topps, 17 Regency Sq., BN1 2FG, ✆ 729334 – 🛗 📺 ☎. 🔼 AE ⓪ VISA. 🛇 BZ i
closed Christmas and New Year – **M** *(closed Sunday and Wednesday)* (dinner only) 13.95 **st.**
▯2.85 – **12 rm** ⊡ 39.00/85.00 **st.** – SB (weekends only) 65.95/81.95 **st.**

Dove, 18 Regency Sq., BN1 2FG, ✆ 779222 – ⤢ rest 📺 ☎. 🔼 AE VISA. 🛇 BZ e
closed last week December – **M** (dinner only)(by arrangement) 10.50 **st.** ▯2.50 – **8 rm** ⊡ 30.00/72.00 **st.** – SB (weekends only) 65.00/86.00 **st.**

Adelaide, 51 Regency Sq., BN1 2FF, ✆ 205286 – ⤢ rest 📺 ☎. 🔼 AE ⓪ VISA. 🛇 BZ z
closed 22 December-17 January – **M** *(closed Sunday and Wednesday)* (bar lunch)/dinner 11.50 **st.** and a la carte ▯3.00 – **12 rm** ⊡ 30.00/70.00 **st.** – SB (weekends only) (except Bank Holidays) 63.00/80.00 **st.**

Prince Regent without rest., 29 Regency Sq., BN1 2FH, ✆ 29962 – ⤢ rest 📺 ☎. 🔼 ⓪ BZ u VISA. 🛇
closed 24 and 31 December – **19 rm** ⊡ 26.00/58.00 **t.**

Dudley House without rest., 10 Madeira Pl., BN2 1TN, ✆ 676794 – ⤢ 📺. 🛇 CZ a
6 rm ⊡ 35.00/55.00 **st.**

Harveys without rest., 1 Broad St., BN2 1TJ, ✆ 699227 – ⤢ 📺 🛇 CZ x
closed Christmas – **8 rm** ⊡ 32.00/50.00 **st.**

Hayward's, 51-52 North St., BN1 1RH, ✆ 24261 – 🔼 AE VISA CZ e
closed Sunday lunch July and August, Sunday dinner and 25-26 December – **M** 12.00/15.00 **t.** and a la carte 11.35/19.00 **t.**

Langan's Bistro, 1 Paston Pl., Kemp Town, BN2 1HA, ✆ 606933 – 🔼 AE ⓪ VISA CV a
closed Saturday lunch, Sunday dinner, Monday, 1 to 16 January and last 2 weeks August – **M** a la carte 12.95/16.25 **t.**

Stubbs, 14 Ship St., BN1 1AD, ✆ 204005 – 🔼 AE ⓪ VISA CZ v
closed lunch Saturday to Monday – **M** 14.50/19.50 **st.** and a la carte 18.60/23.60 **t.**

La Marinade, 77 St. Georges Rd, Kemp Town, BN2 1EF, ✆ 600992, French rest. – 📧. 🔼 CV c AE VISA
closed Saturday lunch, Sunday dinner and Monday – **M** 10.95 **st.** (lunch)/dinner a la carte 15.80/19.50 **st.** ▯4.50.

Whytes, 33 Western St., BN1 2PG, ✆ 776618 – 🔼 AE ⓪ VISA BZ o
closed Sunday and Monday – **M** (dinner only and Sunday lunch)/dinner 14.50 **t.** ▯3.00.

Foggs, 5 Little Western St., BN1 2PU, ✆ 735907 – 🔼 AE VISA BY a
M *(closed lunch Saturday and Sunday)* a la carte 9.90/15.40 **t.** ▯2.60.

Le Grandgousier, 15 Western St., BN1 2PG, ✆ 772005, French rest. – 🔼 AE VISA BY x
closed Saturday lunch, Sunday and 24 December-4 January – **M** 15.00 **st.** ▯3.00.

BRIGHTON AND HOVE

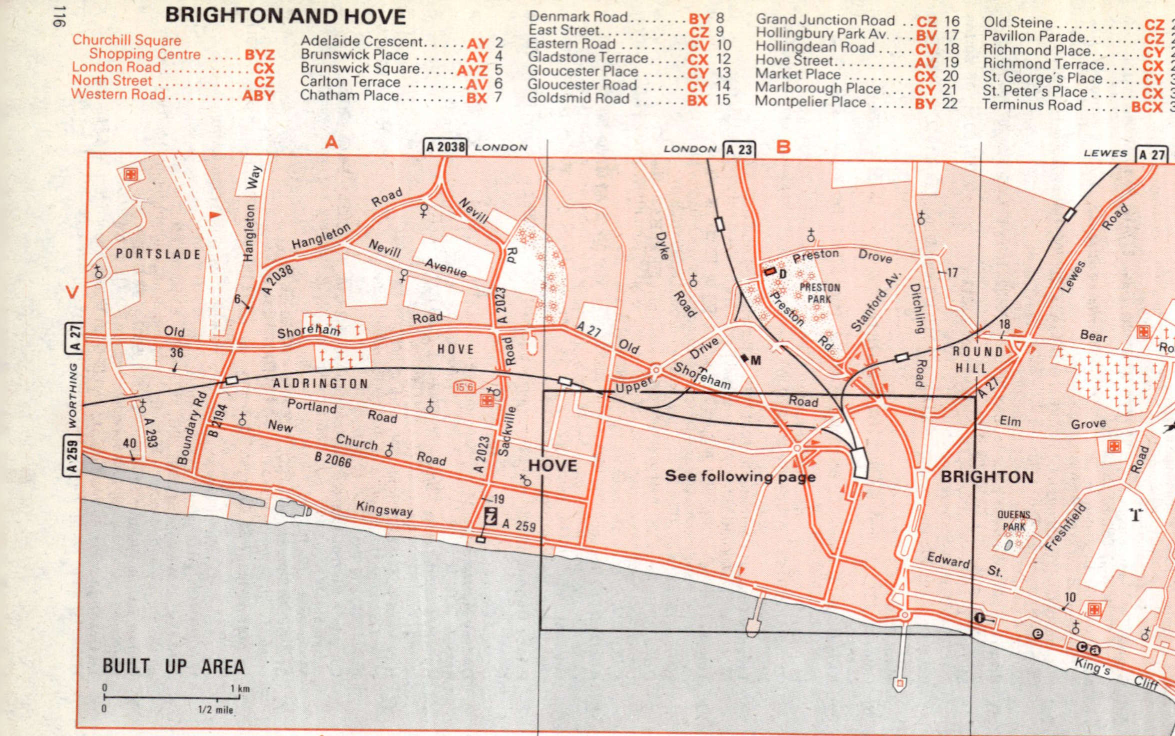

BRIGHTON AND HOVE
CENTRE
300 m
300 yards
For names of numbered streets, see previous page.
HOVE
BRIGHTON
ST. ANN'S WELL GARDENS
CHURCHILL SQ. SHOPPING CENTRE
THE BRIGHTON CENTRE
ROYAL PAVILION
THE LANES
Cromwell Road
Eaton Road
Norton Rd
Tisbury Road
The Drive
Wilbury Road
Selborne Rd
Palmeira Avenue
Lansdowne Road
Holland Road
Western Road
Montpelier St.
Preston St.
Kingsway
King's Road
Fourth Av.
Third Av.
Grand Avenue
Second Av.
First Avenue
Church Road
Davigdor Road
Shoreham Road
Dyke Rd
Vernon Ter.
Clifton Hill
Dyke Road
Buckingham Pl.
Buckingham Road
New England St.
England Rd
London Road
Viaduct Road
Ditchling Road
Southover St.
Albion Hill
Street
Sussex St.
Carlton Hill
John St.
Trafalgar Street
North Road
Church St.
Queen's Road
West St.
Grand Parade
St. James's St.
Marine Parade
Madeira Drive
Edward Street
STATION
B 2185
A 27
A 23
A 27
A 2010
A 2010
A 23
A 259
A 259
B 2066
B 2120
B 2122
B 2121
B 2119
B 2122
B 2118
POL.
POL.
117

at Hove – ✉ Hove – ☎ 0273 Brighton :

🏨 **Dudley** (T.H.F.), Lansdowne Pl., BN3 1HQ, ℰ 736266, Telex 87537, Fax 729802 – 🛗 ⇔ rm
📺 ☎ ⇔ 🅿 – 🕭 80. 🔄 AE ⓘ VISA
M 11.50/17.50 **st.** and a la carte 🍷 3.95 – ☐ 7.60 – **80 rm** 65.00/85.00 **st.**, **2 suites** 120.00 **st.**
– SB (weekends only) 80.00/100.00 **st.**
AY o

🏨 **Whitehaven**, 34 Wilbury Rd, BN3 3JP, ℰ 778355, Fax 731177, 🚗 – 📺 ☎ . 🔄 AE ⓘ VISA .
⇔
M *(closed lunch Saturday and Sunday)* 15.00 **t.** 🍷 3.40 – **17 rm** ☐ 48.00/65.00 **t.** – SB (week-
ends only) 65.00/75.00 **st.**
AX c

⌂ **Claremont House**, Second Av., BN3 2LL, ℰ 735161, Fax 24764, 🚗 – 📺 ☎ . 🔄 AE ⓘ
VISA
M 10.00 **st.** 🍷 2.50 – **12 rm** ☐ 37.50/62.50 **st.** – SB (weekends only) 65.00/72.50 **st.**
AY c

XXX **Eaton Garden**, 13 Eaton Gdns, BN3 3TN, ℰ 738921, Fax 779075, English rest. – 🅿 . 🔄 AE
ⓘ VISA
closed Sunday dinner – **M** 14.00/19.00 **t.** and a la carte 16.00/20.50 **t.** 🍷 4.50.
AX a

X **Le Classique**, 37 Waterloo St., BN3 1AY, ℰ 734140 – 🔄 AE VISA
closed Sunday – **M** (dinner only) 12.75 **t.** and a la carte 12.80/19.00 **t.**
BY i

AUSTIN-ROVER 200 Dyke Rd ℰ 553061
CITROEN, HYUNDAI, RENAULT Old Shoreham Rd,
Portslade ℰ 411020
FIAT, LANCIA 100 Lewes Rd ℰ 508966
FORD 90-96 Preston Rd ℰ 550211
MAZDA 373 Kingsway, Hove ℰ 413833

MERCEDES-BENZ Victoria Rd ℰ 430787
RENAULT Stephenson Rd ℰ 692111
VAUXHALL Old Shoreham Rd, Portslade ℰ 422552

ⓦ ATS 40 Bristol Gdns ℰ 680150/686344

BRIMFIELD Heref. and Worc. 🗺 403 404 L 27 – ✉ Ludlow (Shropshire) – ☎ 058 472.
♦London 149 – ♦Birmingham 41 – Hereford 21 – Shrewsbury 32 – Worcester 33.

XX **Poppies** (at The Roebuck), SY8 4NE, ℰ 230 – ⇔ 🅿 . 🔄 VISA
closed Sunday dinner, Monday, 2 weeks February and 1 week October – **M** a la carte
16.00/27.90 **t.** 🍷 5.00.

BRIMSCOMBE Glos. 🗺 403 404 N 28 – see Stroud.

BRISTOL Avon 🗺 403 404 M 29 The West Country G. – pop. 413 861 – ECD : Wednesday and
Saturday – ☎ 0272.

See : Site★★ – Clifton Suspension Bridge★★★ AY – Cabot Tower Area★★ (The Georgian
House★ *AC* CZ – Theatre Royal★★ DZ T – St. Mary Redcliffe Church★★ DZ – Bristol Zoological
Garden★★ *AC* AY – Clifton Roman Catholic Cathedral of SS Peter and Paul★★ AY B – Floating
Harbour★★ EZ – Clifton★★ AY – Industrial Museum★ *AC* AY M2 – Cathedral★ DZ – City Museum
and Art Gallery★ *AC* CZ M – S.S Great Britain★ *AC* AY A – Envir. : Blaise Castle House
Museum★ *AC* AX M3 Blaise Hamlet★, NW : 5 m. by B4057 AX – at Chew Magna★ Stanton Drew
Stone Circles★ *AC*, S : 8 m. by A37 BY – Clevedon Court★, W : 10 ½ m. by A369 AY.

🏌 Mangotsfield, Carsons Rd ℰ 565501, NE : 6 m. by B 4465 BX.

✈ Bristol Airport : ℰ 027 587 (Lulsgate) 4441/6, SW : 7 m. by A 38 AY.

🚗 ℰ 0345 090700.

🎫 14 Narrow Quay ℰ 260767 – Bristol Airport, Lulsgate ℰ 027 587 (Lulsgate) 4441.
♦London 121 – ♦Birmingham 91.

Plans on following pages

🏨 **Holiday Inn** (Holiday Inn), Lower Castle St., Old Market, BS1 3AD, ℰ 294281, Telex
449720, Fax 225838, 🔄 – 🛗 ⇔ rm 🖩 📺 ☎ 🅰 🅿 – 🕭 600. 🔄 AE ⓘ VISA
M (buffet lunch) 14.95 **s.** /dinner a la carte 🍷 6.00 – ☐ 5.95 – **284 rm** 77.00/182.00 **st.** –
SB (weekends only) 132.00/192.00 **st.**
EZ s

🏨 **Hilton International Bristol** (Hilton), Redcliffe Way, BS1 6NJ, ℰ 260041, Telex 449240,
Fax 230089, 🔄 – 🛗 ⇔ rm 🖩 rest 📺 ☎ 🅿 – 🕭 400. 🔄 AE ⓘ VISA
M *(closed Saturday lunch)* 13.50/15.50 **st.** and a la carte 15.90/23.25 **st.** 🍷 6.00 – ☐ 8.95 –
197 rm 78.00/110.00 **st.**, **2 suites** 120.00/165.00 **st.** – SB (except weekdays in summer)
95.00/145.00 **st.**
DEZ n

🏨 **Grand** (Mt. Charlotte), Broad St., BS1 2EL, ℰ 291645, Telex 449889, Fax 227619 – 🛗 📺 ☎ –
🕭 600
178 rm, 3 suites.
DZ a

🏨 **Unicorn** (Rank), Prince St., BS1 4QF, ℰ 230333, Telex 44315, Fax 230300 – 🛗 ⇔ rm 📺 ☎
⇔ – 🕭 300. 🔄 AE ⓘ VISA
M 10.25/13.75 **t.** and a la carte 🍷 4.25 – ☐ 8.00 – **215 rm** 48.50/80.75 **t.**, **2 suites** 80.75 **t.** –
SB (weekends only) 77.00 **st.**
DZ i

🏨 **Avon Gorge** (Mt. Charlotte), Sion Hill, Clifton, BS8 4LD, ℰ 738955, Telex 444237, Fax 238125,
≼ – 🛗 📺 ☎ – 🕭 100
74 rm, 2 suites.
AY x

🏨 **St. Vincent Rocks** (T.H.F.), Sion Hill, Clifton, BS8 4BB, ℰ 739251, Telex 444932, Fax
238139, ≼ – ⇔ rm 📺 ☎ 🅿 – 🕭 50. 🔄 AE ⓘ VISA
M *(closed Saturday lunch)* 10.50/16.95 **st.** and a la carte 🍷 3.95 – ☐ 7.00 – **46 rm**
62.00/72.00 **st.** – SB (weekends only) 68.00/76.00 **st.**
AY c

⬠ **Downlands**, 33 Henleaze Gdns, BS9 4HH, ℘ 621639 – 📺   AX **s**
M (by arrangement) 7.50 **st.** – **10 rm** ⊇ 17.00/35.00 **st.**

⬠ Park House without rest., 19 Richmond Hill, Clifton, BS8 1BA, ℘ 736331 – 📺 Ⓟ   CZ **z**
4 rm.

XXX **Harvey's**, 12 Denmark St., BS1 5DQ, ℘ 277665, « 18C cellars » – 🍽. 🔲 AE ⓪ VISA
closed Saturday lunch, Sunday and Bank Holidays – **M** 13.75 **t.** (lunch) and a la carte
16.00/23.00 **t.**   DZ **c**

XX **Lettonie**, 9 Druid Hill, Stoke Bishop, BS9 1EW, ℘ 686456, French rest. – 🔲 AE VISA
closed Sunday, Monday, 2 weeks summer, 1 week Christmas and Bank Holidays – **M**
(booking essential) 12.50/17.95 **t.**   AX **a**

XX **Marwick & Hunt**, 43-45 Coin St., BS1 1HT, ℘ 262658 – 🔲 VISA   DZ **i**
*closed Saturday, Sunday, 1 week Easter, 27 August-2 September, 1 week Christmas and
Bank Holidays* – **M** 14.50 **st.** (lunch) and a la carte 17.25/21.25 **st.** 🍾 4.50.

XX **Du Gourmet**, 43 Whiteladies Rd, BS8 2LS, ℘ 736230 – 🔲 AE ⓪ VISA   AY **v**
closed Saturday lunch, Sunday, Monday and 24 December-2 January – **M** a la carte
13.65/20.40 **t.** 🍾 2.85.

XX **Rajdoot**, 83 Park St., BS1 5PJ, ℘ 268033, Indian rest. – 🔲 AE ⓪ VISA   CZ **u**
closed lunch Sunday and Bank Holidays – **M** 14.00 **t.** and a la carte 10.35/13.20 **t.** 🍾 3.00.

XX **China Palace**, 18a Baldwin St., BS1 1SE, ℘ 262719, Chinese rest. – ⬒✗. 🔲 AE VISA
M 16.00 **t.** and a la carte 10.00/13.50 **t.** 🍾 3.00.   DZ **x**

XX **La Taverna Dell'Artista**, 33 King St., BS1 4DZ, ℘ 297712, Italian rest. – 🔲 AE VISA
closed Sunday, Monday, 29 July-13 August and Bank Holidays – **M** a la carte 11.00/18.20 **t.**
🍾 3.25.   DZ **s**

XX **Thai House**, 52 Park Row, BS1 5LH, ℘ 253079, Thai rest. – 🔲 AE ⓪ VISA   CZ **a**
closed Sunday – **M** 20.00 **st.** and a la carte 10.30/18.75 **st.**

X **Plum Duff**, 6 Chandos Rd, Redland, BS6 6PE, ℘ 238450 – 🔲 VISA   AY **n**
M *(closed Sunday, Monday and 2 weeks Christmas)* 13.50 **t.** 🍾 3.00.

X **Bistro Twenty One**, 21 Cotham Road South, Kingsdown, BS6 5TZ, ℘ 421744 – 🔲 VISA
closed Saturday lunch, Sunday and 1 week Christmas – **M** (booking essential) a la carte
13.50/15.75 **t.**   AY **z**

X **Danton**, 2 Upper Byron Pl., The Triangle, BS8 1JY, ℘ 268314 – 🔲 AE ⓪ VISA   CZ **e**
*closed Saturday lunch, Tuesday dinner and Sunday, 1 week Easter, Christmas-New Year and
Bank Holidays* – **M** a la carte 15.00/20.10 **t.** 🍾 3.85.

X **Ganges**, 368 Gloucester Rd, Horfield, BS7 8TP, ℘ 245234, Indian rest. – 🔲 AE ⓪ VISA
closed 25 and 26 December – **M** 12.95 **t.** and a la carte 11.30/19.95 **t.** 🍾 5.95.   AX **e**

at Patchway N : 6 ½ m. on A 38 – BX – ✉ Bristol – ☎ 0454 Almondsbury :

🏨 Stakis Leisure Lodge (Stakis), Woodlands Lane, off A 38, BS12 4JF, ℘ 201144, Telex 445774,
Fax 612022, 🔲, 🐎 – ⬒✗ rm 🍽 rest 📺 ☎ 🚻 Ⓟ – 🏛 80. 🔲 AE ⓪ VISA
M *(closed Saturday lunch)* – ⊇ 7.25 – **112 rm** 64.00/91.00 **st.**

at Hambrook NE : 5 ½ m. by M 32 on A 4174 – BX – ✉ ☎ 0272 Bristol :

🏨 **Crest** (Crest), Filton Rd, BS16 1QX, ℘ 564242, Telex 449376, Fax 569735, 🔲, park – 🛗
⬒✗ rm 🍽 rest 📺 ☎ Ⓟ – 🏛 500. 🔲 AE ⓪ VISA   BX **o**
M *(closed Sunday lunch)* 13.95/15.95 **st.** and a la carte 19.25/30.85 **st.** – ⊇ 7.95 – **193 rm**
77.50/90.00 **st.**, **4 suites** 175.00 **st.** – SB 92.00/96.00 **st.**

at Chelwood S : 8 ½ m. by A 37 – BY – on A 368 – ✉ Bristol – ☎ 076 18 Compton
Dando :

🏛 **Chelwood House**, BS18 4NH, SW : ¾ m. on A 37 ℘ 730, ≤, 🐎 – ⬒✗ rest 📺 ☎ Ⓟ. 🔲
AE ⓪ VISA. 🐕
closed Christmas-New Year – **M** *(closed Sunday to non-residents)* (dinner only) 16.00 **st.**
and a la carte 🍾 3.50 – **8 rm** ⊇ 55.00/89.00 **st.** – SB (weekends only) (except summer)
89.00 **st.**

MICHELIN Distribution Centre, Pennywell Rd, BS5 0UD, ℘ 559802, FAX 553820 BY

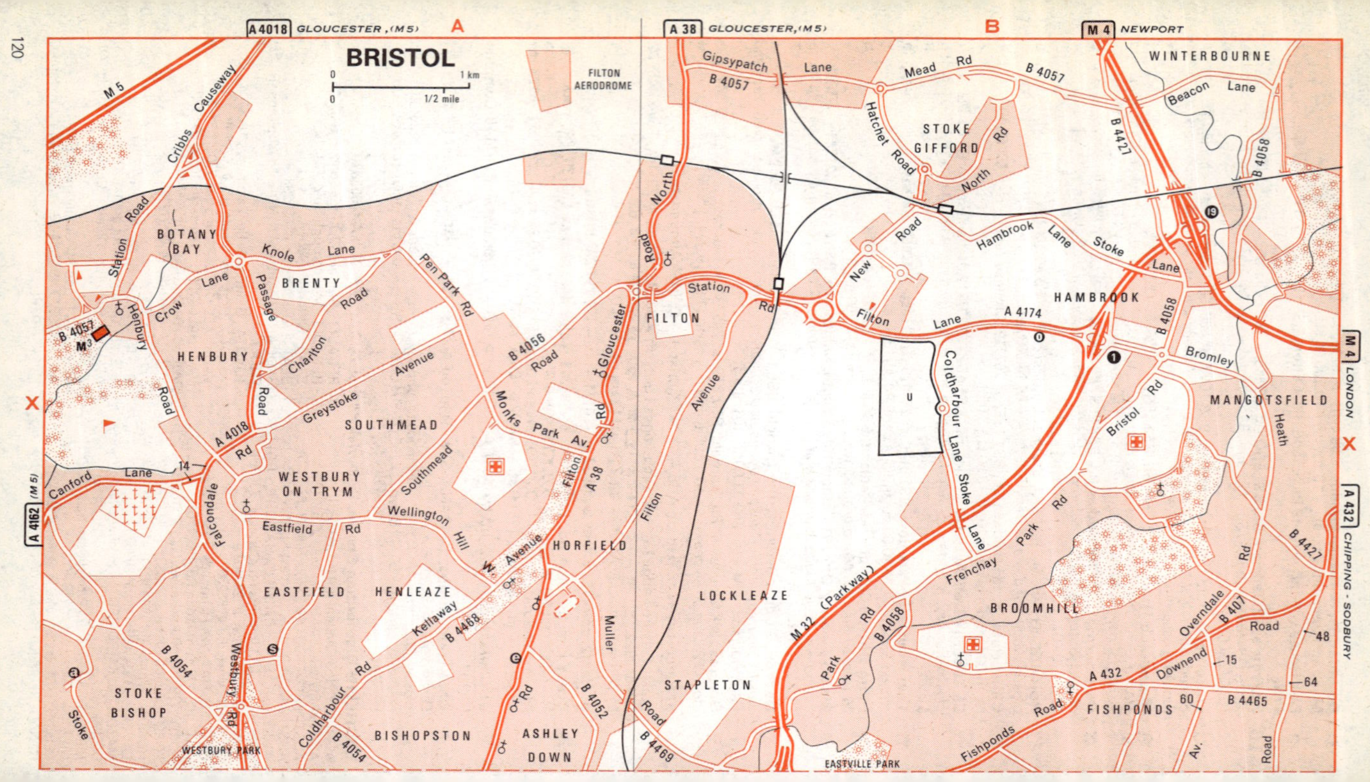
BRISTOL
1 km
1/2 mile
A 4018 GLOUCESTER, (M5)
A
A 38 GLOUCESTER, (M5)
B
M 4 NEWPORT
M 4 LONDON
A 432 CHIPPING - SODBURY
A 4162 (M5)
120
M 5
Cribbs Causeway
Station Road
BOTANY BAY
Knole Lane
Crow
Henbury
B 4057
M 3
HENBURY
Passage
Charlton Road
Greystoke Rd
A 4018 Rd
Canford Lane
14
BRENTY
Pen Park Rd
Avenue
SOUTHMEAD
WESTBURY ON TRYM
Eastfield Rd
EASTFIELD
HENLEAZE
Wellington Hill
Kellaway
B 4468
STOKE BISHOP
B 4054
Westbury Rd
Coldharbour Rd
B 4054
BISHOPSTON
WESTBURY PARK
B 4056 Road
Monks Park Av.
Gloucester Rd
W. Avenue
HORFIELD
Muller
B 4052
ASHLEY DOWN
FILTON AERODROME
Gipsypatch Lane
B 4057
North Road
Station Rd
FILTON
Filton Rd
A 38
Filton Avenue
Avenue
LOCKLEAZE
STAPLETON
Road
B 4469
EASTVILLE PARK
Mead Rd
B 4057
Hatchet Road
STOKE GIFFORD
North Road
Hambrook Lane
Stoke Lane
New Road
Filton Lane
A 4174
Coldharbour Lane Stoke Lane
U
HAMBROOK
M 32 (Parkway)
Park Rd
B 4058
Frenchay
Park Rd
M 32
WINTERBOURNE
Beacon Lane
B 4057
B 4427
B 4058
M 4
Bromley
Bristol Rd
MANGOTSFIELD
Heath
Bristol
Rd
BROOMHILL
Overndale B 407 Road
48
A 432
Downend
15
60 B 4465
64
FISHPONDS
Fishponds Road
Av.
Road
Stoke
B 4058

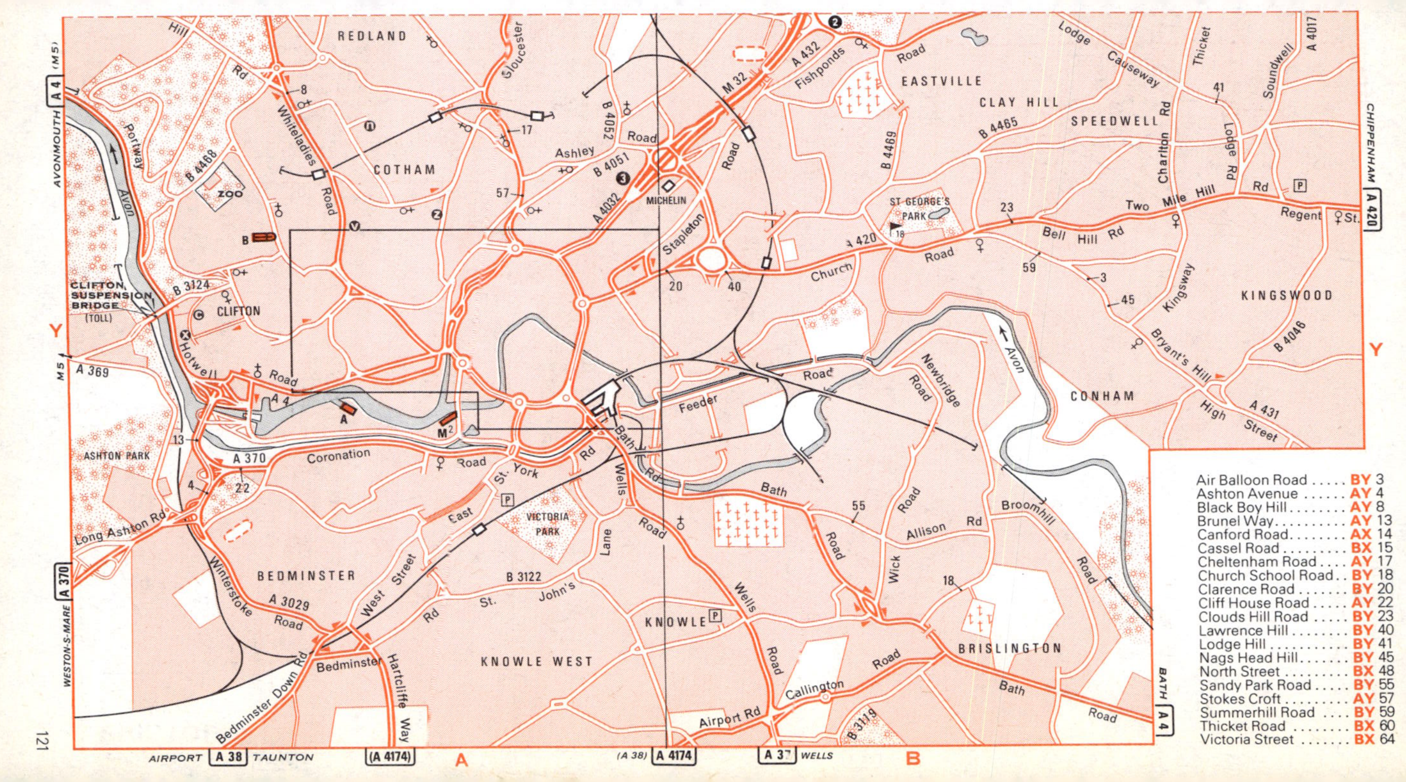

REDLAND
Hill
Rd
Gloucester
AVONMOUTH A 4 (M5)
Portway
Avon
B 4468
ZOO
Whiteladies
Road
COTHAM
8
17
Ashley
B 4052
Road
B 4051
57
A 4032
MICHELIN
Stapleton
M 32
A 432
Fishponds
Road
EASTVILLE
CLAY HILL
B 4469
B 4465
SPEEDWELL
Lodge Causeway
Thicket
41
Soundwell
A 4017
CHIPPENHAM A 420
Charlton Rd
Lodge Rd
Rd
P
Two Mile Hill
Regent St.
23
Bell Hill Rd
59
3
Kingsway
45
Bryant's Hill
KINGSWOOD
B 4046
ST GEORGE'S PARK
18
A 420
Church
Road
20
40
CLIFTON SUSPENSION BRIDGE (TOLL)
B 3124
CLIFTON
Hotwell
Road
M5
A 369
A 4
B
A 4
Newbridge
Road
Avon
CONHAM
A 431
High Street
Feeder
Bath
Road
Broomhill
Allison Rd
Wick Road
18
55
Bath Rd
Bath
Road
ASHTON PARK
13
A 370
Coronation
Road
St. York
East
P
Victoria Park
Long Ashton Rd
4
22
Wells Rd
Road
Wells
Lane
B 3122
St. John's Rd
KNOWLE
P
Callington
Road
Airport Rd
B 3119
BRISLINGTON
Bath
Road
A 4
WESTON-S-MARE A 370
BEDMINSTER
West Street
A 3029
Winterstoke Road
Bedminster Down Rd
Bedminster
Hartcliffe Way
KNOWLE WEST
AIRPORT A 38 TAUNTON
(A 4174)
A
(A 38) A 4174
A 37 WELLS
BATH A 4
Air Balloon Road ..... BY 3
Ashton Avenue ...... AY 4
Black Boy Hill .... AY 8
Brunel Way.......... AY 13
Canford Road .... AX 14
Cassel Road .... BX 15
Cheltenham Road .... AY 17
Church School Road.. BY 18
Clarence Road .... BY 20
Cliff House Road ..... AY 22
Clouds Hill Road ..... BY 23
Lawrence Hill .... BY 40
Lodge Hill .... BY 41
Nags Head Hill....... BY 45
North Street .... BX 48
Sandy Park Road ..... BY 55
Stokes Croft .... AY 57
Summerhill Road .... BY 59
Thicket Road .... BX 60
Victoria Street .... BX 64

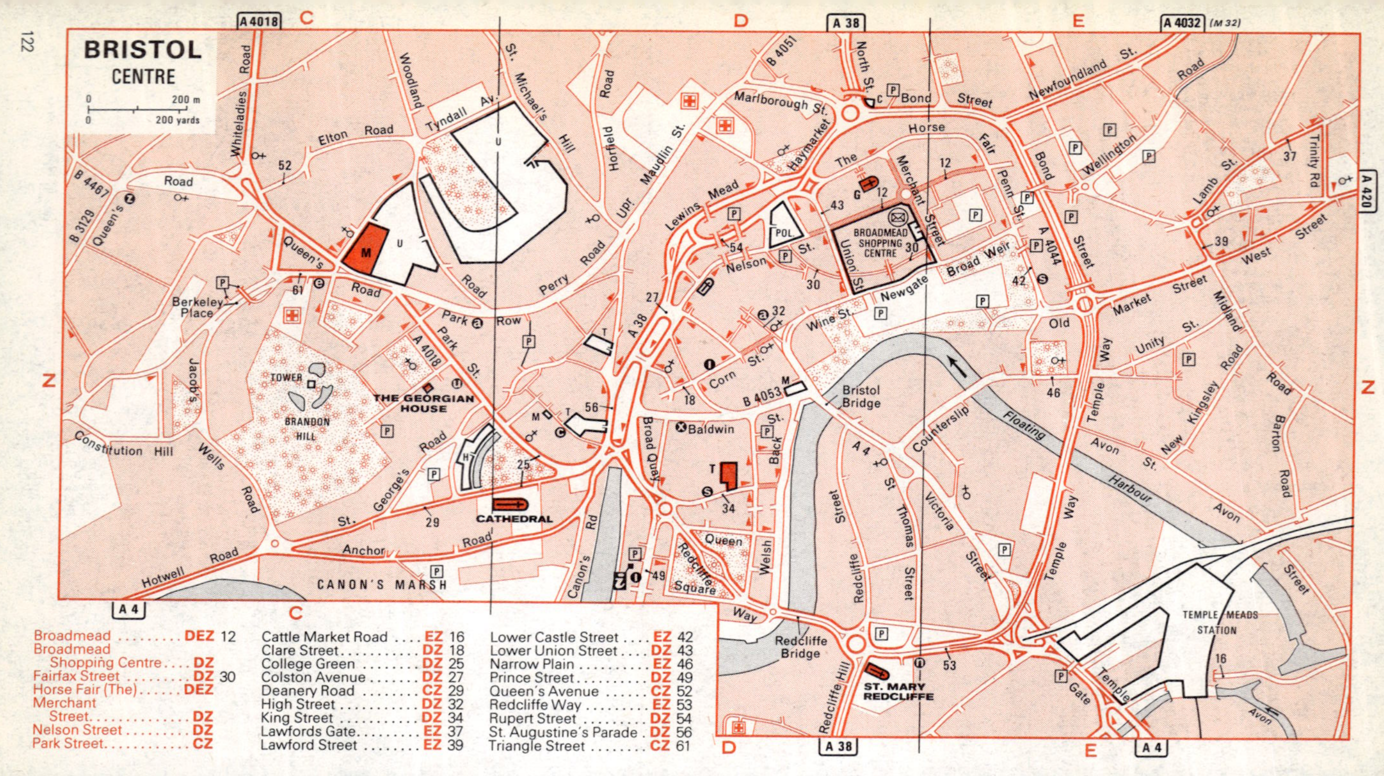

Broadmead .... DEZ 12
Broadmead
  Shopping Centre .... DZ 30
Fairfax Street ...... DZ 30
Horse Fair (The) ...... DEZ
Merchant
  Street .... DZ
Nelson Street .... DZ
Park Street .... CZ

Cattle Market Road .... EZ 16
Clare Street .... DZ 18
College Green .... DZ 25
Colston Avenue .... DZ 27
Deanery Road .... CZ 29
High Street .... DZ 32
King Street .... DZ 34
Lawfords Gate .... EZ 37
Lawford Street .... EZ 39

Lower Castle Street .... EZ 42
Lower Union Street .... DZ 43
Narrow Plain .... EZ 46
Prince Street .... DZ 49
Queen's Avenue .... CZ 52
Redcliffe Way .... EZ 53
Rupert Street .... DZ 54
St. Augustine's Parade . DZ 56
Triangle Street .... CZ 61

BRIXHAM Devon **403** J 32 **The West Country** G. – pop. 15 171 – ECD : Wednesday – ☎ 080 45 (4 & 5 fig.) or 0803 (6 fig.).

Envir. : Berry Head★ (≤★★★), E : 2 m.

🛈 The Old Market House, The Quay ℰ 2861.

♦London 230 – Exeter 30 – ♦Plymouth 32 – Torquay 8.

   🏨 **Quayside**, 41-49 King St., TQ5 9TJ, ℰ 55751, Fax 882733, ≤ harbour – 📺 ☎ 🅿. 🖼 AE ⓪ VISA. ⅜
       closed Christmas and New Year – M 8.95/13.25 **t.** and a la carte 🍾 3.70 – **30 rm**
       ⅏ 32.00/70.00 **st.** – SB 81.00/90.00 **st.**

AUSTIN-ROVER Milton St. ℰ 882474   RENAULT New Rd ℰ 882266
FORD Churston Ferrers ℰ 842245

BROAD CAMPDEN Glos. – see Chipping Campden.

BROAD CHALKE Wilts. **403 404** O 30 – see Salisbury.

BROADSTAIRS Kent **404** Y 29 – pop. 21 551 (inc. St. Peter's) – ECD : Wednesday – ☎ 0843 Thanet.

See : Bleak House (stayed in by Charles Dickens) *AC*.

🛈 Pierremont Hall, 67 High St. ℰ 68399.

♦London 78 – ♦Dover 21 – Maidstone 47.

   🏨 **Castlemere**, 15 Western Esplanade, CT10 1TD, ℰ 61566, ≤, 🚗 – 📺 ☎ 🅿. 🖼 VISA
       M (bar lunch April-October)/dinner 10.50 **st.** – **36 rm** ⅏ 29.00/66.00 **st.** – SB (Thurs-
       day to Sunday) 64.00/73.00 **st.**

   🏨 **Royal Albion**, Albion St., CT10 1LU, ℰ 68071, ≤, 🚗 – 📺 ☎ 🅿 – 🛎 30. 🖼 AE ⓪ VISA
       M (at **Marchesi rest.**, see below) – **18 rm** ⅏ 50.00/60.00 **st.**, **1 suite** 90.00/100.00 **st.** –
       SB 70.00/80.00 **st.**

   🏠 Bay Tree, 12 Eastern Esplanade, CT10 1DR, ℰ 62502, ≤ – ⅍ rest 📺 🅿
       11 rm.

   XX **Marchesi**, 18 Albion St., CT10 1LU, ℰ 62481, ≤ – 🅿. 🖼 AE ⓪ VISA
       closed 1 to 14 November and 26 to 28 December – M 9.50/12.00 **t.** and a la carte 14.25/18.75 **t.**
       🍾 3.00.

AUDI-VW St. Peter's Rd ℰ 62333   HYUNDAI Ramsgate Rd ℰ 63531

BROADSTONE Dorset **403 404** O 31 – see Wimborne Minster.

BROADWATER Herts. – see Stevenage.

BROADWAY Heref. and Worc. **403 404** O 27 – pop. 1 931 – ECD : Thursday – ☎ 0386.

🛈 1 Cotswold Court ℰ 852937 (summer only).

♦London 93 – ♦Birmingham 36 – Cheltenham 15 – Worcester 22.

   🏨 **Lygon Arms**, High St., WR12 7DU, ℰ 852255, Telex 338260, Fax 858611, « Part 15C inn »,
       🚗, 🍴 – 📺 ☎ 🅿 – 🛎 80. 🖼 AE ⓪ VISA
       M 14.75/22.50 **t.** and a la carte 22.25/35.50 **t.** – ⅏ 7.00 – **61 rm** 90.00/135.00 **t.**, **5 suites**
       105.00/265.00 **t.** – SB (except Christmas and New Year) 160.00/185.00 **st.**

   🏨 **Broadway**, The Green, WR12 7AB, ℰ 852401, 🚗 – ⅍ rm 📺 ☎ 🅿. 🖼 AE ⓪ VISA. ⅜
       M *(closed Sunday dinner)* (bar lunch Monday to Saturday)/dinner 14.95 **t.** and a la carte
       🍾 3.00 – **24 rm** ⅏ 35.00/66.00 **st.** – SB (except Christmas) 75.00/95.00 **st.**

   🏠 **Collin House** ⑤, Collin Lane, WR12 7PB, NW : 1 ¼ m. by A 44 ℰ 858354, ≤, 🏊, 🚗 – 🅿.
       🖼 VISA. ⅜
       closed 24 to 28 December – M *(closed Sunday dinner to non-residents)* 10.00/16.50 **st.**
       and a la carte 🍾 3.25 – **7 rm** ⅏ 35.00/72.00 **st.** – SB (November-March) 82.50/92.50 **st.**

   🏠 **Whiteacres** without rest., Station Rd, WR12 7DE, ℰ 852320, 🚗 – ⅍ rm 📺 🅿. ⅜
       March-October – **6 rm** ⅏ 25.00/34.00 **st.**

   🏠 **Mill Hay House** ⑤ without rest., Snowshill Rd, WR12 7JS, S : ½ m. ℰ 852498, ≤, 🚗 –
       ⅍ 🅿. 🖼 VISA. ⅜
       3 rm ⅏ 17.50/50.00 **s.**

   🏠 **Half Way House** without rest., 89 High St., WR12 7AL, ℰ 852237 – ⅍ 🅿. ⅜
       5 rm ⅏ 25.00/40.00 **st.**

   🏠 **Windrush House**, Station Rd, WR12 7DE, ℰ 853577, 🚗 – ⅍ rest 📺 🅿
       M 11.50 **st.** – **4 rm** ⅏ –/32.00 **st.**

   XX **Hunters Lodge**, High St., WR12 7DT, ℰ 853247, 🚗 – 🅿. 🖼 AE ⓪ VISA
       closed Sunday dinner, Monday, first 2 weeks February and first 2 weeks August – M 12.00 **t.**
       (lunch) and a la carte 11.25/18.75 **t.** 🍾 3.50.

     at Willersey (Glos.) N : 2 m. on B 4632 – ✉ ☎ 0386 Broadway :

   🏠 **Old Rectory** ⑤ without rest., Church St., WR12 7PM, ℰ 853729, 🚗 – ⅍ 📺 ☎ 🅿. 🖼
       VISA. ⅜
       closed Christmas – **6 rm** ⅏ 49.00/89.00 **t.**

at Willersey Hill (Glos.) E : 2 m. by A 44 – ✉ ☎ 0386 Broadway :

Dormy House, WR12 7LF, ☎ 852711, Telex 338275, Fax 858636, – TV ☎ P – 200. AE VISA
closed 2 days at Christmas – **M** (bar lunch Saturday) 16.00/24.00 **t.** and a la carte 24.00/32.25 **t.** 4.75 – **45 rm** 49.00/115.00 **t.**, **3 suites** 125.00/160.00 **t.** – SB (weekends only) 132.00 **st.**

at Buckland (Glos.) SW : 2 ¼ m. by B 4632 – ✉ ☎ 0386 Broadway :

Buckland Manor, WR12 7LY, ☎ 852626, ←, « Country house atmosphere », heated, , park, – TV ☎ P. VISA.
closed 16 January-9 February – **M** a la carte 17.65/26.60 **t.** 3.50 – **10 rm** 115.00/180.00 **t.**

AUSTIN-ROVER Willersey ☎ 852338

BROCKENHURST Hants. 403 404 P 31 – pop. 2 939 – ECD : Wednesday – ☎ 0590 Lymington.
♦London 99 – Bournemouth 17 – ♦Southampton 14 – Winchester 27.

Rhinefield House, Rhinefield Rd, SO42 7QB, W : 3 ½ m. on Rhinefield Way ☎ 22922, Telex 477617, Fax 22800, « Victorian country mansion », heated, , , park – TV ☎ P – 100. AE VISA
M 8.50/12.50 **t.** and a la carte – **32 rm** –/120.00 **t.** – SB 90.00 **st.**

Balmer Lawn (Hilton), Lyndhurst Rd, SO42 7ZB, ☎ 23116, Telex 477649, Fax 23864, ←, heated, , , , squash – rm TV ☎ P – 100. AE VISA
M *(closed Saturday lunch)* 10.00/18.00 **st.** and a la carte – **58 rm** 70.00/90.00 **st.**

Carey's Manor, Lyndhurst Rd, SO42 7RH, ☎ 23551, Telex 47442, Fax 22799, Dancing Friday and Saturday, , – rm TV ☎ P – 150. AE VISA.
M 12.90/21.90 **t.** and a la carte 4.95 – **80 rm** 79.90/119.00 **t.** – SB (except Bank Holidays) 97.70/127.70 **st.**

Forest Park, Rhinefield Rd, SO42 7ZG, ☎ 22844, Telex 47572, heated, , – rm TV ☎ P
38 rm.

Whitley Ridge, Beaulieu Rd, SO42 7QL, E : 1 m. on B 3055 ☎ 22354, ←, , – TV ☎ P. AE VISA
M (bar lunch Monday to Saturday)/dinner 15.00 **t.** and a la carte 3.00 – **11 rm** 46.00/65.00 **t.** – SB 84.00/88.00 **st.**

Cottage, Sway Rd, SO42 7SH, ☎ 0590 (Lymington) 22296, – TV P. VISA.
M (bar lunch)/dinner 12.00 **t.** and a la carte 3.50 – **6 rm** 38.00/56.00 **t.** – SB (except Bank Holidays) 70.00/80.00 **st.**

Le Poussin with rm, 57-59 Brookley Rd, SO42 7RB, ☎ 23063, French rest. – . VISA
closed 3 weeks January and 1 week June – **M** *(closed Sunday dinner and Monday)* (booking essential) 9.95/25.00 **t.** and a la carte 23.00/29.00 **t.** – **4 rm** 30.00/50.00.

AUSTIN-ROVER Sway Rd ☎ 23344
HONDA 24 Brookley Rd ☎ 23464
MAZDA Brookley Rd ☎ 23122
PEUGEOT-TALBOT Waters Green ☎ 23113

BROMBOROUGH Merseyside 402 403 L 24 – pop. 14 901 – ✉ Wirral – ☎ 051 Liverpool.
Raby Hall Rd ☎ 334 2155.
♦London 210 – Chester 14 – ♦Liverpool 6.5 – ♦Manchester 46.

Cromwell (Lansbury), High St., L62 7HZ, ☎ 334 2917, Telex 628225, Fax 346 1175 – rm TV ☎ P – 180. AE VISA.
M 8.50/12.50 **t.** and a la carte – **31 rm** 55.00/65.00 **t.** – SB (weekends only) 56.00/64.00 **st.**

Dibbinsdale (B.C.B.), Dibbinsdale Rd, L63 0HJ, off Allport Rd ☎ 334 5171 – TV ☎ P
19 rm.

BROME Suffolk 404 X 26 – see Diss (Norfolk).

BROMLEY CROSS Greater Manchester 402 404 M 23 – see Bolton.

BROMPTON BY SAWDON North Yorks. 402 S 21 – pop. 1 827 – ✉ ☎ 0723 Scarborough.
♦London 242 – ♦Kingston-upon-Hull 44 – Scarborough 8 – York 31.

Brompton Forge, YO13 9DP, ☎ 85409 – P
closed lunch Tuesday, Friday and Saturday, Sunday dinner, Monday and 2 weeks February – **M** 9.50/16.00 **st.** 3.90.

Non dimenticate che in Gran Bretagna esistono limiti di velocità oltre a quelli indicati sui cartelli :

– 60 mph (= 96 km/ora) su strada
– 70 mph (= 112 km/ora) su strada a carreggiate separate e autostrada.

BROMSGROVE Heref. and Worc. 🟦**403** 🟦**404** N 26 – pop. 24 576 – ECD : Thursday – ☎ 0527.
🛈 47-49 Worcester Rd ℰ 31809.
♦London 117 – ♦Birmingham 14 – ♦Bristol 71 – Worcester 13.

🏨 **Perry Hall** (Embassy), 13 Kidderminster Rd, B61 7JN, ℰ 579976, Fax 575998, 🛋 – 📺 ☎ ℗ – 🛎 100. 🅰 🅰🅴 ⓪ 𝗩𝗜𝗦𝗔
M (closed Saturday lunch) 10.50 **st.** and a la carte ₿ 4.40 – ☕ 6.50 – **55 rm** 55.00/85.00 **st.** – SB (weekends only) 54.00/59.00 **st.**

🏠 Pine Lodge (Best Western), 85 Kidderminster Rd, B61 9AB, W : 1 m. on A 448 ℰ 33033, Telex 335072, Fax 78981, 🛋 – 📺 ☎ ℗ – 🛎 200. 🎾
59 rm.

🏠 **Bromsgrove Country,** Stoke Heath, B61 7JA, SW : 2 m. on Worcester Rd ℰ 35522, 🛋 – 📺 ℗. 🅰 𝗩𝗜𝗦𝗔 🎾
closed first week January – **M** (closed Saturday and Sunday) (buffet lunch by arrangement)/dinner 8.00 **st.** ₿ 3.00 – ☕ 4.00 – **9 rm** 35.00/44.00 **st.** – SB (weekends only) 50.00 **st.**

XXX **Grafton Manor** with rm, Grafton Lane, B61 7HA, SW : 1 ¾ m. by Worcester Rd ℰ 579007, Fax 575221, « 16C and 18C manor », 🍲, 🛋, park – 📺 ☎ ℗. 🅰 🅰🅴 ⓪ 𝗩𝗜𝗦𝗔 🎾
M (closed Saturday lunch) 16.50/23.00 **t.** ₿ 3.95 – ☕ 6.95 – **7 rm** 61.00/98.00 **t.**, **2 suites** 145.00 **t.**

PEUGEOT-TALBOT 184 Worcester Rd ℰ 575157   VAUXHALL-OPEL 137 Birmingham Rd ℰ 71244
RENAULT 17-21 Worcester Rd ℰ 79898

BROMYARD Heref and Worc. 🟦**403** 🟦**404** M 27 – pop. 2 783 – ✉ ☎ 0885.
🛈 1 Rowberry St. ℰ 82341.
♦London 138 – ♦Birmingham 39 – Gloucester 41 – Hereford 17 – Worcester 14.

🏠 Falcon, Broad St., HR7 4BT, ℰ 483034 – 📺 ☎ ℗ – 🛎
5 rm.

BROOK Hants. 🟦**403** 🟦**404** P 31 – ECD : Tuesday – ✉ Lyndhurst – ☎ 0703 Southampton.
🛈, 🛈 Bramshaw Brook ℰ 813433, on B 3079.
♦London 92 – Bournemouth 24 – ♦Southampton 14.

🏠 **Bell**, SO34 7HE, ℰ 812214, Fax 813958, 🛈, 🛋 – 📺 ℗ – 🛎 50. 🅰 🅰🅴 ⓪ 𝗩𝗜𝗦𝗔
M (bar lunch)/dinner 16.25 **t.** and a la carte ₿ 3.20 – **12 rm** ☕ 39.00/58.00 **t.** – SB 38.95/49.95 **st.**

BROOKMANS PARK Herts. 🟦**404** T 28 – pop. 4 020 – ☎ 0707 Potters Bar.
♦London 21 – Luton 21.

XX **Villa Rosa,** 3 Great North Rd, AL9 6LB, SE : 1 ¾ m. on A 1000 ℰ 51444, Italian rest. – ℗.
🅰 🅰🅴 ⓪ 𝗩𝗜𝗦𝗔
closed Sunday – **M** a la carte 13.90/20.60 **t.** ₿ 3.75.

BROUGHTON Lancs. 🟦**402** L 22 – see Preston.

BROXTED Essex – see Thaxted.

BROXTON Cheshire 🟦**402** 🟦**403** L 24 – pop. 384 – ☎ 082 925 (from February : 0829).
♦London 197 – ♦Birmingham 68 – Chester 12 – ♦Manchester 44 – Stoke-on-Trent 29.

🏨 **Frogg Manor,** Barn Hill, Nantwich Rd, CH3 9JH, on A 534 ℰ 629 (from February : 782629), 🔲, 🛋, 🍽 – 🍽 rest 📺 ☎ ℗. 🅰 🅰🅴 ⓪ 𝗩𝗜𝗦𝗔
M 12.50/27.00 **st.** and a la carte ₿ 4.80 – ☕ 5.50 – **6 rm** 43.25/76.50 **t.** – SB 84.40/163.40 **st.**

🏠 Broxton Hall Whitchurch Rd, CH3 9JS, at Junction A 41 with A 534 ℰ 321, 🛋 – 🍽 📺 ☎ ℗. 🅰 𝗩𝗜𝗦𝗔 🎾
closed 25 December – **M** (closed Sunday dinner and Monday to non-residents) 10.00/15.00 **t.** – **10 rm** ☕ 45.00/55.00 **t.** – SB (weekdays only) 60.00/80.00 **st.**

BRUSHFORD Somerset 🟦**403** J 30 – pop. 486 – ✉ ☎ 0398 Dulverton.
♦London 195 – Exeter 24 – Minehead 18 – Taunton 24.

🏨 **Carnarvon Arms,** TA22 9AE, ℰ 23302, Fax 24022, 🔲 heated, 🍲, 🛋, park, 🍽 – 🍽 rest 📺 ☎ 🚻 ℗. 🅰 𝗩𝗜𝗦𝗔
closed 3 weeks February – **M** 8.50/15.50 **st.** ₿ 3.00 – **24 rm** ☕ 32.00/68.00 **st.**, **1 suite** 80.00 **st.** – SB 90.00/125.00 **st.**

BRUTON Somerset 🟦**403** 🟦**404** M 30 – pop. 1 759 – ☎ 0749.
♦London 118 – ♦Bristol 27 – Bournemouth 44 – Salisbury 35 – Taunton 36.

X **Claire de Lune** with rm, 2-4 High St., BA10 0EQ, ℰ 813395 – 📺. 🅰 🎾
M (closed Saturday lunch, Sunday dinner, Monday, 1 week September and 26 to 30 December) (booking essential) (lunch by arrangement)/dinner 16.75 **st.** ₿ 3.75 – **3 rm** ☕ 20.00/30.00 **st.**

X **Truffles,** 95 High St., BA10 0AR, ℰ 812255
closed Sunday dinner, Monday, 1 week March and 3 weeks September – **M** (booking essential) 10.50/15.95 **t.** ₿ 3.50.

BRYHER Cornwall **403** ㉚ – see Scilly (Isles of).

BRYNBUGA = Usk.

BUCKDEN Cambs. **404** T 27 – pop. 2 605 – ✉ ☎ 0480 Huntingdon.
♦London 65 – Bedford 15 – ♦Cambridge 20 – Northampton 31.

  🏠 **George**, Old Great North Rd, PE18 9XA, ℰ 810307 – TV ☎ P
  15 rm.

BUCKHURST HILL Essex **404** ㊸ – pop. 11 147 – ECD : Wednesday – ☎ 01 London.
♦London 13 – Chelmsford 25.

Plan : see Greater London (North-East)

  🏨 **Roebuck** (T.H.F.), North End, IG9 5QY, ℰ 505 4636, Fax 504 7826 – ⇔ rm TV ☎ P – 🏖.
  🖼 AE ① VISA
  M 12.00/14.50 **st.** and a la carte ↕ 3.95 – 🍵 7.00 – **29 rm** 59.00/80.00 **st.** – SB (week-
  ends only) 64.00/72.00 **st.**   HT u

  ✗ **Meghna**, Station Approach, 40 Victoria Rd., ℰ 504 2671, Indian rest.   HT e

BUCKINGHAM Bucks. **403 404** Q 27 – pop. 6 439 – ECD : Thursday – ☎ 0280.
Envir. : Claydon House★ (Rococo interior★★ : Chinese Room★★ staircase★★★, Florence Nightingale Museum) *AC*, SE : 8 m. – Stowe School (18C) (south front★, Marble Saloon★, park : monu-
ments★ (18C), ≤★ from the Lake Pavilions) *AC*.
♦London 64 – ♦Birmingham 61 – Northampton 20 – ♦Oxford 25.

  🏨 **White Hart** (T.H.F.), Market Sq., MK18 1NL, ℰ 815151 – ⇔ rm TV ☎ P – 🏖 40. 🖼 AE
  ① VISA
  M 8.00 **st.** and a la carte – **19 rm** 🍵 (dinner included) 40.00/58.00 **st.** – SB (weekends
  only) 62.00/72.00 **st.**

AUSTIN-ROVER Motorworks ℰ 812121   VAUXHALL-OPEL School Lane ℰ 814242
FORD Main St Tingewick ℰ (02804) 7071

BUCKLAND Glos. **403 404** O 27 – see Broadway (Heref. and Worc.).

BUCKLERS HARD Hants. **403 404** P 31 – see Beaulieu.

BUCKLOW HILL Cheshire **402 403 404** M 24 – see Knutsford.

BUDE Cornwall **403** G 31 *The West Country* G. – pop. 2 679 – ECD : Thursday – ☎ 0288.
See : The breakwater★★ – ≤ from Compass Point★.
Envir. : Poughill★ (Church★★) N : 2 ½ m. – at Poundstock★ (≤★★, church★★, Gildhouse★) S :
4 ½ m. – Morwenstowe Church★ (cliffs★★) N : 11 m. – Stratton Church★, E : 1 ½ m. – Launcells
Church★, E : 3 m. – Kilkhampton Church★, NE : 5 ½ m. – Jacobstowe Church★, S : 7 m.
🔢 Burn View ℰ 2006.
🅿 The Crescent car park ℰ 4240 and 3576 (summer only) – A 39, Stamford Hill, Stratton ℰ 3781 (summer
only).
♦London 252 – Exeter 51 – ♦Plymouth 44 – Truro 53.

  🏨 **Hartland**, Hartland Terr., EX23 8JY, ℰ 55661, ≤, ⌇ heated – ⏛ TV ☎ P
  April-mid November and Christmas – **M** 13.80/15.50 t. ↕ 3.50 – **29 rm** 🍵 31.05/55.20 t. –
  SB (except summer) 73.60 **st.**

  🏠 **Camelot**, Downs View, EX23 8RS, ℰ 2361, ⇆ – ⇔ rest TV ☎ P. 🖼 VISA ⚓
  M (bar lunch)/dinner 12.00 **st.** and a la carte ↕ 3.00 – **18 rm** 🍵 20.00/60.00 **st.**

  🏠 **Bude Haven**, Flexbury Av., EX23 8NS, ℰ 2305, ⇆ – TV P. 🖼 VISA
  M (bar lunch)/dinner 7.00 **st.** ↕ 2.25 – **13 rm** 🍵 17.00/34.00 **st.** – SB (except June-September) 39.00/43.00 **st.**

  🏠 **Reeds** ⚜, Northcott Mouth rd, Poughill, EX23 9EL, NE : 1 ¼ m. ℰ 2841, ⇆, park – P. ⚓
  closed Tuesday to Friday and 25 December – **M** (dinner only) (residents only) 17.50 **st.** ↕ 3.00
  – **3 rm** 🍵 35.00/60.00 **st.**

  🏠 **Teeside** without rest., 2 Burn View, EX23 8BY, ℰ 2351 – ⚓
  March-September – **6 rm** 🍵 11.00/24.00 **st.**

  🏠 **Meva Gwin**, Upton, EX23 0LY, S : 1¼ m. on coast rd ℰ 352347, ≤ – ⇔ rest P. ⚓
  closed January-15 April – **M** 6.50 **st.** ↕ 2.80 – **13 rm** 🍵 14.00/32.00 **st.**

AUSTIN-ROVER Bencoolen Rd ℰ 2146   FORD Bencoolen Rd ℰ 4616

BUILTH WELLS (LLANFAIR-YM-MUALLT) Powys **403** J 27 – pop. 2 225 – ☎ 0982.
🅿 Groe car park ℰ 553307 (summer only).
♦London 197 – Brecon 22 – ♦Cardiff 63 – ♦Swansea 63 – Shrewsbury 70.

  🏠 **Llanfair**, 1 The Strand, LD2 3BG, ℰ 553253, ⇆ – TV P. VISA ⚓
  April-November – **M** 11.00 ↕ 4.00 – **8 rm** 🍵 12.00/26.00.

FIAT Garth ℰ 05912 287   PEUGEOT Hay Rd ℰ 553647
FORD Station Rd ℰ 552639

BUNWELL Norfolk **404** X 26 – pop. 797 – ECD : Monday and Wednesday – ✪ 095 389.

♦London 102 – ♦Cambridge 51 – ♦Norwich 16.

   Bunwell Manor ⓢ, Bunwell St., NR16 1QU, NW : 1 m. ☎ 8304, 🍴 – 📺 ☎ 🅿. 🆕 VISA
M 10.50 **t.** and a la carte ♦ 3.25 – **10 rm** ☕ 40.00/55.00 **t.** – SB (except Christmas) 65.00/70.00 **st.**

BURFORD Oxon. **403 404** P 28 – pop. 1 371 – ECD : Wednesday – ✪ 099 382 (4 fig.) or 0993 (6 fig.).

See : St. John's Church★ (12C-14C).

Envir. : Swinbrook (church : Fettiplace Monuments★) 3 ½ m. – Cotswold Wildlife Park★ AC, S : 2 m. – Northleach : SS. Peter and Paul's Church : South Porch and the brasses★ (Perpendicular) NW : 7 ½ m.

📍 Swindon Rd ☎ 2583, S : ½ m. on A 361.

🛈 The Brewery, Sheep St. ☎ 3558.

♦London 76 – ♦Birmingham 55 – Gloucester 32 – ♦Oxford 20.

   Bay Tree, Sheep St., OX8 4LW, ☎ 823137, Fax 823008, « 16C house, antique furnishings »,
🍴 – ✖ rest 📺 ☎ 🅿. 🆕 AE ⓞ VISA
April-December – **M** 13.00/17.00 **t.** and a la carte ♦ 4.25 – **20 rm** ☕ 60.00/95.00 **t.**, **2 suites** 95.00/125.00 **t.** – SB (except summer) (weekends only) 120.00/150.00 **st.**

   Inn For All Seasons, The Barringtons, OX8 4TN, W : 3 ¼ m. on A 40 ☎ 045 14 (Windrush) 324, 🍴 – 📺 ☎ 🅿. 🆕 AE VISA. ✖
M *(closed Sunday dinner)* (bar lunch Monday to Saturday)/dinner 12.75 **t.** ♦ 3.10 – **10 rm** ☕ 37.50/65.00 **t.** – SB 73.00/78.00 **st.**

   Lamb Inn, Sheep St., OX8 4LR, ☎ 3155, « Part 14C inn », 🍴 –
13 rm.

   Golden Pheasant, 91 High St., OX8 4RJ, ☎ 3223 – ✖ rm 📺 ☎ 🅿. 🆕 ⓞ VISA
M 12.95/14.95 **st.** and a la carte ♦ 4.25 – **12 rm** ☕ 43.00/85.50 **st.** – SB 77.50/87.50 **st.**

   Andrews without rest., High St., OX8 4RJ, ☎ 3151, 🍴 – ✖ 📺. 🆕 AE ⓞ VISA. ✖
9 rm ☕ 18.75/48.75 **st.**

   Bull, 105 High St., OX8 4RH, ☎ 2220 – 📺 ☎ 🅿. 🆕 AE ⓞ VISA
M 10.95/15.95 **t.** and a la carte 11.50/17.95 **t.** ♦ 3.00 – **12 rm** ☕ 35.00/59.50 **t.**

   Highway, 117 High St., OX8 4RG, ☎ 2136 – 📺 ☎. 🆕 AE ⓞ VISA
M (bar meals) a la carte 10.70/12.75 **st.** ♦ 3.50 – **10 rm** ☕ 32.00/48.00 **t.** – SB (weekends only) 61.00/72.00 **st.**

   at Fulbrook NE : ¾ m. on A 361 – ✪ 099 382 Burford :

   Elm Farm House, Meadow Lane, OX8 4BW, ☎ 3611, 🍴 – 📺 ☎ 🅿. 🆕 AE VISA. ✖
closed 14 December-January – **M** 13.50 **st.** ♦ 2.95 – **7 rm** ☕ 23.00/45.00 **st.** – SB (except summer) 50.00/62.00 **st.**

   at Taynton NW : 1 ½ m. by A 424 – ✪ 099 382 Burford :

   Manor Farm Barn ⓢ without rest., OX8 4UH, ☎ 2069, ≤, « Tastefully renovated barn »,
🍴 – 📺 🅿. ✖
3 rm ☕ 28.00/45.00 **st.**

BURGHFIELD Berks. **403 404** Q 29 – see Reading.

BURLEY Hants. **403 404** O 31 – pop. 1 492 – ECD : Wednesday – ✉ Ringwood – ✪ 042 53.

📍 Burley, Ringwood ☎ 2431.

♦London 102 – Bournemouth 17 – ♦Southampton 17 – Winchester 30.

   Burley Manor ⓢ, Ringwood Rd, BH24 4BS, ☎ 3522, Telex 41565, Fax 3227, ≤, ⛲ heated,
🐎, 🍴, park – ✖ rm 📺 ☎ 🅿 – 🛎. 🆕 AE ⓞ VISA
M (bar lunch Monday to Saturday)/dinner 16.50 **t.** and a la carte – **30 rm** ☕ 60.00/75.00 **t.** – SB 90.00/100.00 **st.**

BURN BRIDGE North Yorks. – see Harrogate.

BURNHAM Bucks. **404** S 29 – ECD : Thursday – ✪ 062 86 (4 & 5 fig.) or 0628 (6 fig.).

📍 Burnham Beeches, Green Lane ☎ 61448.

♦London 33 – ♦Oxford 37 – Reading 17.

   Burnham Beeches Moat House (Q.M.H.) ⓢ, Grove Rd, Burnham Beeches, SL1 8DP,
NW : 1 m. by Britwell Rd ☎ 603333, Fax 603994, ◱, 🍴, park, ✖ – 🛎 📺 ☎ 🅿 – 🛎. 🆕 ⓞ VISA
M *(closed lunch Saturday and Bank Holidays)* 16.50/18.50 **st.** and a la carte 19.45/34.95 **st.**
♦ 5.00 – **73 rm** ☕ 80.00/95.00 **st.**, **2 suites** 175.00 **st.** – SB (weekends only) 100.00 **st.**

   Grovefield ⓢ, Taplow Common Rd, SL1 8LP, ☎ 603131, Telex 846873, 🍴 – 🛎 📺 ☎ 🅿 –
🛎
42 rm.

CITROEN 46-48 High St. ☎ 5255   VAUXHALL-OPEL 71-73 Stomp Rd ☎ 4994

BURNHAM MARKET Norfolk 404 W 25 – pop. 943 – ✆ 0328 Fakenham.
♦London 128 – ♦Cambridge 71 – ♦Norwich 36.

  ✗ **Forbes,** North St., PE31 8HG, ✆ 738824 – 🅿. 🔄 *VISA*
  closed Wednesday and 10 January-7 February – **M** a la carte 11.65/18.25 t. ⬧ 3.25.

BURNHAM-ON-CROUCH Essex 404 W 29 – pop. 6 268 – ECD : Wednesday – ✆ 0621 Maldon.
🏌 Ferry Lane, Creeksea ✆ 782282, W : 1 ¼ m. by B 1010.
♦London 52 – Chelmsford 19 – Colchester 32 – Southend-on-Sea 25.

  ✗✗ **Contented Sole,** 80 High St., CM0 8AA, ✆ 782139
  closed Sunday, Monday, last 2 weeks July and 23 December-20 January – **M** 8.50 **st.** (lunch)
  and a la carte 15.45/18.50 **st.**

BURNLEY Lancs. 402 N 22 – pop. 76 365 – ✆ 0282.
Envir. : Towneley Hall★ (16C-18C) SE : 1 m.

🏌 Towneley, Towneley Park, Todmorden Rd ✆ 38473, E : 1 ½ m. – 🏌 Glen View ✆ 21045 – 🏌
Marsden Park, Townhouse Rd, Walton Lane, Nelson ✆ 0282 (Nelson) 67525, N : 4 m..
🎫 Burnley Mechanics, Manchester Rd ✆ 30055.
♦London 236 – Bradford 32 – ♦Leeds 37 – ♦Liverpool 55 – ♦Manchester 25 – ♦Middlesbrough 104 – Preston 22
– ♦Sheffield 68.

  🏨 **Oaks,** Colne Rd, Reedley, BB10 2LF, NE : 2 ½ m. on A 56 ✆ 414141, Telex 635309, Fax
  33401, 🔄, ⧖ – 🔄 rm 📺 ☎ 🅿 – 🔔 120. 🔄 AE ⓪ *VISA*
  M *(closed Saturday lunch)* 7.35/14.95 t. and a la carte ⬧ 3.95 – **58 rm** � 58.00/76.00 st. –
  SB (weekends only) 78.00/84.00 st.

  🏠 **Rosehill House,** Rosehill Av., Manchester Rd, BB11 2PW, ✆ 53931, ⧖ – 🔄 rm 📺 ☎
  🅿. 🔄 AE *VISA* ❄
  Accommodation closed 1 week at Christmas – **M** 10.25 st. and a la carte ⬧ 3.80 – **18 rm**
  ⊡ 34.50/40.00 st. – SB (weekends only) 52.00 st.

  🏠 **Travelodge** without rest., Cavalry Barracks, Barracks Rd, BB11 4AS, W : ½ m. at Junction
  of A 671 and A 679 ✆ 416039 – 📺 ⅙ 🅿. 🔄 AE *VISA*
  32 rm 21.50/27.00 t.

MAZDA Todmorden Rd ✆ 36131   🅦 ATS Healey Wood Rd ✆ 22409/38423/51624
RENAULT Trafalgar St. ✆ 33311
VAUXHALL Accrington Rd ✆ 27321

BURNSALL North Yorks. 402 O 21 – pop. 116 – ECD : Monday and Thursday – ✉ Skipton –
✆ 075 672.
♦London 223 – Bradford 26 – ♦Leeds 29.

  ♨ **Red Lion,** BD23 6BU, ✆ 204 – 🅿. ❄
  M (dinner   only)   8.00 t. ⬧ 3.50   –   **12   rm** ⊡ 25.00/33.00 t.   –   SB (November-
  March) 40.00/50.00 **st.**

  ⚲ Manor House, BD23 6BW, ✆ 231, ↘, ⧖ – 🅿
  7 rm.

BURPHAM West Sussex 404 S 30 – see Arundel.

BURRINGTON Devon 403 I 31 – pop. 482 – ECD : Saturday – ✆ 0769 High Bickington.
♦London 260 – Barnstaple 14 – Exeter 28 – Taunton 50.

  🏨 **Northcote Manor** (Best Western) ↘, EX37 9LZ, NW : 1 m. ✆ 60501, ≤, ⧖ – 🔄 rest 📺
  ☎ 🅿. 🔄 AE ⓪ *VISA*
  March-October – **M** (booking essential) 11.95/17.00 t. ⬧ 3.95 – **12 rm** ⊡ 44.00/110.00 t. –
  SB 84.00/92.00 **st.**

BURTON-UPON-TRENT Staffs. 402 403 404 O 25 – pop. 59 040 – ECD : Wednesday –
✆ 0283.
🏌 Branston, Burton Rd ✆ 43207, SW : 1½ m. on A 5121 – 🏌 Ashby Rd, East ✆ 44551, E : 2 m. on
A 50.
🎫 Town Hall, King Edward Square ✆ 45454.
♦London 128 – ♦Birmingham 29 – ♦Leicester 27 – ♦Nottingham 27 – Stafford 27.

  🏨 **Stanhope** (Lansbury), Ashby Rd, East, DE15 0PU, SE : 2 ½ m. on A 50 ✆ 217954, Telex
  347185, Fax 226199 – 🔄 rm 📺 ☎ 🅿 – 🔔 150. 🔄 AE ⓪ *VISA* ❄
  M 8.00/13.50 t. and a la carte ⬧ 3.50 – **21 rm** ⊡ 50.00/60.00 t. – SB (weekends
  only) 64.00/71.00 **st.**

  ⚲ **Edgecote,** 179 Ashby Rd, DE15 0LB, SE : 1 m. on A 50 ✆ 68966, ⧖ – 📺 🅿
  M (by arrangement) 7.00 **st.** ⬧ 3.00 – **12 rm** ⊡ 15.50/36.00 **st.**

  at Stretton N : 3 ½ m. by A 50 off A 5121 – ✉ ✆ 0283 Burton-upon-Trent :

  ✗✗✗ **Dovecliff Hall** ↘ with rm, Dovecliff Rd, DE13 0DJ, ✆ 31818, ≤, « Carefully restored
  Georgian house », ⧖, park – 📺 ☎ 🅿. 🔄 *VISA* ❄
  M *(closed Monday and Saturday lunch and Sunday dinner)* 10.00/19.00 t. ⬧ 5.00 – **6 rm**
  ⊡ 65.00/85.00 t.

at Rolleston-on-Dove N : 3 ¾ m by A 50 on Rolleston Rd – ✉ ☎ 0283 Burton-upon-Trent :

XXX **Brookhouse Inn** with rm, Brookside, DE13 9AA, ✆ 814188, Fax 813644, « Tastefully furnished part 17C house », 🚗 – TV ☎ P. AE ⓓ VISA
M *(closed Saturday lunch and Sunday dinner)* 7.95 t. (lunch) and a la carte 13.35/21.85 t.
🍷 3.75 – **19 rm** ☕ 55.00/69.00 st. – SB (weekends only) 80.00 st.

at Newton Solney NE : 3 m. by A 50 on B 5008 – ✉ ☎ 0283 Burton-upon-Trent :

🏠 **Newton Park** (Embassy) ⌖, DE15 0SS, ✆ 703568, ≤, 🚗 – ⃟ TV ☎ P – 🏛 100. AE ⓓ VISA
M 9.95/17.50 st. 🍷 4.00 – ☕ 6.50 – **46 rm** 48.00/78.00 st. – SB 55.00/62.00 st.

at Branston SW : 1 ½ m. on A 5121 – ✉ ☎ 0283 Burton-upon-Trent :

🏠 **Riverside Inn** ⌖, Riverside Drive, off Warren Lane, DE14 3EP, ✆ 511234, Fax 511441, 🚗
– TV ☎ P. AE VISA
M 10.75/11.90 t. and a la carte 🍷 3.75 – **20 rm** ☕ 23.00/57.00 t.

at Barton-under-Needwood SW : 5 m. by A 5121 on A 38 – ✉ Burton-upon-Trent –
☎ 0283 Barton-under-Needwood :

🏠 **Travelodge** without rest., A 38 Northbound, DE13 0ED, ✆ 716343 – TV 🦽 P. AE VISA
20 rm 21.50/27.00 t.

AUSTIN-ROVER Moor St. ✆ 45353
CITROEN Tollgate ✆ 212454
FORD Horninglow St. ✆ 61081
LADA Woodside Rd ✆ 760363
NISSAN Scalpcliffe Rd ✆ 66677
RENAULT 118 Horninglow Rd ✆ 67811

SCIMITAR, LOTUS, CITROEN Station Rd ✆ 813593
VOLVO New St. ✆ 31331
VW-AUDI Tutbury Rd ✆ 31336

🛞 ATS All Saints Rd ✆ 65994/63170

BURY Greater Manchester 402 N 23 403 ② 404 N 23 – pop. 61 785 – ECD : Tuesday – ☎ 061
Manchester.

🏌 Unsworth Hall, Blackford Bridge ✆ 766 4897 – 🏌 Lowes Park, Hill Top ✆ 764 1231.

♦London 211 – ♦Leeds 45 – ♦Liverpool 35 – ♦Manchester 9.

🏠 **Normandie** ⌖, Elbut Lane, Birtle, BL9 6UT, E : 3 m. by B 6222 ✆ 764 3869, ≤ – ⃟ TV ☎
P. AE ⓓ VISA 🚫
closed 26 December-8 January and Bank Holidays – M (see **Normandie rest.** below) – ☕
6.00 – **24 rm** 49.00/69.00 st.

XXX **Normandie** (at Normandie H.), Elbut Lane, BL9 6UT, ✆ 764 3869 – P. AE ⓓ VISA
closed 26 December-8 January and Bank Holidays – M *(closed Monday and Saturday lunch
and Sunday)* (booking essential) 16.95 st. (dinner) and a la carte 18.15/29.70 st.

🛞 ATS John St. ✆ 764 2830/6860

BURY ST. EDMUNDS Suffolk 404 W 27 – pop. 30 563 – ECD : Thursday – ☎ 0284.

See : Abbey★★ – St. Mary's Church★ (15C) (the Angel roof★★).

Envir. : Ickworth House★ (18C) *AC*, SW : 3 m.

🏌 Fornham Park, Fornham St. Martin ✆ 7563426, by A 134 on B 1106 – 🏌 Tuthill ✆ 755979, NW :
2 m. on B 1106 by A 45.

🛈 6 Angel Hill ✆ 763233 and 764667 (evenings and weekends).

♦London 79 – ♦Cambridge 27 – ♦Ipswich 26 – ♦Norwich 41.

🏠 **Angel**, 3 Angel Hill, IP33 1LT, ✆ 753926, Telex 81630, Fax 750092 – ➰ rest TV ☎ P 🏛
150. AE ⓓ VISA 🚫
M 12.50 t. and a la carte – ☕ 6.50 – **39 rm** 55.00/80.00 t., **1 suite** 95.00/130.00 t.

🏠 **Butterfly**, Symonds Rd, by A 45, IP32 7BW, E : 1 ½ m. by A 1302 at junction of A 1302 and
A 45 ✆ 760884, Telex 818360, Fax 755476 – TV ☎ P – 🏛 50. AE ⓓ VISA 🚫
M 9.00 st. and a la carte 🍷 2.95 – ☕ 4.50 – **50 rm** 48.50/80.00 st. – SB (weekends
only) 63.00 st.

🏠 **Suffolk** (T.H.F.), 38 The Buttermarket, IP33 1DL, ✆ 753995, Fax 750 937 – ➰ rm TV ☎ –
🏛 . AE ⓓ VISA
M 9.50/14.00 st. and a la carte 🍷 7.25 – ☕ 7.50 – **31 rm** 58.00/65.00 st. – SB (weekends only) 60.00/78.00 st.

🏠 **Chantry**, 8 Sparhawk St., IP33 1RY, ✆ 767427 – ➰ rest TV ☎ P. AE VISA
M *(dinner only Monday to Thursday)* 10.00 st. and a la carte 🍷 2.95 – **13 rm** ☕ 24.00/
44.00 st.

🏚 **White Hart** without rest., 35 Southgate St., IP33 2AZ, ✆ 755547 – TV ☎ P. AE
VISA 🚫
8 rm ☕ 30.00/44.00 st.

at Rougham Green E : 4 m. by A 1302 off A 45 – ✉ Bury St. Edmunds – ☎ 0359 Beyton:

🏠 **Ravenwood Hall**, IP30 9JA, on A 45 ✆ 70345, Fax 70788, ☀ heated, 🚗, park, ✗ – TV ☎
P. AE ⓓ VISA
M 13.50 t. and a la carte 🍷 3.85 – **7 rm** ☕ 50.00/75.00 t. – SB (weekends only) 145.00 st.

at Bradfield Combust SE : 4 ½ m. on A 134 – ✉ Bury St. Edmunds – ✆ 028 486 Sickles-
mere :

XX **Bradfield House** with rm, Sudbury Rd, IP30 0LR, ✆ 301, 🎨 – TV ☎ P. 🅰 VISA
M *(closed Sunday dinner, Monday and Tuesday)* 10.25 **st.** and a la carte 11.80/16.50 **st.** 🍾 3.90
– **4 rm** ⊆ 35.00/50.00 **st.** – SB (weekdays only) 65.00/80.00 **st.**

AUSTIN-ROVER 76 Risbygate St. ✆ 753101
FIAT Mildenhall Rd ✆ 750001
FORD 5 Fornham Rd ✆ 752332
NISSAN Bury Rd, Horringer ✆ 028 488 (Horringer)
362
VAUXHALL-OPEL Cotton Lane ✆ 755621

VOLVO, MAZDA Out Risbygate ✆ 762444
VW-AUDI Northern Way ✆ 763441

Ⓜ ATS Southgate Av., Mildenhall ✆ 713841/713891
ATS Unit 1, Ailwin Rd, Moreton Hall Ind. Est. ✆
705610

BUTTERMERE Cumbria 402 K 20 – pop. 194 – ✉ Cockermouth – ✆ 059 685.
See : Lake★.

♦London 306 – ♦Carlisle 35 – Kendal 43.

🏠 **Bridge**, CA13 9UZ, ✆ 266, ← – ⤧ rest ☎ P
M (bar lunch)/dinner 13.25 **t.** 🍾 3.20 – **22 rm** ⊆ 42.00/90.00 **t.** – SB 64.00/90.00 **st.**

BUXTON Derbs. 402 403 404 O 24 – pop. 19 502 – ECD : Wednesday – ✆ 0298.
Envir. : Tideswell (Parish Church★ 14C) NE : 9 m.
🏌 Buxton and High Peak, Town End ✆ 3453, NE : on A 6 – 🏌 Cavendish, Gadley Lane ✆ 3494,
¾ m. Buxton Station.
🏢 The Cresent ✆ 25106.
♦London 172 – Derby 38 – ♦Manchester 25 – ♦Stoke-on-Trent 24.

🏨 **Lee Wood** (Best Western), 13 Manchester Rd, SK17 6TQ, on A 5004 ✆ 23002, Telex
669848, 🎨 – 📳 TV ☎ P – 🔔 110. 🅰 AE ① VISA
M (bar lunch Monday to Saturday)/dinner 13.75 **st.** and a la carte 🍾 4.00 – **38 rm**
⊆ 48.50/66.00 **st.** – SB 72.00/88.00 **st.**

🏠 **Hartington**, 18 Broad Walk, SK17 6JR, ✆ 22638 – TV &. 🅰 VISA. 🎨
closed 16 to 22 July and 24 December-3 January – **M** 8.00 **t.** 🍾 3.50 – **17 rm** ⊆ 18.00/42.00 **t.**

SAAB Leek Rd ✆ 2494

Ⓜ ATS Staden Lane off Ashbourne Rd ✆ 5608/5655

BWLCHTOCYN Gwynedd 402 403 G 25 – see Abersoch.

CADNAM Hants. 403 404 P 31 – pop. 1 882 – ECD : Wednesday – ✆ 0703 Southampton.
♦London 91 – Salisbury 16 – ♦Southampton 8 – Winchester 19.

🏢 **Bartley Lodge** 🍴, Lyndhurst Rd, SO4 2NR, on A 337 ✆ 812248, ←, ⤢ heated, 🎨, park –
⤧ rm TV P. 🅰 AE ① VISA
M (dinner only and Sunday lunch)/dinner 10.00 **st.** and a la carte 🍾 3.15 – **18 rm**
⊆ 45.00/110.00 **st.**

🏠 **Walnut cottage** without rest., Old Romsey Rd, SO4 2NP, off A 31 ✆ 812275, 🎨 – TV P.
🎨
closed 23 to 28 December – **3 rm** ⊆ 17.00/32.00 **st.**

CAERDYDD = Cardiff.

CAERFFILI = Caerphilly.

CAERFYRDDIN = Carmarthen.

CAERGYBI = Holyhead.

CAERNARFON Gwynedd 402 403 H 24 – pop. 9 271 – ECD : Thursday – ✆ 0286 Llanwnda.
See : Castle★★★ (13C-14C) (Royal Welsh Fusiliers Regimental museum★) AC – City walls★.
Envir. : SE : Snowdon (ascent and ❄★★★) 1 h 15 mn by Snowdon Mountain Railway (AC) from
Llanberis (Pass★★) SE : 13 m. – Dinas Dinlle★, SW : 5 m.
🏌 Llanfaglan ✆ 3783, SW : 1 ¾ m – 🅱 Oriel Pendeitsh ✆ 2232 (summer only).
♦London 249 – Birkenhead 76 – Chester 68 – Holyhead 30 – Shrewsbury 85.

🏨 **Seiont Manor** 🍴, Llanrug, LL55 2AQ, E : 3 m. on A 4086 ✆ 76887, Fax 2840, 🔳, 🎨, park
– ⤧ TV ☎ P – 🔔 100. 🅰 AE ① VISA 🎨
M 16.50/22.00 **t.** and a la carte – **28 rm** ⊆ 60.00/125.00 **t.** – SB 100.00/110.00 **st.**

🏠 **Pengwern** 🍴, Saron, LL54 5UH, SW : 3 ¼ m. on Llandwrog rd ✆ 830717, « Working
farm » – P. 🎨
April-October – **M** 7.00 **st.** – **3 rm** ⊆ 14.00/28.00 **st.** – SB (except
July and August) 38.00/42.00 **st.**

🏠 **Isfryn** without rest., 11 Church St., LL55 1SW, ✆ 5628 – TV
March-November – **6 rm** ⊆ 12.50/32.00 **s.**

Ⓜ ATS Bangor Rd ✆ 673110

CAERPHILLY (CAERFFILI) Mid Glam. 403 K 29 – pop. 28 681 – ECD : Wednesday – ۞ 0222.
See : Castle✶✶ (13C).
🏌 Castell Heights, Blaengwynlais ℰ 886666, SW : 2 m.
🛈 Old Police Station, Park Lane ℰ 851378 (summer only).
♦London 157 – ♦Cardiff 8 – Newport 11.

  Hotels and restaurants see : *Cardiff* S : 8 m., *Newport (Gwent)* E : 11 m.

CALCOT Glos. – see Tetbury.

CALDBECK Cumbria 401 402 K 19 – pop. 606 – ✉ Wigton – ۞ 069 98.
♦London 308 – ♦Carlisle 13 – Keswick 16 – Workington 23.
 🏠 Park End ⤵, Park End, CA7 8HH, SW : 1 ½ m. on B 5299 ℰ 494, « Converted 17C farm-house », 🛥 – ⤸ rest 📺 🅿
  3 rm.

CALLINGTON Cornwall 403 H 32 – pop. 2 579 – ECD : Wednesday – ۞ 0579 Liskeard.
♦London 252 – Exeter 51 – Penzance 67 – ♦Plymouth 14.
 ♤ **Coachmakers Arms,** Newport Sq., PL17 7AS, ℰ 82567 – 📺 🅿. 🌇 *VISA*. 🍽
  M 13.00 **st.** and a la carte 8.95/13.75 **st.** ₰ 3.00 – **4 rm** ☕ 22.50/35.00 **st.** – SB 50.00 **st.**

CALNE Wilts. 403 404 O 29 – pop. 10 235 – ECD : Wednesday – ۞ 0249.
♦London 91 – ♦Bristol 33 – Swindon 17.
 🏠 **Chilvester Hill House,** SN11 OLP, W : ¾ m. on A 4 ℰ 813981, ⛱ heated, 🛥 – ⤸ rest
  📺 🅿. 🌇 AE ⓪ *VISA*. 🍽
  M (lunch by arrangement)/dinner 20.00 **st.** ₰ 3.00 – **3 rm** ☕ 35.00/55.00 **st.**

AUSTIN-ROVER Main Rd, Cherhill ℰ 812254

CALSTOCK Cornwall 403 H 32 – pop. 4 079 – ✉ – ۞ 0822 Tavistock.
♦London 246 – Exeter 48 – ♦Plymouth 22.
 🏠 **Danescombe Valley** ⤵, Lower Kelly, PL18 9RY, W : ½ m. ℰ 832414, ≼ River Tamar,
  « Country house atmosphere » – ⤸ rest 🅿. 🍽
  closed 4 November-Easter – **M** *(closed Wednesday and Thursday)* (dinner only) 22.00 **st.**
  ₰ 3.30 – **5 rm** ☕ 55.00/66.00 **st.**

CAMBERLEY Surrey 404 R 29 – pop. 45 108 – ECD : Wednesday – ۞ 0276.
Envir. : Sandhurst (Royal Military Academy : Royal Memorial Chapel✶) NW : 1 ½ m.
♦London 40 – Reading 13 – ♦Southampton 48.
 🏨 **Frimley Hall** (T.H.F.) ⤵, off Portsmouth Rd via Lime Av., GU15 2BG, E : ¾ m. off
  A 325 ℰ 28321, Telex 858446, Fax 691253, 🛥 – ⤸ rm 📺 ☎ 🅿 – 🛎 80. 🌇 AE ⓪
  VISA
  M 12.75/15.75 **st.** and a la carte ₰ 3.95 – ☕ 7.60 – **66 rm** 69.00/102.00 **st.** – SB (week-ends only) 88.00/110.00 **st.**

AUSTIN-ROVER London Rd ℰ 63443

CAMBRIDGE Cambs. 404 U 27 – pop. 87 111 – ECD : Thursday – ۞ 0223.
See : Colleges Quarter✶✶✶ : King's College✶✶ (King's Chapel✶✶✶) Z – St. John's College✶✶✶
(Gateway✶) Y – The Backs✶✶ YZ – Fitzwilliam Museum✶✶ AC Z M1 – Trinity College✶✶ (Wren
Library✶✶, Chapel✶, Great Court and Gate✶) Y – Clare College✶ Z B – Senate House✶ Z S –
Holy Sepulchre✶ (12C round church) Y E – Jesus College (Chapel✶) Y K – Kettle's Yard✶ Y M2 –
Queen's College✶ (Cloister Court) Z.

Envir. : Anglesey Abbey (12C) (interior✶✶ and park✶ AC) NE : 6 m. by A 1303 X and B 1102.
 ✈ Cambridge Airport : ℰ 61133, E : 2 m. on A 1303 X.
🛈 Wheeler St. ℰ 322640.
 ♦London 55 – ♦Coventry 88 – ♦Kingston-upon-Hull 137 – ♦Ipswich 54 – ♦Leicester 74 – ♦Norwich 61 –
♦Nottingham 88 – ♦Oxford 100.

Plan on next page

 🏨 **Garden House** (Best Western), Granta Pl., off Mill Lane, CB2 1RT, ℰ 63421, Telex 81463,
  Fax 316605, ≼, 🛥 – ▐ 📺 ☎ 🅿 – 🛎 180. 🌇 AE ⓪ *VISA*. 🍽   Z **n**
  M 13.25/15.75 **t.** and a la carte ₰ 3.25 – ☕ 5.50 – **113 rm** 67.00/135.00 **t.**, **4 suites** 195.00 **t.** –
  SB (weekends only) 106.00/113.00 **st.**

 🏨 **University Arms** (De Vere), Regent St., CB2 1AD, ℰ 351241, Telex 817311, Fax 315256 –
  ▐ ⤸ rm 📺 ☎ & 🅿 – 🛎 200. 🌇 AE ⓪ *VISA*   Z **e**
  M 10.00/14.00 **st.** and a la carte – **114 rm** ☕ 65.00/80.00 **st.**, **1 suite** 130.00 **st.** – SB (week-ends only) 68.00/74.00 **st.**

P.T.O. →

131

CAMBRIDGE

Grafton Centre .... Y
Lion Yard Centre .. Z
Market Hill .... Z 18
Market Street ..... Y 19
Petty Cury .... Z 27
St. Andrew's St. ... Z 28
Sidney Street ..... Y 32
Trinity Street ..... Y 36

Bridge Street ..... Y 2
Corn Exchange St.. Z 6
Downing Street ... Z 7
Free School Lane.. Z 12
Hobson Street .... Y 14

King's Parade ..... Z 15
Madingley Rd .. X, Y 16
Magdalene St ..... Y 17
Milton Road ...... Y 20
Newmarket Road . Y 21
Northampton St .. Y 22
Parker Street ..... Z 23
Peas Hill .... Z 25
Pembroke Street . Z 26
St. John's Street .. Y 29
Short Street ...... Y 30
Tennis Court Road. Z 35
Trumpington Road Z 37
Wheeler Street.... Z 39

COLLEGES

CHRIST'S — Y A
CHURCHILL — X B
CLARE — Z B
CORPUS CHRISTI — Z G
DARWIN — Z D
DOWNING — Z E
EMMANUEL — Z F
FITZWILLIAM COLLEGE — X G
GONVILLE AND CAIUS — Y G
HARVEY COURT — Z K
HUGHES HALL — Z J
JESUS — Y K
KING'S — Z
LUCY CAVENDISH — Y O
MAGDALENE — Y N

NEW HALL — X D
NEWNHAM — X E
PEMBROKE — Z N
PETERHOUSE — Z O
QUEENS' — Z
RIDDLEY HALL — Z Q
ST-CATHARINE'S — Z R
ST-EDMUNDS HOUSE — Y U
ST-JOHN'S — Y Y
SELWYN — X F
SIDNEY SUSSEX — Y P
TRINITY — Y
TRINITY HALL — Y V
WESTMINSTER — Y W
WOLFSON — X U

(A 604), HUNTINGDON
(A 10)
A 1309 ELY
A 1307
Huntingdon Rd
B 1049
Gilbert Rd
Milton Rd
(A 45)
A 1303 NEWMARKET
A 1303
BEDFORD (A 45)
Grange Road
Madingley Rd
Newmarket Rd
A 603
Mill Rd
X
Barton Road
NEWTOWN X
STATION
Coleridge Rd
(M 11)
Trumpington
Hills Road
0   1 km
1/2 mile
Long
Road
A 1134
(A 10, M 11)
LONDON
A 1309
(A 604)
COLCHESTER
A 1307

A 1309
0   400 m
0   400 yards
A 1307
Victoria Rd
Road
20
A 1303
Castle
Chesterton
JESUS GREEN
Victoria
Cam or Granta
De Freville Av.
Elizabeth
Y
Street
MIDSUMMER COMMON
Way
Y
22 17
K
Avenue
21
A 1303
2
Jesus
Lane
Maid's Causeway
Newmarket Rd
ST. JOHN'S COLLEGE
29
King   St.
30
New Sq.
Fitzroy
GRAFTON CENTRE
New St.
36 32 14
19
18
TRINITY COLLEGE
G
A
Emmanuel Rd.
THE
V
27
23
Norfolk St.
B
S
LION YARD CENTRE
28
BACKS
15 25 39
KING'S COLLEGE
12 6
F
Parkside
POL
Road
QUEENS' COLLEGE
R   M
26
M
PARKER'S PIECE
East
K
N
35 E
Regent
Mill Road
J
Silver St.
Trumpington
Road
Gonvile
Gresham
Barnabas Rd
Gwydir St.
Newnham
The Fen Causeway
Lensfield Rd
Hills Rd
Glisson Rd
Lyndewode Rd   St.
A 603
37
A 1309
A 1307

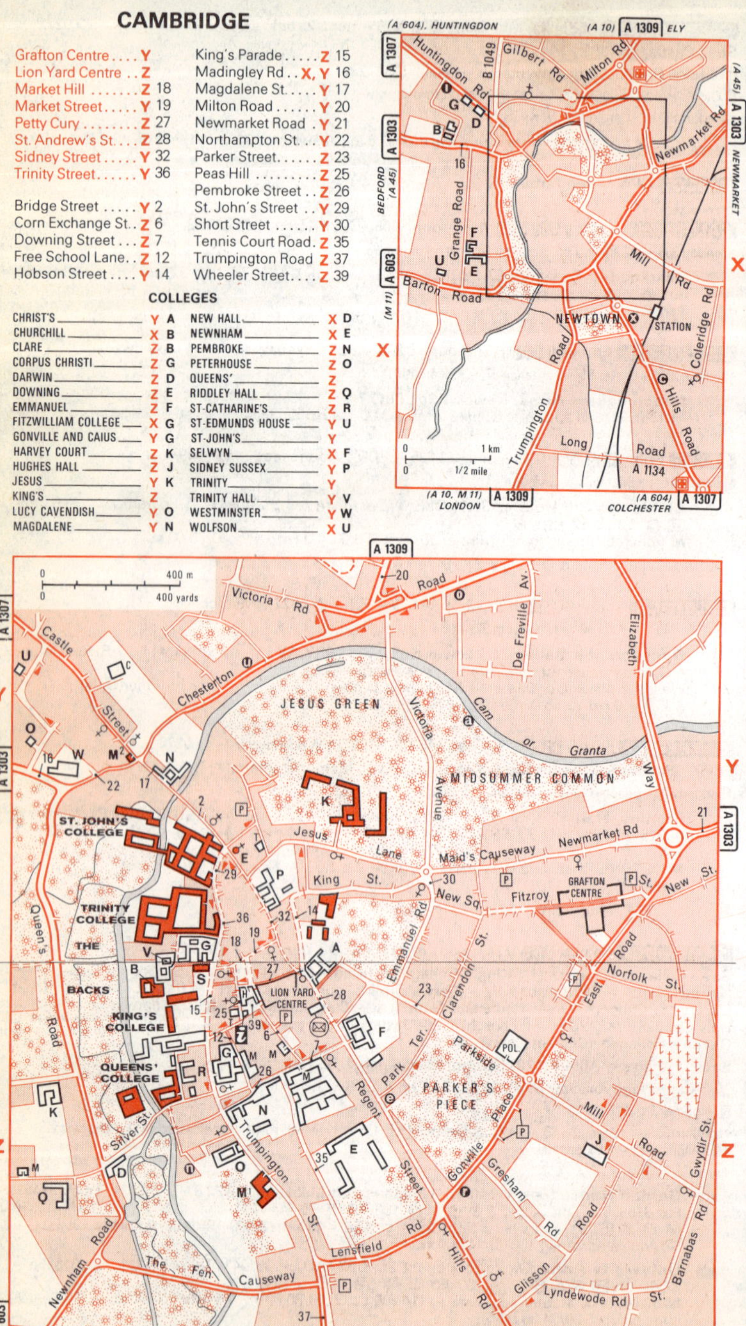

Arundel House, 53 Chesterton Rd, CB4 3AN, ☎ 67701 – ⇔ rest 📺 ☎ 🅿 – 🔥 35. 🔼 AE ⓪ VISA 🛷 **Y u**
closed 25 and 26 December – **M** 7.50/10.50 **t.** and a la carte 🍾 2.20 – ☕ 2.25 – **88 rm** 25.00/58.00 **t.** – SB (weekends only) 67.00 **st.**

Gonville, Gonville Pl., CB1 1LY, ☎ 66611 – 🛎 🔳 rest 📺 ☎ 🅿 – 🔥 60. 🔼 AE VISA **Z r**
closed 4 days at Christmas – **M** 7.45/9.50 **st.** and a la carte – **62 rm** ☕ 53.00/70.00 **st.** – SB (weekends only) 70.00/75.00 **st.**

Centennial, 63-69 Hills Rd, CB2 1PG, ☎ 314652, Telex 817019 – ⇔ rest 📺 ☎ 🅿. 🔼 AE ⓪ VISA 🛷 **X x**
closed 23 December-2 January – **M** 10.00/15.00 **t.** and a la carte – **22 rm** ☕ 45.00/60.00 **t.** – SB (October-March) (weekends only) 80.00/90.00 **st.**

Helen, 167-169 Hills Rd, CB2 2RJ, ☎ 246465, Telex 81365 – 📺 ☎ 🅿. 🔼 AE VISA **X c**
closed 17 December-7 January – **M** *(closed Sunday dinner)* (bar lunch)/dinner 10.00 **st.** 🍾 3.75 – **27 rm** ☕ 25.00/47.00 **st.**

Dykelands, 157 Mowbray Rd, on A 1134, CB1 4SP, ☎ 244300, 🛲 – ⇔ rest 📺 🅿. 🛷 **Y** *by A 1303*
M (by arrangement) 8.00 **t.** – **8 rm** ☕ 19.00/34.00 **t.**

Ashley, 74 Chesterton Rd, CB4 1ER, ☎ 350059, 🛲 – 📺 ☎ 🅿 **Y o**
10 rm.

Midsummer House, Midsummer Common, CB4 1HA, ☎ 69299, « Riverside setting », 🛲 **Y a**
– 🔼 ⓪ VISA
closed Sunday dinner, Monday and Christmas – **M** 16.00/26.50 **st.**

Cambridge Lodge with rm, 139 Huntingdon Rd, CB3 0DQ, ☎ 352833, Telex 817438, 🛲 – **X i**
📺 ☎ 🅿. 🔼 AE ⓪ VISA
M *(closed Saturday lunch)* 14.95/19.95 **st.** and a la carte 16.50/27.00 **st.** 🍾 4.50 – **11 rm** ☕ 39.00/70.00 **st.**

at Impington N : 2 m. on B 1049 at junction of A 45 – X – ✉ Cambridge – ☎ 022 023 Histon :

Post House (T.H.F.), Lakeview, Bridge Rd, CB4 4PH, ☎ 237000, Telex 817123, Fax 233426, 🔼, 🛲 – ⇔ rm 📺 ☎ 🔥 🅿 – 🔥 60. 🔼 AE ⓪ VISA
M 9.50/14.75 **st.** and a la carte 🍾 3.95 – ☕ 6.45 – **119 rm** 78.00/98.00 **st.**, **1 suite** 155.00/220.00 **st.** – SB (weekends only) 96.00/104.00 **st.**

at Fowlmere S : 8 ¾ m. by A 1309 – X – and A 10 on B 1368 – ✉ Royston (Herts.) – ☎ 076 382 Fowlmere :

Maguire's, High St., SG8 7SR, ☎ 444 – 🅿. 🔼 AE ⓪ VISA
closed Sunday dinner and 25-26 December – **M** 18.50 **t.** and a la carte 14.45/18.70 **t.** 🍾 3.40.

Chequers Inn, High St., SG8 7SR, ☎ 369 – 🅿. 🔼 AE ⓪ VISA
closed Christmas Day – **M** a la carte 14.20/23.75 **st.** 🍾 3.10.

at Duxford S : 9 ½ m. by A 1309 – X – A 1301 and A 505 on B 1379 – ✉ Duxford – ☎ 0223 Cambridge :

Duxford Lodge with rm., Ickleton Rd, CB2 4RU, ☎ 836444, Group Telex 817438, Fax 355166, 🛲 – 📺 ☎ 🅿 – 🔥 25. 🔼 AE ⓪ VISA
M *(closed Saturday lunch)* 12.50/14.00 **st.** and a la carte 15.00/19.00 **st.** 🍾 4.95 – **16 rm** ☕ 45.00/75.00 **st.**

at Madingley W : 4 ½ m. by A 1303 – X – ✉ ☎ 0954 Madingley :

Three Horseshoes, 1 High St., CB3 8AB, ☎ 210221, 🛲 – 🔳 🅿.

at Bar Hill NW : 5 ½ m. by A 1307 – X – on A 604 – ✉ Bar Hill – ☎ 0954 Crafts Hill :

Cambridgeshire Moat House (Q.M.H.), Huntingdon Rd, CB3 8EU, ☎ 780555, Telex 817141, Fax 780010, 🔼, 🏌, 🛲, 🎿, squash – 📺 ☎ 🅿 – 🔥 200. 🔼 AE ⓪ VISA 🛷
M *(closed lunch Saturday and Bank Holidays)* 13.50 **st.** and a la carte 🍾 4.25 – **100 rm** ☕ 65.00/82.00 **st.** – SB (weekends only) 87.00 **st.**

at Dry Drayton NW : 5 ¾ m. by A 1307 – X – off A 604 – ✉ Cambridge – ☎ 0954 Madingley :

Coach House 🛇 without rest., Scotland Rd, CB3 8BX, ☎ 782439, 🛲 – ⇔ 🅿. 🛷
Mid March-mid December – **3 rm** ☕ 26.00/40.00 **st.**

at Lolworth Service Area NW : 6 m. by A 1307 – Y – on A 604 – ✉ Cambridge – ☎ 0954 Crafts Hill :

Travelodge without rest., CB3 8DR, Northbound carriageway ☎ 81335 – 📺 🔥 🅿. 🔼 AE VISA
20 rm 21.50/27.00 **t.**

AUSTIN-ROVER 400 Newmarket Rd ☎ 65111
BEDFORD, OPEL-VAUXHALL 137 Histon Rd ☎ 66751
CITROEN Newmarket Rd, Duxford ☎ 832136
DAIMLER-JAGUAR Cherry Hinton Rd ☎ 411114
FORD 350 New Market Rd ☎ 315435
HONDA Cheddars Lane ☎ 359151
LANCIA, SUZUKI, FIAT 315-349 Mill Rd ☎ 242222
MERCEDES-BENZ 121-129 Perne Rd ☎ 411511

NISSAN Babraham Rd ☎ 245456
RENAULT 217 Newmarket Rd ☎ 351616
TOYOTA 1 Union Lane ☎ 356225
VAUXHALL-OPEL Elizabeth Way ☎ 321321
VOLVO Harston ☎ 870123
VW-AUDI 383 Milton Rd ☎ 354472

☎ ATS 143 Histon Rd ☎ 61695 and 351431/2

CANNOCK Staffs. 402 403 404 N 25 – pop. 54 503 – ECD : Thursday – ☎ 054 35 (4 & 5 fig.) or 0543 (6 fig.).

🛈 Prince of Wales Centre, Church St. ✆466543.

♦London 135 – ♦Birmingham 20 – Derby 36 – ♦Leicester 51 – Shrewsbury 32 – ♦Stoke-on-Trent 28.

  🏨 **Roman Way**, Watling St., Hatherton, WS11 1SH, SW : 1 ¼ m. by A 460 on A 5 ✆ 72121, Fax 2749 – 📺 ☎ Ⓟ – 🛎 120. 🔺 AE VISA
  M (closed Saturday lunch) 6.95/9.75 **st.** and a la carte – **24 rm** ⚏ 44.00/52.00 **st.**

  🏠 **Travel Inn** without rest., Walting St., at junction with A 5, WS11 1SJ, SW : 1 m. ✆ 72721 – 📺 ♿ Ⓟ. 🔺 AE ⓄD VISA ✂
  39 rm 24.50/27.50 **t.**

AUSTIN-ROVER Wolverhampton Rd ✆ 466646
FORD PO Box 13 Watling St. ✆ 0922 (Cheslyn Hay) 417014
PEUGEOT-TALBOT 40 Longford Rd. Bridgetown ✆ 4111

VAUXHALL-OPEL Hatherton ✆ 466466
VW-AUDI Delta Way ✆ 6216

◉ ATS Cannock Rd, Chadsmoor ✆ 4985/74580
ATS Cannock Rd, Heath Hayes ✆ 74200

CANON PYON Heref. and Worc. 403 L 27 – see Hereford.

CANTERBURY Kent 404 X 30 – pop. 34 546 – ECD : Thursday – ☎ 0227.

See : Christ Church Cathedral★★★ (Norman crypt★★, Bell Harry Tower★★, Great Cloister★★, ≼★ from Green Court) Y – King's School★ Y B – Mercery Lane★ Y – Weavers★ (old houses) Y D – Eastbridge Hospital★ Y E – Poor Priests Hospital★ Y M1 – St. Augustines Abbey★★ Y K – St. Martin's Church★ Y N – West Gate★ Y R.

Envir. : Patrixbourne (St. Mary's Church : south door★) SE : 3 m. by A 2 Z.

🏌18 Scotlands Hills, Littlebourne Rd ✆ 63586/453532 Z and A 257.

🛈 34 St. Margarets St. ✆ 766567.

♦London 59 – ♦Brighton 76 – ♦Dover 15 – Maidstone 28 – Margate 17.

Plan opposite

  🏨 **County**, High St., CT1 2RX, ✆ 766266, Telex 965076, Fax 451512 – 🛗 📺 ☎ 🚗 Ⓟ – 🛎 50. 🔺 AE ⓄD VISA ✂   **Y n**
  M (see **Sullys** below) – ⚏ 6.50 – **73 rm** 55.00/75.00 **t.**, **1 suite** 130.00 **t.**

  🏨 **Chaucer** (T.H.F.), Ivy Lane, CT1 1TT, ✆ 464427, Telex 965096, Fax 450397 – ✂ rm 📺 ☎ Ⓟ – 🛎 80. 🔺 AE ⓄD VISA   **Z c**
  M 9.50/12.50 **st.** and a la carte 🍷3.95 – ⚏ 7.00 – **45 rm** 64.00/85.00 **st.** – SB (weekends only) 76.00/96.00 **st.**

  🏨 **Falstaff** (Lansbury), 8-12 St. Dunstan's St., CT2 8AF, ✆ 462138, Telex 96394, Fax 463525 – 📺 ☎ Ⓟ – 🛎 50. 🔺 AE ⓄD VISA. ✂   **Y a**
  M 8.50/12.50 **t.** and a la carte – **25 rm** ⚏ 55.00/65.00 **t.**

  🏠 **Thanington** without rest., 140 Wincheap, CT1 3RY, ✆ 453227, 🚿 – 📺 ☎ Ⓟ. 🔺 VISA   **Z s**
  10 rm ⚏ 42.00/50.00 **t.**

  🏠 Victoria (B.C.B.), 59 London Rd, CT2 8JY, ✆ 459333, 🚿 – 📺 ☎ Ⓟ. 🔺 AE ⓄD VISA ✂   **Y i**
  M (grill rest.) a la carte 7.50/15.00 **t.** – **34 rm**.

  🏠 **Canterbury**, 71 New Dover Rd, CT1 3DZ, ✆ 450551, Telex 965809, Fax 450873 – 🛗 📺 ☎ Ⓟ. 🔺 AE ⓄD VISA   **Z u**
  M 10.50 **t.** and a la carte 🍷3.00 – **27 rm** ⚏ 42.00/52.00 **t.** – SB (except summer) 56.00/58.00 **st.**

  🏠 **Ebury**, 65-67 New Dover Rd, CT1 3DX, ✆ 768433, 🔲, 🚿 – 📺 ☎ Ⓟ. 🔺 AE VISA   **Z r**
  closed 24 December-14 January – **M** (closed Sunday) (dinner only) a la carte 9.10/11.00 **t.** 🍷3.90 – **15 rm** ⚏ 36.00/50.00 **t.** – SB (except Sunday) 55.00/65.00 **st.**

  🏠 Miller's Arms, Mill Lane, CT1 2AA, ✆ 456057 – 📺 ☎   **Y x**
  13 rm.

  🏠 **Pointers**, 1 London Rd, CT2 8LR, ✆ 456846 – 📺 ☎ Ⓟ. 🔺 AE ⓄD VISA   **Y e**
  closed Christmas and New Year – **M** (dinner only) 11.00 **st.** 🍷2.80 – **14 rm** ⚏ 26.00/44.00 **st.** – SB 44.00/54.00 **st.**

  ♈ Three Tuns (B.C.B.), 24 Watling St., CT1 2UD, ✆ 67371 – 📺 ☎ Ⓟ. ✂   **Z i**
  8 rm.

  ⋔ **Ann's** without rest., 63 London Rd, CT2 8JZ, ✆ 768767, 🚿 – 📺 Ⓟ. ✂   **Y r**
  17 rm ⚏ 25.00/40.00 **st.**

  ⋔ **Magnolia House** without rest., 36 St. Dunstan's Terr., CT2 8AX, ✆ 765121, 🚿 – ✂   **Y s**
  6 rm ⚏ 18.00/40.00 **st.**

  ⋔ **Alexandra House** without rest., 1 Roper Rd, CT2 7EH, ✆ 767011, 🚿 – 📺 Ⓟ   **Y u**
  9 rm ⚏ 13.00/30.00 **st.**

  ⋔ **Highfield** without rest., Summer Hill, Harbledown, CT2 8NH, ✆ 462772, 🚿 – 📺 Ⓟ. 🔺 VISA ✂   by Rheims way **Y**
  closed December and January – **8 rm** ⚏ 20.00/41.00.

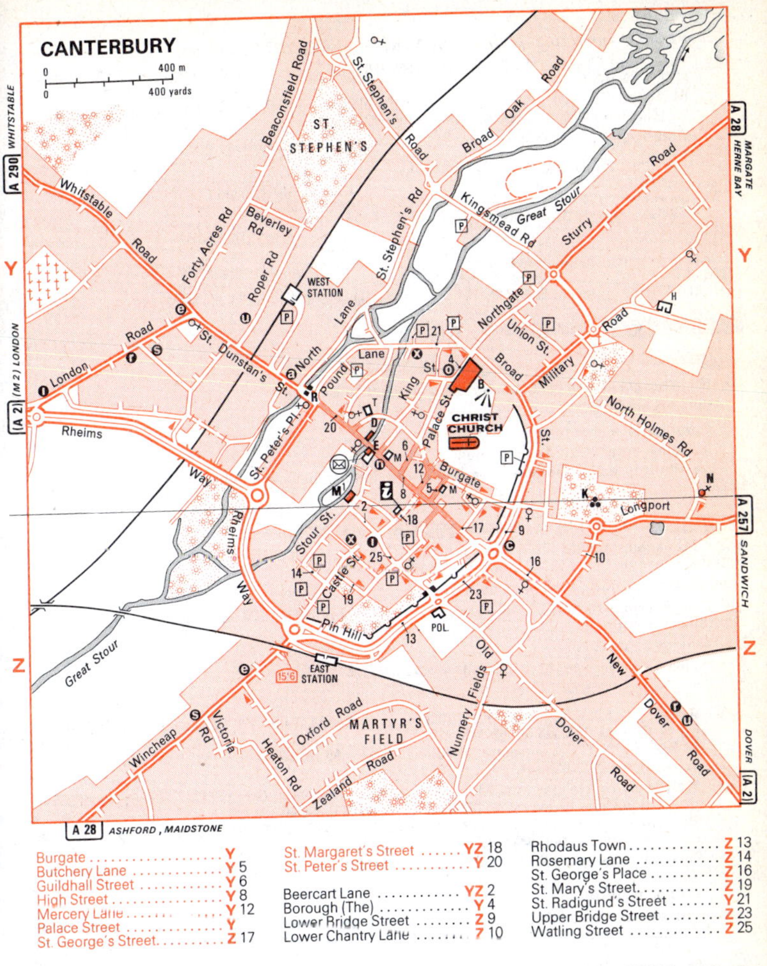

Burgate . . . . **Y**
Butchery Lane . . . . **Y** 5
Guildhall Street . . . . **Y** 6
High Street . . . . **Y** 8
Mercery Lane . . . . **Y** 12
Palace Street . . . . **Y** 17
St. George's Street . . . . **Z**

St. Margaret's Street . . . . . . **YZ** 18
St. Peter's Street . . . . **Y** 20

Beercart Lane . . . . **YZ** 2
Borough (The) . . . . **Y** 4
Lower Bridge Street . . . . **Z** 9
Lower Chantry Lane . . . . **Z** 10

Rhodaus Town . . . . **Z** 13
Rosemary Lane . . . . **Z** 14
St. George's Place . . . . **Z** 16
St. Mary's Street . . . . **Z** 19
St. Radigund's Street . . . . . . **Y** 21
Upper Bridge Street . . . . **Z** 23
Watling Street . . . . **Z** 25

XXX **Sully's,** (at County H.) High St., CT1 2RX, ℰ 766266, Telex 965076, Fax 451512 – ▱ ☞ **Y n**
P. 🅟 AE ⓄⒹ VISA
M 11.50/16.00 **t.** and a la carte 18.00/25.50 **t.**

XX **Michael's,** 74 Wincheap, CT1 3RS, ℰ 767411 – 🅟 AE VISA **Z e**
closed Saturday lunch, Sunday and 7 to 21 January – **M** 12.00/18.00 **t.** and a la carte
14.95/20.00 **t.** 🍷 4.00.

XX **Tuo e Mio,** 16 The Borough, CT1 2JD, ℰ 761471, Italian rest. – 🅟 AE ⓄⒹ VISA **Y o**
closed Tuesday lunch, Monday and 15 August-4 September – **M** a la carte 15.70/18.00 **st.**
🍷 2.75.

X **George's Brasserie,** 71-72 Castle St., CT1 2QD, ℰ 65658 – 🅟 AE VISA **Z x**
closed Sunday – **M** 6.95/9.95 **t.** and a la carte 8.85/16.85 **t.** 🍷 3.00.

at Fordwich NE : 3 m. by A 28 – **Y** – ✉ ☎ 0227 Canterbury :

🏠 **George and Dragon,** King St., CT2 0BX, ℰ 710661, ⛳ – TV ☎ **P.** 🅟 AE ⓄⒹ VISA
M (grill rest.) a la carte 8.45/13.90 **t.** 🍷 3.75 – **12 rm** ⚌ 20.00/40.00 **t.**

at Chartham SW : 3 ¼ m. by A 28 – **Z** – ✉ ☎ 0227 Canterbury :

🏠 **Thruxted Oast** ⚘ without rest., Mystole, CT4 7BX, SW : 1 ¼ m. by Bakers Lane and
Mystole Rd ℰ 730080, ≤, ⛳ – ✕ TV **P.** 🅟 AE VISA. ⚘
3 rm ⚌ 50.00/60.00 **st.**

P.T.O. →

at Chartham Hatch W : 3 ¼ m. by A 28 – Z – ✉ ☎ 0227 Canterbury :

🏨 **Howfield Manor,** Howfield Lane, CT4 7HQ, SE : 1 m. ℰ 738294, 🚗 – 📺 ☎ 🅿 – 🛎 30.
M 13.95/15.95 **st.** and a la carte 14.85/24.25 **st.** 🍾 4.50 – **13 rm** 🍽 55.00/70.00 **st.** –
SB (November-March) (except Christmas) 90.00 **st.**

ALFA-ROMEO, LOTUS The Street, Boughton ℰ 751223

AUSTIN-ROVER, DAIMLER-JAGUAR 28-30 St. Peters St. ℰ 66161

BMW Vauxhall Rd ℰ 454341

FIAT, CITROEN, VAUXHALL 41 St. Georges Pl. ℰ 66131

HONDA Vauxhall Rd ℰ 67781

HYUNDAI Westminster Rd ℰ 453314

MERCEDES-BENZ Mill Rd, Sturry ℰ 710481

PEUGEOT-TALBOT The Pavilion ℰ 451791

PORSCHE Vauxhall Rd ℰ 67781

RENAULT Northgate ℰ 65561

SAAB Westminster Rd ℰ 69100

SUBARU, SEAT Island Rd ℰ 710431

TOYOTA Union St. ℰ 455553

VAUXHALL-OPEL Ashford Rd, Chartham ℰ 731331

VOLVO, MERCEDES-BENZ Mill Rd, Sturry ℰ 710481

YUGO Pound Lane ℰ 463349

◍ ATS 29 Sturry Rd ℰ 464867/765021

CARBIS BAY Cornwall **403** D 33 – see St. Ives.

Gli alberghi o ristoranti ameni sono indicati nella guida
con un simbolo **rosso**.

Contribuite a mantenere
la guida aggiornata segnalandoci
gli alberghi ed i ristoranti dove avete soggiornato piacevolmente.

🏨🏨 ... 🏠

XXXXX ... ✗

CARDIFF (CAERDYDD) South Glam. **403** K 29 – pop. 262 313 – ECD : Wednesday – ☎ 0222.
See : St. Fagan's Castle (Folk Museum)*** AC, by St. Fagans Rd AY – Cardiff Castle** BZ –
National Museum** BY M – Llandaff Cathedral* AY B.
Envir. : Castell Loch*, NW : 4 m. by A470 AY.
✈ Cardiff-Wales Airport ℰ 0446 (Rhoose) 711911, Telex 49235, SW : 8 m. by A 48 AZ – Terminal :
Central Bus Station.
🛈 8-14 Bridge St. ℰ 227281.
♦London 155 – ♦Birmingham 110 – ♦Bristol 46 – ♦Coventry 124.

Plans on following pages

🏨🏨 **Angel** (Norfolk Cap.), Castle St., CF1 2QZ, ℰ 232633, Telex 498132, Fax 396212 – 🛗 ⇷ rm
📺 ☎ 🅿 – 🛎 250. 🅂 🅰🅴 ⓞ 𝗩𝗜𝗦𝗔. 🚫
M 13.00/17.00 **t.** and a la carte 🍾 5.50 – 🍽 5.00 – **89 rm** 66.50/78.50 **st.**, **2 suites** 95.00/140.00
st. – SB 103.00/132.50 **st.**
BZ **a**

🏨🏨 **Holiday Inn** (Holiday Inn), Mill Lane, CF1 1EZ, ℰ 399944, Group Telex 497365, Fax 395578,
≤, 🅂, squash – 🛗 ⇷ rm 🍽 📺 ☎ ♿ 🅿 – 🛎 300. 🅂 🅰🅴 ⓞ 𝗩𝗜𝗦𝗔
M 12.00/14.00 **st.** and a la carte 🍾 6.50 – 🍽 8.50 – **178 rm** 80.00/94.00 **st.**, **4 suites** 195.00 **st.**
– SB (weekends only) 93.00 **st.**
BZ **s**

🏨🏨 **Park** (Mt. Charlotte), Park Pl., CF1 3UD, ℰ 383471, Telex 497195, Fax 399309 – 🛗 📺 ☎ 🅿 –
🛎
102 rm, **6 suites**.
BZ **c**

🏨🏨 **Inn on the Avenue** (Stakis), Circle Way East, Llanedeyrn, CF3 7XF, NE : 3 m. on A 48
ℰ 732520, Telex 497582, Fax 549092, 🅂 – 🛗 ⇷ rm 🍽 rest 📺 ☎ 🅿 – 🛎 200. 🅂 🅰🅴
ⓞ 𝗩𝗜𝗦𝗔
M 12.50 **st.** and a la carte – 🍽 7.25 – **142 rm** 60.00/82.00 **st.**, **2 suites** 115.00 **st.** –
SB 56.00/76.00 **st.**
AY **n**

🏨🏨 **Celtic Bay,** Schooner Way, Atlantic Wharf, Cardiff Bay, CF1 5RT, ℰ 465888, Fax 481491 –
🛗 🍽 rest 📺 ☎ 🅿 – 🛎 250. 🅂 🅰🅴 ⓞ 𝗩𝗜𝗦𝗔. 🚫
M 18.95 **t.** and a la carte – **64 rm** 🍽 64.00/120.00 **t.** – SB (weekends only) 93.50 **st.**
BZ **x**

🏨🏨 **Crest** (Crest), Castle St., CF1 2XB, ℰ 388681, Telex 497258, Fax 371495 – 🛗 ⇷ rm 📺 ☎
🅿 – 🛎 180. 🅂 🅰🅴 ⓞ 𝗩𝗜𝗦𝗔
M 9.50/13.95 **st.** and a la carte – 🍽 7.35 – **157 rm** 67.00/79.00 **st.**, **1 suite** 100.00 **st.** –
SB 80.00/98.00 **st.**
BZ **i**

🏨🏨 **Post House** (T.H.F.), Pentwyn Rd, CF2 7XA, NE : 4 m. by A 48 ℰ 731212, Telex 497633, Fax
549147, 🅂 – 🛗 ⇷ rm 📺 ☎ 🅿 – 🛎 120. 🅂 🅰🅴 ⓞ 𝗩𝗜𝗦𝗔
M 8.50/12.50 **st.** and a la carte 🍾 4.20 – 🍽 7.50 – **150 rm** 66.00/77.00 **st.** – SB (weekends only) 77.00 **st.**
on A 48 AY

🏠 **Riverside,** 55-59 Despencer St., Riverside, CF1 8RG, ℰ 378866, Fax 388306 – 📺 ☎
🅿
36 rm.
BZ **u**

🏠 **Campanile,** Caxton Pl., Pentwyn, CF2 7HA, NE : 4 m. by A 48 ℰ 549044, Telex 497553 –
⇷ rm 📺 ☎ ♿ 🅿
47 rm.
on A 48 AY

🏠 **Beverley,** 75-77 Cathedral Rd, CF1 9PG, ℰ 343443 – 📺 ☎ 🅿
18 rm.
AZ **o**

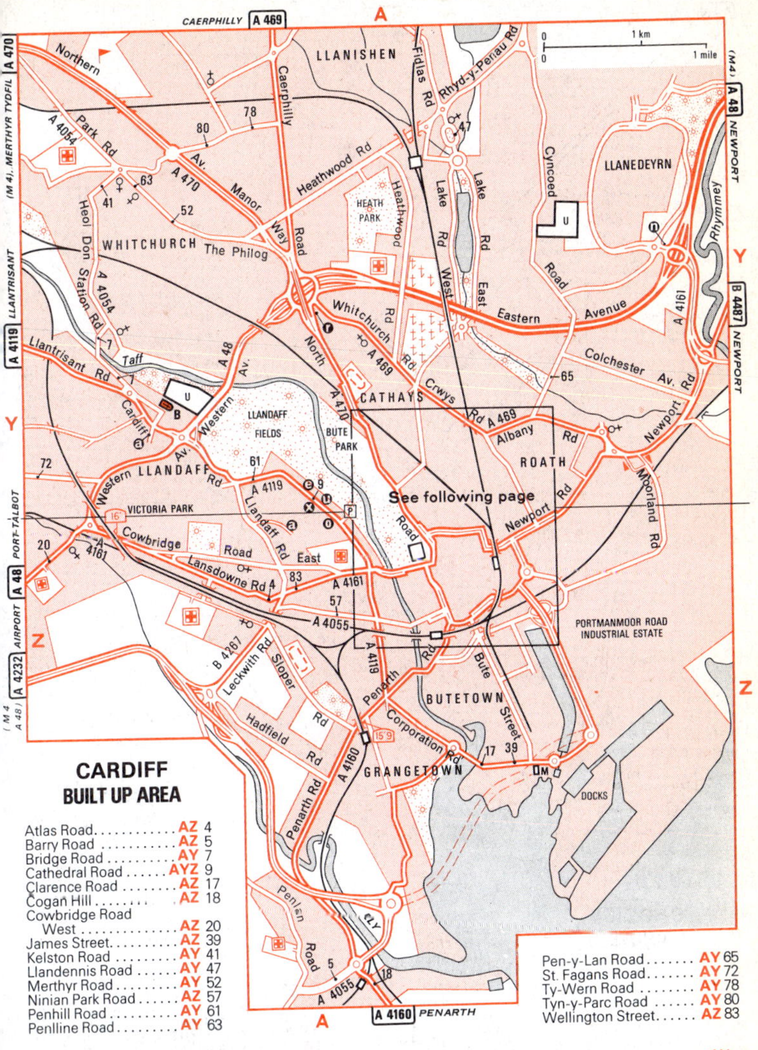

CARDIFF
BUILT UP AREA

Atlas Road . . . . **AZ** 4
Barry Road . . . . **AZ** 5
Bridge Road . . . . **AY** 7
Cathedral Road . . . . . **AYZ** 9
Clarence Road . . . . **AZ** 17
Cogan Hill . . . . **AZ** 18
Cowbridge Road
   West . . . . **AZ** 20
James Street . . . . **AZ** 39
Kelston Road . . . . **AY** 41
Llandennis Road . . . . . . **AY** 47
Merthyr Road . . . . **AY** 52
Ninian Park Road . . . . . . **AZ** 57
Penhill Road . . . . **AY** 61
Penlline Road . . . . **AY** 63
Pen-y-Lan Road . . . . **AY** 65
St. Fagans Road . . . . **AY** 72
Ty-Wern Road . . . . **AY** 78
Tyn-y-Parc Road . . . . . **AY** 80
Wellington Street . . . . . . **AZ** 83

⋔ **Penrhys** without rest., 127 Cathedral Rd, CF1 9JB, ℰ 230548 – TV ☎ P — **AY** x
13 rm.

⋔ **Ferrier's**, 130-132 Cathedral Rd, CF1 9LQ, ℰ 383413 – TV ☎ P. ◫ AE ① VISA — **AY** e
closed 2 weeks Christmas-New Year – **M** (by arrangement) approx. 9.25 t. – **26 rm**
� 22.00/44.00 t.

⋔ **Annedd Lon** without rest., 3 Dyfrig St., off Cathedral Rd, CF1 9LR, ℰ 223349 – ⇥ TV. ⊷ — **AY** u
6 rm � 14.00/28.00 st.

XX **Trillium**, 40 City Rd, CF2 3DL, ℰ 463665 – ◫ AE ① VISA — **BY** e
closed Saturday lunch, dinner Sunday and Monday and Bank Holidays – **M** 10.00 t. (lunch)
and a la carte 14.70/21.50 t.

XX **Indian Ocean**, 290 North Rd, Gabalfa, CF4 3BN, ℰ 621349, Indian rest. – ⊷ ▤. ◫ AE ① — **AY** r
VISA
M 8.95/11.95 t. and a la carte approx. 14.75 t.

XX **Noble House**, 9-11 St. David's House, Wood St., CF1 1ER, ℰ 388430, Chinese rest. – ◫ — **BZ** e
AE ①
M a la carte approx. 11.40 t.

P.T.O. →

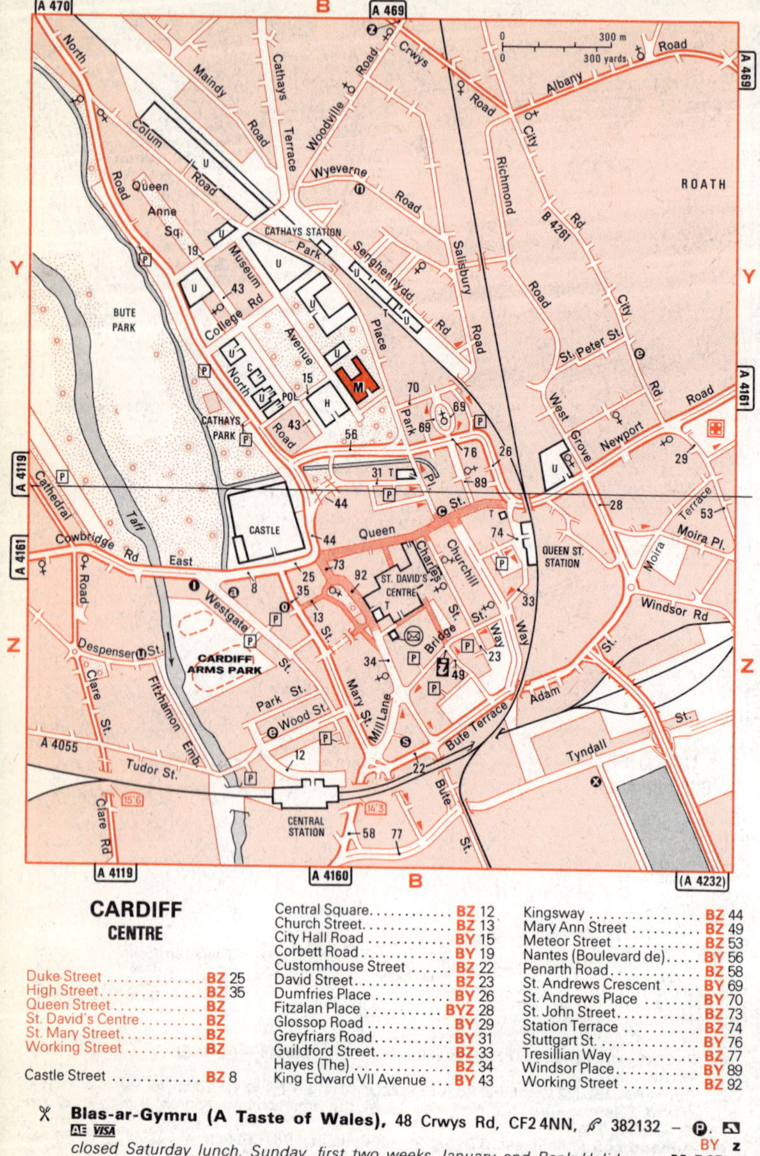

CARDIFF
CENTRE

Duke Street . . . . **BZ** 25
High Street . . . . **BZ** 35
Queen Street . . . . **BZ**
St. David's Centre . . . . **BZ**
St. Mary Street . . . . **BZ**
Working Street . . . . **BZ**

Castle Street . . . . **BZ** 8

Central Square . . . . **BZ** 12
Church Street . . . . **BZ** 13
City Hall Road . . . . **BY** 15
Corbett Road . . . . **BY** 19
Customhouse Street . . . . . . **BZ** 22
David Street . . . . **BZ** 23
Dumfries Place . . . . **BY** 26
Fitzalan Place . . . . **BYZ** 28
Glossop Road . . . . **BY** 29
Greyfriars Road . . . . **BY** 31
Guildford Street . . . . **BZ** 33
Hayes (The) . . . . **BZ** 34
King Edward VII Avenue . . . **BY** 43

Kingsway . . . . **BZ** 44
Mary Ann Street . . . . **BZ** 49
Meteor Street . . . . **BZ** 53
Nantes (Boulevard de) . . . . . **BY** 56
Penarth Road . . . . **BZ** 58
St. Andrews Crescent . . . . . **BY** 69
St. Andrews Place . . . . **BY** 70
St. John Street . . . . **BZ** 73
Station Terrace . . . . **BZ** 74
Stuttgart St. . . . . **BY** 76
Tresillian Way . . . . **BZ** 77
Windsor Place . . . . **BY** 89
Working Street . . . . **BZ** 92

✖ **Blas-ar-Gymru (A Taste of Wales)**, 48 Crwys Rd, CF2 4NN, ✆ 382132 – Ⓟ. △
AE VISA
closed Saturday lunch, Sunday, first two weeks January and Bank Holidays – **M** 7.95 t.
(lunch) and a la carte 12.45/16.40 ▯ 3.00.
BY z

✖ **Gibson's**, 8 Romilly Cres., Canton, CF1 9NR, ✆ 341264, Bistro – △ AE ⓞ VISA
closed Sunday and Monday dinner, Tuesday, and Bank Holidays – **M** (booking essential)
10.50/18.00 **t.** and a la carte ▯ 3.40.
AZ a

✖ **Armless Dragon**, 97 Wyeverne Rd, Cathays, CF2 4BG, ✆ 382357 – △ AE ⓞ
VISA
closed Sunday, Christmas, New Year and Bank Holidays – **M** a la carte 11.20/14.90 **t.**
▯ 2.40.
BY n

✖ **Thai House**, 23 High St., CF1 2BZ, ✆ 387404, Thai rest. – △ AE ⓞ VISA
closed Sunday – **M** approx. 20.00 **st.**
BZ o

at Castleton (Cas-Bach) (Gwent) NE : 7 m. on A 48 – AY – ⊠ Cardiff – ✆ 0633 Castleton :

🏨 **Wentloog Castle**, CF3 8UQ, ✆ 680591, Fax 681287 – ✖ 📺 ☎ 🅿. ◪ AE ⓪ VISA
M *(closed Saturday lunch)* (grill rest.) (buffet lunch)/dinner 12.50 **t.** and a la carte ₰ 3.50 –
55 rm � 45.00/60.00 **t.** – SB 68.00 **st.**

🏨 **Travel Inn** without rest., Newport Rd, CF3 8UQ, ✆ 680070 – 📺 ♿ 🅿. ◪ AE ⓪
VISA
49 rm 24.50/27.50 **t.**

ALFA-ROMEO Newport Rd, St. Mellons ✆ 777183
AUSTIN-ROVER 52 Penarth Rd ✆ 343571
FORD 505 Newport Rd ✆ 490511
FORD 281 Penarth Rd ✆ 223100
RENAULT 325 Penarth Rd ✆ 383122

SKODA Braeval St. ✆ 485725
VAUXHALL-OPEL, CITROEN Sloper Rd ✆ 387221

◉ ATS Hadfield Rd ✆ 228251/226336

CARDIGAN (ABERTEIFI) Dyfed 🅟🅞🅔 G 27 – pop. 3 815 – ECD : Wednesday – ✆ 0239.
Envir. : Mwnt (site★) N : 6 m. – Gwbert-on-Sea (cliffs ≼★) NW : 3 m. – Teifi Valley★, S : 3 m.

🏌 Gwbert-on-Sea ✆ 612035, NW : 3 m.

🛈 Prince Charles Quay ✆ 613230 (summer only).

♦London 250 – Carmarthen 30 – Fishguard 19.

🏨 **Penbontbren Farm** ⟿, Glynarthen, SA44 6PE, NE : 9 ½ m. by A 487 and Brongest rd
✆ 810248, park – 📺 ♿ 🅿. ◪ VISA
M (dinner only) 10.00 **t.** and a la carte ₰ 2.60 – **10 rm** � 27.00/46.00 **t.** – SB 52.00/58.00 **st.**

at St. Dogmaels W : 1 m. by A 487 on B 4568 – ⊠ ✆ 0239 Cardigan :

⌂ **Berwyn** without rest., Cardigan Rd, SA43 3HS, ✆ 613555, ≼, 🐎 – ✖ 🅿. 🐾
3 rm � 12.50/28.00 **s.**

at Gwbert-on-Sea NW : 3 m. on B 4548 – ⊠ ✆ 0239 Cardigan :

🏰 **Cliff** ⟿, SA43 1PP, ✆ 613241, Telex 48440, ≼ bay and countryside, ⌸ heated, 🏌₉, 🐎, 🐎,
squash – 📺 ☎ 🅿 – 🔏 150. ◪ AE ⓪ VISA
closed January – **M** (bar lunch Monday to Saturday)/dinner 11.50 **t.** ₰ 3.50 – **70 rm**
� 27.00/70.00 **t.** – SB (except weekends) 65.00/100.00 **st.**

AUSTIN-ROVER, LAND-ROVER, RANGE ROVER,
JAGUAR-DAILMER Aberystwyth Rd ✆ 612365
FIAT St. Dogmaels ✆ 612025

◉ ATS Bath House Rd ✆ 612917

CARLISLE Cumbria 🅠🅞🅟 🅠🅞🅠 L 19 – pop. 72 206 – ECD : Thursday – ✆ 0228.
See : Cathedral★ (12C-14C) AY E – Tithe Barn★ BY A.
Envir. : Hadrian's Wall★★ (starts NE : 1 ½ m.) by B 5307 AY.

🏌 Aglionby ✆ 022 872 (Scotby) 303, E : 2 m. by A 69 BY – 🏌 Stoney Holme ✆ 34856, E : 1 m. by
St. Aidan's Rd BY.

✈ ✆ 022 873 (Crosby-on-Eden) 641, Telex 64476 by A 7 BY and B 6264 – **Terminal** : Bus Station,
Lowther Street.

🚗 ✆ 49433.

🛈 The Old Town Hall, Greenmarket ✆ 512444.

♦London 317 – ♦Blackpool 95 – ♦Edinburgh 101 – ♦Glasgow 100 – ♦Leeds 124 – ♦Liverpool 127 – ♦Manchester
122 – ♦Newcastle-upon-Tyne 59.

Plan on next page

🏰 **Swallow Hilltop** (Swallow), London Rd, CA1 2PQ, SE : 1 m. on A 6 ✆ 29255, Telex 64292,
Fax 25238, ◪ – ▯ ✖ rm 📺 ☎ 🅿 – 🔏 500. ◪ AE ⓪ VISA   by A 6   BZ
M 8.00/13.25 **st.** and a la carte ₰ 4.75 – **97 rm** � 60.00/85.00 **st.**

🏨 **Cumbria Park**, 32 Scotland Rd, CA3 9DG, N : 1 m. on A 7 ✆ 22887, Telex 64330 – 📺 ☎
🅿 – 🔏 100. ◪ AE VISA. 🐾   by A 7   BY
closed 25 and 26 December – **M** 8.50/10.50 **t.** and a la carte ₰ 4.50 – **42 rm** � 42.00/90.00 **t.**
– SB (except summer) 54.00/102.00 **st.**

at Kingstown N : 3 m. at junction 44 of A 7 – BY – and M 6 – ⊠ ✆ 0228 Carlisle :

🏰 **Crest** (Crest), Kingstown, CA3 0HR, ✆ 31201, Telex 64201, Fax 43178 – ✖ 📺 ☎ 🅿
🔏 60. ◪ AE ⓪ VISA
M *(closed Saturday lunch)* 7.95/14.35 **st.** and a la carte – � 7.05 – **93 rm** 65.00/77.00 **st.** –
SB 68.00/88.00 **st.**

at Crosby-on-Eden NE : 4 ½ m. by A 7 – BY – on B 6264 – ⊠ Carlisle – ✆ 022 873
Crosby-on-Eden :

XX **Crosby Lodge** ⟿ with rm, High Crosby, CA6 4QZ, ✆ 618, Fax 428, ≼, « 18C country
mansion », 🐎 – 📺 ☎ 🅿. AE ⓪ VISA. 🐾
closed 24 December-20 January – **M** *(closed Sunday dinner)* 12.75/18.50 **t.** and a la carte
₰ 4.00 – **11 rm** � 51.00/70.00 **t.** – SB (weekends only) (except summer) 85.00 **st.**

CARLISLE

Botchergate.............. **BZ**
Castle Street .... **BY** 6
English Street .... **BY** 13
Scotch Street............ **BY** 19

Annetwell Street......... **AY** 2

Bridge Street............. **AY** 3
Brunswick Street......... **BZ** 4
Caldcotes................ **AY** 5
Charlotte Street.......... **AZ** 7
Chiswick Street........... **BY** 8
Church Street............ **AY** 10
Eden Bridge.............. **BY** 12
Lonsdale Street.......... **BY** 14
Lowther Street........... **BY** 15

Port Road................. **AY** 16
St. Aidan's Road .... **BY** 17
St. Nicholas Street .... **BZ** 18
Spencer Street .... **BY** 20
Tait Street............... **BZ** 21
Victoria Viaduct .... **ABZ** 24
West Tower Street .... **BY** 26
West Walls .... **ABY** 27
Wigton Road.............. **AZ** 29

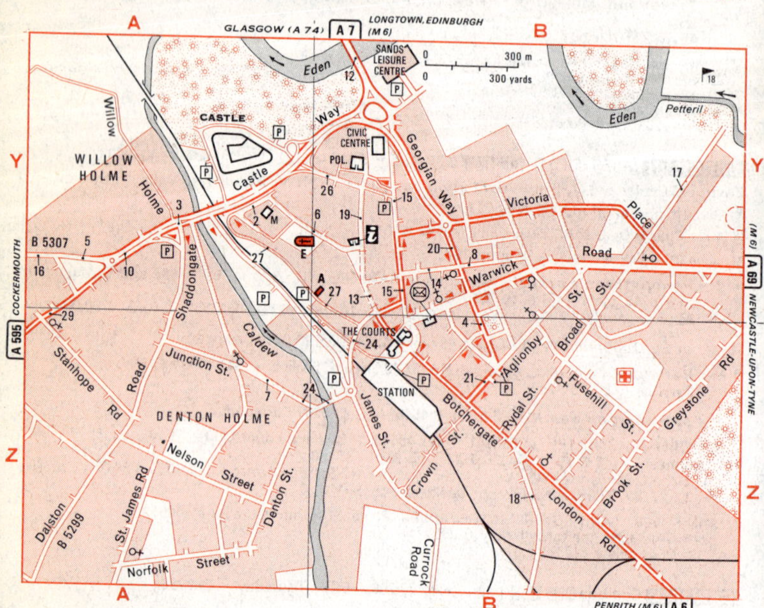

at *Faugh* E : 8 ¼ m. by A 69 – BY – ✉ Carlisle – ✆ 022 870 Hayton :

String of Horses Inn, Heads Nook, CA4 9EG, ✆ 297, « Elaborately furnished 17C inn »,
heated – rest TV ☎ **P.** AE ① VISA
M 8.50/13.95 t. and a la carte – **14 rm** ☲ 50.00/84.00 t.

at *Wetheral* SE : 6 ¼ m. by A 6 – BZ – on B 6263 – ✉ Carlisle – ✆ 0228 Wetheral :

Crown (Best Western), CA4 8ES, ✆ 61888, Telex 64175, Fax 61637, , , squash – ⇥ rm
TV ☎ **P** – 150. AE ① VISA
49 rm ☲ 66.50/85.00 st.. **1 suite** 113.00/125.00 st.

AUSTIN-ROVER, DAIMLER-JAGUAR Rosehill
Estate ✆ 24387
CITROEN, SAAB Willowholme Estate ✆ 26617
FIAT Church St., Caldewgate ✆ 25092
FORD Hardwick Circus ✆ 24234
LADA Cecil St. ✆ 25051
LANCIA, SUZUKI King St. ✆ 47722
MERCEDES-BENZ Victoria Viaduct ✆ 41111

NISSAN Lowther St. ✆ 25555
RENAULT Church St. ✆ 22423
TOYOTA Lonsdale St. ✆ 42041
VAUXHALL-OPEL Viaduct Estate ✆ 29401
VOLVO Victoria Viaduct ✆ 28234

ATS 85 London Rd ✆ 31737
ATS Rosehill Ind. Est., Montgomery Way. ✆ 25277

CARLYON BAY Cornwall **403** F 33 – see St. Austell.

CARMARTHEN (CAERFYRDDIN) Dyfed **403** G 28 – pop. 13 860 – ECD : Thursday – ☎ 0267.

☐ Blaenycoed Rd ✆ 87493, NW : 4 m.

i Lammas St. ✆ 231557 (summer only).

♦London 220 – Fishguard 45 – ♦Swansea 27.

   Ivy Bush Royal (T.H.F.), 11-13 Spilman St., SA31 1LG, ✆ 235111, Telex 48520, Fax 234914
   – 🛗 📺 ☎ 🅿 – 🔺 200. 🔼 AE ⑩ VISA
   M 8.50/12.00 **st.** and a la carte ⑧ 3.95 – ☕ 7.00 – **78 rm** 46.00/60.00 **st.**, **1 suite** 65,00/
   90.00 **st.** – SB 56.00/70.00 **st.**

   at Felingwm Uchaf NE : 7 m. by A 40 on B 4310 – ✉ Carmarthen – ☎ 026 788 Nantgaredig :

   Plough Inn, SA32 7PR, ✆ 220 – 📺 🅿. 🔼 AE ⑩ VISA. 🍽
   closed 25 and 26 December – **M** a la carte 13.45/19.50 **st.** ⑧ 2.95 – **5 rm** ☕ 28.00/45.00 **st.**

   at Nantgaredig E : 5 m. on A 40 – ✉ Carmarthen – ☎ 026 788 Nantgaredig :

   Cwmtwrch Farm ⑤, SA32 7NY, N : ¼ m. on B 4310 ✆ 238, park – 📺 🅿
   closed 10 to 24 March – **M** 13.50 **t.** ⑧ 2.75 – **6 rm** ☕ 18.00/40.00 **t.**

FIAT, VAUXHALL Pensarn ✆ 236633   TOYOTA Priory St. ✆ 234171
FORD The Bridge ✆ 236482
NISSAN Penguin Court ✆ 237356   ⓪ ATS Pensarn Rd ✆ 236996/235456

Per spostarvi più rapidamente utilizzate le carte Michelin "Grandi Strade" :

*n° **920** Europa, n° **980** Grecia, n° **984** Germania, n° **985** Scandinavia-Finlanda,*

*n° **986** Gran Bretagna-Irlanda, n° **987** Germania-Austria-Benelux, n° **988** Italia,*

*n° **989** Francia, n° **990** Spagna-Portogallo, n° **991** Jugoslavia.*

CARNFORTH Lancs. **402** L 21 – ☎ 0524.

♦London 249 – ♦Blackpool 31 – ♦Carlisle 59 – Lancaster 6.

   New Capernwray Farm ⑤, Capernwray, LA6 1AD, NE : 3 m. by B 6254 ✆ 734284, ≤, 🍴
   – ✦🍽 📺 🅿
   M 16.00 **st.** – **3 rm** ☕ 37.00/55.00 **st.**

CARTMEL Cumbria **402** L 21 – see Grange-over-Sands.

CAS-BACH = Castleton.

CAS-BLAIDD = Wolf's Castle.

CASNEWYDD-AR-WYSG = Newport.

CASTELL-NED = Neath.

CASTLE ACRE Norfolk **404** W 25 – pop. 777 – ☎ 076 05.

See : Priory★★ (ruins 11C - 14C) AC.

♦London 101 – King's Lynn 20 – ♦Norwich 31.

   Hotels see : King's Lynn NW : 20 m., *Swaffham* S : 4 m.

CASTLE ASHBY Northants. **404** R 27 – pop. 142 – ✉ Northampton – ☎ 060 129 Yardley
Hastings.

♦London 76 – Bedford 15 – Northampton 11.

   Falcon ⑤, NN7 1LF, ✆ 200, Fax 673, 🍴 – 📺 ☎ 🅿. 🔼 AE VISA 🍽
   closed Christmas and New Year – **M** a la carte 16.30/23.15 **st.** ⑧ 4.90 – **14 rm**
   ☕ 45.00/60.00 **st.** – SB (weekends only) 60.00/80.00 **st.**

CASTLE BROMWICH West Midlands **403 404** O 26 – see Birmingham.

CASTLE CARY Somerset **403 404** M 30 – pop. 2 599 – ECD : Thursday – ☎ 0963.

♦London 125 – ♦Bristol 28 – Taunton 31 – Yeovil 13.

   George, Market Pl., BA7 7AH, ✆ 50761 – 📺 ☎ 🅿. 🔼 VISA
   M *(closed Sunday and Monday)* (dinner only and Sunday lunch)/dinner 15.50 **t.** ⑧ 3.00 –
   16 rm ☕ 30.00/45.00 **t.** – SB (weekends only) (except summer) 55.00/66.00 **st.**

   Bond's with rm, Ansford Hill, Ansford, BA7 7JP, N : ¾ m. on A 371 ✆ 50464, 🍴 – 📺 🅿.
   🔼 AE VISA 🍽
   M *(closed to non-residents Sunday and Monday)* (dinner only) 15.50 **st.** and a la carte ⑧ 3.50
   – ☕ 4.00 – **6 rm** 29.00/49.00 **st.** – SB 62.00/68.00 **st.**

CASTLE COMBE Wilts. 403 404 N 29 The West Country G. – pop. 347 – ⊠ Chippenham – ☎ 0249.

See : Site★★.

♦London 110 – ♦Bristol 23 – Chippenham 6.

🏨 **Manor House** (Best Western) ⑤, SN14 7HR, ☎ 782206, Telex 449931, Fax 782159, « Part 14C manor house in park », ⌱ heated, ⚑, 🐎, ✗ – 📺 ☎ Ⓟ – 🛎 40. 🔳 AE ⓞ VISA
M 19.50/25.00 t. and a la carte – ⊑ 8.50 – **33 rm** 85.00/250.00 t. – SB (November-March) 160.00/220.00 st.

at Ford S : 1 ¾ m. – ⊠ Chippenham – ☎ 0249 Castle Combe :

⚘ **White Hart Inn**, SN14 8RP, ☎ 782213, ⌱ heated – 📺 Ⓟ. 🔳 VISA
M (dinner only and Sunday lunch)/dinner a la carte approx. 8.90 t. ⱬ 3.60 – **11 rm** ⊑ 38.50/53.00 t. – SB (except Bank Holidays) 74.00 st.

at Nettleton W : 2 m. by B 4039 – ⊠ Chippenham – ☎ 0249 Castle Combe :

⌂ **Fosse Farmhouse** ⑤, Nettleton Shrub, SN14 7NJ, ☎ 782286, 🐎 – 📺 Ⓟ. AE VISA
M 18.00 t. – **3 rm** ⊑ 33.50/60.00 t. – SB (weekdays only) 90.00/95.00 st.

CASTLE DONINGTON Leics. 402 403 404 P 25 – pop. 5 854 – ⊠ ☎ 0332 Derby.
✈ East Midlands, ☎ 810621, Telex 37543.

♦London 123 – ♦Birmingham 38 – ♦Leicester 23 – ♦Nottingham 13.

🏨 **Donington Thistle** (Thistle), East Midlands Airport, DE7 2SH, SE : 3 ¼ m. by B 6540 on A 453 ☎ 850700, Telex 377632, Fax 850823, 🔳 – ✗ rm 🍴 rest 📺 ☎ ♿ Ⓟ – 🛎. 🔳 AE ⓞ VISA. ✇
M 9.75/13.95 st. and a la carte – ⊑ 7.25 – **106 rm** 59.00/81.00 st., **4 suites** 95.00 st. – SB 86.00/100.00 st.

🏨 **Donington Manor**, High St., DE7 2PP, ☎ 810253 – 📺 ☎ Ⓟ – 🛎 100. 🔳 AE ⓞ VISA ✇
closed 27 to 30 December – **M** 6.00/8.00 st. and a la carte ⱬ 3.20 – **38 rm** ⊑ 45.00/60.00 st.

at Isley Walton SW : 2 ¼ m. by B 6540 on A 453 – ⊠ Derby – ☎ 0332 Melbourne :

⌂ **Park Farmhouse**, Melbourne Rd, DE7 2RN, W : ¾ m. ☎ 862409, ⇐ – 📺 Ⓟ. 🔳 AE ⓞ VISA
closed 1 week Christmas – **M** a la carte 5.60/10.85 ⱬ 3.00 – **5 rm** ⊑ 25.00/45.00 st.

VAUXHALL-OPEL Station Rd ☎ 810221

CASTLE HEDINGHAM Essex 404 V 28 – ⊠ Halstead – ☎ 0787.

♦London 53 – ♦Cambridge 30 – Chelmsford 20 – Colchester 18.

⌂ **Old School House**, St. James St., CO9 3EW, ☎ 61370, 🐎 – ✗. ✇
M (by arrangement) 12.50 s. – **4 rm** ⊑ 25.00/45.00 s.

CASTLETON Derbs 402 403 404 O 23 – pop. 881 – ECD : Wednesday – ⊠ Sheffield (South Yorks.) – ☎ 0433 Hope Valley.

Envir. : Blue John Caverns★ *AC*, W : 1 m.

♦London 181 – Derby 49 – ♦Manchester 30 – ♦Sheffield 16 – ♦Stoke-on-Trent 39.

🏠 **Ye Olde Nags Head**, S30 2WH, ☎ 20248 – 📺 ☎ Ⓟ. 🔳 AE ⓞ VISA ✇
M 11.50/15.00 t. and a la carte – **8 rm** ⊑ 39.50/68.00 t.

CASTLETON (CAS-BACH) Gwent 403 K 29 – see Cardiff (South Glam.).

CASTLETON North Yorks. 402 R 20 – ⊠ Whitby – ☎ 0287.

♦London 258 – ♦Middlesbrough 18 – York 61.

⚘ **Moorlands**, 55 High St., YO21 2DB, ☎ 60206, ⇐ – Ⓟ
closed January-mid March – **M** (bar meals Sunday to Thursday, dinner Friday and Saturday) a la carte approx. 12.65 t. – **10 rm** ⊑ 17.00/19.00 t.

CATLOWDY Cumbria 401 402 L 18 – ⊠ Carlisle – ☎ 022 877 Nicholforest.

♦London 333 – ♦Carlisle 16 – ♦Dumfries 36 – Hawick 31 – ♦Newcastle 65.

⌂ **Bessietown Farm** ⑤, CA6 5QP, ☎ 219, 🔳, 🐎, park – ✗ Ⓟ. ✇
M (by arrangement) 9.00 s. ⱬ 2.50 – **7 rm** ⊑ 18.50/31.00 s. – SB (October-April) (except Bank Holidays) 43.00 st.

CAWSAND Cornwall 403 H 33 – ⊠ ☎ 0752 Plymouth.

♦London 253 – ♦Plymouth 10 – Truro 53.

🏠 Criterion ⑤, Garrett St., PL10 1PD, ☎ 822244, ⇐ Plymouth Sound, « Converted fishermen's cottages » – 📺 – **8 rm**.

CAWSTON Norfolk 404 X 25 – pop. 1 218 – ⊠ ☎ 0603 Norwich.

♦London 122 – Cromer 15 – King's Lynn 42 – ♦Norwich 13.

🏠 **Grey Gables** ⑤, Norwich Road, NR10 4EY, S : 1 m. ☎ 871259, 🐎, ✗ – ✗ rest 📺 ☎ Ⓟ
closed 25 and 26 December – **M** (lunch by arrangement)/dinner 16.50 t. ⱬ 5.00 – **6 rm** ⊑ 28.00/48.00 t. – SB 50.00/58.00 st.

CEINEWYDD = New Quay.

CERRIGYDRUDION Clwyd 402 403 J 24 – pop. 701 – ⊠ Corwen – ☺ 049 082.
♦London 215 – Chester 40 – Holyhead 54 – Shrewsbury 52.

- 🏠 Saracens Head, LL21 9SY, ⌂ 684, ⤳ – TV ☎ P
  15 rm.

CHADDESLEY CORBETT Heref. and Worc. 403 404 N 26 – see Kidderminster.

CHADLINGTON Oxon. 403 404 P 28 – pop. 749 – ☺ 060 876.
♦London 74 – Cheltenham 32 – ♦Oxford 18 – Stratford-upon-Avon 25.

- 🏠 **Manor** ⑤, OX7 3LX, ⌂ 711, ≼, 🐎, park – TV ☎ P. 🔲 AE VISA. ⚒
  M (dinner only) 21.50 **st.** 🍾 3.50 – **7 rm** � 60.00/110.00 **st.**
- 🏠 **Chadlington House**, OX7 3LZ, ⌂ 437, 🐎 – ⤬ rest TV P. 🔲 VISA. ⚒
  closed January and February – **M** (dinner only) 15.00 **t.** and a la carte 🍾 3.00 – **10 rm**
  � 29.50/65.00 **t.**, **1 suite** 70.00/95.00 **t.** – SB (except spring and autumn) 69.00/75.00 **st.**

CHAGFORD Devon 403 I 31 The West Country G. – pop. 1 400 – ECD : Wednesday – ☺ 064 73
(4 fig.) or 0647 (5 fig.).
Envir. : Castle Drogo★AC, NE : 2 m.
♦London 218 – Exeter 17 – ♦Plymouth 28.

- 🏠 **Gidleigh Park** ⑤, TQ13 8HH, NW : 2 m. by Gidleigh Rd ⌂ 2367, Telex 42643, Fax 2574
  ≼ Vale and woodland, « Timbered country house, water garden », park, ⚒ – TV ☎ P.
  🔲 VISA
  M (booking essential) 33.00/40.00 **s.** 🍾 6.00 – � 7.00 – **15 rm** 84.00/165.00 **s.**
- 🏠 **Teignworthy** ⑤, Frenchbeer, TQ13 8EX, SW : 2 ½ m. by Fernworthy Rd, off Thornworthy
  Rd ⌂ 33355, Fax 3359, ≼ Teign valley and woodland, « Country house atmosphere », 🐎,
  park, ⚒ – ⤬ rest TV ☎ P. 🔲 VISA ⚒
  M (booking essential) 30.00 **st.** and a la carte 30.50/36.50 **st.** 🍾 5.00 – � 5.00 – **9 rm**
  59.50/100.00 **st.** – SB (winter only) (except Christmas and New Year) 147.00/159.00 **st.**
- 🏠 **Thornworthy House** ⑤, Thornworthy, TQ13 8EY, SW : 3 m. by Fernworthy Rd on
  Thornworthy Rd ⌂ 3297, ≼, « Country house atmosphere », 🐎, park, ⚒ – P
  M (dinner only) 16.00 **t.** 🍾 2.50 – **6 rm** � 30.00/60.00 **t.** – SB 84.00 **st.**
- 🏠 **Bly House** ⑤ without rest., Nattadon Hill, TQ13 8BW, E : ¼ m. ⌂ 2404, « Antiques », 🐎,
  park – TV P
  closed November and December – **7 rm** � 20.00/35.50 **t.**
- 🏠 **Torr House** ⑤, Thorn, TQ13 8DX, SW : 1 ½ m. by Fernworthy Rd on Thornworthy Rd
  ⌂ 2228, 🐎 – ⤬ rest P. 🔲 AE VISA
  M (dinner only) 10.00 **t.** 🍾 3.25 – **5 rm** � 20.00/38.00 **t.** – SB 52.50/56.00 **st.**
- 🏠 **Claremont**, 13 Mill St., TQ13 8AW, ⌂ 3304 – TV 🚗. ⚒
  closed February – **M** (by arrangement) 10.00 – **5 rm** � 18.00/38.00.

  at Sandypark NE : 1 ½ m. on A 382 – ⊠ ☺ 064 73 Chagford :

- 🏠 **Mill End** ⑤, TQ13 8JN, on A 382 ⌂ 2282, « Country house with water mill », ⤳, 🐎 – TV
  ☎ 🚗 P. 🔲 AE ① VISA
  closed 12 to 22 December – **M** 18.00/22.50 **t.** 🍾 4.50 – � 4.50 – **17 rm** 30.00/65.00 **t.** –
  SB 90.00/110.00 **st.**
- 🏠 **Great Tree** (Best Western) ⑤, TQ13 8JS, on A 382 ⌂ 2491, ≼, « Country house atmos-
  phere », 🐎, park – ⤬ rest TV ☎ P. 🔲 AE ① VISA
  M 8.50/18.50 **t.** 🍾 2.90 – **12 rm** � 42.50/76.00 **t.** – SB 95.00/110.00 **st.**

  at Easton Cross NE : 1 ½ m. – ⊠ ☺ 064 73 Chagford :

- 🏠 Easton Court, TQ13 8JL, on A 382 ⌂ 3469, « 15C thatched house », 🐎 – P
  8 rm.

CHALE I.O.W. – see Wight (Isle of).

CHALFONT ST. PETER Bucks. 404 S 29 – pop. 14 135 – ☺ 024 07 (4 and 5 fig.) or 0494 (6 fig.)
Chalfont St. Giles.
♦London 24 – ♦Oxford 43.

- XXX **Water Hall**, Amersham Rd, SL9 OPA, N : ½ m. on A 413 ⌂ 3430, Chinese (Peking) rest.,
  🐎 – P. 🔲 AE ① VISA
  closed 25 December-7 January – **M** 19.00 **t.** and a la carte 23.00/33.00 **t.** 🍾 4.00.

CHANCERY (RHYDGALED) Dyfed 403 H 26 – see Aberystwyth.

CHAPELTOWN North Yorks. 402 403 404 P 23 – see Sheffield.

CHARINGWORTH Glos. – see Chipping Campden.

CHARLBURY Oxon. 403 404 P 28 – pop. 2 637 – ☎ 0608.
♦London 72 – ♦Birmingham 50 – ♦Oxford 15.

   🏠 **Bell** (Best Western), Church St., OX7 3AP, ℰ 810278, Fax 811447 – TV ☎ P. ◩ AE
      ◑ VISA
      M 15.00/24.00 **t.** and a la carte ⌂ 4.00 – **14 rm** ⌂ 45.00/70.00 **t.** – SB 86.00 **st.**

CHARLTON West Sussex 404 R 31 – see Chichester.

CHARMOUTH Dorset 403 L 31 – pop. 1 121 – ECD : Thursday – ✉ Bridport – ☎ 0297.
♦London 157 – Dorchester 22 – Exeter 31 – Taunton 27.

   🏠 **White House,** 2 Hillside, The Street, DT6 6PJ, ℰ 60411 – TV ☎ P. ◩ VISA. ✻
      M 15.00 **st.** (dinner) and a la carte 14.40/16.55 **st.** ⌂ 4.10 – **7 rm** ⌂ 23.50/57.00 **st.** –
      SB 80.00/84.00 **st.**

   🏠 Fernhill, Lyme Rd, DT6 6BX, W : ¾ m. by A 35 on A 3052 ℰ 60492, ⌇ heated, ✿ – P
      15 rm.

   🏠 **Newlands House,** Stonebarrow Lane, DT6 6RA, ℰ 60212, ✿ – ✕ TV P
      March-October – **M** 8.50 **st.** ⌂ 2.50 – **12 rm** ⌂ 16.25/37.00 **st.**

   🏠 **Hensleigh,** Lower Sea Lane, DT6 6LW, ℰ 60830 – ✕ rest TV P
      March-October – **M** 7.75 **t.** – **10 rm** ⌂ 17.00/34.00 **t.** – SB (except summer) 46.00 **st.**

CHARTHAM Kent 404 X 30 – see Canterbury.

CHARTHAM HATCH Kent 404 X 30 – see Canterbury.

CHEDINGTON Dorset 403 L 31 – pop. 96 – ✉ Beaminster – ☎ 093 589 Corscombe.
♦ London 148 – Dorchester 17 – Taunton 25.

   🏛 **Chedington Court** ♨ , DT8 3HY, ℰ 265, Fax 442, ≤ countryside, « Country house in
      landscaped gardens» , park – TV ☎ P. ◩ AE VISA ✻
      closed 4 weeks January-February – **M** (bar lunch) (residents only)/dinner 24.50 **st.** ⌂ 3.40 –
      10 rm ⌂ 36.00/102.00 **st.** – SB 110.00/140.00 **st.**

CHELFORD Cheshire 402 403 404 N 24 – see Macclesfield.

CHELMSFORD Essex 404 V 28 – pop. 91 109 – ECD : Wednesday – ☎ 0245.
⛳ Channels Belstead, Farm Lane, Little Waltham ℰ 440005, NE : 3 ½ m. off A 130.
🅱 E Block, County Hall ℰ 283400.
♦London 33 – ♦Cambridge 46 – ♦Ipswich 40 – Southend-on-Sea 19.

   🏛 **South Lodge,** 196 New London Rd, CM2 0AR, ℰ 264564, Telex 99452, Fax 492827 –
      ✕ rm TV ☎ P – ⚖ 60. ◩ AE ◑ VISA ✻
      M 22.50 **st.** (dinner) and a la carte 13.50/18.50 **st.** ⌂ 3.50 – ⌂ 5.75 – **41 rm** 50.00/
      65.00 **st.**

   🏠 **County,** 29 Rainsford Rd, CM1 2QA, ℰ 491911 – TV ☎ P – ⚖ 60. ◩ AE ◑ VISA
      closed 27 to 30 December – **M** 8.50/11.00 **t.** and a la carte ⌂ 4.50 – **53 rm** ⌂ 26.00/
      62.00 **t.**

   🏠 **Tanunda,** 217-219 New London Rd, CM2 0AJ, ℰ 354295, ✿ – TV P. ◩ VISA
      closed 2 weeks Christmas – **M** (by arrangement) 10.50 **st.** – **20 rm** ⌂ 20.80/42.30 **st.**

   ✗ **Rose of India,** 30 Rainsford Rd, CM1 2QD, ℰ 352990, Indian rest. – ◩ ◑ VISA
      M 9.50 **t.** and a la carte ⌂ 3.75.

      at Great Baddow SE : 3 m. by A 130 – ✉ ☎ 0245 Chelmsford :

   🏰 **Pontlands Park** ♨ , West Hanningfield Rd, CM2 8HR, ℰ 76444, Telex 995256, Fax 478393,
      ≤, ⌇, ✿, park – TV ☎ P – ⚖ 45. ◩ AE ◑ VISA ✻
      closed 1 to 7 January – **M** *(closed lunch Monday and Saturday and Sunday dinner)*
      23.00 **t.** and a la carte approx. 30.00 **t.** ⌂ 5.00 – ⌂ 8.00 – **16 rm** 56.00/88.00 **st.**, **1 suite**
      88.00 **st.**

AUSTIN-ROVER 74 Main Rd, Broomfield ℰ 440571
CITROEN Galley Wood ℰ 268366/269465
FORD 39 Robjohns Rd ℰ 264111
RENAULT Southend Rd, Sandon ℰ 71113
VAUXHALL-OPEL Eastern Approach ℰ 466333
VAUXHALL-OPEL Moulsham Lodge ℰ 351611

VOLVO Colchester Rd, Springfield ℰ 468151

◍ ATS 375 Springfield Rd ℰ 257795
ATS Chelmer Village Centre, Springfield ℰ 465676
ATS Town Centre, Inchbonnie Rd, South Wood-
ham Ferrers ℰ 324999

CHELSWORTH Suffolk – pop. 133 – ✉ – ☎ 0449 Bildeston.
♦London 68 – Colchester 21 – ♦Ipswich 16.

   🏠 **Peacock Inn,** The Street, ✉ Ipswich, IP7 7HU, ℰ 740758 – TV P. ✻
      M (buffet lunch)/dinner 12.00 **t.** and a la carte ⌂ 3.50 – **5 rm** ⌂ 19.00/38.00.

See : Site★.

Envir. : Elkstone (Parish Church : doorway★ and arches★ 12C) SE : 7 m. by A 435 A – Sudeley Castle★ (12C - 15C) *AC*, NE : 6 m. by A 46. A.

🏌 Cleeve Hill ✆ 024 267 (Bishop's Cleeve) 2592, N : 3 m. by A 46. A.

🛈 Municipal Offices, The Promenade ✆ 522078.

♦London 99 – ♦Birmingham 48 – ♦Bristol 40 – Gloucester 9 – ♦Oxford 43.

Plan on next page

Queen's (T.H.F.), Promenade, GL50 1NN, ✆ 514724, Telex 43381, Fax 224145, 🚗 – 🛗 ⊱ rm 📺 ☎ 🅿 – 🏛 200. 🆎 🗚 ⑩ *VISA* — **B n**
M 11.75/16.50 **st.** and a la carte 🍷 3.75 – ☕ 7.70 – **77 rm** 68.00/89.00 **st.** – SB (weekends only) 104.00/114.00 **st.**

Golden Valley Thistle (Thistle), Gloucester Rd, GL51 0TS, W : 2 m. on A 40 ✆ 232691, Telex 43410, Fax 221846 – 🛗 ⊱ rm 🍽 rest 📺 ☎ 🅿 – 🏛 200. 🆎 🗚 ⑩ *VISA*
M 11.50/14.50 **t.** and a la carte 🍷 3.75 – ☕ 7.25 – **96 rm** 62.00/115.00 **st.**, **1 suite** 95.00 **st.** – SB (weekends only) 84.00/125.00 **st.** — by A 40 **A**

Cheltenham Park, Cirencester Rd, Charlton Kings, GL53 8EA, ✆ 222021, Telex 437364, Fax 226935, 🚗 – 📺 ☎ 🅿 – 🏛 70. 🆎 🗚 ⑩ *VISA*. 🞨 — **A e**
M 14.50/30.00 **st.** and a la carte 🍷 6.00 – ☕ 9.00 – **41 rm** 69.00/190.00 **st.** – SB (weekends only) 93.00/100.00 **st.**

Lansdown (B.C.B.), Lansdown Rd, GL50 2LB, ✆ 522700 – ⊱ rest 📺 ☎ 🅿. 🆎 🗚 ⑩ *VISA*. 🞨 — **B r**
M 9.00 **t.** and a la carte 🍷 3.35 – **14 rm** ☕ 41.50/51.00 **t.** – SB (weekends only) 58.00 **st.**

Lypiatt House, Lypiatt Rd, GL50 2QW, ✆ 224994, Fax 224996 – ⊱ rest 📺 ☎ 🅿. 🆎 *VISA*. 🞨 — **B c**
closed 23 December-3 January – **M** (closed Saturday dinner) (lunch by arrangement)/dinner 12.95 **t.** – **10 rm** ☕ 30.00/55.00 **t.**

Travel Inn without rest., Tewkesbury Rd, Uckington, GL51 9SL, at junction of A 4019 and B 4063 ✆ 233847 – ⊱ 📺 ♿ 🅿. 🆎 🗚 ⑩ *VISA*. 🞨 — **A a**
☕ 3.95 – **40 rm** 24.50/27.50 **t.**

Hannaford's, 20 Evesham Rd, GL52 2AB, ✆ 515181 – 📺. 🆎 *VISA*. 🞨 — **C u**
M (by arrangement) approx. 10.15 **t.** 🍷 2.25 – **10 rm** ☕ 18.00/40.00 **st.**

Milton House without rest., 12 Royal Parade, Bayshill Rd, GL50 3AY, ✆ 582601 – ⊱ rm 📺 ☎. 🆎 🗚 *VISA*. 🞨 — **B e**
9 rm ☕ 24.00/45.00 **t.**

Abbottslee, Priory Walk, GL52 6DU, ✆ 515255 – ⊱ 🅿. 🞨 — **C a**
closed 2 weeks August – **M** 8.50 **st.** – **5 rm** ☕ 18.00/30.00 **st.**

Hollington House, 115 Hales Rd, GL52 6ST, ✆ 519718, 🚗 – ⊱ 📺 🅿. 🆎 🗚 *VISA*. 🞨 — **A s**
M (by arrangement) 9.95 **t.** – **7 rm** ☕ 25.00/50.00 **t.** – SB (October-March) (except Christmas) (weekends only) 35.00/45.00 **st.**

Beaumont House, 56 Shurdington Rd, GL53 0JE, ✆ 245986, 🚗 – ⊱ rest 📺 🅿. 🆎 🗚 *VISA* — **A u**
M (by arrangement) 8.00 **t.** 🍷 2.25 – **14 rm** ☕ 13.50/40.00 **t.** – SB (weekends only) (except summer) 41.00/55.00 **st.**

✗✗ **Le Champignon Sauvage,** 24-26 Suffolk Rd, GL50 2AQ, ✆ 573449 – 🆎 🗚 *VISA* — **B a**
closed Saturday lunch, Sunday, Easter, 2 weeks June, 1 week Christmas-New Year, and Bank Holidays – **M** 13.30/20.45 **t.** 🍷 3.40.

✗✗ **Twelve,** 12 Suffolk Par., GL50 2AB, ✆ 584544 – 🆎 🗚 ⑩ *VISA* — **B i**
closed Saturday lunch, Sunday dinner and Monday – **M** 9.25/17.00 **t.** and a la carte approx. 15.50 **t.** 🍷 3.25.

at Southam NE : 3 m. on A 46 – A – ✉ 📞 0242 Cheltenham :

De La Bere (T.H.F.), GL52 3NH, NE : 3 m. on B 4632 ✆ 237771, Telex 43232, Fax 236016, « Tudor manor house », 🏊 heated, 🚗, park, ✗, squash – ⊱ rm 📺 ☎ 🅿. 🆎 🗚
⑩ *VISA*
M 10.75/14.25 **st.** and a la carte 🍷 4.25 – ☕ 7.60 – **57 rm** 59.00/102.00 **st.** – SB (weekends only) 92.00/107.00 **st.**

at Cleeve Hill NE : 4 m. on A 46 – A – ✉ Cheltenham – 📞 024 267 Bishop's Cleeve :

Rising Sun (Lansbury), GL52 3PX, ✆ 672002, Telex 437410, Fax 673069, ≤, 🚗 – 📺 ☎ 🅿 – 🏛 50. 🆎 🗚 ⑩ *VISA*. 🞨
M 8.50/12.50 **t.** and a la carte – **24 rm** ☕ 55.00/65.00 **t.**

✗✗ **Redmond's at Malvern View,** GL52 3PR, NE : 4 m. on B 4632 ✆ 2017, ≤ – 🅿. 🆎 *VISA* — **B c**
closed Saturday lunch, Sunday dinner, Monday and first week January – **M** 15.50/23.50 **st.** 🍷 3.50.

at Andoversford SE : 6 m. on A 40 – A – ✉ 📞 0242 Cheltenham :

Old Comfort, Dowdeswell, GL54 4LR, SW : 1 ½ m. on A 436 ✆ 820349, ≤, 🚗 – ⊱ rest 📺 🅿. 🆎 🗚 ⑩ *VISA*. 🞨
M 16.00 **t.** – **5 rm** ☕ 25.00/50.00 **t.**

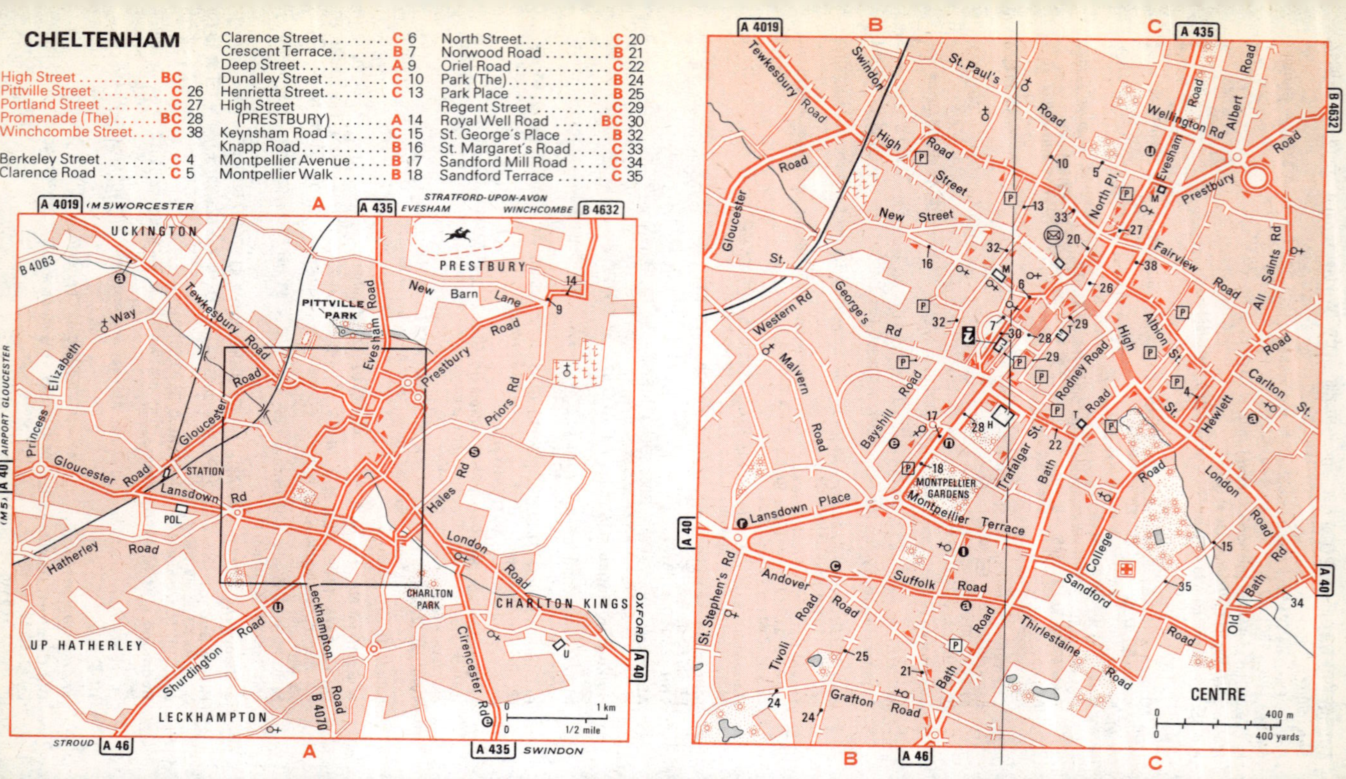

CHELTENHAM
High Street . . . . BC
Pittville Street . . . . C 26
Portland Street . . . . C 27
Promenade (The) . . . . . . BC 28
Winchcombe Street . . . . . C 38
Berkeley Street . . . . C 4
Clarence Road . . . . C 5
Clarence Street . . . . C 6
Crescent Terrace . . . . B 7
Deep Street . . . . A 9
Dunalley Street . . . . C 10
Henrietta Street . . . . C 13
High Street (PRESTBURY) . . . . A 14
Keynsham Road . . . . . C 15
Knapp Road . . . . B 16
Montpellier Avenue . . . . . B 17
Montpellier Walk . . . . . . B 18
North Street . . . . C 20
Norwood Road . . . . B 21
Oriel Road . . . . C 22
Park (The) . . . . B 24
Park Place . . . . B 25
Regent Street . . . . C 29
Royal Well Road . . . . . . BC 30
St. George's Place . . . . . . B 32
St. Margaret's Road . . . . . C 33
Sandford Mill Road . . . . . C 34
Sandford Terrace . . . . . . C 35
A 4019 (M5) WORCESTER
A 435 EVESHAM
STRATFORD-UPON-AVON WINCHCOMBE B 4632
UCKINGTON
B 4063
PRESTBURY
PITTVILLE PARK
New Barn Lane
Tewkesbury Road
Evesham Road
Prestbury Road
Priors Rd
Gloucester Road
Western Rd
Princess Elizabeth Way
STATION
Lansdown Rd
POL.
Hatherley Road
UP HATHERLEY
Shurdington Road
Leckhampton Road
LECKHAMPTON
B 4070
Hales Rd
London Road
Cirencester Rd
CHARLTON PARK
CHARLTON KINGS
OXFORD A 40
(M5) A 40 AIRPORT GLOUCESTER
STROUD A 46
A 435 SWINDON
1 km
1/2 mile
A 4019
B
C A 435
B 4632
Tewkesbury Road
Swindon
St. Paul's Road
Wellington Rd
Evesham
Prestbury
High Street
New Street
Gloucester Road
St. George's Rd
Western Rd
North Pl.
Fairview Road
All Saints Rd
Albion St.
Carlton St.
Hewlett Road
London Road
High St.
Rodney Road
Bayshill Road
Malvern Road
Trafalgar St.
Bath
Lansdown Place
MONTPELLIER GARDENS
Montpellier Terrace
St. Stephen's Rd
Andover Road
Suffolk Road
College Road
Sandford Road
Thirlestaine Road
Old Bath Rd
Tivoli
Grafton Road
Bath
A 40
A 46
A 40
CENTRE
400 m
400 yards

at Shurdington SW : 3 ¾ m. on A 46 – A – ✉ ☎ 0242 Cheltenham :

Greenway ⸙, GL51 5UG, ☎ 862352, Telex 437216, Fax 862780, ≼, « Country house, gardens », park – 📺 ☎ 🅿. 🔳 AE ⓪ VISA. ⚓
closed 27 December-12 January – **M** *(closed lunch Saturday and Bank Holidays)*
15.00/25.00 t. 🍾 6.50 – **18 rm** ☕ 80.00/170.00 t. – SB (except Christmas) 122.50/182.50 **st.**

Allards without rest., Shurdington Rd, GL51 5XA, ☎ 862498, 🚒 – 📺 ☎ 🅿. 🔳 VISA. ⚓
11 rm ☕ 17.00/36.00 **st.**

AUSTIN-ROVER Princess Elizabeth Way ☎ 520441
CITROEN 16-28 Bath Rd ☎ 515391
FORD 71-93 Winchcombe St. ☎ 527061
HONDA 172 Leckhampton Rd ☎ 524348
LADA, PROTON Stoke Orchard ☎ 680428
LANCIA Swindon Rd ☎ 232167
MERCEDES-BENZ Princess Elizabeth Way ☎ 580777
MITSUBISHI 84 Fairview Rd ☎ 513880
RENAULT Montpellier Spa Rd ☎ 521651
ROLLS-ROYCE, BENTLEY Rutherford Way ☎ 515374
SAAB, SUZUKI High St., Prestbury ☎ 224477

SEAT Charlton Kings ☎ 521131
SUBARU, ISUZU Bouncers Lane, Prestbury ☎ 235705
TOYOTA 38 Suffolk Rd ☎ 527778
VAUXHALL-OPEL 379 High St. ☎ 522666
VAUXHALL-OPEL Albion St. ☎ 525252
VOLVO Manor Rd ☎ 222400
VW-AUDI Oddington ☎ (0451) 30422
YUGO Coombe Hill ☎ 680817

🅜 ATS Chosen View Rd ☎ 521288
ATS 99-101 London Rd ☎ 519814

CHELWOOD Avon – see Bristol.

CHENIES Bucks. **404** S 28 – pop. 2 240 – ECD : Thursday – ✉ Rickmansworth (Herts.) –
☎ 092 78 Chorleywood.
♦London 30 – Aylesbury 18 – Watford 7.

Bedford Arms Thistle (Thistle), WD3 6EQ, ☎ 3301, Telex 893939, Fax 4825, « 16C inn »,
🚒 – ⇔ rm 📺 ☎ 🅿. 🔳 AE ⓪ VISA
M a la carte 14.80/32.10 t. 🍾 5.50 – ☕ 7.50 – **10 rm** 65.00/85.00 **st.**

CHEPSTOW Gwent **403** **404** M 29 – pop. 9 039 – ECD : Wednesday – ☎ 029 12 (4 & 5 fig.) or
0291 (6 fig.).

See : Castle⋆ (stronghold) *AC*.

🅉 The Gatehouse, High St. ☎ 3772 (summer only).

♦London 131 – ♦Bristol 17 – ♦Cardiff 28 – Gloucester 34.

George (T.H.F.), Moor St., NP6 5DB, ☎ 625363 – 📺 🕾 🅿 – 🛄 40. 🔳 AE ⓪ VISA
M 9.50 st. (lunch) and a la carte 🍾 3.95 – ☕ 7.00 – **15 rm** 55.00/75.00 st. – SB (weekends only) 68.00/88.00 **st.**

Beaufort, Beaufort Sq., NP6 5EP, ☎ 622497 – 📺 ☎ 🅿. 🔳 AE VISA
M (bar lunch)/dinner 16.00 t. and a la carte 🍾 3.95 – **18 rm** ☕ 25.00/50.00 t. – SB (weekends only) 70.00 **st.**

Castle View, 16 Bridge St., NP6 5EZ, ☎ 70349, 🚒 – 📺 ☎. 🔳 AE ⓪ VISA
M 7.50 t. (lunch) and a la carte 10.20/14.45 t. 🍾 2.80 – **11 rm** ☕ 37.00/56.00 t. –
SB 62.00/70.00 **st.**

AUSTIN-ROVER Station Rd ☎ 3159
FORD Newport Rd ☎ 8155

PEUGEOT, TALBOT Tutshill ☎ 3131

CHERITON BISHOP Devon **403** I 31 – pop 587 – ECD : Wednesday – ✉ Exeter – ☎ 064 724.
♦London 211 – Exeter 10 – ♦Plymouth 51.

Old Thatch Inn, EX6 6HG, ☎ 204 – 📺 🅿. 🔳 VISA. ⚓
M *(closed first 2 weeks November)* a la carte 5.15/7.90 st. 🍾 2.95 – **3 rm** ☕ 26.50/37.50 **st.**

CHESHAM Bucks. **404** S 28 – pop. 20 772 – ☎ 0494.
♦London 32 – Luton 25 – ♦Oxford 42.

Chesham Tandoori, 48 Broad St., HP5 3DX, ☎ 782669, Indian rest. – 🔳 AE ⓪ VISA
closed 25 and 26 December – **M** a la carte 10.25/16.10 t. 🍾 3.75.

 Cheshire 402 403 L 24 – pop. 80 154 – ECD : Wednesday – ☎ 0244.
See : Site★★ – The Rows★★ – Cathedral★ (14C-16C) (choir stalls and misericords★★) – City Walls★ – Grosvenor Museum (Roman gallery★) M1 – **Envir.** : Upton (Chester Zoo★) AC, N : 3 m. by A 5116 – ⌐8 Upton-by-Chester, Upton Lane ℰ 381183, by A 5116 – ⌐8 Vicars Cross, Littleton ℰ 335174, E : 2 m. by A 51.
🛈 Town Hall, Northgate St. ℰ 324324 ext 2111/2250 – Chester Visitor Centre, Vicars Lane ℰ 351609.
◆London 207 – Birkenhead 7 – ◆Birmingham 91 – ◆Liverpool 19 – ◆Manchester 40 – Preston 52 – ◆Sheffield 76 – ◆Stoke-on-Trent 38.

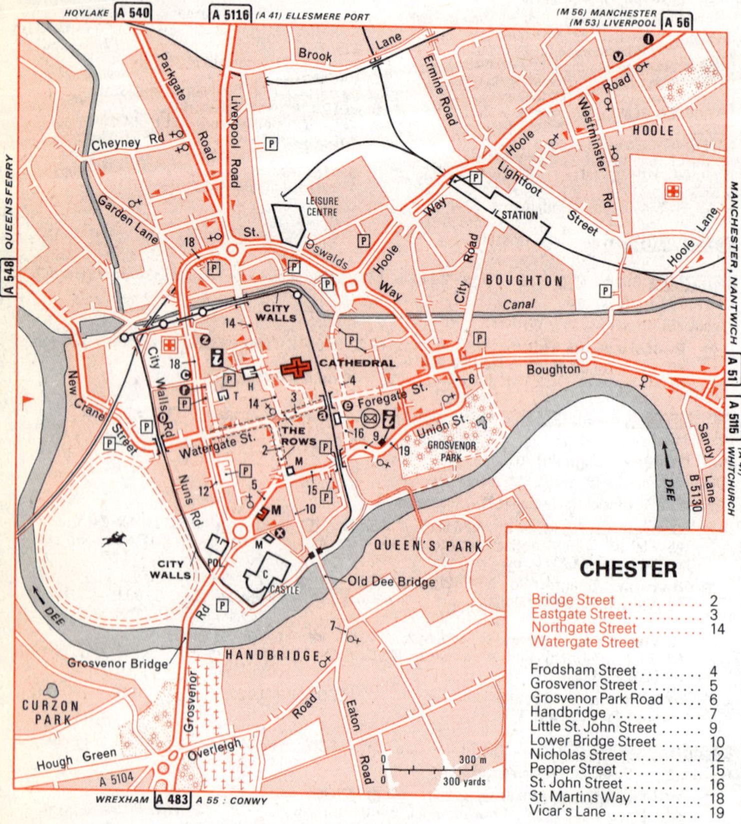

Chester Grosvenor, Eastgate St., CH1 1LT, ℰ 324024, Telex 61240, Fax 313246 – ⇕ ⇄ rest 🍽 TV ☎ & 🅿 – 🔌 150. 🌂 AE ⓪ VISA ⇙
a
closed 25 and 26 December – **M** – (see also **Arkle** below) – La Brasserie 10.45/15.00 t. and a la carte ⌁ 5.45 – ⊡ 7.95 – **83 rm** 98.00/145.00 t., **3 suites** 195.00 t. – SB (weekends only) 140.00/190.00 **st.**

Crabwall Manor ⑤, Parkgate Rd, Mollington, CH1 6NE, NW : 2 ¼ m. on A 540 ℰ 851666, Telex 61220, Fax 851400, « Tastefully furnished manor with 16C origins », 🐎 – ⇄ 🍽 rest TV ☎ & 🅿 – 🔌 100. 🌂 AE ⓪ VISA ⇙
closed 27 to 31 December – **M** 12.95/21.00 t. and a la carte ⌁ 5.00 – ⊡ 7.50 – **42 rm** 77.00/117.00 t., **6 suites** 137.00/175.00 t. – SB (except Easter, Christmas and New Year) 145.00/195.00 **st.**

Mollington Banastre (Best Western), Parkgate Rd, CH1 6NN, NW : 2 m. on A 540 ℰ 851471, Telex 61686, Fax 851165, 🖾, 🐎, squash – ⇕ ⇄ rm TV ☎ 🅿 – 🔌 250. 🌂 AE ⓪ VISA
M 9.00/16.00 st. and a la carte ⌁ 5.25 – **65 rm** ⊡ 68.75/85.90 st., **2 suites** 100.00/120.00 st. – SB (except Christmas and Bank Holidays) 96.00 **st.**

Chester International (Q.M.H.), Trinity St., CH1 2BD, ℰ 322330, Telex 61251, Fax 316118 – ⇕ ⇄ rest TV ☎ & 🅿 – 🔌 375. 🌂 AE ⓪ VISA
r
M 15.00/20.00 st. and a la carte 19.10/26.20 st. ⌁ 4.25 – **146 rm** ⊡ 85.00/120.00 st., **6 suites** 120.00/185.00 **st.** – SB (weekends only) 96.00 **st.**

🏨 **Hoole Hall,** Warrington Road, Hoole, CH2 3PD, NE : 2 m. on A 56 ✆ 350011, Telex 61292, Fax 320251 – ▯ ▤ rest 📺 ☎ ♿ ℗ – 🏛 100. ⬛ AE VISA
M (closed lunch Saturday and Bank Holidays) 10.00/14.00 **t.** and a la carte 🍷 4.00 – **98 rm** ⊇ 63.00/76.00 **t.**

🏨 Post House (T.H.F.), Wrexham Rd, CH4 9DL, S : 2 m. on A 483 ✆ 680111, Telex 61450, Fax 674100, 🔲, 🚗 – ⇆ rm 📺 ☎ ℗ – 🏛 50
104 rm, 3 suites.

🏨 **Redland** without rest., 64 Hough Green, CH4 8JY, SW : 1 m. by A 483 on A 549 ✆ 671024, « Victorian town house » – 📺 ☎ ℗
11 rm ⊇ 30.00/45.00 **t.**

🏨 **Blossoms** (T.H.F.), St. John St., CH1 1HL, ✆ 323186, Telex 61113, Fax 46433 – ▯ 📺 ☎ – 🏛 110. ⬛ AE ⓪ VISA   **e**
M 9.50/15.00 **t.** and a la carte 🍷 4.25 – ⊇ 7.60 – **61 rm** 64.00/93.00 **st.**, **1 suite** 119.00 **st.** – SB 86.00/92.00 **st.**

🏨 **Green Bough,** 60 Hoole Rd, CH2 3NL, ✆ 326241 – 📺 ☎ ℗. ⬛ VISA   **i**
closed Christmas – **M** (lunch residents only)/dinner 10.00 **t.** 🍷 3.50 – **11 rm** ⊇ 23.00/45.00 **t.** – SB (weekends only) 52.00/60.00 **st.**

🏨 **City Walls,** City Walls Rd, CH1 2LU, ✆ 313416 – 📺 ☎. ⬛ AE VISA   **o**
M (closed Sunday) (dinner only) 11.50 **t.** and a la carte 🍷 3.95 – **16 rm** ⊇ 35.00/50.00 **t.** – SB (weekends only) 59.50/62.00 **st.**

🏨 **Cromwell Court** without rest., 5-7 St. Martin's Way, CH1 2NR, ✆ 349202 – 📺 ☎ ℗. ⬛ AE VISA   **c**
⊇ 3.95 – **9 rm** 32.00/60.00 **t.**

🏨 Chester Court, 48 Hoole Rd, CH2 3NL, ✆ 320779, Fax 44795 – 📺 ☎ ℗   **v**
20 rm.

🏨 **Gloster Lodge,** 44 Hoole Rd, CH2 3NL, ✆ 48410 – ⇆ rest 📺 ☎ ℗. ⬛ VISA. 🚫   **v**
closed 24 to 31 December – **M** (closed Sunday) (dinner only) 9.50 **st.** – **8 rm** ⊇ 28.00/34.00 **st.**

🏠 **Edwards House,** 61-63 Hoole Rd, CH2 3NJ, ✆ 318055 – 📺 ℗. ⬛ VISA. 🚫
M 10.00 **s.** – **8 rm** ⊇ 26.00/34.00 **st.** – SB (November-mid May) (weekends only) (except Bank Holidays) 49.00/65.00 **st.**

🏠 **Chester Town House** without rest., 23 King St., CH1 2AH, ✆ 350021, 🚗 – ⇆ 📺 ☎ ℗.   **z**
⬛ VISA
closed 21 December-6 January – **4 rm** ⊇ 32.50/45.00 **s.**

🏠 **Castle House** without rest., 23 Castle St., CH1 2DS, ✆ 350354, « Part Elizabethan town house » – 📺. ⬛ VISA   **x**
5 rm ⊇ 18.00/36.00 **s.**

XXXX ❀ **Arkle** (at Chester Grosvenor H.), Eastgate St., CH1 1LT, ✆ 324024, Telex 61240, Fax 313246 – ▤ ℗. ⬛ AE ⓪ VISA
closed Monday lunch, Sunday and 25-26 December – **M** (booking essential) 17.50/35.00 **t.** and a la carte 25.35/40.40 **t.** 🍷 8.75
Spec. Crisp pastry purses of scallops dressed on a sauce of morels, Sirloin of veal glazed with pistachio nuts and sweet wine, Iced orange and chocolate soufflé.

at Mickle Trafford NE : 2 ½ m. by A 56 – ✉ Chester – ☎ 0244 Mickle Trafford :

🏨 **Royal Oak,** Warrington Rd, CH2 4EX, on A 56 ✆ 301391, Telex 61536, Fax 301948 – ⇆ rest 📺 ☎ ℗. ⬛ AE ⓪ VISA
M 0.75 **t.** and a la carte – **36 rm** ⊇ 41.50/51.50 **t.**

at Christleton E : 2 m. on A 41 – ✉ ☎ 0244 Chester :

🏨 **Abbots Well** (Embassy), Whitchurch Rd, CH3 5QL, ✆ 332121, Telex 61561, Fax 335287, 🔲, 🚗 – ⇆ rm 📺 ☎ ℗ – 🏛 200. ⬛ AE ⓪ VISA
M (closed Saturday lunch) 8.95/13.75 **st.** and a la carte 🍷 4.40 – ⊇ 6.50 – **127 rm** 60.00/86.00 **st.** – SB (weekends only) 60.00/68.00 **st.**

at Rowton SE : 3 m. by A 41 – ✉ ☎ 0244 Chester :

🏨 **Rowton Hall,** Rowton Lane, CH3 6AD, ✆ 335262, Telex 61172, Fax 335464, 🔲, 🚗 – 📺 ☎ ℗ – 🏛 150. ⬛ AE ⓪ VISA
M 9.90/12.65 **t.** and a la carte – **42 rm** ⊇ 60.00/110.00 **t.** – SB (weekends only) 90.00/118.00 **st.**

MICHELIN Distribution Centre, Sandycroft Industrial Estate, Glendale Av., Sandycroft, Deeside, CH5 2QP, ✆ 537373, FAX 537453 by A 548

AUSTIN-ROVER Victoria Rd ✆ 381246
BMW Chester Rd ✆ 311404
CITROEN Border House ✆ 672977
COLT Chester Rd ✆ 534347
DAIHATSU, MITSUBISHI Chester Rd ✆ 534347
DAIMLER-JAGUAR, ROLLS-ROYCE, RENAULT, LO-TUS 8 Russell St. ✆ 25262
FIAT, SUZUKI, RENAULT Sealand Rd ✆ 390909
FORD Bridge Gate ✆ 20444
FORD Station Rd ✆ 813414
FORD Station Rd, Queensferry ✆ 813414
MERCEDES-BENZ 36 Tarvin Rd ✆ 47441

NISSAN Hamilton Pl. ✆ 317661
SAAB Western Av. ✆ 375744
SEAT 159 Boughton ✆ 310344
TOYOTA Welsh Rd ✆ 813633
VAUXHALL-OPEL Boughton ✆ 24611
VAUXHALL-OPEL 21-25 Garden Lane ✆ 46955
VAUXHALL-OPEL Parkgate Rd ✆ 372666
VOLVO Stadium Way ✆ 372199
VW-AUDI Sealand Rd ✆ 379889

🛞 ATS 7 Bumpers Lane, Sealand Trading Est. ✆ 375154

CHESTERFIELD Derbs. 402 403 404 P 24 – pop. 73 352 – ECD : Wednesday – ✆ 0246.
Envir. : Chatsworth★★★ : site★★, house★★★ (Renaissance), garden★★★ *AC*, W : 7 m. – Hardwick Hall★★ (16C) (Tapestries and embroideries★★) *AC*, SE : 8 m. – Bolsover Castle★ (17C) *AC*, E : 6 m. – Worksop (Priory Church : Norman nave★) NE : 14 m.

ⓘ8 Tapton Park, Murray House, Crow Lane, Tapton ✆ 273887.

🛈 The Peacock Tourist Information and Heritage Centre, Low Pavement ✆ 207777.

♦London 152 – Derby 24 – ♦Nottingham 25 – ♦Sheffield 12.

🏨 **Chesterfield** (Best Western), Malkin St., S41 7UA, ✆ 271141, Telex 547492, Fax 220719 – ⧉ ⧙TV⧘ ☎ ⓟ – ⫶ 200. ◪ ⒶⒺ *VISA*
M 6.50/9.95 t. and a la carte ♙2.95 – **60 rm** ⋤ 45.00/64.00 t., **2 suites** 60.00/75.00 t. – SB (weekends only) 62.00/66.00 st.

AUDI-VW, PORSCHE Sheerbridge Ind Est. ✆ 260060
AUSTIN-ROVER 221 Sheffield Rd ✆ 220888
BMW Pottery Lane ✆ 208681
FIAT 300 Northwingfield Rd ✆ 850686
FORD Chatsworth Rd ✆ 209999
LADA 34 Chatsworth Rd ✆ 271029
NISSAN High St., Brimington ✆ 209171
PEUGEOT-TALBOT 361 Sheffield Rd ✆ 260383

RENAULT Chesterfield Rd ✆ 473286
SAAB, TOYOTA 2 Lockoford Lane ✆ 221100
VAUXHALL 464 Chatsworth Rd ✆ 79201
VAUXHALL, RENAULT Chesterfield Rd, Staveley ✆ 473286
VOLVO Whittington Moor ✆ 260100

Ⓦ ATS 512 Sheffield Rd ✆ 452281

CHESTER-LE-STREET Durham 401 402 P 19 – pop. 34 776 – ECD : Wednesday – ✆ 0385 (6 fig.) or 091 (7 fig.).
Envir. : Lumley Castle★ (13C), E : 1 m. – Beamish (North of England open Air Museum★) *AC*, NW : 3 m.

ⓘ8 Lumley Park ✆ 388 3218, E : 1 m. off B 1284.

♦London 275 – Durham 7 – ♦Newcastle-upon-Tyne 8.

🏨 **Lumley Castle**, DH3 4NX, E : 1 m. on B 1284 ✆ 389 1111, Telex 537433, Fax 387 1437, « 13C castle », 🛋, park – ⇌ rm ⧙TV⧘ ☎ ⓟ. ◪ ⒶⒺ ⓞ *VISA*. ⛟
closed 25-26 December and 1 January – **M** 9.50/16.95 st. and a la carte ♙5.95 – **65 rm** ⋤ 49.50/69.50 st., **1 suite** 148.00 st. – SB (weekends only) 74.50/94.50 st.

MICHELIN Distribution Centre, Drum Rd Industrial Estate, Drum Rd, DH3 2AF, ✆ 410 7762, FAX 492 0717

AUSTIN-ROVER Newcastle Rd ✆ 388 2267
FORD 187 Front St. ✆ 388 4221

PEUGEOT Newfield ✆ 370 0355
VAUXHALL Hopgarth ✆ 388 0818

CHICHESTER West Sussex 404 R 31 – pop. 26 050 – ECD : Thursday – ✆ 0243.
See : Site★ – Cathedral★★ (11C-15C) BZ **A** – Market Cross★ BZ **B** – St. Mary's Hospital★ BY **D** – Pallant House★ BZ **E** – Mechanical Music and Doll Museum★, Church Rd.
Envir. : Fishbourne Roman Palace (mosaics★) *AC*, W : 2 m. AZ **R** – Weald and Downland open Air Museum★ N : 5 m. by A 286 AY.

ⓘ8 Goodwood ✆ 774968, NE : 4 ½ m. off A 27.

🛈 St. Peter's Market, West St. ✆ 775888.

♦London 69 – ♦Brighton 31 – ♦Portsmouth 18 – ♦Southampton 30.

Plan opposite

🏨 **Dolphin and Anchor** (T.H.F.), West St., PO19 1QE, ✆ 785121, Fax 533408 – ⇌ rm ⧙TV⧘ ☎ – ⫶ 200. ◪ ⒶⒺ ⓞ *VISA*
M 10.25/13.00 st. ♙3.75 – ⋤ 7.00 – **51 rm** 60.50/77.00 st. – SB 72.00/99.00 st.   BZ **a**

🏨 **Suffolk House,** 3 East Row, PO19 1PD, ✆ 778899, 🛋 – ⇌ rm ⧙TV⧘ ☎. ◪ ⓞ *VISA*. ⛟
M a la carte 15.75/22.45 st. ♙3.50 – **12 rm** ⋤ 50.00/95.00 st.   BY **a**

🏨 **Bedford,** Southgate, PO19 1DP, ✆ 785766 – ⧙TV⧘. ◪ ⒶⒺ ⓞ *VISA*   BZ **i**
M *(closed Sunday)* (dinner only) a la carte 8.75/13.25 st. ♙3.00 – **24 rm** ⋤ 27.50/55.00 st. – SB 70.00/95.00 st.

⌂ **Crouchers Bottom,** Birdham Rd, Apuldram, PO20 7EH, SW : 2 m. on A 286 AZ ✆ 784995, ≼, 🛋 – ⇌ ⓟ. ◪ *VISA*. ⛟
M 14.00 st. ♙2.50 – **4 rm** ⋤ 30.00/46.00 st.

XX **Comme ça,** 149 St. Pancras, PO19 1SH, ✆ 788724, French rest. – ◪ *VISA*   BZ **e**
closed Saturday lunch, Sunday dinner, Monday and Bank Holidays – **M** a la carte 13.10/19.50 t.

XX **Confucius,** 2 Cooper St., off South St., PO19 1EB, ✆ 783158, Chinese rest.   BZ **c**

at Charlton N : 6 ¼ m. by A 286 – AY – ✉ Chichester – ✆ 024 363 Singleton :

🏨 **Woodstock House,** PO18 0HU, ✆ 666, 🛋 – ⧙TV⧘ ⓟ. ◪ ⓞ
M (dinner only) – **11 rm** ⋤ 30.00/63.00 t. – SB (except summer) 65.00 st.

at Chilgrove N : 6 ½ m. by A 286 – AY – on B 2141 – ✉ Chichester – ✆ 024 359 (from August : 0243) East Marden :

XX **White Horse Inn,** 1 High St., PO18 9HX, ✆ 219 (from August : 535219), English rest. – ⓟ. ◪ ⓞ *VISA*
closed Sunday dinner, Monday, last 3 weeks February and 22 to 31 October – **M** 13.50/18.50 t. ♙3.50.

CHICHESTER

East Street .... **BZ**
North Street .... **BYZ**
South Street........... **BZ**

Birdham Road............ **AZ** 2
Bognor Road............. **AZ** 3
Cathedral Way .... **AZ** 4
Chapel Street........... **BY** 6

Chichester Arundel Road .. **AY** 7
Florence Road........... **AZ** 10
Hornet (The)............ **BZ** 12
Kingsham Road........... **BZ** 13
Lavant Road............. **AY** 14
Little London .... **BY** 15
Market Road .... **BZ** 16
Northgate............... **BY** 17
North Pallant .... **BZ** 19
Priory Lane .... **BY** 20
St. James's .... **AZ** 21

St. John's Street .... **BZ** 23
St. Martin's Square....... **BY** 24
St. Pancras............... **BY** 25
St. Paul's Road .... **BY** 27
Sherborne Road .... **AZ** 28
Southgate .... **BZ** 29
South Pallant .... **BZ** 31
Spitalfield Lane .... **BY** 32
Stockbridge Road......... **AZ** 33
Tower Street .... **BY** 35
Westhampnett Road..... **AYZ** 36

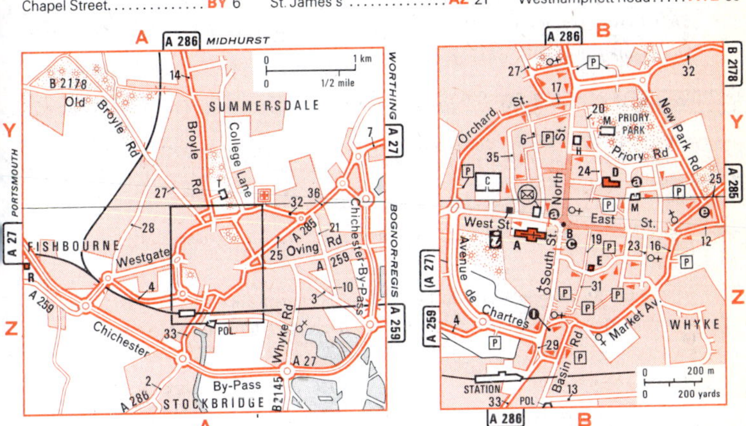

at Goodwood NE : 3 ½ m. by A 27 – **AY** – on East Dean Rd – ✉ ☎ 0243 Chichester :

Goodwood Park, PO18 0QB, ✆ 775537, Telex 869173, Fax 533802, 🏊, 🏌, 🎾, squash – 📺 ☎ 🚫 🅿 – 🛥 120. 🔺 AE ⓪ *VISA*
M 11.95/18.95 **t.** and a la carte 🍷 4.50 – **90 rm** ⊊ 75.00/125.00 **t.**

at Bosham W : 4 m. by A 259 - **AZ** – ✉ ☎ 0243 Chichester :

Millstream, Bosham Lane, PO18 8HL, ✆ 573234, Fax 573459, 🎋 – 📺 ☎ 🅿. 🔺 AE ⓪ *VISA*
M 14.50/15.50 **t.** and a la carte 🍷 4.50 – **29 rm** ⊊ 45.00/75.00 **t.** – SB (except Easter and Christmas) 76.00/86.00 **st.**

XX **Wishing Well Tandoori,** Bosham Roundabout, PO18 8GP, N : ¾ m. on A 259 ✆ 572234, Indian rest. – 🅿. 🔺 AE ⓪ *VISA*
M 12.00 **t.** (lunch) and a la carte 15.00/35.00 **t.** 🍷 3.00.

AUSTIN-ROVER Westhampnett Rd ✆ 781331
FIAT Terminus Rd Ind Est ✆ 784844
FIAT Tangmere By-Pass (A 27) ✆ 773855
FORD The Hornet ✆ 700100
MERCEDES-BENZ Quarry Lane ✆ 776111
PEUGEOT-TALBOT, CITROEN 113 The Hornet ✆ 782293

RENAULT Delling Lane, Bosham ✆ 573271
VAUXHALL-OPEL, NISSAN City Service Centre, Terminus Rd ✆ 774321
VW-AUDI 51-54 Bognor Rd ✆ 787684

🅐 ATS Terminus Rd Ind Est ✆ 773100

CHIDDINGFOLD Surrey **404** S 30 – pop. 2 209 – ☎ 042 879 Wormley.

♦London 45 – ♦Brighton 40 – Guildford 12.

XXX **Crown Inn** with rm, The Green, Petworth Rd, GU8 4TX, ✆ 2255, « 13C inn » – 📺 ☎ 🅿.
🔺 AE ⓪ *VISA*. 🦌
M 12.50 **t.** (lunch) and a la carte 16.35/22.95 **t.** 🍷 4.00 – ⊊ 4.00 – **7 rm** 40.00/65.00 **st.**,
1 suite 75.00 **st.**

CHIDEOCK Dorset **403** L 31 – see Bridport.

CHILCOMPTON Somerset **403** **404** M 30 – ECD : Saturday – ✉ Bath – ☎ 0761 Stratton-on-the-Fosse.

♦London 125 – ♦Bristol 17 – Taunton 35.

🏠 Court, The Broadway, BA3 4SA, W : 1 ¼ m. on B 3139 ✆ 232237, 🎋, 🎾 – 📺 ☎ 🅿.
10 rm.

CHILGROVE West Sussex **404** R 31 – see Chichester.

CHILLINGTON Devon **403** I 33 – see Kingsbridge.

CHINNOR Oxon. 404 R 28 – pop. 5 432 – ✆ 0844 Kingston Blount.
◆London 45 – ◆Oxford 19.

🏠 **Peacock** ⑤, Henton, OX9 4AH, NE : 1 ¾ m. by B 4009 ℰ 53519 – TV ☎ P. ⑤ AE VISA
M a la carte 11.95/19.75 t. – **12 rm** ☲ 40.00/70.00 t.

🏠 **Plough and Harrow**, Sydenham, OX9 4LD, NW : 1 ¼ m. on B 4445 ℰ 51367 – ⇥ rm TV
☎ P. ⑤ AE ① VISA. ※
M (closed Sunday dinner to non-residents) a la carte 10.40/18.40 t. ▮ 2.75 – **7 rm**
☲ 40.00/60.00 st. – SB (weekends only) 60.00/90.00 st.

✗ **Sir Charles Napier Inn**, Sprigg's Alley, by Bledlow Ridge Rd, OX9 4BX, SE : 2 ½ m.
ℰ 3011, ☞ – P. ⑤ AE VISA
closed Sunday dinner and Monday – M 16.00 t. (lunch) and a la carte 18.00/22.00 t. ▮ 3.50.

CHIPPENHAM Wilts. 403 404 N 29 The West Country G. – pop. 21 325 – ECD : Wednesday –
✆ 0249.
See : Yelde Hall★AC – Envir. : Biddestone★, W : 4 ½ m. – Sheldon Manor★AC, W : 1 ½ m. –
Bowood House★AC (Library ≤★ of the Park) SE : 5 m.
🛈 The Neeld Hall, High St. ℰ 657733.
◆London 106 – ◆Bristol 27 – ◆Southampton 64 – Swindon 21.

🏨 Angel (Norfolk Cap.), 8 Market Pl., SN15 3HD, ℰ 652615, Group Telex 23241, Fax 443210 –
TV ☎ P. – 🛎 60
46 rm.

at Stanton St. Quintin N : 4 ¾ m. by A 429 – ✉ Chippenham – ✆ 0666 Malmesbury :

🏛 **Stanton Manor**, SN14 6DQ, ℰ 837552, Fax 837022, ☞ – TV ☎ P. ⑤ AE ① VISA. ※
M (closed Sunday dinner and Monday) 10.50 t. (lunch) and a la carte 16.15/22.45 t. ▮ 4.25 –
5 rm ☲ 62.00/79.00 t. – SB (weekends only) 115.00 st.

CITROEN Bristol Rd ℰ 444000
FIAT New Rd ℰ 655757
FORD Cocklebury Rd ℰ 653255
RENAULT London Rd ℰ 651131
SAAB London Rd ℰ 655871

TOYOTA London Rd ℰ 444888
VAUXHALL-OPEL 16-17 The Causeway ℰ 654321
VOLVO Malmesbury Rd ℰ 652016

🅰 ATS Cocklebury Rd ℰ 653541

CHIPPERFIELD Herts. 404 ㊷ – pop. 1 764 – ECD : Wednesday – ✉ ✆ 092 77 Kings Langley.
◆ London 27 – Hemel Hempstead 5 – Watford 6.

🏨 **Two Brewers** (T.H.F.), The Common, WD4 9BS, ℰ 65266, Fax 61884 – TV ☎ P. ⑤ AE ①
VISA
M 11.25/14.50 st. and a la carte ▮ 4.45 – ☲ 7.00 – **20 rm** 72.00/88.00 st. – SB (weekends
only) 76.00/80.00 st.

CHIPPING Lancs. 402 M 22 – pop. 1 376 – ✉ Preston – ✆ 0995.
◆London 233 – Lancaster 30 – ◆Leeds 54 – ◆Manchester 40 – Preston 12.

🏨 **Gibbon Bridge Country House** ⑤, PR3 2TQ, E : 1 m. on Clitheroe rd ℰ 61456, Fax
61277, ≤, ☞, ✗ – 🛗 TV ☎ & P. ⑤ VISA. ※
M 7.00 t. (lunch) and a la carte 9.90/15.95 t. – **31 rm** ☲ 45.00/90.00 t.

CHIPPING CAMPDEN Glos. 403 404 O 27 – pop. 1 936 – ECD : Thursday – ✆ 0386 Evesham.
See : High Street★.
Envir. : Hidcote Manor Garden★★ AC, NE : 2 ½ m.
🛈 Woolstaplers Hall Museum, High St. ℰ 840289 (summer only).
◆London 93 – Cheltenham 21 – ◆Oxford 37 – Stratford-upon-Avon 12.

🏨 **Cotswold House**, The Square, GL55 6AN, ℰ 840330, Telex 336810, Fax 840310, « Attractively converted Regency townhouse, staircase », ☞ – ⇥ rest TV ☎ P. ⑤ AE ① VISA
※
closed 24 to 27 December – M (dinner only and Sunday lunch)/dinner 18.95 t. – **15 rm**
☲ 45.00/99.00 t. – SB 85.00/122.50 st.

🏠 **Noel Arms**, High St., GL55 6AT, ℰ 840317 – TV ☎ P. ⑤ AE VISA. ※
M (bar lunch)/dinner 12.95 t. and a la carte ▮ 3.95 – **18 rm** ☲ 32.50/62.50 t. – SB 68.50 st.

✗✗ **Bagatelle**, Island House, High St., GL55 6AL, ℰ 840598, French rest. – ⑤ VISA
closed Monday – M 10.95 t. and a la carte 12.55/21.85 t. ▮ 4.50.

✗✗ **Caminetto**, Old Kings Arms Pantry, High St., GL55 6HR, ℰ 840934, Italian rest. – ⑤ VISA
closed Monday lunch and Sunday – M a la carte 7.65/17.45 t. ▮ 4.10.

at Mickleton N : 3 ¼ m. by B 4035 and B 4081 on B 4632 – ✉ Chipping Campden –
✆ 0386 Mickleton :

🏨 **Three Ways**, GL55 6SB, ℰ 438429, Fax 438118, ☞ – TV ☎ P – 🛎 60. ⑤ AE ① VISA
M (bar lunch)/dinner 16.00 st. and a la carte – **40 rm** ☲ 32.00/63.00 st. –
SB (except Bank Holidays) (weekends only) 58.00/72.00 st.

at Charingworth E : 3 ¼ m. by B 4081 off B 4085 – ⊠ ⊕ 038678 Paxford :

Charingworth Manor ⑤, GL55 6NS, on B 4085 ℰ 555, Telex 333444, Fax 353, ≤, « Early 14C manor house with Jacobean additions and 17C courtyard », 禁, park – TV ☎ ℗ – 益 30. 🔄 AE Ⓞ VISA 🛱
closed 14 to 26 January – **M** 16.95/23.00 t. and a la carte 21.50/36.00 t. – **18 rm** 立 80.00/155.00 t., **1 suite** 175.00 t. – SB (except Christmas and New Year) 128.00/198.00 **st.**

at Broad Campden S : 1 ¼ m. by B 4081 – ⊠ Chipping Campden – ⊕ 0386 Evesham :

Malt House, GL55 6UU, S : ¼ m. ℰ 840295, 禁 – TV. 🔄 VISA 🛱
closed 24 December-1 January – **M** *(closed Sunday)* (dinner only) 35.00 t. ⓘ 4.50 – **5 rm** 立 20.00/79.00 t. – SB (weekdays only) (except Bank Holidays) 100.00/145.00 **st.**

AUSTIN-ROVER London Rd ℰ 2014   FORD High St. ℰ 840213
CITROEN Sheep St. ℰ 840221   VAUXHALL Burford Rd ℰ 2461

CHIPPING SODBURY Avon 403 404 M 29 – pop. 26 981 – ⊕ 0454.
Ⓘ8 Chipping Sodbury ℰ 319042, N : ½ m – ♦London 113 – ♦Bristol 11 – Gloucester 30 – Swindon 32.

Dornden ⑤, Church Lane, Old Sodbury, BS17 6NB, SE : 1 ¾ m. by B 4060 and A 43 ℰ 313325, ≤, 禁 – TV ℗
closed 3 weeks October, Christmas and New Year – **M** 6.75 t. – **9 rm** 立 19.00/44.00 t.

MAZDA Sodbury Rd ℰ 294316   ⓦ ATS Wickwar Rd ℰ 318496

CHIPSTEAD Surrey 404 T 30 – pop. 7 177 (inc. Hooley and Woodmanster – ⊕ 0737 Burgh Heath – ♦London 15 – Reigate 6.

XXX **Dene Farm,** Outwood Lane, CR3 3NP, on B 2032 ℰ 552661, 禁 – ℗. 🔄 AE Ⓞ VISA
closed Saturday lunch, Sunday dinner and 26 December-8 January – **M** 14.75/22.50 t. ⓘ 4.80.

BMW Outwood Lane ℰ 556789

CHISLEHAMPTON Oxon. 404 Q 28 – ⊠ Oxford – ⊕ 0865 Stadhampton.
♦London 55 – ♦Oxford 7.

Coach and Horses, OX9 7UX, ℰ 890255 – TV ☎ ℗. 🔄 AE Ⓞ VISA. 🛱
M *(closed Sunday dinner)* (buffet lunch Saturday and Sunday in summer) 11.50 **st.** and a la carte – **9 rm** 立 48.50/65.00 **st.** – SB (except Christmas and New Year) (weekends only) 62.50/87.00 **st.**

CHITTLEHAMHOLT Devon 403 I 31 – pop. 259 – ⊠ Umberleigh – ⊕ 076 94.
♦London 216 – Barnstaple 14 – Exeter 28 – Taunton 45.

Highbullen ⑤, EX37 9HD, ℰ 561, Fax 492, ≤, ⓢ heated, 🔄, Ⓘ9, ⑤, 禁, park, ✗, squash – ⊱✕ rest TV ☎ ℗. 🛱
M (bar lunch)/dinner 13.50 **st.** ⓘ 4.00 – 立 2.50 – **35 rm** 40.00/80.00 **st.**

CHOLLERFORD Northumb. 401 402 N 18 – ⊠ Hexham – ⊕ 043 481 Humshaugh.
♦London 303 – ♦Carlisle 36 – ♦Newcastle-upon-Tyne 21.

George (Swallow), NE46 4EW, ℰ 611, Group Telex 53168, Fax 727, ≤, « Riverside gardens », 🔄, ⑤ – ⊱✕ rm TV ☎ ℗ – 益 . 🔄 AE Ⓞ VISA
M (buffet lunch Monday to Saturday)/dinner 14.95 **st.** and a la carte ⓘ 4.75 – **54 rm** 立 68.00/80.00 **st.** – SB (except Christmas and New Year) 84.00/96.00 **st.**

CHORLEY Lancs. 402 404 M 23 – pop. 33 465 – ECD : Wednesday – ⊕ 025 72.
Ⓘ8 Duxbury Park ℰ 65380 – ♦London 222 – ♦Blackpool 30 – ♦Liverpool 32 – ♦Manchester 26.

Hartwood Hall, Preston Rd, PR6 7AX, on A 6 ℰ 69966, Fax 41678 – TV ☎ ℗ – 益 100. 🔄 AE Ⓞ VISA
closed 25 to 29 December and 1 January – **M** (bar lunch Saturday) 7.00/11.50 **st.** and a la carte ⓘ 3.50 – **20 rm** 立 30.00/50.00 **st.**

at Whittle-le-Woods N : 2 m. on A 6 – ⊠ ⊕ 025 72 Chorley :

Shaw Hill H. Golf and Country Club ⑤, Preston Rd, PR6 7PP, ℰ 69221, Fax 61223, ≤, Ⓘ8 – TV ☎ ℗ – 益 60. 🔄 AE Ⓞ VISA
M *(closed Saturday lunch)* 10.50 t. (lunch) and a la carte 15.80/27.50 t. ⓘ 3.50 – **22 rm** 立 52.50/74.50 t.

ⓦ ATS 18 Westminster Rd ℰ 62000/65472

CHRISTCHURCH Dorset 403 404 O 31 – pop. 32 854 – ECD : Wednesday – ⊕ 0202.
See : Site★ – Priory★ – Envir. : Hengistbury Head★ (≤★★) SW : 4 m. by B 3059.
Ⓘ9 Iford Bridge, Barrack Rd ℰ 473817, W: on A 5 – 🅱 30 Saxon Sq. ℰ 471780.
♦London 111 – Bournemouth 6 – Salisbury 26 – ♦Southampton 24 – Winchester 39.

King's Arms, 18 Castle St., BH23 1DT, ℰ 484117 – 🛗 ⊱✕ rm TV ☎ ℗ – 益 200 – **32 rm.**

X **Splinters,** 12 Church St., BH23 1BW, ℰ 483454 – ⊱✕. AE Ⓞ VISA
closed Sunday and 25-26 December – **M** (dinner only) a la carte 14.80/19.45 t. ⓘ 3.50.

at Mudeford SE : 2 m. – ✉ ☎ 0202 Christchurch :

🏨 **Avonmouth** (T.H.F.), BH23 3NT, ℰ 483434, ≼ Christchurch harbour, ⌁ heated, 🚗 –
⤝ rm 📺 ☎ 🅿 – 🛋 50. 🝙 AE ① VISA
M (buffet lunch Monday to Saturday)/dinner 13.50 **st.** and a la carte ⌁ 3.60 – ⬚ 7.00 –
41 rm 62.00/100.00 **st.** – SB 100.00/140.00 **st.**

🏨 **Waterford Lodge** (Best Western), 87 Bure Lane, Friars CLiff, BH23 4DN, ℰ 042 52 (High-
cliffe) 72948, Fax 79130, 🚗 – 📺 ☎ 🅿. 🝙 AE ① VISA
M (bar lunch)/dinner 12.00 **t.** and a la carte ⌁ 2.90 – **20 rm** ⬚ 45.00/70.00 **t.** –
SB 84.00/90.00 **st.**

↑ **The Pines**, 39 Mudeford, BH23 3NQ, ℰ 475121 – ⤝ rest 📺 ☎ 🅿. 🝙 AE VISA
M 6.00 **st.** ⌁ 2.70 – **14 rm** ⬚ 20.00/50.00 **st.**

AUSTIN-ROVER Highcliffe ℰ 042 52 (Highcliffe)
77703

FORD Lyndhurst Rd ℰ 042 52 (Highcliffe) 71371
VW-AUDI 105 Summerford Rd ℰ 476871

CHRISTLETON Cheshire 402 403 L 24 – see Chester.

CHURCHILL Oxon. 403 404 P 28 – pop. 421 – ✉ ☎ 060871 Kingham.
◆London 79 – ◆Birmingham 46 – Cheltenham 29 – ◆Oxford 23 – Swindon 31.

↑ **Forge House** without rest., OX7 6NJ, ℰ 8173 – 📺 🅿. 🚲
4 rm ⬚ 25.00/45.00 **st.**

CHURCH STRETTON Shropshire 403 L 26 – pop. 2 932 – ECD : Wednesday – ☎ 0694.
🏌 Trevor Hill ℰ 722281 – 🛈 Church St. ℰ 723133 (summer only).
◆London 166 – ◆Birmingham 46 – Hereford 39 – Shrewsbury 14.

🏛 **Stretton Hall** 🦢, Old Shrewsbury Rd, All Stretton, SY6 6HG, NE : 1 m. on B 4370 ℰ 723224,
🚗 – 📺 📠 🅿 – 🛋 25. 🝙 AE ① VISA
13 rm ⬚ 34.00/65.00 **t.**

🏛 **Mynd House**, Ludlow Rd, Little Stretton, SY6 6RB, SW : 1 m. on B 4370 ℰ 722212, Fax
724180, 🚗 – 📺 ☎ 🅿. 🝙 VISA
closed January – **M** 12.00 **st.** ⌁ 5.00 – **9 rm** ⬚ 25.00/65.00 **st.**

◍ ATS Crossways ℰ 722526/722112

CHURT Surrey 404 R 30 – see Farnham.

CIRENCESTER Glos. 403 404 O 28 – pop. 13 491 – ECD : Thursday – ☎ 0285.
See : Site★ – St. John The Baptist Parish Church★ (Perpendicular) – Corinium Museum★.
Envir. : Chedworth *AC*, N : 7 m.
🏌 Cheltenham Rd ℰ 652465, N : 1 ½ m. on A 435 – 🛈 Corn Hall, Market Pl. ℰ 654180.
◆London 97 – ◆Bristol 37 – Gloucester 19 – ◆Oxford 37.

🏨 **Fleece** (Best Western), Market Pl., GL7 2NZ, ℰ 658507, Fax 651017 – 📺 ☎ 🅿. 🝙 AE ①
VISA
M 13.95/15.95 **t.** and a la carte ⌁ 4.50 – ⬚ 5.95 – **23 rm** 55.00/85.00 **st.** – SB (week-
ends only) 76.00 **st.**

🏛 **Crown of Crucis**, Ampney Crucis, GL7 5RS, E : 2 ¾ m. on A 417 ℰ 806, Fax 735, 🐟 –
⤝ rm 📺 ☎ 🅿. 🝙 AE VISA
M (buffet lunch)/dinner a la carte approx. 10.80 **t.** ⌁ 2.40 – **26 rm** ⬚ 43.00/55.00 **t.** –
SB (weekends only) 57.00/64.00 **st.**

🏛 **Corinium Court**, 12 Gloucester St., GL7 2DG, ℰ 659711, Fax 885807 – 📺 ☎ 🅿. 🝙 AE
VISA
M *(closed Sunday)* 7.60/16.50 **t.** and a la carte ⌁ 3.50 – **15 rm** ⬚ 42.00/55.00 **t.**

↑ **Wimborne House**, 91 Victoria Rd, GL7 1ES, ℰ 653890 – ⤝ 📺 🅿. 🚲
closed 25 December-1 January – **M** 7.00 **st.** – **5 rm** ⬚ 25.00/30.00 **st.**

at Barnsley NE : 4 m. by A 429 on A 433 – ✉ Cirencester – ☎ 028 574 Bibury :

⚑ **Village Pub**, GL7 5EF, ℰ 421 – 📺 🅿. 🝙 VISA
closed 25 December – **M** a la carte 7.85/12.45 **t.** ⌁ 3.25 – **6 rm** ⬚ 27.50/37.50 **st.**

at Ewen SW : 3 ¼ m. by A 429 – ✉ Cirencester – ☎ 0285 Kemble :

⚑ Wild Duck Inn, GL7 6BY, ℰ 770310, 🚗 – 📺 🅿
9 rm, 1 suite.

at Stratton NW : 1 ¼ m. on A 417 – ✉ ☎ 0285 Cirencester :

🏨 **Stratton House**, Gloucester Rd, GL7 2LE, ℰ 651761, Fax 640024, 🚗 – 📺 ☎ 🅿 – 🛋 60.
🝙 AE ① VISA
M 9.25/14.95 **st.** and a la carte ⌁ 3.50 – **26 rm** ⬚ 39.00/56.00 **st.** – SB 99.00/106.00 **st.**

AUSTIN-ROVER Tetbury Rd ℰ 652614
CITROEN Perrotts Brook ℰ 028 583 (North Cerney)
219
FORD Chesterton Lane ℰ 640000
MITSUBISHI Love Lane ℰ 655799

RENAULT Gloucester Rd ℰ 658007
VAUXHALL Love Lane Trading Estate ℰ 653314

◍ ATS 1 Mercian Close, Watermoor End ℰ 657761

CLACTON-ON-SEA Essex 404 X 28 – pop. 39 618 – ECD : Wednesday – ✆ 0255.

See : Sea front (gardens)★.

🛈 23 Pier Av. ✆ 423400.

♦London 71 – Chelmsford 38 – Colchester 16.

🏰 **Kings Cliff**, 55 Kings Par., Esplanade, Holland-on-Sea, CO15 5JB, NE : 1 ½ m. ✆ 812343, ≼ – 📺 ☎ 🅿. 🔼 AE VISA
M *(closed Sunday dinner)* a la carte 6.25/16.20 t. 🍷 3.30 – **15 rm** ⌁ 38.50/54.50 st.

AUSTIN-ROVER 107 Old Rd ✆ 424128
CITROEN 67 Frinton Rd ✆ 812205
FORD Valleybridge Rd ✆ 432555

VAUXHALL-OPEL 65 High St. ✆ 222444

🅐 ATS 46 High St. ✆ 420659

CLANFIELD Oxon. 403 404 P 28 – pop. 822 – ECD : Wednesday and Saturday – ✆ 036 781.

♦London 76 – ♦Oxford 20 – Swindon 17.

XXX **Plough at Clanfield** with rm, Bourton Rd, OX8 2RB, on A 4095 ✆ 222, Group Telex 437334, Fax 596, « Small Elizabethan manor house », ⇙ – ⇤ rest 📺 ☎ 🅿. 🔼 AE ⓞ VISA. ⇙
M 15.00/29.00 t. 🍷 6.00 – **6 rm** ⌁ 66.00/110.00 t. – SB 98.00/185.00 st.

CLAPHAM Beds. 404 S 27 – see Bedford.

CLAPPERSGATE Cumbria – see Ambleside.

CLAUGHTON Lancs. 402 M 21 – see Lancaster.

CLAVERING Essex 404 U 28 – pop. 1 076 – ✆ 0799 Saffron Walden.

♦London 44 – ♦Cambridge 25 – Colchester 44 – Luton 29.

X **Cricketers**, CB11 4QT, ✆ 550442, Fax 550882 – 🅿. 🔼 VISA
M (buffet lunch)/dinner 16.00 t. and a la carte 10.90/12.90 t. 🍷 3.00.

CLAWTON Devon 403 H 31 – pop. 300 – ✉ Holsworthy – ✆ 040 927 North Tamerton.

♦London 240 – Exeter 39 – ♦Plymouth 36.

🏰 **Court Barn** ⚘, EX22 6PS, W : ½ m. ✆ 219, « Gardens » – ⇤ rm 🅿. 🔼 AE ⓞ VISA
M 7.50/15.50 t. and a la carte 🍷 2.95 – **8 rm** ⌁ 28.00/50.00 t. – SB 68.00 st.

CLAYDON Suffolk 404 X 27 – pop. 2 516 – ✉ ✆ 0473 Ipswich.

♦London 78 – ♦Cambridge 50 – ♦Ipswich 4 – ♦Norwich 38.

🏰 **Claydon Country House**, Ipswich Rd, IP6 0AR, ✆ 830382, ⇙ – ⇤ rest 📺 ☎ 🅿. 🔼 AE ⓞ VISA. ⇙
M *(closed Saturday lunch)* 9.50/11.95 st. and a la carte 🍷 3.00 – **14 rm** ⌁ 36.50/49.50 st. – SB (weekends only) 52.50/57.50 st.

CLAYGATE Surrey 404 ㊵ – see Esher.

CLAYTON-LE-MOORS Lancs 402 M 22 – pop. 5 484 – ECD : Wednesday – ✉ ✆ 0254 Accrington.

♦London 232 – Blackburn 3.5 – Lancaster 37 – ♦Leeds 44 – Preston 14.

🏰 **Dunkenhalgh**, Blackburn Rd, BB5 5JP, W : 1 ½ m. on A 678 ✆ 398021, Telex 63282, Fax 872230, 🔽, ⇙, park – 📺 ☎ 🅿 – 🔚 400. 🔼 AE ⓞ VISA
M *(closed Saturday)* 7.50/15.95 t. and a la carte 🍷 7.50 – **61 rm** ⌁ 62.00/80.00 st., **2 suites** 85.00/100.00 st. – SB (weekends only) 73.00/83.00 st.

CLAYTON-LE-WOODS Lancs. – pop. 8 002 (inc. Cuerden) – ✉ Chorley – ✆ 0772 Leyland.

♦London 220 – ♦Liverpool 31 – ♦Manchester 26 – Preston 5.5.

🏰 **Pines**, Preston Rd, PR6 7ED, on A 6 ✆ 38551, Telex 67308, ⇙ – 📺 ☎ 🅿. 🔼 AE ⓞ VISA. ⇙
closed 25 and 26 December – M 9.25/18.00 t. and a la carte – **24 rm** ⌁ 30.00/60.00 t. – SB (weekends only) 75.00 st.

CLAYWORTH Notts. 402 404 R 23 – pop. 275 – ✉ ✆ 0777 Retford.

♦London 150 – ♦Leeds 49 – Lincoln 26 – ♦Nottingham 38 – ♦Sheffield 29.

🏰 **Royston Manor** ⚘, St. Peters Lane, DN22 9AA, ✆ 817484, Fax 817155, ≼, ⇙ – 📺 ☎ 🅿. 🔼 AE ⓞ VISA
M 7.25/11.25 st. and a la carte 17.90/24.10 st. 🍷 3.25 – **22 rm** ⌁ 35.00/45.00 st.

CLEARWELL Glos. – see Coleford.

CLEETHORPES Humberside 402 404 U 23 – pop. 33 238 – ECD : Thursday – ✆ 0472.

🛈 43 Alexandra Rd ✆ 200220.

♦London 171 – Boston 49 – Lincoln 38 – ♦Sheffield 77.

Plan : see Great Grimsby

🏨 **Kingsway**, Kingsway, DN35 0AE, ✆ 601122, Telex 527920, ≼ – 🛗 📺 ☎ 🚗 Ⓟ – 🛝 . 🔾 AE ⓪ VISA 🛇
BZ a
closed 25 and 26 December – **M** 10.00/12.75 **t.** and a la carte 🍶 3.50 – **53 rm** ☕ 49.00/75.00 **t.** – SB (weekends only) 75.00 **st.**

🏠 Wellow, Kings Rd, DN35 0AQ, ✆ 695589 – 📺 ☎ Ⓟ – **10 rm**.   by Kingsway BZ

CLEEVE HILL Glos. 403 404 N 28 – see Cheltenham.

CLEOBURY MORTIMER Shropshire 403 404 M 26 – pop. 1 883 – ✆ 0299.

♦London 147 – ♦Birmingham 29 – Shrewsbury 35.

🏠 **Redfern**, Lower St., DY14 8AA, ✆ 270395, Telex 335176, Fax 271011 – 📺 ☎ Ⓟ. 🔾 AE ⓪ VISA
M 10.00/13.50 **st.** and a la carte 🍶 4.00 – **11 rm** ☕ 35.00/50.50 **st.** – SB 64.00/72.00 **st.**

CLEY NEXT THE SEA Norfolk 404 X 25 – see Blakeney.

CLIFTON HAMPDEN Oxon. 403 404 Q 29 – see Abingdon.

CLIMPING West Sussex 404 S 31 – pop. 925 – ✉ ✆ 0903 Littlehampton.

♦London 64 – Bognor Regis 5 – ♦ Brighton 23.

🏨 Bailiffscourt 🦢, Climping St., BN17 5RW, ✆ 723511, Telex 877870, Fax 723107, « Reconstructed medieval house », 🏊, 🐎, park, 🎾 – 📺 ☎ Ⓟ – 🛝 – **20 rm**.

CLIVEDEN Berks. 404 R 29 – see Maidenhead.

CLOWNE Derbs. 402 403 404 Q 24 – pop. 6 846 – ECD : Wednesday – ✆ 0246 Chesterfield.

♦London 156 – Derby 40 – Lincoln 35 – ♦Nottingham 30 – ♦Sheffield 12.

🏨 **Van Dyk**, Worksop Rd, S43 4TD, N : ¾ m. by A 618 on A 619 ✆ 810219 – 📺 ☎ Ⓟ 🛝 80. 🔾 AE VISA
M 13.25 **t.** and a la carte – **16 rm** ☕ 45.00/65.00 **st.** – SB (except Christmas and New Year) (weekends only) 35.85/42.00 **st.**

CLUN Shropshire 403 KL 26 – pop. 817 – ✉ Craven Arms – ✆ 058 84.

♦London 178 – ♦Birmingham 60 – Shrewsbury 29.

✕✕ **Old Post Office** with rm, 9 The Square, SY7 8JA, ✆ 687, ≼ – 🔾 VISA 🛇
closed 14 January-23 March, 4 to 14 September and 22 to 30 December – **M** (closed Monday and Tuesday except Bank Holidays) (booking essential) (lunch by arrangement)/dinner 19.50 **t.** 🍶 5.50 – **2 rm** ☕ 22.00/37.00 **t.**

COATHAM MUNDEVILLE Durham 402 P 20 – see Darlington.

COBHAM Kent 404 V 29 – ✉ ✆ 0474 Gravesend.

♦London 27 – Maidstone 13 – Rochester 6.

🏛 **Leather Bottle** (B.C.B.), The Street, DA12 3BZ, ✆ 814327, 🐎 – 📺 ☎ Ⓟ. 🔾 AE ⓪ VISA 🛇
M 9.85/16.45 and a la carte 🍶 3.40 – **7 rm** ☕ 29.50/58.50 **t.**

COBHAM Surrey 404 S 30 – pop. 13 920 – ECD : Wednesday – ✆ 0932.

Envir. : Wisley gardens★★ AC, SW : 4 m. by A 3 AZ.

♦London 24 – Guildford 10.

Plan : see Greater London (South-West)

🏨 **Hilton National** (Hilton), Seven Hills Rd South, KT11 1EW, W : 1 ½ m. by A 245 ✆ 64471, Telex 929196, Fax 68017, 🏊, 🐎, park, 🎾, squash – 🛗 ⇥ rm 📺 ☎ Ⓟ – 🛝 350. 🔾 AE ⓪ VISA 🛇
by A 3 AZ
M 16.50/30.00 **t.** and a la carte 🍶 4.15 – ☕ 8.50 – **149 rm** 84.00/104.00 **st.**, **3 suites** 140.00/180.00 **st.** – SB (weekends only) (except Easter and Christmas) 58.50/78.50 **st.**

🏠 **Cedar House**, Mill Rd, KT11 3AN, ✆ 63424, 🐎 – ⇥ rest 📺 ☎ Ⓟ. 🔾 VISA 🛇
closed 25 to 30 December – **M** (closed Sunday and Monday) (dinner only) 18.50 **st.** and a la carte 🍶 3.50 – **6 rm** ☕ 35.00/60.00 **st.**

at Stoke D'Aberon S : 1 ½ m. on A 245 – ✉ Cobham – ✆ 037 284 Oxshott :

🏨 Woodlands Park, Woodlands Lane, KT11 3QB, ✆ 3933, Telex 919246, Fax 2704, 🐎, park – 🛗 🖿 rest 📺 ☎ Ⓟ – 🛝 – **59 rm**, **1 suite**

AUDI-VW 42 Portsmouth Rd ✆ 64493   BMW 18-22 Portsmouth Rd ✆ 67141
AUSTIN-ROVER Stoke Rd ✆ 64244

COCKERMOUTH Cumbria 401 402 J 20 – pop. 7 074 – ECD : Thursday – 🕿 0900.

🛆 Embleton ☎ 059681 (Bassenthwaite) 223, E : 3 m. off A 66.

🛈 Riverside Car Park, Market St. ☎ 822634 (summer only).

♦London 306 – ♦Carlisle 25 – Keswick 13.

🏛 **Trout,** Crown St., CA13 0EJ, ☎ 823591, 🌱, 🛱 – 📺 ☎ 🅿. 🔃 VISA
M 8.00/13.00 t. and a la carte ⌕5.00 – **22 rm** ☲ 35.00/47.00 t. – SB (except Bank Holidays) (weekends only) 58.00/60.00 **st.**

at Great Broughton W : 2 ¾ m. by A 66 – ⊠ 🕿 0900 Cockermouth :

🏛 **Broughton Craggs** 🌭, CA13 0XW, ☎ 824400, 🌱, 🛱 – 📺 ☎ 🅿. 🔃 AE VISA. 🌱
M 12.75 t. and a la carte ⌕3.25 – **10 rm** ☲ 35.00/55.00 **st.** – SB (weekends only) 65.00/67.50 **st.**

BMW, VOLVO Derwent St. ☎ 823666   FORD Lorton St. ☎ 822033

COGGESHALL Essex 404 W 28 – pop. 3 505 – ECD : Wednesday – ⊠ Colchester – 🕿 0376.

♦London 49 – Braintree 6 – Chelmsford 16 – Colchester 9.

🏛 **White Hart,** Market End, CO6 1NH, ☎ 561654, Fax 561789, « Part 14C Guild Hall » – 📺
☎ 🅿. 🔃 AE ⓞ VISA. 🌱
M 15.00 **st.** and a la carte 20.45/24.70 **st.** ⌕4.50 – **18 rm** ☲ 50.00/85.00 **st.** – SB 115.00/135.00 **st.**

COLCHESTER Essex 404 W 28 – pop. 87 476 – ECD : Thursday – 🕿 0206.

See : Castle and Museum★.

Envir. : Layer Marney (Marney Tower★ 16C) SW : 7 m. – Stair Valley★ NE : 6 m.

🛆 Birch Grove, Layer Rd ☎ 020 634 (Layer-de-la-Haye) 276, S : 2 m.

🛈 1 Queen St. ☎ 712233.

♦London 52 – ♦Cambridge 48 – ♦Ipswich 18 – Luton 76 – Southend-on-Sea 41.

🏛 **George** (Q.M.H.), 116 High St., CO1 1TD, ☎ 578494, Fax 761732 – 📺 ☎ 🅿 – 🏌. 🔃 AE
ⓞ VISA
M 9.75 **st.** ⌕3.00 – **47 rm** ☲ 52.00/70.00 **st.** – SB (weekends only) 57.50 **st.**

🏛 **Rose and Crown,** Eastgates, CO1 2TZ, ☎ 866677, « Part 15C inn » – 📺 ☎ 🅿. 🔃 AE ⓞ
VISA. 🌱
M a la carte 12.65/20.65 **st.** ⌕3.50 – **26 rm** ☲ 27.50/52.50 **st.**, **3 suites** 52.50/54.50 **st.**

MICHELIN Distribution Centre, Gosbecks Rd, CO2 9JT, ☎ 578451, FAX 45337

AUDI-VW Wyncol Rd ☎ 855000
AUSTIN-ROVER East Gates ☎ 867484
AUSTIN-ROVER Elmstead Rd ☎ 862811
BMW Ipswich Rd ☎ 751100
CITROEN Butt Rd ☎ 576803
DAIMLER-JAGUAR Cowdrey Av. ☎ 764764
FERRARI, PORSCHE Auto Way, Ipswich Rd ☎ 855500
FIAT, SAAB Sheepen Rd ☎ 563311
FORD Magdalen St. ☎ 571171

HONDA, SEAT, MITSUBISHI, HYUNDAI ☎ 855455
RENAULT 78 Military Rd ☎ 577295
TALBOT-PEUGEOT Wimpole Rd ☎ 570197
TOYOTA Gosbecks Rd ☎ 46455
VAUXHALL-OPEL Ipswich Rd ☎ 844422
VOLVO Autoway, Ipswich Rd ☎ 855055

🅐 ATS East Hill ☎ 866484/867471
ATS 451 Ipswich Rd ☎ 841404

COLD CHRISTMAS Herts. – see Ware.

COLEFORD Glos. 403 404 M 28 – pop. 8 246 – ECD : Thursday – 🕿 0594 Dean.

🛆 Royal Forest of Dean, Lords Hills ☎ 32583, ½ m. on Parkend Rd

🛈 24 Market Pl. ☎ 36307.

♦London 143 – ♦Bristol 28 – Gloucester 19 – Newport 29.

🏛 **Speech House** (T.H.F.), Forest of Dean, GL16 7EL, NE : 3 m. on B 4226 ☎ 22607, 🛱 –
🚭 rm 📺 ☎ 🅿. 🔃 AE ⓞ VISA
M 10.50/16.95 **st.** and a la carte ⌕3.65 – ☲ 7.00 – **14 rm** 47.00/67.00 **st.** – SB 70.00/92.00 **st.**

🏛 **Lambsquay** 🌭, Perrygrove Rd, GL16 8QB, S : 1 m. on B 4228 ☎ 33127, 🛱 – 📺 ☎ 🅿. 🔃
ⓞ VISA
closed January – M *(closed lunch and Sunday dinner to non-residents)* (bar lunch)/dinner 15.00 **st.** and a la carte approx 11.75 **st.** ⌕3.00 – **9 rm** ☲ 25.00/60.00 t. – SB (except Bank Holidays) 51.00/60.00 **st.**

at Clearwell S : 2 m. by B 4228 – ⊠ Coleford – 🕿 0594 Dean :

🏛 **Clearwell Castle** 🌭, GL16 8LG, ☎ 32320, Fax 35523, ≼, « Neo-Gothic mansion », 🛱, park – 📺 ☎ 🅿 – 🏌 180. 🔃 AE ⓞ VISA. 🌱
M 15.00/19.00 t. – **17 rm** ☲ 55.00/130.00 t. – SB 115.00/160.00 **st.**

🏛 **Tudor Farmhouse,** GL16 8JS, ☎ 33046 – 📺 ☎ 🅿. 🔃 AE VISA. 🌱
M *(closed Sunday to non-residents)* 9.95 t. and a la carte approx. 17.00 t. ⌕3.95 – **9 rm** ☲ 28.50/50.00 t.

AUSTIN-ROVER, LAND-ROVER, RANGE-ROVER
Market Pl. ☎ 32468

FORD High St ☎ 32747
HYUNDAI, SUBARU Five Acres ☎ 33517

COLERNE Wilts. 403 404 M 29 – see Bath (Avon).

COLESHILL Warw. 408 404 O 26 – pop. 6 038 – ECD : Monday and Thursday – ⊠ Birmingham – ✆ 0675.

 Maxstoke Park, Castle Lane 🖉 62158, E : 2 m.

♦London 113 – ♦Birmingham 8 – ♦Coventry 11.

 Coleshill (Lansbury), 152 High St., B46 3BG, 🖉 65527, Telex 333868, Fax 64013 – 📺 ☎ 🅿 – 🛎 150. 🔄 AE ⓪ VISA ⋙
 M 7.70/12.40 t. and a la carte 🍷 3.50 – **15 rm** � 50.00/60.00 t.

 Swan, High St., B46 3BL, 🖉 64107 – 📺 ☎ 🅿
 32 rm.

COLLYWESTON Northants. 402 404 S 26 – see Stamford (Lincs.).

COLNE Lancs. 402 N 22 – ✆ 0282.

♦London 234 – ♦Manchester 29 – Preston 26.

 West Lynn Country House, Barrowford Rd, BB8 9QW, W : ½ m. on B 6247 🖉 896199, ⋑ – 📺 ☎ 🅿
 12 rm.

COLTISHALL Norfolk 404 Y 25 – ⊠ ✆ 0603 Norwich.

♦London 133 – ♦Norwich 8.

 Norfolk Mead ⋙, Church St., NR12 7DN, 🖉 737531, ⌁ heated, ⋑, ⋑ – 📺 ☎ 🅿. 🔄 AE ⓪ VISA. ⋙
 closed 25 to 28 December and 1 to 3 January – **M** *(closed Sunday dinner and Bank Holidays)* *(dinner only and Sunday lunch)*/dinner 20.00 t. and a la carte – **10 rm** ⊐ 43.00/75.00 st. – SB (weekends only) (except Bank Holidays) 72.00/82.00 **st.**

COLWYN BAY (BAE COLWYN) Clwyd 402 408 I 24 – pop. 27 002 – ECD : Wednesday – ✆ 0492.

See : Zoo★ – Envir. : Bodnant gardens★★ *AC*, SW : 6 m.

 Abergele and Pensarn, Tan-y-Goppa Rd, Abergele 🖉 0745 (Abergele) 824034, E : 6 m. – ⌁ Old Colwyn, Woodland Av. 🖉 515581.

🏢 Station Rd. 🖉 530478 – The Promenade. Rhos-on-sea 🖉 48778.

♦London 237 – Birkenhead 50 – Chester 42 – Holyhead 41.

 Norfolk House, 36 Princes Drive, LL29 8PF, 🖉 531757, ⋑ – ⃗ ⤢ rest 📺 ⊗ 🅿 – 🛎 40. 🔄 AE ⓪ VISA
 M (bar lunch)/dinner 15.00 t. and a la carte 🍷 4.00 – **24 rm** ⊐ 37.50/55.00 t. – SB (weekends only) 66.00 **st.**

 Hopeside, 63-67 Prince's Drive, West End, LL29 8PW, 🖉 533244, Telex 61254 – ⤢ rm 📺 ☎ 🅿. 🔄 AE ⓪ VISA
 M *(closed Sunday dinner to non-residents)* 6.50/11.95 t. and a la carte 🍷 3.50 – **16 rm** ⊐ 29.50/50.00 t. – SB 58.00/68.00 **st.**

 Lyndale, 410 Abergele Rd, Old Colwyn, LL29 9AB, E : 1 ¾ m. on A 547 🖉 515429 – 📺 ☎ 🅿. 🔄 AE ⓪ VISA. ⋙
 M (bar lunch Monday to Saturday)/dinner 12.50 t. and a la carte 🍷 3.50 – **14 rm** ⊐ 29.50/46.00 t. – SB 54.50/64.50 **st.**

⬆ **West Point,** 102 Conway Rd, LL29 7LE, 🖉 530331, ⋑ – 🅿. 🔄 VISA
 closed January – **M** 10.00 st. 🍷 3.35 – **10 rm** ⊐ 12.75/29.50 **st.**

 at Penmaenhead E : 2 ¼ m. on A 547 – ⊠ ✆ 0492 Colwyn Bay :

 Hotel 70° (Best Western), Old Colwyn, LL29 9LD, 🖉 516555, Telex 61362, Fax 515565, ≤ – 📺 ☎ 🅿 – 🛎 60. 🔄 AE ⓪ VISA
 M 10.50/16.75 t. and a la carte – **43 rm** ⊐ 50.00/85.00 st., **1 suite** 95.00 t. – SB 75.00/95.00 **st.**

 at Rhos-on-Sea (Llandrillo-yn-Rhos) NW : 1 m. – ⊠ ✆ 0492 Colwyn Bay :

 Ashmount, 18 College Av., LL28 4NT, 🖉 45479 – 📺 ☎ 🅿. 🔄 AE ⓪ VISA
 M 5.95/8.25 t. and a la carte 🍷 2.85 – **18 rm** ⊐ 24.00/40.50 t. – SB (October-April) 48.50/60.50 **st.**

⬆ **Cabin Hill,** 12 College Av., LL28 4NT, 🖉 44568 – 📺 🅿. ⋙
 March-October – **M** 7.00 st. – **10 rm** ⊐ 13.50/30.00 st. – SB 40.00 **st.**

AUSTIN-ROVER 394 Abergele Rd 🖉 515292
FORD Conwy Rd 🖉 532201
PEUGEOT 268 Conwy Rd 🖉 44278

PORSCHE Abergele Rd 🖉 530456
VAUXALL Conwy Rd 🖉 530271
VW-AUDI Penrhyn Av. 🖉 46722

COLYTON Devon 408 K 31 The West Country G. – pop. 2 435 – ✆ 0297.

See : Site★ – St. Andrew's Church★.

♦London 160 – Exeter 23 – Lyme Regis 7.

 Old Bakehouse, Lower Church St., EX13 6ND, 🖉 52518 – 📺 🅿. VISA
 M 7.00/10.00 t. and a la carte 10.20/14.65 t. 🍷 3.50 – **6 rm** ⊐ 26.00/42.00 t.

⬆ **Grove,** South St., EX13 6ER, 🖉 52438, ⋑ – ⤢ rest 🅿
 closed 20 December-4 January – **M** 6.50 s. 🍷 2.40 – **7 rm** ⊐ 12.00/27.00 s.

COMBE MARTIN Devon 403 H 30 The West Country G. – pop. 2 279 – ECD : Wednesday – ⊠ Ilfracombe – ☏ 027 188.

🛈 Sea Cottage, Cross St. ☏ 3319 and 2692 (summer only).

♦London 218 – Exeter 56 – Taunton 58.

  🏠 **Coulsworthy Country House** ⏳, EX34 0PD, SE : 2 ½ m. by A 399 on road to Hunters Inn ☏ 882463, ≼, « Country house atmosphere », ⌧ heated, 🛲, ⅋ – 🆃🆅 🅿. 🄯 𝗩𝗜𝗦𝗔
    closed mid December-mid February – **M** *(closed Sunday dinner)* (dinner only and Sunday lunch)/dinner 16.00 **st.** ⬧ 3.50 – **10 rm** ⊊ 32.00/74.00 **st.** – SB 72.00/104.00 **st.**

  🏠 **Rone House**, King St., EX34 0AD, ☏ 3428 – 🆃🆅 🅿. 🄯
    closed November-18 December – **M** *(closed Monday)* (bar lunch)/dinner 9.50 **t.** and a la carte
    – **11 rm** ⊊ 14.50/34.00 **t.**

AUSTIN-ROVER Borough Rd ☏ 2391   VAUXHALL-OPEL Borough Rd ☏ 3257

CONGLETON Cheshire 402 403 404 N 24 – pop. 23 482 – ECD : Wednesday – ☏ 0260.

🛈₉ Biddulph Rd ☏ 273540 – 🛈 Town Hall, High St. ☏ 271095.

♦London 183 – ♦Liverpool 50 – ♦Manchester 25 – ♦Sheffield 46 – ♦Stoke-on-Trent 13.

  🏠 **Lion and Swan**, Swan Bank, CW12 1JR, ☏ 273115, « 16C inn » – 🆃🆅 ☎ 🅿. 🄯 🄰🄴 ⓘ 𝗩𝗜𝗦𝗔
    M 8.50/11.95 **st.** and a la carte ⬧ 3.85 – ⊊ 5.95 – **21 rm** 45.00/76.00 **st.** – SB (weekends only) 60.00/72.00 **st.**

🆖 ATS Brookside ☏ 273720

CONISTON Cumbria 402 K 20 – pop. 1 713 – ☏ 053 94.

🛈 16 Yewdale Rd ☏ 41533 (summer only).

♦London 285 – ♦Carlisle 55 – Kendal 22 – Lancaster 42.

  🏠 **Sun** ⏳, LA21 8HQ, ☏ 41248, ≼, 🛲 – ⇥ rest 🆃🆅 ☎ 🅿. 𝗩𝗜𝗦𝗔
    closed January and February – **M** (bar lunch)/dinner 15.50 **t.** ⬧ 3.50 – **11 rm** ⊊ 30.00/60.00 **t.**

CONSTANTINE BAY Cornwall 403 E 32 – see Padstow.

CONWY Gwynedd 402 403 I 24 – pop. 3 649 – ECD : Wednesday – ☏ 0492 Aberconway.

See : Site✶ – Castle✶✶ (13C) *AC* – St. Mary's Church✶ (14C).

Envir. : Bodnant Gardens✶✶ SE : 5 m.

🛈₉ Penmaenmawr ☏ 623330, W : 4 m – 🛈₁₈ The Morfa ☏ 593400, W : 1 m. on A 55.

🛈 Snowdonia National Park, Visitor Centre, Castle St. ☏ 592248 (summer only).

♦London 241 – Caernarfon 22 – Chester 46 – Holyhead 37.

  🏰 **Bryn Cregin Garden**, Ty Mawr Rd, Deganwy, LL31 9UR, NE : 2 m. by A 55 on A 546 ☏ 85266, ≼, 🛲 – 🆃🆅 ☎ 🅿. 🄯 𝗩𝗜𝗦𝗔. ⅋
    M 8.00/15.00 **t.** and a la carte ⬧ 4.50 – **16 rm** ⊊ 44.00/72.00 **t.** – SB 88.00/112.00 **st.**

  🏰 **Castle** (T.H.F.), High St., LL32 8DB, ☏ 592324 – 🆃🆅 ☎ 🅿 – 🛦 25. 🄯 🄰🄴 ⓘ 𝗩𝗜𝗦𝗔
    M (bar lunch Monday to Saturday)/dinner 12.50 **st.** and a la carte ⬧ 3.95 – ⊊ 7.00 – **29 rm** 49.00/69.00 **st.** – SB 40.00/43.00 **st.**

  🏠 **Castle Bank**, Mount Pleasant, LL32 8NY, ☏ 593888, ≼ – 🆃🆅 🅿. 🄯 𝗩𝗜𝗦𝗔. ⅋
    accommodation closed January-mid February – **M** *(restricted service December-February)* (dinner only and Sunday lunch)/dinner 12.50 **t.** ⬧ 3.50 – **9 rm** ⊊ 21.00/42.00 **t.** – SB 57.00/61.00 **st.**

  at Roewen S : 3 m. by B 5100 – ⊠ Conwy – ☏ 0492 Tyn-y-Groes :

  ↑ **Tir-y-Coed** ⏳, LL32 8TP, ☏ 650219, ≼, 🛲 – ⇥ rest 🆃🆅 🅿
    closed Christmas and restricted service November-January – **M** 8.00 **t.** ⬧ 3.00 – **7 rm** ⊊ 20.50/37.50 **t.** – SB (October-April) 43.00 **st.**

  at Tal-y-Bont S : 5 ¾ m. on B 5106 – ⊠ Conwy – ☏ 049 269 Dolgarrog :

  🏠 **Lodge**, LL32 8LX, ☏ 766 – 🆃🆅 ☎ 🅿. 🄯 𝗩𝗜𝗦𝗔
    closed January – **M** *(closed Sunday dinner)* 9.95 **st.** and a la carte 10.30/13.20 **st.** ⬧ 3.50 – **10 rm** ⊊ 25.00/40.00 **st.** – SB (November-February) 40.00/55.00 **st.**

COOKHAM Berks. 404 R 29 – pop. 5 865 – ECD : Wednesday and Thursday – ⊠ Maidenhead – ☏ 062 85 Bourne End – Envir. : Cliveden House✶ (19C) (Park✶✶) *AC*, SE : 2 m.

🛈₁₈ Winter Hill, Grange Lane ☏ 27613, NW: 1 m. by B 4447.

♦London 32 – High Wycombe 7 – Reading 16.

  ✕ **Peking Inn**, 49 High St., SL6 9SL, ☏ 20900, Chinese (Peking) rest. – 🄯 🄰🄴 ⓘ 𝗩𝗜𝗦𝗔
    M 15.00/20.00 **t.** and a la carte.

  ✕ **Cookham Tandoori**, High St., SL6 9SL, ☏ 22584, Indian rest – 🄯 🄰🄴 ⓘ 𝗩𝗜𝗦𝗔
    M 12.00/18.00 **t.** and a la carte ⬧ 3.50.

CITROEN High St. ☏ 22984

COPDOCK Suffolk 404 X 27 – see Ipswich.

COPTHORNE West Sussex 404 T 30 – see Crawley.

CORBRIDGE Northumb. 401 402 N 19 – pop. 2 757 – ECD : Thursday – ☎ 043 471 (4 fig.) or
0434 (Hexham)(6 fig.).

Envir. : Corstopitum Roman Fort★ *AC*, NW : 1 ½ m.

🛈 Vicar's Pele Tower, Market Pl. ☎ 2815 (summer only).

◆London 300 – Hexham 3 – ◆Newcastle-upon-Tyne 18.

　　🕎　**Riverside**, Main St., NE45 5LE, ☎ 632942 – 📺 🅿
　　　closed January – **M** *(closed Sunday)* (booking essential) (lunch by arrangement)/dinner
　　　11.95 **st.** ⌀ 4.00 – **11 rm** ⧉ 23.00/43.00 **st.**

　　↑　**Clive House** without rest., Appletree Lane, NE45 5DN, ☎ 632617, 🚘 – ⤬ 📺 🅿. 🔌 *VISA*
　　　🦚
　　　3 rm ⧉ 25.00/37.00 **s.**

　　XXX　**Ramblers Country House,** Tinklers Bank, Farnley, NE45 5RN, S : 1 m. on Riding Mill Rd
　　　☎ 2424, German rest. – 🅿. 🔌 AE ⓪ *VISA*
　　　closed Sunday and Monday – **M** (lunch by arrangement)/dinner a la carte 14.20/18.00 **t.**
　　　⌀ 3.45.

LANCIA Princes St. ☎ 3480

CORFE CASTLE Dorset 403 404 N 32 – ✉ Wareham – ☎ 0929.

◆London 129 – Bournemouth 18 – Weymouth 23.

　　🏛　**Mortons House,** 45 East St., BH20 5EE, ☎ 480988, « Elizabethan manor », 🚘 – ⤬ rest
　　　📺 ☎ 🅿. 🔌 *VISA*
　　　M 16.00/22.00 **st.** and a la carte ⌀ 4.20 – **17 rm** ⧉ 40.00/140.00 **st.**

CORNHILL-ON-TWEED Northumb. 401 402 N 17 – pop. 312 – ECD : Thursday – ☎ 0890
Coldstream.

◆London 345 – ◆Edinburgh 49 – ◆Newcastle-upon-Tyne 59.

　　↑　**Coach House,** Crookham, TD12 4TD, E : 4 m. on A 697 ☎ 089 082(Crookham) 293, 🚘 –
　　　⤬ rest ♿ 🅿
　　　April-October – **M** 10.50 **st.** ⌀ 2.55 – **10 rm** ⧉ 19.00/42.00 **st.**

CORPUSTY Norfolk 404 X 25 – pop. 1 234 – ✉ Heydon – ☎ 026 387 Saxthorpe.

◆London 134 – ◆Cambridge 77 – ◆Norwich 16.

　　↑　Cropton Hall 🦚, NR11 6RX, S : 1 m. on Heydon Rd ☎ 869, 🔌, 🚘 – 📺 🅿
　　　8 rm.

CORRIS Gwynedd 402 403 I 26 – see Machynlleth (Powys).

CORSE LAWN Heref. and Worc. – see Tewkesbury (Glos.).

CORSHAM Wilts. 403 404 N 29 The West Country G. – pop. 11 259 – ECD : Wednesday –
☎ 0249.

See : Corsham Court★★ *AC*.

🏌 Kingsdown ☎ 742530 – 🛈 Arnold House, 31 High St. ☎ 714660 (summer only).

◆London 110 – ◆Bristol 22 – Swindon 25.

　　🏛　**Rudloe Park,** Leafy Lane, SN13 0PA, W : 2 m. by B 3353 on A 4 ☎ 0225 (Bath) 810555, Fax
　　　811412, ≼, 🚘 – ⤬ rest 📺 ☎ 🅿 – 🔬 50. 🔌 AE ⓪ *VISA*. 🦚
　　　M 11.50/13.75 **t.** and a la carte ⌀ 4.00 – **11 rm** ⧉ 47.50/85.00 **t.** – SB 101.75/118.25 **st.**

　　🏛　**Methuen Arms,** 2 High St., SN13 0HB, ☎ 714867, Fax 712004, 🚘 – 📺 ☎ 🅿. 🔌 *VISA*. 🦚
　　　accommodation closed 4 days at Christmas – **M** (bar meals Sunday evening) a la carte
　　　12.05/18.75 **t.** – **25 rm** ⧉ 33.00/53.00 **st.** – SB (except Bank Holidays) 68.00 **st.**

　　↑　**Spiders Barn** without rest., 13 Cross Keys, SN13 0DT, N : ½ m. by A 4 ☎ 712012, 🚘 – 🅿
　　　🦚
　　　4 rm ⧉ 12.00/24.00 **st.**

FORD 101 Pickwick Rd ☎ 712166

CORTON Wilts. 403 404 N 30 – see Warminster.

COSGROVE Northants. – see Stony Stratford (Bucks.).

COSHAM Hants. 403 404 Q 31 – see Portsmouth and Southsea.

COUNTESTHORPE Leics. 403 404 Q 26 – pop. 6 133 – ☎ 0533 Leicester.

◆London 97 – ◆Coventry 25 – ◆Leicester 7 – Northampton 35.

　　XX　**Old Bakery,** Main St., LE8 3QX, ☎ 778777 – 🅿. 🔌 *VISA*
　　　closed Saturday lunch, Sunday dinner and Monday – **M** 8.95/14.95 **t.**

COUNTISBURY Devon – see Lynton.

COUNTY OAK West Sussex – see Crawley.

See : St. Michael's Cathedral★★★ (1962) : tapestry★★★ AV – Old Cathedral★ (ruins) AV A –
St. John's Church★ (14C-15C) AV B – Old houses★ (16C-17C) AV DEF.

📍 Brandon Wood, Brandon Lane ℰ 0203 (Wolston) 543141, SE : 6 m. by A 428 BY – 📍 Sphinx,
Siddeley Av. ℰ 458890 BY – 📍 Grange Copsewood ℰ 451465 BY.

✈ Coventry Airport : ℰ 301717, Telex 31646, S : 3 ½ m. by Coventry Rd BZ.

🛈 Central Library, Smithford Way ℰ 832311.

♦London 100 – ♦Birmingham 18 – ♦Bristol 96 – ♦Nottingham 52.

Plans on following pages

De Vere (De Vere), Cathedral Sq., CV1 5RP, ℰ 633733, Telex 31380, Fax 225299 – 🛗 📺 ☎
📞 – 🚗 500. 🅿 AE ⓞ VISA
AV n
M 11.50/25.00 t. and a la carte – **180 rm** ⚏ 71.50/107.50 t., **10 suites** 114.00/142.00 t. –
SB 65.00/75.00 st.

Hylands (Best Western), 153 Warwick Rd, CV3 6AU, ℰ 501600, Telex 312388, Fax 501027
– 🍽 rest 📺 ☎ 📞 – 🚗 50. 🅿 AE ⓞ VISA
AYZ z
M *(closed Saturday lunch)* (carving rest.) 7.75/10.75 **st.** and a la carte 🍷 3.10 – **55 rm**
⚏ 54.00/72.00 st. – SB (weekends only) (except Christmas and New Year) 59.50/69.50 st.

Merrick Lodge, 80-82 St. Nicholas St., CV1 4BP, ℰ 553940, Fax 550112 – 📺 ☎ 📞. 🅿 AE
VISA. 🚭
AV a
M 7.50/9.50 **st.** and a la carte – **14 rm** ⚏ 34.00/45.00 st.

Victoria House without rest., 39 St. Patricks Rd, CV1 2LP, ℰ 221378 – 🚭
AV e
5 rm ⚏ 12.00/24.00 s.

Brymar without rest., 39a St. Patricks Rd, CV1 2LP, ℰ 225969 – 🚭
AV e
4 rm ⚏ 13.00/24.00 s.

Hearsall Lodge, 1-3 Broad Lane, Whoberley, CV5 7AA, W : 2 m. by B 4101 ℰ 674543 –
📺 📞
AY a
M (by arrangement) 5.50 **st.** – **18 rm** ⚏ 22.50/40.00 st.

Fairlight without rest., 14 Regent St., CV1 3EP, ℰ 224215
AV i
closed 24 December-1 January – **11 rm** ⚏ 12.00/32.00 st.

at Longford N : 4 m. on A 444 – ✉ ✆ 0203 Coventry :

Novotel, Wilsons Lane, CV6 6HL, ℰ 365000, Telex 31545, Fax 362422, 🏊 heated – 🛗 🍽
📺 ☎ ♿ 📞 – 🚗 200. 🅿 AE ⓞ VISA
BV v
M a la carte 12.75/14.00 st. 🍷 4.50 – ⚏ 5.75 – **100 rm** 52.00 st.

at Walsgrave on Sowe NE : 3 m. on A 46 – ✉ ✆ 0203 Coventry :

Crest (Crest), Hinckley Rd, CV2 2HP, NE : ½ m. on A 46 ℰ 613261, Telex 311292, Fax 621736
– 🛗 🚭 rm 🍽 rest 📺 ☎ ♿ 📞 – 🚗 450
BX e
147 rm, 2 suites.

Campanile, Wigston Rd off Hinckley Rd, CV2 2SD, NE : ½ m. on A 46 ℰ 622311, Telex
317454 – 📺 ☎ 📞 – **47 rm**.
BX a

at Ansty (Warw.) NE : 5 ¾ m. by A 46 – BY – on B 4065 – ✉ ✆ 0203 Coventry :

Ansty Hall, CV7 9HZ, ℰ 612222, Fax 602155, « 17C mansion », 🌲, park – 🚭 rm 📺 ☎
📞. 🅿 AE ⓞ VISA
M *(closed Saturday lunch and Sunday dinner)* 15.00/20.00 st. and a la carte 🍷 3.50 – ⚏ 7.00
– **13 rm** 70.00/100.00 st. – SB (weekends only) (except Christmas and New Year) 180.00 st.

at Brandon (Warw.) E : 6 m. on A 428 – BZ – ✉ ✆ 0203 Coventry :

Brandon Hall (T.H.F.) 🏊, Main St., CV8 3FW, ℰ 542571, Fax 544909, 🌲, park, squash –
📺 ☎ 📞 – 🚗 100. 🅿 AE ⓞ VISA
M *(closed Saturday lunch)* 9.95/13.50 st. and a la carte 🍷 3.95 – ⚏ 7.60 – **59 rm**
65.00/85.00 st., **1 suite** 105.00 st. – SB (weekends only) 68.00/80.00 st.

at Willenhall SE : 3 m. on A 423 – ✉ ✆ 0203 Coventry :

Chace Crest (Crest), London Rd, CV3 4EQ, ℰ 303398, Telex 311993, Fax 301816, 🌲 –
🚭 rm 📺 ☎ 📞 – 🚗 50. 🅿 AE ⓞ VISA
BZ u
M 9.00/15.00 st. and a la carte – ⚏ 7.60 – **67 rm** 67.00/79.00 st.

at Baginton (Warw.) S : 3 m. by A 444 off A 45 (off Westbound carriageway and Howes
Lane turning) – ✉ ✆ 0203 Coventry :

Old Mill (B.C.B.) 🏊, Mill Hill, CV8 2BS, ℰ 303588, « Attractively converted former corn
mill », 🌲 – 🚭 rest 📺 ☎ 📞. 🅿 AE ⓞ VISA. 🚭
BZ e
M 11.95 st. and a la carte 8.85/17.15 st. 🍷 3.40 – **20 rm** ⚏ 46.00/56.00 st. – SB (weekends only) 42.00 st.

at Berkswell W : 6 ½ m. by B 4101 – AY – ✉ ✆ 0203 Coventry :

Nailcote Hall 🏊 with rm, Nailcote Lane, CV7 7DE, S : 1 ½ m. on B 4101 ℰ 466174, Fax
470720, 🌲 – 📺 📞. 🅿 AE ⓞ VISA. 🚭
M 18.00 t. and a la carte 20.50/29.00 t. 🍷 4.50 – **5 rm** ⚏ 70.00/125.00 st. – SB (weekends only) (except Christmas) 90.00/100.00 st.

at Balsall Common W : 6 ¾ m. by B 4101 – AY – ✉ Coventry – ✆ 0676 Berkswell :

Haigs, 273 Kenilworth Rd, CV7 7EL, ℰ 33004, Fax 34572, 🌲 – 📺 📞. 🅿 AE ⓞ VISA. 🚭
closed 24 December-3 January – **M** (dinner only and Sunday lunch) 8.80/11.40 st.
and a la carte 🍷 3.15 – **14 rm** ⚏ 28.00/52.00 st.

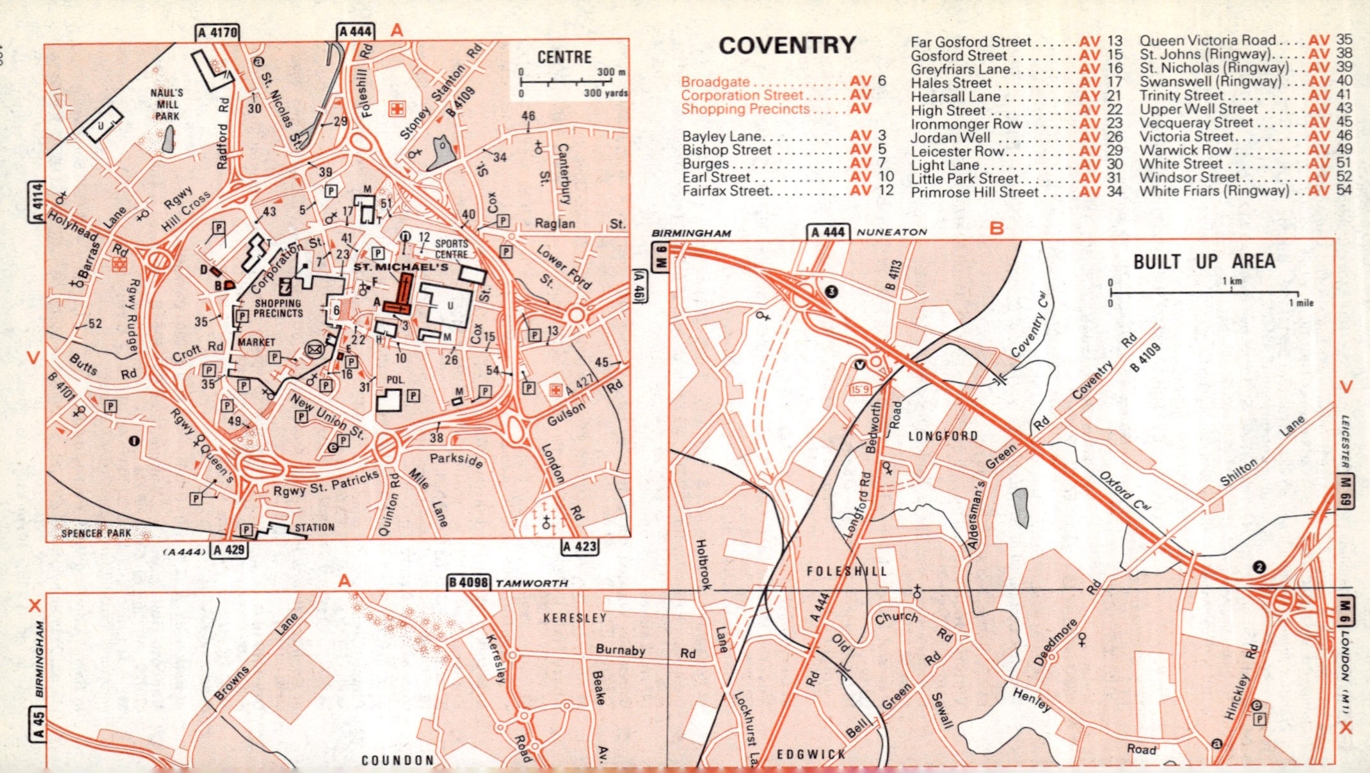

COVENTRY

Broadgate............. AV 6
Corporation Street...... AV 7
Shopping Precincts..... AV

Bayley Lane........... AV 3
Bishop Street......... AV 5
Burges............... AV 7
Earl Street........... AV 10
Fairfax Street......... AV 12

Far Gosford Street...... AV 13
Gosford Street......... AV 15
Greyfriars Lane........ AV 16
Hales Street.......... AV 17
Hearsall Lane......... AV 21
High Street........... AV 22
Ironmonger Row....... AV 23
Jordan Well........... AV 26
Leicester Row......... AV 29
Light Lane............ AV 30
Little Park Street...... AV 31
Primrose Hill Street.... AV 34

Queen Victoria Road.... AV 35
St. Johns (Ringway)..... AV 38
St. Nicholas (Ringway)... AV 39
Swanswell (Ringway).... AV 40
Trinity Street......... AV 41
Upper Well Street...... AV 43
Vecqueray Street...... AV 45
Victoria Street........ AV 46
Warwick Row......... AV 49
White Street.......... AV 51
Windsor Street........ AV 52
White Friars (Ringway)... AV 54

CENTRE
0   300 m
0   300 yards

BUILT UP AREA
0   1 km
0   1 mile

A 4170
A 444
A 4114
A 46
A 444
A 429
A 423
B 4098 TAMWORTH
A 45 BIRMINGHAM

NAUL'S MILL PARK
St. Nicolas St.
Foleshill Rd
Stoney Stanton Rd
B 4109
Radford Rd
Canterbury St.
Raglan St.
Lower Ford St.
Cox St.
Holyhead Rd
Rgwy Hill Cross
Barras Lane
Rgwy Rudge
Butts Rd
B 4101
Corporation St.
ST. MICHAEL'S
SPORTS CENTRE
SHOPPING PRECINCTS
MARKET
Croft Rd
New Union St.
Rgwy Queen's
Rgwy St. Patricks
SPENCER PARK
STATION
Quinton Rd
Mile Lane
Parkside
Gulson Rd
London Rd
A 427
POL.

BIRMINGHAM
A 444 NUNEATON
B
BUILT UP AREA
B 4113
Coventry Cal
Coventry Rd
B 4109
Shilton Lane
LEICESTER
M 69
M 6 LONDON (M1)
Longford Rd
Bedworth Road
LONGFORD
Aldersman's Green Rd
Oxford Cal
FOLESHILL
A 444
Holbrook Lane
Lockhurst La.
Old Rd
Church Rd
Bell Green Rd
Sewall
Deedmore
Henley Road
Hinckley Rd
EDGWICK
KERESLEY
Burnaby Rd
Beake Av.
Keresley
Browns Lane
Road
COUNDON

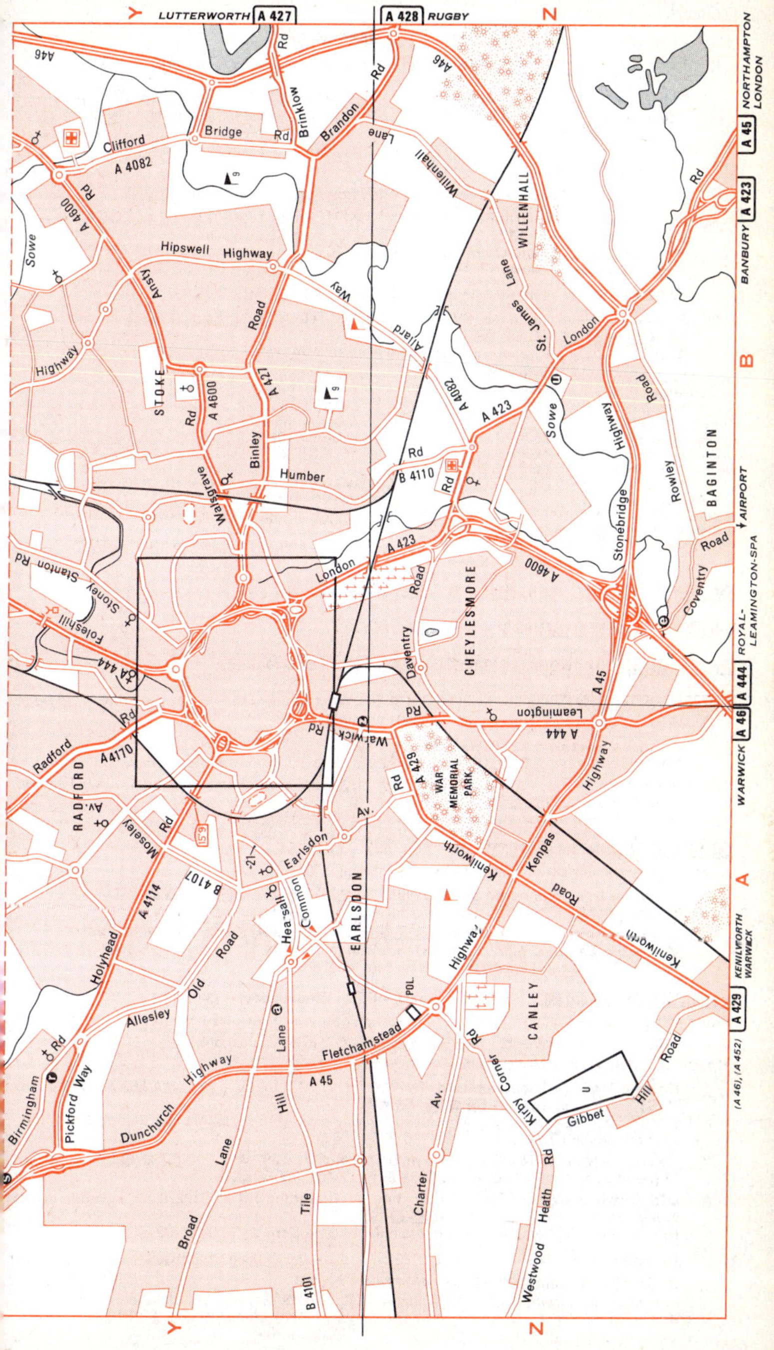

LUTTERWORTH A 427
A 428 RUGBY
Y
N
NORTHAMPTON
LONDON
A 45
BANBURY A 423
Rd
A 46
Rd
Clifford
A 4082
Bridge
Rd
Brinklow
Brandon
Lane
Willenhall
Lane
WILLENHALL
James
St.
London
B
Sowe
A 4600
Rd
Hipswell
Highway
Ansty
Road
A 427
Way
Allard
A 4082
Sowe
Highway
Highway
STOKE
A 4600
Rd
Binley
Humber
A 423
Rd
B 4110
Rd
A 423
Stonebridge
Highway
Rowley
Road
BAGINTON
Wexgrave
London
Road
A 423
Road
CHEYLESMORE
A 4600
Coventry
Road
AIRPORT
ROYAL-
LEAMINGTON-SPA
Stoney Stanton Rd
Foleshill
Daventry
A 444
Rd
Rd
A 45
A 444
A 444
WARWICK A 46
A 4170
Radford
Leamington
Highway
Warwick Rd
A 428
WAR
MEMORIAL
PARK
Kenilworth
Road
Kenpas
Highway
RADFORD
Av.
Moseley
Rd
Rd
Earlsdon
Av.
EARLSDON
Kenilworth
Road
Warwick
KENILWORTH
WARWICK
B 4107
Earlsdon
Common
A
A 114
Holyhead
Old
Road
Hea-salt
Lane
Charter
Av.
Kirby
Corner
Rd
CANLEY
A 429
Birmingham
Rd
Pickford Way
Allesley
Highway
Dunchurch
Broad
Lane
Tile
Hill
Lane
Fletchamstead
Highway
A 45
POL.
Rd
Westwood
Heath
Rd
Gibbet
Hill
Road
B 4101
(A 46), (A 452)

at Allesley NW : 3 m. on A 4114 – ✉ ☎ 0203 Coventry :

🏨 **Post House** (T.H.F.), Rye Hill, CV5 9PH, ℰ 402151, Telex 31427, Fax 402235 – ▐░▌ ⇆ rm 📺
☎ 🅿 – 🔥 120. 🔼 AE ⓞ VISA   AXY s
M 9.50/13.50 **st.** and a la carte – ⇌ 7.50 – **184 rm** 65.00/75.00 **st.** – SB 52.00/68.00 **st.**

🏨 **Allesley**, Birmingham Rd, CV5 9GT, ℰ 403272, Telex 311446, Fax 405190 – ▐░▌ 📺 ☎ 🅿 –
🔥 . 🔼 AE ⓞ VISA   AY r
M (closed Saturday lunch) 11.25 **st.** and a la carte ▮ 3.75 – **79 rm** ⇌ 65.00/75.00 **st.** –
SB (weekends only) 60.00/65.00 **st.**

at Keresley NW : 3 m. on B 4098 – AX – ✉ Coventry – ☎ 0203 Coventry :

🏨 **Royal Court**, Tamworth Rd, CV7 8JG, ℰ 334171, Group Telex 312549, Fax 333478, ⇆ – ▐░▌
📺 ☎ ⅙ 🅿 – 🔥 200. 🔼 AE ⓞ VISA
M (closed lunch Saturday and Bank Holidays) 10.80/13.00 **st.** and a la carte ▮ 3.50 – **98 rm**
⇌ 65.00/75.00 **st.**, **1 suite** 77.00/87.00 **st.** – SB (weekends only) 60.00/65.00 **st.**

at Meriden NW : 6 m. by A 45 on B 4102 – AX – ✉ Coventry – ☎ 0676 Meriden :

🏨 **Manor** (De Vere), Main Rd, CV7 7NH, ℰ 22735, Telex 311011, Fax 22186, ⅄ heated, ⇆ –
📺 ☎ 🅿 – 🔥 . 🔼 AE ⓞ VISA
M (closed Saturday lunch) 13.50 **st.** and a la carte – **74 rm** ⇌ 65.00/80.00 **s.**

AUSTIN-ROVER Lockhurst Lane ℰ 688851
AUSTIN-ROVER Warwick Rd ℰ 633661
AUSTIN-ROVER, LAND-ROVER, RANGE-ROVER
Kenpas Highway ℰ 411515
BMW Holyhead Rd ℰ 591223
CITROEN Lockhurst Lane ℰ 686699
DAIHATSU Goodyers End Lane ℰ 362259
FIAT 324 Station Rd Balsall Common ℰ 0676
(Berkswell) 33145
FORD London Rd ℰ 502000
FORD Pickford Brook, Allesley ℰ 402177
HYUNDAI 149 Far Gosford St. ℰ 224552
JAGUAR Dunchurch Highway ℰ 404641

LADA Brandon Rd ℰ 452777
MAZDA Browns Lane ℰ 402493
MERCEDES-BENZ Humber Rd ℰ 306234
NISSAN 105 Foleshill Rd ℰ 555399
PEUGEOT-TALBOT 136 Daventry Rd ℰ 503522
RELIANT 90 Paynes Lane ℰ 220475
TOYOTA Bennetts Rd, Keresley ℰ 334204
VAUXHALL-OPEL Raglan St. ℰ 225361
VOLVO London Rd ℰ 303132
VW-AUDI Spon End ℰ 525555

⊚ ATS Mile Lane, Cheylesmore ℰ 228727/8

COWAN BRIDGE Cumbria 402 M 21 – see Kirkby Lonsdale.

COWES I.O.W. 403 404 P Q 31 – see Wight (Isle of).

COYCHURCH (LLANGRALLO) Mid Glam. 403 J 29 – see Bridgend.

CRACKINGTON HAVEN Cornwall 403 G 31 The West Country G. – ECD : Tuesday – ✉ Bude
– ☎ 084 03 St. Gennys – ♦London 262 – Bude 11 – Truro 42.

🏠 **Coombe Barton**, EX23 0JG, ℰ 345, ⩽ – 🅿
March-September – M 10.00/15.00 **t.** and a la carte ▮ 3.15 – **7 rm** ⇌ 16.50/40.00 **t.**

⌂ **Manor Farm** ⑤, EX23 0JW, SE: 1 ¼ m. by Tresparrett Posts Rd and Church Park Rd
ℰ 304, « Part 11C manor », ⇆, park – ⇆ 🅿. ⅍
M (unlicensed) (dinner only) 9.00 **s.** – **4 rm** ⇌ 19.00/38.00 **s.**

CRANBORNE Dorset 403 404 O 31 – pop. 596 – ☎ 072 54.
♦London 107 – Bournemouth 21 – Salisbury 18 – ♦Southampton 30.

🏛 **Fleur De Lys**, Wimborne St., BH21 5PP, on B 3078 ℰ 282 – 📺 🅿. 🔼 AE VISA
M (bar lunch)/dinner 10.00 **t.** and a la carte ▮ 2.65 – **8 rm** ⇌ 23.50/39.00 **t.**

XX **La Fosse** with rm, London House, The Square, BH21 5PR, ℰ 604 – 📺. 🔼 AE VISA ⅍
M (closed Saturday lunch, Sunday and Monday) 5.00/20.50 **t.** and a la carte 14.50/20.50 **t.**
▮ 2.75 – **3 rm** ⇌ 25.00/40.00 **t.** – SB (except weekends) 60.40/83.60 **st.**

CRANBROOK Kent 404 V 30 – pop. 3 593 – ECD : Wednesday – ☎ 0580.
Envir. : Sissinghurst : castle★ (16C) (⩽★, 78 steps), gardens★★ AC, NE : 1 ½ m.
🔞 Benenden Rd ℰ 712833 – 🄳 Vestry Hall, Stone St. ℰ 712538 (summer only).
♦London 53 – Hastings 19 – Maidstone 15.

🏠 **Kennel Holt** ⑤, Goudhurst Rd, TN17 2PT, NW : 2 ¼ m. by A 229 on A 262 ℰ 712032, Fax
712931, ⩽, « Gardens » – 📺 ☎ 🅿. 🔼 VISA
closed first week January – M (closed Sunday dinner) 18.75/19.75 **t.** ▮ 4.50 – **9 rm** ⇌ (dinner included) 85.00/150.00 **s.** – SB 115.00/345.00 **st.**

🏠 **Hartley Mount**, TN17 3QX, S : ½ m. on A 229 ℰ 712230, ⇆ – ⇆ 📺 ☎ 🅿. ⅍
M (bar lunch)/dinner 16.00 **st.** ▮ 2.75 – **5 rm** ⇌ 45.00/80.00 **st.**

🏠 **Old Cloth Hall** ⑤, TN17 3NR, E : 1 m. by Tenterden Rd ℰ 712220, ⩽, « Tudor manor
house, gardens », ⅄, park, ⅍ – 📺 🅿. ⅍
M (unlicensed) (dinner only, residents only) 20.00 – **3 rm** ⇌ 35.00/85.00.

at Sissinghurst NE : 1 ¾ m. by B 2189 on A 262 – ✉ ☎ 0580 Cranbrook :

X **Rankins**, The Street, TN17 2JH, ℰ 713964 – 🔼 VISA
closed Sunday dinner, Monday, Tuesday, first 2 weeks May, 1 week October, Christmas Day
and Bank Holidays – M (dinner only and Sunday lunch)/dinner/21.00 **t.** ▮ 3.10.

FORD Stone St. ℰ 712121   RENAULT Wilsley Pound ℰ 713262

CRANLEIGH Surrey **404** S 30 – ECD : Wednesday – ✆ 0483.
♦London 42 – ♦Brighton 36 – Reading 36 – ♦Southampton 58.
　　✕✕　**Restaurant Bonnett,** High St., GU6 8AE, ✆ 273889, French rest. – 🅐 🅐🅔 **VISA**
　　　　　closed Saturday lunch, Sunday dinner and Monday – **M** 12.50/23.50 t. 🍷 3.50.

CRANTOCK Cornwall **403** E 32 – see Newquay.

CRAVEN ARMS Shropshire **403** L 26 – ✆ 058 87 Little Brompton.
♦London 170 – ♦Birmingham 47 – Hereford 32 – Shrewsbury 21.
　　↑　**Old Rectory** ⌂, Hopesay, SY7 8HD, W : 3 ¾ m. by B 4368 ✆ 245, ≼, « Part 17C », 🐎 –
　　　📺 🅿 – *closed 23 to 30 December* – **M** 13.00 t. – **3 rm** ⊑ 38.00/55.00 t.

CRAWLEY West Sussex **404** T 30 – pop. 80 113 – ECD : Wednesday – ✆ 0293.
　📍18 Cottesmore, Buchan Hill ✆ 28256, S : 4 m. on plan of Gatwick Z – 🏴9 Gatwick Manor ✆ 24470,
　N : 5 m. on plan of Gatwick Y – ♦London 33 – ♦Brighton 21 – Lewes 23 – Royal Tunbridge Wells 23.

Plan of enlarged Area : see Gatwick

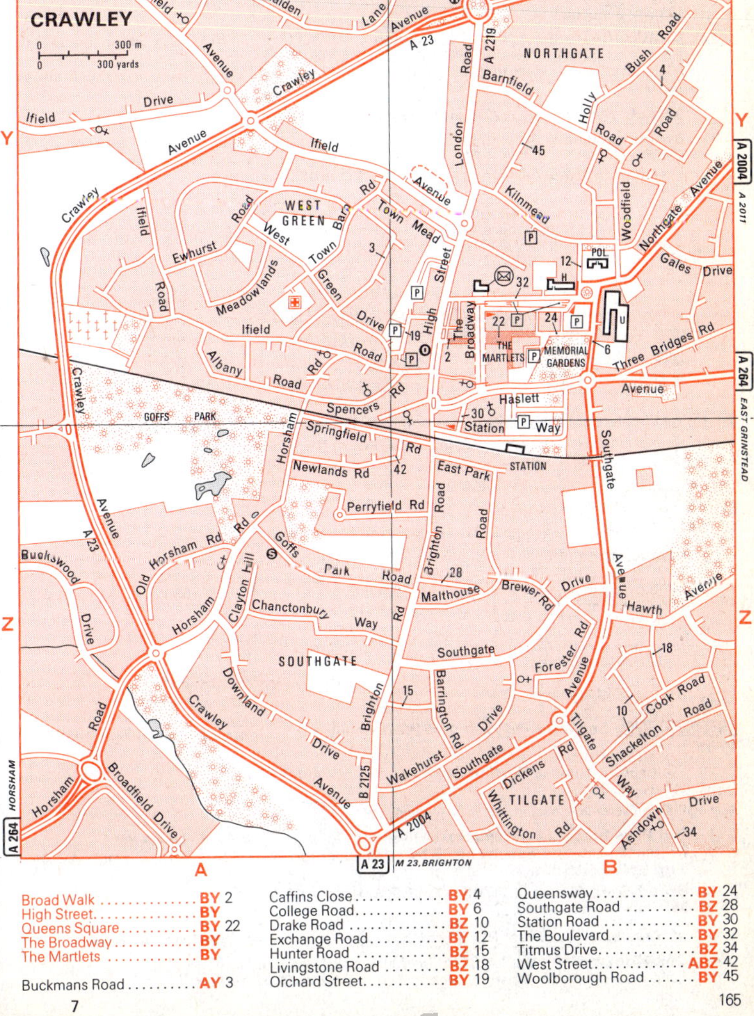

Broad Walk	**BY** 2	Caffins Close	**BY** 4
High Street	**BY**	College Road	**BY** 6
Queens Square	**BY** 22	Drake Road	**BZ** 10
The Broadway	**BY**	Exchange Road	**BY** 12
The Martlets	**BY**	Hunter Road	**BZ** 15
		Livingstone Road	**BZ** 18
Buckmans Road	**AY** 3	Orchard Street	**BY** 19

Queensway	**BY** 24
Southgate Road	**BZ** 28
Station Road	**BY** 30
The Boulevard	**BY** 32
Titmus Drive...........	**BZ** 34
West Street............	**ABZ** 42
Woolborough Road	**BY** 45

🏨 **George** (T.H.F.), High St., RH10 1BS, ✆ 24215, Telex 87385, Fax 553411 – ⊱✕ rm 📺 ☎ 🅿
– 🛎 35. 🆂 AE ⓄＤ VISA
M 11.95/13.95 **st.** and a la carte ❘ 3.95 – 🖂 7.00 – **76 rm** 73.00/120.00 **st.** – SB (weekends only) 85.00 **st.**
BY o

🏨 **Crest** (Crest), Langley Drive, Tushmore Roundabout, RH11 7SX, ✆ 29991, Telex 877311,
Fax 515913, 🆂 – 🛗 ⊱✕ rm 📺 ☎ 🅿 – 🛎 200. 🆂 AE ⓄＤ VISA
M 11.50/14.50 **st.** and a la carte – 🖂 7.70 – **225 rm** 81.00/95.00 **st.** – SB (weekends
only) 96.00/110.00 **st.**
BY n

🏨 **Goffs Park,** Goffs Park Rd, Southgate, RH11 8AX, ✆ 35447, Group Telex 87415, Fax
542050, 🍴 – 📺 ☎ 🅿 – 🛎 120. 🆂 AE ⓄＤ VISA
M (closed Saturday lunch) 9.50/12.50 **st.** and a la carte ❘ 4.20 – **64 rm** 🖂 70.00/90.00 **st.**
AZ s

at County Oak N : 1 ½ m. by A 2219 on A 23 – 🖂 ☎ 0293 Crawley :

🏠 Gatwick Manor, London Rd, RH10 2ST, ✆ 26301, Telex 87529, 🍴 – 📺 ☎ 🅿 – 🛎
M (grill rest.) – **30 rm**.
Y n

at Copthorne NE : 4 ½ m. on A 264 – BY – 🖂 Crawley – ☎ 0342 Copthorne :

🏨 Effingham Park, West Park Rd, RH10 3EU, ✆ 714994, ≤, 🆂, ⛳, 🍴, park – 🛗 ▤ rest 📺 ☎
🦽 🅿 – 🛎
118 rm, 3 suites.

🏨 **Copthorne** (Best Western), Copthorne Rd, RH10 3PG, ✆ 714971, Telex 95500, Fax 717375,
🍴, park, squash – ⊱✕ rm 📺 ☎ 🅿 – 🛎 90. 🆂 AE ⓄＤ VISA 🈺
M 12.50 **st.** and a la carte 26.00/36.00 **t.** ❘ 5.00 – 🖂 7.95 – **255 rm** 80.00/100.00 **t.**, **5 suites**
200.00 **t.**

at Ifield NW : 2 m. by A 2219 off Ifield Av. – AY – 🖂 ☎ 0293 Crawley :

🏠 **Brooklyn Manor** ⬥ without rest., Bonnetts Lane, RH11 0NY, ✆ 546024, 🍴 – 📺 🅿. 🆂
AE VISA 🈺
closed 24 December–4 January – 🖂 3.00 – **11 rm** 18.00/36.00 **st.**

AUSTIN-ROVER Copthorne ✆ 713933
CITROEN 163-165 Three Bridges Rd ✆ 25533
FORD Worth Park Av., Three Bridges ✆ 28381
OPEL-VAUXHALL Fleming Way ✆ 29771
PEUGEOT-TALBOT Barton ✆ 543232
RENAULT Orchard St. ✆ 23323

SAAB Turners Hill ✆ 715467
SKODA Balcombe Rd ✆ 882620
VW-AUDI Overdene Drive ✆ 515551

◍ ATS Reynolds Rd, West Green ✆ 33151/2

☛ *When in a hurry use the Michelin Main Road Maps :*
920 *Europe,* **980** *Greece,* **984** *Germany,* **985** *Scandinavia-Finland,*
986 *Great Britain and Ireland,* **987** *Germany-Austria-Benelux,* **988** *Italy,*
989 *France,* **990** *Spain-Portugal and* **991** *Yugoslavia.*

CREWE Cheshire **402 403 404** M 24 – pop. 59 097 – ECD : Wednesday – ☎ 0270.
Envir. : Sandbach (Two Crosses★ 7C, in Market Place) NE : 10 m.
⛳ Fields Rd ✆ 584099, E : 2 ¼ m. by A 534.
🚗 ✆ 214343.
🅸 Market Hall, Earle St. ✆ 583191 ext 691.
◆London 174 – Chester 24 – ◆Liverpool 49 – ◆Manchester 36 – ◆Stoke-on-Trent 15.

🏨 **Crewe Arms** (Embassy), Nantwich Rd, CW1 1DW, ✆ 213204, Fax 588615 – ⊱✕ rm 📺 ☎
🅿 – 🛎 80. 🆂 AE ⓄＤ VISA
M (carving rest.) 9.50/10.50 **st.** and a la carte ❘ 3.80 – 🖂 6.50 – **53 rm** 45.00/70.00 **st.** –
SB (weekends only) 52.00 **st.**

CITROEN Woolstanwood ✆ 213495
FIAT Cross Green ✆ 500437
PEUGEOT-TALBOT 613 Crewe Rd, Wistaston ✆
664111
SEAT West St. ✆ 214317

VOLVO Earle St. ✆ 587711
VW-AUDI Oak St. ✆ 213241

◍ ATS Gresty Rd ✆ 256285/6

CREWKERNE Somerset **403** L 31 The West Country G. – pop. 6 018 – ECD : Thursday –
☎ 0460.
Envir. : Cricket St. Thomas Wildlife Park★, W: 5 m. – Forde Abbey★, SW: 7 m. – Clapton Court
Gardens★ AC, S: 5 m.
◆London 145 – Exeter 38 – ◆Southampton 81 – Taunton 20.

🏠 **Old Parsonage,** 55-59 Barn St., TA18 8BP, ✆ 73516 – 📺 ☎ 🅿. 🆂 AE ⓄＤ VISA
M (dinner only and Sunday lunch by arrangement)/dinner 11.95 **t.** and a la carte ❘ 2.75 –
9 rm 🖂 37.50/55.00 **t.** – SB 80.00 **st.**

🏠 **Broadview,** 43 East St., TA18 7AG, ✆ 73424, 🍴 – 📺 🅿
M 7.95 – **3 rm** 🖂 22.50/27.00.

at Haselbury Plucknett NE : 2 ¾ m. by A 30 on A 3066 – 🖂 ☎ 0460 Crewkerne :

🏠 **Oak House,** North St., TA18 7RB, ✆ 73625, « 16C thatched cottage », 🍴 – 🅿
Easter-October – **M** (by arrangement) 8.00 – **8 rm** 🖂 16.00/38.00 **st.**

CRICCIETH Gwynedd **402** **403** H 25 – pop. 1 535 – ECD : Wednesday – ✆ 076 671 (4 fig.) or 0766 (6 fig.).

See : Castle ≼⋆⋆ *AC* – ⊞₁₈ Ednyfed Hill ✆ 2154.

♦London 249 – Caernarfon 17 – Shrewsbury 85.

🏠 **Plas Isa**, Porthmadog Rd, LL52 0HP, ✆ 522443 – TV ☎ P. ⛔ ⑩ VISA
M *(closed Sunday dinner)* (dinner only and Sunday lunch)/dinner 10.00 **st.** and a la carte
⌀ 3.00 – **12 rm** ⌁ 25.00/40.00 **st.** – SB 50.00/60.00 **st.**

↑ **Glyn-y-Coed**, Porthmadog Rd, LL52 0HP, ✆ 522870 – TV P
closed Christmas and New Year – **M** 6.75 **st.** ⌀ 2.25 – **10 rm** ⌁ 13.50/34.00 **t.**

↑ **Craig-y-Môr**, West Par., LL52 0EN, ✆ 522830, ≼ – TV ☎ P
closed November and December – **M** 6.00 **st.** – **7 rm** ⌁ 12.50/29.00 **st.**

AUDI-VW. MERCEDES-BENZ Caernarfon Rd ✆ 2516

FIAT Ala Rd, Pwllheli ✆ 612827
VOLVO Penamser Rd ✆ (Portmadoc) 3717

CRICK Northants. **403** **404** Q 26 – see Rugby.

CRICKHOWELL Powys **403** K 28 – pop. 1 979 – ECD : Wednesday – ✆ 0873.

Envir. : Tretower Court and Castle⋆, NW : 2 ½ m.

♦London 169 – Abergavenny 6 – Brecon 14 – Newport 25.

🏛 **Gliffaes Country House** ⟆, NP8 1RH, W : 3 ¾ m. by A 40 ✆ 0874 (Bwlch) 730371, ≼,
« Country house and gardens on the banks of the River Usk », ⟆, park, ✗ – ⟞✗ rest ☎
P. ⛔ AE ⑩ VISA ⛬
closed 31 December-10 March – **M** (buffet lunch)/dinner 13.00 **st.** and a la carte ⌀ 3.50 –
19 rm ⌁ 24.00/64.00 **st.** – SB 42.00/50.00 **st.**

🏛 **Bear**, High St., NP8 1BW, ✆ 810408, Fax 811696 – TV ☎ P. ⛔ AE VISA
M *(closed Sunday)* (bar lunch)/dinner a la carte 13.25/19.00 **t.** ⌀ 3.50 – **29 rm** ⌁ 34.00/58.00 **t.**

CRICKLADE Wilts **403** **404** O 29 – pop. 3 574 – ECD : Wednesday and Saturday – ✆ 0793 Swindon.

♦London 90 – ♦Bristol 45 – Gloucester 27 – ♦Oxford 34 – Swindon 6.

🏛 **Cricklade H. & Country Club,** Common Hill, SN6 6HA, SW : 1 m. on B 4040 ✆ 750751,
Fax 751767, ≼, ⛿, ⊺₉, park, ✗ – TV ☎ P – 🏌 120. ⛔ AE VISA ⛬
M 10.50/15.00 **t.** and a la carte ⌀ 4.20 – **45 rm** ⌁ 65.00/90.00 **t.**

✗✗ **White's,** 93 High St., SN2 6DF, ✆ 751110 – ⛔ VISA
closed Sunday, 2 weeks August and Christmas-New Year – **M** a la carte 16.50/25.00 **t.**
and a la carte ⌀ 4.00.

CRIPP'S CORNER East Sussex – see Sedlescombe.

CROMER Norfolk **404** X 25 – ECD : Wednesday – ✆ 0263.

♦London 132 – ♦Norwich 23.

↑ **Morden House**, 20 Cliff Av., NR27 0AN, ✆ 513396 – ⟞✗ rest
M 7.50 **st.** ⌀ 3.00 – **7 rm** ⌁ 14.50/33.00 **st.** – SB 36.00/42.00 **st.**

↑ **Danum House** without rest., 22 Pauls Lane, Overstrand, NR27 0PE, E : 1 ½ m. on B 1159
✆ 026 378 (Overstrand) 327, ⧖ – TV – **6 rm**.

↑ **Birch House** without rest., 34 Cabbell Rd, NR27 9HX, ✆ 512521 – ⟞✗ TV. ⛬
7 rm ⌁ 11.00/22.00 **st.**

CROOK Durham **401** **402** O 19 – ✉ ✆ 0388 Bishop Auckland.

♦London 261 – ♦Carlisle 65 – ♦Middlesbrough 34 – ♦Newcastle-upon-Tyne 27.

🏛 Helme Park Hall ⟆, DL13 4NW, NW : 3¼ m. by A 689 on A 68 ✆ 730970, ≼, ⧖, park – TV
☎ P – **10 rm**.

↑ **Greenhead,** Fir Tree, Bishop Auckland Rd, DL15 8BL, SW : 3 ½ m. by A 689 off A 68
✆ 763143, « 18C house », ⧖ – TV P. ⛔ VISA ⛬
M 8.50 **s.** ⌀ 3.50 – **6 rm** ⌁ 25.00/35.00 **st.**

CROSBY-ON-EDEN Cumbria **401** **402** L 29 – see Carlisle.

CROSCOMBE Somerset **403** **404** M 30 – see Shepton Mallet.

CROSSGATES Powys **403** J 27 – ✉ Llandrindod Wells – ✆ 059 787 Penybont.

♦London 172 – ♦Birmingham 81 – Hereford 39 – Shrewsbury 60.

↑ **Guidfa House** without rest., LD1 6RF, ✆ 241, ⧖ – P. ⛬
7 rm ⌁ 17.00/35.00 **st.**

CROSS HANDS Dyfed **403** H 28 – ✆ 0269.

♦London 208 – Fishguard 63 – ♦Swansea 19.

🏛 **Travelodge** without rest., SA14 6NW, on A 48 ✆ 845700 – TV ☎ ♿ P. ⛔ AE VISA
32 rm 21.50/27.00 **t.**

CROWBOROUGH East Sussex **404** U 30 – pop. 17 008 – ECD : Wednesday – ☎ 0892 Tunbridge Wells – ◆London 45 – ◆Brighton 25 – Maidstone 26.

  🏨 **Winston Manor,** Beacon Rd, TN6 1AD, on A 26 ℰ 652772, Fax 665537, ☒ – 🛗 📺 ☎ 🅿
    – 🔺 150. 🆎 AE ⑩ VISA
    M (bar lunch Saturday) 8.50/9.50 **t.** and a la carte – **50 rm** � 50.00/70.00 **t.** – SB (weekends only) 67.00 **st.**

AUSTIN-ROVER Beacon Rd ℰ 652777
FORD Crowborough Hill ℰ 652175
TALBOT Church Rd ℰ 653424

          〇 ATS Church Rd ℰ 662100

CROWTHORNE Berks. **404** R 29 – pop. 19 166 – ECD : Wednesday – ☎ 0344.
◆London 42 – Reading 15.

  🏨 **Waterloo** (T.H.F.), Dukes Ride, RG11 7NW, on B 3348 ℰ 777711, Telex 848139, Fax 778913
    – ⇆ rm 📺 ☎ 🅿 – 🔺 45. 🆎 AE ⑩ VISA
    M 12.95/15.95 **st.** and a la carte 🍾 3.60 – ⊆ 7.00 – **58 rm** 70.00/95.00 **st.** – SB (weekends only) (except Easter and Christmas-New Year) 70.00/96.00 **st.**

  ⌂ **Dial House,** 62 Dukes Ride, RG11 6DL, ℰ 776941, ☞ – ⇆ rest 📺 ☎ 🅿. 🆎 VISA 🛇
    M 12.00 **st.** 🍾 2.20 – **15 rm** ⊆ 27.00/62.00 **st.**

  XX **Beijing,** 103 Old Wokingham Rd, RG11 6LH, NE : ¾ m. by A 3095 ℰ 778802, Chinese rest.
    – 🍽 🅿. 🆎 AE ⑩ VISA
    closed Sunday lunch – **M** approx. 17.80 **t.**

CROXDALE Durham – see Durham.

CROYDE Devon **403** H 30 The West Country G. – ✉ Braunton – ☎ 0271.
◆London 232 – Barnstaple 10 – Exeter 50 – Taunton 61.

  🏠 **Baggy Point** 🐾, Baggy Point, EX33 1PA, ℰ 890204, ≼ Appledore, Lundy Island and cliff,
    ☞ – 📺 🅿. 🛇 – **10 rm**.

  🏠 **Whiteleaf,** Hobbs Hill, EX33 1PN, ℰ 890266, ☞ – 📺 ☎ 🅿. 🆎 VISA
    M (dinner only) 15.00 **st.** 🍾 3.00 – **5 rm** ⊆ 27.00/44.00 **st.**

  🏨 **Kittiwell House,** St. Mary's Rd, EX33 1PG, ℰ 890247, « 16C thatched Devon longhouse »
    – ⇆ rm 📺 🅿. 🆎 AE VISA
    closed mid January-mid February – **M** (dinner only and Sunday lunch)/dinner 12.50 **t.**
    and a la carte 🍾 3.50 – **12 rm** ⊆ 33.00/56.00 **t.** – SB (except summer) 68.00/80.00 **st.**

CRUDWELL Wilts. **403 404** N 29 – see Malmesbury.

CRUG-Y-BAR Dyfed **403** I 27 – ECD : Saturday – ✉ Llanwrda – ☎ 0558 Talley.
◆London 213 – Carmarthen 26 – ◆Swansea 36.

  ♔ **Glanrannell Park** 🐾, SA19 8SA, SW : ½ m. by B 4302 ℰ 685230, ≼, ⤚, ☞, park – 🅿
    April-October – **M** (dinner only and Saturday lunch)/dinner 14.00 **t.** 🍾 2.25 – **8 rm**
    ⊆ 25.00/50.00 **t.** – SB 60.00/66.00 **st.**

CRYMMYCH Dyfed **403** G 28 – ✉ Whitland – ☎ 099 47 Hebron.
◆London 245 – Carmarthen 25 – Fishguard 19.

  ⌂ **Preseli Farm Stud** 🐾, SA34 0YP, S : 4 m. by A 478 and lane opposite disused quarry
    ℰ 425, ≼, ☞, park – 🅿
    closed January – **M** (communal dining) 12.50 **st.** 🍾 3.50 – **4 rm** ⊆ 28.00/50.00 **st.**

CUCKFIELD West Sussex **404** T 30 – pop. 2 650 – ECD : Wednesday – ☎ 0444 Haywards
Heath – ◆London 40 – ◆Brighton 15.

  🏨 **Ockenden Manor** 🐾, Ockenden Lane, RH17 5LD, ℰ 416111, Fax 415549, « Part 16C
    manor », ☞ – 📺 ☎ 🅿. 🆎 AE ⑩ VISA 🛇
    M 13.50/26.00 **t.** 🍾 4.50 – ⊆ 2.75 – **12 rm** 55.00/120.00 **t.**, **2 suites** 120.00/130.00 **t.** –
    SB (weekends only) (except Christmas and New Year) 103.00/120.00 **st.**

CUFFLEY Herts. **404** T 28 – pop. 4 875 – ECD : Thursday – ☎ 0707 Potters Bar.
◆London 16 – ◆Cambridge 44 – Luton 26.

  XX **Gable House** with rm, 14-16 Newgate Street Village, SG13 8RA, N : 3 m. by B 157
    ℰ 873899 – 📺 ☎ 🅿. 🆎 AE ⑩ VISA 🛇
    M 11.00/14.50 **t.** and a la carte 22.00/25.50 **t.** 🍾 5.00 – ⊆ 6.50 – **2 rm** 45.00 **t.**

CUMNOR Oxon. **403 404** P 28 – see Oxford.

CWMBRAN Gwent **403** K 29 – pop. 44 592 – ECD : Wednesday – ☎ 063 33.
🛈 Greenmeadow, Treherbert Rd ℰ 69321 – ◆London 149 – ◆Bristol 35 – ◆Cardiff 17 – Newport 5.

  🏨 **Parkway,** Cwmbran Drive, NP44 3UW, S : 1 m. by A 4051 ℰ 71199, Telex 497887, Fax
    69160 – ⇆ rm 📺 ☎ & 🅿 – 🔺 300. 🆎 AE ⑩ VISA
    M *(closed Saturday lunch)* 10.40 **st.** and a la carte 12.55/22.40 **st.** – **89 rm** ⊆ 36.25/59.25 **s.**
    1 suite 61.85/82.45 **s.**

〇 ATS Station Rd ℰ 4964

DALLINGTON East Sussex **404** V 31 – pop. 286 – ⊠ Heathfield – ✆ 042 482 Brightling.

◆London 59 – ◆Brighton 26 – Hastings 14 – Maidstone 34.

✗ **Little Byres,** Christmas Farm, Battle Rd, Wood's Corner, TN21 9LE, on B 2096 ✆ 230, « Converted timber framed barn », 🚗 – 🅿. 🅰 *VISA*
closed Sunday and January – **M** (dinner only) 19.50 **t.** ⌁ 3.95.

DARESBURY Cheshire **402 403 404** M 23 – pop. 353 – ⊠ ✆ 0925 Warrington.

◆London 197 – Chester 16 – ◆Liverpool 22 – ◆Manchester 25.

🏰 **Lord Daresbury** (De Vere), Chester Rd, WA4 4BB, on A 56 ✆ 67331, Telex 629330, Fax 65615, 🔾, squash – 🛗 🚪 rm 📺 ☎ 🅿 – 🕍 500. 🅰 🅰🅴 ⑩ *VISA* 🕸
M 13.95 **st.** and a la carte ⌁ 4.00 – **138 rm** ☕ 55.00/110.00 **st.**, **3 suites** 105.00/125.00 **st.** – SB (weekends only) 80.00/100.00 **st.**

DARLASTON West Midlands **402** ⑨ **404** ⑲ – pop. 13 322 – ⊠ Darlaston – ✆ 021 Birmingham.

◆London 131 – ◆Birmingham 9 – Wolverhampton 5.

🏠 **Petite** without rest., Stafford Rd, Alma Industrial Estate, WS10 8UA, ✆ 526 5482 – 📺 🅿. 🅰 🅰🅴 ⑩ *VISA*
☕ 3.00 – **10 rm** 25.00/32.00 **st.**

🛞 ATS Pinfold St., Wednesbury ✆ 2520/3456

DARLINGSCOTT Warw. – see Shipston-on-Stour.

DARLINGTON Durham **402** P 20 – pop. 85 519 – ECD : Wednesday – ✆ 0325.

🏌 Blackwell Grange, Briar Close ✆ 464464, S : 1 m. on A 66 – 🏌 Stressholme, Snipe Lane ✆ 461002, S : 2 m. on A 67.

✈ Tees-side Airport : ✆ 332811, E : 6 m. by A 67.

🛈 District Library, Crown St. ✆ 469858.

◆London 251 – ◆Leeds 61 – ◆Middlesbrough 14 – ◆Newcastle-upon-Tyne 35.

🏰 **Blackwell Grange Moat House** (Q.M.H.) 🦢, Blackwell Grange, DL3 8QH, SW : 2 m. on A 66 ✆ 380888, Telex 587272, Fax 380899, 🏌, 🚗, ✗ – 🛗 🚪 📺 ☎ 🅿 – 🕍 150. 🅰 🅰🅴 ⑩ *VISA*
M 8.95/15.95 **st.** and a la carte ⌁ 4.50 – **95 rm** ☕ 65.00/120.00 **st.**, **3 suites** 120.00/155.00 **st.** – SB (weekends only) 88.00 **st.**

🏨 **King's Head** (Swallow), Priestgate, DL1 1NW, ✆ 380222, Telex 587112, Fax 382006 – 🛗 📺 ☎ 🅿 – 🕍 200. 🅰 🅰🅴 ⑩ *VISA*
M 11.75 **st.** and a la carte ⌁ 4.25 – **60 rm** ☕ 54.00/72.00 **st.** – SB (weekends only) 70.00 **st.**

🏨 **Stakis White Horse** (Stakis), Harrowgate Hill, DL1 3AD, N : 2 ¼ m. on A 167 ✆ 382121, Group Telex 778704, Fax 355953 – 🛗 📺 ☎ 🅿 – 🕍 50. 🅰 🅰🅴 ⑩ *VISA*
☕ 7.25 – **40 rm** 55.00/78.00 **st.** – SB 50.00/67.00 **st.**

✗✗ **Bishop's House,** 38 Coniscliffe Rd, DL3 7RG, ✆ 382200 – 🅰 🅰🅴 ⑩ *VISA*
closed Sunday and Bank Holidays – **M** 11.00/18.00 **t.** and a la carte ⌁ 4.00.

at Coatham Mundeville N : 4 m. by A 167 – ⊠ Darlington – ✆ 0325 Aycliffe :

🏨 **Hall Garth Country House** 🦢, DL1 3LU, ✆ 300400, Fax 310083, 🔾 heated, 🚗, ✗ – 🚪 rest 📺 ☎ 🅿. 🅰 🅰🅴 ⑩ *VISA* 🕸
M *(closed Sunday dinner)* 9.50/25.00 **t.** ⌁ 4.10 – **18 rm** ☕ 50.00/77.00 **t.**, **2 suites** 45.00/88.00 **t** – SB (weekends only) 76.00/82.00 **st.**

at Tees-side Airport E : 5 ½ m. by A 67 – ⊠ ✆ 0325 Darlington :

🏨 St. George (Mt. Charlotte), DL2 1RH, ✆ 332631, Telex 587623, squash – 📺 ☎ 🅿 – 🕍 60. 🕸 – **59 rm**, **1 suite**.

at Neasham SE : 6 ½ m. by A 66 off A 167 – ⊠ ✆ 0325 Darlington :

🏨 Newbus Arms (Best Western) 🦢, Hurworth Rd, DL2 1PE, W : ½ m. ✆ 721071, 🚗, squash – 📺 ☎ 🅿 – 🕍 30
15 rm.

at Headlam NW : 6 m. by A 67 – ⊠ Gainford – ✆ 0325 Darlington :

🏨 **Headlam Hall** 🦢, DL2 3HA, ✆ 730238, ≼, « Part Jacobean mansion », 🚗, park, ✗ – 📺 ☎ 🅿. 🅰 🅰🅴 *VISA* 🕸
closed 24 December-2 January – **M** *(closed Sunday dinner)* (dinner only and Sunday lunch)/dinner 19.50 **t.** and a la carte ⌁ 2.50 – **12 rm** ☕ 38.00/57.00 **st.**, **3 suites** 67.00 **st.**

AUSTIN-ROVER Croft Rd ✆ 488888
CITROEN 163 Northgate ✆ 468753
FIAT Woodland Rd ✆ 483251
FORD St. Cuthberts Way ✆ 467581
HONDA Chestnut St. ✆ 485141
LADA Albert Rd ✆ 485759
NISSAN Haughton Rd ✆ 462222
TOYOTA Neasham Rd. ✆ 482141

VAUXHALL Chestnut St. ✆ 466155
VAUXHALL-OPEL Whessoe Rd ✆ 466044
VOLVO Chestnut Street ✆ 353536
VW-AUDI 28-56 West Auckland Rd, Faverdale ✆ 353737

🛞 ATS Albert St., off Neasham Rd ✆ 469271/469693

DARTINGTON Devon **403** I 32 – see Totnes.

DARTMOUTH Devon **403** J 32 **The West Country** G. – pop. 5 282 – ECD : Wednesday and Saturday – ✆ 080 43.

See : Site★★ (≤★) – Dartmouth Castle (≤★★★) AC.

Envir. : Start Point (≤★), S : 15 m. including 1 m. on foot – 🛈 11 Duke St. ✆ 4224 (summer only).

♦London 236 – Exeter 36 – ♦Plymouth 35.

🏨 **Royal Castle**, 11 The Quay, TQ6 9PS, ✆ 4004, Fax 5445, ≤ – 📺 ☎. 🔄 *VISA*
  M (bar lunch Monday to Saturday)/dinner 15.00 **t.** and a la carte ⬧ 3.95 – **20 rm**
  ☲ 33.00/80.00 **t.** – SB 65.00/90.00 **st.**

🏨 **Dart Marina** (T.H.F.), Sandquay, TQ6 9PH, ✆ 2580, ≤ – ✎ rm 📺 ☎ 🅿. 🔄 AE ⑩ *VISA*
  M 13.70/17.75 **st.** – ☲ 7.00 – **33 rm** 56.00/88.00 **st.** **1 suite** 100.00 **st.** – SB 40.00/112.00 **st.**

⌂ **Three Feathers** without rest., 51 Victoria Rd, TQ6 9RT, ✆ 834694 – 📺 🅿. ⅏
  5 rm ☲ 14.00/30.00 **s.**

XX **Mansion House**, Mansion House St., TQ6 9AG, ✆ 5474
  closed Saturday lunch, Sunday, Monday and 2 weeks February – **M** 18.00/26.00 **st.** ⬧ 3.50.

XX **Carved Angel**, 2 South Embankment, TQ6 9BH, ✆ 2465, ≤
  closed Sunday dinner, Monday and January – **M** 21.00/32.00 **st.** and a la carte 23.50/30.50 **st.**
  ⬧ 4.50.

at Stoke Fleming SW : 3 m. on A 379 – ⊠ Dartmouth – ✆ 0803 Stoke Fleming :

🏨 **Stoke Lodge**, Cinders Lane, TQ6 0RA, ✆ 770523, ≤, ⌇ heated, 🔄, 🚗 – 📺 ☎ 🅿
  M 6.95/11.95 **t.** and a la carte ⬧ 2.95 – **24 rm** ☲ 33.00/58.00 **t.** – SB (except summer) 59.00/64.00 **st.**

⌖ **Endsleigh**, New Rd, TQ6 0NR, ✆ 770381 – 🅿
  M (bar lunch Monday to Saturday)/dinner 12.00 **t.** and a la carte – **8 rm** ☲ 15.00/35.00 **t.**

DAWLISH Devon **403** J 32 **The West Country** G. – pop. 8 030 – ECD : Thursday and Saturday – ✆ 0626.

🏌 Warren ✆ 862255, E : 1 ½ m – 🛈 The Lawn ✆ 863589.

♦London 215 – Exeter 13 – ♦Plymouth 40 – Torquay 11.

🏨 **Langstone Cliff**, Dawlish Warren, EX7 0NA, N : 2 m. by A 379 ✆ 865155, Fax 867166,
  ⌇ heated, 🔄, 🚗, ✕ – 🔊 📺 ☎ ⌖ 🅿 – 🔼 400. 🔄 AE ⑩ *VISA*
  M 8.00/10.50 **st.** ⬧ 3.80 – **64 rm** ☲ 36.00/70.00 **st.** – SB 70.00/90.00 **st.**

⌂ **Lynbridge**, 8 Barton Villas, The Bartons, EX7 9QJ, ✆ 862352, 🚗 – ✎ rest 🅿. ⅏
  May-September – **M** 4.00 – **7 rm** ☲ 15.00/30.00 **st.**

DEAL Kent **404** Y 30 – pop. 26 548 – ECD : Thursday – ✆ 0304 – 🛈 Town Hall, High St. ✆ 369576.

♦London 78 – Canterbury 19 – Dover 8.5 – Margate 16.

⌂ **Sutherland House**, 186 London Rd, CT14 9PT, ✆ 362853 – ✎ rm 🅿. ⅏
  M (by arrangement) 10.00 ⬧ 4.95 – **5 rm** ☲ 19.50/30.00.

⌂ **Blencathra Country** without rest., Kingsdown Hill, CT14 8EA, ✆ 373725, 🚗 – 📺 🅿. ⅏
  5 rm ☲ 14.00/30.00 **st.**

at Finglesham NW : 3 ½ m. by A 258 off North Bourne – ⊠ ✆ 0304 Deal :

⌂ **Finglesham Grange** ⌖, CT14 0NQ, NW : ¾ m. ✆ 611314, 🚗 – 🅿
  closed Christmas-New Year – **M** 8.50 **s.** – **3 rm** ☲ 22.50/35.00 **s.** – SB (October-March) 47.00 **st.**

⋓ ATS Gilford Rd ✆ 361543

DEDDINGTON Oxon. **403 404** Q 28 – pop. 1 617 – ✆ 0869.

♦London 72 – ♦Birmingham 46 – ♦Coventry 33 – ♦Oxford 18.

🏦 **Holcombe** (Best Western), High St., OX5 4SL, ✆ 38274, Fax 37167, 🚗 – 📺 ☎ 🅿. 🔄 AE ⑩ *VISA*
  M 15.50/16.50 **st.** and a la carte ⬧ 4.95 – **17 rm** ☲ 49.50/95.00 **st.** – SB 75.00/85.00 **st.**

X **Tiffany's**, Market Pl., OX5 4SE, ✆ 38813 – 🔄 ⑩ *VISA*
  closed Sunday, Monday, 2 weeks September and 1 week Christmas – **M** (dinner only) a la carte approx. 17.05 **t.** ⬧ 3.00.

DEDHAM Essex **404** W 28 – pop. 1 905 – ECD : Wednesday – ⊠ ✆ 0206 Colchester.

🛈 Countryside Centre, Duchy Barn, The Drift ✆ 323447 (summer only).

♦London 63 – Chelmsford 30 – Colchester 8 – ♦Ipswich 12.

🏨 **Maison Talbooth** ⌖ without rest., Stratford Rd, CO7 6HN, W : ½ m. ✆ 322367, Group Telex 987083, Fax 322752, ≤, 🚗 – 📺 ☎ 🅿. 🔄 *VISA* ⅏
  ☲ 5.00 – **9 rm** 70.00/120.00 **st.** **1 suite** 95.00/120.00 **st.**

XXX **Le Talbooth**, Gun Hill, CO7 6HP, W : 1 m. ✆ 323150, Group Telex 987083, Fax 322752, ≤,
  « Tudor house in attractive riverside setting », 🚗 – 🅿. 🔄 *VISA*
  M 15.00 **t.** (lunch) and a la carte 26.25/31.25 **t.** ⬧ 4.90.

XX **Dedham Vale H. and Terrace Rest.** with rm, Stratford Rd, CO7 6HW, W : ¾ m.
  ✆ 322273, Group Telex 987083, Fax 322752, ≤, 🚗 – 📺 ☎ 🅿. 🔄 *VISA* ⅏
  M *(closed Saturday lunch and Sunday dinner)* (buffet lunch)/dinner 26.00 **t.** ⬧ 3.60 – ☲ 5.50 – **6 rm** 65.00/85.00 **st.**

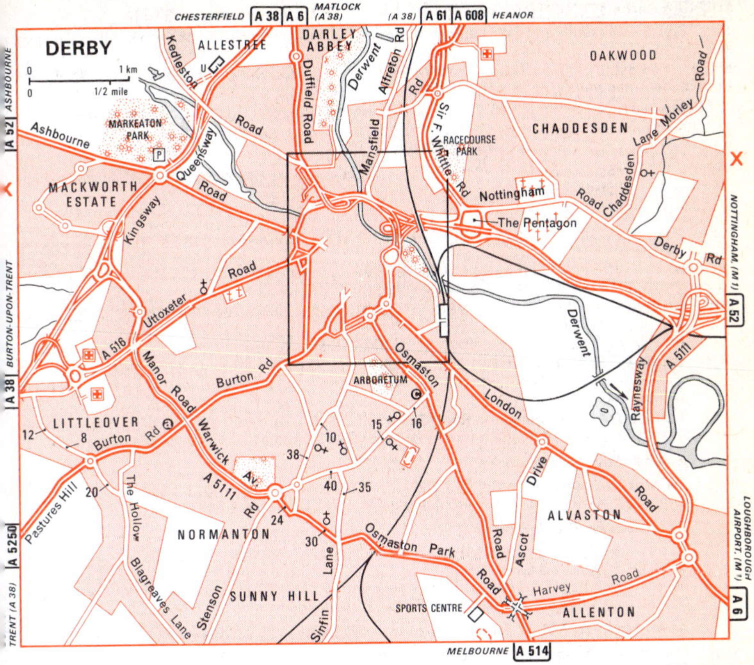

Corn Market . . . . Z 13
Iron Gate . . . . Y 22
Shopping Centre . . . . Z
Victoria Street . . . . Z 39

Albert Street . . . . Z 2
Babington Lane . . . . Z 3
Bold Lane . . . . Y 4
Bradshaw Way . . . . Z 5
Cathedral Road . . . . Y 7
Chain Lane . . . . X 8
Charnwood Street . . . . . . Z 9
Church Street . . . . X 10
Corden Avenue . . . . X 12
Corporation Street . . . . . YZ 14
Dairy House Road . . . . . . X 15
Douglas Street . . . . X 16
Duffield Road . . . . Y 17
East Street . . . . Z 18
Full Street . . . . Y 19
Hillsway . . . . X 20
Jury Street . . . . Y 23
Kenilworth Avenue . . . . . X 24
King Street . . . . Y 25
Leopold Street . . . . Z 26
Market Place . . . . YZ 27
Midland Road . . . . Z 28
Mount Street . . . . Z 29
Newdigate Street . . . . . . X 30
Normanton Road . . . . Z 31
Queen Street . . . . Y 32
St. Mary's Gate . . . . Z 33
St. Peter's Street . . . . . . Z 34
St. Thomas Road . . . . . . X 35
Sacheveral Street . . . . . . Z 36
Stafford Street . . . . Z 37
Upper Dale Road . . . . . . X 38
Walbrook Road . . . . X 40
Wardwick . . . . Z 41

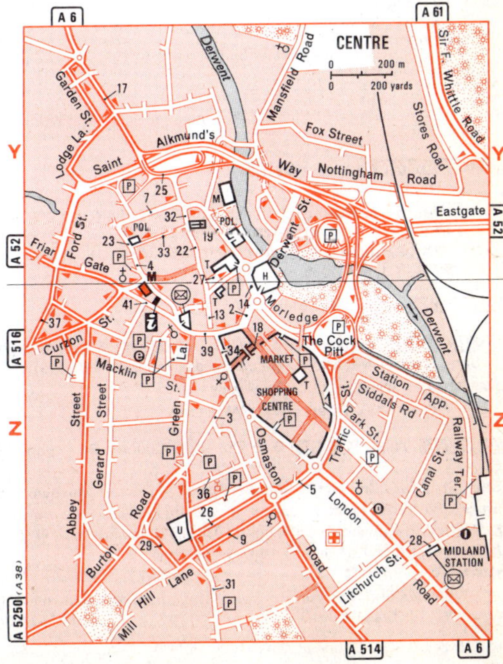

DERBY Derbs. 402 403 404 P 25 – pop. 218 026 – ECD : Wednesday – ☎ 0332.

See : Site★ – Museum and Art Gallery★ (Porcelain collection★, Wright of Derby collection★) YZ M.

Envir. : Kedleston Hall★★ (18C) AC, NW : 5 m. by Kedleston Rd X – Melbourne (St. Michael's Church : Norman nave★) S : 8 m. by A 514 X.

↟18 Shakespeare St., Sinfin ✆ 766323 X – ↟18 Mickleover, Uttoxeter Rd ✆ 513339, W : 3 m. X.

✈ East Midlands, Castle Donington ✆ 810621, Telex 37543, SE : 12 m. by A 6 X.

🛈 Central Library, The Wardwick ✆ 290664.

♦London 132 – ♦Birmingham 40 – ♦Coventry 49 – ♦Leicester 29 – ♦Manchester 62 – ♦Nottingham 16 – ♦Sheffield 47 – ♦Stoke-on-Trent 35.

Plan on preceding page

🏨 **Pennine** (De Vere), Macklin St., DE1 1LF, ✆ 41741, Fax 294549 – ▯ TV ☎ – 🏊 300. 🗗 AE ① VISA
Z e
M *(closed lunch Saturday and Sunday)* (carving lunch) 4.00/9.00 **st.** and a la carte ₪ 4.00 – **95 rm** ☟ 51.00/75.00 **st.** – SB (weekends only) 55.00/130.00 **st.**

🏨 **Midland**, Midland Rd, DE1 2SQ, ✆ 45894, Telex 378373, Fax 293522, 🐎 – TV ☎ P
🏊 150. 🗗 AE ① VISA
Z i
M 17.50 **st.** and a la carte – **60 rm** ☟ 52.00/67.00 **st.**

🏨 **Gables**, 119 London Rd, DE1 2QR, ✆ 40633, Fax 293502 – TV ☎ P. 🗗 AE VISA. 🐕
Z o
closed 25 December-1 January – **M** 6.50/9.50 **st.** and a la carte ₪ 5.95 – **77 rm** ☟ 29.50/68.00 **st.**

XX **La Gondola**, 220 Osmaston Rd, DE3 8JX, ✆ 32895 – P. 🗗 AE ① VISA
X c
closed Sunday – **M** (Dancing Saturday) 6.25/9.00 **st.** and a la carte 13.10/18.50 **st.** ₪ 3.75.

at Shardlow S : 6 m. on A 6 – X – ✉ ☎ 0332 Derby :

X **La Marina**, 134 London Rd, DE7 2GP, ✆ 792553, Italian rest. – P. 🗗 VISA
closed Monday – **M** 5.75 **t.** (lunch) and a la carte 9.00/14.50 **t.** ₪ 2.95.

at Littleover SW : 2 ½ m. on A 5250 – ✉ ☎ 0332 Derby :

🏨 **Crest** (Crest), Pastures Hill, DE3 7BA, ✆ 514933, Telex 377081, Fax 518668, 🐎 – ⇌ rm TV
☎ & P – 🏊 80. 🗗 AE ① VISA
X a
M *(closed lunch Saturday and Bank Holidays)* 7.15/14.30 **st.** and a la carte – ☟ 7.35 – **66 rm** 65.00/77.00 **st.**, **2 suites** 110.00 **st.** – SB (weekends only) 80.00 **st.**

at Mackworth NW : 2 ¾ m. by A 52 – X – ✉ Derby – ☎ 033 124 Kirk Langley :

🏨 **Mackworth**, Ashbourne Rd, DE3 4LY, on A 52 ✆ 324, 🐎 – TV ☎ P
M (grill rest.) – **14 rm**.

AUDI-VW 23-33 Sir Frank Whittle Rd ✆ 290022
AUSTIN-ROVER Derwent St. ✆ 31166
BMW King St. ✆ 369511
CITROEN, DAIHATSU Alfreton Rd ✆ 381502
FORD Normanton Rd ✆ 40271
MAZDA 574-576 Burton Rd ✆ 369723
NISSAN Mansfield Rd ✆ 292525
PEUGEOT-TALBOT 4 Chequers Rd, Pentagon Island ✆ 361626

RENAULT 1263 London Rd, Alvaston ✆ 571847
SUZUKI 34-39 Duffield Rd ✆ 32706
TOYOTA St. Alkmunds Way ✆ 49536
VAUXHALL-OPEL Pentagon Island, Nottingham Rd ✆ 362661
VOLVO Kedleston Rd ✆ 32625

🜛 ATS Gosforth Rd off Ascot Drive ✆ 40854
ATS 67 Bridge St. ✆ 47327

DERSINGHAM Norfolk 402 404 V 25 – pop. 3 263 – ☎ 0485.

♦London 110 – ♦Cambridge 53 – ♦Norwich 46.

⌂ **Westdene House**, 60 Hunstanton Rd, PE31 6HQ, ✆ 40395, 🐎 – TV P. 🗗 VISA
M (by arrangement) – **5 rm** ☟ 16.00/32.00 **st.**

⌂ **White House** without rest., 44 Hunstanton Rd, PE31 6HQ, ✆ 41895 – P
4 rm ☟ 11.00/26.00.

DETHICK Derbs. – see Matlock.

DEVIL'S BRIDGE (PONTARFYNACH) Dyfed 403 I 26 – ✉ Aberystwyth – ☎ 097 085 Ponterwyd – See : Site★ – Nature Trail (Mynach Falls and Devil's Bridge)★★.

♦London 230 – Aberystwyth 12 – Shrewsbury 66.

Hotels see : Aberystwyth W : 12 m.

DEVIZES Wilts. 403 404 O 29 The West Country G. – pop. 12 430 – ECD : Wednesday – ☎ 0380.

See : St. John's Church★★ – Market Place★ – Devizes Museum★ AC.

Envir. : Potterne : Porch House★★, S : 2 m. on A 360.

↟18 North Wilts., Bishop's Cannings ✆ 038 086 (Cannings) 627, N : 5 m.

🛈 Wharf Centre, Couch Lane ✆ 71069 (summer only).

♦London 98 – ♦Bristol 38 – Salisbury 25 – Swindon 19.

Hotels and Restaurants see : Melksham, W : 10 m. by A 361 and A 365

AUDI-VW The Green ✆ 3667
FORD New Park St. ✆ 3456
PEUGEOT-TALBOT Chirton ✆ 038 084 (Chirton) 281

RENAULT Bath Rd ✆ 2032
SEAT Market Lavington ✆ 812761
VAUXHALL-OPEL Lydeway ✆ 038 084 (Chirton) 456

DIDDLEBURY Shropshire **403** L 26 – pop. 526 – ⊠ Craven Arms – ✆ 058 476 Munslow.
Envir. : Wenlock Edge★ NW : 2 ½ m.
♦London 169 – ♦Birmingham 46.

⌂ **Glebe Farm** ⑤, SY7 9DH, ℰ 221, « Part Elizabethan house », 屛 – ⑁ rest ℗. ⌖
March-November – **M** (by arrangement) 10.95 **st.** ⌀ 3.00 – **6 rm** ⌷ 20.00/46.00 **st.** –
SB (weekends only) 59.90/67.90 **st.**

DINBYCH-Y-PSYGOD = Tenby.

DINNINGTON South Yorks. **402 403 404** Q 23 – pop. 1 870 – ⊠ Sheffield – ✆ 0909.
♦London 166 – Lincoln 37 – ♦Sheffield 12.

🏛 **Dinnington Hall** ⑤, Falcon Way, S31 7NY, off B 6060 ℰ 569661, Fax 563411, 屛 – Ⅳ ☎
℗. ◪ ⒶⒺ **VISA**
M (closed Sunday dinner) (lunch by arrangement)/dinner 15.50 **t.** and a la carte ⌀ 4.40 – ⌷
6.50 – **10 rm** 40.00/65.00 **t.**

DISLEY Cheshire **402 403 404** N 23 – pop. 3 425 – ECD : Wednesday – ⊠ Stockport –
✆ 066 32 (4 fig.) or 0663 (5 fig.).
🅕₁₈ Stanley Hall Lane ℰ 62071.
♦London 187 – Chesterfield 35 – ♦Manchester 12.

🏛 **Moorside** (Best Western) ⑤, Mudhurst Lane, Higher Disley, SK12 2AP, SE : 2 m.
by Buxton Old Rd ℰ 64151, Telex 665170, Fax 62794, ≤ – Ⅳ ☎ ℗ – 🏌 200. ◪ ⒶⒺ
⑩ **VISA**
M (bar lunch Saturday) 14.00/18.00 **st.** and a la carte ⌀ 6.00 – ⌷ 6.00 – **88 rm** 60.00/80.00 **st.**,
2 suites 110.00/170.00 **st.** – SB (weekends only) 56.00 **st.**

DISS Norfolk **404** X 26 – pop. 5 463 – ECD : Tuesday – ✆ 0379.
🅕₉ Stuston Common ℰ 2847.
♦London 98 – ♦Ipswich 25 – ♦Norwich 21 – Thetford 17.

🏠 Park (B.C.B.), 29 Denmark St., IP22 3LE, ℰ 642244, 屛 – Ⅳ ☎ ℗ – 🏌 . ⌖
17 rm.

※※ **Salisbury House** with rm, 84 Victoria Rd, IP22 3JG, ℰ 644738, « Stylishly decorated
Victorian house, garden » – Ⅳ ℗. ◪ **VISA** ⌖
closed Saturday lunch, Sunday, Monday, 2 weeks summer and 1 week Christmas –
M 11.00 **t.** (lunch) and a la carte 14.40/19.00 **t.** ⌀ 3.75 – ⌷ 3.00 – **2 rm** 36.00/62.00 **t.**

at Scole E : 2 m. by A 1066 on A 143 – ⊠ ✆ 0379 Diss :

🏛 Scole Inn (Best Western), Main St., IP21 4DR, ℰ 740481, Fax 740762, « 17C inn » – Ⅳ ☎ ℗
23 rm.

at Brome (Suffolk) SE : 2 ¾ m. by A 143 on B 1077 – ⊠ ✆ 0379 Eye :

🏛 **Oaksmere** ⑤, IP23 8AJ, ℰ 870326, Fax 870051, « Part 16C country house and gardens »,
park – Ⅳ ☎ ℗. ◪ ⒶⒺ ⑩ **VISA**
M a la carte 11.15/13.15 **t.** ⌀ 4.50 – **11 rm** ⌷ 36.00/53.00 **t.** – SB 75.00 **st.**

at South Lopham W : 5 ½ m. on A 1066 – ⊠ Diss – ✆ 037 988 Bressingham :

⌂ **Malting Farm** ⑤, Blo' Norton Rd, IP22 2HT, ℰ 201, ≤, « Working farm » – ⑁ ℗. ⌖
closed Christmas and New Year – **M** (by arrangement) – **3 rm** ⌷ 15.00/28.00 **st.**

at Fersfield NW : 7 m. by A 1066 – ⊠ Diss – ✆ 037 988 Bressingham :

⌂ **Strenneth Farmhouse** ⑤, Old Airfield Rd, IP22 2BP, ℰ 8182, 屛 – ℗. ◪ **VISA**
M 9.00 **st.** ⌀ 2.40 – **9 rm** ⌷ 14.00/36.00 **st.** – SB (November-March) 44.00/52.00 **st.**

AUSTIN-ROVER Victoria Rd ℰ 643141
FORD Park Rd ℰ 642311
VAUXHALL-OPEL 142-144 Victoria Rd ℰ 642241

ⓦ ATS Shelfanger Rd ℰ 642861/2

DITTON PRIORS Shropshire **403 404** M 26 – pop. 550 – ⊠ Bridgnorth – ✆ 074 634.
♦London 154 – ♦Birmingham 34 – Ludlow 13 – Shrewsbury 21.

※※ **Howard Arms**, WV16 6SQ, ℰ 200, 屛 – ℗. ◪ **VISA**
closed Sunday dinner, Monday, 2 weeks August and 2 weeks September – **M** (dinner only
and Sunday lunch)/dinner 15.00/21.00 **t.** ⌀ 3.70.

DOCKING Norfolk **404** V 25 – pop. 1 193 – ⊠ King's Lynn – ✆ 048 58.
♦London 118 – ♦Cambridge 63 – ♦Norwich 39.

⌂ **Holland House** without rest., Chequers St., PE31 8LH, ℰ 295, 屛 – Ⅳ ℗
closed 2 weeks Christmas-New Year – **5 rm** ⌷ 13.00/30.00 **st.**

DODDISCOMBSLEIGH Devon – see Exeter.

DOLGELLAU Gwynedd **402 403** I 25 – pop. 2 261 – ECD : Wednesday – ☎ 0341.
Envir. : N : Precipice walk★★, Torrent walk★, Rhaiadr Ddu (Black waterfalls★), Coed-y-Brenin
Forest★ – E : Bwlch Oerddrws★ on road★ from Cross Foxes Hotel to Dinas Mawddwy –
S : Cader Idris (road★★ to Cader Idris : Cregenneu lakes) – Tal-y-Llyn Lake★★.
🏌 Pencefn Rd ☎ 422603.
🛈 Snowdonia National Park Visitor Centre, The Bridge ☎ 422888 (summer only).
◆London 221 – Birkenhead 72 – Chester 64 – Shrewsbury 57.

🏛 **Royal Ship,** Queen Sq., LL40 1AR, ☎ 422209 – ▯ TV P. ◪ VISA
   M (bar lunch Monday to Saturday)/dinner 10.00 t. and a la carte – **24 rm** ☲ 16.50/48.00 t. –
   SB 48.00/62.00 st.

   at Llanfachreth NE : 3 ¾ m. by A 494 – ✉ ☎ 0341 Dolgellau :

🏠 **Tŷ Isaf** ⟐, LL40 2EA, ☎ 423261, ≼, 🚗 – P
   M 8.00 st. – **3 rm** ☲ 28.00/36.00 st.

   at Penmaenpool W : 2 m. on A 493 – ✉ ☎ 0341 Dolgellau :

🏨 **George III,** LL40 1YD, ☎ 422525, ≼ Mawddach estuary and mountains – TV ☎ P. ◪ AE
   VISA 🚫
   closed 2 weeks Christmas-New Year – **M** *(closed Sunday dinner to non-residents) (bar
   lunch Monday to Saturday)/dinner a la carte 11.60/30.20 t.* – **12 rm** ☲ 45.00/77.00 t. –
   SB (except summer and Bank Holidays) 88.00 st.

   at Bontddu W : 5 m. on A 496 (Barmouth Rd) – ✉ Dolgellau – ☎ 034 149 Bontddu :

🏰 **Bontddu Hall,** LL40 2SU, ☎ 661, Fax 284, ≼ Mawddach estuary and mountains, « Victorian
   mansion in large gardens » – ✑ rest TV ☎ P. ◪ AE ⓿ VISA 🚫
   closed January-March – **M** 7.50/16.50 t. and a la carte 16.50/24.00 t. ⦙ 3.50 – **19 rm**
   ☲ 37.50/65.00 t., **3 suites** 80.00/95.00 t. – SB (except summer) 85.00 st.

XX **Borthwnog Hall** with rm, LL40 2TT, E : 1 m. on A 496 ☎ 271, ≼, « Part Regency house on
   banks of Mawddach estuary », 🚗, park – ✑ rest TV P. ◪ AE VISA 🚫
   closed 24 to 27 December – **M** *(closed lunch Monday to Saturday except July and August)
   (booking essential) 7.25/11.25 t.* and a la carte ⦙ 3.00 – **3 rm** ☲ 60.00/85.00 t. –
   SB (October-May) 74.50 st.

FORD Arran Rd ☎ 423441   NISSAN Bala Rd ☎ 422681

DOLWYDDELAN Gwynedd **402 403** I 24 – pop. 480 – ECD : Thursday – ☎ 069 06.
◆London 232 – Holyhead 51 – Dolgellau 24 – LLandudno 27.

🏛 **Elen's Castle,** LL25 0EJ, on A 470 ☎ 207, ≼, 🚲, 🚗 – ✑ rest P. 🚫
   M (bar lunch)/dinner approx. 8.00 st. ⦙ 2.90 – **10 rm** ☲ 17.90/39.90 st. –
   SB (except July and August) 71.80/79.80 st.

DONCASTER South Yorks. **402 403 404** Q 23 – pop. 74 727 – ECD : Thursday – ☎ 0302.
🏌 Crookhill Park, Conisbrough ☎ 0709 (Rotherham) 862979, W : 3 m. on A 630 – 🏌 Doncaster
Town Moor, Neatherds House ☎ 535286 – 🏌 Bawtry Rd, Bessacarr ☎ 868316, SE : 5 m. on A 638.
🛈 Central Library, Waterdale ☎ 734309.
◆London 173 – ◆Kingston-upon-Hull 46 – ◆Leeds 30 – ◆Nottingham 46 – ◆Sheffield 19.

🏰 **Doncaster Moat House** (Q.M.H.), Warmsworth, DN4 9UX, SW : 2 ¾ m. on A 630 ☎
   310331, Telex 547963, Fax 310197 – ✑ ▤ rest TV ☎ & P. – 🏊 . ◪ AE ⓿ VISA
   M *(closed Saturday lunch)* 10.50/12.50 st. and a la carte – **70 rm** ☲ 59.00/69.00 st. –
   SB (weekends only) 66.00 st.

🏛 **Grand St. Leger** (Best Western), Racecourse Roundabout, Bennetthorpe, DN2 6AX,
   SE : 1 ½ m. on A 638 ☎ 329865, Fax 329865 – TV ☎ P. – 🏊 60. ◪ AE ⓿ VISA 🚫
   M 8.95/11.95 st. and a la carte ⦙ 4.00 – **13 rm** ☲ 45.00/70.00 t. – SB (weekends only) 65.00 st.

🏛 **Punch's,** Bawtry Rd, Bessacarr, DN4 7BS, SE : 3 m. on A 638 ☎ 370037, Telex 547137 –
   TV ☎ & P. – 🏊 50. ◪ AE ⓿ VISA
   M (grill rest.) a la carte 7.75/11.35 st. ⦙ 3.00 – **24 rm** ☲ 38.00/58.00 st. – SB (week-
   ends only) 48.00 st.

🏛 **Danum** (Swallow), High St., DN1 1DN, ☎ 342261, Telex 547533, Fax 329034 – ▯ ✑ rm TV
   ☎ P. – 🏊 . ◪ AE ⓿ VISA
   M *(closed Saturday lunch)* 8.75/11.75 st. and a la carte – **64 rm** ☲ 56.00/70.00 st., **2 suites**
   – SB (weekends only) 70.00 st.

🏠 **Ashlea** without rest., 81 Thorne Rd, DN1 2ES, ☎ 363374 – TV P. 🚫
   12 rm ☲ 18.00/35.00 st.

   at Rossington SE : 6 m. on A 638 – ✉ ☎ 0302 Doncaster :

🏛 **Mount Pleasant,** Great North Rd, DN11 0HP, on A 638 ☎ 868219, Fax 865130, 🚗 – TV ☎
   & P. – 🏊 45. ◪ VISA 🚫
   closed Christmas Day – **M** 8.50/12.00 t. and a la carte ⦙ 3.10 – **38 rm** ☲ 35.00/45.00 t.

BMW Wheatley Hall Rd ☎ 369191   TOYOTA Old Thorn Rd, Hatfield ☎ 840348
LANCIA Springwell Lane ☎ 854674   VW-AUDI York rd Roundabout ☎ 364141
RENAULT Selby Rd, Thorne ☎ 0405 (Thorne)
8121100
                                                 ⦿ ATS Carr Hill, Balby ☎ 67337/66997

DONYATT Somerset 403 L 37 – pop. 311 – ✉ ⊙ 046 05 Ilminster.

Envir. : Ilminster (site ★); St. Mary's Church ★★, E : 2 m. – Barrington Court ★ *AC*, NE : 5 m.

♦London 147 – Exeter 33 – Taunton 11 – Yeovil 17.

✗ **Thatchers Pond,** TA19 0RG, ℘ 53210, Buffet rest., « 15C thatched cottage », ⌑ – ℗.
🔲 VISA
closed Sunday, Monday and 26 December-mid February – **M** 11.50/12.50 t.

DORCHESTER Dorset 403 404 M 31 The West Country G. – pop. 13 734 – ECD : Thursday –
⊙ 0305 – **See :** Site ★ – Dorset County Museum ★ *AC*.

Envir. : Bere Regis : St. John the Baptist Church ★★★, NE : 11 m. by A 35 – Maiden Castle ★★ (≼★)
AC, SW : 2 m. by A 354 – Puddletown Church ★, NE : 5 m. by A 35 – Athelhampton ★ *AC*, NE :
6 m. on A 35 – Moreton Church ★, E : 10 m – Cerne Abbas ★ N : 7 m.

🏌 Came Down ℘ 030 581 (Upwey) 2531, S : 2 m – 🄩 7 Acland Rd ℘ 67992.

♦London 135 – Bournemouth 27 – Exeter 53 – ♦Southampton 53.

🏨 **King's Arms,** 30 High East St., DT1 1HF, ℘ 65353, Fax 60269 – 🛗 📺 ☎ ℗ – 🔄 80. 🔲 AE
VISA
M a la carte 9.70/22.70 t. 🍶 3.50 – **31 rm** 🍵 49.00/125.00 t. – SB (weekends
only) 75.00/85.00 st.

🏚 **Casterbridge** without rest., 49 High East St., DT1 1HU, ℘ 64043 – 📺 ☎. 🔲 AE ① VISA
🍴
closed 25 and 26 December – **15 rm** 🍵 26.00/48.00 t.

🏚 **Yalbury Cottage** 🍴, Lower Bockhampton, DT2 8PZ, S : 2 ¼ m. by B 3150 and Bockhampton rd, ⌑ – 📺 ☎ ℗. 🔲 VISA. 🍴
closed January – **M** (dinner only) 20.50 st. – **8 rm** 🍵 –/72.00 st. – SB 77.00/99.00 st.

✗ **Mock Turtle,** 34 High West St., DT1 1UP, ℘ 264011 – 🔲 VISA
closed Sunday lunch and Monday – **M** 8.75/14.25 t. 🍶 4.50.

at Frampton NW : 5 m. by A 37 on A 356 – ✉ Dorchester – ⊙ 0300 Maiden Newton :

⌂ The Court 🍴, DT2 9NH, S : ½ m. by Southever rd ℘ 20242, ≼, ⌑, park – ℗ – **4 rm**.

AUSTIN-ROVER 21-26 Trinity St. ℘ 63031
CITROEN, LAND-ROVER, RANGE-ROVER Puddle-
town ℘ 845456
FORD Great Western Industrial Est. ℘ 62211
MERCEDES-BENZ Millers Close , The Grove ℘
64494

PEUGEOT London Rd ℘ 66066
VAUXHALL 6 High East St. ℘ 03913
VOLVO Bridport Rd ℘ 65555

⊕ ATS Unit 4, Great Western Ind. Centre (South)
℘ 64756

DORCHESTER Oxon. 403 404 Q 29 – pop. 1 045 – ⊙ 0865 Oxford.
See : Abbey Church ★ (14C).

♦London 51 – Abingdon 6 – ♦Oxford 8 – Reading 17.

🏨 **White Hart,** 26 High St., OX9 8HN, ℘ 340074, Fax 341082, « Tastefully converted 17C
coaching inn » – 📺 ☎ ℗. 🔲 AE ① VISA. 🍴
M 12.40/17.00 st. and a la carte 🍶 5.50 – **15 rm** 🍵 57.20/79.20 st., **5 suites** 85.00/95.00 st. –
SB (October-March) (weekends only) 80.00/85.00 st.

🏚 **George,** 23 High St., OX9 8HH, ℘ 340404, Telex 83147 – 📺 ☎ ℗ – 🔄 40. 🔲 AE ① VISA
closed 24 to 31 December – **M** 18.00 t. and a la carte 🍶 3.50 – **17 rm** 🍵 55.00/85.00 t. –
SB (weekends only) 92.50 st.

DORDON Staffs. 402 403 404 P 26 – pop. 9 641 (inc. Polesworth) – ✉ ⊙ 0827 Tamworth.

♦London 124 – ♦Birmingham 18 – ♦Coventry 19 – ♦Leicester 26.

⌂ **Hall End Hall** without rest., Watling St., B78 1SZ, on A 5 ℘ 899200, ⌑ – ℗. 🍴
3 rm 🍵 18.50/30.00 s.

DORKING Surrey 404 T 30 – pop. 14 602 – ECD : Wednesday – ⊙ 0306.

Envir. : Box Hill ≼★★, NE : 2 ½ m. – Polesden Lacey ★★ (19C) *AC*, NW : 4 ½ m.

♦London 26 – ♦Brighton 39 – Guildford 12 – Worthing 33.

🏨 **Burford Bridge** (T.H.F.), Box Hill, RH5 6BX, N : 1 ½ m. on A 24 ℘ 884561, Telex 859507,
Fax 880386, 🏊 heated, ⌑ – ⇥ rm 📺 ☎ ℗ – 🔄 250. 🔲 AE ① VISA
M 17.00/18.00 st. and a la carte 🍶 5.00 – 🍵 7.50 – **48 rm** 80.00/120.00 st. – SB 100.00 st.

🏨 **White Horse** (T.H.F.), High St., RH4 1BE, ℘ 881138, Fax 887241, 🏊 heated – ⇥ rm 📺 ☎
℗ – 🔄 60. 🔲 AE ① VISA
M a la carte 9.15/15.85 st. 🍶 3.75 – 🍵 7.00 – **68 rm** 61.00/76.00 st. – SB (weekends
only) 76.00/90.00 st.

🏚 **Travelodge** without rest., Reigate Rd, RH4 1QB, E : ½ m. on A 25 ℘ 740361 – 📺 ⅙ ℗. 🔲
AE VISA
29 rm 21.50/27.00 t.

✗ **Le Bistro,** 84 South St., RH4 2EZ, ℘ 883239, French rest. – 🔲 AE ① VISA
closed Saturday lunch, Sunday, 27 December-6 January and Bank Holidays – **M** a la carte
14.40/25.40 st. 🍶 3.70.

AUSTIN-ROVER 105 South St. ℘ 882244

VAUXHALL-OPEL Reigate Rd ℘ 885022

DORMINGTON Heref. and Worc. – see Hereford.

DORRINGTON Shropshire 402 403 L 26 – see Shrewsbury.

DOULTING 403 404 M 30 – see Shepton Mallet.

DOVER Kent 404 Y 30 – pop. 33 461 – ECD : Wednesday – ☎ 0304.
See : Castle★★ (12C) (≤★) *AC* Y.
Envir. : Barfreston (Norman Church★ (11C) : carvings★★) NW : 6 ½ m. by A 2 Z –
Bleriot Memorial, E : 1 ½ m. Z A.
🚢 Shipping connections with the Continent : to France (Boulogne and Calais) (P & O European Ferries) (Hoverspeed) – to France (Calais) (Sealink) – to Belgium (Oostende) (P & O European Ferries) – to Belgium (Zeebrugge) (P & O European Ferries).
🚤 to Belgium (Oostende) (P & O European Ferries, Jetfoil).
🛈 Townwall St. ☎ 205108.
♦London 76 – ♦Brighton 84.

DOVER

Bench Street. . . . . Y 3
Biggin Street. . . . . Y 4
Cannon Street . . . . Y 5
High Street . . . . Y
King Street . . . . Y 13
Pencester Road . . . . Y

Barton Road . . . . Y 2
Castle Street . . . . Y 6
Charlton Green . . . . Y 7
Crabble Hill . . . . Z 9
Eaton Road . . . . Z 10
Ladywell, Park Street. . . . . Y 15
London Road . . . . Y 17
Priory Road . . . . Z 19
Priory Street . . . . Y 20
Sandwich Road . . . . Z 21
Tower Street . . . . Z 24
Worthington Street . . . . Y 25

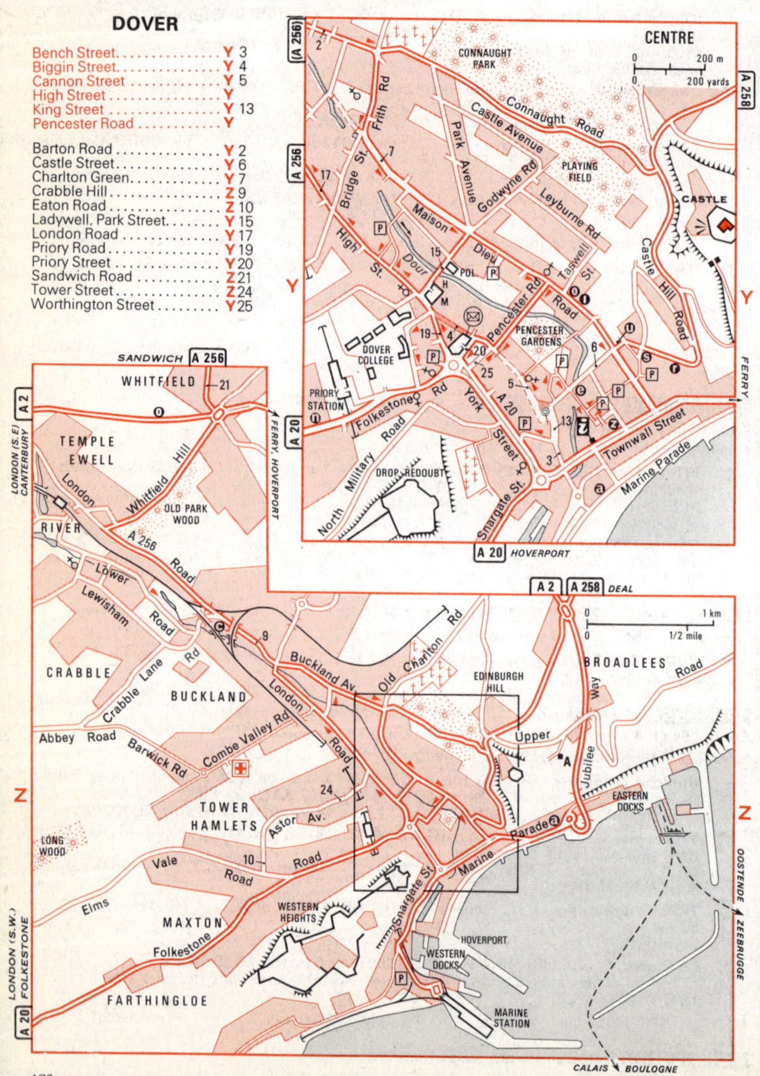

Dover Moat House (Q.M.H.), Townwall St., CT16 1SZ, ℰ 203270, Telex 96458, Fax 213230, ⌕ – ▯ ⇆ rm ▭ ▭ ☎ – ▵ 100. ⚑ AE ⓪ VISA — **Y** z
M 14.50 **st.** and a la carte – ⚏ 6.75 – **79 rm** 63.00/71.00 **st.** – SB (weekends only) 77.00/86.00 **st.**

White Cliffs, Seafront, CT17 9BW, ℰ 203633, Telex 965422, Fax 216320, ≼ – ▯ ▭ ☎ ⇔. ⚑ AE ⓪ VISA. ⚘ — **Y** a
closed 25 and 26 December – **M** (bar lunch Monday to Saturday)/dinner 7.25 **t.** and a la carte ᵇ 4.25 – **54 rm** ⚏ 40.00/64.00 **t.** – SB 56.00/70.00 **st.**

Mildmay, 78 Folkestone Rd, CT17 9SF, ℰ 204278 – ▭ ☎ ⓟ. ⚑ AE ⓪ VISA. ⚘ — **Y** n
closed January – **M** (bar lunch)/dinner a la carte 10.30/13.20 **st.** – **21 rm** ⚏ 34.00/50.00 **st.**

Cliffe Court, 25-27 East Cliff, Marine Par., CT16 1LU, ℰ 211001, ≼ – ▭ ☎ ⓟ – ▵. ⚑ AE ⓪ VISA. ⚘ — **Z** a
M (lunch by arrangement)/dinner 8.75 **t.** and a la carte ᵇ 2.95 – **25 rm** ⚏ 26.00/39.00 **st.**

Hubert House, 9 Castle Hill Rd, CT16 1QW, ℰ 202253 – ▭ ⓟ — **Y** s
closed 2 weeks September-October – **M** (closed Sunday) (dinner only) 7.95 **st.** and a la carte ᵇ 3.00 – **8 rm** ⚏ 22.00/35.50 **t.** – SB (except Sundays) 45.50/50.00 **st.**

East Lee without rest., 108 Maison Dieu Rd, CT16 1RT, ℰ 210176 – ⇆ ☎. ⚑ VISA. ⚘ — **Y** o
4 rm ⚏ 20.00/35.00 **st.**

Number One without rest., 1 Castle St., CT16 1QH, ℰ 202007, ⇚ – ▭ ⇔. ⚘ — **Y** u
5 rm ⚏ 18.00/30.00.

Penny Farthing without rest., 109 Maison Dieu Rd, CT16 1RT, ℰ 205563 – ▭ ⓟ. ⚘ — **Y** i
6 rm ⚏ 15.00/32.00 **s.**

Beulah House without rest., 94 Crabble Hill, London Rd, CT17 0SA, ℰ 824615, ⇚ – ⇔ ⓟ. ⚘ — **Z** c
8 rm ⚏ 17.00/30.00 **s.**

St. Martins and Ardmore without rest., 17 Castle Hill Rd, CT16 1QW, ℰ 205938 – ▭. ⚑. ⚘ — **Y** r
closed Christmas – **8 rm** ⚏ 20.00/30.00 **st.**

Dino's, 58 Castle St., CT16 1PJ, ℰ 204678, Italian rest. – ⚑ AE ⓪ VISA — **Y** e
closed Monday and first 2 weeks October – **M** a la carte 10.90/14.50 **t.** ᵇ 3.00.

at St. Margaret's Bay NE : 4 m. by A 258 – **Z** – on B 2058 – ✉ ☏ 0304 Dover :

Cliffe Tavern, High St., CT15 6AT, ℰ 852400, ⇚ – ▭ ⓟ. ⚑ AE ⓪ VISA
M 12.30 **t.** and a la carte – ⚏ 3.80 – **12 rm** 24.00/30.00 **t.**

Wallet's Court ⑊ with rm, West Cliffe, CT15 6EW, NW : ¾ m. on B 2058 ℰ 852424, « Part 17C manor house, 13C cellars », ⇚ – ▭ ⓟ. ⚑. ⚘
closed 2 weeks January, 2 weeks November and 24 to 27 December – **M** (closed Sunday and Monday) (dinner only) 23.00 **t.** and a la carte 13.50/20.00 **t.** ᵇ 4.50 – **7 rm** ⚏ 35.00/60.00 **t.**

at Whitfield NW : 3 ½ m. on A 256 – ✉ ☏ 0304 Dover :

Crest H. Dover (Crest), Singledge Lane, CT16 3LF, ℰ 821222, Telex 965866, Fax 825576 – ▭ rest ▭ ☎ ὸ ⓟ – ▵ — **Z** o
67 rm.

FORD Woolcomber St. ℰ 206518
RELIANT South Rd ℰ 206160
TOYOTA Poulton Close, Buckland Ind. Est. ℰ 201235

VW-AUDI 1 Crabble Hill ℰ 206710

DOWNTON Wilts. 400 404 ∩ 31 – see Salisbury.

DRENEWYDD = Newtown.

DRENEWYDD YN NOTAIS (NOTTAGE) Mid Glam. – see Porthcawl.

DRIFFIELD Humberside 402 S 21 – see Great Driffield.

DROITWICH Heref. and Worc. 403 404 N 27 – pop. 18 025 – ECD : Thursday – ☏ 0905.
ᵣ₈ Droitwich, Ford Lane ℰ 774344/770207, N : 1 ½ m. by A 38 – 🄱 Heritage Way ℰ 774312.
♦London 129 – ♦Birmingham 20 – ♦Bristol 66 – Worcester 6.

Raven, St. Andrews St., WR9 8DU, ℰ 772224, Group Telex 336673, ⇚ – ▯ ▭ ☎ ⓟ – ▵ 400. ⚑ AE ⓪ VISA
closed Christmas – **M** (closed Saturday lunch and Sunday dinner) 10.00/15.00 **st.** and a la carte ᵇ 4.50 – ⚏ 7.95 – **55 rm** 29.95/89.95 **st.**

Travelodge without rest., Rashwood Hill, WR9 8DA, NE : 1 ½ m. on A 38 ℰ 052 786 (Wychbold) 545 – ▭ ὸ ⓟ. ⚑ AE VISA
32 rm 21.50/27.00 **t.**

Little Lodge Farm ⑊ without rest., Broughton Green, WR9 7EE, ℰ 052 784 (Hanbury) 305, « Attractive 17C timbered farmhouse », ⇚ – ⓟ. ⚘
April-October – **3 rm** ⚏ 20.00/38.00 **s.**

AUSTIN-ROVER St. Georges Sq. ℰ 794000

FORD 141-149 Worcester Rd ℰ 772132

DRONFIELD Derbs. 402 403 404 P 24 – pop. 22 641 – ECD : Wednesday – ⊠ Sheffield (South Yorks) – ✆ 0246.
◆ London 158 – Derby 30 – ◆ Nottingham 31 – ◆ Sheffield 6.

🏠 **Manor**, 10-15 High St., S18 6PY, ℰ 413971 – TV P. 🔾 AE ① VISA
M (closed Sunday dinner) 6.95/12.95 t. and a la carte ╠ 4.85 – **9 rm** ⌇ 42.50/56.00 t.

DRY DRAYTON Cambs. – see Cambridge.

DUDLEY West Midlands 402 403 404 N 26 – ECD : Wednesday – ⊠ ✆ 0384.
🅖 Himley Hall, Cabin, Himley Hall Park ℰ 0902 (Himley) 895207, W : 4 ½ m. on B 4176 – 🅖18 Swindon, Bridgnorth Rd ℰ 0902 (Wombourne) 897031.
🅱 39 Churchill Precinct ℰ 50333.
◆London 132 – ◆Birmingham 10 – Wolverhampton 6.

Plan : see Birmingham p. 2

🏠 **Himley House** (B.C.B.), Himley, DY3 4LD, W : 4 m. by B 4176 on A 449 ℰ 0902 (Wolverhampton) 892468, Fax 892604, 🚗 – TV ☎ P. 🔾 AE ① VISA. 🕸
M (buffet meals) 5.50/9.40 t. and a la carte – **24 rm** ⌇ 40.00/63.00 st. – SB (weekends only) 42.00 st.   AU e

DULVERTON Somerset 403 J 30 The West Country G. – pop. 1 301 – ECD : Thursday – ✆ 0398.
See : Site★.
Envir. : Tarr Steps★★, NW : 6 m. by B 3223.
◆London 198 – Barnstaple 27 – Exeter 26 – Minehead 18 – Taunton 27.

🏠 **Ashwick House** 🕭, TA22 9QD, NW : 4 ¼ m. by B 3223 ℰ 23868, ≼, « Country house atmosphere », 🚗 – 🐩 rest TV P. 🕸
M (dinner only and Sunday lunch)/dinner 16.95 t. ╠ 3.50 – **6 rm** ⌇ (dinner included) 48.50/54.25 t. – SB 75.50/99.00 st.

DUNCHURCH Warw. 403 404 Q 26 – pop. 2 409 – ⊠ ✆ 0788 Rugby.
◆London 90 – ◆Coventry 12 – ◆Leicester 24 – Northampton 26.

🏠 **Dun Cow**, The Green, CV22 6NJ, ℰ 810233, Telex 94013861, « 16C inn » – TV ☎ P. 🔾 AE ① VISA
M 19.95 st. and a la carte ╠ 4.50 – **24 rm** ⌇ 31.00/55.00 st., **1 suite** 65.00/95.00 st. – SB (weekends only) (except Bank Holidays) 89.00/129.00 st.

🏠 **Travelodge** without rest., London Rd, Thurslaston, CV23 9LG, NW : 2 ½ m. on A 45 ℰ 521538 – TV ㏿ P.
40 rm.

VW-AUDI Drayton Fields, Daventry ℰ (0327) 77777

DUNSLEY North Yorks. – see Whitby.

DUNSTABLE Beds. 404 S 28 – pop. 48 436 – ECD : Thursday – ✆ 0582.
See : Priory Church of St. Peter (West front★).
Envir. : Whipsnade Park★ (zoo) ≼★★ AC, S : 3 m.
🅖 Tilsworth, Dunstable Rd ℰ 0525 (Leighton Buzzard) 210721, N : 2 m. on A 5.
🅱 Vernon Pl. ℰ 471012.
◆London 40 – Bedford 24 – Luton 4.5 – Northampton 35.

🏠 **Old Palace Lodge**, Church St., LU5 4RT, ℰ 662201, Fax 696422 – ▮ ☰ rest TV ☎ P – 🛋 40. 🔾 AE ① VISA
M (closed Saturday lunch) a la carte 19.25/27.25 st. – ⌇ 7.25 – **49 rm** 61.50/82.00 st.

🏠 **Highwayman**, London Rd, LU6 3DX, SE : 1 m. on A 5 ℰ 601122, Telex 825562, Fax 471131 – TV ☎ P. 🔾 AE ① VISA
M (closed Sunday lunch) (bar lunch)/dinner 12.00 t. and a la carte ╠ 3.50 – **37 rm** ⌇ 42.00/52.00 t.

✗ **Rajput**, 31 High St. South, ℰ 606065, Indian rest. – 🔾 AE ① VISA
M approx. 12.00 st. and a la carte.

AUSTIN-ROVER London Rd ℰ 666111
FIAT Poynters Rd ℰ 667742
FORD 55 London Rd ℰ 667811
RENAULT Tring Rd ℰ 609605
VW-AUDI Common Rd, Kensworth ℰ 872182

DUNSTER Somerset **403** J 30 The West Country G. – pop. 793 – ECD : Wednesday –
✉ Minehead – ☎ 0643.

See : Site★★ – Castle★★*AC* (upper rooms ≤★ from window) – Dunster Castle Water Mill★*AC* –
Dovecote★ – St. Georges Church★.

Envir. : Exmoor National Park★★ (Dunkery Beacon★★★ – Tarr Steps Clapper Bridge★★ –
Watersmeet★ – Valley of the Locks★) – Cleeve Abbey★★*AC*, SE : 5 m. on A 39.

♦London 184 – ♦Bristol 61 – Exeter 40 – Taunton 22.

Luttrell Arms (T.H.F.), 36 High St., TA24 6SG, ℰ 821555, ☞ – ⤢ rm 📺 ☎ . 🅰 AE ⑩ VISA
M 7.50/12.50 **st.** and a la carte 🍷 3.95 – ☑ 7.00 – **25 rm** 65.00/87.00 **st.** – SB 106.00/118.00 **st.**

Exmoor House, 12 West St., TA24 6SN, ℰ 821268, ☞ – ⤢ 📺 🅰 AE ⑩ VISA
closed December and January – **M** (bar lunch residents only)/dinner 13.00 **st.** 🍷 2.85 – **6 rm**
☑ 28.00/41.00 **st.**

at Blue Anchor SE : 3 ½ m. by A 39 on B 3191 – ✉ Minehead – ☎ 0643 Dunster :

Langbury, TA24 6LB, ℰ 821375, ⅃, ☞ – 📺 🅿
March-October – **M** 9.00 **st.** 🍷 3.50 – **9 rm** ☑ 14.50/32.00 **st.** – SB 42.00/48.00 **st.**

DURHAM Durham **401 402** P 19 – pop. 38 105 – ECD : Wednesday – ☎ 0385 (5 and 6 fig.) or
091 (7 fig.).

See : Cathedral★★★ (Norman) (Chapel of the Nine Altars★★) B – University (Gulbenkian Museum
of Art and Archaeology★★ *AC*) by Elvet Hill Rd A – Castle★ (Norman chapel★) *AC* B.

📗 Littleburn Farm, Langley Moor ℰ 378 0069, SW : 2 m. by A 690 A – 📗 Mount Oswald, South Rd
ℰ 67527 A

🛈 Market Pl. ℰ 384 3720.

♦London 267 – ♦Leeds 77 – ♦Middlesbrough 23 – Sunderland 12.

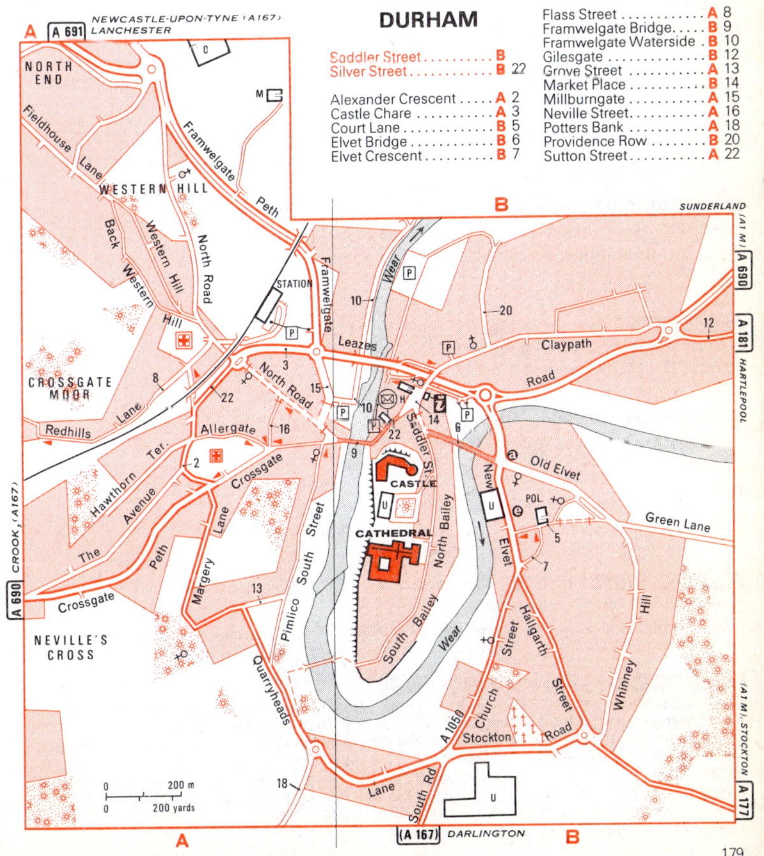

🏨 **Royal County** (Swallow), Old Elvet, DH1 3JN, ℘ 386 6821, Group Telex 538238, Fax 386 0704, 🖾 – 🛏 ⤢ rm 🍽 rest 📺 ☎ ♿ 🅿 – 🛎 100. 🖾 AE ⓞ VISA
M 10.75/17.00 **st.** and a la carte ▯ 4.65 – **149 rm** ☕ 70.00/200.00 **st.**, **1 suite** – SB (week-ends only) 85.00/105.00 **st.**
    B a

🏨 **Three Tuns** (Swallow), New Elvet, DH1 3AQ, ℘ 386 4326, Fax 386 1406 – ⤢ rm 📺 ☎ 🅿 – 🛎 50. 🖾 AE ⓞ VISA
M (closed Saturday lunch) 11.00 **st.** (dinner) and a la carte ▯ 4.65 – **54 rm** ☕ 52.00/70.00 **st.** – SB 75.00 **st.**
    B e

at Croxdale S : 3 m. by A 1050 on A 167 – **B** – ⊠ ☏ 091 Tyneside :

🏠 Bridge, DH1 3SP, ℘ 378 0524, Telex 538156 – 📺 ☎ 🅿 – 🛎 50 – **46 rm**.

AUSTIN-ROVER Gilesgate Moor ℘ 3867231
CITROEN Croxdale ℘ 0388 (Spennymoor) 814671
FORD Nevilles Cross ℘ 3861155
HONDA Bearpark ℘ 3862227
LADA Framwellgate Moor ℘ 386 9499
LANCIA 81 New Elvet ℘ 3847777
MAZDA Framwellgate Moor ℘ 384 1925

VAUXHALL Sacriston ℘ 371 0422
VOLVO · Sawmills Lane ℘ 780866
VW-AUDI 20 Alma Rd, Gilesgate Moor ℘ 3867215

🅐 ATS Finchale Rd, Newton Hall ℘ 3841810/3841835
ATS Mill Rd, Langley Moor ℘ 3780262

DUXFORD Cambs. 404 U 27 – see Cambridge.

DYFFRYN ARDUDWY Gwynedd 402 403 H 25 – pop. 1 122 (inc. Tal-y-bont) – ☏ 034 16 Ardudwy.

♦London 237 – Dolgellau 16 – Caernarfon 44.

🏠 **Ael-Y-Bryn**, LL44 2BE, on A 496 ℘ 701, 🐎, ⤢ – 📺 🅿. 🖾 VISA 🐾
M (bar lunch Monday to Sunday)/dinner 7.25 **t.** and a la carte ▯ 3.45 – **7 rm** ☕ 30.00/55.00 **t.**

MITSUBISHI Smithy Garage ℘ 279

EAGLESCLIFFE Cleveland 402 P 20 – see Stockton-on-Tees.

EARL SHILTON Leics. 403 404 Q 26 – pop. 16 484 – ECD : Wednesday – ⊠ Leicester – ☏ 0455.

♦London 107 – ♦Birmingham 35 – ♦Coventry 16 – ♦Leicester 9 – ♦Nottingham 35.

🏠 **Fernleigh**, 32 Wood St., LE9 7ND, ℘ 47011 – 📺 ☎ 🅿. 🖾 VISA
M 3.50/8.50 **st.** and a la carte ▯ 2.95 – **27 rm** ☕ 25.00/60.00 **st.** – SB (week-ends only) 25.00/35.00 **st.**

EARL STONHAM Suffolk 404 X 27 – ⊠ Stowmarket – ☏ 0449 Stonham.

♦London 81 – ♦Cambridge 47 – ♦Ipswich 10 – ♦Norwich 33.

XX **Mr. Underhill's**, IP14 5DW, Junction of A 140 and A 1120 ℘ 711206 – ⤢ 🅿. 🖾 AE VISA
closed Sunday, Monday and Bank Holidays – **M** (lunch by arrangement) (booking essential) 20.00/25.50 **t.** ▯ 5.00.

EASINGWOLD North Yorks. 402 Q 21 – pop. 3 468 – ⊠ York – ☏ 0347.
⛳ Stillington Rd ℘ 21486 – 🄱 The Galtres, Chapel Lane ℘ 21530 (summer only).
♦London 217 – ♦Middlesbrough 37 – York 14.

🏠 George, Market Pl., YO6 3AD, ℘ 21698 – 📺 ☎ 🅿 – **18 rm**.

at Raskelf W : 2 ¾ m. – ⊠ York – ☏ 0347 Easingwold :

🏠 **Old Farmhouse**, YO6 3LF, ℘ 21971 – 🅿
closed 23 December-25 January – **M** (closed Sunday and Monday to non-residents) (dinner only) 12.00 **t.** ▯ 3.00 – **10 rm** ☕ 23.00/40.00 **t.** – SB (November-March) 50.00 **st.**

at Thormanby NW : 4 ¼ m. on A 19 – ⊠ York – ☏ 0845 Thirsk :

↑ **Old Rectory** without rest., YO6 3NN, ℘ 401417, 🐎 – 🅿
closed Christmas – **3 rm** ☕ 15.00/23.00 **st.**

EAST BERGHOLT Suffolk 404 X 28 – pop. 2 757 – ⊠ ☏ 0206 Colchester (Essex).
♦London 59 – Colchester 9 – ♦Ipswich 8.5.

XX **Fountain House**, The Street, CO7 6TB, ℘ 298232, « 15C cottage » – 🅿. 🖾 VISA
closed Sunday dinner, Monday and 2 weeks February – **M** 10.95/12.95 **t.**

EASTBOURNE East Sussex 404 U 31 – pop. 86 715 – ECD : Wednesday – ☏ 0323.
See : Grand Parade★ X – Sea Front★ – Envir. : Beachy Head★★★ (cliff), ❊★, SW : 3 m. Z – Seven Sisters★ (cliffs) from Birling Gap, SW : 5 m. Z – Charleston Manor★ AC, W : 8 m. by A 259 Z – W : scenic road★, from East Dean by A 259 Z up to Wilmington by West Dean – Wilmington : The Long Man★ : prehistoric giant figure, NW : 7 m. by A 27 Y.
⛳, ⛳ Royal Eastbourne, Paradise Drive ℘ 29738 Z – ⛳ Eastbourne Downs, East Dean Rd ℘ 20827 Z – 🄱 3 Cornfield Terr. ℘ 27474 – The Pier, Marine Parade, ℘ 27474 (summer only) – at Pevensey, Castle Car Park, High St. ℘ 0323 (Eastbourne) 761444.
♦London 68 – ♦Brighton 25 – ♦Dover 61 – Maidstone 49.

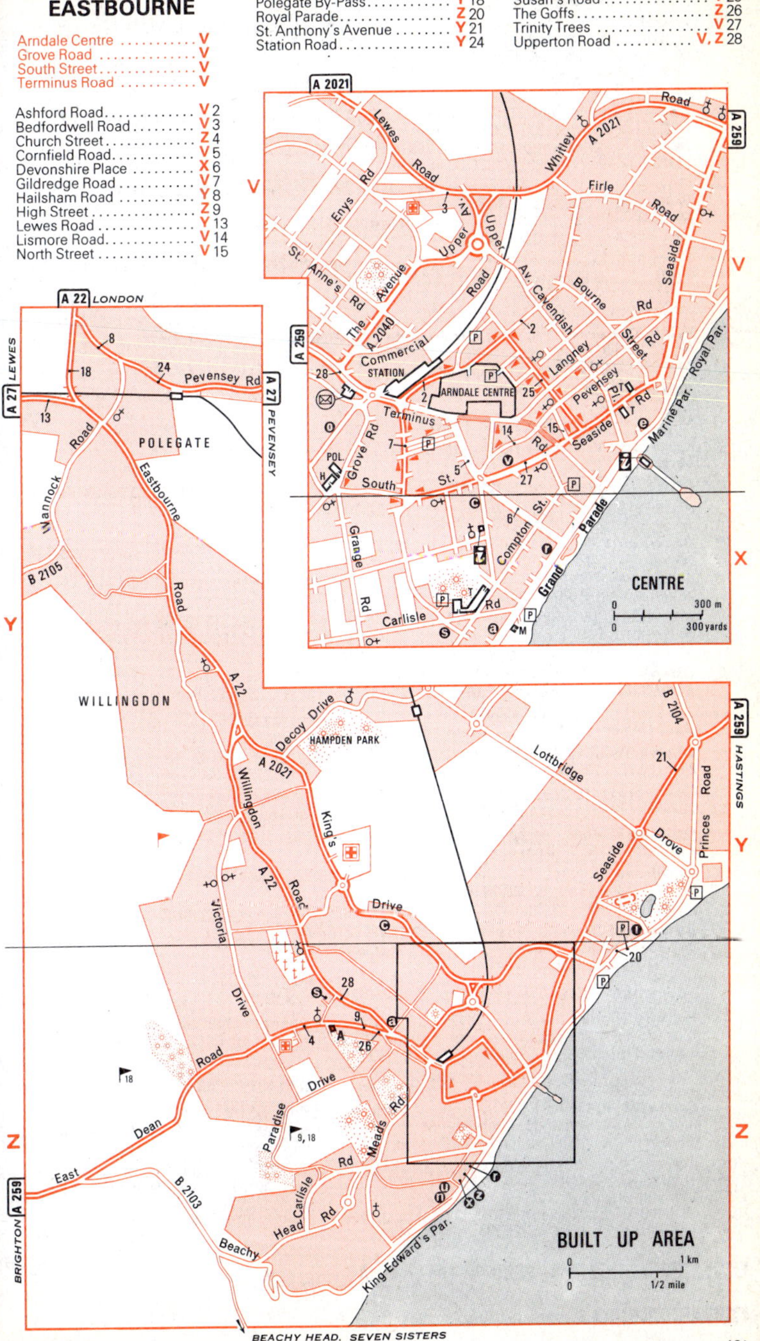

EASTBOURNE

Arndale Centre V
Grove Road V
South Street V
Terminus Road V

Ashford Road .... V 2
Bedfordwell Road .... V 3
Church Street .... Z V 4
Cornfield Road .... V 5
Devonshire Place .... X 6
Gildredge Road .... V 7
Hailsham Road .... Y 8
High Street .... Z 9
Lewes Road .... V 13
Lismore Road .... V 14
North Street .... V 15

Polegate By-Pass .... Y 18
Royal Parade .... Z 20
St. Anthony's Avenue .... Y 21
Station Road .... Y 24

Susan's Road .... V 25
The Goffs .... Z 26
Trinity Trees .... V 27
Upperton Road .... V, Z 28

A 2021
A 259
A 22 LONDON
A 27 LEWES
A 27 PEVENSEY
A 259
A 2040
A 259
A 22
A 2021
A 259 HASTINGS
B 2105
B 2104
B 2103
A 259 BRIGHTON

Lewes Road
Enys Rd
St. Anne's Rd
The Avenue
Upper Avenue
Upper Road
Whitley
Firle Road
Seaside
Bourne Street Rd
Cavendish Av.
Langney
Pevensey Rd
Commercial Road
STATION
ARNDALE CENTRE
Terminus
Grove Rd
South St.
Compton St.
Grange Rd
Carlisle Rd
Seaside
Grand Parade
Marine Par.
Royal Par.
POL.
CENTRE
300 m
300 yards

Wannock Road
Eastbourne Road
Pevensey Rd
POLEGATE
PEVENSEY

WILLINGDON
Decoy Drive
HAMPDEN PARK
A 2021
Willingdon Road
Victoria Drive
A 22
King's Drive
Lottbridge
Seaside
Drove
Princes Road
Paradise Drive
Meads Rd
Carlisle Rd
Head
Dean
East
Beachy
King Edward's Par.
BUILT UP AREA
1 km
1/2 mile

BEACHY HEAD, SEVEN SISTERS

Grand (De Vere), King Edward's Par., BN21 4EQ, ℰ 412345, Telex 87332, Fax 412233, ≼, ⏋ heated, ⏚, ⇘ – ⫯ TV ☎ ⅋ ⚇ ℗ – ⛌ 400. ◪ 🄰🄴 Ⓞ *VISA*   **Z x**
M (see also **Mirabelle rest.** below) 15.00/21.00 **st.** and a la carte ⏐9.50 – **149 rm** ⊏ 70.00/140.00 **st.**, **15 suites** 190.00/270.00 **st.** – SB (October-May) (weekends only) 130.00/230.00 **st.**

Cavendish (De Vere), 37-40 Grand Par., BN21 4DH, ℰ 410222, Telex 87579, Fax 410941, ≼ – ⫯ TV ☎ ℗ – ⛌ 200. ◪ 🄰🄴 Ⓞ *VISA*   **X r**
M 10.00/16.00 **st.** and a la carte – **110 rm** ⊏ 65.00/140.00 **st.**, **4 suites** 125.00/200.00 **st.** – SB (weekends only) 110.00/170.00 **st.**

Queen's (De Vere), Marine Par., BN21 3DY, ℰ 22822, Telex 877736, Fax 30156, ≼ – ⫯ TV ☎ ℗ – ⛌ 150. ◪ 🄰🄴 Ⓞ *VISA*   **V e**
M 10.50/14.00 **st.** and a la carte – **106 rm** ⊏ 60.00/110.00 **st.**, **2 suites** 165.00 **st.** – SB (weekends only) 100.00/115.00 **st.**

Lansdowne (Best Western), King Edward's Par., BN21 4EE, ℰ 25174, Telex 878624, Fax 39721, ≼ – ⫯ TV ☎ ⇛ – ⛌ 80. ◪ 🄰🄴 Ⓞ *VISA*   **Z z**
closed 1 to 13 January – **M** (a la carte lunch)/dinner 12.50 **st.** ⏐4.25 – **130 rm** ⊏ 35.50/84.00 **st.** – SB 63.00/75.00 **st.**

Wish Tower (T.H.F.), King Edward's Par., BN21 4EB, ℰ 22676, Fax 21474, ≼ – ⫯ ⤧ TV ☎. ◪ 🄰🄴 Ⓞ *VISA*   **Z r**
M 8.00/13.50 **st.** and a la carte ⏐3.95 – ⊏ 7.00 – **67 rm** 60.00/78.00 **st.** – SB 70.00/96.00 **st.**

Sussex, 25-26 Cornfield Terr., BN21 4NS, ℰ 27681, Fax 646077 – ⫯ ⤧ rm TV ☎ – ⛌ 50. ◪ 🄰🄴 Ⓞ *VISA*   **X c**
M (carving rest.) 6.95 ⏐3.45 – **27 rm** ⊏ 39.50/49.50 **t.**

Farrar's, 3-5 Wilmington Gdns, BN21 4JN, ℰ 23737, ⇘ – ⫯ TV ℗   **X s**
44 rm.

Croft, 18 Prideaux Rd, BN21 2NB, ℰ 642291, ⏋ heated, ⇘, ⚒ – TV ℗. ◪ 🄰🄴 Ⓞ *VISA*. ⅌   **Y c**
M *(closed Saturday lunch)* 9.50 **st.** (lunch) and a la carte 17.75/21.50 **st.** ⏐4.70 – **11 rm** ⊏ 28.50/64.00 **t.** – SB 66.00/81.00 **st.**

Brownings, 28 Upperton Rd, BN21 1JS, ℰ 24358, Fax 31288, ⏋ heated – TV ☎ ℗. ◪ 🄰🄴 Ⓞ *VISA*. ⅌   **Z a**
closed mid December-mid January – **M** *(closed Sunday dinner)* (dinner only and Sunday lunch)/dinner 11.00 **t.** and a la carte ⏐2.50 – **10 rm** ⊏ 28.00/50.00 **t.**

Mandalay, 16 Trinity Trees, BN21 3LE, ℰ 29222, ⇘ – ⤧ rest TV ℗. ◪ *VISA*. ⅌   **V v**
M *(closed Saturday lunch, Monday dinner and Sunday)* 12.00/15.00 **t.** ⏐3.00 – **12 rm** ⊏ 18.00/50.00 **t.** – SB (except summer) 48.00/60.00 **st.**

Oban, King Edward's Par., BN21 4DS, ℰ 31581 – ⫯ TV   **X a**
Mid March-mid November – **M** 4.50/7.50 **t.** ⏐3.00 – **31 rm** ⊏ 24.00/50.00 **t.**

Far End, 139 Royal Par., BN22 7LH, ℰ 25666 – ⤧ rest TV ℗. ⅌   **Y i**
April-October – **M** 5.50 **t.** – **10 rm** ⊏ 15.00/35.00 **t.**

Cherry Tree, 15 Silverdale Rd, BN20 7AJ, ℰ 22406 – ⤧ rest TV ☎. ◪ *VISA*. ⅌   **Z u**
M 13.00 **t.** – **10 rm** ⊏ 19.00/40.00 **t.** – SB (except summer) 77.00/88.00 **st.**

Southcroft, 15 South Cliff Av., BN20 7AH, ℰ 29071 – ⤧ rest. ⅌   **Z n**
April-September and November – **M** 6.00 **st.** ⏐2.00 – **6 rm** ⊏ 17.00/34.00 **st.**

Orchard House without rest., 10 Old Orchard Rd, BN21 1DB, ℰ 23682, ⇘ – TV. ⅌   **V o**
April-November – **6 rm** ⊏ 25.00/35.00 **st.**

XXXX **Mirabelle** (De Vere), (at Grand H.), King Edward's Par., BN21 4EQ, ℰ 410771, Telex 87332, Fax 412233 – ▤ ℗. ◪ 🄰🄴 Ⓞ *VISA*   **Z x**
closed Sunday – **M** (booking essential) 15.00/25.00 **st.** and a la carte approx. 33.50 **st.**

X **Byron's**, 6 Crown St., Old Town, BN21 1NX, ℰ 20171 – 🄰🄴 Ⓞ *VISA*   **Z s**
closed Sunday, 1 week at Christmas and Bank Holidays – **M** (dinner only) a la carte 14.10/18.65 **t.** ⏐3.25.

at Jevington NW : 6 m. by A 259 – **Z** – on B 2105 – ✉ ☏ 032 12 Polegate :

XX **Hungry Monk**, The Street, BN26 5QF, ℰ 2178, « Part Elizabethan cottages », ⇘ – ℗
closed 24 to 26 December, 1 January and Bank Holidays – **M** (booking essential) (dinner only and Sunday lunch)/dinner 15.95 **t.** ⏐3.80.

at Wilmington NW : 6 ½ m. by A 22 on A 27 – **Y** – ✉ ☏ 032 12 Polegate :

⋔ **Crossways**, Lewes Rd, BN26 5SG, ℰ 2455, ⇘ – TV ℗. ◪ *VISA*. ⅌
closed 24 December-15 January – **M** 15.95 **t.** ⏐3.50 – **7 rm** ⊏ 21.00/49.00 **st.** – SB (weekdays only) (except summer) 65.00/69.00 **st.**

EAST BUCKLAND Devon 🔢 l 30 – see South Molton.

EAST CHINNOCK Somerset – see Yeovil.

EAST DEREHAM Norfolk **404** W 25 – pop. 11 798 – ✆ 0362 Dereham.

◆London 109 – ◆Cambridge 57 – King's Lynn 27 – ◆Norwich 16.

🏨 **Phoenix** (T.H.F.), Church St., NR19 1DL, ✆ 692276 – ↤ rm 📺 ☎ Ⓟ – 🎱 150. 🔼 AE ⓪ VISA
M 4.75/10.25 **st.** and a la carte 🍾 3.95 – ☕ 7.00 – **23 rm** 36.00/72.00 **st.** – SB 62.00/72.00 **st.**

🏨 George (B.C.B.), Swaffham Rd, NR19 2AZ, ✆ 696801 – 📺 ☎ Ⓟ
8 rm.

🏨 **King's Head,** 42 Norwich St., NR19 1AD, ✆ 693842, ⟏, ※ – 📺 ☎ Ⓟ. 🔼 AE ⓪ VISA
M 10.00/11.00 **t.** and a la carte 🍾 3.00 – **15 rm** ☕ 29.50/45.00 **t.** – SB (winter only) (week-ends only) 50.00/54.00 **st.**

AUSTIN-ROVER Norwich Rd ✆ 692293   SEAT Two Oaks Garage Beetley ✆ 860219
FORD High St. ✆ 692281

EAST GRINSTEAD West Sussex **404** T 30 – pop. 23 867 – ECD : Wednesday – ✆ 0342.
Envir. : Hever Castle★ (13C-20C) and gardens★★ *AC*, NE : 10 m.

◆London 32 – ◆Brighton 29 – Eastbourne 33 – Lewes 21 – Maidstone 32.

🏨 **Felbridge,** London Rd, RH19 2BH, NW : 1 ½ m. on A 22 ✆ 326992, Telex 95156, Fax 410778, 🏊 heated, 🔼, ⟏ – ↤ 📺 ☎ Ⓟ – 🎱 . 🔼 AE ⓪ VISA
M 8.95/11.50 **st.** and a la carte 🍾 3.95 – ☕ 6.50 – **50 rm** 55.00/85.00 **st.** – SB (wee-kends only) (except Easter and Christmas) 75.00/95.00 **st.**

※※ **Woodbury House (Garden Room R.)** with rm, Lewes Rd, RH19 3UD, SE : ½ m. on A 22 ✆ 313657, Fax 314801, ⟏ – 📺 ☎ Ⓟ. 🔼 AE ⓪ VISA
closed 25 and 26 December – M *(closed Saturday lunch and Sunday dinner)* 12.50/13.50 **t.** and a la carte 18.75/23.50 **t.** 🍾 3.55 – **14 rm** ☕ 48.00/75.00 **t.**

at Gravetye SW : 4 ½ m. by B 2110 taking second turn left towards West Hoathly – ✉ East Grinstead – ✆ 0342 Sharpthorne :

🏨 **Gravetye Manor** 🕊, Vowels Lane, RH19 4LJ, ✆ 810567, Telex 957239, Fax 810080, ≼, « 16C manor house with gardens and grounds by William Robinson », 🕊, park – ↤ rest 📺 Ⓟ. ※
M *(closed Christmas Night to non residents)* (booking essential) 15.00/19.00 **s.** and a la carte 23.50/33.50 **s.** 🍾 7.00 – ☕ 9.00 – **14 rm** 68.25/154.00 **s.**

FORD 220 London Rd ✆ 324344   ⦿ ATS London Rd, North End ✆ 410740
VAUXHALL King St. ✆ 324666

EASTHAM Merseyside **402 403** L 24 – pop. 16 228 – ✉ Wirral – ✆ 051 Liverpool.
◆London 209 – ◆Birmingham 45 – Chester 13 – ◆Liverpool 7.5 – ◆Manchester 45.

🏨 **Travelodge** without rest., New Chester Rd, Junction of M 53 with A 41, L62 9AQ, ✆ 327 2489 – 📺 ♿ Ⓟ. 🔼 AE VISA
30 rm 21.50/27.00 **t.**

EAST HORNDON Essex – ✆ 0277 Brentwood.
◆London 21 – Chelmsford 13 – Southend-on-Sea 17.

🏨 **Travelodge** without rest., CM13 3LL, on A 127 ✆ 810819 – 📺 ♿ Ⓟ. 🔼 AE VISA
20 rm 21.50/27.00 **t.**

EAST HORSLEY Surrey **404** S 30 – pop. 5 864 – ECD : Thursday – ✉ Leatherhead – ✆ 048 65.
◆London 29 – Guildford 7.

🏨 **Thatchers,** Epsom Rd, KT24 6TB, on A 246 ✆ 4201, Telex 946249, Fax 4222, 🏊 heated, ⟏ – 📺 ☎ Ⓟ – 🎱 60. 🔼 AE ⓪ VISA
M *(closed Saturday lunch)* 14.50/25.00 **t.** 🍾 3.90 – ☕ 5.95 – **59 rm** 65.00/85.00 – SB (weekends only) 76.00/80.00 **st.**

EAST LANGTON Leics. – see Market Harborough.

EASTLEIGH Devon **403** H 30 – see Bideford.

EASTLEIGH Hants. **403** P 31 – pop. 58 585 – ECD : Wednesday – ✆ 0703.
🏌 Fleming Park, Magpie Lane ✆ 612797.
🅸 Town Hall Centre, Leigh Rd ✆ 641261.

◆London 74 – Winchester 8 – ◆Southampton 4.

🏨 **Crest** (Crest), Leigh Rd, SO5 5PG, ✆ 619700, Telex 47606, Fax 643945 – 🛗 ↤ rm 🍽 rest 📺 ☎ ♿ Ⓟ – 🎱 300. 🔼 AE ⓪ VISA
M (bar lunch Saturday) 10.50/15.50 **st.** and a la carte 17.35/19.45 **st.** – ☕ 7.45 – **117 rm** 75.00/89.00 **st.**, **3 suites** 120.00 **st.** – SB (weekends only) 88.00/108.00 **st.**

⦿ ATS Duttons Lane, Bishopstoke Rd ✆ 613027/613393

EAST MOLESEY Surrey **404** ㊷ – see Esher.

EASTON CROSS Devon **403** I 31 – see Chagford.

EASTON GREY Wilts. 408 404 N 29 – see Malmesbury.

EAST PORTLEMOUTH Devon 408 I 33 – see Kingsbridge.

EAST PRESTON West Sussex 404 S 31 – see Worthing.

EAST WITTERING West Sussex 404 R 31 – pop. 3 503 – ✆ 0243 Chichester.
♦London 74 – ♦Brighton 37 – ♦Portsmouth 25.

  ✗ **Clifford's Cottage,** Bracklesham Lane, Bracklesham Bay, PO20 8JA, E : 1 m. by B 2179
on B 2198 ℰ 670250, 🏧 – ⓟ. 🅰 AE ⓪ VISA
closed Sunday dinner, first 2 weeks February and first 3 weeks November – **M** (dinner only
and Sunday lunch)/dinner 15.00 and a la carte 13.35/23.50 **t.** ⌕ 3.95.

EBBERSTON North Yorks. 402 S 21 – pop. 425 – ✉ ✆ 0723 Scarborough.
♦London 243 – Scarborough 9 – York 31.

  ⌂ **Foxholm,** Main St., YO13 9NJ, off A 170 ℰ 85550, 🏧 – ⓟ
April-October – **M** 7.00 **t.** ⌕ 2.80 – **9 rm** ⌁ 17.00/34.00 **t.**

ECCLES Greater Manchester 402 408 404 M 23 – pop. 37 792 – ✉ ✆ 061 Manchester.
♦London 204 – ♦Liverpool 31 – ♦Manchester 4 – Preston 32.

  ⌂ **Ashdene,** 48 Wellington Rd, M30 9QW, ℰ 789 4762 – TV ☎ ⓟ. 🅰 VISA 🦅
M 8.50 **st.** ⌕ 4.00 – **7 rm** ⌁ 33.00/46.00 **st.**

EDENBRIDGE Kent 404 U 30 – pop. 7 674 – ✉ ✆ 0732 – ⛳ Crouch House Rd ℰ 865097.
♦London 35 – ♦Brighton 36 – Maidstone 29.

  ✗✗✗ **Honours Mill,** 87 High Street, TN8 5AU, ℰ 866757, « Carefully restored 18C mill » – 🅰
VISA
*closed Saturday lunch, Sunday dinnner, Monday, 2 weeks in June, 2 weeks after Christmas
and Bank Holidays.* – **M** approx. 25.95 **st.** ⌕ 4.00.

AUSTIN-ROVER Marlpit Hill ℰ 866202
AUSTIN-ROVER, LAND-ROVER, FORD Stanford
Rd, Hartfield End ℰ 863366

HONDA High St. ℰ 862031
VAUXHALL-OPEL Station Rd ℰ 866822

EGERTON Greater Manchester 402 ㉑ 408 ② 404 ⑨ – see Bolton.

EGHAM Surrey 404 S 29 – pop. 21 337 – ECD : Thursday – ✆ 0784.
♦London 29 – Reading 21.

  🏨 **Runnymede,** Windsor Rd, TW20 0AG, on A 308 ℰ 436171, Telex 934900, Fax 436340, ≼ –
🍴 TV ☎ ⓟ – ⚐ 350. 🅰 AE ⓪ VISA
M *(closed Saturday lunch)* (Dancing Saturday) 16.75/17.75 **t.** and a la carte ⌕ 5.00 – ⌁ 8.00
– **125 rm** 80.00/220.00 **t.**

  🏨 **Great Fosters,** Stroude Rd, TW20 9UR, S : 1 ¼ m. by B 388 ℰ 433822, Telex 944441, ≼,
« Elizabethan mansion with extensive gardens », ⊒ heated, park, ✗ – TV ☎ ⓟ – ⚐ 50.
🅰 AE ⓪ VISA 🦅
M 14.50/19.50 **t.** and a la carte ⌕ 4.00 – **42 rm** ⌁ 55.00/120.00 **t.**, **2 suites** 125.00 **t.**

  ✗✗ **La Bonne Franquette,** 5 High St., TW20 9EA, ℰ 439494, French rest., 🏧 – ⓟ. 🅰 AE ⓪
VISA
closed Saturday lunch and Bank Holidays – **M** 12.50/19.50 **st.** and a la carte 16.75/26.30 **st.**
⌕ 3.25.

  ✗ **Trattoria il Borgo,** 15 The Precinct, TW20 9HN, ℰ 433544, Italian rest. – 🅰 AE VISA
closed Saturday lunch and Sunday – **M** 12.00/18.00 **st.** ⌕ 4.00.

FERRARI Egham-by-pass ℰ 36431/36222
VOLVO The Causeway ℰ 36191

EGLWYSFACH Dyfed 408 I 26 – see Machynlleth (Powys).

EGTON BRIDGE North Yorks. – see Goathland.

ELLAND West Yorks. 402 O 22 – see Halifax.

ELSING Norfolk 404 X 25 – ✉ Dereham – ✆ 036 283 Swanton Morley.
♦London 138 – Fakenham 12 – ♦Norwich 17.

  ⌂ Church Farm Motel 🐾, Church Farm, NR20 3EA, ℰ 8236, 🏧 – TV ☎ ⓟ – **7 rm**.

ELSTEAD Surrey 404 R 30 – pop. 2 633 – ✆ 0252.
♦London 43 – Guildford 9 – ♦Portsmouth 41.

  ✗✗✗ **Bentleys,** Elstead Mill, GU8 6LE, on B 3001 ℰ 703333, Fax 702310, « Converted watermill »,
🏧 – ✂ ▤ ⓟ. 🅰 AE ⓪ VISA
closed Saturday lunch and Sunday dinner – **M** 14.10 **st.** (lunch) and a la carte 13.75/23.50 **t.**
⌕ 3.75.

ELY Cambs. **404** U 26 – pop. 9 006 – ECD : Tuesday – ✆ 0353.
See : Cathedral★★★ (11C-16C) (Norman nave★★★, lantern★★★).
Envir. : Wicken Fen★, 5 : 8 ½ m.
🛈 Public Library, Palace Green ✆ 662062.
♦London 74 – ♦Cambridge 16 – ♦Norwich 60.

- 🏠 **Lamb** (Q.M.H.), 2 Lynn Rd, CB7 4EJ, ✆ 663574 – 📺 ☎ Ⓟ. ⟡ AE ⓪ VISA
  M 8.75/10.00 **t.** and a la carte – **32 rm** ⌣ 50.00/65.00 **t.** – SB (weekends only) 65.00/70.00 **st.**

- 🏠 **Fenlands Lodge,** Soham Rd, Stuntney, CB7 5TR, SE : 3 m. on A 142 ✆ 667047 – 📺 ☎
  Ⓟ. ⟡ AE ⓪ VISA
  M (closed Sunday dinner) 11.00/13.00 **t.** and a la carte – **9 rm** ⌣ 45.00/57.00 **t.** – SB
  (weekends only) 60.00 **st.**

- ✗ **Old Fire Engine House,** 25 St. Mary's St., CB7 4ER, ✆ 662582, English rest., 🎴 – Ⓟ
  closed Sunday dinner, 2 weeks at Christmas and Bank Holidays – **M** (booking essential) a la
  carte 11.70/16.95 **t.** 🍶 3.80.

- ✗ **Peking Duck,** 26 Fore Hill, CB7 4AF, ✆ 662948, Chinese rest. – AE
  closed Tuesday lunch, Monday and 25-26 December – **M** 10.50 **t.** and a la carte 10.20/13.40 **t.**
  🍶 3.90.

     at Littleport N : 5 ¾ m. on A 10 – ✉ ✆ 0353 Ely :

- ✗✗ **Fen House,** 2 Lynn Rd, CB6 1QG, ✆ 860645 – ⟡ AE VISA
  (closed Sunday) – **M** (dinner only) a la carte 14.00/20.70 **st.** 🍶 3.75.

AUSTIN-ROVER Lynn Rd ✆ 662981
FORD Southern By-pass ✆ 661181
VOLVO The Slade, Witcham ✆ 778403

VW-AUDI 16-18 St. Mary's St. ✆ 661272

🛞 ATS 11 Broad St. ✆ 662758/662807

EMSWORTH Hants. **404** R 31 – pop. 17 604 (inc. Southbourne) – ECD . Wednesday – ✆ 0243.
♦London 75 – ♦Brighton 37 – ♦Portsmouth 10.

- 🏠 **Brookfield,** 93-95 Havant Rd, PO10 7LF, ✆ 373363, 🎴 – 📺 ☎ Ⓟ – 🛗 50. ⟡ AE ⓪ VISA
  🏊
  closed 24 December-2 January – **M** 9.95 **t.** and a la carte 🍶 3.40 – **31 rm** ⌣ 43.00/57.00 **st.** –
  SB (weekends only) 65.00 **st.**

- ✗✗ **36 on the Quay,** The Quay, South St., PO10 7EG, ✆ 375592 – ⟡ AE ⓪ VISA
  closed Sunday and first 2 weeks January – **M** (dinner only) a la carte 23.95/26.95 **t.** 🍶 3.95.

- ✗ **Spencer's,** 36 North St., PO10 7DG, ✆ 372744 – ⟡ VISA
  closed Sunday and Monday – **M** (dinner only) 15.50 **t.**

EPPING Essex **404** U 28 – pop. 10 148 – ECD : Wednesday – ✆ 0378.
See : Forest★.
Envir. : Waltham Abbey (Abbey★) W : 6 m.
♦London 20 – ♦Cambridge 40 – Chelmsford 18.

- 🏠 **Post House** (T.H.F.), High Rd, Bell Common, CM16 4DG, S : ¾ m. on B 1393 ✆ 73137,
  Telex 81617, Fax 560402, 🎴 – 🍴 rm 📺 ☎ Ⓟ – 🛗 70. ⟡ AE ⓪ VISA
  M 9.50/14.50 **st.** and a la carte – ⌣ 7.00 – **82 rm** 65.00/85.00 **st.** – SB 76.00/90.00 **st.**

FORD 24 High St. ✆ 72281

RENAULT High Rd ✆ 72266

EPSOM Surrey **404** ㉚ – pop. 65 830 (inc. Ewell) – ECD : Wednesday – ✆ 037 27.
Envir. : Chessington Zoo★ AC, NW : 3 ½ m.
🏌 Longdown Lane South, Epsom Downs ✆ 21666.
♦London 17 – Guildford 16.

Plan : see Greater London (South-West)

- ⚑ **White House,** Downs Hill Rd, off Ashley Rd, KT18 5HW, ✆ 22472, 🎴 – 📺 ☎ Ⓟ. ⟡ VISA.
  🏊   CZ
  M (by arrangement) 12.00 **st.** 🍶 3.00 – **15 rm** ⌣ 32.50/52.00 **st.**

- ⚑ **Epsom Downs,** 9 Longdown Rd, KT17 3PT, ✆ 740643, Fax 723259 – 📺 ☎ Ⓟ. ⟡ AE ⓪
  VISA
  M 14.50 🍶 3.00 – **16 rm** ⌣ 59.50/70.00 **t.** – SB (weekends only) 70.00/90.00 **st.**

- ✗ **River Kwai II,** 4 East St., KT17 1HH, ✆ 41475, Thai rest – ⟡ AE ⓪ VISA   CZ a
  M 7.00/12.00 **t.** and a la carte approx. 19.20 **t.** 🍶 3.20.

CITROEN Walton-on-the-Hill ✆ 073 781 (Tadworth)
3811
FIAT 38 Upper High St. ✆ 44444
FORD East St. ✆ 26246

NISSAN 5 Ruxley Lane, Ewell ✆ 01 394 1667
RENAULT Nonsuch Ind Est ✆ 28391
VW-AUDI Reigate Rd ✆ 073 73 (Burgh Heath)
60111

ERMINGTON Devon **403** I 32 – pop. 881 – ⊠ Ivybridge – ☎ 0548 Modbury.
◆London 233 – Exeter 37 – ◆Plymouth 13 – Torquay 23.

   Ermewood House, Totnes Rd, PL21 9NS, on B 3210 ℰ 830741, 🐎 – ⤬ rest 📺 ☎ ℗. 🔲 *VISA*
   closed 2 weeks Christmas – **M** *(closed Sunday)* (dinner only) 14.50 **t.** ▯ 3.75 – **12 rm** ☲ 35.00/50.00 **t.** – SB (weekends only) 65.00/75.00 **st.**

ESHER Surrey **404** S 29 – pop. 46 688 (inc. Molesey) – ECD : Wednesday – ☎ 0372.
🔼9 Moore Place, Portsmouth Rd ℰ 63533 BZ – 🔼18 Thames and Ditton, Marquis of Gransby, Portsmouth Rd ℰ 398 1551 BZ.
◆London 20 – ◆Portsmouth 58.

Plan : see Greater London (South-West)

  XX **Good Earth**, 14-18 High St., KT10 9RT, ℰ 62489, Chinese rest. – ▤. 🔲 AE ⓪ *VISA* BZ **e**
   closed 24 to 27 December – **M** 16.00/20.00 **t.** and a la carte 13.50/20.50.

   at East Molesey N : 2 m. by A 309 – ⊠ East Molesey – ☎ 01 London (from 6 May : 081) :

  XX **Le Chien Qui Fume**, 107 Walton Rd, KT8 0DR, ℰ 979 7150, French rest. – 🔲 AE ⓪ *VISA*
   closed Sunday, last 3 weeks February and Bank Holiday Mondays – **M** 13.50/19.50 **t.** and a la carte 18.95/25.00 **t.** ▯ 3.95. BY **c**

  X **New Anarkali**, 160 Walton Rd, KT8 OHP, ℰ 979 5072, Indian rest. – 🔲 AE ⓪ *VISA* BY **a**
   M 7.00 **t.** and a la carte approx 7.95 **t.** ▯ 3.10.

   at Claygate SE : 1 m. by A 244 – ⊠ ☎ 0372 Esher :

  XXX ❀ **Les Alouettes**, 7 High St., KT10 OJW, ℰ 64882, French rest. – ▤. 🔲 AE ⓪ *VISA*
   closed Saturday lunch, Sunday, 13 to 16 April, 12 to 28 August and Bank Holidays – **M** 23.00/29.00 **t.** ▯ 4.50 BZ **n**
   Spec. Cassolette de coquilles St. Jacques et langoustines, Tronçonnettes de lotte braisées au gingembre, Framboisine au chocolat sur son coulis.

  X **Reads**, 4 The Parade, KT10 0NU, ℰ 65105 – 🔲 AE *VISA* BZ **r**
   closed Sunday, Monday and 24 December-4 January – **M** 13.95/18.95 **t.** and a la carte 18.95/20.95 **t.** ▯ 3.95.

ESKDALE GREEN Cumbria **402** K 20 – pop. 457 – ECD : Wednesday and Saturday – ⊠ Holmrook – ☎ 094 03.
◆London 312 – ◆Carlisle 59 – Kendal 60.

   Bower House Inn 🦢, CA19 1TD, W : ¾ m. ℰ 244, 🐎 – 📺 ℗. 🔲 *VISA* 🐕
   M (bar lunch)/dinner 15.50 **st.** ▯ 3.30 – **22 rm** ☲ 32.50/45.00 **st.** – SB (except autumn) 65.00/80.00 **st.**

ETON Berks. **404** S 29 – see Windsor.

EVERSHOT Dorset **403** **404** M 31 – pop. 224 – ⊠ Dorchester – ☎ 093 583.
◆London 149 – Bournemouth 39 – Dorchester 12 – Salisbury 53 – Taunton 30 – Yeovil 10.

   Summer Lodge 🦢, Summer Lane, DT2 0JR, ℰ 424, « Country house atmosphere », 🌊 heated, 🐎, % – ☎ & ℗. 🔲 AE *VISA*
   closed 1 to 19 January – **M** 13.50/21.00 **t.** ▯ 3.25 – **17 rm** ☲ 60.00/120.00 **t.** – SB (except summer) 110.00/150.00 **st.**

   Acorn Inn, 28 Fore St., DT2 0JW, ℰ 83228 – 📺 ☎ ℗. *VISA*
   M 13.50 **t.** and a la carte ▯ 3.00 – **8 rm** ☲ 24.00/60.00 **t.** – SB (except Bank Holidays) 55.00/75.00 **t.**

EVESHAM Heref. and Worc. **403** **404** O 27 – pop. 15 069 – ECD : Wednesday – ☎ 0386.
🅹 The Almonry Museum, Abbey Gate ℰ 6944.
◆London 99 – ◆Birmingham 30 – Cheltenham 16 – ◆Coventry 32.

   Evesham, Coopers Lane, off Waterside (A 44), WR11 6DA, ℰ 765566, Telex 339342, Fax 765443, 🔲, 🐎 – 📺 ☎ ℗ – 🔾 25. 🔲 AE ⓪ *VISA*
   closed 25 and 26 December – **M** (buffet lunch)/dinner a la carte 11.70/19.45 **st.** ▯ 3.80 – **40 rm** ☲ 48.00/80.00 **st.**

   Northwick Arms (Lansbury), Waterside (A 44), WR11 6BT, ℰ 40322, Telex 333686, Fax 41070 – 📺 ☎ ℗ – 🔾 60. 🐕
   M 8.50/12.50 **t.** and a la carte 11.50/19.00 **t.** – **25 rm** ☲ 55.00/65.00 **t.**

   Waterside, 56-59 Waterside (B 4035), WR11 6JZ, ℰ 442420 – ⤬ rest 📺 ☎ ℗. 🔲 AE *VISA*
   M 9.50/11.50 **t.** – **10 rm** ☲ 21.40/49.80 **t.** – SB (weekends only) 52.00/58.00 **st.**

EWEN Glos. **403** **404** O 28 – see Cirencester.

EXETER Devon **403** J 31 The West Country G. – pop. 88 235 – ✆ 0392.
See : Site★★ – Cathedral★★ AZ **A** – Maritime Museum★★*AC* AZ – Royal Albert Memorial
Museum★*AC* AZ **M2**.
Envir. : Killerton House★★*AC*, N : 7 m. by B 3181 BY – Crediton (Holy Cross Church★), NW : 8 m.
by A 377 AY – Cullompton★, St. Andrews Church★, NE : 14 m. by B 3181 BY.

🏌 Fingle Glen, Union Rd ✆ 064 76 (Tedburn St. Mary) 81718, 5 m. on A 30 AY – 🏌 Downes
Crediton ✆ 036 32 (Crediton) 3991, NW : 7 ½ m. by A 377 AY.

✈ Exeter Airport : ✆ 68807, Telex 42648, E : 5 m. by A 30 BY – Terminal : St. David's and Central
Stations.

🛈 Civic Centre, Paris St. ✆ 265297 – M 5 Service Area, Junction 30, Sandygate ✆ 37581/79088.

♦London 201 – Bournemouth 83 – ♦Bristol 83 – ♦Plymouth 46 – ♦Southampton 110.

Plan on next page

🏨 **Royal Clarence** (Norfolk Cap.), Cathedral Yard, EX1 1HD, ✆ 58464, Group Telex 42919,
Fax 439423 – 📶 ⇔ rm 📺 ☎ – 🛠 80. 🅂 AE ⓞ VISA. 🧺   AZ **z**
M 9.95/15.00 **t.** and a la carte 16.40/24.10 **t.** – ☕ 5.50 – **52 rm** 60.00/120.00 **t.**, **4 suites** –
SB (weekends only) 70.00/189.00 **st.**

🏨 **Buckerell Lodge** (Crest), Topsham Rd, EX2 4SQ, SE : 1 m. on B 3182 ✆ 52451, Telex
42410, Fax 412114, 🌲 – ⇔ rm 📺 ☎ & 🅿 – 🛠 60. 🅂 AE ⓞ VISA   BY **a**
M (carving lunch Saturday) 8.50/15.00 **st.** and a la carte 🍷 6.25 – ☕ 7.70 – **54 rm**
63.00/75.00 **st.** – SB (weekends only) 92.00/100.00 **st.**

🏨 **St. Olaves Court,** Mary Arches St., EX4 3AZ, ✆ 217736, 🌲 – 📺 ☎ 🅿. 🅂 AE ⓞ VISA.
🧺   AZ **e**
M (closed lunch Saturday and Sunday) 9.95/14.95 **t.** and a la carte 🍷 3.95 – **17 rm**
☕ 33.00/65.00 **t.** – SB (weekends only) 33.95 **st.**

🏨 **White Hart,** 65-66 South St., EX1 1EE, ✆ 79897, Telex 42521, Fax 50159, « Part 14C inn »
– 📶 📺 ☎ 🅿 – 🛠 70. 🅂 AE ⓞ VISA. 🧺   AZ **n**
accommodation closed 24-25 December – **M** 7.00/8.00 **t.** and a la carte – **59 rm**
☕ 27.00/58.00 **t.**, **2 suites** 58.00/100.00 **t.**

🏨 **Rougemont** (Mt. Charlotte), Queen St., EX4 3SP, ✆ 54982, Telex 42455 – 📶 📺 ☎ 🅿
🛠 200   AZ **x**
95 rm.

🏨 **Imperial,** St. David's Hill, EX4 4JX, ✆ 211811, Telex 42551, Fax 420906, 🌲 – 📺 ☎ 🚗 🅿
– 🛠 200. 🅂 AE ⓞ VISA   AZ **v**
M 11.25/13.95 **t.** and a la carte 🍷 4.00 – **26 rm** ☕ 30.00/60.00 **t.**

🏨 Countess Wear Lodge (Q.M.H.), 398 Topsham Rd, EX2 6HE, S : 2 ½ m. at junction of A 379
and B 3182 ✆ 875441, Telex 42551, Fax 876174 – ⇔ rm 📺 ☎ 🅿 – 🛠. 🅂 AE ⓞ VISA
M (closed lunch Saturday and Bank Holidays) – **44 rm** ☕ 39.00/70.00 **st.**   BY **o**

🏨 **St. Andrews,** 28 Alphington Rd, EX2 8HN, ✆ 76784 – 📺 ☎ 🅿. 🅂 AE VISA. 🧺   AY **a**
closed Christmas-New Year – **M** (dinner only) a la carte 9.70/14.65 **st.** 🍷 2.85 – **17 rm**
☕ 34.00/57.00 **st.**

🏨 **Red House,** 2 Whipton Village Rd, EX4 8AR, ✆ 56104 – 📺 ☎ 🅿. 🅂 VISA   BY **r**
M 6.95/9.95 **t.** and a la carte 🍷 3.00 – **12 rm** ☕ 24.00/45.00 **t.** – SB (weekends
only) 42.00/50.00 **st.**

🏠 **Sylvania House** without rest., 64 Pennsylvania Rd, EX4 6DF, ✆ 75583 – 📺 🅿   AY **e**
closed November-February – **8 rm** ☕ 13.50/29.50 **st.**

🏠 **Glendale** without rest., 8 St. Davids Hill, EX4 3RQ, ✆ 74350 – 📺 🅿. 🅂 VISA   AZ **o**
10 rm ☕ 18.00/32.00 **st.**

🏠 **Park View** without rest., 8 Howell Rd, EX4 4LG, ✆ 71772 – 📺 ☎ 🅿. 🅂 VISA   AZ **i**
15 rm ☕ 15.00/40.00 **t.**

🏠 **Trenance House,** 1 Queens Cres., York Rd, EX4 6AY, ✆ 73277 – 📺 🅿. 🅂 VISA   BZ **o**
M 6.00 **st.** – **15 rm** ☕ 16.00/30.00 **t.**

at Huxham N : 5 m. by A 377 – AY – off A 396 – ✉ Exeter – ✆ 0392 Stoke Canon :

XX **Barton Cross** 🔈 with rm, EX5 4EJ, ✆ 841245, « Part 16C thatched cottage », 🌲 – 📺 ☎
🅿. 🅂 AE ⓞ VISA
M (closed Sunday lunch) a la carte 15.50/18.50 **st.** 🍷 3.75 – **6 rm** ☕ 35.00/70.00 **st.** –
SB (weekends only) (except Christmas) 79.00 **st.**

at Pinhoe NE : 2 m. by A 30 – BY – ✉ ✆ 0392 Exeter :

🏨 Gipsy Hill 🔈, Gipsy Hill Lane, via Pinn Lane, EX1 3RN, ✆ 65252, 🌲 – 📺 ☎ 🅿 – 🛠 150
21 rm, **1 suite**.

at Whimple NE : 9 m. by A 30 – BY – ✉ Exeter – ✆ 0404 Whimple :

🏠 **Woodhayes** 🔈, EX5 2TD, ✆ 822237, « Country house atmosphere », 🌲, 🍴 – 📺 ☎
🚗 🅿. 🅂 AE ⓞ VISA. 🧺
M (booking essential) (lunch by arrangement) (residents only) 14.00/15.00 **st.** 🍷 4.40 – **6 rm**
☕ 55.00/75.00 **st.**

at Kennford S : 5 m. on A 38 – AY – ✉ ✆ 0392 Exeter :

🏨 **Exeter Court** (Best Western), Kennford Services, EX6 7UX, ✆ 832121, Telex 42443, Fax
833590, 🍴 – 📺 ☎ 🅿 – 🛠 60. 🅂 AE ⓞ VISA
M 9.00/11.50 **st.** and a la carte 🍷 4.00 – **61 rm** ☕ 38.00/58.00 **st.** – SB 70.00/80.00 **st.**

🏠 **Fairwinds,** EX6 7UD, ✆ 832911 – ⇔ 📺 ☎ 🅿. 🅂 VISA. 🧺
closed 8 to 31 December – **M** (residents only)(bar lunch)/dinner 10.00 **t.** and a la carte 🍷 2.50
– **8 rm** ☕ 19.50/39.00 **t.** – SB 46.00/52.00 **st.**

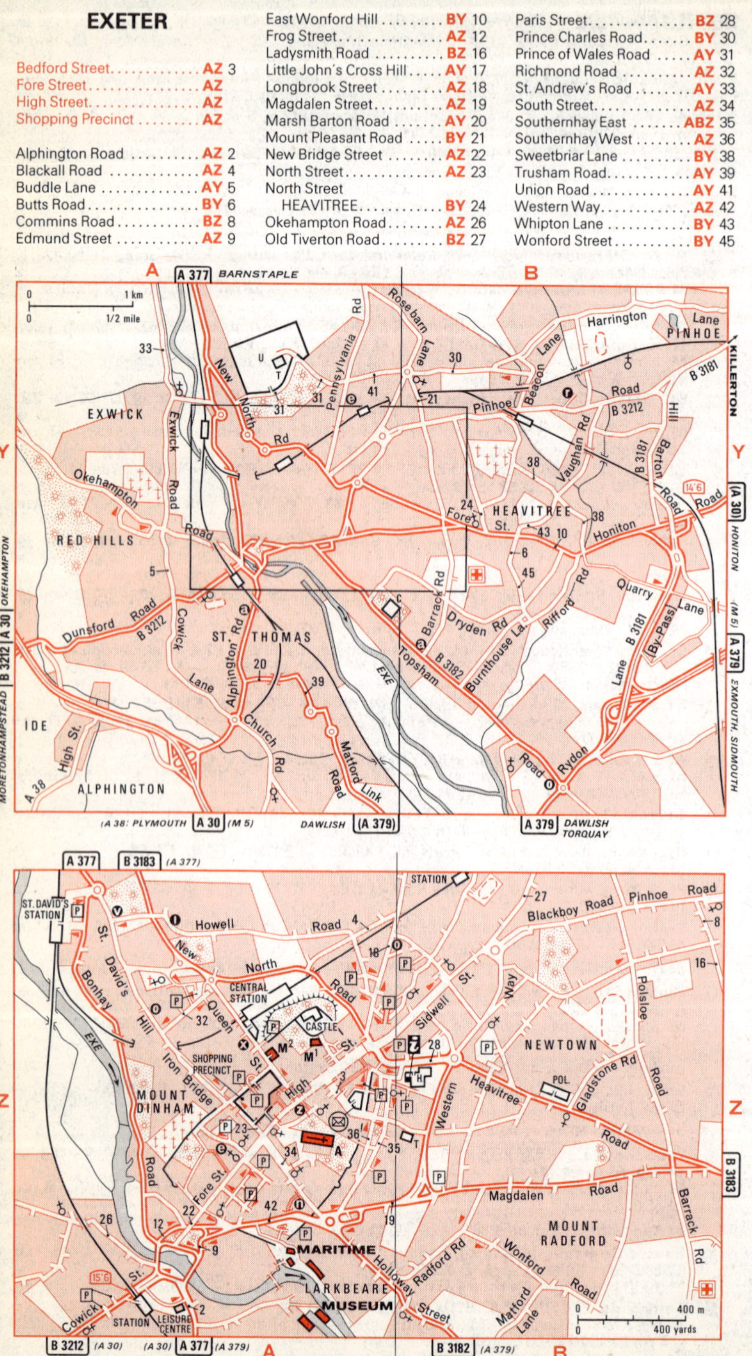

EXETER

Bedford Street............AZ 3
Fore Street...............AZ
High Street...............AZ
Shopping Precinct.........AZ

Alphington Road...........AZ 2
Blackall Road.............AZ 4
Buddle Lane...............AY 5
Butts Road................BY 6
Commins Road..............BZ 8
Edmund Street.............AZ 9
East Wonford Hill.........BY 10
Frog Street...............AZ 12
Ladysmith Road............BZ 16
Little John's Cross Hill..AY 17
Longbrook Street..........AZ 18
Magdalen Street...........AZ 19
Marsh Barton Road.........AY 20
Mount Pleasant Road.......BY 21
New Bridge Street.........AZ 22
North Street..............AZ 23
North Street
  HEAVITREE...............BY 24
Okehampton Road...........AZ 26
Old Tiverton Road.........BZ 27
Paris Street..............BZ 28
Prince Charles Road.......BY 30
Prince of Wales Road......AY 31
Richmond Road.............AZ 32
St. Andrew's Road.........AY 33
South Street..............AZ 34
Southernhay East..........ABZ 35
Southernhay West..........AZ 36
Sweetbriar Lane...........BY 38
Trusham Road..............AY 39
Union Road................AY 41
Western Way...............AZ 42
Whipton Lane..............BY 43
Wonford Street............BY 45

at Doddiscombsleigh SW : 7 ½ m. by A 38 – AY – ⊠ Exeter – ☎ 0647 Christow :

⚲ **Nobody Inn** ⑤, EX6 7PS, ☏ 52394, ≤, « 16C inn », 🐎 – TV P. ⚑ VISA. 🛇
closed 8 to 15 January and Christmas Night – **M** *(closed dinner Sunday and Monday)* (bar lunch)/dinner a la carte 11.80/14.20 **st.** ⌑ 2.50 – **7 rm** ⊇ 15.00/43.00 **st.**

at Ide W : 3 m. by A 30 – AY – ⊠ ☎ 0392 Exeter :

XX **Old Mill,** 20 High St., EX2 9RW, ☏ 59480 – P. ⚑ AE VISA
closed Sunday and 25-26 December – **M** 6.95/11.95 **st.** and a la carte 13.35/25.35 **st.** ⌑ 2.50.

MICHELIN Distribution Centre, Kestrel Way, Sowton Industrial Estate, EX2 7LH, ☏ 77246, FAX 444302 by Honiton Road BY

AUSTIN-ROVER 55 Sidwell St. ☏ 78342
AUSTIN-ROVER Honiton Rd ☏ 68187
BMW Budlake Rd., Marsh Barton Industrial Estate ☏ 69595
DAIMLER-JAGUAR, LAND-ROVER, RANGE-ROVER Marsh Barton Rd ☏ 37152
FIAT 84-88 Sidwell St. ☏ 54923
FORD 9 Marsh Barton Rd ☏ 50141
MAZDA Alphinbrook Rd ☏ 57737
MERCEDES-BENZ Trusham Rd, Marsh Barton ☏ 77311

RENAULT Haven Rd ☏ 30321
TOYOTA 37 Marsh Green Rd, Marsh Barton ☏ 34761
VAUXHALL-OPEL 8 Marsh Barton Rd, Marsh Barton Trading Estate ☏ 34851
VOLVO Longbrook Terr. ☏ 215691

◍ ATS Exe St. ☏ 55465

EXETER SERVICE AREA Devon 403 J 31 – ⊠ ☎ 0392 Exeter

🏨 Granada Lodge, Moor Lane, Sandygate, EX2 4AR, M 5 Junction 30 ☏ 74044, Fax 410406 – TV ☎ ♿ P – 🏊 40
M (grill rest.) – **52 rm**.

EXFORD Somerset 403 J 30 **The West Country G.** – pop. 409 – ECD : Thursday – ⊠ Minehead – ☎ 064 383.

See : Exmoor National Park★★ – Church▲.

Envir. : Dunkery Beacon★★★ (≤★★★), N : 4 ½ m. – Winsford★, SE : 8 m. – at Oare, Doone Valley★, NW : 8 m. plus 6 m. return on foot – Luccombe★ (Church★), NE : 9 m.

◆London 194 – Exeter 35 – Minehead 13 – Taunton 32.

🏨 Crown, TA24 7PP, ☏ 554 – ⤨ rest TV ☎ P
17 rm.

EXMOUTH Devon 403 J 32 **The West Country G.** – pop. 28 037 – ECD : Wednesday – ☎ 0395.

Envir. : A La Ronde★AC, N : 2 m. – Bicton★, The Gardens★AC, NE : 8 m.

🛈 Alexandra Terr. ☏ 263744 (summer only).

◆London 210 – Exeter 11.

🏨 **Imperial** (T.H.F.), The Esplanade, EX8 2SW, ☏ 274761, ≤, ⌇ heated, 🐎, ⚔ – 🛗 TV ☎ P. ⚑ AE ⓪ VISA
M (buffet lunch Monday to Saturday)/dinner 12.75 **st.** and a la carte ⌑ 3.95 – ⊇ 7.25 – **57 rm** 61.00/85.00 **st.** – SB 80.00/110.00 **st.**

🏨 **Royal Beacon** (Best Western), The Beacon, EX8 2AF, ☏ 264886, Telex 94016961, Fax 268890, ≤ – 🛗 ⤨ TV ☎ ⇔ P. ⚑ AE ⓪ VISA
M 7.50/11.75 **t.** and a la carte ⌑ 5.00 – **30 rm** ⊇ 36.00/70.00 **st.**

🏠 **Balcombe House** ⑤, 7 Stevenstone Rd, EX8 2EP, NE : 1 m. by A 376 ☏ 260349, 🐎 – TV P. 🛇
April-October – **M** (bar lunch)/dinner 9.50 **t.** ⌑ 2.50 – **12 rm** ⊇ 20.00/44.00 **t.** – SB 58.00/61.20 **st.**

⚲ **Carlton Lodge,** Carlton Hill, EX8 2AJ, ☏ 263314 – TV P. ⚑ VISA
M (bar lunch)/dinner a la carte 6.15/11.15 **st.** ⌑ 3.45 – **6 rm** ⊇ 19.00/34.00 **st.**

at Lympstone N : 3 m. by A 376 – ⊠ ☎ 0395 Exmouth :

XXX **River House** with rm, The Strand, EX8 5EY, ☏ 265147, ≤ Exe Estuary – TV. ⚑ AE VISA 🛇
M *(closed Sunday dinner and Monday)* 27.50 **t.** and a la carte ⌑ 3.95 – ⊇ 5.50 – **2 rm** 48.00/62.00 **t.**

AUSTIN-ROVER The Parade ☏ 272258

FORD Withycombe Village Rd ☏ 277633/272617

EYAM Derbs. 403 404 O 24 – pop. 923 – ⊠ Sheffield (South Yorks.) – ☎ 0433 Hope Valley.

See : Celtic Cross★ (8C).

◆London 163 – Derby 29 – ◆Manchester 32 – ◆Sheffield 12.

⚲ **Miners Arms,** Water Lane, S30 1RG, ☏ 30853 – TV P. 🛇
M *(closed Sunday dinner and Monday)* 4.95/13.50 **st.** ⌑ 4.00 – **6 rm** ⊇ 24.00/35.00 **st.**

EYTON Heref. and Worc. – see Leominster.

FACCOMBE Hants. – see Hurstbourne Tarrant.

FAIRFORD Glos. 403 404 O 28 – pop. 2 408 – ECD : Saturday – ☎ 0285 Cirencester.
See : St. Mary's Church (stained glass windows★★ 15C-16C).

♦London 99 – ♦Bristol 46 – Gloucester 28 – ♦Oxford 27.

⌂ **Hyperion House,** London St., GL7 4AH, ✆ 712349, Fax 713126, ⇔ – ⇔ rm TV ☎ P –
⚓ . ⟋ AE ⓪ VISA
closed 27 December-4 January – **M** (bar lunch)/dinner 13.50 **t.** and a la carte ⌁ 3.00 – **26 rm**
⌖ 48.00/65.00 **t.** – SB 80.00 **st.**

AUSTIN-ROVER The Bridge, Milton St. ✆ 712222

FAIRY CROSS Devon 403 H 31 – see Bideford.

FAKENHAM Norfolk 404 W 25 – pop. 5 554 – ☎ 0328.
🄳 Red Lion House, 37 Market Pl. ✆ 51981 (summer only).

♦London 108 – King's Lynn 22 – ♦Norwich 27.

⌂ **Crown** (B.C.B.), 6 Market Pl., NR21 9BP, ✆ 51418 – TV ☎ P. ⟋
M (grill rest.) – **11 rm**.

AUSTIN-ROVER, PEUGEOT Norwich Rd ✆ 4035   VOLVO Holt Rd ✆ 4222
VAUXHALL Greenway Lane ✆ 2200

FALMOUTH Cornwall 403 E 33 The West Country G. – pop. 17 810 – ECD : Wednesday –
☎ 0326.

See : Site★ – Pendennis Castle★ (⩻★★)AC B.

Envir. : Glendurgan Garden★★AC, S : 3 ½ m. by Swanpool Rd A – Helston Flora Day Flurry
Dance★★, SW : 11 m. by A 39 A – Mawnan Parish Church★, (⩻★★), SW : 4 m. by Trescobeas Rd
A – at Gweek, Seal Sanctuary★, setting★AC, SW : 8 m. by A 39 A – Carn Brea (⩻★), NW : 9 m.
by A 39 A – at Wendron, Poldark Mine★, W : 9 m. by A 39 A – at Culdrose, Cornwall Aero
Park★AC, SW : 10 m. by A 39 A – at Redruth, Tolgus Tin Streaming★AC, NW : 11 m. by A 39 A.

🅘🅖 Swanpool Rd ✆ 311262 A.

🄳 47 Killigrew St. ✆ 312300.

♦London 308 – Penzance 26 – ♦Plymouth 65 – Truro 11.

Plan opposite

🏨 **Greenbank,** Harbourside, TR11 2SR, ✆ 312440, Telex 45240, Fax 211, ⩻ harbour – 🛗 TV
☎ ⇔ P. ⟋ AE ⓪ VISA   **A a**
closed 24 to 31 December – **M** 8.00/13.25 **t.** and a la carte ⌁ 4.00 – **43 rm** ⌖ 32.00/100.00 **t.**
– SB (weekends only) 88.00/96.00 **st.**

🏨 **Royal Duchy,** Cliff Rd, TR11 4NX, ✆ 313042, Fax 319420, ⩻, ⟋, ⇔ – 🛗 TV ☎ P. ⟋ AE
⓪ VISA ⟋   **B a**
M 6.50/12.00 **t.** and a la carte – **50 rm** ⌖ 37.00/175.00 **t.** – SB (except Easter,
spring Bank Holiday and Christmas) 69.00/109.00 **st.**

🏨 **Green Lawns,** Western Terr., TR11 4QJ, ✆ 312734, Telex 45169, Fax 211427, ⟋ – TV ☎
P – ⚓ 100. ⟋ AE ⓪ VISA   **A i**
closed 24 to 30 December – **M** 8.50/13.50 **t.** and a la carte ⌁ 3.25 – **40 rm** ⌖ 39.10/80.50 **t.** –
SB 73.00/83.00 **st.**

🏨 **Penmere Manor** (Best Western) ⟋, Mongleath Rd, TR11 4PN, ✆ 211411, Telex 45608,
Fax 317588, ⟋ heated, ⟋, ⇔ – ⇔ TV ☎ P. ⟋ AE ⓪ VISA   **A e**
closed 24 to 28 December – **M** (bar lunch)/dinner 15.00 **st.** ⌁ 3.50 – **32 rm** ⌖ 42.00/85.00 **st.**
– SB 88.00/109.00 **st.**

🏨 St. Michael's, Gyllyngvase Beach, Seafront, TR11 4NB, ✆ 312707, Telex 45540, Fax 319147,
⩻, ⟋, ⟋, ⇔ – ⇔ rest TV ☎ P   **A z**
75 rm.

⌂ **Crill Manor** ⟋, Roscarrack Rd, TR11 5BL, SW : 2 ½ m. by Swanpool Rd ✆ 312994,
⟋ heated, ⇔ – TV P. ⟋ AE ⓪ VISA ⟋   by Boslowick Rd   **A**
M 12.50/18.50 **st.** and a la carte ⌁ 4.00 – **11 rm** ⌖ 39.50/99.00 **st.** – SB (October-
June) 98.00/118.00 **st.**

⌂ **Broadmead,** 68 Kimberley Park Rd, TR11 2DD, ✆ 315704 – TV ☎ P. ⟋ VISA   **A u**
closed Christmas and New Year – **M** (dinner only) 10.50 **st.** ⌁ 2.95 – **12 rm** ⌖ 17.00/40.00 **st.**
– SB (except summer) 42.00/50.00 **st.**

⌂ **Carthion,** Cliff Rd, TR11 4AP, ✆ 313669, ⩻, ⇔ – ⇔ rest TV P. ⟋ AE ⓪ VISA   **B v**
March-September – **M** (bar lunch)/dinner 9.00 **t.** ⌁ 3.00 – **18 rm** ⌖ 25.00/56.00 **t.**

⌂ Melvill House, 52 Melvill Rd, TR11 4DQ, ✆ 316645 – ⇔ TV P. ⟋   **B e**
7 rm.

⌂ **Costwold House,** 49 Melvill Rd, TR11 4DF, ✆ 312077 – ⇔ rest TV P. ⟋   **B o**
M (by arrangement) – **10 rm** ⌖ 15.50/30.00 **st.**

⌂ **Rosemullion,** Gyllyngvase Hill, TR11 4DF, ✆ 314690, ⇔ – ⇔ P. ⟋   **B c**
May-September – **M** 6.60 **st.** – **13 rm** ⌖ 14.95/29.90 **st.** – SB (October-May) 19.55/20.40 **st.**

P.T.O. →

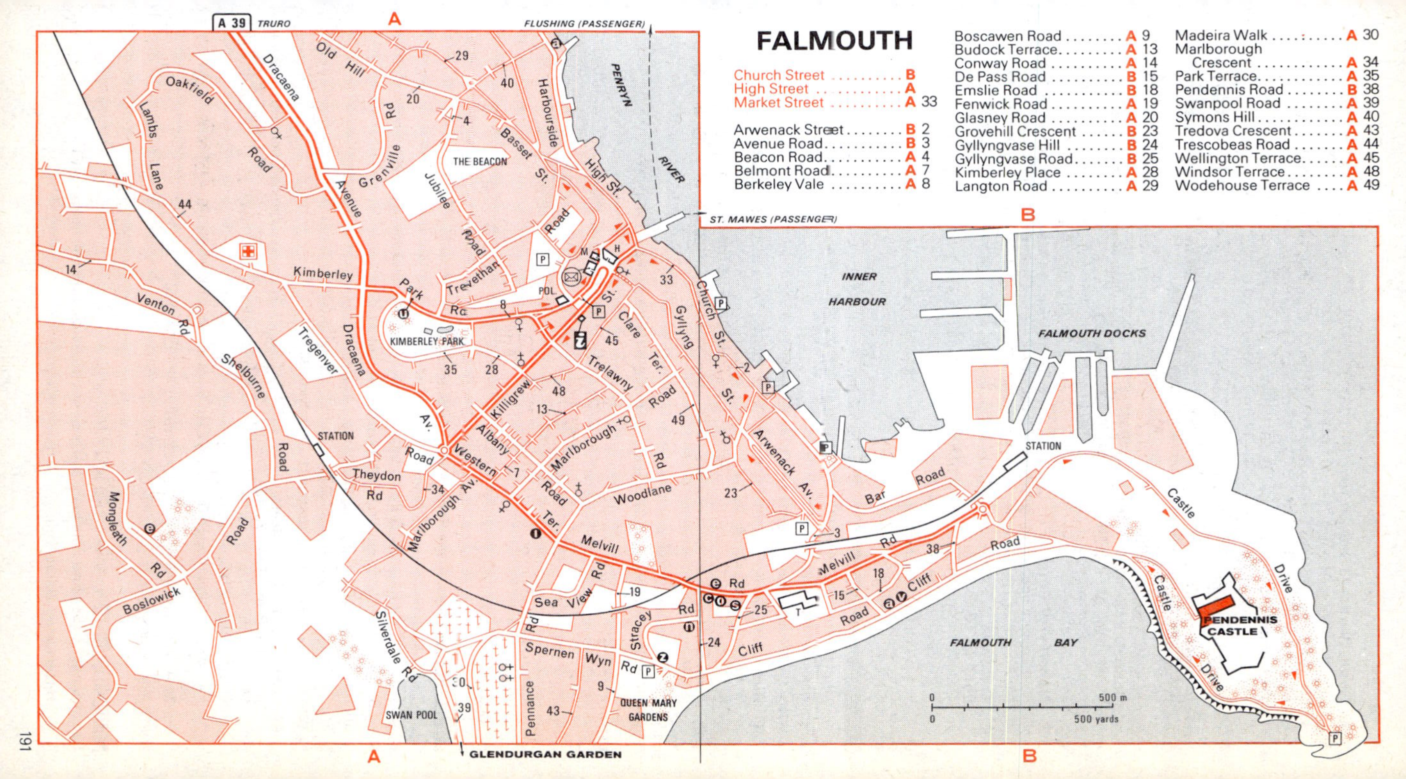

FALMOUTH

Church Street — B
High Street — A
Market Street — A 33

Arwenack Street — B 2
Avenue Road — B 3
Beacon Road — A 4
Belmont Road — A 7
Berkeley Vale — A 8

Boscawen Road — A 9
Budock Terrace — A 13
Conway Road — A 14
De Pass Road — B 15
Emslie Road — B 18
Fenwick Road — A 19
Glasney Road — A 20
Grovehill Crescent — B 23
Gyllyngvase Hill — B 24
Gyllyngvase Road — B 25
Kimberley Place — B 28
Langton Road — A 29

Madeira Walk — A 30
Marlborough Crescent — A 34
Park Terrace — A 35
Pendennis Road — B 38
Swanpool Road — A 39
Symons Hill — A 40
Tredova Crescent — A 43
Trescobeas Road — A 44
Wellington Terrace — A 45
Windsor Terrace — A 48
Wodehouse Terrace — A 49

A 39 TRURO
FLUSHING (PASSENGER)
PENRYN
RIVER
ST. MAWES (PASSENGER)
INNER HARBOUR
FALMOUTH DOCKS
FALMOUTH BAY
PENDENNIS CASTLE
Castle Drive
STATION
GLENDURGAN GARDEN
SWAN POOL
QUEEN MARY GARDENS
Oakfield
Old Hill
Dracaena
Lambs Lane
Grenville Rd
THE BEACON
Basset St.
Harbourside
High St.
Avenue
Road
Kimberley
Park Rd
KIMBERLEY PARK
Trevethan
Jubilee
Tregenver
Dracaena
Shelburne Road
Venton Rd
Mongleath Rd
Boslowick
Silverdale Rd
Spernen Wyn Rd
Pennance
Sea View Rd
Stracey Rd
Western Road
Albany
Marlborough Av.
Theydon Rd
Killigrew
Trelawny
Clare Ter.
Gyllyng
Church St.
Arwenack Av.
Marlborough Road
Woodlane
Melvill
Bar Road
Melvill Road
Cliff Road
Castle Drive
500 m
500 yards

FALMOUTH

↑ **Good-Winds,** 13 Stratton Terr., TR11 2SY, ✆ 313200, ≤ – Ⓟ   by Harbourside   A
April-October – **M** 3.25 ₰ 3.00 – **11 rm** � 16.00/32.00.

↑ **Gyllyngvase House,** Gyllyngvase Rd, TR11 4DJ, ✆ 312956, 🐎 – ⤢ rest ☎ Ⓟ   B s
M (bar lunch)/dinner 8.00 st. ₰ 3.00 – **15 rm** ⊏ 14.50/33.00 st.

↑ **Tresillian House,** 3 Stracey Rd, TR11 4DW, ✆ 312425 – ⤢ rest 📺 ☎ Ⓟ. ⅏   A n
March-October – **M** 9.00 t. ₰ 3.00 – **12 rm** ⊏ 18.50/37.00 t. – SB 39.00/45.00 st.

at Mawnan Smith SW : 5 m. by Trescobeas Rd – A – off B 3291 – ✉ ✆ 0326 Falmouth :

🏨 **Meudon** ⅏, TR11 5HT, E : ½ m. ✆ 250541, Telex 45478, Fax 250500, « ≤ Terraced gardens landscaped by Capability Brown » – 📺 ☎ Ⓟ. ◪ ⓞ VISA
closed January and February – **M** 14.00/26.00 t. and a la carte ₰ 5.50 – **30 rm** ⊏ 55.00/135.00 t. – SB 96.00/110.00 st.

🏨 **Budock Vean Golf and Country House** ⅏, TR11 5LG, ✆ 250288, Fax 250892, ≤, ◪, ⌐9, 🐎, park, ✂ – ▮ 📺 ☎ Ⓟ – ◭ 50. ◪ AE ⓞ VISA
closed 3 January-12 February – **M** (dinner only and Sunday lunch)/dinner 15.75 t. and a la carte ₰ 3.95 – **53 rm** ⊏ 32.00/140.00 t. – SB 78.00/125.00 st.

🏨 **Nansidwell Country House** ⅏, TR11 5HU, SE : ¼ m. on Mawnan Church rd ✆ 250340, ≤, « Country house atmosphere, gardens », park, ✂ – 📺 ☎ Ⓟ. ◪ AE ⓞ VISA
closed 1 to 14 January – **M** 12.75/17.75 t. and a la carte ₰ 4.00 – **13 rm** ⊏ 35.00/100.00 t.

🏠 **Trelawne** ⅏, Maenporth Rd, TR11 5HS, E : ¾ m. ✆ 250226, Fax 250909, ◪, 🐎 – ⤢ rest 📺 ☎ Ⓟ. ◪ AE ⓞ VISA
closed January and February – **M** (bar lunch)/dinner 14.50 t. ₰ 3.50 – **14 rm** ⊏ 35.00/64.00 t. – SB 68.00/82.00 st.

BMW Falmouth Rd, Penryn ✆ 032 67 (Penryn) 2641   ⑩ ATS Dracaena Av. ✆ 319233
FORD Ponsharden ✆ 72011

FAREHAM Hants. �403 �404 Q 31 – pop. 55 563 (inc. Portchester) – ECD : Wednesday – ✆ 0329.
Envir. : Portchester castle★ (ruins 3C - 12C), Keep ≤★ *AC*, SE : 2 ½ m.
🔢 Ferneham Hall, Osborn Rd ✆ 221342.
♦London 77 – ♦Portsmouth 9 – ♦Southampton 13 – Winchester 19.

🏨 **Red Lion** (Lansbury), East St., PO16 0BP, ✆ 822640, Telex 86204, Fax 823579 – ⤢ rm 📺 ☎ Ⓟ – ◭ 80. ◪ AE ⓞ VISA. ⅏
M 8.50/12.50 t. and a la carte – **44 rm** ⊏ 55.00/65.00 t. – SB (weekends only) 70.00/78.00 st.

🏠 **Avenue House** without rest., 22 The Avenue, PO14 1NS, ✆ 232175, 🐎 – 📺 ☎ ♿ Ⓟ. ◪ AE VISA
10 rm ⊏ 27.00/47.00 t.

AUSTIN-ROVER Newgate Lane ✆ 282811   ⑩ ATS Queens Rd ✆ 234941/280032

FARINGDON Oxon. �403 �404 P 29 – pop. 4 646 – ECD : Thursday – ✆ 0367.
🔢 The Pump House, 5 Market Pl. ✆ 22191 (summer only).
♦London 79 – ♦Bristol 55 – ♦Oxford 17 – Reading 34.

🏠 **Faringdon,** 1 Market Pl., SN7 7HL, ✆ 20536 – 📺 ☎. ◪ AE ⓞ VISA
M (dinner only) 20.00 t. and a la carte ₰ 7.50 – **18 rm** ⊏ 38.00/48.00.

PEUGEOT-TALBOT Marlborough St. ✆ 21212   TOYOTA Church St. ✆ 22070

FARLINGTON Hants. – see Portsmouth and Southsea.

FARNBOROUGH Hants. �404 R 30 – pop. 48 063 – ECD : Wednesday – ✆ 0252.
See : St. Michael's Abbey church★ (19C) (Imperial crypt *AC*).
⌐9 Southwood, Ively Rd ✆ 548700, W : 1 m.
🔢 Country Library, Pinehurst Av. ✆ 513838.
♦London 41 – Reading 17 – ♦Southampton 44 – Winchester 33.

🏨 **Queen's** (T.H.F.), Lynchford Rd, GU14 6AZ, S : 1 ½ m. on Farnborough Rd (A 325) ✆ 545051, Group Telex 859637, Fax 377210, ◪ – ⤢ rm 📺 ☎ Ⓟ – ◭ 150. ◪ AE ⓞ VISA
M 18.75 st. and a la carte ₰ 3.95 – ⊏ 7.00 – **110 rm** 72.00/94.00 st. – SB (weekends only) 76.00/80.00 st.

🏠 **Falcon,** 68 Farnborough Rd, GU14 6TH, S : ¾ m. on A 325 ✆ 545378 – 📺 ☎ Ⓟ – ◭ . ◪ VISA ⅏
M 10.50 st. and a la carte ₰ 3.50 – **30 rm** ⊏ 48.00/58.00 st.

FORD Elles Rd ✆ 544344

FARNE ISLANDS Northumb. �401 �402 P 17.
See : Islands★★ (Sea Bird Sanctuary and grey seals, by boat from Seahouses *AC*).

Hotels see : Bamburgh.

FARNHAM Surrey 404 R 30 – pop. 34 541 – ECD : Wednesday – 🕿 0252.

See : Castle keep (12C) (square tower★) *AC*.

Envir. : Birdworld★ (zoological bird gardens) *AC*, SW : 3 ½ m.

🏌₉ Farnham Park, Folly Hill ℰ 715216.

🛈 Locality Office, South St. ℰ 048 68 (Godalming) 4104 ext 543.

◆London 45 – Reading 22 – ◆Southampton 39 – Winchester 28.

🏨 **Bush** (T.H.F.), The Borough, GU9 7NN, ℰ 715237, Telex 858764, Fax 733530, 🐾 – ⇔ rm 📺 ☎ Ⓟ – 🛎 60. 🔼 AE ⓪ VISA
 M *(closed Saturday lunch)* 10.95/13.00 **st.** and a la carte ┃ 3.50 – ☲ 7.00 – **68 rm** 65.00/98.00 **st.** – SB (weekends only) 84.00 **st.**

🏨 **Bishop's Table** (Best Western), 27 West St., GU9 7DR, ℰ 710222, Telex 94016743, 🐾 – 📺 ☎. 🔼 AE ⓪ VISA 🛇
 closed 26 December-5 January – **M** *(closed lunch Saturday and Bank Holidays)* 15.00 **t.** and a la carte – **18 rm** ☲ 44.80/71.50 **t.** – SB (weekends only) 72.00/84.00 **st.**

🏨 **Trevena House** ⌚, Alton Rd, GU10 5ER, SW : 1 ¾ m. on A 31 ℰ 716908, Telex 94013011, ≤, 𝄃 heated, 🐾, 🕆 – 📺 ☎ Ⓟ. 🔼 AE ⓪ VISA 🛇
 closed 21 December-7 January – **M** *(closed Sunday and Bank Holidays)* (bar lunch, residents only)/dinner a la carte 9.60/12.55 **t.** ┃ 3.25 – **20 rm** ☲ 44.00/60.00 **st.**

🍴🍴 Chik's, 68 Castle St., GU9 7LN, ℰ 715666, Chinese (Peking, Szechuan) rest.

🍴🍴 **Krug's,** 84 West St., GU9 7EN, ℰ 723277, Austrian rest. – 🔼 VISA
 closed Sunday and Monday – **M** (dinner only) a la carte 14.00/17.50 **t.** ┃ 5.20.

 at Seale E : 4 m. on A 31 – ✉ Farnham – 🕿 025 18 Runfold :

🏨 **Hog's Back** (Embassy), GU10 1EX, on A 31 ℰ 2345, Telex 859352, Fax 3113, ≤, 🐾 – 📺 ☎ ♿ Ⓟ – 🛎 . 🔼 AE ⓪ VISA
 M 10.50 **st.** and a la carte ┃ 3.90 – ☲ 6.00 – **50 rm** 55.00/75.00 **st.**

 at Frensham S : 3 m. on A 287 – ✉ Farnham – 🕿 025 125 Frensham :

🏨 **Mariners,** Millbridge, GU10 3DJ, N : 1 m. on A 287 ℰ 2050, Fax 2649 – 📺 ☎ Ⓟ. 🔼 AE ⓪ VISA
 M 7.50 **t.** (lunch) and a la carte ┃ 3.25 – **21 rm** ☲ 38.00/50.00 **t.** – SB (weekends only) 56.00 **st.**

 at Churt S : 5 ¾ m. on A 287 – ✉ Farnham – 🕿 025 125 Frensham :

🏨 **Frensham Pond** ⌚, GU10 1QB, N : 1 ½ m. by A 287 ℰ 3175, Telex 858610, Fax 2631, ≤, « Lake-side setting », 𝄃, 🐾, squash – 📺 ☎ Ⓟ – 🛎 . 🔼 AE ⓪ VISA 🛇
 M 14.25/15.95 **t.** and a la carte ┃ 3.50 – **19 rm** ☲ 55.00/65.00 **t.** – SB (except Christmas) (weekends only) 84.00/90.00 **st.**

🏨 **Pride of the Valley** (Best Western), Tilford Rd, GU10 2LE, E : 1 ½ m. via Hale House Lane ℰ 042 873 (Hindhead) 5799, Telex 858893, Fax 5875, 🐾 – 📺 ☎ Ⓟ. 🔼 AE ⓪ VISA
 M 12.50/15.00 **t.** and a la carte – **11 rm** ☲ 51.50/62.00 **st.**, **1 suite** 75.00/77.00 **st.** – SB (weekends only) 77.00/91.00 **st.**

AUSTIN-ROVER, DAIMLER-JAGUAR   East St. ℰ   VW-AUDI   West St. and Crondall Lane ℰ 715616 716201

FARRINGTON GURNEY Avon 403 404 M 30 – pop. 587 – ✉ Bristol – 🕿 0761 Temple Cloud.

◆London 132 – Bath 13 – ◆Bristol 12 – Wells 8.

🏨 **Country Ways** ⌚, Marsh Lane, BS18 5TT, ℰ 52449, 🐾 – ⇔ rest 📺 ☎ Ⓟ. 🔼 AE ⓪ VISA 🛇
 M *(closed Sunday)* a la carte 15.75/19.65 **st.** ┃ 3.25 – **6 rm** ☲ 41.25/52.25 **st.** – SB 75.00/117.00 **st.**

 at Ston Easton S : 1 ¼ m. on A 37 – ✉ Bath – 🕿 076 121 Chewton Mendip :

🏰 **Ston Easton Park** ⌚, BA3 4DF, ℰ 631, Fax 377, ≤, « Palladian country house », 🐾, park – 📺 ☎ Ⓟ. 🔼 AE ⓪ VISA
 M 19.50/30.00 **t.** ┃ 5.00 – ☲ 6.50 – **19 rm** 85.00/275.00 **t.** – SB (November-March) 150.00/210.00 **st.**

FAR SAWREY Cumbria 402 L 20 – see Hawkshead.

FARTHING CORNER SERVICE AREA Kent – ✉ Gillingham – 🕿 0634 Medway.

🛈 Farthing Corner Motorway Services ℰ 360323.

◆London 39 – Canterbury 22 – Maidstone 11.

🏨 **Farthing Corner Lodge** (Rank) without rest., ME8 8PW, at Farthing Corner Service Area on M 2 ℰ 377337 – ⇔ rm 📺 ♿ Ⓟ – 🛎 30. 🔼 AE ⓪ VISA
 58 rm 24.75/31.75 **st.**

FAUGH Cumbria – see Carlisle.

FAVERSHAM Kent 404 W 30 – pop. 15 914 – ECD : Thursday – ☎ 0795.
🛈 Fleur de Lis Heritage Centre, 13 Preston St. ℘ 534542.
◆London 52 – ◆Dover 26 – Maidstone 21 – Margate 25.

XX **Reads,** Painters Forstal, ME13 0EE, SW : 2 ¼ m. by A 2 ℘ 535344 – ⇔ 🅿. 🔂 AE ⓪ VISA
closed Sunday, Monday and first week January – **M** 12.00 **st.** (lunch) and a la carte 19.50/26.50 **st.** ⅃ 5.00.

at Boughton SE : 3 m. by A 2 – ✉ Faversham – ☎ 0227 Canterbury :

White Horse, The Street, ME13 9AX, ℘ 751343, Fax 751090 – TV ☎ 🅿. 🔂 AE ⓪ VISA
M 8.45 **t.** and a la carte ⅃ 2.75 – **13 rm** � 35.00/45.00 **st.** – SB (weekends only) 81.00/92.00 **st.**
FORD West St. ℘ 532255

FAWKHAM Kent – see Brands Hatch.

FAWLEY Bucks. 404 R 29 – see Henley-on-Thames (Oxon.).

FELINDRE FARCHOG (VELINDRE) Dyfed 403 F 27 – see Newport (Dyfed).

FELINGWM UCHAF Dyfed – see Carmarthen.

FELINHELI = Port Dinorwic.

FELIXSTOWE Suffolk 404 Y 28 – pop. 24 207 – ECD : Wednesday – ☎ 0394.
🚢 Shipping connections with the Continent : to Belgium (Zeebrugge) (P & O European ferries).
🚢 to Harwich (Orwell & Harwich Navigation Co.) 4-7 daily (except Sunday) (15 mn).
🛈 Leisure Centre, Sea Front ℘ 282126 and 276770.
◆London 84 – ◆Ipswich 11.

Orwell Moat House (Q.M.H.), Hamilton Rd, IP11 7DX, ℘ 285511, Group Telex 987676, Fax 670687, 🚑 – 🛗 TV ☎ 🅿 – 🔔 250. 🔂 AE ⓪ VISA
M a la carte 13.30/23.50 **st.** ⅃ 4.30 – ⊊ 6.50 – **56 rm** 49.50/65.00 **st.**, **4 suites** 70.00/75.00 **st.** – SB (weekends only) 80.00/90.00 **st.**

Brook, Orwell Rd, IP11 7PS, ℘ 278441, Fax 670422 – TV ☎ 🅿 – 🔔 30. 🔂 AE ⓪ VISA
M 15.00/20.00 **t.** and a la carte ⅃ 4.00 – ⊊ 6.00 – **20 rm** 40.00/49.50 **st.** – SB (weekends only) 60.00/76.00 **st.**

Marlborough, Sea Rd, IP11 8BJ, ℘ 285621, Telex 987047, Fax 670724, ≼ – 🛗 TV ☎ – 🔔 100. 🔂 AE ⓪ VISA
M 9.95/11.00 **t.** and a la carte ⅃ 3.30 – ⊊ 5.25 – **47 rm** 35.00/56.00 **t.** – SB (weekends only) 60.00/77.00 **st.**

XX **Sherebangla,** 7-9 Hamilton Rd, IP11 7AX, ℘ 274343, Indian rest – 🔂 AE VISA
M 20.00 **t.** and a la carte 6.55/14.05 **t.**

AUSTIN-ROVER Crescent Rd ℘ 283221
Ⓜ ATS 4-8 Sunderland Rd, Carr Rd Ind. Est. ℘ 675604
ATS St. Andrews Rd ℘ 277596/277888

FELMINGHAM Norfolk 404 Y 25 – see North Walsham.

FENNY BRIDGES Devon – ✉ ☎ 0404 Honiton.
◆London 166 – Exeter 12.

Greyhound Inn (B.C.B.), EX14 0BJ, on A 30 ℘ 850380, « 17C thatched inn » – ⇔ rest TV ☎ 🅿. 🔂 AE ⓪ VISA 🚑
closed Christmas Night – **M** 7.95 **st.** ⅃ 3.85 – **10 rm** ⊊ 30.50/41.50 **st.** – SB (weekends only) 53.90 **st.**

FERNDOWN Dorset 403 404 O 31 – pop. 23 921 – ECD : Wednesday – ☎ 0202.
◆London 108 – Bournemouth 6 – Dorchester 27 – Salisbury 23.

Dormy (De Vere), New Rd, BH22 8ES, on A 347 ℘ 872121, Telex 418301, Fax 895388, 🔂, 🚑, X, squash – 🛗 ▤ rest TV ☎ & 🅿 – 🔔 220. 🔂 AE ⓪ VISA
M 15.00/20.00 **t.** and a la carte ⅃ 4.00 – **124 rm** ⊊ 85.00/110.00 **t.**, **5 suites** 185.00/235.00 **t.** – SB (except Bank Holidays) (weekends only) 130.00/145.00 **st.**

CITROEN Ringwood Rd ℘ 893589
MITSUBISHI Victoria Rd ℘ 871131
TOYOTA Ringwood Rd ℘ 872201
VAUXHALL-OPEL Wimborne Rd East ℘ 872055
VOLVO 539 Ringwood Rd ℘ 872212

FERSFIELD Norfolk – see Diss.

FINDON West Sussex 404 S 31 – see Worthing.

FINGLESHAM Kent – see Deal.

FISHBOURNE I.O.W. 403 404 Q 31 – Shipping Services : see Wight (Isle of).

FISHGUARD (ABERGWAUN) Dyfed **403** F 28 – pop. 2 903 – ECD : Wednesday – ☎ 0348.
Envir. : Porthgain (cliffs ✹★★★) SW : 10 m. – Goodwick (≤★★) NW : 1 ½ m. – Strumble Head
(≤★★ from the lighthouse) NW : 5 m. – Trevine (≤★★) SW : 8 m. – Bryn Henllan (site★) NE : 5 m.
🚢 to Ireland (Rosslare) (Sealink) 1-2 daily (3 h 30 mn).
🛈 Town Hall ℰ 873484 (summer only).
♦London 265 – ♦Cardiff 114 – Gloucester 176 – Holyhead 169 – Shrewsbury 136 – ♦Swansea 76.

  🏛 **Plas Glyn-Y-Mel** ⑤, Lower Town, SA65 9LY, ℰ 872296, ≤, ☞, park – 🅿. ◪ 𝘝𝘐𝘚𝘈
     Mid March-October – **M** (lunch by arrangement)/dinner 15.00 **t.** and a la carte ▯ 4.50 – **6 rm**
     ☲ 35.00/60.00 **t.**

  ⋔ **Cartref,** High St., SA65 9AW, ℰ 872430 – ⤢ 🅿
     M 5.50/8.00 **st.** and a la carte ▯ 3.00 – **13 rm** ☲ 17.50/37.00 **st.** – SB 49.00/60.00 **st.**

  ⋔ Blair Athol, Windy Hall, SA65 9DP, ℰ 873147 – 📺 🅿. ❀
     8 rm.

     at Llanychaer SE : 2 ¼ m. on B 4313 – ✉ ☎ 0348 Fishguard :

  ✗ **Penlan Oleu** ⑤ with rm, SA65 9TL, SE : 2 m. by B 4313 off Puncheston rd ℰ 881314, ≤,
     « Converted farmhouse », ☞ – ⤢ rest 🅿. ◪ 𝘝𝘐𝘚𝘈. ❀
     closed Sunday lunch and 25-26 December – **M** (booking essential) a la carte approx. 10.50 **st.**
     ▯ 2.45 – **5 rm** ☲ 16.00/32.00 **st.**

     at Welsh Hook SW : 7 ½ m. by A 40 – ✉ Haverfordwest – ☎ 0348 Letterston :

  ✗✗ **Stone Hall** ⑤ with rm, SA62 5NS, ℰ 840212, « Part 14C manor house with 17C extension »,
     ☞ – 📺 🅿. ◪ 𝖠𝖤 𝘝𝘐𝘚𝘈. ❀
     M *(closed Monday dinner December to March)* (lunch by arrangement)/dinner 12.50 **t.** and a
     la carte 9.90/16.70 **t.** ▯ 3.80 – **5 rm** ☲ 32.00/43.00 **t.**

     at Goodwick (Wdig) NW : 1 ½ m. – ✉ ☎ 0348 Fishguard :

  🏛🏛 **Fishguard Bay,** Quay Rd, SA64 0BT, ℰ 873571, Telex 48602, park – ▮ ☎ ⅃ .🅿 – 🛏 300.
     ◪ 𝖠𝖤 ① 𝘝𝘐𝘚𝘈
     M (bar lunch Monday to Saturday)/dinner 14.00 **t.** and a la carte ▯ 3.00 – **62 rm**
     ☲ 28.00/70.00 **t.** – SB 50.00/60.00 **st.**

  🏛 **Glanmoy** ⑤, SA64 0JX, E : 1 ¼ m. by A 487 ℰ 872844, ☞ – 📺 🅿. ◪ 𝘝𝘐𝘚𝘈. ❀
     M *(closed Monday)* 8.00 **t.** (dinner) a la carte – **3 rm** ☲ 26.50/46.00 **t.**

FORD   Clive Rd ℰ 872253

FLAMSTEAD Herts. **404** S 28 – pop. 1 407 – ✉ St. Albans – ☎ 0582 Luton.
♦London 32 – Luton 5.

  🏛🏛 **Hertfordshire Moat House** (Q.M.H.), London Rd, AL3 8HH, on A 5 ℰ 840840, Fax
     842282 – 📺 ☎ 🅿 – 🛏 . ◪ 𝖠𝖤 ① 𝘝𝘐𝘚𝘈
     M (bar lunch Saturday) 13.50/16.00 **st.** and a la carte ▯ 4.25 – **95 rm** ☲ 72.00/82.00 **st.** –
     SB (weekends only) (except Christmas) 80.00/90.00 **st.**

FLEET Hants. **404** R 30 – pop. 27 406 – ECD : Wednesday – ☎ 0252.
🛈 Gurkha Sq., Fleet Rd ℰ 811151.
♦London 46 – Guildford 14 – Reading 16 – ♦Southampton 42.

  🏛🏛 **Lismoyne** ⑤, Church Rd, GU13 8NA, ℰ 628555, Fax 811761, ☞ – 📺 ☎ 🅿. ◪ 𝖠𝖤 ① 𝘝𝘐𝘚𝘈
     M 10.60/11.60 **st.** and a la carte ▯ 4.10 – **40 rm** ☲ 42.00/67.00 **st.** – SB 105.20/139.20 **st.**

AUSTIN-ROVER 66 Albert St. ℰ 613303   ◎ ATS 113-115 Kings Rd ℰ 616412/620028

FLEETWOOD Lancs. **402** K 22 – pop. 27 899 – ECD : Wednesday – ☎ 039 17.
🛈 Fleetwood, Princes Way ℰ 3661, W : from Promenade.
🚢 to the Isle of Man : Douglas (Isle of Man Steam Packet Co.) July-August, 2 weekly
(3 h 15 mn).
🛈 Marine Hall, The Esplanade ℰ 71141 (summer only).
♦London 245 – ♦Blackpool 10 – Lancaster 28 – ♦Manchester 53.

  🏛🏛 **North Euston,** The Esplanade, FY7 6BN, ℰ 6525 – ▮ 📺 ☎ 🅿 – 🛏 200. ◪ 𝖠𝖤 ① 𝘝𝘐𝘚𝘈
     ❀
     M *(closed Saturday lunch)* 7.35/10.35 **t.** and a la carte ▯ 3.25 – **57 rm** ☲ 33.00/49.00 **t.** –
     SB (winter only) (weekends only) 60.00 **st.**

FORD   Hatfield Av. ℰ 2292   ◎ ATS 238 Dock St. ℰ 71211/2

When travelling for business or pleasure
in England, Wales, Scotland and Ireland :

– *use the series of five maps*
   (nos **401**, **402**, **403**, **404** *and* **405***) at a scale of 1:400 000*

– *they are the perfect complement to this Guide*
   as towns underlined in red on the maps will be found in this Guide.

FLITWICK Beds. 404 S 27 – pop. 8 421 – ☎ 0525.
♦London 45 – Bedford 13 – Luton 12 – Northampton 28.

Flitwick Manor, Church Rd, off Dunstable Rd, MK45 1AE, ☎ 712242, Telex 825562, Fax 712242, ≤, « 18C manor house », park, – TV ☎ ♿ P. AE VISA.
closed 24 to 28 December – **M** (seafood) 29.50 **t.** and a la carte 26.55/35.00 **t.** 6.00 – **15 rm** 70.00/160.00 **st.** – SB (weekends only) 200.00/350.00 **st.**

FOLKESTONE Kent 404 X 30 – pop. 42 949 – ECD : Wednesday and Saturday – ☎ 0303.
See : Site★ – Envir. : The Warren★ (cliffs) E : 2 m. by A 20 X – Acrise Place★ *AC*, NW : 6 m. by A 260 X.
Shipping connections to France (Boulogne) (Sealink).
Harbour St. ☎ 58594 – Pedestrian Precinct, Sandgate Rd ☎ 53840/58594 (summer only).
♦London 76 – ♦Brighton 76 – ♦Dover 8 – Maidstone 33.

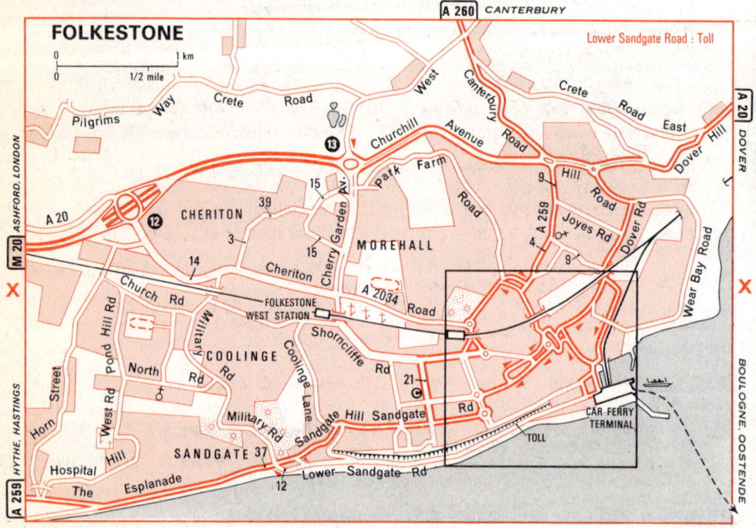

Guildhall Street . . . . Y 23
Rendezvous Street . . YZ 35
Sandgate Road . . . . Z
Tontine Street . . . . Y

Ashley Avenue . . . . X 3
Black Bull Road . . . . X, Y 4
Bouverie Place . . . . Z 6
Bouverie Road East . . . Z 7
Bradstone Road . . . . . . Y 8
Canterbury Road . . . . . X 9
Castle Road . . . . X 12
Cheriton Place . . . . Z 13
Cheriton High Street . . . X 14
Cherry Garden Lane . . . X 15
Clifton Crescent . . . . . . Z 16
Clifton Road . . . . Z 17
Durlocks (The) . . . . Y 20
Earl's Av. . . . . X 21
Grace Hill . . . . Y 22
Harbour Street . . . . Z 24
Harbour App. Road . . . . Z 25
Langhorne Gardens . . . . Z 27
Manor Road . . . . Z 28
Marine Terrace . . . . Z 29
Morrison Road . . . . Y 31
North Street . . . . Y 32
Radnor Bridge Road . . . . Y 33
Remembrance (Rd of) . . Z 34
Ryland Place . . . . Y 36
Sandgate High Street . . X 37
Shorncliffe Road . . . . . . Y 38
Tilekiln Lane . . . . X 39
Trinity Gardens . . . . Z 41
Victoria Grove . . . . Y 43
Wear Bay Road . . . . Y 44
West Terrace . . . . Z 45

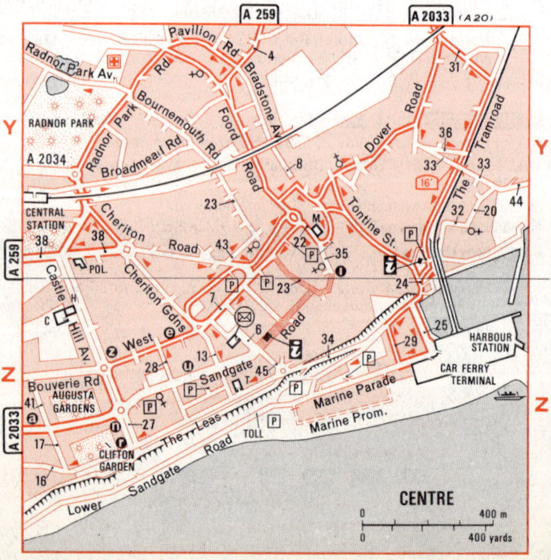

🏠 **Clifton,** The Leas, CT20 2EB, ✆ 851231, Fax 851231, ⬉, ⟤ – 🛗 📺 ☎ – 👥 120. 🅰 AE ⑩ VISA   Z r
M 8.75/13.50 **st.** and a la carte ▮ 3.50 – **84 rm** ⌑ 39.00/63.00 **st.** – SB (except summer) 59.00/75.00 **st.**

🏠 **Wards,** 39 Earls Av., CT20 2HB, ✆ 45166 – 📺 ☎ ⓟ – 👥 40. 🅰 AE ⑩ VISA. 🐾   X c
M 9.50 **t.** (lunch) and a la carte ▮ 3.45 – **10 rm** ⌑ 39.50/79.50 **t.**

🏠 **Garden House,** 142 Sandgate Rd, CT20 2TE, ✆ 52278, Fax 41376 – 🛗 📺 ☎ ⓟ – 👥 60. 🅰 AE ⑩ VISA   Z a
M 6.50/11.50 **st.** and a la carte ▮ 3.85 – **42 rm** ⌑ 35.00/55.00 **t.** – SB 33.00/40.50 **st.**

🏠 **Banque** without rest., 4 Castle Hill Av., CT20 1XD, ✆ 53797 – 📺 ☎. 🅰 AE ⑩ VISA   Z z
12 rm ⌑ 20.00/40.00 **st.**

XX **La Tavernetta,** Leaside Court, Clifton Gdns, CT20 2ED, ✆ 54955, Italian rest. – 🅰 AE ⑩ VISA   Z n
closed Sunday and Bank Holidays – M 8.20 **t.** (lunch) and a la carte 12.50/17.50 **t.** ▮ 3.75.

XX **Emilio,** 124a Sandgate Rd, CT20 2BW, ✆ 55762, Italian rest. – 🅰 AE ⑩ VISA   Z u
M 7.50/8.50 **t.** and a la carte approx. 10.60 **t.** ▮ 3.30.

X **Paul's,** 2a Bouverie Rd West, CT20 2RX, ✆ 59697 – ⓟ. 🅰 VISA   Z e
closed Sunday and 25-26 December – M 12.45 **st.** and a la carte approx. 12.45 **st.** ▮ 3.35.

X **India,** 1 Old High St., CT20 1RJ, ✆ 59155, Indian rest. – 🅰 AE ⑩ VISA   YZ i
closed Monday and 25-26 December – M 6.00/12.00 **t.** and a la carte 5.95/11.60 **t.** ▮ 3.50.

AUSTIN-ROVER 141-143 Sandgate Rd ✆ 850066   VAUXHALL Caesars Way, Cheriton ✆ 53103
COLT, MITSUBISHI 1-3 Park Rd ✆ 275114   YUGO Cheriton High St. ✆ 275795
RENAULT Sandgate Rd ✆ 55331
VAUXHALL Sandgate Rd ✆ 53103   Ⓜ ATS 318-324 Cheriton Rd ✆ 275198/275121

FONTMELL MAGNA Dorset 403 404 N 30 – see Shaftesbury.

FONTWELL West Sussex – ✉ Arundel – ☎ 0243 Eastergate.
♦London 60 – Chichester 6 – Worthing 15.

🏠 **Travelodge** without rest., BN18 0SB, at A 27/29 roundabout ✆ 683973 – 📺 ♿ ⓟ. 🅰 AE VISA
32 rm 21.50/27.00 **t.**

FORD Wilts. – see Castle Combe.

FORDINGBRIDGE Hants. 403 404 O 31 – pop. 3 026 – ECD : Thursday – ☎ 0425.
See : St. Mary's Church★ (13C) – Envir. : Breamore House★ (Elizabethan) *AC*, N : 2 m.
♦London 101 – Bournemouth 17 – Salisbury 11 – Winchester 30.

XX **Hour Glass,** Salisbury Rd, Burgate, SP6 1LX, N : 1 m. on A 338 ✆ 52348, « 14C thatched cottage » – ⓟ. 🅰 AE ⑩ VISA
closed Monday lunch and Sunday dinner – M a la carte 7.95/15.95 **t.** ▮ 3.75.

at Stuckton SE : 1 m. by B 3078 – ✉ ☎ 0425 Fordingbridge :

X **Three Lions,** Stuckton Rd, SP6 2HF, ✆ 52489 – ⓟ. 🅰 VISA
closed Sunday, Monday, 3 weeks July-August, Christmas and New Year – M (booking essential) a la carte 14.65/24.55 **t.** ▮ 3.50.

at Rockbourne NW : 4 m. by B 3078 – ✉ Fordingbridge – ☎ 072 53 Rockbourne :

↑ **Shearings** 🦢, SP6 3NA, ✆ 250, « Picturesque 16C thatched cottage », ⟤ – ⓟ. 🐾
closed mid December-7 February – M (dinner by arrangement) 19.00 **st.** – **3 rm** ⌑ 22.00/39.00 **st.**

FORDWICH Kent 404 X 30 – see Canterbury.

FOREST ROW East Sussex 404 U 30 – pop. 3 842 – ECD : Wednesday – ☎ 034 282.
🏌, 🏌 Royal Ashdown Forest, Chapel Lane ✆ 2018.
♦London 35 – ♦Brighton 26 – Eastbourne 30 – Maidstone 32.

🏠 **Chequers Inn,** The Square, RH18 5ES, ✆ 4394, Fax 5454 – 📺 ☎ 🚗 ⓟ. 🅰 AE ⑩ VISA. 🐾
M 5.45/12.95 **t.** and a la carte ▮ 4.65 – ⌑ 5.00 – **17 rm** 40.00/65.00 **st.** – SB (week-ends only) 98.00 **st.**

at Wych Cross S : 2 ½ m. on A 22 – ✉ ☎ 034 282 Forest Row :

🏠 **Roebuck** (Embassy), RH18 5JL, ✆ 3811, Telex 957088, ⟤ – 📺 ☎ ⓟ – 👥 – **28 rm.**

FOSSEBRIDGE Glos. 403 404 O 28 – pop. 1 706 – ✉ ☎ 028 572.
♦London 88 – Gloucester 23 – ♦Oxford 31 – Swindon 21.

🏠 **Fossebridge Inn,** GL54 3JS, ✆ 72721, « Attractively furnished », ⟤ – 📺 ☎ ⓟ. 🅰 AE ⑩ VISA
M 21.50/25.00 **t.** and a la carte ▮ 4.25 – **12 rm** ⌑ 40.00/70.00 **t.** – SB (except Christmas) 90.00/125.00 **st.**

FOUR MARKS Hants. 408 404 Q 30 – pop. 2 429 – ⊠ ✆ 0420 Alton.
♦London 58 – Guildford 24 – Reading 29 – ♦Southampton 24.

     Travelodge without rest., 156 Winchester Rd, GU34 5HZ, on A 31 ✆ 62659 – TV ⅙ 🅿. ⌧
AE VISA
31 rm 21.50/27.00 t.

FOWEY Cornwall 408 G 32 **The West Country G.** – pop. 2 092 – ECD : Wednesday – ✆ 072 683.
See : Site★★.
🛈 The Post Office, 4 Custom House Hill ✆ 3616.
♦London 277 – Newquay 24 – ♦Plymouth 34 – Truro 22.

     Marina, The Esplanade, PL23 1HY, ✆ 833315, ⩽ Fowey river and harbour – ⤫ rest TV
☎. ⌧ AE ⓪ VISA
March-October – **M** (bar lunch)/dinner 17.00 **t.** and a la carte ◊ 2.90 – **11 rm** ⊇ 26.00/60.00 **t.**
– SB 60.00/74.00 **st.**

     Carnethic House ⚲, Lambs Barn, PL23 1HQ, NW : ¾ m. on A 3082 ✆ 3336, 🛋 heated,
🌳, ✗ – ⤫ TV 🅿. ⌧ AE ⓪ VISA. ⚲
closed December and January – **M** (bar lunch)/dinner 10.00 **st.** ◊ 2.50 – **8 rm**
⊇ 21.00/40.00 **st.** – SB (except July and August) 52.00/58.00 **st.**

     Ocean View without rest., 24 Tower Park, PL23 1JB, ✆ 832283, ⩽ – ⚲
April-October – **4 rm** ⊇ 15.00/30.00 **st.**

     Food for Thought, 4 Town Quay, PL23 1AT, ✆ 2221, ⩽ – ⌧ VISA
closed Sunday, January-February and Christmas – **M** (booking essential) (dinner only)
15.95 **t.** and a la carte 21.00/26.00 **t.** ◊ 3.95.

     at Golant N : 3 m. by B 3269 – ⊠ ✆ 072 683 Fowey :

     Cormorant ⚲, PL23 1LL, ✆ 833426, ⩽ River Fowey, 🛋, 🌳 – TV ☎ 🅿. ⌧ VISA
M a la carte 20.50/25.50 **t.** ◊ 4.00 – **11 rm** ⊇ 44.00/72.00 **t.** – SB (summer only)
115.00/135.00 **st.**

     at Bodinnick-by-Fowey E : ¼ m. via car ferry – ⊠ Fowey – ✆ 072 687 Polruan :

     Old Ferry Inn, PL23 1LX, ✆ 237, ⩽ Fowey Estuary and town, « Part 16C inn » – TV 🅿. ⌧
VISA
M *(March-October)* (bar lunch)/dinner 16.50 **t.** and a la carte ◊ 3.75 – **12 rm** ⊇ 25.00/63.00 **st.**

FOWLMERE Cambs. 404 U 27 – see Cambridge.

FOWNHOPE Heref. and Worc. 408 404 M 27 – pop. 1 362 – ⊠ Hereford – ✆ 043 277.
♦London 132 – ♦Cardiff 46 – Hereford 6 – Gloucester 27.

     Green Man Inn, HR1 4PE, ✆ 243 – TV 🅿. ⌧ VISA
M (bar lunch Monday to Saturday)/dinner 11.00 **t.** and a la carte ◊ 3.50 – **15 rm**
⊇ 27.00/36.50 **t.** – SB (summer only) 56.50 **st.**

     Bowens Country, HR1 4PS, on B 4224 ✆ 430, 🌳 – ⤫ rest TV 🅿. ⌧ VISA. ⚲
closed Christmas – **M** (by arrangement) – **10 rm** ⊇ 15.75/40.00 **t.**

FRAMLINGHAM Suffolk 404 X 27 – pop. 1 830 – ECD : Wednesday – ⊠ Woodbridge –
✆ 0728.
See : Castle ramparts★ (Norman ruins) *AC.*
♦London 92 – ♦Ipswich 19 – ♦Norwich 42.

     Crown (T.H.F.), Market Hill, IP13 9AN, ✆ 723521, « 16C inn » – ⤫ rm TV ☎ 🅿. ⌧ AE ⓪
VISA
M a la carte 14.45/22.00 **st.** ◊ 4.25 – ⊇ 7.00 – **14 rm** 52.00/100.00 **st.** – SB 84.00/110.00 **st.**
FORD Market Hill ✆ 723215

FRAMPTON Dorset 408 404 M 31 – see Dorchester.

FRANKLEY West Midlands 408 404 ⑲ – see Birmingham.

FRENSHAM Surrey 404 R 30 – see Farnham.

FRESHWATER BAY I.O.W. 408 404 P 31 – see Wight (Isle of).

FRESSINGFIELD Suffolk 404 X 26 – pop. 831 – ⊠ Eye – ✆ 037 986.
♦London 103 – ♦Ipswich 30 – ♦Norwich 23.

     Fox and Goose, IP21 5PB, ✆ 247 – 🅿. ⌧ AE ⓪ VISA
closed 2 weeks January-February, 2 weeks September and 4 days at Christmas – **M** *(closed
Sunday dinner except Bank Holidays and Tuesday)* (booking essential) 16.50 **st.** and a la
carte 16.00/27.00 **st.** ◊ 5.00.

FRIETH Bucks. – see Henley-on-Thames (Oxon.).

FRIMLEY Surrey 404 R 30 – ⊠ ✆ 0276 Camberley.
♦London 39 – Reading 17 – ♦Southampton 47.

XX Ancient Raj, 9 The Parade, High St., ✆ 26042, Indian rest..

at Frimley Green SE : 1 ¼ m. by Church Rd – ⊠ Camberley – ✆ 0252 Deepcut :

Lakeside International, Wharf Rd, GU16 6JR, ✆ 838000, Telex 858095, ⋖, 💺 – TV ☎ Ⓟ –
96 rm.

FRINTON-ON-SEA Essex 404 X 28 – pop. 12 507 (inc. Walton) – ECD : Wednesday – ✆ 0255.
The Esplanade ✆ 674618.
♦London 72 – Chelmsford 39 – Colchester 17.

Maplin, 3 The Esplanade, CO13 9EL, ✆ 673832, ⋖, 💺 heated – TV ☎ Ⓟ. 🅿 AE ⓪ VISA
closed January – **M** (closed Sunday dinner and Monday to non-residents) 13.75/14.75
st. and a la carte ▯ 3.95 – **10 rm** ⊊ 30.00/68.00 st.

Uplands, 41 Hadleigh Rd, CO13 9HQ, ✆ 674889, 💺 – ⥱ Ⓟ. 💈
M 8.75 – **8 rm** ⊊ 16.00/41.50.

AUSTIN-ROVER, FORD Connaught Av. ✆ 674311
PEUGEOT-TALBOT Thorpe Rd ✆ 674383

TOYOTA Frinton Rd, Kirby Cross ✆ 679191
VOLVO, SEAT Connaught Av. ✆ 679123/674341

FRODSHAM Cheshire 402 403 404 L 24 – pop. 9 143 – ⊠ Warrington – ✆ 0928.
♦London 203 – Chester 11 – ♦Liverpool 21 – ♦Manchester 29 – ♦Stoke-on-Trent 42.

Old Hall, Main St., WA6 9LY, ✆ 32052, Telex 629794, 💺 heated – TV ☎ Ⓟ. 🅿 AE ⓪ VISA
M 9.50/13.50 **st.** and a la carte ▯ 3.95 – **22 rm** ⊊ 49.50/60.50 st., **1 suite** 77.00 st.

ATS 63 Main St. ✆ 33555

FULBROOK Oxon. 403 404 P 28 – see Burford.

FULWOOD Lancs. 402 L M 22 – see Preston.

GAINSBOROUGH Lincs. 402 404 R 23 – pop. 20 326 – ECD : Wednesday – ✆ 0427.
See : Old Hall★★ (15C) *AC*.
Thonock, The Belt ✆ 3088, N : 1 m. by A 159.
♦London 150 – Lincoln 19 – ♦Nottingham 42 – ♦Sheffield 34.

Hotels and Restaurant see : Bawtry NW : 12 m., **Scunthorpe** NE : 17 m.

AUSTIN-ROVER North St. ✆ 2251
FORD Lea Rd ✆ 810018

VAUXHALL-OPEL 35 Trinity St. ✆ 611570

GALMPTON Devon – ⊠ ✆ 0803 Brixham.
♦London 229 – ♦Plymouth 32 – Torquay 6.

Lost and Found ⤳, Maypool, TQ5 0ET, by Greenway Rd ✆ 842442, ⋖River Dart and
valley, 💺 – TV ☎ Ⓟ. 🅿 AE VISA
M (bar lunch)/dinner 16.95 t. ▯ 2.50 – **16 rm** ⊊ 50.00/90.00 t.

GARFORTH West Yorks. 402 P 22 – see Leeds.

GATESHEAD Tyne and Wear 401 402 P 19 – pop. 91 429 – ECD : Wednesday – ✆ 091 Tyne-
side.
Ravensworth, Mossheaps, Wrekenton ✆ 487 6014/487 2843.
🛈 Central Library, Prince Consort Rd ✆ 477 3478/9.
♦London 282 – Durham 16 – ♦Middlesbrough 38 – ♦Newcastle-upon-Tyne 1 – Sunderland 11.

Plan : see Newcastle-upon-Tyne

Springfield (Embassy), Durham Rd, NE9 5BT, S : ½ m. on A 6127 ✆ 477 4121, Fax 477 7213
– ⥱ rm TV ☎ Ⓟ – 🔥 150. 🅿 AE ⓪ VISA   BX s
M (closed Saturday lunch) 7.95/10.95 **st.** and a la carte ▯ 4.10 – ⊊ 6.50 – **60 rm** 48.50/69.50 st.
– SB (weekends only) 30.50 **st.**

Swallow (Swallow), High West St., NE8 1PE, ✆ 477 1105, Telex 53534, Fax 478 7214, 🅿 –
▤ ⥱ rm TV ☎ Ⓟ – 🔥 200. 🅿 AE ⓪ VISA   CZ r
M (closed Saturday lunch) 9.95/13.50 **st.** and a la carte ▯ 3.50 – **106 rm** ⊊ 63.00/96.00 st. –
SB (weekends only) 73.00/85.00 **st.**

AUSTIN-ROVER Low Fell ✆ 487 2118
FORD Eslington Park ✆ 460 7464
NISSAN Lobley Hill Rd ✆ 460 0000
PEUGEOT-TALBOT Team Valley ✆ 482 6969
TOYOTA St. James Sq. ✆ 490 0112

VAUXHALL St James Sq. ✆ 477 8595

ATS Earlsway/First Av., Team Valley Trading Est.
✆ 4910081/2

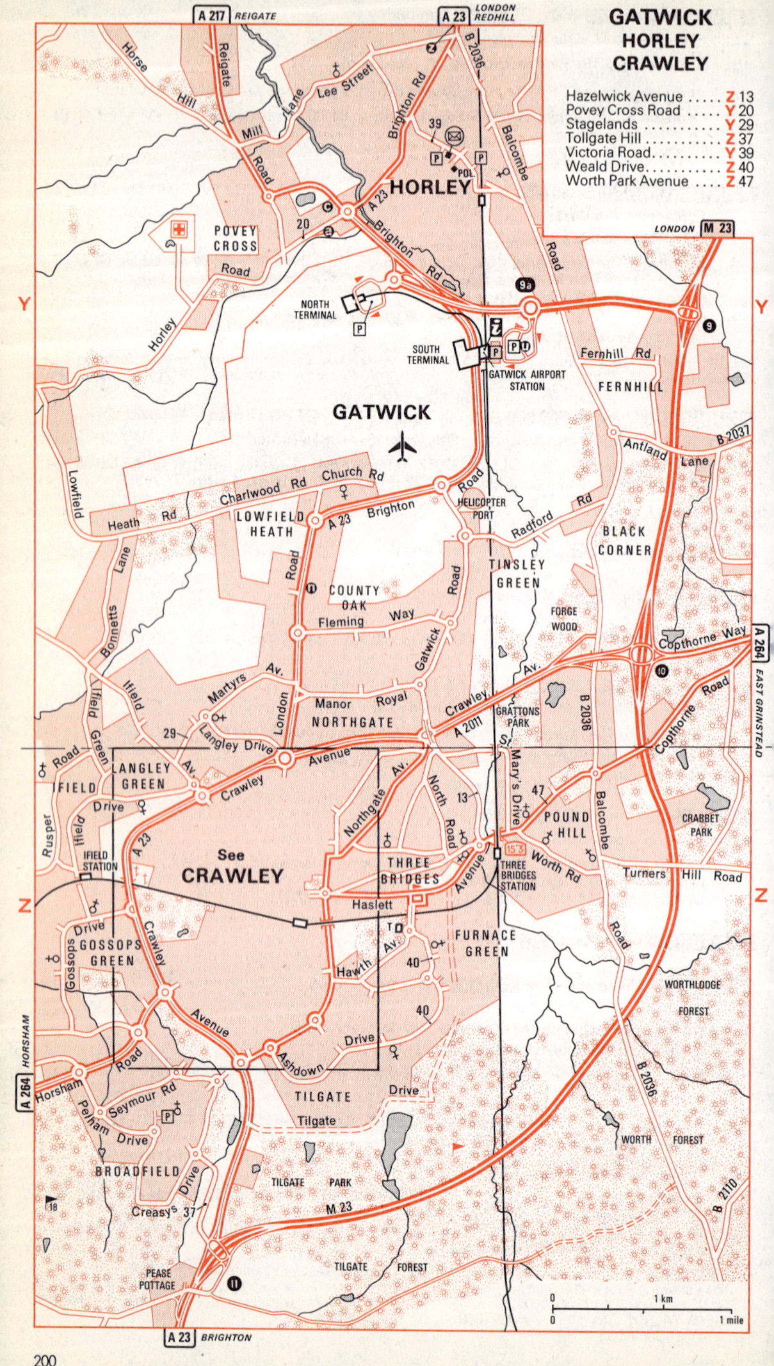

GATWICK
HORLEY
CRAWLEY

Hazelwick Avenue ..... Z 13
Povey Cross Road ..... Y 20
Stagelands .... Y 29
Tollgate Hill .... Z 37
Victoria Road .... Y 39
Weald Drive .... Z 40
Worth Park Avenue .... Z 47

A 217 REIGATE
A 23 LONDON REDHILL
Reigate Lane
Lee Street
Brighton Rd
B 2036
39
HORLEY
POL
A 23
Balcombe Road
LONDON M 23
9a
Horse Hill
Mill Road
POVEY CROSS
20
Brighton Rd
9
Horley Road
NORTH TERMINAL
SOUTH TERMINAL
Gatwick Airport Station
Fernhill Rd
FERNHILL
GATWICK
Antland Lane
B 2037
Lowfield
Heath Rd
Charlwood Rd
Church Rd
LOWFIELD HEATH
A 23 Brighton
Road
HELICOPTER PORT
Radford Rd
BLACK CORNER
Bonnetts Lane
Ifield Green
COUNTY OAK
Fleming Way
Gatwick Road
TINSLEY GREEN
FORGE WOOD
Copthorne Way
A 264 EAST GRINSTEAD
10
Martyrs Av.
London Road
Manor Royal
NORTHGATE
Crawley
A 2011
Av.
B 2036
GRATTONS PARK
Copthorne Road
29
Langley Drive
Avenue
IFIELD
LANGLEY GREEN
Crawley
Northgate Av.
North Road
13
St. Mary's Drive
47
POUND HILL
Balcombe
CRABBET PARK
Rusper Road
Ifield Drive
IFIELD STATION
See CRAWLEY
A 23
THREE BRIDGES
Avenue
15 3
THREE BRIDGES STATION
Worth Rd
Turners Hill Road
Gossops Drive
GOSSOPS GREEN
Crawley
Haslett
T
Av.
FURNACE GREEN
40
Hawth
40
WORTHLODGE FOREST
Avenue
Drive
Ashdown
Drive
TILGATE
Tilgate Drive
WORTH FOREST
B 2036
18
BROADFIELD
Horsham Road
A 264 HORSHAM
Pelham Drive
Seymour Rd
Creasys 37
TILGATE PARK
M 23
B 2110
PEASE POTTAGE
11
TILGATE FOREST
A 23 BRIGHTON
0   1 km
0   1 mile

GATWICK AIRPORT West Sussex 👁👁👁 T 30 – ✉ West Sussex – ☎ 0293 Gatwick.
✈ ☏ 0293 (Crawley) 503089/515011 and ☏ 01 (London) 668 42111.
🛈 International Arrivals Concourse ☏ 560108.
♦ London 29 – ♦Brighton 28.

Plan on preceding page

🏨 **Gatwick Hilton International** (Hilton), Gatwick Airport, RH6 0LL, ☏ 518080, Telex 877021, Fax 28980, 🏊 – 🛗 ⇥ rm ▤ 📺 ☎ 👤 – 🛎 500. 🗚 AE ⓞ VISA   Y u
M 13.60/20.30 t. and a la carte 16.00/34.00 t. ⓘ 5.50 – ☕ 9.10 – **549 rm** 90.00/100.00 t., **3 suites** 180.00/250.00 t.

🏨 **Gatwick Penta**, Povey Cross Rd ✉Horley (Surrey), RH6 0BE, ☏ 820169, Telex 87440, Fax 820259, 🏊, squash – 🛗 ⇥ rm ▤ 📺 ☎ 👤 – 🛎 150. 🗚 AE ⓞ VISA   Y a
M 13.25/15.50 st. and a la carte – ☕ 6.95 – **256 rm** 78.00/94.00 st., **4 suites** 150.00/160.00 st.

🏨 **Post House** (T.H.F.), Povey Cross Rd ✉Horley (Surrey), RH6 0BA, ☏ 771621, Telex 877351, Fax 771054, 🏊 – 🛗 ⇥ rm ▤ 📺 ☎ 👤 – 🛎 100. 🗚 AE ⓞ VISA   Y c
M (closed Saturday lunch) a la carte 15.50/21.00 st. ⓘ 3.65 – ☕ 7.50 – **216 rm** 72.00/98.00 st. – SB (October-April) (weekends only) 74.00/98.00 st.

GERRARDS CROSS Bucks. 👁👁👁 S 29 – pop. 19 447 (inc. Chalfont St.Peter) – ECD : Wednesday – ☎ 0753.
♦London 22 – Aylesbury 22 – ♦Oxford 36.

🏨 **Bull** (De Vere), Oxford Rd, SL9 7PA, on A 40 ☏ 885995, Telex 847747, Fax 885504, 🌱 – 🛗 ⇥ rm ▤ rest 📺 ☎ 👤 – 🛎 200. 🗚 AE ⓞ VISA. ✂
M 14.25/16.50 st. and a la carte – **96 rm** ☕ 75.00/135.00 st. – SB (July and August) (weekends only) 74.00 st.

🏠 **Ethorpe** (B.C.B.), Packhorse Rd, SL9 8HY, ☏ 882039, Fax 887012, 🌱 – 📺 ☎ 👤. 🗚 AE ⓞ VISA. ✂
M a la carte 7.20/14.40 t. ⓘ 3.55 – **29 rm** ☕ 58.00/85.00 t.

✗ **Monsoon**, 1a Packhorse Rd, SL9 7QA, ☏ 888910, Indian rest. – 🗚 AE VISA
M 8.50/10.50 t. and a la carte ⓘ 2.95.

BMW 31-33 Station Rd ☏ 889606   PEUGEOT-TALBOT Oxford Rd ☏ 882545

GIGGLESWICK North Yorks. – see Settle.

GILLAN Cornwall 👁👁👁 E 33 The West Country G. – see Helford.

GILLINGHAM Dorset 👁👁👁 👁👁👁 N 30 – pop. 5 379 – ☎ 074 76.
♦London 116 – Bournemouth 34 – ♦Bristol 46 – ♦Southampton 52.

🏨 **Stock Hill House** 🦢, Wyke, SP8 5NR, W : 1 ½ m. on B 3081 ☏ 823626, « Victorian country house », 🌱, park – ⇥ rest 📺 ☎ 👤. 🗚 VISA. ✂
closed 2 weeks June – M (closed Sunday dinner and Monday except Bank Holidays) 18.00/25.00 t. ⓘ 4.50 – **7 rm** ☕ (dinner included) 70.00/140.00 t. – SB (except summer) (weekdays only) 130.00 st.

at Milton on Stour N : 1 ½ m. by B 3095 on B 3092 – ✉ ☎ 074 76 Gillingham :

🏚 **Milton Lodge** 🦢, SP8 5QD, ☏ 822262, 🏊 heated, 🌱 – 📺 ☎ 👤. 🗚 VISA. ✂
M (closed Sunday dinner) 0.00/13.00 st. and a la carte – **11 rm** ☕ 30.00/70.00 st. – SB 70.00/80.00 st.

GISBURN Lancs. 👁👁👁 N 22 – pop. 435 – ECD : Wednesday – ✉ Clitheroe – ☎ 020 05.
♦London 243 – ♦Manchester 37 – Preston 25.

🏨 **Stirk House**, BB7 4LJ, SW : 1 m. on A 59 ☏ 581, Telex 635238, Fax 744, 🏊, 🌱, squash – 📺 ☎ 👤 – 🛎 250. 🗚 AE ⓞ VISA. ✂
M 9.95/21.50 st. and a la carte ⓘ 4.00 – **50 rm** ☕ 60.00/70.00 st. – SB (weekends only) 62.00/75.00 st.

GISLINGHAM Suffolk 👁👁👁 X 27 – pop. 589 – ✉ Eye – ☎ 037 983 Mellis.
♦London 93 – ♦Cambridge 45 – ♦Ipswich 20 – ♦Norwich 30.

🏠 **Old Guildhall**, Mill St., IP23 8JT, ☏ 361, 🌱 – 📺 👤. ✂
closed January – M (by arrangement) 12.00 ⓘ 2.00 – **4 rm** ☕ 24.00/36.00 st. – SB 45.00/55.00 st.

GITTISHAM Devon 👁👁👁 K 31 – pop. 233 – ECD : Thursday – ✉ ☎ 0404 Honiton.
♦London 164 – Exeter 14 – Sidmouth 9 – Taunton 21.

🏨 **Combe House** 🦢, EX14 0AD, ☏ 42756, ←, « Country house atmosphere », 🐟, 🌱, park – 📺 ☎ 👤. 🗚 AE ⓞ VISA
closed 7 January-2 March – M (bar lunch, residents only)/dinner a la carte 20.35/28.60 st. ⓘ 3.95 – **10 rm** ☕ 52.00/103.50 st., **1 suite** 112.00 st.

GLASBURY Powys 403 K 27 – pop. 289 – ✆ 049 74.
◆London 184 – ◆Birmingham 74 – Brecon 12 – Hereford 25.

   🏛 Llwynaubach Lodge, HR3 5PT, on B 4350 ℰ 473, ⌁, ⌁, ⇌ – TV ☎ P
   6 rm.

GLASTONBURY Somerset 403 L 30 The West Country G. – pop. 6 751 – ECD : Wednesday –
✆ 0458.

See : Site★★★ – Abbey★★★ AC – St. John the Baptist Church★★ – Somerset Rural Life
Museum★ AC – Glastonbury Tor★ (←★★★).

🛈 1 Marchant's Buildings, Northload St. ℰ 32954 (summer only).

◆London 136 – ◆Bristol 26 – Taunton 22.

   🏛 **George and Pilgrims**, 1 High St., BA6 9DP, ℰ 31146, « Part 15C inn » – ⥄ rest TV ☎.
   ⚞ AE ① VISA
   M *(closed Sunday dinner)* (bar lunch)/dinner a la carte 8.95/17.95 t. – **12 rm** ⊡ 38.00/70.00 t.

   XX **Number Three** with rm, 3 Magdalene St., BA6 9EW, ℰ 32129, « Georgian house », ⇌ –
   ⥄ rest TV ☎ P. AE VISA. ⌗
   closed Sunday, Monday and 3 weeks January – **M** (booking essential) (dinner only) 30.00 t.
   🛆 4.00 – **3 rm** ⊡ 38.00/55.00 t.

   at West Pennard E : 3 ½ m. on A 361 – ✉ ✆ 0458 Glastonbury :

   ☎ Red Lion, BA6 8NN, ℰ 32941 – TV ☎ P
   7 rm.

RENAULT Beckery Rd ℰ 34370

GLEMSFORD Suffolk 404 V 27 – pop. 2 406 – ✉ Sudbury – ✆ 0787.
◆London 65 – ◆Cambridge 32 – Colchester 21 – ◆Ipswich 28.

   XX **Barretts**, 31 Egremont St., CO10 7SA, ℰ 281573 – P. ⚞ VISA
   closed Sunday dinner and Monday – **M** (dinner only and Sunday lunch)/dinner a la carte
   20.75/25.70 st.

GLEN PARVA Leics. – see Leicester.

GLEWSTONE Heref. and Worc. – see Ross-on-Wye.

GLOOSTON Leics. – see Market Harborough.

GLOSSOP Derbs. 402 403 404 O 23 – ECD : Wednesday – ✆ 0457.
◆London 194 – ◆Manchester 18 – ◆Sheffield 25.

   🏛 **Wind in the Willows** ⌁, Derbyshire Level, SK13 9PT, off A 57 ℰ 868001, ⇌ – TV ☎ P.
   ⚞ AE VISA. ⌗
   closed Christmas and New Year – **M** (residents only) (dinner only) 17.50 st. 🛆 4.00 – **8 rm**
   ⊡ 45.00/85.00 st.

GLOUCESTER Glos. 403 404 N 28 – pop. 106 526 – ECD : Thursday – ✆ 0452.

See : Site★ – Cathedral★★★ (12C-14C) (Great Cloister★★★ 14C) Y – Docks★ Y – Bishop Hooper's
Lodging (Folk Museum)★ (15C) Y M.

🛈₈ Gloucester Hotel and Country Club, Matson Lane ℰ 25653, S : 2 m. Z.

🛈 St Michael's Tower, The Cross ℰ 421188.

◆London 106 – ◆Birmingham 52 – ◆Bristol 38 – ◆Cardiff 66 – ◆Coventry 57 – Northampton 83 – ◆Oxford 48 –
◆Southampton 98 – ◆Swansea 92 – Swindon 35.

Plan opposite

   🏛 **Crest** (Crest), Crest Way, Barnwood, GL4 7RX, E : 3 m. on A 417 ℰ 613311, Telex 437273,
   Fax 371036, ⚞ – ⥄ ▤ rest TV ☎ & P – 🛆 . ⚞ AE ① VISA   by A 417   Z
   M *(closed lunch Saturday and Bank Holidays)* 10.95/15.95 st. and a la carte 🛆 5.95 – ⊡ 7.95
   – **123 rm** 70.00/125.00 st. – SB (weekends only) 68.00/92.00 st.

   🏛 **Gloucester H. and Country Club** (Embassy), Robinswood Hill, Matson Lane, GL4 9EA,
   SE : 3 m. by B 4073 ℰ 25653, Telex 43571, Fax 307212, ⚞, 🛈₈, ⌗, squash – ⥄ rm TV ☎ P
   – 🛆 120. ⚞ AE ① VISA   Z c
   M 10.50/15.75 st. and a la carte 🛆 4.05 – ⊡ 6.50 – **111 rm** 68.00/79.00 st. **5 suites** 105.00 st.
   – SB 91.00/140.00 st.

   🏛 **Travel Inn** without rest., Tewkesbury Rd, Longford, GL2 9BE, N : 1 ¾ m. on A 38 Z ℰ 23519
   – TV & P
   40 rm.

   🛖 **Rotherfield House**, 5 Horton Rd, GL1 3PX, ℰ 410500 – ⥄ rest TV P. ⚞ AE ① VISA
   closed 22 December-5 January – **M** 7.25 st. – **9 rm** ⊡ 16.95/35.10 st.   Z n

   X **College Green**, 7-11 College St., GL1 2NE, ℰ 20739 – ⚞ AE VISA   Y a
   closed dinner Monday and Tuesday, Sunday and Bank Holidays – **M** 11.00 st. and a la carte
   11.75/18.50 st. 🛆 3.25.

GLOUCESTER

Eastgate Shopping
  Centre . . . . Y
Eastgate Street . . . . Y 10
Northgate Street . . . . Y 16
Southgate Street . . . . Y

Barnwood By-Pass . . . . . . Z 3
Black Dog Way . . . . Y 5
Commercial Road . . . . Y 6
Cotteswold Road . . . . Z 8
Derby Road . . . . Z 9
Great Western Road . . . . . Y 12
Heathville Road . . . . Y 13
King Edward's Avenue . . . Z 14
Lower Westgate Street . . . Y 15
Parkend Road . . . . Z 17
Parliament Street . . . . Y 18
Pitt Street . . . . Y 19
Quay Street . . . . Y 20
Royal Oak Road . . . . Y 21
St. Aldate Street . . . . Y 22
St. Johns Lane . . . . Y 23
Southern Avenue . . . . Z 24
Spa Road . . . . Z 26
Stroud Road . . . . Z 28
Tredworth Road . . . . Z 30
Worcester Street . . . . Y 31

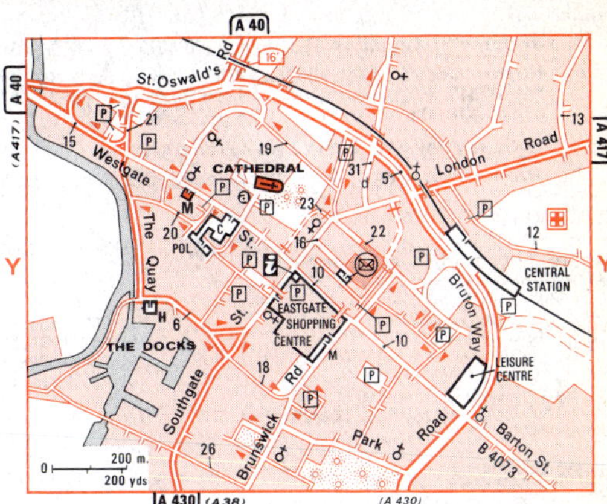

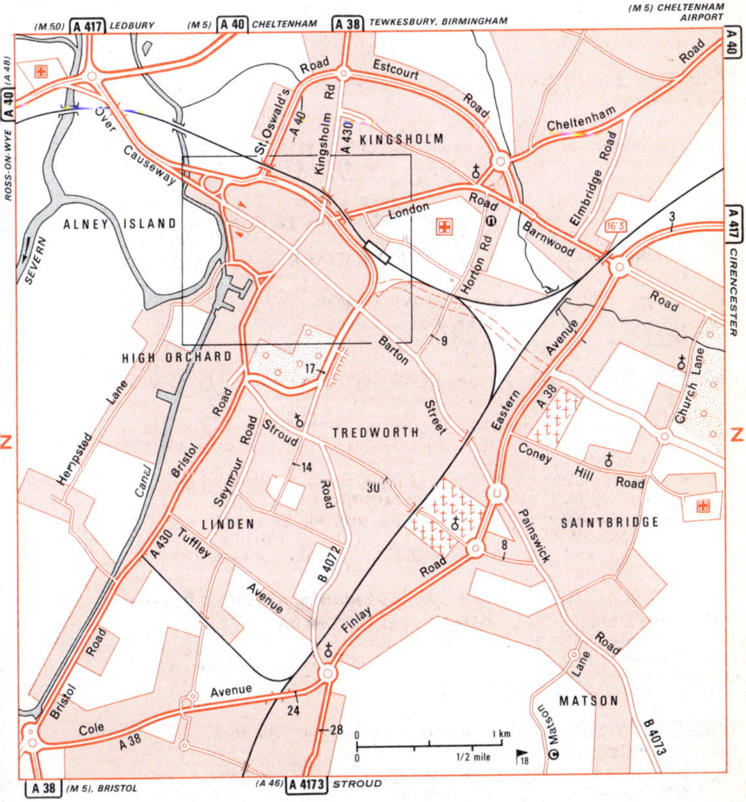

at Upton St. Leonards SE : 3 ½ m. on B 4073 – Z – ⊠ ✆ 0452 Gloucester :

🏠 **Hatton Court**, Upton Hill, GL4 8DE, S : ¾ m. on B 4073 ✆ 617412, Group Telex 437334, Fax 612945, ≤, ⌂ heated, 🐎 – ▤ rest 📺 ☎ Ⓟ – 🛄 35. ⚑ AE ⓪ VISA. ✺
M 14.00/18.00 t. and a la carte – **46 rm** ⊑ 66.00/105.00 t. – SB 98.00/120.00 st.

at Quedgeley SW : 2 ¾ m. by A 430 on B 4008 – Z – ⊠ ✆ 0452 Gloucester :

⌂ **The Retreat** without rest., 116 Bristol Rd, GL2 6NA, ✆ 728296, ⌂ heated, 🐎 – 📺 ☎ Ⓟ. ✺
9 rm ⊑ 13.50/30.00 st.

AUDI-VW Eastern Av. ✆ 25177
AUSTIN-ROVER Mercia Rd ✆ 416565
BMW Kingsholm Rd ✆ 23456
CITROEN 143 Westgate St. ✆ 23252
FIAT Old Bristol Rd ✆ 720107
FORD Bristol Rd ✆ 21731
LAND-ROVER, RANGE-ROVER Wotton-under-Edge ✆ 0453 (Dursley) 844131
NISSAN Eastern Av. ✆ 423691
PANTHER-LIMA, VAUXHALL Shepherd Rd, Cole Av. ✆ 26711

PEUGEOT-TALBOT, DAIHATSU, FIAT Bristol Rd ✆ 29755
RENAULT St. Oswalds Rd ✆ 305051
SAAB Montpelier ✆ 22404
TOYOTA London Rd ✆ 21555
VAUXHALL-OPEL Cole Av. ✆ 26711
VAUXHALL-OPEL Priory Rd ✆ 24912
VOLVO Shepherd Rd ✆ 25291

🅐 ATS St. Oswald's Rd ✆ 27329

GLYN CEIRIOG Clwyd 402 403 K 25 – ⊠ Llangollen – ✆ 069 172.
♦London 194 – Shrewsbury 30 – Wrexham 17.

🏰 **Golden Pheasant** ⑤, Llwynmawr, LL20 7BB, ✆ 281, Telex 35664, ≤, 🐎 – 📺 ☎ Ⓟ. ⚑
AE ⓪ VISA
M 9.50/15.95 st. – **18 rm** ⊑ 28.00/78.00 t. – SB (weekends only) (except Easter and Christmas) 89.00/112.00 st.

GOATHLAND North Yorks. 402 R 20 – pop. 442 – ECD : Wednesday and Saturday – ⊠ ✆ 0947 Whitby.
♦London 248 – ♦Middlesbrough 36 – York 38.

🏛 **Mallyan Spout** ⑤, The Common, YO22 5AN, ✆ 86206, 🐎 – 📺 Ⓟ. ⚑ AE ⓪ VISA
M (bar lunch)/dinner 15.00 t. and a la carte ⅃ 3.50 – **22 rm** ⊑ 35.00/85.00 t. – SB (except Bank Holidays) 42.50/52.50 st.

⌂ **Whitfield House** ⑤, Darnholm, YO22 5LA, NW : ¾ m. ✆ 86215, 🐎 – ✕ rest
closed mid November-mid January – M 10.50 st. ⅃ 3.00 – **10 rm** ⊑ 17.50/35.00 st. – SB (except summer) 45.00/47.00 st.

⌂ **Heatherdene** ⑤, The Common, Y022 5AN, ✆ 86334, ≤, 🐎 – ✕ 📺 Ⓟ
M 7.00 – **6 rm** ⊑ 13.75/25.75.

at Egton Bridge NW : 4 ¾ m. – ⊠ ✆ 0947 Whitby :

⚘ **Horseshoe Inn** ⑤, YO21 1XE, ✆ 85245, 🐎 – Ⓟ
M (bar lunch)/dinner a la carte 6.20 st. ⅃ 3.50 – **6 rm** ⊑ 18.00/30.00 st.

GODALMING Surrey 404 S 30 – pop. 18 758 – ECD : Wednesday – ✆ 048 68.
♦London 38 – Guildford 5 – ♦Southampton 51.

🏛 **Kings Arms and Royal**, High St., GU7 1EB, ✆ 21545 – 📺 ☎ Ⓟ. ⚑ VISA. ✺
closed 25 December – M (closed Sunday dinner) a la carte 8.25/13.60 t. – **17 rm** ⊑ 40.00/50.00 st.

⌂ **Meads**, 65 Meadrow, GU7 3HS, N : ½ m. on A 3100 ✆ 21800 – 📺 Ⓟ. AE VISA
M (by arrangement) 8.50 t. – **15 rm** ⊑ 24.00/45.00 t.

XXX **Inn on the Lake** with rm, Ockford Rd, GU7 1RH, on A 3100 ✆ 5575, 🐎 – 📺 ☎ Ⓟ
🛄 80. ⚑ AE ⓪ VISA
M 12.50 t. and a la carte 14.65/20.75 t. – **20 rm** ⊑ 45.00/70.00 t. – SB (weekends only) 110.00 st.

at Hascombe SE : 3 ½ m. on B 2130 – ⊠ Godalming – ✆ 048 632 Hascombe :

X **White Horse**, GU8 4JA, ✆ 258, 🐎 – Ⓟ. ⚑ AE ⓪ VISA
closed Sunday dinner – M 11.20/22.90 t. ⅃ 3.95.

NISSAN The Wharf ✆ 5201
RENAULT Farncombe ✆ 7743/23169
VAUXHALL Portsmouth Rd ✆ 5666

🅐 ATS Meadrow ✆ 21845/22219

GODSTONE Surrey 404 T 30 – pop. 2 567 – ✆ 0342 South Godstone.
♦London 22 – ♦Brighton 36 – Maidstone 28.

XXX **La Bonne Auberge**, Tilburstow Hill, South Godstone, RH9 8JY, S : 2 ¼ m. ✆ 893184, Fax 893435, French rest., 🐎 – Ⓟ. ⚑ AE VISA
closed Sunday dinner and Monday – M 21.00/32.00 st. and a la carte ⅃ 4.00.

GOLANT Cornwall 403 G 32 – see Fowey.

GOLCAR West Yorks. – see Huddersfield.

GOODWICK (WDIG) Dyfed **403** F 27 – see Fishguard.

GOODWOOD West Sussex **404** R 31 – see Chichester.

GORDANO SERVICE AREA Avon – ✉ Bristol – ☎ 027 581 Pill

    Travelodge without rest., BS20 9XG, M 5 : junction 19 ℘ 3709 – 📺 ⅙ 🅿. ◿ AE VISA
    40 rm 21.50/27.00 t.

GORLESTON-ON-SEA Norfolk **404** Z 26 – see Great Yarmouth.

GOSFORTH Tyne and Wear **401 402** P 18 – see Newcastle-upon-Tyne.

GOUDHURST Kent **404** V 30 – pop. 2 673 – ECD : Wednesday – ✉ Cranbrook – ☎ 0580.
♦London 45 – Hastings 22 – Maidstone 13.

    Star and Eagle (Lansbury), High St., TN17 1AL, ℘ 211512, « 14C inn » – 📺 ☎ 🅿. ◿ AE
    VISA
    M a la carte 13.15/19.65 t. ⓵ 4.50 – **10 rm** ☲ 50.00/66.00 t.

GOVETON Devon **403** I 33 – see Kingsbridge.

GRANGE-IN-BORROWDALE Cumbria **402** K 20 – see Keswick.

GRANGE-OVER-SANDS Cumbria **402** L 21 – pop. 3 864 – ECD : Thursday – ☎ 044 84 (4 fig.)
or 053 95 (5 fig.).
Envir. : Cartmel (Priory Church★ 12C chancel★★) NW : 3 m.
🏌 Meathop Rd ℘ 3180, ½ m. from station – 🏌 Grange Fell, Fell Rd ℘ 32536.
🛈 Victoria Hall, Main St. ℘ 4026 (summer only).
♦London 268 – Kendal 13 – Lancaster 24.

    Graythwaite Manor ⑤, Fernhill Rd, LA11 7JE, ℘ 32001, ⋸ gardens and sea, « Extensive
    flowered gardens », park, ℀ – 📺 ☎ 🚗 🅿. ◿ VISA. ⚘
    M 9.00/17.00 t. ⓵ 2.50 – **22 rm** ☲ 35.00/60.00 **st.** – SB 80.00/90.00 **st.**

    Cumbria Grand (T.H.F), Lindale Rd, LA11 6EN, ℘ 2331, Telex 65446, Fax 4534, ⋸, 🐎,
    park, ℀ – 🛗 ⥃ rm 📺 ☎ ⅙ 🅿 – 🛶 . ◿ AE ⓪ VISA
    M 7.50/11.00 t. and a la carte ⓵ 4.00 – ☲ 6.50 – **120 rm** 39.00/56.00 **st.**

    Netherwood ⑤, Lindale Rd, LA11 6ET, ℘ 32552, ⋸, 🐎 – 📺 ☎ 🅿
    M 10.25 t. (dinner) and a la carte ⓵ 2.75 – **23 rm** ☲ 24.50/57.00 t.

    at Witherslack NE : 5 m. by B 5277 off A 590 – ✉ ☎ 044 852 Witherslack :

    Old Vicarage ⑤, Church Rd, LA11 6RS, ℘ 381, Fax 852373, 🐎, ℀ – ⥃ rest 📺 ☎ 🅿.
    ◿ AE ⓪ VISA
    closed Christmas week – **M** (booking essential)(dinner only) 19.50 t. – **13 rm** ☲ 40.00/85.00 t.

    at Cartmel NW : 3 m. – ✉ Grange-over-Sands – ☎ 044 854 (3 fig.) or 053 95 (5 fig.)
    Cartmel :

    Aynsome Manor ⑤, LA11 6HH, NE : ½ m. ℘ 36653, « Country house atmosphere », 🐎
    – ⥃ rest 📺 ☎ 🅿. ◿ AE VISA
    closed 2 to 25 January – **M** *(closed Sunday dinner to non-residents)* (dinner only) 16.00 t.
    ⓵ 3.60 – **13 rm** ☲ 22.50/45.00 t. – SB (October-mid May) 55.00/65.00 **st.**

    Uplands ⑤ with rm, Haggs Lane ✉ Cartmel, LA11 6HD, E : 1 m. ℘ 36240, ⋸, 🐎 –
    ⥃ rest 📺 ☎ 🅿. ◿ AE
    closed 1 January-25 February – **M** *(closed Monday)* (booking essential) 12.00/18.50 t. –
    5 rm ☲ (dinner included) 58.00/108.00 t. – SB (November-March) (weekdays only)
    85.00/100.00 **st.**

BMW Lindale Hill ℘ 3751   VW-AUDI Lindale ℘ 4242
SUBARU, SEAT Lindale Corner ℘ 2282

GRANTHAM Lincs. **402 404** S 25 – pop. 30 700 – ECD : Wednesday – ☎ 0476.
See : St. Wulfram's Church★ (13C).
Envir. : Belton House★ (Renaissance) *AC*, NE : 2 m. – Belvoir Castle★★ (19C) (interior★) W : 8 m.
🏌 Stoke Rochford, Great North Rd ℘ 047 683 (Great Ponton) 275, S : 6 m. on A 1.
🛈 The Museum, St. Peters Hill ℘ 66444.
♦London 113 – ♦Leicester 31 – Lincoln 29 – ♦Nottingham 24.

    Angel and Royal (T.H.F.), High St., NG31 6PN, ℘ 65816, « Part 13C » – ⥃ rm 📺 ☎ 🅿
    – 🛶 60. ◿ AE ⓪ VISA
    M 8.00/13.00 **st.** and a la carte ⓵ 3.95 – ☲ 7.60 – **23 rm** 56.00/72.50 **st.**, **1 suite** 81.00 **st.** –
    SB (weekends only) 84.00/90.00 **st.**

    King's, 130 North Par., NG31 6BN, ℘ 590800 – 📺 ☎ 🅿. ◿ AE ⓪ VISA
    M 8.95 t. (lunch) and a la carte 11.30/18.35 t. ⓵ 3.10 – **15 rm** ☲ 23.00/45.00 **st.** – SB
    (weekends only) 50.00 **st.**

at Barkston N : 3 ¾ m. on A 607 – ⊠ Grantham – ✆ 0400 Loveden :

XX **Barkston House** with rm, NG32 2NH, ℰ 50555, ⌇, 🐴 – 🔲 ☎ 🅿. 🔊 AE ⓞ *VISA*. ✄
closed 2 weeks June and 25 to 30 December – **M** *(closed Monday and Saturday lunch and Sunday)* 8.25 **t.** (lunch) and a la carte approx. 14.25 **t.** 🍷 2.95 – **2 rm** ☑ 34.00/48.00 **t.** – SB (weekends only) 64.00 **st.**

at Grantham Service Area NW : 3 m on B 1174 at junction with A 1 – ⊠ ✆ 0476 Grantham :

🏠 **Travelodge** without rest., NG32 2AB, ℰ 77500 – 🔲 ⅋ 🅿. 🔊 AE *VISA*
40 rm 21.50/27.00 **t.**

FORD 30-40 London Rd ℰ 65195
NISSAN Barrowby High Rd ℰ 64443
PEUGEOT-TALBOT 66 London Rd ℰ 62595
RENAULT London Rd ℰ 61338
TOYOTA Great Ponton ℰ 047 683 (Great Ponton) 261

VOLVO Barrowby Rd ℰ 64114
VW-AUDI, SUBARU, CITROEN Spittlegate ℰ 66416

⓪ ATS East St. ℰ 590222
ATS Elmer St. South ℰ 590444

GRASMERE Cumbria **402** K 20 – ECD : Thursday – ✆ 096 65.
See : Dove Cottage★ plan of Ambleside AY A – 🛈 Red Bank Rd ℰ 245 (summer only).
♦London 282 – ♦Carlisle 43 – Kendal 18.

Plans : see Ambleside

🏰 **Wordsworth**, Stock Lane, LA22 9SW, ℰ 592, Group Telex 65329, ⌇, 🐴 – 🛗 ▤ rest 🔲 ☎ 🅿 – 🏊 100. 🔊 AE ⓞ *VISA*. ✄   BZ **s**
M 16.00/26.00 **t.** and a la carte 🍷 3.75 – **35 rm** ☑ 44.00/110.00 **t.**, **2 suites** 145.00/155.00 **t.**

🏰 **Michaels Nook Country House** ⑤, LA22 9RP, NE : ½ m. off A 591 ℰ 496, Group Telex 65329, ≼ mountains and countryside, « Antiques and gardens » – ✄ rest 🔲 ☎ 🅿. 🔊 AE ⓞ *VISA*. ✄   AY **n**
M (booking essential) 21.00/31.00 **t.** 🍷 6.15 – **9 rm** ☑ (dinner included) 95.00/210.00 **st.**, **2 suites** (dinner included) 240.00/280.00 **st.** – SB (weekdays only) (except May, September, October and Bank Holidays) 285.00 **st.**

🏰 **Swan** (T.H.F.), LA22 9RF, on A 591 ℰ 551, ≼, 🐴 – 🔲 ☎ 🅿. 🔊 AE ⓞ *VISA*   AY **r**
M 9.50/15.00 **st.** and a la carte 🍷 3.95 – ☑ 8.00 – **36 rm** 64.00/80.00 **st.** – SB 80.00/110.00 **st.**

🏠 **White Moss House**, Rydal Water, LA22 9SE, S : 1 ½ m. on A 591 ℰ 295, 🐴 – ✄ rest 🔲 ☎ 🅿. ✄   BY **v**
Early March-late November – **M** *(closed Sunday except Easter)* (booking essential) (dinner only) 21.00 **t.** 🍷 3.50 – **6 rm** ☑ 39.00/100.00 **t.**

🏠 **Rothay Garden**, Broadgate, LA22 9RJ, ℰ 334, 🐴 – ✄ rest 🔲 ☎ 🅿. 🔊 AE *VISA*   AY **e**
February-November and New Year – **M** (dinner only) 17.50 **t.** 🍷 3.00 – **20 rm** ☑ (dinner included) 35.00/110.00 **t.** – SB (except April-October) 66.00/110.00 **st.**

🏠 **Oak Bank**, Broadgate, LA22 9TA, ℰ 217, 🐴 – ✄ rest 🔲 ☎ 🅿. 🔊 *VISA*   BZ **e**
Mid February-mid December – **M** (bar lunch)/dinner 12.50 **st.** – **14 rm** ☑ 24.00/56.00 **st.** – SB (except summer) 55.00/60.00 **st.**

🏠 **Grasmere**, Broadgate, LA22 9TA, ℰ 277, 🐴 – 🔲 ☎ 🅿. 🔊 *VISA*   BZ **r**
closed January – **M** (bar lunch)/dinner 12.50 **t.** 🍷 4.50 – **12 rm** ☑ 34.00/70.00 **t.** – SB (winter only) 48.00/54.00 **st.**

⌂ **Bridge House** ⑤, Stock Lane, LA22 9SN, ℰ 425, 🐴 – 🅿. 🔊 *VISA*. ✄   BZ **n**
Mid March-mid November – **M** 10.50 **t.** 🍷 3.50 – **12 rm** ☑ (dinner included) 33.00/70.00 **t.** – SB 60.00/72.00 **st.**

⌂ **Lancrigg Vegetarian Country House** ⑤, Easedale Rd, LA22 9QN, W : ½ m. on Easedale Rd ℰ 317, ≼, 🐴, park – ✄ rest 🔲 🅿. ✄   AY **u**
M (by arrangement) 8.50/12.75 **t.** 🍷 3.60 – **10 rm** ☑ (dinner included) 35.00/49.50 **t.** – SB (winter only) (weekdays only) 50.00/70.00 **st.**

⌂ **Banerigg** without rest., Lake Rd, LA22 9PW, S : ¾ m. on A 591 ℰ 204, ≼, 🐴 – 🅿   AY **a**
closed January – **6 rm** ☑ 14.50/34.00 **st.**

⌂ **Rothay Lodge** ⑤, White Bridge, LA22 9RH, ℰ 341, 🐴 – ✄ 🅿. ✄   AY **o**
April-October – **M** (by arrangement) 7.00 **st.** – **6 rm** ☑ 18.00/32.00 **st.**

GRASSINGTON North Yorks. **402** O 21 – pop. 1 220 – ECD : Thursday – ⊠ Skipton – ✆ 0756.
🛈 Colvend, Hebden Rd ℰ 752748 (weekends but not evenings).
♦London 240 – Bradford 30 – Burnley 28 – ♦Leeds 37.

⚓ Grassington House, The Square, BD23 5AQ, ℰ 752406 – 🅿 – **18 rm**.

⌂ **Ashfield House**, BD23 5AE, ℰ 752584, 🐴 – ✄ 🅿. 🔊 *VISA*. ✄
closed December and January – **7 rm** ☑ (dinner included) 28.00/63.00 **st.** – SB (except May-October) 45.00 **st.**

⌂ **Lodge**, 8 Wood Lane, BD23 5LU, ℰ 752518 – ✄ rest 🅿
March-October and December – **M** 7.00 **st.** – **7 rm** ☑ 15.00/35.00 **st.**

at Threshfield SW : ½ m. on B 6265 – ⊠ Skipton – ✆ 0756 Grassington :

🏰 **Wilson Arms**, Station Rd, BD23 5ET, ℰ 752666, 🐴 – 🛗 ✄ rest 🔲 ☎ 🅿. 🔊 AE *VISA*
M 8.50/13.00 **t.** 🍷 3.85 – **19 rm** ☑ 31.50/63.00 **st.** – SB 80.00 **st.**

⌂ **Greenways** ⑤, Wharfeside Av., BD23 5BS, ℰ 752598, ≼, 🐴 – ✄ rest 🅿
April-October – **M** 9.00 **st.** – **5 rm** ☑ 16.50/20.00 **st.**

GRAVESEND Kent 404 V 29 – pop. 53 450 – ECD : Wednesday – ☎ 0474.

🚢 to Tilbury (Sealink) frequent services daily (5 mn).

🛈 10 Parrock St. ☏ 337600.

♦London 25 – ♦Dover 54 – Maidstone 16 – Margate 53.

🏨 **Overcliffe**, 15-16 Overcliffe, DA11 0EF, ☏ 322131, Telex 965117 – 📺 ☎ 🅿. 🔄 AE ⓪ VISA
M (dinner only) a la carte 12.50/17.00 t. ⌕ 3.00 – **29 rm** ☷ 52.00/70.00 t.

🏠 **Cromer** without rest., 194 Parrock St., DA12 1EW, ☏ 361935 – 📺 🅿. ⚭
closed 24 December-2 January – **11 rm** ☷ 12.00/27.00 st.

AUSTIN-ROVER The Grove ☏ 322111   VW-AUDI Old Rd West ☏ 357925
SKODA Meopham ☏ 813562

GRAVETYE East Sussex – see East Grinstead.

GRAYSHOTT Hants. 404 R 30 – pop. 2 048 – ✉ Hindhead (Surrey) – ☎ 042 873 Hindhead.
See : Devils Punch Bowl (≤★).

♦London 47 – Chichester 23 – Farnham 9 – Guildford 14 – ♦Portsmouth and Southsea 31.

✗ **Woods**, Headley Rd, GU26 6LB, ☏ 5555 – 🔄 AE ⓪ VISA
closed Sunday and Monday – **M** (dinner only) a la carte 18.70/22.80 st. ⌕ 3.25.

LANCIA, MASSERATI, SUBARU Headley Rd ☏ 5363

GREASBY Merseyside 402 ㉜ 403 ⑫ – ✉ Wirral – ☎ 051 Liverpool.

♦London 220 – ♦Liverpool 9.

🏨 **Twelfth Man Lodge** without rest., Greasby Rd, ☏ 677 5445, Fax 678 5085 – 📺 ☎ ♿ 🅿
30 rm.

GREAT AYTON North Yorks. 402 Q 20 – pop. 4 690 – ✉ ☎ 0642 Middlesbrough.

🛈 High Green ☏ 722835.

♦London 245 – ♦Leeds 63 – ♦Middlesbrough 7 – York 48.

✗✗✗ **Ayton Hall** ⚶ with rm, Low Green, TS9 6BW, ☏ 723595, « Tasteful decor », 🚗, ✗ – 📺
☎ 🅿. 🔄 AE VISA ⚭
M 12.00/18.95 t. and a la carte approx. 29.50 t. – **9 rm** ☷ 65.00/99.00 t.

GREAT BADDOW Essex 404 V 28 – see Chelmsford.

GREAT BARR West Midlands 403 404 O 26 – see Birmingham.

GREAT BROUGHTON Cumbria 401 402 J 19 – see Cockermouth.

GREAT DRIFFIELD Humberside 402 S 21 – pop. 8 970 – ECD : Wednesday – ✉ York – ☎ 0377.

Envir. : Sledmere House★ NW : 7 ½ m..

🛈 Driffield, Sunderlandwick ☏ 43116.

♦London 201 – ♦Kingston-upon-Hull 21   Scarborough 22 – York 29.

🏨 **Bell** (Best Western), 46 Market Pl., YO25 7AP, ☏ 46661, 🔲, squash – ⟠ rest 📺 ☎ ♿ 🅿
– 🔺 150. 🔄 AE ⓪ VISA ⚭
M (buffet lunch)/dinner a la carte 12.10/16.50 t. ⌕ 3.50 – **13 rm** ☷ 52.00/71.50 t., **1 suite**
76.50 t. – SB (except Christmas and New Year) (weekends only) 90.00/115.00 st.

at North Dalton SW : 7 m. by A 164 and A 163 on B 1246 – ✉ York – ☎ 037 781
Middleton-on-the-Wolds :

🏠 **Star Inn**, Warter Rd, YO25 9UX, ☏ 688 – 📺 ☎ 🅿. 🔄 VISA ⚭
M (bar lunch Monday-Saturday)/dinner a la carte 10.55/16.65 t. – **7 rm** ☷ 37.50/49.00 t. –
SB 69.00 t.

GREAT DUNMOW Essex 404 V 28 – pop. 4 026 – ECD : Wednesday – ☎ 0371.

🛈 Council Offices, High St. ☏ 4533.

♦London 42 – ♦Cambridge 27 – Chelmsford 13 – Colchester 24.

🏨 **Saracen's Head** (T.H.F.), High St., CM6 1AG, ☏ 3901, Fax 5743 – ⟠ rm 📺 ☏ 🅿
🔺 40. 🔄 AE ⓪ VISA
M 9.50 st. and a la carte ⌕ 3.75 – ☷ 7.00 – **23 rm** 59.00/74.00 st., **1 suite** 84.00 st. –
SB (weekends only) 76.00/90.00 st.

✗✗✗ **Starr** with rm, Market Pl., CM6 1AX, ☏ 874321 – ⟠ rm 📺 ☎ 🅿. 🔄 AE ⓪ VISA ⚭
closed 3 weeks August and 26 December-8 January – **M** (closed Saturday lunch and
Sunday dinner) 16.50/30.00 t. ⌕ 5.25 – **8 rm** ☷ 55.00/110.00 t.

BMW 81 High St. ☏ 2884

Envir. : Thornton Curtis (St. Lawrence's Church★ : Norman and Gothic) NW : 16 m. by A 18 Y and B 1211 – Thornton Abbey (ruins 14C) : the Gatehouse★ AC, NW : 18 m. by A 18 Y and B 1211.

✈ Humberside Airport : ✆ 0652 (Barnetby)688456, W : 13 m. by A 8 Y.

🛈 Central Library, Town Hall Square ✆ 240410.

◆London 172 – Boston 50 – Lincoln 36 – ◆Sheffield 75.

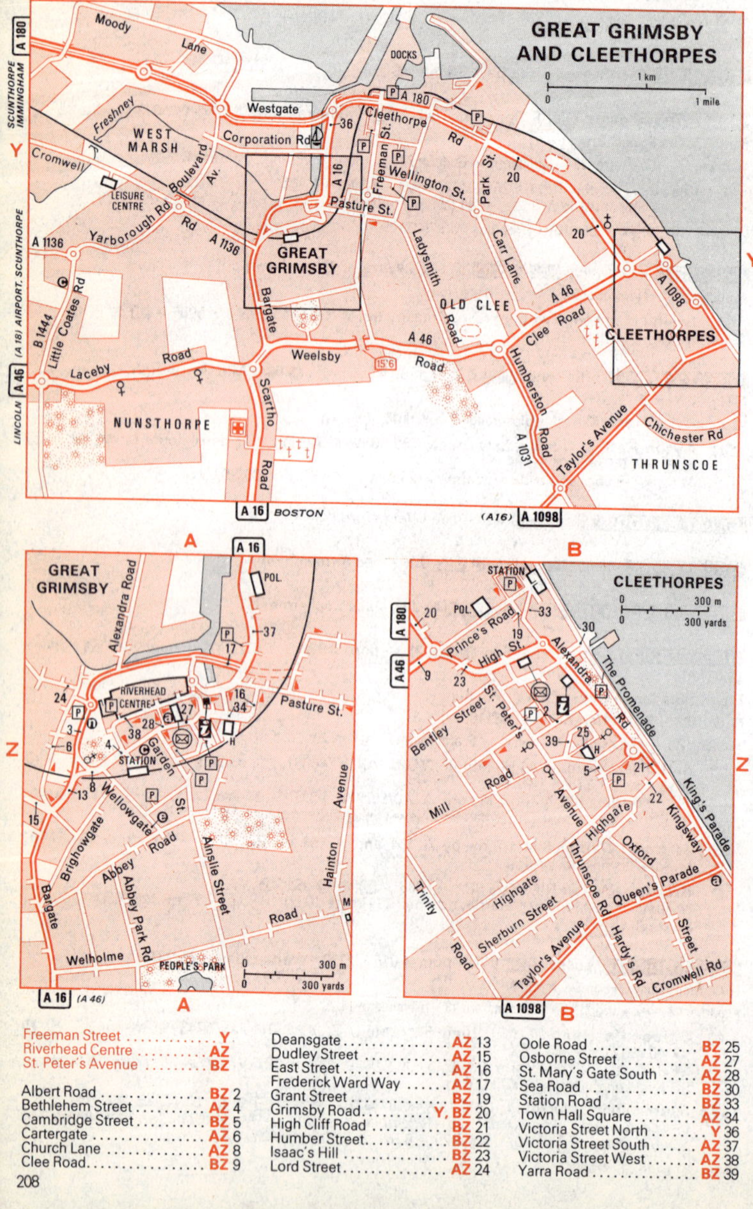

Freeman Street . . . . Y
Riverhead Centre . . . . AZ
St. Peter's Avenue . . . . BZ

Albert Road . . . . BZ 2
Bethlehem Street . . . . AZ 4
Cambridge Street . . . . BZ 5
Cartergate . . . . AZ 6
Church Lane . . . . AZ 8
Clee Road. . . . . BZ 9

Deansgate . . . . AZ 13
Dudley Street . . . . AZ 15
East Street . . . . AZ 16
Frederick Ward Way . . . . . . AZ 17
Grant Street . . . . BZ 19
Grimsby Road. . . . . Y, BZ 20
High Cliff Road . . . . BZ 21
Humber Street . . . . BZ 22
Isaac's Hill . . . . BZ 23
Lord Street . . . . AZ 24

Oole Road . . . . BZ 25
Osborne Street . . . . AZ 27
St. Mary's Gate South . . . . . AZ 28
Sea Road . . . . BZ 30
Station Road . . . . BZ 33
Town Hall Square . . . . AZ 34
Victoria Street North . . . . Y 36
Victoria Street South . . . . . . AZ 37
Victoria Street West . . . . . . AZ 38
Yarra Road . . . . BZ 39

🏨 **Humber Royal** (Crest), Littlecoates Rd, DN34 4LX, ☏ 350295, Telex 527776, Fax 241354, ≼,
🍴 – 📶 ⠯ rm 📺 ☎ 🅿 – 🛆 285. 🅢 🅰🅴 ⓪ 𝗩𝗜𝗦𝗔   Y   c
M 7.50/12.50 **st.** and a la carte 16.00/20.50 **st.** – ☕ 7.35 – **52 rm** 68.00/80.00 **st.** – SB
70.00 **st.**

🏨 **Crest** (Crest), St. James Sq., DN31 1EP, ☏ 359771, Telex 527741, Fax 241427 – 📶 ⠯ 📺 ☎
🅿 – 🛆 70. 🅢 🅰🅴 ⓪ 𝗩𝗜𝗦𝗔   AZ   n
closed 1 week Christmas – **M** 9.00/20.00 **st.** and a la carte ⫶6.00 – ☕ 8.00 – **128 rm**
58.00/70.50 **st.** – SB (weekends only) 64.00/72.00 **st.**

🏨 **Yarborough**, Bethlehem St., DN31 1LY, ☏ 242266, Fax 242266 – 📺 ☎ 🅿 – 🛆 100. 🅢 🅰🅴
⓪ 𝗩𝗜𝗦𝗔   AZ   c
closed 1 week Christmas – **M** 6.95/10.00 **st.** and a la carte ⫶4.50 – **52 rm** ☕ 47.50/57.50 **st.**

XX **Regines**, 2 Osborne St., DN31 1EY, ☏ 356737 – 🅢 𝗩𝗜𝗦𝗔   AZ   a
(closed 1 to 14 February and 1 to 14 August) – **M** *(closed Monday lunch and Sunday)*
10.95 **t.** and a la carte 12.85/19.35 **t.** ⫶3.00.

XX **Brit's**, 29 Abbey Rd, DN32 0HG, ☏ 354442 – 🅢 𝗩𝗜𝗦𝗔   AZ   e
closed 1 to 14 January – **M** *(closed Saturday lunch, Sunday and Monday)* 6.95/15.00 **t.** and a
la carte 15.20/21.20 **t.** ⫶3.00.

AUSTIN-ROVER 415 Victoria St. ☏ 356161
BMW Laceby Rd ☏ 71835
FIAT Wellowgate ☏ 355951
FORD Corporation Rd ☏ 358941
HONDA Alexandra Rd ☏ 358625
MERCEDES-BENZ Bradley Cross Rd ☏ 79274
MITSUBISHI Rendel St. ☏ 362021
NISSAN 210-212 Victoria St. ☏ 353572 and 41281

RENAULT Chelmsford Av. ☏ 70111
SAAB 226 Victoria St. ☏ 48527
TOYOTA Cromwell Rd ☏ 352191
VAUXHALL 123 Cromwell Rd ☏ 46066
VAUXHALL-OPEL Brighowgate ☏ 358486
VW-AUDI Convamore Rd ☏ 355451

🝕 ATS 2 Abbey Rd ☏ 358151

GREAT HANWOOD Shropshire 🐧🐧🐧 L 25 – see Shrewsbury.

GREAT HOCKHAM Norfolk 🐧🐧🐧 W 26 – ✉ Attleborough – ☎ 095 382.
♦London 86 – ♦Cambridge 41 – ♦Norwich 23.

⌂ **Church Cottage** without rest., Breckles, NR17 1EW, N : 1 ½ m. by A 1075 ☏ 286, ⊠ heated,
⥋, 🍴 – 🅿. 🕸
closed 20 December-5 January – **3 rm** ☕ 14.00/28.00 **s.**

GREAT LONGSTONE Derbs. 🐧🐧🐧🐧 O 24 – see Bakewell.

GREAT MALVERN Heref. and Worc. 🐧🐧🐧🐧 N 27 – pop. 30 153 – ECD : Wednesday –
☎ 068 45 (4 fig.) or 0684 (6 fig.).

See : Priory Church★ (11C) B B.

🛈 Winter Gdns, Grange Rd ☏ 892289.

♦London 127 – ♦Birmingham 34 – ♦Cardiff 66 – Gloucester 24.

Plan on next page

🏨 **Foley Arms** (Best Western), Worcester Rd, WR14 4QS, ☏ 573397, ≼, 🍴 – ⠯ rm 📺 ☎
🅿 – 🛆 120. 🅢 🅰🅴 ⓪ 𝗩𝗜𝗦𝗔   B   a
M (bar lunch Monday-Saturday)/dinner 14.95 **st.** and a la carte ⫶4.00 – **26 rm**
☕ 49.50/110.00 **st.**

🏨 **Mount Pleasant**, Belle Vue Terr., WR14 4PZ, ☏ 561837, ≼, 🍴 – 📺 ☎ ⓝ – 🛆 90. 🅢 🅰🅴
⓪ 𝗩𝗜𝗦𝗔. 🕸   B   e
closed 25 and 26 December – **M** 8.95/9.95 **t.** and a la carte ⫶3.75 – ☕ 5.00 – **15 rm**
35.75/47.50 **t.** – SB 62.00/67.50 **st.**

🏠 **Priory Park**, 4 Avenue Rd, WR14 3AG, ☏ 565194, 🍴 – 📺 ☎ 🅿. 🅢   B   x
M (booking essential) 16.00/20.00 **st.** ⫶5.50 – **6 rm** ☕ 40.00/64.00 **st.**

🏠 **Cotford**, 51 Graham Rd, WR14 2JW, ☏ 574680, 🍴 – ⠯ rest 📺 ☎ 🅿. 🅢 𝗩𝗜𝗦𝗔   B   o
closed 26 December-12 January – **M** (dinner only) 13.50 **st.** ⫶5.00 – **16 rm** ☕ 25.00/48.00 **st.**

⌂ **Red Gate**, 32 Avenue Rd, WR14 3BJ, ☏ 565013, 🍴 – ⠯ 📺 🅿. 🕸   B   r
closed 2 weeks March – **M** 9.50 **st.** – **7 rm** ☕ 17.00/36.00 **st.**

⌂ **Elm Bank**, 52 Worcester Rd, WR14 4AB, ☏ 566051, ≼, 🍴 – ⠯ rest 📺 🅿   B   v
M (by arrangement) 9.00 **st.** ⫶3.50 – **6 rm** ☕ 21.00/38.00 **st.** – SB (except summer)
(weekdays only) 54.00/60.00 **st.**

⌂ **Sidney House**, 40 Worcester Rd, WR14 4AA, ☏ 574994, ≼ – ⠯ rest 📺 🅿. 🅢 🅰🅴 𝗩𝗜𝗦𝗔
🕸   B   s
M (by arrangement) 11.50 **st.** ⫶2.25 – **7 rm** ☕ 17.00/46.00 **st.**

at Welland SE : 4 ½ m. by A 449 on A 4104 – ✉ Great Malvern – ☎ 0684 Hanley Swan :

🏠 **Holdfast Cottage** ⑳, Marlbank Rd, WR13 6NA, W : ¾ m. on A 4104 ☏ 310288, « 17C
country cottage », 🍴 – ⠯ rest 📺 🅿. 🅢. 🕸   A   x
closed January – **M** (bar lunch, residents only)/dinner a la carte 17.65/20.75 **st.** ⫶4.45 –
8 rm ☕ 32.00/78.00 **st.** – SB (except Bank Holidays) 94.00/104.00 **st.**

GREAT MALVERN

Church Street .... B
Wells Road .... B

Albert Road South ...... B 3
Blackmore
Park Road .... A 5
Clerkenwell Crescent.... B 6
Cockshot Road .... B 8
Court Road............ B 12
Croft Bank .... A 13
Happy Valley
off St. Ann's Road .... B 15
Imperial Road .... B 16
Jubilee Drive.......... A 17
Lygon Bank .... B 18
Madresfield Road....... B 20
Moorlands Road........ B 22
North Malvern Road..... B 23
Orchard Road .... B 24
Richmond Road .... B 26
Upper Welland
Road .... A 27
Walwyn Road .... A 29
Wells Road .... A 30
Zetland Road........... B 31

Town plans roads most used by traffic and those on which guide listed hotels and restaurants stand are fully drawn ; the beginning only of lesser roads is indicated.

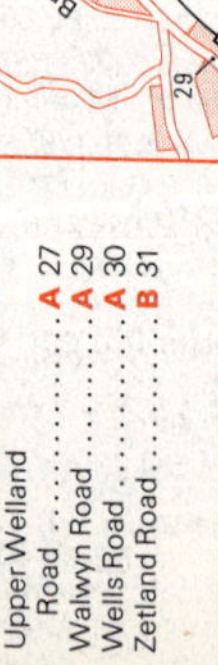

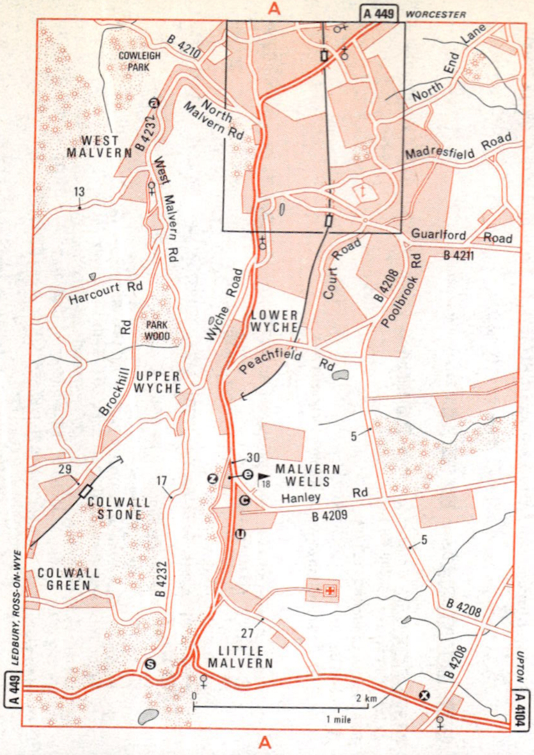

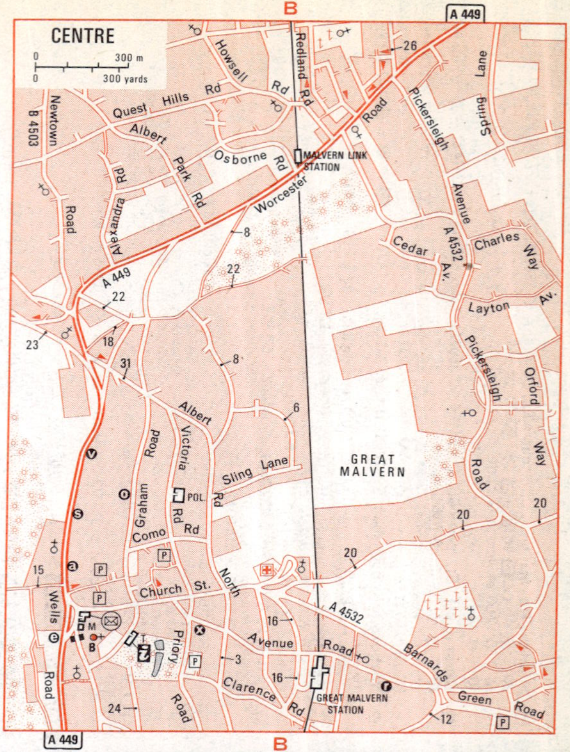

at Malvern Wells S : 2 m. on A 449 – ⊠ ☎ 0684 Great Malvern :

🏨 **Cottage in the Wood** 🦢, Holywell Rd, WR14 4LG, ℰ 573487, Fax 560662, ≤ Severn and Evesham Vales, 🛲 – 📺 ☎ 🅿. 🔌 VISA
M 14.50 st. (lunch) and a la carte ⓑ 3.95 – **20 rm** � 46.00/95.00 st. – SB 60.00/106.00 st.
A z

🏨 **Essington** 🦢, Holywell Rd, WR14 4LQ, ℰ 561177, ≤, 🛲 – ⊱⊰ rest 📺 🅿. 🔌 VISA
M (dinner only) 14.00 t. ⓑ 3.75 – **10 rm** ⊑ 25.00/46.00 t. – SB 60.00/65.00 st.
A e

🏠 **Old Vicarage**, Hanley Rd, WR14 4PH, ℰ 572585, ≤, 🛲 – 📺 🅿
closed Christmas – **M** (by arrangement) 12.50 t. ⓑ 4.00 – **6 rm** ⊑ 25.00/40.00 st.
A c

XX ❀ **Croque-en-Bouche** (Marion Jones), 221 Wells Rd, WR14 4HF, ℰ 565612 – ⊱⊰. 🔌 VISA
closed Sunday to Tuesday and Christmas – **M** (dinner only)(booking essential) 27.00 st.
ⓑ 3.80
A u
Spec. Cannelloni with crab, avocado, coriander and tomato, Leg of lamb, roast as venison with a lovage stuffing; port sauce, Toffee rice pudding with wild strawberries (July-September).

at Wynds Point S : 4 m. on A 449 – ⊠ Great Malvern – ☎ 0684 Colwall :

🏨 **Malvern Hills**, British Camp, WR13 6DW, ℰ 40237, Fax 40327, 🛲 – ⊱⊰ rm 📺 ☎ 🅿. 🔌
AE VISA
A s
M 8.00/12.00 st. and a la carte ⓑ 4.00 – **16 rm** ⊑ 35.00/54.00 st. – SB 80.00/85.00 st.

at West Malvern W : 2 m. on B 4232 – ⊠ ☎ 0684 Great Malvern :

🏠 **One Eight Four** without rest., 184 West Malvern Rd, WR14 4AZ, ℰ 566544, ≤ hills and countryside, « Attractively furnished » – ⊱⊰ 🅿. 🔌 VISA. 🛲
A a
closed 25 December-21 January – **5 rm** ⊑ 23.50/38.50 s.

CITROEN 62 Court Rd ℰ 573391
FORD 203-207 Worcester Rd ℰ 892345
HONDA 157 Wells Rd ℰ 892792

VAUXHALL-OPEL Linktop ℰ 573336
VOLVO Pickersleigh Rd ℰ 892255
VW-AUDI Worcester Rd ℰ 892606

GREAT MILTON Oxon. 403 404 Q 28 – see Oxford.

GREAT MISSENDEN Bucks. 404 R 28 – pop. 7 429 (inc. Prestwood) – ECD : Thursday – ☎ 024 06 – ◆London 34 – Aylesbury 10 – Maidenhead 19 – ◆Oxford 35.

XXX **Graziemille** (at Cock and Rabbit Inn), The Lee, HP16 9LZ, N : 2 ½ m. by A 413 ℰ 024 020 (The Lee) 512, Italian rest., 🛲 – ▤ 🅿. 🔌 AE VISA
closed Sunday dinner and Monday – **M** a la carte 14.05/23.30 t. ⓑ 3.40.

GREAT RISSINGTON Glos. – see Bourton-on-the-Water.

GREAT SNORING Norfolk 404 W 25 – pop. 180 – ⊠ Fakenham – ☎ 0328 Fakenham.
◆London 115 – ◆Cambridge 68 – ◆Norwich 28.

🏨 **Old Rectory** 🦢, Barsham Rd, NR21 0HP, ℰ 820597, « Country house atmosphere », 🛲 – ⊱⊰ rm 📺 ☎ 🅿. AE ⓪. 🛲
closed 24 to 27 December – **M** (booking essential)(dinner only) 14.50 t. – **7 rm** ⊑ 39.00/70.00 t. – SB (November-March) (except Bank Holidays) 85.00 st.

GREAT TEW Oxon. 403 404 P 28 – ☎ 060 883.
◆London 75 – ◆Birmingham 50 – Gloucester 42 – ◆Oxford 21.

🏠 **Falkland Arms** without rest., OX7 4DB, ℰ 653, « 17C inn in picturesque village » – ⊱⊰
📺. 🛲
5 rm ⊑ 25.00/40.00 st.

GREAT WITCHINGHAM Norfolk 404 X 25 – see Lenwade Great Witchingham.

GREAT YARMOUTH Norfolk 404 Z 26 – pop. 54 777 – ECD : Thursday – ☎ 0493.
⛴ Shipping connections with the Continent : to The Netherlands (Scheveningen) (Norfolk Line) – ⓩ 1 South Quay ℰ 846345 – Marine Par. ℰ 842195 (summer only).
◆London 126 – ◆Cambridge 81 – ◆Ipswich 53 – ◆Norwich 20.

🏨 **Carlton**, 1-5 Kimberley Terr., Marine Par., NR30 3JE, ℰ 855234, Telex 975642, Fax 852220 – 🛗 📺 ☎ 🚗. 🔌 AE ⓪ VISA
M (bar lunch Monday to Saturday)/dinner 11.95 st. and a la carte ⓑ 4.95 – **83 rm** ⊑ 46.75/70.50 st., **3 suites** 88.00/145.00 st. – SB 79.20/86.00 st.

🏨 **Two Bears** (B.C.B.), Southtown Rd, NR31 0HU, on A 12 ℰ 603198 – 📺 ☎ 🅿. 🔌 AE ⓪
VISA. 🛲
11 rm ⊑ 31.50/41.50 t.

at Gorleston-on-Sea S : 3 m. on A 12 – ⊠ ☎ 0493 Great Yarmouth :

🏨 **Cliff** (Best Western), Cliff Hill, NR31 6DH, ℰ 662179, Telex 975608, Fax 653617, 🛲 – 📺 ☎
🅿. 🔌 AE ⓪ VISA
M 8.50/11.00 t. and a la carte ⓑ 4.00 – **30 rm** ⊑ 44.00/68.00 t. – SB (weekends only) 60.00/65.00 st.

FIAT North Quay ℰ 844266
FORD South Gates Rd ℰ 844922
FORD 134 Lowestoft Rd, Gorleston-on-Sea ℰ 664151

⊛ ATS Suffling Rd ℰ 858211

GREAT YELDHAM Essex **404** V 27 – pop. 1 440 – ECD : Wednesday – ✉ Halstead – ☎ 0787.
Envir. : Hedingham Castle (Norman Keep★) AC, SE : 2 ½ m.
♦London 56 – ♦Cambridge 27 – Chelmsford 23 – Colchester 21.

XX **White Hart**, Poole St., CO9 4HJ, ℰ 237250, « 15C timbered inn », ☞ – ℗. ◪ *VISA*
M *(closed Sunday dinner)* (bar lunch Monday to Saturday)/dinner a la carte 13.15/20.20 t.

GRETA BRIDGE Durham **402** O 20 – ✉ Barnard Castle – ☎ 0833 Teesdale.
♦London 253 – ♦Carlisle 63 – ♦Leeds 63 – ♦Middlesbrough 32.

🏠 **Morritt Arms**, DL12 9SE, ℰ 27232, ◄, ☞ – ⊺ ⇋ ℗. ◪ AE ⓞ *VISA*
M (bar lunch Monday to Saturday)/dinner 15.50 st. ⅃ 2.95 – **23 rm** ⊑ 33.00/50.00 st. –
SB 60.00/70.00 st.

GRIMSBY Humberside **402 404** T 23 – see Great Grimsby.

GRIMSTHORPE Lincs. **402 404** S 25 – ✉ Bourne – ☎ 077 832 Edenham.
♦London 105 – Lincoln 43 – ♦Nottingham 38.

X **Black Horse Inn** with rm, PE10 0LY, ℰ 247, English rest. – ℗. ◪ AE *VISA*
closed Sunday, 2 weeks Christmas and Bank Holidays – M 12.95/20.00 t. and a la carte –
4 rm ⊑ 36.00/60.00 t. – SB (except summer) (weekends only) 65.00 st.

GRIMSTON Norfolk – see King's Lynn.

GRINDLEFORD Derbs. **402 403 404** P 24 – ✉ Sheffield (South Yorks.) – ☎ 0433 Hope
Valley.
♦London 165 – Derby 31 – ♦Manchester 34 – ♦Sheffield 10.

🏠 **Maynard Arms**, Main Rd, S30 1HP, ℰ 30321, ◄, ☞ – ⊺ ☎ ℗ – ⅍ 100. ◪ AE ⓞ *VISA*
M 9.25/14.50 t. ⅃ 2.80 – **13 rm** ⊑ 43.00/65.00 t. – SB 67.00/70.00 st.

GRINDLETON Lancs. **402** M 22 – pop. 1 451 (inc. West Bradford) – ✉ ☎ 020 07 Bolton-
by-Bowland.
♦London 241 – ♦Blackpool 38 – Lancaster 25 – ♦Leeds 45 – ♦Manchester 33.

🏠 **Harrop Fold Country Farmhouse** ⑤, Harrop Fold, BB7 4PJ, N : 2 ¾ m. by Slaidburn
Rd ℰ 600, ◄, « 17C Longhouse » – ⇴ rest ⊺ ☎ ℗. ◪ *VISA* ⇅
closed January – M (dinner only) 16.50 st. ⅃ 3.50 – **7 rm** ⊑ 35.00/55.00 st. –
SB 70.00/100.00 st.

GRIZEDALE Cumbria **402** K 20 – see Hawkshead.

GUILDFORD Surrey **404** S 30 – pop. 61 509 – ECD : Wednesday – ☎ 0483.
See : Cathedral★ (1961) Z A – Envir. : Clandon Park★★ (Renaissance House) AC, E : 3 m. by A
246 Z – 🛈 Civic Hall, London Rd ℰ 575857.
♦London 33 – ♦Brighton 43 – Reading 27 – ♦Southampton 49.

Plan opposite

🏠 **Post House** (T.H.F.), Egerton Rd, GU2 5XZ, ℰ 574444, Telex 858572, Fax 302960, ◪, ☞ –
⇴ rm ⊺ ☎ ⅋ ℗ – ⅍ 120. ◪ AE ⓞ *VISA*
                                                                          Z v
M 9.95/11.95 st. and a la carte ⅃ 3.75 – ⊑ 7.60 – **111 rm** 80.00/95.00 st., **2 suites** 120.00/
145.00 st. – SB (weekends only) 80.00 st.

🏠 **Manor at Newlands** ⑤, Newlands Corner, GU4 8SE, E : 5 ½ m. by A 246 on A 25
ℰ 222624, ☞, park – ⊺ ☎ ℗ – ⅍ 100. ◪ AE ⓞ *VISA* ⇅
                                                           on A 25   Z
closed 1 week at Christmas – M 11.00/15.00 st. and a la carte ⅃ 3.50 – **20 rm** ⊑ 70.00/98.00 st.
– SB (weekends only) 85.00 st.

🏠 **Angel** (T.H.F.), High St., GU1 3DR, ℰ 64555, « 16C coaching inn » – ⇴ rm ⊺ ☎ – ⅍ 80.
◪ AE ⓞ *VISA*
                                                                          Y a
M (bar lunch)/dinner 12.50 st. and a la carte ⅃ 3.75 – ⊑ 7.00 – **25 rm** 59.00/74.00 st., **2 suites**
99.00 st. – SB (weekends only) 72.00/84.00 st.

🏠 Quinns, 78 Epsom Rd, GU1 2BX, on A 246 ℰ 60422, ☞ – ⊺ ☎ ℗ – **11 rm**.   Z e

X **Cafe de Paris**, 35 Castle St., GU1 3UQ, ℰ 34896, French rest. – ◪ AE ⓞ *VISA*   Y u
closed Saturday lunch, Monday dinner, Sunday and Bank Holidays – M 9.20/10.20 and a la
carte 6.60/24.50.

at Shere E : 5 ¾ m. on A 25 – Z – ✉ Guildford – ☎ 048 641 Shere :

XX **Frederick's**, Gomshall Lane, GU5 9HE, ℰ 2168 – ℗. ◪ AE ⓞ *VISA*
closed Saturday lunch, Sunday dinner and Monday – M 10.90/17.00 t. ⅃ 3.50.

at Bramley S : 3 m. on A 281 – Z – ✉ ☎ 0483 Guildford :

🏠 **Bramley Grange** (Best Western), Horsham Rd, GU5 0BL, ℰ 893434, Telex 859948, Fax
893835, ☞, ⚒ – ⇴ rm ⊺ ☎ ℗ – ⅍ . ◪ AE *VISA* ⇅
M 15.00/17.50 t. and a la carte – **48 rm** ⊑ 79.00/120.00 t. – SB (weekends only)
(except Christmas and Bank Holidays) 110.00 st.

XX **La Baita**, High St., GU5 0HB, ℰ 893392, Italian rest. – ℗. ◪ AE ⓞ *VISA*
closed Sunday – M a la carte 13.60/23.50 t.

GUILDFORD

Friary Centre . . . . Y
High Street . . . . Y
Market Street . . . . Y 18
North Street . . . . Y

Bedford Road . . . . Y 2
Bridge Street . . . . Y 3
Castle Street . . . . Y 5
Chertsey Street . . . . Y 6
College
   Road Link . . . . Y 7
Commercial Road . . . . . . Y 8
Eastgate Gardens . . . . Y 9
Friary Bridge . . . . Y 12
Ladymead . . . . Z 13
Leapale Lane . . . . Y 15
Leapale Road . . . . Y 16
Leas Road . . . . Y 17
Mary Road . . . . Y 19
Midleton Road . . . . Z 20
Millbrook . . . . Y 21
New Inn Lane . . . . Z 22
One Tree
   Hill Road . . . . Z 24
Onslow Street . . . . Y 25
Park Street . . . . Y 27
Quarry Street . . . . Y 28
Stoughton Road . . . . Z 30
Trood's Lane . . . . Z 31
Tungsgate . . . . Y 33
Warwick's Bench . . . . Y 34
Woodbridge Road . . . . . . Z 37

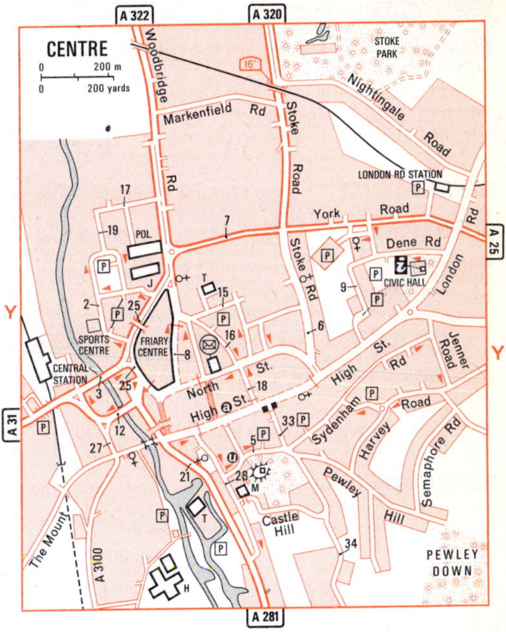

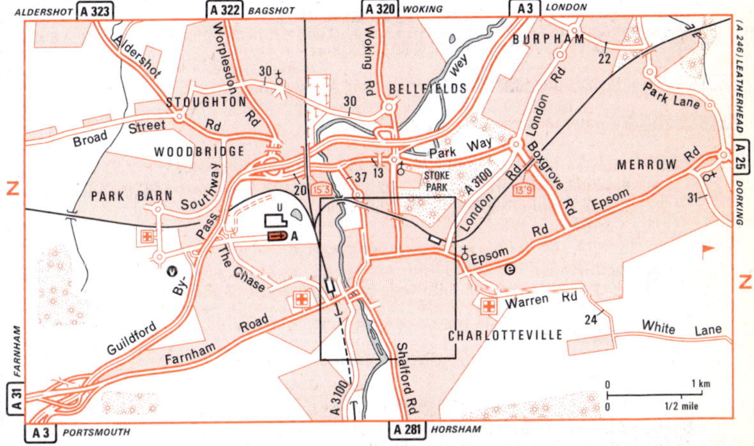

AUSTIN-ROVER, JAGUAR, ROLLS-ROYCE Wood-bridge Rd ℘ 69231
BMW Moorfield Rd ℘ 69944
FORD Woodbridge Meadow ℘ 60601

MERCEDES-BENZ Aldershot Rd ℘ 60751
RENAULT Walnut Tree Close ℘ 577371
TOYOTA Pitch Pl. Worplesdon ℘ 234242
VAUXHALL-OPEL Woking Rd ℘ 37731

GUIST Norfolk **404** W 25 – pop. 209 – ✉ Fakenham – ✆ 036 284 Foulsham.
♦London 119 – ♦Cambridge 67 – King's Lynn 29 – ♦Norwich 20.

XX **Tollbridge**, Dereham Rd, NR20 5NU, S : ½ m. on B 1110 ℘ 359, ≼, « Attractive setting on banks of River Wensum », 🚗 – 🅿 **VISA**
closed Saturday lunch, Sunday, Monday except dinner on Bank Holidays and first 3 weeks January – **M** (booking essential) 10.50/17.50 t. 🍷 3.50.

AUSTIN-ROVER Norwich Rd ℘ 0328 (Fakenham) 4035
FORD Oak St. ℘ 0328 (Fakenham) 2317

VAUXHALL-OPEL Greenway Lane ℘ 0328 (Fakenham) 2200

GULWORTHY Devon 曜3 H 32 – see Tavistock.

GUNNISLAKE Cornwall 曜3 H 32 The West Country G. – pop. 2 154 – ECD : Wednesday –
✆ 0822 Tavistock.
Envir. : Cotehele House★★ AC, SW : 2 ½ m.
♦London 244 – Bude 37 – Exeter 43 – ♦Plymouth 20 – Tavistock 5.

  ⚗ **Cornish Inn**, The Square, PL18 9BW, ℰ 832475 – TV P. 🄰 AE ⓪ VISA
  M a la carte 6.00/12.95 t. ﹩ 2.55 – **6 rm** ⌁ 14.00/33.00 st.

GWBERT-ON-SEA Dyfed 曜3 F 27 – see Cardigan.

HACKNESS North Yorks. 曜2 S 21 – see Scarborough.

HADLEIGH Suffolk 曜4 W 27 – pop. 5 858 – ✆ 0473.
🛈 Toppesfield Hall ℰ 822922 (summer only).
♦London 72 – ♦Cambridge 49 – Colchester 17 – ♦Ipswich 10.

  ↑ **Edgehill**, 2 High St., IP7 5AP, ℰ 822458, 🐎 – ✕ TV P
  M 12.00 st. ﹩ 3.50 – **9 rm** ⌁ 30.00/60.00 st.

  ↑ **Gables**, 63-67 Angel St., IP7 5EY, ℰ 827169, 🐎 – TV P. ✕
  closed Christmas and New Year – **M** 16.00 st. ﹩ 2.20 – **4 rm** ⌁ 18.00/52.00 st. –
  SB (except August) 50.00/60.00 st.

  ✗ **Spinning Wheel**, 117-119 High St., IP7 5EJ, ℰ 822175 – ✕. 🄰 AE ⓪ VISA
  M 7.50/12.95 t. and a la carte 12.35/19.65 t. ﹩ 3.00.

HAILSHAM East Sussex 曜4 U 31 – pop. 12 774 – ECD : Thursday – ✉ ✆ 0323.
🛈 Area Library, Western Rd ℰ 840604.
♦London 57 – ♦Brighton 23 – Eastbourne 7 – Hastings 20.

  🏨 **Boship Farm**, Lower Dicker, BN27 4AT, NW : 3 m. by A 295 on A 22 ℰ 844826, Telex
  878400, Fax 843945, 🏊 heated, 🐎, ✕ – ✕ rm TV ☎ P – 🔬 120. 🄰 AE ⓪ VISA
  M 9.75 t. (lunch)/dinner a la carte 12.55/17.35 t. ﹩ 3.25 – **43 rm** ⌁ 55.00/65.00 t., **2 suites**
  85.00 t. – SB (weekends only) 75.00 st.

  at Magham Down NE : 2 m. by A 295 on A 271 – ✉ Hailsham – ✆ 0323 Eastbourne :

  🏛 **Olde Forge**, BN27 1PN, ℰ 842893 – TV P. 🄰 AE ⓪ VISA
  M *(closed lunch to non-residents)* 9.50 t. (dinner) and a la carte 10.50/14.50 t. ﹩ 3.00 – **8 rm**
  ⌁ 22.50/44.00 st. – SB (October-May) 50.00/55.00 st.

HALE Greater Manchester 曜2 曜3 曜4 M 23 – see Altrincham.

HALEBARNS Greater Manchester – see Altrincham.

HALIFAX West Yorks. 曜2 O 22 – pop. 76 675 – ECD : Thursday – ✆ 0422.
🛆 Halifax Bradley Hall, Holywell Green ℰ 0422 (Elland) 74108 – 🛆 West End, Highroad Well
ℰ 53608, N : 3 m. – 🛆 Ryburn, Norland ℰ 831355, S : 3 m.
🛈 The Piece Hall ℰ 68725.
♦London 205 – Bradford 8 – Burnley 21 – ♦Leeds 15 – ♦Manchester 28.

  🏨 **Holdsworth House**, Holmfield, HX2 9TG, N : 3 m. by A 629 ℰ 240024, Telex 51574, Fax
  245174, « Part 17C house », 🐎 – TV ☎ 🚻 P – 🔬 30. 🄰 AE ⓪ VISA
  closed 1 week at Christmas – **M** *(closed lunch Saturday and Sunday)* a la carte
  approx. 19.50 **st.** ﹩ 3.75 – **36 rm** ⌁ 60.00/75.00 st., **4 suites** 65.00/85.00 st. – SB (weekends only) 90.00/120.00 st.

  🏛 Milans, 6 Carlton Pl., HX1 2SB, ℰ 330539, Telex 517587 – TV ☎
  22 rm.

  at Elland S : 3 ½ m. by A 629 – ✉ ✆ 0422 Halifax :

  ✗ **Berties Bistro**, 7-9 Town Hall Buildings, HX5 0EU, ℰ 71724 – ▤
  closed Monday and 25-26 December – **M** (dinner only) a la carte 8.25/13.95 st. ﹩ 5.75.

AUSTIN-ROVER Huddersfield Rd ℰ 365944
FIAT Skircoat Rd ℰ 53701
FORD Skircoat Rd ℰ 365790
FSO Rochdale Rd ℰ 365036
RENAULT Hanson Lane ℰ 59442
VAUXHALL Northgate ℰ 362851

VAUXHALL-OPEL 7 Horton St. ℰ 365846
VOLVO 31 Pellon New Rd ℰ 361961
VW-AUDI Denholme Gate Rd, Hipperholme ℰ
205611

🛞 ATS Hope St. ℰ 365892

HALLAND East Sussex 曜4 U 31 – ECD : Wednesday – ✉ Lewes – ✆ 082 584.
♦London 48 – ♦Brighton 16 – Eastbourne 16 – Royal Tunbridge Wells 19.

  🏨 **Halland Forge**, BN8 6PW, on A 22 ℰ 456, Fax 773, 🐎, park – TV ☎ P. 🄰 AE ⓪ VISA
  M 8.95/13.50 t. and a la carte ﹩ 3.50 – ⌁ 6.50 – **20 rm** 37.00/46.00 t. – SB 66.00/70.00 st.

HALSE TOWN Cornwall 曜3 D 33 – see St. Ives.

214

HALTWHISTLE Northumb. 401 402 M 19 – pop. 3 522 – ☎ 0434.

🛈 Sycamore St. ℰ 20351 (summer only).

♦London 335 – ♦Carlisle 22 – ♦Newcastle 37.

  ↑ **Ashcroft** without rest., Lantys Lonnen, NE49 0DA, ℰ 320213, 🚗 – 🕸 🅿. 🛁
    closed 20 December-6 January – **6 rm** � 13.00/30.00 **s.**

AUSTIN-ROVER West End Garage ℰ 20294

HAMBLETON Leics. – see Oakham.

HAMBROOK Avon 403 404 M 29 – see Bristol.

HAMPTON LOADE Shropshire – see Bridgnorth.

HAMSTERLEY Durham 401 402 O 19 – ✉ ☎ 0388 Bishop Auckland.

♦London 260 – ♦Carlisle 75 – ♦Middlesbrough 30 – ♦Newcastle upon Tyne 22.

  ↑ **Grove House** 🦌, Hamsterley Forest, DL13 1NL, W : 3 ¾ m. via Bedburn ℰ 88203, 🚗 –
    🕸 🅿. 🛁
    closed 2 weeks August, Christmas and New Year – **M** 8.50 **st.** – **4 rm** ⊑ 16.00/32.00 **st.**

HANDFORTH Cheshire 402 403 404 N 23 – see Wilmslow.

HANLEY Staffs. 402 403 404 N 24 – see Stoke-on-Trent.

HANMER Clwyd 402 403 L 25 – ✉ Whitchurch – ☎ 094 874.

♦London 237 – Chester 26 – Shrewsbury 27 – ♦Stoke-on-Trent 28.

  🏠 Hanmer Arms, SY13 3DE, ℰ 532 – 📺 ☎ &. 🅿 – **7 rm**, **4 suites**.

HANWOOD Shropshire 402 403 L 25 – see Shrewsbury.

HAREWOOD West Yorks. 402 P 22 – pop. 3 429 – ✉ Leeds – ☎ 0532.

♦London 214 – Harrogate 9 – ♦Leeds 10 – York 20.

  🏠🏠 **Harewood Arms**, Harrogate Rd, LS17 9LH, on A 61 ℰ 886566, 🚗 – 📺 ☎ 🅿. 🔳 🆎 ⓪
    VISA
    M 8.95/12.95 **t.** and a la carte – **24 rm** ⊑ 56.00/74.00 **t.**

HARLECH Gwynedd 402 403 H 25 – pop. 1 292 – ECD : Wednesday – ☎ 0766.

See : Castle★★ (13C) AC, site and ≤ from the castle★ – Envir. : Llanbedr (Cwm Bychan★)
S : 3 ½ m. – Vale of Ffestiniog★, NE : 9 m.– 🏌 Royal St. David's ℰ 780203.

🛈 Snowdonia National Park Visitor Centre, High St. ℰ 780658 (summer only).

♦London 241 – Chester 72 – Dolgellau 21.

  🏠🏠 **Maes-y-Neuadd** 🦌, Talsarnau, LL47 6YA, NE : 3 ½ m. by B 4573 ℰ 780200, Fax 780211,
    ≤, « Part 14C country house », 🚗, park – 🕸 rest 📺 ☎ 🅿. 🔳 🆎 ⓪ **VISA**
    closed January – **M** 12.50/22.00 **t.** ⅃ 3.05 – **14 rm** ⊑ 38.00/108.00 **t.**, **1 suite** 99.00/116.00 **t.**
    – SB 160.00/210.00 **st.**

  ↑ **Gwrach Ynys**, LL47 6TS, N : 2 ¼ m. on A 496 ℰ 780742, 🚗 – 🕸 rest 🅿
    February-October – **M** 7.00 **st.** – **7 rm** ⊑ 13.00/30.00 **st.** – SB 40.00/44.00 **st.**

  ✗ **The Cemlyn**, High St., LL46 2YA, ℰ 780425, ≤ Harlech Castle, Cardigan Bay and Lleyn
    Peninsula – 🔳 **VISA**
    March-October – **M** (lunch by arrangement)/dinner 17.50 **t.** ⅃ 3.50.

HARLOW Essex 404 U 28 – pop. 79 150 – ECD : Wednesday – ☎ 0279.

♦London 22 – ♦Cambridge 37 – ♦Ipswich 60.

  🏠 **Churchgate Manor** (Best Western), Churchgate St., Old Harlow, CM17 OJT, E : 3 ¼ m.
    by A 414 and B 183 ℰ 20246, Telex 818289, Fax 37720, 🔲, 🚗 – 📺 ☎ 🅿 – 🛎 200. 🔳 🆎
    ⓪ **VISA**
    M (closed Saturday lunch) 14.95 **t.** (dinner) and a la carte 17.95/25.00 **t.** ⅃ 4.95 – **71 rm**
    ⊑ 48.00/120.00 **t.** – SB (weekends only) 72.00 **st.**

  🏠 **Green Man** (T.H.F.), Mulberry Green, Old Harlow, CM17 0ET, E : 2 ¼ m. by A 414 and B 183
    ℰ 442521, Telex 817972, Fax 626113 – 🕸 rm 📺 ☎ 🅿 – 🛎 50. 🔳 🆎 ⓪ **VISA**
    M (closed Saturday lunch) 10.00/13.00 **st.** and a la carte ⅃ 4.00 – ⊑ 7.00 – **55 rm**
    60.00/70.00 **st.** – SB (weekends only) 72.00/84.00 **st.**

  🏠 **Harlow Moat House** (Q.M.H.), Southern Way, CM18 7BA, SE : 2 ¼ m. by A 1025 on A 414
    ℰ 22441, Telex 81658, Fax 635094 – 🕸 rm 📺 ☎ 🅿 – 🛎 250. 🔳 🆎 ⓪ **VISA**. 🛁
    closed Christmas – **M** (bar lunch Saturday)/dinner 12.50 **t.** and a la carte ⅃ 5.50 – **120 rm**
    ⊑ 70.00/80.00 **t.** – SB (weekends only) 64.00 **st.**

  🏠 **Travel Inn** without rest., Cambridge Rd, Old Harlow, CM20 2EP, NE : 3 ¼ m. by A 414 on
    A 1184 ℰ 442545 – 📺 &. 🅿 – **38 rm**.

FORD Edinburgh Way ℰ 21166   ⓜ ATS 14 Burnt Mill ℰ 21965
VOLVO Crowngate ℰ 39541

HARNHAM Wilts. 🄣🄣🄣 🄣🄣🄣 O 30 – see Salisbury.

HAROME North Yorks. – see Helmsley.

HARPENDEN Herts. 🄣🄣🄣 S 28 – pop. 28 589 – ECD : Wednesday – ✪ 058 27.
♦London 32 – Luton 6.

🏨🏨 **Harpenden Moat House** (Q.M.H.), 18 Southdown Rd, AL5 1PE, ℰ 64111, Telex 826938, Fax
69858, 🚗 – ⊷ rm 📺 ☎ 🅿 – 🔬 100
51 rm, 3 suites.

🏨 **Glen Eagle**, 1 Luton Rd, AL5 2PX, ℰ 60271, Telex 825828, Fax 460819, 🚗 – 🛗 🔲 rest 📺
☎ 🅿 – 🔬 50. 🄰 🄰🄴 🄾 🆅🅸🆂🅰
M 13.50/15.50 **st.** and a la carte 🍶 3.75 – **51 rm** 🍵 64.50/94.50 **st.** – SB (weekends
only) 75.00/111.00 **st.**

AUSTIN-ROVER Lower Luton Rd ℰ 66463
FORD, RELIANT, SCIMITAR 100 Southdown Rd
ℰ 5217
RENAULT 74 High St. ℰ 0582 (Luton) 460545

VAUXHALL-OPEL 17 Luton Rd ℰ 0582 (Luton)
460111
VOLVO Station Rd ℰ 64311

HARROGATE North Yorks. 🄣🄣🄣 P 22 – pop. 63 637 – ECD : Wednesday – ✪ 0423.
Envir. : Fountains Abbey★★★ (ruins 12C-13C, floodlit in summer), Studley Royal Gardens★★ –
Fountains Hall★ (17C) *AC*, NW : 9 m. by A 61 AY – Harewood House★★ S : 10 ½ m. by A 61 BZ.
🄢 Crimple Valley, Hookstone Wood Rd ℰ 883485, by A 661 CZ – 🄸🄸 Forest Lane Head ℰ 862999,
E : 2 m. on A 59 BY – 🄩 Royal Baths Assembly Rooms, Crescent Rd ℰ 525666/7/8.
♦London 211 – Bradford 18 – ♦Leeds 15 – ♦Newcastle-upon-Tyne 76 – York 22.

Plan opposite

🏨🏨 **Old Swan** (Norfolk Cap.), Swan Rd, HG1 2SR, ℰ 500055, Telex 57922, Fax 501154, 🚗, park,
✗ – 🛗 📺 ☎ 🅿 – 🔬 400   AY **e**
127 rm, 10 suites.

🏨🏨 **Majestic** (T.H.F.), Ripon Rd, HG1 2HU, ℰ 568972, Telex 57918, Fax 502283, 🄼, 🚗, ✗,
squash – 🛗 ⊷ rm 📺 ☎ 🅿 – 🔬 300. 🄰 🄰🄴 🄾 🆅🅸🆂🅰   AY **c**
M 12.25/15.75 **st.** and a la carte 🍶 3.95 – 🍵 7.60 – **146 rm** 74.50/96.50 **st., 10 suites**
140.00/160.00 **st.** – SB (weekends only) 92.00/96.00 **st.**

🏨🏨 **Moat House International** (Q.M.H.), Kings Rd, HG1 1XX, ℰ 500000, Telex 57575, Fax
524435, ⪡ – 🛗 ⊷ rm 🔲 📺 ☎ 🔍 🅿 – 🔬 300. 🄰 🄰🄴 🄾 🆅🅸🆂🅰   BY **x**
M 10.00/16.00 **t.** and a la carte 🍶 4.50 – **205 rm** 🍵 77.00/95.00 **t., 9 suites** 130.00 **t.** –
SB (weekends only) 80.00 **st.**

🏨🏨 **Crown** (T.H.F.), Crown Pl., HG1 2RZ, ℰ 567755, Telex 57652, Fax 502284 – 🛗 ⊷ rm 📺 ☎
🅿 – 🔬 350. 🄰 🄰🄴 🄾 🆅🅸🆂🅰   AZ **i**
M 9.20/15.00 **st.** and a la carte 🍶 4.00 – 🍵 7.95 – **116 rm** 70.00/87.00 **st., 5 suites** 110.00/
135.00 **st.** – SB 80.00/92.00 **st.**

🏨 **Imperial**, Prospect Pl., HG1 1LA, ℰ 565671, Telex 57606, Fax 500082 – 🛗 📺 ☎ 🅿
🔬 150. 🄰 🄰🄴 🄾 🆅🅸🆂🅰   BZ **a**
M 9.00/14.50 **st.** and a la carte 🍶 3.50 – **84 rm** 🍵 60.00/80.00 **st., 1 suite** 110.00/135.00 **st.** –
SB 59.00/85.00 **st.**

🏨 **St. George** (Swallow), 1 Ripon Rd, HG1 2SY, ℰ 561431, Telex 57995, Fax 530037, 🄼 – 🛗
📺 ☎ 🅿 – 🔬 350. 🄰 🄰🄴 🄾 🆅🅸🆂🅰   AY **o**
M 10.50/15.00 **st.** and a la carte – **92 rm** 🍵 70.00/95.00 **st., 1 suite** 165.00/170.00 **st.** –
SB (except Christmas and New Year) 92.00/98.00 **st.**

🏨 **Studley**, 28 Swan Rd, HG1 2SE, ℰ 560425, Telex 57506, Fax 530967 – 🛗 🔲 rest 📺 ☎ 🅿.
🄰 🄰🄴 🄾 🆅🅸🆂🅰. 🍴   AZ **x**
M *(closed Saturday lunch)* 16.00 **t.** (dinner) and a la carte 🍶 3.25 – **34 rm** 🍵 49.50/75.00 **st.,**
2 suites 80.00 **st.** – SB (weekends only) (except Christmas) 72.00 **st.**

🏨 **Balmoral**, 16-18 Franklin Mount, HG1 5EJ, ℰ 508208, Fax 530652, « Antique furnishings »
– 📺 ☎ 🅿. 🄰 🄰🄴 🆅🅸🆂🅰   BY **v**
M (bar lunch residents only)/dinner 20.00 **st.** and a la carte 🍶 3.60 – 🍵 6.00 – **19 rm**
45.00/65.00 **st., 1 suite** 75.00/110.00 **st.** – SB (weekends only) 72.00/112.00 **st.**

🏨 **Grants**, Swan Rd, HG1 2SS, ℰ 560666, Fax 502550 – 🛗 🔲 rest 📺 ☎ 🔍 🅿. 🄰 🄰🄴 🄾 🆅🅸🆂🅰
M 8.95/12.95 **t.** and a la carte 🍶 3.95 – **37 rm** 🍵 50.00/100.00 **t.** – SB (weekends
only) 75.00/105.00 **st.**   AY **s**

🏨 **Russell**, 29-35 Valley Drive, HG2 0JN, ℰ 509866, Fax 506185 – 🛗 📺 ☎. 🄰 🄰🄴 🄾 🆅🅸🆂🅰
closed 27 to 30 December – **M** (see **Hodgsons** below) – **32 rm** 🍵 42.95/65.50 **t., 2 suites**
78.50 **t.** – SB 77.00/84.00 **st.**   AZ **e**

🏨 **Hospitality Inn** (Mt. Charlotte), Prospect Pl., West Park, HG1 1LB, ℰ 564601, Telex 57530 –
🛗 📺 ☎ 🅿   BZ **v**
66 rm, 5 suites.

🏨 **Fern**, Swan Rd, HG1 2SS, ℰ 523866, Telex 57583, Fax 501825 – 📺 ☎ – 🔬 35. 🄰 🄰🄴 🄾
🆅🅸🆂🅰. 🍴   AY **z**
M 10.00/13.45 **t.** and a la carte 🍶 3.95 – 🍵 7.00 – **32 rm** 29.90/76.95 **t., 2 suites** 60.00/
120.00 **t.** – SB 100.00/182.00 **st.**

🏨 **Alexandra Court** without rest., 8 Alexandra Rd, HG1 5JS, ℰ 502764 – 📺 ☎ 🅿. 🄰 🆅🅸🆂🅰
🍴   BY **o**
12 rm 🍵 28.00/42.00 **t.**

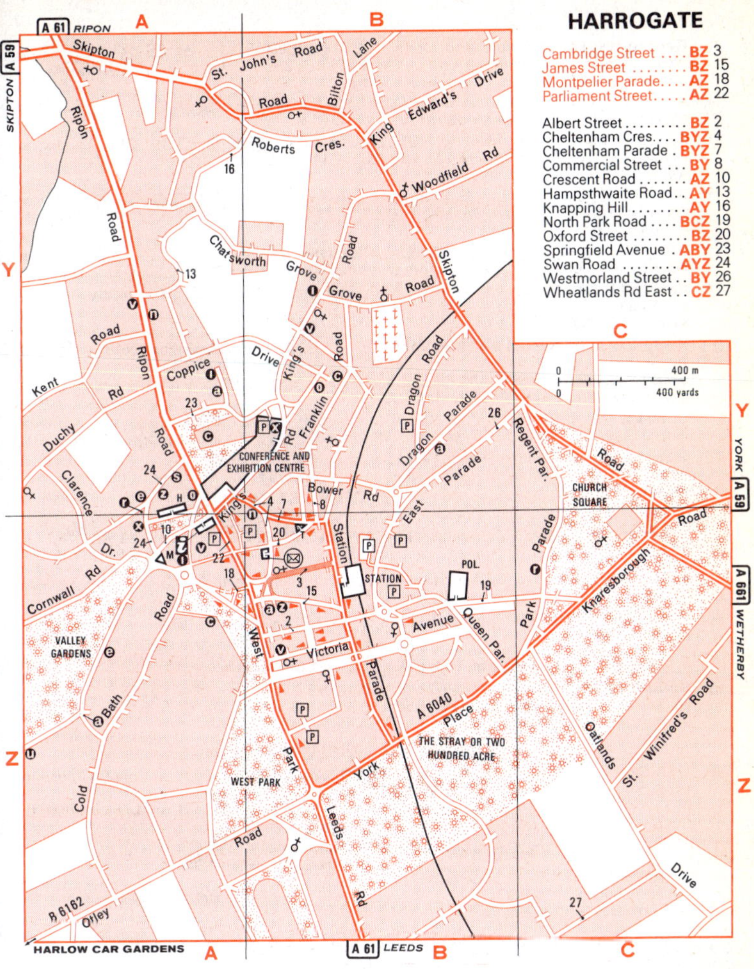

Beech without rest., 1 Esplanade, HG2 0LN, ℰ 531431 – ✗ TV ☎. ⌧ VISA — AZ c
11 rm ⌸ 28.00/45.00 t.

Green Park, Valley Drive, HG2 0JT, ℰ 504681, Fax 530811 – |≋| ✗ rest TV ☎ P – ⌂ 40. — AZ a
⌧ AE ① VISA
M (bar lunch)/dinner 10.25 st. and a la carte – **43 rm** ⌸ 42.00/80.00 st. – SB (weekends only) 63.50/68.50 st.

Gables, 2 West Grove Rd, HG1 2AD, ℰ 505625 – TV ☎ P. ⌧ VISA — BY i
M (bar lunch)/dinner a la carte approx. 9.50 t. ⅋ 2.85 – **9 rm** ⌸ 19.50/46.00 t. – SB 50.00/55.00 st.

White House, 10 Park Par., HG1 5AH, ℰ 501388 – TV ☎ P. ⌧ AE ① VISA — CZ r
M (dinner only and Sunday lunch)/dinner 9.50 t. and a la carte ⅋ 3.50 – **13 rm** ⌸ 35.00/60.00 t. – SB (weekends only) 68.00/90.00 st.

Britannia Lodge, 16 Swan Rd, HG1 2SA, ℰ 508482 – ✗ rest TV ☎ P. ⌧ VISA. ⌘ — AYZ r
M 6.00/13.00 t. ⅋ 3.00 – **12 rm** ⌸ 35.00/48.00 t.

Ashwood House without rest., 7 Spring Grove, HG1 2HS, ℰ 560081 – TV. ⌘ — AY a
closed Christmas-New Year – **9 rm** ⌸ 16.00/38.00 t.

Stoney Lea without rest., 13 Spring Grove, HG1 2HS, ℰ 501524 – TV. ⌘ — AY i
26 February-21 December – **6 rm** ⌸ 20.00/35.00 st.

Crescent Lodge without rest., 20 Swan Rd, HG1 2SA, ℰ 503688 – ⌘ — AZ x
closed 14 January-18 February – **4 rm** ⌸ 13.00/30.00 st.

⌂ **Garden House,** 14 Harlow Moor Drive, HG2 0JX, ✆ 503059 – ⑃ rest ☑ ⌾   AZ **u**
closed Christmas and New Year – **M** 8.00 **st.** ⌾ 2.75 – **7 rm** ⌷ 17.00/32.00 **st.** –
SB (November-April) (weekends only) 42.00 **st.**

⌂ **Alexa House** without rest., 26 Ripon Rd, HG1 2JJ, ✆ 501988 – ☑ ⓟ. ⌾   AY **n**
closed Christmas-New Year – **13 rm** ⌷ 17.00/40.00 **st.**

⌂ **Arden House,** 69-71 Franklin Rd, HG1 5EH, ✆ 509224 – ☑ ☎ ⓟ. ◪ 𝗩𝗜𝗦𝗔. ⌾   BY **c**
closed 2 weeks Christmas – **M** 9.25 **st.** ⌾ 3.50 – **14 rm** ⌷ 17.50/39.00 **st.** – SB (November-
April) 49.50/55.50 **st.**

⌂ **Abbey Lodge** without rest., 29-31 Ripon Rd, HG1 2JL, ✆ 569712 – ☑ ⓟ. ⌾   AY **v**
closed 1 week Christmas – **M** 8.50 **st.** ⌾ 2.50 – **17 rm** ⌷ 18.00/36.00 **st.** – SB (November-
April) 46.00 **st.**

⌂ **Daryl House,** 42 Dragon Par., HG1 5DA, ✆ 502775 – ☑. ⌾   BY **a**
closed 1 week Christmas – **M** (by arrangement) 6.00 **st.** – **6 rm** ⌷ 12.00/20.00 **st.**

⌂ **Knox Mill House** ⌾ without rest., Knox Mill Lane, HG3 2AE, N : 1 ½ m. by A 61 AY
✆ 560650, ≤ – ⓟ. ⌾
3 rm ⌷ 25.00/30.00 **s.**

XXX **Hodgson's,** (at Russell H.) 29-35 Valley Drive, HG2 0JN, ✆ 509866, Fax 506185 – ⑃. ◪
◭ ⓞ 𝗩𝗜𝗦𝗔   AZ **e**
closed 27 to 30 December – **M** *(closed Sunday and Monday to non-residents)* (dinner only)
13.95 **t.** and a la carte 16.35/25.20 **st.** ⌾ 3.35.

XXX **Shabab,** 1 John St., HG1 1JZ, ✆ 500250, Indian rest. – ◪ ◭ ⓞ 𝗩𝗜𝗦𝗔   BZ **z**
closed Sunday lunch and 25 December – **M** 4.90 **t.** (lunch) and a la carte approx. 9.70/13.70 **t.**

XX **Grundy's,** 21 Cheltenham Cres., HG1 1DH, ✆ 502610 – ◪ ◭ 𝗩𝗜𝗦𝗔   BYZ **n**
closed Sunday and Bank Holidays – **M** (dinner only) 10.75 **t.** and a la carte 12.45/19.70 **t.**

X **Millers,** 1 Montpellier Mews, HG1 2TC, ✆ 530708 – ◪ 𝗩𝗜𝗦𝗔   AZ **v**
closed Monday dinner and Sunday – **M** a la carte 16.50/22.40 **t.** ⌾ 3.85.

X **Drum and Monkey,** 5 Montpellier Gdns, HG1 2TF, ✆ 502650, Seafood – ◪ 𝗩𝗜𝗦𝗔   AZ **v**
closed Sunday and 24 December-3 January – **M** (booking essential) a la carte 8.45/17.75 **t.**

at Burn Bridge S : 4 m. by A 61 (turn right before junction with A 658) – BZ – ✉ ✆ 0423
Harrogate :

XX **Roman Court,** 55 Burn Bridge Rd, HG3 1PB, ✆ 879933, Italian rest. – ⓟ
M (dinner only).

at Beckwithshaw W : 2 ½ m. on B 6162 – AZ – ✉ ✆ 0423 Harrogate :

🏛 **Sandringham,** HG2 0NN, ✆ 500722, ≤, « Antiques » – ⑃ rest ☑ ☎ ⓟ. ◪. ⌾
M *(closed Sunday dinner)* 11.00/18.50 **t.** ⌾ 3.50 – **6 rm** ⌷ 45.00/95.00 **t.** – SB (weekends only) 90.00/110.00 **st.**

at Markington NW : 8 ¾ m. by A 61 – AY – ✉ ✆ 0423 Harrogate :

🏛 **Hob Green** ⌾, HG3 3PJ, SW : ½ m. ✆ 770031, Group Telex 57780, ≤, « Country house in
extensive parkland », ☞ – ☑ ☎ ⓟ. ◪ ◭ ⓞ 𝗩𝗜𝗦𝗔
M (bar lunch Monday to Saturday)/dinner approx. 14.50 **st.** ⌾ 4.00 – **11 rm** ⌷ 53.00/78.00 **t.** –
1 suite 95.00 **t.** – SB (weekdays only) (October-April) 95.00 **st.**

AUSTIN-ROVER, DAIMLER-JAGUAR 91 Leeds Rd   RENAULT Stacey Houses, Pannal ✆ 879231
✆ 871263   VW-AUDI Ripon Rd ✆ 505141
CITROEN, LANCIA Cheltenham Mount ✆ 568151
FORD Knaresborough Rd ✆ 88593   ⊛ ATS Leeds Rd, Pannal ✆ 879194
MERCEDES Leeds Rd, Pannal ✆ 879236

HARTFORD Cheshire 402 403 404 M 24 – pop. 4 000 – ✆ 0606 Northwich.
⌸ Delamere Forest ✆ 0606 (Sandiway) 882807, SW : 2 m.
♦London 188 – Chester 15 – ♦Liverpool 31 – ♦Manchester 25.

🏛 Hartford Hall, 81 School Lane, CW8 1PW, ✆ 75711, ☞ – ☑ ☎ ⓟ – ⌂ 35
20 rm, 1 suite.

AUDI-VW Station Rd, Northwich ✆ 0606 (North-   RENAULT Runcorn Rd, Barnton ✆ 0606 (North-
wich) 46061   wich) 77137
CITROEN Manchester Rd, Northwich ✆ 0606   PEUGEOT-TALBOT 322 Chester Rd ✆ 0606 (Sandi-
(Northwich) 43816   way) 888188
FORD Chesterway, Northwich ✆ 0606 (Northwich)   VAUXHALL-OPEL 9 London Rd, Northwich ✆ 0606
46141   (Northwich) 43434

HARTINGTON Derbs. 402 403 404 O 24 – ✉ Buxton – ✆ 0298 Buxton.
♦London 168 – Derby 36 – ♦Manchester 40 – ♦Sheffield 34 – Stoke-on-Trent 22.

⌂ Biggin Hall ⌾, Biggin, SK17 0DH, SE : 2 m. by B 5054 ✆ 84451, ≤, « 17C hall », ☞ –
⑃ rest ☑ ⓟ. ⌾
11 rm.

EUROPE **on a single sheet**
Michelin map no 920

HARTLEPOOL Cleveland **402** Q 19 – pop. 91 749 – ECD : Wednesday – ☎ 0429.

☒ Seaton Carew, Tees Rd ✆ 266249 – ☒ Castle Eden and Peterlee ✆ 836510.

✈ Teesside Airport ✆ 0325 (Darlington) 332811, SW : 20 m.

☑ Civic Centre, Victoria Rd ✆ 869706.

♦London 263 – Durham 19 – ♦Middlesbrough 9 – Sunderland 21.

Grand, Swainson St., TS24 8AA, ✆ 266345, Fax 273896 – ⌘ 📺 ☎ – 🪑 50. 🅰 AE ⓞ VISA
closed 25-26 December and 1 January – **M** *(closed Bank Holiday lunch)* a la carte 8.55/17.95 **t.**
🍷 3.25 – **41 rm** ☕ 36.50/75.00 **st.** – SB (weekends only) 59.00 **st.**

at Seaton Carew SE : 2 m. on A 178 – ☎ 0429 Hartlepool :

✕ **Krimo's**, 8 The Front, TS25 1BS, ✆ 266120 – 🅰 VISA
closed Saturday lunch, Sunday, Monday, 25-26 December, 1 January and 2 weeks August –
M 5.00 **st.** (lunch) and a la carte 8.50/18.25 **st.** 🍷 3.10.

AUDI-VW Brenda Rd ✆ 221619
AUSTIN-ROVER York Rd ✆ 274431
CITROEN Longhill Ind. Est. ✆ 233031
FORD Stockton Rd ✆ 264311

MAZDA Westview Rd ✆ 236783
VAUXHALL Oxford Rd ✆ 273672

🅖 ATS York Rd ✆ 275552

HARTOFT END North Yorks. **402** R 21 – pop. 62 – ✉ Pickering – ☎ 075 15 Lastingham.

♦London 243 – Scarborough 26 – York 32.

Blacksmith's Arms, YO18 8EN, ✆ 331, ≼, 🛋 – 📺 ☎ 🅿. 🅰 VISA. 🕸
M 12.50/16.50 **t.** and a la carte 15.00/20.00 **t.** 🍷 3.30 – **12 rm** ☕ 40.00/70.00 **t.**

HARWICH and DOVERCOURT Essex **404** X 28 – pop. 17 245 – ECD : Wednesday – ☎ 0255.

🚢 Shipping connections with the Continent : to Germany (Hamburg) (Scandinavian Seaways)
– to Denmark (Esbjerg) (Scandinavian Seaways) – from Parkeston Quay to The Netherlands
(Hoek van Holland) (Sealink) – to Sweden (Göteborg) (Scandinavian Seaways).

🚢 to Felixstowe (Orwell & Harwich Navigation Co.) 4-7 daily (except Sunday) (15 mn).

☑ Parkeston Quay ✆ 506139/502426.

♦London 78 – Chelmsford 41 – Colchester 20 – ♦Ipswich 23.

Tower, Main Rd, Dovercourt, CO12 3PJ, ✆ 504952 – 📺 ☎ 🅿. 🅰 AE ⓞ VISA
closed 24 to 26 December – **M** 8.50/20.00 **t.** and a la carte 10.40/21.70 **t.** 🍷 5.65 – **14 rm**
☕ 35.00/50.00 **t.**

Cliff, Marine Par., Dovercourt, CO12 3RE, ✆ 503345, ≼ – ⤢ rest 📺 ☎ 🅿. 🅰 AE ⓞ VISA
M 10.00/11.00 **t.** and a la carte – **29 rm** ☕ 35.00/50.00 **t.**, **1 suite** 48.00/70.00 **t.**

✕✕ **Pier at Harwich** with rm, The Quay, CO12 3HH, ✆ 241212, ≼, Seafood – 📺 ☎ 🅿. 🅰
VISA 🕸
M 9.50 **t.** (lunch) and a la carte 13.20/16.40 **t.** 🍷 6.30 – ☕ 4.00 – **6 rm** 35.00/55.00 **st.** –
SB 80.00 **st.**

SKODA 113 High St., Dovercourt ✆ 502537

🅖 ATS 723 Main Rd, Dovercourt ✆ 508314

HASCOMBE Surrey – see Godalming.

HASELBURY PLUCKNETT Somerset **403** L 31 – see Crewkerne.

HASLEMERE Surrey **404** R 30 – pop. 10 544 – ECD : Wednesday – ☎ 0428.

Envir. : Petworth House★★★ (17C) (paintings★★★ and carved room★★★) *AC*, SE : 11 m.

♦London 47 – ♦Brighton 46 – ♦Southampton 44.

Lythe Hill, Petworth Rd, GU27 3BQ, E : 1 ½ m. on B 2131 ✆ 51251, Telex 858402, Fax 4131,
≼, 🛋, park, ✕ – 📺 ☎ 🅿 – 🪑 50. 🅰 AE VISA
M 14.50 **t.** and a la carte 15.00/32.00 **t.** 🍷 4.50 – ☕ 6.25 – **26 rm** 72.00/120.00 **t.**, **12 suites**
110.00/150.00 **t.** – SB (weekends only) 91.00 **st.**

✕✕✕ **Morels**, 23-27 Lower St., GU27 2NY, ✆ 51462, French rest. – 🅰 AE ⓞ VISA
*closed 2 weeks late February, 2 weeks late September and Bank Holidays except Good
Friday* – **M** *(closed Saturday lunch, Sunday and Monday)* 15.00/18.00 **t.** and a la carte
26.50/33.50 **t.** 🍷 5.00.

✕✕✕ **Auberge de France** (at Lythe Hill H.), Petworth Rd, GU27 3BQ, E : 1 ½ m. on B 2131 ✆
51251, Telex 858402, Fax 4131, ≼, French rest., « Tudor building », 🛋 – 🅿. 🅰 AE VISA
closed Monday – **M** (dinner only and Sunday lunch)/dinner 16.50/17.50 **t.** and a la carte
🍷 4.50.

✕ **Shrimptons**, 2 Grove Cottages, Midhurst Rd, Kingsley Green, GU27 3LF, SW : 1 ¼ m.
on072 A 286 ✆ 3539 – 🅰 AE ⓞ VISA
closed Saturday lunch, Sunday, Christmas-New Year and Bank Holidays – **M** 12.50 **t.** (lunch)
and a la carte 17.50/25.00 **t.** 🍷 6.00.

AUSTIN-ROVER Grayswood Rd ✆ 2303
FORD Havenford ✆ 3222
PEUGEOT-TALBOT High St. ✆ 52552

VAUXHALL-OPEL West St. ✆ 3333
VW-AUDI Hindhead Rd ✆ 53811

HASSOP Derbs. – see Bakewell.

See : Norman Castle (ruins) ※★★ *AC* BZ – Alexandra Park★ AY – White Rocks gardens ⇐★ ABZ
– Public Museum and Art Gallery (Pottery★, Durbar Hall★) BZ **M**.

📍 Beauport Park, St. Leonards, ✆ 52977, NW : 3 m. by B 2159 AY.

🛈 4 Robertson Terr. ✆ 722022 – The Fishmarket ✆ 721201 (summer only).

♦London 65 – ♦Brighton 37 – Folkestone 37 – Maidstone 34.

HASTINGS
AND ST. LEONARDS

King's Road	AZ	22
London Road	AZ	
Norman Road	AZ	
Queen's Road	BZ	
Robertson Street	BZ	27
Wellington Place	BZ	35

Bourne (The)	BY	4
Cambridge Gardens	BZ	5
Castle Street	BZ	7
Castle Hill Road	BZ	8
Cornwallis Gardens	BZ	9
Cornwallis Terrace	BZ	10
Denmark Place	BZ	13
Dorset Place	BZ	15
Gensing Road	AZ	16
George Street	BY	18

Grosvenor Crescent	AY	19
Harold Place	BZ	20
Marine Court	AZ	23
Rock-a-Nore Road	BY	30
St. Helen's Park Road	BY	31
Sedlescombe Road South	AY	32
Silchester Road	AY	33
Warrior Square	AZ	34
Wellington Square	BZ	36
White Rock Road	BZ	38

🏨 **Beauport Park** (Best Western) 🐾, Battle Rd, TN38 8EA, NW : 3 ½ m. at junction A 2100 and B 2159 ℘ 851222, Telex 957126, Fax 52465, ≼, « Formal garden », ⅃ heated, park, ✗ – 🍴 rest 📺 ☎ 🅿 – 🕍 80. 🔌 AE ⓪ VISA   by B 2159   AY
M 11.00/12.00 st. and a la carte ₰ 3.90 – **23 rm** � 42.00/80.00 st. – SB (weekends only) 68.00/75.00 st.

🏨 **Cinque Ports,** Summerfields, Bohemia Rd, TN34 1ET, ℘ 439222, Telex 957584, Fax 437277 – 📺 ☎ 🅿 – 🕍 120. 🔌 AE ⓪ VISA. ✗   AZ   **a**
M 11.00/15.00 t. and a la carte ₰ 3.75 – **40 rm** ⊻ 48.00/70.00 t. – SB (except Bank Holidays) 88.00/94.00 st.

↑ **Norton Villa** without rest., Hill St., Old Town, TN34 3HU, ℘ 428168, ≼, ⛛ – ⇥ 🅿 ✗   BY   **n**
4 rm ⊻ 18.00/34.00 s.

↑ **Chimes,** 1 St. Matthews Gdns, Silverhill, TN38 0TS, ℘ 434041, ⛛ – 📺. ✗   AY   **a**
M (by arrangement) 7.00 t. – **9 rm** ⊻ 15.00/33.00 t.

✗✗ **Röser's,** 64 Eversfield Pl., TN37 6DB, ℘ 712218 – 🔌 AE ⓪ VISA   BZ   **i**
closed lunch Monday and Saturday, Sunday, first 3 weeks January and Bank Holidays – **M** 15.50 st. and a la carte 16.85/27.40 t. ₰ 3.75.

AUSTIN-ROVER 5-9 Western Rd ℘ 721111
FORD Bohemia Rd ℘ 422727
MITSUBISHI Sedlescombe Rd North ℘ 440511
PEUGEOT-TALBOT Bexhill Rd ℘ 431276
RENAULT 109-111 Sedlescombe Rd North ℘ 432982

VAUXHALL 36-39 Western Rd, St. Leonards ℘ 424545
VOLVO 100 Battle Rd ℘ 423451

🅦 ATS Menzies Rd, St. Leonards-on-Sea ℘ 427780/424567

HATCH BEAUCHAMP Somerset 🔢 K 30 – see Taunton.

HATFIELD Herts. 🔢 T 28 – pop. 33 174 – ECD : Monday and Thursday – ☎ 0707.
See : Hatfield House★★★ *AC* (gardens★ and Old Palace★).
ᚋ Bedwell Park, Essendon ℘ 0707 (Potters Bar) 42624, E : 3 m.
♦London 27 – Bedford 38 – ♦Cambridge 39.

🏨 Comet (Embassy), 301 St. Albans Rd West, AL10 9RH, SW : 1 m. by A 1057 at junction with A 1 ℘ 265411, Fax 64019 – 📺 ☎ 🅿 – 🕍 40. 🔌 AE ⓪ VISA
M *(closed Saturday lunch)* 9.95 st. and a la carte 10.75/21.60 t. ₰ 4.10 – ⊻ 6.50 – **57 rm** 55.00/65.00 st. – SB (weekends only) 59.00 st.

🏨 **Hazel Grove,** on A 1001, AL10 9AF, S : 2 m. by B 6426 on A 1001 ℘ 275701, Telex 916580, Fax 66033 – ⇥ rm 📺 ☎ ⅙ 🅿 – 🕍 100. 🔌 AE ⓪ VISA. ✗
M 15.00 t. and a la carte ₰ 3.50 – **28 rm** ⊻ 60.00/80.00 t. – SB 84.00/105.00 st.

ALFA-ROMEO, PEUGEOT-TALBOT By-Pass ℘ 64521

AUSTIN-ROVER 1 Great North Rd ℘ 64366
LANCIA, SUZUKI 42 Beaconsfield Rd ℘ 71226

HATFIELD HEATH Essex. 🔢 U 28 – see Bishop's Stortford (Herts.).

HATHERLEIGH Devon 🔢 H 31 – pop. 1 355 – ECD : Wednesday – ✉ ☎ 0837 Okehampton.
ᚋ at Okehampton, Tors Rd, ℘ 2113, SE : 7 m.
♦London 230 – Exeter 29 – ♦Plymouth 38.

🏛 **Half Moon Inn,** The Square, Sheepwash ✉ Beaworthy, EX21 5NE, NW : 5 ½ m. by A 3072 ℘ 040 923 (Black Torrington) 376, « 17C inn », 🐾 – 📺 ☎ 🅿. 🔌 VISA
closed January – **M** (bar lunch)/dinner 13.00 t. ₰ 3.50 – **14 rm** ⊻ 22.00/50.00 t. – SB (except June-September) 66.00/72.00 st.

HATHERSAGE Derbs. 🔢 🔢 🔢 P 24 – pop. 1 966 – ECD : Wednesday – ✉ Sheffield (South Yorks.) – ☎ 0433 Hope Valley.
♦London 165 – ♦Manchester 33 – ♦Sheffield 10.

🏨 **George** (Lansbury), Main Rd, S30 1BB, ℘ 50436, Telex 547196, Fax 50099 – ⇥ rm 📺 ☎ 🅿 – 🕍 30. 🔌 AE ⓪ VISA. ✗
M 8.00/14.00 t. and a la carte ₰ 3.50 – **18 rm** ⊻ 52.00/64.00 t. – SB (weekends only) 77.00/86.00 st.

↑ **Highlow Hall** 🐾 without rest., S30 1AX, S : 1 ½ m. by B 6001 on Abney rd ℘ 50393, ≼, ⛛ – 🅿
Mid March-mid November – **6 rm** ⊻ 15.00/36.00 st.

HATTON Warw. – see Warwick.

HAVANT Hants. 🔢 R 31 – pop. 50 098 – ECD : Wednesday – ☎ 0705.
🚹 1 Park Rd South ℘ 480024.
♦London 70 – ♦Brighton 39 – ♦Portsmouth 9 – ♦Southampton 22.

🏨 **Bear** (Lansbury), 15 East St., PO9 1AA, ℘ 486501, Telex 869136 – 📲 ⇥ rm 📺 ☎ 🅿 – 🕍 100. 🔌 AE ⓪ VISA. ✗
M 8.50/12.50 t. and a la carte – **42 rm** ⊻ 58.00/68.00 t. – SB (spring and autumn only) (weekends only) 66.00/76.00 st.

FORD New Rd ℘ 482161

🅦 ATS 60-62 Bedhampton Rd ℘ 483018

HAVERFORDWEST (HWLFFORDD) Dyfed 408 F 28 – pop. 13 572 – ECD : Thursday – ☺ 0437.
Envir. : SW : Martin's Haven ❄️★★ – St. Ann's Head★★ by Dale ⇐★ – 🏌 Arnolds Down ✆ 3565.
🛈 Pembrokeshire Coast National Park Centre, 40 High St. ✆ 820144 (summer only).
♦London 250 – Fishguard 15 – ♦Swansea 57.

   🏨 **Mariners**, Mariners Sq., SA61 2DU, ✆ 3353 – 📺 ☎ 🅿. 🔄 AE ⓘ VISA
     closed 25 to 27 December and 1 January – **M** (bar lunch)/dinner 9.00/14.00 t. 🍷 3.50 – **27 rm**
     ⚏ 35.00/52.00 t. – SB (weekends only) 60.00 **st.**

   🏠 **Sutton Lodge** ⑤, Portfield Gate, SA62 3LN, W : 3 m. by B 4327 off B 4341 ✆ 768548, Fax
     760826 – 📺 🅿
     closed January-February – **M** (dinner only) 13.50 t. 🍷 2.85 – **6 rm** ⚏ 27.50/50.00 t. –
     SB (weekends only) (except summer) 73.00/77.50 **st.**

AUSTIN-ROVER, DAIMLER-JAGUAR Salutation   VAUXHALL-OPEL Perrotts Rd ✆ 2717
Sq. ✆ 764511
FORD Dew St. ✆ 3772   Ⓜ ATS Back Lane, Prendergast ✆ 3756/7
RENAULT Fishguard Rd ✆ 2468

HAWES North Yorks. 402 N 21 – pop. 1 177 – ☺ 0969.
🛈 National Park Centre, Station Yard ✆ 450 (summer only).
♦London 253 – Kendal 27 – ♦Leeds 72 – ♦York 65.

   🏨 **Simonstone Hall** ⑤, Simonstone, DL8 3LY, N : 1 ½ m. on Muker rd ✆ 667255, ⇐,
     « Country house atmosphere », 🌳 – 📺 🅿. 🔄 AE ⓘ VISA
     M (bar lunch Monday to Saturday)/dinner 16.50 **t.** and a la carte 🍷 4.30 – **10 rm**
     ⚏ 45.50/80.00 t. – SB 91.50/107.00 **st.**

   🏠 **Rookhurst Georgian Country House** ⑤, Gayle, DL8 3RT, S : ½ m. ✆ 454, « Antique
     furnishings », 🌳 – 🍴 📺 🅿. ⑯
     closed Christmas and New Year – **M** (residents only) (dinner only) a la carte 13.00/20.50 t.
     🍷 2.95 – **5 rm** ⚏ (dinner included) 48.00/96.00 t. – SB (except summer and autumn) 68.00 t.

   🏠 **Stone House** ⑤, Sedbusk, DL8 3PT, N : 1 m. by Muker rd on Askrigg rd ✆ 571, 🌳 –
     🍴 rest 📺 🅿. 🔄 VISA
     closed mid-November-mid March except weekends, Christmas and New Year – **M** (dinner
     only) 11.50 t. 🍷 3.50 – **15 rm** ⚏ 22.50/55.00 t. – SB (October-Easter) 55.00/65.00 **st.**

   🏛 **Herriot's**, Main St., DL8 3QU, ✆ 667536 – 📺
     March-October – **M** 5.50/11.00 t. and a la carte 🍷 3.15 – **6 rm** ⚏ 26.00/38.00 t. –
     SB (October-March) 44.00 **st.**

   ✗ **Cockett's** with rm, Market Pl., DL8 3RD, ✆ 312 – 📺. 🔄 VISA
     M (dinner only) 13.95 st. 🍷 3.50 – **8 rm** ⚏ 42.00 **st.**

HAWKCHURCH Devon 408 L 31 – see Axminster.

HAWKHURST Kent 404 V 30 – pop. 3 192 – ECD : Wednesday – ☺ 0580.
Envir. : Bodiam Castle★★, SE : 3 ½ m. – Bedgebury Pinetum★ AC, NW : 2 m.
🛈 High St. ✆ 2396 – ♦London 47 – Folkestone 34 – Hastings 14 – Maidstone 19.

   🏨 **Tudor Court** (Best Western), Rye Rd, TN18 5DA, E : ¾ m. on A 268 ✆ 752312, ⇐, « Gar-
     dens » – 🍴 rm 📺 ☎ 🅿 – 🔥 50. 🔄 AE ⓘ VISA
     M 9.50/12.00 **st.** and a la carte – **18 rm** ⚏ 49.00/83.00 **st.** – SB (except Christmas
     and New Year) 100.00/105.00 **st.**

HAWKRIDGE Somerset 408 J 30 – ✉ Dulverton – ☺ 064 385 Winsford.
♦London 203 – Exeter 32 – Minehead 17 – Taunton 32.

   🏨 **Tarr Steps** ⑤, TA22 9PY, NE : 1 ½ m. ✆ 293, ⇐, 🎣, 🌳, park – 🅿. 🔄 AE VISA
     Mid March-December – **M** (bar lunch Monday to Saturday)/dinner 15.50 t. 🍷 3.00 – **15 rm**
     ⚏ 26.00/55.00 t.

HAWKSHEAD Cumbria 402 L 20 – pop. 660 – ECD : Thursday – ✉ Ambleside – ☺ 096 66.
🛈 Brown Cow Laithe (near car park) ✆ 525 (summer only) – ♦London 283 – ♦Carlisle 52 – Kendal 19.

   🏠 **Field Head House** ⑤, Outgate, LA22 0PY, N : 1 m. by B 5285 off B 5286 ✆ 240, ⇐, 🌳 –
     🍴 🅿
     closed last 2 weeks January and 1 week before Christmas – **M** (closed Tuesday) (dinner
     only) 18.00 st. – **7 rm** ⚏ 33.00/66.00 st. – SB (mid November-mid March) (except Christ-
     mas and New Year) 77.00/82.40 **st.**

   🏛 **Queen's Head**, Main St., LA22 0NS, ✆ 271 – 📺. 🔄 AE VISA ⑯
     M (bar lunch)/dinner a la carte 8.45/15.50 t. 🍷 3.95 – **12 rm** ⚏ 24.50/43.00 t.

   🏠 **Highfield House** ⑤, Hawkshead Hill, LA22 0PN, W : ½ m. on B 5285 (Coniston rd) ✆ 344,
     ⇐ Kirkstone Pass and Fells, 🌳 – 🍴 rest 📺 🅿
     closed Christmas and New Year – **M** 10.50 st. 🍷 3.00 – **11 rm** ⚏ 19.50/43.00 st. –
     SB (mid November-Easter) 45.00/50.50 **st.**

   🏠 **Ivy House**, Main St., LA22 0NS, ✆ 204 – 🅿
     March-October – **M** 8.50 t. 🍷 2.40 – **11 rm** ⚏ 15.50/39.50 t.

   🏠 **Rough Close** ⑤, LA22 0QF, S : 1 ½ m. on Newby Bridge rd ✆ 370, 🌳 – 🍴 rest 🅿. 🔄
     VISA ⑯
     April-October – **M** 9.00 t. 🍷 3.50 – **6 rm** ⚏ 17.50/35.00 t.

at Near Sawrey SE : 2 m. on B 5285 – ⊠ Ambleside – ☎ 096 66 Hawkshead :

⋔ Garth ⌛, LA22 0JZ, ✆ 373, ⇄ – 📺 🅿
7 rm.

at Far Sawrey SE : 2 ½ m. on B 5285 – ⊠ Ambleside – ☎ 096 62 Windermere :

⋔ West Vale, LA22 0LQ, ✆ 2817, ≼ – ⊁⨯ rest 🅿. 🕸
M 7.50 t. 🍷 2.75 – **8 rm**.

at Grizedale SW : 2 ¾ m. – ⊠ Ambleside – ☎ 096 66 Hawkshead :

✕✕ **Grizedale Lodge** ⌛ with rm, LA22 0QL, ✆ 532 – ⊁⨯ 📺 🅿. 🔲 VISA. 🕸
closed January-mid February – **M** *(closed Monday lunch)* (bar lunch)/dinner 14.50 t. 🍷 3.00
– **6 rm** ⌸ 30.00/48.00 t. – SB 60.00/70.00 st.

HAWORTH West Yorks. 402 O 22 – pop. 5 041 – ECD : Tuesday – ⊠ Keighley – ☎ 0535.
See : Brontë Parsonage Museum⋆ *AC*.
🛈 2-4 West Lane ✆ 42329/45864.
♦London 213 – Burnley 22 – ♦Leeds 22 – ♦Manchester 34.

♔ **Old White Lion,** 6 West Lane, BD22 8DU, ✆ 42313 – 📺 🅿. 🔲 AE ⓪ VISA. 🕸
M (bar lunch)/dinner 8.50 **st.** and a la carte 9.10/13.75 t. 🍷 3.50 – **12 rm** ⌸ 26.00/38.50 t. –
SB (except Bank Holidays) (weekends only) 44.00 **st.**

⋔ **Ferncliffe,** Hebden Rd, BD22 8RS, ✆ 43405, ≼ – 📺 🅿. VISA
M 10.00 t. 🍷 3.25 – **6 rm** ⌸ 17.50/35.00 t. – SB (November-February) (weekends only)
37.50/40.00 **st.**

✕ **Weaver's** with rm, 15 West Lane, BD22 8DU, ✆ 43822 – 📺. 🔲 AE ⓪ VISA
closed 3 weeks July and 1 week Christmas – **M** *(closed dinner Sunday and Monday)* (dinner
only and Sunday lunch in winter) 10.50 **t.** and a la carte 10.25/19.75 t. 🍷 3.50 – **3 rm**
⌸ 40.00/50.00 t.

HAYDOCK Merseyside 402 403 404 M 23 pop. 17 372 – ⊠ Newton-le-Willows – ☎ 0942
Ashton-in-Makerfield.
♦London 198 – ♦Liverpool 17 – ♦Manchester 18.

🏨 **Post House** (T.H.F.), Lodge Lane, WA12 0JG, NE : 1 m. on A 49 ✆ 717878, Telex 677672,
Fax 718419, 🔲 – 🛗 ⊁⨯ rm 📺 ☎ 🅿 – 🔬 50. 🔲 AE ⓪ VISA
M 7.50/10.50 **st.** and a la carte – ⌸ 7.00 – **99 rm** 60.00/80.00 **st.**

⊚ ATS Legh Rd, St. Helens ✆ 50551

HAYLING ISLAND Hants. 404 R 31 – pop. 12 410 – ECD : Wednesday – ☎ 0705.
🛈 32 Seafront ✆ 467111 (summer only).
♦London 77 – ♦Brighton 45 – ♦Southampton 28.

🏨 **Post House** (T.H.F.), Northney Rd, PO11 0NQ, ✆ 465011, Telex 86620, Fax 823201, ≼, 🔲
– ⊁⨯ rm 📺 ☎ 🅿 – 🔬 . 🔲 AE ⓪ VISA
M *(closed Saturday lunch)* 12.50/14.50 **st.** and a la carte 🍷 3.60 – ⌸ 7.00 – **96 rm**
65.00/83.00 **st.**

🏛 **Newtown House,** Manor Rd, PO11 0QR, ✆ 466131, Fax 461366, 🏊 heated, ⇄, ✕✕ – 📺
☎ 🅿. 🔲 AE ⓪ VISA
M 6.95/9.45 t. and a la carte 🍷 3.65 – **28 rm** ⌸ 38.00/57.50 t. – SB (weekends only)
50.00/62.00 **st.**

⋔ **Cockle Warren Cottage,** 36 Seafront, PO11 9HL, ✆ 464961, ⇄ – ⊁⨯ 📺 ☎ 🅿. 🔲 VISA.
🕸
M 18.50 s. 🍷 3.00 – **5 rm** ⌸ 30.00/60.00 **st.**

HAY-ON-WYE Powys 403 K 27 – pop. 1 578 – ECD : Tuesday – ☎ 0497.
🛈 The Car Park ✆ 820912.
♦London 154 – Brecon 16 – Hereford 21 – Newport 62.

🏨 **Swan,** Church St., HR3 5DQ, ✆ 821188 – 📺 ☎ 🅿. 🔲 VISA
M 10.00 t. and a la carte 🍷 3.50 – **15 rm** ⌸ 25.00/45.00 t. – SB (except Bank Holidays)
70.00/75.00 **st.**

🏛 **Old Black Lion,** 6 Lion St., HR3 5AD, ✆ 820841 – 📺 ☎ 🅿. 🔲 VISA
M 6.00/11.00 **st.** and a la carte 11.10/14.35 **st.** 🍷 3.50 – **10 rm** ⌸ 16.50/36.50 **st.** –
SB 59.50/61.50 **st.**

AUSTIN-ROVER, LAND-ROVER, RANGE-ROVER FORD Broad St. ✆ 820548
Church St. ✆ 820404

HAYTOR Devon – see Bovey Tracey.

HEACHAM Norfolk 402 404 V 25 – see Hunstanton.

HEADLAM Durham – see Darlington.

HEATHFIELD East Sussex **404** U 31 – pop. 4 848 – ⊠ ✆ 043 52.
♦London 51 – ♦Brighton 23 – Eastbourne 16.

⚲ **Risingholme**, 38 High St., TN21 8LS, ✆ 4645, 🚗 – ⛛ 📺 Ⓟ. ❄
M (by arrangement) – **3 rm** ☲ 25.00/35.00 s.

HEATHROW AIRPORT – see Hillingdon (Greater London).

HEBDEN BRIDGE West Yorks. **402** N 22 – pop. 4 167 – ECD : Tuesday – ⊠ ✆ 0422 Halifax.
🏌 Mount Skip, Wadsworth ✆ 842896.
🛈 1 Bridge Gate ✆ 843831.
♦London 223 – Burnley 13 – ♦Leeds 24 – ♦Manchester 25.

🏨 **Carlton**, Albert St., HX7 8ES, ✆ 844400, Telex 518176 – 🛗 📺 ☎ – 🔬 100. 🅰 AE VISA. ❄
closed 25 to 29 December and 1 January – **M** (dinner only) 13.00 t. and a la carte 11.25/17.05 t.
🍷 4.25 – **18 rm** ☲ 37.00/47.00 t. – SB (weekends only) 63.00/66.50 st.

HEDON Humberside **402** T 22 – ⊠ ✆ 0482 Kingston-upon-Hull.
♦London 189 – ♦Kingston upon Hull 6 – Lincoln 60 – York 34.

🏨 **Kingstown**, Hull Rd, HU12 9DJ, W : 1 m. on A 1033 ✆ 890461, Fax 890713 – 📺 ☎ 🖐 Ⓟ.
🅰 VISA. ❄
M *(closed Saturday lunch)* 9.95 st. and a la carte 12.15/15.15 st. 🍷 3.50 – **18 rm**
☲ 50.00/60.00 st.

HELFORD Cornwall **403** E 33 – ⊠ Helston – ✆ 032 623 Manaccan.
♦London 324 – Falmouth 15 – Penzance 22 – Truro 27.

XX **Riverside** ⚲ with rm, TR12 6JU, ✆ 443, Fax 443, ≼, « Converted cottages in picturesque
setting », 🚗 – 📺 Ⓟ. ❄
March-October – **M** *(closed lunch Monday to Thursday) (booking essential)/dinner*
24.00 st. and a la carte 🍷 4.25 – ☲ 2.50 – **7 rm** 75.00/90.00 st.

at Gillan S : 3 m. – ⊠ Helston – ✆ 032 623 Manaccan :

🏠 **Tregildry** ⚲, TR12 6HG, ✆ 378, ≼ Gillan Creek, sea, 🚗 – Ⓟ. 🅰 VISA
Easter-mid October – **M** (bar lunch)/dinner 13.50 st. 🍷 3.50 – **10 rm** ☲ 39.00/66.00 st.

HELMSLEY North Yorks. **402** Q 21 – pop. 1 399 – ECD : Wednesday – ✆ 0439.
See : Castle* (ruins 12C) *AC.*
Envir. : Rievaulx Abbey** (ruins 12C-13C) *AC,* NW : 2 ½ m. – Byland Abbey* (ruins 12C) SW :
6 m. by Ampleforth.
🛈 Town Hall, Market Pl. ✆ 70173 (summer only).
♦London 234 – ♦Middlesbrough 29 – York 24.

🏨 **Black Swan** (T.H.F.), Market Pl., YO6 5BJ, ✆ 70466, Telex 57538, Fax 70174, « 16C inn »,
🚗 – 📺 ☎ Ⓟ – 🔬 35. 🅰 AE ⓞ VISA
M 9.50/25.00 st. and a la carte 🍷 6.35 – ☲ 7.00 – **38 rm** 70.00/105.00 st. – SB 64.00/
70.00 st.

🏨 **Feversham Arms** (Best Western), 1 High St., YO6 5AG, ✆ 70766, 🛁 heated, 🚗, ✗ – 📺
☎ Ⓟ – 🔬 40. 🅰 AE ⓞ VISA
M (bar lunch Tuesday to Saturday)/dinner 20.00 t. and a la carte 🍷 4.00 – **18 rm**
☲ 44.00/76.00 t. – SB (except Christmas) 66.00/84.00 st.

🏛 **Feathers**, Market Pl., YO6 5BH, ✆ 70275, 🚗 – 📺 Ⓟ. 🅰 AE ⓞ VISA
closed Christmas – **M** 6.75/14.00 st. 🍷 3.75 – **18 rm** ☲ 18.50/46.00 st. – SB (October-
June) 57.00/60.00 st.

🏛 **Crown**, Market Pl., YO6 5BJ, ✆ 70297, 🚗 – 📺 Ⓟ. 🅰 VISA
M 6.75/12.50 t. and a la carte 🍷 3.00 – **14 rm** ☲ 25.00/50.00 t. – SB (October-May) 63.50 st.

⚲ **Beaconsfield** without rest., Bondgate, YO6 5BW, ✆ 71346 – 📺 Ⓟ. ❄
6 rm ☲ 20.00/35.00 s.

at Harome E : 2 ¾ m. by A 170 – ⊠ York – ✆ 0439 Helmsley :

🏨 **Pheasant**, YO6 5JG, ✆ 71241, 🚗 – ⛛ rest 📺 ☎ 🖐 Ⓟ. ❄
closed January and February – **M** (bar lunch)/dinner 15.50 t. 🍷 4.50 – **12 rm** ☲ (dinner included) 45.00/100.00 t. – SB 64.00/70.00 t.

at Nawton E : 3 ¼ m. on A 170 – ⊠ York – ✆ 0439 Helmsley :

⚲ **Plumpton Court**, High St., YO6 5TT, ✆ 71223, 🚗 – Ⓟ. ❄
Mid March-October – **M** 7.25 st. – **8 rm** ☲ 20.00/33.00 st.

at Nunnington SE : 6 ¼ m. by A 170 off B 1257 – ⊠ York – ✆ 043 95 Nunnington :

XX **Ryedale Lodge** ⚲ with rm, YO6 5XB, W : 1 m. ✆ 246, ≼, « Converted railway station »,
🍴, 🚗 – ⛛ rest 📺 ☎ Ⓟ. 🅰 VISA. ❄
M (lunch by arrangement)/dinner 22.50 t. 🍷 3.50 – **7 rm** ☲ 46.75/71.50 t. – SB (except
Christmas and New Year) 99.00/109.00 st.

HELSTON Cornwall **403** E 33 – pop. 8 543 – ECD : Wednesday – ☼ 0326.
♦London 311 – Falmouth 13 – Penzance 13 – ♦Plymouth 71.

   ⌂ **Nansloe Manor** 🦢, Meneage Rd, TR13 0SB, ℰ 574691, ⇆ – 📺 ☎ 🅿. 🔳 **VISA**
   closed 25 to 30 December – **M** (bar lunch Monday to Saturday)/dinner 16.00 **t.** and a la carte
   � 3.35 – **7 rm** ⊐ 32.00/72.00 **t.**

AUDI-VW Meneage St. ℰ 564771 ⁣   ⓦ ATS Clodgey Lane, Helston ℰ 62656

HEMEL HEMPSTEAD Herts. **404** S 28 – pop. 80 110 – ECD : Wednesday – ☼ 0442.
🏌 Little Hay, Box Lane, Bovington ℰ 833798, off A 41.
🛈 Pavilion, Marlowes ℰ 64451.
♦London 30 – Aylesbury 16 – Luton 10 – Northampton 46.

   🏨 **Post House** (T.H.F.), Breakspear Way, HP2 4UA, E : 2 ½ m. on A 414 ℰ 51122, Telex
   826902, Fax 211812, ⇆ – 🔧 ⇥ rm 📺 ☎ 🅿 – 🔼 100. 🔳 **AE** ⓞ **VISA**
   M *(closed Saturday lunch)* 10.50/18.50 **st.** and a la carte � 3.95 – ⊐ 7.00 – **107 rm**
   71.00/85.00 **st.** – SB 64.00/70.00 **st.**

   ⌂ **Midland** (B.C.B.) without rest., Midland Rd, HP2 5BH, ℰ 53218 – 📺 ☎ 🅿. 🔳 **AE** ⓞ **VISA**.
   🦢
   7 rm ⊐ 36.00/47.00 **st.**

   ✕ **Casanova**, 75 Waterhouse St., HP1 1ED, ℰ 47482, Italian rest. – 🔳 **AE** ⓞ **VISA**
   closed Saturday lunch, Sunday, Christmas Day and Bank Holidays – **M** a la carte
   10.00/15.65 **t.** ⌐ 3.50.

   at Bourne End W : 2 ¼ m. on A 41 – ✉ Hemel Hempstead – ☼ 044 27 Berkhamsted :

   🏨 **Hemel Hempstead Moat House** (Q.M.H.), London Rd, HP1 2RJ, ℰ 871241, Fax 866130
   – ⇥ rm 📺 ☎ 🅿 – 🔼 . 🔳 **AE** ⓞ **VISA**
   M *(closed Saturday lunch)* 10.25 **st.** and a la carte ⌐ 3.95 – **61 rm** ⊐ 55.00/68.00 **st.** –
   SB (weekends only) 63.50/68.50 **st.**

AUSTIN-ROVER London Rd ℰ 42841 ⁣   TOYOTA Waterend ℰ 51466
FIAT, VAUXHALL-OPEL Two Waters Rd ℰ 51212
FORD Redbourne Rd ℰ 63013 ⁣   ⓦ ATS Lyon Way, Hatfield Rd, St Albans ℰ 52314
PEUGEOT-TALBOT Queensway ℰ 54561/50401 ⁣   ATS Grimston Rd, St. Albans ℰ 35174

HENDY-GWYN = Whitland.

HENLADE Somerset – see Taunton.

HENLEY-IN-ARDEN Warw. **403 404** O 27 – pop. 2 636 – ECD : Thursday – ☼ 056 42.
♦London 104 – ♦Birmingham 15 – Stratford-upon-Avon 8 – Warwick 8.5.

   ⌂ **Ashleigh House** without rest., Whitley Hill, B95 5DL, E : 1 ¾ m. on B 4095 ℰ 2315, ⇆ –
   📺 ☎ 🅿. 🔳 **VISA**. 🦢
   10 rm ⊐ 35.00/45.00 **st.**

   ✕✕ **Le Filbert Cottage,** 64 High St., B95 5BX, ℰ 2700, French rest. – 🔳 **AE** ⓞ **VISA**
   closed Sunday, Monday and Bank Holidays – **M** 30.00 **t.** and a la carte 13.75/20.00 **t.**

HENLEY-ON-THAMES Oxon. **404** R 29 – pop. 10 910 – ECD : Wednesday – ☼ 0491.
Envir. : Greys Court★ *AC*, NW : 2 ½ m.
🏌 Badgemore Park ℰ 572206 – 🛈 Town Hall, Market Place ℰ 578034.
♦London 40 – ♦Oxford 23 – Reading 9.

   ⌂ **Edwardian,** Station Rd, RG9 1AT, ℰ 578678, Fax 572295 – 📺 ☎. 🔳 **AE** ⓞ **VISA**. 🦢
   M 10.50 **t.** and a la carte – **18 rm** ⊐ 52.50/62.50 **t.** – SB (except 3 weeks June-
   July and Christmas) (weekends only) 56.00/59.00 **st.**

   ⌂ **Regency House,** 4 River Terr., RG9 1BG, ℰ 571133, ⇐ – 📺 ☎. 🔳 **AE** **VISA**. 🦢
   M *(closed Sunday and Monday)* (dinner only) 15.00 **t.** – **5 rm** ⊐ 43.00/55.00 **st.** – SB (weekends only) 85.00 **st.**

   ✕✕ **Beijing,** 25 Duke St., RG9 1UR, ℰ 410001, Chinese (Peking) rest. – 🔳 **AE** ⓞ **VISA**
   M 8.95/15.00 **t.** and a la carte 11.10/16.80 **t.**

   ✕✕ **Flohr's** with rm, 15 Northfield End, RG9 2JG, ℰ 573412 – 📺 ☎. 🔳 **AE** ⓞ **VISA**
   M *(closed Sunday dinner)* a la carte 14.10/18.30 **st.** ⌐ 3.50 – **9 rm** ⊐ 29.50/69.00 **st.**

   ✕ Chef Peking, 10 Market Pl., RG9 2AH, ℰ 578681, Chinese (Peking) rest. – 🗏.

   ✕ **Little Angel,** Remenham, RG9 2LS, E : ¼ m. on A 423 ℰ 574165 – 🅿. 🔳 **AE** ⓞ **VISA**
   closed Sunday dinner and Monday – **M** 27.00 **st.** and a la carte 10.50/20.50 **st.** ⌐ 3.50.

   at Fawley (Bucks.) N : 3 ½ m. by A 4155 – ✉ Henley-on-Thames – ☼ 049 163 Turville
   Heath :

   ✕ **Walnut Tree,** Fawley Green, RG9 6JE, ℰ 360 – 🅿. 🔳 **VISA** .
   M 9.85 **t.** (lunch) and a la carte 9.05/15.70 **t.**

   at Stonor N : 4 m. by A 423 on B 480 – ✉ Henley-on-Thames – ☼ 049 163 Turville Heath :

   ✕✕ **Stonor Arms,** RG9 6HE, ℰ 345 – 🅿. 🔳 **AE** **VISA**
   M (dinner only and Sunday lunch)/dinner 26.25 **t.**

at Frieth (Bucks.) NE : 7 ½ m. by A 4155 – ✉ Henley-on-Thames – ☎ 0494 High Wycombe :

✗ **Yew Tree**, RG9 6RJ, ☎ 882330 – ⇔ Ⓟ. 🔲 AE VISA
M 11.95/14.95 **t.** and a la carte 16.85/24.85 **t.** 🍷 4.95.

BMW 49 Station Rd ☎ 577933
FORD Station Rd ☎ 578331
FIAT 66 Bell St. ☎ 573077
RENAULT Binfield Heath Rd ☎ 574255

HEREFORD Heref. and Worc. **403** L 27 – pop. 48 277 – ECD : Thursday – ☎ 0432.

See : Cathedral** (12C-13C) (the Mappa Mundi* 13C) A A – The Old House* (17C) A B.

Envir. : Abbey Dore* (12C-17C) SW : 12 m. by A 465 B.

📷 Ravens Causeway, Wormsley ☎ 71219 by A 438 B – 📷 Belmont House, Belmont ☎ 352666 by A 465 B.

🛈 Townhall Annexe, 1a St. Owens St. ☎ 268430.

♦London 133 – ♦Birmingham 51 – ♦Cardiff 56.

HEREFORD

Broad Street . . . . A 7
Commercial Street. . . . A 13
High Street . . . . A 19
High Town. . . . . A 20

Belmont Road. . . . . B 5
Blueschool Street . . . . A 6
Castle Street . . . . A 9
Church Street . . . . A 12

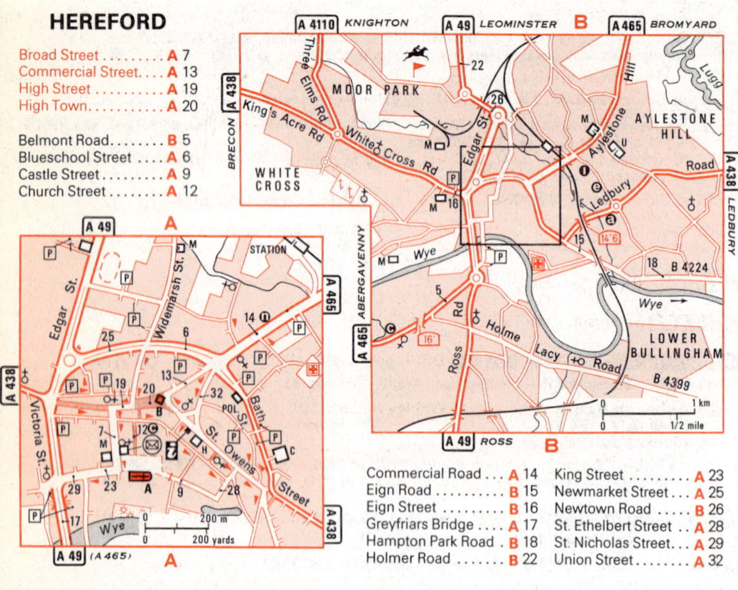

Commercial Road . . . A 14
Eign Road . . . . B 15
Eign Street . . . . B 16
Greyfriars Bridge . . . . A 17
Hampton Park Road . B 18
Holmer Road . . . . B 22
King Street . . . . A 23
Newmarket Street . . . A 25
Newtown Road . . . . . B 26
St. Ethelbert Street . . A 28
St. Nicholas Street. . . A 29
Union Street . . . . A 32

🏰 **Hereford Moat House** (Q.M.H.), Belmont Rd, HR2 7BP, SW : 1 ½ m. on A 465 ☎ 354301, Fax 275114 – TV ☎ Ⓟ – 🛎 300. 🔲 AE ⓞ VISA   B c
M 9.00/15.00 **st.** and a la carte – **60 rm** ⊑ 58.00/70.00 **st.** – SB 80.00 **st.**

🏨 **Merton**, Commercial Rd, HR1 2BD, ☎ 265925 – TV ☎. 🔲 AE ⓞ VISA   A n
closed 25 December-2 January – **M** *(closed Sunday and Bank Holidays non-residents)*
10.00/22.00 **t.** and a la carte 🍷 3.20 – **18 rm** ⊑ 39.00/67.50 **t.** – SB (weekends only) 69.00 **st.**

↑ **Somerville**, 12 Bodenham Rd, HR1 2TS, ☎ 273991, ⚘ – ⇔ rest TV ☎ Ⓟ. ⚘   B i
M 8.95 **st.** 🍷 2.75 – **10 rm** ⊑ 19.00/39.00 **st.**

↑ **Ferncroft**, 144 Ledbury Rd, HR1 2TB, ☎ 265538, ⚘ – TV Ⓟ. 🔲 VISA ⚘   B a
closed mid December-early January – **M** 8.00 **st.** 🍷 3.50 – **11 rm** ⊑ 16.00/40.00 **t.**

✗ **Effy's**, 96 East St., HR1 2LW, ☎ 59754 – 🔲 VISA   A c
closed Sunday, Monday and 1 week Christmas – **M** (dinner only) a la carte 13.85/18.85 **t.**
🍷 2.95.

at Canon Pyon N : 7 m. on A 4110 – B – ✉ Hereford – ☎ 043 271 Canon Pyon :

↑ **Hermitage** ⚘ without rest., HR4 8NR, S : 1 m. on A 4110 ☎ 0432 (Hereford) 760317, ≤
Vale of Hereford, ⚘ – Ⓟ. ⚘
March-mid December – **3 rm** ⊑ 25.00/39.00 **st.**

at Dormington E : 5 ¼ m. on A 438 – B – ✉ ☎ 0432 Hereford :

⚑ **Dormington Court**, HR1 4DA, ☎ 850370, ⚘ – TV Ⓟ. 🔲 VISA
M 11.00/15.00 **t.** and a la carte 🍷 3.00 – **6 rm** ⊑ 28.00/46.00 **t.**

at Much Birch S : 5 ½ m. on A 49 – B – ⊠ Hereford – ☎ 0981 Golden Valley :

🏛 **Pilgrim,** Ross Rd, HR2 8HJ, on A 49 ☎ 540742, Telex 35332, ≼, 🛲 – 📺 ☎ ℗ – ⚒ 40. ◪ AE ⓞ VISA ⅜
M (bar lunch Monday to Saturday)/dinner 15.75 **st.** and a la carte ⓵ 4.50 – **19 rm** ⊊ 34.50/58.00 **st.** – SB (weekends only) 76.00 **st.**

at Ruckhall W : 5 m. by A 49 off A 465 – B – ⊠ Eaton Bishop – ☎ 0981 Golden Valley :

🏠 **Ancient Camp Inn** ⑃, HR2 9QX, ☎ 250449, ≼ River Wye and countryside, « Tastefully renovated inn » – 📺 ☎ ℗. ◪ VISA ⅜
M *(closed Sunday dinner and Monday)* (bar lunch)/dinner a la carte 12.65/16.95 **t.** ⓵ 3.75 – **3 rm** ⊊ 25.00/37.50 **t.**

BMW White Cross Rd ☎ 272589	PEUGEOT-TALBOT 101-105 St. Owen St. ☎ 276268
CITROEN 38 St. Martin St. ☎ 272545	RELIANT, SKODA Bridge St. ☎ 272341
DAIHATSU, ALFA-ROMEO ☎ 054 46 (Eardisley) 441	SAAB Kings Acre Rd ☎ 266974
FIAT Bath St. ☎ 274134	SUBARU, ISUZU, FIAT Conningsby St. ☎ 343471
FORD Commercial Rd ☎ 276494	TOYOTA Mill St. ☎ 276727
HONDA Steels Corner ☎ 267151	VOLVO 14-15 Commercial Rd ☎ 276275
LANCIA, LADA, HYUNDAI Whitestone ☎ 850464	VW-AUDI Roman Rd ☎ 59234
LAND-ROVER, RANGE-ROVER Muchgowarne ☎ 053 186 (Bosbury) 746	
OPEL-VAUXHALL Blackfriars St. ☎ 352352	ⓦ ATS Kyrle St. ☎ 265491

HERNE BAY Kent 404 X 29 – pop. 26 523 – ECD : Thursday – ☎ 0227.

Envir. : Reculver (church twin towers★ *AC*) E : 3 m.

🛆 Herne Bay, Thanet Way ☎ 373964.

🛈 Band Stand, Central Parade ☎ 361911.

♦London 63 – ♦Dover 24 – Maidstone 32 – Margate 13.

🏠 **Northdown** without rest., 14 Cecil Park, CT6 6DL, ☎ 372051, 🛲 – 📺 ☎ ℗. ⅜
5 rm ⊊ 15.00/34.00 **st.**

✗ **L'Escargot,** 22 High St., CT6 5LH, ☎ 372876 – ◪ VISA
closed lunch Saturday and Monday, Sunday except summer, 26 December, 1 week – **M** 8.90/9.95 **t.** and a la carte 12.35/17.00 **t.** ⓵ 3.25.

FORD Sea St. ☎ 374939	SKODA Express Garage ☎ 364077
MAZDA Canterbury Rd ☎ 374772	

HERSTMONCEUX East Sussex 404 U 31 – pop. 2 246 – ☎ 032 181 (4 fig.) or 0323 (6 fig.).

See : Castle (15C) (home of the Royal Greenwich Observatory) site and grounds★★ *AC*.

Envir. : Michelham Priory (site★) *AC*, SW : 6 m.

♦London 63 – Eastbourne 12 – Hastings 14 – Lewes 16.

✗✗ **Sundial,** Gardner St., BN27 4LA, ☎ 832217, French rest., « Converted 16C cottage », 🛲 – ℗. ◪ AE ⓞ VISA
closed Sunday dinner, Monday, mid August-10 September and 25 December-20 January – **M** 14.50/19.50 **t.** and a la carte 18.25/24.00 **t.** ⓵ 3.95.

AUSTIN-ROVER Boreham St. ☎ 832353	FIAT Cowbeech ☎ 833321

HERTFORD Herts. 404 T 28 – pop. 21 350 – ECD : Thursday – ☎ 0992.

🛈 The Castle ☎ 0279 (Bishop's Stortford) 55261.

♦London 24 – ♦Cambridge 35 – Luton 26.

✗ Paddyfields, 3 St. Andrews St., SG14 1HZ, ☎ 550582, Chinese (Peking) rest.

at Letty Green SW : 3 m. on A 414 – ⊠ ☎ 0707 Welwyn Garden City :

🏠 **Cowper Arms,** Cole Green Lane, SG14 2NN, ☎ 330202, 🛲 – 📺 ☎ ℗. ◪ AE ⓞ VISA ⅜
M a la carte 8.40/21.85 **st.** ⓵ 3.65 – **5 rm** ⊊ 37.00/48.00 **st.**

AUSTIN-ROVER First Av. ☎ 0279 (Harlow) 27541	PEUGEOT North Rd ☎ 583044
FORD Gascoyne Way ☎ 551031	

HERTINGFORDBURY Herts. 404 T 28 – pop. 658 – ⊠ ☎ 0992 Hertford.

♦London 26 – Luton 18.

🏛 **White Horse** (T.H.F.), Hertingfordbury Rd, SG14 2LB, ☎ 586791, Fax 550809, 🛲 – ⅏ rm 📺 ☎ ℗ – ⚒ 50. ◪ AE ⓞ VISA
M 10.45/15.95 **st.** and a la carte ⓵ 3.95 – ⊊ 7.00 – **42 rm** 64.00/84.00 **st.** – SB (weekends only) 88.00 **st.**

HETHERSETT Norfolk 404 X 26 – see Norwich.

HETTON North Yorks. – pop. 115 – ⊠ Skipton – ☎ 075 673 Cracoe.

♦London 237 – Burnley 25 – ♦Leeds 33.

✗✗ **Angel Inn,** BD23 6LT, ☎ 263, « Attractive 18C inn » – ℗. ◪
closed Sunday dinner – **M** (dinner only and Sunday lunch) 16.50 **t.** ⓵ 3.45.

HEXHAM Northumb. 401 402 N 19 – pop. 8 914 – ECD : Thursday – ☎ 0434.
See : Abbey Church★ (13C) (Saxon Crypt★★, Leschman chantry★).
Envir. : Hadrian's Wall★★ with its forts and milecastles – Housesteads Fort★, museum★, NW :
14 m.

🏌 Spital Park ✆ 603072 – ⛳ Tynedale, Tyne Green.

🛈 The Manor Office, Hallgate ✆ 605225.

♦London 304 – ♦Carlisle 37 – ♦Newcastle-upon-Tyne 21.

🏨 **Beaumont**, Beaumont St., NE46 3LT, ✆ 602331 – ⇥ rm 📺 ☎ – 🔥 . 🔄 AE ⓪ VISA 🦺
closed 26 December and 1 January – **M** (bar lunch Monday to Saturday)/dinner a la carte
9.50/15.25 t. 🍷 3.00 – **23 rm** ⇆ 35.00/55.00 **st.**

🏨 **County**, Priestpopple, NE46 1PS, ✆ 602030 – 📺 ☎ . 🔄 VISA
M 8.00/15.00 **t.** and a la carte 🍷 3.50 – **9 rm** 30.00/46.00 **t.** – SB (weekends only)
(except summer) 60.00 **st.**

AUSTIN-ROVER Alemouth Rd ✆ 605151   VAUXHALL Parkwell ✆ 602411
MAZDA Tyne Mills Ind. Est. ✆ 607091   VOLVO Dere Park ✆ 605825
PEUGEOT-TALBOT Haugh Lane ✆ 604527
RENAULT, AUDI-VW Station Garage ✆ 606781   🅐 ATS Haugh Lane ✆ 602394
SUZUKI Priestpopple ✆ 603615

HEYSHAM Lancs. 402 L 21 – ECD : Wednesday – ☎ 0524.

🏌 Trumacar Park ✆ 51011.

🚢 to the Isle of Man : Douglas (Isle of Man Steam Packet Co.) 1-2 daily (except Sundays in
winter) (3 h 45 mn to 4 h 30mn).

♦London 251 – ♦Blackpool 33 – ♦Carlisle 74 – Lancaster 8.

HIGHAM Suffolk 404 W 28 – pop. 142 – ✉ Colchester – ☎ 020 637.

♦London 55 – Colchester 10 – ♦Ipswich 11.

↗ **Old Vicarage** 🦢 without rest., CO7 6JY, ✆ 248, ≤, « 16C former vicarage », 🏊 heated,
🐎, 🍴 – 📺 ℗
4 rm ⇆ 18.00/25.00 **st.**

HIGH HALDEN Kent 404 W 30 – see Tenterden.

HIGH OFFLEY Staffs. 402 403 404 N 25 – see Newport (Shropshire).

HIGHWORTH Wilts. 403 404 O 29 – pop. 8 020 – ☎ 0367 Faringdon.

♦London 88 – Gloucester 33 – ♦Oxford 25 – Swindon 5.

XX **Inglesham Forge,** Inglesham, SN6 7QY, N : 2 ½ m. by A 361 ✆ 52298 – ℗ . 🔄 AE ⓪ VISA
closed lunch Monday and Saturday, Sunday dinner, 1 week February, last 2 weeks August
and 1 week Christmas – **M** 24.50 **t.** and a la carte 17.50/24.50 **t.** 🍷 3.50.

HIGH WYCOMBE Bucks. 404 R 29 – pop. 69 575 – ECD : Wednesday – ☎ 0494.
Envir. : Hughenden Manor★ (site★, Disraeli Museum) AC, N : 1 m. – West Wycombe (Manor
House★ (18C) AC, St. Lawrence's Church : from the tower 74 steps, AC, ❄★) NW : 2 ½ m.

🛈 Council Offices, Queen Victoria Rd ✆ 461000.

♦London 34 – Aylesbury 17 – ♦Oxford 26 – Reading 18.

🏨 **Crest** (Crest), Crest Rd, HP11 1TL, SW : 1 ½ m. by A 404 ✆ 442100, Telex 83626, Fax 439071
– ⇥ rm ▤ 📺 ☎ & ℗ – 🔥 100. 🔄 AE ⓪ VISA 🦺
M 13.20/17.50 **st.** and a la carte – ⇆ 7.75 – **110 rm** 78.00/101.00 **st.** – SB (weekends only) 84.00/96.00 **st.**

MICHELIN Distribution Centre, Thomas Rd, Wooburn Green, HP10 0PE, ✆ 062 85 (Bourne End)
27472, FAX 819082

TOYOTA Littleworth Rd, Downley ✆ 35811   VOLVO London Rd ✆ 34511
VAUXHALL London Rd ✆ 30021/445181/27494
VAUXHALL West Wycombe Rd ✆ 32545   🅐 ATS Copyground Lane ✆ 25101/438019

HILLSFORD BRIDGE Devon – see Lynton.

HINCKLEY Leics. 402 403 404 P 26 – pop. 35 510 – ECD : Thursday – ☎ 0455.

🏌 Leicester Rd ✆ 615124, NE : 1 ½ m. on A 47.

🛈 Hinckley Library, Lancaster Rd ✆ 635106/30852.

♦London 103 – ♦Birmingham 31 – ♦Coventry 12 – ♦Leicester 14.

🏨 **Hinckley Island,** Watling St., LE10 3JA, SE : 3 m. by A 447 on A 5 ✆ 631122, Telex 34691,
Fax 634536, 🔄, 🏊 – 📺 ☎ & ℗ – 🔥 400. 🔄 AE ⓪ VISA
M 12.70/14.95 **t.** and a la carte 16.15/23.65 **t.** – ⇆ 5.95 – **131 rm** 69.00/99.00 **st.** – SB
(weekends only) 84.00/92.00 **st.**

🏨 **Sketchley Grange** (Best Western) 🦢, Sketchley Lane, Burbage, LE10 3HU, SE : 2 m. by
A 447 ✆ 251133, Fax 631384, 🐎 – ⇥ rm 📺 ☎ ℗ . 🔄 AE ⓪ VISA 🦺
M a la carte 12.65/18.50 🍷 4.50 – **30 rm** ⇆ 65.00/79.00 **t.** – SB (weekends only) 67.00/78.00 **st.**

AUDI-VW 94-106 Upper Bond St. ☎ 637934
CITROEN Shilton Rd, Barwell ☎ 45091
FORD Watling St. ☎ 38911
NISSAN Roston Drive ☎ 632023
PEUGEOT-TALBOT London Rd ☎ 637152
RENAULT New Building ☎ 635379

SUBARU, ISUZU The Square, Wolvey ☎ 220761
VAUXHALL-OPEL 38 Derby Rd ☎ 636551
VOLVO Station Rd ☎ 632478

ATS 5 Leicester Rd ☎ 632022/635835

HINDON Wilts. **403 404** N 30 – pop. 489 – ECD : Saturday – ✉ Salisbury – ☎ 074 789.
♦London 107 – Bath 28 – Bournemouth 40 – Salisbury 15.

  Lamb at Hindon, SP3 6DP, ☎ 573, 🚗 – ✗ rest TV ☎ P. 🅿 AE VISA
  M 12.50/14.75 t. and a la carte 🍷 3.00 – **16 rm** ☳ 25.00/60.00 t. – SB 65.00/75.00 st.

HINTLESHAM Suffolk **404** X 27 – see Ipswich.

HINTON CHARTERHOUSE Avon – see Bath.

HINWICK Beds. – see Wellingborough (Northants.).

HITCHIN Herts. **404** T 28 – pop. 33 480 – ECD : Wednesday – ☎ 0462.
🛈 Library, Paynes Park ☎ 34738.
♦London 40 – Bedford 14 – ♦Cambridge 26 – Luton 9.

  Sun, Sun St., SG5 1AF, ☎ 36411 – ✗ rm TV ☎ P – 🏛 80. 🐾
  M (carving rest.) – **32 rm**.

  Lord Lister, Park St., SG4 9AH, ☎ 32712 – ✗ rm TV P. 🐾
  20 rm.

  ✗ Raj Douth, 19a Hermitage Rd, SG5 1BT, ☎ 37674, Indian rest.

  at Little Wymondley SF : 2 ½ m. on A 602 – ✉ Hitchin – ☎ 0438 Stevenage :

  ✗✗ **Redcoats Farmhouse** 🐾 with rm, Redcoats Green, SG4 7JR, S : ½ m. by A 602
  ☎ 729500, Telex 83343, Fax 723322, « Part 15C farmhouse », 🚗 – TV ☎ P. 🅿 AE ⓪
  VISA. 🐾
  M *(closed Saturday lunch, Sunday and Bank Holidays)* 8.00 t. (lunch) and a la carte
  17.10/24.50 t. 🍷 5.00 – **14 rm** ☳ 30.00/80.00 t. – SB (weekends only) 101.00/131.00 st.

AUSTIN-ROVER Queen St. ☎ 50311

CITROEN High St., Graveley ☎ 0438 (Stevenage) 316177

HOATH Kent – ✉ Canterbury – ☎ 022 786 Chislet.
♦London 67 – Canterbury 6 – Margate 13.

  Knaves Ash Country Inn, CT3 4JT, ☎ 343 – ✗ rm TV ☎ P. 🅿 AE VISA
  M *(closed Sunday dinner)* a la carte 9.25/16.35 t. 🍷 3.70 – **4 rm** ☳ 42.00/80.00 t. –
  SB (except summer) 60.00/80.00 st.

HOCKLEY HEATH Warw. **403 404** O 26 – pop. 3 507 – ✉ Solihull – ☎ 056 43 Lapworth.
♦London 117 – ♦Birmingham 11 – ♦Coventry 17.

  ✗✗✗ **Nuthurst Grange** 🐾 with rm, Nuthurst Grange Lane, B94 5NL, S : ¾ m. by A 34 ☎ 3972,
  Telex 333185, Fax 3919, ≼, 🚗 – TV ☎ P. 🅿 AE ⓪ VISA. 🐾
  closed 1 week Christmas – M *(closed Saturday lunch)* 15.50/29.50 t. 🍷 4.50 – ☳ 6.90 – **8 rm**
  75.00/105.00 t. – SB (weekends only) 125.00 st.

HODNET Shropshire **402 403 404** M 25 – pop. 1 343 – ☎ 063 084.
♦London 166 – ♦Birmingham 50 – Chester 32 – ♦Stoke-on-Trent 22 – Shrewsbury 14.

  Bear, Shrewsbury St., TF9 3NH, ☎ 84214, Fax 84351 – ✗ rest TV ☎ P. 🅿 VISA. 🐾
  M 9.50/13.00 t. 🍷 3.00 – **6 rm** ☳ 30.00/45.00 t.

HOLDENBY Northants. – see Northampton.

HOLFORD Somerset **403** K 30 – pop. 266 – ✉ Bridgwater – ☎ 027 874.
Envir. : Stogursey Priory Church★★, W : 4 ½ m.
♦London 171 – ♦Bristol 48 – Minehead 15 – Taunton 22.

  Combe House 🐾, TA5 1RZ, SW : 1 m. ☎ 382, « Country house atmosphere », 🅿, 🚗,
  ✗ – ✗ rest TV ☎ P. 🅿 AE VISA
  March-November – M (bar lunch)/dinner 11.00 t. 🍷 2.45 – **22 rm** ☳ 26.00/68.00 t. –
  SB (except summer) 43.00/60.00 st.

  Alfoxton Park 🐾, TA5 1SG, W : 1 ½ m. ☎ 211, ≼, 🏊 heated, 🚗, park, ✗ – TV P
  18 rm.

HOLME West Yorks. – see Holmfirth.

♦London 181 – Chester 25 – ♦Liverpool 41 – ♦Manchester 24 – ♦Stoke-on-Trent 20.

- **Holly Lodge**, 70 London Rd, CW4 7AS, on A 50 ℘ 37033, Fax 35823 – TV ☎ P – 🏊 120. 🖭 AE ⓸ VISA
closed 25 to 31 December – **M** *(closed Saturday lunch and Bank Holidays)* 5.20/9.50 t. and a la carte ▯ 3.50 – **33 rm** ⌑ 41.00/52.00 t.

- **Old Vicarage**, Knutsford Rd, Cranage, CW4 8EF, NW : ½ m. on A 50 ℘ 32041 – ⇔ rm TV ☎ P. 🖭 AE VISA. ⌘
M 9.50/13.50 st. and a la carte 14.15/20.75 st. ▯ 4.50 – **23 rm** ⌑ 42.50/56.00 st. – SB *(weekends only)* 64.00 **st.**

at Twemlow Green NE : 1 ¾ m. on A 535 – ✉ ☎ 0477 Holmes Chapel :

- **Yellow Broom**, Macclesfield Rd, CW4 8BL, ℘ 33289 – P. 🖭 AE VISA
closed Sunday dinner and Monday – **M** *(dinner only and Sunday lunch) (booking essential)*/dinner a la carte 17.50/23.50 t. ▯ 5.50.

at Brereton SE : 2 m. on A 50 – ✉ Sandbach – ☎ 0477 Holmes Chapel :

- **Bear's Head**, Newcastle Rd, CW11 9RS, ℘ 35251, ⚞, ⚒ – TV ☎ P. 🖭 AE ⓸ VISA ⌘
M *(closed Sunday dinner and Bank Holidays)* 8.55 t. (lunch)/dinner a la carte 11.95/20.70 t. ▯ 4.50 – **23 rm** ⌑ 41.50/70.00 st.

🛈 49-51 Huddersfield Rd ℘ 684992/687603.
♦London 195 – ♦Leeds 23 – ♦Manchester 25 – ♦Sheffield 22.

- **Old Bridge**, HD7 1DA, ℘ 681212 – TV ☎ P. 🖭 AE VISA
closed Christmas Night – **M** 8.25/14.25 t. and a la carte ▯ 4.50 – **20 rm** ⌑ 42.50/50.00 t.

at Holme SW : 2 ½ m. on A 6024 – ✉ Huddersfield – ☎ 0484 Holmfirth :

- **Holme Castle**, HD7 1QG, ℘ 686764, ≤ – ⇔ TV P. 🖭 VISA. ⌘
M *(by arrangement)* 16.00 t. – **8 rm** ⌑ 26.00/52.00 t.

♦London 314 – Kendal 52 – Workington 24.

- **Carleton Green** ⚘ without rest., Saltcoats Rd, CA19 1YX, S : 1 m. by A 595 ℘ 608, ⚞ P
March-October – **7 rm** ⌑ 14.00/26.00 s.

♦London 124 – King's Lynn 34 – ♦Norwich 22.

- **Feathers** (B.C.B.), 6 Market Pl., NR25 6BW, ℘ 712318 – TV ☎ P
13 rm.

- **Yetmans**, 37 Norwich Rd, NR25 6SA, ℘ 713320
closed Monday, Tuesday, 1 week May and 2 weeks November – **M** a la carte 11.75/16.75 t.

🅐 ATS Hempstead Rd Ind Est. ℘ 712015

Envir. : South Stack (cliffs★) W : 3 ½ m. – Rhosneigr (site★) SE : 13 m.
⛴ to Ireland (Dun Laoghaire) (Sealink) 2 daily; (3 h 30 mn) – to Ireland (Dublin) (B & I Line) 1-2 daily (3 h 30 mn-4 h.).
🛈 Marine Sq., Salt Island Approach ℘ 2622 (summer only).
♦London 269 – Birkenhead 94 – ♦Cardiff 215 – Chester 88 – Shrewsbury 105 – ♦Swansea 190.

See : Castle (16C) ≤★★ AC – Priory★ (ruins 12C) AC.
♦London 342 – Berwick-upon-Tweed 13 – ♦Newcastle-upon-Tyne 59.

Hotels see : Berwick-upon-Tweed NW : 13 m.

🟆 Holywell, Brynford ℘ 710040.
♦London 217 – Chester 19 – ♦Liverpool 34.

- **Stamford Gate**, Halkyn Rd, CH8 7SJ, ℘ 712942 – TV P. 🖭 VISA ⌘
M 6.50/8.75 t. and a la carte ▯ 3.00 – **12 rm** ⌑ 30.00/45.00 st.

- **Travelodge** without rest., Halkyn, CH8 8RF, SE : 3 ½ m. on A 55 (westbound carriageway) ℘ 780952 – TV 🧩 P. 🖭 AE VISA
31 rm 21.50/27.00 t.

AUSTIN-ROVER Halkyn Rd ℘ 711711   FORD Holway ℘ 711838

HONITON Devon 408 K 31 *The West Country* G. – pop. 6 490 – ECD : Thursday – ✆ 0404.
See : All Hallows Museum ★ *AC*.
Envir. : Farway Countryside Park (≤★) *AC*, S : 3 m.
🛈 Angel Hotel car park, High St. ✆ 3716 (summer only).
♦London 186 – Exeter 17 – ♦Southampton 93 – Taunton 18.

    at Stockland NE : 8 ½ m. by A 30 – ✉ Honiton – ✆ 040 486 Upottery :

🏠 Snodwell Farm ⑤, Stockland Hill, Cotleigh, EX14 9HZ, W : 3 m. ✆ 263, ⤢, ☞ – ℗
10 rm.

    at Weston W : 2 m. by A 30 – ✉ ✆ 0404 Honiton :

🏨 **Deer Park** ⑤, EX14 0PG, ✆ 41266, ≤, ⤢ heated, ⬖, ☞, park, ✂, squash – 📺 ☎ ℗.
🔌 AE ⓞ VISA. ❄
M 13.50/22.00 **st.** and a la carte ⓵ 4.50 – **30 rm** ⌖ 45.00/120.00 **st.** – SB (weekends only) 90.00/140.00 **st.**

HOOK Hants. 404 R 30 – pop. 2 562 – ECD : Thursday – ✆ 0256.
♦London 47 – Reading 13 – ♦Southampton 35.

🏨 **Raven** (Lansbury), Station Rd, RG27 9HS, ✆ 762541, Telex 858901, Fax 768677 – ⤢ rm 📺
☎ ℗ – 🔬 100. 🔌 AE ⓞ VISA. ❄
M 8.50/12.50 **t.** and a la carte – **38 rm** ⌖ 58.00/68.00 **t.** – SB (spring and autumn) (weekends only) 68.00/78.00 **st.**

🏠 White Hart, London Rd, RG27 9DZ, ✆ 762462, Fax 768351, ☞ – 📺 ☎ ℗
20 rm.

⌂ **Oaklea,** London Rd, RG27 9LA, on A 30 ✆ 762673, ☞ – ⤢ ℗
M 9.00 **st.** ⓵ 1.80 – **10 rm** ⌖ 20.50/43.00 **st.**

HOPE COVE Devon 408 I 33 – see Salcombe.

HOPTON WAFERS Shropshire 408 404 M 26 – pop. 948 – ✉ Kidderminster – ✆ 0299 Cleobury Mortimer.
♦London 150 – ♦Birmingham 32 – Shrewsbury 38.

🏦 **Crown Inn,** DY14 0NB, on A 4117 ✆ 270372 – 📺 ☎ ℗. 🔌 VISA
M *(closed Sunday dinner and Monday)* 12.95 **st.** ⓵ 2.50 – ⌖ 4.50 – **7 rm** 29.50/39.50 **st.** – SB (except Christmas and New Year) 65.00 **st.**

HORLEY Surrey 404 T 30 – pop. 17 700 – ECD : Wednesday – ✆ 029 34 (4 and 5 fig.) or 0293 (6 fig.).
♦London 27 – ♦Brighton 26 – Royal Tunbridge Wells 22.

Plan : see Gatwick

🏨 **Chequers Thistle** (Thistle), Brighton Rd, RH6 8PH, ✆ 786992, Telex 877550, Fax 820625,
⤢ – ⤢ rm 📺 ☎ ℗ – 🔬 100. 🔌 AE ⓞ VISA. ❄   **Y z**
M *(closed lunch Saturday and Bank Holidays)* 9.50/15.50 **t.** and a la carte ⓵ 4.50 – ⌖ 7.25 –
78 rm 80.00/90.00 **st.** – SB (weekends only) 88.00 **st.**

AUSTIN-ROVER Massetts Rd ✆ 785176   FORD Reigate Rd, Hookwood ✆ 820110

HORNDON ON THE HILL Essex – ✆ 0375 Stanford-le-Hope.
♦London 24 – Chelmsford 21 – Gravesend 8 – Southend-On-Sea 14.

✗✗ **Hill House** with rm, High Rd, SS17 8LD, ✆ 642463 – 📺 ☎ ℗. 🔌 VISA. ❄
closed 25 to 30 December – **M** *(closed Sunday and Monday)* 14.85 **t.** (lunch)/dinner a la
carte 16.05/20.20 **t.** ⓵ 3.00 – ⌖ 5.25 – **10 rm** 40.00/50.00 **t.**

HORNING Norfolk 404 Y 25 – pop. 1 033 – ECD : Wednesday – ✉ Norwich – ✆ 0692.
♦London 122 – Great Yarmouth 17 – ♦Norwich 11.

🏨 **Petersfield House** ⑤, Lower St., NR12 8PF, ✆ 630741, Fax 630745, ☞ – 📺 ☎ ℗. 🔌 AE
ⓞ VISA
M 12.00/14.00 **t.** and a la carte ⓵ 3.75 – **18 rm** ⌖ 45.00/65.00 **t.** – SB 76.00/80.00 **st.**

🏠 Swan (B.C.B.), Lower St., NR12 8AH, ✆ 630316, ≤, « Riverside setting » – 📺 ☎ ℗
11 rm.

HORNS CROSS Devon 408 H 31 – ECD : Wednesday – ✉ Bideford – ✆ 023 75.
♦London 237 – Barnstaple 15 – Exeter 48.

🏨 **Foxdown Manor** ⑤, Foxdown, EX39 5PJ, S : 1 m. ✆ 325, ≤, « Country house atmosphere », ⤢ heated, ☞, park, ✂ – 📺 ☎ ℗. 🔌 AE VISA
closed January and February – **M** (bar lunch Monday to Saturday)/dinner 12.50 **st.** and a la
carte ⓵ 3.00 – **7 rm** ⌖ 21.00/60.00 **st.** – SB (except August) 64.00/84.00 **st.**

HORSFORTH West Yorks. 402 P 22 – see Leeds.

HORSHAM West Sussex 404 T 30 – pop. 38 356 – ECD : Monday and Thursday – ✆ 0403.
♦London 39 – ♦Brighton 23 – Guildford 20 – Lewes 25 – Worthing 20.

  Ye Olde King's Head, 35 Carfax Rd, RH12 1EG, ✆ 53126 – ⤢ rest TV ✆ P. ⌧ AE ⓪ VISA
  M 9.15/11.50 **t.** and a la carte 🍷 3.80 – **42 rm** ⌑ 54.00/65.00 t. – SB (weekends only)
64.00 **st.**

  at Lower Beeding SE : 3 ½ m. on A 281 – ⌧ Horsham – ✆ 040 376 (3 fig.) or 0403 (6 fig.)
Lower Beeding :

  South Lodge ⌘, Brighton Rd, RH13 6PS, on A 281 ✆ 711, Telex 877765, Fax 766, ≤, ⌘,
🐎, park, ✗ – TV ✆ P – 🛎 80. ⌧ AE ⓪ VISA ✗
  M 17.50/28.00 **t.** and a la carte 28.25/35.75 t. 🍷 6.00 – ⌑ 9.00 – **36 rm** 80.00/125.00 t.,
3 suites 190.00/210.00 **t.** – SB (weekends only) 160.00/200.00 **st.**

  Cisswood House, Sandygate Lane, RH13 6NF, ✆ 891216, Fax 891621, 🐎 – TV ✆ P –
🛎 40. ⌧ AE ⓪ VISA ✗
  closed 1 week August and 1 week December – **M** 25.00/30.00 **t.** and a la carte 🍷 4.00 – ⌑
4.50 – **32 rm** 56.00/78.00 **st.**, **2 suites** 78.00 **st.**

AUSTIN-ROVER Springfield Rd ✆ 54311
CITROEN Guildford Rd ✆ 61393
FIAT Brighton Rd ✆ 65637
FORD The Bishopric ✆ 54331
RENAULT 108 Crawley Rd ✆ 61146
TOYOTA Slinfold ✆ 790766

VAUXHALL-OPEL Broadbridge Heath ✆ 56464
VOLVO Guildford Rd ✆ 56381

🔧 ATS Rear of Brighton Rd Filling Station. ✆
67491/51736

HORSHAM ST. FAITH Norfolk 404 X 25 – see Norwich.

HORTON Dorset 403 404 O 31 – see Wimborne Minster.

HORTON Northants. 404 R 27 – ⌧ ✆ 0604 Northampton.
♦London 66 – Bedford 18 – Northampton 6.

  XX **French Partridge**, Newport Pagnell Rd (B 526), NN7 2AP, ✆ 870033 – ⤢ P
  closed Sunday, Monday, 2 weeks Easter, 3 weeks July-August and 2 weeks Christmas –
M (dinner only) (booking essential) 18.50 **st.** 🍷 4.20.

HORTON-CUM-STUDLEY Oxon. 403 404 Q 28 – ECD : Wednesday – ⌧ Oxford – ✆ 086 735
Stanton St. John.
♦London 57 – Aylesbury 23 – ♦Oxford 7.

  Studley Priory ⌘, OX9 1AZ, ✆ 203, Fax 613, ≤, « Converted priory in park », 🐎, ✗
TV ✆ P – 🛎 30. ⌧ AE ⓪ VISA ✗
  M 25.00 **st.** and a la carte 27.50/31.25 st. 🍷 4.00 – **18 rm** ⌑ 70.00/120.00 st., **1 suite**
150.00 st. – SB 95.00/125.00 st.

HOUGHTON CONQUEST Beds. 404 S 27 – see Bedford.

HOVE East Sussex 404 T 31 – see Brighton and Hove.

HOVINGHAM North Yorks. 402 R 21 – pop. 310 – ECD : Thursday – ⌧ York – ✆ 065 382.
♦London 235 – ♦Middlesbrough 36 – York 25.

  Worsley Arms, YO6 4LA, ✆ 234, 🐎 – ✆ 🚗 P
  closed 25 and 26 December – **14 rm**.

HOWDEN Humberside 402 R 22 – pop. 3 227 – ECD : Thursday – ✆ 0430.
See : St. Peter's Church★ (12C-14C).
🏌 Boothferry, Spaldington Lane ✆ 430364, N : 2 ½ m. by B 1228.
♦London 196 – ♦Kingston-upon-Hull 23 – ♦Leeds 37 – York 22.

  Bowmans, Bridgegate, DN14 7JG, ✆ 430805 – TV 🚗 P. ✗
13 rm.

HOWEY Powys – see Llandrindod Wells.

HOWTOWN Cumbria – see Ullswater.

HUCKNALL Notts. 402 403 404 Q 24 – pop. 27 463 – ✆ 0602 Nottingham.
♦London 134 – Derby 17 – ♦Nottingham 7 – ♦Sheffield 38.

  The Lodge at Hucknall, Nottingham Rd, NG15 7PY, S : 1 m. on A 611 ✆ 634655 – TV
✆ P
33 rm.

HUDDERSFIELD West Yorks. 402 404 O 23 – pop. 147 825 – ECD : Wednesday – ☎ 0484.

☈ Thick Hollins Hall, Meltham ℰ 850227, SW : 5 m. – ☈ Bradley Park, off Bradley Rd ℰ 539988, N : 3 m. – ☈ Longley Park, Maple St., off Somerset Rd ℰ 22304.

🄸 3-5 Albion St. ℰ 22133/23877 (evenings and weekends only).

♦London 191 – Bradford 11 – ♦Leeds 15 – ♦Manchester 25 – ♦Sheffield 26.

🏨 **Pennine Hilton** (Hilton), Ainley Top, HD3 3RH, NW : 2 ½ m. at junction A 629 and A 640 ℰ 0422 (Elland) 375431, Telex 517346, Fax 0422 (Elland) 310067, ⬚ – ▯ ⤢ rm ▤ rest ▣ ☎ ℗ – ⛲ . ⬚ 🅰🄴 ⓞ 𝘝𝘐𝘚𝘈
M (closed lunch Saturday and Bank Holiday Mondays) 12.00/20.00 t. and a la carte ⚱ 4.00 – ☲ 8.50 – **119 rm** 72.00/200.00 t. – SB (weekends only) 100.00/150.00 st.

🏨 **George** (T.H.F.), St. George's Sq., HD1 1JA, ℰ 515444, Fax 435056 – ▯ ⤢ rm ▣ ☎ ℗ – ⛲ 170. ⬚ 🅰🄴 ⓞ 𝘝𝘐𝘚𝘈
M 8.75/12.95 **st.** and a la carte ⚱ 3.50 – ☲ 7.00 – **60 rm** 52.00/67.00 st., **1 suite** 70.00/ 90.00 **st.** – SB (weekends only) 64.00 **st.**

🏩 Briar Court, Halifax Rd, Birchencliffe, HD3 3NT, NW : 2 m. on A 629 ℰ 519902, Telex 518260 – ▣ ☎ ℗ – ⛲ . ⤢
48 rm.

🏩 **Cote Royd**, 7 Halifax Rd, HD3 3AN, ℰ 547588, ⬚, ⇸ – ▣ ☎ ℗. ⬚ 🅰🄴 ⓞ 𝘝𝘐𝘚𝘈. ⤢
closed Christmas – **M** (dinner only) (residents only) 9.50 st. ⚱ 3.50 – **21 rm** ☲ 41.00/51.00 st.

🏩 **Huddersfield**, 37-47 Kirkgate, HD1 1QT, ℰ 512111, Telex 51575, Fax 435262 – ▯ ▣ ☎ ℗. ⬚ 🅰🄴 ⓞ 𝘝𝘐𝘚𝘈
M 6.00/8.00 **st.** and a la carte ⚱ 4.00 – **40 rm** ☲ 39.00/75.00 st.

🏠 **Elm Crest** without rest., 2 Queens Rd, HD2 2AG, ℰ 530990 – ⤢ ℗. ⬚. ⤢
8 rm ☲ 20.00/55.00 st.

XX **Pisces**, 84 Fitzwilliam St., HD1 5BD, ℰ 516773, Seafood – ⬚ 𝘝𝘐𝘚𝘈
closed Sunday, 25-26 December, 1 January and Bank Holidays Mondays – **M** 12.95 t. (dinner) and a la carte 13.95/24.10 t.

at Golcar W : 3 ½ m. by A 62 on B 6111 – ✉ ☎ 0484 Huddersfield :

XX **Weaver's Shed**, Knowl Rd, HD7 4AN, via Scar Lane ℰ 654284. « Converted 18C woollen mill » – ℗. ⬚ 🅰🄴 𝘝𝘐𝘚𝘈
closed Saturday lunch, Sunday, Monday, first 2 weeks January and last 2 weeks July – **M** a la carte 13.85/18.75 t.

at Outlane NW : 4 m. on A 640 – ✉ Huddersfield – ☎ 0422 Elland :

🏨 **Old Golf House** (Lansbury), New Hey Rd, HD3 3YP, ℰ 379311, Telex 51324, Fax 372694 – ⤢ rm ▣ ☎ ℗ – ⛲ . ⬚ 🅰🄴 ⓞ 𝘝𝘐𝘚𝘈. ⤢
M 8.60/12.00 t. and a la carte ⚱ 3.50 – **50 rm** ☲ 50.00/70.00 t. – SB (weekends only) 58.00/62.00 st.

AUSTIN-ROVER Southgate ℰ 535341
BMW Wakefield Rd ℰ 515515
DAIMLER-JAGUAR, LAND-ROVER, RANGE-ROVER Northgate ℰ 535251
TOYOTA Fartown ℰ 514514

VAUXHALL-OPEL 386 Leeds Rd ℰ 518700
VOLVO Northgate ℰ 531362
VW-AUDI Bradford Rd ℰ 542001

🄰 ATS Leeds Rd ℰ 534441

HULL Humberside 402 S 22 – see Kingston-upon-Hull.

HUNGERFORD Berks. 403 404 P 29 – pop. 4 488 – ECD : Thursday – ☎ 0488.

Envir. : Littlecote House★ AC, NW : 3 ½ m.

☈ West Berkshire, Chaddleworth ℰ 048 82 (Chaddleworth) 574, N : 2 ½ m.

♦London 74 – ♦Bristol 57 – ♦Oxford 28 – Reading 26 – ♦Southampton 46.

🏨 **Bear** (Best Western), 17 Charnham St., RG17 0EL, on A 4 ℰ 82512, Fax 84357, ⇸ – ▣ ☎ ℗ – ⛲ 100. ⬚ 🅰🄴 ⓞ 𝘝𝘐𝘚𝘈. ⤢
M 12.95/16.95 t. and a la carte – ☲ 5.95 – **41 rm** 50.00/80.00 t. – SB (weekends only) 75.00 **st.**

🏩 **Marshgate Cottage** without rest., Marsh Lane, RG17 0QX, ¾ m. by Church St. ℰ 682307 – ▣ ☎ ℗. ⬚ 𝘝𝘐𝘚𝘈. ⤢
closed 2 weeks January – **9 rm** ☲ 22.50/43.50 st.

BMW, SUZUKI Bath Rd ℰ 82772

HUNMANBY North Yorks. 402 T 21 – pop. 2 623 – ✉ Filey – ☎ 0723 Scarborough.

♦London 198 – ♦Kingston-upon-Hull 40 – Scarborough 9 – York 41.

🏩 **Wrangham House**, 10 Stonegate, YO14 0NS, ℰ 891333, ⇸ – ⤢ rm ▣ ℗. ⬚ 🅰🄴 ⓞ 𝘝𝘐𝘚𝘈. ⤢
M (dinner only) 10.50 t. ⚱ 3.45 – **9 rm** ☲ (dinner included) 37.00/42.00 t.

HUNSTANTON Norfolk 402 404 V 25 – pop. 3 990 – ECD : Thursday – ✆ 048 53.
Envir. : Holkham Hall★★ (18C) *AC*, W : 14 m.

🛆 Hunstanton ℰ 2811, N : 1 ½ m. by A 149 – 🛈 The Green ℰ 2610.

♦London 120 – ♦Cambridge 60 – ♦Norwich 45.

🏨 **Le Strange Arms**, Golf Course Rd, PE36 6JJ, N : 1 m. by A 149 ℰ 34411, Telex 817403, ≤,
🛥 – TV ☎ P – 🏌 100. 🖂 AE ⓪ VISA
M 13.00 **st.** and a la carte ∤ 2.50 – **28 rm** ⊊ 43.00/75.00 **st.** – SB 68.00/77.00 **st.**

⩗ **Claremont**, 35 Greevegate, PE36 6AF, ℰ 33171 – ⅙✕ rm. VISA. ⅜
M 6.00 **s.** – **7 rm** ⊊ 13.00/26.00 **s.**

⩗ **Deepdene**, 29 Avenue Rd, PE36 5BW, ℰ 2460, 🖂 – P. ⅜
closed October – **M** 8.50 **st.** – **9 rm** ⊊ 19.00/38.00 **st.**

⩗ **Pinewood**, 26 Northgate, PE36 6AP, ℰ 33068 – ⅙✕ TV P. 🖂 VISA
M (by arrangement) 8.95 **t.** ∤ 3.95 – **8 rm** ⊊ 15.00/36.00 **st.** – SB (except August
and Bank Holidays) 40.00/45.00 **st.**

at Heacham S : 3 m. by A 149 – ✉ King's Lynn – ✆ 0485 Heacham :

🏛 **Holly Lodge**, Lynn Rd, PE31 7HY, ℰ 70790, « Country house atmosphere », 🛥 – P. 🖂
VISA. ⅜
closed January and February – **M** *(closed Sunday)* (dinner only) a la carte 13.50/16.45 **t.**
∤ 2.50 – **6 rm** ⊊ 50.00/75.00 **st.** – SB (weekdays only) 80.00/100.00 **st.**

AUSTIN-ROVER 12 Lynn Rd ℰ 33435   CITROEN, ISUZU Westgate ℰ 2508

HUNSTRETE Avon 403 404 M 29 – see Bath.

HUNTINGDON Cambs. 404 T 26 – pop. 14 395 – ECD : Wednesday – ✆ 0480.
See : Cromwell Museum – All Saint's Church (interior★) – Envir. : Hinchingbrooke House★
(Tudor mansion-school) W : 1 m. – Ramsey (Abbey Gatehouse★ 15C) NE : 11 ½ m.

🛈 Huntingdon Library, Princes St. ℰ 425831/425801.

♦London 69 – Bedford 21 – ♦Cambridge 16.

🏨 **Old Bridge**, 1 High St., PE18 6TQ, ℰ 52681, Telex 32706, Fax 411017 – TV ☎ P – 🏌 45.
🖂 AE ⓪ VISA
M a la carte 17.35/26.85 **t.** – **26 rm** ⊊ 63.25/93.50 **st.**

🏛 **George** (T.H.F.), George St., PE18 6AB, ℰ 432444, Fax 453130 – ⅙✕ rm TV ☎ P – 🏌 150.
🖂 AE ⓪ VISA
M 9.50 **st.** and a la carte ∤ 3.95 – ⊊ 7.00 – **24 rm** 56.00/66.00 **st.** – SB (weekends
only) 76.00 **st.**

AUSTIN-ROVER 1-3 Hartford Rd ℰ 56441   ⓦ ATS Nursery Rd ℰ 451031/451515
BMW Stutley Rd ℰ 59551
VAUXHALL-OPEL Brookside ℰ 52694

HURLEY-ON-THAMES Berks. 404 R 29 – ECD : Wednesday – ✉ Maidenhead – ✆ 062 882
Littlewick Green.

♦London 38 – ♦Oxford 26 – Reading 12.

🏛 **Ye Olde Bell** (T.H.F.), High St., SL6 5LX, ℰ 5881, Fax 5939, « Part 12C inn », 🛥 – TV ☎ P
– 🏌 100. 🖂 AE ⓪ VISA
M 14.60/16.50 **st.** and a la carte ∤ 4.25 – ⊊ 7.60 – **25 rm** 69.00/89.00 **st.**, **1 suite** 115.00/
125.00 **st.** – SB (weekends only) 70.00/96.00 **st.**

HURSTBOURNE TARRANT Hants. 403 404 P 30 – pop. 709 – ✉ Andover – ✆ 026 476.
♦London 77 – ♦Bristol 77 – ♦Oxford 38 – ♦Southampton 33.

🏛 **Esseborne Manor** ⑤, SP11 0ER, NE : 1 ½ m. on A 343 ℰ 444, Fax 473, 🛥, ✕ – TV ☎
P. 🖂 AE ⓪ VISA. ⅜
M 11.75/27.50 **st.** ∤ 4.45 – **12 rm** ⊊ 72.00/98.00 **t.** – SB (except Easter, Christmas and
New Year) 126.00/135.00 **st.**

at Faccombe N : 3 ½ m. by A 343 – ✉ Andover – ✆ 026 487 Linkenholt :

⩗ **Jack Russel** ⑤, SP11 0DS, ℰ 315 – TV P. 🖂 VISA. ⅜
M 17.50 **st.** ∤ 3.10 – **3 rm** ⊊ 20.00/35.00 **st.**

HURST GREEN Lancs. 402 M 22 – ✉ Whalley – ✆ 025 486 Stonyhurst.
♦London 236 – Blackburn 12 – Burnley 13 – Preston 12.

🏛 **Shireburn Arms**, Whalley Rd, BB6 9QJ, ℰ 518, 🛥 – TV ☎ P. 🖂 VISA
M a la carte 11.25/15.45 **st.** ∤ 3.50 – **16 rm** ⊊ 29.50/46.00 **st.** – SB 71.00 **st.**

HUSBANDS BOSWORTH Leics. 403 404 Q 26 – pop. 889 – ✉ Lutterworth – ✆ 0858 Market
Harborough.

♦London 88 – ♦Birmingham 40 – ♦Leicester 14 – Northampton 17.

✕✕ **Fernie Lodge** with rm, Berridges Lane, LE17 6LE, ℰ 880551, Fax 88014 – ▤ rest TV ☎ P.
🖂 AE VISA. ⅜
M *(closed Saturday lunch)* 15.95 **t.** and a la carte 8.25/13.50 **t.** ∤ 3.50 – **7 rm** ⊊ 49.00/66.00 **st.**
– SB (weekends only) 72.90/102.90 **st.**

HUTTON-LE-HOLE North Yorks. **402** R 21 – see Lastingham.

HUXHAM Devon – see Exeter.

HUYTON Merseyside **402 403** L 23 – see Liverpool.

HWLFFORDD = Haverfordwest.

HYTHE Kent **404** X 30 – pop. 13 118 – ECD : Wednesday – ✆ 0303.
See : St. Leonard's Church (≼★ from the churchyard) – Canal.
⌐₉ Hythe Imperial, Princes Parade ✆ 67441.
🛈 Prospect Rd Car Park ✆ 67799 (summer only).
♦London 68 – Folkestone 6 – Hastings 33 – Maidstone 31.

 🏨 **Hythe Imperial** (Best Western) ⌂, Princes Par., CT21 6AE, ✆ 67441, Telex 965082, Fax
 264610, ≼, 🏊, ⌐₉, 🛲, ✗, squash – 🛗 TV ✆ & 🅿 – 🔬 250. 🖎 AE ⓪ VISA. ✗
 M 13.00/18.00 **st.** and a la carte ₰ 3.50 – **94 rm** ☲ 60.00/100.00 **t.**, **6 suites** 110.00/140.00 **t.** –
 SB (weekends only) (except Bank Holidays) 85.00/100.00 **st.**

 🏨 **Stade Court** (Best Western), West Par., CT21 6DT, ✆ 68263, Telex 965082, Fax 264610, ≼
 – 🛗 TV ✆ 🅿 – 🔬 35. 🖎 AE ⓪ VISA ☲ 38.00/61.00 **t.** – SB 70.00/80.00 **st.**
 M 9.50/14.00 **t.** and a la carte – **39 rm** ☲ 38.00/61.00 **t.** – SB 70.00/80.00 **st.**

FORD Stade St. ✆ 67726   SAAB 215 Seabrook Rd ✆ 38467

IBSLEY Hants. **403 404** O 31 – see Ringwood.

IDE Devon **403** J 31 – see Exeter.

IFIELD West Sussex – see Crawley.

ILFRACOMBE Devon **403** H 30 **The West Country G.** – pop. 9 966 – ECD : Thursday – ✆ 0271.
See : Capstone Hill★ (≼★) – Hillsborough (≼★★) – St. Nicholas' Chapel AC (≼★).
⌐₁₈ Hele Bay ✆ 62176, E : 1 m.
Access to Lundy Island from Hartland Point by helicopter ✆ 062 882 (Littlewick Green) 3431.
🚢 to Lundy 2-3 weekly (summer only) (Lundy Co.).
🛈 The Promenade ✆ 63001.
♦London 223 – Exeter 54 – Taunton 61.

 🏠 **Langleigh** ⌂, Langleigh Rd, EX34 8EA, ✆ 62629, 🛲 – TV 🅿. 🖎 VISA
 M 8.50 **st.** (dinner) and a la carte – **8 rm** ☲ 20.00/40.00 **st.** – SB (mid September-
 mid July) 45.00 **st.**

 🏠 **St. Helier,** Hillsborough Rd, EX34 9QQ, ✆ 64906 (from spring : 864906) – TV 🅿. 🖎 VISA
 May-September – **M** (dinner only) 7.00 **st.** ₰ 2.80 – **23 rm** ☲ 16.50/40.00 **st.** –
 SB 44.00/55.00 **st.**

 at Lee W : 3 ¼ m. by B 3231 – ✉ ✆ 0271 Ilfracombe :

 🏨 Lee Bay (Best Western) ⌂, EX34 8LP, ✆ 63503, ≼, 🏊 heated, 🛲, park – TV ✆ 🅿
 50 rm.

 🏠 **Lee Manor** ⌂, EX34 8LR, ✆ 63920, 🛲, park – TV 🅿. ✗
 Mid April-mid October – **M** (dinner only) 10.50 **t.** and a la carte ₰ 3.75 – **11 rm** ☲ (dinner included) 30.00/82.00 **t.**

PEUGEOT-TALBOT West Down ✆ 63104   RENAULT Northfield Rd ✆ 62075

ILKLEY West Yorks. **402** O 22 – pop. 13 060 – ECD : Wednesday – ✆ 0943.
⌐₉ Ben Rhydding, High Wood ✆ 608759 – ⌐₁₈ Myddleton ✆ 607277.
🛈 Station Rd ✆ 602319.
♦London 210 – Bradford 13 – Harrogate 17 – ♦Leeds 16 – Preston 46.

 🏨 **Rombalds,** 11 West View, Wells Rd, LS29 9JG, ✆ 603201, Telex 51593, Fax 816586 – TV
 ✆ 🅿. 🖎 AE ⓪ VISA
 closed 27 to 30 December – **M** 8.50 **t.** (lunch) and a la carte 17.00/24.50 **t.** ₰ 4.25 – **11 rm**
 ☲ 56.00/84.00 **t.**, **4 suites** 90.00/125.00 **t.** – SB (except September and October) 90.00/
 130.00 **st.**

 🏠 **Grove,** 66 The Grove, LS29 9PA, ✆ 600298 – ✗ rest TV 🅿. 🖎 VISA
 closed 20 December-4 January – **M** (bar lunch)/dinner 9.00 **st.** and a la carte – **6 rm**
 ☲ 29.00/46.00 **st.**

 🏠 **Cow and Calf,** Cowpasture Rd, LS29 8BT, SE : 1 ¼ m. ✆ 607335, ≼, 🛲 – TV ✆ 🅿. 🖎 AE
 ⓪ VISA
 closed Christmas – **M** 7.50/12.50 **t.** and a la carte 12.00/17.50 **t.** ₰ 3.95 – **17 rm**
 ☲ 47.50/67.50 **t.** – SB 66.00/75.00 **st.**

 🏠 **Moorview,** 104 Skipton Rd, LS29 9HE, W : ¼ m. on A 65 ✆ 600156, ≼, 🛲 – TV 🅿. ✗
 M (by arrangement) 12.95 **st.** ₰ 5.00 **10 rm** ☲ 22.00/42.00 **st.**

P.T.O. →

XXX ❀ **Box Tree**, 35-37 Church St., LS29 9DR, ✆ 608484, Fax 816793, « Ornate decor » – 🔄 AE
    ⑩ VISA
    closed Sunday dinner, Monday, 25-26 December and 1 January – **M** (booking essential)
    (dinner only and Sunday lunch)/dinner 17.50 **t.** and a la carte 24.00/43.70 **t.** ▮ 5.15
    Spec. Soufflé au fromage en robe d'amandes, Pigeonneau de Bresse aux échalotes rôti aux petits navets.
    Timbale de fraise.

X **Roberts**, 60 The Grove, LS29 8PA, ✆ 607307 – 🔄 AE ⑩ VISA
    closed Sunday, Monday and 2 weeks Christmas – **M** 11.95/14.95 **t.** and a la carte 19.95/27.45 **t.**
    ▮ 4.25.

FORD Leeds Rd ✆ 603261
PEUGEOT-TALBOT Bridge Lane ✆ 608966
VAUXHALL Skipton Rd ✆ 607606

VAUXHALL-OPEL Bradford Rd. Menston ✆ 0943
(Menston) 76122

ILLOGAN Cornwall 🔳🔳🔳 E 33 – pop. 11 782 – ✉ ✆ 0209 Redruth.
♦London 305 – Falmouth 14 – Penzance 17 – Truro 11.

🏠 **Aviary Court** ॐ, Mary's Well, TR16 4QZ, NW : ¾ m. by Alexandra Rd ✆ 842256, ⅏
    TV ☎ ℗. AE ⑩. ⅏
    M *(closed Sunday dinner)* (dinner only and Sunday lunch)/dinner 8.50 **t.** and a la carte ▮ 3.50
    – **6 rm** ⊆ 28.50/46.00 **t.**

IMPINGTON Cambs. – see Cambridge.

INGATESTONE Essex 🔳🔳🔳 V 28 – pop. 6 150 – ECD : Wednesday – ✆ 0277.
♦London 27 – Chelmsford 6.

🏠🏠 Ivy Hill, Ivy Barn Lane, Margareting, CM4 0EW, NE : 2 ¼ m. by A 12 ✆ 353040, Telex 995438,
    ⅃ heated, ⅏, X – TV ☎ ℗ – **18 rm**.

INGLETON North Yorks. 🔳🔳🔳 M 21 – pop. 1 769 – ✉ Carnforth – ✆ 052 42.
Envir. : Ribblehead Viaduct★ NE : 6 m..
🄱 Community Centre car park, Main St. ✆ 41049 (summer only).
♦London 266 – Kendal 21 – Lancaster 18 – ♦Leeds 53.

🏠 **Moorgarth Hall Country House**, New Road, LA6 3HL, SE : ¼ m. on A 65 ✆ 41946, ≼,
    ⅏ – ⅌ rm TV ℗. ⅏
    closed 2 to 31 January – **M** (dinner only and Sunday lunch in winter)/dinner 9.00 **st.**
    and a la carte ▮ 2.75 – **8 rm** ⊆ 22.00/44.00 **st.** – SB 58.00/62.00 **st.**

⋔ **Oakroyd**, Main St., LA6 3HJ, ✆ 41258, ⅏ – ⅌ rest ℗. ⅏
    M 8.50 **st.** ▮ 3.95 – **7 rm** ⊆ 15.50/35.00 **st.** – SB (winter only) 40.00/45.00 **st.**

⋔ Pines, LA6 3HN, NW : ¼ m. on A 65 ✆ 41252 – TV ℗ – **4 rm**.

INSTOW Devon 🔳🔳🔳 H 30 – see Bideford.

IPSWICH Suffolk 🔳🔳🔳 X 27 – pop. 129 661 – ECD : Monday and Wednesday – ✆ 0473.
See : St. Margaret's Church (the roof★) X **A** – Christchurch Mansion (Wolsey Art Gallery★) X **B** –
Pykenham House★ (16C) X **E.**
Envir. : Stour Valley★ (Flatford Mill★) (SW : from Ipswich by A 137 **Z**).
🄱🄸 Rushmere Heath ✆ 725648, E : 2 m. **Y.**
✈ Ipswich Airport ✆ 720111 – 🄱 Town Hall, Princes St. ✆ 258070.
♦London 76 – ♦Norwich 43.

Plan opposite

🏠🏠 **Belstead Brook** (Best Western) ॐ, Belstead Rd, IP2 9HB, SW : 2 ½ m. ✆ 684241, Telex
    987674, Fax 681249, ⅏, park – TV ☎ ℗ – 🛋 50. 🔄 AE ⑩ VISA. ⅏   **Z u**
    M *(closed Saturday lunch)* 10.95/15.00 **t.** and a la carte 18.75/27.50 **t.** ▮ 4.00 – ⊆ 6.95 –
    27 rm 64.00/74.00 **st.**, **6 suites** 85.00/105.00 **st.**

🏠🏠 **Marlborough**, Henley Rd, IP1 3SP, ✆ 257677, Fax 226927, ⅏ – TV ☎ ℗ – 🛋 40. 🔄 AE
    ⑩ VISA   **Y e**
    M (see **Marlborough rest.** below) – ⊆ 6.50 – **21 rm** 60.00/80.00 **t.**, **1 suite** 90.00 **t.** –
    SB (weekends only) 68.00/80.00 **st.**

🏠🏠 **Post House** (T.H.F.), London Rd, IP2 0UA, SW : 2 ¼ m. on A 12 ✆ 690313, Telex 987150,
    Fax 680412, ⅃ heated – ⅌ rm TV ☎ ℀ ℗ – 🛋 150. 🔄 AE ⑩ VISA   **Z a**
    M 12.95 **st.** and a la carte ▮ 6.25 – ⊆ 7.00 – **118 rm** 60.00/70.00 **st.** – SB (weekends
    only) 64.00/80.00 **st.**

🏠🏠 **Novotel**, Greyfriars Rd, IP1 1UP, ✆ 232400, Telex 987684, Fax 232414 – 🛗 ⅌ rm ▤ rest
    TV ☎ ℀ ℗ – 🛋 200. 🔄 AE ⑩ VISA   **X c**
    M 10.50/16.00 **st.** and a la carte ▮ 3.25 – ⊆ 5.50 – **101 rm** –/51.50 **st.** – SB (week-
    ends only) 72.00/80.00 **st.**

♤ **Bentley Tower**, 172 Norwich Rd, IP1 2PY, ✆ 212142 – TV ℗. 🔄 VISA. ⅏   **Y o**
    M (dinner only) 12.50 **t.** and a la carte ▮ 4.00 – **10 rm** ⊆ 35.00/45.00 **st.**

⋔ **Highview House**, 56 Belstead Rd, IP2 8BE, ✆ 688659, ⅏ – TV ℗. 🔄 VISA. ⅏   **Z c**
    M (by arrangement) 12.75 **t.** – **11 rm** ⊆ 25.00/40.00 **t.**

IPSWICH

Butter Market .... X 9
Carr Street .... X 10
Corn Hill .... X 16
Tavern Street X
Westgate Street .... X 52

Argyle Street .... X 2
Back Hamlet .... Z 3
Birkfield Drive .... Z 5
Bond Street .... X 6
Bridgwater Road .... Z 7
Chevallier Street .... Y 13
College Street .... X 15
Dogs Head Street .... X 18
Ellenbrook Road .... Z 19
Falcon Street .... X 21
Fore Hamlet .... Z 22
Franciscan Way .... X 24
Friars Street .... X 25
Grey Friars Road .... X 26
Grove Lane .... YZ 28
Handford Road .... X, Y 30
Lloyds Avenue .... X 31
Lower Orwell Street ..... X 32
Northgate Street .... X 33
Orwell Place .... X 34
Queen Street .... X 37
St. Helen's Street .... X, Y 39
St. Margarets Street .... X 40
St. Nicholas Street ..... X 41
St. Peter's Street ...... X 42
Salthouse Street .... X 43
Scrivener Drive .... Z 45
Silent Street .... X 46
Upper Orwell Street ..... X 49
Waterworks Street .... X 51
Yarmouth Road .... Y 54

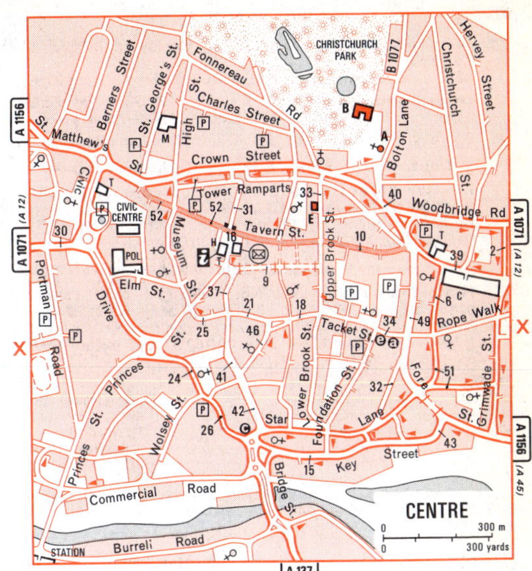

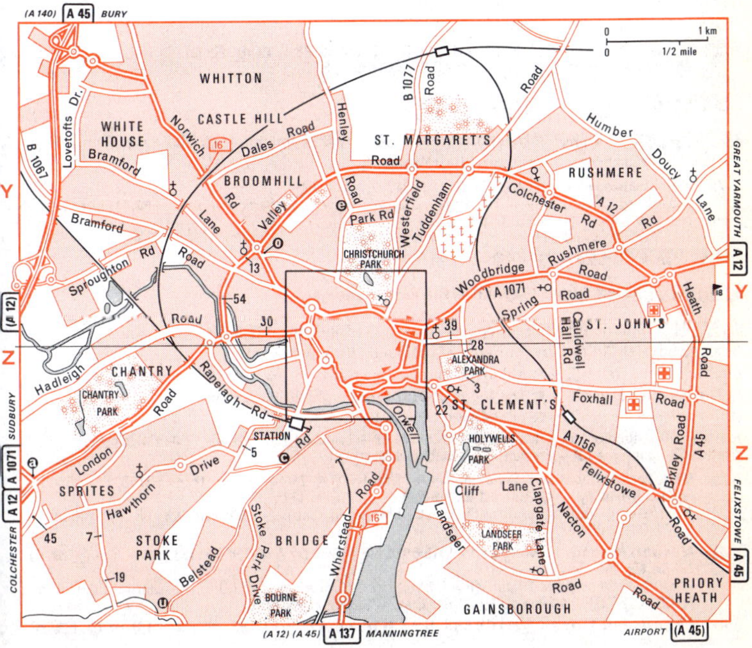

Red Lion

If the name of the hotel

is not in bold type,

on arrival ask the hotelier his prices.

XXX **Marlborough,** (at Marlborough H), Henley Rd, IP1 3SP, *&* 257677, Fax 226927, 🐎 – 🅿.
🔲 AE ⓪ *VISA*
M *(closed Saturday lunch)* 12.50/18.00 **st.** and a la carte 20.50/25.25 **st.** 🍷 3.75.

Y e

XX **Orwell House,** 4 Orwell Pl., IP4 1BB, *&* 230254 – ⇔. 🔲 AE *VISA*
closed Sunday-Monday – **M** a la carte 14.40/27.10 **st.** 🍷 3.80.

X e

XX Bombay, 6 Orwell Pl., IP4 1BB, *&* 251397, Indian rest.

X a

at Copdock SW : 4 m. on A 12 – Z – ✉ Ipswich – 🕿 047 386 Copdock :

🏨 **Ipswich Moat House** (Q.M.H.), Old London Rd, IP8 3JD, *&* 444, Telex 987207, Fax 801,
🐎 – TV ☎ 🅿 – 🔥 450. 🔲 AE ⓪ *VISA*
M *(carving lunch)* 12.20/12.60 **t.** and a la carte 15.65/27.05 🍷 4.20 – 🍽 6.95 – **74 rm**
59.50/85.00 **t.** – SB (weekends only) 70.00 **st.**

at Hintlesham W : 5 m. by A 1214 on A 1071 – Y – ✉ Ipswich – 🕿 047 387 Hintlesham :

🏨 **Hintlesham Hall** 🦢, IP8 3NS, *&* 268, Telex 98340, Fax 463, ≼, « Georgian country house
of 16C origins », 🐎, park, ✗ – ⇔ TV ☎ 🅿. 🔲 AE ⓪ *VISA*. 🐕
M *(closed Saturday lunch to non-residents)* 18.50/35.00 **st.** and a la carte 34.95/43.20 **st.**
🍷 7.50 – 🍽 7.50 – **33 rm** 🍽 85.00/160.00 **st.**, **3 suites** 225.00/300.00 **st.** – SB (except summer) 150.00/250.00 **st.**

AUDI-VW 88 Princes St. *&* 214231
AUSTIN-ROVER Barrack Lane *&* 254202
AUSTIN-ROVER Felixstowe Rd *&* 725431
BMW West End Rd *&* 212456
FIAT, LANCIA Burrel Rd *&* 690321
FORD Princess St. *&* 252525
MAZDA, SEAT Fuchsia Lane *&* 724535
MERCEDES-BENZ Raneleigh Rd *&* 232232
PEUGEOT-TALBOT, ALFA-ROMEO, DAIHATSU
Derby Rd *&* 720101

RENAULT 301-305 Norwich Rd *&* 43021
SAAB Dales Rd *&* 42547
SKODA West End Rd *&* 255461
TOYOTA 301-305 Woodbridge Rd *&* 719221
VAUXHALL-OPEL Knightsdale Rd *&* 43044
VOLVO Woodbridge Rd, Rushmere *&* 626767

🛢 ATS White Elm St. *&* 217157/52815

ISLEY WALTON Leics. – see Castle Donington.

IVINGHOE Bucks. 404 S 28 – pop. 2 517 (inc. Pitstone) – ✉ Leighton Buzzard – 🕿 0296 Cheddington – ┍₉ Wellcroft *&* 668696.
♦London 42 – Aylesbury 9 – Luton 11.

XXX **King's Head** (T.H.F.), Station Rd, LU7 9EB, *&* 668388 – ▤ 🅿. 🔲 AE ⓪ *VISA*
M 18.50 **st.** (lunch) and a la carte 20.25/33.15 **st.** 🍷 5.75.

IVY HATCH Kent – see Sevenoaks.

IXWORTH Suffolk 404 W 27 – pop. 2 121 – ✉ Bury St. Edmunds – 🕿 0359 Pakenham.
♦London 85 – ♦Cambridge 35 – ♦Ipswich 25 – ♦Norwich 36.

XX **Theobalds,** 68 High St., IP31 2HJ, *&* 31707 – 🔲 *VISA*
closed lunch Saturday and Monday, Sunday dinner and Bank Holidays – **M** 11.95 **t.** (lunch)
and a la carte 17.50/20.50 **t.** 🍷 4.25.

JERVAULX ABBEY North Yorks. – see Masham.

JEVINGTON East Sussex 404 U 31 – see Eastbourne.

KENDAL Cumbria 402 L 21 – pop. 23 710 – ECD : Thursday – 🕿 0539.
See : Abbot Hall Art Gallery (Museum of Lakeland Life and Industry★) *AC*.
Envir. : Levens Hall★ (Elizabethan) *AC* and Topiary Garden★ *AC*, SW : 5 ½ m.
┍₁₈ The Heights *&* 24079 – ┍₉ The Riggs *&* 0587 (Sedbergh) 20993, E : 9 m.
🅸 Town Hall, Highgate *&* 25758 or 33333 ext 380 (weekdays).
♦London 270 – Bradford 64 – Burnley 63 – ♦Carlisle 49 – Lancaster 22 – ♦Leeds 72 – ♦Middlesbrough 77 – ♦Newcastle-upon-Tyne 104 – Preston 44 – Sunderland 88.

🏨 **Woolpack** (Swallow), Stricklandgate, LA9 4ND, *&* 23852, Group Telex 53168, Fax 28608 –
⇔ rm TV ☎ 🅿 – 🔥 120. 🔲 AE ⓪ *VISA*
M *(carving lunch)/dinner* 15.00 **st.** and a la carte – **53 rm** 🍽 55.00/70.00 **st.** –
SB 75.00/80.00 **st.**

🏠 **Garden House,** Fowling Lane, LA9 6PH, NE : ½ m. by A 685 *&* 731131, 🐎 – ⇔ TV ☎ 🅿.
🔲 AE ⓪ *VISA*. 🐕
closed 26 December-10 January – **M** *(closed Sunday dinner)* (lunch residents only)/dinner
15.00 **st.** 🍷 3.50 – **10 rm** 🍽 39.00/54.00 **st.** – SB 68.00/75.00 **st.**

🏠 **Lane Head House** 🦢, LA9 5RJ, S : 1 ¾ m. on A 6 *&* 731283, ≼, 🐎 – TV ☎ 🅿. 🔲 *VISA*.
🐕
M (by arrangement) 12.50 **t.** – **7 rm** 🍽 30.00/55.00 **t.** – SB (November-March) (except Sunday, Christmas and New Year) 60.00/75.00 **st.**

XX **Castle Dairy,** 26 Wildman St., LA9 6EN, *&* 21170, English rest., « Part 13C and 16C »
closed Sunday, Monday, Tuesday and August – **M** (booking essential)(dinner only) 15.00
🍷 4.00.

at Underbarrow W : 3 ½ m. on Crosthwaite rd – ✉ Kendal – ☎ 044 88 Crosthwaite :

XX **Tullythwaite House** ⑤ with rm, LA8 8BB, S : ¾ m. by Brigsteer rd ℰ 397, 🚗 – ⊱✕ rest 📺 🅿. 🖅 VISA. 🎇
closed Sunday-Tuesday and February – **M** (dinner only and Sunday lunch)/dinner 20.00 **t.** 🍷 3.50 – **3 rm** ⴾ 45.00/65.00 **t.**

FIAT 113 Stricklandgate ℰ 20967
FORD Mintsfeet Ind. Est. ℰ 23534
FORD, MERCEDES-BENZ Ings ℰ 0539 (Staveley) 821442
RENAULT Kirkland ℰ 22211

VAUXHALL Sandes Av. ℰ 24420
VOLVO Station Rd ℰ 31313
VW-AUDI, NSU, PORSCHE Longpool ℰ 24331

🛞 ATS Mintsfeet Est. ℰ 21559/23802

KENILWORTH Warw. 403 404 P 26 – pop. 18 782 – ECD : Monday and Thursday – ☎ 0926.
See : Castle★ (12C) *AC* – 🏌 Crew Lane ℰ 58517 – 🛈 Library, 11 Smalley Pl. ℰ 52595.
♦London 102 – ♦Birmingham 19 – ♦Coventry 5 – Warwick 5.

🏨 **De Montfort** (De Vere), The Square, CV8 1ED, ℰ 55944, Telex 311012, Fax 57830 – 🛗 ⊱✕ rest 📺 ☎ 🅿 – 🛝. 🖅 AE ⓪ VISA
M 11.00/12.75 **st.** and a la carte 🍷 3.50 – **94 rm** ⴾ 69.00/97.00 **st.**, **1 suite** 166.00 **st.** – SB (weekends only) 59.00 **st.**

🏨 **Clarendon House,** 6-8 High St., Old Town, CV8 1LZ, ℰ 57668, Telex 311240 – 📺 ☎ 🅿 – 🛝 150. 🖅 VISA
M (bar lunch Monday to Saturday)/dinner 13.50 **t.** and a la carte 🍷 4.25 – **30 rm** ⴾ 41.00/60.00 **t.** – SB (weekends only) 65.00/70.00 **st.**

⋔ **Castle Laurels,** 22 Castle Rd, CV8 1NG, ℰ 56179 – ⊱✕ rest 📺 🅿. 🎇
M (by arrangement) 10.00 **st.** 🍷 1.95 – **12 rm** ⴾ 22.00/37.00 **st.**

⋔ **Abbey,** 41 Station Rd, CV8 1JD, ℰ 512707 ⊱✕ rest. 🎇
M 7.00 **s.** – **7 rm** ⴾ 16.00/33.50 **st.**

⋔ **Enderley** without rest., 20 Queens Rd, CV8 1JQ, ℰ 55388 – 🎇
5 rm ⴾ 19.00/30.00.

XX **Bosquet,** 97a Warwick Rd, CV8 1HP, ℰ 52463, French rest. – 🖅 AE VISA
closed Sunday, Monday, 3 weeks July-August, Christmas-New Year and Bank Holidays – **M** (lunch by arrangement)/dinner 15.50 **t.** and a la carte 20.00/25.00.

XX **Diment,** 121-123 Warwick Rd, CV8 1HP, ℰ 53763 – 🅿. 🖅 AE ⓪ VISA
closed Saturday lunch, Sunday, Monday, 1 week Easter, first 3 weeks August and Bank Holidays – **M** 8.25 **t.** (lunch) and a la carte 13.15/18.85 **t.** 🍷 3.95.

X **Portofino,** 14 Talisman Sq., CV8 1JB, ℰ 57186, Italian rest. – 🖅 AE ⓪ VISA
M *(closed Monday lunch, Sunday and Bank Holidays)* 12.00/22.00 **t.** and a la carte 12.30/19.95 **st.** 🍷 3.95.

X **Ana's Bistro,** 121-123 Warwick Rd, CV8 1HP, ℰ 53763 – 🅿. 🖅 AE ⓪ VISA
closed Sunday, Monday, 1 week Easter, first 3 weeks August and Bank Holidays – **M** (dinner only) a la carte 7.45/10.90 **t.** 🍷 2.85.

SUZUKI Whitemoor Rd ℰ 513131

TOYOTA, CITROEN Warwick Rd ℰ 54722

KENNFORD Devon 403 J 32 – see Exeter.

KERESLEY West Midlands 403 404 P 26 – see Coventry.

KESWICK Cumbria 402 K 20 – pop. 4 777 – ECD : Wednesday – ☎ 076 87.
See : Derwent Water★★ Y Envir. : Castlerigg (stone circle) ⁂★, E : 2 m. Y A.
🏌 Threlkeld Hall ℰ 83324, E : 4 m. by A 66 Y – 🛈 Moot Hall, Market Sq. ℰ 74101.
♦London 294 – ♦Carlisle 31 – Kendal 30.

Plan on next page

🏨 **Brundholme Country House** ⑤, Brundholme Rd, CA12 4NL, ℰ 74495, ≤, 🚗 – ⊱✕ rest 📺 ☎ 🅿. 🖅 VISA. 🎇   Y e
closed 20 December-1 February – **M** 12.00/18.00 **t.** and a la carte – **11 rm** ⴾ 30.00/100.00 **t.** – SB 80.00/120.00 **st.**

🏨 **Grange Country House** ⑤, Manor Brow, Ambleside Rd, CA12 4BA, ℰ 72500, ≤, 🚗 – ⊱✕ rest 📺 ☎ 🅿. VISA. 🎇   Y u
closed mid November-mid February except Christmas and New Year – **M** (bar lunch)/dinner 13.50 **t.** 🍷 3.90 – **11 rm** ⴾ 30.00/76.50 **t.** – SB 62.00/72.00 **st.**

🏨 **Dale Head Hall** ⑤, Thirlmere, CA12 4TN, SE : 5 ¾ m. ℰ 72478, ≤ Lake Thirlmere, 🚗 – ⊱✕ ☎ 🅿. 🖅 VISA. 🎇   by A 591   Y
M (dinner only) 15.00 **t.** 🍷 4.50 – **9 rm** ⴾ 53.50/77.00 **t.**

🏨 **Gales Country House** ⑤, Underskiddaw, CA12 4PL, NW : 1 ¾ m. on Ormathwaite rd ℰ 72413, ≤, 🚗 – ⊱✕ rest 🅿. 🖅 VISA. 🎇   by A 591   Y
April-October – **M** (dinner only) 12.00 **st.** 🍷 3.75 – **13 rm** ⴾ 20.00/40.00 **st.**

🏨 **Lyzzick Hall** ⑤, Underskiddaw, CA12 4PY, NW : 2 ½ m. ℰ 72277, ≤, ⌇ heated, 🚗 – 📺 ☎ 🅿. 🖅 AE ⓪ VISA. 🎇   by A 591   Y
closed February – **M** 8.50/15.50 **t.** – **20 rm** ⴾ 22.00/44.00 **t.** – SB (spring and winter) 59.00/66.00 **st.**

P.T.O. →

KESWICK

Main Street . . . . **Z**
Station Street . . . . . . **Z**

Bank Street . . . . **Z** 2
Borrowdale Road . . . **Z** 3
Brackenrigg Drive . . **Z** 5
Brundholme Road . . **Y** 6
Chestnut Hill . . . . . . **Y** 8
Church Street . . . . . . **Z** 10
Crosthwaite Road . . **Y** 12
Derwent Street . . . . . **Z** 13
High Hill . . . . **Z** 14
Manor Brow . . . . . . **Y** 17
Market Square . . . . . **Z** 18
Otley Road . . . . **Z** 20
Police Station
  Court . . . . **Z** 22
Ratcliffe Place . . . . . . **Z** 23
St. Herbert
  Street . . . . **Z** 24
Standish Street . . . . . **Z** 25
Station Street . . . . . . **Z** 26
The Crescent . . . . . . **Z** 27
The Hawthorns . . . . . **Y** 29
The Headlands . . . . . **Z** 31
Tithebarn Street . . . . **Z** 32

**North is at the top
on all town plans.**

*Les plans de villes
sont disposés
le Nord en haut.*

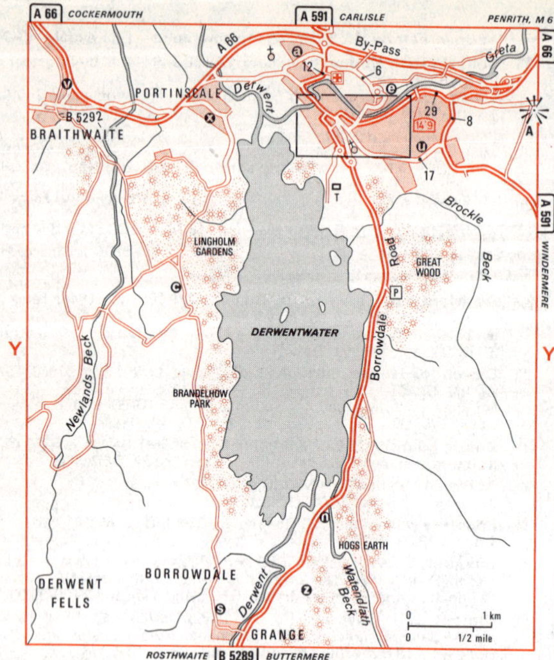

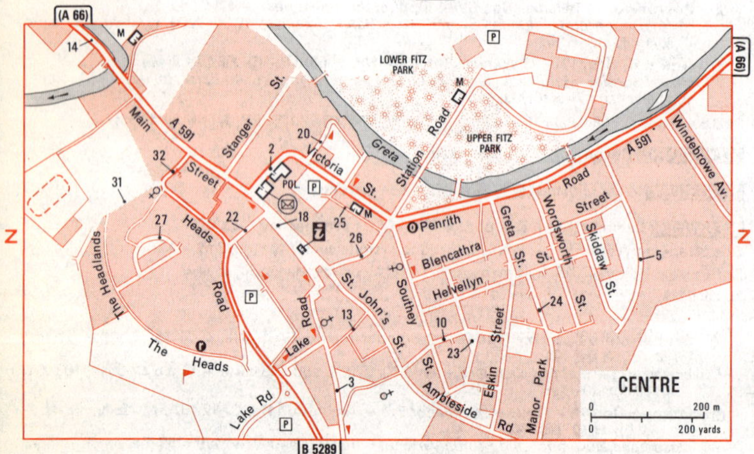

Highfield, The Heads, CA12 5ER, ☎ 72508, ⇐ – ✕ rest **P**   **Z r**
March-October – **M** 10.00 t. ▐ 3.00 – **19 rm** ☲ 14.00/20.50 t.

Brackenrigg Country House, Thirlmere, CA12 4TF, SE : 3 m. ☎ 72258, ⇐ – ✕ rest **P**
⊞   by A 591   **Y**
March-October – **M** 9.50 – **6 rm** ☲ 18.50/40.00.

Linnett Hill, 4 Penrith Rd, CA12 4HF, ☎ 73109 – ✕ TV **P**. ◫ *VISA*   **Z o**
M 8.00 t. ▐ 3.75 – **8 rm** ☲ 18.25/32.50 t. – SB (except summer) 40.00/42.00 st.

Lairbeck ⊗, Vicarage Hill, CA12 5QB, ☎ 73373, ⇐ – ✕ rest TV **P**. ◫ *VISA* ⊞   **Y a**
M 10.00 t. ▐ 3.50 – **15 rm** ☲ 17.50/41.00 t. – SB (except winter) 42.00/48.00 st.

at Borrowdale S : 3 ¼ m. on B 5289 – ⊠ Keswick – ✆ 059 684 Borrowdale :

🏰 Stakis Lodore Swiss (Stakis) ≫, CA12 5UX, ℰ 285, Telex 64305, Fax 343, ≼ Derwent Water and mountains, ⅃ heated, ▨, 🐎, park, ✕, squash – ⊯ ⤬ rest ⊤⊽ ☎ ⇦ ℗. ⛰ ⒜Ⓔ ⓪ *VISA* ℁   Y n
closed 3 January-15 February – ☲ 7.25 – **70 rm** 55.00/75.00 st., **1 suite** 130.00 st.

⋔ **Greenbank** ≫, CA12 5UY, ℰ 215, ≼, 🐎 – ⤬ rm ℗. ℁   Y z
closed December – **M** 9.00 st. 🍾 2.70 – **10 rm** ☲ 16.00/36.00 st. – SB (mid March-December) 42.00/50.00 st.

at Grange-in-Borrowdale S : 4 ¾ m. by B 5289 – ⊠ Keswick – ✆ 059 684 Borrowdale :

🏠 **Borrowdale Gates Country House** ≫, CA12 5UQ, ℰ 204, ≼, 🐎 – ⤬ rest ⊤⊽ ℗. ⛰ ⒜Ⓔ ⓪. ℁   Y s
M (bar lunch)/dinner 13.00 t. 🍾 2.10 – **23 rm** ☲ 25.00/45.00 t. – SB (winter only) 54.00/60.00 st.

at Rosthwaite S : 6 m. on B 5289 – Y – ⊠ Keswick – ✆ 076 87 Borrowdale :

🏠 Scafell ≫, CA12 5XB, ℰ 208, ≼, 🐎 – ☎ ℗
20 rm.

⋔ **Hazel Bank** ≫, CA12 5XB, ℰ 77248, ≼, 🐎 – ⤬ rest ℗
closed November-mid March – **9 rm** ☲ (dinner included) 27.00/58.00 st.

⋔ **Royal Oak**, CA12 5XB, ℰ 214 – ⤬ rest ℗. ⛰
closed last week November-28 December – **12 rm** ☲ (dinner included) 24.00/54.00 t. – SB (January-March) (weekdays only) 36.00 st.

at Seatoller S : 8 m. on B 5289 – Y – ⊠ Keswick – ✆ 059 684 Borrowdale :

⋔ **Seatoller House**, Borrowdale, CA12 5XN, ℰ 218, ≼ Borrowdale, 🐎 – ⤬ ℗
April-October – **9 rm** ☲ (dinner included) 27.50/50.00 t.

at Portinscale W : 1 ½ m. by A 66 – ⊠ ✆ 076 87 Keswick :

⋔ **Derwent Cottage** ≫, CA12 5RF, ℰ 74838, 🐎 – ⤬ rest ℗. ℁   Y x
Mid March-mid November – **M** 11.00 st. 🍾 3.50 – **5 rm** ☲ 25.00/42.00 st.

⋔ **Swinside Lodge** ≫, Newlands, CA12 5UE, S : 1 ½ m. on Grange Rd ℰ 72948, ≼ Catbells and Newlands Valley, 🐎 – ℗. ℁   Y c
February-October – **8 rm** ☲ (dinner included) 25.50/51.00 st.

at Braithwaite W : 2 m. by A 66 on B 5292 – Y – ⊠ Keswick – ✆ 0768778 Braithwaite :

🏰 **Middle Ruddings**, CA12 5RY, on A 66 ℰ 436, 🐎 – ⤬ ⊤⊽ ☎ ℗. ⛰ *VISA* ℁   Y v
M (bar lunch)/dinner 13.50 t. 🍾 3.40 – **13 rm** ☲ 35.00/60.00 t. – SB 68.50/80.00 st.

⋔ **Cottage in The Woods** ≫, Whinlatter Pass, CA12 5TW, NW : 1 ¾ m. on B 5292 ℰ 409, ≼, 🐎 – ⤬ ℗. ℁
closed December and January – **M** 12.50 t. 🍾 2.50 – **7 rm** ☲ 30.00/47.00 t. – SB 56.00/60.00 st.

at Thornthwaite W : 3 ½ m. by A 66 – ⊠ Keswick – ✆ 059 682 Braithwaite :

⋔ **Thwaite Howe** ≫, CA12 5SA, ℰ 281, ≼ Skiddaw and Derwent Valley, 🐎 – ⤬ rest ⊤⊽ ℗. ℁   Y i
April-October – **M** 12.50 t. 🍾 3.00 – **8 rm** ☲ 38.50/52.00 t.

AUSTIN-ROVER High Hill ℰ 72768   FIAT Lake Rd ℰ 72064

KETTERING Northants. 🔢 R 26 – pop. 44 758 – ECD : Thursday – ⊠ ✆ 0536.
🛈 Coach House, Sheep St. ℰ 410266/410333.
♦London 83 – Bedford 25 – ♦Leicester 27 – Northampton 14.

⋔ **Dairy Farm** ≫, 12 St. Andrew's Lane, Cranford St. Andrew, NN14 4AQ, E : 4 m. by A 6 on A 604 ℰ 053 678 (Cranford) 273, « Thatched Jacobean farmhouse » – ℗. ℁
closed Christmas-New Year – **M** 9.00 s. – **3 rm** ☲ 18.00/36.00 st.

FORD Ruswell Rd ℰ 512464   ⓜ ATS Northfield Av. ℰ 512832
NISSAN Northfield Av. ℰ 84848
RENAULT Windmill Av. ℰ 512392

KETTLEWELL North Yorks. 🔢 N 21 – pop. 361 (inc. Starbotton) – ECD : Tuesday and Thursday – ⊠ Skipton – ✆ 075 676.
♦London 237 – Bradford 33 – ♦Leeds 40.

🏠 Racehorses, Town Foot, BD23 5QZ, ℰ 233 – ⊤⊽ ℗
15 rm.

⋔ Bluebell, Town Foot, BD23 5QX, ℰ 230 – ⊤⊽
7 rm.

at Starbotton NW : 1 ¾ m. on B 6160 – ⊠ Skipton – ✆ 075 676 Kettlewell :

⋔ **Hilltop** ≫, BD23 5HY, ℰ 321, « 17C Stone built house », 🐎 – ⤬ rm ⊤⊽ ℗. ⛰ ⒜Ⓔ ⓪ *VISA* ℁
closed January-mid March – **M** 12.50 st. 🍾 3.20 – **5 rm** ☲ 31.00/43.00 st. – SB 63.00 st.

KEXBY North Yorks. – see York.

KEYSTON Cambs. **404** S 26 – pop. 252 (inc. Bythorn) – ⊠ Huntingdon – ✆ 080 14 Bythorn.
♦London 75 – ♦Cambridge 29 – Northampton 24.

  XX **Pheasant Inn**, Village Loop Rd, PE18 0RE, ✆ 241 – ℗. 🔊 AE ① VISA
    M a la carte 8.20/17.90 **st.**

KIDDERMINSTER Heref. and Worc. **403** **404** N 26 – pop. 50 385 – ECD : Wednesday –
✆ 0562.
🛅 Russel Rd ✆ 822303.
♦London 139 – ♦Birmingham 17 – Shrewsbury 34 – Worcester 15.

  🏨 **Gainsborough House** (Best Western), Bewdley Hill, DY11 6BS, SW : 1 m. on A 456
    ✆ 820041, Telex 333058, Fax 66179, 🚗 – 🛏 rm ▤ rest 📺 ☎ ℗ – 🔥 300. 🔊 AE ①
    VISA
    M 7.25/11.95 **st.** and a la carte – **42 rm** � 46.50/72.00 **st.** – SB (wee-
    kends only) 49.00/59.00 **st.**

    at Stone SE : 2 ½ m. on A 448 – ⊠ Kidderminster – ✆ 056 283 Chaddesley Corbett :

  🏰 **Stone Manor** ⑤, DY10 4PJ, ✆ 555, Telex 335661, Fax 834, ≼, ⅃, 🚗, park, ✹ – 📺 ☎
    ℗. 🔊 AE ① VISA
    M 10.25 t. (lunch) and a la carte 11.70/23.10 t. ◊ 4.25 – ⊑ 6.50 – **53 rm** 57.50/85.00 t. –
    SB (weekends only) 88.00 **st.**

    at Chaddesley Corbett SE : 4 ½ m. on A 448 – ⊠ Kidderminster – ✆ 056 283 Chaddesley
    Corbett :

  🏰 **Brockencote Hall** ⑤, DY10 4PY, ✆ 876, Telex 333431, ≼, « 19C mansion in park » – 📺
    ☎ ℗. 🔊 AE ① VISA ✹
    closed 26 December-mid January – **M** (closed Saturday lunch and Sunday dinner) 16.50/
    38.00 **st.** and a la carte 25.50/34.00 **st.** ◊ 6.50 – **9 rm** ⊑ 58.00/95.00 **st.** – SB (week-
    ends only) 113.00/128.00 **st.**

AUSTIN-ROVER Churchfields ✆ 752566
BMW Mustow Green ✆ 056 283 (Chaddesley Cor-
bett) 811
CITROEN, FIAT Worcester Rd ✆ 820202
FORD Worcester Rd ✆ 820028
LADA, PROTON Plimsoll St. ✆ 822145
PEUGEOT-TALBOT Mill St. ✆ 824961

SKODA Mill St. ✆ 823708
VAUXHALL-OPEL Churchfields ✆ 68427
VOLVO Stourport Rd ✆ 515832
VW-AUDI Worcester Rd ✆ 823660

⑩ ATS Park St. ✆ 744668/744843

KIDLINGTON Oxon. **403** **404** Q 28 – see Oxford.

KILSBY Northants. **403** **404** Q 26 – see Rugby (Warw.).

KILVE Somerset – pop. 324 – ✆ 027 874 Holford.
♦London 172 – ♦Bristol 49 – Minehead 13 – Taunton 23.

  🏠 **Meadow House** ⑤, Sea Lane, TA5 1EG, ✆ 546, « Country house atmosphere », 🚗 –
    🛏 rest 📺 ☎ ℗. 🔊 AE VISA ✹
    closed Christmas and New Year – **M** (dinner only) 18.00 **st.** ◊ 3.90 – **5 rm** ⊑ 55.50/74.00 **st.**,
    2 suites 84.00 **st.**

  ♟ **Hood Arms**, TA5 1EA, ✆ 210, 🚗 – 📺 ☎ ℗. 🔊 VISA
    closed Christmas Night – **M** (closed Sunday to Tuesday) a la carte 7.00/12.20 t. ◊ 2.20 –
    5 rm ⊑ 29.00/50.00 t. – SB (weekends only) 60.00 **st.**

KINGHAM Oxon. **403** **404** P 28 – pop. 576 – ECD : Wednesday – ✆ 060 871.
♦London 81 – Gloucester 32 – ♦Oxford 25.

  🏨 **Mill House** ⑤, OX7 6UH, ✆ 8188, Fax 492, 🚗 – 📺 ☎ ℗. 🔊 AE ① VISA ✹
    M 12.00/16.95 t. and a la carte ◊ 5.40 – **21 rm** ⊑ 42.50/85.00 t. – SB 98.00/118.00 **st.**

KINGSBRIDGE Devon **403** I 33 The West Country G. – pop. 4 164 – ECD : Thursday – ✆ 0548.
See : Site★ – Boat Trip to Salcombe★★ *AC*.
🛈 The Quay ✆ 3195.
♦London 236 – Exeter 36 – ♦Plymouth 20 – Torquay 21.

  ♟ **Kings Arms**, Fore St., TQ7 1AB, ✆ 2071, 🔊 – ℗ – 🔥 100. 🔊 VISA
    M 12.00 t. (dinner) and a la carte – **11 rm** ⊑ 25.00/50.00 t. – SB (November-March)
    52.50/66.00 **st.**

    at Goveton NE : 2 ½ m. by A 381 – ⊠ ✆ 0548 Kingsbridge :

  🏨 **Buckland-Tout-Saints** ⑤, TQ7 2DS, ✆ 3055, Fax 6261, ≼, « Queen Anne mansion »,
    🚗, park – 🛏 rest 📺 ☎ ℗. 🔊 AE ① VISA ✹
    M (lunch by arrangement)/dinner 30.00 **st.** ◊ 6.50 – **12 rm** ⊑ 75.00/145.00 **st.** – SB 125.00/
    180.00 **st.**

at Chillington E: 5 m. on A 379 – ⊠ Kingsbridge – ☎ 054 853 Frogmore :

🏠 **White House,** TQ7 2JX, ℰ 0548 (Kingsbridge) 580580, 쿄 – ⋈ rest ⊡ Ⓟ
Easter-October and 23 to 31 December – **M** (bar lunch residents only)/dinner 9.95 **st.** 🍾 1.90
– **8 rm** ☲ 27.60/53.00 **t.**

🏠 **Oddicombe House,** TQ7 2JD, ℰ 53234, ⌁, 쿄 – ⋈ rest Ⓟ
Easter-October – **M** (bar lunch by arrangement)/dinner 12.00 **t.** 🍾 3.50 – **10 rm** ☲ 21.00/
25.00 **t.** – SB 64.00/74.00 **st.**

✗ **Chillington Inn** with rm, TQ7 2JS, ℰ 0548 (Kingsbridge) 580244 – ⊡, ▨ 亜 𝗩𝗜𝗦𝗔
M *(closed Monday)* (bar lunch)/dinner 10.00 **t.** and a la carte 12.50/18.00 **t.** 🍾 3.50 – **3 rm**
16.00/17.50 **t.** – SB (except summer) 54.00/76.00 **st.**

at Torcross E : 7 m. on A 379 – ⊠ ☎ 0548 Kingsbridge :

⋔ **The Venture,** TQ7 2TQ, ℰ 580314, ⬉ – ⊡
March-mid October – **M** 9.35 **t.** 🍾 2.50 – **5 rm** ☲ 15.95/31.90 **t.**

at East Portlemouth S : 6 ½ m. by A 379 – ⊠ ☎ 054 884 Salcombe :

🏠 **Gara Rock** ⬉, TQ8 8PH, SE : ½ m. ℰ 2342, ⬉, ⌁ heated, 쿄, park, ✗ – Ⓟ. ▨ 𝗩𝗜𝗦𝗔
Easter-October – **M** (bar lunch)/dinner 11.50 **t.** and a la carte – **16 rm** ☲ 29.00/68.00 **t.**

at Thurlestone W : 4 m. by A 381 – ⊠ ☎ 0548 Kingsbridge :

🏛 **Thurlestone** (Best Western) ⬉, TQ7 3NN, ℰ 560382, Fax 560382, ⬉, ⌁ heated, ▨, ▨₉,
쿄, park, ✗, squash – 劏 ⋈ rest 🟰 rest ⊡ ☎ Ⓟ – 🏛 50. ▨ 亜 ⓞ 𝗩𝗜𝗦𝗔
closed 3 to 18 January – **M** 9.75/18.50 **st.** and a la carte 🍾 4.25 – **68 rm** ☲ 43.00/145.20 **st.** –
SB (13 November-22 March) 92.00/118.00 **st.**

at Bantham W : 5 m. by A 379 – ⊠ ☎ 0548 Kingsbridge :

⚓ **Sloop Inn,** TQ7 3AJ, ℰ 560489 – ⊡ Ⓟ
M a la carte 9.30/10.90 **t.** 🍾 2.60 – **5 rm** ☲ 22.00/40.00 **t.** – SB 55.00/59.00 **st.**

AUSTIN-ROVER, SUZUKI   The Quay ℰ 2323   ⓐ ATS   Union Rd ℰ 3247

KINGSEY Bucks. – see Thame (Oxon.).

☛ *Pour être inscrit au guide Michelin*
- pas de piston,
- pas de pot-de-vin !

KINGSKERSWELL Devon ▦▦▦ J 32 – pop. 3 471 – ⊠ Torquay – ☎ 080 47.
♦London 219 – Exeter 21 – ♦Plymouth 33 – Torquay 4.

✗✗ **Pitt House,** 2 Church End Rd, TQ12 5DS, ℰ 3374, « 15C Dower house », 쿄 – ⋈ Ⓟ. ▨
亜 𝗩𝗜𝗦𝗔
closed 2 weeks January-February, 2 weeks August-September and Bank Holidays –
M *(closed Monday and Saturday lunch and Sunday)* a la carte 13.50/20.90 **t.** 🍾 4.10.

KING'S LYNN Norfolk ▦▦▦ ▦▦▦ V 25 – pop. 37 323 – ECD : Wednesday – ☎ 0553.
See : St. Margaret's Church★ (17C, chancel 13C) – St. Nicholas' Chapel★ (Gothic).
Envir. : Houghton Hall★★ (18C) *AC*, NE : 15 m. – Sandringham House★ and park★★ *AC*, NE :
6 m. – Holkham Hall★★ – Oxburgh Hall★★ – St. Peter's Church★.
▦ Castle Rising ℰ 87654, NE : 4 m. by A 164.
🛈 The Old Gaol House, Saturday Market Place ℰ 763044.
♦London 103 – ♦Cambridge 45 – ♦Leicester 75 – ♦Norwich 44.

🏛 **Duke's Head** (T.H.F.), Tuesday Market Pl., PE30 1JS, ℰ 774996, Telex 817349, Fax 763556
– 劏 ⋈ rm ⊡ ☎ Ⓟ – 🏛 180. ▨ 亜 ⓞ 𝗩𝗜𝗦𝗔
M 16.00 **st.** (dinner) and a la carte 🍾 3.95 – ☲ 7.60 – **72 rm** 60.00/90.00 **st.** – SB (weekends only) 70.00/90.00 **st.**

🏛 **Knights Hill** (Best Western), Knights Hill Village, PE30 3HQ, NE : 4 ½ m. on A 148 at
junction with A 149 ℰ 675566, Telex 818118, Fax 675568 – ⊡ ☎ Ⓟ – 🏛 300. ▨ 亜
ⓞ 𝗩𝗜𝗦𝗔
M (dinner only) 12.75 **st.** and a la carte 12.45/18.00 **st.** – ☲ 5.95 – **37 rm** 50.00/70.00 **st.** –
SB (weekends only) 60.00/80.00 **st.**

🏛 **Butterfly,** Beveridge Way, PE30 4NB, S : 2 ¼ m. by Hardwick Rd at junction of A 10 and
A 47 ℰ 771707, Telex 818313, Fax 768027 – ⋈ rest ⊡ ☎ Ⓟ – 🏛 40. ▨ 亜 ⓞ 𝗩𝗜𝗦𝗔
ⓢ
M 9.00 **st.** and a la carte 🍾 2.95 – ☲ 4.50 – **50 rm** 49.50/99.00 **st.** – SB (weekends
only) 60.00 **st.**

🏠 Globe (B.C.B.), Tuesday Market Pl., PE30 1EZ, ℰ 772617 – ⊡ ☎ ⇌ Ⓟ. ⓢ
40 rm.

⋔ **Russet House,** 53 Goodwins Rd, PE30 5PE, ℰ 773098, 쿄 – ⋈ rest ⊡ ☎ Ⓟ. ▨ ⓞ 𝗩𝗜𝗦𝗔
ⓢ
closed 22 December-14 January – **M** 12.50 **t.** 🍾 3.50 – **12 rm** ☲ 26.50/55.00 **t.**

at *Grimston* NE : 6 ¼ m. by A 148 – ⊠ King's Lynn – ☎ 0485 Hillington :

🏰 **Congham Hall** ⚘, Lynn Rd, PE32 1AH, ℰ 600250, Telex 81508, ≼, « Country house atmosphere », ⤮ heated, ⚘, park, ✕ – ⤬ rest ⊤⊽ ☎ 🅿. 🔺 🅰🅴 ⓞ 𝘝𝘐𝘚𝘈. ✹
M *(closed lunch Saturday and Bank Holidays)* 12.50/25.00 **t.** and a la carte ⌕ 4.60 – ☲ 2.00 – **10 rm** 65.00/98.00 **t.**, **1 suite** 85.50/130.00 **t.** – SB (weekends only) 125.00/160.00 **st.**

at *Tottenhill* S : 5 ¼ m. on A 10 – ⊠ ☎ 0553 Kings Lynn :

⋔ **Oakwood House,** PE33 0RH, ℰ 810256, ⚘ – ⊤⊽ 🅿. 🔺 𝘝𝘐𝘚𝘈
M 8.80 **st.** ⌕ 3.95 – **8 rm** ☲ 20.00/39.00 **st.** – SB 42.00/68.00 **st.**

AUSTIN-ROVER, LAND-ROVER, RANGE-ROVER   VAUXHALL-OPEL North St. ℰ 773861
Hardwick Ind. Est. ℰ 763133
RELIANT, MAZDA Valingers Rd ℰ 772255   ⓦ ATS 4 Oldmeadow Rd, Hardwick Rd Trading Est.
RENAULT Hardwick Rd ℰ 772644   ℰ 774035/6
TOYOTA Tottenhill ℰ 810306

KING'S NORTON West Midlands 🆂🅾🅸 ⑩ 🆂🅾🆄 ⑳ – see Birmingham.

KINGSTON Devon 🆂🅾🅳 I 33 – pop. 317 – ⊠ ☎ 0548 Kingsbridge.
♦London 237 – Exeter 41 – ♦Plymouth 11.

⋔ **Trebles Cottage** ⚘, TQ7 4PT, ℰ 810268, ⚘ – ⊤⊽ 🅿. 𝘝𝘐𝘚𝘈
M 9.50 **t.** ⌕ 3.25 – **5 rm** ☲ 27.50/38.50 **t.**

When looking for a quiet hotel
use the maps found in the introductory pages
or look for establishments with the sign ⚘ or ⚘.

KINGSTON-UPON-HULL Humberside 🆂🅾🅸 S 22 – pop. 322 144 – ECD : Monday and Thursday – ☎ 0482 Hull.

Envir. : Burton Constable Hall★ (16C) *AC*, NE : 8 m. by A 165 Z – ⛳ Springhead Park, Willerby Rd ℰ 656309, W : by Spring Bank West Z – ⛳ Sutton Park, Salthouse Rd ℰ 781954, E : 3 m. Z.

✈ Humberside Airport : ℰ 0652 (Barnetby) 688456, S : 19 m. by A 63 Z and A 15 via Humber Bridge – Terminal : Coach Service.

⛴ Shipping connections with the Continent : to The Netherlands (Rotterdam) and Belgium (Zeebrugge) (North Sea Ferries).

🄸 Central Library, Albion St. ℰ 223344 – King George Dock, Hedon Rd ℰ 702118 – 75-76 Carr Lane ℰ 223559.

♦London 183 – ♦Leeds 61 – ♦Nottingham 94 – ♦Sheffield 68.

Plan on next page

🏨 Marina Post House (T.H.F.), Castle St., HU1 2BX, ℰ 225221, Telex 592777, Fax 213299, 🔺 –
⬧ ⤬ rm ⊤⊽ ☎ ♿ 🅿 – ⚶ 120. 🔺 🅰🅴 ⓞ 𝘝𝘐𝘚𝘈   Y **n**
M 10.25/14.50 **st.** and a la carte – ☲ 7.60 – **99 rm**.

🏰 Stakis Paragon (Stakis), Paragon St., HU1 3PJ, ℰ 26462, Telex 592431, Fax 213460 – ⬧
⤬ rm ⊤⊽ ☎ ♿ – ⚶   Y **e**
125 rm.

🏛 Campanile, Beverley Rd, Freetown Way, HU2 9AN, ℰ 25530, Telex 592840 – ⊤⊽ ☎ ♿ 🅿 –
⚶   X **a**
49 rm.

⋔ **Earlsmere,** 76-78 Sunnybank, off Spring Bank West, HU3 1LQ, ℰ 41977 – ⊤⊽. ✹   Z **i**
M (by arrangement) 12.00 **st.** ⌕ 3.00 – **15 rm** ☲ 17.25/40.25 **st.**

⋔ **Ashford** without rest., 125 Park Av., HU5 3EX, ℰ 492849 – 🅿. ✹   Z **a**
closed Christmas and New Year – **6 rm** ☲ 13.00/24.00 **s.**

⋔ **Parkwood,** 113 Princes Av., HU5 3JL, ℰ 445610 – ⊤⊽. 🔺 𝘝𝘐𝘚𝘈   Z **c**
M (by arrangement) approx. 12.30 **st.** ⌕ 2.95 – **8 rm** ☲ 15.00/36.00 **st.** – SB (weekends only) 65.00 **st.**

✕✕ **Cerutti's,** 10 Nelson St., HU1 1XE, ℰ 28501, Seafood – 🅿. 🔺 𝘝𝘐𝘚𝘈   Y **o**
closed Saturday lunch, Sunday and Christmas-New Year – **M** a la carte 13.75/19.05 **t.** ⌕ 4.80.

at *Walkington* N : 11 ½ m. by A 1079 – Z – ⊠ Beverley – ☎ 0482 Hull :

✕✕✕ **Manor House** ⚘ with rm, Northlands, Newbald Rd, HU17 8RT, NE : 1 m. ℰ 881645, « Late 19C country house, conservatory », ⚘ – ⊤⊽ ☎ 🅿. 🔺 𝘝𝘐𝘚𝘈. ✹
M *(closed Sunday and Bank Holidays)* (dinner only) 23.50 **t.** ⌕ 4.00 – **5 rm** 55.00/65.00 **t.**

at *North Ferriby* W : 7 m. on A 63 – Z – ⊠ Kingston-upon-Hull – ☎ 0482 Hull :

🏰 **Crest** (Crest), Ferriby High Rd, HU14 3LG, ℰ 645212, Telex 592558, Fax 643332 – ⤬ rm ⊤⊽
☎ 🅿 – ⚶ 100. 🔺 🅰🅴 ⓞ 𝘝𝘐𝘚𝘈
M *(closed Saturday lunch)* 8.95/14.75 **st.** and a la carte ⌕ 4.30 – ☲ 7.35 – **102 rm** 70.00/82.00 **st.** – SB (weekends only) 76.00/80.00 **st.**

KINGSTON-UPON-HULL

Carr Lane .... Y
George Street X
Jameson Street .... XY
King Edward Street..... Y 19
Paragon Street .... Y 29
Prospect Street X
Whitefriargate .... Y 49

Albion Street .... X 2
Bond Street .... X 3
Caroline Street .... X 6
Commercial Road....... Y 8
County Road North..... Z 9
Dock Office Row....... X 10
Dock Street .... X 12
Fairfax Avenue........ X 13
Ferensway .... XY 14
Great Union Street ... X 15
Grimston Street....... X 16
Humber Dock Street ... Y 17
Jarratt Street .... X 18
Lockwood Street ..... X 21
Lowgate .... Y 23
Market Place .... Y 24
Maybury Road........ Z 25
Prince's Avenue ..... Z 31
Prince's Dock Street.. Y 32
Queen's Road .... Z 33
Queen Street .... Y 35
Queen's Dock Avenue.. X 36
Reform Street .... X 37
St. Mark's Street..... X 40
Sculcoates Bridge .... X 42
Southcoates Avenue .. Z 43
Southcoates Lane..... Z 44
Waterhouse Lane..... Y 47
Wilberforce Drive .... X 50
Worship Street ...... X 52

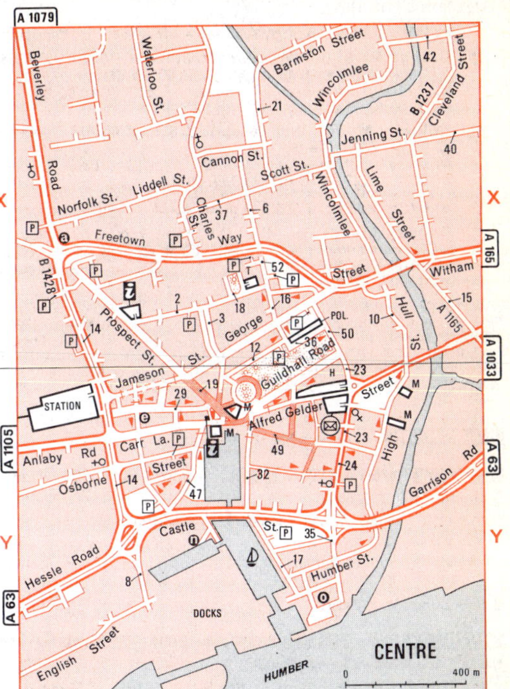

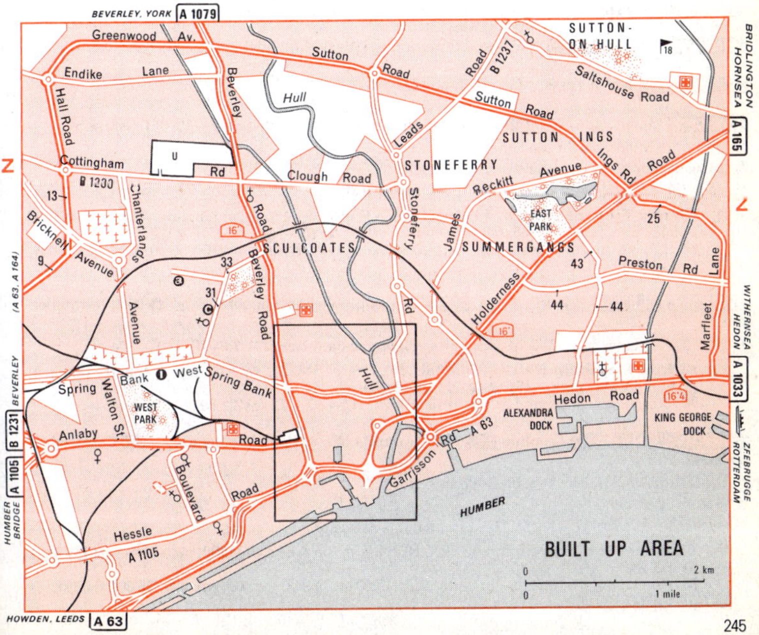

at Willerby NW : 5 m. by A 63 – Z – off A 164 – ✉ Kingston-upon-Hull – ☎ 0482 Hull :

Grange Park (Best Western), Main St., HU10 6EA, ✆ 656488, Telex 592773, Fax 655848, ☒, ⛱ – |‡| TV ☎ ♿ P – 🏛 300. 🏦 AE ⓓ VISA
M 12.50/19.50 **t.** and a la carte 12.75/22.50 **t.** 🍷 3.00 – **50 rm** ☐ 38.00/92.00 **st.** – SB 80.00/89.00 **st.**

Willerby Manor, Well Lane, HU10 6ER, ✆ 652616, Telex 592629, Fax 653901, ⛱ – TV ☎ P – 🏛 . 🏦 AE VISA. ✻
M *(closed Saturday lunch, Sunday dinner and Bank Holidays)* 9.00/10.00 **st.** and a la carte 🍷 3.00 – ☐ 6.25 – **35 rm** 51.00/68.00 **st.**

at Little Weighton NW : 11 m. by A 164 – Z – ✉ Cottingham – ☎ 0482 Hull :

Rowley Manor 🐴, HU20 3XR, SW : ½ m. by Rowley Rd ✆ 848248, Fax 849900, ≤, « Georgian manor house », ⛱ – TV ☎ P – 🏛 . 🏦 AE ⓓ VISA
M 10.00 **t.** and a la carte approx. 14.50 **t.** 🍷 3.75 – **16 rm** ☐ 44.00/85.00 **t.** – SB (weekends only) 70.00 **st.**

BMW 54 Anlaby Rd ✆ 25071
FIAT 96 Boothferry Rd ✆ 506976
FORD 172 Anlaby Rd ✆ 25732
FIAT, PEUGEOT-TALBOT Witham ✆ 24131
HONDA 576 Springbank West ✆ 51250
PEUGEOT-TALBOT Anlaby ✆ 659362
SAAB Anlaby Rd ✆ 23773
TOYOTA Clarence St. ✆ 20039
VAUXHALL-OPEL 230-236 Anlaby Rd ✆ 23681
VW-AUDI Anlaby Rd ✆ 23631

ATS Great Union St. ✆ 29044
ATS Scott St. ✆ 29370/225502

KINGSTOWN Cumbria – see Carlisle.

KINGTON Heref. and Worc. 403 K 27 – pop. 2 040 – ECD : Wednesday – ☎ 0544.

⛳18 Bradnor Hill ✆ 230340.

♦London 152 – ♦Birmingham 61 – Hereford 19 – Shrewsbury 54.

✕ **Penrhos Court,** HR5 3LR, E : 1 ½ m. on A 44 ✆ 230720, « Converted 18C barn » – P
closed Sunday dinner, Monday, Tuesday and January-March – **M** (dinner only and Sunday lunch)/dinner a la carte 13.00/21.00 **t.** 🍷 3.00.

ATS Bridge St. ✆ 230350

KINTBURY Berks. 403 404 P 29 – pop. 2 034 – ✉ Newbury – ☎ 0488.

♦London 73 – Newbury 6 – Reading 23.

✕✕ **Dundas Arms** with rm, Station Rd, RG15 0UT, ✆ 58263, ≤, « Canal and riverside setting », ⛱ – TV ☎ P. 🏦 AE ⓓ VISA. ✻
closed Christmas-New Year – **M** *(closed Sunday, Monday and Bank Holidays)* 14.00/23.50 **t.** 🍷 4.00 – **5 rm** ☐ 48.00/54.00 **t.**

KINVER Staffs. 403 404 N 26 – see Stourbridge (West Midlands).

KIRBY HILL North Yorks. – see Richmond.

KIRKBY Merseyside 402 403 L 23 – pop. 52 825 – ECD : Wednesday – ☎ 051 Liverpool.

⛳ Liverpool Municipal, Ingoe Lane ✆ 546 5435.

ℹ Municipal Buildings, Cherryfield Drive ✆ 443 4025.

♦London 214 – ♦Blackpool 54 – ♦Liverpool 7 – ♦Manchester 31.

Cherry Tree, East Lancs. Rd, Knowsley, L34 9HA, S : 1 ½ m. at junction A 580 and A 5207 ✆ 546 7531, Telex 629769, Fax 549 1069 – ⇔ TV ☎ P – 🏛 . 🏦 AE ⓓ VISA
M 8.75 **st.** and a la carte 10.75/16.60 **st.** 🍷 4.20 – **50 rm** ☐ 46.00/56.00 **st.** – SB (weekends only) 60.00/80.00 **st.**

KIRKBY FLEETHAM North Yorks. 402 P 20 – pop. 406 (inc. Fencote) – ✉ ☎ 0609 Northallerton.

♦London 236 – ♦Leeds 46 – ♦Middlesbrough 31 – ♦Newcastle-upon-Tyne 51 – York 37.

Kirkby Fleetham Hall 🐴, DL7 0SU, N : 1 m. ✆ 748226, ≤, « Georgian country house », ⛱ heated, ⛱, park – TV ☎ P. 🏦 AE ⓓ VISA
M (dinner only and Sunday lunch)/dinner 25.00 🍷 4.50 – **22 rm** ☐ 69.00/130.00 **st.**

KIRKBY LONSDALE Cumbria 402 M 21 – pop. 1 557 – ECD : Wednesday – ✉ Carnforth – ☎ 05242.

⛳9 Casterton Rd ✆ 72085, 1 m. on Sedbergh Rd.

ℹ 18 Main St. ✆ 71603.

♦London 259 – ♦Carlisle 62 – Kendal 13 – Lancaster 17 – ♦Leeds 58.

Pheasant Inn, Casterton, LA6 2RX, NE : 1 ¼ m. on A 683 ✆ 71230, ⛱ – ⇔ rest TV ☎ ♿ P. 🏦 VISA
M (bar lunch)/dinner a la carte 9.25/19.00 **st.** 🍷 3.50 – **13 rm** ☐ 35.00/50.00 **st.** – SB 110.00/130.00 **st.**

at Cowan Bridge SE : ½ m. on A 65 – ⊠ Carnforth – ☎ 052 42 Kirkby Lonsdale :

🏠 **Hipping Hall**, LA6 2JJ, SE : ½ m. on A 65 ✆ 71187, 氣 – 🆃🆅 🅿. 🔊 VISA
March-13 November – **M** (communal dining) (booking essential) (dinner only) 14.00 **st.** –
5 rm � 36.00/52.00 **st.**, **2 suites** 62.00 **st.**

🏠 **Cobwebs Country House** 🦢, Leck, LA6 2HZ, NE : ¼ m. ✆ 72141 – ⇥ rest 🆃🆅 ☎ 🅿.
🔊 🆎 VISA. ✵
Easter-December – **M** *(closed Sunday dinner)* (booking essential) 10.00/15.00 **st.**
and a la carte 🍷 3.00 – **5 rm** ⊋ 20.00/40.00 **st.** – SB (except summer) 60.00/65.00 **st.**

  at Lupton NW : 3 ¾ m. on A 65 – ⊠ Carnforth – ☎ 044 87 Crooklands :

✕ **Lupton Tower** 🦢 with rm, LA6 2PR, ✆ 400, ≤, vegetarian rest., 氣 – ⇥ 🅿
M (booking essential) (dinner only) 11.50 **t.** 🍷 3.00 – **5 rm** ⊋ 21.00/37.00 **t.** –
SB (except winter) 45.00/49.50 **st.**

KIRKBYMOORSIDE North Yorks. 402 R 21 – pop. 2 227 – ECD : Thursday – ☎ 0751.
🇮🇸 Manor Vale ✆ 31525.
♦London 244 – Scarborough 26 – York 33.

🏠 **George and Dragon**, 17 Market Pl., YO6 6AA, ✆ 31637, 氣 – 🆃🆅 ☎ 🅿. 🔊 VISA
M 13.90 **st.** and a la carte 🍷 3.60 – **22 rm** ⊋ 30.00/55.00 **st.**

NISSAN Pickering Rd ✆ 31551   VAUXHALL-OPEL Piercy End ✆ 31434
RENAULT New Rd ✆ 31401

KIRKBY STEPHEN Cumbria 402 M 20 – pop. 1 518 – ECD : Thursday – ☎ 076 83.
Envir. : Brough (Castle ruins 12C-14C : keep ✳ ✱ *AC*) N : 4 m.
🛈 Market Sq. ✆ 71199.
♦London 285 – ♦Carlisle 48 – Kendal 24.

⚓ **King's Arms**, Market Sq., CA17 4QN, ✆ 71378, 氣 – ☎ 🅿. 🔊 VISA
closed Christmas Day – **M** (bar lunch Monday to Saturday)/dinner 14.50 **t.** and a la carte
🍷 3.75 – **9 rm** ⊋ 22.00/45.00 **t.** – SB (November-May) (except Bank Holidays) 55.00 **st.**

KIRKHAM Lancs. 402 L 22 – pop. 8 393 – ⊠ Preston – ☎ 0772.
♦London 240 – ♦Blackpool 9 – Preston 7.

✕✕ **Cromwellian**, 16 Poulton St., PR4 2AB, ✆ 685680. 🔊 🆎 VISA
closed Sunday, Monday, 1 week February and last 2 weeks July – **M** (dinner only and
Sunday lunch)/dinner 9.50/16.00 **t.** 🍷 3.50.

KIRKOSWALD Cumbria 401 402 L 19 – pop. 730 – ⊠ Penrith – ☎ 076 883 Lazonby.
♦London 300 – ♦Carlisle 23 – Kendal 41 – Lancaster 58.

🏠 **Prospect Hill** 🦢, CA10 1ER, N : ¾ m. ✆ 500, ≤, « Converted 18C farm buildings », 氣 –
🅿. 🔊 🆎 ⓪ VISA. ✵
closed February and 25 December – **M** (dinner only) a la carte 9.90/15.40 **t.** 🍷 3.60 – **9 rm**
⊋ 18.00/46.00 **t.**

KNAPTON Norfolk – see North Walsham.

KNARESBOROUGH North Yorks. 402 P 21 – pop. 12 910 – ECD : Thursday – ☎ 0423 Harro-
gate.
🇮🇸 Boroughbridge Rd ✆ 863219, N : 1 ½ m.
🛈 Market Place ✆ 866886 (summer only).
♦London 217 – Bradford 21 – Harrogate 3 – ♦Leeds 18 – York 18.

🏨 **Dower House** (Best Western), Bond End, HG5 9AL, ✆ 863302, Telex 57202, Fax 867665, 🔊,
氣 – 🆃🆅 ☎ 🅿 – 🎣. ✵
31 rm, 1 suite.

✕✕✕ **4 Park Place**, 4 Park Pl., HG5 0ER, ✆ 868002.
FORD York Place ✆ 862291

KNIGHTON (TREFYCLAWDD) Powys 403 K 26 – ☎ 0547.
🇮🇸 The Frydd ✆ 528646.
🛈 The Old School ✆ 528753.
♦London 162 – ♦Birmingham 59 – Hereford 31 – Shrewsbury 35.

🏠 **Milebrook House**, Milebrook, LD7 1LT, E : 2 m. on A 4113 ✆ 528632, ⌇, 氣 – 🆃🆅 🅿. 🔊
VISA. ✵
closed 29 May-12 June – **M** *(closed Monday lunch and Sunday dinner)* 13.50 **t.** and a la
carte 🍷 4.00 – **6 rm** ⊋ 36.00/48.00 **t.**

 Heref. and Worc. **403 404** M 27 – pop. 82 – ECD : Wednesday – ⊠ Worcester – ✆ 0886.

♦London 132 – Hereford 20 – Leominster 18 – Worcester 8.

  🏨   Talbot, WR6 5PH, on B 4197 ✆ 21235, 🎾, squash – **P**. 🅰 *VISA*. ✂
    Accommodation closed 24 and 25 December – **M** *(closed Christmas Night)* – **10 rm**.

KNOWLE Devon – see Braunton.

KNOWL HILL Berks. **404** R 29 – ⊠ Twyford – ✆ 062 882 Littlewick Green.

♦London 38 – Maidenhead 5 – Reading 8.

  🏨   **Bird in Hand,** Bath Rd, RG10 9UP, ✆ 2781, Fax 6748, 🚗 – 📺 ☎ **P**. 🅰 AE ⓞ *VISA*. ✂
    M 12.50/15.00 **st.** and a la carte 🍷 4.25 – **15 rm** ☞ 60.00/80.00 **st.** – SB (weekends only) 65.00/80.00 **st.**

    at Warren Row NW : 1 m. – ⊠ Wargrave – ✆ 062 882 Littlewick Green :

  XX   **Warrener Inn** 🍴 with rm, RG10 8QS, ✆ 2803, Fax 6055, 🚗 – 📺 ☎ **P**. 🅰 AE ⓞ *VISA*. ✂
    closed 2 weeks January – **M** *(closed Sunday dinner and Monday to non-residents)*
    24.00/36.00 **t.** 🍷 5.50 – **5 rm** ☞ 75.00/110.00 **t.** – SB (weekends only) 140.00 **st.**

KNUTSFORD Cheshire **402 403 404** M 24 – pop. 13 628 – ECD : Wednesday – ✆ 0565.
Envir. : Tatton Hall★ (Georgian) and gardens★★ *AC*, N : 2 m. – Jodrell Bank (Concourse building-radiotelescope *AC*) SE : 8 ½ m.
🛈 Council Offices, Toft Rd ✆ 2611.

♦London 187 – Chester 25 – ♦Liverpool 33 – ♦Manchester 18 – ♦Stoke-on-Trent 30.

  🏨   **Cottons,** Manchester Rd, WA16 0SU, NW : 1 ½ m. on A 50 ✆ 50333, Telex 669931, Fax
    55351, 🔲, 🚗, 🍴 – 🛗 ↔ rm 📺 ☎ & **P** – 🔬 200. 🅰 AE ⓞ *VISA*
    M *(closed Saturday lunch)* a la carte approx. 16.00/20.00 **t.** – **77 rm** ☞ 78.00/92.00 **st.**,
    9 suites 116.00/125.00 **st.** – SB (weekends only) 84.00/90.00 **st.**

  🏨   **Royal George** (B.C.B.), King St., WA16 6EE, ✆ 4151, Fax 4955 – 🛗 📺 ☎ **P** – 🔬 80. 🅰 AE
    ⓞ *VISA*. ✂
    31 rm ☞ 50.00/85.00 **t.**

  🏠   **Longview,** 55 Manchester Rd, WA16 0LX, ✆ 2119 – 📺 **P**
    closed Christmas and New Year – **M** *(closed Sunday dinner)* (lunch by arrangement)/dinner
    11.50 **st.** 🍷 3.75 – **23 rm** ☞ 30.00/70.00 **st.**

  🏠   **Travelodge** without rest., A 556 Chester Rd, Tabley, WA16 0PP, NW : 2 ¾ m. by A 5033 on
    A 556 ✆ 52187 – 📺 & **P**. 🅰 AE *VISA*
    32 rm 21.50/27.00 **t.**

  XXX   **La Belle Epoque** with rm, 60 King St., WA16 6DT, ✆ 3060, French rest., « Art nouveau »
    – 📺. 🅰 AE ⓞ *VISA*. ✂
    closed first week January and Bank Holidays – **M** *(closed Sunday)* (dinner only) (booking
    essential) a la carte 15.00/22.45 **t.** 🍷 4.50 – ☞ 3.50 – **5 rm** ☞ 33.00/45.00 **t.**

    at Bucklow Hill NW : 3 ½ m. at junction A 556 and A 5034 – ⊠ Knutsford – ✆ 0565
    Bucklow Hill :

  🏨   **Swan Inn** (De Vere), Bucklow Hill, Chester Rd, WA16 6RD, ✆ 830295, Telex 666911, Fax
    830614 – 📺 ☎ **P** – 🔬 60. 🅰 AE ⓞ *VISA*
    M 11.75 **st.** and a la carte 14.50/22.00 **st.** 🍷 4.10 – **70 rm** ☞ 67.00/75.00 **st.** – SB (weekends only and all July and August) 60.00/80.00 **st.**

FORD Garden Rd ✆ 4141   ⊛ ATS Malt St. ✆ 52224
PEUGEOT Toft Rd ✆ 4294
VOLVO Park Lane, Pickmere ✆ 056 589 (Pickmere)
3254

LACOCK Wilts. **403 404** N 29 The West Country G. – pop. 1 289 – ⊠ Chippenham – ✆ 024 973.
See : Site★ – Lacock Village : High St.★, St. Cyriac Church★, Fox Talbot Museum of Photography★ *AC* – Lacock Abbey★ *AC*.

♦London 109 – Bath 16 – ♦Bristol 30 – Chippenham 3.

  X   **Sign of the Angel** with rm, 6 Church St., SN15 2LA, ✆ 230, English rest., « 14C inn in
    National Trust village », 🚗 – ☎. 🅰 AE *VISA*
    closed 22 December-6 January – **M** *(closed Saturday lunch and Sunday dinner to non-residents)* 18.00/25.00 **t.** – **6 rm** ☞ 55.00/80.00 **t.** – SB (except weekends in summer) 100.00 **st.**

LAKE VYRNWY Powys **402 403** J 25 – ⊠ ✆ 069 173 Llanwddyn.

♦London 204 – Chester 52 – Llanfyllin 10 – Shrewsbury 40.

  🏨   **Lake Vyrnwy** 🍴, SY10 0LY, ✆ 692, Telex 35880, Fax 259, ≤ Lake Vyrnwy, « Country
    house atmosphere », 🎾, 🚗, park, 🍴 – ↔ rm 📺 ☎ 🚗 **P**. 🅰 AE ⓞ *VISA*
    M 10.95/18.50 **t.** 🍷 4.50 – **29 rm** ☞ 40.00/70.00 **t.**, **1 suite** 75.00 **t.** – SB (except Bank Holidays) 93.00 **st.**

LALESTON Mid Glam. 🕮 J 29 – see Bridgend.

LAMBOURN Berks. 🕮 🕮 P 29 – pop. 2 173 – ECD : Thursday – ☎ 0488.
♦London 74 – ♦Oxford 23 – Reading 31 – ♦Southampton 56 – Swindon 12.

  XX **Conways**, East Garston, RG16 7ET, SE : 2 m. by Great Shefford Rd. ✆ 275, Fax 642 – **P**.
      AE VISA
      closed Sunday dinner, Monday, Christmas and New Year – **M** 13.95/24.95 **t.** 🍷 4.50.

LAMORNA COVE Cornwall 🕮 D 33 – ECD : Thursday – ✉ ☎ 0736 Penzance.
Envir. : Land's End★★, W : 7 ½ m.
♦London 323 – Penzance 5 – Truro 31.

  🏨 **Lamorna Cove** ⑤, TR19 6XH, ✆ 731411, ≤, ⤢ heated, 🐴 – ▐ TV ☎ **P**. AE VISA
      closed January – **M** (bar lunch Monday to Saturday)/dinner 15.00 **t.** – **18 rm** ⊿ (dinner
      included) 55.00/120.00 **t.**

LAMPHEY Dyfed – see Pembroke.

LANCASTER Lancs. 🕮 L 21 – pop. 43 902 – ECD : Wednesday – ☎ 0524.
See : Castle★.
🛈 Lansil, Caton Rd ✆ 39269.
🛈 5 Dalton Sq. ✆ 32878.
♦London 252 – ♦Blackpool 26 – Bradford 62 – Burnley 44 – ♦Leeds 71 – ♦Middlesbrough 97 – Preston 26.

  🏨 **Post House** (T.H.F.), Waterside Park, Caton Rd, LA1 3RA, NE : 1 ½ m. on A 683 ✆ 65999,
      Telex 65363, Fax 841265, ⤢, 🐟, 🐴 – ▐ ⤢ rm TV ☎ & **P** – 🛏 120. AE ① VISA
      M 10.50/13.50 **st.** and a la carte 🍷 3.75 – ⊿ 7.00 – **117 rm** 65.00/90.00 **st.** – SB (week-
      ends only) 80.00/100.00 **st.**

  🏨 **Royal Kings Arms**, Market St., CA1 1HP, ✆ 32451, Telex 65481, Fax 841698 – ▐ TV ☎ **P**
      – 🛏 70. AE ① VISA
      M (dinner only and Sunday lunch)/dinner 11.50 **t.** 🍷 3.50 – **55 rm** ⊿ 45.00/75.00 **t.** –
      SB (weekends only) 60.00 **st.**

  ⌂ **Edenbreck House** without rest., Sunnyside Lane, off Ashfield Av., LA1 5ED, via Meeting
      House Lane ✆ 32464, 🐴 – TV **P**
      5 rm ⊿ 20.00/35.00 **st.**

      at Claughton NE : 6 ¾ m. on A 638 – ✉ ☎ 052 42 Kirkby Lonsdale :

  🏨 **Old Rectory**, LA2 9LA, on A 683 ✆ 21455, 🐴 – ⤢ rest TV ☎ **P**. AE VISA ⚞
      M 17.85 **t.** and a la carte – **12 rm** ⊿ 45.00/69.95 **t.** – SB (except Sunday) 70.00/90.00 **st.**

AUSTIN-ROVER King St. ✆ 32233   NISSAN Scotsforth Rd ✆ 36162
FORD Parliament St. ✆ 63553
HYUNDAI, PONY Brookhouse ✆ 0524 (Caton)
770501

LANGSTONE Gwent 🕮 L 29 – see Newport.

LANREATH Cornwall 🕮 G 32 – pop. 449 – ✉ Looe – ☎ 0503.
♦London 269 – ♦Plymouth 26 – Truro 34.

  🏠 **Punch Bowl Inn**, PL13 2NX, ✆ 20218, 🐴 – TV **P**. AE VISA
      M (bar lunch)/dinner 8.50 **t.** and a la carte 7.30/12.35 **t.** 🍷 2.25 – **18 rm** ⊿ 17.50/43.00 **t.**

LARKFIELD Kent 🕮 V 30 – see Maidstone.

LASTINGHAM North Yorks. 🕮 R 21 – pop. 108 – ECD : Wednesday – ✉ York – ☎ 075 15.
🛈 Ryedale Folk Museum ✆ 367.
♦London 244 – Scarborough 26 – York 32.

  🏨 **Lastingham Grange** ⑤, YO6 6TH, ✆ 345, ≤, « Country house atmosphere », 🐴 –
      ⤢ rest TV ☎ **P**. AE ①
      closed December-February – **M** (bar lunch Monday to Saturday)/dinner 17.25 **t.** 🍷 3.50 –
      12 rm ⊿ 45.75/84.75 **t.** – SB 93.00/107.50 **st.**

      at Hutton-le-Hole W : 2 m. – ✉ York – ☎ 075 15 Lastingham :

  ⌂ **Barn**, YO6 6UA, ✆ 311 – ⤢ rm **P**. AE VISA ⚞
      closed January and February – **M** 9.95 **st.** 🍷 3.25 – **8 rm** ⊿ 16.00/40.00 **st.**

Für Ihre Reisen in Großbritannien

  – 5 Karten (Nr. 🕮🕮🕮🕮🕮) im Maßstab 1 : 400 000

  – Die auf den Karten rot unterstrichenen Orte sind im Führer erwähnt,
    benutzen Sie deshalb Karten und Führer zusammen.

LAVENHAM Suffolk **404** W 27 – pop. 1 658 – ECD : Wednesday – ⊠ Sudbury – ✆ 0787.
See : Site★★ – SS. Peter and Paul's Church : the Spring Parclose★ (Flemish).
🛈 Guildhall, Market Pl. ✆ 248207.
♦London 66 – ♦Cambridge 39 – Colchester 22 – ♦Ipswich 19.

🏨 **Swan** (T.H.F.), High St., CO10 9QA, ✆ 247477, Telex 987198, Fax 248286, « Part 14C timbered inn », ⇌ – ⇌ rm 📺 ☎ 🅿 – 🔬 45. 🖃 AE ① VISA
M 13.50/19.00 st. and a la carte – ⊡ 7.50 – **46 rm** 72.00/91.00 st., **2 suites** 125.00 st. – SB 100.00/150.00 st.

at Brent Eleigh SE : 2 ½ m. by A 1141 – ⊠ Sudbury – ✆ 0787 Lavenham :

⋔ **Street Farm** without rest., CO10 9NU, ✆ 247271, ⇌ – ⇌ 🅿. ⨯
closed Christmas-February – **3 rm** ⊡ 15.00/32.00.

XX **Great House** with rm, Market Pl., CO10 9QZ, ✆ 247431, « Part 14C timbered house » – 📺 ☎. 🖃 VISA
closed January – **M** *(closed Sunday dinner and Monday in winter)* 12.00/14.00 t. and a la carte 9.50/25.50 t. ⌘ 6.00 – **2 rm** ⊡ 45.00/75.00 t., **2 suites** 56.00/75.00 t. – SB (week-days only) 82.00 st.

PEUGEOT-TALBOT Sudbury Rd ✆ 247228

LEA Lancs. – see Preston.

LEAMINGTON SPA Warw. **403** **404** P 27 – see Royal Leamington Spa.

LEATHERHEAD Surrey **404** T 30 – pop. 42 399 – ✆ 0372.
🖈 Kingston Rd ✆ 843966, N : 1 ¼ m. on A 244 – 🖈 Tyrells Wood ✆ 376025.
♦London 23 – ♦Brighton 43 – Guildford 15 – Maidstone 41.

XX **Le Pelerin**, Hawk's Hill, Guildford Rd, KT22 9AL, ✆ 373602, Seafood – ▤ 🅿. 🖃 AE ① VISA
M 7.95/10.95 t. and a la carte 11.45/16.05 t. ⌘ 3.95.

◉ ATS 85a and 89 Kingston Rd ✆ 372003

LEDBURY Heref. and Worc. **403** **404** M 27 – pop. 4 985 – ECD : Wednesday – ✆ 0531.
See : Church Lane★.
Envir. : Birtsmorton Court★ (15C) AC, SE : 7 m.
🛈 St. Katherine's, High St. ✆ 2461/5680 (summer only).
♦London 119 – Hereford 14 – Newport 46 – Worcester 16.

🏛 **Feathers**, High St., HR8 1DS, ✆ 5266, « Heavily timbered 16C inn », squash – 📺 ☎ 🅿 – 🔬 150. 🖃 AE ①
M (buffet lunch)/dinner 15.00 st. and a la carte – **11 rm** ⊡ 47.50/75.00 st. – SB (week-ends only) (except Bank Holidays) 97.00 st.

at Wellington Heath N : 2 m. by B 4214 – ⊠ ✆ 0531 Ledbury :

🏛 **Hope End** 🦐, Hope End, HR8 1JQ, N : ¾ m. ✆ 3613, ⇌, park – ⇌ rest ☎ 🅿. 🖃 VISA ⨯
March-November – **M** *(closed Monday and Tuesday)* (booking essential) (dinner only) 25.00 st. ⌘ 5.00 – **9 rm** ⊡ 70.00/118.00 st. – SB 252.00/304.00 st.

AUSTIN-ROVER The Homend ✆ 5561   FORD New St. ✆ 2261

LEE Devon **403** H 30 – see Ilfracombe.

LEEDS West Yorks. **402** P 22 – pop. 445 242 – ECD : Wednesday – ✆ 0532.
See : Site★ – City Art Gallery★ DZ M.
Envir. : Temple Newsam House★ (17C) (interior★★) AC, E : 4 m. CX D – Kirkstall Abbey★ (ruins 12C) AC, NW : 3 m. BV.
🖈, 🖈 The Temple Newsam, Temple Newsam Rd, Halton ✆ 645624, E : 3 m. CX – 🖈 Gotts Park, Armley Ridge Rd, ✆ 638232, W : 2 m. BV – 🖈 Middleton Park Municipal, Town St., Middleton ✆ 700449, S : 3 m. CX – 🖈 Roundhay, Park Lane ✆ 662695.
✈ Leeds and Bradford Airport : ✆ 509696, Telex 557868, NW : 8 m. by A 65 and A 658 BV.
🛈 19 Wellington St. ✆ 462454.
♦London 204 – ♦Liverpool 75 – ♦Manchester 43 – ♦Newcastle-upon-Tyne 95 – ♦Nottingham 74.

Plans on following pages

🏨 **Hilton International** (Hilton), Neville St., LS1 4BX, ✆ 442000, Telex 557143, Fax 433577 – 🛗 ⇌ rm ▤ 📺 ☎ 🔥 🅿 – 🔬 400. 🖃 AE ① VISA   DZ **r**
M 12.00/15.00 st. and a la carte ⌘ 4.50 – ⊡ 9.25 – **225 rm** 78.00/92.00 st., **3 suites** 125.00/150.00 st. – SB (weekends only) 68.00 st.

🏨 **Queen's** (T.H.F.), City Sq., LS1 1PL, ✆ 431323, Telex 55161, Fax 425154 – 🛗 ⇌ rm 📺 ☎ 🔥 – 🔬 700. 🖃 AE ① VISA   DZ **a**
M 11.25/12.50 st. and a la carte ⌘ 4.00 – ⊡ 8.40 – **183 rm** 76.00/110.00 st., **5 suites** 195.00 st. – SB (weekends only) 70.00/80.00 st.

Golden Lion (Mt. Charlotte), Lower Briggate, LS1 4AE, ℰ 436454, Fax 429327 – ⌷ 🄣 ☎ –
🛋 80. ◪ 🄰🄴 ⓞ 𝗩𝗜𝗦𝗔   **DZ v**
M *(closed Sunday lunch)* (bar lunch)/dinner 10.75 **st.** and a la carte ⌂ 3.55 – **89 rm**
⊆ 55.00/75.00 **st.** – SB (weekends only) 61.00/70.00 **st.**

Merrion (Mt. Charlotte), Merrion Centre, 17 Wade Lane, LS2 8NH, ℰ 439191, Telex 55459,
Fax 423527 – ⌷ 🄣 ☎ 🄿 – 🛋   **DZ x**
120 rm.

Metropole, King St., LS1 2HQ, ℰ 450841, Telex 557755, Fax 425156 – ⌷ ⊱ rm 🄣 ☎ 🚗
🄿 – 🛋 . ◪ 🄰🄴 ⓞ 𝗩𝗜𝗦𝗔   **CZ o**
M 6.25/9.25 **st.** and a la carte ⌂ 3.45 – ⊆ 7.00 – **110 rm** 54.00/64.50 **st.**

Butlers, 40 Cardigan Rd, Headingley, LS6 3AG, ℰ 744755 – 🄣 ☎ 🄿 . ◪ 𝗩𝗜𝗦𝗔   **AY a**
M *(closed Sunday)* a la carte 10.10/15.30 **st.** ⌂ 2.40 – **8 rm** ⊆ 38.50/48.50 **st.**

Aragon, 250 Stainbeck Lane, LS7 2PS, ℰ 759306, 🌲 – 🄣 🄿 . ◪ 🄰🄴 ⓞ 𝗩𝗜𝗦𝗔   **CV c**
closed Christmas – **M** 7.50 **s.** ⌂ 3.00 – **13 rm** ⊆ 18.30/34.80 **s.**

Ash Mount without rest., 22 Wetherby Rd, Oakwood, LS8 2QD, ℰ 654263, 🌲 – 🄿   **CV u**
13 rm ⊆ 16.00/33.00 **st.**

Pinewood, 78 Potternewton Lane, LS7 3LW, ℰ 622561, 🌲 – ⊱ rest 🄣 . ◪ . ⍻   **AY s**
closed 22 December-2 January – **M** (by arrangement) 8.00 **t.** – **10 rm** ⊆ 28.00/42.00 **t.**

Mandalay, 8 Harrison St., LS1 6PA, ℰ 446453, Indian rest. – ▤ . ◪ 🄰🄴 ⓞ 𝗩𝗜𝗦𝗔   **DZ e**
closed Saturday lunch, Sunday, 25-26 December and 1 January – **M** 4.95 **st.** (lunch) and a la
carte 8.15/11.15 **t.**

Himalayan Garden, 296 Harrogate Rd, Moortown, LS17 6LY, ℰ 370034, Indian rest.   **CV e**

Sang Sang, 7 The Headrow, LS1 6PN, ℰ 468664, Chinese rest. – ◪ 🄰🄴 ⓞ 𝗩𝗜𝗦𝗔   **DZ u**
closed 24 to 26 December – **M** 9.00 **t.** (dinner) and a la carte 11.30/12.30 **t.** ⌂ 2.50.

at Seacroft NE : 5 ½ m. at junction of A 64 and A 6120 – ✉ ☏ 0532 Leeds :

Stakis Windmill (Stakis), Ring Rd, LS14 5QP, ℰ 732323, Telex 55452, Fax 323018 – ⌷
▤ rest 🄣 ☎ 🄿 – 🛋 300. ◪ 🄰🄴 ⓞ 𝗩𝗜𝗦𝗔 . ⍻   **CV a**
M *(closed Saturday lunch)* – ⊆ 7.25 – **100 rm** 62.00/83.00 **st.** – SB 50.00/67.00 **st.**

at Garforth E : 6 m. at junction of A 63 and A 642 – CV – ✉ ☏ 0532 Leeds :

Hilton National (Hilton), Wakefield Rd, LS25 1LH, ℰ 866556, Telex 556324, Fax 868326,
◪ – ⊱ rm 🄣 ☎ ♿ 🄿 – 🛋 . ◪ 🄰🄴 ⓞ 𝗩𝗜𝗦𝗔
M *(closed Saturday lunch)* (carving rest.) 14.00/25.00 **st.** and a la carte – ⊆ 4.10 – **141 rm**
69.00/101.00 **t.**

at Pudsey W : 5 ¾ m. by A 647 – ✉ Leeds – ☏ 0274 Bradford :

Aagrah, Bradford Rd, on A 647 ℰ 668818, Indian rest. – 🄿 . ◪ 🄰🄴 ⓞ 𝗩𝗜𝗦𝗔   **BV e**
closed Sunday and Christmas Night – **M** a la carte 6.05/26.75 **t.** ⌂ 2.50.

at Horsforth NW : 5 m. by A 65 off A 6120 – ✉ ☏ 0532 Leeds :

Low Hall, Calverley Lane, LS18 4EF, ℰ 588221, « Elizabethan manor », 🌲 – 🄿 . ◪
𝗩𝗜𝗦𝗔   **BV a**
closed Saturday lunch, Sunday, Monday, 26 to 31 December and Bank Holidays –
M 11.50/19.50 **t.** and a la carte 13.75/21.75 **t.**

Roman Garden, Hall Lane, Hall Park, LS18 5JY, ℰ 587962, ≼, Italian rest. – 🄿 . ◪ 𝗩𝗜𝗦𝗔   **BV i**
closed Saturday lunch, Sunday and Monday – **M** a la carte 10.20/17.30 **t.**

at Bramhope NW : 8 m. on A 660 – BV – ✉ ☏ 0532 Leeds :

Post House (T.H.F.), Leeds Rd, LS16 9JJ, ℰ 842911, Telex 556367, Fax 843451, ≼, ◪, 🌲
– ⌷ ⊱ rm 🄣 ☎ 🄿 – 🛋 300. ◪ 🄰🄴 ⓞ 𝗩𝗜𝗦𝗔
M 12.95/15.50 **st.** and a la carte – ⊇ 7.60 – **129 rm** 80.00/95.00 **st.**, **1 suite** 120.00/130.00 **st.**
– SB (weekends only) 72.00/92.00 **st.**

Parkway (Embassy), Otley Rd, LS16 8AG, S : 2 m. on A 660 ℰ 672551, Telex 556614, Fax
674410, ◪, 🌲, ✗ – ⌷ ⊱ rm 🄣 ☎ ♿ 🄿 – 🛋 250. ◪ 🄰🄴 ⓞ 𝗩𝗜𝗦𝗔
M 9.95/12.75 **st.** and a la carte ⌂ 4.50 – ⊇ 6.50 – **103 rm** 65.00/110.00 **st.** – SB (weekends only) 65.00/79.00 **st.**

MICHELIN Distribution Centre, Gelderd Rd, LS12 6EU, ℰ 793911, FAX 794577 BX

ALFA-ROMEO Domestic St. ℰ 468141
AUSTIN-ROVER Town St., Stanningley ℰ 571811
AUSTIN-ROVER Water Lane ℰ 438091
AUSTIN-ROVER, DAIMLER-JAGUAR, ROLLS-
ROYCE, BENTLEY Roseville Rd ℰ 432731
BMW Sheepscar Way ℰ 620641
FORD 83 Roseville Rd ℰ 455955
FORD 54 Dolly Lane ℰ 421222
FORD Whitehall Rd ℰ 634222
MAZDA York Rd ℰ 480093
PEUGEOT South Milford ℰ 0977 (South Milford)
682714
PEUGEOT-TALBOT, CITROEN Meadow Rd ℰ
444531

PORSCHE, SAAB, MAZDA Apperley Lane, Yeadon
ℰ 0532 (Rawdon) 502231
RENAULT Regent St. ℰ 430837
TOYOTA Regent St. ℰ 444223
VAUXHALL 123 Hunslet Rd ℰ 439911
VAUXHALL-OPEL Armley Rd ℰ 434554
VOLVO Harrogate Rd ℰ 694666
VOLVO Wellington Rd ℰ 436412
VW-AUDI Gelderd Rd ℰ 633431

🄰 ATS Cross Green Lane ℰ 459423
ATS 2 Regent St. ℰ 430652

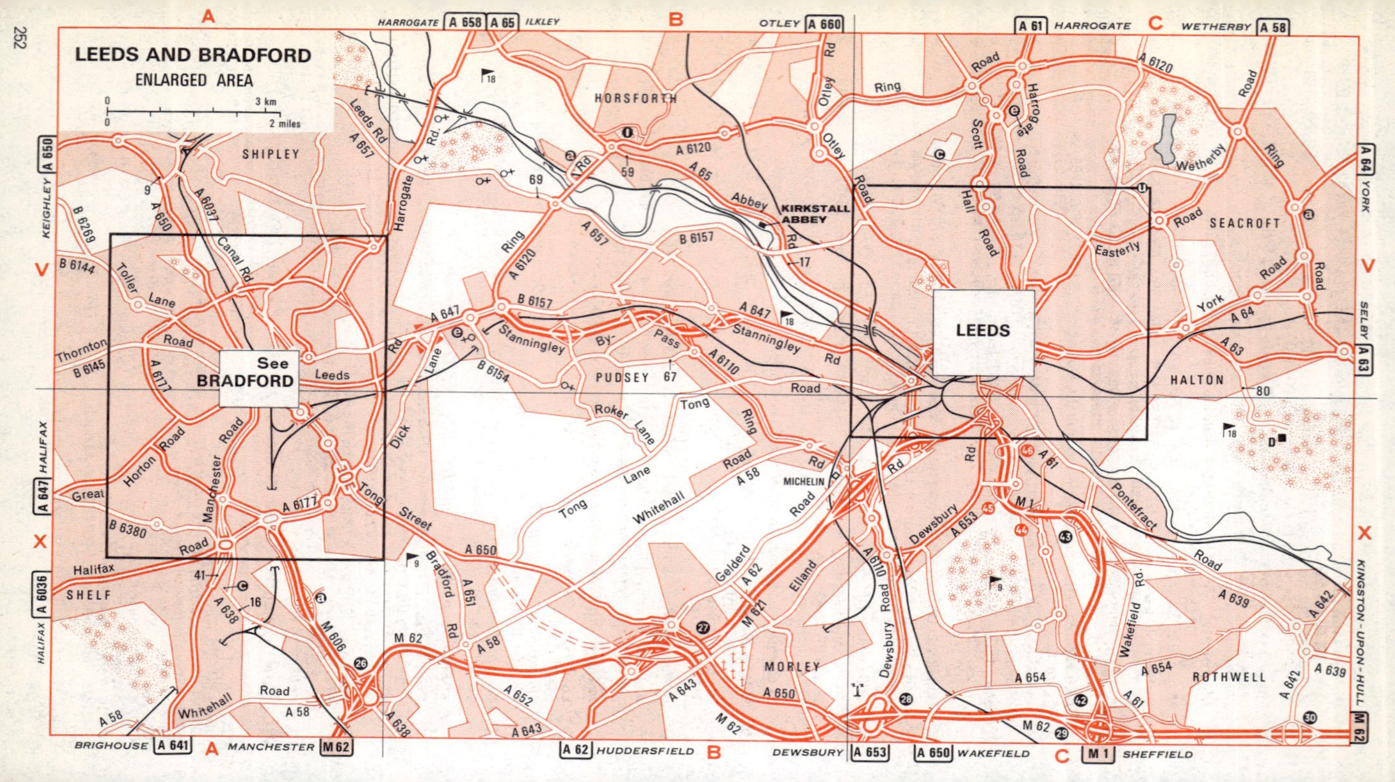

252
LEEDS AND BRADFORD
ENLARGED AREA
3 km
2 miles
HARROGATE A 658 A 65 ILKLEY
OTLEY A 660
A 61 HARROGATE
WETHERBY A 58
KEIGHLEY A 650
HALIFAX A 647
HALIFAX A 6036
BRIGHOUSE A 641
MANCHESTER M 62
A 62 HUDDERSFIELD
DEWSBURY A 653
A 650 WAKEFIELD
M 1 SHEFFIELD
YORK A 64
SELBY A 63
KINGSTON - UPON - HULL
M 62
HORSFORTH
SHIPLEY
SEACROFT
HALTON
MORLEY
ROTHWELL
SHELF
KIRKSTALL ABBEY
See BRADFORD
LEEDS
PUDSEY
Leeds Rd
A 657
A 6120
Otley
Rd
Otley
Ring
Road
Harrogate
Road
Scott
Hall Road
Wetherby
Ring
Road
York
A 64
A 63
Easterly
Road
A 6120
A 650
9
A 6037
A 650
B 6269
B 6144
B 6145
Toller
Lane
Canal Rd
Thornton
Road
Horton
Road
Great
Manchester
Road
B 6380
A 6177
Tong
Street
Dick
Lane
Leeds
Rd
B 6154
A 647
Stanningley
By-
Pass
Stanningley
Rd
A 647
A 6110
69
59
A 65
A 6120
Abbey
Rd
17
A 657
B 6157
Ring
B 6157
Road
Roker
Lane
Tong
Lane
Tong
Ring
Road
A 58
Whitehall
Gelderd
Road
A 62
M 621
Elland
A 58
A 650
Bradford
Rd
A 651
A 650
A 652
A 643
A 643
A 638
M 62
A 58
Whitehall
Road
A 58
41
16
A 638
M 606
M 62
MICHELIN
A 58
Road
Rd
Rd
A 6110
Dewsbury
Road
Dewsbury
A 653
A 61
A 654
A 650
A 654
Wakefield
Rd.
Pontefract
Road
A 61
A 639
A 642
A 639
A 642
M 62
18
D
Halifax
80
York
A 64
A 63

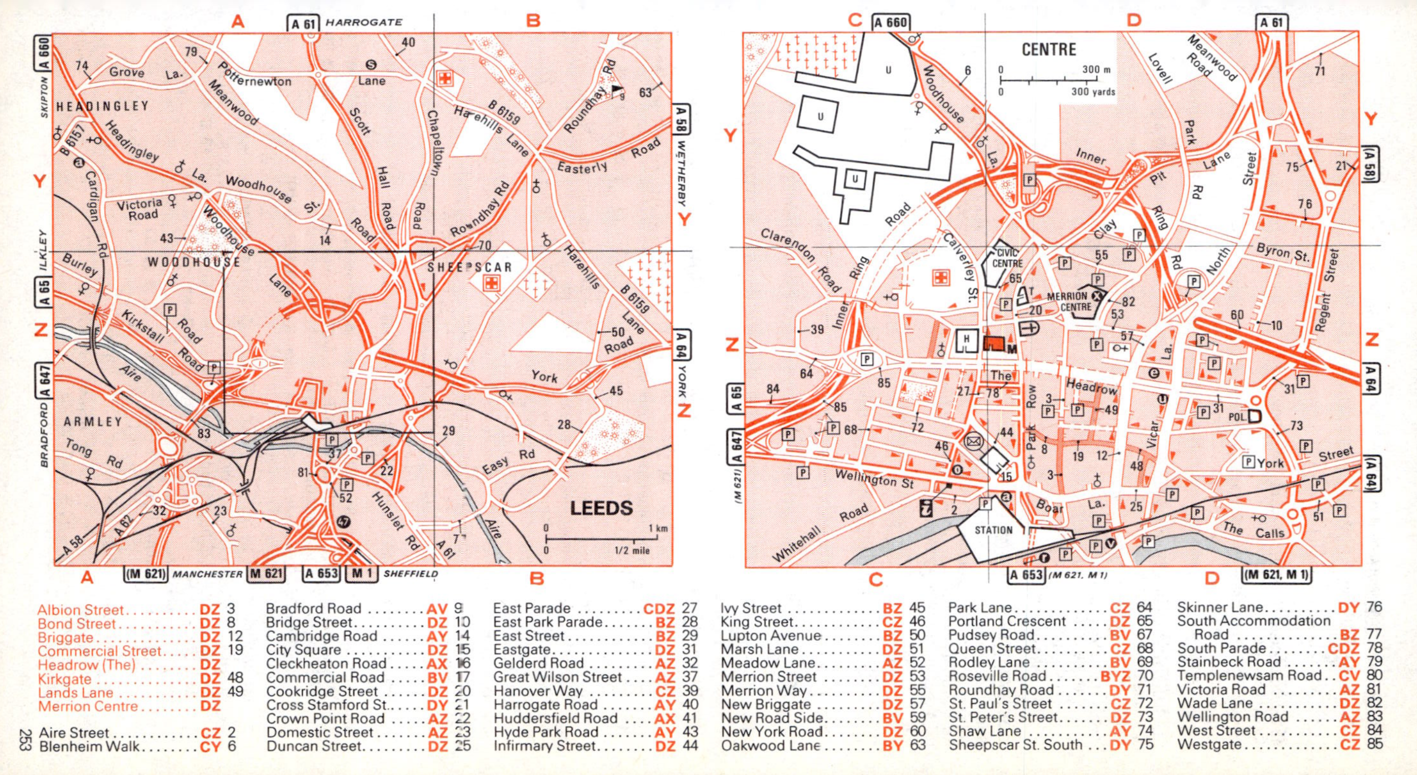

Albion Street .... DZ 3
Bond Street .... DZ 8
Briggate .... DZ 12
Commercial Street ...... DZ 19
Headrow (The) .... DZ
Kirkgate .... DZ 48
Lands Lane .... DZ 49
Merrion Centre .... DZ

Aire Street .... CZ 2
Blenheim Walk .... CY 6

Bradford Road .... AV 9
Bridge Street .... DZ 10
Cambridge Road .... AY 14
City Square .... DZ 15
Cleckheaton Road .... AX 16
Commercial Road .... BV 17
Cookridge Street .... DZ 20
Cross Stamford St. ..... DY 21
Crown Point Road .... AZ 22
Domestic Street .... AZ 23
Duncan Street .... DZ 25

East Parade .... CDZ 27
East Park Parade .... BZ 28
East Street .... BZ 29
Eastgate .... DZ 31
Gelderd Road .... AZ 32
Great Wilson Street .... AZ 37
Hanover Way .... CZ 39
Harrogate Road .... AY 40
Huddersfield Road ...... AX 41
Hyde Park Road .... AY 43
Infirmary Street .... DZ 44

Ivy Street .... BZ 45
King Street .... CZ 46
Lupton Avenue .... BZ 50
Marsh Lane .... DZ 51
Meadow Lane .... AZ 52
Merrion Street .... DZ 53
Merrion Way .... DZ 55
New Briggate .... DZ 57
New Road Side .... BV 59
New York Road .... DZ 60
Oakwood Lane .... BY 63

Park Lane .... CZ 64
Portland Crescent ...... DZ 65
Pudsey Road .... BV 67
Queen Street .... CZ 68
Rodley Lane .... BV 69
Roseville Road .... BYZ 70
Roundhay Road .... DY 71
St. Paul's Street ...... CZ 72
St. Peter's Street ..... DZ 73
Shaw Lane .... AY 74
Sheepscar St. South .... DY 75

Skinner Lane .... DY 76
South Accommodation
  Road .... BZ 77
South Parade .... CDZ 78
Stainbeck Road .... AY 79
Templenewsam Road ...... CV 80
Victoria Road .... AZ 81
Wade Lane .... DZ 82
Wellington Road .... AZ 83
West Street .... CZ 84
Westgate .... CZ 85

LEEK Staffs. 402 403 404 N 24 – ECD : Thursday – ✉ Stoke-on-Trent – ☎ 0782.

↑ **Bank End Farm Motel** ⏴, Longsdon, Leek Old Rd, SW : 2 ½ m. by A 53 ℰ 383638, « Working farm », ◲ – TV P.
M (by arrangement) 13.50 st. ⏴ 3.00 – **8 rm** ⏴ 20.00/33.00 st.

LEEMING BAR North Yorks. 402 P 21 – pop. 1 468 – ECD : Wednesday – ✉ Northallerton – ☎ 0677 Bedale.
♦London 235 – ♦Leeds 44 – ♦Middlesbrough 30 – ♦Newcastle-upon-Tyne 52 – York 37.

🏛 **White Rose**, DL7 9AY, ℰ 22707 – TV ☎ P. ◲ AE ⓸ VISA
M 8.75 t. (dinner) and a la carte 8.45/11.20 t. ⏴ 2.80 – **18 rm** ⏴ 23.00/39.00 t.

LEE-ON-THE-SOLENT Hants. 403 404 Q 31 – pop. 7 068 – ECD : Thursday – ☎ 0705.
⌇18 Brune Lane ℰ 551170.
♦London 81 – ♦Portsmouth 13 – ♦Southampton 15 – Winchester 23.

⚐ **Belle Vue**, 39 Marine Par. East, PO13 9BW, ℰ 550258 – TV P. ◲ VISA
M 8.95 t. (lunch) and a la carte 11.65/16.95 t. ⏴ 3.85 – **27 rm** ⏴ 51.50/60.00 st. – SB (weekends only) 75.00 st.

NISSAN High St. ℰ 551785

LEICESTER Leics. 402 403 404 Q 26 – pop. 324 394 – ECD : Monday and Thursday – ☎ 0533.
See : Guildhall★ BY B – Museum and Art Gallery★ CY M2 – St. Mary de Castro's Church★ (12C) BY A – ⌇18 Leicestershire, Evington Lane ℰ 738825, E : 2 m. AY – ⌇18 Western Park, Scudamore Rd ℰ 876158, W : 4 m. AY – ⌇18 Humberstone Heights, Gypsy Lane ℰ 764674 AX – ⌇9 Cambridge Rd, Whetstone ℰ 862399, by A 426 AZ.

✈ East Midlands Airport : Castle Donington ℰ 0332 (Derby) 810621, Telex 37543, NW : 22 m. by A 50 AX and M1 – 🚌 St. Margaret's Bus Station ℰ 511333 – 2-6 St. Martin's Walk ℰ 549922.
♦London 107 – ♦Birmingham 43 – ♦Coventry 24 – ♦Nottingham 26.

Plans on following pages

🏰 **Holiday Inn**, 129 St. Nicholas Circle, LE1 5LX, ℰ 531161, Telex 341281, Fax 513169, ◲ – ⎪≼⎪ ⤨ rm ▤ TV ☎ ⟐ P – ⏴ 250. ◲ AE ⓸ VISA   BY c
M 17.50 st. (dinner) and a la carte 19.25/25.25 st. – ⏴ 8.00 – **187 rm** 63.00/90.00 st., **1 suite** 150.00/175.00 st.

🏨 **Grand** (Embassy), 73 Granby St., LE1 6ES, ℰ 555599, Group Telex 342244, Fax 544736 – ⎪≼⎪ ⤨ rm ▤ rest TV ☎ P – ⏴   CY o
91 rm, **1 suite**.

🏨 **Belmont** (Best Western), De Montfort St., LE1 7GR, ℰ 544773, Telex 34619, Fax 470804 – ⎪≼⎪ ⤨ rm TV ☎ P – ⏴ 165. ◲ AE ⓸ VISA   CY c
closed 24 to 28 December – M (closed Saturday lunch) 9.95/11.95 t. and a la carte – **56 rm** ⏴ 54.00/72.00 st. – SB (weekends only) 65.00/70.00 st.

🏨 **St. James**, Abbey St., LE1 3TE, ℰ 510666, Telex 342434, Fax 315183 – ⎪≼⎪ TV ☎ P – ⏴ . ⑆   CX a
73 rm.

🏠 **Regency**, 360 London Rd, Stoneygate, LE2 2PL, ℰ 709634 – TV ☎ P. ⑆ – **36 rm**.   AY a

↑ **Spindle Lodge**, 2 West Walk, LE1 7NA, ℰ 551380 – TV P   CY r
closed 21 December-1 January – M (by arrangement) 12.00 st. – **12 rm** ⏴ 18.50/39.50 st.

↑ **Scotia**, 10 Westcotes Drive, LE3 0QR, ℰ 549200, ⌇ – TV   AY e
M (by arrangement) approx. 11.30 st. – **16 rm** ⏴ 18.00/33.00 st.

↑ **Seaforth** without rest., 12 Westcotes Drive, LE3 0QR, ℰ 554895 – ⤨ TV. ⑆   AY c
closed 25 and 26 December – **3 rm** ⏴ 22.00/33.00 st.

↑ Rowans, 290 London Rd, LE2 2AG, ℰ 705364, ⌇ – TV P – **14 rm**.   AY i

XX **Lai's**, 14-16 King St., LE1 6RJ, ℰ 557700, Chinese rest. – ◲ AE ⓸ VISA   CY a
M (closed Sunday) 25.00 st. and a la carte 8.60/13.30 st. ⏴ 4.75.

XX **Flemish House**, 54 Queens Rd, LE2 1TT, ℰ 708408 – ◲ AE ⓸ VISA   AY o
closed Monday, Sunday and 3-16 July – M 10.00/26.00 t. and a la carte 13.75/23.25 t.

XX Curry House, 64 London Rd, LE2 0QD, ℰ 550688, Indian rest.   CY e

XX **Water Margin**, 76-78 High St., LE1 5YP, ℰ 516422, Chinese (Canton) rest. – ◲ AE ⓸ VISA
M 3.50/8.50 t. and a la carte approx. 13.95 t.   BY x

X **Curry Pot**, 78-80 Belgrave Rd, ℰ 538256, Indian Rest. – ◲ AE ⓸ VISA   AX e
closed Sunday lunch – M a la carte 9.80/15.75 t.

at Rothley N: 5 m. by A 6 – AX – on B 5328 – ✉ ☎ 0533 Leicester :

🏨 **Rothley Court** (T.H.F) ⏴, Westfield Lane, LE7 7LG, W : ½ m. on B 5328 ℰ 374141, Fax 374483, ≼, « Part 12C house and chapel », ⌇ – ⤨ rm TV ☎ P – ⏴ 90. ◲ AE ⓸ VISA
M 9.95/17.50 st. and a la carte – ⏴ 7.00 – **35 rm** 65.00/115.00 st. – SB (weekends only) 64.00/114.00 st.

↑ **Limes**, 35 Mountsorrel Lane, LE7 7PS, ℰ 302531 – TV ☎ P. ◲ VISA. ⑆
closed last week August and 1 week Christmas – M 14.50 st. – **11 rm** ⏴ 29.50/35.00 st.

at Thrussington NE : 10 m. by A 46 – AX – ✉ Leicester – ☎ 066 474 Rearsby :

🏠 **Travelodge** without rest., Green Acres Filling Station, LE7 8TF, on A 46 (southbound carriageway) ℰ 525 – TV P. ◲ AE VISA
32 rm 21.50/27.00 t.

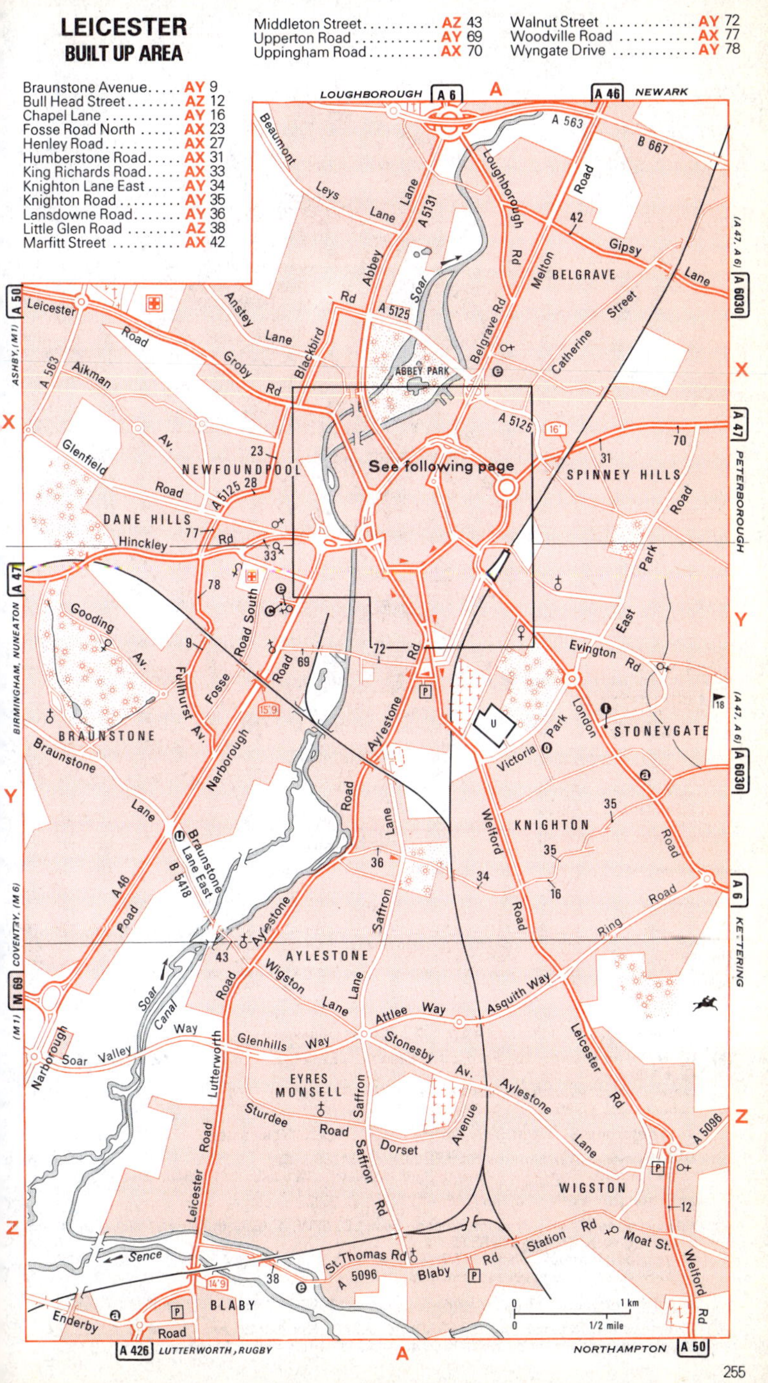

LEICESTER
BUILT UP AREA

Middleton Street AZ 43
Upperton Road AY 69
Uppingham Road AX 70
Walnut Street AY 72
Woodville Road AX 77
Wyngate Drive AY 78

Braunstone Avenue AY 9
Bull Head Street AZ 12
Chapel Lane AY 16
Fosse Road North AX 23
Henley Road AX 27
Humberstone Road AX 31
King Richards Road AX 33
Knighton Lane East AY 34
Knighton Road AY 35
Lansdowne Road AY 36
Little Glen Road AZ 38
Marfitt Street AX 42

LOUGHBOROUGH A 6
A 46 NEWARK
A 563
B 667
ASHBY (M1)
A 50
Leicester
A 563
Aikman
Beaumont
Leys
Lane
Abbey
Lane
Soar
A 5131
Anstey
Lane
Blackbird
Rd
A 5125
Loughborough Rd
Melton Rd
BELGRAVE
Gipsy Lane
Belgrave Rd
Catherine Street
A 6030
X
A 47
PETERBOROUGH
Glenfield
Groby
Rd
Av.
Road
ABBEY PARK
A 5125
16
31
70
NEWFOUNDPOOL
23
A 5125
28
See following page
SPINNEY HILLS
DANE HILLS
Hinckley
Rd
77
33
X
Y
A 47
BIRMINGHAM, NUNEATON
78
Road South
Gooding
Av.
9
Fullhurst Av.
Fosse
Road
69
72
Rd
Evington Rd
East Park Road
Narborough
15.9
BRAUNSTONE
Braunstone
Lane
P
U
Victoria Park
London Road
STONEYGATE
18
A 47, A 6)
A 6030
Aylestone Road
Welford Road
KNIGHTON
35
35
16
34
A 6
KETTERING
COVENTRY (M6)
(M1) M 69
A 46
Road
B 5418
Braunstone
Lane East
Aylestone
Road
43
Soar
Canal
Way
Wigston Lane
AYLESTONE
Saffron Lane
36
Attlee Way
Stonesby
Asquith Way
Leicester Rd
Narborough
Soar Valley Way
Glenhills Way
EYRES MONSELL
Sturdee
Road
Dorset
Saffron Road
Av.
Aylestone
Avenue
Lane
Z
A 5096
WIGSTON
12
P
Sence
14.9
BLABY
Enderby
Road
P
St. Thomas Rd
A 5096
Blaby
Rd
Station Rd
Moat St.
Welford Rd
38
P
A 426 LUTTERWORTH, RUGBY
NORTHAMPTON A 50
0   1 km
0   1/2 mile

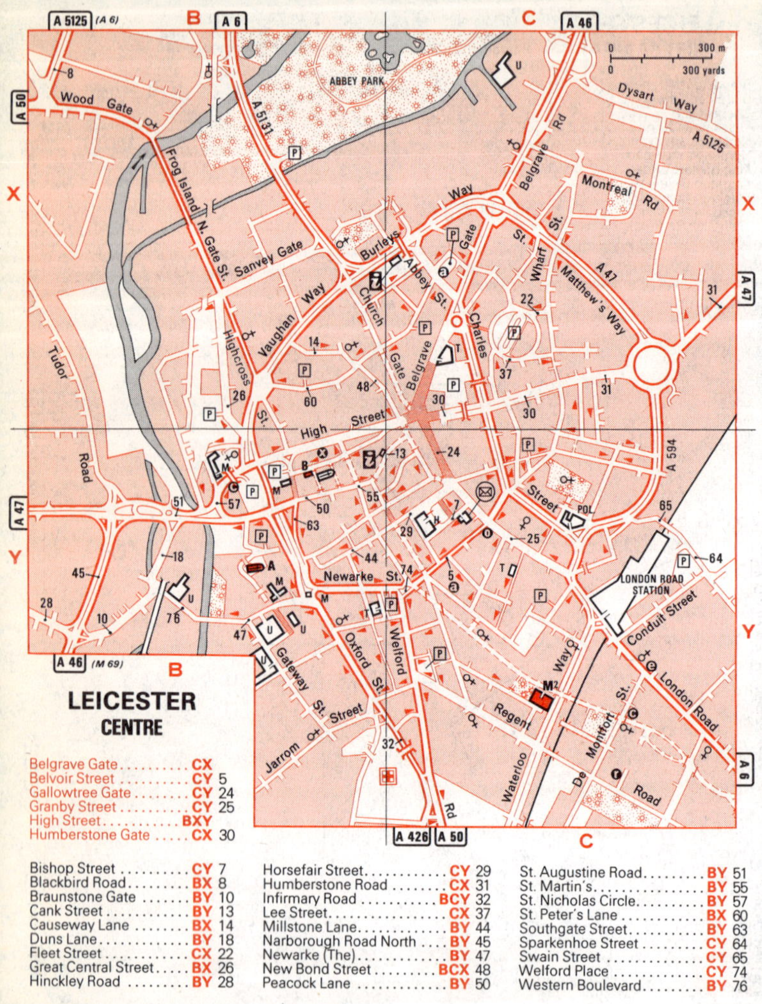

LEICESTER
CENTRE

Belgrave Gate . . . . **CX**
Belvoir Street . . . . **CY** 5
Gallowtree Gate . . . . **CY** 24
Granby Street . . . . **CY** 25
High Street . . . . **BXY**
Humberstone Gate . . . . . **CX** 30

Bishop Street . . . . **CY** 7
Blackbird Road . . . . **BX** 8
Braunstone Gate . . . . **BY** 10
Cank Street . . . . **BY** 13
Causeway Lane . . . . **BX** 14
Duns Lane . . . . **BY** 18
Fleet Street . . . . **CX** 22
Great Central Street . . . . **BX** 26
Hinckley Road . . . . **BY** 28

Horsefair Street . . . . **CY** 29
Humberstone Road . . . . **CX** 31
Infirmary Road . . . . **BCY** 32
Lee Street . . . . **CX** 37
Millstone Lane . . . . **BY** 44
Narborough Road North . . . . **BY** 45
Newarke (The) . . . . **BY** 47
New Bond Street . . . . **BCX** 48
Peacock Lane . . . . **BY** 50

St. Augustine Road . . . . **BY** 51
St. Martin's . . . . **BY** 55
St. Nicholas Circle . . . . **BY** 57
St. Peter's Lane . . . . **BX** 60
Southgate Street . . . . **BY** 63
Sparkenhoe Street . . . . **CY** 64
Swain Street . . . . **CY** 65
Welford Place . . . . **CY** 74
Western Boulevard . . . . **BY** 76

at Glen Parva S : 4 ½ m. on A 426 – ✉ ☎ 0533 Leicester :

XXX **Glen Parva Manor,** The Ford, Little Glen Rd, LE2 9TL, E : ½ m. on A 5096 ☎ 774604, ⌖ – **AZ e**
P. ⌖ AE ⓪
closed Saturday lunch, Sunday dinner and 25-26 December – **M** 10.50/17.50 **t.** and a la carte 19.80/28.65 **t.** ⌖ 3.90.

at Whetstone S : 5 ½ m. by A 426 – **AZ** – ✉ – ☎ 0533 Leicester :

XXX **Old Vicarage,** 123 Enderby Rd, LE8 3JH, ☎ 771195 – P. **AZ a**
closed Saturday lunch, Sunday and Bank Holidays – **M** a la carte 10.25/14.75 **st.** ⌖ 3.00.

at Braunstone SW : 2 m. on A 46 – **BY** – ✉ ☎ 0533 Leicester :

🏨 **Post House** (T.H.F.), Braunstone Lane East, LE3 2FW, ☎ 630500, Telex 341009 – 🛏 ⌖ rm
▤ rest �📺 ☎ & P. – ⌖ 80. ⌖ AE ⓪ VISA **AY u**
M *(closed Saturday lunch)* 10.50/14.00 **st.** and a la carte ⌖ 4.30 – ⌖ 7.00 – **172 rm** 67.00/89.00 **st.** – SB (weekends only) 48.00/72.00 **st.**

at Narborough SW : 6 m. by A 46 – **AZ** – and A 5096 on B 4114 – ✉ ☎ 0533 Leicester :

🏨 **Charnwood,** 48 Leicester Rd, LE9 5DF, ☎ 862218, Fax 750119, ⌖ – 📺 ☎ P. ⌖ AE VISA
M *(closed Sunday dinner)* 10.00/15.00 **st.** and a la carte ⌖ 4.00 – **20 rm** ⌖ 40.00/55.00 **st.**

at Leicester Forest East W : 3 m. on A 47 – AY – ⊠ ☎ 0533 Leicester :

Leicester Forest Moat House (Q.M.H.), Hinckley Rd, LE3 3GH, ✆ 394661, Fax 394952 –
TV ☎ P – 🔔 40. 🅰 AE ⓪ VISA
M *(closed Saturday lunch)* 8.50/10.50 **t.** and a la carte 🍾 3.45 – ⊡ 5.00 – **34 rm** 52.00/62.00 **t.**
– SB (except Christmas) (weekends only) 60.00 **st.**

AUDI-VW Dover St. ✆ 556262
AUSTIN-ROVER Leicester Rd ✆ 881601
AUSTIN-ROVER Parker Drive ✆ 352587
AUSTIN-ROVER 60-62 North Gate St. ✆ 28612
AUSTIN-ROVER Abbey Lane ✆ (05336) 669393
CITROEN Lee Circle ✆ 25285
FORD Belgrave Gate ✆ 510111
FORD Conduit St. ✆ 544301
HONDA 33 St. Matthews Way ✆ 516281
NISSAN Abbey Lane ✆ 666861

PORSCHE Coventry Rd at Narborough ✆ 848270
RENAULT, ROLLS-ROYCE Welford Rd ✆ 548757
SKODA 177 Leicester Rd Mount Sorrel ✆ 303055
TALBOT-PEUGEOT 91 Abbey Lane ✆ 661501
VAUXHALL Main St., Evington ✆ 730421
VOLVO 459 Aylestone Rd ✆ 831052

ATS 16 Wanlip St. ✆ 624281
ATS 31 Woodgate ✆ 625611

LEIGH Heref. and Worc. – see Worcester.

LEIGH DELAMERE Wilts. – ⊠ Chippenham – ☎ 0666 Malmesbury

Granada Lodge without rest., SN14 6LB, on M 4 between junctions 17 and 16 (Eastbound
carriageway) ✆ 837691 – ⇥ TV 👤 P. 🅰 AE ⓪ VISA. 🛇
35 rm 22.50/26.00 **t.**

LEIGHTON BUZZARD Beds. 404 S 28 – pop. 29 554 – ECD : Thursday – ☎ 0525.
♦London 47 – Bedford 20 – Luton 12 – Northampton 30.

Swan, High St., LU7 7EA, ✆ 372148, Fax 370444 – TV ☎ P – 🔔 45. 🅰 AE ⓪ VISA. 🛇
M 14.50/18.00 **t.** and a la carte – **38 rm** ⊡ 66.00/90.00 **t.** – SB (except Christmas and
New Year) (weekends only) 116.00/136.00 **st.**

ALFA-ROMEO Victoria Rd, Linslade ✆ 371102
AUSTIN-ROVER 2 Leighton Rd ✆ 373022

ATS Unit C, Camden Ind Est., 83 Lake St. ✆
376158/379238

LENWADE-GREAT WITCHINGHAM Norfolk 404 X 25 – ECD : Wednesday – ⊠ ☎ 0603
Norwich – ♦London 121 – Fakenham 14 – ♦Norwich 10.

Lenwade House 🏖, Fakenham Rd, NR9 5QP, ✆ 872288, ≤, ⊥ heated, 🐾, 🎾, park, 🍴,
squash – TV ☎ P. 🅰 AE ⓪ VISA
M *(closed Sunday lunch)* 7.95/10.95 **t.** and a la carte 🍾 2.50 – ⊡ 3.95 – **14 rm** 31.00/41.00 **t.**
– SB (October-April)(weekends only) 55.00 **st.**

LEOMINSTER Heref. and Worc. 403 L 27 – pop. 8 637 – ECD : Thursday – ☎ 0568.
See : Priory Church★ (14C) (the north aisle★ 12C).
Envir. : Berrington Hall★ (Georgian) AC, N : 3 m. – Croft Castle★ (15C) AC, NW : 6 m.
🛝 Leominster, Ford Bridge ✆ 2863 – 🚻 6 School Lane ✆ 611100.
♦London 141 – ♦Birmingham 47 – Hereford 13 – Worcester 26.

Talbot (Best Western), West St., HR6 8EP, ✆ 6347 – TV ☎ P – 🔔 150. 🅰 AE ⓪ VISA. 🛇
M 9.00/14.00 **t.** and a la carte – **25 rm** ⊡ 45.00/76.00 **t.** – SB (except Christmas)
74.00/81.00 **st.**

Withenfield, South St., HR6 8JN, ✆ 2011, 🎋 – TV ☎ P. 🅰 VISA. 🛇
M 8.50/11.00 **st.** and a la carte 🍾 2.50 – **4 rm** ⊡ 31.50/52.00 **st.** – SB (except Easter, Christmas and New Year) 57.00/60.00 **st.**

at Stoke Prior SE : 2 m. by A 44 – ⊠ ☎ 0568 Leominster :

✕ **Wheelbarrow Castle** with rm, HR6 0NB, ✆ 2219, ⊥ heated – P. 🅰 AE VISA
closed 25 December – M a la carte 13.10/16.00 **t.** 🍾 2.00 – **3 rm** ⊡ 11.50/35.00 **t.**

at Eyton NW : 2 m. by B 4361 – ⊠ ☎ 0568 Leominster :

The Marsh 🏖, HR6 0AG, ✆ 3952, « Part 14C », 🎋 – TV ☎ P. 🅰 AE VISA. 🛇
M 15.00/22.00 **t.** 🍾 6.75 – **5 rm** ⊡ 62.00/103.00 **st.** – SB (except Christmas-New Year)
80.00/105.00 **st.**

AUSTIN-ROVER South St. ✆ 611879
FORD 3-4 Etnam St. ✆ 2060
PEUGEOT-TALBOT The Bargates ✆ 2337

ATS Market Mill, Dishley St. ✆ 2679/4114

LEONARD STANLEY Glos. 403 404 N 28 – see Stroud.

LETCHWORTH Herts. 404 T 28 – pop. 31 146 – ECD : Wednesday – ☎ 046 26 (4 and 5 fig.) or
0462 (6 fig.) – ♦London 40 – Bedford 22 – ♦Cambridge 22 – Luton 14.

Broadway, The Broadway, SG6 3NZ, ✆ 480111, Telex 84525, Fax 481563 – 🛗 ⇥ rm TV
☎ P – 🔔 180. 🅰 AE ⓪ VISA. 🛇
M 6.90/12.00 **t.** 🍾 3.50 – **35 rm** ⊡ 49.50/59.50 **t.**

AUSTIN-ROVER Works Rd ✆ 73161
FORD 18-22 Station Rd ✆ 83722
HONDA Norton Way North ✆ 78191
VW-AUDI Norton Way North ✆ 686341

ATS Unit 21, Jubilee Trade Centre, Works Rd
✆ 670517/8

LETTY GREEN Herts. – see Hertford.

LEWDOWN Devon 403 H 32 – ⊠ ✆ 056 683.
♦London 238 – Exeter 37 – ♦Plymouth 22.

  🏨 **Lewtrenchard Manor** ⤳, EX20 4PN, S : ¾ m. by Lewtrenchard Rd ✆ 256, Fax 332,
  « Manor house and gardens », ⤳, park – TV ✆ P. ⅀ AE ⓪ VISA ⊗
  closed 8 to 31 January – **M** (dinner only and Sunday lunch by arrangement)/dinner
  25.00 **t.** and a la carte 🍷5.00 – **8 rm** ⊊ 50.00/110.00 **t.** – SB (weekends only) 125.00 **st.**

LEWES East Sussex 404 U 31 – pop. 14 499 – ECD : Wednesday – ✆ 0273.
See : Site★.
Envir. : Glynde Place (pictures★) *AC*, E : 3 ½ m. – Firle Place★ (mansion 15C-16C) *AC*, SE :
4 ½ m. – Ditchling Beacon ≼★, W : 7 ½ m. – Glyndebourne Opera Festival (May-August) *AC*,
E : 3 m.
🛉₈ Chapel Hill ✆ 473245, Opp. Junction Cliffe High/South St.
🛈 Lewes House, 32 High St. ✆ 471600.
♦London 53 – Brighton 8 – Hastings 29 – Maidstone 43.

  🏨 **Shelleys** (Mt. Charlotte), High St., BN7 1XS, ✆ 472361, ⪥ – TV ✆ P – ♿
  21 rm.
  ↑ **Millers** without rest., 134 High St., BN7 1XS, ✆ 475631, ⪥ – ⟜⟜ TV. ⊗
  closed Christmas-New Year – **3 rm** ⊊ 28.00/37.00.
  ↑ **Hillside** without rest., Rotten Row, BN7 1TN, ✆ 473120, ⪥ – ⟜⟜. ⊗
  3 rm ⊊ 12.00/26.00 **s.**
  ⅩⅩ **Kenwards**, 151a High St., Pipe Passage, BN7 1XU, ✆ 472343 – ⅀ AE ⓪ VISA
  closed Saturday lunch, Monday dinner and Sunday – **M** (booking essential) a la carte
  17.50/23.50 **st.** 🍷4.50.
  ⅩⅩ **Trumps**, 19-20 Station St., BN7 2DB, ✆ 473906 – ⅀ VISA
  closed dinner Sunday and Monday – **M** (dinner only and Sunday lunch) 18.25 **st.** and a la
  carte 19.85/26.90 **t.** 🍷3.95.

AUSTIN-ROVER Brooks Rd ✆ 473186   ⊛ ATS 18 North St. ✆ 477972/3
FORD Station St. ✆ 474461
VW Western Rd ✆ 473221

LEYLAND Lancs. 402 L 22 – pop. 36 694 – ECD : Wednesday – ✆ 0772.
Envir. : Rufford Old Hall★ SW : 6 ½ m.
🛉₈ Wigan Rd ✆ 436457.
♦London 220 – ♦Liverpool 31 – ♦Manchester 32 – Preston 6.

  🏨 **Penguin**, Leyland Way, PR5 2JX, E : ¾ m. on B 5256 ✆ 422922, Telex 677651, Fax 622282 –
  ⟜⟜ rm TV ✆ ♿ P – ♿ 250. ⅀ AE ⓪ VISA
  M *(closed Saturday lunch)* 7.95/10.95 **st.** and a la carte 🍷6.95 – ⊊ 6.50 – **93 rm** 49.50/
  61.00 **st.**

PEUGEOT-TALBOT Golden Hill Lane ✆ 23416   ⊛ ATS Leyland Lane ✆ 431021/2
SKODA Wigan Rd ✆ 423797

LICHFIELD Staffs. 402 403 404 O 25 – pop. 25 408 – ECD : Wednesday – ✆ 0543.
See : Cathedral★★ (12C-14C).
🛈 Donegal House, Bore St. ✆ 252109.
♦London 128 – ♦Birmingham 16 – Derby 23 – ♦Stoke-on-Trent 30.

  🏨 **George** (Embassy), Bird St., WS13 6PR, ✆ 414822 – ⟜⟜ rm TV ✆ P – ♿
  39 rm.
  🏨 **Little Barrow**, Beacon St., WS13 7AR, ✆ 414500 – TV ✆ P. ⊗
  24 rm.
  🏨 **Angel Croft**, 3 Beacon St., WS13 7AA, ✆ 258737, ⪥ – TV ✆ P. ⅀ ⓪ VISA. ⊗
  closed 25 and 26 December – **M** (closed Sunday dinner) 16.50 **t.** 🍷3.30 – **21 rm**
  ⊊ 49.00/67.50 **t.**
  ↑ **Gaialands** ⤳ without rest., 9 Gaiafields Rd, off Bulldog Lane, WS13 7LT, ✆ 263764, ⪥ –
  P. ⊗
  4 rm ⊊ 15.00/37.00 **st.**
  ⅩⅩ **Oakleigh House** with rm, 25 St. Chad's Rd, WS13 7LZ, ✆ 262688, ⪥ – ▤ rest TV ✆ P.
  ⅀ VISA. ⊗
  M *(closed Sunday and Monday)* (dinner only) a la carte approx. 17.50 **t.** 🍷3.40 – **10 rm**
  ⊊ 30.00/48.00 **t.**
  Ⅹ **Thrales**, 40-44 Tamworth St. (corner of Backcester Lane), ✆ 255091.

AUSTIN-ROVER St. John St. ✆ 414451   ⊛ ATS Eastern Av. ✆ 414200
FORD Birmingham Rd ✆ 414566
NISSAN Birmingham Rd ✆ 414404

📍 Launceston, St. Stephen ☏ 3442, W : 5 m.

♦London 238 – Bude 24 – Exeter 37 – Launceston 4 – ♦Plymouth 32.

🏰 **Arundell Arms** (Best Western), Fore St., PL16 0AA, on A 30 ☏ 84666, Group Telex 45772, ⟋, 🐟 – ⊱≻ rest 📺 ☎ 🅿 – 🕼 50. 🔼 🆀 ⓪ 𝑽𝑰𝑺𝑨
closed 4 days at Christmas – **M** 12.00/20.00 **t.** and a la carte ⓪ 4.00 – **29 rm** ⍓ 46.00/84.00 **t.**
– SB 80.00/108.00 **st.**

LINCOLN Lincs. **402 404** S 24 – pop. 79 980 – ECD : Wednesday – ☎ 0522.
See : Site★ – Cathedral★★★ (11C-15C) (Angel Choir★★, Library : Magna Carta*AC*) Y – High
Bridge★★ Z A – Usher Gallery★★ YZ M1 – Jews House★ (12C) Y – Castle★ (11C)*AC* Y.
Envir. : Doddington Hall★ (Elizabethan) *AC*, SW : 7 m. by A 15 Z and A 46.

📍 Carholme, Carholme Rd ☏ 23725, 1 m. from town centre.

✈ Humberside Airport : ☏ 0652 (Barnetby) 688456, N : 32 m. by A 15 Y.

🛈 9 Castle Hill ☏ 29828 – 21 The Cornhill ☏ 512971.

♦London 140 – Bradford 81 – ♦Cambridge 94 – ♦Kingston-upon-Hull 44 – ♦Leeds 73 – ♦Leicester 53 – ♦Norwich
104 – ♦Nottingham 38 – ♦Sheffield 48 – York 82.

Plan on next page

🏰 **White Hart** (T.H.F.), Bailgate, LN1 3AR, ☏ 526222, Telex 56304, Fax 531798, « Antique
furniture » – ▤ ⊱≻ rm 📺 ☎ ⥤ 🅿 – 🕼 100. 🔼 🆀 ⓪ 𝑽𝑰𝑺𝑨   Y c
M 6.50/13.50 **st.** and a la carte – ⍓ 5.45 – **36 rm** 65.00/95.00 **st.**, **13 suites** 125.00/150.00 **st.**
– SB (weekends only) 84.00/104.00 **st.**

🏠 **D'Isney Place** without rest., Eastgate, LN2 4AA, ☏ 538881, 🐟 – 📺 ☎. 🔼 🆀 ⓪ 𝑽𝑰𝑺𝑨
18 rm ⍓ 38.00/110.00 **t.**   Y e

🏠 **Hillcrest**, 15 Lindum Terr., LN2 5RT, ☏ 510182, ≤, 🐟 – 📺 ☎ 🅿. 🔼 𝑽𝑰𝑺𝑨   Y o
closed 2 weeks Christmas – **M** (closed Sunday) (bar lunch)/dinner a la carte approx. 9.40 **t.**
⓪ 3.80 – **17 rm** ⍓ 32.50/45.00 **t.** – SB (weekends only) 52.00 **t.**

🏠 **Minster Lodge** without rest., 3 Church Lane, LN2 1QJ, ☏ 513220 – 📺 ☎ 🅿. 🔼 𝑽𝑰𝑺𝑨. ⌘
5 rm ⍓ 40.00/49.00 **t.**   Y a

🏠 Woodcocks, Burton Lane End, Saxilby Rd, LN1, NW : 3 ½ m. on A 57 ☏ 703000, 🐟 – 📺 ☎
🅿 – **8 rm**.   by A 57   Z

🏠 **Grand,** St. Mary's St., LN5 7EP, ☏ 524211, Telex 56401 – 📺 ☎ 🅿. 🔼 🆀 ⓪ 𝑽𝑰𝑺𝑨   Z u
M 6.50/9.00 **t.** and a la carte – **48 rm** ⍓ 34.00/45.00 **t.** – SB (weekends only) 60.00 **st.**

🏠 **Carline** without rest., 3 Carline Rd, LN1 1HN, ☏ 530422 – ⊱≻ 📺 🅿   Y i
closed Christmas and New Year – **11 rm** ⍓ 11.50/25.00.

🏠 **Fircroft,** 396-398 Newark Rd, LN6 8RX, SW : 2 m. on A 1434 ☏ 526522 – 📺 🅿. 🔼 𝑽𝑰𝑺𝑨
closed New Year – **M** (by arrangement) 8.50 **st.** – **15 rm** ⍓ 19.00/36.50 **st.**   by A 15   Z

🏠 **Rowan Lodge** without rest., 58 Pennell St., LN5 7TA, ☏ 29589 – 🅿. ⌘   Z v
4 rm ⍓ 11.00/22.00 **st.**

🏠 **Tennyson,** 7 South Park Av., LN5 8EN, ☏ 521624 – 📺 🅿. 🔼 🆀 𝑽𝑰𝑺𝑨. ⌘ by A 158   Z
closed Christmas-New Year – **M** (by arrangement) 9.50 **st.** ⓪ 3.50 – **8 rm** ⍓ 24.00/40.00 **st.**
– SB 46.00 **st.**

✕✕ **Harveys,** 1 Exchequer Gate, Castle Sq., LN2 1PZ, ☏ 510333 – 🔼 𝑽𝑰𝑺𝑨   Y r
closed Saturday lunch, Sunday dinner and 26 December – **M** 7.95/16.95 **t.** ⓪ 3.40.

✕ Bombay, 6 The Strait, ☏ 23264, Indian rest.   Z a

✕ Newport Arch, 50 Bailsgate, LN1 3AR, ☏ 45006, Chinese rest.   Y n

✕ **White's,** Jews House, 15 The Strait, LN2 1JD, ☏ 24851, « 12C town house » – ⊱≻. 🔼 𝑽𝑰𝑺𝑨
closed Sunday dinner – **M** 5.95/20.00 **t.** and a la carte 6.50/20.00 **t.** ⓪ 4.50.   YZ x

at Washingborough E : 3 m. by B 1188 – Z – on B 1190 – ✉ ☎ 0522 Lincoln :

🏠 **Washingborough Hall** 🐕, Church Hill, LN4 1BE, ☏ 790340, 🏊, 🐟 – ⊱≻ 📺 ☎ 🅿
🕼. 🔼 🆀 ⓪ 𝑽𝑰𝑺𝑨
M (bar lunch Monday to Saturday)/dinner 15.00 **t.** – **12 rm** ⍓ 38.00/55.00 **t.** –
SB (except Christmas and New Year) 54.00/70.00 **st.**

at Branston SE : 3 m. on B 1188 – Z – ☎ 0522 Lincoln :

🏰 **Moor Lodge,** Sleaford Rd, LN4 1HU, ☏ 791366, Fax 510720 – 📺 ☎ ♿ 🅿 – 🕼 160. 🔼 🆀
⓪ 𝑽𝑰𝑺𝑨
M (closed Saturday lunch) 10.25/12.15 **t.** and a la carte – **25 rm** ⍓ 47.50/72.50 **t.** –
SB (except Christmas and New Year) 66.00/76.00 **st.**

MICHELIN Distribution Centre, Tritton Rd, LN6 7RX, ☏ 684023, FAX 500973 by A 1180 Z

AUSTIN-ROVER Outer Circle Rd ☏ 535771
BMW South Park Av. ☏ 521345
CITROEN 300 Wragby Rd ☏ 531195
DAIMLER-JAGUAR 116 High St. ☏ 513410
FIAT 316-322 Wragby Rd ☏ 534805
FORD Wragby Rd ☏ 530101
HONDA, LANCIA Wragby Rd ☏ 531735
LADA Newark Rd, North Hykeham ☏ 681242
MAZDA Tritton Rd ☏ 681094
MITSUBISHI Tritton Rd ☏ 500880

RENAULT 25 Wragby Rd ☏ 521252
SAAB 247 Lincoln Rd ☏ 500200
TALBOT-PEUGEOT 477 High St. ☏ 529131
VAUXHALL Outer Circle Rd ☏ 527127
VOLVO 314 Wragby Rd ☏ 29462/3
VW-AUDI 223 Newark Rd ☏ 531881

⑩ ATS Crofton Rd, Allenby Rd Trading Est. ☏ 27225
ATS Newmark Rd, North Hykeham ☏ 684510

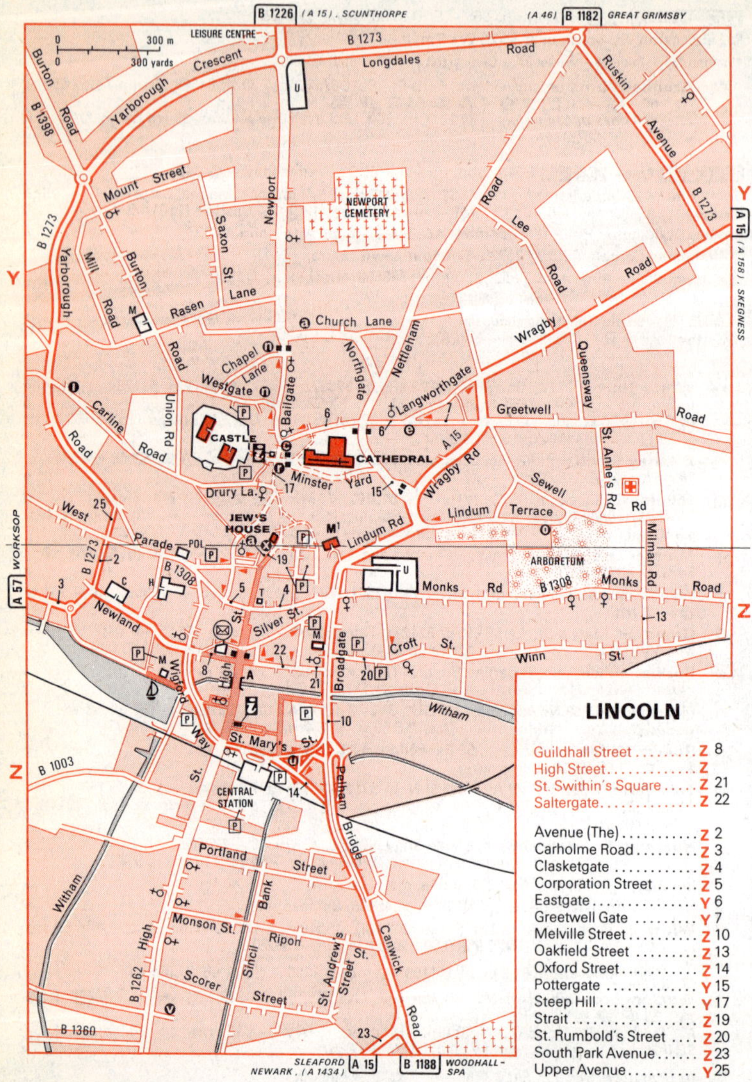

LINCOLN

Guildhall Street . . . . Z 8
High Street . . . . Z
St. Swithin's Square . . . . . Z 21
Saltergate . . . . Z 22

Avenue (The) . . . . Z 2
Carholme Road . . . . Z 3
Clasketgate . . . . Z 4
Corporation Street . . . . . . Z 5
Eastgate . . . . Y 6
Greetwell Gate . . . . Y 7
Melville Street . . . . Z 10
Oakfield Street . . . . Z 13
Oxford Street . . . . Z 14
Pottergate . . . . Y 15
Steep Hill . . . . Y 17
Strait . . . . Z 19
St. Rumbold's Street . . . . Z 20
South Park Avenue . . . . . . Z 23
Upper Avenue . . . . Y 25

LIPHOOK Hants. **404** R 30 – pop. 4 697 – ✆ 0428 – 🏌 Old Thorns, Longmoor Rd ✆ 724555.
◆London 50 – Guildford 17 – ◆Portsmouth 27.

🏨 **Milland Place** ⚓, Milland, GU30 7JW, S : 2 m. by A 3 ✆ 042 876 (Milland) 633, Fax 643,
≼, « Garden » – 📺 ☎ 🅿. 🔺 AE ⓪ VISA. ✦
M 16.50 **t.** (lunch) and a la carte 24.25/39.75 **t.** 🍷 6.00 – 🍽 10.25 – **17 rm** 75.00/115.00 **t.**,
1 suite 150.00 **t.**

🏨 **Old Thorns** ⚓, Longmoor Rd, GU30 7PE, W : 1 m. on B 2131 ✆ 724555, Telex 858293, Fax
725036, 🔲, 🏌, 🛥, ✂ – 📺 ☎ 🅿 – 🔺 60. 🔺 AE ⓪ VISA. ✦
M (see **Nippon-Kan** below) – 🍽 4.00 – **32 rm** 75.00/95.00 **t.** – SB (weekends
only) 115.00/135.00 **st.**

XX **Nippon-Kan** (at Old Thorns H.), Longmoor Rd, GU30 7PE, W : 1 m. on B 2131 ✆ 724555,
Telex 858293, Fax 725036, Japanese rest., 🛥 – 🅿. 🔺 AE ⓪ VISA
closed Monday and 2 weeks Christmas – **M** 16.00/40.00 **t.** and a la carte approx. 14.00 **t.**

LISKEARD Cornwall **403** G 32 The West Country G. – pop. 6 213 – ECD : Wednesday –
◎ 0579 – See : Church★ – Envir. : St. Neot★ (Church★★) NW : 5 m.
♦London 261 – Exeter 59 – ♦Plymouth 18 – Truro 37.

- **Country Castle** ⑤, Station Rd, PL14 4EB, SW : ¾ m. by B 3254 ℘ 42694, 🏊, 🥾 – 📺 ⑳
  P. 🔄 **VISA** – closed November – **M** (lunch by arrangement)/dinner 12.50 **st.** and a la carte
  ⑧ 3.50 – **11 rm** � 33.00/58.00 **st.** – SB 73.00/78.00 **st.**

  at St. Keyne S : 3 m. on B 3254 – ✉ ◎ 0579 Liskeard :

- **Old Rectory** ⑤, Duloe Rd, PL14 4RL, ℘ 42617, 🥾 – ⇔ rest 📺 **P**. 🔄 **VISA**
  closed Christmas – **M** (dinner only) (residents only) a la carte 8.00/16.50 **st.** ⑧ 3.25 – **8 rm**
  ⊠ 31.00/50.00 **st.** – SB (except summer) 55.00 **st.**

- XXX **Well House** ⑤ with rm, PL14 4RN, SE : ¾ m. by St. Keyne Well Rd ℘ 42001, ≤, 🏊 heated,
  🥾, 🍽 – 📺 ☎ **P**. 🔄 **AE** **VISA**
  M (closed Monday to non-residents) 19.50/26.50 **t.** ⑧ 3.50 – ⊠ 6.50 – **7 rm** 60.00/95.00 **t.**

◍ ATS 10 Dean St. ℘ 45489/45247

LISS Hants. **404** R 30 – pop. 5 489 – ◎ 0730 – ♦London 57 – ♦Portsmouth 22 – Reading 34.

- XX Madhuban Tandoori, 94 Station Rd, GU33 7AQ, ℘ 893363, Indian rest., 🥾 – **P**.

LITTLE CHALFONT Bucks. **404** S 29 – pop. 4 093 – ◎ 024 04.
ᵢ₉ Lodge Lane, Amersham ℘ 4877 – ♦London 31 – Luton 20 – ♦Oxford 37.

- XX **Dynasty 1**, 9 Nightingales Corner, HP7 9PZ, ℘ 4038, Chinese (Peking) rest. – 🔄 **AE** **VISA**
  M 18.00/28.00 **t.** and a la carte 15.00/25.00 **t.**

PEUGEOT 4 White Lion Rd ℘ 4666

LITTLE HAVEN Dyfed **403** E 28 – ECD : Thursday – ✉ Haverfordwest – ◎ 0437 Broad Haven.
♦London 258 – Haverfordwest 8.

- **Haven Fort**, Settlands Hill, SA62 3LA, ℘ 781401, ≤ St. Brides Bay, 🥾 – ⇔ **P**. 🐾
  Mid March-mid October – **M** (bar lunch)/dinner 12.95 **t.** and a la carte ⑧3.00 – **15 rm**
  ⊠ 20.50/41.00 **t.**

- ♠ **Pendyffryn**, SA62 3LA, ℘ 781337, ≤ – ⇔ rest 📺 **P** 🐾
  May-October – **M** 8.00 **t.** – **7 rm** ⊠ 15.00/17.00 **t.**

LITTLE LANGDALE Cumbria **402** K 20 – see Ambleside.

LITTLEOVER Derbs. **402** **403** **404** P 25 – see Derby.

LITTLE PETHERICK Cornwall **403** F 32 – see Padstow.

LITTLEPORT Cambs **404** U 26 – see Ely.

LITTLE SINGLETON Lancs. – see Blackpool.

LITTLE THORNTON Lancs. **402** L 22 – see Blackpool.

LITTLE WALSINGHAM Norfolk **404** W 25 – ✉ Walsingham – ◎ 0328 Fakenham.
♦London 117 – ♦Cambridge 67 – Cromer 21 – ♦Norwich 32.

- ⚘ **White Horse Inn**, East Barsham, NR21 0LH, S : 2 ¼ m. on B 1105 ℘ 820645 – 📺 **P**
  M (closed Tuesday lunch, Sunday dinner and Monday) (bar lunch)/dinner a la carte
  approx. 5.95 – **3 rm** ⊠ 28.00/39.00 **st.** – SB 34.00 **st.**

- X **Old Bakehouse** with rm, 33-35 High St., NR22 6BZ, ℘ 820454
  closed February and 3 weeks October-November – **M** (closed Monday dinner and Sunday
  April-October, Wednesday and Sunday November-March) (dinner only and Sunday lunch
  July-August)/dinner a la carte 12.10/15.55 **t.** ⑧ 3.25 – **3 rm** ⊠ 17.00/34.00.

LITTLE WEIGHTON Humberside **402** S 22 – see Kingston-upon-Hull.

LITTLE WYMONDLEY Herts. **404** T 28 – see Hitchin.

LIVERPOOL p. 1

LIVERPOOL Merseyside **402** **403** L 23 – pop. 538 809 – ECD : Wednesday – ◎ 051.
See : Site★ – Walker Art Gallery★★ **CY** M1 – Anglican Cathedral★★ (1904) **CZ** A – Roman
Catholic Cathedral★ (1967) **DZ** B – Albert Dock★ **CZ** – Merseyside Martime Museum★ **CZ** M2 –
Envir. : AC, NE : 8 m. by A 57 **BX** – Speke Hall★ (16C) AC, SE : 7 m. by A 561 **BX**.
ᵢ₁₈ Dunnings Bridge Rd, Bootle ℘ 928 1371, N : 5 m. by A 5036 **AV** – ᵢ₁₈ Allerton Park ℘ 428 8510,
S : 5 m. by B 5180 **BX** – ᵢ₁₈ Childwall, Naylor's Rd, Gateacre ℘ 487 0654, E : 7 m. by B 5178 **BX**.
✈ Liverpool Airport : ℘ 486 8877, Telex 629323, SE : 6 m. by A 561 **BX** – Terminal : Pier Head.
⛴ to Ireland (Dun Laoghaire) (Sealink) 1 daily – to Belfast (Belfast Ferries) 1 daily (9 h) – to
Douglas (Isle of Man Steam Packet Co.) 2-4 weekly (summer only) (4 h) – ⛴ to Birkenhead
(Merseyside Transport) frequent services daily (7-8 mn) – to Wallasey (Merseyside Transport)
frequent services daily (7-8 mn) – 🄯 29 Lime St. ℘ 709 3631 – Atlantic Pavilion, Albert Dock
℘ 708 8854 – ♦London 219 – ♦Birmingham 103 – ♦Leeds 75 – ♦Manchester 35.

Town plans : Liverpool pp. 2-5

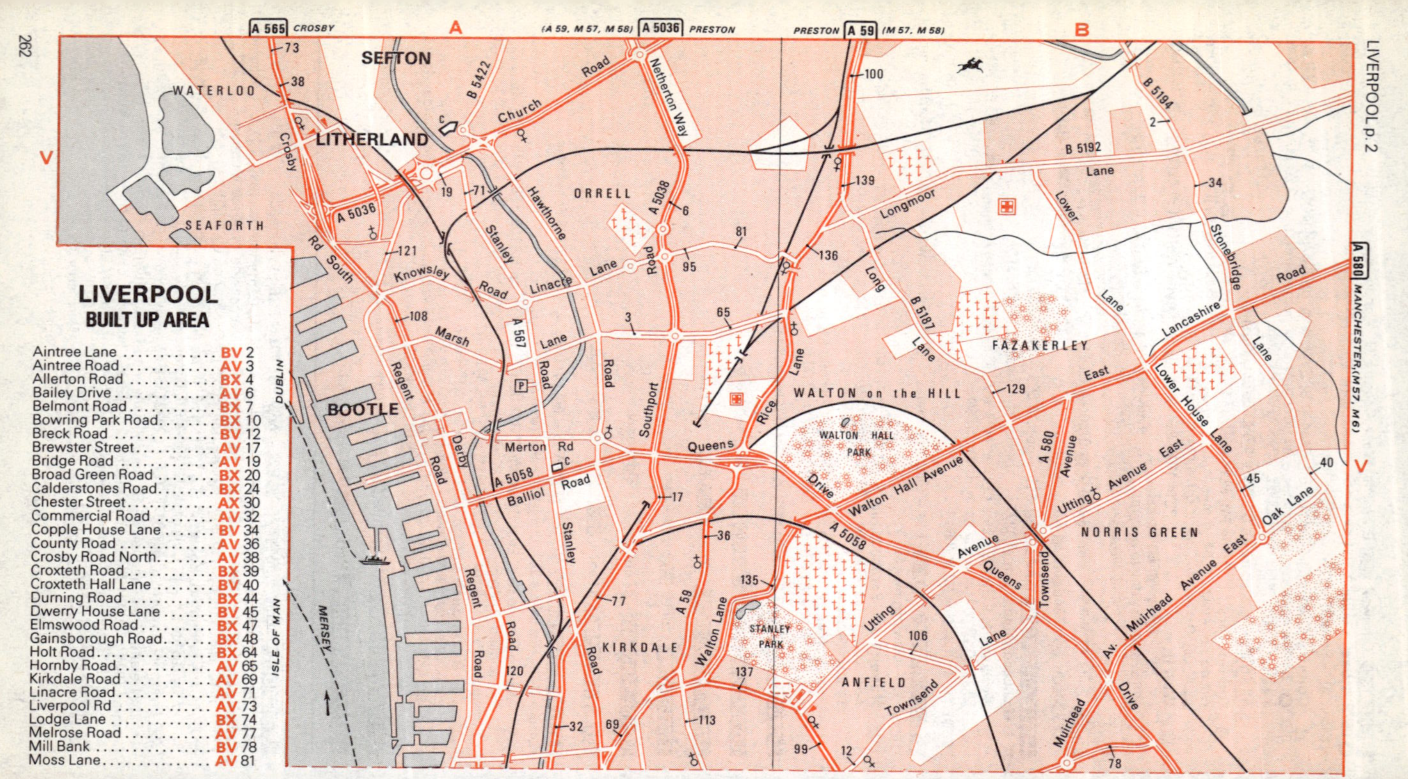
A 565 CROSBY
A
(A 59, M 57, M 58) A 5036 PRESTON
PRESTON A 59 (M 57, M 58)
B
SEFTON
WATERLOO
LITHERLAND
SEAFORTH
BOOTLE
ORRELL
FAZAKERLEY
WALTON on the HILL
WALTON HALL PARK
NORRIS GREEN
KIRKDALE
STANLEY PARK
ANFIELD
A 580 MANCHESTER (M 57, M 6)
B 5422
B 5194
B 5192
B 5187
Church Road
Netherton Way
Hawthorne
Stanley Road
Knowsley Road
Linacre Lane
Marsh Lane
Southport Road
Rice Lane
Long Lane
Longmoor Lane
Lower Lane
Lancashire Lane
Stonebridge Road
Lower House Lane
East
A 580 Avenue
Walton Hall Avenue
Utting Avenue
Oak Lane
Muirhead Avenue East
Queens
Townsend
Utting Lane
Muirhead Drive
Walton Lane
A 59
A 5058
Regent Road
Derby Road
A 5058
Balliol Road
Merton Rd
A 567
Crosby Rd South
A 5036
DUBLIN
ISLE OF MAN
MERSEY
LIVERPOOL
BUILT UP AREA
Aintree Lane .... BV 2
Aintree Road .... AV 3
Allerton Road .... BX 4
Bailey Drive .... AV 6
Belmont Road .... BX 7
Bowring Park Road ...... BX 10
Breck Road .... BV 12
Brewster Street .... AV 17
Bridge Road .... AV 19
Broad Green Road .... BX 20
Calderstones Road ...... BX 24
Chester Street .... AX 30
Commercial Road .... AV 32
Copple House Lane ...... BV 34
County Road .... AV 36
Crosby Road North ...... AV 38
Croxteth Road .... BX 39
Croxteth Hall Lane ..... BV 40
Durning Road .... BX 44
Dwerry House Lane ...... BV 45
Elmswood Road .... BX 47
Gainsborough Road ...... BX 48
Holt Road .... BX 64
Hornby Road .... AV 65
Kirkdale Road .... AV 69
Linacre Road .... AV 71
Liverpool Rd .... AV 73
Lodge Lane .... BX 74
Melrose Road .... AV 77
Mill Bank .... BV 78
Moss Lane .... AV 81

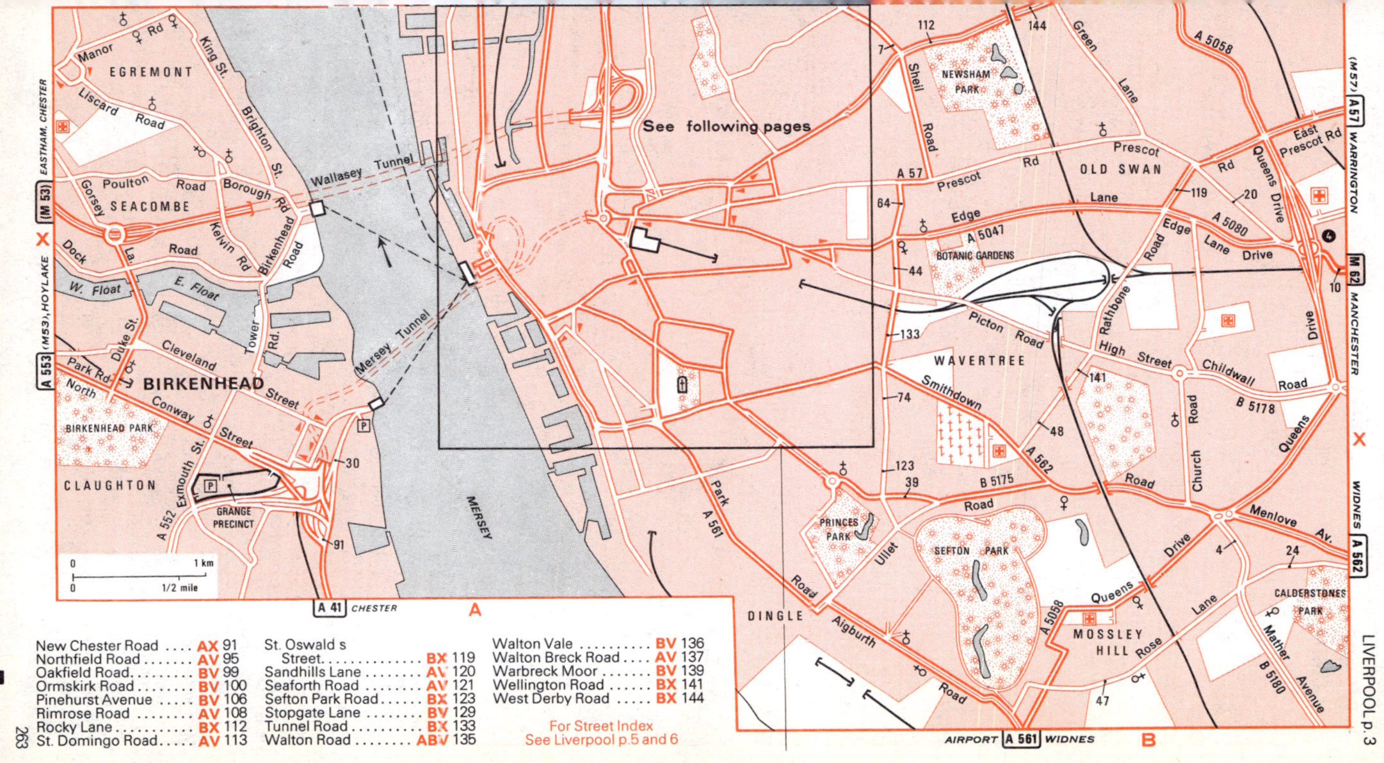
EGREMONT
Manor Rd
Liscard Road
King St.
Brighton St.
Borough Rd
Poulton Road
Gorsey La.
SEACOMBE
Dock
Kelvin Rd
Birkenhead Road
W. Float
E. Float
Tower Rd.
Duke St.
Cleveland Street
Park Rd
North
BIRKENHEAD
Conway Street
Exmouth St.
BIRKENHEAD PARK
CLAUGHTON
A 552
GRANGE PRECINCT
30
91
Wallasey Tunnel
Mersey Tunnel
P
P
MERSEY
See following pages
A 57 Prescot
64
Edge
A 5047
BOTANIC GARDENS
44
133
74
Picton Road
WAVERTREE
Smithdown
123
39
B 5175
Park
A 561
PRINCES PARK
Ullet
SEFTON PARK
Road
Aigburth
DINGLE
Road
112
7
Shell Road
NEWSHAM PARK
Green Lane
Lane
A 5058
Prescot Rd
OLD SWAN
Lane
119
20
Edge Lane Drive
A 5080
Rathbone Road
141
High Street
Edge Lane
Road
Childwall
B 5178
Queens
48
A 562
Road
Church Road
Road
Queens Drive
Menlove Av.
4
24
Rose Lane
A 5058
Queens
MOSSLEY HILL
CALDERSTONES PARK
Mather Avenue
B 5180
47
(M57) A57 WARRINGTON
East Prescot Rd
M62 MANCHESTER
10
WIDNES A562
AIRPORT A 561 WIDNES
A 553 (M53), HOYLAKE
EASTHAM, CHESTER
(M 53)
A 553
A 41 CHESTER
A
B
LIVERPOOL p. 3
0 1 km
0 1/2 mile
New Chester Road .... AX 91
Northfield Road ...... AV 95
Oakfield Road .... BV 99
Ormskirk Road ...... BV 100
Pinehurst Avenue .... BV 106
Rimrose Road .... AV 108
Rocky Lane .... BX 112
St. Domingo Road .... AV 113
St. Oswald's Street ... BX 119
Sandhills Lane ...... AV 120
Seaforth Road ...... AV 121
Sefton Park Road .... BX 123
Stopgate Lane ...... BV 129
Tunnel Road .... BX 133
Walton Road .... ABV 135
Walton Vale .... BV 136
Walton Breck Road ... AV 137
Warbreck Moor ..... BV 139
Wellington Road .... BX 141
West Derby Road ... BX 144
For Street Index
See Liverpool p.5 and 6

LIVERPOOL
CENTRE

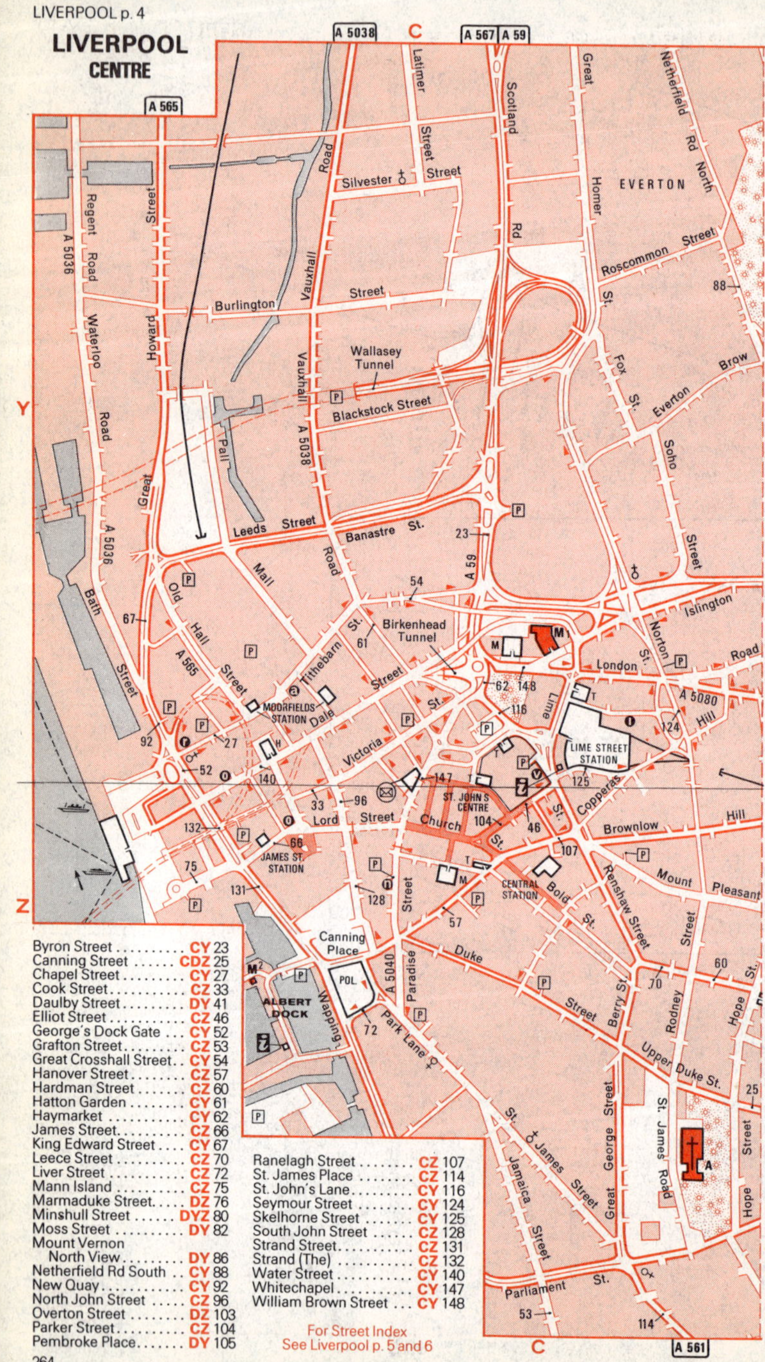

Byron Street .... CY 23
Canning Street ...... CDZ 25
Chapel Street .... CY 27
Cook Street .... CZ 33
Daulby Street .... DY 41
Elliot Street .... CZ 46
George's Dock Gate ... CY 52
Grafton Street .... CZ 53
Great Crosshall Street.. CY 54
Hanover Street .... CZ 57
Hardman Street .... CZ 60
Hatton Garden .... CY 61
Haymarket .... CY 62
James Street .... CZ 66
King Edward Street ... CY 67
Leece Street .... CZ 70
Liver Street .... CZ 72
Mann Island .... CZ 75
Marmaduke Street..... DZ 76
Minshull Street ...... DYZ 80
Moss Street .... DY 82
Mount Vernon
  North View .... DY 86
Netherfield Rd South . CY 88
New Quay .... CY 92
North John Street .... CZ 96
Overton Street .... DZ 103
Parker Street......... CZ 104
Pembroke Place....... DY 105

Ranelagh Street .... CZ 107
St. James Place .... CZ 114
St. John's Lane .... CY 116
Seymour Street .... CY 124
Skelhorne Street .... CY 125
South John Street ...... CZ 128
Strand Street .... CZ 131
Strand (The) .... CZ 132
Water Street .... CY 140
Whitechapel .... CY 147
William Brown Street ... CY 148

For Street Index
See Liverpool p. 5 and 6

STREET INDEX

Church St. . . . . p. 4 **CZ**
Bold St. . . . . p. 4 **CZ**
Lime St. . . . . p. 4 **CY**
London Rd. . . . . p. 4 **CY**
Lord St. . . . . p. 4 **CZ**
Parker St. . . . . p. 4 **CZ** 104
Ranelagh St. . . . . p. 4 **CZ** 107
Renshaw St. . . . . p. 4 **CZ**
St. Johns Centre . . . . . p. 4 **CY**

Aigburth Rd. . . . . p. 3 **BX**
Aintree Lane . . . . p. 2 **BV** 2
Aintree Rd . . . . p. 2 **AV** 3
Allerton Rd . . . . p. 3 **BX** 4
Bailey Drive . . . . p. 2 **AV** 6
Balliol Rd . . . . p. 2 **AV**
Bath St. . . . . p. 4 **CY**
Belmont Rd . . . . p. 3 **BX** 7
Berry St. . . . . p. 4 **CZ**
Birkenhead Rd . . . . p. 3 **AX**
Blackstock St. . . . . p. 4 **CY**
Boaler St. . . . . p. 5 **DY**
Bold St. . . . . p. 4 **CZ**
Borough Rd. . . . . p. 3 **AX**
Bowring Park Rd. . . . . . p. 3 **BX** 10
Breck Rd . . . . p. 5 **DY**
Brewster St. . . . . p. 2 **AV** 17
Bridge Rd . . . . p. 2 **AV** 19
Brighton St. . . . . p. 3 **AX**
Broad Green Rd . . . . . . p. 3 **BX** 20
Brownlow Hill . . . . p. 4 **CZ**
Brunswick Rd . . . . p. 5 **DY**
Burlington St. . . . . p. 4 **CY**
Byron St. . . . . p. 4 **CY** 23
Calderstones Rd. . . . . . p. 3 **BX** 24
Canning Pl. . . . . p. 4 **CZ**
Canning St. . . . . p. 5 **DZ** 25
Catharine St. . . . . p. 5 **DZ**
Chapel St. . . . . p. 4 **CY** 27
Chester St. . . . . p. 3 **AX** 30
Childwall Rd . . . . p. 3 **BX**
Church Rd . . . . p. 3 **BX**
Church Rd
    LITHERLAND . . . . . . p. 2 **AV**
Church St. . . . . p. 4 **CZ**
Cleveland St. . . . . p. 3 **AX**
Commercial Rd . . . . . . p. 2 **AV** 32
Conway St. . . . . p. 3 **AX**
Cook St. . . . . p. 4 **CZ** 33
Copperas Hill . . . . p. 4 **CZ**
Copple House Lane . . . p. 2 **BV** 34
County Rd . . . . p. 2 **AV** 36
Crosby Rd North. . . . . . p. 2 **AV** 38
Crosby Rd South . . . . . p. 2 **AV**
Crown St. . . . . p. 5 **DZ**
Croxteth Rd . . . . p. 3 **BX** 39
Croxteth Hall Lane . . . . p. 2 **BV** 40
Dale St. . . . . p. 4 **CY**
Daulby St. . . . . p. 5 **DY** 41
Derby Rd . . . . p. 2 **AV**
Duke St. . . . . p. 4 **CZ**
Duke St.
    BIRKENHEAD . . . . . p. 3 **AX**
Durning Rd . . . . p. 3 **DX** 44
Dwerry House Lane . . . p. 2 **BV** 45
East Lancashire Rd . . . p. 2 **BV**
East Prescot Rd . . . . . . p. 3 **BX**
Edge Lane . . . . p. 3 **BX**
Edge Lane Drive . . . . . . p. 3 **BX**
Elliot St. . . . . p. 4 **CZ** 46
Elmswood Rd . . . . p. 3 **BX** 47
Erskine St. . . . . p. 5 **DY**
Everton Brow . . . . p. 4 **CY**
Everton Rd. . . . . p. 5 **DY**
Exmouth St. . . . . p. 3 **AX**
Falkner St. . . . . p. 5 **DZ**
Farnworth St. . . . . p. 5 **DY**
Fox St. . . . . p. 4 **CY**
Freeman St. . . . . p. 3 **AX**
Gainsborough Rd . . . . . p. 3 **BX** 48
George's
    Dock Gate . . . . p. 4 **CY** 52
Gorsey Lane . . . . p. 3 **AX**
Grafton St. . . . . p. 4 **CZ** 53
Great Crosshall St. . . . . p. 4 **CY** 54
Great George St. . . . . . p. 4 **CZ**
Great Homer St. . . . . . . p. 4 **CY**
Great Howard St. . . . . . p. 4 **CY**
Green Lane . . . . p. 3 **BX**

STREET INDEX TO LIVERPOOL TOWN PLANS (concluded)

Street	Page	Grid	No.
Grove St.	p. 5	DZ	
Hall Lane	p. 5	DY	
Hanover St.	p. 4	CZ	57
Hardman St.	p. 4	CZ	60
Hatton Garden	p. 4	CY	61
Haymarket	p. 4	CY	62
Hawthorne Rd	p. 2	AV	
Heyworth St.	p. 5	DY	
High St.	p. 3	BX	
Holt Rd.	p. 3	BX	64
Hope St.	p. 4	CZ	
Hornby Rd.	p. 2	AV	65
Islington	p. 4	CY	
Jamaica St.	p. 4	CZ	
James St.	p. 4	CZ	66
Kelvin Rd	p. 3	AX	
Kensington	p. 5	DY	
King St.	p. 3	AX	
King Edward St.	p. 4	CY	67
Kingsley Rd.	p. 5	DZ	
Kirkdale Rd	p. 2	AV	69
Knowsley Rd.	p. 2	AV	
Latimer St.	p. 4	CY	
Leece St.	p. 4	CZ	70
Leeds St.	p. 4	CY	
Lime St.	p. 4	CY	
Linacre Rd.	p. 2	AV	71
Linacre Lane	p. 2	AV	
Liscard Rd.	p. 3	AX	
Liver St.	p. 4	CZ	72
Liverpool Rd	p. 2	AV	73
Lodge Lane	p. 3	BX	74
London Rd	p. 4	CY	
Long Lane	p. 2	BV	
Longmoor Lane	p. 2	BV	
Lord St.	p. 4	CZ	
Lower House Lane	p. 2	BV	
Lower Lane	p. 2	BV	
Low Hill	p. 5	DY	
Manor Rd	p. 3	AX	
Mann Island	p. 4	CZ	75
Marmaduke St.	p. 5	DZ	76
Marsh Lane	p. 2	AV	
Mather Av.	p. 3	BX	
Melrose Rd	p. 2	AV	77
Menlove Av.	p. 3	BX	
Merton Rd.	p. 2	AV	
Mill Bank	p. 2	BV	78
Minshull St.	p. 5	DY	80
Moss Lane	p. 2	AV	81
Moss St.	p. 5	DY	82
Mount Pleasant	p. 4	CZ	
Mount Vernon North View	p. 5	DY	86
Muirhead Av.	p. 2	BV	
Muirhead Av. E.	p. 2	BV	
Myrtle St.	p. 5	DZ	
Netherfield Rd N.	p. 4	CY	
Netherfield Rd S.	p. 4	CY	88
Netherton Way	p. 2	AV	
New Chester Rd.	p. 3	AX	91
New Quay	p. 4	CY	92
Northfield Rd	p. 2	AV	95
North John St.	p. 4	CZ	96
Norton St.	p. 4	CY	
Oakfield Rd.	p. 2	BV	99
Oak Lane	p. 2	BV	
Old Hall St.	p. 4	CY	
Ormskirk Rd	p. 2	BV	100
Overbury St.	p. 5	DZ	
Overton St.	p. 5	DZ	103
Oxford St.	p. 5	DZ	
Pall Mall	p. 4	CY	
Paradise St.	p. 4	CZ	
Parker St.	p. 4	CZ	104
Park Lane	p. 4	CZ	
Park Rd	p. 3	AX	
Park Rd North	p. 3	AX	
Parliament St.	p. 4	CZ	
Pembroke Pl.	p. 5	DY	105
Picton Rd	p. 3	BX	
Pinehurst Av.	p. 2	BV	106
Poulton Rd	p. 3	AX	
Prescot Rd	p. 3	BX	
Prescot St.	p. 5	DY	
Prince's Rd	p. 5	DZ	
Queens Drive	p. 3	BX	
Queensway	p. 3	AX	
Ranelagh St.	p. 4	CZ	107
Rathbone Rd	p. 3	BX	
Regent Rd.	p. 2	AV	
Renshaw St.	p. 4	CZ	
Rice Lane	p. 2	AV	
Rimrose Rd.	p. 2	AV	108
Rocky Lane	p. 3	BX	112
Rodney St.	p. 4	CZ	
Roscommon St.	p. 4	CY	
Rose Lane	p. 3	BX	
St. Domingo Rd	p. 2	AV	113
St. James Pl.	p. 4	CZ	114
St. James Rd	p. 4	CZ	
St. James St.	p. 4	CZ	
St. John's Lane	p. 4	CY	116
St. Johns Centre	p. 4	CY	
St. Oswald's St.	p. 3	BX	119
Sandhills Lane	p. 2	AV	120
Scotland Rd	p. 4	CY	
Seaforth Rd	p. 2	AV	121
Sefton Park Rd	p. 3	BX	123
Seymour St.	p. 4	CY	124
Shaw St.	p. 5	DY	
Sheil Rd.	p. 3	BX	
Silvester St.	p. 4	CY	
Skelhorne St.	p. 4	CY	125
Smithdown Lane	p. 5	DZ	
Smithdown Rd.	p. 3	BX	
Soho St.	p. 4	CY	
South John St.	p. 4	CZ	128
Southport Rd	p. 2	AV	
Stanley Rd	p. 2	AV	
Stonebridge Lane	p. 2	BV	
Stopgate Lane	p. 2	BV	129
Strand St.	p. 4	CZ	131
Strand (The)	p. 4	CZ	132
Tithebarn St.	p. 4	CY	
Townsend Av.	p. 2	BV	
Townsend Lane	p. 2	BV	
Tunnel Rd	p. 3	BX	133
Ullet Rd	p. 3	BX	
Upper Duke St.	p. 4	CZ	
Upper Parliament St.	p. 5	DZ	
Utting Av.	p. 2	BV	
Utting Av. E.	p. 2	BV	
Vauxhall Rd	p. 4	CY	
Victoria St.	p. 4	CY	
Walton Lane	p. 2	AV	
Walton Rd.	p. 2	AV	135
Walton Vale	p. 2	BV	136
Walton Breck Rd	p. 2	AV	137
Walton Hall Av.	p. 2	BV	
Wapping	p. 4	CZ	
Warbreck Moor	p. 2	BV	139
Water St.	p. 4	CY	140
Waterloo Rd	p. 4	CY	
Wellington Rd	p. 3	BX	141
West Derby Rd.	p. 3	BX	144
West Derby St.	p. 5	DY	
Whitechapel	p. 4	CY	147
William Brown St.	p. 4	CY	148

🏨 **Liverpool Moat House** (Q.M.H.), Paradise St., L1 8JD, ✆ 709 0181, Telex 627270, Fax 709 2706, 🔲 – 🛗 🖥 📺 ☎ ♿ – 🏊 400. 🔳 AE ⓞ *VISA*
CZ **n**
closed 25 and 26 December – **M** *(closed Saturday lunch)* 10.00/15.50 **st.** and a la carte 🍶 5.00 – **251 rm** ☲ 70.50/90.00 **st.**, **7 suites** 160.00/200.00 **st.** – SB (weekends only) 74.00/100.00 **st.**

🏨 **Atlantic Tower** (Mt. Charlotte), 30 Chapel St., L3 9RE, ✆ 227 4444, Telex 627070, ≼ – 🛗 🖥 📺 ☎ 🅿 – 🏊
216 rm, **10 suites**.
CY **r**

🏨 **St. George's** (T.H.F.), St. John's Precinct, Lime St., L1 1NQ, ✆ 709 7090, Telex 627630, Fax 709 0137 – 🛗 ✲ rm 📺 ☎ ♿ 🅿 – 🏊 200. 🔳 AE ⓞ *VISA*
CY **v**
M 6.25/9.95 **st.** and a la carte 🍶 3.95 – ☲ 7.60 – **153 rm** 56.00/77.00 **st.**, **2 suites** 87.00 **st.**

🏨 Trials, 62 Castle St., L2 7LQ, ✆ 227 1021 – 🛗 📺 ☎ 🅿. ✲
CZ **o**
20 rm.

🏨 **Crest** (Crest), Lord Nelson St., L3 5QB, ✆ 709 7050, Telex 627954, Fax 709 2193 – 🛗 ✲ rm 📺 ☎ 🅿 – 🏊 500. 🔳 AE ⓞ *VISA*
CY **i**
M 7.00/15.50 **st.** and a la carte 🍶 4.25 – ☲ 7.55 – **159 rm** 58.00/70.00 **st.**, **1 suite** 75.00/85.00 **st.** – SB (weekends only) 72.00/74.00 **st.**

XXX **L'Oriel**, Oriel Chambers, 14 Water St., L2 8TD, ✆ 236 5025 – 🔳 AE ⓞ *VISA*
CY **o**
closed 25-26 December and 1 January – **M** *(closed Saturday lunch and Sunday dinner)* 9.00/11.00 **t.** and a la carte 14.10/19.80 **t.** 🍶 3.95.

XXX **Churchill's**, Churchill House, Tithebarn St., L2 2PB, ✆ 227 3877 – 🔳 AE ⓞ *VISA*
CY **a**
closed Saturday lunch, Sunday and Bank Holidays – **M** 10.25/12.95 **t.** and a la carte 14.95/20.20 🍶 3.95.

at Bootle N : 5 m. by A 565 – AV – ✉ ⊙ 051 Liverpool :

🏨 **Park** (De Vere), Park Lane West, L30 3SU, on A 5036 ✆ 525 7555, Telex 629772, Fax 525 2481 – 🛗 📺 ☎ 🅿 – 🏊 50. 🔳 AE ⓞ *VISA*
M 12.00 **t.** and a la carte 8.00/11.65 **t.** 🍶 3.00 – **58 rm** ☲ 49.50/62.00 **t.** – SB 60.00 **st.**

at Huyton E : 7 m. by M 62 on A 5058 – ✉ ⊙ 051 Liverpool :

🏨 **Derby Lodge**, Roby Rd, L36 4HD, ✆ 480 4440, Telex 629371, Fax 480 8132, ✍ – 📺 ☎ 🅿. 🔳 AE ⓞ *VISA* ✲
M *(closed Saturday lunch)* 10.90/11.95 **t.** and a la carte 🍶 3.00 – **16 rm** ☲ 60.00/72.00 **t.**

at Aigburth SE : 4 m. on A 561 – BX – ✉ ☎ 051 Liverpool :

🏠 **Grange**, 14 Holmefield Rd, L19 3PG, ℰ 427 2950, Fax 427 9055, 🍴 – ⫗ rest 📺 ☎ Ⓟ. 🅢
AE ⓪ VISA. ⫶
M (dinner only and Sunday lunch) (Sunday dinner to residents only)/dinner 15.95 t. and
a la carte ▯ 4.05 – **25 rm** ⚏ 39.70/57.50 st. – SB (weekends only) 69.40 **st.**

AUSTIN-ROVER 72-74 Coronation Rd ℰ 924 6411
AUSTIN-ROVER Kensington ℰ 263 0661
AUSTIN-ROVER Long Lane ℰ 523 3737
BMW Scotland Rd ℰ 207 7213
BMW Aigburth Rd ℰ 427 8086
CITROEN Ullet Rd ℰ 727 1414
FIAT East Prescot Rd ℰ 228 9151
FORD Linacre Lane ℰ 922 0070
FORD Lunts Heath Rd ℰ 424 5781
FORD Speke Hall Rd ℰ 486 2233
HONDA Duke St. ℰ 709 1475
LADA Washington Par. ℰ 922 0481
MAZDA Longmoor Lane ℰ 525 6733
MITSUBISHI Woolton Rd ℰ 737 2138
NISSAN, PEUGEOT Mersey Rd ℰ 924 6575
NISSAN Queen's Drive ℰ 523 9779
NISSAN Mill Lane ℰ 254 1010
PEUGEOT-TALBOT Pilch Lane ℰ 489 4433
RENAULT, SEAT Edge Lane ℰ 228 4737

SAAB 574 Aigburth Rd ℰ 427 3500
SKODA Durning Rd ℰ 263 7374
SKODA Bridge Rd ℰ 928 2515
TOYOTA Gale Rd ℰ 546 8228
TOYOTA 1 Aigburth Rd ℰ 727 2204
VAUXHALL-OPEL 215 Knowsley Rd ℰ 922 7585
VAUXHALL-OPEL Derby Rd ℰ 933 7575
VOLVO Fox St. ℰ 207 4364
VW-AUDI Moor Lane, Thornton ℰ 931 2861
VW-AUDI Edge Lane ℰ 228 0919

⦿ ATS 15/37 Caryl St. ℰ 709 8032/3/4
ATS De Silva St., Huyton ℰ 489 8386/7
ATS 190-194 St. Mary's Rd, Garston ℰ 427 3665/6
ATS 73-77 Durning Rd, Wavertree ℰ 263 7604
ATS 46-50 Lightbody St. ℰ 207 4618
ATS Musker St., Crosby ℰ 931 3166/7/8
ATS 183 Walton Lane, Walton ℰ 207 7042

En saison, *surtout dans les stations fréquentées, il est prudent de retenir à l'avance.*
Cependant, si vous ne pouvez pas occuper la chambre que vous avez retenue,
prévenez immédiatement l'hôtelier.
Si vous écrivez à un hôtel à l'étranger, joignez à votre lettre
un coupon-réponse international (disponible dans les bureaux de poste).

LIZARD Cornwall **403** E 34 The West Country G. – ☎ 0326 The Lizard.
See : Lizard Peninsula★★.
Envir. : Kynance Cove★★★, NW : 1 ½ m. – Landewednack★, Church★, E : ½ m. – Cury★, Church★,
N : 6 ½ m. – Cadgwith★, NE : 4 m. – Ruan Minor (Church★), NE : 4 m. – Gunwalloe Fishing
Cove★, NW : 9 m. – Mawgan In Meneage Church★, N : 10 m.
✦London 326 – Penzance 24 – Truro 29.

🏠 **Housel Bay** ≶, Housel Cove, TR12 7PG, ℰ 290417, Fax 290359, ≼ Housel Cove, 🍴 – 📺
Ⓟ. 🅢 AE VISA
closed 1 January-12 February – **M** (bar lunch)/dinner 12.00 **t.** and a la carte ▯ 3.25 – **23 rm**
⚏ 23.00/66.00 **t.** – SB 55.00/85.00 **st.**

⌂ **Penmenner House** ≶, Penmenner Rd, TR12 7NR, ℰ 290370, ≼, 🍴 – 📺 Ⓟ. 🅢 VISA. ⫶
M 9.35 **st.** ▯ 2.85 – **8 rm** ⚏ 18.00/36.00 **st.** – SB 80.00 **st.**

⌂ **Parc Brawse House** ≶, Penmenner Rd, TR12 7NR, ℰ 290466, ≼, 🍴 – ⫗ rest Ⓟ. 🅢
VISA
(booking essential December-February) – **M** 6.50 – **6 rm** ⚏ 11.50/32.00 – SB (except summer and Bank Holidays) (weekdays only) 32.00/38.00 **st.**

LLANARMON DYFFRYN CEIRIOG Clwyd **402 403** K 25 – pop. 137 – ✉ Llangollen –
☎ 069 176.
✦London 196 – Chester 33 – Shrewsbury 32.

🏰 **West Arms** ≶, LL20 7LD, ℰ 665, Fax 262, ⤸, 🍴, ✕ – ⫗ rm Ⓟ – 🛥 . 🅢 VISA. ⫶
M (bar lunch Monday to Saturday)/dinner 15.95 **t.** ▯ 3.75 – **12 rm** ⚏ 41.00/70.00 **t.**, **2 suites**
80.00 **t.** – SB 90.00/110.00 **st.**

🏠 **Hand** ≶, LL20 7LD, ℰ 666, Fax 262, ⤸, 🍴, ✕ – ⫗ rm Ⓟ. 🅢 VISA. ⫶
closed 1 February-mid March – **M** (bar lunch Monday to Saturday)/dinner 15.95 **t.** ▯ 3.75 –
13 rm ⚏ 41.00/64.00 **t.**, **1 suite** 80.00 **t.** – SB 90.00/100.00 **st.**

LLANBEDR Gwynedd **402 403** H 25 – pop. 486 – ECD : Wednesday – ☎ 034 123.
✦London 262 – Holyhead 54 – Shrewsbury 100.

🏠 **Pensarn Hall** ≶, LL45 2HS, N : ¾ m. on A 496 ℰ 236, ≼, 🍴 – 📺 Ⓟ
M (dinner only) 9.50 **st.** ▯ 2.50 – **7 rm** ⚏ 20.00/38.00 **st.** – SB (October-March) 40.00/45.00 **st.**

⛱ **Ty Mawr** ≶, LL45 2NH, ℰ 440, 🍴 – 📺 Ⓟ
M 7.00/10.00 **t.** and a la carte 6.95/13.50 **t.** ▯ 2.50 – **10 rm** ⚏ 22.00/48.00 **t.** – SB 60.00/62.00 **st.**

LLANBEDROG Gwynedd **402 403** G 25 – ✉ ☎ 0758 Pwllheli.
✦London 263 – Caernarfon 25 – Dolgellau 43.

🏠 **Penarwel Country House** ≶, LL53 7NN, NE : ½ m. on A 499 ℰ 740719, « Edwardian
country house », 🏊, 🍴 – Ⓟ. ⫶
March-November – **M** (bar lunch)/dinner 11.50 **st.** and a la carte ▯ 2.75 – **7 rm**
⚏ 25.00/55.00 **st.**

LLANBERIS Gwynedd **403** H 24 – pop. 1 809 – ECD : Wednesday – ✆ 0286.
🛈 Oriel Eryi ✆ 870765 (summer only).
♦London 243 – Caernarfon 7 – Chester 65 – Shrewsbury 78.

XX **Y Bistro,** 43-45 High St., LL55 4EU, ✆ 871278. ▣ *VISA*
closed Sunday, Monday, 2 weeks February and New Year – **M** (dinner only) (booking
essential) 18.50 **t.**

FIAT Cwm-Y-Go ✆ 870234

LLANDEILO Dyfed **403** I 28 – pop. 1 598 – ECD : Thursday – ✆ 0558.
Envir. : Talley (Abbey and lakes★) N : 7 m.
🛈 Glynhir, Llandybie nr. Ammanford ✆ 0269 (Llandybie) 850472.
♦London 218 – Brecon 34 – Carmarthen 15 – ♦Swansea 25.

🏨 **Cawdor Arms,** Rhosmaen St., SA19 6EN, ✆ 823500, « Tasteful decor » – 📺 ☎ 🅿. ▣ 🄰🄴
🄾 *VISA*. ⚓
M (lunch by arrangement)/dinner 15.50 **t.** ▮3.00 – **17 rm** ⊊ 40.00/60.00 **t.** – SB (week-
ends only) 75.00 **st.**

at Rhosmaen N : 1 m. on A 40 – ✉ ✆ 0558 Llandeilo :

X **Plough Inn,** SA19 6NP, ✆ 823431, Italian rest. – 🅿. ▣ *VISA*
M a la carte 11.00/15.90 **t.** ▮3.50.

FORD 28 Rhosmaen St. ✆ 823221   Ⓜ ATS Towy Terr., Ffairfach ✆ 822567

LLANDEWI SKIRRID Gwent – see Abergavenny.

LLANDOWROR Dyfed **403** G 28 – see St. Clears.

LLANDRILLO Clwyd **402 403** J 25 – ✉ Bala – ✆ 049 084.
♦London 210 – Chester 40 – Dolgellau 26 – Shrewsbury 46.

🏚 **Tyddyn Llan Country House** ⑤, LL21 OST, E : 7 ¾ m. by A 494 on B 4401 ✆ 264,
« Example of 18C rural architecture », ⛟ – ☎ 🅿. ▣ *VISA*
closed February – **M** *(closed lunch Monday and Tuesday)* (bar lunch Wednesday to Saturday)/dinner 18.00 **t.** ▮4.00 – **9 rm** ⊊ 37.00/60.00 **t.** – SB 39.00/41.50 **st.**

LLANDRILLO-YN-RHOS (RHOS-ON-SEA) Clwyd – see Colwyn Bay.

LLANDRINDOD WELLS Powys **403** J 27 – pop. 4 232 – ECD : Wednesday – ✆ 0597.
Envir. : Elan Valley★★ W : from Llandrindod Wells.
🛈 ✆ 2010, E : 1 m.
🛈 Town Hall ✆ 2600.
♦London 204 – Brecon 29 – Carmarthen 60 – Shrewsbury 58.

🏨 **Metropole** (Best Western), Temple St., LD1 5DY, ✆ 2881, Telex 35237, Fax 2881, ▣, ⛟ –
🛗 📺 ☎ 🅿 – 🔔 300. ▣ 🄰🄴 🄾 *VISA*
M 9.50/12.50 **st.** and a la carte – **119 rm** ⊊ 42.00/62.00 **st.**, **2 suites** 68.00/82.00 **st.** –
SB 75.00/105.00 **st.**

↑ **Griffin Lodge,** Temple St., LD1 5HF, ✆ 2432 – 🅿. ▣ *VISA*
M 7.00 **st.** – **8 rm** ⊊ 15.00/32.00 **st.**

↑ **Charis** without rest., Pentrosfa, LD1 5NL, S : ¾ m. by A 483 ✆ 4732, ⛟ – ⚓
March-October – **4 rm** ⊊ 12.00/18.00 **s.**

at Howey S : 1 ½ m. on A 483 – ✉ ✆ 0597 Llandrindod Wells :

↑ **Three Wells Farm** ⑤, LD1 5PB, NE : ½ m. ✆ 2484, ≤, « Working farm », ↝, ⛟ –
⇥ rest 📺 ☎ 🅿. ⚓
M (by arrangement) 7.00 **t.** – **10 rm** ⊊ 12.60/30.00 **t.**, **2 suites** 20.00/40.00 **t.** – SB (March-
October) 40.00/50.00 **st.**

↑ **Corven Hall** ⑤, LD1 5RE, S : ½ m. by A 483 on Hundred House rd ✆ 3368, ⛟ – ⇥ rest
🅿
closed December – **M** 7.00 **st.** ▮2.50 – **7 rm** ⊊ 22.00/27.00 **st.** – SB (except summer) 33.00/36.00 **st.**

AUDI-VW Doldowlod ✆ 810376

See : Great Orme's Head (≤** from the summit) by Ty-Gwyn Rd A – Tour of the Great Orme's Head**.

◻ Rhos-on-Sea Residential, Penryn Bay ✆ 49641, by A 546 A.

◻ Chapel St. ✆ 76413.

♦London 243 – Birkenhead 55 – Chester 47 – Holyhead 43.

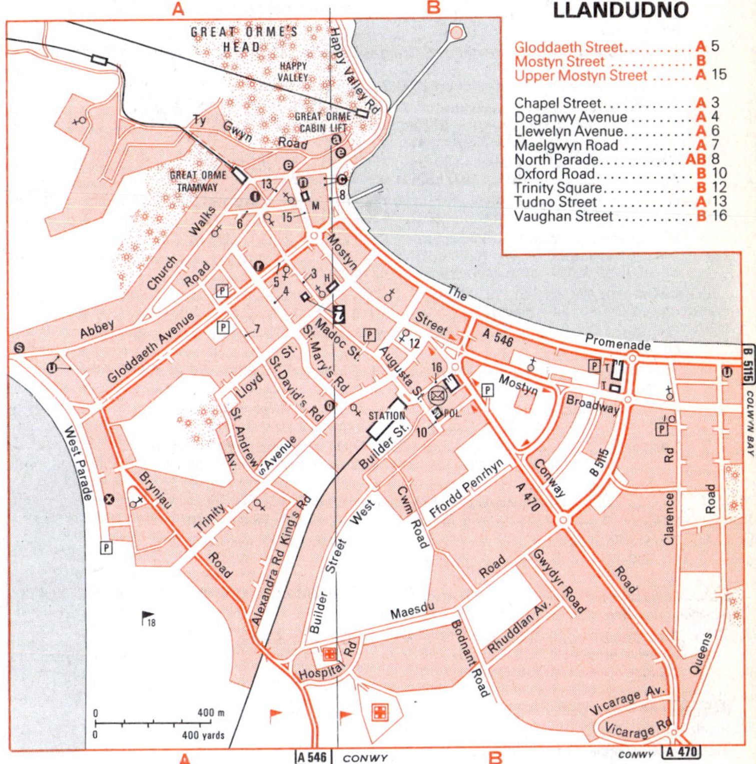

Gloddaeth Street . . . . **A** 5
Mostyn Street . . . . **B**
Upper Mostyn Street . . . . . . **A** 15

Chapel Street . . . . **A** 3
Deganwy Avenue . . . . **A** 4
Llewelyn Avenue . . . . **A** 6
Maelgwyn Road . . . . **A** 7
North Parade . . . . **AB** 8
Oxford Road . . . . **B** 10
Trinity Square . . . . **B** 12
Tudno Street . . . . **A** 13
Vaughan Street . . . . **B** 16

Bodysgallen Hall ⑤, LL30 1RS, SE : 2 m. on A 470 ✆ 584466, Telex 617163, Fax 582519, ≤ gardens and mountains, « Part 17C and 18C hall with terraced gardens », park, ℅ – rest ⊤⊽ ☎ ℗ – 🏌 25. 🖾 AE ① VISA. ℅
on A 470   **B**
M (booking essential) 15.00/25.00 **st.** 🍷 4.50 – � 8.00 – **19 rm** 75.00/125.00 **st.**, **9 suites** 129.00/150.00 **st.** – SB (October-April) 130.00/174.00 **st.**

St. Tudno, Promenade, LL30 2LP, ✆ 74411, Telex 61400, « Tasteful decor », 🖾 – 🛗 ▦ rest ⊤⊽ ☎. 🖾 AE VISA. ℅
A c
closed 23 December-12 January – **M** 12.50/19.50 **t.** and a la carte 🍷 3.95 – **21 rm** ⊑ 37.50/95.00 **t.** – SB 78.00/118.00 **st.**

Empire, 73 Church Walks, LL30 2HE, ✆ 860555, Telex 617161, Fax 860791, ⅃ heated, 🖾 – 🛗 ⊤⊽ ☎ ℗. 🖾 AE ① VISA
A e
closed 2 weeks Christmas-New Year – **M** 9.00/14.00 **st.** and a la carte 🍷 4.00 – **56 rm** ⊑ 42.00/75.00 **st.** – SB 58.00/85.00 **st.**

Annex: **Empire (No 72)**, 72 Church Walks, LL30 2HE, ✆ 860555, Telex 617161, Fax 860791, « Victoriana » – ▦ ⊤⊽ ☎ ℗. 🖾 AE ① VISA. ℅
A e
closed 2 weeks Christmas-New Year – **M** (see **Empire H.**) – **8 rm** ⊑ 55.00/85.00 **st.** – SB 81.00/95.00 **st.**

Gogarth Abbey, West Shore, LL30 2QY, ✆ 76211, ≤, 🖾, 🐎 – ℅ rest ⊤⊽ ☎ ℗. 🖾 AE VISA
A s
Mid January-mid December – **M** (bar lunch)/dinner 16.00 **t.** 🍷 3.75 – **39 rm** ⊑ 32.00/70.00 **t.**, **1 suite** 76.00/100.00 **t.** – SB 66.00/90.00 **st.**

P.T.O. →

Dunoon, Gloddaeth St., LL30 2DW, ℰ 860787 – 🛗 TV ☎. ⟋ VISA   A r
Mid March-October – **M** 7.00/9.00 **st.** ▯ 4.75 – **56 rm** ⟷ 22.50/50.00 **st.** – SB 47.00/63.00 **st.**

Belle Vue, 26 North Par., LL30 2LP, ℰ 79547, ≼ – 🛗 TV ☎ P. ⟋ ⓞ VISA   B e
April-October – **M** (bar lunch)/dinner 8.00 **t.** and a la carte ▯ 3.50 – **17 rm** ⟷ 22.00/48.00 **t.** – SB (except summer) 47.00/52.00 **st.**

Bryn-y-Bia Lodge, Bryn-y-Bia Rd, Craigside, LL30 3AS, E : 1 ½ m. on A 546 ℰ 49644, 🛲   B
– ⇥ rest TV ☎ P. ⟋ AE VISA   by A 546
closed 18 to 31 December – **M** (bar lunch)/dinner 14.90 **t.** ▯ 3.90 – **13 rm** ⟷ 22.50/45.00 **t.** – SB (October-April) 50.00/58.00 **st.**

Bromwell Court, Promenade, 6 Craig-y-Don Par., LL30 1BG, ℰ 78416 – TV ☎. ⟋ VISA   B u
🛇
March-November – **M** (dinner only) 8.00 **st.** ▯ 3.50 – **11 rm** ⟷ 21.00/38.00 **st.**

Headlands, Hill Terr., LL30 2LS, ℰ 77485, ≼ – ⇥ rest TV ☎. ⟋ ⓞ VISA   AB a
closed January and February – **M** (bar lunch)/dinner 13.50 **t.** ▯ 2.75 – **17 rm** ⟷ 21.00/42.00 **t.** – SB (except summer) 50.00/55.00 **st.**

Chandos, 6 Church Walks, LL30 2HD, ℰ 878848 – ⇥ TV ☎. ⟋ VISA. 🛇   A c
M 6.50 **st.** ▯ 3.50 – **6 rm** ⟷ 15.00/30.00 **st.** – SB (Mid September-Easter) 35.00/40.00 **st.**

Craiglands, 7 Carmen Sylva Rd, LL30 1LZ, E : 1 m. by A 546 and B 5115 ℰ 75090 – TV. 🛇   B
April-October – **M** (by arrangement) – **6 rm** ⟷ 16.95/30.00.   by A 546

Sunnymede, West Par., West Shore, LL30 2BD, ℰ 77130 – TV P. ⟋ VISA   A x
March-November – **M** (buffet lunch) 6.00/11.00 **t.** and a la carte ▯ 5.00 – **18 rm** ⟷ 18.00/40.00 **t.** – SB (except summer) 42.00/60.00 **st.**

Leamore, 40 Lloyd St., LL30 2YG, ℰ 75552 – ⇥ rest TV. 🛇   A o
closed Christmas – **M** 8.80 **st.** ▯ 5.00 – **12 rm** ⟷ 16.00/46.00 **st.** – SB 40.00/46.00 **st.**

Clontarf, 1 Great Orme's Rd, West Shore, LL30 2AR, ℰ 77621 – ⇥ rest P. 🛇   A u
10 rm.

Tan Lan, Great Ormes Rd, West Shore, LL30 2AR, ℰ 860221 – TV P. ⟋ AE VISA   A u
April-October – **M** 9.00 **t.** – **18 rm** ⟷ 17.00/40.00 **t.** – SB 48.00/52.00 **st.**

Buile Hill, 46 St. Mary's Rd, LL30 2UE, ℰ 76972, 🛲 – ⇥ rest P   AB o
Mid March-October – **M** 6.00 **st.** ▯ 2.00 – **13 rm** ⟷ 15.00/42.00 **st.**

Lanterns, 7 Church Walks, LL30 2HD, ℰ 77924, Seafood – ⟋ AE ⓞ VISA   A n
closed Monday lunch, Sunday and mid February-mid March – **M** (dinner only) a la carte 15.00/27.00 **t.**

No. 1, 1 Old Rd, LL30 2HA, ℰ 75424, Bistro.. ⟋ VISA   A i
closed Monday lunch, Sunday and 25 to 28 December – **M** a la carte 7.40/14.15 **t.** ▯ 3.50.

BMW Conway Rd ℰ 82441   RENAULT Conway Rd ℰ 85171
CITROEN Herkomer Rd ℰ 77607

LLANDYBIE Dyfed 🄰🄾🄱 H 28 – pop. 2 813 – ✉ Ammanford – ☎ 0269 – ⛳ Glynhir ℰ 850472.
♦London 210 – Brecon 38 – Carmarthen 19 – ♦Swansea 41.

The Cobblers, 3 Church St., SA18 3HZ, ℰ 850540 – ⟋ VISA
closed Thursday lunch, Sunday and Monday except Bank Holidays – **M** 15.00 **t.** (dinner) and a la carte 7.50/13.00 **st.** ▯ 3.00.

LLANELLI Dyfed 🄰🄾🄱 H 29 – pop. 45 336 – ECD : Tuesday – ☎ 0554.
Envir. : Kidwelly (Castle★★) *AC*, NW : 9 m.
♦London 206 – Carmarthen 20 – ♦Swansea 11.

Diplomat, Felinfoel Rd, SA15 3PJ, NE : 1 m. on A 476 ℰ 756156, Fax 751649, ⟋ – 🛗 TV ☎
P – 🛆. ⟋ AE ⓞ VISA
M *(closed Sunday dinner)* 11.95/15.95 **t.** and a la carte – **23 rm** ⟷ 47.50/57.50 **t.** – SB (weekends only) 58.00 **st.**

AUSTIN-ROVER Vauxhall Rd ℰ 773371   🅐 ATS Coldstream St. ℰ 750435

LLANELWY = St. Asaph.

LLANERCHYMEDD Gwynedd 🄰🄾🄼 🄰🄾🄱 G 24 – pop. 613 – ✉ ☎ 0248.
♦London 262 – Bangor 18 – Caernarfon 23 – Holyhead 15.

Llwydiarth Fawr 🐾, LL71 8DF, N : ¾ m. on B 5111 ℰ 0248 (Llanfairfechan) 470321, ≼,
« Georgian farmhouse », 🛲 – ⇥ rest TV P. 🛇
closed December – **M** (by arrangement) 7.50 **st.** – **4 rm** ⟷ 20.00/30.00 **st.** – SB 45.00 **st.**

Drws-Y-Coed 🐾, LL71 8AD, E : 2 ½ m. by B 5111 on Benllech rd ℰ 470473, ≼ – TV P.
🛇
M 7.00 **s.** – **4 rm** ⟷ 18.00/28.00 **s.** – SB 38.00/40.00 **st.**

LLANFACHRETH Gwynedd 🄰🄾🄼 🄰🄾🄱 I 25 – see Dolgellau.

LLANFAIR-YM-MUALLT = Builth Wells.

LLANFIHANGEL Powys 🄰🄾🄼 🄰🄾🄱 J 25 – see Llanfyllin.

LLANFYLLIN Powys **402** **403** K 25 – pop. 1 210 – ECD : Friday – ☎ 069 184.

ℹ High St. ✆ 8868 (summer only).

♦London 188 – Chester 42 – Shrewsbury 24 – Welshpool 11.

  🏨 **Bodfach Hall** ⟿, SY22 5HS, NW : 1 m. on B 4391 ✆ 272, ≼, 🐎, park – 📺 **℗**. 🔄 AE ⓪
    March-mid November – **M** (dinner only and Sunday lunch)/dinner 11.75 **t.** – **9 rm**
    ⊑ 25.00/50.00 **t.** – SB 58.00/64.00 **st.**

      at LLanfihangel SW : 5 m. by A 490 and B 4393 on B 4382 – ✉ ☎ 069 184 LLanfyllin :

  ↑ **Cyfie Farm** ⟿, SY22 5JE, S : 1 ½ m. by B 4382 ✆ 451, ≼, « Working farm, restored 17C
    longhouse », 🐎 – **℗**. 🐾
    M 7.00 **st.** – **2 rm** ⊑ 16.00/26.00 **st.**, **1 suite** 32.00 **st.** – SB 46.00 **st.**

LLANGAMMARCH WELLS Powys **403** J 27 – ECD : Wednesday – ☎ 059 12.

♦London 200 – Brecon 17 – Builth Wells 8.

  🏰 **Lake** ⟿, LD4 4BS, E : ¾ m. ✆ 202, ≼, 🎣, 🏊, 🐎, park, ✂ – ⊱✂ 📺 ☎ **℗**. 🔄 AE **VISA**
    closed January – **M** (bar lunch)/dinner 18.50 **st.** ▯ 4.50 – **10 rm** ⊑ 65.00/75.00 **st.**, **8 suites**
    95.00 **st.** – SB 44.50/55.00 **st.**

LLANGEFNI Gwynedd **402** **403** H 24 – pop. 4 100 – ECD : Tuesday – ✉ ☎ 0248.

🎣 ✆ 722193.

ℹ Penyrorsedd ✆ 724666.

♦London 256 – Chester 75 – Caernarfon 17 – Holyhead 17.

  🏨 **Nant Yr Odyn**, Llanfawr, LL77 7YE, SW : 1 ¼ m. at junction of A 5 and A 5114 ✆ 723354 –
    📺 ☎ **℗**. 🔄 **VISA**. 🐾
    M 6.00/10.50 **st.** and a la carte ▯ 3.50 – **14 rm** ⊑ 28.50/56.00 **st.** – SB 66.00/72.00 **st.**

AUDI, RENAULT Industrial Estate ✆ 724141   ◍ ATS Industrial Est. ✆ 750397
VAUXHALL Argraig Service Station ✆ 750126

LLANGOLLEN Clwyd **402** **403** K 25 – pop. 2 546 – ECD : Thursday – ☎ 0978.

See : Plas Newydd★ (the house of the Ladies of Llangollen) *AC*.

Envir. : Horseshoe Pass★, NW : 4 ½ m. – Chirk Castle★ (gates★)*AC*, SE : 7 ½ m.

🎣 Vale of Llangollen, Holyhead Rd ✆ 860040, E : 1 ½ m.

ℹ Town Hall, ✆ 860828.

♦London 194 – Chester 23 – Holyhead 76 – Shrewsbury 30.

  🏰 **Bryn Howel**, LL20 7UW, E : 2 ¾ m. on A 539 ✆ 860331, Fax 860119, ≼, 🎣, 🐎 – 📺 ☎ **℗**
    – 🛥 300. 🔄 AE **VISA**
    closed 25 December – **M** *(closed Saturday lunch)* 10.00/15.00 **t.** and a la carte ▯ 4.50 –
    38 rm ⊑ 45.00/80.00 **t.**

  🏰 Wild Pheasant, Berwyn Rd, LL20 8AP, on A 5 ✆ 860629, Fax 861837, 🐎 – 📺 ☎ **℗** – 🛥
    33 rm.

  🏰 Royal (T.H.F.), Bridge St., LL20 8PG, ✆ 860202, Fax 861824, ≼, 🎣 – ⊱✂ rm 📺 ☎ **℗** – 🛥
    33 rm.

  ⚘ **Ty'n-y-Wern**, LL20 7PH, E : 1 m. on A 5 ✆ 860252, ≼, 🐎 – 📺 ☎ **℗**. 🔄 **VISA**
    M 9.95 **t.** and a la carte 9.95/14.65 **t.** ▯ 2.75 – **12 rm** ⊑ 29.00/42.00 **st.**

  ✗ **Caesar's**, Deeside Lane, LL20 8PN, ✆ 860133, ≼ – 🔄 **VISA**
    M (dinner only) 14.95 **st.**

FORD Derwyn St. ✆ 860270

LLANGURIG Powys **403** J 26 – pop. 620 – ECD : Thursday – ✉ Llanidloes – ☎ 055 15.

♦London 188 – Aberystwyth 25 – Carmarthen 75 – Shrewsbury 53.

  ↑ **Old Vicarage**, SY18 6RN, ✆ 280 – ⊱✂ **℗**
    M 8.50 **st.** ▯ 3.00 – **4 rm** ⊑ 12.50/32.00 **st.** – SB (October-April) 39.00/45.00 **st.**

LLANGYBI Gwent – see Usk.

LLANGYNIDR Powys **403** K 28 – ✉ Crickhowell – ☎ 0874 Bwlch.

♦London 174 – Abergavenny 14 – Brecon 11 – Newport 30.

  ⚘ **Red Lion**, NP8 1NY, ✆ 730223, « 15C inn » – 📺 **℗**. 🐾
    M *(closed Monday)* a la carte 9.70/16.95 **t.** ▯ 3.50 – **5 rm** ⊑ 27.50/45.00 **st.**

LLANILLTUD FAWR = Llantwit Major.

LLANNEFYDD Clwyd **402** **403** J 24 – ✉ Denbigh – ☎ 074 579.

♦London 225 – Chester 37 – Shrewsbury 63.

  🏨 **Hawk and Buckle Inn**, LL16 5ED, ✆ 249, ≼ – 📺 ☎ **℗**. 🔄 **VISA**. 🐾
    M *(closed Monday and Tuesday lunch and Sunday)* (bar lunch)/dinner 12.50 **t.** and a la carte
    ▯ 3.50 – **10 rm** ⊑ 35.00/45.00 **t.** – SB (weekends only) 55.00/65.00 **st.**

AUSTIN-ROVER Denbigh Rd ✆ 227

LLANRHIDIAN West Glam. – see Swansea.

LLANRWST Gwynedd 402 403 I 24 – pop. 2 908 – ECD : Thursday – ☎ 0492.
See : Gwydir Castle★.
Envir. : Capel Garmon (Burial Chamber★) SE : 6 m.
♦London 230 – Holyhead 50 – Shrewsbury 66.

 🏨 **Maenan Abbey,** N : 2 ½ m. on A 470, LL26 0UL, ℰ 049 269 (Dolgarrog) 247, ⌇, ✒ – 📺
 ☎ 🅿. 🔄 AE ⓪ VISA
 M 8.00/13.00 **t.** and a la carte ₰ 3.25 – **12 rm** ☳ 34.50/55.00 **t.** – SB (except Bank Holi-
 days) 64.00/84.00 **st.**

 XX **Meadowsweet** with rm, Station Rd, LL26 0DS, ℰ 640732, ≼ – ⋈ rest 📺 ☎ 🅿. 🔄 VISA
 M (closed lunch November-May) 12.50/18.50 **t.** ₰ 3.75 – ☳ 6.50 – **10 rm** 30.00/50.00 **t.**

 at Trefriw NW : 2 m. on B 5106 – ⊠ ☎ 0492 Llanrwst :

 🏨 **Hafod House,** LL27 0RQ, ℰ 640029, Fax 641351 – 📺 ☎ 🅿. 🔄 AE ⓪ VISA ⋇
 closed January – **M** (lunch by arrangement)/dinner 12.50 **t.** ₰ 2.75 – **6 rm** ☳ 24.50/49.00 **t.**
 – SB 55.00/65.00 **st.**

AUSTIN-ROVER Kerry Garage ℰ 640381   FORD Betws Rd ℰ 640684

LLANSANFFRAID GLAN CONWY Gwynedd – pop. 1 935 – ⊠ ☎ 0492 Colwyn Bay.
♦London 241 – Colwyn Bay 4 – Holyhead 42.

 🏨 **Old Rectory** ⑤, LL28 5LF, on A 470 ℰ 580611, ≼, « Georgian country house with antique
 furnishings », ✒ – ⋈ 📺 🅿. 🔄 VISA ⋇
 closed 20 December-1 February – **M** (dinner only) 17.50 ₰ 5.90 – **5 rm** ☳ 45.00/60.00.

LLANTWIT MAJOR (LLANILLTUD FAWR) South Glam. 403 J 29 – pop. 13 375 (inc. St. Athan)
– ☎ 044 65.
♦London 175 – ♦Cardiff 18 – ♦Swansea 33.

 🏨 **West House,** West St., CF6 9SP, ℰ 2406, ✒ – 📺 ☎ 🅿. 🔄 AE VISA
 M 5.50/9.50 **t.** and a la carte – **16 rm** ☳ 35.00/45.00 **t.** – SB (weekends only) 55.00 **st.**

TOYOTA 2 Colhugh St. ℰ 3466

LLANWENARTH Gwent – see Abergavenny.

LLANWRTYD WELLS Powys 403 J 27 – pop. 528 – ECD : Wednesday – ☎ 059 13.
See : Cambrian Mountains : road★★, from Llanwrtyd to Tregaron.
Envir. : Rhandir-mwyn (≼★ of Afon Tywi Valley) SW : 12 m.
🛈 The Bookshop ℰ 3391.
♦London 214 – Brecon 32 – Carmarthen 39.

 ⋔ **Lasswade Country House,** Station Rd, LD5 4RW, ℰ 515, ≼, ✒ – ⋈ rest 📺 ☎ 🅿. 🔄
 VISA
 M (by arrangement) 13.95 **t.** ₰ 3.75 – **7 rm** ☳ 32.00/49.00 **t.** – SB (except summer)
 65.00/75.00 **st.**

 at Abergwesyn NW : 4 ¾ m. – ⊠ Builth Wells – ☎ 059 13 Llanwrtyd Wells :

 🏨 Llwynderw ⑤, LD5 4TW, ℰ 238, Fax 632, ≼ countryside and hills, « Georgian house with
 antique furnishings », ✒ – 🅿
 10 rm, 1 suite.

LLANYCHAER Dyfed 403 F 28 – see Fishguard.

LLYSWEN Powys 403 K 27 – ⊠ Brecon – ☎ 087 485.
♦London 188 – Brecon 8 – ♦Cardiff 48 – Worcester 53.

 ☖ **Griffin Inn,** LD3 0UR, on A 470 ℰ 241 – ☎ 🅿. 🔄 AE ⓪ VISA
 M (closed Sunday dinner to non-residents) a la carte 7.40/13.00 **st.** ₰ 3.95 – **6 rm**
 ☳ 19.50/50.00 **st.** – SB (October-March) 65.00/85.00 **st.**

LOFTUS Cleveland 402 R 20 – pop. 5 626 – ECD : Wednesday – ⊠ Saltburn-by-the-Sea –
☎ 0287 Guisborough.
♦London 264 – ♦Leeds 73 – ♦Middlesbrough 17 – Scarborough 36.

 🏨 **Grinkle Park** ⑤, Easington, TS13 4UB, SE : 3 ½ m. by A 174 ℰ 40515, ≼, ✒, park, ✗
 📺 ☎ 🅿. 🔄 AE ⓪ VISA
 M 9.25/13.95 **t.** and a la carte – **20 rm** ☳ 51.50/76.00 **t.** – SB (weekends only) 88.00/108.00 **st.**

LOLWORTH Cambs. – see Cambridge.

LONDON

LONDON (Greater) **404** folds ㊷ to ㊹ — London G. — pop. 7 566 620 — ☎ 01 (until May 6, thereafter 071 or 081, see note on p. 53).

✈ Heathrow, ✆ 759 4321, Telex 934892, p. 8 AX — Terminal : Airbus (A1) from Victoria, Airbus (A2) from Paddington — Underground (Piccadilly line) frequent service daily.

✈ Gatwick, ✆ 0293 (Crawley) 28822 and ✆ 01 (London) 668 4211, Telex 877725, p. 9 : by A 23 EZ and M 23 — Terminal : Coach service from Victoria Coach Station (Flightline 777, hourly service) — Railink (Gatwick Express) from Victoria (24 h service).

✈ London City Airport ✆ 474 2129, Telex 264731, p. 7 : HV.

✈ Stansted, at Bishop's Stortford, ✆ 0279 (Bishop's Stortford) 680757, Telex 818708, NE : 34 m. p. 7 : by M 11 JT and A 120.

British Airways, Victoria Air Terminal : 115 Buckingham Palace Rd, SW1, ✆ 834 9411, p. 32 BX.

🚗 Euston and Paddington ✆ 0345 090700.

🛈 National Tourist Information Centre, Victoria Station Forecourt, SW1, ✆ 730 3488.
British Travel Centre, 12 Regent St., Piccadilly Circus, SW1 ✆ 730 3400.
London Tourist Board and Convention Bureau Telephone Information Service ✆ 730 3488.

Major sights in London and the outskirts . . . . pp. 2 and 3
Maps and lists of streets . . . . pp. 4 to 33
  Greater London . . . . pp. 4 to 11
  Central London . . . . pp. 12 to 27
  Detailed maps of :
  Mayfair, Soho, St. James's, Marylebone . . . . pp. 28 and 29
  South Kensington, Chelsea, Belgravia . . . . pp. 30 and 31
  Victoria, Strand, Bayswater, Kensington . . . . pp. 32 and 33
Hotels and Restaurants
  Alphabetical list of hotels and restaurants . . . . pp. 34 to 37
  Alphabetical list of areas included . . . . p. 38
  Starred establishments in London . . . . p. 39
  Restaurants classified according to type . . . . pp. 40 to 47
  Restaurants open on Sunday and restaurants taking last orders after
  11.30 p.m. . . . . pp. 48 to 52
  Hotels and Restaurants listed by boroughs . . . . pp. 53 to 82
Car dealers and repairers . . . . pp. 83 and 84

SIGHTS

CURIOSITÉS
LE CURIOSITÀ
SEHENSWÜRDIGKEITEN

■ HISTORIC BUILDINGS AND MONUMENTS

Palace of Westminster★★★ : House of Lords★★, Westminster Hall★★ (hammerbeam roof★★★), Robing Room★, Central Lobby★, House of Commons★, Big Ben★, Victoria Tower★ p. 21 LY — Tower of London★★★ (Crown Jewels★★★, White Tower or Keep★★★, St. John's Chapel★★, Beauchamp Tower★) p. 22 PV.

Banqueting House★★ p. 21 LX — Buckingham Palace★★ (Changing of the Guard★★, Royal Mews★★) p. 32 BVX — Kensington Palace★★ p. 19 FX — Lincoln's Inn★★ p. 33 EV — London Bridge★★ p. 22 PX — Royal Hospital Chelsea★★ p. 31 FU — St. James's Palace★★ p. 29 EP — South Bank Arts Centre★★ (Royal Festival Hall★, National Theatre★, County Hall★) p. 21 MX — The Temple★★ (Middle Temple Hall★) p. 17 MV — Tower Bridge★★ p. 22 PX.

Albert Memorial★ p. 30 CQ — Apsley House★ p. 28 BP — Burlington House★ p. 29 EM — Charterhouse★ p. 18 NU — Commonwealth Institute★ p. 19 EY — Design Centre★ p. 29 FM — George Inn★, Southwark p. 22 PX — Gray's Inn★ p. 17 MU — Guildhall★ (Lord Mayor's Show★★) p. 18 NU — Imperial College of Science and Technology★ p. 30 CR — Dr Johnson's House★ p. 17 MUV A — Lancaster House★ p. 29 EP — Leighton House★ p. 19 EY — Linley Sambourne House★ p. 19 EY — Mansion House★ (plate and insignia★★) p. 18 PV P — The Monument★ (✳★) p. 18 PV G — Old Admiralty★ p. 21 LX — Royal Exchange★ p. 18 PV V — Royal Opera Arcade★ (New Zealand House) p. 29 FGN — Royal Opera House★ (Covent Garden) p. 33 DX — Somerset House★ p. 33 EXY — Staple Inn★ p. 17 MU Y — Stock Exchange★ p. 18 PUV — Theatre Royal★ (Haymarket) p. 29 GM — Westminster Bridge★ p. 21 LY.

■ CHURCHES

The City Churches

St. Paul's Cathedral★★★ (Dome ≼★★★) p. 18 NV.

St. Bartholomew the Great★★ (vessel★) p. 18 NU K — St. Dunstan-in-the-East★★ p. 18 PV F — St. Mary-at-Hill★★ (plan★, woodwork★★) p. 18 PV B — Temple Church★★ p. 17 MV.

All Hallows-by-the-Tower (font cover★★, brasses★) p. 18 PV Y — Christ Church★ p. 18 NU E — St. Andrew Undershaft (monuments★) p. 18 PV A — St. Bride★ (steeple★★) p. 18 NV J — St. Clement Eastcheap (panelled interior★★) p. 18 PV E — St. Edmund the King and Martyr (tower and spire★) p. 18 PV D — St. Giles Cripplegate★ p. 18 NU N — St. Helen Bishopsgate★ (monuments★★) p. 18 PUV R — St. James Garlickhythe (tower and spire★, sword rests★) p. 18 NV R — St. Katherine Cree (sword rest★) p. 18 PV J — St. Magnus the Martyr (tower★, sword rest★) p. 18 PV K — St. Margaret Lothbury★ (tower and spire★, woodwork★, screen★, font★) p. 18 PU S — St. Margaret Pattens (woodwork★) p. 18 PV N — St. Martin Ludgate (tower and spire★, door cases★) p. 18 NV B — St. Mary Abchurch★ (tower and spire★, dome★, reredos★) p. 18 PV X — St. Mary-le-Bow (tower and steeple★★) p. 18 NV G — St. Michael Paternoster Royal (tower and spire★) p. 18 NV D — St. Nicholas Cole Abbey (tower and spire★) p. 18 NV F — St. Olave★ p. 18 PV S — St. Peter upon Cornhill (screen★) p. 18 PV L — St. Stephen Walbrook★ (tower and steeple★, dome★) p. 18 PV Z — St. Vedast (tower and spire★, ceiling★) p. 18 NUV E.

Other Churches

Westminster Abbey★★★ (Chapel of Edward the Confessor★★, Henry VII Chapel★★★, Chapter House★★) p. 21 LY.

Southwark Cathedral★★ p. 22 PX.

Queen's Chapel★ p. 29 EP — St. Clement Danes★ p. 33 EX — St. James's★ p. 29 EM — St. Margaret's★ p. 21 LY A — St. Martin-in-the-Fields★ p. 33 DY — St. Paul's★ (Covent Garden) p. 33 DX — Westminster Roman Catholic Cathedral★ p. 21 KY B.

■ PARKS

Regent's Park★★★ p. 16 HJT (terraces★★), Zoo★★★.

Hyde Park★★ p. 20 GHV — St. James's Park★★ p. 21 KX.

Kensington Gardens★ pp. 19-20 FGX (Orangery★ A).

■ STREETS AND SQUARES

The City★★★ p. 18 NV.

Bedford Square★★ p. 17 KU — Belgrave Square★★ p. 32 AVX — Burlington Arcade★★ p. 29 DM — The Mall★★ p. 29 FP — Piccadilly★★ p. 29 EM — The Thames★★ pp. 20-22 — Trafalgar Square★★ p. 33 DY — Whitehall★★ (Horse Guards★) p. 21 LX.

Barbican★ p. 18 NU — Bloomsbury★ p. 17 LMU — Bond Street★ pp. 28-29 CK-DM — Canonbury Square★ p. 18 NS — Carlton House Terrace★ p. 29 GN — Charing Cross★ p. 33 DY — Cheyne Walk★ p. 20 GHZ — Fitzroy Square★ p. 17 KU — Jermyn Street★ p. 29 EN — Merrick Square★ p. 22 NY — Montpelier Square★ p. 31 EQ — Piccadilly Arcade★ p. 29 DEN — Portman Square★ p. 28 AJ — Queen Anne's Gate★ p. 21 KY — Regent Street★ p. 29 EM — St. James's Square★ p. 29 FN — St. James's Street★ p. 29 EN — Shepherd Market★ p. 28 CN — Strand★ p. 33 DY — Trinity Church Square★ p. 22 NY — Victoria Embankment★ p. 33 DEXY — Waterloo Place★ p. 29 FN.

■ MUSEUMS

British Museum★★★ p. 17 LU — National Gallery★★★ p. 29 GM — Science Museum★★★ p. 30 CR — Tate Gallery★★★ p. 21 LZ — Victoria and Albert Museum★★★ p. 31 DR.

Courtauld Institute Galleries★★ p. 17 KU M — Museum of London★★ p. 18 NU M — National Portrait Gallery★★ p. 29 GM — Natural History Museum★★ p. 30 CS — Queen's Gallery★★ p. 32 BV — Wallace Collection★★ p. 28 AH.

Clock Museum★ (Guildhall) p. 18 NU — Geological Museum★ p. 30 CR — Imperial War Museum★ p. 21 MY — London Transport Museum★ p. 33 DX — Madame Tussaud's★ p. 16 JU M — Museum of Mankind★ p. 29 DM — National Army Museum★ p. 31 FU — Percival David Foundation of Chinese Art★ p. 17 KLT M — Sir John Soane's Museum★ p. 17 MU M — Wellington Museum★ p. 28 BP.

■ OUTER LONDON

Hampton Court p. 8 BY (The Palace★★★, gardens★★★) — **Kew** p. 9 CX Royal Botanic Gardens★★★ : Palm House★★, Temperate House★, Kew Palace or Dutch House★★, Orangery★, Pagoda★, Japanese Gateway★ — Windsor (Castle★★★) p. 4 · by M 4 AV.

Blackheath p. 11 HX terraces and houses★, Eltham Palace★ A — **Brentford** p. 8 BX Syon Park★★, gardens★ — **Chiswick** p. 9 CV Chiswick Mall★★, Chiswick House★ D, Hogarth's House★ E — **Greenwich** pp. 10 and 11 : Cutty Sark★★ GV F, National Maritime Museum★★ (Queen's House★★) GV M, Royal Naval College★★ (Painted Hall★, the Chapel★) GV G, Old Royal Observatory★ (Meridian Building : collection★★) HV K, Ranger's House★ GX N — **Hampstead** Kenwood House★★ (Adam Library★★, paintings★★) p. 5 EU P, Fenton House★ p. 15 ES — **Hendon** p. 5 Royal Air Force Museum★★ CT M — **Hounslow** p. 8 BV Osterley Park★★ — **Lewisham** p. 10 GX Horniman Museum★ M — **Richmond** pp. 8 and 9 : Richmond Park★★, ❋★★★ CX, Richmond Bridge★★ BX R, Richmond Green★★ BX S (Maids of Honour Row★★, Trumpeter's House★), Asgill House★ BX B, Ham House★★ BX V.

Dulwich p. 10 Dulwich College Picture Gallery★ FX X — **Shoreditch** p. 6 FU Geffrye Museum★ M — **Tower Hamlets** p. 6 GV St. Katharine Dock★ Y — **Twickenham** p. 8 BX Marble Hill House★ Z, Strawberry Hill★ A.

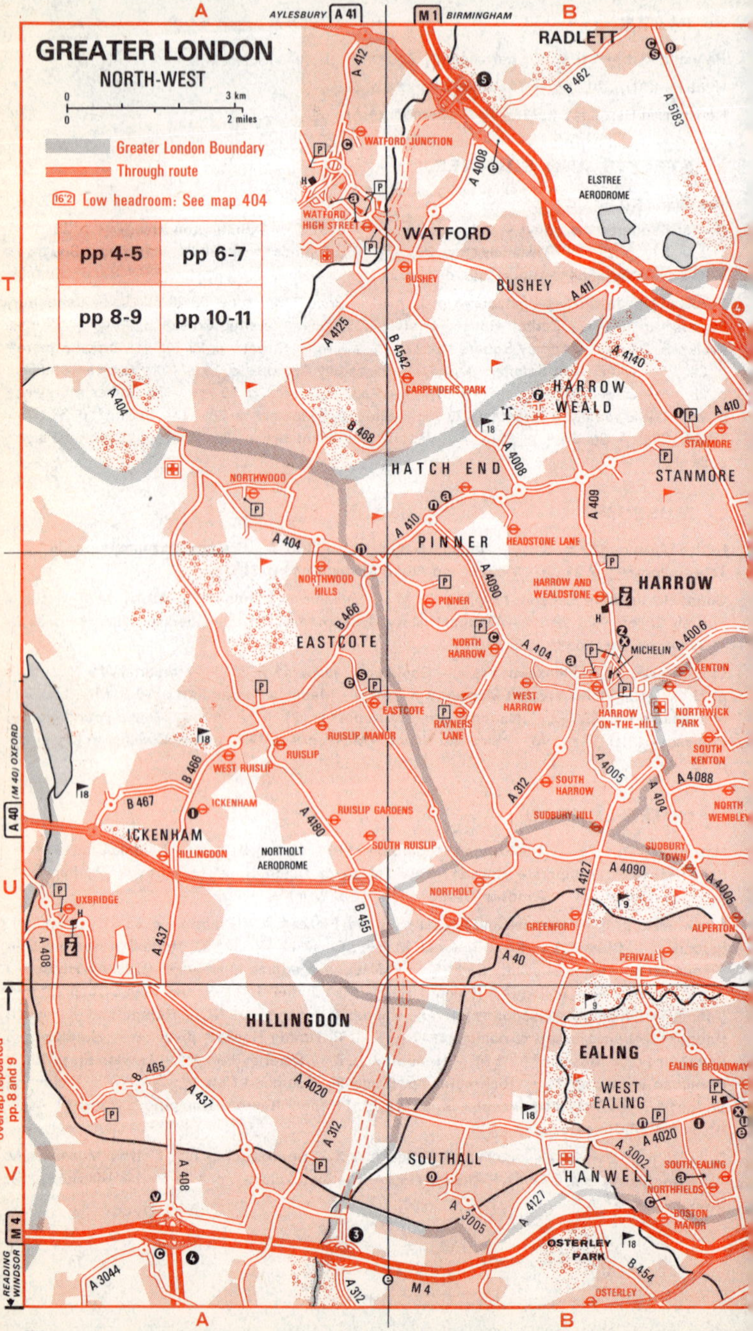
GREATER LONDON
NORTH-WEST
0 3 km
0 2 miles
Greater London Boundary
Through route
16'2 Low headroom: See map 404
pp 4-5
pp 6-7
pp 8-9
pp 10-11
A
B
T
U
V
AYLESBURY A 41
M 1 BIRMINGHAM
A 40 (M 40) OXFORD
M 4 READING WINDSOR
overlap repeated pp. 8 and 9
RADLETT
ELSTREE AERODROME
WATFORD JUNCTION
WATFORD HIGH STREET
WATFORD
BUSHEY
CARPENDERS PARK
HARROW WEALD
STANMORE
HATCH END
NORTHWOOD
PINNER
HEADSTONE LANE
NORTHWOOD HILLS
HARROW AND WEALDSTONE
HARROW
EASTCOTE
NORTH HARROW
MICHELIN
KENTON
WEST HARROW
RAYNERS LANE
HARROW ON-THE-HILL
NORTHWICK PARK
RUISLIP MANOR
RUISLIP
WEST RUISLIP
ICKENHAM
SOUTH KENTON
SOUTH HARROW
NORTH WEMBLEY
RUISLIP GARDENS
SUDBURY HILL
HILLINGDON
NORTHOLT AERODROME
SOUTH RUISLIP
SUDBURY TOWN
UXBRIDGE
NORTHOLT
GREENFORD
ALPERTON
PERIVALE
HILLINGDON
EALING
EALING BROADWAY
WEST EALING
SOUTHALL
HANWELL
SOUTH EALING
NORTHFIELDS
BOSTON MANOR
OSTERLEY PARK
OSTERLEY
M 4
A 412
A 4008
B 462
A 5183
A 411
A 4125
B 4542
A 4140
A 410
A 404
B 468
A 4008
A 409
A 410
A 404
A 4090
B 466
A 404
A 4006
B 466
B 467
A 4180
A 312
A 4005
A 404
A 4088
A 4127
A 4090
A 4005
B 455
A 437
A 408
A 40
B 465
A 437
A 4020
A 312
A 408
A 4020
A 3002
A 3005
A 4127
B 454
A 3044
A 312

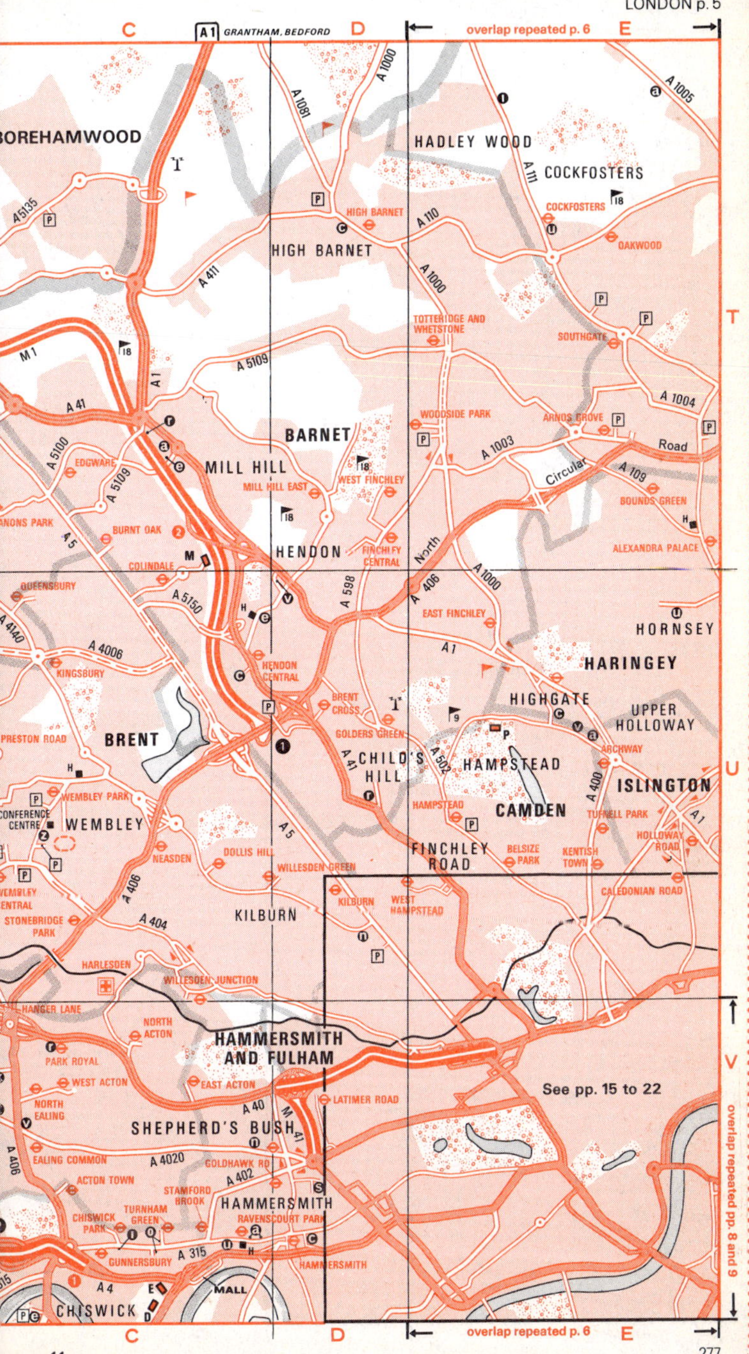
overlap repeated p. 6
A1 GRANTHAM, BEDFORD
C
D
E
T
U
V
A 1000
A 1081
A 1005
A 1005
BOREHAMWOOD
HADLEY WOOD
COCKFOSTERS
A 5135
A 111
COCKFOSTERS
18
HIGH BARNET
OAKWOOD
A 411
HIGH BARNET
A 110
A 1000
M 1
A 1
TOTTERIDGE AND WHETSTONE
SOUTHGATE
A 41
A 1004
A 5100
BARNET
WOODSIDE PARK
ARNOS GROVE
Road
EDGWARE
A 5109
MILL HILL
A 1003
A 109
A 5109
MILL HILL EAST
WEST FINCHLEY
18
Circular
BOUNDS GREEN
ANONS PARK
18
North
ALEXANDRA PALACE
A 5
BURNT OAK
2
HENDON
FINCHLEY CENTRAL
QUEENSBURY
COLINDALE
M
A 5150
A 598
A 406
A 1000
HORNSEY
A 4140
H
EAST FINCHLEY
A 4006
A 1
HARINGEY
KINGSBURY
HENDON CENTRAL
HIGHGATE
UPPER HOLLOWAY
PRESTON ROAD
BRENT CROSS
9
BRENT
GOLDERS GREEN
ARCHWAY
H
CHILD'S HILL
HAMPSTEAD
ISLINGTON
WEMBLEY PARK
A 41
A 502
A 400
A 1
CONFERENCE CENTRE
HAMPSTEAD
TUFNELL PARK
2
WEMBLEY
CAMDEN
HOLLOWAY ROAD
NEASDEN
DOLLIS HILL
FINCHLEY ROAD
BELSIZE PARK
KENTISH TOWN
A 406
WILLESDEN GREEN
WEMBLEY CENTRAL
STONEBRIDGE PARK
A 404
KILBURN
KILBURN
WEST HAMPSTEAD
CALEDONIAN ROAD
HARLESDEN
WILLESDEN JUNCTION
HANGER LANE
NORTH ACTON
HAMMERSMITH AND FULHAM
PARK ROYAL
WEST ACTON
EAST ACTON
See pp. 15 to 22
NORTH EALING
A 40
M 41
LATIMER ROAD
SHEPHERD'S BUSH
EALING COMMON
A 4020
GOLDHAWK RD
ACTON TOWN
A 402
STAMFORD BROOK
HAMMERSMITH
A 406
TURNHAM GREEN
RAVENSCOURT PARK
CHISWICK PARK
GUNNERSBURY
A 315
HAMMERSMITH
A 4
MALL
CHISWICK
C
D
E
overlap repeated p. 6
overlap repeated pp. 8 and 9

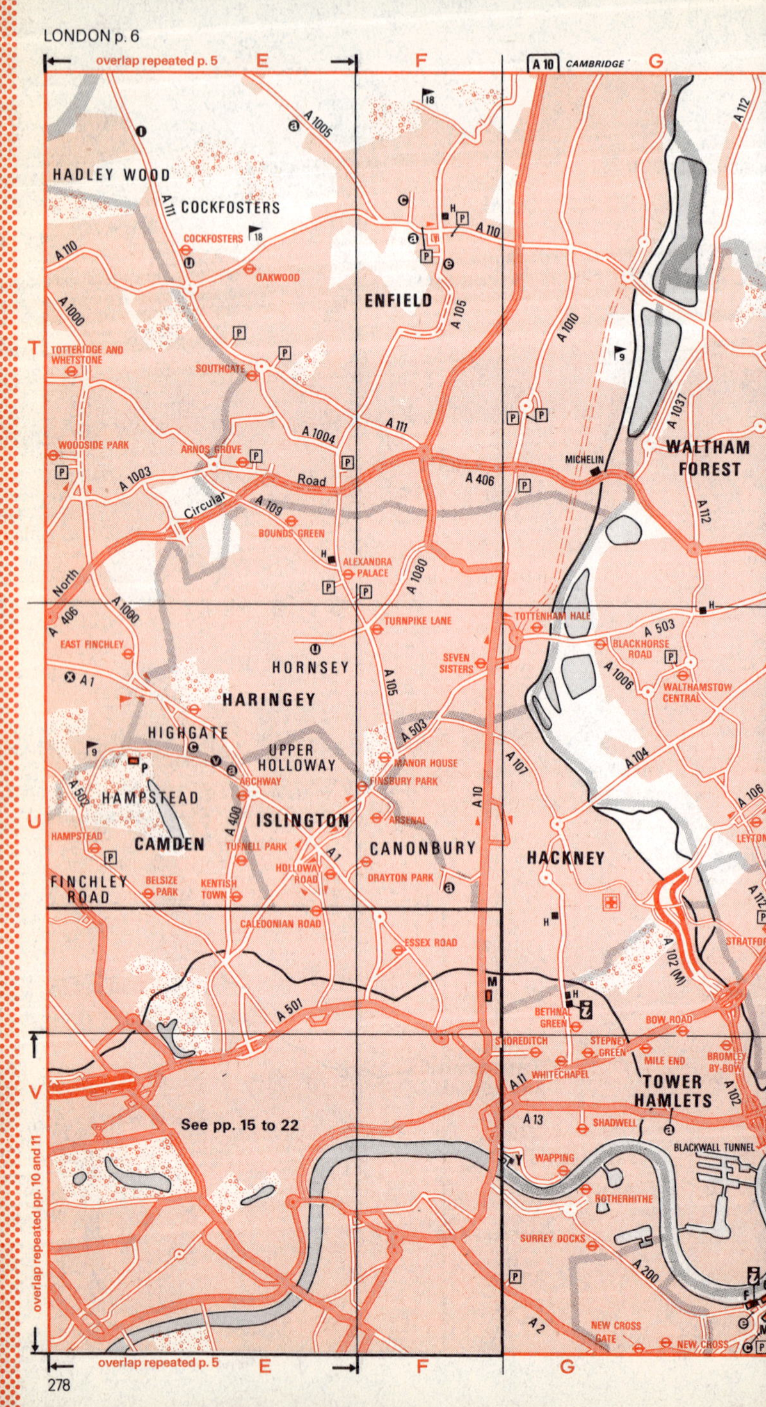
overlap repeated p. 5
E
F
A 10 CAMBRIDGE
G
A 112
18
A 1005
HADLEY WOOD
COCKFOSTERS
A 111
A 110
A 110
COCKFOSTERS 18
OAKWOOD
ENFIELD
A 105
A 1010
A 1037
9
WALTHAM FOREST
A 1000
T
TOTTERIDGE AND WHETSTONE
SOUTHGATE
A 111
A 1004
P
P
MICHELIN
WOODSIDE PARK
ARNOS GROVE
A 1003
Road
A 406
P
A 112
Circular
A 109
BOUNDS GREEN
A 1080
ALEXANDRA PALACE
North
A 406
A 1000
TURNPIKE LANE
TOTTENHAM HALE
A 503
BLACKHORSE ROAD
EAST FINCHLEY
HORNSEY
SEVEN SISTERS
WALTHAMSTOW CENTRAL
A 1
A 105
A 1006
HARINGEY
HIGHGATE
9
UPPER HOLLOWAY
A 503
MANOR HOUSE
FINSBURY PARK
A 107
A 104
A 502
HAMPSTEAD
ARCHWAY
A 400
ISLINGTON
A 10
A 106
U
HAMPSTEAD
CAMDEN
TUFNELL PARK
A 1
ARSENAL
CANONBURY
HACKNEY
LEYTON
FINCHLEY ROAD
BELSIZE PARK
KENTISH TOWN
HOLLOWAY ROAD
DRAYTON PARK
A 112
CALEDONIAN ROAD
STRATFORD
ESSEX ROAD
A 501
M
A 102 (M)
BETHNAL GREEN
BOW ROAD
STEPNEY GREEN
SHOREDITCH
MILE END
BROMLEY BY-BOW
V
See pp. 15 to 22
A 11 WHITECHAPEL
TOWER HAMLETS
A 102
A 13
SHADWELL
BLACKWALL TUNNEL
overlap repeated pp. 10 and 11
WAPPING
ROTHERHITHE
SURREY DOCKS
A 200
F
G
U
M
P
A 2
NEW CROSS GATE
NEW CROSS
overlap repeated p. 5
E
F
G

A 104 CAMBRIDGE, NORWICH
M 11 CAMBRIDGE, NORWICH STANSTED AIRPORT
H
J
GREATER LONDON
NORTH-EAST
0 3 km
0 2 miles
Greater London Boundary
Through route
16'2 Low headroom: See map 404
pp 4-5
pp 6-7
pp 8-9
pp 10-11
THEYDON BOIS
EPPING FOREST
DEBDEN
A 121
A 1168
LOUGHTON
A 113
A 1112
BUCKHURST HILL
A 1069
18
A 110
RODING VALLEY
CHIGWELL
B 173
GRANGE HILL
A 113
A 1009
WOODFORD
A 123
HAINAULT
A 1112
WOODFORD
M 11
FAIRLOP
HAVERING
SOUTH WOODFORD
A 104
A 11
A 1400
REDBRIDGE
BARKINGSIDE
A 12
A 125
H
P
A 113
A 114
SNARESBROOK
REDBRIDGE
NEWBURY PARK
A 118
P
WANSTEAD
A 12
GANTS HILL
P
A 124
LEYTONSTONE
18
A 406
ILFORD
P
A 1083
B 178
LEYTONSTONE
A 116
H
A 123
BARKING AND DAGENHAM
DAGENHAM EAST
A 124
B 1423
A 118
EAST HAM
BARKING
A 124
UPNEY
BECONTREE
DAGENHAM HEATHWAY
P
A 112
NEWHAM
UPTON PARK
P
H
A 123
A 13
PLAISTOW
H
WEST HAM
A 13
A 124
P
A 117
LONDON CITY AIRPORT
THAMES
A 2016
A 2041
P
THAMES BARRIER
H
P
A 206
A 206
A 205
A 102 (M)
GREENWICH
K
H
J
IPSWICH A 12 A 127 : SOUTHEND-ON-SEA
T
U
TILBURY A 13
V
overlap repeated pp. 10 and 11

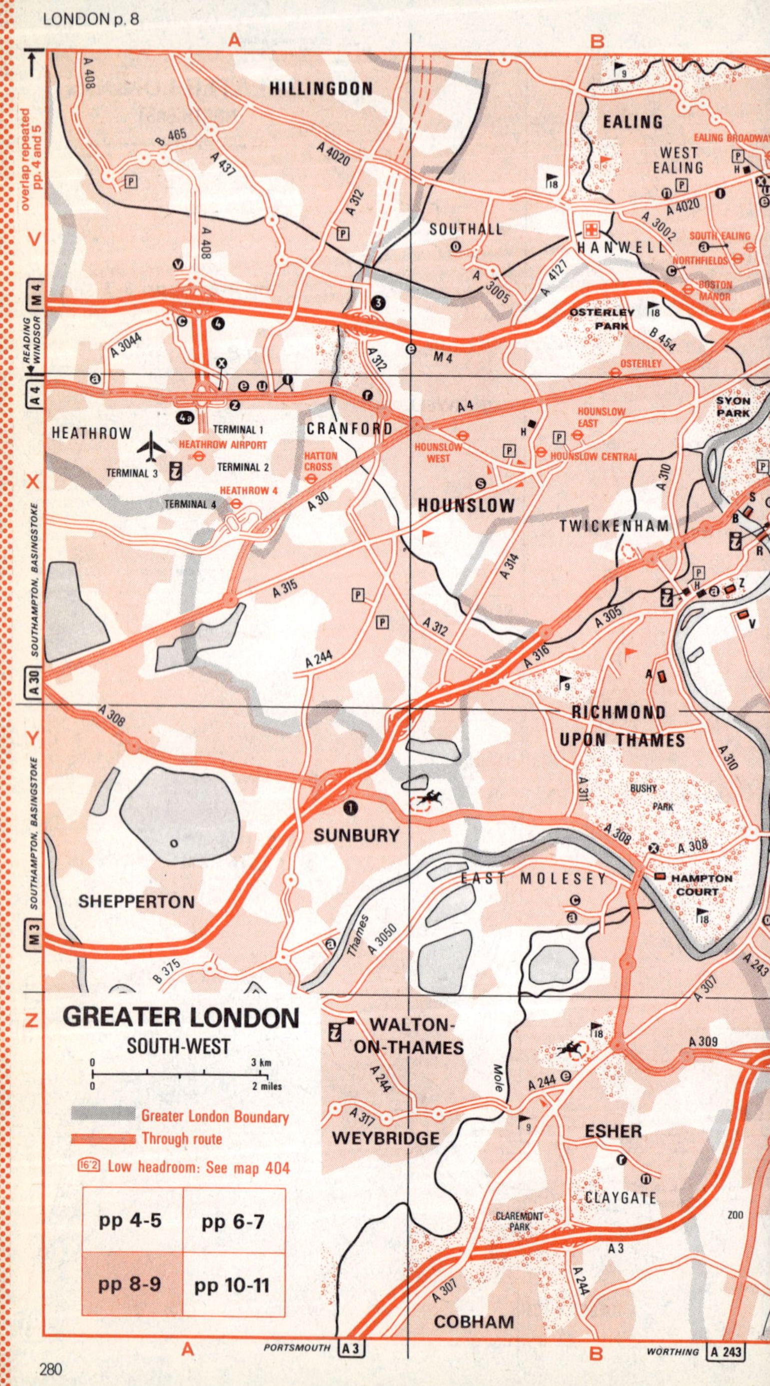

GREATER LONDON
SOUTH-WEST

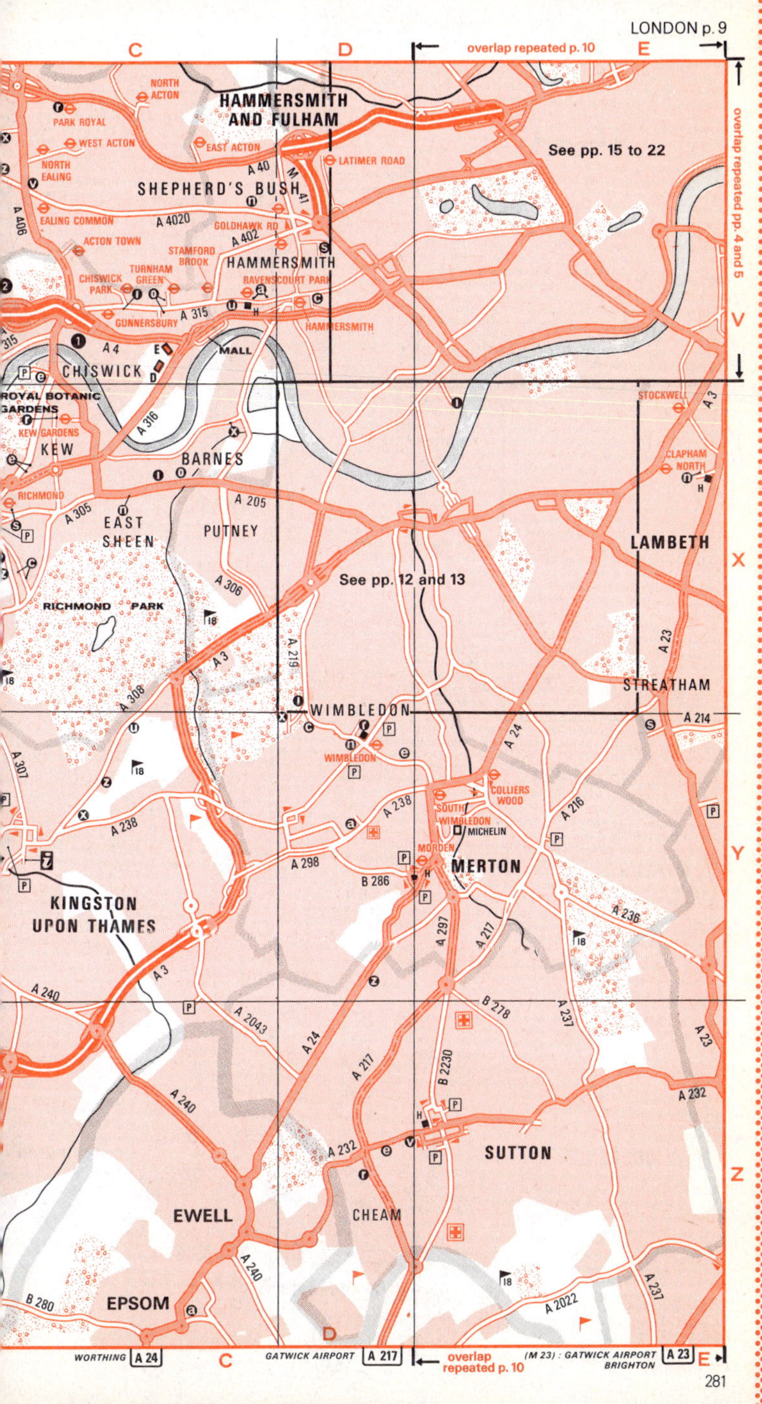

overlap repeated p. 10
overlap repeated pp. 4 and 5
C
D
E
NORTH ACTON
PARK ROYAL
WEST ACTON
EAST ACTON
HAMMERSMITH AND FULHAM
LATIMER ROAD
NORTH EALING
A 40
M 41
SHEPHERD'S BUSH
See pp. 15 to 22
A 406
EALING COMMON
A 4020
GOLDHAWK RD
A 402
ACTON TOWN
STAMFORD BROOK
TURNHAM GREEN
HAMMERSMITH
A 315
CHISWICK PARK
RAVENSCOURT PARK
GUNNERSBURY
HAMMERSMITH
A 315
V
A 4
CHISWICK
MALL
STOCKWELL
A 3
ROYAL BOTANIC GARDENS
A 316
CLAPHAM NORTH
KEW GARDENS
KEW
BARNES
RICHMOND
A 305
A 205
EAST SHEEN
PUTNEY
LAMBETH
X
A 306
See pp. 12 and 13
RICHMOND PARK
A 219
A 3
A 308
A 23
STREATHAM
A 214
WIMBLEDON
WIMBLEDON
A 24
COLLIERS WOOD
A 238
SOUTH WIMBLEDON
A 216
MICHELIN
A 307
A 238
MORDEN
A 298
B 286
MERTON
Y
P
KINGSTON UPON THAMES
A 236
A 297
A 217
A 3
A 240
A 2043
B 278
A 237
A 24
A 23
A 217
B 2230
A 240
A 232
H
P
SUTTON
A 232
Z
EWELL
CHEAM
B 280
EPSOM
A 240
A 2022
A 237
WORTHING A 24
GATWICK AIRPORT A 217
overlap repeated p. 10
(M 23): GATWICK AIRPORT BRIGHTON A 23
C
D
E
281

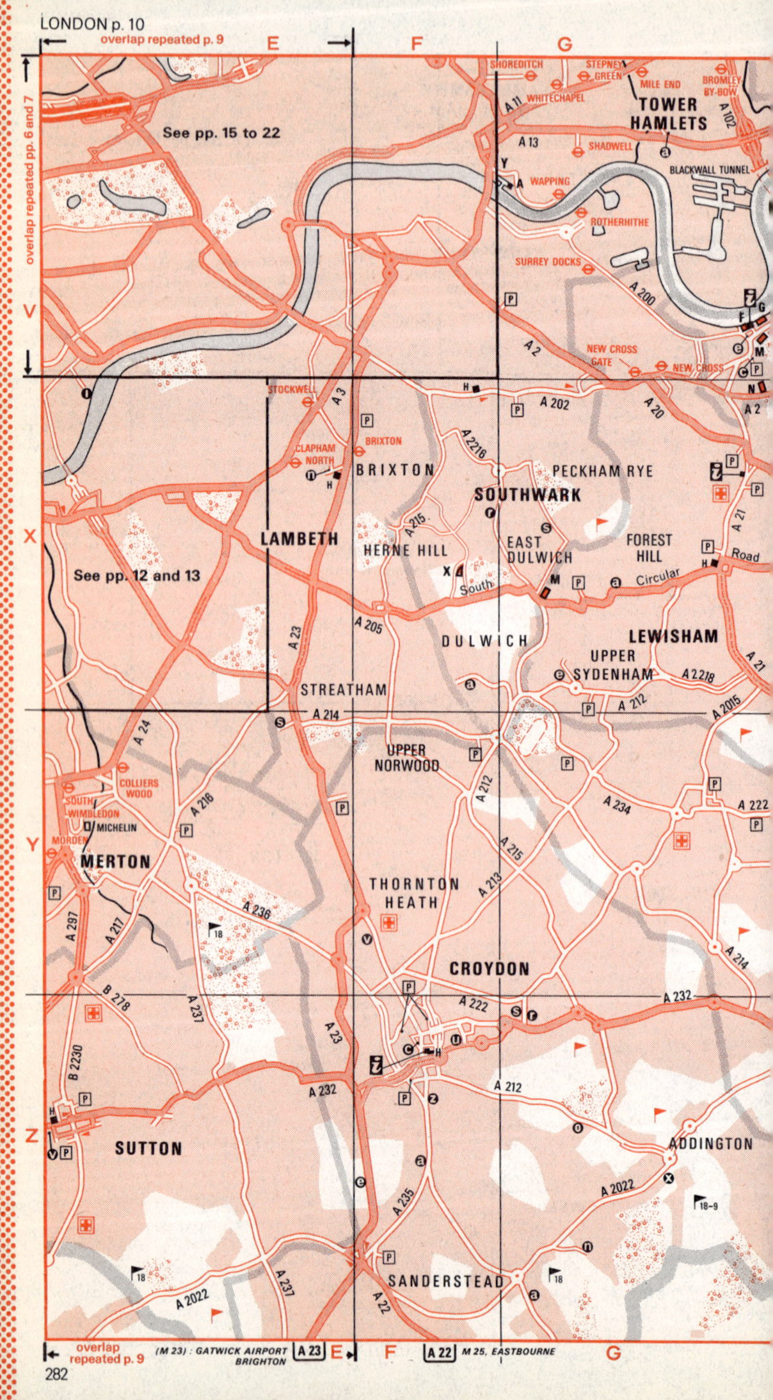

LONDON p. 10
overlap repeated p. 9
See pp. 15 to 22
See pp. 12 and 13
overlap repeated pp. 6 and 7
SHOREDITCH
STEPNEY GREEN
MILE END
BROMLEY BY-BOW
WHITECHAPEL
A 11
TOWER HAMLETS
A 13
SHADWELL
A 102
WAPPING
BLACKWALL TUNNEL
ROTHERHITHE
SURREY DOCKS
A 200
A 2
NEW CROSS GATE
NEW CROSS
STOCKWELL
A 3
A 202
A 20
A 2
CLAPHAM NORTH
BRIXTON
A 2216
PECKHAM RYE
BRIXTON
SOUTHWARK
A 215
LAMBETH
HERNE HILL
EAST DULWICH
FOREST HILL
A 21
South
Road
Circular
A 23
A 205
DULWICH
LEWISHAM
UPPER SYDENHAM
A 2218
A 21
STREATHAM
A 214
A 212
A 2015
A 24
UPPER NORWOOD
A 212
A 234
A 222
COLLIERS WOOD
A 216
SOUTH WIMBLEDON
MICHELIN
A 215
MORDEN
MERTON
THORNTON HEATH
A 213
A 297
A 217
A 236
18
A 214
CROYDON
A 222
A 232
B 278
A 237
A 23
A 212
B 2230
A 232
SUTTON
ADDINGTON
A 235
A 2022
18-9
A 2022
A 237
SANDERSTEAD
18
A 22
overlap repeated p. 9
(M 23) : GATWICK AIRPORT BRIGHTON
A 23   E
F   A 22   M 25, EASTBOURNE   G

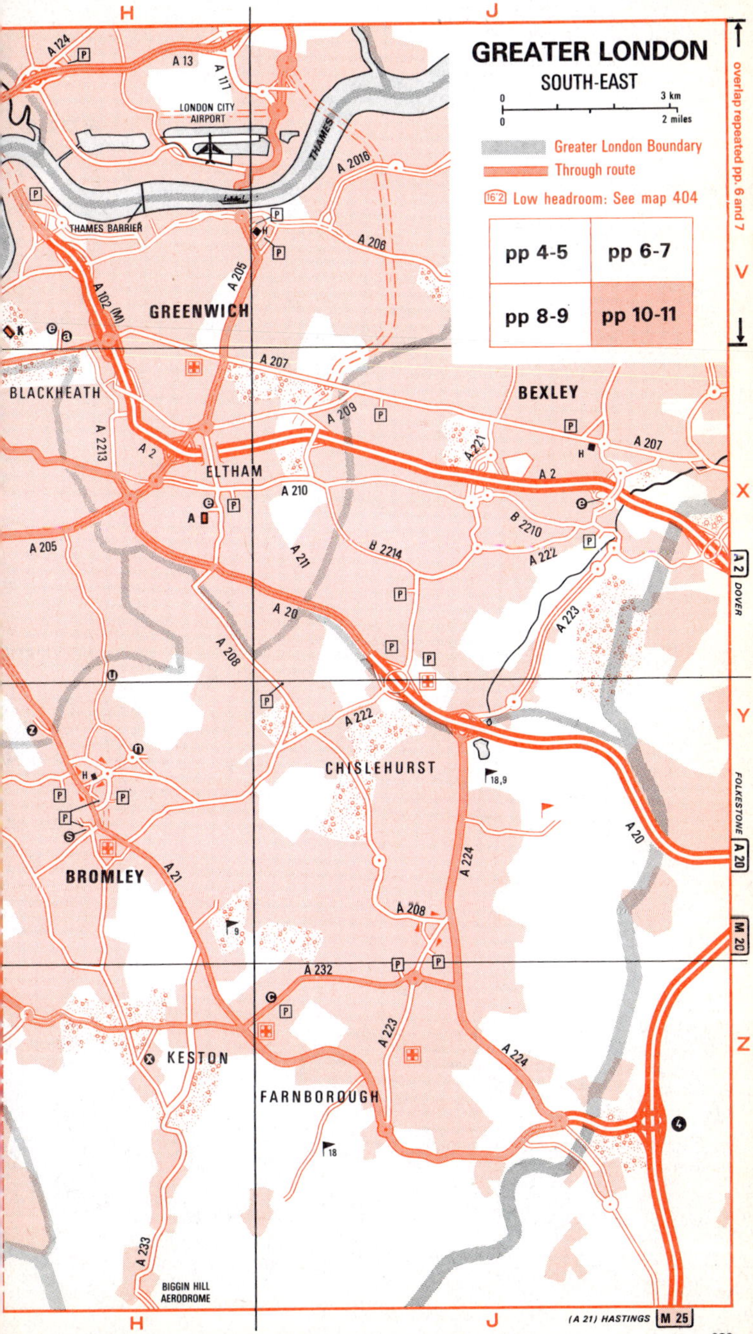

GREATER LONDON
SOUTH-EAST
0 3 km
0 2 miles
Greater London Boundary
Through route
16'2 Low headroom: See map 404
pp 4-5
pp 6-7
pp 8-9
pp 10-11
overlap repeated pp. 6 and 7
A 124
P
A 13
A 111
LONDON CITY AIRPORT
THAMES
A 2016
P
A 206
P
THAMES BARRIER
H
A 205
P
A 102 (M)
GREENWICH
K
a
A 207
BLACKHEATH
A 2213
A 2
A 209
P
BEXLEY
P
A 207
A 221
H
A 2
ELTHAM
A 210
P
A
P
B 2210
e
X
A 205
A 211
B 2214
A 222
A 2
DOVER
A 223
P
A 20
A 208
P
P
P
Y
P
A 222
CHISLEHURST
18,9
z
n
FOLKESTONE
A 20
H
P
P
A 224
A 20
P
S
BROMLEY
A 21
A 208
M 20
9
A 232
P
P
C
P
A 223
N
KESTON
x
A 224
FARNBOROUGH
4
18
A 233
BIGGIN HILL AERODROME
H
J
(A 21) HASTINGS   M 25

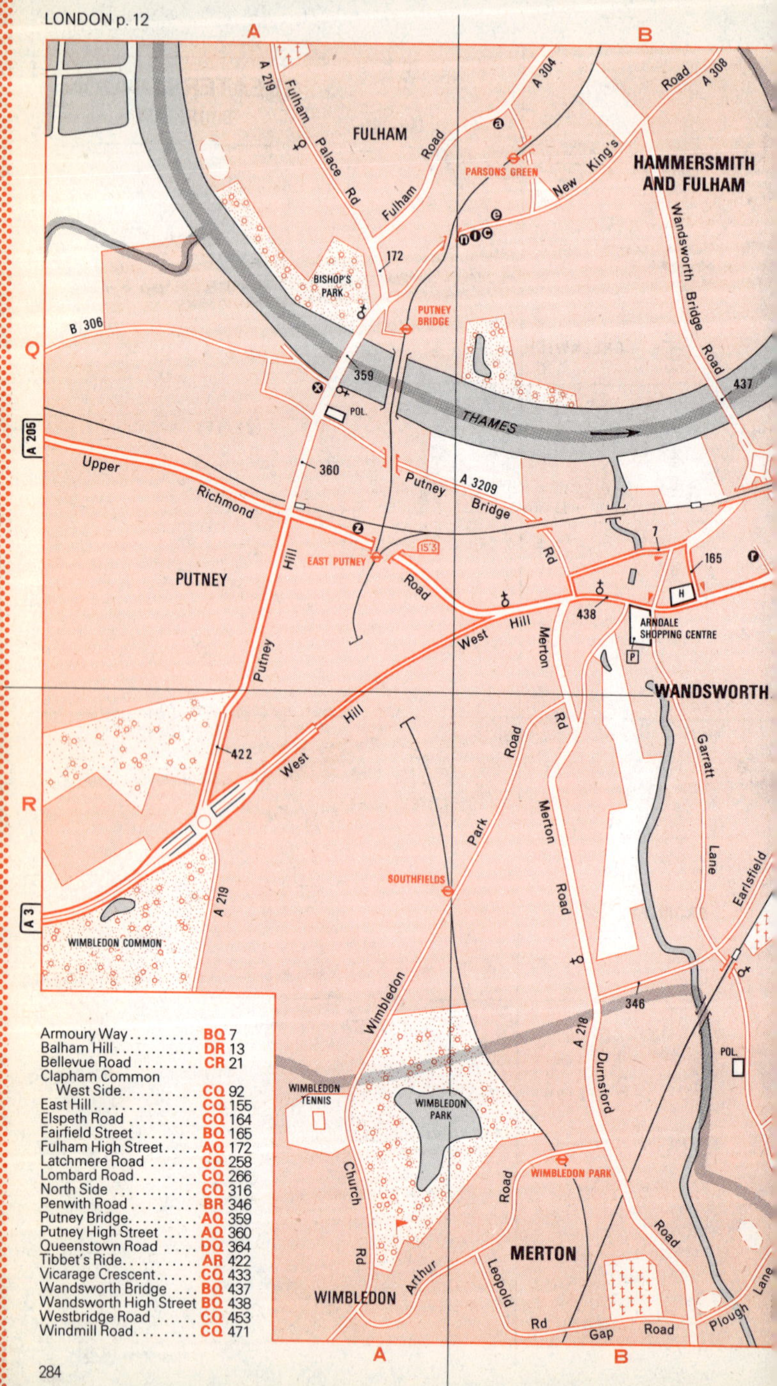

Armoury Way . . . . **BQ** 7
Balham Hill . . . . **DR** 13
Bellevue Road . . . . **CR** 21
Clapham Common
   West Side. . . . . **CQ** 92
East Hill . . . . **CQ** 155
Elspeth Road . . . . **CQ** 164
Fairfield Street . . . . **BQ** 165
Fulham High Street . . . . . **AQ** 172
Latchmere Road . . . . **CQ** 258
Lombard Road . . . . **CQ** 266
North Side . . . . **CQ** 316
Penwith Road . . . . **BR** 346
Putney Bridge. . . . . **AQ** 359
Putney High Street . . . . . **AQ** 360
Queenstown Road . . . . . **DQ** 364
Tibbet's Ride. . . . . **AR** 422
Vicarage Crescent. . . . . . **CQ** 433
Wandsworth Bridge . . . . . **BQ** 437
Wandsworth High Street **BQ** 438
Westbridge Road . . . . **CQ** 453
Windmill Road. . . . . **CQ** 471

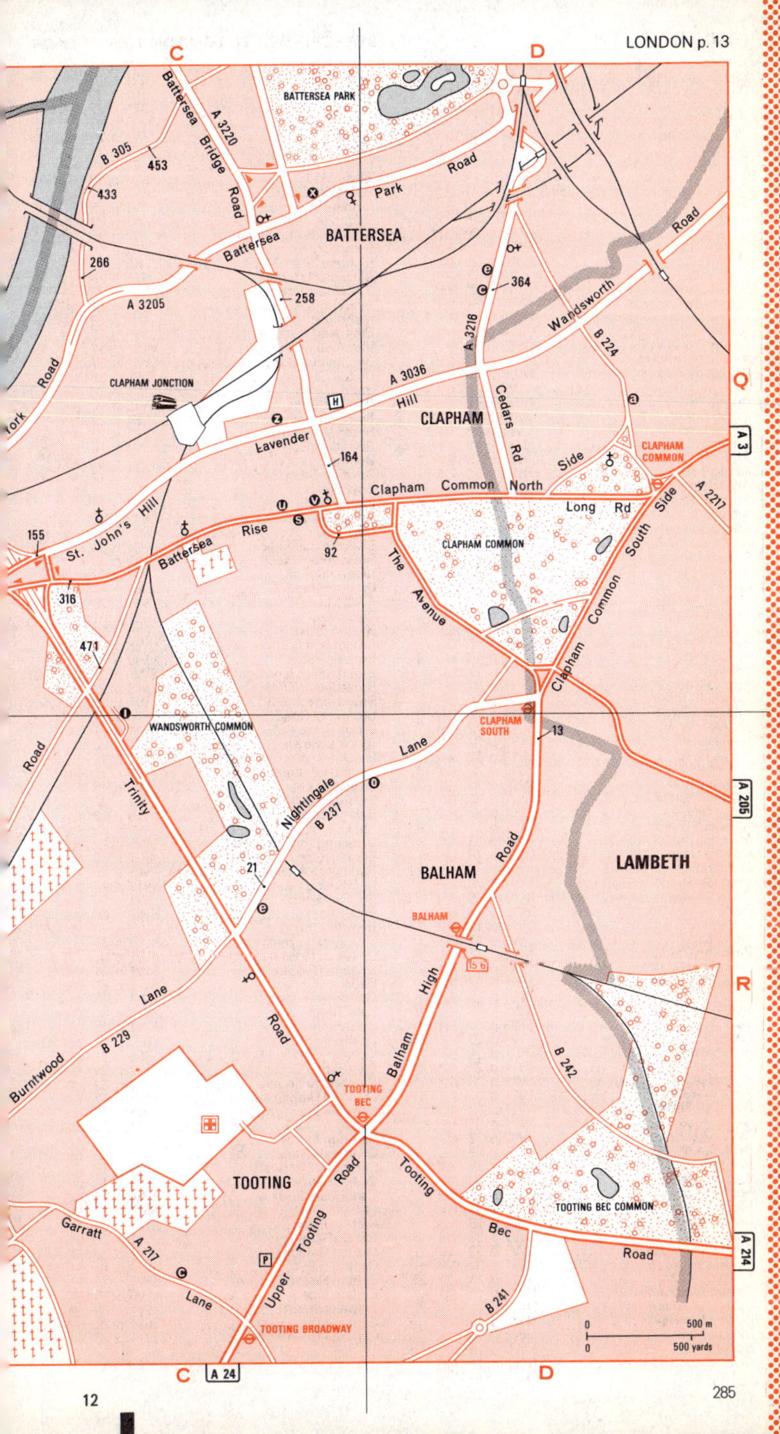

LONDON p. 13
C
D
BATTERSEA PARK
Battersea Bridge Road
A 3220
B 305
453
433
266
A 3205
258
Battersea
Park
Road
BATTERSEA
364
Wandsworth
Road
B 224
A 3216
CLAPHAM JONCTION
A 3036
Hill
CLAPHAM
Cedars Rd
Q
CLAPHAM COMMON
A 3
Lavender
164
Clapham
Common
North
Side
Long Rd
A 2217
St. John's Hill
92
The Avenue
CLAPHAM COMMON
Clapham Common South Side
Battersea
Rise
155
316
471
WANDSWORTH COMMON
Lane
CLAPHAM SOUTH
13
Road
Nightingale
B 237
21
Trinity
Road
Lane
BALHAM
Road
LAMBETH
A 205
Balham High Road
BALHAM
15 b
R
B 242
Burntwood
Lane
B 229
TOOTING BEC
Upper
Tooting
Road
Road
Tooting
TOOTING
Bec
TOOTING BEC COMMON
Garratt
A 217
Lane
P
Bec
Road
A 214
B 241
TOOTING BROADWAY
0   500 m
0   500 yards
C
A 24
D
12
285

STREET INDEX TO LONDON TOWN PLANS

Arndale Shopping Center ...... SW18 p. 12 **BQ**
Beauchamp Place .... SW3 p. 31 **ER**
Brompton Road .... SW1, SW3 p. 31 **DS**
Burlington Arcade .... W1 p. 29 **DM**
Camden Passage .... N1 p. 18 **NS** 70
Carnaby Street .... W1 p. 29 **EK**
Jermyn Street .... SW1 p. 29 **EN**
Kensington High Street ...... W8, W14 p. 19 **EY**
King's Road .... SW3, SW10, SW6 p. 31 **DU**
Knightsbridge .... SW1, SW7 p. 31 **EQ**
Middlesex Street .... E1 p. 18 **PU**
New Bond Street .... W1 p. 28 **CK**
Old Bond Street .... W1 p. 29 **DM**
Oxford Street .... W1 p. 28 **BK**
Piccadilly .... W1 p. 29 **EM**
Portobello Road .... W11, W10 p. 15 **EV**
Regent Street .... W1 p. 29 **EM**
Sloane Street .... SW1 p. 31 **FR**

Abbey Road .... NW8 p. 15 **FS**
Abbey Street .... SE1 p. 22 **PY**
Abbotsbury Road .... W14 p. 19 **EY**
Abercorn Place .... NW8 p. 15 **FT**
Abingdon Road .... W8 p. 19 **EY** 2
Acacia Road .... NW8 p. 16 **GS**
Adam Street .... WC2 p. 33 **DY**
Adam's Row .... W1 p. 28 **BM**
Addison Crescent .... W14 p. 19 **EY** 3
Addison Road .... W14 p. 19 **EY**
Adelaide Road .... NW3 p. 16 **GS**
Agar Grove .... NW1 p. 17 **KS**
Akenside Road .... NW3 p. 15 **ES**
Albany Street .... NW1 p. 16 **JT**
Albert Bridge .... SW3, SW11 p. 20 **HZ**
Albert Bridge Road .... SW11 p. 20 **HZ**
Albert Embankment .... SE1 p. 21 **LZ**
Albion Street .... W2 p. 33 **EZ**
Aldersgate Street .... EC1 p. 18 **NU**
Aldford Street .... W1 p. 28 **BM**
Aldgate High Street .... EC3 p. 18 **PV**
Aldwych .... WC2 p. 33 **EX**
Allitsen Road .... NW8 p. 16 **GS**
Allsop Place .... NW1 p. 16 **HU** 4
Amwell Street .... EC1 p. 17 **MT**
Argyll Street .... W1 p. 29 **DJ**
Arkwright Road .... NW3 p. 15 **ES**
Arlington Street .... SW1 p. 29 **DN** 6
Armoury Way .... SW18 p. 12 **BQ** 7
Artesian Road .... W2 p. 32 **AZ**
Arthur Road .... SW19 p. 12 **AR**
Artillery Row .... SW1 p. 32 **CX** 8
Arundel Street .... WC2 p. 33 **EX**
Ashburn Place .... SW7 p. 30 **BS**
Ashley Place .... SW1 p. 32 **BX**
Atterbury Street .... SW1 p. 21 **LZ** 9
Avenue (The) .... SW4 p. 13 **DQ**
Avenue Road .... NW8, NW3 p. 16 **GS**
Avery Row .... W1 p. 28 **CL** 12
Aybrook Street .... W1 p. 28 **AH**
Baker Street .... W1, NW1 p. 28 **AH**
Balham High Road ..... SW12, SW17 p. 13 **DR**
Balham Hill .... SW13 p. 13 **DR** 13
Bark Place .... W2 p. 32 **BZ**
Barkston Gardens .... SW5 p. 30 **AT** 14
Barnsbury Road .... N1 p. 17 **MS**
Barnsbury Street .... N1 p. 17 **MS**
Baron's Court Road .... W14 p. 19 **EZ**
Bartholomew Road .... NW5 p. 17 **KS** 16
Basil Street .... SW3 p. 31 **ER**
Bateman Street .... W1 p. 29 **FK** 18
Bath Street .... EC1 p. 18 **NT**
Battersea Bridge .... SW3, SW11 p. 20 **GZ**
Battersea Bridge Road .... SW11 p. 20 **GZ**
Battersea Park Road ...... SW8, SW11 p. 21 **KZ** 19
Battersea Rise .... SW11 p. 13 **CQ**
Baylis Road .... SE1 p. 21 **MY**
Bayswater Road .... W2 p. 32 **BZ**
Beak Street .... W1 p. 29 **EL**
Beauchamp Place .... SW3 p. 31 **ER**
Beaufort Street .... SW3 p. 30 **CU**
Bedfort Square .... WC1 p. 17 **KU**
Bedfort Street .... WC2 p. 33 **DX**
Beech Street .... EC2 p. 18 **NU**
Belgrave Place .... SW1 p. 32 **AX**
Belgrave Road .... SW1 p. 32 **BY**
Belgrave Square .... SW1 p. 32 **AV**
Bellevue Road .... SW17 p. 13 **CR** 21
Belsize Avenue .... NW3 p. 15 **ES**
Belsize Crescent .... NW3 p. 15 **ES** 22
Belsize Lane .... NW3 p. 15 **ES**
Belsize Park .... NW3 p. 16 **GS**
Belsize Road .... NW6 p. 15 **FS**
Belsize Park Gardens .... NW3 p. 16 **GS**

Belvedere Road .... SE1 p. 21 **MX** 23
Berkeley Square .... W1 p. 28 **CM**
Berkeley Street .... W1 p. 29 **DN**
Bermondsey Street .... SE1 p. 22 **PY**
Bernard Street .... WC1 p. 17 **LT** 25
Berwick Street .... W1 p. 29 **FK** 26
Bessborough Street .... SW1 p. 21 **KZ** 30
Bethnal Green Road .... E1, E2 p. 18 **PT** 32
Bevis Marks .... EC3 p. 18 **PU** 34
Bina Gardens .... SW5 p. 30 **BT**
Binney Street .... W1 p. 28 **BL** 35
Birdcage Walk .... SW1 p. 32 **CV**
Bishop's Bridge Road .... W2 p. 15 **FU**
Bishopsgate .... EC2 p. 18 **PU** 36
Bishops Road .... N6 p. 19 **EZ**
Blackfriars Bridge .... EC4, SE1 p. 18 **NV** 38
Blackfriars Road .... SE1 p. 22 **NX**
Black Prince Road .... SE11, SE1 p. 21 **MZ**
Blandford Street .... W1 p. 28 **AH**
Blomfield Road .... W9 p. 15 **FU**
Bloomsbury Street .... WC1 p. 17 **LU** 39
Bloomsbury Way .... WC1 p. 17 **LU**
Bolton Gardens .... SW5 p. 30 **AT**
Bolton Street .... W1 p. 28 **CN**
Boltons (The) .... SW10 p. 30 **BU**
Borough High Street .... SE1 p. 22 **NY**
Borough Road .... SE1 p. 22 **NY**
Boundary Road .... NW8 p. 15 **FS**
Bourne Street .... W1 p. 31 **FT**
Bowling Green Lane .... EC1 p. 17 **MT** 43
Bow Street .... WC2 p. 33 **DX**
Braganza Street .... SE17 p. 22 **NZ**
Bramham Gardens .... SW5 p. 30 **AT**
Bray Place .... SW3 p. 31 **ET** 45
Bream's Buildings .... EC4 p. 33 **EV** 47
Bressenden Place .... SW1 p. 32 **BX** 48
Brewer Street .... W1 p. 29 **EM**
Brewery Road .... N7 p. 17 **LS**
Brick Street .... W1 p. 28 **BP**
Bridgefoot .... SE1 p. 21 **LZ** 49
Brixton Road .... E16 p. 21 **MZ**
Broadhurst Gardens .... NW6 p. 15 **FS**
Broadley Street .... NW8 p. 16 **GU**
Broad Sanctuary .... SW1 p. 21 **LY** 52
Broad Walk (The) .... W8 p. 32 **BZ**
Broadwick Street .... W1 p. 29 **EK**
Brompton Road .... SE6 p. 31 **DS**
Brook Drive .... SE11 p. 21 **MY**
Brook's Mews .... W1 p. 28 **CL**
Brook Street .... W1 p. 28 **BL**
Brushfield Street .... E1 p. 18 **PU**
Bruton Street .... W1 p. 28 **CM**
Bryanston Square .... W1 p. 16 **HU**
Bryanston Street .... W1 p. 28 **AK**
Buckingham Gate .... SW1 p. 32 **CV** 56
Buckingham Palace Road ...... SW1 p. 32 **AY**
Bunhill Row .... EC1 p. 18 **PT**
Burlington Arcade .... W1 p. 29 **DM**
Burntwood Lane .... SW17 p. 13 **CR**
Bury Street .... SW1 p. 29 **EN**
Bute Street .... SW7 p. 30 **CS** 59
Byward Street .... EC3 p. 18 **PV** 62
Cadogan Gardens .... SW3 p. 31 **FS**
Cadogan Place .... SW1 p. 31 **FR**
Cadogan Square .... SW1 p. 31 **FS**
Cadogan Street .... SW3 p. 31 **ET**
Caledonian Road .... N1, N7 p. 17 **MS**
Cale Street .... SW3 p. 31 **DT**
Calshot Street .... N1 p. 17 **MT**
Calthorpe Street .... WC1 p. 17 **MT** 65
Camberwell New Road .... SE5 p. 21 **MZ**
Cambridge Circus .... WC2 p. 29 **GK**
Cambridge Square .... W2 p. 33 **EZ** 67
Camden High Street .... NW1 p. 17 **KS**
Camden Passage .... N1 p. 18 **NS** 70
Camden Road .... E11 p. 17 **KS**
Camden Street .... NW1 p. 17 **KS**
Camomile Street .... EC3 p. 18 **PU** 71
Campden Hill Road .... W8 p. 19 **EX**
Cannon Street .... EC4 p. 18 **NV**
Canonbury Square .... N1 p. 18 **NS**
Carey Street .... WC2 p. 33 **EV**
Carlisle Place .... SW1 p. 32 **BX**
Carlos Place .... W1 p. 28 **BM**
Carlton Gardens .... SW1 p. 29 **FP** 74
Carlton Hill .... NW8 p. 15 **FS**
Carlton House Terrace .... SW1 p. 29 **FN**
Carlton Vale .... NW6 p. 15 **ET**
Carnaby Street .... W1 p. 29 **EK**
Carriage Drive East .... SW11 p. 20 **JZ**
Carriage Drive North .... SW11 p. 20 **HZ** 75

Continued p. 23

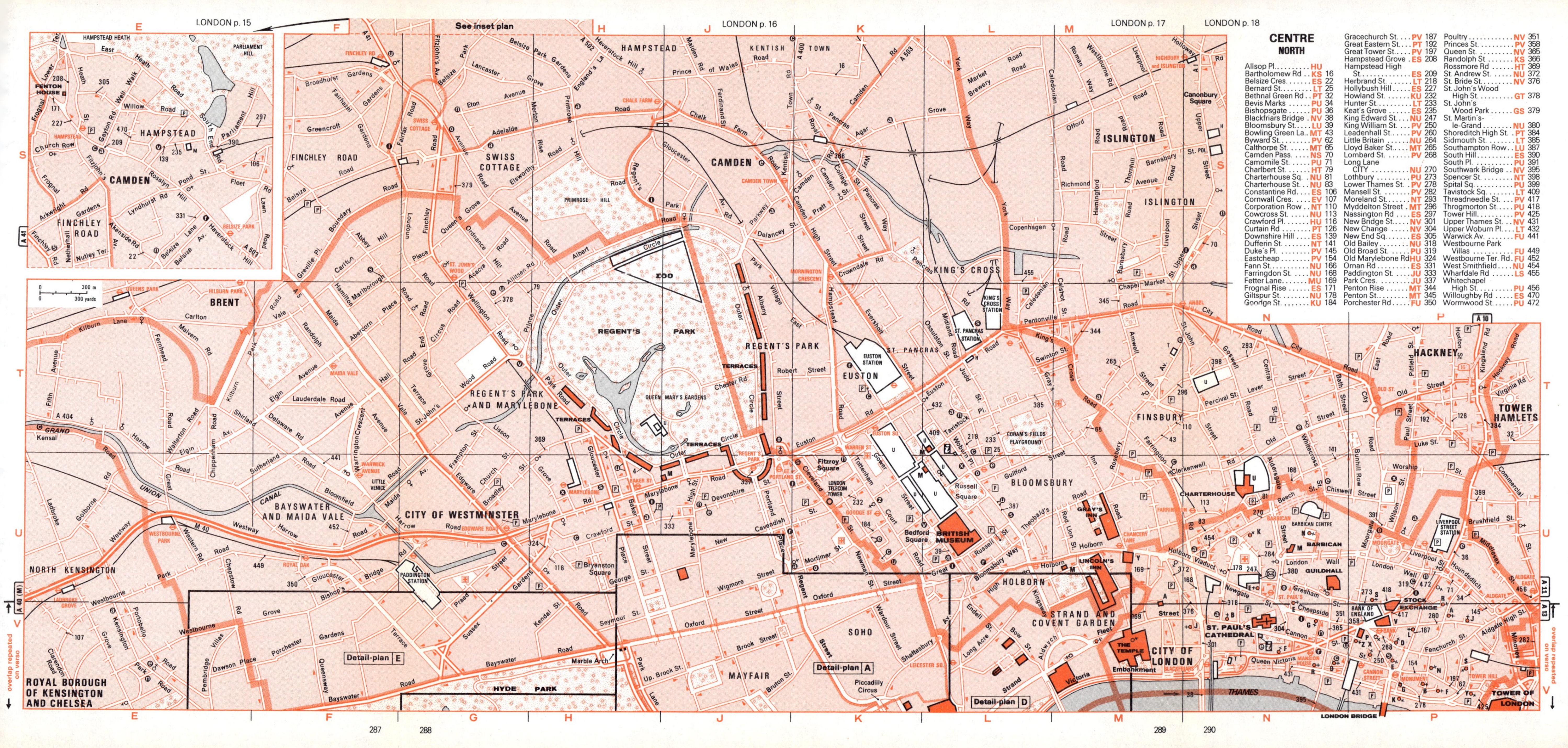

CENTRE
NORTH

Allsop Pl. ... HU
Bartholomew Rd ... KS 16
Belsize Cres. ... ES 22
Bernard St. ... LT 25
Bethnal Green Rd ... PT 32
Bevis Marks ... PU 34
Bishopsgate ... PU 36
Blackfriars Bridge ... NV 38
Bloomsbury St. ... LU 39
Bowling Green La. ... MT 43
Byward St. ... PV 62
Calthorpe St. ... MT 65
Camden Pass ... NS 70
Camomile St. ... PU 71
Charlbert St. ... HT 79
Charterhouse Sq. ... NU 81
Charterhouse St. ... NU 83
Constantine Rd. ... ES 106
Cornwall Cres. ... EV 107
Corporation Row ... NT 110
Cowcross St. ... NU 113
Crawford Pl. ... HU 116
Curtain Rd ... PT 126
Downshire Hill ... ES 139
Dufferin St. ... NT 141
Duke's Pl. ... PV 145
Eastcheap ... PV 154
Fann St. ... NU 166
Farringdon St. ... NU 168
Fetter Lane ... MU 169
Frognal Rise ... ES 171
Giltspur St. ... NU 178
Goodge St. ... KU 184

Gracechurch St. ... PV 187
Great Eastern St. ... PT 192
Great Tower St. ... PV 197
Hampstead Grove ... ES 208
Hampstead High St. ... ES 209
Herbrand St. ... LT 218
Hollybush Hill ... ES 227
Howland St. ... KU 232
Hunter St. ... LT 233
Keat's Grove ... ES 235
King Edward St. ... NU 247
King William St. ... PV 250
Leadenhall St. ... PV 260
Little Britain ... NU 264
Lloyd Baker St. ... MT 265
Lombard St. ... PV 268
Long Lane CITY ... NU 270
Lothbury ... PU 273
Lower Thames St. ... PV 278
Mansell St. ... PV 282
Moreland St. ... NT 293
Myddelton Street ... MT 296
Nassington Rd ... ES 297
New Bridge St. ... NV 301
New Change ... NV 304
New End Sq. ... ES 305
Old Bailey ... NU 318
Old Broad St. ... PU 319
Old Marylebone Rd ... HU 324
Ornan Rd ... ES 331
Paddington St. ... JU 333
Park Cres. ... JU 337
Penton Rise ... MT 344
Penton St. ... MT 345
Porchester Rd. ... FU 350

Poultry ... NV 351
Princes St. ... PV 358
Queen St. ... NV 365
Randolph St. ... KS 366
Rossmore Rd ... HT 369
St. Andrew St. ... NU 372
St. Bride St. ... NV 376
St. John's Wood High St. ... GT 378
St. John's Wood Park ... GS 379
St. Martin's-le-Grand ... NU 380
Shoreditch High St. ... PT 384
Sidmouth St. ... LT 385
Southampton Row ... LU 387
South Hill ... ES 390
South Pl. ... PU 391
Southwark Bridge ... NV 395
Spencer St. ... NT 398
Spital Sq. ... PU 399
Tavistock Sq. ... LT 409
Threadneedle St. ... PV 417
Throgmorton St. ... PU 418
Tower Hill ... PV 425
Upper Thames St. ... NV 431
Upper Woburn Pl. ... LT 432
Warwick Av. ... FU 441
Westbourne Park Villas ... FU 449
Westbourne Ter. Rd. ... FU 452
West Smithfield ... NU 454
Wharfdale Rd ... LS 455
Whitechapel High St. ... PU 456
Willoughby Rd ... ES 470
Wormwood St. ... PU 472

ROYAL BOROUGH OF KENSINGTON AND CHELSEA
NORTH KENSINGTON
BAYSWATER AND MAIDA VALE
CITY OF WESTMINSTER
REGENT'S PARK AND MARYLEBONE
REGENT'S PARK
ZOO
QUEEN MARY'S GARDENS
TERRACES
HYDE PARK
MAYFAIR
SOHO
BLOOMSBURY
BRITISH MUSEUM
STRAND AND COVENT GARDEN
HOLBORN
LINCOLN'S INN
THE TEMPLE
CITY OF LONDON
ST. PAUL'S CATHEDRAL
GUILDHALL
BANK OF ENGLAND
STOCK EXCHANGE
BARBICAN
BARBICAN CENTRE
CHARTERHOUSE
FINSBURY
EUSTON
EUSTON STATION
ST. PANCRAS STATION
KING'S CROSS
KING'S CROSS STATION
LIVERPOOL STREET STATION
PADDINGTON STATION
CAMDEN
CAMDEN TOWN
HAMPSTEAD
HAMPSTEAD HEATH
PARLIAMENT HILL
SWISS COTTAGE
FINCHLEY ROAD
KENTISH TOWN
ISLINGTON
HACKNEY
TOWER HAMLETS
TOWER OF LONDON
BRENT
FITZROY SQUARE
BEDFORD SQUARE
RUSSELL SQUARE
CORAM'S FIELDS PLAYGROUND
LONDON TELECOM TOWER
MARBLE ARCH
PICCADILLY CIRCUS
LEICESTER SQ.
MORNINGTON CRESCENT
PRIMROSE HILL
LITTLE VENICE
WESTBOURNE PARK
ROYAL OAK
CHALK FARM
WARREN ST.
BAKER ST.
GOODGE ST.
CANONBURY SQUARE
HIGHBURY AND ISLINGTON
ANGEL
CANAL
UNION CANAL
THAMES
CANNON STREET
HOXTON
Detail-plan A
Detail-plan D
Detail-plan E

LONDON p. 15
LONDON p. 16
LONDON p. 17
LONDON p. 18
See inset plan
overlap repeated on verso
London Bridge
287 288 289 290

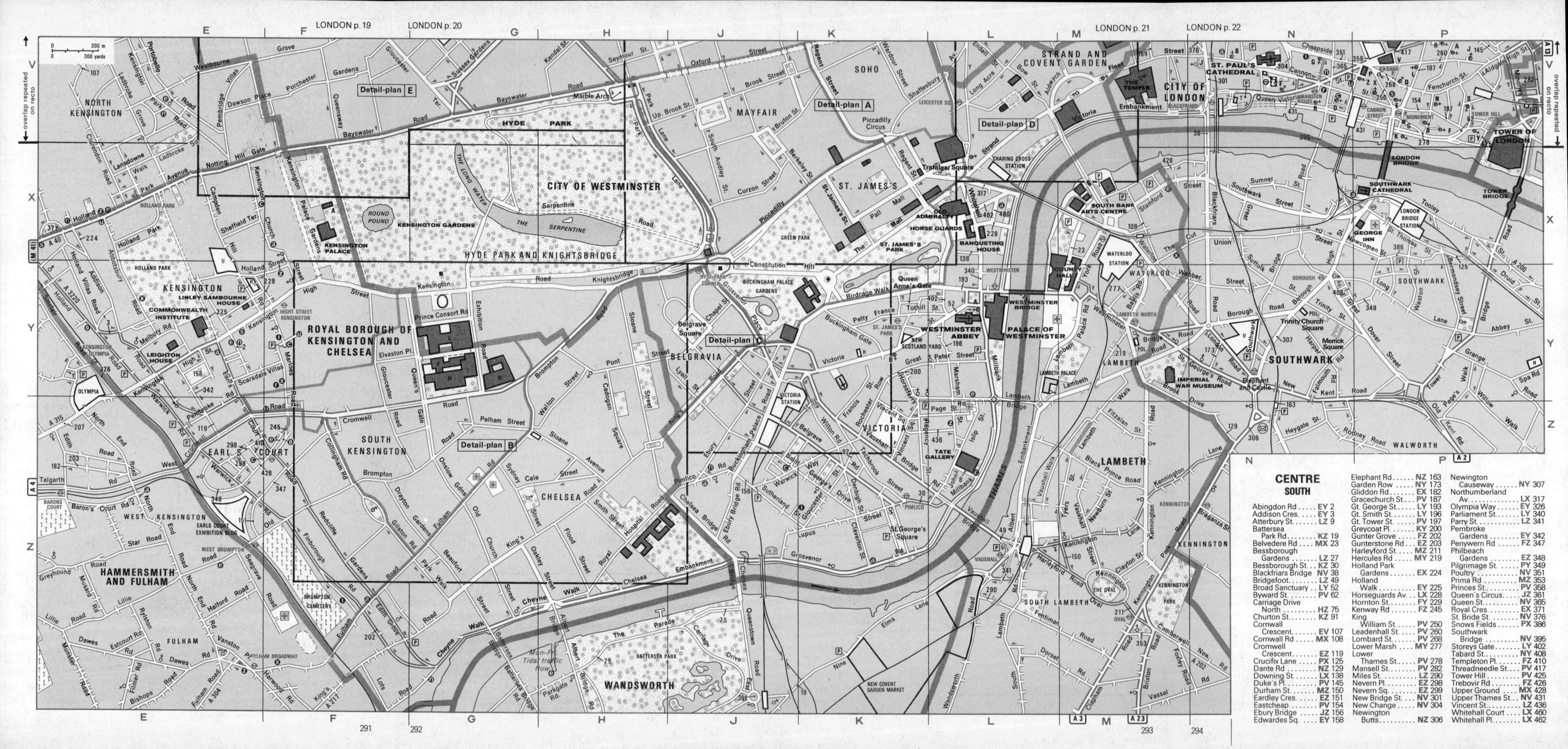

CENTRE
SOUTH

Abingdon Rd ..... EY 2
Addison Cres. ..... EY 3
Atterbury St. ...... LZ 9
Battersea
    Park Rd. .... KZ 19
Belvedere Rd .... MX 23
Bessborough
    Gardens .... LZ 27
Bessborough St. ... KZ 30
Blackfriars Bridge NV 38
Bridgefoot. .... LZ 49
Broad Sanctuary .. LY 52
Byward St. .... PV 62
Carriage Drive
    North .... HZ 75
Churton St. .... KZ 91
Cornwall
    Crescent. ...... EV 107
Cornwall Rd ..... MX 108
Cromwell
    Crescent. ...... EZ 119
Crucifix Lane ..... PX 125
Dante Rd .... NZ 129
Downing St. ...... LX 138
Duke's Pl. .... PV 145
Durham St. ...... MZ 150
Eardley Cres. ..... EZ 151
Eastcheap .... PV 154
Ebury Bridge ..... JZ 156
Edwardes Sq. ..... EY 158

Elephant Rd ...... NZ 163
Garden Row ..... NY 173
Gliddon Rd .... EX 182
Gracechurch St. ... PV 187
Gt. George St. ..... LY 193
Gt. Smith St. ...... LY 196
Gt. Tower St. ..... PV 197
Greycoat Pl. ...... KY 200
Gunter Grove ..... FZ 202
Gunterstone Rd ... EZ 203
Harleyford St. ..... MZ 211
Hercules Rd ..... MY 219
Holland Park
    Gardens .... EX 224
Holland
    Walk .... EY 225
Horseguards Av. ... LX 228
Hornton St. .... FY 229
Kenway Rd .... FZ 245
King
    William St. ..... PV 250
Leadenhall St. ..... PV 260
Lombard St. ...... PV 268
Lower Marsh .... MY 277
Lower
    Thames St. ..... PV 278
Mansell St. .... PV 282
Miles St. .... LZ 290
Nevern Pl. .... EZ 298
Nevern Sq. .... EZ 299
New Bridge St. ... NV 301
New Change ..... NV 304
Newington
    Butts. .... NZ 306

Newington
    Causeway ...... NY 307
Northumberland
    Av. .... LX 317
Olympia Way ...... EY 326
Parliament St. ...... LY 340
Parry St. .... LZ 341
Pembroke
    Gardens .... EY 342
Penywern Rd ..... FZ 347
Philbeach
    Gardens .... EZ 348
Pilgrimage St. ..... PY 349
Poultry .... NV 351
Prima Rd .... MZ 353
Princes St. .... PV 358
Queen's Circus. .... JZ 361
Queen St. .... NV 365
Royal Cres. .... EX 371
St. Bride St. .... NV 376
Snows Fields ..... PX 386
Southwark
    Bridge .... NV 395
Storeys Gate. ...... LY 402
Tabard St. .... NY 408
Templeton Pl. ..... FZ 410
Threadneedle St. ... PV 417
Tower Hill .... PV 425
Trebovir Rd ...... FZ 426
Upper Ground .... MX 428
Upper Thames St. ... NV 431
Vincent St. .... LZ 436
Whitehall Court .... LX 460
Whitehall Pl. ...... LX 462

Carriage Road (the) ..... SW7, SW11 p. 31	EQ		
Castle Lane. .... SW1 p. 32	CX		
Cavendish Square .... W1 p. 28	CJ		
Cedars Road .... SW4 p. 13	DQ		
Central Street .... EC1 p. 18	NT		
Chalk Farm Road .... NW1 p. 16	JS		
Chancery Lane. .... WC2 p. 33	EV		
Chandos Place. .... WC2 p. 33	DY		
Chandos Street .... W1 p. 28	CH		
Chapel Market. .... N1 p. 17	MT		
Chapel Street. .... SW1 p. 32	AV		
Charlbert Street. .... NW8 p. 16	HT	79	
Charles II Street. .... SW1 p. 29	FN		
Charles Street. .... W1 p. 28	CN		
Charing Cross .... SW1 p. 33	DY		
Charing Cross Road .... WC2 p. 29	GJ		
Charterhouse Square .... EC1 p. 18	NU	81	
Charterhouse Street .... EC1 p. 18	NU	83	
Cheapside .... EC2 p. 18	NV		
Chelsea Bridge .... SW1, SW8 p. 20	JZ		
Chelsea Bridge Road .... SW1 p. 20	JZ		
Chelsea Embankment .... SW3 p. 20	HZ		
Chelsea Manor Street. .... SW3 p. 31	EU		
Chelsea Square .... SW3 p. 31	DU		
Cheltenham Terrace .... SW3 p. 31	FT		
Chepstow Crescent .... W11 p. 32	AZ	84	
Chepstow Place .... W2 p. 32	AZ		
Chepstow Road .... W2 p. 32	AZ		
Chesham Place .... SW2 p. 31	FR		
Chesham Street. .... SW1 p. 31	FS		
Chester Road. .... NW1 p. 16	JT		
Chester Row. .... SW1 p. 32	AY		
Chester Square .... SW1 p. 32	AX	88	
Chester Street .... SW1 p. 32	AV		
Cheval Place. .... SW7 p. 31	ER		
Cheyne Walk .... SW3, SW10 p. 20	GZ		
Chilworth Street. .... W2 p. 32	CZ	90	
Chippenham Road .... W9 p. 15	EU		
Chiswell Street .... EC1 p. 18	NU		
Church Road .... SW19 p. 12	AR		
Church Row. .... NW3 p. 15	ES		
Church Street .... NW8, NW2 p. 16	GU		
Churton Street .... SW1 p. 21	KZ	91	
Circus Road .... NW8 p. 16	GT		
City Road .... EC1 p. 18	NT		
Clapham Common			
North Side .... SW4 p. 13	DQ		
Clapham Common			
South Side .... SW4 p. 13	DQ		
Clapham Common			
West Side .... SW4 p. 13	CQ	92	
Clapham Road. .... SW9 p. 21	MZ		
Clarendon Place. .... W2 p. 33	EZ	93	
Clarendon Road. .... W11 p. 15	EV		
Claverton Street. .... SW1 p. 21	KZ		
Clayton Street. .... SE11 p. 21	MZ		
Clerkenwell Road .... EC1 p. 18	NU		
Cleveland Gardens .... W2 p. 32	CZ	94	
Cleveland Square .... W2 p. 32	CZ		
Cleveland Street. .... W1 p. 17	KU		
Cleveland Terrace .... W2 p. 32	CZ		
Clifford Street. .... W1 p. 29	DM		
Cliveden Place. .... SW1 p. 31	FS		
Cockspur Street. .... SW1 p. 20	CN		
Collingham Gardens. .... SW5 p. 30	AT	99	
Collingham Road .... SW5 p. 30	AT	101	
Commercial Street .... E1 p. 18	PU		
Conduit Street .... W1 p. 29	DL		
Connaught Square .... W2 p. 33	EZ	103	
Connaught Street .... W2 p. 33	EZ		
Constantine Road. .... NW3 p. 15	ES	106	
Constitution Hill. .... SW1 p. 32	AV		
Copenhagen Street .... N1 p. 17	LS		
Cork Street .... W1 p. 29	DM		
Cornwall Crescent. .... W11 p. 15	EV	107	
Cornwall Gardens .... SW7 p. 30	AR		
Cornwall Road. .... SE1 p. 21	MX	108	
Corporation Row .... EC1 p. 18	NT	110	
Courtfield Gardens .... SW5 p. 30	AT		
Courtfield Road .... SW7 p. 30	BS		
Coventry Street .... W1 p. 29	FM		
Cowcross Street .... EC1 p. 18	NU	113	
Cranbourn Street. .... WC2 p. 33	DX	115	
Cranley Gardens .... SW7 p. 30	CT		
Craven Hill. .... W2 p. 32	CZ		
Craven Road. .... W2 p. 33	DZ		
Craven Street. .... WC2 p. 33	DY		
Craven Terrace .... W2 p. 33	DZ		
Crawford Place. .... W1 p. 16	HU	116	
Crawford Street. .... W1 p. 16	HU		
Cromwell Crescent .... SW5 p. 19	EZ	119	
Cromwell Place .... SW7 p. 30	CS	120	
Cromwell Road .... SW7, SW5 p. 30	CS		
Crowndale Road. .... NW1 p. 17	KS		
Crucifix Lane .... SE1 p. 22	PX	125	
Culross Street. .... W1 p. 28	AM		
Curtain Road .... EC2 p. 18	PT	126	
Curzon Street .... W1 p. 28	BN		
Cut (The). .... SE1 p. 21	MX		
Dante Road .... SE11 p. 22	NZ	129	
D'Arblay Street. .... W1 p. 29	EK		
Davies Street. .... W1 p. 28	BK		
Dawes Road. .... SW6 p. 19	EZ		
Dawson Place .... W2 p. 32	AZ		
Deanery Street. .... W1 p. 28	BN	132	
Dean Street. .... W1 p. 29	FJ		
Delancey Street .... NW1 p. 16	JS		
Delaware Road .... W9 p. 15	FU		
Denbigh Street. .... SW1 p. 21	KZ		
Denman Street. .... W1 p. 29	FM	133	
Denmark Street. .... WC2 p. 29	GJ	134	
De Vere Gardens .... W8 p. 30	BQ		
Devonshire Street. .... W1 p. 16	JU		
Devonshire Terrace .... W2 p. 32	CZ	136	
Dorset Road. .... SW8 p. 21	LZ		
Dorset Street. .... W1 p. 28	AH		
Dovehouse Street. .... SW3 p. 31	DU		
Dover Street. .... W1 p. 29	DM		
Downing Street. .... SW1 p. 21	LX	138	
Downshire Hill .... NW3 p. 15	ES	139	
Draycott Avenue .... SW3 p. 31	ET		
Draycott Place .... SW3 p. 31	ET		
Drayton Gardens .... SW10 p. 30	BT		
Druid Street .... SE1 p. 22	PY		
Drury Lane .... WC2 p. 33	DV	141	
Dufferin Street. .... EC1 p. 18	NT	142	
Duke of Wellington Place ..... SW1 p. 32	AV	143	
Duke of York Street. .... SW1 p. 29	EN	145	
Duke's Place .... EC3 p. 18	PV		
Duke Street. .... W1 p. 28	BK	146	
Duke Street ST. JAMES .... SW1 p. 29	EN	147	
Duncannon Street. .... WC2 p. 33	DY	149	
Dunraven Street. .... W1 p. 28	AL	150	
Durham Street. .... SE11 p. 21	MZ		
Durnsford Road. .... SW19 p. 12	BR	151	
Eardley Crescent .... SW5 p. 19	EZ	153	
Earlham Street. .... WC2 p. 33	DV		
Earl's Court Road .... W8, SW5 p. 19	EY		
Earlsfield Road .... SW18 p. 12	BR		
Eastbourne Terrace .... W2 p. 33	DZ		
Eastcastle Street .... W1 p. 29	EJ		
Eastcheap .... EC3 p. 18	PV	154	
East Heath Road .... NW3 p. 15	ES	155	
East Hill. .... SW18 p. 13	CQ		
East Road. .... N1 p. 18	PT		
Eaton Place .... SW1 p. 32	AX		
Eaton Square .... SW1 p. 32	AX	156	
Ebury Bridge .... SW1 p. 20	JZ		
Ebury Street. .... SW1 p. 32	AY		
Ebury Bridge Road .... SW1 p. 20	JZ	157	
Eccleston Bridge .... SW1 p. 32	BY		
Eccleston Square .... SW1 p. 32	BY		
Eccleston Street .... SW1 p. 32	AY		
Edgware Road .... W2 p. 16	GU		
Edith Grove. .... SW10 p. 19	FZ		
Edith Road. .... W14 p. 19	EZ		
Edwardes Square .... W8 p. 19	EY	158	
Egerton Gardens .... SW3 p. 31	DS	160	
Egerton Terrace .... SW3 p. 31	DR	161	
Egerton Gardens Mews .... SW3 p. 31	ER	162	
Elephant and Castle .... SE11 p. 22	NY		
Elephant Road .... SE17 p. 22	NZ	163	
Elgin Avenue .... W9 p. 15	FT		
Elizabeth Street .... SW1 p. 32	AY		
Elm Park Gardens .... SW10 p. 30	CU		
Elm Park Road .... SW3 p. 30	CU		
Elspeth Road .... SW11 p. 13	CQ	164	
Elsworthy Road .... NW3 p. 16	GS		
Elvaston Place .... SW7 p. 30	BR		
Elystan Place .... SW3 p. 31	ET		
Elystan Street. .... SW3 p. 31	DT		
Endell Street .... WC2 p. 33	DV		
England's Lane .... NW3 p. 16	HS		
Ennismore Gardens .... SW7 p. 31	DQ		
Essex Street .... WC2 p. 33	EX		
Estcourt Road .... SW6 p. 19	EZ		
Eton Avenue .... NW3 p. 16	GS		
Euston Road .... NW1 p. 17	LT		
Evelyn Gardens .... SW7 p. 30	CU		
Eversholt Street. .... NW1 p. 17	KT		
Exeter Street. .... WC2 p. 33	DX		
Exhibition Road .... SW7 p. 30	CQ		
Fairfax Road. .... NW6 p. 15	FS		
Fairfield Street. .... SW18 p. 12	BQ	165	

Continued on next page

Fairhazel Gardens . . . . NW6 p. 15 **FS**
Falmouth Road . . . . SE1 p. 22 **NY**
Farm Street MAYFAIR . . . . W1 p. 28 **BM**
Fann Street . . . . W1 p. 18 **NU** 166
Farringdon Road . . . . EC1 p. 17 **MT**
Farringdon Street . . . . EC4 p. 18 **NU** 168
Fenchurch Street . . . . EC3 p. 18 **PV**
Fentiman Road . . . . SW8 p. 21 **LZ**
Ferdinand Street . . . . NW1 p. 16 **JS**
Fernhead Road . . . . W9 p. 15 **ET**
Fetter Lane . . . . EC4 p. 17 **MU** 169
Fifth Avenue . . . . W10 p. 15 **ET**
Filmer Road . . . . SW6 p. 19 **EZ**
Finborough Road . . . . SW10 p. 30 **AU**
Finchley Road . . . . NW8, NW3 NW2, NW11 p. 16 **GS**
Fitzalan Street . . . . SE11 p. 21 **MZ**
Fitzjohn's Avenue . . . . NW3 p. 16 **GS**
Fitzroy Square . . . . W1 p. 17 **KU**
Fleet Road . . . . NW3 p. 15 **ES**
Fleet Street . . . . EC4 p. 17 **MV**
Flood Street . . . . SW3 p. 31 **EU**
Floral Street . . . . WC2 p. 33 **DX**
Foulis Terrace . . . . SW7 p. 30 **CT** 170
Foxley Road . . . . SW9 p. 21 **MZ**
Frampton Street . . . . NW8 p. 16 **GT**
Francis Street . . . . SW1 p. 32 **CY**
Franklin's Row . . . . SW3 p. 31 **FU**
Frith Street . . . . W1 p. 29 **FK**
Frognal . . . . NW3 p. 15 **ES**
Frognal Rise . . . . NW3 p. 15 **ES** 171
Fulham High Street . . . . SW6 p. 12 **AQ** 172
Fulham Palace Road . . . . W6, SW6 p. 12 **AQ**
Fulham Road . . . . . SW3, SW10, SW6 p. 19 **EZ**
Gap Road . . . . SW19 p. 12 **BR**
Garden Row . . . . SE1 p. 22 **NY** 173
Garratt Lane . . . . SW17, SW18 p. 12 **BR**
Garrick Street . . . . WC2 p. 33 **DX**
Garway Road . . . . W2 p. 32 **BZ**
Gayton Road . . . . NW3 p. 15 **ES**
George Street . . . . W1 p. 28 **AJ**
Gerrard Street . . . . W1 p. 29 **GL** 174
Gilbert Street . . . . W1 p. 28 **BL** 175
Gillingham Street . . . . SW1 p. 32 **BY**
Gilston Road . . . . SW10 p. 30 **BU**
Giltspur Street . . . . EC1 p. 18 **NU** 178
Glasshouse Street . . . . W1 p. 29 **EM** 179
Glendower Place . . . . SW7 p. 30 **CS** 180
Gliddon Road . . . . W14 p. 19 **EX** 182
Gloucester Avenue . . . . NW1 p. 16 **JS**
Gloucester Place . . . . W1, NW1 p. 16 **HT**
Gloucester Road . . . . SW7 p. 30 **BR**
Gloucester Square . . . . W2 p. 33 **EZ**
Gloucester Street . . . . SW1 p. 21 **KZ**
Gloucester Terrace . . . . W2 p. 32 **CZ**
Golborne Road . . . . W10 p. 15 **EU**
Golden Square . . . . W1 p. 29 **EL**
Goodge Street . . . . W1 p. 17 **KU** 184
Goswell Road . . . . EC1 p. 18 **NT**
Gower Street . . . . WC1 p. 17 **KU**
Gracechurch Street . . . . EC3 p. 18 **PV** 187
Grafton Street . . . . W1 p. 29 **DM**
Grange Road . . . . SE1 p. 22 **PY**
Granville Place . . . . W1 p. 28 **AK** 188
Gray's Inn Road . . . . WC1 p. 17 **LT**
Gt. Castle Street . . . . W1 p. 29 **DJ** 189
Gt. Cumberland Place . . . . W1 p. 33 **EZ** 191
Gt. Dover Street . . . . SE1 p. 22 **PY**
Gt. Eastern Street . . . . EC2 p. 18 **PT** 192
Gt. George Street . . . . SW1 p. 21 **LY** 193
Gt. Marlborough Street . . . . W1 p. 29 **EK**
Gt. Peter Street . . . . SW1 p. 21 **LY**
Gt. Queen Street . . . . WC2 p. 33 **DV**
Gt. Russell Street . . . . WC1 p. 17 **LU**
Gt. Smith Street . . . . SW1 p. 21 **LY** 196
Gt. Suffolk Street . . . . SE1 p. 22 **NX**
Gt. Tower Street . . . . EC3 p. 18 **PV** 197
Gt. Western Road . . . . W9, W11 p. 15 **EU**
Gt. Windmill Street . . . . W1 p. 29 **FM**
Greek Street . . . . W1 p. 29 **GK** 198
Greencroft Gardens . . . . NW6 p. 15 **FS**
Green Street . . . . W1 p. 28 **AL**
Grenville Place . . . . SW7 p. 30 **BS**
Gresham Street . . . . EC2 p. 18 **NU**
Greville Place . . . . NW6 p. 15 **FS**
Greycoat Place . . . . SW1 p. 21 **KY** 200
Greyhound Road . . . . W6, W14 p. 19 **EZ**
Grosvenor Crescent . . . . SW1 p. 32 **AV**
Grosvenor Gardens . . . . SW1 p. 32 **BX**
Grosvenor Place . . . . SW1 p. 32 **AV**
Grosvenor Road . . . . SW1 p. 21 **KZ**
Grosvenor Square . . . . W1 p. 28 **BL**
Grosvenor Street . . . . W1 p. 28 **BL**

Grove End Road . . . . NW8 p. 16 **GT**
Guildhouse Street . . . . SW1 p. 32 **BY** 201
Guilford Street . . . . WC1 p. 17 **LU**
Gunter Grove . . . . SW10 p. 19 **FZ** 202
Gunterstone Road . . . . W14 p. 19 **EZ** 203
Hackney Road . . . . E2 p. 18 **PT**
Half Moon Street . . . . W1 p. 28 **CN**
Halford Road . . . . SW6 p. 19 **EZ**
Halkin Street . . . . SW1 p. 32 **AV**
Hall Road . . . . NW8 p. 15 **FT**
Hamilton Place . . . . W1 p. 28 **BP** 205
Hamilton Terrace . . . . NW8 p. 15 **FT**
Hammersmith Road . . . . W14, W6 p. 19 **EZ** 207
Hampstead Grove . . . . NW3 p. 15 **ES** 208
Hampstead High Street . . . . NW3 p. 15 **ES** 209
Hampstead Road . . . . NW1 p. 17 **KT**
Hanover Square . . . . W1 p. 28 **CK** 210
Hanover Street . . . . W1 p. 29 **DK**
Hans Crescent . . . . SW1 p. 31 **ER**
Hans Place . . . . SW1 p. 31 **ER**
Hans Road . . . . SW3 p. 31 **ER**
Harcourt Terrace . . . . SW10 p. 30 **AU**
Harley Street W1
    WESTMINSTER . . . . p. 28 **CH**
Harleyford Road . . . . SE11 p. 21 **LZ**
Harleyford Street . . . . SE11 p. 21 **MZ** 211
Harper Road . . . . SE1 p. 22 **NY**
Harriet Street . . . . SW1 p. 31 **FQ** 214
Harrington Gardens . . . . SW7 p. 30 **BT**
Harrington Road . . . . SW7 p. 30 **CS** 215
Harrow Road . . . . W2, W9 W10, NW10 p. 15 **FU**
Harwood Road . . . . SW6 p. 19 **FZ**
Hasker Street . . . . SW3 p. 31 **ES**
Haverstock Hill . . . . NW3 p. 16 **HS**
Haymarket . . . . SW1 p. 29 **FM**
Hay's Mews . . . . W1 p. 28 **BN**
Heath Street . . . . NW3 p. 15 **ES**
Hemingford Road . . . . N1 p. 17 **MS**
Henrietta Place . . . . W1 p. 28 **BJ**
Henrietta Street . . . . WC2 p. 33 **DX** 217
Herbrand Street . . . . WC1 p. 17 **LT** 218
Hercules Road . . . . SE1 p. 21 **MY** 219
Hereford Road . . . . W2 p. 32 **AZ**
Hertford Street . . . . W1 p. 28 **BP** 220
Heygate Street . . . . SE17 p. 22 **NZ**
High Holborn . . . . WC1 p. 17 **LU**
Hill Street . . . . W1 p. 28 **BN**
Hobart Place . . . . SW1 p. 32 **AX**
Holbein Place . . . . SW1 p. 31 **FT**
Holbein Mews . . . . SW1 p. 31 **FT** 223
Holborn . . . . EC1 p. 17 **MU**
Holborn Viaduct . . . . EC1 p. 18 **NU**
Holland Park . . . . W11 p. 19 **EX**
Holland Park Avenue . . . . W11 p. 19 **EX**
Holland Park Gardens . . . . W11 p. 19 **EX** 224
Holland Road . . . . W14 p. 19 **EY**
Holland Street . . . . W8 p. 19 **EY**
Holland Walk . . . . W8 p. 19 **EY** 225
Holland Villas Road . . . . W14 p. 19 **EY**
Holles Street . . . . W1 p. 28 **CJ**
Holloway Road . . . . N7, N19 p. 17 **MS**
Hollybush Hill . . . . E11 p. 15 **ES** 227
Hollywood Road . . . . SW10 p. 30 **BU**
Horseferry Road . . . . SW1 p. 21 **KY**
Horseguards Avenue . . . . SW1 p. 21 **LX** 228
Hornton Street . . . . W8 p. 19 **FY** 229
Houndsditch . . . . EC3 p. 18 **PU**
Howick Place . . . . SW1 p. 32 **CX**
Howland Street . . . . W1 p. 17 **KU** 232
Hoxton Street . . . . N1 p. 18 **PT**
Hudson's Place . . . . SW1 p. 32 **BY**
Hugh Street . . . . SW1 p. 32 **BY**
Hunter Street . . . . WC1 p. 17 **LT** 233
Hyde Park Gardens . . . . W2 p. 33 **DZ**
Hyde Park Square . . . . W2 p. 33 **EZ** 234
Hyde Park Street . . . . W2 p. 33 **EZ**
Ifield Road . . . . SW10 p. 30 **AU**
Inverness Terrace . . . . W2 p. 32 **BZ**
Ixworth Place . . . . NW6 p. 31 **DT**
James Street . . . . W1 p. 28 **BJ**
James Street
    SOHO . . . . WC2 p. 29 **EL**
Jermyn Street . . . . SW1 p. 29 **EN**
John Adam Street . . . . WC2 p. 33 **DY**
John Islip Street . . . . SW1 p. 21 **LZ**
Jubilee Place . . . . SW3 p. 31 **ET**
Judd Street . . . . WC1 p. 17 **LT**
Keat's Grove . . . . NW3 p. 15 **ES** 235
Kemble Street . . . . WC2 p. 33 **EV**
Kendal Street . . . . W2 p. 33 **EZ**
Kennington Lane . . . . SE11 p. 21 **MZ**
Kennington Oval . . . . SE11 p. 21 **MZ**

TOWN PLANS (continued)

Kennington Park Road.......... SE11 p. 21 MZ
Kennington Road....... SE1, SE11 p. 21 MZ
Kensal Road .... W10 p. 15 ET
Kensington Church Street .... W8 p. 32 AZ 238
Kensington Court.............. W8 p. 30 AQ 241
Kensington Court Place .... W8 p. 30 AR 242
Kensington Gardens Square ..... W2 p. 32 BZ 243
Kensington Gore.............. SW7 p. 30 CQ
Kensington High Street .... W8, W14 p. 30 EY
Kensington Palace Gardens...... W8 p. 19 FX
Kensington Park Road .... W11 p. 15 EV
Kensington Place.............. W8 p. 32 AZ
Kensington Road.......... W8, SW7 p. 30 BQ
Kensington Square .... W8 p. 30 AQ
Kentish Town Road ...... NW1, NW5 p. 16 JS
Kenway Road................. SW5 p. 19 FZ 245
Kilburn Lane .... W10, W9 p. 15 ET
Kilburn Park Road .... NW6 p. 15 ET
King Edward Street........... EC1 p. 18 NU 247
Kingly Street................. W1 p. 29 DK
King's Cross Road............ WC1 p. 17 LT
Kingsland Road............ E2, E8 p. 18 PT
King's Road....... SW3, SW10, SW6 p. 31 DU
King Street ST. JAMES'S .... SW1 p. 29 EN
King Street WC2
    STRAND .... p. 33 DX
Kingsway .... WC2 p. 33 EV
King William Street.......... EC4 p. 18 PV 250
Knaresborough Place.......... SW5 p. 30 AS
Knightsbridge .... SW1, SW7 p. 31 EQ
Ladbroke Grove .... W10, W11 p. 15 EU
Lambeth Bridge .... SW1, SE1 p. 21 LY
Lambeth Palace Road .... SE1 p. 21 MY
Lambeth Road............... SE1 p. 21 MY
Lambeth Walk............. SE11 p. 21 MZ
Lancaster Gate .... W2 p. 32 CZ 256
Lancaster Grove .... NW3 p. 16 GS
Lancaster Place .... SW19 p. 33 EX
Lancaster Terrace .... W2 p. 33 DZ 257
Lansdowne Walk............. W11 p. 19 EX
Latchmere Road .... SW11 p. 13 CQ 258
Lauderdale Road .... W9 p. 15 FT
Launceston Place .... W8 p. 30 BR 259
Lavender Hill .... SW11 p. 13 CQ
Lawn Road.................. NW3 p. 15 ES
Leadenhall Street .... EC3 p. 18 PV 260
Lees Place .... W1 p. 28 AL
Leicester Square...........WC2 p. 29 GM 261
Leinster Gardens .... W2 p. 32 CZ
Leinster Square .... W2 p. 32 AZ
Leinster Terrace .... W2 p. 32 CZ
Lennox Gardens .... NW10 p. 31 ES
Lennox Gardens Mews .... SW3 p. 31 ES 263
Leopold Road .... SW19 p. 12 BR
Lever Street .... EC1 p. 18 NT
Lexham Gardens .... W8 p. 30 AS
Lexington Street.............. W1 p. 29 EL
Lillie Road.................. SW6 p. 19 EZ
Lincoln's Inn Fields .... WC2 p. 33 EV
Lisle Street .... WC2 p. 29 GL
Lisson Grove............ NW1, NW8 p. 16 GT
Little Boltons (The) .... SW10 p. 30 BU
Little Britain .... EC1 p. 18 NU 264
Liverpool Road............ N1, N7 p. 17 MS
Liverpool Street............. EC2 p. 18 PU
Lloyd Baker Street............ WC1 p. 17 MT 265
Lombard Road.............. SW11 p. 13 CQ 266
Lombard Street.............. EC3 p. 18 PV 268
London Bridge .... SE1, EC4 p. 22 PX
London Road................ SE1 p. 22 NY
London Street............... W2 p. 33 DZ
London Wall .... EC2 p. 18 NU
Long Acre.................. WC2 p. 33 DX
Long Lane CITY............ EC1 p. 18 NU 270
Long Lane SE1
    SOUTHWARK .... p. 22 PY
Long Road................ SW11 p. 13 DQ
Lothbury................... EC2 p. 18 PU 273
Lots Road................. SW10 p. 19 FZ
Loudoun Road .... NW8 p. 16 GS
Lower Belgrave Street .... SW1 p. 32 AX
Lower Grosvenor Place .... SW1 p. 32 BX 274
Lower Marsh .... SE1 p. 21 MY 277
Lower Sloane Street .... SW1 p. 31 FT
Lower Terrace .... NW3 p. 15 ES
Lower Thames Street .... EC3 p. 18 PV 278
Lowndes Square .... SW1 p. 31 FQ
Lowndes Street .... SW1 p. 31 FR
Luke Street................. EC2 p. 18 PT
Lupus Street............... SW1 p. 21 KZ
Lyall Street .... SW1 p. 31 FR
Lyndhurst Road............. NW3 p. 15 ES
Macklin Street.............. WC2 p. 33 DV

Maddox Street .... W1 p. 29 DK
Maida Avenue .... W2 p. 15 FU
Maida Vale .... W9 p. 15 FT
Maiden Lane .... WC2 p. 33 DY
Malden Road .... E15 p. 16 JS
Mall (The) .... SW1 p. 29 FP
Malvern Road .... NW6 p. 15 ET
Manchester Square........... W1 p. 28 AJ 281
Manchester Street............ W1 p. 28 AH
Manresa Road .... SW3 p. 31 DU
Mansell Street .... E1 p. 18 PV 282
Marble Arch .... W1 p. 33 EZ
Margaret Street .... W1 p. 29 DJ
Market Place................ W1 p. 29 DJ 286
Market Road .... N7 p. 17 LS
Markham Street............. SW3 p. 31 ET
Marlborough Place........... NW8 p. 15 FT
Marloes Road .... W8 p. 19 FY
Marshall Street .... W1 p. 29 EK
Marsham Street............. SW1 p. 21 LY
Marylebone High Street .... W1 p. 16 JU
Marylebone Lane............. W1 p. 28 BJ 287
Marylebone Road............ NW1 p. 16 HU
Melbury Road .... W14 p. 19 EY
Merrick Square .... SE1 p. 22 NY
Merton Rise .... NW3 p. 16 HS
Merton Road .... SW18 p. 12 BR
Middlesex Street .... E1 p. 18 PU
Midland Road .... NW1 p. 17 LT
Miles Street .... SW8 p. 21 LZ 290
Millbank .... SW1 p. 21 LY
Milner Street .... SW3 p. 31 ES
Minories.................... EC3 p. 18 PV
Monmouth Street .... WC2 p. 33 DX
Montagu Square .... W1 p. 28 AH
Montpelier Square .... SW7 p. 31 EQ
Montpelier Street .... SW7 p. 31 ER
Montpelier Walk .... SW7 p. 31 DR
Moore Street .... SW3 p. 31 ES
Moorgate................... EC2 p. 18 PU
Moreland Street .... EC1 p. 18 NT 293
Mortimer Street .... W1 p. 17 KU
Moscow Road .... W2 p. 32 BZ
Mossop Street .... SW3 p. 31 ES
Mount Row .... W1 p. 28 BM
Mount Street .... W1 p. 28 BM
Munster Road .... SW6 p. 19 EZ
Musard Road .... W6 p. 19 EZ
Museum Street .... WC1 p. 33 DV 294
Myddelton Street .... EC1 p. 17 MT 296
Nassington Road .... NW3 p. 15 ES 297
Neal Street .... WC2 p. 33 DV
Netherhall Gardens .... NW3 p. 15 ES
Nevern Place .... SW5 p. 19 EZ 298
Nevern Square .... SW5 p. 19 EZ 299
Neville Terrace .... SW7 p. 30 CT 300
New Bond Street .... W1 p. 28 CK
New Bridge Street .... EC4 p. 18 NV 301
Newburn Street............ SE11 p. 21 MZ
New Cavendish Street .... W1 p. 28 BH
New Change .... EC4 p. 18 NV 304
Newcomen Street........... SE1 p. 22 PX
New End Square .... NW3 p. 15 ES 305
Newgate Street.............. EC1 p. 10 NU
Newington Butts .... SE1, SE11 p. 22 NZ 306
Newington Causeway .... SE1 p. 22 NY 307
New Kent Road .... SE1 p. 22 NY
Newman Street .... W1 p. 17 KU
New Oxford Street .... WC1 p. 33 DV 308
New King's Road .... SW6 p. 12 BQ
New Row .... WC2 p. 33 DX
New Square .... WC2 p. 33 EV
Newton Road .... W2 p. 32 BZ
Newton Street .... WC2 p. 33 DV 309
Nightingale Lane ...... SW4, SW12 p. 13 CR
Nine Elms Lane .... SW8 p. 21 KZ
Noel Street .... W1 p. 29 EJ
Norfolk Crescent .... W2 p. 33 EZ 310
Norfolk Square............... W2 p. 33 DZ 313
North Audley Street........... W1 p. 28 AK 314
North Carriage Drive .... W2 p. 33 EZ
North End Road......... W14, SW6 p. 19 EZ
North Row.................. W1 p. 28 AL
North Side .... SW18 p. 13 CQ 316
Northumberland Avenue....... WC2 p. 21 LX 317
Notting Hill Gate .... W11 p. 32 AZ
Nutley Terrace .... NW3 p. 15 ES
Oakley Street .... SW3 p. 31 DU
Offord Road................. N1 p. 17 MS
Old Bailey................. EC4 p. 18 NU 318
Old Bond Street .... W1 p. 29 DM

Continued on next page

Street	Postcode	Page	Grid	Ref
Old Broad Street	EC2	p. 18	PU	319
Old Brompton Road	SW7, SW5	p. 30	BT	
Old Burlington Street	W1	p. 29	DM	322
Old Church Street	SW3	p. 30	CU	
Old Compton Street	W1	p. 29	GK	323
Old Kent Road	SE1, SE15	p. 22	PZ	
Old Marylebone Road	NW1	p. 16	HU	324
Old Park Lane	W1	p. 28	BP	
Old Street	EC1	p. 18	NT	
Olympia Way	W14	p. 19	EY	326
Onslow Gardens	SW7	p. 30	CT	
Onslow Square	SW7	p. 30	CT	
Orange Street	WC2	p. 29	GM	
Orchard Street	W1	p. 28	AK	
Ordnance Hill	NW8	p. 16	GS	
Orme Court	W2	p. 32	BZ	328
Ormonde Gate	SW3	p. 31	FU	329
Ornan Road	NW3	p. 15	ES	331
Ossulton Street	NW1	p. 17	LT	
Outer Circle	NW1	p. 16	HT	
Oxford Circus	W1	p. 29	DJ	
Oxford Square	W2	p. 33	EZ	332
Oxford Street	W1	p. 28	BK	
Paddington Street	W1	p. 16	JU	333
Page Street	SW1	p. 21	LZ	
Page's Walk	SE1	p. 22	PY	
Palace Court	W2	p. 32	BZ	
Palace Gardens Terrace	W8	p. 32	AZ	335
Palace Gate	W8	p. 30	BQ	
Palace Street	SW1	p. 32	BX	
Pall Mall	SW1	p. 29	FN	
Palmer Street	SW1	p. 32	CV	
Pancras Road	NW1	p. 17	KS	
Panton Street	SW1	p. 29	FM	336
Parade (The)	SW11	p. 20	HZ	
Park Crescent	W1	p. 16	JU	337
Parker Street	WC2	p. 33	DV	
Parkgate Road	SW11	p. 20	HZ	
Park Lane	W1	p. 28	AM	
Park Road	NW1, NW8	p. 16	HT	
Park Street	W1	p. 28	AL	
Park Village East	NW1	p. 16	JS	
Park Walk	SW10	p. 30	CU	
Parkway	NW1	p. 16	JS	
Parliament Hill	NW3	p. 15	ES	
Parliament Street	SW1	p. 21	LY	340
Parry Street	SW8	p. 21	LZ	341
Paul Street	EC2	p. 18	PT	
Pelham Street	SW7	p. 31	DS	
Pembridge Gardens	W2	p. 32	AZ	
Pembridge Road	W11	p. 32	AZ	
Pembridge Square	W2	p. 32	AZ	
Pembridge Villas	W11	p. 32	AZ	
Pembrocke Gardens	W8	p. 19	EY	342
Pembrocke Road	W8	p. 19	EZ	
Penton Rise	WC1	p. 17	MT	344
Penton Street	N1	p. 17	MT	345
Pentonville Road	N1	p. 17	LT	
Penwith Road	SW18	p. 12	BR	346
Penywern Road	SW5	p. 19	FZ	347
Percival Street	EC1	p. 18	NT	
Petty France	SW1	p. 32	CV	
Philbeach Gardens	SW5	p. 19	EZ	348
Piccadilly	W1	p. 29	EM	
Piccadilly Circus	W1	p. 29	FM	
Pilgrimage Street	SE1	p. 22	PY	349
Pimlico Road	SW1	p. 20	JZ	
Pitfield Street	N1	p. 18	PT	
Plough Lane	SW17, SW19	p. 12	BR	
Poland Street	W1	p. 29	EJ	
Pond Street	NW3	p. 15	ES	
Pont Street	SW1	p. 31	ER	
Porchester Gardens	W2	p. 32	BZ	
Porchester Road	W2	p. 15	FU	350
Porchester Terrace	W2	p. 32	CZ	
Portland Place	W1	p. 16	JU	
Portman Square	W1	p. 28	AJ	
Portman Street	W1	p. 28	AK	
Portobello Road	W11, W10	p. 15	EV	
Portugal Street	WC2	p. 33	EV	
Poultry	EC2	p. 18	NV	351
Praed Street	W2	p. 16	GU	
Pratt Street	NW1	p. 17	KS	
Prima Road	SW9	p. 21	MZ	353
Primrose Hill Road	NW3	p. 16	HS	
Prince Albert Road	NW1, NW8	p. 16	HS	
Prince Consort Road	SW7	p. 30	CR	
Prince of Wales Road	NW5	p. 16	JS	
Prince's Gardens	SW7	p. 30	CR	357
Prince's Street	W1	p. 29	DK	
Princes Street	EC2	p. 18	PV	358
Putney Bridge	SW6	p. 12	AQ	359
Putney Bridge Road	SW15, SW18	p. 12	AQ	
Putney High Street	SW15	p. 12	AQ	360
Putney Hill	SW15	p. 12	AQ	
Queen Anne's Gate	SW1	p. 21	KY	
Queen Anne Street	W1	p. 28	BH	
Queensberry Place	SW7	p. 30	CS	361
Queensborough Terrace	W2	p. 32	CZ	
Queen's Circus	SW8	p. 20	JZ	361
Queen's Gardens	W2	p. 32	CZ	362
Queen's Gate	SW7	p. 30	BQ	
Queen's Gate Gardens	SW7	p. 30	BR	
Queen's Gate Place	SW7	p. 30	BR	363
Queen's Gate Terrace	SW7	p. 30	BR	
Queen's Grove	NW8	p. 16	GS	
Queenstown Road	SW8	p. 13	DQ	364
Queen Street	EC4	p. 18	NV	365
Queen's Walk	SW1	p. 29	DN	
Queensway	W2	p. 32	BZ	
Queen Victoria Street	EC4	p. 18	NV	
Radnor Place	W2	p. 33	DZ	
Radnor Walk	SW3	p. 31	EU	
Randolph Avenue	W9	p. 15	FT	
Randolph Street	NW1	p. 17	KS	366
Rawlings Street	SW3	p. 31	ES	
Redcliffe Gardens	SW10	p. 30	AU	
Redcliffe Square	SW10	p. 30	AU	
Redesdale Street	SW3	p. 31	EU	367
Red Lion Street	WC1	p. 17	MU	
Reeves Mews	W1	p. 28	AM	
Regency Street	SW1	p. 21	KZ	
Regent's Park Road	NW1	p. 16	HS	
Regent Street	SW1, W1	p. 29	EM	
Richmond Avenue	N1	p. 17	MS	
Robert Street	NW1	p. 16	JT	
Rochester Row	SW1	p. 32	CY	
Rodney Road	N1	p. 22	PZ	
Roland Gardens	SW7	p. 30	BT	
Roman Way	N7	p. 17	MS	
Romilly Street	W1	p. 29	GL	368
Rosebery Avenue	EC1	p. 17	MT	
Rosslyn Hill	NW3	p. 15	ES	
Rossmore Road	NW1	p. 16	HT	369
Royal College Street	NW1	p. 17	KS	
Royal Crescent	W11	p. 19	EX	371
Royal Hospital Road	SW3	p. 31	FU	
Rupert Street	W1	p. 29	FL	
Russell Square	WC1	p. 17	LU	
Russell Street	WC2	p. 33	DX	
Rutland Gate	SW7	p. 31	DQ	
Rylston Road	SW6	p. 19	EZ	
Sackville Street	W1	p. 29	EM	
St. Albans Grove	W8	p. 28	AR	
St. Andrews Street	EC4	p. 18	NU	372
St. Bride Street	EC4	p. 18	NV	376
St. George's Drive	SW1	p. 21	KZ	
St. George's Road	SE1	p. 22	NY	
St. George's Square	SW1	p. 21	KZ	
St. George Street	W1	p. 29	DL	
St. Giles Circus	W1, WC1, WC2	p. 29	GJ	
St. Giles High Street	WC2	p. 33	DV	377
St. James's Place	SW1	p. 29	EN	
St. James's Square	SW1	p. 29	FN	
St. James's Street	SW1	p. 29	EN	
St. James Street	E17	p. 33	DX	
St. John's Hill	SW11	p. 13	CQ	
St. John Street	EC1	p. 18	NT	
St. John's Wood High Street	NW8	p. 16	GT	378
St. John's Wood Park	NW8	p. 16	GS	379
St. John's Wood Road	NW8	p. 16	GT	
St. Leonard's Terrace	SW3	p. 31	FU	
St. Martin's Lane	WC2	p. 33	DY	
St. Martin's-le-Grand	EC1	p. 18	NU	380
St. Pancras Way	NW1	p. 17	KS	
St. Petersburgh Place	W2	p. 32	BZ	
St. Thomas Street	SE1	p. 22	PX	
Sardinia Street	WC2	p. 33	EV	381
Savile Row	W1	p. 29	DM	
Savoy Place	WC2	p. 33	DY	
Savoy Street	WC2	p. 33	EX	
Scarsdale Villas	W8	p. 19	EY	
Seagrave Road	SW6	p. 19	EZ	
Serle Street	WC2	p. 33	EV	
Serpentine Road	W2	p. 28	AP	
Seymour Street	W1, W2	p. 28	AK	
Shaftesbury Avenue	W1, WC2	p. 29	FL	
Sheffield Terrace	W8	p. 19	EX	
Shelton Street	WC2	p. 33	DX	
Shepherd Market	W1	p. 28	CN	
Shepherd Street	W1	p. 28	BP	
Shirland Road	W9	p. 15	ET	
Shoreditch High Street	E1	p. 18	PT	384
Shorts Gardens	WC2	p. 33	DV	
Sidmouth Street	WC1	p. 17	LT	385
Sinclair Road	W14	p. 19	EY	

Sloane Avenue . . . . SW3 p. 31 ET
Sloane Square . . . . SW1 p. 31 FT
Sloane Street . . . . SW1 p. 31 FR
Smith Street . . . . SW3 p. 31 EU
Snows Fields . . . . SE1 p. 22 PX 386
Soho Square . . . . W1 p. 29 FJ
Southampton Row . . . . WC1 p. 17 LU 387
Southampton Street . . . . WC2 p. 33 DX 388
South Audley Street . . . . W1 p. 28 BM
South Eaton Place . . . . SW1 p. 32 AY 389
South End Road . . . . NW3 p. 15 ES
South Hill . . . . NW3 p. 15 ES 390
South Lambeth Road . . . . SW8 p. 21 LZ
South Molton Street . . . . W1 p. 28 BK
South Parade . . . . SW3 p. 30 CU
South Place . . . . EC2 p. 18 PU 391
South Street . . . . W1 p. 28 BN
South Terrace . . . . SW7 p. 31 DS
Southwark Bridge . . . . SE1, EC4 p. 18 NV 395
Southwark Bridge Road . . . . SE1 p. 22 NY
Southwark Street . . . . SE1 p. 22 NX
Southwick Street . . . . W2 p. 33 EZ
Spa Road . . . . SE16 p. 22 PY
Spencer Street . . . . EC1 p. 18 NT 398
Spital Square . . . . E1 p. 18 PU 399
Spring Street . . . . W2 p. 33 DZ
Stamford Street . . . . SE1 p. 21 MX
Stanhope Gardens . . . . SW7 p. 30 BS
Stanhope Place . . . . W2 p. 33 EZ 400
Stanhope Terrace . . . . W2 p. 33 DZ
Star Road . . . . W14 p. 19 EZ
Storeys Gate . . . . SW1 p. 21 LY 402
Strand . . . . WC2 p. 33 DY
Stratton Street . . . . W1 p. 29 DN
Sumner Place . . . . SW7 p. 30 CT
Sumner Street . . . . SE1 p. 22 NX
Surrey Street . . . . WC2 p. 33 EX
Sussex Gardens . . . . W2 p. 33 DZ
Sussex Place . . . . W2 p. 33 DZ
Sussex Square . . . . W2 p. 33 DZ 404
Sutherland Avenue . . . . W9 p. 15 FU
Sutherland Street . . . . SW1 p. 20 JZ
Swinton Street . . . . WC1 p. 17 LT
Sydney Place . . . . SW7 p. 31 DT 405
Sydney Street . . . . SW3 p. 31 DT
Symons Street . . . . SW3 p. 31 FT 407
Tabard Street . . . . SE1 p. 22 NY 408
Tachbrook Street . . . . SW1 p. 21 KZ
Talgarth Road . . . . W14, W6 p. 19 EZ
Tavistock Place . . . . WC1 p. 17 LT
Tavistock Square . . . . WC1 p. 17 LT 409
Tavistock Street . . . . WC2 p. 33 DX
Tedworth Square . . . . SW3 p. 31 EU
Temple Place . . . . WC2 p. 33 EX
Templeton Place . . . . SW5 p. 19 FZ 410
Terminus Place . . . . SW1 p. 32 BX 412
Thayer Street . . . . W1 p. 28 BJ 413
Theobald's Road . . . . WC1 p. 17 LU
Thirleby Road . . . . SW1 p. 32 CX 416
Thornhill Road . . . . N1 p. 17 MS
Threadneedle Street . . . . EC2 p. 18 PV 417
Throgmorton Street . . . . EC2 p. 18 PU 418
Thurloe Place . . . . SW7 p. 30 CS 420
Thurloe Square . . . . SW7 p. 31 DS
Tibbet's Ride . . . . SW15 p. 12 AR 422
Tilney Street . . . . W1 p. 28 BN 421
Tite Street . . . . SW3 p. 31 EU
Tooley Street . . . . SE1 p. 22 PX
Tooting Bec Road . . . . . . SW16, SW17 p. 13 DR
Tothill Street . . . . SW1 p. 21 KY
Tottenham Court Road . . . . W1 p. 17 KU
Tower Bridge . . . . E1 p. 22 PX
Tower Bridge Road . . . . SE1 p. 22 PY
Tower Hill . . . . EC3 p. 18 PV 425
Trafalgar Square . . . . WC2, SW1 p. 33 DY
Trebovir Road . . . . SW5 p. 19 FZ 426
Tregunter Road . . . . SW10 p. 30 BU
Trevor Place . . . . SW7 p. 31 EQ
Trevor Square . . . . SW7 p. 31 ER
Trinity Church Square . . . . SE1 p. 22 NY
Trinity Road . . . . SW17, SW18 p. 13 CR
Trinity Street . . . . SE1 p. 22 NY
Tyers Street . . . . SE11 p. 21 MZ
Union Street . . . . SE1 p. 22 NX
Upper Belgrave Street . . . . SW1 p. 32 AX
Upper Berkeley Street . . . . W1 p. 33 EZ
Upper Brook Street . . . . W1 p. 28 AM
Upper Grosvenor Street . . . . W1 p. 28 AM
Upper Ground . . . . SE1 p. 21 MX 428
Upper Richmond Road . SW14, SW15 p. 12 AQ
Upper St. Martin's Lane . . . . WC2 p. 33 DX 430
Upper Street . . . . N1 p. 18 NS
Upper Thames Street . . . . EC4 p. 18 NV 431

Upper Tooting Road . . . . SW17 p. 13 CR
Upper Woburn Place . . . . WC1 p. 17 LT 432
Vale (The) . . . . SW3 p. 30 CU
Vanston Place . . . . SW6 p. 19 EZ
Vassal Road . . . . SW9 p. 21 MZ
Vauxhall Bridge . . . . SW1, SE1 p. 21 LZ
Vauxhall Bridge Road . . . . SW1 p. 32 BY
Vauxhall Street . . . . SE11 p. 21 MZ
Vauxhall Walk . . . . SE11 p. 21 LZ
Vere Street . . . . W1 p. 28 BJ
Vicarage Crescent . . . . SW11 p. 13 CQ 433
Victoria Embankment SW1
                     WC2, EC4 p. 33 DY
Victoria Grove . . . . W8 p. 30 BR
Victoria Road W8
     KENSINGTON . . . . p. 30 BQ
Victoria Street . . . . SW1 p. 32 BX
Vigo Street . . . . W1 p. 29 EM
Villiers Street . . . . WC2 p. 33 DY
Vincent Square . . . . SW1 p. 21 KZ
Vincent Street . . . . SW1 p. 21 LZ 436
Virginia Road . . . . E2 p. 18 PT
Walterton Road . . . . W9 p. 15 ET
Walton Street . . . . SW3 p. 31 ES
Wandsworth Bridge . . . . SW6 p. 12 BQ 437
Wandsworth Bridge Road . . . . . . SW6 p. 12 BQ
Wandsworth High Street . . . . . . SW18 p. 12 BQ 438
Wandsworth Road . . . . SW8 p. 21 LZ
Wardour Street . . . . W1 p. 29 FJ
Warrington Crescent . . . . W9 p. 15 FT
Warwick Avenue . . . . W2, W9 p. 15 FU 441
Warwick Road . . . . SW5, W14 p. 19 EZ
Warwick Street . . . . W1 p. 29 EM 444
Warwick Way . . . . SW1 p. 20 JZ
Waterloo Bridge . . . . WC2, SE1 p. 33 EY
Waterloo Place . . . . SW1 p. 29 FN
Waterloo Road . . . . SE1 p. 21 MX
Waverton Street . . . . W1 p. 28 BN
Webber Street . . . . SE1 p. 22 NY
Weighhouse Street . . . . W1 p. 28 BK
Welbeck Street . . . . W1 p. 28 BH
Wellington Road . . . . NW8 p. 16 GT
Wellington Street . . . . WC2 p. 33 DX
Wells Street . . . . W1 p. 29 EJ
Well Walk . . . . NW3 p. 15 ES
Westbourne Crescent . . . . W2 p. 33 DZ 448
Westbourne Grove . . . . W2, W11 p. 32 AZ
Westbourne Park Road . . . W2, W11 p. 15 EU
Westbourne Park Villas . . . . W2 p. 15 FU 449
Westbourne Street . . . . W2 p. 33 DZ 450
Westbourne Terrace . . . . W2 p. 33 DZ
Westbourne Road . . . . N7 p. 17 MS
Westbourne
    Terrace Road . . . . W2 p. 15 FU 452
Westbridge Road . . . . SW11 p. 13 CQ 453
West Cromwell Road . . . . . SW5, W14 p. 19 EZ
West Halkin Street . . . . SW1 p. 31 FR
West Hill . . . . SW15, SW18 p. 12 AR
Westminster Bridge . . . . SW1, SE1 p. 21 LY
Westminster Bridge Road . . . . SE1 p. 21 MY
Weston Street . . . . SE1 p. 22 PY
West Smithfield . . . . EC1 p. 18 NU 454
Westway . . . . N18 p. 15 EU
Wetherby Gardens . . . . SW5 p. 30 RT
Wharfdale Road . . . . N1 p. 17 LS 455
Whitcomb Street . . . . WC2 p. 29 GM
Whitechapel High Street . . . . E1 p. 18 PU 456
Whitecross Street . . . . EC1, EC2 p. 18 NT
Whitehall . . . . SW1 p. 21 LX
Whitehall Court . . . . SW1 p. 21 LX 460
Whitehall Place . . . . SW1 p. 21 LX 462
Whitehead's Grove . . . . SW3 p. 31 ET 463
Wigmore Street . . . . W1 p. 28 BJ
Wild Street . . . . WC2 p. 33 DV
William IV Street . . . . WC2 p. 33 DY 467
William Street . . . . SW1 p. 31 FQ 468
Willoughby Road . . . . NW3 p. 15 ES 470
Willow Road . . . . NW3 p. 15 ES
Willow Walk . . . . SE1 p. 22 PZ
Wilson Street . . . . EC2 p. 18 PU
Wilton Place . . . . SW1 p. 31 FQ
Wilton Road . . . . SW1 p. 32 BY
Wilton Street . . . . SW1 p. 32 AX
Wimbledon Park Road . SW18, SW19 p. 12 AR
Windmill Road . . . . SW18 p. 13 CQ 471
Wimpole Street . . . . W1 p. 28 BH
Woburn Place . . . . WC1 p. 17 LT
Woods Mews . . . . W1 p. 28 AL
Wormwood Street . . . . EC2 p. 18 PU 472
Worship Street . . . . EC2 p. 18 PU
York Road . . . . SE1 p. 21 MY
York Way . . . . N1, N7 p. 17 LS
Young Street . . . . W8 p. 30 AQ

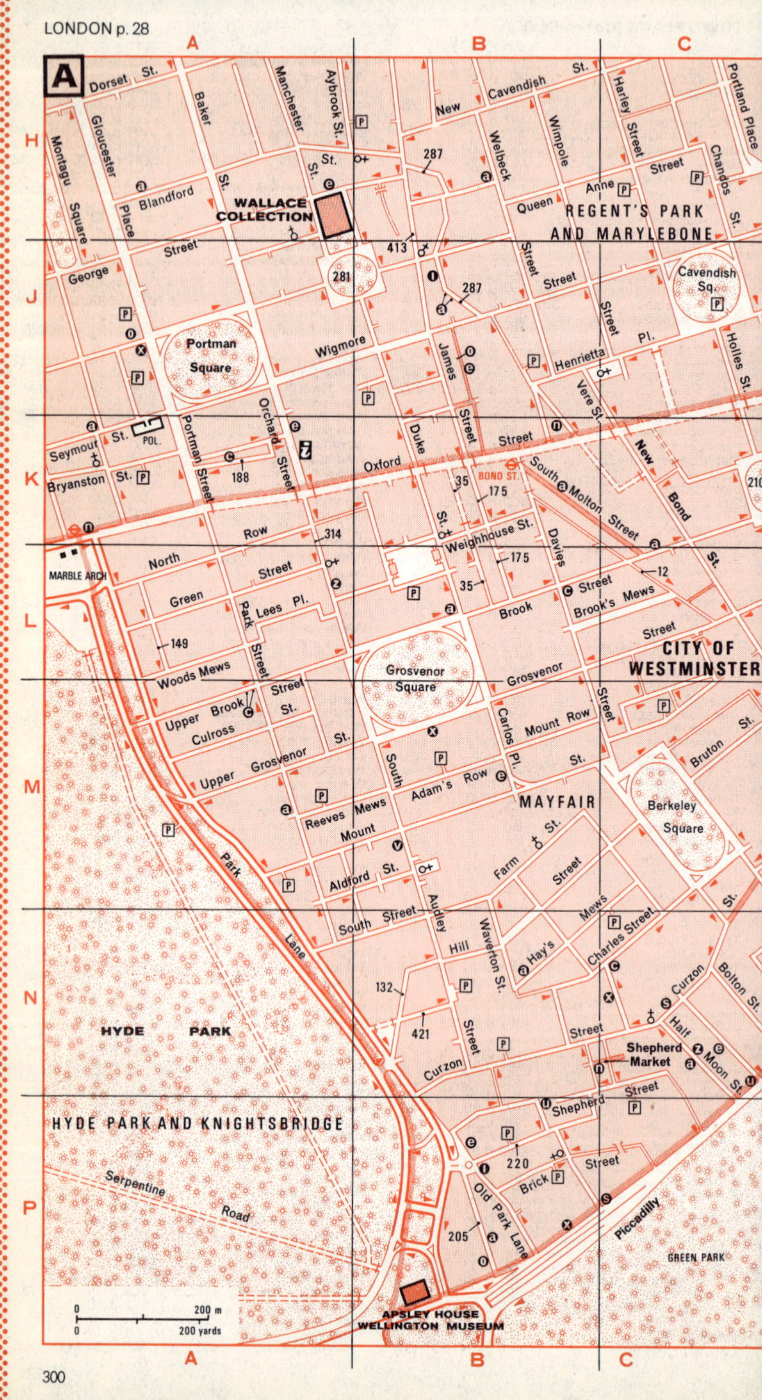
A
Dorset St.
Manchester
Baker
Montagu Square
Gloucester Place
Blandford
George
Aybrook St.
St.
St.
P
WALLACE COLLECTION
Street
281
Portman Square
Wigmore
P
P
Orchard Street
Portman Street
Seymour St.
POL.
Bryanston St.
188
New
Cavendish
St.
Welbeck
Wimpole
Harley Street
Portland Place
Chandos St.
287
Queen
Anne
REGENT'S PARK AND MARYLEBONE
Cavendish Sq.
413
287
Street
Street
Henrietta
Pl.
Holles St.
James
Vere St.
Duke
Street
Street
New Bond St.
Oxford
Street
BOND ST.
35
175
South
Molton Street
210
Bond
St.
Row
314
35
St.
Weighhouse St.
175
Davies
12
North
Street
Green
Lees Pl.
Street
Brook
C Street
Brook's Mews
Street
CITY OF WESTMINSTER
149
Park Street
Woods Mews
Street
Grosvenor Square
Grosvenor
Upper Brook
Culross
St.
South
Carlos Pl.
Mount Row
St.
Bruton St.
MARBLE ARCH
Upper Grosvenor
Reeves Mews
Adam's Row
MAYFAIR
Berkeley Square
Park Lane
Mount
Farm St.
St.
Aldford St.
South Street
Audley
Street
Charles Street
Mews
St.
132
Hill
Waverton St.
Hay's
Street
Curzon
421
Street
Street
Half
Curzon
Shepherd Market
Moon St.
HYDE PARK
Shepherd Street
Street
HYDE PARK AND KNIGHTSBRIDGE
220
Brick
Street
Serpentine
Road
205
Piccadilly
GREEN PARK
0   200 m
0   200 yards
APSLEY HOUSE
WELLINGTON MUSEUM
A
B
C
H
J
K
L
M
N
P

Arlington Street . . . . **DN** 6
Avery Row . . . . **CL** 12
Bateman Street . . . . **FK** 18
Berwick Street . . . . **FK** 26
Binney Street . . . . **BL** 35
Carlton Gardens . . . . **FP** 74
Deanery Street . . . . **BN** 132
Denman Street . . . . **FM** 133
Denmark Street . . . . **GJ** 134
Duke of York Street . . . . . . **EN** 143
Duke Street ST. JAMES . . **EN** 146

Dunraven Street . . . . **AL** 149
Gerrard Street . . . . **GL** 174
Gilbert Street . . . . **BL** 175
Glasshouse Street . . . . . . **EM** 179
Granville Place . . . . **AK** 188
Great Castle Street . . . . . . **DJ** 189
Greek Street . . . . **GK** 198
Hamilton Place . . . . **BP** 205
Hanover Square . . . . **CK** 210
Hertford Street . . . . **BP** 220
Leicester Square . . . . **GM** 261

Manchester Square . . . . . . **AJ** 281
Market Place . . . . **DJ** 286
Marylebone Lane . . . . **BJ** 287
North Audley Street . . . . . . **AK** 314
Old Burlington Street . . . . **DM** 322
Old Compton Street . . . . . **GK** 323
Panton Street . . . . **FM** 336
Romilly Street . . . . **GL** 368
Thayer Street . . . . **BJ** 413
Tilney Street . . . . **BN** 421
Warwick Street . . . . **EM** 444

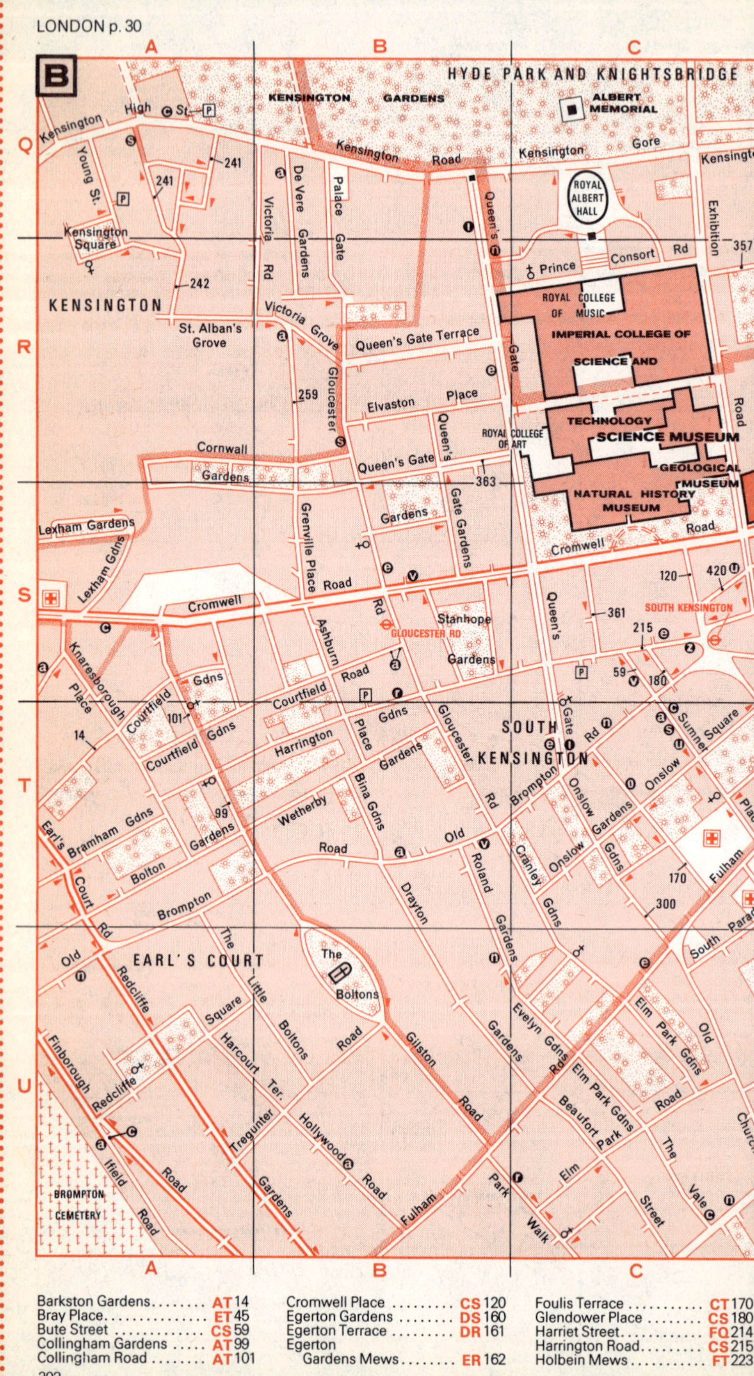

Barkston Gardens .... AT 14
Bray Place .... ET 45
Bute Street .... CS 59
Collingham Gardens ...... AT 99
Collingham Road .... AT 101
Cromwell Place .... CS 120
Egerton Gardens .... DS 160
Egerton Terrace .... DR 161
Egerton Gardens Mews .... ER 162
Foulis Terrace .... CT 170
Glendower Place .... CS 180
Harriet Street .... FQ 214
Harrington Road .... CS 215
Holbein Mews .... FT 223

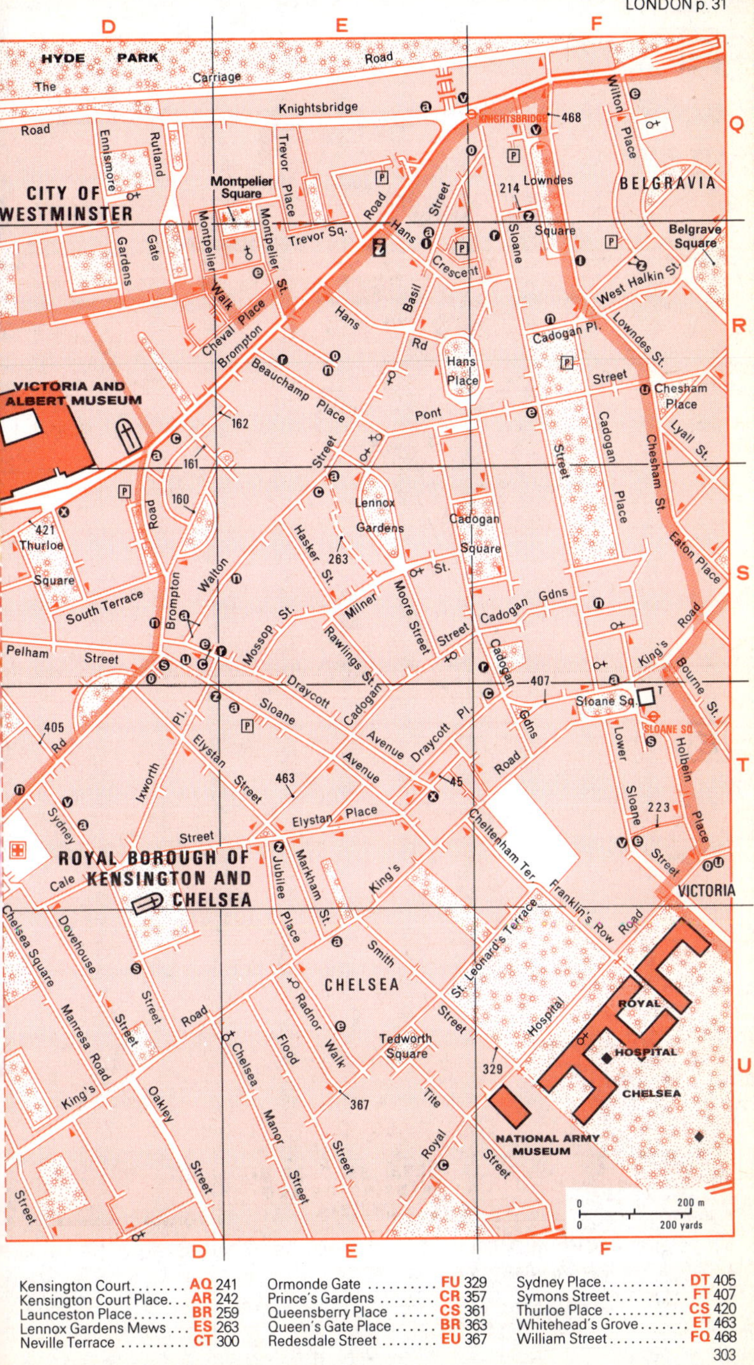

Kensington Court	AQ	241
Kensington Court Place	AR	242
Launceston Place	BR	259
Lennox Gardens Mews	ES	263
Neville Terrace	CT	300
Ormonde Gate	FU	329
Prince's Gardens	CR	357
Queensberry Place	CS	361
Queen's Gate Place	BR	363
Redesdale Street	EU	367
Sydney Place	DT	405
Symons Street	FT	407
Thurloe Place	CS	420
Whitehead's Grove	ET	463
William Street	FQ	468

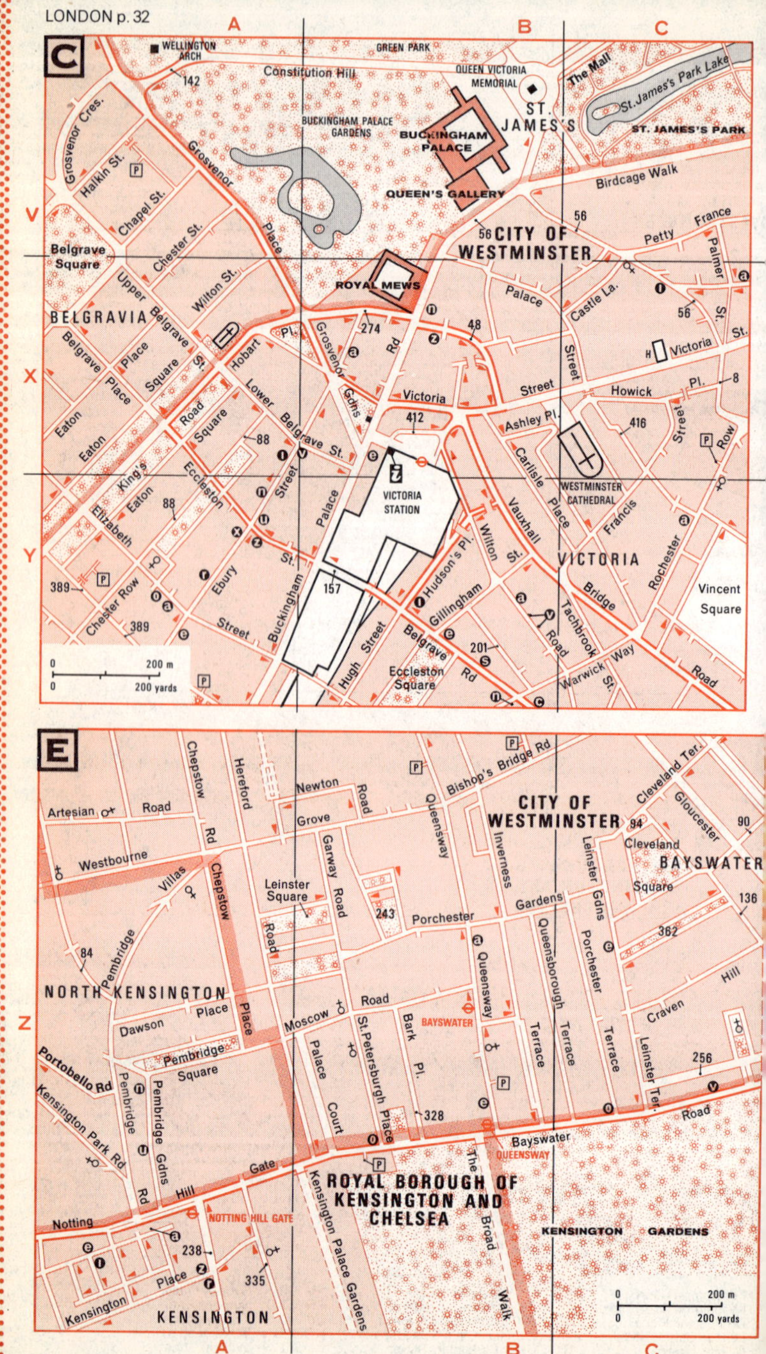
WELLINGTON ARCH
142
Constitution Hill
GREEN PARK
QUEEN VICTORIA MEMORIAL
The Mall
St. James's Park Lake
ST. JAMES'S
BUCKINGHAM PALACE GARDENS
BUCKINGHAM PALACE
ST. JAMES'S PARK
Grosvenor Cres.
Halkin St.
Chapel St.
Chester St.
Grosvenor
Place
Birdcage Walk
QUEEN'S GALLERY
56
Petty
France
Palmer
Belgrave Square
Upper Belgrave St.
Wilton St.
Hobart Pl.
Grosvenor Gdns
274
ROYAL MEWS
48
Palace
Castle La.
CITY OF WESTMINSTER
56
St.
St.
56
Victoria
BELGRAVIA
Belgrave Place
Belgrave Square
Road
Lower Belgrave St.
Street
Street
Howick
Pl.
8
Eaton
Eaton
King's
Square
88
Victoria
412
Ashley Pl.
Carlisle Place
416
P Row
Eccleston
88
Palace
Street
Buckingham
VICTORIA STATION
157
St.
Hudson's Pl.
Wilton St.
Vauxhall
WESTMINSTER CATHEDRAL
Francis
Street
VICTORIA
Rochester
Elizabeth
389
Chester Row
389
Ebury
Street
Hugh Street
Belgrave
Eccleston Square
Gillingham
Belgrave Rd
201
Tachbrook
Bridge
Road
Warwick St.
Vincent Square
Road
Way
0   200 m
0   200 yards
NORTH KENSINGTON
Artesian
Road
Chepstow
Rd
Hereford
Road
Newton
Grove
Garway
Road
Queensway
Bishop's Bridge Rd
Inverness
CITY OF WESTMINSTER
94
Cleveland Ter.
Gloucester
90
Westbourne
Villas
Chepstow
Leinster Square
243
Porchester
Gardens
Leinster Gdns
Cleveland Square
BAYSWATER
136
84
Pembridge
Road
Place
Moscow
Road
Queensway
Queensborough
Porchester
Terrace
362
Dawson
Pembridge Square
Palace Court
St.Petersburg Place
Bark Pl.
BAYSWATER
Terrace
Leinster Ter.
Craven
Hill
256
Portobello Rd
Pembridge
Pembridge Gdns
328
Queensway
Road
Kensington Park Rd
Gate
The
Broad
Bayswater
QUEENSWAY
ROYAL BOROUGH OF KENSINGTON AND CHELSEA
KENSINGTON GARDENS
Notting
238
Place
335
NOTTING HILL GATE
Kensington Palace Gardens
Hill
Kensington
KENSINGTON
Walk
0   200 m
0   200 yards

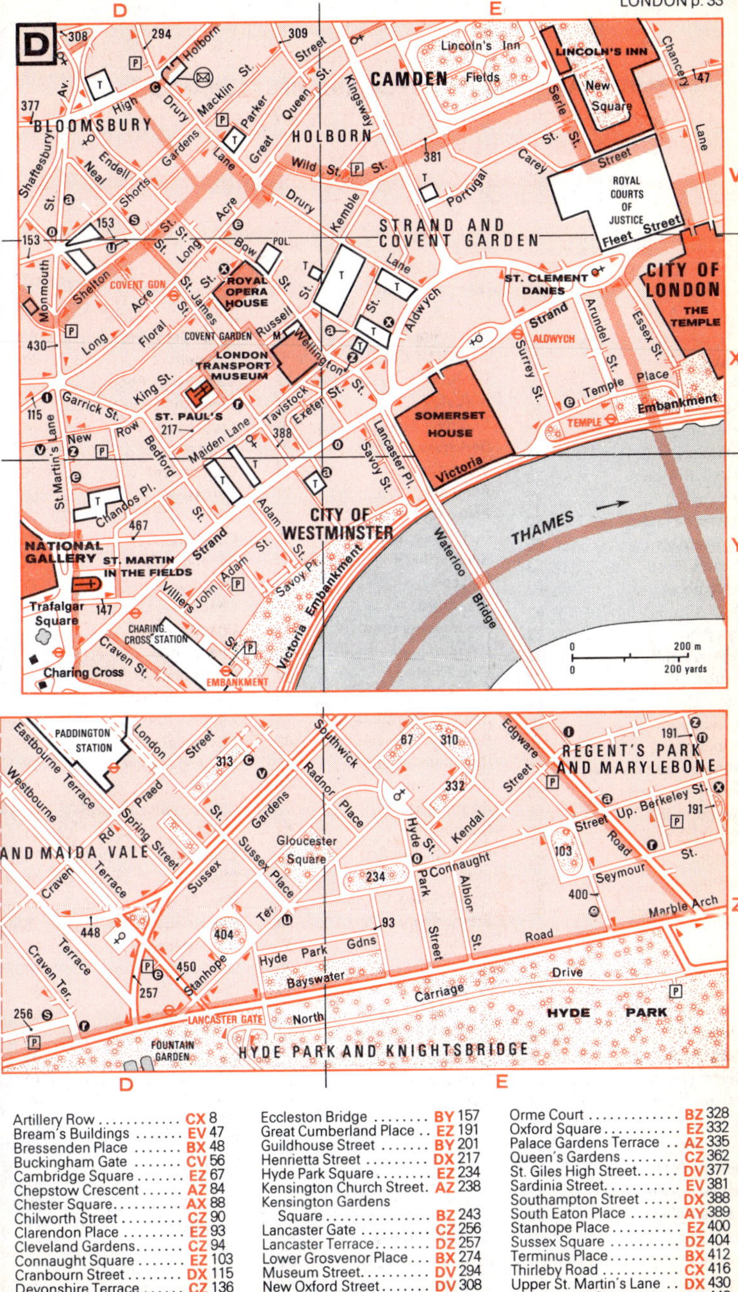

Artillery Row	**CX**	8
Bream's Buildings	**EV**	47
Bressenden Place	**BX**	48
Buckingham Gate	**CV**	56
Cambridge Square	**EZ**	67
Chepstow Crescent	**AZ**	84
Chester Square	**AX**	88
Chilworth Street	**CZ**	90
Clarendon Place	**EZ**	93
Cleveland Gardens	**CZ**	94
Connaught Square	**EZ**	103
Cranbourn Street	**DX**	115
Devonshire Terrace	**CZ**	136
Duke of Wellington Place	**AV**	142
Duncannon Street	**DY**	147
Earlham Street	**DV**	153
Eccleston Bridge	**BY**	157
Great Cumberland Place	**EZ**	191
Guildhall Street	**BY**	201
Henrietta Street	**DX**	217
Hyde Park Square	**EZ**	234
Kensington Church Street	**AZ**	238
Kensington Gardens Square	**BZ**	243
Lancaster Gate	**CZ**	256
Lancaster Terrace	**DZ**	257
Lower Grosvenor Place	**BX**	274
Museum Street	**DV**	294
New Oxford Street	**DV**	308
Newton Street	**DV**	309
Norfolk Crescent	**EZ**	310
Norfolk Square	**DZ**	313
Orme Court	**BZ**	328
Oxford Square	**EZ**	332
Palace Gardens Terrace	**AZ**	335
Queen's Gardens	**CZ**	362
St. Giles High Street	**DV**	377
Sardinia Street	**EV**	381
Southampton Street	**DX**	388
South Eaton Place	**AY**	389
Stanhope Place	**EZ**	400
Sussex Square	**DZ**	404
Terminus Place	**BX**	412
Thirleby Road	**CX**	416
Upper St. Martin's Lane	**DX**	430
Westbourne Crescent	**DZ**	448
Westbourne Street	**DZ**	450
William IV Street	**DY**	467

ALPHABETICAL LIST OF HOTELS AND RESTAURANTS
LISTE ALPHABÉTIQUE DES HOTELS ET RESTAURANTS
ELENCO ALFABETICO DEGLI ALBERGHI E RISTORANTI
ALPHABETISCHES HOTEL- UND RESTAURANTVERZEICHNIS

A

	page pagina Seite
Abbey Court	67
Academy	55
Alastair Little	80
Alexander	68
Al Hamra	76
Alpha Royale	73
Amico (L')	82
Amoureux (Les)	70
Amsterdam	65
Anna's Place	63
Antonio's	62
Ariel	62
Ark (The)	67
Arlequin (L')	72
Asuka	78
Aster House	68
Athenaeum	75
Auberge (L')	72
Auberge de Provence	82
Auntie's	55
Aventure (L')	78
Aykoku Kaku	57
Ayudhya	69
Azami	81
Aziz	60

B

	page pagina Seite
Bailey's	68
Bangkok	69
Barbarella	60
Barbino (Il)	78
Bardon Lodge	59
Barrow House	69
Barton's	58
Basil Street	63
Bastide (La)	79
Bayee House	72
Bayee Village	70
Bay Leaf	60
Beaufort	64
Beccofino	65
Belgravia-Sheraton	74
Bellini	71

	page pagina Seite
Belvedere	66
Bengal Lancer	56
Benihana	56
Berkeley	74
Berkeley Arms	62
Berkshire	77
Bibendum	64
Bingham	71
Bistro (Le)	60
Bistroquet (Le)	55
Bill Bentley's	57
Blakes	68
Blandford	77
Bloomsbury Crest	54
Bloomsbury Park	55
Blue Elephant	60
Bois St. Jean (Au)	78
Bombay Bicycle Club	73
Bombay Brasserie	68
Bombay Palace	73
Bonnington	55
Bouffe (La)	72
Bougie (La)	55
Bouillabaisse (La)	65
Boulestin	80
Boyd's Glass Garden	66
Brasserie de la Paix	68
Briarley	57
Brilliant	58
Brinkley's	65
Brittania	75
Bromley Court	54
Brown's	75
Bryanston Court	77
Bubb's	57
Burt's	80
Bustan (Al)	74

C

	page pagina Seite
Cadogan Thistle	64
Café Pelican	81
Café Rouge	63
Café St. Pierre	63
Camelot	73

	page pagina Seite
Canal Brasserie	67
Canaletto 2	61
Candlewick Room	57
Cannizaro House	70
Capisano	54
Capital	63
Caprice (Le)	79
Carnarvon	58
Cassis	72
Cavaliers'	72
Cavendish	79
Cézanne	71
Chada	72
Chambeli	78
Chanterelle	69
Chaopraya	78
Charles Bernard	55
Chateau (Le)	76
Chateaubriand	56
Chateau Napoleon	57
Chelsea	64
Chesa (Swiss Centre)	80
Chesham House	81
Chesterfield	75
Chez Max	69
Chez Moi	67
Chez Nico	78
Chez Solange	80
Chin's	60
Chinon	60
Chow Shings	59
Churchill	76
Ciboure	82
Claridges's	74
Clarke's	66
Claverley	64
Clifton Ford	77
Clive	56
Coach House	61
Collin House	81
Concorde	77
Connaught	74
Copper Chimney	76
Corney and Barrow	57
Cranley Place	68
Crest (Bexley)	53

Croisette (La) 66
Crowther's 71
Crystal Palace 66
Cumberland 61
Cumberland 77

D

Dan's 65
Daphne's 65
Delhi Brasserie 69
Delmere 73
Dene 72
Dewanian 70
Dijonnais 57
Dining Room 72
Dordogne (La) 62
Dorset Square 77
Draycott 63
**Drury Lane Moat
  House** 56
Dukes 79
Dunheved 58
Durrants 77
Dynasty II 64

E

Eatons 82
Ebury Court 81
Eccleston 81
Edward Lear 77
Eleven Park Walk 64
Elio 58
Elizabeth 81
Embassy House 68
English Garden 64
Equities 60
Escargot (L') 80
Etoile (l') 55
Evergreen 71
Excelsior 62

F

Fakhreldine 76
Fenja 64
Fifty-One, Fifty-One ... 64
Finezza (La) 64
Flemings 75
Flounders 81
Fontana (La) 82
Fontana Amorosa 78
Fortune Cookie 73
Fortyseven Park Street 74
Four Seasons 75
Frederick's 63
Frith's 80
Fung Shing 80

G

Gallery Rendezvous ... 80
Gamin (Le) 57
Garden 60
Gavroche (Le) 75
Gavvers 64
Gay Hussar 80
Gaylord 78
Giannino's 54
Gino's 58
Giralda (La) 61
Gloucester 68
Golden Chopsticks 69
Good Earth 53
Good Earth 65
Good Earth 65
Good Friends 72
Gore 68
Goring 81
Gothique (Le) 73
Grafton 54
Grafton (The) 69
Granada Lodge 63
Gran Paradiso 82
Gravier 69
Great Northern 56
Greenhouse 76
Green's 79
Green Leaves 78
Green Park 75
Grianan 54
Grosvenor 81
Grosvenor House 74
Grove Park 62

H

Halcyon 66
Hallam 77
Hamilton House 81
Hampshire 79
Happiness Garden 58
Happy Wok 81
Harcourt House 81
Harewood 77
Harlingford 55
Harrow 61
Harvey's 73
Hazlitt's 79
Heals 55
Heathrow Park 62
Heathrow Penta 62
Hees 53
Hendon Hall 53
Herisson (L') 70
Hiders 60
Hilaire 68
Hilton International ... 77

**Hilton International
  Kensington** 66
**Hilton Mews
  at Park Lane** 75
Hilton National 53
Hilton National 61
Hiroko 66
Hogarth 65
Hoizin 82
Ho-Ho 70
Ho-Ho 76
Holiday Inn 56
Holiday Inn 57
Holiday Inn 62
Holiday Inn 75
Holiday Inn 77
Holtwhites 59
Hornimans 70
Hospitality Inn 73
**Hospitality Inn
  Piccadilly** 79
Hotel (L') 64
Howard 80
Hunan 82
Hyatt Carlton Tower ... 63
Hyde Park 74

I

Ibis 62
Ibis Euston 55
I Ching 67
Ikeda 76
Incontro (L') 82
Inn of Happiness 82
Inn on the Park 74
Inter-Continental 75

J

Jamdani 55
**Jardin des Gourmets
  (Au)** 80
Jasmin 72
Jason's Court 78
**Jasper's Bun
  in the Oven** 71
John Howard 68
Joy King Lau 80
Julius's 63

K

Kaifeng 53
Kalamaras Taverna ... 73
Kaya 80
Keats 56
Kenilworth 54

Ken Lo's Memories of China 64
Ken Lo's Memories of China 82
Kennedy 55
Kensington Close 66
Kensington Palace Thistle 66
Kensington Place 67
Kensington Plaza 68
Kenton House 58
Kew Rendezvous 71
Kingsley 54
Kingston Lodge 69
Koh-I-Noor 60
Koto 56
Kym's 82

L

Laguna 81
Laguna Tandoori 58
Lakorn 63
Langans Bistro 78
Langan's Brasserie 76
Launceston Place 66
Left Bank 66
Leith's 67
Lena's 72
Liaison 73
Lichfields 71
Lindsay House........ 79
Liongate 71
Lockets 82
Loggia (La) 78
Lok Zen 53
Londonderry 75
London Embassy 73
London Hilton on Park Lane 75
London Metropole 73
London Ryan 63
London Tara 66
Lowndes Thistle 74
Luigi's 71

M

Ma Cuisine 65
Magic Dragon 64
Magno's Brasserie 81
Malabar 67
Mandarin 67
Mandarin Palace 70
Mange Tout (Le) 71
Mansion House at Grims Dyke 61
Mao Tai........... 60
Mario............. 64

Marlborough 54
Marriott 75
Martin's 78
Masako............. 78
Maxim 58
May Fair 75
Mazarin (Le)........ 82
Memories of India 69
Mentone 55
Meridien Londres (Le) 74
Mesurier (Le) 63
Michel's 67
Mijanou 82
Mimmo d'Ischia 82
Ming 65
Ming 80
Miyama............. 57
Miyama............. 76
Mr Kai 76
Mr Liu 71
Mr Tang's Mandarin ... 61
Mon 78
Monkey's 65
Mon Plaisir 55
Monsieur Thompson's . 67
Montcalm........... 77
Montpeliano 74
Mornington 73
Motcombs 74
Mountbatten 54
M'sieur Frog 63

N

Nakamura 78
Nayab 60
Neal Street 55
New Diamond 80
New Matahari 58
Ninety Park Lane 75
Norfolk 59
Norfolk 68
Noughts 'N' Crosses .. 58
Novotel London 60
Number Sixteen 68
Number 10 76
Nusa Dua 80

O

Oak Room 75
Oakwood 57
Odette's 56
Odins............. 78
Oh Boy 57
Oh Boy 73

Old Bangkok Rattanakosin 66
Ombrello (L') 54
One Sixteen 74
Onslow 68
Opera (L') 56
Orso 80
Otters 60

P

Paesana (La) 67
Paolo's 58
Park Lane 75
Parkwood 73
Partners 23 72
Pastoria 79
Peacehaven 53
Peking Diner 54
Pembridge Court 67
Peter's 56
P'tit Montmartre (Le) .. 78
Petersham 71
Phoenicia 66
Plaza on Hyde Park.... 73
Pleasure Diner........ 61
Poissonnerie de l'Avenue 64
Pollyanna's........... 72
Pomegranates 82
Pomme d'Amour (La).. 66
Poons of Russell Square . 55
Poons (Soho)........ 80
Ponte Nuovo 65
Portman Inter-Continental ... 76
Portobello 67
Ports 65
Post House........... 56
Post House 57
Post House 62
Poulbot (Le) (basement) 57
Poule au Pot (La)...... 82
Primula (La) 66
Prince 68
Prince Regent 70
Princess Garden 76
P'tit Montmartre (Le) .. 78

Q - R

Quai St. Pierre (Le) 67
Queens 58
Quincy's 53
Raj Vogue 63
Ramada H. London.... 77
Ramada Inn West London 60
Ransomes 72

Red Fort 79
Reeds 68
Regent Crest 77
Regency 68
Rembrandt 68
Résidence (La) 66
Richmond Gate 71
Richmond Park 71
Ritz 79
Rive Gauche (La) 69
Roberto's 62
Rock Fort 61
Rouxl Britannia 63
Royal Chace 59
Royal Court 64
Royal Garden 66
Royal Horseguards
   Thistle 81
Royal Lancaster 73
Royal Trafalgar
   Thistle 79
Royal Westminster
   Thistle 81
RSJ 69
Rubens 81
Rushmore............. 65
Ruelle (La) 66
Rue St. Jacques 78
Russell 54
Russel House......... 55

S

Saga 76
Saigon 80
Sailing Junk 67
St. George's.......... 77
St. Germain 82
St. James Court 81
St. Quentin........... 65
Salotto 58
Sambuca 61
San Carlo 60
San Frediano 65
San Lorenzo Fuoriporta 70
San Marino 73
San Ruffillo 65
Santini 82
San Vincenzo (Al) 72

Savoy 80
Savoy Court 77
Scandic Crown 81
Selfridge 76
Selsdon Park 58
Shalimar 63
Shanghai 66
Shares 57
Sheekey's 80
Sheraton Heathrow ... 62
Sheraton Park Tower .. 63
Sheraton Skyline 62
Sherlock Holmes 77
Shireen 60
Shogun 76
Simpson's-in-the
   Strand 80
Skyway 62
Smith's 55
Sonar Goan 61
Sonny's.............. 71
Soufflé (Le) 76
Spread Eagle 59
Stafford 79
Stakis St. Ermins...... 81
Stephen Bull 78
Stone House in London 64
Suntory 79
Sutherland's 80
Suquet (Le) 65
Swallow International . 68
Swan 61
Swiss Cottage 56

T

Tagliatelle (Le) 71
T'ang 65
Tandoori Nights 59
Tandoori Nights 60
Tante Claire (La) 64
Taste of China 61
Taste of Raj 71
Tate Gallery Rest...... 82
Thai Castle 61
Thatched House 72
Thierry's 65
Thirty four Surrey Street . 57
Tiger Lee 65
Tino's 78

Topo d'Oro........... 67
Toto 65
Trattoo 67
Treasure of China 59
Trois Plats (Les) 65
Tui 69
Turner's 64
Twenty Trinity Gardens . 69

V

Vanbrugh 59
Vanderbilt 68
Van Long 80
Venezia............. 80
Very Simply Nico 82
Vijay 53
Villa Bianca 56
Villa Medici 82

W - Z

Wakaba 55
Waldorf 80
Waltons 64
Washington 75
Waterfront 65
Waverley House 54
Westbury 75
West Lodge Park 59
Wheeler's 57
White House 56
Whites 73
White Tower 55
Whittington's 57
Wilbraham 64
Willett 64
Willow 57
Wimbledon Palace 70
Winchester 81
Woodford Moat House 70
Worcester House 70
Yardley Court 59
Zai'qa Tandoori....... 53
Zen 64
Zen Central 76
Zen W3 56
Ziani 65

ALPHABETICAL LIST OF AREAS INCLUDED
LISTE ALPHABÉTIQUE DES QUARTIERS CITÉS
ELENCO ALFABETICO DEI QUARTIERI CITATI
LISTE DER ERWÄHNTEN BEZIRKE

	page / pagina / seite		page / pagina / seite		page / pagina / seite
Addington	57	Forest Hill	70	North Kensington	67
Barnes	71	Fulham	60	Peckham Rye	72
Battersea	72	Greenwich	59	Pinner	61
Bayswater and Maida Vale	73	Hadley Wood	59	Putney	72
Belgravia	74	Hammersmith	60	Regent's Park	56
Bexley	53	Hampstead	56	Regent's Park and Marylebone	76
Blackheath	59	Hampton Court	71	Richmond	71
Bloomsbury	54	Hanwell	58	Romford	61
Brixton	69	Harrow Weald	61	St. James's	79
Bromley	54	Hatch End	61	Sanderstead	58
Camden Town	55	Heathrow Airport	62	Shepherd's Bush	60
Canonbury	63	Hendon	53	Soho	79
Central Harrow	61	High Barnet	53	Southall	58
Cheam	72	Highgate	60	South Kensington	68
Chelsea	63	Holborn	56	Southwark	72
Child's Hill	53	Hornchurch	61	South Woodford	70
Chiswick	62	Hornsey	60	Stanmore	61
City of London	57	Hounslow	63	Strand and Covent Garden	80
Clapham	72	Hyde Park and Knightsbridge	74	Streatham	69
Clapham Common	69	Ickenham	62	Surbiton	69
Cockfosters	59	Ilford	70	Sutton	72
Cranford	62	Islington	63	Swiss Cottage	56
Croydon	57	Kensington	66	Thornton Heath	58
Dulwich Village	71	Kentish Town	56	Tooting	73
Ealing	58	Keston	54	Twickenham	71
Earl's Court	65	Kew	71	Upper Holloway	63
Eastcote	61	Kilburn	53	Upper Norwood	58
East Dulwich	71	King's Cross	56	Upper Sydenham	70
East Sheen	71	Kingston	69	Victoria	81
Eltham	59	Limehouse	72	Wandsworth	73
Enfield	59	Liverpool Street	60	Waterloo	69
Euston	55	Mayfair	74	Wembley	53
Farnborough	54	Merton	70	West Ealing	58
Finchley Road	55	Mill Hill	53	West Kensington	60
Finsbury	63	North Harrow	61	Wimbledon	70
				Woodford	70

STARRED ESTABLISHMENTS IN LONDON
LES ÉTABLISSEMENTS A ÉTOILES DE LONDRES
GLI ESERCIZI CON STELLE A LONDRA
DIE STERN-RESTAURANTS LONDONS

	Area	Page
XXXX Le Gavroche	Mayfair	75

	Area	Page
XXXX La Tante Claire	Chelsea	64
XXX Harvey's	Wandsworth	73
XXX Chez Nico	Regents Park and Marylebonne	78

	Area	Page			Area	Page
Connaught	Mayfair	74		XXX Suntory	St. James's	79
Capital	Chelsea	63		XXX L'Arlequin	Battersea	72
XXXXX Oak Room	Mayfair	75		XXX Cavaliers'	Battersea	72
XXXX Four Seasons	Mayfair	75		XX Sutherlands	Soho	80
XXXX Le Soufflé	Mayfair	76				

FURTHER ESTABLISHMENTS WHICH MERIT YOUR ATTENTION
AUTRES TABLES QUI MÉRITENT VOTRE ATTENTION
ALTRE TAVOLE PARTICOLARMENTE INTERESSANTI
WEITERE EMPFEHLENSWERTE HÄUSER

M

	Area	Page			Area	Page
XXX Keat's	Hampstead	56		XX Le Caprice	St. James's	79
XXX Martin's	Regent's Park and Marylebone	78		XX Hilaire	South Kensington	68
XXX Red Fort	Soho	79		XX Partners 23	Sutton	72
XXX Turner's	Chelsea	64		X Chinon	Shepherd's Bush	60
XXX Zen Central	Mayfair	76		X Kensington Place	Kensington	67
XX Candlewick Room	City	57				

RESTAURANTS CLASSIFIED ACCORDING TO TYPE
RESTAURANTS CLASSÉS SUIVANT LEUR GENRE
RISTORANTI CLASSIFICATI SECONDO IL LORO GENERE
RESTAURANTS NACH ART UND EINRICHTUNG GEORDNET

Borough	Area	Restaurant	Page

BISTRO

Borough	Area	Restaurant	Page
Camden	Camden Town	✗ Bougie (La)	56
Islington	Islington	✗ M'sieur Frog	63
Kensington & Chelsea (Royal Borough of)	Chelsea	✗ Thierry's	65
Westminster (City of)	Regent's Park & Marylebone	✗ Langan's Bistro	78

DANCING

Borough	Area	Restaurant	Page
Hammersmith	Fulham	✗✗ Barbarella	60

SEAFOOD

Borough	Area	Restaurant	Page
City of London	City of London	✗✗✗ Wheeler's	57
—	—	✗✗ Bill Bentley's	57
Croydon	Croydon	✗ 34 Surrey Street	57
Kensington & Chelsea (Royal Borough of)	Chelsea	✗✗ Poissonnerie de l'Avenue	64
—	—	✗✗ Suquet (Le)	65
—	Earl's Court	✗✗ Bouillabaisse (La)	65
—	—	✗✗ Croisette (La)	66
—	—	✗✗ Tiger Lee	65
—	Kensington	✗ Quai St. Pierre (Le)	67
Kingston-upon-Thames	Kingston	✗✗ Gravier	69
Westminster (City of)	Strand & Covent Garden	✗✗ Sheekey's	80
—	—	✗ Flounders	81
—	Victoria	✗✗ Hoizin	82

Borough	Area		Restaurant	Page

			CAJUN - CREOLE	
Kensington & Chelsea (Royal Borough of)	Chelsea	XX	Fifty-One Fifty-One	64

			CALIFORNIAN	
Croydon	Croydon	XX	34 Surrey Street	57

			CHINESE	
Barnet	Hendon	XX	Kaifeng	53
–	Mill Hill	XX	Good Earth	53
–	–	XX	Lok Zen	53
Bromley	Bromley	X	Peking Diner	54
Camden	Bloomsbury	XX	Poons of Russell Square	55
–	Hampstead	XX	Zen W3	56
Croydon	Addington	XX	Willow	57
Ealing	Ealing	XX	Maxim	58
–	Hanwell	X	Happiness Garden	58
Enfield	Enfield	XX	Chow Shings	59
Greenwich	Greenwich	XX	Treasure of China	59
Hammersmith	Fulham	XX	Chin's	60
–	–	XX	Mao Tai	60
Harrow	Central Harrow	X	Taste of China	61
–	Hatch End	X	Pleasure Diner	61
–	–	X	Swan	61
–	Stanmore	X	Mr Tang's Mandarin	61
Hounslow	Chiswick	XX	Grove Park	62
Kensington & Chelsea (Royal Borough of)	Chelsea	XXX	Zen	64
		XX	Good Earth	65
–		XX	Good Earth	65
–	–	XX	Ken Lo's Memories of China	64
–	–	XX	Magic Dragon	64
–	–	XX	Ming	65
–	Earl's Court	XX	Tiger Lee	65
–	–	X	Crystal Palace	66
–	Kensington	XX	I Ching	67
–	–	XX	Sailing Junk	67
–	–	XX	Shanghai	66
–	–	X	Mandarin	67
–	South Kensington	XX	Golden Chopsticks	69
Merton	Wimbledon	XX	Bayee Village	70
–	–	XX	Wimbledon Palace	70
Redbridge	Ilford	XX	Mandarin Palace	70
–	South Woodford	XX	Ho-Ho	70
Richmond-upon-Thames	Richmond	XX	Evergreen	71
–	–	XX	Kew Rendezvous	71

Borough	Area		Restaurant	Page

CHINESE (continued)

Borough	Area		Restaurant	Page
Southwark	East Dulwich	X	Mr Liu	71
Tower Hamlets	Limehouse	X	Good Friends	72
Wandsworth	Clapham	X	Jasmin	72
—	Putney	XX	Bayee House	72
Westminster (City of)	Bayswater & Maida Vale	X	Fortune Cookie	73
—	Mayfair	XXX	Princess Garden	76
—	—	XXX	Zen Central	76
—	—	XX	Ho-Ho	76
—	—	XX	Mr Kai	76
—	Regent's Park & Marylebone	X	Green Leaves	78
—	Soho	XX	Ming	80
—	—	X	Fung Shing	80
—	—	X	Gallery Rendezvous	80
—	—	X	Joy King Lau	80
—	—	X	New Diamond	80
—	—	X	Poons	80
—	Strand & Covent Garden	X	Happy Wok	81
—	Victoria	XXX	Inn of Happiness	82
—	—	XX	Hoizin	82
—	—	XX	Hunan	82
—	—	XX	Ken Lo's Memories of China	82
—	—	XX	Kym's	82

ENGLISH

Borough	Area		Restaurant	Page
Kensington & Chelsea (Royal Borough of)	Chelsea	XX	English Garden	64
Westminster (City of)	Mayfair	XX	Number 10	76
—	—	XXX	Jason's Court	78
—	St. James's	XX	Greens	79
—	—	XXX	Lindsay House	79
—	Strand & Covent Garden	XXX	Simpson's-in-the-Strand	80
—	Victoria	XXX	Lockets	82
—	—	X	Tate Gallery Rest.	82

FRENCH

Borough	Area		Restaurant	Page
Camden	Bloomsbury	XXX	Etoile (L')	55
—	—	XX	Mon Plaisir	55
City of London	City of London	XX	Poulbot (Le) (basement)	57
—	—	X	Bubb's	57
—	—	X	Gamin (Le)	57
Croydon	Croydon	X	Dijonnais	57

Borough	Area		Restaurant	Page
FRENCH (continued)				
Hounslow	Chiswick	✗	**Dordogne (La)**	62
Kensington & Chelsea (Royal Borough of)	Chelsea	✗✗✗✗ ❀❀	**Tante Claire (La)**	64
—	—	✗✗	**Gavvers**	64
—	—	✗✗	**Ma Cuisine**	65
—	—	✗✗	**Poissonnerie de l'Avenue**	64
—	—	✗✗	**St. Quentin**	65
—	—	✗✗	**Suquet (Le)**	65
—	—	✗✗	**Trois Plats (Les)**	65
—	Earl's Court	✗✗	**Bouillabaisse (La)**	65
—	—	✗✗	**Croisette (La)**	66
Kensington & Chelsea (Royal Borough of)	Kensington	✗✗✗	**Belvedere**	66
—	—	✗✗✗	**Ruelle (La)**	66
—	—	✗✗	**Pomme d'Amour (La)**	66
—	—	✗✗	**Résidence (La)**	66
—	—	✗	**Ark (The)**	67
—	—	✗	**Quai St. Pierre (Le)**	67
—	North Kensington	✗✗	**Chez Moi**	67
—	—	✗✗	**Monsieur Thompson's**	67
Kingston-upon-Thames	Kingston	✗✗	**Gravier**	69
Lambeth	Clapham Common	✗✗	**Grafton (The)**	69
Southwark	Peckham Rye	✗✗	**Auberge (L')**	72
Wandsworth	Battersea	✗✗✗ ❀	**Arlequin (L')**	72
Westminster (City of)	Mayfair	✗✗✗✗✗ ❀	**Oak Room**	75
—	—	✗✗✗✗	**Chateau (Le)**	76
—	—	✗✗✗✗	**Four Seasons**	75
—	—	✗✗✗✗ ❀❀❀	**Gavroche (Le)**	75
—	Regents Park & Marylebone	✗✗✗✗✗ ❀❀	**Chez Nico**	78
—	—	✗✗✗	**Rue St. Jacques**	78
—	—	✗✗	**P'tit Montmartre (Le)**	78
—	—	✗	**Aventure (L')**	78
—	—	✗	**Bois St. Jean (Au)**	78
—	Soho	✗✗	**Jardin des Gourmets (Au)**	80
—	Strand & Covent Garden	✗✗✗✗	**Boulestin**	80
—	—	✗✗	**Chez Solange**	80
—	—	✗	**Café Pelican**	81
—	—	✗	**Magno's Brasserie**	81
—	Victoria	✗✗✗	**Auberge de Provence**	82
—	—	✗✗	**Ciboure**	82
—	—	✗✗	**Mazarin (Le)**	82
—	—	✗	**Poule au Pot (La)**	82
GREEK				
Camden	Bloomsbury	✗✗✗	**White Tower**	55
Westminster (City of)	Bayswater & Maida Vale	✗	**Kalamaras Taverna**	73

Borough	Area	Restaurant	Page

HUNGARIAN

Borough	Area	Restaurant	Page
Westminster (City of)	Soho	XX Gay Hussar	80

INDIAN & PAKISTANI

Borough	Area	Restaurant	Page
Barnet	High Barnet	XX Zai'qa Tandoori	53
Brent	Kilburn	X Vijay	53
Camden	Bloomsbury	XX Jamdani	55
—	Kentish Town	XX Bengal Lancer	56
Ealing	Ealing	XX Laguna Tandoori	58
—	Southall	X Brilliant	58
Enfield	Cockfosters	XX Tandoori Nights	59
Hammersmith	Fulham	XX Nayab	60
—	Hammersmith	XX Tandoori Nights	60
—	—	X Aziz	60
—	Shepherd's Bush	XX Shireen	60
—	West Kensington	X Koh-I-Noor	60
Haringey	Highgate	X Bayleaf	60
Hillingdon	Eastcote	X Rock Fort	61
Islington	Upper Holloway	X Raj Vogue	63
Kensington & Chelsea (Royal Borough of)	Kensington	X Malabar	67
—	South Kensington	XXX Bombay Brasserie	68
—	—	XX Delhi Brasserie	69
—	—	XX Memories of India	69
Lewisham	Forest Hill	X Dewanian	70
Richmond-upon-Thames	East Sheen	X Taste of Raj	71
Wandsworth	Wandsworth	X Bombay Bicycle Club	73
Westminster (City of)	Bayswater & Maida Vale	XXX Bombay Palace	73
—	Mayfair	XX Copper Chimney	76
—	Regent's Park & Marylebone	XX Chambeli	78
—	—	XX Gaylord	78
—	Soho	XXX Red Fort	79

ITALIAN

Borough	Area	Restaurant	Page
Bromley	Bromley	XX Capisano	54
—	Farnborough	X Ombrello (L')	54
—	Keston	XX Giannino's	54
Camden	Hampstead	X Villa Bianca	56
Croydon	Sanderstead	X Elio	58
Ealing	Ealing	XX Salotto	58
—	—	X Gino's	58
—	—	X Paolo's	58
Hammersmith	Fulham	XX Barbarella	60

Borough	Area		Restaurant	Page
			ITALIAN (continued)	
Haringey	Highgate	XX	San Carlo	60
Harrow	Hatch End	XX	Canaletto 2	61
Hillingdon	Eastcote	X	Sambuca	61
—	Ickenham	X	Roberto's	62
Hounslow	Chiswick	XX	Antonio's	62
Kensington & Chelsea (Royal Borough of)	Chelsea	XX	Beccofino	65
—	—	XX	Eleven Park Walk	64
—	—	XX	Finezza (La)	64
—	—	XX	Mario	64
—	—	XX	Ponte Nuovo	65
—	—	XX	San Frediano	65
—	—	XX	Toto	65
—	—	XX	Waterfront	65
—	—	X	San Ruffillo	65
—	—	X	Ziani	65
—	Earl's Court	XX	Primula (La)	66
—	Kensington	XX	Paesana (La)	67
—	—	XX	Topo d'Oro	67
—	—	XX	Trattoo	67
Merton	Wimbledon	XX	San Lorenzo Fuoriporta	70
Richmond-upon-Thames	East Sheen	X	Tagliatelle (Le)	71
—	Richmond	XX	Bellini	71
Southwark	Dulwich Village	XX	Luigi's	71
Sutton	Cheam	X	San Vincenzo (Al)	72
Westminster (City of)	Bayswater & Maida Vale	XX	San Marino	73
—	Hyde Park & Knightsbridge	XX	Montpeliano	74
—	Regent's Park & Marylebone	XX	Fontana Amorosa	78
—	—	XX	Loggia (La)	78
—	—	X	Barbino (Il)	78
—	Soho	XX	Venezia	80
—	Strand & Covent Garden	XX	Orso	80
—	—	X	Laguna	81
—	Victoria	XXX	L'Incontro	82
—	—	XXX	Santini	82
—	—	XX	Amico (L')	82
—	—	XX	Gran Paradiso	82
—	—	X	Fontana (La)	82
—	—	X	Mimmo d'Ischia	82
—	—	X	Villa Medici	82
			JAPANESE	
Camden	Finchley Road	X	Wakaba	55
—	Hampstead	XXX	Benihana	56
—	Regents Park	X	Koto	56
City of London	City of London	XX	Aykoku Kaku	57
—	—	XX	Miyama	57
Kensington & Chelsea (Royal Borough of)	Kensington	XX	Hiroko	66

Borough	Area	Restaurant	Page

JAPANESE (continued)

Borough	Area	Restaurant	Page
Westminster (City of)	Mayfair	XX **Miyama**	76
–	–	XX **Shogun**	76
–	–	X **Ikeda**	76
–	–	X **Saga**	76
–	Regent's Park & Marylebone	XX **Asuka**	78
–	–	XX **Masako**	78
–	–	XX **Mon**	78
–	–	X **Nakamura**	78
–	St. James's	XXX ❀ **Suntory**	79
–	Strand & Covent Garden	X **Azami**	81

KOREAN

Borough	Area	Restaurant	Page
Hammersmith	Hammersmith	X **Garden**	60
Westminster (City of)	Soho	XX **Kaya**	80

LEBANESE

Borough	Area	Restaurant	Page
Kensington & Chelsea (Royal Borough of)	Kensington	XX **Phoenicia**	66
Westminster (City of)	Belgravia	XX **Al Bustan**	74
–	Mayfair	XX **Al Hamra**	76
–	–	XX **Fakhreldine**	76

ORIENTAL

Borough	Area	Restaurant	Page
Barnet	Mill Hill	XX **Hees**	53
Ealing	West Ealing	X **New Matahari**	58
Kensington & Chelsea (Royal Borough of)	Chelsea	XX **Dynasty II**	64
–	–	XX **T'ang**	65
Westminster (City of)	Soho	X **Nusa Dua**	80

PORTUGUESE

Borough	Area	Restaurant	Page
Kensington & Chelsea (Royal Borough of)	Chelsea	XX **Ports**	65

SPANISH

Borough	Area	Restaurant	Page
Westminster (City of)	Regent's Park	XX **Tino's**	78

SWEDISH

Borough	Area	Restaurant	Page
Islington	Canonbury	X **Anna's Place**	63

Borough	Area	Restaurant		Page

THAI

Borough	Area		Restaurant	Page
Croydon	Croydon	✗	Oh Boy	73
Hammersmith	Fulham	✗✗	Blue Elephant	60
Harrow	North Harrow	✗	Thai Castle	61
Islington	Finsbury	✗	Lakorn	63
Kensington & Chelsea (Royal Borough of)	Kensington	✗✗	Old Bangkok Rattanakasin	66
–	South Kensington	✗✗	Tui	69
–	–	✗	Bangkok	69
Kingston upon Thames	Kingston	✗	Ayudhya	69
Wandsworth	Battersea	✗✗	Chada	72
–	–	✗✗	Lena's	72
–	Tooting	✗	Oh Boy	73
Westminster (City of)	Regent's Park & Marylebone	✗	Chaopraya	78

VEGETARIAN

Borough	Area		Restaurant	Page
Southwark	Southwark	✗	Dining Room	72

VIETNAMESE

Borough	Area		Restaurant	Page
Westminster (City of)	Soho	✗	Saigon	80
–	–	✗	Van Long	80

RESTAURANTS OPEN ON SUNDAY (L : lunch - D : dinner) AND RESTAU-RANTS TAKING LAST ORDERS AFTER 11.30 p.m.

RESTAURANTS OUVERTS LE DIMANCHE (L : déjeuner - D : dîner) ET RESTAURANTS PRENANT LES DERNIÈRES COMMANDES APRÈS 23 h 30

RISTORANTI APERTI LA DOMENICA (L : colazione - D : pranzo) E RISTO-RANTI CHE ACCETTANO ORDINAZIONI DOPO LE 23. 30

RESTAURANTS, DIE SONNTAGS GEÖFFNET SIND (L : Mittagessen - D : Abendessen), BZW. BESTELLUNGEN AUCH NACH 23. 30 UHR ANNEHMEN

Borough	Area	Restaurant		Sunday	11.30 p. m.	Page
Barnet	High Barnet	XX	Zai'qa Tandoori	L D	x	53
—	Mill Hill	XX	Good Earth	L D		53
Brent	Kilburn	X	Vijay	L D		53
Bromley	Bromley	X	Peking Diner		x	54
Camden	Bloomsbury	XX	Jamdani	L D	x	55
—	—	XX	Poons	L D	x	55
—	—	X	Smith's		x	55
—	Camden Town	X	Bistroquet (Le)	L D		55
—	—	X	Bougie (La)	L D		55
—	Hampstead	XXX	Benihana (12.00)	L D	x	56
—	—	XXX	Zen W3 (11.15)	L D	x	56
—	—	X	Chateaubriand (12.00)		x	56
—	Holborn	XXX	Opera (L')		x	56
—	Kentish Town	XX	Bengal Lancer (12.30)	L D	x	56
—	Swiss Cottage	XX	Peters	L D		56
Croydon	Addington	XX	Willow	L D		57
—	Croydon	XXX	Chateau Napoleon	L		57
—	—	X	Oh Boy	L D		57
Ealing	Ealing	XX	Barton's	L		58
—	—	XX	Laguna Tandoori (12.00)	L D	x	58
—	—	XX	Maxim (12.00)	D	x	58
—	Hanwell	X	Happiness Garden		x	58
—	Southall	X	Brilliant	D		58
Enfield	Enfield	XX	Chow Shings	L D	x	59
Greenwich	Greenwich	XX	Treasure of China	L D	x	59
—	—	X	Spread Eagle	L		59

Borough	Area		Restaurant	Sunday	11.30 p. m.	Page
Hammersmith	Fulham	XX	Barbarella (1.00)		x	60
—	—	XX	Blue Elephant (12.30)	L D	x	60
—	—	XX	Hiders		x	60
—	—	XX	Nayab (11.45)	L D	x	60
—	—	XX	Otters	L		60
—	Hammersmith	XX	Tandoori Nights (11.45)	L D	x	60
—	—	X	Aziz (11.45)	L D	x	60
—	West Kensington	X	Koh-I-Noor	L D	x	60
Haringey	Highgate	X	San Carlo	L D	x	60
Harrow	Hatch End	X	Swan	L D		61
—	North Harrow	X	Thai Castle	L D		61
Hounslow	Chiswick	XX	Antonio's	L D		62
—	—	XX	Grove Park	L D	x	62
Islington	Islington	XX	Frederick's		x	63
—	Upper Holloway	X	Raj Vogue (11.45)	L D	x	63
Kensington & Chelsea (Royal Borough of)	Chelsea	🏛	Hyatt Carlton Tower (Chelsea Room) (Rib Room)	L D L D		63
—	—	XXXX	Waltons	L D	x	64
—	—	XXX	Turner's	L D		64
—	—	XX	Beccofino		x	65
—	—	XX	Daphne's (12.00)		x	65
—	—	XX	Dynasty II	L D	x	64
—	—	XX	Eleven Park Walk (12.00)	L D	x	64
—	—	XX	English Garden	L D	x	64
—	—	XX	Fifty-One Fifty-One	L D		64
—	—	XX	Finezza (La)		x	64
—	—	XX	Good Earth	L D		65
—	—	XX	Ken Lo's Memories of China	L		64
—	—	XX	Magic Dragon	L D		64
—	—	XX	Mario	L D	x	64
—	—	XX	Ming	L D	x	65
—	—	XX	Poissonnerie de l'Avenue		x	64
—	—	XX	St. Quentin (12.00)	L D	x	65
—	—	XX	San Frediano	L D	x	65
—	—	XX	Suquet (Le)	L D	x	65
—	—	XX	Toto	L D		65
—	—	XX	Waterfront		x	65
—	—	X	Monkey's		x	65
—	—	X	Thierry's		x	65
—	—	X	Ziani	L D	x	65
—	Earl's Court	XX	Bouillabaisse (La)		x	65
—	—	XX	Brinkley's		x	63
—	—	XX	Croisette (La)	L D	x	66
—	—	XX	Left Bank (12.00)	L	x	66
—	—	XX	Primula (La)	L D		66
—	—	XX	Tiger Lee	D		65
—	—	X	Crystal Palace	L D		66

Borough	Area	Restaurant		Sunday	11.30 p. m.	Page
Kensington & Chelsea (Royal Borough of)	Kensington	🏰	Royal Garden (Royal Roof)		x	66
—	—	🏠	Halcyon (Kingfisher)	L D	x	66
—	—	XXX	Ruelle (La)		x	66
—	—	XX	Hiroko	L D		66
—	—	XX	I Ching	L D	x	67
—	—	XX	Launceston Place	L	x	64
—	—	XX	Paesana (La) (11.45)		x	67
—	—	XX	Phoenicia	L D	x	66
—	—	XX	Residence (La)	L D		66
—	—	XX	Shanghai	L D	x	66
—	—	X	Ark (The)	D		67
—	—	X	Kensington Place (11.45)	L D	x	67
—	—	X	Malabar	L D		67
—	—	X	Quai St. Pierre (Le)		x	67
—	North Kensington	XXX	Leith's	D	x	67
—	—	XX	Monsieur Thompson's		x	67
—	—	X	Canal Brasserie	L		67
—	South Kensington	XX	Brasserie de la Paix	L D		68
—	—	XX	Delhi Brasserie	L D	x	69
—	—	XX	Golden Chopsticks	L D	x	69
—	—	XX	Memories of India	L D	x	69
—	—	XX	Tui	L D		69
—	—	X	Chanterelle	L D	x	69
Kingston	Kingston	X	Ayudhya	L D		69
Lambeth	Clapham Common	XX	Grafton (The)	L		69
Lewisham	Upper Sydenham	XX	Hornimans	L D		70
Merton	Wimbledon	XX	Wimbledon Palace	L D		70
Redbridge	Ilford	XX	Mandarin Palace (12.00)	L D	x	70
—	South Woodford	XX	Ho Ho	L D		70
Richmond-upon-Thames	Barnes	XX	Sonnys	L		71
—	East Sheen	X	Taste of Raj (11.45)	L D	x	71
—	Richmond	XX	Evergreen	L D	x	71
Southwark	Peckham Rye	XX	Auberge (L')	L D		72
Tower Hamlets	Limehouse	X	Good Friends	L D		72
Wandsworth	Battersea	XX	Lena's	D	x	72
—	Clapham	X	Bouffe (La)	L D		72
—	—	X	Jasmin	L D	x	72
—	—	X	Pollyanna's (12.00)	L	x	72
—	Wandsworth	X	Bombay Bicycle Club		x	73

Borough	Area	Restaurant		Sunday	11.30 p. m.	Page
Westminster (City of)	Bayswater & Maida Vale	XXX	Bombay Palace	L D		73
—		XX	San Marino		x	73
—	—	X	Fortune Cookie	L D		73
—	—	X	Kalamaras Taverna (12.00)		x	73
—	Belgravia	⛪	Berkeley (Restaurant)	L D		74
—	—	XX	Al Bustan	L D	x	74
—	Mayfair	⛪	Claridges (Causerie)	L D		74
—	—	⛪	Inn on the Park (Lanes 12.00)	L D	x	74
—	—	XXXX ❀	Four Seasons	L D		75
—	—	XXXX	Chateau (Le)	L D		76
—	—	XXXX ❀	Soufflé (Le)	L D	x	76
—	—	XXX	Princess Garden	L D		76
—	—	XXX	Zen Central	L D	x	76
—	—	XX	Al Hamra	L D		76
—	—	XX	Greenhouse	L D		76
—	—	XX	Langan's Brasserie (11.45)		x	76
—	—	XX	Mr. Kai	L D		76
—	—	XX	Shogun	D		76
—	Regent's Park & Marylebone	XXX	Odins		x	78
—		XX	Fontana Amorosa		x	78
—	—	XX	Gaylord	L D	x	78
—	—	XX	Loggia (La)		x	78
—	—	XX	Tino's	L D	x	78
—	—	X	Bois St. Jean (Au)	L D	x	78
—	—	X	Barbino (Il) (11.45)		x	78
—	—	X	Langans Bistro		x	78
—	—	X	Nakamura	D		78
—	St. Jame's	XX	Caprice (Le) (12.00)	L D	x	79
—	—	XX	Green's	L		79
—	Soho	XXX	Bastide (La)		x	79
—	—	XXX	Lindsay House (12.00)	L D	x	79
—	—	XXX	Red Fort	L D	x	79
—	—	XX	Burt's		x	80
—	—	XX	Kaya	D		80
—	—	XX	Ming (11.45)	L D	x	80
—	—	X	Fung Shing	L D	x	80
—	—	X	Gallery Rendezvous	L D		80
—	—	X	Saigon		x	80
—	—	X	Poons	D	x	80

Borough	Area	Restaurant		Sunday	11.30 p. m.	Page
Westminster (City of)	Strand & Covent Garden	⌂⌂⌂⌂	Savoy (River)	L D		80
—		XX	Chez Solange (12.15)		x	80
—	—	XX	Orso (11.45)	L D	x	80
—	—	X	Azami	D		81
—	—	X	Café Pelican (12.30)	L D	x	81
—	—	X	Happy Wok		x	81
—	—	X	Magno's Brasserie		x	77
—	Victoria	XXX	Incontro (L')	L D	x	82
—	—	XXX	Inn of Happiness	L D	x	82
—	—	XXX	St. Germain	L D	x	82
—	—	XXX	Santini	D	x	82
—	—	XX	Kym's	L D		82
—	—	X	Fontana (La)	L D		82
—	—	X	Villa Medici (11.45)		x	82

BOROUGHS and AREAS

Greater London is divided, for administrative purposes, into 32 boroughs plus the City ; these sub-divide naturally into minor areas, usually grouped around former villages or quarters, which often maintain a distinctive character.

London telephone numbers
The dialling codes for all London telephone and Fax numbers will change.
From May 6 the codes will be as indicated in the heading of each area within a borough, either ☎ 071 or ☎ 081, except special cases (also indicated).
Until May 6 continue to use the code ☎ 01.

BARNET pp. 4 and 5.
⌐18 The Manor House, Friern, Barnet Lane ℰ 445 1604.

Child's Hill – ✉ NW2 – ☎ 071.

✗ **Quincy's,** 675 Finchley Rd, NW2 2JP, ℰ 794 8499 – ▤. 🄰 VISA   DU   r
closed Sunday, Monday, 2 weeks August and 2 weeks Christmas – **M** (booking essential) (dinner only) 19.50 **t.** ⌐ 3.50.

Hendon – ✉ NW4 – ☎ 081.
⌐18 off Sanders Lane ℰ 346 6023.

🏠 Hendon Hall (Mt. Charlotte), Ashley Lane, NW4 1HF, ℰ 203 3341, Telex 8956088, 🚗 – ▭
TV ☎ ℗ – 🔺 300   DU   v
51 rm, 1 suite.

↑ **Peacehaven** without rest., 94 Audley Rd, NW4 3HB, ℰ 202 9758, 🚗 – TV. 🄰 AE VISA 🐾
14 rm ⬡ 32.00/60.00 **st.**   CU   c

✗✗ Kaifeng, 51 Church Rd, NW4 4DU, ℰ 203 1168, Kosher Chinese rest.   CU   e

High Barnet – ✉ Herts – ☎ 081.

✗✗ **Zai'qa Tandoori,** 7d High St., EN5 5UE, ℰ 441 6375, Indian rest. – 🄰 ⓪ VISA   DT   c
closed 25 and 26 December – **M** 9.50 **t.** and a la carte.

Mill Hill – ✉ NW7 – ☎ 081.
⌐18 100 Barnet Way ℰ 959 2339.

✗✗ **Good Earth,** 143-145 The Broadway, NW7 4RN, ℰ 959 7011, Chinese rest. – ▤. 🄰 AE ⓪
VISA   CT   a
closed 24 to 27 December – **M** 16.00/20.00 **t.** and a la carte 13.50/20.50 **t.** ⌐ 3.00.

✗✗ Lok Zen, 655 Watford Way, Apex Corner, NW7 3JR, ℰ 906 2632, Chinese (Peking, Canton) rest. – ▤   CT   r

✗✗ Hees, 27 The Broadway, NW7 3DA, ℰ 959 7109, Chinese (Peking, Szechuan) rest. – ▤   CT   e

BEXLEY pp. 10 and 11.

Bexley – ✉ Kent – ☎ 0322 Crayford.

🏠 **Crest** (Crest), Black Prince Interchange, Southwold Rd, DA5 1ND, on A 2 ℰ 526900, Telex 8956539, Fax 526113 – ▭ ✑ rm ▤ rest TV ☎ ♿ ℗ – 🔺 80. 🄰 AE ⓪ VISA   JX   e
M (closed Saturday lunch) 12.50/15.75 **st.** and a la carte ⌐ 2.95 – ⬡ 7.35 – **104 rm** 77.00/89.00 **st., 2 suites** 120.00 **st.** – SB (weekends only) 72.00/92.00 **st.**

BRENT pp. 4 and 5.

Kilburn – ✉ NW6 – ☎ 071.

✗ **Vijay,** 49 Willesden Lane, NW6 7RF, ℰ 328 1087, South Indian rest. – ▤. 🄰 AE ⓪ VISA
M 5.00 **st.** and a la carte.   DU   n

Wembley – ✉ Middx – ☎ 081.

🏠 **Hilton National** (Hilton), Empire Way, HA9 8DS, ℰ 902 8839, Telex 24837, Fax 900 2201 –
▭ ✑ rm ▤ rest TV ☎ ℗ – 🔺 350. 🄰 AE ⓪ VISA. 🐾   CU   z
M 13.75/15.00 **t.** and a la carte 17.20/25.90 **t.** ⌐ 4.20 – ⬡ 8.50 – **301 rm** 92.50/250.00 **t.**

BROMLEY pp. 10 and 11.

▮18, ▮9 Cray Valley, Sandy Lane ✆ 0689 (Orpington) 37909, NE : by A 224.

Bromley – ✉ Kent – ☎ 081.

▮9 Magpie Hall Lane ✆ 462 7014.

🏨 **Bromley Court**, Bromley Hill, BR1 4JD, ✆ 464 5011, Telex 896310, Fax 460 0899, 🚗 – 🛗
📺 ☎ ℗ – 🛐 150. 🅂 𝗔𝗘 ⓞ 𝗩𝗜𝗦𝗔 ⚘   HY z
M 11.00/12.50 **st.** and a la carte ♦ 3.95 – **122 rm** ⌷ 64.00/86.00 **st.** – SB (weekends only) 40.00/50.00 **st.**

⥮ **Grianan** without rest., 23 Orchard Rd, BR1 2PR, ✆ 460 1795 – 📺 ℗. ⚘   HY n
12 rm ⌷ 18.00/35.00 **st.**

✗ **Capisano**, 9 Simpsons Rd, BR2 9AP, ✆ 464 8036, Italian rest. – 🅂 𝗔𝗘 𝗩𝗜𝗦𝗔   HY s
closed Sunday, Monday and 3 weeks August – **M** a la carte 10.00/16.90 **t.** ♦ 3.60.

✗ **Peking Diner**, 71 Burnt Ash Lane, BR1 5AA, ✆ 464 7911, Chinese rest. – 🅂 𝗔𝗘 ⓞ
𝗩𝗜𝗦𝗔   HX u
closed Sunday and 25-26 December – **M** 12.50 **t.** and a la carte 10.30/14.50 **t.** ♦ 3.50.

Farnborough – ✉ Kent – ☎ 0689 Farnborough.

▮18 High Elms, High Elms Rd ✆ 58175, off A 21 via Shire Lane.

✗ **L'Ombrello**, 360 Crofton Rd, Locks Bottom, BR6 7XX, ✆ 52286, Italian rest. – 🅂 𝗔𝗘 ⓞ
𝗩𝗜𝗦𝗔   JZ c
closed Sunday – **M** 7.95 **t.** (lunch) and a la carte 10.20/15.65 **t.** ♦ 3.00.

Keston – ✉ Kent – ☎ 0689 Farnborough.

✗✗ **Giannino's**, 6 Commonside, BR4 2TS, ✆ 56410, Italian rest. – 🅂 𝗔𝗘 ⓞ 𝗩𝗜𝗦𝗔   HZ x
closed Sunday, Monday, August and 24 December-3 Janaury – **M** 12.75/20.00 **t.** and a la carte 20.00/24.25 ♦ 3.50.

Groß-London (GREATER LONDON) besteht aus der City und 32 Verwaltungsbezirken (Borough). Diese sind wiederum in kleinere Bezirke (Area) unterteilt, deren Mittelpunkt ehemalige Dörfer oder Stadtviertel sind, die oft ihren eigenen Charakter bewahrt haben.

CAMDEN Except where otherwise stated see pp. 15-18.

Bloomsbury – ✉ NW1/W1/WC1 – ☎ 071.

🛈 35 Woburn Pl., WC1 ✆ 580 4599.

🏨 **Russell** (T.H.F.), Russell Sq., WC1B 5BE, ✆ 837 6470, Telex 24615, Fax 837 2857 – 🛗 ⥮ rm
📺 ☎ – 🛐 450. 🅂 𝗔𝗘 ⓞ 𝗩𝗜𝗦𝗔 ⚘   LU o
M (carving rest.) 13.50 **t.** (lunch) and a la carte ♦ 4.55 – ⌷ 8.25 – **317 rm** 95.00/115.00 **st.**,
3 suites 142.00/190.00 **st.** – SB (weekends only) 98.00/110.00 **st.**

🏨 **Mountbatten**, 20 Monmouth St., WC2H 9HD, ✆ 836 4300, Telex 298087, Fax 240 3540 –
🛗 ▤ rest 📺 ☎ – 🛐 90. 🅂 𝗔𝗘 ⓞ 𝗩𝗜𝗦𝗔 ⚘   p.33 DV o
M *(closed Saturday lunch)* 20.00/22.00 **st.** and dinner a la carte ♦ 5.50 – ⌷ 10.00 – **122 rm**
123.00/170.00 **st.**, **5 suites** 200.00/320.00 **st.**

🏨 **Marlborough** (Crest), Bloomsbury St., WC1B 3QD, ✆ 636 5601, Telex 298274, Fax 636 0532
– 🛗 ⥮ ▤ rest 📺 ☎ 🔧 – 🛐 100. 🅂 𝗔𝗘 ⓞ 𝗩𝗜𝗦𝗔 ⚘   LU i
M 14.25 **st.** and a la carte ♦ 4.75 – ⌷ 9.95 – **167 rm** 129.00/159.00 **st.**, **2 suites** 185.00/
300.00 **st.**

🏨 **Grafton**, 130 Tottenham Court Rd, W1P 9HP, ✆ 388 4131, Telex 297234, Fax 387 7394 – 🛗
⥮ rm ▤ rest 📺 ☎ – 🛐 60. 🅂 𝗔𝗘 ⓞ 𝗩𝗜𝗦𝗔   KU n
M 16.50 **st.** and a la carte ♦ 6.00 – ⌷ 8.00 – **232 rm** 85.00/112.00 **st.**, **4 suites** 150.00/
195.00 **st.**

🏨 **Kenilworth**, 97 Great Russell St., WC1B 3LB, ✆ 637 3477, Telex 25842, Fax 631 3133 – 🛗
▤ rest 📺 ☎ – 🛐 160. 🅂 𝗔𝗘 ⓞ 𝗩𝗜𝗦𝗔 ⚘   LU a
M 13.00 **st.** and a la carte 15.85/18.95 **st.** ♦ 4.50 – ⌷ 8.00 – **181 rm** 85.00/112.00 **st.**, **1 suite**
200.00 **st.**

🏨 **Waverley House**, 130-134 Southampton Row, WC1B 5AG, ✆ 833 3691, Telex 296270, Fax
837 3485 – 🛗 📺 ☎ – 🛐 40   LU u
107 rm, 2 suites.

🏨 **Kingsley** (Mt. Charlotte), Bloomsbury Way, WC1A 2SD, ✆ 242 5881, Telex 21157 – 🛗 📺 ☎
– 🛐 80   LU r
143 rm, 2 suites.

🏨 **Bloomsbury Crest** (Crest), Coram St., WC1N 1HT, ✆ 837 1200, Telex 22113, Fax 837 5374
– 🛗 ⥮ ▤ rest 📺 ☎. 🅂 𝗔𝗘 ⓞ 𝗩𝗜𝗦𝗔 ⚘   LT c
M 12.50/14.50 **st.** and a la carte 21.45/35.75 **st.** ♦ 5.10 – ⌷ 8.40 – **282 rm** 92.00/113.00 **t.**,
2 suites 200.00/300.00 **t.** – SB (weekends only) 92.00/100.00 **st.**

🏨 **Bloomsbury Park** (Mt. Charlotte), 126 Southampton Row, WC1B 5AD, ✆ 430 0434, Telex 25757 – 🛗 ⇌ rm 📺 ☎ – 🛎 30   LU **u**
95 rm.

🏨 **Bonnington,** 92 Southampton Row, WC1B 4BH, ✆ 242 2828, Telex 261591, Fax 831 9170 – 🛗 ⇌ rm 📺 ☎ – 🛎 150. 🖸 🆎 ⑩ 𝖵𝖨𝖲𝖠   LU **s**
M (buffet lunch)/dinner 12.00 **t.** and a la carte 🍷 3.80 – **215 rm** ☕ 66.50/88.00 **t.** – SB (weekends only) 95.00/110.00 **st.**

🏦 **Academy** without rest., 17-21 Gower St., WC1E 6HG, ✆ 631 4115, Fax 636 3442 – 📺 ☎. 🖸 🆎 ⑩ 𝖵𝖨𝖲𝖠. 🛇   KLU **v**
☕ 6.25 – **32 rm** 38.00/75.00 **st.**

↥ **Harlingford** without rest., 61-63 Cartwright Gdns, WC1H 9EL, ✆ 387 1551, 🎾 – 📺. 🖸 𝖵𝖨𝖲𝖠. 🛇   LT **n**
43 rm ☕ 30.00/50.00 **st.**

↥ **Mentone** without rest., 54-55 Cartwright Gdns, WC1H 9EL, ✆ 387 3927, 🎾 – 📺. 🛇   LT **a**
27 rm ☕ 28.00/48.00 **t.**

↥ **Russell House** without rest., 11 Bernard St., WC1N 1LN, ✆ 837 7686 – 📺. 🛇   LU **e**
10 rm ☕ 38.00 **st.**

XXX **White Tower,** 1 Percy St., W1P 0ET, ✆ 636 8141, Greek rest. – 🍽. 🖸 🆎 ⑩ 𝖵𝖨𝖲𝖠   KU **u**
closed Saturday, Sunday, 3 weeks August and 1 week Christmas – **M** a la carte 15.00/24.75 **t.** 🍷 3.75.

XXX **L'Etoile,** 30 Charlotte St., W1P 1HJ, ✆ 636 7189, French rest. – 🖸 🆎 ⑩ 𝖵𝖨𝖲𝖠   KU **e**
closed Saturday, Sunday, August and Bank Holidays – **M** a la carte 25.00/27.50 **t.** 🍷 5.00.

XX **Jamdani,** 34 Charlotte St., W1P 1HJ, ✆ 636 1178, Indian rest. – ⇌ 🍽. 🖸 🆎 ⑩ 𝖵𝖨𝖲𝖠   KU **e**
M a la carte 14.30/20.60 **st.**

XX **Neal Street,** 26 Neal Street, WC2 9PH, ✆ 836 8368 – 🍽. 🖸 🆎 ⑩ 𝖵𝖨𝖲𝖠   p. 33 DV **s**
closed Saturday, Sunday, Christmas-New Year and Bank Holidays – **M** a la carte 23.50/32.50 **t.** 🍷 5.50.

XX **Heals,** First floor, Heal's Department Store, 196 Tottenham Court Rd, W1P 9LD, ✆ 636 1666 ext. 5513, Fax 631 3091 – 🍽. 🖸 🆎 ⑩ 𝖵𝖨𝖲𝖠   KU **z**
closed Sunday and Bank Holidays – **M** (lunch only) 25.50 **t.**

XX **Mon Plaisir,** 21 Monmouth St., WC2H 9DD, ✆ 836 7243, French rest. – 🖸 🆎 ⑩ 𝖵𝖨𝖲𝖠   p. 33 DV **a**
closed Saturday lunch, Sunday and Bank Holidays – **M** 12.95 **t.** and a la carte 14.70/23.80 **t.** 🍷 4.50.

XX **Poons of Russell Square,** 50 Woburn Pl., WC1H 0JE, ✆ 580 1188, Chinese rest. – 🍽. 🖸 🆎 ⑩ 𝖵𝖨𝖲𝖠   LU **x**
closed Christmas and Bank Holidays – **M** 12.00/18.00 **t.** and a la carte 6.00/15.00 **t.**

X **Smith's,** 33 Shelton St., WC2 9HT, ✆ 379 0310 – 🖸 🆎 ⑩ 𝖵𝖨𝖲𝖠   p. 33 DVX **u**
closed Saturday lunch, Sunday and 27 August-3 September – **M** a la carte 17.05/22.50 **t.**

X **Auntie's,** 126 Cleveland St., W1P 5DN, ✆ 387 1548 – 🖸 🆎 ⑩ 𝖵𝖨𝖲𝖠   KU **s**
closed Saturday lunch, Sunday, 2 weeks August, Christmas and Bank Holidays – **M** approx. 16.50 **t.** 🍷 4.50.

Camden Town – ✉ NW1 – ☎ 071.

X **Le Bistroquet,** 273-275 Camden High St., NW1 7BX, ✆ 485 9607 – 🖸 🆎 𝖵𝖨𝖲𝖠   JS **e**
M a la carte approx. 19.35 **t.** 🍷 4.65.

X **La Bougie,** 7 Murray St., NW1 9RE, ✆ 485 6400, Bistro   KS **a**
closed last 2 weeks August and 1 week Christmas – **M** *(closed Saturday lunch and Monday)* a la carte 10.45/11.15 **t.**

Euston – ✉ NW1 – ☎ 071.

🏨 **Kennedy** (Mt. Charlotte), 43 Cardington St., NW1 2LP, ✆ 387 4400, Telex 28250, Fax 387 5122 – 🛗 🍽 📺 ☎ – 🛎 100   KT **r**
360 rm.

🏦 **Ibis Euston,** 3 Cardington St., NW1 2LW, ✆ 388 7777, Telex 22115, Fax 388 0001 – 🛗 🍽 rest 📺 ☎ 🛇 – 🛎 200. 🖸 🆎 ⑩ 𝖵𝖨𝖲𝖠   KT **c**
M 8.75 **st.** and a la carte 🍷 4.00 – ☕ 5.75 – **300 rm** 48.00/53.00 **st.**

Finchley Road – ✉ NW3/NW6 – ☎ 071.

🏦 **Charles Bernard,** 5-7 Frognal, NW3 6AL, ✆ 794 0101, Telex 23560, Fax 794 0100 – 🛗 📺 ☎ 🅿. 🖸 🆎 ⑩ 𝖵𝖨𝖲𝖠. 🛇   ES **s**
M (bar lunch)/dinner a la carte 8.50/14.25 **st.** 🍷 4.00 – **57 rm** ☕ 47.50/77.50 **st.** – SB (weekends only) 85.50/111.00 **st.**

X **Wakaba,** 122a Finchley Rd, NW3 5HT, ✆ 586 7960, Japanese rest. – 🍽   FS **u**

Hampstead – ⊠ NW3 – ☏ 071.

🏨 **Clive** (Hilton), Primrose Hill Rd, NW3 3NA, ℰ 586 2233, Telex 22759, Fax 586 1659 – 🛗 📺 ☎ 🅿 – 🔬 350. 🔼 🆎 ⓪ 𝑉𝐼𝑆𝐴
HS a
M *(closed Saturday lunch)* 15.00 t. 🍷 4.20 – ☷ 8.50 – **93 rm** 79.00/93.00 st., **3 suites** 110.00/115.00 st.

🏨 **Swiss Cottage**, 4 Adamson Rd, NW3 3HP, ℰ 722 2281, Telex 297232, Fax 483 4588, « Antique furniture collection » – 🛗 📺 ☎ – 🔬 40. 🔼 🆎 ⓪ 𝑉𝐼𝑆𝐴 ⚡
GS n
M 9.50/12.95 t. and a la carte 🍷 3.75 – **61 rm** 50.00/90.00 t., **3 suites** 96.00/130.00 t.

🏨 **Post House** (T.H.F.), 215 Haverstock Hill, NW3 4RB, ℰ 794 8121, Telex 262494, Fax 435 5586 – 🛗 ⇆ rm 📺 ☎ 🅿 – 🔬 . 🔼 🆎 ⓪ 𝑉𝐼𝑆𝐴
ES r
M a la carte 13.50/20.00 st. 🍷 3.70 – ☷ 6.95 – **140 rm** 79.00/95.00 st. – SB (weekends only) 94.00/110.00 st.

XXX **Keats**, 3a Downshire Hill, NW3 1NR, ℰ 435 3544 – 🔼 🆎 𝑉𝐼𝑆𝐴
ES v
closed Saturday lunch, Sunday, August and Bank Holidays – **M** 18.00 st. (lunch) and a la carte 29.00/34.50 st. 🍷 4.00.

XXX **Benihana**, 100 Avenue Rd, NW3 3HF, ℰ 586 9508, Japanese Teppan-Yaki rest. – 🍽. 🔼 🆎 ⓪ 𝑉𝐼𝑆𝐴
GS o
closed Monday lunch – **M** 18.50/26.50 t. and a la carte approx. 26.75 t.

XX **Zen W3**, 83-84 Hampstead High St., NW3 1RE, ℰ 794 7863, Chinese rest. – 🔼 🆎 ⓪ 𝑉𝐼𝑆𝐴
ES a
closed 25 and 26 December – **M** 6.80/32.00 t. and a la carte 14.50/28.30 t.

X **Villa Bianca**, 1 Perrin's Court, NW3 1QR, ℰ 435 3131, Italian rest.
ES c

X **Chateaubriand**, 48 Belsize Lane, NW3 5AR, ℰ 435 4882 – 🔼 🆎 ⓪ 𝑉𝐼𝑆𝐴
ES n
closed Sunday, 24 to 26 December and 1 January – **M** (dinner only) a la carte 12.00/19.00 t. 🍷 2.75.

Holborn – ⊠ WC2 – ☏ 071.

🏨 **Drury Lane Moat House** (Q.M.H.), 10 Drury Lane, High Holborn, WC2B 5RE, ℰ 836 6666, Telex 8811395, Fax 831 1548 – 🛗 🍽 📺 ☎ – 🔬 150. 🔼 🆎 ⓪ 𝑉𝐼𝑆𝐴
p. 33 DV c
M 11.50/13.50 st. and a la carte 🍷 7.50 – ☷ 8.25 – **151 rm** 99.00/139.00 st., **2 suites** 200.00/300.00 st. – SB (weekends only) 110.00 st.

XXX **L'Opera**, 32 Great Queen St., WC2B 5AA, ℰ 405 9020 – 🔼 🆎 ⓪ 𝑉𝐼𝑆𝐴
p. 33 DV n
closed Saturday lunch, Sunday and Bank Holidays – **M** 15.00 t. and a la carte 14.75/22.25 t. 🍷 3.75.

Kentish Town – ⊠ NW5 – ☏ 071.

XX **Bengal Lancer**, 253 Kentish Town Rd, NW5 2JT, ℰ 485 6688, Indian rest. – 🍽. 🔼 🆎 ⓪ 𝑉𝐼𝑆𝐴
JS c
closed 25 and 26 December – **M** 5.95 t. and a la carte 10.00/12.00 t. 🍷 3.50.

King's Cross – ⊠ N1 – ☏ 071.

🏨 **Great Northern**, N1 9AN, ℰ 837 5454, Telex 299041, Fax 278 5270 – 🛗 📺 ☎ 🅿 – 🔬 100. 🔼 🆎 ⓪ 𝑉𝐼𝑆𝐴 ⚡
LT s
M 11.50/13.00 st. and a la carte 🍷 3.75 – **88 rm** ☷ 75.00/95.00 st. – SB 98.00/111.50 st.

Regent's Park – ⊠ NW1 – ☏ 071.

🏨 **White House** (Rank), Albany St., NW1 3UP, ℰ 387 1200, Telex 24111, Fax 388 0091 – 🛗 ⇆ rm 🍽 rest 📺 ☎ ♿ – 🔬 70. 🔼 🆎 ⓪ 𝑉𝐼𝑆𝐴 ⚡
JT o
M 20.00 t. and a la carte 11.25/21.45 t. 🍷 4.25 – ☷ 9.00 – **558 rm** 95.00/140.00 t., **9 suites** 235.00/295.00 t.

XX **Odette's**, 130 Regent's Park Rd, NW1 8XL, ℰ 586 5486 – 🔼 🆎 𝑉𝐼𝑆𝐴
HS i
closed Saturday lunch, Sunday, last 2 weeks August, 8 days at Christmas and Bank Holidays – **M** a la carte 15.95/21.90 t. 🍷 5.50.

X **Koto**, 75 Parkway, NW1 7PP, ℰ 482 2036, Japanese rest. – 🔼 🆎 ⓪ 𝑉𝐼𝑆𝐴
JS a
closed Sunday and Bank Holidays – **M** 12.80/22.00 t. and a la carte 14.80/20.80 t. 🍷 4.30.

Swiss Cottage – ⊠ NW3 – ☏ 071.

🏨 **Holiday Inn** (Holiday Inn), 128 King Henry's Rd, NW3 3ST, ℰ 722 7711, Telex 267396, Fax 586 5822, 🏊 – 🛗 ⇆ rm 🍽 📺 ☎ ♿ 🅿 – 🔬 300. 🔼 🆎 ⓪ 𝑉𝐼𝑆𝐴
GS a
M 15.50/16.00 st. and a la carte 🍷 6.25 – ☷ 9.25 – **297 rm** 119.00/142.00 st., **5 suites** 170.00/450.00 st.

XX **Peter's**, 65 Fairfax Rd, NW6 4EE, ℰ 624 5804 – 🔼 🆎 ⓪ 𝑉𝐼𝑆𝐴
FS i
M 13.50 t. (lunch) and a la carte approx. 18.50 t. 🍷 4.00.

La Grande Londra (GREATER LONDON) è composta dalla City e da 32 distretti amministrativi (Borough) divisi a loro volta in quartieri o villaggi che hanno conservato il loro proprio carattere (Area).

CITY OF LONDON – ✆ 071 Except where otherwise stated see p. 18.

🛈 St. Paul's Churchyard, EC4, ✆ 606 3030 ext 2456.

XXX **Wheeler's,** 33 Foster Lane, EC2V 6HD, ✆ 606 0896, Seafood – ⬛ AE ⓞ VISA   NU o
M (lunch only) a la carte 13.00/26.75 t. 🍷 4.45.

XX **Candlewick Room,** 45 Old Broad St., EC2N 1HT, ✆ 628 7929 – ⬛ AE ⓞ VISA   PU n
closed Saturday, Sunday and Bank Holidays – M (lunch only) 22.95 t. and a la carte
18.95/22.95 t. 🍷 4.25.

XX **Le Poulbot** (basement), 45 Cheapside, EC2V 6AR, ✆ 236 4379, French rest. – ▣. ⬛ AE
ⓞ VISA   NV i
closed Saturday, Sunday, Christmas-New Year and Bank Holidays – M (lunch only) 28.50 st.

XX **Corney and Barrow,** 109 Old Broad St., EC2N 1AP, ✆ 638 9308 – ▣. ⬛ AE ⓞ VISA
closed Saturday, Sunday and Bank Holidays – M (lunch only) 23.95 t. and a la carte
24.45/29.40 t. 🍷 6.50.   PU c

XX **Corney and Barrow,** 118 Moorgate, EC2M 6UR, ✆ 628 2898 – ▣. ⬛ AE ⓞ VISA   PU o
closed Saturday, Sunday and Bank Holidays – M (lunch only) a la carte 20.00/28.00 t. 🍷 7.50.

XX **Corney and Barrow,** 44 Cannon St., EC4N 6JJ, ✆ 248 1700 – ▣. ⬛ AE ⓞ VISA   NV r
closed Saturday, Sunday and Bank Holidays – M (lunch only) a la carte 19.85/21.65 t. 🍷 7.00.

XX **Bill Bentley's,** Swedeland Court, 202-204 Bishopsgate, EC2M 4NR, ✆ 283 1763, Seafood
– ⬛ ⓞ VISA   PU e
closed Saturday, Sunday and Bank Holidays – M (lunch only) a la carte 19.70/26.85 t. 🍷 3.50.

XX **Shares,** 12-13 Lime St., EC3M 7AA, ✆ 623 1843 – ⬛ AE ⓞ VISA   PV s
closed Sunday and Bank Holidays – M (lunch only) 24.00 t.

XX Aykoku Kaku, 9 Walbrook, EC4, ✆ 236 9020, Japanese rest.   NVP u

XX **Miyama,** 17 Godliman St., EC4V 5BD, ✆ 489 1937, Japanese rest. – ▣. ⬛ AE ⓞ VISA
closed Saturday and Sunday – M 13.00/38.00 t. and a la carte 13.70/38.50 t.   NV e

XX **Bill Bentley's,** 18 Old Broad St., EC2N 1DP, ✆ 588 2655, Seafood – ⬛ AE ⓞ VISA   PU i
closed Saturday, Sunday and Bank Holidays – M (lunch only) a la carte 17.70/22.50 t. 🍷 3.25.

X **Bubb's,** 329 Central Market, Farringdon St., EC1A 9NB, ✆ 236 2435, French rest.   NU a
closed Saturday, Sunday, 2 weeks August, 1 week Christmas and Bank Holidays –
M (booking essential) a la carte 17.15/21.55 t. 🍷 3.50.

X **Le Gamin,** 32 Old Bailey, EC4M 7HS, ✆ 236 7931, French rest. – ⬛ AE ⓞ VISA   NV a
closed Saturday, Sunday and Bank Holidays – M (lunch only) 25.50 st. 🍷 4.00.

X **Whittington's,** 21 College Hill, EC4R 2RP, ✆ 248 5855 – ▣. ⬛ AE ⓞ VISA   NV c
closed Saturday, Sunday and Bank Holidays – M (lunch only) a la carte 16.00/20.35 t. 🍷 3.50.

CROYDON pp. 10 and 11.

Addington – ✉ Surrey – ✆ 081.

🛈₁₈, 🛈₁₈, 🛈₉ Addington Court, Featherbed Lane ✆ 657 0281.

XX **Willow,** 88 Selsdon Park Rd, CR2 8JT, ✆ 657 4656, Chinese (Peking, Szechuan) rest. – ▣
🅿. ⬛ AE ⓞ VISA   GZ x
closed 25 to 27 December – M a la carte 13.15/21.00 t. 🍷 4.50.

Croydon – ✉ Surrey – ✆ 081.

🛈₁₈ Coulsdon Court Municipal ✆ 660 0468.

🛈 Central Library, Katherine St. ✆ 760 5400 ext 2984.

🏨 **Holiday Inn** (Holiday Inn), 7 Altyre Rd, CR9 5AA, ✆ 680 9200, Telex 8956268, Fax 760 0426,
⬛, squash – 🛗 ⇄ rm ▣ TV ☎ & 🅿 – 🔺 300. ⬛ AE ⓞ VISA   F7 u
M 16.00/18.00 t. and a la carte 18.50/30.00 t. – ☕ 7.50 – **212 rm** 89.00/99.00 st., **2 suites**
210.00/220.00 st.

🏨 **Post House** (T.H.F.), Purley Way, CR9 4LT, ✆ 688 5185, Telex 893814, Fax 681 6438, 🚗 –
⇄ rm TV ☎ 🅿 – 🔺 180. ⬛ AE ⓞ VISA   FZ e
M (bar lunch Saturday) 10.95/14.50 st. and a la carte 🍷 3.95 – ☕ 7.00 – **85 rm** 69.00/79.00 st.
– SB (weekends only) 68.00/76.00 st.

🏨 **Briarley,** 8-10 Outram Rd, CR0 6XE, ✆ 654 1000, Fax 656 6084, 🚗 – TV ☎ 🅿. ⬛ AE ⓞ
VISA   GZ r
M *(closed Sunday dinner)* (dinner only and Sunday lunch)/dinner 10.00 t. – **28 rm**
☕ 49.50/59.50 t. – SB (weekends only) 55.00/70.00 st.

🏨 **Oakwood,** 69-71 Outram Rd, CR0 6XJ, ✆ 654 2835, 🚗 – TV ☎ 🅿. ⬛ AE ⓞ VISA   GZ s
M *(closed Saturday and Sunday)* (dinner only) 10.50 st. 🍷 4.50 – **17 rm** ☕ 45.00/55.00 st.

XXX **Chateau Napoleon,** Coombe Lane, CR0 5RE, ✆ 680 6027, 🚗 – 🅿. ⬛ AE ⓞ VISA   GZ o
M *(closed Sunday dinner)* 10.95/13.75 t. and a la carte 15.95/19.95 t.

XX **Thirty Four Surrey Street,** 34 Surrey St., CR0 1RJ, ✆ 686 0586, California fish rest., Live
jazz – ⬛ AE ⓞ VISA   FZ c
closed Sunday and Bank Holidays – M a la carte 10.70/16.85 t. 🍷 3.50.

X **Oh Boy,** 18 South End, CR0 1DN, ✆ 760 0278, Thai rest. – ▣. ⬛ AE ⓞ VISA   FZ a
M 5.95/8.95 t. and a la carte 9.45/11.25 t. 🍷 3.40.

X **Dijonnais,** 299 High St., CR0 1QL, ✆ 686 5624, French rest. – ⬛ AE ⓞ VISA   FZ z
*closed Saturday lunch, Monday dinner, Sunday, 1 week March and 3 weeks August-Septem-
ber* – M 7.50/15.00 t. and a la carte 16.35/20.10 t. 🍷 3.50.

Sanderstead – ⊠ Surrey – ☎ 081.

⌐₁₈ Selsdon Park Hotel, Addington Rd ℰ 657 8811.

🏨 **Selsdon Park** (Best Western), Addington Rd, CR2 8YA, ℰ 657 8811, Telex 945003, Fax 651 6171, ≼, ⊒ heated, ⊠, ⌐₁₈, ℱ, park, ✕, squash – ⃰ ⇥ rest �📺 ☎ 🅿 – 🔏 150. 🔼 🄰🄴 ⓪ 𝗩𝗜𝗦𝗔   GZ n
M 15.50/16.50 st. and a la carte – **163 rm** ⊒ 83.00/140.00 st., **7 suites** 210.00/245.00 st. – SB (weekends only) (except Christmas and New Year) 130.00/140.00 st.

✕ **Elio,** 17 Limpsfield Rd, CR2 9LA, ℰ 657 2953, Italian rest. – 🔼 🄰🄴 ⓪ 𝗩𝗜𝗦𝗔   GZ a
closed Saturday lunch, Sunday and 1 week August – M 20.00 t. and a la carte 10.70/12.90 t. ⓵ 3.60.

Thornton Heath – ⊠ Surrey – ☎ 081.

↑ Dunheved, 639-641 London Rd, CR4 6AZ, ℰ 684 2009, ℱ – 📺 ☎ 🅿   FY v
21 rm.

Upper Norwood – ⊠ SE19 – ☎ 081.

🏨 **Queens,** 122 Church Rd, SE19 2UG, ℰ 653 6622, Telex 8951656, Fax 771 1506 – ⃰ 📺 ☎ 🅿 – 🔏 400. 🔼 🄰🄴 ⓪ 𝗩𝗜𝗦𝗔. ✑   FY
M (bar lunch)/dinner 12.50 **st.** – **149 rm** ⊒ 58.00/91.00 **st.** – SB (weekends only) 51.00 st.

EALING pp. 4 and 5.

Ealing – ⊠ W5 – ☎ 081.

⌐₉ Horsenden Hill, Woodland Rise ℰ 902 4555.

🏨 **Carnarvon,** Ealing Common, W5 3HN, ℰ 992 5399, Telex 935114, Fax 992 7082 – ⃰ ⇥ rm 📺 ☎ 🅿 – 🔏 210. 🔼 🄰🄴 ⓪ 𝗩𝗜𝗦𝗔. ✑   CV v
M a la carte 15.85/18.65 **st.** ⓵ 3.95 – ⊒ 7.50 – **145 rm** 75.00/95.00 st.

🏛 **Kenton House,** 5 Hillcrest Rd, Hanger Hill, W5 2JL, ℰ 997 8436, Telex 8812544, Fax 998 0037 – 📺 ☎ 🅿. 🔼 🄰🄴 ⓪ 𝗩𝗜𝗦𝗔. ✑   CV x
M (bar lunch)/dinner a la carte 10.75/14.20 **st.** ⓵ 2.45 – **51 rm** ⊒ 45.75/62.75 st. – SB (weekends only) 65.50/67.50 **st.**

✕✕ Salotto, 11 High St., W5 5DD, ℰ 840 7669, Italian rest.   BV x

✕✕ **Barton's,** 7a The Green, High St., W5 5DA, ℰ 840 3297 – 🔼 🄰🄴 ⓪ 𝗩𝗜𝗦𝗔   BV e
closed Easter, Christmas and Bank Holidays – **M** *(closed Sunday dinner)* 11.45 **t.** and a la carte 11.75/19.35 t.

✕✕ **Laguna Tandoori,** 1-4 Culmington Par., Uxbridge Rd, W13, ℰ 579 9992, Indian rest. – ▤. 🔼 🄰🄴 ⓪ 𝗩𝗜𝗦𝗔   BV i
closed 25 December – **M** 9.25 **t.** and a la carte 9.00/14.35 t. ⓵ 2.75.

✕✕ **Maxim,** 153-155 Northfield Av., W13 9QT, ℰ 567 1719, Chinese (Peking) rest. – ▤. 🔼 🄰🄴 ⓪ 𝗩𝗜𝗦𝗔   BV a
closed Sunday lunch and 25 to 28 December – **M** 19.80 **t.** and a la carte 18.00/23.00 t.

✕ **Noughts 'N' Crosses,** 77 The Grove, W5 5LL, ℰ 840 7568 – 🔼 🄰🄴 𝗩𝗜𝗦𝗔   BV u
closed Sunday dinner, Monday and August – **M** *(dinner only and Sunday lunch)/dinner* 15.90 **t.** ⓵ 3.45.

✕ **Gino's,** 4 The Mall, W5 2PJ, ℰ 567 3681, Italian rest. – 🔼 🄰🄴 ⓪ 𝗩𝗜𝗦𝗔   CV z
closed Saturday lunch, Sunday, 25 December and 1 January – **M** a la carte 20.00/25.00 t. ⓵ 3.50.

✕ **Paolo's,** 7 Hanger Green, W5 3EL, ℰ 997 8560, Italian rest. – 🔼 🄰🄴 ⓪ 𝗩𝗜𝗦𝗔   CV r
closed Saturday lunch, Sunday and Bank Holidays – **M** a la carte 11.60/16.80 t. ⓵ 3.00.

Hanwell – ⊠ W7 – ☎ 081.

⌐₁₈ Brent Valley, Church Rd, ℰ 567 1287.

✕ **Happiness Garden,** 22 Boston Par., Boston Rd, W7 2DG, ℰ 567 9314, Chinese rest. – 🔼 🄰🄴 ⓪ 𝗩𝗜𝗦𝗔   BV c
closed Monday lunch, Sunday, 25-26 December and 1 January – **M** 14.00/20.00 **t.** and a la carte 11.70/16.10 t. ⓵ 3.00.

Southall – ⊠ Middx – ☎ 081.

⌐₁₈ West Middlesex, Greenford Rd ℰ 574 3450.

✕ **Brilliant,** 72-74 Western Rd, UB2 5DZ, ℰ 574 1928, Indian rest. – ⇥. 🔼 🄰🄴 ⓪ 𝗩𝗜𝗦𝗔   BV o
closed Saturday and Sunday lunch, Monday and August – **M** 7.50/10.00 t.

West Ealing – ⊠ W13 – ☎ 081.

✕ New Matahari, 146 The Broadway, W13 0TL, ℰ 567 6821, Indonesian rest.   BV n

__Le Grand Londres__ (GREATER LONDON) est composé de la City et de 32 arrondissements administratifs (Borough) eux-mêmes divisés en quartiers ou villages ayant conservé leur caractère propre (Area).

ENFIELD pp. 6 and 7.

Leaside Picketts Lock Sports Centre, Edmonton ℰ 803 3611.

Cockfosters – ⊠ Herts. – ☎ 081.

XX Tandoori Nights, 27 Station Par., Cockfosters Rd, EN4 0DW, ℰ 441 2131, Indian rest. – ▤   ET u

Enfield – ⊠ Middx – ☎ 081.

Enfield Municipal, Beggars Hollow ℰ 363 4454, N : 1 m.

🏨 Royal Chase, 162 The Ridgeway, EN2 8AR, ℰ 366 6500, Telex 266628, Fax 367 7191, ≤, 🏊, 🛲 – TV ☎ P – 🕴 300. ❀   ET a
91 rm, 1 suite.

🏨 Holtwhites, 92 Chase Side, EN2 0QN, ℰ 363 0124, Telex 299670, Fax 366 9089 – TV ☎ P. 🅂 AE ① VISA. ❀   FT c
closed 23 to 28 December – **M** *(closed dinner Friday to Sunday)* (bar lunch)/dinner a la carte 11.25/18.55 **t.** ⓘ 2.95 – **30 rm** 🍽 48.00/75.00 **t.** – SB (weekends only) 35.00/85.00 **st.**

XXX Norfolk, 80 London Rd, EN2 6HU, ℰ 363 0979 – 🅂 AE ① VISA   FT e
closed Saturday lunch, Monday dinner, Sunday, first 3 weeks August and Bank Holidays – **M** a la carte 13.70/22.10 **t.** ⓘ 3.40.

XX Chow Shings, 2-4 Sarnesfield Rd, EN2 6AS, ℰ 363 5252, Chinese (Peking) rest. – AE ① VISA   FT a
M 15.00/25.00 **st.** and a la carte 11.20/18.90 **st.** ⓘ 2.50.

Hadley Wood – ⊠ Herts – ☎ 081.

🏨 West Lodge Park 🦢, off Cockfosters Rd, ⊠ Barnet, EN4 0PY, ℰ 440 8311, Telex 24734, Fax 449 3698, ≤, 🛲, park – 📶 TV ☎ P – 🕴 70. 🅂 AE ① VISA. ❀   ET i
M a la carte 12.45/20.50 **t.** ⓘ 4.95 – **50 rm** 🍽 75.00/130.00 **st.** – SB (weekends only) (except Christmas) 102.50/115.00 **st.**

MICHELIN Distribution Centre, Eley's Estate, Angel Rd, N18 3DQ, ℰ 803 7341, FAX 807 0889

GREENWICH pp. 10 and 11.

Blackheath – ⊠ SE3 – ☎ 081.

🏨 Bardon Lodge, 15-17 Stratheden Rd, SE3 7TH, ℰ 853 4051, Fax 858 7387, 🛲 – TV ☎ P. 🅂 AE VISA. ❀   HV a
M *(closed Friday dinner)* (bar lunch)/dinner 9.25 **t.** and a la carte ⓘ 3.50 – **39 rm** 🍽 39.00/64.00 **st.**

🏨 Vanbrugh, 21-23 St. John's Park, SE3, ℰ 853 5505, 🛲 – TV ☎ P   HV e
30 rm.

Eltham – ⊠ SE9 – ☎ 081.

🏠 Yardley Court without rest., 18 Court Yard, SE9 5PZ, ℰ 850 1850, 🛲 – TV P. 🅂 VISA. ❀   HX e
closed 1 week Christmas – **9 rm** 🍽 29.00/48.00 **st.**

Greenwich – ⊠ SE10 – ☎ 081.

🛈 46 Greenwich Church St. ℰ 858 6376.

XX Treasure of China, 10 Nelson Rd, SE10 9JB, ℰ 858 9884, Chinese (Peking, Szechuan) rest. – ▤. 🅂 AE ① VISA   GV e
closed 25 and 26 December – **M** 16.00 **t.** and a la carte 5.95/9.50 **t.** ⓘ 3.00.

X Spread Eagle, 1-2 Stockwell St., SE10 9JN, ℰ 853 2333 – 🅂 AE ① VISA   GV c
closed Saturday lunch, Sunday dinner, last 2 weeks August and 25 to 30 December – **M** 10.75 **t.** (lunch) and a la carte 16.75/22.00 **t.** ⓘ 3.25.

HACKNEY – p.18.

Liverpool Street – ✉ EC2 – ☎ 071.

XX **Equities**, 1 Finsbury Av., EC2M 2PA, ☎ 247 1051 – 🔲. 🔳 AE ⓪ VISA   PU a
closed Saturday, Sunday and Bank Holidays – **M** (lunch only) 26.00 **t.**

HAMMERSMITH and FULHAM Except where otherwise stated see pp. 19-20.

Fulham – ✉ SW6 – ☎ 071.

XX **Hiders**, 755 Fulham Rd, SW6, ☎ 736 2331 – 🔳 VISA   p. 12 BQ a
closed Saturday lunch, Sunday, 1 week Christmas and Bank Holidays – **M** 16.00/18.50 **t.**
🍷 3.25.

XX **Otters**, 271 New Kings Rd, SW6, ☎ 371 0434 – 🔲. 🔳 AE ⓪ VISA   p. 12 BQ c
closed Sunday dinner, Christmas and Bank Holidays – **M** 10.75 **t.** (lunch) and a la carte
12.45/19.25 **t.**

XX **Blue Elephant**, 4-5 Fulham Broadway, SW6 1AA, ☎ 385 6595, Thai rest. – 🔲. 🔳 AE ⓪
VISA   EZ z
closed Saturday lunch and 24 to 27 December – **M** (booking essential) 12.95/25.00 **t.** and a
la carte 18.95/27.45 **t.** 🍷 3.95.

XX **Mao Tai**, 58 New Kings Rd., Parsons Green, SW6, ☎ 731 2520, Chinese (Szechuan) rest. –
🔲   p. 12 BQ e

XX **Chin's**, 311-313 New Kings Rd, SW6 4RF, ☎ 736 8833, Chinese rest. – 🔲. 🔳 AE ⓪ VISA
M 13.50 **t.** and a la carte 11.30/19.80 **t.**   p. 12 BQ n

XX **Nayab**, 309 New Kings Rd, SW6 4RF, ☎ 731 6993, Indian rest. – 🔳 AE ⓪ VISA
closed 24 to 26 December and 1 January – **M** 8.50 **t.** (lunch) and a la carte 8.60/17.80 **t.**
🍷 3.50.   p. 12 BQ i

XX **Barbarella**, 428 Fulham Rd, SW6 1DU, ☎ 385 9434, Italian rest., Dancing – 🔳 AE ⓪
VISA   FZ x
closed Sunday and Bank Holidays – **M** (dinner only) 16.00 **t.** and a la carte 16.25/20.75 **t.**
🍷 3.75.

Hammersmith – ✉ W6/W12/W14 – ☎ 081.

🏨 **Novotel London**, 1 Shortlands, W6 8DR, ☎ 741 1555, Telex 934539, Fax 748 8061 – 🔰
✻ rm 🔲 📺 ☎ ⅙ 🅿 – 🔺 900. 🔳 AE ⓪ VISA   p. 9 DV c
M a la carte 15.85/22.85 **st.** 🍷 3.90 – 🍵 8.25 – **636 rm** 78.00/85.00 **st.**, **4 suites** 140.00 **st.** –
SB (weekends only) 68.50/95.20 **st.**

XX **Tandoori Nights**, 319-321 King St., W6 9NH, ☎ 741 4328, Indian rest. – 🔲. 🔳 AE
⓪ VISA   CV u
closed 25 and 26 December – **M** 4.95 **t.** (lunch) and a la carte 6.25/9.85 **t.** 🍷 3.45.

X **Garden**, 210 King St., W6 0RA, ☎ 748 5058, Korean rest.   p. 9 CV a
closed Sunday – **M** 18.50 **t.** (dinner) and a la carte approx. 9.10 **t.**

X **Aziz**, 116 King St., W6 0QP, ☎ 748 1826, Indian rest. – 🔳 AE ⓪ VISA   p. 9 CV a
M a la carte approx. 6.90 **t.** 🍷 3.70.

Shepherd's Bush – ✉ W12/W14 – ☎ 071.

XX **Shireen**, 270 Uxbridge Rd, W12 8NR, ☎ 749 5927, Indian rest. – 🔲   p. 9 CV n
X **Chinon**, 25 Richmond Way, W14, ☎ 602 5968 – 🔲. 🔳 AE VISA   p. 9 DV s
closed Sunday, Monday, Easter, 2 weeks August and 25 to 28 December – **M** a la carte
approx. 25.00 **t.**

West Kensington – ✉ SW6/W14 – ☎ 071.

🏨 **Ramada Inn West London**, Lillie Rd, SW6 1UQ, ☎ 385 1255, Telex 917728, Fax 381 4450
– 🔰 ✻ rm 📺 ☎ 🅿 – 🔺 2 000. 🔳 AE ⓪ VISA. 🛠   EZ e
M 9.50/11.95 **st.** and a la carte 🍷 4.15 – 🍵 7.95 – **497 rm** 70.00/80.00 **st.**, **4 suites** 150.00 **st.**

X **Koh-I-Noor**, 197-199 North End Rd, W14 9NL, ☎ 381 1364, Indian rest. – 🔳 VISA   EZ a
M a la carte approx. 8.95 **st.** 🍷 3.25.

HARINGEY pp. 6 and 7.

Highgate – ✉ N6 – ☎ 081.

XX **San Carlo**, 2 High St., N6 5JL, ☎ 340 5823, Italian rest. – 🔳 AE ⓪ VISA   EU v
closed Monday and Bank Holidays – **M** a la carte 16.00/22.00 **t.**

X Bayleaf, 2 North Hill, N6 4PU, ☎ 340 1719, Indian rest.   EU c

Hornsey – ✉ N8 – ☎ 081.

X **Le Bistro**, 36 The High St., N8 7NX, ☎ 340 2116 – 🔳 VISA   EU u
closed Sunday, Monday, 2 weeks June and 1 week Christmas – **M** (dinner only) a la carte
10.90/13.30 **t.** 🍷 2.70.

HARROW pp. 4 and 5.

Central Harrow – ⊠ Middx – ☎ 081.
🛈 Civic Centre, Station Rd ℘ 863 5611 ext 2102.

🏨 **Cumberland**, 1 St. John's Rd, HA1 2EF, ℘ 863 4111, Telex 917201 – ⇔ rm 📺 ☎ 🄿. 🔺
🖭 ⓪ *VISA*. 🕸   BU x
M 7.95/12.95 **t.** and a la carte 🍶 4.50 – **77 rm** ⊆ 45.00/77.00 **st.**

🏨 **Harrow**, 12-22 Pinner Rd, HA1 4HZ, ℘ 427 3435, Telex 917898, Fax 861 1370 – ⇔ rm 📺
☎ 🄿 – 🛎 100. 🔺 🖭 ⓪ *VISA*. 🕸   BU a
M 14.95 **t.** and a la carte 🍶 3.75 – **100 rm** ⊆ 48.00/150.00 **st.**

✕ Taste of China, 174 Station Rd, HA1 2RD, ℘ 863 2080, Chinese rest. – 🍽   BU z

Harrow Weald – ⊠ Middx – ☎ 081.

🏰 **Mansion House at Grims Dyke** (Best Western) ⑤, Old Redding, HA3 6SH, ℘ 954 4227,
Fax 954 4560, ☞, park – 📺 ☎ 🄿 – 🛎 50. 🔺 🖭 ⓪ *VISA*   BT r
M *(closed Saturday lunch)* 18.00/20.00 **t.** and a la carte 🍶 3.50 – ⊆ 6.50 – **43 rm** 72.00/150.00 **t.**
– SB (weekends only) 85.00/93.00 **st.**

Hatch End – ⊠ Middx – ☎ 081.
🏌 Grimsdyke, Oxhey Lane ℘ 428 4539.

✕✕ **Canaletto 2**, 302 Uxbridge Rd, HA5 4HR, ℘ 428 4232, Italian rest. – 🍽. 🔺 ⓪ *VISA*   BT a
closed Saturday lunch, Sunday and Bank Holidays – **M** a la carte 14.85/20.80 **t.** 🍶 4.95.

✕ Pleasure Diner, 310 Uxbridge Rd, HA5 4HR, ℘ 421 3130, Chinese rest. – 🍽   BT a

✕ **Swan**, 322 Uxbridge Rd, HA5 4RH, ℘ 428 8821, Chinese (Peking) rest. – 🍽. 🔺 🖭 ⓪
M 15.00/20.00 **t.** and a la carte.   BT n

North Harrow – ⊠ Middx. – ☎ 081.

✕ **Thai Castle**, 28 The Broadwalk, Pinner Rd, HA2 6ED, ℘ 427 4732, Thai rest. – 🔺 *VISA*
closed 25 and 26 December – **M** (dinner only and Sunday lunch)/dinner 18.00 **st.**
and a la carte 🍶 3.75.   BU c

✕ Sonar Gaon, 25 The Broadwalk, Pinner Rd, HA2 6ED, ℘ 427 1991, Indian rest.   BU c

Pinner – ⊠ Middx – ☎ 081.

✕ **La Giralda**, 66-68 Pinner Green, HA5 2AB, ℘ 868 3429 – 🔺 🖭 ⓪ *VISA*   ATU n
closed Sunday, Monday and August – **M** 8.50/12.00 **t.** 🍶 3.00.

Stanmore – ⊠ Middx – ☎ 081.

✕ Mr Tang's Mandarin 28 The Broadway, ℘ 954 0339, Chinese rest.   BT i

This Guide is not a comprehensive list of all hotels and restaurants,
nor even of all good hotels and restaurants in Great Britain and Ireland.

Since our aim is to be of service to all motorists,
we must show establishments in all categories and so we have made a
selection of some in each.

HAVERING pp. 6 and 7.

Hornchurch by A 12 – JT – on A 127 – ⊠ Essex – ☎ 040 23 Ingrebourne.

🏰 **Hilton National** (Hilton), Southend Arterial Rd (A 127), RM11 3UJ, ℘ 46789, Telex 897315,
Fax 41719, ☞ – ⇔ rm 📺 ☎ 🖔 🄿 – 🛎 . 🔺 🖭 ⓪ *VISA*. 🕸
M a la carte 11.10/25.30 **st.** 🍶 4.20 – ⊆ 6.50 – **136 rm** 70.00/80.00 **t.**

Romford by A 118 – JU – ⊠ Essex – ☎ 0708.

🏠 **Coach House** without rest., 48 Main Rd, RM1 3DB, on A 118 ℘ 751901, Fax 730290 – 📺
🄿. 🕸
28 rm ⊆ 27.00/52.00 **st.**

HILLINGDON pp. 4 and 8.
🏌 Haste Hill, The Drive ℘ 092 74 (Northwood) 22877 – 🏌 Harefield Pl., The Drive ℘ 0895
(Uxbridge) 31169, by B 467.

Eastcote – ⊠ Middx – ☎ 081.
🏌 Ruislip, Ickenham Rd ℘ 089 56 (Ruislip) 32004.

✕ Sambuca, 113 Field End Rd, HA5 1QG, ℘ 866 7500, Italian rest.   AU s
✕ Rock Fort, 134 Field End Rd, HA5 1RJ, ℘ 866 8020, Indian rest. – 🍽   AU e

Heathrow Airport – ⊠ Middx – ✆ 081.

🛈 Heathrow Central Station, London Airport ✆ (071) 730 3488.

Sheraton Skyline, Bath Rd, Hayes, UB3 5BP, ✆ 759 2535, Telex 934254, Fax 750 9150, « Exotic indoor garden with 🏊 » – 📶 ⇔ rm 🗏 📺 ☎ & ℗ – 🕍 500. 🔄 🖭 ⓪ *VISA*. ⅌
M 13.00/16.00 **st.** and a la carte 🍷 6.50 – 🍵 9.75 – **347 rm** 100.00/135.00, **5 suites**.　　AX u

Excelsior (T.H.F.), Bath Rd, West Drayton, UB7 0DU, ✆ 759 6611, Telex 24525, Fax 759 3421, 🏊 – 📶 ⇔ rm 🗏 📺 ☎ & ℗ – 🕍 700. 🔄 🖭 ⓪ *VISA*　　AX x
M *(closed Saturday lunch)* 12.50/22.50 **st.** and a la carte 🍷 4.15 – 🍵 8.00 – **573 rm** 110.00/130.00 **st.**, **7 suites** 180.00/200.00 **st.**

Holiday Inn (Holiday Inn), Stockley Rd, West Drayton, UB7 9NA, ✆ 0895 (West Drayton) 445555, Telex 934518, Fax 445122, 🏊, 🐟, ※ – 📶 ⇔ rm 🗏 📺 ☎ & ℗ – 🕍 170. 🔄 🖭 ⓪ *VISA*　　AV v
M 13.95 **t.** and a la carte 🍷 5.65 – 🍵 8.25 – **398 rm** 80.00/112.00 **st.**, **2 suites** 225.00/450.00 **st.**

Post House (T.H.F.), Sipson Rd, West Drayton, UB7 0JU, ✆ 759 2323, Telex 934280, Fax 897 8659 – 📶 ⇔ rm 🗏 📺 ☎ ℗ – 🕍 170. 🔄 🖭 ⓪ *VISA*　　AV c
M 12.50 **st.** and a la carte 🍷 3.60 – 🍵 7.00 – **569 rm** 80.00/100.00 **st.** – SB (weekends only) 81.00/85.00 **st.**

Sheraton Heathrow, Colnbrook by-pass, West Drayton, UB7 0HJ, ✆ 759 2424, Telex 934331, Fax 759 2091, 🛥 – 📶 ⇔ rm 🗏 📺 ☎ ℗ – 🕍 70. 🔄 🖭 ⓪ *VISA*. ⅌　　AVX a
M 9.00 **st.** and a la carte 🍷 4.50 – 🍵 8.75 – **436 rm**, **4 suites**.

Heathrow Penta, Bath Rd, Hounslow, TW6 2AQ, ✆ 897 6363, Telex 934660, Fax 897 1113, ⅏, 🏊 – 📶 🗏 📺 ☎ ℗ – 🕍 500　　AX z
638 rm, **6 suites**.

Skyway (T.H.F.), 140 Bath Rd, Hayes, UB3 5AW, ✆ 759 6311, Telex 23935, Fax 759 4559, 🏊 heated – 📶 ⇔ rm 🗏 rest 📺 ☎ ℗ – 🕍 200. 🔄 🖭 ⓪ *VISA*　　AX e
M (carving rest.) 10.75 **st.** 🍷 3.60 – 🍵 7.25 – **443 rm** 59.00/72.00 **st.**, **3 suites**.

Heathrow Park (Mt. Charlotte), Bath Rd, Longford, West Drayton, UB7 0EQ, ✆ 759 2400, Telex 934093, Fax 759 5278 – 🗏 📺 ☎ ℗ – 🕍 600　　off A 4　AX
306 rm.

Ariel (T.H.F.), Bath Rd, Hayes, UB3 5AJ, ✆ 759 2552, Telex 21777, Fax 564 9265 – 📶 ⇔ 🗏 📺 ☎ ℗ – 🕍 40. 🔄 🖭 ⓪ *VISA*　　AX i
M 15.00/17.50 **st.** and a la carte 🍷 3.65 – 🍵 8.00 – **177 rm** 85.00/120.00 **st.** – SB (weekends only) 82.50 **st.**

Ibis, 112-114 Bath Rd, Hayes, UB3 5AL, ✆ 759 4888, Telex 929014, Fax 564 7894 – 📶 📺 ☎ & ℗ – 🕍 120. 🔄 🖭 ⓪ *VISA*　　AX i
M 8.50 **st.** and a la carte 🍷 3.75 – 🍵 5.75 – **244 rm** 48.00/53.00 **st.**

Ickenham – ⊠ Middx. – ✆ 089 56 Ruislip

Roberto's, 15 Long Lane, UB10 8TB, ✆ 632519, Italian rest. – 🔄 🖭 ⓪ *VISA*　　AU i
closed Sunday – **M** 15.00/18.00 **t.** and a la carte 12.00/17.00 **t.** 🍷 3.95.

HOUNSLOW pp. 8 and 9.

🏌 Wyke Green, Syon Lane, Isleworth ✆ (081) 560 8777, ½ m. from Gillettes Corner (A 4).

Chiswick – ⊠ W4 – ✆ 081.

Antonio's, 6-8 Elliott Rd, W4 1PE, ✆ 742 1485, Italian rest. – 🔄 🖭 *VISA*　　CV o
closed Bank Holidays – **M** a la carte 13.70/19.20 **t.** 🍷 3.50.

Grove Park, 313 Chiswick High Rd, W4 4HH, ✆ 995 3354, Chinese (Peking) rest. – 🔄 🖭 *VISA*　　CV i
closed Saturday lunch and Bank Holidays – **M** 18.50 **t.** and a la carte 14.50/15.50 **t.** 🍷 3.50.

La Dordogne, 5 Devonshire Rd, W4 2EU, ✆ 747 1836, French rest. – 🔄 🖭 *VISA*　　CV o
closed Saturday lunch, Sunday and Bank Holidays – **M** a la carte 15.65/22.65 **t.**

Cranford – ⊠ Middx. – ✆ 081.

Berkeley Arms (Embassy), Bath Rd, TW5 9QE, ✆ 897 2121, Telex 935728, Fax 897 7014, 🛥 – 📶 📺 ☎ ℗ – 🕍 60. 🔄 🖭 ⓪ *VISA*. ⅌　　AX r
M (carving rest.) 14.00 **t.** and a la carte 🍷 4.00 – 🍵 6.50 – **56 rm** 60.00/80.00 **t.** – SB (weekends only) 56.00/200.00 **st.**

Heston Service Area – ⊠ Middx. – ☎ 081.

🏨 Granada Lodge without rest., on M 4 (westbound carriageway), TW5 9NA, ℰ 574 5875, Fax
574 1891 – 📺 & 🅿 – **46 rm**.   ABV **e**

Hounslow – ⊠ Middx. – ☎ 081.

↑ Shalimar without rest., 219-221 Staines Rd, TW3 3JJ, ℰ 572 2816, 🚗 – 📺 ☎. ⚿   BX **s**
14 rm.

ISLINGTON Except where otherwise stated see pp. 15-18.

Canonbury – ⊠ N1 – ☎ 071.

✗ **Anna's Place**, 90 Mildmay Park, N1 4PR, ℰ 249 9379, Swedish rest.   p. 6 FU **a**
closed Sunday and Monday – **M** (booking essential) a la carte 10.80/15.25 **t.**

Finsbury – ⊠ WC1/EC1/EC2 – ☎ 071.

🏨 London Ryan (Mt. Charlotte), Gwynne Pl., King's Cross Rd, WC1X 9QN, ℰ 278 2480, Telex
27728 – 🛗 🗐 rest 📺 ☎ 🅿 – 🔺 45   MT **a**
210 rm.
✗✗ **Café St. Pierre**, 29 Clerkenwell Green (1st floor), EC1R ODU, ℰ 253 0994 – 🔺 AE ⓞ VISA
closed Saturday and Sunday – **M** a la carte 9.00/20.00 **t.** ▮ 4.50.   MU **c**
✗✗ **Café Rouge**, 2c Cherry Tree Walk, Whitecross St., EC1Y ONX, ℰ 588 0710 – 🔺 AE ⓞ
VISA   NU **e**
closed Saturday, Sunday and 2 weeks Christmas – **M** 14.95 **t.** and a la carte 17.85/23.85 **st.**
✗ **Le Mesurier**, 113 Old St., EC1V 9JR, ℰ 251 8117 – 🔺 AE VISA   NT **e**
closed Saturday, Sunday, 3 weeks August, 1 week Christmas and Bank Holidays – **M** (lunch
only) (booking essential) a la carte 16.50/22.50 **t.** ▮ 3.50.
✗ **Rouxl Britannia**, Triton Court, 14 Finsbury Sq., EC2A 1RR, ℰ 256 6997 – 🗐. 🔺 AE ⓞ VISA
M Le Restaurant *(closed Saturday, Sunday, 25 December-2 January and Bank Holidays)*
(lunch only) 18.50 **st.** ▮ 4.00 – **Le Café** *(closed Saturday, Sunday and Bank Holidays)* (lunch
only) a la carte 14.00/17.00 **st.** ▮ 4.00.   PU **x**
✗ **Lakorn**, 197-199 Rosebery Av., EC1R 4TJ, ℰ 837 5048, Thai rest. – 🔺 AE VISA   MNT **e**
closed Saturday lunch, Sunday and Bank Holidays – **M** a la carte 11.50/15.15 **t.** ▮ 3.25.

Islington – ⊠ N1 – ☎ 071.

✗✗ **Frederick's**, Camden Passage, N1 8EG, ℰ 359 2888, « Conservatory and walled garden »
– 🗐. 🔺 AE ⓞ VISA   NS **a**
closed Sunday, 25-26 December, 1 January and Bank Holidays – **M** 9.95 **st.** (lunch) and a la
carte 15.60/22.15 **t.** ▮ 3.95.
✗✗ **Julius's**, 39 Upper St., N1 0PN, ℰ 226 4380 – 🗐. 🔺 AE ⓞ VISA   MNS **i**
closed Saturday lunch, Sunday and Bank Holidays – **M** a la carte 18.45/20.75 **t.** ▮ 3.65.
✗ **M'sieur Frog**, 31a Essex Rd, N1 2SE, ℰ 226 3495, Bistro   NS **n**

Upper Holloway – ⊠ N19 – ☎ 071.

✗ **Raj Vogue**, 34 Highgate Hill, N19 5NL, ℰ 272 9091, Indian rest. – 🔺 AE ⓞ VISA
M 12.50/15.50 **st.** and a la carte ▮ 6.00.   p.6 EU **a**

KENSINGTON and CHELSEA (Royal Borough of).

Chelsea – ⊠ SW1/SW3/SW10 – ☎ 071 – Except where otherwise stated see pp. 30
and 31.

🏨 **Hyatt Carlton Tower**, 2 Cadogan Pl., SW1X 9PY, ℰ 235 5411, Telex 21944, Fax 245 6570,
≼, 🚗, ✗✗ – 🛗 ⇥ rm 🗐 📺 ☎ 🚙 – 🔺 350. 🔺 AE ⓞ VISA. ⚿   FR **n**
M Chelsea Room 36.00/45.00 **st.** and a la carte 30.50/39.50 **st.** – **Rib Room** 32.00/40.00 **st.**
and a la carte 24.50/36.00 **st.** – **194 rm** 190.00/210.00 **t.**, **30 suites** 320.00/1500.00 **t.**
🏨 **Sheraton Park Tower**, 101 Knightsbridge, SW1X 7RN, ℰ 235 8050, Telex 917222, Fax
235 8231 – 🛗 ⇥ rm 🗐 📺 ☎ & 🅿 – 🔺 80. 🔺 AE ⓞ VISA. ⚿   FQ **v**
M a la carte 14.75/28.50 **t.** – ☕ 10.50 – **280 rm** 154.00/170.00, **15 suites** 300.00/660.00 –
SB (weekends only) 308.00/392.40.
🏨 ✿ **Capital**, 22-24 Basil St., SW3 1AT, ℰ 589 5171, Telex 919042, Fax 225 0011 – 🛗 🗐 📺 ☎.
🔺 AE ⓞ VISA. ⚿   ER **a**
M 18.50 **st.** (lunch) and a la carte 32.00/36.50 **st.** ▮ 7.00 – ☕ 8.75 – **48 rm** 135.00/240.00 **st.**
Spec. Gâteau of fresh foie gras served with toasted brioche, Roasted rack of lamb encrusted with mixed herbs
set on a shallot sauce, Gâteau of oranges, bitter sweet orange coulis.
🏨 **Basil Street**, 8 Basil St., SW3 1AH, ℰ 581 3311, Telex 28379, Fax 581 3693 – 🛗 📺 ☎.
🔺 80. 🔺 AE ⓞ VISA   FQ **o**
M *(closed Saturday lunch)* 14.00/17.50 **st.** and a la carte 20.00/22.75 **st.** ▮ 5.75 – ☕ 7.30 –
91 rm 92.00/119.00 **st.**, **1 suite** 195.00 **st.**
🏨 **Draycott**, 24-26 Cadogan Gdns, SW3 2RP, ℰ 730 6466, Telex 914947, Fax 730 0236 – 🛗 📺
☎. 🔺 AE ⓞ VISA. ⚿   FT **c**
M (room service only) a la carte 13.95/25.50 **t.** – ☕ 8.50 – **26 rm** 65.00/210.00 **t.**

Fenja without rest., 69 Cadogan Gdns, SW3 2RB, ℰ 589 7333, Telex 934272, Fax 581 4958 – 劇 ⊤⊽ ☎. ᔕ AE ① *VISA*. ⅍
⇌ 8.75 – **13 rm** 89.25/175.00 **st.** FS r

Chelsea, 17-25 Sloane St., SW1X 9NU, ℰ 235 4377, Telex 919111, Fax 235 3705 – 劇 ⇌ rm ▤ ⊤⊽ ☎ – 🛗 125. ᔕ AE ① *VISA*. ⅍ FR r
M a la carte 18.00/22.65 **st.** ₰ 5.00 – ⇌ 9.75 – **214 rm** 118.00/148.00 **st.**, **6 suites** 245.00 **st.**

Cadogan Thistle (Thistle), 75 Sloane St., SW1X 9SG, ℰ 235 7141, Telex 267893, Fax 245 0994 – 劇 ⇌ rm ⊤⊽ ☎ – 🛗 40. ᔕ AE ① *VISA*. ⅍ FR e
M 11.75/16.00 **t.** and a la carte ₰ 4.75 – **64 rm** 115.00/160.00 **st.**, **5 suites** 180.00 **st.**

Royal Court (Norfolk Cap.), Sloane Sq., SW1W 8EG, ℰ 730 9191, Telex 296818, Fax 824 8381 – 劇 ▤ rest ⊤⊽ ☎ – 🛗 40. ᔕ AE ① *VISA*. ⅍ FST a
M 14.50/19.50 **t.** and a la carte 16.25/30.75 **t.** ₰ 4.25 – ⇌ 8.00 – **100 rm** 105.00/130.00 **st.**, **2 suites** 190.00 **st.** – SB (weekends only) 89.00/99.00 **st.**

Beaufort without rest., 33 Beaufort Gdns, SW3 1PP, ℰ 584 5252, Telex 929200, Fax 589 2834 – 劇 ⊤⊽ ☎. ᔕ AE ① *VISA*. ⅍ ER n
closed 23 December-3 January – **28 rm** ⇌ 135.00/225.00 **st.**

L'Hotel without rest., 28 Basil St., SW3 1AT, ℰ 589 6286, Telex 919042, Fax 225 0011 – 劇 ⊤⊽ ☎. ᔕ AE *VISA* ER i
12 rm ⇌ 100.00 **st.**

Stone House in London without rest., 16 Sydney St., SW3, ℰ 0435 (Rushlake Green) 830553 – ⊤⊽ ☎. ⅍ DT a
closed 22 December-2 January – ⇌ 8.00 – **3 rm** 60.00/80.00 **t.**

Claverley without rest., 13-14 Beaufort Gdns, SW3 1PS, ℰ 589 8541, Fax 584 3410 – 劇 ⊤⊽ ☎. ⅍ – **36 rm**. ER o

Wilbraham without rest., 1-5 Wilbraham Pl., Sloane St., SW1X 9AE, ℰ 730 8296 – 劇 ☎. ⅍ FS n
⇌ 5.50 – **53 rm** 33.00/72.00.

Willett without rest., 32 Sloane Gdns, Sloane Sq., SW1W 8DJ, ℰ 824 8415, Telex 926678, Fax 824 8415 – ⊤⊽ ☎. ᔕ AE ① *VISA*. ⅍ FT s
18 rm ⇌ 44.95/59.95.

❀❀ **La Tante Claire** (Koffman), 68-69 Royal Hospital Rd, SW3 4HP, ℰ 352 6045, French rest. – ▤. ᔕ AE ① *VISA* EU c
closed Saturday, Sunday, 10 days Easter, 3 weeks August, 10 days Christmas-New Year and Bank Holidays – **M** 19.00 **st.** (lunch) and a la carte 39.70/44.80 **st.**
Spec. Coquilles St. Jacques à l'encre, Confit de saumon à la graisse d'oie, Filet de chevreuil au chocolat amer et vinaigre de framboise.

Waltons, 121 Walton St., SW3 2HP, ℰ 584 0204 – ▤. ᔕ AE ① *VISA* DS a
closed Easter and Christmas – **M** 13.00/19.50 **t.** and a la carte 24.00/38.50 **t.**

Turner's, 87-89 Walton St., SW3 3HP, ℰ 584 6711 – ▤. ᔕ AE ① *VISA* ES n
closed Saturday lunch and 25 to 30 December – **M** 17.50/24.50 **st.** and a la carte ₰ 6.00.

Bibendum, Michelin House, 81 Fulham Rd, SW3 6RD, ℰ 581 5817 – ▤. ᔕ *VISA* DS s
closed 5 days at Christmas and Bank Holidays – **M** 20.50 **t.** (lunch) and dinner a la carte 25.75/50.00 **t.** ₰ 4.95.

Zen, Chelsea Cloisters, Sloane Av., SW3 3DW, ℰ 589 1781, Chinese rest. – ▤ ET a

Ken Lo's Memories of China, Harbour Yard, Chelsea Harbour, SW10 0QJ, ℰ 352 4953, Chinese rest. – 🅿. ᔕ AE ① *VISA* p. 9 EX i
closed Sunday dinner, 25-26 December and 1 January – **M** 13.50/25.00 **t.** and a la carte 13.60/21.00 **t.** ₰ 8.00.

Fifty-One Fifty-One, Chelsea Cloisters, Sloane Av., SW3 3DW, ℰ 730 5151, Cajun-Creole rest. – ▤. ᔕ AE ① *VISA* DET z
closed Bank Holidays – **M** a la carte approx. 22.00 **t.** ₰ 4.80.

Eleven Park Walk, 11 Park Walk, SW10 0PZ, ℰ 352 3449, Italian rest. – ▤. ᔕ AE *VISA*
closed Bank Holidays – **M** (buffet lunch Sunday) 14.00/16.00 **t.** and a la carte 15.50/24.30 **t.** ₰ 3.50. CU r

Mario, 260-262a Brompton Rd, SW3 2AS, ℰ 584 1724, Italian rest. – ᔕ AE ① *VISA* DS n
closed Monday – **M** 16.50/25.00 and a la carte 20.50/28.00 **t.** ₰ 4.25.

La Finezza, 62-64 Lower Sloane St., SW1N 8BP, ℰ 730 8639, Italian rest. – ▤. ᔕ AE ① *VISA* FT v
closed Sunday – **M** a la carte 21.00/35.50 **t.** ₰ 3.50.

Dynasty II, Chelsea Wharf, 15 Lots Rd, SW10 0QJ, ℰ 351 1020, Oriental cuisine – ▤ 🅿. ᔕ AE *VISA* p. 20 GZ n
M 18.00/30.00 **t.** and a la carte 18.00/28.00 **t.**

Gavvers, 61-63 Lower Sloane St., SW1W 8DH, ℰ 730 5983, French rest. – ᔕ AE ① *VISA*
closed Sunday and Bank Holidays – **M** 17.00/28.50 **st.** and a la carte ₰ 4.00. FT e

English Garden, 10 Lincoln St., SW3 2TS, ℰ 584 7272, English rest. – ▤. ᔕ *VISA* ET x
closed 13 April and 25-26 December – **M** 15.00 **t.** (lunch) and a la carte 14.75/25.00 **t.** ₰ 4.00.

Poissonnerie de l'Avenue, 82 Sloane Av., SW3 3DZ, ℰ 589 5774, Fax 581 3360, French Seafood rest. – ▤. ᔕ AE ① *VISA* DS u
closed Sunday and Bank Holidays – **M** a la carte 19.60/28.75 **t.** ₰ 4.50.

Magic Dragon, 99-103 Fulham Rd, SW3, ℰ 225 2244, Chinese rest. – ▤. ᔕ AE ① *VISA* DS o
closed 25-26 December and Bank Holidays – **M** 26.00 **t.** and a la carte ₰ 3.00.

XX **Les Trois Plats,** 4 Sydney St., SW3 6PP, ℰ 352 3433, French rest. – ▤. ⊠ AE ◑ VISA DT v
closed Sunday and Bank Holidays – **M** 28.50 **st.** (dinner) and a la carte 16.00/17.70 ▮ 4.00.

XX **Good Earth,** 233 Brompton Rd, SW3 2EP, ℰ 584 3658, Chinese rest. – ▤. ⊠ AE ◑ VISA
closed 23 to 26 December – **M** 18.75 **t.** and a la carte 10.25/19.00 **t.** ▮ 2.75. DR c

XX Good Earth, 91 King's Rd, SW3 4PA, ℰ 352 9231, Chinese rest. – ▤ EU a

XX **St. Quentin,** 243 Brompton Rd, SW3 2EP, ℰ 589 8005, Fax 584 6064, French rest. – ▤. ⊠ AE ◑ VISA DR a
M 11.90/14.90 **st.** and a la carte 16.50/21.00 **t.**

XX **Ma Cuisine,** 113 Walton St., SW3 2HP, ℰ 584 7585, French rest. – ⊠ AE ◑ VISA DS a
closed Saturday lunch, Sunday and Bank Holidays – **M** (booking essential) a la carte 15.00/23.20 **t.** ▮ 7.50.

XX **Waterfront,** Harbour Yard, Chelsea Harbour, SW10 0QJ, ℰ 352 4562, Italian rest. – ⊠ AE VISA p. 9 EX i
closed Sunday and Bank Holidays – **M** 14.00/16.00 **t.** and a la carte 16.00/23.00 **t.** ▮ 3.50.

XX Ports, 11 Beauchamp Pl., SW3 1NQ, ℰ 581 3837, Portuguese rest. – ▤ ER r

XX **Toto,** Walton House, Walton St., SW3 2JH, ℰ 589 0075, Italian rest. – ⊠ AE VISA ES a
closed 3 days at Easter and 24 to 27 December – **M** a la carte approx. 21.50 **t.**

XX Ponte Nuovo, 126 Fulham Rd, SW3 6HU, ℰ 370 6656, Italian rest. CU e

XX **Ming,** 338 Kings Rd, SW3 5ES, ℰ 351 0775, Chinese rest. – ▤. ⊠ AE ◑ VISA CU n
M 5.90/22.50 **t.** and a la carte 9.80/13.80 **t.** ▮ 3.00.

XX **T'ang,** 294 Fulham Rd, SW10 9EW, ℰ 351 2599, Oriental cuisine. – ▤. ⊠ VISA
closed Saturday lunch, Sunday, 24 December-14 January and Bank Holidays – **M** a la carte 16.80/38.80 **st.** p. 19 FZ a

XX **Daphne's,** 110-112 Draycott Av., SW3 3AE, ℰ 589 4257 – ⊠ AE ◑ VISA DS e
closed Saturday lunch, Sunday and Bank Holidays – **M** a la carte 16.00/34.50 **t.** ▮ 5.00.

XX **Beccofino,** 100 Draycott Av., SW3 3AD, ℰ 584 3600, Italian rest. – ⊠ AE VISA ES r
closed Sunday and Bank Holidays – **M** a la carte 12.10/20.00 **t.** ▮ 3.45.

XX **Le Suquet,** 104 Draycott Av., SW3 3AE, ℰ 581 1785, French Seafood rest. – ⊠ AE ◑ VISA
M a la carte 17.50/25.00 **t.** DS c

XX **San Frediano,** 62-64 Fulham Rd, SW3 6HL, ℰ 584 8375, Fax 589 8860, Italian rest. – ⊠ AE ◑ VISA DT n
closed Bank Holidays – **M** a la carte 10.05/15.90 **st.** ▮ 3.25.

XX **Dan's,** 119 Sydney St., SW3 6NR, ℰ 352 2718 – AE ◑ VISA DU s
closed Saturday lunch, Sunday, 1 week at Christmas and Bank Holidays – **M** 19.00 **t.** (dinner) and lunch a la carte 14.10/15.40 **t.** ▮ 4.00.

X **Ziani,** 45-47 Radnor Walk, SW3, ℰ 351 5297, Italian rest. – ⊠ AE ◑ VISA EU e
M a la carte 12.40/15.90 **t.** ▮ 3.75.

X **Monkey's,** 1 Cale St., Chelsea Green, SW3 3QT, ℰ 352 4711 – ▤. AE VISA ET z
closed Saturday, Sunday, 2 weeks at Easter and 3 weeks August – **M** 15.00/25.00 **t.** and a la carte 21.50/29.00 **t.** ▮ 3.75.

X **San Ruffillo,** 8 Harriet St., SW1 9JW, ℰ 235 3969, Italian rest. – ⊠ AE ◑ VISA FQ z
closed Sunday and Bank Holidays – **M** 17.50 **st.**

X **Thierry's,** 342 King's Rd, SW3 5UR, ℰ 352 3365, Bistro – AE ◑ VISA CU c
closed Sunday, 15 August-1 September, Easter and Christmas – **M** 9.50 **t.** (lunch) and a la carte 14.00/18.25 **t.** ▮ 3.25.

Earl's Court – ✉ SW5/SW10 – ☎ 071 – Except where otherwise stated see pp. 30 and 31.

🏨 **Hogarth,** 27-35 Hogarth Rd, SW5 0QQ, ℰ 370 6831, Telex 8951994, Fax 373 6179 – |‡| ▤ rest TV ☎ – 🏛 40. ⊠ AE ◑ VISA AS a
closed 24 to 28 December – **M** 9.00/10.50 **t.** and a la carte ▮ 3.00 – ☕ 5.50 – **85 rm** 59.50/150.00 **t.**

🏨 **Rushmore** without rest., 11 Trebovir Rd, SW5 9LS, ℰ 370 3839, Fax 370 0274 – TV ☎. ⊠ AE VISA. ✻ p. 19 EZ c
22 rm ☕ 28.00/48.00 **st.**

🏨 **Amsterdam** without rest., 7 Trebovir Rd, SW5 9LS, ℰ 370 2814, Fax 244 7608 – |‡| TV ☎. ⊠ AE ◑ VISA. ✻ p. 19 EZ c
21 rm ☕ 42.00/64.00 **st.**

XX **La Bouillabaisse,** 116 Finborough Rd, SW10 9ED, ℰ 370 4183, French Seafood rest. – ⊠ AE ◑ VISA AU c
closed Sunday – **M** (dinner only) 17.50 **t.** and a la carte 17.50/25.00 **t.**

XX **Tiger Lee,** 251 Old Brompton Rd, SW5 9HP, ℰ 370 2323, Chinese Seafood rest. – ▤. ⊠ AE ◑ VISA AU n
closed 25 and 26 December – **M** (dinner only) 38.00 **t.** and a la carte 20.50/38.00 **t.**

XX **Brinkley's,** 47 Hollywood Rd, SW10 9HY, ℰ 351 1683 – ▤. ⊠ VISA BU a
closed Sunday, Christmas and Bank Holidays – **M** (dinner only) 20.00 **t.** and a la carte 16.80/23.70 **t.**

P.T.O. →

XX **La Croisette**, 168 Ifield Rd, SW10 9AF, ℰ 373 3694, French Seafood rest. – ⌧ AE ⓪ VISA
closed Tuesday lunch, Monday and Christmas – **M** 25.00 **t.** (dinner) and a la carte
17.50/25.00 **t.**
AU **a**

XX **La Primula**, 12 Kenway Rd, SW5 0RR, ℰ 370 5958, Italian rest. – ⌧ AE ⓪ VISA
closed Easter, Christmas and Bank Holidays – **M** 18.50 **t.** and a la carte 17.50/20.50 **t.**
▮ 3.80.
p. 19 FZ **e**

X **Left Bank**, 88 Ifield Rd, SW10 9AD, ℰ 352 0970 – ▤. ⌧ AE VISA
p. 19 FZ **i**
closed lunch Monday to Friday and Sunday dinner – **M** 13.00 **t.** (dinner) and a la carte
15.15/22.90 **t.** ▮ 3.75.

X **Crystal Palace**, 10 Hogarth Pl., SW5 0QT, ℰ 373 0754, Chinese (Peking, Szechuan) rest.
– ⌧ AE ⓪ VISA
p. 19 FZ **o**
M 13.50 **t.** and a la carte ▮ 3.25.

▮Kensington▮ – ✉ SW7/W8/W11/W14 – ☎ 071 – Except where otherwise stated see
pp. 19-22.

🏨 **Royal Garden** (Rank), Kensington High St., W8 4PT, ℰ 937 8000, Telex 263151, Fax
938 4532, ≼ – ▮⅊▮ ⅙ rm ▤ TV ☎ ℗ – 🛆 900. ⌧ AE ⓪ VISA. ⅗
p. 30 AQ **c**
M Royal Roof *(closed Saturday lunch and Sunday)* (Dancing) 22.00/32.00 **t.** and a la carte
30.00/37.50 **t.** – ⌕ 9.75 – **369 rm** 127.50/175.00 **t.**, **15 suites** 225.00/850.00 **t.**

🏨 **Halcyon**, 81 Holland Park, W11 3RZ, ℰ 727 7288, Telex 266721, Fax 229 8516 – ▮⅊▮ ▤ TV
☎. ⌧ AE ⓪ VISA. ⅗
EX **u**
M Kingfisher 19.25/25.00 **st.** and a la carte 21.40/31.45 **st.** ▮ 4.75 – ⌕ 12.25 – **42 rm**
140.00/210.00 **st.**, **2 suites** 235.00/450.00 **st.**

🏨 **London Tara** (Best Western), Scarsdale Pl., W8 5SR, ℰ 937 7211, Telex 918834, Fax
937 7100 – ▮⅊▮ ⅙ rm ▤ TV ☎ ⅋ ℗ – 🛆 600. ⌧ AE ⓪ VISA. ⅗
FY **u**
M 10.15 **t.** and a la carte ▮ 4.35 – ⌕ 8.00 – **823 rm** 80.00/110.00 **st.**, **8 suites** 200.00/
300.00 **st.** – SB (weekends only) 100.00/250.00 **st.**

🏨 **Hilton International Kensington** (Hilton), 179-199 Holland Park Av., W11 4UL,
ℰ 603 3355, Telex 919763, Fax 602 9397 – ▮⅊▮ ▤ TV ☎ ⅋ ℗ – 🛆 250. ⌧ AE ⓪ VISA
EX **s**
M 40.00 **st.** and a la carte approx. 21.20 **st.** ▮ 5.00 – ⌕ 9.50 – **605 rm** 104.00/225.00 **st.**

🏨 **Kensington Palace Thistle** (Thistle), De Vere Gdns, W8 5AF, ℰ 937 8121, Telex 262422,
Fax 937 2816 – ▮⅊▮ ⅙ rm ▤ rest TV ☎ – 🛆 200. ⌧ AE ⓪ VISA. ⅗
p. 30 BQ **a**
M 17.50 **st.** and a la carte – ⌕ 8.25 – **297 rm** 83.00/130.00 **st.**, **1 suite** 140.00 **st.**

🏨 **Kensington Close** (T.H.F.), Wrights Lane, W8 5SP, ℰ 937 8170, Telex 23914, Fax 937 8289,
⌧, ⅔, squash – ▮⅊▮ ⅙ rm ▤ rest TV ☎ ℗ – 🛆 200. ⌧ AE ⓪ VISA
FY **c**
M 12.50 **st.** and a la carte ▮ 4.50 – ⌕ 8.00 – **524 rm** 75.00/110.00 **st.**

XXX **La Ruelle**, 14 Wright's Lane, W8 6TF, ℰ 937 8525, French rest. – ⌧ AE ⓪ VISA
FY **i**
closed Sunday, Monday and 3 weeks August – **M** 19.00 **t.** and a la carte 22.95/45.45 **t.**
▮ 4.30.

XXX **Belvedere**, Holland House, Holland Park, W8 6LU, ℰ 602 1238, ≼, French rest., « 19C
orangery in park », ⅔ – ℗. ⌧ AE ⓪ VISA
EY **x**
closed Saturday lunch, Sunday and Bank Holidays – **M** 18.75 **st.** (lunch) and a la carte
26.75/32.25 **st.** ▮ 4.50.

XX **Clarke's**, 124 Kensington Church St., W8 4BH, ℰ 221 9225 – ▤. ⌧ VISA
EX **c**
*closed Saturday, Sunday, 4 days at Easter, 3 weeks August-September, 1 week Christmas-
New Year and Bank Holidays* – **M** 16.00/28.00 **st.**

XX **Shanghai**, 38c Kensington Church St., W8 4BX, ℰ 938 2501, Chinese rest. – ▤. ⌧ AE ⓪
VISA
FX **a**
M 10.00/18.50 **t.** and a la carte 9.90/16.30 **t.** ▮ 3.40.

XX **Launceston Place**, la Launceston Pl., W8 5RL, ℰ 937 6912 – ▤. ⌧ VISA
p. 30 BR **a**
closed Saturday lunch, Sunday dinner and Bank Holidays – **M** 12.75 **t.** and a la carte
18.90/24.85 **t.** ▮ 3.95.

XX **Boyd's Glass Garden**, 135 Kensington Church St., W8 7LP, ℰ 727 5452 – ⌧ AE
VISA
p. 32 AZ **r**
closed Saturday, Sunday, 1 week Christmas and Bank Holidays – **M** 15.75/29.00 **st.** ▮ 5.50.

XX **La Pomme d'Amour**, 128 Holland Park Av., W11 4UE, ℰ 229 8532, French rest. – ▤. ⌧
AE ⓪ VISA
EX **e**
closed Saturday lunch, Sunday and Bank Holidays – **M** 12.75 **st.** (lunch) and a la carte
15.25/21.05 **t.** ▮ 3.45.

XX **La Residence**, 148 Holland Park Av., W11 4UE, ℰ 221 6090, French rest. – ▤. ⌧ AE ⓪
VISA
EX **z**
closed Saturday lunch and Bank Holidays – **M** 10.00/14.00 **t.** and a la carte 10.80/15.50 **t.**
▮ 3.10.

XX **Old Bangkok Rattanakosin**, 11 Russell Gdns, W14, ℰ 602 0312, Thai rest.
EY **o**

XX **Phoenicia**, 11-13 Abingdon Rd, W8, ℰ 937 0120, Lebanese rest. – ▤. ⌧ AE ⓪ VISA
M 16.95 **st.** and a la carte ▮ 3.50.
EY **n**

XX **Hiroko** (at Hilton International Kensington H.), 179-199 Holland Park Av., W11 4UL,
ℰ 603 5003, Japanese rest. – ℗. ⌧ AE ⓪ VISA
EX **s**
closed Monday – **M** 14.00/28.00 **t.** and a la carte 12.50/19.00 **t.** ▮ 6.50.

XX **Sailing Junk,** 59 Marloes Rd, W8 6LE, ☎ 937 5833, Chinese rest. – ▣. ⟐ AE ⓪ *VISA*
FY x
closed Sunday and 25-26 December – **M** 10.00/15.00 **t.** and a la carte 8.50/12.50 **t.** ⓵ 3.00.

XX Trattoo, 2 Abingdon Rd, W8 6AF, ☎ 937 4448, Italian rest. – ▣
EY e

XX **La Paesana,** 30 Uxbridge St., W8 7TA, ☎ 229 4332, Italian rest. – ▣. AE ⓪ *VISA*
closed Sunday, Easter, 25-26 December and Bank Holidays – **M** a la carte 11.45/13.05 **t.**
⓵ 2.90.
p. 32 AZ i

XX Topo D'oro, 39 Uxbridge St., W8, ☎ 727 5813, Italian rest. – ▣
p. 32 AZ a

XX **I Ching,** 40 Earls Court Rd, W8 6EJ, ☎ 937 0409, Chinese rest. – ▣. ⟐ AE ⓪ *VISA*
EY a
M 18.00/25.00 **t.** and a la carte ⓵ 4.00.

X **Kensington Place,** 201-205 Kensington Church St., W8 7LX, ☎ 727 3184 – ▣. ⟐ *VISA*
closed 3 days at Easter, August, Christmas and Bank Holidays – **M** 11.50 **t.** and a la carte
14.00/24.25 **t.** ⓵ 3.25.
p. 32 AZ z

X **The Ark,** Kensington Court, 35 Kensington High St., W8 5BA, ☎ 937 4294, French rest. –
⟐ AE ⓪ *VISA*
p. 30 AQ s
closed Sunday lunch, 4 days at Easter and 4 days at Christmas – **M** a la carte 12.75/16.10 **t.**
⓵ 3.70.

X **Malabar,** 27 Uxbridge St., W8 7TQ, ☎ 727 8800, Indian rest. – ⟐ *VISA*
p. 32 AZ e
closed 26 August-3 September and 25 to 27 December – **M** a la carte 10.85/18.90 **st.** ⓵ 3.50.

X **Le Quai St. Pierre,** 7 Stratford Rd, W8 3JS, ☎ 937 6388, French Seafood rest. – ⟐ AE
⓪ *VISA*
FY r
closed Monday lunch, Sunday and Christmas – **M** a la carte 17.50/25.00 **t.**

X Mandarin, 197c Kensington High St., W8 6BA, ☎ 937 1551, Chinese rest. – ▣
EY s

X Michel's, 6 Holland St., W8 4LT, ☎ 937 3367
FY z

North Kensington – ✉ W2/W10/W11 – ✆ 071 – Except where otherwise stated see
pp. 15-18.

🏨 **Abbey Court** without rest., 20 Pembridge Gdns, W2 4DU, ☎ 221 7518, Telex 262167, Fax
792 0858, « Tastefully furnished Victorian town house » – ⟐ TV ☎. ⟐ AE ⓪ *VISA*. ⟐
⟐ 7.50 – **22 rm** 75.00/140.00 **t.**
p. 32 AZ u

🏠 **Portobello,** 22 Stanley Gdns, W11 2NG, ☎ 727 2777, Telex 268349, Fax 792 9641, « Attrac-
tive town house in Victorian terrace » – ⟐ TV ☎. ⟐ AE ⓪ *VISA*. ⟐
EV n
M (residents only) 15.00 **t.** and a la carte – ⟐ 6.00 – **24 rm** 50.00/85.00 **t.**, **1 suite** 140.00 **t.**

🏠 **Pembridge Court,** 34 Pembridge Gdns, W2 4DX, ☎ 229 9977, Telex 298363, Fax 727 4982
– ⟐ ⟐ rest ▣ rest TV ☎. ⟐ AE ⓪ *VISA*
p. 32 AZ n
M *(closed Sunday)* (dinner only) a la carte 12.00/18.10 **t.** ⓵ 3.95 – **25 rm** ⟐ 60.00/95.00.

XXX **Leith's,** 92 Kensington Park Rd, W11 2PN, ☎ 229 4481 – ▣. ⟐ AE ⓪ *VISA*
EV e
closed 4 days at Christmas and August Bank Holiday – **M** (dinner only) 38.50 **st.** ⓵ 6.25.

XX **Chez Moi,** 1 Addison Av., Holland Park, W11 4QS, ☎ 603 8267, French rest. – ⟐ AE ⓪
VISA
p. 19 EX n
closed Saturday lunch, Sunday, 1 week at Christmas and Bank Holidays – **M** 12.50 **t.** (lunch)
and a la carte 15.00/24.50 **t.** ⓵ 3.75.

XX **Monsieur Thompson's,** 29 Kensington Park Rd, W11 2EU, ☎ 727 9957, French rest. –
⟐ AE ⓪ *VISA*
EV a
closed Sunday, 23 December-3 January and Bank Holidays – **M** 14.90/15.50 **t.** and a la carte
16.20/25.20 **t.** ⓵ 3.75.

X **Canal Brasserie,** Canalot Studios, 222 Kensal Rd, W10 5BN, ☎ 960 2732 – ⟐ *VISA*
ET c
closed Saturday lunch, Sunday dinner and Bank Holidays – **M** a la carte 8.95/16.25 **t.**

Do not mix up :

Comfort of hotels	: 🏨🏨🏨 ... 🏠, ⚘, ⌂
Comfort of restaurants	: XXXXX X
Quality of the cuisine	: ❀❀❀, ❀❀, ❀, **M**

South Kensington – ⊠ SW5/SW7/W8 – ☎ 071 – Except where otherwise stated see pp. 30 and 31.

Blakes, 33 Roland Gdns, SW7 3PF, ℰ 370 6701, Telex 8813500, Fax 373 0442, « Oriental antique furnishings » – 🛗 📺 ☎. 🖎 AE ⓪ VISA
BU n
M a la carte 38.00/51.50 **t.** ▮ 5.75 – � 11.00 – **41 rm** 115.00/165.00 **st.**, **10 suites** 195.00/540.00 **st.**

Norfolk (Norfolk Cap.), 2-10 Harrington Rd, SW7 3ER, ℰ 589 8191, Telex 268852, Fax 581 1874 – 🛗 🔳 rest 📺 ☎ – 🚗 80. 🖎 AE ⓪ VISA. ⚘
CS e
M (see **Brasserie de la Paix** below) – ⊒ 8.00 – **94 rm** 105.00/135.00 **st.**, **3 suites** 170.00 **st.** – SB 63.00/70.50 **st.**

Gloucester (Rank), 4-18 Harrington Gdns, SW7 4LH, ℰ 373 6030, Telex 917505, Fax 373 0409 – 🛗 ✂ rm 🔳 📺 ☎ 🚗 🅿 – 🚗 500. 🖎 AE ⓪ VISA. ⚘
BS r
M 16.50/18.50 **st.** and a la carte ▮ 6.00 – ⊒ 9.90 – **529 rm** 115.00/150.00 **st.**, **6 suites** 300.00/715.00 **st.**

Swallow International (Swallow), 147c Cromwell Rd, SW5 0TH, ℰ 370 4200, Telex 27260, Fax 244 8194 – 🛗 🔳 rest 📺 ☎ 🅿 – 🚗 . 🖎 AE ⓪ VISA
AS c
M 12.50/13.50 **st.** and a la carte ▮ 4.00 – ⊒ 4.95 – **417 rm** 80.00/105.00 **st.** – SB 88.00/102.50 **st.**

Rembrandt, 11 Thurloe Pl., SW7 2RS, ℰ 589 8100, Telex 295828, Fax 225 3363, 🖎 – 🛗 ✂ rm 🔳 rest 📺 ☎ – 🚗 120. 🖎 AE ⓪ VISA. ⚘
DS x
M 14.25 **st.** and a la carte – ⊒ 7.75 – **200 rm** 85.00/105.00 **t.** – SB (weekends only) 54.00/80.00 **st.**

Gore (Best Western), 189 Queen's Gate, SW7 5EX, ℰ 584 6601, Telex 296244, Fax 589 8127, « Attractive decor » – 🛗 📺 ☎. 🖎 AE ⓪ VISA. ⚘
BR n
M a la carte 13.50/17.00 **t.** ▮ 3.50 – ⊒ 7.00 – **54 rm** 76.00/150.00 **st.**

Regency, 100 Queen's Gate, SW7 5AG, ℰ 370 4595, Telex 267594, Fax 370 5555 – 🛗 ✂ rm 🔳 rest 📺 ☎ – 🚗 60. 🖎 AE ⓪ VISA. ⚘
CT e
M 15.00/20.00 **st.** and a la carte ▮ 4.00 – ⊒ 9.00 – **187 rm** 85.00/99.00 **st.**, **5 suites** 140.00 **st.** – SB (weekends only) 177.00/204.00 **st.**

Vanderbilt, 68-86 Cromwell Rd, SW7 5BT, ℰ 589 2424, Telex 946944, Fax 225 2293 – 🛗 🔳 rest 📺 ☎ – 🚗 120. 🖎 AE ⓪ VISA
BS v
M 11.00/13.00 **st.** and a la carte ▮ 4.50 – ⊒ 7.50 – **224 rm** 75.00/95.00 **st.**

Onslow (T.H.F.), 109-113 Queen's Gate, SW7 5LR, ℰ 589 6300, Telex 262180, Fax 589 6300 – 🛗 🔳 rest 📺 ☎ – 🚗 80. 🖎 AE ⓪ VISA. ⚘
CT i
M a la carte 13.95/16.50 **st.** ▮ 4.50 – ⊒ 8.50 – **173 rm** 73.00/145.00 **st.** – SB 68.00/72.00 **st.**

John Howard (Best Western), 4 Queen's Gate, SW7 5EH, ℰ 581 3011, Telex 8813397, Fax 589 8403 – 🛗 🔳 📺 ☎. 🖎 AE ⓪ VISA. ⚘
BQ i
M 15.00/18.00 **st.** and a la carte ▮ 5.00 – ⊒ 10.00 – **40 rm** 75.00/160.00 **st.**

Bailey's, 140 Gloucester Rd, SW7 4HQ, ℰ 373 6000, Telex 264221, Fax 370 3760 – 🛗 📺 ☎ – 🚗 60
BS a
162 rm.

Embassy House (Embassy), 31-33 Queen's Gate, SW7 5JA, ℰ 584 7222, Telex 914893, Fax 589 8193 – 🛗 📺 ☎. 🖎 AE ⓪ VISA. ⚘
BR e
M (closed lunch Saturday, Sunday and Bank Holidays) (buffet lunch)/dinner 14.50 **st.** and a la carte 12.50/19.75 **st.** ▮ 5.00 – ⊒ 5.00 – **68 rm** 66.00/79.00 **st.**, **1 suite** 230.00 **st.** – SB (weekends only) 92.00/110.00 **st.**

Kensington Plaza, 61 Gloucester Rd, SW7 4PE, ℰ 584 8100, Telex 8950993 – 🛗 📺 ☎ – 🚗 30. 🖎 AE ⓪ VISA. ⚘
BS e
M (Indian rest.) a la carte 7.70/24.40 **t.** ▮ 3.50 – ⊒ 6.00 – **51 rm** 58.00/120.00 **st.**

Alexander, 9 Sumner Pl., SW7 3EE, ℰ 581 1591, Telex 917133, Fax 581 0824, « Attractively furnished Victorian town houses », 🌳 – 🛗 📺 ☎. 🖎 AE ⓪ VISA. ⚘
CT a
M approx. 10.00 **st.** ▮ 2.00 – **37 rm** ⊒ 75.00/110.00 **st.**, **1 suite**

Number Sixteen without rest., 14-17 Sumner Pl., SW7 3EG, ℰ 589 5232, Telex 266638, Fax 584 8615, « Attractively furnished Victorian town houses », 🌳 – 🛗 📺 ☎. 🖎 AE ⓪ VISA. ⚘
CT c
33 rm ⊒ 60.00/140.00 **t.**

Cranley Place without rest., 1 Cranley Pl., SW7 3AB, ℰ 589 7944, Fax 225 3931, « Tasteful decor » – 📺 ☎. 🖎 AE ⓪ VISA. ⚘
CT o
10 rm 75.00/120.00 **s.**

Aster House without rest., 3 Summer Pl., SW7 3EE, ℰ 581 5888, Fax 584 4925 – 📺 ☎
CT u
12 rm 50.00/85.00.

Prince without rest., 6 Sumner Pl., SW7 3AB, ℰ 589 6488, 🌳 – 📺 ☎. 🖎 AE VISA. ⚘
CT s
20 rm ⊒ 35.00/80.00 **st.**

XXX **Bombay Brasserie,** Courtfield Close, 140 Gloucester Rd, SW7 4QH, ℰ 370 4040, Indian rest., « Raj-style decor, conservatory garden »
BS a

XX **Hilaire,** 68 Old Brompton Rd, SW7 3LQ, ℰ 584 8993 – 🔳. 🖎 AE ⓪ VISA
CT n
closed Saturday lunch and Sunday – **M** (booking essential) 15.50/23.50 **t.** ▮ 4.25.

XX **Reeds,** 152 Old Brompton Rd, SW5 0BE, ℰ 373 2445 – 🔳
BT a

XX **Brasserie de la Paix** (at Norfolk H.), 10 Harrington Rd, SW7 3ER, ℰ 581 5542, Telex 268852, Fax 581 1874 – 🔳. 🖎 AE ⓪ VISA
CS e
M (closed Saturday lunch) 14.50/16.75 **t.** and a la carte 18.50/23.50 **t.** ▮ 7.75.

XX **Tui,** 19 Exhibition Rd, SW7 2HE, ✆ 584 8359, Thai rest. – 🖼 AE ⓪ VISA   CS **u**
closed 25-26 December and Bank Holidays – **M** a la carte 12.00/17.00 **t.** ⏧ 3.75.

XX **Delhi Brasserie,** 134 Cromwell Rd, SW7 4HA, ✆ 370 7617, Indian rest. – 🗏. 🖼 AE ⓪
VISA   p. 19 EFZ **z**
closed 25 and 26 December – **M** 13.95 **t.** and a la carte 8.20/10.65 **t.**

XX **Golden Chopsticks,** 1 Harrington Rd, SW7 3ES, ✆ 584 0855, Chinese rest. – 🗏. 🖼 AE
⓪ VISA   CS **z**
closed Christmas – **M** 15.00 **t.** and a la carte 9.50/14.50 **t.** ⏧ 4.00.

XX **Memories of India,** 18 Gloucester Rd, SW7 4RB, ✆ 589 6450, Telex 265196, Fax 581 5980,
Indian rest. – 🖼 AE ⓪ VISA   BR **s**
M 11.50 **t.** and a la carte 8.80/14.35 **t.**

X **Chanterelle,** 119 Old Brompton Rd, SW7 3RN, ✆ 373 5522 – 🖼 AE ⓪ VISA   BT **v**
closed 4 days at Christmas – **M** 8.00/14.50 **t.** ⏧ 4.20.

X **Bangkok,** 9 Bute St., SW7 3EY, ✆ 584 8529, Thai bistro – 🗏. 🖼 AE VISA   CS **v**
closed Sunday, 1 week August and Bank Holiday Mondays – **M** a la carte 10.50/18.50 **t.**

KINGSTON UPON THAMES pp. 9 and 10.

🏌 Hampton Wick ✆ (081) 977 2433, by A 308 – 🏌 Coombe Wood, George Rd ✆ (081) 942 0388,
NE : 1 ¼ m. on A 308.
🛈 Wheatfield Way ✆ (081) 546 5386.

Kingston – ✉ Surrey – ☎ 081.
🏌 Malden, Traps Lane ✆ 942 0654.

🏨 **Kingston Lodge** (T.H.F.), Kingston Hill, KT2 7NP, ✆ 541 4481, Telex 936034, Fax 547 1013,
🚗 – ⇤ rm 📺 ☎ ⅙ Ⓟ – 🛋 70. 🖼 AE ⓪ VISA   CY **u**
M *(closed Saturday lunch)* 11.95/19.75 **st.** and a la carte ⏧ 3.50 – ⊊ 7.60 – **61 rm**
77.00/129.00 **st.** – SB (weekends only) 80.00 **st.**

XX **Gravier,** 9 Station Rd, Norbiton, KT2 7AA, ✆ 549 5557, French Seafood rest. – 🖼 AE ⓪
VISA   CY **x**
*closed Saturday lunch, Sunday, first week January, 1 week Easter, 24 July-8 August and 26 to
30 December* – **M** a la carte 17.15/31.45 **t.** ⏧ 3.25.

X **Ayudhya,** 14 Kingston Hill, KT2 7NH, ✆ 549 5984, Thai rest. – 🖼 AE ⓪ VISA   CY **z**
closed Saturday lunch, 25-26 December, 1 January and Bank Holidays – **M** a la carte
14.70/16.75 **st.** ⏧ 2.95.

Surbiton – ✉ Surrey – ☎ 081.

XX **Chez Max,** 85 Maple Rd, KT6 4AW, ✆ 399 2365 – 🖼 AE ⓪ VISA   BY **o**
closed Saturday lunch, Sunday, Monday and 2 weeks summer – **M** (booking essential)
16.50/23.50 **t.** and a la carte 15.85/21.50 **t.** ⏧ 4.25.

LAMBETH Except where otherwise stated see pp.10 and 11.

Brixton – ✉ SW9 – ☎ 071.

X **Twenty Trinity Gardens,** 20 Trinity Gdns., SW9 8DP, ✆ 733 8838 – 🖼 VISA   EX **n**
closed Saturday lunch, Sunday and 25 to 30 December – **M** 10.95/14.95 **t.** ⏧ 3.75.

Clapham Common – ✉ SW4 – ☎ 071.

XX **The Grafton,** 45 Old Town, SW4 0JL, ✆ 627 1048, French rest. – 🖼 AE ⓪ VISA
closed Saturday lunch, Sunday dinner, Monday, last 3 weeks August and 25 to 30 December
– **M** 12.50/22.50 **t.** and a la carte.   p. 13 DQ **a**

Streatham – ✉ SW16 – ☎ 081.

↑ **Barrow House** without rest., 45 Barrow Rd, SW16 5PE, ✆ 677 1925, 🚗 – ⇤. 🕱   EY **s**
closed 20 December-15 January – **5 rm** ⊊ 15.00/28.00 **st.**

Waterloo – ✉ SE1 – ☎ 071.

XX **La Rive Gauche,** 61 The Cut, SE1 8LL, ✆ 928 8645 – 🖼 AE ⓪ VISA   p. 21 MX **x**
closed Saturday lunch, Sunday, 24 December-3 January and Bank Holidays – **M** 16.50 **t.** and
a la carte 19.20/26.35 **t.** ⏧ 4.50.

XX **RSJ,** 13a Coin St., SE1 8YQ, ✆ 928 4554 – 🗏. 🖼 AE VISA   p. 21 MX **e**
closed Saturday lunch, Sunday and 24 to 27 December – **M** 13.75 **t.** and a la carte
15.75/19.25 **t.** ⏧ 4.75.

LEWISHAM – pp. 10 and 11.

Forest Hill – ⊠ SE23 – ☎ 081.

✗ Dewanian, 133-135 Stanstead Rd, SE23 1HH, ℰ 291 4778, Indian rest. – ▤   GX **a**

Upper Sydenham – ⊠ SE26 – ☎ 081.

🛈 Borough Mall, Lewisham Centre ℰ 318 5421 – Lewisham Library, High St. ℰ 690 8325.

✗✗ **Hornimans,** 124 Kirkdale, SE26 4BB, ℰ 291 2901 – ▣ *VISA*   GX **e**
closed lunch Monday, Tuesday and Saturday – **M** (lunch by arrangement)/dinner 10.95 **st.**
and a la carte 11.30/14.05 **st.** ◊ 2.60.

LONDON HEATHROW AIRPORT – see Hillingdon, London p. 61.

MERTON pp. 8 and 9.

Merton – ⊠ SW19 – ☎ 081.

🛈 Mitcham, Carshalton Rd ℰ 648 4197.

✗ Les Amoureux, 156 Merton Hall Rd, SW19 3PZ, ℰ 543 0567   DY **a**
M (dinner only).

Wimbledon – ⊠ SW19 – ☎ 081.

🏰 **Cannizaro House** (Thistle) ⤜, West Side, Wimbledon Common, SW19 4UF, ℰ 879 1464,
Telex 9413837, Fax 879 7338, ≤, « 18C country house overlooking Cannizaro Park », 🚗,
▤ 🖳 ☎ 🅿 – 🕍 25. ▣ 🆎 ⑩ *VISA*. ⅜   DXY **x**
M 16.50 **t.** and a la carte 23.90/46.00 **t.** – ⊊ 7.50 – **46 rm** 79.00/130.00 **st.**, **2 suites** 160.00 **t.**

⌂ **Worcester House** without rest., 38 Alwyne Rd, SW19 7AE, ℰ 946 1300 – 🖳 ☎. ▣ ⑩   DY **r**
VISA. ⅜
9 rm ⊊ 39.00/59.50 **st.**

✗✗ L'Herisson, 8 High St., SW19 5DX, ℰ 947 6477 – ▤   DY **c**

✗✗ Bayee Village, 24 High St., SW19 5DX, ℰ 947 3533, Chinese (Peking, Szechuan)
rest.   DX **i**

✗✗ San Lorenzo Fuoriporta, 38 Worple Rd Mews, SW19 4DB, ℰ 946 8463, Italian rest.   DY **n**

✗✗ **Wimbledon Palace,** 88 The Broadway, SW19 1RH, ℰ 540 4505, Chinese (Peking, Szechuan) rest. – ▤. ▣ 🆎 ⑩ *VISA*   DY **e**
closed Saturday lunch and 25-26 December – **M** 18.00 **t.** and a la carte 9.80/14.30 **t.** ◊ 3.80.

MICHELIN Distribution Centre, Deer Park Rd, Merton, SW19 3UN, ℰ 540 9034/7, FAX 542 7448
South London Branch (Merton) p. 9

REDBRIDGE pp. 6 and 7.

Ilford – ⊠ Essex.

🛈 Wanstead Park Rd ℰ 554 2930, by A 12.

✗✗ **Mandarin Palace,** 559 Cranbrook Rd, Gants Hill, IG2 6JZ, ℰ 550 7661, Chinese (Peking,
Canton) rest. – ▤. ▣ 🆎 ⑩ *VISA*   HU **e**
M a la carte 15.50/25.10 **st.** ◊ 2.70.

South Woodford – ⊠ Essex.

✗✗ **Ho-Ho,** 20 High Rd, E18 2QL, ℰ 989 1041, Chinese rest. – ▤. ▣ 🆎 ⑩ *VISA*   HU **c**
M 19.00 **t.** and a la carte.

Woodford – ⊠ Essex.

🏛 **Woodford Moat House** (Q.M.H.), 30 Oak Hill, Woodford Green, IG8 9NY, ℰ 505 4511,
Telex 264428, Fax 506 0941, 🚗 – ▤ 🖳 ☎ 🅿 – 🕍 250. ▣ 🆎 ⑩ *VISA*. ⅜   HT **c**
M (bar lunch Saturday) 15.00 **t.** and a la carte – **99 rm** ⊊ 69.00/85.00 **st.** – SB (weekends
only) 76.00/84.00 **st.**

🏛 **Prince Regent,** Manor Rd, Woodford Bridge, IG8 8AE, E : ¾ m. ℰ 504 7635, Fax 506 0807,
🚗 – ▤ rest 🖳 ☎ 🅿 – 🕍 175. ▣ 🆎 ⑩ *VISA*. ⅜   HT **a**
M 12.95/15.95 **t.** and a la carte ◊ 3.95 – **10 rm** ⊊ 59.00/77.50 **st.** – SB (weekends
only) 95.00/145.00 **st.**

Dans ce guide
un même symbole, un même mot,
imprimé en **noir** ou en rouge, en maigre ou en **gras,**
n'ont pas tout à fait la même signification.
Lisez attentivement les pages explicatives.

RICHMOND-UPON-THAMES pp. 8 and 9.

Barnes – ⊠ SW13 – ✆ 081.

XX **Sonny's,** 94 Church Rd, SW13 0DQ, ✆ 748 0393 – 🗐. 🔄 *VISA*   **CX x**
closed Saturday lunch, Sunday dinner, 25 to 30 December and Bank Holidays – **M** 9.50 **t.**
and a la carte 12.70/14.65 **t.** ◊ 2.85.

East Sheen – ⊠ SW14 – ✆ 081.

XX **Crowther's,** 481 Upper Richmond Rd West, SW14 7PU, ✆ 876 6372 – 🗐. 🔄 AE *VISA*
closed Monday and Saturday lunch, Sunday, 1 week Christmas-New Year and Bank Holidays
– **M** (booking essential) 15.00/23.00 **t.** ◊ 4.25.   **CX n**

X Le Tagliatelle, 180 Upper Richmond Road West, SW14 8AW, ✆ 876 6559, Italian
rest.   **CX i**

X **Taste of Raj,** 130 Upper Richmond Rd West, SW14 8DS, ✆ 876 8271, Indian rest. – 🔄 AE
⓪ *VISA*   **CX o**
M 9.00/11.00 **t.** *and a la carte* 8.50/10.45 **t.**

Hampton Court – ⊠ Surrey – ✆ 081.

🏨 Liongate, Hampton Court Rd, KT8 9BZ, ✆ 977 8121, Telex 928415 – 📺 ☎ 🅿 – 🔥 40. 🚫
24 rm.   **BY x**

Kew – ⊠ Surrey – ✆ 081.

XX **Le Mange Tout,** 3 Royal Par. (Station Approach), TW9 3QD, ✆ 940 9304 – 🗐. 🔄 AE ⓪
VISA   **CX r**
closed Saturday and Bank Holiday lunch, Sunday, 25-26 December and 1-2 January –
M 19.50 **t.** ◊ 4.25.

X **Jasper's Bun in the Oven,** 11 Kew Green, TW9 3AA, ✆ 940 3987 – 🔄 AE ⓪ *VISA*
closed Sunday and Bank Holidays – **M** (booking essential) 10.95 **t.** *and a la carte* 14.55/22.55 **t.**
◊ 3.55.   **CV e**

Richmond – ⊠ Surrey – ✆ 081.

🏌 , 🏌 Richmond Park ✆ 940 3205 – 🏌 Sudbrook Park ✆ 940 4351.
🗓 Old Town Hall, Whittaker Av. ✆ 940 9125.

🏨 **Petersham** 🐾, Nightingale Lane, Richmond Hill, TW10 6UZ, ✆ 940 7471, Group Telex
928556, Fax 940 9998, ≤, 🍴 – 📶 📺 ☎ 🅿 – 🔥 40. 🔄 AE ⓪ *VISA*. 🚫   **CX c**
M 19.00 **t.** *and a la carte* ◊ 5.00 – **54 rm** 🍵 80.00/150.00 **st.** – SB (weekends
only) 100.00/130.00 **st.**

🏨 Richmond Gate without rest., Richmond Hill, TW10 6RP, ✆ 940 0061, Group Telex 928556,
Fax 940 9998, 🍴 – 📺 ☎ 🅿 – 🔥 40. 🚫   **CX c**
51 rm.

🏨 Bingham, 61-63 Petersham Rd, TW10 6UT, ✆ 940 0902, Fax 948 8737, 🍴 – 📺 ☎   **CX z**
19 rm.

🏨 **Richmond Park** without rest., 3 Petersham Rd, TW10 6UH, ✆ 948 4666, Fax 940 7376 –
📺 ☎. 🔄 AE ⓪ *VISA*. 🚫   **CX v**
24 rm 🍵 58.00/73.00 **st.**

XX Kew Rendezvous, 110 Kew Rd, TW9 2PQ, ✆ 948 4343, Chinese (Peking) rest. – 🗐   **CX e**

XX **Lichfields,** 13 Lichfield Terr,. Sheen Rd, TW9 1AS, ✆ 940 5236 – 🔄 AE *VISA*   **CX s**
closed Saturday lunch, Sunday, Monday and 24 December-1 January – **M** 16.50 **st.** *and a la*
carte 21.50/26.00 **st.** ◊ 5.00.

XX **Evergreen,** 102-104 Kew Rd, TW9 2PQ, ✆ 940 9044, Chinese rest. – 🗐. 🔄 AE ⓪ *VISA*
closed 25 to 27 December – **M** *a la carte* 8.50/14.60 **t.**   **CX e**

XX **Bellini,** 12 The Quadrant, TW9 1DN, ✆ 940 0086, Italian rest. – 🔄 ⓪ *VISA*   **BX e**
closed Saturday lunch and Sunday – **M** 15.00/18.00 **st.** *and a la carte.*

Twickenham – ⊠ Middx. – ✆ 081.

🏌 Staines Rd ✆ 979 6946, W : 2 m. on A 305 – 🗓 District Library, Garfield Rd ✆ 892 0032.

XX **Cézanne,** 68 Richmond Rd, TW1 3BE, ✆ 892 3526 – 🔄 AE *VISA*   **BX a**
closed Saturday lunch, Sunday, 1 week Christmas and Bank Holidays – **M** *a la carte*
15.90/17.00 **t.** ◊ 3.50.

SOUTHWARK Except where otherwise stated see pp. 10 and 11.

Dulwich – ⊠ SE19 – ✆ 081.

XX **Luigi's,** 129 Gipsy Hill, SE19 1QS, ✆ 670 1843, Italian rest. – 🗐. 🔄 AE ⓪ *VISA*   **FX a**
closed Saturday lunch, Sunday and Bank Holidays – **M** *a la carte* 13.95/18.20 **t.** ◊ 4.25.

East Dulwich – ⊠ SE22 – ✆ 081.

X Mr Liu, 148 Lordship Lane, SE22, ✆ 693 8266, Chinese (Peking) rest. – 🗐   **FX r**
M (dinner only).

Peckham Rye – ⊠ SE22 – ☎ 081.

XX **L'Auberge,** 44 Forest Hill Rd, SE22 0RS, ℰ 299 2211, French rest. – ⬛ *VISA*   GX s
closed Sunday dinner and Monday – **M** *(dinner only and Sunday lunch)/dinner* 19.00 **t.**
♦ 3.50.

Southwark – ⊠ SE1 – ☎ 081.

X **Dining Room,** 1 Winchester Walk, London Bridge, SE1, off Cathedral St. ℰ 407 0337,
Vegetarian rest.   pp. 19-20. NPX a
closed Saturday, Sunday, Monday, Christmas and Bank Holidays – **M** 10.00 **t.**

SUTTON pp. 8 and 9.

Cheam – ⊠ Surrey – ☎ 081.

X **Al San Vincenzo,** 52 Upper Mulgrave Rd, SM2 7AJ, ℰ 661 9763, Italian rest. – ⬛ *VISA*
*closed Sunday, Monday, 1 week Easter, 3 weeks July-August and 1 week Christmas-New
Year* – **M** *(booking essential)* 21.00 **t.** ♦ 5.50.   DZ r

Sutton – ⊠ Surrey – ☎ 081.
ⓘ₈, ⓘ₉ Oak Sports Centre, Woodmansterne Rd ℰ 643 8363, E : 1 ¼ m. on B 278.

🏛 **Thatched House,** 135-139 Cheam Rd, SM1 2BN, ℰ 642 3131, 🛋 – ⬛ TV ☎ Ⓟ. ⬛
VISA   DZ e
M *(closed Saturday and Sunday)* (dinner only) 10.75 **st.** ♦ 3.25 – **29 rm** 立 32.50/55.00 **st.**

⌂ **Dene** without rest., 39 Cheam Rd, SM1 2AT, ℰ 642 3170, 🛋 – TV ☎ Ⓟ. ❄   DEZ v
28 rm 立 18.40/55.20 **t.**

XX **Partners 23,** 23 Stonecot Hill, SM3 9HB, ℰ 644 7743 – ⬛. ⬛ AE ⓿ *VISA*   DY z
closed Saturday lunch, Sunday, Monday, and 25 December-2 January – **M** *(booking essential)* 17.75/25.95 **t.** ♦ 4.00.

TOWER HAMLETS – pp. 6 and 7.

Limehouse – ⊠ E14 – ☎ 071 – 🅱 Mayfield House, Cambridge Heath Rd, ℰ 980 4831 ext
5313/5.

X **Good Friends,** 139-141 Salmon Lane, E14 7PG, ℰ 987 5541, Chinese (Canton, Peking)
rest. – ⬛ AE ⓿ *VISA*   GV a
M 15.00 **st.** and a la carte ♦ 3.50.

WANDSWORTH Except where otherwise stated see pp. 12 and 13.

Battersea – ⊠ SW8/SW11 – ☎ 071.

XXX ❀ **L'Arlequin** (Delteil), 123 Queenstown Rd, SW8 3RH, ℰ 622 0555, French rest. – ⬛. ⬛
AE ⓿ *VISA*   DQ c
closed Saturday, Sunday, 3 weeks August and 1 week at Christmas – **M** *(booking essential)*
17.50 **st.** *(lunch) and a la carte approx.* 50.00 **st.**
Spec. Petit chou farci à l'ancienne, Aiguillettes de canard en deux services, Soufflé chaud aux pruneaux
d'Agen.

XXX ❀ **Cavaliers'** (Cavalier), 129 Queenstown Rd, SW8 3RH, ℰ 720 6960 – ⬛ AE ⓿ *VISA*
closed Sunday, Monday, 2 weeks August and 2 weeks Christmas – **M** 16.50/29.50 **t.** ♦ 4.85
Spec. Lobster ravioli infused with it's oil and spiked with herbs, Bourride of fish in it's own juices lightly
thickened with aïoli, Wild crispy tuile with apricot ice cream and fresh fruit.   DQ e

XX **Lena's,** 196 Lavender Hill, SW11 1JA, ℰ 228 3735, Thai rest. – ⬛. ⬛ AE ⓿ *VISA*   CQ z
M *(dinner only)* 12.00 **t.** and a la carte approx. 16.20 **t.** ♦ 3.95.

XX **Ransome's,** Ransome's Dock, 35-37 Parkgate Rd, SW11 4NP, ℰ 223 1611 – Ⓟ. ⬛ AE ⓿
VISA   p. 20 HZ e
closed Saturday lunch, Sunday, 25-26 December, 1 January and Bank Holidays –
M 14.75/19.75 **t.**

XX **Chada,** 208-210 Battersea Park Rd, SW11 4ND, ℰ 622 2209, Thai rest. – ⬛. ⬛ AE ⓿ *VISA*
closed Saturday lunch, Sunday and Bank Holidays – **M** a la carte 10.00/16.45 **t.**   CQ x

Clapham – ⊠ SW11 – ☎ 071.

X **Pollyanna's,** 2 Battersea Rise, SW11 1ED, ℰ 228 0316 – ⬛ *VISA*   CQ v
closed Sunday dinner, 24 to 27 December and 1 January – **M** *(dinner only and Sunday
lunch)/dinner a la carte* 16.30/22.95 **t.** ♦ 4.50.

X **Jasmin,** 50 Battersea Rise, SW11 1EG, ℰ 228 0336, Chinese (Peking, Canton) rest. – ⬛
AE ⓿ *VISA*   CQ u
M 12.00/16.00 **st.** and a la carte approx. 15.00 **st.** ♦ 3.50.

X **La Bouffe,** 13 Battersea Rise, SW11 1HG, ℰ 228 3384 – ⬛. ⬛ *VISA*   CQ s
closed 24 to 30 December – **M** *(dinner only and Sunday lunch)/dinner* 15.95 **t.** ♦ 4.95.

Putney – ⊠ SW15 – ☎ 081.

XX **Bayee House,** 100 Upper Richmond Rd, SW15 2SP, ℰ 789 3161, Chinese (Peking, Szechuan)
rest. – ⬛   AQ z

X **Cassis,** 30 Putney High St., SW15, ℰ 788 8668 – ⬛ AE ⓿ *VISA*   AQ x
closed Saturday lunch, Sunday and 1 week at Christmas – **M** 15.50 **t.** ♦ 3.70.

Tooting – ✉ SW17 – ☎ 081.

✗ **Oh Boy,** 843 Garratt Lane, SW17 0PG, ✆ 947 9760, Thai rest. – 🗏. 🖂 AE ⑩ VISA   CR c
closed Sunday – **M** (booking essential) (dinner only) 15.50 **t.** and a la carte 9.45/11.95 **t.**
🍷 3.40.

Wandsworth – ✉ SW12/SW17/SW18 – ☎ 081.

✗✗✗ ❀❀ **Harvey's** (White), 2 Bellevue Rd, SW17 7EG, ✆ 672 0114 – 🗏. 🖂 VISA   CR e
closed Sunday – **M** (booking essential) 20.00/35.00 **t.**
Spec. Panaché de foie gras et St. Jacques au Sauternes, Canard challandais rôti aux baies de surreau, Poire
caramelisée et sa glace au miel.

✗✗ **Le Gothique,** Royal Victoria and Patriotic Building, Fitzhugh Grove, SW18 3SX, off Trinity
Rd ✆ 870 6567 – 🖂 AE ⑩ VISA   CQR i
closed Saturday lunch, Sunday and Bank Holidays – **M** 15.95 **t.** and a la carte 12.65/22.35 **t.**
🍷 3.50.

✗✗ **Liaison,** 11 Alma Rd, SW18 1AA, ✆ 870 4588 – 🖂 VISA   BQ r
closed Saturday lunch, Sunday, Monday, 25-26 December and Bank Holidays –
M 10.00/19.95 **t.** 🍷 4.75.

✗ **Bombay Bicycle Club,** 95 Nightingale Lane, SW12, ✆ 673 6217, Indian rest. – 🖂
VISA   DR o
closed Sunday, Christmas and Bank Holidays – **M** (dinner only) 14.00 **t.** and a la carte 🍷 4.00.

WESTMINSTER (City of)

Bayswater and Maida Vale – ✉ W2/W9 – ☎ 071 – Except where otherwise stated
see pp. 32 and 33.

🏨 **Royal Lancaster** (Rank), Lancaster Terr., W2 2TY, ✆ 262 6737, Telex 24822, Fax 724 3191,
≤ – 🛗 🗏 TV ☎ P – 🍴 1 400. 🖂 AE ⑩ VISA. 🛁   DZ e
M 17.00/23.00 **t.** and a la carte 🍷 5.00 – 🍵 10.50 – **398 rm** 125.00/190.00 **t., 20 suites**
275.00/800.00 **t.**

🏨 **Whites** (Mt. Charlotte), Bayswater Rd, 90-92 Lancaster Gate, W2 3NR, ✆ 262 2711, Telex
24771, Fax 262 2147 – 🛗 🗏 TV ☎ P   CZ v
52 rm, 2 suites.

🏨 **London Metropole,** Edgware Rd, W2 1JU, ✆ 402 4141, Telex 23711, Fax 724 8866, ≤ – 🛗
🗏 TV ☎ – 🍴 220. 🖂 AE ⑩ VISA. 🛁   p. 16 GU c
M (carving lunch) 13.90/18.75 **t.** and a la carte 14.95/32.65 **t.** 🍷 4.75 – 🍵 9.95 – **567 rm**
99.00/135.00 **t., 4 suites** 250.00/295.00 **t.**

🏨 **Plaza on Hyde Park** (Hilton), Lancaster Gate, W2 3NA, ✆ 262 5022, Telex 8954372, Fax
724 8666 – 🛗 ↔ rm TV ☎. 🖂 AE ⑩ VISA   DZ r
M 14.00 **t.** and a la carte 🍷 3.95 – 🍵 8.75 – **358 rm** 74.00/135.00 **st.**

🏨 **London Embassy** (Embassy), 150 Bayswater Rd, W2 4RT, ✆ 229 1212, Telex 27727, Fax
229 2623 – 🛗 ↔ rm 🗏 TV ☎ P – 🍴 120. 🖂 AE ⑩ VISA   BZ o
M (carving rest.) 6.75/10.95 **st.** and a la carte 🍷 4.40 – 🍵 6.75 – **192 rm** 75.00/97.50 **st.,**
1 suite 140.00 **st.** – SB (weekends only) 91.90 **st.**

🏨 **Hospitality Inn** (Mt. Charlotte), 104 Bayswater Rd, W2 3HL, ✆ 262 4461, Telex 22667, Fax
706 4560, ≤ – 🛗 🗏 TV ☎ P – **174 rm, 1 suite**.   CZ o

🏨 **Mornington** (Best Western) without rest., 12 Lancaster Gate, W2 3LG, ✆ 262 7361, Telex
24281, Fax 706 1028 – 🛗 TV ☎. 🖂 AE ⑩ VISA   DZ s
🍵 3.00 – **68 rm** 64.00/84.00 **st**

🏨 **Alpha Royale,** 35-39 Leinster Gdns, W2 2AR, ✆ 258 0269, Telex 268613 – 🛗 TV ☎ – 🍴 80
100 rm.   CZ o

🏨 **Delmere,** 130 Sussex Gdns., W2 1UB, ✆ 706 3344, Telex 8953857, Fax 262 1863 – TV ☎.
🖂 AE ⑩ VISA. 🛁   DZ v
M 6.75/9.95 **st.** and a la carte 🍷 3.95 – 🍵 5.50 – **40 rm** 61.60/75.50 **st.** – SB (weekends
only) 65.00 **st.**

🏨 **Camelot** without rest., 45-47 Norfolk Sq., W2 1RX, ✆ 262 1980, Telex 268312 – 🛗 TV. 🖂
VISA. 🛁   DZ c
43 rm 🍵 32.00/62.00 **st.**

🏨 **Parkwood** without rest., 4 Stanhope Pl., W2 2HB, ✆ 402 2241, Fax 402 1574 – ↔ TV ☎.
🖂 VISA. 🛁   EZ e
18 rm 🍵 38.75/63.75 **st.**

✗✗✗ **Bombay Palace,** 50 Connaught St., Hyde Park Sq., W2 2AA, ✆ 723 8855, North Indian
rest. – 🖂 AE ⑩ VISA   EZ o
M 9.95/20.00 **t.** and a la carte 16.55/21.75 **t.**

✗✗ **San Marino,** 26 Sussex Pl., W2 2TH, ✆ 723 8395, Italian rest. – 🖂 AE ⑩ VISA   DZ u
closed Sunday and Bank Holidays – **M** a la carte 16.00/23.50 **t.** 🍷 3.50.

✗ **Fortune Cookie,** 1 Queensway, W2 4QJ, ✆ 727 7260, Chinese rest. – 🖂 VISA   BZ e
M 8.00 **t.** and a la carte.

✗ **Kalamaras Taverna,** 76-78 Inverness Mews, W2 3JQ, ✆ 727 9122, Greek rest. – 🖂 AE
⑩ VISA   BZ a
closed Sunday and Bank Holidays – **M** (dinner only) 14.50 **t.** and a la carte 12.70/16.00 **t.**
🍷 3.30.

Belgravia – ⌧ SW1 – ☎ 071 – Except where otherwise stated see pp. 30 and 31.

Berkeley, Wilton Pl., SW1X 7RL, ☎ 235 6000, Telex 919252, Fax 235 4330, 🖾 – ⁅ ▤ 📺 ☎ 🅫 ⇆ – 🔬 220. 🆘 AE ⓪ VISA 🛇   FQ e
M *Restaurant (closed Saturday)* – **Buttery** *(closed Sunday)* – **133 rm** 140.00/240.00 st., **27 suites** 390.00/700.00 st.

Belgravia-Sheraton, 20 Chesham Pl., SW1X 8HQ, ☎ 235 6040, Telex 919020, Fax 259 6243 – ⁅ ⇆ rm ▤ 📺 ☎. 🆘 AE ⓪ VISA 🛇   FR u
M *(closed lunch Saturday and Bank Holidays)* 20.25/25.00 t. and a la carte 🍶 5.50 – 🍵 11.00 – **82 rm** 140.00/205.00 s., **7 suites** 245.00/280.00 s. – SB (weekends only) (except December, January and summer) 96.00/193.00 st.

Lowndes Thistle (Thistle), 21 Lowndes St., SW1X 9ES, ☎ 235 6020, Telex 919065, Fax 235 1154 – ⁅ ⇆ rm ▤ rest 📺 ☎. 🆘 AE ⓪ VISA 🛇   FR i
M 17.50 t. (lunch) and a la carte 🍶 4.75 – 🍵 8.50 – **74 rm** 115.00/160.00 st., **5 suites** 215.00 st.

Al Bustan, 27 Motcomb St., SW1X 8JU, ☎ 235 1668, Lebanese rest. – ▤. 🆘 AE ⓪ VISA
M a la carte 13.25/22.75 t. 🍶 5.00.   FR z

Motcombs, 26 Motcomb St., SW1X 8JU, ☎ 235 6382   FR z

Hyde Park and Knightsbridge – ⌧ SW1/SW7 – ☎ 071 – pp. 30 and 31.
🛈 Harrods, Knightsbridge, SW1 ☎ 730 3488.

Hyde Park (T.H.F.), 66 Knightsbridge, SW1Y 7LA, ☎ 235 2000, Telex 262057, Fax 235 4552, ⇆ – ⁅ ⇆ rm ▤ 📺 ☎ – 🔬 230. 🆘 AE ⓪ VISA   EQ v
M 19.50/40.00 st. and a la carte 30.00/36.50 st. – 🍵 13.00 – **167 rm** 200.00/270.00 st., **19 suites** 425.00/1 050.00 st. – SB (weekends only) 180.00/240.00 st.

One Sixteen, 116 Knightsbridge, SW1X 7PJ, ☎ 823 9983 – 🆘 AE ⓪ VISA   EQ a
closed Sunday, 1 week Easter, 2 weeks August, 1 week Christmas and Bank Holidays –
M 20.00/40.00 st. and a la carte 29.00/36.00 st. 🍶 8.50.

Montpeliano, 13 Montpelier St., SW7 1HQ, ☎ 589 0032, Italian rest.   ER e

Mayfair – ⌧ W1 – ☎ 071 – pp. 28 and 29.

Claridge's, Brook St., W1A 2JQ, ☎ 629 8860, Telex 21872, Fax 499 2210 – ⁅ ▤ 📺 ☎. 🆘 AE ⓪ VISA 🛇   BL c
M a la carte 28.00/55.00 st. 🍶 4.10 – **Causerie** 14.50 st. (lunch) and a la carte 21.30/35.50 st. – 🍵 12.50 – **138 rm** 175.00/250.00 st., **53 suites** 425.00/900.00 st.

Grosvenor House (T.H.F.), Park Lane, W1A 3AA, ☎ 499 6363, Telex 24871, Fax 493 3341, 🖾 – ⁅ ⇆ rm ▤ 📺 ☎ 🅫 🅿 – 🔬 2 000. 🆘 AE ⓪ VISA 🛇   AM a
M (see **90 Park Lane** below) – 🍵 9.75 – **397 rm** 160.00/185.00 st., **57 suites** 285.00/620.00 st.

Inn on the Park, Hamilton Pl., Park Lane, W1A 1AZ, ☎ 499 0888, Telex 22771, Fax 493 1895 – ⁅ ⇆ rm ▤ 📺 ☎ ⇆ – 🔬 600. 🆘 AE ⓪ VISA 🛇   BP a
M – **Lanes** 27.00/32.00 st. and dinner a la carte 29.00/33.50 st. 🍶 6.00 – see also **Four Seasons** rest. below) – **209 rm** 175.00/215.00 s., **19 suites** 330.00/700.00 s.

Le Meridien Londres, Piccadilly, W1V 0BH, ☎ 734 8000, Telex 25795, Fax 437 3574, 🖾, squash – ⁅ ▤ 📺 ☎ 🅫 – 🔬 250. 🆘 AE ⓪ VISA 🛇   EM a
M (see **Oak Room** below) – 🍵 9.50 – **265 rm** 160.00/200.00, **19 suites** 230.00/290.00.

❀ **Connaught**, 16 Carlos Pl., W1Y 6AL, ☎ 499 7070 – ⁅ ▤ rest 📺 ☎. 🆘. 🛇   BM e
M (booking essential) – **90 rm, 24 suites**
Spec. Pâté de turbot froid au homard, sauce pudeur, Rendez-vous du pêcheur, sauce légère au parfum d'Armorique, Salmis de canard strasbourgeoise en surprise.

Fortyseven Park Street, 47 Park St., W1Y 4EB, ☎ 491 7282, Telex 22116, Fax 491 7281 – ⁅ ▤ 📺 ☎. 🆘 AE ⓪ VISA 🛇   AM c
M (see **Le Gavroche** below) – , **52 suites** 225.00/335.00 s.

Brown's (T.H.F.), 29-34 Albemarle St., W1A 4SW, ℰ 493 6020, Telex 28686, Fax 493 9381 – 🛗 ⇔ rm 📺 ☎ – 🔥 70. 🆘 AE ⓞ VISA. 🕸
DM e
M 24.75/29.00 **st.** and a la carte ▯5.75 – ⊒ 9.75 – **127 rm** 145.00/190.00 **st.**, **6 suites** 310.00/380.00 **st.**

May Fair (Inter-Con.), Stratton St., W1A 2AN, ℰ 629 7777, Telex 262526, Fax 629 1459 – 🛗 ▤ 📺 ☎ – 🔥 300. 🆘 AE ⓞ VISA. 🕸
DN z
M (see Le Chateau below) – ⊒ 10.50 – **283 rm** 162.00/232.50 **t.**, **24 suites** 385.00/1 075.00 **t.**

Westbury (T.H.F.), Conduit St., W1A 4UH, ℰ 629 7755, Telex 24378, Fax 495 1163 – 🛗 ⇔ rm ▤ 📺 ☎ ♿ Ⓟ – 🔥 120 – **228 rm**, **15 suites**.
DM a

Inter-Continental (Inter-Con.), 1 Hamilton Pl., Hyde Park Corner, W1V 0QY, ℰ 409 3131, Telex 25853, Fax 409 7460 – 🛗 ⇔ rm ▤ 📺 ☎ ⇔ – 🔥 500. 🆘 AE ⓞ VISA. 🕸
BP o
M (see Le Soufflé below) – ⊒ 11.00 – **472 rm** 170.00/185.00, **19 suites** 270.00/1 025.00.

Britannia (Inter-Con.), Grosvenor Sq., W1A 3AN, ℰ 629 9400, Telex 23941, Fax 629 7736 – 🛗 ⇔ rm ▤ 📺 ☎ – 🔥 80. 🕸
BM x
M (see Shogun below) – ⊒ 9.70 – **342 rm**, **11 suites**.

Londonderry (T.H.F.), Park Lane, W1Y 8AP, ℰ 493 7292, Telex 263292, Fax 495 1395 – 🛗 ▤ 📺 ☎ ⇔ – 🔥 170. 🆘 AE ⓞ VISA. 🕸
BP i
M 17.50/25.00 **st.** and a la carte 18.50/30.50 **st.** ▯5.00 – ⊒ 9.75 – **135 rm** 140.00/185.00 **st.**, **13 suites** 250.00/525.00 **st.**

Marriott, Duke St., Grosvenor Sq., W1A 4AW, ℰ 493 1232, Telex 268101, Fax 491 3201 – 🛗 ▤ 📺 ☎ ♿ – 🔥 1 000. 🆘 AE ⓞ VISA. 🕸
BL a
M (closed Saturday lunch and Sunday dinner) 18.00 **t.** (lunch) and a la carte 19.90/28.20 **t.** – ⊒ 8.50 – **206 rm** 170.00/200.00, **17 suites** 310.00/390.00.

London Hilton on Park Lane (Hilton), 22 Park Lane, W1A 2HH, ℰ 493 8000, Telex 24873, Fax 493 4957, ≼London – 🛗 ⇔ rm ▤ 📺 ☎ ♿ – 🔥 900. 🆘 AE ⓞ VISA. 🕸
BP e
M 25.50/60.00 **st.** and a la carte ▯7.00 – **392 rm** 155.00/200.00 **s.**, **54 suites** 280.00/1 050.00 **s.**

Park Lane, Piccadilly, W1Y 8BX, ℰ 499 6321, Telex 21533, Fax 499 1965 – 🛗 ⇔ rm 📺 ☎ Ⓟ – 🔥 750. 🆘 AE ⓞ VISA
BP x
M 17.50/27.00 **st.** and a la carte 16.25/30.50 **st.** ▯5.50 – ⊒ 9.25 – **266 rm** 149.00/189.00 **st.**, **54 suites** 200.00/500.00 **st.**

Athenaeum (Rank), 116 Piccadilly, W1V 0BJ, ℰ 499 3464, Telex 261589, Fax 493 1860 – 🛗 ⇔ rm ▤ 📺 ☎ – 🔥 45. 🆘 AE ⓞ VISA. 🕸
CP s
M 20.00/35.00 **t.** and a la carte 23.50/30.00 **t.** ▯5.75 – ⊒ 10.00 – **104 rm** 140.00/180.00 **t.**, **8 suites** 225.00/270.00 **t.** – SB (weekends only) 126.00/138.00 **st.**

Holiday Inn (Holiday Inn), 3 Berkeley St., W1X 6NE, ℰ 493 8282, Telex 24561, Fax 629 2827 – 🛗 ⇔ rm ▤ 📺 ☎ – 🔥 70. 🆘 AE ⓞ VISA. 🕸
DN r
M (closed Saturday lunch) 13.75/18.50 **st.** and a la carte 11.95/26.50 **st.** – ⊒ 9.25 – **179 rm** 140.00/185.00 **st.**, **7 suites** 300.00/550.00 **st.** – SB (weekends only) 78.50/108.50 **st.**

Chesterfield, 35 Charles St., W1X 8LX, ℰ 491 2622, Telex 269394, Fax 491 4793 – 🛗 📺 ☎ – 🔥 100. 🆘 AE ⓞ VISA. 🕸 – **M** 16.50/19.50 **t.** and a la carte 17.25/28.95 **t.** ▯5.00 – ⊒ 8.50 – **106 rm** 100.00/140.00 **st.**, **4 suites** 165.00/225.00 **st.**
CN c

Washington, Curzon St., W1 8DT, ℰ 499 7000, Telex 24540, Fax 495 6172 – 🛗 ▤ 📺 ☎ – 🔥 80. 🆘 AE ⓞ VISA. 🕸 – **M** 15.50 **t.** (lunch) and dinner a la carte ▯4.50 – ⊒ 9.95 – **169 rm** 128.00/208.00 **st.**, **4 suites** 225.00/325.00 **st.**
CN s

Green Park, Half Moon St., W1Y 8BP, ℰ 629 7522, Telex 28856, Fax 491 8971 – 🛗 ⇔ rm ▤ rest 📺 ☎ – 🔥 70. 🆘 AE ⓞ VISA. 🕸
CN a
M 14.00 **t.** and a la carte – ⊒ 7.95 – **160 rm** 85.00/160.00 **st.**

Hilton Mews at Park Lane (Hilton) without rest., 2 Stanhope Row, W1Y 7HE, ℰ 493 7222, Telex 24665, Fax 629 9423 – 🛗 ⇔ ▤ 📺 ☎ – 🔥 55. 🆘 AE ⓞ VISA
BP u
70 rm ⊒ 106.00/128.00 **st.**, **1 suite** 250.00/290.00 **st.**

Flemings, 7-12 Half Moon St., W1Y 7RA, ℰ 499 2964, Telex 27510, Fax 629 4063 – 🛗 ⇔ rest 📺 ☎. 🆘 AE ⓞ VISA. 🕸
CN z
M 14.50 **st.** and a la carte ▯5.00 – ⊒ 8.95 – **137 rm** 82.50/145.00 **st.**

XXXXX 90 Park Lane (T.H.F.), (at Grosvenor House H.), Park Lane, W1A 3AA, ℰ 499 6363, Telex 24871, Fax 493 3341 – ▤. 🆘 AE ⓞ VISA
AM a
closed Saturday lunch and Sunday – **M** a la carte approx. 35.00 **st.** ▯5.95.

XXXXX ❁ Oak Room (at Le Meridien Londres H.), Piccadilly, W1V 0BH, ℰ 734 8000, Telex 25795, Fax 437 3574, French rest. – ▤. 🆘 AE ⓞ VISA
EM a
closed Saturday lunch, Sunday and Bank Holidays – **M** 19.50 **t.** (lunch) and a la carte 24.50/36.00 **t.**
Spec. Gazpacho de langoustines à la crème de courgettes, Suprême de canard et son petit farci de chou truffé, Saint-Jacques poêlées sur lit de pommes et olives noires.

XXXX ❁ Four Seasons (at Inn on the Park H.), Hamilton Pl., Park Lane, W1A 1AZ, ℰ 499 0888, Telex 22771, Fax 493 1895, French rest. – ▤ ⇔. 🆘 AE ⓞ VISA
BP a
M 21.00/38.00 **st.** and a la carte 32.50/39.00 **st.** ▯6.00
Spec. Coquilles St. Jacques grillées et grecque de légumes, Poulet de Bresse rôti au jus, sa cuisse cuite à la vapeur, Nougat glacé, salade de fruits au gingembre.

XXXX ❁❁❁ Le Gavroche (Roux), 43 Upper Brook St., W1P 1PF, ℰ 408 0881, French rest. – ▤. 🆘 AE ⓞ VISA
AM c
closed Saturday, Sunday, 22 December-2 January and Bank Holidays – **M** (booking essential) 22.50/50.00 **st.** and a la carte 36.30/69.30 **st.**
Spec. Soufflé suissesse, Assiette du boucher, Sablé aux fraises.

XXXX ❀ **Le Soufflé** (at Inter-Continental H.), 1 Hamilton Pl., Hyde Park Corner, W1V 0QY, ℰ 409 3131, Telex 25853, Fax 493 3476 – 🔲 🚗. 🔺 AE ⓞ VISA
M 22.50/36.50 and a la carte ♦ 5.50   BP o
Spec. Soufflé de saumon fumé aux morilles, sauce cressonnette, Croustade soufflée au fromage Beaufort et
jambon de canard, Rouelles de volaille de Bresse aux langoustines et truffes.

XXXX **Le Chateau** (Inter-Con), (at Mayfair H.) Stratton St., W1A 2AN, ℰ 629 7777, Telex 262526,
Fax 629 1459, French rest. – 🔲. 🔺 AE ⓞ VISA   DN z
closed Saturday lunch – **M** 18.50/28.50 t. and a la carte ♦ 6.50.

XXX **Princess Garden,** 8-10 North Audley St., W1Y 1WF, ℰ 493 3223, Fax 938 4694, Chinese
(Peking) rest. – 🔲. 🔺 AE ⓞ VISA   AL z
M 40.00 t. (dinner) and a la carte 20.00/30.00 ♦ 6.00.

XXX **Zen Central,** 20 Queen St., W1X 7PJ, ℰ 629 8089, Fax 437 0641, Chinese rest. – 🔲. 🔺 AE
ⓞ VISA   CN x
M a la carte approx. 16.00 t. ♦ 10.00.

XX **Greenhouse,** 27a Hay's Mews, W1X 7RJ, ℰ 499 3331 – 🔺 AE ⓞ VISA   BN a
closed 24 December-2 January and Bank Holidays – **M** a la carte 14.90/22.50 t. ♦ 6.95.

XX **Number 10,** 10 Old Burlington St., W1X 1LA, ℰ 439 1099, English rest. – 🔲. 🔺 AE ⓞ VISA
closed Saturday, Sunday and Bank Holidays – **M** 17.95 t. (lunch) and a la carte 18.95/31.45 t.
♦ 4.50.   DM c

XX **Copper Chimney,** 13 Heddon St., W1R 7LF, ℰ 439 2004, Indian rest. – 🔲. 🔺 AE ⓞ VISA
closed Sunday – **M** 18.00/22.00 **st.** and a la carte 18.00/24.00 **st.** ♦ 5.00.   EM e

XX **Langan's Brasserie,** Stratton St., W1X 5FD, ℰ 491 8822 – 🔺 AE ⓞ VISA   DN e
closed Saturday lunch, Sunday, Easter, Christmas and Bank Holidays – **M** (booking essential)
a la carte 13.65/22.60 t. ♦ 4.50.

XX Fakhreldine, 85 Piccadilly, W1V 9HD, ℰ 493 3424, Lebanese rest. – 🔲   CN u

XX **Al Hamra,** 31-33 Shepherd Market, W1Y 7RJ, ℰ 493 1954, Lebanese rest. – 🔺 AE ⓞ VISA
closed 25 December and 1 January – **M** a la carte 12.40/25.00 t. ♦ 5.00.   BCN n

XX **Miyama,** 38 Clarges St., W1Y 7PJ, ℰ 499 2443, Japanese rest. – 🔲. 🔺 AE ⓞ VISA   CN e
closed Saturday lunch, Sunday and Bank Holidays – **M** 12.00/38.00 t. and a la carte
14.30/28.50 t. ♦ 8.00.

XX **Mr. Kai,** 65 South Audley St., W1Y 5FD, ℰ 493 8988, Chinese (Peking) rest. – 🔲. 🔺 AE
ⓞ VISA   BM v
M a la carte 24.00/40.00 **st.** ♦ 5.00.

XX **Ho-Ho,** 29 Maddox St., W1R 9LD, ℰ 493 1228, Chinese rest. – 🔲. 🔺 AE ⓞ VISA   DL x
closed Sunday and Bank Holidays – **M** 24.00 **st.** and a la carte 16.00/26.50 t. ♦ 7.00.

XX **Shogun** (at Britannia H.), Adams Row, W1Y 5DE, ℰ 493 1255, Japanese rest. – 🔺 AE ⓞ
VISA   BM x
closed Monday and Christmas – **M** (dinner only) 25.00 t. and a la carte 11.50/22.00 t. ♦ 8.00.

X Saga, 43-44 South Molton St., W1Y 1HB, ℰ 408 2236, Japanese rest. – 🔲   BK a

X **Ikeda,** 30 Brook St., W1Y 1AG, ℰ 629 2730, Japanese rest. – 🔲. 🔺 AE ⓞ VISA   CKL a
closed Saturday and Sunday – **M** 12.00/30.00 t. and a la carte 17.40/27.50 t.

🛈 Selfridges, Oxford St., W1 ℰ 730 3488.

🏨 **Churchill,** 30 Portman Sq., W1A 4ZX, ℰ 486 5800, Telex 264831, Fax 935 0431, ✗ – 🛗 🔲
📺 ☎ & 🅿 – 🔬 250. 🔺 AE ⓞ VISA   AJ x
M *(closed Sunday)* 25.00 t. (lunch) and a la carte 23.00/44.00 t. – ☲ 11.50 – **422 rm**
150.00/210.00, **30 suites** 275.00/750.00.

🏨 **Portman Inter-Continental** (Inter-Con.), 22 Portman Sq., W1H 9FL, ℰ 486 5844, Telex
261526, Fax 935 0537, ✗ – 🛗 ✗ rm 🔲 📺 ☎ & 🅿 – 🔬 400. 🔺 AE ⓞ VISA. ✿   AJ o
M 17.00/28.50 t. and a la carte ♦ 6.80 – ☲ 9.50 – **266 rm** 135.00/155.00 s., **8 suites**
265.00/600.00 s.

🏨 **Selfridge** (Thistle), 400 Orchard St., W1H 0JS, ℰ 408 2080, Telex 22361, Fax 629 8849 – 🛗
✗ rm 🔲 📺 ☎ – 🔬 220. 🔺 AE ⓞ VISA. ✿   AK e
M 16.95 t. and a la carte 15.00/30.00 t. – ☲ 8.50 – **298 rm** 115.00/185.00 st.

Berkshire, 350 Oxford St., W1N 0BY, ℰ 629 7474, Telex 22270, Fax 629 8156 – 闤 ⇔ rm 囯 TV ☎. ◪ AE ⓪ VISA — BK n
M 17.95/21.00 t. and a la carte 25.00/35.00 t. 📶 5.00 – � 12.00 – **137 rm** 142.00/180.00 st., **3 suites** 350.00/395.00 st.

Holiday Inn (Holiday Inn), 134 George St., W1H 6DN, ℰ 723 1277, Telex 27983, Fax 402 0666, ◪ – 闤 ⇔ rm 囯 TV ☎ ⚐ ℗ – 齒 120. ◪ AE ⓪ VISA — p. 33 EZ i
M 14.50/20.00 t. and a la carte 📶 6.25 – ⊐ 9.25 – **239 rm** 136.00/152.00 st., **2 suites** 395.00/495.00 st.

Ramada H. London, 10 Berners St., W1A 3BE, ℰ 636 1629, Telex 25759, Fax 580 3972 – 闤 ⇔ rm TV ☎ ⚐ – 齒 300. ◪ AE ⓪ VISA. 猋 — EJ r
M 13.75 st. and a la carte 📶 5.00 – ⊐ 8.50 – **232 rm** 76.00/140.00 st., **3 suites** 192.00/230.00 st.

Clifton Ford, 47 Welbeck St., W1M 8DN, ℰ 486 6600, Telex 22569, Fax 486 7492 – 闤 TV ☎. ◪ AE ⓪ VISA — BH a
M (light lunch)/dinner a la carte 19.00/26.50 t. 📶 5.00 – ⊐ 9.50 – **222 rm** 95.00/175.00, **3 suites** 200.00/500.00.

Dorset Square, 39-40 Dorset Sq., NW1 6QN, ℰ 723 7874, Telex 263964, Fax 724 3328, « Attractively furnished Regency town houses » – 闤 囯 TV ☎. ◪ AE VISA — p. 16 HU s
M 15.00 t. and a la carte 📶 4.50 – ⊐ 9.00 – **37 rm** 70.00/140.00 st., **12 suites** 150.00 st. – SB 133.00/188.00 st.

Montcalm, Great Cumberland Pl., W1A 2LF, ℰ 402 4288, Telex 28710, Fax 724 9180 – 闤 囯 TV ☎ — p. 33 EZ x
101 rm, 15 suites.

St. George's (T.H.F.), Langham Pl., W1N 8QS, ℰ 580 0111, Telex 27274, Fax 436 7997, ⇐ – 闤 ⇔ rm 囯 rest TV ☎. ◪ AE ⓪ VISA — pp. 16-17 JKU a
M 16.00/25.00 st. and a la carte 📶 6.00 – ⊐ 9.25 – **83 rm** 90.00/120.00 st., **3 suites** 150.00/275.00 st.

Hilton International (Hilton), 18 Lodge Rd, NW8 7JT, ℰ 722 7722, Telex 23101, Fax 483 2408 – 闤 ⇔ rm 囯 TV ☎ ℗ – 齒. ◪ AE ⓪ VISA — p. 16 GT v
M (carving rest.) 18.50/23.50 t. and a la carte 12.30/24.85 t. 📶 4.35 – ⊐ 8.50 – **374 rm** 95.00/120.00 t., **3 suites** 165.00/175.00 st.

Cumberland (T.H.F.), Marble Arch, W1A 4RF, ℰ 262 1234, Telex 22215, Fax 724 4621 – 闤 ⇔ rm 囯 rest TV ☎ – 齒 1 000 — AK n
M (see **Mon** below) – **898 rm, 9 suites**.

Durrants, 26-32 George St., W1H 6BJ, ℰ 935 8131, Telex 894919, Fax 487 3510, « Converted Georgian houses with Regency façade » – 闤 TV ☎ – 齒 50. ◪ AE VISA. 猋 — AH e
M a la carte 18.00/22.50 t. 📶 4.50 – ⊐ 7.50 – **93 rm** 50.00/92.00 st., **3 suites** 175.00 st.

Sherlock Holmes (Hilton) without rest., 108 Baker St., W1M 1LB, ℰ 486 6161, Telex 8954837, Fax 486 0884 – 闤 ⇔ rm TV ☎ – 齒 70. ◪ AE ⓪ VISA — p. 16 HU a
M (bar lunch)/dinner 14.50 st. 📶 4.95 – ⊐ 9.50 – **126 rm** 105.00/135.00 st.

Regent Crest (Crest), Carburton St., W1P 8EE, ℰ 388 2300, Telex 22453, Fax 387 2806 – 闤 ⇔ rm 囯 rest TV ☎ ℗ – 齒 500. ◪ AE ⓪ VISA. 猋 — pp. 16-17 JKU i
M (closed Sunday lunch and Bank Holidays) 15.00 st. and a la carte 📶 5.40 – ⊐ 9.60 – **311 rm** 97.00/123.00 st., **6 suites** 220.00/262.50 st.

Savoy Court, 13-25 Granville Pl., W1H 0EH, ℰ 408 0130, Telex 8955515, Fax 493 2070 – 闤 TV 猂. ◪ AE ⓪ VISA 猋 — AK c
M 5.00/8.00 st. and a la carte 📶 4.50 – ⊐ 7.50 – **97 rm** 69.00/96.00 st.

Harewood (Best Western), Harewood Row, NW1 6SE, ℰ 262 2707, Telex 297226, Fax 262 2975 – 闤 TV ☎. ◪ AE ⓪ VISA. 猋 — p. 16 HU x
M (closed lunch Saturday and Sunday) (grill rest.) 11.95/16.95 t. 📶 5.25 – ⊐ 6.95 – **93 rm** 65.00/100.00 st. – SB (weekends only) 60.00/90.00 st.

Bryanston Court (Best Western), 56-60 Great Cumberland Pl., W1H 7FD, ℰ 262 3141, Group Telex 262076, Fax 262 7248 – 闤 TV ☎. ◪ AE ⓪ VISA — p. 33 EZ z
M (closed Saturday and Sunday) (grill rest.) (dinner only) – ⊐ 6.00 – **54 rm** 65.00/80.00 st.

Hallam without rest., 12 Hallam St., W1N 5LJ, ℰ 580 1166 – 闤 TV ☎. ◪ AE ⓪ VISA 猋 — pp. 16-17 JKU r
23 rm ⊐ 45.00/66.00 st.

Blandford without rest., 80 Chiltern St., W1M 1PS, ℰ 486 3103, Telex 262594, Fax 487 2786 – 闤 TV ☎. ◪ AE ⓪ VISA. 猋 — p. 16 HU i
33 rm ⊐ 53.00/66.35 st.

Concorde without rest., 50 Great Cumberland Pl., W1H 7FD, ℰ 402 6169, Group Telex 262076, Fax 262 7248 – 闤 TV ☎. ◪ AE ⓪ VISA. 猋 — p. 33 EZ n
closed 22 December-2 January – ⊐ 6.00 – **28 rm** 60.00/70.00 st.

Edward Lear without rest., 28-30 Seymour St., W1H 5WD, ℰ 402 5401, Fax 706 3766 – TV ☎. ◪ VISA. 猋 — AK a
30 rm ⊐ 37.50/49.50 st.

P.T.O. →

XXXX ✿✿ **Chez Nico** (Ladenis), 35 Great Portland St., W1N 5DD, ✆ 436 8846, French rest. – ▤. ◪ ◑ **VISA**
DJ c
closed Bank Holiday lunch, Saturday, Sunday, 4 days at Easter and 3 weeks August –
M (booking essential) 25.00/42.00 **st.** ▮ 8.00
Spec. Mille-feuille de langoustines aux épinards, Turbot aux pommes croquantes, Coupe de framboises à la vanille.

XXX **Jason's Court,** Jason's Court, 76 Wigmore St., ✆ 224 2992, English rest. – ▤. ◪ AE ◑ **VISA**
BJ a
closed Saturday lunch, Sunday, 19 August-4 September, 25 December-2 January and Bank Holidays – **M** 15.00 **t.** (lunch) and a la carte 20.50/33.50 **t.** ▮ 4.75.

XXX **Rue St. Jacques,** 5 Charlotte St., W1P 1HD, ✆ 637 0222, French rest. – ▤. ◪ AE ◑ **VISA**
p. 17 KU c
closed Saturday lunch, Sunday, Christmas-New Year and Bank Holidays – **M** 19.50/32.00 **t.**

XXX **Martin's,** 239 Baker St., NW1 6XE, ✆ 935 3130 – ▤. ◪ AE ◑ **VISA**
p. 16 HU u
closed Saturday lunch, Sunday, Christmas and Bank Holidays – **M** 17.50 **t.** (lunch) and a la carte 19.00/27.50 **t.** ▮ 5.00.

XXX **Odins,** 27 Devonshire St., W1N 1RJ, ✆ 935 7296 – ◪ AE ◑ **VISA**
p. 16 JU n
closed Saturday lunch, Sunday, Easter, Christmas and Bank Holidays – **M** a la carte 19.85/26.85 **t.**

XX **Gaylord,** 79-81 Mortimer St., W1N 7TB, ✆ 580 3615, Indian and Pakistani rest. – ▤. ◪ AE ◑ **VISA**
p. 17 KU o
M 10.50 **t.** and a la carte 8.85/10.85 **t.** ▮ 3.50.

XX **Masako,** 6-8 St. Christopher's Pl., W1M 5HB, ✆ 935 1579, Japanese rest. – ◪ AE ◑ **VISA**
BJ e
closed Sunday – **M** 20.00/30.00 **t.** and a la carte 24.30/31.10 **t.**

XX **Mon,** (at Cumberland H.) Marble Arch, W1A 4RF, ✆ 262 6528, Japanese rest.
AK n

XX **Asuka,** Berkeley Arcade, 209a Baker St., NW1 6AB, ✆ 486 5026, Japanese rest. – ◪ AE ◑ **VISA**
p. 16 HU u
closed Saturday lunch, Sunday, 1 week Christmas and Bank Holidays – **M** a la carte 23.00/31.00 **st.**

XX **Le P'tit Montmartre,** 15 Marylebone Lane, W1M 5FE, ✆ 935 9226, French rest. – ▤. ◪ AE ◑ **VISA**
BJ a
closed Saturday lunch, Sunday, 4 days Easter, 4 days Christmas and Bank Holidays – **M** a la carte 20.40/23.70 **t.** ▮ 4.00.

XX **Tino's,** 128 Allitsen Rd, NW8 7AU, ✆ 586 6264, Spanish rest. – ◪ AE ◑ **VISA**
closed 25 December and 1 January – **M** a la carte 12.45/16.95 **t.** ▮ 3.95.
p. 16 GT u

XX **La Loggia,** 68 Edgware Rd, W2 2EG, ✆ 723 0554, Italian rest. – ▤. ◪ AE ◑ **VISA**
closed Sunday and Bank Holidays – **M** a la carte 14.70/23.70 **t.** ▮ 3.30.
p. 33 EZ a

XX **Chambeli,** 12 Great Castle St., W1N 7AD, ✆ 636 0662, Indian rest.
DJ a

XX **Fontana Amorosa,** 1 Blenheim Terr., NW8 0EH, ✆ 328 5014, Italian rest. – ◪ AE ◑ **VISA**
p. 15 FS s
closed Monday lunch, Sunday and mid August-mid September – **M** a la carte 14.50/22.40 **t.**

XX **Stephen Bull,** 5-7 Blandford St., W1H 3AA, ✆ 486 9696 – ◪ **VISA**
AH a
closed Saturday lunch, Sunday and 23 December-3 January – **M** a la carte 15.00/23.25 **t.** ▮ 4.00.

X **L'Aventure,** 3 Blenheim Terr., NW8 4JS, ✆ 624 6232, French rest.
p. 15 FS s

X **Au Bois St. Jean,** 122 St. John's Wood High St., NW8 7SG, ✆ 722 0400, French rest. – ◪ AE **VISA**
p. 16 GT e
closed Saturday lunch and Christmas – **M** 18.75 **t.** ▮ 3.50.

X **Langan's Bistro,** 26 Devonshire St., W1N 1RJ, ✆ 935 4531 – ◪ AE ◑ **VISA** p. 16 JU e
closed Saturday lunch, Sunday, Easter, Christmas and Bank Holidays – **M** a la carte 12.90/15.40 **t.**

X **Nakamura,** 31 Marylebone Lane, W1M 5FH, ✆ 935 2931, Japanese rest. – ◪ AE ◑ **VISA**
closed Sunday lunch, Saturday and Bank Holidays – **M** 9.50/35.00 **t.** and a la carte 20.10/26.40 **t.**
BJ i

X **Chaopraya,** 22 St. Christopher's Pl., W1M 5HD, ✆ 486 0777, Thai rest. – ◪ AE ◑ **VISA**
closed Saturday lunch, Sunday and Bank Holidays – **M** 13.80 **st.** and a la carte 12.00/15.50 **st.** ▮ 3.75.
BJ o

X **Il Barbino,** 64 Seymour St., W1H 5AF, ✆ 402 6866, Italian rest. – ◪ AE ◑ **VISA**
closed Saturday lunch, Sunday and Bank Holidays – **M** a la carte 15.00/19.70 **t.** ▮ 3.20.
p. 33 EZ r

X **Green Leaves,** 77 York St., W1H 1PQ, ✆ 262 8164, Chinese (Peking, Szechuan) rest. – ◪ AE ◑ **VISA**
p. 16 HU c
closed Saturday lunch and Sunday – **M** 19.80 **st.** and a la carte 10.50/12.30 **st.** ▮ 3.40.

N'oubliez pas qu'il existe des limitations de vitesse au Royaume Uni en dehors de celles mentionnées sur les panneaux.

– 60 mph (= 96 km/h) sur route.

– 70 mph (= 112 km/h) sur route à chaussées séparées et autoroute.

St. James's – ✉ W1/SW1/WC2 – ☎ 071 – pp. 28 and 29.

Ritz, Piccadilly, W1V 9DG, ✆ 493 8181, Telex 267200, Fax 493 2687, « Elegant restaurant in Louis XV style » – 🛗 🗖 📺 ☎. 🖂 AE ⓸ VISA. ✠   DN a
M 23.50/39.50 **st.** and a la carte 35.00/46.50 **st.** 🍾 5.75 – ☕ 10.75 – **111 rm** 165.00/235.00 **st.**, **17 suites** 560.00 **st.**

Dukes ⑤, 35 St. James's Pl., SW1A 1NY, ✆ 491 4840, Telex 28283, Fax 493 1264 – 🛗 📺 ☎. 🖂 AE ⓸ VISA. ✠   EP x
M 18.50 **st.** (lunch) and a la carte 32.00/38.00 **st.** – ☕ 11.00 – **36 rm** 160.00/189.00 **st.**, **26 suites** 355.00/570.00 **st.**

Stafford ⑤, 16-18 St. James's Pl., SW1A 1NJ, ✆ 493 0111, Telex 28602, Fax 493 7121 – 🛗 🗖 rest 📺 ☎ – 🔥 40   DN u
56 rm, 6 suites.

Cavendish (T.H.F.), 81 Jermyn St., SW1Y 6JF, ✆ 930 2111, Telex 263187, Fax 839 2125 – 🛗 ✂ rm 🗖 rest 📺 ☎ Ⓟ – 🔥 90. 🖂 AE ⓸ VISA   EN i
M (closed Saturday lunch) 16.50/18.50 **st.** and a la carte – ☕ 10.25 – **254 rm** 105.00/150.00 **st.** – SB (weekends only) 70.00/100.00 **st.**

Hospitality Inn Piccadilly (Mt. Charlotte), 31-39 Coventry St., W1V 8EL, ✆ 930 4033, Telex 8950058 – 🛗 📺 ☎   FGM a
92 rm.

Royal Trafalgar Thistle (Thistle), Whitcomb St., WC2H 7HG, ✆ 930 4477, Telex 298564, Fax 925 2149 – 🛗 ✂ rm 📺 ☎. 🖂 AE ⓸ VISA   GM r
M 12.50 **st.** and a la carte 12.65/24.95 **st.** 🍾 4.95 – ☕ 8.25 – **108 rm** 79.00/108.00 **st.**

Pastoria, 3-6 St. Martin's St., WC2H 7HL, ✆ 930 8641, Telex 25538, Fax 925 0551 – 🛗 ✂ rm 📺 ☎ – 🔥 50. 🖂 AE ⓸ VISA. ✠   GM v
M (closed Saturday lunch, Sunday and Bank Holidays) 13.40/17.80 **t.** and a la carte – ☕ 7.25 – **58 rm** 85.00/105.00 **t.**

XXX ❀ **Suntory**, 72-73 St. James's St., SW1A 1PH, ✆ 409 0201, Japanese rest. – 🗖. 🖂 AE ⓸ VISA   EP z
closed Sunday and Bank Holidays – **M** 44.00 **t.** and a la carte 22.50/53.50 **t.** 🍾 5.00
Spec. Teppan-Yaki, Shabu-Shabu, Sushi.

XX **Le Caprice**, Arlington House, Arlington St., SW1A 1RT, ✆ 629 2239, Fax 493 9040 – 🗖. 🖂 AE ⓸ VISA   DN c
closed 24 December-2 January – **M** a la carte 14.75/21.75 **t.** 🍾 3.75.

XX **Green's**, 36 Duke St., St. James's, SW1Y 6DF, ✆ 930 4566, Fax 930 1383, English rest. – 🗖. 🖂 AE ⓸ VISA   EN n
closed Sunday dinner, Easter, Christmas and Bank Holidays – **M** a la carte 17.00/22.50 **t.**

Soho – ✉ W1/WC2 – ☎ 071 – pp. 28 and 29.

Hampshire, Leicester Sq., WC2H 7LH, ✆ 839 9399, Telex 914848, Fax 930 8122 – 🛗 🗖 📺 ☎ – 🔥 30   GM s
118 rm, 5 suites.

Hazlitt's without rest., 6 Frith St., W1V 5TZ, ✆ 434 1771, Fax 439 1524 – 📺 ☎. 🖂 AE ⓸ VISA. ✠   FK u
closed 25 and 26 December – **22 rm** 65.00/75.00, **1 suite** 120.00.

XXX **Lindsay House**, 21 Romilly St., W1V 5TG, ✆ 439 0450, English rest. – 🗖. 🖂 ⓸ VISA   GL i
closed 13 April and 25-26 December – **M** 15.00 **t.** (lunch) and a la carte 19.75/28.25 **t.** 🍾 4.00.

XXX **Red Fort**, 77 Dean St., W1V 5HA, ✆ 437 2525, Indian rest. – 🗖. 🖂 AE ⓸ VISA   FJK r
M a la carte 13.85/21.90 **st.**

XXX **La Bastide**, 50 Greek St., W1V 5LQ, ✆ 734 3300 – 🖂 AE ⓸ VISA   GK e
closed Saturday lunch, Sunday and Bank Holidays – **M** 18.50 **t.** and a la carte 16.50/28.40 **t.** 🍾 4.00.

P.T.O. →

XX **Au Jardin des Gourmets,** 5 Greek St., Soho Sq., W1V 5LA, ℰ 437 1816, Fax 437 0043,
French rest. – 🍽. 🔄 AE ⓪ VISA
GJ a
closed lunch Saturday and Bank Holidays, Sunday, Easter and Christmas – **M** 15.00 **t.** and a
la carte 16.20/27.40 **t.** ▯ 3.50.

XX **L'Escargot,** 48 Greek St., W1V 5LQ, ℰ 437 2679, Fax 437 0790 – 🔄 AE ⓪ VISA
GK e
closed Saturday lunch, Sunday, Easter, Christmas and Bank Holidays – **M** a la carte
17.10/25.20 **t.** ▯ 3.65.

XX **Burt's,** 42-43 Dean St., W1V 5AP, ℰ 734 3339 – 🔄 AE ⓪ VISA
FK n
closed Saturday lunch, Sunday and Bank Holidays – **M** a la carte 15.15/19.65 **t.** ▯ 3.25.

XX ❀ **Sutherlands,** 45 Lexington St., W1R 3LG, ℰ 434 3401, Fax 287 2997 – 🍽. 🔄 AE VISA
closed Saturday lunch and Sunday – **M** 25.00 **t.** (lunch) and a la carte 32.50 **t.** ▯ 4.75
EK u
Spec. Ravioli of lobster in a dark lobster sauce, Panache of veal fillet and roast kidney in a sauce of morels,
Rose petal and white chocolate mousse with a peach champagne sauce.

XX **Gay Hussar,** 2 Greek St., W1V 6NB, ℰ 437 0973, Hungarian rest. – 🍽
GJ c
closed Sunday and Bank Holidays – **M** 13.50 **st.** (lunch) and a la carte 16.00/21.25 **st.** ▯ 2.75.

XX **Ming,** 35-36 Greek St., W1V 5LN, ℰ 734 2721, Chinese rest. – 🔄 AE ⓪ VISA
GK c
closed 25-26 December – **M** 13.80 **t.** and a la carte 8.10/14.00 **t.** ▯ 4.00.

XX **Chesa** (Swiss Centre), 2 New Coventry St., W1V 3HG, ℰ 734 1291 – 🍽
GM n

XX **Venezia,** 21 Great Chapel St., W1V 3AQ, ℰ 437 6506, Italian rest. – 🔄 AE ⓪ VISA
FJ a
closed Saturday lunch and Sunday – **M** a la carte 13.20/18.75 **t.** ▯ 3.15.

XX **Kaya,** 22-25 Dean St., W1V 5AL, ℰ 437 6630, Korean rest. – 🍽. 🔄 AE ⓪ VISA
FJ i
closed Sunday lunch – **M** 12.00/35.00 **t.** and a la carte ▯ 7.80.

X **Alastair Little,** 49 Frith St., W1V 5TE, ℰ 734 5183
FK o
closed Saturday lunch, Sunday, 1 week Christmas and Bank Holidays – **M** a la carte
17.25/32.00 ▯ 4.00.

X **Frith's,** 14 Frith St., W1V 5TS, ℰ 439 3370 – 🔄 VISA
FGK s
closed Saturday lunch, Sunday, Easter, Christmas-New Year and Bank Holidays – **M** a la
carte approx. 6.35 **t.**

X **Fung Shing,** 15 Lisle St., WC2H 7BE, ℰ 437 1539, Chinese (Canton) rest. – 🔄 AE ⓪ VISA
closed 25 and 26 December – **M** 21.00 **st.** and a la carte 9.00/18.15 **st.**
GL a

X **Gallery Rendezvous,** 53-55 Beak St., W1R 3LF, ℰ 734 0445, Chinese (Peking) rest. – 🍽.
🔄 AE ⓪ VISA
EL a
M 15.00/35.00 **st.** and a la carte ▯ 4.00.

X Joy King Lau, 3 Leicester St., WC2H 7BL, ℰ 437 1132, Chinese rest.
GM e

X **Saigon,** 45 Frith St., W1V 5TE, ℰ 437 7109, Vietnamese rest. – 🔄 AE ⓪ VISA
FGK x
closed Sunday and Bank Holidays – **M** 15.20 **t.** and a la carte.

X New Diamond, 23 Lisle St., WC2, ℰ 437 2517, Chinese (Canton) rest. – 🍽
GL a

X Van Long, 40 Frith St., W1, ℰ 439 1835, Vietnamese rest.
GK u

X **Poons,** 4 Leicester St., WC2H 7BL, ℰ 437 1528, Chinese rest. – 🍽
GM i
closed Sunday and Christmas – **M** a la carte 4.50/11.00 **t.**

X Nusa Dua, 11-12 Dean St., W1, ℰ 437 3559, Indonesian rest.
FJ e

Strand and Covent Garden – ✉ WC2 – ☎ 071 – Except where otherwise stated see
p. 33.

🏨 **Savoy,** Strand, WC2R 0EU, ℰ 836 4343, Telex 24234, Fax 240 6040 – 🛗 ⤢ rm 🍽 📺 ☎
🚗 – 🔧 500. 🔄 AE ⓪ VISA. 🐾
DEY a
M Grill *(closed Saturday lunch, Sunday and Bank Holidays)* 21.00/24.00 **st.** and a la carte –
River 21.75/31.75 **st.** and a la carte ▯ 8.25 – **152 rm** 155.00/240.00 **st.**, **48 suites** 260.00/
550.00 **st.**

🏨 **Howard,** 12 Temple Pl., WC2R 2PR, ℰ 836 3555, Telex 268047, Fax 379 4547 – 🛗 🍽 📺 ☎
🚗 – 🔧 140. 🔄 AE ⓪ VISA. 🐾
EX e
M a la carte 21.25/53.50 **st.** ▯ 8.50 – � 12.50 – **135 rm** 177.50/239.00 **st.**, **2 suites**
239.00/390.00 **st.** – SB (weekends only) 135.00 **st.**

🏨 **Waldorf** (T.H.F.), Aldwych, WC2B 4DD, ℰ 836 2400, Telex 24574, Fax 836 7244 – 🛗 ⤢ rm
🍽 rest 📺 ☎ – 🔧 300. 🔄 AE ⓪ VISA. 🐾
EX x
M 19.50/24.00 **st.** and a la carte ▯ 10.50 – ⊷ 9.95 – **291 rm** 120.00/150.00 **st.**, **19 suites**
225.00/375.00 **st.** – SB (weekends only) 135.00/155.00 **st.**

XXXX **Boulestin,** 1a Henrietta St., WC2E 8PS, ℰ 836 7061, French rest. – 🍽. 🔄 AE ⓪ VISA
closed Saturday lunch, Sunday, Christmas and Bank Holidays – **M** 22.75/37.50 **st.** and a la
carte ▯ 7.50.
DX r

XXX **Simpson's-in-the-Strand,** 100 Strand, WC2R 0EW, ℰ 836 9112, English rest. – 🍽. 🔄
AE ⓪ VISA
EX o
closed Sunday and Bank Holidays – **M** 14.00 **t.** and a la carte 14.75/24.75 **t.** ▯ 3.95.

XX **Orso,** 27 Wellington St., WC2E 7DA, ℰ 240 5269, Fax 497 2148, Italian rest. – 🍽
EX z
closed 25 and 26 December – **M** (booking essential) a la carte 21.00/28.50 **t.** ▯ 4.00.

XX **Sheekey's,** 28-32 St. Martin's Court, WC2N 4AL, ℰ 240 2565, Seafood – 🍽. 🔄 AE ⓪
VISA
DX v
closed Saturday lunch, Sunday and 22 December-2 January – **M** a la carte 17.00/28.65 **t.**

XX **Chez Solange,** 35 Cranbourn St., WC2H 7AD, ℰ 836 5886, French rest. – 🍽. 🔄 AE ⓪
VISA – *closed Sunday* – **M** 13.50 **t.** and a la carte 15.50/20.60 **t.** ▯ 8.50.
DX i

✗ **Café Pelican,** 45 St. Martins Lane, WC2N 4FJ, ℰ 379 0309, French rest., « Art deco » –
▤. ◪ AE ◑ VISA
DY e
closed 24 December-1 January – **M** 15.95 **t.** and a la carte 12.95/20.45 **t.** 4.00.

✗ **Magno's Brasserie,** 65a Long Acre, WC2E 9JH, ℰ 836 6077, French rest. – ◪ AE
◑ VISA
DV e
closed Saturday lunch, Sunday, Christmas-New Year and Bank Holidays – **M** 14.50 **st.**
(dinner) and a la carte 15.30/18.60 **t.** 4.50.

✗ **Azami,** 13-15 West St., WC2H 9BL, ℰ 240 0634, Japanese rest. – ◪ AE ◑ VISA
closed Saturday and Sunday lunch, Monday and 24 December-5 January – **M** a la carte
30.80/39.00 **st.** 4.80.
p. 29 GK z

✗ Flounders, 19 Tavistock St., WC2E 7PA, ℰ 836 3925, Seafood – ▤
EX a

✗ **Laguna,** 50 St. Martin's Lane, WC2N 4EA, ℰ 836 0960, Italian rest. – ▤. ◪ AE ◑
VISA
DX z
closed Saturday lunch, Sunday and Bank Holidays – **M** a la carte 10.85/14.90 **t.** 2.95.

✗ **Happy Wok,** 52 Floral St., WC2E 9DA, ℰ 836 3696, Chinese (Peking) rest. – ◪ AE ◑
VISA
DX x
closed Sunday – **M** 24.50 **t.** and a la carte 11.95/17.10 **st.**

Victoria – ✉ SW1 – ☎ 071 – Except where otherwise stated see p. 32.

🛈 Victoria Station Forecourt ℰ 730 3488.

🏨 **St. James Court,** Buckingham Gate, SW1E 6AF, ℰ 834 6655, Telex 938075, Fax 630 7587
– ▐ ⇥ rm ▤ rest TV ☎ – 🕮 180. ◪ AE ◑ VISA. ✿
CX i
M (see **Auberge de Provence** and **Inn of Happiness** below) – ☲ 7.50 – **373 rm**
110.00/155.00 **s.**, **18 suites** 165.00/225.00 **s.**

🏨 **Stakis St. Ermin's** (Stakis), 2 Caxton St., SW1H 0QW, ℰ 222 7888, Telex 917731, Fax
222 6914 – ▐ ⇥ rm ▤ rest TV ☎ – 🕮 140. ◪ AE ◑ VISA. ✿
CX a
M (carving rest.) 15.00/16.00 **st.** and a la carte 23.50/29.90 **st.** 4.95 – ☲ 8.50 – **282 rm**
104.00/156.00 **st.**, **8 suites** 220.00/230.00 **st.** – SB 110.00/182.00 **st.**

🏨 **Royal Horseguards Thistle** (Thistle), 2 Whitehall Court, SW1A 2EJ, ℰ 839 3400, Telex
917096, Fax 925 2263 – ▐ ⇥ rm ▤ rest TV ☎ – 🕮 90. ◪ AE ◑ VISA. ✿
p. 21 LX a
M 15.75/19.50 **t.** and a la carte 19.95/27.00 **t.** 4.80 – ☲ 8.25 – **373 rm** 87.00/130.00 **st.**,
3 suites 160.00 **st.**

🏨 **Goring,** 15 Beeston Pl., Grosvenor Gdns, SW1W 0JW, ℰ 834 8211, Telex 919166, Fax
834 4393 – ▐ TV ☎ – 🕮 50. ◪ AE ◑ VISA. ✿
BX a
M 18.00/21.00 **t.** and a la carte 5.50 – ☲ 8.50 – **83 rm** 105.00/150.00 **st.**, **4 suites** 190.00 **st.**

🏨 **Royal Westminster Thistle** (Thistle), 49 Buckingham Palace Rd, SW1W 0QT, ℰ 834 1821,
Telex 916821, Fax 931 7542 – ▐ ⇥ rm ▤ TV ☎ – 🕮 200. ◪ AE ◑ VISA. ✿
BX z
M (see **St. Germain** below) – ☲ 8.50 – **134 rm** 105.00/160.00 **st.**

🏨 **Grosvenor** (Mt. Charlotte), 101 Buckingham Palace Rd, SW1W 0SJ, ℰ 834 9494, Telex
916006, Fax 630 1978 – ▐ ⇥ rm ▤ rest TV ☎ – 🕮 200. ◪ AE ◑ VISA. ✿
BX e
M 12.00 **t.** and a la carte 3.90 – ☲ 7.75 – **363 rm** 77.00/93.50 **st.**, **3 suites**.

🏨 **Rubens,** 39-41 Buckingham Palace Rd, SW1W 0PS, ℰ 834 6600, Telex 916577, Fax 828 5401
– ▐ ⇥ rm ▤ rest TV ☎ – 🕮 100. ◪ AE ◑ VISA. ✿
BX n
M 14.95 **st.** and a la carte – ☲ 7.95 – **191 rm** 79.00/99.00 **st.**

🏨 **Scandic Crown,** 2 Bridge Pl., SW1V 1QA, ℰ 834 8123, Telex 914973, Fax 828 1099 – ▐
⇥ rm ▤ TV ☎ & – 🕮 200. ◪ AE ◑ VISA ✿
BY i
M 15.75/25.00 **t.** and a la carte 4.50 – ☲ 8.50 – **205 rm** 95.00/125.00 **st.**, **5 suites** 205.00 **st.**

🏨 **Eccleston,** 82-83 Eccleston Sq., SW1V 1PS, ℰ 834 8042, Telex 8955775, Fax 630 8942 – ▐
TV ☎ – 🕮 120. ◪ AE ◑ VISA
BY e
M (dinner only) 10.50 **t.** and a la carte 4.50 – ☲ 4.75 – **107 rm** 51.50/71.50 **st.**

🏨 **Winchester** without rest., 17 Belgrave Rd, SW1V 1RB, ℰ 828 2972, Telex 269674 – TV
✿
BY s
18 rm ☲ –/56.00 **st.**

🏨 **Hamilton House,** 60-64 Warwick Way, SW1V 1SA, ℰ 821 7113 – TV ☎. ◪ VISA
✿
BY n
M (grill rest.) (bar lunch)/dinner 12.00 **st.** and a la carte 2.80 – **40 rm** ☲ 34.00/55.00 **st.**

🏨 Ebury Court, 26 Ebury St., SW1W 0LU, ℰ 730 8147 – ▐ ☎
AX i
39 rm.

🏠 **Harcourt House** without rest., 50 Ebury St., SW1W 0LU, ℰ 730 2722 – TV. AE. ✿ AY n
closed 24 December-5 January – **9 rm** ☲ 40.00/55.00 **st.**

🏠 **Collin House** without rest., 104 Ebury St., SW1W 9QD, ℰ 730 8031 – ✿
AY r
13 rm ☲ 30.00/45.00 **t.**

🏠 **Elizabeth** without rest., 37 Eccleston Sq., SW1V 1PB, ℰ 828 6812 – ✿
p. 20 JZ c
24 rm ☲ 28.00/64.00 **st.**

🏠 **Chesham House** without rest., 64-66 Ebury St., SW1W 9QD, ℰ 730 8513 – TV. ◪ AE ◑
VISA. ✿
AY x
23 rm ☲ 28.00/43.00 **st.**

XXX **Auberge de Provence,** (at St. James Court H.) Buckingham Gate, SW1E 6AF, ℘ 834 6655, Telex 938075, French rest. – ▤. ◩ AE ① VISA   CX i
    closed Saturday lunch and Sunday – **M** 19.50 **t.** (lunch) and a la carte 29.00/44.00 **t.** ▯ 6.50.

XXX **Inn of Happiness,** (at St James Court H.) Buckingham Gate, SW1E 6AF, ℘ 821 1931, Telex 938075, Chinese rest. – ▤. ◩ AE ① VISA   CX i
    M 14.50 **t.** (lunch) and a la carte 19.00/32.00 **t.** ▯ 6.50.

XXX **Santini,** 29 Ebury St., SW1W 0NZ, ℘ 730 4094, Fax 730 0544, Italian rest. – ▤. ◩ AE ①
VISA   ABX v
    closed Saturday and Sunday lunch, 25-26 December, 1 January and Bank Holidays –
    M 13.75 **t.** (lunch) and a la carte 25.15/33.95 **t.**

XXX **L'Incontro,** 87 Pimlico Rd, SW1W 8PH, ℘ 730 6327, Fax 730 5062, Italian rest. – ▤. ◩ AE
① VISA   FT u
    closed 25-26 December, 1 January and Bank Holidays – **M** 14.50 **t.** (lunch) and a la carte
    26.00/34.00 **t.**

XXX **St. Germain** (Thistle), (at Royal Westminster Thistle H.) 49 Buckingham Palace Rd, SW1W
    0QT, ℘ 834 1821, Telex 916821, Fax 931 7542 – ▤. ◩ AE ① VISA   BX z
    M 15.95 **st.** and a la carte 17.50/29.00 **st.** ▯ 4.95.

XXX **Lockets,** Marsham Court, Marsham St., SW1P 4JY, ℘ 834 9552, English rest. – ▤. ◩ AE
① VISA   p. 21   LZ z
    closed Saturday lunch and Sunday – **M** a la carte 16.15/23.00 **t.** ▯ 3.60.

XX Hoizin, 72-73 Wilton Rd, SW1V 1DE, ℘ 630 5108, Chinese (Canton) Seafood rest. –
    ▤   BY v

XX **Le Mazarin,** 30 Winchester St., SW1V 4NE, ℘ 828 3366, French rest. – ▤. ◩ AE ① VISA
    closed Sunday, Monday, 1 week Easter, 20 August-2 September, 24 December-1 January
    and Bank Holidays – **M** 16.00/35.00 **t.**   pp. 20-21   JK i

XX **Ken Lo's Memories of China,** 67-69 Ebury St., SW1W 0NZ, ℘ 730 7734, Chinese rest.
    – ▤. ◩ AE ① VISA   AY u
    closed Sunday and Bank Holidays – **M** 25.00/40.00 **st.** and a la carte ▯ 4.00.

XX **Mijanou,** 143 Ebury St., SW1W 9QN, ℘ 730 4099 – ⤢ ▤. ◩ AE ①   AY e
    closed Saturday, Sunday, 1 week at Easter, 3 weeks August, 2 weeks at Christmas and Bank
    Holidays – **M** 15.00/34.00 **t.** ▯ 5.25.

XX **Very Simply Nico,** 48a Rochester Row, SW1P 1JU, ℘ 630 8061 – ◩ ① VISA   CY a
    closed Saturday lunch, Sunday, 3 weeks summer and 10 days at Christmas – **M** (booking
    essential) 21.00 **st.**

XX **Kym's,** 70-71 Wilton Rd, SW1V 1DE, ℘ 828 8931, Chinese (Szechuan, Hunan) rest. – ▤.
    ◩ AE VISA   BY v
    M 7.50/15.00 **t.** and a la carte 15.00/25.00 **t.** ▯ 3.00.

XX **Pomegranates,** 94 Grosvenor Rd, SW1V 3LG, ℘ 828 6560 – ◩ AE ① VISA   p. 21   KZ a
    closed Saturday lunch, Sunday, Easter and Christmas – **M** 15.75/23.50 **t.** ▯ 5.60.

XX Hunan, 51 Pimlico Rd, SW1W 8NE, ℘ 730 5712, Chinese (Hunan) rest.   p. 20   JZ a

XX **Eatons,** 49 Elizabeth St., SW1W 9PP, ℘ 730 0074 – ◩ AE ① VISA   AY a
    closed Saturday, Sunday and Bank Holidays – **M** a la carte 16.00/18.60 **s.** ▯ 4.00.

XX **Ciboure,** 21 Eccleston St., SW1W 9LX, ℘ 730 2505, French rest. – ▤. ◩ AE ① VISA
    closed Saturday, Sunday and 15 August-4 September – **M** 15.00/18.50 **t.** and a la carte
    7.30/22.05 **t.** ▯ 3.90.   AY z

XX L'Amico, 44 Horseferry Rd, SW1P 2AF, ℘ 222 4680, Italian rest.   p. 21   LY e
    M (booking essential).

XX **Gran Paradiso,** 52 Wilton Rd, SW1V 1DE, ℘ 828 5818, Italian rest. – ◩ AE ① VISA
    closed Saturday lunch, Sunday and last 2 weeks August – **M** 20.00 **t.** and a la carte
    12.80/16.80 **t.** ▯ 3.00.   BY a

X **Tate Gallery Rest.,** Tate Gallery, Millbank, SW1P 4RG, ℘ 834 6754, English rest., « Rex
    Whistler murals » – ▤   p. 21   LZ c
    closed Sunday, 24 to 26 December, 1 January and Bank Holidays – **M** (lunch only) (booking
    essential) 16.50 **t.** and a la carte 12.65/16.50 **t.** ▯ 4.75.

X La Poule au Pot, 231 Ebury St., SW1W 8UT, ℘ 730 7763, French rest.   p. 20   JZ n

X **Mimmo d'Ischia,** 61 Elizabeth St., SW1W 9PP, ℘ 730 5406, Italian rest. – ◩ AE ① VISA
    closed Sunday and Bank Holidays – **M** a la carte 19.75/28.50.   AY o

X **La Fontana,** 101 Pimlico Rd, SW1W 8PH, ℘ 730 6630, Italian rest. – ◩ AE ① VISA
    closed Bank Holidays – **M** a la carte 18.00/23.00 **t.** ▯ 4.40.   p. 31   FT o

X **Villa Medici,** 35 Belgrave Rd, SW1 5AX, ℘ 828 3613, Italian rest. – ◩ AE ① VISA   BY c
    closed Saturday lunch, Sunday and Bank Holidays – **M** a la carte 15.00/19.70 **t.** ▯ 3.20.

Pleasant hotels and restaurants
are shown in the Guide by a **red** sign.   血血 ... 仚

Please send us the names
of any where you have enjoyed your stay.   XXXXX ... X

Your Michelin Guide will be even better.

CAR REPAIRS IN LONDON

RÉPARATION DE VOITURES A LONDRES

RIPARAZIONE DI VETTURA A LONDRA

KFZ-REPARATUR IN LONDON

In the event of a breakdown in London, the location of the nearest dealer for your make of car can be obtained by calling the following numbers between 9am and 5pm.

En cas de panne à Londres, vous pouvez obtenir l'adresse du plus proche concessionnaire de votre marque d'automobile en appelant les numéros suivants entre 9 heures et 17 heures.

In caso di guasto a Londra, Vi sara' possibile ottenere l'indirizzo del concessionario della vostra marca di automobile, chiamando i seguenti numeri dalle ore 9.00 alle ore 17.00.

Im Pannenfall können sie die Adresse der nächstgelegenen Reparaturwerkstatt ihrer Automarke zwischen 9 Uhr und 17 Uhr unter folgenden Telefon-Nr. erfahren.

ALFA ROMEO	Alfa Romeo (GB) Ltd P.O. Box 5 Poulton Close Dover, Kent CT17 OHP (0304) 212 500	**AUSTIN ROVER**	(includes Morris, Triumph, MG, Vanden Plas) Austin Rover Group Ltd Canley Rd Coventry West Midlands (0203) 70111
BMW	BMW (GB) Ltd Ellesfield Av. Bracknell Berks. RG12 4TA (0344) 426 565	**CITROEN**	Citroen (UK) Ltd Mill St. Slough Berks. SL2 5DE (0800) 282671
COLT-MITSUBISHI	Colt Car Co. Ltd Watermore Cirencester Glos. GL7 1LS (0285) 655777 ext 204/5	**DATSUN-NISSAN**	Nissan (UK) Ltd Nissan House Columbia Drive Durrington Worthing West Sussex (0903) 68561 ext 571
FIAT	Fiat Information Service Telephone Operator Services (100) and ask for Freephone Fiat	**FORD**	Ford Motor Co. Ltd Becket House Chapel High Brontwood Essex CM14 4BY (0277) 251100
HONDA	Honda (UK) Ltd 4 Power Rd Chiswick London W4 5YT (01 until May 6. Thereafter 081) 747 1400	**JAGUAR**	H.R. Owen Ltd Lyttleton Rd Hampstead London N2 OEF (01 until May 6. Thereafter 081) 458 7111
LAND ROVER-RANGE ROVER	Land Rover Ltd Lode Lane Solihull West Midlands B92 8NW (021) 722 2424	**MAZDA**	Mazda Cars (UK) Ltd 77 Mount Ephraim Tunbridge Wells Kent TN4 8BS (0892) 40123
MERCEDES Benz	Mercedes Benz (UK) Ltd 403 Edgware Rd Colindale London NW9 0HX (01 until May 6. Thereafter 081) 205 1212	**PORSCHE**	Porsche Cars (GB) Ltd Bath Rd Calcot Reading Berks. RG3 7SE (0734) 303 666

RELIANT Reliant Motor PLC
Basin Lane
Kettlebrook Tamworth
Staffs. B77 1HN
(0827) 63521

RENAULT Renault Ltd
Western Av.
Acton
London W3 ORZ
(0800) 400415

SAAB Saab (GB) Ltd
Saab House
Globe Park
Marlow
Bucks. SL7 1LY
(06284) 6977

SKODA Skoda (GB) Ltd
150 Goswell Rd
London EC1V 7DS
(01 until May 6.
Thereafter 071) 253 7441

TALBOT-PEUGEOT Warwick Wright Motors
Ltd
Chiswick Roundabout
Chiswick
London W4 5QO
(01 until May 6.
Thereafter 081)
995 1466

TOYOTA Toyota (GB) Ltd
The Quadrangle
Station Rd
Redhill
Surrey RH1 1PS
(0737) 768585

VAUXHALL-OPEL Dutton Forshaw
(West End)
466-480 Edgware Rd
London W2 1EL
(01 until May 6.
Thereafter 071)
723 0022

VOLKSWAGEN-AUDI V.A.G. (UK) Ltd
Yeomans Drive
Blakelands
Milton Keynes
Bucks. MK14 5AN
(0908) 679121

VOLVO Volvo Concessionnaires
Ltd
Raeburn Rd South
Ipswich
Suffolk IP3 OES
(0473) 270270 ext 3459

TYRE DEALERS

SPECIALISTES DU PNEU

SPECIALISTA IN PNEUMATICI

REIFENSPEZIALISTEN

The address of the nearest ATS tyre dealer can be obtained by contacting the address below between 9am and 5pm.

Des renseignements sur le plus proche point de vente de pneus ATS pourront être obtenus en s'informant entre 9 h et 17 h à l'adresse indiquée ci-dessous.

Potrete avere informazioni sul più vicino punto vendita di pneumatici ATS presso l'indirizzo indicato qui di seguito, tra le ore 9 e le 17.

Die Anschrift der nächstegelegenen ATS-Verkaufsstelle erhalten Sie auf Anfrage (9-17 Uhr) bei nachstehender Adresse.

ATS HOUSE 180-188 Northolt Rd.
Harrow, Middlesex HA2 0ED
(01 until May 6. Thereafter 081) 423 2000

LONGBRIDGE Warw. – see Warwick.

LONG EATON Derbs. 402 403 404 Q 25 – see Nottingham (Notts.).

LONGFORD West Midlands 403 404 P 26 – see Coventry.

LONGFRAMLINGTON Northumb. 401 402 O 18 – pop. 890 – ECD : Wednesday – ⊠ Morpeth
– ☎ 066 570.
♦London 304 – ♦Edinburgh 99 – ♦Newcastle-upon-Tyne 25.

🏠 **Embleton Hall** ⤸, NE65 8DT, on A 697 ℰ 249, « Country house atmosphere », 🐎 – 📺
☎ 🅿. 🔊 ᴁ ⓪ 𝗩𝗜𝗦𝗔
M 8.50/15.50 t. ◊ 3.50 – **10 rm** ⊠ 38.00/65.00 t. – SB 75.00 st.

LONG MARSTON Warw. – see Stratford-upon-Avon.

LONG MELFORD Suffolk 404 W 27 – pop. 2 739 – ECD : Thursday – ☎ 0787 Sudbury.
See : Holy Trinity Church★ (15C) – Melford Hall★.
♦ London 62 – ♦Cambridge 34 – Colchester 18 – ♦Ipswich 24.

🏠 **Bull** (T.H.F.), Hall St., CO10 9JG, ℰ 78494, Fax 880307, « Part 15C coaching inn » – ⇆ rm
📺 ☎ 🅿. 🔊 ᴁ ⓪ 𝗩𝗜𝗦𝗔
M 13.00/20.00 st. and a la carte ◊ 3.95 – ⊠ 7.00 – **27 rm** 60.00/90.00 st. – SB 90.00/100.00 st.
🏠 **Black Lion**, The Green, CO10 9DN, ℰ 312356, 🐎 – 📺 ☎ 🅿. 🔊 𝗩𝗜𝗦𝗔
M (closed Monday lunch and Sunday dinner) 15.00/25.00 t. ◊ 4.00 – **9 rm** ⊠ 40.00/60.00 t.,
1 suite 75.00 t.
🏨 Crown Inn, Hall St., CO10 9JL, ℰ 77666 – 📺. 🔊 𝗩𝗜𝗦𝗔
11 rm ⊠ 29.50/47.50 st. – SB (except Christmas and Bank Holidays) 50.00 st.
✕✕✕ **Chimneys**, Hall St., CO10 9JR, ℰ 79806, « Part 16C cottage », 🐎 – 🔊 𝗩𝗜𝗦𝗔
closed Sunday dinner and Monday – **M** 11.25 t. (lunch) and a la carte 20.75/25.25 t. ◊ 3.75.

LONGNOR Staffs. 402 403 404 O 24 – pop. 381 – ⊠ Buxton – ☎ 029 883.
♦London 161 – Derby 29 – ♦Manchester 31 – ♦Stoke-on-Trent 22.

🏨 **Ye Old Cheshire Cheese**, High St., SK17 0NS, ℰ 218 – 📺 🅿. 🔊 ᴁ ⓪ 𝗩𝗜𝗦𝗔. 🐾
M (closed Sunday dinner and Monday) 9.50 t. and a la carte ◊ 3.60 – **3 rm** ⊠ 20.00/25.00 t.

LOOE Cornwall 403 G 32 The West Country G. – pop. 4 279 – ECD : Thursday – ☎ 050 36.
See : Site★ – Monkey Sanctuary★AC.
🏌 Looe Bin Down ℰ 050 34 (Widegates) 247, E : 3 m.
🛈 The Guildhall, Fore St. ℰ 2072 (summer only).
♦London 264 – ♦Plymouth 21 – Truro 39.

🏩 **Klymiarven** ⤸, Barbican Hill, East Looe, PL13 1BH, ℰ 2333, ≼ Looe and harbour,
⅃ heated, 🐎 – 📺 🅿. 🔊 𝗩𝗜𝗦𝗔
March-December – **M** (bar lunch)/dinner 11.00 **st.** and a la carte ◊ 2.75 – **14 rm**
⊠ 31.00/60.00 st.
🏠 **Harescombe Lodge** ⤸, Watergate, PL13 2NE, NW : 4 ½ m. by A 387 and B 3359 ℰ 3158,
🐎
M (dinner only) 8.50 – **3 rm** ⊠ 16.50/33.00 st.

at Sandplace N : 2 ¼ m. on A 387 – ⊠ ☎ 050 36 Looe :

🏩 **Polraen Country House**, PL13 1PJ, ℰ 3956, 🐎 – 📺 🅿. 🔊 𝗩𝗜𝗦𝗔
M (bar lunch)/dinner 12.50 **st.** ◊ 4.50 – **5 rm** ⊠ 30.00/50.00 st. – SB 55.00/62.00 st.

at Widegates NE : 3 ½ m. on B 3253 – ⊠ Looe – ☎ 050 34 Widegates :

🏠 **Coombe Farm** ⤸, PL13 1QN, ℰ 223, ≼ countryside, ⅃ heated, 🐎, park – 🅿. 🐾
March-October – **M** 10.00 **st.** ◊ 1.90 – **8 rm** ⊠ 14.50/37.00 st. – SB 45.00/52.00 st.

at Talland Bay SW : 4 m. by A 387 – ⊠ Looe – ☎ 0503 Polperro :

🏩 **Talland Bay** ⤸, PL13 2JB, ℰ 72667, ≼, « Country house atmosphere », ⅃ heated, 🐎 –
📺 ☎ ♿ 🅿. 🔊 ᴁ ⓪ 𝗩𝗜𝗦𝗔
closed 2 January-18 February – **M** (bar lunch in winter) (buffet lunch in summer)/dinner
15.50 t. and a la carte ◊ 3.25 – **22 rm** ⊠ (dinner included) 35.00/130.00 t., **1 suite** –
SB (November-mid April) 69.00/75.00 st.
🏩 **Allhays Country House** ⤸, PL13 2JB, ℰ 72434, ≼, 🐎 – ⇆ rm 📺 ☎ 🅿. 🔊 𝗩𝗜𝗦𝗔
M (closed Sunday) (dinner only) (residents only) 10.50 t. and a la carte ◊ 3.50 – **7 rm**
⊠ 17.50/59.00 t.

☞ *When in a hurry use the* Michelin Main Road Maps :
920 *Europe,* 980 *Greece,* 984 *Germany,* 985 *Scandinavia-Finland,*
986 *Great Britain and Ireland,* 987 *Germany-Austria-Benelux,* 988 *Italy,*
989 *France,* 990 *Spain-Portugal and* 991 *Yugoslavia.*

LOSTWITHIEL Cornwall **403** G 32 **The West Country G.** – pop. 1 972 – ECD : Wednesday –
✪ 0208 Bodmin.

Envir. : Restormel Castle★*AC* (❋★), N : 1 ½ m.

🛈 Community Centre, Liddicoat Rd ☎ 872207.

◆London 273 – ◆Plymouth 30 – Truro 23.

   🏨 **Restormel Lodge,** 17 Castle Hill, PL22 0DD, on A 390 ☎ 872223, ⌁ heated – 📺 ☎ 🅿. ⌁
      AE ① *VISA*
      M (bar lunch)/dinner 15.00 **t.** and a la carte ⌁3.00 – ⌁ 4.00 – **32 rm** 29.00/40.00 **t.** –
      SB 56.00/60.00 **st.**

   ✕ **Trewithen,** 3 Fore St., PL22 0AD, ☎ 872373 – ⌁ ① *VISA*
      closed 1 to 25 May and 25 December-2 January – **M** *(closed Sunday except Bank Holidays,*
      Monday except 23 July-24 September and Bank Holidays) (dinner only) a la carte 14.00/20.00 **t.**
      ⌁ 3.50.

LOUGHBOROUGH Leics. **402 403 404** Q 25 – pop. 44 895 – ECD : Wednesday – ✪ 0509.

🏌 Longcliffe, Snells Nook Lane, Nanpantan ☎ 239129, SW : 3 m. by B 5350.

🛈 John Storer House, Wards End ☎ 230131.

◆London 117 – ◆Birmingham 41 – ◆Leicester 11 – ◆Nottingham 15.

   🏨 **Cedars,** Cedar Rd, LE11 2AB, S : 1 m. off Leicester Rd ☎ 214459, Fax 233573, ⌁ heated,
      🐎 – 📺 ☎ 🅿. ⌁ AE ① *VISA*
      closed 26 to 29 December – **M** *(closed Saturday lunch and Sunday dinner)* a la carte
      6.55/14.25 **st.** ⌁ 2.95 – **37 rm** ⌁ 22.00/48.00 **st.** – SB (weekends only) 48.00 **st.**

   🏨 **King's Head** (Embassy), High St., LE11 2QL, ☎ 233222 – 🛗 ⌁ rm 📺 ☎ 🅿 – 🕮 70. ⌁
      AE ① *VISA*. 🐎
      M *(bar lunch Saturday)* 7.95/8.95 **st.** and a la carte ⌁ 3.60 – ⌁ 6.50 – **86 rm** 48.00/68.00 **st.** –
      SB (weekends only) 55.00/59.00 **st.**

   ✕✕✕ **Roger Burdell,** The Manor House, 11-12 Sparrow Hill, LE11 1BT, ☎ 231813 – ⌁ AE *VISA*
      closed Monday lunch, Sunday and Bank Holidays – **M** 23.50 **st.** (dinner) and a la carte ⌁ 4.75.

      at Quorn SE : 3 m. on A 6 – ✉ ✪ 0509 Loughborough :

   🏨 **Quorn Country,** 66 Leicester Rd, LE12 8BB, ☎ 415050, Telex 347166, Fax 415557, 🐎 – 🖥
      📺 ☎ 🅿 – 🕮 70. ⌁ AE ① *VISA*
      M *(closed Saturday lunch)* 10.95/14.95 **st.** and a la carte – ⌁ 6.00 – **16 rm** 64.00/78.00 **st.**,
      3 suites 90.00/110.00 **st.** – SB (Friday and Saturday only) 83.00/93.00 **st.**

   🏨 **Quorn Grange,** 88 Wood Lane, LE12 8DB, ☎ 412167, Fax 415621, 🐎 – 📺 ☎ 🅿. ⌁ AE
      ① *VISA*
      M *(closed Sunday and Bank Holidays to non-residents)* (lunch by arrangement)/dinner
      30.00 **st.** and a la carte ⌁3.00 – **6 rm** ⌁ 45.00/70.00 **st.** – SB (except Christmas)
      (weekends only) 90.00/146.00 **st.**

AUSTIN-ROVER Woodgate ☎ 611211
FIAT Station Rd ☎ 05097 (Kegworth) 2523
MAZDA Clarence St. ☎ 266901
PEUGEOT Nottingham Rd ☎ 212949
RENAULT Nottingham Rd ☎ 267657
SEAT Southfield Rd ☎ 212330

TOYOTA Pinfold Gate ☎ 215731
VAUXHALL-OPEL Woodgate ☎ 213030
VOLVO Derby Rd ☎ 611777
VW-AUDI 28 Market St. ☎ 217080

⑩ ATS Bridge St. ☎ 218447

LOUTH Lincs. **402 404** U 23 – pop. 13 019 – ECD : Thursday – ✪ 0507.

See : St. James' Church★ (15C).

🏌 Crowtree Lane ☎ 603681.

◆London 155 – Boston 33 – Great Grimsby 17 – Lincoln 26.

      at North Ormsby NW : 6 ½ m. by A 16 – ✉ Louth – ✪ 0472 Great Grimsby :

   🏠 **Abbey Farm** 🐦, LN11 0TJ, ☎ 840272, ≼, 🐎, park – ⌁ 🅿. 🐎
      closed Christmas and New Year – **M** (dinner only) 8.50 **st.** – **4 rm** ⌁ 12.50/24.00 **st.** –
      SB (except summer) 35.00/38.00 **st.**

AUSTIN-ROVER 155 Newmarket ☎ 605661
FORD Northolme Rd ☎ 600911
PEUGEOT-TALBOT Newbridge Hill ☎ 600422
VOLVO Grimsby Rd ☎ 603451

VW-AUDI Orme Lane ☎ 605284

⑩ ATS 179 Newmarket ☎ 601975/6

LOWER BEEDING West Sussex **404** T 30 – see Horsham.

LOWER BRAILES Warw. **403 404** P 27 – see Shipston-on-Stour.

LOWER BROADHEATH Heref. and Worc. **403 404** N 27 – see Worcester.

LOWER SLAUGHTER Glos. **403 404** O 28 – see Stow-on-the-Wold.

LOWER SWELL Glos. **403 404** O 28 – see Stow-on-the-Wold.

LOWESTOFT Suffolk **404** Z 26 – pop. 59 430 – ECD : Thursday – ✆ 0502.
🛈 The Esplanade ✆ 565989.
♦London 116 – ♦Ipswich 43 – ♦Norwich 30.

- **Rockville**, 6 Pakefield Rd, NR33 0HS, ✆ 581011 – ✖ rest 📺. 🄰 🆅🅸🆂🅰. ✖
  M 7.50 **st.** 🍾 2.50 – **8 rm** ☕ 14.00/29.00 **st.** – SB 33.50/42.50 **st.**
- **Shanghai Coolie**, 215 London Rd, South, NR33 0DS, ✆ 514573, Chinese (Peking, Sze-chuan) rest. – 🄰 🄰🄴 🆅🅸🆂🅰
  closed Sunday lunch – **M** 13.50 **st.** (dinner) and a la carte 8.70/12.60 **st.** 🍾 3.00.

  at Oulton NW : 2 m. by B 1074 – ✉ ✆ 0502 Lowestoft :

- **Parkhill**, Parkhill, NR32 5DQ, N : ½ m. on A 1117 ✆ 730322, Telex 975391, Fax 731695, ✐
  – 📺 ☎ 🅿 – 🕍 80. 🄰 🄰🄴 🆅🅸🆂🅰
  M *(closed Saturday lunch and Sunday)* 10.00 **t.** and a la carte 12.10/20.30 **t.** 🍾 3.00 – **14 rm**
  ☕ 40.00/50.00 **t.** – SB (weekends only) 50.00/90.00 **st.**

AUSTIN-ROVER 95-101 London Rd South ✆ 561711   〰 ATS 263 Whapload Rd ✆ 561581
FORD Whapload Rd ✆ 565353
VW-AUDI Cooke Rd, South Lowestoft Industrial
Estate ✆ 572583

LOWESWATER Cumbria **402** K 20 – pop. 231 – ECD : Thursday – ✉ Cockermouth – ✆ 090 085
Lorton.
♦London 305 – ♦Carlisle 33 – Keswick 12.

- **Scale Hill** ✎, CA13 9UX, ✆ 232, ≤, ✐ – 🅿
  closed December-February except Christmas and New Year – **M** (bar lunch residents
  only)/dinner 14.00 **st.** 🍾 3.60 – **14 rm** ☕ 36.00/64.00 **st.**

LOWICK GREEN Cumbria **402** K 21 – see Ulverston.

LOW LAITHE North Yorks. – see Pateley Bridge.

LUDLOW Shropshire **403** L 26 – pop. 7 496 – ECD : Thursday – ✆ 0584.
See : Site★★ – Castle★★ (ruins 11C-16C)*AC* – Feathers Hotel★ (early 17C) – Broad Street★
(17C) – St. Lawrences Parish Church★ (13C).
Envir. : Stokesay Castle★ (13C) *AC*, NW : 6 ½ m.
🏌 Bromfield ✆ 058 477 (Bromfield) 285, N : 2 m. on A 49.
🛈 Castle St. ✆ 5053 (summer only).
♦London 162 – ♦Birmingham 39 – Hereford 24 – Shrewsbury 29.

- **Feathers**, Bull Ring, SY8 1AA, ✆ 875261, Telex 35637, Fax 876030, « Part Elizabethan
  house » – 🖃 ✖ rest 📺 ☎ 🅿 – 🕍 50. 🄰 🄰🄴 🅾 🆅🅸🆂🅰
  M 9.50 **st.** (lunch) and a la carte 🍾 3.50 – **36 rm** ☕ 60.00/102.00 **st.** – SB 95.00/125.00 **st.**
- **Overton Grange**, Overton Rd, SY8 4AD, S : 1 ¾ m. on old A 49 ✆ 873500, Fax 873524, ✐
  – 📺 ☎ 🅿 – 🕍 80. 🄰 🄰🄴 🅾 🆅🅸🆂🅰. ✖
  M a la carte 12.95/20.45 **st.** 🍾 3.75 – ☕ 8.00 – **15 rm** 30.00/70.00 **st.** – SB (except Christ-
  mas) 56.00/88.00 **st.**
- **Angel**, 8 Broad St., SY8 1NG, ✆ 2581 – 📺 ☎ 🅿
  17 rm.
- **Cecil**, Sheet Rd, SY8 1LR, ✆ 872442, ✐ – ✖ rest 🅿. 🄰 🆅🅸🆂🅰
  M 7.50 **st.** 🍾 3.00 – **10 rm** ☕ 14.00/33.00 **st.** – SB (November-Easter) 32.50/38.00 **st.**

AUSTIN-ROVER Corve St. ✆ 2001   VOLVO, SUBARU, ISUZU Bromfield Rd ✆ 4666
FORD Temeside Ind Est. ✆ 5553
NISSAN Sheet Rd Ind. Est. ✆ 2774   〰 ATS 141 Corve St. ✆ 2401

LUDWELL Wilts. – see Shaftesbury (Dorset).

LUNDY (Isle of) Devon **403** FG 30 **The West Country G.** – pop. 52 – ✆ 062 882 Littlewick
Green.
See : Site★★.
Helicopter service to Ilfracombe (Hartland Point) ✆ 3431.
🚢 to Bideford (Lundy Co.) 1-2 weekly (2 h) – to Ilfracombe (Lundy Co.) 2-3 weekly (summer
only).

LUPTON Cumbria **402** L 21 – see Kirkby Lonsdale.

LUTON Beds. **404** S 28 – pop. 163 209 – ECD : Wednesday – ✆ 0582.
See : Luton Hoo★ (Wernher Collection★★) and park★ *AC* X.
🏌 Stockwood Park, London Rd ✆ 413704, S : 1 m. on A 6 X.
🛩 Luton International Airport : X – ✆ 405100, Telex 826409, E : 1 ½ m. – **Terminal :** Luton Bus
Station.
🛈 Grosvenor House, 45-47a Alma St. ✆ 401579.
♦London 35 – ♦Cambridge 36 – ♦Ipswich 93 – ♦Oxford 45 – Southend-on-Sea 63.

Strathmore Thistle (Thistle), Arndale Centre, LU1 2TR, ℰ 34199, Telex 825763, Fax 402528 – 🛗 ⤡ rm ▤ rest �📺 ☎ ♿ 🅿 – 🛎 250. ◪ AE ⑩ *VISA*. 🛠
M 12.50/16.00 **st.** and a la carte – ☕ 7.25 – **147 rm** 63.00/93.00 **t.**. **3 suites** 95.00 **st.** – SB 80.00/110.00 **st.** Y n

Chiltern (Crest), Waller Av., Dunstable Rd, LU4 9RU, NW : 2 m. on A 505 ℰ 575911, Telex 825048, Fax 581859 – 🛗 ⤡ rm ▤ rest �📺 ☎ ♿ 🅿 – 🛎 250. ◪ AE ⑩ *VISA*. 🛠
M (closed Saturday lunch) 10.95/11.95 **st.** and a la carte 14.50/21.65 **st.** – ☕ 7.45 – **93 rm** 79.00/100.00 **st.** – SB (weekends only) 94.00/104.00 **st.** V r

Red Lion (Lansbury), Castle St., LU1 3AA, ℰ 413881, Telex 826856, Fax 23864 – �📺 ☎ 🅿 – 🛎 40. ◪ AE ⑩ *VISA*. 🛠
M a la carte 9.00/16.55 **t.** 🍾 3.50 – **38 rm** ☕ 58.00/68.00 **t.** Z e

Crest (Crest), 641 Dunstable Rd, LU4 8RQ, NW : 2 ¾ m. on A 505 ℰ 575955, Telex 826283, Fax 490065 – 🛗 ⤡ rm �📺 ☎ 🅿 – 🛎. ◪ AE ⑩ *VISA*
M 12.50/15.50 **st.** and a la carte 🍾 4.00 – ☕ 7.95 – **117 rm** 69.00/88.00 **st.** – SB (weekends only) 78.00/90.00 **st.** V u

Leaside, 72 New Bedford Rd, LU3 1BT, ℰ 417643 – �📺 ☎ 🅿. ◪ AE ⑩ *VISA*. 🛠 Y a
closed 25 and 26 December – **M** (closed Saturday lunch, Sunday dinner and Bank Holidays) 18.50 **st.** and a la carte 🍾 3.00 – **13 rm** ☕ 38.00/58.00 **st.**

Humberstone, 616-618 Dunstable Rd, LU4 8RT, NW : 2 ½ m. on A 505 ℰ 574399, Fax 491424 – ⤡ rest �📺 ☎ 🅿. ◪ AE ⑩ *VISA*. 🛠 V s
M (closed Bank Holidays) (dinner only) 11.50 **s.** and a la carte 🍾 2.50 – **21 rm** ☕ 32.00/48.00 **s.**

Ibis Luton, Luton Airport, Spittlesea Rd, LU2 9NZ, SE : 2 m. by A 505 ℰ 424488 – �📺 ☎ ♿ 🅿 – 🛎 100
98 rm.

✗ Man Ho, 80 Dunstable Rd, LU1 1EH, ℰ 23366, Chinese (Peking) rest V v

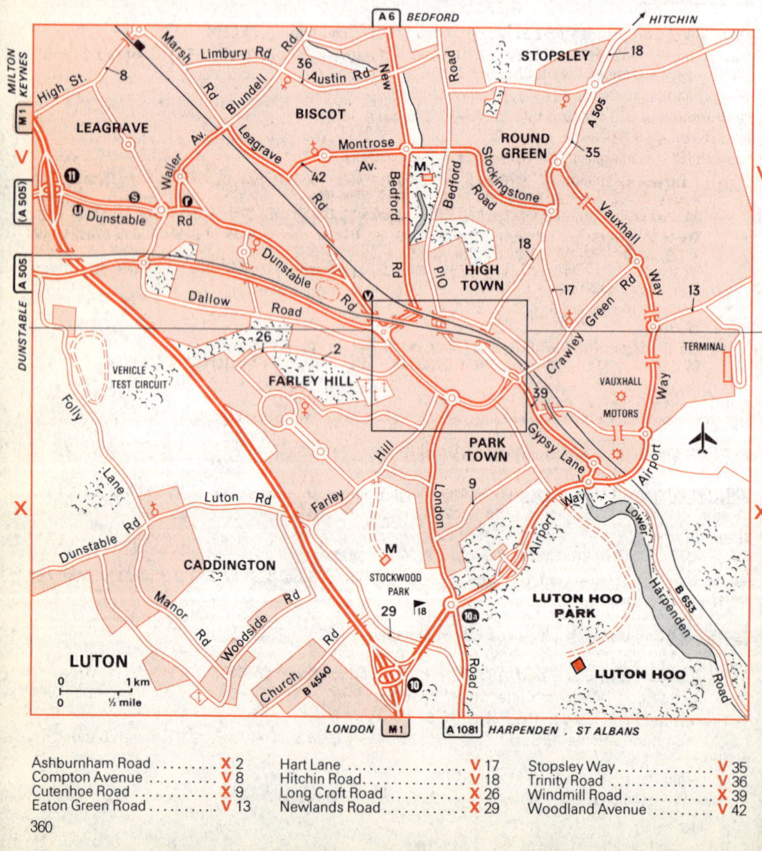

Ashburnham Road	X 2	Hart Lane	V 17
Compton Avenue	V 8	Hitchin Road	V 18
Cutenhoe Road	X 9	Long Croft Road	X 26
Eaton Green Road	V 13	Newlands Road	X 29

Stopsley Way	V 35
Trinity Road	V 36
Windmill Road	X 39
Woodland Avenue	V 42

LUTON

George St .... Z
Arndale Centre .... YZ

Bute Street .... Y 3

Chapel Viaduct .... Z 5
Church Street .... Y 6
Dunstable Road .... Y 12
Hastings Street .... Z 16
King Street .... Z 19
Latimer Road .... Z 23
Liverpool Road .... Y 24

Mill Street .... Y 27
Park St West .... Z 30
Park Viaduct .... Z 32
Silver Street .... Y 33
Upper George Street .... Z 37
Windmill Road .... Z 39
Winsdon Road .... Z 40

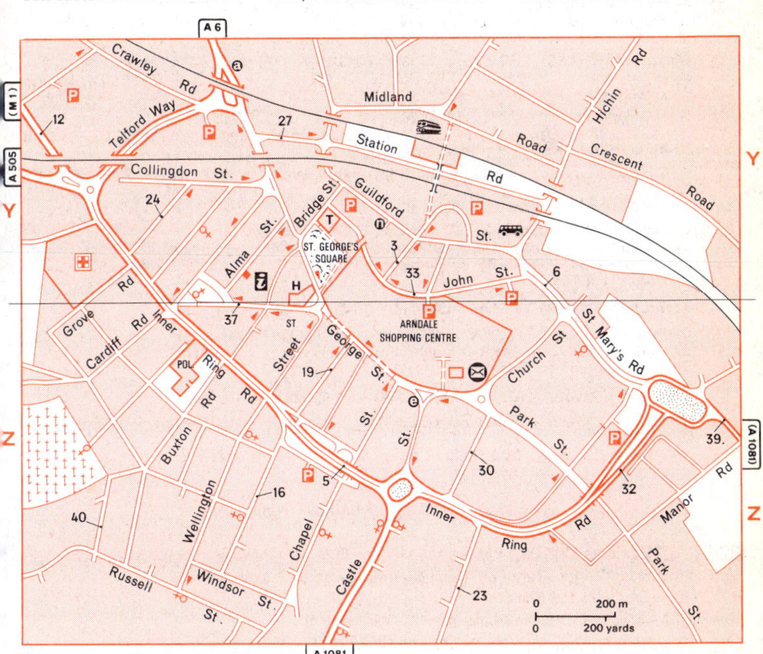

BMW 76-88 Marsh Rd ✆ 576622
FORD 326-340 Dunstable Rd ✆ 31133
LAND-ROVER, JAGUAR Latimer Rd ✆ 411311
MAZDA High St. Markgate ✆ 840474
NISSAN Leagrave Rd ✆ 571221
RENAULT 619 Hitchin Rd ✆ 35332
VAUXHALL-OPEL 15 Hitchin Rd ✆ 454666

VAUXHALL-OPEL 540-550 Dunstable Rd ✆ 575944
VAUXHALL Memorial Rd ✆ 572577
VW-AUDI Castle St. ✆ 417505

ATS 67 Kingsway ✆ 597519
ATS High St., Oakley Rd, Leagrave ✆ 507020/592381

LUTTERWORTH Leics. **403 404** Q 26 – pop. 6 673 – ECD : Wednesday – ☎ 0455 (6 fig.) or 045 55 (5 fig.).

� Rugby Rd ✆ 2532, on A 426.

♦London 93 – ♦Birmingham 34 – ♦Coventry 14 – ♦Leicester 16.

Denbigh Arms, 24 High St., LE17 4AD, ✆ 553537, Telex 342545, Fax 556627 – 📺 ☎ 🅿 – ⚿ . 🖾 🆎 ⓪ **VISA** 🛇
M 14.00/18.00 **st.** and a la carte ⌇ 3.25 – **34 rm** ⌂ 66.50/90.00 **st.**

LADA Leicester Rd ✆ 53217

SAAB Ashby Parva ✆ 209191

LYDDINGTON Leics. – see Uppingham.

LYDFORD Devon **403** H 32 The West Country G. – pop. 1 762 – ✉ Okehampton – ☎ 082 282.

♦London 234 – Exeter 33 – ♦Plymouth 24.

⌂ **Castle Inn,** EX20 4BH, ✆ 242, « 16C inn », ⇜ – 📺 🅿. 🖾 **VISA**
closed 25 December – **M** (bar lunch)/dinner a la carte 12.50/15.00 **st.** – **8 rm** ⌂ 25.00/38.00 **st.** – SB 61.00/66.00 **st.**

LYME REGIS Dorset **403** L 31 The West Country G. – pop. 4 510 – ECD : Thursday – ☎ 029 74.

See : Site★ – The Cobb★ – ⅛ Timber Hill ℰ 2043.

🛈 The Guildhall, Bridge St. ℰ 2138.

◆London 160 – Dorchester 25 – Exeter 31 – Taunton 27.

🏨 **Alexandra**, Pound St., DT7 3HZ, ℰ 2010, ≤, ☞ – 📺 ☎ 🅿. ⚠ 𝘝𝘐𝘚𝘈
closed 16 December-2 February – **M** 7.25/13.95 **t.** and a la carte ▯1.90 – **24 rm**
⊊ 35.00/76.00 **t.** – SB (November-April) 70.00/76.00 **st.**

🏨 **Mariners**, Silver St., DT7 3HS, ℰ 2753, Fax 2431, ☞ – 📺 ☎ 🅿. ⚠ 𝖠𝖤 ⓞ 𝘝𝘐𝘚𝘈
closed 2 January-15 February – **M** 7.50/12.95 **t.** ▯2.95 – **15 rm** ⊊ 43.00/86.00 **t.**, **1 suite**
50.00/93.00 **t.** – SB 60.00/74.00 **st.**

⚓ **Kersbrook**, Pound Rd, DT7 3HX, ℰ 2596, ☞ – ↔ rm 🅿. ⚠ 𝖠𝖤 𝘝𝘐𝘚𝘈
closed December-January – **M** (bar lunch)/dinner 15.00 **t.** and a la carte ▯2.60 – **12 rm**
⊊ 33.00/65.00 **t.** – SB (November-May) 68.00 **st.**

⌂ **Red House** without rest., Sidmouth Rd, DT7 3ES, W : ¾ m. on A 3052 ℰ 2055, ☞ – 📺
🅿. ⚜
March-November – **3 rm** ⊊ –/38.00 **s.**

✗ **Drakes**, 14-15 Monmouth St., DT7 3PX, ℰ 2079 – ⚠ 𝖠𝖤 𝘝𝘐𝘚𝘈
*closed Tuesday and Wednesday February-March, Monday except Easter and Sunday except
lunch February-October* – **M** (booking essential) (buffet lunch)/dinner 15.95 **t.** and a la carte
12.65/18.40 **t.** ▯4.05.

at Rousdon (Devon) W : 3 m. on A 3052 – ✉ ☎ 029 74 Lyme Regis :

🏨 **Orchard Country**, DT7 3XW, ℰ 2972, ☞ – ↔ rest 🅿. ⚠ 𝘝𝘐𝘚𝘈
29 March-30 October – **M** (bar lunch)/dinner 11.00 **st.** ▯3.75 – **11 rm** ⊊ 24.00/48.00 **st.** –
SB (June-September) 51.00 **st.**

at Uplyme (Devon) NW : 1 ¼ m. on A 3070 – ✉ ☎ 029 74 Lyme Regis :

🏨 **Devon** (Best Western), Lyme Rd, DT7 3TQ, ℰ 3231, ≤, ⊥ heated, ☞, park – 📺 ☎ 🅿. ⚠
𝖠𝖤 ⓞ 𝘝𝘐𝘚𝘈
Mid March-October – **M** 5.75/10.25 **t.** and a la carte ▯3.95 – **21 rm** ⊊ (dinner included)
43.00/86.00 **t.** – SB 78.00/82.00 **st.**

Ask your bookseller for the catalogue of Michelin Publications.

LYMINGTON Hants. **403 404** P 31 – pop. 11 614 – ECD : Wednesday – ☎ 0590.

⛴ to the Isle of Wight : Yarmouth (Sealink) frequent services daily (30 mn).

🛈 St. Thomas St., Car Park ℰ 672522.

◆London 104 – Bournemouth 18 – ◆Southampton 19 – Winchester 32.

🏨 **Stanwell House**, 15 High St., SO41 9AA, ℰ 677123, Telex 477463, Fax 677756, ☞ – 📺
☎. ⚠ 𝘝𝘐𝘚𝘈. ⚜
M 10.50/17.50 **t.** and a la carte – **35 rm** ⊊ 52.50/75.00 **t.** – SB (November-March) 92.50 **st.**

🏨 **Passford House** ⚘, Mount Pleasant Lane, Mount Pleasant, SO41 8LS, NW : 2 m. by
A 337 and Sway Rd ℰ 682398, Telex 47502, ≤, ⊥ heated, ⚑, ☞, park, ✗ – 📺 ☎ 🅿
♨ 40. ⚠ 𝖠𝖤 𝘝𝘐𝘚𝘈
M 9.50/16.50 **t.** and a la carte ▯4.00 – **53 rm** ⊊ 60.00/85.00 **t.**, **1 suite** 160.00 **t.** –
SB (November-May) 92.00/110.00 **st.**

⌂ **Albany House**, Highfield, SO41 9GB, ℰ 671900, ☞ – ↔ rest 📺 🅿. ⚜
M 10.50 **s.** – **6 rm** ⊊ 14.50/39.00 **s.**

✗ **Limpets**, 9 Gosport St., SO41 9BG, ℰ 675595 – ⚠ 𝖠𝖤 𝘝𝘐𝘚𝘈
closed Sunday and Monday October-May and December – **M** (dinner only) a la carte
13.00/17.60 **t.** ▯3.80.

SEAT Sway ℰ 059 068 (Sway) 2212   ⓪ ATS Marsh Lane ℰ 75938

LYMM Cheshire **402 403 404** M 23 – pop. 10 036 – ECD : Wednesday – ☎ 092 575.

⅛ Whitbarrow Rd ℰ 5020.

◆London 193 – Chester 24 – ◆Liverpool 23 – ◆Manchester 15.

🏨 **Lymm** (De Vere), Whitbarrow Rd, WA13 9AQ, ℰ 2233, Telex 629455, Fax 6035, ☞ – 📺 ☎
🅿 – ♨ 120. ⚠ 𝖠𝖤 ⓞ 𝘝𝘐𝘚𝘈
M (*closed Saturday lunch*) 12.50 **st.** and a la carte ▯4.50 – **69 rm** ⊊ 64.00/78.00 **st.** –
SB (weekends only) (except summer) 70.00 **st.**

LYMPSTONE Devon **403** J 32 – see Exmouth.

LYNDHURST Hants. **403 404** P 31 – pop. 2 828 – ECD : Wednesday – ☎ 042 128.

See : New Forest★ (Rhinefield Ornamental Drive★★★ – Bolderwood Ornamental Drive★★★ –
Oberwater Walk★★).

⅛ New Forest, Southampton Rd ℰ 2450.

🛈 Main Car Park ℰ 2269 (summer only).

◆London 95 – Bournemouth 20 – ◆Southampton 10 – Winchester 23.

🏨 **Parkhill** 🦢, Beaulieu Rd, SO43 7FZ, SE : 1 ¼ m. by B 3056 ℰ 2944, Fax 3268, ≤, « Tastefully furnished country house », ⅃ heated, ⇗, park – ⇤✕ rest 📺 ☎ 🅿 – 🔥 30. ⬛ 🆎 ⓞ 𝘝𝘐𝘚𝘈
M 12.50/20.00 **t.** and a la carte – **20 rm** ⊇ 67.00/100.00 **t.** – SB (weekends only) 95.00/110.00 **st.**

🏨 **Crown** (Best Western), 9 High St., SO43 7NF, ℰ 2922 – |❙| 📺 ☎ 🅿 – 🔥 . ⬛ 🆎 ⓞ 𝘝𝘐𝘚𝘈
M *(closed Saturday lunch)* 13.25 **t.** and a la carte – **42 rm** ⊇ 50.00/78.00 **t.,** **1 suite** 103.00 **t.**
– SB 94.00 **st.**

🏠 **The Forest Lodge,** Pikes Hill, Romsey Rd, SO43 7AS, ℰ 3677, ⅃ heated, ⇗ – ⇤✕ rm
📺 ☎ ౬ 🅿 . ⬛ 🆎 ⓞ 𝘝𝘐𝘚𝘈
M (dinner only) 10.00 **st.** and a la carte ⏐ 3.15 – **19 rm** ⊇ 45.00/110.00 **st.**

⋔ **Whitemoor House** without rest., Southampton Rd, SO43 7BU, ℰ 2186 – 📺 🅿
5 rm ⊇ 20.00/30.00 **st.**

VAUXHALL-OPEL Romsey Rd ℰ 2609

LYNMOUTH Devon 🆪🅾🅱 I 30 – see Lynton.

LYNTON Devon 🆪🅾🅱 I 30 **The West Country G.** – pop. 2 075 (inc. Lynmouth) – ECD : Thursday – 🕾 0598.

See : Site★ (≤★★) – **Envir. :** Valley of the Rocks★, W : 1 m. – Watersmeet★, E : 1 ½ m.

🛈 Town Hall, Lee Rd ℰ 52225.

♦London 206 – Exeter 59 – Taunton 44.

🏨 **Lynton Cottage** 🦢, North Walk, EX35 6ED, ℰ 52342, Fax 52597, ≤ bay and Countisbury hill, ⇗ – 📺 ☎ 🅿 . ⬛ 🆎 ⓞ 𝘝𝘐𝘚𝘈
closed January – **M** *(closed Monday lunch)* 11.75/17.75 **t.** and a la carte ⏐ 3.75 – **17 rm** ⊇ 62.00/130.00 **t.**

🏠 **Hewitt's** 🦢, North Walk, EX35 6HJ, ℰ 52293, ≤ bay and Countisbury hill, « Country house atmosphere » – ⇤✕ rm 📺 ☎ 🅿 . ⬛ 🆎 ⓞ 𝘝𝘐𝘚𝘈
March–October – **M** (bar lunch)/dinner 16.95 **st.** and a la carte – **11 rm** ⊇ 39.00/78.00 **st.** – SB 75.00/105.00 **st.**

🏠 **Crown,** Sinai Hill, EX35 6AG, ℰ 52253 – 📺 ☎ 🅿 – **13 rm**, **3 suites**.

🏠 **Chough's Nest** 🦢, North Walk, EX35 6HJ, ℰ 53315, ≤ bay and Countisbury hill – ⇤✕
📺 . ⌗
Easter–October – **M** (bar lunch)/dinner 7.50 **st.** ⏐ 2.50 – **12 rm** ⊇ 17.00/34.00 – SB 25.30/ 26.00 **st.**

🏠 **Neubia House,** Lydiate Lane, EX35 6AH, ℰ 52309 – ⇤✕ rest 📺 🅿 . ⬛ 𝘝𝘐𝘚𝘈
9 February–25 November – **M** (dinner only) 10.00 **t.** – **12 rm** ⊇ 22.00/43.50 **t.** – SB (except Bank Holidays) 52.00/55.00 **st.**

🏡 **Seawood** 🦢, North Walk, EX35 6HJ, ℰ 52272, ≤ – ⇤✕ rest 📺 🅿
Mid March–October – **M** (bar lunch)/dinner 12.00 **t.** ⏐ 3.50 – **12 rm** ⊇ 20.00/38.00 **t.**

🏡 **Rockvale,** Lee Rd, EX35 6HW, off Lee Rd ℰ 52279 – 📺 ☎ 🅿 . ⬛ 𝘝𝘐𝘚𝘈
closed 6 to 21 February, 1 to 14 November and 23 to 30 December – **M** (bar lunch)/dinner 9.00 **st.** ⏐ 3.00 – **8 rm** ⊇ 16.00/33.00 **st.** – SB 48.00/55.00 **st.**

⋔ **Pine Lodge** 🦢, Lynway, EX35 6AX, ℰ 53230, ≤, ⇗ – ⇤✕ rest 🅿 . ⌗
Mid May–September – **M** (by arrangement) – **8 rm** ⊇ 15.00/34.00 **st.**

at Lynmouth – ✉ Lynmouth – 🕾 0598 Lynton :

🏨 **Tors** 🦢, EX35 6NA, ℰ 53236, ≤ Lynmouth and bay, ⅃ heated, ⇗ – |❙| 📺 ☎ 🅿 – **36 rm**.

🏠 **Rising Sun,** The Harbour, EX35 6EQ, ℰ 53223, « Part 14C inn », ⇗ – ⇤✕ 📺 . ⬛ 🆎 𝘝𝘐𝘚𝘈
⌗
closed 2 January–10 February – **M** (bar lunch)/dinner 14.50 **t.** and a la carte ⏐ 4.25 – **15 rm** ⊇ 29.50/75.00 **st.,** **1 suite** 90.00 **st.** – SB (except summer and Bank Holidays) 76.00/84.00 **st.**

🏠 **Bath,** EX35 6EL, ℰ 52238 – 📺 ☎ 🅿 – **24 rm**.

🏡 **Beacon** 🦢, Countisbury Hill, EX35 6ND, E : ½ m. on A 39 ℰ 53268, ≤, ⇗ – 📺 🅿 . ⌗
Easter–mid October – **M** 8.00/13.00 **st.** and a la carte ⏐ 2.95 – **7 rm** ⊇ 21.00/46.00 **st.** – SB 56.00/63.00 **st.**

⋔ **Countisbury Lodge** 🦢, Tors Park, Countisbury Hill, EX35 6NB, ℰ 52388, ≤ – ⇤✕ rest 🅿 .
⬛ 𝘝𝘐𝘚𝘈
M 6.50 **st.** ⏐ 2.50 – **8 rm** ⊇ 17.00/38.00 **st.**

⋔ **Heatherville** 🦢, Tors Park, EX35 6NB, by Tors Rd ℰ 52327 – ⇤✕ rest 🅿 . ⌗
Easter–October – **M** 8.00 **st.** – **8 rm** ⊇ 23.00/24.75 **st.** – SB 44.00/47.50 **st.**

at Countisbury E : 2 ¼ m. on A 39 – ✉ Lynton – 🕾 059 87 Brendon :

🏠 Exmoor Sandpiper Inn, Countisbury Hill, EX35 6NE, ℰ 263 – 📺 🅿 – **11 rm**.

at Brendon E : 4 m. by A 39 – ✉ Lynton – 🕾 059 87 Brendon :

🏡 **Stag Hunters** 🦢, High St., EX35 1PS, ℰ 222, ⇗ – 📺 🅿 . ⬛ 🆎 ⓞ 𝘝𝘐𝘚𝘈
M (bar lunch)/dinner 12.75 **st.** – **21 rm** ⊇ 35.00/65.00 **st.** – SB 60.00/70.00 **st.**

at Hillsford Bridge S : 4 ½ m. by A 39 – ✉ 🕾 0598 Lynton :

🏡 Combe Park 🦢, EX35 6LE, ℰ 52356, ⇗ – ⇤✕ rest 🅿 – **9 rm**.

at Woody Bay W : 3 ¼ m. on Coast road – ⌧ ✆ 059 83 Parracombe :

🏠 **Woody Bay** ⌂, EX31 4QX, ✆ 264, ⋖ Woody Bay – ⤫ rest 🅿. ⌦ VISA
closed January-mid February – **M** (bar lunch)/dinner 11.00 **t.** and a la carte ⌑ 3.00 – **14 rm**
⌷ 30.00/60.00 **t.** – SB 66.00/82.00 **st.**

at Martinhoe W : 4 ¼ m. via Coast road – ⌧ ✆ 059 83 Parracombe :

🏠 **Old Rectory** ⌂, EX31 4QT, ✆ 368, ⇜ – ⤫ rest 📺 🅿
March-November – **M** (dinner only) 13.00 **t.** ⌑ 4.30 – **9 rm** ⌷ 31.00/62.00 **t.**

LYTHAM ST ANNE'S Lancs. 402 L 22 – pop. 39 599 – ECD : Wednesday – ✆ 0253 St. Anne's.
See : Site★.

🏌 Lytham Green Drive, Ballam Rd ✆ 737390 – 🏌 Fairhaven, Lytham Hall Park ✆ 736741 – 🏌 St.
Annes Old Links, Highbury Rd ✆ 723597.

🛈 The Square, St. Anne's ✆ 725610 and 721222.

◆London 237 – ◆Blackpool 7 – ◆Liverpool 44 – Preston 13.

🏨 **Dalmeny**, 19-33 South Promenade, FY8 1LX, ✆ 712236, ▨, squash – ⫴ 📺 ✆ 🅿 – ♿
200. ⌦ VISA ⌇
closed 24 to 26 December – **M** *(closed Monday lunch)* (lunch by arrangement)/dinner
15.90 **t.** and a la carte ⌑ 3.00 – ⌷ 4.75 – **91 rm** 25.00/96.00 **t.** – SB 41.00/45.00 **st.**

🏨 **Grand Osprey**, 77 South Promenade, FY8 1NB, ✆ 721288, Telex 67481 – ⫴ 📺 ✆ 🅿 – ♿
150 – **40 rm**.

at Lytham SE : 3 m. – ⌧ ✆ 0253 Lytham :

🏨 **Clifton Arms** (Lansbury), West Beach, FY8 5QJ, ✆ 739898, Telex 677463, Fax 730657 – ⫴
📺 ✆ 🅿 – ♿ 150. ⌦ AE ⓪ VISA ⌇
M 8.50/12.50 and a la carte – **40 rm** ⌷ 70.00/80.00 **t.**, **1 suite** – SB (weekends only) 42.00 **st.**

FORD Preston Rd ✆ 733261   VAUXHALL Heeley Rd ✆ 726714

MACCLESFIELD Cheshire 402 403 404 N 24 – pop. 47 525 – ECD : Wednesday – ✆ 0625.
🏌 The Hollins ✆ 23227, SE : by A 523.
🛈 Town Hall, Market Pl. ✆ 21955 ext 114/5.
◆London 186 – Chester 38 – ◆Manchester 18 – ◆Stoke-on-Trent 21.

🏠 Sutton Hall ⌂, Bullocks Lane, Sutton, SK11 0HE, SE : 2 m. by A 523 ✆ 02605 (Sutton) 3211,
Fax 2538, ⇜ – 📺 ✆ 🅿 – **9 rm**.

🏚 **Fourways Diner Motel**, Cleulow Cross, Wincle, on A 54, SK11 0QL, SE : 4 ½ m. on A 523
✆ 0260 (Congleton) 227228, ⋖, ⇜ – 📺 🅿. ⌦ VISA
M (by arrangement) 8.00 **t.** ⌑ 3.50 – **7 rm** ⌷ 24.00/40.00 **t.**

at Bollington N : 3 ½ m. by A 523 on B 5090 – ✆ 0625 Bollington :

✗ **Mauro's**, 88 Palmerston St., SK10 5LF, ✆ 73898, Italian rest. – ⌦ AE VISA
closed Sunday, Monday and 25-26 December – **M** a la carte 9.75/17.15 **t.** ⌑ 3.50.

✗ **Randall's**, 22 High St., Old Market Pl., SK10 5PH, ✆ 75058 – ⌦ AE ⓪ VISA
closed Monday and Saturday lunch and Sunday dinner – **M** 7.95/13.75 **t.** and a la carte
12.20/17.45 ⌑ 3.00.

at Chelford W : 7 m. on A 537 – ⌧ Macclesfield – ✆ 0625 Chelford :

🏠 **Dixon Arms**, Knutsford Rd, SK11 9AZ, on A 537 ✆ 861313 – 📺 ✆ 🅿. ⌦ AE ⓪ VISA
closed 24 December-1 January – **M** *(closed Sunday dinner to non-residents)* (bar
lunch)/dinner 6.75/16.55 **t.** ⌑ 3.50 – **11 rm** ⌷ 40.00/46.00 **st.**

FIAT, AUDI-VW, VAUXHALL London Rd ✆ 28866   PEUGEOT-TALBOT Waters Green ✆ 22226
FORD Sence Av. ✆ 27766   VAUXHALL, OPEL 98 Chestergate ✆ 22909
HONDA Beech Lane ✆ 23592
MERCEDES-BENZ Crossall St. ✆ 23036   ⓜ ATS 115 Hurdsfield Rd ✆ 25481/25233/24237

MACHYNLLETH Powys 402 403 I 26 – pop. 1 952 – ECD : Thursday – ✆ 0654.
Envir. : NW : Cader Idris (road★★ to Cader Idris : Cregenneu lakes) – Aberangell Clipiau (site★)
NE : 10 m. – SE : Llyfnant Valley★ via Glaspwll.
🏌 Newtown Rd ✆ 2000.
🛈 Canolfan Owain Glyndwr ✆ 2407.
◆London 220 – Shrewsbury 56 – Welshpool 37.

🏠 **Dolguog Hall** ⌂, SY20 8UJ, E : 1 ½ m. by A 489 ✆ 2244 (from February : 702244), ⋖,
« 17C country house », ⌇, ⇜ – ⤫ rest 📺 ✆ 🅿. ⌦ ⓪ VISA ⌇
M (lunch by arrangement Monday to Saturday)/dinner 12.50 **t.** and a la carte ⌑ 3.00 – **9 rm**
⌷ 32.00/58.00 **t.**

🏚 **Bacheiddon Farm** ⌂ without rest., Aberhosan, SY20 8SG, SE : 5 ¼ m. on Dylife rd
✆ 70229, « Working farm » – 🅿
3 rm ⌷ 15.00/30.00 **s.**

at Corris (Gwynedd) N : 5 ¼ m. on A 487 – ⌧ Machynlleth (Powys) – ✆ 065 473 Corris :

🏨 **Braich Goch**, SY20 9RD, on A 487 ✆ 229, ⋖, ⇜ – ⤫ rest 🅿. ⌦ VISA
M a la carte 4.25/11.75 **t.** ⌑ 3.75 – **7 rm** ⌷ 15.00/34.00 **t.** – SB (April-October) 40.00/44.00 **st.**

at Eglwysfach (Dyfed) SW : 6 m. on A 487 – ⊠ Machynlleth (Powys) – ☎ 065 474
Glandyfi :

🏠 **Ynyshir Hall** ॐ, SY20 8TA, ☎ 209, ≤, « Country house in large gardens », park –
⇥ rest 📺 ☎ 🅿. 🔼 🄰🄴 **VISA**
M 15.00 **st.** (dinner) and a la carte ⌁ 4.00 – **9 rm** ⊐ 30.00/60.00 **t.**

AUSTIN-ROVER Station Garage ☎ 2108   FORD ☎ 065 04 (Dinas Mawddwy) 326

MACKWORTH Derbs. – see Derby.

MADINGLEY Cambs. 🏷️ U 27 – see Cambridge.

MAENORBYR = Manorbier.

MAGHAM DOWN East Sussex – see Hailsham.

MAIDENCOMBE Devon 🏷️ J 32 – see Torquay.

MAIDENHEAD Berks. 🏷️ R 29 – pop. 59 809 – ECD : Thursday – ☎ 0628.
🅱 Central Library, St. Ives Rd ☎ 781110 – ♦London 33 – ♦Oxford 32 – Reading 13.

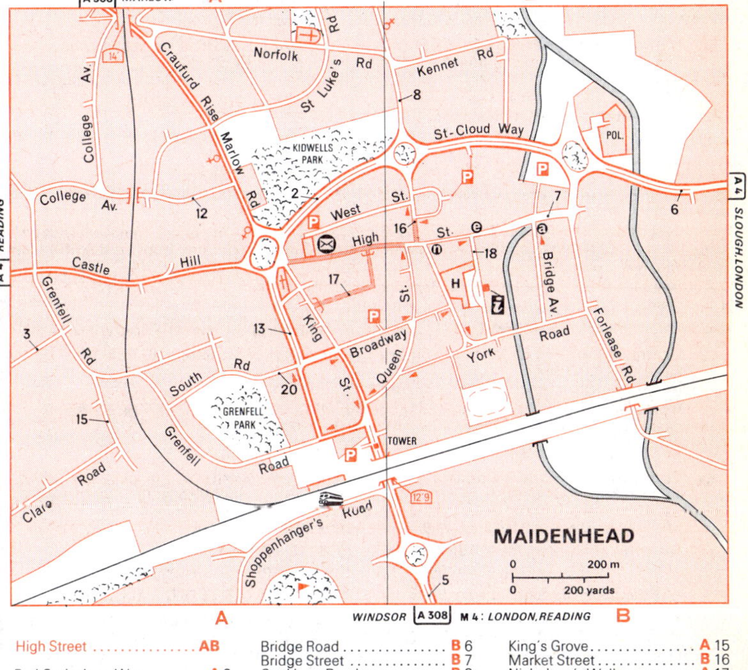

High Street .... **AB**		
	Bridge Road .... **B** 6	King's Grove .... **A** 15
	Bridge Street .... **B** 7	Market Street .... **B** 16
Bad Godesberg Way .... **A** 2	Cookham Road .... **B** 8	Nicholson's Walk .... **A** 17
Boyn Hill Avenue .... **A** 3	Crescent (The) .... **A** 12	St. Ives Road .... **B** 18
Braywick Road .... **B** 5	Frascati Way .... **A** 13	Victoria Street .... **A** 20

🏠 **Crest** (Crest), Manor Lane, SL6 2RA, ☎ 23444, Telex 847502, Fax 770035, 🔼, 🐎, squash –
⊠ ⇥ rm 📺 ☎ ර 🅿 – 🔼 200. 🔼 🄰🄴 ⓞ **VISA**
M (rest. see **Shoppenhangers Manor** A – below) – ⊐ 7.35 – **187 rm** 80.00/95.00 **st.**,
2 suites 110.00/120.00 **st.** – SB (weekends only) 102.00 **st.**

🏠 **Fredrick's**, Shoppenhangers Rd – A –, SL6 2PZ, ☎ 35934, Telex 849966, Fax 771054, 🐎
– 📺 ☎ 🅿 – 🔼 150. 🔼 🄰🄴 ⓞ **VISA**. ⅜
closed 24 to 30 December – **M** (rest. see **Fredrick's** below) – **37 rm** ⊐ 75.00/145.00 **st.**,
1 suite 195.00 **st.**

🏠 **Thames Riviera**, at the bridge, Bridge Rd – B –, SL6 8DW, ☎ 74057, Telex 846687, Fax
776586, ≤ – 📺 ☎ 🅿 – 🔼 50. 🔼 🄰🄴 ⓞ **VISA**. ⅜
M 13.50 **t.** and a la carte 15.05/22.65 **t.** – ⊐ 6.25 – **51 rm** 75.00/105.00 **st.**

XXX **Fredrick's** (at Fredrick's H.), Shoppenhangers Rd – A –, SL6 2PZ, ℰ 35934, Telex 849966, Fax 771054, ⌖ – ▤ ℗. ▨ AE ⑩ VISA
closed Saturday lunch and 24 to 30 December – **M** 32.50/39.50 **st.** ⌗ 5.50.

XXX **Shoppenhangers Manor** (Crest) (at Crest H.) – A, Manor Lane, SL6 2RA, ℰ 23444, Telex 847502, Fax 770035, ⌖ – ℗. ▨ AE ⑩ VISA
closed Saturday lunch and Sunday – **M** 23.95 **st.** and a la carte 21.00/36.00 **st.** ⌗ 4.25.

XX Jasmine Peking, 29 High St., SL6 1JG, ℰ 20334, Chinese rest. – ▤   **B n**

X **Peking Diner**, 1a Glynwood House, Bridge Av., SL6 1RR, ℰ 73655, Chinese rest.   **B a**
M 15.00 **t.** and a la carte.

at Cliveden NE : 4 ½ m. – B – by A 4 via Berry Hill – ✉ Taplow – ☎ 0628 Burnham :

🏰 **Cliveden** ⤸, SL6 0JF, ℰ 668561, Telex 846562, Fax 661837, « Mid-Victorian stately home – ◁ National Trust Gardens and parterre », ⌇ heated, ▨, ✖, squash – ▣ TV ☎ ℗. ▨ AE ⑩ VISA
M 30.00/45.00 **st.** and a la carte – **28 rm** ⊇ 130.00/280.00 **st.**, **3 suites** 330.00/375.00 **st.**

AUSTIN-ROVER 128 Bridge Rd ℰ 33188
BMW 84 Altwood Rd ℰ 37611
FORD Bath Rd, Taplow ℰ 29711
HONDA 14-20 Bath Rd ℰ 21331
MAZDA 7 Bath Rd ℰ 32339

ROLLS-ROYCE Burnham ℰ 06286 (Burnham) 68361
VAUXHALL Braywick Rd ℰ 75461 27575

◍ ATS Denmark St., Cordwallis Est. ℰ 20161

MAIDEN NEWTON Dorset ④⓪③ ④⓪④ M 31 – pop. 777 – ECD : Thursday – ☎ 0300.
♦London 143 – Bournemouth 35 – ♦Bristol 55 – Taunton 34 – Weymouth 16.

🏛 **Maiden Newton House** ⤸, ✉ Dorchester, DT2 0AA, ℰ 20336, « Attractively converted 19C medieval style manor house », ⌇, ⌖, park – ✖← rm ℗. ▨ VISA
closed January-mid February – **M** (communal dining) (booking essential) (dinner only) 22.00 **st.** ⌗ 6.00 – **6 rm** ⊇ 60.00/120.00 **st.**

X **Le Petit Canard**, Dorchester Rd, DT2 0BE, ℰ 20536 – ▨ VISA
closed 2 weeks November – **M** *(closed Monday and Sunday)* (dinner only) 14.95 **t.** ⌗ 4.25.

MAIDSTONE Kent ④⓪④ V 30 – pop. 86 067 – ECD : Wednesday – ☎ 0622.
See : All Saints' Church★ – Carriage Museum★ *AC* – Chillington Manor (Museum and Art Gallery★).
Envir. : Leeds Castle★ *AC*, SE : 4 ½ m. – Aylesford (The Friars carmelite priory : great courtyard★) NW : 3 ½ m. – Coldrum Long Barrow (prehistoric stones) site★ : NE : 1 m. from Trottiscliffe plus 5 mn walk, NW : 12 m.

🏌 Cobtree Manor Park, Chatham Park, Sandling ℰ 681560, N : ¼ m..

🛈 The Gatehouse, Old Palace Gardens, Mill St. ℰ 673581/602169.

♦London 36 – ♦Brighton 64 – ♦Cambridge 84 – Colchester 72 – Croydon 36 – ♦Dover 45 – Southend-on-Sea 49.

🏠 **Grange Moor**, 4-8 St. Michael's Rd (off Tonbridge Rd), ME16 8BS, ℰ 677623, ⌖ – TV ☎ ℗ – 🛎 100. ▨ VISA
M 10.00 **st.** and a la carte ⌗ 3.45 – **36 rm** ⊇ 42.00/57.20 **t.**

↑ **Rock House** without rest., 102 Tonbridge Rd, ME16 8SL, ℰ 751616 – TV ℗. ▨ VISA. ✾
closed 24 December-2 January – **12 rm** ⊇ 22.00/36.00 **st.**

at Bearsted E : 3 m. by A 249 on A 20 – ✉ ☎ 0622 Maidstone :

🏰 **Tudor Park H. Golf & Country Club**, Ashford Rd, ME14 4NQ, E : 1 m. on A 20 ℰ 34334, Telex 966655, Fax 35360, ≤, ▨, 🏌, ⌖, park, squash – ✖← rm TV ☎ ♿ ℗ – 🛎 250. ▨ AE ⑩ VISA
M 11.50/15.00 **t.** and a la carte – **120 rm** ⊇ 85.00/100.00 **t.** – SB (weekends only) 100.00 **st.**

XX **Sueffle**, The Green, ME14 4DN, ℰ 37065 – ℗. ▨ AE ⑩ VISA
closed Saturday lunch, Sunday, Monday and 25 December-7 January – **M** 25.00 **t.** ⌗ 3.75.

at Boughton Monchelsea S : 4 ½ m. by A 229 on B 2163 – ✉ ☎ 0622 Maidstone :

🏠 **Tanyard** ⤸, Wierton Hill, ME17 4JT, S : 1 ½ m. by Park Lane ℰ 744705, ≤, « 14C Tannery standing in orchards », ⌖ – TV ☎ ℗. ▨ AE ⑩ VISA. ✾
closed mid December-early March – **M** (dinner only) 16.10 **t.** ⌗ 5.00 – **5 rm** ⊇ 48.30/82.80 **t.**

at Wateringbury SW : 4 ½ m. on A 26 – ✉ ☎ 0622 Maidstone :

🏛 **Wateringbury** (Lansbury), Tonbridge Rd, ME18 5NS, ℰ 812632, Fax 812720, ⌖ – TV ☎ ℗ – 🛎 80. ▨ AE ⑩ VISA. ✾
M 8.50/12.50 **t.** and a la carte – **28 rm** ⊇ 60.00/70.00 **t.** – SB (weekends only) 70.00/78.00 **st.**

at Larkfield W : 3 ¼ m. on A 20 – ✉ Larkfield – ☎ 0732 West Malling :

🏛 **Larkfield** (T.H.F.), 812 London Rd, ME20 6HJ, ℰ 846858, Telex 957420, Fax 846786 – ✖← rm ▤ rest TV ☎ ℗ – 🛎 70. ▨ AE ⑩ VISA
M *(closed Saturday lunch)* 10.50/15.00 **st.** and a la carte ⌗ 3.95 – ⊇ 7.00 – **52 rm** 62.00/74.00 **st.** – SB (weekends only) 80.00 **st.**

ALFA-ROMEO, CITROEN Bow Rd, Wateringbury ℰ 812358
AUSTIN-ROVER, DAIMLER-JAGUAR Bircholt Rd ℰ 65461
BMW Broadway ℰ 686666

COLT Forstal Rd, Aylesford ℰ 76421
FORD Ashford Rd ℰ 56781
LADA Loose Rd ℰ 52584
NISSAN Ashford Rd, Harrietsham ℰ 859363
PEUGEOT-TALBOT Mill St. ℰ 53333

PORSCHE Broadway ☎ 686666
RENAULT Ashford Rd ☎ 54744
ROLLS-ROYCE, LAND-ROVER Bucholt Rd ☎ 65461
SAAB Linton Rd, Loose ☎ 46629
VAUXHALL-OPEL, MERCEDES-BENZ Park Wood, Sutton Rd ☎ 55531

VAUXHALL London Rd, Ditton ☎ 0732 (West Malling) 844922
VOLVO Cavendish Way ☎ 3953
VW-AUDI Upper Stone St. ☎ 50821

ATS 165 Upper Stone St. ☎ 58738/58664

MALDON Essex **404** V 28 – pop. 14 638 – ECD : Wednesday – 0621.

Forrester Park, Beckingham Rd ☎ 891406.

Oakwood Arts Centre, Whitehorse Lane ☎ 56503.

London 42 – Chelmsford 9 – Colchester 17.

Blue Boar (T.H.F.), Silver St., CM9 7QE, ☎ 852681 – rm TV P – 40. AE VISA
M 15.00/18.50 **st.** and a la carte 4.95 – 7.50 – **28 rm** 55.00/68.00 **st.** – SB (weekends only) 72.00/80.00 **st.**

Benbridge, The Square, Heybridge, CM9 7LT, ☎ 857666 – TV P. AE VISA
M (closed Sunday dinner) 10.00 **t.** and a la carte 12.50/16.50 **t.** 3.60 – **13 rm** 30.00/42.50 **t.** – SB (weekends only) 52.00 **st.**

AUSTIN-ROVER Heybridge ☎ 852468
BMW Spital Rd ☎ 852131
FORD 1 Spital Rd ☎ 852345

VAUXHALL-OPEL 127-131 High St. ☎ 852424

ATS 143-147 High St. ☎ 856541

MALHAM North Yorks. **402** N 21 – pop. 130 – Skipton – 072 93 Airton.

London 231 – Burnley 32 – Leeds 42 – York 58.

Buck Inn, BD23 4DA, ☎ 317 – TV P
M (bar lunch)/dinner 15.00 **st.** and a la carte 3.15 – **10 rm** 28.00/50.00 **st.** – SB (except May-September) 50.00/65.00 **st.**

MALMESBURY Wilts. **403 404** N 29 – pop. 4 220 – ECD : Thursday – 0666.

See : Site★ – Market Cross★★ – Abbey★ – Town Hall, Cross Hayes ☎ 822143/823748.

London 108 – Bristol 28 – Gloucester 24 – Swindon 19.

Old Bell, Abbey Row, SN16 0BW, ☎ 822344, Fax 825145, « Part 13C building », – TV P. VISA
M 10.50/17.50 **t.** and a la carte – **35 rm** 55.00/75.00 **t.** – SB (2 October-March) 92.50 **st.**

at Crudwell N : 4 m. on A 429 – 066 67 Crudwell :

Crudwell Court, SN16 9EP, ☎ 7194, Fax 7853, « Former 17C vicarage », heated, – TV P. AE VISA
M 15.00/19.00 **t.** 3.50 – **15 rm** 40.00/90.00 **t.** – SB (except Christmas-New Year and Bank Holidays) 100.00/120.00 **st.**

Mayfield House, SN16 9EW, ☎ 409, – TV P. AE VISA
M (bar lunch Monday to Saturday)/dinner 15.00 **t.** and a la carte 3.50 – **20 rm** 39.50/52.00 **t.** – SB 60.00/70.00 **st.**

at Easton Grey W : 2 m. on B 4040 – 0666 Malmesbury :

Whatley Manor , SN16 0RB, E : ½ m. on B 4040 ☎ 822888, Telex 449380, Fax 826120, «, « 18C Manor house », heated, , park, – TV P – 30. AE VISA
M 12.50/23.00 **t.** 6.00 – **26 rm** 66.00/105.00 **t.** – SB (weekends only) 110.00/125.00 **st.**

FORD Corston ☎ 3317
PEUGEOT TALBOT Gloucester Rd ☎ 823434

RENAULT 26 High St. ☎ 822787

MALPAS Cheshire **402 403** L 24 – pop. 1 522 – 0948.

London 177 – Birmingham 60 – Chester 15 – Shrewsbury 26 – Stoke-on-Trent 30.

Market House, Church St., SY14 8NU, ☎ 860400, – VISA
closed Sunday dinner, Monday, 1 week March, 2 weeks August and Bank Holidays – M (dinner only and Sunday lunch)/dinner a la carte 8.85/14.85 **t.** 4.75.

MALTON North Yorks. **402** R 21 – pop. 4 033 – ECD : Thursday – 0653.

Envir. : Castle Howard★★ (18C) AC, SW : 6 m. – Flamingo Park Zoo★ AC, N : 4 ½ m.

Malton and Norton, Welham Park ☎ 692959.

Old Town Hall, Market Pl. ☎ 600048 (summer only).

London 229 – Kingston-upon-Hull 36 – Scarborough 24 – York 17.

Greenacres Country, Amotherby, YO17 0TG, W : 2 ½ m. on B 1257 ☎ 693623, –
P. VISA
April-November – M (by arrangement) 7.00 **t.** – **6 rm** 18.00/36.00 **t.** – SB (October and November) 42.00 **st.**

AUSTIN-ROVER Wintringham ☎ 09442 (Rillington)

ATS 27 Commercial St., Norton ☎ 692567/693525

242

MALVERN Heref. and Worc. **403 404** N 27 – see Great Malvern.

MALVERN WELLS Heref. and Worc. **403 404** N 27 – see Great Malvern.

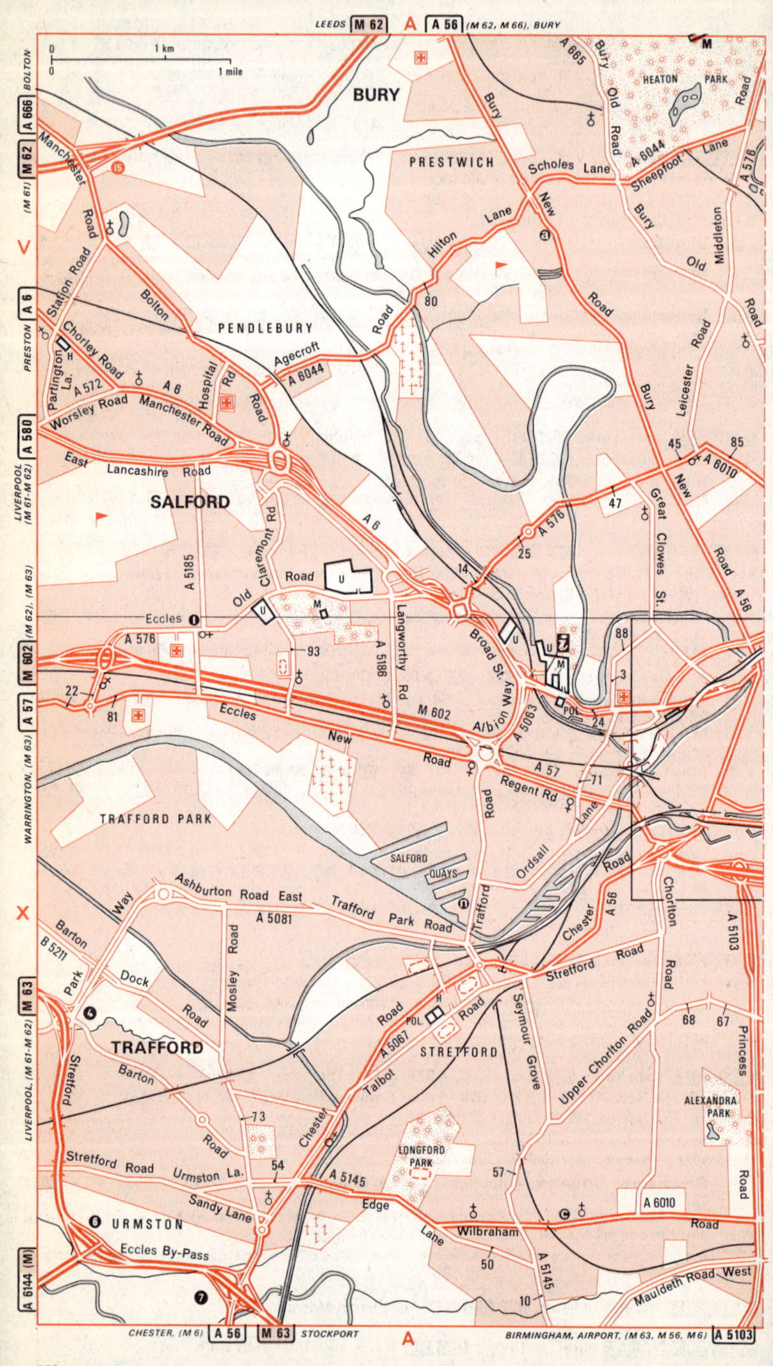

LEEDS M 62
A 56 (M 62, M 66), BURY
0 1 km
0 1 mile
BURY
PRESTWICH
HEATON PARK
Scholes Lane
Sheepfoot Lane
A 6044
A 665
Bury Old Road
Old Road
Middleton Road
A 576
BOLTON A 666
M 62
Manchester
(M 61)
Station Road
Bolton
Chorley Road
PENDLEBURY
Agecroft
A 6044
Hilton
Lane
New
Road
80
Bury
Road
Leicester Road
Old Road
A 56
Bury
PRESTON A 6
Partington La.
Hospital Rd
A 572
A 6
Worsley Road
Manchester Road
East Lancashire Road
Road
New Road
A 6010
85
45
47
A 56
LIVERPOOL A 580
(M 61-M 62)
SALFORD
A 5185
Old Claremont Rd
Road
A 6
A 576
25
14
Great Clowes St.
(M 62), (M 63)
Eccles
A 576
Langworthy Rd.
Broad St.
88
U
M
3
93
A 5186
Albion Way
A 5063
POL
24
M 602 A 57
M 602
22
81
Eccles
New Road
Regent Rd.
71
WARRINGTON. (M 63) A 57
TRAFFORD PARK
SALFORD QUAYS
Ordsall
Trafford Road
Chester Road
A 56
Chorlton Road
A 5103
Way
Ashburton Road East
A 5081
Mosley Road
Dock Road
Trafford Park Road
Stretford Road
Seymour Grove
Upper Chorlton Road
68
67
Princess Road
X
Barton
B 5211
Park
LIVERPOOL. (M 61-M 62) M 63
Stretford
Barton
TRAFFORD
73
Road
Chester Road
Road
A 5067
POL.
Road
Talbot Road
STRETFORD
Longford Park
ALEXANDRA PARK
54
A 5145
Urmston La.
Sandy Lane
Edge Lane
Wilbraham
57
A 6010 Road
URMSTON
Eccles By-Pass
A 6144 (M)
50
A 5145
10
Mauldeth Road West
7
CHESTER. (M 6) A 56 M 63 STOCKPORT
BIRMINGHAM, AIRPORT, (M 63, M 56, M 6) A 5103

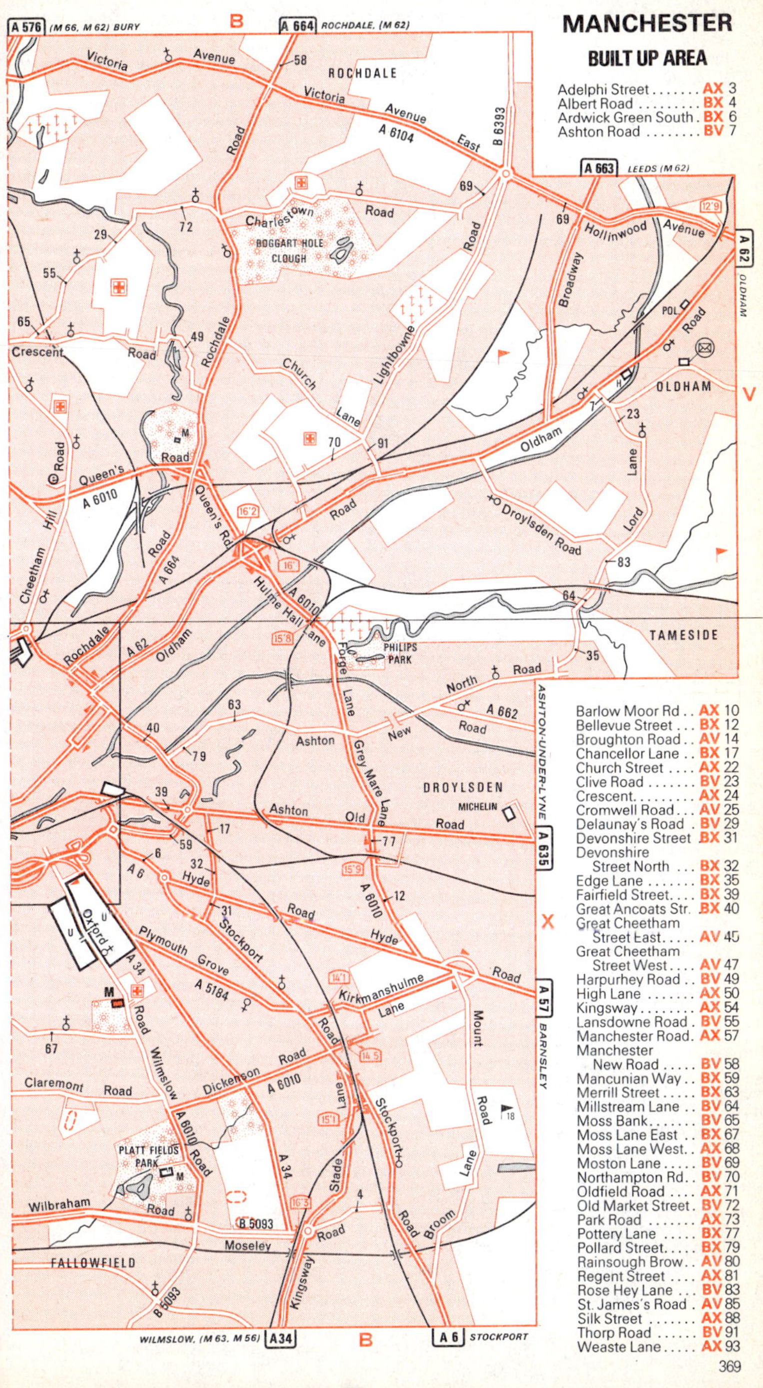

MANCHESTER

BUILT UP AREA

Adelphi Street . . . . **AX** 3
Albert Road . . . . **BX** 4
Ardwick Green South . **BX** 6
Ashton Road . . . . **BV** 7

Barlow Moor Rd . . **AX** 10
Bellevue Street . . . **BX** 12
Broughton Road . . **AV** 14
Chancellor Lane . . **BX** 17
Church Street . . . . **AX** 22
Clive Road . . . . **BV** 23
Crescent . . . . **AX** 24
Cromwell Road . . . **AV** 25
Delaunay's Road . **BV** 29
Devonshire Street **BX** 31
Devonshire
  Street North . . . **BX** 32
Edge Lane . . . . . . **BX** 35
Fairfield Street. . . . **BX** 39
Great Ancoats Str. **BX** 40
Great Cheetham
  Street East. . . . . **AV** 45
Great Cheetham
  Street West . . . . **AV** 47
Harpurhey Road . . **BV** 49
High Lane . . . . **AX** 50
Kingsway . . . . **AX** 54
Lansdowne Road . **BV** 55
Manchester Road . **AX** 57
Manchester
  New Road . . . . . **BV** 58
Mancunian Way . . **BX** 59
Merrill Street . . . . . **BX** 63
Millstream Lane . . **BV** 64
Moss Bank . . . . . . **BV** 65
Moss Lane East . . **BX** 67
Moss Lane West . . **AX** 68
Moston Lane . . . . . **BV** 69
Northampton Rd. . **BV** 70
Oldfield Road . . . . **AX** 71
Old Market Street . **BV** 72
Park Road . . . . **AX** 73
Pottery Lane . . . . . **BX** 77
Pollard Street. . . . . **BX** 79
Rainsough Brow . . **AV** 80
Regent Street . . . . **AX** 81
Rose Hey Lane . . . **BV** 83
St. James's Road . **AV** 85
Silk Street . . . . **AX** 88
Thorp Road . . . . . . **BV** 91
Weaste Lane . . . . . **AX** 93

See : Site★ – Town Hall★ (19C) **DYZ** H – Whitworth Art Gallery★ **BX** M – Cathedral 15C (chancel★) **DY** B – John Ryland's Library (manuscripts★) **CY** A.

Envir. : Heaton Hall★ (18C) *AC*, N : 5 m. **AV** M.

⛳ Heaton Park, ✆ 798 0295, N : by A 576 **ABV** – ⛳ Fairfield Golf and Sailing, Booth Rd, Audenshaw, ✆ 370 1641, E : by A 635 **BX** – ⛳ Houldsworth, Wingate House, Higher Levenshulme ✆ 224 5055 **BX**.

✈ Manchester International Airport ✆ (061) 489 3000 (British Airways) Telex 665457, S : 10 m. by A 5103 **AX** and M 56 – Terminal : Coach service from Victoria Station.

🛈 Town Hall Extension, Lloyd St. ✆ 234 3157/8 – Manchester International Airport, International Arrivals Hall ✆ 436 3344.

◆London 202 – ◆Birmingham 86 – ◆Glasgow 221 – ◆Leeds 43 – ◆Liverpool 35 – ◆Nottingham 72.

MANCHESTER
CENTRE

Deansgate .... **CYZ**
Lower Mosley Street ...... **DZ** 56
Market Place .... **CDY**
Market Street .... **DY**
Mosley Street .... **DYZ**
Princess Street .... **DZ**

Addington Street .... **DY** 2
Albert Square .... **CDYZ** 5

Aytoun Street .... **DZ** 8
Blackfriars Street .... **CY** 13
Cannon Street .... **DY** 15
Cateaton Street .... **DY** 16
Cheetham Hill Road .... **DY** 18
Chepstow Street .... **DZ** 19
Chorlton Street .... **DZ** 20
Church Street .... **DY** 21
Dale Street .... **DY** 27
Dawson Street .... **CZ** 28
Ducie Street .... **DYZ** 33
Egerton Street .... **CZ** 36
Fairfield Street .... **DZ** 39

Great Bridgewater Street... **CZ** 41
Great Ducie Street .... **CY** 48
High Street .... **DY** 51
John Dalton Street .... **CY** 52
King Street .... **DY** 53
Parker Street .... **DY** 75
Peter Street .... **CZ** 76
St. Ann's Street .... **CY** 84
St. Peter's Square .... **DZ** 87
Spring Gardens........... **DY** 89
Viaduct Street .... **CY** 92
Whitworth Street West ... **CZ** 95
Withy Grove............. **DY** 97

Holiday Inn Crowne Plaza Midland (Holiday Inn), 16 Peter St., M60 2DS, ℰ 236 3333, Telex 667550, Fax 228 2241, ⊠, squash – 🛗 ⇔ rm 🍽 TV ☎ ⅋ – 🛦 500. 🔼 AE ⓪ VISA
M French rest. (dinner only) 27.50 t. 🍷 4.00 – **Trafford Room** (carving rest.) 14.50 t. – ⌸ 8.95
– **296 rm** 95.00/113.00 **st.**, **7 suites** 186.00/390.00 **st.**   DZ x

Ramada Renaissance, Blackfriars St., Deansgate, M3 2EQ, ℰ 835 2555, Telex 669699, Fax 835 3077 – 🛗 ⇔ rm 🍽 rest TV ☎ ⅋ – 🛦 400   CY v
200 rm, **5 suites**.

Piccadilly (Embassy), Piccadilly Plaza, M60 1QR, ℰ 236 8414, Telex 668765, Fax 228 1568, ⇐ – 🛗 ⇔ rm 🍽 rest TV ☎ ⅋ – 🛦 800. 🔼 AE ⓪ VISA ⅋   DY s
M 15.50 **t.** and a la carte 16.50/24.80 **t.** 🍷 3.90 – ⌸ 7.75 – **246 rm** 85.00/110.00 **st.**, **9 suites** 195.00/210.00 **st.** – SB (weekends only) 95.00 **st.**

Copthorne Manchester (Best Western), Clippers Quay, Salford Quays, M5 3DL, ℰ 873 7321, Telex 669090, Fax 873 7318, ⊠ – 🛗 ⇔ rm 🍽 rest TV ☎ ⅋ ⅋ – 🛦 75. 🔼 AE ⓪ VISA ⅋   AX n
M 12.95 **t.** and a la carte 17.50/23.00 **t.** 🍷 4.00 – ⌸ 7.25 – **166 rm** 67.50/85.00 **t.** – SB (weekends only) 94.50/114.50 **st.**

Portland Thistle (Thistle), Portland St., Piccadilly Gdns., M1 6DP, ℰ 228 3400, Telex 669157, Fax 228 6347 – 🛗 ⇔ rm 🍽 rest TV ☎ ⅋ – 🛦 300. 🔼 AE ⓪ VISA   DY a
M 11.95/13.95 **st.** and a la carte – **205 rm** 75.00/95.00 **st.**, **3 suites** 105.00 **st.** – SB (weekends only) 56.00/130.00 **st.**

Hazeldean, 467 Bury New Rd, M7 ONX, ℰ 792 6667 – TV ☎ ⅋   AV a
25 rm.

New Central, 144-146 Heywood St., M8 7PD, ℰ 205 2169 – ⅋. ⅋   BV e
M 9.00 **st.** 🍷 3.20 – **10 rm** ⌸ 19.50/32.00 **st.**

Sabre D'or, 392 Wilbraham Rd, Chorlton-cum-Hardy, M21 1UH, S : 5 m. by A 5103 on A 6010 ℰ 881 5055 – ⇔ rm TV ⅋   AX c
M 6.00 **st.** 🍷 3.00 – **13 rm** ⌸ 20.00/32.00 **st.**

XXX **Isola Bella**, Dolefield, Crown Sq., M3 3EN, ℰ 831 7099, Italian rest. – 🔼 VISA   CY e
closed Sunday and Bank Holidays – **M** a la carte 16.30/27.00 **st.** 🍷 4.20.

XXX **Giulio's Terrazza**, 14 Nicholas St., M1 4FE, ℰ 236 4033, Italian rest. – 🔼 AE ⓪ VISA
closed Sunday and Bank Holidays – **M** 8.25/14.80 **t.** and a la carte 11.55/21.25 **t.** 🍷 3.95.   DZ r

XX **Gaylord**, Amethyst House, Marriott's Court, Spring Gdns, M2 1EA, ℰ 832 6037, Indian rest. – 🍽. 🔼 AE ⓪ VISA   DY c
closed 25 December and 1 January – **M** 5.95/11.50 **t.** and a la carte 7.75/13.15 **t.** 🍷 4.25.

X **Yang Sing**, 34 Princess St., M1 4JY, ℰ 236 2200, Chinese (Canton) rest. – 🔼 AE VISA   DZ a
closed 25 December – **M** (booking essential) 10.75 **t.** and a la carte.

X **Market**, 104 High St., M4 1HQ, ℰ 834 3743, Bistro – 🔼 AE VISA   DY o
closed Monday, Sunday, 1 week Easter, August and 1 week after Christmas – **M** (dinner only) a la carte 9.80/17.15 **t.** 🍷 3.50.

X Little Yang Sing, 17 George St., M1 4HE, ℰ 228 7722, Chinese (Canton) rest.   DZ e

X **Koreana**, Kings House, 40 King St. West, M3 2WY, ℰ 832 4330, Korean rest. – 🔼 VISA
closed Saturday lunch, Sunday and Bank Holidays – **M** 5.50/15.50 **st.** and a la carte 13.40/19.95 **st.** 🍷 3.65.   CY r

at Manchester Airport S : 9 m. by A 5103 – AX – off M 56 – ⊠ ☏ 061 Manchester :

Hilton International (Hilton), Outwood Lane, Ringway, M22 5WP, ℰ 436 4404, Telex 668361, Fax 436 1621 – 🛗 ⇔ rm TV ☎ ⅋ ⅋ – 🛦 130. 🔼 AE ⓪ VISA
M *(closed Monday, Saturday lunch and Sunday)* a la carte 14.20/31.45 **st** 🍷 5.25 – ⌸ 8.50 – **226 rm** 82.50/125.00 **st.**

Excelsior (T.H.F.), Ringway Rd, Wythenshawe, M22 5NS, ℰ 437 5811, Telex 668721, Fax 436 2346, ⊠ – 🛗 ⇔ rm 🍽 TV ☎ ⅋ – 🛦 200. 🔼 AE ⓪ VISA
M *(closed Saturday lunch)* 9.95/14.95 **st.** and a la carte 🍷 3.95 – ⌸ 7.60 – **300 rm** 81.00/107.00 **st.**, **4 suites** 160.00/250.00 **st.** – SB (weekends only) 76.00/84.00 **st.**

XXX **Moss Nook**, Ringway Rd, Moss Nook, M22 5NA, ℰ 437 4778 – ⅋. 🔼 AE ⓪ VISA
closed Saturday lunch, Sunday, Monday and 2 weeks Christmas – **M** 24.00 **st.** and a la carte 24.00/33.50 **st.** 🍷 5.50.

at Worsley W : 7 ¼ m. by M 602 – AX – off M 62 East – ⊠ ☏ 061 Manchester :

Novotel Manchester West, Worsley Brow, at junction 13 of M 62, M28 4YA, ℰ 799 3535, Telex 669586, Fax 703 8207, ⊠ heated – 🛗 ⇔ rm 🍽 TV ☎ ⅋ ⅋ – 🛦 200. 🔼 AE ⓪ VISA
M 9.20 **st.** and a la carte 🍷 3.50 – ⌸ 6.50 – **119 rm** 52.00/104.00 **st.**

MICHELIN Distribution Centre, Ferris St., off Louisa St., Openshaw, M11 1BS, ℰ 223 2010, FAX 220 8852 BX

ALFA-ROMEO 123a/b Jersey St. ℰ 205 2213	FORD Oxford Rd ℰ 224 7301
AUSTIN-ROVER 208 Bury New Rd ℰ 792 4343	FORD 660 Chester Rd ℰ 872 2201
BMW 325-327 Deansgate ℰ 832 8781	FORD 3-5 New Wakefield St. ℰ 236 4168
BMW 45 Upper Brook St. ℰ 273 1571	HONDA Liverpool St. ℰ 737 3540
CITROEN, FIAT, LANCIA Ashton Old Rd ℰ 273 4411	MAZDA Oldham Rd, Ashton ℰ 330 8135
FIAT Ashton Old Rd ℰ 273 4411	MERCEDES-BENZ Upper Brook St. ℰ 273 8123
FORD 271 Bury New Rd ℰ 792 6161	MORGAN, RENAULT Ashley Rd, Hale ℰ 941 1916
FORD 391 Palatine Rd ℰ 998 3427	NISSAN Victoria Rd ℰ 330 3840

MANCHESTER
NISSAN Windsor St. Salford ℰ 745 7737
NISSAN Chancellor Lane, Ardwick ℰ 273 8198
PEUGEOT-TALBOT Chester Rd ℰ 834 6677
PEUGEOT Waterloo Rd ℰ 792 4220
PORSCHE Bury New Rd at Whitefield ℰ 796 7414
RENAULT Blackfriars Rd ℰ 832 6121
SAAB Water St. ℰ 832 6566
SUBARU, ISUZU, HYUNDAI Greenside Lane ℰ
370 2145
TOYOTA Moseley Rd ℰ 224 6265
VAUXHALL-OPEL 292 Bury New Rd ℰ 792 4321

VAUXHALL-OPEL Blackfriars Rd ℰ 834 8200
VAUXHALL-OPEL 799 Chester Rd ℰ 872 2141
VAUXHALL-OPEL Ashton Old Rd ℰ 273 4361
VOLVO Rowsley St. ℰ 223 7272
VW-AUDI Stamford Rd ℰ 320 5454

⑩ ATS 85 Liverpool Rd ℰ 832 4089 and 834 7039
ATS 98 Wilmslow Rd. Rusholme ℰ 224 6296/7
ATS Warren Rd, Trafford Park ℰ 872 7631
ATS 122 Higher Rd. Urmston ℰ 748 6990/5923
ATS 20-28 Waterloo Rd ℰ 832 7752

MANNINGTREE Essex 404 X 28 – pop. 3 909 – ⚙ 0206 Colchester.

♦London 67 – Colchester 9 – ♦Ipswich 12.

  ✗ **Clodd's,** 3-5 South St., CO11 1BA, ℰ 394102 – 🆅 VISA
    closed Sunday dinner, Monday and 1 to 15 October – **M** 12.95 **t.** and a la carte approx. 8.70 **t.**
    🍾 4.20.

MANORBIER (MAENORBYR) Dyfed 403 F 29 – pop. 1 136 – ECD : Saturday – ⚙ 0834 (6 fig.)
or 0834 871 (3 fig.).

♦London 253 – Carmarthen 33 – Fishguard 33.

  🏨 **Castlemead,** SA70 7TA, ℰ 871358, 🚗 – TV 🅿. 🆅 AE VISA
    March-November – **M** (dinner only) 8.00 **t.** 🍾 2.50 – **8 rm** � 22.00/48.00 **t.**

MARAZION Cornwall 403 D 33 The West Country G. – pop. 1 366 – ECD : Wednesday – ✉
⚙ 0736 Penzance.

♦London 318 – Penzance 3 – Truro 26.

  🏨 **Mount Haven,** Turnpike Rd, TR17 0DQ, on A 394 ℰ 710249, ≼ St. Michael's Mount and
    Mount's Bay – ✗ rest TV ☎ 🅿. 🆅 AE VISA
    closed 20 December-6January – **M** 12.00 **st.** and a la carte 13.50/17.00 **st.** 🍾 3.50 – **17 rm**
    ⊆ 24.00/52.00 **st.** – SB (except summer) 49.00/57.00 **st.**

    at Perranuthnoe SE : 1 ¾ m. by A 394 – ✉ ⚙ 0736 Penzance :

  ↑ **Ednovean House** 🦢, TR20 9LZ, ℰ 711071, ≼ St. Michael's Mount and Mount's Bay, 🚗
    – ✗ rest 🅿. 🆅 AE VISA
    M 9.00 **st.** 🍾 3.15 – **9 rm** ⊆ 14.30/39.00 **st.**

MARKET DEEPING Lincs. 402 404 T 25 – pop. 9 621 – ⚙ 0778.

♦London 94 – ♦Cambridge 44 – ♦Leicester 41 – Lincoln 42.

  🏠 **Deeping Stage,** 16 Market Pl., PE6 8EA, ℰ 343234, 🚗 – TV 🅿. 🆅 AE ⓞ VISA 🦱
    M 8.95 **st.** (lunch) and a la carte 🍾 4.25 – **7 rm** ⊆ 20.00/40.00 **st.** – SB (weekends
    only) 69.00/78.00 **st.**

PEUGEOT-TALBOT High St. ℰ 342461

MARKET DRAYTON Shropshire 402 403 404 M 25 – pop. 9 003 – ECD : Thursday – ⚙ 0630.
🏌 Sutton ℰ 2266.

♦London 161 – ♦Birmingham 44 – Chester 33 – Shrewsbury 19 – ♦Stoke-on-Trent 16.

  🏠 **Corbet Arms,** 8 High St., TF9 1PY, ℰ 2037, Telex 94070685, Fax 2961 – TV ☎ 🅿. 🆅 AE
    ⓞ VISA
    M (carving lunch)/dinner 8.75 **t.** and a la carte 🍾 2.20 – **12 rm** ⊆ 28.00/40.00 **t.** –
    SB 22.00/25.00 **st.**

    at Tern Hill SW : 2 ¾ m. on A 53 – ✉ Market Drayton – ⚙ 063 083 Tern Hill :

  🏨 **Tern Hill Hall** 🦢, TF9 3PU, SW : ¼ m. on A 53 ℰ 310, ≼, 🚗 – TV 🅿. 🆅 AE VISA 🦱
    closed 25-26 December and 1 January – **M** *(closed Sunday dinner and Bank Holidays)* (bar
    lunch Monday to Friday)/dinner 12.00 **st.** and a la carte 🍾 3.00 – **12 rm** ⊆ 30.00/40.00 **st.**

FORD Shrewsbury Rd ℰ 2027
RENAULT Shrewsbury Rd ℰ 4257
VAUXHALL, VOLVO Cheshire St. ℰ 2444

⑩ ATS 71-73 Shrewsbury Rd ℰ 58446

MARKET HARBOROUGH Leics. 404 R 26 – pop. 15 852 – ECD : Wednesday – ⚙ 0858.
🖼 Pen Lloyd Library, Adam and Eve St. ℰ 62649/62699.

♦London 88 – ♦Birmingham 47 – ♦Leicester 15 – Northampton 17.

  🏨 **Three Swans** (Best Western), 21 High St., LE16 7NJ, ℰ 66644, Telex 342375, Fax 33101 –
    ✗ rm TV ☎ 🅿. 🆅 AE ⓞ VISA 🦱
    M *(closed Sunday dinner)* 9.95/13.95 **t.** – **38 rm** ⊆ 58.00/74.00 **st.** – SB (weekends
    only) 79.00/89.00 **st.**

  ✗✗ **Freeman's,** 4 Roman Way, LE16 7PQ, ℰ 65453 – 🆅 AE ⓞ
    closed 2 weeks September-October – **M** (dinner only Friday and Saturday and Sunday
    lunch).

at East Langton N : 4 m. by A 6 off B 6047 – ✉ ☎ 0858 84 East Langton :

✗ **Bell Inn,** Main St., LE16 7TW, ✆ 567 – **Ⓟ**. 🅰 *VISA*
closed Sunday dinner and Monday – **M** approx. 17.00 **t.** ⌕ 3.50.

at Glooston NE : 7 ½ m. by A 6 and B 6047 off Hallaton Rd – ✉ Market Harborough –
☎ 0858 84 East Langton :

✗ **Old Barn Inn** ⌂ with rm, LE16 7ST, ✆ 215, 🚗 – 📺 ☎ **Ⓟ**. 🅰 *VISA*. ⌇
M *(closed Monday lunch and Sunday dinner)* (bar lunch)/dinner a la carte 8.75/14.25 **t.**
⌕ 3.25 – **3 rm** ⌑ 29.50/39.50 **t.** – SB (weekends only) 40.00 **st.**

at Marston Trussell (Northants.) W : 3 ½ m. by A 427 – ✉ ☎ 0858 Market Harborough :

🏠 **Sun Inn** ⌂, Main St., LE16 9TY, ✆ 65531 – 📺 ☎ **Ⓟ**. 🅰 🆎 *VISA*
M 8.95/12.95 **t.** and a la carte ⌕ 3.95 – **10 rm** ⌑ 32.50/42.50 **st.** – SB (weekends only) 55.00 **st.**

FIAT Main St. ✆ 66984   VW-AUDI Northampton Rd ✆ 65511
SKODA Abbey St. ✆ 32530
VAUXHALL-OPEL Springfield St. ✆ 67177   ⓪ ATS 47-49 Kettering Rd ✆ 64535

MARKFIELD Leics. 🄯🄯🄯 **402 403 404** Q 25 – ☎ 0530.
♦London 113 – ♦Birmingham 45 – ♦Leicester 6 – ♦Nottingham 24.

🏠 **Granada Lodge** without rest., Little Show Lane, LE6 0PP, on A 50 ✆ 244237, Fax 244580 –
📺 **Ⓟ**
39 rm.

MARKHAM MOOR Notts. – ✉ ☎ 0777 Retford.
♦London 143 – Lincoln 18 – ♦Nottingham 28 – ♦Sheffield 27.

🏠 **Travelodge** without rest., A 1 North Bound, DN22 0QH, ✆ 838091 – 📺 ⴷ **Ⓟ**. 🅰 🆎 *VISA*
40 rm 21.50/27.00 **t.**

MARKINGTON North Yorks. **402** P 21 – see Harrogate.

MARLBOROUGH Wilts. **403 404** O 29 The West Country G. – pop. 5 330 – ECD : Wednesday
– ☎ 0672.

See : Site★.

Envir. : Savernake Forest★★ (Grand Avenue★★★), SE : 2 m. by A 346 – The Ridgeway Path★★,
85 miles starting from Overton Hill near Avebury including White Horse ⩤★ – West Kennett
Long Barrow★, W : 4 ½ m. – Silbury Hill★, W : 6 m. – Pewsey : Vale of Pewsey★, S : 7 m. on A
3455 – at Avebury★★, The Stones★, Church★, W : 7 m. – Wilton Windmill★ *AC*, S : 9 m. by A 346
on A 338 – at Great Bedwyn, Crofton Beam Engines★ *AC*, on Kennet and Avon Canal, SE : 10 m.

🏌 The Common ✆ 52147, N : 1 m.

🛈 St. Peter's Church, High St. ✆ 53989 (summer only).

♦London 84 – ♦Bristol 47 – ♦Southampton 40 – Swindon 12.

🏨 **Ivy House** (Best Western), High St., SN8 1HJ, ✆ 515333, Fax 515338 – 📺 ☎. 🅰 🆎 ⓪
VISA
M (see **Garden** below) – ⌑ 6.50 – **30 rm** 45.00/75.00 **st.** – SB 90.00/120.00 **st.**

🏨 **Castle and Ball** (T.H.F.), High St., SN8 1LZ, ✆ 55201, Fax 55895 – ⴳ rm 📺 ☎ **Ⓟ** – 🎿
40. 🅰 🆎 ⓪ *VISA*
M 11.00/15.00 **st.** and a la carte ⌕ 3.05   ⌑ 7.00 – **36 rm** 70.00/90.00 **st.** – SB (weekends only) 80.00/96.00 **st.**

✗✗ **Garden** (at Ivy House H.), High St., SN8 1HJ, ✆ 515333, Fax 515338 – **Ⓟ**. 🅰 🆎 ⓪ *VISA*
M 12.00 **st.** (lunch) and a la carte 13.50/25.00 **st.** ⌕ 5.00.

AUSTIN-ROVER 80-83 High St. ✆ 52076   ⓪ ATS 120-121 London Rd ✆ 52274
CITROEN Granham Hill ✆ 54461
PORSCHE London Rd ✆ 52001

MARLOW Bucks. **404** R 29 – pop. 18 584 – ECD : Wednesday – ☎ 062 84.

🛈 Caravan, Higginson Park, Pound Lane ✆ 3597 (summer only).

♦London 35 – Aylesbury 22 – ♦Oxford 29 – Reading 14.

🏯 **Compleat Angler** (T.H.F.), Marlow Bridge, Bisham Rd, SL7 1RG, ✆ 4444, Telex 848644,
Fax 6388, ⩤ River Thames, « Riverside setting and grounds », ⌇, ✗ – ⴳ rm 📺 ☎ **Ⓟ** –
🎿 150. 🅰 🆎 ⓪ *VISA*
M 19.50 **st.** (lunch) and a la carte 29.00/36.50 **st.** ⌕ 5.75 – ⌑ 8.65 – **42 rm** 90.00/120.00 **st.**,
4 suites 220.00/250.00 **st.** – SB (November-April) (weekends only) 150.00/250.00 **st.**

🏠 **Country House** without rest., Bisham Rd, SL7 1RP, ✆ 890606, 🚗 – 📺 ☎ ⴷ **Ⓟ**. 🅰 🆎
VISA. ⌇
8 rm ⌑ 45.00/65.00 **st.**

✗ **Hare and Hounds,** Henley Rd, SL7 2DF, SW : ¾ m. on A 4155 ✆ 3343 – **Ⓟ**. 🅰 🆎 *VISA*
closed Sunday dinner – **M** a la carte 16.10/19.70 **t.** ⌕ 4.80.

FORD Oxford Rd ✆ 890101

MARPLE Gtr Manchester 402 403 404 N 23 – ✪ 061 Manchester.
♦London 190 – Chesterfield 35 – ♦Manchester 11.

    Springfield, 99 Station Rd, SK6 6PA, ✆ 449 0721, ☞ – TV ☎ P. ⌧ AE ① VISA . ⌧
    M 7.50/12.50 **st.** ⌧ 2.50 – **6 rm** ⌧ 33.00/46.00 **st.**

MARSTON MORETAINE Beds. 404 S 27 – see Bedford.

MARSTON TRUSSELL Northants. – see Market Harborough (Leics.).

MARTINHOE Devon – see Lynton.

MARYPORT Cumbria 401 402 J 19 – pop. 9 890 – ECD : Wednesday – ⌧ ✪ 0900.
🇫9 Bank End ✆ 812605.
🇿 1 Senhouse St. ✆ 813738.
♦London 334 – ♦Carlisle 28 – Workington 6.

    at Birkby NE : 1 ½ m. on A 596 – ⌧ ✪ 0900 Maryport :

    Retreat, CA15 6RG, ✆ 814056, ☞ – ⌧ P. ⌧ VISA
    closed Monday lunch – **M** 13.50 **t.** and a la carte 7.40/14.00 **t.** ⌧ 3.50.
CITROEN Church Rd ✆ 812823   VAUXHALL Ellenborough ✆ 815555
FORD Mealpot Rd ✆ 812184

MASHAM North Yorks. 402 P 21 – pop. 976 – ECD : Thursday – ⌧ Ripon – ✪ 0677 Bedale.
🇫9 Burnholme, Swinton Rd ✆ 0765 (Ripon) 89379.
♦London 231 – ♦Leeds 38 – ♦Middlesbrough 37 – York 32.

    King's Head, Market Pl., HG4 4EF, ✆ 0765 (Ripon) 89295 – TV. ⌧
    10 rm.

    Bank Villa, HG4 4DB, on A 6108 ✆ 0765 (Ripon) 89605, ☞ – ⌧ rest
    April-October – **M** 11.00 **st.** ⌧ 4.00 – **7 rm** ⌧ 16.00/27.00 **st.**

    at Jervaulx Abbey NW : 5 ½ m. on A 6108 – ⌧ Ripon – ✪ 0677 Bedale :

    Jervaulx Hall ⌧, HG4 4PH, ✆ 60235, ≤, « Converted manor house, country house
    atmosphere », ☞, park – ⌧ rest ⌧ P
    Mid March-mid November – **M** (dinner only) 15.00 **t.** ⌧ 3.00 – **8 rm** ⌧ 42.00/78.00 **t.** –
    SB (except May-September) 78.00/96.00 **st.**

    Old Hall ⌧, HG4 4PH, ✆ 60313 – P
    M (dinner only)(residents only)(communal dining) 14.00 **st.** – **3 rm** ⌧ 25.00/50.00 **st.**

MATLOCK Derbs. 402 403 404 P 24 – pop. 13 706 – ECD : Thursday – ✪ 0629.
See : Site★.
Envir. : Riber Castle (ruins) ≤★ (Fauna Reserve and Wildlife Park AC) SE : 2 ½ m.
🇫18 Chesterfield Rd ✆ 582191.
🇿 The Pavilion ✆ 55082.
♦London 153 – Derby 17 – ♦Manchester 46 – ♦Nottingham 24 – ♦Sheffield 24.

    Riber Hall ⌧, Riber, DE4 5JU, SE : 3 m. by A 615 ✆ 582795, Fax 580475, ≤, « Elizabethan
    manor house », ☞, ⌧ – TV ☎ P. ⌧ AE ① VISA. ⌧
    M 12.50 **t.** (lunch) and a la carte 21.50/26.00 **t.** ⌧ 4.00 – ⌧ 4.00 – **11 rm** 58.00/78.00 **t.** –
    SB (mid October-April) 105.00/129.00 **st.**

    at Dethick SE : 4 m. by A 615 – ⌧ ✪ 0629 Matlock :

    Manor Farm ⌧, DE4 5GG, ✆ 534246, ≤, ☞, park – P. ⌧
    closed 2 weeks at Christmas – **M** 8.50 **st.** – **4 rm** ⌧ 13.00/30.00 **st.**

    at Matlock Bath S : 1 ½ m. on A 6 – ⌧ ✪ 0629 Matlock :

    New Bath (T.H.F.), New Bath Rd, DE4 3PX, ✆ 583275, Fax 580268, ⌧ heated, ⌧, ☞, ⌧
    – ⌧ rm TV ☎ P – ⌧ 100. ⌧ AE ① VISA
    M 9.00/13.00 **st.** and a la carte ⌧ 4.25 – ⌧ 8.00 – **55 rm** 60.00/86.00 **st.** – SB (except Christ-
    mas) 90.00/120.00 **st.**

FORD 41 Causeway Lane ✆ 582231

MATLOCK BATH Derbs. 402 403 404 P 24 – see Matlock.

MAWGAN Cornwall 403 E 33 – ⌧ Helston – ✪ 032 622.
♦London 317 – Falmouth 18 – Penzance 19 – Truro 22.

    Yard Bistro, Trelowarren, TR12 6AF, SE : 1 ½ m. by B 3293 ✆ 595, « Converted coach
    house » – P

MAWGAN PORTH Cornwall **403** E 32 – ECD : Wednesday – ⊠ Newquay – ✆ 0637 St. Mawgan.

♦London 293 – Newquay 7 – Truro 20.

🏠 **Tredragon,** Tredragon Rd, TR8 4DQ, ✆ 860213, Telex 860269, ≼ Mawgan Porth, 🔲, 🚗 – 📺 ☎ 🅿. 🔼 VISA
M (bar lunch Monday to Saturday)/dinner 8.50 t. ♨ 3.00 – **29 rm** ☟ 20.00/60.00 t. – SB 55.00/70.00 st.

MAWNAN SMITH Cornwall **403** E 33 – see Falmouth.

MAYFIELD East Sussex **404** U 30 – pop. 1 784 – ECD : Wednesday – ✆ 0435.

♦London 46 – ♦Brighton 25 – Eastbourne 22 – Lewes 17 – Royal Tunbridge Wells 9.

⚘ **Middle House,** High St., TN20 6AB, ✆ 872146, 🚗 – 📺 ☎ 🅿. 🔼 AE ⓞ VISA
M (closed Sunday dinner) 19.95 t. ♨ 4.25 – **8 rm** ☟ 42.50/75.00 t. – SB (except April-September) (weekends only) 71.50/96.50 st.

⚘ **Rose and Crown,** Fletching St., TN20 6TE, ✆ 872200 – 📺. 🔼 VISA 🚭
closed 25 December – **M** 6.50/10.50 t. and a la carte – **3 rm** ☟ 31.00/44.00.

MEADOW HEAD South Yorks. – see Sheffield.

MELBOURN Cambs. **404** U 27 – pop. 3 846 – ⊠ ✆ 0763 Royston (Herts.).

♦London 44 – ♦Cambridge 10.

🏠 **Melbourn Bury** ⑤, SG8 6DE, SW : ¾ m. on London rd ✆ 261151, ≼, « Tastefully furnished country house of Tudor origin », 🚗, park – 🅿. AE VISA 🚭
closed Easter and Christmas – **M** (closed Sunday) (communal dining) (dinner only) 15.00 st. ♨ 2.75 – **3 rm** ☟ 45.00/70.00 st.

XX **Pink Geranium,** 25 Station Rd, SG8 6DX, ✆ 60215, 🚗 – ⦿ 🅿. 🔼 VISA
closed Sunday dinner and Monday – **M** 12.95 t. (lunch) and a la carte 20.40/27.10 t. ♨ 4.25.

XX **Sheen Mill** with rm, Station Rd, SG8 6DH, ✆ 261393, ≼, 🚗 – 📺 ☎ 🅿. 🔼 AE ⓞ VISA. 🚭
closed Bank Holidays – **M** (closed Sunday dinner) (dancing, Saturday) 12.00 t. (lunch) and a la carte 18.90/25.50 t. ♨ 3.50 – **7 rm** ☟ 40.00/60.00 st.

MELKSHAM Wilts. **403 404** N 29 – pop. 13 248 – ECD : Wednesday – ✆ 0225.
🛈 Roundhouse, 25 Church St. ✆ 707424.

♦London 113 – ♦Bristol 25 – Salisbury 35 – Swindon 28.

🏰 **Beechfield House,** Beanacre, SN12 7PU, N : 1 m. on A 350 ✆ 703700, Fax 790118, ≼, « Country house and gardens », ⛆ heated, ⚓, park, ✖ – ⤢ rest 📺 ☎ 🅿. 🔼 AE ⓞ VISA. 🚭
M (closed Saturday lunch) 15.95 t. (lunch) and a la carte 20.40/29.20 st. ♨ 3.50 – **24 rm** ☟ 60.00/100.00 st. – SB (except summer) 97.50 st.

🏠 **Shurnhold House** without rest., Shurnhold, SN12 8DG, NW : 1 m. on A 365 ✆ 790555, « Jacobean Manor House », 🚗 – 📺 ☎ 🅿. 🚭
M (dinner only) a la carte approx. 15.00 st. ♨ 3.00 – **6 rm** ☟ 28.00/45.00 st.

at Westbrook E : 3 ½ m. on A 3102 – ⊠ Chippenham – ✆ 0380 Devizes :

⌂ **Cottage** without rest., on A 3102, SN15 2EE, ✆ 850255, 🚗 – 📺 🅿. 🚭
3 rm ☟ 20.00/35.00 s.

at Shaw NW : 1 ½ m. on A 365 – ⊠ Melksham – ✆ 0225 Shaw :

🏠 **Shaw Country,** Bath Rd, SN12 8EF, on A 365 ✆ 702836, Fax 790275, ⛆ heated, 🚗 – 📺 ☎ 🅿. 🔼 AE VISA. 🚭
closed 24 to 26 December – **M** 7.00/9.50 t. and a la carte 12.75/17.50 t. – **10 rm** ☟ 36.00/60.00 t. – SB (weekends only) 60.00/70.00 st.

AUSTIN-ROVER Lancaster Rd ✆ 702256   RENAULT Semington Rd ✆ 702182
FORD Beanacre Rd ✆ 702230

MELLOR Lancs. – see Blackburn.

MELTHAM West Yorks. **402 404** O 23 – pop. 7 098 – ⊠ ✆ 0484 Huddersfield.
🛈 Thick Hollins Hall ✆ 850227, E : 1 m.

♦London 192 – ♦Leeds 21 – ♦Manchester 23 – ♦Sheffield 26.

🏰 **Durker Roods,** Bishops Way, HD7 3AG, ✆ 851413, Telex 517429, 🚗 – 📺 ☎ 🅿 – 🔬 80. 🔼 AE ⓞ VISA
M (closed Saturday lunch and Sunday dinner) 7.00/10.00 t. and a la carte ♨ 3.70 – **31 rm** ☟ 35.00/55.00 st. – SB (weekends only) 65.00 st.

👉 *Pour voyager rapidement, utilisez les cartes Michelin "Grandes Routes" :*
920 *Europe,* **980** *Grèce,* **984** *Allemagne,* **985** *Scandinavie-Finlande,*
986 *Grande-Bretagne-Irlande,* **987** *Allemagne-Autriche-Benelux,* **988** *Italie,*
989 *France,* **990** *Espagne-Portugal,* **991** *Yougoslavie.*

MELTON MOWBRAY Leics. 402 404 R 25 – pop. 23 379 – ECD : Thursday – ☎ 0664.
🏌 Thorpe Arnold ✆ 62118, NE : 2 m.
🖼 Carnegie Museum, Thorpe End, ✆ 69946.
♦London 113 – ♦Leicester 15 – Northampton 45 – ♦Nottingham 18.

🏰 **Stapleford Park** 🦢, LE14 2EF, E : 5 m. by B 676 on Stapleford rd ✆ 057 284 (Wymondham) 522, Telex 342319, Fax 057 284 651, ≼, « Part 16C and 19C mansion in park », 🦢, 🚗, 🍴 – 🍽 rest 🍲 rest 🆃🆅 ☎ 🅿 – 🧘 300. 🔤 🆎 ⓞ 𝘝𝘐𝘚𝘈
M a la carte 21.75/29.20 t. 🍾 5.95 – 🍽 8.00 – **33 rm** 95.00 t., **2 suites** 175.00/325.00 t.

🏨 George, High St., LE13 0TR, ✆ 62112 – 🆃🆅 ☎ 🅿 – 🧘
20 rm.

⌂ **Westbourne House**, Nottingham Rd, LE13 0NP, ✆ 69456, 🚗 – 🍽 rest 🆃🆅 🅿
closed 24 December-4 January – **M** (by arrangement) 12.00 t. 🍾 3.50 – **16 rm** 🍽 15.50/32.00 t.

XX **Rumours**, 44-46 Sherrard (first floor) St., LE13 1XJ, ✆ 67871 – 🔤 𝘝𝘐𝘚𝘈
closed Saturday lunch, Sunday dinner and Monday – **M** 7.30/12.50 t. and a la carte 17.40/27.95 t. 🍾 3.00.

AUSTIN-ROVER ✆ 60266   VOLVO   Leicester Rd ✆ 63241
FIAT   Mill St. ✆ 60141
RENAULT   Victoria St. ✆ 62235   ⚙ ATS   Leicester Rd ✆ 62072

MENAI BRIDGE (PORTHAETHWY) Gwynedd 402 403 H 24 – pop. 2 972 – ECD : Wednesday – ✉ ☎ 0248.
♦London 250 – Caernarfon 11 – Chester 69 – Holyhead 24.

⚓ **Gazelle**, Glyn Garth, LL59 5PD, NE : 2 m. on A 545 ✆ 713364, ≼ – 🆃🆅 ☎ 🅿. 🔤 𝘝𝘐𝘚𝘈
M 8.50 t. and a la carte 🍾 3.50 – **9 rm** 🍽 27.50/45.00 t.

HYUNDAI, SUZUKI   Four Crosses Motor Centre ✆   MAZDA   Henffordd Garage ✆ 712002
712353

MENTMORE Bucks. 404 R 28 – pop. 196 – ✉ Leighton Buzzard – ☎ 0296 Cheddington.
♦London 46 – Aylesbury 10 – Luton 15.

🏠 **The Stable Yard** without rest., LU7 0QG, ✆ 661488, « Attractive 19C stable and coach yard » – 🆃🆅 🅿. 🚫
4 rm 🍽 32.00/58.00 st.

XX **Stag Inn,** The Green, LU7 0QF, ✆ 668423, 🚗 – 🅿. 🔤 🆎 𝘝𝘐𝘚𝘈
M 12.50 t. (lunch) and a la carte 15.40/22.20 t. 🍾 3.90.

MERE Wilts. 403 404 N 30 The West Country G. – pop. 2 201 – ECD : Wednesday – ☎ 0747.
Envir. : Stourhead House★★★ AC, NW : 3 m.
🖼 The Square, ✆ 860341.
♦London 113 – Exeter 65 – Salisbury 26 – Taunton 40.

🏨 **Old Ship,** Castle St., BA12 6JE, ✆ 860258, Fax 860501 – 🆃🆅 ☎ 🅿. 🔤 𝘝𝘐𝘚𝘈
M a la carte 10.70/17.90 – **23 rm** 🍽 27.00/44.00 t. – SB 28.00/32.00 st.

CITROEN   Castle St. ✆ 860404

MERE BROW Lancs. 402 L 23 – ✉ Preston – ☎ 077 473 (4 fig.) and 0772 (6 fig.) Hesketh Bank.
♦London 221 – ♦Liverpool 22 – Preston 11 – Southport 6.

X **Crab and Lobster,** behind the Leigh Arms, Tarleton, PR4 6LA, ✆ 812734, Seafood – 🅿.
🔤 𝘝𝘐𝘚𝘈
closed Sunday, Monday and Christmas-late January – **M** (dinner only) a la carte 14.25/23.00 t. 🍾 3.50.

MERIDEN West Midlands 403 404 P 26 – see Coventry.

MERTHYR TYDFIL Mid Glam. 403 J 28 – ☎ 0685.
♦London 179 – ♦Cardiff 25 – Gloucester 59 – ♦Swansea 33.

🏨 **Tregenna**, Park Terr., CF47 8RF, ✆ 723627, Fax 721951 – 🆃🆅 ☎ 🅿. 🔤 🆎 𝘝𝘐𝘚𝘈
M 13.50 t. and a la carte 🍾 3.00 – **21 rm** 🍽 30.00/43.00 t. – SB 49.00 st.

MEVAGISSEY Cornwall 403 F 33 The West Country G. – pop. 1 896 – ECD : Thursday – ☎ 0726.
See : Site★★.
♦London 287 – Newquay 21 – ♦Plymouth 44 – Truro 20.

⌂ **Mevagissey House** 🦢, Vicarage Hill, PL26 6SZ, ✆ 842427, 🚗 – 🆃🆅 🅿. 🔤 𝘝𝘐𝘚𝘈 🚫
March-October – **M** 9.50 t. – **6 rm** 🍽 22.50/37.00 – SB (except summer) 45.00/50.00 st.

MICKLETON Glos. 403 404 O 27 – see Chipping Campden.

MICKLE TRAFFORD Cheshire – see Chester.

MIDDLEHAM North Yorks. **402** O 21 – pop. 737 – ECD : Thursday – ☎ 0969 Wensleydale.
♦London 233 – Kendal 45 – ♦Leeds 47 – York 45.

- 🏠 **Miller's House,** Market Pl., DL8 4NR, ℘ 22630, 🐎 – ⊀✕ rest 📺 ☎ Ⓟ. 🔼 *VISA* 🦐
  closed 2 to 31 January – **M** (bar lunch residents only)/dinner 13.50 **st.** 🍷 3.50 – **7 rm**
  ☕ 26.00/76.00 **st.** – SB 66.00/72.00 **st.**

  at West Scrafton SW : 6 m. by Coverdale Rd – ✉ Leyburn – ☎ 0969 Wensleydale :

- ↟ **Coverdale Country** 🐾, Swineside, DL8 4RX, ℘ 40601, ≼, 🐎 – ⊀✕ rest 📺 Ⓟ. 🔼 *VISA*
  🦐
  M 9.25 **st.** 🍷 3.60 – **8 rm** ☕ 25.00/54.00 **t.** – SB (except summer) 49.00/52.00 **st.**

MIDDLESBROUGH

Cleveland Centre . . . . **ABY**
Corporation Road . . . . **BY** 8
Dundas Street . . . . **ABY** 12
Grange Road . . . . **ABY**
Hill Street Centre . . . . **AY**
Linthorpe Road . . . . **AY**
Newport Road . . . . **AY**

Albert Road . . . . **BY** 2
Ayresome Green Lane . . . . **AZ** 3
Bridge Street West . . . . **AY** 4
Bright Street . . . . **BY** 5
Clairville Road . . . . **BZ** 6
Cleveland Street . . . . **BY** 7
Devonshire Road . . . . **AZ** 10
Eastbourne Road . . . . **AZ** 14
Ferry Road . . . . **BY** 15

Finsbury Street . . . . **AZ** 16
Gresham Road . . . . **AZ** 18
Hartington Road . . . . **AY** 19
Longford Street . . . . **AZ** 22
Ormesby Road . . . . **BZ** 24
Princes Road . . . . **AZ** 26
St. Barnabas Road . . . . **AZ** 27
Saltersgill Avenue . . . . **BZ** 28

Smeaton Street . . . . **BY** 30
Tees Bridge
  Approach Road . . . . **AZ** 34
West Terrace . . . . **BZ** 35
Westbourne Grove . . . . **BZ** 36
Wilson Street . . . . **AY** 38
Woodlands Road . . . . **BZ** 39
Zetland Street . . . . **ABY** 41

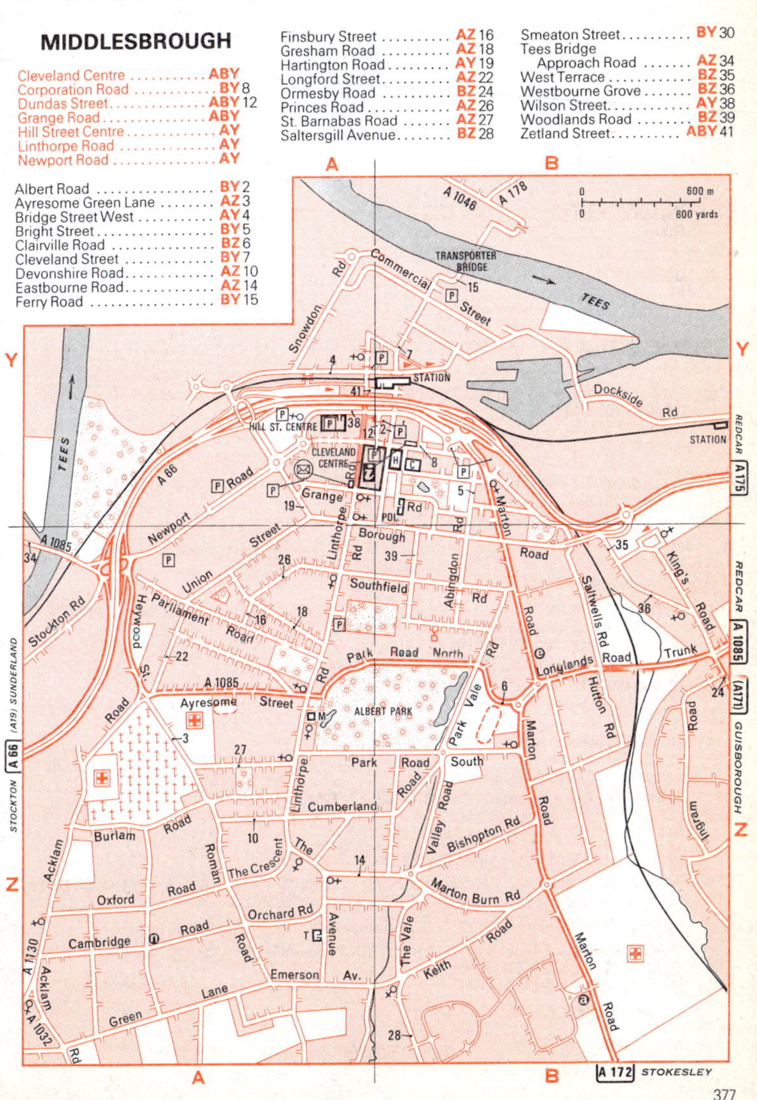

MIDDLESBROUGH Cleveland 402 Q 20 – pop. 158 516 – ECD : Wednesday – ✆ 0642.

🏌 Middlesbrough Municipal, Ladgate Lane ✆ 315533, S : by Acklam Rd AZ – 🏌 Brass Castle Lane, Marton ✆ 316430, by A 172 BZ.

✈ Teesside Airport : ✆ 0325 (Darlington) 332811, SW : 13 m. by A 66 AZ and A 19 on A 67.

🛈 51 Corporation Rd ✆ 245432 ext 3580 or 243425.

◆London 246 – ◆Kingston-upon-Hull 89 – ◆Leeds 66 – ◆Newcastle-upon-Tyne 41.

Plan on preceding page

🏨 **Baltimore,** 250 Marton Rd, TS4 2EZ, ✆ 224111, Telex 58517 – TV ☎ P. 🔲 AE ⓪ VISA 🛪
M (*closed lunch Saturday and Sunday*) 8.50 **st.** and a la carte ▯2.50 – ☕ 5.45 – **30 rm** 39.00/49.00 **st.**, **1 suite** 75.00/95.00 **st.**
  BZ **e**

🏨 **Marton Way Motel,** Marton Rd, TS4 3BS, S : 2 m. on A 172 ✆ 817651, Telex 587783, Fax 829409 – ❌ rm TV ☎ P. 🔲 AE ⓪ VISA
  BZ **a**
M (*carving rest.*) 6.95 **t.** and a la carte – **52 rm** ☕ 24.50/44.50 **st.** – SB (weekends only) 27.00/33.50 **st.**

↑ **Grey House,** 79 Cambridge Rd, TS5 5NL, ✆ 817485, 🛋 – TV P
  AZ **n**
M 7.00 **st.** – **7 rm** ☕ 25.00/39.00 **st.**

AUSTIN-ROVER 336 Stokesley Rd, Marton ✆ 317171
AUSTIN-ROVER 237 Acklam Rd ✆ 817741
BMW, VAUXHALL Stokesley ✆ 710566
CITROEN Linthorpe Rd ✆ 822884
FORD Ormesby ✆ 242451
NISSAN Trunk Rd ✆ 461451
RENAULT Newport Rd ✆ 249346

SKODA Eston Grange ✆ 452436
TALBOT, PEUGEOT Marton Rd ✆ 242873
TOYOTA Eastbourne Rd ✆ 816658
VAUXHALL-OPEL Marton Rd ✆ 243415
VW-AUDI Park End ✆ 317971

🛞 ATS Murdock Rd (off Sotherby Rd), Cargo Fleet ✆ 249245/6

MIDDLETON STONEY Oxon. 403 404 Q 28 – pop. 238 – ECD : Saturday – ✉ Bicester – ✆ 086 989.

◆London 66 – Northampton 30 – ◆Oxford 12.

🏨 **Jersey Arms Inn,** Ardley Rd, OX6 8SE, ✆ 234 – TV ☎ P. 🔲 AE ⓪ VISA 🛪
M (*closed Sunday dinner*) a la carte 14.65/22.95 **t.** ▯3.95 – **10 rm** ☕ 49.50/60.00 **t.**, **3 suites** 85.00 **st.** – SB 82.50/89.50 **st.**

MIDDLE WALLOP Hants. 403 404 P 30 – ✉ Stockbridge – ✆ 0264 Andover.

◆London 80 – Salisbury 11 – ◆Southampton 21.

🏨 **Fifehead Manor,** SO20 8EG, on A 343 ✆ 781565, « Converted 16C manor house », 🛋 – TV ☎ ♿ P. 🔲 AE ⓪ VISA
closed 2 weeks Christmas-New Year – **M** 13.50/23.50 **t.** and a la carte ▯4.00 – **16 rm** ☕ 45.00/85.00 **t.** – SB (November-Easter) 90.00/110.00 **st.**

MIDHURST West Sussex 404 R 31 – pop. 5 991 – ECD : Wednesday – ✆ 073 081.

See : Cowdray House (Tudor ruins)★ *AC.*

Envir. : Upark★ (17C-18C) *AC*, SW : 12 m.

🏌 Cowdray Park ✆ 2088, NE : 1 m. on A 272 – 🏌 at Petersfield, The Heath ✆ 0730 (Petersfield) 63725, W : 10 m.

◆London 57 – ◆Brighton 38 – Chichester 12 – ◆Southampton 41.

🏨 **Spread Eagle** (Best Western), South St., GU29 9NH, ✆ 6911, Telex 86853, Fax 5668, « 15C hostelry, antique furnishings » – ❌ rm TV ☎ P – 🔬 40. 🔲 AE ⓪ VISA
M 17.50/23.50 **st.** ▯5.00 – **41 rm** ☕ 63.00/150.00 **st.** – SB 90.00/140.00 **st.**

XX Asha Tandoori, Rumbolds Hill, GU29 9BX, ✆ 4748, Indian rest.

X **Mida,** Wool Lane, GU29 9BY, ✆ 3284
closed last week May and last week October – **M** (*booking essential*) a la carte approx. 30.35 **t.**

X **Hindle Wakes,** 1 Church Hill, GU29 9NX, ✆ 3371 – 🔲
closed 2 weeks September and 24 to 27 December – **M** (*closed Tuesday lunch, Sunday and Monday*) 12.50/16.50 **t.** ▯3.15.

X **Maxine's,** Red Lion St., GU29 9PB, ✆ 6271 – 🔲 AE ⓪ VISA
closed Monday lunch, Tuesday, 2 weeks February and 2 weeks October – **M** 8.95/20.00 **st.** and a la carte 13.00/19.50 **st.** ▯3.95.

at Bepton SW : 2 ½ m. by A 286 – ✉ ✆ 073 081 Midhurst :

🏠 **Park House** ⌂, South Bepton, GU29 0JB, ✆ 2880, ⏛ heated, 🛋, 🛪 – TV ☎ P. 🔲 VISA
M (*by arrangement*) 12.50/15.00 **st.** ▯2.70 – **11 rm** ☕ 35.00/80.00 **st.**

at Trotton W : 3 ¼ m. on A 272 – ✉ Petersfield (Hants.) – ✆ 073 080 Rogate :

🏨 **Southdowns** ⌂, GU31 5JN, S : 1 m. ✆ 521, Telex 86658, Fax 790, 🔲, 🛋 – ❌ rm 🍽 rest TV ☎ ♿ P – 🔬 150. 🔲 AE VISA 🛪
M 10.00/20.00 **t.** and a la carte ▯3.50 – **21 rm** ☕ 45.00/120.00 **t.** – SB 75.00/90.00 **st.**

RENAULT Rumbolds Hill ✆ 2162

If you find you cannot take up a hotel booking you have made,
please let the hotel know immediately.

MILDENHALL Suffolk **404** V 26 – pop. 9 794 – ECD : Thursday – ✪ 0638.

♦London 73 – ♦Cambridge 22 – ♦Ipswich 38 – ♦Norwich 41.

🏠 **Bell** (Best Western), High St., IP28 7EA, ℘ 717272, Telex 94011647, Fax 717057 – 📺 ☎ Ⓟ – 🔥 100. 🔌 AE ⓞ VISA
M a la carte 10.55/14.85 **t.** 🍷 3.00 – **17 rm** ☕ 36.00/58.00 **t.** – SB 66.00/72.00 **st.**

⑩ ATS Southgate Av. ℘ 713841/713891

MILFORD HAVEN (ABERDAUGLEDDAU) Dyfed **403** E 28 – pop. 13 927 – ECD : Thursday ✪ 064 62.

🏌 Woodbine House, Hubberstone ℘ 2368.

♦London 258 – Carmarthen 39 – Fishguard 23.

🏨 Lord Nelson, Hamilton Terr., SA73 3AL, ℘ 5341, 🚗 – ⇴ rm 📺 ☎ Ⓟ
29 rm.

MILFORD-ON-SEA Hants. **403** **404** P 31 – pop. 3 953 – ECD : Wednesday – ✉ Lymington – ✪ 0590.

♦London 109 – Bournemouth 15 – ♦Southampton 24 – Winchester 37.

🏨 **South Lawn,** Lymington Rd, SO41 0RF, ℘ 43911, 🚗 – ⇴ rest 📺 ☎ Ⓟ. 🔌 VISA. 🐾
closed mid-December-mid January – **M** *(closed dinner Sunday and Monday to non-residents)* (dinner only and Sunday lunch)/dinner 12.75 **t.** and a la carte 🍷 4.50 – **24 rm** ☕ 47.00/80.00 **t.** – SB (November-May) 72.00/77.00 **st.**

🏨 **Westover Hall,** Park Lane, SO41 OPT, ℘ 43044, Fax 44490, ≼ Solent and the Needles, « Restored Victorian mansion » – 📺 ☎ Ⓟ. 🔌 AE ⓞ VISA. 🐾
M 16.95 **st.** and a la carte 🍷 3.25 – **13 rm** ☕ 32.00/110.00 **st.** – SB (except September, Easter and Christmas) 39.00/58.00 **st.**

MILTON ABBAS Dorset **403** **404** N 31 The West Country G. – pop. 433 – ✉ Blandford – ✪ 0258.

See : Village★.

♦London 127 – Bournemouth 23 – Weymouth 19.

🏠 **Milton Manor** 🦃, DT11 0AZ, ℘ 880254, ≼, « Country house atmosphere », 🚗, park – Ⓟ. 🔌 VISA. 🐾
M 9.50/13.50 **t.** 🍷 3.00 – **12 rm** ☕ 38.00/66.00 **t.** – SB 70.00/78.00 **st.**

🏠 **Old Bakery** without rest., DT11 OBW, ℘ 880327, « Late 18C bakehouse in attractive conservation village », 🚗 – Ⓟ
closed Christmas – **3 rm** ☕ 10.00/40.00 **st.**

MILTON KEYNES Bucks. **404** R 27 – pop. 93 305 – ✪ 0908.

🏌 Abbey Hill, Two Mile Ash ℘ 563845, W : 2 m. by A 5.

🄩 Saxon Court, 502 Avebury Boulevard ℘ 691995.

♦London 56 – ♦Birmingham 72 – Bedford 16 – Northampton 18 – ♦Oxford 37.

🏨 **Post House** (T.H.F.), 500 Saxon Gate West, Milton Keynes Central, MK9 2HQ, ℘ 667722, Telex 826842, Fax 674714, 🔲 – 🛗 ⇴ rm 🍽 📺 ☎ ♿ Ⓟ – 🔥 160. 🔌 AE ⓞ VISA
M 14.50 **st.** (dinner) – ☕ 7.60 – **161 rm** 80.00/95.00 **st.**, **2 suites** 160.00 **st.** – SB (weekends only) 66.00/76.00 **st.**

🏨 **Broughton,** Broughton Village, MK10 9AA, E : 4 m. by A 509 off A 5130 ℘ 667726, Telex 826730, Fax 604844, 🚗 – 📺 ☎ ♿ Ⓟ. 🔌 AE ⓞ VISA
M a la carte 7.50/17.00 **st.** 🍷 2.60 – **30 rm** ☕ 55.00/65.00 **st.**

🏨 **Moorings Toby,** Milton Keynes Marina, Waterside, Peartree Bridge, MK6 3PE, SE : 1 ¾ m. by A 509 off A 4146 (Marlborough St.) ℘ 691515, Telex 826244, Fax 690274, « Marina setting alongside the Grand Union Canal » – ⇴ rm 📺 ☎ ♿ Ⓟ. 🔌 AE ⓞ VISA. 🐾
M (grill rest.) a la carte 7.05/12.05 **t.** – **40 rm** ☕ 52.50/62.50 **t.**

🏨 **Friendly Lodge,** Monks Way, Two Mile Ash, MK8 8LY, NW : 2 m. by A 509 and A5 at junction with A 422 ℘ 561666, Telex 826152, Fax 568303 – ⇴ 🍽 rest 📺 ☎ ♿ Ⓟ – 🔥 120. 🔌 AE ⓞ VISA
M *(closed lunch Saturday and Bank Holidays)* (carving rest.) 9.50/12.50 **st.** and a la carte 🍷 4.00 – ☕ 4.75 – **50 rm** 49.50/69.50 **st.** – SB (weekends only) 60.00 **st.**

🏨 Wayfarer, Willen Lake, MK15 ODS, E : 2 m. by A 509 off Brickhill St. ℘ 675222, Fax 674679, ≼, « Lakeside setting » – ⇴ rm 📺 ☎ ♿ Ⓟ – 🔥 50. 🐾
41 rm.

🍴 **Jaipur,** Elder House, 502 Eldergate, Station Sq., MK9 1LR, ℘ 669796, Indian rest. – 🔌 AE ⓞ VISA
M a la carte 10.05/13.45 **t.**

MILTON ON STOUR Dorset 403 404 N 30 – see Gillingham.

MILTON-UNDER-WYCHWOOD Oxon – ✆ 0993 Shipton-under-Wychwood.
♦London 83 – ♦Birmingham 52 – Gloucester 35 – ♦Oxford 27.

  Hillborough, The Green, OX7 6JH, ✆ 830501 – TV P. ⬛ AE ⓞ VISA
  closed 2 to 31 January – **M** *(closed Sunday dinner)* 9.00/11.00 **t.** and a la carte 11.85/18.40 **t.**
  🍷 2.95 – **6 rm** ⊑ 32.00/42.00 **t.** – SB (except Bank Holidays) 36.00/52.00 **st.**

MINEHEAD Somerset 403 J 30 **The West Country G.** – pop. 8 449 – ECD : Wednesday –
✆ 0643.
See : Site★ – Higher Town : Church Steps★ – St. Michael's Church★ – West Somerset Railway★.
Envir. : Selworthy★ : Church★★ (≼★★★ from Church of Dunkery Beacon), W : 4 ½ m. – Timbers-
combe Church★, S : 5 m.

🏌 Warren Rd ✆ 2057.
🛈 Market House, The Parade ✆ 2624.
♦London 187 – ♦Bristol 64 – Exeter 43 – Taunton 25.

  Benares ⑤, Northfield Rd, TA24 5PT, ✆ 704911, ≼, « Gardens » – ⤬ rest TV ☎ P. ⬛
  AE ⓞ VISA
  Mid March-7 November and Christmas – **M** (bar lunch)/dinner 12.90 **t.** 🍷 3.95 – **20 rm**
  ⊑ 33.00/62.00 **t.** – SB 69.00/80.00 **st.**

  Northfield (Best Western) ⑤, Northfield Rd, TA24 5PU, ✆ 5155, « ≼ gardens », ⬛ – 🛗
  ⤬ rest TV ☎ P. – 🔬 80. ⬛ AE ⓞ VISA
  M 4.00/11.75 **t.** 🍷 2.75 – **26 rm** ⊑ 39.00/68.00 **t.** – SB 78.00/102.00 **st.**

  Beach, The Avenue, TA24 5AP, ✆ 2193, Fax 4145, 🛝 heated – ⤬ TV ☏ P. ⬛ AE ⓞ VISA
  M 7.50/9.50 **t.** and a la carte 10.50/13.25 **t.** 🍷 3.00 – **34 rm** ⊑ 23.50/59.00 **t.** – SB 58.00/66.00 **st.**

  Beacon Country House ⑤, Beacon Rd, TA24 5SD, ✆ 703476, 🛝, ⚘, park – TV P. ⬛
  VISA. ❄
  M 12.95/17.50 **st.** – **7 rm** ⊑ 56.50/73.00 **st.**

  Beaconwood ⑤, Church Rd, North Hill, TA24 5SB, ✆ 2032, ≼ sea and Minehead,
  🛝 heated, ⚘ – ⤬ rest TV P. ⬛ VISA
  closed Christmas and New Year – **M** (bar lunch)/dinner 11.00 **t.** 🍷 3.00 – **14 rm**
  ⊑ 21.00/48.00 **t.** – SB (October-March) 40.00/50.00 **st.**

  Remuera, Northfield Rd, TA24 5QH, ✆ 702611, ⚘ – ⤬ rest TV P. ⬛ VISA
  March-October – **M** 12.00 (dinner) and a la carte 🍷 4.25 – **8 rm** ⊑ 20.00/60.00 –
  SB (except summer) 50.00/68.00 **st.**

  York, 48 The Avenue, TA24 5AN, ✆ 5151 – TV ☎ P. ⬛ AE ⓞ VISA ❄
  closed Christmas – **M** (dinner only) a la carte 5.10/12.00 **t.** – **21 rm** ⊑ 14.00/38.00 **t.**

  Mentone, The Parks, TA24 8BS, ✆ 705229, ⚘ – ⤬ rest TV. ❄
  April-October – **M** 6.50 **t.** 🍷 2.50 – **9 rm** ⊑ 19.00/38.00 **t.** – SB 37.00/45.00 **st.**

  Woodbridge, 12-14 The Parks, TA24 8BS, ✆ 704860 – P. ⬛ AE ⓞ VISA
  closed January and February – **M** 7.00 **t.** 🍷 2.50 – **9 rm** ⊑ 12.65/27.60 **t.** – SB 29.10/35.65 **st.**

    at Middlecombe W : 1 ½ m. on A 39 – ✉ ✆ 0643 Minehead:

  Periton Park ⑤, TA24 8SW, ✆ 6885, ≼, ⚘, park – ⤬ rest TV ☎ 🚻 P. ⬛ AE ⓞ VISA
  ❄
  closed January – **M** (restricted lunch, residents only)/dinner 20.00 **t.** and a la carte – **7 rm**
  ⊑ 52.50/90.00 **st.** – SB (except Bank Holidays) 67.50/105.00 **st.**

FIAT Alcombe Rd ✆ 3379   ⓦ ATS Bampton St. ✆ 4808

MINSTER-IN-THANET Kent 404 Y 29 – see Ramsgate.

MINSTER LOVELL Oxon. 403 404 P 28 – pop. 1 364 – ✉ ✆ 0993 Witney.
♦London 72 – Gloucester 36 – ♦Oxford 16.

  Old Swan ⑤, Main St., Old Minster, OX8 5RN, ✆ 775614, « 14C inn », ⚘ – TV ☎ P. ❄
  10 rm.

MISKIN Mid Glam. – ✉ Cardiff – ✆ 0443 Pontypridd.
♦London 169 – ♦Cardiff 22 – ♦Swansea 31.

  Miskin Manor, CF7 8ND, E : 1 ¾ m. by A 4119 (Groes Faen rd) ✆ 224204, Fax 237606, ≼,
  « Local stone building in attractive formal grounds », ⬛, ⚘, park, squash – TV ☎ P. –
  🔬 150. ⬛ AE ⓞ VISA ❄
  closed 5 days Christmas – **M** 16.50 **t.** and a la carte – ⊑ 6.00 – **34 rm** 60.00/95.00 **t.**, **1 suite**
  120.00 **t.** – SB (except Christmas) 200.00 **st.**

MITHIAN Cornwall 403 E 33 – see St. Agnes.

MOLD (YR WYDDGRUG) Clwyd **402 403** K 24 – pop. 8 487 – ECD : Thursday – ☎ 0352.
 Pant-y-Mwyn ℘ 740318, W : 4 m. – Old Padeswood, Station Rd ℘ 0244 (Buckley) 547401, E : 2 m. on A 5118.
 Town Hall, Earl St. ℘ 59331 (summer only).
♦ London 211 – Chester 12 – ♦ Liverpool 29 – Shrewsbury 45.

   Soughton Hall ⑤, CH7 6AB, N : 2 ½ m. by A 494 and A 5119 on Alltami rd ℘ 035 286 (Northrop) 207, Telex 61267, Fax 382, ≤, « Early 18C Italianate mansion », ☞ – ✗ rest TV
   ☎ P. ⑤ AE VISA. ⑤
   closed first 2 weeks January – M (closed Sunday dinner Christmas-Easter) (lunch by arrangement Monday and Saturday) 18.00/26.00 t. ⑤ 5.00 – **11 rm** ⥥ 80.00/130.00 t. – SB (weekends only) 125.00/150.00 **st.**

   Beaufort Palace, Alltami Rd, New Brighton, CH7 6RQ, ℘ 58646, Fax 57132 – TV ☎ P –
   ⑤ 300. ⑤ VISA
   M 6.50/10.50 **st.** and a la carte – ⥥ 4.95 – **102 rm** 49.00/85.00 **st.** – SB (weekends only) 60.00/65.00 **st.**

   Bryn Awel, Denbigh Rd, CH7 1BL, on A 541 ℘ 58622 – TV ☎ P. ⑤ VISA
   M (closed Saturday lunch and Sunday dinner) 7.95 t. and a la carte ⑤ 3.50 – **17 rm** ⥥ 32.00/45.00 t. – SB 44.00/60.00 **st.**

  ATS Wrexham Rd ℘ 3682

MONK FRYSTON North Yorks. **402** Q 22 – pop. 737 – ✉ Lumby – ☎ 0977 South Milford.
Envir. : Selby Abbey Church★★ (12C-16C) E : 8 ½ m. – Carlton Towers★ (19C) AC, SE : 14 ½ m.
♦London 190 – ♦Kingston-upon-Hull 42 – ♦Leeds 13 – York 20.

   Monk Fryston Hall, LS25 5DU, ℘ 682369, Telex 556634, Fax 683544, « Italian garden »,
   park – ✗ rest TV ☎ P – ⑤ 50. ⑤ AE VISA
   M 9.50/14.00 **st.** and a la carte ⑤ 6.00 – **29 rm** ⥥ 50.00/85.00 **st.** – SB (except Christmas and New Year)(weekends only) 73.00/82.00 **st.**

   Selby Fork Post House (T.H.F.), South Milford, LS25 5LF, W : 2 ¼ m. by A 63 on A 1
   ℘ 682711, Telex 557074, Fax 685462, ⑤, ✗ – ✗ rm ☰ rest TV ☎ P – ⑤ 300
   109 rm.

MONKTON COMBE Avon – see Bath.

MONMOUTH (TREFYNWY) Gwent **403** L 28 – pop. 7 379 – ECD : Thursday – ☎ 0600.
Envir. : SE : Wye Valley★ – Raglan (castle★ 15C) SW : 7 m. – Skenfrith (castle and church★) NW : 6 m.
 Rolls of Monmouth, The Hendre ℘ 5353, W : 4 m. on B 4233 – Leasebrook Lane ℘ 2212.
 National Trust Visitor Centre, Church St. ℘ 3899.
♦London 147 – Gloucester 26 – Newport 24 – ♦Swansea 64.

   King's Head, Agincourt Sq., NP5 3DY, ℘ 2177, Telex 497294 – TV ☎ P – ⑤ 80. ⑤ AE
   ⑩ VISA
   M 12.00/22.00 t. and a la carte ⑤ 3.60 – ⥥ 7.00 – **29 rm** 34.00/62.00 – SB (except Christmas and New Year) 72.00/84.00 **st.**

   at Whitebrook SE : 8 ½ m. by A 466 – ✉ ☎ 0600 Monmouth :

  Crown at Whitebrook ⑤ with rm, NP5 4TX, ℘ 860254, ☞ – TV ☎ P. ⑤ AE ⑩ VISA
   closed January – **M** 10.95/19.75 t. ⑤ 3.40 – **12 rm** ⥥ 36.00/67.00 t. – SB 86.00/96.00 **st.**

   at Trelleck S : 5 ½ m. on B 4293 – ✉ ☎ 0600 Monmouth :

  Village Green, NP5 4DA, ℘ 860119 – ⑭.

AUSTIN-ROVER St. James Sq. ℘ 2773   SUZUKI, CITROEN Wonastow Rd ℘ 2896
FORD Redbrook Rd ℘ 2366
MERCEDES-BENZ 8 Wonastow Rd ℘ 3118   ATS Wonastow Rd, Ind. Est. ℘ 6832

MONTACUTE Somerset **403** L 31 – see Yeovil.

MONTGOMERY (TREFALDWYN) Powys **403** K 26 – pop. 1 035 – ☎ 068 681.
♦London 194 – ♦Birmingham 71 – Chester 53 – Shrewsbury 30.

   Dragon, Town Square, SY15 6AA, ℘ 359, ⑤ – TV ☎ P. ⑤ VISA. ⑤
   M 10.75/11.75 t. and a la carte ⑤ 3.00 – **15 rm** ⥥ 29.00/54.00 t. – SB (except Christmas) 65.00/76.00 **st.**

MORECAMBE Lancs. **402** L 21 – pop. 41 432 – ECD : Wednesday – ☎ 0524.
See : Marineland★ AC – Clubhouse ℘ 412841, on sea front.
 Marine Rd Central ℘ 414110.
♦London 248 – ♦Blackpool 29 – ♦Carlisle 66 – Lancaster 4.

   Strathmore (Best Western), Marine Rd, East Promenade, LA4 5AP, ℘ 421234, Telex 65452,
   Fax 414242, ≤ – ⑤ ✗ rest TV ☎ P – ⑤ 100. ⑤ AE ⑩ VISA. ⑤
   M 7.25/11.50 t. and a la carte ⑤ 3.95 – **51 rm** ⥥ 42.00/80.00 t. – SB 70.00/85.00 **st.**

   Prospect, 363 Marine Rd, East Promenade, LA4 5AQ, ℘ 417819 – TV. VISA
   Easter-November – **M** 6.00 st. ⑤ 4.00 – **14 rm** ⥥ 15.00/27.00 st. – SB 32.00/35.00 **st.**

MORECAMBE
AUSTIN-ROVER Marine Drive Central ✆ 414078
CITROEN-LADA West Gate ✆ 413891
VAUXHALL-OPEL Bare Lane ✆ 410205
VOLVO Marlborough Rd ✆ 417437

VW. AUDI Heysham Rd ✆ 415833

⓪ ATS Westgate ✆ 68075/62011

MORETON-IN-MARSH Glos. **403 404** O 28 – pop. 2 545 – ECD : Wednesday – ✆ 0608.
Envir. : Chastleton House★★ (Elizabethan) *AC*, SE : 3 ½ m.

♦London 86 – ♦Birmingham 40 – Gloucester 31 – ♦Oxford 29.

🏛 **Manor House,** High St., GL56 0LJ, ✆ 50501, Telex 837151, Fax 51481, « 16C manor house, gardens », ⬜ – 🛗 📺 ☎ Ⓟ – 🚗 90. 🅰 ⒶⒺ ⓪ *VISA* 🛇
   M 12.00/17.00 st. 🍾 3.15 – **38 rm** ⟷ 45.50/105.00 st.

🏠 Redesdale Arms, High St., GL56 0AW, ✆ 50308, Fax 51843 – 📺 ☎ Ⓟ – **15 rm. 2 suites**.

🏠 **White Hart Royal** (T.H.F.), High St., GL56 0BA, ✆ 50731 – 📺 ☎ Ⓟ – 🚗 25. 🅰 ⒶⒺ ⓪
   VISA
   M 9.50/17.50 st. 🍾 3.75 – ⟷ 7.00 – **18 rm** 38.00/68.00 st. – SB 68.00/108.00 st.

⋔ **Moreton House,** High St., GL56 0LQ, ✆ 50747 – 📺. 🅰 *VISA*
   M 9.25 t. 🍾 3.25 – **12 rm** ⟷ 17.00/38.00 t.

XX **Annies,** 3 Oxford St., GL56 0LA, ✆ 51981 – 🅰 ⒶⒺ ⓪ *VISA*
   closed 29 January-12 February – **M** *(closed lunch Monday and Saturday and Sunday dinner)*
   a la carte 15.25/21.70 st. 🍾 3.50.

PEUGEOT-TALBOT London Rd ✆ 50585

RENAULT Little Compton ✆ 74202

MORPETH Northumb. **401 402** O 18 – pop. 14 301 – ECD : Thursday – ✆ 0670.
Envir. : Brinkburn Priory (site★, church★ : Gothic) *AC*, NW : 10 m – Wallington House★ W :
11 m.

🏌 Newbiggin-by-the-Sea ✆ 817344, E : 9 m.
🛈 The Chantry, Bridge St. ✆ 511323.

♦London 301 – ♦Edinburgh 93 – ♦Newcastle-upon-Tyne 15.

🏰 **Linden Hall** 🐾, Longhorsley Rd, NE65 8XF, NW : 7½ m. by A 192 on A 697 ✆ 516611,
   Telex 538224, Fax 88544, ≤, « Country house in extensive grounds », 🍽, park, ✗ – 🛗 📺
   ☎ ⓴ Ⓟ – 🚗 180. 🅰 ⒶⒺ ⓪ *VISA* 🛇
   M 11.25/17.50 st. and a la carte 18.25/24.50 st. – **45 rm** ⟷ 80.00/145.00 st.

AUSTIN-ROVER Hillgate ✆ 517441
CITROEN Pegswood ✆ 512189
FORD 53-55 Bridge St. ✆ 519611
PEUGEOT, TALBOT Ellington ✆ 860327
RENAULT Clifton ✆ 512538

VAUXHALL Bridge End ✆ 512115
VW 12 Castle Sq. ✆ 519011

⓪ ATS Coopies Lane Ind Est. ✆ 514627

MORSTON Norfolk – see Blakeney.

MORTEHOE Devon **403** H 30 – see Woolacombe.

MOULSFORD Oxon. **403 404** Q 29 – pop. 494 – ✆ 0491 Cholsey.

♦London 58 – ♦Oxford 17 – Reading 13 – Swindon 37.

🏠 **Beetle and Wedge** 🐾, Ferry Lane, OX10 9JF ✆ 651381, ≤, 🍽 – 📺 ☎ Ⓟ. 🅰 ⒶⒺ *VISA*
   M *(closed Sunday dinner)* 23.50 t. and a la carte 🍾 3.75 – **13 rm** ⟷ 50.00/65.00 t. –
   SB (except Christmas and Bank Holidays) (weekends only) 90.00 t.

MOULTON Northants. **404** R 27 – see Northampton.

MOULTON North Yorks. **402** P 20 – ✉ Richmond – ✆ 032 577 Barton.

♦London 243 – ♦Leeds 53 – ♦Middlesbrough 25 – ♦Newcastle-upon-Tyne 43.

XX **Black Bull Inn,** DL10 6QJ, ✆ 377289, Fax 377422, « Brighton Belle Pullman coach » – Ⓟ.
   🅰 ⒶⒺ *VISA*
   closed Saturday lunch, Sunday and 24 to 31 December – **M** 8.75 t. (lunch) and a la carte
   13.25/24.95 t. 🍾 3.50.

MOUSEHOLE Cornwall **403** D 33 The West Country G. – ECD : Wednesday except summer –
✉ ✆ 0736 Penzance.
See : Site★.

♦London 321 – Penzance 3 – Truro 29.

🏠 **Lobster Pot,** South Cliff, TR19 6QX, ✆ 731251, Fax 731140, ≤ – 📺 ☎
   closed January – **M** (bar lunch)/dinner 14.00 st. and a la carte 🍾 4.50 – **26 rm**
   ⟷ 20.50/66.00 st.

🏠 **Carn Du** 🐾, Raginnis Hill, TR19 6SS, ✆ 731233, ≤ Mounts Bay, 🍽 – 🛏 rest Ⓟ. 🅰 ⒶⒺ
   VISA 🛇
   closed 5 February-9 March – **M** (bar lunch)/dinner 13.45 t. 🍾 3.95 – **7 rm** ⟷ 28.00/46.00 t. –
   SB (November-February) 55.00/61.00 st.

⋔ **Tavis Vor,** The Parade, TR19 6PR, ✆ 731306, ≤ Mounts Bay, 🍽 – Ⓟ 🛇
   M 8.00 st. 🍾 3.60 – **7 rm** ⟷ 16.50/37.00 st.

MUDEFORD Dorset **403 404** O 31 – see Christchurch.

MUCH BIRCH Heref. and Worc. – see Hereford.

MUKER North Yorks. **402** N 21 – ✉ ☎ 0748 Richmond.
♦London 262 – ♦Carlisle 63 – Kendal 38.

  🏠 Old Vicarage ⟷, DL11 6QH, ☎ 86498, ≼, 🚗 – ᴚ 📺 ☎ 🅿. 🐾
     March-October – **5 rm**.

MULLION Cornwall **403** E 33 **The West Country G.** – pop. 1 958 – ECD : Wednesday – ✉ Hel-
ston – ☎ 0326.
See : Mullion Cove★★★ (Church★).
♦London 323 – Falmouth 21 – Penzance 21 – Truro 26.

  🏨 **Polurrian** ⟷, TR12 7EN, SW : ½ m. ☎ 240421, Telex 94015906, Fax 240083, ≼ Mounts Bay,
     🏊 heated, 🎾, 🚗, ✵, squash – ᴚ rest 📺 ☎ 🅿. 🔏 AE ⓪ VISA
     closed mid December-mid March – **M** (bar lunch)/dinner 12.00 **st.** and a la carte ▯ 3.00 –
     40 rm ⊇ 34.00/128.00 **st.**, **1 suite** 73.00/146.00 **st.**

MUMBLES West Glam. **403** I 29 – ECD : Wednesday – ✉ ☎ 0792 Swansea.
See : Mumbles Head★.
Envir. : Cefn Bryn (✳★★★ from the reservoir) W : 12 m. – Rhosili (site and ≼★★★) W : 18 m. –
W : Oxwich Bay★.
♦London 202 – ♦Swansea 6.

  🏨 **Langland Court** (Best Western), 31 Langland Court Rd, Langland Bay, SA3 4TD, W : 1 m.
     ☎ 361545, Fax 362302, 🚗 – ᴚ rm 📺 ☎ 🚘 🅿 – 🔥 160. 🔏 AE ⓪ VISA. 🐾
     M 8.75/13.00 **t.** and a la carte ▯ 4.25 – **21 rm** ⊇ 42.00/60.00 **t.** – SB 70.00/85.00 **st.**

  🏨 **Osborne** (Embassy), Rotherslade Rd, Langland Bay, SA3 4QL, W : ¾ m. ☎ 366274, Fax
     363100, ≼ – 🛗 📺 ☎ 🅿 – 🔥 50. 🔏 AE ⓪ VISA
     M 8.50/11.50 **st.** and a la carte ▯ 4.75 – **36 rm** ⊇ 55.00/65.00 **st.** – SB 29.50/36.00 **st.**

  🏨 **Norton House**, 17 Norton Rd, SA3 5TQ, ☎ 404891 – 📺 ☎ 🅿. 🔏 AE ⓪ VISA. 🐾
     M (dinner only) 17.50 **t.** and a la carte – ⊇ 7.50 – **15 rm** 40.00/70.00 **t.**

  🏠 **Old School House**, 37 Nottage Rd, Newton, SA3 4SU, W : 1 m. ☎ 361541 – 📺 ☎ 🅿. 🔏
     VISA. 🐾
     closed 24 to 30 December – **M** 8.95/10.95 **t.** and a la carte ▯ 3.50 – **7 rm** ⊇ 38.00/48.00 **t.**

  🏠 **Wittemberg**, 2 Rotherslade Rd, Langland, SA3 4QN, W : ¾ m. ☎ 369696 – ᴚ rm 📺 🅿.
     🔏 VISA. 🐾
     closed Christmas – **M** 9.50 **st.** – **11 rm** ⊇ 25.00/40.00 **st.**

MUNGRISDALE Cumbria **401 402** L 19 20 – pop. 336 – ✉ Penrith – ☎ 059 683 Threlkeld.
♦London 301 – ♦Carlisle 33 – Keswick 8.5 – Penrith 13.

  ⚘ **Mill** ⟷, CA11 0XR, ☎ 79659, 🚗 – ᴚ rest 📺 🅿
     closed November-February – **M** (dinner only) 13.50 **t.** ▯ 3.40 – **7 rm** ⊇ 24.50/53.00 **t.**

  ⚘ **Mill Inn** ⟷, CA11 0XR, ☎ 79632, 🚗 – ᴚ rest 🅿
     closed mid December-mid February – **M** (bar lunch)/dinner 8.50 **st.** ▯ 2.80 – **7 rm**
     ⊇ 14.50/34.00 **st.**

NANTGAREDIG Dyfed **403** H 28 – see Carmarthen.

NANTWICH Cheshire **402 403 404** M 24 – pop. 11 867 – ECD : Wednesday – ☎ 0270.
🛈 Beam St. ☎ 623914.
♦London 176 – Chester 20 – ♦Liverpool 45 – ♦Stoke-on-Trent 17.

  🏨🏨 **Rookery Hall** ⟷, Worleston, CW5 6DQ, N : 2 ½ m. by A 51 on B 5074 ☎ 626866, Telex
     367169, Fax 626027, ≼, « 19C country house », ⟷, 🚗, park, ✵ – ᴚ rest 📺 ☎ 🅿. 🔏 AE
     ⓪ VISA. 🐾
     M (booking essential) 15.00/30.00 **t.** and a la carte – **10 rm** ⊇ 75.00/190.00 **t.**, **1 suite**
     230.00 **t.** – SB (January-March and July-August) 75.00/135.00 **st.**

  🏨 **Crown**, High St., CW5 5AS, ☎ 625283, Fax 628047, « 16C inn » – 📺 ☎ 🅿 – 🔥 140. 🔏 AE
     ⓪ VISA
     M *(closed 25 December)* (bar lunch)/dinner 12.95 **t.** ▯ 3.50 – **18 rm** ⊇ 38.00/49.00 **t.** –
     SB (weekends only) 88.00 **st.**

AUSTIN-ROVER London Rd ☎ 623151
FORD Crewe Rd ☎ 623739
HONDA Whitchurch Rd ☎ 780300

SAAB Welsh Row ☎ 627678
VAUXHALL-OPEL Station Rd ☎ 0270 (Crewe)
258822

    '' Short Breaks '' (SB)

Molti alberghi propongono delle condizioni vantaggiose
per un soggiorno di due notti
comprendente la camera, la cena e la prima colazione.

NARBERTH (ARBERTH) Dyfed **403** F 28 – pop. 1 077 – ECD : Wednesday – ✉ ☎ 0834.
♦London 241 – Carmarthen 21 – Fishguard 26.

  🏠 **Plas Hyfryd**, Moorfield Rd, SA67 7AB, ℰ 860653, ⌇ heated, 🚗 – TV ☎ Ⓟ. 🖂 AE ①
  VISA
  M 6.75/10.25 st. ⅄ 2.80 – **12 rm** ⊂⊃ 24.50/34.50 st. – SB (October-June) (except Christ-
  mas, New Year and Spring Bank Holidays) 39.00/42.00 **st.**

NARBOROUGH Leics. **403** **404** Q 26 – see Leicester.

NASSINGTON Northants. **404** S 26 – see Peterborough (Cambs.).

NATELY SCURES Hants. – see Basingstoke.

NATIONAL EXHIBITION CENTRE West Midlands **403** **404** O 26 – see Birmingham.

NAWTON North Yorks. – see Helmsley.

NEAR SAWREY Cumbria **402** L 20 – see Hawkshead.

NEASHAM Durham **402** P 20 – see Darlington.

NEATH (CASTELL-NED) West Glam. **403** I 29 – ☎ 0639.
🏌 Swansea Bay, Jersey Marine ℰ 814153.
♦London 188 – ♦Cardiff 40 – ♦Swansea 8.

  🏰 **Castle** (Lansbury), The Parade, SA11 1RB, ℰ 641119, Telex 48119, Fax 641624 – ⇌ rm TV
  ☎ 🚗 Ⓟ – 🔬 150. 🖂 AE ① VISA. ✂
  M 8.50/12.50 t. and a la carte – **28 rm** ⊂⊃ 48.00/58.00 t. – SB (weekends only) 54.00/58.00 **st.**

NEATISHEAD Norfolk **404** Y 25 – pop. 524 – ☎ 0692 Horning.
♦London 122 – North Walsham 8.5 – ♦Norwich 11.

  🏡 **Regency** without rest., Neatishead Post Office, NR12 8AD, ℰ 630233 – TV. VISA
  5 rm ⊂⊃ 17.00/27.00 **s.**

NEEDHAM MARKET Suffolk **404** X 27 – pop. 3 420 – ECD : Tuesday – ✉ ☎ 0449.
♦London 77 – ♦Cambridge 47 – ♦Ipswich 8.5 – ♦Norwich 38.

  🏠 Limes, 99 High St., IP6 8DQ, ℰ 720305 – TV 🐾 Ⓟ – 🔬 200
  11 rm.

  🏡 **Pipps Ford**, Norwich Rd Roundabout, IP6 8LJ, SE : 1 ¾ m. by B 1078 at junction of A 45
  and A 140 ℰ 044 979 (Coddenham) 208, « Elizabethan farmhouse », ⌇, 🚗, ⚲ – ⇌ Ⓟ.
  ✂
      closed Christmas-mid January – **M** (by arrangement) 14.00 **st.** – **6 rm** ⊂⊃ 15.00/50.00 **st.**

NEFYN Gwynedd **402** **403** G 25 – pop. 2 236 – ECD : Wednesday – ☎ 0758.
See : Site★.
♦London 265 – Caernarfon 20.

  ♟ **Caeau Capel** ⌁, Rhodfa Mor, LL53 6EB, ℰ 720240, 🚗 – Ⓟ. 🖂 VISA
  March-October – **M** (bar lunch)/dinner 9.50 t. ⅄ 1.80 – **20 rm** ⊂⊃ 15.75/40.00.
AUSTIN-ROVER Church St. ℰ 720206

NETTLECOMBE Dorset – see Bridport.

NETTLETON Wilts. **403** **404** N 29 – see Castle Combe.

NEW ALRESFORD Hants. **403** **404** Q 30 – pop. 4 117 – ✉ ☎ 0962.
♦London 63 – ♦Portsmouth 40 – Reading 33 – ♦Southampton 20.

  ✕✕ **Old School House**, 60 West St., SO24 9AU, ℰ 732134 – ⇌. 🖂 VISA
      closed Sunday dinner and Monday – **M** (dinner only and Sunday lunch) 10.95/18.95 t.
      ⅄ 3.50.

NEWARK-ON-TRENT Notts. **402** **404** R 24 – pop. 33 143 – ECD : Thursday – ☎ 0636.
See : St. Mary Magdalene Church★.
🏌 Coddington ℰ 84282.
🛈 The Ossington, Beast Market Hill, Castlegate ℰ 78962.
♦London 127 – Lincoln 16 – ♦Nottingham 20 – ♦Sheffield 42.

Grange, 73 London Rd, at corner of Charles St., NG24 1RZ, ☎ 703399, 🐎 – 📺 ℗. 🔌 VISA. 🌿
closed 23 December-1 January – **M** (bar lunch)/dinner 15.00 **t.** and a la carte – **8 rm** 🍵 33.00/40.00 **t.**

Clinton Arms, 44 Market Pl., NG24 1EG, ☎ 72299 – 📺. 🔌 AE VISA. 🌿
11 rm 🍵 25.00/35.00 **t.**

at North Muskham N : 4 m. by A 6065 – ✉ ☏ 0636 Newark-on-Trent :

Travelodge without rest., NG23 6HT, N : ½ m. on A1 (Southbound carriageway) ☎ 703635 – 📺 🚻 ℗. 🔌 AE VISA
30 rm 21.50/27.00 **t.**

AUSTIN-ROVER 69 Northgate ☎ 703413
FORD Farndon Rd ☎ 704131
RENAULT Clinton St. ☎ 704619
SKODA London Rd ☎ 705845

VAUXHALL 116 Farndon Rd ☎ 705431
VW, AUDI Northern Rd ☎ 704484

🛞 ATS 70 William St. ☎ 77531

NEWBRIDGE Cornwall – see Penzance.

NEWBURY Berks. **403** **404** Q 29 – pop. 31 488 – ECD : Wednesday – ☏ 0635.
🛈 District Museum, The Wharf ☎ 30267.
♦London 67 – ♦Bristol 66 – ♦Oxford 28 – Reading 17 – ♦Southampton 38.

Foley Lodge, Stockcross, RG16 8JU, NW : 2 m. by A 4 on B 4000 ☎ 528770, Fax 528398, 🔲, 🐎 – 🔰 ⤬ 📺 ☎ ℗ – 🔬 200. 🔌 AE VISA. 🌿
M 15.50/18.50 **t.** and a la carte 15.80/20.95 **t.** 🍾 5.00 – **67 rm** 🍵 79.00/99.00 **t.**, **3 suites** 115.00/165.00 **t.** – SB (weekends only) 115.00/135.00 **st.**

Hilton National (Hilton), Pinchington Lane, RG14 7HL, S : 2 m. by A 34 on Pinchington Lane ☎ 529000, Telex 848247, Fax 529337, 🔲 – ⤬ rm 📺 ☎ 🚻 ℗ – 🔬 190. 🔌 AE ⓞ VISA
M *(closed lunch Saturday and Bank Holiday Mondays)* (buffet lunch)/dinner a la carte 19.00/24.75 **st.** 🍾 4.50 – 🍵 8.50 – **120 rm** 82.00/102.00 **st.** – SB (weekends only) 100.00/110.00 **st.**

Stakis Newbury (Stakis), Oxford Rd, RG16 8XY, N : 3 ¼ m. on A 34 ☎ 247010, Telex 848694, Fax 247010, 🔲 – ⤬ rm 📺 ☎ 🚻 ℗ – 🔬 60. 🔌 AE ⓞ VISA
M (carving lunch)/dinner a la carte 11.40/18.50 **t.** – **110 rm**, **2 suites**.

Chequers (T.H.F.), 7-8 Oxford St., RG13 1JB, ☎ 38000, Telex 849205, Fax 37170 – ⤬ rm 📺 ☎ ℗ – 🔬 50. 🔌 AE ⓞ VISA
M 11.50/12.95 **st.** and a la carte – **56 rm**.

Enborne Grange 🌿, Enborne St., Wash Common, RG14 6RP, SW : 2 ½ m. by A 343 ☎ 40046, 🐎 – 📺 ☎ ℗. 🔌 AE VISA. 🌿
M *(closed Sunday dinner)* 11.95 **t.** and a la carte 🍾 3.00 – **25 rm** 🍵 40.00/60.00 **t.** – SB (weekends only) 35.00 **st.**

at North Heath N : 4 m. on B 4494 – ✉ ☏ 0635 Newbury :

Blue Boar Inn, RG16 8UE, ☎ 248236 – 📺 ☎ ℗. 🔌 AE ⓞ VISA. 🌿
M 12.95 **t.** and a la carte 🍾 2.95 – **16 rm** 🍵 28.00/58.00 **t.**

at Speen W : 1 ¾ m. on A 4 – ✉ ☏ 0635 Newbury :

Hare & Hounds, Bath Rd, RG13 1QY, ☎ 521152, Telex 847662 – 📺 ☎ ℗. 🔌 AE ⓞ VISA. 🌿
M a la carte 11.90/16.90 **t.** 🍾 3.75 – **30 rm** 🍵 44.00/55.00 **st.**, **1 suite** 55.00/65.00 **st.** – SB (weekends only) 60.00/80.00 **st.**

AUSTIN-ROVER London Rd ☎ 41100
RENAULT London Rd ☎ 41020
VW-AUDI 22 Newtown Rd ☎ 41911

🛞 ATS 30 Queens Rd ☎ 42250

NEWBY BRIDGE Cumbria **402** L 21 – ECD : Saturday – ✉ Ulverston – ☏ 05395.
♦London 270 – Kendal 16 – Lancaster 27.

Whitewater, The Lakeland Village, LA12 8PX, SW : 1 ½ m. by A 590 ☎ 31133, Fax 31881, 🔲, squash – 🔰 📺 ☎ ℗ – 🔬 80. 🔌 AE ⓞ VISA. 🌿
M (bar lunch Monday to Saturday)/dinner 7.50/13.50 **t.** and a la carte 🍾 3.20 – **35 rm** 🍵 59.50/82.00 **t.** – SB 79.50/95.00 **st.**

Swan, LA12 8NB, ☎ 31681, Telex 65108, Fax 31917, ≼, 🎣, 🐎 – 📺 ☎ ℗ – 🔬 65. 🔌 AE ⓞ VISA. 🌿
closed 2 to 9 January – **M** (bar lunch Monday to Saturday)/dinner 15.00 **t.** and a la carte 🍾 4.25 – **36 rm** 🍵 42.00/90.00 **t.**, **1 suite** 98.00 **t.**

NEWBY WISKE North Yorks. – see Northallerton.

NEWCASTLE-UNDER-LYME Staffs. **402** **403** **404** N 24 – pop. 73 208 – ECD : Thursday – ☏ 0782 – Envir. : Wedgewood Visitor's Centre S : 4 ½ m. by A 519.
🛈 Newcastle Municipal, Keele Rd ☎ 627596, NW : 2 m. on A 525 V.
🛈 Area Reference Library, Ironmarket ☎ 618125.
♦London 161 – ♦Birmingham 46 – ♦Liverpool 56 – ♦Manchester 43.

Plan of Built up Area : see Stoke-on-Trent

NEWCASTLE-UNDER-LYME
CENTRE

High Street . . . . YZ

Albert Street . . . . Y
Barracks Road . . . . YZ
Blackfriars Road . . . . Z 9
Brook Lane . . . . Z
Brunswick Street . . . . Y
Church Street . . . . Y 20
Friarswood Road . . . . Z
George Street . . . . Y
Hassell Street . . . . YZ
Higherland . . . . Z 37
Iron Market . . . . Y 38
King Street. . . . . Y
Lancaster Road . . . . Z
Liverpool Road . . . . Z 41
Lower Street . . . . YZ
Merrial Street . . . . Y 47
North Street . . . . Y 51
Parkstone Avenue . . . . Z
Pool Dam . . . . Z
Queen Street . . . . Y
Ryecroft . . . . Y
Vessey Terrace . . . . Z 73
Victoria Road . . . . Z

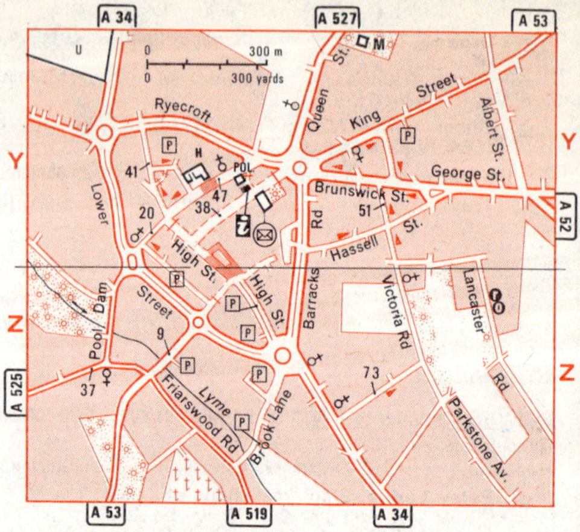

🏨 **Post House** (T.H.F.), Clayton Rd, Clayton, ST5 4DL, S : 2 m. on A 519 ℰ 717171, Telex 36531, Fax 717138 – ⇔ rm TV ☎ P – 🔬 70. 🆚 AE ⓪ VISA
M *(closed Saturday lunch)* 7.95/16.50 **st.** and a la carte – ☲ 7.00 – **126 rm** 65.00/83.00 **st.** – SB (weekends only) 64.00/84.00 **st.**   **V n**

🏨 **Clayton Lodge** (Embassy), Clayton Rd, Clayton, ST5 4AF, S : 1 ¼ m. on A 519 ℰ 613093, Telex 36547, Fax 711896 – ⇔ rm TV ☎ P – 🔬 300. 🆚 AE ⓪ VISA
M 9.75/10.75 **st.** and a la carte ⌔ 4.40 – ☲ 6.50 – **50 rm** 22.00/80.00 **st.** – SB (weekends only) 58.00/62.00 **st.**   **V e**

🏠 **Deansfield**, 98 Lancaster Rd, ST5 1DS, ℰ 619040 – ⇔ rest TV ☎ P. 🆚 AE ⓪ VISA
M 10.50 **st.** ⌔ 2.55 – **11 rm** ☲ 24.90/35.80 **st.** – SB (weekends only) 27.25/49.00 **st.**   **Z r**

🏠 **Grove Court**, 100 Lancaster Rd, ST5 1DS, ℰ 614406, 🚗 – ⇳ ⇔ TV P
M (by arrangement) – **11 rm**.   **Z o**

AUSTIN-ROVER Brook Lane ℰ 618461
BMW Pool Dam ℰ 711000
CITROEN, PEUGEOT-TALBOT Hassell St. ℰ 614621
FIAT Higherland ℰ 622141
FORD London Rd ℰ 717799
RENAULT High St., Wolstanton ℰ 626284

VAUXHALL-OPEL Higherland ℰ 610941
VOLVO Knutton Rd, Wolstanton ℰ 625333
VW, AUDI Brunswick St. ℰ 617321

🅐 ATS Lower St. ℰ 622431

NEWCASTLE-UPON-TYNE Tyne and Wear 📖 📖 0 19 – pop. 199 064 – ECD : Monday and Wednesday – 🕿 091 Tyneside.

See : Site★★ – Cathedral★ 14C **CZ A** – City Centre★ – Grey Street★ **CYZ** – Quayside★ **CZ** – Castle Keep★ **CZ B** – Laing Art Gallery and Museum★ **CY M**.

🟦 High Gosforth Park ℰ 285 6710 **AV** – 🟦 Whorlton Grange, Westerhope, ℰ 286 9125, W : 5 m. by B 6324 **AV**.

✈ Newcastle Airport : ℰ 2860966, Telex 537831 NW : 5 m. by A 696 **AV** – Terminal : Bus Assembly : Central Station Forecourt.

🚗 ℰ 261 1234 ext 2621.

🚢 Shipping connections with the Continent : to Norway (Bergen, Stavanger) (Norway Line) March-December – to Denmark (Esbjerg) (Scandinavian Seaways) summer only – to Sweden (Götenborg) (Scandinavian Seaways) summer only – to Norway (Kristiansand) (Fred Olsen Lines KDS) – to Norway (Oslo) via Denmark (Hirtshals) (Fred Olsen Lines KDS).

🄸 Central Library, Princess Sq. ℰ 261 0691 – Blackfriars, Monk St. ℰ 261 5367 – Newcastle Airport, Woolsington ℰ 271 1929.

♦London 276 – ♦Edinburgh 105 – ♦Leeds 95.

Plans on following pages

🏨 **County Thistle** (Thistle), Neville St., NE99 1AH, ℰ 232 2471, Telex 537873, Fax 232 1285 – ⇳ ⇔ rm TV ☎ – 🔬 150. 🆚 AE ⓪ VISA
M 8.45/14.00 **st.** and a la carte – ☲ 7.25 – **115 rm** 60.00/90.00 **st.** – SB 74.00 **st.**   **CZ a**

🏨 **Crest** (Crest), New Bridge St., NE1 8BS, ℰ 232 6191, Telex 53467, Fax 261 8529 – ⇳ ⇔ rm ▤ rest TV ☎ & P – 🔬 400. 🆚 AE ⓪ VISA
M 12.00/15.00 **st.** and a la carte ⌔ 6.50 – ☲ 7.25 – **165 rm** 69.00/81.00 **st.**, **1 suite** 160.00 **st.** – SB (weekends only) 76.00/84.00 **st.**   **CY n**

🏨 **Swallow** (Swallow), 1 Newgate Arcade, Newgate St., NE1 5SX, ℰ 232 5025, Telex 538230, Fax 232 8428 – ⇳ ⇔ rm TV ☎ P – 🔬 80. 🆚 AE ⓪ VISA
M 9.50/15.00 **st.** and a la carte ⌔ 4.25 – **93 rm** ☲ 63.00/72.00 **st.** – SB (weekends only) (except July and August) 68.00/156.00 **st.**   **CZ o**

🏨 **Imperial** (Swallow), Jesmond Rd, NE2 1PR, ℰ 281 5511, Telex 537972, Fax 281 8472, 🔲 –
🛗 ⇤ rm 📺 ☎ 🅿 – 🔥 100. 🔼 AE ⓪ VISA   **CY** **c**
M *(closed Saturday lunch)* 8.00/13.00 **st.** and a la carte ▮ 4.25 – **129 rm** ☕ 64.00/74.00 **st.** –
SB (weekends only) 73.00/85.00 **st.**

🏨 **Hospitality Inn** (Mt. Charlotte), Osborne Rd, Jesmond, NE2 2AT, ℰ 281 7881, Telex 53636,
Fax 281 6241 – 🛗 📺 ☎ 🅿 – 🔥 80   **BV** **a**
86 rm, 1 suite.

🏨 **New Kent**, 127 Osborne Rd, Jesmond, NE2 2TB, ℰ 281 1083, Fax 281 3369 – 📺 ☎ 🅿 🔼
AE ⓪ VISA. 彩   **BV** **c**
M *(closed Sunday)* (dinner only) 12.90 **t.** and a la carte ▮ 4.00 – **32 rm** ☕ 35.00/69.90 **t.**

🏨 **Travelodge** without rest., Whitemare Pool, NE10 8YB, at junction of A 1 (M) **BX** and A 194
ℰ 438 3333 – 📺 🅿. 🔼 AE VISA
41 rm 21.50/27.00 **t.**

🏨 **Whites,** 38-40 Osborne Rd, Jesmond, NE2 2AL, ℰ 281 5126 – 📺 ☎ 🅿. 🔼 AE ⓪ VISA
彩   **BV** **u**
M *(closed Sunday dinner)* (bar lunch)/dinner 8.95 **st.** and a la carte – **25 rm** ☕ 25.00/43.00 **st.**

🏠 **Avenue,** 2 Manor House Rd, Jesmond, NE2 2LU, ℰ 281 1396 – ⇤ rest 📺 ☎. 🔼
AE   **BV** **x**
closed 23 December-7 January – **M** (by arrangement) 6.00 **st.** ▮ 1.80 – **8 rm** ☕ 19.00/36.00 **st.**

🏠 **Westland,** 27 Osborne Av., Jesmond, NE2 1JR, ℰ 281 0412 – ⇤ rest   ✓**BV** **z**
M (by arrangement) 6.50 **t.** ▮ 3.00 – **14 rm** ☕ 19.75/38.00 **t.**

XX **Fisherman's Wharf,** 15 The Side, NE1 3JE, ℰ 232 1057, Seafood – 🔼 AE ⓪ VISA   **CZ** **v**
closed Saturday lunch, Sunday, 25-26 December and 1 January – **M** 11.50/30.00 **t.** and a la
carte 19.60/31.40 **t.** ▮ 4.40.

XX **Fisherman's Lodge,** Jesmond Dene, Jesmond, NE7 7BQ, ℰ 281 3281, Seafood – 🅿. 🔼
AE ⓪ VISA   **BV** **a**
closed Saturday lunch, Sunday and Bank Holidays – **M** 13.50 **t.** (lunch) and a la carte
19.50/29.50 **t.** ▮ 4.50.

XX **Le Roussillon,** 52-54 St. Andrew's St., NE1 5SF, ℰ 261 1341 – ⇤. 🔼 AE ⓪ VISA   **CY** **a**
closed Saturday lunch and Sunday – **M** 8.95/13.00 **t.** and a la carte 14.50/21.75 **t.** ▮ 4.05.

XX **Ming Dynasty,** 41 Stowell St., NE1 4YB, ℰ 261 5787, Chinese (Peking) rest. – 🔼 AE ⓪
VISA   **CY** **i**
closed Sunday lunch, 25 to 26 December, 1 January and 9 February – **M** 6.50/14.00 **t.** and a
la carte 10.00/12.70 **t.** ▮ 3.95.

at Gosforth N : 4 ¾ m. on A 6125 – **AV** – ✉ ☺ 091 Tyneside:

🏨 **Gosforth Park Thistle** (Thistle), High Gosforth Park, NE3 5HN, on B 1318 ℰ 236 4111,
Telex 53655, Fax 236 8192, ⩽, 🔲, 🎿, park, 🎱, squash – 🛗 ⇤ rm 📺 ☎ ♿ 🅿 – 🔥 200.
🔼 AE ⓪ VISA
M 12.50/18.95 **st.** and a la carte – ☕ 8.25 – **173 rm** 78.00/98.00 **st.**, **5 suites** 145.00 **st.** –
SB 94.00/104.00 **st.**

at Seaton Burn N : 8 m. on A 6125 – **AV** – ✉ Newcastle-upon-Tyne – ☺ 091 Tyneside:

🏨 **Holiday Inn** (Holiday Inn), Great North Rd, NE13 6BP, N : ¾ m. at junction with A 1
ℰ 236 5432, Telex 53271, Fax 236 8091, 🔲 – ⇤ rm 🍽 📺 ☎ ♿ 🅿 – 🔥 200. 🔼 AE ⓪ VISA
M (buffet lunch)/dinner 15.50 **t.** and a la carte 17.55/21.95 **t.** ▮ 5.50 – ☕ 7.95 – **149 rm**
75.00/105.00 **t.**, **1 suite** 184.00/210.00 **t.** – SB (weekends only) 97.00 **st.**

at Wallsend NE : 6 m. on A 1058 – **BV** – ✉ Newcastle-upon-Tyne – ☺ 091 Tyneside :

🏨 **Newcastle Moat House** (Q.M.H.), Coast Rd, NE28 9HP, at junction with A 1 ℰ 262 8989,
Telex 53583, Fax 263 4172 – 🛗 ⇤ 📺 ☎ 🅿 – 🔥 400. 🔼 AE ⓪ VISA
closed 22 December-3 January – **M** *(closed Saturday lunch)* 11.50 **t.** and a la carte ▮ 3.25 –
150 rm ☕ 57.50/80.00 **st.** – SB (weekends only) 72.00/90.50 **st.**

at Newcastle Airport NW : 6 m. on A 696 – **AV** – ✉ Woolsington – ☺ 0661 Ponteland :

🏨 Stakis Airport (Stakis), Woolsington, NE13 8DJ, ℰ 24911, Telex 537121, Fax 860157 – 🛗 📺
☎ ♿ 🅿 – 🔥 200. 🔼 AE ⓪ VISA
☕ 7.25 – **98 rm** 59.00/79.00 **st.**, **2 suites**.

ALFA-ROMEO Diana St. ℰ 273 0700
AUSTIN-ROVER Etherstone Av. ℰ 266 3311
AUSTIN-ROVER Westgate Rd ℰ 273 7901
BMW Fenham Barracks ℰ 261 7366
CITROEN Westgate Rd ℰ 273 7821
FIAT Railway St. ℰ 273 2131
FORD Scotswood Rd ℰ 273 0747
FORD Melbourn St. ℰ 261 1471
HONDA Warwick St. ℰ 261 1519
HONDA Gosforth ℰ 284 1928
LAND-ROVER Comington ℰ 267 6271
MAZDA, DAIHATSU Jesmond ℰ 237 0658
MERCEDES-BENZ Swalwell ℰ 414 2882
MITSUBISHI, SEAT Longbenton ℰ 266 8223
NISSAN Benfield Rd ℰ 226 0333

NISSAN Stoddart St. ℰ 232 3838
PEUGEOT-TALBOT Benton Rd ℰ 266 6361
PORSCHE Melbourne St. ℰ 261 2591
RENAULT Scotswood Rd ℰ 273 0101
SAAB Whitley Rd ℰ 266 8223
SUBARU 87 Osborne Rd ℰ 281 1677
TOYOTA Brunton Lane ℰ 286 8611
VAUXHALL Two Ball Lonnen ℰ 274 1000
VAUXHALL Great North Rd ℰ 236 3176
VOLVO Brunton Lane ℰ 286 7111
VW, AUDI Byker ℰ 265 7121

☺ ATS 80-90 Blenheim St. ℰ 2323921/2325031
ATS Newton Park Garage, Newton Rd ℰ 2812243
ATS White St, Walker ℰ 2620811

NEWCASTLE-UPON-TYNE

Adelaide Terrace .... **AX** 2
Askew Road .... **AX** 3
Atkinson Road .... **AX** 4
Bath Street .... **BX** 6
Bensham Road .... **AX** 7
Benton Bank .... **BV** 8
Buddle Street .... **BV** 13
Byker Bridge .... **BV** 15
Church Avenue .... **AV** 17

Church Road .... **AV** 18
Clayton Road .... **BV** 21
Coldwell Lane .... **BX** 26
Coldwell Street .... **BX** 27
Condercum Road .... **AX** 30
Fossway .... **BV** 35
Haddrick's Mill Road ..... **BV** 41
High Street West .... **BV** 44
Jesmond Dene Road ...... **BV** 45
Killingworth Road .... **BV** 46
Lobley Hill Road .... **AX** 48
Matthew Bank .... **BV** 53
Neptune Road .... **BV** 60

Red Hall Drive .... **BV** 71
Saltwell Road .... **BX** 80
Shipdon Road .... **AX** 82
Springfield Road .... **AV** 85
Station Road .... **BX** 87
Stephenson Road .... **BV** 90
Sunderland Road .... **BX** 93
Sutton Street .... **BV** 95
Swalwell Bank .... **AX** 96
Waverdale Avenue ...... **BV** 102
West Farm Avenue ..... **BV** 104
Whickham Bank .... **AX** 105
Windy Nook Road ...... **BX** 106

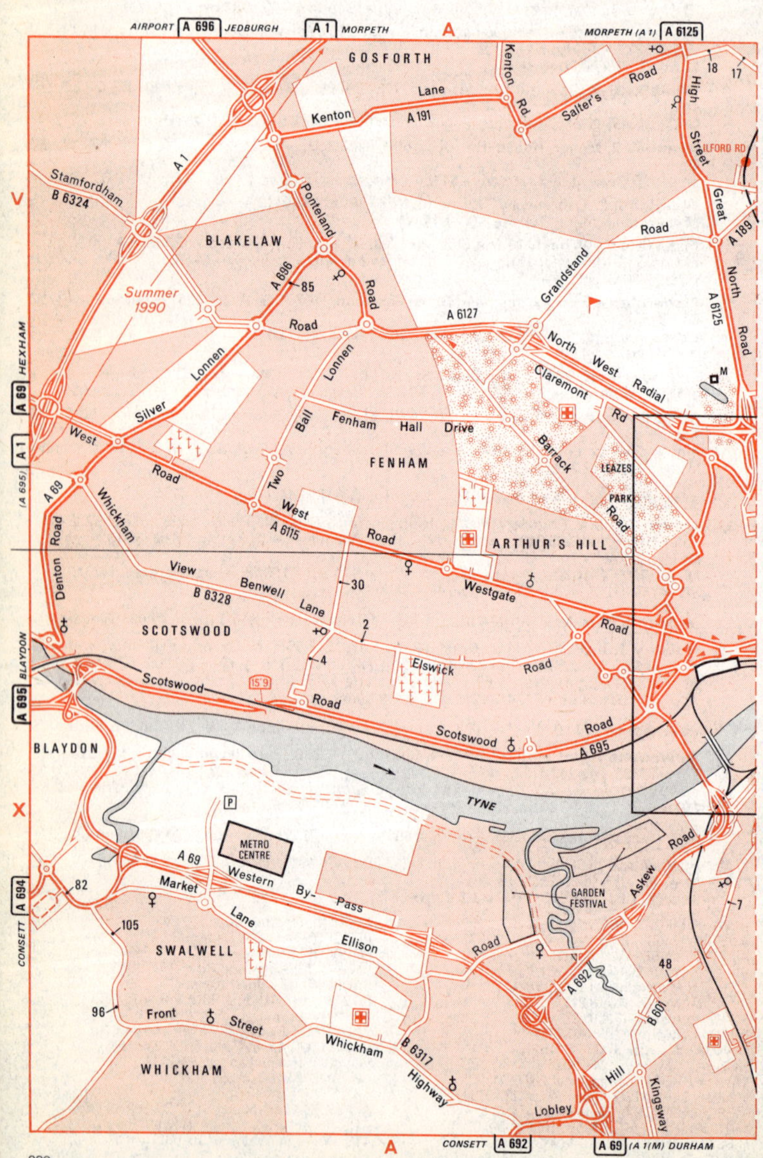

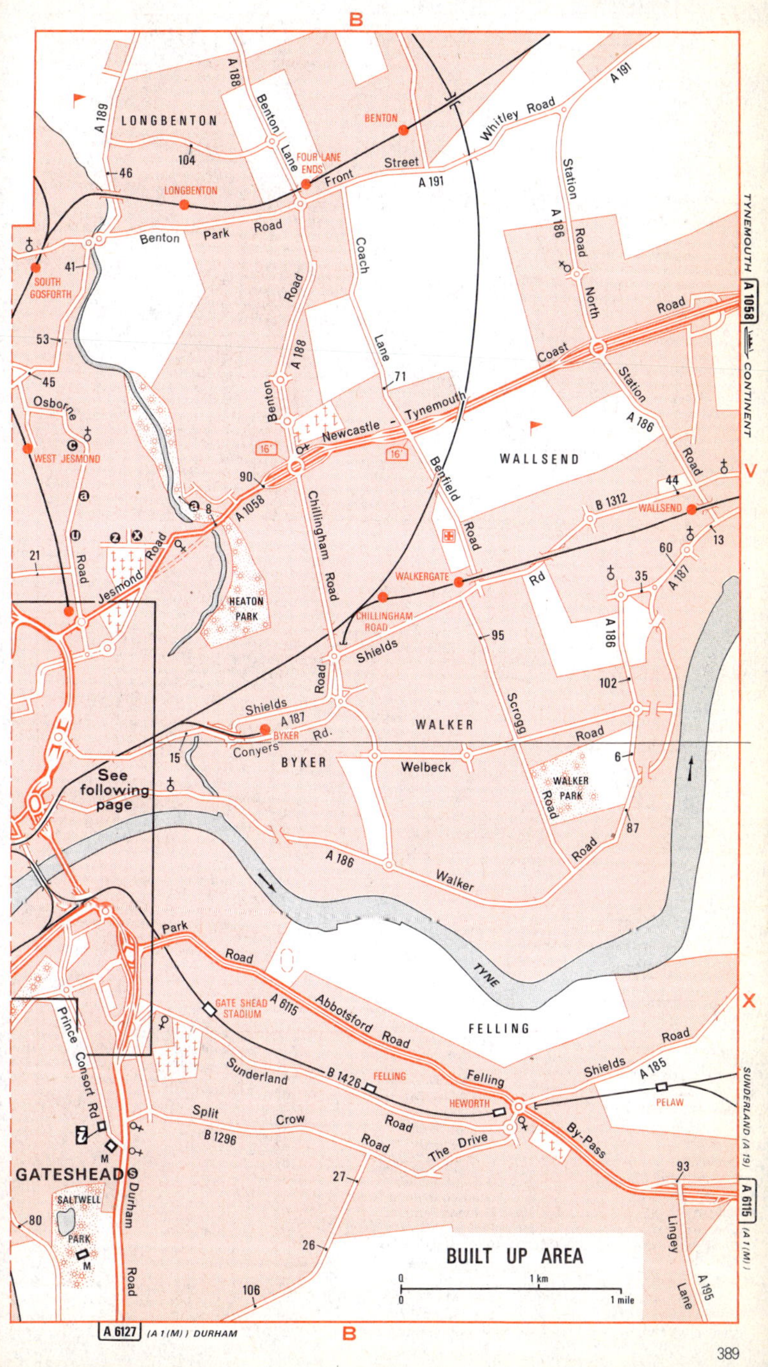

B
A 188
A 189
LONGBENTON
BENTON
104
46
FOUR LANE ENDS
Benton Lane
A 191
Whitley Road
A 191
Station Road North
Front Street
LONGBENTON
Benton Park Road
Coach Lane
A 186
Road
Coast Road
A 1058
TYNEMOUTH
CONTINENT
SOUTH GOSFORTH
41
53
45
Osborne
Benton Road
A 188
71
Newcastle - Tynemouth
Benfield Road
Station Road
A 186
Coast
WALLSEND
V
WEST JESMOND
90
16'
16'
A 1058
8
44
B 1312
WALLSEND
60
13
21
Jesmond Road
Road
Chillingham Road
WALKERGATE
Rd
35
A 187
HEATON PARK
CHILLINGHAM ROAD
95
A 186
102
Shields
Road
Shields
A 187
BYKER
Conyers Rd.
WALKER
Scrogg Road
6
15
BYKER
Welbeck
WALKER PARK
87
See following page
A 186
Walker Road
Road
TYNE
Park
Road
Prince Consort Rd
GATE SHEAD STADIUM
A 6115
Abbotsford Road
FELLING
X
Shields Road
A 185
SUNDERLAND (A 19)
Sunderland
B 1426
FELLING
Felling
PELAW
GATESHEAD
Split Crow Road
B 1296
Road
HEWORTH
The Drive
By-Pass
93
SALTWELL
Durham Road
27
A 6115
(A 1 (M))
PARK
M.
26
BUILT UP AREA
80
106
0   1 km
0   1 mile
A 195
Lingey Lane
A 6127   (A 1 (M)) DURHAM
B

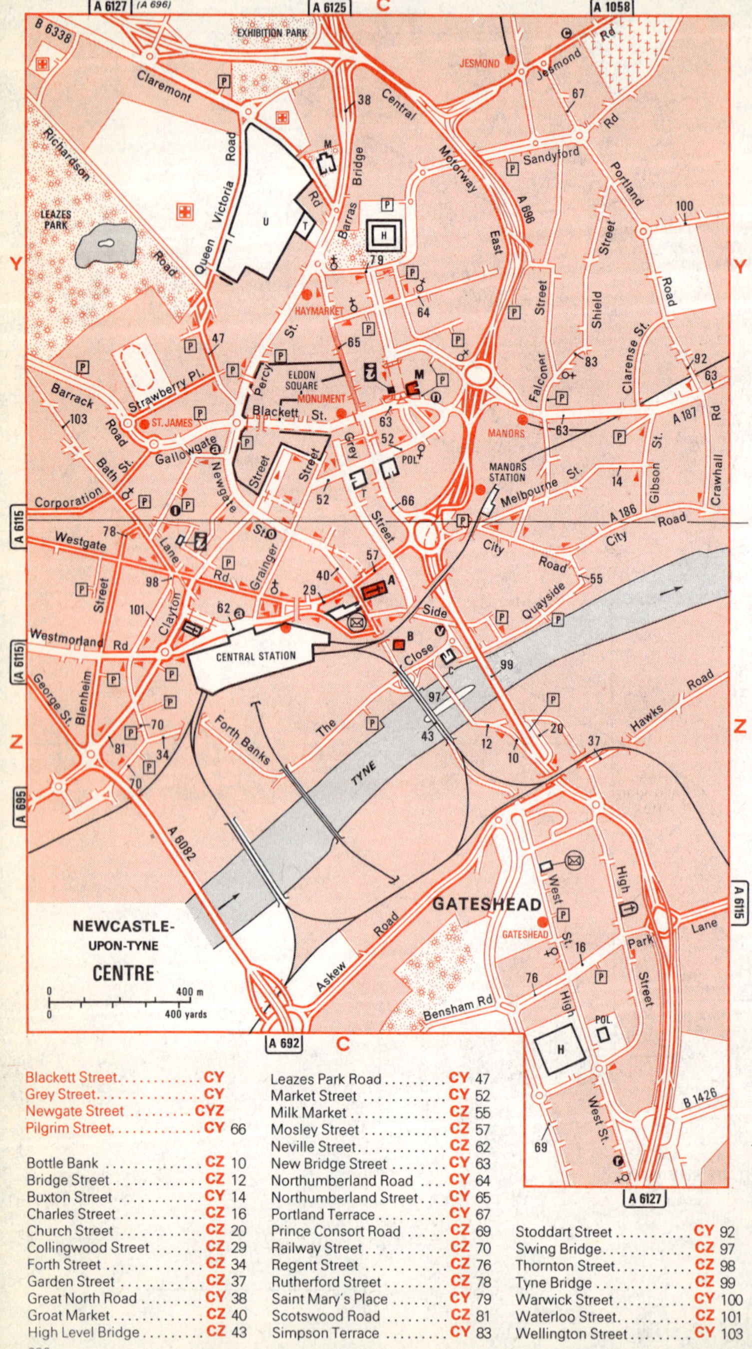

Blackett Street............	**CY**	
Grey Street..............	**CY**	
Newgate Street	**CYZ**	
Pilgrim Street............	**CY** 66	
Bottle Bank	**CZ** 10	
Bridge Street	**CZ** 12	
Buxton Street	**CY** 14	
Charles Street	**CZ** 16	
Church Street	**CZ** 20	
Collingwood Street	**CZ** 29	
Forth Street	**CZ** 34	
Garden Street	**CZ** 37	
Great North Road	**CY** 38	
Groat Market	**CZ** 40	
High Level Bridge	**CZ** 43	
Leazes Park Road	**CY** 47	
Market Street	**CY** 52	
Milk Market	**CZ** 55	
Mosley Street	**CZ** 57	
Neville Street	**CZ** 62	
New Bridge Street	**CY** 63	
Northumberland Road	**CY** 64	
Northumberland Street ...	**CY** 65	
Portland Terrace	**CY** 67	
Prince Consort Road	**CZ** 69	
Railway Street	**CZ** 70	
Regent Street	**CZ** 76	
Rutherford Street	**CZ** 78	
Saint Mary's Place	**CY** 79	
Scotswood Road	**CZ** 81	
Simpson Terrace	**CY** 83	
Stoddart Street	**CY** 92
Swing Bridge	**CZ** 97
Thornton Street	**CZ** 98
Tyne Bridge	**CZ** 99
Warwick Street	**CY** 100
Waterloo Street	**CZ** 101
Wellington Street	**CY** 103

NEWHAVEN East Sussex 📗📗 U 31 – pop. 10 697 – ECD : Wednesday – ☎ 0273.
🏌 Peacehaven, Brighton Rd ☎ 514049.
⛴ Shipping connections with the Continent : to France (Dieppe) (Sealink).
♦London 63 – ♦Brighton 9 – Eastbourne 14 – Lewes 7.

NEWLYN Cornwall 📗📗 D 33 – see Penzance.

NEWMARKET Suffolk 📗📗 V 27 – pop. 15 861 – ECD : Wednesday – ☎ 0638.
🏌 Links, Cambridge Rd ☎ 663000, SW : 1 m.
♦London 64 – ♦Cambridge 13 – ♦Ipswich 40 – ♦Norwich 48.

- **Newmarket Moat House** (Q.M.H.), Moulton Rd, CB8 8DY, ☎ 667171, Fax 666533 – 📶 📺 ☎ 🅿 – 🔥 100. 🌊 AE ⓪ VISA
  closed Christmas – **M** *(closed Saturday lunch)* 14.95 st. and a la carte ⎸3.50 – **44 rm** ⎘ 55.00/125.00 st. – SB (weekends only) 70.00 st.

- **White Hart,** High St., CB8 8JP, ☎ 663051, Fax 667284 – 📺 ☎ 🅿 – 🔥 80. 🌊 AE ⓪ VISA
  M 8.25/10.45 t. and a la carte – **21 rm** ⎘ 45.00/70.00 t. – SB (weekends only) 70.00 st.

  at Six Mile Bottom (Cambs.) SW : 6 m. on A 1304 – ✉ Newmarket – ☎ 063 870 Six Mile Bottom :

- **Swynford Paddocks,** CB8 0UE, ☎ 234, Telex 817438, Fax 283, ⬳, « Country house », 🐎, park, 🍴 – 📺 ☎ 🅿 – 🔥 25. 🌊 AE ⓪ VISA
  M *(closed Saturday lunch)* 13.50/18.50 t. and a la carte 18.00/25.00 st. ⎸ 4.95 – **15 rm** ⎘ 55.00/110.00 st. – SB (weekends only) 100.00/120.00 st.

AUSTIN-ROVER Dullingham ☎ 063 876 (Stetch-worth) 244
TOYOTA Bury Rd ☎ 662130

VAUXHALL-OPEL All Saints Rd ☎ 663121

⊚ ATS 2 Exeter Rd ☎ 662088/662521

NEW MILTON Hants. 📗📗 📗📗 P 31 – ECD : Wednesday – ☎ 0425.
♦London 106 – Bournemouth 12 – ♦Southampton 21 – Winchester 34.

- ❀ **Chewton Glen** ⌁, Christchurch Rd, BH25 6QS, W : 2 m. by A 337 and Ringwood Rd on Chewton Farm Rd ☎ 275341, Telex 41456, Fax 272310, ⬳, « Gardens », ☲ heated, 🏌, park, 🍴 – 📺 ☎ 🅿 – 🔥 40. 🌊 AE ⓪ VISA. ⌁
  M 20.00/40.00 st. and a la carte 35.00/45.50 st. ⎸3.80 – ⎘ 12.00 – **35 rm** 151.00/187.00 st., **11 suites** 220.00/370.00 st. – SB (December-February) (weekdays only) 256.00/301.00 st.
  Spec. Mille-feuille de saumon aux epinards, sauce raifort, Ravioli de fenouil aux herbes de notre jardin, Piccata de ris de veau au vinaigre.

AUSTIN-ROVER Old Milton Rd ☎ 614665
COLT Christchurch Rd ☎ 611198

NISSAN 25 Station Rd ☎ 620660
RENAULT 53 Lymington Rd ☎ 612296

NEWPORT Essex 📗📗 U 28 – ✉ ☎ 0799 Saffron Walden.
♦London 38 – ♦Cambridge 21 – Colchester 41.

- **Village House,** High St., CB11 3PF, ☎ 41560 – 🅿. 🌊 VISA
  closed Sunday, Monday and January – **M** (dinner only) a la carte 16.20/22.90 t. ⎸3.25.

NEWPORT I.O.W. 📗📗 📗📗 Q 31 – see Wight (Isle of).

NEWPORT (CASNEWYDD-AR-WYSG) Gwent 📗📗 L 29 – pop. 115 896 – ECD : Thursday – ☎ 0633.
Envir. : Caerleon : Roman Amphitheatre* *AC*, NE · 3 m.
🏌 Tredegar Park, Bassaleg Rd ☎ 894433, SW : 2 m. by A 467.
🅘 Museum and Art Gallery, John Frost Sq. ☎ 842962.
♦London 145 – ♦Bristol 31 – ♦Cardiff 12 – Gloucester 48.

- **Celtic Manor,** Coldra Woods, NP6 2YA, E : 3 m. on A 48 ☎ 413000, Telex 497557, Fax 412910, ☲, park – ⇌ rm 🍽 📺 ☎ 🅿 – 🔥 200. 🌊 AE ⓪ VISA. ⌁
  M (see **Hedley's** below) – ⎘ 7.00 – **72 rm** 72.00/92.00 t., **3 suites** 150.00/200.00 t. – SB (weekends only) 80.00/125.00 st.

- **Hilton National** (Hilton), The Coldra, NP6 2YG, E : 3 m. on A 48 ☎ 412777, Telex 497205, Fax 413087 – ⇌ rm 📺 ☎ 🅿 – 🔥 350. 🌊 AE ⓪ VISA
  M *(closed Saturday lunch)* 8.95/20.00 t. and a la carte ⎸3.75 – ⎘ 7.50 – **119 rm** 70.00/85.00 st.

- **Kings,** High St., NP9 1QU, ☎ 842020, Telex 497330 – 📶 📺 ☎ 🅿 – 🔥 200. 🌊 AE ⓪ VISA ⌁
  closed 25 to 30 December – **M** *(closed Saturday lunch)* 9.95/12.95 t. and a la carte ⎸4.50 – **47 rm** ⎘ 54.00/75.00 st. – SB (weekends only) 62.00 st.

- **Anderley Lodge,** 216 Stow Hill, NP9 4HA, ☎ 266781 – ⇌ 📺. ⌁
  M 10.50 st. – **6 rm** ⎘ 22.00/34.00 st. – SB (weekends only) 50.00/58.00 st.

- **Hedley's,** (at Celtic Manor H.) Coldra Woods, NP6 2YA, E : 3 m. on A 48 ☎ 413000, Fax 412910, 🐎 – 🅿. 🌊 AE ⓪ VISA
  closed Saturday lunch and Sunday – **M** 16.00/20.00 t. and a la carte 21.00/32.45 t.

- **Fratelli,** 173b Caerleon Rd, NP9 7FX, E : 1 m. on B 4596 ☎ 264602, Italian rest. – 🌊 AE VISA
  closed Saturday lunch, Sunday, 3 weeks August and Bank Holiday Mondays – **M** a la carte 9.20/20.55 t. ⎸3.75.

at Langstone E : 4 ½ m. on A 48 – ⊠ Newport – ✆ 0633 Llanwern :

🏨 **New Inn,** Chepstow Rd, NP6 2JN, ✆ 412426, Fax 413679 – 📺 ☎ 🅿. 🔼 AE Ⓞ VISA. ⚓
M (grill rest.) 8.00 **t.** (dinner) and a la carte 6.90/15.95 **t.** ▯ 5.00 – **34 rm** ⌣ 40.00/55.00 **t.** –
SB (weekends only) 54.00/102.00 **st.**

AUSTIN-ROVER Bassaleg Rd ✆ 263717
NISSAN Spytty Rd ✆ 273414
PEUGEOT-TALBOT Bassaleg Rd ✆ 265488

⬤ ATS 101 Corporation Rd ✆ 216115/216117
ATS Ruskin Av., High Cross ✆ 896112

NEWPORT (TREFDRAETH) Dyfed **403** F 27 – pop. 1 224 – ECD : Wednesday – ✆ 0239.
See : Site★.
Envir. : Pentre Ifan (burial chamber★) SE : 4 ½ m.
🏌 Newport ✆ 820244.
🛈 East St. ✆ 820912.
◆London 258 – Fishguard 7.

✕ **Cnapan** with rm, East St., on A 487, SA42 0WF, ✆ 820575, 🛲 – ⋐⊱ rest 📺 🅿. 🔼 VISA
⚓
closed Tuesday March-October, February and 25-26 December – **M** (wholefood lunch only)
(booking essential) a la carte 12.10/14.00 **t.** ▯ 3.95 – **5 rm** ⌣ 23.00/36.00 **t.**

at Velindre (Felindre Farchog) E : 2 ¾ m. on A 487 – ⊠ Cardigan – ✆ 0239 Newport :

🏨 **Salutation Inn,** Felindre Farchog, SA41 3UY, ✆ 820564, 🛲 – ⋐⊱ rest 📺 🅿. 🔼 VISA
M (closed Monday) (bar lunch)/dinner 11.50 **t.** and a la carte ▯ 3.00 – **9 rm** ⌣ 24.00/44.00 **t.**
– SB (except Bank Holidays) 56.00 **st.**

NEWPORT Shropshire **402 403 404** M 25 – pop. 10 339 – ECD : Thursday – ✆ 0952.
Envir. : Weston Park★★ SE : 6 ½ m..
🛈 9 St. Mary's St. ✆ 814109.
◆London 150 – ◆Birmingham 33 – Shrewsbury 18 – ◆Stoke-on-Trent 21.

🏨 **Royal Victoria,** St. Mary's St., TF10 7AB, ✆ 820331 – 📺 ☎ 🅿. 🔼 AE VISA
M (carving rest.) 8.95/20.00 **t.** and a la carte ▯ 5.80 – **24 rm** ⌣ 39.00/53.00 **t.** –
SB 55.50/67.50 **st.**

at High Offley (Staffs.) NE : 7 ¼ m. by A 519 – ⊠ ✆ 0785 Woodseaves :

✕ **Royal Oak,** Grubb St., ST20 0NE, ✆ 284579 – 🅿. 🔼 AE Ⓞ VISA
closed Monday, 3 weeks September and Bank Holidays – **M** (dinner only and Sunday
lunch)/dinner 18.00 **t.** ▯ 5.00.

FORD Browns Garage ✆ 811076

NEWPORT PAGNELL Bucks. **404** R 27 – pop. 10 733 – ECD : Thursday – ✆ 0908.
◆London 57 – Bedford 13 – Luton 21 – Northampton 15.

🏰 Welcome Lodge (T.H.F.), M 1 Service Area 3, MK16 8DS, W : 1 ¼ m. by Wolverton Rd and
Little Linfold Lane on M 1 ✆ 610878, Telex 826186 – ⋐⊱ rm 📺 ☎ 🅿 – 🔏 30
92 rm.

🏨 **Swan Revived,** High St., MK16 8AR, ✆ 610565, Telex 826801, Fax 210995 – ▯ 📺 ☎ 🅿 –
🔏 40. 🔼 AE Ⓞ VISA
M a la carte 9.15/11.70 **t.** ▯ 3.50 – **31 rm** ⌣ 48.00/60.00 **st.**

PEUGEOT High St. ✆ 611715

NEWQUAY Cornwall **403** E 32 The West Country G. – pop. 13 905 – ECD : Wednesday –
✆ 063 73 (4 and 5 fig.) or 0637 (6 fig.).
Envir. : Pentire Points and Kelsey Head★ (≤★★) SW : 5 m. by A 3075 Y – Trerice Manor★ AC
3 ½ m. by A 392 Y.
✈ Newquay Civil Airport : ✆ 063 74 (St. Mawgan) 860551, NE : 6 m. by A 3059 Y.
🛈 Cliff Rd ✆ 871345.
◆London 291 – Exeter 83 – Penzance 34 – ◆Plymouth 48 – Truro 14.

Plan opposite

🏰 **Bristol,** Narrowcliff, TR7 2PQ, ✆ 875181, Fax 879347, ≤, 🔼 – ▯ 📺 ☎ 🅿 – 🔏 30. 🔼 AE
Ⓞ VISA
M 8.50/13.50 **t.** and a la carte ▯ 3.50 – **86 rm** ⌣ 35.00/70.00 **t.** – SB (October-April) (week-
ends only) 75.00 **st.** Z r

🏰 **Trebarwith,** Trebarwith Cres., TR7 1BZ, ✆ 872288, ≤ bay and coast, 🔼, 🛲 – 📺 ☎ 🅿.
🔼 VISA ⚓
April-mid October – **M** (bar lunch)/dinner 12.00 **st.** ▯ 4.00 – **43 rm** ⌣ 24.00/35.00 **st.** Z a

🏰 Windsor, Mount Wise, TR7 2AY, ✆ 875188, 🏊 heated, 🔼, 🛲, squash – ⋐⊱ rest 📺 ☎ 🅿.
⚓ Z n
45 rm.

Kilbirnie, Narrowcliff, TR7 2RS, ☎ 875155, 🔲 – 📺 ☎ 🅿. 🔄 *VISA*   Z e
M (bar lunch)/dinner 10.50 t. – **69 rm** ☲ 28.00/52.00 st. – SB 52.00/68.00 st.

New Garth, Narrowcliff, TR7 2PG, ☎ 873250, ≼ – ⧉ 📺 ☎ 🅿. 🔄 *VISA* ✏   Z c
M (bar lunch Monday to Saturday)/dinner 9.50 t. and a la carte ⅋ 3.45 – **48 rm**
☲ 19.00/52.60 t. – SB (except summer) 49.95/55.95 st.

Corisande Manor 🕭, Riverside Av., Pentire, TR7 1PL, ☎ 872042, ≼ Gannel Estuary, 🐎
– 🅿. 🔄 *VISA*   Y n
5 May-15 October – **M** (bar lunch)/dinner 9.00 t. ⅋ 4.00 – **19 rm** ☲ 18.00/53.00 t. –
SB 34.00/51.00 st.

Water's Edge, Esplanade Rd, Pentire, TR7 1QA, ☎ 872048, ≼ Fistral Bay, 🐎 – ✕ rest
📺 ☎ 🅿. 🔄 *VISA* ✏   Y u
May-October – **M** (bar lunch)/dinner 11.95 st. ⅋ 3.50 – **20 rm** ☲ 33.00/66.00 st. – SB (May-
November) (weekends only) 50.00/66.00 st.

Porth Veor Manor, 56 Porth Way, TR7 3LW, ☎ 873274, 🐎, ⚒ – ✕ rest 📺 🅿. 🔄
VISA   Y e
closed November – **M** (bar lunch Monday to Saturday)/dinner a la carte 12.50/18.00 t. ⅋ 3.50
– **16 rm** ☲ 27.00/58.00 t. – SB (except summer, Christmas and Bank Holidays) 49.00 st.

Whipsiderry, Trevelgue Rd, Porth, TR7 3LY, NE : 2 m. by A 392 -Y- on B 3276 ☎ 874777,
≼, 🔄 heated, 🐎 – 📺 🅿
April-September – **M** (bar lunch)/dinner 9.50 st. ⅋ 3.90 – **20 rm** ☲ 17.00/39.50 st.

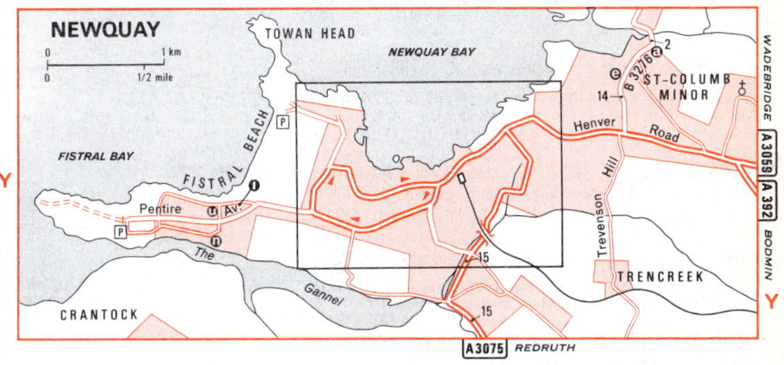

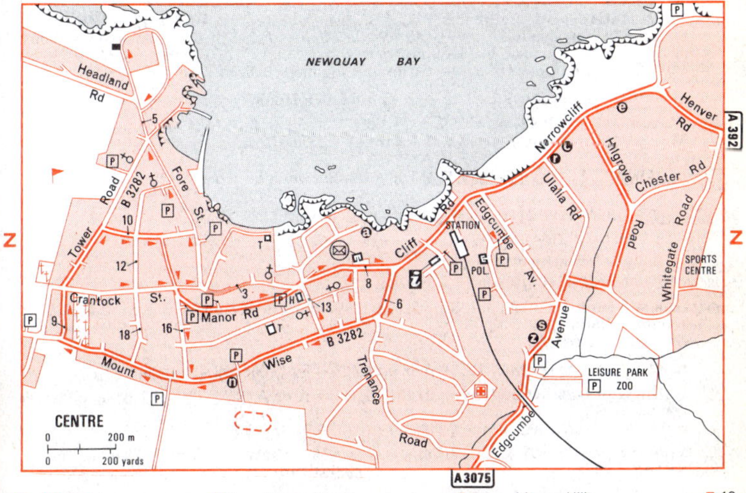

Bank Street .... Z 3
East Street .... Z 8
Fore Street .... Z
Alexander Road .... Y 2
Beacon Road .... Z 5
Berry Road .... Z 6
Higher Tower Road ...... Z 9
Hope Terrace .... Z 10
Jubilee Street .... Z 12
Marcus Hill .... Z 13
Porth Way .... Y 14
Trevemper Road .... Y 15
St. Georges Road ...... Z 16
St. John's Road .... Z 18

↑ **Porth Enodoc,** 4 Esplanade Rd, Pentire, TR7 1PY, ℰ 872372, ≤ Fistral Bay – ⑰ rest **℗**. 🎿   Y i
Easter-October – **M** (by arrangement) – **12 rm** 🖾 15.50/30.00 t.

↑ **Copper Beech,** 70 Edgcumbe Av., TR7 2NN, ℰ 873376 – ⑰ rest **℗**. 🎿   Z s
Easter-mid October – **M** 7.50 – **15 rm** 🖾 18.50/40.00 st.

↑ **Wheal Treasure** without rest., 72 Edgcumbe Av., TR7 2NN, ℰ 874136 – **℗**. 🎿   Z z
Easter-September – **11 rm** 🖾 17.00/34.00 st.

↑ **Pendeen,** 7 Alexandra Rd, Porth, TR7 3ND, ℰ 873521, 🚗 – ⑰ 🆅 **℗**. 🎿   Y a
April-October – **M** 7.00 st. ▯ 2.60 – **15 rm** 🖾 14.50/32.20 st. – SB (except July and August) 32.00/40.00 st.

at St. Columb Minor NE : 3 m. by A 3059 – Y – ✉ ☎ 0637 Newquay :

☨ Cross Mount, 58-60 Church St., TR7 3EX, ℰ 872669 – **℗**. 🎿
12 rm.

at Crantock SW : 4 m. by A 3075 – Y – ✉ Newquay – ☎ 0637 Crantock :

🏛 **Crantock Bay** 🦢, West Pentire, TR8 5SE, W : ¾ m. ℰ 830229, ≤ Crantock Bay, 🚗, 🎾 –
⑰ **℗**. 🅰 🆎 ⓪ 𝗩𝗜𝗦𝗔
5 March-11 November – **M** (buffet lunch)/dinner 10.25 st. ▯ 3.00 – **31 rm** 🖾 19.00/72.00 st.

AUSTIN-ROVER Quintrell Downs ℰ 872410   FIAT Tower Rd ℰ 872378
DAF Newlyn East ℰ 0872 (Mitchell) 510347

NEW QUAY (CEINEWYDD) Dyfed �403 G 27 – pop. 775 – ECD : Wednesday – ✉ ☎ 0545.
See : site★.
🛈 Church St. ℰ 560865 (summer only).
♦London 234 – Aberystwyth 24 – Carmarthen 31 – Fishguard 39.

☨ **Black Lion,** Glanmor Terr., SA45 9PT, ℰ 560209, ≤, 🚗 – ⑰ **℗**. 🅰 🆎 ⓪ 𝗩𝗜𝗦𝗔
closed January-February – **M** (bar lunch)/dinner 15.00 st. and a la carte ▯ 3.25 – **8 rm**
🖾 24.00/45.00 st. – SB (October-April) 54.00/60.00 st.

NEW ROMNEY Kent �404 W 31 – pop. 4 547 – ECD : Wednesday – ☎ 0679.
Envir. : Lydd (All Saints' Church tower : groined vaulting★) SW : 3 ½ m. – Brookland (St. Augustine's Church : belfry★ 15C, Norman font★) W : 6 m.
🛈 2 Littlestone Rd ℰ 64044.
♦London 71 – Folkestone 14 – Hastings 23 – Maidstone 33.

☨ **Blue Dolphins,** Dymchurch Rd, TN28 8BE, ℰ 63224 – ⑰ **℗**. 🎿
M (dinner only) 13.95 st. – **8 rm** 🖾 19.50/36.00 st.

NEWTON FERRERS Devon �403 H 33 The West Country G. – pop. 1 609 – ☎ 0752 Plymouth.
♦London 242 – Exeter 42 – ♦Plymouth 11.

🏛 **Court House** 🦢, Court Rd, PL8 1AQ, ℰ 872324, ⊼ heated, 🚗 – ⑰ ☎ **℗**. 🅰 𝗩𝗜𝗦𝗔
closed 23 December-15 January – **M** (closed Sunday dinner to non-residents) (bar lunch residents only Monday to Saturday)/dinner a la carte 17.00/24.00 t. ▯ 3.50 – **9 rm**
🖾 40.00/60.00 t., **1 suite** 80.00 t. – SB (except summer) 70.00/85.00 st.

at Battisborough Cross E : 3 m. – ✉ ☎ 075 530 Holbeton :

🏛 **Alston Hall** 🦢, PL8 1HN, ℰ 259, ≤, ⊼, 🚗, 🎾 – ⑰ ☎ **℗**. 🅰 𝗩𝗜𝗦𝗔. 🎿
M 12.50/20.45 t. and a la carte ▯ 3.25 – **9 rm** 🖾 45.00/84.00 st.

NEWTON SOLNEY Derbs. �402 �403 �404 P 25 – see Burton-upon-Trent (Staffs.).

NEWTOWN (DRENEWYDD) Powys �403 K 26 – pop. 8 906 – ECD : Thursday – ☎ 0686.
🏌 St. Giles, Pool Rd ℰ 25844 NE : ½ m.
🛈 Central Car Park ℰ 25580 (summer only).
♦London 196 – Aberystwyth 44 – Chester 56 – Shrewsbury 32.

↑ Highgate Farm 🦢, Highgate, SY16 3LF, N : 2 ¾ m. by B 4568 on Llanfair rd ℰ 625981, ≤,
« Working farm », 🚗 – **℗**. 🎿
M 7.00 st. – **3 rm**.

at Abermule (Aber-Miwl) NE : 4 ½ m. on A 483 – ✉ ☎ 068 686 Abermule :

🏛 **Dolforwyn Hall** 🦢, Dolforwyn, SY15 6JG, N : ½ m. on A 483 ℰ 221 – ⑰ ☎ **℗**. 🅰 🆎 ⓪
𝗩𝗜𝗦𝗔. 🎿
M 15.00/20.00 st. and a la carte ▯ 3.00 – **7 rm** 🖾 29.50/47.00 st.

AUDI, VW Abermule ℰ 068 686 (Abermule) 615   ⓦ ATS   Dulas Garage. Llanidloes Rd ℰ
FORD Pool Rd ℰ 25514   626069/27532

NITON I.O.W. �403 �404 Q 32 – see Wight (Isle of).

NORMAN CROSS Cambs. �404 T 26 – see Peterborough.

NORMANTON PARK Leics. - see Stamford.

NORTHALLERTON North Yorks. 𝟰𝟬𝟮 P 20 – pop. 13 566 – ECD : Thursday – ☎ 0609.
Envir. : Bedale, Leyburn Rd (Parish church★ 13C-14C) SW : 7 ½ m.
🛈 at Bedale, Leyburn Rd ℘ 0677 (Bedale) 22451, SW : 7 ½ m.
🅿 Applegarth Car Park ℘ 6864.
♦London 238 – ♦Leeds 48 – ♦Middlesbrough 24 – York 33.

- 🏨 **Golden Lion** (T.H.F.), 114 High St., DL7 8PP, ℘ 777411 – ⊱×⊰ rm 📺 ☎ 🅿 – 🔥 100. 🖾 🖭
  🖸 VISA
  M 9.50 **st.** (lunch) and a la carte 11.15/15.50 **st.** ⍾ 3.75 – ⌷ 7.00 – **28 rm** 54.00/70.00 **st.** –
  SB 68.00/84.00 **st.**

  at Staddlebridge NE : 7 ½ m. by A 684 on A 19 at junction with A 172 – ✉ Northallerton
  – ☎ 060 982 East Harlsey :

- ✗✗ **McCoys at the Tontine** with rm, DL6 3JB, ℘ 671, « 1930's decor » – ▤ 📺 ☎ 🅿. 🖾 🖭
  🖸 VISA
  M *(closed Sunday)* (dinner only) a la carte 21.80/32.50 **t.** ⍾ 4.00 – **6 rm** ⌷ 59.00/75.00 **t.**

  at Newby Wiske S : 2 ½ m. by A 167 – ✉ ☎ 0609 Northallerton :

- 🏨 **Solberge Hall** (Best Western) ⑤, DL7 9ER, ℘ 779191, Fax 780472, ≼, 🐎, park – 📺 ☎ 🅿
  15 rm.

AUDI-VW Darlington Rd ℘ 771011
AUSTIN-ROVER Brompton Rd ℘ 3891
FORD South Par. ℘ 2621

PEUGEOT-TALBOT 2-3 Tannery Lane ℘ 71376
RENAULT Leeming Bar ℘ 0677 (Bedale) 22388

NORTHAMPTON Northants. 𝟰𝟬𝟰 R 27 – pop. 154 172 – ☎ 0604.
See : Church of the Holy Sepulchre★ 12C X A – Central Museum and Art Gallery (collection of
footwear★) X M.
Envir. : Brixworth (All Saints Church★ 7C Saxon) N : 7 m. by A 508 Y – Earls Barton (All Saints
Church : 10C Saxontower★) NE : 5 m. by A 45 Y – Castle Ashby★ (16C-17C) *AC*, NE : 8 m. by A
428 Z – Boughton House★ N : 3 ½ m..
🛈 Delapre, Eagle Drive ℘ 764036 Z.
🅸 21 St. Giles St. ℘ 22677/34881 ext 404.
♦London 69 – ♦Cambridge 53 – ♦Coventry 34 – ♦Leicester 42 – Luton 35 – ♦Oxford 41.

Plan on next page

- 🏨 **Swallow** (Swallow), Eagle Drive, NN4 0HW, SE : 2 m. by A 428 on A 45 ℘ 768700, Telex
  31562, Fax 769011, 🖾 – ⊱×⊰ ▤ rest 📺 ☎ 👤 🅿 – 🔥 200. 🖾 🖭 🖸 VISA   Z a
  M 12.00/18.00 **st.** and a la carte – **122 rm** ⌷ 73.00/110.00 **st.** – SB (weekends only) 90.00 **st.**

- 🏨 **Northampton Moat House** (Q.M.H.), Silver St., NN1 2TA, ℘ 22441, Telex 311142, Fax
  230614 – 🛗 📺 ☎ 🅿 – 🔥 600. 🖾 🖭 🖸 VISA   X n
  M 10.50/11.00 **st.** and a la carte ⍾ 3.95 – **134 rm** ⌷ 64.50/79.50 **st.**, **4 suites** 98.00 **st.** –
  SB (weekends only) 64.00 **st.**

- 🏨 **Queen Eleanor** (B.C.B), Newport Pagnell Rd, Wootton, NN4 0JJ, S : 1 ¾ m. by A 508 on
  B 526 ℘ 762468, 🐎 – 📺 ☎ 🅿 – 🔥 60. 🖾 🖭 🖸 VISA. 🛇   Z u
  M (carving rest.) 6.95 **st.** ⍾ 3.25 – **20 rm** ⌷ 45.00/52.00 **st.** – SB (weekends only) 42.00 **st.**

- 🏨 Thorplands Toby, Talavera Way, Round Spinney, NN3 4RN, NE : 3 ½ m. by A 43 ℘ 494241
  – 📺 ☎ 🅿   Y e
  M (grill rest.) – **31 rm**.

- 🏨 **Travelodge** without rest., Upton Way (Ring Rd), NN5 6EG, W : 1 ½ m. by A 45 ℘ 758395 –
  📺 ⅋ 🅿. 🖾 🖭 VISA   Z e
  40 rm 21.50/27.00 **t.**

- 🏨 Travel Inn without rest., Harpole Turn, Weedon Rd, NN7 4DD, W : ¼ m. on A 45 ℘ 831807
  – 📺 ⅋ 🅿   Z
  51 rm.

- ✗✗ **Dunkley's**, Castle Ashby Station, Cogenhoe, NN7 1NP, E : 8 ¼ m. by A 428 and A 45 on
  Castle Ashby rd ℘ 810546, « Converted station warehouse » – 🅿. 🖾 🖭 🖸 VISA
  closed Sunday – **M** (dinner only and Sunday lunch)/dinner 13.95 **t.** and a la carte
  14.90/16.35 **t.** ⍾ 3.50.

  at Spratton N : 7 m. by A 508 off A 50 – Y – ✉ ☎ 0604 Northampton :

- 🏨 **Broomhill** ⑤, Holdenby Rd, NN6 8LD, SW : 1 m. by A 50 ℘ 845959, Fax 845834, ≼,
  🏊 heated, 🐎, park, ✗ – 📺 ☎ 🅿. 🖾 🖭 🖸 VISA. 🛇
  M a la carte 15.65/23.15 **t.** ⍾ 3.75 – **12 rm** ⌷ 47.00/60.00 **t.**

  at Weston Favell NE : 3 ½ m. by A 4500 – ✉ ☎ 0604 Northampton :

- 🏨 **Westone Moat House** (Q.M.H.), Ashley Way, NN3 3EA, ℘ 406262, Telex 312587, Fax
  415023, 🐎 – 🛗 ▤ rest 📺 ☎ 🅿 – 🔥 100. 🖾 🖭 🖸 VISA   Y a
  closed Christmas-New Year – **M** *(closed Saturday lunch)* 9.00/10.50 **st.** and a la carte ⍾ 3.25
  – **64 rm** ⌷ 59.00/69.00 **st.**, **1 suite** 89.00 **st.** – SB (weekends only) 65.00 **st.**

  at Moulton NE : 4 ½ m. by A 43 – Y – ✉ ☎ 0604 Northampton :

- ⌂ **Poplars**, 33 Cross St., NN3 1RZ, ℘ 643983, 🐎 – 📺 🅿. 🖾 VISA
  closed 1 week at Christmas – **M** (by arrangement) 9.00 **t.** ⍾ 2.75 – **21 rm** ⌷ 22.50/30.00 **st.** –
  SB (weekends only) 50.00/57.00 **st.**

NORTHAMPTON

Abington Street X
Drapery .... X 18
Gold Street X
Grosvenor Centre X
Weston
  Favell Centre .... Y

Abington Square ...... X 2
Ashley Way .... Y 3
Bewick Road .... X 4
Billing Road .... X 7
Bridge Street .... X 8
Campbell Street ...... X 9
Charnwood Avenue .... Y 10
Church Lane .... X 13
College Street .... X 14
Derngate .... X 15
Earl Street .... X 19
Greyfriars.......... X 23
Guildhall Road ...... X 24
Horse
  Shoe Street .... X 28
Kenmuir Avenue....... Y 29
Kettering Road ...... X 30
Kingsthorpe Grove ... X 34
Lower Mounts....... X 35
Mare Fair .... X 37
Oaklands Drive....... Y 38
Overstone Road ..... X 39
Park Avenue North..... Y 40
Park Avenue South..... Z 43
Rushmere Road ..... Z 44
St. Andrew's Road ..... Y 45
St. Edmund's Road .... X 48

St. James's Road .... X 49
St. John's Street .... X 50
St. Leonard's Road .... Z 52
St. Michael's Road .... X 53
Sheep Street .... X 54
Silver Street............... X 55

Spencer Bridge Road .... X, Z 57
Towcester Road .... Z 58
Upper Mounts............... X Y 59
Waveney Way............... Y 60
West Bridge .... X Y 62
Windrush Way .... Y 63

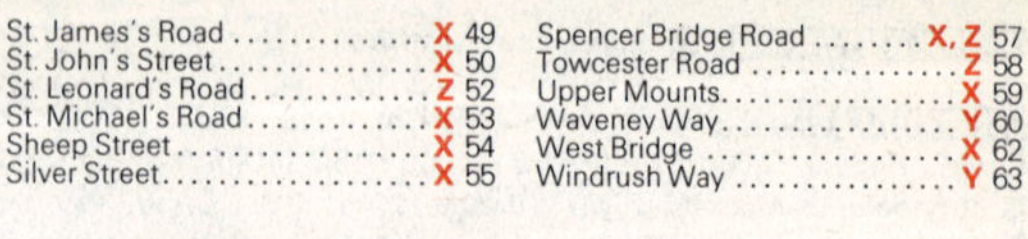

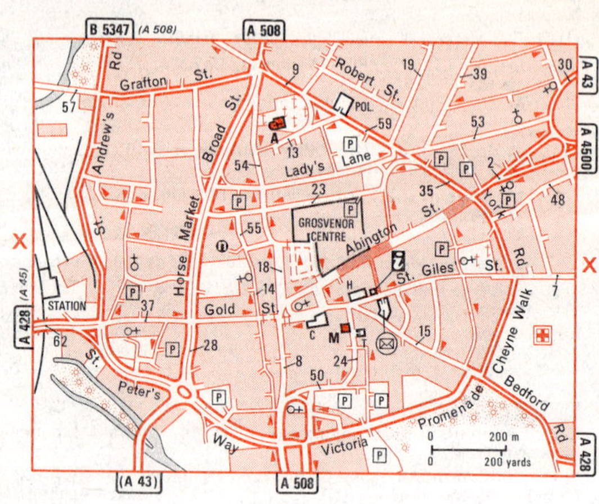

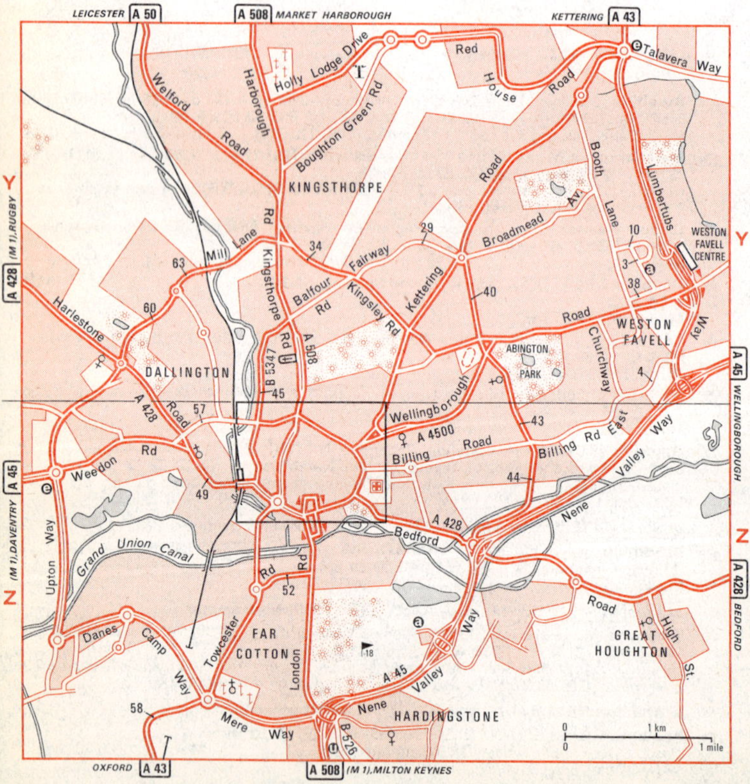

at Holdenby NW : 6 ½ m. by A 508 – Y – off A 50 – ✉ ☎ 0604 Northampton :

XX **Lynton House** ♫ with rm, NN6 8DJ, ✆ 770777, Italian rest., 🚗 – 📺 ☎ 🅿. 🔂 VISA ✗
closed 1 week February and 2 weeks August – **M** *(closed lunch Monday and Saturday, Sunday dinner and Bank Holidays)* 11.75/17.50 **st.** ⌂ 4.50 – **5 rm** ⬚ 52.00/65.00 **st.** – SB *(weekdays only)* 115.00 **st.**

AUSTIN-ROVER Weedon Rd ✆ 54041
FIAT 74 Kingsthorpe Rd ✆ 714555
FORD Weston Favell Centre ✆ 404211
MERCEDES-BENZ Bedford Rd ✆ 250151
NISSAN, SAAB 592 Wellingborough Rd ✆ 401141

RENAULT Bedford Rd ✆ 39645
TOYOTA 348 Wellingborough Rd ✆ 31086
VOLVO Bedford Rd ✆ 21363

ⓐ ATS Kingsthorpe Rd ✆ 713303

NORTH BOVEY Devon 403 I 32 – pop. 368 – ✉ Newton Abbot – ☎ 0647 Moretonhampstead.
♦London 214 – Exeter 13 – ♦Plymouth 31 – Torquay 21.

ⓜ **Glebe House** ♫, TQ13 8RA, ✆ 40544, ≼, 🚗, park – ☎ 🅿. 🔂 VISA
closed 7 January-March – **M** *(bar lunch residents only)*/dinner 17.90 **t.** and a la carte ⌂ 3.50 – **9 rm** ⬚ *(dinner included)* 36.00/72.00 **t.**

⌂ **Blackaller House** ♫ without rest., TQ13 8QY, ✆ 40322, ≼, 🚗 – 🅿. 🔂 AE VISA
April-October – **5 rm** ⬚ 14.85/36.30 **t.**

NORTH DALTON Humberside 402 S 22 – see Great Driffield.

NORTH FERRIBY Humberside 402 S 22 – see Kingston-upon-Hull.

NORTHFIELD West Midlands 403 ㉒ 404 ⑳ – see Birmingham.

NORTH HEATH Berks. – see Newbury.

NORTH HUISH Devon – see South Brent.

NORTHIAM East Sussex 404 V 31 – pop. 1 657 – ECD : Wednesday – ✉ Rye – ☎ 079 74.
♦London 55 – Folkestone 36 – Hastings 12 – Maidstone 27.

ⓜ **Hayes Arms,** Village Green, TN31 6NN, ✆ 3142, « Part Tudor and Georgian country house », 🚗 – 📺 ☎ 🅿. 🔂 AE VISA ✗
M *(bar lunch)*/dinner a la carte 9.05/12.25 **t.** ⌂ 3.50 – **7 rm** ⬚ 30.00/60.00 **t.** – SB 65.00/69.00 **st.**

NORTHLEACH Glos. 403 404 O 28 – pop. 1 043 – ECD : Thursday – ☎ 0451 Cotswold.
🛈 Cotswold Countryside Collection ✆ 60715.
♦London 84 – ♦Birmingham 63 – Gloucester 21 – ♦Oxford 28 – Swindon 24.

XX **Wickens,** Market Pl., GL54 3EJ, ✆ 60421 – ⏴✗.

NORTH MUSKHAM Notts. 402 404 R 24 – see Newark-on-Trent.

NORTH NEWINGTON Oxon – see Banbury.

NORTH ORMSBY Lincs. – see Louth.

NORTH PETHERTON Somerset 403 K 30 – see Bridgwater.

NORTH STIFFORD Essex 404 ㊹ – ✉ Grays – ☎ 0375 Grays Thurrock.
♦London 22 – Chelmsford 24 – Southend-on-Sea 20.

ⓜ **Stifford Moat House** (Q.M.H), High Rd, RM16 1UE, ✆ 390909, Telex 995126, Fax 390426, 🚗, XX – 📺 ☎ 🅿 – 🔔 200. 🔂 AE ⓞ VISA
M *(closed Saturday lunch)* 14.50 **st.** and a la carte – ⬚ 6.50 – **64 rm** 60.00/80.00 **st.** – SB *(weekends only)* 64.00 **st.**

NORTH STOKE Oxon. – see Wallingford.

NORTH WALSHAM Norfolk 403 404 Y 25 – pop. 7 929 – ECD : Wednesday – ☎ 0692.
♦London 125 – ♦Norwich 16.

⌂ **Beechwood,** 20 Cromer Rd, NR28 0HD, ✆ 403231, 🚗 – ⏴✗ rest 🅿
closed 24 December-1 January – **M** 8.00 **t.** ⌂ 2.50 – **11 rm** ⬚ 17.00/39.00 **t.** – SB 37.00/47.00 **st.**

at Knapton NE : 3 ½ m. on B 1145 – ✉ North Walsham – ☎ 0263 Mundesley :

ⓜ **Knapton Hall,** The Street, NR28 0SB, ✆ 720405, 🔲, 🚗 – 📺 ☎ 🅿. 🔂 AE VISA ✗
closed 1 week January – **M** 12.00/14.00 **st.** and a la carte ⌂ 3.50 – **9 rm** ⬚ 40.00/56.00 **st.** – SB *(weekends only)* 65.00 **st.**

NORTH WALSHAM

at Felmingham S : 1 ½ m. on B 1145 – ⊠ North Walsham – ☎ 069 269 Swanton Abbott :

🏨 **Felmingham Hall** 🦢, NR28 0LP, S : 1 ½ m. by Skeyton Rd ℰ 631, Fax 320, ⬍, ☒ heated, 🎋, park – TV ☎ P. ⬛ AE ⓞ VISA. ⬚
M 11.50/30.00 t. and a la carte 15.50/21.50 ▯6.50 – **12 rm** ⊊ 45.00/100.00.

AUSTIN ROVER Bacton Rd ℰ 403401

NORTH WALTHAM Hants. 🆘🆘 Q 30 – pop. 692 – ⊠ Basingstoke – ☎ 025 675 Dummer.
♦London 59 – Reading 24 – Southampton 24 – Swindon 52.

🏨 **Wheatsheaf** (Lansbury), RG25 2BB, on A 30 ℰ 398282, Telex 859775, Fax 398253 – ⬱⬲ rm
TV ☎ ♿ P – ⬛ 80. ⬛ AE ⓞ VISA. ⬚
M 8.50/12.50 t. and a la carte – **28 rm** ⊊ 58.00/68.00 t. – SB (spring and autumn) (week-
ends only) 70.00/78.00 **st.**

NORTON Shropshire – see Telford.

NORTON ST PHILIP Somerset 🆘🆘 N 30 – see Bath (Avon).

NORWICH Norfolk 🆘 Y 26 – pop. 169 814 – ☎ 0603.
See : Site⋆⋆ – Cathedral⋆⋆ 11C-12C (bosses⋆⋆ of nave vaulting) Y – Castle ⋆*AC* Z M – St.
Peter Mancroft's Church⋆ (Perpendicular) Z B – Sainsbury Centre for Visual Arts⋆ (University of
East Anglia) *AC*, by B 1108 X – Market Place⋆ Z A.
Envir. : Norfolk Wildlife Park⋆ *AC*, NW : 12 m. by A 1067 V – Blickling Hall⋆⋆ (Jacobean) N :
12 m. by A 140 V – The Broads⋆ (East : from Norwich).
🏌 Royal Norwich, Hellesdon ℰ 49928 V.
✈ ℰ 411923, Telex 97209, N : 3 ½ m. by A 140 V.
🛈 Guildhall, Gaol Hill ℰ 666071/761082 (evenings).
♦London 109 – ♦Kingston-upon-Hull 148 – ♦Leicester 117 – ♦Nottingham 120.

Plan opposite

🏨 **Maid's Head** (Q.M.H.), Tombland, NR3 1LB, ℰ 761111, Telex 975080, Fax 613688 – ▯ TV
☎ P – ⬛ 60. ⬛ AE ⓞ VISA   Y u
M (carving lunch)/dinner 11.45 t. and a la carte ▯6.95 – **80 rm** ⊊ 59.00/95.00 **st.**, **1 suite**
115.00 **st.** – SB (weekends only) 86.00 **st.**

🏨 **Nelson**, Prince of Wales Rd, NR1 1DX, ℰ 760260, Telex 975203, Fax 620008, ⬍ – ▯ ▤ rest
TV ☎ ♿ P – ⬛ 90. ⬛ AE ⓞ VISA. ⬚   Z a
M (closed lunch Saturday and Bank Holidays) 9.00/12.50 st. and a la carte ▯ 4.00 – **118 rm**
⊊ 60.00/80.00 **st.**, **3 suites** 80.00/110.00 **st.** – SB 73.00/83.00 **st.**

🏨 **Post House** (T.H.F.), Ipswich Rd, NR4 6EP, S : 2 ¼ m. on A 140 ℰ 56431, Telex 975106, Fax
506400, ☒ – ⬱⬲ rm TV ☎ P – ⬛ 100. ⬛ AE ⓞ VISA   on A 140   X
M (closed lunch Saturday and Bank Holidays) 7.95/9.25 **st.** and a la carte ▯ 3.95 – ⊊ 7.00 –
116 rm 62.00/72.00 **st.** – SB (weekends only) 76.00/84.00 **st.**

🏨 **Norwich** (Best Western), 121-131 Boundary Rd, NR3 2BA, on A 47 ℰ 787260, Telex 975337,
Fax 400466 – ⬱⬲ rm TV ☎ ♿ P – ⬛ 300. ⬛ AE ⓞ VISA. ⬚   V r
M (carving lunch) 5.50/10.50 **st.** and a la carte – **99 rm** ⊊ 53.00/63.00 **st.**, **3 suites** 67.00 st.
– SB (weekends only) 64.00 **st.**

🏨 **Sprowston Manor**, Wroxham Rd, Sprowston, NR7 8RP, NE : 3 ¼ m. on A 1151 – V –
ℰ 410871, Telex 975356, Fax 423911, 🎋 – TV ☎ P – ⬛ 200
38 rm.

🏨 **Lansdowne** (Embassy), 116 Thorpe Rd, NR1 1RU, ℰ 620302, Fax 761706 – ▯ ⬱⬲ rm TV ☎
P – ⬛ 120. ⬛ AE ⓞ VISA   X i
M (closed Saturday lunch) 9.00/10.00 **st.** and a la carte – ⊊ 6.50 – **44 rm** 45.00/66.00 st. –
SB (weekends only) 60.00/70.00 **st.**

🏠 **Cumberland**, 212-216 Thorpe Rd, NR1 1TJ, ℰ 34550 – ⬱⬲ rm TV ☎ P. ⬛ VISA. ⬚
M 8.95 st. ▯ 3.25 – **28 rm** ⊊ 29.00/60.00 **st.** – SB (weekends only) 46.00/73.70 **st.**   X a

XX ❀ **Adlard's** (Adlard), 79 Upper St. Giles St., NR2 1AB, ℰ 633522 – ⬛ VISA   Z e
closed Sunday and Monday – **M** (dinner only) 24.50 **st.**
Spec. Young pigeon with a pigeon sausage and madeira sauce, English lamb with a herb crust, jerusalem
artichoke mousse (winter), Scallops with oyster mushrooms and a spaghetti of courgettes (summer).

XX **By Appointment**, 27 St. Georges St., NR3 1AB, ℰ 630730 – ⬛ VISA   Y a
closed Sunday and Monday – **M** (dinner only) 20.00 t. ▯ 3.75.

XX **Brasted's**, 8-10 St. Andrew's Hill, NR2 1AD, ℰ 625949 – ⬛ AE ⓞ VISA   Y c
closed Saturday lunch, Sunday and Bank Holidays – **M** a la carte 14.75/20.00 t.

XX **Marco's**, 17 Pottergate, NR2 1DS, ℰ 624044, Italian rest. – ⬛ AE ⓞ VISA   YZ e
closed Sunday, Monday and mid August-mid September – **M** 12.00 t. (lunch) and a la carte
14.80/20.20 t. ▯ 4.00.

X **Bombay**, 9-11 Magdalen St., NR3 1LE, ℰ 666618, Indian rest. – ⬛ AE ⓞ VISA   Y x
closed 25 December – **M** a la carte approx. 7.35 t.

X **Bombay**, 43 Timber Hill, NR1 3LA, ℰ 620305, Indian rest. – ⬛ AE ⓞ VISA   Z n
closed 25 December – **M** a la carte approx. 7.35 **t.**

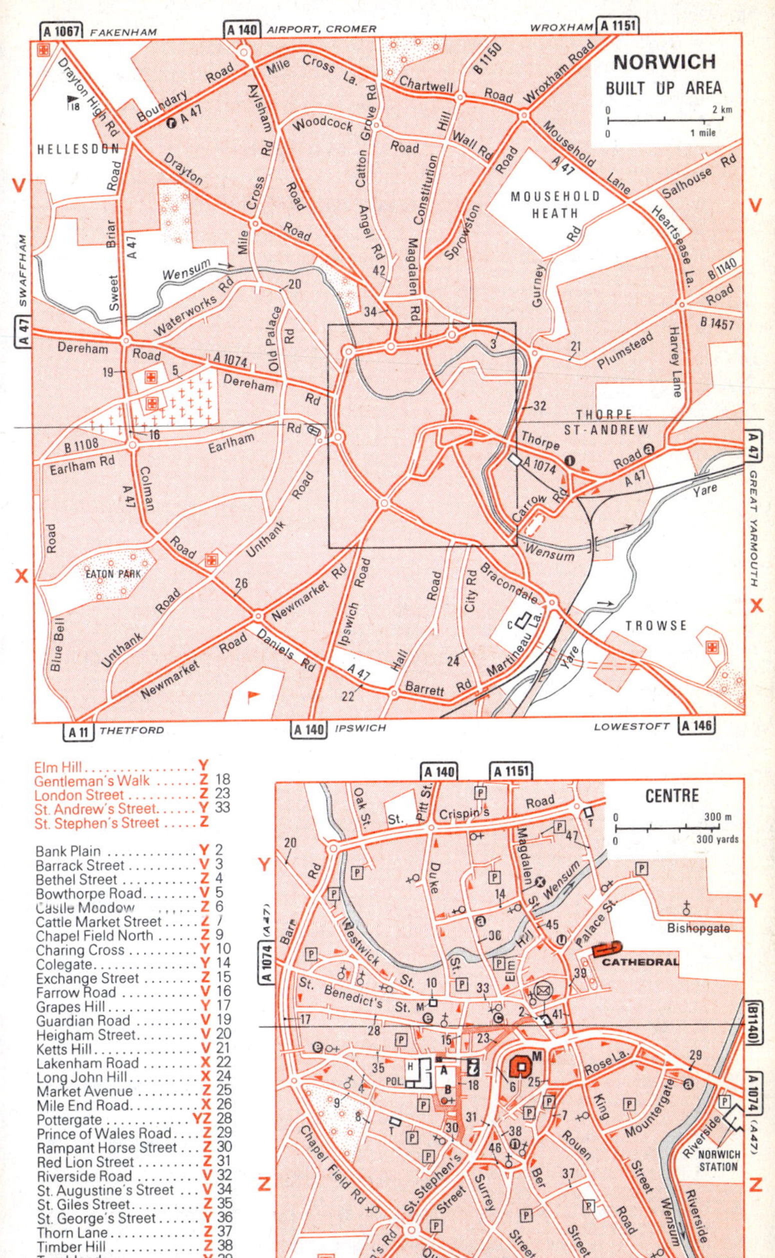

A 1067 FAKENHAM
A 140 AIRPORT, CROMER
WROXHAM A 1151
NORWICH
BUILT UP AREA
0 2 km
1 mile
Drayton High Rd
18
Boundary
Road
Mile Cross La.
Chartwell
B 1150
Road
Wroxham Road
Mousehold Lane
Salhouse Rd
Aylsham Rd
Woodcock
Catton Grove Rd
Hill
Wall Rd
Road
A 47
Heartsease La.
HELLESDON
Drayton
Road
Angel Rd
Constitution
Sprowston
Road
MOUSEHOLD
HEATH
Gurney Rd
B 1140
SWAFFHAM
A 47
Briar
Sweet
Wensum
Mile
Cross
Road
Waterworks Rd
20
Old Palace Rd
Magdalen Rd
42
34
21
Plumstead
Harvey Lane
B 1457
A 47
Dereham
Road
5
A 1074
Dereham Rd
32
THORPE
ST-ANDREW
A 47
19
16
Earlham
Rd
Thorpe
A 1074
Carrow Rd
Road
A 47
Yare
GREAT YARMOUTH
B 1108
Earlham Rd
Colman
Road
Unthank
Road
Road
Wensum
EATON PARK
26
Newmarket Rd
Ipswich Road
Road
City Rd
Bracondale
Martineau La.
c
TROWSE
Blue Bell
Road
Unthank
Newmarket
Road
Daniels Rd
A 47
Hall
Barrett Rd
24
Yare
22
A 11 THETFORD
A 140 IPSWICH
LOWESTOFT A 146

at Horsham St. Faith N : 4 ½ m. by A 140 – **V** – ✉ ☎ 0603 Norwich :

⌂ **Elm Farm Chalet,** 55 Norwich Rd, NR10 3HH, ✆ 898366, 🚗 – ✗ rest 📺 ☎ 🅿. 🔼 AE
VISA 🛇
M (by arrangement) 12.50 t. ▮ 2.65 – **19 rm** ⊐ 22.50/38.50 t. – SB (November-March except Bank Holidays) 52.50/54.50 st.

at Thorpe St. Andrew E : 2 ½ m. on A 47 – **X** – ✉ ☎ 0603 Norwich :

🏨 **Oaklands,** 89 Yarmouth Rd, NR7 0HH, ✆ 34471, Fax 700318, 🚗 – 📺 ☎ 🅿 – 🏛 60. 🔼
AE ① VISA
M 9.00/12.00 st. and a la carte ▮ 3.00 – **41 rm** ⊐ 42.00/85.00 st. – SB 70.00/90.00 st.

at Hethersett SW : 6 m. by A 11 – **X** – ✉ ☎ 0603 Norwich :

🏨 **Park Farm** 🐾, on B 1172, NR9 3DL, ✆ 810264, Fax 812104, ≤, 🔼, 🚗, ✗ – 📺 ☎ 🅿 –
🏛 80. 🔼 AE ① VISA. 🛇
closed 25 to 30 December – **M** (closed Sunday dinner to non-residents) 8.00/10.00 st.
and a la carte ▮ 3.95 – **35 rm** ⊐ 45.00/95.00 st.

AUDI-VW 79 Mile Cross Lane ✆ 410661
ASTON-MARTIN, AUSTIN-ROVER Ipswich Rd,
Long Stratton ✆ 0508 (Long Stratton) 30491
AUSTIN-ROVER Norwich Rd, Stoke Holy Cross ✆
05086 (Framingham Earl) 2218
AUSTIN-ROVER Mile Cross Lane ✆ 483001
AUSTIN-ROVER, DAIMLER-JAGUAR, ROLLS-
ROYCE 5 Prince of Wales Rd ✆ 628383
BMW 26-29 Cattlemarket St. ✆ 621471
CITROEN Earlham Rd ✆ 621393
FORD 39 Palace St. ✆ 624144
HONDA 36 Duke St. ✆ 629825
MERCEDES-BENZ, VW, AUDI Heigham Causeway,
Heigham St. ✆ 612111

NISSAN Constitution Hill ✆ 43944
PORSCHE Vulcan Rd South ✆ 616716
RENAULT 22 Heigham St. ✆ 628911
TALBOT, PEUGEOT 116 Prince of Wales Rd ✆
628811
TOYOTA Rouen Rd ✆ 629655
VAUXHALL-OPEL Aylsham Rd, Mile Cross ✆
414321
VAUXHALL-OPEL Mountergate ✆ 623111
VOLVO Westwick St. ✆ 626192

⊚ ATS Mason Rd, Mile Cross Lane ✆ 43471/2
ATS Aylsham Rd, Aylsham Way ✆ 46316/7

NOTTAGE (DRENEWYDD YN NOTAIS) Mid Glam. 🔳 I 29 – see Porthcawl.

NOTTINGHAM Notts. 🔳 🔳 🔳 Q 25 – pop. 273 300 – ECD : Thursday – ☎ 0602.

See : Castle★ (Renaissance) and Art Gallery★ AC **CZ M.**

Envir. : Newstead Abbey★ (16C) and gardens★★ AC, N : 9 m. by B 683 **AY** – Wollaton Hall★ (16C)
AC, W : 3 ½ m. **AZ M.**

🏌 Bulwell Forest ✆ 278008, NW : 4 m. on A 611 **AY** – 🏌 Bulwell Hall Park Links ✆ 278021, N : 5 m.
AY – 🏌 Mapperley, Central Av. ✆ 265611 **BY.**

✈ East Midlands Airport : Castle Donington ✆ 0332 (Derby) 810621, SW : 15 m. by A 453 **AZ.**

🛈 16 Wheeler Gate ✆ 470661 – 🛈 at West Bridgford: County Hall ✆ 823823.

♦London 135 – ♦Birmingham 50 – ♦Leeds 74 – ♦Manchester 72.

Plans on following pages

🏨 **Albany** (T.H.F.), St. James St., NG1 6BN, ✆ 470131, Telex 37211, Fax 484366 – 🛗 ✗ rm ▤
📺 ☎ – 🏛 500. 🔼 AE ① VISA
M (carving meals Saturday lunch and Sunday) 9.95 st. and a la carte ▮ 3.95 – ⊐ 7.60 – **CYZ a**
137 rm 72.00/87.00 st., **1 suite** 174.00/246.00 st. – SB (weekends only) 60.00/80.00 st.

🏨 **Royal Moat House International** (Q.M.H.), Wollaton St., NG1 5RH, ✆ 414444, Telex 37101,
Fax 475667, squash – 🛗 ✗ ▤ 📺 ☎ – 🏛 450. 🔼 AE ① VISA. 🛇
closed 25 and 26 December – ⊐ 6.50 – **200 rm** 56.00/170.00 st. **CY e**

🏨 **Strathdon Thistle** (Thistle), 44 Derby Rd, NG1 5FT, ✆ 418501, Telex 377185, Fax 483725 –
🛗 ✗ rm ▤ rest 📺 ☎ – 🏛 150. 🔼 AE ① VISA
M 9.40/10.75 st. and a la carte – ⊐ 7.25 – **69 rm** 52.00/95.00 st. – SB 56.00/84.00 st. **CY c**

🏨 **Savoy,** Mansfield Rd, NG5 2BT, ✆ 602621, Telex 377429, Fax 691506 – 🛗 ✗ rm 📺 ☎ ♿
🅿 – 🏛 200. 🔼 AE VISA. 🛇
closed 25 and 26 December – **M** 8.00/11.00 st. and a la carte ▮ 2.90 – ⊐ 5.75 – **170 rm** **BY u**
51.00/64.00 st., **3 suites** 85.00 st.

🏨 **Stakis Victoria** (Stakis), Milton St., NG1 3PZ, ✆ 419561, Telex 37401, Fax 484736 – 🛗 ✗ rm
▤ rest 📺 ☎ – 🏛 200. 🔼 AE ① VISA
M (bar lunch) – ⊐ 7.25 – **166 rm** 56.00/80.00 st. – SB 50.00/67.00 st. **DY a**

🏨 **Priory,** Derby Rd, Wollaton Vale, NG8 2NR, W: 3 m. on A 52 ✆ 221691 – ✗ 📺 ☎ ♿ 🅿.
🔼 AE ① VISA. 🛇
M (grill rest.) a la carte 6.05/11.00 st. – **31 rm** ⊐ 48.50/55.50 st. – SB (weekends only) **AZ s**
49.00/58.00 st.

🏨 **George,** George St., NG1 3BP, ✆ 475641, Telex 378150, Fax 483292 – 🛗 ✗ rm 📺 ☎ – 🏛
150. 🔼 AE ① VISA
M 9.25/10.50 st. and a la carte ▮ 4.00 – ⊐ 4.75 – **69 rm** 49.50/69.50 st. – SB (week- **DY e**
ends only) 55.00 st.

🏠 **Lucieville,** 349 Derby Rd, NG7 2DZ, ✆ 787389, 🚗 – ✗ rm 📺 🅿. 🔼 VISA. 🛇 **AZ c**
M 10.00/13.50 st. ▮ 3.75 – **8 rm** ⊐ 38.00/60.00 st.

🏠 **Westminster,** 312 Mansfield Rd, NG5 2EF, ✆ 623023, Fax 691156 – 📺 ☎ 🅿. 🔼 VISA. 🛇
M (dinner only) 10.95 st. and a la carte ▮ 3.20 – **45 rm** ⊐ 38.00/48.00 st. **BY a**

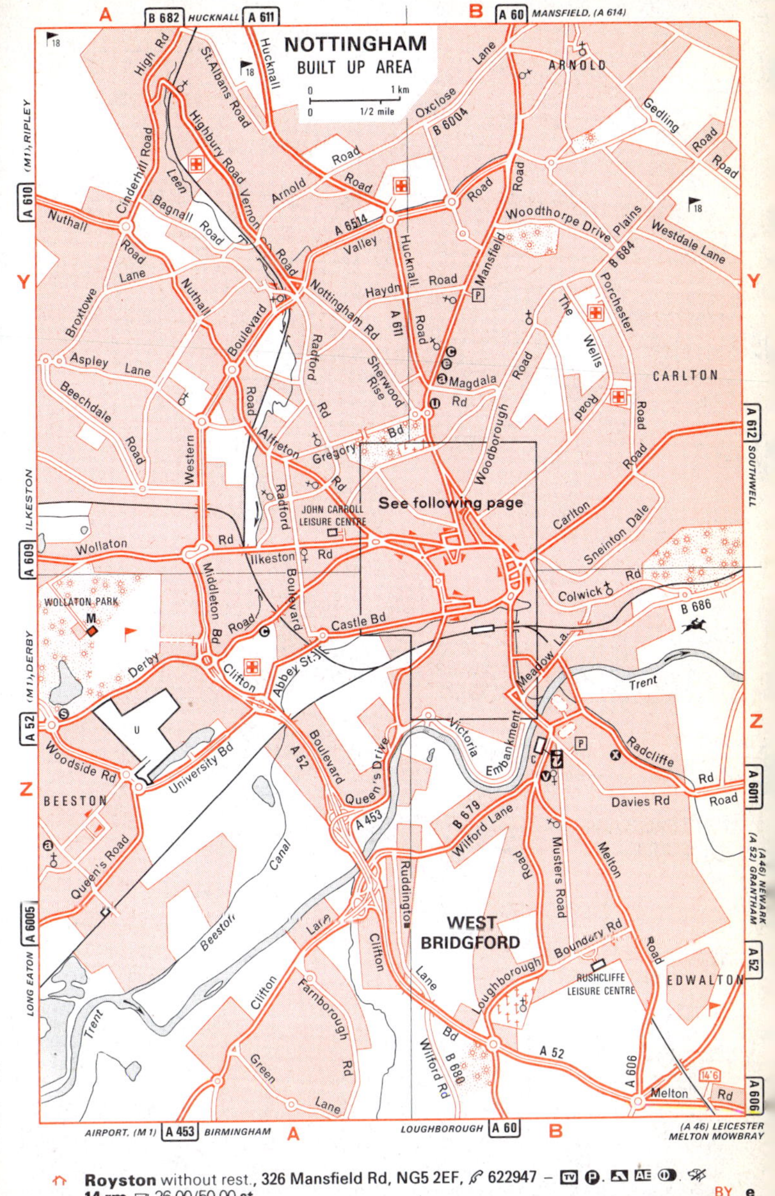

Royston without rest., 326 Mansfield Rd, NG5 2EF, ✆ 622947 – TV P. AE ⓘ BY e

14 rm ⌷ 26.00/50.00 st.

Cotswold, 330-332 Mansfield Rd, NG5 2EF, ✆ 623547, Fax 609910 – TV ☎ P. AE ⓘ BY c
VISA

M 25.00 st. ⌷ 3.00 – **21 rm** ⌷ 18.00/42.00 t.

Ocean City, 100-104 Derby Rd, ✆ 410041, Chinese (Canton) rest. CY u

Chand, 26 Mansfield Rd, NG1 3GX, ✆ 474103, Indian rest. – AE ⓘ VISA DY i
M 3.50 t. (lunch) and a la carte approx. 7.40 t. ⌷ 3.50.

P.T.O. →

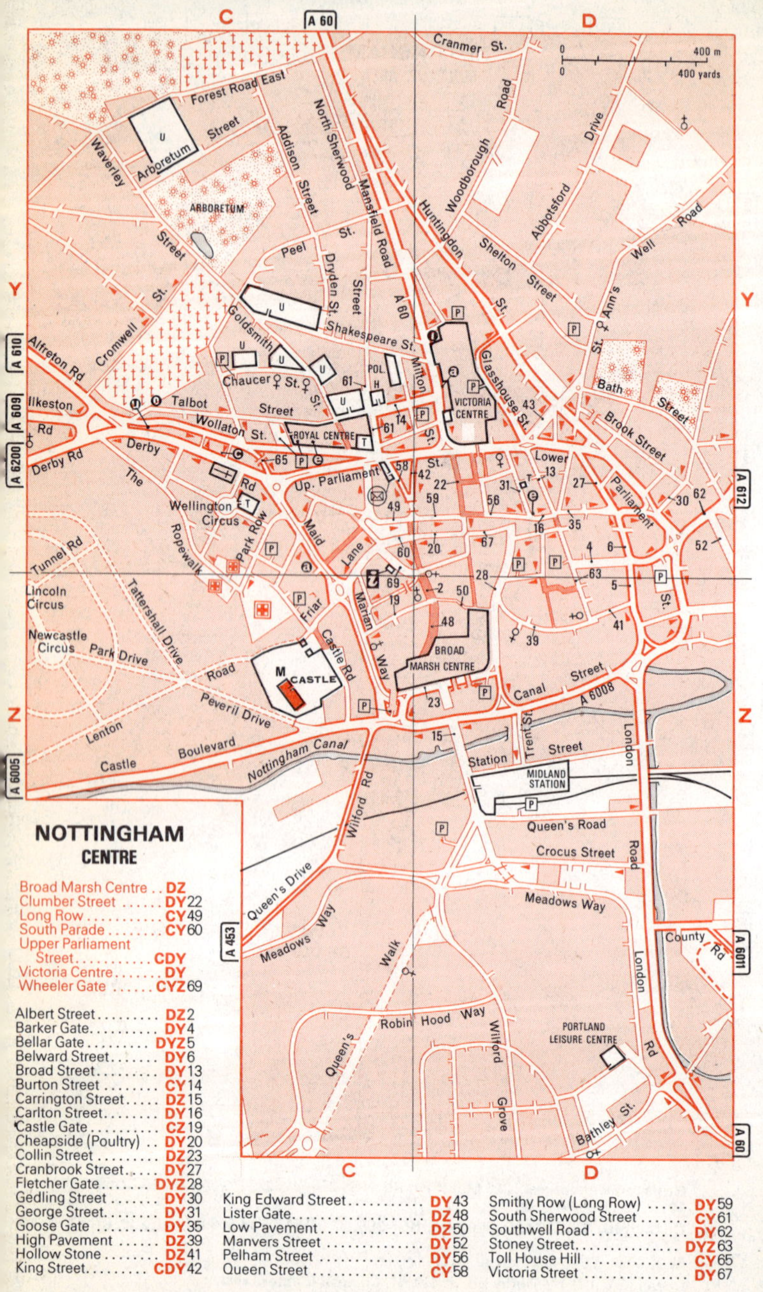

NOTTINGHAM
CENTRE

Broad Marsh Centre .. **DZ**
Clumber Street ...... **DY** 22
Long Row .... **CY** 49
South Parade .... **CY** 60
Upper Parliament
   Street........... **CDY**
Victoria Centre....... **DY**
Wheeler Gate ...... **CYZ** 69

Albert Street......... **DZ** 2
Barker Gate......... **DY** 4
Bellar Gate .... **DYZ** 5
Belward Street....... **DY** 6
Broad Street .... **DY** 13
Burton Street ...... **CY** 14
Carrington Street..... **DZ** 15
Carlton Street ...... **DY** 16
Castle Gate .... **CZ** 19
Cheapside (Poultry) .. **DY** 20
Collin Street .... **DZ** 23
Cranbrook Street.... **DY** 27
Fletcher Gate ...... **DYZ** 28
Gedling Street ..... **DY** 30
George Street...... **DY** 31
Goose Gate .... **DY** 35
High Pavement ..... **DZ** 39
Hollow Stone ...... **DZ** 41
King Street........ **CDY** 42

King Edward Street........... **DY** 43
Lister Gate................. **DZ** 48
Low Pavement .... **DZ** 50
Manvers Street .... **DY** 52
Pelham Street .... **DY** 56
Queen Street .... **CY** 58

Smithy Row (Long Row) ...... **DY** 59
South Sherwood Street .... **CY** 61
Southwell Road .... **DY** 62
Stoney Street............. **DYZ** 63
Toll House Hill .... **CY** 65
Victoria Street .... **DY** 67

*If you find you cannot take up a hotel booking you have made,
please let the hotel know immediately.*

at West Bridgford SE : 2 m. on A 52 – ✉ ☎ 0602 Nottingham :

🏠 **Windsor,** 112-118 Radcliffe Rd, NG2 5HG, ℰ 813773, Fax 819405 – 📺 ☎ 🅿. 🔼 AE ⓪ VISA. ❄️
BZ **x**
closed 25 and 26 December – **M** *(closed Friday to Sunday)* (bar lunch)/dinner 9.50 **st.** 🍾 3.00 – **50 rm** ⊑ 28.75/46.00 **st.**

🏠 **Cambridge,** 63-65 Loughborough Rd, NG2 7LA, on A 60 ℰ 811455 – 📺 🅿. 🔼 AE ⓪ VISA. ❄️
BZ **v**
M *(closed Friday to Sunday)* (dinner only) a la carte 9.30/13.15 **t.** 🍾 3.20 – **18 rm** ⊑ 26.00/48.00 **st.**

at Plumtree SE : 5 ¾ m. by A 60 and A 606 – BZ – ✉ Nottingham – ☎ 060 77 Plumtree :

✕ **Perkins,** Station Rd, Old Railway Station, NG12 5NA, ℰ 3695, Bistro – 🅿. 🔼 AE
closed Sunday, 1 week Christmas and Bank Holidays – **M** a la carte 10.55/15.60 **t.**

at Beeston SW : 4 ½ m. by A 52 on B 6006 – ✉ ☎ 0602 Nottingham :

✕ **Les Artistes Gourmands,** 61 Wollaton Rd, NG9 2NG, ℰ 228288, French rest. – ❄️. 🔼
AE ⓪ VISA
AZ **a**
closed lunch Monday and Saturday, Sunday and 2 weeks August – **M** 16.00/20.00 **st.** and a la carte 14.90/19.90 **st.** 🍾 5.00.

at Toton SW : 6 ½ m. on A 6005 – AZ – ✉ Nottingham – ☎ 0602 Long Eaton :

🏠 **Manor,** 350 Nottingham Rd, NG9 6EF, junction with B 6003 ℰ 733487 – 📺 🅿. 🔼 VISA
M (by arrangement) 9.50 **st.** 🍾 2.25 – **14 rm** ⊑ 20.50/38.50 **st.** – SB (weekends only) 25.50/32.50 **st.**

at Long Eaton (Derbs.) SW : 8 m. by A 52 on B 6002 – AZ – ✉ Nottingham – ☎ 0602 Long Eaton :

🏨 **Novotel Nottingham,** Bostock Lane, NG10 4EP, ℰ 720106, Telex 377585, ☒ heated, 🐎 – 🛗 🖥 📺 ☎ ♿ 🅿 – 🛎 100. 🔼 AE ⓪ VISA
M 10.00/12.00 **st.** and a la carte – ⊑ 5.50 – **110 rm** 50.00/55.00 **st.**

at Sandiacre (Derbs.) SW : 8 m. on A 52 – AZ – ✉ ☎ 0602 Nottingham :

🏨 **Post House** (T.H.F.), Bostocks Lane, NG10 5NJ, ℰ 397800, Telex 377378, Fax 490469 – ❄️ rm 📺 ☎ 🅿 – 🛎 80. 🔼 AE ⓪ VISA
M *(closed Saturday lunch)* 9.50/12.95 **st.** and a la carte 🍾 3.60 – ⊑ 7.00 – **107 rm** 62.00/72.00 **st.** – SB (weekends only) 60.00/80.00 **st.**

AUDI Vernon Rd, Basford ℰ 789291
AUSTIN-ROVER 136 Burton Rd, Carlton ℰ 617111
AUSTIN-ROVER 199 Mansfield Rd
AUSTIN-ROVER Derby Rd ℰ 787701
AUSTIN-ROVER 199 Mansfield Rd, Arnold ℰ 204141
BMW 165 Huntingdon St. ℰ 582831
CITROEN, FIAT 333 Mansfield Rd ℰ 621000
COLT 61a Mansfield Rd ℰ 475635
DAIMLER, ROLLS-ROYCE, BENTLEY Derby Rd ℰ 780730
FIAT Wilford Rd, Ruddington ℰ 844114
FORD Derby Rd ℰ 476111
FORD Nottingham Rd, Stapleford ℰ 395000
FORD London Rd ℰ 506282
HYUNDAI, SUBARU Greasley St., Bulwell ℰ 272228
LADA Woodborough Rd ℰ 623324
MAZDA Station Rd, Plumtree ℰ Plumtree (060 77) 5111
MERCEDES-BENZ Loughborough Rd ℰ 822333

PEUGEOT-TALBOT Pasture Rd, Stapleford ℰ 394444
PEUGEOT-TALBOT Clifton Lane, Clifton ℰ 211228
RENAULT Ilkeston Rd ℰ 781938
RENAULT Sawley, Long Eaton ℰ 0602 (Long Eaton) 733121
SAAB 152 Beechdale Rd ℰ 293023
SKODA 134-138 Loughborough Rd ℰ 814320
TOYOTA North Sherwood St. ℰ 474568
VAUXHALL-OPEL 5 Haywood Rd, Mapperley ℰ 603231
VAUXHALL-OPEL Main St., Bulwell ℰ 770777
VOLVO 50 Plains Rd ℰ 266336
VOLVO 131 Alfreton Rd ℰ 708181
VW, AUDI 180 Loughborough Rd ℰ 813813

🅼 ATS 116 Highbury Rd, Bulwell ℰ 278824
ATS 66 Castle Boulevard ℰ 476678
ATS 126-132 Derby Rd, Stapleford ℰ 392986

NUNEATON Warw. 403 404 P 26 – pop. 60 377 – ECD : Thursday – ☎ 0203.
Envir. : Arbury Hall★ (Gothic house 18C) *AC*, SW : 4 m – 🅹 Public Library, Church St. ℰ 384027.
♦London 107 – ♦Birmingham 25 – ♦Coventry 10 – ♦Leicester 18.

🏨 Chase, Higham Lane, CV11 6AG, NE : 1 m. by A 47 ℰ 341013, 🐎 – 📺 ☎ 🅿 – 🛎 300. ❄️ **28 rm.**

🏨 Longshoot Toby, Watling St., CV11 6JH, NE : 2 ½ m. on A 47 at junction with A 5 ℰ 329711, Telex 311100 – ❄️ 📺 ☎ 🅿 – 🛎 40. ❄️
M (carving rest.) – **47 rm.**

at Sibson (Leics.) N : 7 m. on A 444 – ✉ Nuneaton – ☎ 0827 Tamworth :

🏠 **Millers',** Main Rd, CV13 6LB, ℰ 880223, Fax 880223, «Reconstructed early 19C bakery and water-mill » – 📺 ☎ 🅿 – 🛎 30. 🔼 AE ⓪ VISA
M 9.95/11.95 **st.** and a la carte 🍾 3.00 – **22 rm** ⊑ 45.00/55.00 **st.**

AUSTIN-ROVER Weddington Rd ℰ 383471
FIAT Haunchwood Rd ℰ 382807
HYUNDAI Midland Rd ℰ 346351
HYUNDAI, LADA 208-214 Edward St. ℰ 383339

RENAULT Nuneaton Rd, Bulkington ℰ 383344
SEAT 45 Attleborough Rd ℰ 382241

🅼 ATS Weddington Rd ℰ 341130/341139

NUNNINGTON North Yorks. 402 R 21 – see Helmsley.

OAKFORDBRIDE Devon – see Tiverton.

OAKHAM Leics. 402 404 R 25 – pop. 7 914 – ECD : Thursday – ✆ 0572.
🛈 Public Library, Catmos St. ✆ 724329.
♦London 103 – ♦Leicester 26 – Northampton 35 – ♦Nottingham 28.

🏨 **Whipper-In**, Market Pl., LE15 6DT, ✆ 756971, Fax 757759 – TV ☎ – 🔥 60. 🔄 AE ① VISA
M 9.95/17.95 t. and a la carte – **24 rm** 🍽 45.00/92.00 s. – SB (weekends only) 93.00/125.00 st.

🏠 **Crown**, Crown Walk, High St., LE15 6AP, ✆ 723631, Fax 724635 – TV ☎ P. 🔄 AE VISA
M a la carte 11.15/26.05 t. 🍷 4.75 – **16 rm** 🍽 40.00/55.00 t. – SB (weekends only) 70.00/80.00 st.

🏠 **Boultons**, 4 Catmose St., LE15 6HW, ✆ 722844, 🍴 – ✱ rm TV ☎ P. 🔄 AE ① VISA
M 10.00 st. (dinner) and a la carte 🍷 3.75 – **14 rm** 🍽 40.00/48.00 st. – SB (except Christmas) 62.50 st.

at Hambleton E : 3 m. by A 606 – ✉ ✆ 0572 Oakham :

🏰 ❀ **Hambleton Hall** ⚜, LE15 8TH, ✆ 756991, Telex 342888, Fax 724721, ← Rutland water, 🍴, 🌳, park, ✻ – 📶 TV ☎ P. 🔄 AE ① VISA 🍴
M 30.00/35.00 t. and a la carte 31.50/35.00 t. 🍷 6.50 – 🍽 3.50 – **15 rm** 95.00/195.00 t.
Spec. Mousse of green pea and mint, coriander vinaigrette (spring and summer), Lambs kidneys roasted in their suet, served with gnocchi, Toasted marshmallow flavoured with rose petals.

AUSTIN-ROVER, LAND-ROVER, RANGE-ROVER Burley Rd ✆ 722657

OBORNE Dorset 403 404 M 31 – see Sherborne.

OCKHAM Surrey 404 ㊷ – ✉ Ripley – ✆ 0483 Guildford.
♦London 27 – Guildford 9.

❌❌❌ **Hautboy** with rm, Ockham Lane, GU23 6NP, ✆ 225355, 🍴 – TV ☎ P. 🔄 AE ① VISA. 🍴
closed first 2 weeks January – **M** *(closed Sunday dinner)* 10.50 st. (lunch) and a la carte 16.25/22.25 st. 🍷 3.50 – 🍽 4.95 – **5 rm** 68.00/88.00 st.

ODIHAM Hants. 404 R 30 – pop. 3 002 – ECD : Wednesday – ✆ 025 671.
♦London 51 – Reading 16 – Winchester 25.

🏠 **George**, 100 High St., RG25 1LP, ✆ 72081, Fax 704213 – TV ☎ P. 🔄 ① VISA
M (bar lunch Monday to Saturday)/dinner a la carte 14.00/18.30 – **14 rm** 🍽 48.00/55.00 t.

✻ **King's**, 65 High St., RG25 1LF, ✆ 2559, Chinese rest. – 🔄 AE ① VISA
closed 25-26 December and 1 January – **M** 16.00 t. (dinner) and a la carte 10.90/16.70 t.

MERCEDES-BENZ The Square ✆ 2294

OKEHAMPTON Devon. 403 H 31 – pop. 4 113 – ECD : Wednesday – ✉ ✆ 0837.
⛳ Tors Rd. ✆ 2113 – 🛈 3 West St. ✆ 3020 (summer only).
♦London 226 – Exeter 25 – ♦Plymouth 30.

🏠 **Travelodge** without rest., Sourton Cross, EX20 4LY, W : 4 m. on A 30 ✆ 52124 – TV ♿ P.
🔄 AE VISA
32 rm 21.50/27.00 t.

FIAT Exeter Rd ✆ 2255
FORD East St. ✆ 2776
⊚ ATS Crediton Rd ✆ 3277/2799

OLDHAM Greater Manchester 402 404 N 23 – pop. 107 095 – ECD : Tuesday – ✆ 061 Manchester – ⛳ Crompton and Royton, High Barn ✆ 624 2154 – ⛳ Saddleworth, Uppermill ✆ 045 77 (Saddleworth) 3653 E : 5 m.
🛈 Local Studies Library, 84 Union St. ✆ 678 4654.
♦London 212 – ♦Leeds 36 – ♦Manchester 7 – ♦Sheffield 38.

🏨 **Bower** (De Vere), Hollinwood Av., Chadderton, OL9 8DE, SW : 3 ¼ m. by A 62 on A 6104 ✆ 682 7254, Telex 666883, Fax 683 4605, 🍴 – TV ☎ ♿ P. – 🔥 200. 🔄 AE ① VISA
M *(closed Saturday lunch)* 10.75 st. and a la carte 🍷 4.00 – **66 rm** 🍽 65.00/70.00 st. – SB (weekends only) 65.00 st.

FIAT Lees Rd ✆ 624 8046
MAZDA Oldham Rd, Springhead ✆ 624 3620
NISSAN Huddersfield Rd ✆ 624 6042
⊚ ATS 169-171 Huddersfield Rd ✆ 633 1551
ATS 179-185 Hollins Rd ✆ 627 0180

OLLERTON Notts. 402 403 404 Q 24 – pop. 11 303 (inc. Boughton) – ECD : Thursday – ✉ Newark – ✆ 0623 Mansfield – ⛳ Woodhouse ✆ 0623 (Mansfield) 23521, SW : 7 m.
🛈 Sherwood Heath, Ollerton Roundabout, Newark ✆ 824545.
♦London 151 – ♦Leeds 53 – Lincoln 25 – ♦Nottingham 19 – ♦Sheffield 27.

🏠 **Old Rectory**, Main St., Kirton, NG22 9LP, NE : 3 m. on A 6075 ✆ 861540, 🍴 – P. 🔄 VISA
🍴
closed 22 December-7 January – **M** 8.50 t. – **10 rm** 🍽 19.50/45.00 t.

ORFORD Suffolk 404 Y 27 – pop. 665 – ECD : Wednesday – ✉ Woodbridge – ✆ 0394.
♦London 93 – ♦Ipswich 20 – ♦Norwich 48.

🏠 **Crown and Castle** (T.H.F.), Market Hill, IP12 2LJ, ✆ 450205, 🍴 – TV ☎ P. 🔄 AE ① VISA
M (bar lunch Monday to Saturday)/dinner 11.00 st. 🍷 3.60 – 🍽 7.00 – **19 rm**

ORMESBY ST.MARGARET Norfolk 404 Z 25 – ✉ ☎ 0493 Great Yarmouth.
- ◆London 146 – ◆Cambridge 81 – ◆Ipswich 63 – ◆Norwich 20.

    Ormesby Lodge, Decoy Rd., NR29 3LG, ☎ 730910 – TV ☎ P. 🖅 AE ① VISA
    M 15.00/30.00 **st.** and a la carte ⌀ 3.60 – **8 rm** ⌑ 34.50/46.00 **st.** – SB (weekends only) 60.00 **st.**

OSWESTRY Shropshire 402 403 K 25 – pop. 13 200 – ECD : Thursday – ☎ 0691.
- 🛈 Mile End Service Area A 5 ☎ 662488 – Library, Arthur St. ☎ 654411.
- ◆London 182 – Chester 28 – Shrewsbury 18.

    Ashfield, Llwyn-y-Maen, Trefonen Rd, SY10 9DD, SW : 1 ½ m. ☎ 655200, ≤, 🚲 – ⛝ rest
    TV ☎ P. 🖅
    M 10.00/18.00 **t.** and a la carte ⌀ 4.00 – **12 rm** ⌑ 50.00/60.00 **t.** – SB 70.00/80.00 **st.**

    Sweeney Hall ⌂, Morda, SY10 9EU, S : 1 ¾ m. by B 5069 on A 483 ☎ 652450, ≤, 🚲, park – P. 🖅 VISA
    M 10.00 **t.** and a la carte ⌀ 2.40 – **9 rm** ⌑ 26.00/54.00 **t.**

    Travelodge without rest., Mile End service area, SY11 4JA, SE : 1 ¼ m. by B 4579 at junction of A 5 and A 483 ☎ 658178 – TV 🅰 P. 🖅 AE VISA
    40 rm 21.50/27.00 **t.**

AUSTIN-ROVER Lower Brook St. ☎ 652242
BMW Victoria Rd ☎ 652413
FORD Salop Rd ☎ 654141
HONDA ☎ 653491
PEUGEOT-TALBOT Willow St. ☎ 652301

VAUXHALL-OPEL Smithfield St. ☎ 652235
VOLVO West Felton ☎ 069 188 (Queens Head) 451

ATS Oswald Rd ☎ 653540/653256

OTLEY Suffolk 404 X 27 – pop. 627 – ✉ Ipswich – ☎ 047 339 Helmingham.
- ◆London 83 – ◆Ipswich 7.5 – ◆Norwich 43.

    Otley House ⌂, IP6 9NR, ☎ 253, ≤, « Part 17C manor house », 🚲 – ⛝ P. 🛪
    April- November – **M** (communal dining) (dinner only Monday to Saturday) 14.00 **st.** ⌀ 3.20 – **4 rm** ⌑ 32.00/44.00 **st.**

OTLEY West Yorks. 402 O 22 – pop. 14 136 – ☎ 0943 – 🛆 off West Busk Lane ☎ 461015.
- 🛈 8 Boroughgate ☎ 465151.
- ◆London 216 – Harrogate 14 – ◆Leeds 12 – York 28.

    Chevin Lodge ⌂, Yorkgate, LS21 3NU, S : 2 m. by East Chevin Rd ☎ 467818, Telex 51538, Fax 850335, « Pine log cabin village », 🚲, park – 🍽 rest TV ☎ 🅰 P – 🛆 40. 🖅 AE VISA
    M (closed Saturday lunch) 8.95/13.95 **st.** and a la carte – **40 rm** ⌑ 49.00/85.00 **st.** – SB (weekends only) 72.50 **st.**

OTTERBURN Northumb. 401 402 N 18 – pop. 1 506 – ECD : Thursday – ☎ 0830.
- 🛈 Percy Arms Hotel ☎ 20261.
- ◆London 314 – ◆Carlisle 54 – ◆Edinburgh 74 – ◆Newcastle-upon-Tyne 31.

    Percy Arms, Main St., NE19 1NR, ☎ 20261, 🚲 – TV ☎ P – 🛆 50. 🖅 AE ① VISA
    M 8.00/16.00 **t.** and a la carte – **28 rm** ⌑ 39.00/80.00 **t.** – SB 60.00/80.00 **st.**

OTTERY ST MARY Devon 403 K 31 The West Country G. – pop. 3 957 – ECD : Wednesday – ☎ 040 481 – See : Site★ – St. Mary's Church★★.
- 🛈 Old Town Hall, The Flexton ☎ 3964 (summer only).
- ◆London 167 – Exeter 12 – Bournemouth 71 – ◆Plymouth 53 – Taunton 23.

    The Lodge, 17 Silver St., EX11 1DB, ☎ 2356
    M (booking essential).

FORD Brook St. ☎ 2007

ATS Alansway, Station Yard ☎ 3444

OULTON Suffolk – see Lowestoft.

OUNDLE Northants. 404 S 26 – pop. 3 225 – ECD : Wednesday – ✉ Peterborough – ☎ 0832.
- 🛆 Benefield Rd ☎ 73267.
- 🛈 Market Hall, Market Pl. ☎ 74333.
- ◆London 89 – ◆Leicester 37 – Northampton 30.

    Talbot (T.H.F.), New St., PE8 4EA, ☎ 73621, Telex 32364, Fax 74545, 🚲 – ⛝ rm TV ☎ 🅰 P – 🛆 120. 🖅 AE ① VISA
    M 9.50/14.00 **st.** and a la carte ⌀ 3.95 – ⌑ 7.00 – **38 rm** 59.00/82.00 **st.**

AUSTIN-ROVER 1 Benefield Rd ☎ 73519

FORD 1 Station Rd ☎ 73542

OUTLANE West Yorks. – see Huddersfield.

OWER Hants 403 404 P 31 – see Romsey.

OWERMOIGNE Dorset 403 404 N 32 – see Dorchester.

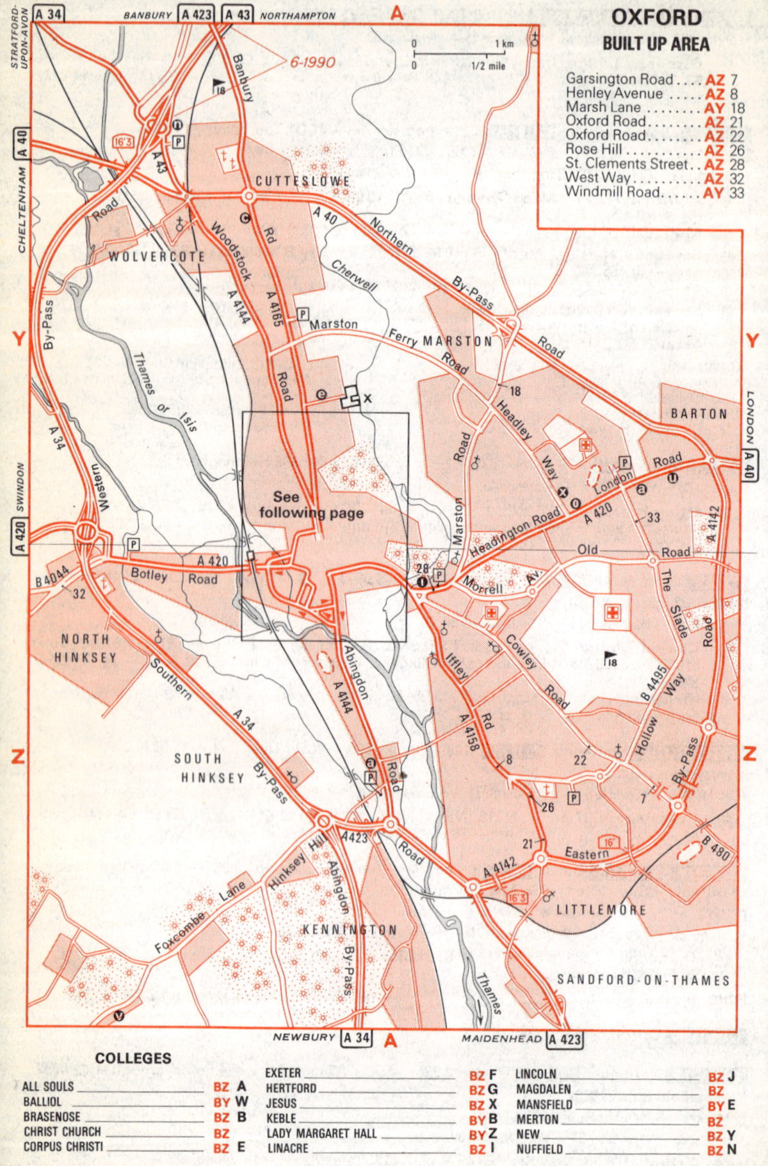

COLLEGES

ALL SOULS	BZ A	EXETER	BZ F	LINCOLN	BZ J	
BALLIOL	BY W	HERTFORD	BZ G	MAGDALEN	BZ	
BRASENOSE	BZ B	JESUS	BZ X	MANSFIELD	BY E	
CHRIST CHURCH	BZ	KEBLE	BY B	MERTON	BZ	
CORPUS CHRISTI	BZ E	LADY MARGARET HALL	BY Z	NEW	BZ Y	
		LINACRE	BZ I	NUFFIELD	BZ N	

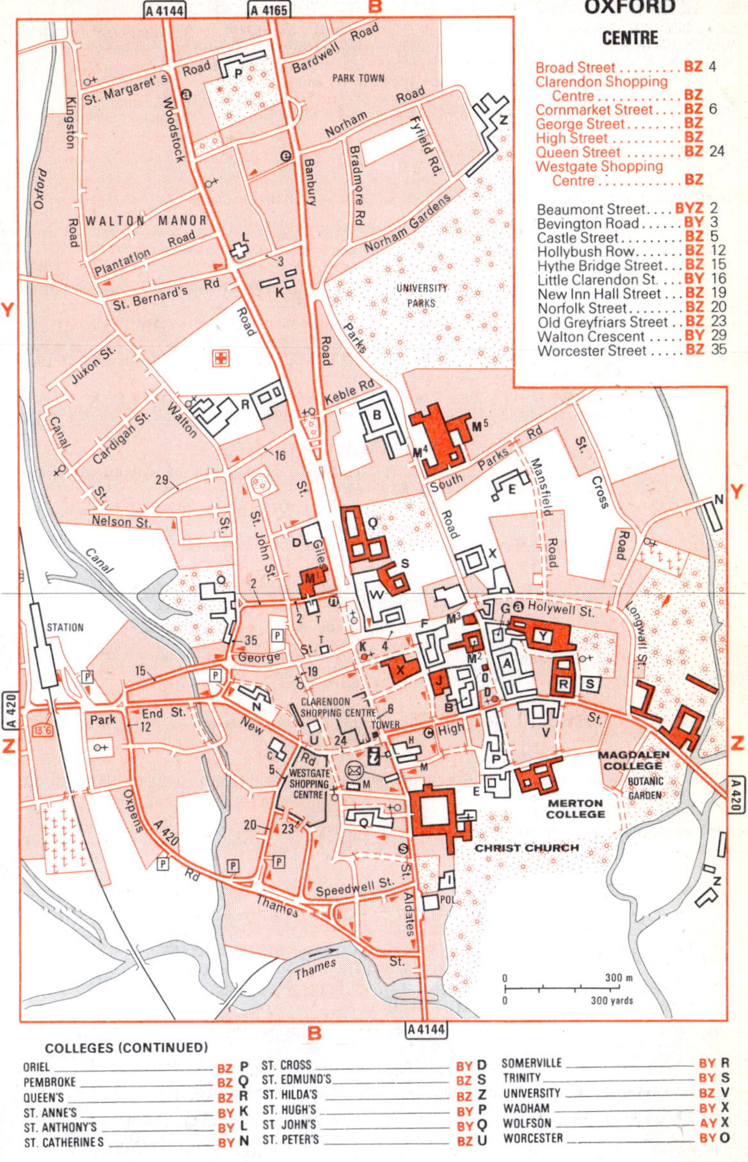

COLLEGES (CONTINUED)

ORIEL	BZ P	ST. CROSS	BY D	SOMERVILLE	BY R
PEMBROKE	BZ Q	ST. EDMUND'S	BZ S	TRINITY	BY S
QUEEN'S	BZ R	ST. HILDA'S	BZ Z	UNIVERSITY	BZ V
ST. ANNE'S	BY K	ST. HUGH'S	BY P	WADHAM	BY X
ST. ANTHONY'S	BY L	ST. JOHN'S	BY Q	WOLFSON	AY X
ST. CATHERINE'S	BY N	ST. PETER'S	BZ U	WORCESTER	BY O

"Short Breaks" (SB)

De nombreux hôtels proposent des conditions avantageuses
pour un séjour de deux nuits
comprenant la chambre, le dîner et le petit déjeuner.

Entrez à l'hôtel le Guide à la main, vous montrerez ainsi,
qu'il vous conduit là en confiance.

See : Site★★★ – Radcliffe Square★★★ BZ **O** – Colleges : Trinity★★ BY **S** – Queens★★ BZ **R** – New★★ (Cloister★, Chapel★) BZ **Y** – Magdalene★★ (Cloister★★, Chapel★) BZ – Lincoln★ BZ **J** – Jesus★ BZ **X** – Merton★ (Old Library★★★, Hall★, Quadrangle★, Chapel windows and glass★)BZ – St. John's★ BY **Q** – Bodleian Library★★ (Painted Ceiling★★) BZ **M2** – Ashmolean Museum★★ **M1** – Churches : St. Mary The Virgin★★ BZ **D** – Christ Church★★ (Tom Quad Tower★) BZ – St. Michael at Northgate★ BZ **K** – Sheldonian Theatre★ BZ **M3** – University Museum★ BY **M4** – Pitt Rivers Museum★ BY **M5**.

₁₈ Banbury Rd ✆ 54415, N : by A 423 AY – ₁₈ Southfield, Hill Top Rd ✆ 242158 and B 480 AZ.

🛈 St. Aldates Chambers, St. Aldates ✆ 726873/4.

♦London 59 – ♦Birmingham 63 – ♦Brighton 105 – ♦Bristol 73 – ♦Cardiff 107 – ♦Coventry 54 – ♦Southampton 64.

Plans on preceding pages

Randolph (T.H.F.), Beaumont St., OX1 2LN, ✆ 247481, Telex 83446, Fax 791678 – 🛗 rm
🍽 rest TV ☎ 🚗 – 🍴 300. 🅰 AE Ⓞ VISA
BZ **n**
M 14.00/20.00 **st.** and a la carte ⅄ 3.95 – ☷ 8.50 – **105 rm** 77.00/108.00 **st.**, **4 suites**
137.00/190.00 **st.** – SB (weekends only) 92.00/104.00 **st.**

Linton Lodge (Hilton), 9-13 Linton Rd, off Banbury Rd, OX2 6UJ, ✆ 53461, Telex 837093,
Fax 310365, 🚗 – 🛗 rm TV ☎ 🅿 – 🍴 100. 🅰 AE Ⓞ VISA
AY **e**
M (closed Saturday lunch) 10.75/14.95 **t.** and a la carte ⅄ 4.20 – ☷ 8.50 – **71 rm** 70.00/90.00 **t.**
– SB (weekends only) 90.00/110.00 **st.**

Welcome Lodge (T.H.F.), Pear Tree Roundabout, Woodstock Rd, OX2 8JZ, N : 3 m. at
junction of A 34 and A 43 ✆ 54301, Telex 83202, Fax 513474, ⊿ heated – rm TV ☎ 🅿.
🅰 AE Ⓞ VISA
AY **n**
M (bar lunch)/dinner 14.50 **st.** ⅄ 4.35 – **95 rm** ☷ 49.00/59.00 **st.**

Foxcombe Lodge, Fox Lane, Boars Hill, OX1 5DP, SW : 3 ¼ m. by A 4144 and A 423
✆ 730746, Fax 730628, 🚗 – TV ☎ 🅿. 🅰 AE Ⓞ VISA
AZ **v**
closed 26 December-2 January – **M** 13.50 **st.** and a la carte ⅄ 3.10 – **20 rm** ☷ 45.00/95.00 **st.**
– SB (weekends only) 65.00/75.00 **st.**

Cotswold House without rest., 363 Banbury Rd, OX2 7PL, ✆ 310558, 🚗 – TV 🅿. ⛬
5 rm ☷ 20.00/48.00 **st.**
AY **c**

Dial House without rest., 25 London Rd, Headington, OX3 7RE, ✆ 69944, 🚗 – TV 🅿
closed Christmas and New Year – **8 rm** ☷ 35.00/42.00 **st.**
AY **o**

Pickwicks without rest., 15-17 London Rd, Headington, OX3 7SP, ✆ 750487, Fax 742208 –
TV ☎ 🅿. 🅰 VISA
AY **x**
18 rm ☷ 18.00/45.00 **st.**

Chestnuts without rest., Davenant Rd, OX2 8BW, ✆ 53375 – TV 🅿. ⛬
4 rm ☷ 18.00/43.00 **st.**
BY **a**

Mount Pleasant, 76 London Rd., Headington, OX3 9AJ, ✆ 62749 – TV ☎ 🅿. 🅰 AE
Ⓞ VISA ⛬
AY **a**
M 15.00 **st.** ⅄ 4.50 – **8 rm** ☷ 45.00/55.00 **st.**

Green Gables without rest., 326 Abingdon Rd, OX1 4TE, ✆ 725870, 🚗 – TV ♿ 🅿. 🅰
VISA ⛬
AZ **a**
8 rm ☷ 16.00/38.00 **st.**

XXX **Elizabeth,** 84 St. Aldates, OX1 1RA, ✆ 242230 – 🅰 AE Ⓞ VISA
BZ **s**
closed Monday, 13 April and 24 to 31 December – **M** 12.95 **st.** (lunch) and a la carte
10.75/25.25 **st.** ⅄ 5.00.

XX **Bath Place** with rm, 4-5 Bath Pl., OX1 3SU, ✆ 791812 – rest TV ☎ 🅿. 🅰 AE Ⓞ VISA
M (closed Monday) 22.50/32.50 **t.** and a la carte ⅄ 4.50 – **8 rm** ☷ 60.00/100.00 **st.** –
SB (October-March) 150.00/225.00 **st.**
BZ **a**

XX **Fifteen North Parade,** 15 North Parade, OX2 6LX, ✆ 513773 – 🅰 VISA
BY **e**
closed Sunday dinner – **M** 10.75/16.75 **t.** and a la carte 15.75/29.25 **t.** ⅄ 3.75.

XX **Café Français,** 146 London Rd, Headington, OX3 9ED, ✆ 62587 – 🍽. 🅰 AE VISA
AY **u**
closed 24 and 26 December – **M** 9.95/16.95 **t.**

XX **La Sorbonne,** 1st floor, 130a High St., OX1 4DH, ✆ 241320, French rest. – 🅰 AE Ⓞ
VISA
BZ **c**
closed 3 weeks August-September – **M** 20.00 **st.** and a la carte 17.00/23.00 **st.** ⅄ 3.90.

at Kidlington N : 4 ½ m. on A 423 – AY – ✉ Oxford – ✆ 0865 Oxford :

Bowood House, 238 Oxford Rd, OX5 1EB, ✆ 842288, 🚗 – TV ☎ 🅿. 🅰 VISA ⛬
closed 24 to 26 December – **M** (closed Sunday) (dinner only) a la carte 8.60/13.95 **st.** –
20 rm ☷ 28.00/57.00 **st.**

at Great Milton SE : 12 m. by A 40 off A 329 – AY – ✉ Oxford – ✆ 0844 Great Milton :

XXXX ❀❀ **Le Manoir aux Quat' Saisons** (Blanc) ⌘ with rm, Church St., OX9 7PD, ✆ 278881,
Telex 837552, Fax 278847, ≤, « 15C and 16C manor house », ⊿ heated, 🚗, park, ⛬ –
rest TV ☎ 🅿 – 🍴 25. 🅰 AE Ⓞ VISA ⛬
closed 1 January-19 February – **M** (closed Tuesday lunch and Monday to non-residents)
55.00 **st.** and a la carte 53.50/64.50 **st.** – **9 rm** 150.00/220.00 **st.**, **1 suite** 300.00 **st.** –
SB (November-April) (weekdays only) 200.00 **st.**
Spec. Tiân d'aubergines, tomates et artichauts, queues de langoustines et homard, Croustillant de rouget de
roche et son jus parfumé aux langues d'oursins, Assiette aux parfums de caramel (all seasonal).

at Cumnor SW : 4 ½ m. by A 420 – **AY** – off B 4017 – ✉ ✆ 0865 Oxford :

XX **Bear and Ragged Staff,** Appleton Rd, OX2 9QH, ✆ 862329 – **P**. **N** **AE** **O** **VISA**
M 14.95 **t.** and a la carte 16.40/21.40 **t.**

AUSTIN-ROVER Oxford Rd, Kidlington ✆ 086 75
(Kidlington) 4363/78187
CITROEN 281 Banbury Rd ✆ 512277
MERCEDES-BENZ Banbury Rd, Shipton-on-Cher-
well ✆ 086 75 (Kidlington) 71011
NISSAN 72 Rose Hill ✆ 774696
SAAB 75 Woodstock Rd ✆ 57028

VAUXHALL-OPEL Woodstock Rd ✆ 59955/722455
VW Abingdon Rd ✆ 242241

ATS Pony Rd, Horspath Trading Est. Cowley ✆
777188
ATS 2 Stephen Rd, Headington ✆ 61732

PADSTOW Cornwall **403** F 32 The West Country G. – pop. 2 256 – ECD : Wednesday –
✆ 0841.

See : Site★.

Envir. : Bedruthan Steps★★*AC*, SW : 8 m. – Trevone (Cornwall Coast Path★★), W : 3 m. – Trevose
Head★ (≤★★), W : 6 m.

◆London 288 – Exeter 78 – ◆Plymouth 45 – Truro 23.

🏠 Metropole (T.H.F.), Station Rd, PL28 8DB, ✆ 532486, Fax 532867, ≤ Camel Estuary, ⅃ hea-
ted, 🚗 – |‡| ⇔ rm TV ⊛ & **P**. **N** **AE** **O** **VISA**
M (bar lunch Monday to Saturday)/dinner 15.00 **st.** and a la carte 🍶 3.60 – ⚬ 7.00 – **43 rm**,
1 suite.

🏠 Old Custom House Inn, South Quay, PL28 8ED, ✆ 532359, ≤ harbour and Camel Estuary –
TV ✆
25 rm.

↑ **Woodlands,** Treator, PL28 8RU, W : 1 ¼ m. by A 389 on B 3276 ✆ 532426, 🚗 – ⇔ rm **P**
March-November – **M** (dinner only) 6.50 **st.** 🍶 3.00 – **9 rm** ⚬ 22.50/36.00 **st.**

XX **Seafood** with rm, Riverside, PL28 8BY, ✆ 532485, ≤, Seafood, « Attractively converted
granary on quayside » – TV ✆. **N** **AE** **VISA**
closed mid December-March – **M** *(closed Sunday)* (booking essential) (dinner only) 21.00 **t.**
and a la carte 26.00/32.00 **t.** 🍾 4.50 – **9 rm** 30.00/85.00 **t.**, **1 suite** 60.00 **t.**

at Little Petherick S : 3 m. on A 389 – ✉ Wadebridge – ✆ 0841 Rumford :

↑ **Old Mill Country House,** PL27 7QT, ✆ 540388, « Part 16C corn mill » – ⇔ rm **P**. 🐾
closed January-February – **M** 9.25 **t.** 🍾 2.75 – **6 rm** ⚬ 34.00/41.00 **t.**

at Constantine Bay SW : 4 m. by B 3276 – ✉ ✆ 0841 Padstow :

🏠 **Treglos** 🐦, PL28 8JH, ✆ 520727, Fax 521163, ≤, 🏊, 🚗 – |‡| ⇔ rest 🍽 rest TV ✆ 🚗 **P**
15 March-5 November – **M** 8.95/15.25 **t.** and a la carte 🍾 4.00 – **41 rm** ⚬ (dinner included) 46.50/99.00 **t.**, **3 suites** 120.00/132.00 **t.** – SB 86.00/115.00 **st.**

at Treyarnon Bay SW : 4 ¾ m. by B 3276 – ✉ ✆ 0841 Padstow :

🏠 **Waterbeach** 🐦, PL28 8JW, ✆ 520292, ≤, 🚗, 🍴 – ✆ **P**. **N** **AE** **VISA**. 🐾
March-November – **M** (bar lunch residents only)/dinner 12.50 **t.** 🍾 1.70 – **21 rm**
⚬ 30.00/66.00 **t.**

During the season, particularly in resorts, it is wise to book in advance.

PAIGNTON Devon **403** J 32 The West Country G. – pop. 39 565 – ECD : Wednesday – ✆ 0803
See : Paignton Zoo★★*AC*, by A 385 Z – Kirkham House★*AC* Y B.

🛈 Festival Hall, Esplanade Rd ✆ 558383.

◆London 226 – Exeter 26 – ◆Plymouth 29.

Plan of Built up Area : see Torbay

Plan on next page

🏠 **Palace** (T.H.F.), Esplanade Rd, TQ4 6BJ, ✆ 555121, Fax 527974, ⅃ heated, 🚗, 🍴, squash
– |‡| ⇔ rm TV **P**. **N** **AE** **O** **VISA**   Y **e**
M (buffet lunch Monday to Saturday)/dinner 12.00 **st.** and a la carte 🍶 3.95 – ⚬ 7.00 –
52 rm 52.00/72.00 **st.** – SB 80.00/103.00 **st.**

🏠 **Redcliffe,** 4 Marine Drive, TQ3 2NL, ✆ 526397, ≤ Torbay, ⅃ heated, 🚗 – |‡| TV ✆ **P**.
🐾   Y **n**
M (bar lunch Monday to Saturday)/dinner 10.75 **t.** and a la carte 🍶 3.50 – **63 rm** ⚬ 35.00/
70.00 **t.** – SB 68.00/80.00 **st.**

↑ **Sea Crest** 🐦, Roundham Cres., TQ4 6DF, ✆ 559849 – ⇔ rest **P**. 🐾   Z **c**
May-September – **M** 4.00 **st.** – **8 rm** ⚬ 9.00/20.00 **st.**

XX **Luigi,** 59 Torquay Rd, TQ3 3DT, ✆ 556185, Italian rest. – **N** **VISA**. 🐾   Y **i**
closed Monday lunch and Sunday – **M** 13.75 **t.** (dinner) and a la carte 11.65/19.45 **t.** 🍶 3.45.

BMW 349 Totnes Rd ✆ 558567
HONDA 45 Totnes Rd ✆ 554484
MERCEDES-BENZ 59 Totnes Rd ✆ 559362
SEAT Bishop's Pl. ✆ 556234

TOYOTA 288-290 Torquay Rd ✆ 553415

ATS Orient Rd ✆ 556888

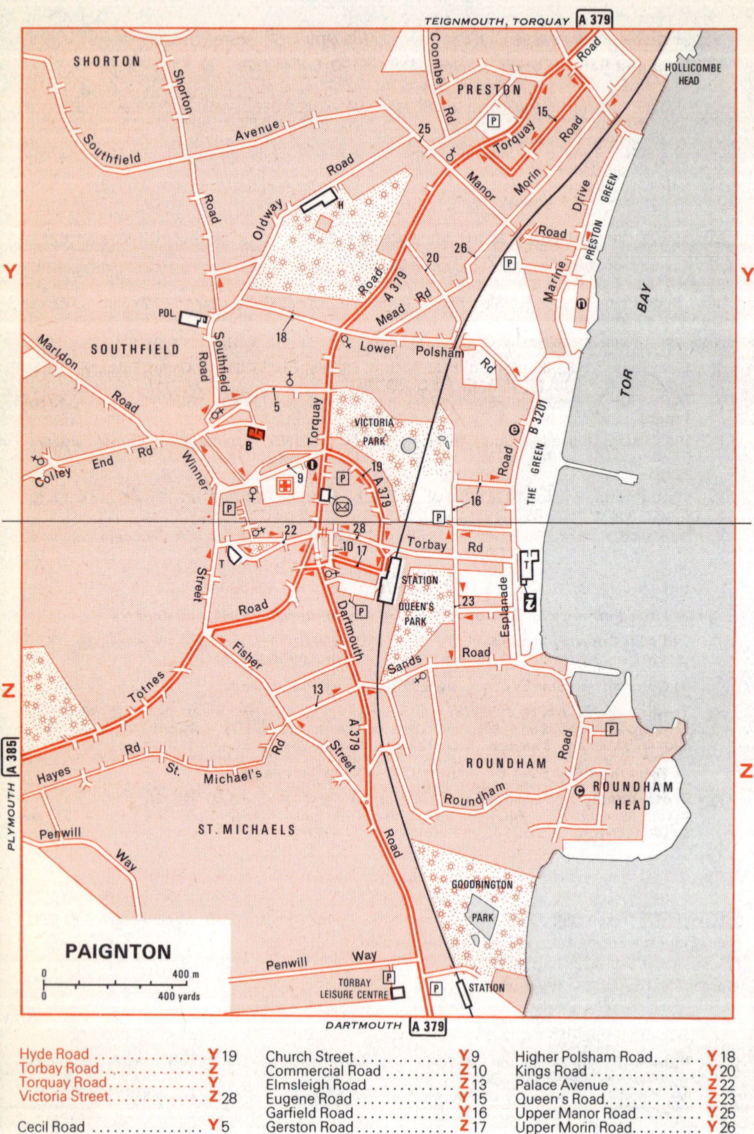

Hyde Road	Y 19	Church Street	Y 9	Higher Polsham Road	Y 18
Torbay Road	Z	Commercial Road	Z 10	Kings Road	Y 20
Torquay Road	Y	Elmsleigh Road	Z 13	Palace Avenue	Z 22
Victoria Street	Z 28	Eugene Road	Y 15	Queen's Road	Z 23
		Garfield Road	Y 16	Upper Manor Road	Y 25
Cecil Road	Y 5	Gerston Road	Z 17	Upper Morin Road	Y 26

PAINSWICK Glos. 403 404 N 28 – pop. 1 757 – ECD : Saturday – ✉ Stroud – ☎ 0452.

🏌 Painswick ☎ 812180.

🛈 The Library, Stroud Rd ☎ 812569.

◆London 107 – ◆Bristol 35 – Cheltenham 10 – Gloucester 7.

🏨 **Painswick** ⏦, Kemps Lane, Tibiwell, GL6 6YB, ☎ 812160, Telex 43605, Fax 812160, 🚲 –
📺 ☎ 🅿 . 🅰 AE ⓪ VISA
M *(closed Sunday dinner)* (dinner only and Sunday lunch)/dinner 25.00 **t.** and a la carte
🍷 3.50 – **15 rm** ⏦ 45.00/70.00 **t.** – SB (weekends only) 75.00/95.00 **st.**

⌂ **Damsell's Cross** ⑤ without rest., The Park, GL6 6SR, N : 1 m. by A 46 on Sheepscombe Rd ℰ 813197, ≼, ⌁, 🌳 – 📺 🅿. 🐾
– **3 rm** ⌷ 20.00/36.00 **s.**

⌂ **Damsell's Lodge** ⑤ without rest., GL6 6SR, N : 1 m. by A 46 on Sheepscombe Rd ℰ 813777, ≼, 🌳 – 📺 🅿. 🐾
3 rm ⌷ 20.00/35.00 **st.**

✕ **Country Elephant,** New St., GL6 6XH, ℰ 813564, 🌳 – 🅽 ⓘ 𝘝𝘐𝘚𝘈
closed Sunday and Monday – **M** (dinner only) 20.00 **t.** ⏧ 3.25.

PANGBOURNE Berks. **403** **404** Q 29 – pop. 3 445 (inc. Whitchurch) – ECD : Thursday – ✆ 073 57.

♦London 56 – ♦Oxford 22 – Reading 6.

🏨 **Copper Inn** (Best Western), 2 Church Rd, RG8 7AR, ℰ 2244, Fax 5542, 🌳 – 📺 ☎ 🅿 –
🔧 60. 🅽 🅰🅴 ⓘ 𝘝𝘐𝘚𝘈. 🐾
M 12.50/23.75 **t.** and a la carte ⏧ 5.50 – ⌷ 5.95 – **21 rm** 55.00/80.00 **st.** – SB (weekends only) 68.00/80.00 **st.**

AUSTIN-ROVER Reading Rd ℰ 2376

PANT MAWR Powys **403** I 26 – ✉ ✆ 055 15 Llangurig.

♦London 219 – Aberystwyth 21 – Shrewsbury 55.

🏠 **Glansevern Arms,** SY18 6SY, on A 44 ℰ 240, ≼, ⌁ – 📺 🅿
closed 1 week Christmas – **M** *(closed Sunday dinner)* (booking essential) (dinner only and Sunday lunch)/dinner 15.00 **t.** ⏧ 3.40 – **8 rm** ⌷ 30.00/47.00 **t.** – SB (weekends only) 64.00/70.00 **st.**

PARKGATE Cheshire **402** **403** K 24 – pop. 3 480 – ECD : Wednesday – ✉ Wirral – ✆ 051 Liverpool.

♦London 206 – Birkenhead 10 – Chester 11 – ♦Liverpool 12.

🏨 **Ship** (T.H.F.), The Parade, L64 6SA, ℰ 336 3931 – 📺 ☎ 🅿. 🅽 🅰🅴 ⓘ 𝘝𝘐𝘚𝘈
M 7.95/11.50 **st.** and a la carte ⏧ 3.95 – ⌷ 7.00 – **26 rm** 46.00/61.00 **st.**

🏨 **Parkgate** (Lansbury), Boat House Lane, L64 6RD, N : ½ m. on B 5135 ℰ 336 5001, Telex 629469, Fax 336 8504, 🌳 – ↞ rm 📺 ☎ 🅿 – 🔧 150. 🅽 🅰🅴 ⓘ 𝘝𝘐𝘚𝘈. 🐾
M 8.50/12.50 **t.** and a la carte – **27 rm** ⌷ 55.00/65.00 **t.** – SB (weekends only) 58.00/64.00 **st.**

PATCHWAY Avon **403** **404** M 29 – see Bristol.

PATELEY BRIDGE North Yorks. **402** O 21 – ✉ ✆ 0423 Harrogate.

Envir. : Brimham Rocks★ E : 4 ½ m.

🛈 Southlands Car Park, off High St. ℰ 711147 (summer only).

♦London 225 – ♦Leeds 28 – ♦Middlesbrough 46 – York 32.

🏠 **Grassfields Country House** ⑤, Ramsgill Rd, HG3 5HL, ℰ 711412, 🌳 – 🅿
Easter-October – **M** (dinner only) 9.00 **st.** ⏧ 2.75 – **9 rm** ⌷ 22.00/42.00 **st.**

at Low Laithe SE : 2 ¾ m. on B 6165 – ✉ ✆ 0423 Harrogate :

✕✕ **Dusty Miller,** Main Rd, HG3 4BU, ℰ 780837 – 🅿. 🅽 𝘝𝘐𝘚𝘈
closed Sunday, first 2 weeks August, 25 December and 1 January – **M** (dinner only) a la carte 17.00/28.40 **t.** ⏧ 4.20.

at Wath-in-Nidderdale NW : 2 ¼ m. – ✉ ✆ 0423 Harrogate :

✕✕ **Sportsman's Arms** ⑤ with rm, HG3 5PP, ℰ 711306, 🌳 – ↞ rm 📺 🅿. 🅽 🅰🅴 ⓘ 𝘝𝘐𝘚𝘈
closed Christmas and New Year – **M** (bar lunch Monday to Saturday)/dinner 14.90 **st.** and a la carte 12.95/27.50 **t.** ⏧ 3.60 – **6 rm** ⌷ 27.00/45.00 **t.** – SB 52.00/70.00 **st.**

PATRICK BROMPTON North Yorks. **402** P 21 – pop. 145 – ✉ ✆ 0677 Bedale.

♦London 228 – ♦Leeds 48 – ♦Newcastle 33 – York 41.

⌂ **Elmfield House** ⑤, Arrathorne, DL8 1NE, NW : 2 ¼ m. by A 684 on Richmond Rd
ℰ 50558 – 📺 ♿ 🅿. 🐾
M 8.00 **st.** ⏧ 2.50 – **9 rm** ⌷ 20.00/40.00 **st.**

PATTINGHAM Staffs. **402** **403** **404** N 26 – see Wolverhampton (W. Midlands).

PEASMARSH East Sussex **404** W 31 – see Rye.

PEMBROKE (PENFRO) Dyfed **403** F 28 – pop. 15 284 – ECD : Wednesday – ✆ 0646.

See : Site★ – Castle★★.

Envir. : Lamphey (Bishop's palace★) *AC*, E : 2 m. – Carew (castle★ 13C) *AC*, NE : 4 ½ m.

🏌 Defensible Barracks, Pembroke Dock ℰ 683817.

⚓ to Rosslare (B & I Line) 1-2 daily.

♦London 252 – Carmarthen 32 – Fishguard 26.

Underdown Country House, Grove Hill, SA71 5PR, ✆ 683350, Fax 621229, « Antiques and gardens » – TV ☎ P. VISA
closed 23 December-3 January – **M** (booking essential) (dinner only) a la carte 13.95/18.70 **t.** 3.00 – **6 rm** 32.50/52.50 **t.** – SB 64.90/75.90 **st.**

Coach House, 116 Main St., SA71 4HN, ✆ 684602, – TV ☎ P. AE VISA
closed 25 and 26 December – **M** (bar lunch)/dinner 12.00 **st.** and a la carte 3.75 – **14 rm** 32.00/42.00 **st.** – SB 52.00 **st.**

High Noon, Lower Lamphey Rd, SA71 4AB, ✆ 683736 – TV P
M 5.50 **st.** – **9 rm** 10.00/25.00 **st.**

at Lamphey E : 1 ¾ m. on A 4139 – ✉ Pembroke – 0646 Lamphey :

Court (Best Western), SA71 5NT, ✆ 672273, Telex 48587, Fax 672480, – TV ☎ P – 80. AE VISA
M (bar lunch)/dinner 14.00 **st.** and a la carte 4.00 – **23 rm** 44.00/84.00 **st.**, **7 suites** 84.00/90.00 **st.** – SB 78.00/102.00 **st.**

Bethwaite's Lamphey Hall, SA71 5NR, ✆ 672394, – TV ☎ P. VISA
M (bar lunch)/dinner 15.00 **t.** and a la carte 2.75 – **10 rm** 35.00/67.00 **t.** – SB (November-February) 70.00 **st.**

at Pembroke Dock NW : 2 m. on A 4139 – ✉ 0646 Pembroke :

Cleddau Bridge, Essex Rd, SA72 6UT, NE : 1 m. by A 4139 on A 477 (at Toll Bridge) ✆ 685961, Fax 685746, heated – TV ☎ P – 180. AE VISA
M 9.00/13.00 **t.** and a la carte 3.50 – **21 rm** 50.00/60.00 **t.**, **3 suites** – SB (weekends only except Bank Holidays) 72.00 **st.**

AUSTIN-ROVER London Rd ✆ 0646 683143 | ATS Well Hill Garage ✆ 683217

PEMBROKESHIRE (Coast) ** Dyfed 403 E 27 28.

See : From Cemaes Head to Strumble Head** : Newport (site*) – Bryn Henllan (site*) – Goodwick <** – Strumble Head (<** from the lighthouse). From Strumble Head to Solva** : Trevine <** – Porthgain (cliffs ***) – Abereiddy (site*) – St. David's Head** – Whitesand Bay** – Solva (site*). From Solva to Dale** : Newgale <** – Martin's Haven ** – St. Ann's Head <** – Dale <*. From Dale to Freshwater West* : Freshwater West (site*). From Freshwater West to Pendine Sands** (Stack Rocks**) – St. Govan's Chapel (site*) – Freshwater East (site*) – Manorbier (castle*) – Tenby (site**) – Amroth (site*) – Pendine Sands*.

PENALLY (PENALUN) Dyfed 403 F 29 – see Tenby.

PENALUN (PENALLY) Dyfed 403 F 29 – see Tenby.

PENCOED Mid Glam. 403 J 29 – 0656.
♦London 173 – ♦Cardiff 16 – ♦Swansea 27.

Travelodge without rest., CF35 5HU, E : 1 ¼ m. on Felindre rd ✆ 864404 – TV ☎ P. AE VISA
40 rm 21.50/27.00 **t.**

PENCRAIG Heref. and Worc. – see Ross-on-Wye.

PENDOGGETT Cornwall 403 F 32 – ✉ – 0208 Bodmin.
♦London 264 – Newquay 22 – Truro 30.

Cornish Arms, PL30 3HH, on B 3314 ✆ 880263, « Retaining 16C features », – P.
7 rm.

PENFRO = Pembroke.

PENMAENHEAD Clwyd – see Colwyn Bay.

PENMAENPOOL Gwynedd 402 403 I 25 – see Dolgellau.

PENN STREET Bucks. 404 S 29 – see Amersham.

PENRITH Cumbria **401 402** L 19 – pop. 12 086 – ECD : Wednesday – ☎ 0768.
🏛 Robinson's School, Middlegate ℰ 67466.
♦London 290 – ♦Carlisle 24 – Kendal 31 – Lancaster 48.

🏨 **North Lakes Gateway,** Ullswater Rd, CA11 8QT, S : 1 m. at M 6 junction 40 ℰ 68111, Telex 64257, Fax 68291, ⬜, squash – 🛏 ✎ rm 📺 ☎ ₺ 🅿 – 🚲 200. 🔄 AE ⑩ VISA
M *(closed Saturday lunch)* 9.50 t. and a la carte 16.10/25.20 t. ₫ 3.95 – **85 rm** ☲ 68.00/120.00 st. – SB 74.00/102.00 st.

🏨 **George,** Devonshire St., CA11 7SU, ℰ 62696, Fax 68223 – 📺 ☎ 🅿 – 🚲 . 🔄 VISA
closed 25, 26 and 31 December-1 January – **M** 3.55/9.25 t. ₫ 3.60 – **31 rm** ☲ 30.00/55.00 t. – SB (November-May) (weekends only) 110.00 st.

🏠 **Travelodge** without rest., Redhills, CA11 0DT, SW : 1 ½ m. by A 592 on A 66 ℰ 66958 – 📺 ₺ 🅿. 🔄 AE VISA
32 rm 21.50/27.00 t.

✕ **Passepartout,** 51 Castlegate, CA11 7HY, ℰ 65852 – ✎. 🔄 VISA
M *(closed Sunday)* (dinner only) 7.00 **t.** and a la carte 10.40/14.40 **t.** ₫ 2.70.

AUDI-VW, CITROEN Ullswater Rd ℰ 64545
AUSTIN-ROVER Victoria Rd ℰ 63666
FORD Old London Rd ℰ 64571
RENAULT 11 King St. ℰ 62371

TOYOTA 15 Victoria Rd ℰ 64555

🛞 ATS Gilwilly Ind Est. ℰ 65656/7

PENSHURST Kent **404** U 30 – pop. 1 749 – ☎ 0892 Tunbridge Wells.
See : Penshurst Place★ (and Tudor gardens★★ 14C) *AC*.
Envir. : Chiddingstone (castle : Egyptian and Japanese collections★ *AC*) NW : 5 m. – Hever Castle★ (13C) *AC*, W : 6 m.
♦London 38 – Maidstone 19 – Royal Tunbridge Wells 6.

🏠 Leicester Arms (Lansbury), High St., TN11 8BT, ℰ 870551 – 📺 ☎ 🅿 – **7 rm**.
↑ **Swale Cottage** 🦢 without rest., Old Swaylands, Tonbridge, TN11 8AH, SE : 1 m. by B 2176 off Poundsbridge Lane ℰ 870738, ≼, 🚜 – ✎ 📺 🅿. 🛇
3 rm ☲ 26.00/42.00 **st.**

PENYBONT Powys **403** K 27 – ✉ Llandegley – ☎ 059 787.
♦London 170 – ♦Birmingham 79 – Hereford 37 – Shrewsbury 58.

✕ **Ffaldau Country House** with rm, LD1 5UD, E : 1 ¼ m. on A 44 ℰ 421, 🚜 – 🅿. 🛇
M *(closed Sunday and Monday dinner to non-residents)* (bar lunch Tuesday-Friday)/dinner a la carte 12.00/14.00 t. ₫ 3.50 – **3 rm** ☲ 20.00/33.00 **t.**

PEN-Y-BONT = Bridgend.

PENZANCE Cornwall **403** D 33 The West Country G. – pop. 18 501 – ECD : Wednesday – ☎ 0736.
See : Site★ – Outlook★★★ – Western Promenade (≼★★★) YZ – Chapel St.★ Y – Museum of Nautical Art★ *AC* Y M1.
Envir. : St. Michael's Mount★★★, (≼★★) E : 5 m. by A 30 Y – Sancreed Church★★, Celtic Crosses★★, W : 4 m. by A 30 Z – St. Buryan★★ (Church Tower★★), SW : 4 ½ m. by A 30 Z – Chysauster★★ *AC*, N : 4 ½ m. by B 3311 Y – Morvah, North Cornwall Coast Path (≼★★), NW : 6 ½ m. by B 3312 Y – Trengwainton Garden★★ *AC*, NW : 2 m. by B 3312 Y – Prussia Cove★, SE : 9 m. by A 30 and A 394 Y – Land's End★ (cliff scenery★★★), SW : 10 m. by A 30 Z.
Access to the Isles of Scilly by helicopter ℰ 63871
🚗 ℰ 0345 090700.
🚢 to the Isles of Scilly : Hugh Town, St.Mary's (Isles of Scilly Steamship Co.) summer Monday to Saturday 1-2 daily ; winter 4 weekly (2 h 30 mn).
🏛 Station Rd ℰ 62207.
♦London 319 – Exeter 113 – ♦Plymouth 77 – Taunton 155.

Plan on next page

🏨 **Mount Prospect,** Briton's Hill, TR18 3AE, ℰ 63117, Fax 50970, ≼, ⬜ heated, 🚜 – 📺 ☎ 🅿. 🔄 AE ⑩ VISA   Y e
M (bar lunch)/dinner 10.35 **st.** and a la carte ₫ 3.50 – **26 rm** ☲ 32.20/52.90 **t.** – SB (March-November) 57.50/77.30 **st.**

🏠 **Abbey,** Abbey St., TR18 4AR, ℰ 66906, « Attractively furnished 17C house », 🚜 – 📺 🅿   Y u
M (dinner only) 15.00 **st.** ₫ 3.00 – **6 rm** ☲ 45.00/80.00 **st.**, **1 suite** 80.00/90.00 **st.** – SB (November-March) 73.00/91.00 **st.**

🏠 **Sea and Horses,** 6 Alexandra Terr., TR18 4NX, ℰ 61961 – 📺 🅿. 🔄 VISA. 🛇   Z s
M (bar lunch)/dinner 8.00 **st.** ₫ 2.50 – **11 rm** ☲ 16.00/36.00 **st.**

↑ **Tarbert,** 11 Clarence St., TR18 2NU, ℰ 63758, 🚜 – 📺. 🔄 AE VISA   Y i
closed 1 December-15 January – **M** (bar lunch)/dinner 11.50 t. and a la carte ₫ 2.95 – **12 rm** ☲ 21.50/49.00 t. – SB (October-mid May except Easter week) 55.00/66.00 **st.**

↑ **Estoril,** 46 Morrab Rd, TR18 4EX, ℰ 62468 – ✎ rest 📺 ☎. 🔄 VISA. 🛇   Y o
closed January-mid February – **M** (lunch by arrangement) 8.50 **st.** ₫ 2.50 – **10 rm** ☲ 29.00/58.00 **st.** – SB 48.00/56.00 **st.**

413

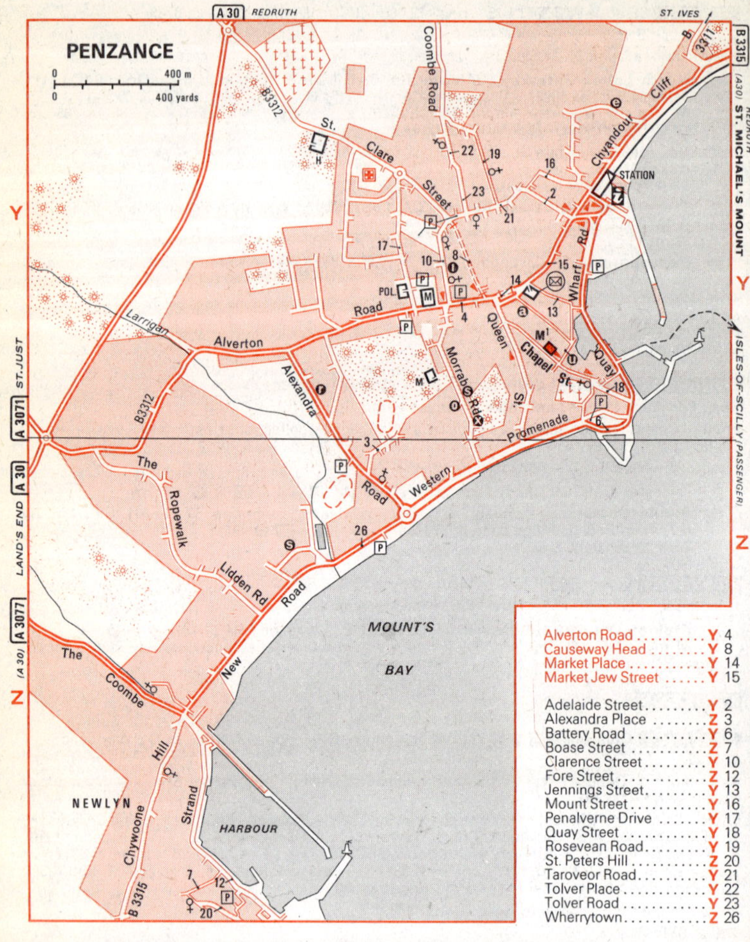

Alverton Road . . . . Y 4
Causeway Head . . . . Y 8
Market Place . . . . Y 14
Market Jew Street . . . . . . Y 15

Adelaide Street . . . . Y 2
Alexandra Place . . . . Z 3
Battery Road . . . . Z 6
Boase Street . . . . Z 7
Clarence Street . . . . Z Y 10
Fore Street . . . . Z 12
Jennings Street . . . . Y 13
Mount Street . . . . Y 16
Penalverne Drive . . . . Y 17
Quay Street . . . . Y 18
Rosevean Road . . . . Y 19
St. Peters Hill . . . . Z 20
Taroveor Road . . . . Y 21
Tolver Place . . . . Y 22
Tolver Road . . . . Y 23
Wherrytown . . . . Z 26

Kimberley House, 10 Morrab Rd, TR18 4EZ, 62727 – VISA. *February-November* – **M** 7.00 st. 3.00 – **9 rm** 12.00/24.00 st.   Y s

Dunedin, Alexandra Rd, TR18 4LZ, 62652 – TV *February-November* – **M** 7.00 t. – **9 rm** 12.00/30.00 t.   Y r

Woodstock, 29 Morrab Rd, TR18 4EZ, 69049 – TV. AE. VISA. **M** 6.50 st. – **5 rm** 11.00/25.00 st.   Y x

Harris's, 46 New St., TR18 2LZ, 64408 – AE. VISA *closed Monday November-May, Sunday, 1 week February-March, 2 weeks November, 25 -26 December and 1 January* – **M** (restricted lunch) a la carte 14.90/23.45 **t.** 3.25.   Y a

at Newbridge NW : 3 m. on A 3071 – Y – 0736 Penzance :

Enzo, TR20 8QH, 63777 – P. AE. VISA *closed 2 weeks February and 2 weeks November* – **M** (dinner only) a la carte 8.55/15.80 t. 3.20.

at Newlyn SW : 1 ½ m. on B 3315 – Z – 0736 Penzance :

Higher Faugan, TR18 5NS, SW : ¾ m. on B 3315 62076, Fax 51648, heated, park, – TV P. AE. VISA **M** (bar lunch)/dinner 13.50 t. 3.30 – **11 rm** 37.00/75.00 t. – SB (October-May) (except Bank Holidays) 70.00 **st.**

AUSTIN-ROVER Newlyn 61998/62038
FORD Coinage Hall St. 69169

ATS Eastern Green 62768

PERRANUTHNOE Cornwall ▨ D 33 – see Marazion.

PERSHORE Heref. and Worc. ▨ ▨ N 27 – pop. 6 850 – ECD : Thursday – ☎ 0386.
🛈 Council Offices, 37 High St. ✆ 554711.
♦London 106 – ♦Birmingham 32 – Cheltenham 22 – Stratford-on-Avon 21 – Worcester 9.

🏠 **Angel**, 9 High St., WR10 1AF, ✆ 552046, Fax 552581, ☞ – 📺 ☎ 🅿. ◪ AE ⓪ VISA
closed Christmas – **M** *(closed Sunday dinner)* (carving lunch)/dinner a la carte 12.40/20.75 **t.**
– **16 rm** ⇆ 44.00/60.00 **t.** – SB (weekends only) 74.00/80.00 **t.**

at Wyre Piddle NE : 2 m. by B 4082 and B 4083 on B 4084 – ⊠ ☎ 0386 Pershore :

🏠 **Avonside**, Main Rd, WR10 2JB, ✆ 552654, ≤, ⤬ heated, ⤬, ☞ – 📺 ☎ 🅿. ◪ VISA. ⌘
M (bar lunch)/dinner 15.00 **st.** – **7 rm** ⇆ 40.00/60.00 **st.** – SB (except Christmas) 70.00 **st.**

AUSTIN-ROVER 3 Spring Rd ✆ 552817   ⓜ ATS Cherry Orchard ✆ 554494
FORD   Pinvin ✆ 552691

PETERBOROUGH Cambs. ▨ ▨ T 26 – pop. 113 404 – ECD : Monday and Thursday –
☎ 0733.
See : Cathedral★★ 12C-13C (nave : painted roof★★★) Y.
Envir. : Crowland : Abbey Church★ (8C ruins), Triangular Bridge★ 13C, NE : 8 m.
🏌 Thorpe Wood, Nene Parkway ✆ 267701, W : 3 m. on A 47 – 🏌 Ramsey ✆ 0487 (Ramsey)
812600, SE : 12 m – 🏌 Orton Meadows, Ham Lane ✆ 380489.
🛈 Central Library, Broadway ✆ 48343 and 43146 – Town Hall, Bridge St. ✆ 63141 or 317336.
♦London 85 – ♦Cambridge 35 – ♦Leicester 41 – Lincoln 51.

Plan on next page

🏨 **Peterborough Moat House** (Q.M.H.), Thorpe Wood, PE3 6SG, SW : 2 ¼ m. at Roundabout 33 ✆ 260000, Telex 32708, Fax 262737, ◪ – 📱 ⤬ rm 📺 ☎ ♿ 🅿 – 🔏 300. ◪ AE ⓪
VISA   BX **s**
M 10.95/11.95 **st.** and a la carte ▯ 3.50 – ⇆ 6.75 – **121 rm** 59.00/68.00 **st.**, **4 suites** 80.00/
90.00 **st.** – SB (weekends only) 70.00 **st.**

🏨 **Bull**, Westgate, PE1 1RP, ✆ 61364, Group Telex 329265 – 📺 ☎ 🅿 – 🔏 100. ◪ AE ⓪ VISA
M 10.50 **st.** and a la carte ▯ 3.95 – **112 rm** ⇆ 56.00/68.00 **st.**, **1 suite** 85.00 **st.** – SB
(weekends only) 54.00 **st.**   Y **Z**

🏠 **Thorpe Lodge**, 83 Thorpe Rd, PE3 6JQ, ✆ 48759 – 📺 🅿. ◪ VISA. ⌘   BX **C**
M *(closed Friday to Sunday)* (bar lunch)/dinner 9.50 **t.** ▯ 3.00 – ⇆ 4.50 – **22 rm** 40.00/49.00 **t.**
– SB (weekends only) 68.00/70.00 **st.**

XX **Grain Barge**, The Quayside, Embankment Rd, PE1 1EG, ✆ 311967, Chinese (Peking) rest.
– ◪ AE ⓪ VISA   Z **V**
M 19.00 **st.** and a la carte 13.00/25.00 **st.**

at Norman Cross S : 5 ¾ m. on A 15 at junction with A 1 – BX – ⊠ ☎ 0733 Peterborough :

🏨 **Crest** (Crest), Great North Rd, PE7 3TB, ✆ 240209, Telex 32576, Fax 244455 – ⤬ rm 📺 ☎
♿ 🅿 – 🔏 60. ◪ AE ⓪ VISA   BX **r**
M 13.50 **st.** and a la carte ▯ 5.50 – ⇆ 7.75 – **97 rm** 66.00/78.00 **st.** – SB (weekends
only) 68.00/80.00 **st.**

at Alwalton SW : 5 ¾ m. on A 605 – AX – ⊠ ☎ 0733 Peterborough :

🏨 **Swallow** (Swallow), Lynch Wood (opposite East of England Showground), PE2 0GB, on
A 605 ✆ 371111, Telex 32422, Fax 236725, ◪, ☞ – ⤬ rm ▤ rest 📺 ☎ ♿ 🅿 – 🔏 275. ◪
AE ⓪ VISA   AX **u**
M 10.50/17.00 **st.** and a la carte 12.30/22.50 **st.** ▯ 4.50 – **160 rm** ⇆ 69.00/90.00 **st.**, **3 suites**
120.00/145.00 **st.**

🏠 **Travelodge** without rest., A 1 Great North Rd (Southbound), PE7 3UR, ✆ 231109 – 📺 ♿
🅿. ◪ AE VISA   AX **x**
32 rm 21.50/27.00 **t.**

at Nassington (Northants.) SW : 10 ¾ m. by A 47 – AX – ⊠ Peterborough – ☎ 0780
Stamford :

XX **Black Horse Inn**, 2 Fotheringhay Rd, PE8 6QU, ✆ 782324, ☞ – 🅿. ◪ AE ⓪ VISA   AX **a**
M a la carte 9.15/14.30 **t.** ▯ 3.95.

at Wansford W : 8 ½ m. by A 47 – AX – ⊠ Peterborough – ☎ 0780 Stamford :

🏨 **Haycock**, PE8 6JA, ✆ 782223, Telex 32710, Fax 783031, ☞ – 📺 ☎ 🅿 – 🔏 120. ◪ AE ⓪
VISA   AX **e**
M a la carte approx. 19.00 **st.** ▯ 4.50 – **51 rm** ⇆ 68.00/105.00 **st.**

🏠 **Sibson House** (B.C.B.), Great North Rd, PE8 6ND, SE : 1 ¾ m. on A 1 ✆ 782227, ⤬ heated –
📺 ☎ 🅿 – 🔏. ⌘ – **19 rm**.   AX **n**

AUSTIN-ROVER, LAND-ROVER, FREIGHT-ROVER   PEUGEOT-TALBOT 343 Eastfield Rd ✆ 310900
7 Oundle Rd ✆ 66011   RENAULT Sturrock Way ✆ 330030
BMW Helpston Rd, Glinton ✆ 253333   VAUXHALL-OPEL, BEDFORD Sturrock Way ✆
FIAT Midland Rd ✆ 314431   264981
FORD 27-53 New Rd ✆ 40104   VW-AUDI Newark Rd ✆ 312213
LANCIA, SUZUKI 659 Lincoln Rd ✆ 52141
MAZDA 50-64 Burghley Rd ✆ 65787   ⓜ ATS Wareley Rd (off George St.) ✆ 67112/3
MERCEDES-BENZ High St., Eye ✆ 222363

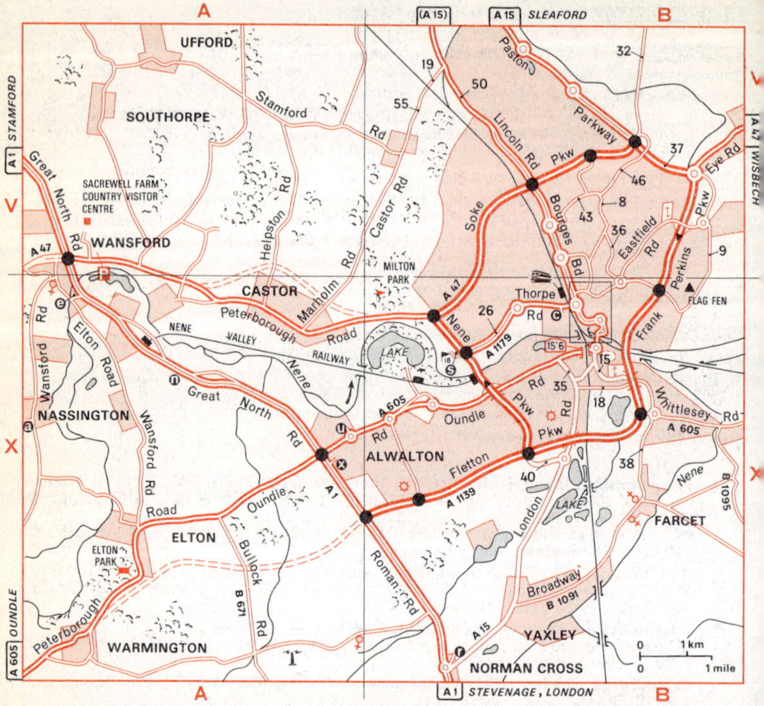

PETERBOROUGH

Bridge Street .... **Z**
Church Street .... **YZ**
Long Causeway .... **Y** 25
Queensgate
  Shopping Centre .... **Y**

Cattle Market
  Road .... **Y** 2
City Road .... **Y** 3
Cowgate .... **Y** 5
Cross Street .... **Z** 6
Dogsthorpe Road .... **BV** 8
Edgerley Drain
  Road .... **BV** 9
Embankment Road .... **Z** 12
Exchange Street .... **Y** 13
Fletton Road .... **BX** 15
Geneva Street .... **Y** 16
High Street .... **BX** 18
Hurn Road .... **BV** 19
Longthorpe
  Parkway .... **BX** 26
Market Way .... **Y** 28
Midgate .... **Y** 29
Newborough Road .... **BV** 32
New Road .... **Y** 34
New Road .... **BX** 35
Park Road .... **BV** 36
Paston Parkway .... **BV** 37
Peterborough Road ...... **BX** 38
Phorpres Way .... **BX** 40
Rivergate .... **Z** 42
St Paul's Road .... **BV** 43
Thorpe Road .... **Y** 45
Welland Road .... **BV** 46
Wentworth
  Street .... **Z** 48
Werrington
  Parkway .... **BV** 50
Wheelyard .... **Y** 52
Woodcroft Road .... **BV** 55

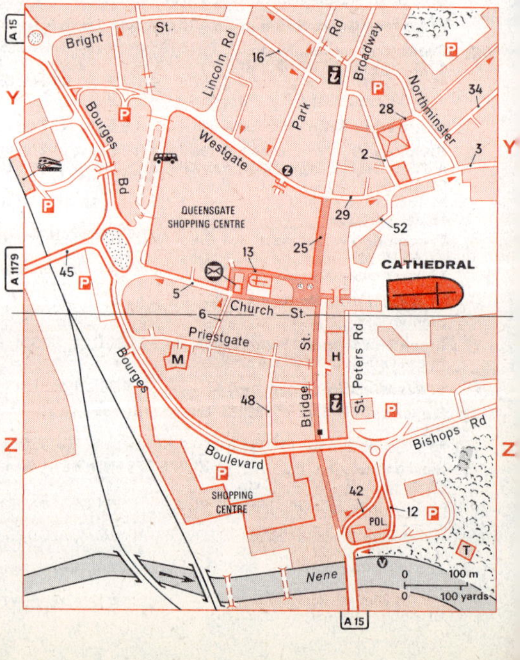

PETERSFIELD Hants. **404** R 30 – pop. 10 078 – ECD : Thursday – ✪ 0730.

ⁱ₈ The Heath ✆ 63725, E : ½ m..

🛈 Library, 27 The Square ✆ 68829.

♦London 59 – ♦Brighton 45 – Guildford 25 – ♦Portsmouth 19 – ♦Southampton 32 – Winchester 19.

🏰 **Langrish House** ⌂, Langrish, GU32 1RN, W : 3 ½ m. by A 272 ✆ 66941, ≼, 絪, park –
📺 ☎ 🅿 – 🔄 40. 🔼 AE ⑩. 🛇
M *(closed Sunday and Bank Holidays)* (dinner only) a la carte 11.85/12.00 t. ⌁ 2.80 – ⌣ 3.50
– **18 rm** 32.50/60.00 t. – SB (November-April) (weekends only) 60.00 **st.**

AUDI-VW Station Rd ✆ 62992
HONDA Alton Rd, Steep ✆ 66341
PEUGEOT-TALBOT 38 Collace St. ✆ 62266
SKODA Alton Rd, Froxfield ✆ 073 084 (Hawkley)
401

VOLVO 23 London Rd ✆ 64541

◍ ATS 15 Dragon St. ✆ 65151

PETERSTOW Heref. and Worc. **403** **404** M 28 – see Ross-on-Wye.

PETWORTH West Sussex **404** S 31 – pop. 2 003 – ECD : Wednesday – ✪ 0798.

See : Petworth House★★★, 17C (paintings★★★ and carved room★★★) *AC*.

♦London 54 – ♦Brighton 31 – ♦Portsmouth 33.

XX **Soanes**, Grove Lane, GU28 0HY, S : ½ m. by High St. ✆ 43659, ≼ – 🅿. 🔼 VISA
closed 10 days February and 10 days October – **M** *(closed Sunday dinner, Monday and
Tuesday)* (dinner only and Sunday lunch)/dinner 15.00 **st.** and a la carte 22.00 **st.** ⌁ 4.50.

PICKERING North Yorks. **402** R 21 – pop. 5 316 – ECD : Wednesday – ✪ 0751.

See : SS. Peter and Paul's Church (wall paintings★ 15C) – Norman castle★ (ruins) : ≼★ *AC*.

🛈 7 Eastgate Sq. ✆ 73791 (summer only).

♦London 237 – ♦Middlesbrough 43 – Scarborough 19 – York 25.

🏨 **White Swan**, Market Pl., YO18 7AA, ✆ 72288 – 📺 ☎ 🅿. 🔼 VISA
M (bar lunch Monday to Saturday)/dinner 12.50 t. ⌁ 3.50 – **12 rm** ⌣ 35.00/55.00 t., **1 suite**
65.00/75.00 t. – SB (except September and Bank Holidays) (weekdays only) 64.00/74.00 t.

🏨 **Forest and Vale**, Malton Rd, YO18 7DL, ✆ 72722, 絪 – 📺 ☎ 🅿. 🔼 AE ⑩ VISA
M 8.60/13.20 t. and a la carte ⌁ 3.90 – **17 rm** ⌣ 40.00/73.00 t. – SB 78.00/88.00 **st.**

FORD, MERCEDES-BENZ Eastgate ✆ 72251   FORD Middleton ✆ 72331

PICKHILL North Yorks. **402** P 21 – pop. 300 (inc. Roxby) – ✉ ✪ 0845 Thirsk.

♦London 229 – ♦Leeds 41 – ♦Middlesbrough 30 – York 34.

🏠 **Nags Head**, YO7 4JG, ✆ 567391 – ≼✕ rest 📺 ☎ 🅿. 🔼 VISA
M 9.00/15.00 **st.** and a la carte – **10 rm** ⌣ 25.00/36.00 **st.**

PIMPERNE Dorset. **403** **404** N 31 – see Blandford Forum.

PINHOE Devon **403** J 31 – see Exeter.

PITTON Wilts. – see Salisbury.

PLAYDEN East Sussex – see Rye.

PLUCKLEY Kent **404** W 30 – pop. 1 109 – ✪ 023 384.

♦London 53 – Folkestone 25 – Maidstone 18.

🏠 **Elvey Farm** ⌂, TN27 0SU, W : 3 m. by B 2077 off Mundy Bois Rd ✆ 442, ≼, 絪 – 📺 🅿.
⑩ VISA
restricted service October-March – **M** (by arrangement) 12.95 t. ⌁ 3.75 – **10 rm** ⌣ 39.50/
49.50 t.

PLUMTREE Notts. – see Nottingham.

PLYMOUTH Devon **403** H 32 The West Country G. – pop. 238 583 – ECD : Wednesday –
✪ 0752.

See : Site★★ – Smeaton's Tower (≼★★) *AC* BZ – Royal Citadel★ *AC* (The Ramparts ≼★★) BZ –
City Museum and Art Gallery★ *AC* BZ M – Envir. : Buckland Abbey★★ *AC*, N : 7 m. by A 386 ABY
– Saltram House★★ *AC*, E : 3 ½ m. BY A – Antony House★ *AC*, W : 5 m. by A 374 AY – Yelverton
Paperweight Centre★ *AC*, N : 9 m. on A 386 ABY – Mount Edgcumbe (≼★) *AC*, W : 9 m. by car
ferry from Cremyll or passenger ferry from Stonehouse.

ⁱ₈ Whitsand Bay Hotel, Portwrinkle, Torpoint ✆ 0503 (St. Germans) 30276, W : 6 m. by A 374 AY –
ⁱ₉ Elfordleigh, Plympton, ✆ 336428, E : 6 m. by A 374 BY.

✈ Roborough Airport : ✆ 772752/3, N : 3 ½ m. by A 386 ABY.

⚓ Shipping connections with the Continent : to France (Roscoff)(Brittany Ferries) – to Spain
(Santander)(Brittany Ferries).

🛈 Civic Centre, Royal Parade ✆ 264851 and 264849 – 12 The Barbican ✆ 223806.

♦London 242 – Bristol 124 – ♦Southampton 161.

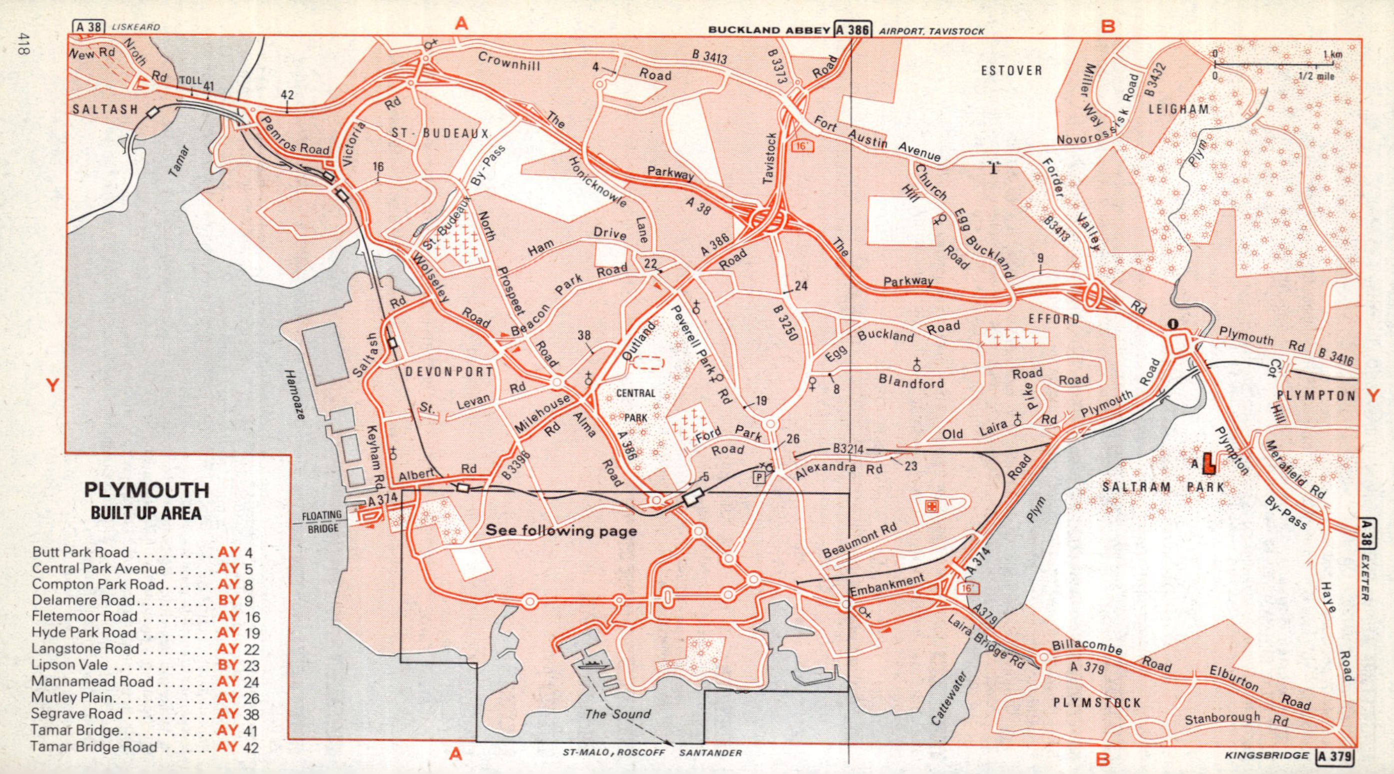

PLYMOUTH
BUILT UP AREA

Butt Park Road . . . . AY 4
Central Park Avenue . . . . . . AY 5
Compton Park Road . . . . . . AY 8
Delamere Road . . . . BY 9
Fletemoor Road . . . . AY 16
Hyde Park Road . . . . AY 19
Langstone Road . . . . AY 22
Lipson Vale . . . . BY 23
Mannamead Road . . . . AY 24
Mutley Plain . . . . AY 26
Segrave Road . . . . AY 38
Tamar Bridge . . . . AY 41
Tamar Bridge Road . . . . . . AY 42

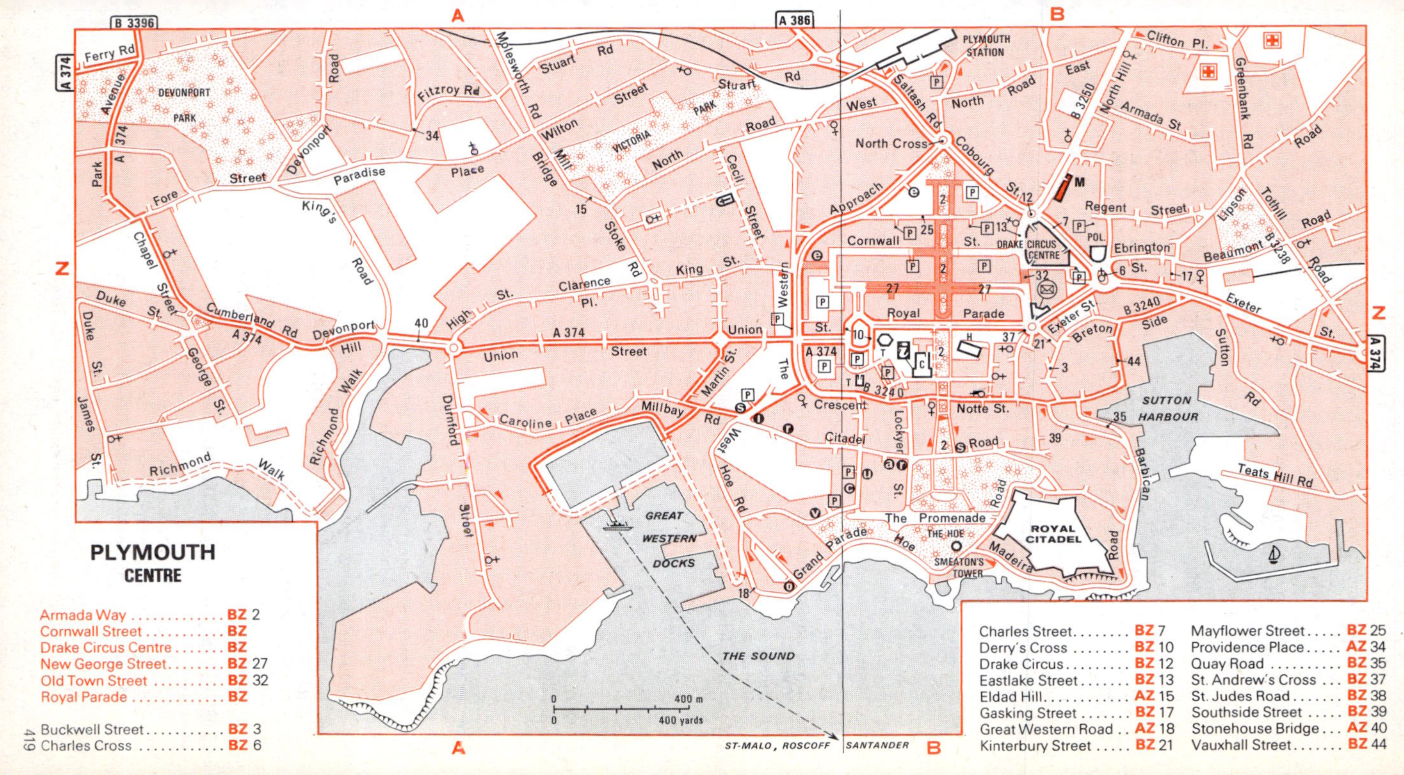

PLYMOUTH CENTRE

Armada Way .... BZ 2
Cornwall Street .... BZ
Drake Circus Centre .... BZ
New George Street ...... BZ 27
Old Town Street .... BZ 32
Royal Parade .... BZ
Buckwell Street .... BZ 3
Charles Cross .... BZ 6

Charles Street .... BZ 7
Derry's Cross .... BZ 10
Drake Circus .... BZ 12
Eastlake Street .... BZ 13
Eldad Hill .... AZ 15
Gasking Street .... BZ 17
Great Western Road .. AZ 18
Kinterbury Street ..... BZ 21

Mayflower Street ..... BZ 25
Providence Place ..... AZ 34
Quay Road .... BZ 35
St. Andrew's Cross ... BZ 37
St. Judes Road .... BZ 38
Southside Street ..... BZ 39
Stonehouse Bridge ... AZ 40
Vauxhall Street .... BZ 44

DEVONPORT PARK
VICTORIA PARK
PLYMOUTH STATION
DRAKE CIRCUS CENTRE
GREAT WESTERN DOCKS
SUTTON HARBOUR
ROYAL CITADEL
THE HOE
SMEATON'S TOWER
THE SOUND
THE PROMENADE

Ferry Rd
Avenue
Park
Fore
Duke St.
George St.
James St.
Chapel Street
Cumberland Rd
Devonport Hill
Richmond Walk
Durnford Street
King's Road
Paradise Place
Fitzroy Rd
Molesworth Rd
Stuart Rd
Wilton
Mill Bridge
Stoke Rd
Cecil Street
North Road
Saltash Rd
West Approach
North Cross
West
Cobourg St.
North Hill
East
Armada St
Clifton Pl.
Greenbank Rd
Lipson
Tothill Road
Regent Street
Ebrington
Beaumont Road
Exeter
Exeter St.
Breton Side
Sutton Rd
Barbican
Teats Hill Rd
Clarence Pl.
King St.
High St.
Union Street
Martin St.
Caroline Place
Millbay Rd
West Hoe Rd
Grand Parade
Crescent
Citadel
Lockyer St.
Notte St.
Cornwall St.
Royal Parade
Madeira Road
Hoe

A 374
A 386
A 374
B 3396
B 3250
B 3238
B 3240

ST-MALO, ROSCOFF   SANTANDER

400 m
400 yards

419

Holiday Inn, Armada Way, PL1 2HJ, ☎ 662866, Telex 45637, Fax 673816, ≤ city and Sound, ⅃ – 🛗 ⇔ rm TV ☎ & 🅿 – 🛎   BZ s
215 rm, 2 suites.

Copthorne Plymouth (Best Western), Armada Centre, Armada Way, PL1 1AR, (via Western Approach) Southbound ☎ 224161, Telex 45756, Fax 670688, ⅃ – ⇔ rm TV ☎ & 🅿 – 🛎 150. ⚠ AE ⑩ VISA   BZ e
M 15.95/18.95 **st.** and a la carte ⌽ 4.45 – ⊒ 7.00 – **131 rm** 68.00/82.00 **st.**, **4 suites** 134.50/145.00 **st.** – SB (weekends only) 43.50/58.50 **st.**

Mayflower Post House (T.H.F.), Cliff Rd, The Hoe, PL1 3DL, ☎ 662828, Telex 45442, Fax 660974, ≤ Plymouth Sound, ⅃ heated – 🛗 ⇔ rm TV ☎ & 🅿 – 🛎 100. ⚠ AE ⑩ VISA
M (closed Saturday lunch) 9.50/13.00 **st.** and a la carte ⌽ 3.85 – ⊒ 7.00 – **102 rm** 65.00/75.00 **st.**, **4 suites** 87.00/107.00 **st.** – SB (weekends only) 72.00/96.00 **st.**   AZ v

Novotel Plymouth, 270 Plymouth Rd., Marsh Mills Roundabout, PL6 8NH, ☎ 221422, Telex 45711, Fax 221422, ⅃ – 🛗 ▤ rest TV ☎ & 🅿 – 🛎 250. ⚠ AE ⑩ VISA   BY i
M 10.50 **st.** and a la carte – ⊒ 6.00 – **100 rm** 49.00/56.00 **st.** – SB (weekends only) 80.00 **st.**

Astor (Mt. Charlotte), 14-22 Elliott St., The Hoe, PL1 2PS, ☎ 225511, Telex 45652 – 🛗 TV ☎ – 🛎 50   BZ c
56 rm.

New Continental, Millbay Rd, PL1 3LD, ☎ 220782, Telex 45193, Fax 227013, ⅃ – 🛗 TV ☎ 🅿 – 🛎 150. ⚠ AE ⑩ VISA ⌖   AZ s
M (closed lunch Saturday and Bank Holidays) 8.50/13.25 **st.** and a la carte – **76 rm** ⊒ 40.00/65.00 **t.** – SB (weekends only) (except 24 December-3 January) 65.00/75.00 **st.**

Georgian House, 51 Citadel Rd, The Hoe, PL1 3AU, ☎ 663237 – TV ☎. ⚠ AE ⑩ VISA ⌖   AZ r
closed 15 December-10 January – **M** (closed Sunday) (dinner only) a la carte approx. 12.25 **t.** – **12 rm** ⊒ 26.00/37.00 **t.**

Grosvenor, 9 Elliott St., The Hoe, PL1 2PP, ☎ 260411, Fax 668878 – TV ☎. ⌖   BZ u
14 rm ⊒ 30.00/44.00 **st.**

Sea Breezes, 28 Grand Par., West Hoe, PL1 3DJ, ☎ 667205 – TV   AZ o
M 7.00 **st.** ⌽ 2.90 – **7 rm** ⊒ 10.00/24.00 **st.**

Cranbourne without rest., 282 Citadel Rd, The Hoe, PL1 2PZ, ☎ 263858 – TV. ⚠ VISA
10 rm ⊒ 13.00/35.00 **st.**   BZ r

Chichester without rest., 280 Citadel Rd, The Hoe, PL1 2PZ, ☎ 662746 – TV   BZ a
10 rm ⊒ 12.00/26.00 **st.**

✗ ❀ **Chez Nous** (Marchal), 13 Frankfort Gate, PL1 1QA, ☎ 266793, French rest. – ⚠ AE ⑩ VISA   AZ e
closed Sunday, Monday, first 3 weeks February, first 3 weeks September and Bank Holidays – **M** (booking essential) 21.00 **t.** and a la carte 26.00/32.50 **t.** ⌽ 4.00
Spec. Cassolette d'escargots aux champignons, Escalope de foie gras aux choux verts et cassis, Blanc de Barbue aux girolles (seasonal).

AUSTIN-ROVER, LAND-ROVER Union St. ☎ 263355
BMW Union St. ☎ 669202
CITROEN Colebrook Rd ☎ 336606
FORD Millbay Rd ☎ 668040
HONDA, SEAT Albert Rd ☎ 564171/561810
MERCEDES-BENZ Crown Hill ☎ 785611
PEUGEOT-TALBOT 241 Union St. ☎ 673553

VAUXHALL-OPEL Normandy Way ☎ 361251
VAUXHALL-OPEL Bretonside ☎ 667111
VAUXHALL-OPEL Cobourg St. ☎ 668886
VOLVO Valley Rd, Plympton ☎ 338306

⦿ ATS Teats Hill Rd ☎ 266217/227964
ATS Market Rd, Plympton ☎ 330250

POCKLINGTON Humberside 🛈🛈🛈 R 22 – pop. 5 051 – ECD : Wednesday – ✉ York – ☏ 075 92 (4 fig.) or 0759 (6 fig.).
♦London 213 – ♦Kingston-upon-Hull 25 – York 13.

Feathers, 56 Market Pl., YO4 2JN, ☎ 303155 – TV ☎ 🅿. ⚠ AE ⑩ VISA ⌖
M 8.50 **t.** and a la carte ⌽ 3.25 – **12 rm** ⊒ 28.50/43.00 **t.** – SB (October-March) (weekends only) 58.00 **st.**

at Barmby Moor W : 2 m. on B 1246 – ✉ York – ☏ 0759 Pocklington :

Barmby Moor, Hull Rd, YO4 5EZ, on A 1079 ☎ 302700, ⅃ heated, ⇔ – TV ☎ 🅿. ⚠ AE VISA. ⌖
M (closed Sunday dinner) (dinner only and Sunday lunch)/dinner 14.00 **st.** ⌽ 2.50 – **10 rm** ⊒ 40.00/50.00 **st.** – SB (except Bank Holidays) 62.00/66.00 **st.**

FORD Hallgate ☎ 302768   VAUXHALL Kilnwick Rd ☎ 303221

POLKERRIS Cornwall 🛈🛈🛈 F 32 The West Country G. – ✉ Fowey – ☏ 072 681 Par.
See : Site★.
♦London 277 – Newquay 22 – ♦Plymouth 34 – Truro 20.

✗ **Rashleigh Inn**, PL24 2TL, ☎ 3991, ≤ – 🅿. VISA
M (buffet lunch)/dinner 12.00 **st.** and a la carte ⌽ 4.00.

☞ *Michelin puts no plaque or sign*
on the hotels and restaurants mentioned in this Guide.

See : Site★ – ♦London 271 – ♦Plymouth 28.

⋔ **Lanhael House** without rest., Langreek Rd, PL13 2PW, ℰ 72428, ≼, ⤓, ⚓ – ⇆ **P**. ◪
VISA. ⅷ
March-October – **6 rm** ⊡ 17.00/32.00 **s.**

⋔ **Claremont**, Fore St., PL13 2RG, ℰ 72241 – **P**. ◪ **VISA**
closed 5 January-15 March – **M** 9.75 **st.** ⅃ 3.20 – **9 rm** ⊡ 17.00/41.00 **st.** – SB (except July and August) (weekdays only) 47.50/57.00 **st.**

✗ **Kitchen**, Fish Na Bridge, The Coombes, PL13 2RQ, ℰ 72780 – ◪ **VISA**
closed Sunday to Thursday in winter except Christmas-New Year – **M** (lunch by arrangement)/dinner 19.00 **t.** ⅃ 5.00.

PONTARFYNACH = Devil's Bridge.

PONTSHAEN Dyfed – ⊠ Llandyssul – ☎ 054 555.
♦London 239 – Carmarthen 19 – Fishguard 37.

✗ **Farmhouse**, Castell Howell, SA44 4UA, N : 1 ½ m. by B 4459 ℰ 209, ◪, park, squash – **P**. ◪
M *(closed dinner Sunday, Monday and Wednesday)* (bar lunch)/dinner a la carte 11.05/14.00 **st.** ⅃ 2.60.

PONT-Y-PANT Gwynedd – see Betws-y-Coed.

POOLE Dorset **403** **404** O 31 The West Country G. – pop. 122 815 – ECD : Wednesday – ☎ 0202 – See : Site★ – The Three Museums★ *AC* by A 35 **AX**.
Envir. : Compton Acres Gardens★★, (≼★★★) *AC*, SE : 3 m. **AX** – Brownsea Island★, Baden Powell Stone (≼★★) *AC*, by boat from Poole Quay or Sandbanks *AC*.
⛴ Shipping connections with the continent : to France (Cherbourg) (Truckline Ferries) summer only – to The Channel Islands : Jersey (St. Helier) and Guernsey (St. Peter Port) (British Channel Island Ferries) summer : 1-2 daily, winter : 4-5 weekly (9 h to 11 ½ h).
🛈 Enefco House, Poole Quay ℰ 673322 – Arndale Centre.
♦London 116 – Bournemouth 4 – Dorchester 23 – Weymouth 28.

Plan : see Bournemouth

🏨 **Haven**, Banks Rd, Sandbanks, BH13 7QL, SE : 4 ¼ m. on B 3369 ℰ 707333, Telex 41338, Fax 708796, ≼ Ferry, Old Harry Rocks and Poole Bay, ⤓ heated, ◪, squash – ▯ ⊡ ☎ **P** – ⚏ 180. ◪ **AE** ⓄⒹ **VISA**. ⅷ   by B 3369 **AX**
M (buffet lunch)/dinner 15.95 ⅃ 4.85 – **97 rm** ⊡ 35.00/100.00 **t.**

🏨 **Mansion House**, 11 Thames St., BH15 1JN, ℰ 685666, Telex 41495, « 18C town house, staircase » – 🍽 rest ⊡ ☎ **P** – ⚏ 25. ◪ **AE** Ⓞ **VISA**   by A 35 **AX**
closed 25 December-7 January – **M** *(closed Saturday lunch)* 15.50/21.00 **t.** and a la carte ⅃ 4.00 – **28 rm** ⊡ 65.00/165.00 **t.** – SB (weekends only) 98.00/108.00 **st.**

🏨 **Salterns** (Best Western), 38 Salterns Way, Lilliput, BH14 8JR, ℰ 707321, Telex 41259, Fax 707488, ≼, squash – ⊡ ☎ **P** – ⚏ 120. ◪ **AE** Ⓞ **VISA**. ⅷ   by B 3369 **AX**
M 11.50/15.00 and a la carte ⅃ 3.50 – ⊡ 6.50 – **16 rm** 54.00/92.00 **t.** – SB 90.00/120.00 **st.**

🏨 **Hospitality Inn** (Mt. Charlotte), The Quay, BH15 1HD, ℰ 666800, Telex 418374, ≼ – ▯ ⊡ ☎ **P** – ⚏ 60 – **68 rm**.   by A 35 **AX**

🏨 **Antelope**, 8 High St., BH15 1BP, ℰ 672029, Telex 418387, Fax 678286 – ⊡ ☎ **P**. ◪ **AE** Ⓞ
VISA. ⅷ   by A 35 **AX**
M a la carte 9.40/13.25 **t.** ⅃ 3.95 – **21 rm** ⊡ 50.00/60.00 **t.** – SB (weekends only) 74.00 **st.**

🏠 **Sea Witch**, 47 Haven Rd, Canford Cliffs, BH13 7LH, ℰ 707697 – ⊡ ☎ **P**. ◪ **VISA**. ⅷ
M *(closed Monday lunch and Sunday dinner)* 7.95/11.95 **st.** and a la carte ⅃ 3.25 – **9 rm**
⊡ 32.00/48.00 **st.** – SB (October-June) (weekends only) 54.00/62.00 **st.**   **AX** o

🏠 **Arndale Court**, 62-64 Wimborne Rd, BH15 2BY, ℰ 683746 – ⊡ **P**. ◪ **AE** Ⓞ **VISA**
M (bar lunch)/dinner 9.50 **st.** and a la carte ⅃ 3.00 – **16 rm** ⊡ 32.00/42.00 **st.** – SB (weekends only) 55.00/76.00 **st.**   by A 3049 **AV**

✗✗ **Warehouse**, Poole Quay, BH15 1HJ, ℰ 677238, ≼ – ◪ **AE** Ⓞ **VISA**   by A 35 **AX**
M 15.00 **t.** and a la carte 16.35/32.50 **t.** ⅃ 3.00.

✗ **Le Chateau**, 13 Haven Rd, Canford Cliffs, BH13 7LE, ℰ 707400 – ◪ **AE** **VISA**   **AX** r
closed Sunday and Monday – **M** a la carte 12.75/18.20 **t.** ⅃ 3.95.

✗ **Isabel's**, 32 Station Rd, Lower Parkstone, BH14 8UD, ℰ 747885 – ◪ **AE** Ⓞ **VISA**   **AX** a
closed Sunday, 25-26 December and 1 January – **M** (lunch by arrangement)/dinner a la carte 13.10/16.90 **t.**

✗ **Le Select**, 129 Parkstone Rd, Parkgates, BH15 2PB, ℰ 740223 – ⇆. ◪ **AE** Ⓞ **VISA**
closed Sunday, Monday, 30 January-13 February and 2 to 16 October – **M** (dinner only) a la carte 13.30/19.10 **t.** ⅃ 3.00.   by A 35 **AX**

✗ **John B's**, 20 Old High St., BH15 1BP, ℰ 672440 – ◪ **AE** Ⓞ **VISA**   by A 35 **AX**
closed February and March – **M** *(closed Sunday September-June)* (dinner only) 13.95 **t.** ⅃ 3.00.

AUDI-VW Cabot Lane ℰ 745000   VAUXHALL-OPEL Poole Rd, Branksome ℰ 763361
CITROEN, PEUGEOT-TALBOT Blandford Rd ℰ
623636   🅖 ATS 1 Fernside Rd ℰ 733301/733326
RENAULT The Quay ℰ 674187

POOLEY BRIDGE Cumbria 401 402 L 20 – see Ullswater.

POOL IN WHARFEDALE West Yorks. 402 P 22 – pop. 1 706 – ⊠ Otley – ✆ 0532 Leeds.
♦London 204 – Bradford 10 – Harrogate 8 – ♦Leeds 10.

XXX **Pool Court** with rm, Pool Bank, LS21 1EH, ✆ 842288, Fax 843115, 🌲 – ▤ rest TV ☎ P.
⚑ AE ⓪ VISA. 🍴
closed Sunday, Monday, 2 weeks August and 10 days Christmas-New Year – **M** (dinner only)(booking essential) 10.00 **t.** and a la carte 19.50/28.75 **t.** ∮8.25 – � 6.75 – **6 rm** 60.00/110.00 **t.** – SB (weekends only) 95.00/133.00 **st.**

PORLOCK Somerset 403 J 30 The West Country G. – pop. 1 453 (inc. Oare) – ECD : Wednesday – ✆ 0643 – See : Site★ – St. Dubricius Church★.
Envir. : St. Culbone★, NW : 5 m. including 3 m. return on foot.
♦London 190 – ♦Bristol 67 – Exeter 46 – Taunton 28.

🏠 **Oaks**, TA24 8ES, ✆ 862265, 🌲 – ⇌ rest TV ☎ P
M (dinner only) 14.00 **st.** ∮3.85 – **11 rm** ⊊ 32.50/50.00 **st.** – SB 65.00/75.00 **st.**

at Porlock Weir NW : 1 ½ m. – ⊠ Minehead – ✆ 0643 Porlock :

🏰 **Anchor and Ship**, TA24 8PB, ✆ 862636, ≼, 🌲 – TV ☎ P. ⚑ AE VISA
M (bar lunch)/dinner 12.45 **st.** and a la carte ∮3.75 – **25 rm** ⊊ 30.00/87.00 **st.** – SB 76.00/107.50 **st.**

PORT DINORWIC (FELINHELI) Gwynedd 402 403 H 24 – ✆ 0248.
♦London 249 – Caernarfon 4 – Holyhead 23.

↑ **Ty'n Rhos Farm** ⚘, Seion. Llanddeiniolen, LL55 3AE, E : 2 ½ m. by A 487 and B4547 ✆ 670489, ≼, 🌲 – ⇌ rest TV P
closed 1 week November and 20 December-7 January – **M** (by arrangement) 11.00 **st.** ∮3.00 – **11 rm** ⊊ 19.00/38.00 **st.** – SB (except mid July-August) 49.00/55.00 **st.**

PORTHAETHWY = Menai Bridge.

PORTHALLOW Cornwall – ⊠ St. Keverne – ✆ 0326 Falmouth.
♦London 325 – Falmouth 26 – Penzance 27.

↑ **Gallen Treath** ⚘, TR12 6PL, ✆ 280400, ≼ – TV P – *April-October* – **5 rm**.

PORTHCAWL Mid Glam. 403 I 29 – pop. 15 162 – ECD : Wednesday – ✆ 065 671.
🛈 The Old Police Station, John St. ✆ 6639 (summer only).
♦London 183 – ♦Cardiff 28 – ♦Swansea 18.

🏨 **Seabank** (Lansbury), The Promenade, CF36 3LU, ✆ 2261, Telex 497797, Fax 5363, ≼ – 🛗
⇌ rm TV ☎ P – 🔁 220. ⚑ AE ⓪ VISA. 🍴
M 8.50/12.50 **t.** and a la carte – **64 rm** ⊊ 55.00/65.00 **t.** – SB (weekends only) 62.00/68.00 **st.**

🏨 **Atlantic**, West Drive, CF36 3LT, ✆ 5011, ≼ – 🛗 TV ☎ P. ⚑ AE ⓪ VISA
M (bar lunch)/dinner 8.95 **t.** and a la carte ∮3.20 – **20 rm** ⊊ 39.50/59.00 **t.** – SB (weekends only) 60.00 **st.**

↑ **Minerva**, 52 Esplanade Av., CF36 3YU, ✆ 2428 – ⇌ rest TV
M 7.00 **s.** – **8 rm** ⊊ 12.00/32.00 **s.**

at Nottage (Drenewydd yn Notais) N : 1 m. by A 4229 – ⊠ ✆ 065 671 Porthcawl :

🏠 **Rose and Crown** (B.C.B.), Heol-y-Capel, CF36 3ST, ✆ 4850 – TV ☎ P. ⚑ AE ⓪ VISA. 🍴
M 7.95 **t.** ∮3.45 – **8 rm** ⊊ 34.00/45.50 **t.** – SB (weekends only) 57.90 **st.**

PORTHMADOG Gwynedd 402 403 H 25 – pop. 2 865 – ECD : Wednesday – ✆ 0766.
🛈 Morfa Bychan ✆ 512037, W : 2 m.
🛈 High St. ✆ 512981 (summer only).
♦London 245 – Caernarfon 20 – Chester 70 – Shrewsbury 81.

🏠 **Bwlch-y-Fedwen Country House**, Penmorfa, LL49 9RY, NW : 2 m. on A 487 ✆ 512975,
« Tastefully renovated 17C inn » – ⇌ rest P. 🍴
April-October – **5 rm** ⊊ (dinner included) 41.00/62.00 **t.**

VOLVO Penamser Rd ✆ 513717

PORTINSCALE Cumbria – see Keswick.

PORT ISAAC Cornwall 403 F 32 The West Country G. – ECD : Wednesday – ✆ 0208 Bodmin.
♦London 266 – Newquay 24 – Tintagel 14 – Truro 32.

🏨 **Port Gaverne**, Port Gaverne, PL29 3SQ, S : ½ m. ✆ 880244, Fax 880151, « Retaining 17C features » – TV ☎ P. ⚑ AE ⓪ VISA
closed 8 January-17 February – **M** (buffet lunch)/dinner 12.00 **st.** and a la carte ∮2.95 –
18 rm ⊊ 34.50/72.00 **st.** – SB (except summer) 70.00/78.00 **st.**

↑ **Archer Farm** ⚘, Trewetha, PL29 3RU, SE : ½ m. by B 3276 ✆ 880522, ≼, 🌲 – P
April-October – **M** 10.50 ∮3.25 – **8 rm** ⊊ 16.00/39.00.

PORTLAND Dorset **403 404** M 32 The West Country G. – pop. 12 405 – ECD : Wednesday –
✆ 0305.

See : Site★ (vantage point★★).

🛈 St. George's Centre, Reforne ℰ 823406.

♦London 149 – Dorchester 14 – Weymouth 6.

🏨 Portland Heights (Best Western), Yeates Corner, DT5 2EN, ℰ 821361, Telex 418493, Fax
860081, ≼, ⌶ heated, **squash** – ⇥ rm 📺 ☎ 🅿 – 🛋 180. 🖭 AE ⓞ VISA
M (carving lunch) – **66 rm** � 49.00/64.00 **t.** – SB (weekends only) 80.00/104.00 **st.**

FORD Easton Lane ℰ 820483

PORTLOE Cornwall **403** F 33 – ✉ ✆ 0872 Truro.

♦London 296 – St. Austell 15 – Truro 15.

🏠 **Lugger,** TR2 5RD, ℰ 501322, Fax 501691, ≼ – ⇥ rest 📺 ☎ 🅿. 🖭 AE ⓞ VISA. ⅏
Mid March-mid November – **M** (bar lunch Monday to Saturday)/dinner 13.50 **t.** and a la carte
🍾 2.20 – **20 rm** ⊆ 34.00/78.00 **t.**

PORTMEIRION Gwynedd **402 403** H 25 – ✆ 0766 Porthmadog.

See : Site★.

♦London 245 – Caernarfon 23 – Colwyn Bay 40 – Dolgellau 24.

🏰 **Portmeirion** ⅌, LL48 6ER, ℰ 770228, Telex 61540, Fax 771331, ≼ village and estuary,
« Private Italianate village, antiques », ⌶ heated, 🏕, park, ⅍ – ⇥ rest 📺 ☎ 🅿 – 🛋
200. 🖭 AE ⓞ VISA. ⅏
closed 15 January-9 February – **M** *(closed lunch Monday)* (buffet lunch)/dinner 19.50 **t.**
🍾 5.00 – **28 rm** ⊆ 50.00/110.00 **st.,** **6 suites** 75.00/135.00 **t.** – SB 70.00/100.00 **st.**

PORTSCATHO Cornwall **403** F 33 – ECD : Wednesday and Saturday – ✉ Truro – ✆ 087 258.

♦London 298 – ♦Plymouth 55 – Truro 16.

🏨 **Rosevine** ⅌, Porthcurnick Beach, TR2 5EW, N : 2 m. by A 3078 ℰ 206, ≼, 🏕 – ☎ 🅿. 🖭
VISA
April-mid October – **M** (bar lunch)/dinner 17.00 **st.** 🍾 2.50 – **14 rm** ⊆ 27.50/61.00 **st.**

🏠 **Gerrans Bay,** Tregassick Rd, TR2 5ED, ℰ 338, 🏕 – 🅿. 🖭 AE VISA
Easter-October and Christmas – **M** (bar lunch Monday to Saturday)/dinner 12.50 **t.** 🍾 3.50 –
14 rm ⊆ 23.00/46.00 **st.**

🏠 **Roseland House** ⅌, Rosevine, TR2 5EW, N : 2 m. by A 3078 ℰ 644, ≼ Gerrans Bay, 🏕 –
⇥ rest 🅿. ⅏
March-October and Christmas – **M** (bar lunch)/dinner – **18 rm.**

PORTSMOUTH and SOUTHSEA Hants. **403 404** Q 31 – pop. 174 218 – ECD : Monday, Wednesday and Thursday – ✆ 0705.

See : Site★ – Naval Portsmouth★★★ BY : H.M.S. Victory★★★ A, H.M.S. Warrior★★★ B, The Mary
Rose★★★ D, Royal Naval Museum★★★ M1*AC* – Royal Marines' Museum★, at Eastney AZ M2 –
Old Town★ BZ – St. Thomas Cathedral★ BZ E.

Envir. : Southsea Castle★ SE : ½ m. BZ K – Portchester Castle★ NW : 6 m. by A 27 AY.

🏌 Great Salterns ℰ 664549. AY – 🏌 Crookhorn Lane, Widley ℰ 372210 AY.

🛳 Shipping connections with the Continent : to France (Cherbourg) (P & O European Ferries)
(Sealink) – to France (Le Havre) (P & O European Ferries) – to France (Saint-Malo and Caen)
(Brittany Ferries) – to the Isle of Wight : Fishbourne (Sealink) frequent services daily (35 mn).

🚢 to the Isle of Wight : Ryde (Sealink from Portsmouth Harbour) frequent services daily (15 mn)
– from Southsea to the Isle of Wight : Ryde (Hovertravel from Southsea Clarence Pier) summer
frequent services daily; winter 8-12 daily (restricted Sundays) (9 mn).

🛈 The Hard ℰ 826722/3 – The Pyramids, Clarence Pier ℰ 832464 – Continental Ferryport, Rudmore
Roundabout ℰ 698111 (summer only).

♦London 78 – ♦Southampton 21.

Plans on following pages

🏨 **Crest** (Crest), Pembroke Rd, PO1 2TA, ℰ 827651, Telex 86397, Fax 756715, 🖭 – 🛗 ⇥ rm
📺 ☎ 🅿 – 🛋 600. 🖭 AE ⓞ VISA   BZ **o**
M a la carte 14.75/20.45 **t.** – ⊆ 7.75 – **163 rm** 70.00/105.00 **st.** – SB 90.00/110.00 **st.**

🏨 Hospitality Inn (Mt. Charlotte), South Par., Southsea, PO4 0RN, ℰ 731281, Telex 86719, ≼ –
🛗 📺 ☎ 🅿 – 🛋 260   BZ **r**
115 rm.

🏠 **Keppel's Head** (T.H.F.), 24-26 The Hard, PO1 3DT, ℰ 833231 – 🛗 ⇥ rm 📺 ☎ 🅿 – 🛋.
🖭 AE ⓞ VISA   BY **a**
M (carving lunch)/dinner 11.50 **st.** and a la carte 🍾 3.95 – ⊆ 7.00 – **25 rm** 49.00/52.00 **st.** –
SB 76.00/80.00 **st.**

🏡 **Goodwood House,** 1 Taswell Rd, Southsea, PO5 2RG, ℰ 824734 – 📺. ⅏   BZ **e**
closed Christmas and New Year – **M** 7.00 **s.** 🍾 2.00 – **8 rm** ⊆ 12.00/28.00 **s.** –
SB (except summer) (weekends only) 30.00/34.00 **st.**

🏡 **Fortitude Cottage** without rest., 51 Broad St., Old Portsmouth, PO1 2JD, ℰ 823748 – 📺
closed 25 and 26 December – **3 rm** ⊆ 21.00/28.00 **st.**   BZ **c**

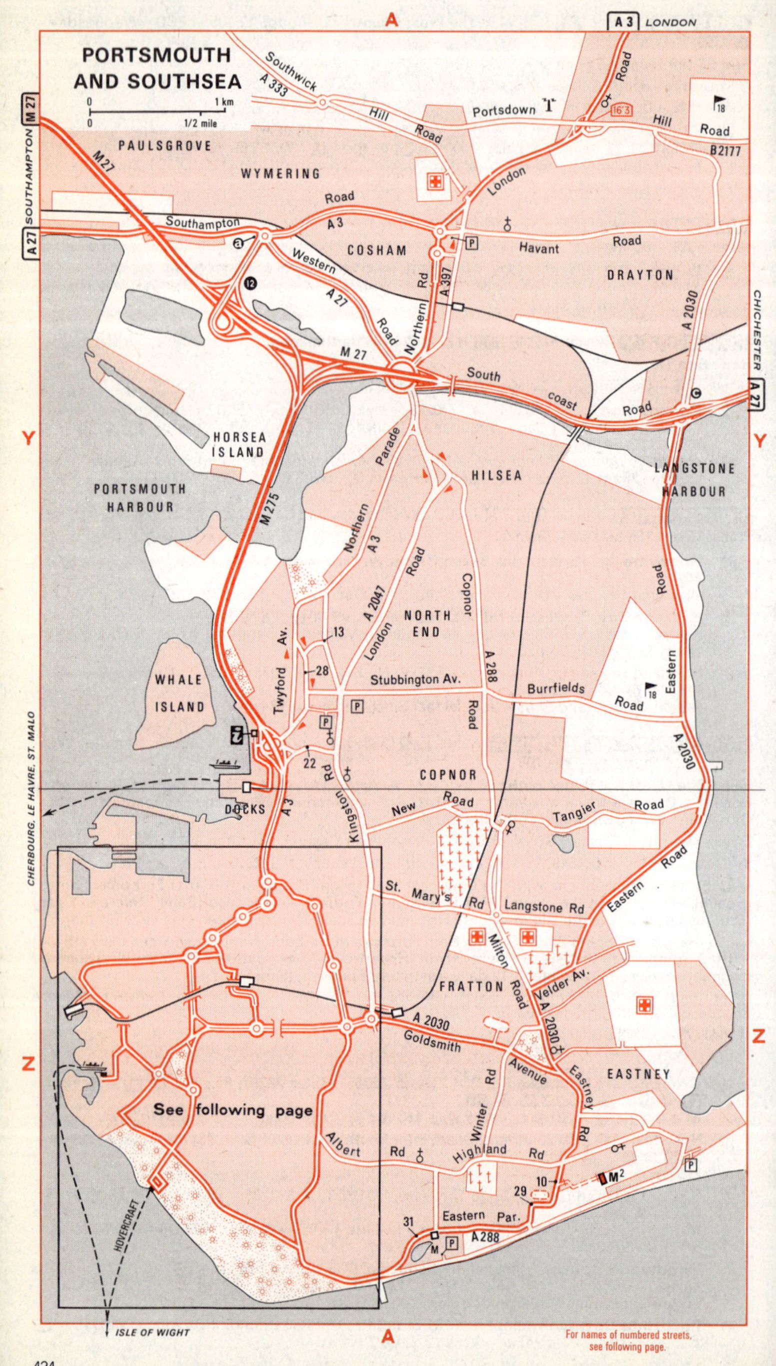

For names of numbered streets, see following page.

PORTSMOUTH AND SOUTHSEA

Arundel Street............**BY**
Charlotte Street............**BY** 9
Commercial Road ....**BY**
Palmerston Road ....**BZ**
Tricorn Centre ....**BY**

Alec Rose Lane............**BY** 2
Alfred Road ....**BY** 5

Anglesea Road ....**BY** 6
Bellevue Terrace ....**BZ** 7
Bradford Road............**AZ** 8
Cromwell Road ....**AZ** 10
Edinburgh Road ....**BY** 12
Gladys Avenue ....**AY** 13
Gordon Road ....**BZ** 14
Grove Road South........**BZ** 15
Guildhall Walk ....**BY** 16
Gunwharf Road ....**BZ** 17
Hampshire Terrace........**BY** 18
Hard (The) ....**BY** 19

Isambard Brunel Road.....**BY** 20
King's Terrace ....**BZ** 21
Kingston Crescent ....**AY** 22
Landport Terrace..........**BZ** 23
Lennox Road South ....**BZ** 24
Ordnance Row ....**BY** 26
Stamshaw Road ....**AY** 28
St. George's Road.........**AZ** 29
St. Helen's Parade ....**AZ** 31
St. Michael's Road ....**BY** 33
Southsea Terrace ....**BZ** 36
Stanhope Road...........**BY** 37

PORTSMOUTH and SOUTHSEA

✗ **Bistro Montparnasse,** 103 Palmerston Rd, Southsea, PO5 3PS, ℰ 816754 – ▨ AE ⓪ VISA

BZ **a**

closed Sunday, first 2 weeks January and Bank Holidays – **M** (dinner only) a la carte 12.40/16.00 **t.** 🍾 4.50.

✗ **Le Talisman,** 123 High St., Old Portsmouth, PO1 2HW, ℰ 811303 – ▨ AE ⓪ VISA   BZ **v**
closed Saturday lunch, Sunday and Monday – **M** 17.25/20.00 **t.** and a la carte 15.75/29.45 **t.**

at Cosham N : 3 ¾ m. by A 3, M 275, M 27 and A 27 – ✉ Portsmouth – ☎ 0705 Cosham :

🏨 **Holiday Inn,** North Harbour, PO6 4SH, ℰ 383151, Telex 86611, Fax 388701, ▨, squash –
|\$| ✗ rm ▤ TV ☎ & P – 🛎 300. ▨ AE ⓪ VISA   AY **a**
M 14.95/30.00 **st.** and a la carte 🍾 6.25 – ☕ 7.95 – **169 rm** 70.00/78.00 **t.**, **1 suite** 82.00/172.00 **t.** – SB (weekends only) 81.00/93.00 **st.**

at Farlington NE : 4 ½ m. by A 3, M 275, M 27 and A 27 on A 2030 – ✉ ☎ 0705 Portsmouth :

🏨 **Hilton National** (Hilton), Eastern Rd, PO6 1UN, ℰ 219111, Telex 86598, Fax 210762, 🚗,
✗ – ▤ rest TV ☎ & P – 🛎 230. ▨ AE ⓪ VISA   AY **c**
M *(closed Saturday lunch)* 13.00/15.00 **t.** and a la carte 10.50/17.00 **t.** 🍾 3.95 – ☕ 7.95 –
118 rm 72.00/92.00 **st.**, **4 suites** 120.00/150.00 **st.**

AUSTIN-ROVER Hambledon Rd ℰ 262641
BMW 135-153 Fratton Rd ℰ 827551
FIAT 117 Copnor Rd ℰ 691621
FORD Southampton Rd ℰ 370944
NISSAN Granada Rd, Southsea ℰ 735311
PEUGEOT-TALBOT Grove Rd South, Southsea ℰ 823261

RENAULT 128 Milton Rd ℰ 815151
SEAT Gamble Rd ℰ 660734
VAUXHALL-OPEL London Rd, Hilsea ℰ 661321
VW-AUDI 226 Haslemere Rd, Southsea ℰ 815111

🛞 ATS 3 Margate Rd ℰ 827544

PORT TALBOT West Glam. ⁜⁜⁜ I 29 – pop. 40 078 – ECD : Thursday – ☎ 0639.
♦London 187 – ♦Cardiff 32 – ♦Swansea 9.

🏰 Twelve Knights, Margam Rd, SA13 1DB, SE : 2 m. on A 48 ℰ 882381 – TV ☎ P – 🛎
11 rm.

AUDI-VW Dan-y-Bryn Rd ℰ 883733
AUSTIN-ROVER Fletchers of Cwmafon Rd ℰ 896378

VAUXHALL-OPEL Talbot Rd ℰ 881962

🛞 ATS 137 Water St. ℰ 883895

POWBURN Northumb. ⁜⁜⁜ ⁜⁜⁜ O 17 – ✉ Alnwick – ☎ 066 578.
♦London 312 – ♦Edinburgh 73 – ♦Newcastle-upon-Tyne 36.

🏨 **Breamish House** 🍴, NE66 4LL, ℰ 266, Fax 500, ≼, 🚗 – ✗ rest TV ☎ P
closed January – **M** (dinner only and Sunday lunch)/dinner 17.50 **t.** 🍾 3.95 – **10 rm**
☕ 38.50/112.00 **t.** – SB (April-October) 43.00/50.00 **st.**

POWERSTOCK Dorset ⁜⁜⁜ L 31 – see Bridport.

PRESTBURY Cheshire ⁜⁜⁜ ⁜⁜⁜ ⁜⁜⁜ N 24 – pop. 2 970 – ☎ 0625.
Envir. : Adlington Hall★ (15C) *AC*, N : 3 ½ m.
♦London 184 – ♦Liverpool 43 – ♦Manchester 17 – ♦Stoke-on-Trent 25.

🏨 **Mottram Hall** (De Vere) 🍴, Wilmslow Rd, Mottram St. Andrew, SK10 4QT, NW : 2 ¼ m.
on A 538 ℰ 828135, Telex 668181, Fax 582635, ≼, « Part 18C mansion in park », ▨, 🚗, ✗,
squash – ✗ rm TV ☎ & P – 🛎 . ▨ AE ⓪ VISA 🍴
M *(closed Sunday lunch)* 10.50/16.00 **st.** and a la carte 🍾 4.30 – **92 rm** ☕ 85.00/100.00 **st.**,
3 suites 155.00/165.00 **st.**

✗✗ **White House,** The Village, SK10 4DG, ℰ 829376 – P . ▨ AE ⓪ VISA 🍴
closed Monday and 2 to 17 January – **M** 9.95 **t.** (lunch) and a la carte 19.70/25.70 **t.** 🍾 3.75.

✗✗ **Legh Arms and Black Boy,** The Village, SK10 4DG, ℰ 829130 – P . ▨ AE ⓪ VISA
closed dinner 25 December and 1 January – **M** 9.50/12.95 **t.** and a la carte 16.00/29.95 **t.**
🍾 4.50.

PRESTEIGNE Powys ⁜⁜⁜ K 27 – pop. 1 490 – ECD : Thursday – ☎ 0544.
See : Church (Flemish Tapestry★).
Envir. : Old Radnor (church★) SW : 7 ½ m.
🏌 at Kington ℰ 0544 (Kington) 230340, S : 7 m.
🛈 Old Market Hall ℰ 260193.
♦London 159 – Llandrindod Wells 20 – Shrewsbury 39.

🏨 **Radnorshire Arms** (T.H.F.), High St., LD8 2BE, ℰ 267406, 🚗 – TV ☎ P – 🛎 25. ▨ AE
⓪ VISA
M 16.60 **st.** (dinner) and lunch a la carte approx. 12.65 **st.** 🍾 3.95 – ☕ 7.00 – **16 rm**
52.00/67.00 **st.** – SB (except Easter, Christmas and New Year) 70.00/90.00 **st.**

Prévenez immédiatement l'hôtelier si vous ne pouvez pas occuper la chambre que vous avez retenue.

PRESTON Lancs. **402** L 22 – pop. 166 675 – ECD : Thursday – ☎ 0772.

Envir. : Samlesbury Old Hall★ (14C) *AC*, E : 2 ½ m.

[18] Fulwood Hall Lane, Fulwood ℰ 700011 – [18] Longridge, Fell Barn, Jeffrey Hill ℰ 077 478 (Longridge) 3291, NE : 8 m. by B 6243 – [18] Fishwick Hall, Glenluce Drive, Farringdon Park, ℰ 795870 – [18] Ingol, Tanterton Hall Rd ℰ 734556.

🛈 Guildhall, Lancaster Rd ℰ 53731.

◆London 226 – ◆Blackpool 18 – Burnley 22 – ◆Liverpool 30 – ◆Manchester 34 – ◆Stoke-on-Trent 65.

🏨 **Crest** (Crest), The Ring Way, PR1 3AU, ℰ 59411, Telex 677147, Fax 201923 – 📶 ⤢ 📺 ☎ 🅿 – 🏊 100. 🆑 AE ① VISA
M 7.95/14.30 **st.** and a la carte 🍷 7.75 – �☕ 7.35 – **126 rm** 64.00/135.00 **st.** – SB 68.00/80.00 **st.**

at Fulwood N : 1 ½ m. on A 6 – ✉ ☎ 0772 Preston :

🏠 **Briarfield** without rest., 147 Watling Street Rd, off Garstang Rd, PR2 4AE, ℰ 700917 – 📺 🅿. ⤢
closed Christmas-New Year – **9 rm** �☕ 20.00/40.00 **st.**

at Broughton N : 3 m. on A 6 – ✉ ☎ 0772 Preston :

🏨 **Broughton Park,** 418 Garstang Rd, PR3 5JB, ℰ 864087, Group Telex 67180, Fax 861728, 🆑, 🛁, squash – 📶 ⤢ rm 📺 ☎ 🅆 🅿 – 🏊. 🆑 AE ① VISA ⤢
M (see **Courtyard** below) – **98 rm** ⊊ 73.00/93.00 **t.** – SB (weekends only) 90.00 **st.**

XXX **Courtyard** (at Broughton Park H.), 418 Garstang Rd, PR3 5JB, ℰ 864087, Group Telex 67180, Fax 861728 – 🅿. 🆑 AE ① VISA
M (booking essential) 10.95/25.50 **t.** and a la carte 14.50/22.00 **t.** 🍷 4.00.

at Samlesbury E : 2 ½ m. at junction M 6 and A 59 – ✉ Preston – ☎ 0772 Preston :

🏨 **Swallow Trafalgar** (Swallow), Preston New Rd, PR5 0UL, E : 1 m. at junction A 59 and A 677 ℰ 877351, Telex 677362, Fax 877424, 🆑, squash – 📶 ⤢ rm 📺 ☎ 🅿 – 🏊 150. 🆑 AE ① VISA
M *(closed lunch Sunday and Bank Holidays)* 7.25/11.25 **st.** and a la carte – **80 rm** ⊊ 57.00/69.00 **st.** – SB (weekends only) (except Christmas) 74.00 **st.**

🏨 **Tickled Trout,** Preston New Rd, PR5 0UJ, ℰ 671, Telex 677625, Fax 463, ≼, 🛶 – 📺 ☎ 🅿 – 🏊 100. 🆑 AE ① VISA
M 14.00/16.00 **t.** and a la carte 🍷 5.00 – **66 rm** ⊊ 60.00/82.00 **t.** – SB (weekends only) 65.00/68.00 **st.**

at Bamber Bridge S : 5 m. on A 6 – ✉ ☎ 0772 Preston :

🏨 Novotel, Reedfield Place, Walton Summit, PR5 6AB, SE : ¾ m. by A 6 at junction with M 6 ℰ 313331, Telex 677164, 🏊 heated, 🛶 – 📶 📺 ☎ 🅆 🅿 – 🏊 100 rm.

at Lea W : 3 ½ m. on A 583 – ✉ ☎ 0772 Preston :

🏠 **Travel Inn** without rest., Blackpool Rd, PR4 0XL, on A 583 ℰ 720476, Fax 729971 – ⤢ 📺 🅆 🅿. 🆑 AE ① VISA ⤢
⊊ 3.95 – **38 rm** 24.50/27.50 **t.**

MICHELIN Distribution Centre, Unit 20, Roman Way, Longbridge Rd, Ribbleton, PR2 5RB, ℰ 651411, FAX 655108

BMW Blackpool Rd, Ashton ℰ 724391
COLT, YUGO Preston Rd ℰ 652323
FIAT 306-310 Ribbleton Lane ℰ 792823
FORD Penwortham ℰ 744471
HONDA Corporation St. ℰ 58802
LADA Watling Street Rd ℰ 717262
NISSAN Ribbleton Lane ℰ 704704
PEUGEOT-TALBOT. Blackpool Rd ℰ 735811

RELIANT Blackpool Rd ℰ 726066
SKODA New Hall Lane ℰ 794491
TOYOTA 350 Blackpool Rd ℰ 719841
VAUXHALL Blackpool Rd ℰ 793054
VOLVO Strand Rd ℰ 50501
VW-AUDI ℰ 702288

⊚ ATS 296-298 Aqueduct St. ℰ 57688/57689

PRIORS HARDWICK Warw. **403 404** Q 27 – pop. 167 – ✉ Rugby – ☎ 0327 Byfield.

◆London 94 – ◆Coventry 17 – Northampton 26 – Warwick 15.

XXX **Butchers Arms,** CV23 8SN, ℰ 60504, English rest., 🛶 – 🅿
closed Saturday lunch and Sunday dinner – **M** 10.00 **s.** (lunch) and a la carte 11.65/20.30 **s.** 🍷 3.00.

PUCKRUP Glos. – see Tewkesbury.

PUDDINGTON Cheshire **402 403** K 24 – pop. 318 – ✉ South Wirral – ☎ 051 Liverpool.

◆London 204 – Birkenhead 12 – Chester 8.

XXX **Craxton Wood** 🍃 with rm, Parkgate Rd, L66 9PB, on A 540 ℰ 339 4717, Fax 339 1740, ≼, « Gardens », park – 📺 ☎ 🅆 🅿. 🆑 AE ① VISA ⤢
closed Sunday, last 2 weeks August and Bank Holidays – **M** a la carte 17.20/21.85 **s.** – **13 rm** ⊊ 38.50/62.50 **s.**, **1 suite** 60.00/77.50 **s.**

PUDSEY West Yorks. **402** P 22 – see Leeds.

PULBOROUGH West Sussex **404** S 31 – pop. 3 197 – ECD : Wednesday – ☎ 079 82.
Envir. : Hardham (church : wall paintings★ 12C) S : 1 m.
☌ West Sussex, Hurston Lane ℘ 2563.
♦London 49 – ♦Brighton 25 – Guildford 25 – ♦Portsmouth 35.

 ☖ **Chequers**, Church Pl., RH20 1AD, NE : ¼ m. on A 29 ℘ 2486, Fax 2715, ⋉ – ⇔ rest 📺 ☎ ℗. 🖎 AE ⓪ VISA
  M (bar lunch Monday to Saturday)/dinner 13.50 st. ₰ 3.50 – **11 rm** � 39.50/52.00 st. –
  SB 59.00/64.00 st.

 XX **Stane Street Hollow**, Codmore Hill, RH20 1BG, NE : 1 m. on A 29 ℘ 2819, Swiss rest. –
  ⇔ ℗
  closed third week February, last 2 weeks May, last 2 weeks October and 23 to 28December –
  M (closed Saturday lunch and Sunday to Tuesday) (booking essential) 7.00 t. (lunch) and a
  la carte 14.85/20.05 t. ₰ 4.00.

HONDA London Rd ℘ 0798 (Petworth) 831691   ROLLS-ROYCE, JAGUAR, DAIMLER, RANGE-
                                          ROVER,LAND-ROVER London Rd ℘ 2407

PURFLEET Essex – ☎ 040 26 (4 fig.) or 0708 (6 fig.).
♦London 16 – Maidstone 30 – Southend-on-Sea 22.

 ☖☖ **Royal**, High St., RM16 1QA, ℘ 865432, ≼ – 📺 ☎ ℗ – 🔯 60. 🖎 AE ⓪ VISA. ⋙
  M 10.00 t. and a la carte ₰ 3.50 – **31 rm** ⊒ 45.00/55.00 t.

PURTON Wilts. **403 404** O 29 – see Swindon.

PWLLHELI Gwynedd **402 403** G 25 – ☎ 0758.
☌ Golf Rd ℘ 612520.
🛈 Y Maes ℘ 613000 (summer only).
♦London 261 – Aberystwyth 73 – Caernarfon 21.

 XXX **Plas Bodegroes** ⅀ with rm, LL53 5TH, NW : 1 ¾ m. on A 497 ℘ 612363, « Georgian
  country house », ⋉, park – ⇔ rest 📺 ☎ ℗. 🖎 VISA
  closed 2 January-February – **M** (closed lunch and Tuesday to non-residents) 19.00 st.
  (dinner) and a la carte approx. 14.50 st. ₰ 3.25 – **5 rm** ⊒ 37.50/75.00 st. – SB (except May-
  October) 80.00/100.00 st.

 at Bodfuan NW : 3 ¾ m. on A 497 – ✉ ☎ 0758 Pwllheli :

 ☖ **Old Rectory**, LL53 6DT, ℘ 720923, ⋉ – 📺 ☎ ℗. 🖎
  M (dinner only) a la carte 12.50/15.00 t. ₰ 3.00 – **4 rm** ⊒ 14.00/28.00 t.

FORD The Garage ℘ 0766 (Chwilog) 810240

*Your recommendation is self-evident if you always walk into a
hotel Guide in hand.*

QUEDGELEY Glos. **403 404** N 28 – see Gloucester.

QUORN Leics. – see Loughborough.

RADLETT Herts. **404** T 28 – pop. 7 749 – ECD : Wednesday – ☎ 0923.
☌ at Aldenham, Radlett Rd ℘ 853929, SW : 3 m. by B462 BT.
♦London 21 – Luton 15.

Plan : see Greater London (North-West)

 ☖ Red Lion, Watling St., WD7 7NP, ℘ 855341 – 📺 ☎ ℗ – 🔯 35. ⋙   BT c
  15 rm.
 XX **Tai Chi**, Conway House, Watling St., WD7 7AA, ℘ 852344, Chinese (Peking, Szechuan)
  rest. – ▤. 🖎 AE ⓪ VISA   BT s
  M 25.00 t. and a la carte.
 XX **Tim's Table**, 335 Watling St., WD7 7LB, ℘ 854388, Chinese (Peking, Szechuan) rest. –
  ▤. 🖎 AE ⓪ VISA   BT o
  M 7.50/15.00 t. and a la carte ₰ 3.00.

BMW 74-76 Watling St. ℘ 854802   VAUXHALL 411 Watling St. ℘ 855681
FORD 203-205 Watling St. ℘ 854851

RAMPSIDE Cumbria **402** K 21 – see Barrow-in-Furness.

RAMSBOTTOM Greater Manchester **402** N 23 – pop. 16 334 – ☎ 0706.
♦London 223 – ♦Blackpool 39 – Burnley 12 – ♦Leeds 46 – ♦Manchester 13 – ♦Liverpool 39.

 ☖ **Old Mill**, Springwood St., off Carr St., BL0 9DS, ℘ 822991, Fax 822291, 🖾 – 📺 ☎ ℗. 🖎
  AE ⓪ VISA ⋙
  M 7.00/11.00 t. and a la carte ₰ 3.75 – **36 rm** ⊒ 39.50/54.00 t. – SB 65.00/75.00 st.
 X **Village**, 16 Market Pl., BL0 9HT, ℘ 825070 – ⇔. 🖎 VISA
  closed Sunday to Tuesday – **M** (booking essential)(dinner only) 22.00 st. ₰ 3.00.

RAMSGATE Kent **404** Y 30 – pop. 36 678 – ECD : Thursday – ☎ 0843 Thanet.

See : St. Augustine's Abbey Church (interior★).

Envir. : Minster-in-Thanet (abbey : remains★ 7C-12C) W : 4 ½ m. – Birchington-on-Sea : in Quex Park (Powell-Cotton Museum★ of African and Asian natural history and ethnology, *AC*) NW : 9 m.

🚢 Shipping connections with the Continent : to France (Dunkerque) (Sally Line).

🛈 Argyle Centre, Queen St. ℰ 591086 – Ferry Terminal ℰ 589830 (summer only).

◆London 77 – ◆Dover 19 – Maidstone 45 – Margate 4.5.

 🏨 **Marina Resort**, Harbour Par., CT11 9DS, ℰ 588276, Fax 586866, ≤, 🏊 – 🗏 rest 📺 ☎ –
 🏊 100. 🖭 **AE** ⓪ **VISA**. 🛠
 M (carving lunch)/dinner 12.50 **t.** and a la carte ↨ 4.25 – **59 rm** ☐ 50.95/86.90 **t.** –
 SB (except summer) (weekends only) 60.00/70.00 **st.**

 🏠 **Savoy**, 43 Grange Rd, CT11 9NA, ℰ 592637 – 📺 ☎ ℗. 🖭 **AE** ⓪ **VISA**. 🛠
 M 8.00 **st.** (lunch) and a la carte 10.00/15.00 **st.** ↨ 3.60 – **26 rm** ☐ 32.00/43.00 **st.**

 ↑ **Abbeygail** without rest., 17 Penshurst Rd, East Cliff, CT11 8EG, ℰ 594154 – 🛠
 11 rm ☐ 10.00/20.00.

 at Minster-in-Thanet W : 5 ½ m. by A 253 on B 2048 – ✉ Ramsgate – ☎ 0843 Thanet :

 XX **Old Oak Cottage**, 53 High St., CT12 4BT, ℰ 821229, �_ – ℗. 🖭 **AE** ⓪ **VISA**
 closed Sunday dinner and Monday – **M** 10.50 **t.** and a la carte 11.70/15.75 **t.** ↨ 2.75.

AUSTIN-ROVER Grange Rd ℰ 583541   VAUXHALL West Cliff Rd ℰ 593877
FIAT Wilson Rd ℰ 593465
FORD Boundary Rd ℰ 593784   ⓪ ATS 82-84 Bellevue Rd ℰ 595829
RENAULT Margate Rd ℰ 592629

RASKELF North Yorks. – – see Easingwold.

RAVENSTONEDALE Cumbria **402** M 20 – pop. 501 – ECD : Thursday – ✉ Kirkby Stephen –
☎ 058 73 Newbiggin-on-Lune.

◆London 280 – ◆Carlisle 43 – Kendal 19 – Kirkby Stephen 5.

 🏠 **Black Swan**, CA17 4NG, ℰ 204, « Attractive country inn », 🌿 – ⤢ rest ☎ ℗. 🖭 **AE** **VISA**
 restricted service January – **M** (bar lunch Monday to Saturday)/dinner 14.50 **t.** and a la carte
 ↨ 3.50 – **14 rm** ☐ 33.00/44.00 **t.** – SB (October-May) (weekends only) 75.00 **st.**

 ⚘ **Fat Lamb**, Crossbank, Fell End, CA17 4LL, SE : 1 ¾ m. on A 683 ℰ 242, ≤, 🌿 – ℗
 M 12.50 **t.** and a la carte ↨ 2.40 – **10 rm** ☐ 27.00/42.00 **t.** – SB 61.00/66.00 **st.**

READING Berks. **403** **404** Q 29 – pop. 194 727 – ☎ 0734 – **Envir.** : Stratfield Saye Park★ *AC*,
S : 7 m. by A 33 X – Mapledurham House★ *AC*, NW : 3 ½ m. by A 329 X.

🛈 Civic Offices, Civic Centre ℰ 575911 and 592388.

◆London 43 – ◆Brighton 79 – ◆Bristol 78 – Croydon 47 – Luton 62 – ◆Oxford 28 – ◆Portsmouth 67 – ◆Southampton 46.

Plan on next page

 🏨 **Ramada**, Oxford Rd, RG1 7RH, ℰ 586222, Telex 847785, Fax 597842, 🏊 – 🛗 ⤢ rm 🗏 📺
 ☎ ℗ – 🏊 150. 🖭 **AE** ⓪ **VISA**. 🛠   Z i
 M 13.50/25.00 **st.** and a la carte – ☐ 7.25 – **195 rm** 45.00/97.00 **st.**, **1 suite** 180.00 **st.** –
 SB (weekends only) 100.00 **st.**

 🏨 **Caversham** (Norfolk Cap.), Caversham Bridge, Richfield Av., RG1 8BD, ℰ 391818, Telex
 846933, Fax 391665, ≤, « Thames-side setting », 🏊 – 🛗 🗏 📺 ☎ ﬗ ℗ – 🏊 200. 🖭 **AE** ⓪
 VISA. 🛠   X e
 M 15.75/18.75 **st.** and a la carte 21.00/28.00 **st.** ↨ 5.25 – ☐ 8.50 – **100 rm** 96.00/192.00 **st.**,
 8 suites 195.00/215.00 **st.** – SB (weekends only) 116.00/124.00 **st.**

 🏨 **Post House** (T.H.F.), Basingstoke Rd, RG2 0SL, S : 2 ½ m. on A 33 ℰ 875485, Telex 849160,
 Fax 311958, 🏊 – ⤢ rm 📺 ☎ ℗ – 🏊 100. 🖭 **AE** ⓪ **VISA**   X a
 M *(closed Saturday lunch and Bank Holidays)* 19.75 **st.** and a la carte ↨ 3.95 – ☐ 7.00 –
 143 rm 82.00/105.00 **st.** – SB (weekends only) 64.00/78.00 **st.**

 🏠 **George** (B.C.B.), King St., RG1 2HE, ℰ 573445 – 📺 ☎. 🛠 – **68 rm** ☐ 42.00/52.00 **t.**

 🏠 **Upcross**, 68 Berkeley Av., RG1 6HY, ℰ 590796, Fax 576517, 🌿 – 📺 ☎ ℗. 🖭 **AE** **VISA**
 closed 26 to 30 December – **M** *(closed Saturday lunch)* 12.95/14.00 **st.** and a la carte ↨ 4.00
 – **27 rm** ☐ 45.00/65.00 **t.**   Z c

 at Sindlesham SE : 5 m. by A 329 on B 3030 – X – ✉ Wokingham – ☎ 0734 Reading :

 🏨 **Reading Moat House** (Q.M.H.), Mill Lane, RG11 5DF, NW : ½ m. via Mole Rd ℰ 351035,
 Telex 846360, Fax 666530 – 🛗 🗏 rest 📺 ☎ ﬗ ℗ – 🏊 80. 🖭 **AE** ⓪ **VISA**. 🛠
 M 15.95/29.95 **t.** and a la carte ↨ 4.85 – ☐ 7.00 – **92 rm** 88.00/96.00 **st.**, **4 suites** 160.00 **st.**

 at Shinfield S : 4 ¼ m. on A 327 – X – ✉ ☎ 0734 Reading :

 XXX ❀ **L'Ortolan** (Burton-Race), The Old Vicarage, Church Lane, RG2 9BY, ℰ 883783, Fax
 885391, French rest., 🌿 – ℗. 🖭 **AE** **VISA**
 closed Sunday dinner, Monday, last 2 weeks February and last 2 weeks August – **M**
 23.00/43.00 **t.**
 Spec. Tagliatelle de ris de veau et écrevisses aux cèpes, Paupiettes de beatilles de veau pôelées, jus au foie
 gras et champignons, Tarte sablée à la noix de coco caramélisée au rhum et banane.

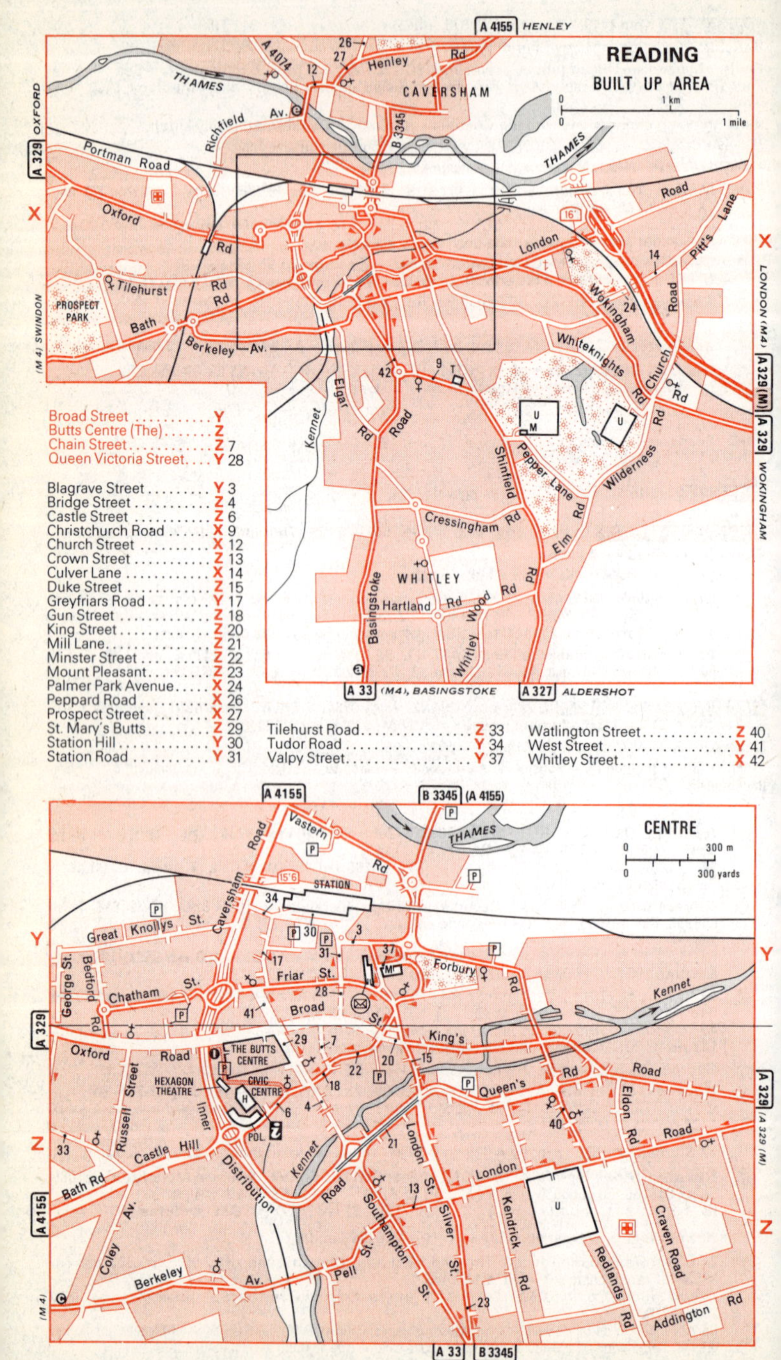

Broad Street .... Y
Butts Centre (The) ...... Z
Chain Street .... Z 7
Queen Victoria Street.... Y 28

Blagrave Street .... Y 3
Bridge Street .... Y Z 4
Castle Street .... Z 6
Christchurch Road ...... X 9
Church Street .... X 12
Crown Street .... X 13
Culver Lane .... X 14
Duke Street .... Z 15
Greyfriars Road .... Y 17
Gun Street .... Z 18
King Street .... Z 20
Mill Lane .... Z 21
Minster Street ...... Z 22
Mount Pleasant ..... Z 23
Palmer Park Avenue ... X 24
Peppard Road ...... X 26
Prospect Street ..... X 27
St. Mary's Butts ...... Z 29
Station Hill .... Y 30
Station Road .... Y 31
Tilehurst Road .... Z 33
Tudor Road .... Y 34
Valpy Street .... Y 37
Watlington Street .... Z 40
West Street .... Y 41
Whitley Street .... X 42

at Burghfield SW : 5 m. by A 4 – X – ✉ ☎ 0734 Reading :

XX **Knight's Farm,** Berrys Lane, RG3 3XE, NE : 2 m. ☎ 572366 – **P**. ⌧ AE ⓪ VISA
closed Saturday lunch and Sunday dinner – **M** 15.00/25.00 **st.** ⌾ 5.50.

AUSTIN-ROVER, FREIGHT-ROVER Basingstoke Rd ☎ 323383
BMW 209-211 Shinfield Rd ☎ 866161
FIAT Eaton Pl., Chatham St. ☎ 582521
FORD Bath Rd ☎ 412021
FORD 160 Basingstoke Rd ☎ 312550
JAGUAR 38 Portman Rd ☎ 585011/875151
PEUGEOT-TALBOT Christchurch Rd ☎ 875242
RENAULT Chatham St. ☎ 583322

RENAULT Wokingham Rd ☎ 669456
TOYOTA 569-575 Basingstoke Rd ☎ 871278
VAUXHALL Vastern Rd ☎ 55501
VOLVO 406-412 London Rd ☎ 67321
VW-AUDI Erleigh Rd ☎ 666111/861176
VW-AUDI Oxford Rd ☎ 418181

⓪ ATS Basingstoke Rd ☎ 580651

REDCAR Cleveland 402 Q 20 – pop. 35 373 – ✉ ☎ 0642 Middlesbrough.

🏌 Wilton Castle ☎ 465265, W : 3 m. on A 174.

🛈 Regent Cinema Building, Newcomen Terr. ☎ 471921.

◆London 255 – ◆Middlesbrough 9 – Scarborough 43.

🏨 **Park,** Granville Terr., TS10 3AR, ☎ 490888, Fax 490888 – TV ☎. ⌧ AE ⓪ VISA. 🍽
M 8.20 **t.** and a la carte ⌾ 3.20 – **24 rm** ⌷ 30.00/75.00 **t.** – SB (weekends only) 43.10/67.90 **st.**

AUDI-VW Park Av. ☎ 488222
AUSTIN-ROVER Longbeck Estate, Marske ☎ 480823
FORD Corporation Rd ☎ 490909

VAUXHALL Trunk Rd ☎ 486161

⓪ ATS Limerick Rd ☎ 477100
ATS 162 Lord St. ☎ 484013

REDDITCH Heref. and Worc. 403 404 O 27 – pop. 61 639 – ECD : Wednesday – ☎ 0527.

🏌 Abbey Park, Dagnell End Rd ☎ 63918 – 🏌 Pitcheroak, Plymouth Rd ☎ 41054.

🛈 Civic Square, Alcester St. ☎ 60806.

◆London 111 – ◆Birmingham 15 – Cheltenham 33 – Stratford-upon-Avon 15.

🏨 **Southcrest** (Best Western) 🐦, Pool Bank, Southcrest District, B97 4JG, ☎ 41511, Telex 338455, Fax 402600, 🌳 – 🍽 rest TV ☎ **P** – 🔥 80. ⌧ AE ⓪ VISA
closed 24 December-2 January – **M** *(closed Saturday lunch, Sunday dinner and Bank Holiday Mondays)* 10.00/12.00 **st.** and a la carte ⌾ 4.30 – **58 rm** ⌷ 54.00/64.00 **st.** – SB (weekends only) 58.00/70.00 **st.**

🏠 **Old Rectory** 🐦, Ipsley Lane, Ipsley, B98 0AP, ☎ 23000, 🌳 – 🍽 rest ☎ **P**. ⌧ AE VISA. 🍽 – **M** *(closed Friday)* (dinner only) 12.00 **st.** – **10 rm** ⌷ 30.00/57.00 **t.**

at Studley (Warw.) SE : 4 ½ m. by A 441 and A 448 on B 4092 – ✉ Redditch – ☎ 052 785 Studley :

XX **Pepper's,** 45 High St., B80 7HN, ☎ 3183, Indian rest. – ⌧ AE VISA
closed 25 and 26 December – **M** (dinner only) 10.00 **t.** and a la carte 10.90/16.05 **t.** ⌾ 5.55.

AUSTIN-ROVER Washford Drive ☎ 25055
CITROEN Birmingham Rd ☎ 63636
FORD Battens Drive ☎ 21212
VOLVO Clive Rd ☎ 69111

VW-AUDI 530 Evesham Rd, Crabe Cross ☎ 44554

⓪ ATS Pipers Rd, Park Farm Ind Est:, Park Farm South ☎ 502002

REDHILL Surrey 404 T 30 – pop. 48 241 (inc. Reigate) – ECD : Wednesday – ☎ 0737.

🏌 Pendleton Rd ☎ 240777 – ◆London 22 – ◆Brighton 31 – Guildford 20 – Maidstone 34.

🏨 Nutfield Priory, Nutfield, RH1 4EN, E : 2 m. on A 25 ☎ 822066, Fax 823321, ≤, 🏊, park, 🍽, squash – 🛗 TV ☎ **P** – 🔥 – **38 rm**.

🏨 **Lakers Toby,** 2 Redstone Hill, OI11 4BL, on A 25 ☎ 768434, Fax 768828 – 🍽 rest TV ☎ ♿ **P** – 🔥 50. ⌧ AE ⓪ VISA. 🍽
M 5.95 **t.** and a la carte ⌾ 3.00 – **37 rm** ⌷ 49.50/59.50 **st.** – SB (weekends only) 52.00/62.00 **st.**

🏠 **Ashleigh House** without rest., 39 Redstone Hill, RH1 4BG, on A 25 ☎ 764763, 🏊 heated, 🌳 – **P**. 🍽
closed Christmas and New Year – **9 rm** ⌷ 22.00/38.00 **st.**

at Salfords S : 2 ½ m. on A 23 – ✉ ☎ 0737 Redhill :

🏨 Travel Inn without rest., Brighton Rd, RH1 5BT, ☎ 767277 – TV ♿ **P** – **21 rm.**

REDLYNCH Wilts. 403 404 O 31 – see Salisbury.

REIGATE Surrey 404 T 30 – pop. 48 241 (inc. Redhill) – ECD : Wednesday – ☎ 073 72 (5 fig.) or 0737 (6 fig.) – 🏌 Reigate Heath ☎ 242610.

◆London 26 – ◆Brighton 33 – Guildford 20 – Maidstone 38.

🏨 **Bridge House,** Reigate Hill, RH2 9RP, ☎ 246801, Telex 268810, Fax 223756 – TV ☎ **P** – 🔥 45. ⌧ AE ⓪ VISA. 🍽
M *(dancing Tuesday to Saturday)(closed Bank Holidays to non-residents)* 12.50/17.00 **t.** and a la carte – ⌷ 5.50 – **37 rm** 40.00/85.00 **st.**

🏠 **Cranleigh,** 41 West St., RH2 9BL, ☎ 223417, 🏊 heated, 🌳 – TV ☎ **P**. ⌧ AE ⓪ VISA. 🍽
M 14.00 **st.** ⌾ 4.00 – ⌷ 3.00 – **10 rm** 34.00/55.00 **st.** – SB (weekends only) 70.00/75.00 **st.**

X **La Barbe,** 71 Bell St., RH2 7AN, ☎ 241966, French Bistro – ⌧ AE VISA
closed lunch Monday and Saturday, Sunday and Bank Holidays – **M** 16.75/26.50 **st.** ⌾ 4.00.

RENISHAW Derbs. **402 403 404** P 24 – pop. 1 809 – ✉ Sheffield (South Yorks.) – ☎ 0246 Eckington.

⌘ Golf House ☎ 432044.

♦London 157 – Derby 33 – ♦Nottingham 31 – ♦Sheffield 8.

🏨 Sitwell Arms, 39 Station Rd, S31 9WE, ☎ 435226, Telex 547303 – 📺 ☎ 🅿 – 🛥
29 rm.

RHAEADR = Rhayader.

RHAYADER (RHAEADR) Powys **403** J 27 – ☎ 0597.

♦London 180 – Brecon 34 – Hereford 46 – Shrewsbury 60.

🏠 Elan Valley, Elan Valley, LD6 5HN, SW : 2 ½ m. on B 4518 ☎ 810448, 🚲 – 🅿
10 rm.

⚐ Elan, West St., LD6 5AF, ☎ 810662 – 📺 🅿. 🔲 **VISA**
M *(closed Sunday and Monday to non-residents)* (bar lunch Monday to Saturday)/dinner
8.25 **t.** and a la carte 🍷 3.75 – **11 rm** 16.00/38.50 **t.** – SB 46.00/50.50 **st.**

RHOSCOLYN Gwynedd **402 403** G 24 – pop. 543 – ✉ Holyhead – ☎ 0407 Trearddur Bay.

♦London 269 – Bangor 25 – Caernarfon 30 – Holyhead 5.5.

↑ **Old Rectory** ⌂, LL65 2DQ, ☎ 860214, ≤ – ✖ rest 📺 🅿. **VISA**. ✂
closed January and December – **M** 10.00 **st.** 🍷 3.15 – **5 rm** ⌷ 19.50/39.00 **st.** – SB 57.00 **st.**

RHOSMAEN Dyfed **403** I 28 – see Llandeilo.

RHOS-ON-SEA (LLANDRILLO-YN-RHOS) Clwyd **402 403** I 24 – see Colwyn Bay.

RHUTHUN = Ruthin.

RHYDAMAN = Ammanford.

RHYDGALED (CHANCERY) Clwyd **403** H 26 – see Aberystwyth (Dyfed).

RICHMOND North Yorks. **402** O 20 – pop. 7 596 – ECD : Wednesday – ☎ 0748.

See : Castle ★ (Norman ruins) *AC* – Georgian Theatre ★.

Envir. : Bolton Castle ★ (15C) *AC*, ≤ ★, SW : 13 m.

⌘ Bend Hagg ☎ 2457 – ⌘ Catterick Garrison, Leyburn Rd ☎ 833268, S : 3 m.

🛈 Friary Gardens, Victoria Rd ☎ 850252 (summer only).

♦London 243 – ♦Leeds 53 – ♦Middlesbrough 26 – ♦Newcastle-upon-Tyne 44.

🏠 **Howe Villa** ⌂, Whitcliffe Mill, DL10 4TJ, S : ½ m. by A 6108 ☎ 850055, ≤, 🚲 – ✖ rest
📺 🅿. ✂
Mid March-November – **M** (dinner only) 13.50 **t.** – **4 rm** ⌷ 33.50 **t.**

🏠 **Frenchgate**, 59-61 Frenchgate, DL10 7AE, ☎ 2087, 🚲 – 📺 ☎ 🅿. 🔲 AE ⓪ **VISA**
closed mid December-mid February – **M** *(closed Sunday lunch)* (lunch by arrangement)/dinner 9.50 **t.** and a la carte 🍷 2.80 – **13 rm** ⌷ 22.50/48.00 **t.** – SB (except mid May-
September) 51.50/57.50 **st.**

↑ **Whashton Springs Farm** ⌂, DL11 7JS, NW : 3 ½ m. by Ravensworth rd ☎ 2884,
« Working farm », 🚲 – ✖ 📺 🅿. ✂
closed Christmas-New Year – **M** (by arrangement) 9.00 **st.** 🍷 2.00 – **8 rm** ⌷ 21.00/32.00 **st.**
– SB (November-March) (except Christmas and New Year) 47.00/50.00 **st.**

↑ **Pottergate** without rest., 4 Pottergate, DL10 4AB, ☎ 3826 – ✖ 📺 🅿
5 rm ⌷ 12.00/22.00 **s.**

at Kirby Hill NW : 4 ½ m. by Ravensworth Rd – ✉ ☎ 0748 Richmond :

⚐ **Shoulder of Mutton Inn**, DL11 7JH, ☎ 2772 – 📺 🅿
M *(closed Sunday dinner and Monday to non-residents)* (bar lunch)/dinner a la carte
8.50/11.50 **t.** – **5 rm** ⌷ 14.00/17.00 **t.** – SB (except April-October) 48.50/51.50 **st.**

AUSTIN-ROVER Victoria Rd ☎ 2539   ⊚ ATS Reeth Rd ☎ 4182/3

RIDGEWAY Derbs. – see Sheffield (South Yorks.).

RINGWOOD Hants. **403 404** O 31 – pop. 10 941 – ECD : Monday and Thursday – ☎ 042 54
(4 and 5 fig.) or 0425 (6 fig.).

⌘ Ringwood ☎ 042 53 (Burley) 2431, NE : 4 m.

🛈 Furlong Lane Car Park ☎ 470896 (summer only).

♦London 102 – Bournemouth 11 – Salisbury 17 – ♦Southampton 20.

⚐ **Moortown Lodge**, 244 Christchurch Rd, BH24 3AS, ☎ 471404 – 📺 ☎ 🅿. 🔲 AE **VISA** ✂
closed 1 to 14 January – **M** *(closed Sunday)* (dinner only) 11.75 **t.** and a la carte 12.75 **t.**
🍷 3.50 – **6 rm** ⌷ 22.00/42.00 **t.** – SB 57.00/73.00 **st.**

at Ibsley N : 2 ½ m. on A 338 – ✉ ☎ 0425 Ringwood :

✗ **Old Beams**, Salisbury Rd, BH24 1AS, ☎ 473387, « 14C thatched cottage » – Ⓟ
M 9.40/12.00 st. ⓵ 4.05.

at Avon S : 4 m. on B 3347 – ✉ Christchurch – ☎ 0425 Bransgore :

🏨 **Tyrrells Ford** ♨, BH23 7BH, ☎ 72646, Fax 72262, ☞, park – 📺 ☎ Ⓟ – 🔬 25. 🅰 VISA
🚫
M 9.95/15.95 t. and a la carte – **16 rm** ☒ 40.00/75.00 t.

at St Leonards (Dorset) SW : 3 m. on A 31 – ✉ ☎ 0425 Ringwood :

🏨 **St. Leonards** (Lansbury), 185 Ringwood Rd, BH24 2NP, ☎ 471220, Telex 418215, Fax
480274 – ⌁ rm 📺 ☎ ₺ Ⓟ. 🅰 AE ⓪ VISA. 🚫
M 8.50/12.50 t. and a la carte – **33 rm** ☒ 53.00/63.00 t. – SB (spring and autumn) (weekends only) 72.00/82.00 st.

FIAT Salisbury Rd ☎ 476111   FORD Christchurch Rd ☎ 470707

━━━

RIPLEY Surrey 🄬 S 30 – pop. 1 903 – ECD : Wednesday – ☎ 0483 Guildford.
♦London 28 – Guildford 6.

✗✗✗ **Michels'**, 13 High St., GU23 6AQ, ☎ 224777, ☞ – 🅰 AE ⓪ VISA
closed Saturday lunch, Sunday dinner and Monday – **M** 17.50/16.00 t. and a la carte
17.50/27.50 t. ⓵ 4.00.

⓪ ATS Meadow Rd ☎ 47478

━━━

RIPON North Yorks. 🄬 P 21 – pop. 13 036 – ECD : Wednesday – ☎ 0765.
See : Cathedral★ (12C-15C).
Envir. : Fountains Abbey★★★ (ruins 12C-13C, floodlit in summer) – Studley Royal Gardens★★ and
Fountains Hall★ (17C) *AC*, SW : 3 m. – Newby Hall★ (18C) *AC* (the tapestry room★★ and gardens★
AC) SE : 3 ½ m.
🏌 Palace Rd ☎ 3640, N : 1 m. on A 6108.
🛈 Minster Rd ☎ 4625 (summer only).
♦London 222 – ♦Leeds 26 – ♦Middlesbrough 35 – York 23.

🏨 **Ripon Spa** (Best Western), Park St., HG4 2BU, ☎ 2172, Telex 57780, ☞ – 🛗 📺 ☎ ₺ Ⓟ.
🅰 AE ⓪ VISA
M 13.00/16.00 t. and a la carte ⓵ 4.00 – **40 rm** ☒ 44.00/80.00 t. – SB 76.00/88.00 st.

⌂ **Crescent Lodge** without rest., 42 North St., HG4 1EN, ☎ 2331 – 📺. 🚫
closed Christmas and New Year – **10 rm** ☒ 13.00/32.00 t.

AUSTIN-ROVER Blossom Gate ☎ 707074   ⓪ ATS Dallamires Lane ☎ 701579/701570
FORD 30 North St. ☎ 2324
VOLVO Palace Rd ☎ 2461

━━━

ROADE Northants. – pop. 2 703 – ☎ 0604.
♦London 66 – ♦Coventry 36 – Northampton 5.5.

✗ **Roadhouse**, 16 High St., NN7 2NW, ☎ 863372 – Ⓟ. 🅰 VISA
closed Saturday lunch, Sunday, Monday and 3 weeks summer – **M** 12.00 st. (lunch) and a la
carte 14.00/19.50 st. ⓵ 4.00.

━━━

ROBERTSBRIDGE East Sussex 🄬 V 31 – ☎ 0580.
♦London 49 – ♦Brighton 39 – Folkestone 44 – Maidstone 24.

✗ **Bough House**, 43 High St., TN32 5AL, ☎ 880440 – 🅰 VISA
closed Saturday lunch, Sunday dinner, Monday, 2 weeks April-May and last week August –
M 10.50/18.50 t. and a la carte 10.50/18.50 t. ⓵ 3.50.

━━━

ROCHESTER Kent 🄬 V 29 – pop. 23 840 – ECD : Wednesday – ✉ Chatham – ☎ 0634
Medway.
See : Castle★, ❄★★ (142 steps) *AC* – Cathedral★ (interior★★) – Eastgate House★ (1590) – Fort
Pitt Hill ⩶★ – Envir. : Cobham Hall (Gilt Hall★) *AC*, W : 4 m.
🛈 Eastgate Cottage, High St. ☎ 43666.
♦London 30 – ♦Dover 45 – Maidstone 8 – Margate 46.

🏨 **Bridgewood Manor**, Maidstone Rd, ME5 9AX, SE : 3 m. by A 2 on A 229 ☎ 201333, Telex
965864, Fax 201330, 🏊 – 🛗 🍴 rest 📺 ☎ ₺ Ⓟ – 🔬 150. 🅰 AE ⓪ VISA
M 12.00/15.00 st. and a la carte 15.10/24.30 st. – **94 rm** ☒ 55.00/80.00 st., **4 suites**
100.00/120.00 st. – SB (weekends only) 75.00/100.00 st.

🏨 **Crest** (Crest), Maidstone Rd, ME5 9SF, SE : 2 ½ m. by A 2 on A 229 ☎ 687111, Telex
965933, Fax 684512, ☞ – 🛗 ⌁ rm 🍴 rest 📺 ☎ ₺ Ⓟ – 🔬 120. 🅰 AE ⓪ VISA
M 10.75/14.50 t. and a la carte ⓵ 5.00 – ☒ 7.35 – **105 rm** 70.00/85.00 st. – SB 80.00/95.00 st.

AUSTIN-ROVER, JAGUAR 16 Medway St., Cha-   RENAULT Hoath Lane, Wigmore ☎ 31688
tham ☎ 41122   TOYOTA High St. ☎ 407788
FIAT, LANCIA Pier Rd, Gillingham ☎ 52333   VAUXHALL Station Rd, Strood ☎ 721021
PEUGEOT-TALBOT High St. ☎ 42231   VOLVO Wood St., Gillingham ☎ 402777
RELIANT Gundulph Rd, Chatham ☎ 41279

ROCHFORD Essex 404 W 29 – pop. 13 426 – ECD : Wednesday – ✉ ⊛ 0702 Southend-on-Sea.

♦London 43 – Southend-on-Sea 4.

🏨 **Hotel Renouf**, Bradley Way, SS4 1BU, ℰ 541334, Telex 995158, Fax 549563, 🚗 – ▤ rest 📺 ☎ 🅿. 🅰 AE ⓓ VISA
M (dinner only and lunch Sunday and Monday) 14.00/22.00 **st.** and a la carte ⬧ 4.00 – **24 rm** � 48.00/75.00 **st.**

✕✕ **Renouf's**, 1 South St., SS4 1BL, ℰ 544393 – 🅰 AE ⓓ VISA
closed Saturday lunch, Sunday, Monday, first 3 weeks January and 2 weeks June-July –
M 13.00/22.00 **st.** and a la carte 14.60/21.50 **st.** ⬧ 4.10.

ROCK Cornwall 403 F 32 – ECD : Wednesday – ✉ Wadebridge – ⊛ 020 886 Trebetherick.
🏌, 🏌 St. Enodoc ℰ 3216.
♦London 288 – Newquay 22 – ♦Plymouth 45 – Truro 30.

🏠 **St. Enodoc** 🍷, PL27 6LA, ℰ 3394, Fax 3394, ≤, 🚗, squash – 📺 ☎ 🅿. 🅰 AE VISA
M (bar lunch)/dinner 12.50 **t.** and a la carte ⬧ 2.75 – ⊏ 4.50 – **13 rm** 28.00/40.00 **st.** –
SB 60.00/74.00 **st.**

ROCKBOURNE Hants. 403 404 O 31 – see Fordingbridge.

ROCK FERRY Merseyside – ✉ Wirral – ⊛ 051 Liverpool.
♦London 212 – Chester 15 – ♦Liverpool 5.

🏠 **Yew Tree**, 58 Rock Lane West, L42 4PA, ℰ 645 4112 – 📺 🅿. 🅰 VISA 🚲
M 8.50 **st.** – **14 rm** ⊏ 18.00/38.00 **st.** – SB (weekends only) 47.00/49.00 **st.**

RODBOROUGH Glos. – see Stroud.

ROEWEN Gwynedd – see Conwy.

ROGATE West Sussex 404 R 30 – pop. 1 459 – ✉ Petersfield (Hants.) – ⊛ 073 080 (from May : 0730).
♦London 63 – ♦Brighton 42 – Guildford 29 – ♦Portsmouth 23 – ♦Southampton 36.

🏠 **Mizzards Farm** 🍷 without rest., GU31 5HS, SW : 1 m. by Harting Rd ℰ 656 (from May 821656), ≤, « 17C farmhouse », ⛱ heated, 🚗 – 🍽 📺 🅿. 🚲
closed 10 days at Christmas – **3 rm** ⊏ 24.00/36.00 **s.**

ROLLESTON-ON-DOVE Staffs. 402 403 404 P 25 – see Burton-upon-Trent.

ROMALDKIRK Durham 402 N 20 – see Barnard Castle.

ROMSEY Hants. 403 404 P 31 – pop. 14 818 – ECD : Wednesday – ⊛ 0794.
See : Abbey Church★★ (12C-13C).
Envir. : Broadlands House★ S : 1 m.
🏌 Dunwood Manor, Shootash Hill ℰ 0794 (Lockerley) 40549, SE : 4 m. on A 27.
🛈 Bus Station car park, Broadwater Rd ℰ 512987 (summer only).
♦London 82 – Bournemouth 28 – Salisbury 16 – ♦Southampton 8 – Winchester 10.

🏨 **White Horse** (T.H.F.), Market Pl., SO51 8ZJ, ℰ 512431, Fax 517485 – 🍽 rm 📺 ☎ ⅋ 🅿.
🅰 AE ⓓ VISA
M 10.00/15.00 **st.** and a la carte ⬧ 3.95 – ⊏ 7.00 – **33 rm** 59.00/74.00 **st.**

✕✕ **Old Manor House**, 21 Palmerston St., SO51 8GF, ℰ 517353 – 🅿. 🅰 VISA
closed Sunday dinner, Monday, last 3 weeks August and 24 to 31 December – **M**
18.50/27.50 **t.** ⬧ 3.75.

at Ower SW : 3 ¼ m. on A 31 – ✉ Romsey – ⊛ 0703 Southampton :

🏨 **New Forest Heathlands**, Romsey Rd, SO51 6ZJ, on A 31 ℰ 814333, Fax 812123, 🚗 –
📺 ☎ 🅿 – 🔬 200. 🅰 AE ⓓ VISA
M 11.50/14.50 **t.** and a la carte ⬧ 4.00 – **48 rm** ⊏ 57.00/90.00 **t.** – SB (weekends only)
(except Easter and Christmas) 75.00/90.00 **st.**

AUSTIN-ROVER Winchester Rd ℰ 512850
CITROEN Industrial Est., Greatbridge ℰ 830100
PEUGEOT 45-55 Winchester Hill ℰ 513185
VAUXHALL-OPEL 24 Middlebridge St. ℰ 513806

ROSEDALE ABBEY North Yorks. 402 R 20 – ✉ Pickering – ⊛ 075 15 Lastingham.
♦London 247 – ♦Middlesbrough 27 – Scarborough 25 – York 36.

🏠 **Milburn Arms**, YO18 8RA, ℰ 312, 🚗 – 🍽 rest 📺 ☎ 🅿. 🅰 VISA
M (bar lunch)/dinner a la carte 10.15/15.40 **t.** ⬧ 2.70 – **12 rm** ⊏ 37.50/69.00 **t.** – SB (October-April) 45.00/65.00 **st.**

🏠 **Sevenford House** 🍷 without rest., Thorgill, YO18 8SE, NW : ¾ m. ℰ 283, 🚗 – 🍽 🅿
4 rm ⊏ 17.00/35.00 **st.**

ROSSETT (YR ORSEDD) Clwyd **402** **403** L 24 – pop. 2 323 – ✆ 0244.

♦London 203 – Chester 8 – Shrewsbury 39.

🏨 **Llyndir Hall** ⤵, Llyndir Lane, LL12 0AY, NE : ¾ m. by B 5445 ℰ 571648, Fax 571648, « Strawberry Gothic country house », ☞ – ⇆ rest 📺 ☎ 🅿. 🅰 🆀 🔘 *VISA* ⤫
M 11.50/20.00 **st.** and a la carte – ⌑ 4.50 – **7 rm** 55.00/160.00 **t.** – SB (except Christmas and New Year) 98.00 **st.**

ROSSINGTON South Yorks. **402** **403** **404** Q 23 – see Doncaster.

ROSS-ON-WYE Heref. and Worc. **403** **404** M 28 – pop. 8 281 – ECD : Wednesday – ✆ 0989.
Envir. : Goodrich (Castle★ : ruins 12C-14C) AC, SW : 3 ½ m.

🛈 20 Broad St. ℰ 62768.

♦London 118 – Gloucester 15 – Hereford 15 – Newport 35.

🏨 **Chase**, Gloucester Rd, HR9 5LH, on A 40 ℰ 763161, Fax 768330, ☞ – 📺 ☎ 🅿 – 🏛 200. ⤫
40 rm.

🏨 **Royal** (T.H.F.), Palace Pound, Royal Par., HR9 5HZ, ℰ 65105, Fax 768058, ≼, ☞ – ⇆ rm 📺 ☎ 🅿 – 🏛 80
M 9.75/14.25 **st.** and a la carte ◊ 3.95 – **40 rm**.

🏠 **Chasedale**, Walford Rd, HR9 5PQ, ℰ 62423, ☞ – 📺 ☎ 🅿. 🅰 🔘 *VISA*
M 7.75/15.00 **st.** ◊ 2.60 – **11 rm** ⌑ 28.50/45.00 **st.** – SB 50.50/63.00 **st.**

↑ **Woodlands** ⤵ without rest., HR9 6QJ, W : 2 m. by A 49 on Hoarwithy Rd ℰ 62972, ≼, ☞, park, ⚒ – ⇆ 📺 🅿. ⤫
closed 15 December-31 January – **3 rm** ⌑ 20.00/34.00 **st.**

↑ **Sunnymount** ⤵, Ryefield Rd, off Gloucester Rd (A 40), HR9 5LU, ℰ 63880 – 🅿. 🅰 *VISA*
closed 21 December-1 January – **M** 9.50 **st.** ◊ 3.00 – **6 rm** ⌑ 16.00/40.50 **st.** – SB (November-May) (except Bank Holidays) 40.00/47.00 **st.**

at Glewstone SW : 3 ¼ m. by A 40 – ✉ Ross-on-Wye – ✆ 098 984 Llangarron :

🏠 **Glewstone Court** ⤵, HR9 6AW, ℰ 367, ≼, ☞ – 🅿. 🅰 🅰 *VISA*
closed 25 and 26 December – **M** (bar lunch Monday to Saturday)/dinner 15.00 **st.** ◊ 2.50 – **6 rm** ⌑ 36.00/52.00 **st.** – SB (except New Year and Bank Holidays) 73.00/80.00 **st.**

at Pencraig SW : 3 ¾ m. on A 40 – ✉ Ross-on-Wye – ✆ 098 984 Llangarron :

🏠 **Pencraig Court**, HR9 6HR, ℰ 306, ☞ – 🅿. 🅰 🅰 🔘 *VISA*. ⤫
April-December – **M** (dinner only) 12.00 **st.** and a la carte ◊ 2.95 – **11 rm** ⌑ 32.00/44.00 **st.** – SB 60.00/64.00 **st.**

at Peterstow W : 2 ½ m. on A 49 – ✉ Ross-on-Wye – ✆ 098 987 Harewood End :

🏨 **Pengethley Manor** (Best Western) ⤵, HR9 6LL, NW : 1 ½ m. on A 49 ℰ 211, Fax 238, ≼, « Georgian country manor », ⚊ heated, ☞, park – 📺 ☎ 🅿 – 🏛 35. 🅰 🅰 🔘 *VISA*
M 12.50/20.00 **st.** and a la carte ◊ 5.50 – **19 rm** ⌑ 65.00/110.00 **st.**, **3 suites** 160.00 **st.** – SB 120.00/180.00 **st.**

AUSTIN-ROVER Cantilupe Rd ℰ 62400
PEUGEOT-TALBOT High St. ℰ 62447
RENAULT Overross St. ℰ 63666

VW-AUDI Whitchurch ℰ 0600 (Monmouth) 890235

◍ ATS Ind Est., Alton Rd ℰ 64638

ROSTHWAITE Cumbria **402** K 20 – see Keswick.

ROTHAY BRIDGE Cumbria – see Ambleside.

ROTHBURY Northumb. **401** **402** O 18 – pop. 1 694 – ECD : Wednesday – ✉ Morpeth – ✆ 0669.

🛈 Old Race Course, S : off B 6342 ℰ 20718.

♦London 311 – ♦Edinburgh 84 – ♦Newcastle-upon-Tyne 29.

↑ **Orchard**, High St., NE65 7TL, ℰ 20684, ☞ – 📺. ⤫
March-November – **M** 9.50 **t.** ◊ 3.50 – **6 rm** ⌑ 17.00/34.00 **t.**

ROTHERHAM South Yorks. **402** **403** **404** P 23 – pop. 122 374 – ECD : Thursday – ✆ 0709.

🛇 Thrybergh Park ℰ 850812, E : 3 m. – 🛇 Sitwell Park, Shrogs Wood Rd ℰ 541046, E : 2 ½ m. – 🛇 Grange Park, Upper Wortley Rd ℰ 559497, NW : 3 m. by A 629 – 🛇 Phoenix, Pavilion Lane, Brinsworth ℰ 363864.

🛈 Central Library and Arts Centre, Walker Pl. ℰ 382121 ext 3611/3612.

♦London 166 – ♦Kingston-upon-Hull 61 – ♦Leeds 36 – ♦Sheffield 6.

🏨 **Rotherham Moat House** (Q.M.H.), 102-104 Moorgate Rd, S60 2BG, ℰ 364902, Telex 547810, Fax 368960 – 📳 ⇆ rm ▤ rest 📺 ☎ 🅿 – 🏛 100. 🅰 🅰 🔘 *VISA*
M (closed Saturday lunch) 7.50/13.50 **st.** – ⌑ 5.75 – **81 rm** 55.00/110.00 **st.** – SB (weekends only) 71.00 **st.**

ROTHERHAM

AUDI Brampton Rd ✆ 873366
AUSTIN-ROVER Doncaster Rd ✆ 373991
CITROEN 106 Barnsley Rd, Goldthorpe ✆ 893864
FIAT 126 Fitzwilliam Rd ✆ 361666
FORD Sheffield Rd ✆ 860151
LANCIA Wortley Rd ✆ 551155
MAZDA West Bawtry Rd, Brinsworth ✆ 364204
PEUGEOT-TALBOT 132-138 Fitzwilliam Rd ✆ 382213

TOYOTA 7-9 Canklow Rd ✆ 820681
VAUXHALL-OPEL 128 Wellgate ✆ 828484
VW Bawtry Rd. Wickersley ✆ 0709 (Wickersley) 543462
VW-AUDI Brampton Rd. Wath ✆ 873366

ⓦ ATS Eastwood Works. Fitzwilliam Rd ✆ 371556/372391

ROTHERWICK Hants – see Basingstoke.

ROTHLEY Leics. 402 403 404 Q 25 – see Leicester.

ROTTINGDEAN East Sussex 404 T 31 – pop. 10 888 (inc. Saltdean) – ECD : Wednesday – ⊠ ✆ 0273 Brighton.

◆London 58 – ◆Brighton 4 – Lewes 9 – Newhaven 5.

🏰 **Rottingdean Olde Place,** High St., BN2 7HE, ✆ 301051, Fax 300021 – TV ☎ Ⓟ
M *(closed Sunday dinner)* a la carte 15.45/24.60 t. 🍷 4.50 – **10 rm** ☲ 50.00/80.00 st.

🏠 **Braemar** without rest., Steyning Rd, BN2 7GA, ✆ 304263, 🚗
15 rm ☲ 12.00/26.00 t.

ROUGHAM GREEN Suffolk – see Bury St. Edmunds.

ROUSDON Devon 403 L 31 – see Lyme Regis.

ROWSLEY Derbs. 402 403 404 P 24 – pop. 200 – ECD : Thursday – ⊠ Matlock – ✆ 0629 Matlock.

◆London 157 – Derby 23 – ◆Manchester 40 – ◆Nottingham 30.

🏨 **Peacock** (Embassy), Bakewell Rd, DE4 2EB, ✆ 733518, « 17C stone house with antiques »,
🐟, 🚗 – ⇔ rm TV ☎ Ⓟ. 🐾 – **20 rm**.

ROWTON Cheshire 402 403 L 24 – see Chester.

ROYAL LEAMINGTON SPA Warw. 403 404 P 27 – pop. 56 552 – ECD : Monday and Thursday – ✆ 0926.

▸18 Newbold-Comyn, Newbold Terrace East ✆ 21157, plan of Warwick – Z – ▸18 Leamington and Country, Golf Lane, Whitnash ✆ 25961 by A 452 V.

🛈 Jephson Lodge. The Parade ✆ 311470.

◆London 99 – ◆Birmingham 23 – ◆Coventry 9 – Warwick 3.

Plan opposite

🏨 **Manor House** (T.H.F.), Avenue Rd, CV31 3NJ, ✆ 423251, Fax 425933 – 🛗 ⇔ rm TV ☎ Ⓟ –
🪑 100. 🔻 AE ⓪ VISA
M a la carte 14.25/23.25 st. – ☲ 7.00 – **53 rm**.
V i

🏨 **Inchfield,** 64 Upper Holly Walk, CV32 4JL, ✆ 883777, Fax 316686, 🚗 – TV ☎ Ⓟ – 🪑 40.
🔻 AE VISA 🐾
M *(closed Saturday lunch)* 15.00/20.00 t. and a la carte 🍷 3.00 – **22 rm** ☲ 55.00/90.00 t. –
SB (weekends only) 120.00/190.00 st.
U o

🏨 **Angel,** 143 Regent St., CV32 4NZ, ✆ 881296, Fax 881296 – 🛗 TV ☎ Ⓟ. 🔻 AE VISA 🐾
M *(closed Saturday lunch and Sunday dinner)* 7.95/9.95 t. and a la carte 🍷 3.25 – **37 rm**
☲ 42.50/55.00 t.
U c

🏨 **Regent** (Best Western), 77 The Parade, CV32 4AX, ✆ 427231, Telex 311715, Fax 450728 –
🛗 TV ☎ Ⓟ – 🪑 250. 🔻 AE ⓪ VISA
M 9.25/12.85 t. and a la carte 🍷 4.25 – **78 rm** ☲ 50.00/78.00 t., **2 suites** 123.00 t. –
SB 61.00/85.00 st.
V r

🏠 **Lansdowne,** 87 Clarendon St., CV32 4PF, ✆ 450505 – TV ☎ Ⓟ. 🔻 VISA 🐾
M *(closed Sunday to non-residents)* (dinner only) 12.95 st. 🍷 3.45 – **15 rm** ☲ 24.95/53.90 t.
– SB (except Christmas) 57.90/69.90 st.
U a

🏠 **Adams,** 22 Avenue Rd, CV31 3PQ, ✆ 450742, 🚗 – ⇔ rm TV ☎ Ⓟ. 🔻 AE ⓪ VISA 🐾
M *(closed Saturday, Sunday and Bank Holidays)* (bar lunch)/dinner 15.00 t. and a la carte
🍷 4.90 – **11 rm** ☲ 29.00/46.00 t. – SB (except January, July and August) (weekends only)
70.00/95.00 st.
V n

🏠 **Beech Lodge,** 28 Warwick New Rd, CV32 5JJ, ✆ 422227 – TV ☎ Ⓟ. 🔻 AE VISA
closed 23 December-3 January – M *(closed lunch Monday to Thursday)* (residents only
Sunday dinner)/dinner 12.50 t. – **12 rm** ☲ 27.00/52.00 t. – SB (weekends only) 30.00 st.
plan of Warwick   Z s

🏠 **Abbacourt,** 40 Kenilworth Rd, CV32 6JF, ✆ 451755, 🚗 – TV ☎ Ⓟ. 🔻 AE ⓪ VISA
M *(closed Sunday lunch)* a la carte 8.95/21.40 t. 🍷 3.50 – **26 rm** ☲ 23.00/65.00 t.
plan of Warwick   Z r

🏠 **Berni Royal** (B.C.B.), Kenilworth Rd, CV32 5TE, ✆ 883561 – 🛗 TV ☎ Ⓟ. 🔻 AE ⓪ VISA 🐾
M (grill rest.) a la carte 6.55/15.05 t. – **31 rm** ☲ 27.00/78.00 t.
U x

ROYAL
LEAMINGTON SPA

Parade . . . . UV
Regent Street . . . . UV
Royal Priors Shopping Centre . . . U
Warwick Street . . . . U

Adelaïde Road V
Avenue Road . . . . V 2
Bath Street . . . . V 3
Beauchamp Avenue . . . . U
Beauchamp Hill . . . . U 4
Binswood Street . . . . U 6
Brandon Parade . . . . U 10
Church Hill . . . . UV 16
Clarendon Avenue . . . . U
Clarendon Place . . . . U 18
Dale Street . . . . UV
Hamilton Terrace . . . . V 21
High Street . . . . V 22
Holly Walk . . . . UV
Kenilworth Road . . . . U
Leam Terrace V
Leicester Street . . . . U
Lillington Avenue . . . . U
Lillington Road . . . . U
Lower Avenue . . . . V 28
Newbold Terrace . . . . V 30
Northumberland Road . . . . U 33
Old Warwick Road . . . . V 37
Priory Terrace V
Radford Road V
Regent Grove . . . . UV 40
Rugby Road . . . . U
Russell Terrace V
Spencer Street . . . . V 44
Tachbrook Road . . . . V 47
Victoria Terrace . . . . V 49
Willes Road . . . . UV

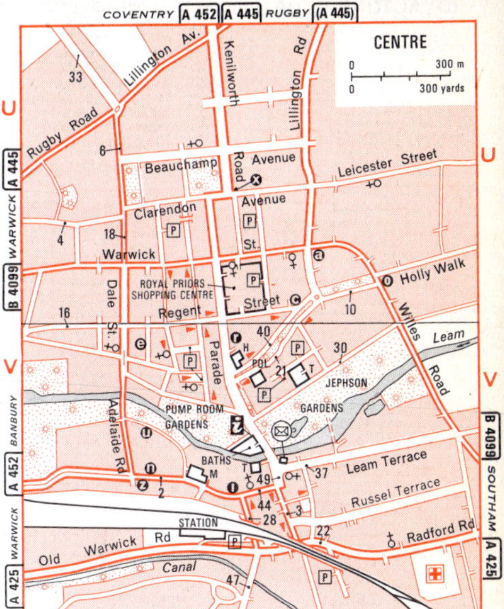

↑ **Flowerdale House** without rest., 58 Warwick New Rd, CV32 6AA, ☎ 426002, 🚗 – ✈ · plan of Warwick Z c
📺 🅿 . 🔄 VISA 🎨
6 rm ☕ 19.00/36.00 s.

↑ **Coverdale** without rest., 8 Portland St., CV32 5HE, ☎ 330400 – 📺 ☎ V e
8 rm ☕ 25.00/35.00 t.

↑ **York House,** 9 York Rd, CV31 3PR, ☎ 424671 – ✈ 📺 ☎ 🅿 V u
closed 23 December-1 January – **M** 10.00 t. 🍷 2.75 – **8 rm** ☕ 15.00/40.00 st.

↑ **Buckland Lodge,** 35 Avenue Rd, CV31 3PG, ☎ 423843 – ✈ rest 📺 ☎ 🅿 . 🔄 AE ⓪ VISA
closed Christmas and New Year – **M** (by arrangement) 7.50 st. 🍷 3.00 – **10 rm** V z
☕ 17.00/37.00 st.

XXX ❀ **Mallory Court** 🦢 with rm, Harbury Lane, Bishop's Tachbrook, CV33 9QB, S : 2 ¼ m.
by B 4087 (Tachbrook Rd) ☎ 330214, Telex 317294, Fax 451714, ≤, 🏊, 🚗, park, 🎿, squash
– 📺 ☎ 🚗 🅿 . 🔄 VISA 🎨 · plan of Warwick Z
M (booking essential) 19.50/36.00 **st.** 🍷 4.50 – ☕ 8.50 – **9 rm** 95.00/165.00 **st.**, **1 suite** (dinner included) 265.00 **st.**
Spec. Mousseline of lobster with champagne sauce, Roast saddle and braised leg of rabbit, grain mustard and
tarragon sauces, Passion fruit soufflé with raspberry sorbet.

AUDI-VW Dormer Pl. ☎ 336511
AUSTIN-ROVER Station Approach ☎ 427156
FORD Sydenham Drive ☎ 314466
JAGUAR Rugby Rd ☎ 833181
MITSUBISHI Wood St. ☎ 424681
RENAULT Russell St. ☎ 421171

SAAB Lime Av. ☎ 423221
SKODA, FORD, VAUXHALL 4 Court St. ☎ 426011
VAUXHALL-OPEL Old Warwick Rd ☎ 420861

Ⓜ ATS 52-54 Morton St. ☎ 339643

ROYAL TUNBRIDGE WELLS Kent 404 U 30 – pop. 57 699 – ECD : Wednesday – ✆ 0892.
See : The Pantiles★ (promenade 18C) B – Town Hall Museum (wood-mosaic articles★) B M.
Envir. : Scotney Castle Gardens (trees★, Bastion view★) AC, SE : 8 m. by B 2169 A.
🖸 Town Hall ☎ 26121.
♦London 36 – ♦Brighton 33 – Folkestone 46 – Hastings 27 – Maidstone 18.

Plan on next page

🏨 **Spa** (Best Western), Mount Ephraim, TN4 8XJ, ☎ 20331, Telex 957188, Fax 510575, ≤, 🔄,
🚗, park, 🎿 – 📳 📺 ☎ 🅿 🅿 – 🛄 300. 🔄 AE ⓪ VISA 🎨 A v
M 15.00/18.00 t. – ☕ 6.50 – **72 rm** 55.00/73.00 st., **4 suites** 80.00/95.00 st. – SB (weekends only) 50.00 st.

🏨 **Royal Wells Inn,** Mount Ephraim, TN4 8BE, ☎ 511188, Fax 511908 – 📳 🖿 📺 ☎ 🅿 . 🔄
AE ⓪ VISA B r
closed 25-26 December, 1 January, 13 April and Bank Holidays – **M** 10.75/25.00 st. and a la
carte 🍷 3.60 – **24 rm** ☕ 47.00/67.00 st. – SB (weekends only) 80.00/90.00 st.

🏨 **Russell,** 80 London Rd, TN1 1DZ, ☎ 544833, Telex 95177, Fax 515846 – ✈ rm 📺 ☎ 🅿 .
🔄 AE ⓪ VISA 🎨 B a
M (bar lunch)/dinner 16.00 t. 🍷 5.00 – **21 rm** ☕ 54.00/66.00 t. – SB 75.00/110.00 st.

ROYAL TUNBRIDGE WELLS

Calverley Road.................... **B**
High Street...................... **B** 14
Mount Pleasant Road............. **B** 25
Pantiles (The).................. **B** 26

Benhall Mill Road .... **A** 3
Bishop's Down .... **A** 4
Calverley Park Gardens .... **B** 7

Clarence Road.......... **B** 8
Crescent Road.......... **B** 9
Fir Tree Road .... **A** 10
Grosvenor Road......... **B** 12
Hall's Hole Road ...... **A** 13
High Rocks Lane .... **A** 16
Hungershall Park Road ... **A** 17
Lansdowne Road .... **B** 18
Lower Green Road ...... **A** 20
Major York's Road ..... **A** 22

Mount Ephraim.......... **A** 23
Mount Ephraim Road..... **B** 24
Prospect Road.......... **A** 27
Rusthall Road .... **A** 28
St. John's Road........ **B** 29
Tea Garden Lane .... **A** 30
Upper Grosvenor Road ... **B** 31
Vale Road.............. **B** 33
Victoria Road.......... **B** 34
Warwick Park........... **B** 35

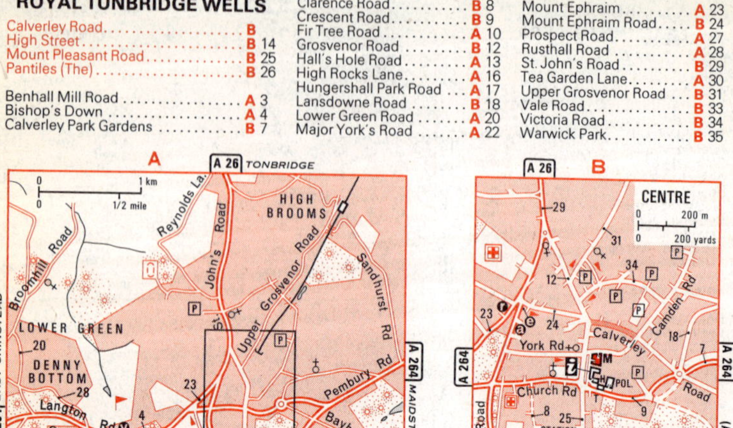

XXX **Thackeray's House**, 85 London Rd, TN1 1EA, ☎ 511921, « Tastefully converted Regency town house », 🦐 – ▨ VISA
B e
closed Sunday and Monday – **M** 15.75/26.50 **st.** ⌀ 4.50.

XX **Cheevers**, 56 High St., TN1 1XF, ☎ 545524 – ▨ VISA
B c
closed Sunday, Monday, 2 weeks Easter, 1 week September and 1 week Christmas – **M** 18.00 **t.** (dinner) and a la carte 11.90/16.20 **t.** ⌀ 2.90.

XX **Eglantine**, 65 High St., TN1 1XX, ☎ 24957 – ▨ AE VISA
B s
closed Sunday, Monday, 2 weeks January and 2 weeks September – **M** 10.00/18.00 **t.** ⌀ 3.60.

X **Xian**, 54 High St., TN1 1XF, ☎ 22930, Chinese rest. – ▨ AE ⓞ VISA
B c
closed Sunday, 1 week Easter, 25 to 27 December and Bank Holidays – **M** 6.50/13.00 **t.** and a la carte 12.65/18.30 **t.** ⌀ 3.00.

at Speldhurst NW : 3 ½ m. by A 26 – **A** – ✉ Royal Tunbridge Wells – ☎ 089 286 Langton :

XX **George and Dragon Inn**, Barden Rd, TN3 0NN, ☎ 3125, « 13C inn » – **P**. ▨ AE ⓞ VISA
closed Saturday lunch, Sunday dinner and Monday – **M** 9.00/16.75 **t.** and a la carte 12.00/17.45 **t.** ⌀ 3.15.

BMW St. John's Rd ☎ 39355
COLT, RELIANT Grosvenor Rd ☎ 27174
FORD Commercial Rd, Paddock Wood ☎ (089 283) Paddock Wood 6388

LANCIA 319 St. Johns Rd ☎ 511522
RENAULT Langton Rd ☎ 39466

RUAN-HIGH-LANES Cornwall **403** F 33 – see Veryan.

RUCKHALL Heref. and Worc. – see Hereford.

RUGBY Warw. 408 404 Q 26 – pop. 59 039 – ECD : Wednesday – ☎ 0788.
Envir. : Stanford-on-Avon (castle 17C : park★ *AC*) NE : 5 m.
🛈 Public Library, St. Matthew's St. ℰ 71813/535348.
♦London 88 – ♦Birmingham 33 – ♦Leicester 21 – Northampton 20 – Warwick 17.

🏨 **Grosvenor**, Clifton Rd, CV21 3QQ, ℰ 535686, Fax 541297 – 📺 ☎ 🅿 – 🎇 60. 🔼 🆎 ⓞ **VISA**
   M *(closed Saturday lunch)* 8.95/21.80 **t.** and a la carte ⓘ 3.95 – **16 rm** ⊆ 55.00/75.00 **t.** – SB (weekends only) 60.00/80.00 **st.**

🏨 **Carlton**, 130 Railway Terr., CV21 3HE, ℰ 543076, Fax 546091 – 📺 ☎ 🅿. 🔼 🆎 **VISA**
   closed 1 week Christmas – **M** *(closed Saturday lunch, Sunday dinner and Bank Holidays)* 8.00/10.50 **t.** and a la carte ⓘ 3.65 – **16 rm** ⊆ 39.00/47.00 **t.**

at Kilsby SE : 6 ¼ m. by A 428 on A 5 – ✉ ☎ 0788 Rugby :

🍴🍴 **Hunt House**, Main Rd, CV23 8XR, ℰ 823282, 🚗 – 🅿. 🔼 **VISA**
   closed Sunday and Monday – **M** (dinner only) 16.50 **t.** ⓘ 4.25.

at Crick SE : 6 m. on A 428 – ✉ ☎ 0788 Crick :

🏰 **Post House** (T.H.F.), NN6 7XR, W : ½ m. on A 428 ℰ 822101, Telex 311107, Fax 823955 – ⇥ rm 📺 ☎ 🅿 – 🎇 220. 🔼 🆎 ⓞ **VISA**
   M *(closed Saturday lunch)* 11.00/15.00 **st.** and a la carte ⓘ 3.95 – ⊆ 7.00 – **96 rm** 65.00/83.00 **st.** – SB (weekends only) (except Christmas and New Year) 70.00/80.00 **st.**

at West Haddon (Northants.) SE : 10 m. on A 428 – ✉ ☎ 078 887 West Haddon :

🏨 **Pytchley**, 23 High St., NN6 7AP, ℰ 426, 🚗 – 📺 ☎ 🅿. 🔼 🆎 ⓞ **VISA** 🙅
   M *(closed Sunday dinner)* 9.95/16.95 **t.** and a la carte ⓘ 4.50 – **17 rm** ⊆ 45.00/55.00 **t.**

at Stretton Under Fosse NW : 7 ½ m. by A 426 and B 4112 on A 427 – ✉ ☎ 0788 Rugby :

🏨 **Ashton Lodge** ⚸, CV23 0PJ, N : 1 m. by A 427 on B 4112 ℰ 832278, 🚗 – 📺 ☎ 🅿. 🔼 🆎 ⓞ **VISA**
   M *(closed Sunday, Christmas-New Year and Bank Holidays)* (dinner only) 16.50 **t.** ⓘ 2.50 – **11 rm** ⊆ 21.00/37.00 **t.**

CITROEN 50 Albert St. ℰ 73671
HONDA Leicester Rd ℰ 60333
PEUGEOT-TALBOT Leicester Rd ℰ 62731

ATS 73 Bath St. ℰ 74705

RUGELEY Staffs. 402 408 404 O 25 – pop. 23 751 – ECD : Wednesday – ☎ 088 94 (4 and 5 fig.) or 0889 (6 fig.).
♦London 134 – ♦Birmingham 31 – Derby 29 – ♦Stoke-on-Trent 22.

🏨 **Travelodge** without rest., Western Springs Rd, WS15 2AS, (at junction A 51 and A 460) ℰ 70096 – 📺 ♿ 🅿. 🔼 🆎 **VISA**
   32 rm 21.50/27.00 **t.**

RUNCORN Cheshire 402 408 L 23 – pop. 63 995 – ECD : Wednesday – ☎ 092 85 (5 fig.) or 0928 (6 fig.) – 🏌 Dundalk Rd ℰ 051 (Liverpool) 424 6230.
🛈 57-61 Church St. ℰ 76776 and 69656.
♦London 202 – ♦Liverpool 14 – ♦Manchester 29.

🏨 **Crest** (Crest), Wood Lane, Beechwood, WA7 3HA, SE : ½ m. off junction 12 of M 56 ℰ 714000, Telex 627426, Fax 714611, 🔼 – 🛗 ⇥ rm 📺 ☎ 🅿 – 🎇 500. 🔼 🆎 ⓞ **VISA**
   M *(closed Saturday lunch)* 10.50/15.50 **st.** and a la carte – ⊆ 7.75 – **127 rm** 72.00/98.00 **st.** – SB (weekends only) (except July and August) 94.00/108.00 **st.**

AUSTIN-ROVER Balfour St. ℰ 72271
FORD Victoria Rd ℰ 74333
MAZDA Picow Farm Rd ℰ 63099

ATS Sandy Lane, Weston Point ℰ 67715/6

RUSHLAKE GREEN East Sussex 404 U 31 – ✉ Heathfield – ☎ 0435.
♦London 54 – ♦Brighton 26 – Eastbourne 13.

🏨 **Stone House** ⚸, TN21 9QJ, ℰ 830553, « Part 14C and part Georgian country house, antiques », 🎣, 🚗, park – 📺 ☎ 🅿
   closed 19 December-19 January and 2 weeks August-September – **M** (lunch by arrangement)(residents only)/dinner 22.95 **t.** ⓘ 4.00 – **7 rm** ⊆ 50.00/150.00 **t.**

RUSPER West Sussex 404 T 30 – pop. 2 678 – ☎ 029 384.
♦London 30 – ♦Brighton 35 – Horsham 6.

🏨 **Ghyll Manor** (T.H.F.), High St., RH12 4PX, ℰ 871571, Telex 877557, Fax 871419, « Part Elizabethan house », 🏊 heated, 🚗, park, 🍴 – 📺 ☎ 🅿 – 🎇 80. 🔼 🆎 ⓞ **VISA**
   M 14.50/19.00 **st.** and a la carte ⓘ 4.75 – ⊆ 7.50 – **25 rm** 72.00/90.00 **st.**, **3 suites** 125.00/135.00 **st.** – SB 108.00/116.00 **st.**

RUTHIN (RHUTHUN) Clwyd 402 408 K 24 – pop. 4 417 – ECD : Thursday – ☎ 082 42.
See : Church★ – 🏌 Pwllglas ℰ 4658, S : 2 ½ m.
🛈 Ruthin Craft Centre ℰ 3992.
♦London 210 – Birkenhead 31 – Chester 23 – Shrewsbury 46.

🏰 **Ruthin Castle** (Best Western) 🐾, Corwen Rd, LL15 2NU, ℰ 2664, Telex 61169, Fax 5978, ≼, « Reconstructed medieval castle », 🐾, 🍴, park – 🛗 📺 ☎ 🅿. 🔊 AE ⓪ VISA 🐾
  M (bar lunch Monday to Saturday)/dinner 12.95 t. and a la carte – **58 rm** ☲ 39.00/90.00 t. – SB 69.00/86.00 st.

🏰 **Castle**, St. Peters Sq., LL15 1AA, ℰ 2479, Telex 617074 – 📺 ☎ 🅿 – 🔥 40. 🔊 AE ⓪ VISA
  M (bar lunch)/dinner 14.00 t. and a la carte ▮2.50 – **25 rm** ☲ 26.00/60.00 t. – SB 60.00/65.00 st.

XX **Llanbedr Hall,** Llanbedr Hall Estate, LL15 1YA, NE : 1 ½ m. by A 494 off B 5429 ℰ 4204 – 🅿. 🔊 VISA
  closed Sunday dinner, Monday, 3 weeks January and Bank Holidays – M 10.00/18.00 t. ▮3.00.

CITROEN Well St. ℰ 2645

RYARSH Kent – see Wrotham Heath.

RYDAL Cumbria 🔢 L 20 – see Ambleside.

RYE East Sussex 🔢 W 31 – pop. 4 127 – ECD : Tuesday – ✆ 0797.
See : Old Town★★ (chiefly : Mermaid Street) – Ypres Tower ≼★.
Envir. : Winchelsea★ (Church of St. Thomas the Martyr★ 1283 : Tombs★★ 12C) SW : 3 m. – Small Hythe (Ellen Terry's House★ *AC*) N : 7 ½ m.
🛈 48 Cinque Ports St. ℰ 222293.
♦London 61 – ♦Brighton 49 – Folkestone 27 – Maidstone 33.

🏨 **George** (T.H.F.), High St., TN31 7JP, ℰ 222114 – ⇆ rm 📺 ☎ 🅿 – 🔥 70. 🔊 AE ⓪ VISA
  M 8.95/11.95 st. and a la carte ▮3.25 – ☲ 7.00 – **22 rm** 56.00/81.00 st. – SB 88.00/96.00 st.

🏨 **Mermaid,** Mermaid St., TN31 7EU, ℰ 223065, Group Telex 957141, « 15C inn » – ☎ 🅿. 🔊 AE ⓪ VISA 🐾
  M 11.50/13.50 t. and a la carte ▮4.00 – **28 rm** ☲ 44.00/75.00 t. – SB (except Christmas and Bank Holidays) 84.00/88.00 st.

⌂ **Old Vicarage** without rest., 66 Church Sq., TN31 7HF, ℰ 222119, 🍴 – ⇆ 📺. 🐾
  closed Christmas – **5 rm** ☲ 24.00/42.00 st.

⌂ **Jeake's House** without rest., Mermaid St., TN31 7ET, ℰ 222828 – 📺
  9 rm ☲ 17.00/42.00 st.

XX **Flushing Inn,** Market St., TN31 7LA, ℰ 223292, Seafood, « 15C inn with 16C mural » – ⇆. 🔊 AE ⓪ VISA
  closed Monday dinner, Tuesday, first 2 weeks January and 2 weeks June – M 11.00/19.50 t. and a la carte 11.70/26.40 t. ▮4.30.

X **Landgate Bistro,** 5-6 Landgate, TN31 7LH, ℰ 222829 – 🔊 AE ⓪ VISA
  closed Sunday, Monday, 2 weeks June, 1 week October and 1 week Christmas – M (dinner only) a la carte 11.90/16.90 st. ▮2.75.

  at Playden N : 1 m. on A 268 – ✉ ✆ 0797 Rye :

🏨 **Playden Oasts,** Peasmarsh Rd, TN31 7UL, on A 268 ℰ 223502, 🍴 – 📺 ☎ 🅿. 🔊 AE ⓪ VISA
  M 7.95 t. (lunch) and a la carte – **8 rm** ☲ 25.00/56.00 t. – SB 62.00/72.00 st.

  at Stone-in-Oxney (Kent) N : 6 ½ m. by A 268 off B 2082 – ✉ Tenterden – ✆ 023 383 Appledore :

⌂ **Tighe Farm** 🐾 without rest., Military Canal Rd, TN30 7JU, S : ¾ m. ℰ 251, ≼, « 17C farmhouse », 🍴, park – 🅿. 🐾
  March-November – **3 rm** ☲ 26.00 s.

  at Udimore W : 2 ¾ m. on B 2089 – ✉ ✆ 0797 Rye :

🏛 **Hammonds Country** 🐾, B 2089 Udimore Rd, TN31 6AJ, ℰ 223167, ≼, « Gardens », ⌇ heated, park, ✕ – ⇆ rest 📺 🅿. 🔊 VISA 🐾
  M (*closed dinner Sunday to Wednesday to non-residents and Monday*) a la carte 9.40/15.75 t. – **10 rm** ☲ 31.00/72.00 t.

  at Rye Foreign NW : 2 m. on A 268 – ✉ Rye – ✆ 079 78 Iden :

🏛 **Broomhill Lodge,** TN31 7UN, on A 268 ℰ 421, 🍴 – 📺 ☎ 🅿. 🔊 VISA 🐾
  closed February – M (bar lunch)/dinner 11.95 st. ▮2.95 – **12 rm** ☲ 37.00/68.00 st. – SB (except Easter and Christmas) 69.00/78.00 t.

  at Peasmarsh NW : 4 m. on A 268 – ✉ Rye – ✆ 079 721 Peasmarsh :

🏨 **Flackley Ash** (Best Western), London Rd, TN31 6YH, ℰ 651, Telex 957210, Fax 510, 🔊, 🍴 – 📺 ☎ 🅿. 🔊 AE ⓪ VISA
  M 7.95/13.50 st. and a la carte ▮3.95 – **30 rm** ☲ 49.50/95.00 st., **2 suites** – SB (except Christmas and New Year) 79.00/89.00 st.

AUSTIN-ROVER, LAND-ROVER, RANGE-ROVER Fishmarket Rd ℰ 223334

RYE FOREIGN East Sussex – see Rye.

SAFFRON WALDEN Essex **404** U 27 – pop. 11 879 – ECD : Thursday – ☎ 0799.

See : Parish Church★ (Perpendicular) – Audley End House★ (Jacobean : interior★★) *AC*.

🛈 Corn Exchange, Market Sq. ☎ 24282.

◆London 46 – ◆Cambridge 15 – Chelmsford 25.

🏨 **Saffron,** 10-18 High St., CB10 1AY, ☎ 22676 – TV ☎ P – 🍴 40. 🅰 VISA
M *(closed Saturday lunch and Sunday)* 13.95 **t.** and a la carte 🍷 2.90 – ☕ 3.00 – **21 rm** 25.00/55.00 **t.** – SB (weekends only) 66.40/70.60 **st.**

✕ **Staircase,** 21 High St., CB10 1AT, ☎ 22226 – 🅰 VISA
M a la carte 11.95/23.20 **t.**

AUSTIN-ROVER 66 High St. ☎ 23597   ⊚ ATS Station Rd ☎ 21426/21001
RENAULT High St. ☎ 27909
VAUXHALL-OPEL 13-15 Station St. ☎ 23238

ST. AGNES Cornwall **403** E 33 The West Country G. – pop. 2 421 – ECD : Wednesday – ☎ 087 255.

See : St. Agnes Beacon★★ (❄★★).

◆London 302 – Newquay 12 – Penzance 26 – Truro 9.

🏖 **Trevaunance Point** ⑤, Quay Rd, Trevaunance Cove, TR5 0RZ, ☎ 3235, ≤ bay and cliffs, 🛥 – TV ☎ P. 🅰 AE ⑩ VISA
M 8.25/14.00 **t.** and a la carte 🍷 6.95 – **8 rm** ☕ 44.00/66.00 **t.**

↑ **Sunholme** ⑤, Goonvrea Rd, Goonvrea, TR5 0NW, SW : 1 m. by B 3277 ☎ 2318, ≤, 🛥 – ⇥ rest ☎ P. 🅰 VISA
March-October – **M** 8.00 **st.** 🍷 3.20 – **10 rm** ☕ 18.50/37.00 **st.**

at Mithian E : 2 m. by B 3285 – ✉ ☎ 087 255 St. Agnes :

🏨 **Rose-in-Vale** ⑤, TR5 0QD, ☎ 2202, ≤, ⌿ heated, 🛥 – ⇥ rest ☎ P. 🅰 VISA
March-October – **M** (bar lunch summer only)/dinner 12.50 **t.** and a la carte 🍷 3.15 – **15 rm** ☕ 22.50/45.00 **t.** – SB (except summer) 50.00 **st.**

FORD Trevellas Garage, Trevellas ☎ 2372

ST. ALBANS Herts. **404** T 28 – pop. 76 709 – ECD : Thursday – ☎ 0727.

See : Site★ – Cathedral and Abbey Church★ (Norman Tower★).

Envir. : Hatfield House★★★ *AC* (gardens★ and Old Palace★) E : 6 m. – Verulamium Park★ (Roman remains and Museum★)*AC*, W : 2 m.

🏌 Batchwood Hall ☎ 33349.

🛈 Town Hall, Market Pl. ☎ 726871.

◆London 27 – ◆Cambridge 41 – Luton 10.

🏨 **Noke Thistle** (Thistle) Watford Rd, AL2 3DS, SW : 2 ½ m. at junction A 405 and B 4630 ☎ 54252, Telex 893834, Fax 41906 – ⇥ rm TV ☎ ⅚ P – 🍴 70. 🅰 AE ⑩ VISA
M 15.50/17.50 **st.** and a la carte – ☕ 7.25 – **57 rm** 70.00/85.00 **st.**

🏨 **St. Michael's Manor,** Fishpool St., AL3 4RY, ☎ 64444, Telex 917647, « Manor house, lake, ≤ garden », park – TV ☎ P – 🍴 . 🛥
closed 27 to 30 December – **M** 16.00/17.50 **t.** and a la carte 🍷 3.95 – **26 rm** ☕ 60.00/80.00 **st.**

🏨 **Sopwell House** (Best Western) ⑤, Cottonmill Lane, AL1 2HQ, SE : 1 ½ m. by A 1081 and Mile House Lane ☎ 64477, Fax 41741, 🛥, park – ⇥ TV ☎ P – 🍴 . 🅰 AE ⑩ VISA
M 14.50/17.50 **t.** and a la carte 🍷 5.25 – ☕ 7.50 – **70 rm** 57.00/100.00 **t.** – SB (weekends only) (except Christmas) 70.00/80.00 **st.**

🏨 Pré, Redbourn Rd, AL3 6JZ, NW : 1 ¼ m. by A 4147 on A 5183 ☎ 55259, ≤, 🛥, park – TV ☎ P – 🍴 45
13 rm.

🏨 Black Lion Inn, 198 Fishpool St., AL3 4SB, ☎ 51786 – TV ☎ P
8 rm.

↑ **Ardmore House** without rest., 54 Lemsford Rd, AL1 3PR, ☎ 59313 – TV P
14 rm ☕ 28.75/46.00 **t.**

↑ **Melford House** without rest., 24 Woodstock Rd North, AL1 4QQ, ☎ 53642, 🛥 – P
12 rm ☕ 23.00/43.70 **st.**

✕✕ **Cinta,** 20-26 High St., AL3 4EN, ☎ 37606, Chinese rest. – 🅰 AE ⑩ VISA
M 9.50/25.00 **t.** and a la carte 10.90/13.50 **t.** 🍷 3.50.

✕ **Koh-I-Noor,** 8 George St., AL3 4ER, ☎ 53602, Indian rest – 🅰 AE ⑩ VISA
M 8.75 **t.** and a la carte 9.95/14.15 **t.** 🍷 3.20.

AUSTIN-ROVER Acrewood Way, Hatfield Rd ☎ 66522
AUSTIN-ROVER Park St., Frogmore ☎ 72626
CITROEN, VAUXHALL-OPEL 68-70 High St., Potters Bar ☎ 0707 (Potters Bar) 42391
CITROEN 101 Holywell Hill ☎ 65756
FIAT Beech Rd ☎ 50871
FORD Ashley Rd ☎ 59155

HONDA Catherine St. ☎ 54342
RENAULT 220 London Rd ☎ 63377
TOYOTA Watford Rd ☎ 34376
VAUXHALL-OPEL 100 London Rd ☎ 50601
VW-AUDI Valley Rd ☎ 36236

⊚ ATS Grimston Rd ☎ 35174
ATS Lyon Way, Hatfield Rd ☎ 52314

ST. ASAPH (LLANELWY) Clwyd 402 403 J 24 – pop. 3 156 – ECD : Thursday – ☎ 0745.
Envir. : Rhuddlan (castle★★ 13C) *AC*, NW : 3 m – Denbigh Castle★ S : 5 m..
◆London 225 – Chester 29 – Shrewsbury 59.

   🏛 **Oriel House,** Upper Denbigh Rd, LL17 0LW, S : ¾ m. on A 525 ℰ 582716, Fax 582716, 🚗 – 📺 ☎ 🅿 – 🏛 200. 🔄 AE ⓘ VISA
     closed 26 December – **M** 8.50/9.50 **t.** and a la carte 9.00/17.00 **t.** – **19 rm** ☲ 33.00/60.00 **t.** – SB (weekends only) 63.20/74.00 **st.**

   🏛 **Plas Elwy,** The Roe, LL17 0LT, N : ½ m. at junction of A 525 and A 55 ℰ 582263 – 📺 ☎ 🅿. 🔄 AE ⓘ VISA 🛇
     closed 26 December-1 January – **M** *(closed Sunday dinner)* (dinner only and Sunday lunch) 9.50 **t.** and a la carte ▯3.40 – **8 rm** ☲ 32.00/44.00 **t.** – SB (weekends only) 98.00 **st.**

FORD Bod Ewr Corner ℰ 582345   RENAULT The Roe ℰ 582233

ST. AUSTELL Cornwall 403 F 32 The West Country G. – pop. 20 267 – ECD : Thursday – ☎ 0726.
See : Holy Trinity★★ – Envir. : St. Austell Bay★★ (Gribbin Head★★), E : 3 m. by A 3601 – Wheal Martyn Museum★★ *AC*, N : 2 m. on A 391 – Polkerris★, E : 9 m. by A 3082.
🛆 Tregongeeves Lane ℰ 72649 SW : 1 m – 🚗 ℰ 01 (London) 723 7000 ext. 3148.
◆London 281 – Newquay 16 – ◆Plymouth 38 – Truro 14.

   🏛 **White Hart,** Church St., PL25 4AT, ℰ 72100 – 📺. 🔄 AE ⓘ VISA
     closed 25 and 26 December – **M** 6.00/10.50 **st.** ▯3.00 – **18 rm** ☲ 31.00/50.00 **st.** – SB (June-November) 45.00/50.00 **st.**

   at Tregrehan E : 2 ½ m. by A 390 – ✉ St. Austell – ☎ 072 681 Par :

   ❌❌ **Boscundle Manor** 🛦 with rm, PL25 3RL, ℰ 3557, « Tastefully converted 18C manor », 🏊 heated, 🚗, park – 📺 ☎ 🅿. 🔄 AE VISA
     Mid January-mid October (restricted service mid January-mid April) – **M** *(closed Sunday dinner to non-residents)* (restricted lunch residents only)/dinner 18.00 **st.** ▯3.25 – **8 rm** ☲ 50.00/90.00 **st.**, **1 suite** 130.00 **st.**

   at Carlyon Bay E : 2 ½ m. by A 3601 – ✉ St. Austell – ☎ 072 681 Par :

   🏛 **Carlyon Bay** 🛦, PL25 3RD, ℰ 2304, Telex 42551, Fax 4938, ⇐ Carlyon Bay, « Extensive gardens », 🏊 heated, 🎾, 🛆, park, ❌ – 📶 📺 🅿 – 🏛 50. 🔄 AE ⓘ VISA 🛇
     M 9.50/15.00 **t.** and a la carte – **69 rm** ☲ 50.00/125.00 **t.** – SB (except summer, Easter and Christmas) 83.00/126.00 **st.**

   🏛 **Porth Avallen** 🛦, Sea Rd, PL25 3SG, ℰ 2802, Fax 7097, ⇐ Carlyon Bay, 🚗 – ⬅✕ rm 📺 ☎ 🅿 – 🏛 40. 🔄 AE ⓘ VISA 🛇
     closed 21 December-3 January – **M** (booking essential) 9.25/11.00 **t.** ▯4.00 – **22 rm** ☲ 42.00/78.00 **t.**

   ⬈ **Wheal Lodge** 🛦, 91 Sea Rd, PL25 3SH, ℰ 5543, 🚗 – 📺 🅿. 🛇
     M approx. 10.00 **st.** ▯2.45 – **7 rm** ☲ 35.00/50.00 **st.** – SB 64.00/80.00 **st.**

AUSTIN-ROVER Carlyon Bay ℰ 072 681 (Par) 4081   🅐 ATS Gover Rd ℰ 65685
CITROEN 77 Fore St. ℰ 850 241
PEUGEOT-TALBOT Gwendra Rd, St. Stephen ℰ 822566

ST. BRIDES-SUPER-ELY South Glam. – ☎ 0446 Peterston-Super-Ely.
◆London 155 – ◆Bristol 51 – ◆Cardiff 9 – Newport 22.

   ⬈ **St.-Y-Nyll House** 🛦, CF5 6EZ, ℰ 760209, ⇐, 🚗, park – 📺 🅿
     M (by arrangement) 12.50 **st.** ▯2.50 – **6 rm** 18.00/30.00 **st.**

ST. CLEARS (SANCLER) Dyfed 403 G 28 – pop. 2 159 – ECD : Wednesday – ☎ 0994.
◆London 229 – Carmarthen 9 – Fishguard 37.

   ♨ **Forge Motel,** E : ½ m. on A 40, SA33 4NA, ℰ 230300 – 📺 ☎ 🅿. 🔄 AE VISA
     closed 25 to 26 December – **M** (grill rest.) a la carte 5.50/10.75 **st.** ▯3.00 – **18 rm** ☲ 30.00/45.00 **st.**

   at Llandowror SW : 2 ½ m. on A 477 – ✉ ☎ 0994 St. Clears :

   ❌❌ **Old Rectory,** SA33 4HH, ℰ 230030, 🚗 – 🅿
     closed Sunday dinner and Monday in winter – **M** 9.50/12.50 **st.** and a la carte 13.90/22.00 **t.** ▯3.10.

ST. COLUMB MINOR Cornwall – see Newquay.

ST. DAVIDS (TYDDEWI) Dyfed 403 E 28 – pop. 1 428 – ECD : Wednesday – ☎ 0437.
See : Cathedral★★ 12C (site★) – Bishops Palace★ *AC*.
Envir. : Porthgain (cliffs ❄★★★) NE : 7 m. – Whitesand Bay★★ and St. David's Head★★ NW : 2 m. – Newgale (⇐★★) by Solva (site★) E : 7 m. – Abereiddy (site★) NE : 5 m.
🛆 St. Davids City, Whitesands ℰ 034 83 (Croesgoch) 607, NW : 2 m. on B 4583.
🛈 City Hall ℰ 720392 (summer only).
◆London 266 – Carmarthen 46 – Fishguard 16.

Warpool Court ⟨...⟩, SA62 6BN, ☎ 720300, Telex 48390, Fax 720300, ≤ sea and countryside, ⟨...⟩ – TV ☎ P. ⟨...⟩ AE ⓘ VISA
M 16.00/25.00 **st.** and a la carte ⟨...⟩ 3.25 – **25 rm** ⟨...⟩ 53.00/120.00 **st.** – SB 84.00/140.00 **st.**

St. Non's, Catherine St., SA62 6RJ, ☎ 720239, Fax 721839, ⟨...⟩ – TV ☎ P. ⟨...⟩ AE ⓘ VISA
M (bar lunch)/dinner 14.40 **t.** and a la carte 15.40/20.95 **t.** – **20 rm** ⟨...⟩ 27.60/55.20 **t.** –
SB 67.50/84.00 **st.**

Old Cross, Cross Sq., SA62 6SP, ☎ 720387, ⟨...⟩ – TV ☎ P. ⟨...⟩ – **17 rm**.

Alandale, 43 Nun St., SA62 6NU, ☎ 720333
M 7.00 s. – **6 rm** ⟨...⟩ 11.50/23.00 s.

ST. DOGMAELS Dyfed **403** G 27 – see Cardigan.

ST. IVES Cornwall **403** D 33 The West Country G. – pop. 9 439 – ECD : Thursday – ✆ 0736
Penzance.

See : Site★★ – Barbara Hepworth Museum★★ *AC* Y **M1** – St. Ia Church★ Y **A** – Barnes Museum
of Cinematography★ *AC* Y **M2**.

🛈 The Guildhall, Street-an-Pol ☎ 796297.
♦London 319 – Penzance 10 – Truro 25.

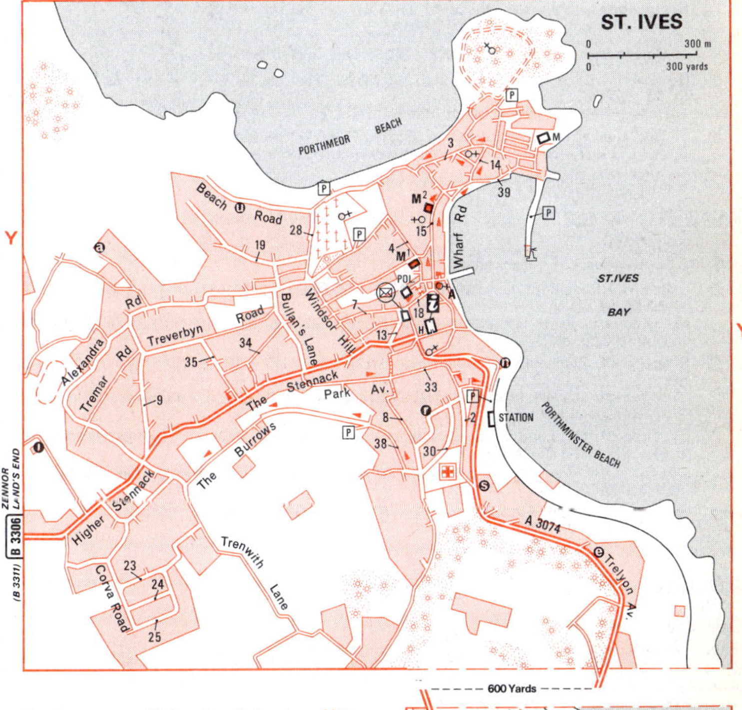

Fore Street .... Y 15
High Street .... Y 18

Albert Road ...... Y 2
Back
  Road West..... Y 3
Barnoon Hill...... Y 4
Bedford Road..... Y 7
Bishop's Road .... Y 8
Carnellis Road .... Y 9
Chapel Street..... Y 13
Fish Street .... Y 14
Orange Lane ..... Y 19
Parc Owles .... Z 20

Penwith Road..... Y 23
Porthia
  Crescent....... Y 24
Porthia Road ..... Y 25
Porthmeor Hill .... Y 28
Porthrepta Road... Z 29
Talland Road ..... Y 30
Tregenna
  Terrace .... Y 33
Trelawney Road... Y 34
Trerice Road...... Y 35
Trewidden Road .. Y 38
Wharf (The) ...... Y 39
Wheal Whidden... Z 40

ST. IVES

🏨 **Porthminster** (Best Western), The Terrace, TR26 2BN, 𝒫 795221, Fax 797043, ≼, ⌇ heated, 🦌 – 📶 TV ☎ 🅿. 🖪 AE ⓞ VISA
M 11.25 t. (dinner) and a la carte 10.75/14.10 t. 🍷 3.65 – **50 rm** ☕ 29.50/90.00 t. – SB (October-May except Easter, Christmas and New Year) 60.00 st.
Y s

🏰 **Garrack** ⑤, Burthallan Lane, TR26 3AA, 𝒫 796199, Fax 798955, ≼, ⌇, 🦌 – ☎ 🅿. 🖪 AE ⓞ VISA 🐾
M 12.00 t. (dinner) and a la carte 9.25/13.40 t. 🍷 3.80 – **19 rm** ☕ 23.00/73.00 t. – SB (except July and August) 58.00/64.00 st.
Y a

🏠 **Pedn-Olva**, The Warren, Porthminster Beach, TR26 2EA, 𝒫 796222, ≼ coastline – TV ☎ 🅿. 🖪 VISA. 🐾
M 10.50 t. (dinner) and a la carte 9.00/17.85 t. 🍷 3.95 – **24 rm** ☕ (dinner included) 38.00/80.00 t. – SB (November-March) 65.00/78.00 st.
Y n

🏠 **Dean Court** without rest., Trelyon Av., TR26 2AD, 𝒫 796023, ≼ St. Ives and bay – TV 🅿. 🐾
April-October – **12 rm**.
Y e

🏠 **Old Vicarage** ⑤, Parc-an-Creet, TR26 2ET, 𝒫 796124, 🦌 – TV 🅿. 🖪 VISA
closed January-February – **M** (by arrangement) 9.00 t. 🍷 2.80 – **8 rm** ☕ 15.00/33.00 t.
Y i

🏠 Pedn Olva Rock, Porthminster Beach, TR26 2EA, 𝒫 796222, ≼ St. Ives and bay – TV. 🐾
10 rm.
Y n

🏠 **Pondarosa**, 10 Porthminster Terr., TR26 2DQ, 𝒫 795875 – TV 🅿. 🐾
M 7.00 s. 🍷 1.75 – **9 rm** ☕ 12.00/30.00 s.
Y r

🏠 **Craigmeor** without rest., Beach Rd, TR26 1JY, 𝒫 796611 – ⎚✕⎚ 🅿
April-September – **4 rm** ☕ 12.00/24.00 s.
Y u

at Carbis Bay S : 1 ¾ m. on A 3074 – ✉ St. Ives – ☎ 0736 Penzance :

🏠 **Boskerris**, Boskerris Rd, TR26 2NQ, 𝒫 795295, Fax 798632, ≼, ⌇ heated, 🦌 – ⎚✕⎚ rest 🅿. 🖪 ⓞ VISA
Easter-November – **M** (bar lunch)/dinner 16.00 t. 🍷 3.10 – **19 rm** ☕ 18.00/44.00 s.
Z x

🏠 St. Uny, Boskerris Rd, TR26 2NQ, 𝒫 795011, ≼, 🦌 – ⎚✕⎚ rest 🅿. 🐾
Easter-October – **M** (bar lunch)/dinner 11.50 t. and a la carte – **29 rm**.
Z z

AUSTIN-ROVER Long Stone Hill, Carbis Bay 𝒫 795188

ST. IVES Cambs. 🗺️404 T 27 – pop. 13 431 – ECD : Thursday – ☎ 0480.
See : Bridge★ 15C.
♦London 75 – ♦Cambridge 14 – Huntingdon 6.

🏨 **Dolphin**, Bridge Foot, London Rd, PE17 4EP, 𝒫 66966, Fax 495597, 🦌 – TV ☎ 🖪 🅿 – 🚴 80. 🖪 AE ⓞ VISA
M 11.50 t. and a la carte 10.65/20.70 t. – **22 rm** ☕ 45.00/55.00 t. – SB (weekends only) 62.50 st.

🏨 **Slepe Hall**, Ramsey Rd, PE17 4RB, 𝒫 63122, Fax 61175 – TV ☎ 🅿 – 🚴 40. 🖪 AE ⓞ VISA
closed 25 and 26 December – **M** 13.50 t. and a la carte 14.70/20.30 t. – **13 rm** ☕ 37.50/62.50 t. – SB (weekends only) 57.50/69.00 st.

🏠 **St. Ives Motel**, London Rd, PE17 4EX, S : ¾ m. on A 1096 𝒫 63857, Fax 492027, 🦌 – TV ☎ 🅿 – 🚴 40. 🖪 AE ⓞ VISA
closed 25 and 26 December – **M** 9.50 t. and a la carte 🍷 3.70 – **16 rm** ☕ 28.50/55.00 t. – SB (weekends only) 60.00 st.

AUSTIN-ROVER The Quadrant 𝒫 62871   🅐 ATS East St. 𝒫 65572
FIAT, LANCIA Station Rd 𝒫 62641
FORD Ramsey Rd 𝒫 63184

ST. JUST Cornwall 🗺️403 C 33 The West Country G. – pop. 1 903 – ECD : Thursday – ☎ 0736 Penzance.
See : Site★ – Church★.
Envir. : Cape Cornwall★ (≼★★), W : 1 ½ m. – Carn Euny★AC, SE : 3 m. – Geevor Tin Mine★AC, N : 3 m. – Sennen (Wayside Cross★, Sennen Cove★ (≼★) SW : 4 ½ m. – Porthcurno (site★) S : 8 m.
♦London 325 – Penzance 7.5 – Truro 35.

🏠 **Boscean** ⑤, TR19 7QP, 𝒫 788748, ≼, 🦌 – 🅿. 🐾
March-October – **M** (bar lunch)/dinner 9.00 t. 🍷 2.90 – **11 rm** ☕ 17.00/30.00 t.

ST. JUST IN ROSELAND Cornwall – see St. Mawes.

ST. KEYNE Cornwall – see Liskeard.

ST. LAWRENCE I.O.W. – see Wight (Isle of) : Ventnor.

ST. LEONARDS East Sussex 🗺️404 V 31 – see Hastings and St. Leonards.

ST. LEONARDS Dorset 403 404 O 31 – see Ringwood (Hants.).

ST. MARGARET'S BAY Kent 404 Y 30 – see Dover.

ST. MARTINS Cornwall 403 ㉚ – see Scilly (Isles of).

ST. MARY'S Cornwall 403 ㉚ – see Scilly (Isles of).

ST. MAWES Cornwall 403 E 33 The West Country G. – ✉ Truro – ☏ 0326.
See : Site★ – Castle★ AC (≼★).
Envir. : St. Just-in-Roseland Church★★, N : 2 ½ m. by A 3078 – St. Anthony-in-Roseland (≼★★),
8 m. round peninsula.
♦London 299 – ♦Plymouth 56 – Truro 18.

- **Tresanton** ⟩, 27 Lower Castle Rd, TR2 5DR, ☏ 270544, ≼ estuary, ⇌ – ☎ ℗. 🗚 AE ⓪ VISA
  March-October and Christmas-New Year – **M** (buffet lunch)/dinner 18.50 t. ⌖ 3.75 – **20 rm** ⊑ 47.00/98.00 t., **1 suite** 147.00 t.
- **Rising Sun,** The Square, TR2 5DJ, ☏ 270233 – TV ☎ ℗. 🗚 AE ⓪ VISA
  closed January-February – **M** (rest. see **Rising Sun** below) – **12 rm** ⊑ 30.00/70.00 st.
- **Idle Rocks,** Tredenham Rd, TR2 5AN, ☏ 270771, ≼ harbour and estuary – TV. 🗚 VISA
  April-December – **M** (bar lunch)/dinner 14.00 t. ⌖ 3.75 – **22 rm** ⊑ 40.00/92.00 t.
- **St. Mawes,** The Seafront, TR2 5DW, ☏ 270266, ≼ – TV. 🗚 VISA
  closed November-January – **M** 10.00/14.00 t. and a la carte ⌖ 3.50 – **7 rm** ⊑ 35.00/70.00 st.
- **Rising Sun** (at Rising Sun H.), The Square, TR2 5DJ, ☏ 270233 – ↝ ℗. 🗚 AE ⓪ VISA
  M (bar lunch)/dinner 16.75 st.

  at St. Just in Roseland N : 2 ½ m. on A 3078 – ✉ Truro – ☏ 0326 St. Mawes :

- **Rose da Mar** ⟩, TR2 5JB, N : ¼ m. on B 3289 ☏ 270450, ≼, ⇌ – ℗. ↝
  April-October – **M** (dinner only) 12.50 t. ⌖ 2.75 – **8 rm** ⊑ 18.80/42.55 t.

ST. MICHAELS-ON-WYRE Lancs. 402 L 22 – ☏ 099 58.
♦London 235 – ♦Blackpool 24 – Burnley 35 – ♦Manchester 43.

- **Mallards,** Garstang Rd, PR3 0TE, ☏ 661 – ℗. 🗚 VISA
  closed first week January and 2 weeks August – **M** *(closed Sunday dinner)* (dinner only and Sunday lunch)/dinner a la carte 14.50/18.50 t. ⌖ 3.25.

ST. NEOTS Cambs. 404 T 27 – pop. 12 468 – ☏ 0480 Huntingdon.
See : St. Mary's Church★ 15C.
⛳ Eynesbury Hardwicke, St. Neots Leisure Centre ☏ 215153, SE : 2 m.
♦London 60 – Bedford 11 – ♦Cambridge 17 – Huntingdon 9.

- **Stephenson's Rocket Motel,** Crosshall Rd, PE19 4AG, NW : 1 m. on A 45 ☏ 72773 – TV ☎ ℗. ↝
  9 rm.
- **Chequers Inn,** St. Mary's St., Eynesbury, PE19 2TA, S : ½ m. on B 1043 ☏ 72116 – ℗. 🗚 AE ⓪ VISA
  closed Christmas Night – **M** a la carte 16.50/26.95 t. ⌖ 4.00.

  at Wyboston (Beds.) SW : 2 ½ m. by A 45 on A 1 – ✉ St. Neots (Cambs.) – ☏ 0480 Huntingdon :

- **Wyboston Lakes Motel** without rest., Great North Rd, MK44 3AL, N : ½ m. at junction of A 45 and A 1 ☏ 219949, Fax 407349 – TV ℗. 🗚 AE VISA
  closed 24 to 29 December – ⊑ 4.00 – **38 rm** 25.00/43.00 t.

AUSTIN-ROVER 42 Huntingdon St. ☏ 73237   ⦿ ATS Brook St. ☏ 72920/1
FORD Cambridge St. ☏ 73321

SALCOMBE Devon 403 I 33 The West Country G. – pop. 1 968 – ECD : Thursday – ☏ 054 884.
Envir. : Kingsbridge★, N : 5 m. by A 381 Y – Prawle Point (≼★★★), E : 16 m. around coast by A 381 Y – Sharpitor Overbecks Museum and garden (≼★★) AC, SW : 2 m. by South Sands Z.
🛈 66 Fore St. ☏ 3927.
♦London 243 – Exeter 43 – ♦Plymouth 27 – Torquay 28.

Plan on next page

- **Marine,** Cliff Rd, TQ8 8JH, ☏ 2251, Fax 42513, ≼ estuary, 🗚 – ⧫ TV ☎ ℗. 🗚 AE ⓪ VISA ↝
  Y e
  M 8.00 t. (lunch) and a la carte 17.50/33.75 t. ⌖ 3.50 – **51 rm** ⊑ 65.00/125.00 t., **1 suite** 88.00/99.00 t. – SB (except Easter, Christmas and New Year) 89.00/105.00 st.
- **Tides Reach,** South Sands, TQ8 8LJ, ☏ 3466, ≼ estuary, 🗚, ⇌, squash – ⧫ TV ☎ ℗. 🗚 AE ⓪ VISA
  Z x
  March-November – **M** (buffet lunch)/dinner 18.25 st. and a la carte ⌖ 3.95 – **42 rm** ⊑ (dinner included) 59.00/150.00 st. – SB (except summer) 98.00/108.00 st.

SALCOMBE

Fore Street .... **Y**

Allenhayes Road .... **Y** 2
Bonaventure Road ...... **Y** 3
Buckley Street .... **Y** 4
Camperdown Road ..... **Y** 7
Church Street .... **Y** 8
Coronation Road ...... **Y** 9
Devon Road .... **Y** 13
Fortescue Road .... **Z** 14
Grenville Road .... **Y** 15
Herbert Road .... **Z** 18
Knowle Road .... **Y** 19
Moult Road .... **Z** 20
Newton Road .... **Y** 23
Sandhills Road .... **Z** 24
Shadycombe Road ..... **Y** 25

Town plans
roads most used
by traffic and those
on which guide listed
hotels and restaurants
stand are fully drawn ;
the beginning only
of lesser roads
is indicated.

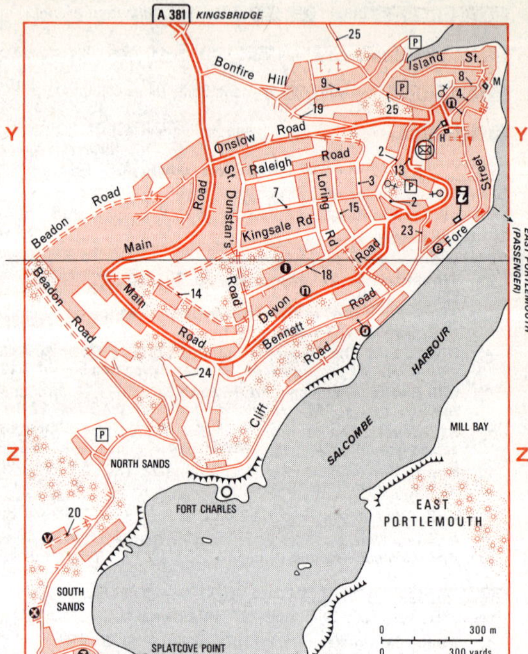

Bolt Head (Best Western) ⤳, South Sands, TQ8 8LL, ℰ 3751, ≤ estuary, ⌇ heated – 🍽 rest 📺 ☎ 🅿. 🖅 AE ① VISA　　**Z z**
April-mid November – **M** (buffet lunch)/dinner 35.00 t. – **28 rm** ⬱ 62.00/124.00 t. – SB (except Bank Holidays) 88.00/124.00 **st.**

Grafton Towers ⤳, Moult Rd, TQ8 8LG, ℰ 2882, ≤ estuary, ⤢ – ⊱ rest 📺 🅿. 🖅 VISA　　**Z v**
Easter-October – **M** (dinner only) 12.50 t. ⌕ 3.20 – **13 rm** ⬱ 24.00/60.00 t.

Bay View without rest., Bennett Rd, TQ8 8JJ, ℰ 2238, ≤ estuary – 🅿. 🖅 VISA. ⤢　　**Z o**
March-October – **4 rm** ⬱ 25.00/48.00.

Woodgrange, Devon Rd, TQ8 8HJ, ℰ 2439, ⤢ – 📺 ☎ 🅿. 🖅 AE ① VISA　　**Z n**
April-November – **M** (bar lunch)/dinner 10.00 t. ⌕ 4.10 – **10 rm** ⬱ 19.00/44.00 t. – SB (except summer) 50.00 **st.**

Penn Torr, Herbert Rd, TQ8 8HN, ℰ 2234 – 🅿　　**Z i**
10 rm.

✕ **Wellingtons**, 84-86 Fore St., TQ8 8BY, ℰ 3385 – 🖅 VISA　　**Y n**
Mid February-October – **M** (dinner only) 9.95 t. and a la carte 11.50/15.35 t. ⌕ 4.25.

at Soar Mill Cove SW : 3 m. via Cliff Rd – **Y** – ✉ Malborough – ☎ 0548 Kingsbridge :

Soar Mill Cove ⤳, TQ7 3DS, ℰ 561566, ≤, ⌇ heated, 🖅, ⤢ – 📺 ☎ 🅿. 🖅 VISA ⤢
closed January-mid February – **M** 16.00/30.00 t. and a la carte – **14 rm** ⬱ 56.00/98.00 t.

at Hope Cove W : 4 m. by A 381 – **Y** – ✉ ☎ 0548 Kingsbridge :

Cottage ⤳, TQ7 3HJ, ℰ 561555, ≤ Bolt Tail and Bigbury Bay, ⤢ – 📺 ☎ 🅿
closed 2 to 30 January – **M** (bar lunch Monday to Saturday)/dinner 13.35 st. and a la carte ⌕ 4.50 – **35 rm** ⬱ 25.00/89.00 **st.** – SB (November-Easter) 45.00/71.00 **st.**

Lantern Lodge ⤳, TQ7 3HE, ℰ 561280, ≤, 🖅, ⤢ – ⊱ rest 📺 🅿. 🖅 AE VISA ⤢
March-November – **M** (bar lunch)/dinner 14.50 t. ⌕ 2.90 – **14 rm** ⬱ 45.40/82.50 t.

Port Light ⤳, Bolberry Down, TQ7 3DY, SE : 1 ¾ m. ℰ 561384, ≤, ⤢ – 🅿
6 rm.

➥ *Benutzen Sie für weite Fahrten in Europa die Michelin-Länderkarten :*
920 *Europa,* **980** *Griechenland,* **984** *Deutschland,* **985** *Skandinavien-Finnland,*
986 *Großbritannien-Irland,* **987** *Deutschland-Österreich-Benelux,* **988** *Italien,*
989 *Frankreich,* **990** *Spanien-Portugal,* **991** *Jugoslawien.*

SALE Greater Manchester **402 403 404** N 23 – pop. 57 993 – ECD : Wednesday – ✉ ☎ 061 Manchester.

🏌 Golf Rd ✆ 973 1638.

♦London 212 – ♦Liverpool 36 – ♦Manchester 6 – ♦Sheffield 43.

🏨 **Amblehurst,** 44 Washway Rd, M33 1QZ, on A 56 ✆ 973 8800, Group Telex 668871, Fax 905 1697, 🚗 – 📺 ☎ Ⓟ. 🔲 AE VISA. 🚫
   M *(closed Saturday lunch and Sunday)* 9.95/10.00 **t.** and a la carte ⅄ 3.95 – **40 rm** ☕ 20.00/52.00 **t.** – SB (weekends only) 65.00/95.00 **st.**

🏨 Normanhurst, 195 Brooklands Rd, M33 1PJ, ✆ 973 1982, Group Telex 668871, 🚗 – 📺 ☎ Ⓟ
   51 rm.

🏨 **Lennox Lea,** Irlam Rd, M33 2BH, ✆ 973 1764, Fax 969 6059, 🚗 – 📺 ☎ Ⓟ. 🔲 AE ① VISA
   M (dinner only) 10.95 **t.** and a la carte approx. 11.50 – **30 rm** ☕ 36.50/46.50 **t.**

SALFORD Greater Manchester **402 403 404** N 23 – pop. 98 343 – ECD : Wednesday – ✉ ☎ 061 Manchester.

ℹ Art Gallery and Museum, The Crescent ✆ 736 3353/2649.

♦London 206 – ♦Liverpool 31 – ♦Manchester 4.

Town plans : see Manchester built up area.

🏨 Inn of Good Hope (B.C.B.), 226 Eccles Old Rd, M6 8AG, ✆ 707 6178 – ⊱ rest 📺 ☎ Ⓟ. 🚫
   8 rm ☕ 35.50/45.00 **t.**   AX i

⦿ ATS Eccles New Rd ✆ 789 4360/3988

SALFORDS Surrey **404** T 30 – see Redhill.

SALISBURY Wilts. **403 404** O 30 The West Country G. – pop. 36 890 – ECD : Wednesday – ☎ 0722.

See : Site✱✱ – Cathedral✱✱✱ *AC* Z – The Close✱ Z : Mompesson House✱*AC* Z A, Military Museum✱✱*AC* Z M1 – Salisbury and South Wiltshire Museum✱*AC* Z M2 – Sarum St. Thomas Church✱ Y B.

Envir. : Stonehenge✱✱✱*AC*, NW : 10 m. by A 345 Y – Wilton House✱✱*AC*, W : 2 ½ m. by A 30 Y – Old Sarum✱*AC* N : 2 m. by A 345 Y – at Wilton Village, Royal Wilton Carpet Factory✱*AC*, W : 2 ½ m. by A 30 Y – Heale House✱*AC* N : 7 m. by Stratford Rd Y – Wardour Castle✱*AC*, W : 10 m. by A 30. Y.

🏌, 🏌 Salisbury and South Wilts., Netherhampton ✆ 742645, by A 3094 Z – 🏌 High Post, Great Durnford ✆ 072 273 (Middle Woodford) 356, N : 4 m. by A 345 Y.

ℹ Fish Row ✆ 334956.

♦London 91 – Bournemouth 28 – ♦Bristol 53 – ♦Southampton 23.

Plan on next page

🏨 **White Hart** (T.H.F.), 1 St. John St., SP1 2SD, ✆ 27476, Fax 412761 – ⊱ rm 📺 ☎ Ⓟ – 🪑 100. 🔲 AE ① VISA   Z s
   M 9.25/13.95 **st.** and a la carte ⅄ 3.60 – ☕ 7.00 – **68 rm** 65.00/95.00 **st.** – SB (except June and September) 65.00/96.00 **st.**

🏨 County (B.C.B.), Bridge St., SP1 2ND, ✆ 20229 – 📺 ☎ Ⓟ – 🪑 110. 🚫   Z n
   31 rm ☕ 35.00/52.00 **t.**

🏨 **Kings Arms** (B.C.B.), 9 St. John's St., SP1 2SB, ✆ 27629, « Part 13C and part 15C inn » – 📺 ☎. 🔲 AE ① VISA. 🚫   Z r
   M a la carte 9.95/14.00 **t.** ⅄ 3.50 – **15 rm** ☕ 35.00/51.00 **st.**

🏨 **Cathedral,** 7 Milford St., SP1 2AJ, ✆ 20144 – 🛗 ▤ rest 📺 ☎. 🔲 VISA. 🚫   Y a
   M *(closed Sunday lunch)* 3.50/8.95 **t.** and a la carte ⅄ 4.50 – **30 rm** ☕ 25.50/59.50 **t.** – SB (except summer) 39.50/62.50 **st.**

🏡 **Old Bell Inn,** 2 St. Ann St., SP1 2DN, ✆ 27958, « Converted 14C inn » – 🔲 AE ① VISA 🚫   Z v
   M *(closed Saturday and Sunday)* 6.50 **t.** (lunch) and a la carte ⅄ 3.00 – **7 rm** ☕ 45.00/55.00 **t.**

🏠 **Stratford Lodge,** 4 Park Lane, Castle Rd Y, SP1 3NP, ✆ 25177, 🚗 – 📺 Ⓟ. 🚫
   closed Christmas and New Year – **M** (by arrangement) 12.50 – **4 rm** ☕ 25.00/40.00 **s.**

🏠 **Byways House** without rest., 31 Fowlers Rd, off Milford Hill, SP1 2QP, ✆ 28364, 🚗 – 📺 Ⓟ   Z e
   17 rm ☕ 15.00/34.00 **st.**

🏠 **Glen Lyn** without rest., 6 Bellamy Lane, Milford Hill, SP1 2SP, ✆ 27880 – ⊱ 📺 Ⓟ. 🚫   YZ x
   6 rm ☕ 15.00/32.00 **st.**

🏠 Cricketfield Cottage without rest., Wilton Rd, SP2 7NS, W : 1 ¼ m. on A 30 Y ✆ 22595, 🚗 – 📺 Ⓟ
   5 rm.

✕ Dutch Mill, 58a Fisherton St., SP2 7RB, ✆ 23447 –   Y i

✕ **Chef Peking,** 39 Catherine St., SP1 2HD, ✆ 26063, Chinese rest. – ▤. 🔲 AE ① VISA   Z c
   M 5.00/10.00 **st.** and a la carte.

P.T.O. →

at Pitton E : 6 m. by A 30 – **Y** – ✉ Salisbury – ☎ 072 272 Farley :

XX **Silver Plough,** White Hill, SP5 1DZ, ☎ 266 – 🅿. 🔼 AE ⓞ VISA
M a la carte 11.25/18.75 **st.** 🍷 2.50.

at Redlynch SE : 8 ½ m. by A 338 – **Z** – off B 3080 – ✉ Salisbury – ☎ 0794 Romsey :

XX **Langley Wood** ⤷ with rm, Hamptworth Rd, SP5 2PB, SE : 1 ½ m. ☎ 390348, 🚗 – 🅿. 🔼
AE ⓞ VISA
closed 3 weeks January-February – **M** _(closed dinner Sunday, Monday and Tuesday to non-residents)_ (lunch by arrangement) a la carte 12.00/19.25 **t.** 🍷 2.50 – **3 rm** � 15.00/ 30.00 **t.**

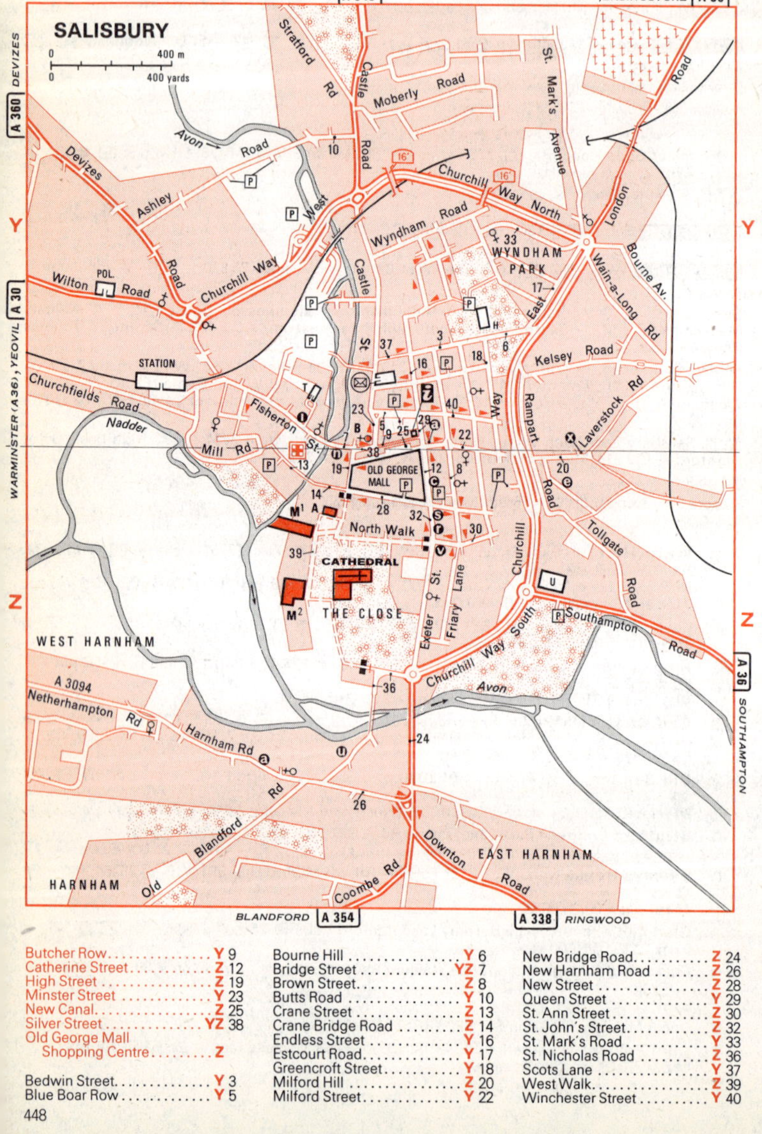

Butcher Row	Y	9	Bourne Hill	Y	6	New Bridge Road	Z 24
Catherine Street	Z	12	Bridge Street	YZ	7	New Harnham Road Romsey	Z 26
High Street	Y	19	Brown Street	Z	8	New Street	Z 28
Minster Street	Y	23	Butts Road	Y	10	Queen Street	Z 29
New Canal	Z	25	Crane Street	Z	13	St. Ann Street	Z 30
Silver Street	YZ	38	Crane Bridge Road	Z	14	St. John's Street	Z 32
Old George Mall			Endless Street	Y	16	St. Mark's Road	Y 33
Shopping Centre	Z		Estcourt Road	Y	17	St. Nicholas Road	Z 36
			Greencroft Street	Y	18	Scots Lane	Y 37
Bedwin Street	Y	3	Milford Hill	Z	20	West Walk	Z 39
Blue Boar Row	Y	5	Milford Street	Y	22	Winchester Street	Y 40

at Downton S : 6 m. by A 338 – Z – on B 3080 – ✉ ☎ 0725 Downton :

⋔ **Warren** without rest., 15 High St., SP5 3PG, ℰ 20263, 🚗 – Ⓟ
closed 15 December-6 January – **6 rm** ☲ 16.00/35.00 **st.**

at Harnham SW : 1 ½ m. by A 3094 – ✉ ☎ 0722 Salisbury :

🏛 Rose and Crown (Q.M.H.), Harnham Rd, SP2 8JQ, ℰ 27908, Telex 47224, ≼, « Riverside
location », 🚗 – 📺 ☎ ⅙ Ⓟ – 🔼 70. 🕸   Z u
28 rm.

🏠 **Grasmere** without rest., 70 Harnham Rd, SP2 8JN, ℰ 338388, ≼, 🚗 – 📺 ☎ Ⓟ. 🕸
5 rm ☲ 38.00/50.00 **st.**   Z a

at Broad Chalke SW : 8 m. by A 354 and Broad Chalke Valley Rd Z – ✉ ☎ 0722 Salisbury

⋔ Stoke Farm ⑊, SP5 5EF, E : ¾ m. ℰ 780209, « Working farm », ⑊ – Ⓟ
3 rm.

AUSTIN-ROVER, ROLLS-ROYCE Southampton Rd
ℰ 335251
BMW Harnham ℰ 24933
CITROEN Stephenson Rd ℰ 413141
FIAT Lower Rd, Churchfield Ind Est. ℰ 336681
FORD Castle St. ℰ 28443
NISSAN 114-120 Wilton Rd ℰ 28328

PEUGEOT-TALBOT Southampton Rd ℰ 335268
VAUXHALL-OPEL Brunell Rd ℰ 23522
VOLVO Telford Rd, Churchfields ℰ 333650
VW-AUDI 16 Lower Rd, Churchfields ℰ 27162

🅖 ATS 155 Wilton Rd ℰ 336789
ATS 28 St. Edmunds Church St. ℰ 22390

SALTASH Cornwall 🐵🐵🐵 H 32 – ☎ 0752.
♦London 246 – Exeter 38 – ♦Plymouth 5 – Truro 49.

🏠 **Granada Lodge** without rest., Callington Rd, Carkeel, PL12 6LF, NW : 1 ½ m. by A 388 on
A 38 at Saltash Service Area ℰ 848408 – ⇔ 📺 ⅙ Ⓟ. 🔼 🆎 ⓪ 𝗩𝗜𝗦𝗔. 🕸
☲ 3.25 – **31 rm** 24.50/27.50 **st.**

SALTBURN-BY-THE-SEA Cleveland 🐵🐵 R 20 – pop. 6 066 – ✉ ☎ 0287 Guisborough.
🅘 4 Station Buildings, Station Sq. ℰ 22422.
♦London 256 – ♦Middlesbrough 13 – Scarborough 40.

🏛 **Rushpool Hall** ⑊, Saltburn Lane, TS12 1HD, S : 1 ¾ m. by A 174 ℰ 24111, 🚗, park – 📺
☎ Ⓟ
15 rm.

SAMLESBURY Lancs. 🐵🐵 M 22 – see Preston.

SANCLÊR = St. Clears.

SANDBACH Cheshire 🐵🐵 🐵🐵 🐵🐵 M 24 – pop. 13 753 – ECD : Tuesday – ☎ 0270.
🅘🅘 Malkins Bank Municipal, Betchton Rd ℰ 762117.
🅘 M 6 Service Area (Northbound) ℰ 760460.
♦London 177 – ♦Liverpool 44 – ♦Manchester 28 – ♦Stoke-on-Trent 16.

🏛 **Chimney House** (Lansbury), Congleton Rd, CW11 OST, E : 1 ½ m. on A 534 ℰ 764141,
Telex 367323, Fax 768916 – 📺 ☎ Ⓟ – 🔼 70. 🔼 🆎 ⓪ 𝗩𝗜𝗦𝗔. 🕸
M 8.50/12.50 **t.** and a la carte – **50 rm** ☲ 65.00/75.00 **t.**

SANDIACRE Derbs. 🐵🐵 🐵🐵 🐵🐵 Q 25 – see Nottingham (Notts.).

SANDOWN I.O.W. 🐵🐵 🐵🐵 Q 32 – see Wight (Isle of).

SANDPLACE Cornwall – see Looe.

SANDRINGHAM Norfolk 🐵🐵 🐵🐵 V 25 – pop. 431 – ✉ King's Lynn – ☎ 0485 Dersingham.
♦London 111 – King's Lynn 8 – ♦Norwich 50.

🏛 **Park House** ⑊, Sandringham Estate, PE35 6EH, ℰ 43000, Restricted to physically disa-
bled, and their carers « Former Royal residence », 🏊 heated, 🚗, park – 🛗 🍽 rest 📺 ☎
⅙ Ⓟ. 🔼 𝗩𝗜𝗦𝗔. 🕸
M (buffet lunch)/dinner/9.00 **s.** 🍷 2.80 – **16 rm** ☲ 22.00/68.00 **s.**

SANDWICH Kent 🐵🐵 Y 30 – pop. 4 184 – ECD : Wednesday – ☎ 030 46 (4 fig.) or 0304 (6 fig.).
See : Site★.
🅘🅘, 🅘🅘 Prince's, Sandwich Bay ℰ 611118.
🅘 St. Peter's Church, Market St. ℰ 613565 (summer only).
♦London 72 – Canterbury 13 – ♦Dover 12 – Maidstone 41 – Margate 9.

🏛 **Bell**, The Quay, CT13 9EF, ℰ 613388, Fax 615308 – ⇔ rm 📺 ☎ Ⓟ – 🔼 50. 🔼 🆎 ⓪ 𝗩𝗜𝗦𝗔
M 12.75 **t.** (dinner) and a la carte 🍷 5.00 – **29 rm** ☲ 50.00/95.00 **t.** – SB 64.00/92.00 **st.**

FORD New St. ℰ 612308

SANDY Beds. **404** T 27 – pop. 7 496 – ECD : Thursday – ☎ 0767.

♦London 49 – Bedford 8 – ♦Cambridge 24 – Peterborough 35.

  ⌂ Sandy Motel without rest., Girtford Bridge, London Rd, SG19 1DH, W : ¾ m. by B 1042 at junction of A 1 and A 603 ℰ 292220 – TV & P. ⑳
38 rm.

  at Tempsford N : 3 ¾ m. by B 1042 on A 1 – ⊠ ☎ 0767 Sandy :

  ⌂ **Anchor** (B.C.B.), Great North Rd, SG19 2AS, on A 1 ℰ 40233, ⌖, ⌖, park – TV ☎ P. ⓹
AE ⓪ VISA ⑳
M a la carte 7.25/9.90 st. ⓵ 2.95 – **10 rm** ⊆ 31.00/49.00 st.

SANDYPARK Devon **403** I 31 – see Chagford.

SARISBURY Hants. **403 404** Q 31 – pop. 5 682 – ⊠ Southampton – ☎ 0489 Locks Heath.

♦London 90 – ♦Portsmouth 16 – ♦Southampton 6.

  ⌂ **Dormy House,** 21 Barnes Lane, Sarisbury Green, SO3 6DA, S : 1 m. ℰ 572626 – TV P.
⑳
M 7.50 st. – **9 rm** ⊆ 15.00/35.00 st.

SARN PARK SERVICE AREA Mid Glam. **403** J 29 – ⊠ ☎ 0656 Bridgend.

♦London 174 – ♦Cardiff 17 – ♦Swansea 20.

  ⌂ **Travelodge** without rest., CF32 9RW, ℰ 59218 – TV & P. ⓹ AE VISA
40 rm 21.50/27.00 t.

SAUNDERSFOOT Dyfed **403** F 28 – pop. 2 196 – ECD : Wednesday – ☎ 0834.

🄸 The Harbour (summer only).

♦London 245 – Carmarthen 25 – Fishguard 34 – Tenby 3.

  🏰 **St. Brides,** St. Brides Hill, SA69 9NH, ℰ 812304, Telex 48350, Fax 813303, ≼ Saundersfoot Bay, ⌖ heated, ⌖ – TV ☎ P – ⓹ 80. ⓹ AE ⓪ VISA
M 10.50/16.95 st. and a la carte ⓵ 4.25 – **44 rm** ⊆ 46.00/70.00 st., **2 suites** 100.00 st. –
SB (weekends only) 58.00/80.00 st.

  ⌂ **Glen Beach** ⌖, Swallow Tree Woods, SA69 9DE, S : ½ m. by B 4316 ℰ 813430, ≼, ⌖ –
TV ☎ P. ⓹ AE ⓪ VISA
M (bar lunch)/dinner 8.75 st. and a la carte ⓵ 3.00 – **13 rm** ⊆ 30.00/60.00 st. –
SB (except July and August) 40.00/70.00 st.

  ⌂ **Malin House,** St. Brides Hill, SA69 9NP, ℰ 812344, ⌖, ⌖ – TV P. ⓹ VISA. ⑳
closed December and January – **M** (bar lunch)/dinner 8.00 st. ⓵ 2.00 – **18 rm**
⊆ 18.00/36.00 st. – SB (October-April) (weekends only) 45.00 st.

SAUNDERTON Bucks. **404** R 28 – ⊠ Aylesbury – ☎ 084 44 Princes Risborough.

♦London 42 – Aylesbury 9 – ♦Oxford 20.

  ⌂ **Rose and Crown,** Wycombe Rd, HP17 9NP, N : on A 4010 ℰ 5299 – TV ☎ P. ⓹ AE ⓪
VISA. ⑳
closed 24 to 30 December – **M** *(closed Monday lunch and Sunday dinner)* 14.50 t. and a la
carte ⓵ 4.25 – **15 rm** ⊆ 25.00/65.00 st. – SB 53.00/63.00 st.

SAUNTON Devon **403** H 30 – ⊠ Braunton – ☎ 0271 Croyde.

♦London 230 – Barnstaple 8 – Exeter 48.

  🏰 **Saunton Sands,** EX33 1LQ, ℰ 890212, Fax 890145, ≼ Saunton Sands, ⌖, ⌖, ⌖, squash
– ⓼ TV ☎ P – ⓹ 200. ⓹ AE ⓪ VISA. ⑳
M 9.00/14.00 t. and a la carte – **90 rm** ⊆ 50.00/106.00 t. – SB (except summer and
Bank Holidays) 74.00/122.00 st.

  ⌂ **Preston House,** EX33 1LG, ℰ 890472, ≼ Saunton Sands, ⌖ – TV ☎ P. ⓹ VISA. ⑳
M (bar lunch)/dinner 15.00 t. and a la carte ⓵ 3.40 – **12 rm** ⊆ 25.00/30.00 t.

SAWBRIDGEWORTH Herts. **404** U 28 – pop. 8 475 – ECD : Thursday and Saturday – ☎ 0279
Bishop's Stortford.

♦London 26 – ♦Cambridge 32 – Chelmsford 17.

  ⌂ Market House, 42 Knight St., CM21 9AX, ℰ 722807 – TV ☎ P
9 rm.

SAWLEY Lancs. **402** M 22 – pop. 179 – ☎ 076 586.

♦London 242 – ♦Blackpool 39 – ♦Leeds 44 – ♦Liverpool 54.

  🏰 **Spread Eagle,** BB7 4NH, ℰ 0200 (Clitheroe) 41202 – TV ☎ & P. ⓹ AE ⓪ VISA. ⑳
M 9.50/13.95 st. and a la carte ⓵ 3.50 – **10 rm** ⊆ 35.00/63.00 st. – SB (weekends
only) 75.00/85.00 st.

SCALBY North Yorks. **402** S 21 – see Scarborough.

North Cliff, North Cliff Av. 360786, NW : 2 m. by A 165 Y.
St. Nicholas Cliff 373333.
◆London 253 – ◆Kingston-upon-Hull 47 – ◆Leeds 67 – ◆Middlesbrough 52.

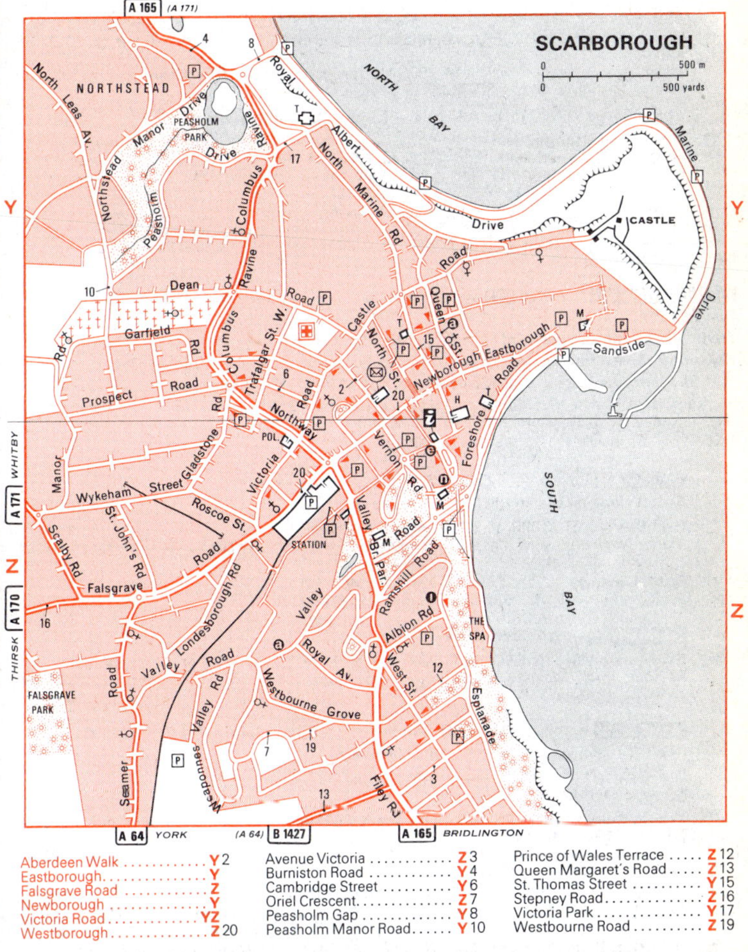

Aberdeen Walk . . . . Y 2	Avenue Victoria . . . . Z 3	Prince of Wales Terrace . . . . . Z 12
Eastborough . . . . Y	Burniston Road . . . . Y 4	Queen Margaret's Road . . . . . Z 13
Falsgrave Road . . . . Z	Cambridge Street . . . . Y 6	St. Thomas Street . . . . Y 15
Newborough . . . . Y	Oriel Crescent . . . . Z 7	Stepney Road . . . . Z 16
Victoria Road . . . . YZ	Peasholm Gap . . . . Y 8	Victoria Park . . . . Y 17
Westborough . . . . Z 20	Peasholm Manor Road . . . . . . Y 10	Westbourne Road . . . . Z 19

Holbeck Hall (Best Western) ⑤, Seacliff Rd, YO11 2XX, 374374, Fax 351114, ⩽, 🚁 –
TV ☎ P. 🅰 AE ⓪ VISA ⌾   by A 165   Z
M 9.95/18.50 t. and a la carte ⌂ 5.50 – **29 rm** ⊡ 40.00/95.00 t., **1 suite** 61.00/66.00 t. –
SB 97.50/107.50 st.

Crown (T.H.F.), 7-11 Esplanade, YO11 2AG, 373491, Telex 52277, Fax 362271, ⩽ – |‡|
⌾✕ rm TV ☎ 🚗 – 🔏 200. 🅰 AE ⓪ VISA   Z i
M 12.00/17.50 st. and a la carte ⌂ 3.95 – ⊡ 7.00 – **82 rm** 46.00/92.00 st., **1 suite** 96.00/
120.00 **st.** – SB 76.00/116.00 st.

St. Nicholas, St. Nicholas Cliff, YO11 2EU, 364101, Telex 52351, Fax 500538, ⩽, 🔲 – |‡|
TV ☎ 🚗 – 🔏 400. 🅰 AE ⓪ VISA   Z n
M (dinner only) 12.00 st. ⌂ 5.00 – **139 rm** ⊡ 50.00/80.00 st., **5 suites** 90.00/100.00 st. –
SB 68.00/80.00 st.

Palm Court, St. Nicholas Cliff, YO11 2ES, 368161, Fax 371547, 🔲 – |‡| TV ☎ – 🔏 100.
🅰 AE ⓪ VISA ⌾   Z e
M 14.00 t. (dinner) and a la carte ⌂ 4.00 – **50 rm** ⊡ 32.00/85.00 t. – SB 68.00/77.00 st.

XX **Grapevine**, 23 Valley Rd, YO11 2LY, ✆ 377088 – 🖼 AE ⓪ VISA   Z a
closed Sunday, 26 to 28 December and 1 to 3 January – **M** (dinner only) a la carte
11.15/18.45 t. 🍷 3.95.

X **Lanterna**, 33 Queen St., YO11 1HQ, ✆ 363616, Italian rest. – 🖼 VISA   Y a
closed Sunday and Monday – **M** (dinner only) a la carte 10.80/13.80 t. 🍷 3.75.

at Scalby NW : 3 m. by A 171 – Z – ✉ ☎ 0723 Scarborough :

🏨 **Wrea Head** ⤴, YO13 0PB, by Barmoor Lane ✆ 378211, ≤, 🌳, park – TV ☎ P. 🖼 AE ⓪
VISA ⌗
closed January and February – **M** 8.50/14.95 t. and a la carte 🍷 5.50 – **19 rm** ⊆ 32.50/100.00 t..
1 suite 110.00/150.00 t. – SB 75.00/125.00 st.

at Hackness NW : 7 m. by A 171 – Z – ✉ ☎ 0723 Scarborough :

🏨 **Hackness Grange** (Best Western) ⤴, YO13 0JW, ✆ 82345, Group Telex 527667, ≤, « 18C
house », 🏊, 🌾, 🌳, park, 🎾 – TV ☎ P. 🖼 AE ⓪ VISA. ⌗
M 7.00/16.50 **st.** and a la carte 🍷 4.25 – **26 rm** ⊆ 49.00/98.00 st. – SB (weekdays only)
89.00/105.00 st.

CITROEN, DATSUN, PEUGEOT-TALBOT Northway
✆ 363533
DAIHATSU Pickering Rd, West Ayton ✆ 862880
FIAT Manor Rd ✆ 364111

FORD Vine St. ✆ 375581
RENAULT Columbus Ravine ✆ 360791
VAUXHALL-OPEL Seamer Rd ✆ 360335

SCILLY (Isles of) Cornwall 🔢 ㉚ The West Country G. – pop. 2 653.

See : Site★★.

Envir. : St. Martin's : Viewpoint★★ – St. Agnes : Horsepoint★.

Helicopter service from St. Mary's and Tresco to Penzance : ✆ 0736 (Penzance) 63871.

✈ St. Mary's Airport : ✆ 0720 (Scillonia) 22677, E : 1 ½ m. from Hugh.

🚢 from Hugh Town, St. Mary's to Penzance (Isles of Scilly Steamship Co.) summer Mon-
day/Saturday 1-2 daily; winter 4 weekly (2 h 30 mn).

🛈 Town Hall, St. Mary's ✆ 0720 (Scillonia) 22536.

Bryher – pop. 66 – ✉ ☎ 0720 Scillonia.

See : Village on Watch Hill (≤★) – Hell Bay★.

🏠 **Hell Bay** ⤴, TR23 0PR, ✆ 22947, 🌳 – TV. 🖼 VISA. ⌗
March-November – **M** (bar lunch)/dinner 14.00 t. 🍷 3.50 – **10 rm** ⊆ 46.00/51.00 t., **4 suites**
– SB 66.00/72.00 st.

🏠 **Bank Cottage** ⤴, TR23 0PR, ✆ 22612, ≤, 🌳 – ⌗
April-October – **5 rm** ⊆ (dinner included) 19.00/42.00 st.

St. Martins – ☎ 0720 Scillonia

🏨 **St. Martins** ⤴, TR25 0QW, ✆ 22092, Fax 22298, ≤, 🏊, 🌳 – TV ☎. 🖼 AE ⓪ VISA
M *(bar lunch Monday to Saturday April-October)* a la carte 17.50/42.50 st. – **24 rm**
⊆ 89.00/208.00 st.

St. Mary's – pop. 2 106 – ECD : Wednesday – ✉ St. Mary's – ☎ 0720 Scillonia.

See : Garrison Walk★ (≤★★) – Peninnis Head★.

🏌 ✆ 22692, N : 1 m. from Hugh Town.

🛈 Town Hall, ✆ 22536.

🏨 **Tregarthen's** (Best Western), Hugh Town, TR21 0PP, ✆ 22540, ≤ harbour and islands –
TV ☎. 🖼 AE ⓪ VISA. ⌗
Late March-late October – **M** (bar lunch Monday to Saturday)dinner/14.00 t. 🍷 4.75 – **33 rm**
⊆ 38.50/109.00 t. – SB 70.00/92.00 st.

🏨 **Star Castle** ⤴, TR21 0JA, ✆ 22317, « Elizabethan fortress », 🏊, 🌳, 🎾 – TV ☎
April-mid October – **M** (bar lunch)/dinner 12.50 st. – **24 rm** ⊆ (dinner included)
40.00/100.00 st.

🏠 **Atlantic**, Hugh St., Hugh Town, TR21 0PL, ✆ 22417, ≤ St. Mary's Harbour – ⌗ rest
April-October – **M** (bar lunch)/dinner 11.75 t. – **24 rm** ⊆ 28.00/37.00 t.

🏠 **Tremellyn** ⤴, Church rd, Hugh Town, TR21 0NA, ✆ 22656, 🌳 – TV P. ⌗
closed November and December – **8 rm** ⊆ (dinner included) 19.00/60.50 st.

🏠 **Carnwethers** ⤴, Pelistry Bay, TR21 0NX, ✆ 22415, 🏊 heated, 🌳 – ⌗ rest. ⌗
Mid March-mid October – **M** 9.00 st. 🍷 2.70 – **8 rm** ⊆ 23.00/46.00 st.

Tresco – pop. 285 – ✉ New Grimsby – ☎ 0720 Scillonia.

See : Site★ – Abbey Gardens★ *AC* – Lighthouse Way (≤★★).

🏨 **Island** ⤴, Old Grimsby, TR24 0PU, ✆ 22883, ≤ St. Martin's and islands, « Sub-tropical
gardens », 🏊 heated, park – TV ☎. ⌗
Mid March-mid October – **M** a la carte lunch 5.95/19.00 st. /dinner 22.00 st. 🍷 4.50 – **23 rm**
⊆ (dinner included) 79.00/170.00 st., **1 suite** (dinner included) 168.00/200.00 st.

🏠 **New Inn** ⤴, TR24 0QQ, ✆ 22844, ≤, 🌳 – ⌗
M (bar lunch)/dinner 14.00 t. – **12 rm** ⊆ (dinner included) 30.25/90.00 t.

SCOLE Norfolk 404 X 26 – see Diss.

SCOTCH CORNER North Yorks. 402 P 20 – ⊠ ✆ 0748 Richmond.
🛏 Scotch Corner Hotel ✆ 2943/4864.
♦London 235 – ♦Carlisle 70 – ♦Middlesbrough 25 – Newcastle 43.

    🏠 **Travelodge** without rest., Skeeby, DL10 5EQ, S : 1 m. on A 1 (Northbound carriageway), ✆ 3768 – TV ⑆ Ⓟ. ⛐ AE VISA
       40 rm 21.50/27.00 t.

SCUNTHORPE Humberside 402 S 23 – pop. 79 043 – ECD : Wednesday – ✆ 0724.
Envir. : Normanby Hall⋆ (Regency) : Wildlife park⋆ *AC*, N : 4 m. – Barton-upon-Humber (St. Mary's Church⋆ 12C, Old St. Peter's Church⋆ 10C-11C) NE : 13 ½ m..
🏌 Kingsway ✆ 840945.
✈ Humberside Airport : ✆ 0652 (Barnetby) 688456, E : 15 m. by A 18.
🛈 Central Library, Carlton St. ✆ 860161.
♦London 167 – ♦Leeds 54 – Lincoln 30 – ♦Sheffield 45.

    🏨 **Royal** (T.H.F.), Doncaster Rd, DN15 7DE, ✆ 282276, Telex 527479 – ⇔ rm TV ⑫ Ⓟ – 🕴.
       ⛐ AE ① VISA
       M *(closed Saturday lunch)* 6.95/18.20 **st.** and a la carte – � 7.00 – **33 rm** 46.00/66.00 **st.** – SB (weekends only) 56.00/60.00 **st.**

    🏨 **Wortley House,** Rowland Rd, DN16 1SU, ✆ 842223, Telex 527837, Fax 280646 – TV ☎ Ⓟ
       – 🕴 250. ⛐ AE ① VISA
       M 12.00/15.00 **st.** and a la carte 🍷 4.50 – **32 rm** ⊑ 50.00/56.00 **st.** – SB (weekends only) 45.00/65.00 **st.**

AUSTIN-ROVER Normanby Rd ✆ 856551
BMW Old Crosby ✆ 281300
FIAT Normanby Rd ✆ 861191
FORD Station Rd ✆ 840655
HYUNDAI Doncaster Rd ✆ 860212
RENAULT Brigg Rd ✆ 842011

VAUXHALL-OPEL Moorwell Rd Industrial Estate ✆ 843284
VAUXHALL Winterton Rd ✆ 861862

⓪ ATS Grange Lane North ✆ 868191
ATS Burringham Rd ✆ 860435

SEACROFT West Yorks. 402 ⑩ – see Leeds.

SEAFORD East Sussex 404 U 31 – pop. 16 367 – ECD : Wednesday – ✆ 0323.
🛈 Station Approach ✆ 897426.
♦London 65 – ♦Brighton 14 – Folkestone 64.

    XX **Quincy's,** 42 High St., BN25 1PL, ✆ 895490 – ⛐ VISA
       closed Sunday and Monday – **M** (dinner only) 18.95 **t.** 🍷 2.75.

SEAHOUSES Northumb. 401 402 P 17 – pop. 1 709 (inc. North Sunderland) – ECD : Wednesday – ✆ 0665.
Envir. : Farne Islands⋆ (by boat from harbour).
🏌 Beadnell Rd ✆ 720794.
🛈 10 Main St. ✆ 720884 (summer only).
♦London 328 – ♦Edinburgh 80 – ♦Newcastle-upon-Tyne 46.

    🏠 **Beach House,** 12a St. Aidans, Seafront, NE68 7SR, ✆ 720337, ≼, 🡒 – ⇔ rest TV ☎ ⑆
       Ⓟ. ⛐ VISA
       April-October – **M** (bar lunch residents only)/dinner 13.50 **t.** – **14 rm** ⊑ 30.00/60.00 **t.** – SB (except summer) 64.00/68.00 **st.**

    🏠 **St. Aidans,** Seafront, ✆ 720355, ≼ – TV Ⓟ
       Mid February-mid November – **M** (bar lunch residents only)/dinner 9.75 **st.** 🍷 4.50 – **10 rm** ⊑ 30.00/50.00 **st.** – SB (mid February-May and mid September-mid November) 55.00/60.00 **st.**

    🍴 **Olde Ship,** 9 Main St., NE68 7RD, ✆ 720200 – TV Ⓟ. ⌘
       Easter-October – **M** (bar lunch)/dinner 9.50 **t.** 🍷 3.50 – **10 rm** ⊑ 21.00/47.00 **t.** – SB 56.00/60.00 **st.**

SEALE Surrey 404 R 30 – see Farnham.

SEATOLLER Cumbria – see Keswick.

SEATON BURN Tyne and Wear 402 P 18 – see Newcastle-upon-Tyne.

SEATON CAREW Cleveland 402 Q 20 – see Hartlepool.

SEAVIEW I.O.W. 403 404 Q 31 – see Wight (Isle of).

SEAVINGTON ST. MARY Somerset 403 L 31 – pop. 321 – ⊠ Ilminster – ☎ 0460 South Petherton.

♦London 142 – Taunton 14 – Yeovil 11.

XX **Pheasant** ⑤ with rm, Water St., TA19 0QH, ℰ 40502, Fax 42388, 淼 – 📺 ☎ 🅿. 🔊 AE ⓪ VISA ⑤
    closed 26 December-10 January – **M** (closed Sunday) (dinner only) 12.95 t. and a la carte
    ₤ 4.00 – **10 rm** ☑ 47.50/75.00 t. – SB 46.50/48.50 st.

SEDGEMOOR SERVICE AREA Somerset – ☎ 0934 Weston-Super-Mare

🏠 **Travelodge** without rest., M 5 (Northbound carriageway) between junctions 21 and 22,
    BS24 0JL, ℰ 750831, Fax 750450 – 📺 � 🅿
    40 rm.

SEDLESCOMBE East Sussex 404 V 31 – pop. 1 315 – ⊠ Battle – ☎ 042 487.

♦London 56 – Hastings 7 – Lewes 26 – Maidstone 27.

🏰 **Brickwall**, The Green, TN33 0QA, ℰ 253, ⏉ heated, 淼 – 📺 ☎ 🅿. 🔊 AE ⓪ VISA
    M 10.00/13.50 t. ₤ 3.15 – **24 rm** ☑ 40.00/51.00 t. – SB 62.00/67.00 st.

at Cripp's Corner N : 2 ¼ m. by A 229 on B 2089 – ⊠ Robertsbridge – ☎ 058 083
Staplecross :

XX **Olivers**, TN32 5RY, ℰ 387, 淼 – 🅿. 🔊 VISA
    closed Monday, Tuesday and first 3 weeks January – **M** 16.50 st. ₤ 3.75.

SELBY North Yorks. 402 Q 22 – ☎ 0757.
See : Selby Abbey Church★★.
🛈 Bus Station, Park St. ℰ 703263.

♦London 202 – ♦Kingston-upon-Hull 36 – ♦Leeds 23 – York 14.

🏠 **Londesborough Arms** (B.C.B.), Market Pl., YO8 0NS, ℰ 707355 – 📺 ☎ 🅿. 🔊 AE ⓪
    VISA ⑤
    M a la carte 9.25/14.35 st. – **27 rm** ☑ 37.50/48.00 st.

⑩ ATS York St., Gowthorpe ℰ 703245/702147

SELLING Kent 404 W 30 – pop. 674 – ⊠ ☎ 022 785 Faversham.
♦London 56 – Canterbury 10 – ♦Dover 28 – Maidstone 25.

↑ **Parkfield House** without rest., Hogben's Hill, ME13 9QX, ℰ 0227 (Canterbury) 752898, 淼
    – ⤬ 🅿. ⑤
    closed 24 to 26 December – **4 rm** ☑ 12.50/25.00 s.

SETTLE North Yorks. 402 N 21 – pop. 3 153 – ECD : Wednesday – ☎ 072 92.
🛈 Giggleswick ℰ 3912.
🛈 Town Hall, Cheapside ℰ 3617 (summer only).

♦London 238 – Bradford 34 – Kendal 30 – ♦Leeds 41.

🏰 **Falcon Manor**, Skipton Rd, BD24 9BD, ℰ 3814, ≤, 淼 – 📺 ☎ 🅿. 🔊 ⓪ VISA
    M (dinner only and Sunday lunch)/dinner 14.75 st. and a la carte ₤ 3.50 – **20 rm**
    ☑ 39.00/82.00 st. – SB 66.00/99.00 st.

🏠 **Royal Oak**, Market Pl., BD24 9ED, ℰ 2561 – 📺 ☎ 🅿. ⑤
    M (bar lunch Monday to Saturday)/dinner a la carte 10.95/15.55 st. ₤ 3.35 – ☑ 6.05 – **6 rm**
    27.50/46.50 st.

at Giggleswick NW : ¾ m. on A 65 – ⊠ ☎ 072 92 Settle :

↑ **Woodlands** ⑤ without rest., The Mains, BD24 0AX, ℰ 2576, ≤, 淼 – 🅿. ⑤
    closed Christmas and New Year – **8 rm** ☑ 21.00/48.00 t.

AUSTIN-ROVER Station Rd ℰ 2323

SEVENOAKS Kent 404 U 30 – pop. 24 493 – ECD : Wednesday – ☎ 0732.
See : Knole★★ (15C-17C) *AC*.
Envir. : Lullingstone (Roman Villa : mosaic panels★) *AC*, N : 6 m.
🛈 Buckhurst Lane ℰ 450305.

♦London 26 – Guildford 40 – Maidstone 17.

XX **Royal Oak** with rm, Upper High St., TN14 5PG, ℰ 451109, Fax 740187 – 🍽 rest 📺 ☎ 🅿.
    🔊 AE ⓪ VISA
    M (closed Saturday lunch and Sunday dinner) 15.00/19.50 t. ₤ 4.50 – **21 rm** ☑ 55.00/85.00 t.
    – SB (weekends only) (except Christmas) 95.00 st.

at Ivy Hatch E : 4 ¾ m. by A25 and A 227 on Coach Rd – ⊠ ☎ 0732 Sevenoaks :

X **Le Chantecler** (at The Plough), TN15 0NL, ℰ 810268, 淼 – 🅿. 🔊 VISA
    closed Sunday dinner – **M** dinner 19.95 t. ₤ 5.00.

CITROEN Tonbridge Rd ℰ 453328
FIAT, MITSUBISHI London Rd ℰ 462800
RENAULT 71 St. Johns Hill ℰ 455174

SAAB Borough Green ℰ 883044
VAUXHALL-OPEL 128 Seal Rd ℰ 451337

LE GUIDE MICHELIN DU PNEUMATIQUE.

En 1889, Edouard Michelin prend la direction de l'entreprise qui porte son nom. Peu de temps après, il dépose le brevet du pneumatique démontable pour bicyclette. Tous les efforts de l'entreprise se concentrent alors sur le développement de la technique du pneumatique. C'est ainsi qu'en 1895, pour la première fois au monde, un véhicule automobile baptisé "l'Eclair" roule sur pneumatiques. Testé sur ce véhicule lors de la course Paris-Bordeaux-Paris, le pneumatique démontre immédiatement sa supériorité sur le bandage plein. Créé en 1898, le Bibendum symbolise l'entreprise qui, de recherche en innovation, du pneu vélocipède au pneu avion, impose le pneumatique à toutes les roues. En 1946, c'est le dépôt du brevet du pneu radial ceinturé acier, l'une des innovations majeures du monde du transport.

C'est cette volonté permanente de battre demain le pneu d'aujourd'hui pour offrir le meilleur service à l'utilisateur qui a permis à Michelin de devenir le leader mondial du pneumatique.

QU'EST - CE QU'UN PNEU ?

Produit de haute technologie, le pneu constitue le seul point de liaison de la voiture avec le sol. Ce contact correspond, pour une roue, à une surface équivalente à celle d'une carte postale. Le pneu doit donc se contenter de ces quelques centimètres carrés de gomme au sol pour remplir un grand nombre de tâches souvent contradictoires dans des conditions très diverses :

Porter le véhicule à l'arrêt, mais aussi résister aux transferts de charge considérables à l'accélération et au freinage.

Transmettre la puissance utile du moteur ainsi que les efforts de freinage.

Rouler régulièrement, plus sûrement, plus longtemps pour un plus grand plaisir de conduire.

Guider le véhicule avec la plus grande précision possible, quels que soient l'état du sol et les conditions climatiques.

Amortir les irrégularités de la route, en assurant le confort du conducteur et des passagers ainsi que la longévité du véhicule.

Durer, c'est-à-dire garder au meilleur niveau ses performances pendant des millions de tours de roue.

Quelques conseils importants: afin de vous permettre d'exploiter au mieux toutes les qualités de vos pneumatiques, nous vous proposons de lire attentivement les informations et les conseils qui suivent :

Le pneu est le seul point de liaison de la voiture avec le sol.

Comment lit-on un pneu ?

① « Bib» repérant l'emplacement de l'indicateur d'usure.

② Marque enregistrée. ③ Largeur du pneu: ≃ 185mm.

④ Série du pneu H/S: 70. ⑤ Structure: R (radial).

⑥ Diamètre intérieur: 14 pouces (correspondant à celui de la jante). ⑦ Type du pneu: MXV. ⑧ Indice de charge: 88 (560kg). ⑨ Symbole de vitesse: H (210 km/h).

⑩ Pneu sans chambre: Tubeless. ⑪ Marque enregistrée.

Symboles de vitesse maximum:

Q : 160km/h

R : 170km/h

S : 180km/h

T : 190km/h

H : 210km/h

V : 240km/h

ZR : supérieure à 240km/h.

GONFLEZ VOS PNEUS, MAIS GONFLEZ-LES BIEN

POUR EXPLOITER AU MIEUX LEURS PERFORMANCES ET ASSURER VOTRE SECURITE.

Contrôlez la pression de vos pneus dans de bonnes conditions :

Un pneu perd régulièrement et naturellement de la pression (en moyenne 0,04 bar par mois). Il vous faut donc contrôler périodiquement (1 fois par mois) la pression de vos pneus, sans oublier la roue de secours. La pression d'un pneu doit toujours être vérifiée à froid, c'est - à-dire une heure au moins après l'arrêt de la voiture ou après avoir parcouru 2 ou 3 km à faible allure. Il ne faut jamais dégonfler un pneu chaud.

Le surgonflage : Si vous devez effectuer un long trajet à vitesse soutenue ou si la charge de votre voiture est particulièrement importante, il est généralement conseillé de majorer la pression de vos pneus. Mais attention, l'écart de pression avant-arrière, nécessaire à l'équilibre du véhicule doit être impérativement respecté. Consultez les tableaux de gonflage Michelin chez tous les professionnels de l'automobile et chez les spécialistes du pneu.

Le sous-gonflage : Lorsque la pression de gonflage est insuffisante, les flancs du pneu travaillent anormalement ; ce qui entraîne une fatigue excessive de la carcasse, une élévation de température et une usure anormale. Le pneu

Vérifiez la pression de vos pneus régulièrement et avant chaque voyage.

subit alors des dommages irréversibles qui peuvent entraîner sa destruction. Le sous-gonflage dégrade la précision de guidage de votre véhicule et met en cause votre sécurité.

Le bouchon de valve : En apparence il s'agit d'un détail: c'est pourtant un élément essentiel de l'étanchéité. Aussi n'oubliez pas de le remettre en place après vérification de la pression en vous assurant de sa parfaite propreté.

Voiture tractant caravane, bateau .....
Dans ce cas particulier, il ne faut jamais oublier que le poids de la remorque accroît considérablement la charge du véhicule. Il est donc nécessaire d'augmenter la pression des pneus arrière de votre voiture en vous conformant aux indications des tableaux de gonflage que Michelin diffuse très largement. Pour de plus amples renseignements, demandez conseil à votre revendeur de pneumatiques, c'est un véritable spécialiste.

POUR FAIRE DURER VOS PNEUS, GARDEZ UN ŒIL SUR EUX .

Afin de préserver longtemps les qualités de vos pneus, il est impératif de les faire contrôler régulièrement et avant chaque grand voyage. Il faut savoir que la durée de vie d'un pneu peut varier dans un rapport de 1 à 4 et parfois plus, selon son entretien, l'état du véhicule, le style de conduite et l'état des routes! Les ensembles roue-pneumatique doivent être parfaitement équilibrés pour éviter les vibrations qui peuvent apparaître à partir d'une certaine vitesse. Ces vibrations, outre leur désagrément, détériorent les suspensions, affectent la tenue de route et endommagent les pneus par une usure irrégulière. Vous confierez l'équilibrage à un professionnel du pneumatique car cette opération nécessite un outillage très spécialisé.

Voici quelques facteurs qui influent sur l'usure et la durée de vie de vos pneumatiques :

les caractéristiques du véhicule (poids, puissance…), le profil des routes (rectilignes, sinueuses), le revêtement (granulométrie: sol lisse ou rugueux), l'état mécanique du véhicule (réglage des trains avant, arrière, état des suspensions et des freins…),le style de conduite (accélérations, freinages, vitesse de passage en courbe…) ,la vitesse (en ligne droite à 120 km/h un pneu s'use deux fois plus vite qu'à 70 km/h), la pression des pneumatiques (si elle est incorrecte, les pneus s'useront beaucoup plus vite et de manière irrégulière).

Une conduite sportive réduit la durée de vie des pneus.

Sans oublier les événements de nature accidentelle (chocs contre trottoirs, nids de poule…) qui, en plus du risque de

Les chocs contre les trottoirs, les nids de poule... peuvent endommager gravement vos pneus.

déréglage et de détérioration de certains éléments du véhicule, peuvent provoquer des dommages internes au pneumatique dont les conséquences ne se manifesteront parfois que bien plus tard. Un contrôle régulier de vos pneus vous permettra donc de détecter puis de corriger rapidement des anomalies telles que: usure anormale, perte de pression... A la moindre alerte, blessure accidentelle par exemple, adressez - vous immédiatement à un revendeur spécialiste qui interviendra pour préserver les qualités de vos pneus, votre confort et votre sécurité.

SURVEILLEZ L'USURE DE VOS PNEUMATIQUES:

Comment ? Tout simplement en observant la profondeur de la sculpture. C'est un facteur de sécurité, en particulier sur sol mouillé. Tous les pneus possèdent des indicateurs d'usure de 1,6 mm d'épaisseur. Ces indicateurs sont repérés par un Bibendum situé aux "épaules"des pneus Michelin. Un examen visuel suffit pour connaître le niveau d'usure de vos pneumatiques. Mais attention, même si vos pneus n'ont pas encore atteint la limite d'usure légale (en France, la profondeur restante de la sculpture doit être supérieure à 1mm sur l'ensemble de la bande de roulement), leur capacité d'évacuer l'eau aura naturellement diminué avec l'usure.

FAITES LE BON CHOIX POUR ROULER EN TOUTE TRANQUILLITE .

Le type de pneumatique qui équipe d'origine votre véhicule a été déterminé pour optimiser ses performances. Il vous est cependant possible d'effectuer un autre choix en fonction de votre style de conduite, des conditions climatiques, de la nature des routes et des trajets effectués.

Dans tous les cas, il est indispensable de consulter un spécialiste du pneumatique, lui seul pourra vous aider à trouver la solution la mieux adaptée à votre utilisation.

Montage, démontage du pneu ; c'est l'affaire d'un spécialiste :
Un mauvais montage ou démontage du pneu peut détériorer celui-ci et mettre en cause votre sécurité : il faut donc confier cette tâche à un spécialiste.

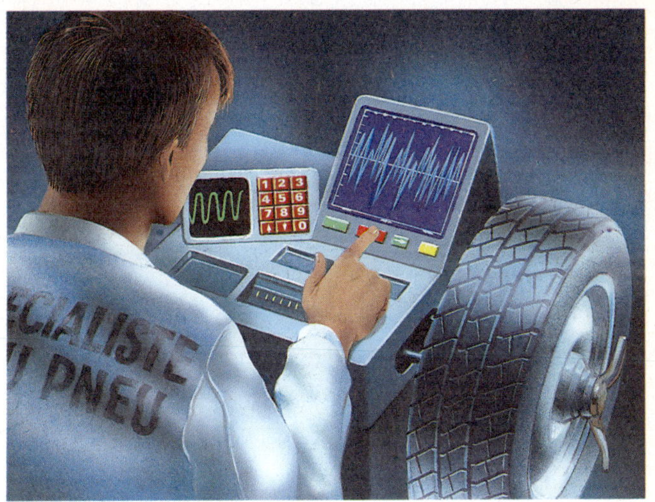

Le montage et l'équilibrage d'un pneu, c'est l'affaire d'un spécialiste.

Il est conseillé de monter le même type de pneu sur l'ensemble du véhicule. Pour obtenir la meilleure tenue de route, les pneumatiques neufs ou les moins usés doivent être montés à l'arrière de votre voiture.

En cas de crevaison, seul un professionnel du pneu saura effectuer les examens nécessaires et décider de son éventuelle réparation.

Il est recommandé de changer la valve ou la chambre à chaque intervention.

Nous déconseillons de monter une chambre à air avec un pneu tubeless.

INNOVER POUR ALLER PLUS LOIN

Concevoir les pneus qui font avancer tous les jours 2 milliards de roues sur la terre, faire évoluer sans relâche plus de 3000 types de pneus différents, c'est ce que font chaque jour 4500 chercheurs dans les centres de recherche Michelin.

Leurs outils : des ordinateurs qui calculent à la vitesse de 100 millions d'opérations par seconde, des laboratoires et des centres d'essais installés sur 6000 hectares en France, en Espagne et aux Etats-Unis pour parcourir quotidiennement 25 fois le tour du monde soit plus d'un million de kilomètres. Leur volonté : écouter, observer puis optimiser chaque fonction du pneumatique et tester sans relâche les solutions qui permettront de battre demain le pneu d'aujourd'hui.

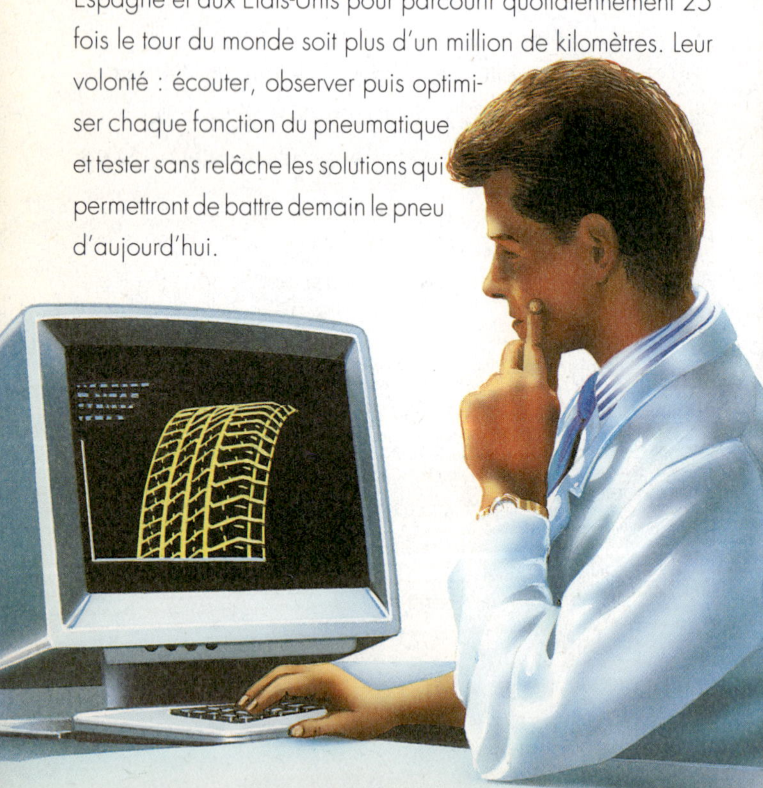

AU SERVICE DU CONDUCTEUR : LES CARTES ET LES GUIDES MICHELIN

Depuis la naissance de l'automobile, les Cartes et les Guides Michelin sont les compagnons les plus précieux de l'usager de la route. Vendus chaque année à 16 millions d'exemplaires les Guides Rouges hôteliers, les cartes routières et les Guides Verts touristiques apportent des informations précises et pratiques régulièrement mises à jour. Ils offrent par leur complémentarité et leur indépendance de jugement un service particulièrement bien adapté à l'automobiliste.

RENSEIGNEMENTS UTILES.

Vous avez des observations, vous souhaitez des précisions concernant l'utilisation de vos pneumatiques Michelin, écrivez-nous à: Manufacture Française des Pneumatiques Michelin. Boîte postale consommateurs .

63040 Clermont-Ferrand cedex.

Assistance Michelin Itinéraires :

Minitel: 3615 code Michelin.

- Centre de Renseignements Autoroutes , tél: (1) 47 05 90 01

Minitel: 3614 code ASFA.

- Centre National d'Informations Routières, tél:(1) 48 94 33 33

Minitel: 3615 code Route.

- Centres Régionaux d'Information et de Coordination Routière.

Bordeaux	56 96 33 33
Ile-de-France-Centre	(1) 48 99 33 33
Lille	20 47 33 33
Lyon	78 54 33 33
Marseille	91 78 78 78
Metz	87 63 33 33
Rennes	99 32 33 33

DATE	CHIFFRE COMPTEUR	OPERATIONS

 Dorset **403 404** N 30 **The West Country G.** – pop. 4 831 – ECD : Wednesday and Saturday – ✆ 0747.

See : ≤★ – Gold Hill★ – Local History Museum★ *AC*.

Envir. : Wardour Castle★ *AC*, NE : 5 m.

🛈 Bell St. ✆ 3514 (summer only).

♦London 115 – Bournemouth 31 – ♦Bristol 47 – Dorchester 29 – Salisbury 20.

Grosvenor (T.H.F.), The Commons, SP7 8JA, ✆ 52282 – ⇔ rm 📺 ⊛ – 🏊 120. 🅰 AE ⓞ VISA
M 9.95 **st.** (dinner) ⦚ 3.60 – ☲ 7.00 – **47 rm** 40.00/58.00 **st.** – SB 76.00/83.00 **st.**

Royal Chase (Best Western), Royal Chase Roundabout, SP7 8DB, junction of A 30 and A 350 ✆ 53355, Telex 418414, Fax 51969, 🅂, 🚗 – 📺 ☎ ⓟ – 🏊 50. 🅰 AE ⓞ VISA
M a la carte 14.70/18.80 **st.** ⦚ 4.70 – **31 rm** ☲ 52.00/170.00 **st.** – SB 78.00/106.00 **st.**

at Ludwell (Wilts.) E : 3 m. on A 30 – ✉ Shaftesbury (Dorset) – ✆ 074 788 Donhead :

Grove House, SP7 9ND, on A 30 ✆ 365, ≤, 🚗 – ⇔ rest 📺 ⓟ. 🅰 VISA
closed January – **M** (bar lunch)/dinner 15.00 **t.** ⦚ 3.00 – **11 rm** ☲ 23.00/46.00 **t.** – SB 63.00/70.00 **st.**

at Fontmell Magna S : 5 ¼ m. on A 350 – ✉ Shaftesbury – ✆ 0747 Fontmell Magna :

Estyard House, SP7 0PB, ✆ 811460, 🚗 – ⇔ ⓟ. 🛇
closed November – **6 rm** ☲ (dinner only) 16.00/30.00 **st.**

AUSTIN-ROVER Salisbury Rd ✆ 52295

 Devon **403** J 32 – see Teignmouth.

 I.O.W. **403 404** Q 32 – see Wight (Isle of).

 Derbs. **402 403 404** P 25 – see Derby.

 Wilts. **403 404** N 29 – see Melksham.

 Hants. **403 404** Q 31 – pop. 3 291 – ✉ Southampton – ✆ 0329 Wickham.

♦London 75 – ♦Portsmouth 13 – ♦Southampton 10.

Meon Valley Golf and Country Club (Best Western), Sandy Lane, SO3 2HQ, off A 334 ✆ 833455, Telex 86272, Fax 833411, ≤, 🅂, 🛅, 🚗, park, 🎾, squash – 📺 ☎ ⓟ – 🏊 . 🅰 AE ⓞ VISA 🛇
M (closed Saturday lunch) 10.00/14.00 **t.** and a la carte ⦚ 4.25 – **84 rm** ☲ 80.00/110.00 **t.**

 Kent **404** W 29 – pop. 11 087 – ECD : Wednesday – ✆ 0795.

See : ≤★ from the pier.

Envir. : Minster (abbey : brasses★, effigied tombs★) SE : 2 ½ m.

⛴ Shipping connections with the Continent : to the Netherlands (Vlissingen) (Olau).

🛈 Bridge Rd Car Park ✆ 665324.

♦London 52 – Canterbury 24 – Maidstone 20.

*Hotels and Restaurants see : **Sittingbourne** SW : 9 m., **Maidstone** SW : 20 m.*

AUSTIN-ROVER New Rd ✆ 664329   SKODA Granville Pl., Granville Rd ✆ 662730
FORD High St. ✆ 580058

 South Yorks. **402 403 404** P 23 – pop. 470 685 – ECD : Thursday – ✆ 0742.

See : Cutler's Hall★ CZ A.

🛅 Tinsley Park ✆ 42237, E : by A 57 BZ – 🛅 Beauchief, Abbey Lane ✆ 620040, SW : by B 6068 AZ – 🛅 Birley Wood, Birley Lane ✆ 397979, SE : 4 ½ m. by A 616 BZ – 🛅 Concorde Park, Shiregreen Lane ✆ 613605, N : 3 ½ m. by A 6135 BY.

🛈 Town Hall Extension, Union St. ✆ 734671/2.

♦London 174 – ♦Leeds 36 – ♦Liverpool 80 – ♦Manchester 41 – ♦Nottingham 44.

Plans on following pages

Hallam Tower Post House (T.H.F.), Manchester Rd (A 57), S10 5DX, ✆ 670067, Telex 547293, Fax 682620, ≤, 🅂 – 🛗 ⇔ rm 📺 ☎ ⓟ – 🏊 300. 🅰 AE ⓞ VISA   AZ o
M 9.25/13.25 **st.** and a la carte ⦚ 3.60 – ☲ 7.00 – **136 rm** 62.00/80.00 **st.**, **2 suites** 99.00/119.00 **st.** – SB (weekends only) 55.00/80.00 **st.**

St. George (Swallow), Kenwood Rd, S7 1NQ, ✆ 583811, Telex 547030, Fax 500138, 🅂, 🚗, park – 🛗 📺 ☎ 🤰 ⓟ – 🏊 200. 🅰 AE ⓞ VISA   AZ r
M 9.25/12.00 **st.** and a la carte ⦚ 4.90 – **141 rm** ☲ 66.00/80.00 **st.**, **1 suite** 86.00 – SB (weekends only) 82.00/85.00 **st.**

Beauchief (Lansbury), 161 Abbeydale Rd South, S7 2QW, SW : 3 ½ m. ✆ 620500, Telex 54164, Fax 368721 – ⇔ rm 📺 ☎ ⓟ – 🏊 110. 🅰 AE ⓞ VISA 🛇   on A 625 AZ
M 8.50/14.00 **t.** and a la carte 10.45/19.90 **t.** ⦚ 3.50 – **41 rm** ☲ 58.00/68.00 **t.**

P.T.O. →

SHEFFIELD
BUILT UP AREA

Barrow Road .... **BY** 4
Bawtry Road .... **BY** 5
Bradfield Road .... **AY** 7

Brocco Bank .... **AZ** 8
Broughton Lane .... **BY** 10
Burngreave Road .... **AY** 12
Handsworth Road .... **BZ** 24
Hollinsend Road .... **BZ** 28
Holywell Road .... **BY** 29
Main Road .... **BZ** 32
Meadow Hall Road .... **BY** 33

Middlewood Road .... **AY** 34
Newhall Road .... **BY** 36
Rustlings Road .... **AZ** 39
Westbourne Road .... **AZ** 47
Western Bank .... **AZ** 48
Whitham Road .... **AZ** 49
Woodbourn Road .... **BYZ** 50
Woodhouse Road .... **BZ** 51

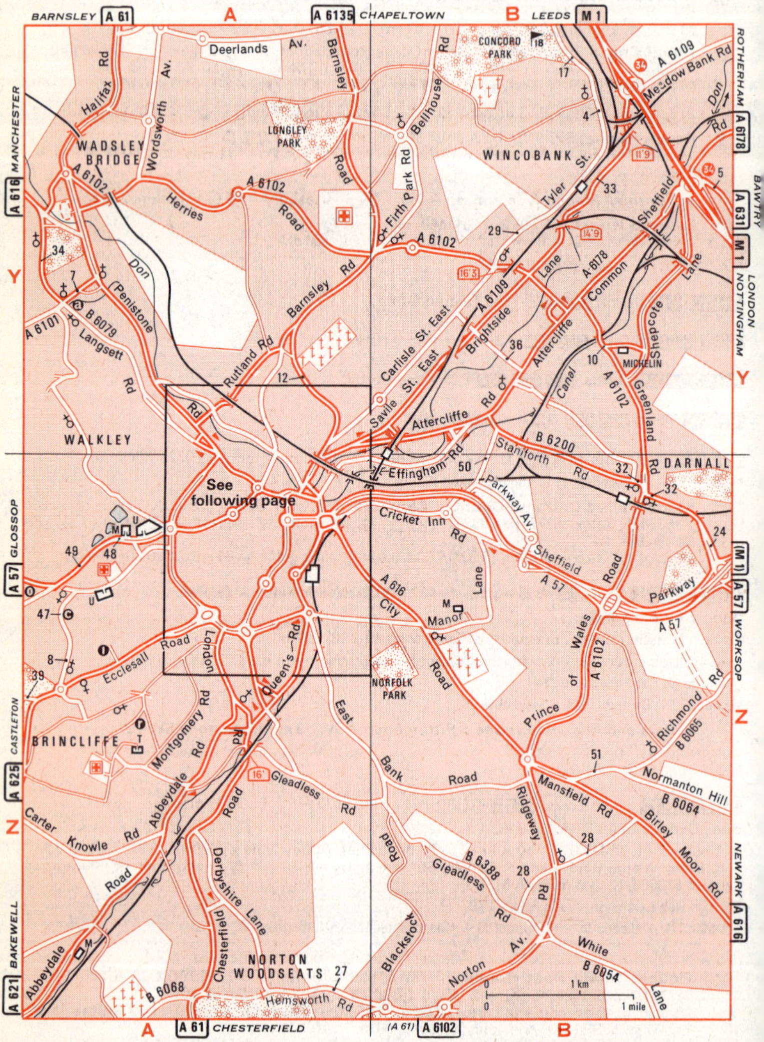

Do not mix up:

Comfort of hotels :
Comfort of restaurants :
Quality of the cuisine : ✿✿✿, ✿✿, ✿, **M**

SHEFFIELD
CENTRE

Angel Street . . . . **DY** 3
Commercial Street . . . . **DZ** 15
Fargate . . . . **CZ**
High Street . . . . **DZ**
Leopold Street . . . . **CZ** 31

West Street . . . . **CZ**
Blonk Street . . . . **DY** 6
Castle Gate . . . . **DY** 13
Charter Row . . . . **CZ** 14
Cumberland Street . . . . **CZ** 16
Fitzwilliam Gate . . . . **CZ** 19
Flat Street . . . . **DZ** 20
Furnival Gate . . . . **CZ** 21
Furnival Street . . . . **CZ** 22

Gibraltar Street . . . . **CY** 23
Haymarket . . . . **DY** 25
Moorfields . . . . **CY** 35
Pinstone Street . . . . **CZ** 37
Queen Street . . . . **CY** 38
St. Mary's Gate . . . . **CZ** 40
Shalesmoor . . . . **CY** 41
Snig Hill . . . . **DY** 42
Waingate . . . . **DY** 44
West Bar Green . . . . **CY** 45

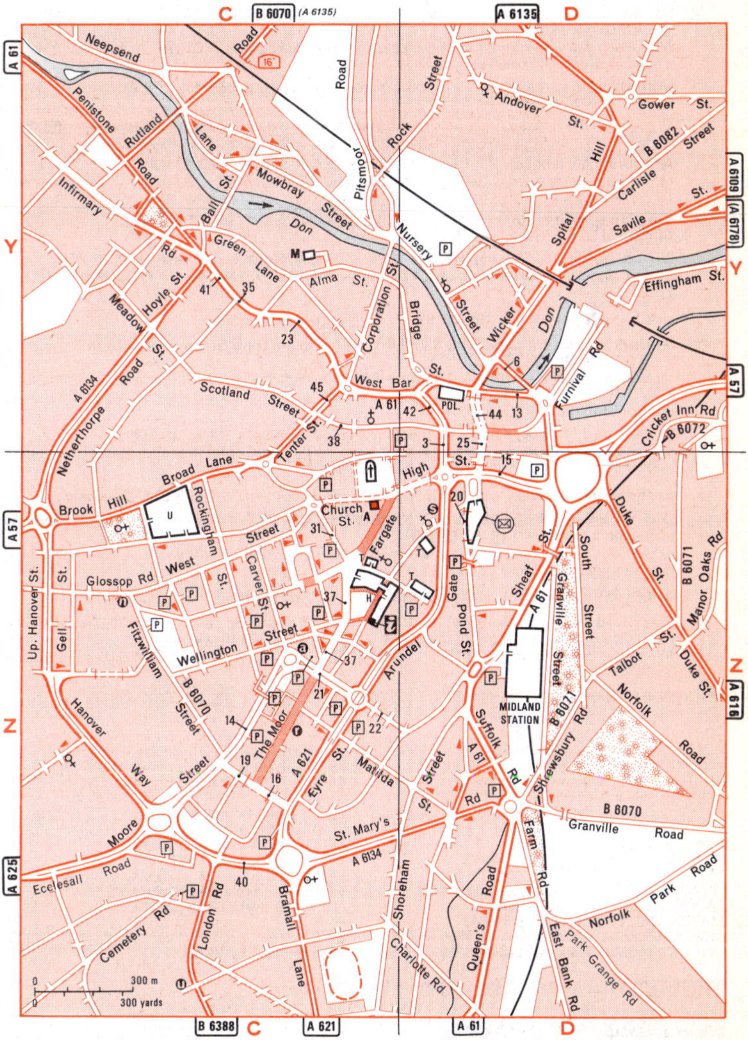

Ne confondez pas :

Confort des hôtels

Confort des restaurants

Qualité de la table

🏨 **Grosvenor House** (T.H.F.), Charter Sq., S1 3EH, ℘ 720041, Telex 54312, Fax 757199 – 🛗
⇥ rm 📺 ☎ 🅿 – 🎪 400. 🔼 AE ⓪ *VISA*   CZ **a**
M 9.50 **st.** (lunch) and a la carte 15.40/23.20 **st.** 🍷 4.25 – ⊊ 8.00 – **102 rm** 80.00/100.00 **st.**,
1 suite 135.00/150.00 **st.** – SB (weekends only) 60.00/72.00 **st.**

🏨 **Charnwood,** 10 Sharrow Lane, S11 8AA, ℘ 589411, Fax 555107 – ⇥ rest 📺 ☎ 🅿 – 🎪
80. 🔼 AE ⓪ *VISA* 🛇   CZ **u**
M 9.95/15.95 **t.** and a la carte 🍷 4.75 – **21 rm** ⊊ 71.00/87.00 **st.**

🏨 **St. James** (Best Western), George St., S1 2PF, ℘ 739939, Fax 768332 – 🛗 ▤ rest 📺 ☎ –
🎪 . 🔼 AE ⓪ *VISA*   DZ **s**
M (closed Saturday lunch) 5.95/9.50 **st.** and a la carte 🍷 3.95 – **32 rm** ⊊ 52.00/63.00 **st.** –
SB (weekends only) 54.00 **st.**

⌂ **Millingtons** without rest., 70 Broomgrove Rd, S10 2NA, ℘ 669549 – 📺 🅿 🛇   AZ **i**
6 rm ⊊ 20.00/38.00 **st.**

⌂ **Westbourne House** without rest., 25 Westbourne Rd, S10 2QQ, ℘ 660109, 🚗 – 📺 🅿
closed last week December and first week January – **9 rm** ⊊ 24.00/45.00 **st.**   AZ **c**

✗ **Arcadia,** 560 Langsett Rd, Hillsborough, S6 2LX, ℘ 323382 – 🔼 AE ⓪ *VISA*   AY **a**
closed Saturday lunch, Sunday, Monday and 23 December-1 January – **M** a la carte
13.75/17.25 **t.**

✗ **Zing Vaa,** 55 The Moor, S1 4PF, ℘ 722432, Chinese rest. – ▤. 🔼 AE ⓪ *VISA*   CZ **r**
M 4.10/14.50 **t.** and a la carte 8.40/16.60 **t.**

✗ **Nirmal's,** 189-193 Glossop Rd, S10 2GN, ℘ 724054, North Indian rest. – 🔼 AE *VISA*   CZ **n**
closed Sunday lunch and 25-26 December – **M** 12.50/13.50 **t.** and a la carte 5.40/11.20 **t.**
🍷 3.00.

at Chapeltown N : 6 m. on A 6135 – AY – ✉ ✆ 0742 Sheffield :

🏨 **Staindrop Lodge,** Lane End, S30 4UH, NW : ½ m. on High Green rd ℘ 846727 – 📺 ☎ 🅿
– 🎪 130. 🔼 AE ⓪ *VISA* 🛇
closed 25 and 26 December – **M** (closed Saturday lunch, Sunday dinner and Bank Holidays)
9.50/18.50 **t.** and a la carte 🍷 4.25 – **13 rm** ⊊ 50.00/70.00 **t.** – SB (weekends only)
(except Christmas) 57.00/65.00 **st.**

✗✗ **Greenhead House,** 84 Buncross Rd, S30 4SF, ℘ 469004 – ⇥ 🅿. AE *VISA*
closed Sunday, Monday, 2 weeks April-May, first 2 weeks September and 24 to 31 December
– **M** (booking essential)(dinner only) 25.50 **t.** 🍷 4.75.

at Ridgeway (Derbs.) SE : 6 ¾ m. by A 616 off B 6054 – BZ – ✉ ✆ 0742 Sheffield :

✗✗✗ **Old Vicarage,** Ridgeway Moor, S12 3XW, on Marsh Lane rd ℘ 475814, « Attractively
furnished », 🚗 – ⇥ 🅿. 🔼 AE *VISA*
closed Sunday dinner, Monday, last week August, and 26 December-3 January – **M** (lunch
by arrangement)/dinner 25.00 **t.** 🍷 7.00.

at Meadow Head S : 5 ¼ m. on A 61 – ✉ – ✆ 0708 Sheffield :

🏨 **Sheffield Moat House** (Q.M.H.), Chesterfield Rd South, S8 8BW, ℘ 375376, Telex 547890,
Fax 378140, 🔼 – 🛗 ⇥ rm ▤ rest 📺 ☎ 🅿 🅿 – 🎪 500. 🔼 AE ⓪ *VISA*
M (closed Saturday lunch) 10.50/12.50 **st.** 🍷 3.80 – ⊊ 7.25 – **89 rm** 58.00/68.00 **st.**, **5 suites**
90.00/130.00 **st.**

MICHELIN Distribution Centre, 12 Tinsley Park Close, S9 DE, ℘ 433264, FAX 439279 BY

AUDI 1 Eccleshall Rd, South ℘ 670670	MITSUBISHI Scotland St. ℘ 760567/ 731836
AUSTIN-ROVER Penistone Rd ℘ 348801	NISSAN 1-7 Meersbrook Rd ℘ 57315
AUSTIN-ROVER Tenter St. ℘ 761141	PEUGEOT-TALBOT Fitzwilliam St. ℘ 756324
AUSTIN-ROVER 286 Sandygate Rd ℘ 302021	PEUGEOT-TALBOT Langsett Rd ℘ 342368
AUSTIN-ROVER Broadfield Rd ℘ 588121	RENAULT Abbeydale Rd Sth. ℘ 369041
BMW Broad Lane ℘ 755077	SAAB 115 Eccleshall Rd South ℘ 369946
CITROEN, FIAT Suffolk Rd ℘ 721378	SEAT Shalesmoor ℘ 750000
FORD 53-67 London Rd ℘ 751515	SKODA 39-45 Infirmary Rd ℘ 701971
FORD Eccleshall Rd ℘ 686986	SKODA 21 Mansfield Rd ℘ 396001
HONDA 918 Chesterfield Rd ℘ 748029	TOYOTA Ellin St. ℘ 768717
HYUNDAI, RENAULT 252 Crookes ℘ 669202	VAUXHALL Saville St. ℘ 766600
JAGUAR-DAIMLER 200 Sharrow Vale ℘ 684741	VAUXHALL Eccleshall Rd ℘ 685922
LADA 178-184 London Rd ℘ 557394	VOLVO Eccleshall Rd ℘ 753151
MAZDA 872 Chesterfield Rd ℘ 748643	
MERCEDES-BENZ 300 Cemetery Rd ℘ 663468	⊚ ATS 87-91 Clifton St., Attercliffe ℘ 449750/449759
MERCEDES-BENZ Hanover Way ℘ 753391	ATS Herries Rd ℘ 343986/7

SHELDON West Midlands 🗺 ㉒ 🗺 ⑳ – see Birmingham.

SHENINGTON Oxon – see Banbury.

SHEPPERTON Surrey 🗺 S 29 – pop. 9 643 – ✆ 0932 Walton-on-Thames.
♦London 25.

Plan : see Greater London (South-West)

🏨 **Shepperton Moat House** (Q.M.H.), Felix Lane, TW17 8NP, E : 1 ¼ m. on B 375 ℘ 241404,
Telex 928170, Fax 245231, 🚗 – 🛗 📺 ☎ 🅿 – 🎪 400. 🔼 AE ⓪ *VISA*   AY **a**
closed 26 to 30 December – **M** 12.75/13.50 **st.** and a la carte 🍷 3.95 – **156 rm**
⊊ 65.00/105.00 **st.** – SB (weekends only) 72.00 **st.**

SHEPTON MALLET Somerset 403 404 M 30 The West Country G. – pop. 6 197 – ECD : Wednesday – ☎ 0749 – **See** : Site★ – SS. Peter and Paul's Church★.

Envir. : Oakhill Manor★*AC*, N : 4 m. off A 37 – Evercreech Church Tower★, SE : 4 m. – Downside Abbey★*AC*, N : 5 m. by A 37 on A 367 – Nunney★, W : 9 m. on A 361.

🛈 2 Petticoat Lane ℰ 5258 (summer only).

♦London 127 – ♦Bristol 20 – ♦Southampton 63 – Taunton 31.

 XX **Bowlish House** with rm, Wells Rd, BA4 5JD, W : ½ m. on A 371 ℰ 342022, ☞ – 📺 P. 🅿 VISA
   closed 24 to 27 December – **M** (booking essential) (dinner only) 16.50 **st.** – ♨ 3.50 – **4 rm** 42.00 **st.**

 X **Blostin's,** 29 Waterloo Rd, BA4 5HH, ℰ 343648 – 🅿 VISA
   closed Sunday, Monday, 2 weeks January and 2 weeks June – **M** (lunch by arrangement)/dinner 12.95 **st.** and a la carte 14.75/16.00 **st.** 🍷 4.25.

  at Doulting E : 1 ½ m. on A 361 – ✉ Shepton Mallet – ☎ 074 988 Cranmore :

 XX **Brottens Lodge** 🅂 with rm, BA4 4RB, S : 1 m. ℰ 352, ≼, ☞ – 📺 ☎ P. 🅿 AE ⓓ VISA ⌿
   closed first 2 weeks January – **M** (closed Saturday lunch, Sunday and Monday) 13.50/16.50 **t.** – ♨ 4.50 – **3 rm** 48.00/65.00 **st.** – SB (weekdays only) 84.00 **st.**

  at Croscombe W : 2 ¼ m. on A 371 – ✉ Wells – ☎ 0749 Shepton Mallet :

 🏠 **The Bull Terrier,** Wells, BA5 3QJ, ℰ 343658 – 📺. 🅿 VISA ⌿
   M (closed Sunday dinner January-April and Monday November-December) a la carte 5.90/10.20 **t.** 🍷 3.55 – **3 rm** ♨ 15.00/35.00 **t.**

HONDA Townsend Rd ℰ 4422   VW-AUDI Station Rd ℰ 4091

SHERBORNE Dorset 403 404 M 31 The West Country G. – pop. 7 405 – ECD : Wednesday – ☎ 0935.

See : Site★ – Abbey★★ – Sherborne Castle★*AC* – **Envir.** : Sandford Orcas Manor House★*AC*, N : 4 m. by B 3148 – Purse Caundle Manor★*AC*, NE : 5 m. by A 30.

🏌 Clatcombe ℰ 814431, N : 1 m.

🛈 Hound St. ℰ 815341 (summer only).

♦London 128 – Bournemouth 39 – Dorchester 19 – Salisbury 36 – Taunton 31.

 🏨 **Eastbury,** Long St., DT9 3BY, ℰ 813131, Telex 46644, ☞ – 📺 ☎ P. 🅿 – 🕍 60. 🅿 VISA ⌿
   M 10.50/17.50 **t.** and a la carte – **12 rm** ♨ 52.50/75.00 **t.** – SB (October-March) 92.50 **st.**

 🏨 **Half Moon,** Half Moon St., DT9 3LN, ℰ 812017 – ↪ 📺 ☎ P. 🅿 AE ⓓ VISA
   M 6.45 **st.** and a la carte – **15 rm** ♨ 41.50/51.50 **st.**

  at Oborne NE : 2 m. by A 30 – ✉ ☎ 0935 Sherborne :

 XX **Grange** 🅂 with rm, DT9 4LA, ℰ 813463, ≼, ☞ – 📺 ☎ P. 🅿 VISA ⌿
   closed Sunday dinner, Monday and 2 weeks August-September – **M** (dinner only and Sunday lunch) a la carte 11.50/16.50 **t.** 🍷 4.00 – **3 rm** ♨ 38.00/45.00 **t.**

ALFA-ROMEO, LANCIA Long St. ℰ 3262   MERCEDES-BENZ Yeovil Rd ℰ 3350
AUSTIN-ROVER Digby Rd ℰ 2436

SHERBOURNE Warw. – see Warwick.

SHERE Surrey 404 S 30 – see Guildford.

SHERIFF HUTTON North Yorks. 402 Q 21 – pop. 884 – ✉ York – ☎ 034 77.

♦London 313 – York 10.

 🏠 **Rangers House** 🅂, The Park, YO6 1RH, S : 1 ¼ m. by Strensall rd ℰ 397, ☞ – 🅿 ⌿
   M (dinner only) 16.50 🍷 2.50 – **6 rm** ♨ 25.00/50.00 – SB (October-March except Christmas and New Year) 60.00/66.00 **st.**

SHERINGHAM Norfolk 404 X 25 – pop. 6 861 – ECD : Wednesday – ☎ 0263 Cromer.
Envir. : Cromer : SS. Peter and Paul's Church (tower ≼★).

🛈 Station Approach ℰ 824329 (summer only).

♦London 128 – Cromer 4 – ♦Norwich 27.

 🏠 **Beacon,** 1 Nelson Rd, NR26 8BT, ℰ 822019, ☞ – ↪ rest P. 🅿 VISA ⌿
   April-October – **6 rm** ♨ (dinner included) 21.00/46.00.

SHIFNAL Shropshire 402 403 404 M 25 – pop. 6 094 – ECD : Thursday – ✉ ☎ 0952 Telford.
See : St. Andrew's Church★ 12C-16C – **Envir.** : Weston Park★ 17C (paintings★★) *AC*, NE : 5 m.

♦London 150 – ♦Birmingham 28 – Shrewsbury 16.

 🏨 **Park House,** Park St., TF11 9BA, ℰ 460128, Fax 461658, 🏊, ☞ – 🛗 📺 ☎ ⅙ P. 🅿 – 🕍 80. 🅿 AE ⓓ VISA
   M (closed lunch Monday and Saturday and Sunday) 10.50/12.50 **t.** and a la carte – **52 rm** ♨ 66.00/77.00 **t.**, **2 suites** 85.00/95.00 **t.** – SB (weekends only) 82.00 **st.**

AUSTIN-ROVER Chepside ℰ 460412   FORD Park St. ℰ 460631

SHINFIELD Berks. 404 R 29 – see Reading.

SHIPDHAM Norfolk 404 W 26 – pop. 1 974 – ⊠ Thetford – ✆ 0362 Dereham.
♦London 102 – East Dereham 5 – ♦Norwich 21 – Watton 6.

XX **Shipdham Place** with rm, Church Close, IP25 7LX, on A 1075 ✆ 820303, ⇄ – ⤬ rest
☎ P. 🄯 *VISA*
M 9.50/20.50 st. ⋀ 2.70 – **8 rm** ⊒ 30.00/77.00 st. – SB 73.00/105.00 st.

SHIPLEY West Yorks. 402 O 22 – pop. 28 815 – ECD : Wednesday – ✆ 0274 Bradford.
⌐18 Northcliffe, High Bank Lane ✆ 584085, SW : 1 ¼ m. by A 650.
♦London 216 – Bradford 4 – ♦Leeds 12.

X **Aagrah**, 27 Westgate, BD18 3QX, ✆ 594660, Indian rest. – 🄯 AE ⓪ *VISA*
closed Sunday and Christmas Night – **M** (booking essential) (dinner only) a la carte
6.05/26.75 t. ⋀ 2.50.

SHIPSTON-ON-STOUR Warw. 403 404 P 27 – pop. 3 072 – ✆ 0608.
♦London 85 – ♦Birmingham 34 – ♦Oxford 29.

☨ **White Bear**, High St., CV35 4AJ, ✆ 61558 – TV P. ⤬
9 rm.

XX **Old Mill** with rm, 8 Mill St., CV36 4AW, on B 4035 ✆ 61880, ⇄ – TV P. 🄯 AE ⓪
VISA
M *(closed dinner Sunday and Bank Holidays)* a la carte 13.20/21.00 t. ⋀ 3.50 – **5 rm**
⊒ 32.00/45.00 t.

at Lower Brailes E : 4 ½ m. on B 4035 – ⊠ Banbury (Oxon.) – ✆ 060 885 Brailes :

X **Feldon House** with rm, OX15 5HW, ✆ 580, « Part 17C and part 19C country house », ⇄
– P. 🄯 *VISA*. ⤬
M *(closed Sunday dinner)* 14.75/18.00 st. ⋀ 3.75 – **3 rm** ⊒ 26.00/48.00 st.

at Darlingscott NW : 2 ¼ m. by B 4035 – ⊠ Shipston-on-Stour – ✆ 060 882 Ilmington :

⋔ **Longdon Manor** , CV36 4PW, W : 1 m. ✆ 235, ≤, « Elizabethan manor, country house
atmosphere », ⇄ – ⤬ P. ⤬
March-November – **M** (by arrangement) 15.00 s. – **3 rm** ⊒ 22.00/50.00 s.

FORD Church St. ✆ 61425   SUBARU, ISUZU Tredington ✆ 61544

SHIPTON GORGE Dorset – see Bridport.

SHIPTON-UNDER-WYCHWOOD Oxon. 403 404 P 28 – pop. 2 558 – ECD : Wednesday –
✆ 0993.
♦London 81 – ♦Birmingham 50 – Gloucester 37 – ♦Oxford 25.

🏛 **Shaven Crown**, OX7 6BA, ✆ 830330, « 14C hospice » – TV P. 🄯 *VISA*. ⤬
M (bar lunch Monday to Saturday)/dinner 20.00 t. ⋀ 3.00 – **9 rm** ⊒ 24.00/58.00 t. –
SB (except Bank Holidays) 75.00 st.

SHIRLEY West Midlands 403 404 O 26 – see Solihull.

SHORNE Kent 404 V 29 – pop. 2 565 – ⊠ Gravesend – ✆ 047 482.
♦London 27 – Gravesend 4 – Maidstone 12 – Rochester 4.

🏛 **Inn on the Lake**, DA12 3HB, on A 2 ✆ 3333, Telex 966356, Fax 3175, ≤, ⤬, ⇄, park – TV
☎ P. – 🛦 150. 🄯 AE ⓪ *VISA*. ⤬
M 10.45 t. and a la carte 13.40/21.70 t. ⋀ 4.50 – **78 rm** ⊒ 60.00/85.00 t.

SHRAWLEY Heref. and Worc. – ⊠ ✆ 0905 Worcester.
♦London 152 – ♦Birmingham 45 – Leominster 3.

🏛 **Lenchford**, WR6 6TB, SE : ½ m. on B 4196 ✆ 620229, ≤, « Riverside setting », ⤬ heated,
⇄ – TV ☎ P. 🄯 AE ⓪ *VISA*. ⤬
closed 25 December-1 January – **M** *(closed Sunday dinner)* (dinner only and Sunday
lunch)/dinner 14.95 st. ⋀ 5.50 – **11 rm** ⊒ 39.50/55.50 st.

SHREWSBURY Shropshire 402 403 L 25 – pop. 57 731 – ECD : Thursday – ✆ 0743.
See : Site* – Abbey Church* (11C-14C) D – St. Mary's Church* (Jesse Tree window*) A –
Grope Lane* (15C).
Envir. : Wroxeter* (Roman city and baths) *AC*, SE : 6 m. by A 5 on B 4380 – Condover Hall*
(15C) *AC*, S : 5 m. by A 49 – Much Wenlock Priory*, SE : 12 m. by A 49 AZ and A 458.
⌐5 Meole Brace ✆ 64050, S : by A 49.
🄯 The Square ✆ 50761.
♦London 164 – ♦Birmingham 48 – ♦Cardiff 10 – Chester 43 – Derby 67 – Gloucester 93 – ♦Manchester 68 –
♦Stoke-on-Trent 39 – ♦Swansea 124.

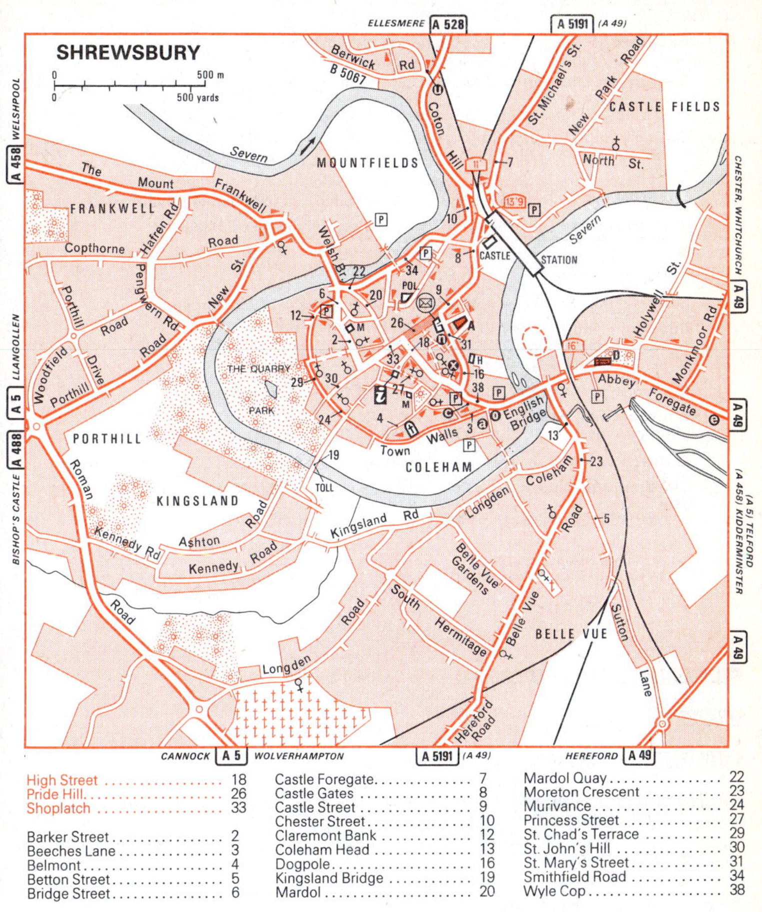

High Street 18
Pride Hill 26
Shoplatch 33

Barker Street 2
Beeches Lane 3
Belmont 4
Betton Street 5
Bridge Street 6

Castle Foregate 7
Castle Gates 8
Castle Street 9
Chester Street 10
Claremont Bank 12
Coleham Head 13
Dogpole 16
Kingsland Bridge 19
Mardol 20

Mardol Quay 22
Moreton Crescent 23
Murivance 24
Princess Street 27
St. Chad's Terrace 29
St. John's Hill 30
St. Mary's Street 31
Smithfield Road 34
Wyle Cop 38

Rowton Castle, SY5 9EP, W : 7 ½ m. on A 458 ℰ 884044, Fax 884949, ≋, park – ⊡ ☎ Ⓟ – 🏊 150. ◪ Ⓐ🄴 𝗩𝗜𝗦𝗔
M 18.00 **st.** and a la carte 13.00/17.95 **st.** ↥ 5.15 – **18 rm** ⊑ 55.00/75.00 **st.** – SB (weekends only) 106.00/146.00 **st.**

Prince Rupert (Q.M.H.), Butcher Row, SY1 1UQ, ℰ 236000, Telex 351000, Fax 57306 – ▣
▤ rest ⊡ ☎ Ⓟ – 🏊 70. ◪ Ⓐ🄴 ⓞ 𝗩𝗜𝗦𝗔   n
M 9.00/12.75 **t.** and a la carte ↥ 3.75 – **63 rm** ⊑ 54.00/69.00 **t.**, **3 suites** 80.00 **t.** – SB (weekends only) 70.00/80.00 **st.**

Lion (T.H.F.), Wyle Cop, SY1 1UY, ℰ 53107, Fax 52744 – ▣ ⊡ ☎ Ⓟ – 🏊 200. ◪ Ⓐ🄴 ⓞ
𝗩𝗜𝗦𝗔   c
M 9.80/12.50 **st.** and a la carte ↥ 3.95 – ⊑ 7.00 – **59 rm** 52.00/100.00 **st.** – SB (weekends only) 84.00/88.00 **st.**

Lord Hill (De Vere), **131 Abbey Foregate**, SY2 6AX, ℰ 232601, Telex 35104 – ⊡ ☎ Ⓟ – 🏊
150   e
46 rm.

Radbrook Hall (B.C.B.), Radbrook Rd, SY3 9BQ, SW : 1 ½ m. on A 488 ℰ 236676, Fax
59194, ≋, squash – ⊡ ☎ Ⓟ – 🏊 120. ◪ Ⓐ🄴 ⓞ 𝗩𝗜𝗦𝗔. ✻
M a la carte 8.05/11.40 **st.** – **28 rm** ⊑ 41.50/53.50 **st.**

Fieldside without rest., 38 London Rd, SY2 6NX, E : 1 ¼ m. via Abbey Foregate on A 5112
ℰ 53143, ≋ – ⊡ Ⓟ. ◪ 𝗩𝗜𝗦𝗔. ✻
9 rm ⊑ 16.00/38.00 **st.**

Cromwells, 11 Dogpole, SY1 1EN, ℰ 61440 – ⊡   u
9 rm.

461

⌂ **Sandford House,** St. Julians Friars, SY1 1XL, ✆ 3829 – TV   **a**
M (by arrangement) 8.00 **st.** – **9 rm** ⌷ 16.50/33.00 **st.**

⌂ **Sydney House,** Coton Cres., off Coton Hill, SY1 2LJ, ✆ 54681 – ⊱⊰ rest TV P. *VISA*
⊗   **x**
closed 23 to 30 December – **M** 9.00 **st.** ⦙ 2.40 – **7 rm** ⌷ 23.00/44.00 **st.**

✕ **Cornerhouse,** 59a Wyle Cop. (1st floor), SY1 1XB, ✆ 231991 – ▣ *VISA*   **o**
closed 25 December and Bank Holiday Mondays – **M** 13.95 **t.** and a la carte 12.00/15.00 **t.**
⦙ 2.80.

at Albrighton N : 3 m. on A 528 – ✉ Shrewsbury – ✆ 0939 Bomere Heath :

🏰 **Albrighton Hall,** Ellesmere Rd, SY4 3AG, ✆ 291000, Fax 291123, ⇗, ✕ – TV ☎ P.
⛨ 250. ▣ AE ⓞ *VISA*
M 9.50/12.00 **st.** and a la carte 17.75/23.25 **st.** ⦙ 4.25 – **33 rm** ⌷ 65.00/90.00 **st.** – SB (weekends only) 78.00 **st.**

at Dorrington S : 7 m. on A 49 – ✉ Shrewsbury – ✆ 074 373 Dorrington :

✕✕ **Country Friends,** SY5 7JD, ✆ 707, ⇗ – P. ▣ AE *VISA*
closed Sunday, Monday, 2 weeks July-August, last week October and 4 days Christmas –
M 14.00 **t.** and a la carte 14.90/19.00 **t.**

at Great Hanwood SW : 4 m. on A 488 – ✉ ✆ 0743 Shrewsbury :

⌂ **White House,** SY5 8LP, ✆ 860414, ⇗ – P. ⊗
M (by arrangement) 10.75 **st.** ⦙ 3.00 – **5 rm** ⌷ 15.50/38.00 **st.** – SB 52.50/59.50 **st.**

at Baschurch NW : 8 ½ m. by A 528 on B 5067 – ✉ Shrewsbury – ✆ 0939 Baschurch :

🏠 **Old Vicarage Country** ⟍, Church Lane, SY4 2EF, ✆ 260135, Fax 261124, ⇗ – TV P. ▣
VISA
M 9.50/13.50 **t.** and a la carte ⦙ 4.15 – **6 rm** ⌷ 25.00/46.00 **t.**

AUSTIN-ROVER Harlescott ✆ 236050
CITROEN 159 Abbey Foregate ✆ 231234
CITROEN, DAIHATSU, SAAB Featherbed Lane ✆
241445
FORD Coton Hill ✆ 3631
LADA Featherbed Lane ✆ 60303
PEUGEOT-TALBOT Featherbed Lane ✆ 235611

SAAB Westbury Garage ✆ 241445
VAUXHALL-OPEL Greyfriars ✆ 231321
VOLVO Featherbed Lane ✆ 231251
VW-AUDI English Bridge ✆ 52471

🝆 ATS Lancaster Rd, Harlescott ✆ 3954/232231

SHURDINGTON Glos. 🆘🆘 N 28 – see Cheltenham.

SIBSON Leics. – see Nuneaton (Warw.).

SIDFORD Devon 🆘 K 31 – see Sidmouth.

SIDMOUTH Devon 🆘 K 31 The West Country G. – pop. 10 808 – ECD : Thursday – ✆ 0395
(6 fig.) or 039 55 (4 and 5 fig.).

Envir. : Seaton, headlands (⩽★★), E : 9 m. – Branscombe★, E : 9 m. – Colyton★, E : 10 m –
Bicton Gardens★ S : S ½ m.

🝆 Cotmaton Rd ✆ 513451.

🎫 The Esplanade ✆ 516441 (summer only).

◆London 170 – Exeter 14 – Taunton 27 – Weymouth 45.

🏰 **Victoria,** The Esplanade, Peak Hill, EX10 8RY, ✆ 512651, Fax 579154, ⩽, ⟍ heated, ▣,
⇗, ✕ – ⊟ TV ☎ P. ▣ AE ⓞ *VISA*. ⊗
M 9.25/17.00 **t.** and a la carte – **60 rm** ⌷ 60.00/140.00 **t.**, **1 suite** 160.00/180.00 **t.** –
SB (except Easter, Whitsun and Christmas) 70.00/130.00 **st.**

🏰 **Riviera,** The Esplanade, EX10 8AY, ✆ 515201, Fax 577775, ⩽ – ⊟ ▤ rest TV ☎ ⅗ ⇔. ▣
AE ⓞ *VISA*
M 8.50/13.50 and a la carte ⦙ 3.50 – **34 rm** ⌷ 46.00/92.00 – SB (week-
ends only) 77.05/81.65 **st.**

🏰 **Belmont,** The Esplanade, EX10 8RX, ✆ 512555, ⩽, ⇗ – ⊟ TV ☎ ⅗ P. ▣ AE ⓞ *VISA*
⊗
M 9.00/14.00 **t.** and a la carte – **54 rm** ⌷ 51.00/120.00 **t.** – SB (except summer, Easter and Christmas) 72.00/100.00 **st.**

🏠 **Salcombe Hill House** ⟍, Beatlands Rd, EX10 8JQ, ✆ 514697, ⟍ heated, ⇗, ✕ – ⊟
⊱⊰ rest TV ☎ P. ▣ ⓞ *VISA*
March-October – **M** 8.00/12.00 **t.** and a la carte ⦙ 3.95 – **32 rm** ⌷ 39.00/80.00 **t.** –
SB (except summer) 52.00/80.00 **st.**

🏠 **Fortfield,** Station Rd, EX10 8NU, ✆ 512403, ▣, ⇗ – ⊟ ⊱⊰ rest TV ☎ ⅗ P. ▣ AE *VISA*
M (bar lunch)/dinner 10.50 **t.** and a la carte ⦙ 3.00 – **52 rm** ⌷ 42.00/88.00 **t.** –
SB (October-11 May except Easter, Christmas and New Year) 64.00/68.00 **t.**

🏠 **Royal Glen,** Glen Rd, EX10 8RW, ✆ 513221, « 17C house », ▣, ⇗ – TV ☎ ⇔ P. ▣ AE
VISA
closed 2 weeks November – **M** 5.25/7.95 **t.** and a la carte – **36 rm** ⌷ 26.60/76.90 **t.**

⌂ **Littlecourt,** Seafield Rd, EX10 8HF, ℰ 515279, ⌁ heated, ⌂ – ⓧ rest 📺 🅿. 🔝 *VISA*
M (bar lunch Monday to Saturday)/dinner 9.50 t. ♟ 2.75 – **21 rm** ☕ 29.00/76.00 t. –
SB (except summer and Bank Holidays) 44.50/57.50 st.

⌂ **Abbeydale,** Manor Rd, EX10 8RP, ℰ 512060, ⌂ – ⓧ ⓧ rest 📺 🅿. ⌂
closed January and February – **M** (bar lunch)/dinner 12.00 t. ♟ 2.70 – **18 rm** ☕ 37.00/74.00 t.

⌂ **Mount Pleasant,** Salcombe Rd, EX10 8JA, ℰ 514694, ⌂ – ⓧ rest 📺 🅿. ⌂
Easter-October – **M** (bar lunch)/dinner 7.00 st. ♟ 3.50 – **16 rm** ☕ 24.00/56.00 st. –
SB (November-April) 50.00/56.00 st.

⌂ **Woodlands,** Station Rd, Cotmaton Cross, EX10 8HG, ℰ 513120, ⌂ – 🅿. 🔝 *VISA*
M 3.75/5.25 t. ♟ 3.00 – **29 rm** ☕ 25.90/57.75 t. – SB (except summer) 41.10/57.00 st.

⌂ **Torbay,** Station Rd, EX10 8NW, ℰ 513456 – ⌂ 📺 ☎. 🔝 *VISA*
M 5.00/8.00 t. and a la carte ♟ 3.25 – **30 rm** ☕ 27.00/54.00 t. – SB (November-
April) 36.30/41.80 st.

↑ **Barrington Villa,** Salcombe Rd, EX10 8PU, ℰ 514252, ⌂ – 🅿
closed mid October-24 December – **M** (by arrangement) 5.50 st. – **9 rm** ☕ 23.10/50.85 st.

↑ **Salcombe Cottage** without rest., Hillside Rd, EX10 8JF, ℰ 516829, « 18C thatched cottage », ⌂ – ⓧ 🅿
4 rm ☕ 17.00/30.00 st.

at Sidford N : 2 m. – ✉ ☎ 039 55 Sidmouth :

⌂ **Applegarth,** Church St., EX10 9QP, E : on A 3052 ℰ 513174, « Garden » – 📺 🅿. 🔝 *VISA*.
⌂
M *(closed Sunday dinner and Monday)* 7.95 st. (lunch) and a la carte 11.60/14.70 t. ♟ 3.75 –
7 rm ☕ 21.50/45.00 t. – SB (October-February) 45.00/52.00 st.

AUSTIN-ROVER Salcombe Rd ℰ 512522 ⓦ ATS Vicarage Rd ℰ 512433
FIAT Crossways, Sidford ℰ 513595

SILCHESTER Hants. 🕮 🕮 Q 29 – pop. 1 072 – ✉ Reading (Berks.) – ☎ 0734.
♦London 62 – Basingstoke 8 – Reading 14 – Winchester 26.

🏨 **Romans** (Best Western) ⌂, Little London Rd, RG7 2PN, ℰ 700421, Fax 700691, ⌁ heated,
⌂, ⌂ – 📺 ☎ 🅿 – ⌂. 🔝 AE ⓪ *VISA*
closed Christmas-New Year – **M** *(closed Saturday lunch and Sunday dinner)* 13.00/17.50 st.
♟ 4.00 – **24 rm** ☕ 54.00/72.00 st. – SB (weekends only) 75.00/90.00 st.

SIMONSBATH Somerset 🕮 I 30 The West Country G. – ✉ Minehead – ☎ 064 383 Exford.
♦London 200 – Exeter 40 – Minehead 19 – Taunton 38.

🏨 **Simonsbath House,** TA24 7SH, ℰ 259, ⬌, « Tastefully converted 17C country house »,
⌂ – ⓧ rest 📺 ☎ 🅿. 🔝 AE ⓪ *VISA*. ⌂
closed December and January – **M** (bar lunch)/dinner 16.50 t. ♟ 3.75 – **7 rm** ☕ 40.00/75.00 t.
– SB 104.00 st.

SINDLESHAM Berks. – see Reading.

SISSINGHURST Kent 🕮 V 30 – see Cranbrook.

SITTINGBOURNE Kent 🕮 W 29 – pop. 35 893 – ECD : Wednesday – ☎ 0795.
🛝 Wormdale, Newington ℰ 842261.
♦London 44 – Canterbury 16 – Maidstone 13.

🏨 **Coniston,** 70 London Rd, ME10 1NT, ℰ 72131 – 📺 ☎ ♿ 🅿 – ⌂ 120. 🔝 AE ⓪ *VISA*
M 11.00 t. and a la carte ♟ 3.70 – **59 rm** ☕ 37.00/60.50 t.

FORD Canterbury Rd ℰ 70711 VAUXHALL-OPEL London Rd, Bapchild ℰ 76222
MAZDA High Newington ℰ 842307
RENAULT Chalkwell Rd ℰ 76361 ⓦ ATS Crown Quay Lane ℰ 72384/72912
TALBOT Teynham ℰ 521286

SIX MILE BOTTOM Cambs. – see Newmarket (Suffolk).

SKEGNESS Lincs. 🕮 🕮 V 24 – pop. 12 645 – ECD : Thursday – ☎ 0754.
🛝 North Shore ℰ 3298.
🅱 Embassy Centre, Grand Parade ℰ 4821 (summer only).
♦London 145 – Lincoln 41.

🏨 **County,** North Par., PE25 2UB, ℰ 2461, ⬌ – ⌂ 📺 ☎ 🅿 – ⌂
44 rm.

AUSTIN-ROVER Roman Bank ℰ 3671 YUGO Clifton Grove ℰ 3589
FIAT Beresford Av. ℰ 67131
FORD Wainfleet Rd ℰ 66019 ⓦ ATS 66 Alexandra Rd ℰ 67272

SKELTON North Yorks. 🕮 Q 22 – see York.

SKIPTON North Yorks. 402 N 22 – pop. 13 009 – ECD : Tuesday – 0756.
See : Castle★ (14C) *AC*.
Envir. : Bolton Priory★ E : 6 m..
Grassington Rd 3922 N : 1 m. on A 65.
8 Victoria Sq. 2809.
◆London 217 – Kendal 45 – ◆Leeds 26 – Preston 36 – York 43.

Unicorn, Devonshire Pl., Keighley Rd, BD23 2LP, 4146 – TV
10 rm.

Travelodge without rest., A 65/A 59 roundabout, Gargrave Rd, BD23 1UD, W : 1 ¾ m. via
Water St., 68091 – TV P. AE VISA
32 rm 21.50/27.00 t.

Oats with rm, Chapel Hill, BD23 1NL, 68118 – TV P. AE VISA
closed 25 to 29 December – **M** *(closed Monday)* 11.50/25.00 t. and a la carte 19.75/24.75 t.
3.25 – **4 rm** 42.00/52.00 t.

ATS Carleton Rd Garage, Carleton Rd 5741/2

SLAIDBURN Lancs. 402 M 22 – pop. 332 – Clitheroe – 020 06.
◆London 249 – Burnley 21 – Lancaster 19 – ◆Leeds 48 – Preston 27.

Parrock Head Farm, BB7 3AH, NW : 1 m. 614, ≤ Bowland Fells, – rest TV
P. AE
closed mid December-early February – **M** (bar lunch)/dinner a la carte 10.70/15.25 t. 3.75
– **9 rm** 30.00/48.00 t.

Hark to Bounty, BB7 3EP, 246 – TV P. AE VISA
M (bar lunch)/dinner 14.00 st. and a la carte 3.00 – **8 rm** 18.00/36.00 st.

SLEAFORD Lincs. 402 404 S 25 – pop. 8 247 – ECD : Thursday – 0529.
See : St. Denis' Church★ 12C-15C.
South Rauceby 052 98 (South Rauceby) 273, W : 1 m. on A 153.
◆London 119 – ◆Leicester 45 – Lincoln 17 – ◆Nottingham 39.

Tally Ho Inn, Aswarby, NG34 8SA, S : 4 ½ m. on A 15 052 95 (Culverthorpe) 205, ≤,
– TV P.
M (bar lunch)/dinner a la carte 5.10/9.70 t. 3.50 – **6 rm** 24.00/36.00 t.

AUSTIN-ROVER Lincoln Rd 303034
FIAT Grantham Rd 052 98 (Sth. Rauceby) 674
FORD London Rd 302921
RENAULT 50 Westgate 305305

SKODA Holdingham 302545

ATS 40 Albion Terr. off Boston Rd 302908

SLOUGH Berks. 404 S 29 – pop. 106 341 – ECD : Wednesday – 0753.
Envir. : Eton (college★★) S : 2 m.
Farnham Park, Park Rd, Stoke Poges 028 14 (Farnham Common) 3332, N : 2 m. – Wexham
Park, Wexham St. 028 16 (Fulmer) 3271, N : 2 m.
◆London 29 – ◆Oxford 39 – Reading 19.

Holiday Inn (Holiday Inn), Ditton Rd, Langley, SL3 8PT, SE : 2 ½ m. on A 4 44244, Telex
848646, Fax 40272, – rm TV P. – 350. AE VISA
M 16.50 st. and a la carte 5.25 – 7.95 – **294 rm** 90.00/110.00 st., **8 suites** 250.00/
350.00 st. – SB (weekends only) 80.00 st.

BMW Petersfield Av. 821821
FORD Petersfield Av. 33321
SAAB Beaconsfield Rd 028 14 (Farnham Com-
mon) 5111

VOLVO Petersfield Av. 23031
VW-AUDI 57 Farnham Rd 33917

ATS 1a Furnival Av. 24214

SNAINTON North Yorks. 402 S 21 – pop. 760 – ECD : Wednesday – 0723 Scarborough.
◆London 240 – Scarborough 10 – York 29.

Coachman Inn, YO13 9PL, 85231 – TV P. AE VISA
M (bar lunch)/dinner 13.50 t. 3.50 – **12 rm** 25.00/40.00 t. – SB (except summer)
50.00/55.00 st.

SNOWDON (YR WYDDFA) Gwynedd 402 403 H 24.
See : Ascent and ★★★ (1 h 15 mn from Llanberis (Pass★★) by Snowdon Mountain Railway *AC*).
Hotels and restaurant see : Beddgelert S : 4 m., *Caernarfon* NW : 9 m.

SOLIHULL West Midlands 403 404 O 26 – pop. 93 940 – ECD : Wednesday – ✆ 021 Birmingham.

🖈 Central Library, Homer Rd ℘ 704 6130.

♦London 109 – ♦Birmingham 7 – ♦Coventry 13 – Warwick 13.

 St. John's Swallow (Swallow), 651 Warwick Rd, B91 1AT, ℘ 711 3000, Telex 339352, Fax 705 6629, ⬛, ⇌ – ⧉ 📺 ☎ Ⓟ – ⚹ 1 000. ◥ 𝔸𝔼 ⓪ 𝗩𝗜𝗦𝗔
 M *(closed Saturday lunch)* 11.00/14.75 **st.** and a la carte ⓵ 4.00 – **202 rm** ⌣ 65.00/85.00 **st.,**
 4 suites 92.00 **st.** – SB (weekends only) 78.00/85.00 **st.**

 George (Embassy), The Square, B91 3RF, ℘ 711 2121, Telex 334134, Fax 711 3374 – ⧉
 ⇌ rm 📺 ☎ Ⓟ – ⚹ 200. ◥ 𝔸𝔼 ⓪ 𝗩𝗜𝗦𝗔
 M 12.00/16.50 **st.** and a la carte ⓵ 4.50 – ⌣ 6.50 – **74 rm** 58.00/160.00 **st.** – SB (weekends only) 59.00/65.00 **st.**

 Liaison, 761 Old Lode Lane, B92 8JE, N : 2 ¾ m. by B 425 (Looe Lane) ℘ 743 3993, French rest. – ◥ 𝔸𝔼 ⓪ 𝗩𝗜𝗦𝗔
 closed Sunday, Monday, August and 2 weeks Christmas – **M** (dinner only) 18.95 **t.** and a la carte 19.40/25.15 **t.** ⓵ 5.95.

 at Shirley W : 2 ½ m. on B 4025 – ⊠ Solihull – ✆ 021 Birmingham :

 Regency, Stratford Rd, B90 4EB, SE : 2 m. on A 34 ℘ 745 6119, Telex 334400, Fax 733 3801
 – ⧉ 📺 ☎ Ⓟ – ⚹ 180. ◥ 𝔸𝔼 𝗩𝗜𝗦𝗔 ⌗
 M 9.50/13.25 **st.** and a la carte ⓵ 3.50 – **57 rm** ⌣ 60.00/75.00 **st.,** **2 suites** 95.00 **st.** – SB (weekends only) 76.00 **st.**

 Saracen's Head, Stratford Rd, B90 3AG, ℘ 733 3888 – ⇌ rest 📺 ☎ Ⓟ – ⚹ 120. ◥ 𝔸𝔼
 ⓪ 𝗩𝗜𝗦𝗔 ⌗
 M 7.25 **st.** and a la carte ⓵ 3.00 – **34 rm** ⌣ 39.00/49.00 **st.** – SB (weekends only) 40.50/63.50 **st.**

AUSTIN-ROVER Stratford Rd, Shirley ℘ 745 5855
BMW 824 Stratford Rd ℘ 733 3444
DAIMLER-JAGUAR 301 Warwick Rd ℘ 706 2801
FIAT The Green ℘ 056 44 (Tanworth) 2218
FORD 361-369 Stratford Rd ℘ 733 3333

MAZDA 270 Stratford Rd, Shirley ℘ 744 1033
NISSAN Stratford Rd, Shirley ℘ 745 5811
PEUGEOT-TALBOT 386 Warwick Rd ℘ 704 1427
SUBARU, ISUZU Station Lane ℘ 056 43 (Lapworth) 2933

SOMERTON Somerset 403 L 30 – pop. 4 339 – ECD : Wednesday – ✆ 0458 – **See :** Site★ – Market place★ (17C Arcaded Cross★) – St Michael's (13C Octagonal South Tower)★.

♦London 138 – ♦Bristol 32 – Taunton 17.

 Lynch Country House, 4 Behind Berry, TA11 7PD, ℘ 72316, ≼, « Attractively converted Regency house », ⇌, park – 📺 ☎ Ⓟ. ◥ 𝗩𝗜𝗦𝗔
 M (dinner only) 16.50 **t.** ⓵ 3.00 – **8 rm** ⌣ 40.00/85.00 **t.** – SB (except Bank Holidays) 75.00/100.00 **st.**

SONNING-ON-THAMES Berks. 404 R 29 – pop. 1 469 – ECD : Wednesday – ✆ 0734 Reading.

♦London 48 – Reading 4.

 The Great House at Sonning, Thames St., RG4 0UT, ℘ 692277, Telex 849031, Fax 441296, ≼, « Rose gardens on river bank » – 📺 ☎ Ⓟ – ⚹ 40. ◥ 𝔸𝔼 ⓪ 𝗩𝗜𝗦𝗔
 M 14.50/19.50 **st.** and a la carte – **25 rm** ⌣ 79.00/140.00 **st.** – SB (weekends only) 95.00/110.00 **st.**

 French Horn with rm, Thames St., RG4 0TN, ℘ 692204, Fax 442210, ≼ River Thames and gardens – 📺 ☎ Ⓟ. ◥ 𝔸𝔼 ⓪ 𝗩𝗜𝗦𝗔 ⌗
 closed 13 April, 26 December and January – **M** 13.50/30.00 **st.** and a la carte 22.00/27.00 **st.** ⓵ 5.00 – **10 rm** ⌣ 67.00/90.00 **st.,** **4 suites** 120.00 **st.**

SOURTON Devon 403 H 31 – ⊠ Okehampton – ✆ 083 766 Bridestowe.

♦London 230 – Exeter 29 – ♦Plymouth 25.

 Collaven Manor ⌂, EX20 4HH, S : ¾ m. on A 386 ℘ 217, Fax 570, « 15C manor house, gardens » – 📺 ☎ Ⓟ. ◥ 𝗩𝗜𝗦𝗔 ⌗
 M 15.95/26.95 **t.** – **9 rm** ⌣ 50.00/95.00 **t.** – SB 72.00/90.00 **st.**

SOUTHAM Glos. 403 404 N 28 – see Cheltenham.

SOUTHAMPTON Hants. 403 404 P 31 – pop. 211 321 – ECD : Monday and Wednesday – ✆ 0703 – **See :** Docks★ AY – Tudor House Museum★ (16C) *AC* AZ **M1** – God's House Tower★ 12C (Museum of Archaelogia) AZ **M2** – Bargate★ AZ **B.**

Envir. : Netley (abbey★ ruins 13C) *AC*, SE : 3 m. BZ A.

🛆, 🛆 West Side Basset Av. ℘ 768407 AY – 🛆 Fleming Park ℘ 0707 (Eastleigh) 612797, N : 6 m. by A 33 AY.

✈ Southampton Airport : ℘ 620021 N : 4 m. BY.

⚓ to America (New York) (Cunard) – to the Isle of Wight : East and West Cowes (Red Funnel Services) frequent services daily (55 mn - 1 h 15 mn).

⚓ to the Isle of Wight : West Cowes (Red Funnel Services : hydrofoil) frequent services daily (20 mn).

🖈 Above Bar Precinct ℘ 221106.

♦London 87 – ♦Bristol 79 – ♦Plymouth 161.

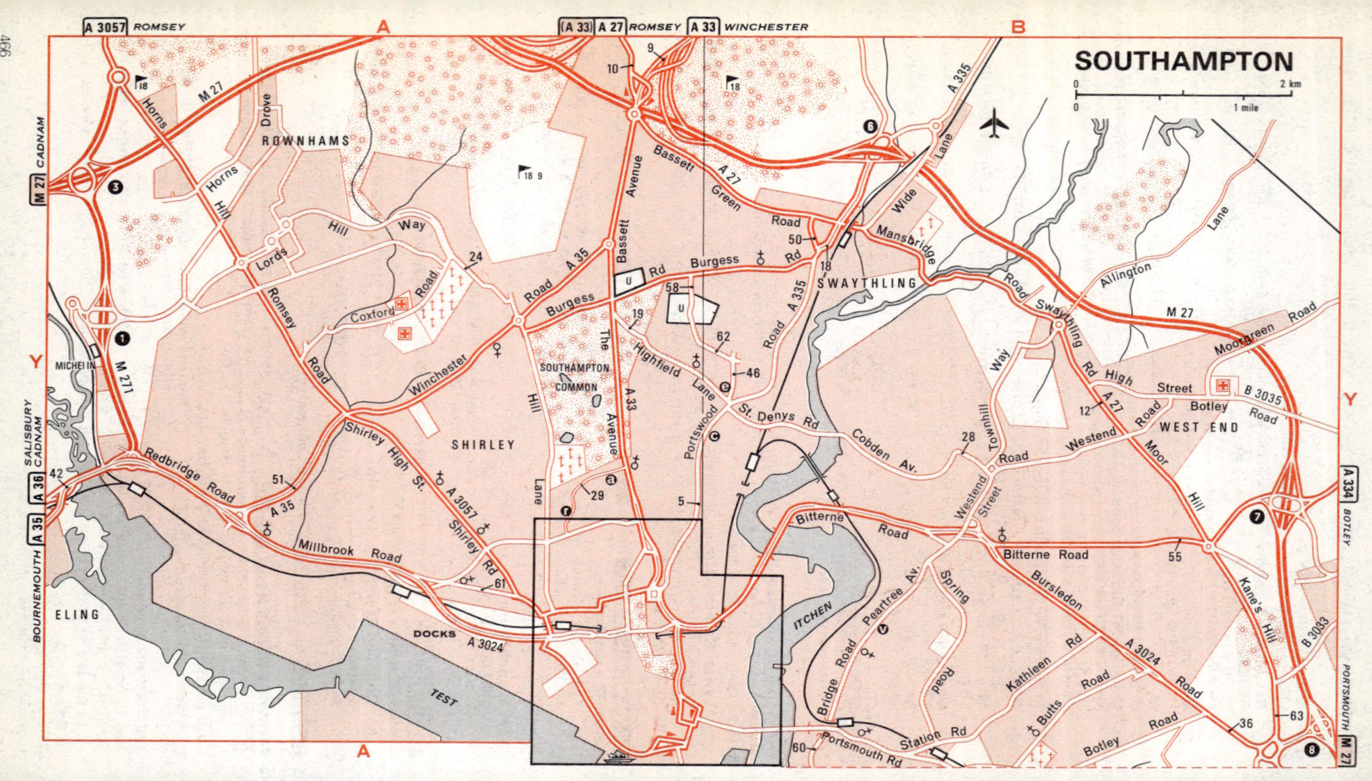

SOUTHAMPTON
466
A 3057 ROMSEY
[A 33] A 27 ROMSEY [A 33] WINCHESTER
A
B
9
10
18
M 27
Horns Drove
ROWNHAMS
Horns Hill
3
M 27 CADNAM
18 9
A 335
6
Wide Lane
Bassett Avenue
Bassett Green Road
A 27
Road
50
Mansbridge
Allington Lane
M 27
Way
Hill
Lords
Winchester Road
Coxford Road
24
Road A 35
Bassett Rd
Burgess Rd
18
SWAYTHLING
Swaythling Rd
Moorgreen Road
Burgess
U Rd
58
U
Road A 335
High Street
12 A 27
Botley Road
B 3035
WEST END
1
MICHELIN
M 271
19
62
Highfield Lane
46
Way
Townhill Road
Westend Road
Moor Hill
Y
A 334 BOTLEY
Y
SALISBURY CADNAM
BOURNEMOUTH
42
A 36
A 35
Redbridge Road
51
A 35
Shirley High St.
A 3057
Shirley Rd
61
Millbrook Road
SHIRLEY
Southampton Common Hill
The Avenue
A 33
Lane
29
5
St. Denys Rd
Portswood
Cobden Av.
28
Westend Street
Bitterne Road
Bitterne Road
55
Kane's Hill
7
DOCKS A 3024
TEST
ELING
ITCHEN
Bridge Road
Peartree Av.
Spring Road
Bursledon
Kathleen Rd
Butts
Road
A 3024 Road
Botley Road
36
63
B 3033
PORTSMOUTH
M 27
8
Station Rd
Portsmouth Rd
60

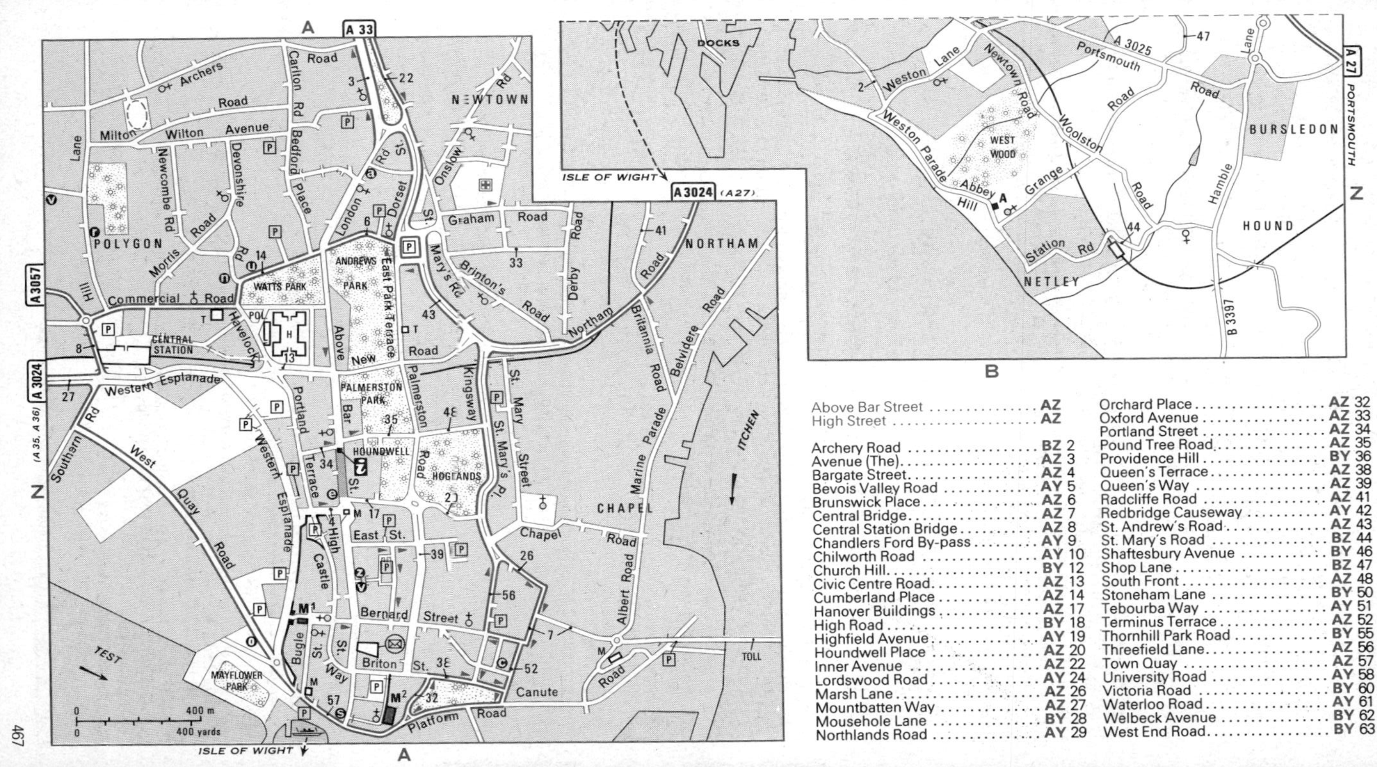

A 33
A 27 PORTSMOUTH
DOCKS
ISLE OF WIGHT
A 3024 (A 27)
BURSLEDON
HOUND
NETLEY
WEST WOOD
Weston Lane
Weston Parade
Abbey
Newtown Road
Woolston Road
Portsmouth Road
Grange Road
Station Rd
Hamble
A 3025
B 3397
B
NEWTOWN
NORTHAM
CHAPEL
POLYGON
WATTS PARK
ANDREWS PARK
PALMERSTON PARK
MAYFLOWER PARK
EAST PARK TERRACE
HOUNDWELL
HOGLANDS
CENTRAL STATION
Archers Road
Milton Lane
Wilton Avenue
Newcombe Rd
Devonshire Road
Morris Rd
Carlton Rd
Bedford Place
Hill
Commercial Road
Havelock
London Rd
Dorset St.
Onslow Rd
Graham Road
Brinton's Road
Derby Road
Northam Road
Britannia Road
Belvidere Road
Albert Road
Marine Parade
Chapel Road
Bugle St.
High St.
Castle Way
Bernard Street
Briton St.
Platform Road
Canute Road
Western Esplanade
Southern Rd
West Quay Road
St. Mary's Rd
St. Mary Street
St. Mary's Pl.
Kingsway
Portland Terrace
Above Bar
New Road
St. Mary's Road
ITCHEN
TEST
TOLL
POL
Briton
East St.
A 3057
A 3024
(A 35, A 36)
ISLE OF WIGHT
N
400 m
400 yards
467
Above Bar Street .... AZ
High Street .... AZ
Archery Road .... BZ 2
Avenue (The) .... AZ 3
Bargate Street .... AZ 4
Bevois Valley Road .... AY 5
Brunswick Place .... AZ 6
Central Bridge .... AZ 7
Central Station Bridge .... AZ 8
Chandlers Ford By-pass ...... AY 9
Chilworth Road .... AY 10
Church Hill .... BY 12
Civic Centre Road .... AZ 13
Cumberland Place .... AZ 14
Hanover Buildings .... AZ 17
High Road .... BY 18
Highfield Avenue .... AY 19
Houndwell Place .... AZ 20
Inner Avenue .... AZ 22
Lordswood Road .... AY 24
Marsh Lane .... AZ 26
Mountbatten Way .... AZ 27
Mousehole Lane .... BY 28
Northlands Road .... AY 29
Orchard Place .... AZ 32
Oxford Avenue .... AZ 33
Portland Street .... AZ 34
Pound Tree Road .... AZ 35
Providence Hill .... BY 36
Queen's Terrace .... AZ 38
Queen's Way .... AZ 39
Radcliffe Road .... AZ 41
Redbridge Causeway .... AY 42
St. Andrew's Road .... AZ 43
St. Mary's Road .... BZ 44
Shaftesbury Avenue .... BY 46
Shop Lane .... BZ 47
South Front .... AZ 48
Stoneham Lane .... BY 50
Tebourba Way .... AY 51
Terminus Terrace .... AZ 52
Thornhill Park Road .... BY 55
Threefield Lane .... AZ 56
Town Quay .... AZ 57
University Road .... AY 58
Victoria Road .... BY 60
Waterloo Road .... AY 61
Welbeck Avenue .... BY 62
West End Road .... BY 63

Polygon (T.H.F.), Cumberland Pl., SO9 4GD, ℰ 330055, Telex 47175, Fax 332435 –
rm TV ☎ ℙ – 500. AE ① VISA   AZ **n**
M 10.95/13.50 st. and a la carte ▮ 4.15 – ☷ 8.20 – **119 rm** 67.00/92.00 st., **2 suites** 121.00 st.
– SB (weekends only) (except Easter and Christmas) 70.00/80.00 st.

Dolphin (T.H.F.), 35 High St., SO9 2DS, ℰ 339955, Telex 477735, Fax 333650 – rm TV
ℙ – . AE ① VISA   AZ **i**
M (closed Saturday lunch) 6.25/11.50 st. and a la carte ▮ 3.95 – ☷ 7.00 – **71 rm**
56.00/71.00 st., **2 suites** 71.00/90.00 st. – SB (weekends only) 68.00/72.00 st.

Post House (T.H.F.), Herbert Walker Av., SO1 0HJ, ℰ 330777, Telex 477368, Fax 332510,
≼, ☒ heated – rm TV ☎ ℙ – . AE ① VISA   AZ **o**
M 9.95/14.95 st. and a la carte – ☷ 7.00 – **130 rm** 75.00/85.00 st., **2 suites** 130.00 st. –
SB (weekends only) 90.00 st.

Southampton Park, 12-13 Cumberland Pl., SO9 4NY, ℰ 223467, Telex 47439, Fax 332538
– rm TV ☎ – 200. AE ① VISA   AZ **u**
M 10.00/20.00 t. and a la carte 10.45/19.65 t. – **75 rm** ☷ 60.00/75.00 t.

Southampton Moat House (Q.M.H.), 119 Highfield Lane, Portswood Junction, SO9 1YQ,
ℰ 559555, Telex 47186, Fax 583910 – TV ☎ ℙ – 180. AE ① VISA   BY **e**
M (dinner only) 15.00 st. and a la carte ▮ 4.00 – **70 rm** ☷ 60.00/85.00 st. – SB (week-
ends only) 55.00/76.00 st.

Wessex, 66-68 Northlands Rd, SO1 2LH, ℰ 631744, Fax 639243, – TV ☎ ℙ. AE VISA
closed 25 and 26 December – **M** (bar lunch)/dinner 10.00 s. and a la carte ▮ 3.50 – **34 rm**
☷ 38.00/49.50 st.   AY **r**

Rosida Garden, 25-27 Hill Lane, S01 5AB, ℰ 228501, Fax 635501, ☒ heated, – TV ☎
ℙ. AE ① VISA   AZ **r**
M (bar lunch)/dinner a la carte 9.50/12.00 t. ▮ 2.95 – **29 rm** ☷ 40.00/63.00 t. – SB (week-
ends only) (except September) 66.00/83.00 st.

Star, 26-27 High St., SO9 4ZA, ℰ 339939, Fax 335291 – rm TV ☎ ℙ – . AE ①
VISA   AZ **z**
closed 24 December-2 January – **M** 5.00/12.00 st. and a la carte – **33 rm** ☷ 20.00/65.00 st.
– SB (November-August) (weekends only) 55.00/65.00 st.

Northlands, Northlands Rd, SO9 3ZW, ℰ 333871 – TV ℙ. AE VISA   AY **a**
M (closed dinner Friday to Sunday) (bar lunch)/dinner 8.50 ▮ 3.20 – **19 rm** ☷ 27.00/49.00 t.

Hunters Lodge, 25 Landguard Rd, SO1 5DL, ℰ 227919 – rm TV ☎ ℙ. AE VISA
          AZ **v**
closed 18 December-4 January – **M** (by arrangement) 6.00 s. – **18 rm** ☷ 19.55/46.00 t.

Earley House, 46 Peartree Av., Bitterne, SO2 7JP, ℰ 448117 – rm ℙ   BY **v**
M 8.00 t. ▮ 2.75 – **9 rm** ☷ 19.00/40.00 st.

Kuti's, 70 London Rd, S01 2AJ, ℰ 221585, Indian rest.   AZ **a**

La Brasserie, 33-34 Oxford St., SO1 1DS, ℰ 221046 – AE VISA   AZ **c**
closed Saturday lunch, Sunday and Bank Holidays – **M** 10.00 st. and a la carte 12.40/24.45 t.
▮ 3.50.

Kohinoor, 2 The Broadway, Portswood, SO2 1WE, ℰ 582770, Indian rest.   BY **c**

Golden Palace, 1st Floor, 17 Above Bar St., SO1 0DX, ℰ 226636, Chinese rest. – AE
① VISA   AZ **e**
M 3.30/11.90 t. and a la carte 11.50/15.70 t. ▮ 3.00.

MICHELIN Distribution Centre, Test Lane, SO1 9JX, ℰ 872344, FAX 663617 AY

AUSTIN-ROVER, DAIMLER-JAGUAR Marsh Lane
ℰ 630911
AUSTIN-ROVER The Causeway ℰ 865021
AUSTIN-ROVER High St., West End ℰ 473773
AUSTIN-ROVER, DAIMLER-JAGUAR The Avenue
ℰ 228811
CITROEN Rochester St. ℰ 331144
FORD 362-364 Shirley Rd ℰ 701700
FORD Palmerston Rd ℰ 228331

PEUGEOT-TALBOT 21-35 St. Denys Rd ℰ 585822
RENAULT Westquay Rd ℰ 639844
VAUXHALL-OPEL Portsmouth Rd, Sholing ℰ
449232
VAUXHALL The Avenue ℰ 226492
VOLVO Millbrook Roundabout ℰ 705600

◍ ATS West Quay Rd ℰ 333231
ATS 88-94 Portswood Rd ℰ 582727

SOUTH BRENT Devon 𝟰𝟬𝟯 I 32 – pop. 2 147 – ECD : Wednesday – ✆ 036 47.

◳ Wrangaton ℰ 3229 SW : 2 ¼ m. by A 38.

♦London 228 – Exeter 28 – ♦Plymouth 16 – Torquay 17.

Glazebrook House, Glazebrook, TQ10 9JE, SW : 1 m. ℰ 3322, , park – rm TV ☎
ℙ. AE VISA .
M 14.50/22.75 st. and a la carte ▮ 3.95 – **10 rm** ☷ 35.00/105.00 st.

at North Huish S : 3 ¼ m. by B 3210 via Avonwick village (turn right opposite Avon Inn) –
✉ South Brent – ✆ 054 882 Gara Bridge :

Brookdale House ﴾, TQ10 9NR, ℰ 402, , park – rest TV ☎ ℙ. AE VISA .
closed 3 to 26 January – **M** (dinner only) 23.50 t. and a la carte ▮ 4.50 – **8 rm** ☷ 60.00/95.00 t.
– SB (November-Easter) 115.00/125.00 st.

SOUTH DALTON Humberside 𝟰𝟬𝟮 S 22 – see Beverley.

SOUTHEND-ON-SEA Essex **404** W 29 – pop. 155 720 – ECD : Wednesday – ✆ 0702.

Envir. : Hadleigh Castle (ruins) ≤★ of Thames *AC*, W : 3 m. – Southend Airport (Historic Aircraft museum) N : 2 m.

☄ Belfairs Park, Eastwood Rd, Leigh-on-Sea ✆ 525345.

✈ ✆ 340201, Telex 995081 N : 2 m.

🛈 High St. Precinct ✆ 355120 – Civic Centre, Victoria Av. ✆ 355122.

♦London 39 – ♦Cambridge 69 – Croydon 46 – ♦Dover 85.

🏨 **Erlsmere**, 24-32 Pembury Rd, Westcliff-on-Sea, SS0 8DS, ✆ 349025, ⌗ heated – 📺 ☎
 P. 🔄 *VISA*. ⅍
 M *(closed Sunday dinner)* (bar lunch)/dinner 14.95 **t.** and a la carte ▯ 2.75 – **21 rm**
 ☷ 34.50/120.00 **t.**

🏨 West Park, 11 Park Rd, Westcliff-on-Sea, SS0 7PQ, ✆ 330729, Fax 338162 – 📺 ☎ **P**. 🔄
 VISA
 21 rm ☷ 27.00/48.00 **t.**

🏨 **Balmoral**, 34-36 Valkyrie Rd, Westcliff-on-Sea, SS0 8BU, ✆ 342947, Fax 337828, ⇌ – 📺
 ⊗ **P**. 🔄 *VISA*. ⅍
 closed 4 days at Christmas – **M** *(closed Sunday dinner)* (bar lunch)/dinner 7.50 **st.** and a
 la carte ▯ 3.00 – **22 rm** ☷ 32.00/48.00 **st.** – SB (weekends only) 52.80/68.00 **st.**

⋔ **Ilfracombe House**, 11-13 Wilson Rd, SS1 1HG, ✆ 351000 – 📺 ☎. 🔄 AE ⓞ *VISA*. ⅍
 M 9.00 **st.** ▯ 2.15 – **13 rm** ☷ 28.00/44.00 **st.**

⋔ **Strand** without rest., 165 Eastern Esplanade, SS1 2YB, ✆ 586611 – ⇥ rm 📺. ⅍
 April-November – **8 rm** ☷ 13.50/35.00 **s.**

AUSTIN-ROVER Priory Cres. ✆ 467766
FIAT 22 Belle Vue Pl. ✆ 610482
PEUGEOT-TALBOT 139-155 West Rd ✆ 347861
RENAULT 536 London Rd., Westcliff-on-Sea ✆
339602
ROLLS-ROYCE, BENTLEY, MERCEDES-BENZ Sta-
tion Rd, Thorpe Bay ✆ 582233

SAAB 661 London Rd. at Westcliff-on-Sea ✆
351471
TOYOTA 57 West Rd ✆ 346288/346296
VW-AUDI 2 Comet Way ✆ 421142

SOUTH LOPHAM Norfolk **404** X 26 – see Diss.

SOUTH MIMMS Herts. **404** T 28 – ECD : Thursday – ✉ ✆ 0707 Potters Bar.

🛈 M 25 Bignalls Corner Service Area, Potters Bar ✆ 43233.

♦London 21 – Luton 17.

🏨 **Crest** (Crest), Bignalls Corner, Potters Bar, EN6 3NH, South Mimms Services, junction of
 A 1 (M), A 6, M 25 on B 197 ✆ 43311, Telex 299162, Fax 46728, 🔲 – ⇥ rm 🍴 rest 📺 ☎ **P**
 – 🛆 200. 🔄 AE ⓞ *VISA*. ⅍
 M *(closed Saturday lunch)* 12.50/17.00 **st.** and a la carte – ☷ 7.75 – **115 rm** 71.50/82.00 **st.**
 – SB (weekends only) 90.00/100.00 **st.**

SOUTH MOLTON Devon **403** I 30 The West Country G. – pop. 3 552 – ECD : Wednesday –
✆ 076 95.

🛈 1 East St. ✆ 4122 and 2378 (summer only).

♦London 210 – Exeter 35 – Taunton 39.

🏨 ❀ **Whitechapel Manor** ⌇, EX36 3EG, NE : 4 m. by B 3227 and unmarked lane off rounda-
 bout junction with A 361 ✆ 3377, Fax 3797, ≤, « Elizabethan manor house built by Robert
 De Bassett », ⇌, park – ⇥ rest 📺 ☎ **P**. 🔄 *VISA*. ⅍
 M 19.50/30.00 **st.** ▯ 5.00 – **9 rm** ☷ 55.00/125.00 **st.**, **1 suite** 150.00 **st.**
 Spec. Cream of carrot and chive soup, Sea Bass cooked in seaweed with a warm olive oil dressing, Sliced fillet
 of Heal Farm lamb with a honey and sherry vinegar sauce.

🏨 **Park House** ⌇, EX36 3ED, N : ½ m. by North Molton rd ✆ 2610, ≤, « Victorian country
 house », ⌇, ⇌, park – ⇥ rest **P**. 🔄 *VISA*. ⅍
 closed 10 to 31 January – **M** *(closed Monday)* 12.75/15.25 **t.** ▯ 3.50 – **7 rm** ☷ 32.00/60.00 **t.**
 – SB (November-March) 70.00/80.00 **st.**

🏨 **Marsh Hall Country House** ⌇, EX36 3HQ, N : 1 ¼ m. by North Molton rd ✆ 2666, ≤,
 ⇌ – 📺 ☎ **P**. 🔄 *VISA*
 M (dinner only) 14.95 **t.** ▯ 3.50 – **7 rm** ☷ 28.00/56.00 **t.**

 at East Buckland NW : 6 ¼ m. by A 361 – ✉ Barnstaple – ✆ 059 86 Filleigh :

XX **Lower Pitt** ⌇ with rm, EX32 0TD, ✆ 243, ⇌ – **P**. 🔄 *VISA*. ⅍
 closed 25-26 December and 1 January – **M** *(closed Sunday and Monday)* (dinner only)(booking essential) a la carte 11.50/16.70 **t.** ▯ 3.20 – **3 rm** ☷ 20.00/40.00 **t.** – SB (weekdays only) 75.00 **st.**

SOUTH NORMANTON Derbs. **402** **403** **404** Q 24 – pop. 11 607 (inc. Pinxton) – ECD : Wednesday – ✆ 0773 Ripley.

♦London 130 – Derby 17 – ♦Nottingham 15 – ♦Sheffield 31.

🏨 **Swallow** (Swallow), Carter Lane East, DE55 2EH, on A 38 ✆ 812000, Telex 377264, Fax
 580032, 🔲 – ⇥ rm 📺 ☎ ᕒ **P** – 🛆 250
 123 rm

SOUTH PETHERTON Somerset **408** L 31 – pop. 2 235 – ✪ 0460.
♦London 138 – ♦Bristol 41 – Exeter 41 – Taunton 19 – Yeovil 7.5.

  XX **Le Tire Bouchon,** 8 Palmer St., TA13 5DB, ✆ 40272, French rest., 🐟 – **P**. 🚗 AE VISA
       closed Sunday to Wednesday to non-residents and November-15 March – **M** (dinner only)
       18.50 **st.** ▯ 3.60.

SOUTHPORT Merseyside **402** K 23 – pop. 88 596 – ECD : Tuesday – ✪ 0704.
Envir. : Rufford Old Hall★ 15C (the Great Hall★★) *AC*, E : 9 m.
🏌 Park Rd ✆ 30133 – 🏌 Hesketh, Cockle Dick's Lane ✆ 36897.
🛈 112 Lord St. ✆ 33133 and 40404.
♦London 221 – ♦Liverpool 20 – ♦Manchester 38 – Preston 19.

  🏰 **Prince of Wales** (T.H.F), Lord St., PR8 1JS, ✆ 36688, Telex 67415, Fax 43488, 🐟 – ▦ TV
       ☎ **P** – 🏊 400. 🚗 AE ① VISA
       M (carving lunch)/dinner 9.95 **st.** and a la carte ▯ 4.00 – 🍵 7.60 – **98 rm** 64.00/90.00 **st.**,
       6 suites 100.00/200.00 **st.** – SB 70.00/100.00 **st.**

  🏰 **Scarisbrick,** 239 Lord St., PR8 1NZ, ✆ 43000, Telex 67107, Fax 33335 – ▦ TV ☎ **P** – 🏊
       120. 🚗 AE ① VISA
       M 6.10/10.50 **st.** and a la carte – **58 rm** 🍵 48.00/85.00 **st.** – SB (weekends only)
       62.00/72.00 **st.**

  🏠 **New Bold,** Lord St., PR9 0BE, ✆ 32578, Fax 32528 – TV ☎ **P** – 🏊 150. 🚗 AE ① VISA 🚫
       M *(closed Sunday dinner)* 6.50/12.50 **t.** and a la carte ▯ 4.95 – 🍵 6.50 – **21 rm** 26.00/47.50 **t.**
       – SB (weekends only) 55.00/70.00 **st.**

  🏠 **Shelbourne,** 1 Lord St. West, PR8 2BH, ✆ 41252, 🐟 – � rm TV ☎ **P**. 🚗 AE VISA
       M (dinner only) 10.95 **st.** and a la carte ▯ 4.00 – **19 rm** 🍵 29.00/45.00 **t.** – SB (week-
       ends only) 40.00/65.00 **st.**

  🏠 **Stutelea,** Alexandra Rd, PR9 0NB, ✆ 44220, Fax 500232, 🚗, 🐟 – TV ☎ **P**. 🚗 AE ① VISA
       🚫 – **M** (bar lunch)/dinner 11.60 **st.** and a la carte – **12 rm** 🍵 30.00/60.00 **st.** –
       SB (except Christmas, New Year and Bank Holidays) 58.00/60.00 **st.**

  🏠 **Crimond,** 28 Knowsley Rd, PR9 0HN, ✆ 36456, 🚗 – � rest TV ☎ **P**. 🚗 AE ① VISA
       M 10.00 **st.** ▯ 2.75 – **14 rm** 🍵 33.00/53.00 **st.** – SB (except summer) (weekends only)
       70.00/80.00 **st.**

  🏠 **Club House,** 15 Leicester St., PR9 0ER, ✆ 33745 – TV **P**. 🚗 AE ① VISA
       M (by arrangement) 8.50 **st.** ▯ 2.50 – **13 rm** 🍵 22.50/35.00 **st.** – SB 50.00/60.00 **st.**

  🏠 **Ambassador,** 13 Bath St., PR9 0DP, ✆ 43998 – � rest TV **P**. 🚗 VISA
       closed first 2 weeks January – **M** 7.00 **st.** ▯ 3.75 – **8 rm** 🍵 15.50/37.00 **st.**

  XX **Squires,** 78-80 King St., PR8 1LG, ✆ 30046 – 🚗 AE ① VISA
       closed lunch Monday to Wednesday and Sunday dinner – **M** 14.95 **st.** and a la carte
       15.80/24.25 **st.** ▯ 5.50.

ALFA-ROMEO, LOTUS, SAAB 609 Liverpool Rd ✆   MITSUBISHI Aughton Rd ✆ 38220
74114   SKODA Portland St. ✆ 34916
CITROEN Liverpool Rd ✆ 74127   TOYOTA Tulketh St. ✆ 30909
COLT Aughton Rd ✆ 67904   VOLVO 51 Weld Rd ✆ 66613
FIAT 89-91 Bath St. North ✆ 35535   VW-AUDI Zetland St. ✆ 31091
FORD Virginia St. ✆ 31550
LADA Liverpool Rd ✆ 77161   ⚙ ATS 69 Shakespeare St. ✆ 34434
MERCEDES 205 Liverpool Rd ✆ 68515

SOUTHSEA Hants. **403 404** Q 31 – see Portsmouth and Southsea.

SOUTH SHIELDS Tyne and Wear **401 402** P 19 – pop. 86 488 – ECD : Wednesday – ✪ 091
Tyneside.
🏌 Cleadon Hill ✆ 456 8942, SE : 3 m. – 🏌 Whitburn, Lizard Lane ✆ 529 2144 SE : 2 ½ m.
🛈 South Foreshore, Sea Rd ✆ 455 7411 (summer only) – The Museum and Art Gallery, Ocean Rd
✆ 454 6612.
♦London 284 – ♦Newcastle-upon-Tyne 9.5 – Sunderland 6.

  🏰 **Sea,** Sea Rd, NE33 2LD, ✆ 427 0999, Telex 53533 – TV ☎ **P**. 🚗 AE ① VISA
       M 5.95/7.80 **st.** and a la carte ▯ 3.05 – **30 rm** 🍵 41.50/52.50 **st.**

ARG Burrow Street ✆ 427 1313   ⚙ ATS Western Approach ✆ 454 1060
FORD ✆ 4552227
NISSAN ✆ 455 2101

SOUTHWAITE SERVICE AREA Cumbria **401 402** L 19 – ✉ Carlisle – ✪ 069 74.
♦London 300 – ♦Carlisle 14 – Lancaster 58 – Workington 48.

  🏠 **Granada Lodge** without rest., CA4 0NT, on M6 (Southbound carriageway) ✆ 73131, Fax
       73669 – TV 🚻 **P** – **39 rm**.

SOUTH WALSHAM Norfolk **404** Y 26 – pop. 543 – ✉ Norwich – ✪ 060 549.
♦London 120 – Great Yarmouth 11 – ♦Norwich 9.

  🏠 **South Walsham Hall H. and Country Club** ⚜, South Walsham Rd, NR13 6DQ, ✆
       378, Fax 519, ≼, 🏊 heated, 🏌, 🐟, park, 🎾 squash – TV ☎ **P**. 🚗 AE ① VISA 🚫
       closed 1 to 15 January – **M** 15.00 **t.** and a la carte ▯ 3.50 – **19 rm** 🍵 36.00/85.00 **st.** –
       SB (weekends only) 75.00/95.00 **st.**

SOUTHWELL Notts. 402 404 R 24 – pop. 6 283 – ECD : Thursday – ✆ 0636.
See : Minster★★ 12C-13C (Chapter house : foliage carving★★ 13C).
♦London 135 – Lincoln 24 – ♦Nottingham 14 – ♦Sheffield 34.

   Saracen's Head (T.H.F.), Market Pl., NG25 0HE, ℰ 812701, Telex 377201, Fax 815408 – ⇆ rm TV ☎ Ⓟ – 🏛 100. 🅢 AE ① VISA
   M 16.95 **st.** and a la carte ⅃ 4.00 – ☕ 7.00 – **27 rm** 57.00/73.00 **st.** – SB (weekends only) 80.00/96.00 **st.**

   Old Forge without rest., 2 Burgage Lane, NG25 0ER, ℰ 812809 – ⇆ TV Ⓟ. 🅢 VISA
   5 rm ☕ 26.00/40.00 **s.**

   ✗ Leos, 12 King St., NG25 0EN, ℰ 812119 – ▤.
FORD Westgate ℰ 813741

SOUTHWOLD Suffolk 404 Z 27 – pop. 3 756 – ECD : Wednesday – ✆ 0502.
🏌 The Common ℰ 723234, W : ½ m. on A 1095.
🛈 Town Hall, Market Place ℰ 722366 (summer only).
♦London 108 – Great Yarmouth 24 – ♦Ipswich 35 – ♦Norwich 34.

   Swan, Market Pl., IP18 6EG, ℰ 722186, Fax 724800, 🚗 – � ⇆ rest TV ☎ Ⓟ – 🏛 40. 🅢 AE VISA
   M 17.50/20.50 **t.** ⅃ 4.50 – **43 rm** ☕ 36.00/80.00 **t.**, **2 suites** 86.00/100.00 **t.** – SB (week-days only) (except summer) 80.00/96.00 **st.**

   Crown, 90 High St., IP18 6DP, ℰ 722275, Telex 97223 – ⇆ rest TV ☎ Ⓟ. 🅢 AE VISA. 🛇
   closed 8 to 14 January – **M** 12.50/15.00 **t.** and a la carte – ☕ 3.20 – **12 rm** 25.50/62.00 **t.**

SOUTH WOODHAM FERRERS Essex 404 V 29 – pop. 6 975 – ✉ ✆ 0245 Chelmsford.
♦London 36 – Chelmsford 12 – Colchester 34 – Southend-on-Sea 13.

   Oakland, 2-6 Reeves Way by Merchant St., CM3 5XE, ℰ 322811 – TV ☎. 🛇 – **34 rm**.

SOUTH ZEAL Devon 403 I 31 The West Country G. – ECD : Thursday – ✉ ✆ 0837 Okehampton.
♦London 218 – Exeter 17 – ♦Plymouth 36 – Torquay 27.

   Oxenham Arms, EX20 2JT, ℰ 840244, « 12C inn », 🚗 – TV ☎ Ⓟ. 🅢 AE ① VISA
   M 8.50/12.50 **t.** ⅃ 2.95 – **8 rm** ☕ 38.00/50.00 **t.**

SOWERBY North Yorks. – see Thirsk.

SPARK BRIDGE Cumbria – see Ulverston.

SPEEN Berks. – see Newbury.

SPELDHURST Kent 404 U 30 – see Royal Tunbridge Wells.

SPRATTON Northants. 404 R 27 – see Northampton.

SPREYTON Devon 403 I 31 – pop. 289 – ✉ Crediton – ✆ 036 33 Bow.
♦London 224 – Exeter 23 – ♦Plymouth 42.

   Downhayes ⑤, EX17 5AR, N : 1 ½ m. on Bow Rd ℰ 378, ≤, « Converted 16C longhouse », park – ⇆ rm Ⓟ. 🛇
   closed 20 to 29 December – **M** 12.50 – **3 rm** ☕ 32.00/45.00.

STADDLEBRIDGE North Yorks. – see Northallerton.

STAFFORD Staffs. 402 403 404 N 25 – pop. 60 915 – ECD : Wednesday – ✆ 0785.
See : High House★ (16C) – St. Mary's Church (Norman font★) Blithfield Hall★ (Elizabethan) AC, W : 8 m.
🏌 Newport Rd ℰ 223821.
🛈 Ancient High House, Greengate St. ℰ 40204.
♦London 142 – ♦Birmingham 26 – Derby 32 – Shrewsbury 31 – ♦Stoke-on-Trent 17.

   Tillington Hall (De Vere), Eccleshall Rd, ST16 1JJ, NW : 1 ½ m. on A 5013 ℰ 53531, Telex 36566, Fax 59223, 🏊, 🛇 – ⇩ TV ☎ Ⓟ – 🏛 200. 🅢 AE ① VISA
   M *(closed Saturday lunch)* 8.00/8.50 **st.** and a la carte ⅃ 3.50 – **90 rm** ☕ 45.00/90.00 **st.** – SB (weekends only) 70.00 **st.**

   Swan (B.C.B.), 46 Greengate St., ST16 2JA, ℰ 58142, Fax 223372 – TV ☎ Ⓟ. 🅢 AE ① VISA 🛇
   closed 25 and 26 December – **M** a la carte 7.50/14.40 **t.** – **32 rm** ☕ 35.00/52.00 **t.**

   Garth, Moss Pit, ST17 9JR, S : 2 m. on A 449 ℰ 56124, Telex 36479, Fax 55152 – ⇆ rm TV ☎ Ⓟ – 🏛. 🅢 AE VISA
   M *(closed Saturday lunch and Bank Holiday Monday lunch)/dinner* 6.35/9.35 **t.** and a la carte – **60 rm** ☕ 43.00/57.00 **t.** – SB (weekends only) 50.00 **st.**

   Vine, Salter St., ST16 2JU, ℰ 44112 – TV ☎ Ⓟ. 🅢 AE VISA
   M 3.50/10.00 **st.** and a la carte ⅃ 5.05 – **27 rm** ☕ 33.00/49.00 **st.**

STAFFORD
AUSTIN-ROVER Lichfield Rd ℰ 51366
BMW Lichfield Rd ℰ 46999
CITROEN Astonfields Rd ℰ 223336
DATSUN Lichfield Rd ℰ 59313
FIAT Milford ℰ 661226
FORD Stone Rd ℰ 51331
HONDA Lichfield Rd ℰ 47221
LADA Sandon Rd ℰ 45299

MAZDA Derby St. ℰ 55486
PEUGEOT-TALBOT Newport Rd ℰ 54495
RENAULT Wolverhampton Rd ℰ 52118
SAAB Yarlet Bank ℰ 088 97 (Sandon) 248
VAUXHALL-OPEL Walton ℰ 661293

ATS Kenworthy Rd. Astonfields Ind Est. ℰ 223832/58118

STAINES Middlesex **404** S 29 – pop. 51 949 – ECD : Thursday – 0784.
♦London 26 – Reading 25.

Thames Lodge (T.H.F.), Thames St., TW18 4SF, ℰ 464433, Group Telex 8812552, Fax 454858, ≼ – rm rest TV ☎ P – 60. AE ① VISA
M *(closed Saturday lunch)* 12.50/13.50 **st.** and a la carte ॥ 3.75 – 7.60 – **47 rm** 72.00/82.00 **st.** – SB (weekends only) 80.00/86.00 **st.**

STAMFORD Lincs. **402 404** S 26 – pop. 16 127 – ECD : Thursday – 0780.
See : Site★★ – St.Martin's Church★ – Lord Burghley's Hospital★ – Browne's Hospital★.
Envir. : Burghley House★★★ (16C) (paintings : Heaven Room★★★)AC.
Burghley Park, St. Martins ℰ 53789 – Museum, Broad St. ℰ 55611.
♦London 92 – ♦Leicester 31 – Lincoln 50 – ♦Nottingham 45.

The George of Stamford, 71 St. Martin's, PE9 2LB, ℰ 55171, Telex 32578, Fax 57070, « 17C coaching inn with walled monastic garden » – rest TV ☎ P – 50. AE VISA
M a la carte 18.50/24.35 **st.** ॥ 3.50 – **46 rm** 64.00/130.00 **t.**, **1 suite** 130.00 **st.** – SB (weekends only) 85.00/130.00 **st.**

Lady Anne's, 37-38 High St., St. Martin's Without, PE9 2LJ, ℰ 53175, 🐎 – TV ☎ P – 100. AE ① VISA
M 8.50/9.50 **t.** and a la carte ॥ 3.95 – **28 rm** 39.50/70.00 **t.** – SB (weekends only) (October-April) 52.50 **st.**

Garden House, 42 High St., St. Martin's, PE9 2LP, ℰ 63359, Telex 329230, 🐎 – TV ☎ P. AE VISA
M *(closed Sunday dinner)* a la carte 15.65/22.50 **st.** ॥ 4.50 – **21 rm** 54.75/100.00 **st.** – SB (except summer) (weekends only) 65.00 **st.**

Welland House without rest., 19 Broad St., PE9 1PG, ℰ 57028, « 18C town house with antiques », 🐎 – .
5 rm 18.00/40.00 **st.**

Candlesticks with rm, 1 Church Lane, PE9 2JU, ℰ 64033 – rest TV P. AE VISA.
M *(closed Tuesday lunch and Monday)* 6.50/11.50 **t.** and a la carte ॥ 3.50 – **4 rm** 25.00/30.00 **t.**

Ram Jam Inn with rm, Great North Rd, Stretton ✉ Oakham (Leics.), LE15 7QX, NW : 8 m. by B 1081 on A 1 ℰ 078 081 (Castle Bytham) 776, Group Telex 342888, Fax 724721, 🐎 – TV ☎ P. AE ① VISA
closed Christmas Day – M (coffee shop) a la carte 8.50/13.00 **t.** ॥ 3.00 – 3.50 – **8 rm** 40.00/50.00 **t.**

at Collyweston (Northants.) SW : 3¾ m. on A43 – ✉ Stamford – 078 083 Duddington

Cavalier, Main St., PE9 3PQ, ℰ 288 – TV P. AE ① VISA.
closed 25 December – M 7.95 **t.** (lunch) and a la carte ॥ 2.75 – **6 rm** 28.00/42.00 **st.** – SB (weekends only) 40.00/50.00 **st.**

at Empingham W : 5 ¾ m. on A 606 – ✉ Oakham – 078 086 Empingham :

White Horse, 2 Main St., LE15 8PR, ℰ 221, Fax 521 – TV ☎ & P – . AE ① VISA
M *(closed Sunday dinner)* 10.00/15.00 **t.** and a la carte ॥ 2.85 – **11 rm** 19.50/49.95 **t.**

at Normanton Park W : 6 ½ m. by A 606 on Edith Weston Rd – ✉ Oakham – 0780 Stamford :

Normanton Park ⑤, South Shore, LE15 8RP, ℰ 720315, ≼, 🚣, 🐎 – TV ☎ & P. AE ① VISA.
M 11.75 **t.** and a la carte ॥ 4.00 – **16 rm** 40.00/65.00 **t.**

AUSTIN-ROVER St. Paul's St. ℰ 52741
FORD Wharf Rd ℰ 55151
PEUGEOT-TALBOT Scotgate ℰ 64741

RENAULT Water St. ℰ 63532
TOYOTA Collyweston ℰ 078 083 (Duddington) 271
VAUXHALL West St. ℰ 62571

STANDISH Greater Manchester **402 404** M 23 – pop. 11 504 – ECD : Wednesday – ✉ Wigan – 0257.
♦London 210 – ♦Liverpool 22 – ♦Manchester 21 – Preston 15.

Kilhey Court (Best Western), Chorley Rd, Worthington, WN1 2XN, E : 1 ¾ m. by B 5239 on A 5106 ℰ 423083, 🐎 – TV ☎ P – 200 – **20 rm.**

The Beeches with rm., School Lane, WN6 0TD, on B 5239 ℰ 426432 – TV P. AE ① VISA.
M *(closed Saturday lunch and Sunday dinner)* 10.00 **st.** and a la carte 14.50/20.50 **st.** ॥ 6.15 – 3.25 – **11 rm** 20.00/42.00 **st.** – SB (weekends only) 50.00/112.00 **st.**

ATS 23 Market St. ℰ 423146/423732

STANDLAKE Oxon. **403 404** P 28 – ✉ Witney – ✆ 086 731.
◆London 69 – ◆Oxford 12 – Swindon 22.

   ↑ **Old Rectory** ⑤ without rest., Church End, OX8 7SG, ✆ 559, « Riverside garden », ⌇ –
     📺 🅿 ⌇
     closed December and January – **4 rm** ☲ 34.00/55.00 **s.**

STANNERSBURN Northumb. – ✉ Hexham – ✆ 0660 Bellingham.
◆London 363 – ◆Carlisle 56 – ◆Newcastle-upon-Tyne 46.

   ⌂ **Pheasant Inn** ⑤, Falstone, NE48 1DD, ✆ 40382 – ⌁ 🅿
     closed 25 December – **M** (bar lunch Monday to Saturday)/dinner 11.50 **t.** and a la carte
     ◊ 2.95 – **11 rm** ☲ 16.00/40.00 **t.** – SB (except summer) 40.00/48.00 **st.**

STANSTEAD ABBOTS Herts. **404** U 28 – pop. 1 906 – ✉ Ware – ✆ 027 979 Roydon.
◆London 22 – ◆Cambridge 37 – Luton 32 – ◆Ipswich 66.

   🏰 **Briggens** (Norfolk Cap.), Stanstead Rd, SG12 8LD, E : 2 m. on A 414 ✆ 2416, Telex 817906,
     Fax 3685, ≤, « Arboretum », ⊠ heated, ┌₉, 🐎, park, ✗ – |🛗| 📺 ☎ 🅿 – 🛱 . ⌇
     53 rm, **1 suite**.

STANTON HARCOURT Oxon **403 404** P 28 – pop. 774 – ✉ ✆ 0865 Oxford.
◆London 71 – Gloucester 45 – ◆Oxford 13 – Swindon 27.

   ✗ **Harcourt Arms**, OX8 1RJ, ✆ 881931 – 🅿. 🆎 AE VISA ⌇
     M 20.00 **t.** and a la carte 11.20/16.50 **t.** ◊ 3.75.

STANTON ST. QUINTIN Wilts. – see Chippenham.

STARBOTTON North Yorks. – see Kettlewell.

STEEPLE ASTON Oxon. **403 404** Q 28 – pop. 1 619 – ECD : Saturday – ✆ 0869.
◆London 69 – ◆Coventry 38 – ◆Oxford 10.

   🏰 **Hopcroft's Holt**, OX5 3QQ, SW : 1 ¼ m. at junction of A 423 and B 4030 ✆ 40259, Fax
     40865 – 📺 ☎ 🅿 – 🛱 . 🆎 AE ① VISA
     M (carving lunch)/dinner 9.50 **t.** and a la carte – **60 rm** ☲ 54.95/69.90 **t.**

   ✗ **Red Lion**, South St., OX5 3RY, ✆ 40225 – 🅿
     closed Sunday, Monday, 1 week February, 2 weeks September and 25 December –
     M (booking essential) (bar lunch)/dinner 15.00/27.00 **t.** ◊ 3.25.

STEVENAGE Herts. **404** T 28 – pop. 74 757 – ECD : Monday and Wednesday – ✆ 0438.
Envir. : Knebworth House (furniture★) S : 3 m.
┌₁₈ Aston Lane ✆ 043 888 (Shephall) 424.
🛈 Central Library, Southgate ✆ 369441.
◆London 36 – Bedford 25 – ◆Cambridge 27.

   🏰 **Novotel**, Knebworth Park, SG1 2AX, SW : 1 ½ m. by A 602 at junction with A 1 (M)
     ✆ 742299, Telex 826132, Fax 723872, ⊠ heated – |🛗| ▤ rest 📺 ☎ & 🅿 – 🛱 . 🆎 AE ① VISA
     M 12.00/15.00 **t.** and a la carte **t.** ◊ 4.50 – ☲ 5.00 – **101 rm** 59.00/67.00 **t.**

   🏰 **Stevenage Moat House** (Q.M.H.), High St., Old Town, SG1 3AZ, ✆ 359111, 🐎 – ⌁ rm
     📺 📽 🅿 🛱 🆎 AE ① VISA
     M 10.75 **st.** and a la carte ◊ 3.95 – **00 rm** ☲ 52.50/65.00 **st.** – SB (weekends only)
     63.00/66.00 **st.**

   ⌂ **Archways**, 15 Hitchin Rd, Old Town, SG1 3BJ, ✆ 316640, 🐎 – 📺 🅿. 🆎 AE ① VISA
     M 10.00/18.00 **st.** and a la carte ◊ 4.00 – **36 rm** ☲ 32.00/48.00 **st.**

     at Broadwater S : 1 ¾ m. by A 602 on B 197 – ✉ ✆ 0438 Stevenage :

   🏰 **Roebuck Post House** (T.H.F.), Old London Rd, SG2 8DS, ✆ 365444, Telex 825505, Fax
     741308, 🐎 – ⌁ rm 📺 ☎ 🅿 – 🛱 . 🆎 AE ① VISA
     M 9.50/14.75 **st.** and a la carte ◊ 3.65 – ☲ 7.00 – **54 rm** 65.00/75.00 **st.** – SB (week-
     ends only) 60.00 **st.**

AUDI-VW Lyton Way ✆ 746400
AUSTIN-ROVER High St. Codicote ✆ 820288
FIAT London Rd ✆ 811011
NISSAN Broadwater Cres. ✆ 315555

PEUGEOT Pound Av. ✆ 356266
VAUXHALL-OPEL 124-6 High St. ✆ 351113

⑩ ATS 4-8 Norton Rd ✆ 313262/353935

STEYNING West Sussex **404** T 31 – pop. 8 318 (inc. Upper Beeding) – ECD : Thursday –
✆ 0903.
See : St. Andrew's Church (the nave★ 12C).
◆London 52 – ◆Brighton 12 – Worthing 10.

   🏰 **Springswells** without rest., 9 High St., BN4 3GG, ✆ 812446, ⊠ heated, 🐎 – 📺 ☎ 🅿. 🆎
     AE ① VISA ⌇
     11 rm ☲ 27.00/68.00 **st.**

STOBOROUGH Dorset – see Wareham.

STOCKBRIDGE Hants. 403 404 P 30 – pop. 524 – ECD : Wednesday – ✆ 0264 Andover.
♦London 75 – Salisbury 14 – Winchester 9.

🏨 **Grosvenor** (Lansbury), High St., SO20 6EU, ✆ 810606, Telex 477677, Fax 810747, 🐎 –
≍ rm 📺 ☎ 🅿 – 🔥 . 🔄 AE ⓞ VISA 🦌
  M 8.50/12.50 **t.** and a la carte 11.25/14.50 **t.** – **23 rm** ⌑ 53.00/63.00 **t.** – SB (spring
  and autumn) (weekends only) 72.00/80.00 **st.**

🏵 **White Hart Inn,** High St., SO20 6HF, ✆ 810475, Fax 810268 – 📺 🅿. 🔄 VISA
  M (closed Sunday dinner and Monday) (dinner only and Sunday lunch)/dinner a la carte
  10.10/16.75 **t.** ▮3.00 – **14 rm** ⌑ 20.00/47.50 **t.**

🏵 **Old Three Cups,** High St., SO20 6HB, ✆ 810527, « 15C inn », 🐎 – 🅿. 🔄 VISA. 🦌
  closed 25 December-31 January – **M** (closed Monday and Sunday dinner to non-residents)
  6.50/7.50 **t.** and a la carte – **8 rm** ⌑ 22.00/42.00 **st.**

⋔ **Carbery,** Salisbury Hill, SO20 6EZ, on A 30 ✆ 810771, ⌇ heated, 🐎 – 🅿. 🦌
  closed 2 weeks at Christmas – **M** (dinner only) 8.05 **st.** – **11 rm** ⌑ 16.10/39.10 **st.**

STOCKLAND Devon – see Honiton.

STOCKPORT Greater Manchester 402 403 404 N 23 – pop. 135 489 – ECD : Thursday –
✆ 061 Manchester.
Envir. : Lyme Park★ (16C-18C) *AC*, SE : 4 ½ m.
🏌 Offerton Rd ✆ 427 2001 – 🏌 Marple, Barnsfold Rd ✆ 427 2311 – 🏌 Heaton Moor ✆ 432 2134.
🛈 9 Princes St. ✆ 480 0315.
♦London 201 – ♦Liverpool 42 – ♦Manchester 6 – ♦Sheffield 37 – ♦Stoke-on-Trent 34.

🏨 **Alma Lodge** (Embassy), 149 Buxton Rd, SK2 6EL, on A 6 ✆ 483 4431, Telex 665026, Fax
  1983 – ≍ rm 📺 ☎ 🅿 – 🔥 200. 🔄 AE ⓞ VISA
  closed Christmas Night – **M** (bar lunch Saturday) 10.50 **t.** and a la carte – ⌑ 6.50 **59 rm**
  29.00/77.50 **t.**

🏨 **Rudyard,** 271 Wellington Rd North, Heaton Chapel, SK4 5BP, ✆ 432 2753, Telex 668594 –
  📺 ☎ 🅿 – 🔥 90 – **21 rm**.

🏠 **Wycliffe Villa,** 74 Edgeley Rd, Edgeley (via Greek St.), SK3 9NQ, ✆ 477 5395 – 📺 ☎ 🅿.
  🔄 AE ⓞ VISA 🦌
  M (closed Saturday lunch, Sunday and Bank Holidays) 5.00 **t.** (lunch) and a la carte ▮3.75 –
  12 rm ⌑ 34.00/41.00 **st.**

ALFA-ROMEO, JAGUAR, LANCIA, LOTUS 5
Marshland St., Hazel Grove ✆ 456 0800
AUSTIN-ROVER 35 Buxton Rd ✆ 480 4244
AUSTIN-ROVER Wellington Rd North ✆ 443 2000
COLT School Lane, Heaton Chapel ✆ 432 4790
FIAT Heaton Lane ✆ 480 6661
FORD Oak St., Hazel Grove ✆ 483 9431
FORD Adswood Rd ✆ 480 0211
MAZDA Wellington Rd North ✆ 442 6466
PEUGEOT-TALBOT 110 Buxton Rd ✆ 480 0831

RANGE-ROVER, DAIMLER, JAGUAR Town Hall Sq.
✆ 480 7966
RENAULT 91 Heaton Moor Rd ✆ 432 9416
SAAB 31-33 Buxton Rd ✆ 483 6271
VAUXHALL-OPEL Wellington Rd South ✆ 480 6146
VAUXHALL-OPEL 398 Wellington Rd North ✆
432 3232
VOLVO Wellington Rd South ✆ 429 7099

🅦 ATS Hollingworth Rd., Bredbury ✆ 430 5221

STOCKTON-ON-TEES Cleveland 402 P 20 – pop. 86 699 – ECD : Thursday – ✆ 0642.
✈ Tees-side Airport : ✆ 0325 (Darlington) 332811, SW : 6 m.
🛈 Theatre Yard ✆ 615080.
♦London 251 – ♦Leeds 61 – ♦Middlesbrough 4.

🏨 **Swallow** (Swallow), 10 John Walker Sq., TS18 1AQ, ✆ 679721, Telex 587895, Fax 601714,
  🔄 – 🛗 ≍ rm 📺 ☎ 🅿 – 🔥 . 🔄 AE ⓞ VISA
  M 10.25/14.25 **st.** and a la carte ▮5.50 – **122 rm** ⌑ 62.00/82.00 **st.** – SB 90.00 **st.**

  at Eaglescliffe S : 3 ½ m. on A 135 – ✉ ✆ 0642 Stockton-on-Tees :

🏨 **Parkmore** (Best Western), 636 Yarm Rd, TS16 0DH, ✆ 786815, Telex 58298, Fax 790485,
  🔄 , 🐎 – 📺 ☎ 🅿 – 🔥 . 🔄 AE ⓞ VISA
  M 8.75/12.50 **st.** and a la carte ▮3.00 – **55 rm** ⌑ 42.00/65.00 **st.**, **1 suite** 60.00/75.00 **st.** –
  SB (weekends only) 67.00/85.00 **st.**

ARG Portrack Lane ✆ 677777
BMW 45 Norton Rd ✆ 675361
FIAT Commercial St. ✆ 675177
MAZDA 87-91 Oxbridge Lane ✆ 671134
NISSAN Middleway Mandale Industrial Estate ✆
672617
RENAULT 110 Yarm Rd ✆ 601393

SAAB, SUBARU Chapel St. ✆ 679781
VAUXHALL-OPEL Boathouse Lane ✆ 607804
VOLVO Prince Regent St. ✆ 673251

🅦 ATS 18 Brunswick St. ✆ 657733
ATS 112 Norton Rd ✆ 604477

STOKE BY NAYLAND Suffolk 404 W 28 – pop. 727 – ✉ ✆ 0206 Colchester (Essex).
♦London 60 – Colchester 8 – Ipswich 15.

🏠 **Angel Inn,** Polstead St., CO6 4SA, ✆ 263245, « Part timbered 17C inn » – 📺 ☎ 🅿. 🔄 AE
  ⓞ VISA 🦌
  closed 25-26 December and 1 January – **M** a la carte 14.35/23.15 **st.** ▮2.75 – **4 rm**
  ⌑ 35.00/45.00 **st.**

STOKE D'ABERNON Surrey 404 ㊷ – see Cobham.

STOKE FLEMING Devon **403** J 33 – see Dartmouth.

STOKE GABRIEL Devon **403** J 32 – see Totnes.

STOKE MANDEVILLE Bucks. **404** R 28 – see Aylesbury.

STOKE-ON-TRENT Staffs. **402** **403** **404** N 24 – pop. 272 446 – ECD : Thursday – ☎ 0782.
See : City Museum and Art Gallery★ Y – Gladstone Pottery Museum★ *AC* V – National Garden Festival site U.
Envir. : Little Moreton Hall★★ (16C) *AC*, NW : 8 m. on A 34 U – Wedgewood Visitor's Centre★ S : 5 ½ m. by A 519 V.
Trentham Park ✆ 658800 V.
1 Glebe St. ✆ 411222 – Cley Museum and Art Gallery, Bethesda St. ✆ 202173.
◆London 162 – ◆Birmingham 46 – ◆Leicester 59 – ◆Liverpool 58 – ◆Manchester 41 – ◆Sheffield 53.

STOKE-ON-TRENT
NEWCASTLE-UNDER-LYME
BUILT UP AREA

Alexandra Road	U 3	Cobridge Road	U 21
Bedford Road	U 4	Davenport Street	U 23
Brownhills Road	U 12	Elder Road	U 24
Church Lane	U 9	Etruria Vale Road	U 27
		Grove Road	V 30
		Hanley Road	U 31
		Heron Street	V 34
		High Street	U 35
		Higherland	V 37
		Manor Street	V 44

Mayne Street	V 45
Moorland Road	U 48
Park Hall Road	V 54
Porthill Road	V 59
Snow Hill	U 63
Stoke Road	U 68
Strand (The)	V 69
Victoria Park Road	U 75
Watlands View	U 76
Williamson Street	U 77

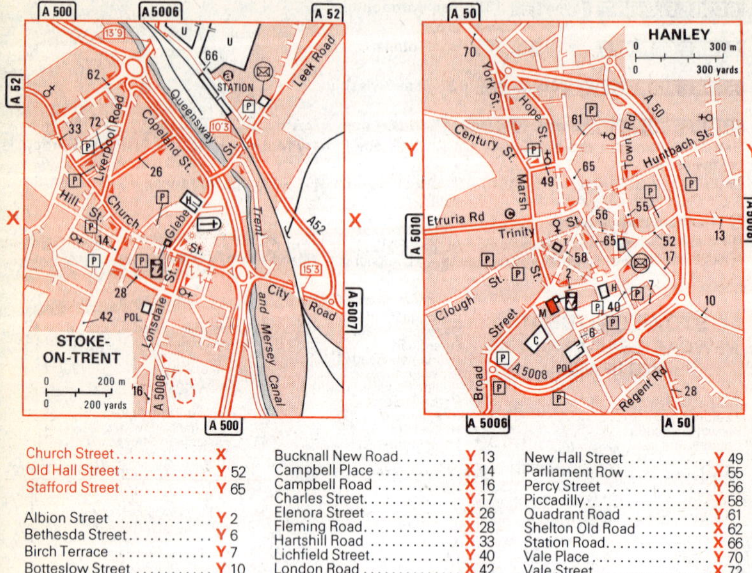

Church Street . . . . **X**
Old Hall Street . . . . **Y** 52
Stafford Street . . . . **Y** 65

Albion Street . . . . **Y** 2
Bethesda Street . . . . **Y** 6
Birch Terrace . . . . **Y** 7
Botteslow Street . . . . **Y** 10

Bucknall New Road . . . . **Y** 13
Campbell Place . . . . **X** 14
Campbell Road . . . . **X** 16
Charles Street . . . . **Y** 17
Elenora Street . . . . **X** 26
Fleming Road . . . . **X** 28
Hartshill Road . . . . **X** 33
Lichfield Street . . . . **Y** 40
London Road . . . . **X** 42

New Hall Street . . . . **Y** 49
Parliament Row . . . . **Y** 55
Percy Street . . . . **Y** 56
Piccadilly . . . . **Y** 58
Quadrant Road . . . . **Y** 61
Shelton Old Road . . . . **X** 62
Station Road . . . . **X** 66
Vale Place . . . . **Y** 70
Vale Street . . . . **X** 72

North Stafford, Station Rd, ST4 2AE, ☎ 744477, Telex 36287, Fax 744580 – 🛗 ⇌ rm 📺 ☎ 🅿 – 🛎 400
67 rm, 2 suites.
X a

White House, 94 Stone Rd, Trent Vale, ST4 6SP, S : 2 ¼ m. on A 34 ☎ 642460 – ☎ 🅿. 🖼
VISA 🛇
V e
closed 2 weeks December-January – **M** (by arrangement) 7.50 **t.** 🍾 2.75 – **10 rm**
⫴ 20.00/44.00 **t.**

at Hanley N : 2 m. by A 5006 – ✉ 🕿 0782 Stoke-on-Trent :

Stakis Grand (Stakis), 66 Trinity St., ST1 5NB, ☎ 202361, Telex 367264, Fax 286464, 🖼 – 🛗
📺 ☎ 🕭 🅿 – 🛎 300
Y c
M *(closed Saturday lunch)* – **128 rm**.

at Basford NW : 1 ¾ m. by A 500 off A 53 – ✉ 🕿 0782 Stoke-on-Trent :

Haydon House, Haydon St., ST4 6JD, ☎ 711311, Telex 36600, Fax 717470 – 📺 ☎ 🅿 –
🛎 30. 🖼 **AE** ⓪ **VISA**
U a
M 9.95/15.00 **st.** and a la carte 🍾 4.50 – ⫴ 5.50 – **19 rm** 48.00/70.00 **st.**, **8 suites** 88.00/
110.00 **st.** – SB (weekends only) 80.00/120.00 **st.**

MICHELIN Distribution Centre, Unit No. 2, Jamage Road Industrial Estate, Talke Pits, ST7 1QF,
☎ 771211, FAX 775782 by A 34 **U**

AUSTIN-ROVER	Leek Rd, Endon ☎ 503160		NISSAN	Victoria Rd, Fenton ☎ 416666
AUSTIN-ROVER	Station Rd, Barlaston ☎ 2014		PEUGEOT-TALBOT	Leek Rd ☎ 214371
AUSTIN-ROVER	Broad St. ☎ 219500		RENAULT	Blue Gates, Biddulph ☎ 514444
AUSTIN-ROVER	King St., Longton ☎ 599456		SAAB, TOYOTA, VW	Leek Rd, Hanley ☎ 264888
AUSTIN-ROVER	Brook Lane, Newcastle ☎ 618461		SKODA	Leek Rd ☎ 261784
BMW	Pool Dam, Newcastle ☎ 711000		SUBARU, HYUNDAI	High St., Tunstall ☎ 838997
CITROEN	Uttoxeter Rd ☎ 599235		VAUXHALL-OPEL	Victoria Rd, Hanley ☎ 202200
DAIHATSU	Ashbank ☎ 2426		VAUXHALL-OPEL	Bullocks House Rd ☎ 513952
FIAT	Lightwood Rd, Longton ☎ 319212		VAUXHALL-OPEL	Lightwood Rd ☎ 599199
FORD	Clough St. ☎ 202591		VOLVO	Duke St. ☎ 599799
FORD	King St. ☎ 599333			
HONDA	Sneyd St., Cobridge ☎ 261593		ATS	25 Smithpool Rd, Fenton ☎ 47081
LADA	292 Waterloo Rd, Cobridge ☎ 202265		ATS	Lower St., Newcastle-under-Lyme ☎ 622431
LADA	Congleton Rd, Biddulph ☎ 512250		ATS	87/89 Waterloo Rd, Burslem ☎ 838493
MERCEDES-BENZ	Clough St. ☎ 202112		ATS	Stone Rd, Hanford ☎ 744281

STOKE PRIOR Heref. and Worc. – see Leominster.

STOKESLEY North Yorks. 🗺 Q 20 – pop. 3 785 – ✉ 🕿 0642 Great Ayton.
◆London 239 – ◆Leeds 59 – ◆Middlesbrough 8 – York 52.

Manor House Farm 🦢, Ingleby Greenhow, TS9 6RB, SE : 4 ¼ m. by B 1257 ☎ 722384, ≤,
🐎 – ⇌ 🅿. 🛇
closed 22 to 30 December – **M** (by arrangement) 10.00 **st.** 🍾 4.50 – **3 rm** ⫴ 15.00/31.00 **st.**

STONE Glos. 403 404 M 29 – pop. 667 (inc. Ham) – ✉ Berkeley – ☎ 0454 Falfield.
♦London 130 – ♦Bristol 17 – Gloucester 18.

🏠 **Elms at Stone,** GL13 9JX, on A 38 ☎ 260279 – ✦✕ rm 📺 ☎ 🅿. ◪ 𝘝𝘐𝘚𝘈
M *(closed Sunday dinner)* 10.95 t. (dinner) and lunch a la carte approx. 9.10 t. ⌢ 3.50 – **8 rm**
⌷ 35.00/45.00 t.

BMW, VAUXHALL   Manor Close ☎ 710566   FORD   Meadowfield Garage ☎ 710386

STONE Heref. and Worc. 403 404 N 26 – see Kidderminster.

STONE Staffs. 402 403 404 N 25 – pop. 12 119 – ECD : Wednesday – ☎ 0785.
♦London 150 – ♦Birmingham 36 – ♦Stoke-on-Trent 9.

🏨 **Stone House** (Lansbury), ST15 0BQ, S : 1 ¼ m. by A 520 on A 34 ☎ 815531, Fax 814764,
◪, 🚤 – ✦✕ rm 📺 ☎ 🅿 – ⌂ 250. ◪ 🄰🄴 ⓪ 𝘝𝘐𝘚𝘈 🐾
M 8.00/12.50 t. and a la carte – **48 rm** ⌷ 65.00/75.00 t., **2 suites**.

🏨 **Crown,** 38 High St., ST15 8AS, ☎ 813535 – 📺 ☎ 🅿 – ⌂ 150. ◪ 🄰🄴 ⓪ 𝘝𝘐𝘚𝘈
M 5.25/7.50 t. and a la carte ⌢ 3.00 – **29 rm** ⌷ 32.50/60.00 t. – SB (weekends only)
37.00/50.00 **st.**

FORD   Darlaston Rd ☎ 813332

STON EASTON Somerset – see Farrington Gurney.

STONEHOUSE Glos. 403 404 N 28 – see Stroud.

STONE-IN-OXNEY Kent – see Rye (East Sussex).

STONOR Oxon. 404 R 29 – see Henley-on-Thames.

STONY STRATFORD Bucks. 404 R 27 – ✉ ☎ 0908 Milton Keynes.
♦London 62 – Bedford 27 – ♦Coventry 34 – Northampton 18 – ♦Oxford 31.

✕✕ **Stratfords,** 7 St. Paul's Court, 118 High St., MK11 1LJ, ☎ 566577, « Converted Victorian
church » – 🅿. ◪ 🄰🄴 𝘝𝘐𝘚𝘈
closed lunch Monday and Saturday, Sunday and 3 weeks January – **M** 14.50/18.50 t.
⌢ 3.50.

✕ **Bekash Tandoori,** 50 High St., MK11 1AQ, ☎ 562249, Indian rest. – ◪ 🄰🄴 ⓪ 𝘝𝘐𝘚𝘈
M 10.00 t. and a la carte 6.75/22.70 t. ⌢ 6.00.

✕ **Akber Tandoori,** 10-12 Wolverton Rd, MK11 1DX, ☎ 562487, Indian rest. – ▤. ◪ 🄰🄴 ⓪
𝘝𝘐𝘚𝘈
M a la carte 10.00/12.50 t. ⌢ 3.20.

at Cosgrove (Northants.) N : 2 ½ m. by A 508 – ✉ ☎ 0908 Milton Keynes (Bucks.) :

⌂ **Old Bakery,** Main St., MK19 7JA, ☎ 564940 – 📺 🅿. ◪ 𝘝𝘐𝘚𝘈 🐾
M 10.00 st. ⌢ 3.00 – **4 rm** ⌷ 29.00/35.00 st.

STORRINGTON West Sussex 404 S 31 – pop. 6 915 – ECD : Wednesday – ☎ 090 66 (4 fig.) or
0903 (6 fig.).

Envir. : Parham House★ (Elizabethan) *AC*, W : 1 ½ m.

♦London 54 – ♦Brighton 20 – ♦Portsmouth 36.

🏨 **Little Thakeham** 🐦, Merrywood Lane, Thakeham, RH20 3HE, N : 1 ¾ m. by B 2139
☎ 744416, ≤, « Lutyens house, gardens by Gertrude Jekyll, country house atmosphere »,
◪ heated, ✕ – 📺 ☎ 🅿. ◪ 🄰🄴 ⓪ 𝘝𝘐𝘚𝘈 🐾
closed 24 December-7 January – **M** *(closed Sunday dinner to non-residents)* (booking
essential) 17.50/23.50 ⌢ 4.00 – **9 rm** ⌷ 65.00/150.00, **1 suite** 175.00.

🏨 **Abingworth Hall** 🐦, Thakeham Rd, RH20 3EF, N : 1 ¾ m. on B 2139 ☎ 079 83 (West
Chiltington) 3636, Telex 877835, ◪ heated, 🚤, ✕ – 📺 ☎ 🅿 – ⌂ 50. ◪ 🄰🄴 ⓪ 𝘝𝘐𝘚𝘈
🐾
M 21.00 t. and a la carte 15.50/28.50 t. ⌢ 3.50 – **22 rm** ⌷ 55.00/120.00 t. – SB 114.00/158.00 **st.**

✕✕✕ **Manley's,** Manleys Hill, RH20 4BT, ☎ 742331 – ✦✕ 🅿. ◪ 🄰🄴 ⓪ 𝘝𝘐𝘚𝘈
closed Sunday dinner, Monday, 2 weeks August-September and first week January –
M 14.50 (lunch) and a la carte 22.40/25.80 **s.**

STOURBRIDGE West Midlands 🅰🅾🅱 🅰🅾🅲 N 26 – pop. 55 136 – ECD : Thursday – ☎ 0384.

🇼 Hagley Country Club ⌀ 0562 (Hagley) 883701 AU.

🇿 The Old House, High St. ⌀ 872940.

♦London 147 – ♦Birmingham 14 – Wolverhampton 10 – Worcester 21.

Plan : see Birmingham p. 2

🏨 **Talbot**, High St., DY8 1DW, ⌀ 394350, Telex 335464, Fax 371318 – 📺 ☎ 🅿. 🅰 AE VISA
M 6.50/8.50 t. and a la carte 🍾4.25 – **25 rm** � 43.00/134.00 t. – SB (weekends only)
32.00/37.50 st.   see plan of Birmingham p.2 AU a

🏠 **Limes**, 260 Hagley Rd, Pedmore, DY9 0RW, SE : 1 ½ m. on A 491 ⌀ 0562 (Hagley) 882689,
🚗 – ☎ 🅿. 🅰 VISA
AU z
closed Christmas – **M** (by arrangement) 7.50 **st.** – **10 rm** ⊆ 19.50/29.00 st.

at Kinver (Staffs.) W : 5 m. by A 458 – AU – ✉ Stourbridge (West Midlands) – ☎ 0384
Kinver :

🍴🍴 **Berkley's (Piano Room)**, High St., DY7 6HG, ⌀ 873679 – 🅿. 🅰 AE � VISA
closed Sunday – **M** (dinner only) 16.85 **t.** 🍾2.75.

AUSTIN-ROVER Hagley Rd ⌀ 393022
FORD Hagley Rd ⌀ 392131
FORD, VOLVO ⌀ 442222
MERCEDES-BENZ, PORSCHE Grange Lane, Lye ⌀
2424575

NISSAN High St ⌀ 393231
RENAULT Norton Rd ⌀ 396655
VAUXHALL-OPEL The Hayes, Lye ⌀ 424665
VAUXHALL-OPEL Bridgnorth Rd ⌀ 394757
VW-AUDI Birmingham St. ⌀ 392626

STOURPORT-ON-SEVERN Heref. and Worc. 🅰🅾🅱 🅰🅾🅲 N 26 – pop. 17 880 – ECD : Wednesday
– ☎ 029 93 (4 and 5 fig.) or 0299 (6 fig.).

♦London 137 – ♦Birmingham 21 – Worcester 12.

🏨 **Stourport Moat House** (Q.M.H.), 35 Hartlebury Rd, DY13 9LT, E : 1 ¼ m. on B 4193
⌀ 827733, Telex 333676, Fax 78520, 🏊, 🚗, park, 🍴, squash – 📺 ☎ 🅿 – 🛎 350. 🅰 AE
ⓓ VISA
M (bar lunch Saturday) 9.00/11.25 t. and a la carte 🍾3.95 – **66 rm** ⊆ 52.00/65.00 st., **2 suites**
70.00/75.00 st. – SB (weekends only) 70.00 st.

🏨 **Swan**, 56 High St., DY13 8BX, ⌀ 71661 – 📺 ☎ 🅿. 🅰 AE ⓓ VISA
M *(closed Saturday lunch and Sunday dinner)* 6.40/9.70 t. and a la carte 🍾2.75 – **32 rm**
⊆ 26.00/52.00 t.

🏠 **Oakleigh**, 17 York St., DY13 9EE, ⌀ 77568, 🚗 – ✁ rm 📺 🅿. 🅰 VISA. 🍴
M 10.00 st. 🍾3.50 – **8 rm** ⊆ 25.00/38.00 st. – SB (weekends only) 32.00/34.00 st.

🍴🍴 **Severn Tandoori**, 11 Bridge St., DY13 8UX, ⌀ 3090, Indian rest. – 🅰 AE ⓓ VISA
M a la carte 8.50/12.35 t. 🍾2.95.

MITSUBISHI Dunley ⌀ 3357

STOW-ON-THE-WOLD Glos. 🅰🅾🅱 🅰🅾🅲 O 28 – pop. 1 596 – ECD : Wednesday – ✉ Cheltenham
– ☎ 0451 Cotswold.

🇿 Talbot Court ⌀ 31082.

♦London 86 – ♦Birmingham 44 – Gloucester 27 – ♦Oxford 30.

🏨 **Wyck Hill House** 🌄, GL54 1HY, S : 2¼ m. by A 429 on A 424 ⌀ 31936, Telex 43611, Fax
32243, ≼, « *Victorian country house* », 🚗, park – 📶 📺 ☎ 🅿. 🅰 AE ⓓ VISA. 🍴
M (bar lunch)/dinner 23.50 t. and a la carte 21.85/26.75 t. 🍾5.85 – **33 rm** ⊆ 65.00/80.00 t.,
1 suite 120.00/150.00 t. – SB (weekends only) 140.00/210.00 st.

🏨 **Unicorn Crest** (Crest), Sheep St., GL54 1HQ, ⌀ 30257, Telex 437186, Fax 31090 – 📺 ☎
🅿. 🅰 AE ⓓ VISA
M (bar lunch Monday to Saturday)/dinner 15.30 st. and a la carte 🍾4.95 – ⊆ 7.35 – **20 rm**
56.00/68.00 t. – SB 86.00/96.00 st.

🏨 **Grapevine** (Best Western), Sheep St., GL54 1AU, ⌀ 30344, Telex 43423, Fax 32278 – ✁
📺 ☎ 🅿. 🅰 AE ⓓ VISA
closed 24 December-12 January – **M** (bar lunch)/dinner 21.95 t. – **17 rm** ⊆ 57.00/92.00 t.

🏨 **Fosse Manor**, Fosse Way, GL54 1JX, S : 1 ¼ m. on A 429 ⌀ 30354, Fax 32486, 🚗 – 📺 ☎
🅿 – 🛎 35. 🅰 AE ⓓ VISA
closed 1 week at Christmas – **M** 15.00/17.00 st. and a la carte 16.20/20.75 st. 🍾3.50 – **20 rm**
⊆ 38.00/87.00 st. – SB (except September) 65.00/100.00 st.

🏨 **Stow Lodge**, The Square, GL54 1AB, ⌀ 30485, 🚗 – ✁ 📺 🅿. AE ⓓ. 🍴
closed 20 December-31 January – **M** (bar lunch Monday to Saturday)/dinner 10.75 t.
and a la carte 11.25/19.25 t. 🍾4.00 – **22 rm** ⊆ 37.00/63.00 t. – SB (November-
Easter except Christmas) 55.00/68.00 st.

🏠 **Limes** without rest., Evesham Rd, GL54 1EJ, ⌀ 30034, 🚗 – 📺 🅿
5 rm ⊆ 12.50/34.00 s.

at Upper Oddington E : 2 ½ m. by A 436 – ✉ Moreton-in-Marsh – ☎ 0451 Cotswold :

🍸 **Horse and Groom**, GL56 OXH, ⌀ 30584 – 📺 🅿. 🅰. 🍴
closed 25 December – **M** (bar lunch)/dinner a la carte 10.95/13.20 t. 🍾3.10 – **7 rm**
⊆ 24.00/42.00 t. – SB (except summer) 55.00/62.00 st.

at Bledington SE : 4 m. by A 436 on B 4450 – ✉ – ☎ 060 871 Kingham (Oxon.) :

⚐ **Kings Head,** OX7 6HD, ℰ 365 – 📺 ☎ 🅿. ⌘
M *(closed Sunday dinner)* (bar lunch)/dinner 14.00 **st.** and a la carte ⬦2.75 – **6 rm**
☕ 24.00/45.00 **st.**

at Lower Slaughter SW : 3 m. by A 429 – ✉ Bourton-on-the-Water – ☎ 0451 Cotswold :

🏰 **Lower Slaughter Manor** ⤳, GL54 2HP, ℰ 20456, Fax 22150, ≼, « 17C manor house and gardens », ◪, ⬳, ✘ – 📺 ☎ 🅿. ◪ 🄐 ⓪ 𝚅𝙸𝚂𝙰. ⌘
M 13.75/25.75 – **19 rm** 75.00/165.00 **st.**

at Lower Swell W : 1 ¼ m. on B 4068 – ✉ Stow-on-the-Wold – ☎ 0451 Cotswold :

🏠 **Old Farmhouse,** GL54 1LF, ℰ 30232, ⌦ – ⤧ rest 📺 🅿. ◪ 𝚅𝙸𝚂𝙰
M (bar lunch Monday to Saturday)/dinner 11.25 **st.** and a la carte – **13 rm** ☕ 18.50/64.50 **st.**

AUDI-VW Oddington, Moreton-in-Marsh ℰ 30422

◼ STRATFIELD TURGIS ◼ Hants – ✉ ☎ 0256 Basingstoke.

♦London 46 – Basingstoke 8 – Reading 11.

🏠 **Wellington Arms,** RG27 0AS, on A 33 ℰ 882214, Telex 265871, Fax 882934, ⌦ – 📺 ☎ 🅿 – ⅙ 80. ◪ 🄐 ⓪ 𝚅𝙸𝚂𝙰
M 12.50/15.75 **st.** and a la carte 12.75/21.60 **st.** ⬦6.50 – **15 rm** ☕ 65.00/90.00 **st.** – SB (week-ends only) 100.00/150.00 **st.**

◼ STRATFORD-UPON-AVON ◼ Warw. ▦▦▦ ▦▦▦ P 27 – pop. 20 941 – ECD : Thursday – ☎ 0789.

See : Site★ – Shakespeare's birthplace★ (16C)*AC*, AB – Hall's Croft★ (16C)*AC*, A B.

Envir. : Charlecote Park (castle 16C : interior★) *AC*, NE : 5 m. by B 4086 B – Wilmcote (Mary Arden's House★★) (16C) *AC*, NW : 5 m. by A 34 A.

🏌 Tiddington Rd ℰ 205749, E : by B 4086 B – 🏌 Warwick Rd ℰ 295252 by A 439 B.

🛈 Judith Shakespeare's House, 1 High St. ℰ 293127.

♦London 96 – ♦Birmingham 23 – ♦Coventry 18 – ♦Oxford 40.

STRATFORD-UPON-AVON

Bridge Street . . . . **B** 8
Henley Street . . . . **A** 29
High Street . . . . **A** 31
Sheep Street . . . . **AB** 35
Wood Street . . . . **A** 47

Banbury Road . . . . **B** 2
Benson Road . . . . **B** 3
Bridge Foot . . . . **B** 6
Chapel Lane . . . . **A** 13
Chapel Street . . . . **A** 14
Church Street . . . . **A** 16
Clopton Bridge . . . . **B** 18
College Lane . . . . **A** 19
Ely Street . . . . **A** 22
Evesham Place . . . . **A** 24
Great William Street . . . . **A** 25
Greenhill Street . . . . **A** 27
Guild Street . . . . **A** 28
Scholars Lane . . . . **A** 33
Tiddington Road . . . . **B** 38
Trinity Street . . . . **A** 40
Warwick Road . . . . **B** 42
Waterside . . . . **B** 43
Windsor Street . . . . **A** 45

Town plans : the names of main shopping streets are indicated in red at the beginning of the list of streets.

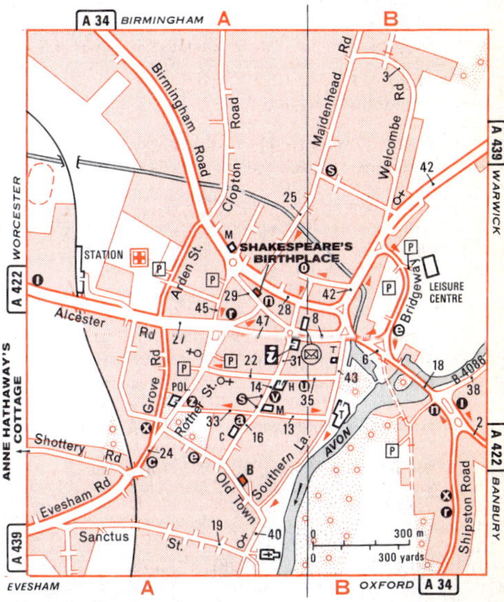

🏰 **Welcombe** ⤳, Warwick Rd, CV37 0NR, NE : 1 ½ m. on A 46/A 439 ℰ 295252, Telex 31347, Fax 414666, ≼, « 19C mansion in grounds », 🏌, ⌦, park – 📺 ☎ 🅿 – ⅙ 30. ◪ 🄐 ⓪ 𝚅𝙸𝚂𝙰
closed 28 December-3 January – M 17.50/25.00 **st.** and a la carte – **70 rm** ☕ 75.00/160.00 **st.**, **5 suites** 140.00/325.00 **st.** – SB (weekends only) 140.00 **st.**   on A 46   B

🏰 **Ettington Park** ⤳, Alderminster, CV37 8BS, SE : 6 ¼ m. on A 34 ℰ 740740, Telex 311825, Fax 87472, ≼, « Victorian Gothic mansion », ◪, ⬳, ⌦, park, ✘ – 🛗 ⤧ rest 📺 ☎ 🅿. ◪ ⓪ 𝚅𝙸𝚂𝙰 ⌘   on A 34   B
M 17.50/27.50 **st.** and a la carte ⬦6.00 – **43 rm** ☕ 95.00/125.00 **st.**, **5 suites** 140.00/175.00 **st.** – SB 150.00/200.00 **st.**

Moat House International (Q.M.H.), Bridgefoot, CV37 6YR, ℰ 414411, Telex 311127, Fax 298589, ☞ – 🛗 🖥 TV ☎ 🅿 – 🛎 400. 🅂 AE ⓞ VISA **B e**
M 15.00/30.00 st. – **245 rm** ☕ 72.50/95.00 st.. **2 suites** 160.00 st. – SB (weekends only) 90.00/100.00 st.

Shakespeare (T.H.F.), Chapel St., CV37 6ER, ℰ 294771, Telex 311181, Fax 415411, « 16C timbered inn » – 🛗 ⤬ rm TV ☎ 🅿 – 🛎 100. 🅂 AE ⓞ VISA **A v**
M 10.00/14.00 st. and a la carte 🍷 5.20 – ☕ 7.00 – **69 rm** 65.00/108.00 st.. **1 suite** 150.00 st. – SB 54.00/65.00 st.

Alveston Manor (T.H.F.), Clopton Bridge, CV37 7HP, ℰ 204581, Telex 31324, Fax 414095, ☞ – ⤬ rm TV ☎ 🅿 – 🛎 150. 🅂 AE ⓞ VISA **B i**
M 10.00/14.00 st. and a la carte 🍷 3.60 – ☕ 7.60 – **105 rm** 65.00/97.00 st.. **3 suites** 110.00/116.00 st. – SB 80.00/100.00 st.

White Swan (T.H.F.), Rother St., CV37 6NH, ℰ 297022 – ⤬ rm TV ☎ – 🛎 60. 🅂 AE ⓞ VISA **A r**
M 9.50 st. (lunch) and a la carte 🍷 3.75 – ☕ 7.00 – **35 rm** 66.00/102.00 st. – SB (weekends only) (except Christmas and New Year) 70.00/96.00 st.

Swan's Nest (T.H.F.), Bridgefoot, CV37 7LT, ℰ 66761, Fax 414547, ☞ – ⤬ rm TV ☎ ♿ 🅿 – 🛎 150. 🅂 AE ⓞ VISA **B n**
M 9.85/15.15 st. and a la carte 🍷 4.35 – ☕ 7.00 – **60 rm** 65.00/117.00 st. – SB 76.00/92.00 st.

Dukes, Payton St., CV37 6UA, ℰ 69300, Fax 414700, ☞ – TV ☎ 🅿. 🅂 AE ⓞ VISA. 🎿
closed Christmas and New Year – **M** *(closed Sunday)* a la carte 12.20/18.50 t. 🍷 3.50 – **17 rm** ☕ 37.50/85.00 t. – SB (October-March) (weekends only) 70.00/85.00 st. **A o**

Falcon (Q.M.H.), Chapel St., CV37 6HA, ℰ 205777, Telex 312522, Fax 414260 – 🛗 TV ☎ 🅿 – 🛎 200. 🅂 AE ⓞ VISA **A s**
M 14.00/16.00 st. and a la carte 🍷 3.50 – **73 rm** ☕ 55.00/86.00 st. – SB 75.00/80.00 st.

Stratford House, 18 Sheep St., CV37 6EF, ℰ 68288, Telex 311612 – TV ☎. 🅂 AE ⓞ VISA. 🎿 **AB u**
closed Christmas – **M** *(closed Sunday and Monday)* a la carte 15.00/17.50 t. – **10 rm** ☕ 57.00/80.00 t. – SB (weekdays only) 95.00/100.00 st.

Moonraker House without rest., 40 Alcester Rd, CV37 9DB, ℰ 67115 – ⤬ TV 🅿 **A i**
24 rm ☕ 28.00/44.00 st.

Sequoia without rest., 51 Shipston Rd, CV37 7LN, ℰ 68852, ☞ – TV ☎ 🅿. 🅂 AE ⓞ VISA 🎿 **B r**
21 rm ☕ 27.50/49.00 st.

Hardwick House without rest., 1 Avenue Rd, CV37 6UY, ℰ 204307 – TV 🅿. 🅂 AE VISA 🎿 **B s**
closed Christmas – **14 rm** ☕ 15.50/48.00 st.

Caterham House without rest., 58-59 Rother St., CV37 6LT, ℰ 67309 – 🅂 VISA **A z**
13 rm ☕ 22.00/40.00 st.

Twelfth Night without rest., Evesham Pl., CV37 6HT, ℰ 414595 – ⤬ TV 🅿. 🎿 **A c**
7 rm ☕ 17.00/40.00 st.

Marlyn without rest., 3 Chestnut Walk, CV37 6HG, ℰ 293752 – 🎿 **A e**
closed Christmas – **8 rm** ☕ 15.00/28.00 t.

Melita without rest., 37 Shipston Rd, CV37 7LN, ℰ 292432, ☞ – TV 🅿. 🅂 VISA **B x**
closed Christmas – **12 rm** ☕ 30.00/50.00 st.

Ashburton House, 27 Evesham Pl., CV37 6HT, ℰ 292444 – ⤬ rest. 🅂 AE VISA **A c**
closed 24 to 27 December – **M** (by arrangement) 12.00 🍷 3.50 – **4 rm** ☕ 13.00/28.00.

Virginia Lodge without rest., 12 Evesham Pl., CV37 6HT, ℰ 292157 – ⤬ TV 🅿 **A x**
closed Christmas – **7 rm** ☕ 12.00/33.00 st.

Hussains, 6a Chapel St., CV37 6EP, ℰ 67506, Indian rest. – 🖥. 🅂 AE ⓞ VISA **A s**
closed 25 December – **M** 10.00/15.00 t. and a la carte 8.15/12.65 t. 🍷 4.95.

Sir Toby's, 8 Church St., CV37 6HB, ℰ 68822 – 🅂 AE VISA **A a**
closed Sunday, 5 February-5 March and 2 weeks August – **M** (lunch by arrangement)/dinner a la carte 12.00/17.00 t. 🍷 3.25.

at Long Marston SW : 7 m. by A 34 – **B** – off A 46 – ✉ ☎ 0789 Stratford-upon-Avon :

Kings Lodge ⌂, CV37 8RL, ℰ 720705, « Country house atmosphere », ☞ – 🅿
closed December and January – **M** (by arrangement) 8.00 st. 🍷 2.00 – **3 rm** ☕ 14.50/40.00 st.

at Billesley W : 4 ½ m. by A 422 – **A** – ✉ Alcester – ☎ 0789 Stratford-upon-Avon :

Billesley Manor (Norfolk Cap.) ⌂, B49 6NF, ℰ 400888, Telex 312599, Fax 764145, ≤, 🅂, ☞, park, 🍴 – TV ☎ 🅿 – 🛎 100. 🅂 AE ⓞ VISA 🎿
M 16.00/23.00 t. and a la carte 21.70/32.75 t. 🍷 5.50 – **38 rm** ☕ 80.00/120.00 t.. **2 suites** 160.00/180.00 t. – SB (weekends only) 120.00/150.00 st.

at Wilmcote NW : 4 m. by A 34 – **A** – ✉ ☎ 0789 Stratford-upon-Avon :

Swan House, The Green, CV37 9XJ, ℰ 67030, ☞ – TV 🅿. 🅂 AE VISA 🎿
closed Christmas – **M** (bar lunch)/dinner a la carte 9.70/15.15 st. – **12 rm** ☕ 30.00/55.00 st. – SB 58.00/62.00 st.

AUDI-VW Western Rd ℰ 294477
CITROEN 23 Weston Rd ℰ 293577
FIAT Western Rd ℰ 67159
FORD Arden St. ℰ 67446
HYUNDAI Wellesbourne ℰ 840279
NISSAN Avenue Farm Industrial Estate ℰ 69894

PEUGEOT-TALBOT Alderminster ℰ 078 987
(Alderminster) 331/419
PEUGEOT-TALBOT Western Rd ℰ 69237
SAAB Birmingham Rd ℰ 205990

ATS Western Rd ℰ 205591

STRATTON Glos. 403 404 O 28 – see Cirencester.

STRATTON ST. MARGARET Wilts. 403 404 O 29 – see Swindon.

STREATLEY Berks. 403 404 Q 29 – pop. 1 055 – ✉ 🕭 0491 Goring.
♦London 56 – ♦Oxford 16 – Reading 11.

🏨 **Swan Diplomat**, High St., RG8 9HR, ℰ 873737, Telex 848259, Fax 872554, « ≼ Thames-side setting », ☞ – 📺 ☎ 👍 ℗ – 🏊 120. 🄰 🄰🄴 🅞 VISA. 🦌
M 14.00/17.00 t. and a la carte – **44 rm** ⌑ 81.00/113.00 t., **1 suite** 170.00/198.00 t.

STREET Somerset 403 L 30 **The West Country** G. – pop. 9 454 – ECD : Wednesday – 🕭 0458.
See : The Shoe Museum ★ AC.
Envir. : at Somerton ★, Market Place ★, St. Michaels Church ★, S : 6 m. – at High Ham (St. Andrews Church ★), SW : 8 m.
♦London 138 – ♦Bristol 28 – Taunton 20.

🏨 **Bear**, 53 High St., BA16 0EF, ℰ 42021 – 📺 ☎ ℗ – 🏊 50. 🄰 🄰🄴 🅞 VISA
M (buffet lunch)/dinner a la carte 11.00/17.00 st. 🍷 4.50 – **15 rm** ⌑ 39.00/60.00 st.

AUSTIN-ROVER Creeches Lane, Walton ℰ 42735
FIAT 84 West End ℰ 42996

FORD 189 High St. ℰ 47147
VAUXHALL-OPEL 12 Main St., Walton ℰ 42275

STRETTON Cheshire 402 403 404 M 23 – see Warrington.

STRETTON Staffs. 402 403 404 P 25 – see Burton-upon-Trent.

STRETTON UNDER FOSSE Warw. 403 404 Q 26 – see Rugby.

STROUD Glos. 403 404 N 28 – pop. 37 791 – ECD : Thursday – 🕭 045 36.
Envir. : Severn Wildfowl Trust ★ AC, W : 11 m – Painswick ★ NE : 3 m.
🏌 Minchinhampton ℰ 045 383 (Nailsworth) 2642 (Old Course) E : 3 m.
🛈 Subscription Rooms, Kendrick St. ℰ 5768.
♦London 113 – ♦Bristol 30 – Gloucester 9.

🏨 **London**, 30-31 London Rd, GL5 2AJ, ℰ 759992 – ⤬ rest 📺 ☎ ℗. 🄰 VISA. 🦌
M (closed Sunday to non-residents) 5.25/10.95 st. and a la carte 🍷 2.75 – **12 rm** ⌑ 22.00/52.00 st.

🏨 Imperial (B.C.B.), Station Rd, GL5 3AP, ℰ 764077 – ⤬ rest 📺 ☎. 🄰 🄰🄴 🅞 VISA. 🦌
closed Christmas – **M** (grill rest.) – **25 rm** ⌑ 35.00/48.00 t.

XX 🌼 **Oakes** (Oakes), 169 Slad Rd, GL5 1RG, ℰ 759950 – ℗. 🄰 VISA
closed Sunday dinner, Monday and January – **M** approx. 32.00 t. 🍷 3.40
Spec. Warm onion tart and tomato sauce with strips of smoked ham, Sliced pigeon breast on rosti potatoes with oyster mushrooms and coriander, Fig and Armagnac ice cream enriched with white chocolate.

at Brimscombe SE : 2 ¼ m. on A 419 – ✉ Stroud – 🕭 0453 Brimscombe :

🏨 **Burleigh Court** ⬧, The Roundabouts, SW : ½ m. by Burleigh Rd off Burleigh Hill, GL5 2PF, ℰ 883804, Fax 886870, ≼, 🛁 heated, ☞ – ⤬ rest 📺 ☎ ℗. 🄰 🄰🄴 🅞 VISA. 🦌
closed 24 December to 6 January – **M** (closed Sunday dinner) 10.95/23.50 st. and a la carte 🍷 3.60 – **17 rm** ⌑ 49.00/120.00 st.

at Rodborough S : ¾ m. by A 46 – ✉ Stroud – 🕭 045 387 Amberley :

🏨 **Bear of Rodborough** (T.H.F.), Rodborough Common, GL5 5DE, E : 1 ½ m. ℰ 878522, Telex 437130, Fax 872523, ☞ – ⤬ rm 📺 ☎ ℗ – 🏊 80. 🄰 🄰🄴 🅞 VISA
M 9.50/14.00 st. and a la carte 🍷 4.00 – ⌑ 7.50 – **47 rm** 65.00/95.00 st. – SB 80.00/95.00 st.

at Amberley S : 3 m. by A 46 – ✉ 🕭 0453 Stroud :

🏨 Amberley Inn (Best Western), GL5 5AF, ℰ 2565, ☞ – 📺 ☎ ℗ – **14 rm**.

at Stonehouse W : 2 m. on A 419 – ✉ 🕭 045 382 Stonehouse :

🏨 **Stonehouse Court**, Bristol Rd, GL10 3RA, ℰ 5155, Fax 4611, ⚓, ☞, park – 📺 ☎ ℗ – 🏊 80. 🄰 VISA. 🦌
M 10.50/17.50 t. and a la carte – **36 rm** ⌑ 60.00/75.00 t. – SB (October-March) 92.50 st.

at Leonard Stanley W : 4 m. by A 419 – ✉ 🕭 045 382 Stonehouse :

🏠 **Grey Cottage** without rest., GL10 3LU, ℰ 2515, (booking essential), ☞ – ⤬ rm 📺 ℗. 🦌
closed 3 weeks January – **3 rm** ⌑ 18.00/38.00 s.

STROUD

ALFA-ROMEO Lansdown Rd ☎ 4845
AUSTIN-ROVER Chestnut Lane ☎ 3671
CITROEN London Rd, Bowbridge ☎ 2861
FIAT Stratford Rd ☎ 4007
FORD London Rd ☎ 71341
MAZDA, HYUNDAI Westward Rd, Ebley ☎ 2000

PEUGEOT-TALBOT Stonehouse ☎ 045 382 (Stone-house) 2139
VAUXHALL-OPEL, BEDFORD Westward Rd ☎ 5522

⒵ ATS Dudbridge Rd ☎ 78156

STUCKTON Hants. – see Fordingbridge.

STUDLAND Dorset 403 404 O 32 **The West Country G.** – pop. 559 – ECD : Thursday – ✉ Swanage – ✹ 092 944.
♦London 130 – Bournemouth 22 – Dorchester 26.

🏨 **Knoll House,** BH19 3AH, ☎ 251, ⚓ heated, ✇, park, ✖ – ☎ Ⓟ
April-October – **M** 11.00/13.00 **st.** 🍵 3.10 – **78 rm** ❐ 32.00/115.00 **st.**

STUDLEY Warw. 403 404 O 27 – see Redditch (Heref. and Worc.).

STURMINSTER NEWTON Dorset 403 404 N 31 – pop. 1 781 – ✹ 0258.
♦London 123 – Bournemouth 30 – ♦Bristol 49 – Salisbury 28 – Taunton 41.

XXX **Plumber Manor** ➡ with rm, DT10 2AF, SW : 1 ¾ m. by A 357 on Hazelbury Bryan rd ☎ 72507, ≤, « 18C manor house », ✇, park, ✖ – TV ☎ Ⓟ. ◆ VISA. ✉
closed 2 weeks February – **M** (dinner only) 25.00 **st.** 🍵 3.75 – **12 rm** ❐ 50.00/90.00 **st.**

MAZDA Station Rd ☎ 72155

STURTON-BY-STOW Lincs. 402 404 S 24 – pop. 1 040 – ✉ Lincoln – ✹ 0427 Gainsborough.
♦London 149 – ♦Kingston-upon-Hull 45 – Lincoln 9 – ♦Sheffield 46.

🏠 **Village Farm,** High St., LN1 2AE, ☎ 788309, ✇ – ✖ rm Ⓟ. ✉
April-October – **M** (by arrangement) 8.00 **st.** – **3 rm** ❐ 12.00/32.00 **st.** – SB 42.00/46.00 **st.**

FSO, DAIHATSU Tillbridge Lane ☎ 788360

SUDBURY Derbs. 402 403 404 O 25 – pop. 839 – ✉ Derby – ✹ 028 372 Marchington.
See : Sudbury Hall★★ (17C) *AC.*
♦London 138 – ♦Birmingham 33 – Derby 13 – ♦Stoke-on-Trent 23.

Hotel and restaurant see : *Tutbury* SE : 6 m., *Uttoxeter* W : 4 ½ m.

To visit a town or region : use the Michelin Green Guides.

SUDBURY Suffolk 404 W 27 – pop. 17 723 – ECD : Wednesday – ✹ 0787.
🛈 Public Library, Market Hill ☎ 72092.
♦London 59 – ♦Cambridge 37 – Colchester 15 – ♦Ipswich 21.

🏨 Four Swans, 10 North St., CO10 6RB, ☎ 78103 – TV ☎ Ⓟ
17 rm.

🏠 **Hill Lodge,** 8 Newton Rd, CO10 6RG, ☎ 77568, ✇ – ✖ rest TV Ⓟ. ✉
closed Christmas week – **M** (by arrangement) 6.00 **s.** – **16 rm** ❐ 17.00/27.00 **s.**

XX **The Friars,** 17 Friars St., CO10 6AA, ☎ 72940 – ▤. ◆ AE Ⓒ VISA
closed Sunday – **M** 10.00/13.50 **st.** and a la carte 14.00/26.50 **st.** 🍵 3.50.

X **Mabey's Brasserie,** 47 Gainsborough St., CO10 7SS, ☎ 74298 – ◆ VISA
closed Sunday and 25 to 28 December – **M** a la carte 10.40/14.95 **t.** 🍵 3.95.

FORD Northern Rd ☎ 73436
VAUXHALL-OPEL Cornard Rd ☎ 72301

⒵ ATS Edgeworthy Rd ☎ 74227

SUNDERLAND Tyne and Wear 401 402 P 19 – pop. 195 064 – ECD : Wednesday – ✹ 0783 (5 and 6 fig.) or 091 (7 fig.).
⛳ Whitburn, Lizard Lane ☎ 529 2144 N : 2 m. by A 183 **A.**
🛈 Crowtree Leisure Centre, Crowtree Rd ☎ 565 0960 and 565 0990.
♦London 272 – ♦Leeds 92 – ♦Middlesbrough 29 – ♦Newcastle-upon-Tyne 12.

Plan opposite

🏨 **Gelt House,** 23 St. Bedes Terr., SR2 8HS, ☎ 567 2990 – ✖ rest TV ☎ Ⓟ. ◆ AE Ⓒ VISA
closed Christmas-New Year – **M** (closed Friday to Sunday) (dinner only) 7.50 **t.** 🍵 2.90 – **22 rm** ❐ 23.00/38.00 **t.**
B a

AUDI-VW, MERCEDES Newcastle Rd ☎ 548 0235
AUSTIN-ROVER Warwick ☎ 521 0838
BMW Ryhope Rd ☎ 523 7373
DAIHATSU, CITROEN Villiers St. ☎ 567 3954
FIAT Villiers St. ☎ 510 0550
FORD Trimdon St. ☎ 514 0311
HONDA Harbour View Garage ☎ 567 7538

MITSUBISHI Nth. Bridge St. ☎ 565 9252
PEUGEOT, SAAB Newcastle Rd ☎ 548 8811
RENAULT Riverside Rd ☎ 549 5260
VAUXHALL 122-129 High St. West ☎ 567 4805
VOLVO Newcastle Rd ☎ 549 1277

⒵ ATS Monkwearmouth Bridge ☎ 565 7694

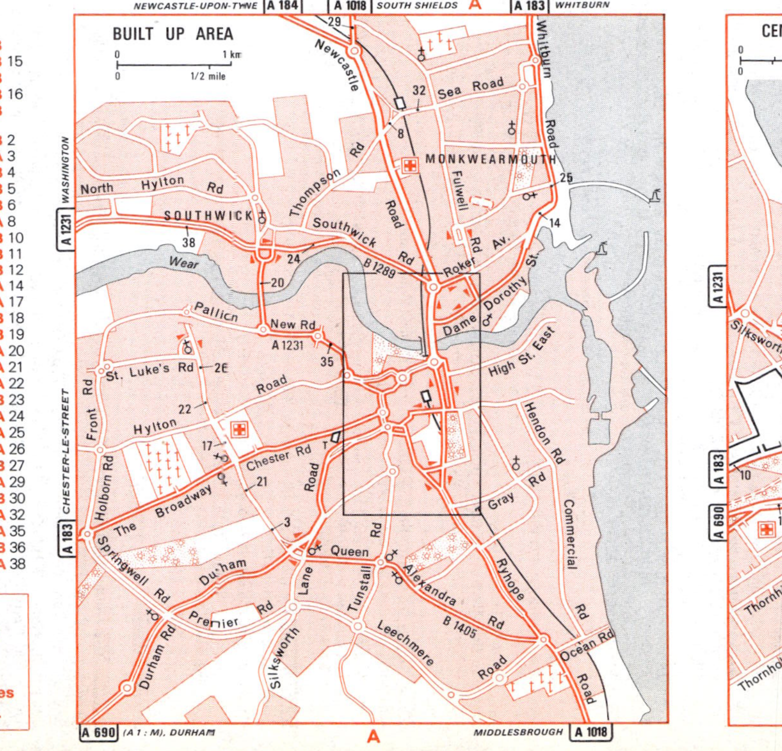

SUNDERLAND

Fawcett Street .... B
High Street West .... B 15
Holmeside .... B
John Street .... B 16
Three Bridges .... B

Albion Place .... B 2
Barnes Park Road .... A 3
Bedford Street .... B 4
Borough Road .... B 5
Bridge Street .... B 6
Charlton Road .... A 8
Chester Road .... B 10
Crowtree Road .... B 11
Derwent Street .... B 12
Harbour View .... A 14
Kayll Road .... A 17
Livingstone Road .... B 18
New Durham Road .... B 19
Northern Way .... A 20
Ormonde Street .... A 21
Pallion Road .... A 22
Park Lane .... B 23
Queens Road .... A 24
Roker Terrace .... A 25
St. Luke's Terrace .... A 26
St. Mary's Way .... B 27
Shields Road .... A 29
Southwick Road .... B 30
Station Road .... A 32
Trimdon Street .... A 35
Vine Place .... B 36
Wessington Way .... A 38

Plans de villes :
Dans la liste des rues des plans de ville les noms en rouge indiquent les principales voies commerçantes.

SUTTON BENGER Wilts. 408 404 N 29 – pop. 839 – ⊠ Chippenham – © 0249 Seagry.
◆London 92 – ◆Bristol 26 – Chippenham 4.5 – Swindon 16.

🏠 Bell House, High St., SN15 4RH, ℰ 720401, 🚗 – 📺 ☎ 🅿 – 🕍 40 – **14 rm**.

SUTTON COLDFIELD West Midlands 408 404 O 26 – © 021 Birmingham.
◆London 124 – ◆Birmingham 8 – ◆Coventry 29 – ◆Nottingham 47 – ◆Stoke-on-Trent 40.

Plan: see Birmingham pp. 2 and 3

🏯 **New Hall** (Thistle) ⤴, Walmley Rd, B76 8QX, SE : 1 ½ m. by Coleshill St., Coleshill Rd
and Reddicap Hill on B 4148 ℰ 378 2442, Telex 333580, Fax 378 4637, « Part 13C moated
manor house », 🚗, park – ⤢ rm 📺 ☎ 🕭 🅿 – 🕍 40. 🔼 🆎 ⓞ 𝘝𝘐𝘚𝘈. 🛠   DT e
M 12.50/19.50 **st.** and a la carte 🍾 7.50 – 🍽 7.50 – **60 rm** 75.00/115.00 **st.**, **5 suites** 150.00 **st.**
– SB (May-November) 114.00/167.00 **st.**

🏯 **Belfry** (De Vere), Lichfield Rd, Wishaw, B76 9PR, E : 6 ½ by A 453 on A 446 ℰ 0675 (Curd-
worth) 70301, Telex 338848, Fax 70178, ≼, 🔼, ⅂₈, 🚗, park, ✂, squash – 🛗 ▤ rest 📺 ☎
🅿 – 🕍 400. 🔼 🆎 ⓞ 𝘝𝘐𝘚𝘈. 🛠   by A 38 DT
M (closed Saturday lunch) 12.50/19.75 **st.** and a la carte 🍾 6.50 – **208 rm** 🍽 90.00/250.00 **st.**,
11 suites – SB (weekends only) 120.00 **st.**

🏯 **Penns Hall** (Embassy) ⤴, Penns Lane, Walmley, B76 8LH, SE : 2 ¾ m. by A 5127
ℰ 351 3111, Telex 335789, Fax 313 1297, 🔼, ⤴, 🚗, squash – 🛗 📺 ☎ 🅿 – 🕍 400. 🔼 🆎
ⓞ 𝘝𝘐𝘚𝘈   DT v
M 18.00 **st.** and a la carte 🍾 4.00 – 🍽 6.50 – **112 rm** 82.00/96.00 **st.**, **3 suites** 150.00 **st.**

🏨 **Sutton Court**, 60-66 Lichfield Rd, B74 2NA, N : ½ m. on A 5127 ℰ 355 6071, Telex 334175
– ⤢ rm 📺 ☎ 🅿 – 🕍 90. 🔼 🆎 ⓞ 𝘝𝘐𝘚𝘈   DT x
M (closed Saturday lunch) 9.95/18.95 **st.** and a la carte 14.95/20.70 **st.** 🍾 5.00 – **64 rm**
🍽 60.00/90.00 **st.** – SB (weekends only) 65.90 **st.**

🏨 **Moor Hall** (Best Western) ⤴, Moor Hall Drive, Four Oaks, B75 6LN, NE : 2 m. by A 453
ℰ 308 3751, Telex 335127, Fax 308 8974, 🚗, park – ⤢ rm 📺 ☎ 🅿 – 🕍 250. 🔼 🆎 ⓞ 𝘝𝘐𝘚𝘈
M (closed Saturday lunch and Sunday dinner) (buffet lunch)/dinner 5.95 **t.** and a la carte
17.00/22.50 **t.** – **75 rm** 🍽 60.00/130.00 **st.**   DT r

🏠 Parson and Clerk without rest., Chester Rd North, Streetly, B73 6SP, W : 3 ½ m. by A 453 on
A 452 ℰ 353 1747 – 📺 ☎ 🅿   CT s
30 rm.

⌂ **Standbridge**, 138 Birmingham Rd, B72 1LY, ℰ 354 3007, 🚗 – ⤢ rest 📺 🅿   DT a
closed 28 May-10 June and 24 December-4 January – **M** (by arrangement) 6.50 **st.** 🍾 3.35 –
9 rm 🍽 17.50/36.00 **st.**

XX **Le Bon Viveur**, 65 Birmingham Rd, B72 1QF, ℰ 355 5836 – ▤. 🔼 🆎 ⓞ 𝘝𝘐𝘚𝘈   DT u
closed Saturday lunch, Sunday and Monday – **M** 7.75/16.50 **t.** and a la carte 15.30/19.15 **t.**
🍾 3.35.

SUTTON SCOTNEY Hants. 408 404 P 30 – ⊠ © 0962 Winchester.
◆London 66 – Reading 32 – Salisbury 21 – ◆Southampton 19.

🏠 **Travelodge** without rest., Sutton Scotney Service Area, SO21 3JY, on A 34 ℰ 760779
(Southside) ℰ 761016 (Northside) – 📺 🕭 🅿. 🔼 🆎 𝘝𝘐𝘚𝘈
71 rm 21.50/27.00 **t.**

SWAFFHAM Norfolk 404 W 26 – pop. 4 742 – ECD : Thursday – © 0760.
Envir. : Oxburgh Hall (15C) : Gate house★ AC, SW : 7 ½ m.
◆London 97 – ◆Cambridge 46 – King's Lynn 16 – ◆Norwich 27.

🏠 **George**, Station St., PE37 7LJ, ℰ 721238 – 📺 ☎ 🅿 – 🕍 180. 🔼 🆎 ⓞ 𝘝𝘐𝘚𝘈
M 10.95 **t.** and a la carte – **28 rm** 🍽 45.00/59.00 **t.**

◍ ATS Unit 2a, Tower Meadow (off Station St.) ℰ 22543

SWALCLIFFE Oxon. – see Banbury.

SWANAGE Dorset 408 404 O 32 The West Country G. – pop. 8 411 – ECD : Thursday –
© 0929.
See : Site★ – Durlston Country Park (≼★★) – The Great Globe★.
Envir. : St. Aldhelm's Head★★ (≼★★★), SW : 4 m. by B 3069 – Corfe Castle★★ (≼★★)AC, NW :
6 m. – Old Harry Rocks★★ (Studland Village - St. Nicholas Church★) N : 4 ½ m. – Studland
Beach (≼★), N : 5 m.
⅂₈ Isle of Purbeck ℰ 44210, NW: on B 3351.
🅱 Shore Rd ℰ 422885.
◆London 130 – Bournemouth 22 – Dorchester 26 – ◆Southampton 52.

🏨 **Grand** (Best Western), 12 Burlington Rd, BH19 1LU, ℰ 423353, Telex 94016947, ≼, 🔼, 🚗
– 🛗 📺 ☎ 🅿. 🔼 🆎 ⓞ 𝘝𝘐𝘚𝘈
M 12.95 **t.** (dinner) and a la carte 12.10/15.85 **t.** 🍾 5.95 – **30 rm** 🍽 35.00/48.00 **t.** –
SB (except summer) 54.00/64.00 **st.**

🏨 **The Pines** ⤴, Burlington Rd, BH19 1LT, ℰ 425211, ≼, 🚗 – 🛗 📺 ☎ 🅿. 🔼 𝘝𝘐𝘚𝘈
M 8.50/13.50 **t.** 🍾 3.25 – **51 rm** 🍽 28.00/66.00 **t.** – SB (winter only) 69.00/71.00 **st.**

⋔ Havenhurst, 3 Cranborne Rd, BH19 1EA, ℰ 424224 – **℗**. ⅋
17 rm.

⋔ Eversden, 5 Victoria Rd, BH19 1LY, ℰ 423276 – **℗**. ⅋
March-November – **M** 8.00 – **12 rm**.

⋔ Crowthorne, 24 Cluny Cres., BH19 2BT, ℰ 422108 – ⤢ rest. ⅋
10 rm.

⋔ Suncliffe, 1 Burlington Rd, BH19 1LR, ℰ 423299, 🛲 – **℗**
14 rm.

FORD 281 High St. ℰ 422877

SWANSEA (ABERTAWE) West Glam. **403** I 29 – pop. 172 433 – ECD : Thursday – ✆ 0792.
See : Maritime Quarter★ B – Maritime and Industrial Museum★ B M.
Envir. : Cefn Bryn (⁂★★★ from the reservoir) W : 12 m. by A 4118 A – Gower Peninsula★ (Rhossili★★★) : West from Swansea by A 4067 A.
Exc. : Rhosili (site and ≤★★★) W : 18 m. by A 4118 A.
🔟 Morriston ℰ 71079, N : 4 m. by A 48 A – 🔟 Clyne, Owls Lodge Lane ℰ 401989, SW : off A 4067 A.

🖪 Singleton St. ℰ 468321 – Ty Croeso, Gloucester Pl. ℰ 465204 – Oystermouth Sq., The Mumbles ℰ 361302 (summer only).

♦London 191 – ♦Birmingham 136 – ♦Bristol 82 – ♦Cardiff 40 – ♦Liverpool 187 – ♦Stoke-on-Trent 175.

Plan on next page

🏨🏨 **Holiday Inn** (Holiday Inn), Maritime Quarter, SA1 3SS, ℰ 642020, Telex 48395, Fax 650345, ≤, 🔲 – �|⤢ rm 🗏 📺 ☎ ⅊ ℗ – 🅰 150. 🔼 🅰🅴 ⓪ **VISA**   B e
M 11.95 **t.** and a la carte approx. 15.75 **t.** 🍾 6.50 – ☕ 7.95 – **117 rm** 68.00/81.00 **st.** –
SB (weekends only) 50.00/95.00 **st.**

🏨🏨 **Dragon** (T.H.F.), 39 The Kingsway, SA1 5LS, ℰ 651074, Telex 48309, Fax 456044 – �|⤢ rm 📺 ☎ ℗ – 🅰 250   B a
117 rm, 1 suite.

🏨 **Fforest** (Lansbury), Pontardulais Rd, Fforestfach, SA5 4BA, NW : 3 ½ m. on A 483 ℰ 588711, Telex 48105, Fax 586219 – ⤢ rm 📺 ☎ ℗ – 🅰 250. 🔼 🅰🅴 ⓪ **VISA**. ⅋
M 8.50/12.50 **t.** and a la carte 8.60/14.70 **t.** – **34 rm** ☕ 60.00/70.00 **t.** – SB (weekends only) 54.00/58.00 **st.**

🏛 **Windsor Lodge,** 15 Mount Pleasant, SA1 6EG, ℰ 642158, « Contemporary decor » – 📺 ☎ ℗. 🔼 🅰🅴 ⓪ **VISA**   B r
closed 23 to 27 December – **M** *(closed Sunday)* (booking essential)(bar lunch)/dinner 18.00 **t.**
🍾 4.00 – **19 rm** ☕ 27.50/48.00 **t.**

🏛 **Beaumont,** 72-73 Walter Rd, SA1 4QA, ℰ 643956, Fax 643044 – 📺 ☎ ℗. 🔼 🅰🅴 ⓪ **VISA**   A n
M *(bar lunch)/dinner* 12.50 **t.** 🍾 4.00 – **18 rm** ☕ 36.00/60.00 **t.**

⋔ **Tredilion House,** 26 Uplands Cres., Uplands, SA2 0PB, ℰ 470766 – 📺 ☎ ℗. 🔼 ⓪ **VISA**. ⅋   A a
M (by arrangement) 10.00 **st.** 🍾 3.00 – **6 rm** ☕ 27.50/45.00 **st.**

⋔ **Alexander,** 3 Sketty Rd, Uplands, SA2 0EU, ℰ 470045 – ⤢ rest 📺 ☎. 🔼 🅰🅴 ⓪ **VISA**. ⅋   A c
closed 24 December-2 January – **M** (by arrangement) 10.00 **st.** – **7 rm** ☕ 25.00/38.00 **st.**

✗ **Annie's,** 56 St. Helen's Rd, SA1 4BE, ℰ 655603 – 🔼 **VISA**   A o
closed Sunday and Monday – **M** (booking essential) (dinner only) 12.80 **st.** and a la carte 13.70/17.00 **st.** 🍾 3.80.

✗ **Jasmine,** 326 Oystermouth Rd, SA1 3UL, ℰ 652912, Chinese rest. – 🔼 🅰🅴 ⓪ **VISA**   A e
M approx. 15.00.

at Swansea Enterprise Park NE : 4 m. by A 4067 off A 48 – ✉ ✆ 0792 Swansea :

🏨🏨 **Hilton National** (Hilton), Phoenix Way, Llansamlet, SA7 9EG, ℰ 310330, Telex 48589, Fax 797535, 🔲 – ⤢ rm 🗏 rest 📺 ☎ ⅊ ℗ – 🅰 140. 🔼 🅰🅴 ⓪ **VISA**
M *(closed Saturday lunch)* (carving rest.) 9.50/13.50 **st.** and a la carte – ☕ 7.50 – **108 rm** 68.00/85.00 **st.**, **6 suites** 100.00 **st.**

at Llanrhidian W : 10 ½ m. by A 4118 A and B 4271 on B 4295 – ✉ Reynoldston – ✆ 0792 Gower :

🏨🏨 **Fairyhill** ⅋, SA3 1BS, W : 2 ½ m. by B 4295 (Llangennith rd) ℰ 390139, « Country house atmosphere », park – ⤢ rest 📺 ☎ ℗. 🔼 **VISA**
closed first 2 weeks January – **M** (dinner only and Sunday lunch) a la carte 15.95/21.40 **t.**
🍾 2.75 – **11 rm** ☕ 55.00/75.00 **t.**

AUSTIN-ROVER 511 Carmarthen Rd ℰ 561166
DAIMLER-JAGUAR Swansea Enterprise Park ℰ 791562
HONDA Valley Way ℰ 771960
PEUGEOT-TALBOT Neath Rd ℰ 310200
RENAULT Swansea Ind. Est. ℰ 701801

VAUXHALL Neath Rd, Morriston ℰ 310111
VW-AUDI, NSU Gorseinon Rd ℰ 0792 (Gorseinon) 894951

🅖 ATS Neath Rd, Hafod ℰ 456379

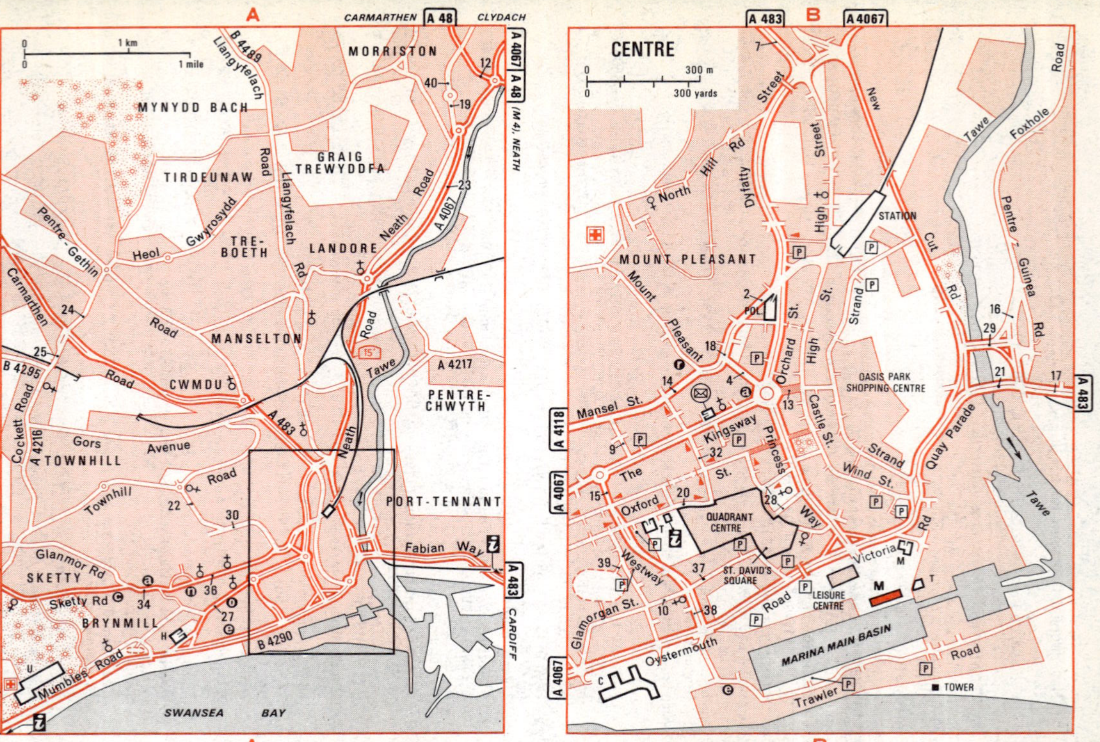

SWANSEA

College Street ... B 13
Kingsway (The) ... B
Oasis Park
 Shopping Centre ... B
Oxford Street ... B
Princess Way ... B
Quadrant Centre ... B
St. David's Square ... B

Alexandra Road ... B 2
Belle Vue Way ... B 4
Carmarthen Road ... B 7
Christina Street ... B 9
Clarence Terrace ... B 10
Clase Road ... A 12
De La Beche Street ... B 14
Dillwyn Street ... B 15
Fabian Way ... B 17
East Bank Way ... B 16
Grove Place ... B 18
Martin Street ... A 19
Nelson Street ... B 20
New Cut Bridge ... B 21
Pen-y-Graig Road ... A 22
Plasmarl By-Pass ... A 23
Ravenhill Road ... A 24
Station Road ... A 25
St. Helen's Road ... A 27
St. Mary's Square ... B 28
Tawe Bridge ... B 29
Terrace Road ... A 30
Union Street ... B 32
Uplands Crescent ... A 34
Walter Road ... B 36
Wellington Street ... B 37
West Way ... B 38
William Street ... B 39
Woodfield Street ... A 40

Zum besseren Verständnis der Stadtpläne lesen Sie bitte die Zeichenerklärung in der Einleitung.

SWINDON Wilts. **403** **404** O 29 **The West Country** G. – pop. 127 348 – ECD : Wednesday – ☎ 0793.

See : Great Western Railway Museum★*AC* – Railway Village Museum★*AC*.

ᵢ₈, ᵢ₉ Broome Manor, Pipers Way ✆ 495761, 2 m. from centre.

🛈 32 The Arcade, David Murray John Building, Brunel Centre ✆ 30328 and 26161.

♦London 83 – Bournemouth 69 – ♦Bristol 40 – ♦Coventry 66 – ♦Oxford 29 – Reading 40 – ♦Southampton 65.

Holiday Inn (Holiday Inn), Pipers Way, SN3 1SH, SE : 1½ m. by Marlborough Road on B 4006 ✆ 512121, Telex 445789, Fax 513114, ☒, ✗, squash – ▯ ✂ rm ▤ ▣ ☎ க ℗ – 🔥 280. ◪ ᴀᴇ ⓞ **VISA**
M *(closed Saturday lunch)* (carving lunch) 13.50 **st.** and dinner a la carte 17.00/25.00 **st.** ◗ 6.00 – ☕ 8.45 – **158 rm** 75.00/150.00 **st.** – SB (weekends only) 96.00/126.00 **st.**

Post House (T.H.F.), Marlborough Rd, SN3 6AQ, SE : 2 ¾ m. on A 4259 ✆ 24601, Telex 444464, Fax 512887, ☒ – ✂ rm ▣ ☎ ℗ – 🔥 70. ◪ ᴀᴇ ⓞ **VISA**
M 9.95/11.95 **st.** and a la carte ◗ 3.95 – ☕ 7.00 – **104 rm** 65.00/75.00 **st.** – SB (weekends only) (except Christmas and New Year) 64.00/72.00 **st.**

Goddard Arms (T.H.F), 1 High St., Old Town, SN1 3EW, ✆ 692313, Telex 444764, Fax 512984 – ✂ rm ▤ rest ▣ ☎ ℗ – 🔥 200. ◪ ᴀᴇ ⓞ **VISA**
M 13.00 **st.** and a la carte ◗ 3.95 – ☕ 7.00 – **65 rm** 62.00/80.00 **st.** – SB (weekends only) 64.00/72.00 **st.**

at Blunsdon N : 4 ½ m. on A 419 – ✉ ☎ 0793 Swindon :

Blunsdon House (Best Western), The Ridge, SN2 4AD, ✆ 721701, Telex 444491, Fax 721056, ☒, ☞, park, ✗, squash – ▯ ▣ ☎ க ℗ – 🔥 300. ◪ ᴀᴇ ⓞ **VISA**. ✗
M 12.00/15.00 **st.** and a la carte 17.75/28.25 **st.** – **89 rm** ☕ 67.00/90.00 **st.** – SB (weekends only) 95.00/100.00 **st.**

at Stratton St. Margaret NE : 2 m. on A 420 – ✉ ☎ 0793 Swindon :

Crest (Crest), Oxford Rd, SN3 4TL, NE : 1 ½ m. on A 420 ✆ 831333, Telex 444456, Fax 831401 – ✂ rm ▤ rest ▣ ☎ க ℗ – 🔥 90. ◪ ᴀᴇ ⓞ **VISA**
M *(closed lunch Saturday and Bank Holidays)* (carving lunch) 13.50/16.00 **st.** and a la carte ◗ 5.50 – ☕ 7.60 – **93 rm** 73.00/83.00 **st.**, **1 suite** 100.00/115.00 **st.** – SB (weekends only) 78.00/90.00 **st.**

at Wanborough SE : 5 ¼ m. by A 4312 off A 419 – ✉ ☎ 0793 Swindon :

Poplars, Lower Wanborough, SN4 0AA, NW : 1 ¼ m. ✆ 790774, Fax 790878 – ▣ ☎ ℗ – 🔥 . ◪ ᴀᴇ ⓞ **VISA**. ✗
M a la carte 13.80/17.75 **t.** ◗ 5.50 – ☕ 5.50 – **14 rm** 54.00/66.00 **st.** – SB (weekends only) 37.00/47.50 **st.**

at Purton W : 5 m. by A 3102 and B 4453 on Purton Rd – ✉ ☎ 0793 Swindon :

✗✗ **The Pear Tree at Purton** with rm, Church End, SN5 9ED, S : ½ m. on Lydiard Millicent Rd ✆ 772100, ≤, « Former vicarage, conservatory », ☞ – ▣ ☎ ℗. ◪ ᴀᴇ ⓞ **VISA**
M *(closed Saturday lunch)* 12.50/18.50 **st.** ◗ 6.00 – **4 rm** ☕ 85.00/95.00 **st.** – SB (weekends only) 85.00/95.00 **st.**

AUSTIN-ROVER, DAIMLER-JAGUAR Dorkan Way ✆ 612091
BMW High St. at Wroughton ✆ 812387
CITROEN Kennedy Drive, Eldean ✆ 642717
FORD 30 Marlborough Rd ✆ 20002
PORSCHE Great Western Way ✆ 615000
RENAULT Elgin Drive ✆ 693841

VAUXHALL 13-21 The Street, Moredon ✆ 23457
VAUXHALL Drove Rd ✆ 20971
VW-AUDI, NSU Eldene Drive ✆ 31333

🅐 ATS Cheney Manor Ind Est. ✆ 21171
ATS 86 Beatrice St. ✆ 34867

SYMONDS YAT Heref. and Worc. **403** **404** M 28 – ✉ Ross-on-Wye – ☎ 0600.

See : Symond's Yat Rock ≤★★.

♦London 126 – Gloucester 23 – Hereford 17 – Newport 31.

⌂ **Woodlea** ⚘, Symonds Yat (West), HR9 6BL, ✆ 890206, ☒, ☞ – ℗. ◪ **VISA**
closed mid January-February – **M** 10.00 **t.** – **9 rm** ☕ 19.00/43.00 **t.** – SB (except summer) (weekdays only) 49.50/67.50 **st.**

TADCASTER North Yorks. **402** Q 22 – pop. 5 877 – ECD : Wednesday – ☎ 0937.

♦London 176 – Harrogate 16 – ♦Kingston-upon-Hull 47 – ♦Leeds 16 – York 10.

⌂ **Shann House** without rest., 47 Kirkgate, LS24 9AQ, ✆ 833931 – ▣ ℗. ◪ **VISA**
8 rm ☕ 17.50/26.00 **st.**

🅐 ATS Station Rd Ind. Est. ✆ 832626/833969

TALKIN Cumbria **401** **402** L 19 – see Brampton.

TALLAND BAY Cornwall **403** G 32 – see Looe.

TAL-Y-BONT Gwynedd **402** **403** I 24 – see Conwy.

TALYBONT-ON-USK Powys. **403** K 28 – ✪ 087 487.

♦London 183 – Abergavenny 14 – Brecon 6 – Newport 39.

- **Aberclydach House** ⏚, Aber Village, LD3 7YS, SW : 1 m. ℘ 361, 🐎 – 🍴 📺 ☎ 🅿 –
  🛥. 🔽 AE ① VISA 🐕
  M 6.50/14.95 **st.** and a la carte ⏸ 3.20 – **11 rm** ⊡ 31.50/53.00 **st.** – SB (except Easter, Christmas and Bank Holidays) 65.00 **st.**

TAL-Y-LLYN Gwynedd **402 403** I 25 – pop. 623 (inc. Corris) – ✉ Tywyn – ✪ 065 477 Abergynolwyn.

♦London 224 – Dolgellau 9 – Shrewsbury 60.

- **Tynycornel,** LL36 9AJ, on B 4405 ℘ 282, ≼ lake and mountains, 🅹 heated, 🐟, 🐎 – 📺
  ☎ 🅿. 🔽 AE ① VISA
  M 8.00/13.00 **t.** and a la carte ⏸ 4.50 – **18 rm** ⊡ 46.00/92.00 **t.**
- **Minffordd,** LL36 9AJ, NE : 2 ¾ m. by B 4405 on A 487 ℘ 065 473 (Corris) 665, ≼, « Converted 18C farmhouse and inn », 🐎 – 🍴 rest ⊛ 🅿. 🔽 ① VISA 🐕
  closed January and February – **M** (closed Sunday dinner) (bar lunch residents only)/dinner 14.25 **st.** ⏸ 5.50 – **7 rm** ⊡ (dinner included) 50.00/90.00 **st.** – SB (except summer and weekdays November-December) 60.00/66.00 **st.**

TAMWORTH Staffs. **402 403 404** O 26 – pop. 63 260 – ECD : Wednesday – ✪ 0827.

🏌 Eagle Drive ℘ 53850.

♦London 128 – ♦Birmingham 12 – ♦Coventry 29 – ♦Leicester 31 – ♦Stoke-on-Trent 37.

- **Castle,** Ladybank, B79 7NB, ℘ 57181 – 📺 ☎ – 🛥 120. 🔽 AE ① VISA
  M 8.50 **st.** (lunch) and a la carte ⏸ 4.50 – **34 rm** ⊡ 55.00/85.00 **st.** – SB (weekends only) (except Christmas and New Year) 65.00/70.00 **st.**

FORD Gungate ℘ 68411   Ⓜ ATS Tame Valley Ind. Est. ℘ 281983
VW-AUDI Coleshill Rd ℘ 288282

TARPORLEY Cheshire **402 403 404** M 24 – pop. 1 774 – ECD : Wednesday – ✪ 0829 Kelsall.

♦London 186 – Chester 11 – ♦Manchester 31 – ♦Stoke-on-Trent 27.

- Willington Hall ⏚, Willington, CW6 0NB, NW : 3 ½ m. by A 51 ℘ 52321, ≼, « Part Jacobean mansion », 🐎, 🍴 – 📺 ☎ 🅿
  10 rm.

TARRANT MONKTON Dorset **403 404** N 31 – see Blandford Forum.

TATTENHALL Cheshire **402 403 404** L 24 – pop. 1 778 – ✪ 0829.

♦London 200 – ♦Birmingham 71 – Chester 10 – ♦Manchester 38 – ♦Stoke-on-Trent 30.

- **Pheasant Inn,** Higher Burwardsley, CH3 9PF, SE : 1 m. ℘ 70434, ≼ – 📺 🅿. 🔽 AE ①
  VISA 🐕
  M (bar lunch)/dinner 10.00 **t.** and a la carte ⏸ 2.50 – **6 rm** ⊡ 30.00/40.00 **t.** – SB (weekends only) 50.00 **st.**

TAUNTON Somerset **403** K 30 The West Country G. – pop. 47 793 – ECD : Thursday – ✪ 0823.

See : Site★ – St. Mary Magdalene's Church★ – Museum★ AC – St. James Church★ – Hammett St.★ – The Crescent★ – Bath Alley★.

Envir. : Muchelney★★ (Parish Church★★), E : 14 ½ m. – Wellington Monument (≼★★), W : 10 m. – Trull : Church★, S : 2 m. – Bishops Lydeard★ (Church★), NW : 5 m. – Combe Florey★, NW : 7 m. – Wellington Church★, W : 8 m. – Gaulden Manor★AC, NW : 9 m. – Midelney Manor★AC, E : 12 m.

🏌 Vivary Park Municipal, Fons George ℘ 333875.

🅱 Public Library, Corporation St. ℘ 274785 and 270479.

♦London 168 – Bournemouth 69 – ♦Bristol 50 – Exeter 37 – ♦Plymouth 78 – ♦Southampton 93 – Weymouth 50.

- ❄ **Castle,** Castle Green, TA1 1NF, ℘ 272671, Telex 46488, Fax 336066, « Part 12C castle with Norman garden » – 🛗 📺 ☎ 🚗 🅿 – 🛥 60. 🔽 AE ① VISA
  M 12.90/31.00 **t.** and a la carte 37.60/42.80 **t.** ⏸ 3.55 – ⊡ 6.50 – **34 rm** 70.00/180.00 **t.**, **1 suite** 250.00 **t.**
  Spec. Foie gras sauté with salad leaves and grilled black pudding, Steamed fillet of turbot with green vegetables, wild mushrooms and ginger, Glazed apple tart with its own sorbet.
- **Crest** (Crest), Deane Gate Av., TA1 2UA, E : 2 ½ m. by A 358 at junction with M 5 ℘ 332222, Telex 46703, Fax 332266 – 🛗 🍴 rm 🍽 rest 📺 ☎ ♿ 🅿 – 🛥 250. 🔽 AE ① VISA
  M (closed Saturday lunch) 14.50/15.50 **st.** and a la carte ⏸ 4.50 – ⊡ 8.50 – **101 rm** 64.00/95.00 **st.** – SB (weekends only) 80.00/84.00 **st.**
- **County** (T.H.F.), East St., TA1 3LT, ℘ 337651, Telex 46484, Fax 334517 – 🛗 🍴 rm 📺 ☎ 🅿 – 🛥 300. 🔽 AE ① VISA
  M 8.95/12.95 **st.** and a la carte ⏸ 3.95 – ⊡ 7.00 – **67 rm** 60.00/91.00 **st.** – SB (weekends only) 74.00 **st.**
- **Corner House,** Park St., TA1 4DQ, ℘ 284683, Telex 46288, Fax 332276 – 📺 ☎ 🅿. 🔽 AE
  VISA 🐕
  M 7.50/20.00 **st.** and la carte ⏸ 3.80 – **32 rm** ⊡ 31.50/57.00 **t.**

at Henlade E : 3 ½ m. on A 358 – ⊠ Taunton – ☎ 0823 Henlade :

🏠 **Falcon**, TA3 5DH, on A 358 ⌂ 442502, 🚗 – ⤢ 📺 ☎ 🅿. 🄽 *VISA*. 🐾
closed 25 and 26 December – **M** *(closed Sunday)* (bar lunch)/dinner 9.50 **t.** and a la carte –
11 rm ⊡ 39.50/55.00 **t.** – SB (weekends only) 57.00 **st.**

at Hatch Beauchamp SE : 6 m. by A 358 – ⊠ Taunton – ☎ 0823 Hatch Beauchamp :

XXX **Farthings Country House** ⑤ with rm, TA3 6SG, ⌂ 480664, « Tastefully decorated
country house », 🚗 – 📺 ⑩ 🅿. 🄽 *VISA*. 🐾
closed late December-mid January – **M** (lunch residents only)/dinner 21.25 **st.** ⑂ 4.60 – **6 rm**
⊡ 60.00/102.00 **st.**

at Bishop's Hull W : 1 ¾ m. by A 38 – ⊠ ☎ 0823 Taunton :

🏠 **Meryan House,** Bishop's Hull Rd, TA1 5EG, ⌂ 337445, 🚗 – ⤢ rm 📺 ☎ 🅿. 🄽 *VISA*
M *(closed dinner Friday to Sunday)* (bar lunch)/dinner 10.00 **st.** ⑂ 2.50 – **8 rm**
⊡ 28.95/45.00 **st.**

AUDI-VW Silver St. ⌂ 88371
AUSTIN-ROVER, DAIMLER-JAGUAR South St. ⌂
88991
FIAT Priory Av. ⌂ 87611
FORD 151-6 East Reach ⌂ 85481

LADA, YUGO 16 Kingston Rd ⌂ 88288
RENAULT 138 Bridgwater Rd, Bathpool ⌂ 412559
SAAB 60 East Reach ⌂ 288351

⑩ ATS 138 Bridgwater Rd, Bathpool ⌂ 412826

TAVISTOCK Devon �403 H 32 The West Country G. – pop. 8 508 – ECD : Wednesday – ☎ 0822.
Envir. : Dartmoor National Park★★ – Lydford★★, Lydford Gorge★★ *AC*, N : 9 m. – Morwell-
ham★*AC*, W : 4 m. – at Launceston★, Castle★ *AC* (⩽★), St. Mary Magdalene Church★ South
Gate★ *AC*, NW : 14 m. – 🏌 Down Rd ⌂ 612049, SW : 1 m.
🅱 Guildhall, Bedford Sq. ⌂ 612938 (summer only).
◆London 239 – Exeter 38 – ◆Plymouth 15.

🏨 **Bedford** (T.H.F.), 1 Plymouth Rd, PL19 8BB, ⌂ 613221 – ⤢ rm 📺 ☎ 🅿 – 🔔 35. 🄽 🄰🄴
⑩ *VISA*. 🐾
M 10.60/10.75 **st.** and a la carte ⑂ 3.95 – ⊡ 7.00 – **31 rm** 58.00/68.00 **st.** – SB 84.00/88.00 **st.**

at Gulworthy W : 3 m. on A 390 – ⊠ ☎ 0822 Tavistock :

XX **Horn of Plenty** ⑤ with rm, PL19 8JD, ⌂ 832528, ⩽ Tamar Valley and Bodmin Moor, 🚗
– 📺 ☎ ⑤ 🅿. 🄽 🄰🄴 *VISA*. 🐾
closed 25 and 26 December – **M** *(closed lunch Thursday and Friday)* 18.50/37.50 **t.**
and a la carte – ⊡ 9.50 – **6 rm** 59.00/79.00 **t.**

AUSTIN-ROVER Plymouth Rd ⌂ 612301

⑩ ATS 2 Parkwood Rd ⌂ 612545

TAYNTON Oxon. – see Burford.

TEESSIDE AIRPORT Durham �402 P 20 – see Darlington.

TEIGNMOUTH Devon �403 J 32 The West Country G. – pop. 11 995 – ECD : Thursday – ☎ 062 67.
🏌 Exeter Rd ⌂ 4194.
🅱 The Den, Sea Front ⌂ 79769.
◆London 216 – Exeter 16 – Torquay 8.

🏠 **London,** 24 Bank St., TQ14 8AW, ⌂ 776336, Fax 778457, 🌊 heated – 🛗 📺 ☎ – 🔔 200.
🄽 🄰🄴 ⑩ *VISA*
M 9.75 **t.** (dinner) and a la carte ⑂ 3.40 – **26 rm** ⊡ 32.00/80.00 **t.**

↑ **Belvedere,** 19 Barnpark Rd, TQ14 8PJ, ⌂ 774561 – 🅿. 🄽 *VISA*. 🐾
M 6.50 **st.** – **13 rm** ⊡ 16.50/37.00 **st.**

at Shaldon S : 1 m. on A 379 – ⊠ Teignmouth – ☎ 0626 Shaldon :

🏠 **Ness House,** Marine Par., TQ14 0HP, ⌂ 873480, Fax 893486, ⩽, 🚗 – 📺 ☎ 🅿. 🄽 🄰🄴 *VISA*
🐾 – **M** a la carte 7.50/15.80 **t.** ⑂ 3.00 – **12 rm** ⊡ 24.50/72.00 **t.**

↑ **Glenside,** Ringmore Rd, TQ14 0EP, W : ½ m. on B 3195 ⌂ 872448, 🚗 – 📺 🅿
closed November – **M** 9.00 **t.** ⑂ 4.00 – **10 rm** ⊡ 16.00/39.50 **t.** – SB (October-
April) 45.00/50.00 **st.**

NISSAN 106 Bitton Park Rd ⌂ 772501

TELFORD Shropshire �402 �403 �404 M 25 – pop. 76 330 – ☎ 0952.
Envir. : Ironbridge Gorge Museum★ (Iron Bridge★★) *AC*, S : 5 m. – Buildwas Abbey★ (ruins 12C)
S : 7 m – 🅱 Shopping Centre ⌂ 291370.
◆London 152 – ◆Birmingham 33 – Shrewsbury 12 – ◆Stoke-on-Trent 29.

🏨 **Telford Moat House** (Q.M.H.), Forgegate, Telford Centre, TF3 4NA, ⌂ 291291, Telex
35588, Fax 292012, 🌊 – 🛗 📺 ☎ 🅿 – 🔔 400. 🄽 🄰🄴 ⑩ *VISA*
closed 25 to 30 December – **M** *(closed Saturday lunch)* 12.50 **t.** and a la carte 13.70/21.40 **t.**
⑂ 3.85 – **144 rm** ⊡ 63.00/84.00 **t.**, **4 suites** 100.00 **t.** – SB (weekends only) 68.00/75.00 **st.**

🏨 Telford H. Golf & C.C. (Q.M.H.), Great Hay, Sutton Hill, TF7 4DT, S : 4 ½ m. by M 54
(Junction 4) and A 442 ⌂ 585642, Telex 35481, ⩽, 🌊, 🏌, squash – 📺 ☎ & 🅿 – 🔔 200
59 rm, **1 suite**.

TELFORD

   Charlton Arms (De Vere), Church St., Wellington, TF1 1DG, ℰ 251351, Fax 222077 – TV
   ☎ Ⓟ – 200. ⚶ AE Ⓞ VISA
   M *(closed Saturday lunch)* 8.00 **st.** and a la carte 4.00 – **26 rm** ⌿ 47.00/59.00 **st.** –
   SB (weekends only) 55.00 **st.**

   Whitehouse, Wellington Rd, Muxton, nr. Donnington, TF2 8NG, N : 4 ½ m. by A 518
   ℰ 604276, ⚶ – TV ☎ Ⓟ. ⚶ AE VISA
   M (bar lunch Saturday) 6.95 **t.** (lunch) and a la carte 10.75/17.45 **t.** – **29 rm** ⌿ 33.50/52.00 **t.**
   – SB (weekends only) 60.00/70.00 **st.**

   at Norton S : 7 m. on A 442 – ✉ Shifnal – ✆ 095 271 Norton :

   Hundred House, Bridgnorth Rd, TF11 9EE, ℰ 353, Fax 355, ⚶ – TV ☎ Ⓟ. ⚶ AE VISA
   M a la carte 11.45/21.90 **t.** – **9 rm** ⌿ 55.00/75.00 **t.** – SB (except Christmas) 85.00/95.00 **st.**

AUSTIN-ROVER, VANDEN-PLAS Market St., Wel-   VAUXHALL-OPEL Holyhead Rd ℰ 618081
lington ℰ 290971
FIAT Trench Rd ℰ 605301   Ⓜ ATS Queen St., Madeley ℰ 582820
PEUGEOT-TALBOT Holyhead Rd ℰ 617272   ATS New St., Oakengates ℰ 613810/612198
TOYOTA Ironbridge Rd ℰ 882100

TEMPLE SOWERBY Cumbria 401 402 M 20 – pop. 341 – ECD : Thursday – ✉ Penrith –
✆ 076 83 Kirkby Thore.
♦London 297 – ♦Carlisle 31 – Kendal 38.

   Temple Sowerby House, CA10 1RZ, ℰ 61578, ⚶ – ⤢ rest TV ☎ & Ⓟ. ⚶ AE VISA
   M 20.00 **t.** 4.00 – **12 rm** ⌿ 37.00/52.00 **t.** – SB (except Bank Holidays) 70.00/90.00 **st.**

TEMPSFORD Beds. 404 T 27 – see Sandy.

TENBY (DINBYCH-Y-PYSGOD) Dyfed 403 F 28 – pop. 5 226 – ECD : Wednesday – ✆ 0834.
See : Site★★ – Harbour and Sea front★★.
Envir. : Caldey Island★ (boat from Tenby harbour Monday to Friday).
🛆 The Burrows ℰ 2978.
🛈 The Norton ℰ 2402.
♦London 247 – Carmarthen 27 – Fishguard 36.

   Imperial, The Paragon, SA70 7HR, ℰ 3737, Fax 4342, ≼ sea and bay – ▣ TV ☎ ⇌ Ⓟ –
   ⚶ 40. ⚶ AE ⓄVISA
   M (bar lunch)/dinner 12.50 **st.** and a la carte 3.50 – **43 rm** ⌿ 29.50/110.00 **st.** –
   SB 55.00/69.00 **st.**

   Fourcroft, Croft Terr., SA70 8AP, ℰ 2886, Fax 2888, ≼, ⛫ heated, ⚶ – ▣ ⤢ rest TV ☎.
   ⚶ VISA
   Easter-October – **M** (bar lunch)/dinner 10.50 **st.** 3.50 – **38 rm** ⌿ 32.50/60.00 **st.** –
   SB 60.00/68.00 **st.**

   Harbour Heights, The Croft, SA70 8AP, ℰ 2132, ≼ – TV. ⚶ AE ⓄVISA. ⚶
   M *(closed Sunday to non-residents)* (dinner only) 16.00 **t.** and a la carte 2.50 – **8 rm**
   ⌿ 34.00/60.00 **t.** – SB 66.00/80.00 **st.**

   Buckingham, Esplanade, SA70 6DU, ℰ 2622, ≼ – TV. ⚶ VISA
   April-October – **M** 8.00 **st.** 2.00 – **8 rm** ⌿ 15.00/40.00 **st.**

   Heywood Lodge, Heywood Lane, SA70 8BN, ℰ 2684, ⚶ – ⤢ rest Ⓟ. ⚶ VISA
   M 10.00 **st.** 2.50 – **13 rm** ⌿ 14.50/37.00 **st.** – SB (October-May) 42.00/48.00 **st.**

   at Penally (Penalun) SW : 2 m. by A 4139 – ✉ ✆ 0834 Tenby :

   Penally Abbey, SA70 7PY, ℰ 3033, ≼, ⛫, ⚶ ⤢ rm TV Ⓟ. ⚶ VISA. ⚶
   M (bar lunch)/dinner 14.50 **st.** 4.20 – **11 rm** ⌿ 42.00/64.00 **st.** – SB 80.00/92.00 **st.**

AUSTIN-ROVER Pembroke Dock ℰ 683143

TENTERDEN Kent 404 W 30 – pop. 5 698 – ECD : Wednesday – ✆ 058 06.
🛆 Woodchurch Rd ℰ 3987.
🛈 Town Hall, High St. ℰ 3572 (summer only).
♦ London 57 – Folkestone 26 – Hastings 21 – Maidstone 19.

   Little Silver Country, Ashford Rd, St. Michaels, TN30 6SP, N : 1 m. on A 28
   ℰ 023 385 (High Halden) 321, ⚶ – ⤢ rest TV ☎ & Ⓟ. ⚶
   M (booking essential) (lunch by arrangement)/dinner 13.00 **st.** and a la carte 3.90 – **10 rm**
   ⌿ 40.00/80.00 **st.**

   White Lion, High St., TN30 6BD, ℰ 2921 – TV ☎ Ⓟ – ⚶ 35. ⚶ AE ⓄVISA. ⚶
   M 9.00/15.00 **t.** and a la carte – **16 rm** ⌿ 40.00/60.00 **t.** – SB (weekends only) 58.00 **st.**

   Collina House, 5 East Hill, TN30 6RL, ℰ 4852, ⚶ – TV Ⓟ. ⚶ ⓄVISA. ⚶
   M 10.00/15.00 **st.** 5.00 – **11 rm** ⌿ 20.00/34.00 **st.**

   West Cross House, 2 West Cross, TN30 6JL, ℰ 2224, ⚶ – Ⓟ
   March-October – **M** 7.50 **st.** 2.75 – **7 rm** ⌿ 13.00/28.00 **st.**

at High Halden NE : 3 ½ m. on A 28 – ⊠ Tenterden – ✆ 023 385 High Halden :

XX **Durrants** with rm, Hookstead House, TN26 3NE, ✆ 670, ☞ – **P**. 🅰 AE ⓞ VISA. ✖
M *(closed Sunday dinner, Monday and Bank Holidays)* (lunch by arrangement)/dinner
14.95 **st.** 🍷 3.95 – **4 rm** ⊡ 25.00/42.00 **st.**

AUSTIN-ROVER High St. ✆ 4444

TERN HILL Shropshire 402 403 404 M 25 – see Market Drayton.

TETBURY Glos. 403 404 N 29 – pop. 4 467 – ECD : Thursday – ✆ 0666.
Envir. : Westonbirt Arboretum★ *AC*, SW : 3 ½ m.

🏌 Westonbirt 066 688 (Westonbirt) 242, S : 3 m.

🛈 The Old Court House, 63 Long St. ✆ 53552 (summer only).

♦London 113 – ♦Bristol 27 – Gloucester 19 – Swindon 24.

🏛 **The Close,** 8 Long St., GL8 8AQ, ✆ 502272, Fax 504401, « 16C town house with walled
garden » – ✖ rest TV ☎ **P** – 🔔 35. 🅰 AE ⓞ VISA. ✖
closed 2 to 16 January – **M** 16.95/29.50 **t.** 🍷 4.70 – **15 rm** ⊡ 75.00/160.00 **t.** – SB 140.00/
180.00 **st.**

🏠 Snooty Fox, Market Pl., GL8 8DD, ✆ 502436, Group Telex 437334, Fax 503479 – TV ☎. ✖
12 rm.

at Avening N : 3 m. on B 4014 – ⊠ Tetbury – ✆ 045 383 Nailsworth :

XX Gibbons, High St., GL8 8NF, ✆ 3070 – **P** – **M** (booking essential).

at Westonbirt SW : 2 ½ m. on A 433 – ⊠ Tetbury – ✆ 066 688 Westonbirt :

🏠 **Hare and Hounds** (Best Western), GL8 8QL, ✆ 233, Fax 241, ☞, park, ✖, squash – TV
☎ **P** – 🔔 40. 🅰 AE VISA
M 10.00/16.00 **st.** and a la carte 🍷 3.00 – **29 rm** ⊡ 46.00/70.00 **st.**

at Calcot W : 3 ½ m. on A 4135 – ⊠ Tetbury – ✆ 066 689 Leighterton :

🏠 ❀ **Calcot Manor** ⑤, GL8 8YJ, ✆ 391, Fax 394, « Converted Cotswold farm buildings »,
⚓ heated, ☞ – ✖ rest TV ☎ **P**. 🅰 AE ⓞ VISA. ✖
closed 2 to 10 January – **M** *(closed Sunday dinner to non-residents)* 27.50/35.00 **st.** 🍷 3.75 –
13 rm ⊡ 65.00/115.00 **st.** – SB 140.00/155.00 **st.**
Spec. Terrine of rabbit and goose liver on a creamed apple and hazelnut sauce, Noisettes of lamb on carrot
flavoured with rosemary, Calcot's Speciality Apple Dessert.

VW-AUDI London Rd ✆ 52473

TEWKESBURY Glos. 403 404 N 28 – pop. 9 454 – ECD : Thursday – ✆ 0684.
See : Site★ – Abbey Chruch★★ (12C-14C) — **Envir. :** St. Mary's Church★, Deerhurst S : 6 m.

🏌 Lincoln, Green Lane ✆ 295405.

🛈 Tewkesbury Museum, 64 Barton St. ✆ 295027 (summer only).

♦London 108 – ♦Birmingham 39 – Gloucester 11.

🏛 **Royal Hop Pole** (Crest), Church St., GL20 5RT, ✆ 293236, Telex 437176, Fax 296680, ☞ –
✖ TV ☎ **P** – 🔔 50. 🅰 AE ⓞ VISA
M 9.00/15.75 **st.** and a la carte 🍷 4.00 – ⊡ 8.00 – **29 rm** 63.00/80.00 **st.** – SB 90.00/94.00 **st.**

🏠 **Tewkesbury Park Hotel, Golf and Country Club** ⑤, Lincoln Green Lane, GL20 7DN,
S : 1 ¼ m hy A 38 ✆ 295405, Telex 43563, Fax 292386, ≤, 🏊, 🏌, park, ✖, squash – TV ☎
P – 🔔 250. 🅰 AE ⓞ VISA. ✖
M (bar lunch Saturday) 10.00/15.00 **st.** and a la carte 🍷 4.00 – **78 rm** ⊡ 78.00/105.00 **st.** –
SB (weekends only) (except Christmas and Bank Holidays) 160.00/200.00 **st.**

🏠 **Bell** (Best Western), 52 Church St., GL20 5SA, ✆ 293293, Telex 43535 – ✖ rm TV ☎ **P** –
🔔 50. 🅰 AE ⓞ VISA
M (bar lunch Monday to Saturday)/dinner 14.95 **t.** and a la carte 🍷 4.00 – **25 rm**
⊡ 53.00/75.00 **t.**, **1 suite** 85.00/110.00 **t.** – SB (weekends only) (except Christmas)
66.00/80.00 **st.**

🏠 **Tudor House,** 51 High St., GL20 5BH, ✆ 297755, « Part Tudor town house » – TV ☎ **P**.
🅰 AE ⓞ VISA. ✖
M *(closed Sunday dinner)* (bar lunch)/dinner 11.75 **t.** and a la carte 🍷 3.20 – **16 rm**
⊡ 30.00/54.00 **t.** – SB 56.00/66.00 **st.**

at Puckrup N : 2 ½ m. on A 38 – ⊠ ✆ 0684 Tewkesbury :

🏛 **Tewkesbury Hall** ⑤, GL20 6EL, ✆ 296200, Fax 850855, ☞, park – ✖ rest TV ☎ **P** –
🔔 180. 🅰 AE ⓞ VISA
M 14.00/19.00 **st.** and a la carte 20.00/25.00 **st.** 🍷 3.65 – **16 rm** ⊡ 70.00/115.00 **st.** – SB (weekends only) 85.00 **st.**

at Bredon NE : 3 m. on B 4080 – ⊠ Tewkesbury – ✆ 0684 Bredon :

🏠 **Bredon Manor** ⑤, GL20 7EG, ✆ 72293, ≤, « Manor house, gardens », ⚓, 🎣, ✖ – TV
☎ **P**. 🅰 AE ⓞ VISA. ✖
M (dinner only) 16.00 **st.** 🍷 6.00 – **4 rm** ⊡ 54.00/79.00 **st.** – SB (except Christmas and
New Year) 92.00 **st.**

at Corse Lawn SW : 6 m. by A 38 and A 438 on B 4211 – ⊠ Gloucester – ☎ 045 278 Tirley :

XXX **Corse Lawn House** with rm, GL19 4LZ, ℰ 479, Telex 437348, Fax 840, « Queen Anne house », ☞ – TV ☎ P. ☒ AE ⓘ VISA
M 15.50/21.75 **st.** and a la carte 22.50/27.75 **st.** ◊ 3.00 – **10 rm** ☞ 60.00/85.00 **st.**

AUSTIN-ROVER Gloucester Rd ℰ 293122   PEUGEOT-TALBOT Bredon Rd ℰ 297575/293122
FORD Ashchurch Rd ℰ 292398
NISSAN Bredon ℰ 72333   ⓦ ATS Oldbury Rd ℰ 292461

THAME Oxon. 404 R 28 – pop. 8 300 – ECD : Wednesday – ☎ 084 421.
See : St. Mary's Church★ (13C) – **Envir. :** Rycote Chapel★ (15C) AC, W : 3 ½ m.
🛈 Town Hall, High St. ℰ 2834.
♦London 48 – Aylesbury 9 – ♦Oxford 13.

🏛 **Spread Eagle,** 16 Cornmarket, OX9 2BW, ℰ 3661 – TV ☎ P – 🛦 200. ☒ AE ⓘ VISA
closed 28 to 30 December – **M** (bar lunch Saturday) 12.35/14.55 **st.** and a la carte ◊ 7.10 –
☞ 6.55 – **22 rm** 61.55/80.30 **st.** – SB (weekends only) (except Christmas) 42.50/45.00 **st.**

⛫ **Essex House,** Chinnor Rd., OX9 3LS, ℰ 7567, Fax 6420 – ⇔ TV ☎ P. ☒ VISA ⚒
closed Christmas and New Year – **M** (by arrangement) 11.95 **st.** ◊ 2.95 – **16 rm**
☞ 30.00/50.00 **st.**

X **Thatchers** with rm, 29-30 Lower High St., OX9 2AA, ℰ 2146, Fax 7413 – TV ☎ P. ☒ VISA
closed 25 and 26 December – **M** *(closed Saturday lunch and Sunday)* 16.50 **t.** and a la carte
15.50/23.85 **t.** ◊ 3.50 – **10 rm** ☞ 46.50/75.00 **st.**

at Towersey E : 2 m. by A 4129 off B 4012 – ⊠ ☎ 084 421 Thame :

⛫ **Upper Green Farm** ⚘ without rest., Manor Rd, OX9 3QR, ℰ 2496, « Part 15C, part 16C thatched farmhouse », ☞ – ⇔ TV P. ⚒
closed Christmas – **3 rm** ☞ 14.00/40.00 **st.**

at Kingsey (Bucks.) E : 2 ½ m. on A 4129 – ⊠ Aylesbury – ☎ 0844 Haddenham :

⛫ **Foxhill Farm** without rest., on A 4129, HP17 8LZ, ℰ 291650, ☒ heated, ☞ – ⇔ P. ⚒
closed December and January – **3 rm** ☞ 17.00/32.00 **s.**

VAUXHALL Park St. ℰ 5566

THATCHAM Berks. 403 404 Q 29 – ⊠ ☎ 0635 Newbury.
♦London 69 – ♦Bristol 68 – ♦Oxford 30 – Reading 15 – ♦Southampton 40.

🏛 **Regency Park,** Bowling Green Rd., RG13 3RP, W : 1¾ m. by A 4 and Henwick Lane
ℰ 71555, Telex 847844, Fax 71571 – TV ☎ ᴦ P – 🛦 60. ☒ AE ⓘ VISA
M 15.00/20.00 **st.** and a la carte 16.75/30.40 **st.** ◊ 4.00 – ☞ 7.25 – **50 rm** 75.00/185.00 **st.** –
SB (weekends only) (except Christmas) 99.00/110.00 **st.**

THAXTED Essex 404 V 28 – pop. 2 177 – ☎ 0371.
♦London 44 – ♦Cambridge 24 – Colchester 31 – Chelmsford 20.

🏠 **Four Seasons,** Walden Rd, CM6 2RE, NW : ½ m. on B 184 ℰ 830129 – ⇔ rest TV P. ☒
AE VISA ⚒
M *(closed Sunday dinner)* 15.00/25.00 **t.** and a la carte – ☞ 5.50 – **9 rm** 50.00/60.00 **t.**

⛫ **The Folly** without rest., Watling Lane, CM6 2QY, ℰ 830618 – ⇔ TV P. ⚒
3 rm ☞ 15.00/30.00.

at Broxted SW : 3 ¾ m. by B 1051 – ⊠ Great Dunmow – ☎ 0279 Bishop's Stortford :

🏛 **Whitehall,** Church End, CM6 2BZ, on B 1051 ℰ 850603, Fax 850385, ≼, « Part 12C and 15C manor house with walled garden », ☒ heated, ※ – TV ☎ P. ☒ AE ⓘ VISA. ⚒
M *(closed Sunday dinner to non-residents)* (dinner only and Sunday lunch)/dinner 27.50 **t.**
◊ 5.00 – **10 rm** ☞ 65.00/105.00 **t.**

THETFORD Norfolk 404 W 26 – pop. 19 591 – ECD : Wednesday – ☎ 0842.
🛈 Ancient House Museum, 21 White Hart St. ℰ 2599.
♦London 83 – ♦Cambridge 32 – ♦Ipswich 33 – King's Lynn 30 – ♦Norwich 29.

🏛 **Bell** (T.H.F.), King St., IP24 2AZ, ℰ 754455, Telex 818868, Fax 755552 – ⇔ rm TV ☎ P –
🛦 70. ☒ AE ⓘ VISA
M 8.25/15.50 **t.** and a la carte 9.40/18.20 ◊ 3.95 – ☞ 7.50 – **47 rm** 55.00/90.00 **t.** – SB (weekends only) 76.00/86.00 **st.**

🏠 **The Historical Thomas Paine** (Best Western), 33 White Hart St., IP24 1AA, ℰ 755631 –
TV ☎ P. ☒ AE ⓘ VISA. ⚒
M *(closed lunch Monday and Saturday)* 9.50/12.00 **st.** and a la carte – **14 rm** ☞ 38.00/55.00 **st.**
– SB 66.00/75.00 **st.**

🏠 **Anchor** (B.C.B.), Bridge St., IP24 3AE, ℰ 763925 – TV ☎ P – 🛦. ⚒
M (carving rest.) – **17 rm.**

⛫ **Wilderness** without rest., Earl St., IP24 2AF, ℰ 764646, ☞ – TV P. ⚒ – **4 rm.**

AUSTIN-ROVER Guildhall St. ℰ 754427   ⓦ ATS Canterbury Way ℰ 755529/755520

THIRSK North Yorks. 402 P 21 – pop. 7 174 – ECD : Wednesday – ☼ 0845.

See : St. Mary's Church★ (Gothic).

Envir. : Sutton Bank (≼★★) E : 6 m. on A 170.

🛈 Thirsk Museum, 16 Kirkgate ⌀ 22755 (summer only).

♦London 227 – ♦Leeds 37 – ♦Middlesbrough 24 – York 24.

⌂ **St. James House** without rest., 36 The Green, YO7 1AQ, ⌀ 24120, ⇗ – ⇔ TV. ⌘
April-October – **4 rm** ⊡ 22.00/34.00.

⌂ **Brook House** without rest., Ingramgate, YO7 1DD, ⌀ 22240, ⇗ – TV Ⓟ. ⌘
3 rm.

at Sowerby S : ½ m. – ⊠ ☼ 0845 Thirsk :

✗ **Sheppard's** with rm, Front St., YO7 1JF, ⌀ 23655 – TV Ⓟ. ◪ VISA. ⌘
closed 1 to 5 January – **M** (lunch by arrangement Monday to Saturday)/dinner a la
carte 11.80/16.95 t. ⌬ 3.95 – **7 rm** ⊡ 40.00/50.00 st.

CITROEN Ingramgate ⌀ 22243   ⓦ ATS Long St. ⌀ 22982/22923
PEUGEOT Station Rd ⌀ 22370

THORMANBY North Yorks. – see Easingwold.

THORNABY-ON-TEES Cleveland 402 Q 20 – pop. 26 319 – ⊠ ☼ 0642 Middlesbrough.

♦London 250 – ♦Leeds 62 – ♦Middlesbrough 3 – York 49.

🏨 Post House (T.H.F.), Low Lane, Stainton Village, TS17 9EW, SE : 3 ½ m. by A 1045 on A 1044
⌀ 591213, Telex 58426, Fax 594989 – ⇔ rm TV ☎ Ⓟ – 🛆 120
135 rm.

VAUXHALL Acklam Rd ⌀ 593333

THORNBURY Avon 403 404 M 29 **The West Country G.** – pop. 11 948 – ECD : Thursday –
⊠ Bristol – ☼ 0454.

♦London 128 – ♦Bristol 12 – Gloucester 23 – Swindon 43.

🏰 **Thornbury Castle** ⑤, Castle St., BS12 1HH, ⌀ 418511, Telex 449986, Fax 418166, « 16C
castle, gardens », park – ⇔ rest TV ☎ Ⓟ. ◪ AE ⓪ VISA. ⌘
closed 2 to 12 January – **M** 16.50/25.50 st. and a la carte ⌬ 4.55 – ⊡ 5.00 – **17 rm**
75.00/180.00 st., **1 suite** 180.00 st. – SB (November-mid March) 134.50/225.50 st.

THORNTHWAITE Cumbria 402 K 20 – see Keswick.

THORNTON CLEVELEYS Lancs. 402 L 22 – ☼ 0253 Blackpool.

♦London 244 – ♦Blackpool 6 – Lancaster 20 – ♦Manchester 44.

🏠 **Victorian House**, Trunnah Rd, FY5 4HF, ⌀ 860619, ⇗ – TV ☎ Ⓟ. ◪ VISA
M (lunch by arrangement)/dinner 15.50 st. ⌬ 3.50 – **3 rm** ⊡ 35.00/65.00 st. – SB (weekends only) 66.00 st.

THORPE Derbs. 402 403 404 O 24 – pop. 227 – ⊠ Ashbourne – ☼ 033 529 Thorpe Cloud.

Envir. : N : Dovedale (valley)★★ – Ashbourne (St. Oswald's Church★ 13C) SE : 3 m.

🏌 at Ashbourne ⌀ 0335 (Ashbourne) 42078, SE : 5 m.

♦London 151 – Derby 16 – ♦Sheffield 33 – ♦Stoke-on-Trent 26.

🏨 **Peveril of the Peak** (T.H.F.) ⑤, DE6 2AW, ⌀ 333, Fax 507, ≼, ⏞, ⅍ – ⇔ rm TV ☎ Ⓟ
– 🛆 60. ◪ AE ⓪ VISA
M 9.95/14.00 st. and a la carte ⌬ 3.95 – ⊡ 7.00 – **41 rm** 61.00/78.00 st.

🏨 **Izaak Walton** ⑤, Dovedale, DE6 2AY, W : 1 m. ⌀ 555, Telex 378406, Fax 539, ≼ Dovedale,
🐟, ⇗ – TV ☎ ⅋ Ⓟ – 🛆 30. ◪ AE ⓪ VISA
M 8.50/12.50 st. and a la carte ⌬ 4.00 – **34 rm** ⊡ 41.50/69.00 t. – SB 84.50/90.50 st.

THORPE MARKET Norfolk 404 X 25 – pop. 221 – ⊠ North Walsham – ☼ 026 379 Southrepps.

♦London 130 – ♦Norwich 21.

🏠 **Green Farm**, North Walsham Rd., NR11 8TH, ⌀ 602 – TV Ⓟ. ◪ VISA
M (lunch by arrangement in winter) 11.50/14.75 t. and a la carte ⌬ 3.60 – **5 rm** ⊡ 38.00/65.00 t.
– SB 70.00/85.00 st.

🏠 **Elderton Lodge** ⑤, Cromer Rd, NR11 8TZ, S : 1 m. on A 149 ⌀ 547, ⇗ – TV Ⓟ. ◪ VISA
M 10.50 t. and a la carte ⌬ 3.65 – **8 rm** ⊡ 18.00/40.00 t. – SB 53.00/63.00 st.

THORPE ST. ANDREW Norfolk 404 Y 26 – see Norwich.

THREE COCKS (ABERLLYNFI) Powys 403 K 27 – ⊠ Brecon – ☼ 049 74 Glasbury.

♦London 184 – Brecon 11 – Hereford 25 – ♦Swansea 55.

✗✗ **Three Cocks** with rm, LD3 0SL, on A 438 ⌀ 215, ⇗ – Ⓟ. ◪ VISA. ⌘
closed January and December – **M** *(closed Sunday lunch and Tuesday)* (bar lunch)/dinner
18.00 **st.** and a la carte 13.25/18.00 st. ⌬ 3.75 – **7 rm** ⊡ 40.00/48.00 st. – SB (except
Bank Holidays) 72.00 st.

THRESHFIELD North Yorks. 402 N 21 – see Grassington.

THRUSSINGTON Leics. 402 403 404 Q 25 – see Leicester.

THURLESTONE Devon 403 I 33 – see Kingsbridge.

TICKTON Humberside – see Beverley.

TILBURY Essex 404 V 29 – pop. 11 430 – ✪ 037 52.
⬳ to Gravesend (Sealink) frequent services daily (5 mn).
♦London 24 – Southend-on-Sea 20.

> *Hotels and restaurants see : London* W : 24 m.

⬤ ATS 6-8 Whitehall Lane, Grays, Essex ✆ 372407/375822

TIMPERLEY Greater Manchester 402 ㉒ 403 ③ 404 ⑨ – see Altrincham.

TINTAGEL Cornwall 403 F 32 The West Country G. – pop. 1 566 – ECD : Wednesday except summer – ✪ 0840 Camelford.
See : Arthur's Castle : site★★★ *AC* – Tintagel Church★ – Old Post Office★ *AC*.
Envir. : Delabole Quarry★ *AC*, SE : 4 m. by B 3263 – Camelford★, SE : 6 m. by B 3263 and B 3266.
♦London 264 – Exeter 63 – ♦Plymouth 49 – Truro 41.

   🏠 **Bossiney House,** Bossiney, PL34 0AX, NE : ½ m. on B 3263 ✆ 770240, 🔲, 🛲 – 🅿. 🔃 AE
     ① VISA
     April-October – **M** (bar lunch)/dinner 9.90 t. ⬧ 3.25 – **19 rm** ⊐ 28.00/59.00 t. – SB (except July and August) 50.00/60.00 st.

   ⚘ Mill House Inn, Trebarwith, PL34 0HD, S : 1 ¼ m. by B 3263 via Treknow ✆ 770200, « Former corn mill » – 📺 🅿
     9 rm.

   ⚘ **Trewarmett Lodge,** Trewarmett, PL34 0ET, SW : 1 ½ m. on B 3263 ✆ 770460, 🛲 –
     ⤢ rm 🅿. 🔃 ① VISA
     March-October – **M** (booking essential) 8.50 t. and a la carte ⬧ 3.50 – **5 rm** ⊐ 14.50/30.00 t.
     – SB 41.00/49.00 st.

   ↑ **Old Millfloor** 🦢, Trebarwith, PL34 0HA, S : 1 ¾ m. by B 3263 ✆ 770234, « Former flour mill », 🛲, park – 📺 🅿. 🦢
     April-November – **M** (by arrangement) 9.50 and a la carte – **3 rm** ⊐ 13.50/27.00.

   ↑ **Old Borough House,** Bossiney Rd, PL34 0AY, NE : ½ m. on B 3263 ✆ 770475 – ⤢ rest
     🅿. 🦢
     M (by arrangement) 8.00 s. ⬧ 3.75 – **6 rm** ⊐ 21.00/32.00 s.

TINTERN (TYNDYRN) Gwent 403 404 L 28 – pop. 816 – ECD : Wednesday – ✉ Chepstow –
✪ 0291.
See : Abbey★★ (ruins) *AC*.
🛈 Tintern Abbey ✆ 689431 (summer only).
♦London 137 – ♦Bristol 23 – Gloucester 40 – Newport 22.

   🏨 **Beaufort** (Embassy), NP6 6SF, on A 466 ✆ 689777, Fax 689727, 🛲 – 📺 ☎ 🅿 – 🔧 . 🔃
     AE ① VISA
     M (bar lunch Monday to Saturday)/dinner 14.95 **st.** and a la carte ⬧ 5.40 – **24 rm**
     ⊐ 55.00/75.00 **st.** – SB (except Easter, Christmas and New Year) 69.00/79.00 **st.**

   🏠 **Royal George,** NP6 6SF, on A 466 ✆ 689205, 🛲 – 📺 ☎ 🅿. 🔃 AE ① VISA
     M (bar lunch)/dinner 11.50 t. and a la carte ⬧ 3.00 – **17 rm** ⊐ 28.50/66.00 t. – SB 71.50 st.

   ↑ **Parva Farmhouse,** NP6 6SQ, on A 466 ✆ 689411 – 📺 ☎ 🅿
     M 14.00 st. ⬧ 3.00 – **9 rm** ⊐ 34.00/48.00 st. – SB 52.00/64.00 st.

TIVERTON Devon 403 J 31 The West Country G. – pop. 14 745 – ECD : Thursday – ✪ 0884.
See : Museum★ *AC*.
Envir. : at Bickleigh★★, Mill Craft Centre and farms★★ *AC*, Castle★ *AC*, S : 4 ½ m. – Knightshayes Court★ *AC*, N : 2 m. on A 396 – Coldharbour Mill, Uffculme★ *AC*, E : 11 m. by A 373.
🛈 Pheonix Lane ✆ 255827 – Junction 27 (M 5) ✆ 821242.
♦London 190 – Exeter 14 – Taunton 23.

   🏨 **Tiverton,** Blundells Rd, EX16 4DB, E : ½ m. on B 3391 ✆ 256120, Fax 258101 – ▤ rest 📺
     ☎ ♿ 🅿 – 🔧 . 🔃 AE ① VISA
     M 7.95/14.50 st. and a la carte ⬧ 3.95 – **75 rm** ⊐ 35.00/60.00 t. – SB 54.00/70.00 st.

   🏠 **Travelodge** without rest., EX16 7HD, NE : 6 ¾ m. by A 396 and A 373 on A 38 ✆ 821087 –
     📺 ☎ ♿ 🅿. 🔃 AE VISA
     40 rm 21.50/27.00 t.

at Oakfordbridge NW : 9 m. on A 396 – ⊠ Tiverton – ☎ 039 85 Oakford :

🏠 **Bark House,** EX16 9HZ, ℰ 236, 🐎 – 📺 🅿. 🖸 AE ⓪ VISA
closed January and February – **M** (bar lunch)/dinner 11.50 **st.** ⌀ 3.90 – ⌑ 5.00 – **6 rm** 16.00/50.00 **st.**

at Bolham N : 1 ¼ m. on A 396 – ⊠ ☎ 0884 Tiverton :

🏠 **Hartnoll Country House,** EX16 7RA, ℰ 252777, Fax 259195, 🐎 – 📺 ☎ 🅿. 🖸 AE ⓪
VISA
M 9.50/10.95 **st.** and a la carte ⌀ 3.95 – **16 rm** ⌑ 38.00/49.00 **st.**

CITROEN 31 Leat St. ℰ 252170   🔘 ATS Newport St. ℰ 252062

TODDINGTON SERVICE AREA Beds. 404 S 28 – ⊠ Luton – ☎ 052 55.

🏠 Granada Lodge without rest., LU5 6HR, ℰ 5150, Fax 5358 – 📺 ⅙ 🅿 – **43 rm**.

TODWICK South Yorks. – pop. 1 661 – ⊠ Sheffield – ☎ 0909 Worksop.

♦London 161 – ♦Nottingham 35 – ♦Sheffield 10.

🏨 **Red Lion** (Lansbury), Worksop Rd, S31 0DJ, on A 57 ℰ 771654, Telex 54120, Fax 773704 –
⅙✕ rm 📺 ☎ ⅙ 🅿 – 🔏 70. 🖸 AE ⓪ VISA 🦅
M 9.00/13.00 **t.** and a la carte 9.50/21.10 **t.** ⌀ 3.50 – **29 rm** ⌑ 55.00/65.00 **t.** – SB (week-ends only) 60.00/66.00 **st.**

TONBRIDGE Kent 404 U 30 – pop. 34 407 – ECD : Wednesday – ☎ 0732.

See : Tonbridge School★ (1553).

Envir. : Ightham Mote★ (Manor House 14C-15C) *AC*, site★ N : 7 m.

🏌 Poult Wood, Higham Lane ℰ 364039, N : 2 m. by A 227.

♦London 33 – ♦Brighton 37 – Hastings 31 – Maidstone 14.

🏨 **Rose and Crown** (T.H.F.), 125 High St., TN9 1DD, ℰ 357966, 🐎 – ⅙✕ rm 📺 ☎ 🅿 – 🔏 80. 🖸 AE ⓪ VISA
M 9.50/15.00 **st.** and a la carte ⌀ 3.75 – ⌑ 7.00 – **50 rm** 56.00/71.00 **st.** – SB (week-ends only) 58.00/80.00 **st.**

✕ **The Office,** 163 High St., TN9 1BX, ℰ 353660 – 🖸 AE ⓪ VISA
M *(closed Sunday and Bank Holidays)* a la carte 8.70/10.80 **t.** ⌀ 2.70.

FORD Avebury Av. ℰ 356301
RENAULT Sovereign Way ℰ 350288
VAUXHALL Waterloo Rd ℰ 354035
VOLVO Hildenborough ℰ 832424

VW-AUDI, NSU, MERCEDES-BENZ Vale Rd ℰ 355822

🔘 ATS 61-63 Pembury Rd ℰ 353800/352231

TORCROSS Devon 403 J 33 – see Kingsbridge.

TORQUAY Devon 403 J 32 The West Country G. – pop. 54 430 – ECD : Wednesday and Saturday – ☎ 0803.

See : Kent's Cavern★ *AC* CX A.

Envir. : Cockington★, W : 1 m. AX.

🏌 Petitor Rd, St. Marychurch ℰ 37471 B.

🚢 to Channel Islands: Alderney (Torbay Seaways) summer only – to Channel Islands: St Peter Port, Guernsey (Torbay Seaways) summer only – to Channel Islands: St Helier, Jersey (Torbay Seaways) summer only.

🛈 Vaughan Parade ℰ 279428.

♦London 223 – Exeter 23 – ♦Plymouth 32.

Plan on next page

🏨 **Imperial** (T.H.F.), Park Hill Rd, TQ1 2DG, ℰ 294301, Telex 42849, Fax 298293, ⩽ Torbay, 🏊 heated, 🖸, 🐎, ✕, squash – 📟 ⅙✕ rm 📺 ☎ ⅙ 🚗 🅿 – 🔏. 🖸 AE ⓪ VISA   CZ a
M 13.00/24.00 **st.** and a la carte 25.50/53.00 ⌀ 5.00 – **146 rm** ⌑ 91.00/170.00 **st.**, **17 suites** 105.00/260.00 **st.** – SB 80.00/98.00 **st.**

🏨 **Palace,** Babbacombe Rd, TQ1 3TG, ℰ 200200, Telex 42606, Fax 299899, « Extensive gardens », 🏊 heated, 🖸, 🏌, park, ✕, squash – 📟 📺 ☎ 🚗 🅿 – 🔏. 🖸 AE ⓪ VISA 🦅
M 8.50/15.00 **st.** and a la carte 10.00/24.50 **st.** – **135 rm** ⌑ 49.00/120.00 **st.**, **6 suites** 82.00/110.00 **st.**   CX u

🏨 **Grand,** Seafront, TQ2 6NT, ℰ 296677, Telex 42891, Fax 213462, ⩽, 🏊 heated, 🖸 – 📟 📺 ☎ 🚗 – 🔏. 🖸 AE ⓪ VISA   BZ z
M 12.50/15.00 **st.** and a la carte ⌀ 3.50 – **101 rm** ⌑ 40.00/100.00 **st.**, **11 suites** 70.00/140.00 **st.**

🏨 **Livermead Cliff** (Best Western), Sea Front, TQ2 6RQ, ℰ 299666, Telex 42424, Fax 294496, ⩽, 🏊 heated, 🐎 – 📟 📺 ☎ 🅿. 🖸 AE ⓪ VISA 🦅   BX r
M 7.25/12.25 **st.** and a la carte ⌀ 3.85 – **64 rm** ⌑ 28.50/84.00 **st.** – SB 51.00/88.00 **st.**

🏨 **Livermead House** (Best Western), Sea Front, TQ2 6QJ, ℰ 294361, Telex 42918, ⩽, 🏊 heated, 🐎, ✕, squash – 📟 📺 ☎ 🅿 – 🔏. 🖸 AE ⓪ VISA 🦅   BZ e
M 7.00/11.50 **st.** and a la carte ⌀ 3.60 – **66 rm** ⌑ 26.00/78.00 **st.** – SB (except Christmas and New Year) 68.00/86.00 **st.**

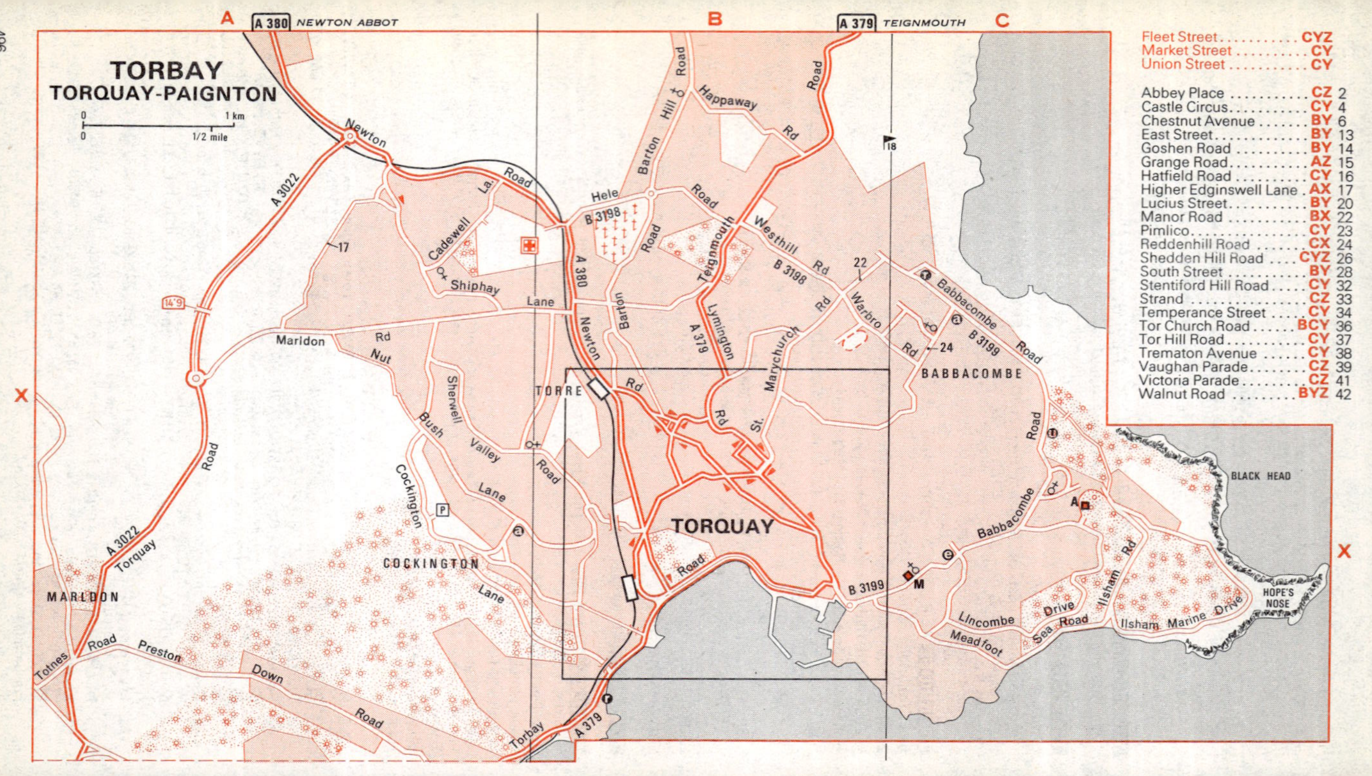

TORBAY
TORQUAY-PAIGNTON
0   1 km
0   1/2 mile
A 380 NEWTON ABBOT
A 379 TEIGNMOUTH
A 3022
Newton
La. Road
Hele
B 3198
Cadewell
17
Shiphay
Lane
Marldon
Rd
Nut
Sherwell
Bush
Valley
Cockington
Lane
P
A 3022
Torquay
MARLDON
Totnes Road
Preston
Down
Road
Torbay
A 379
COCKINGTON
TORRE
Newton
Rd
A 380
Barton
Barton Hill
Road
Happaway
Rd
Road
Road
Teignmouth
Westhill Rd
B 3198
Lymington
A 379
Marychurch
St.
Rd
Rd
Warbro
22
24
Babbacombe
B 3199
BABBACOMBE
Road
18
TORQUAY
Road
B 3199
M
A
Babbacombe
Road
Lincombe
Mead foot
Sea Road
Ilsham
Ilsham Marine Drive
Rd
Drive
BLACK HEAD
HOPE'S NOSE
X
X
A
B
C

Fleet Street . . . . CYZ
Market Street . . . . CY
Union Street . . . . CY
Abbey Place . . . . CZ 2
Castle Circus . . . . CY 4
Chestnut Avenue . . . . BY 6
East Street . . . . BY 13
Goshen Road . . . . BY 14
Grange Road . . . . AZ 15
Hatfield Road . . . . CY 16
Higher Edginswell Lane . . AX 17
Lucius Street . . . . BY 20
Manor Road . . . . BX 22
Pimlico . . . . CY 23
Reddenhill Road . . . . CX 24
Shedden Hill Road . . . . CYZ 26
South Street . . . . BY 28
Stentiford Hill Road . . . . . CY 32
Strand . . . . CZ 33
Temperance Street . . . . . CY 34
Tor Church Road . . . . . . BCY 36
Tor Hill Road . . . . CY 37
Trematon Avenue . . . . . . CY 38
Vaughan Parade . . . . CZ 39
Victoria Parade . . . . CZ 41
Walnut Road . . . . BYZ 42

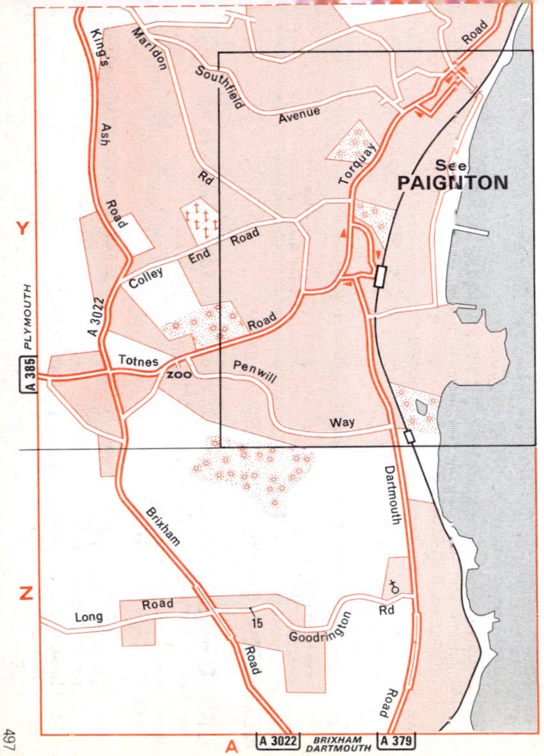

TORQUAY
CENTRE

See
PAIGNTON

PRINCESS GARDENS
UPTON
UPTON UNION PARK
TORRE
TORRE STATION
TORQUAY STATION
CHELSTON
ABBEY GARDENS
The King's Drive
Rathmore
Falkland Road
Belgrave
Mill Lane
Newton Road
Avenue
Lymington
Windsor Road
Ellacombe
Church Rd
Hoxton
Princes Rd
Market St.
St. Marychurch Rd
Warren Road
Fleet St.
Croft Road
Abbey Road
Seaway Lane
Torbay Road
Mill Rd
Old Mill Rd
Dartmouth Road
Goodrington Rd
Brixham Road
Long Road
King's Ash Road
Marldon Road
Southfield Avenue
Colley End Road
Totnes Road
Penwill Way
Torquay Road
ZOO
A 379
A 380
A 385
A 3022
B 3199
B 3202
PLYMOUTH
BRIXHAM
DARTMOUTH
POL.
400 m
400 yards

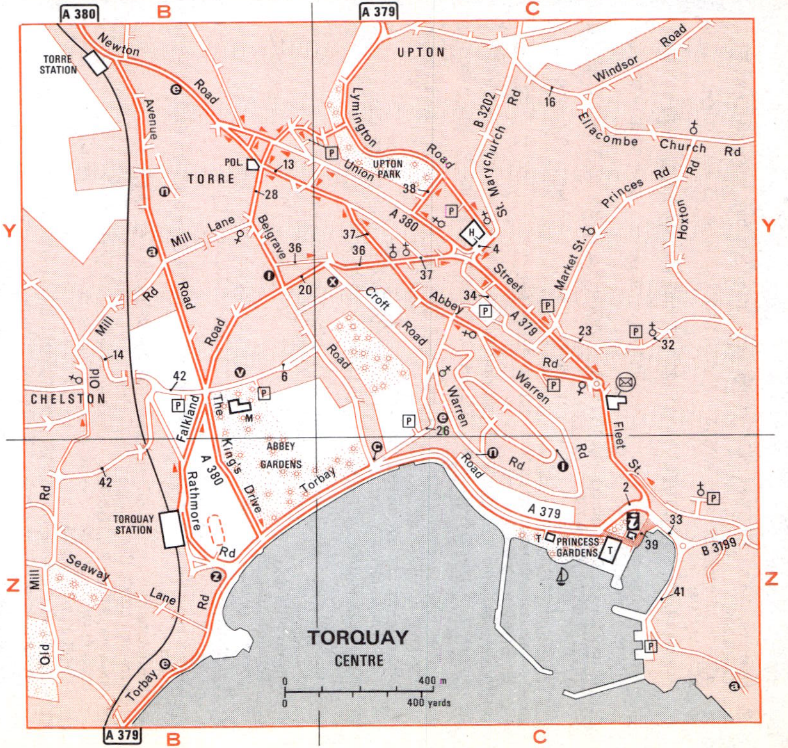

Homers, Warren Rd, TQ2 5TN, ℘ 213456, Fax 213458, ≼ Torbay – ᛒ rest TV ☎. ☒ AE ⓪ VISA. ⚶
CZ n
closed 6 January-4 February – **M** (dinner only) 25.00 t. – **14 rm** ⇆ 45.00/76.00 t., **1 suite** 88.00/130.00 t.

Roseland, Warren Rd, TQ2 5TT, ℘ 213829, ≼ Torbay – ▯ ᛒ rest TV ☎. ☒ AE ⓪ VISA ⚶
CY e
M (bar lunch)/dinner 12.95 st. and a la carte ⅃ 3.75 – **35 rm** ⇆ 30.00/70.00 st. – SB (week-ends only) (except summer) 60.00/70.00 st.

Abbey Lawn, Scarborough Rd, TQ2 5UQ, ℘ 295791, Fax 291460, ≼, ⅃ heated, ⚒ – ▯ ᛒ TV ☎ Ⓟ. ☒ AE ⓪ VISA
M 9.00/14.00 st. ⅃ 3.50 – **64 rm** ⇆ 48.00/110.00 st., **1 suite** 110.00/134.00 st. – SB 78.00/85.00 st.

Toorak, Chestnut Av., TQ2 5JS, ℘ 291444, Fax 291666, ⅃ heated, ⊰, ⚒ – TV ☎ Ⓟ – ⚐ 120. ☒ AE ⓪ VISA
BY v
M (bar lunch)/dinner 11.50 st. ⅃ 2.35 – **41 rm** ⇆ 40.00/150.00 st.

Belgrave, Seafront, Belgrave Rd, TQ2 5HE, ℘ 296666, Telex 211308, ⅃ heated, ⊰ – ▯ TV ☎ Ⓟ – ⚐ 50. ☒ AE ⓪ VISA
CZ c
M (bar lunch)/dinner 9.00 t. – **54 rm** ⇆ 36.00/78.00 t. – SB (October-April) (week-ends only) 59.00/68.00 st.

Glenorleigh, 26 Cleveland Rd, TQ2 5BE, ℘ 292135, ⅃ heated, ⊰ – Ⓟ. ⚶
BY n
M (bar lunch)/dinner 8.00 st. ⅃ 2.50 – **16 rm** ⇆ 16.00/36.00 st. – SB 30.00/68.00 st.

Fairmount House ⌂, Herbert Rd, Chelston, TQ2 6RW, ℘ 605446, ⊰ – ᛒ rest Ⓟ. ☒ AE VISA
AX a
March-October – **M** *(closed Sunday dinner)* (bar lunch)/dinner 8.50 st. ⅃ 3.50 – **7 rm** ⇆ 20.00/40.00 t. – SB (except summer) 50.50/54.50 st.

Mount Nessing, St. Lukes Rd North, TQ2 5PD, ℘ 292970, ≼ – ᛒ rest TV ☎ Ⓟ. ☒ VISA ⚶
CZ i
closed 31 October-15 November – **M** 14.00 t. ⅃ 3.95 – **12 rm** ⇆ 18.00/36.00 t.

Cranborne without rest., 58 Belgrave Rd, TQ2 5HY, ℘ 298046 – TV. ☒ VISA. ⚶
BY i
closed December – **13 rm** ⇆ 14.00/33.00 t.

Concorde without rest., 26 Newton Rd, TQ2 5BZ, ℘ 292330, ⅃ heated – TV Ⓟ
BY e
22 rm.

Elmsdale without rest., 70 Avenue Rd, TQ2 5LF, ℘ 295929 – Ⓟ. ☒ VISA. ⚶
BY a
9 rm ⇆ 12.00/28.00 s.

Remy's, 3 Croft Rd, TQ2 5UN, ℘ 292359, French rest. – AE VISA
CY x
closed Sunday, Monday, 2 weeks August, Christmas and New Year – **M** (booking essential) (dinner only) 15.85 st. ⅃ 3.00.

Yum Sing, Old Torwood Rd, TQ1 1PN, ℘ 293314, Chinese (Canton) rest. – Ⓟ. ☒ VISA
CX e
closed Sunday – **M** (dinner only) 19.50 t. and a la carte 9.50/14.75 t.

at Maidencombe N : 3 ½ m. by A 379 – BX – ✉ ✆ 0803 Torquay :

Orestone Manor ⌂, Rockhouse Lane, TQ1 4SX, ℘ 328098, Fax 328336, ≼, ⅃ heated, ⊰ – ᛒ rest TV ☎ Ⓟ. ☒ AE ⓪ VISA
M (bar lunch)/dinner 18.00 t. and a la carte ⅃ 3.75 – **20 rm** ⇆ 25.00/80.00 t.

at Babbacombe NE : 1 ½ m. – ✉ ✆ 0803 Torquay :

Norcliffe, 7 Babbacombe Downs Rd, TQ1 3LF, ℘ 328456, ≼, ⊰ – ▯ ᛒ rest TV Ⓟ. VISA
M (dinner only and Sunday lunch)/dinner 9.75 t. – **20 rm** ⇆ 20.00/45.00 t. – SB (except summer) 42.00/56.00 st.
CX r

Table, 135 Babbacombe Rd, TQ1 3SR, ℘ 324292
CX a
closed Monday, 1 to 16 February and 1 to 10 September – **M** (booking essential) (dinner only) 18.50/26.50 t. ⅃ 4.50.

AUDI-VW Torwood St. ℘ 298635
AUSTIN-ROVER, MASERATI Lawes Bridge ℘ 62781
FORD Lawes Bridge, Newton Rd ℘ 62021
PEUGEOT-TALBOT 141 Newton Rd ℘ 63626

ROLLS-ROYCE, BENTLEY, FERRARI, VOLVO Lisburne Sq. ℘ 294321

ATS 20 Tor Church Rd ℘ 293985
ATS 100 Teignmouth Rd ℘ 39495

TOTLAND BAY I.O.W. 403 404 P 31 – see Wight (Isle of).

TOTNES Devon 403 I 32 The West Country G. – pop. 6 133 – ECD : Thursday – ✆ 0803.

See : Site★ – St. Mary's Church★ – Butterwalk★ – Castle (≼★★★) *AC*.

🛈 The Plains ℘ 863168 (summer only).

◆London 224 – Exeter 24 – ◆Plymouth 23 – Torquay 9.

Old Forge without rest., Seymour Pl., Bridgetown, TQ9 5AY, ℘ 862174, « 14C working forge », ⊰ – ᛒ TV Ⓟ. ⚶
8 rm ⇆ 40.00/45.00 st.

Elbow Room, 6 North St., TQ9 5NZ, ℘ 863480 – ☒ AE VISA
closed Sunday and Monday – **M** 8.55 t. (lunch) and a la carte 11.20/15.65 t. ⅃ 3.25.

at Stoke Gabriel SE : 4 m. by A 385 – ⊠ Totnes – ✆ 080 428 Stoke Gabriel :

🏨 **Gabriel Court** ⑤, TQ9 6SF, ✆ 206, ⌇ heated, 🚗 – TV ☎ Ⓟ. ◪ AE ⓪ VISA
closed February – **M** (dinner only and Sunday lunch)/dinner 18.00 **st.** ⊓ 3.60 – **21 rm**
⊊ 30.00/64.00 **st.**

at Dartington NW : 2 m. on A 385 – ⊠ ✆ 0803 Totnes :

♔ **Cott Inn,** TQ9 6HE, ✆ 863777, « 14C thatched inn » – ⇥ rm Ⓟ. ◪ AE ⓪ VISA. 彩
M (buffet lunch)/dinner 16.50 **t.** ⊓ 2.95 – **5 rm** ⊊ 40.00/57.00 **t.** – SB (except summer)
60.00/70.00 **st.**

FORD The Stables, Babbage Rd ✆ 862196   ⊕ ATS Babbage Rd ✆ 862086
VAUXHALL The Plains ✆ 862247

TOTON Notts. 🅸🅾🅸 🅸🅾🅸 🅸🅾🅸 Q 25 – see Nottingham.

TOTTENHILL Norfolk – see King's Lynn.

TOWCESTER Northants. 🅸🅾🅸 🅸🅾🅸 R 27 – pop. 5 010 – ✆ 0327.
▨ Woodlands, Farthingstone ✆ 36291, W : 6 m. M 1 junction 16.
◆London 70 – ◆Birmingham 50 – Northampton 9 – ◆Oxford 36.

🏠 Travelodge without rest., A 43, East Towcester by-pass, NN12 0DD, S : ½ m. by Brackley
Rd on A 43 ✆ 359105 – TV ♿ Ⓟ
33 rm.

♔ **Brave Old Oak,** 104 Watling St. East, NN12 7BT, ✆ 50533 – TV 🐕 Ⓟ. ◪ AE ⓪ VISA. 彩
M *(closed Sunday dinner)* (carving lunch) 5.50/9.50 **st.** and a la carte ⊓ 3.50 – **12 rm**
⊊ 21.00/50.00 **st.** – SB (September-May) 55.00/65.00 **st.**

XX **Vine House** with rm, 100 High St., Paulerspury, NN12 7NA, SE : 3 ¼ m. by A 5
✆ 032 733 (Paulerspury) 267, 🚗 – TV ☎ Ⓟ. ◪ VISA
M *(closed Monday and Saturday lunch and Sunday)* 26.00 **t.** and a la carte 18.50/25.40 **t.**
⊓ 3.50 – **6 rm** ⊊ 49.00/59.00 **t.**

AUSTIN-ROVER Quinbury End ✆ 860208

TOWERSEY Oxon. 🅸🅾🅸 R 28 – see Thame.

TRALLWNG = Welshpool.

TREBETHERICK Cornwall 🅸🅾🅸 F 32 – ECD : Wednesday – ⊠ Wadebridge – ✆ 020 886.
◆London 286 – Newquay 22 – ◆Plymouth 46 – Truro 32.

🏠 Bodare ⑤, Daymer Bay Lane, PL27 6SA, ✆ 3210, 🚗 – ☎ Ⓟ
17 rm.

TRECASTLE Powys 🅸🅾🅸 J 28 – ✆ 087 482 Sennybridge.
◆London 183 – Brecon 12.

♔ **Castle,** LD3 8UH, ✆ 354 – ⇥ rm TV Ⓟ. ◪ VISA. 彩
M *(closed Sunday dinner)* (bar lunch)/dinner 15.00 **t.** and a la carte – **8 rm** ⊊ 21.50/45.00 **t.**
– SB 50.00/65.00 **st.**

TREFALDWYN = Montgomery.

TREFDRAETH = Newport (Dyfed).

TREFFYNNON = Holywell.

TREFRIW Gwynedd 🅸🅾🅸 🅸🅾🅸 I 24 – see Llanrwst.

TREFYCLAWDD = Knighton.

TREFYNWY = Monmouth.

TREGONY Cornwall 🅸🅾🅸 F 33 – pop. 670 – ⊠ Truro – ✆ 087 253.
◆London 291 – Newquay 18 – Plymouth 53 – Truro 10.

↑ **Tregony House,** 15 Fore St., TR2 5RN, ✆ 671 – ⇥ rest. 彩
March-October – **6 rm** ⊊ (dinner included) 24.00/54.00.

TREGREHAN Cornwall 🅸🅾🅸 F 32 – see St. Austell.

TRELLECK (TRYLEG) Gwent 🅸🅾🅸 L 28 – see Monmouth.

TRESAITH Dyfed – see Aberporth.

TRESCO Cornwall ▨▨ ㉚ – see Scilly (Isles of).

TREYARNON BAY Cornwall ▨▨ E 32 – see Padstow.

TRING Herts. ▨▨ S 28 – pop. 10 610 – ECD : Wednesday – ✆ 044 282 (4 fig.) or 0442 (6 fig.).
See : Church of St. Peter and St. Paul (interior : stone corbels★).
♦London 38 – Aylesbury 7 – Luton 14.

> 🏨 **Rose and Crown** (Lansbury), High St., HP23 5AH, ℰ 4071, Telex 826538, Fax 890735 –
> ⇆ rm ▣ ☎ Ⓟ – 🕴 70. ◪ 🅰🄴 ⓪ 𝘝𝘐𝘚𝘈. ⅍
> **M** a la carte 9.00/16.55 t. ₰ 3.50 – **28 rm** � 58.00/68.00 t. – SB (weekends only) 73.00/82.00 st.
>
> 🏨 **Travel Inn** without rest., Tring Hill, HP23 4LD, W : 1 ½ m. on A 41 ℰ 4819 – ▣ & Ⓟ
> **30 rm**.

HONDA 110 Western Rd ℰ 4144   SAAB London Rd ℰ 890911

TROTTON West Sussex – see Midhurst.

TROUTBECK Cumbria ▨▨ L 20 – see Windermere.

TROWBRIDGE Wilts. ▨▨ ▨▨ N 30 The West Country G. – pop. 27 299 – ECD : Wednesday –
✆ 022 14 (4 and 5 fig.) or 0225 (6 fig.).
Envir. : Norton St. Philip (The George Inn★★), W : 6 m. – Bratton Castle ❋★★, SE : 7 ½ m. by
B 3098 – Steeple Ashton★, The Green★, E : 7 m. – Edington (St. Mary, St. Catherine and All
Saints Church★),SE : 8 m. – Farleigh Hungerford Castle★ *AC*, (St. Leonards Chapel★), W : 4 m..
🛈 St Stephens Pl. ℰ 777054 (summer only).
♦London 115 – ♦Bristol 27 – ♦Southampton 55 – Swindon 32.

> 🏨 **Old Manor** ⑊, Trowle, BA14 9BL, NW : 1 m. on A 363 ℰ 777393, Fax 765443, 🐎 – ▣ ☎
> Ⓟ. ◪ 🅰🄴 ⓪ 𝘝𝘐𝘚𝘈. ⅍
> **M** (lunch by arrangement) a la carte 10.65/15.85 st. ₰ 2.10 – **14 rm** ⊻ 38.00/44.00 st. –
> SB (weekdays only) 66.00/70.00 st.
>
> 🏨 **Hilbury Court**, Hilperton Rd, BA14 7JW, E : ¼ m. on A 361 ℰ 752949, 🐎 – ⇆ rest ▣ ☎
> Ⓟ. ◪ 𝘝𝘐𝘚𝘈. ⅍
> *closed 24 December-1 January* – **M** *(closed Friday to Sunday)* (bar lunch)/dinner 10.50 st.
> ₰ 3.20 – **13 rm** ⊻ 29.00/36.00 st.

AUSTIN-ROVER Duke St. ℰ 777222   VAUXHALL-OPEL Town Bridge ℰ 66192
CITROEN Bradford Rd ℰ 753297
FORD Bradley Rd ℰ 752525   ⑩ ATS Canal Rd, Ladydown Trading Est. ℰ 753469

TRURO Cornwall ▨▨ E 33 The West Country G. – pop. 17 852 – ECD : Thursday – ✆ 0872.
See : Cornwall County Museum★ *AC*.
Envir. : Trewithen★★★, NE : 7 ½ m. by A 390 – Trelissick garden★★, (←★★) *AC*, S : 8 m. by A 39
and B 3289 – at Probus★ Church Tower★ County Demonstration Garden★, NE : 8 m. – Feock
(Church★), S : 8 ½ m.
🛈₁₈ Treliske ℰ 72640, W : 2 m. on A 390.
🛈 Municipal Building, Boscawen St. ℰ 74555.
♦London 295 – Exeter 87 – Penzance 26 – ♦Plymouth 52.

> 🏨 **Alverton Manor**, Tregolls Rd (A 39), TR1 1XQ, ℰ 76633, Fax 222989, « Mid 19C manor
> house, former Bishops residence and convent », 🐎 – 🛗 ▣ ☎ & Ⓟ – 🕴 30. ◪ 🅰🄴 ⓪
> 𝘝𝘐𝘚𝘈. ⅍
> **M** 10.50/25.00 st. and a la carte ₰ 4.75 – ⊻ 4.50 – **25 rm** 63.00/100.00 st., **6 suites**
> 120.00/140.00 st. – SB (weekends only) 144.00/180.00 st.
>
> 🏨 **Carlton**, 49 Falmouth Rd, TR1 2HL, ℰ 72450 – ▣ ☎ Ⓟ. ◪ 𝘝𝘐𝘚𝘈
> *closed 20 December-6 January* – **M** 7.30 st. (dinner)and a la carte ₰ 3.50 – **31 rm**
> ⊻ 27.50/43.50 st. – SB (weekends only) 52.20/58.10 st.
>
> 🏠 **Laniley House** ⑊ without rest., Newquay rd, nr. Trispen,, TR4 9AU, NE : 3 ½ m. by A 390
> off A 3076 ℰ 75201, 🐎 – ▣ Ⓟ. ⅍
> *March-September* – **3 rm** ⊻ 15.50/31.00.

> **at Blackwater** W : 7 m. by A 390 – ✉ Truro – ✆ 0872 Truro :

> XX **Long's**, TR4 8HH, ℰ 561111 – Ⓟ. ◪ 🅰🄴 𝘝𝘐𝘚𝘈
> *closed Sunday dinner, Monday, Tuesday and 3 weeks January-February* – **M** (dinner only
> and Sunday lunch)/dinner a la carte 17.75/21.70 t.

AUSTIN-ROVER Lemon Quay ℰ 74321   VW-AUDI Three Mile Stone ℰ 79301
FORD Lemon Quay ℰ 73933
MERCEDES-BENZ Moresk ℰ 73949   ⑩ ATS Tabernacle St. ℰ 74083
PEUGEOT-TALBOT Point Mills, Bissoe ℰ 863073   ATS Newham Rd ℰ 40353
VAUXHALL Fairmantle St. ℰ 76231

TRYLEG = Trelleck.

TUDWEILIOG Gwynedd 402 403 G 25 – pop. 882 – ⊠ Pwllheli – ☎ 075 887.
♦London 267 – Caernarfon 25.

   ✗   **Dive Inn,** LL53 8PB, W : 2 m. by B 4417 ℰ 246, Seafood – **Ⓟ**
       closed Sunday dinner and weekdays October-Easter – **M** (booking essential) (bar lunch)/
       dinner 18.50 **t.** ₰ 3.50.

TUNBRIDGE WELLS Kent 404 U 30 – see Royal Tunbridge Wells.

TURNERS HILL West Sussex 404 T 30 – ☎ 0342 Copthorne.
♦London 33 – ♦Brighton 24 – Crawley 7.

   🏨   **Alexander House** ⑤, RH10 4QD, E : 1 m. on B 2110 ℰ 714914, Telex 95611, Fax 717328,
       ≼, « Tastefully decorated country house », ☞, park, ✗ – ▮ TV ☎ Ⓟ. ⓢ AE ① VISA. ⑤
       M a la carte 28.00/36.00 **st.** ₰6.00 – **7 rm** ⊇ 80.00/165.00 **st.**, **5 suites** 185.00/205.00 **st.** –
       SB (weekends only) 197.50/215.00 **st.**

TUTBURY Staffs. 402 403 404 O 25 – pop. 5 099 (inc. Hatton) – ECD : Wednesday – ⊠
☎ 0283 Burton-upon-Trent.
♦London 132 – ♦Birmingham 33 – Derby 11 – ♦Stoke-on-Trent 27.

   🏨   **Ye Olde Dog and Partridge,** High St., DE13 9LS, ℰ 813030, Telex 347220, « Part 15C
       timbered inn », ☞ – TV ☎ Ⓟ. ⓢ AE VISA. ⑤
       closed 25 and 26 December – **M** (carving lunch)/dinner a la carte 14.45/20.00 **t.** ₰ 3.50 –
       17 rm ⊇ 52.00/68.00 **st.**

TUXFORD Notts. 402 404 R 24 – pop. 2 547 – ECD : Wednesday – ⊠ Newark – ☎ 0777.
♦London 141 – ♦Leeds 53 – Lincoln 18 – ♦Nottingham 26 – ♦Sheffield 29.

   🏠   **Newcastle Arms,** Market Pl., NG22 0LA, ℰ 870208 – TV ☎ Ⓟ – ⚐ 90. ⓢ AE ① VISA
       M 12.50 **t.** and a la carte ₰ 3.25 – ⊇ 1.50 – **11 rm** 30.00/55.00 **t.**

TWEMLOW GREEN Cheshire 402 403 404 N 24 – see Holmes Chapel.

TWO BRIDGES Devon 403 I 32 The West Country G. – ⊠ Yelverton – ☎ 0822 Tavistock.
♦London 226 – Exeter 25 – ♦Plymouth 17.

   ⌂   **Cherrybrook** ⑤, PL20 6SP, NE : 1 m. on B 3212 ℰ 88260, ≼, ☞ – ⑤ rest **Ⓟ**
       closed Christmas and New Year – **M** 9.00 **st.** ₰2.75 – **7 rm** ⊇ 18.50/37.00 **st.**

TYDDEWI = St. David's.

TYNDYRN = Tintern.

TYNEMOUTH Tyne and Wear 401 402 P 18 – pop. 17 877 – ECD : Wednesday – ☎ 0632 North
Shields (6 fig.) or 091 Tyneside (7 fig.) – **See** : Priory and castle : ruins★ (11C) *AC*.
⛳ Spital Dene ℰ 257 4578.
♦London 290 – ♦Newcastle-upon-Tyne 8 – Sunderland 7.

   🏠   **Park,** Grand Par., NE30 4JQ, ℰ 257 1406, Fax 257 1716 – ⑤ rm TV ☎ Ⓟ – ⚐ 400. ⓢ AE
       ① VISA
       M *(closed lunch Bank Holidays)* 5.25/11.50 **st.** and a la carte – **49 rm** ⊇ 34.00/54.50 **st.** –
       SB (weekends only) 70.00 **st.**

VAUXHALL Tynemouth Rd ℰ 257 0346

TYWYN Gwynedd 403 H 26 – ☎ 0654.
♦London 234 – Dolgellau 19 – Shrewsbury 72.

   ⌂   **Riverslea,** Aberdovey Rd, LL36 9HS, S : 1 ½ m. on A 493 ℰ 711615, ≼, ☞ – **Ⓟ**. ⑤
       M 10.00 **st.** – **4 rm** ⊇ 19.00/30.00 **st.**

UCKFIELD East Sussex 404 U 31 – pop. 10 938 – ECD : Wednesday – ☎ 0825.
Envir. : Sheffield Park Gardens★ *AC*, W : 6 m.
⛳ Piltdown ℰ 722033, NW : 3 m. by A 272.
♦London 45 – ♦Brighton 17 – Eastbourne 20 – Maidstone 34.

   🏨   **Horsted Place** ⑤, Little Horsted, TN22 5TS, S : 2 ½ m. by B 2102 and A 22 on A 26
       ℰ 75581, Telex 95548, Fax 75459, ≼, « Victorian gothic country house and gardens », ⓢ,
       ✗ – ▮ TV ☎ Ⓟ – ⚐ 25. ⓢ AE ① VISA. ⑤
       closed 1 to 7 January – **M** *(closed Saturday lunch)* 15.00/25.00 **t.** and a la carte 30.90/39.20 **t.**
       ₰ 5.90 – **3 rm** ⊇ 110.00/150.00 **t.**, **14 suites** 175.00/280.00 **t.** – SB (August-May) 195.00 **st.**

   🏠   **Hooke Hall** without rest., High St., TN22 1EN, ℰ 761578, Telex 95228, « Queen Anne town
       house », ☞ – TV ☎ Ⓟ. ⓢ VISA. ⑤
       closed 24 December-1 January – ⊇ 5.75 – **5 rm** 37.50/80.00 **st.**

   ✗   **Thai Fantasy,** Ringles Cross, TN22 1HB, N : 1 m. ℰ 3827, Thai rest., ☞ – ⑤ Ⓟ. ⓢ AE
       VISA
       closed Monday – **M** 16.00/20.00 **t.** and a la carte approx. 8.40 **t.** ₰ 3.00.

AUSTIN-ROVER 84-86 High St. ℰ 4255

UDIMORE East Sussex **404** V 31 – see Rye.

ULLINGSWICK Heref. and Worc. – pop. 261 – ⊠ ✪ 0432 Hereford.
◆London 134 – Hereford 12 – Shrewsbury 52 – Worcester 19.

⌂ **Steppes Country House** ⅋, HR1 3JG, ℰ 820424, « Converted farmhouse of 14C origins », ∰ – ⇠ rest ▥ ☎ ℗
   M (bar lunch)/dinner 17.50 **st.** ⑂ 2.95 – **5 rm** ⊑ 30.00/50.00 **st.** – SB (except Christmas and New Year) 60.00/80.00 **st.**

ULLSWATER Cumbria **402** L 20 – ⊠ Penrith – ✪ 076 84 Pooley Bridge.
See : Lake★ – Lowther Wildlife Park★ *AC*.
🛈 Main Car Park, Glenridding ℰ 085 32 (Glenridding) 414 – at Pooley Bridge, The Square ℰ 530 (summer only).
◆London 296 – ◆Carlisle 25 – Kendal 31 – Penrith 6.

   at Howtown SW : 4 m. of Pooley Bridge – ⊠ Penrith – ✪ 076 84 Pooley Bridge :
🏠 **Howtown** ⅋, CA10 2ND, ℰ 514, ≤, ∰ – ℗. ✗
   April-October – **M** (buffet lunch Monday to Saturday)/dinner 8.50 **t.** – **15 rm** ⊑ 23.25/46.50 **t.**

   at Pooley Bridge on B 5320 – ⊠ Penrith – ✪ 076 84 Pooley Bridge :
🏨 **Sharrow Bay Country House** ⅋, CA10 2LZ, S : 2 m. on Howtown Rd ℰ 86301, Fax 86349, ≤ lake and hills, « Lakeside setting, gardens, tasteful decor » – ⇠ rest ▥ ☎ ℗. ✗
   March-November – **M** (booking essential) 21.50/32.50 **st.** – **22 rm** ⊑ (dinner included) 75.00/220.00 **st.**, **6 suites** 170.00/220.00 **st.**

   at Watermillock on A 592 – ⊠ Penrith – ✪ 076 84 Pooley Bridge :
🏨 **Leeming House** (T.H.F.) ⅋, CA11 0JJ, on A 592 ℰ 86622, Telex 64111, Fax 86443, ≤, ∰, park – ▥ ☎ ℗. ◪ 🄰🄴 ⑩ **VISA**
   M (bar lunch Monday to Saturday)/dinner 27.00 **st.** and a la carte ⑂ 5.30 – ⊑ 7.60 – **25 rm** 60.00/103.00 **st.** – SB 55.00/76.00 **st.**
🏨 **Rampsbeck** ⅋, CA11 0LP, ℰ 442, ≤, ∰, park – ▥ ☎ ℗. ◪ **VISA**
   closed 6 January-mid February – **M** 30.00 **st.** and a la carte ⑂ 3.95 – **19 rm** ⊑ 30.00/80.00 **st.** – SB (except Christmas and Bank Holidays) 90.00/130.00 **st.**
🏠 **Old Church** ⅋, CA11 0JN, ℰ 86204, ≤ lake and hills, « Lakeside setting », ⅌, ∰ – ⇠ rest ☎ ℗. ✗
   March-November – **M** (lunch by arrangement, residents only)/dinner 19.50 **st.** ⑂ 5.50 – **10 rm** ⊑ (dinner included) 70.00/140.00 **st.**

ULVERSTON Cumbria **402** K 21 – pop. 11 976 – ECD : Wednesday – ✪ 0229.
Envir. : Furness Abbey★ (ruins 13C-15C) *AC*, SW : 6 ½ m.
🛈₁₈ Barrow, Rakesmoor, Hawcoat, ℰ 0229 (Barrow-in-Furness) 25444, SW : 7 m.
🛈 Coronation Hall, County Sq. ℰ 57120.
◆London 278 – Kendal 25 – Lancaster 36.

✗ **Bay Horse Inn**, Canal Foot, LA12 9EL, E : 1 ¼ m. ℰ 53972, ≤ – ⇠ ℗. ◪
   closed Sunday dinner, Monday and January-February – **M** (booking essential) 10.50 **t.** (lunch) and a la carte 14.55/18.30 **t.** ⑂ 4.50.

   at Lowick Green N : 5 m. by A 590 on A 5092 – ⊠ Ulverston – ✪ 022 986 Greenodd :
⚘ **Farmers Arms**, LA12 8DT, ℰ 861376 – ▥ ℗. ◪ 🄰🄴 **VISA**
   M a la carte 7.00/16.00 **t.** ⑂ 3.15 – **11 rm** ⊑ 22.00/40.00 **t.**

   at Spark Bridge N : 5 ½ m. by A 590 off A 5092 – ⊠ Ulverston – ✪ 022 985 Lowick Bridge :
🏠 **Bridgefield House** ⅋, LA12 8DA, NW : 1 m. on Nibthwaite Rd ℰ 239, ∰ – ⇠ rest ☎ ℗. ◪
   M (dinner only) (booking essential) 18.50 **t.** – **5 rm** ⊑ 30.00/60.00 **t.**
FORD Argyle St. ℰ 53209   ⓦ ATS The Gill ℰ 53442

UMBERLEIGH Devon **403** I 31 – ✪ 0769 High Bickington.
◆London 215 – Exeter 33 – ◆Plymouth 59 – Taunton 47.
⚘ Rising Sun (B.C.B.), EX37 9DU, ℰ 60447, ⅌ – ▥ ☎ ℗
   6 rm.

UNDERBARROW Cumbria **402** L 21 – see Kendal.

UPLYME Devon **403** L 31 – see Lyme Regis.

UPPER ODDINGTON Glos. – see Stow-on-the-Wold.

UPPINGHAM Leics. **404** R 26 – pop. 2 761 – ECD : Thursday – ✆ 0572.

Envir. : Kirkby Hall★ (ruins 16C), SE : 8 m.

♦London 101 – ♦Leicester 19 – Northampton 28 – ♦Nottingham 35.

   Garden, 16 High St. West, LE15 9QD, ✆ 822352, Fax 821156, 🐎 – ⤞ rest 📺 ☎. 🔃 AE VISA. 🍴
   M *(closed Sunday dinner)* (bar lunch)/dinner 11.75 t. 🍷 3.25 – **12 rm** �🍽 35.00/45.00 t.

   Rutland House without rest., 61 High St., East, LE15 9PY, ✆ 822497, 🐎 – 📺
   4 rm ⍾ 23.00/33.00 t.

   Lake Isle with rm, 16 High St., East, LE15 9PZ, ✆ 822951, Fax 822951, 🐎 – 📺 🚗. 🔃 AE ⓞ VISA
   M *(closed Monday lunch, Sunday dinner and Bank Holidays)* 11.25/19.50 t. 🍷 4.75 – **10 rm** ⍾ 38.00/60.00 st.

   at Lyddington SE : 2 m. by A 6003 – ✉ ✆ 0572 Uppingham :

   Marquess of Exeter (Best Western) ⑤, 52 Main St., LE15 9LT, ✆ 822477, Fax 821343 –
   📺 ☎ Ⓟ. 🔃 AE ⓞ VISA. 🍴
   M *(closed Saturday lunch and Sunday dinner)* 11.95 t. and a la carte 🍷 4.25 – **17 rm** ⍾ 54.00/74.00 t. – SB (weekends only) 72.00/82.00 st.

UPTON ST. LEONARDS Glos. – see Gloucester.

UPTON SNODSBURY Heref. and Worc. **403** **404** N 27 – see Worcester.

UPTON UPON SEVERN Heref. and Worc. **403** **404** N 27 – pop. 1 537 – ECD : Thursday – ✆ 068 46.

🚩 The Pepperpot, Church St. ✆ 4200 (summer only).

♦London 116 – Hereford 25 – Stratford-upon-Avon 29 – Worcester 11.

   White Lion, High St., WR8 0HJ, ✆ 2551 – 📺 ☎ Ⓟ. 🔃 AE ⓞ VISA
   closed 25 and 26 December – **M** 12.75 t. and a la carte 🍷 4.00 – ⍾ 5.50 – **10 rm** 42.00/57.00 t. – SB 70.00/72.00 st.

   Star, High St., WR8 0HQ, ✆ 2300 – 📺 ☎. 🔃 VISA. 🍴
   M a la carte 7.20/12.50 st. 🍷 2.75 – **16 rm** ⍾ 30.00/60.00 st. – SB (weekends only) 48.00 st.

   Pool House, Hanley Rd, WR8 0PA, NW : ½ m. on B 4211 ✆ 2151, ≼, ⅏, 🐎 – ⤞ rm Ⓟ.
   🔃 VISA. 🍴
   closed Christmas – **M** 9.00 st. 🍷 3.50 – **9 rm** ⍾ 26.00/45.00 t. – SB (except summer) 54.00/73.00 st.

USK (BRYNBUGA) Gwent **403** L 28 – pop. 1 783 – ECD : Wednesday – ✆ 029 13.

See : Valley★.

🏌 at Pontypool ✆ 049 55 (Pontypool) 3655, W : 7 m.

♦London 144 – ♦Bristol 30 – Gloucester 39 – Newport 10.

   Glen-yr-Afon House, Pontypool Rd, NP5 1SY, ✆ 2302, 🐎 – ⤞ rest 📺 ☎ Ⓟ. 🔃 VISA
   M (bar lunch)/dinner 18.00 st. and a la carte 🍷 3.60 – **16 rm** ⍾ 26.00/40.00 s. – SB (except summer) (weekends only) 55.00 st.

   at Llangybi S : 2 ½ m. on Llangybi rd – ✉ Usk – ✆ 063 349 Tredunnock :

   Cwrt Bleddyn, NP5 1PG, S : 1 m. ✆ 521, Fax 220, 🔲, 🐎, ⅏, squash – 📺 ☎ Ⓟ – 🛁.
   🔃 AE ⓞ VISA. 🍴
   M 16.95 t. and a la carte 14.85/29.85 t. 🍷 6.75 – **30 rm** ⍾ 58.50/105.00 t. – SB (weekends only) (except Christmas, New Year and Bank Holidays) 95.00/150.00 st.

UTTOXETER Staffs. **402** **403** **404** O 25 – pop. 10 008 – ECD : Thursday – ✆ 088 93 (4 and 5 fig.) or 0889 (6 fig.).

Envir. : Alton Towers (gardens★★) *AC*, NW : 7 ½ m.

♦London 145 – ♦Birmingham 33 – Derby 19 – Stafford 13 – ♦Stoke-on-Trent 16.

   White Hart, Carter St., ST14 8EU, ✆ 562437 – 📺 ☎ Ⓟ. 🔃 AE ⓞ VISA
   M a la carte 8.95/13.00 t. – **26 rm** ⍾ 42.00/46.00 t. – SB (weekends only) 77.50 st.

   Travelodge without rest., Ashbourne Rd, ST14 5AA, junction A 50 and B 5030 ✆ 562043 –
   📺 ᬜ Ⓟ. 🔃 AE VISA
   32 rm 21.50/27.00 t.

FIAT Smithfield Rd ✆ 563838   ⓐ ATS Smithfield Rd ✆ 563848
FORD, ISUZU, VAUXHALL Derby Rd ✆ 562301

VELINDRE (FELINDRE FARCHOG) Dyfed **403** F 27 – see Newport (Dyfed).

VENN OTTERY Devon **403** K 31 – ✉ ✆ 0404 Ottery St. Mary.

♦London 209 – Exeter 11 – Sidmouth 5.

   Venn Ottery Barton ⑤, EX11 1RZ, ✆ 812733, ⅏, 🐎 – ⤞ rest Ⓟ. 🔃 VISA
   M 10.50 st. 🍷 3.00 – **16 rm** ⍾ 20.00/44.00 st.

 I.O.W. 403 404 Q 32 – see Wight (Isle of).

VERYAN Cornwall 403 F 33 The West Country G. – pop. 880 – ✉ ⊗ 0872 Truro.
See : Site★.
♦London 291 – St. Austell 13 – Truro 13.

   Nare ⤴, Carne Beach, TR2 5PF, SW : 1 ¼ m. ✆ 501279, Fax 501856, ⪡ Carne Bay,
   🏊 heated, 🚗, ✗ – 📺 ☎ 🅿 – 🔥 . 🆁 VISA ✾
   M (bar lunch Monday to Saturday)/dinner 17.00 **t.** and a la carte – **38 rm** ☲ 32.00/108.00 **t.**

   at Ruan High Lanes W : 1 ¼ m. on A 3078 – ✉ ⊗ 0872 Truro :

   Hundred House, TR2 5JR, ✆ 501336, 🚗 – ↣ rest 📺 🅿. 🆁 VISA
   March-November – **M** (bar lunch)/dinner 15.00 **st.** – **10 rm** ☲ 34.00/68.00 **st.**

VOWCHURCH Heref. and Worc. 403 L 27 – pop. 160 – ✉ Hereford – ⊗ 0981 Peterchurch.
♦London 144 – Brecon 27 – Hereford 11.

   Croft, HR2 0QE, E : ½ m. on B 4348 ✆ 550226, ⪡, 🚗 – ↣ 📺 🅿. ✾
   M 11.50 **t.** – **8 rm** ☲ 25.50/47.00 **t.**, **1 suite** – SB (winter only) 50.00 **st.**

WADDESDON Bucks. 404 R 28 – pop. 1 644 – ECD : Thursday – ⊗ 029 665.
See : Waddesdon Manor (Rothschild Collection★★★) *AC.*
♦London 52 – Aylesbury 6 – ♦Birmingham 66 – ♦Oxford 25.

   Hotels see : Aylesbury E : 5 m.

WADESMILL Herts. – see Ware.

WADHURST East Sussex 404 U 30 – pop. 3 643 – ECD : Wednesday – ⊗ 089 288.
♦ London 44 – Hastings 21 – Maidstone 24 – Royal Tunbridge Wells 6.

   Spindlewood ⤴, Wallcrouch, TN5 7JG, SE : 2 ¼ m. on B 2099 ✆ 0580 (Ticehurst) 200430,
   ⪡, 🚗 – 📺 ☎ 🅿. 🆁 AE VISA ✾
   closed 4 days at Christmas – **M** *(closed Bank Holiday lunch)* 14.00 **t.** (dinner) and a la carte
   🍷 3.10 – **9 rm** ☲ 42.00/70.00 **t.** – SB (mid October-May) 56.00/80.00 **st.**

   Newbarn ⤴ without rest., Wards Lane, TN5 6HP, E : 3 m. by B 2099 ✆ 2042, ⪡ Bewl
   Water and countryside, 🚗 – ↣ 🅿
   4 rm ☲ 16.00/40.00 **st.**

   Kirkstone without rest., Mayfield Lane, TN5 6HX, ✆ 3204, 🚗 – 🅿
   3 rm ☲ 15.00/25.00 **st.**

FIAT Beech Hill ✆ 2126
FORD Cousley Wood ✆ 2375

VAUXHALL Sparrows Green ✆ 3157
VOLVO High St. ✆ 2128

WAKEFIELD West Yorks. 402 P 22 – pop. 74 764 – ECD : Wednesday – ⊗ 0924.
Envir. : Pontefract (castle★ : ruins 12C-13C) *AC,* E : 9 m – Nostell Priory★ E : 4 ½ m..
🏌 City of Wakefield, Lupset Park, Horbury Rd ✆ 374316, SW : 1 ¼ m. on A 642 – 🏌 Painthorpe
House, Painthorpe Lane ✆ 255083, near junction 39 on M 1.
🛈 Town Hall, Wood St. ✆ 370211 ext 7021/2 and 370700 (evenings and weekends).
♦London 188 – ♦Leeds 9 – ♦Manchester 38 – ♦Sheffield 23.

   Cedar Court, Denby Dale Rd., Calder Grove, WF4 3QZ, SW : 3 m. on A 636 ✆ 276310,
   Telex 557647, Fax 280221 – 🛗 ↣ rm 🍽 📺 ☎ 🅿 – 🔥 500. 🆁 AE ① VISA
   M 10.00/11.00 **t.** and a la carte 🍷 3.50 – **146 rm** ☲ 70.00/97.00 **t.**, **5 suites** 110.00/121.00 **t.** –
   SB (weekends only) 73.50/83.50 **st.**

   Post House (T.H.F.), Queen's Drive, Ossett, WF5 9BE, W : 2 ½ m. on A 638 ✆ 276388,
   Telex 55407, Fax 280277 – 🛗 ↣ rm 🍽 rest 📺 ☎ 🅿 – 🔥 150. 🆁 AE ① VISA
   M *(closed Saturday lunch)* 9.50/14.00 **st.** and a la carte 🍷 4.30 – ☲ 7.50 – **99 rm** 62.00/80.00 **st.**
   – SB 52.00/74.00 **st.**

   Swallow (Swallow), Queen St., WF1 1JU, ✆ 372111, Telex 557464, Fax 383648 – 🛗 ↣ rm
   📺 ☎ 🅿 – 🔥 150. 🆁 AE ① VISA
   M 6.95/10.50 **st.** and a la carte 🍷 4.25 – **63 rm** ☲ 52.00/70.00 **st.** – SB (weekends
   only) 70.00 **st.**

AUSTIN-ROVER Ings Rd ✆ 370100
BMW Ings Rd ✆ 363796
CITROEN Stanley Rd ✆ 291300
FORD Barnsley Rd ✆ 290290
HONDA Westgate ✆ 366261

LANCIA 509 Leeds Rd ✆ 0532 (Leeds) 822254
PEUGEOT-TALBOT Barnsley Rd ✆ 255904
VAUXHALL Doncaster Rd ✆ 376771

⑩ ATS Bethel Pl., Thornes Lane ✆ 371638

WALBERTON West Sussex – see Arundel.

WALKINGTON Humberside 402 S 22 – see Kingston-upon-Hull.

WALLASEY Merseyside **402 403** K 23 – pop. 62 465 – ✆ 051 Liverpool.

☁ Warren, Grove Rd ✆ 691 1024.

⛴ to Liverpool (Merseyside Transport) frequent services daily (7-8 mn).

♦London 226 – Birkenhead 3.5 – ♦Liverpool 4.

WALLINGFORD Oxon. **403 404** Q 29 – pop. 9 041 – ECD : Wednesday – ✆ 0491.

🛈 9 St. Martin's St. ✆ 35351 ext. 3810.

♦London 54 – ♦Oxford 12 – Reading 16.

   🏨 George (Mt. Charlotte), 84 High St., OX10 0BS, ✆ 36665, Telex 847468, Fax 25359 – ⇔ rm
      📺 ☎ 🅿 – 🛅 100
      39 rm.

      at North Stoke S : 2 ¾ m. by A 4130 and A 4074 on B 4009 – ✉ ✆ 0491 Wallingford :

   🏨 Springs ⚘, Wallingford Rd, OX9 6BE, ✆ 36687, Telex 849794, Fax 36877, ≤, ⛱ heated, 🐎,
      park, ⚒ – 📺 ☎ 🅿 – 🛅 65
      35 rm, 3 suites.

AUSTIN-ROVER 8-10 Watlington Rd, Benson, Nr   FORD 43 High St. ✆ 38424
Wallingford ✆ 38308   PEUGEOT-TALBOT Wood St. ✆ 36017

WALLSEND Tyne and Wear **401 402** P 18 – see Newcastle-upon-Tyne.

WALSALL West Midlands **403 404** O 26 – pop. 177 923 – ECD : Thursday – ✆ 0922.

☁ Calderfields, Aldridge Rd ✆ 32243, N : 1 m. CT.

♦London 126 – ♦Birmingham 9 – ♦Coventry 29 – Shrewsbury 36.

Plan of enlarged area : see Birmingham pp. 2 and 3

   🏨 **Crest** (Crest), Birmingham Rd, WS5 3AB, SE : 1 ½ m. on A 34 ✆ 33555, Telex 335479, Fax
      612034 – 🛗 ⇔ rm 🍽 rest 📺 ☎ ♿ 🅿 – 🛅 50. 🅢 AE ⑩ VISA   CT e
      M (*closed Saturday lunch*) 7.95/11.95 **st.** and a la carte ₿4.25 – ⛾ 7.35 – **101 rm**
      67.20/105.00 **st.** – SB (weekends only) 72.00/76.00 **st.**

   🏨 **Friendly Lodge,** 20 Wolverhampton Rd West, Bentley, WS2 0BS, W : 2 ½ m. on A 454 at
      junction 10, M 6 ✆ 724444, Telex 334854, Fax 723148, 🅢 – ⇔ rm 📺 ☎ ♿ 🅿 – 🛅 180. 🅢
      AE ⑩ VISA   BT a
      M (*closed Saturday lunch*) 9.25/11.25 **st.** and a la carte – ⛾ 4.75 – **120 rm** 49.50/75.00 **st.** –
      SB (weekends only) 59.00 **st.**

      at Walsall Wood NE : 3 ½ m. on A 461 – CT – ✉ Walsall – ✆ 0543 Brownhills :

   🏨 **Barons Court** (Best Western), Walsall Rd, WS9 9AH, ✆ 452020, Telex 333061, Fax 361276,
      🅢 – 🛗 ⇔ rm 📺 ☎ 🅿 – 🛅 110. 🅢 AE ⑩ VISA
      M 7.95/12.95 **t.** and a la carte ₿3.95 – **100 rm** ⛾ 49.00/72.00 **t.** – SB (weekends only)
      74.00/82.00 **st.**

FORD Wolverhampton St. ✆ 721212   TOYOTA Lichfield Rd, Willenhall ✆ 0922 (Bloxwich)
FORD Wolverhampton Rd ✆ 402000   493000
LADA 152 Green Lane ✆ 645347   VAUXHALL-OPEL Broadway ✆ 720500
PEUGEOT-TALBOT Paddock Lane, off Charlotte St.
✆ 721188   🅖 ATS Leamore Trading Est., Fryers Rd ✆ 478631
RENAULT Day St. ✆ 720202

WALSGRAVE ON SOWE West Midlands – see Coventry.

WALTHAM ABBEY Essex **404** U 28 – pop. 16 498 – ✆ 0992 Lea Valley.

☁ Royal Epping Forest, Chingford ✆ 01 (London) 529 2195.

♦London 15 – ♦Cambridge 44 – ♦Ipswich 66 – Luton 30 – Southend-on-Sea 35.

   🏨 **Swallow** (Swallow), Old Shire Lane, EN9 3LX, SE : 1 ½ m. on A 121 ✆ 717170, Telex
      916596, Fax 711841, 🅢 – ⇔ rm 🍽 📺 ☎ ♿ 🅿 – 🛅 400. 🅢 AE ⑩ VISA
      M 14.00/18.50 **st.** and a la carte ₿4.25 – **163 rm** ⛾ 80.00/120.00 **st.** – SB (week-
      ends only) 88.00 **st.**

WALTON-ON-THAMES Surrey **404** S 29 – ECD : Wednesday – ✉ ✆ 0932.

🛈 Town Hall, New Zealand Av. ✆ 228844.

♦London 23 – ♦Brighton 54 – ♦Portsmouth 61 – ♦Southampton 65.

Plan : see Greater London (South-West)

   🏨 **Ashley Park,** Ashley Park Rd, KT12 1JP, ✆ 220196, Fax 248721 – 📺 ☎ 🅿 – 🛅 60. 🅢 AE
      ⑩ VISA. ⚒
      M (*closed Sunday dinner*) (bar lunch)/dinner a la carte 8.20/12.65 **st.** ₿4.00 – **28 rm**
      ⛾ 52.00/60.00 **st.**

   XX **La Malmaison,** 17 Queens Rd, Hersham, KT12 5ND, ✆ 227412, French rest. – 🅢 ⑩
      VISA
      closed Saturday lunch and Sunday – M 12.50 **t.** (lunch) and a la carte 19.40/23.30 **t.** ₿3.60.

♦London 19 – ♦Brighton 38.

XX   Ebenezer Cottage, 36 Walton St., KT20 7RT, ✆ 813166, « 17C cottage » – ✖.

WANBOROUGH Wilts. 403 404 O 29 – see Swindon.

WANSFORD Cambs. 404 S 26 – see Peterborough.

WANTAGE Oxon. 403 404 P 29 – pop. 9 708 – ECD : Thursday – ✆ 023 57.

Envir. : White Horse ≤★.

♦London 75 – ♦Bristol 58 – ♦Oxford 15 – Reading 25.

   🏠   Bear, Market Pl., OX12 8AB, ✆ 66366, Group Telex 41363 – 🛗 TV ☎
   34 rm.

   X   Peking Dynasty, Newbury St., OX12 8BS, ✆ 2517, Chinese (Peking) rest.

AUSTIN-ROVER Wallingford St. ✆ 3355   ATS 76 Grove St. ✆ 66466
SAAB East Hanney ✆ 023 587 (West Hanney) 257
VW-AUDI Grove Rd ✆ 65511

WARE Herts. 404 T 28 – pop. 15 344 – ECD : Thursday – ✆ 0920.

♦London 24 – ♦Cambridge 30 – Luton 22.

   🏨   **Ware Moat House** (Q.M.H.), Baldock St., SG12 9DR, N : ½ m. on A 1170 ✆ 465011, Telex
   817417, Fax 468016 – 🛗 ✖ rm TV ☎ P – 🔥 140. 🅰 AE ⓪ VISA
   closed 25 to 31 December – **M** *(closed Saturday lunch)* 11.00/13.75 **t.** and a la carte 🍷 4.25 –
   50 rm 🍽 65.00/75.00 **t.**

      at Wadesmill N : 2 ¼ m. on A 10 – ✉ ✆ 0920 Ware :

   🏠   **Feathers Inn** (B.C.B.), SG1 2ON, ✆ 462606, 🍴 – TV ☎ P – 🔥 70. 🅰 AE ⓪ VISA. ✖
   M (carving rest.) 9.75 **st.** 🍷 3.50 – **10 rm** 🍽 41.00/55.00 **st.**

      at Cold Christmas NE : 3 ¼ m. by A 10 – ✉ ✆ 0920 Ware :

   XX   **Fabdens Park** 🦢 with rm, SG12 0UE, ✆ 463484, ≤, « Attractively furnished 15C house »,
   🍴, park – TV ☎ P
   closed February and September – **M** *(closed Sunday and Monday)* (booking essential)
   (dinner only)/27.50 **t.** – **4 rm** 🍽 65.00/75.00 **st.**

WAREHAM Dorset 403 404 N 31 The West Country G. – pop. 2 771 – ECD : Wednesday –
✆ 092 95 (4 and 5 fig.) or 0929 (6 fig.).

See : Site★ – St. Martin's Church★★.

Envir. : Blue Pool★*AC*, S : 3 m. on A 351 – Smedmore★*AC*, S : 7 m. by A 351 – Bovington : Tank
Museum★*AC*, W : 7 m. on A 352 – Lulworth Cove★, SW : 11 m. by A 352.

🏌 Lakey Hill, Hyde ✆ 471776.

🛈 Town Hall, East St. ✆ 2740.

♦London 123 – Bournemouth 13 – Weymouth 19.

   🏨   **Priory** 🦢, Church Green, BH20 4ND, ✆ 551666, Telex 41143, « Tastefully renovated part
   16C priory with gardens », 🍴 – TV ☎ P. 🅰 AE ⓪ VISA. ✖
   M 12.95/21.00 **t.** and a la carte 🍷 3.50 – **17 rm** 🍽 45.00/115.00 **t.**, **2 suites** 150.00 **t.** –
   SB (October-April) (except Bank Holidays) 122.00/170.50 **st.**

   🏠   **Kemps Country House**, East Stoke, BH20 6AL, W : 2 ¾ m. on A 352 ✆ 0929 (Bin-
   don Abbey) 462563, 🍴 – ✖ rest TV ☎ P. 🅰 AE ⓪ VISA. ✖
   closed 26 to 29 December – **M** 7.50/13.95 **t.** and a la carte – **15 rm** 🍽 25.00/64.00 **t.** –
   SB 65.00/83.00 **st.**

   🏠   **Worgret Manor**, Worgret Rd, BH20 6AB, W : 1 m. on A 352 ✆ 2957, 🍴 – TV P. 🅰 AE
   ⓪ VISA
   M 7.50/12.00 **t.** and a la carte – **9 rm** 🍽 26.00/46.00 **t.** – SB (October-June) 56.00/65.00 **st.**

      at Stoborough S : ½ m. on A 351 – ✉ ✆ 092 95 Wareham :

   🏨   **Springfield Country**, Grange Rd, BH20 5AL, ✆ 2177, Fax 51862, 🏊 heated, 🍴, ✖ – 🛗
   TV ☎ P – 🔥 25. 🅰 AE VISA
   M *(closed Sunday dinner)* (bar lunch)/dinner 12.00 **t.** and a la carte 🍷 3.50 – **32 rm**
   🍽 53.00/82.00 **t.** – SB (except May-June and October-December) 79.00/102.00 **st.**

WARMINSTER Wilts. 403 404 N 30 The West Country G. – pop. 14 826 – ECD : Wednesday –
✆ 0985.

Envir. : Longleat House★★★*AC* SW : 6 m. – Bratton Castle (≤★★), NE : 6 m – Westbury Hill
(White Horse★, ≤★), N : 6 m..

🏌 West Wiltshire, Elm Hill ✆ 212110.

🛈 Library, Three Horseshoes Mall ✆ 218548.

♦London 111 – ♦Bristol 29 – Exeter 74 – ♦Southampton 47.

🏨 **Bishopstrow House** ⚘, Boreham Rd, BA12 9HH, SE : 1 ½ m. on B 3414 𝒫 212312, Telex 444829, Fax 216769, ≼, « Tastefully furnished country house », ⌁ heated, ▨, ⚲, ⚞, park, ✗ – 📺 ☎ 🅿. ⤢ 𝔸𝔼 ⓞ 𝐕𝐈𝐒𝐀
M 12.50/25.00 **t.** and a la carte ▮ 5.50 – ⊡ 5.50 – **25 rm** 73.00/150.00 t., **3 suites** 195.00/ 240.00 **t.**

🏠 **Granada Lodge** without rest., BA12 8PF, NW : 1 m. by B 3414 on A 36 𝒫 219539, Fax 214380 – ↳✗ 📺 ♿ 🅿. ⤢ 𝔸𝔼 ⓞ 𝐕𝐈𝐒𝐀. ⚟
⊡ 2.85 – **32 rm** 24.50/27.50 **st.**

🏠 **Old Bell**, 42 Market Pl., BA12 9AN, 𝒫 216611, Fax 217111 – 📺 ☎ 🅿. ⤢ 𝔸𝔼 𝐕𝐈𝐒𝐀
M (grill rest.) a la carte 7.90/14.70 **t.** ▮ 3.00 – **24 rm** ⊡ 31.00/50.00 **t.** – SB (weekends only) (winter only) 80.00 **st.**

at Corton SE : 5 ¼ m. by A 36 off B 3095 – ✉ ☏ 0985 Warminster :

✗ **Dove Inn**, BA12 0SZ, 𝒫 50378, ⚞ – 🅿. ⤢ 𝐕𝐈𝐒𝐀
closed Sunday dinner, Monday, first week October and 2 weeks January – **M** 12.00 **st.** and a la carte 15.00/23.00 **st.** ▮ 4.00.

AUDI-VW 36 Victoria Rd 𝒫 212893
AUSTIN-ROVER George St. 𝒫 212808
FORD Boreham Rd 𝒫 214777

MERCEDES-BENZ Corsley Heath 𝒫 037 388 (Chapmanslade) 383
VOLVO Fairfield Rd 𝒫 213525

WARREN ROW Berks. – see Knowl Hill.

WARREN STREET Kent – ✉ ☏ 0622 Maidstone.
♦London 51 – Folkestone 28 – Maidstone 12.

⌂ **Harrow Inn**, ME17 2ED, 𝒫 858727, ⚞ – ☎ 🅿. ⤢ 𝐕𝐈𝐒𝐀. ⚟
M a la carte 13.45/24.25 **st.** – **7 rm** ⊡ 30.00/48.00 **st.** – SB (weekends only) 36.90/54.00 **st.**

WARRINGTON Cheshire 402 403 404 M 23 – pop. 81 366 – ECD : Thursday – ☏ 0925.
See : St. Elphin's Church (chancel★ 14C).
🏌18 Hill Warren 𝒫 65431, S : 3 m. – 🏌18 Walton Hall, Warrington Rd 𝒫 630619, S : 2 m. – 🏌18 Kelvin Close, Birchwood 𝒫 0925 (Padgate) 818819.
🛈 80 Sankey St. 𝒫 36501.
♦London 195 – Chester 20 – ♦Liverpool 18 – ♦Manchester 21 – Preston 28.

🏨 **Garden Court Holiday Inn** (Holiday Inn), Woolston Grange Av., Woolston, WA1 4PX, E : 3 ¼ m. by A 57 at junction with M 6 𝒫 838779, Fax 838859 – ▯ ▤ rest 📺 ☎ ♿ 🅿
100 rm.

🏨 **Fir Grove**, Knutsford Old Rd, WA4 2LD, SE : 2 m. by A 50 𝒫 67471, Telex 628117, Fax 601092 – 📺 ☎ 🅿 – ⚗ 150. ⤢ 𝔸𝔼 ⓞ 𝐕𝐈𝐒𝐀
M 9.95 **st.** and a la carte ▮ 3.30 – **40 rm** ⊡ 48.00/68.00 **st.**

at Stretton S : 3 ½ m. by A 49 on B 5356 – ✉ Warrington – ☏ 092 573 Norcott Brook :

🏠 **Old Vicarage**, Stretton Rd, WA4 4NS, 𝒫 706, ⚞ – ▯ 📺 ☎ 🅿. ⤢ 𝔸𝔼 𝐕𝐈𝐒𝐀
M 8.75/12.50 **t.** and a la carte ▮ 3.80 – **30 rm** ⊡ 50.00/70.00 **t.** – SB (weekends only) 60.00 **st.**

AUSTIN-ROVER Winwick St. 𝒫 50011
BMW Farrell St. 𝒫 35987
FORD Winwick Rd 𝒫 51111

HYUNDAI 194-196 Knutsford Rd 𝒫 68444

🛞 ATS Grange Av., Latchford 𝒫 32613/4

WARWICK Warw. 403 404 P 27 – pop. 21 701 – ECD : Thursday – ☏ 0926.
See : Castle★★ (14C) *AC* Y – St. Mary's Church★ (12C-18C) Y A – Lord Leycester's Hospital★ Y B.
🏌9 The Racecourse 𝒫 494316 Y.
🛈 The Court House, Jury St. 𝒫 492212.
♦London 96 – ♦Birmingham 20 – ♦Coventry 11 – ♦Oxford 43.

Plan on next page

🏨 Westgate Arms, 3 Old Bowling Green St., CV34 4DD, 𝒫 492362, ⚞ – 📺 ☎ 🅿. ⚟ Y u
10 rm.

⌂ **Park Cottage** without rest., 113 West St., CV34 6AH, 𝒫 410319 – 📺 ☎ 🅿. ⤢ 𝔸𝔼 ⓞ 𝐕𝐈𝐒𝐀 ⚟ Y e
closed Christmas-New Year – **4 rm** ⊡ 35.00/48.00 **st.**

✗✗ **Randolph's**, 19-21 Coten End, CV34 4NT, 𝒫 491292 – ⤢ 𝔸𝔼 𝐕𝐈𝐒𝐀 Y i
closed Sunday, Monday, 2 weeks May, 1 week September and 24 to 31 December – **M** (dinner only) (booking essential) a la carte 27.00 **t.** and a la carte 23.00 **t.** ▮ 6.00.

at Barford S : 4 ½ m. on A 429 – Z – ✉ ☏ 0926 Warwick :

🏠 **Glebe** ⚘, Church St., CV35 8BS, on B 4462 𝒫 624218, Fax 624625, ⚞ – 📺 ☎ 🅿. ⤢ 𝔸𝔼 ⓞ 𝐕𝐈𝐒𝐀 ⚟
M 12.00/22.00 **t.** ▮ 4.00 – **14 rm** ⊡ 46.00/67.00 **t.** – SB (weekends only) 96.00 **st.**

WARWICK
ROYAL LEAMINGTON SPA

High Street . . . . Y 23
Jury Street . . . . Y
Market Place . . . . Y 29
Smith Street . . . . Y
Swan Street . . . . Y 46

Birmingham Road . . . . Z 7
Bowling Green Street . . . . Y 9
Brook Street . . . . Y 12
Butts (The) . . . . Y 13
Castle Hill . . . . Y 15
Church Street . . . . Y 17
Lakin Road . . . . Y 25
Linen Street . . . . Y 26
North Rock . . . . Y 32
Old Square . . . . Y 35
Old Warwick Road . . . . Z 36
Radford Road . . . . Z 39
St. John's Road . . . . Z 42
St. Nicholas Church Street . . . . . Y 43
Theatre Street . . . . Y 48
West Street . . . . Y 50

*Les plans de villes
sont disposés le Nord en haut.*

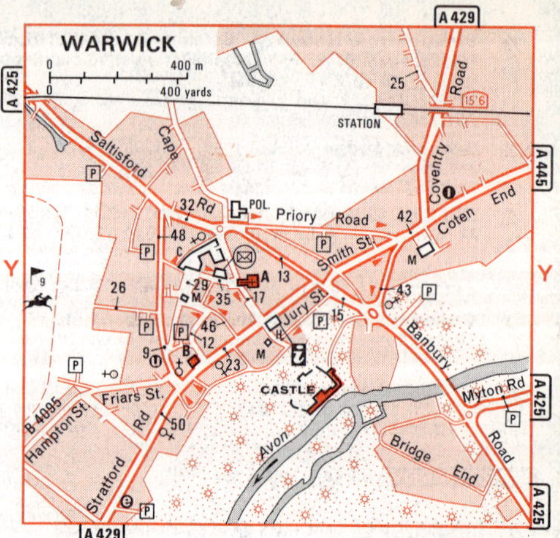

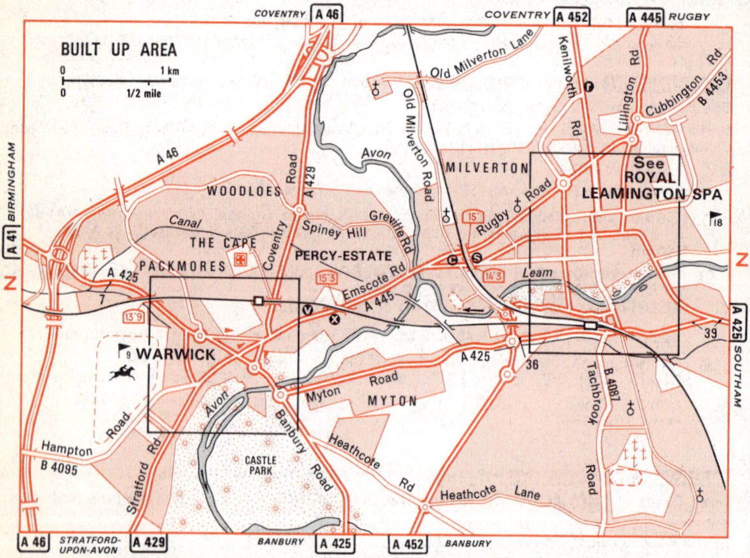

BUILT UP AREA

at Longbridge SW : 2 m. on A 429 – Z – ✉ ☎ 0926 Warwick :

Hilton National (Hilton), Stratford Rd, CV34 6RE, junction of A 429, A 46 and A 41 ℰ 499555, Telex 312468, Fax 410020, ☒ – ☷ ⇌ rm TV ☎ ⅙ P – ⟐ 200. ☒ AE ⑩ VISA
M 11.50/15.95 st. and a la carte ↥ 4.00 – ⊷ 7.95 – **150 rm** 71.00/92.00 st., **1 suite** 100.00/130.00 st. – SB (weekends only) 99.90/109.90 st.

at Sherbourne SW : 2 ¾ m. by A 429 – Z – ✉ ☎ 0926 Warwick :

Old Rectory, Vicarage Lane, CV35 8AB, at junction with A 46 ℰ 624562, ⇌ – TV P
closed 24 to 31 December – **M** (by arrangement) – **8 rm** ⊷ 20.00/38.00 s.

at Hatton NW : 3 m. on A 41 – Z – ✉ Warwick – ☎ 0926 Haseley Knob :

Northleigh House ⇖, Five Ways Rd, CV35 7HZ, NW : 3 m. by A 41, turning left at roundabout with A 4177 ℰ 484203, ⇌ – ⇌ TV P
closed 17 December-5 January – **M** (by arrangement) – **5 rm** ⊷ 24.00/40.00 st.

BMW Heathcote Lane ℰ 452288
FIAT Wharf St. ℰ 496231

PORSCHE Birmingham Rd ℰ 491731
VOLVO Nelson Lane ℰ 400642

WASDALE HEAD Cumbria **402** K 20 – ✉ Gosforth – ✆ 09406 Wasdale.

♦London 324 – Kendal 72 – Workington 30.

  🏠 Wasdale Head Inn ⚞, CA20 1EX, ℰ 229, ≼ Wasdale Head – ☎ ℗ **10 rm**.

WASHINGBOROUGH Lincs. **402 404** S 24 – see Lincoln.

WASHINGTON Tyne and Wear **401 402** P 19 – pop. 48 856 – ECD : Wednesday – ✉ ✆ 091 Tyneside.

🏌 Stone Cellar Rd ℰ 417 8346.

♦London 278 – Durham 13 – ♦Middlesbrough 32 – ♦Newcastle-upon-Tyne 7.

  🏨 **Washington Moat House** (Q.M.H.), Stone Cellar Rd, District 12, NE37 1PH, ℰ 417 2626, Telex 537143, Fax 415 1166, ⬚, 🏌, squash – ⇥ rm 📺 ☎ ℗ – 🛦 180. ⚞ 🆀 ⓞ 💳
    M 12.25 **st.** and a la carte – � 6.75 – **106 rm** 37.00/75.00 **st.** – SB (weekends only) 94.00 **st.**

  🏨 **Post House** (T.H.F.), Emerson, District 5, NE37 1LB, junction A 1 (M) and A 195 ℰ 416 2264, Telex 537574, Fax 415 3371 – |≋| ⇥ rm 📺 ☎ ℗ – 🛦 100. ⚞ 🆀 ⓞ 💳
    M 11.10/14.10 **st.** and a la carte ♪ 3.95 – ⊻ 7.00 – **138 rm** 64.00/75.00 **st.** – SB (weekends only) 76.00/80.00 **st.**

WASHINGTON SERVICE AREA Tyne and Wear – ✉ Washington – ✆ 091 Tyneside

  🏠 **Granada Lodge** without rest., DH3 2SJ, on A 1 (M) ℰ 410 3436 – 📺 ⅙ ℗ **35 rm**.

ARG Village Lane ℰ 415 0066

FORD Parsons Rd ℰ 4167700

WATCHET Somerset **403** J 30 The West Country G. – pop. 3 055 – ECD : Wednesday – ✆ 0984.

Envir. : Cleeve Abbey★★*AC*, SW : 2 m.

♦London 180 – ♦Bristol 57 – Taunton 18.

  🏠 **Downfield**, 16 St. Decuman's Rd, TA23 0HR, ℰ 31267, 🚗 – 📺 ☎ ℗. ⚞ 🆀 ⓞ 💳
    M 6.00/7.00 **t.** and a la carte ♪ 2.00 – **8 rm** ⊻ 28.75/34.50 **t.** – SB 47.05/51.05 **st.**

WATERHEAD Cumbria **402** L 20 – see Ambleside.

WATERHOUSES Staffs. **402 403 404** O 24 – pop. 1 018 – ✉ Stoke-on-Trent – ✆ 0538.

♦London 115 – ♦Birmingham 63 – Derby 23 – ♦Manchester 39 – ♦Stoke-on-Trent 17.

  🏠 **Croft House Farm** ⚞, Waterfall, ST10 3HZ, N : 1 m. by A 523 ℰ 308553, 🚗 – ⇥ rest 📺 ℗. ⋇
    M 16.00 **st.** – **6 rm** ⊻ 15.50/28.00 **st.** – SB 43.00/46.00 **st.**

  XX **Old Beams** with rm, Leek Rd, ST10 3HW, ℰ 308254, 🚗 – 📺 ℗. ⚞ 🆀 ⓞ 💳. ⋇
    closed 14-31 January – **M** *(closed Saturday lunch, Sunday dinner and Tuesday)* (booking essential) 10.95/17.50 **t.** and a la carte 17.75/26.00 **t.** ♪ 5.25 – **6 rm** 45.00/75.00 **t.**

WATERINGBURY Kent **404** V 30 – see Maidstone.

WATERMILLOCK Cumbria **402** L 20 – see Ullswater.

WATERROW Somerset – see Wiveliscombe.

WATFORD Herts. **404** S 29 – pop. 109 503 – ECD : Wednesday – ✆ 0923.

♦London 21 – Aylesbury 23.

Plan : see Greater London (North-West)

  🏨 **Hilton National** (Hilton), Elton Way, WD2 8HA, Watford By-Pass, E : 3 ½ m. on A 41 at junction A 4008 ℰ 35881, Telex 923422, Fax 220836 – |≋| ⇥ rm 📺 ☎ ℗ – 🛦 500. ⚞ 🆀 ⓞ 💳
    BT e
    M *(closed Saturday lunch)* (carving rest.) – ⊻ 7.95 – **169 rm** 75.00/90.00 **t.**, **1 suite** 150.00 **t.**

  🏨 **Dean Park** (Q.M.H.), 30-40 St. Albans Rd, WD1 1RN, ℰ 229212, Telex 8813610, Fax 54638 – |≋| ⇥ rest 📺 ☎ ℗ – 🛦 250. ⚞ 🆀 ⓞ 💳. ⋇
    AT c
    closed 26 December-30 January – **M** *(closed Saturday lunch and Bank Holidays)* 12.50/15.00 **t.** and a la carte ♪ 4.00 – **90 rm** ⊻ 70.00/95.00 **t.** – SB (weekends only) 43.00 **st.**

  XX **Flower Drum**, 16 Market St., WD1 7AD, ℰ 226711, Chinese (Szechuan, Peking) rest. – ▤
    AT a

AUDI-VW 68 Chalk Hill ℰ 55055
FORD 201 High St. ℰ 37211
HONDA, MERCEDES-BENZ High Rd at Bushey Heath ℰ 01 (London) 950 3311
PEUGEOT-TALBOT Aldenham ℰ 852177

VAUXHALL 83-89 High Rd ℰ 01 (London) 950 6146
VAUXHALL-OPEL 329 St. Albans Rd ℰ 31716

Ⓜ ATS Lyon Way, Hatfield Rd, St. Albans ℰ 52314

WATH-IN-NIDDERDALE North Yorks. – see Pateley Bridge.

WATLINGTON Oxon. 403 404 Q 29 – pop. 1 943 – ✪ 049 161.
◆London 45 – ◆Oxford 20 – Reading 15.

   🏛 **Well House,** 34-40 High St., OX9 5PY, ✆ 3333, Fax 2025 – 📺 ☎ 🅿. ⟋ AE ⓪ *VISA*
   ⤨
   M *(closed Saturday lunch, Sunday dinner and Monday to non-residents)* 15.50 **st.** and a la
   carte ▯ 3.50 – ⥿ 3.00 – **9 rm** 30.00/60.00 **st.** – SB (weekends only) 80.00/110.00 **st.**

WDIG (GOODWICK) Dyfed – see Fishguard.

WEEDON BEC Northants. 403 404 Q 27 – pop. 2 361 – ECD : Wednesday – ✉ Northampton
– ✪ 0327 Daventry.
◆London 74 – ◆Coventry 18 – Northampton 8 – ◆Oxford 41.

   🏛 **Heart of England** (B.C.B.), Daventry Rd, NN7 4QD, ✆ 40335, ⇚ – 📺 ☎ 🅿. ⟋ AE ⓪
   VISA. ⤨
   M a la carte 6.00/8.00 **st.** ▯ 3.35 – **12 rm** ⥿ 31.00/48.00 **st.** – SB (weekends only)
   38.00/42.00 **st.**

WELLAND Heref. and Worc. 403 404 N 27 – see Great Malvern.

WELLINGBOROUGH Northants. 404 R 27 – pop. 38 598 – ECD : Thursday – ✪ 0933.
🛈 Library, Pebble Lane ✆ 228101.
◆London 73 – ◆Cambridge 43 – ◆Leicester 34 – Northampton 10.

   🏛 **Hind** (Q.M.H.), Sheep St., NN8 1BY, ✆ 222827, Fax 441921 – ⥺ rest 📺 ☎ 🅿 – ⚏ 80. ⟋
   AE ⓪ *VISA*
   M 7.35/9.50 **st.** and a la carte ▯ 2.70 – **34 rm** ⥿ 49.00/62.00 **st.**

   at Hinwick (Beds.) SE : 6 ½ m. by A 509 (via Wollaston) – ✉ – ✪ 0933 Wellingborough
   (Northants.) :

   XX **Flemish House,** NN9 7JE, ✆ 50012 – 🅿. ⟋ AE ⓪ *VISA*
   closed Sunday dinner and Monday – **M** 33.00 **t.** and a la carte 16.50/31.80 **t.**

AUSTIN-ROVER Finedon Rd ✆ 76651   SKODA Talbot Rd ✆ 223924

WELLINGTON HEATH Heref. and Worc. 403 404 M 27 – see Ledbury.

WELLS Somerset 403 404 M 30 The West Country G. – pop. 9 252 – ECD : Wednesday –
✪ 0749.
See : Site★★★ – Cathedral★★★ – Vicar's Close★ – Bishop's Palace★*AC* (≼★★ of east end of
cathedral).
Envir. : Wookey Hole★★*AC* (Caves★, Papermill★, Fairground collection★), NW : 2 m.
🏌18 East Horrington Rd ✆ 75005.
🛈 Town Hall, Market Pl. ✆ 72552 and 75987.
◆London 132 – ◆Bristol 20 – ◆Southampton 68 – Taunton 28.

   🏛 **Swan** (Best Western), 11 Sadler St., BA5 2RX, ✆ 78877, Telex 449658, Fax 77647 – 📺 ☎
   🅿 – ⚏ 60. ⟋ AE ⓪ *VISA*
   M 17.50 **t.** (dinner) and a la carte ▯ 4.50 – **32 rm** ⥿ 48.75/75.00 **t.** – SB (weekends only)
   85.00/90.00 **st.**

   ♟ **Star,** 14 High St., BA5 2SQ, ✆ 73055, Fax 72654 – 📺. ⟋ AE ⓪ *VISA*
   closed 25 December – **M** 5.95/10.95 **t.** and a la carte ▯ 3.50 – **16 rm** ⥿ 29.50/42.00 **t.**

   at Worth W : 2 ¾ m. by A 371 on B 3139 – ✪ 0749 Wells :

   ♟ **Worth House,** BA5 1LW, ✆ 72041, ⇚ – 🅿
   M 5.50/10.50 **st.** and a la carte ▯ 2.50 – **8 rm** ⥿ 19.00/38.00 **st.** – SB 43.00/53.00 **st.**

AUSTIN-ROVER, LAND-ROVER Glastonbury Rd ✆   CITROEN Long St., Croscombe ✆ 26601
72626   VAUXHALL-OPEL Westfield Rd ✆ 74437

WELLS-NEXT-THE-SEA Norfolk 404 W 25 – ✪ 0328 Fakenham.
◆London 117 – King's Lynn 31 – ◆Norwich 36.

   X **Moorings,** 6 Freeman St., NR23 1BA, ✆ 710949
   *closed Thursday lunch, Tuesday dinner, Wednesday, 4 to 22 June and 26 November-14
   December* – **M** (booking essential) 13.00/15.00 **t.** ▯ 3.00.

Pour vos déplacements en Grande-Bretagne :

– *cinq cartes détaillées nᵒˢ* 401, 402, 403, 404, 405 *à 1/400 000*

– *utilisez-les conjointement avec ce guide,*

   un souligné rouge signale toutes les localités citées dans ce guide.

WELSH HOOK Dyfed – see Fishguard.

WELSHPOOL (TRALLWNG) Powys **402** **403** K 26 – pop. 4 869 – ECD : Thursday – ☏ 0938.
Envir. : Powis Castle★★ S : 1 m..

🏌 Y Golfa Hill ℰ 83249.

🛈 Vicarage Garden Car Park ℰ 2043.

◆London 182 – ◆Birmingham 64 – Chester 45 – Shrewsbury 19.

    🏛 **Royal Oak,** The Cross, SY21 7DG, ℰ 552217 – 📺 ☎ ℗. 🔲 AE VISA. 🙊
    M 8.00/10.00 **t.** and a la carte 🍷 3.20 – **26 rm** ⚏ 27.50/55.00 **t.** – SB (weekends only)
    58.00/60.00 **st.**

    ↑ Gungrog House 🦢, Rhallt, SY21 9HS, NE : 2 m. by A 483 (lane opposite A 458) ℰ 3381, ≤,
    🚗 – ℗
    3 rm.

    ↑ **Tynllwyn Farm** 🦢, SY21 9BW, N : 1 ½ m. on A 490 ℰ 3175, ≤, « Working farm » – 📺
    ℗
    M 6.00 **st.** – **6 rm** ⚏ 14.00/23.00 **st.**

AUSTIN-ROVER Union St. ℰ 3152   VAUXHALL-OPEL Newtown Rd ℰ 4444
FORD Salop Rd ℰ 2391

WELWYN Herts. **404** T 28 – pop. 9 961 (inc. Codicote) – ECD : Wednesday – ☏ 043 871.
◆London 30 – Bedford 31 – ◆Cambridge 32.

    🏨 **Heath Lodge,** Danesbury Park Rd, AL6 9SN, NE : 2 m. by B 197, Canonsfield Rd and
    Potters Heath Rd ℰ 7064, Telex 827618, Fax 8500, 🚗, park – ⟲rm 🍽 rest 📺 ☎ ℗ – 🛝
    120. 🔲 AE Ⓞ VISA. 🙊
    M 25.00/35.00 **st.** 🍷 5.50 – ⚏ 8.95 – **25 rm** 65.00/72.00 **st.**, **8 suites** 135.00/150.00 **st.**

COLT 54 Great North Rd ℰ 5911   FORD By Pass Rd ℰ 6123

WELWYN GARDEN CITY Herts. **404** T 28 – pop. 40 665 – ECD : Wednesday – ☏ 0707 Welwyn
Garden.

🏌 Panshanger ℰ 333350.

🛈 The Campus ℰ 332880.

◆London 28 – Bedford 34 – ◆Cambridge 34.

    🏨 **Crest** (Crest), Homestead Lane, AL7 4LX, by Cole Green Lane ℰ 324336, Telex 261523, Fax
    326447, 🚗 – 📶 ⟲ 📺 ☎ ℗ – 🛝 100. 🔲 AE Ⓞ VISA
    M (bar lunch Saturday) 10.75/14.75 **st.** and a la carte 🍷 4.95 – ⚏ 7.50 – **58 rm** 68.00/81.00 **st.**
    – SB (weekends only) 70.00/90.00 **st.**

LADA Great North Rd ℰ 070 72 (Hatfield) 64567   🛞 ATS 11 Southfield ℰ 371619

WENTBRIDGE West Yorks. **402** **404** Q 23 – ✉ ☏ 0977 Pontefract.
◆London 183 – ◆Leeds 19 – ◆Nottingham 55 – ◆Sheffield 28.

    🏨 **Wentbridge House,** Great North Rd, WF8 3JJ, ℰ 620444, Fax 620148, 🚗 – 📺 ☎ ℗ –
    🛝 . 🔲 AE Ⓤ VISA. 🙊
    closed Christmas Night – M 13.50 **t.** (lunch) and a la carte 20.00/26.25 **t.** 🍷 6.00 – **12 rm**
    60.00/100.00 **st.**

WEOBLEY Heref. and Worc. **403** L 27 – pop. 1 080 – ECD : Wednesday – ✉ Hereford –
☏ 0544.
◆London 145 – Brecon 30 – Hereford 12 – Leominster 9.

    🏮 **Red Lion,** Broad St., HR4 8SE, ℰ 318220, 🚗 – 📺 ⓟ ℗. 🔲 VISA
    M (carving lunch)/dinner 15.00 **t.** and a la carte 🍷 3.50 – **7 rm** ⚏ 39.00/49.50 **t.**

WEST BAY Dorset **403** L 31 – see Bridport.

WEST BEXINGTON Dorset – ✉ Dorchester – ☏ 0308 Burton Bradstock.
◆London 150 – Bournemouth 43 – Bridport 6 – Weymouth 13.

    🏮 **Manor,** Beach Rd, DT2 9DF, ℰ 897616, ≤, 🚗 – 📺 ℗. 🔲 AE VISA. 🙊
    M 12.00/15.45 **t.** 🍷 2.85 – **10 rm** ⚏ 31.50/41.50 **t.** – SB 72.50/86.50 **st.**

WEST BRIDGFORD Notts. **403** **404** Q 25 – see Nottingham.

WEST BROMWICH West Midlands **403** **404** O 26 – see Birmingham.

WESTBROOK Wilts. – see Melksham.

WEST CHILTINGTON West Sussex **404** S 31 – pop. 2 044 – ECD : Wednesday and Thursday – ✉ Pulborough – ✆ 079 83.

◆London 50 – ◆Brighton 22 – Worthing 12.

🏨 **Roundabout** (Best Western), Monkmead Lane, RH20 2PF, S : 1 ¼ m. ✆ 3838, 🚗 – 📺 ☎ 🅿 – 🏊 . 🔄 AE ⓪ VISA 🦿
M 10.00/16.00 **st.** and a la carte 🍷 6.70 – **20 rm** ☲ 49.75/92.00 **st.** – SB 74.00/88.00 **st.**

WEST COKER Somerset **403 404** M 31 – see Yeovil.

WESTERHAM Kent **404** U 30 – pop. 3 392 – ECD : Wednesday – ✆ 0959.
Envir. : Chartwell★ (Sir Winston Churchill's country home, Museum) AC, S : 2 m.
◆London 24 – ◆Brighton 45 – Maidstone 22.

🏨 **Kings Arms,** Market Sq., TN16 1AN, ✆ 62990 – 📺 ☎ 🅿. 🔄 AE ⓪ VISA
M 9.75/15.75 **t.** and a la carte – **17 rm** ☲ 55.00/70.00 **t.**

XXX **Cope's Oyster House,** Quebec Sq., Brasted Rd, TN16 1TE, on A 25 ✆ 62139, 🚗 – 🔄 AE ⓪ VISA
closed Saturday lunch, Sunday dinner, 26 December and 1 January – **M** 18.50 **t.** (lunch) and a la carte 25.00/35.75 **t.**

VW-AUDI London Rd ✆ 64333

WEST HADDON Northants. **403 404** Q 26 – see Rugby.

WEST HUNTSPILL Somerset **403** L 30 – see Bridgwater.

WESTLETON Suffolk **404** Y 27 – pop. 493 – ECD : Wednesday – ✉ Saxmundham – ✆ 072 873.
◆London 72 – ◆Cambridge 72 – ◆Ipswich 28 – ◆Norwich 31.

🏨 Crown, IP17 3AD, ✆ 273, 🚗 – 📺 ☎ 🅿. 🦿 – **14 rm**.

WEST LULWORTH Dorset **403 404** N 32 – pop. 910 – ECD : Wednesday – ✉ Wareham – ✆ 092 941.
See : Lulworth Cove★.
◆London 129 – Bournemouth 21 – Dorchester 17 – Weymouth 19.

🏨 **Cromwell House,** Main Rd, BH20 5RJ, ✆ 253, ≤, 🏊, 🚗 – 📺 🅿
M (dinner only) 8.50 **st.** 🍷 2.95 – **14 rm** ☲ 19.00/38.00 **st.** SB 49.00 **st.**

🏠 Mill House, BH20 5RQ, ✆ 404, 🚗 – 🔄 VISA
9 rm ☲ 21.50/41.00 **t.**

🏠 **Gatton House,** Main Rd, BH20 5RU, ✆ 252, 🚗 – 🦿 rest 📺 🅿. 🔄 VISA
closed January – **M** 10.50 **st.** 🍷 3.25 – **8 rm** ☲ 21.50/47.00 **st.** – SB (weekdays only) (except summer) 55.00/59.50 **st.**

WEST MALVERN Heref. and Worc. **403 404** M 27 – see Great Malvern.

WEST MERSEA Essex **404** W 28 – pop. 5 245 – ✉ Colchester – ✆ 0206.
◆London 58 – Chelmsford 27 – Colchester 9.5.

XX **Blackwater** with rm, 20-22 Church Rd, CO5 8QH, ✆ 383338 – 📺 🅿. 🔄 AE. 🦿
closed 8 January-4 February – **M** (closed Tuesday lunch and Sunday dinner) 10.80/20.00 **t.** and a la carte 12.50/20.15 **t.** 🍷 3.70 – **7 rm** ☲ 24.00/55.00 **t.** – SB (except Sunday, Christmas and Bank Holidays) 60.00/70.00 **st.**

WESTON Devon **403** K 31 – see Honiton.

WESTONBIRT Glos. **403 404** N 29 – see Tetbury.

WESTON FAVELL Northants. **404** R 27 – see Northampton.

WESTON-ON-THE-GREEN Oxon. **403 404** Q 28 – pop. 479 – ✉ ✆ 0869 Bletchington.
◆London 65 – ◆Birmingham 61 – Northampton 33 – ◆Oxford 8.

🏨 **Weston Manor** (Best Western), on A 43, OX6 8QL, ✆ 50621, Telex 83409, Fax 50901, 🏊 heated, 🚗, park, squash – 📺 ☎ 🅿 – 🏊 30. 🔄 AE ⓪ VISA 🦿
M 14.00/20.50 **t.** and a la carte 🍷 4.25 – **36 rm** ☲ 75.00/95.00 **t.**, **1 suite** 105.00 **t.** – SB 95.00/105.00 **st.**

WESTON-SUPER-MARE Avon **403** K 29 The West Country G. – pop. 60 821 – ECD : Thursday – ✆ 0934.
See : Sea front ≤★★.
🏌 Worlebury ✆ 23214, 2 m. from station BY – 🏌 Uphill Rd North ✆ 625789 AZ.
🏢 Beach Lawns ✆ 626838.
◆London 147 – ◆Bristol 24 – Taunton 32.

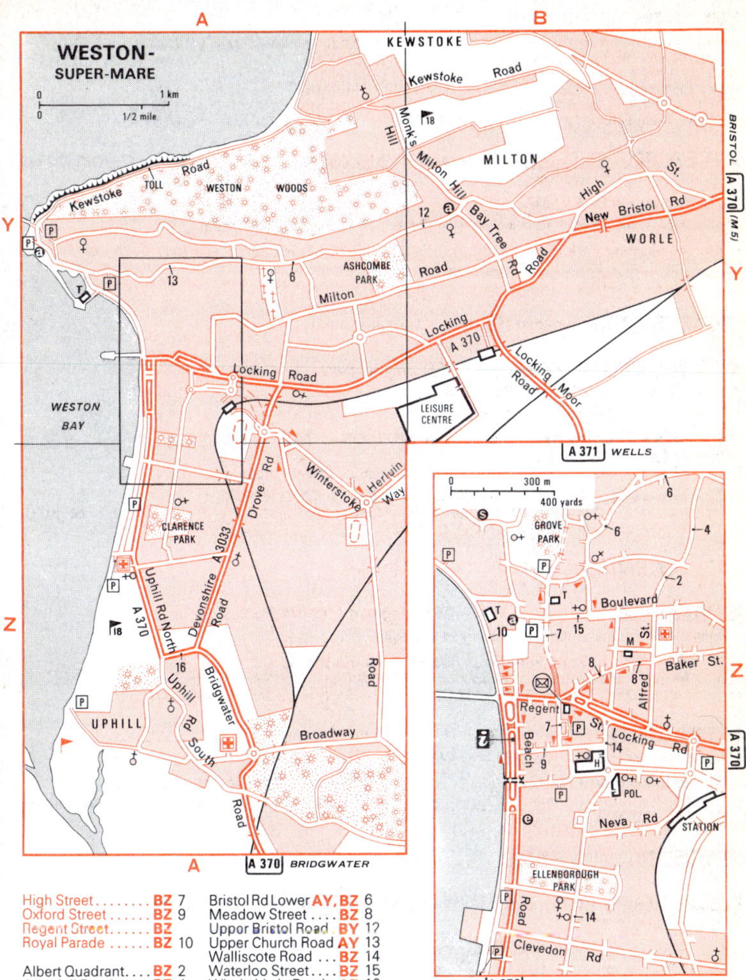

High Street . . . . **BZ** 7	Bristol Rd Lower **AY, BZ** 6
Oxford Street . . . . . **BZ** 9	Meadow Street . . . . **BZ** 8
Regent Street . . . . . . **BZ**	Upper Bristol Road . **BY** 12
Royal Parade . . . . . . **BZ** 10	Upper Church Road **AY** 13
	Walliscote Road . . . **BZ** 14
Albert Quadrant . . . . **BZ** 2	Waterloo Street . . . . **BZ** 15
Arundell Road . . . . . **BZ** 4	Windwhistle Road . **AZ** 16

Grand Atlantic (T.H.F.), Beach Rd, BS23 1BA, ℰ 626543, Fax 415048, ≤, heated, ✎, ✗ – ⬛ rm 🆃🆅 ☎ 🅿 – 🔺 200. 🅰 🆎 🆔 VISA **BZ e**
M 8.50/11.75 **st.** and a la carte ♦ 3.95 – ⬜ 7.00 – **76 rm** 56.00/106.00 **st.** – SB (except Easter, Christmas and New Year) 70.00/96.00 **st.**

Royal Pier (Best Western), 55-57 Birnbeck Rd, BS23 2EJ, ℰ 626644, ≤ Weston Bay and Bristol Channel – ⬛ 🆃🆅 ☎ 🅿 – 🔺 65. 🅰 🆎 🆔 VISA.   **AY a**
M 8.25/13.50 **t.** and a la carte ♦ 3.95 – **38 rm** ⬜ 42.00/68.00 **t.**, **2 suites** 70.00/75.00 **t.** – SB (winter only) (weekends only) 60.00/80.00 **st.**

Berni Royal (B.C.B.), South Par., BS23 1JN, ℰ 623601, ✎ – ⬛ 🆃🆅 ☎ 🅿 – 🔺 40. 🅰 🆎 🆔 VISA.   **BZ a**
M (grill rest.) 8.70/12.70 **t.** ♦ 3.00 – **36 rm** ⬜ 34.00/56.00 **t.** – SB (weekends only) 31.70/38.00 **st.**

Queenswood, 17 Victoria Park, BS23 2HZ, ℰ 416141, ≤ – 🆃🆅 ☎. 🅰 🆎 🆔 VISA   **BZ s**
M 7.50/10.00 **st.** ♦ 3.00 – **18 rm** ⬜ 23.00/50.00 **t.**

✗ **Duets**, 103 Upper Bristol Rd, BS22 8ND, ℰ 413428 – 🅰 VISA   **BY a**
closed Sunday dinner, Monday and first 2 weeks January – **M** (lunch by arrangement)/dinner 11.75 **st.** and a la carte 14.15/16.25 **st.** ♦ 3.95.

WESTON-SUPER-MARE

ALFA-ROMEO Hewish *&* 832078
AUDI-VW Winterstoke Rd *&* 632541
AUSTIN-ROVER Alfred St. *&* 621451
CITROEN Baker St. *&* 623995
FORD Winterstoke Rd *&* 628291
HONDA Bridgwater Rd *&* 0934 (Bleadon) 812244

NISSAN Herwin Way *&* 416454
PEUGEOT-TALBOT Broadway *&* 0934 (Bleadon) 812479
RENAULT Locking Rd *&* 414007
VAUXHALL-OPEL Winterstoke Rd *&* 419526
VOLVO 106-110 Milton Rd *&* 626428

WESTON-UNDER-REDCASTLE Shropshire 402 403 404 M 25 – pop. 256 – ⊠ Shrewsbury – ✆ 093 924 Lee Brockhurst.

ᵣ₈, ᵣ₈ Hawkstone Park *&* 611.

♦London 165 – Chester 31 – ♦Birmingham 48 – Shrewsbury 12 – ♦Stoke-on-Trent 25.

     Hawkstone Park (Best Western), SY4 5UY, *&* 611, Telex 35793, Fax 311, ≤, ⌁, ᵣ₈, ⟋, ⚞, park, ⚟ – ▤ rest 🆃🆅 ☎ Ⓟ – 🏛 200
57 rm, 2 suites.

WEST PENNARD Somerset 403 M 30 – see Glastonbury.

WEST RUNTON Norfolk 404 X 25 – ECD : Wednesday – ⊠ Cromer – ✆ 026 375.

ᵣ₉ Links Country Park Hotel *&* 691.

♦London 135 – King's Lynn 42 – ♦Norwich 24.

     Links Country Park, Sandy Lane, NR27 9QH, *&* 691, Fax 8264, ⌁, ᵣ₉, ⚞, ⚟ – 🛗 🆃🆅 ☎ ⅊ Ⓟ – 🏛 50. 🆁 VISA
M 12.25/15.00 t. and a la carte � 3.75 – **31 rm** 🍽 (dinner included) 45.00/130.00 t.

  XX   **Mirabelle**, 7 Station Rd, NR27 9QD, *&* 396 – Ⓟ. 🆁 AE ⓪ VISA
closed Sunday dinner November-May, Monday and first 2 weeks November – M 10.00/17.50 t. and a la carte 13.00/17.50 t. ♪ 3.25.

WEST SCRAFTON North Yorks. – see Middleham.

WEST STOUR Dorset – pop. 144 – ⊠ Gillingham – ✆ 074 785 East Stour.

♦London 119 – Bournemouth 35 – Salisbury 28 – Yeovil 15.

     Ship Inn, SP8 5RP, on A 30 *&* 640, ⚞ – Ⓟ. 🆁 VISA. ⚟
M *(closed Sunday dinner to non-residents)* (bar lunch Monday to Saturday)/dinner a la carte 10.55/17.75 t. – **6 rm** 🍽 20.00/40.00 t. – SB (except May-September) 55.00 st.

WEST WITTON North Yorks. 402 O 21 – pop. 338 – ⊠ Leyburn – ✆ 0969 Wensleydale.

♦London 241 – Kendal 39 – ♦Leeds 60 – York 53.

     Wensleydale Heifer, Main St., DL8 4LS, *&* 22322 – 🆃🆅 ☎ Ⓟ. 🆁 AE ⓪ VISA
M (bar lunch)/dinner 16.50 st. ♪ 3.50 – **19 rm** 🍽 40.00/70.00 st. – SB (November-May) 70.00 st.

WETHERAL Cumbria 401 402 L 19 – see Carlisle.

WETHERBY West Yorks. 402 P 22 – pop. 9 467 – ECD : Wednesday – ✆ 0937.

ᵣ₈ Linton Lane *&* 62527.

🅱 Council Offices, 24 Westgate *&* 62706.

♦London 208 – Harrogate 8 – ♦Leeds 13 – York 14.

     Wood Hall ⌁, Trip Lane, Linton, LS22 4JA, SW : 3 m. by A 661 and Winton Rd *&* 67271, Fax 64353, ≤, « Part Jacobean and Georgian country house in park », ⚞, ⚟ – 🆃🆅 ☎ Ⓟ. 🆁 AE ⓪ VISA
M *(closed Saturday lunch)* 16.95/29.50 t. and a la carte ♪ 7.00 – **20 rm** 🍽 80.00/115.00 t., **2 suites** 140.00/210.00 t. – SB (weekends only) 140.00/225.00 st.

     Penguin, Leeds Rd, LS22 5HE, junction A 58 and A 1 *&* 63881, Telex 556428, Fax 580062 – ⇤ rm 🆃🆅 ☎ Ⓟ – 🏛 160. 🆁 AE ⓪ VISA
M 8.50/13.00 t. and a la carte ♪ 3.30 – 🍽 6.50 – **72 rm** – SB (weekends only) 68.00/88.00 st.

     Linton Spring ⌁, Sicklinghall Rd, LS22 4AF, W : 1 ¾ m. by A 661 *&* 65353, Fax 67579, ⚞, park – 🆃🆅 ☎ Ⓟ. 🆁 AE ⓪ VISA
M *(closed Saturday lunch)* 11.50 t. (lunch) and a la carte 15.70/25.70 t. ♪ 4.50 – **8 rm** 🍽 75.00/90.00 t., **1 suite** 120.00 t.

AUSTIN-ROVER North St. *&* 62623

WEYBOURNE Norfolk 404 X 25 – pop. 553 – ⊠ Holt – ✆ 026 370.

♦London 128 – Cromer 7.5 – ♦Norwich 26.

     Maltings, The Street, NR25 6SY, on A 149 *&* 731, ⚞ – 🆃🆅 ☎ Ⓟ. 🆁 AE ⓪ VISA
M 6.50/15.00 t. and a la carte ♪ 3.75 – **21 rm** 🍽 33.00/54.00 t. – SB (except Bank Holidays) 60.00/74.00 st.

Plan : see Greater London (South-West)

🏨 **Ship Thistle** (Thistle), Monument Green, High St., KT13 8BQ, ℰ 848364, Telex 894271, Fax
857153 – TV ☎ P – 🏛 110. ⬛ AE ⓞ VISA   by A 3050   AY
    M 9.95/13.75 **st.** and a la carte – ⌤ 7.25 – **39 rm** 75.00/95.00 **st.** – SB 56.00/84.00 **st.**

XXX **Casa Romana,** 2 Temple Hall, Monument Hill, KT13 8RH, ℰ 843470, Italian rest. – P. ⬛
AE VISA   by A 3050   AY
    closed Saturday lunch and Monday – **M** 10.45/30.00 **t.** and a la carte 27.40/38.80 **t.** 🍷 3.75.

XX **Colony,** 3 Balfour Rd, KT13 8HE, ℰ 842766, Chinese (Peking) rest.. ⬛ AE ⓞ VISA
    closed Christmas – **M** a la carte 13.30/17.50 **t.**   by A 317   AZ

X   Gaylord, 73 Queens Rd, KT13 9UQ, E : ¾ m. on A 317 ℰ 842895, Indian rest.
                                              by A 317   AZ

AUSTIN-ROVER 30 Queens Rd ℰ 842233   TOYOTA 51-59 Baker St. ℰ 848247
FORD Brooklands Rd ℰ 093 23 (Byfleet) 52941   VAUXHALL-OPEL New Haw Rd ℰ 853101
MERCEDES Spinney Hill, Addlestone ℰ 093 287   VOLVO 168 Oatlands Drive ℰ 854422
(Ottershaw) 3726

Envir. : Chesil Beach★★ (from Portland★ (S : 1 ½ m.) to Abbotsbury) – at Abbotsbury★★, NW :
9 m. by B 3157 Swannery Gardens★*AC*, Sub Tropical Gardens★*AC*, St. Catherines Chapel★*AC*.
📍₁₈ Links Rd, Westham ℰ 773981.

⛴ Shipping connections with the Continent : to France (Cherbourg) (Sealink) (summer only)
(Weymouth Maritime Services) (restricted service in winter) – to Channel Islands : Jersey
(St. Helier, via Guernsey and Alderney) (Weymouth Maritime Services) 5 weekly.

⛵ to Channel Islands : Guernsey (St. Peter Port) and Jersey (St. Helier) (Condor : hydrofoil)
1-2 daily (summer only).

🛈 Pavilion Theatre Complex, The Esplanade ℰ 785747 (summer only) – King's Statue, The Esplanade
ℰ 785747.

♦London 142 – Bournemouth 35 – ♦Bristol 68 – Exeter 59 – Swindon 94.

🏨 **Streamside,** 29 Preston Rd, Overcombe, DT3 6PX, NE : 2 m. on A 353 ℰ 833121, 🍴 – TV
P. ⬛ AE ⓞ VISA
    M (bar lunch)/dinner 9.95 **t.** and a la carte 🍷 3.75 – **15 rm** ⌤ 36.00/58.00 **t.** –
SB (except summer) 49.50/60.50 **st.**

🏨 **Glenburn,** 42 Preston Rd, Overcombe, DT3 6PZ, NE : 2 m. on A 353 ℰ 832353 – TV P. ⬛
VISA. 🐾
    M 10.00 **t.** and a la carte 🍷 3.75 – **13 rm** ⌤ 27.00/52.00 **t.** – SB (October-March) 65.00/72.00 **st.**

🏨 **Rex,** 29 The Esplanade, DT4 8DN, ℰ 760400 – 🛗 TV ☎ 🚗. ⬛ AE ⓞ VISA
    M (dinner only) 6.50 **t.** and a la carte 🍷 3.00 – **31 rm** ⌤ 33.00/66.00 **t.** – SB 56.00/64.00 **st.**

🏠 **Sou'West Lodge** without rest., Rodwell Rd, DT4 8QT, ℰ 783749 – TV P
    closed 2 weeks Christmas – – **9 rm** ⌤ 15.50/38.00 **st.**

FIAT 172 Dorchester Rd ℰ 786311   FORD 48-62 Dorchester Rd ℰ 782222

📍₉ Long Leese Barn, Portfield Lane ℰ 2236.

♦London 233 – ♦Blackpool 32 – Burnley 12 – ♦Manchester 28 – Preston 15.

🏨 **Mytton Fold Farm,** Whalley Rd., Langho, BB6 8AB, SW : 1 ¾ m. ℰ 0254 (Blackburn)
40662, 🍴 – TV ☎ 🛗 P. ⬛ VISA. 🐾
    M *(closed Saturday lunch)* 6.95 **t.** (lunch) and a la carte 8.85/16.75 **t.** 🍷 3.20 – **27 rm**
⌤ 39.00/54.00 **t.** – SB (weekends only) 57.50 **st.**

XX **Northcote Manor** with rm, Northcote Rd, Langho, BB6 8BE, SW : 2 m. on A 59
ℰ 0254 (Blackburn) 40555, 🍴 – TV ☎ P. ⬛ AE ⓞ VISA
    closed 25-26 December – **M** 9.95 **t.** (lunch) and a la carte 23.00/29.50 **t.** – **6 rm**
⌤ 55.00/65.00 **t.** – SB (weekends only) 47.00/57.00 **st.**

♦London 106 – Lincoln 45 – ♦Leicester 61 – ♦Norwich 60.

🏠 **Guy Wells** 🐾, Eastgate, PE12 6TZ, E : ½ m. by A 151 ℰ 22239, « Queen Anne house », 🍴
– ✖ P. 🐾
    M (by arrangement) 8.00 **st.** – **3 rm** ⌤ 18.00/26.00 **st.** – SB 20.00 **st.**

See : Vantage Point★ – ♦London 191 – Exeter 36 – Taunton 29.

🏨 **Raleigh Manor** 🐾, TA24 7BB, N : ½ m. on A 396 ℰ 0643 (Minehead) 841484, ≼, 🍴 –
✖ rest TV P. VISA
    March-October – **M** (dinner only) 12.00 **st.** 🍷 3.00 – **7 rm** ⌤ 20.00/44.00 **st.**

🏠 **Higherley House** 🐾, TA24 7EB, W : ½ m. on B 3224 ℰ 582, ≼, 🍴 – P. ⬛ VISA
    M 8.50 **st.** – **4 rm** ⌤ 12.75/40.00 **st.** – SB 38.00/48.00 **st.**

 Devon **403** J 31 – see Exeter.

WHITBY North Yorks. **402** S 20 – pop. 12 982 – ECD : Wednesday – ✆ 0947.
See : Abbey ruins★ (13C) *AC*, Old St. Mary's Church★ (12C), East Terrace ⇐★.
🏌 Low Straggleton ✆ 602768.
🛈 New Quay Rd ✆ 602674.
♦London 257 – ♦Middlesbrough 31 – Scarborough 21 – York 45.

　🏠　**Larpool Hall** ⑤, Larpool Lane, YO22 4ND, ✆ 602737, ⇐, 🐎 – ⇔ rm 📺 🅿. 🔼 *VISA*. 🦿
　　　M (bar lunch)/dinner 10.50 **t.** and a la carte ♦ 3.80 – **11 rm** ⌿ 29.00/60.00 **t.** –
　　　SB 59.50/65.00 **st.**

　　　at Sneaton S : 3 m. by A 171 on B 1416 – ✉ ✆ 0947 Whitby :
　🏠　**Sneaton Hall**, YO22 5HP, ✆ 605929, 🐎 – 📺 🅿
　　　M (bar lunch)/dinner 10.00 **t.** ♦ 2.25 – **8 rm** ⌿ 20.50/41.00 **t.** – SB (except summer) 50.00 **st.**

　　　at Dunsley W : 3 ¼ m. by A 171 – ✉ ✆ 0947 Whitby :
　🏠　**Dunsley Hall** ⑤, YO21 3TL, ✆ 83437, ⇐, 🔼, 🐎, 🦿 – 📺 🅿 – **5 rm**.

AUSTIN-ROVER　6 Upgang Lane ✆ 603321
AUSTIN-ROVER　✆ 0287 (Castleton) 60203
FORD　Silver St. ✆ 602237

NISSAN　Castle Park ✆ 602841
RENAULT　18 Silver St. ✆ 602093
VAUXHALL　Argyle Rd ✆ 602898/602238

WHITCHURCH Bucks. **404** R 28 – ✉ ✆ 0296 Aylesbury.
♦London 50 – Luton 27 – ♦Oxford 32.

　XX　**Priory** with rm, 70-72 High St., HP22 4JS, ✆ 641239, « Tudor house », 🐎 – ⇔ rm 📺 ☎
　　　🅿. 🔼 AE ⓪ *VISA*
　　　M *(closed Sunday)* 21.00 **st.** ♦ 4.25 – **11 rm** ⌿ 47.00/80.00 **st.**

WHITCHURCH Shropshire **402 403 404** L 25 – pop. 7 246 – ECD : Wednesday – ✆ 0948.
🏌 Hill Valley, Terrick Rd ✆ 3584, N : 1 m.
🛈 Civic Centre, High St. ✆ 4577.
♦London 171 – ♦Birmingham 54 – Chester 22 – ♦Manchester 43 – Shrewsbury 20.

　🏠　**Redbrook Hunting Lodge,** Wrexham Rd, SY13 3ET, W : 2 ½ m. on A 525 ✆ 094 873
　　　(Redbrook Maelor) 204, 🐎 – 📺 ☎ 🅿. 🔼 AE ⓪ *VISA*. 🦿
　　　M 6.75/8.75 **t.** and a la carte ♦ 2.50 – **12 rm** ⌿ 36.00/50.00 **t.** – SB (except Christ-
　　　mas and New Year) 42.00/50.00 **st.**

AUSTIN-ROVER, LAND-ROVER　Newport Rd ✆
3333
FORD　Dodington ✆ 4471
FORD　Brownlow St. ✆ 2826

RENAULT　Wrexham Rd ✆ 2257

⓪ ATS　The Wharf, Mill St. ✆ 2491/2701

WHITEBROOK Gwent – see Monmouth.

WHITFIELD Kent **404** X 30 – see Dover.

WHITLAND (HENDY-GWYN) Dyfed **403** G 28 – pop. 1 342 – ECD : Wednesday – ✆ 0994.
♦London 235 – Carmarthen 15 – Haverfordwest 17.

　🏠　**Waungron Farm** ⑤, SA34 0QX, SW : 1 m. by B 4328 ✆ 240682, ⇐, « Converted farm
　　　buildings », park – 📺 ⅙ 🅿. 🔼 *VISA*. 🦿
　　　closed Christmas – **M** (lunch by arrangement)/dinner 10.50 **st.** and a la carte – **14 rm**
　　　⌿ 30.00/38.00 **st.** – SB (except Christmas, New Year and Bank Holidays) 50.00 **st.**

　⋔　**Cilpost Farm** ⑤, SA34 0RP, N : 1 ¼ m. by North Rd ✆ 240280, ⇐, « Working dairy
　　　farm », 🔼, 🐎 – 🅿. 🦿
　　　April-September – **7 rm** ⌿ (dinner included) 20.00/40.00 **s.**

BMW　Green Bower ✆ 0437 (Haverfordwest) 86251

⓪ ATS　Emporium Garage, Market St. ✆ 240587

WHITLEY BAY Tyne and Wear **401 402** P 18 – pop. 36 040 – ECD : Wednesday – ✆ 091
Tyneside.
Envir. : Seaton Delaval Hall★ (18C) *AC*, NW: 6 m.
🛈 Central Promenade, ✆ 252 4494 (summer only).
♦London 293 – ♦Newcastle-upon-Tyne 10 – Sunderland 10.

　🏠　**Ambassador,** 38-42 South Par., NE26 2RQ, ✆ 253 1218, Fax 297 0089 – 📺 ☎ 🅿. 🔼 AE
　　　⓪ *VISA*
　　　M *(closed dinner 24 to 26 December)* (lunch by arrangement) 8.50 **st.** and a la carte ♦ 3.00 –
　　　28 rm ⌿ 28.00/48.00 **st.** – SB (weekends only) 55.00/65.00 **st.**

ALFA-ROMEO　Radcliffe St ✆ 252 9347
AUSTIN-ROVER　Cauldwell Lane ✆ 297 0333
CITROEN　Claremont Rd ✆ 252 5909
FIAT　Claremont Rd ✆ 252 3347
FORD　New York Rd ✆ 253 1221
LADA, PEUGEOT-TALBOT　Fox Hunters Rd ✆
252 8282

VAUXHALL　Earsdon Rd, West Monkseaton ✆
252 3355
VW-AUDI　Hillheads Rd ✆ 252 8225

⓪ ATS　John St. Cullercoats ✆ 253 3903

WHITSTABLE Kent ☐☐☐ X 29 – pop. 26 227 – ECD : Wednesday – ☎ 0227.
Envir. : Herne Bay : Reculver (church twin towers★ *AC*), E : 8 ½ m.
☐₁₈ Chestfield Rd ✆ 792365, SE : 2 m. by A 299.
🛈 Horsebridge ✆ 275482.
♦London 59 – ♦Dover 22 – Maidstone 28 – Margate 19.

   ✗   **Shapla**, 36 Harbour St., CT5 1AJ, ✆ 262454, Indian rest – **P**. 🄰 AE ⑩ VISA
      M 10.95 t. and a la carte 🍾 2.95.

FORD Tankerton Rd ✆ 770880   RENAULT Tower Par. ✆ 261477

WHITTLE-LE-WOODS Lancs. ☐☐☐ M 23 – see Chorley.

WHITWELL-ON-THE-HILL North Yorks. ☐☐☐ R 21 – pop. 131 – ✉ York – ☎ 065 381.
♦London 223 – Malton 5 – York 12.

   🏛   **Whitwell Hall Country House** ⚓, YO6 7JJ, ✆ 551, Fax 554, ≤, 🖾, 🏛, park, ✗ –
      ⇌ rest 📺 ☎ **P** – 🔬 40. 🄰 AE VISA. 🛠
      M 12.00/24.00 t. and a la carte 🍾 3.75 – **20 rm** ☲ 45.00/95.00 t. – SB (November-
      March) 76.00/92.00 st.

WICKHAM Hants. ☐☐☐ ☐☐☐ Q 31 – pop. 3 485 – ECD : Wednesday – ☎ 0329.
♦London 74 – ♦Portsmouth 12 – ♦Southampton 11 – Winchester 16.

   🏛   **Old House,** The Square, PO17 5JG, ✆ 833049, Fax 833672, « Tastefully renovated Queen
      Anne house », 🏛 – 📺 ☎ **P**. 🄰 AE ⑩ VISA. 🛠
      closed 2 weeks Easter, 2 weeks July-August and 10 days at Christmas – **M** *(closed lunch*
      Monday and Saturday and Sunday) a la carte 19.50/22.00 **st.** 🍾 5.00 – **9 rm** ☲ 60.00/90.00 **st.**

WICKHAM MARKET Suffolk ☐☐☐ Y 27 – pop. 2 164 – ✉ Woodbridge – ☎ 0728.
♦London 86 – ♦Cambridge 64 – Ipswich 14 – ♦Norwich 41.

   ✗✗   **Old Rectory** ⚓ with rm, Campsea Ashe, IP13 0PU, E : 2 m. on B 1078 ✆ 746524, 🏛 –
      ⇌ rm **P**. 🄰 AE ⑩ VISA. 🛠
      closed 2 weeks February, 1 week November and 25-26 December – **M** *(closed Sunday)*
      (dinner only) 17.50 **t.** – **6 rm** ☲ 27.00/47.00 t.

WIDEGATES Cornwall ☐☐☐ G 32 – see Looe.

WIDNES Cheshire ☐☐☐ ☐☐☐ ☐☐☐ L 23 – ☎ 051 Liverpool.
♦London 205 – ♦Liverpool 19 – ♦Manchester 27 – ♦Stoke-on-Trent 42.

   🏛   Hillcrest, Cronton Lane, Cronton, WA8 9AR, N : 2 m. by A 568 on A 5080 ✆ 424 1616 – 📺
      ☎ **P**
      57 rm.

WIGHT (Isle of) ☐☐☐ ☐☐☐ PQ 31 32 – pop. 118 594.
⛴ from East to West Cowes to Southampton (Red Funnel Services) frequent services daily
(55 mn to 1h 15 mn) – from Yarmouth to Lymington (Sealink) frequent services daily (30 mn) –
from Fishbourne to Portsmouth (Sealink) frequent services daily (35 mn).
🚤 from West Cowes to Southampton (Red Funnel services : hydrofoil) frequent services daily
(20 mn) – from Ryde to Southsea (Hovertravel to Southsea Clarence Pier) summer frequent
services daily ; winter 8-12 daily (restricted Sundays) (9 mn) – from Ryde to Portsmouth (Sealink
to Portsmouth Harbour) frequent services daily (15 mn).

PEUGEOT-TALBOT Church Rd ✆ 872121

     Chale – pop. 561 – ECD : Thursday – ✉ Ventnor – ☎ 0983 Isle of Wight.
     Newport 9.

   🏠   **Clarendon,** Newport Rd, PO38 2HA, ✆ 730431, ≤, 🏛 – 📺 **P**
      M 6.00/14.00 **st.** and a la carte 🍾 2.50 – **13 rm** ☲ 24.15/48.30 t. – SB (October-
      May) 56.00/69.00 **st.**

     Cowes – pop. 16 371 – ECD : Wednesday – ✉ ☎ 0983 Isle of Wight.
     Envir. : Osborne House★ (19C) *AC*, E : 1 m.
     ☐₉ Osborne, East Cowes ✆ 295421, E : by A 3021 – ☐₉ Crossfield Av. ✆ 292303.
     🛈 8 Fountain Yard ✆ 291914 (summer only).
     Newport 4.

   🏛   Fountain (Lansbury), High St., PO31 7AW, ✆ 292397 – 📺 ☎. 🛠
      20 rm.

   🏠   **Cowes,** 260 Arctic Rd, PO31 7PJ, ✆ 291541, Telex 86284 – 📺 ☎ **P**. 🄰 AE ⑩ VISA
      M *(bar meals Saturday and Sunday)* 14.50 **st.** and a la carte 🍾 4.90 – **18 rm** ☲ 34.50/48.30 **st.**
      – SB (weekends only) (except summer) 45.50/63.50 **st.**

WIGHT (Isle of)

Freshwater Bay – pop. 5 073 – ECD : Thursday – ⊠ ✆ 0983 Isle of Wight.
🏌 Afton Down ℰ 752955.
Newport 13.

🏨 **Albion**, Gate Lane, PO40 9RA, ℰ 753631, Fax 755295, ≤ – 📺 ☎ 🅿. 🔼 AE ⓪ VISA
M 9.00/12.00 t. and a la carte ▮ 4.00 – **43 rm** �???? 23.00/56.00 t. – SB 64.00 st.

↑ **Blenheim House**, Gate Lane, PO40 9QD, ℰ 752858, ⊿ heated – ५✕ rm 📺 🅿. ৠ
April-October – **M** 6.50 – **8 rm** ⊡ 15.50/31.00 st.

Newport – pop. 19 758 – ECD : Thursday – ⊠ ✆ 0983 Isle of Wight.
Envir. : Shorwell (St. Peter's Church★ 15C) SW : 5 m. – Carisbrooke Castle★★ (12C-16C)
(keep ≤★) AC, SW : 1 ½ m.
🏌 St. George's Down, Shide ℰ 525076, SE : 1 m.
🛈 Town Lane Car Park ℰ 525450 (summer only).

🏨 **Bugle**, 117 High St., PO30 1TP, ℰ 522800, Telex 86479 – 📺 ☎ 🅿 – 🏛 75. ৠ
26 rm.

at Wootton Common – ⊠ ✆ 0983 Isle of Wight :

✕ **Lugley's** with rm, Stapler's Rd, PO30, NE : 2 ¼ m. by A 3054 ℰ 882202 – 📺 🅿. ৠ
closed 2 weeks March and 2 weeks November – **M** *(closed Sunday dinner)* (lunch by
arrangement in winter) 12.95 t. /dinner a la carte 16.35/24.40 t. ▮ 3.95 – **3 rm** ⊡ 12.00/35.00 t.

AUDI-VW, MERCEDES-BENZ Medina Av. ℰ   ⓪ ATS 44-50 South St. ℰ 522881
523232
SUBARU Blackwater ℰ 523684

Niton – ⊠ Isle of Wight – ✆ 0983 Niton.

↑ **Pine Ridge**, The Undercliff, PO38 2LY, ℰ 730802, ☞ – 📺 🅿
M 10.00 t. – **7 rm** ⊡ 38.50/51.00 t.

AUSTIN-ROVER Elmfield ℰ 62717

Sandown – ⊠ ✆ 0983 Isle of Wight..
🏌 Fairway, Lake ℰ 403217.

↑ **Grange** ॐ, Alverstone, PO36 0EZ, NW : 2 m. ℰ 403729, ☞ – ५✕ rest 🅿. ৠ
March-October – **M** 8.50 st. – **6 rm** ⊡ 15.50/31.00 st.

Seaview – ⊠ ✆ 0983 Isle of Wight

🏨 **Seaview**, High St., PO34 5EX, ℰ 612711 – 📺 🅿. 🔼 AE VISA
M (see **Seaview Rest.** below) – **16 rm** ⊡ 33.00/64.00 t. – SB 72.00/118.00 st.

✕ **Seaview**, (at Seaview H.) High St., PO34 5EX, ℰ 612711 – 🅿. 🔼 AE VISA
closed Sunday dinner – **M** a la carte 12.85/16.85 t. ▮ 3.10.

Shanklin – pop. 8 109 – ECD : Wednesday – ⊠ ✆ 0983 Isle of Wight.
See : Old Village (thatched cottages)★ – The Chine★ AC.
Envir. : Brading★ (Roman Villa : mosaics★ AC) N : 3 ½ m – Brading : St. Mary's Church★.
🛈 67 High St. ℰ 862942.
Newport 9.

🏨 **Cliff Tops** (Best Western), 1-5 Park Rd, PO37 6BB, ℰ 863262, Telex 869441, Fax 867139, ≤,
⊿ heated, ☞ – 🛗 📺 ☎ 🅿 – 🏛. 🔼 AE ⓪ VISA
M (buffet lunch Monday to Saturday)/dinner 12.00 st. and a la carte ▮ 4.00 – **88 rm**
⊡ 54.50/100.00 st. – SB (except Easter, Christmas and New Year) 88.00 st.

🏨 **Bourne Hall Country** ॐ, Luccombe Rd, PO37 6RR, ℰ 862820, ⊿ heated, 🔄, ☞, ৠ
📺 ☎ 🅿. 🔼 AE ⓪ VISA. ৠ
Mid February-late November – **M** (bar lunch)/dinner 15.00 t. ▮ 9.95 – **28 rm** ⊡ 37.20/64.35 t.
– SB (except Easter and summer) 54.00/56.35 st.

🏨 **Chine Lodge** ॐ, Eastcliff Rd, PO37 6AA, ℰ 862358, ☞ – ५✕ rest 📺 🅿. ৠ
closed Christmas and New Year – **M** (dinner only) 7.00 t. – **7 rm** ⊡ 20.00/40.00 t.

🏨 **Queensmead**, 12 Queens Rd, PO37 6AN, ℰ 862342, ⊿ heated, ☞ – ५✕ rest 📺 🅿. 🔼
VISA. ৠ
Mid March-October and Christmas – **M** (bar lunch)/dinner 10.00 st. and a la carte ▮ 2.75 –
31 rm ⊡ 30.00/60.00 st.

🏨 **Carlton**, (entrance on Park Rd) Eastcliff Promenade, PO37 6AY, ℰ 862517, ≤, ☞ – ५✕ rest
📺 🅿
April-October – **14 rm** ⊡ 25.00/30.00 st. – SB 43.00/47.00 st.

↑ **Cavendish House** without rest., Eastmount Rd, PO37 6DN, ℰ 862460 – 📺 🅿. 🔼 VISA ৠ
closed December and January – **3 rm** ⊡ 20.00/45.00.

↑ **Apse Manor Country House** ॐ, Apse Manor Rd, PO37 7PN, W : 1 ½ m. by A 3020
ℰ 866651, ☞ – 📺 ☎ 🅿
M 10.00 t. ▮ 3.50 – **5 rm** ⊡ 40.00/58.00 st. – SB (November-March) 54.00/58.00 st.

↑ **Luccombe Chine Country** ⌂, Luccombe Chine, PO37 6RH, S : 2 ¼ m. by A 3055
 🕿 862037, ≼, 🚗 – 📺 🄿. 🄴 *VISA*. 🛠
 closed 24 December-2 January – **M** 9.95 t. 🛢 4.50 – **8 rm** ⇌ 47.00/66.00 t. – SB 50.00 st.

↑ **Delphi Cliff**, 7 St. Boniface Cliff Rd, PO37 6ET, 🕿 862179, ≼, 🚗 – ↤ rest 🄿. 🛠
 Easter-October – **11 rm** ⇌ (dinner included) 14.00/38.00 st.

Totland Bay – pop. 2 316 – ECD : Wednesday – ✉ ✆ 0983 Isle of Wight.
 Envir. : Alum Bay (coloured sands★) and the Needles★, SW : 1 m.
 Newport 13.

🏠 **Country Garden**, Church Hill, PO39 0ET, on B 3322 🕿 754521, Telex 94017218, ≼, 🚗 –
 📺 🕿 🄿. 🄴 🄰🄴 ⓪ *VISA*
 restricted service November-January – **M** 7.95/12.95 **st.** and a la carte 🛢 3.45 – **18 rm**
 ⇌ 35.00/73.50 t., **1 suite** 60.00/73.50 t. – SB 66.00/78.00 **st.**

🏠 **Sentry Mead**, Madeira Rd, PO39 0BJ, 🕿 753212, 🚗 – 📺 🄿. 🄰🄴
 M (bar lunch)/dinner 8.50 t. 🛢 3.50 – **12 rm** ⇌ 23.00/46.00 t.

↑ **Nodes** ⌂, Alum Bay Old Rd, PO39 0HZ, SW : 1 ½ m. by B 3322 🕿 752859, 🚗 – ↤ rm 🄿
 M 7.50 t. 🛢 2.75 – **11 rm** ⇌ 14.00/40.00 st.

↑ **Westgrange Country** ⌂, Alum Bay Old Rd, PO39 0HZ, SW : 1 ½ m. by B 3322 🕿 752227,
 🚗 – 🄿. 🛠
 April-October – **M** 10.50 st. 🛢 3.50 – **13 rm** ⇌ 15.50/43.00 st. – SB 48.00/60.00 st.

↑ **Littledene Lodge** without rest., Granville Rd, PO39 0AX, 🕿 752411 – 🄿
 March-October – **7 rm** ⇌ 15.50/28.50 t.

Ventnor – pop. 7 956 – ECD : Wednesday – ✉ ✆ 0983 Isle of Wight.
 Envir. : St. Catherine's Point (≼★ from the car park), W : 5 m.
 🏌9 Steep Hill, Drive Rd 🕿 853326.
 🛈 34 High St. 🕿 853625 (summer only).
 Newport 10.

🏠 **Royal** (T.H.F.), Belgrave Rd, PO38 1JJ, 🕿 852186, 🏊 heated, 🚗 – 🛗 ↤ rm 📺 ☏ 🄿. 🄴
 🄰🄴 ⓪ *VISA*
 M (bar lunch)/dinner 10.50 **st.** and a la carte 🛢 3.60 – ⇌ 7.00 – **54 rm** 49.00/69.00 st. –
 SB 78.00/88.00 **st.**

🏠 **Ventnor Towers**, 54 Madeira Rd, PO38 1QT, 🕿 852277, Fax 855536, ≼, 🏊 heated, 🚗, 🎾
 – 📺 🕿 🄿. 🄴 🄰🄴 ⓪ *VISA*
 M 7.50/10.95 t. and a la carte – **27 rm** ⇌ 28.00/56.00 t. – SB 59.00/65.00 st.

↑ **Madeira Hall** ⌂, Trinity Rd, PO38 1NS, 🕿 852624, 🏊 heated, 🚗 – 📺 🄿. 🄴 🄰🄴 *VISA*
 Mid March-October – **M** 7.50 st. 🛢 2.00 – **12 rm** ⇌ 21.00/45.00 st.

 at Bonchurch – ✉ ✆ 0983 Isle of Wight :

🏠 **Winterbourne** ⌂, PO38 1RQ, 🕿 852535, ≼ gardens and sea, « Country house and gardens », 🏊 heated – 📺 🕿 🄿. 🄴 🄰🄴 *VISA*
 March-mid November – **M** (buffet lunch)/dinner 16.00 t. – **19 rm** ⇌ 40.00/88.00 t.

🏠 Highfield, 87 Leeson Rd, Upper Bonchurch, PO38 1PU, on A 3055 🕿 852800, ≼, 🚗 – 📺 🕿
 🄿
 12 rm.

🏠 **Bonchurch Manor** ⌂, Bonchurch Shute, PO38 1NU, 🕿 852868, ≼, 🔲, 🚗 – 📺 🄿. *VISA*
 closed January and February – **M** (dinner only and Sunday lunch)/dinner 12.50 t. and a
 la carte 🛢 3.50 – **11 rm** ⇌ 37.00/74.00 st. – SB (November-April) 64.00 **st.**

🏠 **Lake** ⌂, Shore Rd, PO38 1RF, 🕿 852613, 🚗 – 🄿
 March-October – **M** (bar lunch)/dinner 6.00 st. 🛢 3.00 – **23 rm** ⇌ 13.00/48.00 t.

↑ **Horseshoe Bay** ⌂, Shore Rd, PO38 1RN, 🕿 852487, ≼ – ↤ rest 📺 🄿. 🛠
 April-September – **7 rm** ⇌ (dinner included) 19.50/26.50 st.

 at St. Lawrence – ✉ ✆ 0983 Ventnor :

↑ **Lawyers Rest**, Undercliff Drive, PO38 1XF, 🕿 852610, ≼, 🚗 – ↤ rest 🄿. 🄰🄴 *VISA*. 🛠
 March-October and weekends in winter – **8 rm** ⇌ (dinner included) 29.50/59.00.

AUSTIN-ROVER Mill Rd 🕿 760436   MAZDA Victoria St. 🕿 852650

WILLENHALL West Midlands 🔢🔢 N 26 – see Coventry.

WILLERBY Humberside 🔢 S 22 – see Kingston-upon-Hull.

WILLERSEY Heref. and Worc. 🔢🔢 O 27 – see Broadway.

WILLERSEY HILL Glos. 🔢🔢 O 27 – see Broadway (Heref. and Worc.).

La carta stradale Michelin è costantemente aggiornata.

WILLITON Somerset **403** K 30 The West Country G. – pop. 2 410 – ECD : Saturday – ⊠ Taunton – ✆ 0984.

♦London 177 – Minehead 8 – Taunton 16.

　🏠 **Fairfield House,** 51 Long St., TA4 4QY, ✆ 32636 – **Ⓟ**. 🔄 **VISA**. ✖
　　 March-October – **M** (dinner only) 10.00 **st.** and a la carte ▯ 3.50 – **4 rm** ⊇ 26.00/42.00 st.

　↑ **Curdon Mill** ♨, Lower Vellow, TA4 4LS, SE : 2 ½ m. by A 358 on Stogumber Rd ✆ 56522, ≤, « Converted water mill on working farm », ⌇ heated, 🐾, 🐎, park – ⇖ 🔺📺 **Ⓟ**. ✖
　　 M *(closed Sunday to Tuesday to non-residents)* 20.00 **t.** – **6 rm** ⊇ 23.50/50.00 t.

　XX **White House** with rm, 11 Long St., TA4 4QW, ✆ 32306 – 📺 **Ⓟ**
　　 April-October – **M** (dinner only) 23.50 t. ▯ 5.00 – **13 rm** ⊇ 31.00/60.00 t.

　AUSTIN-ROVER West Quantoxhead ✆ 32437　　　　PEUGEOT-TALBOT High St. ✆ 32761

WILMCOTE Warw. **403** **404** O 27 – see Stratford-upon-Avon.

WILMINGTON East Sussex **404** U 31 – see Eastbourne.

WILMSLOW Cheshire **402** **403** **404** N 24 – pop. 28 827 – ECD : Wednesday – ✆ 0625.

🏌 Great Warford, Mobberley ✆ 056 587 (Mobberley) 2148.

♦London 189 – ♦Liverpool 38 – ♦Manchester 12 – ♦Stoke-on-Trent 27.

　🏰 **Stanneylands** ♨, Stanneylands Rd, SK9 4EY, N : 1 m. by A 34 ✆ 525225, Telex 8950511, Fax 537282, « Gardens » – 🍽 rest 📺 ☎ ᴵ **Ⓟ** – 🔺 90. 🔄 **AE** ⓪ **VISA**. ✖
　　 closed 13 April and 1 January – **M** *(closed Sunday dinner)* 10.00/20.00 t. and a la carte ▯ 3.25 – ⊇ 8.50 – **33 rm** 66.00/80.00 t. – SB (weekends only) 99.00/130.00 **st.**

　🏨 **Wilmslow Moat House** (Q.M.H.), Oversley Ford, Altrincham Rd, SK9 4LR, NW : 2 ¾ m. on A 538 ✆ 529201, Telex 666401, Fax 531876, 🔲, squash – 🍽 📺 ☎ **Ⓟ** – 🔺. ✖
　　 126 rm.

　at Handforth N : 3 m. on A 34 – ⊠ ✆ 0625 Wilmslow :

　🏰 **Belfry,** Stanley Rd, SK9 3LD, ✆ 061 (Manchester) 437 0511, Telex 666358, Fax 499 0597, 🐎 – 🍽 📺 ☎ ᴵ **Ⓟ** – 🔺 100. 🔄 **AE** ⓪ **VISA**. ✖
　　 closed Christmas Night – **M** 9.00/11.00 t. and a la carte – ⊇ 7.50 – **82 rm** 70.00/80.00 t., **3 suites** 85.00/94.00 t.

　BMW Manchester Rd ✆ 529955　　　　　　TOYOTA Station Rd, Styal ✆ 524145
　PORSCHE Green Lane ✆ 526392　　　　　VAUXHALL-OPEL Water Lane ✆ 527311
　RENAULT Knutsford Rd ✆ 523669

WIMBORNE MINSTER Dorset **403** **404** O 31 The West Country G. – pop. 14 193 – ECD : Wednesday – ✆ 0202 Wimborne.

See : Site★.

Envir. : Bere Regis Church★ (Roof★★) W : 11 m.

🏌 Ashley Wood ✆ 0258 (Blandford) 52253, NW : 8 m.

🅱 The Quarter Jack, 6 Cook Row, ✆ 841025.

♦London 112 – Bournemouth 10 – Dorchester 23 – Salisbury 27 – ♦Southampton 30.

　🏨 **King's Head** (T.H.F.), The Square, BH21 1JA, ✆ 880101 – 🍽 ⇖ rm 📺 ⬮ **Ⓟ** – 🔺 30. 🔄 **AE** ⓪ **VISA**
　　 M *(closed Thursday lunch)* 10.50/12.50 st. and a la carte ▯ 3.85 – ⊇ 7.00 – **27 rm** 58.00/79.00 **st.** – SB (except Christmas and New Year) 84.00/92.00 **st.**

　🏠 **Beechleas,** 17 Poole Rd, BH21 1QA, ✆ 841684, 🐎 – 📺 ☎ **Ⓟ**. 🔄 **VISA**. ✖
　　 closed 21 December-31 January – **M** *(closed Monday lunch and Sunday)* 9.50/15.00 st. ▯ 4.00 – ⊇ 7.00 – **5 rm** 40.00/65.00 st.

　↑ **Stour Lodge,** 21 Julians Rd, BH21 1EF, ✆ 888003, 🐎 – 📺 **Ⓟ**
　　 closed 20 December-10 January – **M** 12.00 st. ▯ 2.50 – **3 rm** ⊇ 20.00/50.00 st.

　at Horton N : 6 m. by B 3078 – ⊠ Wimborne Minster – ✆ 0258 Witchampton :

　🏠 **Northill House** ♨, BH21 7HL, NW : ½ m. ✆ 840407, 🐎 – ⇖ rest 📺 ☎ ᴵ **Ⓟ**. 🔄 **VISA**. ✖
　　 closed 20 December-15 February – **M** (bar lunch)/dinner 10.00 st. ▯ 3.00 – **9 rm** ⊇ 23.00/46.00 st.

　🏠 **Horton Inn,** Cranborne Rd, BH21 5AD, NW : 1 m. ✆ 840252 – 📺 **Ⓟ**. 🔄 **VISA**. ✖
　　 M (bar meals Sunday dinner and Monday) a la carte 13.50/17.60 t. ▯ 3.95 – **5 rm** ⊇ 25.00/45.00 t.

　at Broadstone S : 3 ¼ m. by A 349 on B 3074 – ⊠ Poole – ✆ 0202 Broadstone :

　↑ **Fairlight** ♨, 1 Golf Links Rd, BH18 8BE, ✆ 694316, 🐎 – ⇖ rest **Ⓟ**. 🔄 **VISA**
　　 M 15.00 t. ▯ 4.10 – **10 rm** ⊇ 22.00/38.00 t.

　AUSTIN-ROVER West St. ✆ 882261　　　　VAUXHALL-OPEL Walford Bridge ✆ 842414
　FORD Poole Rd ✆ 886211

WINCANTON Somerset 403 404 M 30 – pop. 3 613 – ECD : Thursday – 🕿 0963.

🛈 Public Library, 7 Carrington Way 🖉 32173.

♦London 119 – ♦Bristol 37 – Taunton 34 – Yeovil 16.

🏠 **Holbrook House** 🦢, Holbrook, BA9 8BS, W : 1 ½ m. on A 371 🖉 32377, ≤, « Country mansion », 🏊 heated, 🛲, park, ✗, squash – 🅿. 🔼 AE VISA ✗%
   closed 31 December – **M** 8.00/12.50 **t.** and a la carte 🛢 6.10 – **20 rm** 🖙 –/65.00 **t.** – SB (except Christmas) 60.00/68.00 **st.**

🔘 ATS Bennetts Field Trading Est., Southgate Rd 🖉 33846

WINCHESTER Hants. 403 404 P 30 – pop. 34 127 – ECD : Thursday – 🕿 0962.

See : Site★★ – Cathedral★★★ (11C-13C) B – St. Cross Hospital★★ (12C-15C) A – Winchester College★ (14C) B B – Castle (Great Hall★) B – Pilgrim's Hall★ (14C) B E.

Envir. : Marwell Zoological Park★★ *AC*, SE : 5 m. on A 333 A.

🛈 The Guildhall, The Broadway 🖉 67871.

♦London 72 – ♦Bristol 76 – ♦Oxford 52 – ♦Southampton 12.

WINCHESTER

High Street	**B**	City Road	**B** 10	Park Road	**A** 26
		Clifton Terrace	**B** 12	Quarry Road	**A** 29
Alresford Road	**A** 2	East Hill	**B** 15	St. George's Street	**B** 32
Andover Road	**B** 3	Eastgate Street	**B** 16	St. Paul's Hill	**B** 33
Bereweeke Road	**A** 5	Easton Lane	**A** 18	St. Peter's Street	**B** 34
Bridge Street	**B** 6	Friarsgate	**B** 19	Southgate Street	**B** 35
Broadway (The)	**B** 8	Garnier Road	**A** 20	Stoney Lane	**A** 36
Chilbolton Avenue	**A** 9	Kingsgate Road	**A** 22	Stockbridge Road	**B** 37
		Magdalen Hill	**B** 23	Sussex Street	**B** 38
		Middle Brook Street	**B** 24	Union Street	**B** 39
		Morestead Road	**A** 25	Upper High Street	**B** 40

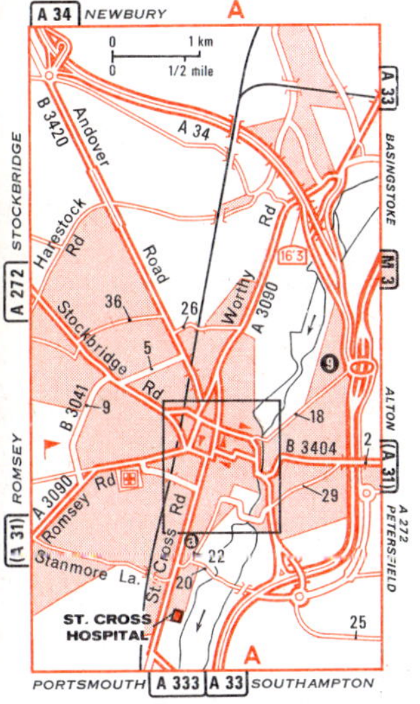
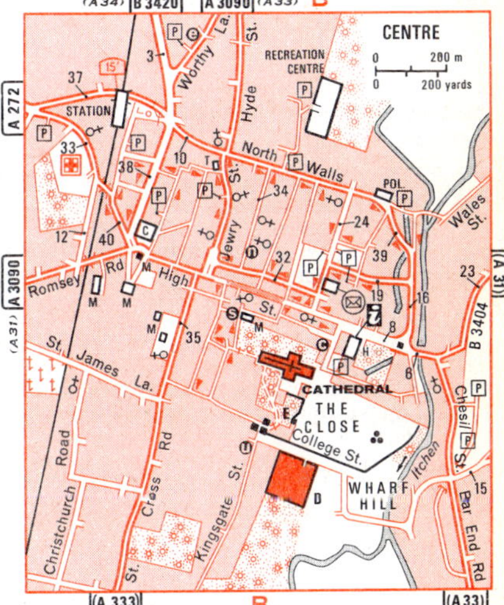

🏰🏰 **Lainston House** 🦢, Sparsholt, SO21 2LT, NW : 3 ½ m. by A 272 🖉 63588, Telex 477375, Fax 72672, ≤, « 17C manor house », 🛲, park, squash – TV 🕿 ⅖ 🅿 – 🔼 60. 🔼 AE ⓓ VISA
   M 18.50/33.00 **t.** and a la carte 🛢 4.00 – 🖙 7.00 – **29 rm** 75.00/125.00 **t.**, **3 suites** 185.00 **t.** – SB (weekends only) 160.00/200.00 **st.**
   by A 272 **A**

🏰🏰 **Wessex** (T.H.F.), Paternoster Row, SO23 9LQ, 🖉 61611, Telex 47419, Fax 841503, ≤ – 🛗
   🛏 rm TV 🕿 🅿 – 🔼 80. 🔼 AE ⓓ VISA
   M 10.50/15.50 **st.** and a la carte 🛢 3.95 – 🖙 7.65 – **93 rm** 72.50/88.00 **st.**, **1 suite** 107.00/112.00 **st.** – SB (weekends only) 84.00/92.00 **st.**
   B c

🏰🏰 **Royal** (Best Western), St. Peter St., SO23 8BS, 🖉 840840, Telex 477071, Fax 841582, 🛲 – TV 🕿 🅿 – 🔼 80
   59 rm.
   B n

🏰🏰 **Saxon Court**, Worthy Lane, SO23 7AB, 🖉 68102, Telex 47383, Fax 840862 – 🛏 rest TV 🕿 ⅖ 🅿. 🔼 AE ⓓ VISA
   M 9.50/13.50 **st.** and a la carte 🛢 3.00 – 🖙 6.50 – **60 rm** 45.00/75.00 **st.** – SB (weekends only) 75.00/95.00 **st.**
   B e

P.T.O. →

☖ **The Wykeham Arms,** 75 Kingsgate St., SO23 9PE, 🖋 53834, 🚗 – ⊱ rest 📺 ☎ 🅿
M *(closed Monday dinner and Sunday)* 12.00/15.00 **st.** and a la carte ⬩2.70 – **7 rm**
⊡ 39.50/55.00 **st.**   **B u**

⌂ **Florum House,** 47 St. Cross Rd, SO23 9PS, 🖋 840427, 🚗 – 📺 🅿   **A a**
M (by arrangement) (communal dining) – **7 rm** ⊡ 30.00/38.00 **st.**

✕✕ **Brann's,** 9 Great Minster St. (1st floor), SO23 9HA, 🖋 64004 – ◫ 𝔸𝔼 𝖵𝖨𝖲𝖠   **B s**
closed Sunday and Bank Holidays – **M** 14.00/23.20 **t.** and a la carte 8.60/20.95 **t.**

ASTON-MARTIN Hursley 🖋 75218   VAUXHALL Stockbridge Rd 🖋 63344
AUSTIN-ROVER Easton Lane, The By-pass 🖋   VOLVO Kingsworthy 🖋 881414
842842   VW-AUDI St. Cross Rd 🖋 66331
FORD Hyde St 🖋 64161
PEUGEOT-TALBOT, CITROEN 2-4 St. Cross Rd 🖋   ⓪ ATS 61 Bar End Rd 🖋 65021
843636

WINDERMERE Cumbria ▦ L 20 – pop. 6 835 – ECD : Thursday – ☏ 096 62.

See : Lake★.

Envir. : Kirkstone Pass (on Windermere ⇐★), N : 7 m. by A 592 Y.

▯₁₈ Cleabarrow 🖋 3123 by A 5074 Z on B 5284.

🛈 The Gateway Centre, Victoria St. 🖋 6490.

🛈 at Bowness : The Glebe 🖋 2895 (summer only).

◆London 274 – ◆Blackpool 55 – ◆Carlisle 46 – Kendal 10.

Plan opposite

🏰 **Merewood Country House** ≫, Ecclerigg, LA23 1LH, NW : 2 ½ m. on A 591 Y 🖋 6484,
Fax 2128, 🚗, park – ⊱ rest 📺 ☎ 🅿 – ♿ 25. ◫ 𝔸𝔼 ⓪ 𝖵𝖨𝖲𝖠. ✾
M 10.95/17.95 **t.** ⬩4.45 – **16 rm** ⊡ 50.00/110.00 **t.** – SB (weekends only) 95.00/120.00 **st.**

🏠 **Cedar Manor,** Ambleside Rd, LA23 1AX, 🖋 3192, 🚗 – ⊱ rest 📺 ☎ 🅿. ◫ 𝖵𝖨𝖲𝖠   **Y i**
M (dinner only) 15.50 **t.** ⬩3.60 – **12 rm** ⊡ 28.00/79.00 **t.** – SB (winter only) (except
Bank Holidays) 54.00/68.00 **st.**

🏠 **Quarry Garth** ≫, Ambleside Rd, LA23 1LF, NW : 2 m. on A 591 🖋 3761, Fax 6584, 🚗,
park – 📺 ☎ 🅿. ◫ 𝔸𝔼 ⓪   by A 591 **Y**
M 8.50 **t.** (lunch) and a la carte ⬩3.25 – **11 rm** ⊡ 30.00/60.00 **t.** – SB 60.00/80.00 **st.**

🏠 **Holbeck Ghyll** ≫, Holbeck Lane, LA23 1LU, NW : 3 ¼ m. by A 591 🖋 05394 (Ambleside) 32375, ⇐, 🚗 – ⊱ rest 📺 ☎ 🅿. ◫ 𝖵𝖨𝖲𝖠   by A 591 **Y**
closed January – **M** (dinner only and Sunday lunch)/dinner 17.00 **st.** ⬩3.25 – **14 rm** ⊡ (dinner included) 50.00/100.00 **st.** – SB (November-May) (except Easter) 62.00/84.00 **st.**

⌂ **Archway,** 13 College Rd, LA23 1BY, 🖋 5613 – ⊱ 📺 ☎. ✾   **Y e**
M 10.00 **st.** – **6 rm** ⊡ 13.00/34.00 **st.** – SB (November-Easter) (weekdays only) 46.00/
51.00 **st.**

⌂ **Glencree,** Lake Rd, LA23 2EQ, 🖋 5822 – ⊱ rest 📺 🅿. ◫ 𝖵𝖨𝖲𝖠. ✾   **Z s**
March-October – **M** 16.50 **st.** ⬩3.20 – **5 rm** ⊡ 39.00/50.00 **st.**

⌂ **Fir Trees** without rest., Lake Rd, LA23 2EQ, 🖋 2272 – 📺 🅿. ◫ 𝔸𝔼 𝖵𝖨𝖲𝖠. ✾   **Z x**
7 rm ⊡ 24.50/39.00 **st.**

⌂ **Braemount House,** Sunny Bank Rd (via Queens Drive), LA23 2EN, 🖋 5967 – ⊱ rest 📺
☎ 🅿. ◫ 𝔸𝔼 ⓪ 𝖵𝖨𝖲𝖠. ✾   **Z u**
closed January and February – **M** 11.50 **st.** ⬩3.90 – **4 rm** ⊡ 29.50/44.00 **st.** –
SB (November-April) 52.00/56.00 **st.**

⌂ Hawksmoor, Lake Rd, LA23 2EQ, 🖋 2110, 🚗 – 📺 🅿   **Z s**
10 rm.

⌂ **Rosemount** without rest., Lake Rd, LA23 2EQ, 🖋 3739 – ⊱ rest 📺 🅿. ◫ 𝖵𝖨𝖲𝖠. ✾
8 rm ⊡ 15.00/39.00 **st.**   **Z z**

✕✕ **Miller Howe** with rm, Rayrigg Rd, LA23 1EY, 🖋 2536, Fax 5664, ⇐ Lake Windermere and
mountains, 🚗 – ⊱ rest ▤ rest 🅿. ◫ 𝔸𝔼 ⓪ 𝖵𝖨𝖲𝖠   **Y s**
March-November – **M** (booking essential) (dinner only) 26.00 **t.** ⬩8.00 – **13 rm** ⊡ (dinner
included) 65.00/110.00 **t.**

✕✕ **Roger's,** 4 High St., LA23 1AF, 🖋 4954 – ◫ 𝔸𝔼 ⓪ 𝖵𝖨𝖲𝖠   **Y o**
closed Sunday and 2 weeks January-February – **M** (lunch by arrangement)/dinner 18.00 **t.**
and a la carte 12.15/19.90 **t.** ⬩3.50.

at Bowness-on-Windermere S : 1 m. – ✉ ☎ 096 62 Windermere :

Old England (T.H.F.), LA23 3DF, ☎ 2444, Telex 65194, Fax 3432, ≼ Lake Windermere and mountains, ☒ heated, 🐎 – 📶 ⇥ rm 📺 ☎ 🅿 – 🍴 . 🖅 AE ⓞ VISA   **Z e**
M 8.50/15.00 **st.** and a la carte 🍷 4.00 – ☕ 8.50 – **80 rm** 62.00/110.00 st., **2 suites** 127.00 st.
– SB 116.00/140.00 **st.**

Linthwaite 🦢, Crook Rd, LA23 3JA, S : ¾ m. by A 5074 on B 5284 ☎ 3688, ≼, « Extensive grounds and private lake », 🦢, 🐎, park – ⇥ rest 📺 ☎ 🅿. 🖅 AE VISA. 🕸
Easter-November – M (dinner only) 14.50 st. 🍷 4.50 – **11 rm** ☕ (dinner included) 43.50/96.00 **st.**   **Z**
by A 5074

Burnside, Kendal Rd, LA23 3EP, ☎ 2211, Telex 65430, Fax 3824, ≼, ☒, 🐎, squash – 📶 📺 ☎ 🅿 – 🍴 80. 🖅 AE ⓞ VISA   **Z c**
M (dinner only and Sunday lunch)/dinner 12.50 **t.** and a la carte 🍷 3.00 – **42 rm** ☕ 38.00/90.00 **t.**, **3 suites** 80.00/110.00 **t.** – SB (November-March) 78.00/82.00 **st.**

P.T.O. →

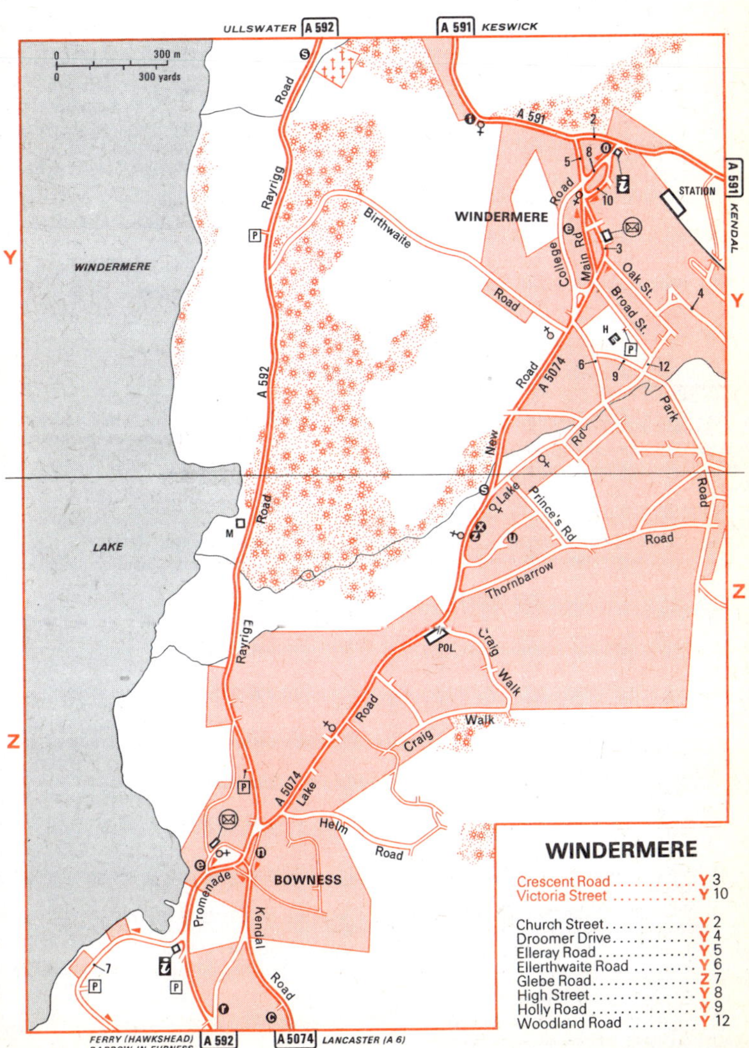

🏨 **Wild Boar** (Best Western), Crook Rd, LA23 3NF, SE : 4 m. by A 5074 on B 5284 ℰ 5225, Telex 65464, Fax 2498, 🚗 – ⤡ rest 📺 ☎ 🅿 – 🔬 40. 🔼 🄰🄴 ⓓ 𝗩𝗜𝗦𝗔. ⋈   by A 5074   Z
M 8.90/17.00 **st.** and a la carte ⦙ 3.50 – **36 rm** � 36.00/90.00 **st.** – SB (except Bank Holidays) 78.00/110.00 **st.**

🏨 **Burn How**, Back Belsfield Rd, LA23 3HH, ℰ 6226, 🚗 – ⤡ rest 📺 ☎ 🅿. 🔼 🄰🄴 𝗩𝗜𝗦𝗔. ⋈
M (bar lunch)/dinner 15.00 **st.** and a la carte ⦙ 4.00 – **26 rm** �}42.00/64.00 **st.** –
SB 65.00/95.00 **st.**   Z r

🏛 **Lindeth Fell Country House** ⌂, Kendal Rd, LA23 3JP, S : 1 m. on A 5074 ℰ 3286, ≤ Lake Windermere and mountains, « Country house atmosphere », 🦢, 🚗, park, ⚹ – ⤡ rest 📺 ☎ 🅿. 🔼 𝗩𝗜𝗦𝗔. ⋈   by A 5074   Z
March-mid November – **M** (bar lunch Monday to Saturday)/dinner 15.00 **t.** 🍾 2.50 – **14 rm** ⊂ (dinner included) 39.00/85.00 **t.**

🏛 **Bordriggs Country House** ⌂, Longtail Hill, LA23 3LD, S : 1 m. by A 592 ℰ 3567, ⌇ heated, 🚗 – ⤡ 📺 ☎ 🅿. ⋈   by A 592   Z
February-October – **M** (lunch by arrangement)/dinner 12.50 **st.** 🍾 3.10 – **11 rm** ⊂ 27.50/55.00 **st.**

↑ **White Foss** ⌂ without rest., Longtail Hill, LA23 3JD, S : ¾ m. by A 592 ℰ 6593, 🚗 – 🅿. ⋈   by A 592   Y
3 rm ⊂ 20.00/36.00 **st.**

↑ **Brooklands**, Ferry View, LA23 3JB, S : ¾ m. on A 5074 ℰ 2344 – ⤡ 🅿
M 14.00 **st.** ⦙ 2.90 – **6 rm** ⊂ 16.00/30.00 **st.**   on A 5074   Z

XXX **Gilpin Lodge Country House** ⌂ with rm, Crook Rd, LA23 3NE, SE : 2 ½ m. by A 5074 on B 5284 ℰ 2295, Fax 88058, ≤, 🚗 – ⤡ rest 📺 ☎ 🅿. 🔼 🄰🄴 ⓓ 𝗩𝗜𝗦𝗔. ⋈   by A 5074   Z
M (dinner only) 19.50 **st.** 🍾 5.25 – **6 rm** ⊂ 50.50/81.00 **st.** – SB (December-March) (weekdays only) 80.00/100.00 **st.**

XX **Porthole Eating House**, 3 Ash St., LA23 3EB, ℰ 2793 – 🔼 🄰🄴 ⓓ 𝗩𝗜𝗦𝗔   Z n
closed Tuesday and mid December-mid February – **M** (dinner only) a la carte 14.30/20.25 **t.** 🍾 3.50.

at Troutbeck N : 4 m. by A 592 – Y – ✉ Windermere – ☏ 053 94 Ambleside :

♨ **Mortal Man**, LA23 1PL, ℰ 33193, ≤ Garburn Hill and Troutbeck Valley, 🚗 – 📺 🅿
Mid February-mid November – **M** (bar lunch Monday to Saturday)/dinner 8.50 **st.** 🍾 3.75 –
12 rm ⊂ (dinner included) 37.50/85.00 **st.**

AUSTIN-ROVER Rayrigg ℰ 2451   PEUGEOT-TALBOT Main Rd ℰ 2441
HONDA Kendal Rd ℰ 2000

WINDSOR Berks. 🔢 S 29 – pop. 30 832 (inc. Eton) – ECD : Wednesday – ☏ 0753.
See : Site★★★ (Town Centre★) – Castle★★★ (St. George's Chapel★★★, State Appartments★★★) Z
– Windsor Park★ – Envir. : Eton (College★) N : 1 m. Z – Runnymede (signing of the Magna Carta, 1215, museum) *AC*, SE : 4 m. by A 308 Y.
🅉 Central Station, Thames St. ℰ 854800.
♦London 28 – Reading 19 – ♦Southampton 59.

Plan opposite

🏰 **Oakley Court** (Norfolk Cap.) ⌂, Windsor Rd, Water Oakley, SL4 5UR, W : 3 m. on A 308 ℰ 0628 (Maidenhead) 74141, Telex 849958, Fax 37011, ≤, « Part Gothic mansion on banks of River Thames », 🚗, park – 📺 ☎ 🅿 – 🔬 100. 🔼 🄰🄴 ⓓ 𝗩𝗜𝗦𝗔. ⋈   by A 308   Y
M 19.50/29.50 **t.** and a la carte ⦙ 6.50 – ⊂ 8.50 – **92 rm** 99.00/295.00 **t.**

🏨 **Castle** (T.H.F.), High St., SL4 1LJ, ℰ 851011, Telex 849220, Fax 830244 – 📲 ⤡ rm 📺 ☎ 🅿 – 🔬 300. 🔼 🄰🄴 ⓓ 𝗩𝗜𝗦𝗔   Z c
M 13.50/18.00 **st.** and a la carte ⦙ 3.25 – ⊂ 7.60 – **84 rm** 72.00/92.00 **st.**, **1 suite** 130.00/165.00 **st.** – SB (weekends only) 100.00 **st.**

🏨 **Sir Christopher Wren's House**, Thames St., SL4 1PX, ℰ 861354, Telex 847938, Fax 860172, ≤, 🚗 – 📺 ☎ 🅿 – 🔬 50. 🔼 🄰🄴 ⓓ 𝗩𝗜𝗦𝗔   Z v
M *(closed Saturday lunch)* 15.00 **st.** (lunch) and a la carte 21.50/25.00 **st.** ⦙ 4.50 – **36 rm** ⊂ 79.00/109.00 **st.**, **1 suite** 120.00 **st.** – SB (except Christmas and Easter) (weekends only) 110.00 **st.**

🏨 **Aurora Garden**, 14 Bolton Av., SL4 3JF, ℰ 868686, 🚗 – 📺 ☎ 🅿 – 🔬 40   Z a
14 rm.

🏨 **Ye Harte and Garter** (B.C.B.), 21 High St., SL4 1LR, ℰ 863426 – 📲 ▤ rest 📺 🕿 – 🔬 60. ⋈   Z e
50 rm.

🏨 **Royal Adelaide**, Kings Rd, SL4 2AG, ℰ 863916, Fax 830682 – 📺 ☎ 🅿 – 🔬 50. ⋈   Z n
42 rm.

↑ **Fairlight Lodge**, 41 Frances Rd, SL4 3AQ, ℰ 861207 – ⤡ rest 📺 🅿. 🔼 𝗩𝗜𝗦𝗔   Z z
M approx. 8.50 **st.** ⦙ 2.50 – **10 rm** ⊂ 30.00/46.00 **st.**

↑ **Trinity** without rest., 18 Trinity Pl., SL4 3AT, ℰ 864186 – 📺. 𝗩𝗜𝗦𝗔   Z i
9 rm ⊂ 16.00/40.00 **st.**

at Eton – ✉ ☏ 0753 Windsor :

🏨 **Christopher**, 110 High St., SL4 6AN, ℰ 852359, Fax 830914 – 📺 ☎ 🅿 – **34 rm**.   Z u

VAUXHALL-OPEL 72-74 Arthur Rd ℰ 860131

WINDSOR

High Street . . . . **Z** 13
King Edward
  Court Centre . . . . **Z**
Peascod Street . . . . **Z**
St. Leonard's Road . . . . **Z**
Thames Street . . . . **Z** 24

Bexley Street . . . . **Z** 2
Bolton Road . . . . **Y** 3
Castle Hill . . . . **Z** 4
Claremont Road . . . . **Z** 6
Clarence Crescent . . . . **Z** 7
Clewer Crescent Road . . . . **Z** 8
Goswell Road . . . . **Z** 9
Grove Road . . . . **Z** 10
High Street (DATCHET) . . . **Y** 12
Horton Road . . . . **Y** 14
Keats Lane . . . . **Z** 16
Peascod Street . . . . **Z** 17
Ragstone Road . . . . **Y** 18
River Street . . . . **Z** 19
Stovell Road . . . . **Z** 20
Thames Avenue . . . . **Z** 22
Trinity Place . . . . **Z** 25
Windsor Bridge . . . . **Z** 26
Windsor Road . . . . **Y** 28

North is at the top on all town plans.

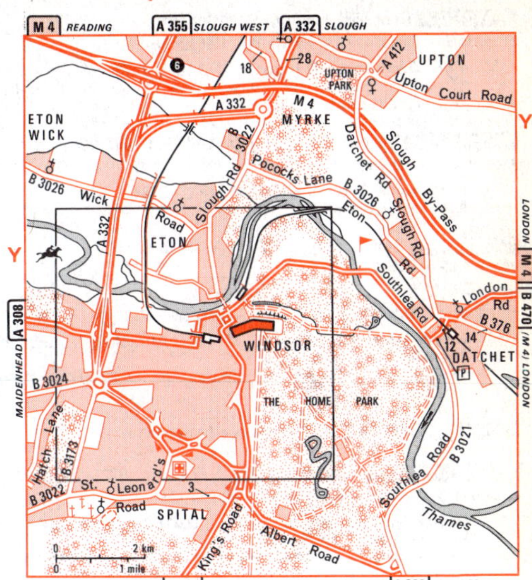

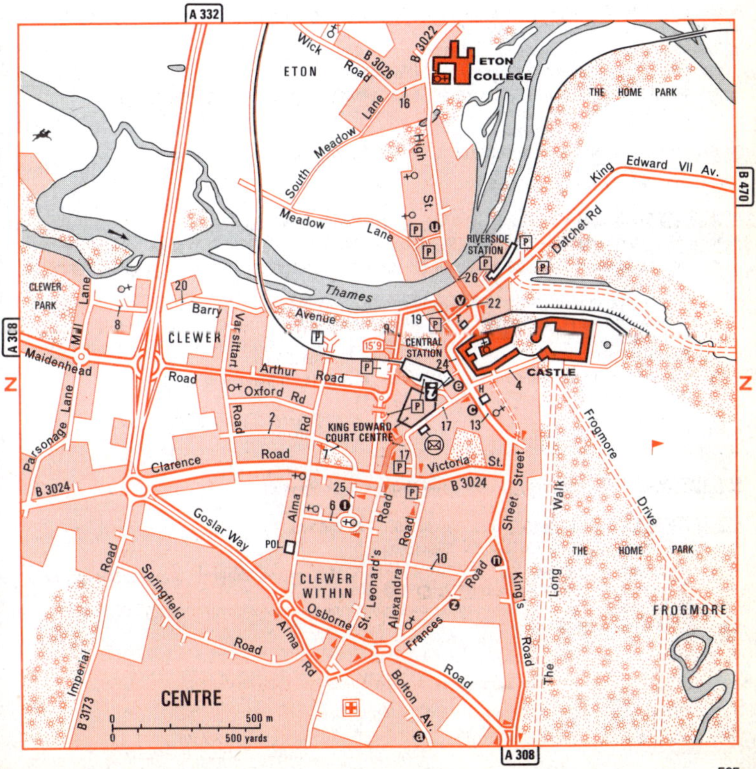

 Kent **404** X 30 – ✿ 0227 Canterbury.
♦London 66 – Canterbury 7 – ♦Dover 19 – Margate 14.

  ✗ **Four Seasons,** 109 High St., CT3 1BU, ℰ 720286, ⇄ – ☒ AE ⓪ *VISA*
    closed Sunday dinner, Tuesday and 25 to 30 December – **M** 8.95/9.95 **t.** and a la
    carte 11.40/13.85 **t.** ▯ 3.95.

WINKLEIGH Devon **403** I 31 – pop. 1 431 – ✿ 083 783.
♦London 214 – Barnstaple 20 – Exeter 22 – ♦Plymouth 41.

  ✗✗ **Kings Arms,** The Square, EX19 8HQ, ℰ 384 – ▤
    M (booking essential).

WINSFORD Somerset **403** J 30 The West Country G. – pop. 340 – ECD : Thursday – ✉ Mine-
head – ✿ 064 385.
See : Site★.
♦London 194 – Exeter 31 – Minehead 10 – Taunton 32.

  🏨 **Royal Oak Inn,** TA24 7JE, ℰ 455, « Attractive 12C thatched inn » – ☒ ☎ ℗. ☒ AE ⓪
    VISA. ⋇
    M (bar lunch Monday to Saturday)/dinner 20.00 **t.** – **14 rm** ⊐ (dinner included) 65.00/
    115.00 **t.**

WINSLEY Wilts. **403** **404** N 29 – see Bath (Avon).

WINTERINGHAM Humberside **402** S 22 – pop. 932 – ✉ ✿ 0724 Scunthorpe.
♦London 176 – ♦Kingston-upon-Hull 16 – ♦Sheffield 67.

  ✗✗✗ **Winteringham Fields** with rm, DN15 9PF, ℰ 733096, « Part 16C manor house », ⇄ –
    ⇔ rm ☒ ☎ ℗. ☒ *VISA*. ⋇
    closed first 2 weeks March and first week August – **M** *(closed Monday lunch, Saturday and
    Sunday)* 12.00 **st.** and a la carte 17.00/23.90 **st.** ▯ 3.75 – ⊐ 3.50 – **4 rm** 50.00/85.00 **st.**

WISBECH Cambs. **402** **404** U 25 – pop. 22 932 – ECD : Wednesday – ✿ 0945.
Envir. : March (St. Wendreda's Church 15C : the Angel roof★) SW : 10 m. – Long Sutton
(St. Mary's Church★ : Gothic) NW : 10 m.
🛈 District Library, Ely Pl. ℰ 583263 and 64009.
♦London 106 – ♦Cambridge 47 – ♦Leicester 62 – ♦Norwich 57.

  🏠 **White Lion,** 5 South Brink, PE13 1JD, ℰ 584813 – ☒ ☎ ℗. ☒ AE ⓪ *VISA*. ⋇
    M *(closed Saturday lunch)* 9.50 **t.** and a la carte ▯ 4.00 – **18 rm** ⊐ 30.80/54.45 **t.** – SB (week-
    ends only) 64.00/68.00 **st.**

AUSTIN-ROVER 46 Norwich Rd ℰ 584342   ⓪ ATS North End ℰ 583214
FORD Elm Rd ℰ 582681
VAUXHALL-OPEL Elm High Rd ℰ 582471

WITHAM Essex **404** V 28 – pop. 21 875 – ECD : Wednesday – ✿ 0376.
♦London 42 – ♦Cambridge 46 – Chelmsford 9 – Colchester 13.

  🏠 **White Hart** (B.C.B.), 39 Newland St., CM8 2AF, ℰ 512245 – ⇔ rest ☒ ☎ ℗. ☒ AE ⓪
    VISA. ⋇
    M (carving lunch)/dinner 11.40 **t.** – **18 rm** ⊐ 37.50/49.50 – SB (weekends only) 60.80 **st.**

  🏠 **Batsford Court,** 100 Newland St., CM8 1AH, ℰ 517777 – ☒ ☎ ℗. ☒ AE ⓪ *VISA*
    M *(closed Saturday lunch, Sunday dinner and Bank Holidays)* 8.95 **t.** and a la carte ▯ 3.50 –
    22 rm ⊐ 38.00/49.50 **t.** – SB (weekends only) 70.00/90.00 **st.**

  ✗✗ **Lian,** High House, Newland St., CM8 2AF, ℰ 510684, Chinese rest. ☒ AE ⓪ *VISA*
    M 8.00/16.00 **st.** and a la carte approx. 16.00 **st.**

AUSTIN-ROVER Newland St. ℰ 513272   ⓪ ATS Moss Rd Ind Est. East, Unit 15 ℰ
FORD Colchester Rd ℰ 513496   518360/515671
NISSAN London Rd ℰ 515575

WITHERSLACK Cumbria **402** L 21 – see Grange-over-Sands.

WITHINGTON Glos. **403** **404** O 28 – pop. 500 – ✿ 024 289.
♦London 91 – Gloucester 15 – ♦Oxford 35 – Swindon 24.

  🏠 **Halewell** ⤢, GL54 4BN, ℰ 238, ≼, « Part 15C manor, country house atmosphere »,
    ⤳ heated, ⤳, ⇄ – ⇔ rest ☒ ⅙ ℗. *VISA*. ⋇
    M (booking essential) (communal dining) (dinner only, residents only) 15.00 **st.** ▯ 3.00 –
    6 rm ⊐ 43.00/66.00 **st.**

WITHYPOOL Somerset 403 J 30 The West Country G. – pop. 231 – ECD : Thursday – ✉ ✆ 064 383 Exford.

♦London 204 – Exeter 34 – Taunton 36.

🏠 **Royal Oak Inn**, TA24 7QP, ✆ 506, 🔖 – 📺 ☎ Ⓟ. 🔲 AE ⑩ VISA
closed 25 and 26 December – **M** (bar lunch)/dinner 19.50 **t.** and a la carte ▯ 3.25 – **8 rm** ⌴ 25.00/56.00 **t.**

🏠 **Westerclose Country House** 🔖, TA24 7QR, NW : ¼ m. ✆ 302, 🚗 – 📺 Ⓟ. 🔲 AE VISA
23 March-6 November – **M** (bar lunch)/dinner 13.00 **t.** and a la carte ▯ 4.50 – **11 rm** ⌴ 25.00/56.00 **t.**

WIVELISCOMBE Somerset 403 K 30 The West Country G. – pop. 1 457 – ECD : Thursday – ✆ 0984.

♦London 185 – Barnstaple 38 – Exeter 37 – Taunton 14.

🏠 **Langley House** 🔖, Langley Marsh, TA4 2UF, NW : ½ m. ✆ 23318, Telex 46648, Fax 23442, « Country house atmosphere », 🚗 – ⇥ rest 📺 ☎ Ⓟ. 🔲 AE
M (booking essential) (lunch by arrangement)/dinner 21.00 **st.** ▯ 4.00 – **8 rm** ⌴ 50.00/ 85.00 **st.** – SB 85.00/120.00 **st.**

at Waterrow SW : 2 ½ m. by A 361 – ✉ ✆ 0984 Wiveliscombe :

🏡 **Hurstone Farmhouse** 🔖, TA4 2AT, E : ½ m. ✆ 23441, ≤ Tone Valley, « Converted farmhouse », 🚗, park – ⇥ 📺 ☎ Ⓟ. 🔲 AE VISA
M 14.00/18.00 **t.** ▯ 3.20 – **5 rm** ⌴ 21.50/57.00 **t.** – SB (weekends only) (except Easter, Christmas, New Year and Bank Holidays) 67.50/77.50 **st.**

WOBURN Beds. 404 S 28 – pop. 824 – ECD : Wednesday – ✉ Milton Keynes – ✆ 0525.
See : Woburn Abbey★★ (18C) *AC*, Wild Animal Kingdom★★ *AC*.
🛈 Heritage Centre, Old St. Mary's Church, 9 Bedford St. (summer only).

♦London 49 – Bedford 13 – Luton 13 – Northampton 24.

🏰 **Bedford Arms** (Mt. Charlotte), 1 George St., MK17 9PX, ✆ 290441, Telex 825205 – 📺 ☎ Ⓟ – 🛏 60
55 rm, 1 suite.

XXX **Paris House**, Woburn Park, MK17 9QP, SE : 2 ¼ m. on A 4012 ✆ 290692, « Reproduction timbered house in Park », 🚗 – Ⓟ. 🔲 AE ⑩ VISA
closed Sunday dinner, Monday and February – **M** 16.50/30.00 **t.** and a la carte 23.00/29.00 **t.** ▯ 4.50.

WOKING Surrey 404 S 30 – pop. 92 667 – ECD : Monday – ✆ 048 62.
🏌, 🏌 Hoebridge Golf Centre, Old Woking Rd ✆ 22611, SE : 1 m.

♦London 31 – Guildford 7 – Reading 24.

✕ **Chez Comus**, 5 High St., Knaphill, GU21 2PG, W : 3 ¼ m. by High St. and Victoria way off A 324 ✆ 048 67 (Brookwood) 89400 – 🔲 VISA
M 8.95 **t.** and a la carte 13.85/17.00 **t.** ▯ 3.25.

WOKINGHAM Berks. 404 R 29 – pop. 30 773 – ECD : Wednesday – ✆ 0734.
🏌 Easthampstead Park ✆ 0344 (Bracknell) 424066.

♦London 43 – Reading 7 – ♦Southampton 52.

🏰 **St. Annes Manor** (Stakis), London Rd, RG11 1ST, E : 1 ½ m. on A 329 ✆ 772550, Telex 847342, Fax 772526, 🔲, 🚗, park, ✕ – 🛗 ⇥ 💢 🍽 rest 📺 ☎ ♿ Ⓟ – 🛏 300. 🔲 AE ⑩ VISA
M 16.00 **st.** (dinner) and a la carte 20.95/29.65 **st.** – ⌴ 7.25 – **126 rm** 75.00/100.00 **st.**, **4 suites** 150.00 **st.** – SB 78.00/92.00 **st.**

🏨 Edward Court, Wellington Rd, RG11 2AN, ✆ 775886, Fax 772018 – 📺 ☎ ♿ Ⓟ – 🛏 . 🔖
25 rm.

AUSTIN-ROVER 82 Goldworth Rd ✆ 61444   FORD 245 Finchampstead Rd ✆ 794776

WOLF'S CASTLE (CAS-BLAIDD) Dyfed 403 F 28 – ✉ Haverfordwest – ✆ 043 787 Treffgarne.
♦London 258 – Fishguard 7 – Haverfordwest 8.

XX **Wolfscastle Country** with rm, SA62 5LZ, on A 40 ✆ 225, ✕, squash – 📺 ☎ Ⓟ. 🔲 AE VISA
M (dinner only and Sunday lunch)/dinner a la carte 13.00/15.50 **t.** ▯ 3.00 – **15 rm** ⌴ 30.80/49.50 **t.** – SB (October-June) (weekends only) 59.00/80.00 **st.**

WOLVERHAMPTON West Midlands 402 403 404 N 26 – pop. 263 501 – ECD : Thursday – ✆ 0902.
See : St. Peter's Church★ (15C) B A.
🏌 Oxley Park, Bushbury ✆ 20506, N : 1 ½ m. A – 🏌 Penn Common ✆ 341142, SW : by A 449 A.
🛈 18 Queen's Sq. ✆ 312051.

♦London 132 – ♦Birmingham 15 – ♦Liverpool 89 – Shrewsbury 30.

Plan of Enlarged Area : see Birmingham pp. 2 and 3

WOLVERHAMPTON

Darlington Street . . . . **B**
Mander Centre . . . . **B**
Victoria Street . . . . **B** 24
Wulfrun Centre . . . . **B**

Alfred Squire Road . . . . **A** 2
Birmingham New Road . . . . . **A** 3
Bridgnorth Road . . . . **A** 6
Cleveland Street . . . . **B** 7
Garrick Street . . . . **B** 8
Lichfield Road . . . . **A** 10
Lichfield Street . . . . **B** 12

Market Street . . . . **B** 14
Princess Street . . . . **B** 15
Queen Square . . . . **B** 17
Railway Drive . . . . **B** 20
Salop Street . . . . **B** 22
Thompson Avenue . . . . **A** 23
Wolverhampton Road . . . . . . **A** 26

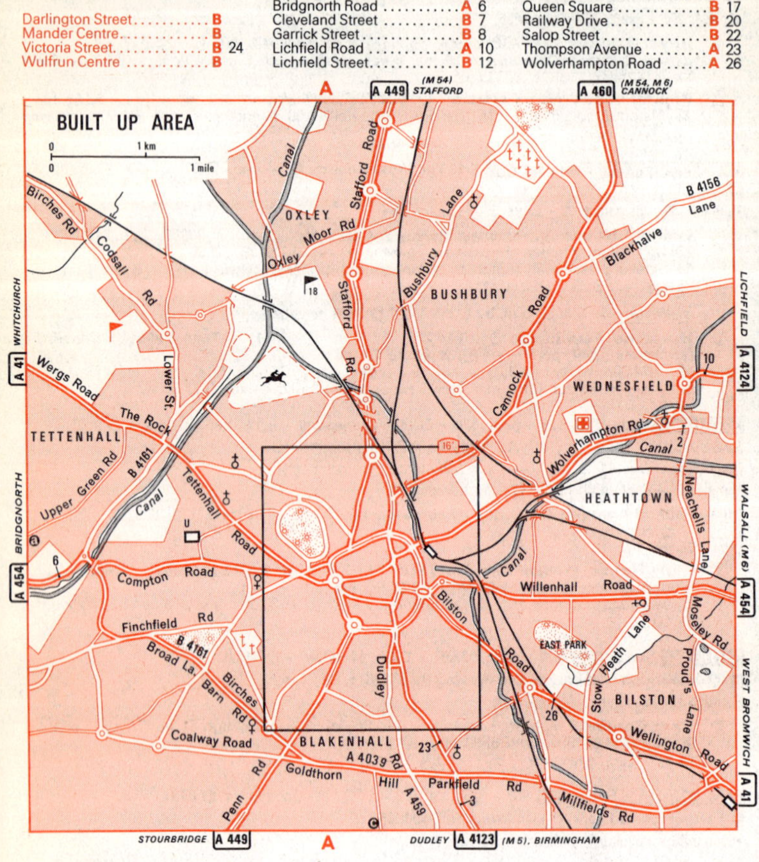

Goldthorn, 126 Penn Rd, WV3 0ER, ✆ 29216, Telex 339516, Fax 710419 – ⊡ ☎ Ⓟ ⚒ 50. ◪ ᴀᴇ ⓞ 𝗩𝗜𝗦𝗔   **B** i
closed 24 to 27 December – **M** *(closed Saturday lunch)* 9.95/10.95 **st.** and a la carte ▮ 3.75 – ⊇ 6.50 – **94 rm** 52.50/75.00 **st.** – SB (weekends only) 77.00/102.00 **st.**

Mount (Embassy) ⤳, Mount Rd, Tettenhall Wood, WV6 8HL, W : 2 ½ m. by A 454 ✆ 752055, Fax 745263, ⌦ – ⇥ rm ⊡ ☎ Ⓟ – ⚒ 200. ◪ ᴀᴇ ⓞ 𝗩𝗜𝗦𝗔   **A** a
M *(closed Saturday lunch)* 10.00/13.00 **st.** and a la carte ▮ 4.40 – ⊇ 6.50 – **48 rm** 63.00/73.00 **st.**, **1 suite** 83.00/94.00 **st.** – SB (weekends only) 62.00/66.00 **st.**

Park Hall (Embassy), Park Drive, off Ednam Rd, Goldthorn Park, WV4 5AJ, S : 2 m. by A 449 ✆ 331121, Telex 333546, Fax 344760, ⌦ – ⇥ rm ⊡ ☎ Ⓟ – ⚒ 400. ◪ ᴀᴇ ⓞ 𝗩𝗜𝗦𝗔
M 9.00/10.50 **st.** and a la carte ▮ 4.50 – ⊇ 6.50 – **56 rm** 46.00/63.00 **st.**, **1 suite** 88.00 **st.** – SB (weekends only) 54.00/59.00 **st.**   **A** c

at Pattingham (Shropshire) W : 6 ¼ m. by A 454 – **A** – ✉ ✆ 0902 Pattingham :

Patshull Park (Best Western) ⤳, Patshull Park, WV6 7HR, W : 1 ¾ m. by Patshull Rd ✆ 700100, Telex 334849, Fax 700874, ≼, ▸, ⤳, park – ⊡ ☎ Ⓟ – ⚒ . ◪ ᴀᴇ ⓞ 𝗩𝗜𝗦𝗔
M 9.50/12.50 **st.** and a la carte ▮ 3.50 – **48 rm** ⊇ 53.00/80.00 **st.** – SB 79.00/115.00 **st.**

ALFA-ROMEO, CITROEN Merridale Lane ✆ 23295
AUSTIN-ROVER Chapel Ash ✆ 311611
AUSTIN-ROVER Wolverhampton Rd, Wednesfield ✆ 731372
BMW, VW-AUDI Rabey St. ✆ 54602
FORD Bilston Rd ✆ 51515
MERCEDES-BENZ Penn Rd ✆ 27897
PEUGEOT-TALBOT Oxford St., Bilston ✆ 353000

RENAULT Bilston Rd ✆ 53111
SKODA, AUSTIN-ROVER Vulcan Rd, Bilston ✆ 402222
VAUXHALL-OPEL Dudley Rd ✆ 58000
VAUXHALL-OPEL 67-71 Bilston Rd ✆ 352352
VOLVO Parkfield Rd ✆ 333211

Ⓜ ATS 35-39 Wednesfield Rd ✆ 55055

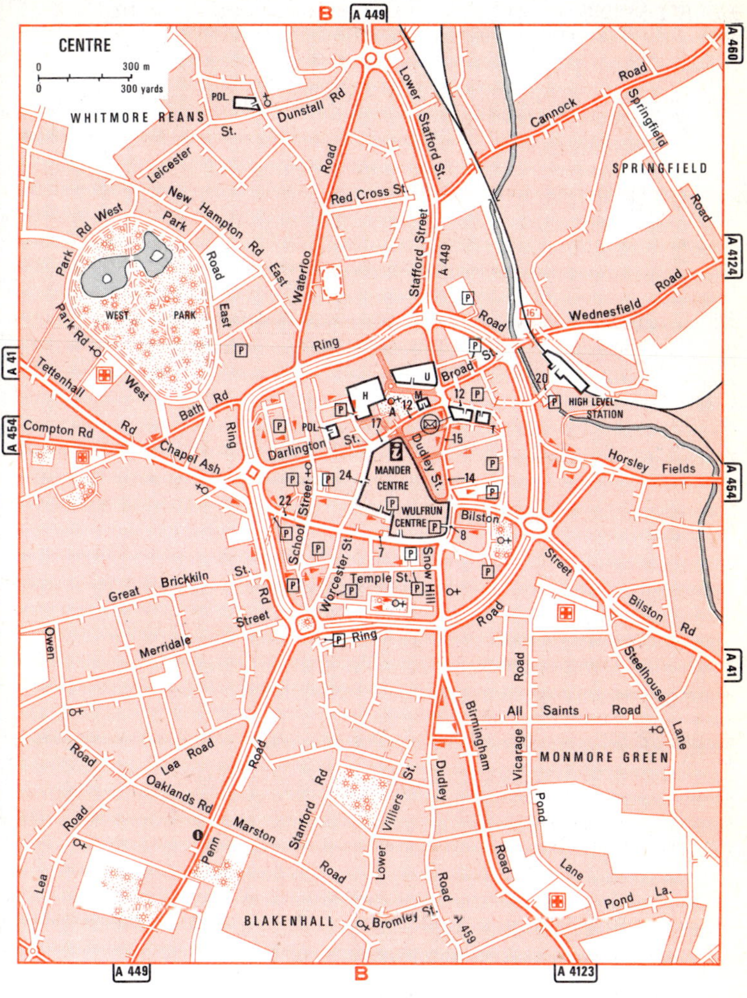

WOODBRIDGE Suffolk ⁴⁰⁴ X 27 – pop. 9 697 – ECD : Wednesday – ☎ 039 43 (4 fig.) or 0394 (6 fig.).

♦London 81 – Great Yarmouth 45 – ♦Ipswich 8 – ♦Norwich 47.

    Seckford Hall ⬧, IP13 6NU, SW : 1 ¼ m. by A 12 ☎ 385678, Telex 987446, Fax 380610, ≤, « Part Tudor country house », ⬧, ≈, park – 📺 ☎ 🅿 – 🔔 100. 🔼 AE ⓞ **VISA**
closed Christmas Day – **M** 9.50 **st.** (lunch) and a la carte 13.05/17.40 **st.** ◊ 3.75 – **24 rm** ⊇ 55.00/100.00 **st.** – SB 94.00/99.00 **st.**

    Crown (T.H.F.), Thoroughfare, IP12 1AD, ☎ 4242, Fax 7192 – ⇥ rm 📺 ☎ 🅿. 🔼 AE ⓞ **VISA**
    M *(closed Sundays in winter)* 8.50/12.95 **st.** and a la carte ◊ 3.95 – ⊇ 7.00 – **20 rm** 52.00/65.00 **st.** – SB 70.00/80.00 **st.**

AUSTIN-ROVER Melton Rd ☎ (039 43) 3456   FORD Bawdsey ☎ 411368
FORD 60 Ipswich Rd ☎ 3333

WOODHALL SPA Lincs. **402 404** T 24 – pop. 2 526 – ECD : Wednesday – ✆ 0526.
Envir. : Tattershall Castle★ (15C Keep) *AC*, SE : 3 ½ m.
🖎 The Broadway ✆ 52511.
♦London 138 – Lincoln 18.

   🏨 **Golf** (T.H.F.), The Broadway, LN10 6SG, ✆ 53535, Telex 56448, Fax 53096, 🐎 – ⇖ rm 📺
      ☎ 🅿 – 🛆 100. 🖎 AE ⑩ *VISA*
      M *(closed Saturday lunch)* 7.50/12.95 **st.** and a la carte ₪ 4.50 – ⇌ 9.00 – **51 rm** 50.00/71.00 **st.**
      – SB 80.00/100.00 **st.**

   🏠 **Dower House** ⑤, Manor Estate, via Spa Rd, LN10 6PY, ✆ 52588, « Country house
      atmosphere », 🐎 – 📺 🅿. 🖎 AE *VISA*
      M (bar lunch)/dinner a la carte 5.60/12.75 **st.** ₪ 3.00 – **7 rm** ⇌ 36.00/48.00 **st.**

   ↑ **Oglee**, 16 Stanhope Av., LN10 6SP, ✆ 53512, 🐎 – 📺 🅿. 🖎. 🐾
      M 10.50 **s.** ₪ 3.00 – **5 rm** ⇌ 16.00/34.00 **st.**

   ↑ **Duns** without rest., The Broadway, LN10 6SQ, ✆ 52969 – 🅿
      6 rm ⇌ 13.00/35.00 **s.**

WOODSTOCK Oxon. **403 404** P 28 – pop. 3 057 – ECD : Wednesday – ✆ 0993.
See : Blenheim Palace★★★ (18C) (park and gardens★★★) *AC*.
Envir. : Rousham (Manor House gardens : statues★) NE : 5 m. – Ditchley Park★ (Renaissance)
AC, NW : 6 m.
🛈 Library, Hensington Rd ✆ 811038.
♦London 65 – Gloucester 47 – ♦Oxford 8.

   🏨 **Bear** (T.H.F.), Park St., OX7 1SZ, ✆ 811511, Telex 837921, Fax 813380, « Part 16C inn » – 📺
      ☎ 🅿 – 🛆 30. 🖎 AE ⑩ *VISA*
      M 15.75/16.95 **st.** and a la carte – ⇌ 7.60 – **41 rm** 69.00/99.00 **st.**, **4 suites** 150.00 **st.** –
      SB (weekends only) (except August) 58.00/68.00 **st.**

   🏨 **Feathers**, Market St., OX7 1SX, ✆ 812291, Fax 813158, « Tastefully furnished » – 📺 ☎.
      🖎 AE ⑩ *VISA*
      M 14.50 **t.** (lunch) and a la carte 18.00/28.50 **t.** – **15 rm** ⇌ 55.00/115.00 **t.** – SB (November-
      March) 98.00/115.00 **st.**

   🏨 **Kings** (T.H.F.), Market St., OX7 1ST, ✆ 811592, Telex 837921, Fax 813380 – 📺 ☎. 🖎 AE
      ⑩ *VISA*
      M (Seafood) 11.95/15.50 **st.** and a la carte ₪ 4.00 – ⇌ 7.00 – **9 rm** 46.00/61.00 **st.** – SB (wee-
      kends only) 60.00/70.00 **st.**

AUSTIN-ROVER 2 Oxford St. ✆ 811286

WOODY BAY Devon **403** I 30 – see Lynton.

WOOLACOMBE Devon **403** H 30 The West Country G. – pop. 1 171 – ECD : Wednesday –
✆ 0271.
Envir. : Mortehoe★★ – Morte Point (vantage point★) – Mortehoe Church★.
🛈 Hall 70, Beach Rd ✆ 870553 (summer only).
♦London 237 – Barnstaple 15 – Exeter 55.

   🏠 **Waters Fall**, Beach Rd, EX34 7AD, ✆ 870365, ≤, 🐎 – 🅿. 🖎 *VISA*
      March-October and December – **M** (dinner only and Sunday lunch)/dinner 9.00 **t.** ₪ 2.70 –
      17 rm ⇌ (dinner included) 26.00/68.00 **t.** – SB (except summer) 44.00/50.00 **st.**

   🏠 **Little Beach**, The Esplanade, EX34 7DJ, ✆ 870398, ≤ – 📺 🅿. 🖎 *VISA*
      February-October – **M** (bar lunch)/dinner 10.50 **st.** – **10 rm** ⇌ 21.50/49.00 **st.** –
      SB (except summer) 52.00/55.00 **st.**

   🏠 **Whin Bay**, Bay View Rd, EX34 7DQ, ✆ 870475, ≤ – 📺 ☎ 🅿
      17 rm ⇌ 25.00/50.00 **t.**

      at Mortehoe N : ½ m. – ✉ ✆ 0271 Woolacombe :

   🏨 **Watersmeet**, The Esplanade, EX34 7EB, ✆ 870333, Fax 870890, ≤ Morte Bay, ⌇ heated,
      ✻ – 📺 ☎ 🅿. 🖎 AE ⑩ *VISA*. 🐾
      closed January – **M** (bar lunch)/dinner 18.50 **st.** and a la carte ₪ 3.55 – **21 rm** ⇌ (dinner
      included) 41.00/120.00 **st.**

   🏠 **Sunnycliffe**, Chapel Hill, EX34 7EB, ✆ 870597, ≤ – ⇖ 📺 🅿. 🐾
      closed December and January – **M** (dinner only) 11.00 **st.** – **8 rm** ⇌ 23.00/46.00 **st.** –
      SB 52.00/60.00 **st.**

WOOLER Northumb. **401 402** N 17 – pop. 1 925 – ECD : Thursday – ✆ 0668.
Envir. : Chillingham Wild Cattle★ in Chillingham Park E : 6 m.
🖎 Doddington ✆ 81408, NE : 2 m.
🛈 Bus Station Car Park, High St. ✆ 81602 (summer only).
♦London 332 – ♦Edinburgh 62 – ♦Newcastle-upon-Tyne 46.

   ⚘ **Ryecroft**, 28 Ryecroft Way, NE71 6AB, ✆ 81459 – ☎ 🅿. 🖎 *VISA*
      closed 2 to 16 November and 24 to 29 December – **M** (bar lunch Monday to Saturday)/dinner
      16.00 **t.** ₪ 3.95 – **9 rm** ⇌ 30.00/52.00 **t.** – SB 70.00/82.00 **st.**

FORD Haughead ✆ 81316

♦London 127 – Gloucester 25 – Hereford 8 – Worcester 25.

⌖ **Butchers Arms,** HR1 4RF, E : ½ m. on Putley rd ☎ 281, ≼, ⇶ – 📺 ℗. ⊛
M (bar meals) (dinner only Wednesday to Saturday) a la carte approx. 10.65 **t.** ⌀ 2.75 – **3 rm**
⊡ 20.50/33.00 **t.** – SB (October-March) 43.50 **st.**

🏠 **Granada Lodge** without rest., WF4 4LQ, M 1 between junctions 38 and 39 ☎ 830371, Fax
830609 – ⇶ rm 📺 ⴟ ℗. ⟋ 𝖠𝖤 ⓞ 𝘝𝘐𝘚𝘈. ⊛
31 rm 24.50/27.00 **st.**

See : Cathedral★★ (13C-15C) (crypt★★ 11C) – The Commandery★ (15C) *AC* **B.**

Envir. : Great Witley : Witley Court (ruins) and the Parish Church of St. Michael and All Saints
(Baroque interior★★) NW : 12 m. by A 443.

🔃 Guildhall, High St. ☎ 723471 ext 201.

♦London 124 – ♦Birmingham 26 – ♦Bristol 61 – ♦Cardiff 74.

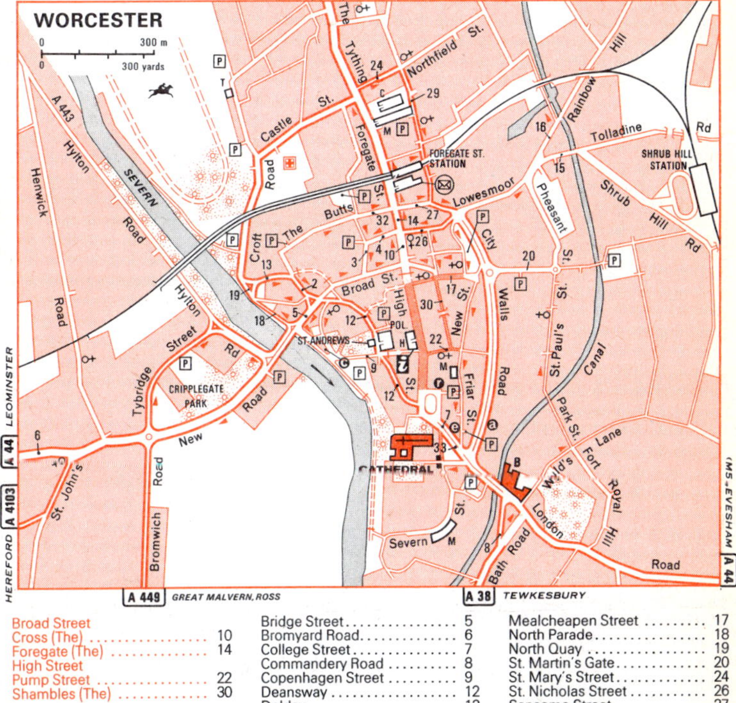

Broad Street
Cross (The) 10
Foregate (The) 14
High Street
Pump Street 22
Shambles (The) 30

All Saints Road 2
Angel Place 3
Angel Street 4

Bridge Street 5
Bromyard Road 6
College Street 7
Commandery Road 8
Copenhagen Street 9
Deansway 12
Dolday 13
Lowesmoor Place 15
Lowesmoor
   Terrace 16

Mealcheapen Street 17
North Parade 18
North Quay 19
St. Martin's Gate 20
St. Mary's Street 24
St. Nicholas Street 26
Sansome Street 27
Sansome Walk 29
Shaw Street 32
Sidbury 33

🏰 **Fownes,** City Walls Rd, WR1 2AP, ☎ 613151, Telex 335021, Fax 23742, « Converted glove
factory » – 🕼 📺 ☎ ⴟ ℗ – 🛦 125. ⟋ 𝖠𝖤 ⓞ 𝘝𝘐𝘚𝘈. ⊛   **a**
M *(closed Monday and Saturday lunch and Sunday dinner)* 11.00/15.95 **t.** and a la
carte 15.10/24.95 **t.** ⌀ 5.95 – ⊡ 7.50 – **58 rm** 70.00/85.00 **t.**, **3 suites** 115.00/145.00 **t.** – SB
(weekends only) 88.00/92.00 **st.**

P.T.O. →

🏨 **Giffard** (T.H.F.), High St., WR1 2QR, ☎ 726262, Telex 338869, Fax 723458 – 🛗 ✂ rm 📺 ☎
🅿 – 🏧 150. 🖪 AE ⑩ VISA
M 12.95/14.95 st. and a la carte ⌀ 4.25 – ⌷ 7.00 – **101 rm** 59.00/76.00 st., **2 suites** 115.00 st.
– SB (weekends only) 68.00/80.00 st.

🏨 **Ye Olde Talbot** (Lansbury), Friar St., WR1 2NA, ☎ 23573, Telex 333315, Fax 612760 –
✂ rm 📺 ☎. 🖪 AE ⑩ VISA. ✳
M 8.50/12.50 t. and a la carte – **29 rm** ⌷ 54.00/64.00 t. – SB (weekends only) 64.00/70.00 st.

🏠 **Park House**, 12 Droitwich Rd, WR3 7LJ, N : 1 m. on A 38 ☎ 21816, Fax 612178 – ✂ rm
📺 🅿
by A 38
M 10.00 st. ⌀ 3.50 – **7 rm** ⌷ 20.00/38.00 st.

XX **Brown's**, 24 Quay St., WR1 2JN, ☎ 26263, « Converted corn mill » – 🖪 AE ⑩ VISA
c
closed Saturday lunch, Sunday dinner, 24 to 30 December and Bank Holidays – **M**
16.00/24.00 t. ⌀ 3.00.

at Upton Snodsbury E : 6 m. by A 44 on A 422 – ✉ Worcester – ✆ 090 560 Upton
Snodsbury :

🏠 **Upton House**, WR7 4NR, on B 4082 ☎ 226, « Tastefully furnished », 🚗 – ✂ rm 📺 🅿.
✳
closed Christmas – **M** (by arrangement) 17.50 st. – **3 rm** ⌷ 27.50/49.00 st.

at Leigh W : 5 m. by A 4103 – ✉ Worcester – ✆ 0886 Leigh Sinton :

🏠 **Leigh Court** 🦢, WR6 5LB, ☎ 32275, 🦢 – 🅿
Mid March-mid October – **M** (by arrangement) 10.00 st. – **3 rm** ⌷ 17.00/28.00 st.

at Lower Broadheath NW : 3 ½ m. by A 443 on B 4204 – ✉ ✆ 0905 Worcester :

XX **Mariners** with rm, Sailors Bank, WR2 6QT, ☎ 641120 – ✂ rest 🅿. 🖪 AE VISA. ✳
closed 2 weeks January – **M** *(closed Sunday dinner, Monday and Tuesday)* 8.50/12.50 st.
and a la carte 16.00/21.00 st. ⌀ 3.50 – ⌷ 3.00 – **2 rm** 20.00/30.00 st. – SB 58.00/75.00 st.

MICHELIN Distribution Centre, Blackpole Trading Estate, WR3 8TJ, ☎ **55626**, FAX 754188 by
A 38

AUSTIN-ROVER Castle St. ☎ 723100
DAIMLER, JAGUAR Castle St. ☎ 726116
FIAT Malvern Rd, Powick ☎ 830361
FORD Bath Rd ☎ 763123
HONDA Pershore Rd, Stoulton ☎ 840661
LADA Droitwich Rd ☎ 58538
LADA Ombersley Rd ☎ 754140
MERCEDES-BENZ Cranham Drive ☎ 754854
NISSAN Bransford Rd ☎ 428101
PEUGEOT-TALBOT Bath Rd ☎ 820777
RENAULT St. Martins Gate ☎ 21215

RENAULT The Butts ☎ 24252
SAAB Kempsey ☎ 821132
SKODA Bromsgrove St. ☎ 23532
SUBARU, SEAT, ISUZU Pierpoint St. ☎ 25786
VAUXHALL-OPEL Hallow ☎ 640228
VAUXHALL-OPEL Brook St. ☎ 726222
VOLVO Farrier St. ☎ 23338
VW-AUDI Hallow Rd ☎ 640512

⬤ ATS Little London, Barbourne ☎ 24009/28543

WORFIELD Shropshire – see Bridgnorth.

WORSLEY Greater Manchester 402 403 404 MN 23 – see Manchester.

WORSTEAD Norfolk 404 Y 25 – ✆ 069 260 Smallburgh.
♦London 128 – ♦Norwich 19.

🏠 **Geoffrey The Dyer House,** Church Plain, NR28 9AL, ☎ 562 – ✂ rm 📺 🅿. ✳
M 7.00 – **4 rm** ⌷ 15.00/32.00.

WORTH Somerset – see Wells.

WORTHING West Sussex 404 S 31 – pop. 90 687 – ECD : Wednesday – ✆ 0903.
Envir. : Shoreham-by-Sea (St. Mary of Haura's Church★ 12C-13C – St. Nichola's Church carved
arches★ 12C) E : 5 m. by A 259 BY.
🏌 Worthing Hill Barn, Hill Barn Lane ☎ 37301 BY.
✈ Shoreham Airport : ☎ 079 17 (Shoreham-by-Sea) 2304, E : 4 m. by A 27 BY.
🛈 Town Hall, Chapel Rd ☎ 210022 – Marine Parade ☎ 210022.
♦London 59 – ♦Brighton 11 – ♦Southampton 50.

Plan opposite

🏨 **Beach**, Marine Par., BN11 3QJ, ☎ 34001, Fax 34567, ≤ – 🛗 📺 ☎ 🅿 – 🏧 . 🖪 AE ⑩ VISA.
✳
AZ e
M 11.00/15.00 t. and a la carte ⌀ 4.00 – **86 rm** ⌷ 40.00/65.00 t., **3 suites** 90.00/100.00 t. –
SB (October-April) 63.50/87.00 st.

🏨 **Chatsworth**, Steyne, BN11 3DU, ☎ 36103, Telex 877046, Fax 823726 – 🛗 📺 ☎ – 🏧 . 🖪
AE ⑩ VISA. ✳
BZ x
M 9.85/12.50 t. and a la carte ⌀ 3.50 – **105 rm** ⌷ 43.00/68.00 t. – SB (except winter) (week-
ends only) 70.00/82.00 st.

WORTHING

Chapel Road . . . . **BZ**
Guildbourne Centre . . . . **BZ**
Montague Street . . . . **BZ**
Liverpool Road . . . . **BZ** 22
South Street (WORTHING) . **BZ**

Broadwater Road . . . . . . **BZ** 3
Broadwater Street West . . . **BY** 5
Broadway (The) . . . . **BZ** 6
Brougham Road . . . . **BY** 7
Brunswick Road . . . . **AZ** 8
Christchurch Road . . . . **BZ** 10

Church Road . . . . **AY** 12
Cowper Road . . . . **AZ** 13
Crockhurst Hill . . . . **AY** 14
Durrington Hill . . . . **AY** 15
Eriswell Road . . . . **ABZ** 16
Goring Street . . . . **AY** 17
Goring Way . . . . **AY** 18
Grafton Road . . . . **BZ** 20
High Street . . . . **BZ** 21
Montague Place . . . . **BZ** 23
Mulberry Lane . . . . **AY** 24
Portland Road . . . . **BZ** 25
Rectory Road . . . . **AY** 26
Reigate Road . . . . **AY** 27
Sompting Avenue . . . . **BY** 28

Sompting Road . . . . **BY** 29
South Street
(WEST TARRING) . **AY, AZ** 30
Southfarm Road . . . . **ABZ** 31
Steyne (The) . . . . **BZ** 32
Steyne Garden . . . . **BZ** 33
Stoke Abbot Road . . . . **BZ** 34
Tennyson Road . . . . **AZ** 36
Thorn Road . . . . **AZ** 37
Union Place . . . . **BZ** 38
Warwick Road . . . . **BZ** 40
Warwick Street . . . . **BZ** 41
West Street . . . . **BZ** 42
Western Place . . . . **BZ** 44
Wykeham Road . . . . **AZ** 45

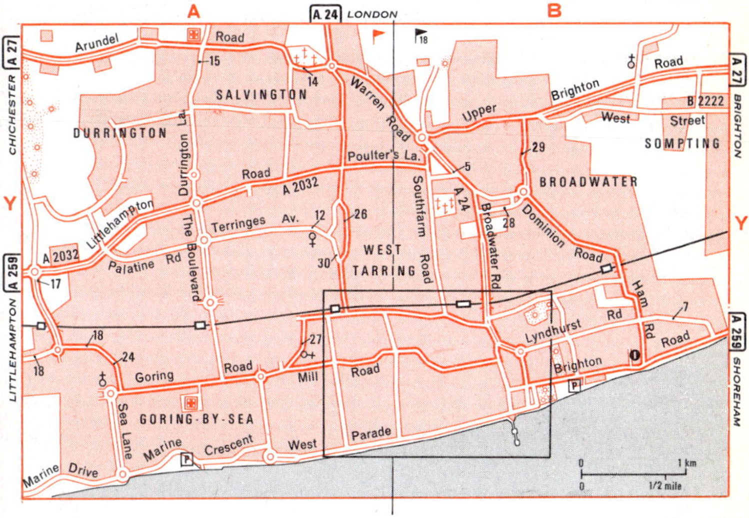

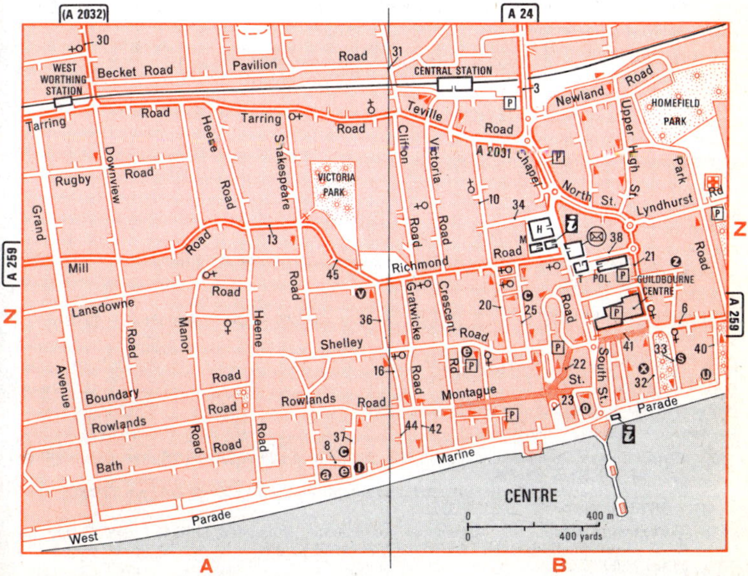

Eardley, 3-10 Marine Par., BN11 3PW, ☏ 34444, Group Telex 877046, ⇐ – 🛗 TV ☏ ℗ – 🏊 . ⊠ AE ⓘ VISA — **M** (carving lunch) 9.50/11.50 **t.** and a la carte ▮ 3.50 – **76 rm** ⊡ 39.00/75.00 **t.** – SB (October-April) (weekends only) 60.00/80.00 **st.**
BZ u

Burlington, Marine Par., BN11 3QL, ☏ 211222 – 🛗 TV ☏ – 🏊
30 rm.
AZ a

Kingsway, 117-119 Marine Par., BN11 3QQ, ☏ 37542, Fax 204173 – 🛗 TV ☏ ℗ . ⊠ AE ⓘ VISA — **M** (carving rest.) 9.50/13.90 **t.** and a la carte ▮ 3.25 – **21 rm** ⊡ 39.00/60.00 **t.** – SB (weekends only) 55.00/90.00 **st.**
AZ i

Ardington, Steyne Gdns, BN11 3DZ, ☏ 30451 – TV ☏ – 🏊 . ⊠ AE ⓘ VISA — **M** 9.50 **t.** (dinner) and a la carte 7.85/14.50 **t.** ▮ 4.00 – **54 rm** ⊡ 27.00/57.00 **t.** – SB (weekends only) 60.00/75.00 **t.**
BZ s

Windsor House, 14-20 Windsor Rd, BN11 2LX, ☏ 39655, 🌇 – TV ☏ ℗ . ⚲ — **M** (carving rest.) (bar lunch)/dinner 10.25 **t.** ▮ 3.50 – **33 rm** ⊡ 20.50/55.00 **t.**
BY i

Bonchurch, 1 Winchester Rd, BN11 4DJ, ☏ 202492 – ⇥ rest TV ℗ . ⚲ — *closed 1 week May and 3 weeks October* – **M** (by arrangement) 7.00 **st.** ▮ 1.80 – **7 rm** ⊡ 12.00/34.00 **st.**
AZ v

Beacons, 18 Shelley Rd, BN11 1TV, ☏ 30948 – TV ℗ . ⊠ VISA — **M** 6.50 **st.** ▮ 2.00 – **3 rm** ⊡ 17.00/35.00 **st.**
BZ e

South Dene, 41 Warwick Gdns, BN11 1PF, ☏ 32909 – TV . ⚲ — **M** 5.50 – **6 rm** ⊡ 13.00/30.00.
BZ z

Trenchers, 118-120 Portland Rd, BN11 1QA, ☏ 820287 – ⊠ AE ⓘ VISA — *closed Saturday lunch, Sunday and Monday* – **M** 17.50 **t.** and a la carte 23.00/33.50 **t.**
BZ c

Paragon, 9-10 Brunswick Rd, BN11 3NG, ☏ 33367 – ⊠ AE ⓘ VISA — *closed Sunday and Bank Holidays* – **M** 9.50/13.50 **st.** and a la carte 13.45/21.70 **st.** ▮ 3.25.
AZ c

Grapes, 3 Bath Pl., BN11 3BA, ☏ 32424, Bistro – ⊠ AE VISA — *closed Saturday lunch and Sunday* – **M** 13.00 **t.** (dinner) and a la carte 6.00/12.50 **t.** ▮ 3.30.
BZ o

at Findon N : 4 m. by A 24 – AY – ⊠ Worthing – ✆ 0903 Findon :

Findon Manor 🐿, High St., BN14 0TA, ☏ 872733, « Part 16C stone and flint house », 🌇 – TV ☏ ℗ . ⊠ AE ⓘ VISA — *closed 25 to 31 December* – **M** *(closed Monday and Saturday lunch and Sunday dinner)* 10.00 **t.** and a la carte 11.10/19.70 **t.** ▮ 3.50 – **10 rm** ⊡ 45.00/85.00 **t.** – SB (September-March) (weekends only) 130.00 **st.**

at East Preston W : 6 ½ m. by A 259 – AY – off B 2225 – ⊠ Littlehampton – ✆ 0903 Rustington :

Old Forge, The Street, BN16 1JJ, ☏ 782040, « 17C cottage » – ℗ . ⊠ AE ⓘ VISA — *closed Sunday dinner and Monday* – **M** 9.50 **t.** (lunch) and a la carte 11.40/26.80 **t.** ▮ 3.60.

ALFA-ROMEO Lancing ☏ 766981
AUSTIN-ROVER Broadwater Rd ☏ 31111
FIAT 123 Upper Brighton Rd ☏ 36065
NISSAN Broadwater Rd ☏ 206091
RENAULT Portland Rd ☏ 200820/823442
SAAB, PEUGEOT-TALBOT St. Lawrence Av. ☏ 207703

SKODA Tarring ☏ 34363
TALBOT Broadwater Rd ☏ 262338
VAUXHALL-OPEL Goring Rd ☏ 42389
VOLVO 187 Findon Rd ☏ 090 671 (Findon) 3022

🅐 ATS 34 Thorn Rd ☏ 37640/820971

WRAFTON Devon 403 H 30 – see Braunton.

WRAY Lancs. 402 M 21 – ⊠ Lancaster – ✆ 052 42 Lancaster.
♦London 258 – ♦Blackpool 44 – Kendal 24 – Lancaster 10.

Lane Head 🐿, Millhouses, LA2 8NF, E : 1 ¼ m. ☏ 21148, 🌇 – TV ℗ . ⚲ — **M** 15.00 **st.** ▮ 2.50 – **4 rm** ⊡ 25.00/40.00 **s.**

WREXHAM (WRECSAM) Clwyd 402 403 L 24 – pop. 39 929 – ECD : Wednesday – ✆ 0978.
See : St. Giles' Church★.
Envir. : Erddig House★ (17C-18C) AC, SW : 2 m.
🏌 Holt Rd ☏ 364268, NE : 1 ¾ m.
🛈 Memorial Hall, Town Centre ☏ 357845 (summer only).
♦London 192 – Chester 12 – Shrewsbury 28.

Cross Lanes, Marchwiel, LL13 0TF, SE : 3 ½ m. on A 525 ☏ 780555, ⊠, 🌇, park – TV ☏ ℗ – 🏊 100. ⊠ AE ⓘ VISA — **M** *(closed Sunday dinner)* 9.50/12.95 **t.** and a la carte ▮ 3.75 – ⊡ 5.00 – **16 rm** 32.00/62.00 **st.** – SB (weekends only) 58.00/82.00 **st.**

Travelodge without rest., Croes-Foel roundabout, Rhostyllen, LL14 4EJ, SW : 3 ½ m. on A 483 (Wrexham by-pass) ☏ 365705 – TV 🕭 ℗ . ⊠ AE VISA — **31 rm** 21.50/27.00 **t.**

AUDI-VW Rhosrobin ☎ 291177
AUSTIN-ROVER Hightown Rd ☎ 291151
CITROEN Holt Rd ☎ 356707
FORD Holt Rd ☎ 290690
HYUNDAI, SUBARU, ISUZU New Broughton ☎ 757838
LADA Rhostyllen ☎ 357996
MAZDA Market Pl. ☎ 351648
PEUGEOT-TALBOT Castle St. ☎ 270271
RENAULT Regent St. ☎ 356822

SEAT Llay New Rd ☎ 720074
SKODA, HYUNDAI Wrexham Rd ☎ 263438
TOYOTA Wrexham Rd ☎ 840578
VAUXHALL-OPEL Mold Rd ☎ 290077
VW-AUDI Llay New Rd ☎ 291177
YUGO Wrexham Rd ☎ 350328

ATS Dolydd Rd, Croesnewydd ☎ 352301/352928
ATS Eagles Meadow, Clwyd ☎ 366510

WRIGHTINGTON BAR Lancs. 402 404 L 23 – pop. 3 160 – ✉ Wigan – ❂ 025 75 Appley Bridge.

♦London 210 – ♦Liverpool 24 – ♦Manchester 30 – Preston 15.

XXX **Highmoor,** High Moor Lane, WN6 9QA, SW : 3 ½ m. by B 5250, A 5209 and Robin Hood Lane ☎ 2364 – **P.** AE O VISA
closed Saturday lunch, Sunday dinner and Monday – **M** 10.00 **t.** (lunch) and a la carte 16.75/20.75 **t.** 4.50.

WROTHAM HEATH Kent 404 U 30 – pop. 1 669 – ✉ ❂ 0732 Sevenoaks.

♦London 35 – Maidstone 10.

Post House (T.H.F.), London Rd, TN15 7RS, ☎ 883311, Telex 957309, Fax 885850, – rm TV ☎ ♿ **P.** – 60. AE O VISA
M 11.00/14.00 **st.** and a la carte 3.95 – 7.60 – **116 rm** 75.00/98.00 **st.**, **2 suites** 120.00/140.00 **st.** – SB (weekends only) 92.00/102.00 **st.**

at Ryarsh NE : 3 ½ m. by A 20 – ✉ ❂ 0732 West Malling :

Heavers Farm ♦, Chapel St., ME19 5JU, N : ½ m. ☎ 842074, – ⊲ **P.**
closed Christmas and New year – **M** 12.00 **st.** – **3 rm** 17.20/34.00 **st.**

WROXHAM Norfolk 404 Y 25 – pop. 2 954 (inc. Hoveton) – ECD : Wednesday – ✉ ❂ 0603 Norwich.

♦London 118 – Great Yarmouth 21 – ♦Norwich 7.

Kings Head (B.C.B.), Station Rd, NR12 8UR, ☎ 782429 – TV ☎ **P.**
8 rm.

Broads, Station Rd, NR12 8UR, ☎ 782869, Fax 784066 – TV ☎ **P.** AE O VISA
M (bar lunch)/dinner a la carte 9.90/14.95 **t.** 2.95 – **26 rm** 20.00/48.00 **t.** – SB (November-mid May) 48.50/56.50 **st.**

Staitheway House without rest., Staitheway Rd, The Avenue, NR12 8TH, SW : ½ m. by A 1151 ☎ 783347, – **P.**
closed Christmas and New Year – **3 rm** 16.00/28.00 **s.**

WROXTON Oxon. 403 404 P 27 – see Banbury.

WYBOSTON Beds. – see St. Neots (Cambs.).

WYCH CROSS East Sussex 404 U 30 – see Forest Row.

WYE Kent 404 W 30 – pop. 1 396 – ECD : Wednesday – ✉ Ashford – ❂ 0233.

♦London 61 – Folkestone 21 – Maidstone 24 – Margate 28.

Woodmans Arms Auberge ♦, Hassell Street, TN25 5JE, E : 4 m. via Hastingleigh rd off Waltham rd ☎ 023 375 (Elmsted) 250, – ⊲ TV **P.** AE.
closed 19 to 30 April and 1 to 26 September – **M** (booking essential) (dinner only, residents only) 12.50 **st.** 3.50 – **3 rm** 47.50/65.00 **st.**

AUSTIN-ROVER Bridge St. ☎ 812331

WYMONDHAM Norfolk 404 X 26 – pop. 9 088 – ECD : Wednesday – ❂ 0953.

♦London 110 – ♦Cambridge 53 – ♦Norwich 9.

Sinclair, 28 Market St., NR18 0BB, ☎ 606721, Fax 601361 – rm TV ☎ **P.** AE VISA
M 8.00/10.00 **st.** and a la carte 3.85 – **20 rm** 37.00/47.00 **t.**

X **Jennings,** Damgate St., NR18 0BQ, ☎ 603533. AE VISA
closed Sunday and Monday – **M** (booking essential) (lunch by arrangement)/dinner 21.00 **t.** 3.50.

WYNDS POINT Heref. and Worc. 403 404 M 27 – see Great Malvern.

WYRE PIDDLE Heref. and Worc. – see Pershore.

YARCOMBE Devon 403 K 31 – pop. 418 – ✉ Honiton – ❂ 040 486 Upottery.

♦London 157 – Exeter 25 – Taunton 12 – Weymouth 42.

Yarcombe Inn, EX14 9BD, ☎ 218 – TV **P.** – **5 rm**.

YARM Cleveland **402** P 20 – pop. 6 360 – ✆ 0642 Middlesbrough.
♦London 242 – Middlesbrough 8.

🏰 **Crathorne Hall** ⑤, Crathorne, TS15 0AR, S : 3 ½ m. by A 67 ℰ 700398, Telex 587426, Fax 700814, « Converted Edwardian mansion », ⪥, park – 📺 ☎ ℗ – 🏛 150. 🌫 AE ⑩ VISA
M 9.00/13.75 **t.** and a la carte – **38 rm** 😐 63.00/75.00 **st.**, **1 suite** 102.00/155.00 **st.** – SB (weekends only) 80.00 **st.**

YATELEY Surrey **404** R 29 – ✉ Camberley – ✆ 0252.
♦London 37 – Reading 12 – ♦Southampton 58.

🏠 **Casa Dei Cesari**, Handford Lane, Cricket Hill, GU17 7BA, ℰ 873275, ⪥ – 📺 ☎ ℗
M (Italian rest.) – **26 rm**.

YATTENDON Berks. **403 404** Q 29 – pop. 568 – ECD : Saturday – ✉ Newbury – ✆ 0635 Hermitage – ♦London 62 – Newbury 8 – Reading 12.

XX **Royal Oak** with rm, The Square, RG16 0UF, ℰ 201325, ⪥ – 📺 ☎ ℗. 🌫 AE VISA ※
M *(closed Sunday dinner)* (booking essential) a la carte 16.00/27.50 **t.** ⍭ 3.75 – **5 rm** 😐 50.00.70.00 **t.** – SB (weekends only) (except Easter and Christmas) 90.00 **st.**

YELVERTON Devon **403** H 32 – ✆ 0822.
♦London 234 – Exeter 33 – ♦Plymouth 9.

🏰 **Moorland Links** ⑤, PL20 6DA, S : 2 m. on A 386 ℰ 852245, Fax 855004, ≤, ⪥, park, ✗ – ✗ rm 📺 ☎ ℗ – 🏛 200. 🌫 AE ⑩ VISA
closed 24 to 31 December – **M** *(closed Saturday lunch)* a la carte 12.20/21.70 **t.** – **30 rm** 😐 57.75/110.00 **t.** – SB (weekends only) 90.00/110.00 **st.**

⌂ **Overcombe**, Horrabridge, PL20 7RN, N : 1 ¼ m. on A 386 ℰ 853501, ≤, ⪥ – ✗ rest 📺 ⅋ ℗. 🌫 VISA
M 9.75 **t.** ⍭ 2.80 – **11 rm** 😐 22.00/39.00 **t.** – SB (except summer) 49.50/54.50 **st.**

⌂ **Harrabeer Country House**, Harrowbeer Lane, PL20 6EA, ℰ 853302, ⚓ heated, ⪥ – ✗ rest 📺 ℗. 🌫 AE ⑩ VISA ※
M 11.00 **st.** ⍭ 3.25 – **7 rm** 😐 19.00/31.00 **st.** – SB (except summer) 56.00/60.50 **st.**

YEOVIL Somerset **403 404** M 31 The West Country G. – pop. 36 114 – ECD : Monday and Thursday – ✆ 0935.
See : St. John the Baptist Church★.
Envir. : Montacute House★★★*AC*, W : 4 m. on A 3088 – Fleet Air Arm Museum★★*AC*, NW : 8 m. by A 37 – Long Sutton★ (Church★★), NW : 10 m. – Huish Episcopi : Church Tower★★, NW : 13 m. – Martock : All Saints Church★★, W : 7 m. – Cadbury Castle (≤★★), NE : 11 m. by A 359 – Ham Hill (≤★★), W : 4 m. – Tintinhull House★*AC*, NW : 5 m – ⒙ Sherborne Rd ℰ 75949.
🛈 Petters House, Petters Way ℰ 71279.
♦London 136 – Exeter 48 – ♦Southampton 72 – Taunton 26.

🏰 **Yeovil Court**, West Coker Rd., BA20 2NE, SW : 2 m. on A 30 ℰ 093 586 (West Coker) 3746, Fax 3990, ⪥ – 📺 ☎ ℗ – 🏛 50. 🌫 AE ⑩ VISA
M *(closed Saturday lunch)* 9.50/19.00 **t.** and a la carte 12.95/21.75 **st.** ⍭ 4.95 – **18 rm** 😐 44.00/59.00 **st.**, **1 suite** 75.00/85.00 **st.** – SB (weekends only) 55.00/75.00 **st.**

🏰 **Manor Crest** (Crest), Hendford Rd, BA20 1TG, ℰ 23116, Telex 46580, Fax 706607, ⪥ – ✗ rm ▤ rest 📺 ☎ ℗ – 🏛 60. 🌫 AE ⑩ VISA
M 10.20/14.70 **st.** and a la carte – 😐 7.50 – **41 rm** 60.00/73.00 **st.** – SB (weekends only) (except Christmas and New Year) 78.00/94.00 **st.**

🏠 **Travelodge** without rest., Podimore, BA22 8JG, N : 9 ½ m. by A 37 off A 303 ℰ 840074 – 📺 ⅋ ℗. 🌫 AE VISA
31 rm 21.50/27.50 **t.**

at Barwick S : 2 m. by A 30 off A 37 – ✉ ✆ 0935 Yeovil :

XX **Little Barwick House** ⑤ with rm, BA22 9TD, ℰ 23902, ≤, ⪥ – ▤ rest 📺 ℗. 🌫 AE VISA
closed Christmas-New Year – **M** *(closed Sunday to non-residents)* (booking essential)(dinner only) 20.00 **st.** ⍭ 3.75 – **6 rm** 😐 42.50/66.00 **st.** – SB 73.00/94.00 **st.**

at West Coker SW : 3 ½ m. on A 30 – ✉ Yeovil – ✆ 093 586 West Coker :

🏰 **Four Acres**, High St., BA22 9AJ, ℰ 2555, Telex 46666, Fax 3929, ⪥ – 📺 ☎ ℗. 🌫 AE ⑩ VISA
M 16.00 **st.** and a la carte ⍭ 3.25 – **25 rm** 😐 45.00/62.00 **st.** – SB (weekends only) 69.50/74.00 **st.**

at East Chinnock SW : 5 m. on A 30 – ✉ Yeovil – ✆ 093 586 West Coker :

⌂ **Barrows Country House** ⑤, Weston St., BA22 9EJ, ℰ 2390, ⪥ – ℗. ※
closed 24 December-1 January – **M** 6.00 **s.** ⍭ 2.00 – 😐 3.00 – **6 rm** 13.00/30.00 **s.**

at Montacute W : 5 ½ m. on A 3088 – ✉ Yeovil – ✆ 0935 Martock :

🏠 **Kings Arms**, Bishopston, TA15 6UU, ℰ 822513, ⪥ – ✗ rest 📺 ⅋ ℗. 🌫 AE VISA
M (buffet lunch)/dinner a la carte 9.95/13.15 **t.** ⍭ 3.40 – **11 rm** 😐 40.00/55.00 **t.** – SB 70.00/97.00 **st.**

XX **Milk House**, 17 The Borough, TA15 6XB, ℰ 823823 – ✗. 🌫 VISA
closed Sunday dinner, Monday and Tuesday – **M** 16.00/18.00 **st.** ⍭ 3.00.

AUSTIN-ROVER, DAIMLER, JAGUAR   Market St. ✆ 75242
FORD   West Henford ✆ 27421
NISSAN   Marston Magna ✆ 850386
SAAB   12 Oxford Rd ✆ 26701

VAUXHALL-OPEL   Addlewell Lane ✆ 74842
VOLVO   Reckleford ✆ 72381

◎ ATS Penmill Trading Est., Lyde Rd ✆ 75580/71780

Y-FENNI = Abergavenny.

YORK   North Yorks. **402** Q 22 – pop. 123 126 – ECD : Monday and Wednesday – ☺ 0904.
See : Site★★★ – Minster★★★ (13C-15C) (Stained Glass★★★ Chapter House★★★, ☀★★ from tower, *AC*, 275 steps) CDY – City Walls★★ (14C) CDYZ – National Railway Museum★★ CY – Castle Museum★*AC* DZ M2 – Jorvik Viking Centre★ DY M1 – Fairfax House★ DY A – The Shambles★ DY.

🏌 Lords Moor Lane, Strensall ✆ 490304, NE : 6 m. by Huntington Rd BY – 🏌 Heworth, Muncaster Gate ✆ 424618 B.

🛈 De Grey Rooms, Exhibition Sq. ✆ 21756/21757 – York Railway Station, Station Rd ✆ 643700.
♦London 203 – ♦Kingston-upon-Hull 38 – ♦Leeds 26 – ♦Middlesbrough 51 – ♦Nottingham 88 – ♦Sheffield 62.

Plan on next page

Middlethorpe Hall, Bishopthorpe Rd, YO2 1QP, S : 1 m. ✆ 641241, Telex 57802, Fax 620176, ≼, « William and Mary house, gardens », park – 🛗 TV ☎ 🅿 – 🛐 30. 🔺 AE ⓪ VISA. 🕏   by A 19 BZ
M 15.90/24.90 **st.** and a la carte 22.80/35.35 **st.** 🍴 8.50 – **Grill** (dinner only) 21.50 **st.** 🍴 4.50 – 🍽 9.00 – **26 rm** 80.00/120.00 **st.**, **5 suites** 150.00/185.00 **st.** – SB (November-April) (except Easter, Christmas and Bank Holidays) 140.00/156.00 **st.**

Crest (Crest), Cliffords Tower, 1 Tower St., YO1 1SB, ✆ 648111, Telex 57566, Fax 610317 – 🛗 ⤢ rm ▤ rest TV ☎ 🚻 🅿 – 🛐 150. 🔺 AE ⓪ VISA   DY a
M *(restricted service Christmas-New Year)* 9.50/15.75 **t.** and a la carte 🍴 4.35 – 🍽 7.75 – **126 rm** 72.00/84.00 **st.**, **2 suites** 125.00 **t.** – SB (weekends only) 100.00/104.00 **st.**

Viking (Q.M.H.), North St., YO1 1JF, ✆ 659822, Telex 57937, Fax 641793, ≼ – 🛗 ▤ rest TV ☎ 🅿 – 🛐 250. 🔺 AE ⓪ VISA. 🕏   CY n
M 9.00/12.00 **st.** and a la carte – **187 rm** 🍽 65.00/96.00 **st.**, **1 suite** 220.00/260.00 **st.** – SB (weekends only) 88.00/94.00 **st.**

Judges' Lodging, 9 Lendal, YO1 2AQ, ✆ 638733, « Restored 18C judge's lodgings » – TV ☎ 🅿. 🔺 AE ⓪ VISA   CY x
M (bar lunch)/dinner a la carte 15.20/24.40 **t.** 🍴 4.50 – **13 rm** 🍽 45.00/95.00 **t.** – SB (except summer) 97.50/107.50 **st.**

Mount Royale, The Mount, YO2 2DA, ✆ 628856, Telex 57414, Fax 611171, « Tasteful decor and furnishings », ⌇ heated, 🐾 – TV ☎ 🅿. 🔺 AE ⓪ VISA. 🕏   AZ s
closed 23 to 30 December – **M** (bar lunch)/dinner 25.00 **t.** – **20 rm** 🍽 67.50/85.00 **t.**, **1 suite** 90.00/100.00 **t.**

Hudsons, 60 Bootham, YO3 7BZ, ✆ 621267 – 🛗 TV ☎ 🅿. 🕏   CX a
28 rm.

Dean Court (Best Western), Duncombe Pl., YO1 2EF, ✆ 625082, Telex 57584, Fax 620305 – 🛗 TV ☎. 🔺 AE ⓪ VISA. 🕏   CY a
M 10.00/16.00 **t.** and a la carte 🍴 4.25 – **41 rm** 🍽 48.00/110.00 **t.** – SB 106.00/110.00 **st.**

York Pavilion, 45 Main St., Fulford, YO1 4PJ, S : 1 m. on A 19 ✆ 622099, Fax 626939, 🐾 – TV ☎ 🅿. 🔺 AE ⓪ VISA. 🕏   on A19 B
M 12.95 **t.** and a la carte 🍴 4.25 – **21 rm** 🍽 57.50/85.00 **t.** – SB (except Easter, Christmas and Bank Holidays) 95.00/100.00 **st.**

Ambassador, 123-125 The Mount, YO2 2DA, ✆ 641316, 🐾 – 🛗 TV ☎ 🅿. 🔺 VISA   AZ c
M 5.75/11.50 **st.** and a la carte 🍴 3.75 – **19 rm** 🍽 48.00/56.00 **t.** – SB 56.00/70.00 **st.**

Swallow Chase, Tascaster Rd, YO2 2QQ, ✆ 701000, Telex 57582, Fax 702308, 🏊, 🐾 – ⤢ rm TV ☎ 🚻 🅿 – 🛐 100. 🔺 AE ⓪ VISA   AZ a
M 10.00/15.00 **st.** and a la carte 🍴 4.00 – **116 rm** 🍽 64.00/125.00 **st.** – SB (except Christmas) 85.00/95.00 **st.**

Post House (T.H.F.), Tadcaster Rd, YO2 2QF, ✆ 707921, Telex 57798, Fax 702804, 🐾 – 🛗 ⤢ rm TV ☎ 🅿 – 🛐 100. 🔺 AE ⓪ VISA   AZ r
M 11.00/15.00 **st.** and a la carte 🍴 3.95 – 🍽 7.00 – **147 rm** 62.00/77.00 **st.** – SB (except Easter and Christmas) 80.00/98.00 **st.**

Novotel York, Fishergate, YO1 4AD, ✆ 611660, Telex 57556, Fax 610925, ⌇ heated – 🛗 ▤ rest TV ☎ 🚻 🅿 – 🛐 300. 🔺 AE ⓪ VISA   DY o
M 7.95/10.75 **st.** and a la carte 🍴 4.25 – 🍽 5.50 – **124 rm** 48.00/56.00 **st.** – SB 72.00/76.00 **st.**

Arndale, 290 Tadcaster Rd, YO2 2ET, ✆ 702424, 🐾 – ⤢ rest TV 🅿. 🕏   AZ i
closed Christmas and New Year – **M** (dinner only) 10.50 **st.** – **9 rm** 🍽 28.00/52.00 **st.** – SB 47.00/69.00 **st.**

Clifton Bridge, Water End, YO3 6LL, ✆ 610510 – TV ☎ 🅿. 🔺 VISA   AY e
closed 25 December-1 January – **M** *(closed Sunday dinner)* (bar lunch)/dinner 10.50 **t.** and a la carte 🍴 2.90 – **11 rm** 🍽 30.00/48.00 **t.** – SB (November-May) (except Bank Holidays) 52.00 **st.**

Cottage, 3 Clifton Green, YO3 6LH, ✆ 643711 – TV ☎ 🅿. 🔺 AE ⓪ VISA. 🕏   AY v
closed Christmas and New Year – **M** (grill rest.) (dinner only) 9.00 **t.** and a la carte 🍴 4.25 – **19 rm** 🍽 35.00/60.00 **t.** – SB (except Bank Holidays) 69.00/79.00 **st.**

YORK

Blake Street ... CY 5
Coney Street ... CY 13
Davygate ... CY 16
Lendal ... CY 32
Parliament Street ... DY 42
Shambles (The) ... DY 54
Stonegate ... CY 58
Bishopgate Street ... CZ 3
Bishophill Senior ... CZ 4
Campleshon Road ... AZ 7

Church Street ... DY 8
Clifford Street ... DY 10
Colliergate ... DY 12
Cromwell Road ... CZ 15
Deangate ... DY 18
Duncombe Place ... CY 20
Fawcett Street ... DZ 21
Fetter Lane ... CY 22
Goodramgate ... DY 25
High Ousegate ... DY 26
High Petergate ... CY 28
Knavesmire Road ... AZ 29
Leeman Road ... AY, CY 30
Lord Mayor's Walk ... DX 33

Low Petergate ... DY 35
Melrosegate ... BY 36
Museum Street ... CY 39
Pavement ... DY 43
Peasholme Green ... DY 45
Penley's Grove Street ... DX 46
Queen Street ... CZ 49
St. Helen's Road ... AZ 50
St. Leonard's Place ... CY 52
St. Maurice's Road ... DXY 53
Station Road ... CY 55
Stonebow (The) ... DY 56
Tower Street ... DZ 59
University Road ... BZ 60

THIRSK
A 19
HELMSLEY
B 1363
(A 64) SCARBOROUGH
A 1036
MALTON
HARROGATE
A 59
WETHERBY
B 1224
A 1036
LEEDS
A 19
SELBY
A 1079
(A 166) BRIDLINGTON
KINGSTON-UPON-HULL

Shipton Rd
Water La.
Wigginton Rd
Malton Road
Stockton Lane
Ouse
End
CLIFTON
Huntington Rd
Heworth Gr.
HEWORTH
Tang Hall La.
TANG HALL
Boroughbridge Rd
Beckfield Lane
Carr Lane
Acomb Rd
Poppleton Rd
Holgate Rd
Water
Lawrence St.
Hull Rd
ACOMB
Gale Lane
Tadcaster Rd
Bishopthorpe Rd
Fulford Rd
Ouse
POL.
Broadway
Heslington Lane
FULFORD
HESLINGTON

1 km
1/2 mile

B 1363
A 19
A 1036
B 1363
A 1079

Burton Stone Lane
Clifton
Grosvenor Ter.
Bootham
Marygate
Gillygate
Clarence St.
Townend St.
Haxby Rd
Lowther Street
Huntington Rd
Heworth Green
Monkgate
Foss Bank
Layerthorpe
MINSTER
NATIONAL RAILWAY MUSEUM
STATION
Micklegate
Blossom St.
Moss St.
Nunnery Lane
Nunthorpe Rd
Scarcroft Road
Bishopthorpe Rd
Ouse
Fossgate
Walmgate
Foss Islands Road
Navigation Rd
Piccadilly
Hope St.
Paragon St.
Fishergate
Barbican Rd
Cemetery Rd

400 m
400 yards

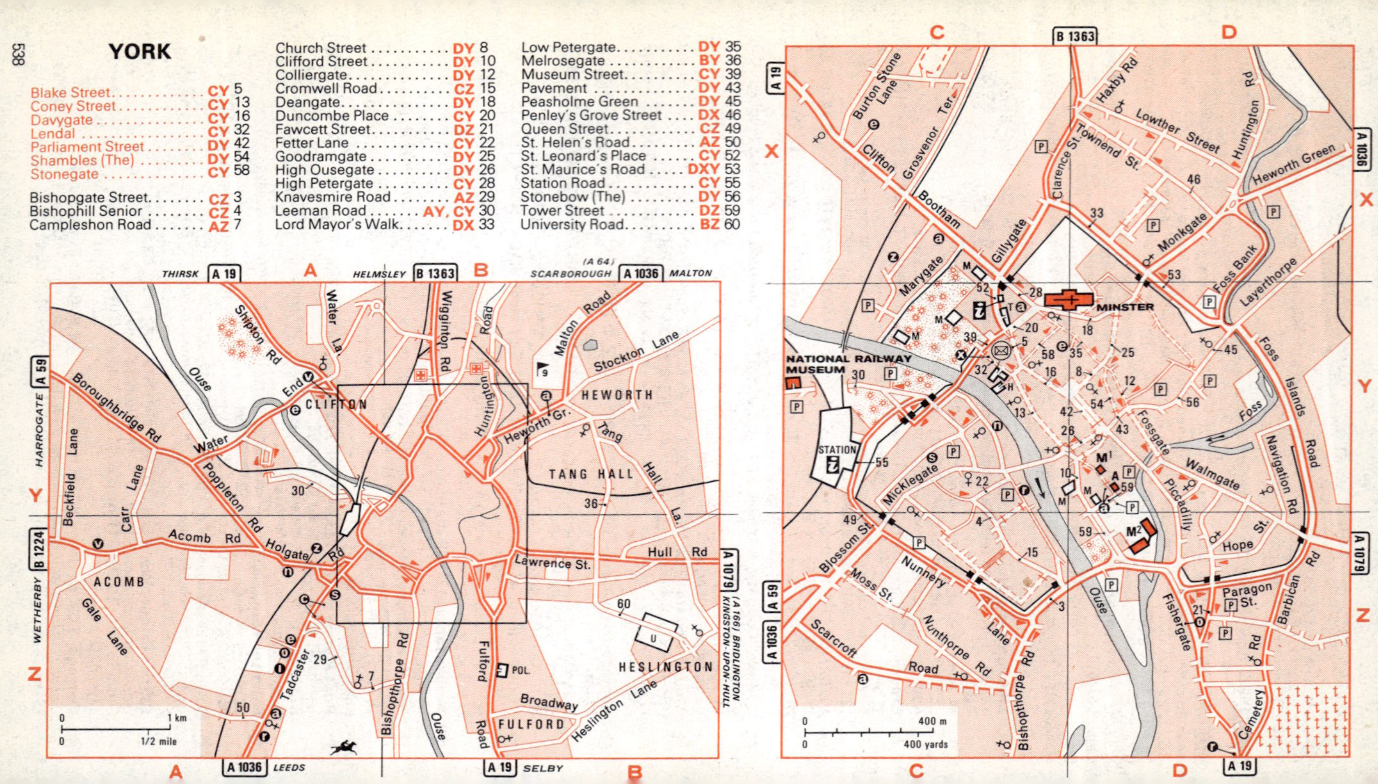

538

Grasmead House without rest., 1 Scarcroft Hill, YO2 1DF, ℘ 629996 – ⊱ rm 📺. ⊠ 𝘝𝘐𝘚𝘈. ⊰
CZ **a**
6 rm ⊆ 42.00/45.00 st.

Heworth Court, 76-78 Heworth Green, YO3 7TQ, ℘ 425156, Telex 57571 – 📺 ☎ ℗. ⊠ AE ⑩ 𝘝𝘐𝘚𝘈. ⊰
BY **a**
M 12.50 t. and a la carte ▮ 4.00 – **16 rm** ⊆ 33.00/56.00 t. – SB 64.00/68.00 st.

Kilima, 129 Holgate Rd, YO2 4DE, ℘ 658844, Telex 57928, ㄹ – ⊱ rest 📺 ☎ � ℗. ⊠ AE ⑩ 𝘝𝘐𝘚𝘈
AZ **n**
M 13.75 t. (dinner) and a la carte ▮ 3.85 – **15 rm** ⊆ 35.00/52.00 t. – SB (except Easter and Christmas) 70.00/76.00 st.

Town House, 98-104 Holgate Rd, YO2 4BB, ℘ 636171 – 📺 ☎ ℗. ⊠ AE ⑩ 𝘝𝘐𝘚𝘈
AZ **z**
closed 24 December-2 January – **M** (bar lunch)/dinner 9.00 t. and a la carte ▮ 2.95 – **23 rm** ⊆ 20.00/45.00 t. – SB (October-April) 50.00/55.00 st.

Field House, 2 St. Georges Pl., YO2 2DR, ℘ 639572, ㄹ – ⊱ rest 📺 ☎ ℗. ⊠ AE 𝘝𝘐𝘚𝘈. ⊰
AZ **e**
closed Christmas – **M** (residents only) (dinner only) 10.00 st. – **17 rm** ⊆ 27.00/50.00 st. – SB 62.00/70.00 st.

Priory, 126 Fulford Rd, YO1 4BE, ℘ 625280, ㄹ – 📺 ℗. ⊠ AE ⑩ 𝘝𝘐𝘚𝘈. ⊰
DZ **r**
closed Christmas – **19 rm** ⊆ 19.00/38.00 st. – SB (November-Easter) 54.00 st.

Hill, 60 York Rd, Acomb, YO2 5LW, ℘ 790777, ㄹ – ⊱ rest 📺 ☎ ℗. ⊠ AE 𝘝𝘐𝘚𝘈. ⊰
AZ **v**
M (bar lunch)/dinner 10.00 st. ▮ 2.60 – **10 rm** ⊆ 31.30/53.00 st. – SB 62.00/68.00 st.

↑ **Fairmount,** 230 Tadcaster Rd, YO2 2ES, ℘ 638298 – ⊱ rest 📺 ℗. ⊠ 𝘝𝘐𝘚𝘈
AZ **o**
M 11.50/12.50 st. ▮ 4.50 – **10 rm** ⊆ 25.00/45.00 st. – SB 56.00/60.00 st.

↑ **Hobbits** without rest., 9 St. Peter's Grove, Clifton, YO3 6AQ, ℘ 624538 – ⊱ 📺 ℗. 𝘝𝘐𝘚𝘈
CX **e**
closed 24 to 26 December – **5 rm** ⊆ 20.00/40.00 st.

↑ **Crook Lodge,** 26 St. Mary's, Bootham, YO3 7DD, ℘ 655614 – 📺 ℗. ⊰
CX **z**
M 8.50 st. ▮ 2.65 – **7 rm** ⊆ 19.50/36.00 st. – SB (November-March) (weekdays only) 39.00/41.00 st.

XX **153 Mount Vale,** 153 Mount Vale, YO2 2DJ, ℘ 620190 – ⊠ AE ⑩ 𝘝𝘐𝘚𝘈
AZ **c**
closed Sunday dinner, Monday and 3 weeks January – **M** 12.00/19.00 t.

X **19 Grape Lane,** 19 Grape Lane, YO1 2HU, ℘ 636366, English rest. – ⊠ 𝘝𝘐𝘚𝘈
CY **e**
closed Sunday, Monday, 2 weeks January and 2 weeks October – **M** 8.50/16.50 t. and a la carte 17.75/20.85 t.

X **Restaurant Français,** 28 Castlegate, YO1 1RP, ℘ 647339 – ⊠ 𝘝𝘐𝘚𝘈
DY **a**
closed Sunday – **M** (dinner only) 15.00 t. and a la carte 15.75/17.75 t.

X **McCoy's,** 17 Skeldergate, YO1 1DH, ℘ 612191. ⊠ AE ⑩ 𝘝𝘐𝘚𝘈
CY **r**
M a la carte 10.30/23.40 t.

X **Tony's,** 39 Tanner Row, YO1 1JP, ℘ 659622, Greek rest. – ⊠ AE 𝘝𝘐𝘚𝘈
CY **s**
closed Sunday and last 3 weeks January – **M** (dinner only) 9.50 t. and a la carte 9.00/11.00 t.

at Kexby E : 6 ¾ m. on A 1079 B – ✉ York – ☏ 075 95 Wilberfoss :

Kexby Bridge, Hull Rd, YO4 5LD, ℘ 8223, ㄹ – ⊱ rm 📺 ☎ ℗. ⊠ 𝘝𝘐𝘚𝘈. ⊰
M 7.50/9.50 st. and a la carte ▮ 3.50 – **32 rm** ⊆ 45.00/64.00 t. – SB 65.00 st.

at Bilbrough SW : 5 ½ m. by A 1036 – AZ – off A 64 – ✉ York – ☏ 0937 Tadcaster :

Bilbrough Manor ⑧, YO2 3PH, ℘ 834002, Fax 834724, ≼, « Tastefully decorated Victorian manor », ㄹ, park – 📺 ☎ ℗. ⊠ AE ⑩ 𝘝𝘐𝘚𝘈. ⊰
M 14.00/29.50 t. and a la carte ▮ 5.00 – **12 rm** ⊆ 75.00/135.00 t. – SB (November-March) (except Christmas and New Year) 103.00/143.00 st.

at Skelton NW : 3 m. on A 19 – AY – ✉ ☏ 0904 York :

Fairfield Manor, Shipton Rd, YO3 6XW, ℘ 625621, ㄹ – 📺 ☎ ℗. ⊰
25 rm.

ALFA-ROMEO Leeman Rd ℘ 622772	MAZDA 17 Layerthorpe ℘ 658809
COLT Fulford ℘ 633139	PEUGEOT-TALBOT The Stonebow ℘ 655118
FIAT Piccadilly ℘ 634321	TOYOTA 172 Fulford Rd ℘ 652947
FORD Piccadilly ℘ 625371	VAUXHALL-OPEL Malton Rd ℘ 426688
FORD, VAUXHALL-OPEL 117 Long St. ℘ 0347 (Easingwold) 21694	VOLVO 88-96 Walmgate ℘ 653798
JAGUAR, DAIMLER Layerthorpe ℘ 658252	ⓦ ATS 2 James St. ℘ 412372/410375
LADA Leeman Rd ℘ 659241	ATS 36 Holgate Rd ℘ 654411

YOXFORD Suffolk 🄴🄾🄴 Y 27 – pop. 690 – ✉ Saxmundham – ☏ 072 877.
♦London 95 – ♦Ipswich 25 – ♦Norwich 55.

Satis House, Brook St., IP17 3EX, ℘ 418, ㄹ – 📺 ☎ ℗. ⊰ – **7 rm**.

YR ORSEDD = Rossett.

YR WYDDFA = Snowdon.

YR WYDDGRUG = Mold.

Scotland

Place with at least :
one hotel or restaurant............................. ● Tongue
one pleasant hotel .... ✕ with rm
one quiet, secluded hotel ....
one restaurant with............................. ✿, ✿✿, ✿✿✿, M
See this town for establishments
  located in its vicinity....................... ABERDEEN

La località possiede come minimo :
una risorsa alberghiera .... ● Tongue
un albergo ameno .... ✕ with rm
un albergo molto tranquillo, isolato ....
un'ottima tavola con............................. ✿, ✿✿, ✿✿✿, M
La località raggruppa nel suo testo
  le risorse dei dintorni....................... ABERDEEN

Localité offrant au moins :
une ressource hôtelière .... ● Tongue
un hôtel agréable .... ✕ with rm
un hôtel très tranquille, isolé....................
une bonne table à............................. ✿, ✿✿, ✿✿✿, M
Localité groupant dans le texte
  les ressources de ses environs .... ABERDEEN

Ort mit mindestens :
einem Hotel oder Restaurant............................. ● Tongue
einem angenehmen Hotel .... ✕ with rm
einem sehr ruhigen und abgelegenen Hotel ......
einem Restaurant mit............................. ✿, ✿✿, ✿✿✿, M
Ort mit Angaben über Hotels und Restaurants
  in seiner Umgebung....................... ABERDEEN

Kinlochbervie
Scourie
ISLE
OF
LEWIS
Uig
Stornoway
Lochinver
Achiltibuie
Ullapool
Tarbert
Scarista
Aultbea
ISLE OF HARRIS
Dundonnell
Poolewe
Gairloch
NORTH
UIST
Culraknock
Balivanich
Kensaleyre
BENBECULA
Skeabost
ISLE
OF
RAASAY
Shieldaig
Strathconon
Dunvegan
Portree
Lochcarron
SOUTH
UIST
ISLE
OF
SKYE
Kyle of
Lochalsh
Plockton
Balmacara
Daliburgh
Dornie
Lochboisdale
Isleornsay
Ardvasar
astlebay
ISLE OF BARRA
Mallaig

SHETLAND ISLANDS
ISLE OF UNST
Hillswick
Brae
MAINLAND
Whiteness
Lerwick
ISLE OF WESTRAY
MAINLAND
Dounby
Loch Harray
Stromness
Kirkwall
ORKNEY
ISLANDS
Thurso
Tongue
Forsinard
Wick
Altnaharra
A 9
Lairg
Rogart
Golspie
Brora
Dornoch
Tain
Lossiemouth
Cromarty
BUCKIE
Cullen
Banff
Pennan
St. Comb
Strathpeffer
A 96
Elgin
Fordyce
Macduff
A 952
Muir of Ord
Forres
A 98
Nairn
Rothes
Peterhead
Beauly
INVERNESS
Aberlour
Farr
A 9
Advie
Ellon
Drumnadrochit
Grantown-on-Spey
Glenlivet
Oldmeldrum
Lewiston
Pitcaple
Newburg
Foyers
Carrbridge
Dulnain Bridge
Inverurie
Invermoriston
Boat of Garten
Kildrummy
Whitebridge
Aviemore
Fort Augustus
Kincraig
ABERDEEN
Newtonmore
Kingussie
Aboyne
Banchory
A 92
Laggan
Ballater

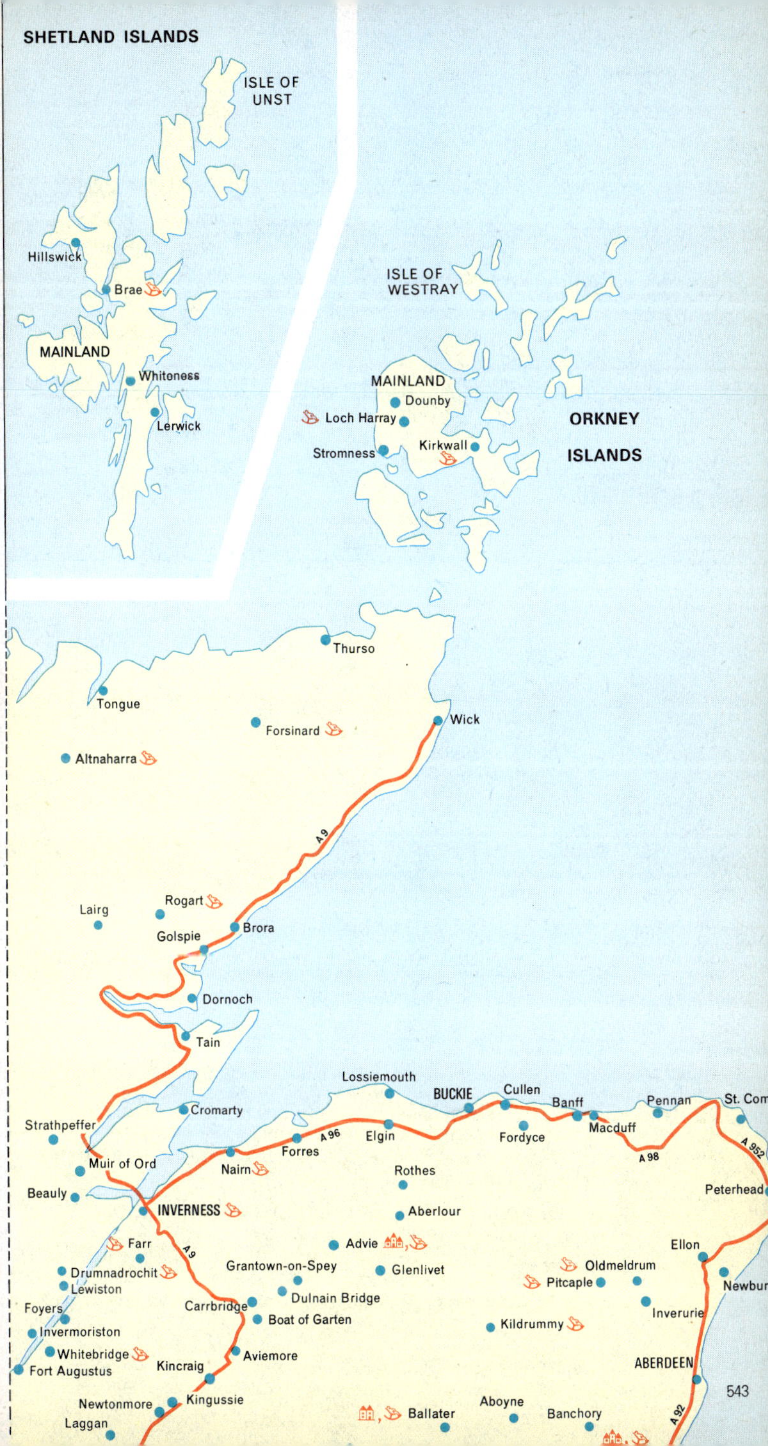

543

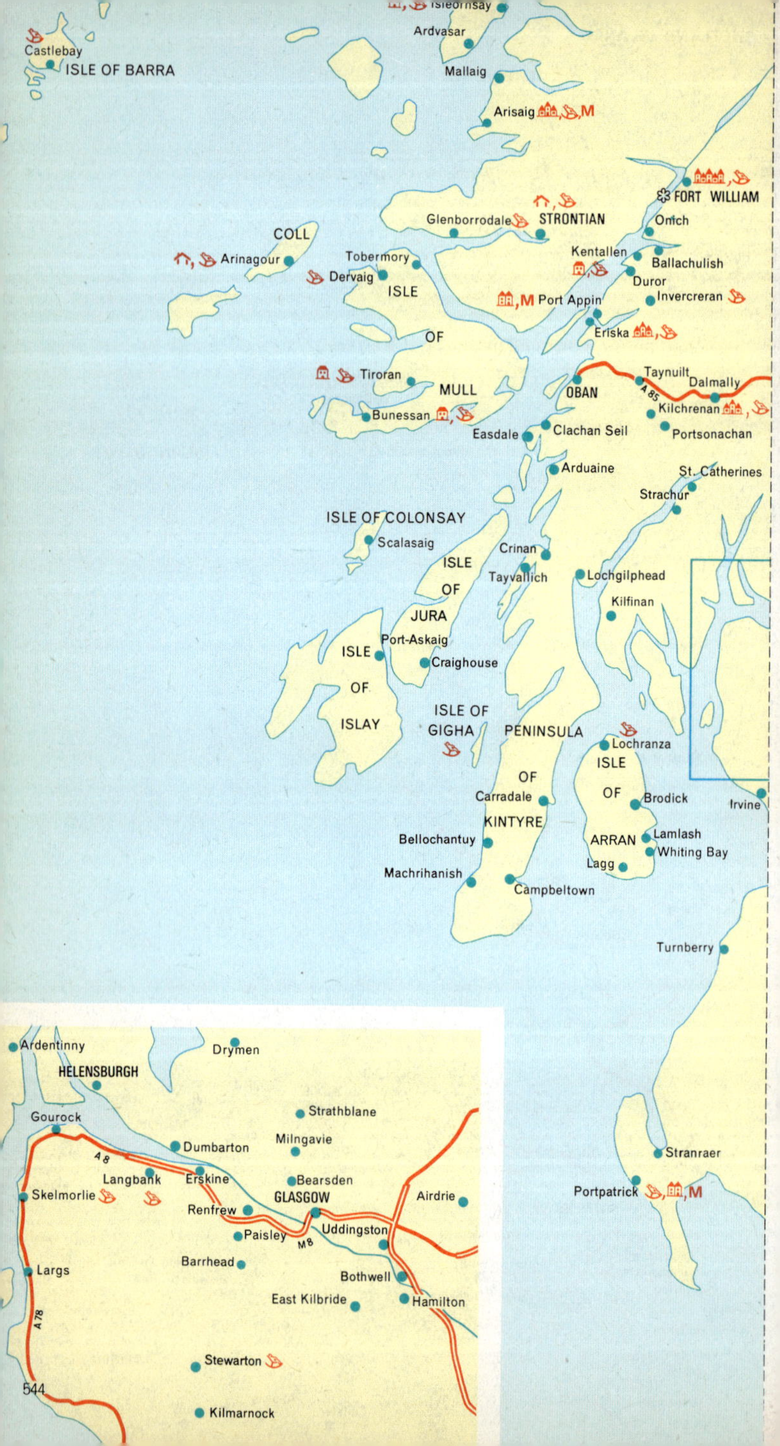
Isleornsay
Ardvasar
Castlebay
ISLE OF BARRA
Mallaig
Arisaig ,M
FORT WILLIAM
Glenborrodale STRONTIAN
Onich
COLL
Kentallen
Ballachulish
Arinagour
Tobermory
Dervaig
Duror
Invercreran
ISLE
Port Appin ,M
Eriska ,
OF
Taynuilt
Tiroran
Dalmally
A 85
MULL
OBAN
Kilchrenan ,
Bunessan ,
Easdale Clachan Seil
Portsonachan
Arduaine
St. Catherines
Strachur
ISLE OF COLONSAY
Scalasaig
Crinan
ISLE
Tayvallich
Lochgilphead
OF
Kilfinan
JURA
Port-Askaig
ISLE
Craighouse
OF
ISLAY
ISLE OF
PENINSULA
GIGHA
Lochranza
ISLE
OF
Carradale
Brodick
Irvine
KINTYRE
OF
Bellochantuy
ARRAN
Lamlash
Whiting Bay
Machrihanish
Lagg
Campbeltown
Turnberry
Ardentinny
Drymen
HELENSBURGH
Gourock
Strathblane
A 8
Milngavie
Dumbarton
Stranraer
Langbank
Erskine
Bearsden
Portpatrick , ,M
Skelmorlie
GLASGOW
Airdrie
Renfrew
Paisley M 8 Uddingston
Barrhead
Largs
Bothwell
A 78
East Kilbride Hamilton
Stewarton
544
Kilmarnock

Whitebridge
Fort Augustus
Kincraig
Aviemore
ABERDEEN
Newtonmore
Kingussie
Aboyne
Banchory
Laggan
Ballater
Stonehaven
A 92
Braémar
Edzell
Blair Atholl
A 9
Montrose
Kirkmichael
PITLOCHRY
A 92
Bridge of Cally
Forfar
With rm. Aberfeldy
Alyth
Blairgowrie
Kenmore
Meigle
Arbroath
Dunkeld
Auchterhouse
KILLIN
Kinclaven
A 85
Crianlarich
DUNDEE
St. Fillans
CRIEFF
PERTH
Wormit
Balquhidder
Lochearnhead
Glencarse
Cupar
STRATHYRE
A 9
St. Andrews
Auchterarder
Brig o'Turk
Peat Inn
Callander
A 84
KINROSS
LEVEN
Doune
Dunblane
Anstruther
Aberfoyle M
Bridge of Allan
GLENROTHES
STIRLING
M 90
KIRKCALDY
DUNFERMLINE
North Berwick
Airth
Burntisland
Denny
Aberdour
GULLANE M,
FALKIRK
Aberlady
Aberdour
Dunbar
South-Queensferry
East Linton
Linlithgow
A 90
Haddington
A 80
Uphall
Edinburgh
Gifford
Livingston
M 8
A 68
Dolphinton
LAUDER
Greenlaw
Lanark
PEEBLES
Walkerburn
Quothquan
Galashiels
KELSO
MELROSE
Troon
Tweedsmuir
Selkirk
Prestwick
AYR
A 74
Hawick
Roberton
Moffat
Beattock
Eskdalemuir
THORNHILL
Dalry
Lockerbie
DUMFRIES
New Galloway
Canonbie
Crocketford
Newton Stewart
Gretna
Castle Douglas
Dalbeattie
Gatehouse of Fleet
Colvend
Sandyhills
Wigtown
Rockcliffe
Kirkcudbright
Auchencairn
Whithorn (Isle of)

SCOTLAND

Towns

ABERDEEN Aberdeen. (Grampian) **401** N 12 **Scotland G** – pop. 186 757 – ECD : Wednesday and Saturday – ✆ 0224.

See : Old Aberdeen★★ X – St. Machar's Cathedral★★ (West front★★★, heraldic ceiling★★★) X A – Mercat Cross★★ Y B – Art Gallery★★ Y M – King's College Chapel★ (Crown spire★★★, medieval fittings★★★) X D – Brig o'Balgownie★ by Don Street X – Maritime Museum★ Z M1 – Provost Skene's House★ (Painted ceiling★★) Y E – Marischal College★ Y U.

Envir. : Deeside★★ and Lin O'Dee★ Tour of 64 m., W : by A 93 X – Grampian Castles★★ (Craigievar★★★) W : 27 m. by A 944 X and B 9119 – Crathes Castle★★, SW : 14 m. by A 93 X – Kildrummy★, NW : 36 m. by A 944 X – Castle Fraser★ (exterior★★) W : 16 m. by A 944 X – Pitmedden Gardens★★, N : 16 m. by A 92 X and B 999 – Haddo House★, NW : 26 m. by A 92 X and B 9005.

🏌 Bon Accord, 19 Golf Rd ✆ 633464 X – 🏌 St. Fittick's Rd, Balnagask ✆ 876407 X – 🏌 Westhill, Westhill Heights Skene ✆ 740159 by A 944 X – 🏌, 🏌, 🏌 Hazelhead ✆ 321830, W : 3 m. by A 944 X – 🏌 Auchmill, Provest Rust Drive ✆ 714577, NW : 3 m. X.

✈ Aberdeen Airport ✆ 722331, NW : 7 m. by A 96 X – Terminal : Bus Station, Guild St. (adjacent to Railway Station) – 🚗 ✆ 0345 090700.

🚢 by P & O Ferries : Orkney & Shetland Services : to Shetland Islands : Lerwick 1 daily Monday/Friday (14 h).

🛈 St. Nicholas House, Broad St. ✆ 632727 – Railway Station, Guild St. (summer only).

◆Edinburgh 130 – ◆Dundee 67.

Plans on following pages

🏨 **Caledonian Thistle** (Thistle), 10-14 Union Terr., AB9 1HE, ✆ 640233, Telex 73758, Fax 641627 – 🛗 ⇆ rm 📺 ☎ 🅿. 🔼 AE ⓪ VISA   Z i
    M 9.00/18.00 t. and a la carte – � 7.25 – **77 rm** 65.00/97.00 st., **3 suites** 105.00 st.

🏨 Stakis Tree Tops (Stakis), 161 Springfield Rd, AB9 2QH, ✆ 313377, Telex 73794, Fax 312028,
🏊 – 🛗 📺 ☎ 🅿 – 👥 600. 🔼 AE ⓪ VISA   X s
    ⊻ 7.25 – **112 rm** 73.00/97.00 st., **2 suites** – SB 58.00/79.00 st.

🏠 Malacca, 349 Great Western Rd, AB1 6NW, ✆ 588901 – 📺 ☎ 🅿   X u
18 rm.

🏠 **Royal**, 1-3 Bath St., AB1 2HY, ✆ 585152, Telex 739018, Fax 583900 – 🛗 📺 ☎ 🅿. 🔼 AE ⓪
VISA   Z a
    M (bar lunch)/dinner 7.90 **st.** and a la carte 🍷 3.50 – **44 rm** ⊻ 18.00/43.00 st., **1 suite** 45.00/60.00 **st.** – SB (weekends only) 46.00/60.00 **st.**

🏠 **Bracklinn** without rest., 348 Great Western Rd, AB1 6LX, ✆ 317060 – 📺. 🦮   X c
6 rm ⊻ 16.00/30.00.

🏠 **Cedars** without rest., 339 Great Western Rd, AB1 6NW, ✆ 583225 – 📺 🅿. AE. 🦮   X e
13 rm ⊻ 25.00/38.00 st.

🏠 Broomfield, 15 Balmoral Pl., AB1 6HR, ✆ 588758, 🦮 – 🅿   X n
M (by arrangement) 7.00 **st.** – **8 rm** ⊻ –/14.00 st.

XX **Atlantis**, 16-17 Bon Accord Cres., AB1 2DE, ✆ 591403, Seafood – 🔼 AE ⓪ VISA   Z r
    closed Saturday lunch and Sunday – M a la carte 17.90/22.50 t. 🍷 4.50.

XX **Aberdeen Rendez-vous**, 218-222 George St., AB1 1BS, ✆ 633610, Chinese (Peking) rest.
– 🍽. 🔼 AE ⓪ VISA   Y c
    M 6.50/15.50 **st.** and a la carte 7.80/11.40 **st.** 🍷 3.80.

XX **Nargile**, 77-79 Skene St., AB1 1QD, ✆ 636093, Turkish rest. – 🔼 AE ⓪ VISA   Y a
    closed 25 December and 1 January – M (dinner only) 12.00 t. and a la carte 8.55/13.60 t.
🍷 3.85.

X **Silver Darling**, Pocra Quay, North Pier, AB2 1DQ, ✆ 576229, French, Seafood rest. – 🔼
AE VISA   X a
    closed lunch Saturday and Sunday and 24 December-8 January – M (booking essential) 12.00 t. (lunch) and a la carte approx. 29.25 t. 🍷 4.00.

at Altens S : 3 m. on A 956 – X – ✉ ✆ 0224 Aberdeen :

🏨 Skean Dhu Altens (Mt. Charlotte), Souterhead Rd, AB1 4LF, ✆ 877000, Telex 739631,
🏊 heated – 🛗 🍽 rest 📺 ☎ 🦽 🅿 – 👥 450 – **221 rm. 1 suite**

at Banchory-Devenick SW : 4½ m. on B 9077 – X – ✉ ✆ 0224 Aberdeen :

🏨 **Ardoe House** 🦢, South Deeside Rd, AB1 5YP, ✆ 867355, Fax 861283, ≤, 🦮, park – 📺
☎ 🅿 – 👥 120. 🔼 AE ⓪ VISA 🦮
    M 15.50 t. and a la carte 15.75/21.75 t. – **17 rm** ⊻ 50.00/100.00 t.

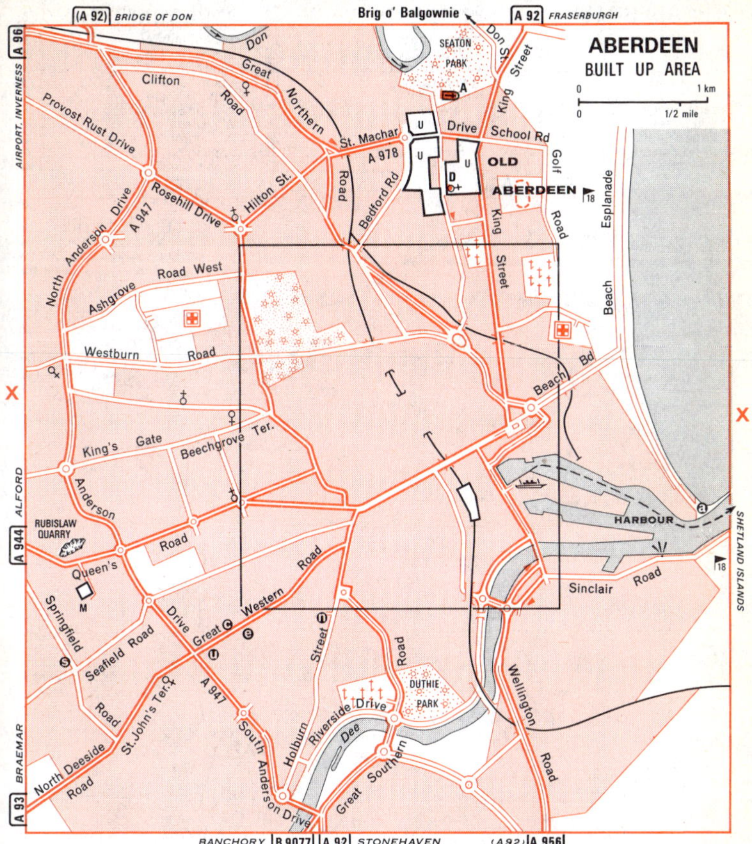

at Maryculter SW : 8 m. on B 9077 – X – ✉ ☎ 0224 Aberdeen :

Maryculter House ⤿, South Deeside Rd, AB1 0BB, ✆ 732124, Fax 733510, « Part 13C house on River Dee », 🐎 – TV ☎ P – 🕴 30
11 rm.

at Westhill W : 6 ½ m. by A 944 – X – ✉ ☎ 0224 Aberdeen :

Westhill, Kinmundy Drive, AB3 6TT, ✆ 740388, Telex 739925, Fax 744354 – 🛗 TV ☎ P – 🕴 250. 🔟 AE ⓘ VISA
M 5.50/11.50 **st.** and a la carte 🍴 3.75 – **52 rm** ☖ 40.00/58.00 **st.** – SB 60.00/65.00 **st.**

at Bucksburn NW : 4 m. by A 96 – X – on A 947 – ✉ ☎ 0224 Aberdeen :

Bucksburn Moat House (Q.M.H.), Oldmeldrum Rd, AB2 9LN, ✆ 713911, Telex 73108, Fax 714020, 🔟 – 🛗 ⤢ rm TV ☎ P – 🕴 200. 🔟 AE ⓘ VISA
closed 25 and 26 December – **M** (closed lunch Saturday and Sunday) 14.00/15.00 **t.** and a la carte 🍴 4.50 – ☖ 6.45 – **97 rm** 71.30/80.50 **t.**, **1 suite** – SB (weekends only) 77.00 **st.**

Craighaar, Waterton Rd, AB2 9HS, ✆ 712275 – TV ☎ P – **41 rm**.

at Dyce NW : 5 ½ m. by A 96 – X – on A 947 – ✉ ☎ 0224 Aberdeen :

Holiday Inn, Riverview Drive, Farburn, AB2 0AZ, ✆ 770011, Telex 739651, Fax 722347, 🔟
– ⤢ rm 🖥 TV ☎ 🕭 P – 🕴 400. 🔟 AE ⓘ VISA
M (buffet lunch)/dinner a la carte 15.50/20.95 **st.** – ☖ 7.95 – **153 rm** 80.00/98.00 **st.**, **1 suite** 85.00/125.00 **st.** – SB (weekends only) 96.00/116.00 **st.**

at Aberdeen Airport NW : 6 m. by A 96 – X – ✉ ☎ 0224 Aberdeen :

Aberdeen Airport Skean Dhu (Mt. Charlotte), Argyll Rd, AB2 0DU, ✆ 725252, Telex 739239, 🏊 heated – 🖥 TV ☎ 🕭 P – 🕴 – **148 rm**.

ABERDEEN

George Street .... Y
St. Nicolas Street .... Y 30
Union Street .... Z

Broad Street .... Y 6
Castle Street .... Y 7
College Street .... Z 9
Craigie Loanings .... Y 12
East North Street ... Y 16

Great Southern Road........ Z 18
Guild Street............. Z 19
Justice Street .... Y 21
Loch Street .... Z 22
Millburn Street .... Z 23
Regent Quay .... Z 24
Rosemount
Terrace .... Y 25
Rosemount Viaduct .... Y 26
St. Andrew Street .... Y 28
St. Swithin Street .... Z 31
School Hill .... YZ 32

South Esplanade West ...... Z 33
South Mount Street......... Y 34
Springbank Terrace .... Z 35
Spring Garden .... Y 36
Trinity Quay .... Z 37
Union Terrace .... Y 39
Upperkirkgate .... Y 40
Victoria Street........... Z 42
Waverley Place .... Z 43
Wellington Place .... Z 45
Wellington Road .... Z 47
Woolmanhill............. Y 48

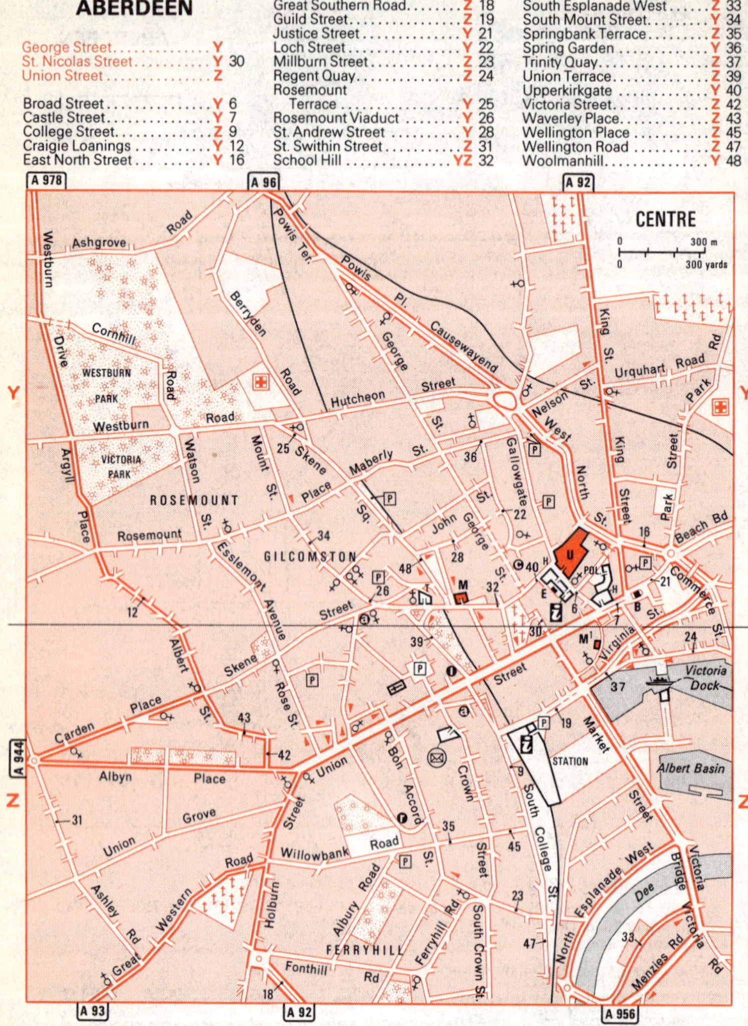

MICHELIN Distribution Centre, Wellington Rd, AB9 2JZ, ☎ 875075, FAX 878474 by A 956 X

ALFA-ROMEO 542 Gt Western Rd ☎ 310181
AUSTIN-ROVER Lang Stracht ☎ 685511
AUSTIN-ROVER 19 Justice Mill Lane ☎ 596151
BMW Grey St. ☎ 313355
FIAT 870 Gt Northern Rd ☎ 695573
FORD Menzies Rd ☎ 248800
FORD Lang Stracht ☎ 697772
FORD Gt Western Rd ☎ 594277

MERCEDES-BENZ, FIAT 366 King St. ☎ 634211
NISSAN North Andason Drive ☎ 681111
PEUGEOT Broadford Rd, Bridge of Don ☎ 826300
RENAULT 78 Powis Terr. ☎ 481313
VAUXHALL-OPEL 16 Dee St. ☎ 589216

ATS Beach Boulevard ☎ 592727
ATS 214 Hardgate ☎ 589461

ABERDOUR Fife. (Fife) 401 K 15 Scotland G – pop. 1 460 – ECD : Wednesday – ☎ 0383.
See : Site★ – Castle★.

Dodhead, Burntisland ☎ 0592 (Burntisland) 874093, E : 5 m. on A 92.

♦Edinburgh 17 – Dunfermline 7.

Woodside, 80 High St., KY3 0SW, ☎ 860328, Fax 860920 – TV ☎ P. AE ① VISA
M 10.50/13.50 t. and a la carte ♦ 3.50 – **20 rm** � 45.50/58.50 t., **1 suite** 50.00/70.00 t.

548

ABERFELDY Perth. (Tayside) **401** I 14 Scotland G – pop. 1 477 – ECD : Wednesday – ☎ 0887.
See : Site★.

Envir. : St. Mary's Church (Painted ceiling★) NE : 2 m. by A 827 – Loch Tay★★, SW : 6 m. by A 827.

☌ Taybridge Rd ℰ 20535.

🛈 District Tourist Association, 8 Dunkeld St. ℰ 20276 (summer only).

◆Edinburgh 76 – ◆Glasgow 73 – ◆Oban 77 – Perth 32.

   🏠 **Guinach House** ⑤, Urlar Rd, PH15 2ET, ℰ 20251, 🚗 – 📺 🅿
    Mid March-October – **M** (dinner only) 15.00 **st.** 🍾 3.75 – **7 rm** ☲ 34.00/60.00 **st.** – SB 50.50/55.00 **st.**

   ⌂ **Balnearn**, Crieff Rd, PH15 2BJ, ℰ 20431, 🚗 – ⥱ rest 🅿
    M 8.05 **t.** – **13 rm** ☲ 12.65/33.00 **t.**

   XXX **Atkins at Farleyer House** ⑤ with rm, PH15 2JE, W : 2 m. on B 846 ℰ 20332, ≤, 🚗, park – 📺 ☎ 🅿. 𝖠𝖤 *VISA*
    M 17.50/25.00 **t.** 🍾 5.00 – **11 rm** ☲ 70.00/200.00 **t.**

SUBARU, FORD   Dunkeld St. ℰ 20254

ABERFOYLE Stirling (Central) **401** G 15 – pop. 546 – ECD : Wednesday – ✉ Stirling – ☎ 087 72.

☌ Braeval ℰ 493.

🛈 Main St. ℰ 352 (summer only).

◆Edinburgh 56 – ◆Glasgow 27.

   X **Braeval Old Mill,** FK8 3UY, E : 1 m. by A 821 on A 81 (Callander Rd) ℰ 711 – 🅿. 𝖠 𝖠𝖤 *VISA*
    closed Monday, 3 weeks January-February, 1 week May and 1 week November – **M** (booking essential) (dinner only and Sunday lunch)/dinner a la carte 13.40/18.85 **t.**

ABERLADY E. Lothian. (Lothian) **401** L 15 – pop. 884 – ECD : Wednesday – ☎ 087 57.

☌ Kilspindie, ℰ 358.

◆Edinburgh 16 – Haddington 5 – North Berwick 7.5.

   🏠 **Green Craig House** ⑤, SW : ¾ m. on A 198, EH32 0PY, ℰ 301, ≤, 🚗 – 📺 ☎ 🅿. 𝖠
    VISA. 𝒮𝒮
    M (bar lunch)/dinner 18.00 **t.** 🍾 3.50 – ☲ 6.50 – **8 rm** 30.00/65.00 **t.**

   ⚐ **Kilspindie House,** Main St., EH32 0RE, ℰ 682 – 📺 ☎ 🅿. 𝖠 *VISA*
    M (bar lunch)/dinner 10.00 **t.** and a la carte 🍾 3.50 – **11 rm** ☲ 30.00/48.00 **t.** – SB 52.00/68.00 **st.**

ABERLOUR Banff. (Grampian) **401** K 11 – pop. 879 – ECD : Wednesday – ☎ 034 05.

Envir. : Dufftown (Glenfiddich Distillery★) SE : 4 m. by A 941 – Huntly Castle (Heraldic carvings★★★) E : 1 ½ m. by A 941 and A 920.

◆Edinburgh 189 – ◆Aberdeen 59 – ◆Inverness 54.

   🏠 **Dowans**, AB3 9LS, SW : ¾ m. by A 95 ℰ 488, ≤, 🚗 – ⥱ rest 🅿
    18 rm.

AUSTIN-ROVER, LAND-ROVER, RANGE-ROVER   15-19 High St. ℰ 505

ABOYNE Aberdeen. (Grampian) **401** L 12 – pop. 1 477 – ECD : Thursday – ☎ 0339 (4 fig.) or 033 98 (5 fig.).

Envir. : Craigievar Castle★★★ (17C) *AC*, NE : 12 m.

☌ Formaston Park ℰ 2328, E : end of Village – ☌ Tarland ℰ 033 981 (Tarland) 413, NW : 5 m.

🛈 Ballater Rd Car Park ℰ 2060 (summer only).

◆Edinburgh 131 – ◆Aberdeen 30 – ◆Dundee 68.

   🏠 **Birse Lodge** ⑤, Charlestown Rd, AB3 5EL, ℰ 86253, 🚗 – ☏ 🅿. 𝖠 *VISA*
    M (bar lunch)/dinner 16.00 **t.** 🍾 3.40 – **16 rm** ☲ 30.00/60.00 **t.**

   X **Hazlehurst Lodge** with rm, Ballater Rd, AB3 5HY, ℰ 86921, 🚗 – ⥱ 🅿. 𝖠 *VISA*
    closed January – **M** a la carte 17.50/18.50 **t.** 🍾 4.95 – **3 rm** ☲ 26.50/38.00 **t.**

AUSTIN-ROVER   Main Rd ℰ 86440

ACHILTIBUIE Ross and Cromarty. (Highland) **401** D 9 – ☎ 085 482.

◆Edinburgh 243 – ◆Inverness 84 – Ullapool 25.

   🏠 **Summer Isles** ⑤, IV26 2YG, ℰ 282, « ≤ Picturesque setting overlooking Summer Isles », 🦢 – ⥱ rest 🅿
    10 April-14 October – **M** (dinner only) 25.00 **st.** – **12 rm** ☲ 40.00/85.00 **st.**

Les cartes Michelin sont constamment tenues à jour.

ADVIE Moray. (Highland) **401** J 11 – ✉ Grantown-on-Spey – ✆ 080 75.
♦Edinburgh 153 – ♦Inverness 46.

⛪ **Tulchan Lodge** ⑤, PH26 3PW, on B 9102 ✆ 200, Telex 75405, Fax 234, ≤ Spey Valley, « Victorian sporting lodge », ⌙, 🐴, park, 🎣 – ☎ ℗. 🐕
Mid April-October – **M** (booking essential for non-residents) (communal dining) 17.00/32.00 t. – **11 rm** ⊠ 138.00/182.00 t.

AIRDRIE Lanark. (Strathclyde) **401 402** I 16 – pop. 45 320 – ECD : Wednesday – ✆ 0236.
☗ Easter Moffat, Plains ✆ 842878.
♦Edinburgh 32 – ♦Glasgow 14 – Motherwell 6.5 – Perth 53.

🏠 **Staging Post**, 8-10 Anderson St., ML6 0AA, ✆ 67525 – 📺 ⊜. ⛁ 𝔸𝔼 ⓪ 𝑽𝑰𝑺𝑨. 🐕
closed 25 December and 1 January – **M** (*closed Sunday*) 6.75/9.75 t. and a la carte 8.70/23.35 t. ⊓ 3.60 – **9 rm** ⊠ 30.00/42.00 t.

⓪ ATS Motherwell St. ✆ 65426

AIRTH Stirling. (Central) **401** I 15 – pop. 972 – ✉ Falkirk – ✆ 0324.
♦Edinburgh 30 – Dunfermline 14 – Falkirk 7 – Stirling 8.

⛪ **Airth Castle** ⑤, FK2 8JF, ✆ 83411, Telex 777975, Fax 83419, ≤, « Castle and stables in extensive grounds », ⌙, 🐴, park – 📺 ☎ ৬ ℗ – ☖ 300. ⛁ 𝔸𝔼 ⓪ 𝑽𝑰𝑺𝑨. 🐕
M a la carte 8.85/20.40 t. ⊓ 3.90 – **47 rm** ⊠ 60.00/80.00 t. – SB (October-April) (weekends only) 74.50/79.50 **st.**

ALLOWAY Ayr. (Strathclyde) **401 402** G 17 – see Ayr.

ALTENS Aberdeen. (Grampian) – see Aberdeen.

ALTNAHARRA Sutherland. (Highland) **401** G 9 – ✉ Lairg – ✆ 054 981.
♦Edinburgh 239 – ♦Inverness 83 – Thurso 61.

🏠 **Altnaharra** ⑤, IV27 4UE, ✆ 222, ≤, ⌙, 🐴 – 🍴 rest ℗. ⛁ 𝑽𝑰𝑺𝑨
March-October – **M** (bar lunch)/dinner 12.50 t. ⊓ 4.50 – **20 rm** ⊠ 43.00/45.00 t. – SB (except summer) 39.00/45.00 **st.**

ALYTH Perth. (Tayside) **401** K 14 – pop. 2 258 – ECD : Wednesday – ✆ 082 83.
☗ Pitcrocknie ✆ 2268.
♦Edinburgh 63 – ♦Aberdeen 69 – ♦Dundee 16 – Perth 21.

🏠 **Lands of Loyal** ⑤, Loyal Rd, Blairgowrie, PH11 8JQ, N : ½ m. by B 952 ✆ 3151, ≤, 🐴, park – ☎ ℗. ⛁ 𝔸𝔼 𝑽𝑰𝑺𝑨
M (bar lunch)/dinner 12.50 t. ⊓ 3.50 – **11 rm** ⊠ 23.50/40.00 t. – SB 60.00 **st.**

ANSTRUTHER Fife. (Fife) **401** L 15 – pop. 2 865 – ECD : Wednesday – ✆ 0333.
See : Scottish Fisheries Museum✶✶ – Crail, NE : 5 m. (Site✶✶) – Old Town✶✶ – Upper Crail✶.
Envir. : The East Neuk✶✶ (coastline from Crail to St. Monance by A 917) – Kellie Castle✶, NW : 7 m. by A 959.
☗ Marsfield ✆ 310956.
🛈 Scottish Fisheries Museum, St. Ayles ✆ 310628.
♦Edinburgh 46 – ♦Dundee 23 – Dunfermline 34.

⛪ **Craw's Nest**, Bankwell Rd, KY10 3DS, ✆ 310691, Telex 727049, 🐴 – 📺 ☎ ℗ – ☖ 180. ⛁ 𝔸𝔼 ⓪ 𝑽𝑰𝑺𝑨. 🐕
M 8.00/14.00 st. and a la carte ⊓ 4.00 – **50 rm** ⊠ 40.00/70.00 st. – SB 65.00/85.00 **st.**

✗ **Cellar**, 24 East Green, KY10 3AA, ✆ 310378, Seafood – 🍴. ⛁ 𝔸𝔼 𝑽𝑰𝑺𝑨
closed Monday lunch, Sunday, 1 week May and 1 week Christmas-New Year – **M** 18.95/23.50 t. and lunch a la carte 9.00/12.25 t. ⊓ 4.00.

ARBROATH Angus. (Tayside) **401** M 14 Scotland G – pop. 23 934 – ECD : Wednesday – ✆ 0241.
See : Site✶ – Abbey✶ *AC*.
Envir. : St. Vigeans Museum✶ by A 92.
☗ Elliot ✆ 72272, S : 1 m..
🛈 Market Pl., ✆ 72609 and 76680.
♦Edinburgh 72 – ♦Aberdeen 51 – .♦Dundee 16.

⛪ Letham Grange ⑤, Colliston, DD11 4RL, NW : 4 ¾ m. by A 933 ✆ 024 189 (Gowanbank) 373, Fax 414, ≤, ☗, 🐴, park – 📺 ☎ ℗ – ☖ 30
19 rm, 1 suite.

✗✗ **Carriage Room**, Montrose Rd, DD11 5RA, N : 1 m. on A 92 ✆ 75755 – 🍴 ℗. ⛁ 𝔸𝔼 ⓪ 𝑽𝑰𝑺𝑨
closed Saturday lunch, Sunday, Monday and first week January – **M** 10.00/17.00 t. ⊓ 3.25.

AUSTIN-ROVER Montrose Rd ✆ 72919   FORD Millgate ✆ 73051

 Argyll. (Strathclyde) **401** F 15 – ECD : Wednesday – ✉ Dunoon – ✆ 036 981.
♦Edinburgh 107 – Dunoon 13 – ♦Glasgow 64 – ♦Oban 71.

   🏨 **Ardentinny** ⑤, PA23 8TR, ℰ 209, ⩽ Loch Long, 🍴 – ✗ rest 📺 Ⓟ. 🔇 AE ⓞ VISA
      Mid March-October – **M** 17.00 **t.** (dinner) and a la carte 9.50/16.00 **t.** 🍷 4.20 – **11 rm**
      ⚏ 24.00/65.00 **t.** – SB (except summer) 64.00/90.00 **st.**

 Perth. (Central) **401** H 14 – see Killin.

 Ayr. (Strathclyde) **401** **402** F 17 – pop. 11 386 – ECD : Wednesday – ✆ 0294.
⛴ by Caledonian MacBrayne : to the Isle of Arran : Brodick, summer : 3-5 daily, winter :
4 weekly (55 mn).
♦Edinburgh 75 – ♦Ayr 18 – ♦Glasgow 32.

      Hotels see : Kilmarnock SE : 11 ½ m., *Largs* N : 11 ½ m.

 Argyll. (Strathclyde) **401** D 15 – ECD : Wednesday – ✉ Oban – ✆ 085 22 Kilmel-
ford.
♦Edinburgh 142 – ♦Oban 20.

   🏰 **Loch Melfort** ⑤, PA34 4XG, ℰ 233, Fax 214, ⩽ Sound of Jura, 🍴, park – 📺 ☎ Ⓟ. 🔇
      VISA
      Restricted service November; closed January and February – **M** (bar lunch)/dinner 19.00 **t.**
      🍷 3.75 – **23 rm** ⚏ 35.00/90.00 **t.**

 Inverness. (Highland) **401** C 12 – see Skye (Isle of).

 Argyll. (Strathclyde) **401** A 14 – see Coll (Isle of).

 Inverness. (Highland) **401** C 13 – ECD : Thursday – ✆ 068 75.
See : Site★ – ⩽★ of Sound of Arisaig.
Envir. : Silver Sands of Morar★, N : 6 m. by A 830.
♦Edinburgh 172 – ♦Inverness 102 – ♦Oban 88.

   🏰 **Arisaig House** ⑤, Beasdale, by Arisaig, PH39 4NR, SE : 3 ¼ m. on A 830 ℰ 622, Telex
      777279, ⩽, 🍴, park – ✗ rest 📺 ☎ Ⓟ. 🔇 VISA. 🐾
      10 April-1 November – **M** (booking essential) (restricted lunch)/dinner 27.50 **t.** 🍷 9.25 –
      14 rm ⚏ 45.00/165.00 **t.**
   🏨 **Arisaig**, PH39 4NH, ℰ 210, ⩽ – ✗ rest ☎ Ⓟ
      M (bar lunch)/dinner 19.00 **t.** 🍷 3.85 – **15 rm** ⚏ 27.00/102.50 **t.**
   ✗ **Old Library Lodge** with rm, High St., PH39 4NH, ℰ 651, ⩽ Loch nan Ceall and Inner
      Hebridean Isles – Ⓟ. 🐾
      April-October – **M** (restricted lunch) a la carte 13.30/15.60 **t.** 🍷 3.75 – **7 rm** ⚏ 15.00/40.00 **t.**

 Inverness. (Highland) **401** C 12 – Shipping Services : see Skye (Isle of).

 Bute. (Strathclyde) **401** **402** DE 16 17 **Scotland G** – pop. 4 726.
See : Site★★ – Brodick Castle★★.
⛴ by Caledonian MacBrayne : from Brodick to Ardrossan summer : 3-5 daily, winter : 4 weekly
(55 mn) – from Lochranza to Claonaig (Kintyre Peninsula) summer only : 8-10 daily (30 mn).

      Brodick – pop. 884 – ECD : Wednesday – ✉ ✆ 0770 Brodick.
      🏌 ℰ 2349, ½ m. from Pier.
      🛈 The Pier ℰ 2401/2140.
   🏰 **Auchrannie Country House** ⑤, KA27 8BZ, ℰ 2234, 🍴 – 📺 ☎ Ⓟ. 🔇 VISA. 🐾
      M 14.00 **st.** and a la carte 13.00/18.45 **st.** 🍷 3.00 – **12 rm** ⚏ 59.00/71.00 **st.** – SB 65.00/80.00 **st.**

      Lagg – ✉ Kilmory – ✆ 077 087 Sliddery
   🏨 **Lagg**, KA27 8PQ, ℰ 255, 🍴 – Ⓟ
      11 March-October – **M** 8.00/14.50 **t.** 🍷 3.00 – **15 rm** ⚏ 28.00/60.00 **t.**

      Lamlash – pop. 908 – ECD : Wednesday except summer – ✉ Brodick – ✆ 077 06
      Lamlash.
      🏌 ℰ 296.
   🏨 **Glenisle**, Shore Rd, KA27 8LS, ℰ 258, ⩽, 🍴 – 📺 ☎ Ⓟ. VISA
      M (bar lunch)/dinner 12.00 **st.** 🍷 3.30 – **13 rm** ⚏ 21.00/42.00 **st.**

      Lochranza – ✉ ✆ 077 083 Lochranza
   🏠 **Butt Lodge** ⑤, KA27 8JF, SE : ½ m. by Brodick Rd ℰ 240, ⩽, 🍴 – Ⓟ. VISA. 🐾
      February-October – **M** 12.00 **st.** – **5 rm** ⚏ 17.00/50.00 **st.**

ARRAN (Isle of)

Whiting Bay – ECD : Wednesday except summer – ⊠ Brodick – ✆ 077 07 Whiting Bay – ⌦ ✆ 487.

↑ **Royal**, Shore Rd, KA27 8PZ, ✆ 286, ≤, ⇌ – ☎ 🅿
M 7.00 st. – **6 rm** ⊊ 19.00/44.00 st. – SB (except July and August) 47.00/55.00 st.

↑ **View Bank** ⑤, Golf Course Rd, KA27 8QT, ✆ 326, ≤, ⇌ – ⊱ rest 🅿
M 6.50 st. – **7 rm** ⊊ 12.00/24.00 st.

AUCHENCAIRN Kirkcudbright. (Dumfries and Galloway) 🚗🚗 I 19 – ⊠ Castle Douglas – ✆ 055 664.

◆Edinburgh 98 – ◆Dumfries 21 – Stranraer 62.

🏰 **Balcary Bay** ⑤, Balcary, DG7 1QZ, SE : 2 m. by A 711 ✆ 217, ≤ Auchencairn bay, hills and countryside, ⇌ – 📺 ☎ 🅿. ☒ *VISA*
Early March-early November – M (bar lunch)/dinner 14.00 st. and a la carte 12.00/21.00 st. ⓑ 3.50 – **13 rm** ⊊ 35.00/66.00 st. – SB (except early March-25 May) 65.00/78.00 st.

↑ **Bluehill Farm** ⑤ without rest., DG7 1QW, W : 1 m. by A 711 ✆ 228, ≤, ⇌, park – ⊱ 🅿. ⊗
3 rm ⊊ 13.00/27.00.

AUCHTERARDER Perth. (Tayside) 🚗 I 15 – pop. 2 838 – ECD : Wednesday – ✆ 0764.
⌦ Orchil Rd ✆ 2804, SW : 1 ½ m. – ⌦, ⌦, ⌦, ⌦ Gleneagles ✆ 62804/63543.
🅳 90 High St. ✆ 63450.

◆Edinburgh 55 – ◆Glasgow 45 – Perth 14.

🏰🏰🏰 **Gleneagles**, PH3 1NF, SW : 1 ½ m. by A 9 ✆ 62231, Telex 76105, Fax 62134, ≤, « Championship golf courses and extensive leisure facilities », ☒, ⌦, ⚲, ⇌, park, ✗, squash – 🛗 ⊱ rm 🍽 rest 📺 ☎ ⅃ 🅿 – 🎪 300. ☒ AE ⓞ *VISA*
M 19.00/24.00 st. – ⊊ 10.00 – **221 rm** 85.00/170.00 st., **20 suites** 240.00/310.00 st. – SB (midweek only) 165.00/185.00 st.

🏰 **Auchterarder House** ⑤, PH3 1DZ, N : 1 ½ m. on B 8062 ✆ 63646, Fax 62939, « Scottish Jacobean house », ⇌, park – ⊱ rest 📺 ☎ 🅿. ☒ AE ⓞ *VISA*
M (booking essential) 31.50/40.00 t. ⓑ 4.00 – **10 rm** ⊊ 70.00/150.00 t. 1 suite.

🏰 **Cairn Lodge** ⑤, Orchill Rd, PH3 1LX, ✆ 62634, ⇌ – 📺 ☎ 🅿. ⊗
M 13.50/27.50 t. and a la carte 18.60/24.75 t. ⓑ 3.50 – **5 rm** ⊊ 45.00/70.00 t.

🏰 **Collearn House**, PH3 1DF, ✆ 63553, Fax 63059, ⇌ – 📺 ☎ 🅿. ☒ AE ⓞ *VISA*. ⊗
M 11.00/15.00 t. and a la carte 12.25/21.80 t. ⓑ 3.70 – **8 rm** ⊊ 35.00/65.00 t. – SB 76.00/90.00 st.

AUCHTERHOUSE Angus. (Tayside) 🚗 K 14 – ⊠ Dundee – ✆ 082 626.
◆Edinburgh 69 – ◆Dundee 7 – Perth 24.

XXX **Old Mansion House** ⑤ with rm, DD3 0QN, ✆ 366, Fax 400, ≤, « 15-17C country house », ☒ heated, ⇌, park, ✗, squash – 📺 ☎ 🅿. ☒ AE ⓞ *VISA*
closed first week January – M 13.95 t. (lunch) and a la carte 16.85/25.80 t. ⓑ 3.50 – **6 rm** ⊊ 55.00/80.00 t.

AULTBEA Ross and Cromarty. (Highland) 🚗 D 10 – ECD : Wednesday – ✆ 044 582.
◆Edinburgh 234 – ◆Inverness 79 – Kyle of Lochalsh 80.

🏠 **Aultbea**, IV22 2HX, ✆ 201, ≤ – 📺 ☎ 🅿. ☒ *VISA*
M (bar lunch)/dinner 14.00 t. and a la carte ⓑ 2.75 – **8 rm** ⊊ 25.00/50.00 t. – SB (except summer) 50.00 st.

AVIEMORE Inverness. (Highland) 🚗 I 12 Scotland G – pop. 1 510 – ECD : Wednesday – Winter Sports – ✆ 0479.

See : Site★ – Envir. : ❋★★★ from Cairn Gorm (alt. 4 084 ft.) SE : 8 ½ m. by B 970 (chair lift *AC*) – Highland Wildlife Park★, S : by A 9.

🅳 Main Rd ✆ 810363.

◆Edinburgh 129 – ◆Inverness 29 – Perth 85.

🏰 Stakis Four Seasons (Stakis), Aviemore Centre, PH22 1PF, ✆ 810681, Telex 75213, Fax 810862, ≤ Cairngorms, ☒ – 🛗 📺 ☎ 🅿 – 🎪. ☒ AE ⓞ *VISA*
M (dancing Saturday) – ⊊ 7.25 – **88 rm** 65.00/90.00 st. – SB 68.00/102.00 st.

🏰 Stakis Coylumbridge Resort (Stakis), PH22 1QN, SE : 1 ¾ m. by B 970 ✆ 810661, Telex 75272, Fax 811309, ≤, ☒, ⇌, ✗ – ⊱ rm 📺 ☎ 🅿 – 🎪. ☒ AE ⓞ *VISA*
⊊ 7.25 – **171 rm** 60.00/85.00 st., **4 suites** 130.00 st. – SB 62.00/98.00 st.

🏰 **Post House** (T.H.F.), Aviemore Centre, PH22 1PJ, ✆ 810771, Telex 75597, Fax 811473, ≤ – 🛗 ⊱ rm 📺 ☎ 🅿 – 🎪 80. ☒ AE ⓞ *VISA*
M (bar lunch)/dinner 10.50 st. and a la carte ⓑ 3.45 – ⊊ 7.00 – **103 rm** 50.00/70.00 st. – SB 68.00/84.00 st.

🏰 Stakis Badenoch (Stakis), Aviemore Centre, PH22 1PF, ✆ 810261, Fax 810862, ≤ – 🛗 ⊱ rm 📺 ☎ 🅿. ☒ AE ⓞ *VISA*
M (dinner only) – ⊊ 7.25 – **72 rm** 48.00/75.00 st. – SB 52.00/80.00 st.

FORD 62 Grampian Rd ✆ 810232

AYR Ayr. (Strathclyde) 401 402 G 17 **Scotland G** – pop. 48 493 – ECD : Wednesday – ✆ 0292.

Envir. : Alloway★ (Burns' Cottage and Museum★) S : 3 m. by B 7024 BZ – Culzean Castle★ (Setting★★★, Oval staircase★★) SW : 14 m. by A 719 BZ.

18 Belleisle ✆ 41258 BZ – **18 Dalmilling, Westwood Av., Whitletts** ✆ 63893 BZ.

i 39 Sandgate ✆ 284196.

♦Edinburgh 81 – ♦Glasgow 35.

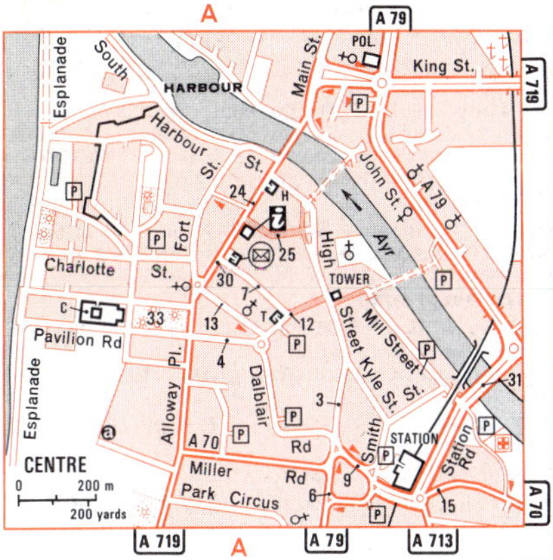

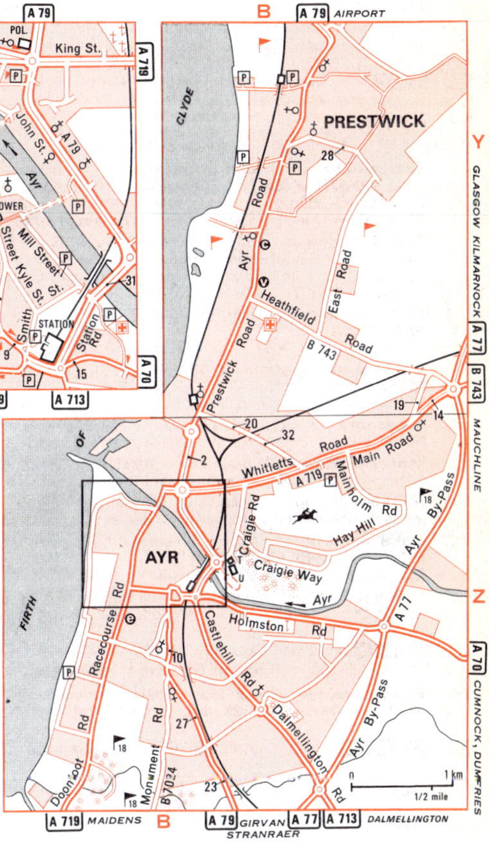

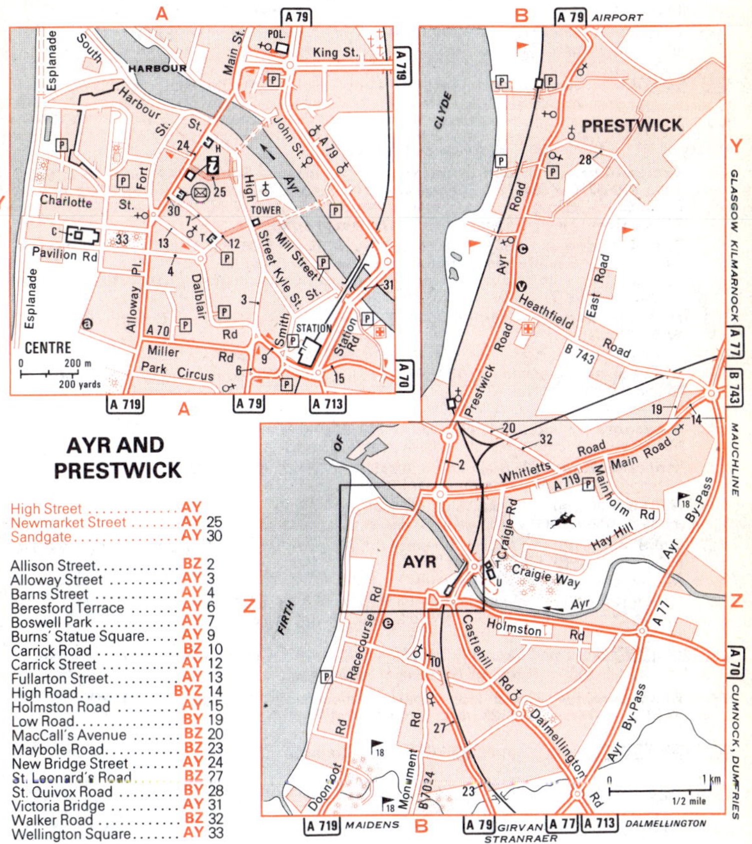

AYR AND PRESTWICK

High Street	AY	
Newmarket Street	AY	25
Sandgate	AY	30
Allison Street	BZ	2
Alloway Street	AY	3
Barns Street	AY	4
Beresford Terrace	AY	6
Boswell Park	AY	7
Burns' Statue Square	AY	9
Carrick Road	BZ	10
Carrick Street	AY	12
Fullarton Street	AY	13
High Road	BYZ	14
Holmston Road	AY	15
Low Road	BY	19
MacCall's Avenue	BZ	20
Maybole Road	BZ	23
New Bridge Street	AY	24
St. Leonard's Road	BZ	27
St. Quivox Road	BY	28
Victoria Bridge	AY	31
Walker Road	BZ	32
Wellington Square	AY	33

Pickwick, 19 Racecourse Rd, KA7 2TD, ✆ 260111 – TV ☎ P. BZ **e**
15 rm.

Fairfield House, 12 Fairfield Rd, KA7 2AR, ✆ 267461, Telex 778833, Fax 261456, – rm TV ☎ P. AE VISA. AY **a**
M 12.50/32.50 **st.** and a la carte 5.00 – **26 rm** 75.00/150.00 **st.**

at Alloway S : 3 m. on A 719 – BZ – ✉ ✆ 0292 Ayr :

Balgarth, 8 Dunure Rd, Doonfoot, KA7 4HR, on A 719 ✆ **42441,** – TV ☎ P
15 rm.

ALFA-ROMEO, FIAT Galloway Av. ✆ 260416
DAIMLER, JAGUAR 18 Holmston Rd ✆ 266944
LANCIA Cambuslea Rd ✆ 266146
MERCEDES-BENZ Heathfield Industrial Estate ✆ 282727
PEUGEOT-TALBOT Alloway Pl. ✆ 263140
TOYOTA 65 Peebles St. ✆ 267606
VAUXHALL 196 Prestwick Rd ✆ 261631
VOLVO Burn's Statue Sq. ✆ 282711
VW-AUDI 24 Dalblair Rd ✆ 269522

Envir. : Glen Coe★★, E : 6 m. by A 82.

🛈 ✆ 296 (summer only).

♦Edinburgh 117 − ♦Inverness 80 − Kyle of Lochalsh 90 − ♦Oban 38.

🏨 **Ballachulish,** PA39 4JY, W : 2 ¼ m. by A 82 on A 828 ✆ 606, Group Telex 9401369, Fax 629, ≤, 🐎 − ⇥ rest 📺 ☎ 🅿. 🔄 **VISA**
M 4.50/13.00 **st.** and a la carte 🍷6.50 − **30 rm** ⌸ 36.50/75.00 **st.** − SB (November-March) 55.00 **st.**

🏠 **Lyn Leven** without rest., White St., PA39 4JW, ✆ 392, ≤, 🐎 − ⇥ 📺 🅿
closed Christmas − **8 rm** ⌸ −/32.00 **st.**

BALLATER Aberdeen. (Grampian) **401** K 12 − pop. 1 051 − ECD : Thursday − ✆ 033 97.

🏌 Victoria Rd ✆ 55567.

🛈 Station Sq. ✆ 55306 (summer only).

♦Edinburgh 111 − ♦Aberdeen 41 − ♦Inverness 70 − Perth 67.

🏨 **Craigendarroch H. and Country Club** 🏊, Braemar Rd, AB3 5XA, on A 93 ✆ 55858, Telex 739952, Fax 55447, ≤ Dee Valley and Grampians, 🔄, 🐎, squash − 🛗 📺 ☎ 🅿 − 🔄 80. 🔄 **AE** ⓘ **VISA**. 🛥
M (see **Oaks** below) − **49 rm** ⌸ 75.00/275.00 **st.**, **1 suite**

🏨 **Tullich Lodge** 🏊, AB3 5SB, E : 1 ½ m. on A 93 ✆ 55406, Fax 55397, ≤ Dee Valley and Grampians, « Country house atmosphere », 🐎 − ☎ 🅿. 🔄 **AE**
April-October − **M** (booking essential) (bar lunch)/dinner 18.00 **st.** 🍷6.00 − **10 rm** ⌸ (dinner included) 72.00/154.00 **st.** − SB 67.00/70.00 **st.**

🏨 **Darroch Learg,** Braemar Rd, AB3 5UX, ✆ 55443, ≤ Dee Valley and Grampians, 🐎 − 📺 ☎ 🅿. 🔄 **VISA**
February-October − **M** 12.00/16.00 **st.** 🍷3.50 − **23 rm** ⌸ 21.00/60.00 **st.**

🏨 **Glen Lui,** 14 Invernauld Rd, AB3 5RP, ✆ 55402, Fax 55545, ≤, 🐎 − 📺 🅿. 🔄 **AE** **VISA**
M (bar lunch)/dinner 15.00 **st.** 🍷2.75 − **9 rm** ⌸ 25.00/50.00 **st.**, **3 suites** 50.00/60.00 **st.** − SB (except Christmas and New Year) 69.00 **st.**

🏠 **Alexandra,** 12 Bridge Sq., AB3 5QJ, ✆ 55376 − ⇥ rest 📺 🅿. 🔄 **AE** ⓘ **VISA**
M (bar lunch)/dinner 16.00 **st.** and a la carte − **6 rm** ⌸ 14.00/40.00 **st.** − SB 46.00/56.00 **st.**

🏠 **Moorside House,** 26 Braemar Rd, AB3 5RL, ✆ 55492, 🐎 − 📺 🅿. 🔄 **VISA**. 🛥
March-October − **M** (by arrangement) 10.00 **st.** 🍷5.00 − **9 rm** ⌸ 19.00/30.00 **st.**

🏠 **Morvada,** Braemar Rd, AB3 5RL, ✆ 55501, 🐎 − 📺 🅿
April-October − **M** (by arrangement) 8.00 **st.** − **7 rm** ⌸ 15.00/30.00 **st.**

XX **Oaks** (at Craigendarroch H.), Braemar Rd, AB3 5XA, on A 93 ✆ 55858, Telex 739952, Fax 55447 − ⇥ 🍽 🅿. 🔄 **AE** ⓘ **VISA**
M 9.95/27.50 **st.** and a la carte 🍷8.00.

X **Green Inn** with rm, 9 Victoria Rd, AB3 5QQ, ✆ 55701 − 📺. 🔄 **VISA**
March-October − **M** 7.80/17.50 **t.** and a la carte 9.70/17.65 **t.** 🍷4.95 − **3 rm** ⌸ −/35.00 **t.**

BALMACARA Ross and Cromarty. (Highland) **401** D 12 − ECD : Wednesday − ✉ Kyle of Lochalsh − ✆ 059 986 − ♦Edinburgh 197 − Kyle of Lochalsh 4.5.

🏨 **Balmacara,** IV40 8DH, ✆ 283, ≤ coast and mountains − 📺 ☎ 🅿. 🔄 **AE** ⓘ **VISA**
M 8.00/14.00 **st.** 🍷3.00 − **29 rm** ⌸ 27.00/47.00 **st.**

BALQUHIDDER Perth. (Central) **401** G 14 − see Strathyre.

BANAVIE Inverness. (Highland) **401** E 13 − see Fort William.

BANCHORY Kincardine. (Grampian) **401** M 12 − pop. 4 683 − ECD : Thursday − ✆ 033 02.
Envir. : Crathes Castle★★, E : 2 m. by A 93 − Craigievar Castle★★★, N : 17 m. by A 980 − Castle Fraser★ (exterior★★), N : 14 m. by A 980 and B 977.

🏌 Kinneskie ✆ 2365 − 🏌 Torphins ✆ 033 982 (Torphins) 493, NW : 6 m.

🛈 Dee St. Car Park ✆ 2000 (summer only).

♦Edinburgh 118 − ♦Aberdeen 17 − ♦Dundee 55 − ♦Inverness 94.

🏨 **Invery House** 🏊, Bridge of Feugh, AB3 3NJ, S : 1 ½ m. on B 974 ✆ 4782, Telex 73737, Fax 4712, ≤, « Georgian mansion, gardens », 🐟, park − 📺 ☎ 🅿 − 🔄 30. 🔄 **AE** ⓘ **VISA**. 🛥
M 15.50/27.50 **st.** 🍷5.00 − **14 rm** ⌸ 75.00/220.00 **st.** − SB 130.00/180.00 **st.**

🏨 **Raemoir House** 🏊, AB3 4ED, N : 2 ½ m. on A 980 ✆ 4884, Fax 2171, ≤, « 18C mansion with 16C Ha-House », 🐎, park − 📺 ☎ ♿ 🅿. 🔄 **AE** ⓘ **VISA**
M (bar lunch Monday to Saturday)/dinner 18.50 **t.** and a la carte 🍷3.75 − **22 rm** ⌸ 50.00/80.00 **t.**, **6 suites** 120.00/160.00 **t.** − SB (except Christmas and New Year) 85.00/95.00 **st.**

🏨 **Banchory Lodge** 🏊, Dee St., AB3 3HS, ✆ 2625, ≤, « Part 18C house on River Dee », 🐟, 🐎 − 📺 ☎ 🅿. 🔄 **AE** ⓘ **VISA**
closed mid December-January − **M** 10.50/18.50 **st.** and a la carte 🍷3.85 − **24 rm** ⌸ 40.00/80.00 **s.**

RENAULT North Deeside Rd ✆ 2847

BANCHORY-DEVENICK Aberdeen. (Grampian) – see Aberdeen.

BANFF Banff. (Grampian) **401** M 10 **Scotland G** – pop. 3 843 – ECD : Wednesday – ✆ 026 12.
See : Site★ – Duff House★ – Mercat Cross★.
🛇 Duff House Royal, The Barnyards ✆ 2062, S : ½ m.
🄯 Collie Lodge ✆ 2419.
◆Edinburgh 177 – ◆Aberdeen 47 – Fraserburgh 26 – ◆Inverness 74.

　🏰　**Banff Springs**, Golden Knowes Rd, AB4 2JE, W : ¾ m. on A 98 ✆ 2881, ≤ – TV ☎ P –
　　　🏊 300. ⚑ AE ① VISA
　　　M (bar lunch)/dinner 10.50 t. and a la carte ↥ 3.75 – **30 rm** ⚏ 27.60/44.00 t., **2 suites** 58.00 t.
　　　– SB (weekends only) 50.00 st.

　🏠　**County**, 32 High St., AB4 1AE, ✆ 5353, 🚗 – ↦ rest TV ☎ P. ⚑ AE ① VISA. ⅍
　　　M 8.00/20.00 t. and a la carte ↥ 2.80 – **7 rm** ⚏ 27.00/40.00 t. – SB 28.00/30.00 st.

　🏠　**Fife Lodge**, Sandyhill Rd, AB4 1BE, ✆ 2436, ≤, 🚗 – ↦ rest TV P. ⚑ VISA
　　　M (bar lunch)/dinner a la carte 10.60/20.50 t. ↥ 2.75 – **7 rm** ⚏ 27.00/40.00 t.

FORD Bridge Rd ✆ 2673　　　　　　　　　　🅜 ATS Carmelite St. ✆ 2234

BARRA (Isle of) Inverness. (Outer Hebrides) (Western Isles) **401** X 12 13 – pop. 1 232.
✈ at North Bay ✆ 041 889 1311/3181.
🛳 by Caledonian MacBrayne : from Castlebay to Oban : 3-8 weekly (6 h) – to Lochboisdale
(South Uist) 2-8 weekly (2 h).
🛥 by Western Isles Council : to Vatersay 2-4 daily except Sunday (10 mn).

　　　Castlebay – ✉ ✆ 087 14 Castlebay.
　　　🄯 ✆ 336 (summer only).

　🏰　**Isle of Barra** ⑳, Tangusdale Beach, PA80 5XY, NW : 2 m. on A 888 ✆ 383, Fax 385, ≤ sea
　　　and mountains – P. ⚑ VISA
　　　April-October – **M** (bar lunch)/dinner 13.50 st. and a la carte – **36 rm** ⚏ 30.00/50.00 st. –
　　　SB 70.00 st.

BARRHEAD Renfrew. (Strathclyde) **401 402** G 16 – pop. 18 419 – ECD : Tuesday – ✉ ✆ 041
Glasgow.
◆Edinburgh 56 – ◆Ayr 32 – ◆Glasgow 10.

　🏠　**Dalmeny Park**, Lochlibo Rd, G78 1LG, SW : ½ m. on A 736 ✆ 881 9211, « Gardens » –
　　　↦ rm TV ☎ P. ⚑ AE ① VISA
　　　closed 26 December and 1-2 January – **M** (closed Saturday lunch and Sunday dinner)
　　　5.50/15.00 t. and a la carte ↥ 4.95 – **18 rm** ⚏ 35.50/57.00 t. – SB (weekends only) 64.00 st.

VW-AUDI Blackburn Rd ✆ 52948　　　　　　🅜 ATS Glasgow Rd, Crossmill ✆ 881 5651

BEARSDEN Dunbarton. (Strathclyde) **401** G 16 – pop. 27 146 – ECD : Tuesday and Saturday –
✉ ✆ 041 Glasgow.
🛇 Windyhill ✆ 942 2349.
◆Edinburgh 51 – ◆Glasgow 5.

　XX　**October**, 128 Drymen Rd, G61 3RB, ✆ 942 7272 – ⚑ VISA
　　　closed Sunday, 1 week Easter, 2 weeks August and Bank Holidays – **M** 8.70 st. (lunch) and a
　　　la carte 13.40/18.50 st.

　X　**La Bavarde**, 19 New Kirk Rd, G61 9JS, ✆ 942 2202 – ⚑ AE ① VISA
　　　closed Sunday and Monday – **M** 7.50/22.00 t. and a la carte 12.50/22.35 t. ↥ 4.00.

　X　Amritsar Tandoori, 9 Kirk Rd, G61 3RG, ✆ 942 7710, Indian rest.

PORSCHE, FERRARI Maxwell Av. ✆ 943 1155

BEATTOCK Dumfries. (Dumfries and Galloway) **401 402** J 18 – ✉ Moffat – ✆ 068 33.
◆Edinburgh 60 – ◆Carlisle 41 – ◆Dumfries 20 – ◆Glasgow 59.

　🏰　**Auchen Castle** ⑳, DG10 9SH, N : 2 m. by A 74 ✆ 407, ≤, ❀, 🚗, park – TV ☎ P – 🏊
　　　30. ⚑ AE ① VISA
　　　closed 20 December-8 January – **M** (bar lunch)/dinner 15.00 st. ↥ 3.30 – **25 rm**
　　　⚏ 36.00/56.00 st. – SB 56.00/72.00 st.

　🏠　**Beattock House**, DG10 9QB, ✆ 403, 🚗 – TV P. ⚑ AE ① VISA
　　　M 7.95/14.50 t. and a la carte – **7 rm** ⚏ 22.50/48.50 t.

BEAULY Inverness. (Highland) **401** G 11 – pop. 1 135 – ECD : Thursday – ✆ 0463.
◆Edinburgh 169 – ◆Inverness 13 – ◆Wick 125.

　🏠　**Priory**, The Square, IV4 7BX, ✆ 782309, Fax 782531 – TV ☎. ⚑ AE ① VISA
　　　M a la carte 5.30/10.95 t. ↥ 2.70 – **11 rm** ⚏ 24.95/42.50 t. – SB (October-April) 40.50/68.50 st.

　↑　**Chrialdon**, Station Rd, IV4 7EH, ✆ 782336, 🚗 – ↦ rest TV P. VISA. ⅍
　　　M 11.50 st. ↥ 2.25 – **7 rm** ⚏ 15.00/34.00 st. – SB 40.00/50.00 st.

SUBARU High St. ✆ 782266

BELLOCHANTUY Argyll. (Strathclyde) **401** C 17 – see Kintyre (Peninsula).

BENBECULA Inverness. (Western Isles) **401** X 11 – see Uist (Isles of).

BIRSAY Orkney (Orkney Islands) **401** K 6 – see Orkney Islands (Mainland).

BLAIR ATHOLL Perth. (Tayside) **401** I 13 – pop. 516 – ✆ 079 681.
See : Blair Castle★★★.
Envir. : Queens View★★ S : 9 m. by A 9 and B 8019 – Falls of Bruar★ W : 3 m..
₉ ✆ 407, S : ½ m.
♦Edinburgh 78 – ♦Inverness 78 – Perth 34.

🏨 Atholl Arms, PH18 5SG, ✆ 205 – TV ☎ P
30 rm.

BLAIRGOWRIE Perth. (Tayside) **401** J 14 – pop. 7 028 – ✆ 0250.
🛈 Wellmeadow ✆ 2960.
♦Edinburgh 60 – ♦Dundee 19 – Perth 16.

🏨 **Kinloch House** ⏎, PH10 6SG, W : 3 m. on A 923 ✆ 025 084 (Essendy) 237, Fax 333, ≤,
« Country house atmosphere », 🐎, park – ⇔ rest ☎ P. 🔄 AE ⓪ VISA
closed 3 to 29 December – **M** (bar lunch Monday to Saturday)/dinner 17.50 t. ₤ 3.20 – **13 rm**
⊏ 38.50/88.00 t.

🏨 **Altamount House** ⏎, Coupar Angus Rd, PH10 6JN, on A 923 ✆ 3512, 🐎 – TV ☎ P. 🔄
AE ⓪ VISA. ⅍
closed 4 January-14 February – **M** (bar lunch Monday to Saturday)/dinner 14.50 t. ₤ 5.90 –
7 rm ⊏ 27.50/50.00 t. – SB (November-May) 55.00 **st.**

🏨 **Rosemount Golf,** Golf Course Rd, PH10 6LJ, SE : 1 ¾ m. by A 923 ✆ 2604, 🐎 – TV P.
🔄 VISA. ⅍
M (bar lunch)/dinner 12.25 **st.** and a la carte ₤ 2.70 – **12 rm** ⊏ 27.00/40.00 **st.** –
SB (except summer) 50.00 **st.**

BLAIRLOGIE Stirling. (Central) – see Stirling.

Le Guide change,
changez de guide Michelin tous les ans.

BOAT OF GARTEN Inverness. (Highland) **401** I 12 – ECD : Thursday – ✆ 047 983.
₁₈ ✆ 282.
♦Edinburgh 133 – ♦Inverness 28 – ♦Perth 89.

🏨 **The Boat** (Best Western), PH24 3BH, ✆ 258, Telex 94013436, Fax 414, 🐎 – TV ☎ P. 🔄 AE
⓪ VISA
M 11.00/14.50 **st.** and a la carte ₤ 4.20 – **32 rm** ⊏ 39.00/75.00 **st.** – SB 76.00/83.00 **st.**

🏠 **Moorfield House,** Deshar Rd, PH24 3BN, ✆ 646, 🐎 – ⇔ rest P
closed November-27 December – **M** 10.50 t. ₤ 3.60 – **6 rm** ⊏ 16.00/39.00 t.

BOTHWELL Lanark. (Strathclyde) **401** **402** H 16 Scotland G – ✆ 0698.
See : Castle★.
Envir. : Blantyre : David Livingstone Centre (Museum★) off A 724.
₁₈ Blantyre Rd ✆ 853177.
♦Edinburgh 39 – ♦Glasgow 8.5.

🏨 **Silvertrees,** 27-29 Silverwells Cres., G71 8DP, ✆ 852311, 🐎 – TV ☎ P – 🏛 180. 🔄 AE
⓪ VISA
M *(closed Sunday dinner)*8.50/10.50 t. and a la carte ₤ 3.90 – **26 rm** ⊏ 50.00/55.00 t., **2 suites**
50.00/65.00 t.

BRAE Shetland (Shetland Islands) **401** P 2 – see Shetland Islands (Mainland).

BRAEMAR Aberdeen. (Grampian) **401** J 12 – ECD : Thursday except summer – ✆ 033 97
(5 fig.) or 033 83 (3 fig.).
Envir. : Lin O' Dee★, W : 7 m.
₁₈ Cluniebank Rd ✆ 618.
🛈 Balnellan Rd ✆ 600 (summer only).
♦Edinburgh 85 – ♦Aberdeen 58 – ♦Dundee 51 – Perth 51.

🏨 **Braemar Lodge,** Glenshee Rd, AB3 5YQ, ✆ 41627, 🐎 – ⇔ rest TV P. 🔄 VISA
March-November – **M** (dinner only) 15.00 **st.** ₤ 2.50 – **8 rm** ⊏ 21.50/55.00 **st.**

BRESSAY (Isle of) Shetland (Shetland Islands) **401** Q 3 – Shipping services : see Shetland
Islands.

BRIDGE OF ALLAN Stirling. (Central) 401 I 15 – pop. 4 551 – ECD : Wednesday – ℡ 0786.
Envir. : Dollar (Castle Campbell★ (site★★★) E : 12 m. by A 91 – Wallace Monument (✳★★)
S : 2 m. by A 9 – Doune★ (Castle★, Motor Museum★) NW : 7 m. by A 9 and B 824.
⌐ Sunnylaw ℰ 83233, N : ½ m. by A 9.
◆Edinburgh 21 – ◆Dundee 54 – ◆Glasgow 33.

    Royal, 55 Henderson St., FK9 4HG, ℰ 832284, ⇆ – ⓘ TV ☎ Ⓟ
    32 rm.

BRIDGE OF CALLY Perth. (Tayside) 401 J 14 – ✉ Blairgowrie – ℡ 025 086.
◆Edinburgh 66 – ◆Dundee 25 – Perth 22.

    Bridge of Cally, PH10 7JJ, on A 93 ℰ 231, ⇖, ⇆ – Ⓟ. ◨ ① VISA
    closed November and first week December – **M** 6.70/16.25 t. and a la carte ⌁ 3.30 – **9 rm**
    ☲ 22.00/42.00 t.

BRIG O'TURK Perth. (Central) 401 G 15 – ✉ Callander – ℡ 08776.
◆Edinburgh 58 – ◆Glasgow 36 – Perth 47.

    Dundarroch and the Byre ⇖, Trossachs, FK17 8HT, ℰ 200, ⇐, ⇖, ⇆ – TV Ⓟ. ✳
    March-November – **M** a la carte 8.40/15.20 t. ⌁ 3.40 – **3 rm** ☲ 26.00/52.00 t.

BRODICK Bute. (Strathclyde) 401 402 E 17 – see Arran (Isle of).

BRORA Sutherland. (Highland) 401 I 9 – pop. 1 728 – ECD : Wednesday – ℡ 0408.
⌐ Golf Rd ℰ 21417.
◆Edinburgh 234 – ◆Inverness 78 – ◆Wick 49.

    Royal Marine ⇖, Golf Rd, KW9 6QS, ℰ 21252, ◨, ⇆ – TV ☎ Ⓟ. ◨ AE ① VISA
    M 8.00/15.00 st. ⌁ 3.30 – **11 rm** ☲ 40.00/70.00 st. – SB 100.00/120.00 st.

BROUGHTY FERRY Angus. (Tayside) 401 L 14 – see Dundee.

BUCKIE Banff. (Grampian) 401 L 10 – pop. 7 869 – ECD : Wednesday – ℡ 0542.
⌐ Buckpool, Barrhill Rd ℰ 32236 – ⌐ Strathlene ℰ 31798, E : ½ m.
🛈 High St. ℰ 34853.
◆Edinburgh 195 – ◆Aberdeen 66 – ◆Inverness 56.

    Cluny, 2 High St., AB5 1AL, ℰ 32922 – TV ☎ Ⓟ. ◨ AE ① VISA
    closed 1 and 2 January – **M** (bar lunch)/dinner 15.00 t. and a la carte 7.00/13.00 t. ⌁ 3.00 –
    16 rm ☲ 16.00/36.00 t. – SB (weekends only) 50.00/60.00 st.

    at Drybridge S : 2 m. by A 942 – ✉ Drybridge – ℡ 0542 Buckie :

    Old Monastery, AB2 5JB, SW : 2 m. ℰ 32660, ⇐, « Former chapel overlooking Spey
    Bay » – ✂ rest Ⓟ. ◨ AE ① VISA
    closed Sunday, Monday, 2 weeks November and 3 weeks January – **M** a la carte 8.75/18.75 t.
    ⌁ 4.50.

    at Tynet SW : 4 m. by A 942 on A 98 – ✉ Fochabers – ℡ 054 27 Clochan :

    Mill, AB5 2HJ, on A 98 ℰ 233 – TV ☎ Ⓟ – **15 rm**.

VAUXHALL-OPEL Marine Place ℰ 32327

BUCKSBURN Aberdeen. (Grampian) 401 N 12 – see Aberdeen.

BUNCHREW Inverness. (Highland) – see Inverness.

BUNESSAN Argyll. (Strathclyde) 401 B 15 – see Mull (Isle of).

BURNTISLAND Fife. (Fife) 401 K 15 – ℡ 0592.
◆Edinburgh 20 – Dunfermline 10 – Kirkcaldy 6.

    Inchview, 69 Kinghorn Rd, KY3 9EB, ℰ 872239 – TV ☎ Ⓟ. ◨ AE VISA
    M 7.50/12.50 t. and a la carte ⌁ 4.20 – **10 rm** ☲ 28.50/43.00 t. – SB 49.50/65.00 st.

BUSBY Lanark. (Strathclyde) 401 402 H 16 – see Glasgow.

BUTE (Isle of) Bute. (Strathclyde) 401 402 E 16 – pop. 7 733.
⛴ by Caledonian MacBrayne : from Rothesay to Wemyss Bay : frequent services daily (30 mn)
– from Rhubodach to Colintraive : frequent services daily (5 mn).
🛈 Rothesay : The Pier ℰ 0700 (Rothesay) 2151.

CAIRNGORM (Mountains) Inverness. (Highland) 401 J 12 Scotland G.
See : Mountains★★ (✳★★ from Cairn Gorm) (alt. 4 048 ft.) (chairlift *AC*) Highland wildlife Park★.

    Hotels see : Aviemore NW, Braemar SE.

CAIRNRYAN Wigtown. (Dumfries and Galloway) **401 402** E 19.

by P & O European Ferries : to Larne 4-6 daily (2 h 15 mn).

♦ Edinburgh 126 – ♦ Ayr 45 – Stranraer 6.5.

Hotel see : *Stranraer* S : 6 ½ m.

CALLANDER Perth. (Central) **401** H 15 Scotland G – pop. 2 286 – ECD : Wednesday except summer – ✆ 0877.

See : Site★.

Envir. : The Trossachs★★★ : Loch Katrine★★ – Hilltop Viewpoint (✱★★★) W : 10 m. by A 821 – Inchmahone Priory (Monument★) S : 6 m. by A 81 and B 8034.

☐ Aveland Rd ✆ 30090.

☑ Leny Rd ✆ 30342.

♦Edinburgh 52 – ♦Glasgow 43 – ♦Oban 71 – Perth 41.

Roman Camp ⌂, Main St., FK17 8BG, ✆ 30003, Fax 0764 (Auchterarder) 62939, ≼, « 17C hunting lodge in extensive gardens », ⌐, park – ⊱ rest ⊡ ☎ ᕕ ℗ **11 rm, 3 suites**.

Lubnaig, Leny Feus, FK17 8AS, ✆ 30376, ⇗ – ⊱ rest ℗ *Easter-October* – **M** (dinner only) (residents only) – **10 rm** ⊿ (dinner included) 43.00/66.00 t.

Brook Linn ⌂, Leny Feus, FK17 8AU, ✆ 30103, ≼, ⇗ – ⊱ ⊡ ℗ *Easter-October* – **M** 8.00 st. 1 3.50 – **7 rm** ⊿ 13.00/32.00 st.

Highland House, 8 South Church St., FK17 8BN, ✆ 30269 – ⊱ *March-November* – **M** 12.50 t. 1 3.00 – **10 rm** ⊿ 15.50/35.50 t.

East Mains House without rest., Bridgend, FK17 8AG, ✆ 30080, ⇗ – ℗ **5 rm** ⊿ 12.00/25.00 s.

CAMPBELTOWN Argyll. (Strathclyde) **401** D 17 – see Kintyre (Peninsula).

CANNA (Isle of) Inverness. (Highland) **401** A 12 – Shipping Services : see Mallaig.

CANONBIE Dumfries. (Dumfries and Galloway) **401 402** L 18 – ✆ 038 73 (5 fig.) or 054 15 (3 fig.).

♦Edinburgh 80 – ♦Carlisle 15 – ♦Dumfries 34.

XX Riverside Inn with rm, DG14 0UX, ✆ 71295 – ⊱ rest ⊡ ℗. ⊠ VISA ⇗ *closed last 2 weeks February and first 2 weeks November* – **M** (*closed Sunday dinner*) (booking essential) (bar lunch)/dinner 17.50 t. 1 3.95 – **6 rm** ⊿ 44.00/55.00 st. – SB (November-April) 62.00 **st.**

CARFRAEMILL Berwick. (Borders) **401 402** L 16 – see Lauder.

CARRADALE Argyll. (Strathclyde) **401** D 17 – see Kintyre (Peninsula).

CARRBRIDGE Inverness. (Highland) **401** I 12 – ECD : Wednesday – ✆ 047 984.

☑ Village Car Park ✆ 630 (summer only).

♦Edinburgh 135 – ♦Aberdeen 92 – ♦Inverness 23.

Struan House, PH23 3AS, ✆ 242, ⇗ – ℗. ⊠ AE ⓪ VISA **M** (buffet lunch summer and bar lunch winter)/dinner 11.50 t. and a la carte 1 4.40 – **16 rm** ⊿ 19.00/38.00 t. – SB (except summer) 52.00/58.00 **st.**

Keeper's House, PH23 3AT, ✆ 621, ≼, ⇗ – ⊱ rest ℗ *closed November-20 December* – **M** 8.00 t. – **5 rm** ⊿ 28.00/31.00 t.

CASTLEBAY Inverness. (Outer Hebrides) (Western Isles) **401** X 13 – see Barra (Isle of).

CASTLE DOUGLAS Kirkcudbright. (Dumfries and Galloway) **401 402** I 19 Scotland G – pop. 3 546 – ECD : Thursday – ✆ 0556.

Envir. : Threave Garden★★ and Castle★, SW : 3 m. by A 75.

☐ Abercromby Rd ✆ 2801.

☑ Markethill ✆ 2611 (summer only).

♦Edinburgh 98 – ♦Ayr 49 – ♦Dumfries 18 – Stranraer 57.

King's Arms, St. Andrew St., DG7 1EL, ✆ 2626 – ⊱ rest ⊡ ℗. ⊠ AE ⓪ VISA **M** 4.50/13.00 st. and a la carte 1 2.75 – **14 rm** ⊿ 17.00/45.00 st. – SB 56.00/62.00 **st.**

AUSTIN-ROVER Morris House ✆ 2560
FORD, LADA Oakwell Rd ✆ 2805
VAUXHALL-OPEL King St. ✆ 2038

Ⓜ ATS Station Yard ✆ 3121/2

CLACHAN SEIL Argyll. (Strathclyde) **401** D 15 – ECD : Wednesday – ⊠ Oban – ✆ 085 23 Balvicar – ♦Edinburgh 137 – ♦Oban 14.

⚲ **Willowburn** ⟋, Isle of Seil, PA34 4TJ, ✆ 276, ≤, 🍴 – 📺 🅿. ⑊ *VISA*. ⚙
April-October – **M** 9.50 t. ⬩3.80 – **6 rm** ⊡ 22.50/39.00 t.

⚲ **Old Clachan Farmhouse** ⟋, Clachan, PA34 4RH, ✆ 493, ≤, « 18C former drovers inn »
– 🅿
closed 21 December-7 January – **M** 17.50 st. – **3 rm** ⊡ 15.00/45.00 st.

CLAONAIG (Cap) Argyll. (Strathclyde) **401** **402** D 16 – Shipping Services : see Kintyre (Peninsula).

CLARENCEFIELD Dumfries. (Dumfries and Galloway) – see Dumfries.

CLEISH Fife. (Tayside) **401** J 15 – see Kinross.

CLOSEBURN Dumfries. (Dumfries and Galloway) **401** **402** I 18 – see Thornhill.

COLINTRAIVE Argyll. (Strathclyde) **401** **402** E 16 – ✆ 070 084.
⛴ by Caledonian MacBrayne : to Rhubodach (Isle of Bute) : frequent services daily (5 mn).
♦Edinburgh 127 – ♦Glasgow 81 – ♦Oban 81.

COLL (Isle of) Argyll. (Strathclyde) **401** A 14 – pop. 153.
⛴ by Caledonian MacBrayne : from Arinagour to Oban : 4 weekly (3 h 30 mn) – from Arinagour to Tobermory (Isle of Mull) 3 weekly (1 h 20 mn) – from Arinagour to Isle of Tiree : 3-4 weekly (1 h to 1 h 15 mn).

Arinagour – ⊠ ✆ 087 93 Coll
⚲ **Tigh-Na-Mara** ⟋, PA78 6SY, ✆ 354, ≤ Mull and Treshnish Isles, « Idyllic Hebridean setting », ⟍, 🍴 – ⤬ 🅿
closed December-mid January – **M** (communal dining) 6.00/9.90 st. and a la carte – **8 rm** ⊡ (dinner included) 24.50/54.00 st.

COLONSAY (Isle of) Argyll. (Strathclyde) **401** B 15 – pop. 132 – ✆ 095 12 Colonsay.
📋 ✆ 316.
⛴ by Caledonian MacBrayne : summer only, from Scalasaig to Oban 3-4 weekly (2 h 30 mn).

Scalasaig – ECD : Wednesday – ⊠ ✆ 095 12 Colonsay
🏠 **Isle of Colonsay** ⟋, PA61 7YP, ✆ 316, Fax 353, ≤, « 18C inn », 🍴 – ⤬ rest 🅿. ⑊ **AE** ⓄⒹ *VISA*
restricted service 12 January-28 February – **M** (bar lunch)/dinner 14.00 st. ⬩4.00 – **11 rm** ⊡ 39.50/79.00 st. – SB 76.00/95.00 st.

COLVEND Kircudbright. (Dumfries and Galloway) – ⊠ Dalbeattie – ✆ 055 663 Rockcliffe.
📋 ✆ 398, E : 1 ¼ m – ♦Edinburgh 99 – ♦Dumfries 19.
⚲ **Clonyard House**, DG5 4QW, NW : 1 m. on A 710 ✆ 372, 🍴 – 📺 ☎ & 🅿. ⑊ *VISA*
M (bar lunch)/dinner 12.00 t. and a la carte 7.70/14.60 t. ⬩2.90 – **10 rm** ⊡ 17.00/44.00 t. – SB (November-March) 50.00 **st.**

CRAIGHOUSE Argyll. (Strathclyde) **401** C 16 – see Jura (Isle of).

CRIANLARICH Perth. (Central) **401** G 16 – ✆ 083 83.
♦Edinburgh 82 – ♦Glasgow 52 – Perth 53.
⚲ **Allt-Chaorain House** ⟋, FK20 8RU, NW : 1 m. on A 82 ✆ 283, ≤, 🍴 – ⤬ 📺 🅿. ⑊ *VISA*
20 March-4 November – **M** 12.00 t. – **9 rm** ⊡ 28.00/64.00 t.

CRIEFF Perth. (Tayside) **401** I 14 Scotland G – pop. 5 101 – ECD : Wednesday – ✆ 0764.
See : Site★ – Envir. : Drummond Castle★ *AC*, S : 2 m. by A 822 – Tullibardine Chapel★, S : 6 m. by – Upper Strathearn★ (Loch Earn★★) NW : 12 m. by A B5.
📋 Perth Rd ✆ 2909 – 📋 Peat Rd, Muthill ✆ 3319, S : 3 m. on A 822.
🛈 High St. ✆ 2578 (summer only).
♦Edinburgh 60 – ♦Glasgow 50 – ♦Oban 76 – Perth 18.
🏠 **Murraypark**, Connaught Terr., PH7 3DJ, ✆ 3731, Fax 5311, 🍴 – ☎ 🅿. ⑊ **AE** Ⓓ *VISA*
M 11.00/19.00 t. and a la carte ⬩3.75 – **13 rm** ⊡ 24.00/56.00 t., **1 suite** 51.00/64.00 t. – SB (November-April) 60.00/68.00 st.

⚲ **Gwydyr House**, Comrie Rd, PH7 4BP, on A 85 ✆ 3277, ≤, 🍴 – 📺 🅿
Easter-October – **M** 8.15 t. ⬩2.90 – **10 rm** ⊡ 13.50/27.00 t.

⚲ **Leven House**, Comrie Rd, PH7 4BA, on A 85 ✆ 2529, ≤ – ⤬ rest 🅿
M 8.00 st. ⬩1.80 – **10 rm** ⊡ 13.00/20.00 st. – SB 40.00/50.00 st.

at Sma'Glen NE : 4 m. by A 85 on A 822 – ✉ ☎ 0764 Crieff :

🏛 **Foulford Inn** ⌂, PH7 3LN, ☏ 2407, ≼ – 🅿 *VISA*
closed February – **M** 7.00/10.00 **t.** and a la carte ⌾ 4.00 – **11 rm** �) 13.00/32.00 **t.** –
SB 35.00/57.00 **st.**

VAUXHALL, SUZUKI Comrie Rd ☏ 2125

CRINAN Argyll. (Strathclyde) **401** D 15 – ✉ Lochgilphead – ☎ 054 683.
See : Site*.
Envir. : Kilmory Knap (Macmillan's Cross*) SW : 14 m.
♦Edinburgh 137 – ♦Glasgow 91 – ♦Oban 36.

🏛 **Crinan**, PA31 8SR, ☏ 261, Fax 292, « ≼ commanding setting, overlooking Loch Crinan and
Sound of Jura », ⌂, 🛥 – ▦ TV ☎ 🅿 🔌 *VISA*
M (buffet lunch)/dinner 22.50 **st.** (rest. see also **Lock 16** below) – **22 rm** �) 37.50/80.00 **st.**

XX **Lock 16** (at Crinan H.), PA31 8SR, ☏ 261, Seafood, « ≼ commanding setting, overlooking
Loch Crinan and Sound of Jura » – 🅿 🔌 *VISA*
closed Monday – **M** (booking essential) (dinner only) 30.00 **st.**

CROCKETFORD Kirkcudbright. (Dumfries and Galloway) **401 402** I 18 – ☎ 055 669.
♦Edinburgh 86 – ♦Dumfries 9 – ♦Stranraer 67.

🏛 **Galloway Arms**, DG2 8RA, ☏ 240 – TV 🅿 ⌖ – **11 rm**.

CROMARTY Ross and Cromarty. (Highland) **401** H 10 – pop. 685 – ECD : Wednesday –
☎ 038 17.
♦Edinburgh 182 – ♦Inverness 26 – ♦Wick 126.

🏛 **Royal**, Marine Terr., IV11 8YN, ☏ 217, ≼ – 🅿 *AE* *VISA*
M *(closed Sunday dinner)* 8.00/13.50 **st.** ⌾ 3.00 – **10 rm** �) 20.00/38.00 **st.**

X **Le Chardon**, 20 Church St., IV11 8XA, ☏ 471 – ⌖. 🔌 *AE* *VISA*
closed Sunday dinner and Monday – **M** 10.00/22.00 **t.**

CROSSFORD Fife. (Fife) **401** J 15 – see Dunfermline.

CULLEN Banff. (Grampian) **401** L 10 Scotland G – pop. 1 378 – ECD : Wednesday – ☎ 0542.
See : Auld Kirk* (Sacrament house*, carved panels*).
Envir. : Deskford Church (Sacrament house*) S : 4 m. by B 9018 – Portsoy*, E : 5 ½ m. by A 98.
🏴 The Links ☏ 40685.
🛈 20 Seafield St. ☏ 40757 (summer only).
♦Edinburgh 189 – ♦Aberdeen 59 – Banff 12 – ♦Inverness 61.

🏛 **Seafield Arms**, 19 Seafield St., AB5 2SG, ☏ 40791 – TV ☎ 🅿
22 rm.

CULLODEN Inverness. (Highland) **401** H 11 – see Inverness.

CULNAKNOCK Inverness. (Highland) **401** B 11 – see Skye (Isle of).

CUPAR Fife. (Fife) **401** K 15 – pop. 6 662 – ECD : Thursday – ☎ 0334.
🛈 Fluthers car park ☏ 55555 (summer only).
♦Edinburgh 45 – ♦Dundee 15 – Perth 23.

X **Ostler's Close**, Bonnygate, KY15 4BU, ☏ 55574 – 🔌 *VISA*
closed Sunday and Monday – **M** a la carte 15.75/20.75 **t.** ⌾ 3.25.

◎ ATS St. Catherine St. ☏ 54003

DALBEATTIE Kirkcudbright. (Dumfries and Galloway) **401 402** I 19 – pop. 3 891 – ☎ 0556.
🛈 Car Park ☏ 610117.
♦Edinburgh 94 – ♦Ayr 56 – ♦Dumfries 14 – Stranraer 62.

↟ **Auchenskeoch Lodge**, DG5 4PG, SE : 5 m. on B 793 ☏ 038 778 (Southwick) 277, ⌂, 🛥,
park – 🅿 🔌 *VISA*
Easter-October – **M** 10.00 **st.** – **5 rm** �) 23.00/40.00 **st.** – SB (except summer) 55.60 **st.**

DALIBURGH Inverness. (Outer Hebrides) (Western Isles) **401** X 12 – see Uist (South)
(Isles of).

DALMALLY Argyll. (Strathclyde) **401** F 14 – ✉ ☎ 083 82.
♦Edinburgh 99 – ♦Glasgow 69 – ♦Oban 24 – Perth 70.

↟ **Craig Villa**, PA33 1AX, on A 85 ☏ 255, ≼, 🛥 – 🅿 ⌖
Easter-October – **M** 8.50 **st.** – **6 rm** �) 30.00 **s.**

DALRY (ST. JOHN'S TOWN OF) Kirkcudbright. (Dumfries and Galloway) 401 402 H 18 – ⊠ Castle Douglas – ☎ 064 43.
♦Edinburgh 82 – ♦Dumfries 27 – ♦Glasgow 66 – Stranraer 47.

🏠 **Lochinvar**, Main St., DG7 3UP, ✆ 210 – ℗. 🔄 AE VISA
M 14.50 t. (dinner) and a la carte 11.75/17.85 t. ⌾ 3.15 – **16 rm** ⊏ 16.00/30.00 t. – SB (week-days only) 40.00/60.00 **st.**

DENNY Stirling. (Central) 401 I 15 – pop. 23 172 – ☎ 0324.
♦Edinburgh 34 – ♦Glasgow 25 – Stirling 7.

↑ **Topps Farm** ♫, Fintry Rd., FK6 5JF, W : 4 m. on B 818 ✆ 822471, ≼ – ⇖ ℗
M 12.00 **st.** ⌾ 4.00 – **4 rm** ⊏ 18.00/36.00 **st.** – SB 50.00/60.00 **st.**

DERVAIG Argyll. (Strathclyde) 401 B 14 – see Mull (Isle of).

DIRLETON E. Lothian. (Lothian) 401 402 L 15 – see Gullane.

DOLPHINTON Lanark. (Strathclyde) 401 J 16 – ⊠ West Linton – ☎ 0968.
♦Edinburgh 26 – Hawick 43 – ♦Glasgow 41.

🏨 **Dolphinton House** ♫, EH46 7AB, ✆ 82286, 🐎 – ⇖ TV ☎ ℗. 🔄 AE ① VISA
M 11.00/19.75 t. ⌾ 4.00 – **12 rm** ⊏ 41.50/89.75 **st.** – SB 98.75 **st.**

DORNIE Ross and Cromarty. (Highland) 401 D 12 – ⊠ Kyle of Lochalsh – ☎ 059 985.
♦Edinburgh 212 – ♦Inverness 74 – Kyle of Lochalsh 8.

🏠 **Loch Duich**, IV40 8DY, ✆ 213, ≼ Eilean Donan Castle and hills, 🐎 – ⇖ ℗. 🔄 VISA. 🍸
Early March-mid November – M (bar lunch)/dinner 15.00 t. ⌾ 2.95 – **18 rm** ⊏ 22.00/44.00 t.

DORNOCH Sutherland. (Highland) 401 H 10 Scotland G – pop. 1 006 – ECD : Thursday – ☎ 0862 – ⛳ Royal Dornoch, Golf Rd ✆ 810219.
🛈 The Square, ✆ 810400.
♦Edinburgh 219 – ♦Inverness 63 – ♦Wick 65.

🏨 **Dornoch Castle**, Castle St., IV25 3SD, ✆ 810216, « Former bishop's palace, part 16C »,
🐎 – ⇖ rest ℗. 🔄 AE VISA
Mid April-mid November – M 16.25 **st.** (dinner) and a la carte ⌾ 3.50 – **19 rm** ⊏ 29.00/64.00 **st.** – SB 72.00/89.00 **st.**

PEUGEOT St. Gilbert St. ✆ 810341   PEUGEOT Evelix Service Station (on A 9) ✆ 810255

DOUNBY Orkney. (Orkney Islands) 401 K 6 – see Orkney Islands (Mainland).

DOUNE Perth. (Central) 401 H 15 Scotland G – pop. 1 020 – ECD : Wednesday – ☎ 0786.
See : Site* – Castle* – Envir. : Doune Motor Museum*, NW : 1 m. by A 84.
♦Edinburgh 45 – ♦Glasgow 35 – Perth 33 – Stirling 8.

✗ **Broughton's**, Blair Drummond, FK9 4XE, S : 3 m. by A 84 on A 873 ✆ 841897, 🐎 – ⇖
℗. 🔄 VISA
closed Sunday dinner, Monday, last 2 weeks January and first 2 weeks February – M (booking essential) 9.15/16.25 t. and lunch a la carte approx. 6.80 t. ⌾ 3.50.

DRUMNADROCHIT Inverness. (Highland) 401 G 11 – pop. 542 – ⊠ Milton – ☎ 045 62.
Envir. : Loch Ness** – Loch Ness Monster Exhibition*.
♦Edinburgh 172 – ♦Inverness 16 – Kyle of Lochalsh 66.

🏨 **Polmaily House** ♫, IV3 6XT, W : 2 m. on A 831 ✆ 343, « Country house atmosphere »,
🏊, 🐎, park, ✗ – ⇖ rest ℗. 🔄 VISA. 🍸
Easter-mid October – M (bar lunch, residents only)/dinner 15.00 **st.** ⌾ 3.75 – **9 rm** ⊏ 35.00/80.00 **st.**

DRYBRIDGE Banff. (Grampian) – see Buckie.

DRYMEN Stirling. (Central) 401 G 15 – pop. 771 – ECD : Wednesday – ☎ 0360.
Envir. : Loch Lomond**, W : 3 m – ♦Edinburgh 64 – ♦Glasgow 18 – Stirling 22.

🏨 **Buchanan Arms**, Main St., G63 0BQ, ✆ 60588, Fax 60943, 🏊, 🐎, squash – TV ☎ ℗ –
🔥 150. 🔄 AE ① VISA
M 8.95/15.95 t. and a la carte ⌾ 3.50 – **35 rm** ⊏ 50.00/80.00 t. – SB (except wee-kends November-March) 28.00/46.00 **st.**

DULNAIN BRIDGE Inverness. (Highland) 401 J 12 – ECD : Wednesday – ⊠ Grantown-on-Spey (Moray Highland) – ☎ 047 985 – ♦Edinburgh 140 – ♦Inverness 31 – Perth 96.

🏠 **Muckrach Lodge**, PH26 3LY, W : ½ m. on A 938 ✆ 257, ≼, 🐎 – TV ☎ ℗. 🔄 AE ① VISA
🍸
M (bar lunch)/dinner 17.75 t. ⌾ 3.75 – **10 rm** ⊏ 26.25/62.50 t. – SB (January-March and October-22 December) 72.00 **st.**

See : Dumbarton Castel site★.

Envir. : Loch Lomond★★ N : 6 m. by A 82 – Helensburgh (Hill House★) NW 10 m. by A 814.

♦Edinburgh 64 – ♦Glasgow 12 – Greenock 17.

🏠 **Travelodge** without rest., Milton, G82 2TY, E : 2 ½ m. by A 814 on A 82 ✆ 65202 – 📺 ♿
P. 🅿 **AE** **VISA**
32 rm 21.50/27.00 **t.**

DUMFRIES Dumfries. (Dumfries and Galloway) **401** **402** J 18 **Scotland G** – pop. 31 307 – ECD : Thursday – ✆ 0387.

See : Site★ – Midsteeple★ **A A** – Lincluden College (Tomb★) by College Str. **A.**

Envir. : Sweetheart Abbey★, S : 8 ¼ m. by A 710 **A** – Caerlaverock Castle★, SE : 9 m. by B 725 **B**
– Ruthwell Cross★, SE : 16 m. by B 725 **B** – Glenkiln (Sculptures★) E : 10 m. by A 75 **B** – Kippford★,
SW : 18 m. by A 710 or A 711 **A** – Drumlanrig Castle★★, NW : 18 m. by A 76 **A.**

🏌18 Laurieston Av. ✆ 53582 **A** – 🏌9 Lochmaben ✆ 81552, NE : 8 m. by A 709 **B** – 🏌18 Dumfries and County, Edinburgh rd ✆ 53585, NE : 1 m. **B.**

🚉 Whitesands ✆ 53862 (summer only).

♦Edinburgh 80 – ♦Ayr 59 – ♦Carlisle 34 – ♦Glasgow 79 – ♦Manchester 155 – ♦Newcastle-upon-Tyne 91.

DUMFRIES

High Street................ **A** 18

Aldermanhill Road........ **B** 2	Eastfield Rd.............. **B** 12	St. Michael's Bridge Road....... **A** 30
Bank Street.............. **A** 3	Friars Vennel............ **A** 13	Shakespeare Street............ **B** 31
Buccleuch Street........ **A** 4	Galloway Street.......... **A** 14	Union Street................. **A** 32
Cardoness Street........ **B** 5	Glebe Street............. **B** 15	Whitesands................. **A** 34
Cassalands .... **A** 6	Great King Street........ **A** 16	
Castle Street............ **A** 7	Hermitage Drive......... **A** 17	
Castle Douglas Road.... **A** 8	Laurieknowe .... **A** 20	
Catherine Street .... **B** 9	Loreburn Street......... **A** 21	
Corberry Avenue......... **A** 10	Nith Street.............. **AB** 22	
	Queen Street............ **B** 23	
	Queensberry Street ...... **A** 24	
	Rae Street.............. **B** 26	
	St. Mary's Street......... **B** 27	
	St. Michael Street .... **B** 28	

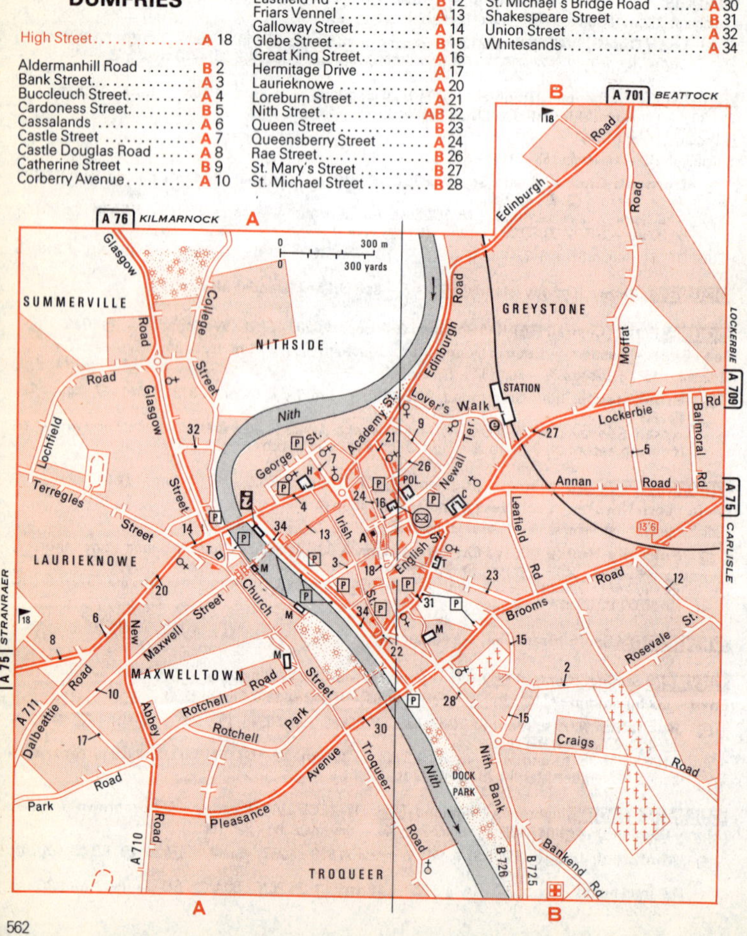

🏨 **Station,** 49 Lovers Walk, DG1 1LT, 🖉 54316, Fax 50388 – 🛗 📺 ☎ 🅿 – 🔬 70. 🔼 AE ⓪ VISA
B e
closed 26 December and 1 January – **M** (carving lunch)/dinner 13.75 **t.** and a la carte
11.75/18.75 **t.** 🍾 3.50 – **32 rm** ☕ 49.50/58.00 **t.** – SB (weekends only) 64.00 **st.**

at Clarencefield SE : 9 ½ m. by A 75 – B – on B 724 – ✉ ⚙ 038 787 Clarencefield :

🏰 **Comlongon Castle** 🦯, DG1 4NA, 🖉 283, ≼, « Part 16C castle, 13C origins », 🦰, �,
park – ✵ rest 📺 🅿. 🔼 VISA 🦮
closed January and February – **M** (dinner only) 16.00 **t.** 🍾 4.00 – **8 rm** ☕ 25.00/80.00 **t.**

🏰 **Kirklands** 🦯, Ruthwell, DG1 4NP, SE : 1 m. by B 724 🖉 284, 🚂 – 📺 ☎ 🅿. 🔼 VISA. 🦮
M a la carte 6.50/11.00 **t.** 🍾 2.75 – **5 rm** ☕ 20.00/36.00 **t.** – SB (except summer) 50.00/60.00 **st.**

FIAT 123 Whitesands 🖉 64875   ⓦ ATS Glasgow St. 🖉 63837/8
FORD Main Rd 🖉 710491
VOLVO Annan Rd 🖉 61437

DUNAIN PARK Inverness. (Highland) – see Inverness.

DUNBAR E. Lothian. (Lothian) 🔟 M 15 Scotland G   pop. 5 795 – ECD : Wednesday –
⚙ 0368.
See : Tolbooth★ – John Muir's Birthplace★.
Envir. : Museum of Flight★, W : 5 m. by A 1087 and A 1 – Preston Mill★, W : 6 m. by A 1087, A 1
and B 1407 – Tyninghame★, NW : 6 m. by A 1 and A 198 – Tantallon Castle★★, NW : 10 m. by
A 1087, A 1 and A 198.
🏌 Winterfield, North Rd 🖉 63562 – 🏌 East Links 🖉 62317, S : ½ m.
🛈 Town House, High St. 🖉 63353.
♦Edinburgh 28 – ♦Newcastle-upon-Tyne 90.

🏰 **Redheuch,** Bayswell Park, EH42 1AE, 🖉 62793 – 📺 ☎. 🔼 AE VISA
M a la carte 9.30/13.00 **t.** 🍾 3.30 – **10 rm** ☕ 30.80/39.50 **t.**

🏰 **Courtyard,** Woodbrush Brae, EH42 1HB, 🖉 64169 – 📺 🅿. 🔼 VISA
closed 1 to 21 January – **M** 6.50/16.00 **t.** 🍾 3.65 – **7 rm** ☕ 14.50/48.00 **t.**

↑ **St Beys,** 2 Bayswell Rd, EH42 1AB, 🖉 63571 – 📺. VISA
M 8.00 **st.** – **6 rm** ☕ 15.50/29.00 **st.**

↑ **Marine,** 7 Marine Rd, EH42 1AR, 🖉 63315, ≼ – ✵ rest
M 5.00 **st.** – **9 rm** ☕ 12.00/24.00 **st.**

DUNBLANE Perth. (Central) 🔟 I 15 Scotland G – pop. 6 783 – ECD : Wednesday – ⚙ 0786.
See : Site★ – Cathedral★★.
🛈 Stirling Rd 🖉 824428 (summer only).
♦Edinburgh 42 – ♦Glasgow 33 – Perth 29.

🏩 **Cromlix House** 🦯, Kinbuck, FK15 9JT, N : 3 ¼ m. by A 9 on B 8033 🖉 822125, Telex
779959, Fax 825450, ≼, « Antique furnishings », 🦰, 🚂, park, 🎾 – ✵ rest 📺 ☎ 🅿. 🔼 AE
⓪ VISA
closed 1 to 14 February – **M** (booking essential) 19.00/30.00 **st.** 🍾 3.75 – **6 rm**
☕ 75.00/110.00 **st.**, **8 suites** 145.00/185.00 **st.** – SB (November-March) 160.00 **st.**

AUSTIN-ROVER Stirling Rd 🖉 823271

DUNDEE Angus. (Tayside) 🔟 L 14 Scotland G   pop. 172 294 – ECD : Wednesday – ⚙ 0382.
See : The Frigate Unicorn★ Y A – R. RS Discovery★ Y B.
🏌 Caird Park 🖉 453606 off Kingsway Bypass at Mains Loan Z – 🏌 Camperdown Park 🖉 621145,
NW : 2 m. by A 923 Z.
✈ Dundee Airport : 🖉 643242, SW : 1 ½ m. Z.
🛈 4 City Sq. 🖉 27723.
♦Edinburgh 63 – ♦Aberdeen 67 – ♦Glasgow 83.

Plan on next page

🏩 Stakis Earl Grey (Stakis), Earl Grey Pl., DD1 4DE, 🖉 29271, Telex 76569, Fax 200072, ≼, 🔽 –
🛗 🍴 rest 📺 ☎ 🦽 🅿 – 🔬 220. 🔼 AE ⓪ VISA. 🦮
Y a
☕ 7.25 – **102 rm** 62.00/94.00 **st.**, **2 suites** 125.00 **st.** – SB 58.00/79.00 **st.**

🏩 **Angus Thistle** (Thistle), 101 Marketgait, DD1 1QU, 🖉 26874, Telex 76456, Fax 22564 – 🛗
✵ rm 📺 ☎ 🅿 – 🔬 600. 🔼 AE ⓪ VISA
Y c
M 7.75/12.95 **st.** and a la carte – ☕ 7.25 – **53 rm** 55.00/80.00 **st.**, **5 suites** 85.00 **st.** –
SB 64.00/72.00 **st.**

🏨 **Swallow** (Swallow), Kingsway West (Dundee Ring Rd), DD2 5JT, W : 4 ¾ m. at junction A
85 and A 972 Z 🖉 641122, Telex 76694, Fax 568340, 🔽, 🚂 – ✵ rm 🍴 rest 📺 ☎ 🦽 🅿. 🔼
AE ⓪ VISA
M 9.25/14.50 **st.** and a la carte 🍾 5.00 – **110 rm** ☕ 65.00/120.00 **st.** – SB 70.00/75.00 **st.**

🏨 **Queen's,** 160 Nethergate, DD1 4DU, 🖉 22515, Fax 202668 – 🛗 📺 ☎ 🅿 – 🔬 150. 🔼 AE
⓪ VISA. 🦮
Y e
M 7.00/13.50 **st.** and a la carte 🍾 3.50 – **30 rm** ☕ 27.50/90.00 **st.**

DUNDEE

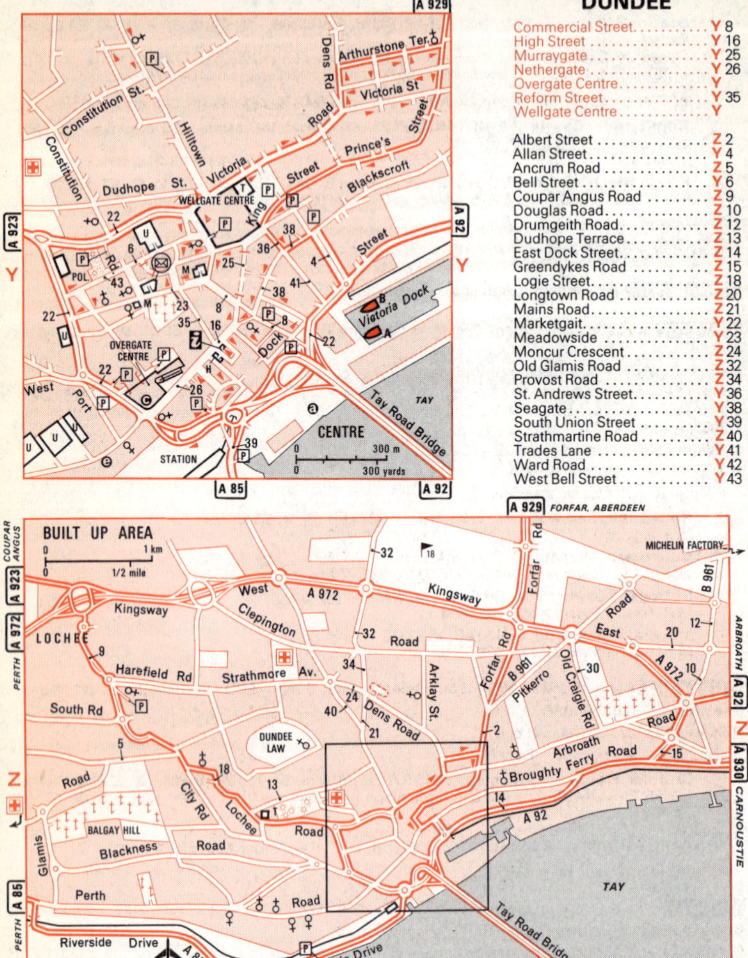

Commercial Street . . . . Y 8
High Street . . . . Y 16
Murraygate . . . . Y 25
Nethergate . . . . Y 26
Overgate Centre . . . . Y
Reform Street . . . . Y 35
Wellgate Centre . . . . Y

Albert Street . . . . Z 2
Allan Street . . . . Y 4
Ancrum Road . . . . Z 5
Bell Street . . . . Y 6
Coupar Angus Road . . . . Z 9
Douglas Road . . . . Z 10
Drumgeith Road . . . . Z 12
Dudhope Terrace . . . . Z 13
East Dock Street . . . . Z 14
Greendykes Road . . . . Z 15
Logie Street . . . . Z 18
Longtown Road . . . . Z 20
Mains Road . . . . Z 21
Marketgait . . . . Y 22
Meadowside . . . . Y 23
Moncur Crescent . . . . Z 24
Old Glamis Road . . . . Z 32
Provost Road . . . . Y 34
St. Andrews Street . . . . Y 36
Seagate . . . . Y 38
South Union Street . . . . Y 39
Strathmartine Road . . . . Z 40
Trades Lane . . . . Y 41
Ward Road . . . . Y 42
West Bell Street . . . . Y 43

at Broughty Ferry E : 4 ½ m. by A 930 – Z – (Dundee Rd) – ⊠ ☎ 0382 Dundee :

Tayview without rest., 71-73 St. Vincent St., DD5 2EZ, ℘ 79438 – ⇔. ◪. ⅌
11 rm ⇆ 25.00/55.00 t.

AUSTIN-ROVER 64 Ward Rd ℘ 24013		RENAULT Riverside Drive ℘ 644401
CITROEN 3 Roseangle ℘ 28483		TOYOTA East Kingsway ℘ 457667
FIAT, LADA MacAlpine Rd ℘ 818004		VAUXHALL East Dock St. ℘ 26521
FORD Balfield Rd ℘ 60191		VOLVO Riverside Drive ℘ 643295
HONDA Queen St., Broughty Ferry ℘ 77257		
HYUNDAI 25 Rosebank St. ℘ 25406		ATS 332 Clepington Rd ℘ 88327
MAZDA 166 Seagate ℘ 25007		

DUNDONNELL Ross and Cromarty. (Highland) 401 E 10 – ⊠ Garve – ☎ 085 483.

♦Edinburgh 215 – ♦ Inverness 59.

Dundonnell, IV23 2QS, ℘ 204, ⟨ Dundonnell Valley – ⅋ ☎ ℗. ◪ VISA
April-October – **M** (bar lunch)/dinner 14.50 **t.** and a la carte ⅃ 3.95 – **24 rm** ⇆ 34.50/59.00 **t.**
– SB 70.00/85.00 **st.**

DUNFERMLINE Fife. (Fife) **401** J 15 Scotland G – pop. 52 105 – ECD : Wednesday – ☎ 0383.

See : Site★ – Abbey★ (Norman nave★★).

Envir. : Culross★★★ (Palace★★ and Study★) E : 7 m. by A 994.

🏌 Canmore, Venturefair ℘ 724969, N : 1 m. – 🏌 Pitreavie, Queensferry Rd ℘ 722591.

🛈 Glen Bridge Car Park ℘ 720999 (summer only).

♦Edinburgh 16 – ♦Dundee 48 – Motherwell 39.

🏨 **King Malcolm Thistle** (Thistle), Queensferry Rd, KY11 5DS, S : 1 m. on A 823 ℘ 722611, Telex 727721, Fax 730865 – ⇥ rm ▤ rest 📺 ☎ 🅿 – 🔬 150. 🔼 🅰🅴 ⓞ 𝘝𝘐𝘚𝘈
M 15.50 **st.** and a la carte – ☲ 7.25 – **48 rm** 45.00/65.00 **st.** – SB 74.00/78.00 **st.**

at Crossford SW : 1 ¾ m. on A 994 – ✉ ☎ 0383 Dunfermline :

🏨 **Keavil House** (Best Western) ⑤, Main St., KY12 8NY, ℘ 736258, Telex 728227, Fax 612600, ☞, ✀ – 📺 ☎ 㘴 🅿 – 🔬 200. 🔼 🅰🅴 ⓞ 𝘝𝘐𝘚𝘈
M 9.50/14.50 **st.** and a la carte 8.00/15.00 **st.** 🍾 3.25 – **32 rm** ☲ 42.50/65.00 **st.** – SB 75.00/85.00 **st.**

AUSTIN-ROVER 18 Halbeath Rd ℘ 731041　　　　VAUXHALL 3 Carnock Rd ℘ 721511
FIAT 128-140 Pittencrieff St. ℘ 722565
PEUGEOT-TALBOT 206 Rumbingwell ℘ 731791　　⑩ ATS 14 Dickson St , Elgin St. Est. ℘ 722802
RENAULT Headwell Av. ℘ 721914

DUNKELD Perth. (Tayside) **401** J 14 Scotland G – ECD : Thursday – ☎ 035 02.

See : Site★ – Cathedral Street★.

🏌 Fungarth ℘ 524, N : 1 m. on A 923.

🛈 The Cross ℘ 688 (summer only).

♦Edinburgh 58 – ♦Aberdeen 88 – ♦Inverness 98 – Perth 14.

🏰 Stakis Dunkeld House (Stakis) ⑤, PH8 0HX, ℘ 771, Telex 76657, Fax 8924, ≤, « Tayside setting », 🔲, ☞, ✀, park, ✀ – 🛗 ⇥ rm 📺 ☎ 🅿 – 🔬 100. 🔼 🅰🅴 ⓞ 𝘝𝘐𝘚𝘈. ✿
☲ 7.25 – **89 rm** 70.00/100.00 **st.**, **3 suites** 130.00 **st.** – SB 90.00/130.00 **st.**

🏠 **Bheinne Mhor,** Perth Rd, Birnam, PH8 0DH, S : ¾ m. by A 923 ℘ 779, ☞ – ⇥ rest 🅿. ✿
closed Christmas-New Year – **M** 8.50 **st.** – **4 rm** ☲ 12.00/28.00 **st.** – SB (October-April) 38.50/42.50 **st.**

XXX **Kinnaird House,** Dalguise, PH8 0LB, NW : 6 ¾ m. by A 9 on B 898 ℘ 440, Fax 289, ≤, ☞ – 🅿
closed Sunday dinner, Monday and February – **M** 19.00 **st.** (lunch) and a la carte 24.00/28.00 **st.** 🍷 4.50.

DUNOON Argyll. (Strathclyde) **401** F 16 – pop. 8 797 – ECD : Wednesday – ☎ 0369.

🏌 Cowal, Ardenslate Rd ℘ 5673, NE : boundary.

🚢 by Caledonian MacBrayne : from Dunoon Pier to Gourock Railway Pier : frequent services daily (20 mn) – by Western Ferries : from Hunters Quay to McInroy's Point, Gourock : frequent services daily (20 mn).

🛈 7 Alexandra Par. ℘ 3785.

♦Edinburgh 73 – ♦Glasgow 27 – ♦Oban 77.

🏠 **Enmore,** Marine Par., Kirn, PA23 8HH, N : 1 m. on A 815 ℘ 2230, ≤ Firth of Clyde, ☞, squash – ⇥ rest 📺 ☎ 🅿. 🔼 ⓞ 𝘝𝘐𝘚𝘈
closed 1 to 11 January – **M** 16.50 **st.** (dinner) 🍷 4.00 – **12 rm** ☲ 25.00/91.00 **st.** – SB (November-March) 70.00/110.00 **st.**

AUSTIN-ROVER, LAND-ROVER, FORD East Bay　　⑩ ATS 247 Argyll St. ℘ 2853
Promenade ℘ 3094
RENAULT Shore St., Inverary ℘ 0499 (Inverary) 2150

DUNVEGAN Inverness. (Highland) **401** A 11 – see Skye (Isle of).

DUROR Argyll. (Strathclyde) **401** E 14 – ✉ Appin – ☎ 063 174.

♦Edinburgh 125 – Fort William 19 – ♦Oban 31.

🏠 **Stewart** (Best Western) ⑤, Glen Duror, PA38 4BW, ℘ 268, ≤, ☞ – ⇥ rest 📺 ☎ 🅿. 🔼 🅰🅴 ⓞ 𝘝𝘐𝘚𝘈
Easter-November – **M** (bar lunch)/dinner 22.00 **t.** 🍷 4.00 – **19 rm** ☲ 32.50/65.00 **t.** – SB 88.00 **st.**

DYCE Aberdeen. (Grampian) **401** N 12 – see Aberdeen.

EASDALE Argyll. (Strathclyde) **401** D 15 – ✉ Oban – ☎ 085 23 Balvicar.

♦Edinburgh 140 – ♦Glasgow 120 – ♦Oban 17.

🏠 **Easdale Inn** ⑤, Isle of Seil, PA34 4RF, ℘ 256, ≤ – ⇥ 📺 🅿
April-October – **M** (bar lunch)/dinner 11.50 **t.** – **7 rm** ☲ 22.50/49.00 **t.**

♦Edinburgh 46 – ♦Ayr 35 – ♦Glasgow 10.

🏨 Bruce (Swallow), 35 Cornwall St., G74 1AF, ✆ 29771, Telex 778428, Fax 42216 – 🕮 ⇷ rm 📺 ☎ 🅿 – 🕭 200 – **84 rm**.

🏨 Stuart, 2 Cornwall Way, G74 1JR, ✆ 21161, Telex 778504, Fax 64410 – 🕮 📺 ☎ – 🕭 200. 🔲 AE ⑪ VISA
closed 25 December-1 January – **M** 5.75/10.75 **t.** and a la carte 🍾 3.25 – **38 rm** 🍽 40.00/51.00 **t.**, **1 suite** 53.00/65.00 **t.** – SB (weekends only) 64.00/104.00 **st.**

🏨 Crutherland Country House ⏃, Strathaven Rd, G75 0QZ, SE : 2 m. on A 726 ✆ 37633, Fax 37633, ⛀, park – 📺 ☎ 🅿. ⚒
19 rm.

♦Edinburgh 22 – ♦Newcastle-upon-Tyne 96.

🏨 **Harvesters**, Station Rd, EH40 3DP, ✆ 860395, ⛀ – 📺 ☎ 🅿. 🔲 AE ⑪ VISA
M (closed Sunday and Monday) (bar lunch)/dinner 10.50 **st.** and a la carte 🍾 4.00 – **11 rm** 🍽 25.00/56.00 **st.** – SB (weekends only) 66.00/70.00 **st.**

See : Site★★★ – International Festival★★★ (August) – Castle★★ (Site★★★, ⇐★★ ✳★★★, Great Hall: hammerbeam roof★★, Palace block: Honours of Scotland★★★) DZ – Abbey and Palace of Holyroodhouse★★ (Plasterwork ceilings★★★) BV – Royal Mile★★ : Gladstone's Land★ EYZ A, St. Giles' Cathedral★★ (Crown Spire★★★) EZ – Canongate Tolbooth★ EY B Victoria Street★ EZ 84 – Royal Museum of Scotland★★, EZ M2 – New Town★★ : Charlotte Square★★★ CY 14, Royal Museum of Scotland (Antiquities★★) EY M3 – The Georgian House★ CY D – National Portrait Gallery★ EY M3 – Princes Street and Gardens : National Gallery of Scotland★★★ DY M4 – Scott Monument★ EY F Calton Hill EY : ✳★★★ from Nelson Monument – Royal Botanic Gardens★★★ AV – Edinburgh Zoo★★ AV – Scottish Agricultural Museum★ by A 90 AV – Craigmillar Castle★ BX.

Envir. : Rosslyn Chapel★★, Apprentice Pillar★★★, S : 7 m. by A 701 BX – Hopetoun House★★ W : 10 ½ m. by A 90 AV – Forth Bridges★★ W : 7 ½ m. by A 90 AV – Dalmeny (site★) W : 7 m. by A 90 AV.

🏌18 Silverknowes, Parkway, ✆ 336 3843, W : 4 m. AV – 🏌18 Liberton, Gilmerton Rd ✆ 664 3009, SE : 3 m. on A 7 B – 🏌18 Craigmillar Park, Observatory Rd ✆ 667 2837 BX – 🏌18 Carrick Knowe, Glendevon Park ✆ 337 1096, W : 5 m. AX – 🏌18 Swanston Rd, Fairmilehead ✆ 445 2239, S : 4 m. by A 702 AX – 🏌18 Lothianburn, Biggar Rd ✆ 445 2206, S : 4 ½ m. by A 702 B – 🏌9 Ravelston Dykes Rd ✆ 315 2486, W : 3 m. by A 90 AV.

✈ ✆ 333 1000, Telex 727615, W : 6 m. by A 8 AV – **Terminal** : Waverley Bridge.

🚗 ✆ 0345 090700.

🛈 Waverley Market, 3 Princes St., ✆ 557 1700 – Edinburgh Airport ✆ 333 2167.

♦Glasgow 46 – ♦Newcastle-upon-Tyne 105.

Plans on following pages

🏨🏨 **Caledonian** (Norfolk Cap.), Princes St., EH1 2AB, ✆ 225 2433, Telex 72179, Fax 225 6632 – 🕮 ⇷ rm 📺 ☎ 🕭 🅿 – 🕭 150. 🔲 AE ⑪ VISA ⚒   CY n
M (see **Pompadour** below) – 🍽 8.50 – **221 rm** 95.00/145.00 **st.**, **16 suites** – SB (weekends only) 140.00 **st.**

🏨🏨 **Sheraton**, 1 Festival Square, EH3 9SR, ✆ 229 9131, Telex 72398, Fax 228 4510, 🔲 – 🕮 ▤ 📺 ☎ 🕭 🅿 – 🕭 450. ⚒   CDZ v
247 rm, 16 suites.

🏨🏨 **George** (Inter-Continental), 19-21 George St., EH2 2PB, ✆ 225 1251, Telex 72570, Fax 226 5644 – 🕮 ⇷ rm ▤ rest 📺 ☎ 🕭 🅿 – 🕭 250. 🔲 AE ⑪ VISA   DY z
M 17.95/23.95 **t.** and a la carte 12.25/24.25 **t.** 🍾 3.75 – 🍽 9.50 – **193 rm** 85.00/132.00 **t.**, **2 suites** 205.00/340.00 **t.** – SB (weekends only) 85.00 **st.**

🏨🏨 **Carlton Highland**, 1-29 North Bridge, EH1 1SD, ✆ 556 7277, Telex 727001, Fax 556 2691, 🔲, squash – 🕮 ▤ rest 📺 ☎ 🕭 – 🕭 350   EY s
201 rm, 4 suites.

🏨🏨 **Roxburghe** (Best Western), 38 Charlotte Sq., EH2 4HG, ✆ 225 3921, Telex 727054, Fax 220 2518 – 🕮 📺 ☎ 🕭 – 🕭 200. 🔲 AE ⑪ VISA   DY o
M (closed Saturday lunch) 8.00/13.00 **t.** and a la carte 13.70/23.70 **t.** 🍾 3.50 – 🍽 6.50 – **75 rm** 65.00/110.00 **t.**, **2 suites** 130.00 **t.**

🏨🏨 **Capital**, Clermiston Rd, EH12 6UG, W : 3 ½ m. by A 90 and Clermiston Rd North ✆ 334 3391, Telex 728284, Fax 334 3391, 🔲 – 🕮 📺 ☎ 🕭 🅿 – 🕭 400. 🔲 AE ⑪ VISA AV n
M (closed Sunday lunch) 8.50/14.25 **st.** and a la carte 14.00/24.00 **st.** 🍾 3.95 – **98 rm** 🍽 62.00/105.00 **st.** – SB (weekends only) 70.00/84.00 **st.**

🏨🏨 **Hilton National** (Hilton), Bells Mills, 69 Belford Rd, EH4 3DG, ℰ 332 2545, Telex 727979, Fax 332 3805 – 🛗 ⤧ rm 📺 ☎ & 🅿 – 🛥 . 🅂 AE ⓞ VISA   CY i
M 9.75/13.75 **st.** and a la carte 16.50/24.25 **st.** 🍾 3.75 – ☕ 7.50 – **146 rm** 70.00/120.00 **st.**, **3 suites** 150.00 **st.**

🏨🏨 **Royal Scott** (Swallow), 111 Glasgow Rd, EH12 8NF, W : 4 ½ m. on A 8 ℰ 334 9191, Telex 727197, Fax 316 4507, 🅂 – 🛗 ⤧ rm ▤ rest 📺 ☎ 🅿 – 🛥 250. 🅂 AE ⓞ VISA
M 13.70 **st.** and a la carte 🍾 4.00 – **252 rm** ☕ 72.00/92.00 **st.** – SB (weekends only) 80.00/90.00 **st.**   by A 8 AV

🏨 King James Thistle (Thistle), 1 Leith St., EH1 3SW, ℰ 556 0111, Telex 727200, Fax 557 5333 – 🛗 ⤧ rm ▤ rest 📺 ☎ 🅿 – 🛥 300. 🅂 AE ⓞ VISA   EY u
☕ 7.25 – **142 rm** 60.00/108.00 **st.**, **5 suites** 90.00 **st.** – SB 96.00/138.00 **st.**

🏨 Howard, 32-36 Gt. King St., EH3 6QH, ℰ 557 3500, Telex 727887, Fax 557 6515 – 🛗 📺 ☎ 🅿 – 🛥 35. 🅂 AE ⓞ VISA. 🦺   DY s
closed January-March – **25 rm** ☕ 65.00/120.00 **t.** – SB (except August and Christmas) (weekends only) 85.00/120.00 **st.**

🏨 **Bruntsfield** (Best Western), 69-74 Bruntsfield Pl., EH10 4HH, ℰ 229 1393, Telex 727897, Fax 229 5634 – 🛗 📺 ☎ 🅿 – 🛥 80. 🅂 AE ⓞ VISA   DZ e
M 6.50/15.00 **st.** and a la carte 6.70/13.50 **st.** 🍾 3.35 – ☕ 5.00 – **52 rm** 52.50/85.00 **st.** – SB 75.00/100.00 **st.**

🏨 **Ellersly House** (Embassy), 4 Ellersly Rd, EH12 6HZ, W : 2 ½ m. by A 8 ℰ 337 6888, Telex 727860, Fax 313 2543, 🌳 – 🛗 ⤧ rm 📺 ☎ 🅿. 🅂 AE ⓞ VISA   AV v
M 9.00/13.75 **st.** and a la carte 🍾 3.95 – ☕ 7.00 – **55 rm** 62.00/95.00 **st.** – SB (weekends only) 60.00/86.00 **st.**

🏨 **Crest** (Crest), Queens Ferry Rd, EH4 3HL, NW : 2 m. on A 90 ℰ 332 2442, Telex 72541, Fax 332 3408 – 🛗 ⤧ rm ▤ rest 📺 ☎ 🅿 – 🛥 400. 🅂 AE ⓞ VISA. 🦺   AV x
M (closed Saturday lunch) 9.75/15.75 **st.** and a la carte – ☕ 7.75 – **118 rm** 80.00/99.00 **st.**, **1 suite** 150.00 **st.** – SB 66.00/94.00 **st.**

🏨 **Barnton Thistle** (Thistle), 562 Queensferry Rd, EH4 6AS, NW : 4 ¾ m. on A 90 ℰ 339 1144, Telex 727928, Fax 339 5521 – 🛗 📺 ☎ 🅿 – 🛥 100. 🅂 AE ⓞ VISA   AV o
M 8.95 **t.** (lunch) and a la carte 10.00/25.00 **t.** – ☕ 7.25 – **47 rm** 59.00/88.00 **st.**, **3 suites** 90.00 **st.** – SB 84.00/110.00 **st.**

🏨 **Post House** (T.H.F.), Corstorphine Rd, EH12 6UA, W : 3 m. on A 8 ℰ 334 0390, Telex 727103, Fax 334 9237, ⩽ – 🛗 ⤧ rm 📺 ☎ 🅿 – 🛥 150. 🅂 AE ⓞ VISA   AV u
M 9.90/15.00 **st.** and a la carte 🍾 4.35 – ☕ 7.50 – **206 rm** 60.00/70.00 **st.**, **1 suite** 140.00 **st.** – SB 56.00/108.00 **st.**

🏨 Stakis Grosvenor (Stakis), Grosvenor St., EH12 5EF, ℰ 226 6001, Telex 72445, Fax 220 2387 – 🛗 📺 ☎ – 🛥 300. 🅂 AE ⓞ VISA   CZ a
☕ 7.25 – **135 rm** 69.00/102.00 **st.**, **1 suite** 130.00 **st.** – SB 54.00/104.00 **st.**

🏨 Albany, 39-43 Albany St., EH1 3QY, ℰ 556 0397, Telex 727079 – 📺 ☎. 🅂 AE ⓞ VISA
20 rm.   EY v

🏨 Lady Nairne (B.C.B.), 228 Willowbrae Rd, EH8 7NG, ℰ 661 3396 – 🛗 📺 ☎ 🅿. 🅂 AE ⓞ VISA. 🦺 – **33 rm**.   BV u

🏠 **Old Waverley,** 43 Princes St., EH2 2BY, ℰ 556 4648, Telex 727050, Fax 557 6316 – 🛗 📺 ☎. 🅂 AE ⓞ VISA   EY r
M 6.50/11.50 **t.** and a la carte 🍾 4.00 – **66 rm** ☕ 45.00/50.00 **t.** – SB (except August) (weekends only) 66.00/100.00 **st.**

🏠 **Hotel de France,** South St. Andrew St., EH2 2AZ, ℰ 556 8774, Telex 727539, Fax 556 2965 – 🛗 📺 ☎. 🅂 AE ⓞ VISA. 🦺   DEY a
M (closed lunch Saturday and Sunday) 6.95/9.75 **st.** and a la carte 🍾 3.20 – **31 rm** ☕ 55.00/65.00 **st.**

🏠 Clarendon, 22 Grosvenor St., EH12 5EG, ℰ 337 7033 – 🛗 📺 ☎ – 🛥   CZ e
51 rm.

🏠 Christopher North House, 6 Gloucester Pl., EH3 6EF, ℰ 225 2720 – 📺 ☎. 🅂 AE ⓞ VISA 🦺   CY s
11 rm ☕ 35.00/66.00 **st.**

🏠 **Kildonan Lodge,** 27 Craigmillar Park, EH16 5PE, ℰ 667 2793 – 📺 🅿. AE VISA 🦺   BX r
M (dinner only) a la carte 8.10/10.80 **t.** 🍾 3.60 – **13 rm** ☕ 14.50/35.00 **t.**

⚘ **Iona,** 17 Strathearn Pl., EH9 2AL, ℰ 447 6264 – 📺 ☎ 🅿. 🅂 VISA   BX u
M 5.60/13.00 **t.** and a la carte 🍾 3.50 – **21 rm** ☕ 26.75/54.60 **t.**

⌂ **International** without rest., 37 Mayfield Gdns, EH9 2BX, ℰ 667 2511 – 📺. 🦺   BX s
7 rm ☕ 15.00/37.00 **st.**

⌂ **Buchan** without rest., 3 Coates Gdns, EH12 5LG, ℰ 337 1045 – 📺   CZ o
10 rm ☕ 18.00/44.00 **st.**

⌂ **Dorstan,** 7 Priestfield Rd, EH16 5HJ, ℰ 667 6721 – ⤧ rest 📺 ☎ 🅿   BX e
closed Christmas and New Year – **M** 9.00 **t.** – **14 rm** ☕ 15.00/36.00 **t.**

⌂ **Greenside** without rest., 9 Royal Terr., EH7 5AB, ℰ 557 0022, 🌳 –   EY a
closed November and December – **12 rm** ☕ 19.55/43.70 **t.**

⌂ **Ravensdown** without rest., 248 Ferry Rd, CH5 3AN, ℰ 552 5438 – 📺. 🦺   BV e
7 rm ☕ –/30.00 **st.**

⌂ **Southdown** without rest., 20 Craigmillar Park, EH16 5PS, ℰ 667 2410 – 📺 🅿. 🦺   BX n
closed Christmas and New Year – **6 rm** ☕ 25.00/32.00 **st.**

⌂ **Galloway** without rest., 22 Dean Park Cres., EH4 1PH, ℰ 332 3672   CY a
10 rm ☕ 15.00/36.00 **st.**

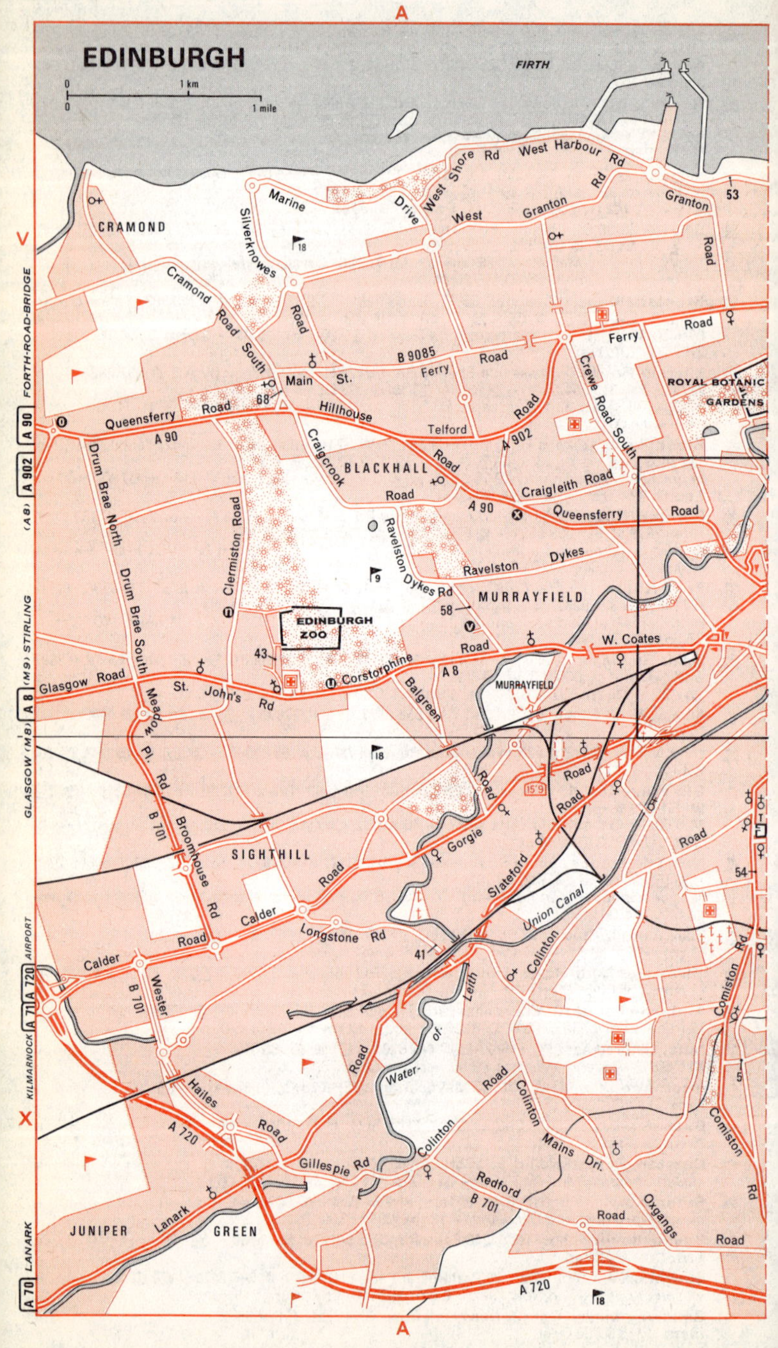

EDINBURGH
0   1 km
0   1 mile
FIRTH
A
V
X
A
FORTH-ROAD-BRIDGE
A 90
A 902
(A 8)
GLASGOW (M8) STIRLING (M9)
A 8
KILMARNOCK A 71 A 720 AIRPORT
LANARK
A 70
West Shore Rd
West Harbour Rd
Marine
Drive
West
Granton
Rd
Granton
53
CRAMOND
Silverknowes
18
Cramond Road South
Road
West Granton Road
Ferry
Road
Crewe Road South
ROYAL BOTANIC
GARDENS
Queensferry
Road
Main St.
68
Hillhouse
B 9085
Ferry
Road
Telford
Road
A 902
A 90
Drum Brae North
Craigcrook
Road
BLACKHALL
Road
A 90
Craigleith Road
Queensferry
Road
Clermiston Road
Ravelston Dykes Rd
9
Ravelston
Dykes
MURRAYFIELD
Drum Brae South
58
EDINBURGH
ZOO
43
Road
V
Road
W. Coates
Glasgow   Road
St. John's Rd
Corstorphine
A 8
Balgreen
MURRAYFIELD
Meadow
Pl. Rd
18
Road
15'9
Road
Road
B 701
Broomhouse Rd
SIGHTHILL
Road
Gorgie
Slateford
Union Canal
Road
54
Calder
Longstone Rd
41
Leith
Colinton
Road
Calder
Wester
B 701
Water-
of-
Colinton
Road
Road
Comiston Rd
5
Hailes
Road
A 720
Gillespie Rd
Colinton
Mains Dri.
Oxgangs
Road
JUNIPER   Lanark   GREEN
Redford
B 701
Road
Comiston
Road
A 720
18
A

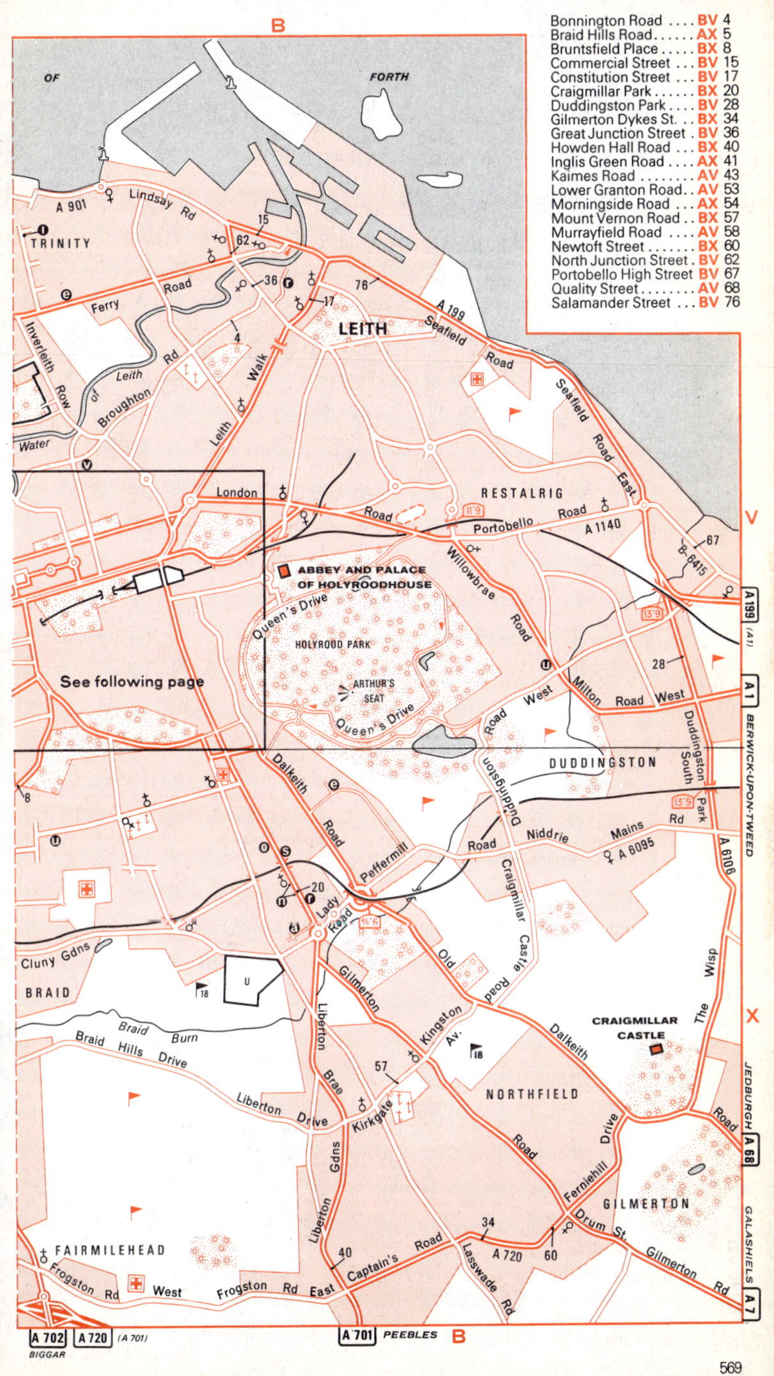

Bonnington Road .... BV 4
Braid Hills Road..... AX 5
Bruntsfield Place ..... BX 8
Commercial Street ... BV 15
Constitution Street ... BV 17
Craigmillar Park ...... BX 20
Duddingston Park .... BV 28
Gilmerton Dykes St. . BX 34
Great Junction Street . BV 36
Howden Hall Road ... BX 40
Inglis Green Road .... AX 41
Kaimes Road .... AV 43
Lower Granton Road.. AV 53
Morningside Road ... AX 54
Mount Vernon Road .. BX 57
Murrayfield Road .... AV 58
Newtoft Street .... BX 60
North Junction Street . BV 62
Portobello High Street BV 67
Quality Street .... AV 68
Salamander Street ... BV 76

OF
FORTH
A 901
Lindsay Rd
15
TRINITY
62
36
17
Ferry
Road
4
76
A 199
Inverleith Row
Leith
of
Broughton
Rd
Walk
LEITH
Seafield
Road
Water
Leith
RESTALRIG
Seafield Road East
London
Road
Portobello Road
A 1140
V
67
B 6415
ABBEY AND PALACE
OF HOLYROODHOUSE
Willowbrae Road
A 199 (A1)
Queen's Drive
13'9
See following page
HOLYROOD PARK
28
A 1
ARTHUR'S
SEAT
Road West
Milton Road West
BERWICK-UPON-TWEED
Queen's Drive
DUDDINGSTON
Duddingston South
Dalkeith
8
Road
Duddingston Park
13'9
A 6106
Peffermill
Road
Niddrie
Mains
Rd
20
A 6095
Lady
Road
Old
Craigmillar Castle Road
Cluny Gdns
BRAID
Gilmerton
U
18
CRAIGMILLAR
CASTLE
Braid Burn
Liberton Brae
Kingston
Av.
18
Dalkeith Drive
The Wisp
X
Braid Hills Drive
Braid Hills Drive
57
NORTHFIELD
Road
JEDBURGH A 68
Liberton Drive
Gdns
Kirkgate
Road
Ferniehill Drive
GILMERTON
GALASHIELS
FAIRMILEHEAD
40
Captain's
34
Drum St.
Gilmerton Rd
Frogston Rd
West
Frogston Rd East
Lasswade Rd
A 720
60
A 7
A 702
A 720
(A 701)
BIGGAR
A 701
PEEBLES
B

EDINBURGH
CENTRE

Castle Street .... DY
Frederick Street .... DY
George Street .... DY
Hanover Street .... DY
High Street .... EYZ 37
Lawnmarket .... EYZ 46
Princes Street .... DY
St. James Centre .... EY
Waverley Market .... EY

Bernard Terrace .... EZ 3
Bread Street .... DZ 6
Bristo Place .... EZ 7
Candlemaker Row .... EZ 9
Castlehill .... DZ 10
Chambers Street .... EZ 12
Chapel Street .... EZ 13
Charlotte Square .... CY 14
Deanhaugh Street .... CY 23
Douglas Gardens .... CY 25
Drummond Street .... EZ 27
Forrest Road .... EZ 31
Gardner's Crescent ..... CZ 32
George IV Bridge .... EZ 33
Grassmarket .... DZ 35
Home Street .... DZ 38
Hope Street .... CY 39
Johnston Terrace .... DZ 42
King's Bridge .... DZ 44
King's Stables Road .... DZ 45
Leith Street .... EY 47
Leven Street .... DZ 48
Lothian Street .... EZ 51
Mound (The) .... DY 55
North Bridge .... EY 61
North St. Andrew Street EY 66
Raeburn Place .... CY 69
Randolph Crescent ...... CY 71
St. Andrew Square ...... EY 73
St. Mary's Street ...... EY 75
Shandwick Place .... CYZ 77
South Charlotte Street   DY 78
South St. David Street   DEY 79
Spittal Street .... DZ 83
Victoria Street .... EZ 84
Waterloo Place .... EY 87
Waverley Bridge .... EY 89
West Maitland Street ... CZ 92

⌂ **St. Margarets** without rest., 18 Craigmillar Park, EH16 5PS, ☎ 667 2202 – 📺 Ⓟ. ✗ BX n
closed January and February – **8 rm** ☐ 18.00/28.00 **st.**

⌂ **Glenisla,** 12 Lygon Rd, EH16 5QB, ☎ 667 4098 – BX a
M 12.00 **t.** 🍷 3.00 – **8 rm** ☐ 15.00/38.00 **t.** – SB (except Winter) 40.00/50.00 **st.**

⌂ **Parklands** without rest., 20 Mayfield Gdns, EH9 2BZ, ☎ 667 7184. ✗ BX o
6 rm ☐ 20.00/36.00.

XXXX **Pompadour** (at Caledonian H.), Princes St., OH1 2AB, ☎ 225 2433 – Ⓟ. AE VISA CY n
M 14.50/29.75 **t.** and a la carte 🍷 5.00.

XX **L'Auberge,** 56 St. Mary's St., EH1 1SX, ☎ 556 5888, French rest. – AE VISA EYZ c
closed 25-26 December and 1-2 January – **M** 8.00/18.00 **t.** and a la carte 19.90/28.00 **t.** 🍷 3.85.

XX **Martins,** 70 Rose St., North Lane, EH2 3DX, ☎ 225 3106 – AE VISA DY n
closed Saturday lunch, Sunday, Monday and 24 December-8 January – **M** (booking essential) 12.00 **t.** (lunch) and a la carte 18.10/23.90 **t.** 🍷 4.50.

XX **Cosmo,** 58a North Castle St., EH2 3LU, ☎ 226 6743, Italian rest. – VISA DY r
closed Saturday lunch, Sunday and Monday – **M** a la carte 16.10/23.40 **t.** 🍷 3.70.

XX **Raffaelli,** 10-11 Randolph Pl., EH3 7TA, ☎ 225 6060, Italian rest. – AE VISA CY c
closed Saturday lunch, Sunday, 25-26 December and 1-2 January – **M** a la carte 9.70/17.00 **t.**

XX **Merchants,** 17 Merchant St., EH1 2QD, ☎ 225 4009 – AE VISA EZ x
closed Sunday and 25 to 27 December – **M** (booking essential) 15.00/25.00 **t.** and a la carte 15.00/19.00 **t.** 🍷 3.50.

XX **Vintners Room,** The Vaults, 87 Giles St., Leith, EH6 6BZ, ☎ 554 6767 – AE VISA BV r
closed Sunday and 23 December-9 January – **M** a la carte approx. 17.50 **t.** 🍷 4.50.

XX **Lancer's Brasserie,** 5 Hamilton Pl., Stockbridge, EH3 5BA, ☎ 332 3444, North Indian rest. – AE VISA CY r
M 11.95 **t.** (lunch) and a la carte 10.90/22.10 **t.**

XX **Umberto,** 29 Dublin St., EH3 6NL, ☎ 556 2231, Italian rest. – AE VISA EY e
closed Saturday lunch and Sunday – **M** 7.50 **t.** (lunch) and a la carte 10.30/17.60 **t.** 🍷 3.95.

XX **Premier Mandarin,** 8b Abercromby Pl., EH3 6LB, ☎ 556 2321, Chinese rest. – AE VISA – *closed Saturday lunch* – **M** 4.50/10.90 **t.** and a la carte 6.70/16.50 **t.** 🍷 3.75. EY x

X **Alp-Horn,** 167 Rose St., EH2 4LS, ☎ 225 4787, Swiss rest. – VISA DY x
closed Sunday, 1 week January and 2 weeks July – **M** 9.30 **t.** (lunch) and a la carte 13.50/16.70 **t.** 🍷 3.80.

X **Verandah,** 17 Dalry Rd, EH11 2BQ, ☎ 337 5828, North Indian rest. – AE VISA CZ z
M 11.95 **t.** and a la carte 8.80/14.80 **t.** 🍷 4.00.

ALFA-ROMEO, DAIHATSU 22 Canning St. ☎ 229 5561
AUSTIN-ROVER, LAND-ROVER, RANGE-ROVER Westfield Av. ☎ 337 3222
AUSTIN-ROVER Lanark Rd ☎ 443 2936
AUSTIN-ROVER 70 Slateford Rd ☎ 337 1252
CITROEN 13 Lauriston Gdns ☎ 229 4207
FORD Baileyfield Rd ☎ 669 6261
FORD Fountainbridge ☎ 229 3331
FORD 12 West Mayfield ☎ 667 1900
FORD Craighall Rd ☎ 552 5524
HYUNDAI Westfield Rd ☎ 337 7204
PEUGEOT-TALBOT Lochrin Tollcross ☎ 229 8911
PORSCHE, FERRARI 300 Colinton Rd ☎ 441 6805
RENAULT 553 Gorgie Rd ☎ 444 1673
VOLVO 38 Seafield Rd East ☎ 669 8301
VOLVO Bankhead ☎ 442 3333
VW-AUDI-NSU 454 Gorgie Rd ☎ 346 1661
VW-AUDI-NSU Marionville Rd ☎ 652 1691

ATS 167 Bonnington Rd, Leith ☎ 554 6617
ATS 6 Gylemuir Rd, Montagu Ind. Est. ☎ 334 6174

EDZELL Angus. (Tayside) 401 M 13 **Scotland G** – pop. 751 – ECD : Thursday – ☎ 035 64.
Envir. : Castle★ (The Pleasance★★★) W : 1 ¼ m.
18 ☎ 236 18 at Brechin ☎ 035 62 (Brechin) 2383, S : 5 ½ m.
♦Edinburgh 94 – ♦Aberdeen 36 – ♦Dundee 31.

🏨 Glenesk, High St., DD9 7TF, ☎ 319, 🏊, 🌳 – 📺 ☎ Ⓟ – 🎪 100. AE VISA
25 rm ☐ 32.00/55.00 **t.**

EGILSAY (Isle of) Orkney. (Orkney Islands) 401 L 6 – Shipping Services : see Orkney Islands (Mainland : Kirkwall).

EIGG (Isle of) Inverness. (Highland) 401 B 13 – Shipping Services : see Mallaig.

ELGIN Moray. (Grampian) 401 K 11 **Scotland G** – pop. 18 702 – ECD : Wednesday – ☎ 0343.
See : Site★ – Cathedral★ (Chapter House★★) – 18 Hardhillock, Birnie Rd ☎ 2338, S : 1 m. – 9 Hopeman ☎ 830578, N : 7 m – ℹ 17 High St. ☎ 3388 and 2666.
♦Edinburgh 198 – ♦Aberdeen 68 – Fraserburgh 61 – ♦Inverness 39.

🏨 **Mansion House,** The Haugh, IV30 1AW, via Haugh Rd and Murdocks Wynd ☎ 548811, Fax 547916, 🌳 – 📺 ☎ Ⓟ. AE VISA. ✗
M 7.50/15.00 **st.** and a la carte 🍷 3.90 – **12 rm** ☐ 45.00/150.00 **st.** – SB (weekends only) 150.00 **st.**

🏨 **Park House,** South St., IV30 1JB, ☎ 547695 – 📺 ☎ Ⓟ. AE VISA
M 5.20 **t.** (lunch) and a la carte 15.00/19.60 **t.** 🍷 3.20 – **6 rm** ☐ 31.00/50.00 **st.**

FORD East Rd ☎ 2176
PEUGEOT 27 Greyfriars St. ☎ 7416
VAUXHALL-OPEL Edgar Rd ☎ 7688
VW-AUDI Blackfriars Rd ☎ 44977

ATS Moycroft ☎ 46333

ELLON Aberdeen. (Grampian) 401 N 11 – pop. 6 304 – ECD : Wednesday – ✆ 0358.
Envir. : Pitmedden Gardens★★, SW : 5 m. by A 920 – Haddo House★, NW : 8 m. by B 9005 –
Fyvie Castle★ NW : 14 m. by B 9005 and A 947.

⌨ McDonald ✆ 20576.

🛈 Market St. Car Park ✆ 20730 (summer only).
♦Edinburgh 147 – ♦Aberdeen 17 – Fraserburgh 27.

🏨 Mercury (Mt. Charlotte), South Rd, AB4 9NP, ✆ 20666, Telex 739200 – 📺 🅟 – 🕍
40 rm.

FORD 99 Station Rd ✆ 20206

ERISKA (Isle of) Argyll. (Strathclyde) 401 D 14 – ✉ Oban – ✆ 063 172 Ledaig

🏨 Isle of Eriska 🦢, PA37 1SD, ✆ 371, Telex 777040, ≤ Lismore and mountains, « Country
house atmosphere », 🐎, park, 🍴 – 📺 ☎ ६ 🅟. 🖾 AE VISA. 🛠
March-October – M (buffet lunch)/dinner 30.50 t. ὰ 4.30 – 16 rm ⌷ 98.00/126.00 t.

ERSKINE Renfrew. (Strathclyde) 401 402 G 16 – ✆ 041 Glasgow.
♦Edinburgh 55 – ♦Glasgow 9.

🏨 Crest (Crest) 🦢, Erskine Bridge, PA8 6AN, on A 726 ✆ 812 0123, Telex 777713, Fax 812 7642,
≤, 🐎 – 🕸 ⅙ ⅗ rm ▤ rest 📺 ☎ ६ 🅟 – 🕍 . 🖾 AE ⓞ VISA. 🛠
M 11.50/16.00 st. and a la carte – ⌷ 8.00 – 166 rm 69.00/98.00 st. – SB 80.00/90.00 st.

ESKDALEMUIR Dumfries. (Dumfries and Galloway) 401 402 K 18 – ✉ Langholm – ✆ 054 16.
♦Edinburgh 71 – ♦Carlisle 33 – ♦Dumfries 28.

⚓ Hart Manor 🦢, DG13 0QQ, S : ½ m. on B 709 ✆ 73217, ≤ – ⅗ rest 🅟
closed Christmas Day – M (bar lunch)/dinner 15.00 t. and a la carte ὰ 3.50 – 7 rm
⌷ 24.50/48.00.

FALKIRK Stirling. (Central) 401 I 16 – pop. 36 372 – ECD : Wednesday – ✆ 0324.
⌨ Grangemouth ✆ 0324 (Polmont) 711500, E : 3 m.

🛈 The Steeple, High St. ✆ 20244.
♦Edinburgh 26 – Dunfermline 18 – ♦Glasgow 25 – Motherwell 27 – Perth 43.

🏨 Stakis Park (Stakis), Camelon Rd, Arnothill, FK1 5RY, ✆ 28331, Telex 776502, Fax 611593
– 🕸 📺 ☎ 🅟 – 🕍 250. 🖾 AE ⓞ VISA
M a la carte 14.10/19.30 st. – ⌷ 7.25 – 55 rm 55.00/68.00 st. – SB 50.00/67.00 st.

✗ Pierre's, 140 Grahams Rd, FK2 7BQ, ✆ 35843, French rest. – 🅟. 🖾 AE ⓞ VISA
closed Saturday lunch, Sunday, Monday and 1 to 5 January – M 6.75/11.75 t. and a la carte
12.70/20.45 ὰ 3.50.

at Grangemouth NE : 3 m. on A 904 – ✉ ✆ 0324 Grangemouth :

🏨 Grange Manor, Glensburgh Rd, FK3 8XJ, SW : 1 m. by A 904 on A 905 ✆ 474836, Telex
777620 – 📺 ☎ 🅟 – 🕍 130
7 rm.

at Polmont SE : 3 m. on A 803 – ✉ ✆ 0324 Polmont :

🏨 Inchyra Grange (Best Western), Grange Rd, via Boness Rd – Kirk entry, FK2 0YB, ✆
711911, Telex 777693, Fax 716134, 🐎 – 📺 ☎ 🅟 – 🕍 250. 🖾 AE ⓞ VISA
M *(closed Saturday lunch)* 8.50/12.50 t. and a la carte ὰ 3.50 – 31 rm ⌷ 57.00/100.00 t.

FORD Callendar Rd ✆ 21511
HYUNDAI, SAMBURA, ISUZU, TOYOTA, MAZDA
High Station Rd ✆ 24221
MAZDA Main St. ✆ 22584
TOYOTA, SUBARU, HYUNDAI, MAZDA Lady's Mill
✆ 35935

TOYOTA Winchester Av., Denny ✆ 824387
VAUXHALL-OPEL 76-80 Grahams Rd ✆ 21234
VOLVO West End ✆ 613333

Ⓜ ATS Burnbank Rd ✆ 22958

FARR Inverness. (Highland) 401 H 11 – ✉ Inverness – ✆ 080 83.
♦Edinburgh 155 – ♦Inverness 10.

⚲ Dunlichity Lodge 🦢, Dunlichity, IV1 2AN, W : 2 m. ✆ 282, ≤, 🎣, 🐎 – 🅟
April-19 October – M 10.50 st. ὰ 2.80 – 4 rm ⌷ 16.50/40.00 st.

FEOLIN Argyll. (Strathclyde) 401 B 16 – Shipping Services : see Jura (Isle of).

FETLAR (Isle of) Shetland. (Shetland Islands) 401 R 2 – Shipping Services : see Shetland
Islands.

FIONNPHORT Argyll. (Strathclyde) 401 A 15 – Shipping Services : see Mull (Isle of).

FISHNISH Argyll. (Strathclyde) 401 C 14 – Shipping Services : see Mull (Isle of).

FLOTTA (Isle of) Orkney. (Orkney Islands) 401 K 7 – Shipping Services : see Orkney Islands.

FORDYCE Banff. (Grampian) 401 L 11 – pop. 145 – ۞ 0261 Portsoy.
◆Edinburgh 187 – ◆Aberdeen 57 – ◆Inverness 65.

   ✕ **Hawthorne**, Church St., AB4 2SL, ✆ 43003 – **P**. 🔄 VISA
      closed Sunday dinner and Monday – **M** a la carte 7.70/16.35 **t**. 🍷 3.50.

FORFAR Angus. (Tayside) 401 L 14 – pop. 12 652 – ECD : Thursday – ۞ 0307.
Envir. : Glamis★ (Castle★★, Angus Folk Museum★) SW : 5 ½ m. by A 94.
🏌 Cunninghill, Arbroath Rd ✆ 62120, E : 1 m. on A 932.
🛈 The Myre ✆ 67876 (summer only).
◆Edinburgh 75 – ◆Aberdeen 55 – ◆Dundee 12 – Perth 31.

   🏨 **Royal**, Castle St., DD8 3AE, ✆ 62691, Fax 62691, 🔲 – 📺 ☎ **P**. 🔄 AE ⓞ VISA. ⌘
      M 10.00/15.00 **st**. and a la carte 🍷 3.25 – **19 rm** 🍽 35.00/65.00 **st**. – SB (week-
      ends only) 60.00/65.00 **st**.

AUSTIN-ROVER 128 Castle St. ✆ 62542   ⓦ ATS Queenswell Rd ✆ 64501/2
FORD Kirriemuir Rd ✆ 62347
PEUGEOT-TALBOT Lochside Rd ✆ 62676

FORRES Moray. (Grampian) 401 J 11 Scotland G. – pop. 8 346 – ECD : Wednesday – ۞ 0309.
See : Sueno's Stone★★ – **Envir. :** Brodie Castle★ W : 4 m. by A 96.
🏌 Muiryshade ✆ 72949, SE : by B 9010.
🛈 Falconer Museum, Talbooth St. 72938 (summer only).
◆Edinburgh 165 – ◆Aberdeen 80 – ◆Inverness 27.

   🏨 **Ramnee**, Victoria Rd, IV36 0BN, ✆ 72410, 🚗 – 📺 ☎ **P** – 🔥 70. 🔄 AE ⓞ VISA
      M 7.50/12.75 **st**. and a la carte 🍷 2.40 – **21 rm** 🍽 30.50/70.00 **st**.

AUSTIN-ROVER Greshop Ind Estate ✆ 74709   FORD Market St. ✆ 72677
FIAT Tytler St. ✆ 72122

FORSINARD Sutherland. (Highland) – ۞ 064 17 Halladale.
◆Edinburgh 271 – Thurso 30 – ◆Wick 51.

   🏧 **Forsinard** 🦌, KW13 6YT, ✆ 221, ⩽, 🎣 – ⤢ rest **P**. 🔄 VISA
      Mid April-mid October – **M** (bar lunch)/dinner 14.50 **t**. 🍷 2.95 – **10 rm** 🍽 26.00/52.00 **t**.

FORT AUGUSTUS Inverness. (Highland) 401 F 12 – pop. 573 – ✉ ۞ 0320.
🛈 Car Park ✆ 6367.
◆Edinburgh 166 – Fort William 32 – ◆Inverness 36 – Kyle of Lochalsh 57.

   🏨 **Lovat Arms**, PH32 2BE, ✆ 6206, 🚗 – 📺 ☎ **P**. 🔄 VISA
      M 7.50/13.50 **st**. and a la carte 🍷 3.50 – **25 rm** 🍽 26.00/52.00 **st**.

FORT WILLIAM Inverness. (Highland) 401 E 13 Scotland G – pop. 10 805 – ECD : Wednesday
except summer – ۞ 0397.
See : Site★.
Envir. : Ben Nevis★★, SE : 4 m. – Road to the Isles★★ (Glenfinnan★, Arisaig★ (⩽★ of Sound of
Arisaig), Silver Sands of Morar★, Mallaig★) NW : 46 m. by A 830 – Glen Nevis★, SE.
🏌 Torlundy ✆ 4464, N : 3 m. on A 82.
🛈 ✆ 3781
◆Edinburgh 133 – ◆Glasgow 104 – ◆Inverness 68 – ◆Oban 50.

   🏰🏰🏰 ☸ **Inverlochy Castle** 🦌, Torlundy, PH33 6SN, NE : 3 m. on A 82 ✆ 2177, Telex 776229,
      Fax 2953, ⩽ garden, loch and mountains, « Victorian castle in extensive grounds », 🎣, 🚗,
      park, ✕ – 📺 ☎ **P**. 🔄 VISA. ⌘
      Mid March-mid November – **M** (booking essential) 25.00/45.00 **t**. 🍷 5.00 – **15 rm** 🍽 121.00/
      185.00 **t**., **1 suite** 210.00/230.00 **t**.
      Spec. Mille feuille of scallop mousseline with champagne and chive sauce, Grilled cannon of lamb with shallot
      and basil sauce, Tears of bitter chocolate filled with whisky mousse.

   🏨 **Mercury** (Mt. Charlotte), Achintore Rd, PH33 6RW, SW : 2 m. on A 82 ✆ 3117, Telex 778454,
      ⩽ – 🛗 📺 ☎ **P**
      M (carving rest.) – **86 rm**.

   🏠 **Guisachan**, Alma Rd, PH33 6HA, ✆ 3797, ⩽, 🚗 – ⤢ rm **P**. ⌘
      closed 20 December-4 January – **M** 9.00 **t**. – **15 rm** 🍽 14.00/32.00 **st**.

   🏠 **Cabana House** without rest., Union Rd, PH33 6RB, ✆ 5991 – **3 rm**.

   ✕✕ **Factor's House** with rm, Torlundy, PH33 6SN, NE : 3 ½ m. on A 82 ✆ 5767, Telex 776229,
      Fax 2953, 🚗 – 📺 ☎ **P**. 🔄 AE ⓞ VISA. ⌘
      closed mid December-mid January – **M** *(closed lunch and Monday to non-residents)* (bar
      lunch)/dinner 20.00 **t**. 🍷 4.40 – **7 rm** 🍽 40.25/69.00 **t**.

      at Banavie N : 3 m. by A 82 and A 830 on B 8004 – ✉ Fort William – ۞ 039 77 Corpach :

   🏨 **Moorings**, PH33 7LY, ✆ 797, ⩽, 🚗 – ⤢ rest 📺 ☎ **P**. 🔄 AE ⓞ VISA. ⌘
      M (bar lunch)/dinner 16.00 **t**. and a la carte 🍷 3.50 – **21 rm** 🍽 45.00/68.00 **t**.

AUSTIN-ROVER Gordon Sq. ✆ 2345/2346

 Inverness. (Highland) **401** G 12 – ✆ 045 63 Gorthleck.

See : Loch Ness★★.

◆Edinburgh 176 – ◆Inverness 18.

   🏨 **Foyers**, IV1 2XT, N : ½ m. on B 852 ☎ 216, ≤ Loch Ness and mountains, ⤸, ☞ – ⇚ **P**.
          🅰 VISA ⤸
          M 7.50/14.50 **t.** and a la carte 🍷3.00 – **9 rm** ☲ 25.00/50.00 **t.** – SB (November-March)
          (except Christmas and New Year) 27.50 **st.**

GAIRLOCH Ross and Cromarty. (Highland) **401** C 10 – ECD : Wednesday except summer –
✆ 0445.

Envir. : Inverewe Gardens★★★, NE : 8 m. by A 832 – Wester Ross★★★ (Gairloch to Ullapool★ via
Loch Maree★★★, Inverewe Gardens★★★, Falls of Measach★ and Loch Broom★★) NE : 56 m. by A
832 and A 835 – Wester Ross★★★ (Gairloch to Kyle of Lochalsh via Victoria Falls★ Loch Maree★★★,
and Plockton★) S : 102 m. by A 832, A 896 and A 890.

🏌 Gairloch ☎ 2407, S : 1 m. on A 832.

🛈 Achtercairn ☎ 2130.

◆Edinburgh 228 – ◆Inverness 72 – Kyle of Lochalsh 68.

   🏨 **Shieldaig Lodge** ⤸, IV21 2AW, S : 4 ½ m. by A 832 on B 8056 ☎ 044 583 (Badachro) 250,
       ≤ Gair Loch, « Former hunting lodge on lochside », ⤸, ☞ – ⇚ rest **P**. ⤸
       April-October – **M** (bar lunch)/dinner 14.50 **t.** 🍷3.50 – **13 rm** ☲ 27.50/50.00 **t.**

   🏠 **Kerrysdale House** without rest., IV21 2AL, S : 3 m. on A 832 ☎ 2292, ☞ – ⇚ rm **P**. ⤸
       March-October – **3 rm** ☲ 16.00/32.00 **st.**

GALASHIELS Selkirk. (Borders) **401** **402** L 17 – pop. 12 206 – ECD : Wednesday – ✆ 0896.

Envir. : Abbotsford★★ SE : 2 m. by A 7 – Melrose Abbey★★ SE : 4 m. by A 7 and A 6091.

🏌 Ladhope, ☎ 3724, NE : ¼ m. – 🏌 Torwoodlee, ☎ 2260, N : 1 m. on A 7.

🛈 Bank St. ☎ 55551 (summer only).

◆Edinburgh 34 – ◆Carlisle 61 – ◆Glasgow 71 – ◆Newcastle-upon-Tyne 74.

   🏨 **Woodlands House**, Windyknowe Rd, TD1 1RQ, NW : ¾ m. by A 72 and Hall St. ☎ 4722,
       ☞ – 📺 ☎ **P**. 🅰 VISA
       M 6.95 **t.** (lunch) and dinner a la carte approx. 15.80 **t.** 🍷3.00 – **9 rm** ☲ 38.00/56.00 **t.** –
       SB (weekends only) 70.00/80.00 **st.**

   🏨 **Kingsknowes**, Selkirk Rd, TD1 3HY, SE : 1 ½ m. on A 7 ☎ 58375, ≤, ☞, ✕ – 📺 ☎ **P**.
       🅰 AE ⓪ VISA
       M 12.50 **t.** and a la carte 🍷3.50 – **11 rm** ☲ 35.00/60.00 **t.** – SB (October-May) 74.00/90.00 **st.**

⑩ ATS Paton St. ☎ 3271/2

GATEHOUSE OF FLEET Kirkcudbright. (Dumfries and Galloway) **401** **402** H 19 – pop. 894 –
ECD : Thursday – ✆ 055 74.

🏌 Laurieston Rd ☎ 654.

🛈 Car Park ☎ 212 (summer only).

◆Edinburgh 113 – ◆Dumfries 33 – Stranraer 42.

   🏨 **Cally Palace** ⤸, DG7 2DL, S : 1 ½ m. by A 75 ☎ 341, Fax 522, ≤, ☒ heated, ⤸, ☞, park,
       ✕ – 📧 ⇚ rest 📺 ☎ **P**. VISA
       closed 3 January-4 March – **M** 6.50/16.00 **st.** 🍷2.70 – **58 rm** ☲ 45.00/50.00 **st.**, **1 suite**
       50.00 **st.**

   🏨 **Murray Arms** (Best Western), High St., DG7 2HY, ☎ 207, Fax 370, ⤸, ☞, ✕ – 📺 ☎ **P**.
       🅰 AE ⓪ VISA
       M (bar lunch)/dinner 15.00 **st.** 🍷3.20 – **12 rm** ☲ 30.00/66.00 **st.**, **1 suite** 60.00/70.00 **st.** –
       SB 84.00/90.00 **st.**

GATTONSIDE Roxburgh. (Borders) – see Melrose.

GIFFNOCK Renfrew. (Strathclyde) **401** ④ **402** ⑨ – see Glasgow.

GIFFORD E. Lothian. (Lothian) **401** L 16 – pop. 665 – ECD : Monday and Wednesday –
✉ Haddington – ✆ 062 081.

🏌 Cawdor Cottage ☎ 267, SW : 1 m.

◆Edinburgh 20 – Hawick 50.

   🏨 Tweeddale Arms, High St., EH41 4QU, ☎ 240 – 📺 ☎
       15 rm.

GIGHA (Isle of) Argyll. (Strathclyde) **401** C 16 – pop. 176 – ✆ 058 35.

⛴ by Caledonian MacBrayne : from Ardminish to Tayinloan : 4-6 daily (20 mn).

   🏨 **Gigha** ⤸, PA41 7AD, ☎ 254, ≤ Sound of Gigha and Kintyre Peninsula, « Tastefully reno-
       vated inn and farmhouse », ⤸, ☞ – **P**. 🅰 VISA
       M (buffet lunch)/dinner 15.00 **t.** – **9 rm** ☲ 24.00/54.00 **t.**

GLASGOW Lanark. (Strathclyde) **401 402** H 16 **Scotland G** – pop. 754 586 – ✆ 041.

See : Site★★★ – Burrell Collection★★★ AX M1 – Cathedral★★★ DYZ – Tolbooth Steeple★ DZ A – Hunterian Art Gallery★★ (Whistler Collection★★★, Mackintosh wing★★★) CY M2 – Art Gallery and Museum Kelvingrove★★ CY – City Chambers★ DZ C – Glasgow School of Art★ CY B – Museum of Transport★★ (Scottish cars★★★, Clyde Room of Ship Models★★★) AV M3 – Pollok House★ (Spanish paintings★★) AX D.

Envir. : Trossachs★★★, N : by A 739 AV and A 81 – Loch Lomond★★, NW : by A 82 AV – Clyde Estuary★ (Dumbarton Castle Site★, Hill House★, Helensburgh) by A 82, AV – Bothwell Castle★ and David Livingstone Centre (Museum★) SE : 9 m. by A 724 BX.

ⁱₛ Linn Park, Simshill Rd ✆ 637 5871, S : 4 m. BX – ⁱₛ Lethamhill, Cumbernauld Rd ✆ 770 6220 BV – ₉ Knightswood, Lincoln Av. ✆ 959 2131, W : 4 m. AV – ₉ Kings Park, Croftpark Av., S : 4 m. by B 766 BX – ₉ Alexandra Park, Alexandra Par. ✆ 556 3211 BV.

Access to Oban by helicopter.

✈ Glasgow Airport : ✆ 887 1111, W : 8 m. by M 8 AV – **Terminal :** Coach service from Glasgow Central and Queen Street main line Railway Stations and from Anderston Cross and Buchanan Bus Stations.

✈ see also Prestwick.

🛈 35-39 St. Vincent Pl. ✆ 227 4880 – Inchinnon Rd ✆ 848 4440.

♦Edinburgh 46 – ♦Manchester 221.

Plans on following pages

Holiday Inn (Holiday Inn), 500 Argyle St., Anderston, G3 8RR, ✆ 226 5577, Telex 776355, Fax 221 9202, ⌧, squash – |$| ⤢ rm ▤ TV ☎ ⅋ P – △ 800. ◩ AE ⓪ VISA   CZ **a**
M (buffet meals) 16.00 **t.** and a la carte 24.35/31.75 **st.** – ☲ 8.25 – **291 rm** 84.00/99.00 **st.**, **5 suites** 200.00 **st.**

Albany (T.H.F.), Bothwell St., G2 7EN, ✆ 248 2656, Telex 77440, Fax 221 8986, ⇐ – |$| ⤢ rm ▤ TV ☎ P – △ . ◩ AE ⓪ VISA   CZ **z**
M (carving lunch Saturday) 10.95/19.75 **st.** and a la carte ♭ 3.95 – ☲ 7.50 – **251 rm** 72.00/92.00 **st.**, **3 suites** 170.00/220.00 **st.** – SB (weekends only) 70.00/80.00 **st.**

One Devonshire Gardens, 1 Devonshire Gdns, G12 0UX, ✆ 339 2001, Fax 337 1663, « Opulent interior design » – TV ☎. ◩ AE ⓪ VISA   AV **a**
closed 1 to 4 January and 25-26 December – **M** (closed Saturday lunch) 25.00 **t.** (dinner) and a la carte 12.00/15.05 **t.** – ☲ 3.50 – **8 rm** 94.00/135.00 **t.**

Hospitality Inn (Mt. Charlotte), 36 Cambridge St., G2 3HN, ✆ 332 3311, Telex 777334, Fax 332 4050 – |$| TV ☎ & P – △ 1 500   DY **z**
313 rm, **3 suites**.

Stakis Grosvenor (Stakis), Grosvenor Terr., Great Western Rd, G12 0TA, ✆ 339 8811, Telex 776247, Fax 334 0710 – |$| TV ☎ P – △ 350. ◩ AE ⓪ VISA   CY **r**
M a la carte 17.00/24.20 **st.** ♭ 3.25 – ☲ 7.25 – **93 rm** 77.00/105.00 **st.**, **2 suites** 150.00 **st.** – SB 58.00/80.00 **st.**

White House without rest., 12 Cleveden Cres., G12 0PA, ✆ 339 9375, Telex 777582, Fax 337 1430 – TV ☎ – △ 25. ◩ AE ⓪ VISA. ✄   AV **r**
M (room service only) a la carte 10.95/22.75 **t.** ♭ 4.50 – ☲ 5.95 – **21 rm** 57.00/69.00 **t.**, **11 suites** 57.00/115.00 **t.** – SB (weekends only) 127.80/171.80 **st.**

Copthorne (Best Western), George Sq., G2 1DS, ✆ 332 6711, Telex 778147, Fax 332 4264 – |$| ⤢ rm TV ☎ – △ 100. ◩ AE ⓪ VISA. ✄   DZ **n**
M (closed lunch Saturday and Sunday) (carving rest.) 12.95/13.95 **t.** and a la carte ♭ 3.95 – ☲ 7.25 – **136 rm** 78.00/96.00 **st.**, **5 suites** 105.00/120.00 **st.** – SB (weekends only) 83.00/91.00 **st.**

Tinto Firs Thistle (Thistle), 470 Kilmarnock Rd, G43 2BB, ✆ 637 2353, Telex 778329, Fax 633 1340 – ⤢ rm TV ☎ P – △ . ◩ AE ⓪ VISA   AX **c**
M 7.75/12.50 **st.** and a la carte – ☲ 7.25 – **25 rm** 60.00/75.00 **st.**, **2 suites** 100.00 **st.** – SB 82.00/90.00 **st.**

Kelvin Park Lorne (Q.M.H.), 923 Sauchiehall St., G3 7TE, ✆ 334 4891, Telex 778935 – |$| TV ☎ P – △ 50 – **80 rm**.   CY **a**

Swallow (Swallow), 517 Paisley Rd West, G51 1RW, ✆ 427 3146, Telex 778795, Fax 427 4059, ⌧ – |$| ⤢ rm TV ☎ P – △ 200. ◩ AE ⓪ VISA   AX **a**
M 9.50/15.00 **st.** and a la carte ♭ 4.75 – **119 rm** ☲ 65.00/85.00 **st.** – SB (weekends only) 75.00/85.00 **st.**

Stakis Pond (Stakis), 2-4 Shelley Rd, Great Western Rd, G12 0XP, ✆ 334 8161, Telex 776573, Fax 334 3846, ⌧ – |$| TV ☎ P – △ 50. ◩ AE ⓪ VISA   AV **i**
☲ 7.25 – **137 rm** 66.00/84.00 **st.** – SB 58.00/80.00 **st.**

Crest (Crest), 377 Argyle St., G2 8LL, ✆ 248 2355, Telex 779652, Fax 221 1014 – |$| ⤢ TV ☎ P – △ 80. ◩ AE ⓪ VISA   CZ **x**
M (closed lunch Saturday and Sunday) 9.50/14.50 **st.** and a la carte – ☲ 8.00 – **121 rm** 69.00/81.90 **st.** – SB (weekends only) 84.00/90.00 **st.**

Stakis Ingram (Stakis), 201 Ingram St., G1 1DQ, ✆ 248 4401, Telex 776470, Fax 226 5149 – |$| TV ☎ – △ 200. ◩ AE ⓪ VISA   DZ **c**
M a la carte 15.25/22.70 **st.** – ☲ 7.25 – **90 rm** 63.00/85.00 **st.** – SB 50.00/70.00 **st.**

Albion without rest., 405-407 North Woodside Rd, G20 6NN, ✆ 339 8620 – TV. AE ✄   CY **u**
16 rm ☲ 30.00/40.00 **st.**

GLASGOW
BUILT UP AREA

Aikenhead Road .... **BX** 2
Alexandra Parade .... **BV** 3
Balgrayhill Road .... **BV** 4
Ballater Street .... **BX** 6
Balornock Road .... **BV** 8

Balshagray Avenue .... **AV** 9
Battlefield Road .... **BX** 12
Berryknowes Road......... **AX** 15
Bilsland Drive .... **BV** 16
Blairbeth Road .... **BX** 18
Braidcraft Road.......... **AX** 20
Broomloan Road .... **AV** 26
Burnhill Chapel Street .... **BX** 28
Byres Road .... **AV** 29
Caledonia Road .... **BX** 30

Carmunnock Road......... **BX** 33
Cook Street .... **BV** 38
Cumbernauld Road .... **BV** 40
Edmiston Drive .... **AV** 48
Farmeloan Road.......... **BX** 53
Fenwick Road .... **AX** 55
Glasgow Road
(PAISLEY) .... **AX** 62
Gorbals Street .... **BX** 63
Grange Road............. **BX** 67

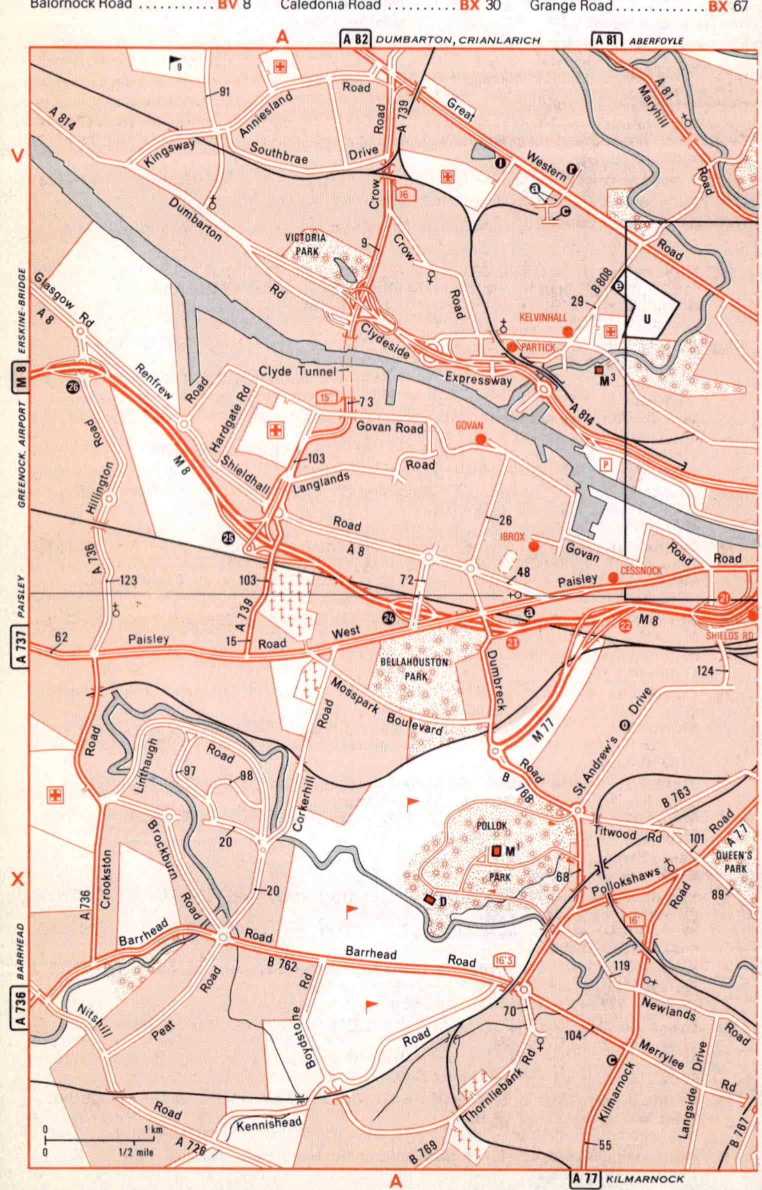

Haggs Road	**AX** 68	
Harriet Street	**AX** 70	
Helen Street	**AV** 72	
Holmfauld Road	**AV** 73	
Holmlea Road	**BX** 75	
Hospital Street	**BX** 75	
James Street	**BX** 79	
King's Drive	**BX** 83	
King's Park Road	**BX** 84	
Lamont Road	**BV** 88	
Langside Av.	**AX** 89	
Langside Road	**BX** 90	
Lincoln Avenue	**AV** 91	
Lyoncross Road	**AX** 97	
Meiklerig Crescent	**AX** 98	
Minard Rd	**AX** 101	
Moss Road	**AV** 103	
Nether Auldhouse Road	**AX** 104	
Prospecthill Road	**BX** 112	
Provan Road	**BV** 114	
Red Road	**BV** 118	
Riverford Road	**AX** 119	
Sandwood Road	**AV** 123	
Shields Road	**AX** 124	
Todd Street	**BV** 131	
Westmuir Place	**BX** 136	
Westmuir Street	**BX** 138	

For Street Index see Glasgow p. 6

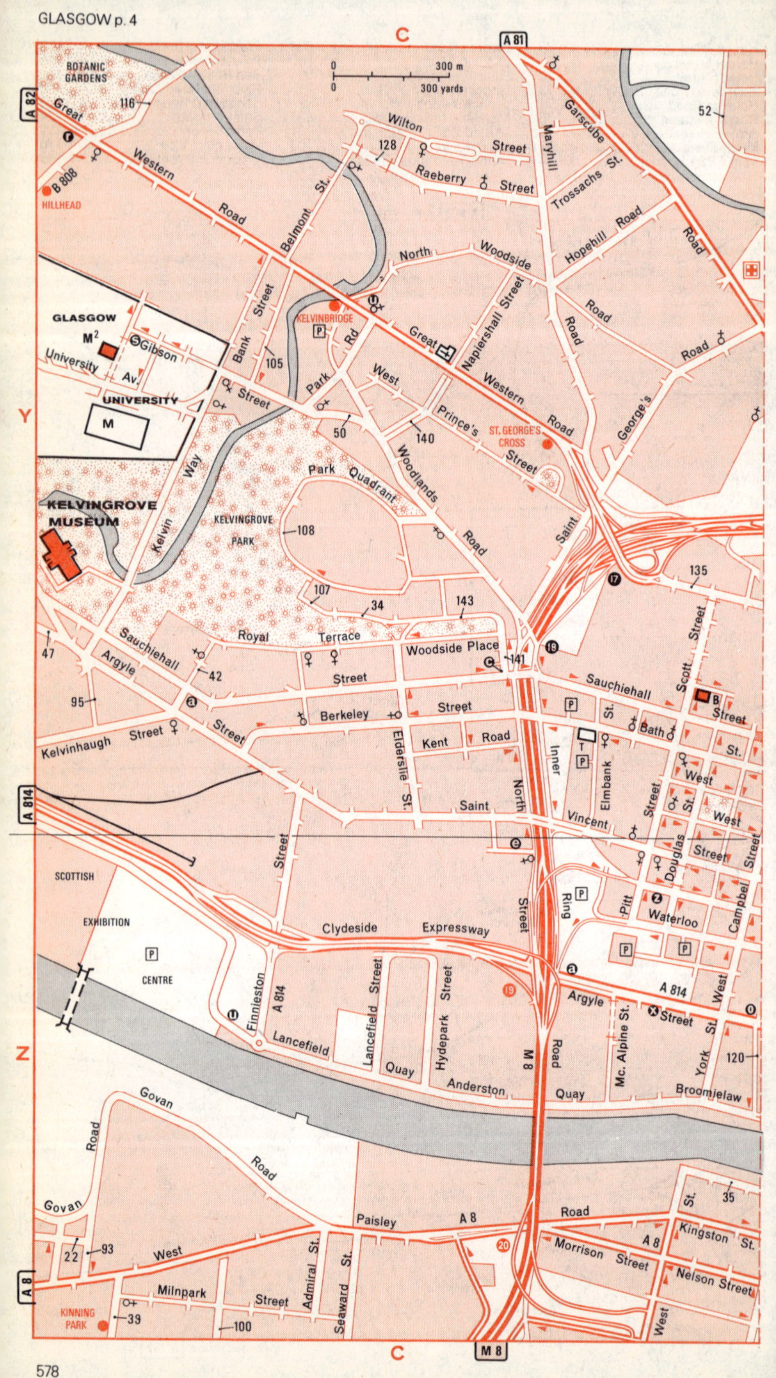
C
A 81
BOTANIC GARDENS
116
52
A 82
Great
Western
Road
Wilton
Street
128
Raeberry
Street
Garscube
Maryhill
Trossachs St.
Hopehill
Road
Road
r
B 808
HILLHEAD
North
Woodside
Street
Napiershall Street
Road
Road
GLASGOW
M²
Gibson
Bank
Street
Belmont St.
KELVINBRIDGE
P
Park Rd
Great
Western
Road
George's
Road
University
Av.
105
West
Prince's
ST. GEORGE'S CROSS
UNIVERSITY
M
50
140
Street
Y
Kelvin Way
Park
Quadrant
Woodlands
Road
Saint.
KELVINGROVE MUSEUM
KELVINGROVE PARK
108
135
107
34
143
17
Royal
Terrace
Woodside Place
19
Scott
Street
47
Sauchiehall
42
141
Sauchiehall
B
95
Street
a
Berkeley
Street
P
Bath
St.
St.
Kelvinhaugh
Street
Street
Kent
Road
Inner
P
Elmbank
West
Elderslie St.
Saint
North
Street
Douglas
West
A 814
Vincent
Street
Street
e
SCOTTISH
EXHIBITION
Street
Clydeside
Expressway
Ring
P
P
Pitt
Waterloo
Campbell
CENTRE
P
Finnieston
A 814
Lancefield
Street
Hydepark
Street
Street
19
Argyle
a
A 814
Street
York St.
West
Lancefield
Quay
Mc. Alpine St.
X
120
Z
Anderston
Quay
M 8
Road
Broomielaw
Govan
Road
Road
Govan
Road
St.
35
Govan
Paisley
A 8
Road
Kingston St.
A 8
20
Morrison
Street
A 8
Nelson Street
22
93
West
Admiral St.
Seaward St.
West
A 8
Milnpark
Street
KINNING PARK
39
100
578
C
M 8

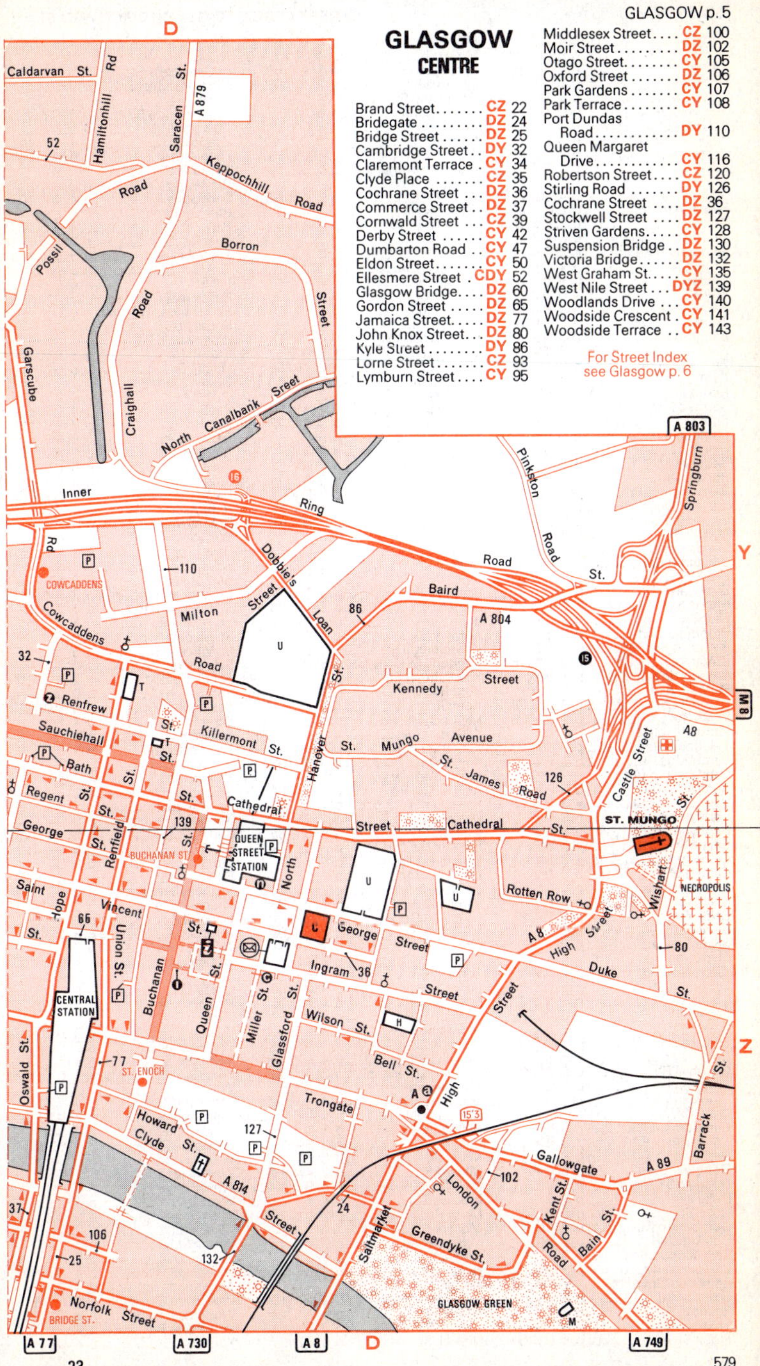

GLASGOW p. 5

GLASGOW
CENTRE

Brand Street....... CZ 22
Bridegate .... DZ 24
Bridge Street ...... DZ 25
Cambridge Street .. DY 32
Claremont Terrace . CY 34
Clyde Place .... CZ 35
Cochrane Street ... DZ 36
Commerce Street .. CZ 37
Cornwald Street ... CZ 39
Derby Street ...... CY 42
Dumbarton Road .. CY 47
Eldon Street....... CY 50
Ellesmere Street . CDY 52
Glasgow Bridge.... DZ 60
Gordon Street ..... DZ 65
Jamaica Street .... DZ 77
John Knox Street... DZ 80
Kyle Street .... DY 86
Lorne Street ...... CZ 93
Lymburn Street .... CY 95

Middlesex Street.... CZ 100
Moir Street .... DZ 102
Otago Street....... CY 105
Oxford Street ...... DZ 106
Park Gardens ..... CY 107
Park Terrace .... CY 108
Port Dundas
   Road........... DY 110
Queen Margaret
   Drive.......... CY 116
Robertson Street.... CZ 120
Stirling Road ...... DY 126
Cochrane Street ... DZ 36
Stockwell Street ... DZ 127
Striven Gardens ... CY 128
Suspension Bridge . DZ 130
Victoria Bridge .... DZ 132
West Graham St.... CY 135
West Nile Street ... DYZ 139
Woodlands Drive .. CY 140
Woodside Crescent . CY 141
Woodside Terrace .. CY 143

For Street Index
see Glasgow p. 6

D
A 879
Caldarvan St.
Hamiltonhill Rd
Saracen St.
Keppochhill Road
52
Road
Borron
Possil
Road
Craighall
Garscube
North Canalbank Sreet
A 803
Inner
16
Ring
Pinkston
Springburn
Road
Road
St.
Y
M 8
Rd
P
110
COWCADDENS
Cowcaddens
Milton
Dobbie's
Street
Baird
A 804
15
32
Road
Loan
86
Kennedy
Street
A 8
P
Renfrew
T
St.
St.
Killermont St.
St.
Mungo
Avenue
Castle Street
Sauchiehall
Bath
Hanover
St. James
Road
126
St.
Regent
St.
St.
Cathedral
Cathedral
ST. MUNGO
George
St.
139
Street
St.
Renfield
St.
BUCHANAN ST.
QUEEN
STREET
STATION
North
U
NECROPOLIS
Saint
Hope
Vincent
66
Union St.
St.
U
U
Rotten Row
80
George
Street
A 8
High
Street
CENTRAL
STATION
Buchanan
Queen
St.
Miller St.
Glassford St.
Ingram
Street
Duke
St.
Oswald St.
77
ST. ENOCH
Wilson St.
H
Z
Bell St.
Barrack St.
Howard
Clyde St.
127
Trongate
High
15'3
Saltmarket
A 814
102
London
Gallowgate
A 89
37
Street
24
Kent St.
Bain
St.
Road
106
132
Greendyke St.
25
Norfolk Street
GLASGOW GREEN
M
BRIDGE ST.
A 77
A 730
A 8
D
A 749

23
579

STREET INDEX TO GLASGOW TOWN PLAN

Argyle St. .... p. 4 **CZ**
Buchanan St. .... p. 5 **DZ**
Gordon St. .... p. 5 **DZ** 65
Jamaica St. .... p. 5 **DZ** 77
Oswald St. .... p. 5 **DZ**
Renfield St. .... p. 5 **DZ**
St. Vincent St. ...... p. 5 **DZ**
Sauchiehall St. ...... p. 5 **DY**
Trongate .... p. 5 **DZ**
Union St. .... p. 5 **DZ**

Admiral St. .... p. 4 **CZ**
Aikenhead Rd. ...... p. 3 **BX** 2
Alexandra Par. ..... p. 3 **BV** 3
Anderston Quay. .... p. 4 **CZ**
Anniesland Rd ...... p. 2 **AV**
Argyle St. .... p. 4 **CZ**
Bain St. .... p. 5 **DZ**
Baird St. .... p. 5 **DY**
Balgrayhill. .... p. 3 **BV** 4
Ballater St. .... p. 3 **BX** 6
Balmore Rd. .... p. 3 **BV**
Balornock Rd .... p. 3 **BV** 8
Balshagray Av. ..... p. 2 **AV** 9
Bank St. .... p. 4 **CY**
Barrack St. .... p. 5 **DZ**
Barrhead Rd .... p. 2 **AX**
Bath St. .... p. 4 **CY**
Battlefield Rd ...... p. 3 **BX** 12
Bell St. .... p. 5 **DZ**
Belmont St. .... p. 4 **CY**
Berkeley St. .... p. 4 **CY**
Berryknowes Rd. .... p. 2 **AX** 15
Bilsland Drive ...... p. 3 **BV** 16
Blairbeth Rd .... p. 3 **BX** 18
Borron St. .... p. 5 **DY**
Boydstone Rd. ...... p. 2 **AX**
Braidcraft Rd. ...... p. 2 **AX** 20
Brand St. .... p. 4 **CZ** 22
Bridegate .... p. 5 **DZ** 24
Bridge St. .... p. 5 **DZ** 25
Brockburn Rd ...... p. 2 **AX**
Broomfield Rd ...... p. 3 **BV**
Broomielaw .... p. 4 **CZ**
Broomloan Rd ...... p. 2 **AV** 26
Brownside Rd. ...... p. 3 **BX**
Buchanan St. .... p. 5 **DZ**
Burnhill Chapel St. .. p. 3 **BX** 28
Byres Rd .... p. 2 **AV** 29
Caldarvan St. ...... p. 5 **DY**
Caledonia Rd ...... p. 3 **BX** 30
Cambridge St. ..... p. 5 **DY** 32
Cambuslang Rd. .... p. 3 **BX**
Cardowan Rd ...... p. 3 **BV**
Carmunnock Rd. ... p. 3 **BX** 33
Carntyne Rd .... p. 3 **BV**
Carntynehall Rd .... p. 3 **BV**
Castle St. .... p. 5 **DY**
Cathcart Rd. .... p. 3 **BX**
Cathedral St. .... p. 5 **DY**
Claremont Ter. ...... p. 4 **CY** 34
Clarkston Rd. ...... p. 3 **BX**
Clyde Place .... p. 4 **CZ** 35
Clyde St. .... p. 5 **DZ**
Clyde Tunnel. ...... p. 2 **AV**
Clydeside
   Expressway ...... p. 2 **AV**
Cochrane St. .... p. 5 **DZ** 36
Commerce St. ...... p. 5 **DZ** 37
Cook St. .... p. 3 **BV** 38
Corkerhill Rd. ...... p. 2 **AX**
Cornwald St. .... p. 4 **CZ** 39
Cowcaddens St. ..... p. 5 **DY**
Craighall Rd .... p. 5 **DY**
Croftfoot Rd .... p. 3 **BX**
Crookston Rd ...... p. 2 **AX**
Crow Rd. .... p. 2 **AV**
Cumbernauld Rd ... p. 3 **BV** 40
Dalmarnock Rd .... p. 3 **BX**
Derby St. .... p. 4 **CY** 42
Dobbie's Loan ..... p. 5 **DY**
Douglas St. .... p. 4 **CZ**
Duke's Rd .... p. 3 **BX**
Duke St. .... p. 5 **DZ**
Dumbarton Rd ...... p. 4 **CY** 47
Dumbreck Rd. ...... p. 2 **AX**
East Kilbride Rd .... p. 3 **BX**
Edinburgh Rd. ...... p. 3 **BV**
Edmiston Drive ..... p. 2 **AV** 48
Eglinton Rd. .... p. 3 **BX**
Eglinton St. .... p. 3 **BX**
Elderslie St. .... p. 4 **CY**
Eldon St. .... p. 4 **CY** 50

Ellesmere St. .... p. 5 **DY** 52
Elmbank St. .... p. 4 **CY**
Farmeloan Rd ...... p. 3 **BX** 53
Fenwick Rd. .... p. 2 **AX** 55
Finnieston St. .... p. 4 **CZ**
Gallowgate. .... p. 5 **DZ**
Garscube Rd .... p. 5 **DY**
George St. .... p. 5 **DZ**
Gibson St. .... p. 4 **CY**
Glasgow Bridge ..... p. 5 **DZ** 60
Glasgow Rd
   (PAISLEY). .... p. 2 **AX** 62
Glasgow Rd
   (RENFREW). ..... p. 2 **AV**
Glasgow Rd
   (RUTHERGLEN) .. p. 3 **BX**
Glassford St. .... p. 5 **DZ**
Gorbals St. .... p. 3 **BX** 63
Gordon St. .... p. 5 **DZ** 65
Govan Rd. .... p. 4 **CZ**
Grange Rd. .... p. 3 **BX** 67
Great Western Rd ... p. 4 **CY**
Greendyke St. ...... p. 5 **DZ**
Haggs Rd .... p. 2 **AX** 68
Hamiltonhill Rd ..... p. 5 **DY**
Hardgate Rd .... p. 2 **AV**
Harriet St. .... p. 2 **AX** 70
Helen St. .... p. 2 **AV** 72
High St. .... p. 5 **DZ**
Hillington Rd .... p. 2 **AV**
Holmfauld Rd. ...... p. 2 **AV** 73
Holmlea Rd .... p. 3 **BX** 74
Hope St. .... p. 5 **DZ**
Hopehill Rd. .... p. 4 **CY**
Hospital St. .... p. 3 **BX** 75
Howard St. .... p. 5 **DZ**
Hydepark St. .... p. 4 **CZ**
Ingram St. .... p. 5 **DZ**
Inner Ring Rd ...... p. 5 **DY**
Jamaica St. .... p. 5 **DZ** 77
James St. .... p. 3 **BX** 79
John Knox St. ...... p. 5 **DZ** 80
Kelvin Way .... p. 4 **CY**
Kelvinhaugh St. ..... p. 4 **CY**
Kennedy St. .... p. 5 **DY**
Kennishead Rd ..... p. 2 **AX**
Kent Rd .... p. 4 **CY**
Kent St. .... p. 5 **DZ**
Keppoch Hill Rd. .... p. 5 **DY**
Killermont St. ...... p. 5 **DY**
Kilmarnock Rd ..... p. 2 **AX**
King's Drive .... p. 3 **BX** 83
King's Park Av. ..... p. 3 **BX**
King's Park Rd ..... p. 3 **BX** 84
Kingston St. .... p. 4 **CZ**
Kingsway .... p. 2 **AV**
Kyle St. .... p. 5 **DY** 86
Lamont Rd .... p. 3 **BV** 88
Lancefield Quay. .... p. 4 **CZ**
Lancefield St. ...... p. 4 **CZ**
Langlands Rd. ...... p. 2 **AV**
Langside Av. .... p. 2 **AX** 89
Langside Drive. ..... p. 2 **AX**
Langside Rd .... p. 3 **BX** 90
Lincoln Av. .... p. 2 **AV** 91
Linthaugh Rd ...... p. 2 **AX**
London Rd .... p. 3 **BX**
Lorne St. .... p. 4 **CZ** 93
Lymburn St. .... p. 4 **CY** 95
Lyoncross Rd ...... p. 2 **AX** 97
McAlpine St. .... p. 4 **CZ**
Main St. .... p. 3 **BX**
Maryhill Rd .... p. 4 **CY**
Meiklerig Crescent .. p. 2 **AX** 98
Merrylee Rd .... p. 2 **AX**
Middlesex St. ...... p. 4 **CZ** 100
Milnpark St. .... p. 4 **CZ**
Milton St. .... p. 5 **DY**
Mill St. .... p. 3 **BX**
Miller St. .... p. 5 **DZ**
Minard Rd. .... p. 2 **AX** 101
Moir St. .... p. 5 **DZ** 102
Morrison St. .... p. 4 **CZ**
Moss Rd .... p. 2 **AV** 103
Mosspark
   Boulevard. .... p. 2 **AX**
Napiershall St. ..... p. 4 **CY**
Nelson St. .... p. 4 **CZ**
Nether
   Auldhouse Rd .... p. 2 **AX** 104
Newlands Rd ...... p. 2 **AX**
Nitshill Rd .... p. 2 **AX**
Norfolk St. .... p. 5 **DZ**

North St. .... p. 4 **CY**
North
   Canalbank St. .... p. 5 **DY**
North Hanover St. ... p. 5 **DY**
North
   Woodside Rd .... p. 4 **CY**
Oswald St. .... p. 5 **DZ**
Otago St. .... p. 4 **CY** 105
Oxford St. .... p. 5 **DZ** 106
Paisley Rd .... p. 2 **AV**
Paisley Rd West. .... p. 2 **AX**
Park Gdns .... p. 4 **CY** 107
Park Quadrant ..... p. 4 **CY**
Park Ter. .... p. 4 **CY** 108
Peat Rd .... p. 2 **AX**
Petershill Rd .... p. 3 **BV**
Pinkston Rd .... p. 5 **DY**
Pitt St. .... p. 4 **CZ**
Pollokshaws Rd .... p. 2 **AX**
Port Dundas Rd .... p. 5 **DY** 110
Possil Rd. .... p. 5 **DY**
Prospecthill Rd. ..... p. 3 **BX** 112
Provan Rd .... p. 3 **BV** 114
Queen St. .... p. 5 **DZ**
Queen Margaret
   Drive .... p. 4 **CY** 116
Raeberry St. .... p. 4 **CY**
Red Rd. .... p. 3 **BV** 118
Renfield St. .... p. 5 **DZ**
Renfrew Rd. .... p. 2 **AV**
Renfrew St. .... p. 5 **DY**
Ring Rd. .... p. 3 **BV**
Riverford Road. ..... p. 2 **AX** 119
Robertson St. ...... p. 4 **CZ** 120
Robroyston Rd. ..... p. 3 **BV**
Rotten Row. .... p. 5 **DZ**
Royal Ter. .... p. 4 **CY**
Royston Rd. .... p. 3 **BV**
Rutherglen Rd ..... p. 3 **BX**
St. Andrew's Drive .. p. 2 **AX**
St. George's Rd .... p. 4 **CY**
St. James Rd ...... p. 5 **DY**
St. Mungo Av. ..... p. 5 **DY**
St. Vincent St. ...... p. 5 **DZ**
Saltmarket .... p. 5 **DZ**
Sandwood Rd ..... p. 2 **AV** 123
Saracen St. .... p. 5 **DY**
Sauchiehall St. ...... p. 5 **DY**
Scott St. .... p. 4 **CY**
Seaward St. .... p. 4 **CZ**
Shettleston Rd ..... p. 3 **BX**
Shieldhall Rd ...... p. 2 **AV**
Shields Rd .... p. 2 **AX** 124
Southbrae Drive .... p. 2 **AV**
Springburn Rd ..... p. 3 **BV**
Springfield Rd ..... p. 3 **BX**
Stirling Rd. .... p. 5 **DY** 126
Stockwell St. .... p. 5 **DZ** 127
Stonelaw Rd. ...... p. 3 **BX**
Striven Gdns. ...... p. 4 **CY** 128
Suspension Bridge .. p. 5 **DZ** 130
Thornliebank Rd .... p. 2 **AX**
Titwood Rd .... p. 2 **AX**
Todd St. .... p. 3 **BV** 131
Tollcross Rd .... p. 3 **BX**
Trongate .... p. 5 **DZ**
Trossachs St. ...... p. 4 **CY**
Union St. .... p. 5 **DZ**
University Av. ...... p. 4 **CY**
Victoria Bridge ..... p. 5 **DZ** 132
Victoria Rd .... p. 3 **BX**
Wallacewell Rd .... p. 3 **BV**
Waterloo St. .... p. 4 **CZ**
West St. .... p. 4 **CZ**
West
   Campbell St. ..... p. 4 **CZ**
West George St. .... p. 5 **DZ**
West Graham St. ... p. 4 **CY** 135
Westmuir Place ..... p. 3 **BX** 136
Westmuir St. ...... p. 3 **BX** 138
West Nile St. ...... p. 5 **DYZ** 139
West Paisley Rd. .... p. 4 **CZ**
West Prince's St. .... p. 4 **CY**
West Regent St. .... p. 5 **DY**
Wilson St. .... p. 5 **DZ**
Wilton St. .... p. 4 **CY**
Wishart St. .... p. 5 **DZ**
Woodlands Drive ... p. 4 **CY** 140
Woodlands Rd. ..... p. 4 **CY**
Woodside Crescent . p. 4 **CY** 141
Woodside Place .... p. 4 **CY**
Woodside Ter. ...... p. 4 **CY** 143
York St. .... p. 4 **CZ**

↑ **Dalmeny,** 62 St. Andrews Drive, Nithsdale Cross, Pollokshields, G41 5EZ, ☎ 427 1106 –
📺 🅿️   AX o
M (by arrangement) – **8 rm** � 25.00/48.00 **st.**

↑ **Kirklee** without rest., 11 Kensington Gate, G12 9LG, ☎ 334 5555 – 📺 ☎. 🐾   AV c
9 rm � 32.50/45.00 **st.**

↑ **Town House,** 4 Hughenden Terr., G12 9XR, ☎ 357 0862, 🛋 – ⇆ rest 📺. 🐾   AV a
M 7.50 **st.** – **10 rm** � 31.00/42.00 **st.**

XXX **North Rotunda,** 28 Tunnel St. (2nd floor), G3 8HL, ☎ 204 1238, Fax 226 4264, French rest.
– 🅿️. 🔳 AE ⓞ VISA   CZ u
closed Saturday lunch, Sunday, 25 December, 1 January and Bank Holidays – **M** 10.50/
17.95 **t.** and a la carte 12.70/21.60 **t.** 🍷 3.95.

XXX **Killermont House,** 2022 Maryhill Rd, Maryhill Park, G20 0AB, ☎ 946 5412, 🛋 – 🅿️. 🔳
AE VISA   by A 81 AV
closed Sunday dinner, Monday and 6 to 31 August – **M** 10.00/18.50 **st.**

XXX **Fountain,** 2 Woodside Cres., G3 7UL, ☎ 332 6396 – 🔳 AE ⓞ VISA   CY c
closed Saturday lunch and Sunday – **M** 9.00/13.95 **t.** and a la carte 14.15/33.60 **t.** 🍷 3.90.

XX **Buttery,** 652 Argyle St., G3 8UF, ☎ 221 8188 – 🅿️. 🔳 AE ⓞ VISA   CZ e
closed Saturday lunch, Sunday and Bank Holidays – **M** 12.50 **st.** (lunch) and a la carte
15.70/21.10 **t.**

XX **Rogano,** 11 Exchange Pl., G1 3AN, ☎ 248 4055, Seafood, « Art deco » – 🔳 AE ⓞ VISA
closed Sunday and Bank Holidays – **M** a la carte 18.15/27.85 **t.**   DZ i

XX **Colonial,** 25 High St., G1 1LX, ☎ 552 1923 – 🔳 AE VISA   DZ a
closed Saturday lunch, Sunday and Bank Holidays – **M** 9.95/28.00 **t.** and a la carte
18.45/23.85 **t.** 🍷 3.75.

X **Ubiquitous Chip,** 12 Ashton Lane, off Byres Rd, G12 8SJ, ☎ 334 5007 – 🔳 AE ⓞ VISA
closed Sunday, 25 and 31 December-1 January – **M** 17.95 **t.** and a la carte 12.05/20.95 **t.**
🍷 2.75.   AV e

X **Shish Mahal,** 45 Gibson St., G12 8NW, ☎ 339 8256, Indian and Pakistani rest. – ⇆. 🔳
AE ⓞ VISA   CY s
M 6.00/8.00 **t.** and a la carte 🍷 3.75.

at Giffnock (Renfrew.) (Strathclyde) S : 5 ¼ m. by A 77 – AX – ✉ 🕲 041 Glasgow :

🏨 **MacDonald Thistle** (Thistle), Eastwood Toll, G46 6RA, at intersection of A 77 and A 726
☎ 638 2225, Telex 779138, Fax 638 6231 – 📺 ☎ 🅿️ – 🏄 . 🔳 AE ⓞ VISA
M 7.50/13.95 **st.** and a la carte – � 7.25 – **52 rm** 55.00/75.00 **st.,** **4 suites** 95.00 **st.** –
SB 72.00/120.00 **st.**

🏨 Redhurst (B.C.B.), 77 Eastwoodmains Rd, G46 6QE, ☎ 638 6465 – ⇆ rm 📺 ☎ 🅿️
19 rm.

at Busby S : 5 ½ m. by A 727 – AX – on A 726 – ✉ 🕲 041 Glasgow :

🏨 **Busby,** 1 Field Rd, Clarkston, G76 8RX, ☎ 644 2661 – 🔁 📺 ☎ 🅿️. 🔳 AE ⓞ VISA
closed 25 December and 1 January – **M** (bar lunch)/dinner 7.65 **t.** and a la carte 🍷 4.95 –
14 rm ⊑ 37.00/45.00 **t.** – SB (weekends only) 91.10/121.10 **st.**

at Glasgow Airport (Renfrew.) (Strathclyde) W : 8 m. by M 8 – AV – ✉ 🕲 041 Glasgow :

🏨 **Excelsior** (T.H.F.), Abbotsinch, PA3 2TR, ☎ 887 1212, Telex 777733, Fax 887 3738 – 🔁
⇆ rm 📺 ☎ 🅿️ – 🏄 400. 🔳 AE ⓞ VISA
M 8.50/11.50 **st.** and a la carte 19.75/25.25 **st.** 🍷 3.85 – ⊑ 7.50 – **283 rm** 72.00/92.00 **st.,**
7 suites 115.00 **st.**   SB 80.00 **st.**

MICHELIN Distribution Centre, 60 Cunningham Rd, Rutherglen, G73 1PP, ☎ 643 2101,
FAX 647 5267 p. 3 BX

AUSTIN-ROVER, MAZDA 215 Queensborough
Gdns ☎ 357 1234
AUSTIN-ROVER, VAUXHALL Vineycombe St. ☎
334 4761
FORD Hilton Gdns ☎ 954 1500
FORD 34 Fenwick Rd ☎ 637 7161
FORD Pollockshaws Rd ☎ 423 6644
HONDA Maxwell Rd ☎ 429 4298
NISSAN 77-81 Dumbarton Rd ☎ 334 1241
OPEL-VAUXHALL 10 Holmbank Av. ☎ 649 9321
PORSCHE Maxwell Av. Bearsden ☎ 943 1155

RENAULT 64 Kirkintilloch Rd ☎ 772 6481
SAAB 162 Crow Rd ☎ 334 4661
VAUXHALL-OPEL St. Georges Rd ☎ 332 2626
VOLVO 2413-2493 London Rd ☎ 778 8501
VOLVO Bothwell Rd, Hamilton ☎ 728 4100
VW-AUDI 512 Kilmarnock Rd ☎ 637 2241

🅖 ATS 192 Finnieston St. ☎ 248 6761
ATS Rutherglen Ind Est., Glasgow Rd, Rutherglen
☎ 647 9341
ATS 1 Sawmillfield St., off Garscube Rd ☎ 332 1945

---

*When travelling for business or pleasure
in England, Wales, Scotland and Ireland :*

*– use the series of five maps
  (nos* **401**, **402**, **403**, **404** and **405***) at a scale of 1:400 000*

*– they are the perfect complement to this Guide
  as towns underlined in red on the maps will be found in this Guide.*

GLENBORRODALE Argyll. (Highland) **401** C 13 – ✉ Acharacle – ✆ 097 24.
◆Edinburgh 151 – ◆Inverness 108 – ◆Oban 72.

🏰 **Glenborrodale Castle** ⑤, Ardnamurchan, PH36 4JP, ℰ 266, Telex 778815, Fax 224, ≤ Loch Sunart and gardens, « Victorian castle in extensive gardens », ᗡ, park, ✗ – TV ☎ ℗. 🔄 AE VISA. ⑤⑤
Easter-October – **M** (booking essential) (buffet lunch, residents only)/dinner 30.00 t. – **15 rm** ☑ 90.00/200.00 t.

GLENCARSE Perth. (Tayside) **401** K 14 – ECD : Wednesday – ✉ Perth – ✆ 073 886.
◆Edinburgh 47 – ◆Dundee 16 – Perth 6.5.

🏠 **Newton House**, PH2 7LX, ℰ 250, Fax 717, 🚗 – TV ☎ ℗. 🔄 ① VISA
M a la carte approx. 16.50 t. ◊ 3.75 – **10 rm** ☑ 33.00/52.00 t. – SB 37.00/49.00 st.

GLENCRIPESDALE Argyll. (Highland) – see Strontian.

GLENLIVET Banff. (Grampian) **401** J 11 – ✉ ✆ 080 73.
◆Edinburgh 173 – ◆Aberdeen 67 – ◆Inverness 50.

🏠 **Blairfindy Lodge** ⑤, Ballindalloch, AB3 9DJ, ℰ 376, ≤, 🚗 – ℗. 🔄 AE VISA
M *(closed Sunday and Monday)* 10.50/16.50 t. – **12 rm** ☑ 26.00/56.00 t. – SB (except summer) 36.00/42.00 st.

GLENROTHES Fife. (Fife) **401** K 15 – pop. 33 639 – ECD : Tuesday – ✆ 0592.
Envir. : Falkland (Palace of Falkland★ ; village★) N : 5 m. by A 92 and A 912.
🏌 Thornton ℰ 771111, S : 3 m. – 🏌 Golf Course Rd ℰ 758686 – 🏌 Leslie ℰ 741449, W : 3 m. on A 911.
🛈 Kingdom Centre, Lyon Sq. ℰ 754954.
◆Edinburgh 33 – ◆Dundee 25 – Stirling 36.

🏨 **Stakis Albany** (Stakis), 1 North St., KY7 5NA, ℰ 752292 – 📶 TV 📠 ℗ – 🔌 200
29 rm.

at Leslie W : 3 m. by A 911 – ✉ Leslie – ✆ 0592 Glenrothes :

🏨 **Balgeddie House** ⑤, Balgeddie Way, KY6 3ET, NE : 1 ¾ m. by A 911 and B 969 via Formonthills Rd ℰ 742511, Fax 621702, ≤, 🚗 – TV ☎ ℗. 🔄 AE VISA. ⑤⑤
closed 1 and 2 January – **M** 11.00 st. and a la carte ◊ 7.15 – ☑ 6.05 – **18 rm** 45.10/71.50 st. – SB (weekends only) 49.50 st.

🏠 **Rescobie** ⑤, Valley Drive, KY6 3BQ, ℰ 742143, 🚗 – TV ☎ ℗. 🔄 AE ① VISA. ⑤⑤
M 8.50/13.50 t. and a la carte – **8 rm** ☑ 38.00/60.00 t. – SB (weekends only) 65.00 st.

PEUGEOT-TALBOT North St. ℰ 752262

GLENSHEE Perth. (Tayside) **401** J 13 – see Spittal of Glenshee.

GOLSPIE Sutherland. (Highland) **401** I 10 – pop. 1 385 – ECD : Wednesday – ✉ ✆ 040 83.
🏌 Ferry Rd ℰ 3266.
◆Edinburgh 228 – ◆Inverness 72 – ◆Wick 54.

🏨 **Golf Links**, Church St., KW10 6TT, ℰ 3408, ≤, 🚗 – TV ℗
M 6.00/12.50 t. and dinner a la carte ◊ 2.00 – **8 rm** ☑ 23.00/40.00 t.

AUSTIN-ROVER Station Rd ℰ 3205   FIAT Old Bank Rd ℰ 3411

GOUROCK Renfrew. (Strathclyde) **401** F 16 – pop. 11 087 – ECD : Wednesday – ✆ 0475.
⛴ by Caledonian MacBrayne : from Railway Pier to Dunoon Pier: frequent services daily (20 mn) – by Western Ferries : from McInroy's Point to Hunters Quay, Dunoon: frequent services daily (20 mn).
⛴ by Caledonian MacBrayne and Clyde Marine Motoring Co. Ltd. to Helensburgh via Kilcreggan : 3-8 daily (40 mn).
🛈 Municipal Buildings, Shore St., ℰ 39404 (summer only).
◆Edinburgh 71 – ◆Ayr 47 – ◆Glasgow 27.

🏨 **Stakis Gantock** (Stakis), Cloch Rd, PA15 1AR, SW : 2 m. on A 78 ℰ 34671, Telex 778584, Fax 32490, ≤ Firth of Clyde, 🏊 – TV ☎ ℗ – 🔌 180. 🔄 AE ① VISA
M a la carte 17.05/24.70 st. – ☑ 7.25 – **99 rm** 60.00/85.00 st., **1 suite** 130.00 st. – SB 50.00/88.00 st.

🏠 **Claremont** without rest., 34 Victoria Rd, PA19 1DF, ℰ 31687, ≤ Firth of Clyde – TV ℗
6 rm ☑ 12.50/27.00 st.

FIAT Manor Cres. ℰ 32356

GRAEMSAY (Isle of) Orkney. (Orkney Islands) **401** K 7 – Shipping Services : see Orkney Islands.

GRANGEMOUTH Stirling. (Central) **401** I 15 – see Falkirk.

 Moray. (Highland) 401 J 12 – pop. 1 800 – ECD : Thursday – ☎ 0479.

�)8 Golf Course Rd ℰ 2079, East town boundary.

🔋 54 High St. ℰ 2773.

◆Edinburgh 143 – ◆Inverness 34 – Perth 99.

🏠 **Garth,** The Square, PH26 3HN, ℰ 2836, ☜ – ✕ rest 📺 ☎ 🅿. 🔳 ⓞ *VISA*. ❄
M (bar lunch)/dinner 15.00 **t.** and a la carte ⑂ 3.25 – **14 rm** ☷ 30.00/60.00 **t.**

⌂ **Crann Tara,** High St., PH26 3EN, ℰ 2197, ☜ – ✕ rest 🅿. ❄
closed November – **M** 6.00 **s.** – **6 rm** ☷ 9.50/20.00 **s.**

AUSTIN-ROVER   Chapel Rd ℰ 2037   FORD   Woodland Service Centre ℰ 2289

 Bute. (Strathclyde) 401 402 F 16 – pop. 1 611 – ☎ 047 553 Millport.

🛥 by Caledonian MacBrayne : from Cumbrae Slip to Largs frequent services daily (10 mn).

 Berwick. (Borders) 401 402 M 16 – pop. 608 – ✉ Duns – ☎ 089 084 Leitholm.
Envir. : Manderston★, NE : 9 m. by B 6355 and A 6105.

◆Edinburgh 39 – ◆Newcastle-upon-Tyne 70.

🏛 **Purves Hall** 🦢, TD10 6UJ, SE : 4 m. by A 697 ℰ 558, 🏊 heated, ☜, park, ✕ – 📺 ☎ 🅿.
🔳 *VISA*. ❄
M 8.00/14.00 **t.** and a la carte ⑂ 4.00 – **7 rm** ☷ 28.00/58.00 **t.** – SB (November-June) 75.60/77.40 **st.**

 Dumfries. (Dumfries and Galloway) 401 K 19 – pop. 2 737 – ECD : Wednesday –
☎ 046 13 (3 fig.) or 0461 (5 fig.).

🔋 Annan Rd ℰ 37834 (summer only).

◆Edinburgh 91 – ◆Carlisle 10 – ◆Dumfries 24.

🏠 **Gretna Chase,** CA6 5JB, S : ¼ m. on B 721 ✉ Carlisle (Cumbria) ℰ 37517, ☜ – 📺 🅿.
🔳 ㏂ ⓞ *VISA*. ❄
M *(closed Bank Holidays lunch and Sunday)* a la carte 9.20/14.50 **t.** ⑂ 2.55 – **9 rm**
☷ 30.00/70.00 **t.**

🏠 **Travelodge** without rest, A 74 Trunk Rd, Gretna Green ✉ Carlise (Cumbria), CA6 5HQ,
NW : 1 ½ m. by B 721 on A 74 ℰ 37566 – 📺 ♿ 🅿. 🔳 ㏂ *VISA*
31 rm 21.50/27.00 **t.**

 E. Lothian. (Lothian) 401 L 15 – pop. 2 124 – ECD : Wednesday – ☎ 0620.
Envir. : Dirleton★ (Castle★) E : 2 m. by A 198.

�)8, 🇠8, 🇠8 ℰ 843115.

◆Edinburgh 19 – North Berwick 5.

🏛 **Greywalls** 🦢, Duncur Rd, Muirfield, EH31 2EG, ℰ 842144, Telex 72294, Fax 842241, ≤
gardens and golf course, « Lutyens house, gardens by Gertrude Jekyll », ✕ – ✕ rest 📺
☎ 🅿. 🔳 ㏂ ⓞ *VISA*
M 12.50/25.00 **t.** ⑂ 5.00 – **22 rm** ☷ 60.00/115.00 **t.**

✗ **La Potinière,** Main St., EH31 2AA, ℰ 843214 – 🅿
closed Saturday lunch, Wednesday, 1 week June and October – **M** (lunch only and Saturday
dinner)(booking essential) 13.50/21.00 **t.** ⑂ 3.50

at Dirleton NE : 2 m. by A 198 – ✉ ☎ 062 085 Dirleton :

✗✗ **Open Arms** with rm, EH39 5BG, ℰ 241, Fax 570, « Tastefully converted stone cottages »,
☜ – 📺 ☎ 🅿. 🔳 ㏂ ⓞ *VISA*
M 9.50/17.00 **t.** and a la carte ⑂ 5.50 – **7 rm** ☷ 55.00/88.00 **t.** – SB (30 October-
9 May) 80.00/90.00 **st.**

 E. Lothian. (Lothian) 401 L 16 Scotland G – pop. 7 988 – ECD : Thursday –
☎ 062 082.

See : Site★ – High Street★.

Envir. : Gifford★, S : 4 m. by B 8369 – Stenton★, E : 7 m. – Lennoxlove★, S : 1 m.

🇠8 Amisfield Park, ℰ 3627.

◆Edinburgh 17 – Hawick 53 – ◆Newcastle-upon-Tyne 101.

✗✗ **Brown's** with rm, 1 West Rd, EH41 3RD, ℰ 2254, ☜ – 📺 ☎ 🅿. 🔳 ㏂ *VISA*. ❄
M (dinner only and Sunday lunch)(booking essential)/dinner 18.50 **t.** – **5 rm** ☷ 42.75/56.75 **t.**

 Lanark. (strathclyde) 401 402 H 16 – ☎ 0698.
◆Edinburgh 38 – ◆Glasgow 12.

🏠 **Roadchef Lodge** without rest., M74 between junctions 6 and 5 (Northbound carriagway)
ℰ 891904, Fax 891682 – ✕ 📺 ☎ ♿ – ⛽ 30. 🔳 ㏂ ⓞ *VISA*. ❄
closed 25 December – **36 rm** 29.00/35.00 **st.**

HARRIS (Isle of) Inverness. (Outer Hebrides) (Western Isles) **401** Z 10 – pop. 2 137.
See : St. Clement's Church, Rodel (tomb★).

⛴ by Caledonian MacBrayne : from Kyles Scalpay to the Isle of Scalpay : Monday/Saturday 6-13 daily (restricted in winter) (10 mn) – from Tarbert to Uig (Isle of Skye) summer only : Monday/Saturday 1-2 daily (1 h 45 mn) – from Tarbert to Lochmaddy (Isle of Uist) summer only : Monday/Saturday 1-3 weekly (1 h 45 mn).

Scarista – ✉ ☎ 085 985 Scarista

Scarista House ⑤, PA85 3HX, from Tarbert, SW : 15 m. on A 859 ⌀ 238, ≤ beach and mountains, ☞ – ⇥ rest ☎ ℗
May-September – **M** *(closed lunch to non-residents)* (booking essential) (bar lunch)/dinner 18.00 **t.** ⛴ 3.50 – **7 rm** ⊑ 47.00/70.00 **t.**

Tarbert – pop. 479 – ECD : Thursday – ✉ ☎ 0859 Harris.
🛈 ⌀ 2011 (summer only).

Harris, PA85 3DL, ⌀ 2154, Fax 2281, ☞ – ⇥ rest ℗. *VISA*
M 7.00/13.50 **st.** and a la carte ⛴ 2.95 – **24 rm** ⊑ 22.00/49.50 **t.** – SB (except June-August) (weekends only) 58.50/66.40 **st.**

HAWICK Roxburgh. (Borders) **401** **402** L 17 Scotland G – pop. 16 213 – ECD : Tuesday – ☎ 0450.

Envir. : Jedburgh★ (Abbey★★-Mary Queen of Scots House★-Canongate Bridge★) NE : 11 m. by A 698 and B 6358 – Waterloo Monument (❊★★) NE : 12 m. by A 698, A 68 and B 6400 – Hermitage Castle★, S : 16 m. by B 6399.

🛈 Vertish Hill ⌀ 72293, S : 1 ½ m.
🛈 Common Haugh, Car Park ⌀ 72547 (summer only).
♦Edinburgh 51 – ♦Ayr 122 – ♦Carlisle 44 – ♦Dumfries 63 – Motherwell 76 – ♦Newcastle-upon-Tyne 62.

Kirklands, West Stewart Pl., TD9 8BH, ⌀ 72263, ☞ – 📺 ☎ ℗. 🖅 AE ⓄⅠ *VISA*
closed 25-26 December and 1 January – **M** 7.95/11.95 **t.** and a la carte ⛴ 3.50 – **13 rm** ⊑ 30.00/50.00 **t.** – SB (October-June) (weekends only) 48.00/50.00 **st.**

PEUGEOT-TALBOT 29 Commercial Rd ⌀ 72287   ⓦ ATS Victoria Rd ⌀ 73369
VW-AUDI Commercial Rd ⌀ 73211

HEITON Roxburgh. (Borders) – see Kelso.

HELENSBURGH Dunbarton. (Strathclyde) **401** F 15 – pop. 16 432 – ECD : Wednesday – ☎ 0436.
See : Hill House★.
Envir. : Loch Lomond★★, NE : 5 m. by B 832.
⛴ by Caledonian MacBrayne and Clyde Marine Motoring Co. Ltd. to Gourock via Kilcreggan : 3-8 daily (40 mn).
🛈 The Clock Tower, ⌀ 2642 (summer only).
♦Edinburgh 68 – ♦Glasgow 22.

Commodore, 112 West Clyde St., G84 8ES, ⌀ 6924, Telex 778740, ≤ – 🛗 📺 ☎ ℗ – 🕭 150
45 rm, **1 suite**.

at Rhu NW : 2 m. on A 814 – ✉ ☎ 0436 Rhu :

Rosslea Hall (Best Western) ⑤, Ferry Rd, G84 8NF, ⌀ 820684, Telex 778695, Fax 820897, ≤, ☞ – 📺 ☎ � ℗ – 🕭 70. 🖅 AE Ⓞ *VISA*
M 6.95/12.75 **t.** and a la carte ⛴ 3.00 – **31 rm** ⊑ 52.00/69.00 **t.** – SB (weekends only) 84.00 **st.**

RENAULT 103 East Clyde St. ⌀ 76021   TOYOTA 5-7 John Street ⌀ 72779

HILLSWICK Shetland. (Shetland Islands) **401** P 2 – see Shetland Islands (Mainland).

HOY (Isle of) Orkney. (Orkney Islands) **401** K 7 – see Orkney Islands.

INVERCRERAN Argyll. (Strathclyde) **401** E 14 – ✉ ☎ 063 173 Appin.
♦Edinburgh 142 – Fort William 29 – ♦Oban 19.

Invercreran Country House ⑤, Glen Creran, PA38 4BJ, ⌀ 414, ≤ Glen Creran and mountains, ☞, park – ⇥ 📺 ☎ ℗. 🖅 *VISA*
March-November – **M** 14.00/20.00 **st.** ⛴ 5.50 – **7 rm** ⊑ 55.00/100.00 **st.** – SB (October-April) 90.00/103.50 **st.**

INVERMORISTON Inverness. (Highland) **401** G 12 – ☎ 0320 Glenmoriston.
See : Loch Ness★★.
♦Edinburgh 168 – ♦Inverness 29 – Kyle of Lochalsh 56.

Glenmoriston Arms, IV3 6YA, ⌀ 51206, ☜ – 📺 ☎ ℗. 🖅 *VISA*
M a la carte 12.90/14.40 **t.** ⛴ 3.90 – **8 rm** ⊑ 32.00/50.00 **t.** – SB (October-March) (except Christmas and New Year) 60.00/65.00 **st.**

584

INVERNESS Inverness. (Highland) **401** H 11 **Scotland G** – pop. 38 204 – ECD : Wednesday – ✆ 0463 – **See** : Site★ – Museum and Art Gallery★ **M**.

Envir. : Loch Ness★★ by A 82 – Loch Ness Monster Exhibition★ – Cawdor Castle★, E : 14 m. by A 82, A 96 and B 9090 – Clava Cairns★, E : 10 m. by B 9006 – Culloden Moor, E : 6 m. by B 9006 – Fortrose (Cathedral Site★) N : 16 m. by B 865, A 9 and A 832.

⛳ ✆ 239882, S : 1 m. by Culcabock Rd – ⛳ Torvean, Glenurquhart Rd ✆ 237543, W : 1 m.

✈ Dalcross Airport : ✆ 232471, NE : 8 m. by A 96 – 🚗 ✆ 0345 090700.

🛈 23 Church St. ✆ 234353.

♦Edinburgh 156 – ♦Aberdeen 107 – ♦Dundee 134.

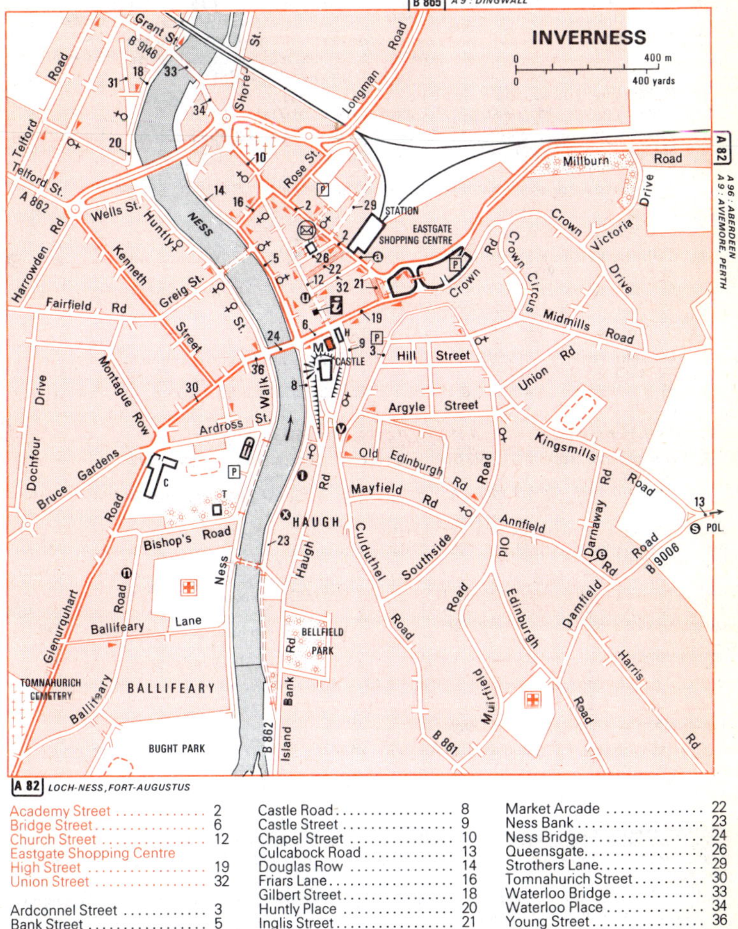

Academy Street	2	Castle Road	8	Market Arcade	22
Bridge Street	6	Castle Street	9	Ness Bank	23
Church Street	12	Chapel Street	10	Ness Bridge	24
Eastgate Shopping Centre		Culcabock Road	13	Queensgate	26
High Street	19	Douglas Row	14	Strothers Lane	29
Union Street	32	Friars Lane	16	Tomnahurich Street	30
		Gilbert Street	18	Waterloo Bridge	33
Ardconnel Street	3	Huntly Place	20	Waterloo Place	34
Bank Street	5	Inglis Street	21	Young Street	36

🏨 **Kingsmills** (Swallow), Culcabock Rd, IV2 3LP, ✆ 237166, Telex 75566, Fax 225208, 🏊, 🐎 – ⛲ rm 📺 ☎ 🅿. 🔒 AE ⓓ VISA   **s**
M (lunch by arrangement)/dinner 14.75 **st.** and a la carte ♟ 4.50 – **62 rm** ⊋ 54.00/92.00 **st.**, **6 suites** 140.00/180.00 **st.** – SB (except Easter, Christmas and New Year) (weekends only) 89.00/100.00 **st.**

🏨 **Caledonian** (Embassy), 33 Church St., IV1 1DX, ✆ 235181, Telex 75232, Fax 711206, 🔲 – 🔁 ⛲ rm 📺 ☎ 🅿 – 🔒 300. 🔒 AE ⓓ VISA   **u**
M (carving lunch) 6.50/13.50 **st.** and a la carte ♟ 6.40 – ⊋ 6.50 – **96 rm** 57.00/76.00 **st.**, **4 suites** 152.00 **st.** – SB (weekends only) 59.00/84.00 **st.**

INVERNESS

Station, 16-18 Academy St., IV1 1LG, ☎ 231926, Telex 75275, Fax 710705 – 🛗 📺 ☎ – 🛎
50. 🅿 AE ⓞ VISA
    a
M (buffet lunch)/dinner 15.50 t. and a la carte ↥ 4.50 – **67 rm** ☲ 55.00/80.00 t.

Mercury (Mt. Charlotte), Millburn Rd, IV2 3TR, E : by A 96 at junction A 9 and A 96
☎ 239666, Telex 75377 – 🛗 📺 ☎ 🅿 – 🛎 250
M (carving rest.) – **120 rm**.

Craigmonie (Best Western), 9 Annfield Rd, IV2 3HX, ☎ 231649, Telex 94013304, Fax 233720
– 🛗 ⇔ rm 📺 ☎ 🅿 – 🛎 100. 🅿 AE ⓞ VISA ⚘
    e
M 11.50/15.00 t. and a la carte ↥ 4.00 – **30 rm** ☲ 51.00/84.00 t., **3 suites** 96.00/110.00 t. –
SB (weekends only) 84.00/92.00 st.

Glenmoriston, 20 Ness Bank, IV2 4SF, ☎ 223777, 🦐 – 📺 ☎ 🅿. 🅿 AE VISA ⚘
    x
M (lunch by arrangement)/dinner 13.50 st. and a la carte ↥ 3.60 – **20 rm** ☲ 37.50/75.00 st.

Glen Mhor, 9-12 Ness Bank, IV2 4SG, ☎ 234308 – 📺 ☎ 🅿. 🅿 AE ⓞ VISA
    i
closed 31 December-2 January – **M** 17.50 t. (dinner) and a la carte – **31 rm** ☲ 20.00/80.00 t.
– SB (mid September-mid June) (weekends only) 30.00/52.00 st.

Ballifeary House, 10 Ballifeary Rd, IV3 5PJ, ☎ 235572, 🦐 – ⇔ 📺 🅿. ⚘
    n
April-October – **M** 9.00 st. ↥ 3.00 – **8 rm** ☲ 19.00/38.00 st.

Firs without rest., Dores Rd, IV2 4QU, S : 1 ¼ m. on B 862 ☎ 225197, ≼, « Antique furnishings », 🦐 – ⇔ 🅿. ⚘
5 rm ☲ 30.00/40.00 st.

Craigside Lodge without rest., 4 Gordon Terr., IV2 3HD, ☎ 231576, ≼ – 📺
    v
6 rm ☲ 20.00/32.00 st.

at Culloden E : 3 m. by A 96 – ✉ ☎ 0463 Inverness :

Culloden House ⑤, IV1 2NZ, ☎ 790461, Telex 75402, Fax 792181, ≼, 🦐, park, 🎾 – 📺
☎ 🅿. 🅿 AE ⓞ VISA ⚘
M 27.50 t. (dinner) and a la carte 12.40/23.80 t. ↥ 4.60 – **19 rm** ☲ 85.00/145.00 t., **1 suite**
155.00 t. – SB (November-April) 130.00/150.00 st.

at Dunain Park SW : 2 ½ m. on A 82 – ✉ ☎ 0463 Inverness :

Dunain Park ⑤, IV3 6JN, ☎ 230512, ≼, « Country house and gardens », park – ⇔ rest
📺 ☎ 🅿. 🅿 AE ⓞ VISA
M 14.50/22.50 t. ↥ 4.00 – **6 rm** ☲ 75.00/99.00 t., **2 suites** 99.00 t. – SB (November-
March) 125.00 st.

at Bunchrew W : 3 m. on A 862 – ✉ ☎ 0463 Inverness :

Bunchrew House ⑤, IV3 6TA, ☎ 234917, ≼ Beauly Firth, 🐟, 🦐, park – ⇔ 📺 ☎ 🅿.
🅿 AE VISA
closed mid November-mid December – **M** 9.50/18.50 t. ↥ 3.50 – **6 rm** ☲ 48.75/95.00 t. –
SB 102.00/150.00 st.

AUSTIN-ROVER, DAIMLER-JAGUAR, LAND-
ROVER, RANGE-ROVER, ROLLS-ROYCE 66 Har-
bour Rd ☎ 220011
BMW Harbour Rd ☎ 236566
FIAT, LANCIA 8 Tomnahurich St. ☎ 235777
FORD Harbour Rd ☎ 710000
LADA, MITSUBISHI Harbour Rd ☎ 226226

PEUGEOT-TALBOT Harbour Rd ☎ 231536
RENAULT 16 Telford St. ☎ 222848
VAUXHALL-OPEL 112 Academy St. ☎ 234311
VOLVO Harbour Rd ☎ 230885
VW-AUDI Harbour Rd ☎ 231313

ⓐ ATS Carsegate Rd North, The Carse ☎ 236167

INVERURIE Aberdeen. (Grampian) 401 M 12 – pop. 7 701 – ECD : Wednesday – ☎ 0467.
Envir. : Fyvie Castle* N 13 m. by B 9170 and A 47 – 🐓 Davah Wood, Blackhall Rd ☎ 24080.
🅹 Town Hall, Market Pl. ☎ 20600.
♦Edinburgh 147 – ♦Aberdeen 17 – ♦Inverness 90.

Strathburn, Burghmuir Drive, AB5 9GY, ☎ 24422, Fax 25133, 🦐 – 📺 ☎ 🦽 🅿. 🅿 AE VISA
⚘
M (bar lunch)/dinner 13.75 st. and a la carte ↥ 3.75 – **15 rm** ☲ 30.00/52.00 st. – SB
(weekends only) 62.75/72.75 st.

IONA (Isle of) Argyll. (Strathclyde) 401 A 15 Scotland G – pop. 268 – ☎ 068 17.
See : Site* – Maclean's Cross* – St. Oran's Chapel* – St. Martin's Cross* – Infirmary
Museum*.

🛳 by Caledonian MacBrayne : to Fionnphort (Isle of Mull) frequent services daily in summer,
restricted service in winter (5 mn).

Argyll ⑤, PA76 6SJ, ☎ 334, ≼ Sound of Iona and Mull, 🦐 – ⇔ rest. 🅿 VISA
Mid April-late October – **M** 11.00 t. (dinner) and a la carte ↥ 3.00 – **19 rm** ☲ 20.00/48.00 t.

IRVINE Ayr. (Strathclyde) 401 402 F 17 – pop. 32 507 – ☎ 0294.
🐓 Bogside ☎ 78139 – 🐓 Kilwinning Rd ☎ 79550 – 🐓 Gailes-by-Irvine ☎ 311357.
♦Edinburgh 75 – Ayr 14 – ♦Glasgow 29.

Hospitality Inn (Mt. Charlotte), Roseholm, Annick Water, KA11 4LD, E : ¾ m. on A 71
☎ 74272, Telex 777097, « Exotic indoor garden with 🏊 » – 📺 ☎ 🦽 🅿 – 🛎 250
128 rm.

ⓐ ATS 9 Kyle Rd, Ind. Est. ☎ 78727

ISLAY (Isle of) Argyll. (Strathclyde) **401** B 16 – pop. 3 997.

✈ Port Ellen Airport : ℰ 0496 (Port Ellen) 2361.

🛥 by Western Ferries : from Port Askaig to Feolin (Isle of Jura) 2-4 daily (5-mn) – by Caledonian MacBrayne : from Port Ellen to Kennacraig (Kintyre Peninsula) 1-2 daily (2 h 20 mn) – from Port Askaig to Kennacraig (Kintyre Peninsula) Monday/Saturday 1-2 daily (2 h).

🛈 at Bowmore, The Square ℰ 049 681 (Bowmore) 254 (summer only).

Port Askaig – ECD : Tuesday – ✉ ☎ 049 684 Port Askaig.

🏠 **Port Askaig**, PA46 7RD, ℰ 245, ← Sound of Islay and Jura, 🚗 – 📺 ℗
M (bar lunch)/dinner 10.00 **st.** ⌕ 3.85 – **9 rm** ⌕ 22.00/44.00 **st.** – SB (weekdays only) 57.00/62.00 **st.**

ISLEORNSAY Inverness. (Highland) **401** C 12 – see Skye (Isle of).

JEDBURGH Roxburgh. (Borders) **401 402** M 17 Scotland G – pop. 4 053 – ECD : Thursday – ☎ 0835.

See : Site★ – Abbey★★ – Mary Queen of Scots House★ – Canongate Bridge★.

Envir. : Waterloo Monument (⚹★★) N : 3 m. by A 68 and B 6400.

🏌 Dunion Rd ℰ 63587, W : 1 m.

🛈 Murray's Green ℰ 63435/63688 (summer only).

♦Edinburgh 48 – ♦Carlisle 54 – ♦Newcastle-upon-Tyne 57.

*Hotel and restaurant see : **Melrose** NW : 12 m.*

JOHN O'GROATS Caithness. (Highland) **401** K 8 – Shipping Services : see Orkney Islands.

JURA (Isle of) Argyll. (Strathclyde) **401** C 15 – pop. 239.

🛥 by Western Ferries : from Feolin to Port Askaig (Isle of Islay) 2-4 daily (5-mn).

Craighouse – ECD : Tuesday – ✉ ☎ 049 682 Jura.

🏠 Jura 🦢, PA60 7XU, ℰ 243, ← Small Isles Bay, 🎣, 🚗 – ℗ – **16 rm, 1 suite**.

KELSO Roxburgh. (Borders) **401 402** M 17 Scotland G – pop. 5 547 – ECD : Wednesday – ☎ 0573.

See : Site★ – Market Square★★ – ←★ from Kelso Bridge.

Envir. : Mellerstain★★ (ceilings★★★-Library★★★) NW : 6 m. by A 6089 – Floors Castle★, NW : 2 m. by A 6089 – Smailholm Tower★ (⚹★★) NW : 6 m. by A 6089 and B 6397 – Ladykirk (Kirk O'Steil★) NE : 16 m. by A 698, A 697, A 6112 and B 6437 – Flodden Field, NE : 11 m. by A 698 and A 697.

🏌 Racecourse Rd ℰ 23009.

🛈 Turret House ℰ 23464 (summer only).

♦Edinburgh 44 – Hawick 21 – ♦Newcastle-upon-Tyne 68.

🏨 **Ednam House**, Bridge St., TD5 7HT, ℰ 24168, ←, 🚗 – 📺 ☎ ℗. **VISA**
closed 24 December-12 January – M (bar lunch Monday to Saturday)/dinner 14.00 **t.** ⌕ 3.00 – **32 rm** ⌕ 27.00/65.00 **t.** – SB 65.00/85.00 **st.**

at Heiton SW : 3 m. by A 698 – ✉ Kelso – ☎ 057 35 Roxburgh :

🏨 **Sunlaws House** 🦢, TD5 8JZ, ℰ 331, Telex 728147, Fax 011, ←, « Victorian country house », 🎣, 🚗, park, ✕ – 📺 ☎ ℗. 🆔 🆎 ⓪ **VISA**. 🐾
M *(closed lunch Saturday and Sunday)* 13.75 **t.** (lunch) and a la carte 18.20/23.85 **t.** ⌕ 3.75 – **21 rm** ⌕ 50.00/130.00 **t.** – SB (except Christmas and New Year) 110.00/125.00 **st.**

at Eckford SW : 4 ½ m. by A 698 – ✉ Kelso – ☎ 057 34 Morebattle :

✕✕ **Marlefield Country House** 🦢 with rm, TD5 8ED, NE : 2 m. on B 6401 ℰ 561, ←, 🚗 – 📺 ☎ ℗. 🆔 🆎 ⓪ **VISA**
M 8.00/13.50 **t.** and a la carte ⌕ 4.95 – **6 rm** ⌕ 45.00/100.00 **t.** – SB (November-March) (except Christmas and New Year) 70.00/90.00 **st.**

AUSTIN-ROVER, JAGUAR Bridge St. ℰ 24345   ⊕ ATS The Butts ℰ 24997/8
PEUGEOT-TALBOT Sheddon Par. Rd ℰ 24488
RENAULT Golf Course Rd ℰ 24720

KENMORE Perth. (Tayside) **401** I 14 – ECD : Thursday except summer – ✉ Aberfeldy – ☎ 088 73.

See : Site★.

Envir. : Loch Tay★★ – Ben Lawers★★, SW : 8 m. by A 827.

🏌 Taymouth Castle ℰ 228.

♦Edinburgh 82 – ♦Dundee 60 – ♦Oban 71 – Perth 38.

🏨 **Kenmore**, PH15 2NU, ℰ 205, Fax 262, 🏌, 🎣, 🚗 – 📧 ✕ rest 📺 ☎ ℗. 🆔 🆎 ⓪ **VISA**. 🐾
M 15.00 **st.** (dinner) and a la carte 7.60/21.25 **st.** ⌕ 4.25 – ⌕ 5.00 – **38 rm** 35.00/75.00 **st.** – SB 75.00/105.00 **st.**

KENNACRAIG Argyll. (Strathclyde) 401 D 16 – Shipping Services : see Kintyre (Peninsula).

KENSALEYRE Inverness. (Highland) 401 B 11 – see Skye (Isle of).

KENTALLEN Argyll. (Highland) 401 E 14 – ✆ 063 174 Duror.
♦Edinburgh 123 – Fort William 17 – ♦Oban 33.

- **Ardsheal House** ⌂, PA38 4BX, SW : ¾ m. by A 828 ☎ 227, ≼, « Country house in lochside setting », ☞, park, ✗ – ✗ rest ⓟ. ◪ ⅍ *VISA*
April-October – **M** 10.50/25.00 t. – **13 rm** � 70.00/136.00 t.

- ✗✗ **Holly Tree** with rm, Kentallen Pier, PA38 4BY, ☎ 292, Fax 345, ≼ Loch Linnhe and mountains, ☞ – ✗ rest ⓣⓥ ☎ ⅌ ⓟ. ◪ *VISA*
April-October – **M** 10.00/21.50 t. and a la carte ⌘ 4.00 – **10 rm** ⊊ 37.00/68.00 t.

KILCHOAN Argyll. (Highland) 401 B 13 – ✉ Acharacle – ✆ 097 23.
⛴ by Caledonian MacBrayne : to Tobermory (Isle of Mull) summer only Monday/Saturday 3-6 daily (35 mn).
♦Edinburgh 163 – ♦Inverness 120 – ♦Oban 92.

KILCHRENAN Argyll. (Strathclyde) 401 E 14 – ✉ Taynuilt – ✆ 086 63.
♦Edinburgh 117 – ♦Glasgow 87 – ♦Oban 18.

- **Ardanaiseig** ⌂, PA35 1HE, NE : 4 m. ☎ 333, Fax 222, ≼ gardens and Loch Awe, « Country house in extensive informal gardens on Loch Awe », ⌕, park, ✗ – ⓣⓥ ☎ ⓟ. ◪ ⅍ ⓓ *VISA*
Easter-late October – **M** 15.00/35.00 t. and a la carte – **13 rm** ⊊ (dinner included) 82.50/180.00 t., **1 suite** – SB 60.50/82.50 st.

- **Taychreggan** ⌂, Lochaweside, PA35 1HQ, SE : 1 ¼ m. ☎ 211, ≼ Loch Awe, « Lochside setting », ⌕, ☞, park – ⓟ. ◪ ⅍ *VISA*
29 March-October – **M** (bar lunch)/dinner 20.00 t. ⌘ 4.50 – **16 rm** ⊊ 56.00/68.00 t.

KILCREGGAN Dunbarton. (Strathclyde) 401 F 16 – Shipping Services : see Gourock.

KILDRUMMY Aberdeen. (Grampian) 401 L 12 Scotland G – ✉ Alford – ✆ 033 65 (from spring : 097 56).
See : Castle★.
Envir. : Craigievar Castle★★★, SE : 13 m. by A 944 and A 980 – Huntly Castle (Heraldic carvings★★) N : 15 m. by A 97.
♦Edinburgh 137 – ♦Aberdeen 35.

- **Kildrummy Castle** (Best Western) ⌂, AB3 8RA, S : 1 ¼ m. on A 97 ☎ 71288, Telex 94012529, Fax 71345, ≼ gardens and Kildrummy Castle, « 19C mansion in extensive park », ⌕ – ✗ rest ⓣⓥ ☎ ⓟ. ◪ ⅍ *VISA*
M 11.00/18.50 t. and a la carte ⌘ 4.00 – **16 rm** ⊊ 43.00/84.00 t. – SB (except summer) 84.00/90.00 st.

KILFINAN Argyll. (Strathclyde) 401 E 16 – ✉ Tighnabruaich – ✆ 070 082.
♦Edinburgh 124 – ♦Glasgow 78 – ♦Oban 78.

- ✗✗ **Kilfinan** ⌂ with rm, Tighnabruaich, PA21 2AP, ☎ 201, Fax 205, ☞ – ✗ rest ⓣⓥ ☎ ⓟ. ◪ ⅍ *VISA*
M 20.00 t. and a la carte 17.50/23.00 t. ⌘ 3.60 – ⊊ 6.00 – **11 rm** 32.00/44.00 t.

KILLIECRANKIE Perth. (Tayside) 401 I 13 – see Pitlochry.

KILLIN Perth. (Central) 401 H 14 – pop. 545 – ECD : Wednesday – ✆ 056 72.
Envir. : Loch Tay★★, Ben Lawers★★, NE : 8 m. by A 827 – Kenmore★, NE : 17 m. by A 827.
🛈 ☎ 312.
🛈 Main St. ☎ 254 (summer only).
♦Edinburgh 72 – ♦Dundee 65 – Perth 43 – ♦Oban 54.

- **Morenish Lodge** ⌂, FK21 8TX, NE : 2 ½ m. on A 827 ☎ 258, ≼ Loch Tay and hills, ⌕, ☞, ✗ – ⓟ. ◪ *VISA* ⌖
Mid April-October – **M** *(closed lunch to non-residents)* (bar lunch)/dinner 14.50 st. ⌘ 2.50 – **13 rm** ⊊ 21.00/42.00 st.

- **Fairview House,** Main St., FK21 8UT, ☎ 667 – ⓟ
M 6.50 t. – **7 rm** ⊊ 11.00/26.00 t.

- **Dall Lodge,** Main St., FK21 8TN, N : ¼ m. on A 827 ☎ 217, ⌕ – ✗ ☎ ⓟ. ◪ *VISA*
M 14.50 st. – **8 rm** ⊊ 20.00/55.00 st.

at Ardeonaig NE : 7 ¼ m. – ✉ ✆ 056 72 Killin :

- **Ardeonaig** ⌂, South Loch Tayside, FK21 8SU, ☎ 400, ⌕, ☞, park – ⓟ. ◪ ⅍ ⓓ *VISA*
closed 15 November-10 January – **M** (bar lunch)/dinner 17.00 t. – **12 rm** ⊊ 22.00/44.00 t. – SB 57.00/67.00 st.

KILMARNOCK Ayr. (Strathclyde) **401 402** G 17 **Scotland G** – pop. 51 799 – ECD : Wednesday – ✆ 0563.

See : Dean Castle (Arms and armour collection* – musical instruments*).

⛳ Annanhill, Irvine Rd ✆ 21644, W : 1 m. – ⛳ Caprington, Ayr Rd ✆ 23702.

🛈 62 Bank St., ✆ 39090.

◆Edinburgh 62 – ◆Ayr 13 – ◆Dumfries 58 – ◆Glasgow 22.

🏨 **Howard Park** (Swallow), 136 Glasgow Rd, KA3 1UT, N : 2 m. on B 7038 ✆ 31211, Group Telex 53168, Fax 27795 – 📺 rm ☎ 🅿 – 🔬 150. 🔼 AE ⓪ VISA
M 7.50 **st.** (lunch) and a la carte 14.25/20.95 **st.** ⓵ 4.50 – **46 rm** ⌁ 45.00/85.00 **st.** – SB (weekends only) 62.00/68.00 **st.**

⊚ ATS Riccarton Rd, Hurlford ✆ 20111

KILNINVER Argyll. (Strathclyde) **401** D 14 – see Oban.

KINCLAVEN Perth. (Tayside) **401** J 14 – ✉ Stanley – ✆ 025 083 Meikleour.

◆Edinburgh 56 – Perth 12.

🏨 **Ballathie House** (Best Western) 🦢, PH1 4QN, ✆ 268, Telex 76216, Fax 396, ≤, « Country house in extensive grounds on banks of River Tay », 🎣, 🛶, park, ✂ – 📺 ☎ 🅿. 🔼 AE ⓪ VISA. 🛥
closed 27 January-10 March – **M** *(restricted service November-March)* 10.75/18.00 **t.** and a la carte 18.00/25.00 **t.** ⓵ 3.80 – **22 rm** ⌁ 38.00/105.00 **t.** – SB (mid October-July) 106.00/137.00 **st.**

KINCRAIG Inverness. (Highland) **401** I 12 – ECD : Wednesday – ✉ Kingussie – ✆ 054 04.

◆Edinburgh 119 – ◆Inverness 37 – Perth 75.

🏨 **Ossian**, PH21 1NA, ✆ 242, ≤, 🛶, 🚲 – 🅿. 🔼 AE VISA
closed January and November – **M** (bar lunch)/dinner 15.00 st. and a la carte ⓵ 3.00 – **9 rm** ⌁ 18.00/36.00 **st.**

KINGUSSIE Inverness. (Highland) **401** H 12 – pop. 1 140 – ECD : Wednesday – ✆ 0540.

⛳ ✆ 661374, N : ½ m. from town shops by A 9.

🛈 Caledonia Buildings, King St. ✆ 661297 (summer only).

◆Edinburgh 117 – ◆Inverness 41 – Perth 73.

↟ **Homewood Lodge**, Newtonmore Rd, PH21 1HD, ✆ 661507, ≤, 🚲 – 📺 rest 🅿
M 11.95 **st.** ⓵ 3.50 – **5 rm** ⌁ 15.00/30.00 **st.**

XX **The Cross** with rm, 25-27 High St., PH21 1HX, ✆ 661762 – 📺. 🛥
closed Sunday, Monday, 3 weeks May and 3 weeks December – **M** (booking essential) (dinner only) 25.00 **t.** ⓵ 2.00 – **3 rm** –/50.00 **t.**

X **Osprey** with rm, Ruthven Rd, PH21 1EN, ✆ 661510 – 🅿. 🔼 AE ⓪ VISA
closed November -27 December – **M** (dinner only) 17.00 **t.** ⓵ 3.00 – **8 rm** ⌁ 22.00/60.00 **t.**

KINLOCHBERVIE Sutherland. (Highland) **401** E 8 – ECD : Wednesday – ✉ Lairg – ✆ 097 182.

Envir. : Cape Wrath★★★ (❄★★) SE : 28 ½ m. by B 801 and A 838.

◆Edinburgh 276 – Thurso 93 – Ullapool 61.

🏨 **Kinlochbervie** 🦢, IV27 4RP, ✆ 275, Fax 438, ≤ Loch Inchard and sea – 📺 rest 📺 ☎ 🅿. 🔼 VISA
closed 2 January-23 February – **M** (booking essential) (bar lunch)/dinner 24.50 **st.** ⓵ 6.50 – **14 rm** ⌁ 53.00/83.00 **st.** – SB 44.00/66.00 **st.**

KINROSS Kinross. (Tayside) **401** J 15 – pop. 3 493 – ECD : Thursday – ✆ 0577.

⛳ Green Hotel, ✆ 63467 – ⛳ Beeches Park ✆ 62237 – ⛳ Milnathort ✆ 64069, N : 2 m.

🛈 Kinross Service Area (off junction 6, M 90) ✆ 63680 (summer only).

◆Edinburgh 28 – Dunfermline 13 – Perth 18 – Stirling 25.

🏨 **Windlestrae**, The Muirs, KY13 7AS, ✆ 63217, Fax 64733, 🚲 – 📺 ☎ 🅿 – 🔬. 🔼 AE ⓪ VISA
M 8.95/12.50 **t.** and a la carte ⓵ 3.20 – **18 rm** ⌁ 44.00/65.00 **t.** – SB (weekends only) (except Easter and New Year) 140.00/170.00 **st.**

🏨 **Green** (Best Western), 2 The Muirs, KY13 7AS, ✆ 63467, Telex 76684, Fax 64525, « Gardens », 🔲, ⛳, 🛶, squash – 📺 ☎ 🅿 – 🔬 120. 🔼 AE ⓪ VISA
M (bar lunch)/dinner 16.00 **st.** and a la carte ⓵ 4.00 – **40 rm** ⌁ 48.00/80.00 **st.** – SB (except Christmas and New Year) 80.00/90.00 **st.**

🏠 Granada Lodge without rest., Kincardine Rd, KY13 7NQ, W : 1 m. by A 922 on A 977 ✆ 64646, Fax 64108 – 📺 rm 📺 ☎ 🅿
34 rm.

at Cleish SW : 4 ½ m. by B 996 off B 9097 – ✉ Kinross – ✆ 057 75 Cleish Hills :

🏨 **Nivingston House** 🦢, KY13 7LS, ✆ 216, Fax 238, ≤, 🚲 – 📺 ☎ 🅿. 🔼 AE VISA
M 13.50/21.50 **t.** ⓵ 4.50 – **17 rm** ⌁ 50.00/100.00 **t.** – SB (weekends only) 80.00/110.00 **st.**

FORD High St. ✆ 62424

KINTYRE (Peninsula) Argyll. (Strathclyde) **401** D 16 17 Scotland G.
See : Carradale★ – Saddell (grave stones★).

✈ at Campbeltown (Machrihanish Airport) : ✆ 0586 (Campbeltown) 53021.

⛴ by Caledonian MacBrayne : from Claonaig to Lochranza (Isle of Arran) summer only 8-10 daily (30 mn) – from Kennacraig to Port Ellen (Isle of Islay) 1-2 daily (2 h 20mn) – from Kennacraig to Port Askaig (Isle of Islay) Monday/Saturday 1-2 daily (2 h).

Bellochantuy – ✉ Campbeltown – ☎ 058 32 Glenbarr.

🏨 Putechan Lodge, PA28 6QE, on A 83 ✆ 323, ≤ – TV ☎ P
12 rm.

Campbeltown – ECD : Wednesday – ✉ ☎ 0586 Campbeltown.
🛈 ✆ 52056.
♦Edinburgh 176.

↑ **Seafield**, Kilkerran Rd, PA28 6JL, ✆ 54385, ⇌ – TV ☎ P. 🅰 VISA. ✵
M 11.50 s. ᛫3.00 – **9 rm** ⚬ 25.00/40.00 t.

🔟 ATS Burnside St. ✆ 54404

Carradale – ECD : Wednesday – ✉ ☎ 058 33 Carradale.
🛈 ✆ 624.
♦Edinburgh 164 – ♦Glasgow 121 – ♦Oban 74.

🏨 **Carradale**, PA28 6RY, ✆ 223, ≤, ⇌, squash – ⇌ rm P. 🅰 VISA
April-mid November – **M** 13.50 st. – **16 rm** ⚬ 26.00/62.00 st. – SB 58.00/80.00 st.

Machrihanish – pop. 540 – ✉ Campbeltown – ☎ 058 681 Machrihanish.
🛈, 🛈 ✆ 213.

↑ **Ardell House**, PA28 6PT, ✆ 235, ≤, ⇌ – TV P
closed Christmas and New Year – **M** 12.00 st. ᛫3.00 – **10 rm** ⚬ 18.00/40.00 st.

KIRKCALDY Fife. (Fife) **401** K 15 Scotland G – pop. 46 356 – ECD : Wednesday – ☎ 0592.
🛈 Balwearie ✆ 260370 – 🛈 Dunnikier Park, Dunnikier Way ✆ 261599, North boundary.
🛈 Esplanade ✆ 267775.
♦Edinburgh 27 – ♦Dundee 32 – ♦Glasgow 54.

at West Wemyss NE : 4 ½ m. by A 955 – ✉ ☎ 0592 Kirkcaldy :

🏨 **Belvedere** ⏚, Coxstool, KY1 4SN, ✆ 54167, ≤ – TV ☎ P. 🅰 VISA. ✵
closed 25 December-4 January – **M** (closed Sunday) 9.50/13.00 t. – **19 rm** ⚬ 36.00/48.00 t.,
1 suite 55.00 t.

AUSTIN-ROVER 27 Rosslyn St. ✆ 51997
BMW Bennochy Rd ✆ 262191
CITROEN, VAUXHALL-OPEL 24 Victoria Rd ✆ 264755

FORD Forth Av. ✆ 261199
HYUNDAI, SUZUKI Meldrum Rd ✆ 200354
SAAB 180-186 St. Clair St. ✆ 52291
VOLVO 8 Abbotshall Rd ✆ 262141

KIRKCUDBRIGHT Kirkcudbright. (Dumfries and Galloway) **401 402** H 19 Scotland G – pop. 3 352 – ECD : Thursday – ☎ 0557.
See : Site★.
Envir. : Dundrennan Abbey★, SE : 5 m. by A 711.
🛈 Stirling Cres. ✆ 30314.
🛈 Harbour Sq. ✆ 30494 (summer only).
♦Edinburgh 108 – ♦Dumfries 28 – Stranraer 50.

☖ **Selkirk Arms**, Old High St., DG6 4JG, ✆ 30402, ⇌ – TV ☎ P. 🅰 AE ⓞ VISA
M 12.00 st. (dinner) and a la carte 8.40/16.20 st. ᛫2.50 – **16 rm** ⚬ 25.00/53.00 st. – SB (except Christmas and New Year) 60.00/70.00 st.

AUSTIN-ROVER Mews Lane ✆ 30412

KIRKMICHAEL Perth. (Tayside) **401** J 13 – ✉ Blairgowrie – ☎ 025 081 Strathardle.
♦Edinburgh 74 – Perth 30 – Pitlochry 12.

🏨 **Log Cabin** ⏚, Blairgowrie, PH10 7NB, W : 1 m. ✆ 288, ≤, « Scandinavian pine chalet », ✵ – ᗃ P. 🅰 AE ⓞ VISA
M 14.95 t. (dinner) and lunch a la carte approx. 7.45 t. – **12 rm** ⚬ 30.95/41.90 t.

KIRKWALL Orkney. (Orkney Islands) **401** L 7 – see Orkney Islands (Mainland).

KYLEAKIN Inverness. (Highland) **401** C 12 – Shipping Services : see Skye (Isle of).

KYLE OF LOCHALSH Ross and Cromarty. (Highland) **401** C 12 **Scotland G** – pop. 803 – ECD : Thursday – ✆ 0599.

Envir. : Eilean Donan Castle★ (Site★★) E : 8 m. by A 87 – Plockton★, N : 6 m.

⛴ by Caledonian MacBrayne : to Kyleakin (Isle of Skye) frequent services daily (5 mn).

⛴ by Caledonian MacBrayne : to Mallaig: 3 weekly (summer only) (2 h).

🛈 ℰ 4276 (summer only).

◆Edinburgh 204 – ◆Dundee 182 – ◆Inverness 82 – ◆Oban 125.

🏨 **Lochalsh**, Ferry Rd, IV40 8AF, ℰ 4202, Telex 75318, ≤ Skye Ferry and hills – 🛗 📺 ☎ 🅿.
🔄 AE ⓪ VISA
M (buffet lunch)/dinner 15.00 **t.** and a la carte ⬧ 5.25 – **38 rm** ⊆ 50.00/125.00 **t.** – SB (except summer) 70.00/90.00 **st.**

FORD Main Rd ℰ 4329

KYLES SCALPAY Inverness. (Western Isles) (Highland) **401** Z 10 – Shipping Services : see Harris (Isle of).

LAGG Bute. (Strathclyde) – see Arran (Isle of).

LAGGAN Inverness. (Highland) **401** H 12 – ✉ Newtonmore – ✆ 052 84.

◆Edinburgh 110 – ◆Inverness 52 – Perth 66.

🏠 **Gaskmore House**, PH20 1BS, E : ¾ m. on A 86 ℰ 250, Fax 207, ≤ – ⇖ rest 📺 ☎ & 🅿.
🔄 AE VISA
M 10.00/17.00 **t.** and a la carte ⬧ 4.00 – **9 rm** ⊆ 25.00/50.00 **t.** – SB 70.00 **st.**

LAIDE Ross and Cromarty. (Highland) **401** D 10 – ✉ Achnasheen – ✆ 044 582 Aultbea.

Envir. : Inverewe Gardens★★★, S : 8 m. by A 832.

◆Edinburgh 232 – ◆Inverness 76.

Hotel see : Aultbea SW : 1 m.

LAIRG Sutherland. (Highland) **401** G 9 – pop. 628 – ECD : Wednesday – ✆ 0549.

🛈 ℰ 2160 (summer only).

◆Edinburgh 218 – ◆Inverness 61 – ◆Wick 72.

🏨 **Sutherland Arms**, IV27 4AT, ℰ 2291, ≤, ⚲, ≉ – 📺 🅿. 🔄 AE ⓪ VISA
March-September – **M** (bar lunch)/dinner 16.00 **t.** ⬧ 3.50 – **25 rm** ⊆ 41.00/71.00 **t.** – SB 74.00/84.00 **st.**

LAMLASH Bute. (Strathclyde) **401** E 17 – see Arran (Isle of).

LANARK Lanark. (Strathclyde) **401** **402** I 16 **Scotland G** – pop. 9 673 – ECD : Thursday – ✆ 0555 – **See : New Lanark★.**

🛈 Horsemarket, Ladyacre Rd ℰ 61661 (summer only).

◆Edinburgh 34 – ◆Carlisle 78 – ◆ Glasgow 28.

✕ **Ristorante La Vigna**, 40 Wellgate, ML11 9DT, ℰ 4320, Italian rest. – 🔄 AE ⓪ VISA
closed Sunday lunch, 8 to 14 January and first 3 weeks September – **M** (booking essential) a la carte 11.75/22.45 **t.** ⬧ 3.65.

CITROEN 30 West Port ℰ 2581

LANGBANK Renfrew. (Strathclyde) **401** G 16 – ECD : Saturday – ✆ 047 554.

◆Edinburgh 63 – ◆Glasgow 17 – Greenock 7.

🏨 **Gleddoch House** ⚘, PA14 6YE, SE : 1 m. by B 789 ℰ 711, Telex 779801, Fax 201, ≤ Clyde and countryside, 🏌, ⚲, ≉, park, squash – 📺 ☎ 🅿. 🔄 AE ⓪ VISA
M *(closed Saturday lunch)* 15.00/27.50 **t.** and a la carte ⬧ 4.50 – **33 rm** ⊆ 75.00/108.00 **t.**, **1 suite** 140.00 **t.**

LARGS Ayr. (Strathclyde) **401** **402** F 16 **Scotland G** – pop. 9 619 – ECD : Wednesday – ✆ 0475.
See : Skelmorlie Aisle★ (Monument★ and ceiling★).

🏌 Irvine Rd ℰ 673594, S : 1 m. – 🏌 Routenburn, ℰ 673230 – ⛴ by Caledonian MacBrayne : to Cumbrae Slip (Great Cumbrae Island) frequent services daily (10 mn).

🛈 Promenade ℰ 673765.

◆Edinburgh 76 – ◆Ayr 32 – ◆Glasgow 30.

🏛 **Glen Eldon**, 2 Barr Cres., KA30 8PX, ℰ 673381 – ⇖ rest 📺 🅿. 🔄 ✾
closed mid January-mid March – **M** (dinner only) 10.00 **t.** ⬧ 3.20 – **9 rm** ⊆ 23.00/42.00 **t.** – SB (except summer) 55.00/65.00 **st.**

↑ **Haylie**, 108 Irvine Rd, KA30 8EY, ℰ 673207, ≤ Firth of Clyde and Islands, ≉ – 📺 🅿. 🔄 AE ⓪ VISA
M (bar lunch)/dinner 15.25 **st.** ⬧ 2.50 – **8 rm** ⊆ 17.00/40.00 **st.** – SB (October-April) 80.00 **st.**

LAUDER Berwick. (Borders) **401** **402** L 16 Scotland G – pop. 799 – ECD : Thursday – ☎ 057 82.
See : Thirlestane Castle (Plasterwork ceilings★★).
ୖ₉ ♟ 381, W : ½ m.
♦Edinburgh 27 – Hawick 31 – ♦Newcastle-upon-Tyne 78.

♙ Black Bull, Market Pl., ♟ 208 – ℗
11 rm.

at Carfraemill N : 4 m. on A 68 – ⊠ Lauder – ☎ 057 85 Oxton :

▥ Carfraemill, TD2 6RA, ♟ 200, Fax 640 – TV ☎ ℗. ⤳ AE ⓞ VISA
accommodation closed 24 and 25 December – M (closed 25 December) a la carte
13.20/18.50 t. ⋀ 3.20 – 10 rm � 30.00/55.00 t. – SB 55.00/65.00 st.

LERWICK Shetland. (Shetland Islands) **401** Q 3 – see Shetland Islands (Mainland).

LESLIE Fife. (Fife) **401** K 15 – see Glenrothes.

LEVEN Fife. (Fife) **401** K 15 – pop. 8 596 – ECD : Thursday – ☎ 0333.
ୖ₁₈ Links Rd ♟ 29096.
🛈 South St. ♟ 29464.
♦Edinburgh 36 – ♦Dundee 23 – ♦Glasgow 65.

at Lundin Links E : 2 m. on A 915 – ⊠ ☎ 0333 Lundin Links :

▤ Old Manor, Leven Rd, KY8 6AJ, ♟ 320368, Telex 727606, ≤, ⤳ – TV ☎ ℗. ⤳ AE VISA
⤳
closed 1 and 2 January – M 8.65/15.10 t. and a la carte ⋀ 3.15 – 18 rm � 33.00/57.50 t. –
SB (winter only) (weekends only) 75.00/87.00 st.

AUSTIN-ROVER The Promenade ♟ 23449   FIAT Scoonie Rd ♟ 27003

LEWIS (Isle of) Ross and Cromarty. (Outer Hebrides) (Western Isles) **401** Z 8 Scotland G.
See : Callanish Standing Stones★★ – Carloway Broch★.
⛴ by Caledonian MacBrayne : from Stornoway to Ullapool Monday/Saturday 1-2 daily (3 h
30 mn).

Stornoway – pop. 8 660 – ECD : Wednesday – ⊠ ☎ 0851 Stornoway.
ୖ₁₈ Lady Lever Park ♟ 2240.
✈ Stornoway Airport : ♟ 2256 and 2281, Telex 75495, E : 2 ½ m. – Terminal : British
Airways, Cromwell St.
🛈 Area Tourist Officer, 4 South Beach St. ♟ 3088.

▥ Crown, Castle St., PA87 2XY, ♟ 3734 – TV ☎
15 rm.

Uig – ECD : Wednesday – ⊠ Uig – ☎ 085 175 Timsgarry.

▥ Baile-Na-Cille ⤳, Timsgarry, PA86 9JD, ♟ 242, ≤ Uig bay and mountains, ⤳ – ⤳ rest
℗
closed 20 October-10 January – M (lunch by arrangement) 15.00/16.00 st. ⋀ 3.25 – 12 rm
� 16.00/38.00 st.

AUSTIN-ROVER 11-16 Bayhead St. ♟ 3246   VAUXHALL-OPEL Bayhead St. ♟ 2888
FORD Sandwick Rd ♟ 5553

LEWISTON Inverness. (Highland) **401** G 12 – ☎ 045 62 Drumnadrochit.
See : Loch Ness★★.
♦Edinburgh 173 – ♦Inverness 17.

♙ Lewiston Arms, IV3 6UN, ♟ 225, ⤳ – ℗. VISA
M (bar lunch)/dinner a la carte 4.80/10.50 t. ⋀ 4.00 – 8 rm � 11.00/28.00 t.

LINLITHGOW W. Lothian. (Lothian) **401** J 16 – pop. 9 524 – ☎ 0506.
See : Site★★ – Linlithgow Palace★★ (gateway★, fountain★★, Great Hall : Fireplace★★) – Old
Town★ – St. Michaels Church★.
Envir. : Cairnpapple Hill★ S : 2 m..
ୖ₁₈ Braehead ♟ 842585, S : 1 m – ୖ₁₈ Avingath Hill ♟ 826030.
🛈 Burgh Halls, The Cross ♟ 844600.
♦Edinburgh 19 – Falkirk 9 – ♦Glasgow 35.

XXX Champany Inn, Champany, EH49 7LU, NE : 2 m. on A 803 at junction with A 904
♟ 050 683 (Philipstoun) 4532, « Converted horse-mill » – ℗. ⤳ AE ⓞ VISA
closed Saturday lunch, Sunday and 2 weeks Christmas – M (grill rest.) a la carte 20.50/30.00 t.

LISMORE (Isle of) Argyll. (Strathclyde) **401** D 14 – pop. 156.
⚓ by Caledonian MacBrayne : from Achnacroish to Oban Monday/Saturday 2-5 daily (50 mn).
⚓ to Port Appin Monday/Saturday 5 daily ; Sunday 4 daily (10 mn).

   Hotels see : Oban.

LIVINGSTON Midlothian. (Lothian) **401** J 16 – pop. 38 594 – ☎ 0506.
⌐₁₈ Carmowdean *ℰ* 38843.
♦Edinburgh 16 – Falkirk 23 – ♦Glasgow 32.

   🏨 **Hilton National** (Hilton), Almondview, Almondvale, EH54 6QB, *ℰ* 31222, Telex 727680, Fax 34666, ⧆ – ⤬ rm 📺 ☎ 🛦 ℗ – 🛎 140. ⚞ ⵄ ⓞ 𝗩𝗜𝗦𝗔
   M (carving lunch)/dinner a la carte 16.75/24.45 **t.** 🍷 4.20 – ⍁ 7.50 – **120 rm** 75.00/100.00 **st.**, **6 suites**.

LOCHALINE Argyll. (Highland) **401** C 14.
⚓ by Caledonian MacBrayne : to Fishnish (Isle of Mull) Monday/Saturday frequent services daily. Sunday, summer only : 6 daily (15 mn).
♦Edinburgh 129 – ♦Inverness 109 – Kyle of Lochalsh 116 – ♦Oban 6.

   Hotels see : Mull (Isle of).

LOCHBOISDALE Inverness. (Western Isles) **401** Y 12 – Shipping Services-: see Uist (South) (Isles of).

LOCHCARRON Ross and Cromarty. (Highland) **401** D 11 **Scotland G** – ECD : Thursday – ☎ 052 02.
Envir. : Plockton★, S : 17 m. by A 896 and A 890.
🛈 Locality Office *ℰ* 241.
♦Edinburgh 221 – ♦Inverness 65 – Kyle of Lochalsh 23.

   ⌂ **Lochcarron**, IV54 8YS, *ℰ* 226, ⇐ Loch Carron – ☎ ℗. ⚞ 𝗩𝗜𝗦𝗔
   M (bar lunch)/dinner 12.50 **t.** and a la carte 🍷 3.50 – **11 rm** ⍁ 20.00/46.00 **t.**

LOCHEARNHEAD Perth. (Central) **401** H 14 – ECD : Wednesday – ☎ 056 73.
♦Edinburgh 65 – ♦Glasgow 56 – ♦Oban 57 – Perth 36.

   ↑ **Mansewood Country House**, FK19 8NS, S : ½ m. on A 84 *ℰ* 213, 🚗 – ⤬ rest ℗
   M 12.00 **st.** 🍷 3.50 – **8 rm** ⍁ 17.00/39.00 **st.**

LOCHGILPHEAD Argyll. (Strathclyde) **401** D 15 – pop. 2 391 – ECD : Tuesday – ☎ 0546.
🛈 Lochnell St. *ℰ* 2344 (summer only).
♦Edinburgh 130 – ♦Glasgow 84 – ♦Oban 38.

   ⌂ **Stag**, Argyll St., PA31 8NE, *ℰ* 2496 – 📺 ☎ ℗. ⚞ 𝗩𝗜𝗦𝗔
   M 8.00/11.50 **t.** and a la carte 🍷 3.50 – **21 rm** ⍁ 23.00/42.00 **t.** – SB (except summer) (weekends only) 23.00/27.50 **st.**

LOCH HARRAY Orkney. (Orkney Islands) **401** K 6 – see Orkney Islands (Mainland).

LOCHINVER Sutherland. (Highland) **401** E 9 – ECD : Tuesday – ✉ Lairg – ☎ 057 14.
🛈 *ℰ* 330 (summer only).
♦Edinburgh 251 – ♦Inverness 95 – ♦Wick 105.

   ↑ **Ardglas** ⤰ without rest., IV27 4LI, *ℰ* 257, ⇐ Loch Inver – ⤬ ℗
   March-November – **8 rm** ⍁ 10.50/23.00 **st.**

LOCHRANZA Bute. (Strathclyde) **401 402** E 16 – see Arran (Isle of).

LOCKERBIE Dumfries. (Dumfries and Galloway) **401 402** J 18 – pop. 3 545 – ECD : Tuesday – ☎ 057 62.
⌐₉ Corrie Rd *ℰ* 3363.
♦Edinburgh 74 – ♦Carlisle 27 – ♦Dumfries 13 – ♦Glasgow 73.

   🏨 **Lockerbie House** ⤰, Boreland Rd, DG11 2RG, N : 1 m. on B 723 *ℰ* 2610, Fax 3046, ⇐, 🚗, park – ⤬ rest 📺 ☎ ℗ – 🛎 80. ⚞ ⵄ ⓞ 𝗩𝗜𝗦𝗔
   M (bar lunch by arrangement)/dinner 9.00 **st.** and a la carte 🍷 3.95 – **25 rm** ⍁ 38.50/75.00 **st.**

   ⌂ **Dryfesdale**, DG11 2SF, NW : 1 m. by A 74 *ℰ* 2427, ⇐, 🚗 – 📺 ☎ ℗. ⚞ ⵄ 𝗩𝗜𝗦𝗔
   closed 26 December-1 January – **M** 8.50/11.95 **t.** and a la carte 🍷 3.50 – **10 rm** ⍁ 36.00/55.00 **t.** – SB (December-March) (weekends only) 84.00 **st.**

LOSSIEMOUTH Moray. (Grampian) **401** K 10 – pop. 6 650 – ECD : Thursday – ☎ 034 381.
⌐₁₈, ⌐₁₈ Stotfield Rd, Moray *ℰ* 2018.
♦Edinburgh 203 – ♦Aberdeen 73 – Fraserburgh 66 – ♦Inverness 44.

   🏨 **Stotfield**, Stotfield Rd, IV31 6QS, *ℰ* 2011 – 📺 ☎ ℗ – **50 rm**.

LUING (Isle of) Argyll. (Strathclyde) **401** D 15 – pop. 183.

⛴ to Isle of Seil (Strathclyde Regional Council) frequent sailings daily (5 mn).

LUNDIN LINKS Fife. (Fife) **401** L 15 – see Leven.

MACDUFF Banff. (Grampian) **401** M 10 – pop. 3 893 – ECD : Wednesday – ✆ 0261.

ᵢ₈ Royal Tarlair ✆ 32897.

♦ Edinburgh 176 – ♦ Aberdeen 46 – Fraserburgh 24 – ♦ Inverness 76.

🏨 **Highland Haven**, Shore St., AB4 1UB, ✆ 32408, ≼ – TV ☎ Ⓟ. 🔽 AE ⓪ VISA
M 5.00/15.00 **st.** and a la carte 🍶 3.00 – **16 rm** ⌷ 28.95/49.50 **st.** – SB (weekends only in summer) 50.00/60.00 **st.**

MACHRIHANISH Argyll. (Strathclyde) **401** C 17 – see Kintyre (Peninsula).

MAINLAND Orkney. (Orkney Islands) **401** KL 6 – see Orkney Islands.

MAINLAND Shetland. (Shetland Islands) **401** PQ 3 – see Shetland Islands.

MALLAIG Inverness. (Highland) **401** C 12 – pop. 998 – ECD : Wednesday – ✆ 0687.
See : Site*.

Envir. : Silver Sands of Morar*, S : by A 830 – Arisaig, S : 9 m. by A 830.

⛴ by Caledonian MacBrayne : to Armadale (Isle of Skye) summer only Monday/Saturday 3-6 daily (30 mn).

⛴ by Caledonian MacBrayne : to Isles of Eigg, Muck, Rhum, Canna, return Mallaig Monday/Saturday 3-5 weekly (7 h) – to Kyle of Lochalsh: 3 weekly (summer only) (2 h).

🛈 Station Buildings ✆ 2170 (summer only).

♦Edinburgh 179 – ♦ Inverness 110 – ♦Oban 96.

MARYCULTER Aberdeen. (Grampian) **401** N 12 – see Aberdeen.

MEIGLE Perth. (Tayside) **401** K 14 – ✆ 082 84.
See : Museum** (Early Christian Monuments**).

Envir. : Glamis Castle** NE : 7 m. by A 94.

♦Edinburgh 62 – ♦Dundee 13 – Perth 18.

🏨 **Kings of Kinloch** ⑤, Coupar Angus Rd, PH12 8QX, W : 1 m. on A 94 ✆ 273, ≼, 🐎 – TV
Ⓟ. 🔽 ⓪ VISA
closed January and February – **M** 6.00/16.00 **st.** and a la carte 🍶 3.25 – **6 rm** ⌷ 40.00/70.00 **st.**

MELROSE Roxburgh. (Borders) **401** **402** L 17 Scotland G – pop. 2 143 – ECD : Thursday – ✆ 089 682.

See : Site* – Abbey** (Decorative sculpture***).

Envir. : Eildon Hill North (❄***) – Scott's View** – Abbotsford**, W : 4 m. by A 6091 – Dryburgh Abbey*** (setting***) SE : 4 m. by A 6091.

ᵢ₉ Dingleton ✆ 2855, South boundary.

🛈 Priorwood Gdns, near Abbey ✆ 2555 (summer only).

♦Edinburgh 38 – Hawick 19 – ♦Newcastle-upon-Tyne 70.

🏨 **Burts**, Market Sq., TD6 9PN, ✆ 2285, Fax 2870, 🐎 – TV ☎ Ⓟ. 🔽 AE ⓪ VISA
M 11.50/16.50 **t.** and a la carte 🍶 3.00 – **21 rm** ⌷ 30.00/52.00 **t.** – SB 37.00/42.00 **st.**

at Gattonside NW : 2 ¼ m. by A 6091 on B 6360 – ✉ ✆ 089 682 Melrose :

✗ **Hoebridge Inn**, TD6 9LZ, ✆ 3082 – Ⓟ. 🔽 AE VISA
closed Monday, last 2 weeks June, first week October, 25 December and 1 January –
M (dinner only) a la carte 10.65/14.75 **t.** 🍶 3.40.

HONDA St. Dunstans ✆ 2048

MILLPORT Bute. (Strathclyde) **401** **402** F 16 – Shipping Services : see Great Cumbrae Island.

MILNGAVIE Dunbarton. (Strathclyde) **401** H 16 – pop. 12 030 – ECD : Tuesday and Saturday – ✉ ✆ 041 Glasgow.

ᵢ₈ Dougalston ✆ 956 5750 – ᵢ₈,ᵢ₈ Hilton Park ✆ 956 4657.

♦Edinburgh 53 – ♦Glasgow 7.

🏨 **Black Bull Thistle** (Thistle), Main St., G62 6BH, ✆ 956 2291, Telex 778323, Fax 956 1896 –
TV ☎ Ⓟ – 🔼 100. 🔽 AE ⓪ VISA
M 6.75/12.75 **t.** and a la carte – ⌷ 7.25 – **27 rm** 50.00/70.00 **st.** – SB 82.00/88.00 **st.**

AUSTIN-ROVER Main St. ✆ 956 2255   VAUXHALL-OPEL Glasgow Rd ✆ 956 1126

MOFFAT Dumfries. (Dumfries and Galloway) 401 402 J 17 Scotland G – pop. 1 990 – ECD : Wednesday – ☎ 0683.

Envir. : Grey Mare's Tail (waterfall)** NE : 9 m. – Tweed Valley** N : 6 m.

🏌 Coasthill ℰ 20020.

🛈 Church Gate ℰ 20620 (summer only).

♦Edinburgh 61 – ♦Dumfries 22 – ♦Carlisle 43 – ♦Glasgow 60.

  🏰 **Beechwood Country House** ⑤, up Harthope Pl., off Academy Rd, DG10 9RS, ℰ 20210, ≼, 🍴 – 🍴 rest 📺 ☎ 🅿. 🅰 AE VISA
    M (lunch by arrangement)/dinner 14.95 **st.** 🍷 3.50 – **7 rm** ☲ 51.15/85.00 **st.**

  🏰 **Moffat House**, High St., DG10 9HL, ℰ 20039, 🍴 – 📺 ☎ 🅿. 🅰 VISA
    accommodation closed January and February – **M** (bar lunch)/dinner a la carte 12.80/15.30 **t.**
    🍷 4.40 – **16 rm** ☲ 32.50/54.00 **t.**

  ↑ **Well View** ⑤, Ballplay Rd, off Holm St., DG10 9JU, ℰ 20184, 🍴 – 🍴 🅿. 🅰 VISA
    M 12.00 **st.** – **7 rm** ☲ 21.00/66.00 **t.**

  ↑ **Hartfell House** ⑤, Hartfell Cres., DG10 9AL, ℰ 20153, 🍴 – 🅿
    March-November – **M** 9.00 **st.** 🍷 3.15 – **9 rm** ☲ 13.50/27.00 **st.** – SB (September-April) 41.00/42.00 **st.**

  ↑ **Arden House**, High St., DG10 9HG, ℰ 20220 – 📺 🅿
    M 6.50 **s.** – **7 rm** ☲ 12.00/28.00 **s.**

MONTROSE Angus. (Tayside) 401 M 13 Scotland G – pop. 12 127 – ECD : Wednesday – ☎ 0674.

Envir. : Brechin (Round Tower*) W : 7 m. by A 935 – Aberlemno Stones* (summer only) W : 13 m. by A 935 and B 9134 – Glen Esk* (via Brechin and Edzell) 29 m. by A 935, B 9667, B 966, B 974 and A 937 – Cairn O'Mount Road* (≼**) N : 20 m. by A 937 and B 974.

🏌, 🏌 Montrose Links Trust, Triall Drive ℰ 72932, E : 1 m. by A 92.

🛈 212 High St ℰ 72000.

♦Edinburgh 92 – ♦Aberdeen 39 – ♦Dundee 29.

  🏨 **Park**, 61 John St., DD10 8RJ, ℰ 73415, Telex 76367, Fax 77091, 🍴 – 📺 ☎ 🅿 – 🔥 150. 🅰
    AE ⓞ VISA
    M 11.50 **t.** (dinner) and a la carte 🍷 2.85 – **59 rm** ☲ 28.00/60.00 **t.** – SB (weekends only) 35.50/40.50 **st.**

MUCK (Isle of) Inverness. (Highland) 401 B 13 – Shipping Services : see Mallaig.

MUIR OF ORD Ross and Cromarty. (Highland) 401 G 11 – ☎ 0463 Inverness.

♦Edinburgh 173 – ♦Inverness 10 – Wick 121.

  🏨 **Dower House**, Highfield, IV6 7XN, N : 1 m. on A 862 ℰ 870090, « Tasteful decor, country house atmosphere », 🍴 – 🍴 ☎ 🅿. 🅰 VISA
    M (lunch by arrangement)/dinner 18.00 **t.** 🍷 3.60 – **4 rm** ☲ 45.00/70.00 **t.**, **1 suite** 90.00 **t.**

MULL (Isle of) Argyll. (Strathclyde) 401 C 14 Scotland G – pop. 2 605.

See : Site* – Calgary Bay** – Isle of Iona* – Torosay Castle (Gardens* – ≼*).

🚢 by Caledonian MacBrayne: from Craignure to Oban: 1-12 daily – from Fishnish to Lochaline Monday/Saturday frequent services daily. Sunday, summer only: 6 daily (15 mn) – from Tobermory to Arinagour (Isle of Coll) 3 weekly (1 h 5 mn) – from Tobermory to Isle of Tiree Monday/Saturday 3 weekly (2 h 45 mn) – from Tobermory to Oban 3 weekly (2 h direct).

🚢 by Caledonian MacBrayne : from Fionnphort to Isle of Iona frequent services daily in summer, restricted service in winter (5 mn) – from Tobermory to Kilchoan summer only Monday/Saturday 3-6 daily (35 mn).

🛈 48 Main St. at Tobermory ℰ 0688 (Tobermory) 2182.

  Bunessan – ECD : Wednesday – ✉ Bunessan – ☎ 068 17 Fionnphort.

  🏰 **Ardfenaig House** ⑤, PA67 6DX, W : 3 m. by A 849 ℰ 210, ≼, « Country house atmosphere », 🍴, park – 🍴 rest 🅿
    Mid May-September – **M** *(closed Sunday to non-residents)* (dinner only) 20.00 **st.** 🍷 2.50 – **5 rm** ☲ (dinner included) 60.00/120.00 **st.**

  Dervaig – ✉ Tobermory – ☎ 068 84 Dervaig.

  🏰 **Druimnacroish** ⑤, PA75 6QW, S : 2 m. by B 8073 and Salen rd ℰ 274, ≼ Bellart Glen, « Converted steading », 🍴 – 🍴 rest 📺 ☎ 🅿. 🅰 AE ⓞ VISA
    May-mid October – **M** (dinner only) 20.00 **st.** 🍷 2.50 – **6 rm** ☲ 40.00/90.00 **st.**

  Tiroran – ✉ ☎ 068 15 Tiroran.

  🏰 **Tiroran House** ⑤, PA69 6ES, ℰ 232, ≼ Loch Scridain, « Country house atmosphere », 🍴, park – 🍴 rest 🅿. 🦌
    Early May-mid October – **M** (light lunch)/dinner 21.50 **st.** 🍷 3.75 – **9 rm** ☲ (dinner included) 70.00/175.00 **st.**

MULL (Isle of)

Tobermory – pop. 843 – ECD : Wednesday – ✉ ☎ 0688 Tobermory.

⌸ Western Isles ℰ 2020.

🛈 48 Main St. ℰ 2182.

🏠 **Harbour House**, 59 Main St., PA75 6NT, ℰ 2209, ≼
M (dinner only) 16.00 st. ▯ 3.15 – **9 rm** ⊈ 19.00/40.00 st.

🏠 **Tobermory**, 53 Main St., PA75 6NT, ℰ 2091, ≼
M (dinner only) 13.50 st. ▯ 3.60 – **15 rm** ⊈ 21.00/50.00 st.

⌂ **Ulva House** ⌂, Strongarbh, PA75 6PR, ℰ 2044, ≼ Tobermory Harbour and Calve Island,
🚗 – ℗
March-October – **M** 13.50 t. ▯ 3.90 – **6 rm** ⊈ 19.50/48.00 t.

NAIRN Nairn. (Highland) 401 I 11 Scotland G – pop. 7 366 – ECD : Wednesday – ☎ 0667.

Envir. : Cawdor Castle★, S : 7 m. by A 9090 – Brodie Castle★, E : 2 m. – Forres (Sueno's Stone★★)
E : 11 m. by A 96 and B 9011 – Fort George★ W : 10 m. by A 96 and B 9006.

⌸, ⌸ Seabank Rd ℰ 53208 – ⌸ Nairn Dunbar, Lochloy Rd ℰ 52741.

🛈 62 King St. ℰ 52753 (summer only).

♦Edinburgh 172 – ♦Aberdeen 91 – ♦Inverness 16.

🏰 **Golf View**, Seabank Rd, IV12 4HD, ℰ 52301, Telex 75134, ≼, ⌇ heated, 🚗, ✕ – 🛗 📺 ☎
℗ – 🏊 100 – **54 rm**, **1 suite**.

🏰 **Newton** ⌂, Inverness Rd, IV12 4RX, off A 96 ℰ 53144, Fax 54026, ≼, « Country house in
extensive grounds », 🚗, park, ✕ – 🛗 📺 ☎ ℗. 🅰 AE ⓞ VISA
M 6.75/13.75 t. ▯ 3.80 – **41 rm** ⊈ 44.00/74.00 t., **3 suites** 90.00 t.

🏠 **Clifton** ⌂, Viewfield St., IV12 4HW, ℰ 53119, Fax 52836, ≼, « Tasteful decor », 🚗 –
✕ rest ℗. 🅰 AE ⓞ VISA
March-November – **M** (booking essential) a la carte 14.00/21.00 t. ▯ 5.00 – **16 rm**
⊈ 48.00/76.00 t.

🏠 **Carnach House**, Delnies, IV12 5NT, W : 2 ¼ m. on A 96 ℰ 52094, 🚗 – ✕ rest 📺 ☎ ℗.
🅰 AE VISA
M (bar lunch Monday to Saturday)/dinner 15.50 t. and a la carte ▯ 3.50 – **12 rm**
⊈ 28.50/57.00 t. – SB (November-February) (weekends only) 44.00 st.

⌂ **Sunny Brae**, Marine Rd, IV12 4EA, ℰ 52309, ≼, 🚗 – 📺 ℗
Easter-October – **M** 6.50 st. ▯ 2.50 – **10 rm** ⊈ 16.00/32.00 st.

⌂ **Greenlawns** without rest., 13 Seafield St., IV12 4HG, ℰ 52738, 🚗 – 📺 ℗. 🅰
6 rm ⊈ 15.50/32.00.

FSO Inverness Rd ℰ 52335

NEWBURGH Aberdeen. (Grampian) 401 N 12 – ☎ 035 86.

♦Edinburgh 144 – ♦Aberdeen 14 – Fraserburgh 33.

🏠 **Udny Arms**, Main St., AB4 0BL, ℰ 89444, Fax 89012 – 📺 ☎ ℗. 🅰 AE VISA
M a la carte 8.05/14.70 t. ▯ 4.00 – ⊈ 3.00 – **26 rm** 36.00/52.00 t. – SB 75.00 st.

🏠 **Foveran House** ⌂, Foveran, AB4 0AP, SW : 1 m. on A 975 ℰ 398, Fax 398, park, ✕ – 📺
☎ ℗ – 🏊 – **18 rm**.

NEW GALLOWAY Kirkcudbright. (Dumfries and Galloway) 401 402 H 18 – pop. 290 – ☎ 064 42
– ⌸, S : on A 762.

♦Edinburgh 88 – ♦Ayr 36 – Dumfries 25.

⌂ **Leamington**, High St., DG7 3RN, ℰ 327 – ℗. 🅰 VISA
closed 29 October-3 December – **M** 9.00 t. ▯ 2.75 – **9 rm** ⊈ 11.00/30.00 t.

NEW SCONE Perth. (Tayside) 401 J 14 – see Perth.

NEWTONMORE Inverness. (Highland) 401 H 12 – pop. 1 010 – ECD : Wednesday – ☎ 054 03.

⌸ Golf Course Rd ℰ 328.

♦Edinburgh 113 – ♦Inverness 43 – Perth 69.

🏠 **Ard-na-Coille**, Kingussie Rd, PH20 1AY, ℰ 214, ≼ – ✕ rest ℗
closed November and December – **M** (lunch by arrangement)/dinner 19.50 t. ▯ 3.50 – **8 rm**
⊈ 17.50/60.00 t. – SB (except July-September and Bank Holidays) 60.00/75.00 st.

⌂ **Pines** ⌂, Station Rd, PH20 1AR, ℰ 271, ≼, 🚗 – ✕ ℗. ✕
May-late October – **M** 8.00 st. ▯ 2.55 – **6 rm** ⊈ 17.00/34.00 st.

NEWTON STEWART Wigtown. (Dumfries and Galloway) 401 402 G 19 – pop. 3 212 – ECD :
Wednesday – ☎ 0671.

Envir. : Galloway Forest Parks★, N : Queen's Way★ (Newton Stewart to New Galloway) 19 m. by
A 712.

⌸ Kirroughtree Av., Minnigaff ℰ 2172.

🛈 Dashwood Sq. ℰ 2431 (summer only).

♦Edinburgh 131 – ♦Dumfries 51 – ♦Glasgow 87 – Stranraer 24.

🏨 **Kirroughtree** 🛐, DG8 6AN, NE : 1 ½ m. on A 712 ☏ 2141, ≤ woodland and River Cree, « Country house and gardens », park – ⤬ rest 📺 ☎ 🅿. ⟋⟍ AE ⓞ *VISA*
closed 4 January-4 February – **M** 12.00/24.00 **t.** and a la carte ⫯ 4.50 – **21 rm** ⌷ 41.00/90.00 **t.**, **1 suite** 100.00 **t.** – SB 96.00/116.00 **st.**

🏨 **Creebridge House** 🛐, Minnigaff, DG8 6NP, ☏ 2121, ⟹ – 📺 ☎ 🅿. ⟋⟍ *VISA*
M (bar lunch)/dinner 15.00 **t.** – **17 rm** ⌷ 30.00/60.00 **t.** – SB 76.00/84.00 **st.**

🏠 **Bruce,** 88 Queen St., DG8 6JL, ☏ 2294 – 📺 ☎ 🅿. ⟋⟍ AE ⓞ *VISA*
closed December and January – **M** 8.50/13.50 **st.** ⫯ 3.40 – **17 rm** ⌷ 32.00/52.00 **st.** – SB 68.00 **st.**

🏠 **Crown,** 101 Queen St., DG8 6JW, ☏ 2727 – ⤬ rest 📺 🅿. ⟋⟍ *VISA*
M (bar lunch)/dinner 10.00 **t.** and a la carte ⫯ 2.50 – **10 rm** ⌷ 16.00/35.00 **t.** – SB 25.00/30.00 **st.**

↑ **Rowallan House** 🛐, Corsbie Rd, DG8 6JB, ☏ 2520, ⟹ – ⤬ rest 📺 🅿. ⠕
closed 22 October-15 November – **M** 11.00 **t.** ⫯ 3.50 – **6 rm** ⌷ 22.00/44.00 **t.**

RENAULT Duncan Park, Wigtown ☏ 098 84 (Wig-town) 3287
VW-AUDI Queen St. ☏ 2112
VOLVO Minnigaff Holm Park Ind Est ☏ 3101

NORTH BERWICK E. Lothian. (Lothian) 🛐🛐🛐 L 15 **Scotland G** – pop. 4 861 – ECD : Thursday – ☎ 0620.

Envir. : Tantallon Castle★★ (Site★★★) E : 3 m. by A 198 – Tyninghame★, S : 6 m. by A 198 – Preston Mill★, S : 8 m. by A 198 and B 1407 – Museum of Flight★, S : 10 m. by A 198 and B 1407.

🛇 New Clubhouse, Beach Rd ☏ 2135 – 🛇 East Links ☏ 2726 – 🛇 Glen, East Links ☏ 2221.

🛈 Quality St. ☏ 2197.

♦Edinburgh 24 – ♦Newcastle-upon-Tyne 102.

🏨 **Marine** (T.H.F.), Cromwell Rd, EH39 4LZ, ☏ 2406, Telex 72550, Fax 4480, ≤ golf course and Firth of Forth, ⊿ heated, ⟹, ✎, squash – ▧ ⤬ rm 📺 ☎ 🅿 – ⽥ 250. ⟋⟍ AE ⓞ *VISA*
M 8.50/11.95 **st.** and dinner a la carte 12.50/22.75 **st.** ⫯ 3.00 – ⌷ 6.95 – **83 rm** 59.00/85.00 **st.**, **5 suites** 100.00/170.00 **st.** – SB (except Christmas and New Year) 38.00/75.00 **st.**

🏠 **Point Garry,** 20 West Bay Rd, EH39 4AW, ☏ 2380, ≤ – 📺 🅿
March-October – **M** (bar lunch)/dinner 10.95 **t.** and a la carte – **16 rm** ⌷ 19.00/36.00 **t.**

🏠 **Blenheim House,** 14 Westgate, EH39 4AF, ☏ 2385, ≤, ⟹ – 📺 🅿. ⟋⟍ *VISA*
11 rm ⌷ 25.00/60.00 **st.**

🏠 **Nether Abbey,** 20 Dirleton Av., EH39 4BQ, ☏ 2802 – 📺. ⟋⟍ *VISA*
M (bar lunch)/dinner a la carte approx. 6.45 ⫯ 3.25 – **15 rm** ⌷ 20.00/28.50 **st.**

↑ **Craigview,** 5 Beach Rd, EH39 4AB, ☏ 2257 – ⤬ 📺. ⠕
M 9.75 **st.** ⫯ 4.25 – **3 rm** ⌷ 15.00/35.00 **st.**, **1 suite** 30.00/45.00 **st.**

FORD 52 Dunbar Rd ☏ 2232

NORTH RONALDSAY (Isle of) Orkney. (Orkney Islands) 🛐🛐🛐 M 5 – Shipping Services : see Orkney Islands (Mainland : Kirkwall).

OBAN Argyll. (Strathclyde) 🛐🛐🛐 D 14 **Scotland G** – pop. 7 476 – ECD : Thursday – ☎ 0631.
See : Site★.

Envir. : Loch Awe★★ – Inverary★★ (Castle★★-Interior★★★) – Loch Fyne★★ – Bonawe Furnace★ – Cruachan Power Station★ – Auchindrain★ – Crinan★, 83 m. by A 85, A 819, A 83 and A 816 – Sea Life Centre★, N : 11 m. by A 828

🛇 Glencruitten Rd ☏ 62868.

Access to Glasgow by helicopter.

⛴ by Caledonian MacBrayne : to Craignure (Isle of Mull) 1-12 daily – to Castlebay (Isle of Barra): 1-4 weekly (5 h 40 mn) – to Lochboisdale (South Uist) 3-6 weekly (6 h direct ; 8 h via Castlebay) – to Arinagour (Isle of Coll) : 4 weekly (2 h 50 mn to 3 h 5 mn) – to Isle of Tiree 3-4 weekly (4 h to 5 h) – to Scalasaig (Isle of Colonsay) summer only: 3-4 weekly (2 h 30 mn) – to Achnacroish (Isle of Lismore) Monday/Saturday 2-5 daily (50 mn) – to Tobermory (Isle of Mull) 3 weekly (1 h 45 mn to 2 h 15 mn).

🛈 Argyll Sq. ☏ 63122.

♦Edinburgh 123 – ♦Dundee 116 – ♦Glasgow 93 – ♦Inverness 118.

🏨 **Columba,** North Pier, PA34 5QD, ☏ 62183, Telex 728256, Fax 64683, ≤ – ▧ 📺 ☎. ⟋⟍ AE *VISA*
M 7.50/15.00 **st.** and a la carte ⫯ 3.00 – **50 rm** ⌷ 50.00/75.00 **st.** – SB (except summer, Whitsun, Easter and Christmas) 60.00/85.00 **st.**

🏠 **Manor House,** Gallanach Rd, PA34 4LS, ☏ 62087, ≤ – ⤬ 📺 ☎ 🅿. ⟋⟍ *VISA*
M 10.00/16.00 **t.** and a la carte ⫯ 3.50 – **11 rm** ⌷ (dinner included) 84.00/100.00 **t.** – SB 50.00/90.00 **st.**

↑ **Dungrianach** 🛐 without rest., Pulpit Hill, PA34 4LX, ☏ 62840, ≤ Oban, Sound and Isle of Kerrara, ⟹ – 🅿. ⠕
Easter-mid October – **3 rm** ⌷ –/30.00 **st.**

↑ **Corriemar,** Esplanade, PA34 5AQ, ☏ 62476, ≤ – ⤬ rest 📺 🅿. ⠕
Easter and May-October – **M** 9.00 **t.** ⫯ 1.80 – **14 rm** ⌷ 22.00/50.00 **t.**

at Kilninver SW : 8 m. on A 816 – ⊠ Oban – ☎ 085 26 Kilninver :

🏨 **Knipoch**, PA34 4QT, NE : 1 ½ m. on A 816 ℰ 251, Fax 249, ≼, « Tastefully furnished », 🐎 – 📺 ☎ 🅿. 🔄 AE ⓪ VISA. 🛇
Mid February-mid November – **M** (lunch by arrangement)/dinner 28.00 t. ⬦ 4.50 – **17 rm** ☲ 48.00/96.00 t.

AUSTIN-ROVER Airds Pl. ℰ 63173   VOLVO, VAUXHALL Breadalbane Pl. ℰ 63066
FORD Soroba Rd ℰ 63061

OLDMELDRUM Aberdeen. (Grampian) 🗺 N 11 – pop. 1 343 – ECD : Wednesday – ☎ 065 12.
Envir. : Pitmedden Gardens★★, E : 5 m. by A 920 – Haddo House★, N : 9 m. by B 9170 and B 9005 – Fyvie Castle★, N : 8 m. by A 947.
🏌₉ ℰ 2648, E : off A 947.
◆Edinburgh 148 – ◆Aberdeen 18 – Fraserburgh 30 – ◆Inverness 89.

🏨 **Meldrum House** 🦢, AB5 0AE, N : 1 ½ m. on A 947 ℰ 2294, ≼, « Country house atmosphere », 🐎, park – 📺 ☎ 🅿. AE ⓪ VISA. 🛇
closed January and February – **M** (bar lunch)/dinner 21.00 st. ⬦ 5.50 – **11 rm** ☲ 50.00/140.00 st.

RENAULT Station Rd ℰ 3928

ONICH Inverness. (Highland) 🗺 E 13 – ECD : Saturday except summer – ⊠ Fort William – ☎ 085 53.
◆Edinburgh 123 – ◆Glasgow 93 – ◆Inverness 79 – ◆Oban 39.

🏨 **Allt-Nan-Ros**, PH33 6RY, on A 82 ℰ 210, Fax 462, ≼ Loch Linnhe and mountains, 🐎 – ⊁ rest 📺 ☎ 🅿. 🔄 AE ⓪ VISA
2 April-2 November – **M** 10.00/19.00 t. ⬦ 4.00 – **21 rm** ☲ 37.50/85.00 t.

🏨 **The Lodge on the Loch**, Creag Dhu, PH33 6RY, on A 82 ℰ 238, Group Telex 94013696, Fax 629, ≼ Loch Linnhe and mountains, 🐎 – ⊁ rest 📺 ☎ 🅊 🅿. 🔄 VISA
April-October – **M** (bar lunch)/dinner 15.00 **st.** and a la carte ⬦ 3.50 – **20 rm** ☲ 26.50/84.00 st. – SB 79.00/104.00 st.

🏨 **Onich**, PH33 6RY, on A 82 ℰ 214, ≼ Loch Linnhe and mountains, 🐎 – 📺 ☎ 🅿. 🔄 AE ⓪ VISA
M (bar lunch)/dinner 13.50 **st.** and a la carte ⬦ 3.50 – **26 rm** ☲ 32.00/58.00 st. – SB (except summer) 64.00 st.

↑ **Cuilcheanna House** 🦢, PH33 6SD, ℰ 226, ≼, 🐎 – ⊁ rest 🅿
Mid March-mid October – **M** 10.50 t. ⬦ 2.25 – **8 rm** ☲ 23.00/42.00 t.

ORKNEY ISLANDS Orkney. (Orkney Islands) 🗺 KL 6 and 7 Scotland G – pop. 19 040.
✈ see Mainland : Kirkwall.
🚢 🚢 see Mainland : Kirkwall and Stromness.
🚢 by Thomas & Bews : from Burwick (South Ronaldsay) to John O'Groats summer only 2-5 daily (45 mn) – by Orkney Islands Shipping Co. : service between Longhope (Isle of Hoy), Lyness (Isle of Hoy), Flotta (Isle of), Houton, Graemsay (Isle of), Stromness and return, daily itinerary varies, consult operator.

HOY

Old Man of Hoy Scotland G.
See : Old Man of Hoy★★★ (sandstone stack).

MAINLAND

Birsay Scotland G – ⊠ ☎ 085 672 Birsay.
See : Brough of Birsay (site★★).

Dounby – ⊠ Dounby – ☎ 085 677 Harray.
⚑ **Smithfield**, KW17 2HT, ℰ 215 – 🅿
M (bar lunch)/dinner 10.00 st. – **7 rm** ☲ 15.00/32.00 s.

Kirkwall Scotland G – pop. 5 947 – ECD : Wednesday – ⊠ ☎ 0856 Kirkwall.
See : Site★★ – St. Magnus Cathedral★★ – Earl's Palace★ – Tankerness House Museum★.
Envir. : Italian Chapel★ – Corrigall Farm Museum★.
🏌₁₈ Grainbank ℰ 2457, W : 1 m.
✈ Kirkwall Airport : ℰ 2421, Telex 75473, S : 3 ½ m.
🚢 by Orkney Islands Shipping Co. : to Westray via Eday, Stronsay, Sanday and Papa Westray 3 weekly (2 to 6 h) – to North Ronaldsay 1 weekly (2 h 30 mn) – to Shapinsay 1-4 daily (25 mn).
🅹 Broad St. ℰ 2856.

🏨 **Kirkwall**, Harbour St., KW15 1LF, ☏ 2232, Telex 9401173, ≼ – 🛗 📺 ☎
44 rm.

🏛 **Foveran** ⑤, St. Ola, KW15 1SF, SW : 3 m. on A 964 ☏ 2389, ≼ sea, « Tranquil setting on the banks of Scapa Flow » – 🅿. 🖸 𝗩𝗜𝗦𝗔
March-October – **M** *(closed Sunday)* (dinner only) 12.50 **st.** and a la carte 9.50/15.30 **st.** 🍾 3.00 – **8 rm** ⊑ 24.00/39.00 **st.**

🏛 **Ayre**, Ayre Rd, KW15 1QX, ☏ 3001 – 📺 ☎ 🅿. 🖸 𝗩𝗜𝗦𝗔
M (bar lunch)/dinner 9.95 **t.** and a la carte 🍾 3.00 – ⊑ 3.70 – **32 rm** 17.00/42.00 **t.**

🏛 **Lynnfield** ⑤, Holm Rd, KW15 1RX, S : 1 ¼ m. on A 961 ☏ 2505, 🛋 – 📺 🅿
8 rm.

⌂ **Bellavista**, Carness Rd, KW15 1TB, N : 1 m. via Cromwell Rd ☏ 2306 – ⟆ 🅿. 🗶
closed October and Christmas – **M** 5.00 **s.** – **8 rm** ⊑ 10.00/30.00 **s.**

COLT, TALBOT Gt Western Rd ☏ 2805
FIAT Junction Rd ☏ 2158
FORD Castle St. ☏ 3212
RENAULT Gt Western Rd ☏ 2601

VAUXHALL Burnmouth Rd ☏ 2950

🛞 ATS Junction Rd ☏ 2361

Loch Harray – ✉ Loch Harray – ☎ 085 677 Harray.

🏛 **Merkister** ⑤, KW17 2LF, ☏ 366, ≼, 🎣, 🛋 – 🅿. 🖸 𝗔𝗘 𝗩𝗜𝗦𝗔
April-September – **M** (bar lunch)/dinner 10.00 **t.** and a la carte 🍾 4.00 – **15 rm** ⊑ 24.00/46.50 **t.**

Stromness Scotland G – pop. 1 816 – ECD : Thursday – ✉ ☎ 0856 Stromness.
See : Site★ – Pier Arts Centre (Collection of abstract art★).
Envir. : Old Man of Hoy★★★ – Maes Howe★★ E : 4 m. – Skara Brae★★ (Prehistoric Village) N : 7 ½ m..
🏌 Ness ☏ 850772.
🚢 by P & O Ferries : Orkney and Shetland Services : to Scrabster Monday/Saturday 1-2 daily. Sunday, summer 1-2 daily (2 h).
🚤 to Moaness (Isle of Hoy) 2-3 daily (except weekends in winter) (25 mn).
🛈 Ferry Terminal Building, Pierhead ☏ 850716 (summer only).

🏛 **Stromness**, Victoria St., KW16 3AA, ☏ 850298, 🛋 – 🛗. 🖸 𝗩𝗜𝗦𝗔. 🗶
M 8.00/14.00 **st.** and a la carte 🍾 3.20 – **42 rm** ⊑ 20.00/50.00 **st.**

*Great Britain and Ireland are covered entirely
at a scale of 16 miles to 1 inch by our map « Main roads »* 🟥🟥🟥.

OUT SKERRIES Shetland. (Shetland Islands) 🟥 R 2 – Shipping Services : see Shetland Islands (Mainland : Lerwick).

PAISLEY Renfrew. (Strathclyde) 🟥 🟥 G 16 Scotland G – pop. 84 330 – ECD : Tuesday – ☎ 041 Glasgow.
See : Museum and Art gallery (Paisley Shawl Section★).
🏌 Barshaw Park ☏ 889 2908, E : 1 m. of Paisley Cross off A 737.
🛈 Town Hall, Abbey Close ☏ 889 0711.
♦Edinburgh 53 – ♦Ayr 35 – ♦Glasgow 7.5 – Greenock 17.

🏨 Stakis Watermill (Stakis), Lonend, PA1 1SR, ☏ 889 3201 – 🛗 📺 ☎ 🅿. 🖸 𝗔𝗘 ⓞ 𝗩𝗜𝗦𝗔
⊑ 7.25 – **51 rm** 54.00/74.00 **st.** – SB 70.00/76.00 **st.**

🏛 **Rockfield**, 125 Renfrew Rd, PA3 4EA, ☏ 889 6182 – 📺 ☎ 🅿. 🖸 𝗔𝗘 ⓞ 𝗩𝗜𝗦𝗔
M (bar lunch)/dinner 11.50 **t.** and a la carte 🍾 3.10 – **20 rm** ⊑ 33.50/53.25 **t.** – SB (weekends only) 80.00/90.00 **st.**

AUSTIN-ROVER 46 New Sneddon St. ☏ 889 7882
CITROEN 92 Glasgow Rd ☏ 889 8526
FIAT 4-8 Lochfield Rd ☏ 884 2281
FORD 37-41 Lonend ☏ 887 0191

HYUNDAI, SUBARU, ISUZU 11-17 Weir St. ☏ 889 6866
PEUGEOT-TALBOT 7 West St. ☏ 889 0011
VAUXHALL-OPEL 69 Espedair St. ☏ 889 5254

PAPA WESTRAY (Isle of) Orkney. (Orkney Islands) 🟥 L 5 – Shipping Services : see Orkney Islands (Mainland : Kirkwall).

PEAT INN Fife. (Fife) 🟥 L 15 – ✉ Cupar – ☎ 033 484.
♦Edinburgh 45 – Dundee 21 – Perth 28.

XXX ❀ **The Peat Inn** (Wilson) ⑤ with rm, KY15 5LH, ☏ 206, 🛋 – ⟆ rest 📺 ☎ ♿ 🅿. 🖸 𝗔𝗘 ⓞ 𝗩𝗜𝗦𝗔. 🗶
closed 2 weeks January and 2 weeks November – **M** *(closed Sunday and Monday)* (booking essential) 14.50/30.00 **st.** and a la carte 20.80/24.20 **st.** 🍾 6.00, **8 suites** 75.00/97.00 **st.**
Spec. Ragout of scallops monkfish and pork, Loin of spring lamb with a lamb charlotte (May-September), A trio of nut desserts.

PEEBLES Peebles. (Borders) 401 402 K 17 – pop. 6 404 – ECD : Wednesday – ✆ 0721.

Envir. : Traquair House★★ SE : 7 m..

🛆 Kirkland St. ✆ 20197 – 🛆 West Linton ✆ 0968 (West Linton) 60589.

🖥 Chambers Institute, High St. ✆ 20138 (summer only).

♦Edinburgh 24 – Hawick 31 – ♦Glasgow 53.

🏨 **Peebles Hydro**, Innerleithen Rd, EH45 8LX, ✆ 20602, Telex 72568, Fax 22999, ≼, 🔲, ☞, park, ※, squash – 📶 TV ☎ P – 🕭 500. 🔼 AE ⓪ VISA ☒
135 rm ☑ 45.00/92.50 st., **2 suites** 105.00/115.00 st.

🏨 **Tweedbridge House**, Chambers Terr., EH45 9DZ, ✆ 20590, Fax 22793, ≼, ☞ – ⇔ rest TV ☎ P. 🔼 AE VISA
M 9.50/16.95 t. and a la carte – **5 rm** ☑ 30.00/70.00 t.

🏨 **Cringletie House** ॐ, EH45 8PL, N : 3 m. on A 703 ✆ 072 13 (Eddleston) 233, ≼, « Country house in extensive grounds », ☞, park, ※ – 📶 TV ☎ P. 🔼 VISA
closed January-mid March – **M** (restricted lunch Monday to Saturday)/dinner 18.50 t. ⌾ 3.50 – **13 rm** ☑ 35.00/65.00 t. – SB (March-April and November-December) (except Christmas) 48.00 st.

🏨 **Park**, Innerleithen Rd, EH45 8BA, ✆ 20451, ☞ – TV ☎ P – **M** (bar lunch) – **25 rm**.

🏨 **Tontine** (T.H.F.), 39 High St., EH45 8AJ, ✆ 20892 – ⇔ TV ☎ P. 🔼 AE ⓪ VISA
M (bar lunch)/dinner 10.50 st. and a la carte ⌾ 3.60 – **36 rm** ☑ 40.00/59.00 st. – SB 59.00/80.00 st.

at Eddleston N : 4 ½ m. on A 703 – ✉ Peebles – ✆ 072 13 Eddleston :

XX **Champany Horse Shoe Inn**, EH45 8QP, ✆ 225 – ⇔ P – **M** (grill rest.).

AUSTIN-ROVER, LAND-ROVER Innerleithen Rd ✆ 20627

CITROEN, LANCIA, SUZUKI George St. ✆ 20545
VAUXHALL-OPEL 104 Old Town ✆ 20886

PENNAN Aberdeen. (Grampian) 401 N 10 – pop. 92 – ✉ ✆ 034 66 New Aberdour.

♦Edinburgh 181 – ♦Aberdeen 51 – Fraserburgh 12 – ♦Inverness 85.

🕭 **Pennan Inn**, 17-19 Main St., AB4 4JB, ✆ 201 – ☒
closed 25-26 December and 1-2 January – **M** (closed dinner Sunday and Monday) (bar lunch)/dinner 20.00 st. and a la carte ⌾ 3.50 – **6 rm** ☑ 30.00/35.00 st.

PERTH Perth. (Tayside) 401 J 14 Scotland G – pop. 41 916 – ECD : Wednesday – ✆ 0738.

See : Black Watch Regimental Museum★ Y M1 – Georgian terraces★ Y – Museum and Art Gallery★ Y M2 – Branklyn Garden★ by A 85 Z – Kinnoull Hill (≼★) by Bowerswell Rd Y.

Envir. : Scone Palace★★, N : 2 m. by A 93 Y – Huntingtower Castle★, NW : 3 m. by A 9 Y – Elcho Castle★, SE : by A 912 Z – Abernethy Round Tower★, SE : 8 m. by A 912 Z and A 913 – Cairnwell (❄★★) N : 40 m. by A 93 Y.

🛆 Craigie Hill, Cherrybank ✆ 22644, West boundary, by A 9 Z – 🛆 King James VI, Moncrieffe Island ✆ 25170.

🖥 The Round House, Marshall Pl. ✆ 38353.

♦Edinburgh 44 – ♦Aberdeen 86 – ♦Dundee 22 – Dunfermline 29 – ♦Glasgow 64 – ♦Inverness 112 – ♦Oban 94.

Plan opposite

🏨 **Hunting Tower** ॐ, Crieff Rd, PH1 3JT, W : 3 ½ m. by A 85 ✆ 83771, Fax 83777, ☞ – TV ☎ P. 🔼 AE VISA
on A 85 Y
M 9.50/16.95 st. and a la carte dinner 20.30 st. ⌾ 3.60 – **24 rm** ☑ 49.00/92.00 st. – SB (weekends only) 87.00 st.

🏨 **Royal George** (T.H.F.), Tay St., PH1 5LD, ✆ 24455, Fax 30345 – ⇔ rm TV ☎ P – 🕭 120. 🔼 AE ⓪ VISA
Y c
M 9.00/13.00 st. and a la carte ⌾ 4.00 – ☑ 7.50 – **43 rm** 48.00/65.00 st. – SB 84.00/100.00 st.

🏨 **Station**, Leonard St., PH2 8HE, ✆ 24141, Telex 76481, Fax 39912, ☞ – 📶 ⇔ rm TV ☎ P – 🕭 300. 🔼 AE ⓪ VISA. ☒
Z n
M 8.50/10.50 st. and a la carte ⌾ 4.50 – ☑ 4.75 – **68 rm** 43.50/62.50 st., **2 suites** 72.50 st.

🏨 **Stakis City Mills** (Stakis), West Mill St., PH1 5QP, ✆ 28281, Fax 43423 – ⇔ rm TV ☎ P – 🕭 200. 🔼 AE ⓪ VISA – ☑ 7.25 – **76 rm** 54.00/95.00 st.
Y a

🏠 **Pitcullen**, 17 Pitcullen Cres., PH2 7HT, NE : ¾ m. on A 94 ✆ 26506 – ⇔ rest TV P. ☒
6 rm ☑ 15.00/27.00 s.
Y r

XX **Coach House**, 8 North Port, PH1 5LU, ✆ 27950 – 🔼 AE VISA
Y s
closed Sunday and Monday – **M** 9.50/19.50 st. ⌾ 3.40.

X **Timothy's**, 24 St. John St., PH1 5SP, ✆ 26641, Smörrebrod – 🔼
Y e
closed Sunday, Monday and 3 weeks July – **M** a la carte 5.75/8.00 t. ⌾ 3.50.

at New Scone NE : 2 ½ m. on A 94 – Y – ✉ ✆ 0738 Perth :

🏨 **Murrayshall House** ॐ, PH2 7PH, E : 1 ½ m. by A 94 ✆ 51171, Telex 76197, Fax 52595, ≼, 🛆, ☞, park, ※ – TV ☎ P. 🔼 AE ⓪ VISA. ☒
M 15.00/27.50 t. and a la carte ⌾ 4.50 – **16 rm** ☑ 60.00/105.00 t., **3 suites** 105.00/185.00 t. – SB (except summer) 105.00 st.

🏨 **Balcraig House** ॐ, PH2 7PG, E : 1 ½ m. by A 94 ✆ 51123, Fax 33449, ≼, ☞, park, ※ – TV ☎ P. 🔼 AE ⓪ VISA
M 9.50/17.50 t. and a la carte ⌾ 3.95 – **10 rm** ☑ 54.50/80.00 st. – SB 46.00/49.00 st.

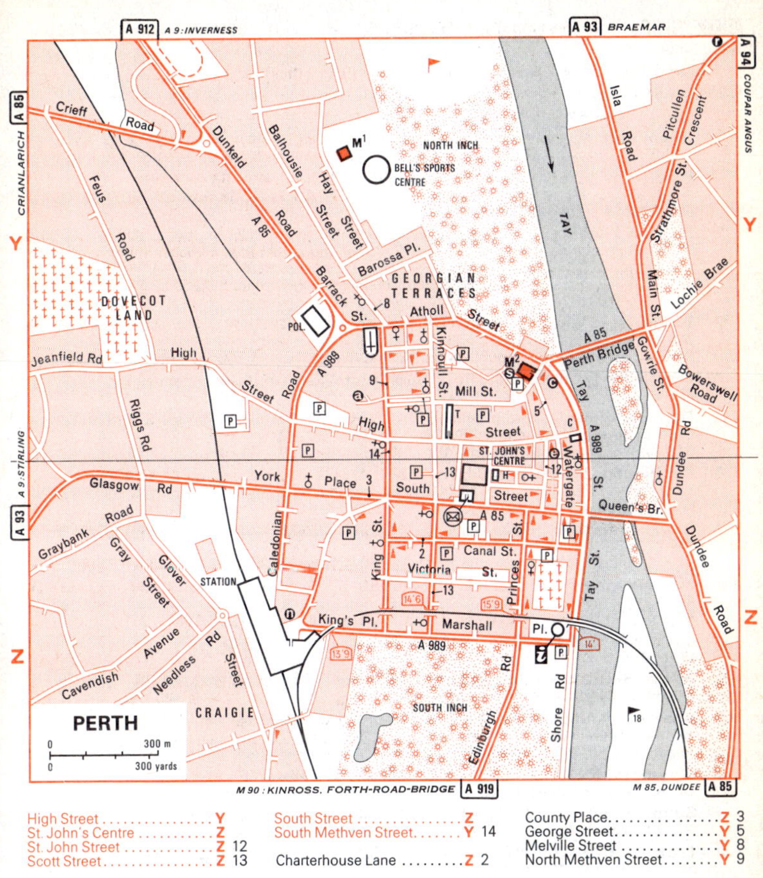

High Street . . . . **Y**
St. John's Centre . . . . **Z**
St. John Street . . . . **Z** 12
Scott Street . . . . **Z** 13

South Street . . . . **Z**
South Methven Street . . . . . . **Y** 14
Charterhouse Lane . . . . **Z** 2

County Place . . . . **Z** 3
George Street . . . . **Y** 5
Melville Street . . . . **Y** 8
North Methven Street . . . . . . **Y** 9

AUSTIN-ROVER Dunkeld Rd ℰ 39993
BMW, ROLLS-ROYCE 50-56 Leonard St. ℰ 30001
CITROEN 60 South St. ℰ 23335
FORD Riggs Rd ℰ 25121/25129
PEUGEOT-TALBOT Glenearn Rd ℰ 20811
VAUXHALL Dunkeld Rd ℰ 26241

VOLVO Arran Rd, North Muirton ℰ 22156
VW-AUDI Dunkeld Rd ℰ 25252

ATS Inveralmond Ind Est., Ruthvenfield Rd ℰ 29481

PETERHEAD Aberdeen. (Grampian) 401 O 11 – pop. 16 804 – ECD : Wednesday – ☎ 0779.
Craigewan Links ℰ 72149.
71 Broad St. ℰ 71904 (summer only).
◆Edinburgh 165 – ◆Aberdeen 35 – Fraserburgh 18.

Waterside Inn, Fraserburgh Rd, AB4 7BN, NW : 2 m. on A 952 ℰ 71121, Telex 739413, Fax 70670, ⬚, ⬚ – TV ☎ P – 150. AE ① VISA
closed 25 and 26 December – **110 rm** ⬚ 35.00/75.00 st.

Palace, Prince St., AB4 6PL, ℰ 74821, Fax 76119 – ⬚ rm TV ☎ P – 50. AE ①
VISA
M 6.00/9.00 t. and a la carte ⬚ 3.20 – **89 rm** ⬚ 26.00/60.00 t. – SB (weekends only) 33.00 st.

VAUXHALL-OPEL West Rd ℰ 72440

PITCAPLE Aberdeen. (Grampian) 401 M 12 – ☎ 046 76.
◆Edinburgh 51 – ◆Aberdeen 21.

Pittodrie House ⬚, AB5 9HS, SW : 1 ¾ m. by Chapel of Garioch Rd ℰ 444, Telex 739935, ≼, « Country house atmosphere », ⬚, park, ※, squash – TV ☎ ⬚ P. AE ①
VISA
M 11.00/21.00 st. ⬚ 3.75 – **12 rm** ⬚ 42.00/80.00 st. – SB (except summer) 100.00 st.

PITLOCHRY Perth. (Tayside) 401 I 13 Scotland G – pop. 2 194 – ECD : Thursday – ✆ 0796.
See : Site★.

🛈 Estates Office ✆ 2114 – ☞ Blair Atholl ✆ 079 681 (Blair Atholl) 407.
🛈 22 Atholl Rd ✆ 2215 and 2751.

◆Edinburgh 71 – ◆Inverness 85 – Perth 27.

🏨 **Green Park** ⤳, Clunie Bridge Rd, PH16 5JY, ✆ 3248, ≤, 🐎 – ⇔ rest 📺 ☎ 🅿. ⟰. 🛇
  20 March-October – **M** (bar lunch)/dinner 13.50 **t.** ⓵ 2.95 – **37 rm** ⌑ 23.50/59.00 **t.**

🏨 **Pine Trees** ⤳, Strathview Terr., PH16 5QR, ✆ 2121, ≤, 🐎 – 📺 🅿. ⟰ VISA 🛇
  April-October – **M** (bar lunch)/dinner 15.00 **t.** ⓵ 3.50 – **18 rm** ⌑ 35.00/64.00 **t.** –
  SB (except summer) 84.00 **st.**

🏨 **Port-an-Eilean** ⤳, Strathtummel, PH16 5RU, NW : 10 ½ m. by A 924 on B 8019
  ✆ 088 24 (Tummel Bridge) 233, ≤ Loch Tummel and mountains, « Lochside Victorian sporting lodge », ⤳, 🐎, park – 🅿
  May-mid October – **M** (bar lunch, residents only)/dinner 12.50 **t.** ⓵ 3.00 – **9 rm**
  ⌑ 28.00/48.00 **t.**

🏨 **Burnside**, 19 West Moulin Rd, PH16 5EA, on A 924 ✆ 2203, 🐎 – ⇔ rest 📺 ⓺ 🅿. AE ⓞ
  VISA
  April-October – **M** (bar lunch)/dinner 12.35 **t.** and a la carte ⓵ 5.90 – **23 rm** ⌑ 25.00/49.90 **t.**

🏨 **Castlebeigh** ⤳, 10 Knockard Rd, PH16 5HJ, off A 924 ✆ 2925, 🐎 – ⇔ rest 🅿
  18 rm.

🏨 **Queen's View** ⤳, Strathtummel, PH16 5NR, NW : 6 ½ m. by A 924 on B 8019 ✆ 3291, ≤
  Loch Tummel and mountains, ⤳, 🐎 – 🅿. ⟰ AE ⓞ VISA
  Mid April-October – **M** 14.30/17.70 **t.** and a la carte ⓵ 4.20 – **11 rm** ⌑ 22.70/54.50 **t.**

🏨 **Birchwood**, 2 East Moulin Rd, PH16 5DW, ✆ 2477, 🐎 – ⇔ rest 📺 🅿. ⟰ VISA
  closed December-February – **M** 7.00/11.25 **st.** and a la carte ⓵ 4.00 – **16 rm** ⌑ (dinner included) 34.75/56.00 **st.**

🏨 **Knockendarroch**, Higher Oakfield, PH16 5HT, ✆ 3473, ≤, 🐎 – ⇔ rest 📺 🅿. ⟰ AE ⓞ
  VISA
  April-October – **M** (dinner only) 10.50 **t.** ⓵ 3.50 – **12 rm** ⌑ 26.25/52.50 **t.** – SB 57.00/67.00 **st.**

🏨 **East Haugh House**, East Haugh, PH16 5SS, SE : 2 m. by A 924 ✆ 3121, 🐎 – 🅿. ⟰ VISA
  🛇
  M (bar lunch)/dinner 16.95 **t.** and a la carte ⓵ 4.95 – **6 rm** ⌑ 37.50/76.00 **t.**

🏨 **Craigvrack**, West Moulin Rd, PH16 5EQ, ✆ 2399 – ⇔ rest 📺 🅿
  19 rm.

🏨 **Airdaniar**, 160 Atholl Rd, PH16 5AR, ✆ 2266, 🐎 – ⇔ rest 📺 ☎ 🅿. ⟰ VISA
  closed January – **M** (bar lunch)/dinner 11.50 **st.** ⓵ 3.20 – **9 rm** ⌑ 33.85/49.70 **st.**

🏨 **Acarsaid**, 8 Atholl Rd, PH16 5BX, ✆ 2389 – ⇔ rest 🅿. ⟰ VISA 🛇
  closed 6 January-February – **M** 12.00 **t.** (dinner) and a la carte lunch approx. 5.00 **t.** ⓵ 2.75 –
  18 rm ⌑ 22.50/45.00 **t.**

🏛 **Claymore**, 162 Atholl Rd, PH16 5AR, ✆ 2888, 🐎 – ⇔ rest 📺 🅿. ⟰ VISA
  closed January-February – **M** (bar lunch)/dinner 13.15 **t.** – **12 rm** ⌑ 24.50/49.00 **t.**

🏠 **Balrobin**, Higher Oakfield, PH16 5HT, ✆ 2901, ≤, 🐎 – ⇔ rest 📺 🅿
  April-October – **M** 9.00 **t.** ⓵ 3.50 – **8 rm** ⌑ 16.00/40.00 **t.**

🏠 **Craig Urrard**, 10 Atholl Rd, PH16 5BX, ✆ 2346, 🐎 – ⇔ rest 📺 🅿. ⟰ AE VISA
  M 9.00 **t.** ⓵ 3.50 – **12 rm** ⌑ 15.50/34.00 **t.**

  at Killiecrankie NW : 4 m. by A 924 and B 8019 on B 8079 – ✉ ✆ 0796 Pitlochry :

🏨 **Killiecrankie** ⤳, PH16 5LG, ✆ 3220, Fax 2451, ≤, 🐎 – ⇔ rest 🅿
  March-November – **M** (bar lunch)/dinner 18.00 **t.** ⓵ 2.55 – **12 rm** ⌑ 32.50/63.00 **t.** –
  SB (except summer) 85.00/91.00 **st.**

FORD, SUBARU Atholl Rd ✆ 2471

PLOCKTON Ross and Cromarty. (Highland) 401 D 11 – pop. 425 – ✆ 059 984.

◆Edinburgh 210 – ◆Inverness 88.

🏨 **Haven**, Innes St., IV52 8TW, ✆ 223, ≤, 🐎 – ⇔ rest 📺 ☎ 🅿. ⟰ VISA
  closed 20 December-1 February – **M** (bar lunch)/dinner 15.50 **t.** ⓵ 4.00 – **13 rm**
  ⌑ 22.00/50.00 **t.**

POLMONT Stirling. (Central) 401 402 I 16 – see Falkirk.

POOLEWE Ross and Cromarty. (Highland) 401 D 10 – ECD : Thursday – ✉ Achnasheen –
✆ 044 586.

See : Inverewe Gardens★★★.

◆Edinburgh 241 – ◆Inverness 85.

🏨 **Pool House** ⤳, IV22 2LD, ✆ 272, ≤ Loch Ewe – ⇔ rest 📺 🅿. ⟰ VISA 🛇
  April-mid October – **M** (bar lunch)/dinner 12.50 **t.** – **13 rm** ⌑ 22.00/50.00 **t.**

EUROPE on a single sheet Michelin map no 920.

PORT APPIN Argyll. (Strathclyde) **401** D 14 – ECD : Thursday – ✆ 063 173 Appin.

⛴ to Lismore (Isle of) Monday/Saturday 5 daily : Sunday 4 daily (10 mn).

♦Edinburgh 136 – Ballachulish 20 – ♦Oban 24.

   Airds ⚜, PA38 4DF, ✆ 236, Fax 535, ← Loch Linnhe and hills of Kingairloch, « Former ferry inn on lochside », ⇘ – ⟨⟩ rest 📺 ☎ 🅿. ⚘
   closed mid November-mid March – **M** (restricted lunch)/dinner 28.00 t. ₰ 5.00 – **13 rm** 🛏 60.00/104.00 t., **1 suite** 124.00 t.

PORT ASKAIG Argyll. (Strathclyde) **401** B 16 – see Islay (Isle of).

PORTPATRICK Wigtown. (Dumfries and Galloway) **401** **402** E 19 – pop. 595 – ECD : Thursday – ✉ Stranraer – ✆ 077 681.

🏌18, 🏌9 Dunskey ✆ 81273.

♦Edinburgh 141 – ♦Ayr 60 – ♦Dumfries 80 – Stranraer 9.

   Knockinaam Lodge ⚜, DG9 9AD, SE : 3 ¼ m. by A 77 off B 7042 ✆ 471, ← garden and sea, park – ⟨⟩ rest 📺 ☎ 🅿. ⚒ ᴀᴇ ⊙ 𝘝𝘐𝘚𝘈
   Easter-January – **M** (booking essential) 24.00 t. (dinner) and a la carte lunch 11.00/14.50 t. ₰ 5.50 – **10 rm** 🛏 (dinner included) 77.00/154.00 t.

   Fernhill, Heugh Rd, DG9 8TD, ✆ 220, ←, ⇘ – 📺 ☎ 🅿. ⚒ ᴀᴇ ⊙ 𝘝𝘐𝘚𝘈
   M 12.50 t. (dinner) and a la carte ₰ 3.00 – **15 rm** 🛏 25.50/60.00 t. – SB 60.00/80.00 st.

   Broomknowe, School Brae, DG9 8LG, ✆ 365, ←, ⇘ – 📺 🅿
   closed December-January – **M** 5.75 s. – **3 rm** 🛏 15.50/21.50 s. – SB 15.75 st.

   Blinkbonnie, School Brae, DG9 8LJ, ✆ 282, ⇘ – ⟨⟩ rest 🅿
   February-October – **M** (by arrangement) 6.50 – **6 rm** 🛏 12.50/22.00.

PORTREE Inverness. (Highland) **401** B 11 – see Skye (Isle of).

PORTSONACHAN Argyll. (Strathclyde) **401** E 14 – ✉ Dalmally – ✆ 086 63 Kilchrenan.

♦Edinburgh 109 – ♦Glasgow 72 – ♦Oban 31 – Perth 80.

   Portsonachan ⚜, South Lochaweside, PA33 1BL, ✆ 224, ← Loch Awe and Ben Cruachan, ⇗, ⇘ – ⟨⟩ rest 📺 ☎. ⚒ ᴀᴇ 𝘝𝘐𝘚𝘈
   M (buffet lunch)/dinner 18.00 t. – **20 rm** 🛏 (dinner included) 38.00/87.00 t.

PRESTWICK Ayr. (Strathclyde) **401** **402** G 17 – pop. 13 355 – ECD : Wednesday – ✆ 0292.

🏌18 St. Nicholas, Grangemuir Rd ✆ 77608 S: off A 79 BY.

✈ ✆ 79822, Telex 778792 – **Terminal** : Buchanan Bus Station.

✈ see also Glasgow.

ℹ Prestwick Airport ✆ 79822 – Boydfield Gdns ✆ 79946.

♦Edinburgh 78 – ♦Ayr 2 – ♦Glasgow 32.

Plan of Built up Area : see Ayr

   Carlton, 187 Ayr Rd, KA9 1TP, ✆ 76811 – ⟨⟩ 📺 ☎ 🅿. ⚒ ᴀᴇ ⊙ 𝘝𝘐𝘚𝘈   BY **v**
   M (carving rest.) 6.35 st. – **36 rm** 🛏 41.50/56.00 st.

   Kincraig, 39 Ayr Rd, KA9 1SY, ✆ 79480 – 🅿   BY **c**
   M 6.00 st. – **6 rm** 🛏 12.00/23.00 st.

AUSTIN-ROVER 1 Monkton Rd ✆ 77415

QUOTHQUAN Lanark. (Strathclyde) **401** J 27 – ✉ ✆ 0899 Biggar.

♦Edinburgh 32 – ♦Dumfries 50 – ♦Glasgow 36.

   Shieldhill ⚜, ML12 6NA, ✆ 20035, Fax 21092, ←, « Victorian country house, 12C origins », ⇘ – ⟨⟩ 📺 ☎ 🅿 – ⚱ 25. ⚒ ᴀᴇ ⊙ 𝘝𝘐𝘚𝘈. ⚘
   closed 25 December-1 March – **M** 20.00/30.00 t. and a la carte ₰ 3.50 – **9 rm** 🛏 82.00/130.00 t. – SB (except summer) 112.00/165.00 st.

RAASAY (Isle of) Inverness. (Highland) **401** B 11 – pop. 182 – see Skye (Isle of).

⛴ by Caledonian MacBrayne : to Sconser (Isle of Skye) Monday/Saturday 3-7 daily (15 mn).

RENFREW Renfrew. (Strathclyde) **401** G 16 – pop. 21 456 – ECD : Wednesday – ✆ 041 Glasgow.

♦Edinburgh 53 – ♦Glasgow 7.

   Stakis Normandy (Stakis), Inchinnan Rd, PA4 9EJ, ✆ 886 4100, Telex 778897, Fax 885 2366 – 🛗 📺 ☎ 🅿 – ⚱ 400. ⚒ ᴀᴇ ⊙ 𝘝𝘐𝘚𝘈
   🛏 7.25 – **141 rm** 62.00/80.00 st.

   Glynhill, 169 Paisley Rd, PA4 8XB, ✆ 886 5555, Telex 779536, Fax 886 5355 – 📺 📠 🅿 – ⚱ 300. ⚒ ᴀᴇ ⊙ 𝘝𝘐𝘚𝘈
   M 8.75/15.95 st. and a la carte ₰ 4.00 – **80 rm** 🛏 47.50/79.00 st. – SB (except Christmas and New Year) (weekends only) 80.00/99.00 st.

PEUGEOT-TALBOT 18-20 Fulbar St. ✆ 886 3354   VAUXHALL-OPEL Porterfield Rd ✆ 886 2777

RHU Dunbarton. (Strathclyde) **401 402** F 15 – see Helensburgh.

RHUBODACH Bute. (Strathclyde) **401 402** E 16 – Shipping Services : see Bute (Isle of).

RHUM (Isle of) Inverness. (Highland) **401** B 13 – Shipping Services : see Mallaig.

ROBERTON Roxburgh. (Borders) **401 402** L 17 – ⊠ Hawick – ☎ 0750 Ettrick Valley.
♦Edinburgh 56 – ♦Carlisle 46 – Hawick 55.

    West Buccleuch ⑤, Ettrick Valley, TD9 7NQ, W : 8 m. on B 711 ℰ 62230, ☒, ☞ – ℗
    VISA
    M (bar lunch)/dinner 8.50 **st.** and a la carte ⫯ 3.00 – **7 rm** � 16.00/37.00 **st.** –
    SB 47.00/52.00 **st.**

ROCKCLIFFE Kirkcudbright. (Dumfries and Galloway) **401 402** I 19 – ⊠ Dalbeattie –
☎ 055 663.
⦗₉⦘ Colvend, Sand Hills ℰ 398.
♦Edinburgh 100 – ♦Dumfries 20 – Stranraer 69.

    Baron's Craig ⑤, DG5 4QF, ℰ 225, ≤, ☞, park – ☒ ☎ ℗. ☒ *VISA*
    Easter-mid October – **M** (bar lunch)/dinner 17.00 **t.** ⫯ 3.00 – **26 rm** ⊏ 42.15/86.40 **t.**

ROGART Sutherland. (Highland) **401** H 9 – ☎ 040 84.
♦Edinburgh 229 – ♦Inverness 73 – ♦Wick 63.

    Rovie Farm ⑤, IV28 3TZ, W : ¾ m. by A 839 ℰ 209, ≤, « Working farm », ☞, park –
    ☒ rest ℗. ☒
    Easter-October – **M** 8.00 **st.** – **6 rm** ⊏ 12.50/25.00 **st.**

ROTHES Moray. (Grampian) **401** K 11 – pop. 1 414 – ECD : Wednesday – ☎ 034 03.
♦Edinburgh 192 – ♦Aberdeen 62 – Fraserburgh 58 – ♦Inverness 49.

    Rothes Glen ⑤, IV33 7AH, N : 3 m. on A 941 ℰ 254, ≤, « Country house atmosphere »,
    ☞, park – ☒ ☎ ℗. ☒ AE ⊙ *VISA*
    closed January – **M** 9.50/19.00 **t.** ⫯ 4.00 – **16 rm** ⊏ 55.00/85.00 **st.** – SB (except sum-
    mer) (weekends only) 80.00 **st.**

ROUSAY (Isle of) Orkney. (Orkney Islands) **401** K 6 – Shipping Services : see Orkney Islands
(Mainland : Kirkwall).

ST. ANDREWS Fife. (Fife) **401** L 14 Scotland G – pop. 10 525 – ECD : Thursday – ☎ 0334.
See : Site★★ – Cathedral★ – West Port★.
Envir. : The East Neuk★★ (coastline from Crail to St. Monance) SE : 16 m. by A 917 – Leuchars
Parish Church★, NW : 6 m. by A 91 and A 919 – Ceres★ (Fife Folk Museum) W : 9 m. by B 939 –
Kellie Castle★, S : 9 m. by B 9131 and B 9171.
⦗₁₈⦘ Old Course, ⦗₁₈⦘ Eden Course, ⦗₁₈⦘ Jubilee Course, ⦗₁₈⦘ New Course, ⦗₉⦘ Balgove Course St Andrews
Links ℰ 75757 – ⦗₉⦘ St. Michaels ℰ 033 483 (Leuchars) 365, N : 5 m.
🛈 South St. ℰ 72021.
♦Edinburgh 51 – ♦Dundee 14 – Stirling 51.

    Old Course Golf and Country Club, Old Station Rd, KY16 9SP, ℰ 74371, Telex 76280,
    Fax 77668, ≤ golf courses and sea – ⧙ ☒ ☎ ♿ ℗ – ⚖ 150. ☒ AE ⊙ *VISA*
    May-December – **M** 15.50/22.00 **st.** and a la carte 18.50/42.25 **st.** ⫯ 7.00 – **108 rm**
    ⊏ 105.00/205.00 **st.**, **17 suites** 240.00/580.00 **st.** – SB (except summer) 130.00 **st.**

    Rusacks (T.H.F.), 16 Pilmour Links, KY16 9JQ, ℰ 74321, Fax 77896, ≤ – ⧙ ⇆ rm ☒ ☎ ℗
    – ⚖ 50. ☒ AE ⊙ *VISA*
    M 10.50/38.00 **st.** ⫯ 4.00 – ⊏ 8.75 – **48 rm** 75.00/138.00 **st.**, **2 suites** 200.00 **st.** –
    SB 90.00/140.00 **st.**

    Rufflets, Strathkinness Low Rd, KY16 9TX, W : 1 ½ m. on B 939 ℰ 72594, ≤, « Country
    house, gardens » – ☒ ☎ ℗. ☒ AE ⊙ *VISA*. ☒
    closed 7 January-19 February – **M** 9.00/17.00 **t.** and a la carte ⫯ 4.00 – **21 rm** ⊏ 46.00/100.00 **t.**
    – SB 76.00/133.10 **st.**

    St. Andrews Golf, 40 The Scores, KY16 9AS, ℰ 72611, Fax 72188, ≤ – ⧙ ☒ ☎ – ⚖
    150. ☒ *VISA*
    M (bar lunch)/dinner 16.50 **t.** and a la carte ⫯ 3.65 – **23 rm** ⊏ 47.50/81.00 **t.** –
    SB 70.00/94.00 **st.**

    The Scores (Best Western), 76 The Scores, KY16 9BB, ℰ 72451, Telex 94012061, Fax
    73947, ≤, ☞ – ⧙ ⇆ rest ☒ ☎. ☒ AE ⊙ *VISA*
    M (dinner only) 14.50 **st.** and a la carte ⫯ 4.00 – **30 rm** ⊏ 52.00/100.00 **st.** –
    SB (except Christmas-New Year) 76.00/110.00 **st.**

    Russell, 26 The Scores, KY16 9AS, ℰ 73447, ≤ – ☒ ☎. ☒ AE *VISA*. ☒
    M 15.00 **t.** (dinner) and a la carte ⫯ 3.50 – **7 rm** ⊏ 50.00/55.00 **t.** – SB (except sum-
    mer) 33.00/35.50 **st.**

AUSTIN-ROVER West Port ℰ 72101

ST. BOSWELLS Roxburgh. (Borders) ⓐⓞⓛ ⓐⓞ❷ L 17 – pop. 1 086 – ☏ 0835.
Envir. : Dryburgh Abbey★★ (Setting★★★).
🇫9 ✆ 22359, off A 68 at St. Boswells Green.
♦Edinburgh 39 – ♦Glasgow 79 – Hawick 17 – ♦Newcastle-upon-Tyne 66.

    Hotels see: Melrose NW : 4½ m.

ST. CATHERINES Argyll. (Strathclyde) ⓐⓞⓛ E 15 – ✉ Cairndow – ☏ 0499 Inveraray.
Envir. : Inveraray★★ (Castle★★-interior★★★) NW : 12 m. by A 815 and A 83 – Auchindrain★, NE :
18 m. by A 815 and A 83 SW.
♦Edinburgh 99 – ♦Glasgow 53 – ♦Oban 53.

  ↑ **Thistle House** without rest., PA25 8AZ, on A 815 ✆ 2209, ≤, 🛋 – 🍽 🅿
     April-September – **6 rm** ☲ 17.50/35.00 st.

ST. COMBS Aberdeen. (Grampian) ⓐⓞⓛ O 11 – pop. 817 – ECD : Wednesday – ✉ Fraserburgh
– ☏ 034 65 Inverallochy.
♦Edinburgh 173 – ♦Aberdeen 43 – Fraserburgh 6.

  🏨 **Tufted Duck** ⑤, AB4 5YS, ✆ 2481, ≤, 🛋 – 🍽 rest 📺 ☎ 🅿. 🔄 AE ⓞ VISA
     M 10.00 st. and a la carte 🍷 3.50 – **15 rm** ☲ 25.50/40.00 st. – SB 45.00/55.00 st.

ST. FILLANS Perth. (Tayside) ⓐⓞⓛ H 14 – ECD : Wednesday – ☏ 076 485.
🇫9 ✆ 312.
♦Edinburgh 67 – ♦Glasgow 57 – ♦Oban 64 – Perth 30.

  🏨 **Four Seasons**, PH6 2NF, ✆ 333, ≤ Loch Earn and mountains – 🍽 rest 📺 ☎ 🅿. 🔄 AE
     VISA
     closed mid January-late February – **M** 10.50/16.95 t. and a la carte 🍷 3.75 – **12 rm**
     ☲ 40.00/62.00 t. – SB 80.00/93.00 st.

  🏨 **Achray House**, PH6 2NF, ✆ 231, ≤ Loch Earn and mountains, 🛋 – 🅿. 🔄 AE VISA. 🛇
     March-October – **M** (bar lunch)/dinner 18.00 **st.** and a la carte 🍷 2.45 – **5 rm** ☲ 23.00/45.00 st.

SANDAY (Isle of) Orkney. (Orkney Islands) ⓐⓞⓛ M 6 – Shipping Services : see Orkney Islands
(Mainland : Kirkwall).

SANDYHILLS Kirkcudbright. (Dumfries and Galloway) ⓐⓞⓛ ⓐⓞ❷ I 19 – ✉ Dalbeattie –
☏ 038 778 Southwick.
♦Edinburgh 99 – ♦Ayr 62 – ♦Dumfries 19 – Stranraer 68.

  ↑ **Cairngill House** ⑤, DG5 4NZ, ✆ 681, ≤, 🛋, 🍴 – 📺 🅿
     closed January and February – **M** 11.00 st. 🍷 2.50 – **8 rm** ☲ 17.00/22.00 st.

SCALASAIG Argyll. (Strathclyde) ⓐⓞⓛ B 15 – see Colonsay (Isle of).

SCALPAY (Isle of) Inverness. (Highland) ⓐⓞⓛ A 10 – Shipping Services : see Harris (Isle of).

SCARISTA Inverness. (Outer Hebrides) (Western Isles) – see Harris (Isle of).

SCOURIE Sutherland. (Highland) ⓐⓞⓛ E 8 – ✉ Lairg – ☏ 0971.
♦Edinburgh 263 – ♦Inverness 107.

  🏨 **Eddrachilles** ⑤, Badcall Bay, IV27 4TH, S : 2 ½ m. on A 894 ✆ 2080, ≤ Badcall Bay and
     islands, 🛋 – 📺 ☎ 🅿. 🛇
     March-October – **M** (bar lunch)/dinner 8.40 t. and a la carte 🍷 2.60 – **11 rm** ☲ 38.75/59.00 t.

  🏨 **Scourie** ⑤, IV27 4SX, ✆ 2396, Fax 2423, ≤, 🐟 – ☎ 🅿. 🔄 AE ⓞ VISA
     Mid March-late October – **M** (bar lunch)/dinner 11.00 t. 🍷 3.00 – **20 rm** ☲ 20.00/48.00 t.

SCRABSTER Caithness. (Highland) ⓐⓞⓛ J 8 – Shipping Services : see Thurso.

SELKIRK Selkirk. (Borders) ⓐⓞⓛ ⓐⓞ❷ L 17 Scotland G – pop. 5 469 – ☏ 0750.
Envir. : Bowhill★★, W : 3 m. by A 708.
🇫9 Selkirk Hills ✆ 21091, S : 1 m.
🅸 Halliwell's House ✆ 20054 (summer only).
♦Edinburgh 40 – ♦Glasgow 73 – Hawick 11 – ♦Newcastle-upon-Tyne 73.

  🏨 **Philipburn House** ⑤, TD7 5LS, W : 1 m. at junction A 707 and A 708 ✆ 20747, Fax 21690,
     🌊 heated, 🛋 – 🍽 rest 📺 ☎ 🅿. 🔄 AE ⓞ VISA. 🛇
     closed 2 weeks January – **M** 10.50/18.50 t. and a la carte 🍷 4.25 – **16 rm** ☲ 41.00/82.00 t. –
     SB (weekends only) 85.00 **st.**

SHAPINSAY (Isle of) Orkney. (Orkney Islands) ⓐⓞⓛ L 6 – Shipping Services : see Orkney
Islands (Mainland : Kirkwall).

SHETLAND ISLANDS Shetland. (Shetland Islands) **401** PQ 3 Scotland G – pop. 27 271.

See : Site★ – Up Helly Aa★★ (last Tuesday in January).

✈ see Mainland : Lerwick and Sumburgh.

✈ Unst Airport : at Baltasound ✆ 095 781 (Baltasound) 404/7.

⛴ Shipping connections with the Continent : from Lerwick to Faroe Islands (Thorshavn) (Smyril Line) summer only – to Norway (Bergen) (Smyril Line) summer only – to Iceland (Seydisfjordur via Thorshavn) (Smyril Line) summer only – by P & O Ferries : Orkney and Shetland Services : from Lerwick to Aberdeen 5 weekly (14 h) – by Shetland Islands Council : from Lerwick (Mainland) to Bressay frequent services daily (5 mn) – from Laxo (Mainland) to Symbister (Isle of Whalsay) 5-8 daily (35 mn) – from Toft (Mainland) to Ulsta (Isle of Yell) frequent services daily (22 mn) – from Gutcher (Isle of Yell) to Belmont (Isle of Unst) frequent services daily (restricted on Sunday) (10 mn) – from Gutcher (Isle of Yell) to Oddsta (Isle of Fetlar) 2-3 daily (25 mn).

⛴ by J.W. Stout : from Fair Isle to Sumburgh (Gruntness) 1-2 weekly (2 h 30 mn) – by Shetland Islands Council : from Lerwick (Mainland) to Skerries 2 weekly (2 h 20 mn).

MAINLAND

Brae – ✉ ☎ 080 622 Brae.

⌂ **Busta House** ⟲, ZE2 9QN, SW : 1 ½ m. ✆ 506, Telex 9312100218, Fax 588, ≤, « Part 16C and 18C country house », ☞ – ⇥ rest �📺 ☎ ℗. ⟋ AE ① VISA
closed 22 December-3 January – **M** (bar lunch)/dinner 16.50 t. – **21 rm** ⊒ 27.50/59.00 t.

Hillswick – ✉ ☎ 080 623 Hillswick.

⌂ **St. Magnus Bay**, ZE2 9RW, ✆ 372, ≤, ☞ – 📺 ℗. ⟋ VISA
M 6.50/14.00 st. and a la carte ⌕ 3.50 – **25 rm** ⊒ 23.00/42.00 st.

Lerwick Scotland G – pop. 7 223 – ECD : Wednesday – ✉ ☎ 0595 Lerwick.

See : Clickhimin Broch★ – Shetland Croft House Museum★ – Mousa Broch★★★ (island site) S : 13 m.

▮ Dale ✆ 369, NW : 3 ½ m. on A 970.

✈ Tingwall Airport : ✆ 3535/2024, NW : 6 ½ m. by A 971.

🛈 Market Cross ✆ 3434.

⌂ **Shetland**, Holmsgarth Rd, ZE1 0PW, ✆ 5515, Telex 75432, Fax 5828, ≤, ⟋ – 🛗 📺 ☎ 🚻 ℗ – ⛣ 200. ⟋ AE ① VISA
M 6.50/12.50 st. ⌕ 3.50 – **64 rm** ⊒ 54.00/62.00 st., **1 suite** 90.00 st.

⌂ **Kveldsro House**, Greenfield Pl., ZE1 0AN, ✆ 2195 – 📺 ☎ ℗. 🦢
M *(closed Sunday to non-residents)* 7.50/8.50 t. and a la carte ⌕ 2.65 – **14 rm** ⊒ 33.35/54.65 t.

AUSTIN-ROVER North Rd ✆ 2709
PEUGEOT-TALBOT, MAZDA Holms Garth ✆ 2896

⊙ ATS 3 Gremista Ind Est. ✆ 3857

Sumburgh – ✉ ☎ 0950 Sumburgh.

See : Jarlshof★★ (prehistoric village).

✈ ✆ 60654, Telex 75451.

Whiteness – ✉ Whiteness – ☎ 059 584 Gott.

⚐ **Westings**, Wormadale, ZE2 9LJ, SE : 2 m. on A 971 ✆ 242, ≤ The Deeps and Islands – 📺 ℗. ⟋ VISA. 🦢
M (bar lunch Monday to Saturday)/dinner 12.50 **st.** and a la carte ⌕ 3.75 – **6 rm** ⊒ 22.50/32.00 st.

SHIELDAIG Ross and Cromarty. (Highland) **401** D 11 – ✉ Strathcarron – ☎ 052 05.
♦Edinburgh 226 – ♦Inverness 70 – Kyle of Lochalsh 36.

⌂ **Tigh-An Eilean**, IV54 8XN, ✆ 251, ≤ Shieldaig Islands and Loch, « Attractively furnished inn » – ℗. VISA
Easter-October – **M** (bar lunch)/dinner 13.00 t. ⌕ 3.25 – **12 rm** ⊒ 23.00/49.50 t.

SKEABOST Inverness. (Highland) **401** B 11 – see Skye (Isle of).

SKELMORLIE Ayr. (Strathclyde) **401** F 16 – pop. 1 606 – ECD : Wednesday – ☎ 0475 Wemyss Bay.
▮ ✆ 520152, E: off A 78.
♦Edinburgh 78 – ♦Ayr 39 – ♦Glasgow 32.

⌂ **Manor Park** ⟲, PA17 5HE, S : 2 ¾ m. on A 78 ✆ 520832, ≤ gardens and Firth of Clyde, « Extensive gardens », park – 📺 ☎ ℗. 🦢
closed 3 January-early March – **M** 18.00 t. (dinner) and a la carte ⌕ 3.85 – **23 rm** ⊒ 45.00/90.00 st. – SB 95.00/105.00 st.

⌂ **Redcliffe**, 25 Shore Rd, PA17 5EH, on A 78 ✆ 521036, Fax 521894, ≤, ☞ – 📺 ☎ ℗. ⟋ AE ①
M 10.00/16.00 st. and a la carte ⌕ 3.95 – **9 rm** ⊒ 38.50/58.50 st. – SB 90.00/110.00 st.

SKYE (Isle of) Inverness. (Highland) **401** B 11 and 12 **Scotland G** – pop. 8 139.

See : Site★★ – Cuillin Hills★★★.

✈ at Broadford : ℱ 047 12 (Broadford) 202.

🛳 by Caledonian MacBrayne : from Kyleakin to Kyle of Lochalsh : frequent services daily (5 mn) – from Armadale to Mallaig summer only Monday/Saturday 1-5 daily (30 mn) – from Uig to Tarbert (Isle of Harris) Monday/Saturday : 1-2 daily 1 h 45 mn direct - 4 h 45 mn via Lochmaddy – from Uig to Lochmaddy (North Uist) Monday/Saturday 1-2 daily (1 h 45 mn direct - 3 h 55 mn via Tarbert) – from Sconser to Isle of Raasay ; Monday/Saturday 3-7 daily (15 mn).

Ardvasar **401** C 12 – ⊠ ✆ 047 14 Ardvasar.

🏛 **Ardvasar,** ⊠ Sleat, IV45 8RS, ℱ 223, 🍴 – **P**. **VISA**
closed January, February and 2 weeks October – **M** 10.00/15.00 t. ⦙ 4.50 – **10 rm** ⪥ 25.00/55.00 t.

Culnaknock **401** B 11 – ⊠ Portree – ✆ 047 062 Staffin.

⌂ Glenview Inn, ℱ 248, ≼ – **TV** **P**
5 rm.

Dunvegan **Scotland G** – ⊠ ✆ 047 022 Dunvegan.

See : Dunvegan Castle★.

🏛 **Harlosh** ⌂, IV55 8ZG, SE : 6 m. by A 863 ℱ 367, ≼ Loch Bracadale and Islands – ⊱⊰ **P**.
◪ **VISA**. 🦌
7 April-October – **M** (dinner only) a la carte 10.80/21.50 t. ⦙ 3.50 – **7 rm** ⪥ 20.50/45.00 t.

✕ **Three Chimneys,** Colbost, IV51 9SY, NW : 5 ¾ m. by A 863 on B 884 ℱ 047 081 (Glendale) 258 – **P**. **◪** **VISA**
April-October – **M** *(closed Sunday except dinner July and August)* (booking essential) (restricted lunch)/dinner a la carte 12.00/20.70 t. ⦙ 3.50.

Isleornsay – ⊠ ✆ 047 13 Isleornsay.

🏰 **Kinloch Lodge** ⌂, IV43 8QY, ⊠ Sleat, N : 3 ½ m. by A 851 ℱ 333, ≼ Loch Na Dal, « Country house atmosphere », 🍴, 🍴 – ⊱⊰ rest **P**. **◪** **VISA**. 🦌
Mid March-November – **M** (dinner only) 26.00 st. ⦙ 4.00 – **10 rm** ⪥ 50.00/100.00 st.

🏛 **Toravaig House** ⌂, IV44 8RJ, ⊠ Sleat, SW : 3 m. on A 851 ℱ 231, 🍴 – ⊱⊰ rest **TV** **P**.
◪ **AE** **①** **VISA**
April-October – **M** (lunch by arrangement)/dinner 15.00 t. ⦙ 3.90 – **9 rm** ⪥ 50.00/80.00 t.

Kensaleyre – ⊠ Portree – ✆ 047 032 Skeabost Bridge.

⌂ **Kensaleyre House** ⌂, IV51 9XE, on A 856 ℱ 210, ≼ Loch Snizort Beag, « Country house atmosphere » – **P**
April-October – **M** 8.00 st. ⦙ 2.80 – **5 rm** ⪥ 15.00/30.00 st.

Portree **Scotland G** – pop. 1 533 – ECD : Wednesday – ⊠ ✆ 0478 Portree.

See : Site★★ – Skye Croft Museum★, N : 18 m. by A 850 and A 856 – Trotternish Peninsula★★, N : 40 m. by A 850, A 856 and A 855.

🛈 Meall House ℱ 2137.

🏛 **Rosedale,** Beaumont Cres., IV51 9DB, ℱ 3131, ≼ harbour – **TV** ☎ **P**
Mid May-September – **M** (bar lunch, residents only)/dinner 14.00 t. – **23 rm** ⪥ 26.00/56.00 t.

⌂ **Kings Haven** without rest., 11 Bosville Terr., IV51 0DJ, ℱ 2290 – **TV** 🦌
closed December-January – **6 rm** ⪥ 30.00/48.00 st.

AUSTIN-ROVER, FORD, RENAULT Dunvegan Rd ℱ 2554

Raasay Isle of – ⊠ Kyle of Lochalsh – ✆ 047 862 Raasay.

🏛 **Isle of Raasay** ⌂, IV40 8PB, ℱ 222, ≼ Narrows of Raasay and Skye, 🍴 – ⊱⊰ rest **TV** ⅖
P
April-September – **M** *(closed Sunday to non-residents)* (bar lunch)/dinner 13.50 t. ⦙ 4.00 – **12 rm** ⪥ 24.00/48.00 t.

Skeabost – ECD : Wednesday – ⊠ ✆ 047 032 Skeabost Bridge.

🏛🏛 **Skeabost House** ⌂, IV51 9NP, ℱ 202, ≼ Loch Snizort Beag, « Country house atmosphere », ⅌, 🍴, 🍴, park – **TV** ☎ **P**
14 April-22 October – **M** (buffet lunch)/dinner 15.00 t. ⦙ 4.50 – **21 rm** ⪥ 26.00/92.00 st.

SMA'GLEN Perth. (Tayside) **401** I 14 – see Crieff.

SOUTH QUEENSFERRY W. Lothian. (Lothian) **401** J 16 **Scotland G** – pop. 7 485 – ECD : Wednesday – ✆ 031 Edinburgh.

See : Forth Bridges★★.

Envir. : Dalmeny (St. Cuthbert's Church★ – Dalmeny House★) E : 2 m. by B 924 – Hopetoun House★★, W : 2 m. by A 904 – Abercorn Parish Church (Hopetoun Loft★) W : 3 m. by A 904.

ⓖ Dundas Parks ✆ 331 1902.

◆Edinburgh 9 – Dunfermline 7 – ◆Glasgow 41.

🏨 Forth Bridges Moat House (Q.M.H.), EH30 9SF, junction A 90 and Forth Bridge ✆ 331 1199, Telex 727430, ≼ Firth of Forth and Bridges, ▨, squash – 📺 ☎ Ⓟ – 🛥 120 **108 rm**.

STEWARTON Ayr. (Strathclyde) **401** **402** G 16 – pop. 6 319 – ECD : Wednesday and Saturday – ✆ 0560.

◆Edinburgh 68 – ◆Ayr 21 – ◆Glasgow 22.

XXX **Chapeltoun House** ⌕ with rm, KA3 3ED, SW : 2 ½ m. by A 735 off B 769 ✆ 82696, Fax 85100, « Country house in extensive grounds », ⌕, 🚗, park, ✀ – 🈁 rest 📺 ☎ Ⓟ. ▨ 🅰🅴 💳 **M** 16.00/23.50 **t.** and a la carte 12.50/17.50 **t.** ♦ 4.50 – **8 rm** ⊇ 65.00/114.00 **t.** – SB (except summer) 112.00/120.00 **st.**

Don't get lost, use **Michelin Maps** which are kept up to date.

STIRLING

Dumbarton Road.......... **B** 10
Murray Place .... **B** 15
Port Street................. **B**
Thistle Centre .... **B**
Upper Craigs .... **B** 29

Barnton Street .... **B** 2

Borestone Crescent .... **A** 3
Causewayhead Road .... **A**, **B** 4
Corn Exchange Road .... **B** 5
Cornton Road.............. **A** 7
Coxithill Road............. **A** 8
Drummond Place .... **B** 9
Goosecroft Road .... **B** 12
King Street .... **B** 13
Newhouse .... **A** 16
Park Place................ **A** 18

Queen Street .... **B** 20
Randolph Terrace .... **A** 22
St. John Street .... **B** 23
St. Mary's Wynd .... **B** 24
Seaforth Place .... **B** 25
Shirra's Brae Road .... **A** 26
Spittal Street.............. **B** 27
Union Street .... **B** 28
Victoria Square .... **B** 30
Weaver Row............... **A** 31

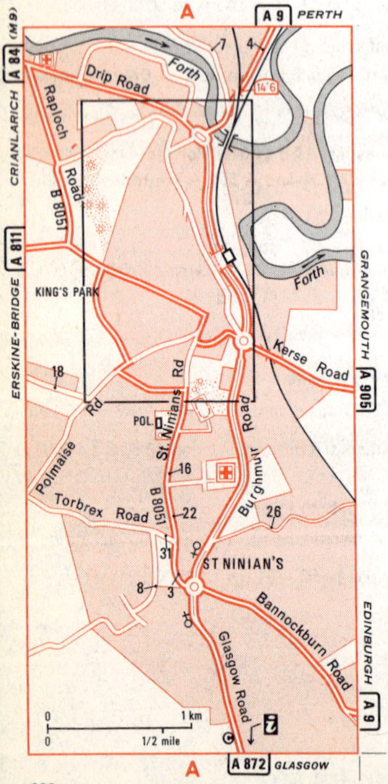

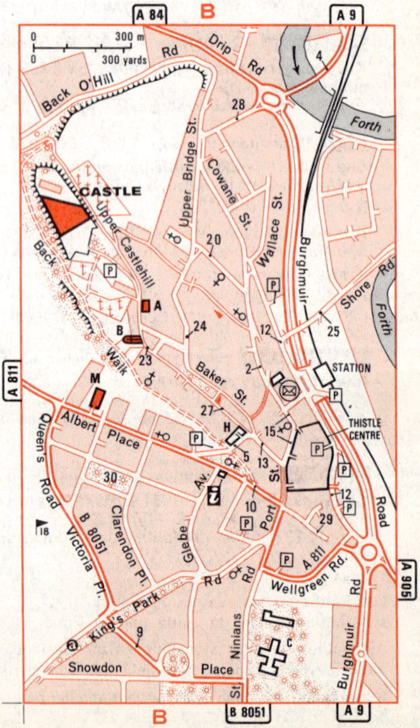

STIRLING Stirling. (Central) **401** I 15 **Scotland G** – pop. 36 640 – ECD : Wednesday – ✆ 0786.
See : Site★★ – Castle★★ (Site★★★-external elevations★★★-Stirling Heads★★★) B – Argyll and Sutherland Highlanders Regimental Museum★ B M – Argyll's Lodging★ (Renaissance decoration★) B A – Church of the Holy Rude★ B B.

Envir. : Wallace Monument (❄★★) N : 2 ½ m. by A 9 – A – and B 998 – Dunblane★ (Cathedral★) N : 6 ½ m. by A 9 – A – Doune★ (Castle★-Motor Museum★) NW : 8 m. by A 84 – A – M 9 and B 824 – Bannockburn, S : 2 m. by A 9 – A.

🏌18 Queens Rd ✆ 64098 – B – 🏌9 Alva Rd, Tillicoultry ✆ 0259 (Tillicoultry) 50741, E : 9 m. by A 9 – A – 🚗 ✆ 73085.

🛈 Dumbarton Rd ✆ 75019 – Broad St. ✆ 79901 (summer only).

♦Edinburgh 37 – Dunfermline 23 – Falkirk 14 – ♦Glasgow 28 – Greenock 52 – Motherwell 30 – ♦Oban 87 – Perth 35.

Plan opposite

🏨 Park Lodge, 32 Park Terr., FK8 2JS, ✆ 74862, « Tastefully decorated Georgian house, antiques », 🌳 – 📺 ☎ 🅿. 🆘 ⓓ 𝗩𝗜𝗦𝗔. 🕸   B **a**
closed Christmas – **9 rm** ☞ 45.00/100.00 **st.**

🏨 Granada Lodge without rest., Pirnhall roundabout, Snabhead, FK7 8EU, S : 3 m. ✆ 813614, Fax 815033 – 📺 ⚐ 🅿
36 rm.

at Blairlogie NE : 4 ½ m. by A 9 on A 91 – A – ✉ Stirling – ✆ 0259 Alva :

🏨 **Blairlogie House,** FK9 5QE, ✆ 61441, 🌳, park – 📺 ☎ 🅿. 🆘 𝗩𝗜𝗦𝗔
closed Christmas-New Year – **M** *(closed Sunday)* a la carte 11.45/17.25 **t.** ▯ 3.50 – **7 rm** ☞ 32.50/60.00 **t.** – SB (weekends only) 70.00 **st.**

CITROEN, VAUXHALL-OPEL 119-139 Glasgow Rd   ⊚ ATS 45 Drip Rd ✆ 50770
✆ 0786 (Bannockburn) 811234
FIAT 44 Causeway Head Rd ✆ 62426

STONEHAVEN Kincardine. (Grampian) **401** N 13 **Scotland G** – pop. 7 834 – ECD : Wednesday – ✆ 0569.

Envir. : Dunnottar Castle★★ (site★★★) S : 2 m. by A 92 – Muchalls Castle (plasterwork ceilings★★) N : 5 m. by A 92.

🏌18 Cowie ✆ 62124, N : 1 m. on Aberdeen Rd.

🛈 The Square ✆ 62806 (summer only).

♦Edinburgh 114 – ♦Aberdeen 16 – ♦Dundee 51.

✕✕ **Lairhillock,** Netherley, AB3 2QS, N : 6 ½ m. by B 979 ✆ 30001 – 🅿. 🆘 AE ⓓ 𝗩𝗜𝗦𝗔
M *(closed Monday dinner)* (bar lunch Monday to Saturday)/dinner 19.35 **t.** ▯ 4.40.

⊚ ATS 64-72 Barclay St. ✆ 62077

STORNOWAY Ross and Cromarty. (Outer Hebrides) (Western Isles) **401** A 9 – see Lewis (Isle of).

STRACHUR Argyll. (Strathclyde) **401** E 15 – ECD : Wednesday – ✉ Cairndow – ✆ 036 986.
♦Edinburgh 104 – ♦Glasgow 58 – ♦Oban 58.

🏨 **Creggans Inn,** PA27 8BX, on A 815 ✆ 279, Telex 778425, ≼ Loch Fyne, 🌳 – ☎ ⚐ 🅿. 🆘 AE ⓓ 𝗩𝗜𝗦𝗔
M 8.00/20.00 **st.** and a la carte ▯ 3.75 – **21 rm** ☞ 35.00/80.00 **st.** – SB (April-October) 88.00 **st.**

STRANRAER Wigtown. (Dumfries and Galloway) **401** **402** E 19 **Scotland G** – pop. 10 766 – ECD : Wednesday – ✆ 0776.

Envir. : Logan Botanic Garden★, S : 13 m. by A 77, A 716 and B 7065.

🏌18 Creachmore by Stranraer, Leswalt ✆ 87245, NW : 2 m.

⛴ by Sealink : to Larne frequent services daily (2 h 15 mn) – to Douglas (Isle of Man) by Isle of Man Steam Packet Co., summer only ; 1 weekly (4 h 45 mn).

🛈 Port Rodie ✆ 2595 (summer only).

♦Edinburgh 132 – ♦Ayr 51 – ♦Dumfries 75.

🏨 **North West Castle,** Portrodie, DG9 8EH, ✆ 4413, Telex 777088, Fax 2646, 🆘 – 🛗 📺 ☎ 🅿 – 🔥 100. 🕸
M 10.00/16.00 **st.** and a la carte – **77 rm** ☞ 36.00/98.00 **st.** – SB 80.00/84.00 **st.**

AUSTIN-ROVER Leswalt Rd ✆ 3636   ⊚ ATS Commerce Rd ✆ 2131

STRATHBLANE Stirling. (Central) **401** H 16 – pop. 1 933 – ECD : Wednesday – ✉ Glasgow – ✆ 0360 Blanefield.
♦Edinburgh 52 – ♦Glasgow 11 – Stirling 26.

🏨 **Country Club** 🦢, 41 Milngavie Rd, G63 9AH, S : ¾ m. on A 81 ✆ 70491, 🌳, park – 📺 ⚐ 🅿. 🆘 AE ⓓ 𝗩𝗜𝗦𝗔
M 9.50/15.10 **t.** and a la carte ▯ 4.25 – **10 rm** ☞ 40.00/65.00 **t.** – SB (weekends only) 60.00/80.00 **st.**

STRATHCONON Ross and Cromarty. (Highland) **401** F 11 – ⊠ Muir of Ord – ✆ 099 77 Strath-conon.

♦Edinburgh 184 – ♦Inverness 28.

  ⚲ **East Lodge** ⏚, IV6 7QQ, W : 11 m. from Marybank off A 832 ℰ 222, ≼, ⤆, ᴙ – ⊤ⱽ ℗.
  ◨ Æ ⓪ 𝘝𝘐𝘚𝘈
  M (bar lunch)/dinner a la carte 6.35/12.50 **t.** – **10 rm** � 18.00/42.00 **t.**

STRATHPEFFER Ross and Cromarty. (Highland) **401** G 11 – pop. 1 244 – ECD : Thursday –
✆ 0997.

🛈 Strathpeffer Spa ℰ 21219.
🛈 The Square ℰ 21415 (summer only).
♦Edinburgh 174 – ♦Inverness 18.

  🏠 **Holly Lodge**, Golf Course Rd, IV14 9AR, ℰ 21254, ᴙ – ⊤ⱽ ℗
  M (bar lunch)/dinner 13.50 **t.** ⦿ 2.50 – **7 rm** � 19.00/38.00 **t.**
  ⚲ **Mackay's**, High St., IV14 9DL, ℰ 21542, ᴙ – ⤇ rest ⊤ⱽ ℗. ◨ 𝘝𝘐𝘚𝘈. ⟡
  February-October – **M** (bar lunch)/dinner 10.50 **st.** and a la carte ⦿ 3.75 – **18 rm**
  ⊠ 18.50/33.00 **st.** – SB (except summer) 23.50/27.50 **st.**

STRATHYRE Perth. (Central) **401** H 15 – ⊠ Callander – ✆ 087 74.
♦Edinburgh 62 – ♦Glasgow 53 – Perth 42.

  ✕ **Creagan House** with rm, FK18 8ND, on A 84 ℰ 638, ≼ – ℗. ◨ 𝘝𝘐𝘚𝘈
  closed February and 1 week October – **M** (booking essential) (dinner only and Sunday
  lunch) 9.50/14.00 **t.** ⦿ 2.50 – **5 rm** ⊠ 18.50/37.00 **t.**

  at Balquhidder NW : 4 m. by A 84 – ⊠ ✆ 087 74 Strathyre :

  🏠 **Stronvar Country House** ⏚, FK19 8PB, ℰ 688, ≼ Loch Voil and Braes of Balquhidder,
  ᴙ – ⊤ⱽ ☎ ℗. ◨ 𝘝𝘐𝘚𝘈. ⟡
  February-October – **M** (bar lunch)/dinner 15.00 **st.** ⦿ 2.50 – **5 rm** ⊠ 36.50/69.00 **st.** –
  SB (October-March) 67.00 **st.**

STROMNESS Orkney. (Orkney Islands) **401** K 7 – see Orkney Islands (Mainland).

STRONSAY (Isle of) Orkney. (Orkney Islands) **401** M 6 – Shipping Services : see Orkney Islands
(Mainland : Kirkwall).

STRONTIAN Argyll. (Highland) **401** D 13 – ⊠ ✆ 0967.
🛈 ℰ 2131 (summer only).
♦Edinburgh 139 – Fort William 23 – ♦Oban 66.

  🏠 **Kilcamb Lodge** ⏚, PH36 4HY, ℰ 2257, ≼, ᴙ, park – ⤇ rest ℗. ⟡
  Easter-20 October – **M** (bar lunch)/dinner 16.50 **t.** ⦿ 4.00 – **9 rm** ⊠ (dinner included) 30.00/92.00 **t.**

  at Glencripesdale W : 15 ½ m. by A 884, Laudale rd and Forestry Commission Track –
  ⊠ Acharacle – ✆ 096 785 Salen :

  ⌂ **Glencripesdale** ⏚, Loch Sunart, Acharacle, PH36 4JH, ℰ 263, ≼ Loch Sunart and Ben
  Laga, ⤆, ᴙ, park – ⤇ rest ℗
  March-October (booking advisable) – **4 rm** ⊠ (dinner included) 51.00/102.00 **st.**

SUMBURGH Shetland. (Shetland Islands) **401** Q 4 – see Shetland Islands (Mainland).

TAIN Ross and Cromarty. (Highland) **401** H 10 – pop. 3 428 – ECD : Thursday – ✆ 0862.
🛈 The Clubhouse ℰ 2314.
♦Edinburgh 191 – ♦Inverness 35 – ♦Wick 91.

  🏠 **Royal,** High St., IV19 1AB, ℰ 2013, Fax 3450 – ⊤ⱽ ☎ ℗. ◨ Æ ⓪ 𝘝𝘐𝘚𝘈
  M (bar lunch)/dinner 25.00 **t.** ⦿ 3.10 – **25 rm** ⊠ 25.00/50.00 **t.** – SB (except summer)
  (weekends only) 60.00 **st.**

VAUXHALL Knockbreck Rd ℰ 2175

TARBERT Inverness. (Outer Hebrides) (Western Isles) **401** Z 10 – see Harris (Isle of).

TAYINLOAN Argyll. (Strathclyde) **401** D 16 – Shipping Services : see Gigha (Isle of).

TAYNUILT Argyll. (Strathclyde) **401** E 14 – ECD : Wednesday – ✆ 086 62.
♦Edinburgh 111 – ♦Glasgow 81 – ♦Oban 12.

  ⚲ **Polfearn** ⏚, PA35 1JQ, N : 1 m. ℰ 251, ≼, ᴙ – ℗. ◨ 𝘝𝘐𝘚𝘈
  M (bar lunch)/dinner 11.50 **t.** ⦿ 3.50 – **16 rm** ⊠ 26.00/46.00 **t.**

TAYVALLICH Argyll. (Strathclyde) **401** D 15 – ⊠ Lochgilphead – ✆ 054 67.
♦Edinburgh 141 – ♦Glasgow 95 – ♦Oban 40.

  X **Tayvallich Inn,** by Lochgilphead, PA31 8PR, ✆ 282, ≼ – **P**. 🆑 _VISA_
    April-October and Friday and Saturday in winter – **M** a la carte 6.50/14.25 **t.** ⓵ 3.00.

THORNHILL Dumfries. (Dumfries and Galloway) **401 402** I 18 **Scotland G** – pop. 1 449 – ECD :
Thursday – ✆ 0848.
Envir. : Drumlanrig Castle★★, NW : 4 m. by A 76.
🇮8 Blacknest ✆ 30546.
♦Edinburgh 64 – ♦Ayr 44 – ♦Dumfries 15 – ♦Glasgow 63.

  🏠 **Buccleuch and Queensberry,** 112 Drumlanrig St., DG3 5LU, ✆ 30215 – **P**. 🆑 _VISA_
    M (bar lunch)/dinner 12.50 **t.** and a la carte ⓵ 3.30 – **12 rm** � 25.00/55.00 **t.** – SB (January-
    May) 80.00/90.00 **st.**

    at Closeburn S : 2 ½ m. on A 76 – ✆ 0848 Thornhill :

  🏠 Trigony House, DG3 5EZ, N : 1 m. on A 76 ✆ 31211, ⌇, 🐎 – **P**
    12 rm � 26.00/42.00 **st.**

THURSO Caithness. (Highland) **401** J 8 **Scotland G** – pop. 8 828 – ECD : Thursday – ✆ 0847.
Envir. : Coast road to Durness via Strathy Point★ (≼★★★) – Torrisdale Bay★ – Ben Loyal★★ –
Coldbackie (≼★★) – Ben Hope★ – Loch Eriboll (≼★★★) W : 74 m. by A 836 and A 838.
🇮8 Newlands of Geise ✆ 63807.
🛥 by P & O Ferries : Orkney and Shetland Services : from Scrabster to Stromness (Orkney
Islands) 1-2 daily (2 h).
🅱 Car Park, Riverside ✆ 62371 (summer only).
♦Edinburgh 289 – ♦Inverness 133 – ♦Wick 21.

  🏠 **Forss House** ⌇, Bridge of Forss, KW14 7XY, W : 5 ½ m. on A 836 ✆ 202, ≼, ⌇, 🐎, park
    – 📺 ☎ **P**. 🆑 _VISA_
    M (bar lunch)/dinner 12.50 **t.** ⓵ 3.00 – **7 rm** � 32.50/60.00 **t.**
CITROEN Couper Sq. Riverside ✆ 62777   FORD Mansons Lane ✆ 63101

TIREE (Isle of) Argyll. (Strathclyde) **401** Z 14 – pop. 780.
🛩 ✆ 087 92 (Scarinish) 456.
🛥 by Caledonian MacBrayne : to Arinagour (Isle of Coll): 3-4 weekly (1 h to 1 h 15 mn) – to
Oban 3-4 weekly (4 h 30 mn to 5 h) – to Tobermory (Isle of Mull) Monday/Saturday 3 weekly (2 h
45 mn).

TIRORAN Argyll. (Strathclyde) **401** B 14 – see Mull (Isle of).

TOBERMORY Argyll. (Strathclyde) **401** B 14 – see Mull (Isle of).

TONGUE Sutherland. (Highland) **401** G 8 – ECD : Saturday – ⊠ Lairg – ✆ 084 755.
Envir. : Coast road east via Coldbackie (≼★★) – Ben Loyal★★ – Torrisdale Bay★ – Strathy
Point★ (≼★★★) E : 24 m. by A 836 – Coast road west via Ben Hope★ – Loch Eriboll (≼★★★) –
Cape Wrath★★★ (≼★★) W : 44 m. by A 838.
♦Edinburgh 257 – ♦Inverness 101 – Thurso 43.

  🏠 **Ben Loyal,** Main St., IV27 4XE, ✆ 216, ≼ – **P**. 🆑 _VISA_
    Mid March-mid October – **M** (bar lunch)/dinner 13.50 **t.** ⓵ 3.05 – **15 rm** � 19.00/33.50 **t.**

TROON Ayr. (Strathclyde) **401 402** G 17 – pop. 14 035 – ECD : Wednesday – ✆ 0292.
🇮8, 🇮8, 🇮8 Harling Drive ✆ 312464 – 🇮8, 🇮8 Royal Troon, Craigend Rd ✆ 311555.
🅱 Municipal Buildings, South Beach ✆ 317696 (summer only).
♦Edinburgh 77 – ♦Ayr 7 – ♦Glasgow 31.

  🏨 **Marine Highland,** 8 Crosbie Rd, KA10 6HE, ✆ 314444, Telex 777595, Fax 316922, ≼, 🆑,
    squash – 🛗 📺 ☎ **P** – 🔔 140. 🆑 AE ⓪ _VISA_
    M 8.95/17.50 **t.** and a la carte ⓵ 4.50 – **65 rm** � 67.00/99.00 **t.**, **6 suites** 132.00 **t.** –
    SB 80.00/116.00 **st.**

  🏨 **Piersland House,** 15 Craigend Rd, KA10 6HD, ✆ 314747, Fax 315613, 🐎 – 📺 ☎ **P**. 🆑
    AE ⓪ _VISA_
    M 16.50 **t.** and a la carte ⓵ 3.75 – **17 rm** � 49.00/86.00 **t.** – SB (winter only except Christ-
    mas) (weekends only) 60.00 **st.**

  🏨 Sun Court (Best Western), 19 Crosbie Rd, KA10 6HF, ✆ 312727, Group Telex 779830, ≼, 🐎,
    🍴, squash – 📺 ☎ **P** – 🔔 30
    20 rm.

  🏮 **Ardneil,** 51 St. Meddans St., KA10 6NU, ✆ 311611 – 📺 **P**. 🆑 AE
    M a la carte 8.35/13.15 **t.** ⓵ 2.25 – **8 rm** � 21.00/45.00 **t.**

  X **Campbell's,** 3 South Beach, KA10 6UG, ✆ 314421, Bistro – 🆑 AE _VISA_
    closed Sunday, Monday and first 3 weeks January – **M** a la carte 12.85/19.95 **t.** ⓵ 3.50.

DAIHATSU St. Meddans St. ✆ 312099   FORD 72-76 Portland St. ✆ 312312

TURNBERRY Ayr. (Strathclyde) **401 402** F 18 – ECD : Wednesday – ⊠ Girvan – ✆ 0655.
⌐₁₈, ⌐₁₈ Turnberry Hotel ℰ 31000.
♦Edinburgh 97 – ♦Ayr 15 – ♦Glasgow 51 – Stranraer 36.

🏨 **Turnberry** ⓢ, Maidens Rd, KA26 9LT, on A 719 ℰ 31000, Telex 777779, Fax 31706, ≤ golf
course and bay, ☒, ⌐₁₈, 🐎, ✗ – ⁅§⁆ 🆃🆅 ☎ ♿ ℗ – 🚣 220. 🅰 AE ⓞ VISA. ✘
M 13.75/24.50 **st.** and a la carte 22.10/37.80 **st.** ₰ 6.40 – **115 rm** ⬚ 130.00/170.00 **st.**, **6 suites**
190.00/325.00 **st.**

TWEEDSMUIR Peebles. (Borders) **401 402** J 17 – ⊠ Biggar (Lanark) – ✆ 089 97.
♦Edinburgh 38 – ♦Carlisle 58 – ♦Dumfries 57 – ♦Glasgow 37.

🏠 **Crook Inn,** ML12 6QN, N : 1 m. on A 701 ℰ 272, ≤, ⤸, 🐎 – ✗ rm ℗. 🅰
M 11.00/15.00 **st.** and a la carte ₰ 3.00 – **8 rm** ⬚ 22.00/52.00 **st.** – SB (weekends only) 60.00/70.00 **st.**

TYNET Banff. (Grampian) – see Buckie.

UDDINGSTON Lanark. (Strathclyde) **401 402** H 16 – pop. 10 681 – ECD : Wednesday –
⊠ Glasgow – ✆ 0698.
♦Edinburgh 41 – ♦Glasgow 10.

🏠 **Redstones,** 8-10 Glasgow Rd, G71 7AS, ℰ 813774, Fax 815319 – 🆃🆅 ☎ ℗. 🅰 AE ⓞ VISA. ✘
closed 25 December and 1-2 January – **M** (closed Sunday dinner) – **14 rm** ⬚ 35.00/53.00 **t.**

✗ **Il Buongustaio,** 84 Main St., ML6 6LT, ℰ 816000, Italian rest. – 🅰 AE ⓞ VISA
M (closed Sunday and Tuesday) 4.95 **t.** (lunch) and a la carte 6.95/35.95 **t.** ₰ 3.50.

UIG Ross and Cromarty. (Outer Hebrides) (Western Isles) **401** Y 9 – see Lewis (Isle of).

UIST (Isles of) Inverness. (Western Isles) **401** XY 11 and 12 – pop. 3 677.
✈ see Benbecula.
⛴ by Caledonian MacBrayne : from Lochboisdale to Oban 2-8 weekly (5 h 30 mn direct; 9 h via
Castlebay) – from Lochmaddy to Uig (Isle of Skye) Monday/Saturday 1-2 daily (1 h 45 mn direct -
3 h 55 mn via Tarbert) – from Lochmaddy to Tarbert (Isle of Harris) summer only: Monday/Satur-
day 1-3 weekly (1 h 45 mn).

Benbecula – ⊠ Liniclate – ✆ 0870 Benbecula.
✈ Benbecula Airport : ℰ 2051.
🏨 **Dark Island,** PA88 5PJ, ℰ 2414 – 🆃🆅 ☎ ℗. 🅰 VISA
M 6.00/24.00 **t.** and a la carte ₰ 3.00 – **42 rm** ⬚ 24.00/95.00 **t.**

Daliburgh (South Uist) – ⊠ ✆ 087 84 Lochboisdale.
🏠 **Borrodale,** PA81 5SS, ℰ 444, Fax 611, ≤, ⤸ – 🆃🆅 ℗. 🅰 VISA
M 6.50/12.50 **t.** ₰ 6.00 – **13 rm** ⬚ 20.00/40.00 **st.** – SB (weekends only) 56.00/61.00 **st.**

ULLAPOOL Ross and Cromarty. (Highland) **401** E 10 Scotland G – pop. 1 006 – ECD : Tuesday
except summer – ✆ 0854.
See : Site★.
Envir. : Falls of Measach★★ in the Corrieshalloch Gorge★, S : 11 m. by A 835 – Loch Broom★★,
Loch Assynt★★ and Lochinver, N : 37 m. by A 835 and A 837.
Exc. : Inverewe Gardens★★★ W : 50 m. by A 835 and A 832.
⛴ by Caledonian MacBrayne : to Stornoway (Isle of Lewis) Monday/Saturday 1-2 daily
(3 h 30 mn).
🅱 ℰ 2135 (summer only).
♦Edinburgh 215 – ♦Inverness 59.

🏨 **Royal** (Best Western), Garve Rd, IV26 2SY, ℰ 2181, ≤ Loch Broom, ⤸, 🐎, park – 🆃🆅 ☎ ♿
℗
57 rm, 1 suite.

🏨 **Mercury** (Mt. Charlotte), North Rd, IV26 2UD, ℰ 2314 – 🆃🆅 ℗
60 rm.

🏡 ❀ **Altnaharrie Inn** (Gunn Eriksen) ⓢ, IV26 2SS, SW : ½ m. via private ferry ℰ 085 483
(Dundonnell) 230, ≤ Loch Broom and Ullapool, « Idyllic setting on bank of Loch Broom »,
⤸, 🐎 – ✗. ✘
Easter-late October – **M** (booking essential) (restricted lunch, residents only)/dinner 40.00 **st.**
₰ 5.00 – **7 rm** ⬚ (dinner included) 95.00/170.00 **st.**
Spec. Crab soup, Breast of wood pigeon with a juniper berry sauce, Ravioli of seafood with a champagne
butter sauce.

🏠 **Ceilidh Place,** 14 West Argyle St., IV26 2TY, ℰ 2103, « Tasteful decor » – ✗ rest ℗. 🅰
AE ⓞ VISA
M (buffet lunch)/dinner 15.00 **st.** and a la carte ₰ 3.50 – **15 rm** ⬚ 25.00/70.00 **st.**

🏠 **Harbour Lights Motel,** Garve Rd, IV26 2SX, ℰ 2222, ≤ Loch Broom, 🐎 – ℗. 🅰 VISA
M (dinner only) 12.00 **t.** ₰ 3.50 – **22 rm** ⬚ 20.00/50.00 **t.** – SB 28.00/33.00 **st.**

🏠 **Ferry Boat Inn,** Shore St., IV26 2UJ, ℰ 2366, ≤ – ✗ rest – **11 rm**.

UNST Shetland. (Shetland Islands) **401** R 1 – Shipping Services : see Shetland Islands.

UPHALL W. Lothian. (Lothian) **401** J 16 – ECD : Wednesday – ⊕ 0506 Broxburn.
ᵢ₈ ☎ 856404.
♦Edinburgh 13 – ♦Glasgow 32.

　🏰　**Houstoun House,** EH52 6JS, ☎ 853831, Telex 727148, Fax 854220, ≤, « Gardens », park
　　– 📺 ☎ 🅿. 🔼 AE ⓪ *VISA*
　　M *(closed Saturday lunch)* 15.00/25.00 **t.** ⌷ 4.00 – **30 rm** ⊂ 70.00/108.00 **t.** – SB (week-
　　ends only) 100.00 **st.**

VATERSAY Inverness. (Western Isles) **401** X 13 – Shipping Services : see Barra (Isle of).

WALKERBURN Peebles. (Borders) **401** **402** K 17 – pop. 713 – ⊕ 089 687.
Envir. : Traquair House★★, W : 4 m.
♦Edinburgh 32 – Galashiels 10 – Peebles 8.

　🏠　**Tweed Valley** ⑤, Galashiels Rd, EH43 6AA, ☎ 636, Telex 13344, Fax 687639, ≤, ❧, 🚗 –
　　⊱✕ rest 📺 ☎ 🅿. 🔼 AE ⓪ *VISA*
　　M 7.50/9.50 **st.** and a la carte ⌷ 3.95 – **15 rm** ⊂ 31.50/63.00 **t.** – SB 69.00/78.00 **st.**

WEMYSS BAY Renfrew. (Strathclyde) **401** **402** F 16 – ECD : Wednesday – ⊕ 0475.
⛴ by Caledonian MacBrayne : to Rothesay (Isle of Bute) : frequent services daily (30 mn).
　　Hotels see : **Largs** S : 4 ½ m., **Skelmorlie** S : 1 ½ m.

WESTHILL Aberdeen. (Grampian) **401** N 12 – see Aberdeen.

WESTRAY (Isle of) Orkney. (Orkney Islands) **401** KL 6 – Shipping Services : see Orkney Islands
(Mainland : Kirkwall).

WEST WEMYSS Fife. (Fife) – see Kirkcaldy.

WHALSAY (Isle of) Shetland. (Shetland Islands) **401** R 2 – Shipping Services : see Shetland
Islands.

WHITEBRIDGE Inverness. (Highland) **401** G 12 – ⊕ 045 63 Gorthleck.
♦Edinburgh 171 – ♦Inverness 23 – Kyle of Lochalsh 67 – ♦Oban 92.

　🏰　**Knockie Lodge** ⑤, IV1 2UP, SW : 3 ½ m. by B 862 ☎ 276, ≤ Loch Nanlann and mountains,
　　« Tastefully converted hunting lodge », ❧, 🚗, park – ⊱✕ rest 🅿. 🔼 AE ⓪ *VISA*
　　May-October – **M** (bar lunch)/dinner 20.00 **t.** ⌷ 4.00 – **10 rm** ⊂ (dinner included)
　　65.00/138.00 **t.**

WHITENESS Shetland. (Shetland Islands) **401** Q 3 – see Shetland Islands (Mainland).

WHITING BAY Bute. (Strathclyde) **401** **402** E 17 – see Arran (Isle of).

WHITHORN (Isle of) Wigtown. (Dumfries and Galloway) **401** **402** G 19 Scotland G – pop. 989
– ECD : Wednesday – ⊕ 098 85.
Envir. : Priory Museum (Early Christian Crosses★★) NW : 4 m. by A 750.
♦Edinburgh 52 – ♦Ayr 72 – ♦Dumfries 72 – Stranraer 34.

　🏠　**Steam Packet,** Harbour Row, DG8 8LL, ☎ 334, ≤, 🚗 – 📺
　　M 7.45/9.50 **t.** and a la carte ⌷ 3.50 – **5 rm** ⊂ 16.50/33.00 **t.**
　♇　Queens Arms, 22 Main St., DG8 8LF, ☎ 369 – ⊱✕ rest 📺 ☎ 🅿. *VISA*
　　9 rm ⊂ 15.50/33.00 **t.**

WICK Caithness. (Highland) **401** K 8 Scotland G – pop. 7 770 – ECD : Wednesday – ⊕ 0955.
Envir. : the Hill O'Many Stanes★, S by A 9 – Grey Cairns of Camster★, S by A 9 – Duncansby
Head★ and the stacks of Duncansby★★, N : 17 m. by A 9.
ᵢ₈ Reiss ☎ 2726, N : 3 m.
✈ ☎ 2215, N : 1 m.
🛈 Caithness Tourist Organisation, Whitechapel Rd off High St. ☎ 2596.
♦Edinburgh 282 – ♦Inverness 126.

　🏠　**Mercury** (Mt. Charlotte), Riverside, KW1 4NL, ☎ 3344 – 📺 ☏ 🅿 – 🛋 150. 🔼 AE ⓪ *VISA*
　　M (bar lunch)/dinner 10.50 **t.** and a la carte ⌷ 3.70 – ⊂ 6.00 – **48 rm** 36.00/50.00 **st.**

DATSUN, VAUXHALL Francis St. ☎ 4123　　　　　　　　FORD Francis St. ☎ 2103

EUROPE on a single sheet

Michelin map no 920

Newton Stewart – 098 84 (4 fig.) or 0988 (5 fig.).

Wigtown and Bladnoch 3354.

Edinburgh 137 – Ayr 61 – Dumfries 61 – Stranraer 26.

Corsemalzie House , DG8 9RL, SW : 6 ½ m. by A 714 on B 7005 098 886 (Mochrum) 254, « Country house atmosphere », , , park – TV P. AE VISA
closed 20 January-6 March – **M** 8.50/13.90 **t.** and a la carte 3.00 – **15 rm** 39.50/62.00 **t.** – SB 66.00/82.00 **st.**

WORMIT Fife. (Fife) **401** L 14 – ECD : Wednesday – 0382 Newport-on-Tay.

Edinburgh 53 – Dundee 6 – St. Andrews 12.

Sandford Hill , DD6 8RG, S : 2 m. at junction of A 914 and B 946 541802, , – TV P. AE VISA
closed 1 and 2 January – **M** 11.55/15.65 **t.** 5.00 – **15 rm** 40.00/60.00 **t.** – SB (week-ends only) 68.00/77.00 **st.**

WYRE (Isle of) Orkney. (Orkney Islands) **401** L 6 – Shipping Services : see Orkney Islands (Mainland : Kirkwall).

YELL (Isle of) Shetland. (Shetland Islands) **401** Q 2 – Shipping Services : see Shetland Islands (Mainland).

Northern Ireland

Place with at least :

one hotel or restaurant .... ● Londonderry
one pleasant hotel .... 🏨 , ✕ with rm
one quiet, secluded hotel .... 🦆
one restaurant with .... ✿, ✿✿, ✿✿✿, M
See this town for establishments located in its vicinity .... BELFAST

La località possiede come minimo :

una risorsa alberghiera .... ● Londonderry
un albergo ameno .... 🏨 , ✕ with rm
un albergo molto tranquillo, isolato .... 🦆
un'ottima tavola con .... ✿, ✿✿, ✿✿✿, M
La località raggruppa nel suo testo le risorse dei dintorni .... BELFAST

Localité offrant au moins :

une ressource hôtelière .... ● Londonderry
un hôtel agréable .... 🏨 , ✕ with rm
un hôtel très tranquille, isolé .... 🦆
une bonne table à .... ✿, ✿✿, ✿✿✿, M
Localité groupant dans le texte les ressources de ses environs .... BELFAST

Ort mit mindestens :

einem Hotel oder Restaurant .... ● Londonderry
einem angenehmen Hotel .... 🏨 , ✕ with rm
einem sehr ruhigen und abgelegenen Hotel .... 🦆
einem Restaurant mit .... ✿, ✿✿, ✿✿✿, M
Ort mit Angaben über Hotels und Restaurants in seiner Umgebung .... BELFAST

NORTHERN IRELAND

Towns

ANNALONG Down 405 O 5 – ✆ 039 67.
♦Belfast 37 – ♦Dundalk 36.

🏠 **Glassdrumman Lodge** ⊱, 85 Mill Rd, BT34 4RH, ℰ 68451, Telex 747717, ≼ Irish Sea and Mourne mountains, « Working farm », 🐎, park – 📺 ☎ 🅿. 🔼 AE ① VISA. 🦺
  M (communal dining) (bar lunch)/dinner 16.50 t. ᵇ 6.50 – **8 rm** ☕ 45.00/65.00 t.

XX **Kitchen Garden,** Glassdrumman House, 224 Glassdrumman Rd, BT34 4QN, N : 1 ¼ m. on A 2 ℰ 68585, 🐎 – 🅿. 🔼 AE ① VISA
  closed Sunday to Tuesday in winter – **M** (dinner only and Sunday lunch)/dinner a la carte 10.00/13.75 t. ᵇ 3.50.

ANTRIM (Coast Road) Antrim 405 O 3.
See : Road★★★ (A 2) from Larne to Portrush.

BALLYCASTLE Antrim 405 N 2 – pop. 3 284 – ✆ 026 57.
See : Site★★.
Envir. : Giant's Causeway★★★ (Chaussée des Géants) basalt formation (from the car-park *AC*, ½ h return on foot) NW : 12 m. – White Park Bay★★, NW : 8 ½ m. – Carrick-a-Rede (≼★★ of Rathlin Island) NW : 5 ½ m.
🛈₁₈ ℰ 62536.
🛈 Sheskburn House, 7 Mary St. ℰ 62024.
♦Belfast 60 – Ballymena 28 – Larne 40.

⚓ **Antrim Arms,** 75 Castle St., BT54 6AS, ℰ 62284 – 🅿
  M *(closed dinner January-March)* (bar lunch Monday to Saturday)/dinner a la carte 8.40/12.20 t. ᵇ 3.00 – **16 rm** ☕ 16.00/35.00 t. – SB 38.00/40.00 **st.**

FORD, NISSAN Sheskburn Garage ℰ 62478   TOYOTA 47-49 Market St. ℰ 62733

BALLYMENA Antrim 405 N 3 – pop. 28 166 – ✆ 0266.
Envir. : Glen of Glenariff★★★ – Glenariff (or Waterfoot) site★, NE : 19 m.
🛈₁₈ 128 Raceview Rd ℰ 861207, E : 2 m. on A 42.
🛈 80 Galgorm Rd ℰ 44111.
♦Belfast 28 – ♦Dundalk 78 – Larne 21 – ♦Londonderry 51 – ♦Omagh 53.

🏠 **Country House** ⊱, 20 Doagh Rd ✉ Kells, BT42 3LZ, SE : 6 m. by A 36 on B 59 ℰ 891663, Fax 891477, 🐎 – 📺 ☎ 🅿 – 🔏 . 🔼 AE ① VISA. 🦺
  M 6.95/15.00 t. and a la carte ᵇ 3.25 – **14 rm** ☕ 30.50/126.00 t.

🏠 **Adair Arms,** 1-5 Ballymoney Rd, BT43 5BS, ℰ 653674, Fax 40436 – 📺 ☎ 🅿 – 🔏 250. 🔼 AE ① VISA. 🦺
  closed 25 December – **M** *(closed Saturday lunch)* 7.00/11.00 t. ᵇ 3.30 – **36 rm** ☕ 38.00/53.00 t. – SB (weekends only) 62.00 **st.**

X **Water Margin,** 8-10 Cully Backey Rd, BT43 5DF, ℰ 48643, Chinese rest. – 🅿. 🔼 AE ① VISA
  M 5.00/20.00 **st.** and a la carte approx. 15.80 **st.** ᵇ 4.00.

X **Manley,** State Cinema Arcade, Ballymoney Rd, BT43 5BY, ℰ 48967, Chinese (Canton, Peking) rest. – 🔼 AE ① VISA
  M a la carte approx. 10.00 t. ᵇ 3.50.

AUSTIN-ROVER 103 Waveney Av. ℰ 653557   ⓦ ATS Antrim Rd ℰ 652888
SEAT Pennybridge Ind Est, Larne Rd ℰ 652161
VW-AUDI 1-5 Railway St. ℰ 6546014

BALLYNAHINCH Down 405 O 4 – pop. 3 721 – ✆ 0238.
🛈₉ 20 Grove Rd ℰ 562365.
♦Belfast 14 – Downpatrick 10.

X **Woodlands,** 29 Spa Rd, BT24 8PT, SW : 1 ½ m. by A 24 on B 175 ℰ 562650, 🐎 – 🅿. 🔼 VISA
  closed Sunday, Monday and 25 December – **M** (dinner only) (booking essential) 16.25 t. ᵇ 3.00.

DAIHATSU-HYUNDAI Lisburn Rd ℰ 562597   FORD 41 Main St. ℰ 562519

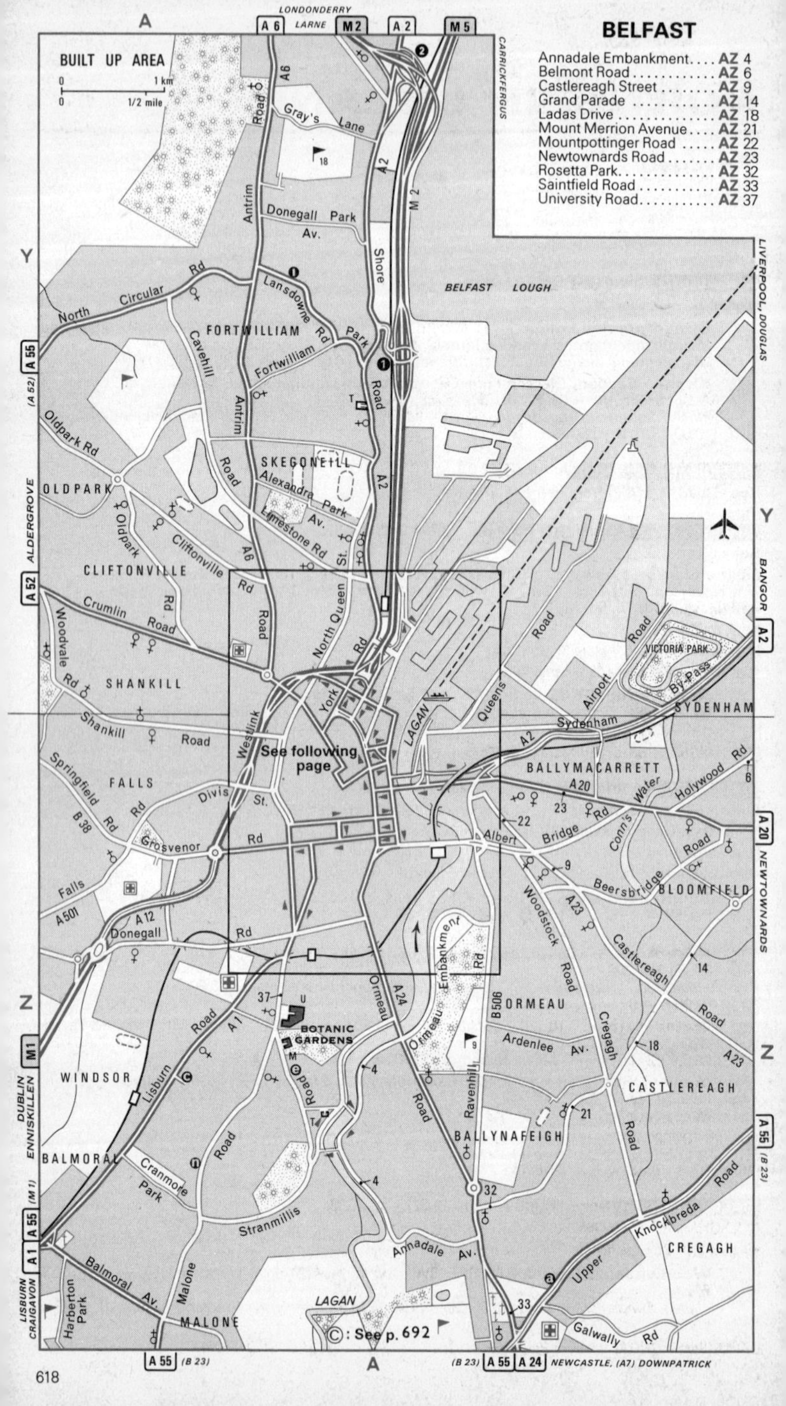

BELFAST

LONDONDERRY
LARNE
CARRICKFERGUS

BUILT UP AREA
0   1 km
0   1/2 mile

Annadale Embankment.... AZ 4
Belmont Road .... AZ 6
Castlereagh Street .... AZ 9
Grand Parade .... AZ 14
Ladas Drive .... AZ 18
Mount Merrion Avenue.... AZ 21
Mountpottinger Road ..... AZ 22
Newtownards Road ...... AZ 23
Rosetta Park............. AZ 32
Saintfield Road .... AZ 33
University Road.......... AZ 37

LIVERPOOL, DOUGLAS

BELFAST LOUGH

Gray's Lane

Donegall Park Av.

Antrim Road

Shore Road

Lansdowne Park

FORTWILLIAM

Fortwilliam

Cavehill Road

Antrim Road

SKEGONEILL
Alexandre Park
Av.

Limestone Rd

OLDPARK
Oldpark Rd

Oldpark Road

CLIFTONVILLE
Cliftonville Road

Crumlin Road

Woodvale Rd

SHANKILL

Shankill Road

North Queen St

York

LAGAN

Queens Road

VICTORIA PARK

Airport Road

Holywood Rd

SYDENHAM

Westlink

See following page

Springfield Rd

FALLS

Divis St.

Grosvenor Road

Falls Road

Donegall Road

BALLYMACARRETT

A20

Conn's Water

Castlereagh Road

BLOOMFIELD

Beersbridge Road

Albert Bridge

Woodstock Road

Cregagh Road

ORMEAU

Embankment

Ormeau Rd

WINDSOR

BOTANIC GARDENS

Lisburn Road

Malone Road

Stranmillis

Ardenlee Av.

CASTLEREAGH

BALLYNAFEIGH

Ravenhill Road

Annadale Av.

BALMORAL

Cranmore Park

Harberton Park

Balmoral Av.

Malone Av.

MALONE

LAGAN

Upper Knockbreda Road

CREGAGH

Galwally Rd

NORTH Circular Rd

ALDERGROVE

DUBLIN ENNISKILLEN

LISBURN CRAIGAVON

BANGOR

NEWTOWNARDS

NEWCASTLE, (A7) DOWNPATRICK

©: See p. 692

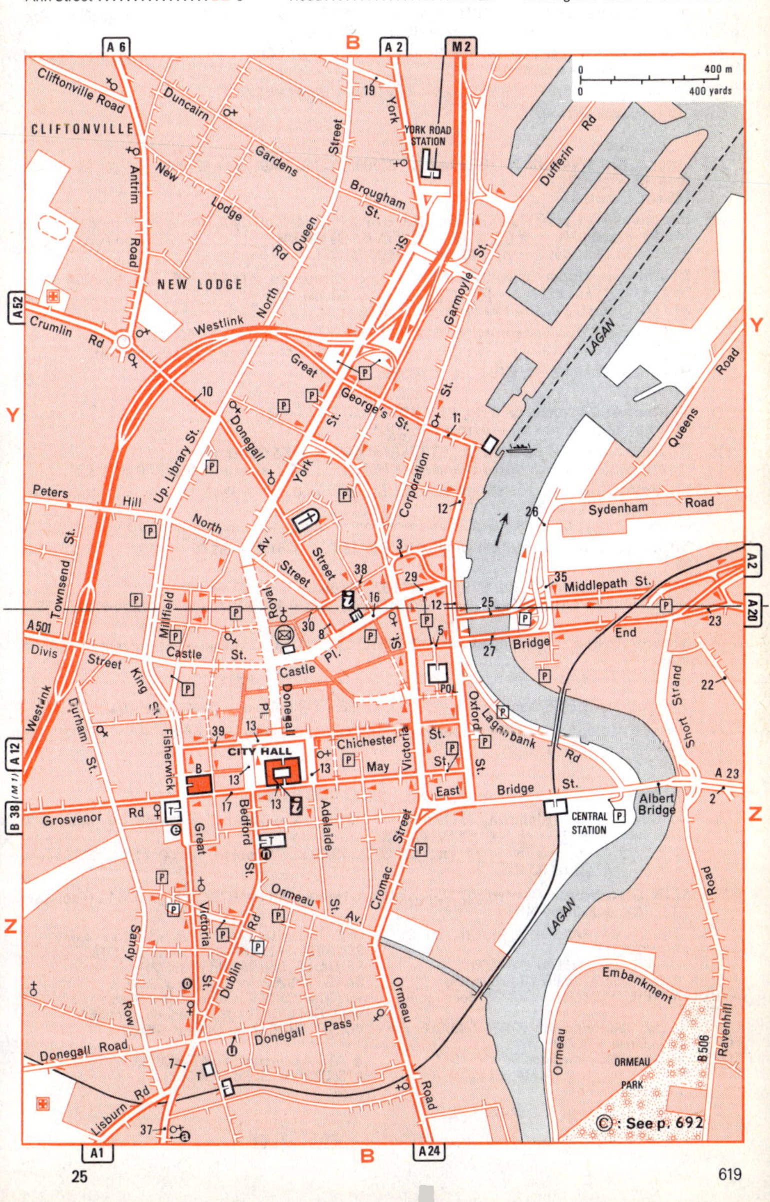

BELFAST
CENTRE

Castle Place .... BZ
Donegal Place .... BZ
Royal Avenue .... BYZ

Albert Bridge Road......... BZ 2
Albert Square .... BY 3
Ann Street .... BZ 5

Bradbury Place .... BZ 7
Bridge Street .... BZ 8
Clifton Street .... BY 10
Corporation Square .... BY 11
Donegall Quay .... BYZ 12
Donegall Square .... BZ 13
High Street .... BYZ 16
Howard Street .... BZ 17
Limestone Road .... BY 19
Mountpottinger
    Road .... BZ 22

Newtownards Road .... BZ 23
Queen Elizabeth
    Bridge............ BZ 25
Queen's Quay Road ...... BY 26
Queen's Bridge .... BZ 27
Queen's Square .... BY 29
Rosemary Street .... BZ 30
Station Street. .... BY 35
University Road .... BZ 37
Waring Street .... BY 38
Wellington Place......... BZ 39

A 6
B
A 2
M 2

Cliftonville Road
CLIFTONVILLE
Duncairn
Gardens
York Street
19
Brougham St.
YORK ROAD STATION
Dufferin Rd
LAGAN
A 52
Antrim Road
New Lodge Rd
Queen
Crumlin Rd
Westlink
NEW LODGE
North
Great George's St.
Garmoyle St.
Y
10
Donegall
Up. Library St.
York
Corporation
11
12
26
Sydenham Road
Queens Road
Peters Hill
North
Street
3
Av.
38
29
35 Middlepath St.
A 2
Townsend St.
16
12
25
23
A 20
A 501
Millfield
Royal
30
8
5
27
Bridge End
Divis Street
Castle St.
Castle Pl.
POL
Oxford St.
Laganbank Rd
22
Westlink
King St.
Donegall Pl.
Short Strand
A 12
Durham St.
39
13
CITY HALL
Chichester
Victoria St.
A 23
2
B 38 (M 1)
Fisherwick
B
13
May St.
East Bridge St.
Albert Bridge
Grosvenor Rd
13
17
13
Adelaide
Cromac Street
CENTRAL STATION
LAGAN
Great
Bedford St.
Ormeau St. Av.
Victoria
Sandy Row
Dublin Rd
Ormeau
Embankment
Ravenhill
B 506
Donegall Road
Donegall Pass
Ormeau
ORMEAU PARK
Lisburn Rd
7
37
Road
© : See p. 692
A1
B
A 24

See : City Hall★★ (1906) BZ – Queen's University★★ (1906) AZ U – Ulster Museum★ AZ M – Church House★ (1905) BZ B – Botanic Gardens (hot houses★) AZ – Bellevue Zoological Gardens (site★, ≤★) AC, by A 6 AY.

Envir. : Stormont (Parliament House★ 1932, terrace : vista★★) E : 4 m. by Belmont Rd AZ – The Giant's Ring★ (prehistoric area) S : 5 m. by Malone Rd AZ – Lisburn (Castle gardens ≤★) SW : 8 m. by A 1 AZ.

🏌 Balmoral, Lisburn Rd ℰ 381514 AZ – 🏌 Fortwilliam, Downview Av. ℰ 370770, N : 2 m. AY – 🏌 Shandon Park ℰ 701799, E : 3 m. by A55 AZ – 🏌 Knockbracken, Ballymaconaghy Rd ℰ 792108 Z – 🏌 Ormeau, Ravenhill Rd ℰ 641069 Z and B 506.

✈ Belfast Airport : ℰ 229271, NW : 12 m. by M 2 Motorway AY – Terminal : Coach service (Ulsterbus Ltd.) from Great Victoria Street Station (40 mn).

⛴ to Liverpool (Belfast Ferries) 1 daily (9 h) – to Isle of Man : Douglas (Isle of Man Steam Packet Co.) 2 weekly (4 h 30 mn).

🛈 River House, 52 High St., BT1 2DS ℰ 246609 – City Hall ℰ 320202 ext 227.

♦Dublin 103 – ♦Londonderry 70.

Plans on preceding pages

🏨 Europa, Great Victoria St., BT2 7AP, ℰ 327000, Telex 74491, Fax 327800, ≤ – 🛗 ⇔ rm 📺 ☎ 👤 – 🏛 600
195 rm, 5 suites.   BZ **e**

🏨 Stormont, 587 Upper Newtownards Rd, BT4 3LP, E : 4 ½ m. by A 2 on A 20 ℰ 658621, Telex 748198, Fax 480240 – 🛗 📺 ☎ 👤 – 🏛 250. 🚫 AE ⓞ VISA   on A 20   AZ
M (closed Saturday lunch) – **67 rm** ☷ 66.00/88.00 t.

🏨 **Drumkeen,** Upper Galwally, off Upper Knockbreda Rd, BT8 4TL, SE : 3 m. by A 24 off A 55 ℰ 491321, Fax 692949 – 📺 ☎ 👤 – 🏛 600. 🚫 VISA. ✗   AZ **a**
M 7.00/10.00 st. ⅄ 4.00 – **28 rm** ☷ 48.00/68.00 st.

↑ **Ash Rowan,** 12 Windsor Av., BT9 6EE, ℰ 661758, ☞ – ⇔ 📺 👤. 🚫 VISA. ✗   AZ **c**
closed 24 to 31 December – **M** (by arrangement) 15.00 st. – **4 rm** ☷ 28.00/50.00 st.

↑ Malone, 79 Malone Rd, BT9 6SH, ℰ 669565 – 📺 👤   AZ **n**
8 rm.

↑ **Somerton,** 22 Lansdowne Rd, BT15 4DB, ℰ 370717 – 📺   AY **i**
M (by arrangement) 7.50 – **8 rm** ☷ 15.00/26.00.

✗ **Restaurant 44,** 44 Bedford St., BT2 7FF, ℰ 244844 – 🚫 AE ⓞ VISA   BZ **n**
closed Saturday lunch, Sunday and Bank Holidays – **M** a la carte 13.55/17.00 st. ⅄ 3.25.

✗ **La Belle Epoque,** 103 Great Victoria St., BT2 7AG, ℰ 323244, Live music Monday to Thursday – 🚫 ⓞ VISA   BZ **o**
closed Sunday, 12-13 July and 25-26 December – **M** (dinner only) a la carte 10.10/15.00 t.

✗ **Saints and Scholars,** 3 University St., BT7 1FY, ℰ 325137 – 🚫 AE ⓞ VISA   BZ **a**
M 10.00 t. ⅄ 2.95.

✗ **Strand,** 12 Stranmillis Rd, BT9 5AA, ℰ 682266, Bistro – 🚫 AE ⓞ VISA   AZ **e**
closed Sunday lunch, 12-13 July and 25-26 December – **M** 10.15 t. and a la carte 8.50/10.35 t. ⅄ 3.15.

✗ **Manor House,** 47 Donegall Pass, BT7 1DQ, ℰ 238755, Chinese (Canton) rest. – 🚫 ⓞ VISA   BZ **u**
closed 25 December – **M** 3.50/10.50 t. and a la carte 10.50/13.50 t.

at Dundonald E : 5 ½ m. by A 2 – BY – on A 20 – ✉ Belfast – ✆ 0247 Comber :

↑ Cottage without rest., 377 Comber Rd, BT16 0XB, SE : 1 ¾ m. on Comber Rd ℰ 878189, ☞ – 👤
3 rm.

at Dunmurry SW : 5 ½ m. on A 1 – AZ – ✉ ✆ 0232 Belfast :

🏨 **Conway** (T.H.F.), Kingsway, BT17 9ES, ℰ 612101, Telex 74281, Fax 626546, ☞, squash – 🛗 ▤ rest 📺 ☎ 👤 – 🏛 300. 🚫 AE ⓞ VISA
M 8.50/11.50 st. ⅄ 3.75 – **77 rm** ☷ 59.00/79.00 st., **1 suite** 135.00 st. – SB (weekends only) 47.00/57.00 st.

MICHELIN Distribution Centre, 40 Mallusk Road, Newtonabbey, BT38 8PX, ℰ 023 13 (Glengormie) 42616, FAX 342732 by N7 AZ

ALFA-ROMEO, DAIHATSU, FERRARI 50 St. Georges St. ℰ 232111
AUSTIN-ROVER Saintfield Rd ℰ 649774
AUSTIN-ROVER 52-80 Shankil Rd ℰ 242456
AUSTIN-ROVER, DAIMLER-JAGUAR Boucher Rd ℰ 381721
CITROEN 357 Albertbridge Rd ℰ 457575 457766
FORD Lislea Drive ℰ 662231
FORD 397 Upper Newtownards Rd ℰ 654687
FORD 58-82 Antrim Rd ℰ 744744

OPEL-VAUXHALL 17-29 Ravenhill Rd ℰ 451422
PEUGEOT-TALBOT 226 York St. ℰ 747133
RENAULT Boucher Rd ℰ 381721
SAAB 250-252 Donegall Rd ℰ 321019
TOYOTA 39-49 Adelaide St. ℰ 328225
VAUXHALL-OPEL 83-87 York Rd ℰ 746960
VOLVO 59-75 Ladas Drive ℰ 705666

⦿ ATS 4 Duncrue St. ℰ 749531
ATS 32 Boucher Rd. ℰ 663623

BUSHMILLS Antrim 𝟜𝟘𝟝 M 2 – pop. 1 381 – ✉ Bushmills – ✆ 026 57 Dervock.

🛉₉ Bushfoot, Portballintrae ✆ 31317.

♦Belfast 57 – Ballycastle 12 – Coleraine 10.

🏛 **Bushmills Inn,** 25 Main St., BT57 8QA, ✆ 32339 – 📺 ✆ ℗ – 🎪 60. ◪ 𝘝𝘐𝘚𝘈
    M a la carte 6.25/13.25 t. 🍷 3.75 – **11 rm** ⌷ 30.00/48.00 t. – SB (weekends only)
    (except July, August and Bank Holidays) 57.00 **st.**

🏛 **Causeway** ⌂, Causeway Head, BT57 8SU, NE : 2 m. by A 2 ✆ 31226, ≤, 🚒 – 📺 ✆ ℗.
    ◪ 𝘝𝘐𝘚𝘈. 🛇
    M 6.30/10.50 **st.** and a la carte – **16 rm** ⌷ 20.00/35.00 **st.** – SB (except July and
    August) 50.00/55.00 **st.**

XX **Auberge de Seneirl** ⌂ with rm, 28 Ballyclogh Rd, BT57 8UZ, SW : 3 m. by B 17 on
    Seneirl rd ✆ 41536, French rest., ◪ – 📺 ℗. ◍. 🛇
    M *(closed Sunday and Monday and Tuesday in winter)* (dinner only) 16.95 **st.** and a la carte
    12.45/15.40 **st.** 🍷 4.15 – **5 rm** ⌷ 18.50/44.00 **st.**

CITROEN Inland Ballycastle Rd ✆ 31748/31452

CARNLOUGH Antrim 𝟜𝟘𝟝 O 3 – pop. 1 462 – ✉ Ballymena – ✆ 0574.

🛈 Post Office, Harbour Rd ✆ 85210.

♦Belfast 37 – Ballymena 16 – Larne 14.

🏛 **Londonderry Arms,** Harbour Rd, BT44 0EU, ✆ 85255, Fax 85263 – 📺 ✆ ℗ – 🎪 35. ◪
    𝘈𝘌 ◍ 𝘝𝘐𝘚𝘈. 🛇
    M 8.45/12.45 **st.** and a la carte 🍷 3.20 – **14 rm** ⌷ 25.00/45.00 **st.** – SB (weekends
    only) (except Easter and Christmas) 49.95/62.20 **st.**

CARRICKFERGUS Antrim 𝟜𝟘𝟝 O 3 – pop. 17 633 – ✆ 096 03.

See : Castle★★ (13C) *AC* – Sea Front★ – St. Nicholas' Church★ (12C-18C).

Envir. : Island Magee Peninsula (Port Muck★, Isle of Muck★, Power Station ≤★) NE : 9 m.

🛉₁₈ 35 North Rd ✆ 63713.

🛈 Castle Green ✆ 51604 (summer only) – Town Hall (winter only).

♦Belfast 10 – Larne 14.

☎ Coast Road, 28 Scotch Quarter, BT38 7DP, ✆ 51021 – 📺 ✆. 🛇
    20 rm.

FORD 30 Joymount Rd ✆ 69933   RENAULT Larne Rd ✆ 63672

Pour l'ensemble de la Grande-Bretagne et de l'Irlande,
procurez-vous la carte Michelin 𝟿𝟪𝟨 à 1/1 000 000.

CASTLEROCK Londonderry – see Coleraine.

COLERAINE Londonderry 𝟜𝟘𝟝 L 2 – pop. 15 967 – ✆ 0265.

Envir. : Giant's Causeway★★★ (Chaussée des Géants) basalt formation (from the car-park *AC*,
½ h return on foot) NE : 9 m. – Downhill Castle (Mussenden Temple★ 18C : ≤★★★ *AC*) NW : 7 m.
– Portrush (site★, ≤★) N : 6 m. – Dunluce Castle (site★, ≤★) NE : 8 m. – W : Benevenagh Moun-
tain★ – 🛉₁₈, 🛉₁₈, 🛉₉ Royal Portrush, Dunluce Rd, Portrush ✆ 822311.

🛈 Swimming Pool, Main St., Castlerock ✆ 848258 (summer only).

♦Belfast 53 – Ballymena 25 – ♦Londonderry 31 – ♦Omagh 65.

🛖 **Greenhill House** ⌂, 24 Greenhill Rd, Aghadowey, BT51 4EU, S : 9 m. by A 29 on B 66
    ✆ 868241, 🚒 – ℗. 🛇
    March-October – **M** 10.00 – **7 rm** ⌷ 17.00/30.00 – SB 49.00/53.00 **st.**

🛖 Camus House ⌂ without rest., 27 Curragh Rd, SE : 3 ¾ m. on A 54 ✆ 42982, 🚒 – 📺 ℗
    3 rm.

XX **MacDuffs** ⌂ with rm, Blackheath House, 112 Killeague Rd, Blackhill, BT51 4HH, S : 8 m.
    by A 29 on Macosquin rd ✆ 868433, « 18C former manse », ◪, 🚒 – 📺 ℗. 🛇
    closed Sunday, Monday, 12 July and 25-26 December – **M** (booking essential) (dinner only)
    a la carte 11.00/15.45 t. 🍷 3.00 – **6 rm** ⌷ 25.00/45.00 t.

    at Castlerock NW : 6 m. by A 2 on B 119 – ✉ ✆ 0265 Castlerock :

🛖 **Maritima** without rest., 43 Main St., BT51 4RA, ✆ 848388, ≤, 🚒 – ℗
    3 rm ⌷ 12.00/24.00 s.

VAUXHALL-OPEL Hanover Pl. ✆ 2386/8788   ◉ ATS Loguestown Ind Est., Bushmills Rd ✆
                                             42329/52817

CRAWFORDSBURN Down 𝟜𝟘𝟝 O 4 – pop. 140 – ✆ 0247 Helen's Bay.

🛉₁₈ Carnalea, Station Rd ✆ 0247 (Bangor) 465004 – 🛉₁₈, 🛉₁₈ Clandeboye, Conlig ✆ 0247 (Bangor)
271767 – 🛉₁₈ Broadway ✆ 0247 (Bangor) 465133.

♦Belfast 10 – Bangor 3.

🏛 **Old Inn,** 15 Main St., BT19 1JH, ✆ 853255, Fax 852775, 🚒 – 📺 ✆ ℗. ◪ 𝘈𝘌 ◍ 𝘝𝘐𝘚𝘈. 🛇
    closed 25 and 26 December – **M** 8.50/12.00 **st.** and a la carte – **25 rm** ⌷ 45.00/70.00 **st.**

DUNADRY Antrim **405** N 3 – ✆ 084 94 Templepatrick.
Envir. : Antrim (round tower★ 10C) NW : 5 m. – Shane's Castle★ (16C ruins) *AC*, NW : 5 ½ m. (access by miniature railway).
♦Belfast 15 – Larne 18 – ♦Londonderry 56.

- **Dunadry Inn**, 2 Islandreagh Drive, BT41 2HA, ✆ 32474, Telex 747245, Fax 33389, ⚲, ⪪ TV ☎ 🅿 – 🕭 250. ⬛ AE Ⓞ VISA ❄
  closed 24 to 26 December – **M** (buffet lunch Saturday) 10.00/14.00 **t.** and a la carte ⬧ 3.75 – **64 rm** ⬄ 70.00/130.00 **t.** – SB (weekends only) 55.00/315.00 **st.**

DUNDONALD Antrim **405** O 4 – see Belfast.

DUNMURRY Antrim **405** N 4 – see Belfast.

ENNISKILLEN Fermanagh **405** J 4 – pop. 10 429 – ✆ 0365.
See : Lough Erne★★★ (Upper and Lower) – On Lower Lough Erne, by boat *AC* : Devenish Island (site★★, monastic ruins : scenery★) and White Island★.
Envir. : Castle Coole★ 18C (site★) E : 1 m. – Florence Court (site★, park★) *AC*, SW : 8 m.
⛳ Castlecoole ✆ 25250.
🛈 Lakeland Visitor Centre, Shore Rd ✆ 23110 and 25050.
♦Belfast 87 – ♦Londonderry 59.

- **Killyhevlin**, Dublin Rd, BT74 4AU, SE : 1 ¾ m. on A 4 ✆ 23481, Fax 24726, ≤, ⪪, park – TV ☎ 🅿 – 🕭 270. ⬛ AE Ⓞ VISA ❄
  closed 25 December – **M** (carving lunch) 8.00/12.50 **t.** and a la carte ⬧ 3.95 – **21 rm** ⬄ 41.25/62.50 **st.**, **1 suite** 85.00/110.00 **st.**
- **Fort Lodge**, 72 Forthill St., ✆ 23275 – ⤢ rest TV ☎ 🅿. ❄ – **11 rm.**
- **Willoughby**, 24 Willoughby Pl., BT74 7EX, ✆ 25275 – ⤢ rest 🅿. ❄ – **14 rm**.

AUSTIN-ROVER Dublin Rd ✆ 23475   VAUXHALL-OPEL Tempo Rd ✆ 24366

GLENARM Antrim **405** O 3 – ✆ 057 484.
♦Belfast 32 – Ballycastle 29 – Ballymena 19 – Larne 12.

- **Drumnagreagh Lodge** ⟡, Coast Rd, BT44 0BB, S : 4 m. on A 2 ✆ 651, ≤, ⪪ – TV ☎ 🅿 – 🕭 250. ⬛ AE Ⓞ VISA
  M 6.50/12.50 **t.** and a la carte ⬧ 4.95 – **16 rm** ⬄ 30.00/49.00 **t.** – SB (weekends only) 56.00/70.00 **st.**

GLENGORMLEY Antrim **405** O 3 – ✉ Newtownabbey – ✆ 023 13 (4 and 5 fig.) or 0232 (6 fig.).
♦Belfast 6 – Larne 15.

- **Chimney Corner**, 630 Antrim Rd, BT36 8RH, NW : 2 m. on A 6 ✆ 44925, Telex 748158, Fax 44352, ⛳, ⪪, ✗ – ⤢ rest TV ☎ 🅿 – 🕭 300. ⬛ AE Ⓞ VISA ❄
  closed 10 days at Christmas and 11 to 13 July – **M** 8.00/13.00 **st.** and a la carte ⬧ 3.25 – **63 rm** ⬄ 52.00/64.00 **st.** – SB (weekends only) 70.00/74.00 **st.**
- **Sleepy Hollow**, 15 Kiln Rd, Ballyhenry, BT36 8SU, N : 2 m. by A 8(M) off B 56 ✆ 342042 – 🅿. ⬛ AE Ⓞ VISA
  closed Sunday to Tuesday – **M** (dinner only) 17.95 **t.** ⬧ 3.95.

AUSTIN-ROVER 144 Antrim Rd ✆ 0232 (Belfast)   RENAULT 612 Antrim Rd ✆ 3496
773606   VW-AUDI 45 Mallusk Rd ✆ 0232 (Belfast) 342111

HILLSBOROUGH Down **405** N 4 – ✆ 0846.
See : Government House★ (18C) – the Fort★ (17C).
Envir. : Legananny Dolmen ≤★, S : 16 m.
🛈 Council Offices, The Square ✆ 682477.
♦Belfast 13.

- **White Gables**, 14 Dromore Rd, BT26 6HU, ✆ 682755, Telex 748060, Fax 689532 – TV ☎ 🅿 – 🕭 200. ⬛ AE Ⓞ VISA. ❄
  M 9.50/10.50 **t.** and a la carte – **25 rm** ⬄ 49.50/75.00 **t.**
- **Hillside**, 21 Main St., BT26 6AE, ✆ 682765 – ⬛ AE Ⓞ VISA
  M *(closed Sunday dinner)* (buffet lunch)/dinner a la carte 14.70/18.15 **t.**

TOYOTA 23 Lisburn Rd ✆ 682188

HOLYWOOD Down **405** O 4 – pop. 9 462 – ✆ 023 17.
Envir. : Craigavad : Ulster Folk and Transport Museum★ (Cultra Manor) *AC*, NE : 3 m.
♦Belfast 5 – Bangor 6.

- **Culloden** ⟡, 142 Bangor Rd, BT18 0EX, E : 1 ½ m. on A 2 ✆ 5223, Telex 74617, Fax 6777, ≤, ⪪, park, ✗, squash – ⧉ TV ☎ ♿ 🅿 – 🕭 500
  84 rm, **7 suites**.
- **Tudor Guest Lodge** ⟡, 60 Demesne Rd, off High St., BT18 9EX, ✆ 5859, ⪪ – ⤢ rest TV 🅿. ❄
  M (residents only) 7.00/8.00 **st.** – **5 rm** ⬄ 33.00/43.00 **st.**

IRVINESTOWN Fermanagh **405** J 4 – pop. 1 827 – ❂ 036 56.

◆Belfast 78 – ◆Dublin 132 – Donegal 27.

   🏛 **Mahon's,** Mill St., BT74 9XX, ℰ 21656 – 📺 ☎ 🅿. 🔼 *VISA*
    closed 25 December – **M** 6.00/9.00 **t.** and a la carte ▮ 3.20 – **18 rm** ⊑ 18.00/36.00 t. –
    SB 33.00/40.00 **st.**

LARNE Antrim **405** O 3 – pop. 18 224 – ❂ 0574.

Exc. : Antrim Coast Road★★★ (A 2) from Larne to Portrush.

🏌 Cairndhu, 192 Coast Rd ℰ 83248, N : 4 m. – 🏌 Larne, 54 Ferris Bay Rd, Islandmagee ℰ 82228.

🛳 to Stranraer (Sealink) frequent services daily (2 h to 2 h 15 mn) – to Cairnryan (P & O European Ferries) 4-6 daily (2 h to 2 h 15 mn).

🛈 Council Offices, Victoria Rd ℰ 72313 – Car Park, Murrayfield Shopping Centre, Broadway ℰ 72313 (summer only) – Larne Harbour ℰ 70517.

◆Belfast 23 – Ballymena 20.

   ↑ Derrin House, 2 Prince's Gdns, BT40 1RQ, off Glenarm Rd (A 2) ℰ 73269 – 🅿
    M (residents only) **7 rm** ⊑ 10.50/25.00 **st.**

AUSTIN-ROVER 104-106 Curran Rd ℰ 2071   ⓜ ATS Narrow Guago Rd ℰ 74491/74659
FORD 39 Glynn Rd ℰ 5411

LONDONDERRY Londonderry **405** K 2-3 – pop. 62 697 – ❂ 0504.

See : City Walls★★ (17C) – Guildhall★ (1908) – Memorial Hall★.

Envir. : Grianan of Aileach★ (Republic of Ireland) (stone fort) ☀★★★, NW : 5 m. – Dungiven (priory : site★) SE : 18 m.

🏌 City of Derry, 49 Victoria Rd, Prehen ℰ 42610.

✈ Eglinton Airport : ℰ 810784, E : 6 m.

🛈 Foyle St. ℰ 267284 (summer only).

◆Belfast 70 – ◆Dublin 146.

   🏨 **Everglades,** Prehen Rd, BT47 2PA, S : 1 ½ m. on A 5 ℰ 46722, Telex 748005, Fax 49200 –
    ✑⇥ rest 📺 ☎ ♿ 🅿 – 🛄 300. 🔼 AE ① *VISA*. ⅝
    closed 25 December – **M** 6.75/11.50 **st.** and a la carte ▮ 3.95 – ⊑ 4.95 – **39 rm** 50.00/125.00 **st.**

   🏛 White Horse Inn, 68 Clooney Rd, BT47 3PA, NE : 5 ¼ m. on A 2 ℰ 0504 (Campsie) 860606 –
    📺 ☎ 🅿. ⅝
    44 rm.

FORD 173 Strand Rd ℰ 367613   VAUXHALL-OPEL Maydown ℰ 860601
PEUGEOT-TALBOT Campsie ℰ 860588   VW-AUDI 24 Buncrana Rd ℰ 265985

NEWCASTLE Down **405** O 5 – pop. 6 246 – ❂ 039 67.

Envir. : Tollymore Forest Park★ *AC*, NW : 2 m. by B 180 – Dundrum (castle★ 13C ruins : top ☀★★, 70 steps) NE : 3 m. – Loughinisland (the 3 churches★ : 1000-1547-1636) NE : 8 m.

Exc. : SW : Mourne Mountains★★ (Slieve Donard★, Silent Valley★, Lough Shannagh★ : reservoir 1948).

🛈 Newcastle Centre, Central Promenade ℰ 22222.

◆Belfast 30 – ◆Londonderry 101.

   🏨 **Burrendale H. and Country Club,** Castlewellan Rd, BT33 0JY, N : 1 m. on A 50
    ℰ 22599, Telex 747377, Fax 22328, 🔽, 🏊 – 📺 ☎ 🅿 – 🛄 150, 🔼 ① *VISA*. ⅝
    M (bar lunch Monday to Saturday)/dinner 12.00 **t.** and a la carte ▮ 3.75 – **40 rm**
    ⊑ 38.00/75.00 **t.** – SB (except July-August, Christmas and Easter) 70.00/90.00 **st.**

   🏛 **Enniskeen** 🦢, 98 Bryansford Rd, BT33 0LF, NW : 1 m. ℰ 22392, Fax 24084, ≤, 🏖, park –
    ✑⇥ rm 📺 ☎ 🅿. 🔼 *VISA*. ⅝
    Mid March-mid November – **M** 7.95/9.50 **st.** and a la carte ▮ 3.75 – **12 rm** ⊑ 32.00/50.00 **st.**
    – SB (except Bank Holidays) 64.00/77.00 **st.**

TOYOTA 23 Bryansford Village ℰ 22382

NEWRY Down **405** M N 5 – pop. 19 026 – ❂ 0693.

Envir. : Slieve Gullion★★, Ring of Gullion : Ballitemple viewpoint★★, Bernish Rock viewpoint★★ – Cam Lough★, Killevy Churches (site★) SW : 5 m. – Derrymore House (site★) *AC*, NW : 2 ½ m. – Rostrevor (Fairy Glen★) SE : 8 ¾ m. – Carlingford Lough★, SE : 10 m.

🏌 Warrenpoint, Dromore Rd ℰ 069 37 (Warrenpoint) 72219, S : 5 m.

🛈 Arts Centre, Bank Parade ℰ 66232.

◆Belfast 39 – Armagh 20 – ◆Dundalk 13.

   🏨 **Mourne Country,** 52 Belfast Rd, BT34 1TR, N : 1 m. on A 1 ℰ 67922, Fax 62659 – 📺 ☎ ♿
    🅿 – 🛄 350. 🔼 AE ① *VISA*. ⅝
    closed 25 December – **M** (carving lunch Monday to Saturday) 7.50/14.00 **st.** and a la carte
    ▮ 4.50 – **44 rm** ⊑ 35.00/50.00 **st.**

PEUGEOT-TALBOT 18 Edward St. ℰ 62877/63393   ⓜ ATS Downshire Rd ℰ 63077/63078
RENAULT 49-53 Merchants Quay ℰ 63626

 Down **405** O 4 – pop. 20 531 – ✆ 0247.

Envir. : Scrabo Tower (site★) SW : 1 m. – Mount Stewart Gardens★ *AC* – Temple of the Winds ⩰★ *AC*, SE : 5 ½ m. – Grey Abbey★ (Cistercian ruins 12C) *AC*, SW : 7 m.

🏌 Kirkistown Castle, 142 Main Rd, Cloughey ✆ 024 77 (Portavogie) 71233, SE : 25 m. – 🏌 Scrabo, 233 Scrabo Rd ✆ 812355, W : 2 m.

♦Belfast 10 – Bangor 5.

🏛 **Strangford Arms,** 92 Church St., BT23 4AL, ✆ 814141, Fax 818846 – 📺 ☎ 🅿 – 🏛 120. 🔄 AE ① VISA 🍴
closed 15-16 April and 25 December – **M** (bar lunch)/dinner 11.50 **t.** and a la carte ▯ 3.70 – ☲ 6.00 – **36 rm** 49.50/68.00 **t.**

FORD Regent St. ✆ 812626
VAUXHALL-OPEL Portaferry Rd ✆ 813376
VW-AUDI 39 Portaferry Rd ✆ 815505

 Tyrone **405** K 4 – pop. 14 627 – ✆ 0662.

Envir. : Gortin Glen Forest Park★, Gortin Gap★ (on B 48) NE : 9 m. – Glenelly Valley★, NE : 17 m. by Plumbridge.

🏌 Dublin Rd ✆ 3160 – 🏌 Fintona ✆ 0662 (Fintona) 841480, S : 5 ½ m.

🛈 1 Market St., ✆ 47831/2.

♦Belfast 68 – ♦Dublin 112 – ♦Dundalk 64 – ♦Londonderry 34 – ♦Sligo 69.

RENAULT Cookstown Rd ✆ 3451
VW-AUDI, VAUXHALL-OPEL 13 Dublin Rd ✆ 3116
Ⓦ ATS Derry Rd ✆ 3266

 Armagh **405** M 4 – ✆ 0762.

Envir. : Ardress House★ 17C (site★, drawing-room plasterwork★★) *AC*, W : 6 m. – Rich Hill (site★, church- : scenery★) SW : 5 m.

♦Belfast 28 – ♦Dundalk 32 – ♦Londonderry 76.

🏛 Seagoe, Upper Church Lane, BT63 5JE, ✆ 333076, Fax 350210, 🌲 – 📺 ☎ 🅿 – 🏛 300. 🍴 **36 rm, 2 suites**.

BMW Seago Rd ✆ 338833
FIAT Mahon Rd, Ind. Est. ✆ 332552
RENAULT Station House, Annaghmore ✆ 851257
TOYOTA Tandragee Rd ✆ 332980
VAUXHALL 128 Bridge St. ✆ 332238

Ⓦ ATS Cecil St ✆ 355865

 Down **405** P 4 – pop. 2 148 – ✆ 024 77.

Envir. : Castle Ward 1765 (great hall★), SW : 4 m. – Portaferry : Strangford (site★, Audley's Castle : top ❋★★, 44 steps) SW : 1 ½ m. – Saul (St. Patrick's Memorial Church : site★, ⩰★) SW : 7 ½ m.

♦ Belfast 29 – Bangor 24.

🏛 **Portaferry,** 10 The Strand, BT22 1PE, ✆ 28231, ⩰ – 🔄 AE ① VISA 🍴
closed 24-25 December – **M** *(closed Sunday dinner)* a la carte 14.30/20.25 **t.** ▯ 3.75 – **5 rm** ☲ 25.00/40.00 **t.** – SB 57.50/60.00 **st.**

 Antrim **405** M 2 – pop. 586 – ✉ ✆ 026 57 Bushmills.

🏌 Portballintrae, Bushmills ✆ 31317, N : 1 m.

🛈 Beach Rd ✆ 31672 (summer only).

♦Belfast 68 – Coleraine 15.

🏛 **Bayview,** 2 Bayhead Rd, BT57 8RZ, ✆ 31453, Fax 32360, ⩰ – 📺 ☎ 🅿. 🔄 VISA 🍴 **M** *(closed Sunday dinner)* 6.75 **t.** (lunch) and a la carte ▯ 4.50 – **16 rm** ☲ 27.00/42.00 **t.** – SB 57.50 **st.**

 Antrim **405** L 2 – pop. 5 114 – ✆ 0265.

🏌 🏌 🏌 Royal Portrush, Dunluce Rd, ✆ 822311.

🛈 Town Hall ✆ 823333 (summer only).

♦Belfast 58 – Coleraine 4 – ♦Londonderry 35.

🏛 Magherabuoy House, 41 Magherabuoy Rd, BT56 8NX, SW : 1 m. by A 29 ✆ 823507, 🌲 – ⟻ rm 📺 ☎ 🅿. 🍴 **38 rm**.

XX **Ramore,** The Harbour, BT56 8DQ, ✆ 824313, ⩰ – 🅿. 🔄 VISA
closed Sunday, Monday, 2 weeks February, 25 December and 1 January – **M** (booking essential) (dinner only) a la carte 13.35/20.90 **t.** ▯ 6.00.

AUSTIN-ROVER 100 Coleraine Rd ✆ 823702
VOLVO 154 Atlantic Rd ✆ 824330

☛ *Per spostarvi più rapidamente utilizzate le **carte** Michelin "Grandi Strade" :*
*nº **920** Europa, nº **980** Grecia, nº **984** Germania, nº **985** Scandinavia-Finlanda,*
*nº **986** Gran Bretagna-Irlanda, nº **987** Germania-Austria-Benelux, nº **988** Italia,*
*nº **989** Francia, nº **990** Spagna-Portogallo, nº **991** Jugoslavia.*

PORTSTEWART Londonderry 405 L 2 – pop. 5 312 – ✆ 026 583.
18, 18 117 Strand Head ✆ 2015, West boundary.
Town Hall, The Crescent ✆ 2286 (summer only).
•Belfast 67 – Coleraine 6.

Edgewater, 88 Strand Rd, BT55 7LZ, ✆ 2224, Fax 3314, ← – TV ☎ P. VISA.
M 6.50/8.25 **st.** and a la carte 3.75 – **31 rm** 34.00/70.00 **st.**

STRABANE Tyrone 405 J 3 – pop. 10 340 – ✆ 0504.
18 Ballycolman ✆ 382271.
Lifford Rd ✆ 883735 (summer only).
•Belfast 87 – Donegal 34 – •Dundalk 98 – •Londonderry 14.

Fir Trees, Melmount Rd, BT82 9JT, ✆ 382382, Fax 885932 – TV ☎ P. AE VISA
closed 25 December – **M** 7.50/11.50 **t.** and a la carte 4.00 – **26 rm** 35.50/51.50 **t.**

AUSTIN-ROVER 4 Derry Rd ✆ 882334
FORD 132 Melmont Rd ✆ 066 26 (Sion Mills) 58275

WARINGSTOWN Armagh 405 N 4 – pop. 1 167 – ✆ 0762.
•Belfast 26 – Craigavon 4.

XX Grange, Main St., BT66 7QH, ✆ 881989, – P

Channel Islands

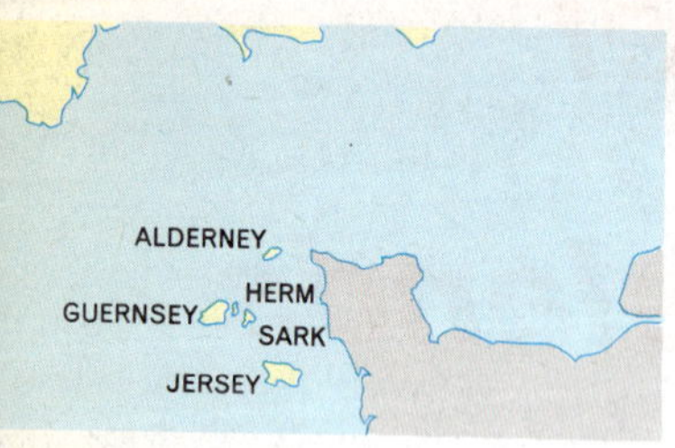

Place with at least :
one hotel or restaurant .... ● Herm
one pleasant hotel .... , ✗ with rm
one quiet, secluded hotel .... ⌂
one restaurant with .... ❀, ❀❀, ❀❀❀, M
See this town for establishments
  located in its vicinity .... GOREY

La località possiede come minimo :
una risorsa alberghiera .... ● Herm
un albergo ameno .... , ✗ with rm
un albergo molto tranquillo, isolato .... ⌂
un'ottima tavola con .... ❀, ❀❀, ❀❀❀, M
La località raggruppa nel suo testo
  le risorse dei dintorni .... GOREY

Localité offrant au moins :
une ressource hôtelière .... ● Herm
un hôtel agréable .... , ✗ with rm
un hôtel très tranquille, isolé .... ⌂
une bonne table à .... ❀, ❀❀, ❀❀❀, M
Localité groupant dans le texte
  les ressources de ses environs .... GOREY

Ort mit mindestens :
einem Hotel oder Restaurant .... ● Herm
einem angenehmen Hotel .... , ✗ with rm
einem sehr ruhigen und abgelegenen Hotel .... ⌂
einem Restaurant mit .... ❀, ❀❀, ❀❀❀, M
Ort mit Angaben über Hotels und Restaurants
  in seiner Umgebung .... GOREY

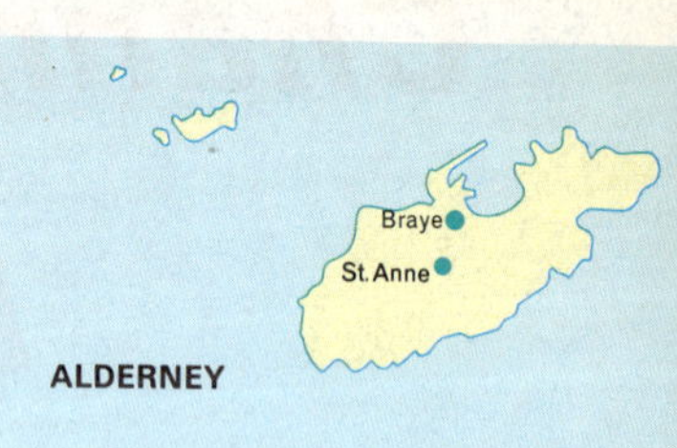

ALDERNEY
GUERNSEY
HERM
SARK
JERSEY
Braye
St. Anne
ALDERNEY

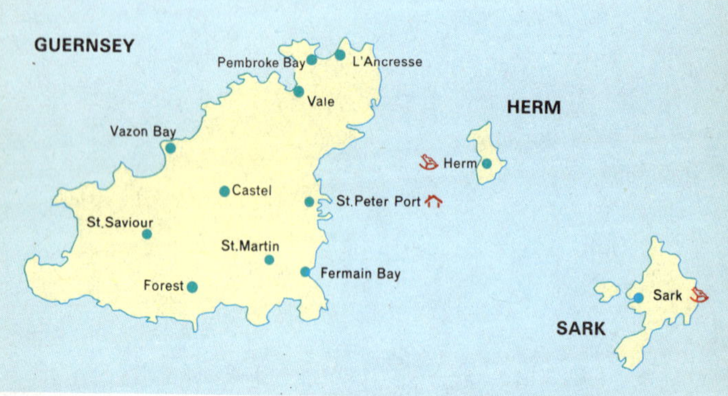

GUERNSEY
Pembroke Bay
L'Ancresse
Vale
Vazon Bay
HERM
Herm
Castel
St. Peter Port
St. Saviour
St. Martin
Fermain Bay
Forest
Sark
SARK

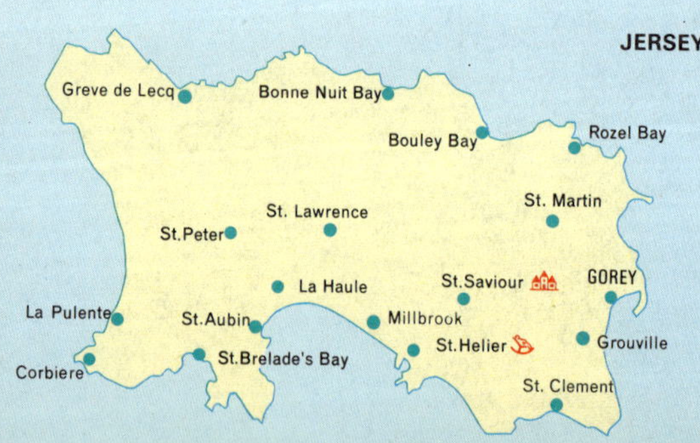

JERSEY
Greve de Lecq
Bonne Nuit Bay
Rozel Bay
Bouley Bay
St. Martin
St. Lawrence
St. Peter
St. Saviour
GOREY
La Haule
La Pulente
Millbrook
St. Aubin
St. Helier
Grouville
Corbiere
St. Brelade's Bay
St. Clement

CHANNEL ISLANDS

Towns

ALDERNEY **403** Q 33 and **230** ⑨ – pop. 2 068 – ECD : Wednesday – ☎ 048 182.
See : Braye Bay★ – Mannez Garenne (≤★ from lighthouse) – Telegraph Bay★ – Vallée des Trois Vaux★ – Clonque Bay★.
✈ ✆ 2851 - Booking Office : Aurigny Air Services ✆ 2889, Air Ferries ✆ 2993.
To Torquay (Torbay Seaways) summer only – to Weymouth (Weymouth Maritime Services) 5 weekly.
Shipping connections with the Continent : to France (Saint-Malo) (via Guernsey, Sark and Jersey) (Condor : hydrofoil) summer only – to Jersey (St. Helier) (Condor : hydrofoil) 4 weekly summer only (1 h 30 mn) – to Guernsey (St. Peter Port) (Condor: hydrofoil) summer only 1 weekly (45 mn).
🛈 States Office, St. Anne ✆ 2994.

St. Anne – ✉ St. Anne – ☎ 048 182 Alderney.
🏌 ✆ 2835, E : 1 m.

🏨 **Inchalla** ⚘, Le Val, ✆ 3220, 🚗 – 📺 ☎ 🅿. 🆎 *VISA*. ⚜
M (dinner only and Sunday lunch)/dinner 9.50 and a la carte ⚱ 2.25 – ☕ 4.50 – **11 rm** 24.00/47.00 – SB (except summer) 126.00/138.00.

🏨 **Chez André**, Victoria St., ✆ 2777 – 📺 ☎ – **11 rm**.

🏛 **Belle Vue**, ✆ 2844 – 📺. 🔲 🆎 ⓓ *VISA*. ⚜
closed 24 December-1 January – **M** *(closed Sunday dinner)* 7.25 and a la carte ⚱ 5.00 –
19 rm ☕ 21.25/42.50.

XX **Nellie Gray's**, Victoria St., ✆ 3333 – 🔲 *VISA*
closed Tuesday and Sunday dinner and Monday October-April, Sunday May-September and January – **M** a la carte 14.50/26.50 ⚱ 2.60.

X **Georgian House** with rm, Victoria St., ✆ 2471 – 📺. 🔲 🆎 ⓓ *VISA*. ⚜
M 10.00/10.50 and a la carte 9.00/18.00 ⚱ 2.50 – **4 rm** ☕ 22.50/45.00 – SB (except summer) 60.00/80.00 **s.**

Braye – ✉ Braye – ☎ 048 182 Alderney.

X **First and Last**, ✆ 3162, ≤ harbour – 🔲 🆎 ⓓ *VISA*
closed Sunday dinner, Monday and October to March – **M** 5.00/12.00 and a la carte 9.95/13.50 ⚱ 3.00.

GUERNSEY **403** OP 33 and **230** ⑨ ⑩ – pop. 53 637 – ☎ 0481.
See : Site★ – Pezeries Point★★ – Icart Point★★   Cobo Bay★★ – St Apollines Chapel★ – Vale Castle★ – Fort Doyle★ – La Gran'mère du Chimiquière★ – Moulin Huet Bay★ – Rocquaine Bay★ – St Martins Point★ – Jerbourg Point★.
✈ La Villiaze, Forest ✆ 37766.
to France (Saint-Malo) (Emeraude Ferries) summer only - (Vedettes Blanches) summer only – to Weymouth (via Alderney) (Weymouth Maritime Services) 5 weekly – to Poole (British Channel Island Ferries) summer : 2 daily, winter : 4-5 weekly (5h to 9h 30 mn) – to Torquay (Torbay seaways) summer only.
Shipping connections with the Continent : to France (Saint-Malo) (Condor : hydrofoil) summer only – to France (Carteret and Cherbourg) (Service Maritime) summer only – to France via Jersey (Granville) (Emeraude Lines) summer only – to Jersey (St. Helier) (Condor : hydrofoil) 1-4 daily in summer (1 h) – to Alderney (Condor : hydrofoil) summer only 1 weekly (45 mn) – to Herm by Herm Seaway, 7 daily (25 mn) – to Sark (Isle of Sark Shipping Co.) summer only 1-6 daily (40 mn) – to Weymouth (Condor : hydrofoil) 1-2 daily (summer only).
🛈 Crown Pier, St. Peter Port ✆ 23552 – The Airport, La Villiaze ✆ 37267.

L'Ancresse – ✉ Vale – ☎ 0481 Guernsey.
🏌 Royal Guernsey ✆ 47022.

🏨 **Lynton Park** ⚘, Hacse Lane, Clos du Valle, ✆ 45418, 🚗 – 🅿 – **14 rm**.

Catel – ✉ Catel – ☎ 0481 Guernsey.

🏠 **Belvoir Farm** without rest., Rue de la Hougue, ✆ 56004, ⚊ heated, 🚗 – 📺 🅿. ⚜
2 April-mid October – **14 rm** ☕ 39.00/58.00 **s.**

Fermain Bay – ⊠ St. Peter Port – ✆ 0481 Guernsey.

🏨 **La Favorita** ⚓, Fermain Lane, ✆ 35666, Telex 94016631, Fax 35413, ≤, ☞ – ⊁ rest 📺
☎ ℗. ⚠ VISA. ⚘
accommodation closed December-February – **M** *(closed 22 December-1 February)* 8.50/
14.00 **s.** and a la carte ♦ 2.40 – **29 rm** ⊊ 23.50/56.00 **s.** – SB 47.00/70.00 **s.**

🏨 **Le Chalet** ⚓, Fermain Lane, ⊠ St. Martin, ✆ 35716, Fax 35718, ≤ – 📺 ☎ ℗. ⚠ AE ①
VISA
Late May-late October – **M** (buffet lunch)/dinner 11.50 and a la carte ♦ 4.50 – **50 rm**
⊊ 28.00/58.00.

Forest – ⊠ Forest – ✆ 0481 Guernsey.

⋔ Tudor Lodge Deer Farm, Forest Rd, ✆ 37849, ☞, park – 📺 ☎ ℗. ⚘ – **5 rm**.

Pembroke Bay – ⊠ Vale – ✆ 0481 Guernsey.
St. Peter Port 5.

🏨 **Pembroke** ⚓, ✆ 47573 – 📺 ☎ ℗. ⚠ AE ① VISA
M (bar lunch)/dinner 9.00 and a la carte ♦ 2.25 – **14 rm** ⊊ 30.00/50.00.

St. Martin – pop. 5 842 – ECD : Thursday – ⊠ St. Martin – ✆ 0481 Guernsey.
St. Peter Port 2.

🏨 **Green Acres** ⚓, Les Hubits, ✆ 35711, Fax 35978, ⊿ heated, ☞ – ⊁ rest ▤ rest 📺 ☎
℗. ⚠ VISA. ⚘
M (bar lunch)/dinner 8.50 and a la carte ♦ 2.20 – **48 rm** ⊊ (dinner included) 33.00/70.00.

🏨 **Bella Luce**, La Fosse, Moulin Huet, ✆ 38764, ⊿ heated, ☞ – 📺 ☎ ℗
M (bar lunch Monday to Saturday)/dinner 14.45 and a la carte ♦ 3.65 – **31 rm** ⊊ 35.50/68.00.

🏠 **Windmill**, Rue Poudreuse, ✆ 35383, ⊿ heated, ☞ – ⊁ rest 📺 ☎ ℗
April-October – **M** (bar lunch, residents only)/dinner 9.00 ♦ 2.30 – **18 rm** ⊊ 28.00/51.00.

🏠 **La Cloche** ⚓, Les Traudes, ✆ 35421, ⊿ heated, ☞ – 📺 ☎ ℗. ⚠ VISA. ⚘
April-October – **M** (bar lunch, residents only)/dinner 9.00 ♦ 2.40 – **10 rm** ⊊ 34.00/58.00.

⋔ **Wellesley** without rest., Sausmarez Rd, ✆ 38028, ☞ – ℗. ⚘
April-October – **9 rm** ⊊ 24.00/46.00.

AUSTIN-ROVER, JAGUAR Ville au Roi ✆ 37661   VOLVO St. Andrews Rd, Bailiffs Cross ✆ 37641

St. Peter Port – pop. 15 587 – ECD : Thursday – ⊠ St. Peter Port – ✆ 0481 Guernsey.
See : Site★ – St. Peter's church★ Z – Hauteville House (Victor Hugo's house)★AC Z –
Castle Cornet★AC Z.
Envir. : Saumarez Park★ – The Little Chapel★.
◦9 St Pierre Park, Rohais ✆ 27039.
🛈 Crown Pier ✆ 23552.

Plan opposite

🏨 **St. Pierre Park,** Rohais, ✆ 28282, Telex 4191662, Fax 712041, ≤, ⊿, ◦9, ☞, park, ✗ – ⃟
📺 ☎ ♿ ℗ – ⛄. ⚠ AE ① VISA. ⚘   by Grange Rd   Z
M (see rest. **Victor Hugo** below) – **131 rm** ⊊ 70.00/104.00, **3 suites** 164.00/184.00.

🏨 **Duke of Richmond,** Cambridge Park, ✆ 26221, Telex 4191462, Fax 28945, ⊿ heated – ⃟
▤ rest 📺 ☎ – ⛄ 60. ⚠ AE ① VISA   Y c
M 10.00/11.00 **s.** and a la carte ♦ 2.75 – **75 rm** ⊊ 35.00/96.00 **s.**, **1 suite** 60.00/110.00 **s.** –
SB (weekends only) 75.00/95.00 **s.**

🏨 **Old Government House,** St. Ann's Pl., ✆ 24921, Telex 4191144, Fax 24429, ⊿ heated,
☞ – ⃟ 📺 ☎ – ⛄ 100. ⚠ AE ① VISA   Y o
M 7.50/10.75 and a la carte ♦ 2.00 – **73 rm** ⊊ 45.50/143.00.

🏨 **De Havelet,** Havelet, ✆ 22199, Fax 714057, ☞ – 📺 ☎ ℗. ⚠ AE ① VISA   Z u
M 11.50 (dinner) and a la carte ♦ 4.50 – **31 rm** ⊊ 35.00/66.00.

🏨 **La Collinette,** St. Jacques, ✆ 710331, Fax 713516, ⊿ heated, ☞ – 📺 ☎ ℗. ⚠ AE ①
VISA. ⚘   Y a
M 7.00/10.00 and a la carte ♦ 2.50 – **22 rm** ⊊ 19.50/59.00.

🏨 **Les Rocquettes,** Les Gravées, ✆ 22146, ☞ – 📺 ☎ ℗. ⚠ ① VISA. ⚘
closed 21 December-6 January – **M** 6.00/10.50 ♦ 2.50 – **26 rm** ⊊ 28.00/50.00 –
SB (except spring and winter) 38.00/56.00.

🏠 **Midhurst House,** Candie Rd, ✆ 24391, ☞ – 📺. ⚘   Y r
Mid April-mid October – **M** (dinner only, residents only) 6.00 **s.** and a la carte ♦ 2.20 – **8 rm**
⊊ 29.00/47.00 **s.**

🏠 Havelet Court, Havelet, ✆ 710110, ≤ gardens and Havelet Bay, ☞ – 📺 ℗   Z x
M (dinner only, residents only) – **12 rm**.

🏠 **Moore's Central,** Le Pollet, ✆ 24452, Telex 4191342, Fax 714037 – ⃟ 📺 ☎. ⚠ AE ① VISA
M 7.50/10.50 and a la carte ♦ 3.75 – **50 rm** ⊊ 30.00/60.00.   Y n

🏠 Abbey Court, Les Gravées, ✆ 20148, ☞ – ℗. ⚘ – **26 rm**.   by Grange Rd   Z

⋔ **Cleveley House** without rest., Cambridge Park, ✆ 21791 – ⊁ 📺 ☎. AE. ⚘   Y u
April-September – ⊊ 2.00 – **3 rm** 33.00/50.00.

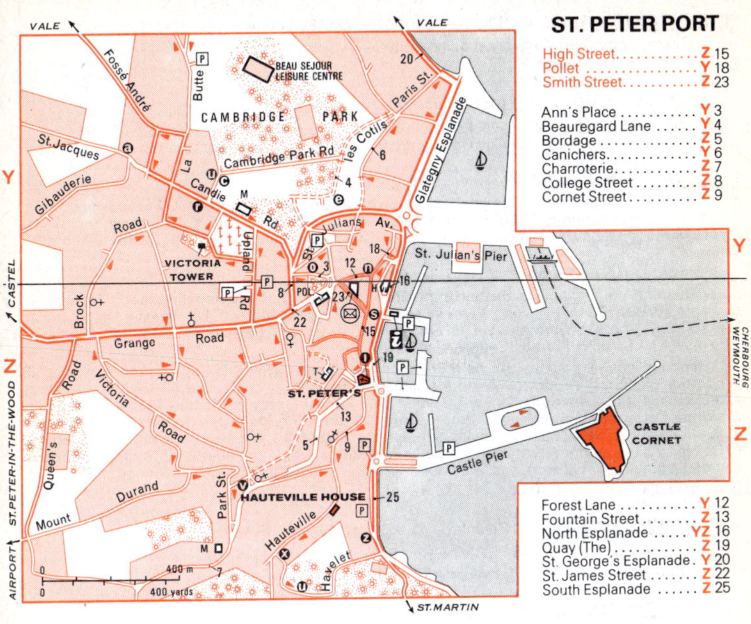

Victor Hugo (at St. Pierre Park H.), Rohais, ℰ 28282, Telex 4191662, Fax 712041 – 🍽 🅿. by Grange Rd — **Z**

🖼 AE ① VISA

closed Saturday lunch and Sunday dinner – M 8.50/18.50 and a la carte 14.00/21.00 🍷 6.00.

La Frégate 🐦 with rm, Les Côtils, ℰ 24624, Fax 20443, ← town and harbour, 🐕 – 🍽 rest — **Y e**

📺 ☎ 🅿. 🖼 AE ① VISA 🐾

M 9.50/14.00 s. and a la carte 14.00/21.00 s. 🍷 2.75 – ☕ 6.00 – **13 rm** 40.00/85.00 s.

Louisiana, South Esplanade, ℰ 713157, ← – 🍽. 🖼 AE ① VISA — **Z z**

M 8.50/15.00 and a la carte 12.75/19.50 🍷 3.00.

La Piazza, Trinity Sq., ℰ 25085, Italian rest. – 🖼 AE VISA — **Z v**

closed Sunday and 24 December-24 January – M a la carte 11.80/20.90 🍷 2.90.

Le Nautique, Quay Steps, ℰ 21714, ← – 🖼 AE ① VISA — **Z s**

closed Sunday and first 2 weeks January – M a la carte 11.00/17.30 s. 🍷 2.75.

Steak and Stilton, 23 The Quay, ℰ 23080 — **Z i**

ASTON-MARTIN, LANCIA, ROLLS-ROYCE, TOYOTA Trinity Sq. ℰ 24201
FORD Les Banques ℰ 24774

HONDA Doyle Rd ℰ 24025
RENAULT The Grange ℰ 26846

St. Saviour – pop. 2 432 – ✉ St. Saviour – ☏ 0481 Guernsey.

St. Peter Port 4.

L'Atlantique, Perelle Bay, ℰ 64056, ←, 🏊 heated, 🐕 – 📺 ☎ 🅿. 🖼 AE ① VISA. 🐾

M (dinner only and Sunday lunch)/dinner 8.25 s. and a la carte 🍷 2.80 – **21 rm** ☕ 18.00/60.00.

La Hougue Fouque Farm, Route-des-Bas-Courtil, ℰ 64181, 🏊 heated – 📺 ☎ 🅿. 🐾

16 rm.

Les Piques Farm 🐦, ℰ 64515, « Part 15C farmhouse », 🐕 – ⤵ rest 📺 🅿. 🐾

April-October – M 7.00 s. 🍷 2.95 – **7 rm** ☕ –/46.00 s.

Vale – ✉ Vale – ☏ 0481 Guernsey.

Novotel, Les Dicqs, ℰ 48400, Telex 4191306, Fax 48706, ←, 🏊 heated, 🐕 – 📶 🍽 rest 📺

☎ & 🅿 – 🛥 . 🖼 AE ① VISA

M 9.00 s. and a la carte 🍷 2.90 – ☕ 5.75 – **99 rm** 54.00/60.00 s.

Vazon Bay – ✉ Vazon Bay – ☏ 0481 Guernsey.

La Grande Mare, ℰ 56576, 🏊 heated, 🐕 – 📶 📺 ☎ 🅿

21 rm, 9 suites.

Les Embruns, Route de la Margion, ✉ Catel, ℰ 64834, 🏊 heated, 🐕 – ⤵ rest 📺 🅿

May-September – M (dinner only, residents only) 12.00 s. 🍷 2.25 – **16 rm** ☕ 20.00/40.00 s.

HERM ISLAND 🗺️ P 33 and 🗺️ ⑩ – pop. 37 – ☎ 0481 Guernsey.
🚢 to Guernsey by Herm Seaway, 6 daily (25 mn).
🛈 Administrative Office ☎ 22377.

Herm – ✉ Herm – ☎ 0481 Guernsey.

🏨 **White House** ⑤, ☎ 22159, Fax 710066, ≤, ⌇, 🐎, park, ✕ – ✕ rest. 🎴 VISA. ⚠
April-7 October – **M** 7.25/12.50 and a la carte ⌐3.00 – **32 rm** ⊇ 30.00/49.00.

JERSEY 🗺️ OP 33 and 🗺️ ⑪ – pop. 72 970 – ☎ 0534.
See : Site★★ – Chapels★ – German Occupation Museum★ – Jersey Zoo★ AC – Grosnez Point★
– St. Matthews Church Millbrook (glasswork★) – La Hougue Bie★ (Neolithic tomb) AC
– St. Catherines Bay (≤★ from lighthouse) – Noirmont Point★ – Millbrook St. Matthew's
Church★.

✈ States of Jersey Airport ☎ 46111, Telex 4192332.

🚢 Shipping connections with the Continent : to France (Saint-Malo) (Emeraude Ferries) –
to Poole (British Channel Island Ferries) summer : 2 daily, winter : 4-5 weekly (7h 45 mn to
12h 45 mn) – to Weymouth (via Guernsey and Alderney) (Weymouth Maritime Services)
5 weekly – to Torquay (Torbay Seaways) summer only.

🚢 Shipping connections with the continent : to France (Saint-Malo) (Condor : hydrofoil)
(Vedettes Blanches) (Vedettes Armoricaines) summer only – to France (Granville) (Vedettes
Armoricaines and Emeraude Lines) summer only - from Gorey to France (Carteret) (Service
Maritime Carteret) summer only – from Gorey to France (Portbail) (Service Maritime Carteret)
summer only – to Sark (Condor : hydrofoil) Monday/Saturday 1-4 daily (1 h 10 mn) – to Guernsey
(St. Peter Port) (Condor : hydrofoil) 1-4 daily in summer (1 h) – to Alderney (Condor : hydrofoil)
summer 4 weekly (1 h 30 mn) – to Weymouth (Condor : hydrofoil) 1-2 daily, summer only.

🛈 Weighbridge, St. Helier ☎ 78000/24779/31958.

Bonne Nuit Bay – ✉ St. John – ☎ 0534 Jersey – St. Helier 6.

🏨 Cheval Roc ⑤, ☎ 62865, ≤ Bonne Nuit Bay, ⌇ heated – 📺 ☎ 🅿 – **39 rm**.

🏠 Idlerocks, ☎ 61633, ≤, ⌇ heated – 📺 – **10 rm**.

Bouley Bay – ✉ Trinity – ☎ 0534 Jersey – St. Helier 5.

🏨 **Water's Edge** ⑤, ☎ 62777, Telex 4192521, Fax 63645, ≤ Bouley Bay, ⌇ heated, 🐎 – 🛗
📺 ☎ 🅿. 🎴 AE ⓪ VISA
April-October – **M** 8.75/14.00 and a la carte ⌐3.50 – **51 rm** ⊇ 47.00/90.00, **3 suites**
112.00/122.00.

Corbiere – ✉ St. Brelade – ☎ 0534 Jersey – St. Helier 8.

✕✕ **Sea Crest** with rm, Petit Port, ☎ 46353, ≤, ⌇, 🐎 – 📺 ☎ 🅿. 🎴 AE VISA ⚠
closed January – **M** (closed Monday) 7.50 **s.** (lunch) and a la carte 13.50/23.50 **s.** ⌐2.50 –
7 rm ⊇ 39.00/58.00 **s.**

Gorey – ✉ St. Martin – ☎ 0534 Jersey.
See : Mont Orgueil Castle★ (≤★★) AC – Jersey Pottery★ AC.
St. Helier 4.

🏨 **Old Court House,** Gorey Village, ☎ 54444, Telex 4192032, ⌇ heated, 🐎 – 🛗 ✕ rest 📺
☎ 🅿. 🎴 AE ⓪ VISA ⚠
March-October – **M** 11.00 **s.** (dinner) and a la carte – **58 rm** ⊇ 41.50/90.00.

🏠 **Trafalgar Bay,** Gorey Village, ☎ 53216, Telex 4192349, ⌇ heated, 🐎 – 📺 🅿. 🎴 VISA. ⚠
June-September – **M** (bar lunch)/dinner 8.00 and a la carte ⌐2.50 – **27 rm** ⊇ 28.00/63.00.

🏠 **Hotel Des Iles,** ☎ 54324 – ⚠
closed January – **8 rm** ⊇ (dinner included) 14.50/43.00 **s.**

at Gorey Pier – ✉ St. Martin – ☎ 0534 Jersey :

🏠 **Moorings,** ☎ 53633, Group Telex 4192085, Fax 56660 – 🍽 rest 📺 ☎. 🎴 AE VISA. ⚠
M 15.00/25.00 **s.** and la carte ⌐2.50 – **16 rm** ⊇ (dinner included) 27.50/87.00 **s.** –
SB (November-February) 65.00/80.00 **s.**

🏠 **Dolphin,** ☎ 53370, Group Telex 4192085, Fax 56660 – 📺 ☎. 🎴 VISA. ⚠
M 11.00/20.00 **s.** and a la carte ⌐2.50 – **16 rm** ⊇ 22.00/74.00 **s.** – SB (November-
February) 55.00/70.00 **s.**

Grève De Lecq – ✉ St. Ouen – ☎ 0534 Jersey.

🏠 **Hotel Des Pierres,** on B 65, ☎ 81858 – 📺 🅿. 🎴 VISA ⚠
closed 15 December-10 January – **M** (dinner only) 6.00 **s.** ⌐2.65 – **14 rm** ⊇ (dinner included)
21.00/46.00 **s.** – SB (March-May and October) 42.00/52.00 **s.**

Grouville – ☎ 0534 Jersey.

🏠 **Lavender Villa,** Rue a Don, on A 3 ☎ 54937, ⌇, 🐎 – ✕ rest 🅿. VISA ⚠
Mid February-mid November – **M** (dinner only) 7.00 ⌐2.00 – **18 rm** ⊇ (dinner included) 18.00/28.00.

🏠 Mon Desir House, Rue Des Prés Grouville, ☎ 54718, 🎴 – 📺 🅿 – **13 rm**.

La Haule – ⊠ St. Brelade – ☎ 0534 Jersey.

🏨 **La Place** ⚐, Route du Coin, by B 25 on B 43 ℰ 44261, Telex 4192522, Fax 45164, ⛝ heated – 📺 ☎ ℗ – **40 rm**.

↟ **Au Caprice**, on A 1 ℰ 22083 – 📺. ⚒
closed January and February – **12 rm** ⌣ (dinner included) 21.00/48.00 **s.**

Millbrook – ⊠ St. Lawrence – ☎ 0534 Jersey.

🏨 **Coralie**, on A 1, ℰ 21877 – 📶 📺 ℗. ◩ **VISA**. ⚒
Mid April-mid October – **M** (dinner only, residents only) – **55 rm** ⌣ (dinner included) 27.75/55.50 **st.**

La Pulente – ⊠ St. Brelade – ☎ 0534 Jersey.
St. Helier 7.

🏨 **Atlantic** ⚐, La Moye, ℰ 44101, Telex 4192405, Fax 44102, ≼, ⛝ heated, 🐎, ✗ – 📶 📺 ☎ ℗ – 🏊 100. ◩ AE ⓪ **VISA** ⚒
closed January-8 March – **M** 10.75/16.50 and a la carte – **46 rm** ⌣ 60.00/275.00.

Rozel Bay – ⊠ St. Martin – ☎ 0534 Jersey.
St. Helier 6.

🏨 **Chateau La Chaire** ⚐, Rozel Valley, ℰ 63354, Fax 65137, 🐎 – 📺 ☎ ℗. ◩ AE ⓪ **VISA**. ⚒
M 11.50/18.50 and a la carte 🍾 3.00 – **13 rm** ⌣ 48.00/95.00.

🏨 **Le Couperon de Rozel,** ℰ 65522, Fax 65332, ⛝ heated – ℗. ◩ AE ⓪ **VISA**. ⚒
Mid April-mid October – **M** 12.50 and a la carte – **32 rm** ⌣ 32.50/71.00 **s.**

✗✗ **Granite Corner**, Rozel Harbour, ℰ 63590 – ◩ AE ⓪ **VISA**
closed Sunday, Monday and December-February – **M** (dinner only) a la carte 15.00/28.00.

St. Aubin – ⊠ St. Aubin – ☎ 0534 Jersey.
St. Helier 4.

🏨 **Panorama** without rest., High St., ℰ 42429, Fax 45940, ≼ St. Aubin's Fort and Bay, 🐎 – 📺. ◩ AE ⓪ **VISA**. ⚒
Late March-mid December – **16 rm** ⌣ 27.00/50.00.

↟ **Tenby**, Market Hill, ℰ 41099, ≼
closed November-December and restricted service January-February – **M** 6.00 🍾 2.30 –
10 rm ⌣ (dinner included) 17.50/39.00.

↟ Porthole Cottage, Market Hill, ℰ 45007 – ℗ – **13 rm**.

✗ **Old Court House Inn** with rm, St. Aubin's Harbour, ℰ 46433 – 📺 ☎. ◩ **VISA**. ⚒
closed February and 25-26 December – **M** a la carte 16.00/26.00 🍾 2.50 – **9 rm** ⌣ 37.50/85.00,
1 suite 100.00/150.00.

St. Brelade's Bay – pop. 8 566 – ⊠ St. Brelade – ☎ 0534 Jersey.
See : Fishermans Chapel (frescoes★).
St. Helier 6.

🏨 **L'Horizon,** ℰ 43101, Telex 4192281, Fax 46269, ≼ St. Brelade's Bay, ⛝ – 📶 📺 ☎ ♿ ℗ –
🏊 70. ◩ **VISA**. ⚒
M 10.50/19.50 and a la carte 16.50/25.95 (see also rest. **Star Grill** below) – **100 rm**
⌣ 50.00/150.00, **4 suites** 180.00/200.00 – SB (except summer and Christmas) 175.00.

🏨 **St. Brelade's Bay,** ℰ 46141, Telex 4192519, ≼, ⛝ heated, 🐎, ✗ – 📶 ✗ rest 📺 ☎ ℗.
◩ AE ⓪ **VISA**. ⚒
mid April-mid October – **M** 9.00/15.50 🍾 3.00 – **72 rm** ⌣ 69.00/79.00, **1 suite** 90.00/150.00.

🏨 **Chateau Valeuse**, Rue de la Valeuse, ℰ 46281, ⛝ heated, 🐎 – 📺 ☎ ℗. ◩ **VISA**. ⚒
closed January-March – **M** 8.00 (lunch)/dinner a la carte 11.50/18.90 🍾 3.00 – **32 rm**
⌣ 29.00/68.00.

✗✗✗ Star Grill, (at L'Horizon H.), ℰ 43101, Telex 4192281, Fax 46269, ≼ St. Brelade's Bay – ℗
M (booking essential).

FORD Airport Rd ℰ 43222 VW-AUDI Airport Rd ℰ 41131
NISSAN La Moye ℰ 45546

St. Clement – pop. 6 541 – ⊠ St. Clement – ☎ 0534 Jersey.
⛳ Jersey recreation grounds ℰ 21938.
St. Helier 2.

🏨 **Ambassadeur,** St. Clement's Coast Rd, ℰ 24455, ≼, ⛝ heated – 📶 📺 ☎ ℗. ◩ AE ⓪
VISA
M 7.15/13.20 **s.** and a la carte 🍾 2.75 – **41 rm** ⌣ 30.00/65.00 **s.**

🏨 **Shakespeare**, Samares, St. Clement's Coast Rd, ℰ 51915, Fax 56269 – 📶 📺 ☎ ℗. ◩ AE
⓪ **VISA**
closed 3 January-2 February – **M** (bar lunch Monday to Saturday)/dinner 12.50 and a la
carte 🍾 2.90 – **30 rm** ⌣ 36.00/72.00.

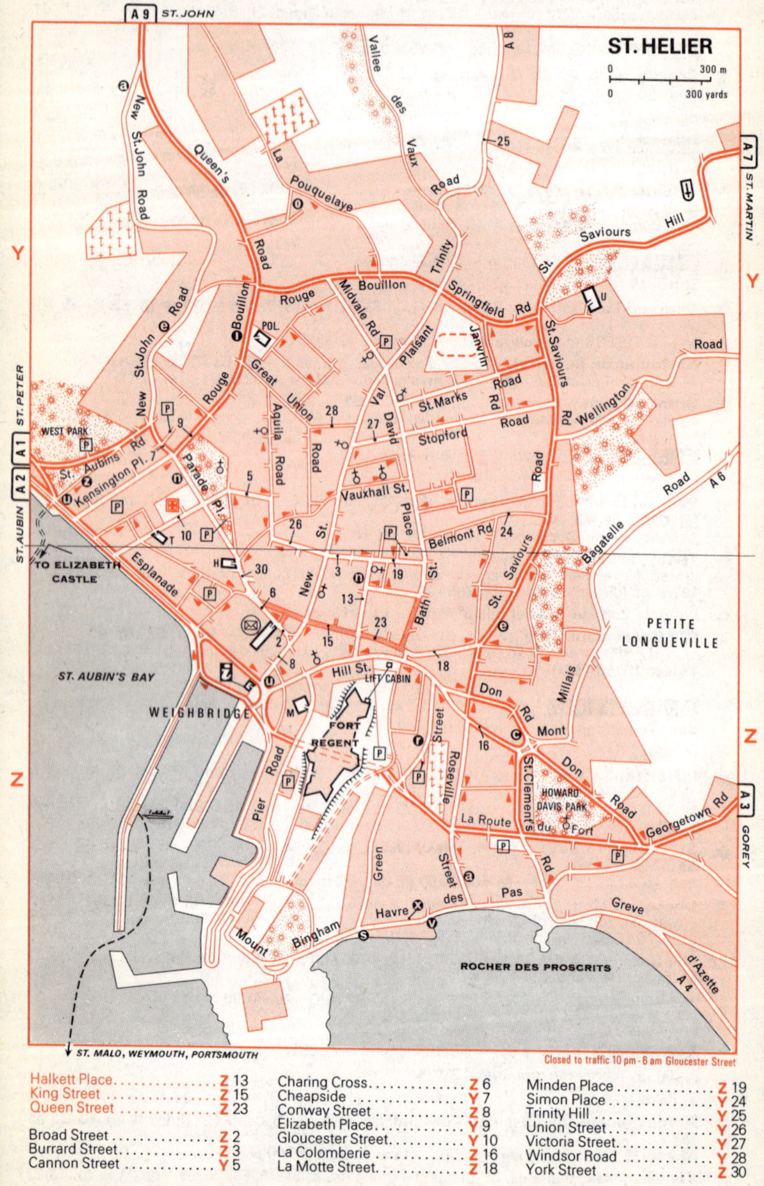

St. Helier – pop. 29 941 – ECD : Thursday and Saturday – ✉ St. Helier – ☎ 0534 Jersey – **See :** Elizabeth Castle ❋ ★ *AC* Z – Fort Regent ❋ ★ *AC* Z.
🛈 Weighbridge ☎ 78000/24779/31958.

Halkett Place .... Z 13	Charing Cross .... Z 6	Minden Place .... Z 19
King Street .... Z 15	Cheapside .... Y 7	Simon Place .... Y 24
Queen Street .... Z 23	Conway Street .... Z 8	Trinity Hill .... Y 25
	Elizabeth Place .... Y 9	Union Street .... Y 26
Broad Street .... Z 2	Gloucester Street .... Y 10	Victoria Street .... Y 27
Burrard Street .... Z 3	La Colomberie .... Z 16	Windsor Road .... Y 28
Cannon Street .... Y 5	La Motte Street .... Z 18	York Street .... Z 30

Town plans : *the names of main shopping streets are indicated in red at the beginning of the list of streets.*

Grand (De Vere), Esplanade, ☎ 22301, Telex 4192104, Fax 37815, ≤, 🏊 – 🛗 📺 ☎ 🅿 – 🎿 70. 🖼 AE ⓪ **VISA** **Y u**
M 13.00/16.00 and a la carte 🍾 2.25 – (see also rest. **Victoria's** below) – **110 rm** ☲ 60.00/135.00 s., **5 suites** 145.00/160.00 s. – SB 109.00/147.00 s.

De la Plage, Havre des Pas, ☎ 23474, Telex 4192328, Fax 68642, ≤ – 🛗 📺 ☎ 🅿. 🖼 AE ⓪ **VISA** ⅍ **Z s**
7 April-October – **M** 12.50/14.00 s. and a la carte 🍾 2.00 – **78 rm** ☲ 46.00/144.00.

Beaufort, Green St., ☎ 32471, Telex 4192160, 🏊 – 🛗 📺 ☎ 🅿. 🖼 AE ⓪ **VISA**. ⅍ **Z r**
M 7.50/10.50 and a la carte 🍾 3.00 – **54 rm** ☲ 39.50/100.00 s.

Pomme d'Or, The Esplanade, ☎ 78644, Telex 4192309, Fax 37781, ≤ – 🛗 🍽 rest 📺 ☎ – 🎿 150. 🖼 AE ⓪ **VISA** **Z u**
M 5.70/10.95 s. and a la carte 🍾 2.45 – **150 rm** ☲ 50.00/73.00 s.

Apollo, 9 St. Saviour's Rd, ☎ 25441, Telex 4192086, Fax 22120, 🏊 – 🛗 📺 ☎ 🅿. 🖼 AE ⓪ **VISA**. ⅍ **Z e**
M 8.50/10.50 s. and a la carte 🍾 4.00 – **79 rm** ☲ 37.50/63.00 s. – SB 83.00 s.

Savoy, Rouge Bouillon, ☎ 27521, 🏊 heated – 🛗 📺 ☎ 🅿 – **61 rm**. **Y i**

Uplands, St. John's Rd, ☎ 73006, Fax 68804, 🏊 heated – 📺 ☎ 🅿. 🖼 **VISA** **Y a**
M (residents only) (bar lunch)/dinner 5.50 s. – **39 rm** ☲ 27.00/54.00 s.

Mornington, 60-68 Don Rd, ☎ 24452 – 📺. 🖼 **VISA** ⅍ **Z c**
Mid April-mid October – **M** (closed Sunday dinner) (dinner only and Sunday lunch)/dinner 5.50 s. 🍾 3.95 – **31 rm** ☲ 27.00/54.00 s.

Mountview, 46 New St. John's Rd, ☎ 78887, Fax 39763 – 🛗 📺 🅿. 🖼 **VISA** **Y e**
April-October – **M** (bar lunch)/dinner 9.50 **s.** and a la carte 🍾 3.00 – **35 rm** ☲ 18.00/66.00 s.

Fort d'Auvergne, Havre des Pas, ☎ 73006, Telex 4192371 – 🛗 ☎. 🖼 **VISA** **Z v**
April-October – **M** (bar lunch, residents only) – **65 rm** ☲ (dinner included) 26.00/52.00 s.

Millbrook House ⑤, Rue de Trachy, W : 1 ¾ m. by A 1 ☎ 33036, 🌳 – 🛗 📺 🅿. ⅍ **Y**
May-first week October – **M** (dinner only) 6.00 🍾 1.95 – **24 rm** ☲ (dinner included) 27.50/55.00. by A 1

La Bonne Vie without rest., Roseville St., ☎ 35955 – 📺. ⅍ **Z a**
closed 20 December-7 January – **10 rm** ☲ 16.50/33.00.

Almorah, 1 Almorah Cres., La Pouquelaye, ☎ 21648, Fax 68600, 🌳 – 🅿. 🖼 **VISA**. ⅍ **Y o**
16 rm ☲ (dinner included) 30.00/60.00 s.

Lorraine, 8 Havre des pas, ☎ 74470, Fax 23462 – 📺. 🖼 AE **VISA**. ⅍ **Z x**
closed 20 to 30 April and 4 to 24 November – **M** 4.50 s. 🍾 1.75 – **10 rm** ☲ 16.50/33.00 s. – SB (except Easter, summer and Christmas) 19.50/25.00 s.

XXX Victoria's, (at Grand H.), Peirson Rd, ☎ 22301, Telex 4192104, Fax 37815 – 🍽 🅿 **Y z**

XX **La Capannina,** 67 Halkett Pl., ☎ 34602, Italian rest. – 🖼 AE ⓪ **VISA** **Z n**
closed Sunday and Bank Holidays – **M** (booking essential) 18.50 and a la carte 11.50/33.00 🍾 2.90.

XX **La Buca,** The Parade, ☎ 34283, Italian rest. – 🖼 AE ⓪ **VISA** **Y n**
M (closed Sunday lunch) 6.00/9.50 and a la carte 8.20/13.00 🍾 2.00.

ASTON-MARTIN, ROLLS-ROYCE, BENTLEY, LAND-ROVER, RANGE-ROVER 33-35 Lamotte St. ☎ 31341
AUSTIN-ROVER Havre des Pas ☎ 33233
CITROEN 10 Devonshire Pl. ☎ 24541
FORD Longueville ☎ 73777
PEUGEOT-TALBOT 17 Esplanade ☎ 33623

St. Lawrence – pop. 3 845 – ✉ St. Lawrence – ☎ 0534 Jersey.
St. Helier 3.

Little Grove ⑤, Rue de Haut, by A 11 ☎ 25321, Fax 25325, 🏊 heated, 🌳 – 📺 ☎ 🅿. 🖼 AE ⓪ **VISA**. ⅍
closed January – **M** 19.50 (dinner) and a la carte 🍾 4.00 – **11 rm** ☲ 93.50/132.00, **2 suites** 162.00 – SB (November-March) 99.50 s.

Villa D'Oro without rest., La Grande Route de St. Laurent, on A 10 ☎ 62262 – 📺. ⅍
April-October – **12 rm** ☲ 14.50/31.00 s.

FIAT, MAZDA Belroyal Corner ☎ 22556

St. Martin – pop. 3 095 – ✉ St. Martin – ☎ 0534 Jersey.
St. Helier 4.

Le Relais de St. Martin, ☎ 53271, 🏊, 🌳 – 🅿. ⅍
24 March-mid November – **M** (dinner only, residents only) 7.50 s. 🍾 2.50 – **11 rm** ☲ 21.00/42.00 s.

St. Peter – pop. 3 713 – ✉ St. Peter – ☎ 0534 Jersey.
St. Helier 5.

Mermaid, Airport Rd, on B 36, ☎ 41255, Telex 4192249, ≤, 🏊, 🌳 – 📺 ☎ 🅿 – 🎿 100. 🖼 AE ⓪ **VISA**. ⅍
M 9.00 (lunch) and dinner a la carte – **68 rm** ☲ 50.00/85.00 s.

Greenhill Country, Coin Varin, Mont de l'Ecole, on C 112 ☎ 81042, 🏊 heated – 📺 ☎ 🅿. 🖼 AE ⓪ **VISA**. ⅍
closed mid December-mid February – **M** 7.50/11.00 and a la carte 🍾 4.00 – **18 rm** ☲ 58.00/116.50 s.

St. Saviour – pop. 10 910 – ECD : Thursday – ✉ St. Saviour – ☎ 0534 Jersey.
St. Helier 1.

🏠 **Longueville Manor,** Longueville Rd, on A 3 ✆ 25501, Telex 4192306, Fax 31613, « Former manor house with Jacobean panelling », ⌇ heated, 🚗, park – 🔄 📺 ☎ ℗. 🅽 AE ⓓ VISA
M 14.75/21.00 **s.** and a la carte ⌽ 3.50 – **32 rm** ⊊ 71.00/147.00 **s., 2 suites** 205.00 **s.** –
SB (mid October-April) (except Christmas-New Year) 85.00/130.00 **s.**

PORSCHE Five Oaks ✆ 26156   RENAULT Bagot Rd ✆ 36471

SARK 403 P 33 and 230 – pop. 560 – ☎ 048 183.
See : Site★★ – La Coupee★★★ – Port du Moulin★★ – La Seigneurie★ AC – Pilcher Monument★ – Hog's Back★.

🚢 Shipping connections with the Continent : to France (Saint-Malo) (Condor : hydrofoil) summer only – to Jersey (St. Helier) (Condor : hydrofoil) Monday/Saturday 1-4 daily (1 h 10 mn) – to Guernsey (St. Peter Port) (Isle of Sark Shipping Co.) summer only 1-8 daily (40 mn).
🇮 ✆ 2345.

🏠 **Petit Champ** ⌂, ✆ 2046, ≼ coast, Herm, Jetou and Guernsey, « Country house atmosphere », ⌇ heated, 🚗 – ⤬ rest. 🅽 AE ⓓ VISA ⚹
May-September – **M** 9.50/13.50 **s.** ⌽ 2.75 – **16 rm** ⊊ 26.00/60.00 **s.**

🏠 **Stocks** ⌂, ✆ 2001, Fax 2130, ⌇, 🚗
12 April-7 October – **M** 12.00/14.50 and a la carte ⌽ 3.00 – **23 rm** ⊊ 23.00/60.00.

🏠 **Aval du Creux,** Harbour Hill, ✆ 2036, Fax 2368, ⌇ heated, 🚗 – 📺
May-September – **M** (booking essential) 13.50 (dinner) and a la carte – **12 rm** ⊊ 21.00/42.00.

✗ **La Sablonnerie** ⌂ with rm, ✆ 2061, 🚗 – 🅽 AE VISA
May-September – **M** 12.00/15.00 ⌽ 3.00 – **21 rm** ⊊ 20.00/50.00.

Isle
of Man

Place with at least :

one hotel or restaurant ____________ ● Douglas

one pleasant hotel ____________ , X with rm

one quiet, secluded hotel ____________

one restaurant with ____________ ✤,✤✤,✤✤✤, M

See this town for establishments
  located in its vicinity ____________

Localité offrant au moins :

une ressource hôtelière ____________ ● Douglas

un hôtel agréable ____________ , X with rm

un hôtel très tranquille, isolé ____________

une bonne table à ____________ ✤,✤✤,✤✤✤, M

Localité groupant dans le texte
  les ressources de ses environs ____________

La località possiede come minimo :

una risorsa alberghiera ____________ ● Douglas

un albergo ameno ____________ , X with rm

un albergo molto tranquillo, isolato ____________

un'ottima tavola con ____________ ✤,✤✤,✤✤✤, M

La località raggruppa nel suo testo
  le risorse dei dintorni ____________

Ort mit mindestens :

einem Hotel oder Restaurant ____________ ● Douglas

einem angenehmen Hotel ____________ X with rm

einem sehr ruhigen und abgelegenen Hotel ____________

einem Restaurant mit ____________ ✤,✤✤,✤✤✤, M

Ort mit Angaben über Hotels und Restaurants
  in seiner Umgebung ____________

ISLE OF MAN
Ramsey
Douglas Onchan
Ballasalla
Castletown

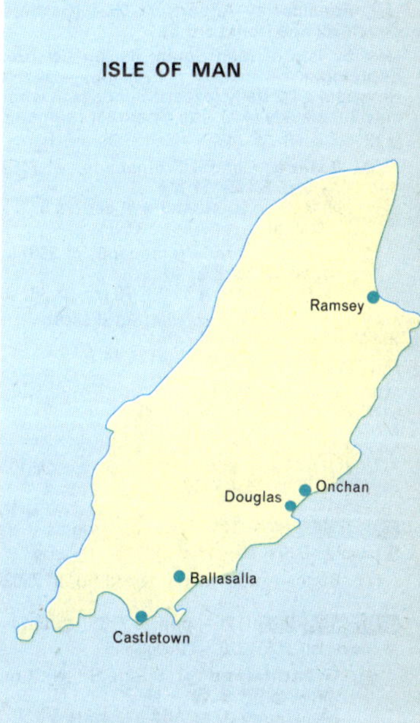

ISLE OF MAN

Towns

BALLASALLA 402 G 21 – ✪ 0624 Douglas – Douglas 8.
- ✕✕ **Silverburn Lodge,** ✆ 822343 – 🅿. ◪ *VISA*
  M *(closed Sunday dinner and Monday)* 10.75 **t.** (lunch) and a la carte 14.75/28.75 **t.** 🍶 4.00.
- ✕ La Rosette, Main Rd, ✆ 822940.

CASTLETOWN 402 G 21 – pop. 3 141 – ECD : Thursday – ✪ 0624.
See : Rushen Castle★★ (13C) *AC* : Keep ❋★ – Port Erin (site★) W : 4 ½ m.
- 🏌 Fort Island ✆ 834422, E : 2 m.
- 🛈 Commissioner's Office, Parliament Sq. ✆ 823518 – Douglas 10.
- 🏨 **Castletown Golf Links** 🦢, Fort Island, E : 2 m. ✆ 822201, Telex 627636, Fax 824633,
  ≼ sea and golf links, ◪, 🏌 – 📺 ☎ 🅿 – 🔼 300. ◪ AE ⓪ *VISA*
  M 14.50 **st.** (dinner)and a la carte 🍶 6.50 – **50 rm** ⊑ 55.00/70.00 **st., 8 suites** 80.00/150.00 **st.**
  – SB 90.00/110.00 **st.**

AUSTIN-ROVER Douglas Rd ✆ 822421   SKODA Alexandra Rd ✆ 823698

DOUGLAS 402 G 21 – pop. 19 944 – ECD : Thursday – ✪ 0624.
See : Manx Museum★★ – The Promenades★ – A 18 Road★★ From Douglas to Ramsey.
Envir. : Snaefell ❋★★★ (by electric railway from Laxey) *AC*, NE : 7 m. – Laxey (waterwheel★ :
Lady Isabella) NE : 6 m. – St. John's (Tynwald Hill) NW : 8 m. – Peel : Castle★ (ruins 13C-16C)
AC, NW : 11 ½ m.
- 🏌 Pulrose Park ✆ 75952, 1 m. from Douglas Pier.
- 🛪 Ronaldsway Airport, ✆ 0624 (Castletown) 823311, Telex 629243, SW : 7 m. – **Terminal :**
Coach service from Lord St.
- 🚢 by Isle of Man Steam Packet Co : to Belfast : 2 weekly (4 h 30 mn) – to Dublin : June-
September 1-4 weekly (4 h 30 mn) – to Fleetwood : July-August, 2 weekly (3 h 15 mn) – to
Heysham : 1-2 daily (except Sundays in winter) (3 h 45 mn to 4 h 30 mn) – to Liverpool : summer
only 2-4 weekly (4 h) – to Stranraer : summer only 1 weekly (4 h 45 mn).
- 🛈 13 Victoria St. ✆ 74323 – Sefton Bureau, Harris Promenade ✆ 28627 – Sea Terminal ✆ 74323.
- 🏨 **Palace,** Central Promenade, ✆ 74521, Telex 627742, Fax 25535, ≼, ◪ – 📶 📺 ☎ 🅿
  🔼 250. ◪ AE ⓪ *VISA*
  M 8.00/15.00 **st.** and a la carte 🍶 5.00 – ⊑ 6.00 – **131 rm** 60.00/75.00 **st., 4 suites** 100.00/
  200.00 **st.**
- 🏨 **Sefton,** Harris Promenade, ✆ 26011, Telex 627519, Fax 76004, ≼, ◪ – 📶 ✖ rest 📺 ☎
  🅿. ◪ AE ⓪ *VISA* ✾
  M 7.50/12.00 **t.** 🍶 3.50 – **79 rm** ⊑ 38.00/55.00 **t., 1 suite** 75.00/90.00 **t.**

AUSTIN-ROVER Westmoreland Rd ✆ 23481
BMW 41-45 Bucks Rd ✆ 73380
CITROEN Kingswood Grove ✆ 24114
DAIHATSU Victoria Rd ✆ 22071
FORD Douglas ✆ 73211
HONDA Kingswood Grove ✆ 73196
MAZDA Kingswood Grove ✆ 24114
MERCEDES-BENZ Douglas Rd ✆ 822884
PEUGEOT-TALBOT, COLT, FIAT Peel Rd ✆ 24519
RENAULT Peel Rd ✆ 73342

TOYOTA Westmoreland Rd ✆ 75556
VAUXHALL-OPEL The Milestone, Peel Rd ✆ 73781
VOLVO New Castletown Rd ✆ 74683
VW-AUDI 1 Main Rd ✆ 75885

◉ ATS Geoff Duke Ltd, Mount Vernon, Peel Rd ✆ 22661
ATS Douglas Tyre and Battery Co., 5-7 South Quay ✆ 76532

ONCHAN 402 G 21 – ✪ 0624 Douglas – 🏌 Howstrake, Groudle Rd ✆ 20430.
- 🛈 Library, 10 Elm Tree Rd ✆ 21228 – Douglas 1.5.
- ✕✕✕ Boncomptes, King Edward Rd, ✆ 75626, ≼ – 🅿.

RAMSEY 402 G 21 – pop. 5 778 – ✪ 0624 – 🏌 4 Abbey Terr. ✆ 812600.
- 🛈 Town Hall ✆ 812228 – Douglas 16.
- 🏨 **Grand Island** 🦢, Bridge Rd, N : 1 m. on A 10 ✆ 812455, Telex 629849, Fax 815291, ≼, ◪,
  ✾ – 📶 📺 ☎ 🅿 – 🔼 200. ◪ AE ⓪ *VISA*
  M 10.00/20.00 **st.** and a la carte 🍶 3.50 – **46 rm** ⊑ 40.00/78.00 **st., 8 suites** 108.00/138.00 **st.**
  – SB 70.00 **st.**
- 🏨 Admiral House, 12 Loch Promenade, ✆ 29551, Fax 75021, ≼ – 📶 📺 ☎ – **12 rm.**

FORD Parliament Sq. ✆ 813000

Republic of Ireland

Ballyliffin
Rosapenna
DUNFANAGHY
Fahar
Rathmullan
Letterkenny
Raphoe
Ballybofey
Ardara
N 15
DONEGAL
Rossnowlagh
N 16
SLIGO
N 59
Dromahair
Riverstown
Crossmolina
Ballina
Doogort
Castlebaldwin
Boyle
Carrick-on-Shannon
ACHILL ISLAND
Cavan
Newport
Lough Gowna
Westport
Virginia
Longford
T 40
N 4
Letterfrack
Cong
Clifden
Ballynahinch
Oughterard
Ballyconneely
Mullingar
Cashel Bay
N 84
Athlone
M, Moycullen
Furbogh
GALWAY
Tyrellspass
Spiddle
Barna
Ballinasloe
Banagher
Ballyvaughan
Birr
Lisdoonvarna
Emo
Feakle
Ballinderry
N 18
Portlaoise
Lahinch
Mountshannon
Dromineer
Ennis
Killaloe
Roscrea
Abbeyleix
Newmarket on Fergus
N 7
Bunratty
Castleconnell
M
Limerick
KILKENNY
AdareM, ,
N 21
N 24
Templeglentan
Tipperary
Glen of Aherlow
NEW ROSS
Caher
Tralee
Charleville
Carrick-on-Suir
(Rath Luirc)
Clonmel
Dingle M
,
Ballymacarbry
Ballyhack
Kanturk
Castletownrocne
WATERFORD
Caragh Lake
Banteer
Cappoquin
Glenbeigh
Killarney
M Mallow
Ballyduff
Dunmore East
Lismore
Waterville
Tahilla
Kenmare
Dungarvan
Parknasilla
Macroom
Blarney
Youghal
N 25
Ardmore
Shanagarry M, with rm
Ahakista M
N 22
640

Place with at least :
one hotel or restaurant
one pleasant hotel
with rm
one quiet, secluded hotel
one restaurant with
M
See this town for establishments
located in its vicinity
SLIGO
Longford

Localité offrant au moins :
une ressource hôtelière
Longford
un hôtel agréable
with rm
un hôtel très tranquille, isolé
une bonne table à
M
Localité groupant dans le texte
les ressources de ses environs
SLIGO

La località possiede come minimo :
una risorsa alberghiera
Longford
un albergo ameno
with rm
un albergo molto tranquillo, isolato
un'ottima tavola con
M
La località raggruppa nel suo testo
le risorse dei dintorni
SLIGO

Ort mit mindestens :
einem Hotel oder Restaurant
Longford
einem angenehmen Hotel
with rm
einem sehr ruhigen und abgelegenen Hotel
einem Restaurant mit
M
Ort mit Angaben über Hotels und Restaurants
in seiner Umgebung
SLIGO

Moville
Red Castle
Castleblayney
Cootehill
Carrickmacross
Carlingford
Dundalk
M 22
M 1
A 1
N 1
Navan
Trim
Drogheda
Skerries
Newbridge
Droichead Nua
Dunlavin
Castledermot
Rathnew
Wicklow
Carlow
Aughrim
Avoca
Ballon
N 11
Gorey
M
Borris
Courtown
N 25
Wexford
Foulksmills
Rosslare
Rosslare Harbour

Maynooth
Malahide
N 1
N 4
Howth
DUBLIN
M
Dun Laoghaire
N 1
Dalkey
Killiney
Blessington
Bray
N 11
Delgany

N 71
Gougane Barra
CORK
N 25
Glengarriff
Ballylickey
Crosshaven
Dunmanway
Kinsale
N 71
Durrus
Ballinascarty
Glandore
Skull
Skibbereen

Towns

ABBEYLEIX Laois **405** J 9 – pop. 1 402 – ECD : Wednesday – ✆ 0502 Portlaoise.
Envir. : Dunamase Rock (castle★★ 13C-16C ruins), site★★, ※★★, NE : 13 ½ m.
🛈 Portlaoise ✆ 31450.
◆Dublin 64 – Kilkenny 21 – ◆Limerick 65 – ◆Tullamore 30.

   Hibernian House, Lower Main St., ✆ 31252 – 🔲 ⓪ **VISA**. ※
   M 6.50/10.00 t. and a la carte 🍾 4.00 – **13 rm** ⌑ 16.00/30.00 **st.** – SB 46.00/52.00 **st.**

ACHILL ISLAND Mayo **405** B 5 and 6.
See : Achill Sound★ – The Atlantic Drive★★★, SW : Coast road from Cloghmore to Dooega –
Keel : (the strand★) – Lough Keel★.
🛈 Achill Sound, Westport, in Keel ✆ 43202.
🅱 ✆ Achill Sound 43249 (July and August).

   Doogort – ✉ Achill Island – ✆ 098 Westport.
   Gray's ⑤, ✆ 43244, 🚗 – ℗. ※
   April-September – **M** 12.00 t. 🍾 4.00 – **15 rm** ⌑ 14.00/26.00 t.

ADARE Limerick **405** F 10 – pop. 785 – ✆ 061 Limerick.
See : ≤★ from the bridge of the River Maigue.
🅱 ✆ 86255 (June-August).
◆Dublin 131 – ◆Killarney 59 – ◆Limerick 10.

   Adare Manor ⑤, ✆ 86566, Telex 70733, Fax 86124, ≤, « 19C Gothic mansion in extensive
   parkland », 🔲, 🚗, 🚗 – 🛗 TV ☎ ℗ – 🔥 50. 🔲 AE ⓪ **VISA**. ※
   M a la carte 19.50/28.00 t. 🍾 10.00 – **64 rm** 95.00/230.00 **st.**

   Dunraven Arms, Main St., ✆ 86209, Telex 70202, Fax 86541, « Attractively furnished,
   antiques », 🚗 – TV ☎ ℗ – 🔥 100. 🔲 AE ⓪ **VISA**. ※
   M 8.50/17.95 t. and a la carte 🍾 3.75 – ⌑ 6.75 – **45 rm** 48.00/110.00 t. – SB 90.00/110.00 **st.**

   Woodlands House, SE : 2 m. by N 21 on Croom rd ✆ 86118, 🚗 – ☎ ℗. 🔲 AE ⓪ **VISA**.
   ※
   closed 25 December – **M** (bar lunch Monday to Saturday)/dinner 13.95 t. 🍾 3.75 – **12 rm**
   ⌑ 15.00/34.00 t. – SB (weekends only) 36.00/39.00 **st.**

   Mustard Seed, Main St., ✆ 86451 – 🔲 ⓪ **VISA**
   closed Monday October-June, Sunday and 28 January-1 March – **M** (dinner only) 21.00 t.
   🍾 5.00.

AHAKISTA Cork **405** D 13 – ✉ ✆ 027 Bantry.
◆Dublin 217 – ◆Cork 63 – ◆Killarney 59.

   Shiro, ✆ 67030, Japanese rest., 🚗 – ℗. 🔲 AE **VISA**
   closed January – **M** (dinner only) (booking essential) 24.00 **st.** 🍾 7.00.

ANNAMOE Wicklow **405** N 8 – ✉ ✆ 0404 Wicklow.
Envir. : Glendalough (ancient monastic city★★ : site★★★, St. Kervin's Church★) and Upper Lake★
in Glendalough Valley★★★, SW : 5 m.
◆Dublin 29 – Wexford 72.

   Hotels see : Rathnew E : 9 m.

ARAN ISLANDS ★★ Galway **405** CD 8.
See : Inishmore Island (Kilronan harbour★).
Access by boat or aeroplane from Galway city or by boat from Kilkieran, or Fisherstreet (Clare).
🅱 ✆ 099 (Kilronan) 61263 (summer only).

   Hotels see : Galway.

ARDARA Donegal **405** G 3 – ✪ 075.
♦Dublin 188 – Donegal 24 – ♦Londonderry 58.

⚓ **Bay View Country House** ⌂, Portnoo Rd, N : ¾ m. ☎ 41145, ≼ Loughros Bay and hills, 🚗 – **🅟**. ✄
March-mid November – **M** 10.00 st. – **7 rm** ⌷ 11.00/22.00 st.

ARDMORE Waterford **405** I 12 – pop. 318 – ✪ 024 Youghal.
♦Dublin 139 – ♦Cork 34 – ♦Waterford 43.

🏠 **Cliff House,** ☎ 94106, ≼, 🚗 – **🅟**. ◪ 🅰🅴 ⓪ *VISA*
May-September – **M** (bar lunch Monday to Saturday)/dinner 15.00 **st.** and a la carte ⌴ 4.10 – **16 rm** ⌷ 23.00/52.00 st.

ATHLONE Westmeath **405** I 7 – pop. 9 444 – ECD : Thursday – ✪ 0902.
Envir. : Clonmacnoise★★ (medieval ruins) SW : 8 m. – N : Lough Ree★.
🏌 Hodson Bay ☎ 2073.
🛈 17 Church St. ☎ 72866.
♦Dublin 75 – ♦Galway 57 – ♦Limerick 75 – Roscommon 20 – ♦Tullamore 24.

🏨 **Prince of Wales,** Church St., ☎ 72626, Telex 53068, Fax 75658 – ⇤ rm 📺 ☎ **🅟** – 🛎 250. ◪ 🅰🅴 ⓪ *VISA*. ✄
closed 24 to 28 December – **M** 9.00/15.00 **st.** and a la carte ⌴ 5.00 – **42 rm** ⌷ 25.00/50.00 st. – SB (weekends only) 49.00/55.00 **st.**

FORD Dublin Rd ☎ 75426

AUGHRIM Wicklow **405** N 9 – pop. 639 – ✪ 0402 Arklow.
♦Dublin 48 – Wexford 52.

⚘ **Lawless's,** ☎ 36146 – **🅟**
10 rm.

AVOCA Wicklow **405** N 9 – pop. 289 – ✪ 0402 Arklow.
See : Vale of Avoca★ from Arklow to Rathdrum on T 7.
♦Dublin 47 – ♦Waterford 72 – Wexford 55.

🏨 **Woodenbridge,** Vale of Avoca, SW : 1 ½ m. ☎ 5146, 🚗 – 📺 🕾 **🅟**. ◪ ⓪ *VISA*
closed 25 December – **M** (bar lunch Monday to Saturday)/dinner 13.50 st. and a la carte ⌴ 3.50 – **12 rm** ⌷ 25.00/52.00 st. – SB 55.00/65.00 st.

BALLINA Mayo **405** E 5 – pop. 6 856 – ECD : Thursday – ✪ 096.
Envir. : Rosserk Abbey★ (Franciscan Friary 15C) N : 4 m. – Ballycastle (cliffs★) NW : 3 m. near Downpatrick Head★, NW : 18 m.
🏌 ☎ 21050, E : 1 m. – 🏌 Belmullet ☎ 097 (Belmullet) 81093.
🛈 ☎ 22422 (July and August).
♦Dublin 150 – ♦Galway 73 – Roscommon 64 – ♦Sligo 37.

🏨 **Downhill,** Sligo Rd, ☎ 21033, Telex 40796, Fax 21338, ◪, 🚗, ✗, squash – 📺 ☎ **🅟**. ◪ 🅰🅴 ⓪ *VISA*. ✄
closed 4 days at Christmas – **M** (buffet lunch)/dinner 18.00 **t.** and a la carte ⌴ 10.00 – **54 rm** ⌷ 38.00/85.00 t. – SB (October-June) (weekends only) 74.00/86.00 **st.**

🏨 **Mount Falcon Castle** ⌂, Foxford Rd, S : 4 m. on Foxford-Ballina rd (T 40/N 57) ☎ 21172, ≼, « Country house atmosphere », ⌇, park, ✗ – **🅟**. ◪ 🅰🅴 ⓪ *VISA*
closed February and March – **M** (bar lunch)/dinner 16.50 t. – **10 rm** ⌷ 37.50/75.00 t.

NISSAN Lord Edward St. ☎ 21037

BALLINASCARTY Cork **405** F 12 – ✉ Clonakilty – ✪ 023 Bandon.
Envir. : Timoleague (Franciscan Abbey★ 16C) NW : 7 m.
♦Dublin 188 – ♦Cork 27.

🏨 **Ardnavaha House** ⌂, SE : 2 m. by L 63 ☎ 49135, Telex 75702, Fax 49316, ≼, ⌇ heated, ⌇, 🚗, park, ✗ – ☎ **🅟**. ◪ 🅰🅴 ⓪ *VISA*
April-October – **M** 10.00/20.00 st. and a la carte ⌴ 7.00 – **36 rm** ⌷ 40.50/80.00 st. – SB (June-September) 80.00/88.00 **st.**

BALLINASLOE Galway **405** H 8 – pop. 6 374 – ECD : Thursday – ✪ 0905.
🏌 ☎ 42126 – 🏌 Mount Belleur ☎ 9259.
🛈 ☎ 42131 (July and August).
♦Dublin 91 – ♦Galway 41 – ♦Limerick 66 – Roscommon 36 – ♦Tullamore 34.

🏨 **Haydens,** Dunlo St., ☎ 42347, Telex 53947, Fax 42895, 🚗 – ⌷ 📺 ☎ **🅟**. ◪ 🅰🅴 ⓪ *VISA*. ✄
closed 24 to 26 December – **M** 9.50/13.90 st. and a la carte ⌴ 3.95 – ⌷ 4.25 – **51 rm** 23.00/40.00 **st.**

FORD Kilmartins ☎ 42204　　　　　　　　　RENAULT Brackernagh ☎ 42420
PEUGEOT Dunlo St. ☎ 42290

BALLINDERRY Tipperary **405** H 8 – ⊠ ✆ 067 Nenagh.
♦Dublin 111 – ♦Galway 53 – ♦Limerick 41.

　⋔　**Gurthalougha House** ⟆, W : 1 ¾ m. ☏ 22080, « ≼ Country house on banks of Lough
　　Derg », ☞, park – **P**. ☒ **AE** **VISA**
　　closed 17 to 30 December – **M** (bar lunch, residents only)/dinner 18.00 **st.** ⓘ 5.00 – **8 rm**
　　⊿ 27.00/54.00 **st.** – SB 83.00 **st.**

BALLON Carlow **405** L 9 – ✆ 0503 Carlow.
♦Dublin 55 – Kilkenny 26 – Wexford 33.

　⯭　**Ballykealey House** ⟆, N : ½ m. on T 16 ☏ 57278, ≼, ⟍, ☞, park, ✗ – ☎ **P**
　　16 rm.

BALLYBOFEY Donegal **405** I 3 – pop. 2 928 – ECD : Wednesday – ✆ 074 Letterkenny.
⌁ ☏ 31093.
♦Dublin 148 – ♦Londonderry 30 – ♦Sligo 58.

　⯭　**Kee's,** Main St., Stranorlar, NE : ½ m. on N 15 ☏ 31018 – **TV** ☏ **P**. ☒ **AE** **①** **VISA**
　　closed 24 and 25 December – **M** 14.00 **t.** (dinner) and a la carte 10.25/13.70 **t.** ⓘ 3.50 – **26 rm**
　　⊿ 20.00/40.00 **t.** – SB 52.00/54.00 **st.**

BALLYCONNEELY Galway **405** B 7 – ⊠ ✆ 095 Clifden.
♦Dublin 189 – ♦Galway 54.

　⯯　**Erriseask House** ⟆, ☏ 23553, ≼ – ☎ **P**. ☒ **AE** **①** **VISA**. ✋
　　April-October – **M** (bar lunch)/dinner 14.00 **st.** and a la carte ⓘ 4.00 – **11 rm** ⊿ 23.00/40.00 **st.**

BALLYDUFF Waterford **405** H 11 – ✆ 058 Dungarvan.
♦Dublin 139 – ♦Cork 32 – ♦Limerick 47 – ♦Waterford 69.

　⯯　**Blackwater Lodge** ⟆, Upper Ballyduff, SW : 1 ½ m. ☏ 60235, ⟍ – **P**
　　16 rm.

BALLYHACK Wexford **405** L 11 – pop. 221 – ⊠ New Ross – ✆ 051 Waterford.
♦Dublin 105 – ♦Waterford 8.5.

　✗　**Neptune,** Ballyhack Harbour, ☏ 89284, Seafood – ☒ **AE** **①** **VISA**
　　closed 20 November-15 March and first 2 weeks October – **M** (closed Sunday dinner and
　　Monday) 10.90/9.90 **t.** and a la carte 12.50/19.50 **t.** ⓘ 5.50.

BALLYLICKEY Cork **405** D 12 – ⊠ ✆ 027 Bantry.
♦Dublin 216 – ♦Cork 55 – ♦Killarney 45.

　⯭　**Sea View House** ⟆, ☏ 50462, ≼, ☞ – ☎ **P**. ☒ **AE** **VISA**
　　March-October – **M** (bar lunch Monday to Saturday)/dinner 16.50 **t.** and a la carte ⓘ 5.50 –
　　10 rm ⊿ 25.00/62.00 **st.** – SB (weekdays only) 75.00/84.00 **st.**

　✗✗　**Ballylickey Manor House** ⟆ with rm, ☏ 50071, Fax 50124, ≼, ⟰ heated, ⟍, ☞, park
　　– **TV** ☎ **P**. **AE** **VISA**. ✋
　　April-October – **M** (closed Wednesday to non-residents) (bar lunch)/dinner 22.50 **t.** ⓘ 6.00 –
　　8 rm ⊿ 50.00/75.00 **t.**, **3 suites** 90.00/115.00 **t.** – SB 57.00/78.75 **st.**

BALLYLIFFIN Donegal **405** J 2 – pop. 260 – ⊠ ✆ 077 Buncrana.
Envir. : Carndonagh (Donagh Cross★) SE : 6 m. – Lough Naminn★, S : 6 m.
⌁ Clonmany ☏ 76119.
♦Dublin 180 – Donegal 83 – ♦Londonderry 35.

　⯭　**Strand,** ⊠ Carndonagh, ☏ 76107, ☞ – **TV** ☎ **P**. ☒ **VISA**. ✋
　　M 8.00/15.00 and dinner a la carte ⓘ 3.75 – **12 rm** ⊿ 25.00/45.00 **t.** – SB (weekends
　　only) 36.50/38.50 **st.**

BALLYMACARBRY Waterford **405** I 11 – ⊠ ✆ 052 Clonmel.
♦Dublin 118 – ♦Cork 49 – Waterford 39.

　⋔　**Clonanav Farm** ⟆, N : 1 m. by T 27 ☏ 36141, ≼, ⟍, ☞, park – **P**
　　10 rm.

BALLYNAHINCH Galway **405** C 7 – ⊠ Recess – ✆ 095 Clifden.
See : Lake★.
♦Dublin 140 – ♦Galway 41 – Westport 49.

　⯭　**Ballynahinch Castle** ⟆, Ballinafad, ☏ 31006, Telex 50809, Fax 31085, ≼ Owenmore
　　River and woods, ⟍, ☞, park, ✗ – ☎ **P**. ☒ **AE** **①** **VISA**. ✋
　　M (bar lunch)/dinner 20.00 **st.** ⓘ 5.00 – **28 rm** ⊿ 48.00/90.00 **st.**

 Clare 405 E 8 – ✆ 065 Ennis – **Envir. : SW : Coast road L 54 from Ailladie to Fanore : Burren District (Burren limestone terraces★★) – Corcomroe Abbey★ (or Abbey of St. Maria de Petra Fertilis : 12C Cistercian ruins) NE : 6 m.**

♦Dublin 149 – Ennis 34 – ♦Galway 29.

🏨 **Gregans Castle** ⑤, SW : 3 ¼ m. on T 69 ℰ 77005, Fax 77111, ≼ countryside and Galway Bay, « Attractively furnished », ⚑ – ☎ ℗. *VISA*. ⍟
7 April-21 October – **M** (bar lunch)/dinner 23.65 **st.** and a la carte ₰ 6.20 – **15 rm** � 62.00/84.00 **st.**, **1 suite** 135.00 **st.**

🏚 **Hylands,** ℰ 77037, Fax 77131 – ☎ ℗. 🖭 AE ⓪ *VISA*. ⍟
Easter-October – **M** (bar lunch)/dinner 18.00 **t.** ₰ 5.00 – **11 rm** ⊡ 22.00/44.00 **t.** – SB 50.40/53.55 **st.**

 Offaly 405 I 8 – pop. 1 378 – ✆ 0902.
See : ≼★ from the bridge of Shannon.
Envir. : Clonfert (St. Brendan's Cathedral : west door★ 12C, east windows★ 13C) NW : 4 ½ m. – Birr : Castle Demesne (arboretum★, gardens★, telescope of Lord Rosse) *AC*, SE : 8 m.

♦Dublin 83 – ♦Galway 54 – ♦Limerick 56 – ♦Tullamore 24.

⌂ **Brosna Lodge,** Main St., ℰ 51350, ⚑ – ℗. 🖭 AE. ⍟
M 5.50/9.50 **st.** and a la carte ₰ 4.00 – **10 rm** ⊡ 12.00/30.00 **st.**

 Cork 405 F 11 – pop. 217 – ✆ 029.
♦Dublin 154 – ♦Cork 34 – ♦Killarney 29 – ♦Limerick 48.

🏰 **Clonmeen Manor House** ⑤, E : 2 m. on Mallow rd ℰ 56008, ⌐, ⚑, park – ☎ ℗. 🖭 AE ⓪ *VISA*. ⍟
May-August – **M** (lunch by arrangement)/dinner 22.00 **t.** and a la carte – ⊡ 2.50 – **9 rm** 38.00/70.00 **t.**, **3 suites** 80.00/92.00 **t.**

⌂ **Clonmeen Lodge** ⑤, E : 2 m. on Mallow rd ℰ 56090, ⌐, park – ℗. 🖭 ⓪ *VISA*. ⍟
closed March and October – **M** (by arrangement) 18.00 **t.** ₰ 3.20 – **6 rm** ⊡ 22.00/50.00 **st.** – SB 58.00/64.00 **st.**

 Cork 405 D 12 – pop. 2 862 – ECD : Wednesday – ✆ 027.
See : Bantry Bay★★ – Bantry House (interior★★, ≼★) *AC*.
Envir. : Glengarrif (site★★★) NW : 8 m. – NE : Shehy Mountains★★.
🏌 Donemark ℰ 50579, on Glengariff rd.
🛈 ℰ 50229 (July and August).
♦Dublin 218 – ♦Cork 57 – ♦Killarney 48.

Hotels and restaurants see : Ballylickey N : 6 m.

RENAULT Barrack St. ℰ 50092   VAUXHALL-OPEL Cork Rd ℰ 50023

 Galway 405 E 8 – ✆ 091 Galway.
♦Dublin 135 – ♦Galway 3.

✗ **Ty Ar Mor,** Sea Point, ℰ 92223, ≼, Seafood – ℗. 🖭 AE ⓪ *VISA*
closed January and February – **M** (dinner only in winter) 10.00/30.00 **st.** and a la carte 16.50/22.00 ₰ 5.00.

 Offaly 405 I 8 – pop. 3 679 – ✆ 0509 – 🏌 Glenns ℰ 20082, N : 2 m.
🛈 ℰ 20206 (June-September).
Athlone 28 – ♦Dublin 87 – Kilkenny 49 – ♦Limerick 49.

🏨 **County Arms,** Railway Rd, ℰ 20791, Fax 21234, ⚑, squash – 📺 ☏ ℗ – 🍽 60. 🖭 AE ⓪ *VISA*. ⍟
M 8.00/13.50 **t.** and a la carte ₰ 5.00 – **18 rm** ⊡ 24.00/48.00 **t.** – SB 60.00/72.00 **st.**

 Cork 405 G 11 – pop. 1 980 – ✉ ✆ 021 Cork.
See : Castle★ (15C) (top ❊★, 112 steps) *AC*.
♦Dublin 167 – ♦Cork 6.

🏨 **Blarney Park,** ℰ 385281, Telex 75022, Fax 381506, ⚑ – 📺 ☎ ₺ ℗ – 🍽 200. 🖭 AE ⓪ *VISA*
M 9.75/14.00 **st.** and a la carte ₰ 5.00 – **74 rm** ⊡ 34.00/56.00 **st.** – SB 49.00/59.00 **st.**

 Wicklow 405 M 8 – pop. 988 – ✆ 045 Naas.
Envir. : Lackan ≼★, SE : 4 ½ m. – SE : Poulaphuca Lake★ (reservoir).
♦Dublin 20.

🏯 **Tulfarris House** ⑤, S : 6 m. by N 81 ℰ 64574, Telex 60915, Fax 64423, ≼, « Georgian country house overlooking Poulaphuca Lake », 🏌, ⌐, ⚑, park – 📺 ☎ ₺ ℗ – 🍽 100. 🖭 AE ⓪ *VISA*
M a la carte 11.00/19.00 **t.** ₰ 5.00 – **19 rm** 45.00/110.00 **st.**, **2 suites** 70.00/120.00 **st.** – SB (except Bank Holidays) 100.00/142.00 **st.**

AUSTIN-ROVER Main St. ℰ 65555

BORRIS Carlow **405** L 10 – ✆ 0503 Carlow.

ᵣ₉ Deerpark 🖉 73143.

♦Dublin 68 – Kilkenny 16 – ♦Waterford 30.

   XX   **Step House** with rm, 🖉 73401, 🍴. **VISA**
   closed Monday except Bank Holidays and February – **M** *(closed dinner Sunday and Monday)*
   (bar lunch Monday to Saturday)/dinner 17.90 **st.** *and a la carte* 10.70/16.90 **t.** ⓘ 3.75 – **4 rm**
   ⌷ 20.00/40.00 **st.** – SB 65.00 **st.**

BOYLE Roscommon **405** H 6 – pop. 1 737 – ✆ 079.

See : Cistercian Abbey★ (12C).

Envir. : NE : Lough Key★.

ᵣ₉ Roscommon Rd 🖉 62594.

🛈 🖉 62145 (June-September).

♦Dublin 107 – Ballina 40 – ♦Galway 74 – Roscommon 26 – ♦Sligo 24.

   🏛   **Royal**, Bridge St., 🖉 62016 – **TV** ☎ **P**. 🔄 **AE** ⓞ **VISA**
   closed 25 and 26 December – **M** 7.40/13.50 **t.** *and a la carte* ⓘ 4.50 – **16 rm** ⌷ 25.00/44.00 **t.**
   – SB (weekends only) 55.00/59.00 **st.**

   🏛   **Forest Park**, Dublin Rd, E : ½ m. on N 4 🖉 62229, 🍴 – **TV** ☎ **P**. 🔄 **AE** ⓞ **VISA**. 🐾
   closed 24 to 26 December – **M** 8.50/15.00 **st.** *and a la carte* ⓘ 4.75 – **12 rm** ⌷ 20.00/50.00 **st.**
   – SB 55.00/75.00 **st.**

BRAY Wicklow **405** N 8 – pop. 22 853 – ECD : Wednesday – ✆ 01 Dublin.

ᵣ₉ Ravenswell Rd 🖉 862484.

🛈 🖉 867128 (July and August).

♦Dublin 13 – Wicklow 20.

   XX   **Tree of Idleness**, Seafront, 🖉 863498, Greek-Cypriot rest. – 🔄 ⓞ **VISA**
   closed Monday, first 2 weeks September, Christmas and Bank Holidays – **M** *(dinner only)*
   19.25 **st.** *and a la carte* 17.50/24.50 **t.** ⓘ 4.75.

BUNRATTY Clare **405** F 9 – ✆ 061 Limerick.

See : Castle (Great Hall★) *AC* – Folk Park★ *AC*.

♦Dublin 129 – Ennis 15 – ♦Limerick 8.

   🏛🏛   **Fitzpatrick's Shannon Shamrock**, 🖉 361177, Telex 72114, Fax 61252, 🔄, 🍴 – ▤ rest
   TV ☎ ♿ **P** – 🔥 50. 🔄 **AE** ⓞ **VISA**. 🐾
   closed 25 December – **M** 7.50/15.00 **t.** *and a la carte* ⓘ 5.00 – ⌷ 7.00 – **105 rm** 54.00/100.00 **t.**
   – SB (weekends only) 70.00 **st.**

   XX   **MacCloskey's**, Bunratty House Mews, 🖉 364082, « Cellars of Georgian house » – **P**.
   🔄 **AE** ⓞ **VISA**
   closed Sunday, Monday and 20 December-21 January – **M** *(dinner only)* 23.00 **t.** ⓘ 10.00.

CAHER Tipperary **405** I 10 – pop. 2 120 – ECD : Thursday – ✆ 052.

See : Castle★ (12C-15C) the most extensive medieval castle in Ireland.

ᵣ₉ Cahir Park, 🖉 41474, S : 1 m.

🛈 🖉 41453 (July and August).

♦Dublin 112 – ♦Cork 49 – Kilkenny 41 – ♦Limerick 38 – ♦Waterford 39.

   🏛🏛   **Kilcoran Lodge**, SW : 4 ¾ m. on N 8 🖉 41288, 🍴 – **TV** ☎ **P** – 🔥 50
   23 rm.

FORD   Dublin Rd 🖉 41432

CAHERDANIEL Kerry **405** B 12.

Envir. : Sheehan's Point ≤★★★, W : 5 m. – Staigue Fort★ (prehistoric stone fort : site★, ≤★) *AC*,
NE : 5 m.

♦Dublin 238 – ♦Killarney 48.

CAPPOQUIN Waterford **405** I 11 – pop. 950 – ✉ Lismore – ✆ 058 Dungarvan.

♦Dublin 136 – ♦Cork 31 – ♦Waterford 40.

   🏠   **Richmond House** ⑤, SE : ½ m. on N 72, 🖉 54278, 🍴, park – **P**. **VISA**. 🐾
   February-October – **M** 9.00 **st.** ⓘ 5.00 – **9 rm** ⌷ 21.00/36.00 **st.**

CARAGH LAKE Kerry **405** C 11 – ✆ 066 Tralee.

See : Lough Caragh★.

♦Dublin 212 – ♦Killarney 22 – Tralee 25.

   🏛🏛   **Caragh Lodge** ⑤, 🖉 69115, ≤, « Country house atmosphere », 🎣, 🍴, park, ✂ – **P**.
   🔄 **AE** ⓞ **VISA**. 🐾
   April-October – **M** *(bar lunch)/dinner* 18.00 **t.** ⓘ 4.50 – **9 rm** ⌷ 34.00/60.00 **t.**

   🏛🏛   **Ard Na Sidhe** ⑤, 🖉 69105, ≤, « Country house atmosphere », 🎣, 🍴, park – **P**
   M *(dinner only)* – **20 rm**.

♦Dublin 66 – ♦Dundalk 13.

⚐ **McKevitt's Village**, Market Sq., 🕻 73116 – 📺 ☎. ▭ AE ① VISA ✻
    closed 25 December – **M** 8.00/14.00 **t.** and a la carte ▯8.00 – **10 rm** ⟷ 22.00/36.00 **s.** –
    SB 45.00/53.00 **st.**

CARLOW Carlow **405** L 9 – pop. 11 722 – ECD : Thursday – 🕸 0503.

▮₁₈ Oak Park 🕻 31695.

▯ 🕻 31554 (July and August).

♦Dublin 52 – Kilkenny 25 – ♦Tullamore 44 – Wexford 46.

🏨 **Royal**, 8-13 Dublin St., 🕻 31621 – 📺 ☎ ℗. ▭ AE ① VISA
    closed 25 and 26 December – **M** 10.00/15.00 **st.** and a la carte ▯4.95 – **28 rm**
    ⟷ 26.50/45.00 **st.**

🏠 Carlow Lodge, Kilkenny Rd, S : 2 m. on N 9 🕻 42002, ⇗ – 📺 ☎ ℗. ✻
    10 rm.

CITROEN, HONDA, PEUGEOT, SAAB Tullow Rd 🕻
31391
MITSUBISHI Tullow Rd 🕻 31955
OPEL Tullow Rd 🕻 31303

TOYOTA Dublin Rd 🕻 31572
VW-AUDI, MAZDA, MERCEDES-BENZ Green Lane
🕻 31047

CARRICKMACROSS Monaghan **405** L 6 – pop. 1 768 – ECD : Wednesday – 🕸 042.

♦Dublin 97 – ♦Dundalk 14.

🏨 Nuremore ⚐, SE : 1 m. on N 2 🕻 61438, ≼, ▭, ▮₉, ⚒, ⇗, park, ✗, squash – 📺 ☎ ℗ –
    ⚐ 200. ✻
    39 rm.

CARRICK-ON-SHANNON Leitrim **405** H 6 – pop. 2 037 – ECD : Wednesday – 🕸 078.

▮₉ Woodbrook 🕻 67015.

▯ 🕻 20170 (summer only).

♦Dublin 97 – Ballina 50 – Roscommon 26 – ♦Sligo 34.

🏠 **County**, Bridge St., 🕻 20042 – 📺 ☎ ℗. ▭ AE VISA
    M 7.50/12.50 **st.** and a la carte ▯4.00 – **17 rm** ⟷ 18.50/44.00 **st.** – SB 27.50/29.75 **st.**

CARRICK-ON-SUIR Tipperary **405** J 10 – pop. 5 566 – 🕸 051 Waterford.

▮₉ Garravone 🕻 40047.

♦Dublin 95 – ♦Cork 68 – ♦Limerick 62 – ♦Waterford 16.

🏠 **Cedarfield House** ⚐, Waterford Rd, E : 1 m. on N 24 🕻 40164, ⇗ – 📺 ☎ ℗. ✻
    closed 6 January-mid March – **M** *(closed Sunday dinner to non-residents)* (dinner only)
    16.50 **st.** ▯4.00 – **5 rm** ⟷ 22.50/55.50 **st.** – SB 70.00/80.00 **st.**

RENAULT Carrigbeg 🕻 40202

CASHEL Tipperary **405** I 10 – pop. 2 436 – ECD : Wednesday – 🕸 062.

See : St. Patrick's Rock★★★ (or Rock of Cashel) : site and ecclesiastical ruins (12C-15C) (❋★★)
AC – Hore Abbey★ ruins (13C) – St. Dominick's Abbey★ ruins (13C).

Envir. : Holycross Abbey★★ (12C) *AC*, N : 9 m.

▯ Town Hall 🕻 61333 (summer only).

♦Dublin 101 – ♦Cork 60 – Kilkenny 34 – ♦Limerick 36 – ♦Waterford 44.

🏨 **Cashel Palace** ⚐, Main St., 🕻 61411, Telex 70638, Fax 61521, « Former Archbishop's
    palace, gardens » – 📺 ☎ ℗ – ⚐ 50. ▭ AE ① VISA. ✻
    closed 25 and 26 December – **M** a la carte 8.65/24.00 **t.** ▯5.50 – ⟷ 10.00 – **20 rm**
    58.00/155.00 **t.**

✗✗ **Chez Hans**, Rockside, 🕻 61177, « Converted 19C church » – ℗
    closed Sunday, Monday and 3 weeks January – **M** (dinner only) a la carte 19.50/21.50 **t.**
    ▯5.00.

PROTON, LADA Cahir Rd 🕻 61155

CASHEL BAY Galway **405** C 7 – 🕸 095 Clifden.

Envir. : SE : Kilkieran Peninsula★★.

♦Dublin 173 – Galway 41.

🏨 **Cashel House** ⚐, 🕻 31001, Telex 50812, Fax 31077, ≼, « Country house atmosphere,
    gardens », ⚒, ✗ – ☎ ℗. ▭ AE ① VISA
    closed 15 January-15 February and 15 November-15 December – **M** 15.00/23.50 **t.** and a la
    carte ▯5.75 – **32 rm** ⟷ 44.00/110.00 **t.** – SB 135.00/146.25 **st.**

🏨 Zetland ⚐, 🕻 31111, Telex 50853, ≼ Cashel Bay, « Country house, gardens », ⚒ – ✗ rm
    ☎ ℗. ▭ AE ① VISA ✻
    April-October – **19 rm** ⟷ 33.00/116.00 **t.**

CASTLEBALDWIN Sligo 405 G 5 – ⊠ Boyle (Roscommon) – ✆ 071 Sligo.
♦Dublin 118 – Longford 42 – ♦Sligo 15.

　✗　**Cromleach Lodge** ⑤ with rm, Ballindoon, SE : 3 ½ m. ✆ 65155, ≼ Loch Arrow, 🐾, 🐎 –
　　☎ Ⓟ. 🌂 AE VISA. ⅏
　　closed 22 to 31 December – **M** (closed Sunday) (dinner only) 18.95 t. ▯5.00 – ⚏ 4.00 –
　　7 rm 16.00/35.00 t. – SB 80.00/120.00 st.

CITROEN Breaffy Rd ✆ 421975

CASTLEBLAYNEY Monaghan 405 L 5 – pop. 2 425 – ✆ 042.
🏌9 ✆ 40197.
♦Dublin 68 – ♦Belfast 58 – ♦Drogheda 39 – ♦Dundalk 17 – ♦Londonderry 80.

　🏨　Glencarn, Monaghan Rd, ✆ 46666, Telex 747415 – TV Ⓟ – 🛏 250
　　15 rm.

CASTLECONNELL Limerick 405 G 9 – pop. 1 053 – ✆ 061 Limerick.
♦Dublin 111 – ♦Limerick 9.

　🏨　**Castle Oaks House** ⑤, ✆ 377666, Telex 70328, ≼, 🐎, park – TV ☎ Ⓟ – 🛏 250. 🌂 AE
　　Ⓞ VISA. ⅏
　　M 10.00/16.00 st. ▯5.00 – **11 rm** ⚏ 54.00/110.00 st. – SB 128.00/148.00 st.

CASTLEDERMOT Kildare 405 L 9 – pop. 805 – ✆ 0503 Carlow.
Envir. : Baltinglass (Abbey ruins : scenery★) NE : 7 m.
♦Dublin 44 – Kilkenny 33 – Wexford 54.

　✗✗　**Doyle's Schoolhouse** with rm, Main St., ✆ 44282 – TV Ⓟ. 🌂 AE Ⓞ VISA
　　closed mid February-mid March – **M** (dinner only and Sunday lunch in summer)/dinner
　　18.00 st. and a la carte ▯8.00 – **4 rm** ⚏ 20.00/45.00 t. – SB (except Christmas) 50.00/70.00 st.

CASTLETOWNROCHE Cork 405 G 11 – pop. 455 – ✆ 022 Mallow.
♦Dublin 138 – ♦Cork 31 – ♦Killarney 50 – ♦Limerick 45 – ♦Waterford 68.

　🏨　**Blackwater Castle** ⑤, ✆ 26333, Telex 75145, Fax 26210, ≼, « Renovated castle with
　　distinctive modern decor », 🐾, 🐎, park, ✗ – TV ☎ Ⓟ – 🛏 35. 🌂 AE Ⓞ VISA. ⅏
　　Mid March-mid November – **M** (bar lunch)/dinner 22.50 t. and a la carte ▯5.50 – **10 rm**
　　⚏ 60.00/180.00 t.

CAVAN Cavan 405 J 6 – pop. 3 240 – ✆ 049.
🏌18 Drumelis ✆ 31283.
🅱 ✆ 31942 (May-September).
♦Dublin 71 – Drogheda 58 – Enniskillen 40.

　🏨　Kilmore, Dublin Rd, E : 2 m. on N 3 ✆ 32288, Fax 32458 – TV ☎ 🖐 Ⓟ – 🛏 400
　　39 rm.

　🏨　Farnham Arms, Main St., ✆ 32577 – TV ☎ Ⓟ. ⅏
　　29 rm.

FIAT Dublin Rd ✆ 31188　　　　　　　　　　　　　　FORD Farnham St. ✆ 31700

CHARLEVILLE (RATH LUIRC) Cork 405 F 10 – pop. 2 874 – ECD : Thursday – ✆ 063 Rathluirc.
Envir. : Kilmallock (Dominican Friary ruins 13C, SS. Peter and Paul church 14C : scenery★)
NE : 6 m. – Kilfinnane (site★) E : 11 m.
🏌18 ✆ 021 (Cork) 81257.
♦Dublin 138 – ♦Cork 38 – ♦Killarney 57 – ♦Limerick 24.

　🏨　**Deerpark**, Limerick Rd, N : ½ m. on N 20 ✆ 81581, 🐎 – TV ☎ Ⓟ. 🌂 VISA
　　M 6.50/12.50 st. and a la carte ▯4.00 – ⚏ 4.50 – **20 rm** 15.50/29.00 t.

CLIFDEN Galway 405 B 7 – pop. 796 – ECD : Thursday – ✆ 095.
Envir. : E : Connemara★★ : The Twelve Pins★ (mountains), Lough Inagh★ – Cleggan (site★★)
NW : 6 m. – Streamstown Bay★, NW : 2 m.
🅱 ✆ 21163 (June-August).
♦Dublin 181 – Ballina 77 – ♦Galway 49.

　🏨　**Rock Glen Country House** ⑤, S : 1 ¼ m. by L 102 ✆ 21035, Telex 50915, Fax 21737, 🐎
　　– ☎ Ⓟ. 🌂 AE Ⓞ VISA
　　Mid March-October – **M** (bar lunch)/dinner 20.00 t. ▯4.50 – **29 rm** ⚏ 38.00/130.00 st. –
　　SB 80.00/146.00 st.

　🏨　**Abbeyglen Castle** ⑤, Sky Rd, W : ½ m. ✆ 21201, Telex 50866, Fax 21797, ≼, ⚊ heated,
　　🐎 – ✗ rm TV ☎ Ⓟ. 🌂 AE Ⓞ VISA
　　closed 10 January-1 February – **M** 11.00/21.00 t. ▯6.00 – ⚏ 6.00 – **40 rm** 25.00/60.00 t.,
　　2 suites 85.00/125.00 t. – SB (September-June) (except Bank Holidays) 80.00/90.00 st.

Ardagh ⑤, Ballyconneely rd, S : 1 ¾ m. on L 102 ℰ 21384, Fax 21314, ≤ Ardbear Bay, ⌐
– TV ☎ ℗. ⚠ AE ⓪ VISA ⚮
Easter-October – **M** (bar lunch)/dinner 17.05 **st.** ⬧ 6.50 – **21 rm** ⚏ 35.20/70.40 **st.** –
SB 72.00/87.00 **st.**

Shades, The Square, ℰ 21215 – ⚠ AE ⓪ VISA
March-October – **M** *(closed Monday except summer)*7.50/15.00 **t.** and a la carte 18.00/22.00 **t.**
⬧ 4.00.

CLONMEL Tipperary **405** I 10 – pop. 12 407 – ECD : Thursday – ☺ 052.

See : The Main Guard★ (1674).

Envir. : Ahenny (2 high crosses★) NE : 16 m. – S : Nire Valley★ (≤★★).

🏌 Lyreanearla, ℰ 21138.

🛈 ℰ 22960 (July and August).

♦Dublin 108 – ♦Cork 59 – Kilkenny 31 – ♦Limerick 48 – ♦Waterford 29.

Knocklofty House ⑤, W : 4 ½ m. by T 27 on L 28 ℰ 38222, Fax 38289, ≤, « Georgian
mansion in extensive parkland on banks of River Suir », ⚠, ⌐, ⇔, ⚟, squash – ☎ ℗.
⚠ VISA ⚮
M 10.00/17.50 **t.** ⬧ 3.80 – **11 rm** ⚏ 40.00/50.00 **t.** – SB 80.00/130.00 **st.**

AUDI-VW, MAZDA, MERCEDES-BENZ, Upper   OPEL Dungarvon Rd ℰ 22399
Irishtown ℰ 22199   TOYOTA Cashel Rd ℰ 21652

CONG Mayo **405** E 7 – pop. 213 – ☺ 092.

See : Ashford Castle (site★).

Envir. : Ross Abbey★★, Franciscan Friary (tower ⁂★, 80 steps) SE : 9 m.

♦Dublin 160 – Ballina 49 – ♦Galway 28.

Ashford Castle ⑤, ℰ 46003, Telex 53749, Fax 46260, ≤ Lough Corrib and countryside,
« Part 13C and 18C converted castle », 🏌, ⌐, ⚟, park, ⚟ – 🛗 TV ☎ ℗ – ⚐ 50. ⚠ AE
⓪ VISA ⚮
M 17.00/29.00 **t.** and a la carte 22.00/27.15 **t.** – (see also **Connaught Room** below) – ⚏ 9.50
– **77 rm** 150.00/170.00 **st.**, **6 suites** 190.00/220.00 **st.** – SB (October-April) 179.00 **st.**

Connaught Room, (at Ashford Castle H.), ℰ 46003, Telex 53749, Fax 46260, ≤ Lough
Corrib, ⚟ – ℗. ⚠ AE ⓪ VISA
M 17.00/35.00 **t.** and a la carte 33.50/45.00 **t.**

COOTEHILL Cavan **405** K 5 – pop. 1 554 – ECD : Tuesday – ☺ 049 Cavan.

Envir. : Bellamont Forest★, N : 1 ½ m.

♦Dublin 68 – ♦Dundalk 33.

White Horse, Market St., ℰ 52124, Fax 52407 – TV ☎ ℗ – ⚐ 500
30 rm.

CORK Cork **405** G 12 – pop. 136 344 – ☺ 021.

See : St. Patrick's Street★ YZ – St. Ann's Shandon Church★ (18C) (steeple ⁂★ *AC*, 134 steps)
Y A – University College★ (1845) X U – The Marina ≤★ X.

🏌 Monkstown ℰ 841225, S : 7 m. by L 66 X.

✈ ℰ 313131, Telex 32085, S : 4 m. by L 42 X – **Terminal :** Bus Station, Parnell Pl.

⚓ Shipping Connections with the continent : to France (Roscoff) (Brittany Ferries) – to France
(Le Havre) (Irish Ferries) summer only.

🛈 Cork City, Tourist House, Grand Parade ℰ 273251 – Cork Airport ℰ 964347 (summer only).

♦Dublin 154.

Plan on next page

Fitzpatrick's Silver Springs, Tivoli, E : 2 ½ m. on N 25 ℰ 507533, Telex 76111, Fax
507641, ⚠, 🏌, ⚟, park, ⚟, squash – 🛗 ▤ rest TV ☎ ℗ – ⚐ 150. ⚠ AE ⓪ VISA ⚮
M *(closed Sunday dinner)*7.50/13.50 **t.** and a la carte ⬧ 4.50 – ⚏ 7.00 – **103 rm** 65.00/84.00 **st.**,
3 suites 105.00/215.00 **st.**   X c

Jury's, Washington St., ℰ 276622, Telex 76073, Fax 274477, ⚒ heated, ⚟, squash – 🛗
TV ☎ ⚭ ℗ – ⚐ 500. ⚠ AE ⓪ VISA ⚮   Z v
closed 24 to 26 December – **M** 9.95/17.25 **t.** and a la carte 15.45/21.75 ⬧ 5.25 – ⚏ 6.25 –
184 rm 67.50/78.50 **t.**, **1 suite** 100.00/200.00 **t.** – SB (weekends only) 84.90/92.90 **st.**

Imperial, South Mall, ℰ 274040, Telex 75126, Fax 274040 – 🛗 TV ☎ – ⚐ 300. ⚠ AE ⓪
VISA ⚮   Z n
closed 1 week at Christmas – **M** 8.50/10.50 **t.** and a la carte – **100 rm** ⚏ 58.00/140.00 **t.**

Arbutus Lodge , Middle Glanmire Rd, Montenotte, ℰ 501237, Telex 75079, Fax 502893,
≤, ⚟ – ▤ rest TV ☎ ℗. ⚠ AE ⓪ VISA ⚮   Y a
closed 24 to 29 December – **M** *(closed Sunday)* 14.95/18.95 **st.** and a la carte 18.95/24.45 **st.**
⬧ 6.95 – **20 rm** ⚏ 30.00/98.00 **st.** – SB (weekends only) 90.00/120.00 **st.**

Lotamore House without rest., Tivoli, E : 3 ¼ m. on N 25 ℰ 822344, ≤, ⚟, park – TV ⚭
℗. ⚠ AE VISA ⚮   X a
21 rm ⚏ 24.00/40.00 **t.**

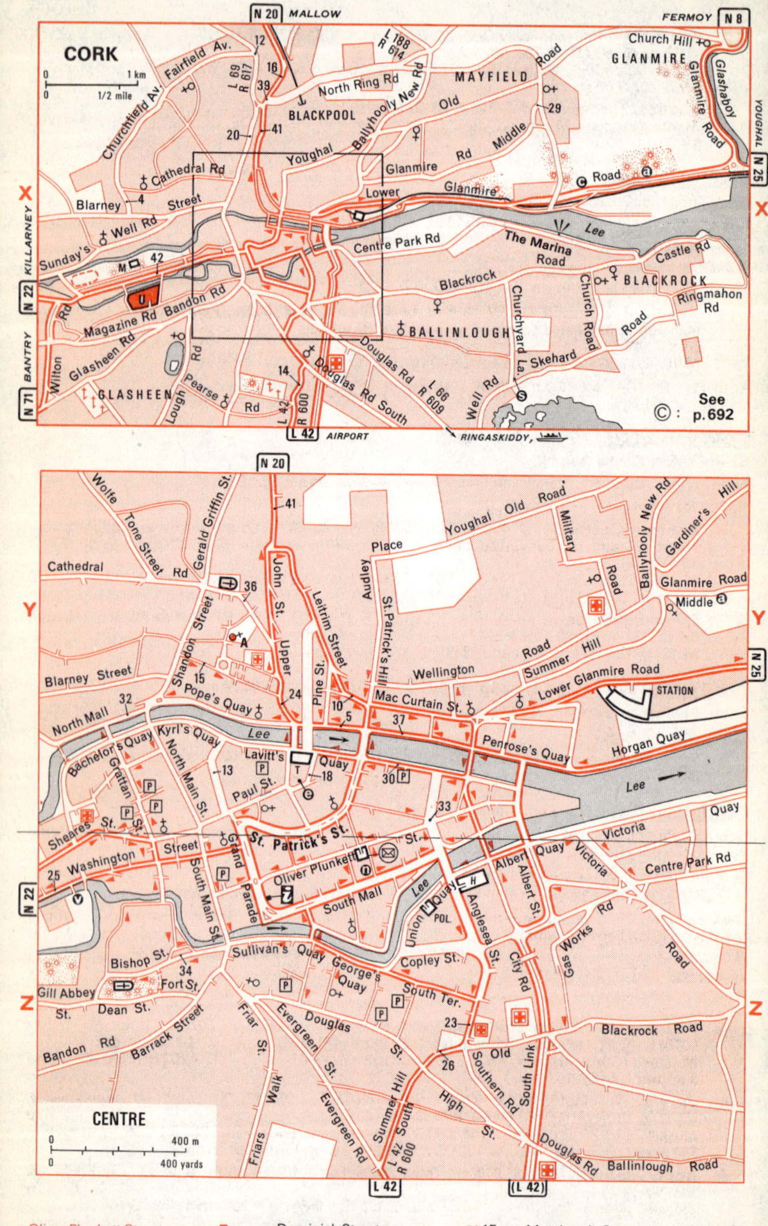

Oliver Plunkett Street .... Z
St. Patrick's Street .... YZ

Baker's Road .... X 4
Camden Place .... Y 5
Coburg Street .... Y 10
Commons Road .... X 12
Corn Market Street .... Y 13
Curragh Road .... X 14
Dominick Street .... Y 15
Dublin Street .... X 16
Emmet Place .... Y 18
Great William O'Brien Street . X 20
Infirmary Road .... Z 23
John Redmond Street .... Y 24
Lancaster Quay .... Z 25
Langford Row .... Z 26
Lower Mayfield Road .... X 29
Merchant's Quay .... Y 30
Newsom's Quay .... Y 32
Parnell Place .... Y 33
Proby's Quay .... Z 34
Roman Street .... Y 36
St. Patrick's Quay .... Y 37
Thomas Davis Street .... X 39
Watercourse Road .... X 41
Western Road .... X 42

XX **Lovett's** with rm, Churchyard Lane, off Well Rd, Douglas, *&* 294909 – TV ☎ **P**. ⚑ AE ⓪
VISA. ⚞   X   s
closed Saturday lunch, Sunday and Bank Holidays – **M** 18.00 **t**. and a la carte 17.00/25.25 **t**.
⚗ 4.75 – **9 suites** 45.00/55.00 **st**.

XX Cliffords, 23 Washington St. West, *&* 275333.

X **Crawford Gallery Café**, Crawford Gallery, Emmet Pl., *&* 274415 – VISA   Y   e
closed dinner Monday, Tuesday and Saturday, Sunday and 24 December-2 January –
M (dinner booking essential) a la carte 10.30/15.50 **t**. ⚗ 5.00.

at Glounthaune E : 7 m. on N 25 – X – ✉ ☺ 021 Cork :

🏠 **Ashbourne House,** *&* 353319, Fax 354338,« Extensive gardens» , ⚊ heated, ⚔ – TV ☎
P. ⚑ AE ⓪ VISA
M 8.00/16.00 **t**. – **26 rm** ⚏ 26.00/90.00 **t**. – SB (except Christmas) 60.00 **st**.

FIAT   24 Watercourse Rd *&* 503228   OPEL   26 St. Patricks Quay *&* 276657
FIAT, LANCIA   11 South Terr. *&* 507344   RENAULT   Bishop's Town Rd *&* 544655
FORD   Dennehys Cross *&* 542846

COURTOWN Wexford 405 N 10 – pop. 337 – ☺ 055 Gorey.

🏌 Courtown Harbour *&* 25166.

♦Dublin 62 – ♦Waterford 59 – Wexford 42.

🏠 **Courtown,** *&* 25108, 🖼 – **P**. ⚑ AE ⓪ VISA. ⚞
closed 2 weeks at Christmas – **M** (bar lunch Monday to Saturday)/dinner 16.50 **t**. and a
la carte – **21 rm** ⚏ 20.00/50.00 **t**. – SB (weekends only) (except summer) 65.00/75.00 **st**.

CROSSHAVEN Cork 405 H 12 – pop. 1 419 – ✉ ☺ 021 Cork.

♦Dublin 173 – ♦Cork 12.

🏠 **Whispering Pines,** *&* 831843, ≤, ⚛, ⚛ – **P**. ⚑ AE ⓪ VISA. ⚞
closed Christmas – **M** (dinner only) 12.00 **t**. ⚗ 4.50 – **15 rm** ⚏ 17.00/32.00 **st**.

CROSSMOLINA Mayo 405 E 5 – pop. 1 335 – ✉ ☺ 096 Ballina.

♦Dublin 157 – ♦Ballina 6.5.

🏠 **Enniscoe House** ⚘ , Castlehill, S : 2 m. on L 140 *&* 31112, ≤,« Georgian country house,
antiques» , ⚛, park – **P**. ⚑ AE VISA. ⚞
April-mid October and January – **M** (dinner only) 16.00 **st**. ⚗ 4.25 – **6 rm** ⚏ 45.00/74.00 **st**.
– SB 96.00/100.00 **st**.

DALKEY Dublin 405 N 8 – ☺ 01 Dublin.

♦Dublin 11.

XX **Guinea Pig,** 17-18 Railway Rd, *&* 859055, Seafood – ⚑ AE ⓪ VISA
M (booking essential) (dinner only and Sunday lunch)/dinner 16.50 **t**. and a la carte
18.75/22.95 **t**. ⚗ 4.50.

DELGANY Wicklow 405 N 8 – pop. 7 442 (inc. Greystones) – ✉ Bray – ☺ 01 Dublin.

🏌 *&* 404 (Wicklow) 874536.

♦Dublin 19.

🏠 **Glenview** ⚘, Glen of the Downs, NW : 2 m. by L 164 on N 11 *&* 877600, Telex 30638, Fax
877511, ≤, ⚛, park – ⚔ rm TV ☎ **P** – ⚖ 30. ⚑ AE VISA. ⚞
closed 24 to 26 December – **M** 12.00 **t**. and a la carte 15.90/19.75 **t**. ⚗ 7.00 – ⚏ 6.00 – **23 rm**
35.00/60.00 **t**. – SB 65.00/80.00 **st**.

DINGLE Kerry 405 B 11 – pop. 1 358 – ECD : Thursday – ☺ 066 Tralee.

See : Dingle Bay★.

Envir. : NE : Conair Pass ☀★ – Fahan : Belvedere (coast road) ≤★, SW : 7 ½ m. – Kilmakedar
(church★ 12C), Gallarus Oratory★ (8C), NW : 5 m.

🅑 *&* 51188 (July and August).

♦Dublin 216 – ♦Killarney 51 – ♦Limerick 95.

🏠 **Skellig,** *&* 51144, Fax 51501, ≤, 🖼, ⚛ – TV ☎ **P**. ⚑ AE ⓪ VISA
March-November – **M** (dinner only and Sunday lunch)/dinner 17.95 **st**. ⚗ 9.00 – **60 rm**
⚏ 39.00/80.00 **st**. – SB 67.00/85.00 **st**.

🏠 **Benners,** Main St., *&* 51638, Telex 73937, Fax 51412, ⚛ – TV ☎. ⚑ AE ⓪ VISA. ⚞
closed 1 January-17 March – **M** (bar lunch Monday to Saturday)/dinner 15.50 **t**. and a la carte
⚗ 6.00 – **24 rm** ⚏ 39.00/66.00 **t**. – SB (weekends only) 55.00/75.00 **st**.

↑ **Milltown House** ⚘ without rest., W : ¾ m. *&* 51372, ≤ – **P**. VISA. ⚞
Easter-October – **7 rm** ⚏ 20.00/24.00 **st**.

↑ **Alpine House** without rest., Mail Rd, *&* 51250, ⚛ – **P**. ⚞
March-October – **14 rm** ⚏ 25.00 **st**.

XX **Beginish,** Green St., ℰ 51588, Seafood, 🦐 – 🔊 🗚 ⓞ 𝘃𝘐𝘚𝘈
closed Monday and December-Easter – **M** (dinner only) a la carte 14.00/20.00 **t.** ⓵ 5.00.

X **Doyle's Seafood Bar** with rm, 4 John St., ℰ 51174 – 📺 ☎. 🔊 🗚 ⓞ 𝘃𝘐𝘚𝘈. 🦐
Mid March-mid November – **M** *(closed Sunday)* a la carte 12.25/19.25 **t.** ⓵ 5.50 – **8 rm**
� 30.00/50.00 **st.**

X Half Door, John St., ℰ 51600, Seafood.

DONEGAL Donegal **405** H 4 – pop. 1 956 – ECD : Wednesday – ⊛ 073.
See : Franciscan Priory (site*, ≤*).
🛇 Murvagh ℰ 073 (Ballintra) 34054.
🅩 ℰ 21148 (summer only).
♦Dublin 164 – ♦Londonderry 48 – ♦Sligo 40.

🏛 **Hyland Central** (Best Western), The Diamond, ℰ 21027, Telex 40522, Fax 22295, 🦐 – 🛗
📺 ☎ Ⓟ – 🔺 250. 🔊 🗚 𝘃𝘐𝘚𝘈. 🦐
closed 25 to 27 December – **M** 9.50/16.50 **t.** and a la carte ⓵ 4.00 – **60 rm** ⊊ 36.00/50.00 **t.**

at St. Ernan's Island SW : 2 ¼ m. by N 15 – ✉ ⊛ 073 Donegal :

🏛 **Ernan's House** 🦢, ℰ 21065, ≤ Donegal Bay, park – 📺 ☎ Ⓟ. 🔊 𝘃𝘐𝘚𝘈. 🦐
Easter-3 November – **M** (dinner only) 16.50 **t.** ⓵ 4.40 – **11 rm** ⊊ 35.00/70.00 **t.**

AUSTIN-ROVER Quay St. ℰ 21039

DROGHEDA Louth **405** M 6 – pop. 23 247 – ECD : Wednesday – ⊛ 041.
See : St. Lawrence's Gate* (13C) – Hill of Slane (site*, ≤*) W : 8 ½ m.
Envir. : Mellifont Abbey** (Cistercian ruins 1142) NW : 4 ½ m. – Monasterboice (3 tall crosses**
10C) NW : 5 ½ m. – Dowth Tumulus ❋*, W : 4 m. – Duleek (priory* 12C ruins) SW : 5 m. –
Newgrange Tumulus* (prehistoric tomb) *AC*, SW : 7 m.
🛇 County Louth, Baltray ℰ 22327, E : 3 m.
🅩 ℰ 37070 (June-August).
♦Dublin 31 – ♦Dundalk 22 – ♦Tullamore 69.

🏠 **Glenside,** Smithstown, SE : 3 m. on N 1 ℰ 29049, 🦐 – 📺 ☎ Ⓟ. 🔊 🗚 ⓞ 𝘃𝘐𝘚𝘈. 🦐
M 7.50/14.00 **st.** and a la carte ⓵ 4.50 – **14 rm** ⊊ 26.00/42.00 **st.** – SB 50.00/60.00 **st.**

FORD North Rd ℰ 31106   PEUGEOT Palace St. ℰ 37303
NISSAN North Rd ℰ 38566

DROMAHAIR Leitrim **405** H 5 – ⊛ 071 Sligo.
♦Dublin 146 – ♦Sligo 13.

🏠 Drumlease Glebe House 🦢, E : 2 m. by Manorhamilton rd ℰ 64141, ⊡ heated, 🦢, 🦐,
park – Ⓟ
M (dinner only, residents only) – **7 rm**.

DROMINEER Tipperary **405** H 9 – ✉ ⊛ 067 Nenagh.
♦Dublin 102 – ♦Galway 69 – ♦Limerick 32.

🏠 Waterside, ℰ 24114, ≤, 🦐 – ⓟ Ⓟ
12 rm.

DUBLIN Dublin **405** N 7 – pop. 528 882 – ⊛ 01.
See : National Gallery*** BY – Castle (State apartments*** *AC*) BY – Christ Church Cathedral**
(12C) BY – National Museum (Irish antiquities, Art and Industrial)** BY M2 – Trinity College*
(Library**) BY – National Museum (Zoological Collection)* BY M1 – Municipal Art Gallery*
BX M3 – O'Connell Street* (and the General Post Office) BXY – St. Stephen's Green* BZ – St.
Patrick's Cathedral (interior*) BZ – Phoenix Park (Zoological Gardens*) AY.
Envir. : St. Doolagh's Church* (13C) (open Saturday and Sunday, afternoon only) NE : 7 m. by
L 87 AY.
🛇 Edmondstown, Rathfarnham ℰ 932461, S : 3 m. by N 81 AZ – 🛇 Elm Park, Nutley House,
Dunnybrook ℰ 693438, S : 3 m. AZ – 🛇 Lower Churchtown Rd, Milltown ℰ 977060, S : by T 43 AZ
– 🛇 Royal Dublin, Bull Island ℰ 336346, E : by L 86 AY.
✈ ℰ 379900, Telex 31266, N : 5 ½ m. by N 1 AY – Terminal : Busaras (Central Bus Station)
Store St.
⛴ to Holyhead (B & I Line) 2-3 daily (3 h 30 mn-4 h 45 mn) – to the Isle of Man : Douglas (Isle
of Man Steam Packet Co.) June-September 1-6 weekly (4 h 30 mn).
🅩 14 Upper O'Connell St. ℰ 747733 – Dublin Airport ℰ 376387.
Baggot St. ℰ 747733 (weekdays only in summer).
♦Belfast 103 – ♦Cork 154 – ♦Londonderry 146.

Plans on following pages

Berkeley Court, Lansdowne Rd, Ballsbridge, ℰ 601711, Telex 30554, Fax 617238, 🏊 – 📶
🍽 rest 📺 ☎ 🚗 Ⓟ – 🛎 300. 🅿 AE ⓪ VISA. 🛇   AZ **c**
M 12.65/15.75 **t.** and a la carte ♦ 4.50 – 😊 6.50 – **200 rm** 110.00/135.00 **t.**, **10 suites** 175.00/750.00 **t.**

Westbury, Grafton St., ℰ 791122, Telex 91091, Fax 797078 – 📶 📺 ☎ Ⓟ – 🛎 150. 🅿 AE
⓪ VISA. 🛇   BY **z**
M 13.50/17.50 **t.** and a la carte ♦ 4.50 – **147 rm**, **4 suites**.

Shelbourne (T.H.F.), 27 St. Stephen's Green, ℰ 766471, Telex 93653, Fax 616006 – 📶 📺
☎ 🚗 Ⓟ – 🛎 500. 🅿 AE ⓪ VISA   BZ **s**
M 16.00/20.00 **t.** and a la carte ♦ 6.00 – 😊 9.00 – **170 rm** 116.00/190.00 **t.**, **6 suites** 224.00/275.00 **t.**

Gresham, O'Connell St., ℰ 746881, Telex 32473 – 📶 🍽 rest 📺 ☎ & Ⓟ – 🛎 300   BY **s**
172 rm, **10 suites**.

Buswells, 25-26 Molesworth St., ℰ 764013, Telex 90622, Fax 762090 – 📶 📺 ☎ – 🛎 100.
🅿 AE ⓪ VISA. 🛇   BY **u**
M (closed Sunday lunch and Saturday) 10.50 **st.** (lunch) and dinner a la carte ♦ 5.00 – 😊 6.50 – **68 rm** 47.00/74.00 **t.**

Russell Court, 21-23 Harcourt St., ℰ 784991, Fax 784066 – 📶 📺 ☎ – 🛎 100   BZ **v**
20 rm, **1 suite**.

Tara Tower, Merrion Rd, SE : 4 m. on T 44 ℰ 694666, Fax 691027 – 📶 📺 ☎ Ⓟ – 🛎 100.
🅿 AE ⓪ VISA. 🛇   on T 44   AZ
M 8.50/11.50 **t.** and a la carte ♦ 3.40 – **82 rm** 😊 50.45/80.45 **st.**

Skylon, Upper Drumcondra Rd, N : 2 ½ m. on N 1 ℰ 379121, Group Telex 90790, Fax 372778
– 📶 📺 ☎ Ⓟ – 🛎 60 – **92 rm**.   AY **e**

Blooms, Anglesea St., ℰ 715622, Telex 31688, Fax 715997 – 📶 📺 ☎ Ⓟ – 🛎 30. 🅿 AE
⓪ VISA. 🛇   BY **e**
M 12.00/17.00 **t.** and a la carte ♦ 5.00 – 😊 8.00 – **86 rm** 80.00/100.00 **t.**

Ariel House without rest., 52 Lansdowne Rd, Ballsbridge, ℰ 685512, Fax 685845, 🚃 – 📺
☎ Ⓟ. 🅿 AE VISA. 🛇   AZ **e**
closed December – **15 rm** 😊 38.50/77.00 **t.**

Abrae Court, 9 Zion Rd, Rathgar, ℰ 979944 – 📺 ☎ Ⓟ – **14 rm**.   AZ **i**

Kilronan House, 70 Adelaide Rd, ℰ 755266 – 📺 ☎. 🅿 VISA. 🛇   BZ **r**
closed 23 to 30 December – **M** (by arrangement) 12.50 **st.** ♦ 4.00 – **11 rm** 😊 32.00/50.00 **t.**

Egans House, 7-9 Iona Park, Glasnevin, ℰ 303611, Fax 303312 – 📺 ☎ Ⓟ. VISA   AY **a**
closed 23 December-3 January – **M** (by arrangement) 14.50 **t.** – 😊 5.20 – **24 rm** 23.00/36.00 **t.**

St. Aiden's, 32 Brighton Rd, Rathgar, ℰ 906178 – 🛏 rm 📺 ☎ Ⓟ. 🅿 AE VISA. 🛇   AZ **r**
M (by arrangement) 15.00 **st.** ♦ 4.00 – **12 rm** 😊 16.00/36.00 **st.**

Anglesea Town House, 63 Anglesea Rd, Ballsbridge, ℰ 683877 – 📺 ☎ – **7 rm**.   AZ **x**

Merrion Hall without rest., 54 Merrion Rd, Ballsbridge, ℰ 681426, 🚃 – 📺 Ⓟ   AZ **v**
6 rm.

XXX **Le Coq Hardi**, 35 Pembroke Rd, ℰ 689070 – Ⓟ. 🅿 AE ⓪ VISA   AZ **n**
closed Saturday lunch, Sunday, 2 weeks August and 2 weeks Christmas – **M** 15.00 **t.** (lunch) and a la carte 25.00/35.00 **t.** ♦ 6.00.

XXX ❀ **Patrick Guilbaud**, 46 St. James' Pl., St. James' St., off Lower Baggot St., ℰ 764192,
French rest. – 🍽. 🅿 AE ⓪ VISA   BZ **n**
closed Saturday lunch, Sunday and Bank Holidays – **M** 14.00/22.00 **t.** and a la carte 19.60/33.90 **t.** ♦ 7.00
Spec. Dos de porcelet rôti et ses croustillons de pommes vertes, Petite marmite de queues de langoustines et homard aux aromates, Assiette d'abats à la sauce poivrade.

XXX **Whites on The Green**, 119 St. Stephen's Green, ℰ 751975 – 🍽. 🅿 AE ⓪ VISA   BZ **a**
closed Saturday lunch, Sunday, 2 days Christmas and Bank Holidays – **M** 14.50/20.00 **t.** and a la carte 20.50/27.50 **t.** ♦ 5.00.

XX **Ernie's**, Mulberry Gdns, Downybrook, ℰ 693300, « Contemporary Irish art collection » –
🍽. 🅿 AE ⓪ VISA   AZ **o**
closed Saturday lunch, Sunday and Monday – **M** 12.50/22.00 **t.** and a la carte 21.75/28.25 **t.** ♦ 5.00.

XX **Locks**, 1 Windsor Terr., Portobello, ℰ 543391 – 🅿 AE ⓪ VISA   BZ **u**
closed Saturday lunch, Sunday and 1 week Christmas-New Year – **M** 12.50/17.50 **t.** and a la carte 18.60/23.85 **t.** ♦ 5.15.

XX **Park**, 40 The Mews, Main St., Blackrock, SE : 4 ½ m. by T 44 ℰ 886177 – 🅿 AE ⓪ VISA
closed Saturday lunch, Sunday, Monday and Tuesday after Bank Holidays – **M** 10.00/21.50 **t.**
♦ 7.00.   by T44   AZ

XX **Stokers**, 16 Harcourt St., ℰ 782441 – 🅿 AE ⓪ VISA   BZ **i**
closed 1 week Easter, 2 weeks July-August, 1 week Christmas and Bank Holidays –
M (closed Saturday lunch, Monday dinner and Sunday) 12.50/20.00 **st.** and a la carte 14.25/19.50 **t.** ♦ 5.00.

XX **Lord Edward**, 23 Christchurch Pl., ℰ 542420, Seafood – 🅿 AE ⓪ VISA   BY **c**
closed Saturday lunch, Sunday, Monday, 12 to 28 August, 1 week Christmas-New Year and Bank Holidays – **M** 13.50/18.50 **t.** and a la carte 15.30/25.90 **t.** ♦ 5.00.

XX **Old Dublin**, 90-91 Francis St., ℰ 542028, Russian-Scandinavian rest. – 🅿 AE ⓪ VISA
closed Saturday lunch, Sunday, Easter, Christmas and Bank Holidays – **M** 11.00/17.50 **t.**
♦ 4.50.   BY **i**

DUBLIN

Anne Street South . . . . . . **BY** 2
Dawson Street . . . . **BY**
Duke Street . . . . **BY** 27
Grafton Street . . . . **BY**
Henry Street . . . . **BY**
Irish Life Mall Centre . . . . **BY**
O'Connell Street . . . . **BXY**

Bath Avenue . . . . **AZ** 3
Belvidere Place . . . . **BX** 4
Benburb Street . . . . **AY** 5
Blessington Street . . . . . . **BX** 6
Botanic Road . . . . **AY** 7
Brunswick Street North . . . . **BY** 8
Bull Alley . . . . **BY** 9
Chancery Street . . . . **BY** 13
Charlotte Street . . . . **BZ** 15
College Street . . . . **BY** 19

Denmark Street. . . . . **BX** 23
D'Olier Street. . . . . **BY** 24
Donnybrook Road . . . . **AZ** 25
Eglinton Road . . . . **AZ** 29
Essex Quay . . . . **BY** 30
Fitzgibbon Street . . . . **BX** 31
Fitzwilliam Place . . . . **BZ** 32
Frederick Street North . . . . **BX** 33
Gardiner Place . . . . **BX** 35
George's Quay . . . . **BY** 36
Golden Lane . . . . **BY** 39
Harrington Street . . . . **BZ** 44
Infirmary Road . . . . **AY** 46
Kevin Street Upper . . . . . . **BZ** 47
Kildare Street . . . . **BYZ** 48
King Street South . . . . **BY** 49
Macken Street. . . . . **AZ** 50
Marlborough Street . . . . . . **BY** 53
Merchants Quay . . . . **BY** 56
Montague Street . . . . **BZ** 59
Morehampton Road. . . . . . . **AZ** 60

Mountjoy Street . . . . **BX** 62
Nicholas Street. . . . . **BY** 64
Parnell Square East . . . . . **BX** 67
Parnell Square North . . . . **BX** 68
Parnell Square West . . . . . **BX** 69
Rathmines Road Upper. . . . **AZ** 73
Ringsend Road . . . . **AZ** 75
Sandford Road . . . . **AZ** 77
Shelbourne Road . . . . **AZ** 79
Stephen Street . . . . **BY** 80
Tara Street . . . . **BY** 81
Terenure Road East . . . . . **AZ** 83
Townsend Street . . . . **BY** 89
Victoria Quay . . . . **AY** 92
Wellington Quay . . . . **BY** 95
Westland Row . . . . **BY** 96
Westmoreland Street . . . . . **BY** 97
Wexford Street . . . . **BZ** 99
Winetavern Street . . . . **BY** 100
Wolfe Tone Quay. . . . . . . **AYZ** 102
Wood Quay . . . . **BY** 103

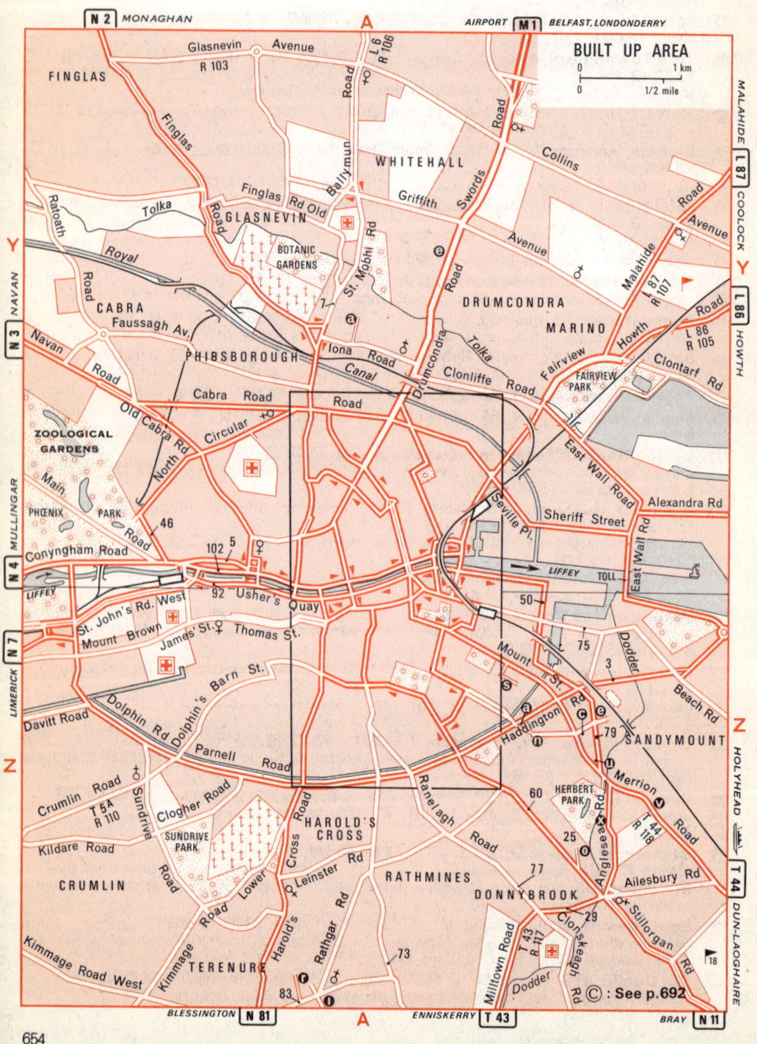

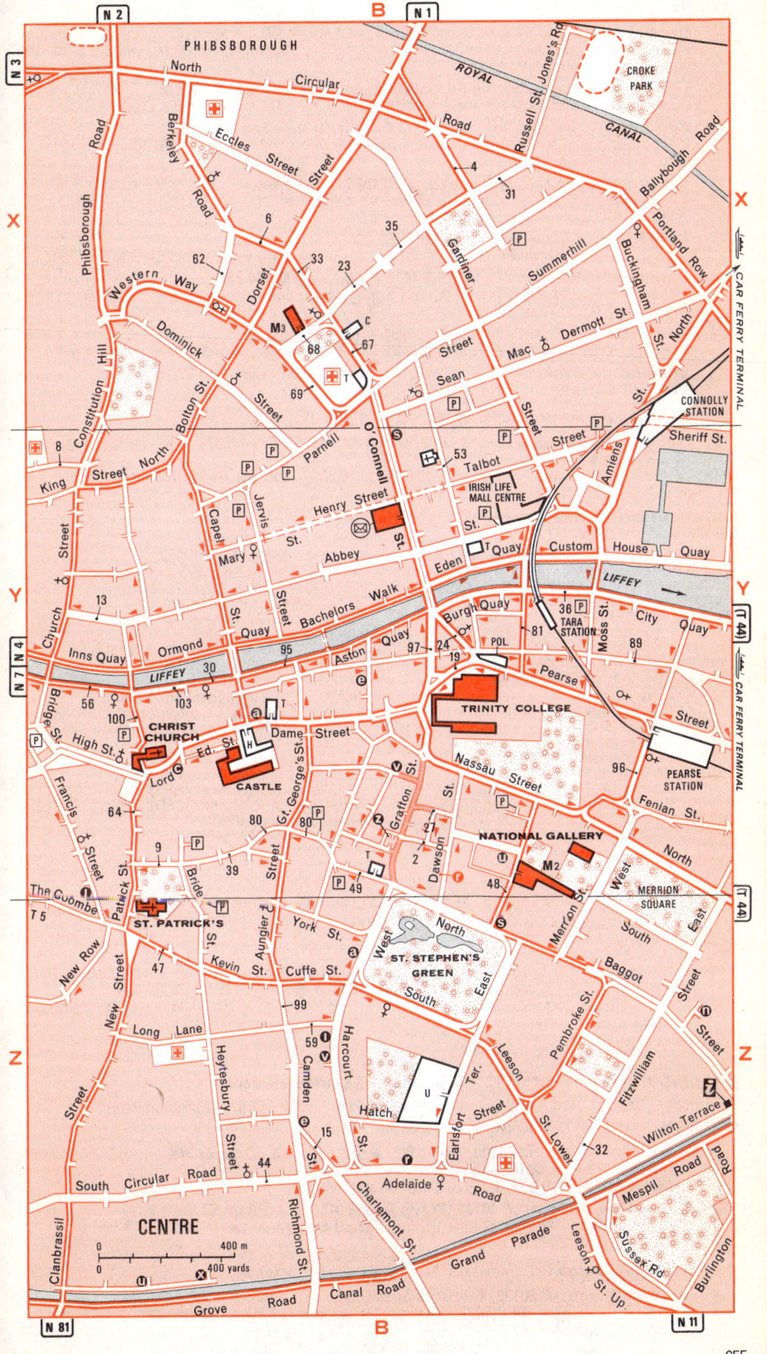

N 2
B
N 1
N 3
PHIBSBOROUGH
ROYAL
Russell St.
St. Jones's Rd.
CROKE
PARK
North
Circular
CANAL
Ballybough
Road
Road
4
31
X
Portland
Row
CAR FERRY TERMINAL
X
Berkeley
Eccles
Street
Street
Street
Road
6
Gardiner
35
Buckingham
Summerhill
Phibsborough
62
33
23
Dorset
Mac
Dermott
St.
St.
North
M3
C
Western
Way
68
67
Street
CONNOLLY
STATION
Dominick
Sean
Sheriff St.
Constitution
Hill
Bolton St.
69
T
Street
Street
Amiens
8
Parnell
O'Connell
S
Talbot
IRISH LIFE
MALL CENTRE
King
Street
North
Capel
Jervis
Henry
Street
53
St.
St.
Custom
House
Quay
Mary
St.
Abbey
Eden
T
Quay
LIFFEY
Y
13
St.
Quay
Bachelors
Walk
Burgh Quay
36
City
Quay
Y
T 44
N 7 N 4
Church
Ormond
Quay
Aston
Quay
97
24
TARA
STATION
81
Moss St.
89
Inns Quay
30
95
19
POL.
Pearse
CAR FERRY TERMINAL
LIFFEY
56
103
e
Street
Bridge St.
100
T
a
TRINITY COLLEGE
96
CHRIST
CHURCH
Dame
Street
Nassau
Street
PEARSE
STATION
High St.
Ed. St.
H
Lord
CASTLE
V
St.
Fenian St.
64
Gt. George's St.
Gratton
27
NATIONAL GALLERY
Francis
80
80
Z
2
Dawson
48
M2
West
North
9
39
Street
T
2
MERRION
SQUARE
Patrick St.
Bride
P
49
r
The Coombe
T 5
S
East
Baggot
ST. PATRICK'S
St.
York
St.
West
North
47
Aungier
St.
Cuffe St.
a
ST. STEPHEN'S
GREEN
East
Pembroke St.
New Row
Kevin
St.
South
Fitzwilliam
New
Street
99
East
Street
Z
Long
Lane
59
Harcourt
Leeson
Z
Heytesbury
Camden
U
Street
St. Lower
32
Wilton Terrace
Hatch
Earlsfort Ter.
15
St.
Street
Mespil
Road
Road
44
Adelaïde
Leeson St. Up.
Sussex Rd.
Burlington
South
Circular
Road
Charlemont St.
Road
CENTRE
Grand
Parade
0   400 m
0   400 yards
N 81
B
Grove
Road
Canal
Road
N 11

XX **Bentleys,** 46 Upper Baggot St., ☎ 682760 – 🔄 AE ① VISA   AZ a
closed Monday dinner, Sunday, 2 weeks July, 1 week Christmas and Bank Holidays – **M** a la carte 13.50/17.70 **t.** ∦ 5.25.

XX **Osprey's,** 41-43 Shelbourne Rd, Ballsbridge, ☎ 608087 – 🔄 AE ① VISA   AZ u
closed Sunday and Bank Holidays – **M** 10.50/15.50 **t.** and a la carte 14.00/19.00 **t.** ∦ 4.50.

XX **Kapriol,** 45 Lower Camden St., ☎ 751235, Italian rest. – 🔄 AE ① VISA   BZ e
closed Sunday, 6 to 27 August, 25-26 December and Bank Holidays – **M** (dinner only) a la carte 16.00/28.50 **t.** ∦ 5.00.

XX **Les Frères Jacques,** 74 Dame St., ☎ 794555 – 🔄 AE VISA   BY a
closed Saturday lunch, Sunday, 25 to 31 December and Bank Holidays – **M** 11.95/18. **t.** and a la carte 20.00/27.50 **t.** ∦ 4.95.

X **Cafe Klara,** 35 Dawson St., ☎ 778611. 🔄 VISA   BY r
closed 25 December and 1 January – **M** 9.50 **t.** (lunch) and a la carte 14.25/18.50 **t.** ∦ 5.90.

X **Dobbin's,** 15 Stephen's Lane, ☎ 764679, Bistro – 🔄 AE ① VISA   AZ s
closed Saturday lunch, Monday dinner, Sunday and Bank Holidays – **M** 13.50/18.50 **st.** and a la carte 18.90/23.70 **st.** ∦ 5.75.

X **Puerto Bella,** 1 Portobello Rd, ☎ 720851 – 🔄 AE ① VISA   BZ x
closed Saturday and Sunday lunch, Easter and 25-26 December – **M** 13.95/19.95 **t.** ∦ 6.95.

X **Imperial,** 12a Wicklow St., ☎ 772580, Chinese (Canton) rest. – 🔄 AE VISA   BY v
M 6.00/16.00 **t.** and a la carte 10.00/16.50 **t.**

at Dublin Airport N : 6 ½ m. by N 1 – AY – ✉ ☎ 01 Dublin :

🏨 **Dublin International** (T.H.F.), ☎ 379211, Telex 32849, Fax 425874 – ⇆ rm 📺 ☎ ☐ ☐ –
♨ . 🔄 AE ① VISA
M 8.95/13.95 **t.** and a la carte ∦ 4.25 – ☲ 6.50 – **192 rm** 64.00/76.00 **st.** – SB (weekends only) 64.00/106.00 **st.**

MICHELIN Distribution Centre, 4 Spilmak Pl., Bluebell Industrial Estate, Naas Rd, Dublin 12, ☎ 509096, FAX 504302 by N7 AZ

AUSTIN-ROVER, NISSAN 48-52 New St. ☎ 780033
AUSTIN-ROVER Northbrook Rd ☎ 970811
AUSTIN-ROVER, JAGUAR, NISSAN Richmond Rd ☎ 379162
BMW, MITSUBISHI Ballygall Rd East ☎ 342577
BMW, TOYOTA Rathgar Av. ☎ 979456
CITROEN, PEUGEOT Buckingham St. ☎ 745821
DAIHATSU, TOYOTA ☎ 401393
FIAT, LANCIA 56 Howth Rd ☎ 332301
FIAT North Rd ☎ 342977
FIAT, LANCIA 84 Prussia St. ☎ 791722
FIAT Milltown Rd ☎ 698577
FORD Herberton Rd ☎ 754216
FORD 172-175 Parnell St. ☎ 747831
FORD Stillorgan Rd ☎ 886821
HONDA Clarince St., Dun Laoghaire ☎ 806467
HONDA, SUZUKI Harolds Cross Rd ☎ 975757
LAND-ROVER, MITSUBISHI Temple Rd ☎ 885085
MERCEDES-BENZ, TOYOTA 54 Glasnevin Hill ☎ 373771
NISSAN Howth Rd ☎ 314066

NISSAN Bluebell Av. ☎ 507887
NISSAN Merrion Rd ☎ 693911
OPEL, BMW Beach Rd ☎ 686011
OPEL 146 Cabra Rd ☎ 385222
OPEL Emmet Rd, Inchicore ☎ 534535
OPEL New Rd ☎ 592438
PEUGEOT, MAZDA Church Pl. ☎ 973999
PEUGEOT-TALBOT, CITROEN 23 Parkgate St. ☎ 710333
RENAULT 19 Conyngnam Rd ☎ 775677
RENAULT 27 Upper Drumcondra Rd ☎ 373706
SUZUKI 232 North Circular Rd, Grangegorman ☎ 300799
TOYOTA Kilbarrack Rd ☎ 322701
TOYOTA Smithfield Market ☎ 721222
VOLVO Townsend St. ☎ 779177
VW-AUDI, MAZDA, MERCEDES-BENZ 218-224 North Circular Rd ☎ 387211
VW-AUDI, MAZDA, MERCEDES-BENZ Ballybough Rd ☎ 723033

DUNDALK Louth 405 M 5 – pop. 25 663 – ECD : Thursday – ☎ 042.

📔 Blackrock ☎ 21379, S : 3 m – 🅱 Market Sq. ☎ 35484.

♦Dublin 53 – Drogheda 22.

🏨 **Ballymascanlon House** (Best Western) 🐾, N : 3 ½ m. by N 1 ☎ 71124, Group Telex 43735, Fax 71598, 🔲, 🍴, park, 🍽, squash – 📺 ☎ ☐ – ♨ 300. 🔄 AE ① VISA
closed 24 to 26 December – **M** 8.80/14.85 **st.** and a la carte ∦ 5.00 – **36 rm** ☲ 35.00/60.00 **t.** – SB (weekends only) 73.00/80.00 **st.**

RENAULT Newry Rd ☎ 34603

DUNFANAGHY Donegal 405 I 2 – pop. 390 – ✉ ☎ 074 Letterkenny.

Envir. : Doe Castle★ (16C ruins) (site★, ≤ ★) SE : 7 ½ m. – SW : Bloody Foreland Head★.

📔 ☎ 36335 – ♦Dublin 172 – Donegal 54 – ♦Londonderry 43.

🏨 **Arnold's,** Main St., ☎ 36208, Fax 36352, ≤, 🍴, 🍽 – ☐. 🔄 AE ① VISA
April-September – **M** (bar lunch Monday to Saturday)/dinner 14.00 **st.** and a la carte ∦ 4.50 – **34 rm** ☲ 24.00/46.50 **t.** – SB 61.00/67.00 **st.**

🏨 **Carrig Rua,** Main St., ☎ 36133, Group Telex 80464, ≤ – 📺 ☐. AE VISA 🐾
Easter-October – **M** (buffet lunch)/dinner 15.00 **t.** and a la carte ∦ 3.90 – **22 rm** ☲ 19.00/46.00 **t.** – SB 60.00/68.00 **st.**

at Port-na-Blagh E : 1 ½ m. on T 72 – ✉ ☎ 074 Letterkenny :

🏨 **Port-na-Blagh,** ☎ 36129, ≤ Sheephaven Bay and harbour, 🐾, 🍴, 🍽 – ☐
Easter-September – **M** 7.50/15.00 **t.** and a la carte ∦ 4.50 – **49 rm** ☲ 20.00/48.00 **t.** – SB 59.50/68.50 **st.**

🏌9 Ballinacourty, ✆ 41605.

🛈 ✆ 41741 (July and August).

♦Dublin 124 – ♦Cork 48 – ♦Killarney 90 – ♦Waterford 29.

XX **Seanachie**, SW : 5 ½ m. by N 25, ✆ 46285 – **P**. ◫ **VISA**
closed Sunday, 25 December and Monday to Wednesday November-March – **M** (bar lunch)/dinner 12.50/17.80 **st.** and a la carte 🍷 5.00.

OPEL Youghal Rd ✆ 42288

DUN LAOGHAIRE Dublin **405** N 8 – pop. 54 496 – ✆ 01 Dublin.

See : Windsor Terrace ⩽★ over Dublin Bay.

🏌18 Eglinton Park ✆ 801055.

🛳 to Holyhead (Sealink) 2 daily (3 h 30 mn) – to Liverpool (Sealink) 1 daily.

🛈 St. Michaels Wharf ✆ 806984.

♦Dublin 9.

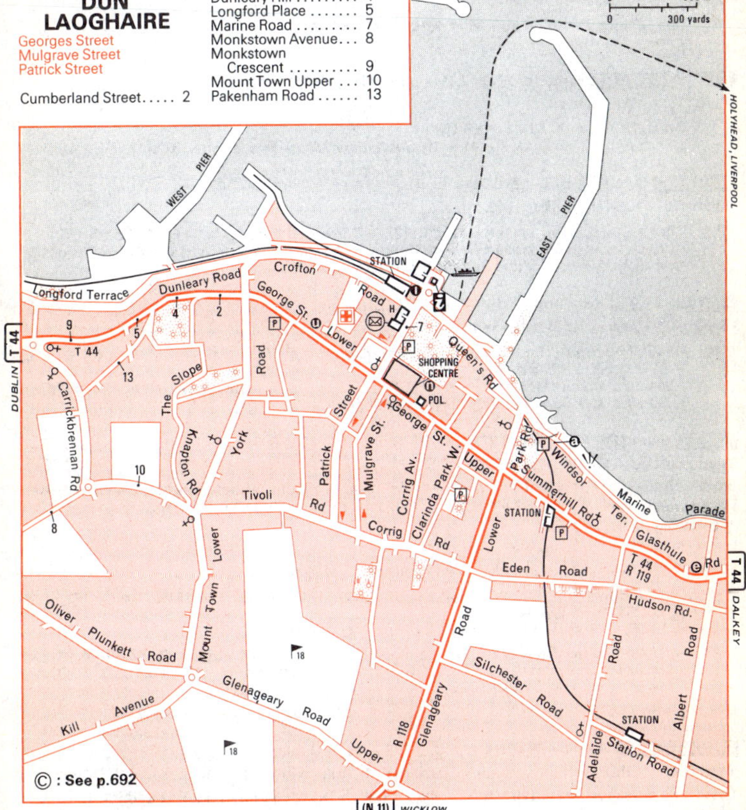

🏨 Royal Marine, Marine Rd, ✆ 801911, Telex 91277, ⩽, 🚗 – 🛗 ▤ rest 📺 ☎ **P** – 🔬 400. ◫
AE ⑩ **VISA**. 🚲   **n**
⊿ 7.00 – **104 rm** 60.00/140.00 **t.**

XXX **na Mara**, 1 Harbour Rd, ✆ 806767, Seafood – ◫ **AE** ⑩ **VISA**   **i**
closed Sunday, 1 week Easter and 1 week Christmas – **M** 12.00/17.50 **t.** and a la carte 19.20/27.50 **t.** 🍷 4.75.

XX **Digby's**, 5 Windsor Terr., ✆ 804600, ⩽ – ◫ **AE** ⑩ **VISA**   **a**
closed Saturday lunch, Tuesday, 13 April and 25-26 December – **M** 10.50 **t.** (lunch) and a la carte 18.50/23.50 **t.** 🍷 4.80.

%   **Trudi's**, 107 Lower George's St., ✆ 805318, Bistro – ⩟ AE ⓪ VISA   u
     closed Sunday and Monday – **M** (dinner only) a la carte 11.55/15.90 t. ⌂ 4.00.

%   **Russell's**, 56 Glasthule Rd, Sandycove, ✆ 808878 – ⩟ VISA   e
     closed Sunday, 13 April and 25-26 December – **M** (dinner only) 9.95 t. and a la carte
     11.50/15.50 t. ⌂ 4.60.

HONDA, OPEL Crofton Pl. ✆ 800341   RENAULT Rochestown Av. ✆ 852555
MITSUBISHI, SUZUKI Glasthule Rd ✆ 802991

DUNLAVIN Wicklow **405** L 8 – pop. 583 – ✆ 045 Naas.
♦Dublin 31 – ♦Kilkenny 44 – Wexford 61.

🏠   **Rathsallagh House** ⑤, SW : 2 m. on Grangecon Rd ✆ 53112, Fax 53343, ≤, « Walled
     garden », 🔲, park, % – ☎ ℗. ⩟ ⓪ VISA. ⋇
     closed 18 December-2 January – **M** (lunch by arrangement Monday to Saturday)/dinner
     21.45 st. ⌂ 5.00 – **8 rm** ⊇ 57.50/92.00 st.

DUNMANWAY Cork **405** E 12 – ✆ 023 Bandon.
♦Dublin 191 – ♦Cork 37 – ♦Killarney 49.

↑   Dun Mhuire, W : ½ m. by T 65 ✆ 45162, 🛱 – TV ℗
     4 rm.

DUNMORE EAST Waterford **405** L 11 – pop. 734 – ✆ 051 Waterford.
♦Dublin 108 – ♦Waterford 12.

%   **Ship**, Bayview, ✆ 83141 – ⩟ VISA
     closed lunch and Sunday to Monday September-May – **M** a la carte 13.95/17.25 t. ⌂ 4.95.

DURRUS Cork **405** D 13 – ✆ 027.
♦Dublin 210 – ♦Cork 56 – ♦Killarney 53.

%%   **Blairs Cove**, SW : 1 m. on L 56 ✆ 61127, « Converted barn », 🛱 – ℗. ⩟ AE ⓪ VISA
     April-October – **M** *(closed Sunday dinner and Monday except July and August)* (booking
     essential) (dinner only and Sunday lunch)/dinner 20.00 t.

EMO Laois **405** K 8 – pop. 200 – ✉ ✆ 0502 Portlaoise.
♦Dublin 49 – ♦Limerick 74 – ♦Tullamore 20.

🏰   **New Montague** (Best Western), E : 1 ¾ m. on N 7 ✆ 26154, Fax 21976, 🛱 – TV ☎ ⓹ ℗
     – 🔺 250. ⩟ AE ⓪ VISA. ⋇
     closed 2 January-14 March – **M** 7.50/13.75 t. and a la carte ⌂ 4.75 – ⊇ 4.50 – **75 rm**
     30.00/70.00 t. – SB (weekends only) 65.00/75.00 st.

ENNIS Clare **405** F 9 – pop. 6 223 – ECD : Thursday – ✆ 065.
See : Franciscan Friary★ (13C ruins).
Envir. : Tulla (site★, ancient church ⋇★★) E : 10 m. – Killone Abbey (site★) S : 4 m. – Dysert
O'Dea (site★) NW : 6 ½ m. – Kilmacduagh monastic ruins★ (site★) NE : 16 ½ m.
🏌 Drumbiggle Rd ✆ 24074.
🛈 Bank Pl. ✆ 28366 (summer only).
♦Dublin 142 – ♦Galway 42 – ♦Limerick 22 – Roscommon 92 – ♦Tullamore 93.

🏨   **Old Ground** (T.H.F.), O'Connell St., ✆ 28127, Telex 70603, Fax 28112, 🛱 – TV ☎ ℗
     🔺 80. ⩟ AE ⓪ VISA. ⋇
     M 10.15/17.15 st. and a la carte ⌂ 4.50 – ⊇ 7.00 – **59 rm** 46.50/126.00 st.

🏨   **Auburn Lodge**, Galway Rd, N : 1 ½ m. on N 18 ✆ 21247, 🛱 – TV ☎ ℗. ⩟ AE ⓪ VISA. ⋇
     closed 24 to 26 December – **M** 7.50/16.50 t. and a la carte ⌂ 6.75 – **45 rm** ⊇ 35.00/50.00 t. –
     SB (weekends only) 64.00/78.00 st.

FIAT Tulla Rd ✆ 22758   FORD Lifford ✆ 21035

ENNISKERRY Wicklow **405** N 8 – pop. 1 179 – ✆ 01 Dublin.
See : Site★ – Powerscourt Demesne (gardens★★★, Araucaria Walk★) AC.
Envir. : Powerscourt Waterfall★ AC, S : 4 m. – Lough Tay★★, SW by T 43, T 61 and L 161.
♦Dublin 17 – ♦Waterford 100.

     *Hotels and restaurants see : **Dublin** N : 17 m.*

FAHAN Donegal **405** J 2 – ✉ Lifford – ✆ 077 Buncrana.
🏌 North West, Lisfannon, ✆ 61027.
♦Dublin 156 – ♦Londonderry 11 – ♦Sligo 95.

%%   **St. John's**, ✆ 60289, « Lough-side setting » – ⋇ ℗. ⩟ AE ⓪ VISA
     closed Monday, 13 April and 24-25 December – **M** (dinner only) 14.50 t. and a la carte
     12.45/21.45 t. ⌂ 3.60.

FEAKLE Clare **405** G 9 – pop. 188 – ✆ 0619.
♦Dublin 125 – ♦Galway 36 – ♦Limerick 25.

🏠 **Smyth's Village** ⟍, ℘ 24002, ⟍, park, ✗ – ℗
May-September – **M** (booking essential) (lunch by arrangement)/dinner 9.00 t. ¾ 3.50 –
12 rm ⟷ 15.00/28.00 t. – SB 21.85 st.

FOULKSMILLS Wexford **405** L 11 – ✆ 051 Waterford.
♦Dublin 94 – ♦Kilkenny 38 – ♦Waterford 26 – Wexford 12.

🏠 **Horetown House** ⟍, E : 1 ½ m. by L 160 ℘ 63633, ≤, « Equestrian centre », ⟜, park –
℗. ⟐
closed mid January-1 March – **M** (lunch by arrangement)/dinner 15.00 t. ¾ 4.10 – **12 rm**
⟷ 12.00/24.00 t.

FURBOGH Galway **405** E 8 – ✆ 091 Galway.
♦Dublin 42 – ♦Galway 7.

🏠🏠 **Connemara Coast,** ℘ 92108, Group Telex 50905, Fax 92065, ≤, ⟐ heated – 📺 ☎ ℗ –
⟐ 50. ⟐ 🆎 ⓪ 𝘝𝘐𝘚𝘈
M (dinner only) 16.50 st. ¾ 4.90 – **54 rm** ⟷ 46.00/200.00 st. – SB (weekends only)
(except Bank Holidays) 60.00/85.00 st.

GALWAY Galway **405** E 8 – pop. 37 835 – ECD : Monday – ✆ 091.
See : Lynch's Castle★ (16C).
Envir. : NW : Lough Corrib★★★ – Claregalway (Franciscan Friary★ 13C) NE : 7 m. – Abbeyknock-
moy (Cistercian Monastery★ 12C ruins) NE : 18 m. – Tuam (St. Mary's Cathedral : chancel arch★
12C) NE : 20 m.

ⁱ₈ Galway, Salthill ℘ 23038, W : 3 m.

✈ Carnmore Airport ℘ 55569/23876, NE : 4 m.

⛵ to Aran Islands: Kilronan (Inishmore), Inishmaan and Inishere (C.I.E) 2 weekly.

🛈 Victoria Pl., Eyre Sq. ℘ 63081.
♦Dublin 135 – ♦Limerick 64 – ♦Sligo 90.

🏠🏠🏠 **Great Southern,** Eyre Sq., ℘ 64041, Telex 50164, Fax 66704, ⟐ – ⧉ 📺 ☎ – ⟐ 400. ⟐
🆎 ⓪ 𝘝𝘐𝘚𝘈
M (bar lunch Monday to Saturday)/dinner 17.00 **t.** and a la carte ¾ 4.50 – **120 rm**
⟷ 60.00/160.00 t.

🏠🏠 **Ardilaun House,** Taylor's Hill, ℘ 21433, Telex 50013, Fax 21546, ⟜ – ⧉ 📺 ☎ ℗ – ⟐
50. ⟐ 🆎 ⓪ 𝘝𝘐𝘚𝘈
closed 1 week Christmas – **M** 8.00/17.00 t. and a la carte ¾ 4.00 – **91 rm** ⟷ 32.00/70.00 t.,
2 suites 75.00/120.00 t. – SB (weekends only) 40.00/60.00 st.

🏠🏠 **Galway Ryan,** Dublin Rd, E : 1 ¼ m. on N 6 ℘ 53181, Telex 50149, Fax 53187, ⟜ – ⧉ 📺
☎ ℗ – ⟐ 50. ⟐ 🆎 ⓪ 𝘝𝘐𝘚𝘈. ⟐
M (dinner only) 12.00 st. and a la carte – ⟷ 6.00 – **96 rm** 50.00/70.00 st.

🏠 **Adare House,** 9 Father Griffin Pl., Lower Salthill, ℘ 62638, Fax 63693 – ℗. ⟐
M 8.00 st. ¾ 3.50 – **11 rm** 16.00/29.00 st.

✗✗ **Casey's Westwood,** Newcastle, NW : 1 ¾ m. on N 59 ℘ 21442 – ℗. ⟐ 🆎 ⓪ 𝘝𝘐𝘚𝘈
closed 13 April and 24 to 27 December – **M** 9.00/15.95 st. and a la carte 14.05/23.00 t. ¾ 4.50.

at Salthill SW : 2 m. – ✉ Salthill – ✆ 091 Galway :

🏠 **Rockbarton Park,** 5-7 Rockbarton Park, ℘ 22018 – 📺 ☎ ℗. ⟐ 🆎 ⓪ 𝘝𝘐𝘚𝘈. ⟐
closed 1 week Christmas – **M** *(closed Sunday)* (bar lunch)/dinner 14.50 t. and a la carte –
⟷ 5.25 – **11 rm** 22.00/35.00 t.

🏠 **Anno Santo,** Threadneedle Rd, ℘ 22110 – 📺 ☎ ℗. ⟐ 🆎 ⓪ 𝘝𝘐𝘚𝘈. ⟐
closed 20 December-20 January – **M** *(closed November-March)* (bar lunch)/dinner a la carte
11.50/14.80 st. ¾ 4.80 – **13 rm** ⟷ 28.00/52.80 st.

CITROEN, PEUGEOT, SAAB Spanish Par. ℘ 62167

GLANDORE Cork **405** E 13 – ✆ 028 Skibbereen.
♦Dublin 198 – ♦Cork 44 – ♦Killarney 75.

⚓ **Marine,** ℘ 33366, Fax 33600 – 📺 ℗
16 rm.

GLENBEIGH Kerry **405** C 17 – pop. 195 – 🕿 066 Tralee.

🏌18 Dooks 🕿 68205.

♦Dublin 200 – ♦Killarney 21 – Tralee 24.

🏠 **Towers,** 🕿 68212 – 📺 🕿 🅿. 🔊 AE ⓞ VISA
Easter-October – **M** (bar lunch)/dinner 18.00 and a la carte 🍾 5.00 – **22 rm** 🍴 32.00/44.00 – SB (weekends only) 68.00/75.00 **st.**

GLENDALOUGH Wicklow **405** MN 8 – 🕿 0404.

See : Ancient monastic city★★ (site★★★, St. Kervin's Church★) and Upper Lake★ in Glendalough Valley★★★.

♦Dublin 34 – Wexford 71.

Hotels see : *Rathnew* E : 13 m.

GLENGARRIFF Cork **405** D 12 – pop. 159 – 🕿 027.

See : Site★★★.

Envir. : S : Garinish Island (20 mn by boat *AC*) : Italian gardens★ – Martello Tower ❄★★ *AC*.

🏌9 🕿 63150, E : 1 m.

🛈 🕿 63084 (July and August).

♦Dublin 224 – ♦Cork 63 – ♦Killarney 37.

🏠 Casey's, 🕿 63010, ☞ – 🅿
Mid May-mid October – **20 rm** 🍴 16.00/33.00 **s.**

GLEN OF AHERLOW Tipperary **405** H 10 – ✉ 🕿 062 Tipperary.

See : Glen of Aherlow★ (statue of Christ the King★★).

♦Dublin 118 – Cahir 6 – Tipperary 9.

🏠 Glen, 🕿 56146, ☞ – 📺 🕿 🅿 – **24 rm**.

GLOUNTHAUNE Cork **405** G 12 – see Cork.

GOREY Wexford **405** N 9 – pop. 2 588 – ECD : Wednesday – 🕿 055.

🛈 🕿 21248 (July and August).

♦Dublin 58 – Waterford 55 – Wexford 38.

🏠 **Marlfield House** 🦢 , Courtown Rd, E : 1 m. 🕿 21124, Telex 80757, Fax 21572, ≤, « Regency house and conservatory », ☞, park – 📺 🕿 🅿. 🔊 AE ⓞ VISA. 🦅
closed 9 to 25 January – **M** (booking essential) 15.00/24.50 **t.** and a la carte 🍾 6.00 – **18 rm** 🍴 45.00/186.00 **t.**, **1 suite** 200.00/310.00 **t.**

PEUGEOT Courtown 🕿 27318

GOUGANE BARRA Cork **405** D 12 – ✉ 🕿 026 Ballingeary.

See : Lake (site★).

♦Dublin 206 – ♦Cork 45.

🏠 Gougane Barra 🦢, 🕿 47069, ≤ lough and mountains, ⚒ – 🅿. 🔊 AE ⓞ VISA. 🦅
Mid April-September – **M** 7.00/15.00 **st.** and a la carte 🍾 4.50 – **26 rm** 🍴 16.00/32.00 **st.**

HOWTH Dublin **405** N 7 – ✉ 🕿 01 Dublin.

See : Howth Summit ≤★★ – Cliff Walk ≤★★ – Harbour★ – St Mary's Abbey★ (ruins 13C, 15C), site★ – Howth Gardens (rhododendrons★, site★, ≤★) *AC*.

🏌18 Deer Park Hotel 🕿 322624.

♦Dublin 10.

🏠 **Howth Lodge** (Best Western), 🕿 390288, Fax 322268, ≤ – 📺 🕿 🅿 – 🔼 150. 🔊 AE ⓞ VISA. 🦅
closed 24 to 28 December – **M** (bar lunch Monday to Saturday)/dinner 18.00 **t.** and a la carte 🍾 4.50 – 🍴 5.50 – **17 rm** 35.00/45.00 **t.**

XX **King Sitric,** Harbour Rd, East Pier, 🕿 325235, Seafood – 🔊 AE ⓞ VISA
closed Saturday lunch, Sunday, 9 to 17 April and Bank Holidays – **M** 12.00/18.75 **t.** and a la carte 17.30/25.25 **t.** 🍾 5.40.

XX **Russells,** Harbour Rd, 🕿 322681, ≤ – 🔊 ⓞ VISA
M 9.75 **st.** (dinner) and a la carte 13.70/16.20 **t.** 🍾 4.50.

KANTURK Cork **405** F 11 – pop. 1 976 – ECD : Wednesday – 🕿 029.

🏌9 Fairyhill 🕿 50534, SW : 1 ½ m.

♦Dublin 161 – ♦Cork 33 – ♦Killarney 31 – ♦Limerick 44.

🏠 **Assolas Country House** 🦢 , E : 3 ¼ m. by L 38 on L 186 🕿 50015, Fax 50795, ≤, « Part 17C and 18C country house, gardens, riverside setting », ⚒, park, 🦅 – 🕿 🅿. 🔊 AE ⓞ VISA. 🦅
closed 1 November-15 March – **M** (booking essential) (dinner only) 22.50 **st.** 🍾 4.75 – **9 rm** 🍴 54.00/118.00 **st.** – SB (weekends only) (except summer) 97.00/117.00 **st.**

KELLS Kilkenny **405** K 10 – pop. 2 623.

See : Augustinian Priory★★ (14C).

Envir. : Kilree's Church (site★, round tower★) S : 2 m.

♦Dublin 86 – Kilkenny 9 – ♦Waterford 23.

Hotels and restaurants see : Kilkenny N : 9 m.

MITSUBISHI, SUZUKI   Bective St. ℘ 40681

KENMARE Kerry **405** D 12 – pop. 1 123 – ECD : Thursday – ✆ 064 Killarney.

Envir. : Kenmare River Valley★★, E : by L 62.

⛳ ℘ 41291.

🛈 ℘ 41233 (July and August).

♦Dublin 210 – ♦Cork 58 – ♦Killarney 20.

❅ **Park** ⏴, ℘ 41200, Telex 73905, Fax 41402, ≤, « Antiques, paintings », ⛲, park, ✎ – 🛗
☎ ᳖ 🅿. 🖭 AE ⓸ VISA. ✂
April-mid November and Christmas – **M** 16.50/33.00 **st.** and a la carte ≬ 7.50 – **44 rm**
⊑ 86.00/180.00 **st.**, **6 suites** 244.00/304.00 **t.**
Spec. Mousse de canard chaude sur du chou rouge, sauce au porto, Saumon cuit au raifort, puree de legumes
verts, Coulis de fruits rouges dans un souffle au Baileys, sauce a la canelle.

⋔ **Hawthorn House** without rest., Shelbourne St., ℘ 41035 – ✂
7 rm ⊑ 15.00/36.00 **t.**

⋔ **Muxnaw Lodge** ⏴, Castletownbere Rd, S : ¾ m. by N 71 ℘ 41252, ⛲, ✎ – 🅿. ✂
M 10.00 **st.** – **5 rm** ⊑ 16.00/24.00 **st.**

✗ **Lime Tree**, Shelbourne St., ℘ 41225, « Converted schoolhouse featuring local crafts » –
🅿
15 March-6 November – **M** *(closed Sunday)* (dinner only) a la carte 16.75/21.25 **t.** ≬ 6.00.

FORD   Henry St. ℘ 41166   NISSAN   Shelbourne St. ℘ 41355

KILKENNY Kilkenny **405** K 10 – pop. 9 466 – ECD : Thursday – ✆ 056.

See : St. Canice's Cathedral★★ (13C) – Grace's Castle (Courthouse)★ – Castle (park★, ≤★).

Envir. : Jerpoint Abbey★★ (ruins 12C-15C) SE : 12 m. – Callan (St. Mary's Church★ 13C-15C)
SW : 13 m.

⛳ Glendine ℘ 22125, N : 1 m.

🛈 Shee Alms House ℘ 21755.

♦Dublin 71 – ♦Cork 86 – ♦Killarney 115 – ♦Limerick 69 – ♦Tullamore 52 – ♦Waterford 29.

🏨 **Kilkenny**, College Rd, ℘ 62000, Fax 65984, 🏊, ⛲, ✎ – 📺 ☎ 🅿 – 🔬 250. 🖭 AE VISA
M 8.00/15.00 **st.** and a la carte ≬ 4.75 – **60 rm** ⊑ 38.00/85.00 **st.** – SB 82.00/90.00 **st.**

🏨 **Newpark**, Castlecomer Rd, N : ¾ m. on N 77 ℘ 22122, Telex 80080, Fax 61111, 🏊, ⛲, ✎
– 📺 ☎ 🅿 – 🔬 300. 🖭 AE ⓸ VISA. ✂
M *(restricted service January and February)* 10.50/15.50 **t.** and a la carte ≬ 4.95 – ⊑ 7.00 –
60 rm 43.00/53.00 **t.** – SB 77.50/85.00 **st.**

✗✗ **Lacken House** with rm, Dublin Rd, ℘ 61085, Fax 62435, ⛲ – 📺 ☎ 🅿. 🖭 AE ⓸ VISA. ✂
closed Sunday, Monday and 1 week Christmas – **M** (dinner only) 17.00 **t.** and a la carte
14.50/21.50 **t.** ≬ 5.00 – **8 rm** ⊑ 22.00/40.00 **t.**

at Knocktopher S · 13 m. on N 10 – ✉ ✆ 056 Kilkenny :

✗✗ **Knocktopher Abbey**, ℘ 28618, Fax 28609, ≤, ⛲ – 🅿. 🖭 VISA
closed Sunday – **M** (dinner only) 15.00 **st.** and a la carte 14.00/21.75 **t.**

NISSAN   Patrick St. ℘ 21016   RENAULT   Irishtown ℘ 21494

KILLALOE Clare **405** G 9 – pop. 1 022 – ECD : Wednesday – ✆ 061.

See : Site★.

Envir. : N : Lough Derg Coast Road★★ (L 12) to Tuamgraney, Lough Derg★★★ (Holy Island :
site★★) – Nenagh : Butler Castle (keep★ 13C) NE : 9 m.

♦Dublin 109 – Ennis 32 – ♦Limerick 13 – ♦Tullamore 58.

🏨 **Lakeside**, ℘ 76122, ≤, 🏊, ⛲ – ☎ 🅿 – 🔬 60. 🖭 AE ⓸ VISA. ✂
closed 24 to 26 December – **M** 8.00/14.00 **st.** and a la carte ≬ 4.25 – **32 rm** ⊑ 21.00/46.00 **st.**
– SB 46.00/54.00 **st.**

KILLARNEY Kerry **405** D 11 – pop. 7 693 – ECD : Thursday – ✆ 064.

Envir. : SW : Killarney District, Ring of Kerry : Lough Leane★★★, Muckross House (gardens★★★)
– Muckross Abbey★ (ruins 13C), Tork Waterfall (Belvedere : ≤★★, 251 steps), Lady's View Belve-
dere★★ – Gap of Dunloe★★.

⛳, ⛳ Mahoney's Point ℘ 31034, W : 3 m.

🛈 Town Hall ℘ 31633.

♦Dublin 189 – ♦Cork 54 – ♦Limerick 69 – ♦Waterford 112.

Europe ⑤, Fossa, W : 3 ½ m. on T 67 ℰ 31900, Telex 73913, Fax 32118, ← lake and mountains, ⬚, ⌇, 🚲, park, ✕ – 🏢 TV ☎ 🅟 – 🏊 40. 🔲 AE ⓞ VISA
April-October – **M** 17.50/21.00 **st.** and a la carte 18.80/28.00 **st.** ⚬ 8.00 – **170 rm** ⌷ 54.00/97.00 **st.**, **6 suites** 120.00/180.00 **st.**

Dunloe Castle ⑤, Beaufort, W : 6 m. by T 67 ℰ 44111, Telex 73913, Fax 32118, ← Gap of Dunloe, countryside and mountains, ⬚, ⌇, 🚲, park, ✕ – 🏢 TV ☎ 🅟 – 🏊 500. 🔲 AE ⓞ VISA
May-September – **M** 17.50/21.00 **st.** and a la carte 18.80/28.00 **st.** ⚬ 8.00 – **139 rm** ⌷ 45.00/97.00 **st.**, **1 suite**.

Great Southern, ℰ 31262, Telex 73998, Fax 31642, ⬚, 🚲, ✕ – 🏢 TV ☎ 🅟 – 🏊 . 🔲 AE ⓞ VISA
closed January and February – **M** (dinner only) 16.00 **t.** and a la carte ⚬ 5.50 – ⌷ 6.50 – **178 rm** 45.00/90.00 **t.**, **2 suites** 140.00/220.00 **t.**

Aghadoe Heights ⑤, NW : 3 ½ m. by N 22 ℰ 31766, Telex 73942, Fax 31345, ← countryside, lake and mountains, 🚲, ✕ – ⊷ rm TV ☎ ⬚ 🅟 – 🏊 . 🔲 AE ⓞ VISA
closed 20 December-20 January – **M** 8.75/17.00 **t.** and a la carte ⚬ 4.50 – ⌷ 6.50 – **59 rm** 33.00/77.00 **t.**, **1 suite** 90.00/120.00 **t.** – SB 80.00/90.00 **st.**

Cahernane, Muckross Rd, S : 1 m. on N 71 ℰ 31895, Telex 73823, ←, ⌇, 🚲, ✕ – ☎ 🅟. 🔲 AE ⓞ VISA. 🦢
Easter-October and 2 weeks Christmas – **M** (bar lunch)/dinner 23.00 **st.** and a la carte ⚬ 6.00 – **50 rm** ⌷ 55.00/95.00 **st.**

Castlerosse (Best Western) ⑤, W : 2 m. on T 67 ℰ 31144, Telex 73910, Fax 31031, ← lake and mountains, 🚲, ✕ – ☎ 🅟. 🔲 AE ⓞ VISA. 🦢
April-October – **M** (bar lunch)/dinner 15.00 **t.** ⚬ 4.50 – **67 rm** ⌷ 41.00/62.00 **t.**

Royal, College St., ℰ 31853 – TV ☎. 🔲 VISA. 🦢
closed Christmas week – **M** (bar lunch Monday to Saturday)/dinner 12.50 **st.** – **28 rm** ⌷ 30.00/60.00 **t.** – SB 60.00/85.00 **st.**

Linden House, New Rd, ℰ 31379 – 🅟. VISA. 🦢
closed December and January – **M** *(closed Monday except Bank Holidays and Wednesday after Bank Holidays)* (dinner only) 13.00 **t.** and a la carte – **11 rm** ⌷ 14.00/24.00 **t.** – SB 65.00/74.00 **st.**

Kathleens Country House, Madams Height, 22 Tralee Rd, N : 2 m. on N 22 ℰ 32810, ←, 🚲 – ⊷ rest TV ☎ 🅟. 🦢
April-October – **M** 15.00 **st.** ⚬ 6.00 – **10 rm** ⌷ 30.00/45.00 **s.** – SB 65.00/80.00 **st.**

Carriglea Farmhouse ⑤ without rest., Muckross Rd, S : 1 ½ m. on N 71 ℰ 31116, ←, 🚲 – 🅟. 🦢
Easter-mid November – **9 rm** ⌷ –/27.00 **t.**

Castle Lodge, Muckross Rd, ℰ 31545 – 🅟 – **17 rm**.

Loch Lein ⑤ without rest., Fossa, W : 4 m. on T 67 ℰ 31260, ←, 🚲 – 🦢
March-October – **10 rm** ⌷ 15.00/27.00 **t.**

✕ **Gaby's,** 17 High St., ℰ 32519, Seafood bistro – 🔲 AE ⓞ VISA
closed mid December-March – **M** *(closed Monday lunch and Sunday)* 4.50/20.00 **t.** and a la carte 15.50/20.50 **t.** ⚬ 5.00.

AUSTIN-ROVER Muckross Rd ℰ 31237   FORD New Rd ℰ 31087

KILLINEY Dublin 405 N 8 – ✆ 01 Dublin – 🏌 ℰ 851983.
♦Dublin 8 – Bray 4.

Fitzpatrick's Castle, ℰ 851533, Telex 30353, Fax 850207, ⬚, 🚲, ✕, squash – 🏢 TV ☎ 🅟 – 🏊 . 🔲 AE ⓞ VISA. 🦢
M 8.50/16.00 **t.** and a la carte ⚬ 5.00 – ⌷ 7.00 – **85 rm** 65.00/90.00 **t.**, **7 suites** 140.00/230.00 **t.**

Court, Killiney Bay, ℰ 851622, Telex 33244, Fax 852085, ←, 🚲 – 🏢 TV ☎ 🅟 – 🏊 200. 🔲 AE ⓞ VISA
M 9.00/14.00 **t.** ⚬ 4.00 – ⌷ 6.00 – **36 rm** 48.00/60.00 **t.** – SB (weekends only) 61.00 **st.**

KILLYBEGS Donegal 405 G 4 – pop. 1 570.
See : Fishing harbour★ – Carpet factory.
Envir. : NW : Glen Bay★★ – Glencolumbkille (site★★, folk village) NW : 14 m. – Portnoo (site★).
♦Dublin 181 – ♦Londonderry 65 – ♦Sligo 57.

KINSALE Cork 405 G 12 – pop. 1 765 – ECD : Thursday – ✆ 021 Cork.
See : St. Multose's Church★ (12C).
🏌 Ringenane, Belgooly ℰ 772197.
🛈 ℰ 772234 (July and August).
♦Dublin 178 – ♦Cork 17.

Acton's (T.H.F.), Pier Rd, ℰ 772135, Telex 75443, Fax 772231, ←, ⬚ – 🏢 TV ☎ 🅟 – 🏊 70. 🔲 AE ⓞ VISA
M (bar lunch)/dinner 16.00 **st.** and a la carte ⚬ 4.75 – **57 rm** ⌷ 50.00/76.00 **st.**

Old Presbytery, Cork St., ℰ 772027, « Memorabilia » – VISA. 🦢
M (by arrangement) 11.50 **st.** ⚬ 4.50 – **5 rm** ⌷ 17.00/29.00 **st.**

XX **Billy Mackesy's Bawnleigh House**, N : 5 ½ m. on Old Cork Rd ℰ 771333 – Ⓟ
closed Sunday, Monday, and last 2 weeks August – **M** (dinner only) 22.00 **t.** and a la carte
15.75/24.50 **st.** ⌑ 4.95.

XX Blue Haven with rm, 3 Pearse St., ℰ 772209, Seafood – ⊡ ☎
10 rm.

XX **Vintage**, 50 Main St., ℰ 772502 – ⊠ AE ⊚ VISA
closed Sunday dinner in winter and 4 weeks January-February – **M** (lunch by arrangement)/dinner a la carte 19.15/21.40 **t.** ⌑ 6.00.

X Man Friday, Scilly, SE : ½ m. ℰ 772260.

X **Cottage Loft**, 6 Main St., Castlepark, ℰ 772803, Seafood – ⊠ VISA
closed Monday in winter – **M** (dinner only and Sunday lunch)/dinner 12.95 **t.** and a la
carte 15.35/19.50 **t.** ⌑ 5.00.

X Bernards, Milk Market St., ℰ 772233.

KNOCKTOPHER Kilkenny 405 K 10 – see Kilkenny.

LAHINCH Clare 405 D 9 – pop. 473 – ✆ 065.
Envir. : Cliffs of Moher★★★ (O'Brien's Tower ⁕★★ N : 1 h return on foot) NW : 5 ½ m.
⌐₁₈, ⌐₁₈ ℰ 81003.
♦Dublin 162 – ♦Galway 49 – ♦Limerick 41.

🏠 **Atlantic House**, Main St., ℰ 81049, Fax 81029 – ⌂. ⊠ VISA
Easter-October – **M** (bar lunch)/dinner 17.50 **t.** and a la carte ⌑ 5.00 – **14 rm** 15.00/42.00 **t.** –
SB 52.50/55.00 **st.**

LEENANE Galway 405 C 7.
See : ≤★ on Killary Harbour★.
Exc. : SE : Joyces Country : by road L 100 from Leenane to Clonbur : Lough Nafooey★ – ⁕★
from the bridge on Lough Mask★★.
♦Dublin 173 – Ballina 56 – ♦Galway 41.

Hotels see : *Clifden* SW : 19 m.

LETTERFRACK Galway 405 C 7 – ✆ 095 Clifden.
Envir. : Kylemore Abbey (site★★) and Kylemore Lake★, E : 4 m. – Renvyle (castle ≤★) NW : 5 m.
♦Dublin 189 – Ballina 69 – ♦Galway 57.

🏰 **Rosleague Manor** ⌖, W : 1 ½ m. on T 71 ℰ 41101, Fax 41168, ≤ Ballynakill harbour and
Tully Mountain, « Country house atmosphere », ⌗, park, ✕ – ⌂ rest ☎ Ⓟ. ⊠ AE VISA
Easter-October – **M** (bar lunch)/dinner 20.00 **t.** and a la carte ⌑ 7.50 – **15 rm** ⌑ 40.00/90.00 **t.**
– SB (except August and Bank Holidays) 90.00/110.00 **st.**

LETTERKENNY Donegal 405 I 3 – pop. 6 444 – ECD : Monday – ✆ 074.
See : St. Eunan's Cathedral ≤★.
Envir. : Grianan of Aileach★ (stone fort) ⁕★★★, NE : 18 m. – Gartan Lake★, NW : 8 ½ m.
⌐₁₈ Barnhill ℰ 21150, NE : 1 m
🛈 Derry Rd ℰ 21160.
♦Dublin 150 – ♦Londonderry 21 – ♦Sligo 72.

🏠 **Gallagher's**, 100 Upper Main St., ℰ 22066, Fax 21016 – ⊡ ☎ Ⓟ. ⊠ AE ⊚ VISA
closed 25 to 30 December – **M** 7.50/12.00 **st.** and a la carte ⌑ 4.00 – **27 rm** ⌑ 21.00/38.00 **st.**
– SB (weekends only) (except Easter and Bank Holidays) 48.00/52.00 **st.**

LIMERICK Limerick 405 G 9 – pop. 60 736 – ECD : Thursday – ✆ 061.
Envir. : Monasteranenagh Abbey★ (ruins 12C) S : 14 m. by N 20 Z.
⌐₁₈ Castleroy ℰ 335261 Z and N 27.
✈ Shannon Airport : ℰ 061 (Shannon) 61444, Telex 72016, W : 16 m. by N 18 Y – Terminal :
Limerick Railway Station.
🛈 The Granary, Michael St. ℰ 317522.
♦Dublin 120 – ♦Cork 58.

Plan on next page

🏨 Jury's, Ennis Rd, ℰ 55266, Telex 28266, Fax 326400, ⌗ – ☰ rest ⊡ ☎ Ⓟ – ⌂   Y z
96 rm.

🏨 **Limerick Inn**, Ennis Rd, NW : 4 m. on N 18 ℰ 51544, Telex 70621, Fax 326281, ⊠, ✕ – ⌷
☰ rest ⊡ ☎ ⌖ Ⓟ – ⌂ 500. ⊠ AE ⊚ VISA. ⌗   on N 18   Y
closed 24 to 26 December – **M** 9.50/19.00 **t.** and a la carte ⌑ 3.50 – ⌑ 6.50 – **149 rm**
65.00/80.00 **t.**, **4 suites** 95.00 **t.** – SB 72.00/76.00 **st.**

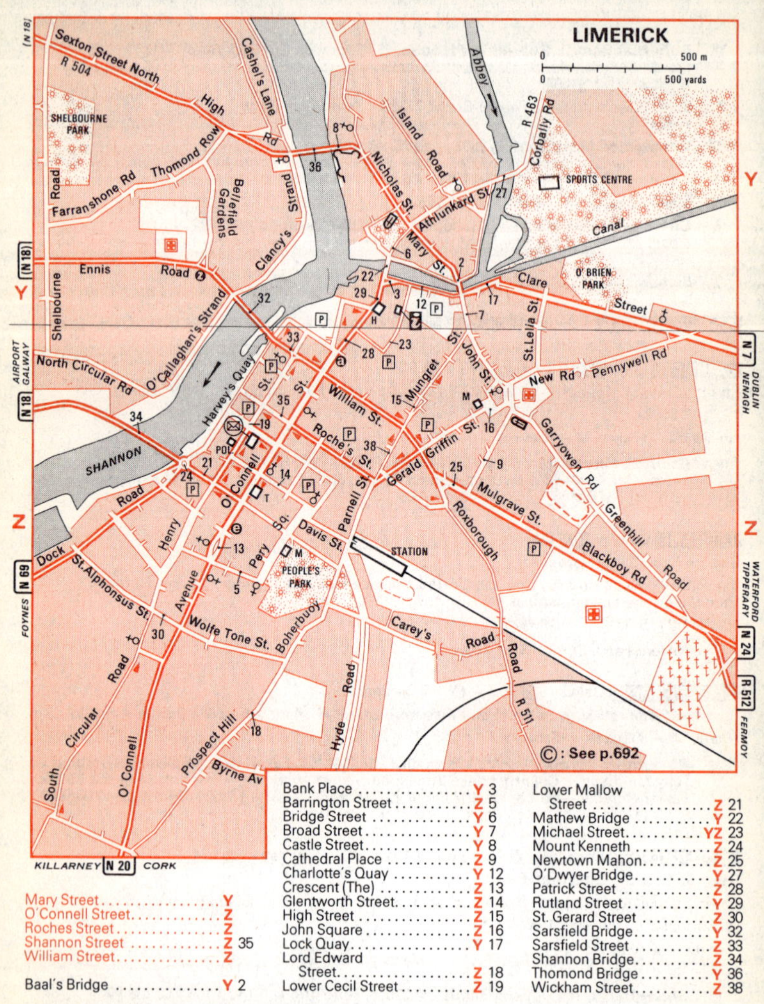

Bank Place . . . . Y	3	
Barrington Street . . . . Z	5	
Bridge Street . . . . Y	6	
Broad Street . . . . Y	7	
Castle Street . . . . Y	8	
Cathedral Place . . . . Z	9	
Charlotte's Quay . . . . Y	12	
Crescent (The) . . . . Z	13	
Glentworth Street . . . . Z	14	
High Street . . . . Z	15	
John Square . . . . Z	16	
Lock Quay . . . . Y	17	
Lord Edward Street . . . . Z	18	
Lower Cecil Street . . . . Z	19	
Lower Mallow Street . . . . Z	21	
Mathew Bridge . . . . Y	22	
Michael Street . . . . YZ	23	
Mount Kenneth . . . . Z	24	
Newtown Mahon . . . . Z	25	
O'Dwyer Bridge . . . . Y	27	
Patrick Street . . . . Z	28	
Rutland Street . . . . Y	29	
St. Gerard Street . . . . Z	30	
Sarsfield Bridge . . . . Y	32	
Sarsfield Street . . . . Z	33	
Shannon Bridge . . . . Z	34	
Thomond Bridge . . . . Y	36	
Wickham Street . . . . Z	38	

Mary Street . . . . Y
O'Connell Street . . . . Z
Roches Street . . . . Z
Shannon Street . . . . Z 35
William Street . . . . Z

Baal's Bridge . . . . Y 2

Limerick Ryan, Ennis Rd, NW : 1 ¼ m. on N 18 ✆ 53922, Fax 326333, �_ – 📶 TV ☎ P –
🛃 30. ◪ AE ⓪ VISA 🚫   on N 18   Y
M (buffet lunch Monday to Saturday)/dinner 12.50 **st.** and a la carte ⑂ 3.75 – **184 rm**
49.00/66.00 **st.**

Greenhills, Ennis Rd, NW : 2 ¼ m. on N 18 ✆ 53033, Telex 70246, Fax 53307, 🌀 – TV ☎
P – 🛃 50. ◪ AE ⓪ VISA 🚫   on N 18   Y
M 11.50/15.50 **st.** and a la carte ⑂ 5.50 – **55 rm** ☲ 47.00/64.00 **t.**

Two Mile Inn, Ennis Rd, NW : 3 ½ m. on N 18 ✆ 53122, Telex 70157, Fax 53783, 🌀 – TV ☎
& P – 🛃 70. 🚫 – **125 rm**.   on N 18   Y

Cruise's Royal, 5-7 O'Connell St., ✆ 44977, Telex 70088 – 📶 TV ☎ – 🛃 50. 🚫   Z a
70 rm.

Silver Plate, 74 O'Connell St., ✆ 316311 – ◪ AE ⓪ VISA   Z e
closed Sunday, 13 April, 25 December and Bank Holidays – **M** (dinner only) 17.00 **t.** and a la
carte 16.50/22.00 **t.** ⑂ 4.00.

BMW, NISSAN Castle St. ✆ 43133
FORD Lansdowne ✆ 52244
MAZDA, VW-AUDI, MERCEDES-BENZ, PORSCHE
Dublin Rd ✆ 46000

OPEL Ennis Rd ✆ 53211
SUZUKI, VOLVO, MITSUBISHI Coonagh Cross ✆ 51577

LISDOONVARNA Clare **405** E 8 – pop. 607 – ✪ 065 Ennis.
Envir. : Cliffs of Moher★★★ (O' Brien's Tower ❄★★ N : 1 h return on foot) SW : 8 m.
🛈 ✆ 74062 (summer only).
◆Dublin 167 – ◆Galway 39 – ◆Limerick 47.

 🏠 **Sheedy's Spa View,** Sulphir Hill, ✆ 74026, ➳, ✖ – 🅿. ◪ AE ⓞ VISA. ⚞
 Mid March-October – **M** (bar lunch)/dinner 15.50 **t.** and a la carte ▯ 8.50 – **11 rm**
 ⌸ 25.00/40.00.

LISMORE Waterford **405** I 11 – pop. 919 – ECD : Thursday – ✪ 058 Dungarvan.
See : Castle (site★) – **Envir. : SE : Blackwater Valley★★** (from Lismore to the Mouth, by a scenic road along the right bank of the River Blackwater).
▮₉ ✆ 54026, N : 1 m.
◆Dublin 143 – ◆Cork 37 – ◆Killarney 74 – ◆Waterford 44.

 🏠 **Ballyrafter House** ⌂, N : ¾ m. by N 72 on L 34 ✆ 54002, ➳, park – 🅿. ◪ ⓞ VISA. ⚞
 Easter-September – **M** (dinner only) 15.00 **t.** ▯ 4.00 – **12 rm** ⌸ 20.00/38.00 **st.** – SB
 (weekends only) 55.00/60.00 **st.**

TOYOTA Lismore ✆ 54147

LONGFORD Longford **405** I 6 – pop. 3 998 – ECD : Thursday – ✪ 043.
Envir. : SE : Lough Derravaragh★ – **Lough Owel★** – **Multyfarman** (Franciscan College park : Stations of the Cross★) – **Lough Lene★** – **Fore** (St. Feichin's Church and ruined priory 13C★) – **Lough Ennell★**.
▮₁₈ Dublin Rd ✆ 46310.
🛈 ✆ 46566 (June-September).
◆Dublin 74 – Roscommon 19 – ◆Sligo 57 – ◆Tullamore 47.

 🏨 Longford Arms, 24 Main St., ✆ 46296 – 📺 ☎ 🅿 – ⛱ 250 – **51 rm**.

FORD Dublin Rd ✆ 46421
NISSAN Drumlish ✆ 24104
RENAULT Athlone Rd ✆ 46615

TOYOTA Lanesboro ✆ 21159
TOYOTA Athlone Rd ✆ 45621
VW-AUDI Dublin Rd ✆ 46321

LOUGH GOWNA Cavan **405** J 6 – pop. 125 – ✪ 043 Longford.
◆Dublin 81 – ◆Tullamore 54.

 ↑ **Robin Hill** ⌂, ✆ 83121, ➳ – 🅿
 M (by arrangement) 11.00 **st.** – **6 rm** ⌸ 11.00/22.00 **st.**

MACROOM Cork **405** F 12 – pop. 2 495 – ECD : Wednesday – ✪ 026.
▮₉ Lackaduve ✆ 41072.
◆Dublin 186 – ◆Cork 25 – ◆Killarney 30.

 🏠 **Castle,** Main St., ✆ 41074 – 📺 ☎. ◪ AE ⓞ VISA. ⚞
 M 7.00/13.00 **st.** and a la carte ▯ 4.00 – **16 rm** ⌸ 17.00/32.00 **st.**

MALAHIDE Dublin **405** N 7 – pop. 9 158 – ✪ 01 Dublin.
Envir. : Swords (St. Columba's Church : towers★) W : 2 ½ m. – **Lusk** (church : round towers★) NW : 8 m.
▮₉ Coast Rd ✆ 450248.
◆Dublin 9 – Drogheda 24.

 🏨 **Grand,** ✆ 450633, Telex 31446, ≼ – 📺 ☎ 🅿 – ⛱ . ◪ AE ⓞ VISA. ⚞
 M 8.50/15.50 **t.** and a la carte ▯ 3.75 – **47 rm** ⌸ 38.50/73.00 **t.**, **3 suites** 73.00/100.00 **t.** –
 SB 104.00/116.00 **st.**

 ✖ Johnny's, 9 James's Terr., ✆ 450314.

FORD Main St. ✆ 452044

MALLOW Cork **405** F 11 – pop. 6 572 – ECD : Wednesday – ✪ 022.
▮₁₈ Balleyellis ✆ 21145, SE : 1 ½ m. from Mallow Bridge.
◆Dublin 149 – ◆Cork 21 – ◆Killarney 40 – ◆Limerick 41.

 🏨 **Longueville House** ⌂, W : 3 ½ m. by N 72 ✆ 47156, Fax 47459, ≼, « Georgian mansion
 in extensive grounds », ⌂, ➳, park – 📺 ☎ 🅿. ◪ AE ⓞ VISA. ⚞
 closed 20 December-1 March – **M** (booking essential) 14.00/26.00 **t.** ▯ 5.50 – **16 rm**
 ⌸ 40.00/114.00 **t.**

OPEL Buttevant ✆ 23338

MAYNOOTH Kildare **405** M 7 – pop. 3 388 – ECD : Wednesday – ✪ 01 Dublin.
◆Dublin 15.

 ✖✖✖ **Moyglare Manor** ⌂ with rm, Moyglare, N : 2 m. ✆ 286351, Telex 90358, Fax 285405, ≼,
 « Georgian country house with antique furnishings », ➳, park – ⚞ rest ☎ 🅿. ◪ AE ⓞ
 VISA. ⚞
 closed 24 to 26 December – **M** *(closed Saturday lunch)* 14.50/26.00 **t.** and a la carte
 approx. 23.25 **t.** ▯ 6.95 – **13 rm** ⌸ 70.00/100.00 **t.**

MOUNTSHANNON Clare **405** G 9 – ✪ 0619.
♦Dublin 129 – ♦Galway 45 – ♦Limerick 30.

   Mountshannon, Main St., ℰ 27162, 🐎 – **AE** ⑩
   Easter-December – **M** 7.00/15.00 **t.** and a la carte ⛴ 5.50 – **11 rm** ⊊ 15.00/42.00 **st.**

MOVILLE Donegal **405** K 2 – pop. 1 252 – ✪ 077.
♦Dublin 165 – ♦Londonderry 19.

   McNamara's, ℰ 82010 – ℗
   13 rm.

MOYCULLEN Galway **405** E 7 – pop. 228 – ✉ Rosscahill – ✪ 091 Galway.
♦Dublin 139 – ♦Galway 7.

   Knockferry Lodge ⌂, Knockferry (on Lough Corrib), NE : 6 ½ m. ℰ 80122, 🐟 – ℗. ⬛
   AE ⑩ **VISA**. ✚
   May-September – **M** (booking essential) (bar lunch)/dinner 13.50 **t.** – **12 rm** ⊊ 18.50/
   32.00 **st.**

   Moycullen House ⌂ without rest., SW : 1 m. on Spiddle Rd ℰ 85566, 🐎 – ⤢ rm ℗
   AE **VISA**. ✚
   March-October – **4 rm** ⊊ 15.00/30.00 **st.**

   Drimcong House, NW : 1 m. on N 59 ℰ 85115, « 17C estate house », 🐎 – ℗. ⬛ **AE** ⑩
   VISA
   closed Sunday, Monday and Christmas-March – **M** (booking essential) 15.50 **t.** and
   a la carte 20.00/27.00 **t.** ⛴ 5.00.

MULLINGAR Westmeath **405** JK 7 – pop. 7 854 – ✪ 044.
Envir. : N : Lough Derravaragah★ – Lough Owel★ – Multyfarman (Franciscan College park :
Stations of the Cross★ – NE : Lough Lene★ – Fore (St. Feichin's Church and ruined priory 13C★)
– S : Lough Ennell.

🏌 Belvedere ℰ48366, S : 3 m.
ℹ Dublin Road ℰ 48761.
♦Dublin 49 – ♦Drogheda 36.

   Greville Arms, Pearse St., ℰ 48563 – **TV** ☎ ℗ – 🛎 100
   28 rm.

FIAT, LANCIA Dublin Rd ℰ 48806   FORD Harbour St. ℰ 48403

NAVAN Meath **405** L 7 – pop. 4 124 – ECD : Thursday – ✪ 046.
Envir. : Bective Abbey★ (12C ruins) S : 3 m.
🏌 Royal Tara, Bellinter Park ℰ 25244.
♦Dublin 30 – Drogheda 16 – ♦Dundalk 34.

   Ardboyne (Best Western), Dublin Rd, SE : 1 m. on N 3 ℰ 23119, Fax 22355, 🐎 – ⤢ **TV** ☎
   ℗ – 🛎 60. ⬛ **AE** ⑩ **VISA**. ✚
   closed 24 and 25 December – **M** 10.95/15.95 **st.** and a la carte ⛴ 4.50 – **27 rm**
   ⊊ 34.50/75.00 **st.**

PEUGEOT-TALBOT Castlemartin ℰ 21949   TOYOTA Kells Rd ℰ 21336
RENAULT Cannon Row ℰ 21312   VW-AUDI, MERCEDES-BENZ Dublin Rd ℰ 21212

NEWBAWN Wexford **405** L 10 – see New Ross.

NEWBRIDGE Kildare **405** L 8 – pop. 5 780 – ECD : Tuesday – ✪ 045 Naas.
Envir. : Kildare (St. Brigid's Cathedral★ 13C-19C and round tower★ 9C-10C) SW : 5 m. – Tully
(National Stud★, Japanese gardens★ AC) SW : 6 m. via Kildare – Old Kilcullen (site★, ✵★).

🏌 Curragh ℰ 045 (Curragh) 41238, S : 3 m. – 🏌 Cill-Dara, ℰ 045 (Kildare) 21433, Kildare Town,
SW : 5 m.
ℹ ℰ 97636 (July and August).
♦Dublin 28 – Kilkenny 57 – ♦Tullamore 36.

   Keadeen, Ballymany, SW : 1 m. on N 7 ℰ 31666, Telex 60672, Fax 31666, 🐎 – **TV** ☎ ℗
   🛎 250. ⬛ **AE** ⑩ **VISA**
   M 15.00/20.00 **t.** and a la carte ⛴ 4.50 – **36 rm** ⊊ 50.00/70.00 **t.**, **1 suite** 100.00/150.00 **t.**

FORD Moorefield ℰ 31725

NEWMARKET-ON-FERGUS Clare **405** F 7 – pop. 1 348 – ✪ 061 Shannon.
♦Dublin 136 – Ennis 8 – ♦Limerick 15.

   Dromoland Castle ⌂, NW : 1 ½ m. on N 18 ℰ 71144, Telex 70654, Fax 363355, ≤,
   « Converted castle », 🏌, 🐟, 🐎, park, ✖ – **TV** ☎ ℗ – 🛎 250. ⬛ **AE** ⑩ **VISA**. ✚
   M 17.00/29.00 **t.** and dinner a la carte ⛴ 6.50 – ⊊ 10.50 – **67 rm** 160.00/170.00 **st.**, **6 suites**
   200.00/240.00 **st.**

NEWPORT Mayo **405** D 6 – pop. 470 – ✆ 098.
See : St. Patrick's Church★, modern Irish-Romanesque style (site★).
Envir. : Burrishoole Abbey (site★) NW : 2 m.
♦Dublin 164 – Ballina 37 – ♦Galway 60.

🏨 **Newport House** 🦢, ☏ 41222, Telex 53740, Fax 41613, « Country house atmosphere, antiques », 🦢, 🚗, park – ☎ **P**. 🔄 **AE** ⓞ **VISA**. 🛏
18 March-September – **M** (buffet lunch)/dinner 25.00 **st.** and a la carte 🍾 8.00 – **19 rm** 🍽 44.00/88.00 **st.**

NEW ROSS Wexford **405** L 10 – pop. 5 386 – ECD : Wednesday – ✆ 051.
Envir. : St. Mullins Monastery (site★) N : 9 m. – John F. Kennedy Memorial Park★ (1968) (arboretum, ⩽★) S : 7 ½ m. – SW : River Barrow Valley★.
🏌 Tinneranny ☏ 21433.
🛈 ☏ 21857 (July and August).
♦Dublin 88 – Kilkenny 27 – ♦Waterford 15 – Wexford 23.

🏠 **Old Rectory**, Rosbercon, W : ½ m. by N 25 ☏ 21719, 🚗 – ↩ rest **TV** **P**. 🔄 **AE** ⓞ **VISA**. 🛏
closed 3 days at Christmas – **M** 6.50/13.50 **t.** and a la carte 🍾 4.50 – **13 rm** 🍽 24.50/39.00 **t.**

🏠 **Inishross House** without rest., 96 Mary St., ☏ 21335 – **P**. 🛏
6 rm 🍽 14.00/20.00 **st.**

at Newbawn E : 8 m. by N 25 off L 160 – ✉ ✆ 051 New Ross :

🍽🍽 **Cedar Lodge** with rm, Carrigbyrne, N : 1 ½ m. on N 25 ☏ 28386, Fax 28222, 🚗 – **TV** ☏ ♿ **P**. 🔄 **VISA**. 🛏
closed January – **M** 12.00/18.00 **st.** and a la carte 🍾 4.00 – **13 rm** 🍽 35.00/56.00 **t.** – SB 80.00 **st.**

FORD Waterford Rd ☏ 21403

OUGHTERARD Galway **405** E 7 – pop. 748 – ✆ 091 Galway.
See : The northern scenic road (cul-de-sac) ⩽★★ on Lough Corrib★★★.
Envir. : Aughnanure Castle★ (16C) SE : 3 m. – Leckavrea Mountain★, NW : 13 m. – Gortmore (⩽★★ S : on Kilkieran Bay, ⩽★ NW : on the Twelve Pins) SW : 16 m.
🏌 Gurteeva ☏ 82131.
♦Dublin 149 – ♦Galway 17.

🏨 **Connemara Gateway**, SE : ¾ m. on N 59 ☏ 82328, Telex 50905, Fax 82332, 🏊 heated, 🚗, park, 🎾 – **TV** ☎ **P**. 🔄 **AE** ⓞ **VISA**. 🛏
M (bar lunch)/dinner 16.50 **st.** 🍾 4.90 – **62 rm** 🍽 45.00/180.00 **st.** – SB (except Bank Holidays) (weekends only) 60.00/85.00 **st.**

🏠 **Currarevagh House** 🦢, NW : 4 m. ☏ 82313, ⩽, « Country house atmosphere », 🦢, 🚗, park, 🎾 – ↩ rest **P**. 🛏
12 April-5 October – **M** (booking essential) 7.50/15.00 **t.** 🍾 4.00 – **15 rm** 🍽 33.00/66.00 **t.**

🏠 **Sweeney's Oughterard House** 🦢, W : ½ m. on T 71 ☏ 82207, Fax 82161, 🚗 – 🛗 ☎ **P**. 🔄 **AE** ⓞ **VISA**
closed 24 to 27 December – **M** (lunch by arrangement)/dinner 16.50 **t.** and a la carte 16.00/24.00 **t.** 🍾 4.50 – **20 rm** 🍽 43.00/82.00 **t.**

PARKNASILLA Kerry **405** C 12 – ✆ 064 Killarney – 🏌 Parknasilla ☏ 45122.
♦Dublin 224 – ♦Cork 72 – ♦Killarney 34.

🏨 **Great Southern** 🦢, ☏ 45122, Group Telex 73899, Fax 45323, ⩽ Kenmare river, bay and mountains, 🏊, 🏌, 🦢, 🚗, park, 🎾 – **TV** ☎ **P** – 🛎 50. 🔄 **AE** ⓞ **VISA**. 🛏
Easter-1 November – **M** 12.00/18.00 **t.** and a la carte 🍾 5.50 – 🍽 7.00 – **55 rm** 64.00/98.00 **t.**, **1 suite** 160.00/200.00 **t.** – SB (weekends only) 112.00/138.00 **st.**

PORTLAOISE Laois **405** K 8 – pop. 4 049 – ✆ 0502.
🏌 Heath ☏ 46533, E : 4 m.
🛈 ☏ 21178 (summer only).
♦ Dublin 54 – Kilkenny 31 – ♦Limerick 67.

🏨 **Killeshin**, Dublin Rd, E : 1 m. on N 7 ☏ 21663, Telex 60036 – **TV** ♿ **P** – 🛎 120. 🔄 **AE** ⓞ **VISA**
M 7.50/13.75 **t.** and a la carte 🍾 5.00 – **44 rm** 🍽 30.00/52.00 **t.** – SB 65.00/75.00 **st.**

PORT NA BLAGH Donegal **405** I 2 – see Dunfanaghy.

RAPHOE Donegal **405** J 3 – pop. 1 070 – ✆ 074.
Envir. : Beltany Stone Circle★ (site★) from the road 10 mn on foot, S : 2 m.
♦Dublin 139 – Donegal 29 – ♦Londonderry 20 – ♦Sligo 69.

🏠 **Central**, The Diamond, ☏ 45126 – 🛏
closed 24 to 31 December – **M** (closed Sunday lunch) 7.00/10.50 **st.** and a la carte 🍾 3.40 – 🍽 3.50 – **10 rm** 10.00/20.00 **st.**

RATHMULLAN Donegal 405 J 2 – pop. 584 – ⊠ ✆ 074 Letterkenny.
Envir. : Mulroy Bay★★, NW : 8 m. – Fanad Head ≤★, N : 20 m.
☈₉ Otway, Saltpans ℘ 58319.
◆Dublin 165 – ◆Londonderry 36 – ◆Sligo 87.

- 🏨 **Rathmullan House** ॐ, N : ½ m. on R 247 ℘ 58188, Fax 58200, ≤ Lough Swilly and hills, « Country house atmosphere, gardens », ॐ, park, ✵ – 🅿. 🖳 AE ⓞ VISA. ⚓
  April-December – **M** (bar lunch)/dinner 17.50 t. ⓐ 4.00 – **13 rm** ☟ 30.00/75.00 t. – SB 98.00/114.00 st.

RATHNEW Wicklow 405 N 8 – pop. 1 366 – ⊠ ✆ 0404 Wicklow.
◆Dublin 31 – ◆Waterford 82 – Wexford 65.

- 🏨 **Tinakilly House** ॐ, ℘ 69274, Fax 67806, ≤, « Victorian country house », ✿, park, ✵ – 🆃🆅 ☎ 🅿. 🖳 AE ⓞ VISA. ⚓
  M 12.00/23.00 t. ⓐ 5.00 – **14 rm** ☟ 60.00/110.00 t. – SB (except summer) 100.00 st.
- 🏨 **Hunter's**, Newrath Bridge, N : ¾ m. on L 29 ℘ 40106, « Converted 18C inn with garden » – 🅿. 🖳 AE ⓞ VISA. ⚓
  M 11.00/16.00 t. ⓐ 4.50 – **18 rm** ☟ 27.50/55.00 t.

REDCASTLE Donegal 405 K 2 – ECD : Wednesday – ⊠ ✆ 077 Moville.
◆Dublin 160 – ◆Londonderry 14.

- 🏨 Redcastle Country ॐ, ℘ 82073, ≤, ☈₉, ॐ, ✿, park, ✵ – 🆃🆅 ☎ 🅿 – ⚓ 400 – **31 rm**.

RIVERSTOWN Sligo 405 G 5 – pop. 262 – ✆ 071 Sligo.
◆Dublin 123 – ◆Sligo 13.

- 🏠 **Coopershill** ॐ, ℘ 65108, Fax 65466, ≤, ✿, park – ✄ 🅿. 🖳 AE VISA. ⚓
  16 March-October – **M** (dinner only) 16.00 st. ⓐ 3.50 – **6 rm** ☟ 38.00/64.00 st.

ROSAPENNA Donegal 405 I 2 – ✆ 074 Letterkenny.
☈₁₈ Golf Hotel ℘ 55301.
◆Dublin 216 – Donegal 52 – ◆Londonderry 47.

- 🏨 **Rosapenna Golf** (Best Western), Downings, ℘ 55301, Fax 55128, ≤, ☈₁₈, ✵ – ☎ 🅿. 🖳 AE ⓞ VISA
  31 March-29 October – **M** (bar lunch)/dinner 17.00 t. ⓐ 4.50 – **40 rm** ☟ 31.00/55.00 st. – SB 73.00/83.00 st.

ROSCREA Tipperary 405 I 9 – ✆ 0505.
☈₉ Derry Vale, Dublin Rd ℘ 21130.
◆Dublin 75 – ◆Limerick 45.

- ⚐ **Racket Hall**, Dublin Rd, E : 1 ¾ m. on N 7 ℘ 21748, ✿ – ☏ 🅿. 🖳 AE ⓞ VISA. ⚓
  closed 24 to 28 December – **M** 10.00/12.50 st. and a la carte – ☟ 4.50 – **8 rm** 17.50/40.00 st. – SB 42.50/52.50 st.

ROSSES POINT Sligo 405 G 5 – see Sligo.

ROSSLARE Wexford 405 M 11 – pop. 779 – ✆ 053.
☈₁₈ ℘ 32113.
🄴 Harbour ℘ 33232 (summer only).
◆Dublin 104 – ◆Waterford 50 – Wexford 12.

- 🏨 **Kelly's Strand**, Strand Rd, ℘ 32114, Fax 32222, ☒ heated, 🖳, ✿, ✵, squash – ｜$｜ 🆃🆅 ☎ 🅿. ⚓
  2 March-9 December – **M** 9.50/18.00 t. ⓐ 4.50 – **89 rm** 31.00/58.00 t.
- ✕ **Le Gourmet**, Strand Rd, ℘ 32157, French rest.
  June-September – **M** (lunch by arrangement) 17.50 t. (dinner) and a la carte 12.90/18.00 t. ⓐ 6.00.

ROSSLARE HARBOUR Wexford 405 N 11 – pop. 777 – ✆ 053 Wexford.
⛴ Shipping connections with the Continent : to France (Cherbourg), (Le Havre) (Irish Ferries) – to Fishguard (Sealink) 1-2 daily (3 h 30 mn) – to Pembroke (B & I Line) 1-2 daily.
🄴 ℘ 33232 (summer only).
◆Dublin 105 – ◆Waterford 51 – Wexford 13.

- 🏨 **Rosslare**, ℘ 33110, Telex 80772, Fax 33386, ≤, squash – 🆃🆅 ☎ 🅿. 🖳 AE VISA
  closed Christmas Day – **M** 12.00/16.50 st. and a la carte ⓐ 4.20 – **25 rm** ☟ 25.20/58.80 st. – SB 67.40/85.50 st.
- 🏨 **Tuskar House**, St. Martins Rd, ℘ 33363, ≤, ✿ – 🆃🆅 ☎ 🅿. 🖳 AE ⓞ VISA. ⚓
  M (bar lunch Monday to Saturday)/dinner 14.95 t. and a la carte ⓐ 3.95 – ☟ 4.00 – **20 rm** 24.40/40.00 st. – SB 49.00/63.00 st.

ROSSNOWLAGH Donegal 405 H 4 – ◎ 072 Bundoran.
◆Dublin 157 – Donegal 9 – ◆Sligo 33.

🏨 **Sand House** ⑤, ℘ 51777, Telex 40460, ≤ bay, beach and mountains, ⚓, ✗ – ☎ ℗. ◰
AE ⓪ VISA ⁑
Easter-4 October – **M** 9.50/17.50 **t.** and a la carte ⌷4.50 – **40 rm** ☲ 30.00/80.00 **t.** –
SB (except Bank Holidays weekends) 75.00/95.00 **st.**

ST ERNAN'S ISLAND Donegal – see Donegal.

SALTHILL Galway 405 E 8 – see Galway.

SCHULL (SKULL) Cork 405 D 13 – pop. 502 – ◎ 028 Skibbereen.
Envir. : E : Roaringwater Bay★.
◆Dublin 226 – ◆Cork 65 – ◆Killarney 64.

⚐ **Ard-na-Greine Inn** ⑤, SW : 1 ¾ m. by L 57 ℘ 28181, 🚗 – ℗. ◰ AE ⓪ VISA ⁑
April-October – **M** (booking essential) (bar lunch)/dinner 18.50 **t.** ⌷5.00 – **6 rm**
☲ 35.00/90.00 **t.**

SHANAGARRY Cork 405 H 12 – ✉ Midleton – ◎ 021 Cork.
◆Dublin 163 – ◆Cork 25 – ◆Waterford 64.

✗✗ **Ballymaloe House** ⑤ with rm, NW : 1 ¾ m. on L 35 ℘ 652531, Telex 75208, Fax 652021,
≤, « Country house atmosphere », ⌁ heated, 🚗, park, ✗ – ☎ & ℗. ◰ AE ⓪ VISA ⁑
closed 23 to 26 December and 7 to 18 January – **M** (buffet lunch)/dinner 24.00 **t.** ⌷5.00 – ☲
5.50 – **30 rm** 41.00/74.00 **t.** – SB (except 15 March-October) 90.00/96.00 **st.**

SHANNON AIRPORT Clare 405 F 9 – ◎ 061 Limerick.
ⓡ18 ℘ Shannon 61020.
✈ ℘ 61444, Telex 26222 – **Terminal** : Limerick Railway Station ℘ 42433.
🛈 ℘ 61664.
◆Dublin 136 – Ennis 16 – ◆Limerick 15.

SKERRIES Dublin 405 N 7 – pop. 5 793 – ◎ 01 Dublin.
ⓡ18 ℘ 491204.
◆Dublin 19 – Drogheda 15.

⚐ Pier House, Harbour Rd, ℘ 491708, ≤
10 rm.

✗✗ **Red Bank,** 7 Church St., ℘ 491005, Seafood – ◰ AE ⓪ VISA
closed Sunday, Monday and 4 weeks October-November – **M** (dinner only) 18.00 **t.** and a la
carte 18.00/22.00 **t.**

SKIBBEREEN Cork 405 E 13 – pop. 2 130 – ◎ 028.
ⓡ9 ℘ 21227.
🛈 Town Hall ℘ 21766.
◆Dublin 205 – ◆Cork 51 – ◆Killarney 68.

✗✗ **Mill House,** Rineen, E : 5 m. by L 60 on Union Hall rd ℘ 36299, 🚗 – ℗. ◰ AE ⓪ VISA
March-November – **M** *(closed Monday)* (dinner only) (booking essential) 15.95 **t.** ⌷5.00.

SKULL = Schull.

SLIEVERUE Waterford – see Waterford.

SLIGO Sligo 405 G 5 – pop. 17 232 – ◎ 071.
See : Sligo Abbey★ (13C ruins) – Court House★.
Envir. : E : Lough Gill★★★ (Innisfree★) Park's Castle (site★★), Lough Colgagh★★, Drumcliff (High
Cross) ≤★ on Benbulbin Moutains, N : 4 m. – Glencar Lough★, NE : 6 m. – Carrowmore (Megali-
thic cemetery★) SW : 2 m.
ⓡ18 Strandhill ℘ 68188, W : 8 m.
🛈 Aras Reddan, Temple St. ℘ 61201.
◆Dublin 133 – ◆Belfast 126 – ◆Dundalk 106 – ◆Londonderry 86.

🏨 **Sligo Park,** Pearse Rd, S : 1 m. on N 4 ℘ 60291, Telex 40397, Fax 69556, 🚗 – TV ☎ & ℗
– ⚙ 300. ◰ AE ⓪ VISA
M 8.50/15.00 **st.** and a la carte 11.25/16.80 **st.** ⌷4.50 – ☲ 5.50 – **62 rm** 40.00/80.00 **st.**

🏨 **Ballincar House** ⑤, Rosses Point Rd, NW : 2 ½ m. on R 291 ℘ 45361, Telex 91297, Fax
44198, ≤, 🚗, ✗, squash – TV ☎ ℗. ◰ AE ⓪ VISA ⁑
closed 23 December-23 January – **M** 9.50/19.00 **st.** and a la carte – **20 rm** ☲ 40.00/75.00 **st.**
– SB 75.00/85.00 **st.**

at Rosses Point NW : 5 m. on R 291 – ⊠ ✆ 071 Sligo :

XX   **Reveries,** ✆ 77371, ≤ Mount Knocknarae, Sligo Bay and Oyster Island – ⚅ *VISA*
closed Sunday, Monday in winter, 2 weeks November and 5 days at Christmas – **M** (dinner only) 19.25 **t.** ▯ 4.25.

FORD Bundoran Rd ✆ 42610   VW-AUDI Ballisodare ✆ 67291
MAZDA Ballinode ✆ 42188

SPIDDLE Galway **405** E 8 – ✆ 091 Galway.
♦Dublin 143 – ♦Galway 11.

🏠   **Bridge House,** Main St., ✆ 83118, � – 🅿. ⚅ AE ① *VISA*. ✺
closed 23 December-11 January – **M** 10.00/17.00 **t.** and a la carte ▯ 4.95 – **14 rm**
⊊ 30.00/60.00 **t.** – SB (weekdays only) (except 20 July-15 August) 75.00/85.00 **st.**

🏠   **Park Lodge,** E : 1 ¾ m. on L 100 ✆ 83159, ≤ – 🅿. ⚅ AE ① *VISA*
June-September – **M** (dinner only) 13.00 – **23 rm** ⊊ 25.00/44.00.

TAHILLA Kerry **405** C 12 – ✆ 064 Killarney.
♦Dublin 222 – ♦Cork 70 – ♦Killarney 32.

⚘   **Tahilla Cove** ⑤, ✆ 45104, ≤, � – 🅿. ⚅ AE ① *VISA*. ✺
Easter-September – **M** (dinner by arrangement) 14.00 **st.** ▯ 5.00 – **9 rm** ⊊ 22.00/24.00 **t.**

TEMPLEGLENTAN Limerick **405** E 10 – ✆ 069 Newcastle West.
♦Dublin 154 – ♦Killarney 36 – ♦Limerick 33.

🏠   **Devon Inn,** on N 21 ✆ 84122 – TV ✆ 🅿. ⚅ AE ① *VISA*
closed 2 weeks October – **M** 6.50/11.00 **t.** and a la carte ▯ 4.00 – **18 rm** ⊊ 20.00/34.00 **t.**

TIPPERARY Tipperary **405** H 10 – pop. 4 984 – ECD : Wednesday – ✆ 062.
Envir. : S : Glen of Aherlow★ (statue of Christ the King ≤★★).
🏌 Rathanny ✆ 51119, S : 1 m.
♦Dublin 113 – ♦Cork 57 – ♦Limerick 24 – ♦Waterford 53.

🏠   **Ach-na-Sheen House,** Waterford Rd, ✆ 51298 – 🅿. *VISA*
M 12.00 **st.** – **13 rm** ⊊ 14.00/28.00 **st.**

TRALEE Kerry **405** C 11 – pop. 16 495 – ECD : Wednesday – ✆ 066.
🏌 West Barrow ✆ 36379.
🛈 Aras Siamsa, Godfrey Pl. ✆ 21288.
♦Dublin 185 – ♦Killarney 20 – ♦Limerick 64.

🏨   **Ballygarry House,** SE : 1 ½ m. on N 21 ✆ 23305, � – TV ✆ 🅿. ✺
16 rm.

🏨   **Brandon,** Princes Quay, ✆ 23333, Group Telex 73130, Fax 25019, ⚅ – ▤ TV ✆ 🅿 – 🛌
500. ⚅ AE ① *VISA*. ✺
M 9.00/17.50 **st.** and a la carte – **159 rm** ⊊ 28.00/90.00 **st.**, **1 suite** 110.00/135.00 **st.**

FIAT Ashe St. ✆ 21124   TOYOTA Rithiss ✆ 21688
FORD Edward St. ✆ 21555   VW-AUDI The Market and Rock St. ✆ 21193

TRIM Meath **405** L 7 – pop. 2 144 – ECD : Thursday – ✆ 046.
🏌 ✆ 31463, SW : 2 ½ m.
♦Dublin 28 – Drogheda 25 – ♦Dundalk 43.

🏨   **Wellington Court,** Summerhill Rd, ✆ 31516 – TV ✆ 🅿. ⚅ AE ① *VISA*. ✺
M 7.00/14.00 **t.** and a la carte ▯ 3.50 – ⊊ 4.50 – **18 rm** 20.00/30.00 **st.**

TYRELLSPASS Westmeath **405** J 7 – pop. 307 – ✆ 044 Mullingar.
♦Dublin 51 – ♦Tullamore 13.

⚘   **Village,** ✆ 23171 – TV 🅿. ✺
10 rm.

VIRGINIA Cavan **405** K 6 – pop. 657 – ✆ 049 Cavan.
Envir. : Kells : St. Columba's House★ (9C) – St. Columba's Church : old tower★ (1783) – Churchyard (high crosses★) SE : 11 m.
🏌 ✆ 44103.
♦Dublin 52 – ♦Dundalk 39 – Roscommon 56 – ♦Tullamore 59.

🏨   **Park** ⑤, ✆ 47235, ≤, 🏌, ⤢, �, park, XX – TV ✆ 🅿 – 🛌 100. ⚅ AE ① *VISA*. ✺
accommodation closed January-March – **M** 8.50/14.00 **st.** and a la carte ▯ 6.00 – **22 rm**
⊊ 35.50/55.00 **st.** – SB 72.00 **st.**

WATERFORD Waterford **405** K 11 – pop. 38 473 – ✆ 051.

See : Franciscan ruins of the French Church★ (13C-16C) (Grey Friars St.).

🏌 Newrath ✆ 74182.

🛈 41 The Quay ✆ 75788.

◆Dublin 96 – ◆Cork 73 – ◆Limerick 77.

🏰 **Waterford Castle** 🦢, The Island, Ballinakill, E : 2 ½ m. by R 684, Ballinakill Rd and
private ferry ✆ 78203, Telex 80332, Fax 79316, ≤, « 19C castle, river island setting », 🦢,
🚗, park – 🛗 TV ☎ ℗. 🅰 AE ① VISA. 🐾
M 15.50/27.00 t. and a la carte ▯ 8.00 – ☷ 9.50 – **15 rm** 90.00/160.00 t., **4 suites** 220.00/
250.00 t. – SB (October-April) 170.00/220.00 st.

🏨 **Granville**, Meagher Quay, ✆ 55111, Telex 80188 – 🛗 TV ☎ – 🕍 60. 🅰 AE ① VISA. 🐾
closed 25 and 26 December – **M** 8.75/15.95 st. and a la carte ▯ 5.80 – **66 rm** ☷ 43.00/90.00 st.

🏨 **Tower,** The Mall, ✆ 75801, Telex 80699, Fax 70129 – 🛗 TV ☎ – 🕍 300. 🅰 AE ① VISA
closed 24 and 27 December – **M** 10.00/17.00 st. and a la carte ▯ 4.50 – ☷ 6.50 – **81 rm**
38.50/61.00 st. – SB (weekends only) 56.00 st.

   at Slieverue NE : 2 ¼ m. by N 25 – ✉ ✆ 051 Waterford :

🏠 **Diamond Hill**, ✆ 32855, 🚗 – ℗. VISA. 🐾
M (by arrangement) 12.95 t. ▯ 4.00 – **10 rm** ☷ 13.50/30.00 – SB 45.00/60.00 st.

OPEL Catherine St. ✆ 74988   TOYOTA William St. ✆ 74037

WATERVILLE Kerry **405** B 12 – pop. 478 – ✆ 0667.

Envir. : Sheehan's Point ≤★★★, S : 6 m. – Remains of Carhan House (birthplace of Daniel O'Connell) N : 11 m. – Ballinskelligs (Augustinian Monastery ≤★) W : 9 m.

🏌 ✆ 4102, W : 1 m.

◆Dublin 238 – ◆Killarney 48.

🏰 **Waterville Lake** 🦢, ✆ 4133, Telex 73806, Fax 4482, ≤ Lough Currane, Atlantic and
countryside, 🏊, 🏌, 🦢, 🚗, 🍴 – 🛗 ☎ ♿ ℗ – 🕍 50. 🅰 AE ① VISA
Mid April-mid October – **M** (bar lunch)/dinner 19.50 t. and a la carte 16.75/23.95 t. ▯ 5.00 –
76 rm 47.00/80.00 t., **8 suites** 130.00/150.00 t. – SB 88.00/95.00 st.

🏨 **Butler Arms,** ✆ 4144, Group Telex 73826, Fax 4520, 🦢, 🚗, 🍴 – ☎ ℗. 🅰 AE ① VISA. 🐾
12-April-13 October – **M** (bar lunch)/dinner 18.00 t. ▯ 4.75 – **29 rm** ☷ 23.00/60.00 st. –
SB 80.00/93.00 st.

🏠 White House, ✆ 4233 – ⊱✕ rest ℗. 🐾
8 rm.

🍴🍴 **Huntsman** with rm, ✆ 4124, ≤, Seafood – TV ℗. 🅰 AE ① VISA. 🐾
March 16-October – **M** 12.00/16.00 t. and a la carte 13.50/20.80 t. ▯ 4.50 – **2 rm** 16.00/40.00 t.

WESTPORT Mayo **405** D 6 – pop. 3 378 – ECD : Wednesday – ✆ 098 Newport.

See : Westport House★ *AC*.

Envir. : Croagh Patrick Mountain★ (statue of St. Patrick ≤★, pilgrimage) SW : 6 m. – Roonah
Quay ≤★ on Clare Island, W : 15 m.

🏌 Carrowholly ✆ 25113.

🛈 The Mall ✆ 25711.

◆Dublin 163 – ◆Galway 50 – ◆Sligo 65.

🏨 **Westport Ryan,** Louisburgh Rd, W : ¾ m. on T 39 ✆ 25811, Telex 53757, Fax 26212, 🍴 –
TV ☎ ℗. 🅰 AE ① VISA. 🐾
closed late December-mid January – **M** (bar lunch)/dinner 11.00 st. and a la carte ▯ 4.00 –
57 rm ☷ 50.00/70.00 st.

🍴🍴 **Ardmore,** The Quay, W : 1 ½ m. on T 39 ✆ 25994, ≤ – ℗. 🅰 AE ① VISA
closed Sunday, 1 week March, 13 April, 2 weeks November and 24 to 26 December –
M 6.50/15.00 t. and a la carte 14.50/18.50 t. ▯ 4.75.

WEXFORD Wexford **405** M 10 – pop. 11 417 – ECD : Thursday – ✆ 053.

Envir. : Johnstown Castle (the park-arboretum★) SW : 4 m.

🏌 Mulgannon ✆ 42238, SE : 1 m.

🛈 Crescent Quay ✆ 23111.

◆Dublin 88 – Kilkenny 49 – ◆Waterford 38.

🏰 **Ferrycarrig** 🦢, Ferrycarrig Bridge, NW : 2 ¾ m. on N 11 ✆ 22999, Telex 80147, Fax 41982,
≤, 🚗, 🍴 – 🛗 TV ☎ ℗. 🅰 AE ① VISA
M 10.50/21.00 st. and a la carte ▯ 6.00 – **38 rm** ☷ 35.00/95.00 st. – SB 83.50/95.00 st.

🏨 **Talbot**, Trinity St., ✆ 22566, Telex 80658, Fax 23377, 🏊, squash – 🛗 ⊱✕ rest TV ☎ ℗ –
🕍 150. 🅰 AE ① VISA. 🐾
M 12.50/18.00 t. and a la carte ▯ 4.90 – ☷ 7.00 – **103 rm** 33.50/75.50 t. – SB 63.00/82.00 st.

🏨 **White's** (Best Western), George's St., ✆ 22311, Telex 80630, Fax 45000 – 🛗 TV ☎ ℗
🕍 50. 🅰 AE ① VISA. 🐾
closed Christmas Day – **M** 17.50 st. (dinner) and a la carte 14.25/19.60 st. ▯ 4.00 – **75 rm**
☷ 40.00/70.00 st. – SB 79.00/84.00 st.

Whitford House, New Line Rd, SW : 2 m. on L 159 ℰ 43444, ⬚, 🏇, 🏸 – 📺 ☎ 🅿. ⚡
25 rm.

Newbay Country House ⚜, W : 4 m. by N 25 and Clonard rd ℰ 22779, 🏇, park – 🅿
M (communal dining) (dinner only) (residents only) – **5 rm**.

FORD Ferrybank ℰ 23329
MITSUBISHI, SUZUKI The Saythe ℰ 22998
OPEL Ferrybank ℰ 22107

PEUGEOT Drinagh ℰ 22377
TOYOTA Carriglawn, Newtown Rd ℰ 23788

WICKLOW Wicklow **405** N 9 – pop. 5 178 – ECD : Thursday – ✆ 0404.

Envir. : Ashford (Mount Usher or Walpole's Gardens★) *AC*, NW : 4 m.

🏌 Blainroe ℰ 68168, S : 3 ½ m.

🛈 ℰ 67904 (June-September).

◆Dublin 33 – ◆Waterford 84 – Wexford 67.

XX **Old Rectory** with rm, ℰ 67048, 🏇 – ⟲ 🅿. ⬚ AE ⓪ VISA. ⚡
Mid October-mid April – **M** (booking essential) (dinner only) 20.00 **st**. and a la carte ⌁ 10.00
– **5 rm** ⌑ 34.00/68.00 **st**. – SB 92.00/98.00 **st**.

FORD Whitegates ℰ 67331

YOUGHAL Cork **405** I 12 – pop. 5 870 – ECD : Wednesday – ✆ 024.

See : St. Mary's Collegiate Church★ (13C).

Envir. : Ardmore (site★, round tower★ 10C, cathedral ruins★ 12C, ≤★) E : 5 ½ m.

🏌 Knockaverry ℰ 92787.

🛈 ℰ 92390 (July and August).

◆Dublin 146 – ◆Cork 30 – ◆Waterford 47.

XX **Aherne's Seafood Bar,** 163 North Main St., ℰ 92424 – 🅿. ⬚ AE ⓪ VISA
closed Sunday lunch, Monday except Easter, August and Whitsun, and 3 days at Christmas
– **M** 10.50 **st**. (lunch) and a la carte 15.75/22.25 **st**. ⌁ 5.00.

RENAULT North Abbey ℰ 92019/92010

Location	Town	Hotel
M 1		
Junction 5 — S : ½ m. on A 41	**Watford**	Hilton National
Junction 6 — NE : 1 m. on A 405 (this hotel also under M 10)	**St. Albans**	Noke Thistle
Junction 8 — W : ½ m. on A 414	**Hemel Hempstead**	Post House
Junction 9 — NW : 1 m. on A 5	**Flamstead**	Hertfordshire Moat House
Junction 10 — NE : 2 ½ m. by A 505	**Luton**	Ibis Luton
Junction 11 — E : ¾ m. on A 505	**Luton**	Chiltern
Junction 11 — on A 505	**Luton**	Crest
Junction 11 — E : 1 ½ m. on A 505	**Luton**	Humberstone
Newport Pagnell Service Area 3	**Newport Pagnell**	Welcome Lodge
Junction 12 — S : ½ m.	**Toddington**	Granada Lodge
Junction 13 — SW : 1 ½ m. by A 507	**Aspley Guise**	Moore Place
Junction 14 — S : 1 m. by A 509 off A 5130	**Milton Keynes**	Broughton
Junction 14 — SW : 1 ½ m. by A 509	**Milton Keynes**	Wayfarer
Junction 15 — NE : 3 m. by A 508 on A 45	**Northampton**	Swallow
Junction 15 — N : 2 ¼ m. by A 508 on B 526	**Northampton**	Queen Eleanor
Junction 18 — E : 1 m. on A 428	**Rugby (at Crick)**	Post House
Junction 21/21A — NE : 2 ½ m. on A 46	**Leicester (at Braunstone)**	Post House
Junction 22 — E : ¼ m. on A 50	**Markfield**	Granada Lodge
Junction 24 — SW : 2 m. on A 453	**Castle Donington**	Donington Thistle
Junction 25 — W : ¼ m. on A 52	**Nottingham (at Sandiacre)**	Post House
Junction 25 — S : ½ m. on B 6002	**Nottingham (at Long Eaton)**	Novotel Nottingham
Junction 28 — on A 38	**South Normanton**	Swallow
Junction 30 — NW : 1 ½ m. on A 616	**Renishaw**	Sitwell Arms
Junction 30 — E : 1 ¾ m. by A 616 on A 619	**Clowne**	Van Dyk
Junction 31 — E : 1 m. on A 57	**Todwick**	Red Lion
Junction 31 — W : ½ m. by A 57 on A 6067	**Aston**	Aston Hall
Junction 39 — W : ¼ m. on A 636	**Wakefield**	Cedar Court
Junction 40 — E : ¼ m. on A 638	**Wakefield**	Post House
Woolley Edge Service Area		Granada Lodge
A 1 (M)		
Junction 1, A 638 — N : 2 ½ m. on A 1	**Wentbridge (at Barnsdale Bar)**	Travelodge
Junction 3 — S : ½ m. on A 1001	**Hatfield**	Hazel Grove
Junction 7 — W : ¼ m.	**Stevenage**	Novotel
A 1 (M) via A 66 (M) — E : 2 m. on A 66	**Darlington**	Blackwell Grange Moat House
A 1 (M) via A 167 — S : ¾ m. by A 167	**Darlington (at Coatham Mundeville)**	Hall Garth Country House
A 1 (M) via A 630 — SW : ¼ m. on A 630	**Doncaster**	Doncaster Moat House

A 1 (M) Junction with A 195 − E : ½ m. by A 1231	Washington	Post House
A 1 (M) Washington Service Area (Southbound Carriageway)	Washington Service Area	Granada Lodge
A 1 (M) Junction A 6 and M 25 (this hotel also under M 25)	South Mimms	Crest
A 1 (M) − N : 4 ½ m. at Junction with A 6065 (Southbound Carriageway)	Newark-on-Trent (at North Muskham)	Travelodge
A 1 (M) Junction with A 614	Blyth (Notts.)	Granada Lodge
A 1 − NE : ½ m. on A 605	Peterborough (at Alwalton)	Swallow
A 1 (Southbound Carriageway)	Peterborough (at Alwalton)	Travelodge
Farthing Corner Service Area	Farthing Corner	Farthing Corner Lodge

M 2

Junction 1 − W : 1 ½ m. on A 2	Shorne	Inn on the Lake
Junction 3 − N : ½ m. on A 229	Rochester	Bridgewood Manor
Junction 3 − N : 1 m. on A 229	Rochester	Crest

M 3

Junction 3 − N : 1 m. on A 30	Bagshot	Cricketer's
Junction 6 − N : 1 m. at Black Dam roundabout	Basingstoke	Hilton Lodge
Junction 6 − SW : 1 ½ m. at junction A 30 and A 339	Basingstoke	Crest
Junction 7 − SW : 2 m. on A 30	North Waltham	Wheatsheaf

M 4

Leigh Delamere Service Area		Granada Lodge
Heston Service Area (Westbound Carriageway)	Heston (L.B. of Hounslow)	Granada Lodge
Junction 4 − S : ½ m. on B 379	Heathrow Airport	Post House
Junction 4 − N : ¼ m. on B 379	Heathrow Airport	Holiday Inn
Junction 5 − NW : 1 m. by A 287 and 2 m. by A 30	Basingstoke (at Rotherwick)	Tylney Hall
Junction 5 − NW : ¼ m. on A 4	Slough	Holiday Inn
Junction 8-9 − SE : 3 m. by A 308 (M) and A 308	Windsor	Oakley Court
Junction 9 A − NE : ¾ m. by A 423 (M) on Shoppenhangers Rd	Maidenhead	Fredericks
Junction 9 A − NE : ½ m. by A 423 (M) on Shoppenhangers Rd	Maidenhead	Crest
Junction 10 − SE : 2 ½ m. by A 329 (M)	Wokingham	St. Anne's Manor
Junction 11 − N : ½ m. on A 33	Reading	Post House
Junction 13 − S : 5 ¼ m. by A 34 on Pinchington Lane	Newbury	Hilton National
Junction 15 − N : 2 m. by A 419 on A 4259	Swindon	Post House
Junction 17 − NW : 1 m. by A 429	Chippenham (at Stanton St. Quinton)	Stanton Manor
Junction 19 − SW : 2 ½ m. by M 32 on A 4174 (this hotel also under M 32)	Bristol (at Hambrook)	Crest
Junction 24 − S : ½ m. on A 48	Newport (Gwent)	Celtic Manor
Junction 24 − E : 1 ½ m. on A 48	Newport (Gwent) (at Langstone)	New Inn
Junction 24 − S : ¼ m. on A 48	Newport (Gwent)	Hilton National
Junction 34 − N : 1 ¾ m. by A 4119 (Groes Faen road)	Miskin	Miskin Manor
Junction 35 − N : 1 m. by A 473 off Felindre Rd	Pencoed	Travelodge
Junction 36	Sarn Park Service Area	Travelodge
Junction 38 (A 48 m) − NW : 1 m. on A 48	Port Talbot	Twelve Knights
Junction 45 − S : 2 ¼ m. by A 4067 off A 48	Swansea Enterprise Park	Hilton National
Junction 47 − S : 1 m. on A 483	Swansea	Fforest

M 5

| Junction 1 − W : 1 m. by A 41 | Birmingham
(at West Bromwich) | West Bromwich
Moat House |
| Junctions 3-4 (Southbound
Carriageway | Birmingham (at Frankley) | Granada Lodge |

Junction 11 — E : 1 m. on A 40	Cheltenham	Golden Valley Thistle
Junction 13 — SE : 1 ¾ m. on A 419	Stroud (at Stonehouse)	Stonehouse Court
Junction 16 — S : 2 ½ m. by A 38	Bristol (at Patchway)	Stakis Leisure Lodge
Sedgemoor Service Area (Northbound Carriageway)	Sedgemoor	Travelodge
Junction 22 — N : 1 m. on A 38	Brent Knoll	Battleborough Grange
Junction 25 — by approach road	Taunton	Crest
Junction 27 — Sampford Peverell Service Area	Tiverton	Travelodge
Junction 29 — N: 1½ m. by Moor Lane	Exeter (at Pinhoe)	Gipsy Hill
Junction 30 — Exeter Service Area	Exeter	Granada Lodge
Junction 31 — S : 2 ½ m. at junction of A 379 and B 3182	Exeter	Countiswell Lodge

M 6

Junction 2 — SW : ½ m. on A 46	Coventry (at Walsgrave-on-Sowe)	Crest
Junction 2 — SW : ¾ m. on A 46	Coventry (at Walsgrave-on-Sowe)	Campanile
Junction 2 — NE : ¼ m. on B 4065	Coventry (at Ansty)	Ansty Hall
Junction 3 — SE : 1 m. on A 444	Coventry (at Longford)	Novotel
Junction 5 — N : 3 ½ m. by A 452 on B 4148	Sutton Coldfield	New Hall
Junction 7 — N : ¼ m. on A 34	Birmingham (at Great Barr)	Post House
Junction 7 — N : 2 ½ m. on A 34	Walsall	Crest
Junction 10 — SW : 3 m. by A 454 on A 462	Darlaston	Petite
Junction 12 — E : 2 m. on A 5	Cannock	Roman Way
Junction 13 — N : 1 m. on A 449	Stafford	Garth
Junction 14 — SE : ½ m. on A 5013	Stafford	Tillington Hall
Junction 15 — N : ¼ m. on A 519	Newcastle-under-Lyme	Post House
Junction 15 — N : ¾ m. on A 519	Newcastle-under-Lyme	Clayton Lodge
Junction 15 — NE : 1 ½ m. on A 34	Stoke on Trent	White House
Junction 17 — E : ½ m. on A 534	Sandbach	Chimney House
Junction 19 — NE : 2 ½ m. on A 556 (this hotel also under M 56)	Knutsford (at Bucklow Hill)	Swan
Junction 19 — N : on A 556	Knutsford	Travelodge
Junction 21	Warrington	Garden Court Holiday Inn
Junction 23 — N : ½ m. on A 49	Haydock	Post House
Junction 28 — W : ¼ m. on B 5256	Leyland	Penguin
Junction 29 — SE : ¼ m. by A 6	Preston (at Bamber Bridge)	Novotel
Junction 31 — W : ¼ m. on A 59	Preston (at Samlesbury)	Tickled Trout
Junction 31 — E : 1 ¼ m. on A 59	Preston (at Samlesbury)	Swallow Trafalgar
Junction 34 — SW : ¼ m. on A 683	Lancaster	Post House
Junction 40 — on A 592	Penrith	North Lakes Gateway
Junction 40 — W : ½ m. on A 66	Penrith	Travelodge
Junction 44 — N : ¼ m. on A 7	Carlisle (at Kingstown)	Crest
Southwaite Service Area		Granada Lodge

M 8

Junction 3 — SE : 2 ½ m. by A 899	Livingston	Hilton National
Junction 11 — E : 1 ¾ m. by M 898 and on A 726	Erskine	Crest
Junction 27 — N : ¼ m. on A 741	Renfrew	Glynhill
Junction 27 — S : ½ m. on A 741	Paisley	Rockfield

M 9

| Junction 6 — NW : ¼ m. on A 905 | Falkirk (at Grangemouth) | Grange Manor |
| Junction 9 — at junction of M 9 and M 80 | Stirling | Granada Lodge |

M 10

| Junction 1 — SW : 1 m. on A 405 (this hotel also under M 1) | St. Albans | Noke Thistle |

M 11

| Junction 10 — SE : 1 ½ m. by A 505 | Cambridge (at Duxford) | with rm Duxford Lodge |
| Junction 14 with A 604 — NW : 1 ¾ m. on A 604 | Cambridge (at Bar Hill) | Cambridgeshire Moat House |

M 20

Junction 2 A — SE : 1 m. on A 20	Wrotham Heath	Post House
Junction 3 — SE : 3 ½ m. on A 20	Brands Hatch	Brands Hatch Thistle
Junction 3 — SE : 3 ½ m. on A 20	Brands Hatch	Brands Hatch Place
Junction 9 — SE : 1 ½ m. on A 28	Ashford	Post House

M 23

Junction 9 — in Gatwick Airport	Gatwick	Gatwick Hilton International
Junction 9 — W : 1 m. on A 23	Gatwick	Gatwick Penta
Junction 9 — W : 1 m. on A 23	Gatwick	Post House

M 25

Junction 3 — SE : 3 ½ m. on A 20	Brands Hatch	Brands Hatch Thistle
Junction 3 — SE : 3 ½ m. on A 20	Brands Hatch	Brands Hatch Place
Junction 8 — S : ½ m. on A 217	Reigate	Bridge House
Junction 10 — N : 1 ¼ m. by A 3 and A 245	Cobham	Hilton National
Junction 10 — NE : 1 ½ m. by A 3 on A 245	Cobham	Cedar House
Junction 10 — NE : 4 m. by A 3 and A 245	Cobham	Woodlands Park
Junction 13 — S : 1 m. by A 30 on A 308	Egham	Runnymede
Junction 21 A — N : ½ m. on A 405	St. Albans	Noke Thistle
Junction 26 — S : 4 m. on B 1393 and A 121	Epping	Post House
Junction 28 — NE : ¾ m. on A 1023	Brentwood	Brentwood Moat House
Junction 28 — NE : ¼ m. on A 1023	Brentwood	Post House
Junction 29 — E : 3 ½ m.	East Horndon	Travelodge
Junction A 6 and A 1 (M) (this hotel also under A 1 (M))	South Mimms	Crest

M 26

| Junction 2 A — SE : ¼ m. on A 20 | Wrotham Heath | Post House |

M 27

Junction 1 — on A 337 at Junction of A 31 and A 336	Cadnam	Bartley Lodge
Junction 12 — N : at junction of A 3 and A 27	Portsmouth & Southsea (at Cosham)	Holiday Inn
Junction 12 — E : 1 m. on A 27 at junction with A 2030	Portsmouth & Southsea (at Farlington)	Hilton National

M 32

| Junction 1 — W : ½ m. on A 4174 (this hotel also under M 4) | Bristol (at Hambrook) | Crest |

M 40

Junction 2 — E : 1 ¾ m. by A 355 on A 40	Beaconsfield	Bellhouse
Junction 4 — on Crest Road	High Wycombe	Crest
Junction 7 — W : 2 m. by A 329	Oxford (at Great Milton)	with rm Le Manoir aux Quat Saisons

M 42

Junction 1 — S : 2 m. by A 38 on A 448	Bromsgrove	Perry Hall
Junction 4 — S : 3 m. by A 34	Hockley Heath	with rm, Nuthurst Grange
Junction 4 — NW : 1 m. on A 34	Solihull (at Shirley)	Regency
Junction 5 — NW : 1 ¾ m. by A 41 on B 4025	Solihull	George
Junction 5 — NW : 1 ¾ m. by A 41 on B 4025	Solihull	St. Johns Swallow
Junction 6 — NW : 1 m.	Birmingham (at National Exhibition Centre)	Birmingham Metropole
Junction 6 — W : ½ m. on A 45	Birmingham (at National Exhibition Centre)	Arden

M 45

Junction 1 — E : 1 ¼ m. on A 45 | Dunchurch | Dun Cow

M 50

Junction 1 — S : ½ m. on A 38 | Tewkesbury | Tewkesbury Hall

M 53

at Junction 5 and A 41 | Eastham | Travelodge

M 54

Junction 5 — SW : ½ m. | Telford | Telford Moat House

M 55

Junction 1 — N : ¾ m. | Preston (at Broughton) | Broughton Park

M 56

Junction 5 — on Airport Approach Road | Manchester (at Airport) | Hilton National
Junction 5 — on Airport Approach Road | Manchester (at Airport) | Excelsior
Junction 6 — N : ¼ m. on A 538 | Altrincham (at Halebarns) | Four Seasons
Junction 6 — S : 2 m. on A 538 | Wilmslow | Valley Lodge
Junction 7/8 — SW : 2 m. on A 556 (this hotel also under M 6) | Knutsford (at Bucklow Hill) | Swan
Junction 11 — N : ¼ m. on A 56 | Daresbury | Lord Daresbury
Junction 12 — SE : ½ m. by A 557 | Runcorn | Crest

M 57

Junction 2 — E : ½ m. | Kirkby | Cherry Tree

M 61

Junction 5 — NE : 1 m. on A 58 | Bolton | Crest

M 62

Junction 7 — S : 1 ¼ m. by A 569 | Widnes | Hillcrest
Junction 13 — W : ¼ m. on A 572 | Manchester (at Worsley) | Novotel Manchester West
Junction 18-19 | Birch Service Area | Granada Lodge
Junction 24 — SE : 1 ½ m. on A 629 | Huddersfield | Pennine Hilton
Junction 25 — N : ½ m. on A 644 | Brighouse | Forte

M 65

Junction 10 : E at Junction of A 671 and A 679 | Burnley | Travelodge

M 69

Junction with M 1 — NE : 2 ½ m. on A 46 | Leicester (at Braunstone) | Post House
Junction 1 — NW : 1 m. by A 447 | Hinckley | Sketchley Grange
Junction 1 — SE : ¼ m. on A 5 | Hinckley | Hinckley Island

M 74

between Junctions 6 and 5 (Northbound Carriageway) | Hamilton Service Area | Roadchef Lodge

M 80

Junction 9 — at junction of M 9 and M 80 | Stirling | Granada Lodge

M 90

Junction 6 — at junction with A 977 | Kinross | Granada Lodge

M 606

Junction 1 — E : ¼ m. | Bradford | Novotel Bradford

MAJOR HOTEL GROUPS

Abbreviations used in the Guide and central reservation telephone numbers

PRINCIPALES CHAINES HOTELIÈRES

Abréviations utilisées dans nos textes et centraux téléphoniques de réservation

PRINCIPALI CATENE ALBERGHIERE

Abbreviazioni utilizzate nei nostri testi e centrali telefoniche di prenotazione

DIE WICHTIGSTEN HOTELKETTEN

Im Führer benutzte Abkürzungen der Hotelketten und ihre Zentralen für telefonische Reservierung

The dialling codes for London will change.
From May 6 the codes will be as indicated in the entries below, either ☏ 071 or ☏ 081. Until May 6 continue to use the code ☏ 01.

BERNI AND CHEF & BREWER HOTELS	BCB	071 (London) 727 7007
BEST WESTERN HOTELS	BEST WESTERN	081 (London) 541 0033 041 (Glasgow) 204 1794 061 (Manchester) 834 5464
CREST HOTELS LTD	CREST	071 (London) 236 3242
DE VERE HOTELS PLC	DE VERE	0925 (Warrington) 65050
EMBASSY HOTELS	EMBASSY	0345 581237
HILTON INTERNATIONAL	HILTON	071 (London) 734 6000
HOLIDAY INNS INTERNATIONAL	HOLIDAY INN	071 (London) 722 7755
INTER-CONTINENTAL HOTELS LTD	INTER-CON	081 (London) 741 9000 or calls from outside London 0345 581444
LANSBURY HOTELS	LANSBURY	0582 (Luton) 400158
MOUNT CHARLOTTE HOTELS LTD	MT. CHARLOTTE	0532 (Leeds) 444866
NORFOLK CAPITAL HOTELS LTD	NORFOLK CAP.	071 (London) 589 7000
QUEENS MOAT HOUSES PLC	Q.M.H.	0800 289330
RANK HOTELS LTD	RANK	081 (London) 569 7120
STAKIS HOTELS	STAKIS	071 (London) 222 4081 and 0800 833775
SWALLOW HOTELS PLC	SWALLOW	091 (Tyneside) 529 4666
THISTLE HOTELS LTD	THISTLE	071 (London) 937 8033
TRUSTHOUSE FORTE (U.K.) LTD	T.H.F.	081 (London) 567 3444

TRAFFIC SIGNS
A few important signs

Please note: The maximum speed limits in Great Britain are 70 mph (112 km/h) on motorways and dual carriageways and 60 mph (96 km/h) on all other roads, except where a lower speed limit is indicated.

N.B. N'oubliez pas qu'il existe des limitations de vitesse en Grande-Bretagne: 70 mph (112 km/h) sur routes à chaussée séparée et autoroutes, 60 mph (96 km/h) sur autres routes, sauf indication d'une vitesse inférieure.

N.B. In Gran Bretagna esistono dei limiti di velocità: 70 mph (112 km/h) sulle strade a doppia carreggiata e autostrade, 60 mph (96 km/h) sulle altre strade, salvo che sia indicata una velocità inferiore.

Zur Beachtung: In Großbritannien gelten folgende Geschwindigkeitsbegrenzungen: 70 mph (112 km/h) auf Autobahnen und Straßen mit getrennten Fahrbahnen, 60 mph (96 km/h) auf allen anderen Straßen, wenn keine niedrigere Geschwindigkeit angezeigt ist.

Warning signs — *Signaux d'avertissement*
Segnali di avvertimento — Warnzeichen

T junction
Jonction avec autre route
Confluenza con altra strada
Straßeneinmündung

Roundabout
Sens giratoire
Senso rotatorio
Kreisverkehr

Dual carriageway ends

Fin de chaussée à deux voies

Fine di doppia carreggiata

Ende der zweispurigen Fahrbahn

Change to opposite carriageway

Déviation sur chaussée opposée

Deviazione sulla carreggiata opposta

Überleitung auf Gegenfahrbahn

Distance to give way sign ahead
Cédez le passage à 50 yards
Dare la precedenza a 50 iarde
Vorfahrt gewähren in 50 yards Entfernung

Ralentir maintenant

Rallentare subito

Geschwindigkeit verringern

Right-hand lane closed
Voie de droite barrée
Corsia di destra sbarrata
Rechte Fahrbahn gesperrt

Quayside or river bank
Débouché sur un quai ou une berge
Banchina o argine senza sponda
Ufer

Two-way traffic crosses one-way road
Voie à deux sens croisant voie à sens unique
Strada a due sensi che incrocia una strada a senso unico
Straße mit Gegenverkehr kreuzt Einbahnstraße

Level crossing with automatic half barriers ahead
Passage à niveau automatique
Passaggio a livello automatico con semi-barriere
Bahnübergang mit automatischen Halbschranken

Height limit
Hauteur limitée (en pieds et pouces)
Altezza limitata (piedi e pollici)
Maximale Höhe (in Fuß und Zoll)

Opening or swing bridge
Pont mobile
Ponte mobile
Bewegliche Brücke

Signs giving orders

National speed limit applies
Fin de limitation de vitesse
Fine di limitazione di velocità
Ende der Geschwindigkeitsbeschränkung

School crossing patrol
Sortie d'école
Uscita di scolari
Achtung Schule

No stopping (« clearway »)

Arrêt interdit

Fermata vietata

Halteverbot

All vehicles prohibited
(plate gives details)
Circulation interdite à tous véhicules
(plaque donnant détails)
Divieto di transito a tutti i veicoli (la
placca sottostante fornisce dei dettagli)
Verkehrsverbot für Fahrzeuge aller Art
(näherer Hinweis auf Zusatzschild)

Give priority to vehicles from opposite
direction
Priorité aux véhicules venant de face
Dare la precedenza ai veicoli che proven-
gono dal senso opposto
Dem Gegenverkehr Vorrang gewähren

Voie à stationnement réglementé

Sosta regolamentata

Fahrbahn mit zeitlich begrenzter
Parkerlaubnis

Width limit
Largeur limitée (en pieds et pouces)
Larghezza limitata (piedi e pollici)
Breite begrenzt (in Fuß und Zoll)

Plate below sign at end of restriction
Fin d'interdiction
Fine del divieto posta sotto il segnale
Ende einer Beschränkung

Information signs

One-way street
Rue à sens unique
Via a senso unico
Einbahnstraße

No through road
Voie sans issue
Strada senza uscita
Sackgasse

Accès à une chaussée à deux voies

Accesso ad una carreggiata a due corsie

Zufahrt zu einer zweispurigen Fahrbahn

Ring road
Voie de contournement
Strada di circonvallazione
Ringstraße

Warning signs on rural motorways

Maximum advised speed
Vitesse maximum conseillée
Velocità massima consigliata
Empfohlene Höchstgeschwindigkeit

1 Lane closed
1 voie barrée
1 Corsia sbarrata
1 Fahrstreifen gesperrt

Count-down markers at exit from motorway (or primary route if green-backed)

Balises situées sur autoroute ou route principale (fond vert) et annonçant une sortie

Segnali su autostrada o strade principali (fondo verde) annuncianti un'uscita

Hinweise auf Abfahrten an Autobahnen und Hauptverkehrsstraßen (Grünengrund)

End of restriction

Route libre

Strada libera

Straße frei

Direction to service area, with fuel, parking, cafeteria and restaurant facilities.

Indication d'aire de service avec carburant, parc à voitures, cafeteria et restaurant.

Indicazione di area di servizio con carburante, parcheggio, bar e ristorante

Hinweis auf Tankstelle, Parkplatz, Cafeteria und Restaurant

Warning signs on urban motorways
Signaux d'avertissement sur autoroutes urbaines
Segnali di avvertimento su autostrade urbane
Warnzeichen auf Stadtautobahnen

_1_   _2_   _3_

The insets show (flashing amber lights) (1) advised maximum speed, (2) lane to be used; (3) (flashing red lights), you must stop.

L'ensemble de ces panneaux indique : (1) la vitesse maximale conseillée, (2) la voie à utiliser (signaux lumineux jaunes); (3) l'arrêt obligatoire (signaux lumineux rouges).

L'insieme di questi segnali indica : (1) la velocità massima consigliata, (2) la corsia da imboccare (segnali luminosi gialli); (3) la fermata obbligatoria (segnali luminosi rossi).

Diese Schilder (mit blinkenden Ampeln) weisen hin auf : 1. die empfohlene Höchstgeschwindigkeit, 2. die zu befahrende Fahrbahn (gelbes Licht) und 3. Halt (rotes Licht).

In town — En ville
In città — in der Stadt

SIGNALISATION SHOWN ON OR ALONG KERBS

SIGNALISATION MATÉRIALISÉE SUR OU AU LONG DES TROTTOIRS

SEGNALI TRACCIATI SOPRA O LUNGO I MARCIAPIEDI

ZEICHEN AUF ODER AN GEHWEGEN

OTHER ROAD SIGNS

AUTRES PANNEAUX

ALTRI CARTELLI INDICATORI

ZUSÄTZLICHE VERKEHRSZEICHEN

No waiting during every working day
Stationnement interdit tous les jours ouvrables
Sosta vietata nei giorni feriali con indicazioni complementari
Parkverbot an Werktagen

Stationnement interdit de 8 h 30 à 18 h 30 du lundi au samedi
Sosta vietata da lunedì a sabato dalle 8,30 alle 18,30
Parkverbot Montag bis Samstag von 8.30 bis 18.30 Uhr

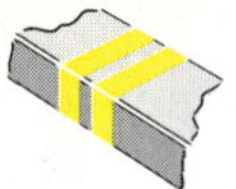

No loading or unloading during every working day

Livraisons interdites tous les jours ouvrables

Carico e scarico vietato nei giorni feriali con indicazioni complementari

Be- und Entladen verboten an allen Werktagen

Livraisons interdites de 8 h 30 à 18 h 30 du lundi au samedi
Carico e scarico vietato da lunedi a sabato dalle 8,30 alle 18,30
Be- und Entladen verboten von Montag bis Samstag von 8.30 bis 18.30 Uhr

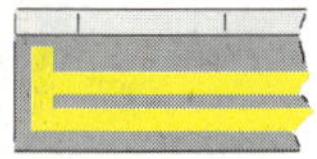

No waiting during every working day and additional times as indicated
Stationnement interdit tous les jours ouvrables plus autres périodes indiquées sur panneaux
Divieto di sosta tutti i giorni feriali e negli altri periodi indicati sul cartello
Parkverbot an Werktagen und den auf Zusatzschildern angegebenen Zeiten

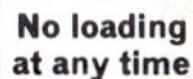

Stationnement interdit en permanence

Divieto permanente di sosta

Parkverbot zu jeder Zeit

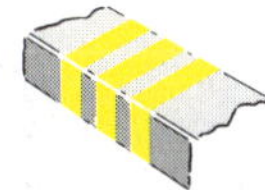

No loading or unloading during every working day and additional times as indicated
Livraisons interdites tous les jours ouvrables plus autres périodes indiquées sur panneaux
Divieto di carico e scarico tutti i giorni feriali e negli altri periodi indicati sul cartello
Be- und Entladen verboten an Werktagen und den auf Zusatzschildern angegebenen Zeiten

Livraisons interdites en permanence

Divieto permanente di carico e scarico

Be- und Entladeverbot zu jeder Zeit

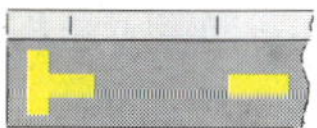

No waiting during any other periods
Stationnement interdit à toute autre période
Sosta vietata in determinate ore
Parkverbot zu bestimmten Zeiten

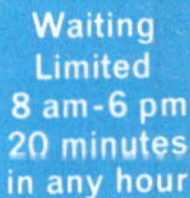

Stationnement limité à 20 mn de 8 h à 18 h
Sosta limitata a 20 mn dalle 8 alle 18
Höchstparkdauer 20 Min. in der Zeit von 8.00 bis 18.00 Uhr

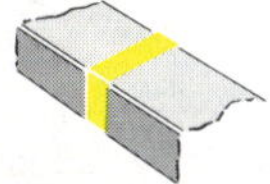

No loading or unloading during any other periods

Livraisons interdites à toute autre période

Divieto di carico e scarico in determinate ore

Be- und Entladeverbot zu bestimmten Zeiten

Livraisons interdites du lundi au vendredi de 8 h à 9 h 30 et de 16 h 30 à 18 h 30
Carico e scarico vietato da lunedi a venerdi dalle 8 alle 9,30 e dalle 16,30 alle 18,30
Be- und Entladeverbot Montag bis Freitag von 8.00 bis 9.30 und von 16.30 bis 18.30 Uhr

Remember : speed limit in Great Britain 70 mph and in Eire 60 mph.

Direction signs on the road network
Panneaux de direction sur le réseau routier
Cartelli direzionali sulla rete stradale
Richtungsschilder auf den Straßen

401	Michelin maps
402	Cartes Michelin
403	Carte Michelin
404	Michelin-Karten

Motorways and A (M) class roads
Sur autoroutes et routes classées A (M)
Sulle autostrade e strade classificate A (M)
Autobahn M und Schnellstraße A (M)

Primary routes

Apart from motorways, « Primary routes » provide the major road network linking towns of local and national traffic importance

Sur grands itinéraires routiers « Primary routes »

En complément du système autoroutier, les grands itinéraires constituent un réseau de routes recommandées reliant les villes selon leur importance dans le trafic national

Sui principali itinerari stradali (Primary routes)

I principali itinerari, unitamente alle autostrade, costituiscono una rete di strade consigliate che collegano le città secondo la loro importanza nel traffico nazionale

Empfohlene Fernverkehrsstraßen (Primary routes)

Sie bilden ein überregionales Straßennetz, das verkehrswichtige Orte verbindet ; sie ergänzen das Autobahnnetz

Other A class roads
Sur autres routes classées A
Sulle altre strade classificate A
Andere Straße der Kategorie A

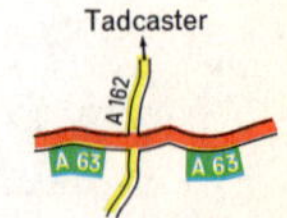

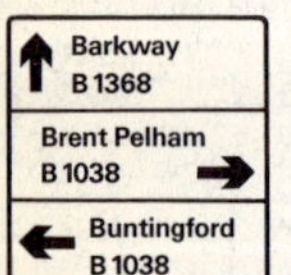

B class roads
Sur routes classées B
Sulle strade classificate B
Straße der Kategorie B

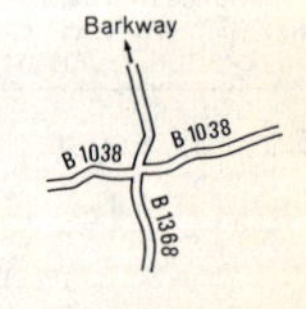

Unclassified roads — Local direction sign
Sur routes non classées — Signalisation locale
Sulle strade non classificate — Segnaletica locale
Nicht klassifizierte Straßen — Örtliche Richtungsschilder

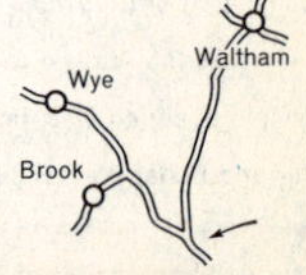

ADDRESSES OF SHIPPING COMPANIES AND THEIR PRINCIPAL AGENTS

ADRESSES DES COMPAGNIES DE NAVIGATION ET DE LEURS PRINCIPALES AGENCES

INDIRIZZI DELLE COMPAGNIE DI NAVIGAZIONE E DELLE LORO PRINCIPALI AGENZIE

ADRESSEN DER SCHIFFAHRTSGESELLSCHAFTEN UND IHRER WICHTIGSTEN AGENTUREN

BELFAST FERRIES

47 Donegal Quay, Belfast, BTI 3ED, ☎ (0232) 326800, 320364, Telex 74268 BELFER, Fax 331239.

Agent : North Brocklebank Dock, Bootle, Merseyside, L20 1DB, ☎ (051) 922 6234, Telex 627167 BELCAR, Fax 9441540.

B & I LINE

16 Westmoreland St., Dublin 2, Eire, ☎ (01) 797977, Telex 30912. Fax 778146.

Agent : 150 New Bond St., London, W1Y 0AQ, ☎ (01) 734 4681, Telex 23523.

BRITISH RAIL see SEALINK and HOVERSPEED

BRITTANY FERRIES

BAI Brittany Ferries, Gare Maritime Roscoff, Port du Bloscon 29211, France, ☎ 98 61 22 11, Telex 940360.

Agents : Millbay Docks, Plymouth, PL1 3EW, Devon, ☎ (0752) 221321, Telex 45380.

The Brittany Centre, Wharf Rd, Portsmouth, PO2 8RU, Hampshire. ☎ (0705) 827701, Telex 86878.

Gare Maritime, F-35400 St-Malo, France, ☎ 99 82 41 41, Telex 740426.

Tourist House, 42 Grand Parade, Cork, Eire, ☎ (021) 277801, Telex 75088.

Modesto Pineiro & Co., 27 Paseo de Pereda, Santander, Spain, ☎ (042) 214500, Telex 35913 MPCIA.

CALEDONIAN MACBRAYNE LTD.

Ferry Terminal, Gourock, PA19 1QP, Renfrewshire, Scotland, ☎ (0475) 34531, Telex 779318, Fax 37607.

BRITISH CHANNEL ISLAND FERRIES

Fairfield House, Kingston Cres., Portsmouth, PO2 8AA, ☎ (0705) 664818.

Agents :

P.O. Box 315, Poole, Dorset, BH15 4DB, ☎ (0202) 681155, Telex 418125.

New North Quay, St. Helier, Jersey, Channel Islands, ☎ (0534) 38300.

White Rock, St. Peter Port, Guernsey, Channel Islands, ☎ (0481) 711111.

CLYDE MARINE MOTORING CO. LTD.

Princess Pier, Greenock, Scotland ☎ (0475) 21281.

CONDOR LTD.

Commodore House, Bulwer Av., St. Sampsons, Guernsey, Channel Islands, ☎ (0481) 48771, Telex 4191289, Fax 45059.

Agents : Commodore Travel Ltd., 28 Conway St., St. Helier, Jersey, Channel Islands, ☎ (0534) 71263, Telex 419 2079, Fax 58194.

Condor Ltd., Morvan Fils, 2 Place du Poids du Roi, F-35402 St. Malo, France, ☎ 99 56 42 29, Telex 950486, Fax 99402366.

Condor Passenger Dept., New Jetty, White Rock, St. Peter Port, Guernsey, Channel Islands. ☎ (0481) 26121, Telex 4191417, Fax 712555.

CORAS IOMPAIR EIREANN.

Ceant Station, Galway, Eire, ☎ (091) 62141.

CUNARD LINE LTD.

South Western House, Canute Rd, Southampton, Hampshire, SO9 1ZA, ✆ (0703) 634166, Telex 477577.

Agents : 30a Pall Mall, London SW1Y 5LS, ✆ (01) 491 3930, Telex 295483.
555 Fifth Av., New York, NY 10017, USA, ✆ (212) 800 7500, Telex 220436.
Compagnie Générale de Croisières, 22 Rue Royale, F-75008 Paris, France, ✆ 42 60 36 63, Telex 215755 F.

EMERAUDE LINES

Gare Maritime du Naye, F-35400, St. Malo, France, ✆ 99 82 83 84, Telex 950271, Fax 99 81 28 73.

Agents : Channel Islands Handling Ltd., 17 York St., St. Helier, Jersey, Channel Islands, ✆ (0534) 74458, Telex 4192311 EMFJER, Fax 59513.
Emeraude Ferries, New Jetty, White Rock, St. Peter Port, Guernsey, ✆ (0481) 711414, Telex 4191571 EMFERY G.

FRED OLSEN LINES KDS

Fergeterminaten, P.O. Box 82, N 4601 Kristiansand, Norway, ✆ (042) 70501, Telex 21969, Fax 24907.

Agents : Fred Olsen Lines, Tyne Commission Quay, Albert Edward Dock, North Shields, NE29 6EA, ✆ (091) 257 9682.
Fred Olsen Lines, PO Box 1159 Centrum, N-0107, Oslo 1, Norway, ✆ (02) 678000, Telex 77538.
Fred Olsen Lines, Postboks 30, DK-9850, Hirtshals, Denmark, ✆ (08) 94 19 66, Telex 67752, Fax (08) 94 37 92.

HERM SEAWAY

Guernseybus Ltd., Picquet House, St. Peter Port, Guernsey, Channel Islands, ✆ (0481) 24677.

HOVERSPEED

Maybrook House, Queens Gardens, Dover, Kent CT17 9UQ, ✆ (0304) 240241, Telex 96323.

Agents : International Hoverport, Boulogne, France, ✆ 21 30 27 26, Telex 110008.
International Hoverport, Calais, France, ✆ 21 96 65 70, Telex 810856.

HOVERTRAVEL LTD.

Quay Road, Ryde, Isle of Wight, P033 2HB.

Agent : Clarence Pier, Southsea, Portsmouth, PO5 3AD, Hampshire, ✆ (0705) 829988.

IRISH FERRIES

2-4 Merrion Row, Dublin 2, Eire, ✆ (01) 610714, Telex 93705 IFD, Fax (01) 610743.

Agent : Transport et Voyages, 40 Rue Kleber, F-92307, Levallois-Perret, France, ✆ 47 59 44 21, Telex 613491 FERYVOY, Fax 47 59 40 33.

ISLE OF MAN STEAM PACKET CO. LTD.

P.O. Box 5, Imperial Buildings, Douglas, Isle of Man, ✆ (0624) 72468, Telex 629414.

Agents : W.E. Williames (N.I.) Ltd., Northern Rd, Belfast, BT3 9AL, Northern Ireland, ✆ (0232) 351009, Telex 747166.
George Bell Agencies Ltd., Bell House, 7-11 Montague St., Dublin 2, Eire ✆ (01) 722100, Telex 93683.
Sea Terminal, Heysham, Lancashire, LA3 2XF, ✆ (0524) 53802.
Sealink British Ferries, Ferry Terminal, Stranraer, Wigtownshire DG9 8EJ, ✆ (0776) 2262, Telex 778125.

ISLE OF SARK SHIPPING CO. LTD.

White Rock, St. Peter Port, Guernsey, Channel Islands, ✆ (0481) 24059, Telex 419 1549, Fax 712081.

ISLES OF SCILLY STEAMSHIP CO. LTD.

Hugh Town, St. Mary's, Isles of Scilly, TR21 OLJ, ✆ 0720 (Scillonia) 22357/8.

Agent : 16 Quay St., Penzance, TR18 4BD, Cornwall, ✆ (0736) 62009/64013.

LUNDY CO.

Lundy, Bristol Channel, via Bideford, Devon, EX39 2LY, ✆ 0271 (Woolacombe) 870870.

MERSEYSIDE PASSENGER TRANSPORT EXECUTIVE

Mersey Ferries, Victoria Pl., Seacombe, Wallasey, Merseyside, ✆ (051) 227 5181.

NORFOLK LINE BV

Kranenburgweg 211, 2583 ER Scheveningen, Netherlands, ✆ (070) 527400, Telex 31515.

Agent : Atlas House, Southgates Rd, Great Yarmouth, Norfolk NR30 3LN, ✆ (0493) 330000, Telex 975741, Fax 335275.

NORTH SEA FERRIES LTD.

Noordzee Veerdiensten, Benel uxhaven, Europoort, P.O. Box 1123, 3180 AC Rozenburg Z.H., Netherlands, ℘ (01819) 55500, Telex 26571.

Agents : King George Dock, Hedon Rd, Hull, HU9 5QA, Humberside, ℘ (0482) 795141, Telex 592349.

Leopold II Dam (Havendam) B8380, Zeebrugge, Belgium, ℘ (050) 543430, Telex 81469.

NORWAY LINE

Postboks 4004, N-5023 Bergen-Dreggen, Norway, ℘ 05-322780, Telex 40425 NLINE.

Agent : Tyne Commission Quay, North Shields, NE29 6EA, ℘ (091) 296 1313, Telex 537275 NLINE, Fax 296 1540.

OLAU-LINE (UK) LTD.

Sheerness, Kent, ME12 1SN, ℘ (0795) 666666, Telex 965605.

Agents : Olau-Line Terminal, Buitenhaven, P.O. Box 231, Vlissingen, Netherlands, ℘ (01184) 88000, Telex 37817.

ORKNEY ISLANDS SHIPPING CO. LTD.

4 Ayre Road, Kirkwall, Orkney Islands, Scotland, ℘ (0856) 2044.

ORWELL & HARWICH NAVIGATION CO. LTD.

The Quay, Harwich, Essex, ℘ (0255) 502004.

P & O EUROPEAN FERRIES

127 Regent Street, London, W1R 8LB, ℘ (01) 734 4431.

Agents : Main Reservation Centre, Enterprise Hse., Channel View Rd Dover, CT17 9TJ, Kent, ℘ (0304) 223000 Reservations : ℘ 203388.
Viking House, Wharf Rd, Portsmouth, Hants., PO2 8TA, ℘ (0705) 772000.
European House, The Docks, Felixstowe, Suffolk, IP11 8TB, ℘ (0394) 604802.
Cairnryan, Stranraer, Wigtownshire, Scotland, ℘ (058 12) 276 and 277.
Larne Harbour, Larne, Co. Antrim, Northern Ireland, BT40 1AQ, ℘ (0574) 74321, Telex 74528.
Regie Voor Martiem Transport, Natienkaai 5, B-8400 Ostend, Belgium, ℘ (059) 70 76 01.
Car Ferry Terminal, Doverlaan 7, B-8380 Zeebrugge, Belgium, ℘ (050) 54.50.50, Telex 81306.
Terminal Car Ferry, 62226 Calais Cedex, France, ℘ 21 97 21 21, Telex 120878.
Gare Maritime, Quai Chanzy BP 309, F-62204, Boulogne, France, ℘ 21 31 78 00, Telex 130187.
9 Place de la Madeleine, F-75008 Paris, France, ℘ 42 66 40 17, Telex 210679.
Gare Maritime, 50101 Cherbourg, France, ℘ 33 44 20 13, Telex 170765.
Quai de Southampton, 76600 Le Havre, France, ℘ 35 21 36 50, Telex 190757.

P & O FERRIES : ORKNEY & SHETLAND SERVICES

P.O. Box 5, P & O Ferry Terminal, Jamieson's Quay, Aberdeen, AB9 8DL, Scotland, ℘ (0224) 58911, Telex 73344.

Agents : Terminal Building, Scrabster, Caithness, KW14 7UJ, Scotland, ℘ (0847) 62052.
Holmsgarth Terminal, Lerwick, Shetland Islands, ZE1 0PW, Scotland, ℘ (0595) 5252, Telex 75294.
Terminal Bldg., Stromness, Orkney Islands, KW16 3AA, Scotland, ℘ (0856) 850 655, Telex 75221.

RED FUNNEL SERVICES

12 Bugle St., Southampton, SO9 4LJ, Hampshire, ℘ (0703) 330333.

Agents : Fountain Pier, West Cowes, Isle of Wight, ℘ (0983) 292101 (car ferry) and 292704 (Hydrofoil).

THE SALLY LINE LTD

Argyle Centre, York St., Ramsgate, Kent, CT11 9DS ℘ (0843) 595522, Telex 96389.

Agents : 81 Piccadilly, London W1, ℘ (01) 409 0536 and 858 1127, Telex 291860.

Sally Line, Dunkerque Port-Ouest, F-59279 Loon Plage, France, ℘ 28.21.43.44, Telex 130078.

SCANDINAVIAN SEAWAYS

DFDS Travel Centre, 15 Hanover St., London, W1R 8HG, ℘ (01) 493 6696, Telex 28257.

Agents : Sankt Annae Plads 30, DK-1295 Copenhagen K, Denmark, ℘ (01) 15 63 00, Telex 19435.
DFDS Travelbureaü (Scandinavian Seaways), Axelborg Vesterbrogade 4a, DK-1620 Copenhagen, Denmark, ℘ (01) 15 63 00, Telex 19435.
Scandinavian Seaways, Tyne Commission Quay, North Shields, NE29 6EE, Tyne and Wear, ℘ (091) 296 0101, Telex 53201.
Scandinavian Seaways, Karl Johansgate 1, Oslo 1, Norway, ℘ (02) 429350, Telex 18129.
Scandinavian Seaways, Skandiahamnen, P.O. Box 8895, S-40272 Gothenburg 8, Sweden, ℘ (031) 65 06 00, Telex 21724.
Scandinavian Seaways, Jessenstrasse 4, 2000 Hamburg 1, West Germany, ℘ (040) 3890371, Telex 02161759.

SEALINK U.K. LTD.

Sealink UK Ltd., 163/203 Eversholt St., London, NW1 1BG, ✆ (01) 387 1234, Telex 269295 SELINK G.

SNCF, 88 Rue Saint-Lazare, 75436 Paris Cedex 09, France, ✆ 15 38 52 29.

Zeeland Steamship Co., Hook of Holland, Netherlands, ✆ (3117) 47 39 44, Telex 31272 ZLDHK NL.

Agents : *For services from all English and Welsh ports contact :*
Sealink UK Ltd., Charter House, Park St., Ashford, Kent, TN24 8EX, ✆ (0233) 47033, Telex 965954, Fax 42024.

For Isle of Wight services contact :
Sealink UK Ltd., Isle of Wight Ferry Services, P.O. Box 59, Portsmouth, Hampshire, PO1 2XB, ✆ (0705) 827744, Telex 86440.

For services between Scotland and Northern Ireland contact :
Sealink (Scotland and Northern Ireland) Ltd., 4-6 South Strand St., Stranraer, Dumfries and Galloway, DG9 7JW, ✆ (0776) 3515, Telex 777578.

Other European Agents : Sealink UK Ltd, Dun Laoghaire Harbour Dun Laoghaire, Dublin, ✆ (01) 801905, Telex 30319.

Sealink, Rosslare Harbour, County Wexford, ✆ (053) 33115, Telex 28389.

GT Link A/S H.C., Ørstedsvej 70, DK-1879, Frederiksberg C, Denmark, ✆ (01) 37 67 57, Telex 19800 VIKING DK, Fax (01) 37 20 28.

Armement Naval SNCF, Gare Maritime BP 27, F-62201 Boulogne-sur-Mer, France, ✆ 21 30 25 11, Telex 110908.

Agence Maritime Tellier, Gare Maritime, F-50100 Cherbourg, France, ✆ 33 20 43 38, Telex 170559.

Armement Naval SNCF, Gare Maritime BP 85, F-76203 Dieppe, France, ✆ 35 84 22 60, Telex 770924.

SMZ, Post Box 2, 3150 AA, Hook of Holland, Netherlands, ✆ 311 747 3944, Telex 31272.

SERVICE MARITIME CARTERET-JERSEY

BP 15, F-50270 Barneville-Carteret, France, ✆ 33 53 87 21, Telex 170477.

Agents : CNTM Ltd., Gorey, Jersey, Channel Islands, ✆ (0534) 53737.
Gare Maritime, F-50580 Portbail, France, ✆ 33 04 86 71, Telex 170477.

SHETLAND ISLANDS COUNCIL

Grantfield, Lerwick, Shetland, ZE1 ONT, ✆ (0595) 2024, Telex 75218.

SMYRIL LINE

P.O. Box 370, Jonas Broncksgøta 25, FR-110 Thorshavn, Faroe Islands, ✆ (298)15900, Telex 81296, Fax 15707.

Agents : P & O Ferries, Orkney & Shetland Services, P.O. Box 5, P & O Ferry Terminal, Aberdeen, AB9 8DL, Scotland, ✆ (0224) 572615, Telex 73344, Fax 574411.

Norraena Ferdaskristofar, Smyril Line Iceland, Langavegur 3, 101 Reykjavik, Iceland, ✆ (91) 62 63 62, Telex 3122, Fax (91) 29450.

Smyril Line (Norge) Postboks 4135, Dreggen, N-5023, Bergen ✆ (05) 320970, Telex 42109.

THOMAS & BEWS FERRIES

Ferry Office, John O'Groats, Caithness, Scotland, ✆ (095 581) 353 (summer).
Windieknap, Brough, Thurso, Caithness, Scotland, ✆ (084 785) 619 (winter).

TORBAY SEAWAYS

Beacon Quay, Torquay, Devon, ✆ (0803) 214397, Telex 42500, Fax 26462.

TRUCKLINE FERRIES POOLE LTD.

New Harbour Rd, Poole, Dorset, BH15 4AJ, ✆ (0705) 827701, Telex 418446.

VEDETTES ARMORICAINES

Gare Maritime de la Bourse, B.P. 180, F-35049 St-Malo, France, ✆ 99 56 48 88, Telex 950196 NAVIPAX.

Agents : Vedettes Armoricaines, Albert Pier, St. Helier, Jersey, ✆ 20361, Telex 4192131 NAVIEX.

Boutins Travel Bureau, Library Pl., St. Helier, Jersey, ✆ 21532/3/4, Telex 4192149.

12 rue Georges-Clemenceau, B.P. 304, F-50403 Granville, France, ✆ 33 50 77 45, Telex 170449 F.

VEDETTES BLANCHES

Les Vedettes Blanches, Gare Maritime, F-35400 St-Malo, France, ✆ 99 82 83 84, Telex 740906, Fax 99 81 28 73.

Agents : Channel Islands Handling Ltd., 17 York St., St. Helier, Jersey, ✆ (0534) 74458, Telex 4192311 EMFJER, Fax 59513.
1-3 Rue Le Campion, F-50400, Granville, France, ✆ 33 50 16 36, Telex 170002.

WESTERN FERRIES (ARGYLL) LTD.

16 Woodside Crescent, Glasgow, Scotland, G3 7UT, ✆ (041) 332 9766, Telex 77203 CLYDE-BUILT.

Agents : Hunters Quay, Dunoon, Argyll, Scotland, ✆ (0369) 4452.
The Pier, Port Askaig, Isle of Islay, Scotland, ✆ (049 684) 681.

WEYMOUTH MARITIME SERVICES LTD.

Ferry Terminal, Weymouth, Dorset, ✆ (0305) 788300.

DISTANCES

All distances in this edition are quoted in miles. The distance is given from each town to other nearby towns and to the capital of each region as grouped in the guide. Towns appearing in the charts are preceded by a diamond ♦ in text.

To avoid excessive repetition some distances have only been quoted once — you may therefore have to look under both town headings.

The distances in miles quoted are not necessarily the shortest but have been based on the roads which afford the best driving conditions and are therefore the most practical.

DISTANCES EN MILES

Pour chaque région traitée, vous trouverez au texte de chacune des localités sa distance par rapport à la capitale et aux villes environnantes. Lorsque ces villes sont celles des tableaux, leur nom est précédé d'un losange noir ♦.

La distance d'une localité à une autre n'est pas toujours répétée aux deux villes intéressées : voyez au texte de l'une ou de l'autre.

Ces distances ne sont pas nécessairement comptées par la route la plus courte mais par la plus pratique, c'est-à-dire celle offrant les meilleures conditions de roulage.

Belfast	Cork	Dublin	Dundalk	Galway	Killarney	Limerick	Londonderry	Omagh	Sligo	Tullamore	Waterford
250											
103	154										
50	200	53									
196	122	135	153								
273	54	189	223	133							
204	58	120	154	64	69						
70	281	146	98	176	300	231					
68	247	112	64	148	266	197	34				
126	200	133	106	90	216	147	86	69			
132	118	60	82	82	141	72	163	129	95		
197	73	96	147	141	112	77	242	208	176	81	

133 Miles

Dublin - Sligo

DISTANZE IN MIGLIA

Per ciascuna delle regioni trattate, troverete nel testo di ogni località la sua distanza dalla capitale e dalle città circostanti. Quando queste città sono comprese nelle tabelle, il loro nome è preceduto da una losanga ♦

La distanza da una località all'altra non è sempre ripetuta nelle due città interessate : vedere nel testo dell'una o dell'altra.

Le distanze non sono necessariamente calcolate seguendo il percorso più breve, ma vengono stabilite secondo l'itinerario più pratico, che offre cioè le migliori condizioni di viaggio.

ENTFERNUNGSANGABEN IN MEILEN

Die Entfernungen der einzelnen Orte zur Landeshauptstadt und zu den nächstgrößeren Städten in der Umgebung sind im allgemeinen Ortstext angegeben. Die Namen der Städte in der Umgebung, die auf der Tabelle zu finden sind, sind durch eine Raute ♦ gekennzeichnet.

Die Entfernung zweier Städte voneinander können Sie aus den Angaben im Ortstext der einen oder der anderen Stadt ersehen.

Die Entfernungsangaben gelten nicht immer für den kürzesten, sondern für den günstigsten Weg.

DISTANCES BETWEEN MAJOR TOWNS
DISTANCES ENTRE PRINCIPALES VILLES
DISTANZE TRA LE PRINCIPALI CITTÀ
ENTFERNUNGEN ZWISCHEN DEN GRÖSSEREN STÄDTEN

Example · Exemple · Esempio · Beispiel
Edinburgh - Southampton
442 Miles

	Aberdeen	Ayr	Birmingham	Blackpool	Brighton	Bristol	Cambridge	Cardiff	Carlisle	Coventry	Dover	Dumfries	Dundee	Edinburgh	Glasgow	Inverness	Ipswich	Kingston upon Hull	Leeds	Leicester	Liverpool	London	Manchester	Middlesbrough	Newcastle	Norwich	Nottingham	Oban	Oxford	Plymouth	Portsmouth	Sheffield	Southampton	Stoke on Trent	Swansea
Ayr	196																																		
Birmingham	442	293																																	
Blackpool	336	187	130																																
Brighton	616	467	180	304																															
Bristol	526	377	91	214	157																														
Cambridge	500	351	110	221	117	166																													
Cardiff	545	396	110	233	191	46	200																												
Carlisle	242	93	201	95	375	285	259	304																											
Coventry	461	311	18	148	158	96	88	124	219																										
Dover	637	488	201	325	84	199	120	233	396	179																									
Dumfries	221	59	234	128	408	318	292	337	34	252	429																								
Dundee	67	129	375	269	549	459	433	478	175	394	570	151																							
Edinburgh	130	81	301	195	475	385	335	404	101	319	459	83	63																						
Glasgow	150	35	300	194	474	384	358	403	100	318	495	73	83	46																					
Inverness	107	207	468	362	642	552	526	571	268	487	663	247	134	156	172																				
Ipswich	553	404	163	274	123	203	54	237	312	141	126	345	486	388	411	579																			
Kingston upon Hull	397	247	139	144	250	230	137	249	155	141	262	188	330	231	254	423	190																		
Leeds	366	216	119	88	262	210	147	229	124	121	272	157	299	200	223	392	200	61																	
Leicester	470	320	43	157	165	121	74	149	228	24	186	261	403	293	327	496	127	96	101																
Liverpool	368	219	103	56	277	187	208	173	127	121	298	160	301	227	226	394	261	131	75	130															
London	558	409	122	246	53	121	55	155	317	100	76	350	491	417	416	584	76	183	204	107	219														
Manchester	363	214	86	51	260	170	163	189	122	105	281	155	296	222	221	389	216	99	43	91	35	202													
Middlesbrough	331	182	177	123	319	267	200	286	90	178	325	123	264	146	189	357	253	89	66	159	141	246	109												
Newcastle	235	150	206	150	349	297	230	316	59	208	354	91	168	105	157	261	283	126	95	188	170	276	139	41											
Norwich	527	377	161	248	170	225	61	259	285	149	173	318	460	361	384	553	43	148	174	117	235	109	190	227	256										
Nottingham	432	282	50	143	193	149	88	166	190	52	214	223	365	266	289	458	141	94	74	26	130	135	72	132	161	120									
Oban	180	127	400	294	574	484	458	503	200	419	595	179	116	123	93	118	511	355	324	428	326	516	321	289	258	485	390								
Oxford	509	360	63	197	105	73	100	107	268	54	146	301	442	368	367	535	138	187	167	70	170	59	153	224	254	160	98	467							
Plymouth	641	492	206	329	222	124	287	161	400	211	320	433	574	500	499	667	324	345	325	236	302	242	285	382	412	346	264	599	194						
Portsmouth	604	455	148	292	48	100	133	143	363	139	142	396	537	463	462	630	157	255	267	171	265	78	248	325	354	192	199	562	85	182					
Sheffield	418	268	89	105	232	180	122	199	176	91	253	209	351	240	275	444	175	68	36	71	80	174	41	105	135	149	44	376	137	295	237				
Southampton	583	434	127	271	61	79	128	122	342	118	152	375	516	442	441	609	166	251	263	166	244	87	227	320	350	188	194	541	64	161	21	233			
Stoke on Trent	397	248	46	85	220	130	133	149	156	65	241	189	330	256	255	423	186	132	95	59	58	162	41	161	190	177	50	355	113	245	208	53	187		
Swansea	542	392	136	229	227	82	236	40	300	149	269	333	475	400	399	568	273	275	255	184	187	191	215	312	342	295	192	500	143	197	179	225	158	175	
Wick	233	333	594	488	768	678	652	697	394	613	789	373	260	282	298	126	705	549	518	622	520	710	515	483	387	679	584	244	661	793	756	570	735	549	694

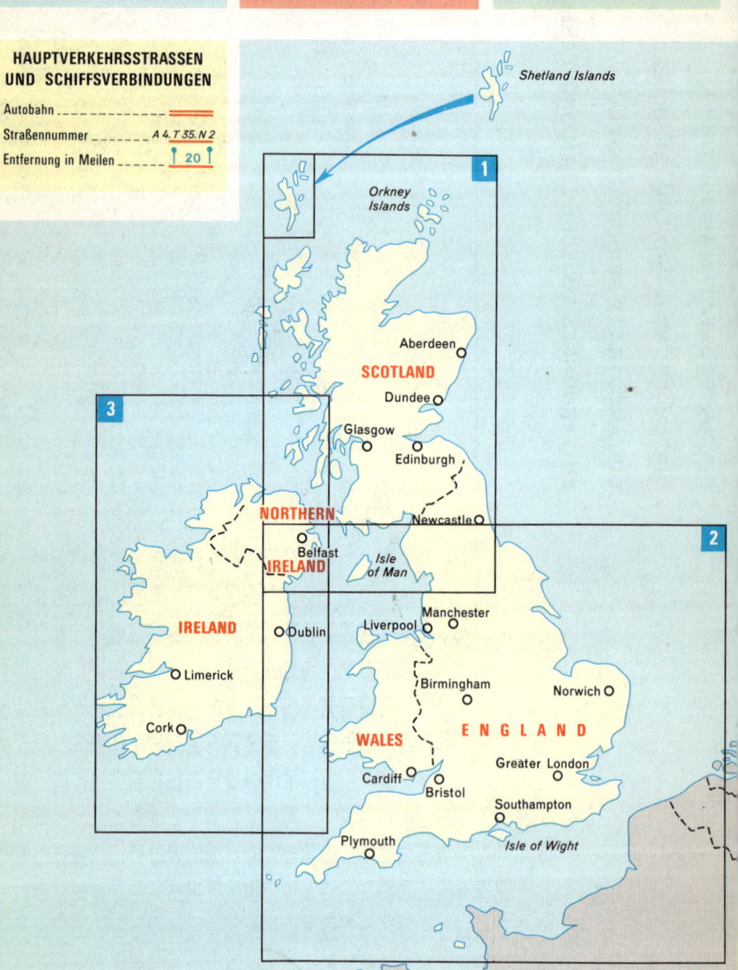

GREAT BRITAIN : the maps and town plans in the Great Britain Section of this Guide are based upon the Ordnance Survey of Great Britain with the permission of the Controller of Her Majesty's Stationery Office. Crown Copyright reserved.

NORTHERN IRELAND : the maps and town plans in the Northern Ireland Section of this Guide are based upon the Ordnance Survey of Northern Ireland with the sanction of the Controller of H.M. Stationery Office, Permit number 289

REPUBLIC OF IRELAND : the maps and town plans in the Republic of Ireland Section of this Guide are based upon the Ordnance Survey of Ireland by permission of the Government of the Republic, Permit number 5172

1
SHETLAND ISLANDS
Unst
Yell
Whalsay
Mainland
Scalloway
Lerwick
Kirkwall
Aberdeen
ORKNEY ISLANDS
Westray
Rousay
Sanday
Stronsay
Mainland
Stromness
Kirkwall
Hoy
Scalloway
Durness
Thurso
27 A 836 16
31 Tongue A 882 Wick
A 897 39 58
A 836 A 9
Stornoway
Lewis
THE MINCH
72
Loch Shin
Brora
Tarbert
Ullapool
89
North Uist
31 A 835
Elgin 35 Banff Fraserbur
Lochmaddy Uig
Garve 26 Nairn 39 17 Keith 21 A 98
A 890 49 A 9 64 A 96 51 68
Skye
Portree
Inverness
Kyle of Lochalsh 43
South Uist
57 A 82 40 A 9 A 95
Lochboisdale 50 Loch Ness Spey ABERDEEN Ler
A 87 Invergarry 52 Kingussie A 93 59 A 92
Ardvasar 25 A 86 105 72 Dee Braemar Stonehave
Castlebay Mallaig Fort William A 9 67 A 94 68
Rhum 46 51 A 92
A 830 S C O T L A N D A 93
Coll 46 52 DUNDEE Arbroath
Tiree Mull A 85 A 82 Loch Tay 22 A 85
Craignure Oban 41 53 A 85 Perth St. Andrews
A 849 Crianlarich 17 Lochearnhead 33 A 9 29 77 30
38 A 84 43 Stirling M 90 A 91
A 816 A 83 49 Tarbet Firth of Forth
Colonsay 41 Falkirk 14 Kirkcaldy
Lochgilphead Greenock 20 Dunfermline
Port Askaig Jura Tarbert GLASGOW 39 13 EDINBURGH 56
Rothesay Largs 69 8 M 8 39
Islay Ardrossan A 77 Motherwell 41 A 7 34 Berwick upon Twe
Port Ellen Brodick 21 31 A 721 Peebles 63 Galashiels
51 Kilmarnock M 74 A 702 A 72 A 698 45
Arran Ayr 13 Abington 17 A 68 Alnwick
Campbeltown A 76 Hawick
NORTH CHANNEL 58 A 701 60 62 63
51 35 46 39 A 74 43 A 7 693
A 2 Coleraine A 77 New Galloway A 702 Dumfries A 696 Tynemo
31 Waterfoot A 713 NEWCASTLE
Londonderry A 26 25 Cairnryan 44 14 18 32 A 75 UPON-TYNE
A 6 90 55 A 75 A 69 59
Ballymena Larne Stranraer Carlisle Sunderlar
ane 70 28 34 20 43
NORTHERN A 8 Bangor A 596 Penrith Durham
15 Lough Neagh BELFAST 42 Workington A 66 38 Keswick Darlingto
Ballygawley Strangford Whitehaven 55 A 66 49
53 M1 Lough M 6
IRELAND 57 A 595 38
17 A 3 Armagh Banbridge A 25 Isle of Man Kendal E N G
Monaghan 37 Douglas 21
N2 32 52 Newcastle Barrow-in-Furness 12 A 65
67 T 24 A 66 Wharfe

NORTHERN
Lough Neagh
Ballygawley
Bangor
BELFAST
IRELAND
Strangford Lough
Armagh
Banbridge
Monaghan
Newcastle
Dundalk / Dun Dealgan
Kells
Drogheda / Droichead Átha
Boyne
DUBLIN / BAILE ÁTHA CLIATH
Naas
Dún Laoghaire
Bray
Wicklow
Arklow
Enniscorthy
Wexford
Rosslare
Isle of Man
Douglas
Barrow-in-Furness
Heysham
IRISH SEA
BLACKPOOL
Preston
Southport
Wigan
LIVERPOOL
Birkenhead
Colwyn Bay / Bae Colwyn
Holyhead / Caergybi
Bangor
Caernarfon
Mold / Yr Wyddgrug
Wrexham / Wrecsam
Chester
Warrington
Workington
Whitehaven
Keswick
Kendal
Lancaster
Blackburn
Burnley
Bolton
Oldham
MANCHESTER
Stockport
Macclesfield
Matlock
STOKE-ON-TRENT
Shrewsbury
Wolverhampton
Dudley
BIRMINGHAM
Walsall
Warwick
Penrith
Durham
Darlington
Harrogate
LEEDS
Bradford
Halifax
ENGLAND
Dolgellau
Welshpool / Y Trallwng
Aberystwyth
Llangurig
Llandrindod Wells
WALES
Ludlow
Hereford
Ross
Worcester
Stratford-upon-Avon
Cheltenham
Gloucester
Fishguard / Abergwaun
Carmarthen / Caerfyrddin
Milford Haven / Aberdaugleddau
Pembroke Dock / Doc Penfro
Brecon / Aberhonddu
Merthyr Tydfil
Swansea / Abertawe
Newport / Casnewydd
CARDIFF / CAERDYDD
BRISTOL
Bath
Swindon
Bristol Channel
Ilfracombe
Barnstaple
Bude
Newquay
Bodmin
Truro
Penzance
Falmouth
Isles of Scilly
Minehead
Bridgwater
Taunton
Wells
Yeovil
Dorchester
EXETER
Honiton
Exmouth
Weymouth
Salisbury
BOURNEMOUTH
Torquay / Torbay
PLYMOUTH
le Havre Cherbourg
ST. GEORGE'S CHANNEL
Santander
Roscoff
ENGLISH
Rosslare
Alderney
Cherbourg
Guernsey
Sark
St. Peter-Port
Jersey
St. Hélier
St. Malo
THAMES

2
Hartlepool
Middlesbrough
Scarborough
York
KINGSTON UPON HULL
Immingham
Rotterdam
Zeebruge
Wakefield
Scunthorpe
Barnley
Great Grimsby
Doncaster
Rotherham
SHEFFIELD
Lincoln
Skegness
Boston
Cromer
Derby
NOTTINGHAM
King's Lynn
NORWICH
Scheveningen
Wisbech
Great Yarmouth
LEICESTER
Stamford
Lowestoft
Peterborough
Coventry
Ely
Rugby
Bury St.Edmunds
Zeebrugge
Northampton
CAMBRIDGE
Bedford
Ipswich
Oslo
Kristiansand
Göteborg
Esbjerg
Hoek van Holland
Hamburg
Stevenage
Colchester
Felixstowe
Luton
Harwich
Aylesbury
Harlow
OXFORD
Chelmsford
GREATER LONDON
NEDERLAN
Vlissinge
Reading
Tilbury
Southend-on-Sea
Windsor
Sheerness
Margate
Zeebrugge
Newbury
Canterbury
Ramsgate
OOSTENDE
BRUGG
Basingstoke
Deal
BELGIË
BELGIQU
Guildford
Maidstone
Winchester
Crawley
Royal-
Tunbridge Wells
Dover
Dunkerque
SOUTHAMPTON
Folkestone
Calais
Gravelines
Chichester
BRIGHTON
Hastings
St-Omer
LILLE
Worthing
Eastbourne
Boulogne
Newhaven
PORTSMOUTH
Newport
Isle of Wight
Arras
Camb
St-Malo
Abbeville
CHANNEL
Rosslare
Dieppe
AMIENS
St-Quentin
Somme
Beauvais
Compiègne
LE HAVRE
FRANCE
Senlis
Soisso
ROUEN
CAEN
Lisieux
SEINE
NORTH
SEA
Swale
Ouse
Trent
Ouse
THAMES

3
ATLANTIC OCEAN
NORTH CHANNEL
ST GEORGE'S CHANNEL
CELTIC SEA
Colonsay
Port Askaig
Jura
Tarbert
Islay
Port Ellen
Campbeltown
Coleraine
A 2
Waterfoot
Letterkenny
31
25
A 26
Londonderry
90
23
30
17
14
A 6
Ballymena
N 56
Donegal
32
Strabane
70
Larne
N 15
A 5
20
28
A 8
T 35
Omagh
37
15
NORTHERN
Belfast
Bangor
26
Ballygawley
Lough Neagh
M 1
N 15 40
53
Strangford Lough
42
N 16
Enniskillen
IRELAND
A 2
Sligo/
31
17
57
Sligeach
42
A 4
A 4
Armagh
Banbridge
A 25
Ballina
29
L. Allen
Monaghan
37
Newcastle
99
N 59
37
N 4
25
29
N 2
52
L 133
40
40
A 3
13
A 2
N 59
26
T 53
52
N 54
A 1
32
Westport
11
Castlebar
Boyle
Cavan
67
T 24
Dundalk/
N 5
26
Dun Dealgan
Clifden
T 40
N 17
26
49
Longford
27
Kells
22
L. Mask
48
N 60
59
19
N 55
T 24
N 51
Drogheda/
52
Roscommon
L.
18
60
71
Droichead Átha
49
N 59
60
50
Ree
26
Mullingar
31
L. Corrib
19
N 6 21
43
DUBLIN/
Galway/
N 84
N 63
Athlone
15
N 4
BAILE ÁTHA CLIATH
Gaillimh
57
N 6
Ballinasloe
25
7
19
38
N 1
Lisdoonvarna
42
T 21
Tullamore
Dún Laoghaire
N 67
IRELAND
68
N 62
72
51
N 7
Naas
N 11
Bray
N 18
River Shannon
40
21
N 80
Ennis/
Roscrea
24
Wicklow
111
Inis
22
N 62
N 7
74
Kilkee
N 7 45
58
31
Carlow
N 68
45
Suir
T 19
N 80
55
Arklow
69
Thurles
N 8
R.
N 9
L 105
N 69
71
N 11
LIMERICK/
Kilkenny/
80
33
LUIMNEACH
Cill Chainnigh
Barrow
L 30
Enniscorthy
N 20
39
N 24
Cashel/
13
35
14
Tralee
N 21
58
Caher
Caiseal
41
N 76
16
Wexford
Dingle
65
74
N 8
38
38
31
23
Carrick
N 24
12
21
Killarney/
N 72
Fermoy
on Suir
Rosslare
Cill Airne
60
R. Blackwater
60
N 72
N 25
Waterford/
90
20
Lismore
77
Port Lairge
N 70
54
22
Glengarriff
N 22
N 25
Youghal
Bantry
CORK/
99
N 71
CORCAIGH
Cobh
Fishguard
Abergwau
Milford Haven
Aberdaugleddau
le Havre
Cherbourg
Roscoff
A 849
A 83
51
A 26
N 54
N 55

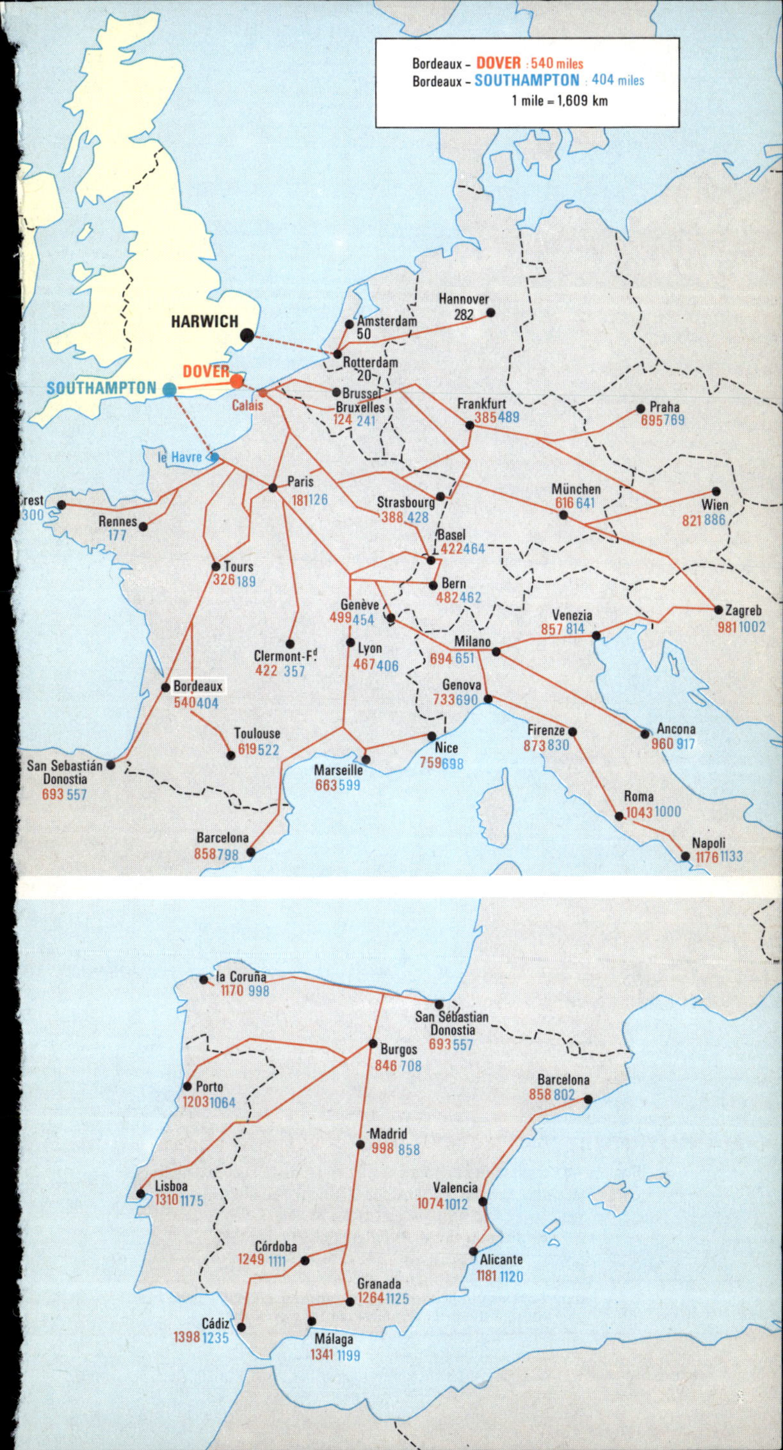

Bordeaux – DOVER : 540 miles
Bordeaux – SOUTHAMPTON : 404 miles
1 mile = 1,609 km
HARWICH
DOVER
SOUTHAMPTON
Calais
le Havre
Hannover 282
Amsterdam 50
Rotterdam 20
Brussel
Bruxelles 124 241
Frankfurt 385 489
Praha 695 769
Paris 181 126
Strasbourg 388 428
München 616 641
Wien 821 886
Brest 300
Rennes 177
Basel 422 464
Tours 326 189
Bern 482 462
Genève 499 454
Venezia 857 814
Zagreb 981 1002
Clermont-F.d 422 357
Lyon 467 406
Milano 694 651
Bordeaux 540 404
Genova 733 690
Toulouse 619 522
Firenze 873 830
Ancona 960 917
Nice 759 698
San Sebastián Donostia 693 557
Marseille 663 599
Roma 1043 1000
Barcelona 858 798
Napoli 1176 1133
la Coruña 1170 998
San Sébastian Donostia 693 557
Burgos 846 708
Barcelona 858 802
Porto 1203 1064
Madrid 998 858
Lisboa 1310 1175
Valencia 1074 1012
Córdoba 1249 1111
Alicante 1181 1120
Granada 1264 1125
Cádiz 1398 1235
Málaga 1341 1199

MANUFACTURE FRANÇAISE DES PNEUMATIQUES MICHELIN

Société en commandite par actions au capital de 875 000 000 de francs

Place des Carmes-Déchaux - 63 Clermont-Ferrand (France)

R.C.S. Clermont-Fd B 855 200 507

© Michelin et Cie, Propriétaires-Éditeurs 1990

Dépôt légal 2-90 — ISBN 2.06.006.509-7

Printed in France — 12-89-55

Photocomposition : S.C.I.A., La Chapelle-d'Armentières - Impression : TARDY QUERCY à Bourges n° 15622

REGIONAL MAPS

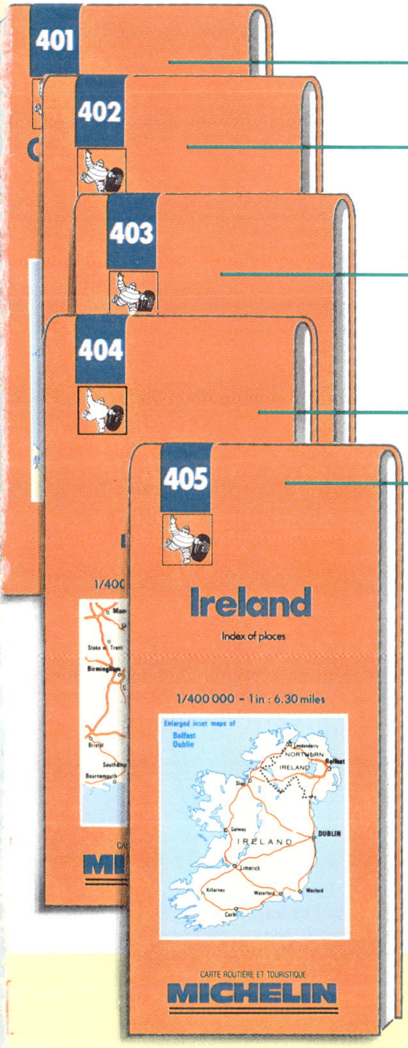

SCOTLAND

MIDLANDS -
THE NORTH

WALES
WEST COUNTRY
MIDLANDS

SOUTH EAST-
MIDLANDS
EAST ANGLIA

IRELAND

With index of places

1/1 000 000
986
Great Britain
Ireland
Grande-Bretagne
Irlande
1 in : 16 miles — 1/1 000 000
Wick
Inverness
SCOTLAND
Aberdeen
Dundee
Shetland I.
Londonderry
Glasgow
Edinburgh
Orkney I.
NORTHERN
IRELAND
Belfast
Carlisle
Newcastle
Galway
IRELAND
DUBLIN
Liverpool
Leeds
Kingston upon Hull
Limerick
Manchester
Cork
Waterford
Nottingham
Birmingham
Norwich
Channel I.
WALES
ENGLAND
Cardiff
Oxford
Cambridge
Bristol
LONDON
Plymouth
Exeter
Southampton
Dover
Bournemouth
Brighton
Calais
MICHELIN
PNEU MICHELIN 46, Av. de Breteuil 75341 PARIS CEDEX 07 - tél. (1) 45.66.12.34